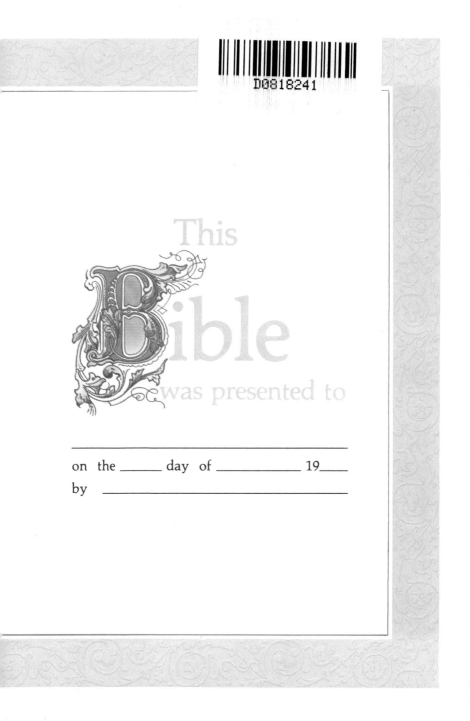

This

Bible

was presented to

_____

on   the _____ day   of _____ 19____

by   _____

THE

HOLY BIBLE

Containing the
OLD and NEW TESTAMENTS

Authorized
King James Version
with
Words of Christ in Red, Maps,
and Selected Helps to Bible Study

Broadman & Holman Publishers
Nashville, Tennessee

Helps to Bible Study
Copyright © 1979 by
Holman Bible Publishers
Nashville, TN 37234

Color	Binding	ISBN	Holman Code
Black	Imitation	0-87981-460-8	4634-01
Blue	Imitation	0-87981-461-6	4634-02
Burgundy	Imitation	0-87981-463-2	4634-04
Dusty Rose	Imitation	1-55819-135-6	4634-10
Teal	Imitation	1-55819-127-5	4634-07
White	Imitation	0-87981-464-0	4634-05
Prepack of 32	Imitation	1-55819-136-4	4634-13

Books of the Bible
Old Testament

New Testament

THE
OLD TESTAMENT

GENESIS

1 IN the beginning God created the heaven and the earth.

2 And the earth was without form, and void; and darkness *was* upon the face of the deep. And the Spirit of God moved upon the face of the waters.

3 ¶ And God said, Let there be light: and there was light.

4 And God saw the light, that *it was* good: and God divided the light from the darkness.

5 And God called the light Day, and the darkness he called Night. And the evening and the morning were the first day.

6 ¶ And God said, Let there be a firmament in the midst of the waters, and let it divide the waters from the waters.

7 And God made the firmament, and divided the waters which *were* under the firmament from the waters which *were* above the firmament: and it was so.

8 And God called the firmament Heaven. And the evening and the morning were the second day.

9 ¶ And God said, Let the waters under the heaven be gathered together unto one place, and let the dry *land* appear: and it was so.

10 And God called the dry *land* Earth; and the gathering together of the waters called he Seas: and God saw that *it was* good.

11 And God said, Let the earth bring forth grass, the herb yielding seed, *and* the fruit tree yielding fruit after his kind, whose seed *is* in itself, upon the earth: and it was so.

12 And the earth brought forth grass, *and* herb yielding seed after his kind, and the tree yielding fruit, whose seed *was* in itself, after his kind: and God saw that *it was* good.

13 And the evening and the morning were the third day.

14 ¶ And God said, Let there be lights in the firmament of the heaven to divide the day from the night; and let them be for signs, and for seasons, and for days, and years:

15 And let them be for lights in the firmament of the heaven to give light upon the earth: and it was so.

16 And God made two great lights; the greater light to rule the day, and the lesser light to rule the night: *he made* the stars also.

17 And God set them in the firmament of the heaven to give light upon the earth,

18 And to rule over the day and over the night, and to divide the light from the darkness: and God saw that *it was* good.

19 And the evening and the morning were the fourth day.

20 And God said, Let the waters bring forth abundantly the moving creature that hath life, and fowl *that* may fly above the earth in the open firmament of heaven.

21 And God created great whales, and every living creature that moveth, which the waters brought forth abundantly, after their kind, and every winged fowl after his kind: and God saw that *it was* good.

22 And God blessed them, saying, Be fruitful, and multiply, and fill the waters in the seas, and let fowl multiply in the earth.

23 And the evening and the morning were the fifth day.

24 ¶ And God said, Let the earth bring forth the living creature after his kind, cattle, and creeping thing, and beast of the earth after his kind: and it was so.

25 And God made the beast of the earth after his kind, and cattle after their kind, and every thing that creepeth upon the earth after his kind: and God saw that *it was* good.

26 ¶ And God said, Let us make man in our image, after our likeness: and let them have dominion over the fish of the sea, and over the fowl of the air, and over the cattle, and over all the earth, and over every creeping thing that creepeth upon the earth.

27 So God created man in his *own* image, in the image of God created he him; male and female created he them.

28 And God blessed them, and God said unto them, Be fruitful, and multiply, and replenish the earth, and subdue it: and have dominion over the fish of the sea, and over the fowl of the air, and over every living thing that moveth upon the earth.

29 ¶ And God said, Behold, I have given you every herb bearing seed, which *is* upon the face of all the earth, and every tree, in the which *is* the fruit of a tree yielding seed; to you it shall be for meat.

30 And to every beast of the earth, and to every fowl of the air, and to every thing that creepeth upon the earth, wherein *there is* life, I *have given* every green herb for meat: and it was so.

31 And God saw every thing that he had made, and, behold, *it was* very good. And the evening and the morning were the sixth day.

2 THUS the heavens and the earth were finished, and all the host of them.

2 And on the seventh day God ended his work which he had made; and he rested on the seventh day from all his work which he had made.

3 And God blessed the seventh day, and sanctified it: because that in it he had rested from all his work which God created and made.

4 ¶ These *are* the generations of the heavens and of the earth when they were created, in the day that the LORD God made the earth and the heavens,

5 And every plant of the field before it was in the earth, and every herb of the field before it grew: for the LORD God had not caused it to rain upon the earth, and *there was* not a man to till the ground.

6 But there went up a mist from the earth, and watered the whole face of the ground.

7 And the LORD God formed man *of* the dust of the ground, and breathed into his nostrils the breath of life; and man became a living soul.

8 ¶ And the LORD God planted a garden eastward in E'den; and there he put the man whom he had formed.

9 And out of the ground made the LORD God to grow every tree that is pleasant to the sight, and good for food; the tree of life also in the midst of the garden, and the tree of knowledge of good and evil.

10 And a river went out of E'den to water the garden; and from thence it was parted, and became into four heads.

11 The name of the first *is* Pi'son: that *is* it

which compasseth the whole land of Hav'i-lah, where *there* is gold;

12 And the gold of that land *is* good: there *is* bdellium and the onyx stone.

13 And the name of the second river *is* Gi'hon: the same *is* it that compasseth the whole land of E-thi-o'pi-a.

14 And the name of the third river *is* Hid'de-kel: that *is* it which goeth toward the east of As-syr'i-a. And the fourth river *is* Eu-phra'tes.

15 And the LORD God took the man, and put him into the garden of E'den to dress it and to keep it.

16 And the LORD God commanded the man, saying, Of every tree of the garden thou mayest freely eat:

17 But of the tree of the knowledge of good and evil, thou shalt not eat of it: for in the day that thou eatest thereof thou shalt surely die.

18 ¶ And the LORD God said, *It is* not good that the man should be alone; I will make him an help meet for him.

19 And out of the ground the LORD God formed every beast of the field, and every fowl of the air; and brought *them* unto Ad'am to see what he would call them: and whatsoever Ad'-am called every living creature, that *was* the name thereof.

20 And Ad'am gave names to all cattle, and to the fowl of the air, and to every beast of the field; but for Ad'am there was not found an help meet for him.

21 And the LORD God caused a deep sleep to fall upon Ad'am, and he slept: and he took one of his ribs, and closed up the flesh instead thereof;

22 And the rib, which the LORD God had taken from man, made he a woman, and brought her unto the man.

23 And Ad'am said, This *is* now bone of my bones, and flesh of my flesh: she shall be called Woman, because she was taken out of Man.

24 Therefore shall a man leave his father and his mother, and shall cleave unto his wife: and they shall be one flesh.

25 And they were both naked, the man and his wife, and were not ashamed.

3 NOW the serpent was more subtil than any beast of the field which the LORD God had made. And he said unto the woman, Yea, hath God said, Ye shall not eat of every tree of the garden?

2 And the woman said unto the serpent, We may eat of the fruit of the trees of the garden:

3 But of the fruit of the tree which *is* in the midst of the garden, God hath said, Ye shall not eat of it, neither shall ye touch it, lest ye die.

4 And the serpent said unto the woman, Ye shall not surely die:

5 For God doth know that in the day ye eat thereof, then your eyes shall be opened, and ye shall be as gods, knowing good and evil.

6 And when the woman saw that the tree *was* good for food, and that it *was* pleasant to the eyes, and a tree to be desired to make *one* wise, she took of the fruit thereof, and did eat, and gave also unto her husband with her; and he did eat.

7 And the eyes of them both were opened, and they knew that they *were* naked; and they sewed fig leaves together, and made themselves aprons.

8 And they heard the voice of the LORD God walking in the garden in the cool of the day: and Ad'am and his wife hid themselves from the presence of the LORD God amongst the trees of the garden.

9 And the LORD God called unto Ad'am, and said unto him, Where *art* thou?

10 And he said, I heard thy voice in the garden, and I was afraid, because I *was* naked; and I hid myself.

11 And he said, Who told thee that thou *wast* naked? Hast thou eaten of the tree, whereof I commanded thee that thou shouldest not eat?

12 And the man said, The woman whom thou gavest *to be* with me, she gave me of the tree, and I did eat.

13 And the LORD God said unto the woman, What *is* this *that* thou hast done? And the woman said, The serpent beguiled me, and I did eat.

14 And the LORD God said unto the serpent, Because thou hast done this, thou *art* cursed above all cattle, and above every beast of the field; upon thy belly shalt thou go, and dust shalt thou eat all the days of thy life:

15 And I will put enmity between thee and the woman, and between thy seed and her seed; it shall bruise thy head, and thou shalt bruise his heel.

16 Unto the woman he said, I will greatly multiply thy sorrow and thy conception; in sorrow thou shalt bring forth children; and thy desire *shall be* to thy husband, and he shall rule over thee.

17 And unto Ad'am he said, Because thou hast hearkened unto the voice of thy wife, and hast eaten of the tree, of which I commanded thee, saying, Thou shalt not eat of it: cursed *is* the ground for thy sake; in sorrow shalt thou eat *of* it all the days of thy life;

18 Thorns also and thistles shall it bring forth to thee; and thou shalt eat the herb of the field;

19 In the sweat of thy face shalt thou eat bread, till thou return unto the ground; for out of it wast thou taken: for dust thou *art*, and unto dust shalt thou return.

20 And Ad'am called his wife's name Eve; because she was the mother of all living.

21 Unto Ad'am also and to his wife did the LORD God make coats of skins, and clothed them.

22 ¶ And the LORD God said, Behold, the man is become as one of us, to know good and evil: and now, lest he put forth his hand, and take also of the tree of life, and eat, and live for ever:

23 Therefore the LORD God sent him forth from the garden of E'den, to till the ground from whence he was taken.

24 So he drove out the man; and he placed at the east of the garden of E'den Cher'u-bims, and a flaming sword which turned every way, to keep the way of the tree of life.

4 AND Ad'am knew Eve his wife; and she conceived, and bare Cain, and said, I have gotten a man from the LORD.

2 And she again bare his brother A'bel. And A'bel was a keeper of sheep, but Cain was a tiller of the ground.

3 And in the process of time it came to pass, that Cain brought of the fruit of the ground an offering unto the LORD.

4 And A'bel, he also brought of the firstlings of his flock and of the fat thereof. And the LORD had respect unto A'bel and to his offering:

5 But unto Cain and to his offering he had not respect. And Cain was very wroth, and his countenance fell.

6 And the LORD said unto Cain, Why art thou wroth? and why is thy countenance fallen?

7 If thou doest well, shalt thou not be accepted? and if thou doest not well, sin lieth at the door. And unto thee *shall be* his desire, and thou shalt rule over him.

8 And Cain talked with A′bel his brother: and it came to pass, when they were in the field, that Cain rose up against A′bel his brother, and slew him.

9 ¶ And the LORD said unto Cain, Where *is* A′bel thy brother? And he said, I know not: *Am* I my brother's keeper?

10 And he said, What hast thou done? the voice of thy brother's blood crieth unto me from the ground.

11 And now *art* thou cursed from the earth, which hath opened her mouth to receive thy brother's blood from thy hand;

12 When thou tillest the ground, it shall not henceforth yield unto thee her strength; a fugitive and a vagabond shalt thou be in the earth.

13 And Cain said unto the LORD, My punishment *is* greater than I can bear.

14 Behold, thou hast driven out this day from the face of the earth; and from thy face shall I be hid; and I shall be a fugitive and a vagabond in the earth; and it shall come to pass, *that* every one that findeth me shall slay me.

15 And the LORD said unto him, Therefore whosoever slayeth Cain, vengeance shall be taken on him sevenfold. And the LORD set a mark upon Cain, lest any finding him should kill him.

16 ¶ And Cain went out from the presence of the LORD, and dwelt in the land of Nod, on the east of E′den.

17 And Cain knew his wife; and she conceived, and bare E′noch: and he builded a city, and called the name of the city, after the name of his son, E′noch.

18 And unto E′noch was born I′rad: and I′rad begat Me-hu′ja-el: and Me-hu′ja-el begat Me-thusa-el: and Me-thusa-el begat La′mech.

19 ¶ And La′mech took unto him two wives: the name of the one *was* A′dah, and the name of the other Zil′lah.

20 And A′dah bare Ja′bal: he was the father of such as dwell in tents, and *of such as have* cattle.

21 And his brother's name *was* Ju′bal: he was the father of all such as handle the harp and organ.

22 And Zil′lah, she also bare Tu′bal-cain, an instructer of every artificer in brass and iron: and the sister of Tu′bal-cain *was* Na′a-mah.

23 And La′mech said unto his wives, A′dah and Zil′lah, Hear my voice; ye wives of La′mech, hearken unto my speech: for I have slain a man to my wounding, and a young man to my hurt.

24 If Cain shall be avenged sevenfold, truly La′mech seventy and sevenfold.

25 ¶ And Ad′am knew his wife again; and she bare a son, and called his name Seth: For God, *said she,* hath appointed me another seed instead of A′bel, whom Cain slew.

26 And to Seth, to him also there was born a son; and he called his name E′nos: then began men to call upon the name of the LORD.

5 THIS *is* the book of the generations of Ad′am. In the day that God created man, in the likeness of God made he him;

2 Male and female created he them; and blessed them, and called their name Ad′am, in the day when they were created.

3 ¶ And Ad′am lived an hundred and thirty years, and begat a *son* in his own likeness, after his image; and called his name Seth:

4 And the days of Ad′am after he had begotten Seth were eight hundred years: and he begat sons and daughters:

5 And all the days that Ad′am lived were nine hundred and thirty years: and he died.

6 And Seth lived an hundred and five years, and begat E′nos:

7 And Seth lived after he begat E′nos eight hundred and seven years, and begat sons and daughters:

8 And all the days of Seth were nine hundred and twelve years: and he died.

9 ¶ And E′nos lived ninety years, and begat Ca-i′nan:

10 And E′nos lived after he begat Ca-i′nan eight hundred and fifteen years, and begat sons and daughters:

11 And all the days of E′nos were nine hundred and five years: and he died.

12 ¶ And Ca-i′nan lived seventy years, and begat Ma-ha′la-le-el:

13 And Ca-i′nan lived after he begat Ma-ha′-la-le-el eight hundred and forty years, and begat sons and daughters:

14 And all the days of Ca-i′nan were nine hundred and ten years: and he died.

15 ¶ And Ma-ha′la-le-el lived sixty and five years and begat Ja′red:

16 And Ma-ha′la-le-el lived after he begat Ja′red eight hundred and thirty years, and begat sons and daughters:

17 And all the days of Ma-ha′la-le-el were eight hundred ninety and five years: and he died.

18 ¶ And Ja′red lived an hundred sixty and two years, and he begat E′noch:

19 And Ja′red lived after he begat E′noch eight hundred years, and begat sons and daughters:

20 And all the days of Ja′red were nine hundred sixty and two years: and he died.

21 ¶ And E′noch lived sixty and five years, and begat Me-thu′se-lah:

22 And E′noch walked with God after he begat Me-thu′se-lah three hundred years, and begat sons and daughters:

23 And all the days of E′noch were three hundred sixty and five years:

24 And E′noch walked with God: and he *was* not; for God took him.

25 And Me-thu′se-lah lived an hundred eighty and seven years, and begat La′mech.

26 And Me-thu′se-lah lived after he begat La′mech seven hundred eighty and two years, and begat sons and daughters:

27 And all the days of Me-thu′se-lah were nine hundred sixty and nine years: and he died.

28 ¶ And La′mech lived an hundred eighty and two years, and begat a son:

29 And he called his name No′ah, saying, This *same* shall comfort us concerning our work and toil of our hands, because of the ground which the LORD hath cursed.

30 And La′mech lived after he begat No′ah five hundred ninety and five years, and begat sons and daughters:

31 And all the days of La′mech were seven hundred seventy and seven years: and he died.

32 And No′ah was five hundred years old: and No′ah begat Shem, Ham, and Ja′pheth.

6 AND it came to pass, when men began to multiply on the face of the earth, and daughters were born unto them,

2 That the sons of God saw the daughters of men that they *were* fair; and they took them wives of all which they chose.

3 And the LORD said, My spirit shall not always strive with man, for that he also *is* flesh: yet his days shall be an hundred and twenty years.

4 There were giants in the earth in those days; and also after that, when the sons of God came in unto the daughters of men, and they bare *children* to them, the same *became* mighty men which *were* of old, men of renown.

5 ¶ And GOD saw that the wickedness of man *was* great in the earth, and *that* every imagination of the thoughts of his heart *was* only evil continually.

6 And it repented the LORD that he had made man on the earth, and it grieved him at his heart.

7 And the LORD said, I will destroy man whom I have created from the face of the earth; both man, and beast, and the creeping thing, and the fowls of the air; for it repenteth me that I have made them.

8 But No'ah found grace in the eyes of the LORD.

9 ¶ These *are* the generations of No'ah: No'ah was a just man *and* perfect in his generations, *and* No'ah walked with God.

10 And No'ah begat three sons, Shem, Ham, and Ja'pheth.

11 The earth also was corrupt before God, and the earth was filled with violence.

12 And God looked upon the earth, and, behold, it was corrupt; for all flesh had corrupted his way upon the earth.

13 And God said unto No'ah, The end of all flesh is come before me; for the earth is filled with violence through them; and, behold, I will destroy them with the earth.

14 ¶ Make thee an ark of gopher wood; rooms shalt thou make in the ark, and shalt pitch it within and without with pitch.

15 And this *is the fashion* which thou shalt make it *of:* The length of the ark *shall be* three hundred cubits, the breadth of it fifty cubits, and the height of it thirty cubits.

16 A window shalt thou make to the ark, and in a cubit shalt thou finish it above; and the door of the ark shalt thou set in the side thereof; *with* lower, second, and third *stories* shalt thou make it.

17 And, behold, I, even I, do bring a flood of waters upon the earth, to destroy all flesh, wherein *is* the breath of life, from under heaven; *and* every thing that *is* in the earth shall die.

18 But with thee will I establish my covenant; and thou shalt come into the ark, thou, and thy sons, and thy wife, and thy sons' wives with thee.

19 And of every living thing of all flesh, two of every *sort* shalt thou bring into the ark, to keep *them* alive with thee; they shall be male and female.

20 Of fowls after their kind, and of cattle after their kind, of every creeping thing of the earth after his kind, two of every *sort* shall come unto thee, to keep *them* alive.

21 And take thou unto thee of all food that is eaten, and thou shalt gather *it* to thee; and it shall be for food for thee, and for them.

22 Thus did No'ah; according to all that God commanded him, so did he.

7 AND the LORD said unto No'ah, Come thou and all thy house into the ark; for thee have I seen righteous before me in this generation.

2 Of every clean beast thou shalt take to thee by sevens, the male and his female: and of beasts that *are* not clean by two, the male and his female.

3 Of fowls also of the air by sevens, the male and the female; to keep seed alive upon the face of all the earth.

4 For yet seven days, and I will cause it to rain upon the earth forty days and forty nights; and every living substance that I have made will I destroy from off the face of the earth.

5 And No'ah did according unto all that the LORD commanded him.

6 And No'ah *was* six hundred years old when the flood of waters was upon the earth.

7 ¶ And No'ah went in, and his sons, and his wife, and his sons' wives with him, into the ark, because of the waters of the flood.

8 Of clean beasts, and of beasts that *are* not clean, and of fowls, and of every thing that creepeth upon the earth,

9 There went in two and two unto No'ah into the ark, the male and the female, as God had commanded No'ah.

10 And it came to pass after seven days, that the waters of the flood were upon the earth.

11 ¶ In the six hundredth year of No'ah's life, in the second month, the seventeenth day of the month, the same day were all the fountains of the great deep broken up, and the windows of heaven were opened.

12 And the rain was upon the earth forty days and forty nights.

13 In the selfsame day entered No'ah, and Shem, and Ham, and Ja'pheth, the sons of No'ah, and No'ah's wife, and the three wives of his sons with them, into the ark;

14 They, and every beast after his kind, and all the cattle after their kind, and every creeping thing that creepeth upon the earth after his kind, and every fowl after his kind, every bird of every sort.

15 And they went in unto No'ah into the ark, two and two of all flesh, wherein *is* the breath of life.

16 And they that went in, went in male and female of all flesh, as God had commanded him: and the LORD shut him in.

17 And the flood was forty days upon the earth; and the waters increased, and bare up the ark, and it was lift up above the earth.

18 And the waters prevailed, and were increased greatly upon the earth; and the ark went upon the face of the waters.

19 And the waters prevailed exceedingly upon the earth; and all the high hills, that *were* under the whole heaven, were covered.

20 Fifteen cubits upward did the waters prevail; and the mountains were covered.

21 And all flesh died that moved upon the earth, both of fowl, and of cattle, and of beast, and of every creeping thing that creepeth upon the earth, and every man:

22 All in whose nostrils *was* the breath of life, of all that *was* in the dry *land,* died.

23 And every living substance was destroyed which was upon the face of the ground, both man, and cattle, and the creeping things, and the fowl of the heaven; and they were destroyed from the earth: and No'ah only remained *alive,* and they that *were* with him in the ark.

24 And the waters prevailed upon the earth an hundred and fifty days.

8 AND God remembered No'ah, and every living thing, and all the cattle that *was* with him in the ark: and God made a wind to pass over the earth, and the waters asswaged;

2 The fountains also of the deep and the windows of heaven were stopped, and the rain from heaven was restrained;

3 And the waters returned from off the earth continually: and after the end of the hundred and fifty days the waters were abated.

4 And the ark rested in the seventh month, on the seventeenth day of the month, upon the mountains of Ar'a-rat.

5 And the waters decreased continually until the tenth month: in the tenth *month*, on the first *day* of the month, were the tops of the mountains seen.

6 ¶ And it came to pass at the end of forty days, that No'ah opened the window of the ark which he had made:

7 And he sent forth a raven, which went forth to and fro, until the waters were dried up from off the earth.

8 Also he sent forth a dove from him, to see if the waters were abated from off the face of the ground;

9 But the dove found no rest for the sole of her foot, and she returned unto him into the ark, for the waters *were* on the face of the whole earth: then he put forth his hand, and took her, and pulled her in unto him into the ark.

10 And he stayed yet other seven days; and again he sent forth the dove out of the ark;

11 And the dove came in to him in the evening; and, lo, in her mouth *was* an olive leaf pluckt off: so No'ah knew that the waters were abated from off the earth.

12 And he stayed yet other seven days; and sent forth the dove; which returned not again unto him any more.

13 ¶ And it came to pass in the six hundredth and first year, in the first *month*, the first *day* of the month, the waters were dried up from off the earth: and No'ah removed the covering of the ark, and looked, and, behold, the face of the ground was dry.

14 And in the second month, on the seven and twentieth day of the month, was the earth dried.

15 ¶ And God spake unto No'ah, saying,

16 Go forth of the ark, thou, and thy wife, and thy sons, and thy sons' wives with thee.

17 Bring forth with thee every living thing that *is* with thee, of all flesh, *both* of fowl, and of cattle, and of every creeping thing that creepeth upon the earth; that they may breed abundantly in the earth, and be fruitful, and multiply upon the earth.

18 And No'ah went forth, and his sons, and his wife, and his sons' wives with him:

19 Every beast, every creeping thing, and every fowl, *and* whatsoever creepeth upon the earth, after their kinds, went forth out of the ark.

20 ¶ And No'ah builded an altar unto the LORD; and took of every clean beast, and of every clean fowl, and offered burnt offerings on the altar.

21 And the LORD smelled a sweet savour; and the LORD said in his heart, I will not again curse the ground any more for man's sake; for the imagination of man's heart *is* evil from his youth; neither will I again smite any more every thing living, as I have done.

22 While the earth remaineth, seedtime and harvest, and cold and heat, and summer and winter, and day and night shall not cease.

9 AND God blessed No'ah and his sons, and said unto them, Be fruitful, and multiply, and replenish the earth.

2 And the fear of you and the dread of you shall be upon every beast of the earth, and upon every fowl of the air, upon all that moveth *upon* the earth, and upon all the fishes of the sea; into your hand are they delivered.

3 Every moving thing that liveth shall be meat for you; even as the green herb have I given you all things.

4 But flesh with the life thereof, *which is* the blood thereof, shall ye not eat.

5 And surely your blood of your lives will I require; at the hand of every beast will I require it, and at the hand of man; at the hand of every man's brother will I require the life of man.

6 Whoso sheddeth man's blood, by man shall his blood be shed: for in the image of God made he man.

7 And you, be ye fruitful, and multiply; bring forth abundantly in the earth, and multiply therein.

8 ¶ And God spake unto No'ah, and to his sons with him, saying,

9 And I, behold, I establish my covenant with you, and with your seed after you;

10 And with every living creature that *is* with you, of the fowl, of the cattle, and of every beast of the earth with you; from all that go out of the ark, to every beast of the earth.

11 And I will establish my covenant with you; neither shall all flesh be cut off any more by the waters of a flood; neither shall there any more be a flood to destroy the earth.

12 And God said, This *is* the token of the covenant which I make between me and you and every living creature that *is* with you, for perpetual generations:

13 I do set my bow in the cloud, and it shall be for a token of a covenant between me and the earth.

14 And it shall come to pass, when I bring a cloud over the earth, that the bow shall be seen in the cloud:

15 And I will remember my covenant, which *is* between me and you and every living creature of all flesh; and the waters shall no more become a flood to destroy all flesh.

16 And the bow shall be in the cloud; and I will look upon it, that I may remember the everlasting covenant between God and every living creature of all flesh that *is* upon the earth.

17 And God said unto No'ah, This *is* the token of the covenant, which I have established between me and all flesh that *is* upon the earth.

18 ¶ And the sons of No'ah, that went forth of the ark, were Shem, and Ham, and Ja'pheth: and Ham *is* the father of Ca'naan.

19 These *are* the three sons of No'ah: and of them was the whole earth overspread.

20 And No'ah began *to be* an husbandman, and he planted a vineyard:

21 And he drank of the wine, and was drunken; and he was uncovered within his tent.

22 And Ham, the father of Ca'naan, saw the nakedness of his father, and told his two brethren without.

23 And Shem and Ja'pheth took a garment, and laid *it* upon both their shoulders, and went backward, and covered the nakedness of their father; and their faces *were* backward, and they saw not their father's nakedness.

24 And No'ah awoke from his wine, and

knew what his younger son had done unto him.

25 And he said, Cursed be Ca'naan; a servant of servants shall he be unto his brethren.

26 And he said, Blessed be the LORD God of Shem; and Ca'naan shall be his servant.

27 God shall enlarge Ja'pheth, and he shall dwell in the tents of Shem; and Ca'naan shall be his servant.

28 ¶ And No'ah lived after the flood three hundred and fifty years.

29 And all the days of No'ah were nine hundred and fifty years: and he died.

10 NOW these are the generations of the sons of No'ah, Shem, Ham, and Ja'pheth: and unto them were sons born after the flood.

2 The sons of Ja'pheth; Go'mer, and Ma'gog, and Mad'a-i, and Ja'van, and Tu'bal, and Me'shech, and Ti'ras.

3 And the sons of Go'mer; Ash'ke-naz, and Ri'phath, and To-gar'mah.

4 And the sons of Ja'van; E-li'shah, and Tar'shish, Kit'tim, and Dod'a-nim.

5 By these were the isles of the Gen-tiles divided in their lands; every one after his tongue, after their families, in their nations.

6 ¶ And the sons of Ham; Cush, and Miz'ra-im, and Phut, and Ca'naan.

7 And the sons of Cush; Se'ba, and Hav'i-lah, and Sab'tah, and Ra'a-mah, and Sab'te-chah: and the sons of Ra'a-mah; She'ba, and De'dan.

8 And Cush begat Nim'rod: he began to be a mighty one in the earth.

9 He was a mighty hunter before the LORD: wherefore it is said, Even as Nim'rod the mighty hunter before the LORD.

10 And the beginning of his kingdom was Ba'bel, and E'rech, and Ac'cad, and Cal'neh, in the land of Shi'nar.

11 Out of that land went forth As'shur, and builded Nin'e-veh, and the city Re-ho'both, and Ca'lah,

12 And Re'sen between Nin'e-veh and Ca'lah: the same is a great city.

13 And Miz'ra-im begat Lu'dim, and An'a-mim, and Le'ha-bim, and Naph'tu-him,

14 And Path-ru'sim, and Cas'lu-him, (out of whom came Phi-lis'tim,) and Caph'to-rim.

15 ¶ And Ca'naan begat Si'don his first born, and Heth,

16 And the Jeb'u-site, and the Am'or-ite, and the Gir'ga-site,

17 And the Hi'vite, and the Ark'ite, and the Sin'ite,

18 And the Ar'vad-ite, and the Zem'a-rite, and the Ha'math-ite: and afterward were the families of the Ca'naan-ites spread abroad.

19 And the border of the Ca'naan-ites was from Si'don, as thou comest to Ge'rar, unto Ga'za; as thou goest, unto Sod'om, and Go-mor'rah, and Ad'-mah, and Ze-bo'im, even unto La'sha.

20 These are the sons of Ham, after their families, after their tongues, in their countries, and in their nations.

21 ¶ Unto Shem also, the father of all the children of E'ber, the brother of Ja'pheth the elder, even to him were children born.

22 The children of Shem; E'lam, and As'shur, and Arphax'ad, and Lud, and A'ram.

23 And the children of A'ram; Uz, and Hul, and Ge'ther, and Mash.

24 And Arphax'ad begat Sa'lah; and Sa'lah begat E'ber.

25 And unto E'ber were born two sons: the name of one was Pe'leg; for in his days was the earth divided; and his brother's name was Jok'tan.

26 And Jok'tan begat Al-mo'dad, and She'leph, and Ha'zar-ma'veth, and Je'rah,

27 And Ha-do'ram, and U'zal, and Dik'lah,

28 And O'bal, and A-bim'a-el, and She'ba,

29 And O'phir, and Hav'i-lah, and Jo'bab: all these were the sons of Jok'tan.

30 And their dwelling was from Me'sha, as thou goest unto Se'phar a mount of the east.

31 These are the sons of Shem, after their families, after their tongues, in their lands, after their nations.

32 These are the families of the sons of No'ah, after their generations, in their nations: and by these were the nations divided in the earth after the flood.

11 AND the whole earth was of one language, and of one speech.

2 And it came to pass, as they journeyed from the east, that they found a plain in the land of Shi'nar; and they dwelt there.

3 And they said one to another, Go to, let us make brick, and burn them thoroughly. And they had brick for stone, and slime had they for morter.

4 And they said, Go to, let us build us a city and a tower, whose top may reach unto heaven; and let us make us a name, lest we be scattered abroad upon the face of the whole earth.

5 And the LORD came down to see the city and the tower, which the children of men builded.

6 And the LORD said, Behold, the people is one, and they have all one language; and this they begin to do: and now nothing will be restrained from them, which they have imagined to do.

7 Go to, let us go down, and there confound their language, that they may not understand one another's speech.

8 So the LORD scattered them abroad from thence upon the face of all the earth: and they left off to build the city.

9 Therefore is the name of it called Ba'bel; because the LORD did there confound the language of all the earth: and from thence did the LORD scatter them abroad upon the face of all the earth.

10 ¶ These are the generations of Shem: Shem was an hundred years old, and begat Arphax'ad two years after the flood:

11 And Shem lived after he begat Arphax'ad five hundred years, and begat sons and daughters.

12 And Arphax'ad lived five and thirty years, and begat Sa'lah:

13 And Arphax'ad lived after he begat Sa'lah four hundred and three years, and begat sons and daughters.

14 And Sa'lah lived thirty years, and begat E'ber:

15 And Sa'lah lived after he begat E'ber four hundred and three years, and begat sons and daughters.

16 And E'ber lived four and thirty years, and begat Pe'leg:

17 And E'ber lived after he begat Pe'leg four hundred and thirty years, and begat sons and daughters.

18 And Pe'leg lived thirty years, and begat Re'u:

19 And Pe'leg lived after he begat Re'u two hundred and nine years, and begat sons and daughters.

20 And Re'u lived two and thirty years, and begat Se'rug:

21 And Re'u lived after he begat Se'rug two hundred and seven years, and begat sons and daughters.

22 And Se'rug lived thirty years, and begat Na'hor:

23 And Se'rug lived after he begat Na'hor two hundred years, and begat sons and daughters.

24 And Na'hor lived nine and twenty years, and begat Te'rah:

25 And Na'hor lived after he begat Te'rah an hundred and nineteen years, and begat sons and daughters.

26 And Te'rah lived seventy years, and begat A'bram, Na'hor, and Ha'ran.

27 ¶ Now these are the generations of Te'rah: Te'rah begat A'bram, Na'hor, and Ha'ran; and Ha'ran begat Lot.

28 And Ha'ran died before his father Te'rah in the land of his nativity, in Ur of the Chal'-dees.

29 And A'bram and Na'hor took them wives: the name of A'bram's wife was Sa'rai; and the name of Na'hor's wife, Mil'cah, the daughter of Ha'ran, the father of Mil'cah, and the father of Is'cah.

30 But Sa'rai was barren; she had no child.

31 And Te'rah took A'bram his son, and Lot the son of Ha'ran his son's son, and Sa'rai his daughter in law, his son A'bram's wife; and they went forth with them from Ur of the Chal'-dees, to go into the land of Ca'naan; and they came unto Ha'ran, and dwelt there.

32 And the days of Te'rah were two hundred and five years: and Te'rah died in Ha'ran.

12 NOW the LORD had said unto A'bram, Get thee out of thy country, and from thy kindred, and from thy father's house, unto a land that I will shew thee:

2 And I will make of thee a great nation, and I will bless thee, and make thy name great; and thou shalt be a blessing:

3 And I will bless them that bless thee, and curse him that curseth thee: and in thee shall all families of the earth be blessed.

4 So A'bram departed, as the LORD had spoken unto him; and Lot went with him: and A'-bram was seventy and five years old when he departed out of Ha'ran.

5 And A'bram took Sa'rai his wife, and Lot his brother's son, and all their substance that they had gathered, and the souls that they had gotten in Ha'ran; and they went forth to go into the land of Ca'naan; and into the land of Ca'-naan they came.

6 ¶ And A'bram passed through the land unto the place of Si'chem, unto the plain of Mo'-reh. And the Ca'naan-ite was then in the land.

7 And the LORD appeared unto A'bram, and said, Unto thy seed will I give this land: and there builded he an altar unto the LORD, who appeared unto him.

8 And he removed from thence unto a mountain on the east of Beth'-el, and pitched his tent, having Beth'-el on the west, and Ha'i on the east: and there he builded an altar unto the LORD, and called upon the name of the LORD.

9 And A'bram journeyed, going on still toward the south.

10 ¶ And there was a famine in the land: and A'bram went down into E'gypt to sojourn there; for the famine was grievous in the land.

11 And it came to pass, when he was come near to enter into E'gypt, that he said unto Sa'-rai his wife, Behold now, I know that thou art a fair woman to look upon:

12 Therefore it shall come to pass, when the E-gyptians shall see thee, that they shall say, This is his wife: and they will kill me, but they will save thee alive.

13 Say, I pray thee, thou art my sister: that it may be well with me for thy sake; and my soul shall live because of thee.

14 ¶ And it came to pass, that, when A'bram was come into E'gypt, the E-gyptians beheld the woman that she was very fair.

15 The princes also of Pha'raoh saw her, and commended her before Pha'raoh: and the woman was taken into Pha'raoh's house.

16 And he entreated A'bram well for her sake: and he had sheep, and oxen, and he asses, and menservants, and maidservants, and she asses, and camels.

17 And the LORD plagued Pha'raoh and his house with great plagues because of Sa'rai A'-bram's wife.

18 And Pha'raoh called A'bram, and said, What is this that thou hast done unto me? why didst thou not tell me that she was thy wife?

19 Why saidst thou, She is my sister? so I might have taken her to me to wife: now therefore behold thy wife, take her, and go thy way.

20 And Pha'raoh commanded his men concerning him: and they sent him away, and his wife, and all that he had.

13 AND A'bram went up out of E'gypt, he, and his wife, and all that he had, and Lot with him, into the south.

2 And A'bram was very rich in cattle, in silver, and in gold.

3 And he went on his journeys from the south even to Beth'-el, unto the place where his tent had been at the beginning, between Beth'-el and Ha'i;

4 Unto the place of the altar, which he had made there at the first: and there A'bram called on the name of the LORD.

5 ¶ And Lot also, which went with A'bram, had flocks, and herds, and tents.

6 And the land was not able to bear them, that they might dwell together: for their substance was great, so that they could not dwell together.

7 And there was a strife between the herdmen of A'bram's cattle and the herdmen of Lot's cattle: and the Ca'naan-ite and the Per'iz-zite dwelled then in the land.

8 And A'bram said unto Lot, Let there be no strife, I pray thee, between me and thee, and between my herdmen and thy herdmen; for we be brethren.

9 Is not the whole land before thee? separate thyself, I pray thee, from me: if thou wilt take the left hand, then I will go to the right; or if thou depart to the right hand, then I will go to the left.

10 And Lot lifted up his eyes, and beheld all the plain of Jor'dan, that it was well watered every where, before the LORD destroyed Sod'-om and Go-mor'rah, even as the garden of the LORD, like the land of E'gypt, as thou comest unto Zo'ar.

11 Then Lot chose him all the plain of Jor'-dan; and Lot journeyed east: and they separated themselves the one from the other.

12 A'bram dwelled in the land of Ca'naan, and Lot dwelled in the cities of the plain, and pitched his tent toward Sod'om.

13 But the men of Sod'om were wicked and sinners before the LORD exceedingly.

14 ¶ And the LORD said unto A'bram, after that Lot was separated from him, Lift up now thine eyes, and look from the place where thou art northward, and southward, and eastward, and westward:

15 For all the land which thou seest, to thee will I give it, and to thy seed for ever.

16 And I will make thy seed as the dust of the earth: so that if a man can number the dust of the earth, then shall thy seed also be numbered.

17 Arise, walk through the land in the length of it and in the breadth of it; for I will give it unto thee.

18 Then A'bram removed his tent, and came and dwelt in the plain of Mam're, which is in He'bron, and built there an altar unto the LORD.

14 AND it came to pass in the days of Am'-ra-phel king of Shi'nar, A'ri-och king of El'la-sar, Ched-or-la'o-mer king of E'lam, and Ti'dal king of nations;

2 That these made war with Be'ra king of Sod'om, and with Bir'sha king of Go-mor'rah, Shi'nab king of Ad'-mah, and Shem'e-ber king of Ze-boi'im, and the king of Be'la, which is Zo'-ar.

3 All these were joined together in the vale of Sid'dim, which is the salt sea.

4 Twelve years they served Ched-or-la'o-mer, and in the thirteenth year they rebelled.

5 And in the fourteenth year came Ched-or-la'o-mer, and the kings that were with him, and smote the Reph'a-ims in Ash'te-roth Kar-na'im, and the Zu'zims in Ham, and the E'mims in Sha'veh Kir-i-a-tha'im,

6 And the Ho'rites in the mount Se'ir, unto El–pa'ran, which is by the wilderness.

7 And they returned, and came to En-mish'-pat, which is Ka'desh, and smote all the country of the Am'a-lek-ites, and also the Am'or-ites, that dwelt in Haz'e-zon–ta'mar.

8 And there went out the king of Sod'om, and the king of Go-mor'rah, and the king of Ad'-mah, and the king of Ze-boi'im, and the king of Be'la (the same is Zo'ar;) and they joined battle with them in the vale of Sid'dim;

9 With Ched-or-la'o-mer the king of E'lam, and with Ti'dal king of nations, and Am'ra-phel king of Shi'nar, and A'ri-och king of El'la-sar; four kings with five.

10 And the vale of Sid'dim was full of slimepits; and the kings of Sod'om and Go-mor'rah fled, and fell there; and they that remained fled to the mountain.

11 And they took all the goods of Sod'om and Go-mor'rah, and all their victuals, and went their way.

12 And they took Lot, A'bram's brother's son, who dwelt in Sod'om, and his goods, and departed.

13 ¶ And there came one that had escaped, and told A'bram the He'brew; for he dwelt in the plain of Mam're the Am'or-ite, brother of Esh'col, and brother of A'ner: and these were confederate with A'bram.

14 And when A'bram heard that his brother was taken captive, he armed his trained servants, born in his own house, three hundred and eighteen, and pursued them unto Dan.

15 And he divided himself against them, he and his servants, by night, and smote them, and pursued them into Ho'bah, which is on the left hand of Da-mas'cus.

16 And he brought back all the goods, and also brought again his brother Lot, and his goods, and the women also, and the people.

17 ¶ And the king of Sod'om went out to meet him after his return from the slaughter of Ched-or-la'o-mer, and of the kings that were with him, at the valley of Sha'veh, which is the king's dale.

18 And Mel-chiz'e-dek king of Sa'lem brought forth bread and wine: and he was the priest of the most high God.

19 And he blessed him, and said, Blessed be A'bram of the most high God, possessor of heaven and earth:

20 And blessed be the most high God, which hath delivered thine enemies into thy hand. And he gave him tithes of all.

21 And the king of Sod'om said unto A'bram, Give me the persons, and take the goods to thyself.

22 And A'bram said to the king of Sod'om, I have lift up mine hand unto the LORD, the most high God, the possessor of heaven and earth,

23 That I will not take from a thread even to a shoelatchet, and that I will not take any thing that is thine, lest thou shouldest say, I have made A'bram rich:

24 Save only that which the young men have eaten, and the portion of the men which went with me, A'ner, Esh'col, and Mam're; let them take their portion.

15 AFTER these things the word of the LORD came unto A'bram in a vision, saying, Fear not, A'bram: I am thy shield, and thy exceeding great reward.

2 And A'bram said, Lord GOD, what wilt thou give me, seeing I go childless, and the steward of my house is this E-li-e'zer of Da-mas'cus?

3 And A'bram said, Behold, to me thou hast given no seed: and, lo, one born in my house is mine heir.

4 And, behold, the word of the LORD came unto him, saying, This shall not be thine heir; but he that shall come forth out of thine own bowels shall be thine heir.

5 And he brought him forth abroad, and said, Look now toward heaven, and tell the stars, if thou be able to number them: and he said unto him, So shall thy seed be.

6 And he believed in the LORD; and he counted it to him for righteousness.

7 And he said unto him, I am the LORD that brought thee out of Ur of the Chal'dees, to give thee this land to inherit it.

8 And he said, Lord GOD, whereby shall I know that I shall inherit it?

9 And he said unto him, Take me an heifer of three years old, and a she goat of three years old, and a ram of three years old, and a turtledove, and a young pigeon.

10 And he took unto him all these, and divided them in the midst, and laid each piece one against another: but the birds divided he not.

11 And when the fowls came down upon the carcases, A'bram drove them away.

12 And when the sun was going down, a deep sleep fell upon A'bram; and, lo, an horror of great darkness fell upon him.

13 And he said unto A'bram, Know of a surety that thy seed shall be a stranger in a land that is not theirs, and shall serve them; and they shall afflict them four hundred years;

14 And also that nation, whom they shall serve, will I judge: and afterward shall they come out with great substance.

15 And thou shalt go to thy fathers in peace; thou shalt be buried in a good old age.

16 But in the fourth generation they shall

come hither again: for the iniquity of the Am'or-ites *is* not yet full.

17 And it came to pass, that, when the sun went down, and it was dark, behold a smoking furnace, and a burning lamp that passed between those pieces.

18 In the same day the LORD made a covenant with A'bram, saying, Unto thy seed have I given this land, from the river of E'gypt unto the great river, the river Eu-phra'tes:

19 The Ken'ites, and the Ken'iz-zites, and the Kad'mon-ites,

20 And the Hit'tites, and the Per'iz-zites, and the Reph'a-ims,

21 And the Am'or-ites, and the Ca'naan-ites, and the Gir'ga-shites, and the Jeb'u-sites.

16 NOW Sa'rai A'bram's wife bare him no children: and she had an handmaid, an E-gyp'tian, whose name *was* Ha'gar.

2 And Sa'rai said unto A'bram, Behold now, the LORD hath restrained me from bearing: I pray thee, go in unto my maid; it may be that I may obtain children by her. And A'bram hearkened to the voice of Sa'rai.

3 And Sa'rai A'bram's wife took Ha'gar her maid the E-gyp'tian, after A'bram had dwelt ten years in the land of Ca'naan, and gave her to her husband A'bram to be his wife.

4 ¶ And he went in unto Ha'gar, and she conceived: and when she saw that she had conceived, her mistress was despised in her eyes.

5 And Sa'rai said unto A'bram, My wrong *be* upon thee: I have given my maid into thy bosom; and when she saw that she had conceived, I was despised in her eyes: the LORD judge between me and thee.

6 But A'bram said unto Sa'rai, Behold, thy maid *is* in thy hand; do to her as it pleaseth thee. And when Sa'rai dealt hardly with her, she fled from her face.

7 ¶ And the angel of the LORD found her by a fountain of water in the wilderness, by the fountain in the way to Shur.

8 And he said, Ha'gar, Sa'rai's maid, whence camest thou? and whither wilt thou go? And she said, I flee from the face of my mistress Sa'rai.

9 And the angel of the LORD said unto her, Return to thy mistress, and submit thyself under her hands.

10 And the angel of the LORD said unto her, I will multiply thy seed exceedingly, that it shall not be numbered for multitude.

11 And the angel of the LORD said unto her, Behold, thou *art* with child, and shalt bear a son, and shalt call his name Ish'ma-el; because the LORD hath heard thy affliction.

12 And he will be a wild man; his hand *will be* against every man, and every man's hand against him; and he shall dwell in the presence of all his brethren.

13 And she called the name of the LORD that spake unto her, Thou God seest me: for she said, Have I also here looked after him that seeth me?

14 Wherefore the well was called Be'er-la-hai'-roi; behold, *it is* between Ka'desh and Be'-red.

15 ¶ And Ha'gar bare A'bram a son: and A'-bram called his son's name, which Ha'gar bare, Ish'ma-el.

16 And A'bram *was* fourscore and six years old, when Ha'gar bare Ish'ma-el to A'bram.

17 AND when A'bram was ninety years old and nine, the LORD appeared to A'bram,.

and said unto him, I *am* the Almighty God; walk before me, and be thou perfect.

2 And I will make my covenant between me and thee, and will multiply thee exceedingly.

3 And A'bram fell on his face: and God talked with him, saying,

4 As for me, behold, my covenant *is* with thee, and thou shalt be a father of many nations.

5 Neither shall thy name any more be called A'bram, but thy name shall be A'bra-ham; for a father of many nations have I made thee.

6 And I will make thee exceeding fruitful, and I will make nations of thee, and kings shall come out of thee.

7 And I will establish my covenant between me and thee and thy seed after thee in their generations for an everlasting covenant, to be a God unto thee, and to thy seed after thee.

8 And I will give unto thee, and to thy seed after thee, the land wherein thou art a stranger, all the land of Ca'naan, for an everlasting possession; and I will be their God.

9 ¶ And God said unto A'bra-ham, Thou shalt keep my covenant therefore, thou, and thy seed after thee in their generations.

10 This *is* my covenant, which ye shall keep, between me and you and thy seed after thee; Every man child among you shall be circumcised.

11 And ye shall circumcise the flesh of your foreskin; and it shall be a token of the covenant betwixt me and you.

12 And he that is eight days old shall be circumcised among you, every man child in your generations, he that is born in the house, or bought with money of any stranger, which *is* not of thy seed.

13 He that is born in thy house, and he that is bought with thy money, must needs be circumcised: and my covenant shall be in your flesh for an everlasting covenant.

14 And the uncircumcised man child whose flesh of his foreskin is not circumcised, that soul shall be cut off from his people; he hath broken my covenant.

15 ¶ And God said unto A'bra-ham, As for Sa'rai thy wife, thou shalt not call her name Sa'-rai, but Sa'rah *shall* her name *be*.

16 And I will bless her, and give thee a son also of her: yea, I will bless her, and she shall be a *mother* of nations; kings of people shall be of her.

17 Then A'bra-ham fell upon his face, and laughed, and said in his heart, Shall a *child* be born unto him that is an hundred years old? and shall Sa'rah, that is ninety years old, bear?

18 And A'bra-ham said unto God, O that Ish'-ma-el might live before thee!

19 And God said, Sa'rah thy wife shall bear thee a son indeed; and thou shalt call his name I'saac: and I will establish my covenant with him for an everlasting covenant, *and* with his seed after him.

20 And as for Ish'ma-el, I have heard thee: Behold, I have blessed him, and will make him fruitful, and will multiply him exceedingly; twelve princes shall he beget, and I will make him a great nation.

21 But my covenant will I establish with I'-saac, which Sa'rah shall bear unto thee at this set time in the next year.

22 And he left off talking with him, and God went up from A'bra-ham.

23 ¶ And A'bra-ham took Ish'ma-el his son, and all that were born in his house, and all that were bought with his money, every male among

the men of A'bra-ham's house; and circumcised the flesh of their foreskin in the selfsame day, as God had said unto him.

24 And A'bra-ham *was* ninety years old and nine, when he was circumcised in the flesh of his foreskin.

25 And Ish'ma-el his son *was* thirteen years old, when he was circumcised in the flesh of his foreskin.

26 In the selfsame day was A'bra-ham circumcised, and Ish'ma-el his son.

27 And all the men of his house, born in the house, and bought with money of the stranger, were circumcised with him.

18 AND the Lord appeared unto him in the plains of Mam're: and he sat in the tent door in the heat of the day;

2 And he lift up his eyes and looked, and, lo, three men stood by him: and when he saw *them*, he ran to meet them from the tent door, and bowed himself toward the ground,

3 And said, My Lord, if now I have found favour in thy sight, pass not away, I pray thee, from thy servant:

4 Let a little water, I pray you, be fetched, and wash your feet, and rest yourselves under the tree:

5 And I will fetch a morsel of bread, and comfort ye your hearts; after that ye shall pass on: for therefore are ye come to your servant. And they said, So do, as thou hast said.

6 And A'bra-ham hastened into the tent unto Sa'rah, and said, Make ready quickly three measures of fine meal, knead *it*, and make cakes upon the hearth.

7 And A'bra-ham ran unto the herd, and fetcht a calf tender and good, and gave *it* unto a young man; and he hasted to dress it.

8 And he took butter, and milk, and the calf which he had dressed, and set *it* before them; and he stood by them under the tree, and they did eat.

9 ¶ And they said unto him, Where *is* Sa'rah thy wife? And he said, Behold, in the tent.

10 And he said, I will certainly return unto thee according to the time of life; and, lo, Sa'rah thy wife shall have a son. And Sa'rah heard *it* in the tent door, which *was* behind him.

11 Now A'bra-ham and Sa'rah *were* old *and* well stricken in age; *and* it ceased to be with Sa'rah after the manner of women.

12 Therefore Sa'rah laughed within herself, saying, After I am waxed old shall I have pleasure, my lord being old also?

13 And the Lord said unto A'bra-ham, Wherefore did Sa'rah laugh, saying, Shall I of a surety bear a child, which am old?

14 Is any thing too hard for the Lord? At the time appointed I will return unto thee, according to the time of life, and Sa'rah shall have a son.

15 Then Sarah denied, saying, I laughed not; for she was afraid. And he said, Nay; but thou didst laugh.

16 ¶ And the men rose up from thence, and looked toward Sod'om: and A'bra-ham went with them to bring them on the way.

17 And the Lord said, Shall I hide from A'bra-ham that thing which I do;

18 Seeing that A'bra-ham shall surely become a great and mighty nation, and all the nations of the earth shall be blessed in him?

19 For I know him, that he will command his children and his household after him, and they shall keep the way of the Lord, to do justice and judgment; that the Lord may bring upon

A'bra-ham that which he hath spoken of him.

20 And the Lord said, Because the cry of Sod'om and Go-mor'rah is great, and because their sin is very grievous;

21 I will go down now, and see whether they have done altogether according to the cry of it, which is come unto me; and if not, I will know.

22 And the men turned their faces from thence, and went toward Sod'om: but A'bra-ham stood yet before the Lord.

23 ¶ And A'bra-ham drew near, and said, Wilt thou also destroy the righteous with the wicked?

24 Peradventure there be fifty righteous within the city: wilt thou also destroy and not spare the place for the fifty righteous that *are* therein?

25 That be far from thee to do after this manner, to slay the righteous with the wicked: and that the righteous should be as the wicked, that be far from thee: Shall not the Judge of all the earth do right?

26 And the Lord said, If I find in Sod'om fifty righteous within the city, then I will spare all the place for their sakes.

27 And A'bra-ham answered and said, Behold now, I have taken upon me to speak unto the Lord, which *am but* dust and ashes:

28 Peradventure there shall lack five of the fifty righteous: wilt thou destroy all the city for *lack of* five? And he said, If I find there forty and five, I will not destroy *it*.

29 And he spake unto him yet again, and said, Peradventure there shall be forty found there. And he said, I will not do *it* for forty's sake.

30 And he said *unto him*, Oh let not the Lord be angry, and I will speak: Peradventure there shall thirty be found there. And he said, I will not do *it*, if I find thirty there.

31 And he said, Behold now, I have taken upon me to speak unto the Lord: Peradventure there shall be twenty found there. And he said, I will not destroy *it* for twenty's sake.

32 And he said, Oh let not the Lord be angry, and I will speak yet but this once: Peradventure ten shall be found there. And he said, I will not destroy *it* for ten's sake.

33 And the Lord went his way, as soon as he had left communing with A'bra-ham: and A'bra-ham returned unto his place.

19 AND there came two angels to Sod'om at even; and Lot sat in the gate of Sod'om: and Lot seeing *them* rose up to meet them; and he bowed himself with his face toward the ground;

2 And he said, Behold now, my lords, turn in, I pray you, into your servant's house, and tarry all night, and wash your feet, and ye shall rise up early, and go on your ways. And they said, Nay; but we will abide in the street all night.

3 And he pressed upon them greatly; and they turned in unto him, and entered into his house; and he made them a feast, and did bake unleavened bread, and they did eat.

4 ¶ But before they lay down, the men of the city, *even* the men of Sod'om, compassed the house round, both old and young, all the people from every quarter:

5 And they called unto Lot, and said unto him, Where *are* the men which came in to thee this night? bring them out unto us, that we may know them.

6 And Lot went out at the door unto them, and shut the door after him,

7 And said, I pray you, brethren, do not so wickedly.

8 Behold now, I have two daughters which have not known man; let me, I pray you, bring them out unto you, and do ye to them as is good in your eyes: only unto these men do nothing; for therefore came they under the shadow of my roof.

9 And they said, Stand back. And they said again, This one fellow came in to sojourn, and he will needs be a judge: now will we deal worse with thee, than with them. And they pressed sore upon the man, even Lot, and came near to break the door.

10 But the men put forth their hand, and pulled Lot into the house to them, and shut to the door.

11 And they smote the men that were at the door of the house with blindness, both small and great: so that they wearied themselves to find the door.

12 ¶ And the men said unto Lot, Hast thou here any besides? son in law, and thy sons, and thy daughters, and whatsoever thou hast in the city, bring them out of this place:

13 For we will destroy this place, because the cry of them is waxen great before the face of the Lord; and the Lord hath sent us to destroy it.

14 And Lot went out, and spake unto his sons in law, which married his daughters, and said, Up, get you out of this place; for the Lord will destroy this city. But he seemed as one that mocked unto his sons in law.

15 ¶ And when the morning arose, then the angels hastened Lot, saying, Arise, take thy wife, and thy two daughters, which are here; lest thou be consumed in the iniquity of the city.

16 And while he lingered, the men laid hold upon his hand, and upon the hand of his wife, and upon the hand of his two daughters; the Lord being merciful unto him: and they brought him forth, and set him without the city.

17 ¶ And it came to pass, when they had brought them forth abroad, that he said, Escape for thy life; look not behind thee, neither stay thou in all the plain; escape to the mountain, lest thou be consumed.

18 And Lot said unto them, Oh, not so, my Lord:

19 Behold now, thy servant hath found grace in thy sight, and thou hast magnified thy mercy, which thou has shewed unto me in saving my life; and I cannot escape to the mountain, lest some evil take me, and I die:

20 Behold now, this city is near to flee unto, and it is a little one: Oh, let me escape thither, (is it now a little one?) and my soul shall live.

21 And he said unto him, See, I have accepted thee concerning this thing also, that I will not overthrow this city, for the which thou hast spoken.

22 Haste thee, escape thither; for I cannot do any thing till thou be come thither. Therefore the name of the city was called Zo'ar.

23 ¶ The sun was risen upon the earth when Lot entered into Zo'ar.

24 Then the Lord rained upon Sod'om and upon Go-mor'rah brimstone and fire from the Lord out of heaven;

25 And he overthrew those cities, and all the plain, and all the inhabitants of the cities, and that which grew upon the ground.

26 ¶ But his wife looked back from behind him, and she became a pillar of salt.

27 ¶ And A'bra-ham gat up early in the morning to the place where he stood before the Lord:

28 And he looked toward Sod'om and Go-mor'rah, and toward all the land of the plain, and beheld, and, lo, the smoke of the country went up as the smoke of a furnace.

29 ¶ And it came to pass, when God destroyed the cities of the plain, that God remembered A'bra-ham, and sent Lot out of the midst of the overthrow, when he overthrew the cities in the which Lot dwelt.

30 ¶ And Lot went up out of Zo'ar, and dwelt in the mountain, and his two daughters with him; for he feared to dwell in Zo'ar: and he dwelt in a cave, he and his two daughters.

31 And the firstborn said unto the younger, Our father is old, and there is not a man in the earth to come in unto us after the manner of all the earth:

32 Come, let us make our father drink wine, and we will lie with him, that we may preserve seed of our father.

33 And they made their father drink wine that night: and the firstborn went in, and lay with her father; and he perceived not when she lay down, nor when she arose.

34 And it came to pass on the morrow, that the firstborn said unto the younger, Behold, I lay yesternight with my father: let us make him drink wine this night also; and go thou in, and lie with him, that we may preserve seed of our father.

35 And they made their father drink wine that night also: and the younger arose, and lay with him; and he perceived not when she lay down, nor when she arose.

36 Thus were both the daughters of Lot with child by their father.

37 And the firstborn bare a son, and called his name Mo'ab: the same is the father of the Mo'ab-ites unto this day.

38 And the younger, she also bare a son, and called his name Ben-am'mi: the same is the father of the children of Am'mon unto this day.

20 AND A'bra-ham journeyed from thence toward the south country, and dwelled between Ka'desh and Shur, and sojourned in Ge'rar.

2 And A'bra-ham said of Sa'rah his wife, She is my sister: and A-bim'e-lech king of Ge'rar sent, and took Sa'rah.

3 But God came to A-bim'e-lech in a dream by night, and said to him, Behold, thou art but a dead man, for the woman which thou hast taken; for she is a man's wife.

4 But A-bim'e-lech had not come near her: and he said, Lord, wilt thou slay also a righteous nation?

5 Said he not unto me, She is my sister? and she, even she herself said, He is my brother: in the integrity of my heart and innocency of my hands have I done this.

6 And God said unto him in a dream, Yea, I know that thou didst this in the integrity of thy heart; for I also withheld thee from sinning against me: therefore suffered I thee not to touch her.

7 Now therefore restore the man his wife; for he is a prophet, and he shall pray for thee, and thou shalt live: and if thou restore her not, know thou that thou shalt surely die, thou, and all that are thine.

8 Therefore A-bim'e-lech rose early in the morning, and called all his servants, and told all these things in their ears: and the men were sore afraid.

9 Then A-bim'e-lech called A'bra-ham, and said unto him, What hast thou done unto us? and what have I offended thee, that thou hast brought on me and on my kingdom a great sin? thou hast done deeds unto me that ought not to be done.

10 And A-bim'e-lech said unto A'bra-ham, What sawest thou, that thou hast done this thing?

11 And A'bra-ham said, Because I thought, Surely the fear of God is not in this place; and they will slay me for my wife's sake.

12 And yet indeed she is my sister; she is the daughter of my father, but not the daughter of my mother; and she became my wife.

13 And it came to pass, when God caused me to wander from my father's house, that I said unto her, This is thy kindness which thou shalt shew unto me; at every place whither we shall come, say of me, He is my brother.

14 And A-bim'e-lech took sheep, and oxen, and menservants, and womenservants, and gave them unto A'bra-ham, and restored him Sa'rah his wife.

15 And A-bim'e-lech said, Behold, my land is before thee: dwell where it pleaseth thee.

16 And unto Sa'rah he said, Behold, I have given my brother a thousand pieces of silver: behold, he is to thee a covering of the eyes, unto all that are with thee, and with all other: thus she was reproved.

17 ¶ So A'bra-ham prayed unto God: and God healed A-bim'e-lech, and his wife, and his maidservants; and they bare children.

18 For the LORD had fast closed up all the wombs of the house of A-bim'e-lech, because of Sa'rah A'bra-ham's wife.

21 AND the LORD visited Sa'rah as he had said, and the LORD did unto Sa'rah as he had spoken.

2 For Sa'rah conceived, and bare A'bra-ham a son in his old age, at the set time of which God had spoken to him.

3 And A'bra-ham called the name of his son that was born unto him, whom Sa'rah bare to him, I'saac.

4 And A'bra-ham circumcised his son I'saac being eight days old, as God had commanded him.

5 And A'bra-ham was an hundred years old, when his son I'saac was born unto him.

6 ¶ And Sa'rah said, God hath made me to laugh, so that all that hear will laugh with me.

7 And she said, Who would have said unto A'bra-ham, that Sa'rah should have given children suck? for I have born him a son in his old age.

8 And the child grew, and was weaned: and A'bra-ham made a great feast the same day that I'saac was weaned.

9 ¶ And Sa'rah saw the son of Ha'gar the E-gyp'tian, which she had born unto A'bra-ham, mocking.

10 Wherefore she said unto A'bra-ham, Cast out this bondwoman and her son: for the son of this bondwoman shall not be heir with my son, even with I'saac.

11 And the thing was very grievous in A'bra-ham's sight because of his son.

12 ¶ And God said unto A'bra-ham, Let it not be grievous in thy sight because of the lad, and because of thy bondwoman; in all that Sa'-rah hath said unto thee, hearken unto her voice; for in I'saac shall thy seed be called.

13 And also of the son of the bondwoman will I make a nation, because he is thy seed.

14 And A'bra-ham rose up early in the morning, and took bread, and a bottle of water, and gave it unto Ha'gar, putting it on her shoulder, and the child, and sent her away: and she departed, and wandered in the wilderness of Be'-er-she'ba.

15 And the water was spent in the bottle, and she cast the child under one of the shrubs.

16 And she went, and sat her down over against him a good way off, as it were a bow-shot: for she said, Let me not see the death of the child. And she sat over against him, and lift up her voice, and wept.

17 And God heard the voice of the lad; and the angel of God called to Ha'gar out of heaven, and said unto her, What aileth thee, Ha'gar? fear not; for God hath heard the voice of the lad where he is.

18 Arise, lift up the lad, and hold him in thine hand; for I will make him a great nation.

19 And God opened her eyes, and she saw a well of water; and she went, and filled the bottle with water, and gave the lad drink.

20 And God was with the lad; and he grew, and dwelt in the wilderness, and became an archer.

21 And he dwelt in the wilderness of Pa'ran: and his mother took him a wife out of the land of E'gypt.

22 ¶ And it came to pass at that time, that A-bim'e-lech and Phi'chol the chief captain of his host spake unto A'bra-ham, saying, God is with thee in all that thou doest:

23 Now therefore swear unto me here by God that thou wilt not deal falsely with me, nor with my son, nor with my son's son: but according to the kindness that I have done unto thee, thou shalt do unto me, and to the land wherein thou hast sojourned.

24 And A'bra-ham said, I will swear.

25 And A'bra-ham reproved A-bim'e-lech because of a well of water, which A-bim'e-lech's servants had violently taken away.

26 And A-bim'e-lech said, I wot not who hath done this thing: neither didst thou tell me, neither yet heard I of it, but to day.

27 And A'bra-ham took sheep and oxen, and gave them unto A-bim'e-lech; and both of them made a covenant.

28 And A'bra-ham set seven ewe lambs of the flock by themselves.

29 And A-bim'e-lech said unto A'bra-ham, What mean these seven ewe lambs which thou hast set by themselves?

30 And he said, For these seven ewe lambs shalt thou take of my hand, that they may be a witness unto me, that I have digged this well.

31 Wherefore he called that place Be'er-she'-ba; because there they sware both of them.

32 Thus they made a covenant at Be'er-she'-ba: then A-bim'e-lech rose up, and Phi'chol the chief captain of his host, and they returned into the land of the Phi-lis'tines.

33 ¶ And A'bra-ham planted a grove in Be'-er-she'ba, and called there on the name of the LORD, the everlasting God.

34 And A'bra-ham sojourned in the Phi-lis'-tines' land many days.

22 AND it came to pass after these things, that God did tempt A'bra-ham, and said unto him, A'bra-ham: and he said, Behold, here I am.

2 And he said, Take now thy son, thine only son I'saac, whom thou lovest, and get thee into the land of Mo-ri'ah; and offer him there for a

burnt offering upon one of the mountains which I will tell thee of.

3 ¶ And A'bra-ham rose up early in the morning, and saddled his ass, and took two of his young men with him, and I'saac his son, and clave the wood for the burnt offering, and rose up, and went unto the place of which God had told him.

4 Then on the third day A'bra-ham lifted up his eyes, and saw the place afar off.

5 And A'bra-ham said unto his young men, Abide ye here with the ass; and I and the lad will go yonder and worship, and come again to you.

6 And A'bra-ham took the wood of the burnt offering, and laid it upon I'saac his son; and he took the fire in his hand, and a knife; and they went both of them together.

7 And I'saac spake unto A'bra-ham his father, and said, My father: and he said, Here am I, my son. And he said, Behold the fire and the wood: but where is the lamb for a burnt offering?

8 And A'bra-ham said, My son, God will provide himself a lamb for a burnt offering: so they went both of them together.

9 And they came to the place which God had told him of; and A'bra-ham built an altar there, and laid the wood in order, and bound I'saac his son, and laid him on the altar upon the wood.

10 And A'bra-ham stretched forth his hand, and took the knife to slay his son.

11 And the angel of the LORD called unto him out of heaven, and said, A'bra-ham, A'bra-ham: and he said, Here am I.

12 And he said, Lay not thine hand upon the lad, neither do thou any thing unto him: for now I know that thou fearest God, seeing thou hast not withheld thy son, thine only son from me.

13 And Abraham lifted up his eyes, and looked, and behold behind him a ram caught in a thicket by his horns: and A'bra-ham went and took the ram, and offered him up for a burnt offering in the stead of his son.

14 And A'bra-ham called the name of that place Je-ho'vah–ji'reh: as it is said to this day, In the mount of the LORD it shall be seen.

15 ¶ And the angel of the LORD called unto A'bra-ham out of heaven the second time,

16 And said, By myself have I sworn, saith the LORD, for because thou hast done this thing, and hast not withheld thy son, thine only son:

17 That in blessing I will bless thee, and in multiplying I will multiply thy seed as the stars of the heaven, and as the sand which is upon the sea shore; and thy seed shall possess the gate of his enemies;

18 And in thy seed shall all the nations of the earth be blessed; because thou hast obeyed my voice.

19 So A'bra-ham returned unto his young men, and they rose up and went together to Be'-er-she'ba; and A'bra-ham dwelt at Be'er-she'-ba.

20 ¶ And it came to pass after these things, that it was told A'bra-ham, saying, Behold, Mil'-cah, she hath also born children unto thy brother Na'hor;

21 Huz his firstborn, and Buz his brother, and Ke-mu'el the father of A'ram,

22 And Che'sed, and Ha'zo, and Pil'dash, and Jid'laph, and Beth-u'el.

23 And Beth-u'el begat Re-bek'ah: these eight Mil'cah did bear to Na'hor, A'bra-ham's brother.

24 And his concubine, whose name was Reu'mah, she bare also Te'bah, and Ga'ham, and Tha'hash, and Ma'a-chah.

23 AND Sa'rah was an hundred and seven and twenty years old: these were the years of the life of Sa'rah.

2 And Sa'rah died in Kir'jath-ar'ba; the same is He'bron in the land of Ca'naan: and A'bra-ham came to mourn for Sa'rah, and to weep for her.

3 ¶ And A'bra-ham stood up from before his dead, and spake unto the sons of Heth, saying,

4 I am a stranger and a sojourner with you: give me a possession of a buryingplace with you, that I may bury my dead out of my sight.

5 And the children of Heth answered A'bra-ham, saying unto him,

6 Hear us, my lord: thou art a mighty prince among us: in the choice of our sepulchres bury thy dead; none of us shall withhold from thee his sepulchre, but that thou mayest bury thy dead.

7 And A'bra-ham stood up, and bowed himself to the people of the land, even to the children of Heth.

8 And he communed with them, saying, If it be your mind that I should bury my dead out of my sight; hear me, and intreat for me to E'-phron the son of Zo'har,

9 That he may give me the cave of Mach-pe'-lah, which he hath, which is in the end of his field; for as much money as it is worth he shall give it me for a possession of a buryingplace amongst you.

10 And E'phron dwelt among the children of Heth: and E'phron the Hit'tite answered A'bra-ham in the audience of the children of Heth, even of all that went in at the gate of his city, saying,

11 Nay, my lord, hear me: the field give I thee, and the cave that is therein, I give it thee; in the presence of the sons of my people give I it thee: bury thy dead.

12 And A'bra-ham bowed down himself before the people of the land.

13 And he spake unto E'phron in the audience of the people of the land, saying, But if thou wilt give it, I pray thee, hear me: I will give thee money for the field; take it of me, and I will bury my dead there.

14 And E'phron answered A'bra-ham, saying unto him,

15 My lord, hearken unto me: the land is worth four hundred shekels of silver; what is that betwixt me and thee? bury therefore thy dead.

16 And A'bra-ham hearkened unto E'phron; and A'bra-ham weighed to E'phron the silver, which he had named in the audience of the sons of Heth, four hundred shekels of silver, current money with the merchant.

17 ¶ And the field of E'phron, which was in Mach-pe'lah, which was before Mam're, the field, and the cave which was therein, and all the trees that were in the field, that were in all the borders round about, were made sure

18 Unto A'bra-ham for a possession in the presence of the children of Heth, before all that went in at the gate of his city.

19 And after this, A'bra-ham buried Sa'rah his wife in the cave of the field of Mach-pe'lah before Mam're: the same is He'bron in the land of Ca'naan.

20 And the field, and the cave that is therein, were made sure unto A'bra-ham for a possession of a buryingplace by the sons of Heth.

24 AND A'bra-ham was old, *and* well stricken in age: and the LORD had blessed A'bra-ham in all things.

2 And A'bra-ham said unto his eldest servant of his house, that ruled over all that he had, Put, I pray thee, thy hand under my thigh:

3 And I will make thee swear by the LORD, the God of heaven, and the God of the earth, that thou shalt not take a wife unto my son of the daughters of the Ca'naan-ites, among whom I dwell:

4 But thou shalt go unto my country, and to my kindred, and take a wife unto my son I'saac.

5 And the servant said unto him, Peradventure the woman will not be willing to follow me unto this land: must I needs bring thy son again unto the land from whence thou camest?

6 And A'bra-ham said unto him, Beware thou that thou bring not my son thither again.

7 ¶ The LORD God of heaven, which took me from my father's house, and from the land of my kindred, and which spake unto me, and that sware unto me, saying, Unto thy seed will I give this land; he shall send his angel before thee, and thou shalt take a wife unto my son from thence.

8 And if the woman will not be willing to follow thee, then thou shalt be clear from this my oath: only bring not my son thither again.

9 And the servant put his hand under the thigh of A'bra-ham his master, and sware to him concerning that matter.

10 ¶ And the servant took ten camels of the camels of his master, and departed; for all the goods of his master *were* in his hand: and he arose, and went to Mes-o-po-ta'mi-a, unto the city of Na'hor.

11 And he made his camels to kneel down without the city by a well of water at the time of the evening, *even* the time that women go out to draw *water*.

12 And he said, O LORD God of my master A'bra-ham, I pray thee, send me good speed this day, and shew kindness unto my master A'-bra-ham.

13 Behold, I stand *here* by the well of water; and the daughters of the men of the city come out to draw water:

14 And let it come to pass, that the damsel to whom I shall say, Let down thy pitcher, I pray thee, that I may drink; and she shall say, Drink, and I will give thy camels drink also: *let the same be* she *that* thou hast appointed for thy servant I'saac; and thereby shall I know that thou hast shewed kindness unto my master.

15 ¶ And it came to pass, before he had done speaking, that, behold, Re-bek'ah came out, who was born to Beth-u'el, son of Mil'cah, the wife of Na'hor, A'bra-ham's brother, with her pitcher upon her shoulder.

16 And the damsel *was* very fair to look upon, a virgin, neither had any man known her: and she went down to the well, and filled her pitcher, and came up.

17 And the servant ran to meet her, and said, Let me, I pray thee, drink a little water of thy pitcher.

18 And she said, Drink, my lord: and she hasted, and let down her pitcher upon her hand, and gave him drink.

19 And when she had done giving him drink, she said, I will draw *water* for thy camels also, until they have done drinking.

20 And she hasted, and emptied her pitcher into the trough, and ran again unto the well to draw *water*, and drew for all his camels.

21 And the man wondering at her held his peace, to wit whether the LORD had made his journey prosperous or not.

22 And it came to pass, as the camels had done drinking, that the man took a golden earring of half a shekel weight, and two bracelets for her hands of ten *shekels* weight of gold;

23 And said, Whose daughter *art* thou? tell me, I pray thee: is there room *in* thy father's house for us to lodge in?

24 And she said unto him, I *am* the daughter of Beth-u'el the son of Mil'cah, which she bare unto Na'hor.

25 She said moreover unto him, We have both straw and provender enough, and room to lodge in.

26 And the man bowed down his head, and worshipped the LORD.

27 And he said, Blessed *be* the LORD God of my master A'bra-ham, who hath not left destitute my master of his mercy and his truth: I *being* in the way, the LORD led me to the house of my master's brethren.

28 And the damsel ran, and told *them* of her mother's house these things.

29 ¶ And Re-bek'ah had a brother, and his name *was* La'ban: and La'ban ran out unto the man, unto the well.

30 And it came to pass, when he saw the earring and bracelets upon his sister's hands, and when he heard the words of Re-bek'ah his sister, saying, Thus spake the man unto me; that he came unto the man; and, behold, he stood by the camels at the well.

31 And he said, Come in, thou blessed of the LORD; wherefore standest thou without? for I have prepared the house, and room for the camels.

32 ¶ And the man came into the house: and he ungirded his camels, and gave straw and provender for the camels, and water to wash his feet, and the men's feet that *were* with him.

33 And there was set *meat* before him to eat: but he said, I will not eat, until I have told mine errand. And he said, Speak on.

34 And he said, I *am* A'bra-ham's servant.

35 And the LORD hath blessed my master greatly; and he is become great: and he hath given him flocks, and herds, and silver, and gold, and menservants, and maidservants, and camels, and asses.

36 And Sa'rah my master's wife bare a son to my master when she was old: and unto him hath he given all that he hath.

37 And my master made me swear, saying, Thou shalt not take a wife to my son of the daughters of the Ca'naan-ites, in whose land I dwell:

38 But thou shalt go unto my father's house, and to my kindred, and take a wife unto my son.

39 And I said unto my master, Peradventure the woman will not follow me.

40 And he said unto me, The LORD, before whom I walk, will send his angel with thee, and prosper thy way; and thou shalt take a wife for my son of my kindred, and of my father's house:

41 Then shalt thou be clear from *this* my oath, when thou comest to my kindred; and if they give not thee *one*, thou shalt be clear from my oath.

42 And I came this day unto the well, and said, O LORD God of my master A'bra-ham, if now thou do prosper my way which I go:

43 Behold, I stand by the well of water; and it shall come to pass, that when the virgin cometh forth to draw *water*, and I say to her, Give me, I

pray thee, a little water of thy pitcher to drink;

44 And she say to me, Both drink thou, and I will also draw for thy camels: *let the same be* the woman whom the LORD hath appointed out for my master's son.

45 And before I had done speaking in mine heart, behold, Re-bek'ah came forth with her pitcher on her shoulder; and she went down unto the well, and drew *water:* and I said unto her, Let me drink, I pray thee.

46 And she made haste, and let down her pitcher from her *shoulder,* and said, Drink, and I will give thy camels drink also: so I drank, and she made the camels drink also.

47 And I asked her, and said, Whose daughter *art* thou? And she said, The daughter of Beth-u'el, Na'hor's son, whom Mil'cah bare unto him: and I put the earring upon her face, and the bracelets upon her hands.

48 And I bowed down my head, and worshipped the LORD, and blessed the LORD God of my master A'bra-ham, which had led me in the right way to take my master's brother's daughter unto his son.

49 And now if ye will deal kindly and truly with my master, tell me: and if not, tell me; that I may turn to the right hand, or to the left.

50 Then La'ban and Beth-u'el answered and said, The thing proceedeth from the LORD: we cannot speak unto thee bad or good.

51 Behold, Re-bek'ah *is* before thee, take *her,* and go, and let her be thy master's son's wife, as the LORD hath spoken.

52 And it came to pass, that, when A'bra-ham's servant heard their words, he worshipped the LORD, *bowing himself* to the earth.

53 And the servant brought forth jewels of silver, and jewels of gold, and raiment, and gave *them* to Re-bek'ah: he gave also to her brother and to her mother precious things.

54 And they did eat and drink, he and the men that *were* with him, and tarried all night; and they rose up in the morning, and he said, Send me away unto my master.

55 And her brother and her mother said, Let the damsel abide with us a *few* days, at the least ten; after that she shall go.

56 And he said unto them, Hinder me not, seeing the LORD hath prospered my way; send me away that I may go to my master.

57 And they said, We will call the damsel, and enquire at her mouth.

58 And they called Re-bek'ah, and said unto her, Wilt thou go with this man? And she said, I will go.

59 And they sent away Re-bek'ah their sister, and her nurse, and A'bra-ham's servant, and his men.

60 And they blessed Re-bek'ah, and said unto her, Thou *art* our sister, be thou *the mother* of thousands of millions, and let thy seed possess the gate of those which hate them.

61 ¶ And Re-bek'ah arose, and her damsels, and they rode upon the camels, and followed the man: and the servant took Re-bek'ah, and went his way.

62 And I'saac came from the way of the well La-hai'roi; for he dwelt in the south country.

63 And I'saac went out to meditate in the field at the eventide: and he lifted up his eyes, and saw, and, behold, the camels *were* coming.

64 And Re-bek'ah lifted up her eyes, and when she saw I'saac, she lighted off the camel.

65 For she *had* said unto the servant, What man *is* this that walketh in the field to meet us? And the servant *had* said, It *is* my master: therefore she took a veil, and covered herself.

66 And the servant told I'saac all things that he had done.

67 And I'saac brought her into his mother Sa'rah's tent, and took Re-bek'ah, and she became his wife; and he loved her: and I'saac was comforted after his mother's *death.*

25 THEN again A'bra-ham took a wife, and her name *was* Ke-tu'rah.

2 And she bare him Zim'ran, and Jok'shan, and Me'dan, and Mid'i-an, and Ish'bak, and Shu'ah.

3 And Jok'shan begat She'ba, and De'dan. And the sons of De'dan were As-shu'rim, and Le-tu'shim, and Le-um'mim.

4 And the sons of Mid'i-an; E'phah, and E'pher, and Ha'noch, and A-bi'dah, and El'da-ah. All these *were* the children of Ke-tu'rah.

5 ¶ And A'bra-ham gave all that he had unto I'saac.

6 But unto the sons of the concubines, which A'bra-ham had, A'bra-ham gave gifts, and sent them away from I'saac his son, while he yet lived, eastward, unto the east country.

7 And these *are* the days of the years of A'bra-ham's life which he lived, an hundred threescore and fifteen years.

8 Then A'bra-ham gave up the ghost, and died in a good old age, an old man, and full of *years;* and was gathered to his people.

9 And his sons I'saac and Ish'ma-el buried him in the cave of Mach-pe'lah, in the field of E'phron the son of Zo'har the Hit'tite, which *is* before Mam're;

10 The field which A'bra-ham purchased of the sons of Heth: there was A'bra-ham buried, and Sa'rah his wife.

11 ¶ And it came to pass after the death of A'bra-ham, that God blessed his son I'saac; and I'saac dwelt by the well La-hai'roi.

12 ¶ Now these *are* the generations of Ish'ma-el, A'bra-ham's son, whom Ha'gar the E-gyp'tian, Sa'rah's handmaid, bare unto A'bra-ham:

13 And these *are* the names of the sons of Ish'ma-el, by their names, according to their generations: the firstborn of Ish'ma-el, Ne-ba'joth, and Ke'dar, and Ad'be-el, and Mib'sam,

14 And Mish'ma, and Du'mah, and Mas'sa,

15 Ha'dar, and Te'ma, Je'tur, Na'phish, and Ked'e-mah:

16 These *are* the sons of Ish'ma-el, and these *are* their names, by their towns, and by their castles; twelve princes according to their nations.

17 And these *are* the years of the life of Ish'ma-el, an hundred and thirty and seven years: and he gave up the ghost and died; and was gathered unto his people.

18 And they dwelt from Hav'i-lah unto Shur, that *is* before E'gypt, as thou goest toward As-syr'i-a: *and* he died in the presence of all his brethren.

19 ¶ And these *are* the generations of I'saac, A'bra-ham's son: A'bra-ham begat I'saac:

20 And I'saac was forty years old when he took Re-bek'ah to wife, the daughter of Beth-u'el the Syr'i-an of Pa'dan-a'ram, the sister to La'ban the Syr'i-an.

21 And I'saac intreated the LORD for his wife, because she *was* barren: and the LORD was intreated of him, and Re-bek'ah his wife conceived.

22 And the children struggled together within her; and she said, If *it be* so, why *am* I thus? And she went to enquire of the LORD.

23 And the LORD said unto her, Two nations

are in thy womb, and two manner of people shall be separated from thy bowels: and *the one* people shall be stronger than *the other* people; and the elder shall serve the younger.

24 ¶ And when her days to be delivered were fulfilled, behold, *there were* twins in her womb.

25 And the first came out red, all over like an hairy garment; and they called his name E'sau.

26 And after that came his brother out, and his hand took hold on E'sau's heel; and his name was called Ja'cob: and I'saac *was* threescore years old when she bare them.

27 And the boys grew: and E'sau was a cunning hunter, a man of the field; and Ja'cob *was* a plain man, dwelling in tents.

28 And I'saac loved E'sau, because he did eat of *his* venison: but Re-bek'ah loved Ja'cob.

29 ¶ And Ja'cob sod pottage: and E'sau came from the field, and he *was* faint:

30 And E'sau said to Ja'cob, Feed me, I pray thee, with that same red *pottage;* for I *am* faint: therefore was his name called E'dom.

31 And Ja'cob said, Sell me this day thy birthright.

32 And E'sau said, Behold, I *am* at the point to die: and what profit shall this birthright do to me?

33 And Ja'cob said, Swear to me this day; and he sware unto him: and he sold his birthright unto Ja'cob.

34 Then Ja'cob gave E'sau bread and pottage of lentiles; and he did eat and drink, and rose up, and went his way: thus E'sau despised *his* birthright.

26 AND there was a famine in the land, beside the first famine that was in the days of A'bra-ham. And I'saac went unto A-bim'e-lech king of the Phi-lis'tines unto Ge'rar.

2 And the LORD appeared unto him, and said, Go not down into E'gypt; dwell in the land which I shall tell thee of:

3 Sojourn in this land, and I will be with thee, and will bless thee; for unto thee, and unto thy seed, I will give all these countries, and I will perform the oath which I sware unto A'bra-ham thy father;

4 And I will make thy seed to multiply as the stars of heaven, and will give unto thy seed all these countries; and in thy seed shall all the nations of the earth be blessed;

5 Because that A'bra-ham obeyed my voice, and kept my charge, my commandments, my statutes, and my laws.

6 ¶ And I'saac dwelt in Ge'rar:

7 And the men of the place asked *him* of his wife; and he said, She *is* my sister: for he feared to say, *She is* my wife; lest, *said he,* the men of the place should kill me for Re-bek'ah; because she *was* fair to look upon.

8 And it came to pass, when he had been there a long time, that A-bim'e-lech king of the Phi-lis'tines looked out at a window, and saw, and, behold, I'saac *was* sporting with Re-bek'ah his wife.

9 And A-bim'e-lech called I'saac, and said, Behold, of a surety she *is* thy wife: and how saidst thou, She *is* my sister? And I'saac said unto him, Because I said, Lest I die for her.

10 And A-bim'e-lech said, What *is* this thou hast done unto us? one of the people might lightly have lien with thy wife, and thou shouldest have brought guiltiness upon us.

11 And A-bim'e-lech charged all *his* people, saying, He that toucheth this man or his wife shall surely be put to death.

12 Then I'saac sowed in that land, and received in the same year an hundredfold: and the LORD blessed him.

13 And the man waxed great, and went forward, and grew until he became very great:

14 For he had possession of flocks, and possession of herds, and great store of servants: and the Phi-lis'tines envied him.

15 For all the wells which his father's servants had digged in the days of A'bra-ham his father, the Phi-lis'tines had stopped them, and filled them with earth.

16 And A-bim'e-lech said unto I'saac, Go from us; for thou art much mightier than we.

17 ¶ And I'saac departed thence, and pitched his tent in the valley of Ge'rar, and dwelt there.

18 And I'saac digged again the wells of water, which they had digged in the days of A'bra-ham his father; for the Phi-lis'tines had stopped them after the death of A'bra-ham: and he called their names after the names by which his father had called them.

19 And Isaac's servants digged in the valley, and found there a well of springing water.

20 And the herdmen of Ge'rar did strive with Isaac's herdmen, saying, The water *is* ours: and he called the name of the well E'sek; because they strove with him.

21 And they digged another well, and strove for that also: and he called the name of it Sit'-nah.

22 And he removed from thence, and digged another well; and for that they strove not: and he called the name of it Re-ho'both; and he said, For now the LORD hath made room for us, and we shall be fruitful in the land.

23 And he went up from thence to Be'er-she'ba.

24 And the LORD appeared unto him the same night, and said, I *am* the God of A'bra-ham thy father: fear not, for I *am* with thee, and will bless thee, and multiply thy seed for my servant A'bra-ham's sake.

25 And he builded an altar there, and called upon the name of the LORD, and pitched his tent there: and there Isaac's servants digged a well.

26 ¶ Then A-bim'e-lech went to him from Ge'rar, and A-huz'zath one of his friends, and Phi'chol the chief captain of his army.

27 And I'saac said unto them, Wherefore come ye to me, seeing ye hate me, and have sent me away from you?

28 And they said, We saw certainly that the LORD was with thee: and we said, Let there be now an oath betwixt us, *even* betwixt us and thee, and let us make a covenant with thee;

29 That thou wilt do us no hurt, as we have not touched thee, and as we have done unto thee nothing but good, and have sent thee away in peace: thou *art* now the blessed of the LORD.

30 And he made them a feast, and they did eat and drink.

31 And they rose up betimes in the morning, and sware one to another: and I'saac sent them away, and they departed from him in peace.

32 And it came to pass the same day, that Isaac's servants came, and told him concerning the well which they had digged, and said unto him, We have found water.

33 And he called it She'bah: therefore the name of the city *is* Be'er-she'ba unto this day.

34 ¶ And E'sau was forty years old when he took to wife Ju'dith the daughter of Be-e'ri the Hit'tite, and Bash'e-math the daughter of E'lon the Hit'tite:

35 Which were a grief of mind unto I'saac and to Re-bek'ah.

27 AND it came to pass, that when I'saac was old, and his eyes were dim, so that he could not see, he called E'sau his eldest son, and said unto him, My son: and he said unto him, Behold, here am I.

2 And he said, Behold now, I am old, I know not the day of my death:

3 Now therefore take, I pray thee, thy weapons, thy quiver and thy bow, and go out to the field, and take me some venison;

4 And make me savoury meat, such as I love, and bring it to me, that I may eat; that my soul may bless thee before I die.

5 And Re-bek'ah heard when I'saac spake to E'sau his son. And E'sau went to the field to hunt for venison, and to bring it.

6 ¶ And Re-bek'ah spake unto Ja'cob her son, saying, Behold, I heard thy father speak unto E'sau thy brother, saying,

7 Bring me venison, and make me savoury meat, that I may eat, and bless thee before the LORD before my death.

8 Now therefore, my son, obey my voice according to that which I command thee.

9 Go now to the flock, and fetch me from thence two good kids of the goats; and I will make them savoury meat for thy father, such as he loveth:

10 And thou shalt bring it to thy father, that he may eat, and that he may bless thee before his death.

11 And Ja'cob said to Re-bek'ah his mother, Behold, E'sau my brother is a hairy man, and I am a smooth man:

12 My father peradventure will feel me, and I shall seem to him as a deceiver; and I shall bring a curse upon me, and not a blessing.

13 And his mother said unto him, Upon me be thy curse, my son: only obey my voice, and go fetch me them.

14 And he went, and fetched, and brought them to his mother: and his mother made savoury meat, such as his father loved.

15 And Re-bek'ah took goodly raiment of her eldest son E'sau, which were with her in the house, and put them upon Ja'cob her younger son:

16 And she put the skins of the kids of the goats upon his hands, and upon the smooth of his neck:

17 And she gave the savoury meat and the bread, which she had prepared, into the hand of her son Ja'cob.

18 ¶ And he came unto his father, and said, My father: and he said, Here am I; who art thou, my son?

19 And Ja'cob said unto his father, I am E'sau thy firstborn; I have done according as thou badest me: arise, I pray thee, sit and eat of my venison, that thy soul may bless me.

20 And I'saac said unto his son, How is it that thou hast found it so quickly, my son? And he said, Because the LORD thy God brought it to me.

21 And I'saac said unto Ja'cob, Come near, I pray thee, that I may feel thee, my son, whether thou be my very son E'sau or not.

22 And Ja'cob went near unto I'saac his father; and he felt him, and said, The voice is Ja'cob's voice, but the hands are the hands of E'sau.

23 And he discerned him not, because his hands were hairy, as his brother E'sau's hands: so he blessed him.

24 And he said, Art thou my very son E'sau? And he said, I am.

25 And he said, Bring it near to me, and I will eat of my son's venison, that my soul may bless thee. And he brought it near to him, and he did eat: and he brought him wine, and he drank.

26 And his father I'saac said unto him, Come near now, and kiss me, my son.

27 And he came near, and kissed him: and he smelled the smell of his raiment, and blessed him, and said, See, the smell of my son is as the smell of a field which the LORD hath blessed:

28 Therefore God give thee of the dew of heaven, and the fatness of the earth, and plenty of corn and wine:

29 Let people serve thee, and nations bow down to thee: be lord over thy brethren, and let thy mother's sons bow down to thee: cursed be every one that curseth thee, and blessed be he that blesseth thee.

30 ¶ And it came to pass, as soon as I'saac had made an end of blessing Ja'cob, and Ja'cob was yet scarce gone out from the presence of I'saac his father, that E'sau his brother came in from his hunting.

31 And he also had made savoury meat, and brought it unto his father, and said unto his father, Let my father arise, and eat of his son's venison, that thy soul may bless me.

32 And I'saac his father said unto him, Who art thou? And he said, I am thy son, thy firstborn E'sau.

33 And I'saac trembled very exceedingly, and said, Who? where is he that hath taken venison, and brought it me, and I have eaten of all before thou camest, and have blessed him? yea, and he shall be blessed.

34 And when E'sau heard the words of his father, he cried with a great and exceeding bitter cry, and said unto his father, Bless me, even me also, O my father.

35 And he said, Thy brother came with subtilty, and hath taken away thy blessing.

36 And he said, Is not he rightly named Ja'cob? for he hath supplanted me these two times: he took away my birthright; and, behold, now he hath taken away my blessing. And he said, Hast thou not reserved a blessing for me?

37 And I'saac answered and said unto E'sau, Behold, I have made him thy lord, and all his brethren have I given to him for servants; and with corn and wine have I sustained him: and what shall I do now unto thee, my son?

38 And E'sau said unto his father, Hast thou but one blessing, my father? bless me, even me also, O my father. And E'sau lifted up his voice, and wept.

39 And I'saac his father answered and said unto him, Behold, thy dwelling shall be the fatness of the earth, and of the dew of heaven from above;

40 And by thy sword shalt thou live, and shalt serve thy brother; and it shall come to pass when thou shalt have the dominion, that thou shalt break his yoke from off thy neck.

41 ¶ And E'sau hated Ja'cob because of the blessing wherewith his father blessed him: and E'sau said in his heart, The days of mourning for my father are at hand; then will I slay my brother Ja'cob.

42 And these words of E'sau her elder son were told to Re-bek'ah: and she sent and called Ja'cob her younger son, and said unto him, Behold, thy brother E'sau, as touching thee, doth comfort himself, purposing to kill thee.

43 Now therefore, my son, obey my voice;

and arise, flee thou to La'ban my brother to Ha'-ran;

44 And tarry with him a few days, until thy brother's fury turn away;

45 Until thy brother's anger turn away from thee, and he forget *that* which thou hast done to him: then I will send, and fetch thee from thence: why should I be deprived also of you both in one day?

46 And Re-bek'ah said to I'saac, I am weary of my life because of the daughters of Heth: if Ja'cob take a wife of the daughters of Heth, such as these *which are* of the daughters of the land, what good shall my life do me?

28 AND I'saac called Ja'cob, and blessed him, and charged him, and said unto him, Thou shalt not take a wife of the daughters of Ca'naan.

2 Arise, go to Pa'dan-a'ram, to the house of Beth-u'el thy mother's father; and take thee a wife from thence of the daughters of La'ban thy mother's brother.

3 And God Almighty bless thee, and make thee fruitful, and multiply thee, that thou mayest be a multitude of people;

4 And give thee the blessing of A'bra-ham, to thee, and to thy seed with thee; that thou mayest inherit the land wherein thou art a stranger, which God gave unto A'bra-ham.

5 And I'saac sent away Ja'cob: and he went to Pa'dan-a'ram unto La'ban, son of Beth-u'el the Syr'i-an, the brother of Re-bek'ah, Ja'cob's and E'sau's mother.

6 ¶ When E'sau saw that I'saac had blessed Ja'cob, and sent him away to Pa'dan-a'ram, to take him a wife from thence; and that as he blessed him he gave him a charge, saying, Thou shalt not take a wife of the daughters of Ca'-naan;

7 And that Ja'cob obeyed his father and his mother, and was gone to Pa'dan-a'ram;

8 And E'sau seeing that the daughters of Ca'-naan pleased not I'saac his father;

9 Then went E'sau unto Ish'ma-el, and took unto the wives which he had Ma'ha-lath the daughter of Ish'ma-el A'bra-ham's son, the sister of Ne-ba'joth, to be his wife.

10 ¶ And Ja'cob went out from Be'er-she'ba, and went toward Ha'ran.

11 And he lighted upon a certain place, and tarried there all night, because the sun was set; and he took of the stones of that place, and put *them for* his pillows, and lay down in that place to sleep.

12 And he dreamed, and behold a ladder set up on the earth, and the top of it reached to heaven: and behold the angels of God ascending and descending on it.

13 And, behold, the LORD stood above it, and said, I am the LORD God of A'bra-ham thy father, and the God of I'saac: the land whereon thou liest, to thee will I give it, and to thy seed;

14 And thy seed shall be as the dust of the earth, and thou shalt spread abroad to the west, and to the east, and to the north, and to the south: and in thee and in thy seed shall all the families of the earth be blessed.

15 And, behold, I am with thee, and will keep thee in all *places* whither thou goest, and will bring thee again into this land; for I will not leave thee, until I have done *that* which I have spoken to thee of.

16 And Ja'cob awaked out of his sleep, and he said, Surely the LORD is in this place; and I knew *it* not.

17 And he was afraid, and said, How dreadful *is* this place! this *is* none other but the house of God, and this *is* the gate of heaven.

18 And Ja'cob rose up early in the morning, and took the stone that he had put *for* his pillows, and set up *for* a pillar, and poured oil upon the top of it.

19 And he called the name of that place Beth'-el: but the name of that city *was called* Luz at the first.

20 And Ja'cob vowed a vow, saying, If God will be with me, and will keep me in this way that I go, and will give me bread to eat, and raiment to put on,

21 So that I come again to my father's house in peace; then shall the LORD be my God:

22 And this stone, which I have set *for* a pillar, shall be God's house: and of all that thou shalt give me I will surely give the tenth unto thee.

29 THEN Ja'cob went on his journey, and came into the land of the people of the east.

2 And he looked, and behold a well in the field, and, lo, there *were* three flocks of sheep lying by it; for out of that well they watered the flocks: and a great stone *was* upon the well's mouth.

3 And thither were all the flocks gathered: and they rolled the stone from the well's mouth, and watered the sheep, and put the stone again upon the well's mouth in his place.

4 And Ja'cob said unto them, My brethren, whence *be* ye? And they said, Of Ha'ran *are* we.

5 And he said unto them, Know ye La'ban the son of Na'hor? And they said, We know *him.*

6 And he said unto them, *Is* he well? And they said, *He is* well: and, behold, Ra'chel his daughter cometh with the sheep.

7 And he said, Lo, *it is* yet high day, neither *is it* time that the cattle should be gathered together: water ye the sheep, and go *and* feed *them.*

8 And they said, We cannot, until all the flocks be gathered together, and *till* they roll the stone from the well's mouth; then we water the sheep.

9 ¶ And while he yet spake with them, Ra'-chel came with her father's sheep: for she kept them.

10 And it came to pass, when Ja'cob saw Ra'-chel the daughter of La'ban his mother's brother, and the sheep of La'ban his mother's brother, that Ja'cob went near, and rolled the stone from the well's mouth, and watered the flock of La'ban his mother's brother.

11 And Ja'cob kissed Ra'chel, and lifted up his voice, and wept.

12 And Ja'cob told Ra'chel that he *was* her father's brother, and that he *was* Re-bek'ah's son: and she ran and told her father.

13 And it came to pass, when La'ban heard the tidings of Ja'cob his sister's son, that he ran to meet him, and embraced him, and kissed him, and brought him to his house. And he told La'ban all these things.

14 And La'ban said to him, Surely thou *art* my bone and my flesh. And he abode with him the space of a month.

15 ¶ And La'ban said unto Ja'cob, Because thou *art* my brother, shouldest thou therefore serve me for nought? tell me, what *shall* thy wages *be?*

16 And La'ban had two daughters: the name of the elder *was* Le'ah, and the name of the younger *was* Ra'chel.

17 Le´ah *was* tender eyed; but Ra´chel was beautiful and well favoured.

18 And Ja´cob loved Ra´chel; and said, I will serve thee seven years for Ra´chel thy younger daughter.

19 And La´ban said, *It is* better that I give her to thee, than that I should give her to another man: abide with me.

20 And Ja´cob served seven years for Ra´chel; and they seemed unto him *but* a few days, for the love he had to her.

21 ¶ And Ja´cob said unto La´ban, Give *me* my wife, for my days are fulfilled, that I may go in unto her.

22 And La´ban gathered together all the men of the place, and made a feast.

23 And it came to pass in the evening that he took Le´ah his daughter, and brought her to him; and he went in unto her.

24 And La´ban gave unto his daughter Le´ah Zil´pah his maid *for* an handmaid.

25 And it came to pass, that in the morning, behold, it *was* Leah: and he said to La´ban, What *is* this thou hast done unto me? did not I serve with thee for Ra´chel? wherefore then hast thou beguiled me?

26 And La´ban said, It must not be so done in our country, to give the younger before the firstborn.

27 Fulfil her week, and we will give thee this also for the service which thou shalt serve with me yet seven other years.

28 And Ja´cob did so, and fulfilled her week: and he gave him Ra´chel his daughter to wife also.

29 And La´ban gave to Ra´chel his daughter Bil´hah his handmaid to be her maid.

30 And he went in also unto Ra´chel, and he loved also Ra´chel more than Le´ah, and served with him yet seven other years.

31 ¶ And when the LORD saw that Le´ah *was* hated, he opened her womb: but Ra´chel *was* barren.

32 And Le´ah conceived, and bare a son, and she called his name Reu´ben: for she said, Surely the LORD hath looked upon my affliction; now therefore my husband will love me.

33 And she conceived again, and bare a son; and said, Because the LORD hath heard that I *was* hated, he hath therefore given me this *son* also: and she called his name Sim´e-on.

34 And she conceived again, and bare a son; and said, Now this time will my husband be joined unto me, because I have born him three sons: therefore was his name called Le´vi.

35 And she conceived again, and bare a son: and she said, Now will I praise the LORD: therefore she called his name Ju´dah; and left bearing.

30 AND when Ra´chel saw that she bare Ja´cob no children, Ra´chel envied her sister; and said unto Ja´cob, Give me children, or else I die.

2 And Ja´cob's anger was kindled against Ra´chel: and he said, *Am* I in God's stead, who hath withheld from thee the fruit of the womb?

3 And she said, Behold my maid Bil´hah, go in unto her; and she shall bear upon my knees, that I may also have children by her.

4 And she gave him Bil´hah her handmaid to wife: and Ja´cob went in unto her.

5 And Bil´hah conceived, and bare Ja´cob a son.

6 And Ra´chel said, God hath judged me, and hath also heard my voice, and hath given me a son: therefore called she his name Dan.

7 And Bil´hah Ra´chel's maid conceived again, and bare Ja´cob a second son.

8 And Ra´chel said, With great wrestlings have I wrestled with my sister, and I have prevailed: and she called his name Naph´ta-li.

9 When Le´ah saw that she had left bearing, she took Zil´pah her maid, and gave her Ja´cob to wife.

10 And Zil´pah Le´ah's maid bare Ja´cob a son.

11 And Le´ah said, A troop cometh: and she called his name Gad.

12 And Zil´pah Le´ah's maid bare Ja´cob a second son.

13 And Le´ah said, Happy am I, for the daughters will call me blessed: and she called his name Ash´er.

14 ¶ And Reu´ben went in the days of wheat harvest, and found mandrakes in the field, and brought them unto his mother Le´ah. Then Ra´chel said to Le´ah, Give me, I pray thee, of thy son's mandrakes.

15 And she said unto her, *Is it* a small matter that thou hast taken my husband? and wouldest thou take away my son's mandrakes also? And Ra´chel said, Therefore he shall lie with thee to night for thy son's mandrakes.

16 And Ja´cob came out of the field in the evening, and Le´ah went out to meet him, and said, Thou must come in unto me; for surely I have hired thee with my son's mandrakes. And he lay with her that night.

17 And God hearkened unto Le´ah, and she conceived, and bare Ja´cob the fifth son.

18 And Le´ah said, God hath given me my hire, because I have given my maiden to my husband: and she called his name Is´sa-char.

19 And Le´ah conceived again, and bare Ja´cob the sixth son.

20 And Le´ah said, God hath endued me *with* a good dowry; now will my husband dwell with me, because I have born him six sons: and she called his name Zeb´u-lun.

21 And afterwards she bare a daughter, and called her name Di´nah.

22 ¶ And God remembered Ra´chel, and God hearkened to her, and opened her womb.

23 And she conceived, and bare a son; and said, God hath taken away my reproach:

24 And she called his name Jo´seph; and said, The LORD shall add to me another son.

25 And it came to pass, when Ra´chel had born Jo´seph, that Ja´cob said unto La´ban, Send me away, that I may go unto mine own place, and to my country.

26 Give *me* my wives and my children, for whom I have served thee, and let me go: for thou knowest my service which I have done thee.

27 And La´ban said unto him, I pray thee, if I have found favour in thine eyes, *tarry: for* I have learned by experience that the LORD hath blessed me for thy sake.

28 And he said, Appoint me thy wages, and I will give *it.*

29 And he said unto him, Thou knowest how I have served thee, and how thy cattle was with me.

30 For *it was* little which thou hadst before I *came,* and it is *now* increased unto a multitude; and the LORD hath blessed thee since my coming: and now when shall I provide for mine own house also?

31 And he said, What shall I give thee? And Ja´cob said, Thou shalt not give me any thing: if thou wilt do this thing for me, I will again feed *and* keep thy flock.

32 I will pass through all thy flock to day, removing from thence all the speckled and spotted cattle, and all the brown cattle among the sheep, and the spotted and speckled among the goats: and *of such* shall be my hire.

33 So shall my righteousness answer for me in time to come, when it shall come for my hire before thy face: every one that *is* not speckled and spotted among the goats, and brown among the sheep, that shall be counted stolen with me.

34 And La'ban said, Behold, I would it might be according to thy word.

35 And he removed that day the he goats that were ringstraked and spotted, and all the she goats that were speckled and spotted, *and* every one that had *some* white in it, and all the brown among the sheep, and gave *them* into the hand of his sons.

36 And he set three days' journey betwixt himself and Ja'cob: and Ja'cob fed the rest of La'ban's flocks.

37 ¶ And Ja'cob took him rods of green poplar, and of the hazel and chesnut tree; and pilled white strakes in them, and made the white appear which *was* in the rods.

38 And he set the rods which he had pilled before the flocks in the gutters in the watering troughs when the flocks came to drink, that they should conceive when they came to drink.

39 And the flocks conceived before the rods, and brought forth cattle ringstraked, speckled, and spotted.

40 And Ja'cob did separate the lambs, and set the faces of the flocks toward the ringstraked, and all the brown in the flock of La'ban; and he put his own flocks by themselves, and put them not unto La'ban's cattle.

41 And it came to pass, whensoever the stronger cattle did conceive, that Ja'cob laid the rods before the eyes of the cattle in the gutters, that they might conceive among the rods.

42 But when the cattle were feeble, he put *them* not in: so the feebler were La'ban's, and the stronger Ja'cob's.

43 And the man increased exceedingly, and had much cattle, and maidservants, and menservants, and camels, and asses.

31 AND he heard the words of La'ban's sons, saying, Ja'cob hath taken away all that *was* our father's; and of *that* which *was* our father's hath he gotten all this glory.

2 And Ja'cob beheld the countenance of La'ban, and, behold, it *was* not toward him as before.

3 And the LORD said unto Ja'cob, Return unto the land of thy fathers, and to thy kindred; and I will be with thee.

4 And Ja'cob sent and called Ra'chel and Le'ah to the field unto his flock,

5 And said unto them, I see your father's countenance, that *is* not toward me as before; but the God of my father hath been with me.

6 And ye know that with all my power I have served your father.

7 And your father hath deceived me, and changed my wages ten times; but God suffered him not to hurt me.

8 If he said thus, The speckled shall be thy wages; then all the cattle bare speckled: and if he said thus, The ringstraked shall be thy hire; then bare all the cattle ringstraked.

9 Thus God hath taken away the cattle of your father, and given *them* to me.

10 And it came to pass at the time that the cattle conceived, that I lifted up mine eyes, and saw in a dream, and, behold, the rams which leaped upon the cattle *were* ringstraked, speckled, and grisled.

11 And the angel of God spake unto me in a dream, *saying,* Ja'cob: And I said, Here *am* I.

12 And he said, Lift up now thine eyes, and see, all the rams which leap upon the cattle *are* ringstraked, speckled, and grisled: for I have seen all that La'ban doeth unto thee.

13 I *am* the God of Beth'-el, where thou anointedst the pillar, *and* where thou vowedst a vow unto me: now arise, get thee out from this land, and return unto the land of thy kindred.

14 And Ra'chel and Le'ah answered and said unto him, *Is there* yet any portion or inheritance for us in our father's house?

15 Are we not counted of him strangers? for he hath sold us, and hath quite devoured also our money.

16 For all the riches which God hath taken from our father, that *is* ours, and our children's: now then, whatsoever God hath said unto thee, do.

17 ¶ Then Ja'cob rose up, and set his sons and his wives upon camels;

18 And he carried away all his cattle, and all his goods which he had gotten, the cattle of his getting, which he had gotten in Pa'dan-a'ram, for to go to I'saac his father in the land of Ca'naan.

19 And La'ban went to shear his sheep: and Ra'chel had stolen the images that *were* her father's.

20 And Ja'cob stole away unawares to La'ban the Syr'i-an, in that he told him not that he fled.

21 So he fled with all that he had; and he rose up, and passed over the river, and set his face *toward* the mount Gil'e-ad.

22 And it was told La'ban on the third day that Ja'cob was fled.

23 And he took his brethren with him, and pursued after him seven days' journey; and they overtook him in the mount Gil'e-ad.

24 And God came to La'ban the Syr'i-an in a dream by night, and said unto him, Take heed that thou speak not to Ja'cob either good or bad.

25 ¶ Then La'ban overtook Ja'cob. Now Ja'cob had pitched his tent in the mount: and La'ban with his brethren pitched in the mount of Gil'e-ad.

26 And La'ban said to Ja'cob, What hast thou done, that thou hast stolen away unawares to me, and carried away my daughters, as captives *taken* with the sword?

27 Wherefore didst thou flee away secretly, and steal away from me; and didst not tell me, that I might have sent thee away with mirth, and with songs, with tabret, and with harp?

28 And hast not suffered me to kiss my sons and my daughters? thou hast now done foolishly in *so* doing.

29 It is in the power of my hand to do you hurt: but the God of your father spake unto me yesternight, saying, Take thou heed that thou speak not to Ja'cob either good or bad.

30 And now, *though* thou wouldest needs be gone, because thou sore longedst after thy father's house, *yet* wherefore hast thou stolen my gods?

31 And Ja'cob answered and said to La'ban, Because I was afraid: for I said, Peradventure thou wouldest take by force thy daughters from me.

32 With whomsoever thou findest thy gods, let him not live: before our brethren discern

thou what is thine with me, and take it to thee. For Ja'cob knew not that Ra'chel had stolen them.

33 And La'ban went into Ja'cob's tent, and into Le'ah's tent, and into the two maidservants' tents; but he found them not. Then went he out of Le'ah's tent, and entered into Ra'chel's tent.

34 Now Ra'chel had taken the images, and put them in the camel's furniture, and sat upon them. And La'ban searched all the tent, but found them not.

35 And she said to her father, Let it not displease my lord that I cannot rise up before thee; for the custom of women is upon me. And he searched, but found not the images.

36 ¶ And Ja'cob was wroth, and chode with La'ban: and Ja'cob answered and said to La'ban, What is my trespass? what is my sin, that thou hast so hotly pursued after me?

37 Whereas thou hast searched all my stuff, what hast thou found of all thy household stuff? set it here before my brethren and thy brethren, that they may judge betwixt us both.

38 This twenty years have I been with thee; thy ewes and thy she goats have not cast their young, and the rams of thy flock have I not eaten.

39 That which was torn of beasts I brought not unto thee; I bare the loss of it; of my hand didst thou require it, whether stolen by day, or stolen by night.

40 Thus I was; in the day the drought consumed me, and the frost by night; and my sleep departed from mine eyes.

41 Thus have I been twenty years in thy house; I served thee fourteen years for thy two daughters, and six years for thy cattle: and thou hast changed my wages ten times.

42 Except the God of my father, the God of A'bra-ham, and the fear of I'saac, had been with me, surely thou hadst sent me away now empty. God hath seen mine affliction and the labour of my hands, and rebuked thee yesternight.

43 ¶ And La'ban answered and said unto Ja'cob, These daughters are my daughters, and these children are my children, and these cattle are my cattle, and all that thou seest is mine: and what can I do this day unto these my daughters, or unto their children which they have born?

44 Now therefore come thou, let us make a covenant, I and thou; and let it be for a witness between me and thee.

45 And Ja'cob took a stone, and set it up for a pillar.

46 And Ja'cob said unto his brethren, Gather stones; and they took stones, and made an heap: and they did eat there upon the heap.

47 And La'ban called it Je'gar-sa-ha-du'tha: but Ja'cob called it Gal'e-ed.

48 And La'ban said, This heap is a witness between me and thee this day. Therefore was the name of it called Gal'e-ed;

49 And Miz'pah; for he said, The LORD watch between me and thee, when we are absent one from another.

50 If thou shalt afflict my daughters, or if thou shalt take other wives beside my daughters, no man is with us; see, God is witness betwixt me and thee.

51 And La'ban said to Ja'cob, Behold this heap, and behold this pillar, which I have cast betwixt me and thee;

52 This heap be witness, and this pillar be witness, that I will not pass over this heap to thee, and that thou shalt not pass over this heap and this pillar unto me, for harm.

53 The God of A'bra-ham, and the God of Na'hor, the God of their father, judge betwixt us. And Ja'cob sware by the fear of his father I'saac.

54 Then Ja'cob offered sacrifice upon the mount, and called his brethren to eat bread: and they did eat bread, and tarried all night in the mount.

55 And early in the morning La'ban rose up, and kissed his sons and his daughters, and blessed them: and La'ban departed, and returned unto his place.

32 AND Ja'cob went on his way, and the angels of God met him.

2 And when Ja'cob saw them, he said, This is God's host: and he called the name of that place Ma-ha-na'im.

3 And Ja'cob sent messengers before him to E'sau his brother unto the land of Se'ir, the country of E'dom.

4 And he commanded them, saying, Thus shall ye speak unto my lord E'sau; Thy servant Ja'cob saith thus, I have sojourned with La'ban, and stayed there until now:

5 And I have oxen, and asses, flocks, and menservants, and womenservants: and I have sent to tell my lord, that I may find grace in thy sight.

6 ¶ And the messengers returned to Ja'cob, saying, We came to thy brother E'sau, and also he cometh to meet thee, and four hundred men with him.

7 Then Ja'cob was greatly afraid and distressed: and he divided the people that was with him, and the flocks, and herds, and the camels, into two bands;

8 And said, If E'sau come to the one company, and smite it, then the other company which is left shall escape.

9 ¶ And Ja'cob said, O God of my father A'bra-ham, and God of my father I'saac, the LORD which saidst unto me, Return unto thy country, and to thy kindred, and I will deal well with thee:

10 I am not worthy of the least of all the mercies, and of all the truth, which thou hast shewed unto thy servant; for with my staff I passed over this Jor'dan; and now I am become two bands.

11 Deliver me, I pray thee, from the hand of my brother, from the hand of E'sau: for I fear him, lest he will come and smite me, and the mother with the children.

12 And thou saidst, I will surely do thee good, and make thy seed as the sand of the sea, which cannot be numbered for multitude.

13 ¶ And he lodged there that same night; and took of that which came to his hand a present for E'sau his brother;

14 Two hundred she goats, and twenty he goats, two hundred ewes, and twenty rams,

15 Thirty milch camels with their colts, forty kine, and ten bulls, twenty she asses, and ten foals.

16 And he delivered them into the hand of his servants, every drove by themselves; and said unto his servants, Pass over before me, and put a space betwixt drove and drove.

17 And he commanded the foremost, saying, When E'sau my brother meeteth thee, and asketh thee, saying, Whose art thou? and whither goest thou? and whose are these before thee?

18 Then thou shalt say, They be thy servant

Ja'cob's; it *is* a present sent unto my lord E'sau: and, behold, also he *is* behind us.

19 And so commanded he the second, and the third, and all that followed the droves, saying, On this manner shall ye speak unto E'sau, when ye find him.

20 And say ye moreover, Behold, thy servant Ja'cob *is* behind us. For he said, I will appease him with the present that goeth before me, and afterward I will see his face; peradventure he will accept of me.

21 So went the present over before him: and himself lodged that night in the company.

22 And he rose up that night, and took his two wives, and his two womenservants, and his eleven sons, and passed over the ford Jab'bok.

23 And he took them, and sent them over the brook, and sent over that he had.

24 ¶ And Ja'cob was left alone; and there wrestled a man with him until the breaking of the day.

25 And when he saw that he prevailed not against him, he touched the hollow of his thigh; and the hollow of Ja'cob's thigh was out of joint, as he wrestled with him.

26 And he said, Let me go, for the day breaketh. And he said, I will not let thee go, except thou bless me.

27 And he said unto him, What *is* thy name? And he said, Ja'cob.

28 And he said, Thy name shall be called no more Ja'cob, but Is'ra-el: for as a prince hast thou power with God and with men, and hast prevailed.

29 And Ja'cob asked *him*, and said, Tell *me*, I pray thee, thy name. And he said, Wherefore *is* it *that* thou dost ask after my name? And he blessed him there.

30 And Ja'cob called the name of the place Pe-ni'el: for I have seen God face to face, and my life is preserved.

31 And as he passed over Pe-nu'el the sun rose upon him, and he halted upon his thigh.

32 Therefore the children of Is'ra-el eat not *of* the sinew which shrank, which *is* upon the hollow of the thigh, unto this day: because he touched the hollow of Ja'cob's thigh in the sinew that shrank.

33 AND Ja'cob lifted up his eyes, and looked, and, behold, E'sau came, and with him four hundred men. And he divided the children unto Le'ah, and unto Ra'chel, and unto the two handmaids.

2 And he put the handmaids and their children foremost, and Le'ah and her children after, and Ra'chel and Jo'seph hindermost.

3 And he passed over before them, and bowed himself to the ground seven times, until he came near to his brother.

4 And E'sau ran to meet him, and embraced him, and fell on his neck, and kissed him: and they wept.

5 And he lifted up his eyes, and saw the women and the children; and said, Who *are* those with thee? And he said, The children which God hath graciously given thy servant.

6 Then the handmaidens came near, they and their children, and they bowed themselves.

7 And Le'ah also with her children came near, and bowed themselves: and after came Jo'seph near and Ra'chel, and they bowed themselves.

8 And he said, What *meanest* thou by all this drove which I met? And he said, *These are* to find grace in the sight of my lord.

9 And E'sau said, I have enough, my brother; keep that thou hast unto thyself.

10 And Ja'cob said, Nay, I pray thee, if now I have found grace in thy sight, then receive my present at my hand: for therefore I have seen thy face, as though I had seen the face of God, and thou wast pleased with me.

11 Take, I pray thee, my blessing that is brought to thee; because God hath dealt graciously with me, and because I have enough. And he urged him, and he took *it*.

12 And he said, Let us take our journey, and let us go, and I will go before thee.

13 And he said unto him, My lord knoweth that the children *are* tender, and the flocks and herds with young *are* with me: and if men should overdrive them one day, all the flock will die.

14 Let my lord, I pray thee, pass over before his servant: and I will lead on softly, according as the cattle that goeth before me and the children be able to endure, until I come unto my lord unto Se'ir.

15 And E'sau said, Let me now leave with thee *some* of the folk that *are* with me. And he said, What needeth it? let me find grace in the sight of my lord.

16 ¶ So E'sau returned that day on his way unto Se'ir.

17 And Ja'cob journeyed to Suc'coth, and built him an house, and made booths for his cattle: therefore the name of the place is called Suc'coth.

18 ¶ And Ja'cob came to Sha'lem, a city of Shechem, which *is* in the land of Ca'naan, when he came from Pa'dan-a'ram; and pitched his tent before the city.

19 And he bought a parcel of a field, where he had spread his tent, at the hand of the children of Ha'mor, She'chem's father, for an hundred pieces of money.

20 And he erected there an altar, and called it El-e-lo'he-Is'ra-el.

34 AND Di'nah the daughter of Le'ah, which she bare unto Ja'cob, went out to see the daughters of the land.

2 And when Shechem the son of Ha'mor the Hi'vite, prince of the country, saw her, he took her, and lay with her, and defiled her.

3 And his soul clave unto Di'nah the daughter of Ja'cob, and he loved the damsel, and spake kindly unto the damsel.

4 And Shechem spake unto his father Ha'mor, saying, Get me this damsel to wife.

5 And Ja'cob heard that he had defiled Di'nah his daughter: now his sons were with his cattle in the field: and Ja'cob held his peace until they were come.

6 ¶ And Ha'mor the father of Shechem went out unto Ja'cob to commune with him.

7 And the sons of Ja'cob came out of the field when they heard *it*: and the men were grieved, and they were very wroth, because he had wrought folly in Is'ra-el in lying with Ja'cob's daughter; which thing ought not to be done.

8 And Ha'mor communed with them, saying, The soul of my son Shechem longeth for your daughter: I pray you give her to him to wife.

9 And make ye marriages with us, *and* give your daughters unto us, and take our daughters unto you.

10 And ye shall dwell with us: and the land shall be before you; dwell and trade ye therein, and get you possessions therein.

11 And Shechem said unto her father and unto her brethren, Let me find grace in your

eyes, and what ye shall say unto me I will give.

12 Ask me never so much dowry and gift, and I will give according as ye shall say unto me: but give me the damsel to wife.

13 And the sons of Ja'cob answered She'chem and Ha'mor his father deceitfully, and said, because he had defiled Di'nah their sister:

14 And they said unto them, We cannot do this thing, to give our sister to one that is uncircumcised; for that were a reproach unto us:

15 But in this will we consent unto you: If ye will be as we be, that every male of you be circumcised;

16 Then will we give our daughters unto you, and we will take your daughters to us, and we will dwell with you, and we will become one people.

17 But if ye will not hearken unto us, to be circumcised; then will we take our daughter, and we will be gone.

18 And their words pleased Ha'mor, and Shechem Ha'mor's son.

19 And the young man deferred not to do the thing, because he had delight in Ja'cob's daughter: and he was more honourable than all the house of his father.

20 ¶ And Ha'mor and Shechem his son came unto the gate of their city, and communed with the men of their city, saying,

21 These men are peaceable with us; therefore let them dwell in the land, and trade therein; for the land, behold it is large enough for them; let us take their daughters to us for wives, and let us give them our daughters.

22 Only herein will the men consent unto us for to dwell with us, to be one people, if every male among us be circumcised, as they are circumcised.

23 Shall not the cattle and their substance and every beast of theirs be ours? only let us consent unto them, and they will dwell with us.

24 And unto Ha'mor and unto Shechem his son hearkened all that went out of the gate of his city; and every male was circumcised, all that went out of the gate of his city.

25 ¶ And it came to pass on the third day, when they were sore, that two of the sons of Ja'cob, Sim'e-on and Le'vi, Di'nah's brethren, took each man his sword, and came upon the city boldly, and slew all the males.

26 And they slew Ha'mor and Shechem his son with the edge of the sword, and took Di'nah out of She'chem's house, and went out.

27 The sons of Ja'cob came upon the slain, and spoiled the city, because they had defiled their sister.

28 They took their sheep, and their oxen, and their asses, and that which was in the city, and that which was in the field,

29 And all their wealth, and all their little ones, and their wives took they captive, and spoiled even all that was in the house.

30 And Ja'cob said to Sim'e-on and Le'vi, Ye have troubled me to make me to stink among the inhabitants of the land, among the Ca'naanites and the Per'iz-zites: and I being few in number, they shall gather themselves together against me, and slay me; and I shall be destroyed, I and my house.

31 And they said, Should he deal with our sister as with an harlot?

35

AND God said unto Ja'cob, Arise, go up to Beth'-el, and dwell there: and make there an altar unto God, that appeared unto thee when thou fleddest from the face of E'sau thy brother.

2 Then Ja'cob said unto his household, and to all that were with him, Put away the strange gods that are among you, and be clean, and change your garments:

3 And let us arise, and go up to Beth'-el; and I will make there an altar unto God, who answered me in the day of my distress, and was with me in the way which I went.

4 And they gave unto Ja'cob all the strange gods which were in their hand, and all their earrings which were in their ears; and Ja'cob hid them under the oak which was by Shechem.

5 And they journeyed: and the terror of God was upon the cities that were round about them, and they did not pursue after the sons of Ja'cob.

6 ¶ So Ja'cob came to Luz, which is in the land of Ca'naan, that is, Bethel, he and all the people that were with him.

7 And he built there an altar, and called the place El-bethel: because there God appeared unto him, when he fled from the face of his brother.

8 But Deb'o-rah Re-bek'ah's nurse died, and she was buried beneath Beth'-el under an oak: and the name of it was called Al'lon-bach'uth.

9 ¶ And God appeared unto Ja'cob again, when he came out of Pa'dan-a'ram, and blessed him.

10 And God said unto him, Thy name is Ja'cob: thy name shall not be called any more Ja'cob, but Is'ra-el shall be thy name: and he called his name Is'ra-el.

11 And God said unto him, I am God Almighty: be fruitful and multiply; a nation and a company of nations shall be of thee, and kings shall come out of thy loins;

12 And the land which I gave A'bra-ham and I'saac, to thee I will give it, and to thy seed after thee will I give the land.

13 And God went up from him in the place where he talked with him.

14 And Ja'cob set up a pillar in the place where he talked with him, even a pillar of stone: and he poured a drink offering thereon, and he poured oil thereon.

15 And Ja'cob called the name of the place where God spake with him, Beth'-el.

16 ¶ And they journeyed from Beth'-el; and there was but a little way to come to Eph'rath: and Ra'chel travailed, and she had hard labour.

17 And it came to pass, when she was in hard labour, that the midwife said unto her, Fear not; thou shalt have this son also.

18 And it came to pass, as her soul was in departing, (for she died) that she called his name Ben-o'ni: but his father called him Ben'ja-min.

19 And Ra'chel died, and was buried in the way to Eph'rath, which is Beth'-le-hem.

20 And Ja'cob set a pillar upon her grave: that is the pillar of Ra'chel's grave unto this day.

21 ¶ And Is'ra-el journeyed, and spread his tent beyond the tower of E'dar.

22 And it came to pass, when Is'ra-el dwelt in that land, that Reu'ben went and lay with Bil'-hah his father's concubine: and Is'ra-el heard it. Now the sons of Ja'cob were twelve:

23 The sons of Le'ah; Reu'ben, Ja'cob's firstborn, and Sim'e-on, and Le'vi, and Ju'dah, and Is'sa-char, and Zeb'u-lun:

24 The sons of Ra'chel; Jo'seph, and Ben'ja-min:

25 And the sons of Bil'hah, Ra'chel's handmaid; Dan, and Naph'ta-li:

26 And the sons of Zil'pah, Le'ah's hand-

maid; Gad, and Ash'er: these *are* the sons of Ja'cob, which were born to him in Pa'dan-a'-ram.

27 ¶ And Ja'cob came unto I'saac his father unto Mam're, unto the city of Ar'bah, which *is* He'bron, where A'bra-ham and I'saac sojourned.

28 And the days of I'saac were a hundred and fourscore years.

29 And I'saac gave up the ghost, and died, and was gathered unto his people, *being* old and full of days: and his sons E'sau and Ja'cob buried him.

36 NOW these *are* the generations of E'-sau, who *is* E'dom.

2 E'sau took his wives of the daughters of Ca'naan; A'dah the daughter of E'lon the Hit'-tite, and A-ho-lib'a-mah the daughter of A'nah the daughter of Zib'e-on the Hi'vite;

3 And Bash'e-math Ish'ma-el's daughter, sister of Ne-ba'joth.

4 And A'dah bare to E'sau El'i-phaz; and Bash'e-math bare Reu'el;

5 And A-ho-lib'a-mah bare Je'ush, and Ja-a'-lam, and Ko'rah: these *are* the sons of E'sau, which were born unto him in the land of Ca'-naan.

6 And E'sau took his wives, and his sons, and his daughters, and all the persons of his house, and his cattle, and all his beasts, and all his substance, which he had got in the land of Ca'naan; and went into the country from the face of his brother Ja'cob.

7 For their riches were more than that they might dwell together; and the land wherein they were strangers could not bear them because of their cattle.

8 Thus dwelt E'sau in mount Se'ir: E'sau *is* E'dom.

9 ¶ And these *are* the generations of E'sau the father of the E'dom-ites in mount Se'ir:

10 These *are* the names of E'sau's sons; El'i-phaz the son of A'dah the wife of E'sau, Reu'el the son of Bash'e-math the wife of E'sau.

11 And the sons of El'i-phaz were Te'man, O'mar, Ze'pho, and Ga'tam, and Ke'naz.

12 And Tim'na was concubine to El'i-phaz E'-sau's son; and she bare to El'i-phaz Am'a-lek: these *were* the sons of A'dah E'sau's wife.

13 And these *are* the sons of Reu'el; Na'hath, and Ze'rah, Sham'mah, and Miz'zah: these were the sons of Bash'e-math E'sau's wife.

14 ¶ And these were the sons ofA-ho-lib'a-mah, the daughter of A'nah the daughter of Zib'e-on, E'sau's wife: and she bare to E'sau Je'-ush, and Ja-a'lam, and Ko'rah.

15 ¶ These *were* dukes of the sons of E'sau: the sons of El'i-phaz the firstborn *son* of E'sau; duke Te'man, duke O'mar, duke Ze'pho, duke Ke'naz,

16 Duke Ko'rah, duke Ga'tam, *and* duke Am'a-lek: these *are* the dukes *that came* of El'i-phaz in the land of E'dom; these *were* the sons of A'dah.

17 ¶ And these *are* the sons of Reu'el E'sau's son; duke Na'hath, duke Ze'rah, duke Sham'-mah, duke Miz'zah: these *are* the dukes *that came* of Reu'el in the land of E'dom; these *are* the sons of Bash'e-math E'sau's wife.

18 ¶ And these *are* the sons of A-ho-lib'a-mah E'sau's wife; duke Je'ush, duke Ja-a'lam, duke Ko'rah: these *were* the dukes *that came* of A-ho-lib'a-mah the daughter of A'nah, E'sau's wife.

19 These *are* the sons of E'sau, who *is* E'dom, and these *are* their dukes.

20 ¶ These *are* the sons of Se'ir the Ho'rite, who inhabited the land; Lo'tan, and Sho'bal, and Zib'e-on, and A'nah,

21 And Di'shon, and E'zer, and Di'shan: these *are* the dukes of the Ho'rites, the children of Se'ir in the land of E'dom.

22 And the children of Lo'tan were Ho'ri and He'mam; and Lo'tan's sister *was* Tim'na.

23 And the children of Sho'bal *were* these; Al'van, and Man'a-hath, and E'bal, She'pho, and O'nam.

24 And these *are* the children of Zib'e-on; both A'jah, and A'nah: this *was that* A'nah that found the mules in the wilderness, as he fed the asses of Zib'e-on his father.

25 And the children of A'nah *were* these; Di'-shon, and A-ho-lib'a-mah the daughter of A'-nah.

26 And these *are* the children of Di'shon; Hem'dan, and Esh'ban, and Ith'ran, and Che'ran.

27 The children of E'zer *are* these; Bil'han, and Za'a-van, and A'kan.

28 The children of Di'shan *are* these; Uz, and A'ran.

29 These *are* the dukes *that came* of the Ho'-rites; duke Lo'tan, duke Sho'bal, duke Zib'e-on, duke A'nah,

30 Duke Di'shon, duke E'zer, duke Di'shan: these *are* the dukes *that came* of Ho'ri, among their dukes in the land of Se'ir.

31 ¶ And these *are* the kings that reigned in the land of E'dom, before there reigned any king over the children of Is'ra-el.

32 And Be'la the son of Be'or reigned in E'-dom: and the name of his city *was* Din'ha-bah.

33 And Be'la died, and Jo'bab the son of Ze'-rah of Boz'rah reigned in his stead.

34 And Jo'bab died, and Hu'sham of the land of Tem'a-ni reigned in his stead.

35 And Hu'sham died, and Ha'dad the son of Be'dad, who smote Mid'i-an in the field of Mo'-ab, reigned in his stead: and the name of his city *was* A'vith.

36 And Ha'dad died, and Sam'lah of Mas're-kah reigned in his stead.

37 And Sam'lah died, and Saul of Re-ho'both *by* the river reigned in his stead.

38 And Saul died, and Ba'al-ha'nan the son of Ach'bor reigned in his stead.

39 And Ba'al-ha'nan the son of Ach'bor died, and Ha'dar reigned in his stead: and the name of his city *was* Pa'u; and his wife's name *was* Me-het'a-bel, the daughter of Ma'tred, the daughter of Mez'a-hab.

40 And these *are* the names of the dukes *that came* of E'sau, according to their families, after their places, by their names; duke Tim'nah, duke Al'vah, duke Je'theth,

41 Duke A-ho-lib'a-mah, duke E'lah, duke Pi'non,

42 Duke Ke'naz, duke Te'man, duke Mib'zar,

43 Duke Mag'di-el, duke I'ram: these *be* the dukes of E'dom, according to their habitations in the land of their possession: he *is* E'sau the father of the E'dom-ites.

37 AND Ja'cob dwelt in the land wherein his father was a stranger, in the land of Ca'naan.

2 These *are* the generations of Ja'cob. Jo'-seph, *being* seventeen years old, was feeding the flock with his brethren; and the lad *was* with the sons of Bil'hah, and with the sons of Zil'pah, his father's wives: and Jo'seph brought unto his father their evil report.

3 Now Is'ra-el loved Jo'seph more than all his

children, because he *was* the son of his old age: and he made him a coat of *many* colours.

4 And when his brethren saw that their father loved him more than all his brethren, they hated him, and could not speak peaceably unto him.

5 ¶ And Jo′seph dreamed a dream, and he told *it* his brethren: and they hated him yet the more.

6 And he said unto them, Hear, I pray you, this dream which I have dreamed:

7 For, behold, we *were* binding sheaves in the field, and, lo, my sheaf arose, and also stood upright; and, behold, your sheaves stood round about, and made obeisance to my sheaf.

8 And his brethren said to him, Shalt thou indeed reign over us? or shalt thou indeed have dominion over us? And they hated him yet the more for his dreams, and for his words.

9 ¶ And he dreamed yet another dream, and told *it* his brethren, and said, Behold, I have dreamed a dream more; and, behold, the sun and the moon and the eleven stars made obeisance to me.

10 And he told *it* to his father, and to his brethren: and his father rebuked him, and said unto him, What *is* this dream that thou hast dreamed? Shall I and thy mother and thy brethren indeed come to bow down ourselves to thee to the earth?

11 And his brethren envied him: but his father observed the saying.

12 ¶ And his brethren went to feed their father's flock in Shechem.

13 And Is′ra-el said unto Jo′seph, Do not thy brethren feed *the flock* in Shechem? come, and I will send thee unto them. And he said to him, Here *am* I.

14 And he said to him, Go, I pray thee, see whether it be well with thy brethren, and well with the flocks; and bring me word again. So he sent him out of the vale of He′bron, and he came to Shechem.

15 ¶ And a certain man found him, and, behold, *he was* wandering in the field: and the man asked him, saying, What seekest thou?

16 And he said, I seek my brethren: tell me, I pray thee, where they feed *their flocks.*

17 And the man said, They are departed hence; for I heard them say, Let us go to Do′than. And Jo′seph went after his brethren, and found them in Do′than.

18 And when they saw him afar off, even before he came near unto them, they conspired against him to slay him.

19 And they said one to another, Behold, this dreamer cometh.

20 Come now therefore, and let us slay him, and cast him into some pit, and we will say, Some evil beast hath devoured him: and we shall see what will become of his dreams.

21 And Reu′ben heard *it*, and he delivered him out of their hands; and said, Let us not kill him.

22 And Reu′ben said unto them, Shed no blood, *but* cast him into this pit that *is* in the wilderness, and lay no hand upon him; that he might rid him out of their hands, to deliver him to his father again.

23 ¶ And it came to pass, when Jo′seph was come unto his brethren, that they stript Jo′seph out of his coat, *his* coat of *many* colours that *was* on him;

24 And they took him, and cast him into a pit: and the pit *was* empty, *there was* no water in it.

25 And they sat down to eat bread: and they lifted up their eyes and looked, and, behold, a company of Ish′me-el-ites came from Gil′e-ad with their camels bearing spicery and balm and myrrh, going to carry *it* down to E′gypt.

26 And Ju′dah said unto his brethren, What profit *is it* if we slay our brother, and conceal his blood?

27 Come, and let us sell him to the Ish′me-el-ites, and let not our hand be upon him; for he *is* our brother *and* our flesh. And his brethren were content.

28 Then there passed by Mid′i-an-ites merchantmen; and they drew and lifted up Jo′seph out of the pit, and sold Jo′seph to the Ish′me-el-ites for twenty *pieces* of silver: and they brought Jo′seph into E′gypt.

29 ¶ And Reu′ben returned unto the pit; and, behold, Jo′seph *was* not in the pit; and he rent his clothes.

30 And he returned unto his brethren, and said, The child *is* not; and I, whither shall I go?

31 And they took Jo′seph's coat, and killed a kid of the goats, and dipped the coat in the blood;

32 And they sent the coat of *many* colours, and they brought *it* to their father; and said, This have we found: know now whether it *be* thy son's coat or no.

33 And he knew it, and said, *It is* my son's coat; an evil beast hath devoured him; Jo′seph *is* without doubt rent in pieces.

34 And Ja′cob rent his clothes, and put sackcloth upon his loins, and mourned for his son many days.

35 And all his sons and all his daughters rose up to comfort him; but he refused to be comforted; and he said, For I will go down into the grave unto my son mourning. Thus his father wept for him.

36 And the Mid′i-an-ites sold him into E′gypt unto Pot′i-phar, an officer of Pha′raoh's, *and* captain of the guard.

38

AND it came to pass at that time, that Ju′dah went down from his brethren, and turned in to a certain A-dul′lam-ite, whose name *was* Hi′rah.

2 And Ju′dah saw there a daughter of a certain Ca′naan-ite, whose name *was* Shu′ah; and he took her, and went in unto her.

3 And she conceived, and bare a son; and he called his name Er.

4 And she conceived again, and bare a son; and she called his name O′nan.

5 And she yet again conceived, and bare a son; and called his name She′lah: and he was at Che′zib, when she bare him.

6 And Ju′dah took a wife for Er his firstborn, whose name *was* Ta′mar.

7 And Er, Ju′dah's firstborn, was wicked in the sight of the Lord; and the Lord slew him.

8 And Ju′dah said unto O′nan, Go in unto thy brother's wife, and marry her, and raise up seed to thy brother.

9 And O′nan knew that the seed should not be his; and it came to pass, when he went in unto his brother's wife, that he spilled *it* on the ground, lest that he should give seed to his brother.

10 And the thing which he did displeased the Lord: wherefore he slew him also.

11 Then said Ju′dah to Ta′mar his daughter in law, Remain a widow at thy father's house, till She′lah my son be grown: for he said, Lest peradventure he die also, as his brethren *did.* And Ta′mar went and dwelt in her father's house.

12 ¶ And in process of time the daughter of Shu'ah Ju'dah's wife died; and Ju'dah was comforted, and went up unto his sheepshearers to Tim'nath, he and his friend Hi'rah the A-dul'-lam-ite.

13 And it was told Ta'mar, saying, Behold thy father in law goeth up to Tim'nath to shear his sheep.

14 And she put her widow's garments off from her, and covered her with a veil, and wrapped herself, and sat in an open place, which is by the way to Tim'nath; for she saw that She'lah was grown, and she was not given unto him to wife.

15 When Ju'dah saw her, he thought her to be an harlot; because she had covered her face.

16 And he turned unto her by the way, and said, Go to, I pray thee, let me come in unto thee; (for he knew not that she was his daughter in law.) And she said, What wilt thou give me, that thou mayest come in unto me?

17 And he said, I will send thee a kid from the flock. And she said, Wilt thou give me a pledge, till thou send it?

18 And he said, What pledge shall I give thee? And she said, Thy signet, and thy bracelets, and thy staff that is in thine hand. And he gave it her, and came in unto her, and she conceived by him.

19 And she arose, and went away, and laid by her veil from her, and put on the garments of her widowhood.

20 And Ju'dah sent the kid by the hand of his friend the A-dul'lam-ite, to receive his pledge from the woman's hand: but he found her not.

21 Then he asked the men of that place, saying, Where is the harlot, that was openly by the way side? And they said, There was no harlot in this place.

22 And he returned to Ju'dah, and said, I cannot find her; and also the men of the place said, that there was no harlot in this place.

23 And Ju'dah said, Let her take it to her, lest we be shamed: behold, I sent this kid, and thou hast not found her.

24 ¶ And it came to pass about three months after, that it was told Ju'dah, saying, Ta'mar thy daughter in law hath played the harlot; and also, behold, she is with child by whoredom. And Ju'dah said, Bring her forth, and let her be burnt.

25 When she was brought forth, she sent to her father in law, saying, By the man, whose these are, am I with child: and she said, Discern, I pray thee, whose are these, the signet, and bracelets, and staff.

26 And Ju'dah acknowledged them, and said, She hath been more righteous than I; because that I gave her not to She'lah my son. And he knew her again no more.

27 ¶ And it came to pass in the time of her travail, that, behold, twins were in her womb.

28 And it came to pass, when she travailed, that the one put out his hand: and the midwife took and bound upon his hand a scarlet thread, saying, This came out first.

29 And it came to pass, as he drew back his hand, that, behold, his brother came out: and she said, How hast thou broken forth? this breach be upon thee: therefore his name was called Pharez.

30 And afterward came out his brother, that had the scarlet thread upon his hand: and his name was called Za'rah.

39 AND Jo'seph was brought down to E'-gypt; and Pot'i-phar, an officer of Pha'-raoh, captain of the guard, an E-gyp'tian, bought him of the hands of the Ish'me-el-ites, which had brought him down thither.

2 And the LORD was with Jo'seph, and he was a prosperous man; and he was in the house of his master the E-gyp'tian.

3 And his master saw that the LORD was with him, and that the LORD made all that he did to prosper in his hand.

4 And Jo'seph found grace in his sight, and he served him: and he made him overseer over his house, and all that he had he put into his hand.

5 And it came to pass from the time that he had made him overseer in his house, and over all that he had, that the LORD blessed the E-gyp'tian's house for Jo'seph's sake; and the blessing of the LORD was upon all that he had in the house, and in the field.

6 And he left all that he had in Jo'seph's hand; and he knew not ought he had, save the bread which he did eat. And Jo'seph was a goodly person, and well favoured.

7 ¶ And it came to pass after these things, that his master's wife cast her eyes upon Jo'-seph; and she said, Lie with me.

8 But he refused, and said unto his master's wife, Behold, my master wotteth not what is with me in the house, and he hath committed all that he hath to my hand;

9 There is none greater in this house than I; neither hath he kept back any thing from me but thee, because thou art his wife: how then can I do this great wickedness, and sin against God?

10 And it came to pass, as she spake to Jo'-seph day by day, that he hearkened not unto her, to lie by her, or to be with her.

11 And it came to pass about this time, that Joseph went into the house to do his business; and there was none of the men of the house there within.

12 And she caught him by his garment, saying, Lie with me: and he left his garment in her hand, and fled, and got him out.

13 And it came to pass, when she saw that he had left his garment in her hand, and was fled forth,

14 That she called unto the men of her house, and spake unto them, saying, See, he hath brought in an He'brew unto us to mock us; he came in unto me to lie with me, and I cried with a loud voice:

15 And it came to pass, when he heard that I lifted up my voice and cried, that he left his garment with me, and fled, and got him out.

16 And she laid up his garment by her, until his lord came home.

17 And she spake unto him according to these words, saying, The He'brew servant, which thou hast brought unto us, came in unto me to mock me:

18 And it came to pass, as I lifted up my voice and cried, that he left his garment with me, and fled out.

19 And it came to pass, when his master heard the words of his wife, which she spake unto him, saying, After this manner did thy servant to me; that his wrath was kindled.

20 And Jo'seph's master took him, and put him into the prison, a place where the king's prisoners were bound: and he was there in the prison.

21 ¶ But the LORD was with Jo'seph, and shewed him mercy, and gave him favour in the sight of the keeper of the prison.

22 And the keeper of the prison committed

to Jo'seph's hand all the prisoners that *were* in the prison; and whatsoever they did there, he was the doer *of it.*

23 The keeper of the prison looked not to any thing *that was* under his hand; because the LORD was with him, and *that* which he did, the LORD made *it* to prosper.

40 AND it came to pass after these things, *that* the butler of the king of E'gypt and *his* baker had offended their lord the king of E'gypt.

2 And Pha'raoh was wroth against two *of* his officers, against the chief of the butlers, and against the chief of the bakers.

3 And he put them in ward in the house of the captain of the guard, into the prison, the place where Jo'seph *was* bound.

4 And the captain of the guard charged Jo'seph with them, and he served them: and they continued a season in ward.

5 ¶ And they dreamed a dream both of them, each man his dream in one night, each man according to the interpretation of his dream, the butler and the baker of the king of E'gypt, which *were* bound in the prison.

6 And Jo'seph came in unto them in the morning, and looked upon them, and, behold, they *were* sad.

7 And he asked Pha'raoh's officers that *were* with him in the ward of his lord's house, saying, Wherefore look ye *so* sadly to day?

8 And they said unto him, We have dreamed a dream, and *there* is no interpreter of it. And Jo'seph said unto them, *Do* not interpretations *belong* to God? tell me *them,* I pray you.

9 And the chief butler told his dream to Jo'seph, and said to him, In my dream, behold, a vine *was* before me;

10 And in the vine *were* three branches: and it *was* as though it budded, *and* her blossoms shot forth; and the clusters thereof brought forth ripe grapes:

11 And Pha'raoh's cup *was* in my hand: and I took the grapes, and pressed them into Pha'raoh's cup, and I gave the cup into Pha'raoh's hand.

12 And Jo'seph said unto him, This *is* the interpretation of it: The three branches *are* three days:

13 Yet within three days shall Pha'raoh lift up thine head, and restore thee unto thy place: and thou shalt deliver Pha'raoh's cup into his hand, after the former manner when thou wast his butler.

14 But think on me when it shall be well with thee, and shew kindness, I pray thee, unto me, and make mention of me unto Pha'raoh, and bring me out of this house:

15 For indeed I was stolen away out of the land of the He'brews: and here also have I done nothing that they should put me into the dungeon.

16 When the chief baker saw that the interpretation was good, he said unto Jo'seph, I also *was* in my dream, and, behold, *I had* three white baskets on my head:

17 And in the uppermost basket *there was* of all manner of bakemeats for Pha'raoh; and the birds did eat them out of the basket upon my head.

18 And Jo'seph answered and said, This *is* the interpretation thereof: The three baskets *are* three days:

19 Yet within three days shall Pha'raoh lift up thy head from off thee, and shall hang thee on a tree; and the birds shall eat thy flesh from off thee.

20 ¶ And it came to pass the third day, *which was* Pha'raoh's birthday, that he made a feast unto all his servants: and he lifted up the head of the chief butler and of the chief baker among his servants.

21 And he restored the chief butler unto his butlership again; and he gave the cup into Pha'raoh's hand:

22 But he hanged the chief baker: as Jo'seph had interpreted to them.

23 Yet did not the chief butler remember Jo'seph, but forgat him.

41 AND it came to pass at the end of two full years, that Pha'raoh dreamed: and, behold, he stood by the river.

2 And, behold, there came up out of the river seven well favoured kine and fatfleshed; and they fed in a meadow.

3 And, behold, seven other kine came up after them out of the river, ill favoured and leanfleshed; and stood by the *other* kine upon the brink of the river.

4 And the ill favoured and leanfleshed kine did eat up the seven well favoured and fat kine. So Pha'raoh awoke.

5 And he slept and dreamed the second time: and, behold, seven ears of corn came up upon one stalk, rank and good.

6 And, behold, seven thin ears and blasted with the east wind sprung up after them.

7 And the seven thin ears devoured the seven rank and full ears. And Pha'raoh awoke, and, behold, *it was* a dream.

8 And it came to pass in the morning that his spirit was troubled; and he sent and called for all the magicians of E'gypt, and all the wise men thereof: and Pha'raoh told them his dream; but *there was* none that could interpret them unto Pha'raoh.

9 ¶ Then spake the chief butler unto Pha'raoh, saying, I do remember my faults this day:

10 Pha'raoh was wroth with his servants, and put me in ward in the captain of the guard's house, *both* me and the chief baker:

11 And we dreamed a dream in one night, I and he; we dreamed each man according to the interpretation of his dream.

12 And *there was* there with us a young man, an He'brew, servant to the captain of the guard; and we told him, and he interpreted to us our dreams; to each man according to his dream he did interpret.

13 And it came to pass, as he interpreted to us, so it was; me he restored unto mine office, and him he hanged.

14 ¶ Then Pha'raoh sent and called Jo'seph, and they brought him hastily out of the dungeon: and he shaved *himself,* and changed his raiment, and came in unto Pha'raoh.

15 And Pha'raoh said unto Jo'seph, I have dreamed a dream, and *there is* none that can interpret it: and I have heard say of thee, *that* thou canst understand a dream to interpret it.

16 And Jo'seph answered Pha'raoh, saying, *It is* not in me: God shall give Pha'raoh an answer of peace.

17 And Pha'raoh said unto Jo'seph, In my dream, behold, I stood upon the bank of the river:

18 And, behold, there came up out of the river seven kine, fatfleshed and well favoured; and they fed in a meadow:

19 And, behold, seven other kine came up after them, poor and very ill favoured and lean-

fleshed, such as I never saw in all the land of E'gypt for badness:

20 And the lean and the ill favoured kine did eat up the first seven fat kine:

21 And when they had eaten them up, it could not be known that they had eaten them; but they *were* still ill favoured, as at the beginning. So I awoke.

22 And I saw in my dream, and, behold, seven ears came up in one stalk, full and good:

23 And, behold, seven ears, withered, thin, *and* blasted with the east wind, sprung up after them:

24 And the thin ears devoured the seven good ears: and I told *this* unto the magicians; but *there was* none that could declare *it* to me.

25 ¶ And Jo'seph said unto Pha'raoh, The dream of Pha'raoh *is* one: God hath shewed Pha'raoh what he *is* about to do.

26 The seven good kine *are* seven years; and the seven good ears *are* seven years: the dream *is* one.

27 And the seven thin and ill favoured kine that came up after them *are* seven years; and the seven empty ears blasted with the east wind shall be seven years of famine.

28 This *is* the thing which I have spoken unto Pha'raoh: What God *is* about to do he sheweth unto Pha'raoh.

29 Behold, there come seven years of great plenty throughout all the land of E'gypt:

30 And there shall arise after them seven years of famine; and all the plenty shall be forgotten in the land of E'gypt; and the famine shall consume the land;

31 And the plenty shall not be known in the land by reason of that famine following; for it *shall be* very grievous.

32 And for that the dream was doubled unto Pha'raoh twice; *it is* because the thing *is* established by God, and God will shortly bring it to pass.

33 Now therefore let Pha'raoh look out a man discreet and wise, and set him over the land of E'gypt.

34 Let Pha'raoh do *this*, and let him appoint officers over the land, and take up the fifth part of the land of E'gypt in the seven plenteous years.

35 And let them gather all the food of those good years that come, and lay up corn under the hand of Pha'raoh, and let them keep food in the cities.

36 And that food shall be for store to the land against the seven years of famine, which shall be in the land of E'gypt; that the land perish not through the famine.

37 ¶ And the thing was good in the eyes of Pha'raoh, and in the eyes of all his servants.

38 And Pha'raoh said unto his servants, Can we find such *a one* as this *is*, a man in whom the Spirit of God *is*?

39 And Pha'raoh said unto Jo'seph, Forasmuch as God hath shewed thee all this, *there is* none so discreet and wise as thou *art*:

40 Thou shalt be over my house, and according unto thy word shall all my people be ruled: only in the throne will I be greater than thou.

41 And Pha'raoh said unto Jo'seph, See, I have set thee over all the land of E'gypt.

42 And Pha'raoh took off his ring from his hand, and put it upon Jo'seph's hand, and arrayed him in vestures of fine linen, and put a gold chain about his neck;

43 And he made him to ride in the second chariot which he had; and they cried before him, Bow the knee: and he made him *ruler* over all the land of E'gypt.

44 And Pha'raoh said unto Jo'seph, I *am* Pha'raoh, and without thee shall no man lift up his hand or foot in all the land of E'gypt.

45 And Pha'raoh called Jo'seph's name Zaph'nath-pa-a-ne'ah; and he gave him to wife As'e-nath the daughter of Po-tiphe-rah priest of On. And Jo'seph went out over *all* the land of E'gypt.

46 ¶ And Jo'seph *was* thirty years old when he stood before Pha'raoh king of E'gypt. And Jo'seph went out from the presence of Pha'raoh, and went throughout all the land of E'gypt.

47 And in the seven plenteous years the earth brought forth by handfuls.

48 And he gathered up all the food of the seven years, which were in the land of E'gypt, and laid up the food in the cities: the food of the field, which *was* round about every city, laid he up in the same.

49 And Jo'seph gathered corn as the sand of the sea, very much, until he left numbering; for *it was* without number.

50 And unto Jo'seph were born two sons before the years of famine came, which As'e-nath the daughter of Po-tiphe-rah priest of On bare unto him.

51 And Jo'seph called the name of the firstborn Ma-nas'seh: For God, *said he*, hath made me forget all my toil, and all my father's house.

52 And the name of the second called E'phraim: For God hath caused me to be fruitful in the land of my affliction.

53 ¶ And the seven years of plenteousness, that was in the land of E'gypt, were ended.

54 And the seven years of dearth began to come, according as Jo'seph had said: and the dearth was in all lands; but in all the land of E'gypt there was bread.

55 And when all the land of E'gypt was famished, the people cried to Pha'raoh for bread: and Pha'raoh said unto all the E-gyptians; Go unto Jo'seph; what he saith to you, do.

56 And the famine was over all the face of the earth: And Jo'seph opened all the storehouses, and sold unto the E-gyptians; and the famine waxed sore in the land of E'gypt.

57 And all countries came into E'gypt to buy of Jo'seph for to buy *corn*; because that the famine was so sore in all lands.

42 NOW when Ja'cob saw that there was corn in E'gypt, Ja'cob said unto his sons, Why do ye look one upon another?

2 And he said, Behold, I have heard that there is corn in E'gypt: get you down thither, and buy for us from thence; that we may live, and not die.

3 ¶ And Jo'seph's ten brethren went down to buy corn in E'gypt.

4 But Ben'ja-min, Jo'seph's brother, Ja'cob sent not with his brethren; for he said, Lest peradventure mischief befall him.

5 And the sons of Is'ra-el came to buy *corn* among those that came: for the famine was in the land of Ca'naan.

6 And Jo'seph *was* the governor over the land, *and* he *it was* that sold to all the people of the land: and Jo'seph's brethren came, and bowed down themselves before him *with* their faces to the earth.

7 And Jo'seph saw his brethren, and he knew them, but made himself strange unto them, and spake roughly unto them; and he said unto

them, Whence come ye? And they said, From the land of Ca'naan to buy food.

8 And Jo'seph knew his brethren, but they knew not him.

9 And Jo'seph remembered the dreams which he dreamed of them, and said unto them, Ye are spies; to see the nakedness of the land ye are come.

10 And they said unto him, Nay, my lord, but to buy food are thy servants come.

11 We are all one man's sons; we are true men, thy servants are no spies.

12 And he said unto them, Nay, but to see the nakedness of the land ye are come.

13 And they said, Thy servants are twelve brethren, the sons of one man in the land of Ca'naan; and, behold, the youngest is this day with our father, and one is not.

14 And Jo'seph said unto them, That is it that I spake unto you, saying, Ye are spies:

15 Hereby ye shall be proved: By the life of Pha'raoh ye shall not go forth hence, except your youngest brother come hither.

16 Send one of you, and let him fetch your brother, and ye shall be kept in prison, that your words may be proved, whether there be any truth in you: or else by the life of Pha'raoh surely ye are spies.

17 And he put them all together into ward three days.

18 And Jo'seph said unto them the third day, This do, and live; for I fear God:

19 If ye be true men, let one of your brethren be bound in the house of your prison: go ye, carry corn for the famine of your houses:

20 But bring your youngest brother unto me; so shall your words be verified, and ye shall not die. And they did so.

21 ¶ And they said one to another, We are verily guilty concerning our brother, in that we saw the anguish of his soul, when he besought us, and we would not hear; therefore is this distress come upon us.

22 And Reu'ben answered them, saying, Spake I not unto you, saying, Do not sin against the child; and ye would not hear? therefore, behold, also his blood is required.

23 And they knew not that Jo'seph understood them; for he spake unto them by an interpreter.

24 And he turned himself about from them, and wept; and returned to them again, and communed with them, and took from them Sim'e-on, and bound him before their eyes.

25 ¶ Then Jo'seph commanded to fill their sacks with corn, and to restore every man's money into his sack, and to give them provision for the way: and thus did he unto them.

26 And they laded their asses with the corn, and departed thence.

27 And as one of them opened his sack to give his ass provender in the inn, he espied his money; for, behold, it was in his sack's mouth.

28 And he said unto his brethren, My money is restored; and, lo, it is even in my sack: and their heart failed them, and they were afraid, saying one to another, What is this that God hath done unto us?

29 ¶ And they came unto Ja'cob their father unto the land of Ca'naan, and told him all that befell unto them; saying,

30 The man, who is the lord of the land, spake roughly to us, and took us for spies of the country.

31 And we said unto him, We are true men; we are no spies:

32 We be twelve brethren, sons of our father;

one is not, and the youngest is this day with our father in the land of Ca'naan.

33 And the man, the lord of the country, said unto us, Hereby shall I know that ye are true men; leave one of your brethren here with me, and take food for the famine of your households, and be gone:

34 And bring your youngest brother unto me: then shall I know that ye are no spies, but that ye are true men: so will I deliver you your brother, and ye shall traffick in the land.

35 ¶ And it came to pass as they emptied their sacks, that, behold, every man's bundle of money was in his sack: and when both they and their father saw the bundles of money, they were afraid.

36 And Ja'cob their father said unto them, Me have ye bereaved of my children: Jo'seph is not, and Sim'e-on is not, and ye will take Ben'-ja-min away: all these things are against me.

37 And Reu'ben spake unto his father, saying, Slay my two sons, if I bring him not to thee: deliver him into my hand, and I will bring him to thee again.

38 And he said, My son shall not go down with you; for his brother is dead, and he is left alone: if mischief befall him by the way in the which ye go, then shall ye bring down my gray hairs with sorrow to the grave.

43 AND the famine was sore in the land.

2 And it came to pass, when they had eaten up the corn which they had brought out of E'gypt, their father said unto them, Go again, buy us a little food.

3 And Ju'dah spake unto him, saying, The man did solemnly protest unto us, saying, Ye shall not see my face, except your brother be with you.

4 If thou wilt send our brother with us, we will go down and buy thee food:

5 But if thou wilt not send him, we will not go down: for the man said unto us, Ye shall not see my face, except your brother be with you.

6 And Is'ra-el said, Wherefore dealt ye so ill with me, as to tell the man whether ye had yet a brother?

7 And they said, The man asked us straitly of our state, and of our kindred, saying, Is your father yet alive? have ye another brother? and we told him according to the tenor of these words: could we certainly know that he would say, Bring your brother down?

8 And Ju'dah said unto Is'ra-el his father, Send the lad with me, and we will arise and go; that we may live, and not die, both we, and thou, and also our little ones.

9 I will be surety for him; of my hand shalt thou require him: if I bring him not unto thee, and set him before thee, then let me bear the blame for ever:

10 For except we had lingered, surely now we had returned this second time.

11 And their father Is'ra-el said unto them, If it must be so now, do this; take of the best fruits in the land in your vessels, and carry down the man a present, a little balm, and a little honey, spices, and myrrh, nuts, and almonds:

12 And take double money in your hand; and the money that was brought again in the mouth of your sacks, carry it again in your hand; peradventure it was an oversight:

13 Take also your brother, and arise, go again unto the man:

14 And God Almighty give you mercy before the man, that he may send away your other

brother, and Ben'ja-min. If I be bereaved *of my children*, I am bereaved.

15 ¶ And the men took that present, and they took double money in their hand, and Ben'-ja-min; and rose up, and went down to E'gypt, and stood before Jo'seph.

16 And when Jo'seph saw Ben'ja-min with them, he said to the ruler of his house, Bring *these* men home, and slay, and make ready; for *these* men shall dine with me at noon.

17 And the man did as Jo'seph bade; and the man brought the men into Jo'seph's house.

18 And the men were afraid, because they were brought into Jo'seph's house; and they said, Because of the money that was returned in our sacks at the first time are we brought in; that he may seek occasion against us, and fall upon us, and take us for bondmen, and our asses.

19 And they came near to the steward of Jo'-seph's house, and they communed with him at the door of the house,

20 And said, O sir, we came indeed down at the first time to buy food:

21 And it came to pass, when we came to the inn, that we opened our sacks, and, behold, ev-ery man's money *was* in the mouth of his sack, our money in full weight: and we have brought it again in our hand.

22 And other money have we brought down in our hands to buy food: we cannot tell who put our money in our sacks.

23 And he said, Peace *be* to you, fear not: your God, and the God of your father, hath giv-en you treasure in your sacks: I had your mon-ey. And he brought Sim'e-on out unto them.

24 And the man brought the men into Jo'-seph's house, and gave *them* water, and they washed their feet; and he gave their asses prov-ender.

25 And they made ready the present against Jo'seph came at noon: for they heard that they should eat bread there.

26 ¶ And when Jo'seph came home, they brought him the present which *was* in their hand into the house, and bowed themselves to him to the earth.

27 And he asked them of *their* welfare, and said, *Is* your father well, the old man of whom ye spake? *Is* he yet alive?

28 And they answered, Thy servant our fa-ther *is* in good health, he *is* yet alive. And they bowed down their heads, and made obeisance.

29 And he lifted up his eyes, and saw his brother Ben'ja-min, his mother's son, and said, *Is* this your younger brother, of whom ye spake unto me? And he said, God be gracious unto thee, my son.

30 And Jo'seph made haste; for his bowels did yearn upon his brother: and he sought *where* to weep; and he entered into *his* cham-ber, and wept there.

31 And he washed his face, and went out, and refrained himself, and said, Set on bread.

32 And they set on for him by himself, and for them by themselves, and for the E-gyptians, which did eat with him, by themselves: because the E-gyptians might not eat bread with the He'brews; for that *is* an abomination unto the E-gyptians.

33 And they sat before him, the firstborn ac-cording to his birthright, and the youngest ac-cording to his youth: and the men marvelled one at another.

34 And he took *and sent* messes unto them from before him: but Ben'ja-min's mess was five times so much as any of theirs. And they drank, and were merry with him.

44 AND he commanded the steward of his house, saying, Fill the men's sacks *with* food, as much as they can carry, and put every man's money in his sack's mouth.

2 And put my cup, the silver cup, in the sack's mouth of the youngest, and his corn money. And he did according to the word that Jo'seph had spoken.

3 As soon as the morning was light, the men were sent away, they and their asses.

4 *And* when they were gone out of the city, *and* not yet far off, Jo'seph said unto his stew-ard, Up, follow after the men; and when thou dost overtake them, say unto them, Wherefore have ye rewarded evil for good?

5 *Is* not this *it* in which my lord drinketh, and whereby indeed he divineth? ye have done evil in so doing.

6 ¶ And he overtook them, and he spake unto them these same words.

7 And they said unto him, Wherefore saith my lord these words? God forbid that thy ser-vants should do according to this thing:

8 Behold, the money, which we found in our sacks' mouths, we brought again unto thee out of the land of Ca'naan: how then should we steal out of thy lord's house silver or gold?

9 With whomsoever of thy servants it be found, both let him die, and we also will be my lord's bondmen.

10 And he said, Now also *let* it *be* according unto your words: he with whom it is found shall be my servant; and ye shall be blameless.

11 Then they speedily took down every man his sack to the ground, and opened every man his sack.

12 And he searched, *and* began at the eldest, and left at the youngest: and the cup was found in Ben'ja-min's sack.

13 Then they rent their clothes, and laded ev-ery man his ass, and returned to the city.

14 ¶ And Ju'dah and his brethren came to Jo'seph's house; for he *was* yet there: and they fell before him on the ground.

15 And Jo'seph said unto them, What deed *is* this that ye have done? wot ye not that such a man as I can certainly divine?

16 And Ju'dah said, What shall we say unto my lord? what shall we speak? or how shall we clear ourselves? God hath found out the iniquity of thy servants: behold, we *are* my lord's ser-vants, both we, and *he* also with whom the cup is found.

17 And he said, God forbid that I should do so: *but* the man in whose hand the cup is found, he shall be my servant; and as for you, get you up in peace unto your father.

18 ¶ Then Ju'dah came near unto him, and said, Oh my lord, let thy servant, I pray thee, speak a word in my lord's ears, and let not thine anger burn against thy servant: for thou *art* even as Pha'raoh.

19 My lord asked his servants, saying, Have ye a father, or a brother?

20 And we said unto my lord, We have a fa-ther, an old man, and a child of his old age, a little one; and his brother is dead, and he alone is left of his mother, and his father loveth him.

21 And thou saidst unto thy servants, Bring him down unto me, that I may set mine eyes upon him.

22 And we said unto my lord, The lad cannot leave his father: for *if* he should leave his fa-ther, *his father* would die.

23 And thou saidst unto thy servants, Except your youngest brother come down with you, ye shall see my face no more.

24 And it came to pass when we came up unto thy servant my father, we told him the words of my lord.

25 And our father said, Go again, *and* buy us a little food.

26 And we said, We cannot go down: if our youngest brother be with us, then will we go down: for we may not see the man's face, except our youngest brother *be* with us.

27 And thy servant my father said unto us, Ye know that my wife bare me two *sons:*

28 And the one went out from me, and I said, Surely he is torn in pieces; and I saw him not since:

29 And if ye take this also from me, and mischief befall him, ye shall bring down my gray hairs with sorrow to the grave.

30 Now therefore when I come to thy servant my father, and the lad *be* not with us; seeing that his life is bound up in the lad's life;

31 It shall come to pass, when he seeth that the lad *is* not *with us,* that he will die: and thy servants shall bring down the gray hairs of thy servant our father with sorrow to the grave.

32 For thy servant became surety for the lad unto my father, saying, If I bring him not unto thee, then I shall bear the blame to my father for ever.

33 Now therefore, I pray thee, let thy servant abide instead of the lad a bondman to my lord; and let the lad go up with his brethren.

34 And for how shall I go up to my father, and the lad *be* not with me? lest peradventure I see the evil that shall come on my father.

45 THEN Jo'seph could not refrain himself before all them that stood by him; and he cried, Cause every man to go out from me. And there stood no man with him, while Jo'seph made himself known unto his brethren.

2 And he wept aloud: and the E-gyptians and the house of Pha'raoh heard.

3 And Jo'seph said unto his brethren, I *am* Jo'seph; doth my father yet live? And his brethren could not answer him; for they were troubled at his presence.

4 And Jo'seph said unto his brethren, Come near to me, I pray you. And they came near. And he said, I *am* Jo'seph your brother, whom ye sold into E'gypt.

5 Now therefore be not grieved, nor angry with yourselves, that ye sold me hither: for God did send me before you to preserve life.

6 For these two years *hath* the famine *been* in the land: and yet *there are* five years, in the which *there shall* neither *be* earing nor harvest.

7 And God sent me before you to preserve you a posterity in the earth, and to save your lives by a great deliverance.

8 So now *it was* not you *that* sent me hither, but God: and he hath made me a father to Pha'-raoh, and lord of all his house, and a ruler throughout all the land of E'gypt.

9 Haste ye, and go up to my father, and say unto him, Thus saith thy son Jo'seph, God hath made me lord of all E'gypt: come down unto me, tarry not:

10 And thou shalt dwell in the land of Go'-shen, and thou shalt be near unto me, thou, and thy children, and thy children's children, and thy flocks, and thy herds, and all that thou hast:

11 And there will I nourish thee; for yet *there are* five years of famine; lest thou, and thy

household, and all that thou hast, come to poverty.

12 And, behold, your eyes see, and the eyes of my brother Ben'ja-min, that *it is* my mouth that speaketh unto you.

13 And ye shall tell my father of all my glory in E'gypt, and of all that ye have seen; and ye shall haste and bring down my father hither.

14 And he fell upon his brother Ben'ja-min's neck, and wept; and Ben'ja-min wept upon his neck.

15 Moreover he kissed all his brethren, and wept upon them: and after that his brethren talked with him.

16 ¶ And the fame thereof was heard in Pha'raoh's house, saying, Jo'seph's brethren are come: and it pleased Pha'raoh well, and his servants.

17 And Pha'raoh said unto Jo'seph, Say unto thy brethren, This do ye; lade your beasts, and go, get you unto the land of Ca'naan;

18 And take your father and your households, and come unto me: and I will give you the good of the land of E'gypt, and ye shall eat the fat of the land.

19 Now thou art commanded, this do ye; take you wagons out of the land of E'gypt for your little ones, and for your wives, and bring your father, and come.

20 Also regard not your stuff; for the good of all the land of E'gypt is yours.

21 And the children of Is'ra-el did so: and Jo'-seph gave them wagons, according to the commandment of Pha'raoh, and gave them provision for the way.

22 To all of them he gave each man changes of raiment; but to Ben'ja-min he gave three hundred *pieces* of silver, and five changes of raiment.

23 And to his father he sent after this *manner;* ten asses laden with the good things of E'-gypt, and ten she asses laden with corn and bread and meat for his father by the way.

24 So he sent his brethren away, and they departed: and he said unto them, See that ye fall not out by the way.

25 ¶ And they went up out of E'gypt, and came into the land of Ca'naan unto Ja'cob their father,

26 And told him, saying, Jo'seph *is* yet alive, and he *is* governor over all the land of E'gypt. And Ja'cob's heart fainted, for he believed them not.

27 And they told him all the words of Jo'-seph, which he had said unto them: and when he saw the wagons which Jo'seph had sent to carry him, the spirit of Ja'cob their father revived:

28 And Is'ra-el said, *It is* enough; Jo'seph my son *is* yet alive: I will go and see him before I die.

46 AND Is'ra-el took his journey with all that he had, and came to Be'er-she'ba, and offered sacrifices unto the God of his father I'saac.

2 And God spake unto Is'ra-el in the visions of the night, and said, Ja'cob, Ja'cob. And he said, Here *am* I.

3 And he said I *am* God, the God of thy father: fear not to go down into E'gypt; for I will there make of thee a great nation:

4 I will go down with thee into E'gypt; and I will also surely bring thee up *again:* and Jo'seph shall put his hand upon thine eyes.

5 And Ja'cob rose up from Be'er-she'ba: and the sons of Is'ra-el carried Ja'cob their father,

and their little ones, and their wives, in the wagons which Pha'raoh had sent to carry him.

6 And they took their cattle, and their goods, which they had gotten in the land of Ca'naan, and came into E'gypt, Ja'cob, and all his seed with him:

7 His sons, and his sons' sons with him, his daughters, and his sons' daughters, and all his seed brought he with him into E'gypt.

8 ¶ And these are the names of the children of Is'ra-el, which came into E'gypt, Ja'cob and his sons: Reu'ben, Ja'cob's firstborn.

9 And the sons of Reu'ben; Ha'noch, and Phal'lu, and Hez'ron, and Car'mi.

10 ¶ And the sons of Sim'e-on; Je-mu'el, and Ja'min, and O'had, and Ja'chin, and Zo'har, and Sha'ul the son of a Ca'naan-it-ish woman.

11 ¶ And the sons of Le'vi; Ger'shon, Ko'hath, and Me-ra'ri.

12 ¶ And the sons of Ju'dah; Er, and O'nan, and She'lah, and Pha'rez, and Za'rah: but Er and O'nan died in the land of Ca'naan. And the sons of Pha'rez were Hez'ron and Ha'mul.

13 ¶ And the sons of Is'sa-char; To'la, and Phu'vah, and Job, and Shim'ron.

14 ¶ And the sons of Zeb'u-lun; Se'red, and E'lon, and Jah'le-el.

15 These be the sons of Le'ah, which she bare unto Ja'cob in Pa'dan–a'ram, with his daughter Di'nah: all the souls of his sons and his daughters were thirty and three.

16 ¶ And the sons of Gad; Ziph'i-on, and Hag'gi, Shu'ni, and Ez'bon, E'ri, and Ar'o-di, and A-re'li.

17 ¶ And the sons of Ash'er; Jim'nah, and Ishu-ah, and Is'u-i, and Be-ri'ah, and Se'rah their sister: and the sons of Be-ri'ah; He'ber, and Mal'chi-el.

18 These are the sons of Zil'pah, whom La'ban gave to Le'ah his daughter, and these she bare unto Ja'cob, even sixteen souls.

19 The sons of Ra'chel Ja'cob's wife; Jo'seph, and Ben'ja-min.

20 ¶ And unto Jo'seph in the land of E'gypt were born Ma-nas'seh and E'phra-im, which As'e-nath the daughter of Po-tiphe-rah priest of On bare unto him.

21 ¶ And the sons of Ben'ja-min were Be'lah, and Be'cher, and Ash'bel, Ge'ra, and Na'a-man, E'hi, and Rosh, Mup'pim, and Hup'pim, and Ard.

22 These are the sons of Ra'chel, which were born to Ja'cob: all the souls were fourteen.

23 ¶ And the sons of Dan; Hu'shim.

24 ¶ And the sons of Naph'ta-li; Jah'ze-el, and Gu'ni, and Je'zer, and Shil'lem.

25 These are the sons of Bil'hah, which La'ban gave unto Ra'chel his daughter, and she bare these unto Ja'cob: all the souls were seven.

26 All the souls that came with Ja'cob into E'gypt, which came out of his loins, besides Ja'cob's sons' wives, all the souls were threescore and six;

27 And the sons of Jo'seph, which were born him in E'gypt, were two souls: all the souls of the house of Ja'cob, which came into E'gypt, were threescore and ten.

28 ¶ And he sent Ju'dah before him unto Jo'seph, to direct his face unto Go'shen; and they came into the land of Go'shen.

29 And Jo'seph made ready his chariot, and went up to meet Is'ra-el his father, to Go'shen, and presented himself unto him; and he fell on his neck, and wept on his neck a good while.

30 And Is'ra-el said unto Jo'seph, Now let me die, since I have seen thy face, because thou art yet alive.

31 And Jo'seph said unto his brethren, and unto his father's house, I will go up, and shew Pha'raoh, and say unto him, My brethren, and my father's house, which were in the land of Ca'naan, are come unto me;

32 And the men are shepherds, for their trade hath been to feed cattle; and they have brought their flocks, and their herds, and all that they have.

33 And it shall come to pass, when Pha'raoh shall call you, and shall say, What is your occupation?

34 That ye shall say, Thy servants' trade hath been about cattle from our youth even until now, both we, and also our fathers: that ye may dwell in the land of Go'shen; for every shepherd is an abomination unto the E-gyptians.

47 THEN Jo'seph came and told Pha'raoh, and said, My father and my brethren, and their flocks, and their herds, and all that they have, are come out of the land of Ca'naan; and, behold, they are in the land of Go'shen.

2 And he took some of his brethren, even five men, and presented them unto Pha'raoh.

3 And Pha'raoh said unto his brethren, What is your occupation? And they said unto Pha'raoh, Thy servants are shepherds, both we, and also our fathers.

4 They said moreover unto Pha'raoh, For to sojourn in the land are we come; for thy servants have no pasture for their flocks; for the famine is sore in the land of Ca'naan: now therefore, we pray thee, let thy servants dwell in the land of Go'shen.

5 And Pha'raoh spake unto Jo'seph, saying, Thy father and thy brethren are come unto thee:

6 The land of E'gypt is before thee; in the best of the land make thy father and brethren to dwell; in the land of Go'shen let them dwell: and if thou knowest any men of activity among them, then make them rulers over my cattle.

7 And Jo'seph brought in Ja'cob his father, and set him before Pha'raoh: and Ja'cob blessed Pha'raoh.

8 And Pha'raoh said unto Ja'cob, How old art thou?

9 And Ja'cob said unto Pha'raoh, The days of the years of my pilgrimage are an hundred and thirty years: few and evil have the days of the years of my life been, and have not attained unto the days of the years of the life of my fathers in the days of their pilgrimage.

10 And Ja'cob blessed Pha'raoh, and went out from before Pha'raoh.

11 ¶ And Jo'seph placed his father and his brethren, and gave them a possession in the land of E'gypt, in the best of the land, in the land of Ra-me'ses, as Pha'raoh had commanded.

12 And Jo'seph nourished his father, and his brethren, and all his father's household, with bread, according to their families.

13 ¶ And there was no bread in all the land; for the famine was very sore, so that the land of E'gypt and all the land of Ca'naan fainted by reason of the famine.

14 And Jo'seph gathered up all the money that was found in the land of E'gypt, and in the land of Ca'naan, for the corn which they bought: and Jo'seph brought the money into Pha'raoh's house.

15 And when money failed in the land of E'gypt, and in the land of Ca'naan, all the E-gyptians came unto Jo'seph, and said, Give us

bread: for why should we die in thy presence? for the money faileth.

16 And Jo'seph said, Give your cattle; and I will give you for your cattle, if money fail.

17 And they brought their cattle unto Jo'-seph: and Jo'seph gave them bread *in exchange* for horses, and for the flocks, and for the cattle of the herds, and for the asses: and he fed them with bread for all their cattle for that year.

18 When that year was ended, they came unto him the second year, and said unto him, We will not hide *it* from my lord, how that our money is spent; my lord also hath our herds of cattle; there is not ought left in the sight of my lord, but our bodies, and our lands:

19 Wherefore shall we die before thine eyes, both we and our land? buy us and our land for bread, and we and our land will be servants unto Pha'raoh: and give *us* seed, that we may live, and not die, that the land be not desolate.

20 And Jo'seph bought all the land of E'gypt for Pha'raoh; for the E-gyptians sold every man his field, because the famine prevailed over them: so the land became Pha'raoh's.

21 And as for the people, he removed them to cities from *one* end of the borders of E'gypt even to the *other* end thereof.

22 Only the land of the priests bought he not; for the priests had a portion *assigned them* of Pha'raoh, and did eat their portion which Pha'-raoh gave them: wherefore they sold not their lands.

23 Then Jo'seph said unto the people, Behold, I have bought you this day and your land for Pha'raoh: lo, *here is* seed for you, and ye shall sow the land.

24 And it shall come to pass in the increase, that ye shall give the fifth *part* unto Pha'raoh, and four parts shall be your own, for seed of the field, and for your food, and for them of your households, and for food for your little ones.

25 And they said, Thou hast saved our lives: let us find grace in the sight of my lord, and we will be Pha'raoh's servants.

26 And Jo'seph made it a law over the land of E'gypt unto this day, *that* Pha'raoh should have the fifth *part;* except the land of the priests only, *which* became not Pha'raoh's.

27 ¶ And Is'ra-el dwelt in the land of E'gypt, in the country of Go'shen; and they had possessions therein, and grew, and multiplied exceedingly.

28 And Ja'cob lived in the land of E'gypt seventeen years: so the whole age of Ja'cob was an hundred forty and seven years.

29 And the time drew nigh that Is'ra-el must die: and he called his son Jo'seph, and said unto him, If now I have found grace in thy sight, put, I pray thee, thy hand under my thigh, and deal kindly and truly with me; bury me not, I pray thee, in E'gypt:

30 But I will lie with my fathers, and thou shalt carry me out of E'gypt, and bury me in their buryingplace. And he said, I will do as thou hast said.

31 And he said, Swear unto me. And he sware unto him. And Is'ra-el bowed himself upon the bed's head.

48 AND it came to pass after these things, that *one* told Jo'seph, Behold, thy father *is* sick: and he took with him his two sons, Ma-nas'seh and E'phra-im.

2 And *one* told Ja'cob, and said, Behold, thy son Jo'seph cometh unto thee: and Is'ra-el strengthened himself, and sat upon the bed.

3 And Ja'cob said unto Jo'seph, God Al-mighty appeared unto me at Luz in the land of Ca'naan, and blessed me,

4 And said unto me, Behold, I will make thee fruitful, and multiply thee, and I will make of thee a multitude of people; and will give this land to thy seed after thee *for* an everlasting possession.

5 ¶ And now thy two sons, E'phra-im and Ma-nas'seh, which were born unto thee in the land of E'gypt before I came unto thee into E'-gypt, *are* mine; as Reu'ben and Sim'e-on, they shall be mine.

6 And thy issue, which thou begettest after them, shall be thine, *and* shall be called after the name of their brethren in their inheritance.

7 And as for me, when I came from Pa'dan, Ra'chel died by me in the land of Ca'naan in the way, when yet *there was* but a little way to come unto Eph'rath: and I buried her there in the way of Eph'rath; the same *is* Beth'-le-hem.

8 And Is'ra-el beheld Jo'seph's sons, and said, Who *are* these?

9 And Jo'seph said unto his father, They *are* my sons, whom God hath given me in this *place*. And he said, Bring them, I pray thee, unto me, and I will bless them.

10 Now the eyes of Is'ra-el were dim for age, *so that* he could not see. And he brought them near unto him; and he kissed them, and embraced them.

11 And Is'ra-el said unto Jo'seph, I had not thought to see thy face: and, lo, God hath shewed me also thy seed.

12 And Jo'seph brought them out from between his knees, and he bowed himself with his face to the earth.

13 And Jo'seph took them both, E'phra-im in his right hand toward Is'ra-el's left hand, and Ma-nas'seh in his left hand toward Is'ra-el's right hand, and brought *them* near unto him.

14 And Is'ra-el stretched out his right hand, and laid *it* upon E'phra-im's head, who *was* the younger, and his left hand upon Ma-nas'seh's head, guiding his hands wittingly; for Ma-nas'-seh *was* the firstborn.

15 ¶ And he blessed Jo'seph, and said, God, before whom my fathers A'bra-ham and I'saac did walk, the God which fed me all my life long unto this day,

16 The Angel which redeemed me from all evil, bless the lads; and let my name be named on them, and the name of my fathers A'bra-ham and I'saac; and let them grow into a multitude in the midst of the earth.

17 And when Jo'seph saw that his father laid his right hand upon the head of E'phra-im, it displeased him: and he held up his father's hand, to remove it from E'phra-im's head unto Ma-nas'seh's head.

18 And Jo'seph said unto his father, Not so, my father: for this *is* the firstborn; put thy right hand upon his head.

19 And his father refused, and said, I know *it*, my son, I know *it*: he also shall become a people, and he also shall be great: but truly his younger brother shall be greater than he, and his seed shall become a multitude of nations.

20 And he blessed them that day, saying In thee shall Is'ra-el bless, saying, God make thee as E'phra-im and as Ma-nas'seh: and he set E'-phra-im before Ma-nas'seh.

21 And Is'ra-el said unto Jo'seph, Behold, I die: but God shall be with you, and bring you again unto the land of your fathers.

22 Moreover I have given to thee one portion above thy brethren, which I took out of the

hand of the Am'or-ite with my sword and with my bow.

49 AND Ja'cob called unto his sons, and said, Gather yourselves together, that I may tell you *that* which shall befall you in the last days.

2 Gather yourselves together, and hear, ye sons of Ja'cob; and hearken unto Is'ra-el your father.

3 ¶ Reu'ben, thou *art* my firstborn, my might, and the beginning of my strength, the excellency of dignity, and the excellency of power:

4 Unstable as water, thou shalt not excel; because thou wentest up to thy father's bed; then defiledst thou *it:* he went up to my couch.

5 ¶ Sim'e-on and Le'vi *are* brethren; instruments of cruelty *are* in their habitations.

6 O my soul, come not thou into their secret; unto their assembly, mine honour, be not thou united: for in their anger they slew a man, and in their selfwill they digged down a wall.

7 Cursed *be* their anger, for *it was* fierce; and their wrath, for it was cruel: I will divide them in Ja'cob, and scatter them in Is'ra-el.

8 ¶ Ju'dah, thou *art he* whom thy brethren shall praise: thy hand *shall be* in the neck of thine enemies; thy father's children shall bow down before thee.

9 Ju'dah *is* a lion's whelp: from the prey, my son, thou art gone up: he stooped down, he couched as a lion, and as an old lion; who shall rouse him up?

10 The sceptre shall not depart from Ju'dah, nor a lawgiver from between his feet, until Shi'-loh come; and unto him *shall* the gathering of the people *be.*

11 Binding his foal unto the vine, and his ass's colt unto the choice vine; he washed his garments in wine, and his clothes in the blood of grapes:

12 His eyes *shall be* red with wine, and his teeth white with milk.

13 ¶ Zeb'u-lun shall dwell at the haven of the sea; and he *shall be* for an haven of ships; and his border *shall be* unto Zi'don.

14 ¶ Is'sa-char *is* a strong ass couching down between two burdens:

15 And he saw that rest *was* good, and the land that *it was* pleasant; and bowed his shoulder to bear, and became a servant unto tribute.

16 ¶ Dan shall judge his people, as one of the tribes of Is'ra-el.

17 Dan shall be a serpent by the way, an adder in the path, that biteth the horse heels, so that his rider shall fall backward.

18 I have waited for thy salvation, O LORD.

19 ¶ Gad, a troop shall overcome him: but he shall overcome at the last.

20 ¶ Out of Ash'er his bread *shall be* fat, and he shall yield royal dainties.

21 ¶ Naph'ta-li *is* a hind let loose: he giveth goodly words.

22 ¶ Jo'seph *is* a fruitful bough, *even* a fruitful bough by a well; *whose* branches run over the wall:

23 The archers have sorely grieved him, and shot *at him*, and hated him:

24 But his bow abode in strength, and the arms of his hands were made strong by the hands of the mighty God of Ja'cob; (from thence *is* the shepherd, the stone of Is'ra-el:)

25 *Even* by the God of thy father, who shall help thee; and by the Almighty, who shall bless

thee with blessings of heaven above, blessings of the deep that lieth under, blessings of the breasts, and of the womb:

26 The blessings of thy father have prevailed above the blessings of my progenitors unto the utmost bound of the everlasting hills: they shall be on the head of Jo'seph, and on the crown of the head of him that was separate from his brethren.

27 ¶ Ben'ja-min shall ravin *as* a wolf: in the morning he shall devour the prey, and at night he shall divide the spoil.

28 ¶ All these *are* the twelve tribes of Is'ra-el: and this *is it* that their father spake unto them, and blessed them; every one according to his blessing he blessed them.

29 And he charged them, and said unto them, I am to be gathered unto my people: bury me with my fathers in the cave that *is* in the field of E'phron the Hit'tite,

30 In the cave that *is* in the field of Mach-pe'lah, which *is* before Mam're, in the land of Ca'naan, which A'bra-ham bought with the field of E'phron the Hit'tite for a possession of a buryingplace.

31 There they buried A'bra-ham and Sa'rah his wife; there they buried I'saac and Re-bek'ah his wife; and there I buried Le'ah.

32 The purchase of the field and of the cave that *is* therein *was* from the children of Heth.

33 And when Ja'cob had made an end of commanding his sons, he gathered up his feet into the bed, and yielded up the ghost, and was gathered unto his people.

50 AND Jo'seph fell upon his father's face, and wept upon him, and kissed him.

2 And Jo'seph commanded his servants the physicians to embalm his father: and the physicians embalmed Is'ra-el.

3 And forty days were fulfilled for him; for so are fulfilled the days of those which are embalmed: and the E-gyptians mourned for him threescore and ten days.

4 And when the days of his mourning were past, Jo'seph spake unto the house of Pha'raoh, saying, If now I have found grace in your eyes, speak, I pray you, in the ears of Pha'raoh, saying,

5 My father made me swear, saying, Lo, I die: in my grave which I have digged for me in the land of Ca'naan, there shalt thou bury me. Now therefore let me go up, I pray thee, and bury my father, and I will come again.

6 And Pha'raoh said, Go up, and bury thy father, according as he made thee swear.

7 ¶ And Jo'seph went up to bury his father: and with him went up all the servants of Pha'-raoh, the elders of his house, and all the elders of the land of E'gypt,

8 And all the house of Jo'seph, and his brethren, and his father's house: only their little ones, and their flocks, and their herds, they left in the land of Go'shen.

9 And there went up with him both chariots and horsemen: and it was a very great company.

10 And they came to the threshingfloor of A'-tad, which *is* beyond Jor'dan, and there they mourned with a great and very sore lamentation: and he made a mourning for his father seven days.

11 And when the inhabitants of the land, the Ca'naan-ites, saw the mourning in the floor of A'tad, they said, This *is* a grievous mourning to the E-gyptians: wherefore the name of it was

called A'bel-miz'ra-im, which is beyond Jor'-dan.

12 And his sons did unto him according as he commanded them:

13 For his sons carried him into the land of Ca'naan, and buried him in the cave of the field of Mach-pe'lah, which A'bra-ham bought with the field for a possession of a buryingplace of E'phron the Hit'tite, before Mam're.

14 ¶ And Jo'seph returned into E'gypt, he, and his brethren, and all that went up with him to bury his father, after he had buried his father.

15 ¶ And when Jo'seph's brethren saw that their father was dead, they said, Jo'seph will peradventure hate us, and will certainly requite us all the evil which we did unto him.

16 And they sent a messenger unto Jo'seph, saying, Thy father did command before he died, saying,

17 So shall ye say unto Jo'seph, Forgive, I pray thee now, the trespass of thy brethren, and their sin; for they did unto thee evil: and now, we pray thee, forgive the trespass of the servants of the God of thy father. And Jo'seph wept when they spake unto him.

18 And his brethren also went and fell down before his face; and they said, Behold, we be thy servants.

19 And Jo'seph said unto them, Fear not: for am I in the place of God?

20 But as for you, ye thought evil against me; but God meant it unto good, to bring to pass, as it is this day, to save much people alive.

21 Now therefore fear ye not: I will nourish you, and your little ones. And he comforted them, and spake kindly unto them.

22 ¶ And Jo'seph dwelt in E'gypt, he, and his father's house: and Jo'seph lived an hundred and ten years.

23 And Jo'seph saw E'phra-im's children of the third generation: the children also of Ma'-chir the son of Ma-nas'seh were brought up upon Jo'seph's knees.

24 And Jo'seph said unto his brethren, I die: and God will surely visit you, and bring you out of this land unto the land which he sware to A'bra-ham, to I'saac, and to Ja'cob.

25 And Jo'seph took an oath of the children of Is'ra-el, saying, God will surely visit you, and ye shall carry up my bones from hence.

26 So Jo'seph died, being an hundred and ten years old: and they embalmed him, and he was put in a coffin in E'gypt.

THE SECOND BOOK OF MOSES
COMMONLY CALLED

EXODUS

1 NOW these are the names of the children of Is'ra-el, which came into E'gypt; every man and his household came with Ja'cob.

2 Reu'ben, Sim'e-on, Le'vi, and Ju'dah,

3 Is'sa-char, Zeb'u-lun, and Ben'ja-min,

4 Dan, and Naph'ta-li, Gad, and Ash'er.

5 And all the souls that came out of the loins of Ja'cob were seventy souls: for Jo'seph was in E'gypt already.

6 And Jo'seph died, and all his brethren, and all that generation.

7 ¶ And the children of Is'ra-el were fruitful, and increased abundantly, and multiplied, and waxed exceeding mighty; and the land was filled with them.

8 Now there arose up a new king over E'-gypt, which knew not Jo'seph.

9 And he said unto his people, Behold, the people of the children of Is'ra-el are more and mightier than we:

10 Come on, let us deal wisely with them; lest they multiply, and it come to pass, that, when there falleth out any war, they join also unto our enemies, and fight against us, and so get them up out of the land.

11 Therefore they did set over them taskmasters to afflict them with their burdens. And they built for Pha'raoh treasure cities, Pi'thom and Ra-am'ses.

12 But the more they afflicted them, the more they multiplied and grew. And they were grieved because of the children of Is'ra-el.

13 And the E-gyptians made the children of Is'ra-el to serve with rigour:

14 And they made their lives bitter with hard bondage, in morter, and in brick, and in all manner of service in the field: all their service, wherein they made them serve, was with rigour.

15 ¶ And the king of E'gypt spake to the He'-brew midwives, of which the name of the one was Shiphrah, and the name of the other Pu'ah:

16 And he said, When ye do the office of a midwife to the He'brew women, and see them upon the stools; if it be a son, then ye shall kill him: but if it be a daughter, then she shall live.

17 But the midwives feared God, and did not as the king of E'gypt commanded them, but saved the men children alive.

18 And the king of E'gypt called for the midwives, and said unto them, Why have ye done this thing, and have saved the men children alive?

19 And the midwives said unto Pha'raoh, Because the He'brew women are not as the E-gyp'tian women; for they are lively, and are delivered ere the midwives come in unto them.

20 Therefore God dealt well with the midwives: and the people multiplied, and waxed very mighty.

21 And it came to pass, because the midwives feared God, that he made them houses.

22 And Pha'raoh charged all his people, saying, Every son that is born ye shall cast into the river, and every daughter ye shall save alive.

2 AND there went a man of the house of Le'-vi, and took to wife a daughter of Le'vi.

2 And the woman conceived, and bare a son: and when she saw him that he was a goodly child, she hid him three months.

3 And when she could not longer hide him, she took for him an ark of bulrushes, and daubed it with slime and with pitch, and put the child therein; and she laid it in the flags by the river's brink.

4 And his sister stood afar off, to wit what would be done to him.

5 ¶ And the daughter of Pha'raoh came down to wash herself at the river; and her maidens walked along by the river's side; and when she saw the ark among the flags, she sent her maid to fetch it.

6 And when she had opened it, she saw the child: and, behold, the babe wept. And she had compassion on him, and said, This is one of the He'brews' children.

7 Then said his sister to Pha'raoh's daughter, Shall I go and call to thee a nurse of the He'brew women, that she may nurse the child for thee?

8 And Pha'raoh's daughter said to her, Go. And the maid went and called the child's mother.

9 And Pha'raoh's daughter said unto her, Take this child away, and nurse it for me, and I will give thee thy wages. And the woman took the child, and nursed it.

10 And the child grew, and she brought him unto Pha'raoh's daughter, and he became her son. And she called his name Moses: and she said, Because I drew him out of the water.

11 ¶ And it came to pass in those days, when Mo'ses was grown, that he went out unto his brethren, and looked on their burdens: and he spied an E-gyp'tian smiting an He'brew, one of his brethren.

12 And he looked this way and that way, and when he saw that there was no man, he slew the E-gyp'tian, and hid him in the sand.

13 And when he went out the second day, behold, two men of the He'brews strove together: and he said to him that did the wrong, Wherefore smitest thou thy fellow?

14 And he said, Who made thee a prince and a judge over us? intendest thou to kill me, as thou killedst the E-gyp'tian? And Mo'ses feared, and said, Surely this thing is known.

15 Now when Pha'raoh heard this thing, he sought to slay Mo'ses. But Mo'ses fled from the face of Pha'raoh, and dwelt in the land of Mid'i-an: and he sat down by a well.

16 Now the priest of Mid'i-an had seven daughters: and they came and drew water, and filled the troughs to water their father's flock.

17 And the shepherds came and drove them away: but Mo'ses stood up and helped them, and watered their flock.

18 And when they came to Reu'el their father, he said, How is it that ye are come so soon to day?

19 And they said, An E-gyp'tian delivered us out of the hand of the shepherds, and also drew water enough for us, and watered the flock.

20 And he said unto his daughters, And where is he? why is it that ye have left the man? call him, that he may eat bread.

21 And Mo'ses was content to dwell with the man: and he gave Mo'ses Zip-po'rah his daughter.

22 And she bare him a son, and he called his name Ger'shom: for he said, I have been a stranger in a strange land.

23 ¶ And it came to pass in process of time, that the king of E'gypt died: and the children of Is'ra-el sighed by reason of the bondage, and they cried, and their cry came up unto God by reason of the bondage.

24 And God heard their groaning, and God remembered his covenant with A'bra-ham, with I'saac, and with Ja'cob.

25 And God looked upon the children of Is'ra-el, and God had respect unto them.

3 NOW Mo'ses kept the flock of Je'thro his father in law, the priest of Mid'i-an: and he led the flock to the backside of the desert, and came to the mountain of God, even to Ho'reb.

2 And the angel of the LORD appeared unto him in a flame of fire out of the midst of a bush:

and he looked, and, behold, the bush burned with fire, and the bush was not consumed.

3 And Mo'ses said, I will now turn aside, and see this great sight, why the bush is not burnt.

4 And when the LORD saw that he turned aside to see, God called unto him out of the midst of the bush, and said, Mo'ses, Mo'ses. And he said, Here am I.

5 And he said, Draw not nigh hither: put off thy shoes from off thy feet, for the place whereon thou standest is holy ground.

6 Moreover he said, I am the God of thy father, the God of A'bra-ham, the God of I'saac, and the God of Ja'cob. And Mo'ses hid his face; for he was afraid to look upon God.

7 ¶ And the LORD said, I have surely seen the affliction of my people which are in E'gypt, and have heard their cry by reason of their taskmasters; for I know their sorrows;

8 And I am come down to deliver them out of the hand of the E-gyptians, and to bring them up out of that land unto a good land and a large, unto a land flowing with milk and honey; unto the place of the Ca'naan-ites, and the Hit'tites, and the Am'or-ites, and the Per'iz-zites, and the Hi'vites, and the Jeb'u-sites.

9 Now therefore, behold, the cry of the children of Is'ra-el is come unto me: and I have also seen the oppression wherewith the E-gyptians oppress them.

10 Come now therefore, and I will send thee unto Pha'raoh, that thou mayest bring forth my people the children of Is'ra-el out of E'gypt.

11 ¶ And Mo'ses said unto God, Who am I, that I should go unto Pha'raoh, and that I should bring forth the children of Is'ra-el out of E'gypt?

12 And he said, Certainly I will be with thee; and this shall be a token unto thee, that I have sent thee: When thou hast brought forth the people out of E'gypt, ye shall serve God upon this mountain.

13 And Mo'ses said unto God, Behold, when I come unto the children of Is'ra-el, and shall say unto them, The God of your fathers hath sent me unto you; and they shall say to me, What is his name? what shall I say unto them?

14 And God said unto Mo'ses, I AM THAT I AM: and he said, Thus shalt thou say unto the children of Is'ra-el, I AM hath sent me unto you.

15 And God said moreover unto Mo'ses, Thus shalt thou say unto the children of Is'ra-el, The LORD God of your fathers, the God of A'bra-ham, the God of I'saac, and the God of Ja'cob, hath sent me unto you: this is my name for ever, and this is my memorial unto all generations.

16 Go, and gather the elders of Is'ra-el together, and say unto them, The LORD God of your fathers, the God of A'bra-ham, of I'saac, and of Ja'cob, appeared unto me, saying, I have surely visited you, and seen that which is done to you in E'gypt:

17 And I have said, I will bring you up out of the affliction of E'gypt unto the land of the Ca'naan-ites, and the Hit'tites, and the Am'or-ites, and the Per'iz-zites, and the Hi'vites, and the Jeb'u-sites, unto a land flowing with milk and honey.

18 And they shall hearken to thy voice: and thou shalt come, thou and the elders of Is'ra-el, unto the king of E'gypt, and ye shall say unto him, The LORD God of the He'brews hath met with us: and now let us go, we beseech thee, three days' journey into the wilderness, that we may sacrifice to the LORD our God.

19 ¶ And I am sure that the king of E'gypt

will not let you go, no, not by a mighty hand.

20 And I will stretch out my hand, and smite E'gypt with all my wonders which I will do in the midst thereof: and after that he will let you go.

21 And I will give this people favour in the sight of the E-gyptians: and it shall come to pass, that, when ye go, ye shall not go empty:

22 But every woman shall borrow of her neighbour, and of her that sojourneth in her house, jewels of silver, and jewels of gold, and raiment: and ye shall put *them* upon your sons, and upon your daughters; and ye shall spoil the E-gyptians.

4 AND Mo'ses answered and said, But, behold, they will not believe me, nor hearken unto my voice: for they will say, The LORD hath not appeared unto thee.

2 And the LORD said unto him, What *is* that in thine hand? And he said, A rod.

3 And he said, Cast it on the ground. And he cast it on the ground, and it became a serpent; and Mo'ses fled from before it.

4 And the LORD said unto Mo'ses, Put forth thine hand, and take it by the tail. And he put forth his hand, and caught it, and it became a rod in his hand:

5 That they may believe that the LORD God of their fathers, the God of A'bra-ham, the God of I'saac, and the God of Ja'cob, hath appeared unto thee.

6 ¶ And the LORD said furthermore unto him, Put now thine hand into thy bosom. And he put his hand into his bosom: and when he took it out, behold, his hand *was* leprous as snow.

7 And he said, Put thine hand into thy bosom again. And he put his hand into his bosom again; and plucked it out of his bosom, and, behold, it was turned again as his *other* flesh.

8 And it shall come to pass, if they will not believe thee, neither hearken to the voice of the first sign, that they will believe the voice of the latter sign.

9 And it shall come to pass, if they will not believe also these two signs, neither hearken unto thy voice, that thou shalt take of the water of the river, and pour *it* upon the dry *land:* and the water which thou takest out of the river shall become blood upon the dry *land.*

10 ¶ And Mo'ses said unto the LORD, O my Lord, I *am* not eloquent, neither heretofore, nor since thou hast spoken unto thy servant: but I *am* slow of speech, and of a slow tongue.

11 And the LORD said unto him, Who hath made man's mouth? or who maketh the dumb, or deaf, or the seeing, or the blind? have not I the LORD?

12 Now therefore go, and I will be with thy mouth, and teach thee what thou shalt say.

13 And he said, O my Lord, send, I pray thee, by the hand *of him whom* thou wilt send.

14 And the anger of the LORD was kindled against Mo'ses, and he said, *Is* not Aar'on the Le'vite thy brother? I know that he can speak well. And also, behold, he cometh forth to meet thee: and when he seeth thee, he will be glad in his heart.

15 And thou shalt speak unto him, and put words in his mouth: and I will be with thy mouth, and with his mouth, and will teach you what ye shall do.

16 And he shall be thy spokesman unto the people: and he shall be, *even* he shall be to thee instead of a mouth, and thou shalt be to him instead of God.

17 And thou shalt take this rod in thine hand, wherewith thou shalt do signs.

18 ¶ And Mo'ses went and returned to Je'-thro his father in law, and said unto him, Let me go, I pray thee, and return unto my brethren which *are* in E'gypt, and see whether they be yet alive. And Je'thro said to Mo'ses, Go in peace.

19 And the LORD said unto Mo'ses in Mid'i-an, Go, return into E'gypt: for all the men are dead which sought thy life.

20 And Mo'ses took his wife and his sons, and set them upon an ass, and he returned to the land of E'gypt: and Mo'ses took the rod of God in his hand.

21 And the LORD said unto Mo'ses, When thou goest to return into E'gypt, see that thou do all those wonders before Pha'raoh, which I have put in thine hand: but I will harden his heart, that he shall not let the people go.

22 And thou shalt say unto Pha'raoh, Thus saith the LORD, Is'ra-el *is* my son, *even* my first-born:

23 And I say unto thee, Let my son go, that he may serve me: and if thou refuse to let him go, behold, I will slay thy son, *even* thy first-born.

24 ¶ And it came to pass by the way in the inn, that the LORD met him, and sought to kill him.

25 Then Zip-po'rah took a sharp stone, and cut off the foreskin of her son, and cast *it* at his feet, and said, Surely a bloody husband *art* thou to me.

26 So he let him go: then she said, A bloody husband *thou art,* because of the circumcision.

27 ¶ And the LORD said to Aar'on, Go into the wilderness to meet Mo'ses. And he went, and met him in the mount of God, and kissed him.

28 And Mo'ses told Aar'on all the words of the LORD who had sent him, and all the signs which he had commanded him.

29 ¶ And Mo'ses and Aar'on went and gathered together all the elders of the children of Is'ra-el:

30 And Aar'on spake all the words which the LORD had spoken unto Mo'ses, and did the signs in the sight of the people.

31 And the people believed: and when they heard that the LORD had visited the children of Is'ra-el, and that he had looked upon their affliction, then they bowed their heads and worshipped.

5 AND afterward Mo'ses and Aar'on went in, and told Pha'raoh, Thus saith the LORD God of Is'ra-el, Let my people go, that they may hold a feast unto me in the wilderness.

2 And Pha'raoh said, Who *is* the LORD, that I should obey his voice to let Is'ra-el go? I know not the LORD, neither will I let Is'ra-el go.

3 And they said, The God of the He'brews hath met with us: let us go, we pray thee, three days' journey into the desert, and sacrifice unto the LORD our God; lest he fall upon us with pestilence, or with the sword.

4 And the king of E'gypt said unto them, Wherefore do ye, Mo'ses and Aar'on, let the people from their works? get you unto your burdens.

5 And Pha'raoh said, Behold, the people of the land now *are* many, and ye make them rest from their burdens.

6 And Pha'raoh commanded the same day the taskmasters of the people, and their officers, saying,

7 Ye shall no more give the people straw to make brick, as heretofore: let them go and gather straw for themselves.

8 And the tale of the bricks, which they did make heretofore, ye shall lay upon them; ye shall not diminish *ought* thereof: for they *be* idle; therefore they cry, saying, Let us go *and* sacrifice to our God.

9 Let there more work be laid upon the men, that they may labour therein; and let them not regard vain words.

10 ¶ And the taskmasters of the people went out, and their officers, and they spake to the people, saying, Thus saith Pha'raoh, I will not give you straw.

11 Go ye, get you straw where ye can find it: yet not ought of your work shall be diminished.

12 So the people were scattered abroad throughout all the land of E'gypt to gather stubble instead of straw.

13 And the taskmasters hasted *them*, saying, Fulfil your works, *your* daily tasks, as when there was straw.

14 And the officers of the children of Is'ra-el, which Pha'raoh's taskmasters had set over them, were beaten, *and* demanded, Wherefore have ye not fulfilled your task in making brick both yesterday and to day, as heretofore?

15 ¶ Then the officers of the children of Is'ra-el came and cried unto Pha'raoh, saying, Wherefore dealest thou thus with thy servants?

16 There is no straw given unto thy servants, and they say to us, Make brick: and, behold, thy servants *are* beaten; but the fault *is* in thine own people.

17 But he said, Ye *are* idle, *ye are* idle: therefore *ye* say, Let us go *and* do sacrifice to the LORD.

18 Go therefore now, *and* work; for there shall no straw be given you, yet shall ye deliver the tale of bricks.

19 And the officers of the children of Is'ra-el did see *that* they *were* in evil *case*, after it was said, Ye shall not minish *ought* from your bricks of your daily task.

20 ¶ And they met Mo'ses and Aar'on, who stood in the way, as they came forth from Pha'-raoh:

21 And they said unto them, The LORD look upon you, and judge; because ye have made our savour to be abhorred in the eyes of Pha'raoh, and in the eyes of his servants, to put a sword in their hand to slay us.

22 And Mo'ses returned unto the LORD, and said, Lord, wherefore hast thou *so* evil entreated this people? why *is* it *that* thou hast sent me?

23 For since I came to Pha'raoh to speak in thy name, he hath done evil to this people; neither hast thou delivered thy people at all.

6 THEN the LORD said unto Mo'ses, Now shalt thou see what I will do to Pha'raoh: for with a strong hand shall he let them go, and with a strong hand shall he drive them out of his land.

2 And God spake unto Mo'ses, and said unto him, I *am* the LORD:

3 And I appeared unto A'bra-ham, unto I'-saac, and unto Ja'cob, by *the name of* God Almighty, but by my name JE-HO'VAH was I not known to them.

4 And I have also established my covenant with them, to give them the land of Ca'naan, the land of their pilgrimage, wherein they were strangers.

5 And I have also heard the groaning of the children of Is'ra-el, whom the E-gyptians keep in bondage; and I have remembered my covenant.

6 Wherefore say unto the children of Is'ra-el, I *am* the LORD, and I will bring you out from under the burdens of the E-gyptians, and I will rid you out of their bondage, and I will redeem you with a stretched out arm, and with great judgments:

7 And I will take you to me for a people, and I will be to you a God: and ye shall know that I *am* the LORD your God, which bringeth you out from under the burdens of the E-gyptians.

8 And I will bring you in unto the land, concerning the which I did swear to give it to A'-bra-ham, to I'saac, and to Ja'cob; and I will give it you for an heritage: I *am* the LORD.

9 ¶ And Mo'ses spake so unto the children of Is'ra-el: but they hearkened not unto Mo'ses for anguish of spirit, and for cruel bondage.

10 And the LORD spake unto Mo'ses, saying,

11 Go in, speak unto Pha'raoh king of E'gypt, that he let the children of Is'ra-el go out of his land.

12 And Mo'ses spake before the LORD, saying, Behold, the children of Is'ra-el have not hearkened unto me; how then shall Pha'raoh hear me, who *am* of uncircumcised lips?

13 And the LORD spake unto Mo'ses and unto Aar'on, and gave them a charge unto the children of Is'ra-el, and unto Pha'raoh king of E'-gypt, to bring the children of Is'ra-el out of the land of E'gypt.

14 ¶ These *be* the heads of their fathers' houses: The sons of Reu'ben the firstborn of Is'-ra-el; Ha'noch, and Pal'lu, Hez'ron, and Car'mi: these *be* the families of Reu'ben.

15 And the sons of Sim'e-on; Je-mu'el, and Ja'min, and O'had, and Ja'chin, and Zo'har, and Sha'ul the son of a Ca'naan-it-ish woman: these *are* the families of Sim'e-on.

16 ¶ And these *are* the names of the sons of Le'vi according to their generations; Ger'shon, and Ko'hath, and Me-ra'ri: and the years of the life of Le'vi *were* an hundred thirty and seven years.

17 The sons of Ger'shon; Lib'ni, and Shi'mi, according to their families.

18 And the sons of Ko'hath; Am'ram, and Iz'-har, and He'bron, and Uz'zi-el: and the years of the life of Ko'hath *were* an hundred thirty and three years.

19 And the sons of Me-ra'ri; Ma'ha-li and Mu'shi: these *are* the families of Le'vi according to their generations.

20 And Am'ram took him Joch'e-bed his father's sister to wife; and she bare him Aar'on and Mo'ses: and the years of the life of Am'ram *were* an hundred and thirty and seven years.

21 ¶ And the sons of Iz'har; Ko'rah, and Ne'-pheg, and Zich'ri.

22 And the sons of Uz'zi-el; Mish'a-el, and El'za-phan, and Zith'ri.

23 And Aar'on took him E-lish'e-ba, daughter of Am-min'a-dab, sister of Na-ash'on, to wife; and she bare him Na'dab, and A-bi'hu, E-le-a'-zar, and Ith'a-mar.

24 And the sons of Ko'rah; As'sir, and El'ka-nah, and A-bi'a-saph: these *are* the families of the Kor'hites.

25 And E-le-a'zar Aar'on's son took him *one* of the daughters of Pu'ti-el to wife; and she bare him Phin'e-has: these *are* the heads of the fathers of the Le'vites according to their families.

26 These *are* that Aar'on and Mo'ses, to whom the LORD said, Bring out the children of

Is'ra-el from the land of E'gypt according to their armies.

27 These are they which spake to Pha'raoh king of E'gypt, to bring out the children of Is'ra-el from E'gypt: these are that Mo'ses and Aar'on.

28 ¶ And it came to pass on the day when the LORD spake unto Mo'ses in the land of E'gypt,

29 That the LORD spake unto Mo'ses, saying, I am the LORD: speak thou unto Pha'raoh king of E'gypt all that I say unto thee.

30 And Mo'ses said before the LORD, Behold, I am of uncircumcised lips, and how shall Pha'-raoh hearken unto me?

7 AND the LORD said unto Mo'ses, See, I have made thee a god to Pha'raoh: and Aar'on thy brother shall be thy prophet.

2 Thou shalt speak all that I command thee: and Aar'on thy brother shall speak unto Pha'-raoh, that he send the children of Is'ra-el out of his land.

3 And I will harden Pha'raoh's heart, and multiply my signs and my wonders in the land of E'gypt.

4 But Pha'raoh shall not hearken unto you, that I may lay my hand upon E'gypt, and bring forth mine armies, and my people the children of Is'ra-el, out of the land of E'gypt by great judgments.

5 And the E-gyptians shall know that I am the LORD, when I stretch forth mine hand upon E'gypt, and bring out the children of Is'ra-el from among them.

6 And Mo'ses and Aar'on did as the LORD commanded them, so did they.

7 And Mo'ses was fourscore years old, and Aar'on fourscore and three years old, when they spake unto Pha'raoh.

8 ¶ And the LORD spake unto Mo'ses and unto Aar'on, saying,

9 When Pha'raoh shall speak unto you, saying, Shew a miracle for you: then thou shalt say unto Aar'on, Take thy rod, and cast it before Pha'raoh, and it shall become a serpent.

10 ¶ And Mo'ses and Aar'on went in unto Pha'raoh, and they did so as the LORD had commanded: and Aar'on cast down his rod before Pha'raoh, and before his servants, and it became a serpent.

11 Then Pha'raoh also called the wise men and the sorcerers: now the magicians of E'gypt, they also did in like manner with their enchantments.

12 For they cast down every man his rod, and they became serpents: but Aar'on's rod swallowed up their rods.

13 And he hardened Pha'raoh's heart, that he hearkened not unto them; as the LORD had said.

14 ¶ And the LORD said unto Mo'ses, Pha'-raoh's heart is hardened, he refuseth to let the people go.

15 Get thee unto Pha'raoh in the morning; lo, he goeth out unto the water; and thou shalt stand by the river's brink against he come; and the rod which was turned to a serpent shalt thou take in thine hand.

16 And thou shalt say unto him, The LORD God of the He'brews hath sent me unto thee, saying, Let my people go, that they may serve me in the wilderness: and, behold, hitherto thou wouldest not hear.

17 Thus saith the LORD, In this thou shalt know that I am the LORD: behold, I will smite with the rod that is in mine hand upon the wa-ters which are in the river, and they shall be turned to blood.

18 And the fish that is in the river shall die, and the river shall stink; and the E-gyptians shall loathe to drink of the water of the river.

19 ¶ And the LORD spake unto Mo'ses, Say unto Aar'on, Take thy rod, and stretch out thine hand upon the waters of E'gypt, upon their streams, upon their rivers, and upon their ponds, and upon all their pools of water, that they may become blood; and that there may be blood throughout all the land of E'gypt, both in vessels of wood, and in vessels of stone.

20 And Mo'ses and Aar'on did so, as the LORD commanded; and he lifted up the rod, and smote the waters that were in the river, in the sight of Pha'raoh, and in the sight of his servants; and all the waters that were in the river were turned to blood.

21 And the fish that was in the river died; and the river stank, and the E-gyptians could not drink of the water of the river; and there was blood throughout all the land of E'gypt.

22 And the magicians of E'gypt did so with their enchantments: and Pha'raoh's heart was hardened, neither did he hearken unto them; as the LORD had said.

23 And Pha'raoh turned and went into his house, neither did he set his heart to this also.

24 And all the E-gyptians digged round about the river for water to drink; for they could not drink of the water of the river.

25 And seven days were fulfilled, after that the LORD had smitten the river.

8 AND the LORD spake unto Mo'ses, Go unto Pha'raoh, and say unto him, Thus saith the LORD, Let my people go, that they may serve me.

2 And if thou refuse to let them go, behold, I will smite all thy borders with frogs:

3 And the river shall bring forth frogs abundantly, which shall go up and come into thine house, and into thy bedchamber, and upon thy bed, and into the house of thy servants, and upon thy people, and into thine ovens, and into thy kneadingtroughs:

4 And the frogs shall come up both on thee, and upon thy people, and upon all thy servants.

5 ¶ And the LORD spake unto Mo'ses, Say unto Aar'on, Stretch forth thine hand with thy rod over the streams, over the rivers, and over the ponds, and cause frogs to come up upon the land of E'gypt.

6 And Aar'on stretched out his hand over the waters of E'gypt; and the frogs came up, and covered the land of E'gypt.

7 And the magicians did so with their enchantments, and brought up frogs upon the land of E'gypt.

8 ¶ Then Pha'raoh called for Mo'ses and Aar'on, and said, Intreat the LORD, that he may take away the frogs from me, and from my people; and I will let the people go, that they may do sacrifice unto the LORD.

9 And Mo'ses said unto Pha'raoh, Glory over me: when shall I intreat for thee, and for thy servants, and for thy people, to destroy the frogs from thee and thy houses, that they may remain in the river only?

10 And he said, To morrow. And he said, Be it according to thy word: that thou mayest know that there is none like unto the LORD our God.

11 And the frogs shall depart from thee, and from thy houses, and from thy servants, and

from thy people; they shall remain in the river only.

12 And Mo'ses and Aar'on went out from Pha'raoh: and Mo'ses cried unto the LORD because of the frogs which he had brought against Pha'raoh.

13 And the LORD did according to the word of Mo'ses; and the frogs died out of the houses, out of the villages, and out of the fields.

14 And they gathered them together upon heaps: and the land stank.

15 But when Pha'raoh saw that there was respite, he hardened his heart, and hearkened not unto them; as the LORD had said.

16 ¶ And the LORD said unto Mo'ses, Say unto Aar'on, Stretch out thy rod, and smite the dust of the land, that it may become lice throughout all the land of E'gypt.

17 And they did so; for Aar'on stretched out his hand with his rod, and smote the dust of the earth, and it became lice in man, and in beast; all the dust of the land became lice throughout all the land of E'gypt.

18 And the magicians did so with their enchantments to bring forth lice, but they could not: so there were lice upon man, and upon beast.

19 Then the magicians said unto Pha'raoh, This is the finger of God: and Pha'raoh's heart was hardened, and he hearkened not unto them; as the LORD had said.

20 ¶ And the LORD said unto Mo'ses, Rise up early in the morning, and stand before Pha'raoh; lo, he cometh forth to the water; and say unto him, Thus saith the LORD, Let my people go, that they may serve me.

21 Else, if thou wilt not let my people go, behold, I will send swarms of flies upon thee, and upon thy servants, and upon thy people, and into thy houses: and the houses of the E-gyptians shall be full of swarms of flies, and also the ground whereon they are.

22 And I will sever in that day the land of Go'shen, in which my people dwell, that no swarms of flies shall be there; to the end thou mayest know that I am the LORD in the midst of the earth.

23 And I will put a division between my people and thy people: to morrow shall this sign be.

24 And the LORD did so; and there came a grievous swarm of flies into the house of Pha'raoh, and into his servants' houses, and into all the land of E'gypt: the land was corrupted by reason of the swarm of flies.

25 ¶ And Pha'raoh called for Mo'ses and for Aar'on, and said, Go ye, sacrifice to your God in the land.

26 And Mo'ses said, It is not meet so to do; for we shall sacrifice the abomination of the E-gyptians to the LORD our God: lo, shall we sacrifice the abomination of the E-gyptians before their eyes, and will they not stone us?

27 We will go three days' journey into the wilderness, and sacrifice to the LORD our God, as he shall command us.

28 And Pha'raoh said, I will let you go, that ye may sacrifice to the LORD your God in the wilderness; only ye shall not go very far away: intreat for me.

29 And Mo'ses said, Behold, I go out from thee, and I will intreat the LORD that the swarms of flies may depart from Pha'raoh, from his servants, and from his people, to morrow: but let not Pha'raoh deal deceitfully any more in not letting the people go to sacrifice to the LORD.

30 And Mo'ses went out from Pha'raoh, and intreated the LORD.

31 And the LORD did according to the word of Mo'ses; and he removed the swarms of flies from Pha'raoh, from his servants, and from his people; there remained not one.

32 And Pha'raoh hardened his heart at this time also, neither would he let the people go.

9 THEN the LORD said unto Mo'ses, Go in unto Pha'raoh, and tell him, Thus saith the LORD God of the He'brews, Let my people go, that they may serve me.

2 For if thou refuse to let them go, and wilt hold them still,

3 Behold, the hand of the LORD is upon thy cattle which is in the field, upon the horses, upon the asses, upon the camels, upon the oxen, and upon the sheep: there shall be a very grievous murrain.

4 And the LORD shall sever between the cattle of Is'ra-el and the cattle of E'gypt: and there shall nothing die of all that is the children's of Is'ra-el.

5 And the LORD appointed a set time, saying, To morrow the LORD shall do this thing in the land.

6 And the LORD did that thing on the morrow, and all the cattle of E'gypt died: but of the cattle of the children of Is'ra-el died not one.

7 And Pha'raoh sent, and, behold, there was not one of the cattle of the Is'ra-el-ites dead. And the heart of Pha'raoh was hardened, and he did not let the people go.

8 ¶ And the LORD said unto Mo'ses and unto Aar'on, Take to you handfuls of ashes of the furnace, and let Mo'ses sprinkle it toward the heaven in the sight of Pha'raoh.

9 And it shall become small dust in all the land of E'gypt, and shall be a boil breaking forth with blains upon man, and upon beast, throughout all the land of E'gypt.

10 And they took ashes of the furnace, and stood before Pha'raoh; and Mo'ses sprinkled it up toward heaven; and it became a boil breaking forth with blains upon man, and upon beast.

11 And the magicians could not stand before Mo'ses because of the boils; for the boil was upon the magicians, and upon all the E-gyptians.

12 And the LORD hardened the heart of Pha'raoh, and he hearkened not unto them; as the LORD had spoken unto Mo'ses.

13 ¶ And the LORD said unto Mo'ses, Rise up early in the morning, and stand before Pha'raoh, and say unto him, Thus saith the LORD God of the He'brews, Let my people go, that they may serve me.

14 For I will at this time send all my plagues upon thine heart, and upon thy servants, and upon thy people; that thou mayest know that there is none like me in all the earth.

15 For now I will stretch out my hand, that I may smite thee and thy people with pestilence; and thou shalt be cut off from the earth.

16 And in very deed for this cause have I raised thee up, for to shew in thee my power; and that my name may be declared throughout all the earth.

17 As yet exaltest thou thyself against my people, that thou wilt not let them go?

18 Behold, to morrow about this time I will cause it to rain a very grievous hail, such as hath not been in E'gypt since the foundation thereof even until now.

19 Send therefore now, and gather thy cattle, and all that thou hast in the field; for upon ev-

ery man and beast which shall be found in the field, and shall not be brought home, the hail shall come down upon them, and they shall die.

20 He that feared the word of the LORD among the servants of Pha'raoh made his servants and his cattle flee into the houses:

21 And he that regarded not the word of the LORD left his servants and his cattle in the field.

22 ¶ And the LORD said unto Mo'ses, Stretch forth thine hand toward heaven, that there may be hail in all the land of E'gypt, upon man, and upon beast, and upon every herb of the field, throughout the land of E'gypt.

23 And Mo'ses stretched forth his rod toward heaven: and the LORD sent thunder and hail, and the fire ran along upon the ground; and the LORD rained hail upon the land of E'gypt.

24 So there was hail, and fire mingled with the hail, very grievous, such as there was none like it in all the land of E'gypt since it became a nation.

25 And the hail smote throughout all the land of E'gypt all that *was* in the field, both man and beast; and the hail smote every herb of the field, and brake every tree of the field.

26 Only in the land of Go'shen, where the children of Is'ra-el *were*, was there no hail.

27 ¶ And Pha'raoh sent, and called for Mo'ses and Aar'on, and said unto them, I have sinned this time: the LORD *is* righteous, and I and my people *are* wicked.

28 Intreat the LORD (for *it is* enough) that there be no *more* mighty thunderings and hail; and I will let you go, and ye shall stay no longer.

29 And Mo'ses said unto him, As soon as I am gone out of the city, I will spread abroad my hands unto the LORD; *and* the thunder shall cease, neither shall there be any more hail; that thou mayest know how that the earth *is* the LORD'S.

30 But as for thee and thy servants, I know that ye will not yet fear the LORD God.

31 And the flax and the barley was smitten: for the barley *was* in the ear, and the flax *was* bolled.

32 But the wheat and the rie were not smitten: for they *were* not grown up.

33 And Mo'ses went out of the city from Pha'raoh, and spread abroad his hands unto the LORD: and the thunders and hail ceased, and the rain was not poured upon the earth.

34 And when Pha'raoh saw that the rain and the hail and the thunders were ceased, he sinned yet more, and hardened his heart, he and his servants.

35 And the heart of Pha'raoh was hardened, neither would he let the children of Is'ra-el go; as the LORD had spoken by Mo'ses.

10 AND the LORD said unto Mo'ses, Go in unto Pha'raoh: for I have hardened his heart, and the heart of his servants, that I might shew these my signs before him:

2 And that thou mayest tell in the ears of thy son, and of thy son's son, what things I have wrought in E'gypt, and my signs which I have done among them; that ye may know how that I *am* the LORD.

3 And Mo'ses and Aar'on came in unto Pha'raoh, and said unto him, Thus saith the LORD God of the He'brews, How long wilt thou refuse to humble thyself before me? let my people go, that they may serve me.

4 Else, if thou refuse to let my people go, behold, to morrow will I bring the locusts into thy coast:

5 And they shall cover the face of the earth, that one cannot be able to see the earth: and they shall eat the residue of that which is escaped, which remaineth unto you from the hail, and shall eat every tree which groweth for you out of the field:

6 And they shall fill thy houses, and the houses of all thy servants, and the houses of all the E-gyptians; which neither thy fathers, nor thy fathers' fathers have seen, since the day that they were upon the earth unto this day. And he turned himself, and went out from Pha'-raoh.

7 And Pha'raoh's servants said unto him, How long shall this man be a snare unto us? let the men go, that they may serve the LORD their God: knowest thou not yet that E'gypt is destroyed?

8 And Mo'ses and Aar'on were brought again unto Pha'raoh: and he said unto them, Go, serve the LORD your God: *but* who *are* they that shall go?

9 And Mo'ses said, We will go with our young and with our old, with our sons and with our daughters, with our flocks and with our herds will we go; for we *must hold* a feast unto the LORD.

10 And he said unto them, Let the LORD be so with you, as I will let you go, and your little ones: look *to it;* for evil *is* before you.

11 Not so: go now ye *that are* men, and serve the LORD; for that ye did desire. And they were driven out from Pha'raoh's presence.

12 ¶ And the LORD said unto Mo'ses, Stretch out thine hand over the land of E'gypt for the locusts, that they may come up upon the land of E'gypt, and eat every herb of the land, *even* all that the hail hath left.

13 And Mo'ses stretched forth his rod over the land of E'gypt, and the LORD brought an east wind upon the land all that day, and all *that* night; *and* when it was morning, the east wind brought the locusts.

14 And the locusts went up over all the land of E'gypt, and rested in all the coasts of E'gypt: very grievous *were they;* before them there were no such locusts as they, neither after them shall be such.

15 For they covered the face of the whole earth, so that the land was darkened; and they did eat every herb of the land, and all the fruit of the trees which the hail had left: and there remained not any green thing in the trees, or in the herbs of the field, through all the land of E'gypt.

16 ¶ Then Pha'raoh called for Mo'ses and Aar'on in haste; and he said, I have sinned against the LORD your God, and against you.

17 Now therefore forgive, I pray thee, my sin only this once, and intreat the LORD your God, that he may take away from me this death only.

18 And he went out from Pha'raoh, and intreated the LORD.

19 And the LORD turned a mighty strong west wind, which took away the locusts, and cast them into the Red sea; there remained not one locust in all the coasts of E'gypt.

20 But the LORD hardened Pha'raoh's heart, so that he would not let the children of Is'ra-el go.

21 ¶ And the LORD said unto Mo'ses, Stretch out thine hand toward heaven, that there may be darkness over the land of E'gypt, even darkness *which* may be felt.

22 And Mo'ses stretched forth his hand toward heaven; and there was a thick darkness in all the land of E'gypt three days:

23 They saw not one another, neither rose

any from his place for three days: but all the children of Is'ra-el had light in their dwellings.

24 ¶ And Pha'raoh called unto Mo'ses, and said, Go ye, serve the LORD; only let your flocks and your herds be stayed: let your little ones also go with you.

25 And Mo'ses said, Thou must give us also sacrifices and burnt offerings, that we may sacrifice unto the LORD our God.

26 Our cattle also shall go with us; there shall not an hoof be left behind; for thereof must we take to serve the LORD our God; and we know not with what we must serve the LORD, until we come thither.

27 ¶ But the LORD hardened Pha'raoh's heart, and he would not let them go.

28 And Pha'raoh said unto him, Get thee from me, take heed to thyself, see my face no more; for in that day thou seest my face thou shalt die.

29 And Mo'ses said, Thou hast spoken well, I will see thy face again no more.

11 AND the LORD said unto Mo'ses, Yet will I bring one plague more upon Pha'-raoh, and upon E'gypt; afterwards he will let you go hence: when he shall let you go, he shall surely thrust you out hence altogether.

2 Speak now in the ears of the people, and let every man borrow of his neighbour, and every woman of her neighbour, jewels of silver, and jewels of gold.

3 And the LORD gave the people favour in the sight of the E-gyptians. Moreover the man Mo'-ses was very great in the land of E'gypt, in the sight of Pha'raoh's servants, and in the sight of the people.

4 And Mo'ses said, Thus saith the LORD, About midnight will I go out into the midst of E'gypt:

5 And all the firstborn in the land of E'gypt shall die, from the firstborn of Pha'raoh that sitteth upon his throne, even unto the firstborn of the maidservant that is behind the mill; and all the firstborn of beasts.

6 And there shall be a great cry throughout all the land of E'gypt, such as there was none like it, nor shall be like it any more.

7 But against any of the children of Is'ra-el shall not a dog move his tongue, against man or beast: that ye may know how that the LORD doth put a difference between the E-gyptians and Is'ra-el.

8 And all these thy servants shall come down unto me, and bow down themselves unto me, saying, Get thee out, and all the people that follow thee: and after that I will go out. And he went out from Pha'raoh in a great anger.

9 And the LORD said unto Mo'ses, Pha'raoh shall not hearken unto you; that my wonders may be multiplied in the land of E'gypt.

10 And Mo'ses and Aar'on did all these wonders before Pha'raoh: and the LORD hardened Pha'raoh's heart, so that he would not let the children of Is'ra-el go out of his land.

12 AND the LORD spake unto Mo'ses and Aar'on in the land of E'gypt, saying,

2 This month shall be unto you the beginning of months: it shall be the first month of the year to you.

3 ¶ Speak ye unto all the congregation of Is'-ra-el, saying, In the tenth day of this month they shall take to them every man a lamb, according to the house of their fathers, a lamb for an house:

4 And if the household be too little for the lamb, let him and his neighbour next unto his house take it according to the number of the souls; every man according to his eating shall make your count for the lamb.

5 Your lamb shall be without blemish, a male of the first year: ye shall take it out from the sheep, or from the goats:

6 And ye shall keep it up until the fourteenth day of the same month: and the whole assembly of the congregation of Is'ra-el shall kill it in the evening.

7 And they shall take of the blood, and strike it on the two side posts and on the upper door post of the houses, wherein they shall eat it.

8 And they shall eat the flesh in that night, roast with fire, and unleavened bread; and with bitter herbs they shall eat it.

9 Eat not of it raw, nor sodden at all with water, but roast with fire; his head with his legs, and with the purtenance thereof.

10 And ye shall let nothing remain until the morning; and that which remaineth of it until the morning ye shall burn with fire.

11 ¶ And thus shall ye eat it; with your loins girded, your shoes on your feet, and your staff in your hand; and ye shall eat it in haste: it is the LORD's passover.

12 For I will pass through the land of E'gypt this night, and will smite all the firstborn in the land of E'gypt, both man and beast; and against all the gods of E'gypt I will execute judgment: I am the LORD.

13 And the blood shall be to you for a token upon the houses where ye are: and when I see the blood, I will pass over you, and the plague shall not be upon you to destroy you, when I smite the land of E'gypt.

14 And this day shall be unto you for a memorial; and ye shall keep it a feast to the LORD throughout your generations; ye shall keep it a feast by an ordinance for ever.

15 Seven days shall ye eat unleavened bread; even the first day ye shall put away leaven out of your houses: for whosoever eateth leavened bread from the first day until the seventh day, that soul shall be cut off from Is'ra-el.

16 And in the first day there shall be an holy convocation, and in the seventh day there shall be an holy convocation to you; no manner of work shall be done in them, save that which every man must eat, that only may be done of you.

17 And ye shall observe the feast of unleavened bread; for in this selfsame day have I brought your armies out of the land of E'gypt: therefore shall ye observe this day in your generations by an ordinance for ever.

18 ¶ In the first month, on the fourteenth day of the month at even, ye shall eat unleavened bread, until the one and twentieth day of the month at even.

19 Seven days shall there be no leaven found in your houses: for whosoever eateth that which is leavened, even that soul shall be cut off from the congregation of Is'ra-el, whether he be a stranger, or born in the land.

20 Ye shall eat nothing leavened; in all your habitations shall ye eat unleavened bread.

21 ¶ Then Mo'ses called for all the elders of Is'ra-el, and said unto them, Draw out and take you a lamb according to your families, and kill the passover.

22 And ye shall take a bunch of hyssop, and dip it in the blood that is in the bason, and strike the lintel and the two side posts with the blood that is in the bason; and none of you shall

go out at the door of his house until the morning.

23 For the LORD will pass through to smite the E-gyptians; and when he seeth the blood upon the lintel, and on the two side posts, the LORD will pass over the door, and will not suffer the destroyer to come in unto your houses to smite you.

24 And ye shall observe this thing for an ordinance to thee and to thy sons for ever.

25 And it shall come to pass, when ye be come to the land which the LORD will give you, according as he hath promised, that ye shall keep this service.

26 And it shall come to pass, when your children shall say unto you, What mean ye by this service?

27 That ye shall say, It is the sacrifice of the LORD's passover, who passed over the houses of the children of Is'ra-el in E'gypt, when he smote the E-gyptians, and delivered our houses. And the people bowed the head and worshipped.

28 And the children of Is'ra-el went away, and did as the LORD had commanded Mo'ses and Aar'on, so did they.

29 ¶ And it came to pass, that at midnight the LORD smote all the firstborn in the land of E'gypt, from the firstborn of Pha'raoh that sat on his throne unto the firstborn of the captive that was in the dungeon; and all the firstborn of cattle.

30 And Pha'raoh rose up in the night, he, and all his servants, and all the E-gyptians; and there was a great cry in E'gypt; for there was not a house where there was not one dead.

31 ¶ And he called for Mo'ses and Aar'on by night, and said, Rise up, and get you forth from among my people, both ye and the children of Is'ra-el; and go, serve the LORD, as ye have said.

32 Also take your flocks and your herds, as ye have said, and be gone; and bless me also.

33 And the E-gyptians were urgent upon the people, that they might send them out of the land in haste; for they said, We be all dead men.

34 And the people took their dough before it was leavened, their kneadingtroughs being bound up in their clothes upon their shoulders.

35 And the children of Is'ra-el did according to the word of Mo'ses; and they borrowed of the E-gyptians jewels of silver, and jewels of gold, and raiment:

36 And the LORD gave the people favour in the sight of the E-gyptians, so that they lent unto them such things as they required. And they spoiled the E-gyptians.

37 ¶ And the children of Is'ra-el journeyed from Ra-me'ses to Suc'coth, about six hundred thousand on foot that were men, beside children.

38 And a mixed multitude went up also with them; and flocks, and herds, even very much cattle.

39 And they baked unleavened cakes of the dough which they brought forth out of E'gypt, for it was not leavened; because they were thrust out of E'gypt, and could not tarry, neither had they prepared for themselves any victual.

40 ¶ Now the sojourning of the children of Is'ra-el, who dwelt in E'gypt, was four hundred and thirty years.

41 And it came to pass at the end of the four hundred and thirty years, even the selfsame day it came to pass, that all the hosts of the LORD went out from the land of E'gypt.

42 It is a night to be much observed unto the LORD for bringing them out from the land of E'gypt: this is that night of the LORD to be observed of all the children of Is'ra-el in their generations.

43 ¶ And the LORD said unto Mo'ses and Aar'on, This is the ordinance of the passover: There shall no stranger eat thereof:

44 But every man's servant that is bought for money, when thou hast circumcised him, then shall he eat thereof.

45 A foreigner and an hired servant shall not eat thereof.

46 In one house shall it be eaten; thou shalt not carry forth ought of the flesh abroad out of the house; neither shall ye break a bone thereof.

47 All the congregation of Is'ra-el shall keep it.

48 And when a stranger shall sojourn with thee, and will keep the passover to the LORD, let all his males be circumcised, and then let him come near and keep it; and he shall be as one that is born in the land: for no uncircumcised person shall eat thereof.

49 One law shall be to him that is homeborn, and unto the stranger that sojourneth among you.

50 Thus did all the children of Is'ra-el; as the LORD commanded Mo'ses and Aar'on, so did they.

51 And it came to pass the selfsame day, that the LORD did bring the children of Is'ra-el out of the land of E'gypt by their armies.

13 AND the LORD spake unto Mo'ses, saying,

2 Sanctify unto me all the firstborn, whatsoever openeth the womb among the children of Is'ra-el, both of man and of beast: it is mine.

3 ¶ And Mo'ses said unto the people, Remember this day, in which ye came out from E'gypt, out of the house of bondage; for by strength of hand the LORD brought you out from this place: there shall no leavened bread be eaten.

4 This day came ye out in the month A'bib.

5 ¶ And it shall be when the LORD shall bring thee into the land of the Ca'naan-ites, and the Hit'tites, and the Am'or-ites, and the Hi'vites, and the Jeb'u-sites, which he sware unto thy fathers to give thee, a land flowing with milk and honey, that thou shalt keep this service in this month.

6 Seven days thou shalt eat unleavened bread, and in the seventh day shall be a feast to the LORD.

7 Unleavened bread shall be eaten seven days; and there shall no leavened bread be seen with thee, neither shall there be leaven seen with thee in all thy quarters.

8 ¶ And thou shalt shew thy son in that day, saying, This is done because of that which the LORD did unto me when I came forth out of E'-gypt.

9 And it shall be for a sign unto thee upon thine hand, and for a memorial between thine eyes, that the LORD's law may be in thy mouth: for with a strong hand hath the LORD brought thee out of E'gypt.

10 Thou shalt therefore keep this ordinance in his season from year to year.

11 ¶ And it shall be when the LORD shall bring thee into the land of the Ca'naan-ites, as he sware unto thee and to thy fathers, and shall give it thee,

12 That thou shalt set apart unto the LORD all that openeth the matrix, and every firstling that cometh of a beast which thou hast; the males shall be the LORD's.

13 And every firstling of an ass thou shalt re-

deem with a lamb; and if thou wilt not redeem it, then thou shalt break his neck: and all the firstborn of man among thy children shalt thou redeem.

14 ¶ And it shall be when thy son asketh thee in time to come, saying, What is this? that thou shalt say unto him, By strength of hand the LORD brought us out from E'gypt, from the house of bondage:

15 And it came to pass, when Pha'raoh would hardly let us go, that the LORD slew all the firstborn in the land of E'gypt, both the first-born of man, and the firstborn of beast: there-fore I sacrifice to the LORD all that openeth the matrix, being males; but all the firstborn of my children I redeem.

16 And it shall be for a token upon thine hand, and for frontlets between thine eyes: for by strength of hand the LORD brought us forth out of E'gypt.

17 ¶ And it came to pass, when Pha'raoh had let the people go, that God led them not through the way of the land of the Phi-lis'tines, although that was near; for God said, Lest peradventure the people repent when they see war, and they return to E'gypt:

18 But God led the people about, through the way of the wilderness of the Red sea: and the children of Is'ra-el went up harnessed out of the land of E'gypt.

19 And Mo'ses took the bones of Jo'seph with him: for he had straitly sworn the children of Is'ra-el, saying, God will surely visit you; and ye shall carry up my bones away hence with you.

20 ¶ And they took their journey from Suc'-coth, and encamped in E'tham, in the edge of the wilderness.

21 And the LORD went before them by day in a pillar of a cloud, to lead them the way; and by night in a pillar of fire, to give them light; to go by day and night:

22 He took not away the pillar of the cloud by day, nor the pillar of fire by night, from be-fore the people.

14 AND the LORD spake unto Mo'ses, say-ing,

2 Speak unto the children of Is'ra-el, that they turn and encamp before Pi-ha-hi'roth, be-tween Mig'dol and the sea, over against Ba'al-ze'phon: before it shall ye encamp by the sea.

3 For Pha'raoh will say of the children of Is'-ra-el, They are entangled in the land, the wilder-ness hath shut them in.

4 And I will harden Pha'raoh's heart, that he shall follow after them; and I will be honoured upon Pha'raoh, and upon all his host; that the E-gyptians may know that I am the LORD. And they did so.

5 ¶ And it was told the king of E'gypt that the people fled; and the heart of Pha'raoh and of his servants was turned against the people, and they said, Why have we done this, that we have let Is'ra-el go from serving us?

6 And he made ready his chariot, and took his people with him:

7 And he took six hundred chosen chariots, and all the chariots of E'gypt, and captains over every one of them.

8 And the LORD hardened the heart of Pha'-raoh king of E'gypt, and he pursued after the children of Is'ra-el: and the children of Is'ra-el went out with an high hand.

9 But the E-gyptians pursued after them, all the horses and chariots of Pha'raoh, and his horsemen, and his army, and overtook them en-

camping by the sea, beside Pi-ha-hi'roth, before Ba'al-ze'phon.

10 ¶ And when Pha'raoh drew nigh, the chil-dren of Is'ra-el lifted up their eyes, and, behold, the E-gyptians marched after them; and they were sore afraid: and the children of Is'ra-el cried out unto the LORD.

11 And they said unto Mo'ses, Because there were no graves in E'gypt, hast thou taken us away to die in the wilderness? wherefore hast thou dealt thus with us, to carry us forth out of E'gypt?

12 Is not this the word that we did tell thee in E'gypt, saying, Let us alone, that we may serve the E-gyptians? For it had been better for us to serve the E-gyptians, than that we should die in the wilderness.

13 ¶ And Mo'ses said unto the people, Fear ye not, stand still, and see the salvation of the LORD, which he will shew to you to day: for the E-gyptians whom ye have seen to day, ye shall see them again no more for ever.

14 The LORD shall fight for you, and ye shall hold your peace.

15 ¶ And the LORD said unto Mo'ses, Where-fore criest thou unto me? speak unto the chil-dren of Is'ra-el, that they go forward:

16 But lift thou up thy rod, and stretch out thine hand over the sea, and divide it: and the children of Is'ra-el shall go on dry ground through the midst of the sea.

17 And I, behold, I will harden the hearts of the E-gyptians, and they shall follow them: and I will get me honour upon Pha'raoh, and upon all his host, upon his chariots, and upon his horsemen.

18 And the E-gyptians shall know that I am the LORD, when I have gotten me honour upon Pha'raoh, upon his chariots, and upon his horse-men.

19 ¶ And the angel of God, which went be-fore the camp of Is'ra-el, removed and went be-hind them; and the pillar of the cloud went from before their face, and stood behind them:

20 And it came between the camp of the E-gyptians and the camp of Is'ra-el; and it was a cloud and darkness to them, but it gave light by night to these: so that the one came not near the other all the night.

21 And Mo'ses stretched out his hand over the sea; and the LORD caused the sea to go back by a strong east wind all that night, and made the sea dry land, and the waters were divided.

22 And the children of Is'ra-el went into the midst of the sea upon the dry ground: and the waters were a wall unto them on their right hand, and on their left.

23 ¶ And the E-gyptians pursued, and went in after them to the midst of the sea, even all Pha'raoh's horses, his chariots, and his horse-men.

24 And it came to pass, that in the morning watch the LORD looked unto the host of the E-gyptians through the pillar of fire and of the cloud, and troubled the host of the E-gyptians,

25 And took off their chariot wheels, that they drave them heavily: so that the E-gyptians said, Let us flee from the face of Is'ra-el; for the LORD fighteth for them against the E-gyptians.

26 ¶ And the LORD said unto Mo'ses, Stretch out thine hand over the sea, that the waters may come again upon the E-gyptians, upon their chariots, and upon their horsemen.

27 And Mo'ses stretched forth his hand over the sea, and the sea returned to his strength when the morning appeared; and the E-gyptians

fled against it; and the LORD overthrew the E-gyptians in the midst of the sea.

28 And the waters returned, and covered the chariots, and the horsemen, *and* all the host of Pha'raoh that came into the sea after them; there remained not so much as one of them.

29 But the children of Is'ra-el walked upon dry *land* in the midst of the sea; and the waters *were* a wall unto them on their right hand, and on their left.

30 Thus the LORD saved Is'ra-el that day out of the hand of the E-gyptians; and Is'ra-el saw the E-gyptians dead upon the sea shore.

31 And Is'ra-el saw that great work which the LORD did upon the E-gyptians: and the people feared the LORD, and believed the LORD, and his servant Mo'ses.

15 THEN sang Mo'ses and the children of Is'ra-el this song unto the LORD, and spake, saying, I will sing unto the LORD, for he hath triumphed gloriously: the horse and his rider hath he thrown into the sea.

2 The LORD *is* my strength and song, and he is become my salvation: he *is* my God, and I will prepare him a habitation; my father's God, and I will exalt him.

3 The LORD *is* a man of war: the LORD *is* his name.

4 Pha'raoh's chariots and his host hath he cast into the sea: his chosen captains also are drowned in the Red sea.

5 The depths have covered them: they sank into the bottom as a stone.

6 Thy right hand, O LORD, is become glorious in power: thy right hand, O LORD, hath dashed in pieces the enemy.

7 And in the greatness of thine excellency thou hast overthrown them that rose up against thee: thou sentest forth thy wrath, *which* consumed them as stubble.

8 And with the blast of thy nostrils the waters were gathered together, the floods stood upright as an heap, *and* the depths were congealed in the heart of the sea.

9 The enemy said, I will pursue, I will overtake, I will divide the spoil; my lust shall be satisfied upon them; I will draw my sword, my hand shall destroy them.

10 Thou didst blow with thy wind, the sea covered them: they sank as lead in the mighty waters.

11 Who *is* like unto thee, O LORD, among the gods? who *is* like thee, glorious in holiness, fearful *in* praises, doing wonders?

12 Thou stretchedst out thy right hand, the earth swallowed them.

13 Thou in thy mercy hast led forth the people *which* thou hast redeemed: thou hast guided *them* in thy strength unto thy holy habitation.

14 The people shall hear, *and* be afraid: sorrow shall take hold on the inhabitants of Pal-es-ti'na.

15 Then the dukes of E'dom shall be amazed; the mighty men of Mo'ab, trembling shall take hold upon them; all the inhabitants of Ca'naan shall melt away.

16 Fear and dread shall fall upon them; by the greatness of thine arm they shall be *as* still as a stone; till thy people pass over, O LORD, till the people pass over, *which* thou hast purchased.

17 Thou shalt bring them in, and plant them in the mountain of thine inheritance, *in* the place, O LORD, *which* thou hast made for thee to dwell in, *in* the Sanctuary, O LORD, *which* thy hands have established.

18 The LORD shall reign for ever and ever.

19 For the horse of Pha'raoh went in with his chariots and with his horsemen into the sea, and the LORD brought again the waters of the sea upon them; but the children of Is'ra-el went on dry *land* in the midst of the sea.

20 ¶ And Mir'i-am the prophetess, the sister of Aar'on, took a timbrel in her hand; and all the women went out after her with timbrels and with dances.

21 And Mir'i-am answered them, Sing ye to the LORD, for he hath triumphed gloriously; the horse and his rider hath he thrown into the sea.

22 So Mo'ses brought Is'ra-el from the Red sea, and they went out into the wilderness of Shur; and they went three days in the wilderness, and found no water.

23 ¶ And when they came to Ma'rah, they could not drink of the waters of Ma'rah, for they *were* bitter: therefore the name of it was called Ma'rah.

24 And the people murmured against Mo'ses, saying, What shall we drink?

25 And he cried unto the LORD; and the LORD shewed him a tree, *which* when he had cast into the waters, the waters were made sweet: there he made for them a statute and an ordinance, and there he proved them,

26 And said, If thou wilt diligently hearken to the voice of the LORD thy God, and wilt do that which is right in his sight, and wilt give ear to his commandments, and keep all his statutes, I will put none of these diseases upon thee, which I have brought upon the E-gyptians: for I *am* the LORD that healeth thee.

27 ¶ And they came to E'lim, where *were* twelve wells of water, and threescore and ten palm trees: and they encamped there by the waters.

16 AND they took their journey from E'-lim, and all the congregation of the children of Is'ra-el came unto the wilderness of Sin, which *is* between E'lim and Si'nai, on the fifteenth day of the second month after their departing out of the land of E'gypt.

2 And the whole congregation of the children of Is'ra-el murmured against Mo'ses and Aar'on in the wilderness:

3 And the children of Is'ra-el said unto them, Would to God we had died by the hand of the LORD in the land of E'gypt, when we sat by the flesh pots, *and* when we did eat bread to the full; for ye have brought us forth into this wilderness, to kill this whole assembly with hunger.

4 ¶ Then said the LORD unto Mo'ses, Behold, I will rain bread from heaven for you; and the people shall go out and gather a certain rate every day, that I may prove them, whether they will walk in my law, or no.

5 And it shall come to pass, that on the sixth day they shall prepare *that* which they bring in; and it shall be twice as much as they gather daily.

6 And Mo'ses and Aar'on said unto all the children of Is'ra-el, At even, then ye shall know that the LORD hath brought you out from the land of E'gypt:

7 And in the morning, then ye shall see the glory of the LORD; for that he heareth your murmurings against the LORD: and what *are* we, that ye murmur against us?

8 And Mo'ses said, *This shall be,* when the LORD shall give you in the evening flesh to eat, and in the morning bread to the full; for that the LORD heareth your murmurings which ye mur-

mur against him: and what *are* we? your murmurings *are* not against us, but against the LORD.

9 ¶ And Mo'ses spake unto Aar'on, Say unto all the congregation of the children of Is'ra-el, Come near before the LORD: for he hath heard your murmurings.

10 And it came to pass, as Aar'on spake unto the whole congregation of the children of Is'ra-el, that they looked toward the wilderness, and, behold, the glory of the LORD appeared in the cloud.

11 ¶ And the LORD spake unto Mo'ses, saying,

12 I have heard the murmurings of the children of Is'ra-el: speak unto them, saying, At even ye shall eat flesh, and in the morning ye shall be filled with bread; and ye shall know that I *am* the LORD your God.

13 And it came to pass, that at even the quails came up, and covered the camp: and in the morning the dew lay round about the host.

14 And when the dew that lay was gone up, behold, upon the face of the wilderness *there lay* a small round thing, *as* small as the hoar frost on the ground.

15 And when the children of Is'ra-el saw *it,* they said one to another, It *is* manna: for they wist not what it *was.* And Mo'ses said unto them, This *is* the bread which the LORD hath given you to eat.

16 ¶ This *is* the thing which the LORD hath commanded, Gather of it every man according to his eating, an omer for every man, *according to* the number of your persons; take ye every man for *them* which *are* in his tents.

17 And the children of Is'ra-el did so, and gathered, some more, some less.

18 And when they did mete *it* with an omer, he that gathered much had nothing over, and he that gathered little had no lack; they gathered every man according to his eating.

19 And Mo'ses said, Let no man leave of it till the morning.

20 Notwithstanding they hearkened not unto Mo'ses; but some of them left of it until the morning, and it bred worms, and stank: and Mo'ses was wroth with them.

21 And they gathered it every morning, every man according to his eating: and when the sun waxed hot, it melted.

22 ¶ And it came to pass, *that* on the sixth day they gathered twice as much bread, two omers for one *man:* and all the rulers of the congregation came and told Mo'ses.

23 And he said unto them, This *is that* which the LORD hath said, To morrow *is* the rest of the holy sabbath unto the LORD: bake *that* which ye will bake *to day,* and seethe that ye will seethe; and that which remaineth over lay up for you to be kept until the morning.

24 And they laid it up till the morning, as Mo'ses bade: and it did not stink, neither was there any worm therein.

25 And Mo'ses said, Eat that to day; for to day *is* a sabbath unto the LORD: to day ye shall not find it in the field.

26 Six days ye shall gather it; but on the seventh day, *which is* the sabbath, in it there shall be none.

27 ¶ And it came to pass, *that* there went out *some* of the people on the seventh day for to gather, and they found none.

28 And the LORD said unto Mo'ses, How long refuse ye to keep my commandments and my laws?

29 See, for that the LORD hath given you the

sabbath, therefore he giveth you on the sixth day the bread of two days; abide ye every man in his place, let no man go out of his place on the seventh day.

30 So the people rested on the seventh day.

31 And the house of Is'ra-el called the name thereof Manna: and it *was* like coriander seed white; and the taste of it *was* like wafers *made* with honey.

32 ¶ And Mo'ses said, This *is* the thing which the LORD commandeth, Fill an omer of it to be kept for your generations; that they may see the bread wherewith I have fed you in the wilderness, when I brought you forth from the land of E'gypt.

33 And Mo'ses said unto Aar'on, Take a pot and put an omer full of manna therein, and lay it up before the LORD, to be kept for your generations.

34 As the LORD commanded Mo'ses, so Aar'-on laid it up before the Testimony, to be kept.

35 And the children of Is'ra-el did eat manna forty years, until they came to a land inhabited; they did eat manna, until they came unto the borders of the land of Ca'naan.

36 Now an omer *is* the tenth *part* of an e-phah.

17 AND all the congregation of the children of Is'ra-el journeyed from the wilderness of Sin, after their journeys, according to the commandment of the LORD, and pitched in Reph'i-dim: and *there was* no water for the people to drink.

2 Wherefore the people did chide with Mo'-ses, and said, Give us water that we may drink. And Mo'ses said unto them, Why chide ye with me? wherefore do ye tempt the LORD?

3 And the people thirsted there for water; and the people murmured against Mo'ses, and said, Wherefore *is* this *that* thou hast brought us up out of E'gypt, to kill us and our children and our cattle with thirst?

4 And Mo'ses cried unto the LORD, saying, What shall I do unto this people? they be almost ready to stone me.

5 And the LORD said unto Mo'ses, Go on before the people, and take with thee of the elders of Is'ra-el; and thy rod, wherewith thou smotest the river, take in thine hand, and go.

6 Behold, I will stand before thee there upon the rock in Ho'reb; and thou shalt smite the rock, and there shall come water out of it, that the people may drink. And Mo'ses did so in the sight of the elders of Is'ra-el.

7 And he called the name of the place Mas'-sah, and Mer'i-bah, because of the chiding of the children of Is'ra-el, and because they tempted the LORD, saying, Is the LORD among us, or not?

8 ¶ Then came Am'a-lek, and fought with Is'ra-el in Reph'i-dim.

9 And Mo'ses said unto Josh'u-a, Choose us out men, and go out, fight with Am'a-lek: to morrow I will stand on the top of the hill with the rod of God in mine hand.

10 So Josh'u-a did as Mo'ses had said to him, and fought with Am'a-lek: and Mo'ses, Aar'on, and Hur went up to the top of the hill.

11 And it came to pass, when Mo'ses held up his hand, that Is'ra-el prevailed: and when he let down his hand, Am'a-lek prevailed.

12 But Mo'ses' hands *were* heavy; and they took a stone, and put *it* under him, and he sat thereon; and Aar'on and Hur stayed up his hands, the one on the one side, and the other on

the other side; and his hands were steady until the going down of the sun.

13 And Josh'u-a discomfited Am'a-lek and his people with the edge of the sword.

14 And the LORD said unto Mo'ses, Write this *for* a memorial in a book, and rehearse *it* in the ears of Josh'u-a: for I will utterly put out the remembrance of Am'a-lek from under heaven.

15 And Mo'ses built an altar, and called the name of it Je-ho'vah-nis'si:

16 For he said, Because the LORD hath sworn *that* the LORD *will have* war with Am'a-lek from generation to generation.

18 WHEN Je'thro, the priest of Mid'i-an, Mo'ses' father in law, heard of all that God had done for Mo'ses, and for Is'ra-el his people, *and* that the LORD had brought Is'ra-el out of E'gypt;

2 Then Je'thro, Mo'ses' father in law, took Zip-po'rah, Mo'ses' wife, after he had sent her back,

3 And her two sons; of which the name of the one *was* Ger'shom; for he said, I have been an alien in a strange land:

4 And the name of the other *was* E-li-e'zer; for the God of my father, *said he, was* mine help, and delivered me from the sword of Pha'-raoh:

5 And Je'thro, Mo'ses' father in law, came with his sons and his wife unto Mo'ses into the wilderness, where he encamped at the mount of God:

6 And he said unto Mo'ses, I thy father in law Je'thro am come unto thee, and thy wife, and her two sons with her.

7 ¶ And Mo'ses went out to meet his father in law, and did obeisance, and kissed him; and they asked each other of *their* welfare; and they came into the tent.

8 And Mo'ses told his father in law all that the LORD had done unto Pha'raoh and to the E-gyptians for Is'ra-el's sake, *and* all the travail that had come upon them by the way, and how the LORD delivered them.

9 And Je'thro rejoiced for all the goodness which the LORD had done to Is'ra-el, whom he had delivered out of the hand of the E-gyptians.

10 And Je'thro said, Blessed *be* the LORD, who hath delivered you out of the hand of the E-gyptians, and out of the hand of Pha'raoh, who hath delivered the people from under the hand of the E-gyptians.

11 Now I know that the LORD *is* greater than all gods: for in the thing wherein they dealt proudly *he was* above them.

12 And Je'thro, Mo'ses' father in law, took a burnt offering and sacrifices for God: and Aar'-on came, and all the elders of Is'ra-el, to eat bread with Mo'ses' father in law before God.

13 ¶ And it came to pass on the morrow, that Mo'ses sat to judge the people: and the people stood by Mo'ses from the morning unto the evening.

14 And when Mo'ses' father in law saw all that he did to the people, he said, What *is* this thing that thou doest to the people? why sittest thou thyself alone, and all the people stand by thee from morning unto even?

15 And Mo'ses said unto his father in law, Because the people come unto me to enquire of God:

16 When they have a matter, they come unto me; and I judge between one and another, and I do make *them* know the statutes of God, and his laws.

17 And Mo'ses' father in law said unto him, The thing that thou doest *is* not good.

18 Thou wilt surely wear away, both thou, and this people that *is* with thee: for this thing *is* too heavy for thee; thou art not able to per-form it thyself alone.

19 Hearken now unto my voice, I will give thee counsel, and God shall be with thee: be thou for the people to God-ward, that thou mayest bring the causes unto God:

20 And thou shalt teach them ordinances and laws, and shalt shew them the way wherein they must walk, and the work that they must do.

21 Moreover thou shalt provide out of all the people able men, such as fear God, men of truth, hating covetousness; and place *such* over them, *to be* rulers of thousands, *and* rulers of hundreds, rulers of fifties, and rulers of tens.

22 And let them judge the people at all sea-sons: and it shall be, *that* every great matter they shall bring unto thee, but every small mat-ter they shall judge: so shall it be easier for thy-self, and they shall bear *the burden* with thee.

23 If thou shalt do this thing, and God com-mand thee *so*, then thou shalt be able to endure, and all this people shall also go to their place in peace.

24 So Mo'ses hearkened to the voice of his father in law, and did all that he had said.

25 And Mo'ses chose able men out of all Is'-ra-el, and made them heads over the people, rulers of thousands, rulers of hundreds, rulers of fifties, and rulers of tens.

26 And they judged the people at all seasons: the hard causes they brought unto Mo'ses, but every small matter they judged themselves.

27 ¶ And Mo'ses let his father in law depart; and he went his way into his own land.

19 IN the third month, when the children of Is'ra-el were gone forth out of the land of E'gypt, the same day came they *into* the wil-derness of Si'nai.

2 For they were departed from Reph'i-dim, and were come *to* the desert of Si'nai, and had pitched in the wilderness; and there Is'ra-el camped before the mount.

3 And Mo'ses went up unto God, and the LORD called unto him out of the mountain, say-ing, Thus shalt thou say to the house of Ja'cob, and tell the children of Is'ra-el;

4 Ye have seen what I did unto the E-gyp-tians, and *how* I bare you on eagles' wings, and brought you unto myself.

5 Now therefore, if ye will obey my voice in-deed, and keep my covenant, then ye shall be a peculiar treasure unto me above all people: for all the earth *is* mine:

6 And ye shall be unto me a kingdom of priests, and an holy nation. These *are* the words which thou shalt speak unto the children of Is'-ra-el.

7 ¶ And Mo'ses came and called for the el-ders of the people, and laid before their faces all these words which the LORD commanded him.

8 And all the people answered together, and said, All that the LORD hath spoken we will do. And Mo'ses returned the words of the people unto the LORD.

9 And the LORD said unto Mo'ses, Lo, I come unto thee in a thick cloud, that the people may hear when I speak with thee, and believe thee for ever. And Mo'ses told the words of the peo-ple unto the LORD.

10 ¶ And the LORD said unto Mo'ses, Go

unto the people, and sanctify them to day and to morrow, and let them wash their clothes.

11 And be ready against the third day: for the third day the LORD will come down in the sight of all the people upon mount Si'nai.

12 And thou shalt set bounds unto the people round about, saying, Take heed to yourselves, *that ye go not* up into the mount, or touch the border of it: whosoever toucheth the mount shall be surely put to death:

13 There shall not an hand touch it, but he shall surely be stoned, or shot through; whether *it be* beast or man, it shall not live: when the trumpet soundeth long, they shall come up to the mount.

14 ¶ And Mo'ses went down from the mount unto the people, and sanctified the people; and they washed their clothes.

15 And he said unto the people, Be ready against the third day: come not at *your* wives.

16 ¶ And it came to pass on the third day in the morning, that there were thunders and lightnings, and a thick cloud upon the mount, and the voice of the trumpet exceeding loud; so that all the people that *was* in the camp trembled.

17 And Mo'ses brought forth the people out of the camp to meet with God; and they stood at the nether part of the mount.

18 And mount Si'nai was altogether on a smoke, because the LORD descended upon it in fire: and the smoke thereof ascended as the smoke of a furnace, and the whole mount quaked greatly.

19 And when the voice of the trumpet sounded long, and waxed louder and louder, Mo'ses spake, and God answered him by a voice.

20 And the LORD came down upon mount Si'-nai, on the top of the mount: and the LORD called Mo'ses *up* to the top of the mount; and Mo'ses went up.

21 And the LORD said unto Mo'ses, Go down, charge the people, lest they break through unto the LORD to gaze, and many of them perish.

22 And let the priests also, which come near to the LORD, sanctify themselves, lest the LORD break forth upon them.

23 And Mo'ses said unto the LORD, The people cannot come up to mount Si'nai: for thou chargedst us, saying, Set bounds about the mount, and sanctify it.

24 And the LORD said unto him, Away, get thee down, and thou shalt come up, thou, and Aar'on with thee: but let not the priests and the people break through to come up unto the LORD, lest he break forth upon them.

25 So Mo'ses went down unto the people, and spake unto them.

20 AND God spake all these words, saying,
2 I *am* the LORD thy God, which have brought thee out of the land of E'gypt, out of the house of bondage.

3 Thou shalt have no other gods before me.

4 Thou shalt not make unto thee any graven image, or any likeness *of any thing* that *is* in heaven above, or that *is* in the earth beneath, or that *is* in the water under earth:

5 Thou shalt not bow down thyself to them, nor serve them: for I the LORD thy God *am* a jealous God, visiting the iniquity of the fathers upon the children unto the third and fourth *generation* of them that hate me;

6 And shewing mercy unto thousands of them that love me, and keep my commandments.

7 Thou shalt not take the name of the LORD thy God in vain; for the LORD will not hold him guiltless that taketh his name in vain.

8 Remember the sabbath day, to keep it holy.

9 Six days shalt thou labour, and do all thy work:

10 But the seventh day *is* the sabbath of the LORD thy God: *in it* thou shalt not do any work, thou, nor thy son, nor thy daughter, thy manservant, nor thy maidservant, nor thy cattle, nor thy stranger that *is* within thy gates:

11 For *in* six days the LORD made heaven and earth, the sea, and all that in them *is*, and rested the seventh day: wherefore the LORD blessed the sabbath day, and hallowed it.

12 ¶ Honour thy father and thy mother: that thy days may be long upon the land which the LORD thy God giveth thee.

13 Thou shalt not kill.

14 Thou shalt not commit adultery.

15 Thou shalt not steal.

16 Thou shalt not bear false witness against thy neighbour.

17 Thou shalt not covet thy neighbour's house, thou shalt not covet thy neighbour's wife, nor his manservant, nor his maidservant, nor his ox, nor his ass, nor any thing that *is* thy neighbour's.

18 ¶ And all the people saw the thunderings, and the lightnings, and the noise of the trumpet, and the mountain smoking: and when the people saw *it*, they removed, and stood afar off.

19 And they said unto Mo'ses, Speak thou with us, and we will hear: but let not God speak with us, lest we die.

20 And Mo'ses said unto the people, Fear not: for God is come to prove you, and that his fear may be before your faces, that ye sin not.

21 And the people stood afar off, and Mo'ses drew near unto the thick darkness where God *was*.

22 ¶ And the LORD said unto Mo'ses, Thus thou shalt say unto the children of Is'ra-el, Ye have seen that I have talked with you from heaven.

23 Ye shall not make with me gods of silver, neither shall ye make unto you gods of gold.

24 ¶ An altar of earth thou shalt make unto me, and shalt sacrifice thereon thy burnt offerings, and thy peace offerings, thy sheep, and thine oxen: in all places where I record my name I will come unto thee, and I will bless thee.

25 And if thou wilt make me an altar of stone, thou shalt not build it of hewn stone: for if thou lift up thy tool upon it, thou hast polluted it.

26 Neither shalt thou go up by steps unto mine altar, that thy nakedness be not discovered thereon.

21 NOW these *are* the judgments which thou shalt set before them.

2 If thou buy an He'brew servant, six years he shall serve: and in the seventh he shall go out free for nothing.

3 If he came in by himself, he shall go out by himself: if he were married, then his wife shall go out with him.

4 If his master have given him a wife, and she have born him sons or daughters; the wife and her children shall be her master's, and he shall go out by himself.

5 And if the servant shall plainly say, I love my master, my wife, and my children; I will not go out free:

6 Then his master shall bring him unto the

judges; he shall also bring him to the door, or unto the door post; and his master shall bore his ear through with an aul; and he shall serve him for ever.

7 ¶ And if a man sell his daughter to be a maidservant, she shall not go out as the menservants do.

8 If she please not her master, who hath betrothed her to himself, then shall he let her be redeemed: to sell her unto a strange nation he shall have no power, seeing he hath dealt deceitfully with her.

9 And if he have betrothed her unto his son, he shall deal with her after the manner of daughters.

10 If he take him another *wife:* her food, her raiment, and her duty of marriage, shall he not diminish.

11 And if he do not these three unto her, then shall she go out free without money.

12 ¶ He that smiteth a man, so that he die, shall be surely put to death.

13 And if a man lie not in wait, but God deliver *him* into his hand; then I will appoint thee a place whither he shall flee.

14 But if a man come presumptuously upon his neighbour, to slay him with guile; thou shalt take him from mine altar, that he may die.

15 ¶ And he that smiteth his father, or his mother, shall be surely put to death.

16 ¶ And he that stealeth a man, and selleth him, or if he be found in his hand, he shall surely be put to death.

17 ¶ And he that curseth his father, or his mother, shall surely be put to death.

18 ¶ And if men strive together, and one smite another with a stone, or with *his* fist, and he die not, but keepeth *his* bed:

19 If he rise again, and walk abroad upon his staff, then shall he that smote *him* be quit: only he shall pay *for* the loss of his time, and shall cause *him* to be thoroughly healed.

20 ¶ And if a man smite his servant, or his maid, with a rod, and he die under his hand; he shall be surely punished.

21 Notwithstanding, if he continue a day or two, he shall not be punished: for he *is* his money.

22 ¶ If men strive, and hurt a woman with child, so that her fruit depart *from her,* and yet no mischief follow: he shall be surely punished, according as the woman's husband will lay upon him; and he shall pay as the judges *determine.*

23 And if *any* mischief follow, then thou shalt give life for life,

24 Eye for eye, tooth for tooth, hand for hand, foot for foot,

25 Burning for burning, wound for wound, stripe for stripe.

26 ¶ And if a man smite the eye of his servant, or the eye of his maid, that it perish; he shall let him go free for his eye's sake.

27 And if he smite out his manservant's tooth, or his maidservant's tooth; he shall let him go free for his tooth's sake.

28 ¶ If an ox gore a man or a woman, that they die: then the ox shall be surely stoned, and his flesh shall not be eaten; but the owner of the ox *shall be* quit.

29 But if the ox were wont to push with his horn in time past, and it hath been testified to his owner, and he hath not kept him in, but that he hath killed a man or a woman; the ox shall be stoned, and his owner also shall be put to death.

30 If there be laid on him a sum of money, then he shall give for the ransom of his life whatsoever is laid upon him.

31 Whether he have gored a son, or have gored a daughter, according to this judgment shall it be done unto him.

32 If the ox shall push a manservant or a maidservant; he shall give unto their master thirty shekels of silver, and the ox shall be stoned.

33 ¶ And if a man shall open a pit, or if a man shall dig a pit, and not cover it, and an ox or an ass fall therein;

34 The owner of the pit shall make *it* good, *and* give money unto the owner of them; and the dead *beast* shall be his.

35 ¶ And if one man's ox hurt another's, that he die; then they shall sell the live ox, and divide the money of it; and the dead ox also they shall divide.

36 Or if it be known that the ox hath used to push in time past, and his owner hath not kept him in; he shall surely pay ox for ox; and the dead shall be his own.

22 IF a man shall steal an ox, or a sheep, and kill it, or sell it; he shall restore five oxen for an ox, and four sheep for a sheep.

2 ¶ If a thief be found breaking up, and be smitten that he die, *there shall* no blood *be shed* for him.

3 If the sun be risen upon him, *there shall be* blood *shed* for him; *for* he should make full restitution; if he have nothing, then he shall be sold for his theft.

4 If the theft be certainly found in his hand alive, whether it be ox, or ass, or sheep; he shall restore double.

5 ¶ If a man shall cause a field or vineyard to be eaten, and shall put in his beast, and shall feed in another man's field; of the best of his own field, and of the best of his own vineyard, shall he make restitution.

6 ¶ If fire break out, and catch in thorns, so that the stacks of corn, or the standing corn, or the field, be consumed *therewith;* he that kindled the fire shall surely make restitution.

7 ¶ If a man shall deliver unto his neighbour money or stuff to keep, and it be stolen out of the man's house; if the thief be found, let him pay double.

8 If the thief be not found, then the master of the house shall be brought unto the judges, *to see* whether he have put his hand unto his neighbour's goods.

9 For all manner of trespass, *whether it be* for ox, for ass, for sheep, for raiment, *or* for any manner of lost thing, which *another* challengeth to be his, the cause of both parties shall come before the judges; *and* whom the judges shall condemn, he shall pay double unto his neighbour.

10 If a man deliver unto his neighbour an ass, or an ox, or a sheep, or any beast, to keep; and it die, or be hurt, or driven away, no man seeing *it:*

11 *Then* shall an oath of the LORD be between them both, that he hath not put his hand unto his neighbour's goods; and the owner of it shall accept *thereof,* and he shall not make *it* good.

12 And if it be stolen from him, he shall make restitution unto the owner thereof.

13 If it be torn in pieces, *then* let him bring it *for* witness, *and* he shall not make good that which was torn.

14 ¶ And if a man borrow *ought* of his neighbour, and it be hurt, or die, the owner thereof *being* not with it, he shall surely make *it* good.

15 *But* if the owner thereof *be* with it, he shall not make *it* good: if it *be* an hired *thing*, it came for his hire.

16 ¶ And if a man entice a maid that is not betrothed, and lie with her, he shall surely endow her to be his wife.

17 If her father utterly refuse to give her unto him, he shall pay money according to the dowry of virgins.

18 ¶ Thou shalt not suffer a witch to live.

19 ¶ Whosoever lieth with a beast shall surely be put to death.

20 ¶ He that sacrificeth unto *any* god, save unto the LORD only, he shall be utterly destroyed.

21 ¶ Thou shalt neither vex a stranger, nor oppress him: for ye were strangers in the land of E'gypt.

22 ¶ Ye shall not afflict any widow, or fatherless child.

23 If thou afflict them in any wise, and they cry at all unto me, I will surely hear their cry;

24 And my wrath shall wax hot, and I will kill you with the sword; and your wives shall be widows, and your children fatherless.

25 ¶ If thou lend money to *any of* my people *that is* poor by thee, thou shalt not be to him as an usurer, neither shalt thou lay upon him usury.

26 If thou at all take thy neighbour's raiment to pledge, thou shalt deliver it unto him by that the sun goeth down:

27 For that *is* his covering only, it *is* his raiment for his skin: wherein shall he sleep? and it shall come to pass, when he crieth unto me, that I will hear; for I *am* gracious.

28 ¶ Thou shalt not revile the gods, nor curse the ruler of thy people.

29 ¶ Thou shalt not delay *to offer* the first of thy ripe fruits, and of thy liquors: the first born of thy sons shalt thou give unto me.

30 Likewise shalt thou do with thine oxen, *and* with thy sheep: seven days it shall be with his dam; on the eighth day thou shalt give it me.

31 ¶ And ye shall be holy men unto me: neither shall ye eat *any* flesh *that is* torn of beasts in the field; ye shall cast it to the dogs.

23 THOU shalt not raise a false report: put not thine hand with the wicked to be an unrighteous witness.

2 ¶ Thou shalt not follow a multitude to *do* evil; neither shalt thou speak in a cause to decline after many to wrest *judgment:*

3 ¶ Neither shalt thou countenance a poor man in his cause.

4 ¶ If thou meet thine enemy's ox or his ass going astray, thou shalt surely bring it back to him again.

5 If thou see the ass of him that hateth thee lying under his burden, and wouldest forbear to help him, thou shalt surely help with him.

6 Thou shalt not wrest the judgment of thy poor in his cause.

7 Keep thee far from a false matter; and the innocent and righteous slay thou not: for I will not justify the wicked.

8 ¶ And thou shalt take no gift: for the gift blindeth the wise, and perverteth the words of the righteous.

9 ¶ Also thou shalt not oppress a stranger: for ye know the heart of a stranger, seeing ye were strangers in the land of E'gypt.

10 And six years thou shalt sow thy land, and shalt gather in the fruits thereof:

11 But the seventh *year* thou shalt let it rest and lie still; that the poor of thy people may eat:

and what they leave the beasts of the field shall eat. In like manner thou shalt deal with thy vineyard, *and* with thy oliveyard.

12 Six days thou shalt do thy work, and on the seventh day thou shalt rest: that thine ox and thine ass may rest, and the son of thy handmaid, and the stranger, may be refreshed.

13 And in all *things* that I have said unto you be circumspect: and make no mention of the name of other gods, neither let it be heard out of thy mouth.

14 ¶ Three times thou shalt keep a feast unto me in the year.

15 Thou shalt keep the feast of unleavened bread: (thou shalt eat unleavened bread seven days, as I commanded thee, in the time appointed of the month A'bib; for in it thou camest out from E'gypt: and none shall appear before me empty:)

16 And the feast of harvest, the firstfruits of thy labours, which thou hast sown in the field: and the feast of ingathering, *which is* in the end of the year, when thou hast gathered in thy labours out of the field.

17 Three times in the year all thy males shall appear before the Lord GOD.

18 Thou shalt not offer the blood of my sacrifice with leavened bread; neither shall the fat of my sacrifice remain until the morning.

19 The first of the firstfruits of thy land thou shalt bring into the house of the LORD thy God. Thou shalt not seethe a kid in his mother's milk.

20 ¶ Behold, I send an Angel before thee, to keep thee in the way, and to bring thee into the place which I have prepared.

21 Beware of him, and obey his voice, provoke him not; for he will not pardon your transgressions: for my name *is* in him.

22 But if thou shalt indeed obey his voice, and do all that I speak; then I will be an enemy unto thine enemies, and an adversary unto thine adversaries.

23 For mine Angel shall go before thee, and bring thee in unto the Am'or-ites, and the Hit'-tites, and the Per'iz-zites, and the Ca'naan-ites, and Hi'vites, and the Jeb'u-sites: and I will cut them off.

24 Thou shalt not bow down to their gods, nor serve them, nor do after their works: but thou shalt utterly overthrow them, and quite break down their images.

25 And ye shall serve the LORD your God, and he shall bless thy bread, and thy water; and I will take sickness away from the midst of thee.

26 ¶ There shall nothing cast their young, nor be barren, in thy land: the number of thy days I will fulfil.

27 I will send my fear before thee, and will destroy all the people to whom thou shalt come, and I will make all thine enemies turn their backs unto thee.

28 And I will send hornets before thee, which shall drive out the Hi'vite, the Ca'naan-ite, and the Hit'tite, from before thee.

29 I will not drive them out from before thee in one year; lest the land become desolate, and the beast of the field multiply against thee.

30 By little and little I will drive them out from before thee, until thou be increased, and inherit the land.

31 And I will set thy bounds from the Red sea even unto the sea of the Phi-lis'tines, and from the desert unto the river: for I will deliver the inhabitants of the land into your hand; and thou shalt drive them out before thee.

32 Thou shalt make no covenant with them, nor with their gods.

33 They shall not dwell in thy land, lest they make thee sin against me: for if thou serve their gods, it will surely be a snare unto thee.

24 AND he said unto Mo'ses, Come up unto the LORD, thou, and Aar'on, Na'-dab, and A-bi'hu, and seventy of the elders of Is'ra-el; and worship ye afar off.

2 And Mo'ses alone shall come near the LORD: but they shall not come nigh; neither shall the people go up with him.

3 ¶ And Mo'ses came and told the people all the words of the LORD, and all the judgments: and all the people answered with one voice, and said, All the words which the LORD hath said will we do.

4 And Mo'ses wrote all the words of the LORD, and rose up early in the morning, and builded an altar under the hill, and twelve pillars, according to the twelve tribes of Is'ra-el.

5 And he sent young men of the children of Is'ra-el, which offered burnt offerings, and sacrificed peace offerings of oxen unto the LORD.

6 And Mo'ses took half of the blood, and put it in basons; and half of the blood he sprinkled on the altar.

7 And he took the book of the covenant, and read in the audience of the people: and they said, All that the LORD hath said will we do, and be obedient.

8 And Mo'ses took the blood, and sprinkled it on the people, and said, Behold the blood of the covenant, which the LORD hath made with you concerning all these words.

9 ¶ Then went up Mo'ses, and Aar'on, Na'-dab, and A-bi'hu, and seventy of the elders of Is'ra-el:

10 And they saw the God of Is'ra-el: and there was under his feet as it were a paved work of a sapphire stone, and as it were the body of heaven in his clearness.

11 And upon the nobles of the children of Is'ra-el he laid not his hand: also they saw God, and did eat and drink.

12 ¶ And the LORD said unto Mo'ses, Come up to me into the mount, and be there: and I will give thee tables of stone, and a law, and commandments which I have written; that thou mayest teach them.

13 And Mo'ses rose up, and his minister Josh'u-a: and Mo'ses went up into the mount of God.

14 And he said unto the elders, Tarry ye here for us, until we come again unto you: and, behold, Aar'on and Hur are with you: if any man have any matters to do, let him come unto them.

15 And Mo'ses went up into the mount, and a cloud covered the mount.

16 And the glory of the LORD abode upon mount Si'nai, and the cloud covered it six days: and the seventh day he called unto Mo'ses out of the midst of the cloud.

17 And the sight of the glory of the LORD was like devouring fire on the top of the mount in the eyes of the children of Is'ra-el.

18 And Mo'ses went into the midst of the cloud, and gat him up into the mount: and Mo'ses was in the mount forty days and forty nights.

25 AND the LORD spake unto Mo'ses, saying,

2 Speak unto the children of Is'ra-el, that they bring me an offering: of every man that giveth it willingly with his heart ye shall take my offering.

3 And this is the offering which ye shall take of them; gold, and silver, and brass,

4 And blue, and purple, and scarlet, and fine linen, and goats' hair,

5 And rams' skins dyed red, and badgers' skins, and shittim wood,

6 Oil for the light, spices for anointing oil, and for sweet incense,

7 Onyx stones, and stones to be set in the ephod, and in the breastplate.

8 And let them make me a sanctuary; that I may dwell among them.

9 According to all that I shew thee, after the pattern of the tabernacle, and the pattern of all the instruments thereof, even so shall ye make it.

10 ¶ And they shall make an ark of shittim wood: two cubits and a half shall be the length thereof, and a cubit and a half the breadth thereof, and a cubit and a half the height thereof.

11 And thou shalt overlay it with pure gold, within and without shalt thou overlay it, and shalt make upon it a crown of gold round about.

12 And thou shalt cast four rings of gold for it, and put them in the four corners thereof; and two rings shall be in the one side of it, and two rings in the other side of it.

13 And thou shalt make staves of shittim wood, and overlay them with gold.

14 And thou shalt put the staves into the rings by the sides of the ark, that the ark may be borne with them.

15 The staves shall be in the rings of the ark: they shall not be taken from it.

16 And thou shalt put into the ark the testimony which I shall give thee.

17 And thou shalt make a mercy seat of pure gold: two cubits and a half shall be the length thereof, and a cubit and a half the breadth thereof.

18 And thou shalt make two cherubims of gold, of beaten work shalt thou make them, in the two ends of the mercy seat.

19 And make one cherub on the one end, and the other cherub on the other end: even of the mercy seat shall ye make the cherubims on the two ends thereof.

20 And the cherubims shall stretch forth their wings on high, covering the mercy seat with their wings, and their faces shall look one to another; toward the mercy seat shall the faces of the cherubims be.

21 And thou shalt put the mercy seat above upon the ark; and in the ark thou shalt put the testimony that I shall give thee.

22 And there I will meet with thee, and I will commune with thee from above the mercy seat, from between the two cherubims which are upon the ark of the testimony, of all things which I will give thee in commandment unto the children of Is'ra-el.

23 ¶ Thou shalt also make a table of shittim wood: two cubits shall be the length thereof, and a cubit the breadth thereof, and a cubit and a half the height thereof.

24 And thou shalt overlay it with pure gold, and make thereto a crown of gold round about.

25 And thou shalt make unto it a border of an hand breadth round about, and thou shalt make a golden crown to the border thereof round about.

26 And thou shalt make for it four rings of gold, and put the rings in the four corners that are on the four feet thereof.

27 Over against the border shall the rings be for places of the staves to bear the table.

28 And thou shalt make the staves of shittim wood, and overlay them with gold, that the table may be borne with them.

29 And thou shalt make the dishes thereof, and spoons thereof, and covers thereof, and bowls thereof, to cover withal: of pure gold shalt thou make them.

30 And thou shalt set upon the table shewbread before me alway.

31 ¶ And thou shalt make a candlestick of pure gold: of beaten work shall the candlestick be made: his shaft, and his branches, his bowls, his knops, and his flowers, shall be of the same.

32 And six branches shall come out of the sides of it; three branches of the candlestick out of the one side, and three branches of the candlestick out of the other side:

33 Three bowls made like unto almonds, with a knop and a flower in one branch; and three bowls made like almonds in the other branch, with a knop and a flower: so in the six branches that come out of the candlestick.

34 And in the candlestick shall be four bowls made like unto almonds, with their knops and their flowers.

35 And there shall be a knop under two branches of the same, and a knop under two branches of the same, and a knop under two branches of the same, according to the six branches that proceed out of the candlestick.

36 Their knops and their branches shall be of the same: all it shall be one beaten work of pure gold.

37 And thou shalt make the seven lamps thereof: and they shall light the lamps thereof, that they may give light over against it.

38 And the tongs thereof, and the snuffdishes thereof, shall be of pure gold.

39 Of a talent of pure gold shall he make it, with all these vessels.

40 And look that thou make them after their pattern, which was shewed thee in the mount.

26 MOREOVER thou shalt make the tabernacle with ten curtains of fine twined linen, and blue, and purple, and scarlet: with cherubims of cunning work shalt thou make them.

2 The length of one curtain shall be eight and twenty cubits, and the breadth of one curtain four cubits: and every one of the curtains shall have one measure.

3 The five curtains shall be coupled together one to another; and other five curtains shall be coupled one to another.

4 And thou shalt make loops of blue upon the edge of the one curtain from the selvedge in the coupling; and likewise shalt thou make in the uttermost edge of another curtain, in the coupling of the second.

5 Fifty loops shalt thou make in the one curtain, and fifty loops shalt thou make in the edge of the curtain that is in the coupling of the second; that the loops may take hold one of another.

6 And thou shalt make fifty taches of gold, and couple the curtains together with the taches: and it shall be one tabernacle.

7 ¶ And thou shalt make curtains of goats' hair to be a covering upon the tabernacle: eleven curtains shalt thou make.

8 The length of one curtain shall be thirty cubits, and the breadth of one curtain four cubits: and the eleven curtains shall be all of one measure.

9 And thou shalt couple five curtains by themselves, and six curtains by themselves, and shalt double the sixth curtain in the forefront of the tabernacle.

10 And thou shalt make fifty loops on the edge of the one curtain that is outmost in the coupling, and fifty loops in the edge of the curtain which coupleth the second.

11 And thou shalt make fifty taches of brass, and put the taches into the loops, and couple the tent together, that it may be one.

12 And the remnant that remaineth of the curtains of the tent, the half curtain that remaineth, shall hang over the backside of the tabernacle.

13 And a cubit on the one side, and a cubit on the other side of that which remaineth in the length of the curtains of the tent, it shall hang over the sides of the tabernacle on this side and on that side, to cover it.

14 And thou shalt make a covering for the tent of rams' skins dyed red, and a covering above of badgers' skins.

15 ¶ And thou shalt make boards for the tabernacle of shittim wood standing up.

16 Ten cubits shall be the length of a board, and a cubit and a half shall be the breadth of one board.

17 Two tenons shall there be in one board, set in order one against another: thus shalt thou make for all the boards of the tabernacle.

18 And thou shalt make the boards for the tabernacle, twenty boards on the south side southward.

19 And thou shalt make forty sockets of silver under the twenty boards; two sockets under one board for his two tenons, and two sockets under another board for his two tenons.

20 And for the second side of the tabernacle on the north side there shall be twenty boards:

21 And their forty sockets of silver; two sockets under one board, and two sockets under another board.

22 And for the sides of the tabernacle westward thou shalt make six boards.

23 And two boards shalt thou make for the corners of the tabernacle in the two sides.

24 And they shall be coupled together beneath, and they shall be coupled together above the head of it unto one ring: thus shall it be for them both; they shall be for the two corners.

25 And they shall be eight boards, and their sockets of silver, sixteen sockets; two sockets under one board, and two sockets under another board.

26 ¶ And thou shalt make bars of shittim wood; five for the boards of the one side of the tabernacle,

27 And five bars for the boards of the other side of the tabernacle, and five bars for the boards of the side of the tabernacle, for the two sides westward.

28 And the middle bar in the midst of the boards shall reach from end to end.

29 And thou shalt overlay the boards with gold, and make their rings of gold for places for the bars: and thou shalt overlay the bars with gold.

30 And thou shalt rear up the tabernacle according to the fashion thereof which was shewed thee in the mount.

31 ¶ And thou shalt make a veil of blue, and purple, and scarlet, and fine twined linen of cunning work: with cherubims shall it be made:

32 And thou shalt hang it upon four pillars of shittim wood overlaid with gold: their hooks shall be of gold, upon the four sockets of silver.

33 ¶ And thou shalt hang up the veil under the taches, that thou mayest bring in thither within the veil the ark of the testimony: and the veil shall divide unto you between the holy place and the most holy.

34 And thou shalt put the mercy seat upon the ark of the testimony in the most holy place.

35 And thou shalt set the table without the veil, and the candlestick over against the table on the side of the tabernacle toward the south: and thou shalt put the table on the north side.

36 And thou shalt make an hanging for the door of the tent, of blue, and purple, and scarlet, and fine twined linen, wrought with needle work.

37 And thou shalt make for the hanging five pillars of shittim wood, and overlay them with gold, and their hooks shall be of gold: and thou shalt cast five sockets of brass for them.

27 AND thou shalt make an altar of shittim wood, five cubits long, and five cubits broad; the altar shall be foursquare: and the height thereof shall be three cubits.

2 And thou shalt make the horns of it upon the four corners thereof: his horns shall be of the same: and thou shalt overlay it with brass.

3 And thou shalt make his pans to receive his ashes, and his shovels, and his basons, and his fleshhooks, and his firepans: all the vessels thereof thou shalt make of brass.

4 And thou shalt make for it a grate of net-work of brass; and upon the net shalt thou make four brasen rings in the four corners thereof.

5 And thou shalt put it under the compass of the altar beneath, that the net may be even to the midst of the altar.

6 And thou shalt make staves for the altar, staves of shittim wood, and overlay them with brass.

7 And the staves shall be put into the rings, and the staves shall be upon the two sides of the altar, to bear it.

8 Hollow with boards shalt thou make it: as it was shewed thee in the mount, so shall they make it.

9 ¶ And thou shalt make the court of the tabernacle: for the south side southward there shall be hangings for the court of fine twined linen of an hundred cubits long for one side:

10 And the twenty pillars thereof and their twenty sockets shall be of brass; the hooks of the pillars and their fillets shall be of silver.

11 And likewise for the north side in length there shall be hangings of an hundred cubits long, and his twenty pillars and their twenty sockets of brass; the hooks of the pillars and their fillets of silver.

12 ¶ And for the breadth of the court on the west side shall be hangings of fifty cubits: their pillars ten, and their sockets ten.

13 And the breadth of the court on the east side eastward shall be fifty cubits.

14 The hangings of one side of the gate shall be fifteen cubits: their pillars three, and their sockets three.

15 And on the other side shall be hangings fifteen cubits: their pillars three, and their sockets three.

16 ¶ And for the gate of the court shall be an hanging of twenty cubits, of blue, and purple, and scarlet, and fine twined linen, wrought with needlework: and their pillars shall be four, and their sockets four.

17 All the pillars round about the court shall be filleted with silver; their hooks shall be of silver, and the sockets of brass.

18 ¶ The length of the court shall be an hundred cubits, and the breadth fifty every where, and the height five cubits of fine twined linen, and their sockets of brass.

19 All the vessels of the tabernacle in all the service thereof, and all the pins thereof, and all the pins of the court, shall be of brass.

20 ¶ And thou shalt command the children of Is'ra-el, that they bring thee pure oil olive beaten for the light, to cause the lamp to burn always.

21 In the tabernacle of the congregation without the veil, which is before the testimony, Aar'on and his sons shall order it from evening to morning before the LORD: it shall be a statute for ever unto their generations on the behalf of the children of Is'ra-el.

28 AND take thou unto thee Aar'on thy brother, and his sons with him, from among the children of Is'ra-el, that he may minister unto me in the priest's office, even Aar'on, Na'dab and A-bi'hu, E-le-a'zar and Ith'a-mar, Aar'on's sons.

2 And thou shalt make holy garments for Aar'on thy brother for glory and for beauty.

3 And thou shalt speak unto all that are wise hearted, whom I have filled with the spirit of wisdom, that they may make Aar'on's garments to consecrate him, that he may minister unto me in the priest's office.

4 And these are the garments which they shall make; a breastplate, and an ephod, and a robe, and a broidered coat, a mitre, and a girdle: and they shall make holy garments for Aar'on thy brother, and his sons, that he may minister unto me in the priest's office.

5 And they shall take gold, and blue, and purple, and scarlet, and fine linen.

6 ¶ And they shall make the ephod of gold, of blue, and of purple, of scarlet, and fine twined linen, with cunning work.

7 It shall have the two shoulderpieces thereof joined at the two edges thereof; and so it shall be joined together.

8 And the curious girdle of the ephod, which is upon it, shall be of the same, according to the work thereof; even of gold, of blue, and purple, and scarlet, and fine twined linen.

9 And thou shalt take two onyx stones, and grave on them the names of the children of Is'-ra-el:

10 Six of their names on one stone, and the other six names of the rest on the other stone, according to their birth.

11 With the work of an engraver in stone, like the engravings of a signet, shalt thou engrave the two stones with the names of the children of Is'ra-el: thou shalt make them to be set in ouches of gold.

12 And thou shalt put the two stones upon the shoulders of the ephod for stones of memorial unto the children of Is'ra-el: and Aar'on shall bear their names before the LORD upon his two shoulders for a memorial.

13 ¶ And thou shalt make ouches of gold;

14 And two chains of pure gold at the ends; of wreathen work shalt thou make them, and fasten the wreathen chains to the ouches.

15 ¶ And thou shalt make the breastplate of judgment with cunning work; after the work of the ephod thou shalt make it; of gold, of blue, and of purple, and of scarlet, and of fine twined linen, shalt thou make it.

16 Foursquare it shall be being doubled; a

span *shall be* the length thereof, and a span *shall be* the breadth thereof

17 And thou shalt set in it settings of stones, *even* four rows of stones: *the first* row *shall be* a sardius, a topaz, and a carbuncle: *this shall be* the first row.

18 And the second row *shall be* an emerald, a sapphire, and a diamond.

19 And the third row a ligure, an agate, and an amethyst.

20 And the fourth row a beryl, and an onyx, and a jasper: they shall be set in gold in their inclosings.

21 And the stones shall be with the names of the children of Is´ra-el, twelve, according to their names, *like* the engravings of a signet; every one with his name shall they be according to the twelve tribes.

22 ¶ And thou shalt make upon the breastplate chains at the ends *of* wreathen work *of* pure gold.

23 And thou shalt make upon the breastplate two rings of gold, and shalt put the two rings on the two ends of the breastplate.

24 And thou shalt put the two wreathen *chains* of gold in the two rings *which are* on the ends of the breastplate.

25 And *the other* two ends of the two wreathen *chains* thou shalt fasten in the two ouches, and put *them* on the shoulderpieces of the e-phod before it.

26 ¶ And thou shalt make two rings of gold, and thou shalt put them upon the two ends of the breastplate in the border thereof, which *is* in the side of the ephod inward.

27 And two *other* rings of gold thou shalt make, and shalt put them on the two sides of the ephod underneath, toward the forepart thereof, over against the *other* coupling thereof, above the curious girdle of the ephod.

28 And they shall bind the breastplate by the rings thereof unto the rings of the ephod with a lace of blue, that *it* may be above the curious girdle of the ephod, and that the breastplate be not loosed from the ephod.

29 And Aar´on shall bear the names of the children of Is´ra-el in the breastplate of judgment upon his heart, when he goeth in unto the holy *place*, for a memorial before the LORD continually.

30 ¶ And thou shalt put in the breastplate of judgment the U´rim and the Thum´mim; and they shall be upon Aar´on's heart, when he goeth in before the LORD: and Aar´on shall bear the judgment of the children of Is´ra-el upon his heart before the LORD continually.

31 ¶ And thou shalt make the robe of the e-phod all *of* blue.

32 And there shall be an hole in the top of it, in the midst thereof: it shall have a binding of woven work round about the hole of it, as it were the hole of an habergeon, that it be not rent.

33 ¶ And *beneath* upon the hem of it thou shalt make pomegranates *of* blue, and *of* purple, and *of* scarlet, round about the hem thereof; and bells of gold between them round about:

34 A golden bell and a pomegranate, a golden bell and a pomegranate, upon the hem of the robe round about.

35 And it shall be upon Aar´on to minister: and his sound shall be heard when he goeth in unto the holy *place* before the LORD, and when he cometh out, that he die not.

36 ¶ And thou shalt make a plate *of* pure

gold, and grave upon it, *like* the engravings of a signet, HOLINESS TO THE LORD.

37 And thou shalt put it on a blue lace, that it may be upon the mitre; upon the forefront of the mitre it shall be.

38 And it shall be upon Aar´on's forehead, that Aar´on may bear the iniquity of the holy things, which the children of Is´ra-el shall hallow in all their holy gifts; and it shall be always upon his forehead, that they may be accepted before the LORD.

39 ¶ And thou shalt embroider the coat of fine linen, and thou shalt make the mitre *of* fine linen, and thou shalt make the girdle *of* needle-work.

40 ¶ And for Aar´on's sons thou shalt make coats, and thou shalt make for them girdles, and bonnets shalt thou make for them, for glory and for beauty.

41 And thou shalt put them upon Aar´on thy brother, and his sons with him; and shalt anoint them, and consecrate them, and sanctify them, that they may minister unto me in the priest's office.

42 And thou shalt make them linen breeches to cover their nakedness; from the loins even unto the thighs they shall reach:

43 And they shall be upon Aar´on, and upon his sons, when they come in unto the tabernacle of the congregation, or when they come near unto the altar to minister in the holy *place*; that they bear not iniquity, and die: *it shall be* a statute for ever unto him and his seed after him.

29 AND this *is* the thing that thou shalt do unto them to hallow them, to minister unto me in the priest's office: Take one young bullock, and two rams without blemish,

2 And unleavened bread, and cakes unleavened tempered with oil, and wafers unleavened anointed with oil: *of* wheaten flour shalt thou make them.

3 And thou shalt put them into one basket, and bring them in the basket, with the bullock and the two rams.

4 And Aar´on and his sons thou shalt bring unto the door of the tabernacle of the congregation, and shalt wash them with water.

5 And thou shalt take the garments, and put upon Aar´on the coat, and the robe of the e-phod, and the ephod, and the breastplate, and gird him with the curious girdle of the ephod:

6 And thou shalt put the mitre upon his head, and put the holy crown upon the mitre.

7 Then shalt thou take the anointing oil, and pour *it* upon his head, and anoint him.

8 And thou shalt bring his sons, and put coats upon them.

9 And thou shalt gird them with girdles, Aar´on and his sons, and put the bonnets on them: and the priest's office shall be theirs for a perpetual statute: and thou shalt consecrate Aar´on and his sons.

10 And thou shalt cause a bullock to be brought before the tabernacle of the congregation: and Aar´on and his sons shall put their hands upon the head of the bullock.

11 And thou shalt kill the bullock before the LORD, *by* the door of the tabernacle of the congregation.

12 And thou shalt take of the blood of the bullock, and put *it* upon the horns of the altar with thy finger, and pour all the blood beside the bottom of the altar.

13 And thou shalt take all the fat that covereth the inwards, and the caul *that is* above the

liver, and the two kidneys, and the fat that *is* upon them, and burn *them* upon the altar.

14 But the flesh of the bullock, and his skin, and his dung, shalt thou burn with fire without the camp: it *is* a sin offering.

15 ¶ Thou shalt also take one ram; and Aar'on and his sons shall put their hands upon the head of the ram.

16 And thou shalt slay the ram, and thou shalt take his blood, and sprinkle *it* round about upon the altar.

17 And thou shalt cut the ram in pieces, and wash the inwards of him, and his legs, and put *them* unto his pieces, and unto his head.

18 And thou shalt burn the whole ram upon the altar: it *is* a burnt offering unto the LORD: it *is* a sweet savour, an offering made by fire unto the LORD.

19 ¶ And thou shalt take the other ram; and Aar'on and his sons shall put their hands upon the head of the ram.

20 Then shalt thou kill the ram, and take of his blood, and put *it* upon the tip of the right ear of Aar'on, and upon the tip of the right ear of his sons, and upon the thumb of their right hand, and upon the great toe of their right foot, and sprinkle the blood upon the altar round about.

21 And thou shalt take of the blood that *is* upon the altar, and of the anointing oil, and sprinkle *it* upon Aar'on, and upon his garments, and upon his sons, and upon the garments of his sons with him: and he shall be hallowed, and his garments, and his sons, and his sons' garments with him.

22 Also thou shalt take of the ram the fat and the rump, and the fat that covereth the inwards, and the caul *above* the liver, and the two kidneys, and the fat that *is* upon them, and the right shoulder; for it *is* a ram of consecration:

23 And one loaf of bread, and one cake of oiled bread, and one wafer out of the basket of the unleavened bread that *is* before the LORD:

24 And thou shalt put all in the hands of Aar'on, and in the hands of his sons; and shalt wave them *for* a wave offering before the LORD.

25 And thou shalt receive them of their hands, and burn *them* upon the altar for a burnt offering, for a sweet savour before the LORD: it *is* an offering made by fire unto the LORD.

26 And thou shalt take the breast of the ram of Aar'on's consecration, and wave it *for* a wave offering before the LORD: and it shall be thy part.

27 And thou shalt sanctify the breast of the wave offering, and the shoulder of the heave offering, which is waved, and which is heaved up, of the ram of the consecration, *even* of *that* which *is* for Aar'on, and of *that* which is for his sons:

28 And it shall be Aar'on's and his sons' by a statute for ever from the children of Is'ra-el: for it *is* an heave offering: and it shall be an heave offering from the children of Is'ra-el of the sacrifice of their peace offerings, *even* their heave offering unto the LORD.

29 ¶ And the holy garments of Aar'on shall be his sons' after him, to be anointed therein, and to be consecrated in them.

30 *And* that son that is priest in his stead shall put them on seven days, when he cometh into the tabernacle of the congregation to minister in the holy *place.*

31 ¶ And thou shalt take the ram of the consecration, and seethe his flesh in the holy place.

32 And Aar'on and his sons shall eat the flesh of the ram, and the bread that *is* in the basket,

by the door of the tabernacle of the congregation.

33 And they shall eat those things wherewith the atonement was made, to consecrate *and* to sanctify them: but a stranger shall not eat *thereof,* because they *are* holy.

34 And if ought of the flesh of the consecrations, or of the bread, remain unto the morning, then thou shalt burn the remainder with fire: it shall not be eaten, because it *is* holy.

35 And thus shalt thou do unto Aar'on, and to his sons, according to all *things* which I have commanded thee: seven days shalt thou consecrate them.

36 And thou shalt offer every day a bullock *for* a sin offering for atonement: and thou shalt cleanse the altar, when thou hast made an atonement for it, and thou shalt anoint it, to sanctify it.

37 Seven days thou shalt make an atonement for the altar, and sanctify it; and it shall be an altar most holy: whatsoever toucheth the altar shall be holy.

38 ¶ Now this *is that* which thou shalt offer upon the altar; two lambs of the first year day by day continually.

39 The one lamb thou shalt offer in the morning; and the other lamb thou shalt offer at even:

40 And with the one lamb a tenth deal of flour mingled with the fourth part of an hin of beaten oil; and the fourth part of an hin of wine *for* a drink offering.

41 And the other lamb thou shalt offer at even, and shalt do thereto according to the meat offering of the morning, and according to the drink offering thereof, for a sweet savour, and offering made by fire unto the LORD.

42 *This shall be* a continual burnt offering throughout your generations *at* the door of the tabernacle of the congregation before the LORD: where I will meet you, to speak there unto thee.

43 And there I will meet with the children of Is'ra-el, and *the tabernacle* shall be sanctified by my glory.

44 And I will sanctify the tabernacle of the congregation, and the altar: I will sanctify also both Aar'on and his sons, to minister to me in the priest's office.

45 ¶ And I will dwell among the children of Is'ra-el, and will be their God.

46 And they shall know that I *am* the LORD their God, that brought them forth out of the land of E'gypt, that I may dwell among them: I *am* the LORD their God.

30 AND thou shalt make an altar to burn incense upon: of shittim wood shalt thou make it.

2 A cubit *shall be* the length thereof, and a cubit the breadth thereof; foursquare shall it be: and two cubits *shall be* the height thereof: the horns thereof *shall be* of the same.

3 And thou shalt overlay it with pure gold, the top thereof, and the sides thereof round about, and the horns thereof; and thou shalt make unto it a crown of gold round about.

4 And two golden rings shalt thou make to it under the crown of it, by the two corners thereof, upon the two sides of it shalt thou make *it;* and they shall be for places for the staves to bear it withal.

5 And thou shalt make the staves *of* shittim wood, and overlay them with gold.

6 And thou shalt put it before the veil that *is* by the ark of the testimony, before the mercy seat that *is* over the testimony, where I will meet with thee.

7 And Aar'on shall burn thereon sweet incense every morning: when he dresseth the lamps, he shall burn incense upon it.

8 And when Aar'on lighteth the lamps at even, he shall burn incense upon it, a perpetual incense before the LORD throughout your generations.

9 Ye shall offer no strange incense thereon, nor burnt sacrifice, nor meat offering; neither shall ye pour drink offering thereon.

10 And Aar'on shall make an atonement upon the horns of it once in a year with the blood of the sin offering of atonements: once in the year shall he make atonement upon it throughout your generations: it is most holy unto the LORD.

11 ¶ And the LORD spake unto Mo'ses, saying,

12 When thou takest the sum of the children of Is'ra-el after their number, then shall they give every man a ransom for his soul unto the LORD, when thou numberest them; that there be no plague among them, when thou numberest them.

13 This they shall give, every one that passeth among them that are numbered, half a shekel after the shekel of the sanctuary: (a shekel is twenty gerahs:) and half shekel shall be the offering of the LORD.

14 Every one that passeth among them that are numbered, from twenty years old and above, shall give an offering unto the LORD.

15 The rich shall not give more, and the poor shall not give less than half a shekel, when they give an offering unto the LORD, to make an atonement for your souls.

16 And thou shalt take the atonement money of the children of Is'ra-el, and shalt appoint it for the service of the tabernacle of the congregation; that it may be a memorial unto the children of Is'ra-el before the LORD, to make an atonement for your souls.

17 ¶ And the LORD spake unto Mo'ses, saying,

18 Thou shalt also make a laver of brass, and his foot also of brass, to wash withal: and thou shalt put it between the tabernacle of the congregation and the altar, and thou shalt put water therein.

19 For Aar'on and his sons shall wash their hands and their feet thereat:

20 When they go into the tabernacle of the congregation, they shall wash with water, that they die not; or when they come near to the altar to minister, to burn offering made by fire unto the LORD:

21 So they shall wash their hands and their feet, that they die not: and it shall be a statute for ever to them, even to him and to his seed throughout their generations.

22 ¶ Moreover the LORD spake unto Mo'ses, saying,

23 Take thou also unto thee principal spices, of pure myrrh five hundred shekels, and of sweet cinnamon half so much, even two hundred and fifty shekels, and of sweet calamus two hundred and fifty shekels,

24 And of cassia five hundred shekels, after the shekel of the sanctuary, and of oil olive an hin:

25 And thou shalt make it an oil of holy ointment, an ointment compound after the art of the apothecary: it shall be an holy anointing oil.

26 And thou shalt anoint the tabernacle of the congregation therewith, and the ark of the testimony,

27 And the table and all his vessels, and the candlestick and his vessels, and the altar of incense,

28 And the altar of burnt offering with all his vessels, and the laver and his foot.

29 And thou shalt sanctify them, that they may be most holy: whatsoever toucheth them shall be holy.

30 And thou shalt anoint Aar'on and his sons, and consecrate them, that they may minister unto me in the priest's office.

31 And thou shalt speak unto the children of Is'ra-el, saying, This shall be an holy anointing oil unto me throughout your generations.

32 Upon man's flesh shall it not be poured, neither shall ye make any other like it, after the composition of it: it is holy, and it shall be holy unto you.

33 Whosoever compoundeth any like it, or whosoever putteth any of it upon a stranger, shall even be cut off from his people.

34 ¶ And the LORD said unto Mo'ses, Take unto thee sweet spices, stacte, and onycha, and galbanum; these sweet spices with pure frankincense: of each shall there be a like weight:

35 And thou shalt make it a perfume, a confection after the art of the apothecary, tempered together, pure and holy:

36 And thou shalt beat some of it very small, and put of it before the testimony in the tabernacle of the congregation, where I will meet with thee: it shall be unto you most holy.

37 And as for the perfume which thou shalt make, ye shall not make to yourselves according to the composition thereof: it shall be unto thee holy for the LORD.

38 Whosoever shall make like unto that, to smell thereto, shall even be cut off from his people.

31 AND the LORD spake unto Mo'ses, saying,

2 See, I have called by name Be-zal'e-el the son of U'ri, the son of Hur, of the tribe of Ju'dah:

3 And I have filled him with the spirit of God, in wisdom, and in understanding, and in knowledge, and in all manner of workmanship,

4 To devise cunning works, to work in gold, and in silver, and in brass,

5 And in cutting of stones, to set them, and in carving of timber, to work in all manner of workmanship.

6 And I, behold, I have given with him A-ho'li-ab, the son of A-his'a-mach, of the tribe of Dan: and in the hearts of all that are wise hearted I have put wisdom, that they may make all that I have commanded thee;

7 The tabernacle of the congregation, and the ark of the testimony, and the mercy seat that is thereupon, and all the furniture of the tabernacle,

8 And the table and his furniture, and the pure candlestick with all his furniture, and the altar of incense,

9 And the altar of burnt offering with all his furniture, and the laver and his foot,

10 And the cloths of service, and the holy garments for Aar'on the priest, and the garments of his sons, to minister in the priest's office,

11 And the anointing oil, and sweet incense for the holy place: according to all that I have commanded thee shall they do.

12 ¶ And the LORD spake unto Mo'ses, saying,

13 Speak thou also unto the children of Is'ra-el, saying, Verily my sabbaths ye shall keep: for

it *is* a sign between me and you throughout your generations; that *ye* may know that I *am* the LORD that doth sanctify you.

14 Ye shall keep the sabbath therefore; for it *is* holy unto you: every one that defileth it shall surely be put to death: for whosoever doeth *any* work therein, that soul shall be cut off from among his people.

15 Six days may work be done; but in the seventh *is* the sabbath of rest, holy to the LORD: whosoever doeth *any* work in the sabbath day, he shall surely be put to death.

16 Wherefore the children of Is'ra-el shall keep the sabbath, to observe the sabbath throughout their generations, *for* a perpetual covenant.

17 It *is* a sign between me and the children of Is'ra-el for ever: for *in* six days the LORD made heaven and earth, and on the seventh day he rested, and was refreshed.

18 ¶ And he gave unto Mo'ses, when he had made an end of communing with him upon mount Si'nai, two tables of testimony, tables of stone, written with the finger of God.

32 AND when the people saw that Mo'ses delayed to come down out of the mount, the people gathered themselves together unto Aar'on, and said unto him, Up, make us gods, which shall go before us; for *as for* this Mo'ses, the man that brought us up out of the land of E'gypt, we wot not what is become of him.

2 And Aar'on said unto them, Break off the golden earrings, which *are* in the ears of your wives, of your sons, and of your daughters, and bring *them* unto me.

3 And all the poeple brake off the golden earrings which *were* in their ears, and brought *them* unto Aar'on.

4 And he received *them* at their hand, and fashioned it with a graving tool, after he had made it a molten calf: and they said, These *be* thy gods, O Is'ra-el, which brought thee up out of the land of E'gypt.

5 And when Aar'on saw *it,* he built an altar before it; and Aar'on made proclamation, and said, To morrow *is* a feast to the LORD.

6 And they rose up early on the morrow, and offered burnt offerings, and brought peace offerings; and the people sat down to eat and to drink, and rose up to play.

7 ¶ And the LORD said unto Mo'ses, Go, get thee down; for thy people, which thou broughtest out of the land of E'gypt, have corrupted *themselves:*

8 They have turned aside quickly out of the way which I commanded them: they have made them a molten calf, and have worshipped it, and have sacrificed thereunto, and said, These *be* thy gods, O Is'ra-el, which have brought thee up out of the land of E'gypt.

9 And the LORD said unto Mo'ses, I have seen this people, and, behold, it *is* a stiffnecked people:

10 Now therefore let me alone, that my wrath may wax hot against them, and that I may consume them: and I will make of thee a great nation.

11 And Mo'ses besought the LORD his God, and said, LORD, why doth thy wrath wax hot against thy people, which thou hast brought forth out of the land of E'gypt with great power, and with a mighty hand?

12 Wherefore should the E-gyptians speak, and say, For mischief did he bring them out, to slay them in the mountains, and to consume them from the face of the earth? Turn from thy fierce wrath, and repent of this evil against thy people.

13 Remember A'bra-ham, I'saac, and Is'ra-el, thy servants, to whom thou swarest by thine own self, and saidst unto them, I will multiply your seed as the stars of heaven, and all this land that I have spoken of will I give unto your seed, and they shall inherit *it* for ever.

14 And the LORD repented of the evil which he thought to do unto his people.

15 ¶ And Mo'ses turned, and went down from the mount, and the two tables of the testimony *were* in his hand: the tables *were* written on both their sides; on the one side and on the other *were* they written.

16 And the tables *were* the work of God, and the writing *was* the writing of God, graven upon the tables.

17 And when Josh'u-a heard the noise of the people as they shouted, he said unto Mo'ses, *There is* a noise of war in the camp.

18 And he said, *It is* not the voice of *them that* shout for mastery, neither *is it* the voice of *them that* cry for being overcome: *but* the noise of *them that* sing do I hear.

19 ¶ And it came to pass, as soon as he came nigh unto the camp, that he saw the calf, and the dancing: and Mo'ses' anger waxed hot, and he cast the tables out of his hands, and brake them beneath the mount.

20 And he took the calf which they had made, and burnt *it* in the fire, and ground *it* to powder, and strawed *it* upon the water, and made the children of Is'ra-el drink *of it.*

21 And Mo'ses said unto Aar'on, What did this people unto thee, that thou hast brought so great a sin upon them?

22 And Aar'on said, Let not the anger of my lord wax hot: thou knowest the people, that they *are* set on mischief.

23 For they said unto me, Make us gods, which shall go before us: for *as for* this Mo'ses, the man that brought us up out of the land of E'gypt, we wot not what is become of him.

24 And I said unto them, Whosoever hath any gold, let them break *it* off. So they gave *it* me: then I cast it into the fire, and there came out this calf.

25 ¶ And when Mo'ses saw that the people *were* naked; (for Aar'on had made them naked unto *their* shame among their enemies:)

26 Then Mo'ses stood in the gate of the camp, and said, Who *is* on the LORD's side? *let him come* unto me. And all the sons of Le'vi gathered themselves together unto him.

27 And he said unto them, Thus saith the LORD God of Is'ra-el, Put every man his sword by his side, *and* go in and out from gate to gate throughout the camp, and slay every man his brother, and every man his companion, and every man his neighbour.

28 And the children of Le'vi did according to the word of Mo'ses: and there fell of the people that day about three thousand men.

29 For Mo'ses had said, Consecrate yourselves to day to the LORD, even every man upon his son, and upon his brother; that he may bestow upon you a blessing this day.

30 ¶ And it came to pass on the morrow, that Mo'ses said unto the people, Ye have sinned a great sin: and now I will go up unto the LORD; peradventure I shall make an atonement for your sin.

31 And Mo'ses returned unto the LORD, and said, Oh, this people have sinned a great sin, and have made them gods of gold.

32 Yet now, if thou wilt forgive their sin—;

and if not, blot me, I pray thee, out of thy book which thou hast written.

33 And the LORD said unto Mo'ses, Whosoever hath sinned against me, him will I blot out of my book.

34 Therefore now go, lead the people unto *the place* of which I have spoken unto thee: behold, mine Angel shall go before thee: nevertheless in the day when I visit I will visit their sin upon them.

35 And the LORD plagued the people, because they made the calf, which Aar'on made.

33 AND the LORD said unto Mo'ses, Depart, *and* go up hence, thou and the people which thou hast brought up out of the land of E'gypt, unto the land which I sware unto A'bra-ham, to I'saac, and to Ja'cob, saying, Unto thy seed will I give it:

2 And I will send an angel before thee; and I will drive out the Ca'naan-ite, the Am'or-ite, and the Hit'tite, and the Per'iz-zite, the Hi'vite, and the Jeb'u-site:

3 Unto a land flowing with milk and honey: for I will not go up in the midst of thee; for thou *art* a stiffnecked people: lest I consume thee in the way.

4 ¶ And when the people heard these evil tidings, they mourned: and no man did put on him his ornaments.

5 For the LORD had said unto Mo'ses, Say unto the children of Is'ra-el, Ye *are* a stiffnecked people: I will come up into the midst of thee in a moment, and consume thee: therefore now put off thy ornaments from thee, that I may know what to do unto thee.

6 And the children of Is'ra-el stripped themselves of their ornaments by the mount Ho'reb.

7 And Mo'ses took the tabernacle, and pitched it without the camp, afar off from the camp, and called it the Tabernacle of the congregation. And it came to pass, *that* every one which sought the LORD went out unto the tabernacle of the congregation, which *was* without the camp.

8 And it came to pass, when Mo'ses went out unto the tabernacle, *that* all the people rose up, and stood every man *at* his tent door, and looked after Mo'ses, until he was gone into the tabernacle.

9 And it came to pass, as Mo'ses entered into the tabernacle, the cloudy pillar descended, and stood *at* the door of the tabernacle, and *the LORD* talked with Mo'ses.

10 And all the people saw the cloudy pillar stand *at* the tabernacle door: and all the people rose up and worshipped, every man *in* his tent door.

11 And the LORD spake unto Mo'ses face to face, as a man speaketh unto his friend. And he turned again into the camp: but his servant Josh'u-a, the son of Nun, a young man, departed not out of the tabernacle.

12 ¶ And Mo'ses said unto the LORD, See, thou sayest unto me, Bring up this people: and thou hast not let me know whom thou wilt send with me. Yet thou hast said, I know thee by name, and thou hast also found grace in my sight.

13 Now therefore, I pray thee, if I have found grace in thy sight, shew me now thy way, that I may know thee, that I may find grace in thy sight: and consider that this nation *is* thy people.

14 And he said, My presence shall go *with* thee, and I will give thee rest.

15 And he said unto him, If thy presence go not *with me*, carry us not up hence.

16 For wherein shall it be known here that I and thy people have found grace in thy sight? *is it* not in that thou goest with us? so shall we be separated, I and thy people, from all the people that *are* upon the face of the earth.

17 And the LORD said unto Mo'ses, I will do this thing also that thou hast spoken: for thou hast found grace in my sight, and I know thee by name.

18 And he said, I beseech thee, shew me thy glory.

19 And he said, I will make all my goodness pass before thee, and I will proclaim the name of the LORD before thee; and will be gracious to whom I will be gracious, and will shew mercy on whom I will shew mercy.

20 And he said, Thou canst not see my face: for there shall no man see me, and live.

21 And the LORD said, Behold, *there is* a place by me, and thou shalt stand upon a rock:

22 And it shall come to pass, while my glory passeth by, that I will put thee in a clift of the rock, and will cover thee with my hand while I pass by:

23 And I will take away mine hand, and thou shalt see my back parts: but my face shall not be seen.

34 AND the LORD said unto Mo'ses, Hew thee two tables of stone like unto the first: and I will write upon *these* tables the words that were in the first tables, which thou brakest.

2 And be ready in the morning, and come up in the morning unto mount Si'nai, and present thyself there to me in the top of the mount

3 And no man shall come up with thee, neither let any man be seen throughout all the mount; neither let the flocks nor herds feed before that mount.

4 ¶ And he hewed two tables of stone like unto the first; and Mo'ses rose up early in the morning, and went up unto mount Si'nai, as the LORD had commanded him, and took in his hand the two tables of stone.

5 And the LORD descended in the cloud, and stood with him there, and proclaimed the name of the LORD.

6 And the LORD passed by before him, and proclaimed, The LORD, The LORD God, merciful and gracious, longsuffering, and abundant in goodness and truth,

7 Keeping mercy for thousands, forgiving iniquity and transgression and sin, and that will by no means clear *the guilty;* visiting the iniquity of the fathers upon the children, and upon the children's children, unto the third and to the fourth *generation.*

8 And Mo'ses made haste, and bowed his head toward the earth, and worshipped.

9 And he said, If now I have found grace in thy sight, O Lord, let my Lord, I pray thee, go among us; for it *is* a stiffnecked people; and pardon our iniquity and our sin, and take us for thine inheritance.

10 ¶ And he said, Behold, I make a covenant: before all thy people I will do marvels, such as have not been done in all the earth, nor in any nation: and all the people among which thou *art* shall see the work of the LORD: for it *is* a terrible thing that I will do with thee.

11 Observe thou that which I command thee this day: behold, I drive out before thee the Am'or-ite, and the Ca'naan-ite, and the Hit'tite,

and the Per'iz-zite, and the Hi'vite, and the Jeb'-u-site.

12 Take heed to thyself, lest thou make a covenant with the inhabitants of the land whither thou goest, lest it be for a snare in the midst of thee:

13 But ye shall destroy their altars, break their images, and cut down their groves:

14 For thou shalt worship no other god: for the LORD, whose name is Jealous, is a jealous God:

15 Lest thou make a covenant with the inhabitants of the land, and they go a whoring after their gods, and do sacrifice unto their gods, and one call thee, and thou eat of his sacrifice:

16 And thou take of their daughters unto thy sons, and their daughters go a whoring after their gods, and make thy sons go a whoring after their gods.

17 Thou shalt make thee no molten gods.

18 ¶ The feast of unleavened bread shalt thou keep. Seven days thou shalt eat unleavened bread, as I commanded thee, in the time of the month A'bib: for in the month A'bib thou camest out from E'gypt.

19 All that openeth the matrix is mine; and every firstling among thy cattle, whether ox or sheep, that is male.

20 But the firstling of an ass thou shalt redeem with a lamb: and if thou redeem him not, then shalt thou break his neck. All the firstborn of thy sons thou shalt redeem. And none shall appear before me empty.

21 ¶ Six days thou shalt work, but on the seventh day thou shalt rest: in earing time and in harvest thou shalt rest.

22 ¶ And thou shalt observe the feast of weeks, of the firstfruits of wheat harvest, and the feast of ingathering at the year's end.

23 ¶ Thrice in the year shall all your menchildren appear before the Lord GOD, the God of Is'ra-el.

24 For I will cast out the nations before thee, and enlarge thy borders: neither shall any man desire thy land, when thou shalt go up to appear before the LORD thy God thrice in the year.

25 Thou shalt not offer the blood of my sacrifice with leaven; neither shall the sacrifice of the feast of the passover be left unto the morning.

26 The first of the firstfruits of thy land thou shalt bring unto the house of the LORD thy God. Thou shalt not seethe a kid in his mother's milk.

27 And the LORD said unto Mo'ses, Write thou these words: for after the tenor of these words I have made a covenant with thee and with Is'ra-el.

28 And he was there with the LORD forty days and forty nights; he did neither eat bread, nor drink water. And he wrote upon the tables the words of the covenant, the ten commandments.

29 ¶ And it came to pass, when Mo'ses came down from mount Si'nai with the two tables of testimony in Mo'ses' hand, when he came down from the mount that Mo'ses wist not that the skin of his face shone while he talked with him.

30 And when Aar'on and all the children of Is'ra-el saw Mo'ses, behold, the skin of his face shone; and they were afraid to come nigh him.

31 And Mo'ses called unto them; and Aar'on and all the rulers of the congregation returned unto him: and Mo'ses talked with them.

32 And afterward all the children of Is'ra-el came nigh: and he gave them in commandment all that the LORD had spoken with him in mount Si'nai.

33 And till Mo'ses had done speaking with them, he put a veil on his face.

34 But when Mo'ses went in before the LORD to speak with him, he took the veil off, until he came out. And he came out, and spake unto the children of Is'ra-el that which he was commanded.

35 And the children of Is'ra-el saw the face of Mo'ses, that the skin of Mo'ses' face shone: and Mo'ses put the veil upon his face again, until he went in to speak with him.

35 AND Mo'ses gathered all the congregation of the children of Is'ra-el together, and said unto them, These are the words which the LORD hath commanded, that ye should do them.

2 Six days shall work be done, but on the seventh day there shall be to you an holy day, a sabbath of rest to the LORD: whosoever doeth work therein shall be put to death.

3 Ye shall kindle no fire throughout your habitations upon the sabbath day.

4 ¶ And Mo'ses spake unto all the congregation of the children of Is'ra-el, saying, This is the thing which the LORD commanded, saying,

5 Take ye from among you an offering unto the LORD: whosoever is of a willing heart, let him bring it, an offering of the LORD; gold, and silver, and brass,

6 And blue, and purple, and scarlet, and fine linen, and goats' hair,

7 And rams' skins dyed red, and badgers' skins, and shittim wood,

8 And oil for the light, and spices for anointing oil, and for the sweet incense,

9 And onyx stones, and stones to be set for the ephod, and for the breastplate.

10 And every wise hearted among you shall come, and make all that the LORD hath commanded;

11 The tabernacle, his tent, and his covering, his taches, and his boards, his bars, his pillars, and his sockets,

12 The ark, and the staves thereof, with the mercy seat, and the veil of the covering,

13 The table, and his staves, and all his vessels, and the shewbread,

14 The candlestick also for the light, and his furniture, and his lamps, with the oil for the light,

15 And the incense altar, and his staves, and the anointing oil, and the sweet incense, and the hanging for the door at the entering in of the tabernacle,

16 The altar of burnt offering, with his brasen grate, his staves, and all his vessels, the laver and his foot,

17 The hangings of the court, his pillars, and their sockets, and the hanging for the door of the court,

18 The pins of the tabernacle, and the pins of the court, and their cords,

19 The cloths of service, to do service in the holy place, the holy garments for Aar'on the priest, and the garments of his sons, to minister in the priest's office.

20 ¶ And all the congregation of the children of Is'ra-el departed from the presence of Mo'ses.

21 And they came, every one whose heart stirred him up, and every one whom his spirit made willing, and they brought the LORD's offering to the work of the tabernacle of the con-

gregation, and for all his service, and for the holy garments.

22 And they came, both men and women, as many as were willing hearted, *and* brought bracelets, and earrings, and rings, and tablets, all jewels of gold: and every man that offered *offered* an offering of gold unto the LORD.

23 And every man, with whom was found blue, and purple, and scarlet, and fine linen, and goats' *hair*, and red skins of rams, and badgers' skins, brought *them*.

24 Every one that did offer an offering of silver and brass brought the LORD's offering: and every man, with whom was found shittim wood for any work of the service, brought *it*.

25 And all the women that were wise hearted did spin with their hands, and brought that which they had spun, *both* of blue, and of purple, *and* of scarlet, and of fine linen.

26 And all the women whose heart stirred them up in wisdom spun goats' *hair*.

27 And the rulers brought onyx stones, and stones to be set, for the ephod, and for the breastplate;

28 And spice, and oil for the light, and for the anointing oil, and for the sweet incense.

29 The children of Is′ra-el brought a willing offering unto the LORD, every man and woman, whose heart made them willing to bring for all manner of work, which the LORD had commanded to be made by the hand of Mo′ses.

30 ¶ And Mo′ses said unto the children of Is′ra-el, See, the LORD hath called by name Be-zal′e-el the son of U′ri, the son of Hur, of the tribe of Ju′dah;

31 And he hath filled him with the spirit of God, in wisdom, in understanding, and in knowledge, and in all manner of workmanship;

32 And to devise curious works, to work in gold, and in silver, and in brass,

33 And in the cutting of stones, to set *them*, and in carving of wood, to make any manner of cunning work.

34 And he hath put in his heart that he may teach, *both* he, and A-ho′li-ab, the son of A-his′-a-mach, of the tribe of Dan.

35 Them hath he filled with wisdom of heart, to work all manner of work, of the engraver, and of the cunning workman, and of the embroiderer, in blue, and in purple, in scarlet, and in fine linen, and of the weaver, *even* of them that do any work, and of those that devise cunning work.

36 THEN wrought Be-zal′e-el and A-ho′li-ab, and every wise hearted man, in whom the LORD put wisdom and understanding to know how to work all manner of work for the service of the sanctuary, according to all that the LORD had commanded.

2 And Mo′ses called Be-zal′e-el and A-ho′li-ab, and every wise hearted man, in whose heart the LORD had put wisdom, *even* every one whose heart stirred him up to come unto the work to do it:

3 And they received of Mo′ses all the offering, which the children of Is′ra-el had brought for the work of the service of the sanctuary, to make it *withal*. And they brought yet unto him free offerings every morning.

4 And all the wise men, that wrought all the work of the sanctuary, came every man from his work which they make;

5 ¶ And they spake unto Mo′ses, saying, The people bring much more than enough for the service of the work, which the LORD commanded to make.

6 And Mo′ses gave commandment, and they caused it to be proclaimed throughout the camp, saying, Let neither man nor woman make any more work for the offering of the sanctuary. So the people were restrained from bringing.

7 For the stuff they had was sufficient for all the work to make it, and too much.

8 ¶ And every wise hearted man among them that wrought the work of the tabernacle made ten curtains *of* fine twined linen, and blue, and purple, and scarlet: *with* cherubims of cunning work made he them.

9 The length of one curtain *was* twenty and eight cubits, and the breadth of one curtain four cubits: the curtains *were* all of one size.

10 And he coupled the five curtains one unto another: and *the other* five curtains he coupled one unto another.

11 And he made loops of blue on the edge of one curtain from the selvedge in the coupling: likewise he made in the uttermost side of *another* curtain, in the coupling of the second.

12 Fifty loops made he in one curtain, and fifty loops made he in the edge of the curtain which *was* in the coupling of the second: the loops held one *curtain* to another.

13 And he made fifty taches of gold, and coupled the curtains one unto another with the taches: so it became one tabernacle.

14 ¶ And he made curtains *of* goats' *hair* for the tent over the tabernacle: eleven curtains he made them.

15 The length of one curtain *was* thirty cubits, and four cubits *was* the breadth of one curtain: the eleven curtains *were* of one size.

16 And he coupled five curtains by themselves, and six curtains by themselves.

17 And he made fifty loops upon the uttermost edge of the curtain in the coupling, and fifty loops made he upon the edge of the curtain which coupleth the second.

18 And he made fifty taches *of* brass to couple the tent together, that it might be one.

19 And he made a covering for the tent *of* rams' skins dyed red, and a covering *of* badgers' skins above *that*.

20 ¶ And he made boards for the tabernacle *of* shittim wood, standing up.

21 The length of a board *was* ten cubits, and the breadth of a board one cubit and a half.

22 One board had two tenons, equally distant one from another: thus did he make for all the boards of the tabernacle.

23 And he made boards for the tabernacle; twenty boards for the south side southward:

24 And forty sockets of silver he made under the twenty boards; two sockets under one board for his two tenons, and two sockets under another board for his two tenons.

25 And for the other side of the tabernacle, which is toward the north corner, he made twenty boards,

26 And their forty sockets of silver; two sockets under one board, and two sockets under another board.

27 And for the sides of the tabernacle westward he made six boards.

28 And two boards made he for the corners of the tabernacle in the two sides.

29 And they were coupled beneath, and coupled together at the head thereof, to one ring: thus he did to both of them in both corners.

30 And there were eight boards; and their sockets *were* sixteen sockets of silver, under every board two sockets.

31 ¶ And he made bars of shittim wood; five

for the boards of the one side of the tabernacle,

32 And five bars for the boards of the other side of the tabernacle, and five bars for the boards of the tabernacle for the sides westward.

33 And he made the middle bar to shoot through the boards from the one end to the other.

34 And he overlaid the boards with gold, and made their rings *of* gold *to be* places for the bars, and overlaid the bars with gold.

35 ¶ And he made a veil *of* blue, and purple, and scarlet, and fine twined linen: *with* cherubims made he it of cunning work.

36 And he made thereunto four pillars *of* shittim *wood*, and overlaid them with gold: their hooks *were of* gold; and he cast for them four sockets of silver.

37 ¶ And he made an hanging for the tabernacle door *of* blue, and purple, and scarlet, and fine twined linen, of needlework;

38 And the five pillars of it with their hooks: and he overlaid their chapiters and their fillets with gold: but their five sockets *were of* brass.

37 AND Be-zal´e-el made the ark *of* shittim wood: two cubits and a half *was* the length of it, and a cubit and a half the breadth of it, and a cubit and a half the height of it:

2 And he overlaid it with pure gold within and without, and made a crown of gold to it round about.

3 And he cast for it four rings of gold, *to be set* by the four corners of it; even two rings upon the one side of it, and two rings upon the other side of it.

4 And he made staves *of* shittim wood, and overlaid them with gold.

5 And he put the staves into the rings by the sides of the ark, to bear the ark.

6 ¶ And he made the mercy seat *of* pure gold: two cubits and a half *was* the length thereof, and one cubit and a half the breadth thereof.

7 And he made two cherubims *of* gold, beaten out of one piece made he them, on the two ends of the mercy seat;

8 One cherub on the end on this side, and another cherub on the *other* end on that side: out of the mercy seat made he the cherubims on the two ends thereof.

9 And cherubims spread out *their* wings on high, *and* covered with their wings over the mercy seat, with their faces one to another; *even* to the mercy seatward were the faces of the cherubims.

10 ¶ And he made the table *of* shittim wood: two cubits *was* the length thereof, and a cubit the breadth thereof, and a cubit and a half the height thereof:

11 And he overlaid it with pure gold, and made thereunto a crown of gold round about.

12 Also he made thereunto a border of an handbreadth round about; and made a crown of gold for the border thereof round about.

13 And he cast for it four rings of gold, and put the rings upon the four corners that *were* in the four feet thereof.

14 Over against the border were the rings, the places for the staves to bear the table.

15 And he made the staves *of* shittim wood, and overlaid them with gold to bear the table.

16 And he made the vessels which *were* upon the table, his dishes, and his spoons, and his bowls, and his covers to cover withal, *of* pure gold.

17 ¶ And he made the candlestick *of* pure gold: *of* beaten work made he the candlestick; his shaft, and his branch, his bowls, his knops, and his flowers, were of the same:

18 And six branches going out of the sides thereof; three branches of the candlestick out of the one side thereof, and three branches of the candlestick out of the other side thereof:

19 Three bowls made after the fashion of almonds in one branch, a knop and a flower; and three bowls made like almonds in another branch, a knop and a flower: so throughout the six branches going out of the candlestick.

20 And in the candlestick *were* four bowls made like almonds, his knops, and his flowers:

21 And a knop under two branches of the same, and a knop under two branches of the same, and a knop under two branches of the same, according to the six branches going out of it.

22 Their knops and their branches were of the same: all of it *was* one beaten work *of* pure gold.

23 And he made his seven lamps, and his snuffers, and his snuffdishes, *of* pure gold.

24 *Of* a talent of pure gold made he it, and all the vessels thereof.

25 ¶ And he made the incense altar *of* shittim wood: the length of it *was* a cubit, and the breadth of it a cubit; *it was* foursquare; and two cubits *was* the height of it; the horns thereof were of the same.

26 And he overlaid it with pure gold, *both* the top of it, and the sides thereof round about, and the horns of it: also he made unto it a crown of gold round about.

27 And he made two rings of gold for it under the crown thereof, by the two corners of it, upon the two sides thereof, to be places for the staves to bear it withal.

28 And he made the staves *of* shittim wood, and overlaid them with gold.

29 ¶ And he made the holy anointing oil, and the pure incense of sweet spices, according to the work of the apothecary.

38 AND he made the altar of burnt offering *of* shittim wood: five cubits *was* the length thereof, and five cubits the breadth thereof; *it was* foursquare; and three cubits the height thereof.

2 And he made the horns thereof on the four corners of it; the horns thereof were of the same: and he overlaid it with brass.

3 And he made all the vessels of the altar, the pots, and the shovels, and the basons, *and* the fleshhooks, and the firepans: all the vessels thereof made he *of* brass.

4 And he made for the altar a brasen grate of network under the compass thereof beneath unto the midst of it.

5 And he cast four rings for the four ends of the grate of brass, *to be* places for the staves.

6 And he made the staves *of* shittim wood, and overlaid them with brass.

7 And he put the staves into the rings on the sides of the altar, to bear it withal; he made the altar hollow with boards.

8 ¶ And he made the laver *of* brass, and the foot of it *of* brass, of the lookingglasses of *the women* assembling, which assembled *at* the door of the tabernacle of the congregation.

9 ¶ And he made the court: on the south side southward the hangings of the court *were of* fine twined linen, an hundred cubits:

10 Their pillars *were* twenty, and their brasen sockets twenty; the hooks of the pillars and their fillets *were of* silver.

11 And for the north side *the hangings were* an hundred cubits, their pillars *were* twenty, and their sockets of brass twenty; the hooks of the pillars and their fillets *of* silver.

12 And for the west side *were* hangings of fifty cubits, their pillars ten, and their sockets ten; the hooks of the pillars and their fillets *of* silver.

13 And for the east side eastward fifty cubits.

14 The hangings of the one side *of the gate were* fifteen cubits; their pillars three, and their sockets three.

15 And for the other side of the court gate, on this hand and that hand, *were* hangings of fifteen cubits; their pillars three, and their sockets three.

16 All the hangings of the court round about *were* of fine twined linen.

17 And the sockets for the pillars *were of* brass; the hooks of the pillars and their fillets *of* silver; and the overlaying of their chapiters *of* silver; and all the pillars of the court *were* filleted with silver.

18 And the hanging for the gate of the court *was* needlework, *of* blue, and purple, and scarlet, and fine twined linen: and twenty cubits *was* the length, and the height in the breadth *was* five cubits, answerable to the hangings of the court.

19 And their pillars *were* four, and their sockets *of* brass four; their hooks *of* silver, and the overlaying of their chapiters and their fillets *of* silver.

20 And all the pins of the tabernacle, and of the court round about, *were of* brass.

21 ¶ This is the sum of the tabernacle, *even* of the tabernacle of testimony, as it was counted, according to the commandment of Mo'ses, *for* the service of the Le'vites, by the hand of Ith'a-mar, son to Aar'on the priest.

22 And Be-zal'e-el the son of U'ri, the son of Hur, of the tribe of Ju'dah, made all that the LORD commanded Mo'ses.

23 And with him *was* A-ho'li-ab, son of A-his'a-mach, of the tribe of Dan, an engraver, and a cunning workman, and an embroiderer in blue, and in purple, and in scarlet, and fine linen.

24 All the gold that was occupied for the work in all the work of the holy *place*, even the gold of the offering, was twenty and nine talents, and seven hundred and thirty shekels, after the shekel of the sanctuary.

25 And the silver of them that were numbered of the congregation *was* an hundred talents, and a thousand seven hundred and threescore and fifteen shekels, after the shekel of the sanctuary:

26 A bekah for every man, *that is*, half a shekel, after the shekel of the sanctuary, for every one that went to be numbered, from twenty years old and upward, for six hundred thousand and three thousand and five hundred and fifty *men*.

27 And of the hundred talents of silver were cast the sockets of the sanctuary, and the sockets of the veil; an hundred sockets of the hundred talents, a talent for a socket.

28 And of the thousand seven hundred seventy and five *shekels* he made hooks for the pillars, and overlaid their chapiters, and filleted them.

29 And the brass of the offering *was* seventy talents, and two thousand and four hundred shekels.

30 And therewith he made the sockets to the door of the tabernacle of the congregation, and the brasen altar, and brasen grate for it, and all the vessels of the altar,

31 And the sockets of the court round about, and the sockets of the court gate, and all the pins of the tabernacle, and all the pins of the court round about.

39 AND of the blue, and purple, and scarlet, they made cloths of service, to do service in the holy *place*, and made the holy garments for Aar'on; as the LORD commanded Mo'ses.

2 And he made the ephod *of* gold, blue, and purple, and scarlet, and fine twined linen.

3 And they did beat the gold into thin plates, and cut *it into* wires, to work *it* in the blue, and in the purple, and in the scarlet, and in the fine linen, *with* cunning work.

4 They made shoulderpieces for it, to couple *it* together: by the two edges was it coupled together.

5 And the curious girdle of his ephod, that *was* upon it, *was* of the same, according to the work thereof; *of* gold, blue, and purple, and scarlet, and fine twined linen; as the LORD commanded Mo'ses.

6 ¶ And they wrought onyx stones inclosed in ouches of gold, graven, as signets are graven, with the names of the children of Is'ra-el.

7 And he put them on the shoulders of the ephod, *that they should be* stones for a memorial to the children of Is'ra-el; as the LORD commanded Mo'ses.

8 ¶ And he made the breastplate *of* cunning work, like the work of the ephod; *of* gold, blue, and purple, and scarlet, and fine twined linen.

9 It was foursquare; they made the breastplate double: a span *was* the length thereof, and a span the breadth thereof, *being* doubled.

10 And they set in it four rows of stones: *the first* row *was* a sardius, a topaz, and a carbuncle: this *was* the first row.

11 And the second row, an emerald, a sapphire, and a diamond.

12 And the third row, a ligure, an agate, and an amethyst.

13 And the fourth row, a beryl, an onyx, and a jasper: *they were* inclosed in ouches of gold in their inclosings.

14 And the stones *were* according to the names of the children of Is'ra-el, twelve, according to their names, *like* the engravings of a signet, every one with his name, according to the twelve tribes.

15 And they made upon the breastplate chains at the ends, *of* wreathen work *of* pure gold.

16 And they made two ouches *of* gold, and two gold rings; and put the two rings in the two ends of the breastplate.

17 And they put the two wreathen chains of gold in the two rings on the ends of the breastplate.

18 And the two ends of the two wreathen chains they fastened in the two ouches, and put them on the shoulderpieces of the ephod, before it.

19 And they made two rings of gold, and put *them* on the two ends of the breastplate, upon the border of it, which *was* on the side of the ephod inward.

20 And they made two *other* golden rings, and put them on the two sides of the ephod underneath, toward the forepart of it, over against the *other* coupling thereof, above the curious girdle of the ephod.

21 And they did bind the breastplate by his

rings unto the rings of the ephod with a lace of blue, that it might be above the curious girdle of the ephod, and that the breastplate might not be loosed from the ephod; as the LORD commanded Mo'ses.

22 ¶ And he made the robe of the ephod *of* woven work, all *of* blue.

23 And *there was* an hole in the midst of the robe, as the hole of an habergeon, *with* a band round about the hole, that it should not rend.

24 And they made upon the hems of the robe pomegranates *of* blue, and purple, and scarlet, *and* twined *linen.*

25 And they made bells *of* pure gold, and put the bells between the pomegranates upon the hem of the robe, round about between the pomegranates;

26 A bell and a pomegranate, a bell and a pomegranate, round about the hem of the robe to minister *in;* as the LORD commanded Mo'ses.

27 ¶ And they made coats *of* fine linen *of* woven work for Aar'on, and for his sons,

28 And a mitre *of* fine linen, and goodly bonnets *of* fine linen, and linen breeches *of* fine twined linen,

29 And a girdle *of* fine twined linen, and blue, and purple, and scarlet, *of* needlework; as the LORD commanded Mo'ses.

30 ¶ And they made the plate of the holy crown *of* pure gold, and wrote upon it a writing, *like to* the engravings of a signet, HOLINESS TO THE LORD.

31 And they tied unto it a lace of blue, to fasten *it* on high upon the mitre; as the LORD commanded Mo'ses.

32 ¶ Thus was all the work of the tabernacle of the tent of the congregation finished: and the children of Is'ra-el did according to all that the LORD commanded Mo'ses, so did they.

33 ¶ And they brought the tabernacle unto Mo'ses, the tent, and all his furniture, his taches, his boards, his bars, and his pillars, and his sockets,

34 And the covering of rams' skins dyed red, and the covering of badgers' skins, and the veil of the covering,

35 The ark of the testimony, and the staves thereof, and the mercy seat,

36 The table, *and* all the vessels thereof, and the shewbread,

37 The pure candlestick, *with* the lamps thereof, *even with* the lamps to be set in order, and all the vessels thereof, and the oil for light,

38 And the golden altar, and the anointing oil, and the sweet incense, and the hanging for the tabernacle door,

39 The brasen altar, and his grate of brass, his staves, and all his vessels, the laver and his foot,

40 The hangings of the court, his pillars, and his sockets, and the hanging for the court gate, his cords, and his pins, and all the vessels of the service of the tabernacle, for the tent of the congregation,

41 The cloths of service to do service in the holy *place,* and the holy garments for Aar'on the priest, and his sons' garments, to minister in the priest's office.

42 According to all that the LORD commanded Mo'ses, so the children of Is'ra-el made all the work.

43 And Mo'ses did look upon all the work, and, behold, they had done it as the LORD had commanded, even so had they done it: and Mo'ses blessed them.

40 AND the LORD spake unto Mo'ses, saying,

2 On the first day of the first month shalt thou set up the tabernacle of the tent of the congregation.

3 And thou shalt put therein the ark of the testimony, and cover the ark with the veil.

4 And thou shalt bring in the table, and set in order the things that are to be set in order upon it; and thou shalt bring in the candlestick, and light the lamps thereof.

5 And thou shalt set the altar of gold for the incense before the ark of the testimony, and put the hanging of the door to the tabernacle.

6 And thou shalt set the altar of the burnt offering before the door of the tabernacle of the tent of the congregation.

7 And thou shalt set the laver between the tent of the congregation and the altar, and shalt put water therein.

8 And thou shalt set up the court round about, and hang up the hanging at the court gate.

9 And thou shalt take the anointing oil, and anoint the tabernacle, and all that *is* therein, and shalt hallow it, and all the vessels thereof: and it shall be holy.

10 And thou shalt anoint the altar of the burnt offering, and all his vessels, and sanctify the altar: and it shall be an altar most holy.

11 And thou shalt anoint the laver and his foot, and sanctify it.

12 And thou shalt bring Aar'on and his sons unto the door of the tabernacle of the congregation, and wash them with water.

13 And thou shalt put upon Aar'on the holy garments, and anoint him, and sanctify him; that he may minister unto me in the priest's office.

14 And thou shalt bring his sons, and clothe them with coats:

15 And thou shalt anoint them, as thou didst anoint their father, that they may minister unto me in the priest's office: for their anointing shall surely be an everlasting priesthood throughout their generations.

16 Thus did Mo'ses: according to all that the LORD commanded him, so did he.

17 ¶ And it came to pass in the first month in the second year, on the first *day* of the month, *that* the tabernacle was reared up.

18 And Mo'ses reared up the tabernacle, and fastened his sockets, and set up the boards thereof, and put in the bars thereof, and reared up his pillars.

19 And he spread abroad the tent over the tabernacle, and put the covering of the tent above upon it; as the LORD commanded Mo'ses.

20 ¶ And he took and put the testimony into the ark, and set the staves on the ark, and put the mercy seat above upon the ark:

21 And he brought the ark into the tabernacle, and set up the veil of the covering, and covered the ark of the testimony; as the LORD commanded Mo'ses.

22 ¶ And he put the table in the tent of the congregation, upon the side of the tabernacle northward, without the veil.

23 And he set the bread in order upon it before the LORD; as the LORD had commanded Mo'ses.

24 ¶ And he put the candlestick in the tent of the congregation, over against the table, on the side of the tabernacle southward.

25 And he lighted the lamps before the LORD; as the LORD commanded Mo'ses.

26 ¶ And he put the golden altar in the tent of the congregation before the veil:

27 And he burnt sweet incense thereon; as the LORD commanded Mo'ses.

28 ¶ And he set up the hanging *at* the door of the tabernacle.

29 And he put the altar of burnt offering by the door of the tabernacle of the tent of the congregation, and offered upon it the burnt offering and the meat offering; as the LORD commanded Mo'ses.

30 ¶ And he set the laver between the tent of the congregation and the altar, and put water there, to wash *withal*.

31 And Mo'ses and Aar'on and his sons washed their hands and their feet thereat:

32 When they went into the tent of the congregation, and when they came near unto the altar, they washed; as the LORD commanded Mo'ses.

33 And he reared up the court round about

the tabernacle and the altar, and set up the hanging of the court gate. So Mo'ses finished the work.

34 ¶ Then a cloud covered the tent of the congregation, and the glory of the LORD filled the tabernacle.

35 And Mo'ses was not able to enter into the tent of the congregation, because the cloud abode thereon, and the glory of the LORD filled the tabernacle.

36 And when the cloud was taken up from over the tabernacle, the children of Is'ra-el went onward in all their journeys:

37 But if the cloud were not taken up, then they journeyed not till the day that it was taken up.

38 For the cloud of the LORD *was* upon the tabernacle by day, and fire was on it by night, in the sight of all the house of Is'ra-el, throughout all their journeys.

THE THIRD BOOK OF MOSES
COMMONLY CALLED

LEVITICUS

1 AND the LORD called unto Mo'ses, and spake unto him out of the tabernacle of the congregation, saying,

2 Speak unto the children of Is'ra-el, and say unto them, If any man of you bring an offering unto the LORD, ye shall bring your offering of the cattle, *even* of the herd, and of the flock.

3 If his offering *be* a burnt sacrifice of the herd, let him offer a male without blemish: he shall offer it of his own voluntary will at the door of the tabernacle of the congregation before the LORD.

4 And he shall put his hand upon the head of the burnt offering; and it shall be accepted for him to make atonement for him.

5 And he shall kill the bullock before the LORD: and the priests, Aar'on's sons, shall bring the blood, and sprinkle the blood round about upon the altar that *is* by the door of the tabernacle of the congregation.

6 And he shall flay the burnt offering, and cut it into his pieces.

7 And the sons of Aar'on the priest shall put fire upon the altar, and lay the wood in order upon the fire:

8 And the priests, Aar'on's sons, shall lay the parts, the head, and the fat, in order upon the wood that *is* on the fire which *is* upon the altar:

9 But his inwards and his legs shall he wash in water: and the priest shall burn all on the altar, *to be* a burnt sacrifice, an offering made by fire, of a sweet savour unto the LORD.

10 ¶ And if his offering *be* of the flocks, *namely*, of the sheep, or of the goats, for a burnt sacrifice; he shall bring it a male without blemish.

11 And he shall kill it on the side of the altar northward before the LORD: and the priests, Aar'on's sons, shall sprinkle his blood round about upon the altar.

12 And he shall cut it into his pieces, with his head and his fat: and the priest shall lay them in order on the wood that *is* on the fire which *is* upon the altar:

13 But he shall wash the inwards and the legs with water: and the priest shall bring *it* all, and burn *it* upon the altar: it *is* a burnt sacrifice,

an offering made by fire, of a sweet savour unto the LORD.

14 ¶ And if the burnt sacrifice for his offering to the LORD *be* of fowls, then he shall bring his offering of turtledoves, or of young pigeons.

15 And the priest shall bring it unto the altar, and wring off his head, and burn *it* on the altar; and the blood thereof shall be wrung out at the side of the altar:

16 And he shall pluck away his crop with his feathers, and cast it beside the altar on the east part, by the place of the ashes:

17 And he shall cleave it with the wings thereof, *but* shall not divide *it* asunder: and the priest shall burn it upon the altar, upon the wood that *is* upon the fire: it *is* a burnt sacrifice, an offering made by fire, of a sweet savour unto the LORD.

2 AND when any will offer a meat offering unto the LORD, his offering shall be *of* fine flour; and he shall pour oil upon it, and put frankincense thereon:

2 And he shall bring it to Aar'on's sons the priests: and he shall take thereout his handful of the flour thereof, and of the oil thereof, with all the frankincense thereof; and the priest shall burn the memorial of it upon the altar, *to be* an offering made by fire, of a sweet savour unto the LORD:

3 And the remnant of the meat offering *shall be* Aar'on's and his sons': *it is* a thing most holy of the offerings of the LORD made by fire.

4 ¶ And if thou bring an oblation of a meat offering baken in the oven, *it shall be* unleavened cakes of fine flour mingled with oil, or unleavened wafers anointed with oil.

5 ¶ And if thy oblation *be* a meat offering *baken* in a pan, it shall be *of* fine flour unleavened, mingled with oil.

6 Thou shalt part it in pieces, and pour oil thereon: it *is* a meat offering.

7 ¶ And if thy oblation *be* a meat offering *baken* in the fryingpan, it shall be made *of* fine flour with oil.

8 And thou shalt bring the meat offering that is made of these things unto the LORD: and

when it is presented unto the priest, he shall bring it unto the altar.

9 And the priest shall take from the meat offering a memorial thereof, and shall burn *it* upon the altar: *it is* an offering made by fire, of a sweet savour unto the LORD.

10 And that which is left of the meat offering *shall be* Aar'on's and his sons': *it is* a thing most holy of the offerings of the LORD made by fire.

11 No meat offering, which ye shall bring unto the LORD, shall be made with leaven: for ye shall burn no leaven, nor any honey, in any offering of the LORD made by fire.

12 ¶ As for the oblation of the firstfruits, ye shall offer them unto the LORD: but they shall not be burnt on the altar for a sweet savour.

13 And every oblation of thy meat offering shalt thou season with salt; neither shalt thou suffer the salt of the covenant of thy God to be lacking from thy meat offering: with all thine offerings thou shalt offer salt.

14 And if thou offer a meat offering of thy firstfruits unto the LORD, thou shalt offer for the meat offering of thy firstfruits green ears of corn dried by the fire, *even* corn beaten out of full ears.

15 And thou shalt put oil upon it, and lay frankincense thereon: it *is* a meat offering.

16 And the priest shall burn the memorial of it, *part* of the beaten corn thereof, and *part* of the oil thereof, with all the frankincense thereof: *it is* an offering made by fire unto the LORD.

3 AND if his oblation *be* a sacrifice of peace offering, if he offer *it* of the herd; whether *it be* a male or female, he shall offer it without blemish before the LORD.

2 And he shall lay his hand upon the head of his offering, and kill it *at* the door of the tabernacle of the congregation: and Aar'on's sons the priests shall sprinkle the blood upon the altar round about.

3 And he shall offer of the sacrifice of the peace offering an offering made by fire unto the LORD; the fat that covereth the inwards, and all the fat that *is* upon the inwards,

4 And the two kidneys, and the fat that *is* on them, which *is* by the flanks, and the caul above the liver, with the kidneys, it shall he take away.

5 And Aar'on's sons shall burn it on the altar upon the burnt sacrifice, which *is* upon the wood that *is* on the fire: *it is* an offering made by fire, of a sweet savour unto the LORD.

6 ¶ And if his offering for a sacrifice of peace offering unto the LORD *be* of the flock; male or female, he shall offer it without blemish.

7 If he offer a lamb for his offering, then shall he offer it before the LORD.

8 And he shall lay his hand upon the head of his offering, and kill it before the tabernacle of the congregation: and Aar'on's sons shall sprinkle the blood thereof round about upon the altar.

9 And he shall offer of the sacrifice of the peace offering an offering made by fire unto the LORD; the fat thereof, *and* the whole rump, it shall he take off hard by the backbone; and the fat that covereth the inwards, and all the fat that *is* upon the inwards,

10 And the two kidneys, and the fat that *is* upon them, which *is* by the flanks, and the caul above the liver, with the kidneys, it shall he take away.

11 And the priest shall burn it upon the altar: *it is* the food of the offering made by fire unto the LORD.

12 ¶ And if his offering *be* a goat, then he shall offer it before the LORD.

13 And he shall lay his hand upon the head of it, and kill it before the tabernacle of the congregation: and the sons of Aar'on shall sprinkle the blood thereof upon the altar round about.

14 And he shall offer thereof his offering, *even* an offering made by fire unto the LORD; the fat that covereth the inwards, and all the fat that *is* upon the inwards,

15 And the two kidneys, and the fat that *is* upon them, which *is* by the flanks, and the caul above the liver, with the kidneys, it shall he take away.

16 And the priest shall burn them upon the altar: *it is* the food of the offering made by fire for a sweet savour: all the fat *is* the LORD's.

17 *It shall be* a perpetual statute for your generations throughout all your dwellings, that ye eat neither fat nor blood.

4 AND the LORD spake unto Mo'ses, saying,
2 Speak unto the children of Is'ra-el, saying, If a soul shall sin through ignorance against any of the commandments of the LORD *concerning things* which ought not to be done, and shall do against any of them:

3 If the priest that is anointed do sin according to the sin of the people; then let him bring for his sin, which he hath sinned, a young bullock without blemish unto the LORD for a sin offering.

4 And he shall bring the bullock unto the door of the tabernacle of the congregation before the LORD; and shall lay his hand upon the bullock's head, and kill the bullock before the LORD.

5 And the priest that is anointed shall take of the bullock's blood, and bring it to the tabernacle of the congregation:

6 And the priest shall dip his finger in the blood, and sprinkle of the blood seven times before the LORD, before the veil of the sanctuary.

7 And the priest shall put *some* of the blood upon the horns of the altar of sweet incense before the LORD, which *is* in the tabernacle of the congregation; and shall pour all the blood of the bullock at the bottom of the altar of the burnt offering, which *is at* the door of the tabernacle of the congregation.

8 And he shall take off from it all the fat of the bullock for the sin offering; the fat that covereth the inwards, and all the fat that *is* upon the inwards,

9 And the two kidneys, and the fat that *is* upon them, which *is* by the flanks, and the caul above the liver, with the kidneys, it shall he take away,

10 As it was taken off from the bullock of the sacrifice of peace offerings: and the priest shall burn them upon the altar of the burnt offering.

11 And the skin of the bullock, and all his flesh, with his head, and with his legs, and his inwards, and his dung,

12 Even the whole bullock shall he carry forth without the camp unto a clean place, where the ashes are poured out, and burn him on the wood with fire: where the ashes are poured out shall he be burnt.

13 ¶ And if the whole congregation of Is'ra-el sin through ignorance, and the thing be hid from the eyes of the assembly, and they have done *somewhat against* any of the commandments of the LORD *concerning things* which should not be done, and are guilty;

14 When the sin, which they have sinned against it, is known, then the congregation shall offer a young bullock for the sin, and bring him before the tabernacle of the congregation.

15 And the elders of the congregation shall lay their hands upon the head of the bullock before the LORD: and the bullock shall be killed before the LORD.

16 And the priest that is anointed shall bring of the bullock's blood to the tabernacle of the congregation:

17 And the priest shall dip his finger *in some* of the blood, and sprinkle *it* seven times before the LORD, *even* before the veil.

18 And he shall put *some* of the blood upon the horns of the altar which *is* before the LORD, that *is* in the tabernacle of the congregation, and shall pour out all the blood at the bottom of the altar of the burnt offering, which *is at* the door of the tabernacle of the congregation.

19 And he shall take all his fat from him, and burn *it* upon the altar.

20 And he shall do with the bullock as he did with the bullock for a sin offering, so shall he do with this: and the priest shall make an atonement for them, and it shall be forgiven them.

21 And he shall carry forth the bullock without the camp, and burn him as he burned the first bullock: it *is* a sin offering for the congregation.

22 ¶ When a ruler hath sinned, and done *somewhat* through ignorance *against* any of the commandments of the LORD his God *concerning things* which should not be done, and is guilty;

23 Or if his sin, wherein he hath sinned, come to his knowledge; he shall bring his offering, a kid of the goats, a male without blemish:

24 And he shall lay his hand upon the head of the goat, and kill it in the place where they kill the burnt offering before the LORD: it *is* a sin offering.

25 And the priest shall take of the blood of the sin offering with his finger, and put *it* upon the horns of the altar of burnt offering, and shall pour out his blood at the bottom of the altar of burnt offering.

26 And he shall burn all his fat upon the altar, as the fat of the sacrifice of peace offerings: and the priest shall make an atonement for him as concerning his sin, and it shall be forgiven him.

27 ¶ And if any one of the common people sin through ignorance, while he doeth *somewhat against* any of the commandments of the LORD *concerning things* which ought not to be done, and be guilty;

28 Or if his sin, which he hath sinned, come to his knowledge: then he shall bring his offering, a kid of the goats, a female without blemish, for his sin which he hath sinned.

29 And he shall lay his hand upon the head of the sin offering, and slay the sin offering in the place of the burnt offering.

30 And the priest shall take of the blood thereof with his finger, and put *it* upon the horns of the altar of burnt offering, and shall pour out all the blood thereof at the bottom of the altar.

31 And he shall take away all the fat thereof, as the fat is taken away from off the sacrifice of peace offerings; and the priest shall burn *it* upon the altar for a sweet savour unto the LORD; and the priest shall make an atonement for him, and it shall be forgiven him.

32 And if he bring a lamb for a sin offering, he shall bring it a female without blemish.

33 And he shall lay his hand upon the head of the sin offering, and slay it for a sin offering in the place where they kill the burnt offering.

34 And the priest shall take of the blood of the sin offering with his finger, and put *it* upon the horns of the altar of burnt offering, and shall pour out all the blood thereof at the bottom of the altar:

35 And he shall take away all the fat thereof, as the fat of the lamb is taken away from the sacrifice of the peace offerings; and the priest shall burn them upon the altar, according to the offerings made by fire unto the LORD: and the priest shall make an atonement for his sin that he hath committed, and it shall be forgiven him.

5 AND if a soul sin, and hear the voice of swearing, and *is* a witness, whether he hath seen or known *of it;* if he do not utter *it,* then he shall bear his iniquity.

2 Or if a soul touch any unclean thing, whether *it be* a carcase of an unclean beast, or a carcase of unclean cattle, or the carcase of unclean creeping things, and *if* it be hidden from him; he also shall be unclean, and guilty.

3 Or if he touch the uncleanness of man, whatsoever uncleanness *it be* that a man shall be defiled withal, and it be hid from him; when he knoweth *of it,* then he shall be guilty.

4 Or if a soul swear, pronouncing with *his* lips to do evil, or to do good, whatsoever *it be* that a man shall pronounce with an oath, and it be hid from him; when he knoweth *of it,* then he shall be guilty in one of these.

5 And it shall be, when he shall be guilty in one of these *things,* that he shall confess that he hath sinned in that *thing:*

6 And he shall bring his trespass offering unto the LORD for his sin which he hath sinned, a female from the flock, a lamb or a kid of the goats, for a sin offering; and the priest shall make an atonement for him concerning his sin.

7 And if he be not able to bring a lamb, then he shall bring for his trespass, which he hath committed, two turtledoves, or two young pigeons, unto the LORD; one for a sin offering, and the other for a burnt offering.

8 And he shall bring them unto the priest, who shall offer *that* which *is* for the sin offering first, and wring off his head from his neck, but shall not divide *it* asunder:

9 And he shall sprinkle of the blood of the sin offering upon the side of the altar; and the rest of the blood shall be wrung out at the bottom of the altar: it *is* a sin offering.

10 And he shall offer the second *for* a burnt offering, according to the manner: and the priest shall make an atonement for him for his sin which he hath sinned, and it shall be forgiven him.

11 ¶ But if he be not able to bring two turtledoves, or two young pigeons, then he that sinned shall bring for his offering the tenth part of an ephah of fine flour for a sin offering; he shall put no oil upon it, neither shall he put *any* frankincense thereon: for it *is* a sin offering.

12 Then shall he bring it to the priest, and the priest shall take his handful of it, *even* a memorial thereof, and burn *it* on the altar, according to the offerings made by fire unto the LORD: it *is* a sin offering.

13 And the priest shall make an atonement for him as touching his sin that he hath sinned in one of these, and it shall be forgiven him: and *the remnant* shall be the priest's, as a meat offering.

14 ¶ And the LORD spake unto Mo'ses, saying,

15 If a soul commit a trespass, and sin through ignorance, in the holy things of the LORD; then he shall bring for his trespass unto the LORD a ram without blemish out of the flocks, with thy estimation by shekels of silver, after the shekel of the sanctuary, for a trespass offering:

16 And he shall make amends for the harm that he hath done in the holy thing, and shall add the fifth part thereto, and give it unto the priest: and the priest shall make an atonement for him with the ram of the trespass offering, and it shall be forgiven him.

17 ¶ And if a soul sin, and commit any of these things which are forbidden to be done by the commandments of the LORD; though he wist it not, yet is he guilty, and shall bear his iniquity.

18 And he shall bring a ram without blemish out of the flock, with thy estimation, for a trespass offering, unto the priest: and the priest shall make an atonement for him concerning his ignorance wherein he erred and wist it not, and it shall be forgiven him.

19 It is a trespass offering: he hath certainly trespassed against the LORD.

6 AND the LORD spake unto Mo'ses, saying,

2 If a soul sin, and commit a trespass against the LORD, and lie unto his neighbour in that which was delivered him to keep, or in fellowship, or in a thing taken away by violence, or hath deceived his neighbour;

3 Or have found that which was lost, and lieth concerning it, and sweareth falsely; in any of all these that a man doeth, sinning therein:

4 Then it shall be, because he hath sinned, and is guilty, that he shall restore that which he took violently away, or the thing which he hath deceitfully gotten, or that which was delivered him to keep, or the lost thing which he found,

5 Or all that about which he hath sworn falsely; he shall even restore it in the principal, and shall add the fifth part more thereto, and give it unto him to whom it appertaineth, in the day of his trespass offering.

6 And he shall bring his trespass offering unto the LORD, a ram without blemish out of the flock, with thy estimation, for a trespass offering, unto the priest:

7 And the priest shall make an atonement for him before the LORD: and it shall be forgiven him for any thing of all that he hath done in trespassing therein.

8 ¶ And the LORD spake unto Mo'ses, saying,

9 Command Aar'on and his sons, saying, This is the law of the burnt offering: It is the burnt offering, because of the burning upon the altar all night unto the morning, and the fire of the altar shall be burning in it.

10 And the priest shall put on his linen garment, and his linen breeches shall he put upon his flesh, and take up the ashes which the fire hath consumed with the burnt offering on the altar, and he shall put them beside the altar.

11 And he shall put off his garments, and put on other garments, and carry forth the ashes without the camp unto a clean place.

12 And the fire upon the altar shall be burning in it; it shall not be put out: and the priest shall burn wood on it every morning, and lay the burnt offering in order upon it; and he shall burn thereon the fat of the peace offerings.

13 The fire shall ever be burning upon the altar; it shall never go out.

14 ¶ And this is the law of the meat offering: the sons of Aar'on shall offer it before the LORD, before the altar.

15 And he shall take of it his handful, of the flour of the meat offering, and of the oil thereof, and all the frankincense which is upon the meat offering, and shall burn it upon the altar for a sweet savour, even the memorial of it, unto the LORD.

16 And the remainder thereof shall Aar'on and his sons eat: with unleavened bread shall it be eaten in the holy place; in the court of the tabernacle of the congregation they shall eat it.

17 It shall not be baken with leaven. I have given it unto them for their portion of my offerings made by fire; it is most holy, as is the sin offering, and as the trespass offering.

18 All the males among the children of Aar'on shall eat of it. It shall be a statute for ever in your generations concerning the offerings of the LORD made by fire: every one that toucheth them shall be holy.

19 ¶ And the LORD spake unto Mo'ses, saying,

20 This is the offering of Aar'on and of his sons, which they shall offer unto the LORD in the day when he is anointed; the tenth part of an ephah of fine flour for a meat offering perpetual, half of it in the morning, and half thereof at night.

21 In a pan it shall be made with oil; and when it is baken, thou shalt bring it in: and the baken pieces of the meat offering shalt thou offer for a sweet savour unto the LORD.

22 And the priest of his sons that is anointed in his stead shall offer it: it is a statute for ever unto the LORD; it shall be wholly burnt.

23 For every meat offering for the priest shall be wholly burnt: it shall not be eaten.

24 ¶ And the LORD spake unto Mo'ses, saying,

25 Speak unto Aar'on and to his sons, saying, This is the law of the sin offering: In the place where the burnt offering is killed shall the sin offering be killed before the LORD: it is most holy.

26 The priest that offereth it for sin shall eat it: in the holy place shall it be eaten, in the court of the tabernacle of the congregation.

27 Whatsoever shall touch the flesh thereof shall be holy: and when there is sprinkled of the blood thereof upon any garment, thou shalt wash that whereon it was sprinkled in the holy place.

28 But the earthen vessel wherein it is sodden shall be broken: and if it be sodden in a brasen pot, it shall be both scoured, and rinsed in water.

29 All the males among the priests shall eat thereof: it is most holy.

30 And no sin offering, whereof any of the blood is brought into the tabernacle of the congregation to reconcile withal in the holy place, shall be eaten: it shall be burnt in the fire.

7 LIKEWISE this is the law of the trespass offering: it is most holy.

2 In the place where they kill the burnt offering shall they kill the trespass offering: and the blood thereof shall he sprinkle round about upon the altar.

3 And he shall offer of it all the fat thereof; the rump, and the fat that covereth the inwards,

4 And the two kidneys, and the fat that is on them, which is by the flanks, and the caul that is above the liver, with the kidneys, it shall he take away:

5 And the priest shall burn them upon the altar for an offering made by fire unto the LORD: it is a trespass offering.

6 Every male among the priests shall eat thereof: it shall be eaten in the holy place: it is most holy.

7 As the sin offering is, so is the trespass offering: there is one law for them: the priest that maketh atonement therewith shall have it.

8 And the priest that offereth any man's burnt offering, even the priest shall have to himself the skin of the burnt offering which he hath offered.

9 And all the meat offering that is baken in the oven, and all that is dressed in the fryingpan, and in the pan, shall be the priest's that offereth it.

10 And every meat offering, mingled with oil, and dry, shall all the sons of Aar'on have, one as much as another.

11 And this is the law of the sacrifice of peace offerings, which he shall offer unto the LORD.

12 If he offer it for a thanksgiving, then he shall offer with the sacrifice of thanksgiving unleavened cakes mingled with oil, and unleavened wafers anointed with oil, and cakes mingled with oil, of fine flour, fried.

13 Besides the cakes, he shall offer for his offering leavened bread with the sacrifice of thanksgiving of his peace offerings.

14 And of it he shall offer one out of the whole oblation for an heave offering unto the LORD, and it shall be the priest's that sprinkleth the blood of the peace offerings.

15 And the flesh of the sacrifice of his peace offerings for thanksgiving shall be eaten the same day that it is offered; he shall not leave any of it until the morning.

16 But if the sacrifice of his offering be a vow, or a voluntary offering, it shall be eaten the same day that he offereth his sacrifice: and on the morrow also the remainder of it shall be eaten:

17 But the remainder of the flesh of the sacrifice on the third day shall be burnt with fire.

18 And if any of the flesh of the sacrifice of his peace offerings be eaten at all on the third day, it shall not be accepted, neither shall it be imputed unto him that offereth it: it shall be an abomination, and the soul that eateth of it shall bear his iniquity.

19 And the flesh that toucheth any unclean thing shall not be eaten; it shall be burnt with fire: and as for the flesh, all that be clean shall eat thereof.

20 But the soul that eateth of the flesh of the sacrifice of peace offerings, that pertain unto the LORD, having his uncleanness upon him, even that soul shall be cut off from his people.

21 Moreover the soul that shall touch any unclean thing, as the uncleanness of man, or any unclean beast, or any abominable unclean thing, and eat of the flesh of the sacrifice of peace offerings, which pertain unto the LORD, even that soul shall be cut off from his people.

22 ¶ And the LORD spake unto Mo'ses, saying,

23 Speak unto the children of Is'ra-el, saying, Ye shall eat no manner of fat, of ox, or of sheep, or of goat.

24 And the fat of the beast that dieth of itself, and the fat of that which is torn with beasts, may be used in any other use: but ye shall in no wise eat of it.

25 For whosoever eateth the fat of the beast, of which men offer an offering made by fire unto the LORD, even the soul that eateth it shall be cut off from his people.

26 Moreover ye shall eat no manner of blood, whether it be of fowl or of beast, in any of your dwellings.

27 Whatsoever soul it be that eateth any manner of blood, even that soul shall be cut off from his people.

28 ¶ And the LORD spake unto Mo'ses, saying,

29 Speak unto the children of Is'ra-el, saying, He that offereth the sacrifice of his peace offerings unto the LORD shall bring his oblation unto the LORD of the sacrifice of his peace offerings.

30 His own hands shall bring the offerings of the LORD made by fire, the fat with the breast, it shall he bring, that the breast may be waved for a wave offering before the LORD.

31 And the priest shall burn the fat upon the altar: but the breast shall be Aar'on's and his sons'.

32 And the right shoulder shall ye give unto the priest for an heave offering of the sacrifices of your peace offerings.

33 He among the sons of Aar'on, that offereth the blood of the peace offerings, and the fat, shall have the right shoulder for his part.

34 For the wave breast and the heave shoulder have I taken of the children of Is'ra-el from off the sacrifices of their peace offerings, and have given them unto Aar'on the priest and unto his sons by a statute for ever from among the children of Is'ra-el.

35 ¶ This is the portion of the anointing of Aar'on, and of the anointing of his sons, out of the offerings of the LORD made by fire, in the day when he presented them to minister unto the LORD in the priest's office;

36 Which the LORD commanded to be given them of the children of Is'ra-el, in the day that he anointed them, by a statute for ever throughout their generations.

37 This is the law of the burnt offering, of the meat offering, and of the sin offering, and of the trespass offering, and of the consecrations, and of the sacrifice of the peace offerings;

38 Which the LORD commanded Mo'ses in mount Si'nai, in the day that he commanded the children of Is'ra-el to offer their oblations unto the LORD, in the wilderness of Si'nai.

8 AND the LORD spake unto Mo'ses, saying,

2 Take Aar'on and his sons with him, and the garments, and the anointing oil, and a bullock for the sin offering, and two rams, and a basket of unleavened bread;

3 And gather thou all the congregation together unto the door of the tabernacle of the congregation.

4 And Mo'ses did as the LORD commanded him; and the assembly was gathered together unto the door of the tabernacle of the congregation.

5 And Mo'ses said unto the congregation, This is the thing which the LORD commanded to be done.

6 And Mo'ses brought Aar'on and his sons, and washed them with water.

7 And he put upon him the coat, and girded him with the girdle, and clothed him with the robe, and put the ephod upon him, and he girded him with the curious girdle of the ephod, and bound it unto him therewith.

8 And he put the breastplate upon him: also he put in the breastplate the U'rim and the Thum'mim.

9 And he put the mitre upon his head; also

upon the mitre, *even* upon his forefront, did he put the golden plate, the holy crown; as the Lord commanded Mo'ses.

10 And Mo'ses took the anointing oil, and anointed the tabernacle and all that *was* therein, and sanctified them.

11 And he sprinkled thereof upon the altar seven times, and anointed the altar and all his vessels, both the laver and his foot, to sanctify them.

12 And he poured of the anointing oil upon Aar'on's head, and anointed him, to sanctify him.

13 And Mo'ses brought Aar'on's sons, and put coats upon them, and girded them with girdles, and put bonnets upon them; as the Lord commanded Mo'ses.

14 And he brought the bullock for the sin offering: and Aar'on and his sons laid their hands upon the head of the bullock for the sin offering.

15 And he slew *it;* and Mo'ses took the blood, and put *it* upon the horns of the altar round about with his finger, and purified the altar, and poured the blood at the bottom of the altar, and sanctified it, to make reconciliation upon it.

16 And he took all the fat that *was* upon the inwards, and the caul *above* the liver, and the two kidneys, and their fat, and Mo'ses burned *it* upon the altar.

17 But the bullock, and his hide, his flesh, and his dung, he burnt with fire without the camp; as the Lord commanded Mo'ses.

18 ¶ And he brought the ram for the burnt offering: and Aar'on and his sons laid their hands upon the head of the ram.

19 And he killed *it;* and Mo'ses sprinkled the blood upon the altar round about.

20 And he cut the ram into pieces; and Mo'ses burnt the head, and the pieces, and the fat.

21 And he washed the inwards and the legs in water; and Mo'ses burnt the whole ram upon the altar: it *was* a burnt sacrifice for a sweet savour, *and* an offering made by fire unto the Lord; as the Lord commanded Mo'ses.

22 ¶ And he brought the other ram, the ram of consecration: and Aar'on and his sons laid their hands upon the head of the ram.

23 And he slew *it;* and Mo'ses took of the blood of it, and put *it* upon the tip of Aar'on's right ear, and upon the thumb of his right hand, and upon the great toe of his right foot.

24 And he brought Aar'on's sons, and Mo'ses put of the blood upon the tip of their right ear, and upon the thumbs of their right hands, and upon the great toes of their right feet: and Mo'ses sprinkled the blood upon the altar round about.

25 And he took the fat, and the rump, and all the fat that *was* upon the inwards, and the caul *above* the liver, and the two kidneys, and their fat, and the right shoulder:

26 And out of the basket of unleavened bread, that *was* before the Lord, he took one unleavened cake, and a cake of oiled bread, and one wafer, and put *them* on the fat, and upon the right shoulder:

27 And he put all upon Aar'on's hands, and upon his sons' hands, and waved them *for* a wave offering before the Lord.

28 And Mo'ses took them from off their hands, and burnt *them* on the altar upon the burnt offering: they *were* consecrations for a sweet savour: it *is* an offering made by fire unto the Lord.

29 And Mo'ses took the breast, and waved it *for* a wave offering before the Lord: *for* of the ram of consecration it was Mo'ses' part; as the Lord commanded Mo'ses.

30 And Mo'ses took of the anointing oil, and of the blood which *was* upon the altar, and sprinkled *it* upon Aar'on, *and* upon his garments, and upon his sons, and upon his sons' garments with him; and sanctified Aar'on, *and* his garments, and his sons, and his sons' garments with him.

31 ¶ And Mo'ses said unto Aar'on and to his sons, Boil the flesh *at* the door of the tabernacle of the congregation: and there eat it with the bread that *is* in the basket of consecrations, as I commanded, saying, Aar'on and his sons shall eat it.

32 And that which remaineth of the flesh and of the bread shall ye burn with fire.

33 And ye shall not go out of the door of the tabernacle of the congregation *in* seven days, until the days of your consecration be at an end: for seven days shall he consecrate you.

34 As he hath done this day, *so* the Lord hath commanded to do, to make an atonement for you.

35 Therefore shall ye abide *at* the door of the tabernacle of the congregation day and night seven days, and keep the charge of the Lord, that ye die not: for so I am commanded.

36 So Aar'on and his sons did all things which the Lord commanded by the hand of Mo'ses.

9 AND it came to pass on the eighth day, *that* Mo'ses called Aar'on and his sons, and the elders of Is'ra-el;

2 And he said unto Aar'on, Take thee a young calf for a sin offering, and a ram for a burnt offering, without blemish, and offer *them* before the Lord.

3 And unto the children of Is'ra-el thou shalt speak, saying, Take ye a kid of the goats for a sin offering; and a calf and a lamb, *both* of the first year, without blemish, for a burnt offering;

4 Also a bullock and a ram for peace offerings, to sacrifice before the Lord; and a meat offering mingled with oil: for to day the Lord will appear unto you.

5 ¶ And they brought *that* which Mo'ses commanded before the tabernacle of the congregation: and all the congregation drew near and stood before the Lord.

6 And Mo'ses said, This *is* the thing which the Lord commanded that ye should do: and the glory of the Lord shall appear unto you.

7 And Mo'ses said unto Aar'on, Go unto the altar, and offer thy sin offering, and thy burnt offering, and make an atonement for thyself, and for the people: and offer the offering of the people, and make an atonement for them; as the Lord commanded.

8 ¶ Aar'on therefore went unto the altar, and slew the calf of the sin offering, which *was* for himself.

9 And the sons of Aar'on brought the blood unto him: and he dipped his finger in the blood, and put *it* upon the horns of the altar, and poured out the blood at the bottom of the altar:

10 But the fat, and the kidneys, and the caul above the liver of the sin offering, he burnt upon the altar; as the Lord commanded Mo'ses.

11 And the flesh and the hide he burnt with fire without the camp.

12 And he slew the burnt offering; and Aar'on's sons presented unto him the blood, which he sprinkled round about upon the altar.

13 And they presented the burnt offering

unto him, with the pieces thereof, and the head: and he burnt *them* upon the altar.

14 And he did wash the inwards and the legs, and burnt *them* upon the burnt offering on the altar.

15 ¶ And he brought the people's offering, and took the goat, which *was* the sin offering for the people, and slew it, and offered it for sin, as the first.

16 And he brought the burnt offering, and offered it according to the manner.

17 And he brought the meat offering, and took an handful thereof, and burnt *it* upon the altar, beside the burnt sacrifice of the morning.

18 He slew also the bullock and the ram *for* a sacrifice of peace offerings, which *was* for the people: and Aar'on's sons presented unto him the blood, which he sprinkled upon the altar round about,

19 And the fat of the bullock and of the ram, the rump, and that which covereth *the inwards,* and the kidneys, and the caul *above* the liver:

20 And they put the fat upon the breasts, and he burnt the fat upon the altar:

21 And the breasts and the right shoulder Aar'on waved *for* a wave offering before the Lord; as Mo'ses commanded.

22 And Aar'on lifted up his hand toward the people, and blessed them, and came down from offering of the sin offering, and the burnt offering, and peace offerings.

23 And Mo'ses and Aar'on went into the tabernacle of the congregation, and came out, and blessed the people: and the glory of the Lord appeared unto all the people.

24 And there came a fire out from before the Lord, and consumed upon the altar the burnt offering and the fat: which when all the people saw, they shouted, and fell on their faces.

10 AND Na'dab and A-bi'hu, the sons of Aar'on, took either of them his censer, and put fire therein, and put incense thereon, and offered strange fire before the Lord, which he commanded them not.

2 And there went out fire from the Lord, and devoured them, and they died before the Lord.

3 Then Mo'ses said unto Aar'on, This *is* it that the Lord spake, saying, I will be sanctified in them that come nigh me, and before all the people I will be glorified. And Aar'on held his peace.

4 And Mo'ses called Mish'a-el and El'za-phan, the sons of Uz'zi-el the uncle of Aar'on, and said unto them, Come near, carry your brethren from before the sanctuary out of the camp.

5 So they went near, and carried them in their coats out of the camp; as Mo'ses had said.

6 And Mo'ses said unto Aar'on, and unto E-le-a'zar and unto Ith'a-mar, his sons, Uncover not your heads, neither rend your clothes; lest ye die, and lest wrath come upon all the people: but let your brethren, the whole house of Is'ra-el, bewail the burning which the Lord hath kindled.

7 And ye shall not go out from the door of the tabernacle of the congregation, lest ye die: for the annointing oil of the Lord *is* upon you. And they did according to the word of Mo'ses.

8 ¶ And the Lord spake unto Aar'on, saying,

9 Do not drink wine nor strong drink, thou, nor thy sons with thee, when ye go into the tabernacle of the congregation, lest ye die: *it shall be* a statute for ever throughout your generations:

10 And that ye may put difference between holy and unholy, and between unclean and clean;

11 And that ye may teach the children of Is'ra-el all the statutes which the Lord hath spoken unto them by the hand of Mo'ses.

12 ¶ And Mo'ses spake unto Aar'on, and unto E-le-a'zar and unto Ith'a-mar, his sons that were left, Take the meat offering that remaineth of the offerings of the Lord made by fire, and eat it without leaven beside the altar: for it *is* most holy:

13 And ye shall eat it in the holy place, because it *is* thy due, and thy sons' due, of the sacrifices of the Lord made by fire: for so I am commanded.

14 And the wave breast and heave shoulder shall ye eat in a clean place; thou, and thy sons, and thy daughters with thee: for *they be* thy due, and thy sons' due, *which* are given out of the sacrifices of peace offerings of the children of Is'ra-el.

15 The heave shoulder and the wave breast shall they bring with the offerings made by fire of the fat, to wave *it for* a wave offering before the Lord; and it shall be thine, and thy sons' with thee, by a statute for ever; as the Lord hath commanded.

16 ¶ And Mo'ses diligently sought the goat of the sin offering, and, behold, it was burnt: and he was angry with E-le-a'zar and Ith'a-mar, the sons of Aar'on *which were* left alive, saying,

17 Wherefore have ye not eaten the sin offering in the holy place, seeing it *is* most holy, and *God* hath given it you to bear the iniquity of the congregation, to make atonement for them before the Lord?

18 Behold, the blood of it was not brought in within the holy *place:* ye should indeed have eaten it in the holy *place,* as I commanded.

19 And Aar'on said unto Mo'ses, Behold, this day have they offered their sin offering and their burnt offering before the Lord; and such things have befallen me: and *if* I had eaten the sin offering to day, should it have been accepted in the sight of the Lord?

20 And when Mo'ses heard *that,* he was content.

11 AND the Lord spake unto Mo'ses and to Aar'on, saying unto them,

2 Speak unto the children of Is'ra-el, saying, These *are* the beasts which ye shall eat among all the beasts that *are* on the earth.

3 Whatsoever parteth the hoof, and is cloven-footed, *and* cheweth the cud, among the beasts, that shall ye eat.

4 Nevertheless these shall ye not eat of them that chew the cud, or of them that divide the hoof: *as* the camel, because he cheweth the cud, but divideth not the hoof; he *is* unclean unto you.

5 And the coney, because he cheweth the cud, but divideth not the hoof; he *is* unclean unto you.

6 And the hare, because he cheweth the cud, but divideth not the hoof; he *is* unclean unto you.

7 And the swine, though he divide the hoof, and be clovenfooted, yet he cheweth not the cud; he *is* unclean to you.

8 Of their flesh shall ye not eat, and their carcase shall ye not touch; they *are* unclean to you.

9 ¶ These shall ye eat of all that *are* in the waters: whatsoever hath fins and scales in the waters, in the seas, and in the rivers, them shall ye eat.

10 And all that have not fins and scales in the

seas, and in the rivers, of all that move in the waters, and of any living thing which is in the waters, they shall be an abomination unto you:

11 They shall be even an abomination unto you; ye shall not eat of their flesh, but ye shall have their carcases in abomination.

12 Whatsoever hath no fins nor scales in the waters, that shall be an abomination unto you.

13 ¶ And these are they which ye shall have in abomination among the fowls; they shall not be eaten, they are an abomination: the eagle, and the ossifrage, and the ospray,

14 And the vulture, and the kite after his kind;

15 Every raven after his kind;

16 And the owl, and the night hawk, and the cuckow, and the hawk after his kind,

17 And the little owl, and the cormorant, and the great owl,

18 And the swan, and the pelican, and the gier eagle,

19 And the stork, the heron after her kind, and the lapwing, and the bat.

20 All fowls that creep, going upon all four, shall be an abomination unto you.

21 Yet these may ye eat of every flying creeping thing that goeth upon all four, which have legs above their feet, to leap withal upon the earth;

22 Even these of them ye may eat; the locust after his kind, and the bald locust after his kind, and the beetle after his kind, and the grasshopper after his kind.

23 But all other flying creeping things, which have four feet, shall be an abomination unto you.

24 And for these ye shall be unclean: whosoever toucheth the carcase of them shall be unclean until the even.

25 And whosoever beareth ought of the carcase of them shall wash his clothes, and be unclean until the even.

26 The carcases of every beast which divideth the hoof, and is not clovenfooted, nor cheweth the cud, are unclean unto you: every one that toucheth them shall be unclean.

27 And whatsoever goeth upon his paws, among all manner of beasts that go on all four, those are unclean unto you: whoso toucheth their carcase shall be unclean until the even.

28 And he that beareth the carcase of them shall wash his clothes, and be unclean until the even: they are unclean unto you.

29 ¶ These also shall be unclean unto you among the creeping things that creep upon the earth; the weasel, and the mouse, and the tortoise after his kind,

30 And the ferret, and the chameleon, and the lizard, and the snail, and the mole.

31 These are unclean to you among all that creep: whosoever doth touch them, when they be dead, shall be unclean until the even.

32 And upon whatsoever any of them, when they are dead, doth fall, it shall be unclean; whether it be any vessel of wood, or raiment, or skin, or sack, whatsoever vessel it be, wherein any work is done, it must be put into water, and it shall be unclean until the even; so it shall be cleansed.

33 And every earthen vessel, whereinto any of them falleth, whatsoever is in it shall be unclean; and ye shall break it.

34 Of all meat which may be eaten, that on which such water cometh shall be unclean: and all drink that may be drunk in every such vessel shall be unclean.

35 And every thing whereupon any part of their carcase falleth shall be unclean; whether it be oven, or ranges for pots, they shall be broken down: for they are unclean, and shall be unclean unto you.

36 Nevertheless a fountain or pit, wherein there is plenty of water, shall be clean: but that which toucheth their carcase shall be unclean.

37 And if any part of their carcase fall upon any sowing seed which is to be sown, it shall be clean.

38 But if any water be put upon the seed, and any part of their carcase fall thereon, it shall be unclean unto you.

39 And if any beast, of which ye may eat, die; he that toucheth the carcase thereof shall be unclean until the even.

40 And he that eateth of the carcase of it shall wash his clothes, and be unclean until the even: he also that beareth the carcase of it shall wash his clothes, and be unclean until the even.

41 And every creeping thing that creepeth upon the earth shall be an abomination; it shall not be eaten.

42 Whatsoever goeth upon the belly, and whatsoever goeth upon all four, or whatsoever hath more feet among all creeping things that creep upon the earth, them ye shall not eat; for they are an abomination.

43 Ye shall not make yourselves abominable with any creeping thing that creepeth, neither shall ye make yourselves unclean with them, that ye should be defiled thereby.

44 For I am the LORD your God: ye shall therefore sanctify yourselves, and ye shall be holy; for I am holy: neither shall ye defile yourselves with any manner of creeping thing that creepeth upon the earth.

45 For I am the LORD that bringeth you up out of the land of E'gypt, to be your God: ye shall therefore be holy, for I am holy.

46 This is the law of the beasts, and of the fowl, and of every living creature that moveth in the waters, and of every creature that creepeth upon the earth:

47 To make a difference between the unclean and the clean, and between the beast that may be eaten and the beast that may not be eaten.

12

AND the LORD spake unto Mo'ses, saying,

2 Speak unto the children of Is'ra-el, saying, If a woman have conceived seed, and born a man child: then she shall be unclean seven days; according to the days of the separation for her infirmity shall she be unclean.

3 And in the eighth day the flesh of his foreskin shall be circumcised.

4 And she shall then continue in the blood of her purifying three and thirty days; she shall touch no hallowed thing, nor come into the sanctuary, until the days of her purifying be fulfilled.

5 But if she bear a maid child, then she shall be unclean two weeks, as in her separation: and she shall continue in the blood of her purifying three-score and six days.

6 And when the days of her purifying are fulfilled, for a son, or for a daughter, she shall bring a lamb of the first year for a burnt offering, and a young pigeon, or a turtledove, for a sin offering, unto the door of the tabernacle of the congregation, unto the priest:

7 Who shall offer it before the LORD, and make an atonement for her; and she shall be cleansed from the issue of her blood. This is the law for her that hath born a male or a female.

8 And if she be not able to bring a lamb, then

she shall bring two turtles, or two young pigeons; the one for the burnt offering, and the other for a sin offering: and the priest shall make an atonement for her, and she shall be clean.

13 AND the LORD spake unto Mo'ses and Aar'on, saying,

2 When a man shall have in the skin of his flesh a rising, a scab, or bright spot, and it be in the skin of his flesh like the plague of leprosy; then he shall be brought unto Aar'on the priest, or unto one of his sons the priests:

3 And the priest shall look on the plague in the skin of the flesh: and when the hair in the plague is turned white, and the plague in sight be deeper than the skin of his flesh, it is a plague of leprosy: and the priest shall look on him, and pronounce him unclean.

4 If the bright spot be white in the skin of his flesh, and in sight be not deeper than the skin, and the hair thereof be not turned white; then the priest shall shut up him that hath the plague seven days:

5 And the priest shall look on him the seventh day: and, behold, if the plague in his sight be at a stay, and the plague spread not in the skin; then the priest shall shut him up seven days more:

6 And the priest shall look on him again the seventh day: and, behold, if the plague be somewhat dark, and the plague spread not in the skin, the priest shall pronounce him clean: it is but a scab: and he shall wash his clothes, and be clean.

7 But if the scab spread much abroad in the skin, after that he hath been seen of the priest for his cleansing, he shall be seen of the priest again:

8 And if the priest see that, behold, the scab spreadeth in the skin, then the priest shall pronounce him unclean: it is a leprosy.

9 ¶ When the plague of leprosy is in a man, then he shall be brought unto the priest;

10 And the priest shall see him: and, behold, if the rising be white in the skin, and it have turned the hair white, and there be quick raw flesh in the rising;

11 It is an old leprosy in the skin of his flesh, and the priest shall pronounce him unclean, and shall not shut him up: for he is unclean.

12 And if a leprosy break out abroad in the skin, and the leprosy cover all the skin of him that hath the plague from his head even to his foot, wheresoever the priest looketh;

13 Then the priest shall consider: and, behold, if the leprosy have covered all his flesh, he shall pronounce him clean that hath the plague: it is all turned white: he is clean.

14 But when raw flesh appeareth in him, he shall be unclean.

15 And the priest shall see the raw flesh, and pronounce him to be unclean: for the raw flesh is unclean: it is a leprosy.

16 Or if the raw flesh turn again, and be changed unto white, he shall come unto the priest;

17 And the priest shall see him: and, behold, if the plague be turned into white; then the priest shall pronounce him clean that hath the plague: he is clean.

18 ¶ The flesh also, in which, even in the skin thereof, was a boil, and is healed,

19 And in the place of the boil there be a white rising, or a bright spot, white, and somewhat reddish, and it be shewed to the priest;

20 And if, when the priest seeth it, behold, it be in sight lower than the skin, and the hair thereof be turned white; the priest shall pronounce him unclean: it is a plague of leprosy broken out of the boil.

21 But if the priest look on it, and, behold, there be no white hairs therein, and if it be not lower than the skin, but be somewhat dark; then the priest shall shut him up seven days:

22 And if it spread much abroad in the skin, then the priest shall pronounce him unclean: it is a plague.

23 But if the bright spot stay in his place, and spread not, it is a burning boil; and the priest shall pronounce him clean.

24 ¶ Or if there be any flesh, in the skin whereof there is a hot burning, and the quick flesh that burneth have a white bright spot, somewhat reddish, or white;

25 Then the priest shall look upon it: and, behold, if the hair in the bright spot be turned white, and it be in sight deeper than the skin; it is a leprosy broken out of the burning: wherefore the priest shall pronounce him unclean: it is the plague of leprosy.

26 But if the priest look on it, and, behold, there be no white hair in the bright spot, and it be no lower than the other skin, but be somewhat dark; then the priest shall shut him up seven days:

27 And the priest shall look upon him the seventh day: and if it be spread much abroad in the skin, then the priest shall pronounce him unclean: it is the plague of leprosy.

28 And if the bright spot stay in his place, and spread not in the skin, but it be somewhat dark; it is a rising of the burning, and the priest shall pronounce him clean: for it is an inflammation of the burning.

29 ¶ If a man or woman have a plague upon the head or the beard;

30 Then the priest shall see the plague: and, behold, if it be in sight deeper than the skin; and there be in it a yellow thin hair; then the priest shall pronounce him unclean: it is a dry scall, even a leprosy upon the head or beard.

31 And if the priest look on the plague of the scall, and, behold, it be not in sight deeper than the skin, and that there is no black hair in it; then the priest shall shut up him that hath the plague of the scall seven days:

32 And in the seventh day the priest shall look on the plague: and, behold, if the scall spread not, and there be in it no yellow hair, and the scall be not in sight deeper than the skin;

33 He shall be shaven, but the scall shall he not shave; and the priest shall shut up him that hath the scall seven days more:

34 And in the seventh day the priest shall look on the scall: and, behold, if the scall be not spread in the skin, nor be in sight deeper than the skin; then the priest shall pronounce him clean: and he shall wash his clothes, and be clean.

35 But if the scall spread much in the skin after his cleansing;

36 Then the priest shall look on him: and, behold, if the scall be spread in the skin, the priest shall not seek for yellow hair; he is unclean.

37 But if the scall be in his sight at a stay, and that there is black hair grown up therein; the scall is healed, he is clean: and the priest shall pronounce him clean.

38 ¶ If a man also or a woman have in the skin of their flesh bright spots, even white bright spots;

39 Then the priest shall look: and, behold, if

the bright spots in the skin of their flesh *be* darkish white; it *is* a freckled spot *that* groweth in the skin; he *is* clean.

40 And the man whose hair is fallen off his head, he *is* bald; *yet is* he clean.

41 And he that hath his hair fallen off from the part of his head toward his face, he *is* forehead bald: *yet is* he clean.

42 And if there be in the bald head, or bald forehead, a white reddish sore; it *is* a leprosy sprung up in his bald head, or his bald forehead.

43 Then the priest shall look upon it: and, behold, *if* the rising of the sore *be* white reddish in his bald head, or in his bald forehead, as the leprosy appeareth in the skin of the flesh;

44 He is a leprous man, he *is* unclean: the priest shall pronounce him utterly unclean; his plague *is* in his head.

45 And the leper in whom the plague *is*, his clothes shall be rent, and his head bare, and he shall put a covering upon his upper lip, and shall cry, Unclean, unclean.

46 All the days wherein the plague *shall be* in him he shall be defiled; he *is* unclean: he shall dwell alone; without the camp *shall* his habitation *be*.

47 ¶ The garment also that the plague of leprosy is in, *whether it be* a woollen garment, or a linen garment;

48 Whether *it be* in the warp, or woof, of linen, or of woollen; whether in a skin, or in any thing made of skin;

49 And if the plague be greenish or reddish in the garment, or in the skin, either in the warp, or in the woof, or in any thing of skin; it *is* a plague of leprosy, and shall be shewed unto the priest:

50 And the priest shall look upon the plague, and shut up *it that hath* the plague seven days:

51 And he shall look on the plague on the seventh day: if the plague be spread in the garment, either in the warp, or in the woof, or in a skin, *or* in any work that is made of skin; the plague *is* a fretting leprosy; it *is* unclean.

52 He shall therefore burn that garment, whether warp or woof, in woollen or in linen, or any thing of skin, wherein the plague is: for it *is* a fretting leprosy; it shall be burnt in the fire.

53 And if the priest shall look, and, behold, the plague be not spread in the garment, either in the warp, or in the woof, or in any thing of skin;

54 Then the priest shall command that they wash *the thing* wherein the plague *is*, and he shall shut it up seven days more:

55 And the priest shall look on the plague, after that it is washed: and, behold, *if* the plague have not changed his colour, and the plague be not spread; it *is* unclean; thou shalt burn it in the fire; it *is* fret inward, *whether it be* bare within or without.

56 And if the priest look, and, behold, the plague *be* somewhat dark after the washing of it; then he shall rend it out of the garment, or out of the skin, or out of the warp, or out of the woof:

57 And if it appear still in the garment, either in the warp, or in the woof, or in any thing of skin; it *is* a spreading *plague:* thou shalt burn that wherein the plague *is* with fire.

58 And the garment, either warp, or woof, or whatsoever thing of skin *it be*, which thou shalt wash, if the plague be departed from them, then it shall be washed the second time, and shall be clean.

59 This *is* the law of the plague of leprosy in a garment of woollen or linen, either in the warp, or woof, or any thing of skins, to pronounce it clean, or to pronounce it unclean.

14 AND the LORD spake unto Mo'ses, saying,

2 This shall be the law of the leper in the day of his cleansing: He shall be brought unto the priest:

3 And the priest shall go forth out of the camp; and the priest shall look, and, behold, *if* the plague of leprosy be healed in the leper;

4 Then shall the priest command to take for him that is to be cleansed two birds alive *and* clean, and cedar wood, and scarlet, and hyssop:

5 And the priest shall command that one of the birds be killed in an earthen vessel over running water:

6 As for the living bird, he shall take it, and the cedar wood, and the scarlet, and the hyssop, and shall dip them and the living bird in the blood of the bird *that was* killed over the running water:

7 And he shall sprinkle upon him that is to be cleansed from the leprosy seven times, and shall pronounce him clean, and shall let the living bird loose into the open field.

8 And he that is to be cleansed shall wash his clothes, and shave off all his hair, and wash himself in water, that he may be clean: and after that he shall come into the camp, and shall tarry abroad out of his tent seven days.

9 But it shall be on the seventh day, that he shall shave all his hair off his head and his beard and his eyebrows, even all his hair he shall shave off: and he shall wash his clothes, also he shall wash his flesh in water, and he shall be clean.

10 And on the eighth day he shall take two he lambs without blemish, and one ewe lamb of the first year without blemish, and three tenth deals of fine flour *for* a meat offering, mingled with oil, and one log of oil.

11 And the priest that maketh *him* clean shall present the man that is to be made clean, and those things, before the LORD, *at* the door of the tabernacle of the congregation:

12 And the priest shall take one he lamb, and offer him for a trespass offering, and the log of oil, and wave them *for* a wave offering before the LORD:

13 And he shall slay the lamb in the place where he shall kill the sin offering and the burnt offering, in the holy place: for as the sin offering *is* the priest's, *so is* the trespass offering: it *is* most holy:

14 And the priest shall take *some* of the blood of the trespass offering, and the priest shall put *it* upon the tip of the right ear of him that is to be cleansed, and upon the thumb of his right hand, and upon the great toe of his right foot:

15 And the priest shall take *some* of the log of oil, and pour *it* into the palm of his own left hand:

16 And the priest shall dip his right finger in the oil that *is* in his left hand, and shall sprinkle of the oil with his finger seven times before the LORD:

17 And of the rest of the oil that *is* in his hand shall the priest put upon the tip of the right ear of him that is to be cleansed, and upon the thumb of his right hand, and upon the great toe of his right foot, upon the blood of the trespass offering:

18 And the remnant of the oil that *is* in the priest's hand he shall pour upon the head of him

that is to be cleansed: and the priest shall make an atonement for him before the LORD.

19 And the priest shall offer the sin offering, and make an atonement for him that is to be cleansed from his uncleanness; and afterward he shall kill the burnt offering:

20 And the priest shall offer the burnt offering and the meat offering upon the altar: and the priest shall make an atonement for him, and he shall be clean.

21 And if he *be* poor, and cannot get so much; then he shall take one lamb *for* a trespass offering to be waved, to make an atonement for him, and one tenth deal of fine flour mingled with oil for a meat offering, and a log of oil;

22 And two turtledoves, or two young pigeons, such as he is able to get; and the one shall be a sin offering, and the other a burnt offering.

23 And he shall bring them on the eighth day for his cleansing unto the priest, unto the door of the tabernacle of the congregation, before the LORD.

24 And the priest shall take the lamb of the trespass offering, and the log of oil, and the priest shall wave them *for* a wave offering before the LORD:

25 And he shall kill the lamb of the trespass offering, and the priest shall take *some* of the blood of the trespass offering, and put *it* upon the tip of the right ear of him that is to be cleansed, and upon the thumb of his right hand, and upon the great toe of his right foot:

26 And the priest shall pour of the oil into the palm of his own left hand:

27 And the priest shall sprinkle with his right finger *some* of the oil that *is* in his left hand seven times before the LORD:

28 And the priest shall put of the oil that *is* in his hand upon the tip of the right ear of him that is to be cleansed, and upon the thumb of his right hand, and upon the great toe of his right foot, upon the place of the blood of the trespass offering:

29 And the rest of the oil that *is* in the priest's hand he shall put upon the head of him that is to be cleansed, to make an atonement for him before the LORD.

30 And he shall offer the one of the turtledoves, or of the young pigeons, such as he can get;

31 *Even* such as he is able to get, the one *for* a sin offering, and the other *for* a burnt offering, with the meat offering: and the priest shall make an atonement for him that is to be cleansed before the LORD.

32 This *is* the law of *him* in whom *is* the plague of leprosy, whose hand is not able to get *that which pertaineth* to his cleansing.

33 ¶ And the LORD spake unto Mo'ses and unto Aar'on, saying,

34 When ye be come into the land of Ca'-naan, which I give to you for a possession, and I put the plague of leprosy in a house of the land of your possession;

35 And he that owneth the house shall come and tell the priest, saying, It seemeth to me *there is* as it were a plague in the house:

36 Then the priest shall command that they empty the house, before the priest go *into* it to see the plague, that all that *is* in the house be not made unclean: and afterward the priest shall go in to see the house:

37 And he shall look on the plague, and, behold, *if* the plague *be* in the walls of the house with hollow strakes, greenish or reddish, which in sight *are* lower than the wall;

38 Then the priest shall go out of the house to the door of the house, and shut up the house seven days:

39 And the priest shall come again the seventh day, and shall look: and, behold, *if* the plague be spread in the walls of the house;

40 Then the priest shall command that they take away the stones in which the plague *is*, and they shall cast them into an unclean place without the city:

41 And he shall cause the house to be scraped within round about, and they shall pour out the dust that they scrape off without the city into an unclean place:

42 And they shall take other stones, and put *them* in the place of those stones; and he shall take other morter, and shall plaister the house.

43 And if the plague come again, and break out in the house, after that he hath taken away the stones, and after he hath scraped the house, and after it is plaistered;

44 Then the priest shall come and look, and, behold, *if* the plague be spread in the house, it *is* a fretting leprosy in the house: it *is* unclean.

45 And he shall break down the house, the stones of it, and the timber therof, and all the morter of the house; and he shall carry *them* forth out of the city into an unclean place.

46 Moreover he that goeth into the house all the while that it is shut up shall be unclean until the even.

47 And he that lieth in the house shall wash his clothes; and he that eateth in the house shall wash his clothes.

48 And if the priest shall come in, and look *upon it*, and, behold, the plague hath not spread in the house, after the house was plaistered: then the priest shall pronounce the house clean, because the plague is healed.

49 And he shall take to cleanse the house two birds, and cedar wood, and scarlet, and hyssop:

50 And he shall kill the one of the birds in an earthen vessel over running water:

51 And he shall take the cedar wood, and the hyssop, and the scarlet, and the living bird, and dip them in the blood of the slain bird, and in the running water, and sprinkle the house seven times:

52 And he shall cleanse the house with the blood of the bird, and with the running water, and with the living bird, and with the cedar wood, and with the hyssop, and with the scarlet:

53 But he shall let go the living bird out of the city into the open fields, and make an atonement for the house: and it shall be clean.

54 This *is* the law for all manner of plague of leprosy, and scall,

55 And for the leprosy of a garment, and of a house,

56 And for a rising, and for a scab, and for a bright spot:

57 To teach when *it is* unclean, and when *it is* clean: this *is* the law of leprosy.

15 AND the LORD spake unto Mo'ses and to Aar'on, saying,

2 Speak unto the children of Is'ra-el, and say unto them, When any man hath a running issue out of his flesh, *because of* his issue he *is* unclean.

3 And this shall be his uncleanness in his issue: whether his flesh run with his issue, or his

flesh be stopped from his issue, it *is* his uncleanness.

4 Every bed, whereon he lieth that hath the issue, is unclean: and every thing, whereon he sitteth, shall be unclean.

5 And whosoever toucheth his bed shall wash his clothes, and bathe *himself* in water, and be unclean until the even.

6 And he that sitteth on *any* thing whereon he sat that hath the issue shall wash his clothes, and bathe *himself* in water, and be unclean until the even.

7 And he that toucheth the flesh of him that hath the issue shall wash his clothes, and bathe *himself* in water, and be unclean until the even.

8 And if he that hath the issue spit upon him that is clean; then he shall wash his clothes, and bathe *himself* in water, and be unclean until the even.

9 And what saddle soever he rideth upon that hath the issue shall be unclean.

10 And whosoever toucheth any thing that was under him shall be unclean until the even: and he that beareth *any of* those things shall wash his clothes, and bathe *himself* in water, and be unclean until the even.

11 And whomsoever he toucheth that hath the issue, and hath not rinsed his hands in water, he shall wash his clothes, and bathe *himself* in water, and be unclean until the even.

12 And the vessel of earth, that he toucheth which hath the issue, shall be broken: and every vessel of wood shall be rinsed in water.

13 And when he that hath an issue is cleansed of his issue; then he shall number to himself seven days for his cleansing, and wash his clothes, and bathe his flesh in running water, and shall be clean.

14 And on the eighth day he shall take to him two turtledoves, or two young pigeons, and come before the LORD unto the door of the tabernacle of the congregation, and give them unto the priest:

15 And the priest shall offer them, the one *for* a sin offering, and the other *for* a burnt offering; and the priest shall make an atonement for him before the LORD for his issue.

16 And if any man's seed of copulation go out from him, then he shall wash all his flesh in water, and be unclean until the even.

17 And every garment, and every skin, whereon is the seed of copulation, shall be washed with water, and be unclean until the even.

18 The woman also with whom man shall lie *with* seed of copulation, they shall *both* bathe *themselves* in water, and be unclean until the even.

19 ¶ And if a woman have an issue, *and* her issue in her flesh be blood, she shall be put apart seven days: and whosoever toucheth her shall be unclean until the even.

20 And every thing that she lieth upon in her separation shall be unclean: every thing also that she sitteth upon shall be unclean.

21 And whosoever toucheth her bed shall wash his clothes, and bathe *himself* in water, and be unclean until the even.

22 And whosoever toucheth any thing that she sat upon shall wash his clothes, and bathe *himself* in water, and be unclean until the even.

23 And if it *be* on *her* bed, or on any thing whereon she sitteth, when he toucheth it, he shall be unclean until the even.

24 And if any man lie with her at all, and her flowers be upon him, he shall be unclean seven days; and all the bed whereon he lieth shall be unclean.

25 And if a woman have an issue of her blood many days out of the time of her separation, or if it run beyond the time of her separation; all the days of the issue of her uncleanness shall be as the days of her separation: she *shall be* unclean.

26 Every bed whereon she lieth all the days of her issue shall be unto her as the bed of her separation: and whatsoever she sitteth upon shall be unclean, as the uncleanness of her separation.

27 And whosoever toucheth those things shall be unclean, and shall wash his clothes, and bathe *himself* in water, and be unclean until the even.

28 But if she be cleansed of her issue, then she shall number to herself seven days, and after that she shall be clean.

29 And on the eighth day she shall take unto her two turtles, or two young pigeons, and bring them unto the priest, to the door of the tabernacle of the congregation.

30 And the priest shall offer the one *for* a sin offering, and the other *for* a burnt offering; and the priest shall make an atonement for her before the LORD for the issue of her uncleanness.

31 Thus shall ye separate the children of Is'-ra-el from their uncleanness; that they die not in their uncleanness, when they defile my tabernacle that *is* among them.

32 This *is* the law of him that hath an issue, and *of him* whose seed goeth from him, and is defiled therewith;

33 And of her that is sick of her flowers, and of him that hath an issue, of the man, and of the woman, and of him that lieth with her that is unclean.

16 AND the LORD spake unto Mo'ses after the death of the two sons of Aar'on, when they offered before the LORD, and died;

2 And the LORD said unto Mo'ses, Speak unto Aar'on thy brother, that he come not at all times into the holy *place* within the veil before the mercy seat, which *is* upon the ark; that he die not: for I will appear in the cloud upon the mercy seat.

3 Thus shall Aar'on come into the holy *place*: with a young bullock for a sin offering, and a ram for a burnt offering.

4 He shall put on the holy linen coat, and he shall have the linen breeches upon his flesh, and shall be girded with a linen girdle, and with the linen mitre shall he be attired: these *are* holy garments; therefore shall he wash his flesh in water, and *so* put them on.

5 And he shall take of the congregation of the children of Is'ra-el two kids of the goats for a sin offering, and one ram for a burnt offering.

6 And Aar'on shall offer his bullock of the sin offering, which *is* for himself, and make an atonement for himself, and for his house.

7 And he shall take the two goats, and present them before the LORD *at* the door of the tabernacle of the congregation.

8 And Aar'on shall cast lots upon the two goats; one lot for the LORD, and the other lot for the scapegoat.

9 And Aar'on shall bring the goat upon which the LORD's lot fell, and offer him *for* a sin offering.

10 But the goat, on which the lot fell to be the scapegoat, shall be presented alive before the LORD, to make an atonement with him, *and* to let him go for a scapegoat into the wilderness.

11 And Aar'on shall bring the bullock of the sin offering, which *is* for himself, and shall make an atonement for himself, and for his house, and shall kill the bullock of the sin offering which *is* for himself:

12 And he shall take a censer full of burning coals of fire from off the altar before the LORD, and his hands full of sweet incense beaten small, and bring *it* within the veil:

13 And he shall put the incense upon the fire before the LORD, that the cloud of the incense may cover the mercy seat that *is* upon the testimony, that he die not:

14 And he shall take of the blood of the bullock, and sprinkle *it* with his finger upon the mercy seat eastward; and before the mercy seat shall he sprinkle of the blood with his finger seven times.

15 ¶ Then shall he kill the goat of the sin offering, that *is* for the people, and bring his blood within the veil, and do with that blood as he did with the blood of the bullock, and sprinkle it upon the mercy seat, and before the mercy seat:

16 And he shall make an atonement for the holy *place,* because of the uncleanness of the children of Is'ra-el, and because of their transgressions in all their sins: and so shall he do for the tabernacle of the congregation, that remaineth among them in the midst of their uncleanness.

17 And there shall be no man in the tabernacle of the congregation when he goeth in to make an atonement in the holy *place,* until he come out, and have made an atonement for himself, and for his household, and for all the congregation of Is'ra-el.

18 And he shall go out unto the altar that *is* before the LORD, and make an atonement for it; and shall take of the blood of the bullock, and of the blood of the goat, and put *it* upon the horns of the altar round about.

19 And he shall sprinkle of the blood upon it with his finger seven times, and cleanse it, and hallow it from the uncleanness of the children of Is'ra-el.

20 ¶ And when he hath made an end of reconciling the holy *place,* and the tabernacle of the congregation, and the altar, he shall bring the live goat:

21 And Aar'on shall lay both his hands upon the head of the live goat, and confess over him all the iniquities of the children of Is'ra-el, and all their transgressions in all their sins, putting them upon the head of the goat, and shall send *him* away by the hand of a fit man into the wilderness:

22 And the goat shall bear upon him all their iniquities unto a land not inhabited: and he shall let go the goat in the wilderness.

23 And Aar'on shall come into the tabernacle of the congregation, and shall put off the linen garments, which he put on when he went into the holy *place,* and shall leave them there:

24 And he shall wash his flesh with water in the holy place, and put on his garments, and come forth, and offer his burnt offering, and the burnt offering of the people, and make an atonement for himself, and for the people.

25 And the fat of the sin offering shall he burn upon the altar.

26 And he that let go the goat for the scapegoat shall wash his clothes, and bathe his flesh in water, and afterward come into the camp.

27 And the bullock *for* the sin offering, and the goat *for* the sin offering, whose blood was brought in to make atonement in the holy *place,* shall *one* carry forth without the camp; and

they shall burn in the fire their skins, and their flesh, and their dung.

28 And he that burneth them shall wash his clothes, and bathe his flesh in water, and afterward he shall come into the camp.

29 ¶ And *this* shall be a statute for ever unto you: *that* in the seventh month, on the tenth *day* of the month, ye shall afflict your souls, and do no work at all, *whether it be* one of your own country, or a stranger that sojourneth among you:

30 For on that day shall *the priest* make an atonement for you, to cleanse you, *that* ye may be clean from all your sins before the LORD.

31 It *shall be* a sabbath of rest unto you, and ye shall afflict your souls, by a statute for ever.

32 And the priest, whom he shall anoint, and whom he shall consecrate to minister in the priest's office in his father's stead, shall make the atonement, and shall put on the linen clothes, *even* the holy garments:

33 And he shall make an atonement for the holy sanctuary, and he shall make an atonement for the tabernacle of the congregation, and for the altar, and he shall make an atonement for the priests, and for all the people of the congregation.

34 And this shall be an everlasting statute unto you, to make an atonement for the children of Is'ra-el for all their sins once a year. And he did as the LORD commanded Mo'ses.

17 AND the LORD spake unto Mo'ses, saying,

2 Speak unto Aar'on, and unto his sons, and unto all the children of Is'ra-el, and say unto them; This *is* the thing which the LORD hath commanded, saying,

3 What man soever *there be* of the house of Is'ra-el, that killeth an ox, or lamb, or goat, in the camp, or that killeth *it* out of the camp,

4 And bringeth it not unto the door of the tabernacle of the congregation, to offer an offering unto the LORD before the tabernacle of the LORD; blood shall be imputed unto that man; he hath shed blood; and that man shall be cut off from among his people:

5 To the end that the children of Is'ra-el may bring their sacrifices, which they offer in the open field, even that they may bring them unto the LORD, unto the door of the tabernacle of the congregation, unto the priest, and offer them *for* peace offerings unto the LORD.

6 And the priest shall sprinkle the blood upon the altar of the LORD *at* the door of the tabernacle of the congregation, and burn the fat for a sweet savour unto the LORD.

7 And they shall no more offer their sacrifices unto devils, after whom they have gone a whoring. This shall be a statute for ever unto them throughout their generations.

8 ¶ And thou shalt say unto them, Whatsoever man *there be* of the house of Is'ra-el, or of the strangers which sojourn among you, that offereth a burnt offering or sacrifice,

9 And bringeth it not unto the door of the tabernacle of the congregation, to offer it unto the LORD; even that man shall be cut off from among his people.

10 ¶ And whatsoever man *there be* of the house of Is'ra-el, or of the strangers that sojourn among you, that eateth any manner of blood; I will even set my face against that soul that eateth blood, and will cut him off from among his people.

11 For the life of the flesh *is* in the blood: and I have given it to you upon the altar to make an

atonement for your souls for it *is* the blood *that* maketh an atonement for the soul.

12 Therefore I said unto the children of Is'ra-el, No soul of you shall eat blood, neither shall any stranger that sojourneth among you eat blood.

13 And whatsoever man *there be* of the children of Is'ra-el, or of the strangers that sojourn among you, which hunteth and catcheth any beast or fowl that may be eaten; he shall even pour out the blood thereof, and cover it with dust.

14 For *it is* the life of all flesh; the blood of it *is* for the life thereof: therefore I said unto the children of Is'ra-el, Ye shall eat the blood of no manner of flesh: for the life of all flesh *is* the blood thereof: whosoever eateth it shall be cut off.

15 And every soul that eateth that which died *of itself*, or that which was torn *with beasts, whether it be* one of your own country, or a stranger, he shall both wash his clothes, and bathe *himself* in water, and be unclean until the even: then shall he be clean.

16 But if he wash *them* not, nor bathe his flesh; then he shall bear his iniquity.

18 AND the LORD spake unto Mo'ses, saying,

2 Speak unto the children of Is'ra-el, and say unto them, I am the LORD your God.

3 After the doings of the land of E'gypt, wherein ye dwelt, shall ye not do: and after the doings of the land of Ca'naan, whither I bring you, shall ye not do: neither shall ye walk in their ordinances.

4 Ye shall do my judgments, and keep mine ordinances, to walk therein: I *am* the LORD your God.

5 Ye shall therefore keep my statutes, and my judgments: which if a man do, he shall live in them: I *am* the LORD.

6 ¶ None of you shall approach to any that is near of kin to him, to uncover *their* nakedness: I *am* the LORD.

7 The nakedness of thy father, or the nakedness of thy mother, shalt thou not uncover: she *is* thy mother; thou shalt not uncover her nakedness.

8 The nakedness of thy father's wife shalt thou not uncover: it *is* thy father's nakedness.

9 The nakedness of thy sister, the daughter of thy father, or daughter of thy mother, *whether she be* born at home, or born abroad, *even* their nakedness thou shalt not uncover.

10 The nakedness of thy son's daughter, or of thy daughter's daughter, *even* their nakedness thou shalt not uncover: for theirs *is* thine own nakedness.

11 The nakedness of thy father's wife's daughter, begotten of thy father, she *is* thy sister, thou shalt not uncover her nakedness.

12 Thou shalt not uncover the nakedness of thy father's sister: she *is* thy father's near kinswoman.

13 Thou shalt not uncover the nakedness of thy mother's sister: for she *is* thy mother's near kinswoman.

14 Thou shalt not uncover the nakedness of thy father's brother, thou shalt not approach to his wife: she *is* thine aunt.

15 Thou shalt not uncover the nakedness of thy daughter in law: she *is* thy son's wife; thou shalt not uncover her nakedness.

16 Thou shalt not uncover the nakedness of thy brother's wife: it *is* thy brother's nakedness.

17 Thou shalt not uncover the nakedness of a woman and her daughter, neither shalt thou take her son's daughter, or her daughter's daughter, to uncover her nakedness; *for* they *are* her near kinswomen: it *is* wickedness.

18 Neither shalt thou take a wife to her sister, to vex *her*, to uncover her nakedness, beside the other in her life *time*.

19 Also thou shalt not approach unto a woman to uncover her nakedness, as long as she is put apart for her uncleanness.

20 Moreover thou shalt not lie carnally with thy neighbour's wife, to defile thyself with her.

21 And thou shalt not let any of thy seed pass through *the fire* to Mo'lech, neither shalt thou profane the name of thy God: I *am* the LORD.

22 Thou shalt not lie with mankind, as with womankind: it *is* abomination.

23 Neither shalt thou lie with any beast to defile thyself therewith: neither shall any woman stand before a beast to lie down thereto: it *is* confusion.

24 Defile not ye yourselves in any of these things: for in all these the nations are defiled which I cast out before you:

25 And the land is defiled: therefore I do visit the iniquity thereof upon it, and the land itself vomiteth out her inhabitants.

26 Ye shall therefore keep my statutes and my judgments, and shall not commit *any* of these abominations; *neither* any of your own nation, nor any stranger that sojourneth among you:

27 (For all these abominations have the men of the land done, which *were* before you, and the land is defiled;)

28 That the land spue not you out also, when ye defile it, as it spued out the nations that *were* before you.

29 For whosoever shall commit any of these abominations, even the souls that commit *them* shall be cut off from among their people.

30 Therefore shall ye keep mine ordinance, that ye commit not *any one* of these abominable customs, which were committed before you, and that ye defile not yourselves therein: I *am* the LORD your God.

19 AND the LORD spake unto Mo'ses, saying,

2 Speak unto all the congregation of the children of Is'ra-el, and say unto them, Ye shall be holy: for I the LORD your God *am* holy.

3 ¶ Ye shall fear every man his mother, and his father, and keep my sabbaths: I *am* the LORD your God.

4 ¶ Turn ye not unto idols, nor make to yourselves molten gods: I *am* the LORD your God.

5 ¶ And if ye offer a sacrifice of peace offerings unto the LORD, ye shall offer it at your own will.

6 It shall be eaten the same day ye offer it, and on the morrow: and if ought remain until the third day, it shall be burnt in the fire.

7 And if it be eaten at all on the third day, it *is* abominable; it shall not be accepted.

8 Therefore *every one* that eateth it shall bear his iniquity, because he hath profaned the hallowed thing of the LORD: and that soul shall be cut off from among his people.

9 ¶ And when ye reap the harvest of your land, thou shalt not wholly reap the corners of thy field, neither shalt thou gather the gleanings of thy harvest.

10 And thou shalt not glean thy vineyard, neither shalt thou gather *every* grape of thy vineyard; thou shalt leave them for the poor and stranger: I *am* the LORD your God.

11 ¶ Ye shall not steal, neither deal falsely, neither lie one to another.

12 ¶ And ye shall not swear by my name falsely, neither shalt thou profane the name of thy God: I am the LORD.

13 ¶ Thou shalt not defraud thy neighbour, neither rob him: the wages of him that is hired shall not abide with thee all night until the morning.

14 ¶ Thou shalt not curse the deaf, nor put a stumblingblock before the blind, but shalt fear thy God: I am the LORD.

15 ¶ Ye shall do no unrighteousness in judgment: thou shalt not respect the person of the poor, nor honour the person of the mighty: but in righteousness shalt thou judge thy neighbour.

16 ¶ Thou shalt not go up and down as a talebearer among thy people: neither shalt thou stand against the blood of thy neighbour: I am the LORD.

17 ¶ Thou shalt not hate thy brother in thine heart: thou shalt in any wise rebuke thy neighbour, and not suffer sin upon him.

18 ¶ Thou shalt not avenge, nor bear any grudge against the children of thy people, but thou shalt love thy neighbour as thyself: I am the LORD.

19 ¶ Ye shall keep my statutes. Thou shalt not let thy cattle gender with a diverse kind: thou shalt not sow thy field with mingled seed: neither shall a garment mingled of linen and woollen come upon thee.

20 ¶ And whosoever lieth carnally with a woman, that is a bondmaid, betrothed to an husband, and not at all redeemed, nor freedom given her; she shall be scourged; they shall not be put to death, because she was not free.

21 And he shall bring his trespass offering unto the LORD, unto the door of the tabernacle of the congregation, even a ram for a trespass offering.

22 And the priest shall make an atonement for him with the ram of the trespass offering before the LORD for his sin which he hath done: and the sin which he hath done shall be forgiven him.

23 ¶ And when ye shall come into the land, and shall have planted all manner of trees for food, then ye shall count the fruit thereof as uncircumcised: three years shall it be as uncircumcised unto you: it shall not be eaten of.

24 But in the fourth year all the fruit thereof shall be holy to praise the LORD withal.

25 And in the fifth year shall ye eat of the fruit thereof, that it may yield unto you the increase thereof: I am the LORD your God.

26 ¶ Ye shall not eat any thing with the blood: neither shall ye use enchantment, nor observe times.

27 Ye shall not round the corners of your heads, neither shalt thou mar the corners of thy beard.

28 Ye shall not make any cuttings in your flesh for the dead, nor print any marks upon you: I am the LORD.

29 ¶ Do not prostitute thy daughter, to cause her to be a whore; lest the land fall to whoredom, and the land become full of wickedness.

30 ¶ Ye shall keep my sabbaths, and reverence my sanctuary: I am the LORD.

31 ¶ Regard not them that have familiar spirits, neither seek after wizards, to be defiled by them: I am the LORD your God.

32 ¶ Thou shalt rise up before the hoary head, and honour the face of the old man, and fear thy God: I am the LORD.

33 ¶ And if a stranger sojourn with thee in your land, ye shall not vex him.

34 But the stranger that dwelleth with you shall be unto you as one born among you, and thou shalt love him as thyself; for ye were strangers in the land of E'gypt: I am the LORD your God.

35 ¶ Ye shall do no unrighteousness in judgment, in meteyard, in weight, or in measure.

36 Just balances, just weights, a just ephah, and a just hin, shall ye have: I am the LORD your God, which brought you out of the land of E'-gypt.

37 Therefore shall ye observe all my statutes, and all my judgments, and do them: I am the LORD.

20 AND the LORD spake unto Mo'ses, saying,

2 Again, thou shalt say to the children of Is'-ra-el, Whosoever he be of the children of Is'ra-el, or of the strangers that sojourn in Is'ra-el, that giveth any of his seed unto Mo'lech; he shall surely be put to death: the people of the land shall stone him with stones.

3 And I will set my face against that man, and will cut him off from among his people; because he hath given of his seed unto Mo'lech, to defile my sanctuary, and to profane my holy name.

4 And if the people of the land do any ways hide their eyes from the man, when he giveth of his seed unto Mo'lech, and kill him not:

5 Then I will set my face against that man, and against his family, and will cut him off, and all that go a whoring after him, to commit whoredom with Mo'lech, from among their people.

6 ¶ And the soul that turneth after such as have familiar spirits, and after wizards, to go a whoring after them, I will even set my face against that soul, and will cut him off from among his people.

7 ¶ Sanctify yourselves therefore, and be ye holy: for I am the LORD your God.

8 And ye shall keep my statutes, and do them: I am the LORD which sanctify you.

9 ¶ For every one that curseth his father or his mother shall be surely put to death: he hath cursed his father or his mother; his blood shall be upon him.

10 ¶ And the man that committeth adultery with another man's wife, even he that committeth adultery with his neighbour's wife, the adulterer and the adulteress shall surely be put to death.

11 And the man that lieth with his father's wife hath uncovered his father's nakedness: both of them shall surely be put to death; their blood shall be upon them.

12 And if a man lie with his daughter in law, both of them shall surely be put to death: they have wrought confusion; their blood shall be upon them.

13 If a man also lie with mankind, as he lieth with a woman, both of them have committed an abomination: they shall surely be put to death; their blood shall be upon them.

14 And if a man take a wife and her mother, it is wickedness: they shall be burnt with fire, both he and they; that there be no wickedness among you.

15 And if a man lie with a beast, he shall surely be put to death: and ye shall slay the beast.

16 And if a woman approach unto any beast, and lie down thereto, thou shalt kill the woman,

and the beast: they shall surely be put to death; their blood *shall be* upon them.

17 And if a man shall take his sister, his father's daughter, or his mother's daughter, and see her nakedness, and she see his nakedness; it *is* a wicked thing; and they shall be cut off in the sight of their people: he hath uncovered his sister's nakedness; he shall bear his iniquity.

18 And if a man shall lie with a woman having her sickness, and shall uncover her nakedness; he hath discovered her fountain, and she hath uncovered the fountain of her blood: and both of them shall be cut off from among their people.

19 And thou shalt not uncover the nakedness of thy mother's sister, nor of thy father's sister: for he uncovereth his near kin: they shall bear their iniquity.

20 And if a man shall lie with his uncle's wife, he hath uncovered his uncle's nakedness: they shall bear their sin; they shall die childless.

21 And if a man shall take his brother's wife, it *is* an unclean thing: he hath uncovered his brother's nakedness; they shall be childless.

22 ¶ Ye shall therefore keep all my statutes, and all my judgments, and do them: that the land, whither I bring you to dwell therein, spue you not out.

23 And ye shall not walk in the manners of the nation, which I cast out before you: for they committed all these things, and therefore I abhorred them.

24 But I have said unto you, Ye shall inherit their land, and I will give it unto you to possess it, a land that floweth with milk and honey: I *am* the LORD your God, which have separated you from *other* people.

25 Ye shall therefore put difference between clean beasts and unclean, and between unclean fowls and clean: and ye shall not make your souls abominable by beast, or by fowl, or by any manner of living thing that creepeth on the ground, which I have separated from you as unclean.

26 And ye shall be holy unto me: for I the LORD *am* holy, and have severed you from *other* people, that ye should be mine.

27 ¶ A man also or woman that hath a familiar spirit, or that is a wizard, shall surely be put to death: they shall stone them with stones: their blood *shall be* upon them.

21 AND the LORD said unto Mo'ses, Speak unto the priests the sons of Aar'on, and say unto them, There shall none be defiled for the dead among his people:

2 But for his kin, that is near unto him, *that is,* for his mother, and for his father, and for his son, and for his daughter, and for his brother,

3 And for his sister a virgin, that is nigh unto him, which hath had no husband; for her may he be defiled.

4 *But* he shall not defile himself, *being* a chief man among his people, to profane himself.

5 They shall not make baldness upon their head, neither shall they shave off the corner of their beard, nor make any cuttings in their flesh.

6 They shall be holy unto their God, and not profane the name of their God: for the offerings of the LORD made by fire, *and* the bread of their God, they do offer: therefore they shall be holy.

7 They shall not take a wife *that is* a whore, or profane; neither shall they take a woman put away from her husband: for he *is* holy unto his God.

8 Thou shalt sanctify him therefore; for he offereth the bread of thy God: he shall be holy unto thee: for I the LORD, which sanctify you, *am* holy.

9 ¶ And the daughter of any priest, if she profane herself by playing the whore, she profaneth her father: she shall be burnt with fire.

10 And *he that is* the high priest among his brethren, upon whose head the anointing oil was poured, and that is consecrated to put on the garments, shall not uncover his head, nor rend his clothes;

11 Neither shall he go in to any dead body, nor defile himself for his father, or for his mother;

12 Neither shall he go out of the sanctuary, nor profane the sanctuary of his God; for the crown of the anointing oil of his God *is* upon him: I *am* the LORD.

13 And he shall take a wife in her virginity.

14 A widow, or a divorced woman, or profane, *or* an harlot, these shall he not take: but he shall take a virgin of his own people to wife.

15 Neither shall he profane his seed among his people: for I the LORD do sanctify him.

16 ¶ And the LORD spake unto Mo'ses, saying,

17 Speak unto Aar'on, saying, Whosoever *he be* of thy seed in their generations that hath *any* blemish, let him not approach to offer the bread of his God.

18 For whatsoever man *he be* that hath a blemish, he shall not approach: a blind man, or a lame, or he that hath a flat nose, or any thing superfluous,

19 Or a man that is brokenfooted, or brokenhanded,

20 Or crookbackt, or a dwarf, or that hath a blemish in his eye, or be scurvy, or scabbed, or hath his stones broken;

21 No man that hath a blemish of the seed of Aar'on the priest shall come nigh to offer the offerings of the LORD made by fire: he hath a blemish; he shall not come nigh to offer the bread of his God.

22 He shall eat the bread of his God, *both* of the most holy, and of the holy.

23 Only he shall not go in unto the veil, nor come nigh unto the altar, because he hath a blemish; that he profane not my sanctuaries: for I the LORD do sanctify them.

24 And Mo'ses told *it* unto Aar'on, and to his sons, and unto all the children of Is'ra-el.

22 AND the LORD spake unto Mo'ses, saying,

2 Speak unto Aar'on and to his sons, that they separate themselves from the holy things of the children of Is'ra-el, and that they profane not my holy name *in those things* which they hallow unto me: I *am* the LORD.

3 Say unto them, Whosoever *he be* of all your seed among your generations, that goeth unto the holy things, which the children of Is'ra-el hallow unto the LORD, having his uncleanness upon him, that soul shall be cut off from my presence: I *am* the LORD.

4 What man soever of the seed of Aar'on *is* a leper, or hath a running issue; he shall not eat of the holy things, until he be clean. And whoso toucheth any thing that is unclean *by* the dead, or a man whose seed goeth from him;

5 Or whosoever toucheth any creeping thing, whereby he may be made unclean, or a man of whom he may take uncleanness, whatsoever uncleanness he hath;

6 The soul which hath touched any such shall be unclean until even, and shall not eat of the

holy things, unless he wash his flesh with water.

7 And when the sun is down, he shall be clean, and shall afterward eat of the holy things; because it *is* his food.

8 That which dieth of itself, or is torn *with beasts,* he shall not eat to defile himself therewith: I *am* the LORD.

9 They shall therefore keep mine ordinance, lest they bear sin for it, and die therefore, if they profane it: I the LORD do sanctify them.

10 There shall no stranger eat *of* the holy thing: a sojourner of the priest, or an hired servant, shall not eat *of* the holy thing.

11 But if the priest buy *any* soul with his money, he shall eat of it, and he that is born in his house: they shall eat of his meat.

12 If the priest's daughter also be *married* unto a stranger, she may not eat of an offering of the holy things.

13 But if the priest's daughter be a widow, or divorced, and have no child, and is returned unto her father's house, as in her youth, she shall eat of her father's meat: but there shall no stranger eat thereof.

14 ¶ And if a man eat *of* the holy thing unwittingly, then he shall put the fifth *part* thereof unto it, and shall give *it* unto the priest with the holy thing.

15 And they shall not profane the holy things of the children of Is'ra-el, which they offer unto the LORD;

16 Or suffer them to bear the iniquity of trespass, when they eat their holy things: for I the LORD do sanctify them.

17 ¶ And the LORD spake unto Mo'ses, saying.

18 Speak unto Aar'on, and to his sons, and unto all the children of Is'ra-el, and say unto them, Whatsoever *he be* of the house of Is'ra-el, or of the strangers in Is'ra-el, that will offer his oblation for all his vows, and for all his freewill offerings, which they will offer unto the LORD for a burnt offering;

19 *Ye shall offer* at your own will a male without blemish, of the beeves, of the sheep, or of the goats.

20 *But* whatsoever hath a blemish, *that* shall ye not offer: for it shall not be acceptable for you.

21 And whosoever offereth a sacrifice of peace offerings unto the LORD to accomplish *his* vow, or a freewill offering in beeves or sheep, it shall be perfect to be accepted; there shall be no blemish therein.

22 Blind, or broken, or maimed, or having a wen, or scurvy, or scabbed, ye shall not offer these unto the LORD, nor make an offering by fire of them upon the altar unto the LORD.

23 Either a bullock or a lamb that hath any thing superfluous or lacking in his parts, that mayest thou offer *for* a freewill offering; but for a vow it shall not be accepted.

24 Ye shall not offer unto the LORD that which is bruised, or crushed, or broken, or cut; neither shall ye make *any offering thereof* in your land.

25 Neither from a stranger's hand shall ye offer the bread of your God of any of these; because their corruption *is* in them, *and* blemishes *be* in them: they shall not be accepted for you.

26 ¶ And the LORD spake unto Mo'ses, saying,

27 When a bullock, or a sheep, or a goat, is brought forth, then it shall be seven days under the dam; and from the eighth day and thenceforth it shall be accepted for an offering made by fire unto the LORD.

28 And *whether it be* cow or ewe, ye shall not kill it and her young both in one day.

29 And when ye will offer a sacrifice of thanksgiving unto the LORD, offer *it* at your own will.

30 On the same day it shall be eaten up; ye shall leave none of it until the morrow: I *am* the LORD.

31 Therefore shall ye keep my commandments, and do them: I *am* the LORD.

32 Neither shall ye profane my holy name; but I will be hallowed among the children of Is'ra-el: I *am* the LORD which hallow you,

33 That brought you out of the land of E'-gypt, to be your God: I *am* the LORD.

23 AND the LORD spake unto Mo'ses, saying,

2 Speak unto the children of Is'ra-el, and say unto them, *Concerning* the feasts of the LORD, which ye shall proclaim *to be* holy convocations, *even* these *are* my feasts.

3 Six days shall work be done: but the seventh day *is* the sabbath of rest, an holy convocation; ye shall do no work *therein*: it *is* the sabbath of the LORD in all your dwellings.

4 ¶ These *are* the feasts of the LORD, *even* holy convocations, which ye shall proclaim in their seasons.

5 In the fourteenth *day* of the first month at even *is* the LORD's passover.

6 And on the fifteenth day of the same month *is* the feast of unleavened bread unto the LORD: seven days ye must eat unleavened bread.

7 In the first day ye shall have an holy convocation: ye shall do no servile work therein.

8 But ye shall offer an offering made by fire unto the LORD seven days: in the seventh day *is* an holy convocation: ye shall do no servile work *therein.*

9 ¶ And the LORD spake unto Mo'ses, saying,

10 Speak unto the children of Is'ra-el, and say unto them, When ye be come into the land which I give unto you, and shall reap the harvest thereof, then ye shall bring a sheaf of the firstfruits of your harvest unto the priest:

11 And he shall wave the sheaf before the LORD, to be accepted for you: on the morrow after the sabbath the priest shall wave it.

12 And ye shall offer that day when ye wave the sheaf an he lamb without blemish of the first year for a burnt offering unto the LORD.

13 And the meat offering thereof *shall be* two tenth deals of fine flour mingled with oil, an offering made by fire unto the LORD *for* a sweet savour: and the drink offering thereof *shall be* of wine, the fourth *part* of an hin.

14 And ye shall eat neither bread, nor parched corn, nor green ears, until the selfsame day that ye have brought an offering unto your God: *it shall be* a statute for ever throughout your generations in all your dwellings.

15 ¶ And ye shall count unto you from the morrow after the sabbath, from the day that ye brought the sheaf of the wave offering; seven sabbaths shall be complete:

16 Even unto the morrow after the seventh sabbath shall ye number fifty days; and ye shall offer a new meat offering unto the LORD.

17 Ye shall bring out of your habitations two wave loaves of two tenth deals: they shall be of fine flour; they shall be baken with leaven; *they are* the firstfruits unto the LORD.

18 And ye shall offer with the bread seven lambs without blemish of the first year, and one

young bullock, and two rams: they shall be *for* a burnt offering unto the LORD, with their meat offering, and their drink offerings, *even* an offering made by fire, of sweet savour unto the LORD.

19 Then ye shall sacrifice one kid of the goats for a sin offering, and two lambs of the first year for a sacrifice of peace offerings.

20 And the priest shall wave them with the bread of the firstfruits *for* a wave offering before the LORD, with the two lambs: they shall be holy to the LORD for the priest.

21 And ye shall proclaim on the selfsame day, *that* it may be an holy convocation unto you: ye shall do no servile work *therein: it shall be* a statute for ever in all your dwellings throughout your generations.

22 ¶ And when ye reap the harvest of your land, thou shalt not make clean riddance of the corners of thy field when thou reapest, neither shalt thou gather any gleaning of thy harvest: thou shalt leave them unto the poor, and to the stranger: I *am* the LORD your God.

23 ¶ And the LORD spake unto Mo'ses, saying,

24 Speak unto the children of Is'ra-el, saying, In the seventh month, in the first *day* of the month, shall ye have a sabbath, a memorial of blowing of trumpets, an holy convocation.

25 Ye shall do no servile work *therein:* but ye shall offer an offering made by fire unto the LORD.

26 ¶ And the LORD spake unto Mo'ses, saying,

27 Also on the tenth *day* of this seventh month *there shall be* a day of atonement: it shall be an holy convocation unto you; and ye shall afflict your souls, and offer an offering made by fire unto the LORD.

28 And ye shall do no work in that same day: for it *is* a day of atonement, to make an atonement for you before the LORD your God.

29 For whatsoever soul *it be* that shall not be afflicted in that same day, he shall be cut off from among his people.

30 And whatsoever soul *it be* that doeth any work in that same day, the same soul will I destroy from among his people.

31 Ye shall do no manner of work: *it shall be* a statute for ever throughout your generations in all your dwellings.

32 *It shall be* unto you a sabbath of rest, and ye shall afflict your souls: in the ninth *day* of the month at even, from even unto even, shall ye celebrate your sabbath.

33 ¶ And the LORD spake unto Mo'ses, saying,

34 Speak unto the children of Is'ra-el, saying, The fifteenth day of this seventh month *shall be* the feast of tabernacles *for* seven days unto the LORD.

35 On the first day *shall be* an holy convocation: ye shall do no servile work *therein.*

36 Seven days ye shall offer an offering made by fire unto the LORD: on the eighth day shall be an holy convocation unto you; and ye shall offer an offering made by fire unto the LORD: it *is* a solemn assembly; *and* ye shall do no servile work *therein.*

37 These *are* the feasts of the LORD, which ye shall proclaim *to be* holy convocations, to offer an offering made by fire unto the LORD, a burnt offering, and a meat offering, a sacrifice, and drink offerings, every thing upon his day:

38 Beside the sabbaths of the LORD, and beside your gifts, and beside all your vows, and beside all your freewill offerings, which ye give unto the LORD.

39 Also in the fifteenth day of the seventh month, when ye have gathered in the fruit of the land, ye shall keep a feast unto the LORD seven days: on the first day *shall be* a sabbath, and on the eighth day *shall be* a sabbath.

40 And ye shall take you on the first day the boughs of goodly trees, branches of palm trees, and the boughs of thick trees, and willows of the brook; and ye shall rejoice before the LORD your God seven days.

41 And ye shall keep it a feast unto the LORD seven days in the year. *It shall be* a statute for ever in your generations: ye shall celebrate it in the seventh month.

42 Ye shall dwell in booths seven days; all that are Is'ra-el-ites born shall dwell in booths:

43 That your generations may know that I made the children of Is'ra-el to dwell in booths, when I brought them out of the land of E'gypt: I *am* the LORD your God.

44 And Mo'ses declared unto the children of Is'ra-el the feasts of the LORD.

24 AND the LORD spake unto Mo'ses, saying,

2 Command the children of Is'ra-el, that they bring unto thee pure oil olive beaten for the light, to cause the lamps to burn continually.

3 Without the veil of the testimony, in the tabernacle of the congregation, shall Aar'on order it from the evening unto the morning before the LORD continually: *it shall be* a statute for ever in your generations.

4 He shall order the lamps upon the pure candlestick before the LORD continually.

5 ¶ And thou shalt take fine flour, and bake twelve cakes thereof: two tenth deals shall be in one cake.

6 And thou shalt set them in two rows, six on a row, upon the pure table before the LORD.

7 And thou shalt put pure frankincense upon *each* row, that it may be on the bread for a memorial, *even* an offering made by fire unto the LORD.

8 Every sabbath he shall set it in order before the LORD continually, *being taken* from the children of Is'ra-el by an everlasting covenant.

9 And it shall be Aar'on's and his sons'; and they shall eat it in the holy place: for it *is* most holy unto him of the offerings of the LORD made by fire by a perpetual statute.

10 ¶ And the son of an Is'ra-el-it-ish woman, whose father *was* an E-gyp'tian, went out among the children of Is'ra-el: and this son of the Is'ra-el-it-ish *woman* and a man of Is'ra-el strove together in the camp;

11 And the Is'ra-el-it-ish woman's son blasphemed the name *of the LORD,* and cursed. And they brought him unto Mo'ses: (and his mother's name *was* Shel'o-mith, the daughter of Dib'ri, of the tribe of Dan:)

12 And they put him in ward, that the mind of the LORD might be shewed them.

13 And the LORD spake unto Mo'ses, saying,

14 Bring forth him that hath cursed without the camp; and let all that heard *him* lay their hands upon his head, and let all the congregation stone him.

15 And thou shalt speak unto the children of Is'ra-el, saying, Whosoever curseth his God shall bear his sin.

16 And he that blasphemeth the name of the LORD, he shall surely be put to death, *and* all the congregation shall certainly stone him: as well the stranger, as he that is born in the land, when

he blasphemeth the name of the LORD, shall be put to death.

17 ¶ And he that killeth any man shall surely be put to death.

18 And he that killeth a beast shall make it good; beast for beast.

19 And if a man cause a blemish in his neighbour; as he hath done, so shall it be done to him;

20 Breach for breach, eye for eye, tooth for tooth: as he hath caused a blemish in a man, so shall it be done to him again.

21 And he that killeth a beast, he shall restore it: and he that killeth a man, he shall be put to death.

22 Ye shall have one manner of law, as well for the stranger, as for one of your own country: for I am the LORD your God.

23 ¶ And Mo'ses spake to the children of Is'ra-el, that they should bring forth him that had cursed out of the camp, and stone him with stones. And the children of Is'ra-el did as the LORD commanded Mo'ses.

25 AND the LORD spake unto Mo'ses in mount Si'nai, saying,

2 Speak unto the children of Is'ra-el, and say unto them, When ye come into the land which I give you, then shall the land keep a sabbath unto the LORD.

3 Six years thou shalt sow thy field, and six years thou shalt prune thy vineyard, and gather in the fruit thereof;

4 But in the seventh year shall be a sabbath of rest unto the land, a sabbath for the LORD: thou shalt neither sow thy field, nor prune thy vineyard.

5 That which groweth of its own accord of thy harvest thou shalt not reap, neither gather the grapes of thy vine undressed: for it is a year of rest unto the land.

6 And the sabbath of the land shall be meat for you; for thee, and for thy servant, and for thy maid, and for thy hired servant, and for thy stranger that sojourneth with thee,

7 And for thy cattle, and for the beast that are in thy land, shall all the increase thereof be meat.

8 ¶ And thou shalt number seven sabbaths of years unto thee, seven times seven years; and the space of the seven sabbaths of years shall be unto thee forty and nine years.

9 Then shalt thou cause the trumpet of the jubile to sound on the tenth day of the seventh month, in the day of atonement shall ye make the trumpet sound throughout all your land.

10 And ye shall hallow the fiftieth year, and proclaim liberty throughout all the land unto all the inhabitants thereof: it shall be a jubile unto you; and ye shall return every man unto his possession, and ye shall return every man unto his family.

11 A jubile shall that fiftieth year be unto you: ye shall not sow, neither reap that which groweth of itself in it, nor gather the grapes in it of thy vine undressed.

12 For it is the jubile; it shall be holy unto you: ye shall eat the increase thereof out of the field.

13 In the year of this jubile ye shall return every man unto his possession.

14 And if thou sell ought unto thy neighbour, or buyest ought of thy neighbour's hand, ye shall not oppress one another:

15 According to the number of years after the jubile thou shalt buy of thy neighbour, and according unto the number of years of the fruits he shall sell unto thee:

16 According to the multitude of years thou shalt increase the price thereof, and according to the fewness of years thou shalt diminish the price of it: for according to the number of the years of the fruits doth he sell unto thee.

17 Ye shall not therefore oppress one another; but thou shalt fear thy God: for I am the LORD your God.

18 ¶ Wherefore ye shall do my statutes, and keep my judgments, and do them; and ye shall dwell in the land in safety.

19 And the land shall yield her fruit, and ye shall eat your fill, and dwell therein in safety.

20 And if ye shall say, What shall we eat the seventh year? behold, we shall not sow, nor gather in our increase:

21 Then I will command my blessing upon you in the sixth year, and it shall bring forth fruit for three years.

22 And ye shall sow the eighth year, and eat yet of old fruit until the ninth year; until her fruits come in ye shall eat of the old store.

23 ¶ The land shall not be sold for ever: for the land is mine; for ye are strangers and sojourners with me.

24 And in all the land of your possession ye shall grant a redemption for the land.

25 ¶ If thy brother be waxen poor, and hath sold away some of his possession, and if any of his kin come to redeem it, then shall he redeem that which his brother sold.

26 And if the man have none to redeem it, and himself be able to redeem it;

27 Then let him count the years of the sale thereof, and restore the overplus unto the man to whom he sold it; that he may return unto his possession.

28 But if he be not able to restore it to him, then that which is sold shall remain in the hand of him that hath bought it until the year of jubile: and in the jubile it shall go out, and he shall return unto his possession.

29 And if a man sell a dwelling house in a walled city, then he may redeem it within a whole year after it is sold; within a full year may he redeem it.

30 And if it be not redeemed within the space of a full year, then the house that is in the walled city shall be established for ever to him that bought it throughout his generations: it shall not go out in the jubile.

31 But the houses of the villages which have no wall round about them shall be counted as the fields of the country: they may be redeemed, and they shall go out in the jubile.

32 Notwithstanding the cities of the Le'vites, and the houses of the cities of their possession, may the Le'vites redeem at any time.

33 And if a man purchase of the Le'vites, then the house that was sold, and the city of his possession, shall go out in the year of jubile: for the houses of the cities of the Le'vites are their possession among the children of Is'ra-el.

34 But the field of the suburbs of their cities may not be sold; for it is their perpetual possession.

35 ¶ And if thy brother be waxen poor, and fallen in decay with thee; then thou shalt relieve him: yea, though he be a stranger, or a sojourner; that he may live with thee.

36 Take thou no usury of him, or increase: but fear thy God; that thy brother may live with thee.

37 Thou shalt not give him thy money upon usury, nor lend him thy victuals for increase.

38 I am the LORD your God, which brought

you forth out of the land of E'gypt, to give you the land of Ca'naan, and to be your God.

39 ¶ And if thy brother that dwelleth by thee be waxen poor, and be sold unto thee; thou shalt not compel him to serve as a bondservant:

40 But as an hired servant, and as a sojourner, he shall be with thee, and shall serve thee unto the year of jubile:

41 And then shall he depart from thee, both he and his children with him, and shall return unto his own family, and unto the possession of his fathers shall he return.

42 For they are my servants, which I brought forth out of the land of E'gypt: they shall not be sold as bondmen.

43 Thou shalt not rule over him with rigour; but shalt fear thy God.

44 Both thy bondmen, and thy bondmaids, which thou shalt have, shall be of the heathen that are round about you; of them shall ye buy bondmen and bondmaids.

45 Moreover of the children of the strangers that do sojourn among you, of them shall ye buy, and of their families that are with you, which they begat in your land: and they shall be your possession.

46 And ye shall take them as an inheritance for your children after you, to inherit them for a possession; they shall be your bondmen for ever: but over your brethren the children of Is'-ra-el ye shall not rule one over another with rigour.

47 ¶ And if a sojourner or stranger wax rich by thee, and thy brother that dwelleth by him wax poor, and sell himself unto the stranger or sojourner by thee, or to the stock of the stranger's family:

48 After that he is sold he may be redeemed again; one of his brethren may redeem him:

49 Either his uncle, or his uncle's son, may redeem him, or any that is nigh of kin unto him of his family may redeem him; or if he be able, he may redeem himself.

50 And he shall reckon with him that bought him from the year that he was sold to him unto the year of jubile: and the price of his sale shall be according unto the number of years, according to the time of an hired servant shall it be with him.

51 If there be yet many years behind, according unto them he shall give again the price of his redemption out of the money that he was bought for.

52 And if there remain but few years unto the year of jubile, then he shall count with him, and according unto his years shall he give him again the price of his redemption.

53 And as a yearly hired servant shall he be with him: and the other shall not rule with rigour over him in thy sight.

54 And if he be not redeemed in these years, then he shall go out in the year of jubile, both he, and his children with him.

55 For unto me the children of Is'ra-el are servants; they are my servants whom I brought forth out of the land of E'gypt: I am the LORD your God.

26 YE shall make you no idols nor graven image, neither rear you up a standing image, neither shall ye set up any image of stone in your land, to bow down unto it: for I am the LORD your God.

2 ¶ Ye shall keep my sabbaths, and reverence my sanctuary: I am the LORD.

3 ¶ If ye walk in my statutes, and keep my commandments, and do them;

4 Then I will give you rain in due season, and the land shall yield her increase, and the trees of the field shall yield their fruit.

5 And your threshing shall reach unto the vintage, and the vintage shall reach unto the sowing time: and ye shall eat your bread to the full, and dwell in your land safely.

6 And I will give peace in the land, and ye shall lie down, and none shall make you afraid: and I will rid evil beasts out of the land, neither shall the sword go through your land.

7 And ye shall chase your enemies, and they shall fall before you by the sword.

8 And five of you shall chase an hundred, and an hundred of you shall put ten thousand to flight: and your enemies shall fall before you by the sword.

9 For I will have respect unto you, and make you fruitful, and multiply you, and establish my covenant with you.

10 And ye shall eat old store, and bring forth the old because of the new.

11 And I will set my tabernacle among you: and my soul shall not abhor you.

12 And I will walk among you, and will be your God, and ye shall be my people.

13 I am the LORD your God, which brought you forth out of the land of E'gypt, that ye should not be their bondmen; and I have broken the bands of your yoke, and made you go upright.

14 ¶ But if ye will not hearken unto me, and will not do all these commandments;

15 And if ye shall despise my statutes, or if your soul abhor my judgments, so that ye will not do all my commandments, but that ye break my covenant:

16 I also will do this unto you; I will even appoint over you terror, consumption, and the burning ague, that shall consume the eyes, and cause sorrow of heart: and ye shall sow your seed in vain, for your enemies shall eat it.

17 And I will set my face against you, and ye shall be slain before your enemies: they that hate you shall reign over you; and ye shall flee when none pursueth you.

18 And if ye will not yet for all this hearken unto me, then I will punish you seven times more for your sins.

19 And I will break the pride of your power; and I will make your heaven as iron, and your earth as brass:

20 And your strength shall be spent in vain: for your land shall not yield her increase, neither shall the trees of the land yield their fruits.

21 ¶ And if ye walk contrary unto me, and will not hearken unto me; I will bring seven times more plagues upon you according to your sins.

22 I will also send wild beasts among you, which shall rob you of your children, and destroy your cattle, and make you few in number; and your high ways shall be desolate.

23 And if ye will not be reformed by me by these things, but will walk contrary unto me;

24 Then will I also walk contrary unto you, and will punish you yet seven times for your sins.

25 And I will bring a sword upon you, that shall avenge the quarrel of my covenant: and when ye are gathered together within your cities, I will send the pestilence among you; and ye shall be delivered into the hand of the enemy.

26 And when I have broken the staff of your bread, ten women shall bake your bread in one oven, and they shall deliver you your bread

again by weight: and ye shall eat, and not be satisfied.

27 And if ye will not for all this hearken unto me, but walk contrary unto me;

28 Then I will walk contrary unto you also in fury; and I, even I, will chastise you seven times for your sins.

29 And ye shall eat the flesh of your sons, and the flesh of your daughters shall ye eat.

30 And I will destroy your high places, and cut down your images, and cast your carcases upon the carcases of your idols, and my soul shall abhor you.

31 And I will make your cities waste, and bring your sanctuaries unto desolation, and I will not smell the savour of your sweet odours.

32 And I will bring the land into desolation: and your enemies which dwell therein shall be astonished at it.

33 And I will scatter you among the heathen, and will draw out a sword after you: and your land shall be desolate, and your cities waste.

34 Then shall the land enjoy her sabbaths, as long as it lieth desolate, and ye *be* in your enemies' land; *even* then shall the land rest, and enjoy her sabbaths.

35 As long as it lieth desolate it shall rest; because it did not rest in your sabbaths, when ye dwelt upon it.

36 And upon them that are left *alive* of you I will send a faintness into their hearts in the lands of their enemies; and the sound of a shaken leaf shall chase them; and they shall flee, as fleeing from a sword; and they shall fall when none pursueth.

37 And they shall fall one upon another, as it were before a sword, when none pursueth: and ye shall have no power to stand before your enemies.

38 And ye shall perish among the heathen, and the land of your enemies shall eat you up.

39 And they that are left of you shall pine away in their iniquity in your enemies' lands; and also in the iniquities of their fathers shall they pine away with them.

40 If they shall confess their iniquity, and the iniquity of their fathers, with their trespass which they trespassed against me, and that also they have walked contrary unto me;

41 And *that* I also have walked contrary unto them, and have brought them into the land of their enemies; if then their uncircumcised hearts be humbled, and they then accept of the punishment of their iniquity:

42 Then will I remember my covenant with Ja'cob, and also my covenant with I'saac, and also my covenant with A'bra-ham will I remember; and I will remember the land.

43 The land also shall be left of them, and shall enjoy her sabbaths, while she lieth desolate without them: and they shall accept of the punishment of their iniquity: because, even because they despised my judgments, and because their soul abhorred my statutes.

44 And yet for all that, when they be in the land of their enemies, I will not cast them away, neither will I abhor them, to destroy them utterly, and to break my covenant with them: for I *am* the Lord their God.

45 But I will for their sakes remember the covenant of their ancestors, whom I brought forth out of the land of E'gypt in the sight of the heathen, that I might be their God: I *am* the Lord.

46 These *are* the statutes and judgments and laws, which the Lord made between him and the children of Is'ra-el in mount Si'nai by the hand of Mo'ses.

27 AND the Lord spake unto Mo'ses, saying,

2 Speak unto the children of Is'ra-el, and say unto them, When a man shall make a singular vow, the persons *shall be* for the Lord by thy estimation.

3 And thy estimation shall be of the male from twenty years old even unto sixty years old, even thy estimation shall be fifty shekels of silver, after the shekel of the sanctuary.

4 And if it *be* a female, then thy estimation shall be thirty shekels.

5 And if *it be* from five years old even unto twenty years old, then thy estimation shall be of the male twenty shekels, and for the female ten shekels.

6 And if *it be* from a month old even unto five years old, then thy estimation shall be of the male five shekels of silver, and for the female thy estimation *shall be* three shekels of silver.

7 And if *it be* from sixty years old and above; if *it be* a male, then thy estimation shall be fifteen shekels, and for the female ten shekels.

8 But if he be poorer than thy estimation, then he shall present himself before the priest, and the priest shall value him; according to his ability that vowed shall the priest value him.

9 And if *it be* a beast, whereof men bring an offering unto the Lord, all that *any man* giveth of such unto the Lord shall be holy.

10 He shall not alter it, nor change it, a good for a bad, or a bad for a good: and if he shall at all change beast for beast, then it and the exchange thereof shall be holy.

11 And if *it be* any unclean beast, of which they do not offer a sacrifice unto the Lord, then he shall present the beast before the priest:

12 And the priest shall value it, whether it be good or bad: as thou valuest it, *who art* the priest, so shall it be.

13 But if he will at all redeem it, then he shall add a fifth *part* thereof unto thy estimation.

14 ¶ And when a man shall sanctify his house *to be* holy unto the Lord, then the priest shall estimate it, whether it be good or bad: as the priest shall estimate it, so shall it stand.

15 And if he that sanctified it will redeem his house, then he shall add the fifth *part* of the money of thy estimation unto it, and it shall be his.

16 And if a man shall sanctify unto the Lord *some part* of a field of his possession, then thy estimation shall be according to the seed thereof: an homer of barley seed *shall be valued* at fifty shekels of silver.

17 If he sanctify his field from the year of jubile, according to thy estimation it shall stand.

18 But if he sanctify his field after the jubile, then the priest shall reckon unto him the money according to the years that remain, even unto the year of the jubile, and it shall be abated from thy estimation.

19 And if he that sanctified the field will in any wise redeem it, then he shall add the fifth *part* of the money of thy estimation unto it, and it shall be assured to him.

20 And if he will not redeem the field, or if he have sold the field to another man, it shall not be redeemed any more.

21 But the field, when it goeth out in the jubile, shall be holy unto the Lord, as a field devoted; the possession thereof shall be the priest's.

22 And if *a man* sanctify unto the Lord a

field which he hath bought, which *is* not of the fields of his possession;

23 Then the priest shall reckon unto him the worth of thy estimation, *even* unto the year of the jubile: and he shall give thine estimation in that day, *as* a holy thing unto the LORD.

24 In the year of the jubile the field shall return unto him of whom it was bought, *even* to him to whom the possession of the land *did* belong.

25 And all thy estimations shall be according to the shekel of the sanctuary: twenty gerahs shall be the shekel.

26 ¶ Only the firstling of the beasts, which should be the LORD's firstling, no man shall sanctify it; whether *it be* ox, or sheep: it *is* the LORD's.

27 And if *it be* of an unclean beast, then he shall redeem *it* according to thine estimation, and shall add a fifth *part* of it thereto: or if it be not redeemed, then it shall be sold according to thy estimation.

28 Notwithstanding no devoted thing, that a man shall devote unto the LORD of all that he hath, *both* of man and beast, and of the field of his possession, shall be sold or redeemed: every devoted thing *is* most holy unto the LORD.

29 None devoted, which shall be devoted of men, shall be redeemed; *but* shall surely be put to death.

30 And all the tithe of the land, *whether* of the seed of the land, *or* of the fruit of the tree, *is* the LORD's: *it is* holy unto the LORD.

31 And if a man will at all redeem *ought* of his tithes, he shall add thereto the fifth *part* thereof.

32 And concerning the tithe of the herd, or of the flock, *even* of whatsoever passeth under the rod, the tenth shall be holy unto the LORD.

33 He shall not search whether it be good or bad, neither shall he change it: and if he change it at all, then both it and the change thereof shall be holy; it shall not be redeemed.

34 These *are* the commandments, which the LORD commanded Mo'ses for the children of Is'-ra-el in mount Si'nai.

THE FOURTH BOOK OF MOSES
COMMONLY CALLED

NUMBERS

1 AND the LORD spake unto Mo'ses in the wilderness of Si'nai, in the tabernacle of the congregation, on the first *day* of the second month, in the second year after they were come out of the land of E'gypt, saying,

2 Take ye the sum of all the congregation of the children of Is'ra-el, after their families, by the house of their fathers, with the number of *their* names, every male by their polls;

3 From twenty years old and upward, all that are able to go forth to war in Is'ra-el: thou and Aar'on shall number them by their armies.

4 And with you there shall be a man of every tribe; every one head of the house of his fathers.

5 ¶ And these *are* the names of the men that shall stand with you: of *the* tribe of Reu'ben; E-li'zur the son of Shed'e-ur.

6 Of Sim'e-on; She-lu'mi-el the son of Zu-ri-shad'da-i.

7 Of Ju'dah; Nah'shon the son of Am-min'a-dab.

8 Of Is'sa-char; Ne-than'e-el the son of Zu'ar.

9 Of Zeb'u-lun; E-li'ab the son of He'lon.

10 Of the children of Jo'seph: of E'phra-im; E-lish'a-ma the son of Am-mi'hud: of Ma-nas'-seh; Ga-ma'li-el the son of Pe-dah'zur.

11 Of Ben'ja-min; Ab'i-dan the son of Gid-e-o'ni.

12 Of Dan; A-hi-e'zer the son of Am-mi-shad'da-i.

13 Of Ash'er; Pa'gi-el the son of Oc'ran.

14 Of Gad; E-li'a-saph the son of Deu'el.

15 Of Naph'ta-li; A-hi'ra the son of E'nan.

16 These *were* the renowned of the congregation, princes of the tribes of their fathers, heads of thousands in Is'ra-el.

17 ¶ And Mo'ses and Aar'on took these men which are expressed by *their* names:

18 And they assembled all the congregation together on the first *day* of the second month, and they declared their pedigrees after their families, by the house of their fathers, according to the number of the names, from twenty years old and upward, by their polls.

19 As the LORD commanded Mo'ses, so he numbered them in the wilderness of Si'nai.

20 And the children of Reu'ben, Is'ra-el's eldest son, by their generations, after their families, by the house of their fathers, according to the number of the names, by their polls, every male from twenty years old and upward, all that were able to go forth to war;

21 Those that were numbered of them, *even* of the tribe of Reu'ben, *were* forty and six thousand and five hundred.

22 ¶ Of the children of Sim'e-on, by their generations, after their families, by the house of their fathers, those that were numbered of them, according to the number of the names, by their polls, every male from twenty years old and upward, all that were able to go forth to war;

23 Those that were numbered of them, *even* of the tribe of Sim'e-on, *were* fifty and nine thousand and three hundred.

24 ¶ Of the children of Gad, by their generations, after their families, by the house of their fathers, according to the number of the names, from twenty years old and upward, all that were able to go forth to war;

25 Those that were numbered of them, *even* of the tribe of Gad, *were* forty and five thousand six hundred and fifty.

26 ¶ Of the children of Ju'dah, by their generations, after their families, by the house of their fathers, according to the number of the names, from twenty years old and upward, all that were able to go forth to war;

27 Those that were numbered of them, *even* of the tribe of Ju'dah, *were* threescore and fourteen thousand and six hundred.

28 ¶ Of the children of Is'sa-char, by their generations, after their families, by the house of their fathers, according to the number of the names, from twenty years old and upward, all that were able to go forth to war;

29 Those that were numbered of them, *even* of the tribe of Is'sa-char, *were* fifty and four thousand and four hundred.

30 ¶ Of the children of Zeb'u-lun, by their generations, after their families, by the house of their fathers, according to the number of the names, from twenty years old and upward, all that were able to go forth to war;

31 Those that were numbered of them, *even* of the tribe of Zeb'u-lun, *were* fifty and seven thousand and four hundred.

32 ¶ Of the children of Jo'seph, *namely,* of the children of E'phra-im, by their generations, after their families, by the house of their fathers, according to the number of the names, from twenty years old and upward, all that were able to go forth to war;

33 Those that were numbered of them, *even* of the tribe of E'phra-im, *were* forty thousand and five hundred.

34 ¶ Of the children of Ma-nas'seh, by their generations, after their families, by the house of their fathers, according to the number of the names, from twenty years old and upward, all that were able to go forth to war;

35 Those that were numbered of them, *even* of the tribe of Ma-nas'seh, *were* thirty and two thousand and two hundred.

36 ¶ Of the children of Ben'ja-min, by their generations, after their families, by the house of their fathers, according to the number of the names, from twenty years old and upward, all that were able to go forth to war;

37 Those that were numbered of them, *even* of the tribe of Ben'ja-min, *were* thirty and five thousand and four hundred.

38 ¶ Of the children of Dan, by their generations, after their families, by the house of their fathers, according to the number of the names, from twenty years old and upward, all that were able to go forth to war;

39 Those that were numbered of them, *even* of the tribe of Dan, *were* threescore and two thousand and seven hundred.

40 ¶ Of the children of Ash'er, by their generations, after their families, by the house of their fathers, according to the number of the names, from twenty years old and upward, all that were able to go forth to war;

41 Those that were numbered of them, *even* of the tribe of Ash'er, *were* forty and one thousand and five hundred.

42 ¶ Of the children of Naph'ta-li, throughout their generations, after their families, by the house of their fathers, according to the number of the names, from twenty years old and upward, all that were able to go forth to war;

43 Those that were numbered of them, *even* of the tribe of Naph'ta-li, *were* fifty and three thousand and four hundred.

44 These *are* those that were numbered, which Mo'ses and Aar'on numbered, and the princes of Is'ra-el, *being* twelve men: each one was for the house of his fathers.

45 So were all those that were numbered of the children of Is'ra-el, by the house of their fathers, from twenty years old and upward, all that were able to go forth to war in Is'ra-el;

46 Even all they that were numbered were six hundred thousand and three thousand and five hundred and fifty.

47 ¶ But the Le'vites after the tribe of their fathers were not numbered among them.

48 For the LORD had spoken unto Mo'ses, saying,

49 Only thou shalt not number the tribe of Le'vi, neither take the sum of them among the children of Is'ra-el:

50 But thou shalt appoint the Le'vites over the tabernacle of testimony, and over all the vessels thereof, and over all things that *belong* to it: they shall bear the tabernacle, and all the vessels thereof; and they shall minister unto it, and shall encamp round about the tabernacle.

51 And when the tabernacle setteth forward, the Le'vites shall take it down: and when the tabernacle is to be pitched, the Le'vites shall set it up: and the stranger that cometh nigh shall be put to death.

52 And the children of Is'ra-el shall pitch their tents, every man by his own camp, and every man by his own standard, throughout their hosts.

53 But the Le'vites shall pitch round about the tabernacle of testimony, that there be no wrath upon the congregation of the children of Is'ra-el: and the Le'vites shall keep the charge of the tabernacle of testimony.

54 And the children of Is'ra-el did according to all that the LORD commanded Mo'ses, so did they.

2 AND the LORD spake unto Mo'ses and unto Aar'on, saying,

2 Every man of the children of Is'ra-el shall pitch by his own standard, with the ensign of their father's house: far off about the tabernacle of the congregation shall they pitch.

3 And on the east side toward the rising of the sun shall they of the standard of the camp of Ju'dah pitch throughout their armies: and Nah'shon the son of Am-min'a-dab *shall be* captain of the children of Ju'dah.

4 And his host, and those that were numbered of them, *were* threescore and fourteen thousand and six hundred.

5 And those that do pitch next unto him *shall be* the tribe of Is'sa-char: and Ne-than'e-el the son of Zu'ar *shall be* captain of the children of Is'sa-char.

6 And his host, and those that were numbered thereof, *were* fifty and four thousand and four hundred.

7 *Then* the tribe of Zeb'u-lun: and E-li'ab the son of He'lon *shall be* captain of the children of Zeb'u-lun.

8 And his host, and those that were numbered thereof, *were* fifty and seven thousand and four hundred.

9 All that were numbered in the camp of Ju'dah *were* an hundred thousand and fourscore thousand and six thousand and four hundred, throughout their armies. These shall first set forth.

10 ¶ On the south side *shall be* the standard of the camp of Reu'ben according to their armies: and the captain of the children of Reu'ben *shall be* E-li'zur the son of Shed'e-ur.

11 And his host, and those that were numbered thereof, *were* forty and six thousand and five hundred.

12 And those which pitch by him *shall be* the tribe of Sim'e-on: and the captain of the children of Sim'e-on *shall be* She-lu'mi-el the son of Zu-ri-shad'da-i.

13 And his host, and those that were numbered of them, *were* fifty and nine thousand and three hundred.

14 Then the tribe of Gad: and the captain of the sons of Gad *shall be* E-li'a-saph the son of Reu'el.

15 And his host, and those that were numbered of them, *were* forty and five thousand and six hundred and fifty.

16 All that were numbered in the camp of Reu'ben *were* an hundred thousand and fifty and one thousand and four hundred and fifty,

throughout their armies. And they shall set forth in the second rank.

17 ¶ Then the tabernacle of the congregation shall set forward with the camp of the Le'vites in the midst of the camp: as they encamp, so shall they set forward, every man in his place by their standards.

18 ¶ On the west side *shall be* the standard of the camp of E'phra-im according to their armies: and the captain of the sons of E'phra-im *shall be* E-lish'a-ma the son of Am-mi'hud.

19 And his host, and those that were numbered of them, *were* forty thousand and five hundred.

20 And by him *shall be* the tribe of Ma-nas'-seh: and the captain of the children of Ma-nas'-seh *shall be* Ga-ma'li-el the son of Pe-dah'zur.

21 And his host, and those that were numbered of them, *were* thirty and two thousand and two hundred.

22 Then the tribe of Ben'ja-min: and the captain of the sons of Ben'ja-min *shall be* Ab'i-dan the son of Gid-e-o'ni.

23 And his host, and those that were numbered of them, *were* thirty and five thousand and four hundred.

24 All that were numbered of the camp of E'phra-im *were* an hundred thousand and eight thousand and an hundred, throughout their armies. And they shall go forward in the third rank.

25 ¶ The standard of the camp of Dan *shall be* on the north side by their armies: and the captain of the children of Dan *shall be* A-hi-e'-zer the son of Am-mi-shad'da-i.

26 And his host, and those that were numbered of them, *were* threescore and two thousand and seven hundred.

27 And those that encamp by him *shall be* the tribe of Ash'er: and the captain of the children of Ash'er *shall be* Pa'gi-el the son of Oc'-ran.

28 And his host, and those that were numbered of them, *were* forty and one thousand and five hundred.

29 ¶ Then the tribe of Naph'ta-li: and the captain of the children of Naph'ta-li *shall be* A-hi'ra the son of E'nan.

30 And his host, and those that were numbered of them, *were* fifty and three thousand and four hundred.

31 All they that were numbered in the camp of Dan *were* an hundred thousand and fifty and seven thousand and six hundred. They shall go hindmost with their standards.

32 ¶ These *are* those which were numbered of the children of Is'ra-el by the house of their fathers: all those that were numbered of the camps throughout their hosts *were* six hundred thousand and three thousand and five hundred and fifty.

33 But the Le'vites were not numbered among the children of Is'ra-el; as the LORD commanded Mo'ses.

34 And the children of Is'ra-el did according to all that the LORD commanded Mo'ses: so they pitched by their standards, and so they set forward, every one after their families, according to the house of their fathers.

3 THESE also *are* the generations of Aar'on and Mo'ses in the day *that* the LORD spake with Mo'ses in mount Si'nai.

2 And these *are* the names of the sons of Aar'on; Na'dab the firstborn, and A-bi'hu, E-le-a'zar, and Ith'a-mar.

3 These *are* the names of the sons of Aar'on,

the priests which were anointed, whom he consecrated to minister in the priest's office.

4 And Na'dab and A-bi'hu died before the LORD, when they offered strange fire before the LORD, in the wilderness of Si'nai, and they had no children: and E-le-a'zar and Ith'a-mar ministered in the priest's office in the sight of Aar'on their father.

5 ¶ And the LORD spake unto Mo'ses, saying,

6 Bring the tribe of Le'vi near, and present them before Aar'on the priest, that they may minister unto him.

7 And they shall keep his charge, and the charge of the whole congregation before the tabernacle of the congregation, to do the service of the tabernacle.

8 And they shall keep all the instruments of the tabernacle of the congregation, and the charge of the children of Is'ra-el, to do the service of the tabernacle.

9 And thou shalt give the Le'vites unto Aar'-on and to his sons: they *are* wholly given unto him out of the children of Is'ra-el.

10 And thou shalt appoint Aar'on and his sons, and they shall wait on their priest's office: and the stranger that cometh nigh shall be put to death.

11 And the LORD spake unto Mo'ses, saying,

12 And I, behold, I have taken the Le'vites from among the children of Is'ra-el instead of all the firstborn that openeth the matrix among the children of Is'ra-el: therefore the Le'vites shall be mine;

13 Because all the firstborn *are* mine; *for* on the day that I smote all the firstborn in the land of E'gypt I hallowed unto me all the firstborn in Is'ra-el, both man and beast: mine shall they be: I *am* the LORD.

14 ¶ And the LORD spake unto Mo'ses in the wilderness of Si'nai, saying,

15 Number the children of Le'vi after the house of their fathers, by their families: every male from a month old and upward shalt thou number them.

16 And Mo'ses numbered them according to the word of the LORD, as he was commanded.

17 And these were the sons of Le'vi by their names; Ger'shon, and Ko'hath, and Me-ra'ri.

18 And these *are* the names of the sons of Ger'shon by their families; Lib'ni, and Shim'e-i.

19 And the sons of Ko'hath by their families; Am'ram, and Iz'e-har, and He'bron, and Uz'zi-el.

20 And the sons of Me-ra'ri by their families; Mah'li, and Mu'shi. These *are* the families of the Le'vites according to the house of their fathers.

21 Of Ger'shon *was* the family of the Lib'-nites, and the family of the Shim'ites: these *are* the families of the Ger'shon-ites.

22 Those that were numbered of them, according to the number of all the males, from a month old and upward, *even* those that were numbered of them *were* seven thousand and five hundred.

23 The families of the Ger'shon-ites shall pitch behind the tabernacle westward.

24 And the chief of the house of the father of the Ger'shon-ites *shall be* E-li'a-saph the son of La'el.

25 And the charge of the sons of Ger'shon in the tabernacle of the congregation *shall be* the tabernacle, and the tent, the covering thereof, and the hanging for the door of the tabernacle of the congregation,

26 And the hangings of the court, and the curtain for the door of the court, which *is* by the tabernacle, and by the altar round about, and the cords of it for all the service thereof.

27 ¶ And of Ko'hath was the family of the Am'ram-ites, and the family of the Iz'e-har-ites, and the family of the He'bron-ites, and the family of the Uz'zi-el-ites: these are the families of the Ko'hath-ites.

28 In the number of all the males, from a month old and upward, were eight thousand and six hundred, keeping the charge of the sanctuary.

29 The families of the sons of Ko'hath shall pitch on the side of the tabernacle southward.

30 And the chief of the house of the father of the families of the Ko'hath-ites shall be E-liz'a-phan the son of Uz'zi-el.

31 And their charge shall be the ark, and the table, and the candlestick, and the altars, and the vessels of the sanctuary wherewith they minister, and the hanging, and all the service thereof.

32 And E-le-a'zar the son of Aar'on the priest shall be chief over the chief of the Le'vites, and have the oversight of them that keep the charge of the sanctuary.

33 ¶ Of Me-ra'ri was the family of the Mah'-lites, and the family of the Mu'shites: these are the families of Me-ra'ri.

34 And those that were numbered of them, according to the number of all the males, from a month old and upward, were six thousand and two hundred.

35 And the chief of the house of the father of the families of Me-ra'ri was Zu'ri-el the son of Ab-i-ha'il: these shall pitch on the side of the tabernacle northward.

36 And under the custody and charge of the sons of Me-ra'ri shall be the boards of the tabernacle, and the bars thereof, and the pillars thereof, and the sockets thereof, and all the vessels thereof, and all that serveth thereto,

37 And the pillars of the court round about, and their sockets, and their pins, and their cords.

38 ¶ But those that encamp before the tabernacle toward the east, even before the tabernacle of the congregation eastward, shall be Mo'-ses, and Aar'on and his sons, keeping the charge of the sanctuary for the charge of the children of Is'ra-el; and the stranger that cometh nigh shall be put to death.

39 All that were numbered of the Le'vites, which Mo'ses and Aar'on numbered at the commandment of the LORD, throughout their families, all the males from a month old and upward, were twenty and two thousand.

40 ¶ And the LORD said unto Mo'ses, Number all the firstborn of the males of the children of Is'ra-el from a month old and upward, and take the number of their names.

41 And thou shalt take the Le'vites for me (I am the LORD) instead of all the firstborn among the children of Is'ra-el; and the cattle of the Le'-vites instead of all the firstlings among the cattle of the children of Is'ra-el.

42 And Mo'ses numbered, as the LORD commanded him, all the firstborn among the children of Is'ra-el.

43 And all the firstborn males by the number of names, from a month old and upward, of those that were numbered of them, were twenty and two thousand two hundred and threescore and thirteen.

44 ¶ And the LORD spake unto Mo'ses, saying,

45 Take the Le'vites instead of all the firstborn among the children of Is'ra-el, and the cattle of the Le'vites instead of their cattle; and the Le'vites shall be mine: I am the LORD.

46 And for those that are to be redeemed of the two hundred and threescore and thirteen of the firstborn of the children of Is'ra-el, which are more than the Le'vites;

47 Thou shalt even take five shekels apiece by the poll, after the shekel of the sanctuary shalt thou take them: (the shekel is twenty gerahs:)

48 And thou shalt give the money, wherewith the odd number of them is to be redeemed, unto Aar'on and to his sons.

49 And Mo'ses took the redemption money of them that were over and above them that were redeemed by the Le'vites:

50 Of the firstborn of the children of Is'ra-el took he the money; a thousand three hundred and threescore and five shekels, after the shekel of the sanctuary:

51 And Mo'ses gave the money of them that were redeemed unto Aar'on and to his sons, according to the word of the LORD, as the LORD commanded Mo'ses.

4 AND the LORD spake unto Mo'ses and unto Aar'on, saying,

2 Take the sum of the sons of Ko'hath from among the sons of Le'vi, after their families, by the house of their fathers,

3 From thirty years old and upward even until fifty years old, all that enter into the host, to do the work in the tabernacle of the congregation.

4 This shall be the service of the sons of Ko'-hath in the tabernacle of the congregation, about the most holy things:

5 ¶ And when the camp setteth forward, Aar'on shall come, and his sons, and they shall take down the covering veil, and cover the ark of testimony with it:

6 And shall put thereon the covering of badgers' skins, and shall spread over it a cloth wholly of blue, and shall put in the staves thereof.

7 And upon the table of shewbread they shall spread a cloth of blue, and put thereon the dishes, and the spoons, and the bowls, and covers to cover withal: and the continual bread shall be thereon:

8 And they shall spread upon them a cloth of scarlet, and cover the same with a covering of badgers' skins, and shall put in the staves thereof.

9 And they shall take a cloth of blue, and cover the candlestick of the light, and his lamps, and his tongs, and his snuffdishes, and all the oil vessels thereof, wherewith they minister unto it:

10 And they shall put it and all the vessels thereof within a covering of badgers' skins, and shall put it upon a bar.

11 And upon the golden altar they shall spread a cloth of blue, and cover it with a covering of badgers' skins, and shall put to the staves thereof:

12 And they shall take all the instruments of ministry, wherewith they minister in the sanctuary, and put them in a cloth of blue, and cover them with a covering of badgers' skins, and shall put them on a bar:

13 And they shall take away the ashes from the altar, and spread a purple cloth thereon:

14 And they shall put upon it all the vessels thereof, wherewith they minister about it, even the censers, the fleshhooks, and the shovels, and the basons, all the vessels of the altar; and they shall spread upon it a covering of badgers' skins, and put to the staves of it.

15 And when Aar'on and his sons have made an end of covering the sanctuary, and all the vessels of the sanctuary, as the camp is to set forward; after that, the sons of Ko'hath shall come to bear it: but they shall not touch any holy thing, lest they die. These things are the burden of the sons of Ko'hath in the tabernacle of the congregation.

16 ¶ And to the office of E-le-a'zar the son of Aar'on the priest pertaineth the oil for the light, and the sweet incense, and the daily meat offering, and the anointing oil, and the oversight of all the tabernacle, and of all that therein is, in the sanctuary, and in the vessels thereof.

17 ¶ And the LORD spake unto Mo'ses and unto Aar'on, saying,

18 Cut ye not off the tribe of the families of the Ko'hath-ites from among the Le'vites:

19 But thus do unto them, that they may live, and not die, when they approach unto the most holy things: Aar'on and his sons shall go in, and appoint them every one to his service and to his burden:

20 But they shall not go in to see when the holy things are covered, lest they die.

21 ¶ And the LORD spake unto Mo'ses, saying,

22 Take also the sum of the sons of Ger'shon, throughout the houses of their fathers, by their families;

23 From thirty years old and upward until fifty years old shalt thou number them; all that enter in to perform the service, to do the work in the tabernacle of the congregation.

24 This is the service of the families of the Ger'shon-ites, to serve, and for burdens:

25 And they shall bear the curtains of the tabernacle, and the tabernacle of the congregation, his covering, and the covering of the badgers' skins that is above upon it, and the hanging for the door of the tabernacle of the congregation,

26 And the hangings of the court, and the hanging for the door of the gate of the court, which is by the tabernacle and by the altar round about, and their cords, and all the instruments of their service, and all that is made for them: so shall they serve.

27 At the appointment of Aar'on and his sons shall be all the service of the sons of the Ger'shon-ites, in all their burdens, and in all their service: and ye shall appoint unto them in charge all their burdens.

28 This is the service of the families of the sons of Ger'shon in the tabernacle of the congregation: and their charge shall be under the hand of Ith'a-mar the son of Aar'on the priest.

29 ¶ As for the sons of Me-ra'ri, thou shalt number them after their families, by the house of their fathers;

30 From thirty years old and upward even unto fifty years old shalt thou number them, every one that entereth into the service, to do the work of the tabernacle of the congregation.

31 And this is the charge of their burden, according to all their service in the tabernacle of the congregation; the boards of the tabernacle, and the bars thereof, and the pillars thereof, and sockets thereof,

32 And the pillars of the court round about, and their sockets, and their pins, and their cords, with all their instruments, and with all their service: and by name ye shall reckon the instruments of the charge of their burden.

33 This is the service of the families of the sons of Me-ra'ri, according to all their service, in the tabernacle of the congregation, under the hand of Ith'a-mar the son of Aar'on the priest.

34 ¶ And Mo'ses and Aar'on and the chief of the congregation numbered the sons of the Ko'hath-ites after their families, and after the house of their fathers,

35 From thirty years old and upward even unto fifty years old, every one that entereth into the service, for the work in the tabernacle of the congregation:

36 And those that were numbered of them by their families were two thousand seven hundred and fifty

37 These were they that were numbered of the families of the Ko'hath-ites, all that might do service in the tabernacle of the congregation, which Mo'ses and Aar'on did number according to the commandment of the LORD by the hand of Mo'ses.

38 And those that were numbered of the sons of Ger'shon, throughout their families, and by the house of their fathers,

39 From thirty years old and upward even unto fifty years old, every one that entereth into the service, for the work in the tabernacle of the congregation,

40 Even those that were numbered of them, throughout their families, by the house of their fathers, were two thousand and six hundred and thirty.

41 These are they that were numbered of the families of the sons of Ger'shon, of all that might do service in the tabernacle of the congregation, whom Mo'ses and Aar'on did number according to the commandment of the LORD.

42 ¶ And those that were numbered of the families of the sons of Me-ra'ri, throughout their families, by the house of their fathers,

43 From thirty years old and upward even unto fifty years old, every one that entereth into the service, for the work in the tabernacle of the congregation,

44 Even those that were numbered of them after their families, were three thousand and two hundred.

45 These be those that were numbered of the families of the sons of Me-ra'ri, whom Mo'ses and Aar'on numbered according to the word of the LORD by the hand of Mo'ses.

46 All those that were numbered of the Le'vites, whom Mo'ses and Aar'on and the chief of Is'ra-el numbered, after their families, and after the house of their fathers,

47 From thirty years old and upward even unto fifty years old, every one that came to do the service of the ministry, and the service of the burden in the tabernacle of the congregation,

48 Even those that were numbered of them, were eight thousand and five hundred and fourscore.

49 According to the commandment of the LORD they were numbered by the hand of Mo'ses, every one according to his service, and according to his burden: thus were they numbered of him, as the LORD commanded Mo'ses.

5 AND the LORD spake unto Mo'ses, saying,

2 Command the children of Is'ra-el, that they put out of the camp every leper, and every one that hath an issue, and whosoever is defiled by the dead:

3 Both male and female shall ye put out, without the camp shall ye put them; that they defile not their camps, in the midst whereof I dwell.

4 And the children of Is'ra-el did so, and put

them out without the camp: as the LORD spake unto Mo'ses, so did the children of Is'ra-el.

5 ¶ And the LORD spake unto Mo'ses, saying,

6 Speak unto the children of Is'ra-el, When a man or woman shall commit any sin that men commit, to do a trespass against the LORD, and that person be guilty;

7 Then they shall confess their sin which they have done: and he shall recompense his trespass with the principal thereof, and add unto it the fifth *part* thereof, and give *it* unto *him* against whom he hath trespassed.

8 But if the man have no kinsman to recompense the trespass unto, let the trespass be recompensed unto the LORD, *even* to the priest; beside the ram of the atonement, whereby an atonement shall be made for him.

9 And every offering of all the holy things of the children of Is'ra-el, which they bring unto the priest, shall be his.

10 And every man's hallowed things shall be his: whatsoever any man giveth the priest, it shall be his.

11 ¶ And the LORD spake unto Mo'ses, saying,

12 Speak unto the children of Is'ra-el, and say unto them, If any man's wife go aside, and commit a trespass against him,

13 And a man lie with her carnally, and it be hid from the eyes of her husband, and be kept close, and she be defiled, and *there be* no witness against her, neither she be taken *with the manner;*

14 And the spirit of jealousy come upon him, and he be jealous of his wife, and she be defiled: or if the spirit of jealousy come upon him, and he be jealous of his wife, and she be not defiled:

15 Then shall the man bring his wife unto the priest, and he shall bring her offering for her, the tenth *part* of an ephah of barley meal; he shall pour no oil upon it, nor put frankincense thereon; for it *is* an offering of jealousy, an offering of memorial, bringing iniquity to remembrance.

16 And the priest shall bring her near, and set her before the LORD:

17 And the priest shall take holy water in an earthen vessel; and of the dust that is in the floor of the tabernacle the priest shall take, and put *it* into the water:

18 And the priest shall set the woman before the LORD, and uncover the woman's head, and put the offering of memorial in her hands, which *is* the jealousy offering: and the priest shall have in his hand the bitter water that causeth the curse:

19 And the priest shall charge her by an oath, and say unto the woman, If no man have lain with thee, and if thou hast not gone aside to uncleanness *with another* instead of thy husband, be thou free from this bitter water that causeth the curse:

20 But if thou hast gone aside *to another* instead of thy husband, and if thou be defiled, and some man have lain with thee beside thine husband:

21 Then the priest shall charge the woman with an oath of cursing, and the priest shall say unto the woman, The LORD make thee a curse and an oath among thy people, when the LORD doth make thy thigh to rot, and thy belly to swell;

22 And this water that causeth the curse shall go into thy bowels, to make *thy* belly to swell, and *thy* thigh to rot: And the woman shall say, Amen, amen.

23 And the priest shall write these curses in a book, and he shall blot *them* out with the bitter water:

24 And he shall cause the woman to drink the bitter water that causeth the curse: and the water that causeth the curse shall enter into her, *and become* bitter.

25 Then the priest shall take the jealousy offering out of the woman's hand, and shall wave the offering before the LORD, and offer it upon the altar:

26 And the priest shall take an handful of the offering, *even* the memorial thereof, and burn *it* upon the altar, and afterward shall cause the woman to drink the water.

27 And when he hath made her to drink the water, then it shall come to pass, *that,* if she be defiled, and have done trespass against her husband, that the water that causeth the curse shall enter into her, *and become* bitter, and her belly shall swell, and her thigh shall rot: and the woman shall be a curse among her people.

28 And if the woman be not defiled, but be clean; then she shall be free, and shall conceive seed.

29 This *is* the law of jealousies, when a wife goeth aside *to another* instead of her husband, and is defiled;

30 Or when the spirit of jealousy cometh upon him, and he be jealous over his wife, and shall set the woman before the LORD, and the priest shall execute upon her all this law.

31 Then shall the man be guiltless from iniquity, and this woman shall bear her iniquity.

6 AND the LORD spake unto Mo'ses, saying,

2 Speak unto the children of Is'ra-el, and say unto them, When either man or woman shall separate *themselves* to vow a vow of a Naz'a-rite, to separate *themselves* unto the LORD:

3 He shall separate *himself* from wine and strong drink, and shall drink no vinegar of wine, or vinegar of strong drink, neither shall he drink any liquor of grapes, nor eat moist grapes, or dried.

4 All the days of his separation shall he eat nothing that is made of the vine tree, from the kernels even to the husk.

5 All the days of the vow of his separation there shall no razor come upon his head: until the days be fulfilled, in the which he separateth *himself* unto the LORD, he shall be holy, *and* shall let the locks of the hair of his head grow.

6 All the days that he separateth *himself* unto the LORD he shall come at no dead body.

7 He shall not make himself unclean for his father, or for his mother, for his brother, or for his sister, when they die: because the consecration of his God *is* upon his head.

8 All the days of his separation he *is* holy unto the LORD.

9 And if any man die very suddenly by him, and he hath defiled the head of his consecration; then he shall shave his head in the day of his cleansing, on the seventh day shall he shave it.

10 And on the eighth day he shall bring two turtles, or two young pigeons, to the priest, to the door of the tabernacle of the congregation:

11 And the priest shall offer the one for a sin offering, and the other for a burnt offering, and make an atonement for him, for that he sinned by the dead, and shall hallow his head that same day.

12 And he shall consecrate unto the LORD the days of his separation, and shall bring a lamb of the first year for a trespass offering: but the

days that were before shall be lost, because his separation was defiled.

13 ¶ And this is the law of the Naz'a-rite, when the days of his separation are fulfilled: he shall be brought unto the door of the tabernacle of the congregation:

14 And he shall offer his offering unto the LORD, one lamb of the first year without blemish for a burnt offering, and one ewe lamb of the first year without blemish for a sin offering, and one ram without blemish for peace offerings,

15 And a basket of unleavened bread, cakes of fine flour mingled with oil, and wafers of unleavened bread anointed with oil, and their meat offering, and their drink offerings.

16 And the priest shall bring them before the LORD, and shall offer his sin offering, and his burnt offering:

17 And he shall offer the ram for a sacrifice of peace offerings unto the LORD, with the basket of unleavened bread: the priest shall offer also his meat offering, and his drink offering.

18 And the Naz'a-rite shall shave the head of his separation at the door of the tabernacle of the congregation, and shall take the hair of the head of his separation, and put it in the fire which is under the sacrifice of the peace offerings.

19 And the priest shall take the sodden shoulder of the ram, and one unleavened cake out of the basket, and one unleavened wafer, and shall put them upon the hands of the Naz'a-rite, after the hair of his separation is shaven:

20 And the priest shall wave them for a wave offering before the LORD: this is holy for the priest, with the wave breast and heave shoulder: and after that the Naz'a-rite may drink wine.

21 This is the law of the Naz'a-rite who hath vowed, and of his offering unto the LORD for his separation, beside that that his hand shall get: according to the vow which he vowed, so he must do after the law of his separation.

22 ¶ And the LORD spake unto Mo'ses, saying,

23 Speak unto Aar'on and unto his sons, saying, On this wise ye shall bless the children of Is'ra-el, saying unto them,

24 The LORD bless thee, and keep thee:

25 The LORD make his face shine upon thee, and be gracious unto thee:

26 The LORD lift up his countenance upon thee, and give thee peace.

27 And they shall put my name upon the children of Is'ra-el; and I will bless them.

7 AND it came to pass on the day that Mo'ses had fully set up the tabernacle, and had anointed it, and sanctified it, and all the instruments thereof, both the altar and all the vessels thereof, and had anointed them, and sanctified them;

2 That the princes of Is'ra-el, heads of the house of their fathers, who were the princes of the tribes, and were over them that were numbered, offered:

3 And they brought their offering before the LORD, six covered wagons, and twelve oxen; a wagon for two of the princes, and for each one an ox: and they brought them before the tabernacle.

4 And the LORD spake unto Mo'ses, saying,

5 Take it of them, that they may be to do the service of the tabernacle of the congregation; and thou shalt give them unto the Le'vites, to every man according to his service.

6 And Mo'ses took the wagons and the oxen, and gave them unto the Le'vites.

7 Two wagons and four oxen he gave unto the sons of Ger'shon, according to their service:

8 And four wagons and eight oxen he gave unto the sons of Me-ra'ri, according unto their service, under the hand of Ith'a-mar the son of Aar'on the priest.

9 But unto the sons of Ko'hath he gave none: because the service of the sanctuary belonging unto them was that they should bear upon their shoulders.

10 ¶ And the princes offered for dedicating of the altar in the day that it was anointed, even the princes offered their offering before the altar.

11 And the LORD said unto Mo'ses, They shall offer their offering, each prince on his day, for the dedicating of the altar.

12 ¶ And he that offered his offering the first day was Nah'shon the son of Am-min'a-dab, of the tribe of Ju'dah:

13 And his offering was one silver charger, the weight thereof was an hundred and thirty shekels, one silver bowl of seventy shekels, after the shekel of the sanctuary; both of them were full of fine flour mingled with oil for a meat offering:

14 One spoon of ten shekels of gold, full of incense:

15 One young bullock, one ram, one lamb of the first year, for a burnt offering:

16 One kid of the goats for a sin offering:

17 And for a sacrifice of peace offerings, two oxen, five rams, five he goats, five lambs of the first year: this was the offering of Nah'shon the son of Am-min'a-dab.

18 ¶ On the second day Ne-than'e-el the son of Zu'ar, prince of Is'sa-char, did offer:

19 He offered for his offering one silver charger, the weight whereof was an hundred and thirty shekels, one silver bowl of seventy shekels, after the shekel of the sanctuary; both of them full of fine flour mingled with oil for a meat offering:

20 One spoon of gold of ten shekels, full of incense:

21 One young bullock, one ram, one lamb of the first year, for a burnt offering:

22 One kid of the goats for a sin offering:

23 And for a sacrifice of peace offerings, two oxen, five rams, five he goats, five lambs of the first year: this was the offering of Ne-than'e-el the son of Zu'ar.

24 ¶ On the third day E-li'ab the son of He'lon, prince of the children of Zeb'u-lun, did offer:

25 His offering was one silver charger, the weight whereof was an hundred and thirty shekels, one silver bowl of seventy shekels, after the shekel of the sanctuary; both of them full of fine flour mingled with oil for a meat offering:

26 One golden spoon of ten shekels, full of incense:

27 One young bullock, one ram, one lamb of the first year, for a burnt offering:

28 One kid of the goats for a sin offering:

29 And for a sacrifice of peace offerings, two oxen, five rams, five he goats, five lambs of the first year: this was the offering of E-li'ab the son of He'lon.

30 ¶ On the fourth day E-li'zur the son of Shed'e-ur, prince of the children of Reu'ben, did offer:

31 His offering was one silver charger of the weight of an hundred and thirty shekels, one

silver bowl of seventy shekels, after the shekel of the sanctuary; both of them full of fine flour mingled with oil for a meat offering:

32 One golden spoon of ten *shekels,* full of incense:

33 One young bullock, one ram, one lamb of the first year, for a burnt offering:

34 One kid of the goats for a sin offering:

35 And for a sacrifice of peace offerings, two oxen, five rams, five he goats, five lambs of the first year: this *was* the offering of E-li'zur the son of Shed'e-ur.

36 ¶ On the fifth day She-lu'mi-el the son of Zu-ri-shad'da-i, prince of the children of Sim'e-on, *did offer:*

37 His offering *was* one silver charger, the weight whereof *was* an hundred and thirty *shekels,* one silver bowl of seventy shekels, after the shekel of the sanctuary; both of them full of fine flour mingled with oil for a meat offering:

38 One golden spoon of ten *shekels,* full of incense:

39 One young bullock, one ram, one lamb of the first year, for a burnt offering:

40 One kid of the goats for a sin offering:

41 And for a sacrifice of peace offerings, two oxen, five rams, five he goats, five lambs of the first year: this *was* the offering of She-lu'mi-el the son of Zu-ri-shad'da-i.

42 ¶ On the sixth day E-li'a-saph the son of Deu'el, prince of the children of Gad, *offered:*

43 His offering *was* one silver charger of the weight of an hundred and thirty *shekels,* a silver bowl of seventy shekels, after the shekel of the sanctuary; both of them full of fine flour mingled with oil for a meat offering:

44 One golden spoon of ten *shekels,* full of incense:

45 One young bullock, one ram, one lamb of the first year, for a burnt offering:

46 One kid of the goats for a sin offering:

47 And for a sacrifice of peace offerings, two oxen, five rams, five he goats, five lambs of the first year: this *was* the offering of E-li'a-saph the son of Deu'el.

48 ¶ On the seventh day E-lish'a-ma the son of Am-mi'hud, prince of the children of E'phra-im, *offered:*

49 His offering *was* one silver charger, the weight whereof *was* an hundred and thirty *shekels,* one silver bowl of seventy shekels, after the shekel of the sanctuary; both of them full of fine flour mingled with oil for a meat offering:

50 One golden spoon of ten *shekels,* full of incense:

51 One young bullock, one ram, one lamb of the first year, for a burnt offering:

52 One kid of the goats for a sin offering:

53 And for a sacrifice of peace offerings, two oxen, five rams, five he goats, five lambs of the first year: this *was* the offering of E-lish'a-ma the son of Am-mi'hud.

54 ¶ On the eighth day *offered* Ga-ma'li-el the son of Pe-dah'zur, prince of the children of Ma-nas'seh:

55 His offering *was* one silver charger of the weight of an hundred and thirty *shekels,* one silver bowl of seventy shekels, after the shekel of the sanctuary; both of them full of fine flour mingled with oil for a meat offering:

56 One golden spoon of ten *shekels,* full of incense:

57 One young bullock, one ram, one lamb of the first year, for a burnt offering:

58 One kid of the goats for a sin offering:

59 And for a sacrifice of peace offerings, two oxen, five rams, five he goats, five lambs of the first year: this *was* the offering of Ga-ma'li-el the son of Pe-dah'zur.

60 ¶ On the ninth day Ab'i-dan the son of Gid-e-o'ni, prince of the children of Ben'ja-min, *offered:*

61 His offering *was* one silver charger, the weight whereof *was* an hundred and thirty *shekels,* one silver bowl of seventy shekels, after the shekel of the sanctuary; both of them full of fine flour mingled with oil for a meat offering:

62 One golden spoon of ten *shekels,* full of incense:

63 One young bullock, one ram, one lamb of the first year, for a burnt offering:

64 One kid of the goats for a sin offering:

65 And for a sacrifice of peace offerings, two oxen, five rams, five he goats, five lambs of the first year: this *was* the offering of Ab'i-dan the son of Gid-e-o'ni.

66 ¶ On the tenth day A-hi-e'zer the son of Am-mi-shad'da-i, prince of the children of Dan, *offered:*

67 His offering *was* one silver charger, the weight whereof *was* an hundred and thirty *shekels,* one silver bowl of seventy shekels, after the shekel of the sanctuary; both of them full of fine flour mingled with oil for a meat offering:

68 One golden spoon of ten *shekels,* full of incense:

69 One young bullock, one ram, one lamb of the first year, for a burnt offering:

70 One kid of the goats for a sin offering:

71 And for a sacrifice of peace offerings, two oxen, five rams, five he goats, five lambs of the first year: this *was* the offering of A-hi-e'zer the son of Am-mi-shad'da-i.

72 ¶ On the eleventh day Pa'gi-el the son of Oc'ran, prince of the children of Ash'er, *offered:*

73 His offering *was* one silver charger, the weight whereof *was* an hundred and thirty *shekels,* one silver bowl of seventy shekels, after the shekel of the sanctuary; both of them full of fine flour mingled with oil for a meat offering:

74 One golden spoon of ten *shekels,* full of incense:

75 One young bullock, one ram, one lamb of the first year, for a burnt offering:

76 One kid of the goats for a sin offering:

77 And for a sacrifice of peace offerings, two oxen, five rams, five he goats, five lambs of the first year: this *was* the offering of Pa'gi-el the son of Oc'ran.

78 ¶ On the twelfth day A-hi'ra the son of E'nan, prince of the children of Naph'ta-li, *offered:*

79 His offering *was* one silver charger, the weight whereof *was* an hundred and thirty *shekels,* one silver bowl of seventy shekels, after the shekel of the sanctuary; both of them full of fine flour mingled with oil for a meat offering:

80 One golden spoon of ten *shekels,* full of incense:

81 One young bullock, one ram, one lamb of the first year, for a burnt offering:

82 One kid of the goats for a sin offering:

83 And for a sacrifice of peace offerings, two oxen, five rams, five he goats, five lambs of the first year: this *was* the offering of A-hi'ra the son of E'nan.

84 This *was* the dedication of the altar, in the day when it was anointed, by the princes of Is'-

ra-el: twelve chargers of silver, twelve silver bowls, twelve spoons of gold:

85 Each charger of silver *weighing* an hundred and thirty *shekels*, each bowl seventy: all the silver vessels *weighed* two thousand and four hundred *shekels*, after the shekel of the sanctuary:

86 The golden spoons *were* twelve, full of incense, *weighing* ten *shekels* apiece, after the shekel of the sanctuary: all the gold of the spoons *was* an hundred and twenty *shekels*.

87 All the oxen for the burnt offering *were* twelve bullocks, the rams twelve, the lambs of the first year twelve, with their meat offering: and the kids of the goats for sin offering twelve.

88 And all the oxen for the sacrifice of the peace offerings *were* twenty and four bullocks, the rams sixty, the he goats sixty, the lambs of the first year sixty. This *was* the dedication of the altar, after that it was anointed.

89 And when Mo'ses was gone into the tabernacle of the congregation to speak with him, then he heard the voice of one speaking unto him from off the mercy seat that *was* upon the ark of testimony, from between the two cherubims: and he spake unto him.

8 AND the LORD spake unto Mo'ses, saying,
2 Speak unto Aar'on, and say unto him, When thou lightest the lamps, the seven lamps shall give light over against the candlestick.

3 And Aar'on did so; he lighted the lamps thereof over against the candlestick, as the LORD commanded Mo'ses.

4 And this work of the candlestick *was of* beaten gold, unto the shaft thereof, unto the flowers thereof, *was* beaten work: according unto the pattern which the LORD had shewed Mo'ses, so he made the candlestick.

5 ¶ And the LORD spake unto Mo'ses, saying,
6 Take the Le'vites from among the children of Is'ra-el, and cleanse them.

7 And thus shalt thou do unto them, to cleanse them: Sprinkle water of purifying upon them, and let them shave all their flesh, and let them wash their clothes, and *so* make themselves clean.

8 Then let them take a young bullock with his meat offering, *even* fine flour mingled with oil, and another young bullock shalt thou take for a sin offering.

9 And thou shalt bring the Le'vites before the tabernacle of the congregation: and thou shalt gather the whole assembly of the children of Is'ra-el together:

10 And thou shalt bring the Le'vites before the LORD: and the children of Is'ra-el shall put their hands upon the Le'vites:

11 And Aar'on shall offer the Le'vites before the LORD for an offering of the children of Is'ra-el, that they may execute the service of the LORD.

12 And the Le'vites shall lay their hands upon the heads of the bullocks: and thou shalt offer the one *for* a sin offering, and the other *for* a burnt offering, unto the LORD, to make an atonement for the Le'vites.

13 And thou shalt set the Le'vites before Aar'on, and before his sons, and offer them *for* an offering unto the LORD.

14 Thus shalt thou separate the Le'vites from among the children of Is'ra-el: and the Le'vites shall be mine.

15 And after that shall the Le'vites go in to do the service of the tabernacle of the congregation: and thou shalt cleanse them, and offer them *for* an offering.

16 For they *are* wholly given unto me from among the children of Is'ra-el; instead of such as open every womb, *even instead of* the firstborn of all the children of Is'ra-el, have I taken them unto me.

17 For all the firstborn of the children of Is'ra-el *are* mine, *both* man and beast: on the day that I smote every firstborn in the land of E'gypt I sanctified them for myself.

18 And I have taken the Le'vites for all the firstborn of the children of Is'ra-el.

19 And I have given the Le'vites *as* a gift to Aar'on and to his sons from among the children of Is'ra-el, to do the service of the children of Is'ra-el in the tabernacle of the congregation, and to make an atonement for the children of Is'ra-el: that there be no plague among the children of Is'ra-el, when the children of Is'ra-el come nigh unto the sanctuary.

20 And Mo'ses, and Aar'on, and all the congregation of the children of Is'ra-el, did to the Le'vites according unto all that the LORD commanded Mo'ses concerning the Le'vites, so did the children of Is'ra-el unto them.

21 And the Le'vites were purified, and they washed their clothes; and Aar'on offered them *as* an offering before the LORD; and Aar'on made an atonement for them to cleanse them.

22 And after that went the Le'vites in to do their service in the tabernacle of the congregation before Aar'on, and before his sons: as the LORD had commanded Mo'ses concerning the Le'vites, so did they unto them.

23 ¶ And the LORD spake unto Mo'ses, saying,

24 This *is it that* belongeth unto the Le'vites: from twenty and five years old and upward they shall go in to wait upon the service of the tabernacle of the congregation:

25 And from the age of fifty years they shall cease waiting upon the service *thereof*, and shall serve no more:

26 But shall minister with their brethren in the tabernacle of the congregation, to keep the charge, and shall do no service. Thus shalt thou do unto the Le'vites touching their charge.

9 AND the LORD spake unto Mo'ses in the wilderness of Si'nai, in the first month of the second year after they were come out of the land of E'gypt, saying,

2 Let the children of Is'ra-el also keep the passover at his appointed season.

3 In the fourteenth day of this month, at even, ye shall keep it in his appointed season: according to all the rites of it, and according to all the ceremonies thereof, shall ye keep it.

4 And Mo'ses spake unto the children of Is'ra-el, that they should keep the passover.

5 And they kept the passover on the fourteenth day of the first month at even in the wilderness of Si'nai: according to all that the LORD commanded Mo'ses, so did the children of Is'ra-el.

6 ¶ And there were certain men, who were defiled by the dead body of a man, that they could not keep the passover on that day: and they came before Mo'ses and before Aar'on on that day:

7 And those men said unto him, We *are* defiled by the dead body of a man: wherefore are we kept back, that we may not offer an offering of the LORD in his appointed season among the children of Is'ra-el?

8 And Mo'ses said unto them, Stand still, and I will hear what the LORD will command concerning you.

9 ¶ And the LORD spake unto Mo'ses, saying,

10 Speak unto the children of Is'ra-el, saying, If any man of you or of your posterity shall be unclean by reason of a dead body, or be in a journey afar off, yet he shall keep the passover unto the LORD.

11 The fourteenth day of the second month at even they shall keep it, and eat it with unleavened bread and bitter herbs.

12 They shall leave none of it unto the morning, nor break any bone of it: according to all the ordinances of the passover they shall keep it.

13 But the man that is clean, and is not in a journey, and forbeareth to keep the passover, even the same soul shall be cut off from among his people: because he brought not the offering of the LORD in his appointed season, that man shall bear his sin.

14 And if a stranger shall sojourn among you, and will keep the passover unto the LORD; according to the ordinance of the passover, and according to the manner thereof, so shall he do: ye shall have one ordinance, both for the stranger, and for him that was born in the land.

15 ¶ And on the day that the tabernacle was reared up the cloud covered the tabernacle, namely, the tent of the testimony: and at even there was upon the tabernacle as it were the appearance of fire, until the morning.

16 So it was alway: the cloud covered it by day, and the appearance of fire by night.

17 And when the cloud was taken up from the tabernacle, then after that the children of Is'ra-el journeyed: and in the place where the cloud abode, there the children of Is'ra-el pitched their tents.

18 At the commandment of the LORD the children of Is'ra-el journeyed, and at the commandment of the LORD they pitched: as long as the cloud abode upon the tabernacle they rested in their tents.

19 And when the cloud tarried long upon the tabernacle many days, then the children of Is'-ra-el kept the charge of the LORD, and journeyed not.

20 And so it was, when the cloud was a few days upon the tabernacle; according to the commandment of the LORD they abode in their tents, and according to the commandment of the LORD they journeyed.

21 And so it was, when the cloud abode from even unto the morning, and that the cloud was taken up in the morning, then they journeyed: whether it was by day or by night that the cloud was taken up, they journeyed.

22 Or whether it were two days, or a month, or a year, that the cloud tarried upon the tabernacle, remaining thereon, the children of Is'ra-el abode in their tents, and journeyed not: but when it was taken up, they journeyed.

23 At the commandment of the LORD they rested in the tents, and at the commandment of the LORD they journeyed: they kept the charge of the LORD, at the commandment of the LORD by the hand of Mo'ses.

10

AND the LORD spake unto Mo'ses, saying,

2 Make thee two trumpets of silver; of a whole piece shalt thou make them: that thou mayest use them for the calling of the assembly, and for the journeying of the camps.

3 And when they shall blow with them, all the assembly shall assemble themselves to thee at the door of the tabernacle of the congregation.

4 And if they blow but with one trumpet, then the princes, which are heads of the thousands of Is'ra-el, shall gather themselves unto thee.

5 When ye blow an alarm, then the camps that lie on the east parts shall go forward.

6 When ye blow an alarm the second time, then the camps that lie on the south side shall take their journey: they shall blow an alarm for their journeys.

7 But when the congregation is to be gathered together, ye shall blow, but ye shall not sound an alarm.

8 And the sons of Aar'on, the priests, shall blow with the trumpets; and they shall be to you for an ordinance for ever throughout your generations.

9 And if ye go to war in your land against the enemy that oppresseth you, then ye shall blow an alarm with the trumpets; and ye shall be remembered before the LORD your God, and ye shall be saved from your enemies.

10 Also in the day of your gladness, and in your solemn days, and in the beginnings of your months, ye shall blow with the trumpets over your burnt offerings, and over the sacrifices of your peace offerings; that they may be to you for a memorial before your God: I am the LORD your God.

11 ¶ And it came to pass on the twentieth day of the second month, in the second year, that the cloud was taken up from off the tabernacle of the testimony.

12 And the children of Is'ra-el took their journeys out of the wilderness of Si'nai; and the cloud rested in the wilderness of Pa'ran.

13 And they first took their journey according to the commandment of the LORD by the hand of Mo'ses.

14 ¶ In the first place went the standard of the camp of the children of Ju'dah according to their armies: and over his host was Nah'shon the son of Am-min'a-dab.

15 And over the host of the tribe of the children of Is'sa-char was Ne-than'e-el the son of Zu'ar.

16 And over the host of the tribe of the children of Zeb'u-lun was E-li'ab the son of He'lon.

17 And the tabernacle was taken down; and the sons of Ger'shon and the sons of Me-ra'ri set forward, bearing the tabernacle.

18 ¶ And the standard of the camp of Reu'-ben set forward according to their armies: and over his host was E-li'zur the son of Shed'e-ur.

19 And over the host of the tribe of the children of Sim'e-on was She-lu'mi-el the son of Zu-ri-shad'da-i.

20 And over the host of the tribe of the children of Gad was E-li'a-saph the son of Deu'el.

21 And the Ko'hath-ites set forward, bearing the sanctuary: and the other did set up the tabernacle against they came.

22 ¶ And the standard of the camp of the children of E'phra-im set forward according to their armies: and over his host was E-lish'a-ma the son of Am-mi'hud.

23 And over the host of the tribe of the children of Ma-nas'seh was Ga-ma'li-el the son of Pe-dah'zur.

24 And over the host of the tribe of the children of Ben'ja-min was Ab'i-dan the son of Gid-e-o'ni.

25 ¶ And the standard of the camp of the children of Dan set forward, which was the rereward of all the camps throughout their hosts: and over his host was A-hi-e'zer the son of Am-mi-shad'da-i.

26 And over the host of the tribe of the children of Ash'er was Pa'gi-el the son of Oc'ran.

27 And over the host of the tribe of the children of Naph'ta-li was A-hi'ra the son of E'nan.

28 Thus were the journeyings of the children of Is'ra-el according to their armies, when they set forward.

29 ¶ And Mo'ses said unto Ho-bab, the son of Ra-gu'el the Mid'i-an-ite, Mo'ses' father in law, We are journeying unto the place of which the LORD said, I will give it you: come thou with us, and we will do thee good: for the LORD hath spoken good concerning Is'ra-el.

30 And he said unto him, I will not go; but I will depart to mine own land, and to my kindred.

31 And he said, Leave us not, I pray thee; forasmuch as thou knowest how we are to encamp in the wilderness, and thou mayest be to us instead of eyes.

32 And it shall be, if thou go with us, yea, it shall be, that what goodness the LORD shall do unto us, the same will we do unto thee.

33 ¶ And they departed from the mount of the LORD three days' journey: and the ark of the covenant of the LORD went before them in the three days' journey, to search out a resting place for them.

34 And the cloud of the LORD was upon them by day, when they went out of the camp.

35 And it came to pass, when the ark set forward, that Mo'ses said, Rise up, LORD, and let thine enemies be scattered; and let them that hate thee flee before thee.

36 And when it rested, he said, Return, O LORD, unto the many thousands of Is'ra-el.

11 AND when the people complained, it displeased the LORD: and the LORD heard it; and his anger was kindled; and the fire of the LORD burnt among them, and consumed them that were in the uttermost parts of the camp.

2 And the people cried unto Mo'ses; and when Mo'ses prayed unto the LORD, the fire was quenched.

3 And he called the name of the place Tab'e-rah: because the fire of the LORD burnt among them.

4 ¶ And the mixt multitude that was among them fell a lusting: and the children of Is'ra-el also wept again, and said, Who shall give us flesh to eat?

5 We remember the fish, which we did eat in E'gypt freely; the cucumbers, and the melons, and the leeks, and the onions, and the garlick:

6 But now our soul is dried away: there is nothing at all, beside this manna, before our eyes.

7 And the manna was as coriander seed, and the colour thereof as the colour of bdellium.

8 And the people went about, and gathered it, and ground it in mills, or beat it in a mortar, and baked it in pans, and made cakes of it: and the taste of it was as the taste of fresh oil.

9 And when the dew fell upon the camp in the night, the manna fell upon it.

10 ¶ Then Mo'ses heard the people weep throughout their families, every man in the door of his tent: and the anger of the LORD was kindled greatly; Mo'ses also was displeased.

11 And Mo'ses said unto the LORD, Wherefore hast thou afflicted thy servant? and wherefore have I not found favour in thy sight, that thou layest the burden of all this people upon me?

12 Have I conceived all this people? have I begotten them, that thou shouldest say unto me, Carry them in thy bosom, as a nursing father beareth the sucking child, unto the land which thou swarest unto their fathers?

13 Whence should I have flesh to give unto all this people? for they weep unto me, saying, Give us flesh, that we may eat.

14 I am not able to bear all this people alone, because it is too heavy for me.

15 And if thou deal thus with me, kill me, I pray thee, out of hand, if I have found favour in thy sight; and let me not see my wretchedness.

16 ¶ And the LORD said unto Mo'ses, Gather unto me seventy men of the elders of Is'ra-el, whom thou knowest to be the elders of the people, and officers over them; and bring them unto the tabernacle of the congregation, that they may stand there with thee.

17 And I will come down and talk with thee there: and I will take of the spirit which is upon thee, and will put it upon them; and they shall bear the burden of the people with thee, that thou bear it not thyself alone.

18 And say thou unto the people, Sanctify yourselves against to morrow, and ye shall eat flesh: for ye have wept in the ears of the LORD, saying, Who shall give us flesh to eat? for it was well with us in E'gypt: therefore the LORD will give you flesh, and ye shall eat.

19 Ye shall not eat one day, nor two days, nor five days, neither ten days, nor twenty days;

20 But even a whole month, until it come out at your nostrils, and it be loathsome unto you: because that ye have despised the LORD which is among you, and have wept before him, saying, Why came we forth out of E'gypt?

21 And Mo'ses said, The people, among whom I am, are six hundred thousand footmen; and thou hast said, I will give them flesh, that they may eat a whole month.

22 Shall the flocks and the herds be slain for them, to suffice them? or shall all the fish of the sea be gathered together for them, to suffice them?

23 And the LORD said unto Mo'ses, Is the LORD's hand waxed short? thou shalt see now whether my word shall come to pass unto thee or not.

24 ¶ And Mo'ses went out, and told the people the words of the LORD, and gathered the seventy men of the elders of the people, and set them round about the tabernacle.

25 And the LORD came down in a cloud, and spake unto him, and took of the spirit that was upon him, and gave it unto the seventy elders: and it came to pass, that, when the spirit rested upon them, they prophesied, and did not cease.

26 But there remained two of the men in the camp, the name of the one was El'dad, and the name of the other Me'dad: and the spirit rested upon them; and they were of them that were written, but went not out unto the tabernacle: and they prophesied in the camp.

27 And there ran a young man, and told Mo'ses, and said, El'dad and Me'dad do prophesy in the camp.

28 And Josh'u-a the son of Nun, the servant of Mo'ses, one of his young men, answered and said, My lord Mo'ses, forbid them.

29 And Mo'ses said unto him, Enviest thou for my sake? would God that all the LORD's people were prophets, and that the LORD would put his spirit upon them!

30 And Mo'ses gat him into the camp, he and the elders of Is'ra-el.

31 ¶ And there went forth a wind from the LORD, and brought quails from the sea, and let

them fall by the camp, as it were a day's journey on this side, and as it were a day's journey on the other side, round about the camp, and as it were two cubits *high* upon the face of the earth.

32 And the people stood up all that day, and all *that* night, and all the next day, and they gathered the quails: he that gathered least gathered ten homers: and they spread *them* all abroad for themselves round about the camp.

33 And while the flesh *was* yet between their teeth, ere it was chewed, the wrath of the LORD was kindled against the people, and the LORD smote the people with a very great plague.

34 And he called the name of that place Kib'-roth–hat-ta'a-vah: because there they buried the people that lusted.

35 *And* the people journeyed from Kib'roth-hat-ta'a-vah unto Ha-ze'roth; and abode at Ha-ze'roth.

12 AND Mir'i-am and Aar'on spake against Mo'ses because of the E-thi-o'pi-an woman whom he had married: for he had married an E-thi-o'pi-an woman.

2 And they said, Hath the LORD indeed spoken only by Mo'ses? hath he not spoken also by us? And the LORD heard *it.*

3 (Now the man Mo'ses *was* very meek, above all the men which *were* upon the face of the earth.)

4 And the LORD spake suddenly unto Mo'ses, and unto Aar'on, and unto Mir'i-am, Come out ye three unto the tabernacle of the congregation. And they three came out.

5 And the LORD came down in the pillar of the cloud, and stood in the door of the tabernacle, and called Aar'on and Mir'i-am: and they both came forth.

6 And he said, Hear now my words: If there be a prophet among you, *I* the LORD will make myself known unto him in a vision, *and* will speak unto him in a dream.

7 My servant Mo'ses *is* not so, who *is* faithful in all mine house.

8 With him will I speak mouth to mouth, even apparently, and not in dark speeches; and the similitude of the LORD shall he behold: wherefore then were ye not afraid to speak against my servant Mo'ses?

9 And the anger of the LORD was kindled against them; and he departed.

10 And the cloud departed from off the tabernacle; and, behold, Mir'i-am *became* leprous, *white* as snow: and Aar'on looked upon Mir'i-am, and, behold, *she was* leprous.

11 And Aar'on said unto Mo'ses, Alas, my lord, I beseech thee, lay not the sin upon us, wherein we have done foolishly, and wherein we have sinned.

12 Let her not be as one dead, of whom the flesh is half consumed when he cometh out of his mother's womb.

13 And Mo'ses cried unto the LORD, saying, Heal her now, O God, I beseech thee.

14 ¶ And the LORD said unto Mo'ses, If her father had but spit in her face, should she not be ashamed seven days? let her be shut out from the camp seven days, and after that let her be received in *again.*

15 And Mir'i-am was shut out from the camp seven days: and the people journeyed not till Mir'i-am was brought in *again.*

16 And afterward the people removed from Ha-ze'roth, and pitched in the wilderness of Pa'-ran.

13 AND the LORD spake unto Mo'ses, saying,

2 Send thou men, that they may search the land of Ca'naan, which I give unto the children of Is'ra-el: of every tribe of their fathers shall ye send a man, every one a ruler among them.

3 And Mo'ses by the commandment of the LORD sent them from the wilderness of Pa'ran: all those men *were* heads of the children of Is'-ra-el.

4 And these *were* their names: of the tribe of Reu'ben, Sham-mu'a the son of Zac'cur.

5 Of the tribe of Sim'e-on, Sha'phat the son of Ho'ri.

6 Of the tribe of Ju'dah, Ca'leb the son of Je-phun'neh.

7 Of the tribe of Is'sa-char, I'gal the son of Jo'seph.

8 Of the tribe of E'phra-im, O-she'a the son of Nun.

9 Of the tribe of Ben'ja-min, Pal'ti the son of Ra'phu.

10 Of the tribe of Zeb'u-lun, Gad'di-el the son of So'di.

11 Of the tribe of Jo'seph, *namely,* of the tribe of Ma-nas'seh, Gad'di the son of Su'si.

12 Of the tribe of Dan, Am'mi-el the son of Ge-mal'li.

13 Of the tribe of Ash'er, Se'thur the son of Mi'chael.

14 Of the tribe of Naph'ta-li, Nah'bi the son of Voph'si.

15 Of the tribe of Gad, Ge-u'el the son of Ma'-chi.

16 These *are* the names of the men which Mo'ses sent to spy out the land. And Mo'ses called O-she'a the son of Nun Je-hosh'u-a.

17 ¶ And Mo'ses sent them to spy out the land of Ca'naan, and said unto them, Get you up this *way* southward, and go up into the mountain:

18 And see the land, what it *is;* and the people that dwelleth therein, whether they *be* strong or weak, few or many;

19 And what the land *is* that they dwell in, whether it *be* good or bad; and what cities *they be* that they dwell in, whether in tents, or in strong holds;

20 And what the land *is,* whether it *be* fat or lean, whether there be wood therein, or not. And be ye of good courage, and bring of the fruit of the land. Now the time *was* the time of the firstripe grapes.

21 ¶ So they went up, and searched the land from the wilderness of Zin unto Re'hob, as men come to Ha'math.

22 And they ascended by the south, and came unto He'bron; where A-hi'man, She'shai, and Tal'mai, the children of A'nak, *were.* (Now He'bron was built seven years before Zo'an in E'gypt.)

23 And they came unto the brook of Esh'col, and cut down from thence a branch with one cluster of grapes, and they bare it between two upon a staff; and *they* brought of the pomegranates, and of the figs.

24 The place was called the brook Esh'col, because of the cluster of grapes which the children of Is'ra-el cut down from thence.

25 And they returned from searching of the land after forty days.

26 ¶ And they went and came to Mo'ses, and to Aar'on, and to all the congregation of the children of Is'ra-el, unto the wilderness of Pa'-ran, to Ka'desh; and brought back word unto them, and unto all the congregation, and shewed them the fruit of the land.

27 And they told him, and said, We came unto the land whither thou sentest us, and surely it floweth with milk and honey; and this *is* the fruit of it.

28 Nevertheless the people *be* strong that dwell in the land, and the cities *are* walled, *and* very great: and moreover we saw the children of A'nak there.

29 The Am'a-lek-ites dwell in the land of the south: and the Hit'tites, and the Jeb'u-sites, and the Am'or-ites, dwell in the mountains: and the Ca'naan-ites dwell by the sea, and by the coast of Jor'dan.

30 And Ca'leb stilled the people before Mo'-ses, and said, Let us go up at once, and possess it; for we are well able to overcome it.

31 But the men that went up with him said, We be not able to go up against the people; for they *are* stronger than we.

32 And they brought up an evil report of the land which they had searched unto the children of Is'ra-el, saying, The land, through which we have gone to search it, *is* a land that eateth up the inhabitants thereof; and all the people that we saw in it *are* men of a great stature.

33 And there we saw the giants, the sons of A'nak, *which come* of the giants: and we were in our own sight as grasshoppers, and so we were in their sight.

14 AND all the congregation lifted up their voice, and cried; and the people wept that night.

2 And all the children of Is'ra-el murmured against Mo'ses and against Aar'on: and the whole congregation said unto them, Would God that we had died in the land of E'gypt! or would God we had died in this wilderness!

3 And wherefore hath the Lord brought us unto this land, to fall by the sword, that our wives and our children should be a prey? were it not better for us to return into E'gypt?

4 And they said one to another, Let us make a captain, and let us return into E'gypt.

5 Then Mo'ses and Aar'on fell on their faces before all the assembly of the congregation of the children of Is'ra-el.

6 ¶ And Josh'u-a the son of Nun, and Ca'leb the son of Je-phun'neh, *which were* of them that searched the land, rent their clothes:

7 And they spake unto all the company of the children of Is'ra-el, saying, The land, which we passed through to search it, *is* an exceeding good land.

8 If the Lord delight in us, then he will bring us into this land, and give it us; a land which floweth with milk and honey.

9 Only rebel not ye against the Lord, neither fear ye the people of the land; for they *are* bread for us: their defence is departed from them, and the Lord *is* with us: fear them not.

10 But all the congregation bade stone them with stones. And the glory of the Lord appeared in the tabernacle of the congregation before all the children of Is'ra-el.

11 ¶ And the Lord said unto Mo'ses, How long will this people provoke me? and how long will it be ere they believe me, for all the signs which I have shewed among them?

12 I will smite them with the pestilence, and disinherit them, and will make of thee a greater nation and mightier than they.

13 And Mo'ses said unto the Lord, Then the E-gyptians shall hear *it*, (for thou broughtest up this people in thy might from among them;)

14 And they will tell *it* to the inhabitants of this land: *for* they have heard that thou Lord *art* among this people, that thou Lord art seen face to face, and *that* thy cloud standeth over them, and *that* thou goest before them, by day time in a pillar of a cloud, and in a pillar of fire by night.

15 ¶ Now *if* thou shalt kill *all* this people as one man, then the nations which have heard the fame of thee will speak, saying,

16 Because the Lord was not able to bring this people into the land which he sware unto them, therefore he hath slain them in the wilderness.

17 And now, I beseech thee, let the power of my Lord be great, according as thou hast spoken, saying,

18 The Lord *is* longsuffering, and of great mercy, forgiving iniquity and transgression, and by no means clearing *the guilty*, visiting the iniquity of the fathers upon the children unto the third and fourth *generation*.

19 Pardon, I beseech thee, the iniquity of this people according unto the greatness of thy mercy, and as thou hast forgiven this people, from E'gypt even until now.

20 And the Lord said, I have pardoned according to thy word:

21 But *as* truly *as* I live, all the earth shall be filled with the glory of the Lord.

22 Because all those men which have seen my glory, and my miracles, which I did in E'-gypt and in the wilderness, and have tempted me now these ten times, and have not hearkened to my voice;

23 Surely they shall not see the land which I sware unto their fathers, neither shall any of them that provoked me see it:

24 But my servant Ca'leb, because he had another spirit with him, and hath followed me fully, him will I bring into the land whereinto he went; and his seed shall possess it.

25 (Now the Am'a-lek-ites and the Ca'naan-ites dwelt in the valley.) To morrow turn you, and get you into the wilderness by the way of the Red sea.

26 ¶ And the Lord spake unto Mo'ses and unto Aar'on, saying,

27 How long *shall I bear with* this evil congregation, which murmur against me? I have heard the murmurings of the children of Is'ra-el, which they murmur against me.

28 Say unto them, *As truly as* I live, saith the Lord, as ye have spoken in mine ears, so will I do to you:

29 Your carcases shall fall in this wilderness; and all that were numbered of you, according to your whole number, from twenty years old and upward, which have murmured against me,

30 Doubtless ye shall not come into the land, *concerning* which I sware to make you dwell therein, save Ca'leb the son of Je-phun'neh, and Josh'u-a the son of Nun.

31 But your little ones, which ye said should be a prey, them will I bring in, and they shall know the land which ye have despised.

32 But *as for* you, your carcases, they shall fall in this wilderness.

33 And your children shall wander in the wilderness forty years, and bear your whoredoms, until your carcases be wasted in the wilderness.

34 After the number of the days in which ye searched the land, *even* forty days, each day for a year, shall ye bear your iniquities, *even* forty years, and ye shall know my breach of promise.

35 I the Lord have said, I will surely do it unto all this evil congregation, that are gathered

together against me: in this wilderness they shall be consumed, and there they shall die.

36 And the men, which Mo'ses sent to search the land, who returned, and made all the congregation to murmur against him, by bringing up a slander upon the land,

37 Even those men that did bring up the evil report upon the land, died by the plague before the LORD.

38 But Josh'u-a the son of Nun, and Ca'leb the son of Je-phun'neh, which were of the men that went to search the land, lived still.

39 And Mo'ses told these sayings unto all the children of Is'ra-el: and the people mourned greatly.

40 ¶ And they rose up early in the morning, and gat them up into the top of the mountain, saying, Lo, we be here, and will go up unto the place which the LORD hath promised: for we have sinned.

41 And Mo'ses said, Wherefore now do ye transgress the commandment of the LORD? but it shall not prosper.

42 Go not up, for the LORD is not among you; that ye be not smitten before your enemies.

43 For the Am'a-lek-ites and the Ca'naan-ites are there before you, and ye shall fall by the sword: because ye are turned away from the LORD, therefore the LORD will not be with you.

44 But they presumed to go up unto the hill top: nevertheless the ark of the covenant of the LORD, and Mo'ses, departed not out of the camp.

45 Then the Am'a-lek-ites came down, and the Ca'naan-ites which dwelt in that hill, and smote them, and discomfited them, even unto Hor'mah.

15 AND the LORD spake unto Mo'ses, saying,

2 Speak unto the children of Is'ra-el, and say unto them, When ye be come into the land of your habitations, which I give unto you,

3 And will make an offering by fire unto the LORD, a burnt offering, or a sacrifice in performing a vow, or in a freewill offering, or in your solemn feasts, to make a sweet savour unto the LORD, of the herd, or of the flock:

4 Then shall he that offereth his offering unto the LORD bring a meat offering of a tenth deal of flour mingled with the fourth part of an hin of oil.

5 And the fourth part of an hin of wine for a drink offering shalt thou prepare with the burnt offering or sacrifice, for one lamb.

6 Or for a ram, thou shalt prepare for a meat offering two tenth deals of flour mingled with the third part of an hin of oil.

7 And for a drink offering thou shalt offer the third part of an hin of wine, for a sweet savour unto the LORD.

8 And when thou preparest a bullock for a burnt offering, or for a sacrifice in performing a vow, or peace offerings unto the LORD:

9 Then shall he bring with a bullock a meat offering of three tenth deals of flour mingled with half an hin of oil.

10 And thou shalt bring for a drink offering half an hin of wine, for an offering made by fire, of a sweet savour unto the LORD.

11 Thus shall it be done for one bullock, or for one ram, or for a lamb, or a kid.

12 According to the number that ye shall prepare, so shall ye do to every one according to their number.

13 All that are born of the country shall do these things after this manner, in offering an offering made by fire, of a sweet savour unto the LORD.

14 And if a stranger sojourn with you, or whosoever be among you in your generations, and will offer an offering made by fire, of a sweet savour unto the LORD; as ye do, so he shall do.

15 One ordinance shall be both for you of the congregation, and also for the stranger that sojourneth with you, an ordinance for ever in your generations: as ye are, so shall the stranger be before the LORD.

16 One law and one manner shall be for you, and for the stranger that sojourneth with you.

17 ¶ And the LORD spake unto Mo'ses, saying,

18 Speak unto the children of Is'ra-el, and say unto them, When ye come into the land whither I bring you,

19 Then it shall be, that, when ye eat of the bread of the land, ye shall offer up an heave offering unto the LORD.

20 Ye shall offer up a cake of the first of your dough for an heave offering: as ye do the heave offering of the threshingfloor, so shall ye heave it.

21 Of the first of your dough ye shall give unto the LORD an heave offering in your generations.

22 ¶ And if ye have erred, and not observed all these commandments, which the LORD hath spoken unto Mo'ses,

23 Even all that the LORD hath commanded you by the hand of Mo'ses, from the day that the LORD commanded Mo'ses, and henceforward among your generations;

24 Then it shall be, if ought be committed by ignorance without the knowledge of the congregation, that all the congregation shall offer one young bullock for a burnt offering, for a sweet savour unto the LORD, with his meat offering, and his drink offering, according to the manner, and one kid of the goats for a sin offering.

25 And the priest shall make an atonement for all the congregation of the children of Is'ra-el, and it shall be forgiven them; for it is ignorance: and they shall bring their offering, a sacrifice made by fire unto the LORD, and their sin offering before the LORD, for their ignorance:

26 And it shall be forgiven all the congregation of the children of Is'ra-el, and the stranger that sojourneth among them; seeing all the people were in ignorance.

27 ¶ And if any soul sin through ignorance, then he shall bring a she goat of the first year for a sin offering.

28 And the priest shall make an atonement for the soul that sinneth ignorantly, when he sinneth by ignorance before the LORD, to make an atonement for him; and it shall be forgiven him.

29 Ye shall have one law for him that sinneth through ignorance, both for him that is born among the children of Is'ra-el, and for the stranger that sojourneth among them.

30 ¶ But the soul that doeth ought presumptuously, whether he be born in the land, or a stranger, the same reproacheth the LORD; and that soul shall be cut off from among his people.

31 Because he hath despised the word of the LORD, and hath broken his commandment, that soul shall utterly be cut off; his iniquity shall be upon him.

32 ¶ And while the children of Is'ra-el were in the wilderness, they found a man that gathered sticks upon the sabbath day.

33 And they that found him gathering sticks

brought him unto Mo'ses and Aar'on, and unto all the congregation.

34 And they put him in ward, because it was not declared what should be done to him.

35 And the LORD said unto Mo'ses, The man shall be surely put to death: all the congregation shall stone him with stones without the camp.

36 And all the congregation brought him without the camp, and stoned him with stones, and he died; as the LORD commanded Mo'ses.

37 ¶ And the LORD spake unto Mo'ses, saying,

38 Speak unto the children of Is'ra-el, and bid them that they make them fringes in the borders of their garments throughout their generations, and that they put upon the fringe of the borders a ribband of blue:

39 And it shall be unto you for a fringe, that ye may look upon it, and remember all the commandments of the LORD, and do them; and that ye seek not after your own heart and your own eyes, after which ye use to go a whoring:

40 That ye may remember, and do all my commandments, and be holy unto your God.

41 I am the LORD your God, which brought you out of the land of E'gypt, to be your God: I am the LORD your God.

16 NOW Ko'rah, the son of Iz'har, the son of Ko'hath, the son of Le'vi, and Da'than and A-bi'ram, the sons of E-li'ab, and On, the son of Pe'leth, sons of Reu'ben, took men:

2 And they rose up before Mo'ses, with certain of the children of Is'ra-el, two hundred and fifty princes of the assembly, famous in the congregation, men of renown:

3 And they gathered themselves together against Mo'ses and against Aar'on, and said unto them, Ye take too much upon you, seeing all the congregation are holy, every one of them, and the LORD is among them: wherefore then lift ye up yourselves above the congregation of the LORD?

4 And when Mo'ses heard it, he fell upon his face:

5 And he spake unto Ko'rah and unto all his company, saying, Even to morrow the LORD will shew who are his, and who is holy; and will cause him to come near unto him: even him whom he hath chosen will he cause to come near unto him.

6 This do; Take you censers, Ko'rah, and all his company;

7 And put fire therein, and put incense in them before the LORD to morrow: and it shall be that the man whom the LORD doth choose, he shall be holy: ye take too much upon you, ye sons of Le'vi.

8 And Mo'ses said unto Ko'rah, Hear, I pray you, ye sons of Le'vi:

9 Seemeth it but a small thing unto you, that the God of Is'ra-el hath separated you from the congregation of Is'ra-el, to bring you near to himself to do the service of the tabernacle of the LORD, and to stand before the congregation to minister unto them?

10 And he hath brought thee near to him, and all thy brethren the sons of Le'vi with thee: and seek ye the priesthood also?

11 For which cause both thou and all thy company are gathered together against the LORD: and what is Aar'on, that ye murmur against him?

12 ¶ And Mo'ses sent to call Da'than and A-bi'ram, the sons of E-li'ab: which said, We will not come up:

13 Is it a small thing that thou hast brought us up out of a land that floweth with milk and honey, to kill us in the wilderness, except thou make thyself altogether a prince over us?

14 Moreover thou hast not brought us into a land that floweth with milk and honey, or given us inheritance of fields and vineyards: wilt thou put out the eyes of these men? we will not come up.

15 And Mo'ses was very wroth, and said unto the LORD, Respect not thou their offering: I have not taken one ass from them, neither have I hurt one of them.

16 And Mo'ses said unto Ko'rah, Be thou and all thy company before the LORD, thou, and they, and Aar'on, to morrow:

17 And take every man his censer, and put incense in them, and bring ye before the LORD every man his censer, two hundred and fifty censers; thou also, and Aar'on, each of you his censer.

18 And they took every man his censer, and put fire in them, and laid incense thereon, and stood in the door of the tabernacle of the congregation with Mo'ses and Aar'on.

19 And Ko'rah gathered all the congregation against them unto the door of the tabernacle of the congregation: and the glory of the LORD appeared unto all the congregation.

20 And the LORD spake unto Mo'ses and unto Aar'on, saying,

21 Separate yourselves from among this congregation, that I may consume them in a moment.

22 And they fell upon their faces, and said, O God, the God of the spirits of all flesh, shall one man sin, and wilt thou be wroth with all the congregation?

23 ¶ And the LORD spake unto Mo'ses, saying,

24 Speak unto the congregation, saying, Get you up from about the tabernacle of Ko'rah, Da'than, and A-bi'ram.

25 And Mo'ses rose up and went unto Da'-than and A-bi'ram; and the elders of Is'ra-el followed him.

26 And he spake unto the congregation, saying, Depart, I pray you, from the tents of these wicked men, and touch nothing of theirs, lest ye be consumed in all their sins.

27 So they gat up from the tabernacle of Ko'-rah, Da'than, and A-bi'ram, on every side: and Da'than and A-bi'ram came out, and stood in the door of their tents, and their wives, and their sons, and their little children.

28 And Mo'ses said, Hereby ye shall know that the LORD hath sent me to do all these works; for I have not done them of mine own mind.

29 If these men die the common death of all men, or if they be visited after the visitation of all men; then the LORD hath not sent me.

30 But if the LORD make a new thing, and the earth open her mouth, and swallow them up, with all that appertain unto them, and they go down quick into the pit; then ye shall understand that these men have provoked the LORD.

31 ¶ And it came to pass, as he had made an end of speaking all these words, that the ground clave asunder that was under them:

32 And the earth opened her mouth, and swallowed them up, and their houses, and all the men that appertained unto Ko'rah, and all their goods.

33 They, and all that appertained to them, went down alive into the pit, and the earth

closed upon them: and they perished from among the congregation.

34 And all Is-ra-el that were round about them fled at the cry of them: for they said, Lest the earth swallow us up also.

35 And there came out a fire from the LORD, and consumed the two hundred and fifty men that offered incense.

36 ¶ And the LORD spake unto Mo'ses, saying,

37 Speak unto E-le-a'zar the son of Aar'on the priest, that he take up the censers out of the burning, and scatter thou the fire yonder; for they are hallowed.

38 The censers of these sinners against their own souls, let them make them broad plates for a covering of the altar: for they offered them before the LORD, therefore they are hallowed: and they shall be a sign unto the children of Is-ra-el.

39 And E-le-a'zar the priest took the brasen censers, wherewith they that were burnt had offered; and they were made broad plates for a covering of the altar:

40 To be a memorial unto the children of Is'-ra-el, that no stranger, which is not of the seed of Aar'on, come near to offer incense before the LORD; that he be not as Ko'rah, and as his company: as the LORD said to him by the hand of Mo'ses.

41 ¶ But on the morrow all the congregation of the children of Is'ra-el murmured against Mo'ses and against Aar'on, saying, Ye have killed the people of the LORD.

42 And it came to pass, when the congregation was gathered against Mo'ses and against Aar'on, that they looked toward the tabernacle of the congregation: and, behold, the cloud covered it, and the glory of the LORD appeared.

43 And Mo'ses and Aar'on came before the tabernacle of the congregation.

44 ¶ And the LORD spake unto Mo'ses, saying,

45 Get you up from among this congregation, that I may consume them as in a moment. And they fell upon their faces.

46 ¶ And Mo'ses said unto Aar'on, Take a censer, and put fire therein from off the altar, and put on incense, and go quickly unto the congregation, and make an atonement for them: for there is wrath gone out from the LORD; the plague is begun.

47 And Aar'on took as Mo'ses commanded, and ran into the midst of the congregation; and, behold, the plague was begun among the people: and he put on incense, and made an atonement for the people.

48 And he stood between the dead and the living; and the plague was stayed.

49 Now they that died in the plague were fourteen thousand and seven hundred, beside them that died about the matter of Ko'rah.

50 And Aar'on returned unto Mo'ses unto the door of the tabernacle of the congregation: and the plague was stayed.

17 AND the LORD spake unto Mo'ses, saying,

2 Speak unto the children of Is'ra-el, and take of every one of them a rod according to the house of their fathers, of all their princes according to the house of their fathers twelve rods: write thou every man's name upon his rod.

3 And thou shalt write Aar'on's name upon the rod of Le'vi: for one rod shall be for the head of the house of their fathers.

4 And thou shalt lay them up in the tabernacle of the congregation before the testimony, where I will meet with you.

5 And it shall come to pass, that the man's rod, whom I shall choose, shall blossom: and I will make to cease from me the murmurings of the children of Is'ra-el, whereby they murmur against you.

6 ¶ And Mo'ses spake unto the children of Is'ra-el, and every one of their princes gave him a rod apiece, for each prince one, according to their fathers' houses, even twelve rods: and the rod of Aar'on was among their rods.

7 And Mo'ses laid up the rods before the LORD in the tabernacle of witness.

8 And it came to pass, that on the morrow Mo'ses went into the tabernacle of witness; and, behold, the rod of Aar'on for the house of Le'vi was budded, and brought forth buds, and bloomed blossoms, and yielded almonds.

9 And Mo'ses brought out all the rods from before the LORD unto all the children of Is'ra-el: and they looked, and took every man his rod.

10 ¶ And the LORD said unto Mo'ses, Bring Aar'on's rod again before the testimony, to be kept for a token against the rebels; and thou shalt quite take away their murmurings from me, that they die not.

11 And Mo'ses did so: as the LORD commanded him, so did he.

12 And the children of Is'ra-el spake unto Mo'ses, saying, Behold, we die, we perish, we all perish.

13 Whosoever cometh any thing near unto the tabernacle of the LORD shall die: shall we be consumed with dying?

18 AND the LORD said unto Aar'on, Thou and thy sons and thy father's house with thee shall bear the iniquity of the sanctuary: and thou and thy sons with thee shall bear the iniquity of your priesthood.

2 And thy brethren also of the tribe of Le'vi, the tribe of thy father, bring thou with thee, that they may be joined unto thee, and minister unto thee: but thou and thy sons with thee shall minister before the tabernacle of witness.

3 And they shall keep thy charge, and the charge of all the tabernacle: only they shall not come nigh the vessels of the sanctuary and the altar, that neither they, nor ye also, die.

4 And they shall be joined unto thee, and keep the charge of the tabernacle of the congregation, for all the service of the tabernacle: and a stranger shall not come nigh unto you.

5 And ye shall keep the charge of the sanctuary, and the charge of the altar: that there be no wrath any more upon the children of Is'ra-el.

6 And I, behold, I have taken your brethren the Le'vites from among the children of Is'ra-el: to you they are given as a gift for the LORD, to do the service of the tabernacle of the congregation.

7 Therefore thou and thy sons with thee shall keep your priest's office for every thing of the altar, and within the veil; and ye shall serve: I have given your priest's office unto you as a service of gift: and the stranger that cometh nigh shall be put to death.

8 ¶ And the LORD spake unto Aar'on, Behold, I also have given thee the charge of mine heave offerings of all the hallowed things of the children of Is'ra-el; unto thee have I given them by reason of the anointing, and to thy sons, by an ordinance for ever.

9 This shall be thine of the most holy things, reserved from the fire: every oblation of theirs,

every meat offering of theirs, and every sin offering of theirs, and every trespass offering of theirs, which they shall render unto me, *shall be* most holy for thee and for thy sons.

10 In the most holy *place* shalt thou eat it; every male shall eat it: it shall be holy unto thee.

11 And this *is* thine; the heave offering of their gift, with all the wave offerings of the children of Is'ra-el: I have given them unto thee, and to thy sons and to thy daughters with thee, by a statute for ever: every one that is clean in thy house shall eat of it.

12 All the best of the oil, and all the best of the wine, and of the wheat, the firstfruits of them which they shall offer unto the LORD, them have I given thee.

13 *And* whatsoever is first ripe in the land, which they shall bring unto the LORD, shall be thine; every one that is clean in thine house shall eat *of* it.

14 Every thing devoted in Is'ra-el shall be thine.

15 Every thing that openeth the matrix in all flesh, which they bring unto the LORD, *whether it be* of men or beasts, shall be thine: nevertheless the firstborn of man shalt thou surely redeem, and the firstling of unclean beasts shalt thou redeem.

16 And those that are to be redeemed from a month old shalt thou redeem, according to thine estimation, for the money of five shekels, after the shekel of the sanctuary, which *is* twenty gerahs.

17 But the firstling of a cow, or the firstling of a sheep, or the firstling of a goat, thou shalt not redeem; they *are* holy: thou shalt sprinkle their blood upon the altar, and shalt burn their fat *for* an offering made by fire, for a sweet savour unto the LORD.

18 And the flesh of them shall be thine, as the wave breast and as the right shoulder are thine.

19 All the heave offerings of the holy things, which the children of Is'ra-el offer unto the LORD, have I given thee, and thy sons and thy daughters with thee, by a statute for ever: it *is* a covenant of salt for ever before the LORD unto thee and to thy seed with thee.

20 ¶ And the LORD spake unto Aar'on, Thou shalt have no inheritance in their land, neither shalt thou have any part among them: I *am* thy part and thine inheritance among the children of Is'ra-el.

21 And, behold, I have given the children of Le'vi all the tenth in Is'ra-el for an inheritance, for their service which they serve, *even* the service of the tabernacle of the congregation.

22 Neither must the children of Is'ra-el henceforth come nigh the tabernacle of the congregation, lest they bear sin, and die.

23 But the Le'vites shall do the service of the tabernacle of the congregation, and they shall bear their iniquity: *it shall be* a statute for ever throughout your generations, that among the children of Is'ra-el they have no inheritance.

24 But the tithes of the children of Is'ra-el, which they offer *as* an heave offering unto the LORD, I have given to the Le'vites to inherit: therefore I have said unto them, Among the children of Is'ra-el they shall have no inheritance.

25 ¶ And the LORD spake unto Mo'ses, saying,

26 Thus speak unto the Le'vites, and say unto them, When ye take of the children of Is'ra-el the tithes which I have given you from them for your inheritance, then ye shall offer up

an heave offering of it for the LORD, *even* a tenth *part* of the tithe.

27 And *this* your heave offering shall be reckoned unto you, as though *it were* the corn of the threshingfloor, and as the fulness of the winepress.

28 Thus ye also shall offer an heave offering unto the LORD of all your tithes, which ye receive of the children of Is'ra-el; and ye shall give thereof the LORD's heave offering to Aar'on the priest.

29 Out of all your gifts ye shall offer every heave offering of the LORD, of all the best thereof, *even* the hallowed part thereof out of it.

30 Therefore thou shalt say unto them, When ye have heaved the best thereof from it, then it shall be counted unto the Le'vites as the increase of the threshingfloor, and as the increase of the winepress.

31 And ye shall eat it in every place, ye and your households: for it *is* your reward for your service in the tabernacle of the congregation.

32 And ye shall bear no sin by reason of it, when ye have heaved from it the best of it: neither shall ye pollute the holy things of the children of Is'ra-el, lest ye die.

19 AND the LORD spake unto Mo'ses and unto Aar'on, saying,

2 This *is* the ordinance of the law which the LORD hath commanded, saying, Speak unto the children of Is'ra-el, that they bring thee a red heifer without spot, wherein *is* no blemish, *and* upon which never came yoke:

3 And ye shall give her unto E-le-a'zar the priest, that he may bring her forth without the camp, and *one* shall slay her before his face:

4 And E-le-a'zar the priest shall take of her blood with his finger, and sprinkle of her blood directly before the tabernacle of the congregation seven times:

5 And *one* shall burn the heifer in his sight; her skin, and her flesh, and her blood, with her dung, shall he burn:

6 And the priest shall take cedar wood, and hyssop, and scarlet, and cast *it* into the midst of the burning of the heifer.

7 Then the priest shall wash his clothes, and he shall bathe his flesh in water, and afterward he shall come into the camp, and the priest shall be unclean until the even.

8 And he that burneth her shall wash his clothes in water, and bathe his flesh in water, and shall be unclean until the even.

9 And a man *that is* clean shall gather up the ashes of the heifer, and lay *them* up without the camp in a clean place, and it shall be kept for the congregation of the children of Is'ra-el for a water of separation: it *is* a purification for sin.

10 And he that gathereth the ashes of the heifer shall wash his clothes, and be unclean until the even: and it shall be unto the children of Is'ra-el, and unto the stranger that sojourneth among them, for a statute for ever.

11 ¶ He that toucheth the dead body of any man shall be unclean seven days.

12 He shall purify himself with it on the third day, and on the seventh day he shall be clean: but if he purify not himself the third day, then the seventh day he shall not be clean.

13 Whosoever toucheth the dead body of any man that is dead, and purifieth not himself, defileth the tabernacle of the LORD; and that soul shall be cut off from Is'ra-el: because the water of separation was not sprinkled upon him, he shall be unclean; his uncleanness *is* yet upon him.

14 This *is* the law, when a man dieth in a tent: all that come into the tent, and all that *is* in the tent, shall be unclean seven days.

15 And every open vessel, which hath no covering bound upon it, *is* unclean.

16 And whosoever toucheth one that is slain with a sword in the open fields, or a dead body, or a bone of a man, or a grave, shall be unclean seven days.

17 And for an unclean *person* they shall take of the ashes of the burnt heifer of purification for sin, and running water shall be put thereto in a vessel:

18 And a clean person shall take hyssop, and dip *it* in the water, and sprinkle *it* upon the tent, and upon all the vessels, and upon the persons that were there, and upon him that touched a bone, or one slain, or one dead, or a grave:

19 And the clean *person* shall sprinkle upon the unclean on the third day, and on the seventh day: and on the seventh day he shall purify himself, and wash his clothes, and bathe himself in water, and shall be clean at even.

20 But the man that shall be unclean, and shall not purify himself, that soul shall be cut off from among the congregation, because he hath defiled the sanctuary of the LORD: the water of separation hath not been sprinkled upon him; he *is* unclean.

21 And it shall be a perpetual statute unto them, that he that sprinkleth the water of separation shall wash his clothes; and he that toucheth the water of separation shall be unclean until even.

22 And whatsoever the unclean *person* toucheth shall be unclean; and the soul that toucheth *it* shall be unclean until even.

20 THEN came the children of Is'ra-el, *even* the whole congregation, into the desert of Zin in the first month: and the people abode in Ka'desh; and Mir'i-am died there, and was buried there.

2 And there was no water for the congregation: and they gathered themselves together against Mo'ses and against Aar'on.

3 And the people chode with Mo'ses, and spake, saying, Would God that we had died when our brethren died before the LORD!

4 And why have ye brought up the congregation of the LORD into this wilderness, that we and our cattle should die there?

5 And wherefore have ye made us to come up out of E'gypt, to bring us in unto this evil place? it *is* no place of seed, or of figs, or of vines, or of pomegranates; neither *is* there any water to drink.

6 And Mo'ses and Aar'on went from the presence of the assembly unto the door of the tabernacle of the congregation, and they fell upon their faces: and the glory of the LORD appeared unto them.

7 ¶ And the LORD spake unto Mo'ses, saying,

8 Take the rod, and gather thou the assembly together, thou, and Aar'on thy brother, and speak ye unto the rock before their eyes; and it shall give forth his water, and thou shalt bring forth to them water out of the rock: so thou shalt give the congregation and their beasts drink.

9 And Mo'ses took the rod from before the LORD, as he commanded him.

10 And Mo'ses and Aar'on gathered the congregation together before the rock, and he said unto them, Hear now, ye rebels; must we fetch you water out of this rock?

11 And Mo'ses lifted up his hand, and with his rod he smote the rock twice: and the water came out abundantly, and the congregation drank, and their beasts *also*.

12 ¶ And the LORD spake unto Mo'ses and Aar'on, Because ye believed me not, to sanctify me in the eyes of the children of Is'ra-el, therefore ye shall not bring this congregation into the land which I have given them.

13 This *is* the water of Mer'i-bah; because the children of Is'ra-el strove with the LORD, and he was sanctified in them.

14 ¶ And Mo'ses sent messengers from Ka'-desh unto the king of E'dom, Thus saith thy brother Is'ra-el, Thou knowest all the travail that hath befallen us:

15 How our fathers went down into E'gypt, and we have dwelt in E'gypt a long time; and the E-gyptians vexed us, and our fathers:

16 And when we cried unto the LORD, he heard our voice, and sent an angel, and hath brought us forth out of E'gypt: and, behold, we *are* in Ka'desh, a city in the uttermost of thy border:

17 Let us pass, I pray thee, through thy country: we will not pass through the fields, or through the vineyards, neither will we drink *of* the water of the wells: we will go by the king's *high* way, we will not turn to the right hand nor to the left, until we have passed thy borders.

18 And E'dom said unto him, Thou shalt not pass by me, lest I come out against thee with the sword.

19 And the children of Is'ra-el said unto him, We will go by the high way: and if I and my cattle drink of thy water, then I will pay for it: I will only, without *doing* any thing *else*, go through on my feet.

20 And he said, Thou shalt not go through. And E'dom came out against him with much people, and with a strong hand.

21 Thus E'dom refused to give Is'ra-el passage through his border: wherefore Is'ra-el turned away from him.

22 ¶ And the children of Is'ra-el, *even* the whole congregation, journeyed from Ka'desh, and came unto mount Hor.

23 And the LORD spake unto Mo'ses and Aar'on in mount Hor, by the coast of the land of E'dom, saying,

24 Aar'on shall be gathered unto his people: for he shall not enter into the land which I have given unto the children of Is'ra-el, because ye rebelled against my word at the water of Mer'i-bah.

25 Take Aar'on and E-le-a'zar his son, and bring them up unto mount Hor:

26 And strip Aar'on of his garments, and put them upon E-le-a'zar his son: and Aar'on shall be gathered *unto his people*, and shall die there.

27 And Mo'ses did as the LORD commanded: and they went up into mount Hor in the sight of all the congregation.

28 And Mo'ses stripped Aar'on of his garments, and put them upon E-le-a'zar his son; and Aar'on died there in the top of the mount: and Mo'ses and E-le-a'zar came down from the mount.

29 And when all the congregation saw that Aar'on was dead, they mourned for Aar'on thirty days, *even* all the house of Is'ra-el.

21 AND *when* king A'rad the Ca'naan-ite, which dwelt in the south, heard tell that Is'ra-el came by the way of the spies; then he fought against Is'ra-el, and took *some* of them prisoners.

2 And Is'ra-el vowed a vow unto the LORD,

and said, If thou wilt indeed deliver this people into my hand, then I will utterly destroy their cities.

3 And the LORD hearkened to the voice of Is'ra-el, and delivered up the Ca'naan-ites; and they utterly destroyed them and their cities: and he called the name of the place Hor'mah.

4 ¶ And they journeyed from mount Hor by the way of the Red sea, to compass the land of E'dom: and the soul of the people was much discouraged because of the way.

5 And the people spake against God, and against Mo'ses, Wherefore have ye brought us up out of E'gypt to die in the wilderness? for there is no bread, neither is there any water; and our soul loatheth this light bread.

6 And the LORD sent fiery serpents among the people, and they bit the people; and much people of Is'ra-el died.

7 ¶ Therefore the people came to Mo'ses, and said, We have sinned, for we have spoken against the LORD, and against thee; pray unto the LORD, that he take away the serpents from us. And Mo'ses prayed for the people.

8 And the LORD said unto Mo'ses, Make thee a fiery serpent, and set it upon a pole: and it shall come to pass, that every one that is bitten, when he looketh upon it, shall live.

9 And Mo'ses made a serpent of brass, and put it upon a pole, and it came to pass, that if a serpent had bitten any man, when he beheld the serpent of brass, he lived.

10 ¶ And the children of Is'ra-el set forward, and pitched in O'both.

11 And they journeyed from O'both, and pitched at Ij'e-ab'a-rim, in the wilderness which is before Mo'ab, toward the sunrising.

12 ¶ From thence they removed, and pitched in the valley of Za'red.

13 From thence they removed, and pitched on the other side of Ar'non, which is in the wilderness that cometh out of the coasts of the Am'or-ites: for Ar'non is the border of Mo'ab, between Mo'ab and the Am'or-ites.

14 Wherefore it is said in the book of the wars of the LORD, What he did in the Red sea, and in the brooks of Ar'non,

15 And at the stream of the brooks that goeth down to the dwelling of Ar, and lieth upon the border of Mo'ab.

16 And from thence they went to Be'er: that is the well whereof the LORD spake unto Mo'ses, Gather the people together, and I will give them water.

17 ¶ Then Is'ra-el sang this song, Spring up, O well; sing ye unto it:

18 The princes digged the well, the nobles of the people digged it, by the direction of the lawgiver, with their staves. And from the wilderness they went to Mat'ta-nah:

19 And from Mat'ta-nah to Na-ha'li-el: and from Na-ha'li-el to Ba'moth:

20 And from Ba'moth in the valley, that is in the country of Mo'ab, to the top of Pis'gah, which looketh toward Jesh'i-mon.

21 ¶ And Is'ra-el sent messengers unto Si'hon king of the Am'or-ites, saying,

22 Let me pass through thy land: we will not turn into the fields, or into the vineyards; we will not drink of the waters of the well: but we will go along by the king's high way, until we be past thy borders.

23 And Si'hon would not suffer Is'ra-el to pass through his border: but Si'hon gathered all his people together, and went out against Is'ra-el into the wilderness: and he came to Ja'haz, and fought against Is'ra-el.

24 And Is'ra-el smote him with the edge of the sword, and possessed his land from Ar'non unto Jab'bok, even unto the children of Am'mon: for the border of the children of Am'mon was strong.

25 And Is'ra-el took all these cities: and Is'ra-el dwelt in all the cities of the Am'or-ites, in Hesh'bon, and in all the villages thereof.

26 For Hesh'bon was the city of Si'hon the king of the Am'or-ites, who had fought against the former king of Mo'ab, and taken all his land out of his hand, even unto Ar'non.

27 Wherefore they that speak in proverbs say, Come into Hesh'bon, let the city of Si'hon be built and prepared:

28 For there is a fire gone out of Hesh'bon, a flame from the city of Si'hon: it hath consumed Ar of Mo'ab, and the lords of the high places of Ar'non.

29 Woe to thee, Mo'ab! thou art undone, O people of Che'mosh: he hath given his sons that escaped, and his daughters, into captivity unto Si'hon king of the Am'or-ites.

30 We have shot at them; Hesh'bon is perished even unto Di'bon, and we have laid them waste even unto No'phah, which reacheth unto Med'e-ba.

31 ¶ Thus Is'ra-el dwelt in the land of the Am'or-ites.

32 And Mo'ses sent to spy out Ja-a'zer, and they took the villages thereof, and drove out the Am'or-ites that were there.

33 ¶ And they turned and went up by the way of Ba'shan: and Og the king of Ba'shan went out against them, he, and all his people, to the battle at Ed're-i.

34 And the LORD said unto Mo'ses, Fear him not: for I have delivered him into thy hand, and all his people, and his land; and thou shalt do to him as thou didst unto Si'hon king of the Am'or-ites, which dwelt at Hesh'bon.

35 So they smote him, and his sons, and all his people, until there was none left him alive: and they possessed his land.

22 AND the children of Is'ra-el set forward, and pitched in the plains of Mo'ab on this side Jor'dan by Jer'i-cho.

2 ¶ And Ba'lak the son of Zip'por saw all that Is'ra-el had done to the Am'or-ites.

3 And Mo'ab was sore afraid of the people, because they were many: and Mo'ab was distressed because of the children of Is'ra-el.

4 And Mo'ab said unto the elders of Mid'i-an, Now shall this company lick up all that are round about us, as the ox licketh up the grass of the field. And Ba'lak the son of Zip'por was king of the Mo'ab-ites at that time.

5 He sent messengers therefore unto Ba'laam the son of Be'or to Pe'thor, which is by the river of the land of the children of his people, to call him, saying, Behold, there is a people come out from E'gypt: behold, they cover the face of the earth, and they abide over against me:

6 Come now therefore, I pray thee, curse me this people; for they are too mighty for me: peradventure I shall prevail, that we may smite them, and that I may drive them out of the land: for I wot that he whom thou blessest is blessed, and he whom thou cursest is cursed.

7 And the elders of Mo'ab and the elders of Mid'i-an departed with the rewards of divination in their hand; and they came unto Ba'laam, and spake unto him the words of Ba'lak.

8 And he said unto them, Lodge here this night, and I will bring you word again, as the

LORD shall speak unto me: and the princes of Mo'ab abode with Ba'laam.

9 And God came unto Ba'laam, and said, What men are these with thee?

10 And Ba'laam said unto God, Ba'lak the son of Zip'por, king of Mo'ab, hath sent unto me, saying,

11 Behold, there is a people come out of E'gypt, which covereth the face of the earth: come now, curse me them; peradventure I shall be able to overcome them, and drive them out.

12 And God said unto Ba'laam, Thou shalt not go with them; thou shalt not curse the people: for they are blessed.

13 And Ba'laam rose up in the morning, and said unto the princes of Ba'lak, Get you into your land: for the LORD refuseth to give me leave to go with you.

14 And the princes of Mo'ab rose up, and they went unto Ba'lak, and said, Ba'laam refuseth to come with us.

15 ¶ And Ba'lak sent yet again princes, more, and more honourable than they.

16 And they came to Ba'laam, and said to him, Thus saith Ba'lak the son of Zip'por, Let nothing, I pray thee, hinder thee from coming unto me:

17 For I will promote thee unto very great honour, and I will do whatsoever thou sayest unto me: come therefore, I pray thee, curse me this people.

18 And Ba'laam answered and said unto the servants of Ba'lak, If Ba'lak would give me his house full of silver and gold, I cannot go beyond the word of the LORD my God, to do less or more.

19 Now therefore, I pray you, tarry ye also here this night, that I may know what the LORD will say unto me more.

20 And God came unto Ba'laam at night, and said unto him, If the men come to call thee, rise up, and go with them; but yet the word which I shall say unto thee, that shalt thou do.

21 And Ba'laam rose up in the morning, and saddled his ass, and went with the princes of Mo'ab.

22 ¶ And God's anger was kindled because he went: and the angel of the LORD stood in the way for an adversary against him. Now he was riding upon his ass, and his two servants were with him.

23 And the ass saw the angel of the LORD standing in the way, and his sword drawn in his hand: and the ass turned aside out of the way, and went into the field: and Ba'laam smote the ass, to turn her into the way.

24 But the angel of the LORD stood in a path of the vineyards, a wall being on this side, and a wall on that side.

25 And when the ass saw the angel of the LORD, she thrust herself unto the wall, and crushed Ba'laam's foot against the wall: and he smote her again.

26 And the angel of the LORD went further, and stood in a narrow place, where was no way to turn either to the right hand or to the left.

27 And when the ass saw the angel of the LORD, she fell down under Ba'laam: and Ba'laam's anger was kindled, and he smote the ass with a staff.

28 And the LORD opened the mouth of the ass, and she said unto Ba'laam, What have I done unto thee, that thou hast smitten me these three times?

29 And Ba'laam said unto the ass, Because thou hast mocked me: I would there were a sword in mine hand, for now would I kill thee.

30 And the ass said unto Ba'laam, Am not I thine ass, upon which thou hast ridden ever since I was thine unto this day? was I ever wont to do so unto thee? And he said, Nay.

31 Then the LORD opened the eyes of Ba'laam, and he saw the angel of the LORD standing in the way, and his sword drawn in his hand: and he bowed down his head, and fell flat on his face.

32 And the angel of the LORD said unto him, Wherefore hast thou smitten thine ass these three times? behold, I went out to withstand thee, because thy way is perverse before me:

33 And the ass saw me, and turned from me these three times: unless she had turned from me, surely now also I had slain thee, and saved her alive.

34 And Ba'laam said unto the angel of the LORD, I have sinned; for I knew not that thou stoodest in the way against me: now therefore, if it displease thee, I will get me back again.

35 And the angel of the LORD said unto Ba'laam, Go with the men: but only the word that I shall speak unto thee, that thou shalt speak. So Ba'laam went with the princes of Ba'lak.

36 ¶ And when Ba'lak heard that Ba'laam was come, he went out to meet him unto a city of Mo'ab, which is in the border of Ar'non, which is in the utmost coast.

37 And Ba'lak said unto Ba'laam, Did I not earnestly send unto thee to call thee? wherefore camest thou not unto me? am I not able indeed to promote thee to honour?

38 And Ba'laam said unto Ba'lak, Lo, I am come unto thee: have I now any power at all to say any thing? the word that God putteth in my mouth, that shall I speak.

39 And Ba'laam went with Ba'lak, and they came unto Kir'jath-hu'zoth.

40 And Ba'lak offered oxen and sheep, and sent to Ba'laam, and to the princes that were with him.

41 And it came to pass on the morrow, that Ba'lak took Ba'laam, and brought him up into the high places of Ba'al, that thence he might see the utmost part of the people.

23 AND Ba'laam said unto Ba'lak, Build me here seven altars, and prepare me here seven oxen and seven rams.

2 And Ba'lak did as Ba'laam had spoken; and Ba'lak and Ba'laam offered on every altar a bullock and a ram.

3 And Ba'laam said unto Ba'lak, Stand by thy burnt offering, and I will go: peradventure the LORD will come to meet me: and whatsoever he sheweth me I will tell thee. And he went to an high place.

4 And God met Ba'laam: and he said unto him, I have prepared seven altars, and I have offered upon every altar a bullock and a ram.

5 And the LORD put a word in Ba'laam's mouth, and said, Return unto Ba'lak, and thus thou shalt speak.

6 And he returned unto him, and, lo, he stood by his burnt sacrifice, he, and all the princes of Mo'ab.

7 And he took up his parable, and said, Ba'lak the king of Mo'ab hath brought me from A'ram, out of the mountains of the east, saying, Come, curse me Ja'cob, and come, defy Is'ra-el.

8 How shall I curse, whom God hath not cursed? or how shall I defy, whom the LORD hath not defied?

9 For from the top of the rocks I see him, and from the hills I behold him: lo, the people shall

dwell alone, and shall not be reckoned among the nations.

10 Who can count the dust of Ja′cob, and the number of the fourth *part* of Is′ra-el? Let me die the death of the righteous, and let my last end be like his!

11 And Ba′lak said unto Ba′laam, What hast thou done unto me? I took thee to curse mine enemies, and, behold, thou hast blessed *them* altogether.

12 And he answered and said, Must I not take heed to speak that which the LORD hath put in my mouth?

13 And Ba′lak said unto him, Come, I pray thee, with me unto another place, from whence thou mayest see them: thou shalt see but the utmost part of them, and shalt not see them all: and curse me them from thence.

14 ¶ And he brought him into the field of Zo′phim, to the top of Pisgah, and built seven altars, and offered a bullock and a ram on *every* altar.

15 And he said unto Ba′lak, Stand here by thy burnt offering, while I meet *the* LORD yonder.

16 And the LORD met Ba′laam, and put a word in his mouth, and said, Go again unto Ba′lak, and say thus.

17 And when he came to him, behold, he stood by his burnt offering, and the princes of Mo′ab with him. And Ba′lak said unto him, What hath the LORD spoken?

18 And he took up his parable, and said, Rise up, Ba′lak, and hear; hearken unto me, thou son of Zip′por:

19 God *is* not a man, that he should lie; neither the son of man, that he should repent: hath he said, and shall he not do *it?* or hath he spoken, and shall he not make it good?

20 Behold, I have received *commandment* to bless: and he hath blessed; and I cannot reverse it.

21 He hath not beheld iniquity in Ja′cob, neither hath he seen perverseness in Is′ra-el: the LORD his God *is* with him, and the shout of a king *is* among them.

22 God brought them out of E′gypt; he hath as it were the strength of an unicorn.

23 Surely *there is* no enchantment against Ja′cob, neither *is there* any divination against Is′ra-el: according to this time it shall be said of Ja′cob and of Is′ra-el, What hath God wrought!

24 Behold, the people shall rise up as a great lion, and lift up himself as a young lion: he shall not lie down until he eat *of* the prey, and drink the blood of the slain.

25 ¶ And Ba′lak said unto Ba′laam, Neither curse them at all, nor bless them at all.

26 But Ba′laam answered and said unto Ba′lak, Told not I thee, saying, All that the LORD speaketh, that I must do?

27 ¶ And Ba′lak said unto Ba′laam, Come, I pray thee, I will bring thee unto another place; peradventure it will please God that thou mayest curse me them from thence.

28 And Ba′lak brought Ba′laam unto the top of Pe′or, that looketh toward Jesh′i-mon.

29 And Ba′laam said unto Ba′lak, Build me here seven altars, and prepare me here seven bullocks and seven rams.

30 And Ba′lak did as Ba′laam had said, and offered a bullock and a ram on *every* altar.

24 AND when Ba′laam saw that it pleased the LORD to bless Is′ra-el, he went not, as at other times, to seek for enchantments, but he set his face toward the wilderness.

2 And Ba′laam lifted up his eyes, and he saw Is′ra-el abiding *in his tents* according to their tribes; and the spirit of God came upon him.

3 And he took up his parable, and said, Ba′laam the son of Be′or hath said, and the man whose eyes are open hath said:

4 He hath said, which heard the words of God, which saw the vision of the Almighty, falling *into a trance,* but having his eyes open:

5 How goodly are thy tents, O Ja′cob, *and* thy tabernacles, O Is′ra-el!

6 As the valleys are they spread forth, as gardens by the river's side, as the trees of lign aloes which the LORD hath planted, *and* as cedar trees beside the waters.

7 He shall pour the water out of his buckets, and his seed *shall be* in many waters, and his king shall be higher than A′gag, and his kingdom shall be exalted.

8 God brought him forth out of E′gypt; he hath as it were the strength of an unicorn: he shall eat up the nations his enemies, and shall break their bones, and pierce *them* through with his arrows.

9 He couched, he lay down as a lion, and as a great lion: who shall stir him up? Blessed *is* he that blesseth thee, and cursed *is* he that curseth thee.

10 ¶ And Ba′lak's anger was kindled against Ba′laam, and he smote his hands together: and Ba′lak said unto Ba′laam, I called thee to curse mine enemies, and, behold, thou hast altogether blessed *them* these three times.

11 Therefore now flee thou to thy place: I thought to promote thee unto great honour; but, lo, the LORD hath kept thee back from honour.

12 And Ba′laam said unto Ba′lak, Spake I not also to thy messengers which thou sentest unto me, saying,

13 If Ba′lak would give me his house full of silver and gold, I cannot go beyond the commandment of the LORD, to do *either* good or bad of mine own mind; *but* what the LORD saith, that will I speak?

14 And now, behold, I go unto my people: come *therefore, and* I will advertise thee what this people shall do to thy people in the latter days.

15 ¶ And he took up his parable, and said, Ba′laam the son of Be′or hath said, and the man whose eyes are open hath said:

16 He hath said, which heard the words of God, and knew the knowledge of the most High, *which* saw the vision of the Almighty, falling *into a trance,* but having his eyes open:

17 I shall see him, but not now: I shall behold him, but not nigh: there shall come a Star out of Ja′cob, and a Sceptre shall rise out of Is′ra-el, and shall smite the corners of Mo′ab, and destroy all the children of Sheth.

18 And E′dom shall be a possession, Se′ir also shall be a possession for his enemies; and Is′ra-el shall do valiantly.

19 Out of Ja′cob shall come he that shall have dominion, and shall destroy him that remaineth of the city.

20 ¶ And when he looked on Am′a-lek, he took up his parable, and said, Am′a-lek *was* the first of the nations; but his latter end *shall be* that he perish for ever.

21 And he looked on the Ken′ites, and took up his parable, and said, Strong is thy dwelling-place, and thou puttest thy nest in a rock.

22 Nevertheless the Kenite shall be wasted, until As′shur shall carry thee away captive.

23 And he took up his parable, and said, Alas, who shall live when God doeth this!

24 And ships *shall come* from the coast of Chit'tim, and shall afflict As'shur, and shall afflict E'ber, and he also shall perish for ever.

25 And Ba'laam rose up, and went and returned to his place: and Ba'lak also went his way.

25 AND Is'ra-el abode in Shit'tim, and the people began to commit whoredom with the daughters of Mo'ab.

2 And they called the people unto the sacrifices of their gods: and the people did eat, and bowed down to their gods.

3 And Is'ra-el joined himself unto Ba'al-pe'-or: and the anger of the LORD was kindled against Is'ra-el.

4 And the LORD said unto Mo'ses, Take all the heads of the people, and hang them up before the LORD against the sun, that the fierce anger of the LORD may be turned away from Is'ra-el.

5 And Mo'ses said unto the judges of Is'ra-el, Slay ye every one his men that were joined unto Ba'al-pe'or.

6 ¶ And, behold, one of the children of Is'ra-el came and brought unto his brethen a Mid'i-an-it-ish woman in the sight of Mo'ses, and in the sight of all the congregation of the children of Is'ra-el, who *were* weeping *before* the door of the tabernacle of the congregation.

7 And when Phin'e-has, the son of E-le-a'zar, the son of Aar'on the priest, saw *it*, he rose up from among the congregation, and took a javelin in his hand;

8 And he went after the man of Is'ra-el into the tent, and thrust both of them through, the man of Is'ra-el, and the woman through her belly. So the plague was stayed from the children of Is'ra-el.

9 And those that died in the plague were twenty and four thousand.

10 ¶ And the LORD spake unto Mo'ses, saying,

11 Phin'e-has, the son of E-le-a'zar, the son of Aar'on the priest, hath turned my wrath away from the children of Is'ra-el, while he was zealous for my sake among them, that I consumed not the children of Is'ra-el in my jealousy.

12 Wherefore say, Behold, I give unto him my covenant of peace:

13 And he shall have it, and his seed after him, *even* the covenant of an everlasting priesthood; because he was zealous for his God, and made an atonement for the children of Is'ra-el.

14 Now the name of the Is'ra-el-ite that was slain, *even* that was slain with the Mid'i-an-it-ish woman, *was* Zim'ri, the son of Sa'lu, a prince of a chief house among the Sim'e-on-ites.

15 And the name of the Mid'i-an-it-ish woman that was slain *was* Coz'bi, the daughter of Zur; he *was* head over a people, *and* of a chief house in Mid'i-an.

16 ¶ And the LORD spake unto Mo'ses, saying,

17 Vex the Mid'i-an-ites, and smite them:

18 For they vex you with their wiles, wherewith they have beguiled you in the matter of Pe'or, and in the matter of Coz'bi, the daughter of a prince of Mid'i-an, their sister, which was slain in the day of the plague for Pe'or's sake.

26 AND it came to pass after the plague, that the LORD spake unto Mo'ses and unto E-le-a'zar the son of Aar'on the priest, saying,

2 Take the sum of all the congregation of the children of Is'ra-el, from twenty years old and upward, throughout their fathers' house, all that are able to go to war in Is'ra-el.

3 And Mo'ses and E-le-a'zar the priest spake with them in the plains of Mo'ab by Jor'dan near Jer'i-cho, saying,

4 Take the sum of the people, from twenty years old and upward; as the LORD commanded Mo'ses and the children of Is'ra-el, which went forth out of the land of E'gypt.

5 ¶ Reu'ben, the eldest son of Is'ra-el: the children of Reu'ben; Ha'noch, *of whom cometh* the family of the Ha'noch-ites: of Pal'lu, the family of the Pal'lu-ites:

6 Of Hez'ron, the family of the Hez'ron-ites: of Car'mi, the family of the Car'mites.

7 These *are* the families of the Reu'ben-ites: and they that were numbered of them were forty and three thousand and seven hundred and thirty.

8 And the sons of Pal'lu; E-li'ab.

9 And the sons of E-li'ab; Ne-mu'el, and Da'-than, and A-bi'ram. This *is that* Da'than and A-bi'ram, *which were* famous in the congregation, who strove against Mo'ses and against Aar'on in the company of Ko'rah, when they strove against the LORD:

10 And the earth opened her mouth, and swallowed them up together with Ko'rah, when that company died, what time the fire devoured two hundred and fifty men: and they became a sign.

11 Notwithstanding the children of Ko'rah died not.

12 ¶ The sons of Sim'e-on after their families: of Ne-mu'el, the family of the Ne-mu'el-ites: of Ja'min, the family of the Ja'min-ites: of Ja'chin, the family of the Ja'chin-ites:

13 Of Ze'rah, the family of the Zar'hites: of Sha'ul, the family of the Sha'ul-ites.

14 These *are* the families of the Sim'e-on-ites, twenty and two thousand and two hundred.

15 ¶ The children of Gad after their families: of Ze'phon, the family of the Ze'phon-ites: of Hag'gi, the family of the Hag'gites: of Shu'ni, the family of the Shu'nites:

16 Of Oz'ni, the family of the Oz'nites: of E'-ri, the family of the E'rites:

17 Of A'rod, the family of the A'rod-ites: of A-re'li, the family of the A-re'lites.

18 These *are* the families of the children of Gad according to those that were numbered of them, forty thousand and five hundred.

19 ¶ The sons of Ju'dah *were* Er and O'nan: and Er and O'nan died in the land of Ca'naan.

20 And the sons of Ju'dah after their families were; of She'lah, the family of the She'lan-ites: of Pha'rez, the family of the Phar'zites: of Ze'-rah, the family of the Zar'hites.

21 And the sons of Pha'rez were; of Hez'ron, the family of the Hez'ron-ites: of Ha'mul, the family of the Ha'mul-ites.

22 These *are* the families of Ju'dah according to those that were numbered of them, threescore and sixteen thousand and five hundred.

23 ¶ *Of* the sons of Is'sa-char after their families: *of* To'la, the family of the To'la-ites: of Pu'-a, the family of the Pu'nites:

24 Of Jash'ub, the family of the Jash'ub-ites: of Shim'ron, the family of the Shim'ron-ites.

25 These *are* the families of Is'sa-char according to those that were numbered of them, threescore and four thousand and three hundred.

26 ¶ *Of* the sons of Zeb'u-lun after their families: of Se'red, the family of the Sar'dites: of

E'lon, the family of the E'lon-ites: of Jah'le-el, the family of the Jah'le-el-ites.

27 These are the families of the Zeb'u-lun-ites according to those that were numbered of them, threescore thousand and five hundred.

28 ¶ The sons of Jo'seph after their families were Ma-nas'seh and E'phra-im.

29 Of the sons of Ma-nas'seh: of Ma'chir, the family of the Ma'chir-ites: and Ma'chir begat Gil'e-ad: of Gil'e-ad come the family of the Gil'-e-ad-ites.

30 These are the sons of Gil'e-ad: of Je-e'zer, the family of the Je-e'zer-ites: of He'lek, the family of the He'lek-ites.

31 And of As'ri-el, the family of the As'ri-el-ites: and of Shechem, the family of the She'-chem-ites.

32 And of She-mi'da, the family of the She-mi'da-ites: and of He'pher, the family of the He'pher-ites.

33 ¶ And Ze-lo'phe-had the son of He'pher had no sons, but daughters: and the names of the daughters of Ze-lo'phe-had were Mah'lah, and No'ah, Hog'lah, Mil'cah, and Tir'zah.

34 These are the families of Ma-nas'seh, and those that were numbered of them, fifty and two thousand and seven hundred.

35 ¶ These are the sons of E'phra-im after their families: of Shu'the-lah, the family of the Shu'thal-hites: of Be'cher, the family of the Bach'rites: of Ta'han, the family of the Ta'han-ites.

36 And these are the sons of Shu'the-lah: of E'ran, the family of the E'ran-ites.

37 These are the families of the sons of E'-phra-im according to those that were numbered of them, thirty and two thousand and five hundred. These are the sons of Jo'seph after their families.

38 ¶ The sons of Ben'ja-min after their families: of Be'la, the family of the Be'la-ites: of Ash'bel, the family of the Ash'bel-ites: of A-hi'ram, the family of the A-hi'ram-ites:

39 Of Shu'pham, the family of the Shu'pham-ites: of Hu'pham, the family of the Hu'pham-ites.

40 And the sons of Be'la were Ard and Na'a-man: of Ard, the family of the Ard'ites: and of Na'a-man, the family of the Na'a-mites.

41 These are the sons of Ben'ja-min after their families: and they that were numbered of them were forty and five thousand and six hundred.

42 ¶ These are the sons of Dan after their families: of Shu'ham, the family of the Shu'-ham-ites. These are the families of Dan after their families.

43 All the families of the Shu'ham-ites, according to those that were numbered of them, were threescore and four thousand and four hundred.

44 ¶ Of the children of Ash'er after their families: of Jim'na, the family of the Jim'nites: of Jes'u-i, the family of the Jes'u-ites: of Be-ri'-ah, the family of the Be-ri'tes.

45 Of the sons of Be-ri'ah: of He'ber, the family of the He'ber-ites: of Mal'chi-el, the family of the Mal'chi-el-ites.

46 And the name of the daughter of Ash'er was Sa'rah.

47 These are the families of the sons of Ash'-er according to those that were numbered of them; who were fifty and three thousand and four hundred.

48 ¶ Of the sons of Naph'ta-li after their families: of Jah'ze-el, the family of the Jah'ze-el-ites: of Gu'ni, the family of the Gu'nites:

49 Of Je'zer, the family of the Je'zer-ites: of Shil'lem, the family of the Shil'lem-ites.

50 These are the families of Naph'ta-li according to their families: and they that were numbered of them were forty and five thousand and four hundred.

51 These were the numbered of the children of Is'ra-el, six hundred thousand and a thousand seven hundred and thirty.

52 ¶ And the LORD spake unto Mo'ses, saying,

53 Unto these the land shall be divided for an inheritance according to the number of names.

54 To many thou shalt give the more inheritance, and to few thou shalt give the less inheritance: to every one shall his inheritance be given according to those that were numbered of him.

55 Notwithstanding the land shall be divided by lot: according to the names of the tribes of their fathers they shall inherit.

56 According to the lot shall the possession thereof be divided between many and few.

57 ¶ And these are they that were numbered of the Le'vites after their families: of Ger'shon, the family of the Ger'shon-ites: of Ko'hath, the family of the Ko'hath-ites: of Me-ra'ri, the family of the Me-ra'rites.

58 These are the families of the Le'vites: the family of the Lib'nites, the family of the He'-bron-ites, the family of the Mah'lites, the family of the Mu'shites, the family of the Ko'rath-ites. And Ko'hath begat Am'ram.

59 And the name of Am'ram's wife was Joch'e-bed, the daughter of Le'vi, whom her mother bare to Le'vi in E'gypt: and she bare unto Am'ram Aar'on and Mo'ses, and Mir'i-am their sister.

60 And unto Aar'on was born Na'dab, and A-bi'hu, E-le-a'zar, and Ith'a-mar.

61 And Na'dab and A-bi'hu died, when they offered strange fire before the LORD.

62 And those that were numbered of them were twenty and three thousand, all males from a month old and upward: for they were not numbered among the children of Is'ra-el, because there was no inheritance given them among the children of Is'ra-el.

63 ¶ These are they that were numbered by Mo'ses and E-le-a'zar the priest, who numbered the children of Is'ra-el in the plains of Mo'ab by Jor'dan near Jer'i-cho.

64 But among these there was not a man of them whom Mo'ses and Aar'on the priest numbered, when they numbered the children of Is'-ra-el in the wilderness of Si'nai.

65 For the LORD had said of them, They shall surely die in the wilderness. And there was not left a man of them, save Ca'leb the son of Je-phun'neh, and Josh'u-a the son of Nun.

27 THEN came the daughters of Ze-lo'phe-had, the son of He'pher, the son of Gil'e-ad, the son of Ma'chir, the son of Ma-nas'seh, of the families of Ma-nas'seh the son of Jo'seph: and these are the names of his daughters; Mah'-lah, No'ah, and Hog'lah, and Mil'cah, and Tir'-zah.

2 And they stood before Mo'ses, and before E-le-a'zar the priest, and before the princes and all the congregation, by the door of the tabernacle of the congregation, saying,

3 Our father died in the wilderness, and he was not in the company of them that gathered themselves together against the LORD in the company of Ko'rah; but died in his own sin, and had no sons.

4 Why should the name of our father be done away from among his family, because he hath no son? Give unto us *therefore* a possession among the brethren of our father.

5 And Mo'ses brought their cause before the LORD.

6 ¶ And the LORD spake unto Mo'ses, saying,

7 The daughters of Ze-lo'phe-had speak right: thou shalt surely give them a possession of an inheritance among their father's brethren; and thou shalt cause the inheritance of their father to pass unto them.

8 And thou shalt speak unto the children of Is'ra-el, saying, If a man die, and have no son, then ye shall cause his inheritance to pass unto his daughter.

9 And if he have no daughter, then ye shall give his inheritance unto his brethren.

10 And if he have no brethren, then ye shall give his inheritance unto his father's brethren.

11 And if his father have no brethren, then ye shall give his inheritance unto his kinsman that is next to him of his family, and he shall possess it: and it shall be unto the children of Is'ra-el a statute of judgment, as the LORD commanded Mo'ses.

12 ¶ And the LORD said unto Mo'ses, Get thee up into this mount Ab'a-rim, and see the land which I have given unto the children of Is'ra-el.

13 And when thou hast seen it, thou also shalt be gathered unto thy people, as Aar'on thy brother was gathered.

14 For ye rebelled against my commandment in the desert of Zin, in the strife of the congregation, to sanctify me at the water before their eyes: that *is* the water of Mer'i-bah in Ka'desh in the wilderness of Zin.

15 ¶ And Mo'ses spake unto the LORD, saying,

16 Let the LORD, the God of the spirits of all flesh, set a man over the congregation,

17 Which may go out before them, and which may go in before them, and which may lead them out, and which may bring them in; that the congregation of the LORD be not as sheep which have no shepherd.

18 ¶ And the LORD said unto Mo'ses, Take thee Josh'u-a the son of Nun, a man in whom *is* the spirit, and lay thine hand upon him;

19 And set him before E-le-a'zar the priest, and before all the congregation; and give him a charge in their sight.

20 And thou shalt put *some* of thine honour upon him, that all the congregation of the children of Is'ra-el may be obedient.

21 And he shall stand before E-le-a'zar the priest, who shall ask *counsel* for him after the judgment of U'rim before the LORD: at his word shall they go out, and at his word they shall come in, *both* he, and all the children of Is'ra-el with him, even all the congregation.

22 And Mo'ses did as the LORD commanded him: and he took Josh'u-a, and set him before E-le-a'zar the priest, and before all the congregation:

23 And he laid his hands upon him, and gave him a charge, as the LORD commanded by the hand of Mo'ses.

28 AND the LORD spake unto Mo'ses, saying,

2 Command the children of Is'ra-el, and say unto them, My offering, *and* my bread for my sacrifices made by fire, *for* a sweet savour unto me, shall ye observe to offer unto me in their due season.

3 And thou shalt say unto them, This *is* the offering made by fire which ye shall offer unto the LORD; two lambs of the first year without spot day by day, *for* a continual burnt offering.

4 The one lamb shalt thou offer in the morning, and the other lamb shalt thou offer at even;

5 And a tenth *part* of an ephah of flour for a meat offering, mingled with the fourth *part* of an hin of beaten oil.

6 *It is* a continual burnt offering, which was ordained in mount Si'nai for a sweet savour, a sacrifice made by fire unto the LORD.

7 And the drink offering thereof *shall be* the fourth *part* of an hin for the one lamb: in the holy *place* shalt thou cause the strong wine to be poured unto the LORD *for* a drink offering.

8 And the other lamb shalt thou offer at even: as the meat offering of the morning, and as the drink offering thereof, thou shalt offer *it*, a sacrifice made by fire, of a sweet savour unto the LORD.

9 ¶ And on the sabbath day two lambs of the first year without spot, and two tenth deals of flour *for* a meat offering, mingled with oil, and the drink offering thereof:

10 *This is* the burnt offering of every sabbath, beside the continual burnt offering, and his drink offering.

11 ¶ And in the beginnings of your months ye shall offer a burnt offering unto the LORD; two young bullocks, and one ram, seven lambs of the first year without spot;

12 And three tenth deals of flour *for* a meat offering, mingled with oil, for one bullock; and two tenth deals of flour *for* a meat offering, mingled with oil, for one ram;

13 And a several tenth deal of flour mingled with oil *for* a meat offering unto one lamb; *for* a burnt offering of a sweet savour, a sacrifice made by fire unto the LORD.

14 And their drink offerings shall be half an hin of wine unto a bullock, and the third *part* of an hin unto a ram, and a fourth *part* of an hin unto a lamb: this *is* the burnt offering of every month throughout the months of the year.

15 And one kid of the goats for a sin offering unto the LORD shall be offered, beside the continual burnt offering, and his drink offering.

16 And in the fourteenth day of the first month *is* the passover of the LORD.

17 And in the fifteenth day of this month *is* the feast: seven days shall unleavened bread be eaten.

18 In the first day *shall be* an holy convocation; ye shall do no manner of servile work *therein*:

19 But ye shall offer a sacrifice made by fire *for* a burnt offering unto the LORD; two young bullocks, and one ram, and seven lambs of the first year: they shall be unto you without blemish:

20 And their meat offering *shall be of* flour mingled with oil: three tenth deals shall ye offer for a bullock, and two tenth deals for a ram;

21 A several tenth deal shalt thou offer for every lamb, throughout the seven lambs:

22 And one goat *for* a sin offering, to make an atonement for you.

23 Ye shall offer these beside the burnt offering in the morning, which *is* for a continual burnt offering.

24 After this manner ye shall offer daily, throughout the seven days, the meat of the sacrifice made by fire, of a sweet savour unto the LORD: it shall be offered beside the continual burnt offering, and his drink offering.

25 And on the seventh day ye shall have an

holy convocation; ye shall do no servile work.

26 ¶ Also in the day of the firstfruits, when ye bring a new meat offering unto the LORD, after your weeks *be out,* ye shall have an holy convocation; ye shall do no servile work:

27 But ye shall offer the burnt offering for a sweet savour unto the LORD; two young bullocks, one ram, seven lambs of the first year;

28 And their meat offering of flour mingled with oil, three tenth deals unto one bullock, two tenth deals unto one ram,

29 A several tenth deal unto one lamb, throughout the seven lambs;

30 *And* one kid of the goats, to make an atonement for you.

31 Ye shall offer *them* beside the continual burnt offering, and his meat offering, (they shall be unto you without blemish) and their drink offerings.

29 AND in the seventh month, on the first day of the month, ye shall have an holy convocation; ye shall do no servile work: it is a day of blowing the trumpets unto you.

2 And ye shall offer a burnt offering for a sweet savour unto the LORD; one young bullock, one ram, *and* seven lambs of the first year without blemish:

3 And their meat offering *shall be of* flour mingled with oil, three tenth deals for a bullock, *and* two tenth deals for a ram,

4 And one tenth deal for one lamb, throughout the seven lambs:

5 And one kid of the goats *for* a sin offering, to make an atonement for you:

6 Beside the burnt offering of the month, and his meat offering, and the daily burnt offering, and his meat offering, and their drink offerings, according unto their manner, for a sweet savour, a sacrifice made by fire unto the LORD.

7 ¶ And ye shall have on the tenth *day* of this seventh month an holy convocation; and ye shall afflict your souls: ye shall not do any work *therein.*

8 But ye shall offer a burnt offering unto the LORD *for* a sweet savour; one young bullock, one ram, *and* seven lambs of the first year; they shall be unto you without blemish:

9 And their meat offering *shall be of* flour mingled with oil, three tenth deals to a bullock, *and* two tenth deals to one ram,

10 A several tenth deal for one lamb, throughout the seven lambs:

11 One kid of the goats *for* a sin offering; beside the sin offering of atonement, and the continual burnt offering, and the meat offering of it, and their drink offerings.

12 ¶ And on the fifteenth day of the seventh month ye shall have an holy convocation; ye shall do no servile work, and ye shall keep a feast unto the LORD seven days:

13 And ye shall offer a burnt offering, a sacrifice made by fire, of a sweet savour unto the LORD; thirteen young bullocks, two rams, *and* fourteen lambs of the first year; they shall be without blemish:

14 And their meat offering *shall be of* flour mingled with oil, three tenth deals unto every bullock of the thirteen bullocks, two tenth deals to each ram of the two rams,

15 And a several tenth deal to each lamb of the fourteen lambs:

16 And one kid of the goats *for* a sin offering; beside the continual burnt offering, his meat offering, and his drink offering.

17 ¶ And on the second day *ye shall offer* twelve young bullocks, two rams, fourteen lambs of the first year without spot:

18 And their meat offering and their drink offerings for the bullocks, for the rams, and for the lambs, *shall be* according to their number, after the manner:

19 And one kid of the goats *for* a sin offering; beside the continual burnt offering, and the meat offering thereof, and their drink offerings.

20 ¶ And on the third day eleven bullocks, two rams, fourteen lambs of the first year without blemish;

21 And their meat offering and their drink offerings for the bullocks, for the rams, and for the lambs, *shall be* according to their number, after the manner:

22 And one goat *for* a sin offering; beside the continual burnt offering, and his meat offering, and his drink offering.

23 ¶ And on the fourth day ten bullocks, two rams, *and* fourteen lambs of the first year without blemish:

24 Their meat offering and their drink offerings for the bullocks, for the rams, and for the lambs, *shall be* according to their number, after the manner:

25 And one kid of the goats *for* a sin offering; beside the continual burnt offering, his meat offering, and his drink offering.

26 ¶ And on the fifth day nine bullocks, two rams, *and* fourteen lambs of the first year without spot:

27 And their meat offering and their drink offerings for the bullocks, for the rams, and for the lambs, *shall be* according to their number, after the manner:

28 And one goat *for* a sin offering; beside the continual burnt offering, and his meat offering, and his drink offering.

29 ¶ And on the sixth day eight bullocks, two rams, *and* fourteen lambs of the first year without blemish:

30 And their meat offering and their drink offerings for the bullocks, for the rams, and for the lambs, *shall be* according to their number, after the manner:

31 And one goat *for* a sin offering; beside the continual burnt offering, his meat offering, and his drink offering.

32 ¶ And on the seventh day seven bullocks, two rams, *and* fourteen lambs of the first year without blemish:

33 And their meat offering and their drink offerings for the bullocks, for the rams, and for the lambs, *shall be* according to their number, after the manner:

34 And one goat *for* a sin offering; beside the continual burnt offering, his meat offering, and his drink offering.

35 ¶ On the eighth day ye shall have a solemn assembly: ye shall do no servile work *therein:*

36 But ye shall offer a burnt offering, a sacrifice made by fire, of a sweet savour unto the LORD: one bullock, one ram, seven lambs of the first year without blemish:

37 Their meat offering and their drink offerings for the bullock, for the ram, and for the lambs, *shall be* according to their number, after the manner:

38 And one goat *for* a sin offering; beside the continual burnt offering, and his meat offering, and his drink offering.

39 These *things* ye shall do unto the LORD in your set feasts, beside your vows, and your freewill offerings, for your burnt offerings, and

for your meat offerings, and for your drink offerings, and for your peace offerings.

40 And Mo'ses told the children of Is'ra-el according to all that the LORD commanded Mo'ses.

30 AND Mo'ses spake unto the heads of the tribes concerning the children of Is'ra-el, saying, This is the thing which the LORD hath commanded.

2 If a man vow a vow unto the LORD, or swear an oath to bind his soul with a bond; he shall not break his word, he shall do according to all that proceedeth out of his mouth.

3 If a woman also vow a vow unto the LORD, and bind herself by a bond, being in her father's house in her youth;

4 And her father hear her vow, and her bond wherewith she hath bound her soul, and her father shall hold his peace at her: then all her vows shall stand, and every bond wherewith she hath bound her soul shall stand.

5 But if her father disallow her in the day that he heareth; not any of her vows, or of her bonds wherewith she hath bound her soul, shall stand: and the LORD shall forgive her, because her father disallowed her.

6 And if she had at all an husband, when she vowed, or uttered ought out of her lips, wherewith she bound her soul;

7 And her husband heard it, and held his peace at her in the day that he heard it: then her vows shall stand, and her bonds wherewith she bound her soul shall stand.

8 But if her husband disallowed her on the day that he heard it; then he shall make her vow which she vowed, and that which she uttered with her lips, wherewith she bound her soul, of none effect: and the LORD shall forgive her.

9 But every vow of a widow, and of her that is divorced, wherewith they have bound their souls, shall stand against her.

10 And if she vowed in her husband's house, or bound her soul by a bond with an oath;

11 And her husband heard it, and held his peace at her, and disallowed her not: then all her vows shall stand, and every bond wherewith she bound her soul shall stand.

12 But if her husband hath utterly made them void on the day he heard them; then whatsoever proceeded out of her lips concerning her vows, or concerning the bond of her soul, shall not stand: her husband hath made them void; and the LORD shall forgive her.

13 Every vow, and every binding oath to afflict the soul, her husband may establish it, or her husband may make it void.

14 But if her husband altogether hold his peace at her from day to day; then he establisheth all her vows, or all her bonds, which are upon her: he confirmeth them, because he held his peace at her in the day that he heard them.

15 But if he shall any ways make them void after that he hath heard them; then he shall bear her iniquity.

16 These are the statutes, which the LORD commanded Mo'ses, between a man and his wife, between the father and his daughter, being yet in her youth in her father's house.

31 AND the LORD spake unto Mo'ses, saying,

2 Avenge the children of Is'ra-el of the Mid'i-an-ites: afterward shalt thou be gathered unto thy people.

3 And Mo'ses spake unto the people, saying, Arm some of yourselves unto the war, and let them go against the Mid'i-an-ites, and avenge the LORD of Mid'i-an.

4 Of every tribe a thousand, throughout all the tribes of Is'ra-el, shall ye send to the war.

5 So there were delivered out of the thousands of Is'ra-el, a thousand of every tribe, twelve thousand armed for war.

6 And Mo'ses sent them to the war, a thousand of every tribe, them and Phin'e-has the son of E-le-a'zar the priest, to the war, with the holy instruments, and the trumpets to blow in his hand.

7 And they warred against the Mid'i-an-ites, as the LORD commanded Mo'ses; and they slew all the males.

8 And they slew the kings of Mid'i-an, beside the rest of them that were slain; namely, E'vi, and Re'kem, and Zur, and Hur, and Re'ba, five kings of Mid'i-an: Ba'laam also the son of Be'or they slew with the sword.

9 And the children of Is'ra-el took all the women of Mid'i-an captives, and their little ones, and took the spoil of all their cattle, and all their flocks, and all their goods.

10 And they burnt all their cities wherein they dwelt, and all their goodly castles, with fire.

11 And they took all the spoil, and all the prey, both of men and of beasts.

12 And they brought the captives, and the prey, and the spoil, unto Mo'ses, and E-le-a'zar the priest, and unto the congregation of the children of Is'ra-el, unto the camp at the plains of Mo'ab, which are by Jor'dan near Jer'i-cho.

13 ¶ And Mo'ses, and E-le-a'zar the priest, and all the princes of the congregation, went forth to meet them without the camp.

14 And Mo'ses was wroth with the officers of the host, with the captains over thousands, and captains over hundreds, which came from the battle.

15 And Mo'ses said unto them, Have ye saved all the women alive?

16 Behold, these caused the children of Is'ra-el, through the counsel of Ba'laam, to commit trespass against the LORD in the matter of Pe'or, and there was a plague among the congregation of the LORD.

17 Now therefore kill every male among the little ones, and kill every woman that hath known man by lying with him.

18 But all the women children, that have not known a man by lying with him, keep alive for yourselves.

19 And do ye abide without the camp seven days: whosoever hath killed any person, and whosoever hath touched any slain, purify both yourselves and your captives on the third day, and on the seventh day.

20 And purify all your raiment, and all that is made of skins, and all work of goats' hair, and all things made of wood.

21 ¶ And E-le-a'zar the priest said unto the men of war which went to the battle, This is the ordinance of the law which the LORD commanded Mo'ses;

22 Only the gold, and the silver, the brass, the iron, the tin, and the lead,

23 Every thing that may abide the fire, ye shall make it go through the fire, and it shall be clean: nevertheless it shall be purified with the water of separation: and all that abideth not the fire ye shall make go through the water.

24 And ye shall wash your clothes on the seventh day, and ye shall be clean, and afterward ye shall come into the camp.

25 ¶ And the LORD spake unto Mo'ses, saying,

26 Take the sum of the prey that was taken, both of man and of beast, thou, and E-le-a'zar the priest, and the chief fathers of the congregation:

27 And divide the prey into two parts; between them that took the war upon them, who went out to battle, and between all the congregation:

28 And levy a tribute unto the LORD of the men of war which went out to battle: one soul of five hundred, both of the persons, and of the beeves, and of the asses, and of the sheep:

29 Take it of their half, and give it unto E-le-a'zar the priest, for an heave offering of the LORD.

30 And of the children of Is'ra-el's half, thou shalt take one portion of fifty, of the persons, of the beeves, of the asses, and of the flocks, of all manner of beasts, and give them unto the Le'vites, which keep the charge of the tabernacle of the LORD.

31 And Mo'ses and E-le-a'zar the priest did as the LORD commanded Mo'ses.

32 And the booty, being the rest of the prey which the men of war had caught, was six hundred thousand and seventy thousand and five thousand sheep,

33 And threescore and twelve thousand beeves,

34 And threescore and one thousand asses,

35 And thirty and two thousand persons in all, of women that had not known man by lying with him.

36 And the half, which was the portion of them that went out to war, was in number three hundred thousand and seven and thirty thousand and five hundred sheep:

37 And the LORD's tribute of the sheep was six hundred and threescore and fifteen.

38 And the beeves were thirty and six thousand; of which the LORD's tribute was threescore and twelve.

39 And the asses were thirty thousand and five hundred; of which the LORD's tribute was threescore and one.

40 And the persons were sixteen thousand; of which the LORD's tribute was thirty and two persons.

41 And Mo'ses gave the tribute, which was the LORD's heave offering, unto E-le-a'zar the priest, as the LORD commanded Mo'ses.

42 And of the children of Is'ra-el's half, which Mo'ses divided from the men that warred,

43 (Now the half that pertained unto the congregation was three hundred thousand and thirty thousand and seven thousand and five hundred sheep,

44 And thirty and six thousand beeves,

45 And thirty thousand asses and five hundred,

46 And sixteen thousand persons;)

47 Even of the children of Is'ra-el's half, Mo'ses took one portion of fifty, both of man and of beast, and gave them unto the Le'vites, which kept the charge of the tabernacle of the LORD; as the LORD commanded Mo'ses.

48 ¶ And the officers which were over thousands of the host, the captains of thousands, and captains of hundreds, came near unto Mo'ses:

49 And they said unto Mo'ses, Thy servants have taken the sum of the men of war which are under our charge, and there lacketh not one man of us.

50 We have therefore brought an oblation for the LORD, what every man hath gotten, of jewels of gold, chains, and bracelets, rings, earrings, and tablets, to make an atonement for our souls before the LORD.

51 And Mo'ses and E-le-a'zar the priest took the gold of them, even all wrought jewels.

52 And all the gold of the offering that they offered up to the LORD, of the captains of thousands, and of the captains of hundreds, was sixteen thousand seven hundred and fifty shekels.

53 (For the men of war had taken spoil, every man for himself.)

54 And Mo'ses and E-le-a'zar the priest took the gold of the captains of thousands and of hundreds, and brought it into the tabernacle of the congregation, for a memorial for the children of Is'ra-el before the LORD.

32 NOW the children of Reu'ben and the children of Gad had a very great multitude of cattle: and when they saw the land of Ja'zer, and the land of Gil'e-ad, that, behold, the place was a place for cattle;

2 The children of Gad and the children of Reu'ben came and spake unto Mo'ses, and to E-le-a'zar the priest, and unto the princes of the congregation, saying,

3 At'a-roth, and Di'bon, and Ja'zer, and Nim'rah, and Hesh'bon, and E-le-a'leh, and She'bam, and Ne'bo, and Be'on,

4 Even the country which the LORD smote before the congregation of Is'ra-el, is a land for cattle, and thy servants have cattle:

5 Wherefore, said they, if we have found grace in thy sight, let this land be given unto thy servants for a possession, and bring us not over Jor'dan.

6 ¶ And Mo'ses said unto the children of Gad and to the children of Reu'ben, Shall your brethren go to war, and shall ye sit here?

7 And wherefore discourage ye the heart of the children of Is'ra-el from going over into the land which the LORD hath given them?

8 Thus did your fathers, when I sent them from Ka'desh-bar'ne-a to see the land.

9 For when they went up unto the valley of Esh'col, and saw the land, they discouraged the heart of the children of Is'ra-el, that they should not go into the land which the LORD had given them.

10 And the LORD's anger was kindled the same time, and he sware, saying,

11 Surely none of the men that came up out of E'gypt, from twenty years old and upward, shall see the land which I sware unto A'braham, unto I'saac, and unto Ja'cob; because they have not wholly followed me:

12 Save Ca'leb the son of Je-phun'neh the Kenez-ite, and Josh'u-a the son of Nun: for they have wholly followed the LORD.

13 And the LORD's anger was kindled against Is'ra-el, and he made them wander in the wilderness forty years, until all the generation, that had done evil in the sight of the LORD, was consumed.

14 And, behold, ye are risen up in your fathers' stead, an increase of sinful men, to augment yet the fierce anger of the LORD toward Is'ra-el.

15 For if ye turn away from after him, he will yet again leave them in the wilderness; and ye shall destroy all this people.

16 ¶ And they came near unto him, and said, We will build sheepfolds here for our cattle, and cities for our little ones:

17 But we ourselves will go ready armed be-

fore the children of Is'ra-el, until we have brought them unto their place: and our little ones shall dwell in the fenced cities because of the inhabitants of the land.

18 We will not return unto our houses, until the children of Is'ra-el have inherited every man his inheritance.

19 For we will not inherit with them on yonder side Jor'dan, or forward; because our inheritance is fallen to us on this side Jor'dan eastward.

20 ¶ And Mo'ses said unto them, If ye will do this thing, if ye will go armed before the LORD to war,

21 And will go all of you armed over Jor'dan before the LORD, until he hath driven out his enemies from before him,

22 And the land be subdued before the LORD: then afterward ye shall return, and be guiltless before the LORD, and before Is'ra-el; and this land shall be your possession before the LORD.

23 But if ye will not do so, behold, ye have sinned against the LORD: and be sure your sin will find you out.

24 Build you cities for your little ones, and folds for your sheep; and do that which hath proceeded out of your mouth.

25 And the children of Gad and the children of Reu'ben spake unto Mo'ses, saying, Thy servants will do as my lord commandeth.

26 Our little ones, our wives, our flocks, and all our cattle, shall be there in the cities of Gil'e-ad:

27 But thy servants will pass over, every man armed for war, before the LORD to battle, as my lord saith.

28 So concerning them Mo'ses commanded E-le-a'zar the priest, and Josh'u-a the son of Nun, and the chief fathers of the tribes of the children of Is'ra-el:

29 And Mo'ses said unto them, If the children of Gad and the children of Reu'ben will pass with you over Jor'dan, every man armed to battle, before the LORD, and the land shall be subdued before you; then ye shall give them the land of Gil'e-ad for a possession:

30 But if they will not pass over with you armed, they shall have possessions among you in the land of Ca'naan.

31 And the children of Gad and the children of Reu'ben answered, saying, As the LORD hath said unto thy servants, so will we do.

32 We will pass over armed before the LORD into the land of Ca'naan, that the possession of our inheritance on this side Jor'dan may be ours.

33 And Mo'ses gave unto them, even to the children of Gad, and to the children of Reu'ben, and unto half the tribe of Ma-nas'seh the son of Jo'seph, the kingdom of Si'hon king of the Am'or-ites, and the kingdom of Og king of Ba'shan, the land, with the cities thereof in the coasts, even the cities of the country round about.

34 ¶ And the children of Gad built Di'bon, and At'a-roth, and Ar'o-er,

35 And At'roth, Sho'phan, and Ja-a'zer, and Jog'-be-hah,

36 And Beth-nim'rah, and Beth-ha'ran, fenced cities: and folds for sheep.

37 And the children of Reu'ben built Hesh'bon, and E-le-a'leh, and Kir-jath-a'im,

38 And Ne'bo, and Ba'al-me'on, (their names being changed,) and Shib'mah: and gave other names unto the cities which they builded.

39 And the children of Ma'chir the son of Ma-nas'seh went to Gil'e-ad, and took it, and dispossessed the Am'or-ite which was in it.

40 And Mo'ses gave Gil'e-ad unto Ma'chir the son of Ma-nas'seh; and he dwelt therein.

41 And Ja'ir the son of Ma-nas'seh went and took the small towns thereof, and called them Ha'voth-ja'ir.

42 And No'bah went and took Ke'nath, and the villages thereof, and called it No'bah, after his own name.

33 THESE are the journeys of the children of Is'ra-el, which went forth out of the land of E'gypt with their armies under the hand of Mo'ses and Aar'on.

2 And Mo'ses wrote their goings out according to their journeys by the commandment of the LORD: and these are their journeys according to their goings out.

3 And they departed from Ra-me'ses in the first month, on the fifteenth day of the first month; on the morrow after the passover the children of Is'ra-el went out with an high hand in the sight of all the Egyptians

4 For the E-gyptians buried all their firstborn, which the LORD had smitten among them: upon their gods also the LORD executed judgments.

5 And the children of Is'ra-el removed from Ra-me'ses, and pitched in Suc'coth.

6 And they departed from Suc'coth, and pitched in E'tham, which is in the edge of the wilderness.

7 And they removed from E'tham, and turned again unto Pi-ha-hi'roth, which is before Ba'al-ze'phon: and they pitched before Mig'dol.

8 And they departed from before Pi-ha-hi'-roth, and passed through the midst of the sea into the wilderness, and went three days' journey in the wilderness of E'tham, and pitched in Ma'rah.

9 And they removed from Ma'rah, and came unto E'lim: and in E'lim were twelve fountains of water, and threescore and ten palm trees; and they pitched there.

10 And they removed from E'lim, and encamped by the Red sea.

11 And they removed from the Red sea, and encamped in the wilderness of Sin.

12 And they took their journey out of the wilderness of Sin, and encamped in Doph'kah.

13 And they departed from Doph'kah, and encamped in A'lush.

14 And they removed from A'lush, and encamped at Reph'i-dim, where was no water for the people to drink.

15 And they departed from Reph'i-dim, and pitched in the wilderness of Si'nai.

16 And they removed from the desert of Si'-nai, and pitched at Kib'roth-hat-ta'a-vah.

17 And they departed from Kib'roth-hat-ta'-a-vah, and encamped at Ha-ze'roth.

18 And they departed from Ha-ze'roth, and pitched in Rith'mah.

19 And they departed from Rith'mah, and pitched at Rim'mon-pa'rez.

20 And they departed from Rim'mon-pa'rez, and pitched in Lib'nah.

21 And they removed from Lib'nah, and pitched at Ris'sah.

22 And they journeyed from Ris'sah, and pitched in Ke-hel'a-thah.

23 And they went from Ke-hel'a-thah, and pitched in mount Sha'pher.

24 And they removed from mount Sha'pher, and encamped in Har'a-dah.

25 And they removed from Har'a-dah, and pitched in Mak-he'loth.

26 And they removed from Mak-he'loth, and encamped at Ta'hath.

27 And they departed from Ta'hath, and pitched at Ta'rah.

28 And they removed from Ta'rah, and pitched in Mith'cah.

29 And they went from Mith'cah, and pitched in Hash-mo'nah.

30 And they departed from Hash-mo'nah, and encamped at Mo-se'roth.

31 And they departed from Mo-se'roth, and pitched in Ben-e-ja'a-kan.

32 And they removed from Ben-e-ja'a-kan, and encamped at Hor-ha-gid'gad.

33 And they went from Hor–ha-gid'gad, and pitched in Jot'ba-thah.

34 And they removed from Jot'ba-thah, and encamped at E-bro'nah.

35 And they departed from E-bro'nah, and encamped at E'zi-on-ga'ber.

36 And they removed from E'zi-on-ga'ber, and pitched in the wilderness of Zin, which is Ka'desh.

37 And they removed from Ka'desh, and pitched in mount Hor, in the edge of the land of E'dom.

38 And Aar'on the priest went up into mount Hor at the commandment of the LORD, and died there, in the fortieth year after the children of Is'ra-el were come out of the land of E'gypt, in the first day of the fifth month.

39 And Aar'on was an hundred and twenty and three years old when he died in mount Hor.

40 And king A'rad the Ca'naan-ite, which dwelt in the south in the land of Ca'naan, heard of the coming of the children of Is'ra-el.

41 And they departed from mount Hor, and pitched in Zal-mo'nah.

42 And they departed from Zal-mo'nah, and pitched in Pu'non.

43 And they departed from Pu'non, and pitched in O'both.

44 And they departed from O'both, and pitched in Ij'e–ab'a-rim, in the border of Mo'ab.

45 And they departed from I'im, and pitched in Di'bon-gad.

46 And they removed from Di'bon-gad, and encamped in Al'mon–dib-la-tha'im.

47 And they removed from Al'mon–dib-la-tha'im, and pitched in the mountains of Ab'a-rim, before Ne'bo.

48 And they departed from the mountains of Ab'a-rim, and pitched in the plains of Mo'ab by Jor'dan near Jer'i-cho.

49 And they pitched by Jor'dan, from Beth-jes'i-moth even unto A'bel–shit'tim in the plains of Mo'ab.

50 ¶ And the LORD spake unto Mo'ses in the plains of Mo'ab by Jor'dan near Jer'i-cho, saying,

51 Speak unto the children of Is'ra-el, and say unto them, When ye are passed over Jor'-dan into the land of Ca'naan;

52 Then ye shall drive out all the inhabitants of the land from before you, and destroy all their pictures, and destroy all their molten images, and quite pluck down all their high places:

53 And ye shall dispossess the inhabitants of the land, and dwell therein: for I have given you the land to possess it.

54 And ye shall divide the land by lot for an inheritance among your families: and to the more ye shall give the more inheritance, and to the fewer ye shall give the less inheritance: every man's inheritance shall be in the place where his lot falleth; according to the tribes of your fathers ye shall inherit.

55 But if ye will not drive out the inhabitants of the land from before you; then it shall come to pass, that those which ye let remain of them shall be pricks in your eyes, and thorns in your sides, and shall vex you in the land wherein ye dwell.

56 Moreover it shall come to pass, that I shall do unto you, as I thought to do unto them.

34 AND the LORD spake unto Mo'ses, saying,

2 Command the children of Is'ra-el, and say unto them, When ye come into the land of Ca'-naan; (this is the land that shall fall unto you for an inheritance, even the land of Ca'naan with the coasts thereof:)

3 Then your south quarter shall be from the wilderness of Zin along by the coast of E'dom, and your south border shall be the outmost coast of the salt sea eastward:

4 And your border shall turn from the south to the ascent of A-krab'bim, and pass on to Zin: and the going forth thereof shall be from the south Ka'desh-bar'ne-a, and shall go on to Ha'-zar-ad'dar, and pass on to Az'mon:

5 And the border shall fetch a compass from Az'mon unto the river of E'gypt, and the goings out of it shall be at the sea.

6 And as for the western border, ye shall even have the great sea for a border: this shall be your west border.

7 And this shall be your north border: from the great sea ye shall point out for you mount Hor:

8 From mount Hor ye shall point out your border unto the entrance of Ha'math; and the goings forth of the border shall be to Zedad:

9 ¶ And the border shall go on to Ziph'ron, and the goings out of it shall be at Ha'zar-e'nan: this shall be your north border.

10 And ye shall point out your east border from Ha'zar-e'nan to She'pham:

11 And the coast shall go down from She'-pham to Rib'lah, on the east side of A'in; and the border shall descend, and shall reach unto the side of the sea of Chin'ne-reth eastward:

12 And the border shall go down to Jor'dan, and the goings out of it shall be at the salt sea: this shall be your land with the coasts thereof round about.

13 And Mo'ses commanded the children of Is'ra-el, saying, This is the land which ye shall inherit by lot, which the LORD commanded to give unto the nine tribes, and to the half tribe:

14 For the tribe of the children of Reu'ben according to the house of their fathers, and the tribe of the children of Gad according to the house of their fathers, have received their inheritance; and half the tribe of Ma-nas'seh have received their inheritance:

15 The two tribes and the half tribe have received their inheritance on this side Jor'dan near Jer'i-cho eastward, toward the sunrising.

16 And the LORD spake unto Mo'ses, saying,

17 These are the names of the men which shall divide the land unto you: E-le-a'zar the priest, and Josh'u-a the son of Nun.

18 And ye shall take one prince of every tribe, to divide the land by inheritance.

19 And the names of the men are these: Of the tribe of Ju'dah, Ca'leb the son of Je-phun'-neh.

20 And of the tribe of the children of Sim'e-on, She-mu'el the son of Am-mi'hud.

21 Of the tribe of Ben'ja-min, E-li'dad the son of Chis'lon.

22 And the prince of the tribe of the children of Dan, Buk′ki the son of Jog′li.

23 The prince of the children of Jo′seph, for the tribe of the children of Ma-nas′seh, Han′ni-el the son of E′phod.

24 And the prince of the tribe of the children of E′phra-im, Ke-mu′el the son of Shiph′tan.

25 And the prince of the tribe of the children of Zeb′u-lun, E-liz′a-phan the son of Par′nach.

26 And the prince of the tribe of the children of Is′sa-char, Pal′ti-el the son of Az′zan.

27 And the prince of the tribe of the children of Ash′er, A-hi′hud the son of Shel′o-mi.

28 And the prince of the tribe of the children of Naph′ta-li, Ped′a-hel the son of Am-mi′hud.

29 These *are they* whom the LORD commanded to divide the inheritance unto the children of Is′ra-el in the land of Ca′naan.

35 AND the LORD spake unto Mo′ses in the plains of Mo′ab by Jor′dan *near* Jer′i-cho, saying,

2 Command the children of Is′ra-el, that they give unto the Le′vites of the inheritance of their possession cities to dwell in; and ye shall give *also* unto the Le′vites suburbs for the cities round about them.

3 And the cities shall they have to dwell in; and the suburbs of them shall be for their cattle, and for their goods, and for all their beasts.

4 And the suburbs of the cities, which ye shall give unto the Le′vites, *shall reach* from the wall of the city and outward a thousand cubits round about.

5 And ye shall measure from without the city on the east side two thousand cubits, and on the south side two thousand cubits, and on the west side two thousand cubits, and on the north side two thousand cubits; and the city *shall be* in the midst: this shall be to them the suburbs of the cities.

6 And among the cities which ye shall give unto the Le′vites *there shall be* six cities for refuge, which ye shall appoint for the manslayer, that he may flee thither: and to them ye shall add forty and two cities.

7 *So* all the cities which ye shall give to the Le′vites *shall be* forty and eight cities: them *shall ye give* with their suburbs.

8 And the cities which ye shall give *shall be* of the possession of the children of Is′ra-el: from *them that have* many ye shall give many; but from *them that have* few ye shall give few: every one shall give of his cities unto the Le′-vites according to his inheritance which he inheriteth.

9 ¶ And the LORD spake unto Mo′ses, saying,

10 Speak unto the children of Is′ra-el, and say unto them, When ye be come over Jor′dan into the land of Ca′naan;

11 Then ye shall appoint you cities to be cities of refuge for you; that the slayer may flee thither, which killeth any person at unawares.

12 And they shall be unto you cities for refuge from the avenger; that the manslayer die not, until he stand before the congregation in judgment.

13 And of these cities which ye shall give six cities shall ye have for refuge.

14 Ye shall give three cities on this side Jor′-dan, and three cities shall ye give in the land of Ca′naan, *which* shall be cities of refuge.

15 These six cities shall be a refuge, *both* for the children of Is′ra-el, and for the stranger, and for the sojourner among them: that every one that killeth any person unawares may flee thither.

16 And if he smite him with an instrument of iron, so that he die, he *is* a murderer: the murderer shall surely be put to death.

17 And if he smite him with throwing a stone, wherewith he may die, and he die, he *is* a murderer: the murderer shall surely be put to death.

18 Or *if* he smite him with an hand weapon of wood, wherewith he may die, and he die, he *is* a murderer: the murderer shall surely be put to death.

19 The revenger of blood himself shall slay the murderer: when he meeteth him, he shall slay him.

20 But if he thrust him of hatred, or hurl at him by laying of wait, that he die;

21 Or in enmity smite him with his hand, that he die: he that smote *him* shall surely be put to death; *for he is* a murderer: the revenger of blood shall slay the murderer, when he meeteth him.

22 But if he thrust him suddenly without enmity, or have cast upon him any thing without laying of wait,

23 Or with any stone, wherewith a man may die, seeing *him* not, and cast *it* upon him, that he die, and *was* not his enemy, neither sought his harm:

24 Then the congregation shall judge between the slayer and the revenger of blood according to these judgments:

25 And the congregation shall deliver the slayer out of the hand of the revenger of blood, and the congregation shall restore him to the city of his refuge, whither he was fled: and he shall abide in it unto the death of the high priest, which was anointed with the holy oil.

26 But if the slayer shall at any time come without the border of the city of his refuge, whither he was fled;

27 And the revenger of blood find him without the borders of the city of his refuge, and the revenger of blood kill the slayer; he shall not be guilty of blood:

28 Because he should have remained in the city of his refuge until the death of the high priest: but after the death of the high priest the slayer shall return into the land of his possession.

29 So these *things* shall be for a statute of judgment unto you throughout your generations in all your dwellings.

30 Whoso killeth any person, the murderer shall be put to death by the mouth of witnesses: but one witness shall not testify against any person *to cause him* to die.

31 Moreover ye shall take no satisfaction for the life of a murderer, which *is* guilty of death: but he shall be surely put to death.

32 And ye shall take no satisfaction for him that is fled to the city of his refuge, that he should come again to dwell in the land, until the death of the priest.

33 So ye shall not pollute the land wherein ye *are*: for blood it defileth the land: and the land cannot be cleansed of the blood that is shed therein, but by the blood of him that shed it.

34 Defile not therefore the land which ye shall inhabit, wherein I dwell: for I the LORD dwell among the children of Is′ra-el.

36 AND the chief fathers of the families of the children of Gil′e-ad, the son of Ma′-chir, the son of Ma-nas′seh, of the families of the sons of Jo′seph, came near, and spake before Mo′ses, and before the princes, the chief fathers of the children of Is′ra-el:

2 And they said, The Lord commanded my lord to give the land for an inheritance by lot to the children of Is'ra-el: and my lord was commanded of the Lord to give the inheritance of Ze-lo'phe-had our brother unto his daughters.

3 And if they be married to any of the sons of the *other* tribes of the children of Is'ra-el, then shall their inheritance be taken from the inheritance of our fathers, and shall be put to the inheritance of the tribe whereunto they are received: so shall it be taken from the lot of our inheritance.

4 And when the jubile of the children of Is'ra-el shall be, then shall their inheritance be put unto the inheritance of the tribe whereunto they are received: so shall their inheritance be taken away from the inheritance of the tribe of our fathers.

5 And Mo'ses commanded the children of Is'-ra-el according to the word of the Lord, saying, The tribe of the sons of Jo'seph hath said well.

6 This *is* the thing which the Lord doth command concerning the daughters of Ze-lo'phe-had, saying, Let them marry to whom they think best; only to the family of the tribe of their father shall they marry.

7 So shall not the inheritance of the children of Is'ra-el remove from tribe to tribe: for every one of the children of Is'ra-el shall keep himself to the inheritance of the tribe of his fathers.

8 And every daughter, that possesseth an inheritance in any tribe of the children of Is'ra-el, shall be wife unto one of the family of the tribe of her father, that the children of Is'ra-el may enjoy every man the inheritance of his fathers.

9 Neither shall the inheritance remove from *one* tribe to another tribe; but every one of the tribes of the children of Is'ra-el shall keep himself to his own inheritance.

10 Even as the Lord commanded Mo'ses, so did the daughters of Ze-lo'phe-had:

11 For Mah'lah, Tir'zah, and Hog'lah, and Mil'cah, and No'ah, the daughters of Ze-lo'phe-had, were married unto their father's brothers' sons:

12 *And* they were married into the families of the sons of Ma-nas'seh the son of Jo'seph, and their inheritance remained in the tribe of the family of their father.

13 These *are* the commandments and the judgments, which the Lord commanded by the hand of Mo'ses unto the children of Is'ra-el in the plains of Mo'ab by Jor'dan *near* Jer'i-cho.

THE FIFTH BOOK OF MOSES
COMMONLY CALLED

DEUTERONOMY

1 THESE *be* the words which Mo'ses spake unto all Is'ra-el on this side Jor'dan in the wilderness, in the plain over against the Red sea, between Pa'ran, and To'phel, and La'ban, and Ha-ze'roth, and Diz'a-hab.

2 (*There are* eleven days' *journey* from Ho'reb by the way of mount Se'ir unto Ka'desh-bar'ne-a.)

3 And it came to pass in the fortieth year, in the eleventh month, on the first *day* of the month, *that* Mo'ses spake unto the children of Is'ra-el, according unto all that the Lord had given him in commandment unto them;

4 After he had slain Si'hon the king of the Am'or-ites, which dwelt in Hesh'bon, and Og the king of Ba'shan, which dwelt at As'ta-roth in Ed're-i:

5 On this side Jor'dan, in the land of Mo'ab, began Mo'ses to declare this law, saying,

6 The Lord our God spake unto us in Ho'reb, saying, Ye have dwelt long enough in this mount:

7 Turn you, and take your journey, and go to the mount of the Am'or-ites, and unto all *the places* nigh thereunto, in the plain, in the hills, and in the vale, and in the south, and by the sea side; to the land of the Ca'naan-ites, and unto Leb'a-non, unto the great river, the river Eu-phra'tes.

8 Behold, I have set the land before you: go in and possess the land which the Lord sware unto your fathers, A'bra-ham, I'saac, and Ja'cob, to give unto them and to their seed after them.

9 ¶ And I spake unto you at that time, saying, I am not able to bear you myself alone:

10 The Lord your God hath multiplied you, and, behold, ye *are* this day as the stars of heaven for multitude.

11 (The Lord God of your fathers make you a thousand times so many more as ye *are*, and bless you, as he hath promised you!)

12 How can I myself alone bear your cumbrance, and your burden, and your strife?

13 Take you wise men, and understanding, and known among your tribes, and I will make them rulers over you.

14 And ye answered me, and said, The thing which thou hast spoken *is* good *for us* to do.

15 So I took the chief of your tribes, wise men, and known, and made them heads over you, captains over thousands, and captains over hundreds, and captains over fifties, and captains over tens, and officers among your tribes.

16 And I charged your judges at that time, saying, Hear *the causes* between your brethren, and judge righteously between *every* man and his brother, and the stranger *that is* with him.

17 Ye shall not respect persons in judgment; *but* ye shall hear the small as well as the great; ye shall not be afraid of the face of man; for the judgment *is* God's: and the cause that is too hard for you, bring *it* unto me, and I will hear it.

18 And I commanded you at that time all the things which ye should do.

19 ¶ And when we departed from Ho'reb, we went through all that great and terrible wilderness, which ye saw by the way of the mountain of the Am'or-ites, as the Lord our God commanded us; and we came to Ka'desh-bar'ne-a.

20 And I said unto you, Ye are come unto the mountain of the Am'or-ites, which the Lord our God doth give unto us.

21 Behold, the Lord thy God hath set the land before thee: go up *and* possess *it*, as the Lord God of thy fathers hath said unto thee; fear not, neither be discouraged.

22 ¶ And ye came near unto me every one of you, and said, We will send men before us, and they shall search us out the land, and bring us word again by what way we must go up, and into what cities we shall come.

23 And the saying pleased me well: and I took twelve men of you, one of a tribe:

24 And they turned and went up into the mountain, and came unto the valley of Esh'col, and searched it out.

25 And they took of the fruit of the land in their hands, and brought it down unto us, and brought us word again, and said, It is a good land which the LORD our God doth give us.

26 Notwithstanding ye would not go up, but rebelled against the commandment of the LORD your God:

27 And ye murmured in your tents, and said, Because the LORD hated us, he hath brought us forth out of the land of E'gypt, to deliver us into the hand of the Am'or-ites, to destroy us.

28 Whither shall we go up? our brethren have discouraged our heart, saying, The people is greater and taller than we; the cities are great and walled up to heaven; and moreover we have seen the sons of the An'a-kims there.

29 Then I said unto you, Dread not, neither be afraid of them.

30 The LORD your God which goeth before you, he shall fight for you, according to all that he did for you in E'gypt before your eyes;

31 And in the wilderness, where thou hast seen how that the LORD thy God bare thee, as a man doth bear his son, in all the way that ye went, until ye came into this place.

32 Yet in this thing ye did not believe the LORD your God,

33 Who went in the way before you, to search you out a place to pitch your tents in, in fire by night, to shew you by what way ye should go, and in a cloud by day.

34 And the LORD heard the voice of your words, and was wroth, and sware, saying,

35 Surely there shall not one of these men of this evil generation see that good land, which I sware to give unto your fathers,

36 Save Ca'leb the son of Je-phun'neh; he shall see it, and to him will I give the land that he hath trodden upon, and to his children, because he hath wholly followed the LORD.

37 Also the LORD was angry with me for your sakes, saying, Thou also shalt not go in thither.

38 But Josh'u-a the son of Nun, which standeth before thee, he shall go in thither: encourage him: for he shall cause Is'ra-el to inherit it.

39 Moreover your little ones, which ye said should be a prey, and your children, which in that day had no knowledge between good and evil, they shall go in thither, and unto them will I give it, and they shall possess it.

40 But as for you, turn you, and take your journey into the wilderness by the way of the Red sea.

41 Then ye answered and said unto me, We have sinned against the LORD, we will go up and fight, according to all that the LORD our God commanded us. And when ye had girded on every man his weapons of war, ye were ready to go up into the hill.

42 And the LORD said unto me, Say unto them, Go not up, neither fight; for I am not among you; lest ye be smitten before your enemies.

43 So I spake unto you; and ye would not hear, but rebelled against the commandment of the LORD, and went presumptuously up into the hill.

44 And the Am'or-ites, which dwelt in that mountain, came out against you, and chased you, as bees do, and destroyed you in Se'ir, even unto Hor'mah.

45 And ye returned and wept before the LORD; but the LORD would not hearken to your voice, nor give ear unto you.

46 So ye abode in Ka'desh many days, according unto the days that ye abode there.

2 THEN we turned, and took our journey into the wilderness by the way of the Red sea, as the LORD spake unto me: and we compassed mount Se'ir many days.

2 And the LORD spake unto me, saying,

3 Ye have compassed this mountain long enough: turn you northward.

4 And command thou the people, saying, Ye are to pass through the coast of your brethren the children of E'sau, which dwell in Se'ir; and they shall be afraid of you: take ye good heed unto yourselves therefore:

5 Meddle not with them; for I will not give you of their land, no, not so much as a foot breadth; because I have given mount Se'ir unto E'sau for a possession.

6 Ye shall buy meat of them for money, that ye may eat; and ye shall also buy water of them for money, that ye may drink.

7 For the LORD thy God hath blessed thee in all the works of thy hand: he knoweth thy walking through this great wilderness: these forty years the LORD thy God hath been with thee; thou hast lacked nothing.

8 And when we passed by from our brethren the children of E'sau, which dwelt in Se'ir, through the way of the plain from E'lath, and from E'zi-on-ga'ber, we turned and passed by the way of the wilderness of Mo'ab.

9 And the LORD said unto me, Distress not the Mo'ab-ites, neither contend with them in battle: for I will not give thee of their land for a possession; because I have given Ar unto the children of Lot for a possession.

10 The E'mims dwelt therein in times past, a people great, and many, and tall, as the An'a-kims;

11 Which also were accounted giants, as the An'a-kims; but the Mo'ab-ites call them E'-mims.

12 The Ho'rims also dwelt in Se'ir beforetime; but the children of E'sau succeeded them, when they had destroyed them from before them, and dwelt in their stead; as Is'ra-el did unto the land of his possession, which the LORD gave unto them.

13 Now rise up, said I, and get you over the brook Ze'red. And we went over the brook Ze'-red.

14 And the space in which we came from Ka'desh-bar'ne-a, until we were come over the brook Ze'red, was thirty and eight years; until all the generation of the men of war were wasted out from among the host, as the LORD sware unto them.

15 For indeed the hand of the LORD was against them, to destroy them from among the host, until they were consumed.

16 ¶ So it came to pass, when all the men of war were consumed and dead from among the people,

17 That the LORD spake unto me, saying,

18 Thou art to pass over through Ar, the coast of Mo'ab, this day:

19 And when thou comest nigh over against the children of Am'mon, distress them not, nor meddle with them: for I will not give thee of the land of the children of Am'mon any possession; because I have given it unto the children of Lot for a possession.

20 (That also was accounted a land of giants: giants dwelt therein in old time; and the Am'-mon-ites call them Zam-zum'mims;

21 A people great, and many, and tall, as the

An'a-kims; but the Lord destroyed them before them; and they succeeded them, and dwelt in their stead:

22 As he did to the children of E'sau, which dwelt in Se'ir, when he destroyed the Ho'rims from before them; and they succeeded them, and dwelt in their stead even unto this day:

23 And the A'vims which dwelt in Ha-ze'rim, *even* unto Az'zah, the Caph'to-rims, which came forth out of Caph'tor, destroyed them, and dwelt in their stead.)

24 ¶ Rise ye up, take your journey, and pass over the river Ar'non: behold, I have given into thine hand Si'hon the Am'or-ite, king of Hesh'-bon, and his land: begin to possess *it*, and contend with him in battle.

25 This day will I begin to put the dread of thee and the fear of thee upon the nations *that are* under the whole heaven, who shall hear report of thee, and shall tremble, and be in anguish because of thee.

26 ¶ And I sent messengers out of the wilderness of Ked'e-moth unto Si'hon king of Hesh'bon with words of peace, saying,

27 Let me pass through thy land: I will go along by the high way, I will neither turn unto the right hand nor to the left.

28 Thou shalt sell me meat for money, that I may eat; and give me water for money, that I may drink: only I will pass through on my feet;

29 (As the children of E'sau which dwelt in Se'ir, and the Mo'ab-ites which dwell in Ar, did unto me;) until I shall pass over Jor'dan into the land which the Lord our God giveth us.

30 But Si'hon king of Hesh'bon would not let us pass by him: for the Lord thy God hardened his spirit, and made his heart obstinate, that he might deliver him into thy hand, as *appeareth* this day.

31 And the Lord said unto me, Behold, I have begun to give Si'hon and his land before thee: begin to possess, that thou mayest inherit his land.

32 Then Si'hon came out against us, he and all his people, to fight at Ja'haz.

33 And the Lord our God delivered him before us; and we smote him, and his sons, and all his people.

34 And we took all his cities at that time, and utterly destroyed the men, and the women, and the little ones, of every city, we left none to remain:

35 Only the cattle we took for a prey unto ourselves, and the spoil of the cities which we took.

36 From Ar'o-er, which *is* by the brink of the river of Ar'non, and *from* the city that *is* by the river, even unto Gil'e-ad, there was not one city too strong for us: the Lord our God delivered all unto us:

37 Only unto the land of the children of Am'-mon thou camest not, *nor* unto any place of the river Jab'bok, nor unto the cities in the mountains, nor unto whatsoever the Lord our God forbad us.

3 THEN we turned, and went up the way to Ba'shan: and Og the king of Ba'shan came out against us, he and all his people, to battle at Ed're-i.

2 And the Lord said unto me, Fear him not: for I will deliver him, and all his people, and his land, into thy hand; and thou shalt do unto him as thou didst unto Si'hon king of the Am'or-ites, which dwelt at Hesh'bon.

3 So the Lord our God delivered into our hands Og also, the king of Ba'shan, and all his people: and we smote him until none was left to him remaining.

4 And we took all his cities at that time, there was not a city which we took not from them, threescore cities, all the region of Ar'gob, the kingdom of Og in Ba'shan.

5 All these cities *were* fenced with high walls, gates, and bars; beside unwalled towns a great many.

6 And we utterly destroyed them, as we did unto Si'hon king of Hesh'bon, utterly destroying the men, women, and children, of every city.

7 But all the cattle, and the spoil of the cities, we took for a prey to ourselves.

8 And we took at that time out of the hand of the two kings of the Am'or-ites the land that *was* on this side Jor'dan, from the river of Ar'-non unto mount Her'mon;

9 (Which Her'mon the Si-do'ni-ans call Sir'i-on; and the Am'or-ites call it She'nir;)

10 All the cities of the plain, and all Gil'e-ad, and all Ba'shan, unto Sal'chah and Ed're-i, cities of the kingdom of Og in Ba'shan.

11 For only Og king of Ba'shan remained of the remnant of giants; behold, his bedstead *was* a bedstead of iron; *is* it not in Rab'bath of the children of Am'mon? nine cubits *was* the length thereof, and four cubits the breadth of it, after the cubit of a man.

12 And this land, *which* we possessed at that time, from Ar'o-er, which *is* by the river Ar'non, and half mount Gil'e-ad, and the cities thereof, gave I unto the Reu'ben-ites and to the Gad'ites.

13 And the rest of Gil'e-ad, and all Ba'shan, *being* the kingdom of Og, gave I unto the half tribe of Ma-nas'seh; all the region of Ar'gob, with all Ba'shan, which was called the land of giants.

14 Ja'ir the son of Ma-nas'seh took all the country of Ar'gob unto the coasts of Gesh'u-ri and Ma-ach'a-thi; and called them after his own name, Ba'shan-ha'voth-ja'ir, unto this day.

15 And I gave Gil'e-ad unto Ma'chir.

16 And unto the Reu'ben-ites and unto the Gad'ites I gave from Gil'e-ad even unto the river Ar'non half the valley, and the border even unto the river Jab'bok, *which is* the border of the children of Am'mon;

17 The plain also, and Jor'dan, and the coast *thereof*, from Chin'ne-reth even unto the sea of the plain, *even* the salt sea, under Ash'doth-pis'gah eastward.

18 ¶ And I commanded you at that time, saying, The Lord your God hath given you this land to possess it: ye shall pass over armed before your brethren the children of Is'ra-el, all *that are* meet for the war.

19 But your wives, and your little ones, and your cattle, (*for* I know that ye have much cattle,) shall abide in your cities which I have given you;

20 Until the Lord have given rest unto your brethren, as well as unto you, and *until* they also possess the land which the Lord your God hath given them beyond Jor'dan: and *then* shall ye return every man unto his possession, which I have given you.

21 ¶ And I commanded Josh'u-a at that time, saying, Thine eyes have seen all that the Lord your God hath done unto these two kings: so shall the Lord do unto all the kingdoms whither thou passest.

22 Ye shall not fear them: for the Lord your God he shall fight for you.

23 And I besought the Lord at that time, saying,

24 O Lord God, thou hast begun to shew thy servant thy greatness, and thy mighty hand: for what God *is there* in heaven or in earth, that can do according to thy works, and according to thy might?

25 I pray thee, let me go over, and see the good land that *is* beyond Jor'dan, that goodly mountain, and Leb'a-non.

26 But the Lord was wroth with me for your sakes, and would not hear me: and the Lord said unto me, Let is suffice thee; speak no more unto me of this matter.

27 Get thee up into the top of Pis'gah, and lift up thine eyes westward, and northward, and southward, and eastward, and behold *it* with thine eyes: for thou shalt not go over this Jor'-dan.

28 But charge Josh'u-a, and encourage him, and strengthen him: for he shall go over before this people, and he shall cause them to inherit the land which thou shalt see.

29 So we abode in the valley over against Beth-pe'or.

4 NOW therefore hearken, O Is'ra-el, unto the statutes and unto the judgments, which I teach you, for to do *them*, that ye may live, and go in and possess the land which the Lord God of your fathers giveth you.

2 Ye shall not add unto the word which I command you, neither shall ye diminish *ought* from it, that ye may keep the commandments of the Lord your God which I command you.

3 Your eyes have seen what the Lord did because of Ba-al-pe'or: for all the men that followed Ba-al-pe'or, the Lord thy God hath destroyed them from among you.

4 But ye that did cleave unto the Lord your God *are* alive every one of you this day.

5 Behold, I have taught you statutes and judgments, even as the Lord my God commanded me, that ye should do so in the land whither ye go to possess it.

6 Keep therefore and do *them;* for this *is* your wisdom and your understanding in the sight of the nations, which shall hear all these statutes, and say, Surely this great nation *is* a wise and understanding people.

7 For what nation *is there so* great, who *hath* God *so* nigh unto them, as the Lord our God *is* in all *things that* we call upon him for?

8 And what nation *is there so* great, that hath statutes and judgments *so* righteous as all this law, which I set before you this day?

9 Only take heed to thyself, and keep thy soul diligently, lest thou forget the things which thine eyes have seen, and lest they depart from thy heart all the days of thy life: but teach them thy sons, and thy sons' sons;

10 *Specially* the day that thou stoodest before the Lord thy God in Ho'reb, when the Lord said unto me, Gather me the people together, and I will make them hear my words, that they may learn to fear me all the days that they shall live upon the earth, and *that* they may teach their children.

11 And ye came near and stood under the mountain; and the mountain burned with fire unto the midst of heaven, with darkness, clouds, and thick darkness.

12 And the Lord spake unto you out of the midst of the fire: ye heard the voice of the words, but saw no similitude; only *ye heard* a voice.

13 And he declared unto you his covenant, which he commanded you to perform, *even* ten commandments; and he wrote them upon two tables of stone.

14 ¶ And the Lord commanded me at that time to teach you statutes and judgments, that ye might do them in the land whither ye go over to possess it.

15 Take ye therefore good heed unto yourselves; for ye saw no manner of similitude on the day *that* the Lord spake unto you in Ho'reb out of the midst of the fire:

16 Lest ye corrupt *yourselves,* and make you a graven image, the similitude of any figure, the likeness of male or female,

17 The likeness of any beast that *is* on the earth, the likeness of any winged fowl that flieth in the air,

18 The likeness of any thing that creepeth on the ground, the likeness of any fish that *is* in the waters beneath the earth:

19 And lest thou lift up thine eyes unto heaven, and when thou seest the sun, and the moon, and the stars, *even* all the host of heaven, shouldest be driven to worship them, and serve them, which the Lord thy God hath divided unto all nations under the whole heaven.

20 But the Lord hath taken you, and brought you forth out of the iron furnace, *even* out of E'gypt, to be unto him a people of inheritance, as *ye are* this day.

21 Furthermore the Lord was angry with me for your sakes, and sware that I should not go over Jor'dan, and that I should not go in unto that good land, which the Lord thy God giveth thee *for* an inheritance:

22 But I must die in this land, I must not go over Jor'dan: but ye shall go over, and possess that good land.

23 Take heed unto yourselves, lest ye forget the covenant of the Lord your God, which he made with you, and make you a graven image, *or* the likeness of any *thing,* which the Lord thy God hath forbidden thee.

24 For the Lord thy God *is* a consuming fire, *even* a jealous God.

25 ¶ When thou shalt beget children, and children's children, and ye shall have remained long in the land, and shall corrupt *yourselves,* and make a graven image, *or* the likeness of any *thing,* and shall do evil in the sight of the Lord thy God, to provoke him to anger:

26 I call heaven and earth to witness against you this day, that ye shall soon utterly perish from off the land whereunto ye go over Jor'dan to possess it; ye shall not prolong *your* days upon it, but shall utterly be destroyed.

27 And the Lord shall scatter you among the nations, and ye shall be left few in number among the heathen, whither the Lord shall lead you.

28 And there ye shall serve gods, the work of men's hands, wood and stone, which neither see, nor hear, nor eat, nor smell.

29 But if from thence thou shalt seek the Lord thy God, thou shalt find *him,* if thou seek him with all thy heart and with all thy soul.

30 When thou art in tribulation, and all these things are come upon thee, *even* in the latter days, if thou turn to the Lord thy God, and shalt be obedient unto his voice;

31 (For the Lord thy God *is* a merciful God;) he will not forsake thee, neither destroy thee, nor forget the covenant of thy fathers which he sware unto them.

32 For ask now of the days that are past, which were before thee, since the day that God created man upon the earth, and *ask* from the one side of heaven unto the other, whether

there hath been *any such thing* as this great thing *is*, or hath been heard like it?

33 Did *ever* people hear the voice of God speaking out of the midst of the fire, as thou hast heard, and live?

34 Or hath God assayed to go *and* take him a nation from the midst of *another* nation, by temptations, by signs, and by wonders, and by war, and by a mighty hand, and by a stretched out arm, and by great terrors, according to all that the LORD your God did for you in E'gypt before your eyes?

35 Unto thee it was shewed, that thou mightest know that the LORD he *is* God; *there is* none else beside him.

36 Out of heaven he made thee to hear his voice, that he might instruct thee: and upon earth he shewed thee his great fire; and thou heardest his words out of the midst of the fire.

37 And because he loved thy fathers, therefore he chose their seed after them, and brought thee out in his sight with his mighty power out of E'gypt;

38 To drive out nations from before thee greater and mightier than thou *art*, to bring thee in, to give thee their land *for* an inheritance, as *it is* this day.

39 Know therefore this day, and consider *it* in thine heart, that the LORD he *is* God in heaven above, and upon the earth beneath: *there is* none else.

40 Thou shalt keep therefore his statutes, and his commandments, which I command thee this day, that it may go well with thee, and with thy children after thee, and that thou mayest prolong *thy* days upon the earth, which the LORD thy God giveth thee, for ever.

41 ¶ Then Mo'ses severed three cities on this side Jor'dan toward the sunrising;

42 That the slayer might flee thither, which should kill his neighbour unawares, and hated him not in times past; and that fleeing unto one of these cities he might live:

43 *Namely*, Be'zer in the wilderness, in the plain country, of the Reu'ben-ites; and Ra'moth in Gil'e-ad, of the Gad'ites; and Go'lan in Ba'-shan, of the Ma-nas'sites.

44 ¶ And this *is* the law which Mo'ses set before the children of Is'ra-el:

45 These *are* the testimonies, and the statutes, and the judgments, which Mo'ses spake unto the children of Is'ra-el, after they came forth out of E'gypt,

46 On this side Jor'dan, in the valley over against Beth-pe'or, in the land of Si'hon king of the Am'or-ites, who dwelt at Hesh'bon, whom Mo'ses and the children of Is'ra-el smote, after they were come forth out of E'gypt:

47 And they possessed his land, and the land of Og king of Ba'shan, two kings of the Am'or-ites, which *were* on this side Jor'dan toward the sunrising;

48 From Ar'o-er, which *is* by the bank of the river Ar'non, even unto mount Si'on, which *is* Her'mon,

49 And all the plain on this side Jor'dan eastward, even unto the sea of the plain, under the springs of Pis'gah.

5 AND Mo'ses called all Is'ra-el, and said unto them, Hear, O Is'ra-el, the statutes and judgments which I speak in your ears this day, that ye may learn them, and keep, and do them.

2 The LORD our God made a covenant with us in Ho'reb.

3 The LORD made not this covenant with our fathers, but with us, *even* us, who *are* all of us here alive this day.

4 The LORD talked with you face to face in the mount out of the midst of the fire,

5 (I stood between the LORD and you at that time, to shew you the word of the LORD: for ye were afraid by reason of the fire, and went not up into the mount;) saying,

6 ¶ I *am* the LORD thy God, which brought thee out of the land of E'gypt, from the house of bondage.

7 Thou shalt have none other gods before me.

8 Thou shalt not make thee *any* graven image, *or* any likeness of *any thing* that *is* in heaven above, or that *is* in the earth beneath, or that *is* in the waters beneath the earth:

9 Thou shalt not bow down thyself unto them, nor serve them: for I the LORD thy God *am* a jealous God, visiting the iniquity of the fathers upon the children unto the third and fourth *generation* of them that hate me,

10 And shewing mercy unto thousands of them that love me and keep my commandments.

11 Thou shalt not take the name of the LORD thy God in vain: for the LORD will not hold *him* guiltless that taketh his name in vain.

12 Keep the sabbath day to sanctify it, as the LORD thy God hath commanded thee.

13 Six days thou shalt labour, and do all thy work:

14 But the seventh day *is* the sabbath of the LORD thy God: *in it* thou shalt not do any work, thou, nor thy son, nor thy daughter, nor thy manservant, nor thy maidservant, nor thine ox, nor thine ass, nor any of thy cattle, nor thy stranger that *is* within thy gates; that thy manservant and thy maidservant may rest as well as thou.

15 And remember that thou wast a servant in the land of E'gypt, and *that* the LORD thy God brought thee out thence through a mighty hand and by a stretched out arm: therefore the LORD thy God commanded thee to keep the sabbath day.

16 ¶ Honour thy father and thy mother, as the LORD thy God hath commanded thee; that thy days may be prolonged, and that it may go well with thee, in the land which the LORD thy God giveth thee.

17 Thou shalt not kill.

18 Neither shalt thou commit adultery.

19 Neither shalt thou steal.

20 Neither shalt thou bear false witness against thy neighbour.

21 Neither shalt thou desire thy neighbour's wife, neither shalt thou covet thy neighbour's house, his field, or his manservant, or his maidservant, his ox, or his ass, or any *thing* that *is* thy neighbour's.

22 ¶ These words the LORD spake unto all your assembly in the mount out of the midst of the fire, of the cloud, and of the thick darkness, with a great voice: and he added no more. And he wrote them in two tables of stone, and delivered them unto me.

23 And it came to pass, when ye heard the voice out of the midst of the darkness, (for the mountain did burn with fire,) that ye came near unto me, *even* all the heads of your tribes, and your elders;

24 And ye said, Behold, the LORD our God hath shewed us his glory and his greatness, and we have heard his voice out of the midst of the fire: we have seen this day that God doth talk with man, and he liveth.

25 Now therefore why should we die? for this great fire will consume us: if we hear the voice of the LORD our God any more, then we shall die.

26 For who *is there of* all flesh, that hath heard the voice of the living God speaking out of the midst of the fire, as we *have,* and lived?

27 Go thou near, and hear all that the LORD our God shall say: and speak thou unto us all that the LORD our God shall speak unto thee; and we will hear *it,* and do *it.*

28 And the LORD heard the voice of your words, when ye spake unto me; and the LORD said unto me, I have heard the voice of the words of this people, which they have spoken unto thee: they have well said all that they have spoken.

29 O that there were such an heart in them, that they would fear me, and keep all my commandments always, that it might be well with them, and with their children for ever!

30 Go say to them, Get you into your tents again.

31 But as for thee, stand thou here by me, and I will speak unto thee all the commandments, and the statutes, and the judgments, which thou shalt teach them, that they may do *them* in the land which I give them to possess it.

32 Ye shall observe to do therefore as the LORD your God hath commanded you: ye shall not turn aside to the right hand or to the left.

33 Ye shall walk in all the ways which the LORD your God hath commanded you, that ye may live, and *that it may be* well with you, and *that* ye may prolong *your* days in the land which ye shall possess.

6 NOW these *are* the commandments, the statutes, and the judgments, which the LORD your God commanded to teach you, that ye might do *them* in the land whither ye go to possess it:

2 That thou mightest fear the LORD thy God, to keep all his statutes and his commandments, which I command thee, thou, and thy son, and thy son's son, all the days of thy life; and that thy days may be prolonged.

3 ¶ Hear therefore, O Is'ra-el, and observe to do *it;* that it may be well with thee, and that ye may increase mightily, as the LORD God of thy fathers hath promised thee, in the land that floweth with milk and honey.

4 Hear, O Is'ra-el: the LORD our God *is* one LORD:

5 And thou shalt love the LORD thy God with all thine heart, and with all thy soul, and with all thy might.

6 And these words, which I command thee this day, shall be in thine heart:

7 And thou shalt teach them diligently unto thy children, and shalt talk of them when thou sittest in thine house, and when thou walkest by the way, and when thou liest down, and when thou risest up.

8 And thou shalt bind them for a sign upon thine hand, and they shall be as frontlets between thine eyes.

9 And thou shalt write them upon the posts of thy house, and on thy gates.

10 And it shall be, when the LORD thy God shall have brought thee into the land which he sware unto thy fathers, to A'bra-ham, to I'saac, and to Ja'cob, to give thee great and goodly cities, which thou buildedst not,

11 And houses full of all good *things,* which thou filledst not, and wells digged, which thou diggedst not, vineyards and olive trees, which thou plantedst not; when thou shalt have eaten and be full;

12 *Then* beware lest thou forget the LORD, which brought thee forth out of the land of E'-gypt, from the house of bondage.

13 Thou shalt fear the LORD thy God, and serve him, and shalt swear by his name.

14 Ye shall not go after other gods, of the gods of the people which *are* round about you;

15 (For the LORD thy God *is* a jealous God among you) lest the anger of the LORD thy God be kindled against thee, and destroy thee from off the face of the earth.

16 ¶ Ye shall not tempt the LORD your God, as ye tempted *him* in Mas'sah.

17 Ye shall diligently keep the commandments of the LORD your God, and his testimonies, and his statutes, which he hath commanded thee.

18 And thou shalt do *that which is* right and good in the sight of the LORD: that it may be well with thee, and that thou mayest go in and possess the good land which the LORD sware unto thy fathers,

19 To cast out all thine enemies from before thee, as the LORD hath spoken.

20 *And* when thy son asketh thee in time to come, saying, What *mean* the testimonies, and the statutes, and the judgments, which the LORD our God hath commanded you?

21 Then thou shalt say unto thy son, We were Pha'raoh's bondmen in E'gypt; and the LORD brought us out of E'gypt with a mighty hand:

22 And the LORD shewed signs and wonders, great and sore, upon E'gypt, upon Pha'raoh, and upon all his household, before our eyes:

23 And he brought us out from thence, that he might bring us in, to give us the land which he sware unto our fathers.

24 And the LORD commanded us to do all these statutes, to fear the LORD our God, for our good always, that he might preserve us alive, as *it is* at this day.

25 And it shall be our righteousness, if we observe to do all these commandments before the LORD our God, as he hath commanded us.

7 WHEN the LORD thy God shall bring thee into the land whither thou goest to possess it, and hath cast out many nations before thee, the Hit'tites, and the Gir'ga-shites, and the Am'-or-ites, and the Ca'naan-ites, and the Per'iz-zites, and the Hi'vites, and the Jeb'u-sites, seven nations greater and mightier than thou;

2 And when the LORD thy God shall deliver them before thee; thou shalt smite them, and utterly destroy them; thou shalt make no covenant with them, nor shew mercy unto them:

3 Neither shalt thou make marriages with them; thy daughter thou shalt not give unto his son, nor his daughter shalt thou take unto thy son.

4 For they will turn away thy son from following me, that they may serve other gods: so will the anger of the LORD be kindled against you, and destroy thee suddenly.

5 But thus shall ye deal with them; ye shall destroy their altars, and break down their images, and cut down their groves, and burn their graven images with fire.

6 For thou *art* an holy people unto the LORD thy God: the LORD thy God hath chosen thee to be a special people unto himself, above all people that *are* upon the face of the earth.

7 The LORD did not set his love upon you, nor choose you, because ye were more in number

than any people; for ye *were* the fewest of all people:

8 But because the LORD loved you, and because he would keep the oath which he had sworn unto your fathers, hath the LORD brought you out with a mighty hand, and redeemed you out of the house of bondmen, from the hand of Pha'raoh king of E'gypt.

9 Know therefore that the LORD thy God, he *is* God, the faithful God, which keepeth covenant and mercy with them that love him and keep his commandments to a thousand generations;

10 And repayeth them that hate him to their face, to destroy them: he will not be slack to him that hateth him, he will repay him to his face.

11 Thou shalt therefore keep the commandments, and the statutes, and the judgments, which I command thee this day, to do them.

12 ¶ Wherefore it shall come to pass, if ye hearken to these judgments, and keep, and do them, that the LORD thy God shall keep unto thee the covenant and the mercy which he sware unto thy fathers:

13 And he will love thee, and bless thee, and multiply thee: he will also bless the fruit of thy womb, and the fruit of thy land, thy corn, and thy wine, and thine oil, the increase of thy kine, and the flocks of thy sheep, in the land which he sware unto thy fathers to give thee.

14 Thou shalt be blessed above all people: there shall not be male or female barren among you, or among your cattle.

15 And the LORD will take away from thee all sickness, and will put none of the evil diseases of E'gypt, which thou knowest, upon thee; but will lay them upon all *them* that hate thee.

16 And thou shalt consume all the people which the LORD thy God shall deliver thee; thine eye shall have no pity upon them: neither shalt thou serve their gods; for that *will be* a snare unto thee.

17 If thou shalt say in thine heart, These nations *are* more than I; how can I dispossess them?

18 Thou shalt not be afraid of them: *but* shalt well remember what the LORD thy God did unto Pha'raoh, and unto all E'gypt;

19 The great temptations which thine eyes saw, and the signs, and the wonders, and the mighty hand, and the stretched out arm, whereby the LORD thy God brought thee out: so shall the LORD thy God do unto all the people of whom thou art afraid.

20 Moreover the LORD thy God will send the hornet among them, until they that are left, and hide themselves from thee, be destroyed.

21 Thou shalt not be affrighted at them: for the LORD thy God *is* among you, a mighty God and terrible.

22 And the LORD thy God will put out those nations before thee by little and little: thou mayest not consume them at once, lest the beasts of the field increase upon thee.

23 But the LORD thy God shall deliver them unto thee, and shall destroy them with a mighty destruction, until they be destroyed.

24 And he shall deliver their kings into thine hand, and thou shalt destroy their name from under heaven: there shall no man be able to stand before thee, until thou have destroyed them.

25 The graven images of their gods shall ye burn with fire: thou shalt not desire the silver or gold *that is* on them, nor take *it* unto thee, lest

thou be snared therein: for it *is* an abomination to the LORD thy God.

26 Neither shalt thou bring an abomination into thine house, lest thou be a cursed thing like it: *but* thou shalt utterly detest it, and thou shalt utterly abhor it; for it *is* a cursed thing.

8 ALL the commandments which I command thee this day shall ye observe to do, that ye may live, and multiply, and go in and possess the land which the LORD sware unto your fathers.

2 And thou shalt remember all the way which the LORD thy God led thee these forty years in the wilderness, to humble thee, *and* to prove thee, to know what *was* in thine heart, whether thou wouldest keep his commandments, or no.

3 And he humbled thee, and suffered thee to hunger, and fed thee with manna, which thou knewest not, neither did thy fathers know; that he might make thee know that man doth not live by bread only, but by every *word* that proceedeth out of the mouth of the LORD doth man live.

4 Thy raiment waxed not old upon thee, neither did thy foot swell, these forty years.

5 Thou shalt also consider in thine heart, that, as a man chasteneth his son, *so* the LORD thy God chasteneth thee.

6 Therefore thou shalt keep the commandments of the LORD thy God, to walk in his ways, and to fear him.

7 For the LORD thy God bringeth thee into a good land, a land of brooks of water, of fountains and depths that spring out of valleys and hills;

8 A land of wheat, and barley, and vines, and fig trees, and pomegranates; a land of oil olive, and honey;

9 A land wherein thou shalt eat bread without scarceness, thou shalt not lack any *thing* in it; a land whose stones *are* iron, and out of whose hills thou mayest dig brass.

10 When thou hast eaten and art full, then thou shalt bless the LORD thy God for the good land which he hath given thee.

11 Beware that thou forget not the LORD thy God, in not keeping his commandments, and his judgments, and his statutes, which I command thee this day:

12 Lest *when* thou hast eaten and art full, and hast built goodly houses, and dwelt *therein;*

13 And *when* thy herds and thy flocks multiply, and thy silver and thy gold is multiplied, and all that thou hast is multiplied;

14 Then thine heart be lifted up, and thou forget the LORD thy God, which brought thee forth out of the land of E'gypt, from the house of bondage;

15 Who led thee through that great and terrible wilderness, *wherein were* fiery serpents, and scorpions, and drought, where *there was* no water; who brought thee forth water out of the rock of flint;

16 Who fed thee in the wilderness with manna, which thy fathers knew not, that he might humble thee, and that he might prove thee, to do thee good at thy latter end;

17 And thou say in thine heart, My power and the might of *mine* hand hath gotten me this wealth.

18 But thou shalt remember the LORD thy God: for *it is* he that giveth thee power to get wealth, that he may establish his covenant which he sware unto thy fathers, as *it is* this day.

19 And it shall be, if thou do at all forget the LORD thy God, and walk after other gods, and serve them, and worship them, I testify against you this day that ye shall surely perish.

20 As the nations which the LORD destroyeth before your face, so shall ye perish; because ye would not be obedient unto the voice of the LORD your God.

9 HEAR, O Is'ra-el: Thou art to pass over Jor'dan this day, to go in to possess nations greater and mightier than thyself, cities great and fenced up to heaven,

2 A people great and tall, the children of the An'a-kims, whom thou knowest, and of whom thou hast heard say, Who can stand before the children of A'nak!

3 Understand therefore this day, that the LORD thy God is he which goeth over before thee; as a consuming fire he shall destroy them, and he shall bring them down before thy face: so shalt thou drive them out, and destroy them quickly, as the LORD hath said unto thee.

4 Speak not thou in thine heart, after that the LORD thy God hath cast them out from before thee, saying, For my righteousness the LORD hath brought me in to possess this land: but for the wickedness of these nations the LORD doth drive them out from before thee.

5 Not for thy righteousness, or for the uprightness of thine heart, dost thou go to possess their land: but for the wickedness of these nations the LORD thy God doth drive them out from before thee, and that he may perform the word which the LORD sware unto thy fathers, A'bra-ham, I'saac, and Ja'cob.

6 Understand therefore, that the LORD thy God giveth thee not this good land to possess it for thy righteousness; for thou art a stiffnecked people.

7 ¶ Remember, and forget not, how thou provokedst the LORD thy God to wrath in the wilderness: from the day that thou didst depart out of the land of E'gypt, until ye came unto this place, ye have been rebellious against the LORD.

8 Also in Ho'reb ye provoked the LORD to wrath, so that the LORD was angry with you to have destroyed you.

9 When I was gone up into the mount to receive the tables of stone, even the tables of the covenant which the LORD made with you, then I abode in the mount forty days and forty nights, I neither did eat bread nor drink water:

10 And the LORD delivered unto me two tables of stone written with the finger of God; and on them was written according to all the words, which the LORD spake with you in the mount out of the midst of the fire in the day of the assembly.

11 And it came to pass at the end of forty days and forty nights, that the LORD gave me the two tables of stone, even the tables of the covenant.

12 And the LORD said unto me, Arise, get thee down quickly from hence; for thy people which thou hast brought forth out of E'gypt have corrupted themselves; they are quickly turned aside out of the way which I commanded them; they have made them a molten image.

13 Furthermore the LORD spake unto me, saying, I have seen this people, and, behold, it is a stiffnecked people:

14 Let me alone, that I may destroy them, and blot out their name from under heaven: and I will make of thee a nation mightier and greater than they.

15 So I turned and came down from the mount, and the mount burned with fire: and the two tables of the covenant were in my two hands.

16 And I looked, and, behold, ye had sinned against the LORD your God, and had made you a molten calf: ye had turned aside quickly out of the way which the LORD had commanded you.

17 And I took the two tables, and cast them out of my two hands, and brake them before your eyes.

18 And I fell down before the LORD, as at the first, forty days and forty nights: I did neither eat bread, nor drink water, because of all your sins which ye sinned, in doing wickedly in the sight of the LORD, to provoke him to anger.

19 For I was afraid of the anger and hot displeasure, wherewith the LORD was wroth against you to destroy you. But the LORD hearkened unto me at that time also.

20 And the LORD was very angry with Aar'on to have destroyed him: and I prayed for Aar'on also the same time.

21 And I took your sin, the calf which ye had made, and burnt it with fire, and stamped it, and ground it very small, even until it was as small as dust: and I cast the dust thereof into the brook that descended out of the mount.

22 And at Tab'e-rah, and at Mas'sah, and at Kib'roth-hat-ta'a-vah, ye provoked the LORD to wrath.

23 Likewise when the LORD sent you from Ka'desh-bar'ne-a, saying, Go up and possess the land which I have given you; then ye rebelled against the commandment of the LORD your God, and ye believed him not, nor hearkened to his voice.

24 Ye have been rebellious against the LORD from the day that I knew you.

25 Thus I fell down before the LORD forty days and forty nights, as I fell down at the first; because the LORD had said he would destroy you.

26 I prayed therefore unto the LORD, and said, O Lord GOD, destroy not thy people and thine inheritance, which thou hast redeemed through thy greatness, which thou hast brought forth out of E'gypt with a mighty hand.

27 Remember thy servants, A'bra-ham, I'saac, and Ja'cob; look not unto the stubbornness of this people, nor to their wickedness, nor to their sin:

28 Lest the land whence thou broughtest us out say, Because the LORD was not able to bring them into the land which he promised them, and because he hated them, he hath brought them out to slay them in the wilderness.

29 Yet they are thy people and thine inheritance, which thou broughtest out by thy mighty power and by thy stretched out arm.

10 AT that time the LORD said unto me, Hew thee two tables of stone like unto the first, and come up unto me into the mount, and make thee an ark of wood.

2 And I will write on the tables the words that were in the first tables which thou brakest, and thou shalt put them in the ark.

3 And I made an ark of shittim wood, and hewed two tables of stone like unto the first, and went up into the mount, having the two tables in mine hand.

4 And he wrote on the tables, according to the first writing, the ten commandments, which the LORD spake unto you in the mount out of the midst of the fire in the day of the assembly: and the LORD gave them unto me.

5 And I turned myself and came down from the mount, and put the tables in the ark which I had made; and there they be, as the LORD commanded me.

6 ¶ And the children of Is'ra-el took their journey from Be-e'roth of the children of Ja'a-kan to Mo-se'ra: there Aar'on died, and there he was buried, and E-le-a'zar his son ministered in the priest's office in his stead.

7 From thence they journeyed unto Gud'go-dah; and from Gud'go-dah to Jot'bath, a land of rivers of waters.

8 ¶ At that time the LORD separated the tribe of Le'vi, to bear the ark of the covenant of the LORD, to stand before the LORD, to minister unto him, and to bless in his name, unto this day.

9 Wherefore Le'vi hath no part nor inheritance with his brethren; the LORD is his inheritance, according as the LORD thy God promised him.

10 And I stayed in the mount, according to the first time, forty days and forty nights; and the LORD hearkened unto me at that time also, and the LORD would not destroy thee.

11 And the LORD said unto me, Arise, take thy journey before the people, that they may go in and possess the land, which I sware unto their fathers to give unto them.

12 ¶ And now, Is'ra-el, what doth the LORD thy God require of thee, but to fear the LORD thy God, to walk in all his ways, and to love him, and to serve the LORD thy God with all thy heart and with all thy soul,

13 To keep the commandments of the LORD, and his statutes, which I command thee this day for thy good?

14 Behold, the heaven and the heaven of heavens is the LORD's thy God, the earth also, with all that therein is.

15 Only the LORD had a delight in thy fathers to love them, and he chose their seed after them, even you above all people, as it is this day.

16 Circumcise therefore the foreskin of your heart, and be no more stiffnecked.

17 For the LORD your God is God of gods, and LORD of lords, a great God, a mighty, and a terrible, which regardeth not persons, nor taketh reward:

18 He doth execute the judgment of the fatherless and widow, and loveth the stranger, in giving him food and raiment.

19 Love ye therefore the stranger: for ye were strangers in the land of E'gypt.

20 Thou shalt fear the LORD thy God; him shalt thou serve, and to him shalt thou cleave, and swear by his name.

21 He is thy praise, and he is thy God, that hath done for thee these great and terrible things, which thine eyes have seen.

22 Thy fathers went down into E'gypt with threescore and ten persons; and now the LORD thy God hath made thee as the stars of heaven for multitude.

11 THEREFORE thou shalt love the LORD thy God, and keep his charge, and his statutes, and his judgments, and his commandments, alway.

2 And know ye this day: for I speak not with your children which have not known, and which have not seen the chastisement of the LORD your God, his greatness, his mighty hand, and his stretched out arm,

3 And his miracles, and his acts, which he did in the midst of E'gypt unto Pha'raoh the king of E'gypt, and unto all his land;

4 And what he did unto the army of E'gypt, unto their horses, and to their chariots; how he made the water of the Red sea to overflow them as they pursued after you, and how the LORD hath destroyed them unto this day;

5 And what he did unto you in the wilderness, until ye came into this place;

6 And what he did unto Da'than and A-bi'-ram, the sons of E-li'ab, the son of Reu'ben: how the earth opened her mouth, and swallowed them up, and their households, and their tents, and all the substance that was in their possession, in the midst of all Is'ra-el:

7 But your eyes have seen all the great acts of the LORD which he did.

8 Therefore shall ye keep all the commandments which I command you this day, that ye may be strong, and go in and possess the land, whither ye go to possess it;

9 And that ye may prolong your days in the land, which the LORD sware unto your fathers to give unto them and to their seed, a land that floweth with milk and honey.

10 ¶ For the land, whither thou goest in to possess it, is not as the land of E'gypt, from whence ye came out, where thou sowedst thy seed, and wateredst it with thy foot, as a garden of herbs:

11 But the land, whither ye go to possess it, is a land of hills and valleys, and drinketh water of the rain of heaven:

12 A land which the LORD thy God careth for: the eyes of the LORD thy God are always upon it, from the beginning of the year even unto the end of the year.

13 ¶ And it shall come to pass, if ye shall hearken diligently unto my commandments which I command you this day, to love the LORD your God, and to serve him with all your heart and with all your soul,

14 That I will give you the rain of your land in his due season, the first rain and the latter rain, that thou mayest gather in thy corn, and thy wine, and thine oil.

15 And I will send grass in thy fields for thy cattle, that thou mayest eat and be full.

16 Take heed to yourselves, that your heart be not deceived, and ye turn aside, and serve other gods, and worship them;

17 And then the LORD's wrath be kindled against you, and he shut up the heaven, that there be no rain, and that the land yield not her fruit; and lest ye perish quickly from off the good land which the LORD giveth you.

18 ¶ Therefore shall ye lay up these my words in your heart and in your soul, and bind them for a sign upon your hand, that they may be as frontlets between your eyes.

19 And ye shall teach them your children, speaking of them when thou sittest in thine house, and when thou walkest by the way, when thou liest down, and when thou risest up.

20 And thou shalt write them upon the door posts of thine house, and upon thy gates:

21 That your days may be multiplied, and the days of your children, in the land which the LORD sware unto your fathers to give them, as the days of heaven upon the earth.

22 ¶ For if ye shall diligently keep all these commandments which I command you, to do them, to love the LORD your God, to walk in all his ways, and to cleave unto him;

23 Then will the LORD drive out all these nations from before you, and ye shall possess greater nations and mightier than yourselves.

24 Every place whereon the soles of your feet shall tread shall be yours: from the wilderness and Leb'a-non, from the river, the river Eu-phra'tes, even unto the uttermost sea shall your coast be.

25 There shall no man be able to stand before you: *for* the LORD your God shall lay the fear of you and the dread of you upon all the land that ye shall tread upon, as he hath said unto you.

26 ¶ Behold, I set before you this day a blessing and a curse;

27 A blessing, if ye obey the commandments of the LORD your God, which I command you this day:

28 And a curse, if ye will not obey the com-mandments of the LORD your God, but turn aside out of the way which I command you this day, to go after other gods, which ye have not known.

29 And it shall come to pass, when the LORD thy God hath brought thee in unto the land whither thou goest to possess it, that thou shalt put the blessing upon mount Ger'i-zim, and the curse upon mount E'bal.

30 *Are* they not on the other side Jor'dan, by the way where the sun goeth down, in the land of the Ca'naan-ites, which dwell in the cham-paign over against Gil'gal, beside the plains of Mo'reh?

31 For ye shall pass over Jor'dan to go in to possess the land which the LORD your God giv-eth you, and ye shall possess it, and dwell therein.

32 And ye shall observe to do all the statutes and judgments which I set before you this day.

12 THESE *are* the statutes and judgments, which ye shall observe to do in the land, which the LORD God of thy fathers giveth thee to possess it, all the days that ye live upon the earth.

2 Ye shall utterly destroy all the places, wherein the nations which ye shall possess served their gods, upon the high mountains, and upon the hills, and under every green tree:

3 And ye shall overthrow their altars, and break their pillars, and burn their groves with fire; and ye shall hew down the graven images of their gods, and destroy the names of them out of that place.

4 Ye shall not do so unto the LORD your God.

5 But unto the place which the LORD your God shall choose out of all your tribes to put his name there, *even* unto his habitation shall ye seek, and thither thou shalt come:

6 And thither ye shall bring your burnt offer-ings, and your sacrifices, and your tithes, and heave offerings of your hand, and your vows, and your freewill offerings, and the firstlings of your herds and of your flocks:

7 And there ye shall eat before the LORD your God, and ye shall rejoice in all that ye put your hand unto, ye and your households, wherein the LORD thy God hath blessed thee.

8 Ye shall not do after all *the things* that we do here this day, every man whatsoever *is* right in his own eyes.

9 For ye are not as yet come to the rest and to the inheritance, which the LORD your God giveth you.

10 But *when* ye go over Jor'dan, and dwell in the land which the LORD your God giveth you to inherit, and *when* he giveth you rest from all your enemies round about, so that ye dwell in safety;

11 Then there shall be a place which the LORD your God shall choose to cause his name to dwell there; thither shall ye bring all that I command you; your burnt offerings, and your sacrifices, your tithes, and the heave offering of your hand, and all your choice vows which ye vow unto the LORD:

12 And ye shall rejoice before the LORD your God, ye, and your sons, and your daughters, and your menservants, and your maidservants, and the Le'vite that *is* within your gates; foras-much as he hath no part nor inheritance with you.

13 Take heed to thyself that thou offer not thy burnt offerings in every place that thou seest:

14 But in the place which the LORD shall choose in one of thy tribes, there thou shalt of-fer thy burnt offerings, and there thou shalt do all that I command thee.

15 Notwithstanding thou mayest kill and eat flesh in all thy gates, whatsoever thy soul lust-eth after, according to the blessing of the LORD thy God which he hath given thee: the unclean and the clean may eat thereof, as of the roe-buck, and as of the hart.

16 Only ye shall not eat the blood; ye shall pour it upon the earth as water.

17 ¶ Thou mayest not eat within thy gates the tithe of thy corn, or of thy wine, or of thy oil, or the firstlings of thy herds or of thy flock, nor any of thy vows which thou vowest, nor thy freewill offerings, or heave offering of thine hand:

18 But thou must eat them before the LORD thy God in the place which the LORD thy God shall choose, thou, and thy son, and thy daugh-ter, and thy manservant, and thy maidservant, and the Le'vite that *is* within thy gates: and thou shalt rejoice before the LORD thy God in all that thou puttest thine hands unto.

19 Take heed to thyself that thou forsake not the Le'vite as long as thou livest upon the earth.

20 ¶ When the LORD thy God shall enlarge thy border, as he hath promised thee, and thou shalt say, I will eat flesh, because thy soul long-eth to eat flesh; thou mayest eat flesh, whatso-ever thy soul lusteth after.

21 If the place which the LORD thy God hath chosen to put his name there be too far from thee, then thou shalt kill of thy herd and of thy flock, which the LORD hath given thee, as I have commanded thee, and thou shalt eat in thy gates whatsoever thy soul lusteth after.

22 Even as the roebuck and the hart is eaten, so thou shalt eat them: the unclean and the clean shall eat *of* them alike.

23 Only be sure that thou eat not the blood: for the blood *is* the life; and thou mayest not eat the life with the flesh.

24 Thou shalt not eat it; thou shalt pour it upon the earth as water.

25 Thou shalt not eat it; that it may go well with thee, and with thy children after thee, when thou shalt do *that which is* right in the sight of the LORD.

26 Only thy holy things which thou hast, and thy vows, thou shalt take, and go unto the place which the LORD shall choose:

27 And thou shalt offer thy burnt offerings, the flesh and the blood, upon the altar of the LORD thy God: and the blood of thy sacrifices shall be poured out upon the altar of the LORD thy God, and thou shalt eat the flesh.

28 Observe and hear all these words which I command thee, that it may go well with thee, and with thy children after thee for ever, when thou doest *that which is* good and right in the sight of the LORD thy God.

29 ¶ When the Lord thy God shall cut off the nations from before thee, whither thou goest to possess them, and thou succeedest them, and dwellest in their land;

30 Take heed to thyself that thou be not snared by following them, after that they be destroyed from before thee; and that thou enquire not after their gods, saying, How did these nations serve their gods? even so will I do likewise.

31 Thou shalt not do so unto the Lord thy God: for every abomination to the Lord, which he hateth, have they done unto their gods; for even their sons and their daughters they have burnt in the fire to their gods.

32 What thing soever I command you, observe to do it: thou shalt not add thereto, nor diminish from it.

13 IF there arise among you a prophet, or a dreamer of dreams, and giveth thee a sign or a wonder,

2 And the sign or the wonder come to pass, whereof he spake unto thee, saying, Let us go after other gods, which thou hast not known, and let us serve them;

3 Thou shalt not hearken unto the words of that prophet, or that dreamer of dreams: for the Lord your God proveth you, to know whether ye love the Lord your God with all your heart and with all your soul.

4 Ye shall walk after the Lord your God, and fear him, and keep his commandments, and obey his voice, and ye shall serve him, and cleave unto him.

5 And that prophet, or that dreamer of dreams, shall be put to death; because he hath spoken to turn *you* away from the Lord your God, which brought you out of the land of E'gypt, and redeemed you out of the house of bondage, to thrust thee out of the way which the Lord thy God commanded thee to walk in. So shalt thou put the evil away from the midst of thee.

6 ¶ If thy brother, the son of thy mother, or thy son, or thy daughter, or the wife of thy bosom, or thy friend, which *is* as thine own soul, entice thee secretly, saying, Let us go and serve other gods, which thou hast not known, thou, nor thy fathers;

7 *Namely,* of the gods of the people which *are* round about you, nigh unto thee, or far off from thee, from the *one* end of the earth even unto the *other* end of the earth;

8 Thou shalt not consent unto him, nor hearken unto him; neither shall thine eye pity him, neither shalt thou spare, neither shalt thou conceal him:

9 But thou shalt surely kill him; thine hand shall be first upon him to put him to death, and afterwards the hand of all the people.

10 And thou shalt stone him with stones, that he die; because he hath sought to thrust thee away from the Lord thy God, which brought thee out of the land of E'gypt, from the house of bondage.

11 And all Is'ra-el shall hear, and fear, and shall do no more any such wickedness as this is among you.

12 ¶ If thou shalt hear *say* in one of thy cities, which the Lord thy God hath given thee to dwell there, saying,

13 *Certain* men, the children of Be'li-al, are gone out from among you, and have withdrawn the inhabitants of their city, saying, Let us go and serve other gods, which ye have not known;

14 Then shalt thou enquire, and make search,

and ask diligently; and, behold, *if it be* truth, *and* the thing certain, *that* such abomination is wrought among you;

15 Thou shalt surely smite the inhabitants of that city with the edge of the sword, destroying it utterly, and all that *is* therein, and the cattle thereof, with the edge of the sword.

16 And thou shalt gather all the spoil of it into the midst of the street thereof, and shalt burn with fire the city, and all the spoil thereof every whit, for the Lord thy God: and it shall be an heap for ever; it shall not be built again.

17 And there shall cleave nought of the cursed thing to thine hand: that the Lord may turn from the fierceness of his anger, and shew thee mercy, and have compassion upon thee, and multiply thee, as he hath sworn unto thy fathers;

18 When thou shalt hearken to the voice of the Lord thy God, to keep all his commandments which I command thee this day, to do *that which is* right in the eyes of the Lord thy God.

14 YE *are* the children of the Lord your God: ye shall not cut yourselves, nor make any baldness between your eyes for the dead.

2 For thou *art* an holy people unto the Lord thy God, and the Lord hath chosen thee to be a peculiar people unto himself, above all the nations that *are* upon the earth.

3 ¶ Thou shalt not eat any abominable thing.

4 These *are* the beasts which ye shall eat: the ox, the sheep, and the goat,

5 The hart, and the roebuck, and the fallow deer, and the wild goat, and the pygarg, and the wild ox, and the chamois.

6 And every beast that parteth the hoof, and cleaveth the cleft into two claws, *and* cheweth the cud among beasts, that ye shall eat.

7 Nevertheless these ye shall not eat of them that chew the cud, or of them that divide the cloven hoof; *as* the camel, and the hare, and the coney: for they chew the cud, but divide not the hoof; *therefore* they *are* unclean unto you.

8 And the swine, because it divideth the hoof, yet cheweth not the cud, it *is* unclean unto you: ye shall not eat of their flesh, nor touch their dead carcase.

9 ¶ These ye shall eat of all that *are* in the waters: all that have fins and scales shall ye eat:

10 And whatsoever hath not fins and scales ye may not eat; it *is* unclean unto you.

11 ¶ *Of* all clean birds ye shall eat.

12 But these *are they* of which ye shall not eat: the eagle, and the ossifrage, and the ospray,

13 And the glede, and the kite, and the vulture after his kind,

14 And every raven after his kind,

15 And the owl, and the night hawk, and the cuckow, and the hawk after his kind,

16 The little owl, and the great owl, and the swan,

17 And the pelican, and the gier eagle, and the cormorant,

18 And the stork, and the heron after her kind, and the lapwing, and the bat.

19 And every creeping thing that flieth *is* unclean unto you: they shall not be eaten.

20 *But of* all clean fowls ye may eat.

21 ¶ Ye shall not eat *of* any thing that dieth of itself: thou shalt give it unto the stranger that *is* in thy gates, that he may eat it; or thou mayest sell it unto an alien: for thou *art* an holy people unto the Lord thy God. Thou shalt not seethe a kid in his mother's milk.

22 Thou shalt truly tithe all the increase of thy seed, that the field bringeth forth year by year.

23 And thou shalt eat before the LORD thy God, in the place which he shall choose to place his name there, the tithe of thy corn, of thy wine, and of thine oil, and the firstlings of thy herds and of thy flocks; that thou mayest learn to fear the LORD thy God always.

24 And if the way be too long for thee, so that thou art not able to carry it; or if the place be too far from thee, which the LORD thy God shall choose to set his name there, when the LORD thy God hath blessed thee:

25 Then shalt thou turn it into money, and bind up the money in thine hand, and shalt go unto the place which the LORD thy God shall choose:

26 And thou shalt bestow that money for whatsoever thy soul lusteth after, for oxen, or for sheep, or for wine, or for strong drink, or for whatsoever thy soul desireth: and thou shalt eat there before the LORD thy God, and thou shalt rejoice, thou, and thine household,

27 And the Le'vite that is within thy gates; thou shalt not forsake him; for he hath no part nor inheritance with thee.

28 ¶ At the end of three years thou shalt bring forth all the tithe of thine increase the same year, and shalt lay it up within thy gates:

29 And the Le'vite, (because he hath no part nor inheritance with thee,) and the stranger, and the fatherless, and the widow, which are within thy gates, shall come, and shall eat and be satisfied; that the LORD thy God may bless thee in all the work of thine hand which thou doest.

15 AT the end of every seven years thou shalt make a release.

2 And this is the manner of the release: Every creditor that lendeth ought unto his neighbour shall release it; he shall not exact it of his neighbour, or of his brother; because it is called the LORD's release.

3 Of a foreigner thou mayest exact it again: but that which is thine with thy brother thine hand shall release;

4 Save when there shall be no poor among you; for the LORD shall greatly bless thee in the land which the LORD thy God giveth thee for an inheritance to possess it:

5 Only if thou carefully hearken unto the voice of the LORD thy God, to observe to do all these commandments which I command thee this day.

6 For the LORD thy God blesseth thee, as he promised thee: and thou shalt lend unto many nations, but thou shalt not borrow; and thou shalt reign over many nations, but they shall not reign over thee.

7 ¶ If there be among you a poor man of one of thy brethren within any of thy gates in thy land which the LORD thy God giveth thee, thou shalt not harden thine heart, nor shut thine hand from thy poor brother:

8 But thou shalt open thine hand wide unto him, and shalt surely lend him sufficient for his need, in that which he wanteth.

9 Beware that there be not a thought in thy wicked heart, saying, The seventh year, the year of release, is at hand; and thine eye be evil against thy poor brother, and thou givest him nought; and he cry unto the LORD against thee, and it be sin unto thee.

10 Thou shalt surely give him, and thine heart shall not be grieved when thou givest unto him: because that for this thing the LORD thy God shall bless thee in all thy works, and in all that thou puttest thine hand unto.

11 For the poor shall never cease out of the land: therefore I command thee, saying, Thou shalt open thine hand wide unto thy brother, to thy poor, and to thy needy, in thy land.

12 ¶ And if thy brother, an He'brew man, or an He'brew woman, be sold unto thee, and serve thee six years; then in the seventh year thou shalt let him go free from thee.

13 And when thou sendest him out free from thee, thou shalt not let him go away empty:

14 Thou shalt furnish him liberally out of thy flock, and out of thy floor, and out of thy winepress: of that wherewith the LORD thy God hath blessed thee thou shalt give unto him.

15 And thou shalt remember that thou wast a bondman in the land of E'gypt, and the LORD thy God redeemed thee: therefore I command thee this thing to day.

16 And it shall be, if he say unto thee, I will not go away from thee; because he loveth thee and thine house, because he is well with thee;

17 Then thou shalt take an aul, and thrust it through his ear unto the door, and he shall be thy servant for ever. And also unto thy maidservant thou shalt do likewise.

18 It shall not seem hard unto thee, when thou sendest him away free from thee; for he hath been worth a double hired servant to thee, in serving thee six years: and the LORD thy God shall bless thee in all that thou doest.

19 ¶ All the firstling males that come of thy herd and of thy flock thou shalt sanctify unto the LORD thy God: thou shalt do no work with the firstling of thy bullock, nor shear the firstling of thy sheep.

20 Thou shalt eat it before the LORD thy God year by year in the place which the LORD shall choose, thou and thy household.

21 And if there be any blemish therein, as if it be lame, or blind, or have any ill blemish, thou shalt not sacrifice it unto the LORD thy God.

22 Thou shalt eat it within thy gates: the unclean and the clean person shall eat it alike, as the roebuck, and as the hart.

23 Only thou shalt not eat the blood thereof; thou shalt pour it upon the ground as water.

16 OBSERVE the month of A'bib, and keep the passover unto the LORD thy God: for in the month of A'bib the LORD thy God brought thee forth out of E'gypt by night.

2 Thou shalt therefore sacrifice the passover unto the LORD thy God, of the flock and the herd, in the place which the LORD shall choose to place his name there.

3 Thou shalt eat no leavened bread with it; seven days shalt thou eat unleavened bread therewith, even the bread of affliction; for thou camest forth out of the land of E'gypt in haste: that thou mayest remember the day when thou camest forth out of the land of E'gypt all the days of thy life.

4 And there shall be no leavened bread seen with thee in all thy coast seven days; neither shall there any thing of the flesh, which thou sacrificedst the first day at even, remain all night until the morning.

5 Thou mayest not sacrifice the passover within any of thy gates, which the LORD thy God giveth thee:

6 But at the place which the LORD thy God shall choose to place his name in, there thou shalt sacrifice the passover at even, at the going

down of the sun, at the season that thou camest forth out of E'gypt.

7 And thou shalt roast and eat *it* in the place which the LORD thy God shall choose: and thou shalt turn in the morning, and go unto thy tents.

8 Six days thou shalt eat unleavened bread: and on the seventh day *shall be* a solemn assembly to the LORD thy God: thou shalt do no work *therein*.

9 ¶ Seven weeks shalt thou number unto thee: begin to number the seven weeks from *such time as* thou beginnest *to put* the sickle to the corn.

10 And thou shalt keep the feast of weeks unto the LORD thy God with a tribute of a freewill offering of thine hand, which thou shalt give *unto the* LORD *thy God*, according as the LORD thy God hath blessed thee:

11 And thou shalt rejoice before the LORD thy God, thou, and thy son, and thy daughter, and thy manservant, and thy maidservant, and the Le'vite that *is* within thy gates, and the stranger, and the fatherless, and the widow, that *are* among you, in the place which the LORD thy God hath chosen to place his name there.

12 And thou shalt remember that thou wast a bondman in E'gypt: and thou shalt observe and do these statutes.

13 ¶ Thou shalt observe the feast of tabernacles seven days, after that thou hast gathered in thy corn and thy wine:

14 And thou shalt rejoice in thy feast, thou, and thy son, and thy daughter, and thy manservant, and thy maidservant, and the Le'vite, the stranger, and the fatherless, and the widow, that *are* within thy gates.

15 Seven days shalt thou keep a solemn feast unto the LORD thy God in the place which the LORD shall choose: because the LORD thy God shall bless thee in all thine increase, and in all the works of thine hands, therefore thou shalt surely rejoice.

16 ¶ Three times in a year shall all thy males appear before the LORD thy God in the place which he shall choose; in the feast of unleavened bread, and in the feast of weeks, and in the feast of tabernacles: and they shall not appear before the LORD empty:

17 Every man *shall give* as he is able, according to the blessing of the LORD thy God which he hath given thee.

18 ¶ Judges and officers shalt thou make thee in all thy gates, which the LORD thy God giveth thee, throughout thy tribes: and they shall judge the people with just judgment.

19 Thou shalt not wrest judgment; thou shalt not respect persons, neither take a gift: for a gift doth blind the eyes of the wise, and pervert the words of the righteous.

20 That which is altogether just shalt thou follow, that thou mayest live, and inherit the land which the LORD thy God giveth thee.

21 ¶ Thou shalt not plant thee a grove of any trees near unto the altar of the LORD thy God, which thou shalt make thee.

22 Neither shalt thou set thee up *any* image; which the LORD thy God hateth.

17 THOU shalt not sacrifice unto the LORD thy God *any* bullock, or sheep, wherein is blemish, *or* any evilfavouredness: for that *is* an abomination unto the LORD thy God.

2 ¶ If there be found among you, within any of thy gates which the LORD thy God giveth thee, man or woman, that hath wrought wick-

edness in the sight of the LORD thy God, in transgressing his covenant,

3 And hath gone and served other gods, and worshipped them, either the sun, or moon, or any of the host of heaven, which I have not commanded;

4 And it be told thee, and thou hast heard *of it*, and enquired diligently, and, behold, *it be* true, *and* the thing certain, *that* such abomination is wrought in Is'ra-el:

5 Then shalt thou bring forth that man or that woman, which have committed that wicked thing, unto thy gates, *even* that man or that woman, and shalt stone them with stones, till they die.

6 At the mouth of two witnesses, or three witnesses, shall he that is worthy of death be put to death; *but* at the mouth of one witness he shall not be put to death.

7 The hands of the witnesses shall be first upon him to put him to death, and afterward the hands of all the people. So thou shalt put the evil away from among you.

8 ¶ If there arise a matter too hard for thee in judgment, between blood and blood, between plea and plea, and between stroke and stroke, *being* matters of controversy within thy gates: then shalt thou arise, and get thee up into the place which the LORD thy God shall choose;

9 And thou shalt come unto the priests the Le'vites, and unto the judge that shall be in those days, and enquire; and they shall shew thee the sentence of judgment:

10 And thou shalt do according to the sentence, which they of that place which the LORD shall choose shall shew thee; and thou shalt observe to do according to all that they inform thee:

11 According to the sentence of the law which they shall teach thee, and according to the judgment which they shall tell thee, thou shalt do: thou shalt not decline from the sentence which they shall shew thee, *to* the right hand, nor *to* the left.

12 And the man that will do presumptuously, and will not hearken unto the priest that standeth to minister there before the LORD thy God, or unto the judge, even that man shall die: and thou shalt put away the evil from Is'ra-el.

13 And all the people shall hear, and fear, and do no more presumptuously.

14 ¶ When thou art come unto the land which the LORD thy God giveth thee, and shalt possess it, and shalt dwell therein, and shalt say, I will set a king over me, like as all the nations that *are* about me;

15 Thou shalt in any wise set *him* king over thee, whom the LORD thy God shall choose: *one* from among thy brethren shalt thou set king over thee: thou mayest not set a stranger over thee, which *is* not thy brother.

16 But he shall not multiply horses to himself, nor cause the people to return to E'gypt, to the end that he should multiply horses: forasmuch as the LORD hath said unto you, Ye shall henceforth return no more that way.

17 Neither shall he multiply wives to himself, that his heart turn not away: neither shall he greatly multiply to himself silver and gold.

18 And it shall be, when he sitteth upon the throne of his kingdom, that he shall write him a copy of this law in a book out of *that which is* before the priests the Le'vites:

19 And it shall be with him, and he shall read therein all the days of his life: that he may learn to fear the LORD his God, to keep all the words of this law and these statutes, to do them:

20 That his heart be not lifted up above his brethren, and that he turn not aside from the commandment, *to* the right hand, or *to* the left: to the end that he may prolong *his* days in his kingdom, he, and his children, in the midst of Is'ra-el.

18 THE priests the Le'vites, *and* all the tribe of Le'vi, shall have no part nor inheritance with Is'ra-el: they shall eat the offerings of the LORD made by fire, and his inheritance.

2 Therefore shall they have no inheritance among their brethren: the LORD *is* their inheritance, as he hath said unto them.

3 ¶ And this shall be the priest's due from the people, from them that offer a sacrifice, whether *it be* ox or sheep; and they shall give unto the priest the shoulder, and the two cheeks, and the maw.

4 The firstfruit *also* of thy corn, of thy wine, and of thine oil, and the first of the fleece of thy sheep, shalt thou give him.

5 For the LORD thy God hath chosen him out of all thy tribes, to stand to minister in the name of the LORD, him and his sons for ever.

6 ¶ And if a Le'vite come from any of thy gates out of all Is'ra-el, where he sojourned, and come with all the desire of his mind unto the place which the LORD shall choose;

7 Then he shall minister in the name of the LORD his God, as all his brethren the Le'vites *do*, which stand there before the LORD.

8 They shall have like portions to eat, beside that which cometh of the sale of his patrimony.

9 ¶ When thou art come into the land which the LORD thy God giveth thee, thou shalt not learn to do after the abominations of those nations.

10 There shall not be found among you *any one* that maketh his son or his daughter to pass through the fire, *or* that useth divination, *or* an observer of times, or an enchanter, or a witch,

11 Or a charmer, or a consulter with familiar spirits, or a wizard, or a necromancer.

12 For all that do these things *are* an abomination unto the LORD: and because of these abominations the LORD thy God doth drive them out from before thee.

13 Thou shalt be perfect with the LORD thy God.

14 For these nations, which thou shalt possess, hearkened unto observers of times, and unto diviners: but as for thee, the LORD thy God hath not suffered thee so *to do.*

15 ¶ The LORD thy God will raise up unto thee a Prophet from the midst of thee, of thy brethren, like unto me; unto him ye shall hearken;

16 According to all that thou desiredst of the LORD thy God in Ho'reb in the day of the assembly, saying, Let me not hear again the voice of the LORD my God, neither let me see this great fire any more, that I die not.

17 And the LORD said unto me, They have well *spoken that* which they have spoken.

18 I will raise them up a Prophet from among their brethren, like unto thee, and will put my words in his mouth; and he shall speak unto them all that I shall command him.

19 And it shall come to pass, *that* whosoever will not hearken unto my words which he shall speak in my name, I will require *it* of him.

20 But the prophet, which shall presume to speak a word in my name, which I have not commanded him to speak, or that shall speak in the name of other gods, even that prophet shall die.

21 And if thou say in thine heart, How shall we know the word which the LORD hath not spoken?

22 When a prophet speaketh in the name of the LORD, if the thing follow not, nor come to pass, that *is* the thing which the LORD hath not spoken, *but* the prophet hath spoken it presumptuously: thou shalt not be afraid of him.

19 WHEN the LORD thy God hath cut off the nations, whose land the LORD thy God giveth thee, and thou succeedest them, and dwellest in their cities, and in their houses;

2 Thou shalt separate three cities for thee in the midst of thy land, which the LORD thy God giveth thee to possess it.

3 Thou shalt prepare thee a way, and divide the coasts of thy land, which the LORD thy God giveth thee to inherit, into three parts, that every slayer may flee thither.

4 ¶ And this *is* the case of the slayer, which shall flee thither, that he may live: Whoso killeth his neighbour ignorantly, whom he hated not in time past;

5 As when a man goeth into the wood with his neighbour to hew wood, and his hand fetcheth a stroke with the ax to cut down the tree, and the head slippeth from the helve, and lighteth upon his neighbour, that he die; he shall flee unto one of those cities, and live:

6 Lest the avenger of the blood pursue the slayer, while his heart is hot, and overtake him, because the way is long, and slay him; whereas he *was* not worthy of death, inasmuch as he hated him not in time past.

7 Wherefore I command thee, saying, Thou shalt separate three cities for thee.

8 And if the LORD thy God enlarge thy coast, as he hath sworn unto thy fathers, and give thee all the land which he promised to give unto thy fathers;

9 If thou shalt keep all these commandments to do them, which I command thee this day, to love the LORD thy God, and to walk ever in his ways; then shalt thou add three cities more for thee, beside these three:

10 That innocent blood be not shed in thy land, which the LORD thy God giveth thee *for* an inheritance, and *so* blood be upon thee.

11 ¶ But if any man hate his neighbour, and lie in wait for him, and rise up against him, and smite him mortally that he die, and fleeth into one of these cities:

12 Then the elders of his city shall send and fetch him thence, and deliver him into the hand of the avenger of blood, that he may die.

13 Thine eye shall not pity him, but thou shalt put away *the guilt of* innocent blood from Is'ra-el, that it may go well with thee.

14 ¶ Thou shalt not remove thy neighbour's landmark, which they of old time have set in thine inheritance, which thou shalt inherit in the land that the LORD thy God giveth thee to possess it.

15 ¶ One witness shall not rise up against a man for any iniquity, or for any sin, in any sin that he sinneth: at the mouth of two witnesses, or at the mouth of three witnesses, shall the matter be established.

16 ¶ If a false witness rise up against any man to testify against him *that which is* wrong;

17 Then both the men, between whom the controversy *is,* shall stand before the LORD, before the priests and the judges, which shall be in those days;

18 And the judges shall make diligent inquisition: and, behold, if the witness be a false witness, and hath testified falsely against his brother;

19 Then shall ye do unto him, as he had thought to have done unto his brother: so shalt thou put the evil away from among you.

20 And those which remain shall hear, and fear, and shall henceforth commit no more any such evil among you.

21 And thine eye shall not pity; but life shall go for life, eye for eye, tooth for tooth, hand for hand, foot for foot.

20 WHEN thou goest out to battle against thine enemies, and seest horses, and chariots, and a people more than thou, be not afraid of them: for the LORD thy God is with thee, which brought thee up out of the land of E'gypt.

2 And it shall be, when ye are come nigh unto the battle, that the priest shall approach and speak unto the people,

3 And shall say unto them, Hear, O Is'ra-el, ye approach this day unto battle against your enemies: let not your hearts faint, fear not, and do not tremble, neither be ye terrified because of them;

4 For the LORD your God is he that goeth with you, to fight for you against your enemies, to save you.

5 ¶ And the officers shall speak unto the people, saying, What man is there that hath built a new house, and hath not dedicated it? let him go and return to his house, lest he die in the battle, and another man dedicate it.

6 And what man is he that hath planted a vineyard, and hath not yet eaten of it? let him also go and return unto his house, lest he die in the battle, and another man eat of it.

7 And what man is there that hath betrothed a wife, and hath not taken her? let him go and return unto his house, lest he die in the battle, and another man take her.

8 And the officers shall speak further unto the people, and they shall say, What man is there that is fearful and fainthearted? let him go and return unto his house, lest his brethren's heart faint as well as his heart.

9 And it shall be, when the officers have made an end of speaking unto the people, that they shall make captains of the armies to lead the people.

10 ¶ When thou comest nigh unto a city to fight against it, then proclaim peace unto it.

11 And it shall be, if it make thee answer of peace, and open unto thee, then it shall be, that all the people that is found therein shall be tributaries unto thee, and they shall serve thee.

12 And if it will make no peace with thee, but will make war against thee, then thou shalt besiege it:

13 And when the LORD thy God hath delivered it into thine hands, thou shalt smite every male thereof with the edge of the sword:

14 But the women, and the little ones, and the cattle, and all that is in the city, even all the spoil thereof, shalt thou take unto thyself; and thou shalt eat the spoil of thine enemies, which the LORD thy God hath given thee.

15 Thus shalt thou do unto all the cities which are very far off from thee, which are not of the cities of these nations.

16 But of the cities of these people, which the LORD thy God doth give thee for an inheritance, thou shalt save alive nothing that breatheth:

17 But thou shalt utterly destroy them; namely, the Hit'tites, and the Am'or-ites, the Ca'naan-ites, and the Per'iz-zites, the Hi'vites, and the Jeb'u-sites; as the LORD thy God hath commanded thee:

18 That they teach you not to do after all their abominations, which they have done unto their gods; so should ye sin against the LORD your God.

19 ¶ When thou shalt besiege a city a long time, in making war against it to take it, thou shalt not destroy the trees thereof by forcing an ax against them: for thou mayest eat of them, and thou shalt not cut them down (for the tree of the field is man's life) to employ them in the siege:

20 Only the trees which thou knowest that they be not trees for meat, thou shalt destroy and cut them down; and thou shalt build bulwarks against the city that maketh war with thee, until it be subdued.

21 IF one be found slain in the land which the LORD thy God giveth thee to possess it, lying in the field, and it be not known who hath slain him:

2 Then thy elders and thy judges shall come forth, and they shall measure unto the cities which are round about him that is slain:

3 And it shall be, that the city which is next unto the slain man, even the elders of that city shall take an heifer, which hath not been wrought with, and which hath not drawn in the yoke;

4 And the elders of that city shall bring down the heifer unto a rough valley, which is neither eared nor sown, and shall strike off the heifer's neck there in the valley:

5 And the priests the sons of Le'vi shall come near; for them the LORD thy God hath chosen to minister unto him, and to bless in the name of the LORD; and by their word shall every controversy and every stroke be tried:

6 And all the elders of that city, that are next unto the slain man, shall wash their hands over the heifer that is beheaded in the valley:

7 And they shall answer and say, Our hands have not shed this blood, neither have our eyes seen it.

8 Be merciful, O LORD, unto thy people Is'ra-el, whom thou hast redeemed, and lay not innocent blood unto thy people of Is'ra-el's charge. And the blood shall be forgiven them.

9 So shalt thou put away the guilt of innocent blood from among you, when thou shalt do that which is right in the sight of the LORD.

10 ¶ When thou goest forth to war against thine enemies, and the LORD thy God hath delivered them into thine hands, and thou hast taken them captive,

11 And seest among the captives a beautiful woman, and hast a desire unto her, that thou wouldest have her to thy wife;

12 Then thou shalt bring her home to thine house; and she shall shave her head, and pare her nails;

13 And she shall put the raiment of her captivity from off her, and shall remain in thine house, and bewail her father and her mother a full month: and after that thou shalt go in unto her, and be her husband, and she shall be thy wife.

14 And it shall be, if thou have no delight in her, then thou shalt let her go whither she will; but thou shalt not sell her at all for money, thou shalt not make merchandise of her, because thou hast humbled her.

15 ¶ If a man have two wives, one beloved,

and another hated, and they have born him children, *both* the beloved and the hated; and *if* the firstborn son be hers that was hated:

16 Then it shall be, when he maketh his sons to inherit *that* which he hath, *that* he may not make the son of the beloved firstborn before the son of the hated, *which is* indeed the firstborn:

17 But he shall acknowledge the son of the hated *for* the firstborn, by giving him a double portion of all that he hath: for he *is* the beginning of his strength; the right of the firstborn *is* his.

18 ¶ If a man have a stubborn and rebellious son, which will not obey the voice of his father, or the voice of his mother, and *that,* when they have chastened him, will not hearken unto them:

19 Then shall his father and his mother lay hold on him, and bring him out unto the elders of his city, and unto the gate of his place;

20 And they shall say unto the elders of his city, This our son *is* stubborn and rebellious, he will not obey our voice; *he is* a glutton, and a drunkard.

21 And all the men of his city shall stone him with stones, that he die: so shalt thou put evil away from among you; and all Is'ra-el shall hear, and fear.

22 ¶ And if a man have committed a sin worthy of death, and he be to be put to death, and thou hang him on a tree:

23 His body shall not remain all night upon the tree, but thou shalt in any wise bury him that day; (for he that is hanged *is* accursed of God;) that thy land be not defiled, which the LORD thy God giveth thee *for* an inheritance.

22 THOU shalt not see thy brother's ox or his sheep go astray, and hide thyself from them: thou shalt in any case bring them again unto thy brother.

2 And if thy brother *be* not nigh unto thee, or if thou know him not, then thou shalt bring it unto thine own house, and it shall be with thee until thy brother seek after it, and thou shalt restore it to him again.

3 In like manner shalt thou do with his ass; and so shalt thou do with his raiment; and with all lost thing of thy brother's, which he hath lost, and thou hast found, shalt thou do likewise: thou mayest not hide thyself.

4 ¶ Thou shalt not see thy brother's ass or his ox fall down by the way, and hide thyself from them: thou shalt surely help him to lift *them* up again.

5 ¶ The woman shall not wear that which pertaineth unto a man, neither shall a man put on a woman's garment: for all that do so *are* abomination unto the LORD thy God.

6 ¶ If a bird's nest chance to be before thee in the way in any tree, or on the ground, *whether they be* young ones, or eggs, and the dam sitting upon the young, or upon the eggs, thou shalt not take the dam with the young:

7 *But* thou shalt in any wise let the dam go, and take the young to thee; that it may be well with thee, and *that* thou mayest prolong *thy* days.

8 ¶ When thou buildest a new house, then thou shalt make a battlement for thy roof, that thou bring not blood upon thine house, if any man fall from thence.

9 ¶ Thou shalt not sow thy vineyard with divers seeds: lest the fruit of thy seed which thou hast sown, and the fruit of thy vineyard, be defiled.

10 ¶ Thou shalt not plow with an ox and an ass together.

11 ¶ Thou shalt not wear a garment of divers sorts, *as* of woollen and linen together.

12 ¶ Thou shalt make thee fringes upon the four quarters of thy vesture, wherewith thou coverest *thyself.*

13 ¶ If any man take a wife, and go in unto her, and hate her,

14 And give occasions of speech against her, and bring up an evil name upon her, and say, I took this woman, and when I came to her, I found her not a maid:

15 Then shall the father of the damsel, and her mother, take and bring forth *the tokens of* the damsel's virginity unto the elders of the city in the gate:

16 And the damsel's father shall say unto the elders, I gave my daughter unto this man to wife, and he hateth her;

17 And, lo, he hath given occasions of speech *against her,* saying, I found not thy daughter a maid; and yet these *are the tokens of* my daughter's virginity. And they shall spread the cloth before the elders of the city.

18 And the elders of that city shall take that man and chastise him;

19 And they shall amerce him in an hundred *shekels* of silver, and give *them* unto the father of the damsel, because he hath brought up an evil name upon a virgin of Is'ra-el: and she shall be his wife; he may not put her away all his days.

20 But if this thing be true, *and the tokens of* virginity be not found for the damsel:

21 Then they shall bring out the damsel to the door of her father's house, and the men of her city shall stone her with stones that she die: because she hath wrought folly in Is'ra-el, to play the whore in her father's house: so shalt thou put evil away from among you.

22 ¶ If a man be found lying with a woman married to an husband, then they shall both of them die, *both* the man that lay with the woman, and the woman: so shalt thou put away evil from Is'ra-el.

23 ¶ If a damsel *that is* a virgin be betrothed unto an husband, and a man find her in the city, and lie with her;

24 Then ye shall bring them both out unto the gate of that city, and ye shall stone them with stones that they die; the damsel, because she cried not, *being* in the city; and the man, because he hath humbled his neighbour's wife: so thou shalt put away evil from among you.

25 ¶ But if a man find a betrothed damsel in the field, and the man force her, and lie with her: then the man only that lay with her shall die:

26 But unto the damsel thou shalt do nothing; *there is* in the damsel no sin *worthy* of death: for as when a man riseth against his neighbour, and slayeth him, even so *is* this matter:

27 For he found her in the field, *and* the betrothed damsel cried, and *there was* none to save her.

28 ¶ If a man find a damsel *that is* a virgin, which is not betrothed, and lay hold on her, and lie with her, and they be found;

29 Then the man that lay with her shall give unto the damsel's father fifty *shekels* of silver, and she shall be his wife; because he hath humbled her, he may not put her away all his days.

30 ¶ A man shall not take his father's wife, nor discover his father's skirt.

23 HE that is wounded in the stones, or hath his privy member cut off, shall not enter into the congregation of the LORD.

2 A bastard shall not enter into the congregation of the LORD; even to his tenth generation shall he not enter into the congregation of the LORD.

3 An Am'mon-ite or Mo'ab-ite shall not enter into the congregation of the LORD; even to their tenth generation shall they not enter into the congregation of the LORD for ever:

4 Because they met you not with bread and with water in the way, when ye came forth out of E'gypt; and because they hired against thee Ba'laam the son of Be'or of Pe'thor of Mes-o-po-ta'mi-a, to curse thee.

5 Nevertheless the LORD thy God would not hearken unto Ba'laam; but the LORD thy God turned the curse into a blessing unto thee, because the LORD thy God loved thee.

6 Thou shalt not seek their peace nor their prosperity all thy days for ever.

7 ¶ Thou shalt not abhor an E'dom-ite; for he *is* thy brother: thou shalt not abhor an E-gyp'-tian; because thou wast a stranger in his land.

8 The children that are begotten of them shall enter into the congregation of the LORD in their third generation.

9 ¶ When the host goeth forth against thine enemies, then keep thee from every wicked thing.

10 ¶ If there be among you any man, that is not clean by reason of uncleanness that chanceth him by night, then shall he go abroad out of the camp, he shall not come within the camp:

11 But it shall be, when evening cometh on, he shall wash *himself* with water: and when the sun is down, he shall come into the camp *again*.

12 ¶ Thou shalt have a place also without the camp, whither thou shalt go forth abroad:

13 And thou shalt have a paddle upon thy weapon; and it shall be, when thou wilt ease thyself abroad, thou shalt dig therewith, and shalt turn back and cover that which cometh from thee:

14 For the LORD thy God walketh in the midst of thy camp, to deliver thee, and to give up thine enemies before thee; therefore shall thy camp be holy: that he see no unclean thing in thee, and turn away from thee.

15 ¶ Thou shalt not deliver unto his master the servant which is escaped from his master unto thee:

16 He shall dwell with thee, *even* among you, in that place which he shall choose in one of thy gates, where it liketh him best: thou shalt not oppress him.

17 ¶ There shall be no whore of the daughters of Is'ra-el, nor a sodomite of the sons of Is'ra-el.

18 Thou shalt not bring the hire of a whore, or the price of a dog, into the house of the LORD thy God for any vow: for even both these *are* abomination unto the LORD thy God.

19 ¶ Thou shalt not lend upon usury to thy brother; usury of money, usury of victuals, usury of any thing that is lent upon usury:

20 Unto a stranger thou mayest lend upon usury; but unto thy brother thou shalt not lend upon usury: that the LORD thy God may bless thee in all that thou settest thine hand to in the land whither thou goest to possess it.

21 ¶ When thou shalt vow a vow unto the LORD thy God, thou shalt not slack to pay it: for the LORD thy God will surely require it of thee; and it would be sin in thee.

22 But if thou shalt forbear to vow, it shall be no sin in thee.

23 That which is gone out of thy lips thou shalt keep and perform; *even* a freewill offering, according as thou hast vowed unto the LORD thy God, which thou hast promised with thy mouth.

24 ¶ When thou comest into thy neighbour's vineyard, then thou mayest eat grapes thy fill at thine own pleasure; but thou shalt not put *any* in thy vessel.

25 When thou comest into the standing corn of thy neighbour, then thou mayest pluck the ears with thine hand; but thou shalt not move a sickle unto thy neighbour's standing corn.

24 WHEN a man hath taken a wife, and married her, and it come to pass that she find no favour in his eyes, because he hath found some uncleanness in her: then let him write her a bill of divorcement, and give *it* in her hand, and send her out of his house.

2 And when she is departed out of his house, she may go and be another man's *wife*.

3 And *if* the latter husband hate her, and write her a bill of divorcement, and giveth *it* in her hand, and sendeth her out of his house; or if the latter husband die, which took her *to be* his wife;

4 Her former husband, which sent her away, may not take her again to be his wife, after that she is defiled; for that *is* abomination before the LORD: and thou shalt not cause the land to sin, which the LORD thy God giveth thee *for* an inheritance.

5 ¶ When a man hath taken a new wife, he shall not go out to war, neither shall he be charged with any business: *but* he shall be free at home one year, and shall cheer up his wife which he hath taken.

6 ¶ No man shall take the nether or the upper millstone to pledge: for he taketh *a man's* life to pledge.

7 ¶ If a man be found stealing any of his brethren of the children of Is'ra-el, and maketh merchandise of him, or selleth him; then that thief shall die; and thou shalt put evil away from among you.

8 ¶ Take heed in the plague of leprosy, that thou observe diligently, and do according to all that the priests the Le'vites shall teach you: as I commanded them, *so* ye shall observe to do.

9 Remember what the LORD thy God did unto Mir'i-am by the way, after that ye were come forth out of E'gypt.

10 ¶ When thou dost lend thy brother any thing, thou shalt not go into his house to fetch his pledge.

11 Thou shalt stand abroad, and the man to whom thou dost lend shall bring out the pledge abroad unto thee.

12 And if the man *be* poor, thou shalt not sleep with his pledge:

13 In any case thou shalt deliver him the pledge again when the sun goeth down, that he may sleep in his own raiment, and bless thee: and it shall be righteousness unto thee before the LORD thy God.

14 ¶ Thou shalt not oppress an hired servant *that is* poor and needy, *whether he be* of thy brethren, or of thy strangers that *are* in thy land within thy gates:

15 At his day thou shalt give *him* his hire, neither shall the sun go down upon it; for he *is* poor, and setteth his heart upon it: lest he cry against thee unto the LORD, and it be sin unto thee.

16 The fathers shall not be put to death for the children, neither shall the children be put to death for the fathers: every man shall be put to death for his own sin.

17 ¶ Thou shalt not pervert the judgment of the stranger, *nor* of the fatherless; nor take a widow's raiment to pledge:

18 But thou shalt remember that thou wast a bondman in E'gypt, and the LORD thy God redeemed thee thence: therefore I command thee to do this thing.

19 ¶ When thou cuttest down thine harvest in thy field, and hast forgot a sheaf in the field, thou shalt not go again to fetch it: it shall be for the stranger, for the fatherless, and for the widow: that the LORD thy God may bless thee in all the work of thine hands.

20 When thou beatest thine olive tree, thou shalt not go over the boughs again: it shall be for the stranger, for the fatherless, and for the widow.

21 When thou gatherest the grapes of thy vineyard, thou shalt not glean *it* afterward: it shall be for the stranger, for the fatherless, and for the widow.

22 And thou shalt remember that thou wast a bondman in the land of E'gypt: therefore I command thee to do this thing.

25 IF there be a controversy between men, and they come unto judgment, that *the judges* may judge them; then they shall justify the righteous, and condemn the wicked.

2 And it shall be, if the wicked man *be* worthy to be beaten, that the judge shall cause him to lie down, and to be beaten before his face, according to his fault, by a certain number.

3 Forty stripes he may give him, *and* not exceed: lest, *if* he should exceed, and beat him above these with many stripes, then thy brother should seem vile unto thee.

4 ¶ Thou shalt not muzzle the ox when he treadeth out *the corn.*

5 ¶ If brethren dwell together, and one of them die, and have no child, the wife of the dead shall not marry without unto a stranger: her husband's brother shall go in unto her, and take her to him to wife, and perform the duty of an husband's brother unto her.

6 And it shall be, *that* the firstborn which she beareth shall succeed in the name of his brother *which* is dead, that his name be not put out of Is'ra-el.

7 And if the man like not to take his brother's wife, then let his brother's wife go up to the gate unto the elders, and say, My husband's brother refuseth to raise up unto his brother a name in Is'ra-el, he will not perform the duty of my husband's brother.

8 Then the elders of his city shall call him, and speak unto him: and *if* he stand *to it,* and say, I like not to take her;

9 Then shall his brother's wife come unto him in the presence of the elders, and loose his shoe from off his foot, and spit in his face, and shall answer and say, So shall it be done unto that man that will not build up his brother's house.

10 And his name shall be called in Is'ra-el, The house of him that hath his shoe loosed.

11 ¶ When men strive together one with another, and the wife of the one draweth near for to deliver her husband out of the hand of him that smiteth him, and putteth forth her hand, and taketh him by the secrets:

12 Then thou shalt cut off her hand, thine eye shall not pity *her.*

13 ¶ Thou shalt not have in thy bag divers weights, a great and a small.

14 Thou shalt not have in thine house divers measures, a great and a small.

15 *But* thou shalt have a perfect and just weight, a perfect and just measure shalt thou have: that thy days may be lengthened in the land which the LORD thy God giveth thee.

16 For all that do such things, *and* all that do unrighteously, *are* an abomination unto the LORD thy God.

17 ¶ Remember what Am'a-lek did unto thee by the way, when ye were come forth out of E'gypt;

18 How he met thee by the way, and smote the hindmost of thee, *even* all *that* were feeble behind thee, when thou *wast* faint and weary; and he feared not God.

19 Therefore it shall be, when the LORD thy God hath given thee rest from all thine enemies round about, in the land which the LORD thy God giveth thee *for* an inheritance to possess it, *that* thou shalt blot out the remembrance of Am'a-lek from under heaven; thou shalt not forget *it.*

26 AND it shall be, when thou *art* come in unto the land which the LORD thy God giveth thee *for* an inheritance, and possessest it, and dwellest therein;

2 That thou shalt take of the first of all the fruit of the earth, which thou shalt bring of thy land that the LORD thy God giveth thee, and shalt put *it* in a basket, and shalt go unto the place which the LORD thy God shall choose to place his name there.

3 And thou shalt go unto the priest that shall be in those days, and say unto him, I profess this day unto the LORD thy God, that I am come unto the country which the LORD sware unto our fathers for to give us.

4 And the priest shall take the basket out of thine hand, and set it down before the altar of the LORD thy God.

5 And thou shalt speak and say before the LORD thy God, A Syr'i-an ready to perish *was* my father, and he went down into E'gypt, and sojourned there with a few, and became there a nation, great, mighty, and populous:

6 And the E-gyptians evil entreated us, and afflicted us, and laid upon us hard bondage:

7 And when we cried unto the LORD God of our fathers, the LORD heard our voice, and looked on our affliction, and our labour, and our oppression:

8 And the LORD brought us forth out of E'-gypt with a mighty hand, and with an outstretched arm, and with great terribleness, and with signs, and with wonders:

9 And he hath brought us into this place, and hath given us this land, *even* a land that floweth with milk and honey.

10 And now, behold, I have brought the firstfruits of the land, which thou, O LORD, hast given me. And thou shalt set it before the LORD thy God, and worship before the LORD thy God:

11 And thou shalt rejoice in every good *thing* which the LORD thy God hath given unto thee, and unto thine house, thou, and the Le'vite, and the stranger that *is* among you.

12 ¶ When thou hast made an end of tithing all the tithes of thine increase the third year, *which is* the year of tithing, and hast given *it* unto the Le'vite, the stranger, the fatherless, and the widow, that they may eat within thy gates, and be filled;

13 Then thou shalt say before the LORD thy

God, I have brought away the hallowed things out of *mine* house, and also have given them unto the Le´vite, and unto the stranger, to the fatherless, and to the widow, according to all thy commandments which thou hast commanded me: I have not transgressed thy commandments, neither have I forgotten *them:*

14 I have not eaten thereof in my mourning, neither have I taken away *ought* thereof for *any* unclean *use*, nor given *ought* thereof for the dead: *but* I have hearkened to the voice of the LORD my God, *and* have done according to all that thou hast commanded me.

15 Look down from thy holy habitation, from heaven, and bless thy people Is´ra-el, and the land which thou hast given us, as thou swarest unto our fathers, a land that floweth with milk and honey.

16 ¶ This day the LORD thy God hath commanded thee to do these statutes and judgments: thou shalt therefore keep and do them with all thine heart, and with all thy soul.

17 Thou hast avouched the LORD this day to be thy God, and to walk in his ways, and to keep his statutes, and his commandments, and his judgments, and to hearken unto his voice:

18 And the LORD hath avouched thee this day to be his peculiar people, as he hath promised thee, and that *thou* shouldest keep all his commandments;

19 And to make thee high above all nations which he hath made, in praise, and in name, and in honour; and that thou mayest be an holy people unto the LORD thy God, as he hath spoken.

27 AND Mo´ses with the elders of Is´ra-el commanded the people, saying, Keep all the commandments which I command you this day.

2 And it shall be on the day when ye shall pass over Jor´dan unto the land which the LORD thy God giveth thee, that thou shalt set thee up great stones, and plaister them with plaister:

3 And thou shalt write upon them all the words of this law, when thou art passed over, that thou mayest go in unto the land which the LORD thy God giveth thee, a land that floweth with milk and honey; as the LORD God of thy fathers hath promised thee.

4 Therefore it shall be when ye be gone over Jor´dan, *that* ye shall set up these stones, which I command you this day, in mount E´bal, and thou shalt plaister them with plaister.

5 And there shalt thou build an altar unto the LORD thy God, an altar of stones: thou shalt not lift up *any* iron *tool* upon them.

6 Thou shalt build the altar of the LORD thy God of whole stones: and thou shalt offer burnt offerings thereon unto the LORD thy God:

7 And thou shalt offer peace offerings, and shalt eat there, and rejoice before the LORD thy God.

8 And thou shalt write upon the stones all the words of this law very plainly.

9 ¶ And Mo´ses and the priests the Le´vites spake unto all Is´ra-el, saying, Take heed, and hearken, O Is´ra-el; this day thou art become the people of the LORD thy God.

10 Thou shalt therefore obey the voice of the LORD thy God, and do his commandments and his statutes, which I command thee this day.

11 ¶ And Mo´ses charged the people the same day, saying,

12 These shall stand upon mount Ger´i-zim to bless the people, when ye are come over Jor´-

dan; Sim´e-on, and Le´vi, and Ju´dah, and Is´sachar, and Jo´seph, and Ben´ja-min:

13 And these shall stand upon mount E´bal to curse; Reu´ben, Gad, and Ash´er, and Zeb´u-lun, Dan, and Naph´ta-li.

14 ¶ And the Le´vites shall speak, and say unto all the men of Is´ra-el with a loud voice,

15 Cursed *be* the man that maketh *any* graven or molten image, an abomination unto the LORD, the work of the hands of the craftsman, and putteth *it* in *a* secret *place.* And all the people shall answer and say, Amen.

16 Cursed *be* he that setteth light by his father or his mother. And all the people shall say, Amen.

17 Cursed *be* he that removeth his neighbour's landmark. And all the people shall say, Amen.

18 Cursed *be* he that maketh the blind to wander out of the way. And all the people shall say, Amen.

19 Cursed *be* he that perverteth the judgment of the stranger, fatherless, and widow. And all the people shall say, Amen.

20 Cursed *be* he that lieth with his father's wife; because he uncovereth his father's skirt. And all the people shall say, Amen.

21 Cursed *be* he that lieth with any manner of beast. And all the people shall say, Amen.

22 Cursed *be* he that lieth with his sister, the daughter of his father, or the daughter of his mother. And all the people shall say, Amen.

23 Cursed *be* he that lieth with his mother in law. And all the people shall say, Amen.

24 Cursed *be* he that smiteth his neighbour secretly. And all the people shall say, Amen.

25 Cursed *be* he that taketh reward to slay an innocent person. And all the people shall say, Amen.

26 Cursed *be* he that confirmeth not *all* the words of this law to do them. And all the people shall say, Amen.

28 AND it shall come to pass, if thou shalt hearken diligently unto the voice of the LORD thy God, to observe *and* to do all his commandments which I command thee this day, that the LORD thy God will set thee on high above all nations of the earth:

2 And all these blessings shall come on thee, and overtake thee, if thou shalt hearken unto the voice of the LORD thy God.

3 Blessed *shalt* thou *be* in the city, and blessed *shalt* thou *be* in the field.

4 Blessed *shall be* the fruit of thy body, and the fruit of thy ground, and the fruit of thy cattle, the increase of thy kine, and the flocks of thy sheep.

5 Blessed *shall be* thy basket and thy store.

6 Blessed *shalt* thou *be* when thou comest in, and blessed *shalt* thou *be* when thou goest out.

7 The LORD shall cause thine enemies that rise up against thee to be smitten before thy face: they shall come out against thee one way, and flee before thee seven ways.

8 The LORD shall command the blessing upon thee in thy storehouses, and in all that thou settest thine hand unto; and he shall bless thee in the land which the LORD thy God giveth thee.

9 The LORD shall establish thee an holy people unto himself, as he hath sworn unto thee, if thou shalt keep the commandments of the LORD thy God, and walk in his ways.

10 And all people of the earth shall see that thou art called by the name of the LORD; and they shall be afraid of thee.

11 And the LORD shall make thee plenteous

in goods, in the fruit of thy body, and in the fruit of thy cattle, and in the fruit of thy ground, in the land which the LORD sware unto thy fathers to give thee.

12 The LORD shall open unto thee his good treasure, the heaven to give the rain unto thy land in his season, and to bless all the work of thine hand: and thou shalt lend unto many nations, and thou shalt not borrow.

13 And the LORD shall make thee the head, and not the tail; and thou shalt be above only, and thou shalt not be beneath; if that thou hearken unto the commandments of the LORD thy God, which I command thee this day, to observe and to do *them:*

14 And thou shalt not go aside from any of the words which I command thee this day, *to* the right hand, or *to* the left, to go after other gods to serve them.

15 ¶ But it shall come to pass, if thou wilt not hearken unto the voice of the LORD thy God, to observe to do all his commandments and his statutes which I command thee this day; that all these curses shall come upon thee, and overtake thee:

16 Cursed *shalt* thou *be* in the city, and cursed *shalt* thou *be* in the field.

17 Cursed *shall be* thy basket and thy store.

18 Cursed *shall be* the fruit of thy body, and the fruit of thy land, the increase of thy kine, and the flocks of thy sheep.

19 Cursed *shalt* thou *be* when thou comest in, and cursed *shalt* thou *be* when thou goest out.

20 The LORD shall send upon thee cursing, vexation, and rebuke, in all that thou settest thine hand unto for to do, until thou be destroyed, and until thou perish quickly; because of the wickedness of thy doings, whereby thou hast forsaken me.

21 The LORD shall make the pestilence cleave unto thee, until he have consumed thee from off the land, whither thou goest to possess it.

22 The LORD shall smite thee with a consumption, and with a fever, and with an inflammation, and with an extreme burning, and with the sword, and with blasting, and with mildew; and they shall pursue thee until thou perish.

23 And thy heaven that *is* over thy head shall be brass, and the earth that *is* under thee *shall be* iron.

24 The LORD shall make the rain of thy land powder and dust: from heaven shall it come down upon thee, until thou be destroyed.

25 The LORD shall cause thee to be smitten before thine enemies: thou shalt go out one way against them, and flee seven ways before them: and shalt be removed into all the kingdoms of the earth.

26 And thy carcase shall be meat unto all fowls of the air, and unto the beasts of the earth, and no man shall fray *them* away.

27 The LORD will smite thee with the botch of E'gypt, and with the emerods, and with the scab, and with the itch, whereof thou canst not be healed.

28 The LORD shall smite thee with madness, and blindness, and astonishment of heart:

29 And thou shalt grope at noonday, as the blind gropeth in darkness, and thou shalt not prosper in thy ways: and thou shalt be only oppressed and spoiled evermore, and no man shall save thee.

30 Thou shalt betroth a wife, and another man shall lie with her: thou shalt build an house, and thou shalt not dwell therein: thou shalt plant a vineyard, and shalt not gather the grapes thereof.

31 Thine ox *shall be* slain before thine eyes, and thou shalt not eat thereof: thine ass *shall be* violently taken away from before thy face, and shall not be restored to thee: thy sheep *shall be* given unto thine enemies, and thou shalt have none to rescue *them.*

32 Thy sons and thy daughters *shall be* given unto another people, and thine eyes shall look, and fail *with longing* for them all the day long: and *there shall be* no might in thine hand.

33 The fruit of thy land, and all thy labours, shall a nation which thou knowest not eat up; and thou shalt be only oppressed and crushed alway:

34 So that thou shalt be mad for the sight of thine eyes which thou shalt see.

35 The LORD shall smite thee in the knees, and in the legs, with a sore botch that cannot be healed, from the sole of thy foot unto the top of thy head.

36 The LORD shall bring thee, and thy king which thou shalt set over thee, unto a nation which neither thou nor thy fathers have known; and there shalt thou serve other gods, wood and stone.

37 And thou shalt become an astonishment, a proverb, and a byword, among all nations whither the LORD shall lead thee.

38 Thou shalt carry much seed out into the field, and shalt gather *but* little in; for the locust shall consume it.

39 Thou shalt plant vineyards, and dress *them,* but shalt neither drink *of* the wine, nor gather *the grapes;* for the worms shall eat them.

40 Thou shalt have olive trees throughout all thy coasts, but thou shalt not anoint *thyself* with the oil; for thine olive shall cast *his fruit.*

41 Thou shalt beget sons and daughters, but thou shalt not enjoy them; for they shall go into captivity.

42 All thy trees and fruit of thy land shall the locust consume.

43 The stranger that *is* within thee shall get up above thee very high; and thou shalt come down very low.

44 He shall lend to thee, and thou shalt not lend to him: he shall be the head, and thou shalt be the tail.

45 Moreover all these curses shall come upon thee, and shall pursue thee, and overtake thee, till thou be destroyed; because thou hearkenedst not unto the voice of the LORD thy God, to keep his commandments and his statutes which he commanded thee:

46 And they shall be upon thee for a sign and for a wonder, and upon thy seed for ever.

47 Because thou servedst not the LORD thy God with joyfulness, and with gladness of heart, for the abundance of all *things;*

48 Therefore shalt thou serve thine enemies which the LORD shall send against thee, in hunger, and in thirst, and in nakedness, and in want of all *things:* and he shall put a yoke of iron upon thy neck, until he have destroyed thee.

49 The LORD shall bring a nation against thee from far, from the end of the earth, *as* swift as the eagle flieth; a nation whose tongue thou shalt not understand;

50 A nation of fierce countenance, which shall not regard the person of the old, nor shew favour to the young:

51 And he shall eat the fruit of thy cattle, and the fruit of thy land, until thou be destroyed: which *also* shall not leave thee *either* corn,

wine, or oil, or the increase of thy kine, or flocks of thy sheep, until he have destroyed thee.

52 And he shall besiege thee in all thy gates, until thy high and fenced walls come down, wherein thou trustedst, throughout all thy land: and he shall besiege thee in all thy gates throughout all thy land, which the LORD thy God hath given thee.

53 And thou shalt eat the fruit of thine own body, the flesh of thy sons and of thy daughters, which the LORD thy God hath given thee, in the siege, and in the straitness, wherewith thine enemies shall distress thee:

54 So that the man that is tender among you, and very delicate, his eye shall be evil toward his brother, and toward the wife of his bosom, and toward the remnant of his children which he shall leave:

55 So that he will not give to any of them of the flesh of his children whom he shall eat: because he hath nothing left him in the siege, and in the straitness, wherewith thine enemies shall distress thee in all thy gates.

56 The tender and delicate woman among you, which would not adventure to set the sole of her foot upon the ground for delicateness and tenderness, her eye shall be evil toward the husband of her bosom, and toward her son, and toward her daughter,

57 And toward her young one that cometh out from between her feet, and toward her children which she shall bear: for she shall eat them for want of all things secretly in the siege and straitness, wherewith thine enemy shall distress thee in thy gates.

58 If thou wilt not observe to do all the words of this law that are written in this book, that thou mayest fear this glorious and fearful name, THE LORD THY GOD;

59 Then the LORD will make thy plagues wonderful, and the plagues of thy seed, even great plagues, and of long continuance, and sore sicknesses, and of long continuance.

60 Moreover he will bring upon thee all the diseases of E'gypt, which thou wast afraid of; and they shall cleave unto thee.

61 Also every sickness, and every plague, which is not written in the book of this law, them will the LORD bring upon thee, until thou be destroyed.

62 And ye shall be left few in number, whereas ye were as the stars of heaven for multitude; because thou wouldest not obey the voice of the LORD thy God.

63 And it shall come to pass, that as the LORD rejoiced over you to do you good, and to multiply you; so the LORD will rejoice over you to destroy you, and to bring you to nought; and ye shall be plucked from off the land whither thou goest to possess it.

64 And the LORD shall scatter thee among all people, from the one end of the earth even unto the other; and there thou shalt serve other gods, which neither thou nor thy fathers have known, even wood and stone.

65 And among these nations shalt thou find no ease, neither shall the sole of the foot have rest: but the LORD shall give thee there a trembling heart, and failing of eyes, and sorrow of mind:

66 And thy life shall hang in doubt before thee; and thou shalt fear day and night, and shalt have none assurance of thy life:

67 In the morning thou shalt say, Would God it were even! and at even thou shalt say, Would God it were morning! for the fear of thine heart wherewith thou shalt fear, and for the sight of thine eyes which thou shalt see.

68 And the LORD shall bring thee into E'gypt again with ships, by the way whereof I spake unto thee, Thou shalt see it no more again: and there ye shall be sold unto your enemies for bondmen and bondwomen, and no man shall buy you.

29 THESE are the words of the covenant, which the LORD commanded Mo'ses to make with the children of Is'ra-el in the land of Mo'ab, beside the covenant which he made with them in Ho'reb.

2 ¶ And Mo'ses called unto all Is'ra-el, and said unto them, Ye have seen all that the LORD did before your eyes in the land of E'gypt unto Pha'raoh, and unto all his servants, and unto all his land;

3 The great temptations which thine eyes have seen, the signs, and those great miracles:

4 Yet the LORD hath not given you an heart to perceive, and eyes to see, and ears to hear, unto this day.

5 And I have led you forty years in the wilderness: your clothes are not waxen old upon you, and thy shoe is not waxen old upon thy foot.

6 Ye have not eaten bread, neither have ye drunk wine or strong drink: that ye might know that I am the LORD your God.

7 And when ye came unto this place, Si'hon the king of Hesh'bon, and Og the king of Ba'shan, came out against us unto battle, and we smote them:

8 And we took their land, and gave it for an inheritance unto the Reu'ben-ites, and to the Gad'ites, and to the half tribe of Ma-nas'seh.

9 Keep therefore the words of this covenant, and do them, that ye may prosper in all that ye do.

10 ¶ Ye stand this day all of you before the LORD your God; your captains of your tribes, your elders, and your officers, with all the men of Is'ra-el,

11 Your little ones, your wives, and thy stranger that is in thy camp, from the hewer of thy wood unto the drawer of thy water:

12 That thou shouldest enter into covenant with the LORD thy God, and into his oath, which the LORD thy God maketh with thee this day:

13 That he may establish thee to day for a people unto himself, and that he may be unto thee a God, as he hath said unto thee, and as he hath sworn unto thy fathers, to A'bra-ham, to I'saac, and to Ja'cob.

14 Neither with you only do I make this covenant and this oath;

15 But with him that standeth here with us this day before the LORD our God, and also with him that is not here with us this day:

16 (For ye know how we have dwelt in the land of E'gypt; and how we came through the nations which ye passed by;

17 And ye have seen their abominations, and their idols, wood and stone, silver and gold, which were among them:)

18 Lest there should be among you man, or woman, or family, or tribe, whose heart turneth away this day from the LORD our God, to go and serve the gods of these nations; lest there should be among you a root that beareth gall and wormwood;

19 And it come to pass, when he heareth the words of this curse, that he bless himself in his heart, saying, I shall have peace, though I walk

in the imagination of mine heart, to add drunkenness to thirst:

20 The LORD will not spare him, but then the anger of the LORD and his jealousy shall smoke against that man, and all the curses that are written in this book shall lie upon him, and the LORD shall blot out his name from under heaven.

21 And the LORD shall separate him unto evil out of all the tribes of Is'ra-el, according to all the curses of the covenant that are written in this book of the law:

22 So that the generation to come of your children that shall rise up after you, and the stranger that shall come from a far land, shall say, when they see the plagues of the land, and the sicknesses which the LORD hath laid upon it;

23 And that the whole land thereof is brimstone, and salt, and burning, that it is not sown, nor beareth, nor any grass groweth therein, like the overthrow of Sod'om, and Go-mor'rah, Ad'-mah, and Ze-bo'im, which the LORD overthrew in his anger, and in his wrath:

24 Even all nations shall say, Wherefore hath the LORD done thus unto this land? what meaneth the heat of this great anger?

25 Then men shall say, Because they have forsaken the covenant of the LORD God of their fathers, which he made with them when he brought them forth out of the land of E'gypt:

26 For they went and served other gods, and worshipped them, gods whom they knew not, and whom he had not given unto them:

27 And the anger of the LORD was kindled against this land, to bring upon it all the curses that are written in this book:

28 And the LORD rooted them out of their land in anger, and in wrath, and in great indignation, and cast them into another land, as it is this day.

29 The secret things belong unto the LORD our God: but those things which are revealed belong unto us and to our children for ever, that we may do all the words of this law.

30 AND it shall come to pass, when all these things are come upon thee, the blessing and the curse, which I have set before thee, and thou shalt call them to mind among all the nations, whither the LORD thy God hath driven thee,

2 And shalt return unto the LORD thy God, and shalt obey his voice according to all that I command thee this day, thou and thy children, with all thine heart, and with all thy soul;

3 That then the LORD thy God will turn thy captivity, and have compassion upon thee, and will return and gather thee from all the nations, whither the LORD thy God hath scattered thee.

4 If any of thine be driven out unto the outmost parts of heaven, from thence will the LORD thy God gather thee, and from thence will he fetch thee:

5 And the LORD thy God will bring thee into the land which thy fathers possessed, and thou shalt possess it; and he will do thee good, and multiply thee above thy fathers.

6 And the LORD thy God will circumcise thine heart, and the heart of thy seed, to love the LORD thy God with all thine heart, and with all thy soul, that thou mayest live.

7 And the LORD thy God will put all these curses upon thine enemies, and on them that hate thee, which persecuted thee.

8 And thou shalt return and obey the voice of the LORD, and do all his commandments which I command thee this day.

9 And the LORD thy God will make thee plenteous in every work of thine hand, in the fruit of thy body, and in the fruit of thy cattle, and in the fruit of thy land, for good: for the LORD will again rejoice over thee for good, as he rejoiced over thy fathers:

10 If thou shalt hearken unto the voice of the LORD thy God, to keep his commandments and his statutes which are written in this book of the law, and if thou turn unto the LORD thy God with all thine heart, and with all thy soul.

11 ¶ For this commandment which I command thee this day, it is not hidden from thee, neither is it far off.

12 It is not in heaven, that thou shouldest say, Who shall go up for us to heaven, and bring it unto us, that we may hear it, and do it?

13 Neither is it beyond the sea, that thou shouldest say, Who shall go over the sea for us, and bring it unto us, that we may hear it, and do it?

14 But the word is very nigh unto thee, in thy mouth, and in thy heart, that thou mayest do it.

15 ¶ See, I have set before thee this day life and good, and death and evil;

16 In that I command thee this day to love the LORD thy God, to walk in his ways, and to keep his commandments and his statutes and his judgments, that thou mayest live and multiply: and the LORD thy God shall bless thee in the land whither thou goest to possess it.

17 But if thine heart turn away, so that thou wilt not hear, but shalt be drawn away, and worship other gods, and serve them;

18 I denounce unto you this day, that ye shall surely perish, and that ye shall not prolong your days upon the land, whither thou passest over Jor'dan to go to possess it.

19 I call heaven and earth to record this day against you, that I have set before you life and death, blessing and cursing: therefore choose life, that both thou and thy seed may live:

20 That thou mayest love the LORD thy God, and that thou mayest obey his voice, and that thou mayest cleave unto him: for he is thy life, and the length of thy days: that thou mayest dwell in the land which the LORD sware unto thy fathers, to A'bra-ham, to I'saac, and to Ja'-cob, to give them.

31 AND Mo'ses went and spake these words unto all Is'ra-el.

2 And he said unto them, I am an hundred and twenty years old this day; I can no more go out and come in: also the LORD hath said unto me, Thou shalt not go over this Jor'dan.

3 The LORD thy God, he will go over before thee, and he will destroy these nations from before thee, and thou shalt possess them: and Josh'u-a, he shall go over before thee, as the LORD hath said.

4 And the LORD shall do unto them as he did to Si'hon and to Og, kings of the Am'or-ites, and unto the land of them, whom he destroyed.

5 And the LORD shall give them up before your face, that ye may do unto them according unto all the commandments which I have commanded you.

6 Be strong and of a good courage, fear not, nor be afraid of them: for the LORD thy God, he it is that doth go with thee; he will not fail thee, nor forsake thee.

7 ¶ And Mo'ses called unto Josh'u-a, and said unto him in the sight of all Is'ra-el, Be strong and of a good courage: for thou must go with this people unto the land which the LORD

hath sworn unto their fathers to give them; and thou shalt cause them to inherit it.

8 And the LORD, he *it is* that doth go before thee; he will be with thee, he will not fail thee, neither forsake thee: fear not, neither be dismayed.

9 ¶ And Mo'ses wrote this law, and delivered it unto the priests the sons of Le'vi, which bare the ark of the covenant of the LORD, and unto all the elders of Is'ra-el.

10 And Mo'ses commanded them, saying, At the end of *every* seven years, in the solemnity of the year of release, in the feast of tabernacles,

11 When all Is'ra-el is come to appear before the LORD thy God in the place which he shall choose, thou shalt read this law before all Is'ra-el in their hearing.

12 Gather the people together, men, and women, and children, and thy stranger that *is* within thy gates, that they may hear, and that they may learn, and fear the LORD your God, and observe to do all the words of this law:

13 And *that* their children, which have not known *any* thing, may hear, and learn to fear the LORD thy God, as long as ye live in the land whither ye go over Jor'dan to possess it.

14 ¶ And the LORD said unto Mo'ses, Behold, thy days approach that thou must die: call Josh'u-a, and present yourselves in the tabernacle of the congregation, that I may give him a charge. And Mo'ses and Josh'u-a went, and presented themselves in the tabernacle of the congregation.

15 And the LORD appeared in the tabernacle in a pillar of a cloud: and the pillar of the cloud stood over the door of the tabernacle.

16 ¶ And the LORD said unto Mo'ses, Behold, thou shalt sleep with thy fathers; and this people will rise up, and go a whoring after the gods of the strangers of the land, whither they go *to be* among them, and will forsake me, and break my covenant which I have made with them.

17 Then my anger shall be kindled against them in that day, and I will forsake them, and I will hide my face from them, and they shall be devoured, and many evils and troubles shall befall them; so that they will say in that day, Are not these evils come upon us, because our God *is* not among us?

18 And I will surely hide my face in that day for all the evils which they shall have wrought, in that they are turned unto other gods.

19 Now therefore write ye this song for you, and teach it the children of Is'ra-el: put it in their mouths, that this song may be a witness for me against the children of Is'ra-el.

20 For when I shall have brought them into the land which I sware unto their fathers, that floweth with milk and honey; and they shall have eaten and filled themselves, and waxen fat; then will they turn unto other gods, and serve them, and provoke me, and break my covenant.

21 And it shall come to pass, when many evils and troubles are befallen them, that this song shall testify against them as a witness; for it shall not be forgotten out of the mouths of their seed: for I know their imagination which they go about, even now, before I have brought them into the land which I sware.

22 ¶ Mo'ses therefore wrote this song the same day, and taught it the children of Is'ra-el.

23 And he gave Josh'u-a the son of Nun a charge, and said, Be strong and of a good courage: for thou shalt bring the children of Is'ra-el into the land which I sware unto them: and I will be with thee.

24 ¶ And it came to pass, when Mo'ses had made an end of writing the words of this law in a book, until they were finished,

25 That Mo'ses commanded the Le'vites, which bare the ark of the covenant of the LORD, saying,

26 Take this book of the law, and put it in the side of the ark of the covenant of the LORD your God, that it may be there for a witness against thee.

27 For I know thy rebellion, and thy stiff neck: behold, while I am yet alive with you this day, ye have been rebellious against the LORD; and how much more after my death?

28 ¶ Gather unto me all the elders of your tribes, and your officers, that I may speak these words in their ears, and call heaven and earth to record against them.

29 For I know that after my death ye will utterly corrupt *yourselves*, and turn aside from the way which I have commanded you; and evil will befall you in the latter days; because ye will do evil in the sight of the LORD, to provoke him to anger through the work of your hands.

30 And Mo'ses spake in the ears of all the congregation of Is'ra-el the words of this song, until they were ended.

32 GIVE ear, O ye heavens, and I will speak; and hear, O earth, the words of my mouth.

2 My doctrine shall drop as the rain, my speech shall distil as the dew, as the small rain upon the tender herb, and as the showers upon the grass:

3 Because I will publish the name of the LORD: ascribe ye greatness unto our GOD.

4 *He is* the Rock, his work *is* perfect: for all his ways *are* judgment: a God of truth and without iniquity, just and right *is* he.

5 They have corrupted themselves, their spot *is* not *the spot* of his children: *they are* a perverse and crooked generation.

6 Do ye thus requite the LORD, O foolish people and unwise? *is* not he thy father *that* hath bought thee? hath he not made thee, and established thee?

7 ¶ Remember the days of old, consider the years of many generations: ask thy father, and he will shew thee; thy elders, and they will tell thee.

8 When the most High divided to the nations their inheritance, when he separated the sons of Ad'am, he set the bounds of the people according to the number of the children of Is'ra-el.

9 For the LORD's portion *is* his people; Ja'cob *is* the lot of his inheritance.

10 He found him in a desert land, and in the waste howling wilderness; he led him about, he instructed him, he kept him as the apple of his eye.

11 As an eagle stirreth up her nest, fluttereth over her young, spreadeth abroad her wings, taketh them, beareth them on her wings:

12 *So* the LORD alone did lead him, and *there was* no strange god with him.

13 He made him ride on the high places of the earth, that he might eat the increase of the fields; and he made him to suck honey out of the rock, and oil out of the flinty rock;

14 Butter of kine, and milk of sheep, with fat of lambs, and rams of the breed of Ba'shan, and goats, with the fat of kidneys of wheat; and thou didst drink the pure blood of the grape.

15 ¶ But Jeshu-run waxed fat, and kicked: thou art waxen fat, thou art grown thick, thou art covered *with fatness;* then he forsook God

which made him, and lightly esteemed the Rock of his salvation.

16 They provoked him to jealousy with strange *gods,* with abominations provoked they him to anger.

17 They sacrificed unto devils, not to God; to gods whom they knew not, to new *gods that* came newly up, whom your fathers feared not.

18 Of the Rock *that* begat thee thou art unmindful, and hast forgotten God that formed thee.

19 And when the LORD saw *it,* he abhorred *them,* because of the provoking of his sons, and of his daughters.

20 And he said, I will hide my face from them, I will see what their end *shall be:* for they *are* a very froward generation, children in whom *is* no faith.

21 They have moved me to jealousy with *that which is* not God; they have provoked me to anger with their vanities: and I will move them to jealousy with *those which are* not a people; I will provoke them to anger with a foolish nation.

22 For a fire is kindled in mine anger, and shall burn unto the lowest hell, and shall consume the earth with her increase, and set on fire the foundations of the mountains.

23 I will heap mischiefs upon them; I will spend mine arrows upon them.

24 *They shall be* burnt with hunger, and devoured with burning heat, and with bitter destruction: I will also send the teeth of beasts upon them, with the poison of serpents of the dust.

25 The sword without, and terror within, shall destroy both the young man and the virgin, the suckling *also* with the man of gray hairs.

26 I said, I would scatter them into corners, I would make the remembrance of them to cease from among men:

27 Were it not that I feared the wrath of the enemy, lest their adversaries should behave themselves strangely, *and* lest they should say, Our hand *is* high, and the LORD hath not done all this.

28 For they *are* a nation void of counsel, neither *is there any* understanding in them.

29 O that they were wise, *that* they understood this, *that* they would consider their latter end!

30 How should one chase a thousand, and two put ten thousand to flight, except their Rock had sold them, and the LORD had shut them up?

31 For their rock *is* not as our Rock, even our enemies themselves *being* judges.

32 For their vine *is* of the vine of Sod'om, and of the fields of Go-mor'rah: their grapes *are* grapes of gall, their clusters *are* bitter:

33 Their wine *is* the poison of dragons, and the cruel venom of asps.

34 *Is* not this laid up in store with me, *and* sealed up among my treasures?

35 To me *belongeth* vengeance, and recompence; their foot shall slide in *due* time: for the day of their calamity *is* at hand, and the things that shall come upon them make haste.

36 For the LORD shall judge his people, and repent himself for his servants, when he seeth that *their* power is gone, and *there is* none shut up, or left.

37 And he shall say, Where *are* their gods, *their* rock in whom they trusted,

38 Which did eat the fat of their sacrifices, *and* drank the wine of their drink offerings? let

them rise up and help you, *and* be your protection.

39 See now that I, *even* I, *am* he, and *there is* no god with me: I kill, and I make alive; I wound, and I heal: neither *is there any* that can deliver out of my hand.

40 For I lift up my hand to heaven, and say, I live for ever.

41 If I whet my glittering sword, and mine hand take hold on judgment; I will render vengeance to mine enemies, and will reward them that hate me.

42 I will make mine arrows drunk with blood, and my sword shall devour flesh; *and that* with the blood of the slain and of the captives, from the beginning of revenges upon the enemy.

43 Rejoice, O ye nations, *with* his people: for he will avenge the blood of his servants, and will render vengeance to his adversaries, and will be merciful unto his land, *and* to his people.

44 ¶ And Mo'ses came and spake all the words of this song in the ears of the people, he, and Ho-she'a the son of Nun.

45 And Mo'ses made an end of speaking all these words to all Is'ra-el:

46 And he said unto them, Set your hearts unto all the words which I testify among you this day, which ye shall command your children to observe to do, all the words of the law.

47 For it *is* not a vain thing for you; because it *is* your life: and through this thing ye shall prolong *your* days in the land, whither ye go over Jor'dan to possess it.

48 And the LORD spake unto Mo'ses that selfsame day, saying,

49 Get thee up into this mountain Ab'a-rim, *unto* mount Ne'bo, which *is* in the land of Mo'ab, that *is* over against Jer'i-cho; and behold the land of Ca'naan, which I give unto the children of Is'ra-el for a possession:

50 And die in the mount whither thou goest up, and be gathered unto thy people; as Aar'on thy brother died in mount Hor, and was gathered unto his people:

51 Because ye trespassed against me among the children of Is'ra-el at the waters of Mer'i-bah–Ka'desh, in the wilderness of Zin; because ye sanctified me not in the midst of the children of Is'ra-el.

52 Yet thou shalt see the land before *thee:* but thou shalt not go thither unto the land which I give the children of Is'ra-el.

33 AND this *is* the blessing, wherewith Mo'ses the man of God blessed the children of Is'ra-el before his death.

2 And he said, The LORD came from Si'nai, and rose up from Se'ir unto them; he shined forth from mount Pa'ran, and he came with ten thousands of saints: from his right hand *went* a fiery law for them.

3 Yea, he loved the people; all his saints *are* in thy hand: and they sat down at thy feet; *every* one shall receive of thy words.

4 Mo'ses commanded us a law, *even* the inheritance of the congregation of Ja'cob.

5 And he was king in Jeshu-run, when the heads of the people *and* the tribes of Is'ra-el were gathered together.

6 ¶ Let Reu'ben live, and not die; and let *not* his men be few.

7 ¶ And this *is the blessing* of Ju'dah: and he said, Hear, LORD, the voice of Ju'dah, and bring him unto his people: let his hands be sufficient for him; and be thou an help *to him* from his enemies.

8 ¶ And of Le'vi he said, *Let* thy Thum'mim and thy U'rim *be* with thy holy one, whom thou didst prove at Mas'sah, *and with* whom thou didst strive at the waters of Mer'i-bah;

9 Who said unto his father and to his mother, I have not seen him; neither did he acknowledge his brethren, nor knew his own children: for they have observed thy word, and kept thy covenant.

10 They shall teach Ja'cob thy judgments, and Is'ra-el thy law: they shall put incense before thee, and whole burnt sacrifice upon thine altar.

11 Bless, LORD, his substance, and accept the work of his hands: smite through the loins of them that rise against him, and of them that hate him, that they rise not again.

12 ¶ *And* of Ben'ja-min he said, The beloved of the LORD shall dwell in safety by him; *and* the LORD shall cover him all the day long, and he shall dwell between his shoulders.

13 ¶ And of Jo'seph he said, Blessed of the LORD *be* his land, for the precious things of heaven, for the dew, and for the deep that coucheth beneath,

14 And for the precious fruits *brought forth* by the sun, and for the precious things put forth by the moon,

15 And for the chief things of the ancient mountains, and for the precious things of the lasting hills,

16 And for the precious things of the earth and fulness thereof, and *for* the good will of him that dwelt in the bush: let *the blessing* come upon the head of Jo'seph, and upon the top of the head of him *that was* separated from his brethren.

17 His glory *is like* the firstling of his bullock, and his horns *are like* the horns of unicorns: with them he shall push the people together to the ends of the earth: and they *are* the ten thousands of E'phra-im, and they *are* the thousands of Ma-nas'seh.

18 ¶ And of Zeb'u-lun he said, Rejoice, Zeb'-u-lun, in thy going out; and, Is'sa-char, in thy tents.

19 They shall call the people unto the mountain; there they shall offer sacrifices of righteousness: for they shall suck *of* the abundance of the seas, and *of* treasures hid in the sand.

20 ¶ And of Gad he said, Blessed *be* he that enlargeth Gad: he dwelleth as a lion, and teareth the arm with the crown of the head.

21 And he provided the first part for himself, because there, *in* a portion of the lawgiver, *was* he seated; and he came with the heads of the people, he executed the justice of the LORD, and his judgments with Is'ra-el.

22 ¶ And of Dan he said, Dan *is* a lion's whelp: he shall leap from Ba'shan.

23 ¶ And of Naph'ta-li he said, O Naph'ta-li, satisfied with favour, and full with the blessing of the LORD: possess thou the west and the south.

24 ¶ And of Ash'er he said, *Let* Ash'er *be* blessed with children; let him be acceptable to his brethren, and let him dip his foot in oil.

25 Thy shoes *shall be* iron and brass; and as thy days, *so shall* thy strength *be*.

26 ¶ *There is* none like unto the God of Je'shu-run, *who* rideth upon the heaven in thy help, and in his excellency on the sky.

27 The eternal God *is thy* refuge, and underneath *are* the everlasting arms: and he shall thrust out the enemy from before thee; and shall say, Destroy *them*.

28 Is'ra-el then shall dwell in safety alone: the fountain of Ja'cob *shall be* upon a land of corn and wine; also his heavens shall drop down dew.

29 Happy *art* thou, O Is'ra-el: who *is* like unto thee, O people saved by the LORD, the shield of thy help, and who *is* the sword of thy excellency! and thine enemies shall be found liars unto thee; and thou shalt tread upon their high places.

34 AND Mo'ses went up from the plains of Mo'ab unto the mountain of Ne'bo, to the top of Pis'gah, that *is* over against Jer'i-cho. And the LORD shewed him all the land of Gil'e-ad, unto Dan,

2 And all Naph'ta-li, and the land of E'phra-im, and Ma-nas'seh, and all the land of Ju'dah, unto the utmost sea,

3 And the south, and the plain of the valley of Jer'i-cho, the city of palm trees, unto Zo'ar.

4 And the LORD said unto him, This *is* the land which I sware unto A'bra-ham, unto I'saac, and unto Ja'cob, saying, I will give it unto thy seed: I have caused thee to see *it* with thine eyes, but thou shalt not go over thither.

5 ¶ So Mo'ses the servant of the LORD died there in the land of Mo'ab, according to the word of the LORD.

6 And he buried him in a valley in the land of Mo'ab, over against Beth-pe'or: but no man knoweth of his sepulchre unto this day.

7 ¶ And Mo'ses *was* an hundred and twenty years old when he died: his eye was not dim, nor his natural force abated.

8 ¶ And the children of Is'ra-el wept for Mo'ses in the plains of Mo'ab thirty days: so the days of weeping *and* mourning for Mo'ses were ended.

9 ¶ And Josh'u-a the son of Nun was full of the spirit of wisdom; for Mo'ses had laid his hands upon him: and the children of Is'ra-el hearkened unto him, and did as the LORD commanded Mo'ses.

10 ¶ And there arose not a prophet since in Is'ra-el like unto Mo'ses, whom the LORD knew face to face,

11 In all the signs and the wonders, which the LORD sent him to do in the land of E'gypt to Pha'raoh, and to all his servants, and to all his land,

12 And in all that mighty hand, and in all the great terror which Mo'ses shewed in the sight of all Is'ra-el.

THE BOOK OF

JOSHUA

1 NOW after the death of Mo'ses the servant of the LORD it came to pass, that the LORD spake unto Josh'u-a the son of Nun, Mo'ses' minister, saying,

2 Mo'ses my servant is dead; now therefore arise, go over this Jor'dan, thou, and all this people, unto the land which I do give to them, *even* to the children of Is'ra-el.

3 Every place that the sole of your foot shall tread upon, that have I given unto you, as I said unto Mo'ses.

4 From the wilderness and this Leb'a-non even unto the great river, the river Eu-phra'tes, all the land of the Hit'tites, and unto the great sea toward the going down of the sun, shall be your coast.

5 There shall not any man be able to stand before thee all the days of thy life: as I was with Mo'ses, so I will be with thee: I will not fail thee, nor forsake thee.

6 Be strong and of a good courage: for unto this people shalt thou divide for an inheritance the land, which I sware unto their fathers to give them.

7 Only be thou strong and very courageous, that thou mayest observe to do according to all the law, which Mo'ses my servant commanded thee: turn not from it *to* the right hand or *to* the left, that thou mayest prosper whithersoever thou goest.

8 This book of the law shall not depart out of thy mouth; but thou shalt meditate therein day and night, that thou mayest observe to do according to all that is written therein: for then thou shalt make thy way prosperous, and then thou shalt have good success.

9 Have not I commanded thee? Be strong and of a good courage; be not afraid, neither be thou dismayed: for the LORD thy God *is* with thee whithersoever thou goest.

10 ¶ Then Josh'u-a commanded the officers of the people, saying,

11 Pass through the host, and command the people, saying, Prepare you victuals; for within three days ye shall pass over this Jor'dan, to go in to possess the land, which the LORD your God giveth you to possess it.

12 ¶ And to the Reu'ben-ites, and to the Gad'ites, and to half the tribe of Ma-nas'seh, spake Josh'u-a, saying,

13 Remember the word which Mo'ses the servant of the LORD commanded you, saying, The LORD your God hath given you rest, and hath given you this land.

14 Your wives, your little ones, and your cattle, shall remain in the land which Mo'ses gave you on this side Jor'dan; but ye shall pass before your brethren armed, all the mighty men of valour, and help them;

15 Until the LORD have given your brethren rest, as *he hath given* you, and they also have possessed the land which the LORD your God giveth them: then ye shall return unto the land of your possession, and enjoy it, which Mo'ses the LORD's servant gave you on this side Jor'dan toward the sunrising.

16 ¶ And they answered Josh'u-a, saying, All that thou commandest us we will do, and whithersoever thou sendest us, we will go.

17 According as we hearkened unto Mo'ses in all things, so will we hearken unto thee: only the LORD thy God be with thee, as he was with Mo'ses.

18 Whosoever *he be* that doth rebel against thy commandment, and will not hearken unto thy words in all that thou commandest him, he shall be put to death: only be strong and of a good courage.

2 AND Josh'u-a the son of Nun sent out of Shit'tim two men to spy secretly, saying, Go view the land, even Jer'i-cho. And they went, and came into an harlot's house, named Ra'hab, and lodged there.

2 And it was told the king of Jer'i-cho, saying, Behold, there came men in hither to night of the children of Is'ra-el to search out the country.

3 And the king of Jer'i-cho sent unto Ra'hab, saying, Bring forth the men that are come to thee, which are entered into thine house: for they be come to search out all the country.

4 And the woman took the two men, and hid them, and said thus, There came men unto me, but I wist not whence they *were:*

5 And it came to pass *about the time* of shutting of the gate, when it was dark, that the men went out: whither the men went I wot not: pursue after them quickly; for ye shall overtake them.

6 But she had brought them up to the roof of the house, and hid them with the stalks of flax, which she had laid in order upon the roof.

7 And the men pursued after them the way to Jor'dan unto the fords: and as soon as they which pursued after them were gone out, they shut the gate.

8 ¶ And before they were laid down, she came up unto them upon the roof;

9 And she said unto the men, I know that the LORD hath given you the land, and that your terror is fallen upon us, and that all the inhabitants of the land faint because of you.

10 For we have heard how the LORD dried up the water of the Red sea for you, when ye came out of E'gypt; and what ye did unto the two kings of the Am'or-ites, that *were* on the other side Jor'dan, Si'hon and Og, whom ye utterly destroyed.

11 And as soon as we had heard *these things,* our hearts did melt, neither did there remain any more courage in any man, because of you: for the LORD your God, he *is* God in heaven above, and in earth beneath.

12 Now therefore, I pray you, swear unto me by the LORD, since I have shewed you kindness, that ye will also shew kindness unto my father's house, and give me a true token:

13 And *that* ye will save alive my father, and my mother, and my brethren, and my sisters, and all that they have, and deliver our lives from death.

14 And the men answered her, Our life for yours, if ye utter not this our business. And it shall be, when the LORD hath given us the land, that we will deal kindly and truly with thee.

15 Then she let them down by a cord through the window: for her house *was* upon the town wall, and she dwelt upon the wall.

16 And she said unto them, Get you to the mountain, lest the pursuers meet you; and hide yourselves there three days, until the pursuers

be returned: and afterward may ye go your way.

17 And the men said unto her, We *will be* blameless of this thine oath which thou hast made us swear.

18 Behold, *when* we come into the land, thou shalt bind this line of scarlet thread in the window which thou didst let us down by: and thou shalt bring thy father, and thy mother, and thy brethren, and all thy father's household, home unto thee.

19 And it shall be, *that* whosoever shall go out of the doors of thy house into the street, his blood *shall be* upon his head, and we *will be* guiltless: and whosoever shall be with thee in the house, his blood *shall be* on our head, if *any* hand be upon him.

20 And if thou utter this our business, then we will be quit of thine oath which thou hast made us to swear.

21 And she said, According unto your words, so *be* it. And she sent them away, and they departed: and she bound the scarlet line in the window.

22 And they went, and came unto the mountain, and abode there three days, until the pursuers were returned: and the pursuers sought *them* throughout all the way, but found *them* not.

23 ¶ So the two men returned, and descended from the mountain, and passed over, and came to Josh'u-a the son of Nun, and told him all *things* that befell them:

24 And they said unto Josh'u-a, Truly the LORD hath delivered into our hands all the land; for even all the inhabitants of the country do faint because of us.

3 AND Josh'u-a rose early in the morning; and they removed from Shit'tim, and came to Jor'dan, he and all the children of Is'ra-el, and lodged there before they passed over.

2 And it came to pass after three days, that the officers went through the host;

3 And they commanded the people, saying, When ye see the ark of the covenant of the LORD your God, and the priests the Le'vites bearing it, then ye shall remove from your place, and go after it.

4 Yet there shall be a space between you and it, about two thousand cubits by measure: come not near unto it, that ye may know the way by which ye must go: for ye have not passed *this* way heretofore.

5 And Josh'u-a said unto the people, Sanctify yourselves: for to morrow the LORD will do wonders among you.

6 And Josh'u-a spake unto the priests, saying, Take up the ark of the covenant, and pass over before the people. And they took up the ark of the covenant, and went before the people.

7 ¶ And the LORD said unto Josh'u-a, This day will I begin to magnify thee in the sight of all Is'ra-el, that they may know that, as I was with Mo'ses, *so* I will be with thee.

8 And thou shalt command the priests that bear the ark of the covenant, saying, When ye are come to the brink of the water of Jor'dan, ye shall stand still in Jor'dan.

9 ¶ And Josh'u-a said unto the children of Is'ra-el, Come hither, and hear the words of the LORD your God.

10 And Josh'u-a said, Hereby ye shall know that the living God *is* among you, and *that* he will without fail drive out from before you the Ca'naan-ites, and the Hit'tites, and the Hi'vites,

and the Per'iz-zites, and the Gir'ga-shites, and the Am'or-ites, and the Jeb'u-sites.

11 Behold, the ark of the covenant of the LORD of all the earth passeth over before you into Jor'dan.

12 Now therefore take you twelve men out of the tribes of Is'ra-el, out of every tribe a man.

13 And it shall come to pass, as soon as the soles of the feet of the priests that bear the ark of the LORD, the Lord of all the earth, shall rest in the waters of Jor'dan, *that* the waters of Jor'dan shall be cut off *from* the waters that come down from above; and they shall stand upon an heap.

14 ¶ And it came to pass, when the people removed from their tents, to pass over Jor'dan, and the priests bearing the ark of the covenant before the people;

15 And as they that bare the ark were come unto Jor'dan, and the feet of the priests that bare the ark were dipped in the brim of the water, (for Jor'dan overfloweth all his banks all the time of harvest,)

16 That the waters which came down from above stood *and* rose up upon an heap very far from the city Ad'am, that *is* beside Zar'e-tan: and those that came down toward the sea of the plain, *even* the salt sea, failed, *and* were cut off: and the people passed over right against Jer'i-cho.

17 And the priests that bare the ark of the covenant of the LORD stood firm on dry ground in the midst of Jor'dan, and all the Is'ra-el-ites passed over on dry ground, until all the people were passed clean over Jor'dan.

4 AND it came to pass, when all the people were clean passed over Jor'dan, that the LORD spake unto Josh'u-a, saying,

2 Take you twelve men out of the people, out of every tribe a man,

3 And command ye them, saying, Take you hence out of the midst of Jor'dan, out of the place where the priests' feet stood firm, twelve stones, and ye shall carry them over with you, and leave them in the lodging place, where ye shall lodge this night.

4 Then Josh'u-a called the twelve men, whom he had prepared of the children of Is'ra-el, out of every tribe a man:

5 And Josh'u-a said unto them, Pass over before the ark of the LORD your God into the midst of Jor'dan, and take you up every man of you a stone upon his shoulder, according unto the number of the tribes of the children of Is'ra-el:

6 That this may be a sign among you, *that* when your children ask *their fathers* in time to come, saying, What *mean* ye by these stones?

7 Then ye shall answer them, That the waters of Jor'dan were cut off before the ark of the covenant of the LORD; when it passed over Jor'dan, the waters of Jor'dan were cut off: and these stones shall be for a memorial unto the children of Is'ra-el for ever.

8 And the children of Is'ra-el did so as Josh'u-a commanded, and took up twelve stones out of the midst of Jor'dan, as the LORD spake unto Josh'u-a, according to the number of the tribes of the children of Is'ra-el, and carried them over with them unto the place where they lodged, and laid them down there.

9 And Josh'u-a set up twelve stones in the midst of Jor'dan, in the place where the feet of the priests which bare the ark of the covenant stood: and they are there unto this day.

10 ¶ For the priests which bare the ark stood

in the midst of Jor'dan, until every thing was finished that the LORD commanded Josh'u-a to speak unto the people, according to all that Mo'ses commanded Josh'u-a: and the people hasted and passed over.

11 And it came to pass, when all the people were clean passed over, that the ark of the LORD passed over, and the priests, in the presence of the people.

12 And the children of Reu'ben, and the children of Gad, and half the tribe of Ma-nas'seh, passed over armed before the children of Is'ra-el, as Mo'ses spake unto them:

13 About forty thousand prepared for war passed over before the LORD unto battle, to the plains of Jer'i-cho.

14 ¶ On that day the LORD magnified Josh'u-a in the sight of all Is'ra-el: and they feared him, as they feared Mo'ses, all the days of his life.

15 And the LORD spake unto Josh'u-a, saying,

16 Command the priests that bear the ark of the testimony, that they come up out of Jor'dan.

17 Josh'u-a therefore commanded the priests, saying, Come ye up out of Jor'dan.

18 And it came to pass, when the priests that bare the ark of the covenant of the LORD were come up out of the midst of Jor'dan, and the soles of the priests' feet were lifted up unto the dry land, that the waters of Jor'dan returned unto their place, and flowed over all his banks, as they did before.

19 ¶ And the people came up out of Jor'dan on the tenth day of the first month, and encamped in Gil'gal, in the east border of Jer'i-cho.

20 And those twelve stones, which they took out of Jor'dan, did Josh'u-a pitch in Gil'gal.

21 And he spake unto the children of Is'ra-el, saying, When your children shall ask their fathers in time to come, saying, What mean these stones?

22 Then ye shall let your children know, saying, Is'ra-el came over this Jor'dan on dry land.

23 For the LORD your God dried up the waters of Jor'dan from before you, until ye were passed over, as the LORD your God did to the Red sea, which he dried up from before us, until we were gone over:

24 That all the people of the earth might know the hand of the LORD, that it is mighty: that ye might fear the LORD your God for ever.

5 AND it came to pass, when all the kings of the Am'or-ites, which were on the side of Jor'dan westward, and all the kings of the Ca'naan-ites, which were by the sea, heard that the LORD had dried up the waters of Jor'dan from before the children of Is'ra-el, until we were passed over, that their heart melted, neither was there spirit in them any more, because of the children of Is'ra-el.

2 ¶ At that time the LORD said unto Josh'u-a, Make thee sharp knives, and circumcise again the children of Is'ra-el the second time.

3 And Josh'u-a made him sharp knives, and circumcised the children of Is'ra-el at the hill of the foreskins.

4 And this is the cause why Josh'u-a did circumcise: All the people that came out of E'gypt, that were males, even all the men of war, died in the wilderness by the way, after they came out of E'gypt.

5 Now all the people that came out were circumcised: but all the people that were born in the wilderness by the way as they came forth out of E'gypt, them they had not circumcised.

6 For the children of Is'ra-el walked forty years in the wilderness, till all the people that were men of war, which came out of E'gypt, were consumed, because they obeyed not the voice of the LORD: unto whom the LORD sware that he would not shew them the land, which the LORD sware unto their fathers that he would give us, a land that floweth with milk and honey.

7 And their children, whom he raised up in their stead, them Josh'u-a circumcised: for they were uncircumcised, because they had not circumcised them by the way.

8 And it came to pass, when they had done circumcising all the people, that they abode in their places in the camp, till they were whole.

9 And the LORD said unto Josh'u-a, This day have I rolled away the reproach of E'gypt from off you. Wherefore the name of the place is called Gil'gal unto this day.

10 ¶ And the children of Is'ra-el encamped in Gil'gal, and kept the passover on the fourteenth day of the month at even in the plains of Jer'i-cho.

11 And they did eat of the old corn of the land on the morrow after the passover, unleavened cakes, and parched corn in the selfsame day.

12 ¶ And the manna ceased on the morrow after they had eaten of the old corn of the land; neither had the children of Is'ra-el manna any more; but they did eat of the fruit of the land of Ca'naan that year.

13 ¶ And it came to pass, when Josh'u-a was by Jer'i-cho, that he lifted up his eyes and looked, and, behold, there stood a man over against him with his sword drawn in his hand: and Josh'u-a went unto him, and said unto him, Art thou for us, or for our adversaries?

14 And he said, Nay; but as captain of the host of the LORD am I now come. And Josh'u-a fell on his face to the earth, and did worship, and said unto him, What saith my lord unto his servant?

15 And the captain of the LORD's host said unto Josh'u-a, Loose thy shoe from off thy foot; for the place whereon thou standest is holy. And Josh'u-a did so.

6 NOW Jer'i-cho was straitly shut up because of the children of Is'ra-el: none went out, and none came in.

2 And the LORD said unto Josh'u-a, See, I have given into thine hand Jer'i-cho, and the king thereof, and the mighty men of valour.

3 And ye shall compass the city, all ye men of war, and go round about the city once. Thus shalt thou do six days.

4 And seven priests shall bear before the ark seven trumpets of rams' horns: and the seventh day ye shall compass the city seven times, and the priests shall blow with the trumpets.

5 And it shall come to pass, that when they make a long blast with the ram's horn, and when ye hear the sound of the trumpet, all the people shall shout with a great shout; and the wall of the city shall fall down flat, and the people shall ascend up every man straight before him.

6 ¶ And Josh'u-a the son of Nun called the priests, and said unto them, Take up the ark of the covenant, and let seven priests bear seven trumpets of rams' horns before the ark of the LORD.

7 And he said unto the people, Pass on, and compass the city, and let him that is armed pass on before the ark of the LORD.

8 ¶ And it came to pass, when Josh'u-a had

spoken unto the people, that the seven priests bearing the seven trumpets of rams' horns passed on before the LORD, and blew with the trumpets: and the ark of the covenant of the LORD followed them.

9 ¶ And the armed men went before the priests that blew with the trumpets, and the rereward came after the ark, *the priests* going on, and blowing with the trumpets.

10 And Josh'u-a had commanded the people, saying, Ye shall not shout, nor make any noise with your voice, neither shall *any* word proceed out of your mouth, until the day I bid you shout; then shall ye shout.

11 So the ark of the LORD compassed the city, going about *it* once: and they came into the camp, and lodged in the camp.

12 ¶ And Josh'u-a rose early in the morning, and the priests took up the ark of the LORD.

13 And seven priests bearing seven trumpets of rams' horns before the ark of the LORD went on continually, and blew with the trumpets: and the armed men went before them; but the rereward came after the ark of the LORD, *the priests* going on, and blowing with the trumpets.

14 And the second day they compassed the city once, and returned into the camp: so they did six days.

15 And it came to pass on the seventh day, that they rose early about the dawning of the day, and compassed the city after the same manner seven times: only on that day they compassed the city seven times.

16 And it came to pass at the seventh time, when the priests blew with the trumpets, Josh'u-a said unto the people, Shout; for the LORD hath given you the city.

17 ¶ And the city shall be accursed, *even* it, and all that *are* therein, to the LORD: only Ra'hab the harlot shall live, she and all that *are* with her in the house, because she hid the messengers that we sent.

18 And ye, in any wise keep *yourselves* from the accursed thing, lest ye make *yourselves* accursed, when ye take of the accursed thing, and make the camp of Is'ra-el a curse, and trouble it.

19 But all the silver, and gold, and vessels of brass and iron, *are* consecrated unto the LORD: they shall come into the treasury of the LORD.

20 So the people shouted when *the priests* blew with the trumpets: and it came to pass, when the people heard the sound of the trumpet, and the people shouted with a great shout, that the wall fell down flat, so that the people went up into the city, every man straight before him, and they took the city.

21 And they utterly destroyed all that *was* in the city, both man and woman, young and old, and ox, and sheep, and ass, with the edge of the sword.

22 But Josh'u-a had said unto the two men that had spied out the country, Go into the harlot's house, and bring out thence the woman, and all that she hath, as ye sware unto her.

23 And the young men that were spies went in, and brought out Ra'hab, and her father, and her mother, and her brethren, and all that she had; and they brought out all her kindred, and left them without the camp of Is'ra-el.

24 And they burnt the city with fire, and all that *was* therein: only the silver, and the gold, and the vessels of brass and of iron, they put into the treasury of the house of the LORD.

25 And Josh'u-a saved Ra'hab the harlot alive, and her father's household, and all that she had; and she dwelleth in Is'ra-el *even* unto this day; because she hid the messengers, which Josh'u-a sent to spy out Jer'i-cho.

26 ¶ And Josh'u-a adjured *them* at that time, saying, Cursed *be* the man before the LORD, that riseth up and buildeth this city Jer'i-cho: he shall lay the foundation thereof in his firstborn, and in his youngest *son* shall he set up the gates of it.

27 So the LORD was with Josh'u-a; and his fame was *noised* throughout all the country.

7 BUT the children of Is'ra-el committed a trespass in the accursed thing: for A'chan, the son of Car'mi, the son of Zab'di, the son of Ze'rah, of the tribe of Ju'dah, took of the accursed thing: and the anger of the LORD was kindled against the children of Is'ra-el.

2 And Josh'u-a sent men from Jer'i-cho to A'i, which *is* beside Beth-a'ven, on the east side of Beth'-el, and spake unto them, saying, Go up and view the country. And the men went up and viewed A'i.

3 And they returned to Josh'u-a, and said unto him, Let not all the people go up; but let about two or three thousand men go up and smite A'i; *and* make not all the people to labour thither; for they *are* but few.

4 So there went up thither of the people about three thousand men: and they fled before the men of A'i.

5 And the men of A'i smote of them about thirty and six men: for they chased them *from* before the gate *even* unto Sheb'a-rim, and smote them in the going down: wherefore the hearts of the people melted, and became as water.

6 ¶ And Josh'u-a rent his clothes, and fell to the earth upon his face before the ark of the LORD until the eventide, he and the elders of Is'ra-el, and put dust upon their heads.

7 And Josh'u-a said, Alas, O Lord GOD, wherefore hast thou at all brought this people over Jor'dan, to deliver us into the hand of the Am'or-ites, to destroy us? would to God we had been content, and dwelt on the other side Jor'dan!

8 O Lord, what shall I say, when Is'ra-el turneth their backs before their enemies!

9 For the Ca'naan-ites and all the inhabitants of the land shall hear *of it*, and shall environ us round, and cut off our name from the earth: and what wilt thou do unto thy great name?

10 ¶ And the LORD said unto Josh'u-a, Get thee up; wherefore liest thou thus upon thy face?

11 Is'ra-el hath sinned, and they have also transgressed my covenant which I commanded them: for they have even taken of the accursed thing, and have also stolen, and dissembled also, and they have put *it* even among their own stuff.

12 Therefore the children of Is'ra-el could not stand before their enemies, *but* turned *their* backs before their enemies, because they were accursed: neither will I be with you any more, except ye destroy the accursed from among you.

13 Up, sanctify the people, and say, Sanctify yourselves against to morrow: for thus saith the LORD God of Is'ra-el, *There is* an accursed thing in the midst of thee, O Is'ra-el: thou canst not stand before thine enemies, until ye take away the accursed thing from among you.

14 In the morning therefore ye shall be brought according to your tribes: and it shall be, *that* the tribe which the LORD taketh shall come according to the families *thereof*: and the

family which the LORD shall take shall come by households; and the household which the LORD shall take shall come man by man.

15 And it shall be, *that* he that is taken with the accursed thing shall be burnt with fire, he and all that he hath: because he hath transgressed the covenant of the LORD, and because he hath wrought folly in Is′ra-el.

16 ¶ So Josh′u-a rose up early in the morning, and brought Is′ra-el by their tribes; and the tribe of Ju′dah was taken:

17 And he brought the family of Ju′dah; and he took the family of the Zar′hites: and he brought the family of the Zar′hites man by man; and Zab′di was taken:

18 And he brought his household man by man; and A′chan, the son of Car′mi, the son of Zab′di, the son of Ze′rah, of the tribe of Ju′dah, was taken.

19 And Josh′u-a said unto A′chan, My son, give, I pray thee, glory to the LORD God of Is′ra-el, and make confession unto him; and tell me now what thou hast done; hide *it* not from me.

20 And A′chan answered Josh′u-a, and said, Indeed I have sinned against the LORD God of Is′ra-el, and thus and thus have I done:

21 When I saw among the spoils a goodly Bab′y-lo-nish garment, and two hundred shekels of silver, and a wedge of gold of fifty shekels weight, then I coveted them, and took them; and, behold, they *are* hid in the earth in the midst of my tent, and the silver under it.

22 ¶ So Josh′u-a sent messengers, and they ran unto the tent; and, behold, *it was* hid in his tent, and the silver under it.

23 And they took them out of the midst of the tent, and brought them unto Josh′u-a, and unto all the children of Is′ra-el, and laid them out before the LORD.

24 And Josh′u-a, and all Is′ra-el with him, took A′chan the son of Ze′rah, and the silver, and the garment, and the wedge of gold, and his sons, and his daughters, and his oxen, and his asses, and his sheep, and his tent, and all that he had: and they brought them unto the valley of A′chor.

25 And Josh′u-a said, Why hast thou troubled us? the LORD shall trouble thee this day. And all Is′ra-el stoned him with stones, and burned them with fire, after they had stoned them with stones.

26 And they raised over him a great heap of stones unto this day. So the LORD turned from the fierceness of his anger. Wherefore the name of that place was called, The valley of A′chor, unto this day.

8 AND the LORD said unto Josh′u-a, Fear not, neither be thou dismayed: take all the people of war with thee, and arise, go up to A′i: see, I have given into thy hand the king of A′i, and his people, and his city, and his land:

2 And thou shalt do to A′i and her king as thou didst unto Jer′i-cho and her king: only the spoil thereof, and the cattle thereof, shall ye take for a prey unto yourselves: lay thee an ambush for the city behind it.

3 ¶ So Josh′u-a arose, and all the people of war, to go up against A′i: and Josh′u-a chose out thirty thousand mighty men of valour, and sent them away by night.

4 And he commanded them, saying, Behold, ye shall lie in wait against the city, *even* behind the city: go not very far from the city, but be ye all ready:

5 And I, and all the people that *are* with me, will approach unto the city: and it shall come to pass, when they come out against us, as at the first, that we will flee before them,

6 (For they will come out after us) till we have drawn them from the city; for they will say, They flee before us, as at the first: therefore we will flee before them.

7 Then ye shall rise up from the ambush, and seize upon the city: for the LORD your God will deliver it into your hand.

8 And it shall be, when ye have taken the city, *that* ye shall set the city on fire: according to the commandment of the LORD shall ye do. See, I have commanded you.

9 ¶ Josh′u-a therefore sent them forth: and they went to lie in ambush, and abode between Beth′-el and A′i, on the west side of A′i: but Josh′u-a lodged that night among the people.

10 And Josh′u-a rose up early in the morning, and numbered the people, and went up, he and the elders of Is′ra-el, before the people to A′i.

11 And all the people, *even the people* of war that *were* with him, went up, and drew nigh, and came before the city, and pitched on the north side of A′i: now *there was* a valley between them and A′i.

12 And he took about five thousand men, and set them to lie in ambush between Beth′-el and A′i, on the west side of the city.

13 And when they had set the people, *even* all the host that *was* on the north of the city, and their liers in wait on the west of the city, Josh′u-a went that night into the midst of the valley.

14 ¶ And it came to pass, when the king of A′i saw *it*, that they hasted and rose up early, and the men of the city went out against Is′ra-el to battle, he and all his people, at a time appointed, before the plain; but he wist not that *there were* liers in ambush against him behind the city.

15 And Josh′u-a and all Is′ra-el made as if they were beaten before them, and fled by the way of the wilderness.

16 And all the people that *were* in A′i were called together to pursue after them: and they pursued after Josh′u-a, and were drawn away from the city.

17 And there was not a man left in A′i or Beth′-el, that went not out after Is′ra-el: and they left the city open, and pursued after Is′ra-el.

18 And the LORD said unto Josh′u-a, Stretch out the spear that *is* in thy hand toward A′i; for I will give it into thine hand. And Josh′u-a stretched out the spear that *he had* in his hand toward the city.

19 And the ambush arose quickly out of their place, and they ran as soon as he had stretched out his hand: and they entered into the city, and took it, and hasted and set the city on fire.

20 And when the men of A′i looked behind them, they saw, and, behold, the smoke of the city ascended up to heaven, and they had no power to flee this way or that way: and the people that fled to the wilderness turned back upon the pursuers.

21 And when Josh′u-a and all Is′ra-el saw that the ambush had taken the city, and that the smoke of the city ascended, then they turned again, and slew the men of A′i.

22 And the other issued out of the city against them; so they were in the midst of Is′ra-el, some on this side, and some on that side: and they smote them, so that they let none of them remain or escape.

23 And the king of A′i they took alive, and brought him to Josh′u-a.

24 And it came to pass, when Is'ra-el had made an end of slaying all the inhabitants of A'i in the field, in the wilderness wherein they chased them, and when they were all fallen on the edge of the sword, until they were consumed, that all the Is-ra-el-ites returned unto A'i, and smote it with the edge of the sword.

25 And *so* it was, *that* all that fell that day, both of men and women, *were* twelve thousand, *even* all the men of A'i.

26 For Josh'u-a drew not his hand back, wherewith he stretched out the spear, until he had utterly destroyed all the inhabitants of A'i.

27 Only the cattle and the spoil of that city Is'ra-el took for a prey unto themselves, according unto the word of the LORD which he commanded Josh'u-a.

28 And Josh'u-a burnt A'i, and made it an heap for ever, *even* a desolation unto this day.

29 And the king of A'i he hanged on a tree until eventide: and as soon as the sun was down, Josh'u-a commanded that they should take his carcase down from the tree, and cast it at the entering of the gate of the city, and raise thereon a great heap of stones, *that remaineth* unto this day.

30 ¶ Then Josh'u-a built an altar unto the LORD God of Is'ra-el in mount E'bal,

31 As Mo'ses the servant of the LORD commanded the children of Is'ra-el, as it is written in the book of the law of Mo'ses, an altar of whole stones, over which no man hath lift up *any* iron; and they offered thereon burnt offerings unto the LORD, and sacrificed peace offerings.

32 ¶ And he wrote there upon the stones a copy of the law of Mo'ses, which he wrote in the presence of the children of Is'ra-el.

33 And all Is'ra-el, and their elders, and officers, and their judges, stood on this side the ark and on that side before the priests the Le'vites, which bare the ark of the covenant of the LORD, as well the stranger, as he that was born among them; half of them over against mount Ger'i-zim, and half of them over against mount E'bal; as Mo'ses the servant of the LORD had commanded before, that they should bless the people of Is'ra-el.

34 And afterward he read all the words of the law, the blessings and cursings, according to all that is written in the book of the law.

35 There was not a word of all that Mo'ses commanded, which Josh'u-a read not before all the congregation of Is'ra-el, with the women, and the little ones, and the strangers that were conversant among them.

9 AND it came to pass, when all the kings which *were* on this side Jor'dan, in the hills, and in the valleys, and in all the coasts of the great sea over against Leb'a-non, the Hit'-tite, and the Am'or-ite, the Ca'naan-ite, the Per'-iz-zite, the Hi'vite, and the Jeb'u-site, heard *thereof:*

2 That they gathered themselves together, to fight with Josh'u-a and with Is'ra-el, with one accord.

3 ¶ And when the inhabitants of Gib'e-on heard what Josh'u-a had done unto Jer'i-cho and to A'i,

4 They did work wilily, and went and made as if they had been ambassadors, and took old sacks upon their asses, and wine bottles, old, and rent, and bound up;

5 And old shoes and clouted upon their feet, and old garments upon them; and all the bread of their provision was dry *and* mouldy.

6 And they went to Josh'u-a unto the camp at Gil'gal, and said unto him, and to the men of Is'ra-el, We be come from a far country: now therefore make ye a league with us.

7 And the men of Is'ra-el said unto the Hi'-vites, Peradventure ye dwell among us; and how shall we make a league with you?

8 And they said unto Josh'u-a, We *are* thy servants. And Josh'u-a said unto them, Who *are* ye? and from whence come ye?

9 And they said unto him, From a very far country thy servants are come because of the name of the LORD thy God: for we have heard the fame of him, and all that he did in E'gypt,

10 And all that he did to the two kings of the Am'or-ites, that *were* beyond Jor'dan, to Si'hon king of Hesh'bon, and to Og king of Ba'shan, which *was* at Ash'ta-roth.

11 Wherefore our elders and all the inhabitants of our country spake to us, saying, Take victuals with you for the journey, and go to meet them, and say unto them, We *are* your servants: therefore now make ye a league with us.

12 This our bread we took hot *for* our provision out of our houses on the day we came forth to go unto you; but now, behold, it is dry, and it is mouldy:

13 And these bottles of wine, which we filled, *were* new; and, behold, they be rent: and these our garments and our shoes are become old by reason of the very long journey.

14 And the men took of their victuals, and asked not *counsel* at the mouth of the LORD.

15 And Josh'u-a made peace with them, and made a league with them, to let them live: and the princes of the congregation sware unto them.

16 ¶ And it came to pass at the end of three days after they had made a league with them, that they heard that they *were* their neighbours, and *that* they dwelt among them.

17 And the children of Is'ra-el journeyed, and came unto their cities on the third day. Now their cities *were* Gib'e-on, and Che-phi'rah, and Be-e'roth, and Kir'jath-je'a-rim.

18 And the children of Is'ra-el smote them not, because the princes of the congregation had sworn unto them by the LORD God of Is'ra-el. And all the congregation murmured against the princes.

19 But all the princes said unto all the congregation, We have sworn unto them by the LORD God of Is'ra-el: now therefore we may not touch them.

20 This we will do to them; we will even let them live, lest wrath be upon us, because of the oath which we sware unto them.

21 And the princes said unto them, Let them live; but let them be hewers of wood and drawers of water unto all the congregation; as the princes had promised them.

22 ¶ And Josh'u-a called for them, and he spake unto them, saying, Wherefore have ye beguiled us, saying, We *are* very far from you; when ye dwell among us?

23 Now therefore ye *are* cursed, and there shall none of you be freed from being bondmen, and hewers of wood and drawers of water for the house of my God.

24 And they answered Josh'u-a, and said, Because it was certainly told thy servants, how that the LORD thy God commanded his servant Mo'ses to give you all the land, and to destroy all the inhabitants of the land from before you, therefore we were sore afraid of our lives because of you, and have done this thing.

25 And now, behold, we *are* in thine hand: as it seemeth good and right unto thee to do unto us, do.

26 And so did he unto them, and delivered them out of the hand of the children of Is'ra-el, that they slew them not.

27 And Josh'u-a made them that day hewers of wood and drawers of water for the congregation, and for the altar of the LORD, even unto this day, in the place which he should choose.

10 NOW it came to pass, when A-don'i-ze'-dec king of Je-ru'sa-lem had heard how Josh'u-a had taken A'i, and had utterly destroyed it; as he had done to Jer'i-cho and her king, so he had done to A'i and her king; and how the inhabitants of Gib'e-on had made peace with Is'ra-el, and were among them;

2 That they feared greatly, because Gib'e-on *was* a great city, as one of the royal cities, and because it *was* greater than A'i, and all the men thereof *were* mighty.

3 Wherefore A-don'i-ze'dec king of Je-ru'sa-lem sent unto Ho'ham king of He'bron, and unto Pi'ram king of Jar'muth, and unto Ja-phi'a king of La'chish, and unto De'bir king of Eg'lon, saying,

4 Come up unto me, and help me, that we may smite Gib'e-on: for it hath made peace with Josh'u-a and with the children of Is'ra-el.

5 Therefore the five kings of the Am'or-ites, the king of Je-ru'sa-lem, the king of He'bron, the king of Jar'muth, the king of La'chish, the king of Eg'lon, gathered themselves together, and went up, they and all their hosts, and encamped before Gib'e-on, and made war against it.

6 ¶ And the men of Gib'e-on sent unto Josh'-u-a to the camp to Gil'gal, saying, Slack not thy hand from thy servants; come up to us quickly, and save us, and help us: for all the kings of the Am'or-ites that 'dwell in the mountains are gathered together against us.

7 So Josh'u-a ascended from Gil'gal, he, and all the people of war with him, and all the mighty men of valour.

8 ¶ And the LORD said unto Josh'u-a, Fear them not: for I have delivered them into thine hand; there shall not a man of them stand before thee.

9 Josh'u-a therefore came unto them suddenly, *and* went up from Gil'gal all night.

10 And the LORD discomfited them before Is'-ra-el, and slew them with a great slaughter at Gib'e-on, and chased them along the way that goeth up to Beth-ho'ron, and smote them to A-ze'kah, and unto Mak-ke'dah.

11 And it came to pass, as they fled from before Is'ra-el, *and* were in the going down to Beth-ho'ron, that the LORD cast down great stones from heaven upon them unto A-ze'kah, and they died: *they were* more which died with hailstones than *they* whom the children of Is'ra-el slew with the sword.

12 ¶ Then spake Josh'u-a to the LORD in the day when the LORD delivered up the Am'or-ites before the children of Is'ra-el, and he said in the sight of Is'ra-el, Sun, stand thou still upon Gib'e-on; and thou, Moon, in the valley of Aj'a-lon.

13 And the sun stood still, and the moon stayed, until the people had avenged themselves upon their enemies. *Is* not this written in the book of Ja'sher? So the sun stood still in the midst of heaven, and hasted not to go down about a whole day.

14 And there was no day like that before it or after it, that the LORD hearkened unto the voice of a man: for the LORD fought for Is'ra-el.

15 ¶ And Josh'u-a returned, and all Is'ra-el with him, unto the camp to Gil'gal.

16 But these five kings fled, and hid themselves in a cave at Mak-ke'dah.

17 And it was told Josh'u-a, saying, The five kings are found hid in a cave at Mak-ke'dah.

18 And Josh'u-a said, Roll great stones upon the mouth of the cave, and set men by it for to keep them:

19 And stay ye not, *but* pursue after your enemies, and smite the hindmost of them; suffer them not to enter into their cities: for the LORD your God hath delivered them into your hand.

20 And it came to pass, when Josh'u-a and the children of Is'ra-el had made an end of slaying them with a very great slaughter, till they were consumed, that the rest *which* remained of them entered into fenced cities.

21 And all the people returned to the camp to Josh'u-a at Mak-ke'dah in peace: none moved his tongue against any of the children of Is'ra-el.

22 Then said Josh'u-a, Open the mouth of the cave, and bring out those five kings unto me out of the cave.

23 And they did so, and brought forth those five kings unto him out of the cave, the king of Je-ru'sa-lem, the king of He'bron, the king of Jar'muth, the king of La'chish, *and* the king of Eg'lon.

24 And it came to pass, when they brought out those kings unto Josh'u-a, that Josh'u-a called for all the men of Is'ra-el, and said unto the captains of the men of war which went with him, Come near, put your feet upon the necks of these kings. And they came near, and put their feet upon the necks of them.

25 And Josh'u-a said unto them, Fear not, nor be dismayed, be strong and of good courage: for thus shall the LORD do to all your enemies against whom ye fight.

26 And afterward Josh'u-a smote them, and slew them, and hanged them on five trees: and they were hanging upon the trees until the evening.

27 And it came to pass at the time of the going down of the sun, *that* Josh'u-a commanded, and they took them down off the trees, and cast them into the cave wherein they had been hid, and laid great stones in the cave's mouth, *which remain* until this very day.

28 ¶ And that day Josh'u-a took Mak-ke'dah, and smote it with the edge of the sword, and the king thereof he utterly destroyed, them, and all the souls that *were* therein; he let none remain: and he did to the king of Mak-ke'dah as he did unto the king of Jer'i-cho.

29 Then Josh'u-a passed from Mak-ke'dah, and all Is'ra-el with him, unto Lib'nah, and fought against Lib'nah:

30 And the LORD delivered it also, and the king thereof, into the hand of Is'ra-el; and he smote it with the edge of the sword, and all the souls that *were* therein; he let none remain in it; but did unto the king thereof as he did unto the king of Jer'i-cho.

31 ¶ And Josh'u-a passed from Lib'nah, and all Is'ra-el with him, unto La'chish, and encamped against it, and fought against it:

32 And the LORD delivered La'chish into the hand of Is'ra-el, which took it on the second day, and smote it with the edge of the sword, and all the souls that *were* therein, according to all that he had done to Lib'nah.

33 ¶ Then Ho'ram king of Ge'zer came up to

help La'chish; and Josh'u-a smote him and his people, until he had left him none remaining.

34 ¶ And from La'chish Josh'u-a passed unto Eg'lon, and all Is'ra-el with him; and they encamped against it, and fought against it:

35 And they took it on that day, and smote it with the edge of the sword, and all the souls that were therein he utterly destroyed that day, according to all that he had done to La'chish.

36 And Josh'u-a went up from Eg'lon, and all Is'ra-el with him, unto He'bron; and they fought against it:

37 And they took it, and smote it with the edge of the sword, and the king thereof, and all the cities thereof, and all the souls that were therein; he left none remaining, according to all that he had done to Eg'lon; but destroyed it utterly, and all the souls that were therein.

38 ¶ And Josh'u-a returned, and all Is'ra-el with him, to De'bir; and fought against it:

39 And he took it, and the king thereof, and all the cities thereof; and they smote them with the edge of the sword, and utterly destroyed all the souls that were therein; he left none remaining: as he had done to He'bron, so he did to De'bir, and to the king thereof; as he had done also to Lib'nah, and to her king.

40 ¶ So Josh'u-a smote all the country of the hills, and of the south, and of the vale, and of the springs, and all their kings: he left none remaining, but utterly destroyed all that breathed, as the LORD God of Is'ra-el commanded.

41 And Josh'u-a smote them from Ka'desh-bar'ne-a even unto Ga'za, and all the country of Go'shen, even unto Gib'e-on.

42 And all these kings and their land did Josh'u-a take at one time, because the LORD God of Is'ra-el fought for Is'ra-el.

43 And Josh'u-a returned, and all Is'ra-el with him, unto the camp to Gil'gal.

11 AND it came to pass, when Ja'bin king of Ha'zor had heard these things, that he sent to Jo'bab king of Ma'don, and to the king of Shim'ron, and to the king of Ach'shaph,

2 And to the kings that were on the north of the mountains, and of the plains south of Chin'ne-roth, and in the valley, and in the borders of Dor on the west,

3 And to the Ca'naan-ite on the east and on the west, and to the Am'or-ite, and the Hit'tite, and the Per'iz-zite, and the Jeb'u-site in the mountains, and to the Hi'vite under Her'mon in the land of Miz'peh.

4 And they went out, they and all their hosts with them, much people, even as the sand that is upon the sea shore in multitude, with horses and chariots very many.

5 And when all these kings were met together, they came and pitched together at the waters of Me'rom, to fight against Is'ra-el.

6 ¶ And the LORD said unto Josh'u-a, Be not afraid because of them: for to morrow about this time will I deliver them up all slain before Is'ra-el: thou shalt hough their horses, and burn their chariots with fire.

7 So Josh'u-a came, and all the people of war with him, against them by the waters of Me'rom suddenly; and they fell upon them.

8 And the LORD delivered them into the hand of Is'ra-el, who smote them, and chased them unto great Zi'don, and unto Mis're-photh-ma'im, and unto the valley of Miz'peh eastward; and they smote them, until they left them none remaining.

9 And Josh'u-a did unto them as the LORD

bade him: he houghed their horses, and burnt their chariots with fire.

10 ¶ And Josh'u-a at that time turned back, and took Ha'zor, and smote the king thereof with the sword: for Ha'zor beforetime was the head of all those kingdoms.

11 And they smote all the souls that were therein with the edge of the sword, utterly destroying them: there was not any left to breathe: and he burnt Ha'zor with fire.

12 And all the cities of those kings, and all the kings of them, did Josh'u-a take, and smote them with the edge of the sword, and he utterly destroyed them, as Mo'ses the servant of the LORD commanded.

13 But as for the cities that stood still in their strength, Is'ra-el burned none of them, save Ha'zor only; that did Josh'u-a burn.

14 And all the spoil of these cities, and the cattle, the children of Is'ra-el took for a prey unto themselves; but every man they smote with the edge of the sword, until they had destroyed them, neither left they any to breathe.

15 ¶ As the LORD commanded Mo'ses his servant, so did Mo'ses command Josh'u-a, and so did Josh'u-a; he left nothing undone of all that the LORD commanded Mo'ses.

16 So Josh'u-a took all that land, the hills, and all the south country, and all the land of Go'shen, and the valley, and the plain, and the mountain of Is'ra-el, and the valley of the same;

17 Even from the mount Ha'lak, that goeth up to Se'ir, even unto Ba'al-gad in the valley of Leb'a-non under mount Her'mon: and all their kings he took, and smote them, and slew them.

18 Josh'u-a made war a long time with all those kings.

19 There was not a city that made peace with the children of Is'ra-el, save the Hi'vites the inhabitants of Gib'e-on: all other they took in battle.

20 For it was of the LORD to harden their hearts, that they should come against Is'ra-el in battle, that he might destroy them utterly, and that they might have no favour, but that he might destroy them, as the LORD commanded Mo'ses.

21 ¶ And at that time came Josh'u-a, and cut off the An'a-kims from the mountains, from He'bron, from De'bir, from A'nab, and from all the mountains of Ju'dah, and from all the mountains of Is'ra-el: Josh'u-a destroyed them utterly with their cities.

22 There was none of the An'a-kims left in the land of the children of Is'ra-el: only in Ga'za, in Gath, and in Ash'dod, there remained.

23 So Josh'u-a took the whole land, according to all that the LORD said unto Mo'ses; and Josh'u-a gave it for an inheritance unto Is'ra-el according to their divisions by their tribes. And the land rested from war.

12 NOW these are the kings of the land, which the children of Is'ra-el smote, and possessed their land on the other side Jor'dan toward the rising of the sun, from the river Ar'non unto mount Her'mon, and all the plain on the east:

2 Si'hon king of the Am'or-ites, who dwelt in Hesh'bon, and ruled from Ar'o-er, which is upon the bank of the river Ar'non, and from the middle of the river, and from half Gil'e-ad, even unto the river Jab'bok, which is the border of the children of Am'mon;

3 And from the plain to the sea of Chin'ne-roth on the east, and unto the sea of the plain, even the salt sea on the east, the way to Beth-

jesh'i-moth; and from the south, under Ash'-doth-pis'gah:

4 ¶ And the coast of Og king of Ba'shan, which was of the remnant of the giants, that dwelt at Ash'ta-roth and at Ed're-i,

5 And reigned in mount Her'mon, and in Sal'cah, and in all Ba'shan, unto the border of the Gesh'u-rites and the Ma-ach'a-thites, and half Gil'e-ad, the border of Si'hon king of Hesh'bon.

6 Them did Mo'ses the servant of the LORD and the children of Is'ra-el smite: and Mo'ses the servant of the LORD gave it for a possession unto the Reu'ben-ites, and the Gad'ites, and the half tribe of Ma-nas'seh.

7 ¶ And these are the kings of the country which Josh'u-a and the children of Is'ra-el smote on this side Jor'dan on the west, from Ba'al-gad in the valley of Leb'a-non even unto the mount Ha'lak, that goeth up to Se'ir; which Josh'u-a gave unto the tribes of Is'ra-el for a possession according to their divisions;

8 In the mountains, and in the valleys, and in the plains, and in the springs, and in the wilderness, and in the south country; the Hit'tites, the Am'or-ites, and the Ca'naan-ites, the Per'iz-zites, the Hi'vites, and the Jeb'u-sites:

9 ¶ The king of Jer'i-cho, one; the king of A'i, which is beside Beth'-el, one;

10 The king of Je-ru'sa-lem, one; the king of He'bron, one;

11 The king of Jar'muth, one; the king of La'chish, one;

12 The king of Eg'lon, one; the king of Ge'zer, one;

13 The king of De'bir, one; the king of Ge'der, one;

14 The king of Hor'mah, one; the king of A'rad, one;

15 The king of Lib'nah, one; the king of A-dul'lam, one;

16 The king of Mak-ke'dah, one; the king of Beth'-el, one;

17 The king of Tap'pu-ah, one; the king of He'pher, one;

18 The king of A'phek, one; the king of La-shar'on, one;

19 The king of Ma'don, one; the king of Ha'zor, one;

20 The king of Shim'ron-me'ron, one; the king of Ach'shaph, one;

21 The king of Ta'a-nach, one; the king of Me-gid'do, one;

22 The king of Ke'desh, one; the king of Jok'ne-am of Car'mel, one;

23 The king of Dor in the coast of Dor, one; the king of the nations of Gil'gal, one;

24 The king of Tir'zah, one: all the kings thirty and one.

13 NOW Josh'u-a was old and stricken in years; and the LORD said unto him, Thou art old and stricken in years, and there remaineth yet very much land to be possessed.

2 This is the land that yet remaineth: all the borders of the Phi-lis'tines, and all Gesh'u-ri,

3 From Si'hor, which is before E'gypt, even unto the borders of Ek'ron northward, which is counted to the Ca'naan-ite: five lords of the Phi-lis'tines; the Ga'zath-ites, and the Ash'doth-ites, the Esh'ka-lon-ites, the Git'tites, and the Ek'ron-ites; also the A'vites:

4 From the south, all the land of the Ca'naan-ites, and Me-a'rah that is beside the Si-do'ni-ans, unto A'phek, to the borders of the Am'or-ites:

5 And the land of the Gib'lites, and all Leb'a-non, toward the sunrising, from Ba'al-gad under mount Her'mon unto the entering into Ha'math.

6 All the inhabitants of the hill country from Leb'a-non unto Mis're-photh-ma'im, and all the Si-do'ni-ans, them will I drive out from before the children of Is'ra-el: only divide thou it by lot unto the Is'ra-el-ites for an inheritance, as I have commanded thee.

7 Now therefore divide this land for an inheritance unto the nine tribes, and the half tribe of Ma-nas'seh,

8 With whom the Reu'ben-ites and the Gad'ites have received their inheritance, which Mo'ses gave them, beyond Jor'dan eastward, even as Mo'ses the servant of the LORD gave them;

9 From Ar'o-er, that is upon the bank of the river Ar'non, and the city that is in the midst of the river, and all the plain of Med'e-ba unto Di'bon;

10 And all the cities of Si'hon king of the Am'or-ites, which reigned in Hesh'bon, unto the border of the children of Am'mon;

11 And Gil'e-ad, and the border of the Gesh'u-rites and Ma-ach'a-thites, and all mount Her'mon, and all Ba'shan unto Sal'cah;

12 All the kingdom of Og in Ba'shan, which reigned in Ash'ta-roth and in Ed're-i, who remained of the remnant of the giants: for these did Mo'ses smite, and cast them out.

13 Nevertheless the children of Is'ra-el expelled not the Gesh'u-rites, nor the Ma-ach'a-thites: but the Gesh'u-rites and the Ma-ach'a-thites dwell among the Is'ra-el-ites until this day.

14 Only unto the tribe of Le'vi he gave none inheritance; the sacrifices of the LORD God of Is'ra-el made by fire are their inheritance, as he said unto them.

15 ¶ And Mo'ses gave unto the tribe of the children of Reu'ben inheritance according to their families.

16 And their coast was from Ar'o-er, that is on the bank of the river Ar'non, and the city that is in the midst of the river, and all the plain by Med'e-ba;

17 Hesh'bon, and all her cities that are in the plain; Di'bon, and Ba'moth-ba'al, and Beth-ba'-al-me'on,

18 And Ja-ha'za, and Ked'e-moth, and Meph'a-ath,

19 And Kir-jath-a'im, and Sib'mah, and Za'reth-sha'har in the mount of the valley,

20 And Beth-pe'or, and Ash'doth-pis'gah, and Beth-jesh'i-moth,

21 And all the cities of the plain, and all the kingdom of Si'hon king of the Am'or-ites, which reigned in Hesh'bon, whom Mo'ses smote with the princes of Mid'i-an, E'vi, and Re'kem, and Zur, and Hur, and Re'ba, which were dukes of Si'hon, dwelling in the country.

22 ¶ Ba'laam also the son of Be'or, the soothsayer, did the children of Is'ra-el slay with the sword among them that were slain by them.

23 And the border of the children of Reu'ben was Jor'dan, and the border thereof. This was the inheritance of the children of Reu'ben after their families, the cities and the villages thereof.

24 And Mo'ses gave inheritance unto the tribe of Gad, even unto the children of Gad according to their families.

25 And their coast was Ja'zer, and all the cities of Gil'e-ad, and half the land of the children of Am'mon, unto Ar'o-er that is before Rab'bah;

26 And from Hesh'bon unto Ra'math-miz'peh, and Bet'o-nim; and from Ma-ha-na'im unto the border of De'bir;

27 And in the valley, Beth-a′ram, and Beth-nim′rah, and Suc′coth, and Za′phon, the rest of the kingdom of Si′hon king of Hesh′bon, Jor′dan and *his* border, *even* unto the edge of the sea of Chin′ne-reth on the other side Jor′dan eastward.

28 This *is* the inheritance of the children of Gad after their families, the cities, and their villages.

29 ¶ And Mo′ses gave *inheritance* unto the half tribe of Ma-nas′seh: and *this* was *the possession* of the half tribe of the children of Ma-nas′seh by their families.

30 And their coast was from Ma-ha-na′im, all Ba′shan, all the kingdom of Og king of Ba′shan, and all the towns of Ja′ir, which *are* in Ba′shan, threescore cities:

31 And half Gil′e-ad, and Ash′ta-roth, and Ed′re-i, cities of the kingdom of Og in Ba′shan, *were pertaining* unto the children of Ma′chir the son of Ma-nas′seh, *even* to the one half of the children of Ma′chir by their families.

32 These *are the countries* which Mo′ses did distribute for inheritance in the plains of Mo′ab, on the other side Jor′dan, by Jer′i-cho, eastward.

33 But unto the tribe of Le′vi Mo′ses gave not *any* inheritance: the LORD God of Is′ra-el *was* their inheritance, as he said unto them.

14 AND these *are the countries* which the children of Is′ra-el inherited in the land of Ca′naan, which E-le-a′zar the priest, and Josh′u-a the son of Nun, and the heads of the fathers of the tribes of the children of Is′ra-el, distributed for inheritance to them.

2 By lot *was* their inheritance, as the LORD commanded by the hand of Mo′ses, for the nine tribes, and *for* the half tribe.

3 For Mo′ses had given the inheritance of two tribes and an half tribe on the other side Jor′dan: but unto the Le′vites he gave none inheritance among them.

4 For the children of Jo′seph were two tribes, Ma-nas′seh and E′phra-im: therefore they gave no part unto the Le′vites in the land, save cities to dwell *in*, with their suburbs for their cattle and for their substance.

5 As the LORD commanded Mo′ses, so the children of Is′ra-el did, and they divided the land.

6 ¶ Then the children of Ju′dah came unto Josh′u-a in Gil′gal: and Ca′leb the son of Je-phun′neh the Ken′ez-ite said unto him, Thou knowest the thing that the LORD said unto Mo′ses the man of God concerning me and thee in Ka′desh-bar′ne-a.

7 Forty years old *was* I when Mo′ses the servant of the LORD sent me from Ka′desh-bar′ne-a to espy out the land; and I brought him word again as *it was* in mine heart.

8 Nevertheless my brethren that went up with me made the heart of the people melt: but I wholly followed the LORD my God.

9 And Mo′ses sware on that day, saying, Surely the land whereon thy feet have trodden shall be thine inheritance, and thy children′s for ever, because thou hast wholly followed the LORD my God.

10 And now, behold, the LORD hath kept me alive, as he said, these forty and five years, even since the LORD spake this word unto Mo′ses, while *the children of* Is′ra-el wandered in the wilderness: and now, lo, I *am* this day fourscore and five years old.

11 As yet I *am as* strong this day as I *was* in the day that Mo′ses sent me: as my strength

was then, even so *is* my strength now, for war, both to go out, and to come in.

12 Now therefore give me this mountain, whereof the LORD spake in that day; for thou heardest in that day how the An′a-kims *were* there, and *that* the cities *were* great *and* fenced: if so be the LORD *will be* with me, then I shall be able to drive them out, as the LORD said.

13 And Josh′u-a blessed him, and gave unto Ca′leb the son of Je-phun′neh He′bron for an inheritance.

14 He′bron therefore became the inheritance of Ca′leb the son of Je-phun′neh the Ken′ez-ite unto this day, because that he wholly followed the LORD God of Is′ra-el.

15 And the name of He′bron before *was* Kir′-jath-ar′ba; *which Ar′ba was* a great man among the An′a-kims. And the land had rest from war.

15 THIS then was the lot of the tribe of the children of Ju′dah by their families; *even* to the border of E′dom the wilderness of Zin southward *was* the uttermost part of the south coast.

2 And their south border was from the shore of the salt sea, from the bay that looketh southward:

3 And it went out to the south side to Ma-al′eh-a-crab′bim, and passed along to Zin, and ascended up on the south side unto Ka′desh-bar′ne-a, and passed along to Hez′ron, and went up to A′dar, and fetched a compass to Kar′ka-a:

4 *From thence* it passed toward Az′mon, and went out unto the river of E′gypt; and the goings out of that coast were at the sea: this shall be your south coast.

5 And the east border *was* the salt sea, *even* unto the end of Jor′dan. And *their* border in the north quarter *was* from the bay of the sea at the uttermost part of Jor′dan:

6 And the border went up to Beth-hog′la, and passed along by the north of Beth-ar′a-bah; and the border went up to the stone of Bo′han the son of Reu′ben:

7 And the border went up toward De′bir from the valley of A′chor, and so northward, looking toward Gil′gal, that *is* before the going up to A-dum′mim, which *is* on the south side of the river: and the border passed toward the waters of En-she′mesh, and the goings out thereof were at En-ro′gel:

8 And the border went up by the valley of the son of Hin′nom unto the south side of the Jeb′u-site; the same *is* Je-ru′sa-lem: and the border went up to the top of the mountain that *lieth* before the valley of Hin′nom westward, which *is* at the end of the valley of the giants northward:

9 And the border was drawn from the top of the hill unto the fountain of the water of Neph′-to-ah, and went out to the cities of mount E′-phron; and the border was drawn to Ba′al-ah, which *is* Kir′jath-je′a-rim:

10 And the border compassed from Ba′al-ah westward unto mount Se′ir, and passed along unto the side of mount Je′a-rim, which *is* Ches′a-lon, on the north side, and went down to Beth-she′mesh, and passed on to Tim′nah:

11 And the border went out unto the side of Ek′ron northward: and the border was drawn to Shi′cron, and passed along to mount Ba′al-ah, and went out unto Jab′ne-el; and the goings out of the border were at the sea.

12 And the west border *was* to the great sea, and the coast *thereof*. This *is* the coast of the children of Ju′dah round about according to their families.

13 ¶ And unto Ca'leb the son of Je-phun'neh he gave a part among the children of Ju'dah, according to the commandment of the LORD to Josh'u-a, *even* the city of Ar'ba the father of A'-nak, which *city is* He'bron.

14 And Ca'leb drove thence the three sons of A'nak, She'shai, and A-hi'man, and Tal'mai, the children of A'nak.

15 And he went up thence to the inhabitants of De'bir: and the name of De'bir before *was* Kir'jath-se'pher.

16 ¶ And Ca'leb said, He that smiteth Kir'-jath-se'pher, and taketh it, to him will I give Ach'sah my daughter to wife.

17 And Oth'ni-el the son of Ke'naz, the brother of Ca'leb, took it: and he gave him Ach'-sah his daughter to wife.

18 And it came to pass, as she came *unto him*, that she moved him to ask of her father a field: and she lighted off *her* ass; and Ca'leb said unto her, What wouldest thou?

19 Who answered, Give me a blessing; for thou hast given me a south land; give me also springs of water. And he gave her the upper springs, and the nether springs.

20 This *is* the inheritance of the tribe of the children of Ju'dah according to their families.

21 And the uttermost cities of the tribe of the children of Ju'dah toward the coast of E'dom southward were Kab'ze-el, and E'der, and Ja'-gur,

22 And Ki'nah, and Di-mo'nah, and Ad'a-dah,

23 And Ke'desh, and Ha'zor, and Ith'nan,

24 Ziph, and Te'lem, and Be'a-loth,

25 And Ha'zor, Ha-dat'tah, and Ke'ri-oth, *and* Hez'ron, which *is* Ha'zor,

26 A'mam, and She'ma, and Mol'a-dah,

27 And Ha'zar-gad'dah, and Hesh'mon, and Beth-pa'let,

28 And Ha'zar-shu'al, and Be'er-she'ba, and Biz-joth'jah,

29 Ba'al-ah, and I'im, and A'zem,

30 And El'to-lad, and Che'sil, and Hor'mah,

31 And Zik'lag, and Mad-man'nah, and San-san'nah,

32 And Leb'a-oth, and Shil'him, and A'in, and Rim'mon: all the cities *are* twenty and nine, with their villages:

33 *And* in the valley, Esh'ta-ol, and Zo're-ah, and Ash'nah,

34 And Za-no'ah, and En-gan'nim, Tap'pu-ah, and E'nam,

35 Jar'muth, and A-dul'lam, So'coh, and A-ze'kah,

36 And Shar-a'im, and Ad-i-tha'im, and Ge-de'rah, and Ged-e-roth-a'im; fourteen cities with their villages:

37 Ze'nan, and Had'a-shah, and Mig'dal-gad,

38 And Dil'e-an, and Miz'peh, and Jok'the-el,

39 La'chish, and Boz'kath, and Eg'lon,

40 And Cab'bon, and Lah'mam, and Kith'-lish,

41 And Ge-de'roth, Beth-da'gon, and Na'a-mah, and Mak-ke'dah; sixteen cities with their villages:

42 Lib'nah, and E'ther, and A'shan,

43 And Jiph'tah, and Ash'nah, and Ne'zib,

44 And Kei'lah, and Ach'zib, and Ma-re'shah; nine cities with their villages:

45 Ek'ron, with her towns and her villages:

46 From Ek'ron even unto the sea, all that *lay* near Ash'dod, with their villages:

47 Ash'dod with her towns and her villages, Ga'za with her towns and her villages, unto the river of E'gypt, and the great sea, and the border *thereof*:

48 ¶ And in the mountains, Sha'mir, and Jat'tir, and So'coh,

49 And Dan'nah, and Kir'jath-san'nah, which *is* De'bir,

50 And A'nab, and Esh'te-moh, and A'nim,

51 And Go'shen, and Ho'lon, and Gi'loh; eleven cities with their villages:

52 A'rab, and Du'mah, and E'she-an,

53 And Ja'num, and Beth-tap'pu-ah, and A-phe'kah,

54 And Hum'tah, and Kir'jath-ar'ba, which *is* He'bron, and Zi'or; nine cities with their villages:

55 Ma'on, Car'mel, and Ziph, and Jut'tah,

56 And Jez're-el, and Jok'de-am, and Za-no'-ah,

57 Cain, Gib'e-ah, and Tim'nah; ten cities with their villages:

58 Hal'hul, Beth'-zur, and Ge'dor,

59 And Ma'a-rath, and Beth-a'noth, and El'-te-kon; six cities with their villages:

60 Kir'jath-ba'al, which *is* Kir'jath-je'a-rim, and Rab'bah; two cities with their villages:

61 In the wilderness, Beth-ar'a-bah, Mid'din, and Sec'a-cah,

62 And Nib'shan, and the city of Salt, and En-ge'di; six cities with their villages.

63 ¶ As for the Jeb'u-sites the inhabitants of Je-ru'sa-lem, the children of Ju'dah could not drive them out: but the Jeb'u-sites dwell with the children of Ju'dah at Je-ru'sa-lem unto this day.

16 AND the lot of the children of Jo'seph fell from Jor'dan by Jer'i-cho, unto the water of Jer'i-cho on the east, to the wilderness that goeth up from Jer'i-cho throughout mount Beth'-el,

2 And goeth out from Beth'-el to Luz, and passeth along unto the borders of Ar'chi to At'-a-roth,

3 And goeth down westward to the coast of Japh-le'ti, unto the coast of Beth-ho'ron the nether, and to Ge'zer: and the goings out thereof are at the sea.

4 So the children of Jo'seph, Ma-nas'seh and E'phra-im, took their inheritance.

5 ¶ And the border of the children of E'phra-im according to their families was *thus:* even the border of their inheritance on the east side was At'a-roth-ad'dar, unto Beth-ho'ron the upper;

6 And the border went out toward the sea to Mich'me-thah on the north side; and the border went about eastward unto Ta'a-nath-shi'loh, and passed by it on the east to Ja-no'hah;

7 And it went down from Ja-no'hah to At'a-roth, and to Na'a-rath, and came to Jer'i-cho, and went out at Jor'dan.

8 The border went out from Tap'pu-ah westward unto the river Ka'nah; and the goings out thereof were at the sea. This *is* the inheritance of the tribe of the children of E'phra-im by their families.

9 And the separate cities for the children of E'phra-im *were* among the inheritance of the children of Ma-nas'seh, all the cities with their villages.

10 And they drave not out the Ca'naan-ites that dwelt in Ge'zer: but the Ca'naan-ites dwell among the E'phra-im-ites unto this day, and serve under tribute.

17 THERE was also a lot for the tribe of Ma-nas'seh; for he *was* the firstborn of Jo'seph; *to wit,* for Ma'chir the firstborn of Ma-nas'seh, the father of Gil'e-ad: because he was a

man of war, therefore he had Gil´e-ad and Ba´-shan.

2 There was also *a lot* for the rest of the children of Ma-nas´seh by their families; for the children of A-bi-e´zer, and for the children of He´lek, and for the children of As´ri-el, and for the children of She´chem, and for the children of He´pher, and for the children of She-mi´da: these *were* the male children of Ma-nas´seh the son of Jo´seph by their families.

3 ¶ But Ze-lo´phe-had, the son of He´pher, the son of Gil´e-ad, the son of Ma´chir, the son of Ma-nas´seh, had no sons, but daughters: and these *are* the names of his daughters, Mah´lah, and No´ah, Hog´lah, Mil´cah, and Tir´zah.

4 And they came near before E-le-a´zar the priest, and before Josh´u-a the son of Nun, and before the princes, saying, The LORD commanded Mo´ses to give us an inheritance among our brethren. Therefore according to the commandment of the LORD he gave them an inheritance among the brethren of their father.

5 And there fell ten portions to Ma-nas´seh, beside the land of Gil´e-ad and Ba´shan, which *were* on the other side Jor´dan;

6 Because the daughters of Ma-nas´seh had an inheritance among his sons: and the rest of Ma-nas´seh's sons had the land of Gil´e-ad.

7 ¶ And the coast of Ma-nas´seh was from Ash´er to Mich´me-thah, that *lieth* before She´-chem; and the border went along on the right hand unto the inhabitants of En-tap´pu-ah.

8 *Now* Ma-nas´seh had the land of Tap´pu-ah: but Tap´pu-ah on the border of Ma-nas´seh *belonged* to the children of E´phra-im;

9 And the coast descended unto the river Ka´nah, southward of the river: these cities of E´phra-im *are* among the cities of Ma-nas´seh: the coast of Ma-nas´seh also *was* on the north side of the river, and the outgoings of it were at the sea:

10 Southward *it was* E´phra-im's, and northward *it was* Ma-nas´seh's, and the sea is his border; and they met together in Ash´er on the north, and in Is´sa-char on the east.

11 And Ma-nas´seh had in Is´sa-char and in Ash´er Beth–she´an and her towns, and Ib´le-am and her towns, and the inhabitants of Dor and her towns, and the inhabitants of En´–dor and her towns, and the inhabitants of Ta´a-nach and her towns, and the inhabitants of Me-gid´do and her towns, *even* three countries.

12 Yet the children of Ma-nas´seh could not drive out *the inhabitants* of those cities; but the Ca´naan-ites would dwell in that land.

13 Yet it came to pass, when the children of Is´ra-el were waxen strong, that they put the Ca´naan-ites to tribute; but did not utterly drive them out.

14 And the children of Jo´seph spake unto Josh´u-a, saying, Why hast thou given me *but* one lot and one portion to inherit, seeing I *am* a great people, forasmuch as the LORD hath blessed me hitherto?

15 And Josh´u-a answered them, If thou *be* a great people, *then* get thee up to the wood *country,* and cut down for thyself there in the land of the Per´iz-zites and of the giants, if mount E´phra-im be too narrow for thee.

16 And the children of Jo´seph said, The hill is not enough for us: and all the Ca´naan-ites that dwell in the land of the valley have chariots of iron, *both* they who *are* of Beth–she´an and her towns, and *they* who *are* of the valley of Jez´re-el.

17 And Josh´u-a spake unto the house of Jo´-seph, *even* to E´phra-im and to Ma-nas´seh, saying, Thou *art* a great people, and hast great power: thou shalt not have one lot *only:*

18 But the mountain shall be thine; for it *is* a wood, and thou shalt cut it down: and the outgoings of it shall be thine: for thou shalt drive out the Ca´naan-ites, though they have iron chariots, *and* though they *be* strong.

18 AND the whole congregation of the children of Is´ra-el assembled together at Shi´loh, and set up the tabernacle of the congregation there. And the land was subdued before them.

2 And there remained among the children of Is´ra-el seven tribes, which had not yet received their inheritance.

3 And Josh´u-a said unto the children of Is´-ra-el, How long *are* ye slack to go to possess the land, which the LORD God of your fathers hath given you?

4 Give out from among you three men for *each* tribe: and I will send them, and they shall rise, and go through the land, and describe it according to the inheritance of them; and they shall come *again* to me.

5 And they shall divide it into seven parts: Ju´dah shall abide in their coast on the south, and the house of Jo´seph shall abide in their coasts on the north.

6 Ye shall therefore describe the land *into* seven parts, and bring *the description* hither to me, that I may cast lots for you here before the LORD our God.

7 But the Le´vites have no part among you; for the priesthood of the LORD *is* their inheritance: and Gad, and Reu´ben, and half the tribe of Ma-nas´seh, have received their inheritance beyond Jor´dan on the east, which Mo´ses the servant of the LORD gave them.

8 ¶ And the men arose, and went away: and Josh´u-a charged them that went to describe the land, saying, Go and walk through the land, and describe it, and come *again* to me, that I may here cast lots for you before the LORD in Shi´loh.

9 And the men went and passed through the land, and described it by cities into seven parts in a book, and came *again* to Josh´u-a to the host at Shi´loh.

10 ¶ And Josh´u-a cast lots for them in Shi´-loh before the LORD: and there Josh´u-a divided the land unto the children of Is´ra-el according to their divisions.

11 ¶ And the lot of the tribe of the children of Ben´ja-min came up according to their families: and the coast of their lot came forth between the children of Ju´dah and the children of Jo´seph.

12 And their border on the north side was from Jor´dan; and the border went up to the side of Jer´i-cho on the north side, and went up through the mountains westward; and the goings out thereof were at the wilderness of Beth-a´ven.

13 And the border went over from thence toward Luz, to the side of Luz, which *is* Beth´-el, southward; and the border descended to At´-a-roth-a´dar, near the hill that *lieth* on the south side of the nether Beth-ho´ron.

14 And the border was drawn *thence,* and compassed the corner of the sea southward, from the hill that *lieth* before Beth–ho´ron southward; and the goings out thereof were at Kir´jath-ba´al, which *is* Kir´jath-je´a-rim, a city of the children of Ju´dah: this *was* the west quarter.

15 And the south quarter *was* from the end of Kir´jath-je´a-rim, and the border went out on

the west, and went out to the well of waters of Neph'to-ah:

16 And the border came down to the end of the mountain that *lieth* before the valley of the son of Hin'nom, *and* which *is* in the valley of the giants on the north, and descended to the valley of Hin'nom, to the side of Je-bu'si on the south, and descended to En-ro'gel,

17 And was drawn from the north, and went forth to En-she'mesh, and went forth toward Gel'i-loth, which *is* over against the going up of A-dum'mim, and descended to the stone of Bo'han the son of Reu'ben,

18 And passed along toward the side over against Ar'a-bah northward, and went down unto Ar'a-bah:

19 And the border passed along to the side of Beth-hog'lah northward: and the outgoings of the border were at the north bay of the salt sea at the south end of Jor'dan: this *was* the south coast.

20 And Jor'dan was the border of it on the east side. This *was* the inheritance of the children of Ben'ja-min, by the coasts thereof round about, according to their families.

21 Now the cities of the tribe of the children of Ben'ja-min according to their families were Jer'i-cho, and Beth-hog'lah, and the valley of Ke'ziz,

22 And Beth-ar'a-bah, and Zem-a-ra'im, and Beth'-el,

23 And A'vim, and Pa'rah, and Oph'rah,

24 And Che'phar-ha-am'mo-nai, and Oph'ni, and Ga'ba; twelve cities with their villages:

25 Gib'e-on, and Ra'mah, and Be-e'roth,

26 And Miz'peh, and Che-phi'rah, and Mo'zah,

27 And Re'kem, and Ir'pe-el, and Tar'a-lah,

28 And Ze'lah, E'leph, and Je-bu'si, which *is* Je-ru'sa-lem, Gib'e-ath, *and* Kir'jath; fourteen cities with their villages. This *is* the inheritance of the children of Ben'ja-min according to their families.

19 AND the second lot came forth to Sim'e-on, *even* for the tribe of the children of Sim'e-on according to their families: and their inheritance was within the inheritance of the children of Ju'dah.

2 And they had in their inheritance Be'er-she'ba, and She'ba, and Mol'a-dah,

3 And Ha'zar-shu'al, and Ba'lah, and A'zem,

4 And El'to-lad, and Be'thul, and Hor'mah,

5 And Zik'lag, and Beth-mar'ca-both, and Ha'zar-su'sah,

6 And Beth-leb'a-oth, and Sha-ru'hen; thirteen cities and their villages:

7 A'in, Rem'mon, and E'ther, and A'shan; four cities and their villages:

8 And all the villages that *were* round about these cities to Ba'al-ath-be'er, Ra'math of the south. This *is* the inheritance of the tribe of the children of Sim'e-on according to their families.

9 Out of the portion of the children of Ju'dah *was* the inheritance of the children of Sim'e-on: for the part of the children of Ju'dah was too much for them: therefore the children of Sim'e-on had their inheritance within the inheritance of them.

10 ¶ And the third lot came up for the children of Zeb'u-lun according to their families: and the border of their inheritance was unto Sa'rid:

11 And their border went up toward the sea, and Mar'a-lah, and reached to Dab'ba-sheth, and reached to the river that *is* before Jok'ne-am;

12 And turned from Sa'rid eastward toward the sunrising unto the border of Chis'loth-ta'bor, and then goeth out to Dab'e-rath, and goeth up to Ja-phi'a,

13 And from thence passeth on along on the east to Git'tah-he'pher, to It'tah-ka'zin, and goeth out to Rem'mon-meth'o-ar to Ne-ah;

14 And the border compasseth it on the north side to Han'na-thon: and the outgoings thereof are in the valley of Jiph'thah-el:

15 And Kat'tath, and Na-hal'lal, and Shim'ron, and I-da'lah, and Beth'-le-hem: twelve cities with their villages.

16 This *is* the inheritance of the children of Zeb'u-lun according to their families, these cities with their villages.

17 ¶ *And* the fourth lot came out to Is'sa-char, for the children of Is'sa-char according to their families.

18 And their border was toward Jez're-el, and Che-sul'loth, and Shu'nem,

19 And Haph-ra'im, and Shi'hon, and An-a-ha'rath,

20 And Rab'bith, and Kish'i-on, and A'bez,

21 And Re'meth, and En-gan'nim, and En-had'dah, and Beth-paz'zez;

22 And the coast reacheth to Ta'bor, and Sha-haz'i-mah, and Beth-she'mesh; and the outgoings of their border were at Jor'dan: sixteen cities with their villages.

23 This *is* the inheritance of the tribe of the children of Is'sa-char according to their families, the cities and their villages.

24 ¶ And the fifth lot came out for the tribe of the children of Ash'er according to their families.

25 And their border was Hel'kath, and Ha'li, and Be'ten, and Ach'shaph,

26 And A-lam'me-lech, and A'mad, and Mi'she-al; and reacheth to Car'mel westward, and to Shi'hor-lib'nath;

27 And turneth toward the sunrising to Beth-da'gon, and reacheth to Zeb'u-lun, and to the valley of Jiph'thah-el toward the north side of Beth-e'mek, and Ne'i-el, and goeth out to Ca'bul on the left hand,

28 And He'bron, and Re'hob, and Ham'mon, and Ka'nah, *even* unto great Zi'don;

29 And *then* the coast turneth to Ra'mah, and to the strong city Tyre; and the coast turneth to Ho'sah; and the outgoings thereof are at the sea from the coast to Ach'zib:

30 Um'mah also, and A'phek, and Re'hob: twenty and two cities with their villages.

31 This *is* the inheritance of the tribe of the children of Ash'er according to their families, these cities with their villages.

32 ¶ The sixth lot came out to the children of Naph'ta-li, *even* for the children of Naph'ta-li according to their families.

33 And their coast was from He'leph, from Al'lon to Za-a-nan'nim, and Ad'a-mi, Ne'keb, and Jab'ne-el, unto La'kum; and the outgoings thereof were at Jor'dan:

34 And *then* the coast turneth westward to Az'noth-ta'bor, and goeth out from thence to Huk'kok, and reacheth to Zeb'u-lun on the south side, and reacheth to Ash'er on the west side, and to Ju'dah upon Jor'dan toward the sunrising.

35 And the fenced cities *are* Zid'dim, Zer, and Ham'math, Rak'kath, and Chin'ne-reth,

36 And Ad'a-mah, and Ra'mah, and Ha'zor,

37 And Ke'desh, and Ed're-i, and En-ha'zor,

38 And I'ron, and Mig'dal-el, Ho'rem, and Beth-a'nath, and Beth-she'mesh; nineteen cities with their villages.

39 This *is* the inheritance of the tribe of the children of Naph'ta-li according to their families, the cities and their villages.

40 ¶ *And* the seventh lot came out for the tribe of the children of Dan according to their families.

41 And the coast of their inheritance was Zo'rah, and Esh'ta-ol, and Ir-she'mesh,

42 And Sha-al-ab'bin, and Aj'a-lon, and Jeth'lah,

43 And E'lon, and Thim'na-thah, and Ek'ron,

44 And El'te-keh, and Gib'be-thon, and Ba'al-ath,

45 And Je'hud, and Ben'e-be'rak, and Gath-rim'mon,

46 And Me-jar'kon, and Rak'kon, with the border before Ja'pho.

47 And the coast of the children of Dan went out *too little* for them: therefore the children of Dan went up to fight against Le'shem, and took it, and smote it with the edge of the sword, and possessed it, and dwelt therein, and called Le'-shem, Dan, after the name of Dan their father.

48 This *is* the inheritance of the tribe of the children of Dan according to their families, these cities with their villages.

49 ¶ When they had made an end of dividing the land for inheritance by their coasts, the children of Is'ra-el gave an inheritance to Josh'u-a the son of Nun among them:

50 According to the word of the LORD they gave him the city which he asked, *even* Tim'-nath-se'rah in mount E'phra-im: and he built the city, and dwelt therein.

51 These *are* the inheritances, which E-le-a'-zar the priest, and Josh'u-a the son of Nun, and the heads of the fathers of the tribes of the children of Is'ra-el, divided for an inheritance by lot in Shi'loh before the LORD, at the door of the tabernacle of the congregation. So they made an end of dividing the country.

20 THE LORD also spake unto Josh'u-a, saying,

2 Speak to the children of Is'ra-el, saying, Appoint out for you cities of refuge, whereof I spake unto you by the hand of Mo'ses:

3 That the slayer that killeth *any* person unawares *and* unwittingly may flee thither: and they shall be your refuge from the avenger of blood.

4 And when he that doth flee unto one of those cities shall stand at the entering of the gate of the city, and shall declare his cause in the ears of the elders of that city, they shall take him into the city unto them, and give him a place, that he may dwell among them.

5 And if the avenger of blood pursue after him, then they shall not deliver the slayer up into his hand; because he smote his neighbour unwittingly, and hated him not beforetime.

6 And he shall dwell in that city, until he stand before the congregation for judgment, *and* until the death of the high priest that shall be in those days: then shall the slayer return, and come unto his own city, and unto his own house, unto the city from whence he fled.

7 ¶ And they appointed Ke'desh in Gal'i-lee in mount Naph'ta-li, and She'chem in mount E'-phra-im, and Kir'jath-ar'ba, which *is* He'bron, in the mountain of Ju'dah.

8 And on the other side Jor'dan by Jer'i-cho eastward, they assigned Be'zer in the wilderness upon the plain out of the tribe of Reu'ben, and Ra'moth in Gil'e-ad out of the tribe of Gad, and Go'lan in Ba'shan out of the tribe of Ma-nas'seh.

9 These were the cities appointed for all the children of Is'ra-el, and for the stranger that sojourneth among them, that whosoever killeth *any* person at unawares might flee thither, and not die by the hand of the avenger of blood, until he stood before the congregation.

21 THEN came near the heads of the fathers of the Le'vites unto E-le-a'zar the priest, and unto Josh'u-a the son of Nun, and unto the heads of the fathers of the tribes of the children of Is'ra-el;

2 And they spake unto them at Shi'loh in the land of Ca'naan, saying, The LORD commanded by the hand of Mo'ses to give us cities to dwell in, with the suburbs thereof for our cattle.

3 And the children of Is'ra-el gave unto the Le'vites out of their inheritance, at the commandment of the LORD, these cities and their suburbs.

4 And the lot came out for the families of the Ko'hath-ites: and the children of Aar'on the priest, *which were* of the Le'vites, had by lot out of the tribe of Ju'dah, and out of the tribe of Sim'e-on, and out of the tribe of Ben'ja-min, thirteen cities.

5 And the rest of the children of Ko'hath *had* by lot out of the families of the tribe of E'phra-im, and out of the tribe of Dan, and out of the half tribe of Ma-nas'seh, ten cities.

6 And the children of Ger'shon *had* by lot out of the families of the tribe of Is'sa-char, and out of the tribe of Ash'er, and out of the tribe of Naph'ta-li, and out of the half tribe of Ma-nas'-seh in Ba'shan, thirteen cities.

7 The children of Me-ra'ri by their families *had* out of the tribe of Reu'ben, and out of the tribe of Gad, and out of the tribe of Zeb'u-lun, twelve cities.

8 And the children of Is'ra-el gave by lot unto the Le'vites these cities with their suburbs, as the LORD commanded by the hand of Mo'ses.

9 ¶ And they gave out of the tribe of the children of Ju'dah, and out of the tribe of the children of Sim'e-on, these cities which are *here* mentioned by name,

10 Which the children of Aar'on, *being* of the families of the Ko'hath-ites, *who were* of the children of Le'vi, had: for theirs was the first lot.

11 And they gave them the city of Ar'ba the father of A'nak, which *city is* He'bron, in the hill country of Ju'dah, with the suburbs thereof round about it.

12 But the fields of the city, and the villages thereof, gave they to Ca'leb the son of Je-phun'-neh for his possession.

13 ¶ Thus they gave to the children of Aar'-on the priest He'bron with her suburbs, *to be* a city of refuge for the slayer; and Lib'nah with her suburbs,

14 And Jat'tir with her suburbs, and Esh-te-mo'a with her suburbs,

15 And Ho'lon with her suburbs, and De'bir with her suburbs,

16 And A'in with her suburbs, and Jut'tah with her suburbs, *and* Beth-she'mesh with her suburbs; nine cities out of those two tribes.

17 And out of the tribe of Ben'ja-min, Gib'e-on with her suburbs, Ge'ba with her suburbs,

18 An'a-thoth with her suburbs, and Al'mon with her suburbs; four cities.

19 All the cities of the children of Aar'on, the priests, *were* thirteen cities with their suburbs.

20 ¶ And the families of the children of Ko'-hath, the Le'vites which remained of the chil-

dren of Ko'hath, even they had the cities of their lot out of the tribe of E'phra-im.

21 For they gave them She'chem with her suburbs in mount E'phra-im, to be a city of refuge for the slayer; and Ge'zer with her suburbs,

22 And Kib'za-im with her suburbs, and Beth-ho'ron with her suburbs; four cities.

23 And out of the tribe of Dan, El'te-keh with her suburbs, Gib'be-thon with her suburbs,

24 Aij'a-lon with her suburbs, Gath-rim'mon with her suburbs; four cities.

25 And out of the half tribe of Ma-nas'seh, Ta'nach with her suburbs, and Gath-rim'mon with her suburbs; two cities.

26 All the cities were ten with their suburbs for the families of the children of Ko'hath that remained.

27 ¶ And unto the children of Ger'shon, of the families of the Le'vites, out of the other half tribe of Ma-nas'seh they gave Go'lan in Ba'shan with her suburbs, to be a city of refuge for the slayer; and Be-esh'-te-rah with her suburbs; two cities.

28 And out of the tribe of Is'sa-char, Ki'shon with her suburbs, Dab'a-reh with her suburbs,

29 Jar'muth with her suburbs, En-gan'nim with her suburbs; four cities.

30 And out of the tribe of Ash'er, Mi'shal with her suburbs, Ab'don with her suburbs,

31 Hel'kath with her suburbs, and Re'hob with her suburbs; four cities.

32 And out of the tribe of Naph'ta-li, Ke'desh in Gal'i-lee with her suburbs, to be a city of refuge for the slayer; and Ham'moth-dor with her suburbs, and Kar'tan with her suburbs; three cities.

33 All the cities of the Ger'shon-ites according to their families were thirteen cities with their suburbs.

34 ¶ And unto the families of the children of Me-ra'ri, the rest of the Le'vites, out of the tribe of Zeb'u-lun, Jok'ne-am with her suburbs, and Kar'tah with her suburbs,

35 Dim'nah with her suburbs, Na'ha-lal with her suburbs; four cities.

36 And out of the tribe of Reu'ben, Be'zer with her suburbs, and Ja-ha'zah with her suburbs,

37 Ked'e-moth with her suburbs, and Meph'-a-ath with her suburbs; four cities.

38 And out of the tribe of Gad, Ra'moth in Gil'e-ad with her suburbs, to be a city of refuge for the slayer; and Ma-ha-na'im with her suburbs,

39 Hesh'bon with her suburbs, Ja'zer with her suburbs; four cities in all.

40 So all the cities for the children of Me-ra'ri by their families, which were remaining of the families of the Le'vites, were by their lot twelve cities.

41 All the cities of the Le'vites within the possession of the children of Is'ra-el were forty and eight cities with their suburbs.

42 These cities were every one with their suburbs round about them: thus were all these cities.

43 ¶ And the LORD gave unto Is'ra-el all the land which he sware to give unto their fathers; and they possessed it, and dwelt therein.

44 And the LORD gave them rest round about, according to all that he sware unto their fathers: and there stood not a man of all their enemies before them; the LORD delivered all their enemies into their hand.

45 There failed not ought of any good thing which the LORD had spoken unto the house of Is'ra-el; all came to pass.

22 THEN Josh'u-a called the Reu'ben-ites, and the Gad'ites, and the half tribe of Ma-nas'seh,

2 And said unto them, Ye have kept all that Mo'ses the servant of the LORD commanded you, and have obeyed my voice in all that I commanded you:

3 Ye have not left your brethren these many days unto this day, but have kept the charge of the commandment of the LORD your God.

4 And now the LORD your God hath given rest unto your brethren, as he promised them: therefore now return ye, and get you unto your tents, and unto the land of your possession, which Mo'ses the servant of the LORD gave you on the other side Jor'dan.

5 But take diligent heed to do the commandment and the law, which Mo'ses the servant of the LORD charged you, to love the LORD your God, and to walk in all his ways, and to keep his commandments, and to cleave unto him, and to serve him with all your heart and with all your soul.

6 So Josh'u-a blessed them, and sent them away: and they went unto their tents.

7 ¶ Now to the one half of the tribe of Ma-nas'seh Mo'ses had given possession in Ba'shan: but unto the other half thereof gave Josh'u-a among their brethren on this side Jor'dan westward. And when Josh'u-a sent them away also unto their tents, then he blessed them,

8 And he spake unto them, saying, Return with much riches unto your tents, and with very much cattle, with silver, and with gold, and with brass, and with iron, and with very much raiment: divide the spoil of your enemies with your brethren.

9 ¶ And the children of Reu'ben and the children of Gad and the half tribe of Ma-nas'seh returned, and departed from the children of Is'-ra-el out of Shi'loh, which is in the land of Ca'-naan, to go unto the country of Gil'e-ad, to the land of their possession, whereof they were possessed, according to the word of the LORD by the hand of Mo'ses.

10 ¶ And when they came unto the borders of Jor'dan, that are in the land of Ca'naan, the children of Reu'ben and the children of Gad and the half tribe of Ma-nas'seh built there an altar by Jor'dan, a great altar to see to.

11 ¶ And the children of Is'ra-el heard say, Behold, the children of Reu'ben and the children of Gad and the half tribe of Ma-nas'seh have built an altar over against the land of Ca'-naan, in the borders of Jor'dan, at the passage of the children of Is'ra-el.

12 And when the children of Is'ra-el heard of it, the whole congregation of the children of Is'-ra-el gathered themselves together at Shi'loh, to go up to war against them.

13 And the children of Is'ra-el sent unto the children of Reu'ben, and to the children of Gad, and to the half tribe of Ma-nas'seh, into the land of Gil'e-ad, Phin'e-has the son of E-le-a'zar the priest,

14 And with him ten princes, of each chief house a prince throughout all the tribes of Is'ra-el; and each one was an head of the house of their fathers among the thousands of Is'ra-el.

15 ¶ And they came unto the children of Reu'ben, and to the children of Gad, and to the half tribe of Ma-nas'seh, unto the land of Gil'e-ad, and they spake with them, saying,

16 Thus saith the whole congregation of the LORD, What trespass is this that ye have committed against the God of Is'ra-el, to turn away this day from following the LORD, in that ye

have builded you an altar, that ye might rebel
this day against the LORD?

17 Is the iniquity of Pe'or too little for us,
from which we are not cleansed until this day,
although there was a plague in the congregation
of the LORD,

18 But that ye must turn away this day from
following the LORD? and it will be, seeing ye
rebel to day against the LORD, that to morrow
he will be wroth with the whole congregation of
Is'ra-el.

19 Notwithstanding, if the land of your possession be unclean, then pass ye over unto the
land of the possession of the LORD, wherein the
LORD's tabernacle dwelleth, and take possession among us: but rebel not against the LORD,
nor rebel against us, in building you an altar
beside the altar of the LORD our God.

20 Did not A'chan the son of Ze'rah commit a
trespass in the accursed thing, and wrath fell on
all the congregation of Is'ra-el? and that man
perished not alone in his iniquity.

21 ¶ Then the children of Reu'ben and the
children of Gad and the half tribe of Ma-nas'seh
answered, and said unto the heads of the thousands of Is'ra-el,

22 The LORD God of gods, the LORD God of
gods, he knoweth, and Is'ra-el he shall know; if
it be in rebellion, or if in transgression against
the LORD, (save us not this day,)

23 That we have built us an altar to turn from
following the LORD, or if to offer thereon burnt
offering or meat offering, or if to offer peace
offerings thereon, let the LORD himself require
it;

24 And if we have not rather done it for fear
of this thing, saying, In time to come your children might speak unto our children, saying,
What have ye to do with the LORD God of Is'ra-
el?

25 For the LORD hath made Jor'dan a border
between us and you, ye children of Reu'ben and
children of Gad; ye have no part in the LORD: so
shall your children make our children cease
from fearing the LORD.

26 Therefore we said, Let us now prepare to
build us an altar, not for burnt offering, nor for
sacrifice:

27 But that it may be a witness between us,
and you, and our generations after us, that we
might do the service of the LORD before him
with our burnt offerings, and with our sacrifices, and with our peace offerings; that your
children may not say to our children in time to
come, Ye have no part in the LORD.

28 Therefore said we, that it shall be, when
they should so say to us or to our generations in
time to come, that we may say again, Behold
the pattern of the altar of the LORD, which our
fathers made, not for burnt offerings, nor for
sacrifices; but it is a witness between us and
you.

29 God forbid that we should rebel against
the LORD, and turn this day from following the
LORD, to build an altar for burnt offerings, for
meat offerings, or for sacrifices, beside the altar
of the LORD our God that is before his tabernacle.

30 ¶ And when Phin'e-has the priest, and the
princes of the congregation and heads of the
thousands of Is'ra-el which were with him,
heard the words that the children of Reu'ben
and the children of Gad and the children of Ma-
nas'seh spake, it pleased them.

31 And Phin'e-has the son of E-le-a'zar the
priest said unto the children of Reu'ben, and to
the children of Gad, and to the children of Ma-

nas'seh, This day we perceive that the LORD is
among us, because ye have not committed this
trespass against the LORD: now ye have delivered the children of Is'ra-el out of the hand of
the LORD.

32 ¶ And Phin'e-has the son of E-le-a'zar the
priest, and the princes, returned from the children of Reu'ben, and from the children of Gad,
out of the land of Gil'e-ad, unto the land of Ca'-
naan, to the children of Is'ra-el, and brought
them word again.

33 And the thing pleased the children of Is'-
ra-el; and the children of Is'ra-el blessed God,
and did not intend to go up against them in battle, to destroy the land wherein the children of
Reu'ben and Gad dwelt.

34 And the children of Reu'ben and the children of Gad called the altar Ed: for it shall be a
witness between us that the LORD is God.

23 AND it came to pass a long time after
that the LORD had given rest unto Is'ra-
el from all their enemies round about, that
Josh'u-a waxed old and stricken in age.

2 And Josh'u-a called for all Is'ra-el, and for
their elders, and for their heads, and for their
judges, and for their officers, and said unto
them, I am old and stricken in age:

3 And ye have seen all that the LORD your
God hath done unto all these nations because of
you; for the LORD your God is he that hath
fought for you.

4 Behold, I have divided unto you by lot
these nations that remain, to be an inheritance
for your tribes, from Jor'dan, with all the nations that I have cut off, even unto the great sea
westward.

5 And the LORD your God, he shall expel
them from before you, and drive them from out
of your sight; and ye shall possess their land, as
the LORD your God hath promised unto you.

6 Be ye therefore very courageous to keep
and to do all that is written in the book of the
law of Mo'ses, that ye turn not aside therefrom
to the right hand or to the left;

7 That ye come not among these nations,
these that remain among you; neither make
mention of the name of their gods, nor cause to
swear by them, neither serve them, nor bow
yourselves unto them:

8 But cleave unto the LORD your God, as ye
have done unto this day.

9 For the LORD hath driven out from before
you great nations and strong: but as for you, no
man hath been able to stand before you unto
this day.

10 One man of you shall chase a thousand:
for the LORD your God, he it is that fighteth for
you, as he hath promised you.

11 Take good heed therefore unto yourselves, that ye love the LORD your God.

12 Else if ye do in any wise go back, and
cleave unto the remnant of these nations, even
these that remain among you, and shall make
marriages with them, and go in unto them, and
they to you:

13 Know for a certainty that the LORD your
God will no more drive out any of these nations
from before you; but they shall be snares and
traps unto you, and scourges in your sides, and
thorns in your eyes, until ye perish from off this
good land which the LORD your God hath given
you.

14 And, behold, this day I am going the way
of all the earth: and ye know in all your hearts
and in all your souls, that not one thing hath
failed of all the good things which the LORD

your God spake concerning you; all are come to pass unto you, *and* not one thing hath failed thereof.

15 Therefore it shall come to pass, *that* as all good things are come upon you, which the LORD your God promised you; so shall the LORD bring upon you all evil things, until he have destroyed you from off this good land which the LORD your God hath given you.

16 When ye have transgressed the covenant of the LORD your God, which he commanded you, and have gone and served other gods, and bowed yourselves to them; then shall the anger of the LORD be kindled against you, and ye shall perish quickly from off the good land which he hath given unto you.

24 AND Josh'u-a gathered all the tribes of Is'ra-el to She'chem, and called for the elders of Is'ra-el, and for their heads, and for their judges, and for their officers; and they presented themselves before God.

2 And Josh'u-a said unto all the people, Thus saith the LORD God of Is'ra-el, Your fathers dwelt on the other side of the flood in old time, *even* Te'rah, the father of A'bra-ham, and the father of Na'chor: and they served other gods.

3 And I took your father A'bra-ham from the other side of the flood, and led him throughout all the land of Ca'naan, and multiplied his seed, and gave him I'saac.

4 And I gave unto I'saac Ja'cob and E'sau: and I gave unto E'sau mount Se'ir, to possess it; but Ja'cob and his children went down into E'gypt.

5 I sent Mo'ses also and Aar'on, and I plagued E'gypt, according to that which I did among them: and afterward I brought you out.

6 And I brought your fathers out of E'gypt: and ye came unto the sea; and the E-gyp'tians pursued after your fathers with chariots and horsemen unto the Red sea.

7 And when they cried unto the LORD, he put darkness between you and the E-gyp'tians, and brought the sea upon them, and covered them; and your eyes have seen what I have done in E'gypt: and ye dwelt in the wilderness a long season.

8 And I brought you into the land of the Am'-or-ites, which dwelt on the other side Jor'dan; and they fought with you: and I gave them into your hand, that ye might possess their land; and I destroyed them from before you.

9 Then Ba'lak the son of Zip'por, king of Mo'-ab, arose and warred against Is'ra-el, and sent and called Ba'laam the son of Be'or to curse you:

10 But I would not hearken unto Ba'laam; therefore he blessed you still: so I delivered you out of his hand.

11 And ye went over Jor'dan, and came unto Jer'i-cho: and the men of Jer'i-cho fought against you, the Am'or-ites, and the Per'iz-zites, and the Ca'naan-ites, and the Hit'tites, and the Gir'ga-shites, the Hi'vites, and the Jeb'u-sites; and I delivered them into your hand.

12 And I sent the hornet before you, which drave them out from before you, *even* the two kings of the Am'or-ites; *but* not with thy sword, nor with thy bow.

13 And I have given you a land for which ye did not labour, and cities which ye built not, and ye dwell in them; of the vineyards and oliveyards which ye planted not do ye eat.

14 ¶ Now therefore fear the LORD, and serve him in sincerity and in truth: and put away the gods which your fathers served on the other side of the flood, and in E'gypt; and serve ye the LORD.

15 And if it seem evil unto you to serve the LORD, choose you this day whom ye will serve; whether the gods which your fathers served that *were* on the other side of the flood, or the gods of the Am'or-ites, in whose land ye dwell: but as for me and my house, we will serve the LORD.

16 And the people answered and said, God forbid that we should forsake the LORD, to serve other gods;

17 For the LORD our God, he *it is* that brought us up and our fathers out of the land of E'gypt, from the house of bondage, and which did those great signs in our sight, and preserved us in all the way wherein we went, and among all the people through whom we passed:

18 And the LORD drave out from before us all the people, even the Am'or-ites which dwelt in the land: *therefore* will we also serve the LORD; for he *is* our God.

19 And Josh'u-a said unto the people, Ye cannot serve the LORD: for he *is* an holy God; he *is* a jealous God; he will not forgive your transgressions nor your sins.

20 If ye forsake the LORD, and serve strange gods, then he will turn and do you hurt, and consume you, after that he hath done you good.

21 And the people said unto Josh'u-a, Nay; but we will serve the LORD.

22 And Josh'u-a said unto the people, Ye *are* witnesses against yourselves that ye have chosen you the LORD, to serve him. And they said, We *are* witnesses.

23 Now therefore put away, *said he*, the strange gods which *are* among you, and incline your heart unto the LORD God of Is'ra-el.

24 And the people said unto Josh'u-a, The LORD our God will we serve, and his voice will we obey.

25 So Josh'u-a made a covenant with the people that day, and set them a statute and an ordinance in She'chem.

26 ¶ And Josh'u-a wrote these words in the book of the law of God, and took a great stone, and set it up there under an oak, that *was* by the sanctuary of the LORD.

27 And Josh'u-a said unto all the people, Behold, this stone shall be a witness unto us; for it hath heard all the words of the LORD which he spake unto us: it shall be therefore a witness unto you, lest ye deny your God.

28 So Josh'u-a let the people depart, every man unto his inheritance.

29 ¶ And it came to pass after these things, that Josh'u-a the son of Nun, the servant of the LORD, died, *being* an hundred and ten years old.

30 And they buried him in the border of his inheritance in Tim'nath-se'rah, which *is* in mount E'phra-im, on the north side of the hill of Ga'ash.

31 And Is'ra-el served the LORD all the days of Josh'u-a, and all the days of the elders that overlived Josh'u-a, and which had known all the works of the LORD, that he had done for Is'ra-el.

32 ¶ And the bones of Jo'seph, which the children of Is'ra-el brought up out of E'gypt, buried they in She'chem, in a parcel of ground which Ja'cob bought of the sons of Ha'mor the father of She'chem for an hundred pieces of silver: and it became the inheritance of the children of Jo'seph.

33 And E-le-a'zar the son of Aar'on died; and they buried him in a hill *that pertained to* Phin'-e-has his son, which was given him in mount E'phra-im.

1 NOW after the death of Josh'u-a it came to pass, that the children of Is'ra-el asked the LORD, saying, Who shall go up for us against the Ca'naan-ites first, to fight against them?

2 And the LORD said, Ju'dah shall go up: behold, I have delivered the land into his hand.

3 And Ju'dah said unto Sim'e-on his brother, Come up with me into my lot, that we may fight against the Ca'naan-ites; and I likewise will go with thee into thy lot. So Sim'e-on went with him.

4 And Ju'dah went up; and the LORD delivered the Ca'naan-ites and the Per'iz-zites into their hand: and they slew of them in Be'zek ten thousand men.

5 And they found A-don'i-be'zek in Be'zek: and they fought against him, and they slew the Ca'naan-ites and the Per'iz-zites.

6 But A-don'i-be'zek fled; and they pursued after him, and caught him, and cut off his thumbs and his great toes.

7 And A-don'i-be'zek said, Threescore and ten kings, having their thumbs and their great toes cut off, gathered *their meat* under my table: as I have done, so God hath requited me. And they brought him to Je-ru'sa-lem, and there he died.

8 Now the children of Ju'dah had fought against Je-ru'sa-lem, and had taken it, and smitten it with the edge of the sword, and set the city on fire.

9 ¶ And afterward the children of Ju'dah went down to fight against the Ca'naan-ites, that dwelt in the mountain, and in the south, and in the valley.

10 And Ju'dah went against the Ca'naan-ites that dwelt in He'bron: (now the name of He'bron before *was* Kir'jath-ar'ba:) and they slew She'shai, and A-hi'man, and Tal'mai.

11 And from thence he went against the inhabitants of De'bir: and the name of De'bir before *was* Kir'jath-se'pher:

12 And Ca'leb said, He that smiteth Kir'jath-se'pher, and taketh it, to him will I give Ach'sah my daughter to wife.

13 And Oth'ni-el the son of Ke'naz, Ca'leb's younger brother, took it: and he gave him Ach'sah his daughter to wife.

14 And it came to pass, when she came to *him*, that she moved him to ask of her father a field: and she lighted from off *her* ass; and Ca'leb said unto her, What wilt thou?

15 And she said unto him, Give me a blessing: for thou hast given me a south land; give me also springs of water. And Ca'leb gave her the upper springs and the nether springs.

16 ¶ And the children of the Ken'ite, Mo'ses' father in law, went up out of the city of palm trees with the children of Ju'dah into the wilderness of Ju'dah, which *lieth* in the south of A'rad; and they went and dwelt among the people.

17 And Ju'dah went with Sim'e-on his brother, and they slew the Ca'naan-ites that inhabited Ze'phath, and utterly destroyed it. And the name of the city was called Hor'mah.

18 Also Ju'dah took Ga'za with the coast thereof, and As'ke-lon with the coast thereof, and Ek'ron with the coast thereof.

19 And the LORD was with Ju'dah; and he drave out *the inhabitants of* the mountain; but could not drive out the inhabitants of the valley, because they had chariots of iron.

20 And they gave He'bron unto Ca'leb, as Mo'ses said: and he expelled thence the three sons of A'nak.

21 And the children of Ben'ja-min did not drive out the Jeb'u-sites that inhabited Je-ru'sa-lem; but the Jeb'u-sites dwell with the children of Ben'ja-min in Je-ru'sa-lem unto this day.

22 ¶ And the house of Jo'seph, they also went up against Beth'-el: and the LORD *was* with them.

23 And the house of Jo'seph sent to descry Beth'-el. (Now the name of the city before *was* Luz.)

24 And the spies saw a man come forth out of the city, and they said unto him, Shew us, we pray thee, the entrance into the city, and we will shew thee mercy.

25 And when he shewed them the entrance into the city, they smote the city with the edge of the sword; but they let go the man and all his family.

26 And the man went into the land of the Hit'tites, and built a city, and called the name thereof Luz: which *is* the name thereof unto this day.

27 ¶ Neither did Ma-nas'seh drive out *the inhabitants of* Beth-she'an and her towns, nor Ta'a-nach and her towns, nor the inhabitants of Dor and her towns, nor the inhabitants of Ib'le-am and her towns, nor the inhabitants of Me-gid'do and her towns: but the Ca'naan-ites would dwell in that land.

28 And it came to pass, when Is'ra-el was strong, that they put the Ca'naan-ites to tribute, and did not utterly drive them out.

29 ¶ Neither did E'phra-im drive out the Ca'naan-ites that dwelt in Ge'zer; but the Ca'naan-ites dwelt in Ge'zer among them.

30 ¶ Neither did Zeb'u-lun drive out the inhabitants of Kit'ron, nor the inhabitants of Na'ha-lol; but the Ca'naan-ites dwelt among them, and became tributaries.

31 ¶ Neither did Ash'er drive out the inhabitants of Ac'cho, nor the inhabitants of Zi'don, nor of Ah'lab, nor of Ach'zib, nor of Hel'bah, nor of A'phik, nor of Re'hob:

32 But the Ash'er-ites dwelt among the Ca'naan-ites, the inhabitants of the land: for they did not drive them out.

33 ¶ Neither did Naph'ta-li drive out the inhabitants of Beth-she'mesh, nor the inhabitants of Beth-a'nath; but he dwelt among the Ca'naan-ites, the inhabitants of the land: nevertheless the inhabitants of Beth-she'mesh and of Beth-a'nath became tributaries unto them.

34 And the Am'or-ites forced the children of Dan into the mountain: for they would not suffer them to come down to the valley:

35 But the Am'or-ites would dwell in mount He'res in Aij'a-lon, and in Sha-al'bim: yet the hand of the house of Jo'seph prevailed, so that they became tributaries.

36 And the coast of the Am'or-ites *was* from the going up to A-krab'bim, from the rock, and upward.

2 AND an angel of the LORD came up from Gil'gal to Bo'chim, and said, I made you to go up out of E'gypt, and have brought you unto

the land which I sware unto your fathers; and I said, I will never break my covenant with you.

2 And ye shall make no league with the inhabitants of this land; ye shall throw down their altars: but ye have not obeyed my voice: why have ye done this?

3 Wherefore I also said, I will not drive them out from before you; but they shall be as thorns in your sides, and their gods shall be a snare unto you.

4 And it came to pass, when the angel of the LORD spake these words unto all the children of Is'ra-el, that the people lifted up their voice, and wept.

5 And they called the name of that place Bo'-chim: and they sacrificed there unto the LORD.

6 ¶ And when Josh'u-a had let the people go, the children of Is'ra-el went every man unto his inheritance to possess the land.

7 And the people served the LORD all the days of Josh'u-a, and all the days of the elders that outlived Josh'u-a, who had seen all the great works of the LORD, that he did for Is'ra-el.

8 And Josh'u-a the son of Nun, the servant of the LORD, died, being an hundred and ten years old.

9 And they buried him in the border of his inheritance in Tim'nath-he'res, in the mount of E'phra-im, on the north side of the hill Ga'ash.

10 And also all that generation were gathered unto their fathers: and there arose another generation after them, which knew not the LORD, nor yet the works which he had done for Is'ra-el.

11¶ And the children of Is'ra-el did evil in the sight of the LORD, and served Ba'al-im:

12 And they forsook the LORD God of their fathers, which brought them out of the land of E'gypt, and followed other gods, of the gods of the people that were round about them, and bowed themselves unto them, and provoked the LORD to anger.

13 And they forsook the LORD, and served Ba'al and Ash'ta-roth.

14 ¶ And the anger of the LORD was hot against Is'ra-el, and he delivered them into the hands of spoilers that spoiled them, and he sold them into the hands of their enemies round about, so that they could not any longer stand before their enemies.

15 Whithersoever they went out, the hand of the LORD was against them for evil, as the LORD had said, and as the LORD had sworn unto them: and they were greatly distressed.

16 ¶ Nevertheless the LORD raised up judges, which delivered them out of the hand of those that spoiled them.

17 And yet they would not hearken unto their judges, but they went a whoring after other gods, and bowed themselves unto them: they turned quickly out of the way which their fathers walked in, obeying the commandments of the LORD; but they did not so.

18 And when the LORD raised them up judges, then the LORD was with the judge, and delivered them out of the hand of their enemies all the days of the judge: for it repented the LORD because of their groanings by reason of them that oppressed them and vexed them.

19 And it came to pass, when the judge was dead, that they returned, and corrupted themselves more than their fathers, in following other gods to serve them, and to bow down unto them; they ceased not from their own doings, nor from their stubborn way.

20 ¶ And the anger of the LORD was hot against Is'ra-el; and he said, Because that this people hath transgressed my covenant which I commanded their fathers, and have not hearkened unto my voice;

21 I also will not henceforth drive out any from before them of the nations which Josh'u-a left when he died:

22 That through them I may prove Is'ra-el, whether they will keep the way of the LORD to walk therein, as their fathers did keep it, or not.

23 Therefore the LORD left those nations, without driving them out hastily; neither delivered he them into the hand of Josh'u-a.

3 NOW these are the nations which the LORD left, to prove Is'ra-el by them, even as many of Is'ra-el as had not known all the wars of Ca'naan;

2 Only that the generations of the children of Is'ra-el might know, to teach them war, at the least such as before knew nothing thereof;

3 Namely, five lords of the Phi-lis'tines, and all the Ca'naan-ites, and the Si-do'ni-ans, and the Hi'vites that dwelt in mount Leb'a-non, from mount Ba'al-her'mon unto the entering in of Ha'math.

4 And they were to prove Is'ra-el by them, to know whether they would hearken unto the commandments of the LORD, which he commanded their fathers by the hand of Mo'ses.

5 ¶ And the children of Is'ra-el dwelt among the Ca'naan-ites, Hit'tites, and Am'or-ites, and Per'iz-zites, and Hi'vites, and Jeb'u-sites:

6 And they took their daughters to be their wives, and gave their daughters to their sons, and served their gods.

7 And the children of Is'ra-el did evil in the sight of the LORD, and forgat the LORD their God, and served Ba'al-im and the groves.

8 ¶ Therefore the anger of the LORD was hot against Is'ra-el, and he sold them into the hand of Chu'shan-rish-a-tha'im king of Mes-o-po-ta'mi-a: and the children of Is'ra-el served Chu'shan-rish-a-tha'im eight years.

9 And when the children of Is'ra-el cried unto the LORD, the LORD raised up a deliverer to the children of Is'ra-el, who delivered them, even Oth'ni-el the son of Ke'naz, Ca'leb's younger brother.

10 And the Spirit of the LORD came upon him, and he judged Is'ra-el, and went out to war: and the LORD delivered Chu'shan-rish-a-tha'im king of Mes-o-po-ta'mi-a into his hand; and his hand prevailed against Chu'shan-rish-a-tha'im.

11 And the land had rest forty years. And Oth'ni-el the son of Ke'naz died.

12 ¶ And the children of Is'ra-el did evil again in the sight of the LORD: and the LORD strengthened Eg'lon the king of Mo'ab against Is'ra-el, because they had done evil in the sight of the LORD.

13 And he gathered unto him the children of Am'mon and Am'a-lek, and went and smote Is'ra-el, and possessed the city of palm trees.

14 So the children of Is'ra-el served Eg'lon the king of Mo'ab eighteen years.

15 But when the children of Is'ra-el cried unto the LORD, the LORD raised them up a deliverer, E'hud the son of Ge'ra, a Ben'ja-mite, a man lefthanded: and by him the children of Is'ra-el sent a present unto Eg'lon the king of Mo'ab.

16 But E'hud made him a dagger which had two edges, of a cubit length; and he did gird it under his raiment upon his right thigh.

17 And he brought the present unto Eg'lon king of Mo'ab: and Eg'lon was a very fat man.

18 And when he had made an end to offer the present, he sent away the people that bare the present.

19 But he himself turned again from the quarries that *were* by Gil'gal, and said, I have a secret errand unto thee, O king: who said, Keep silence. And all that stood by him went out from him.

20 And E'hud came unto him; and he was sitting in a summer parlour, which he had for himself alone. And E'hud said, I have a message from God unto thee. And he arose out of *his* seat.

21 And E'hud put forth his left hand, and took the dagger from his right thigh, and thrust it into his belly:

22 And the haft also went in after the blade; and the fat closed upon the blade, so that he could not draw the dagger out of his belly; and the dirt came out.

23 Then E'hud went forth through the porch, and shut the doors of the parlour upon him, and locked them.

24 When he was gone out, his servants came; and when they saw that, behold, the doors of the parlour *were* locked, they said, Surely he covereth his feet in his summer chamber.

25 And they tarried till they were ashamed: and, behold, he opened not the doors of the parlour; therefore they took a key, and opened *them:* and, behold, their lord *was* fallen down dead on the earth.

26 And E'hud escaped while they tarried, and passed beyond the quarries, and escaped unto Se'i-rath.

27 And it came to pass, when he was come, that he blew a trumpet in the mountain of E'-phra-im, and the children of Is'ra-el went down with him from the mount, and he before them.

28 And he said unto them, Follow after me: for the LORD hath delivered your enemies the Mo'ab-ites into your hand. And they went down after him, and took the fords of Jor'dan toward Mo'ab, and suffered not a man to pass over.

29 And they slew of Mo'ab at that time about ten thousand men, all lusty, and all men of valour; and there escaped not a man.

30 So Mo'ab was subdued that day under the hand of Is'ra-el. And the land had rest fourscore years.

31 ¶ And after him was Sham'gar the son of A'nath, which slew of the Phi-lis'tines six hundred men with an ox goad: and he also delivered Is'ra-el.

4 AND the children of Is'ra-el again did evil in the sight of the LORD, when E'hud was dead.

2 And the LORD sold them into the hand of Ja'bin king of Ca'naan, that reigned in Ha'zor; the captain of whose host *was* Sis'e-ra, which dwelt in Ha-ro'sheth of the Gen'tiles.

3 And the children of Is'ra-el cried unto the LORD: for he had nine hundred chariots of iron; and twenty years he mightily oppressed the children of Is'ra-el.

4 ¶ And Deb'o-rah, a prophetess, the wife of Lap'i-doth, she judged Is'ra-el at that time.

5 And she dwelt under the palm tree of Deb'-o-rah between Ra'mah and Beth'-el in mount E'phra-im: and the children of Is'ra-el came up to her for judgment.

6 And she sent and called Ba'rak the son of A-bin'o-am out of Ke'desh-naph'ta-li, and said unto him, Hath not the LORD God of Is'ra-el commanded, *saying,* Go and draw toward mount Ta'bor, and take with thee ten thousand men of the children of Naph'ta-li and of the children of Zeb'u-lun?

7 And I will draw unto thee to the river Ki'-shon Sis'e-ra, the captain of Ja'bin's army, with his chariots and his multitude; and I will deliver him into thine hand.

8 And Ba'rak said unto her, If thou wilt go with me, then I will go: but if thou wilt not go with me, *then* I will not go.

9 And she said, I will surely go with thee: notwithstanding the journey that thou takest shall not be for thine honour; for the LORD shall sell Sis'e-ra into the hand of a woman. And Deb'o-rah arose, and went with Ba'rak to Ke'-desh.

10 ¶ And Ba'rak called Zeb'u-lun and Naph'-ta-li to Ke'desh; and he went up with ten thousand men at his feet: and Deb'o-rah went up with him.

11 Now He'ber the Ken'ite, *which was* of the children of Ho'bab the father in law of Mo'ses, had severed himself from the Ken'ites, and pitched his tent unto the plain of Za-a-na'im, which *is* by Ke'desh.

12 And they shewed Sis'e-ra that Ba'rak the son of A-bin'o-am was gone up to mount Ta'-bor.

13 And Sis'e-ra gathered together all his chariots, *even* nine hundred chariots of iron, and all the people that *were* with him, from Ha-ro'sheth of the Gen'tiles unto the river of Ki'-shon.

14 And Deb'o-rah said unto Ba'rak, Up; for this *is* the day in which the LORD hath delivered Sis'e-ra into thine hand: is not the LORD gone out before thee? So Ba'rak went down from mount Ta'bor, and ten thousand men after him.

15 And the LORD discomfited Sis'e-ra, and all *his* chariots, and all *his* host, with the edge of the sword before Ba'rak; so that Sis'e-ra lighted down off *his* chariot, and fled away on his feet.

16 But Ba'rak pursued after the chariots, and after the host, unto Ha-ro'sheth of the Gen'tiles: and all the host of Sis'e-ra fell upon the edge of the sword; *and* there was not a man left.

17 Howbeit Sis'e-ra fled away on his feet to the tent of Ja'el the wife of He'ber the Ken'ite: for *there was* peace between Ja'bin the king of Ha'zor and the house of He'ber the Ken'ite.

18 ¶ And Ja'el went out to meet Sis'e-ra, and said unto him, Turn in, my lord, turn in to me; fear not. And when he had turned in unto her into the tent, she covered him with a mantle.

19 And he said unto her, Give me, I pray thee, a little water to drink; for I am thirsty. And she opened a bottle of milk, and gave him drink, and covered him.

20 Again he said unto her, Stand in the door of the tent, and it shall be, when any man doth come and enquire of thee, and say, Is there any man here? that thou shalt say, No.

21 Then Ja'el He'ber's wife took a nail of the tent, and took an hammer in her hand, and went softly unto him, and smote the nail into his temples, and fastened it into the ground: for he was fast asleep and weary. So he died.

22 And, behold, as Ba'rak pursued Sis'e-ra, Ja'el came out to meet him, and said unto him, Come, and I will shew thee the man whom thou seekest. And when he came into her *tent,* behold, Sis'e-ra lay dead, and the nail *was* in his temples.

23 So God subdued on that day Ja'bin the king of Ca'naan before the children of Is'ra-el.

24 And the hand of the children of Is'ra-el prospered, and prevailed against Ja'bin the king-

of Ca'naan, until they had destroyed Ja'bin king of Ca'naan.

5 THEN sang Deb'o-rah and Ba'rak the son of A-bin'o-am on that day, saying,

2 Praise ye the LORD for the avenging of Is'-ra-el, when the people willingly offered themselves.

3 Hear, O ye kings; give ear, O ye princes; I, even I, will sing unto the LORD; I will sing praise to the LORD God of Is'ra-el.

4 LORD, when thou wentest out of Se'ir, when thou marchedst out of the field of E'dom, the earth trembled, and the heavens dropped, the clouds also dropped water.

5 The mountains melted from before the LORD, even that Si'nai from before the LORD God of Is'ra-el.

6 In the days of Sham'gar the son of A'nath, in the days of Ja'el, the highways were unoccupied, and the travellers walked through byways.

7 The inhabitants of the villages ceased, they ceased in Is'ra-el, until that I Deb'o-rah arose, that I arose a mother in Is'ra-el.

8 They chose new gods; then was war in the gates: was there a shield or spear seen among forty thousand in Is'ra-el?

9 My heart is toward the governors of Is'ra-el, that offered themselves willingly among the people. Bless ye the LORD.

10 Speak, ye that ride on white asses, ye that sit in judgment, and walk by the way.

11 They that are delivered from the noise of archers in the places of drawing water, there shall they rehearse the righteous acts of the LORD, even the righteous acts toward the inhabitants of his villages in Is'ra-el: then shall the people of the LORD go down to the gates.

12 Awake, awake, Deb'o-rah: awake, awake, utter a song: arise, Ba'rak, and lead thy captivity captive, thou son of A-bin'o-am.

13 Then he made him that remaineth have dominion over the nobles among the people: the LORD made me have dominion over the mighty.

14 Out of E'phra-im was there a root of them against Am'a-lek; after thee, Ben'ja-min, among thy people; out of Ma'chir came down governors, and out of Zeb'u-lun they that handle the pen of the writer.

15 And the princes of Is'sa-char were with Deb'o-rah; even Is'sa-char, and also Ba'rak: he was sent on foot into the valley. For the divisions of Reu'ben there were great thoughts of heart.

16 Why abodest thou among the sheepfolds, to hear the bleatings of the flocks? For the divisions of Reu'ben there were great searchings of heart.

17 Gil'e-ad abode beyond Jor'dan: and why did Dan remain in ships? Ash'er continued on the sea shore, and abode in his breaches.

18 Zeb'u-lun and Naph'ta-li were a people that jeoparded their lives unto the death in the high places of the field.

19 The kings came and fought, then fought the kings of Ca'naan in Ta'a-nach by the waters of Me-gid'do; they took no gain of money.

20 They fought from heaven; the stars in their courses fought against Sis'e-ra.

21 The river of Ki'shon swept them away, that ancient river, the river Ki'shon. O my soul, thou hast trodden down strength.

22 Then were the horsehoofs broken by the means of the pransings, the pransings of their mighty ones.

23 Curse ye Me'roz, said the angel of the LORD, curse ye bitterly the inhabitants thereof; because they came not to the help of the LORD, to the help of the LORD against the mighty.

24 Blessed above women shall Ja'el the wife of He'ber the Ken'ite be, blessed shall she be above women in the tent.

25 He asked water, and she gave him milk; she brought forth butter in a lordly dish.

26 She put her hand to the nail, and her right hand to the workmen's hammer; and with the hammer she smote Sis'e-ra, she smote off his head, when she had pierced and stricken through his temples.

27 At her feet he bowed, he fell, he lay down: at her feet he bowed, he fell: where he bowed, there he fell down dead.

28 The mother of Sis'e-ra looked out at a window, and cried through the lattice, Why is his chariot so long in coming? why tarry the wheels of his chariots?

29 Her wise ladies answered her, yea, she returned answer to herself,

30 Have they not sped? have they not divided the prey; to every man a damsel or two; to Sis'e-ra a prey of divers colours, a prey of divers colours of needlework, of divers colours of needlework on both sides, meet for the necks of them that take the spoil?

31 So let all thine enemies perish, O LORD: but let them that love him be as the sun when he goeth forth in his might. And the land had rest forty years.

6 AND the children of Is'ra-el did evil in the sight of the LORD: and the LORD delivered them into the hand of Mid'i-an seven years.

2 And the hand of Mid'i-an prevailed against Is'ra-el: and because of the Mid'i-an-ites the children of Is'ra-el made them the dens which are in the mountains, and caves, and strong holds.

3 And so it was, when Is'ra-el had sown, that the Mid'i-an-ites came up, and the Am'a-lek-ites, and the children of the east, even they came up against them;

4 And they encamped against them, and destroyed the increase of the earth, till thou come unto Ga'za, and left no sustenance for Is'ra-el, neither sheep, nor ox, nor ass.

5 For they came up with their cattle and their tents, and they came as grasshoppers for multitude; for both they and their camels were without number: and they entered into the land to destroy it.

6 And Is'ra-el was greatly impoverished because of the Mid'i-an-ites; and the children of Is'ra-el cried unto the LORD.

7 ¶ And it came to pass, when the children of Is'ra-el cried unto the LORD because of the Mid'i-an-ites,

8 That the LORD sent a prophet unto the children of Is'ra-el, which said unto them, Thus saith the LORD God of Is'ra-el, I brought you up from E'gypt, and brought you forth out of the house of bondage;

9 And I delivered you out of the hand of the E-gyp'tians, and out of the hand of all that oppressed you, and drave them out from before you, and gave you their land;

10 And I said unto you, I am the LORD your God; fear not the gods of the Am'or-ites, in whose land ye dwell: but ye have not obeyed my voice.

11 ¶ And there came an angel of the LORD, and sat under an oak which was in Oph'rah, that pertained unto Jo'ash the A'bi-ez'rite: and

his son Gid'e-on threshed wheat by the winepress, to hide *it* from the Mid'i-an-ites.

12 And the angel of the LORD appeared unto him, and said unto him, The LORD *is* with thee, thou mighty man of valour.

13 And Gid'e-on said unto him, Oh my Lord, if the LORD be with us, why then is all this befallen us? and where *be* all his miracles which our fathers told us of, saying, Did not the LORD bring us up from E'gypt? but now the LORD hath forsaken us, and delivered us into the hands of the Mid'i-an-ites.

14 And the LORD looked upon him, and said, Go in this thy might, and thou shalt save Is'ra-el from the hand of the Mid'i-an-ites: have not I sent thee?

15 And he said unto him, Oh my Lord, wherewith shall I save Is'ra-el? behold, my family *is* poor in Ma-nas'seh, and I *am* the least in my father's house.

16 And the LORD said unto him, Surely I will be with thee, and thou shalt smite the Mid'i-an-ites as one man.

17 And he said unto him, If now I have found grace in thy sight, then shew me a sign that thou talkest with me.

18 Depart not hence, I pray thee, until I come unto thee, and bring forth my present, and set *it* before thee. And he said, I will tarry until thou come again.

19 ¶ And Gid'e-on went in, and made ready a kid, and unleavened cakes of an ephah of flour: the flesh he put in a basket, and he put the broth in a pot, and brought *it* out unto him under the oak, and presented *it*.

20 And the angel of God said unto him, Take the flesh and the unleavened cakes, and lay *them* upon this rock, and pour out the broth. And he did so.

21 ¶ Then the angel of the LORD put forth the end of the staff that *was* in his hand, and touched the flesh and the unleavened cakes; and there rose up fire out of the rock, and consumed the flesh and the unleavened cakes. Then the angel of the LORD departed out of his sight.

22 And when Gid'e-on perceived that he *was* an angel of the LORD, Gid'e-on said, Alas, O Lord God! for because I have seen an angel of the LORD face to face.

23 And the LORD said unto him, Peace *be* unto thee; fear not: thou shalt not die.

24 Then Gid'e-on built an altar there unto the LORD, and called it Je-ho'vah-sha'lom: unto this day it *is* yet in Oph'rah of the A'bi-ez'rites.

25 ¶ And it came to pass the same night, that the LORD said unto him, Take thy father's young bullock, even the second bullock of seven years old, and throw down the altar of Ba'al that thy father hath, and cut down the grove that *is* by it:

26 And build an altar unto the LORD thy God upon the top of this rock, in the ordered place, and take the second bullock, and offer a burnt sacrifice with the wood of the grove which thou shalt cut down.

27 Then Gid'e-on took ten men of his servants, and did as the LORD had said unto him: and *so* it was, because he feared his father's household, and the men of the city, that he could not do *it* by day, that he did *it* by night.

28 ¶ And when the men of the city arose early in the morning, behold, the altar of Ba'al was cast down, and the grove was cut down that *was* by it, and the second bullock was offered upon the altar *that was* built.

29 And they said one to another, Who hath done this thing? And when they enquired and asked, they said, Gid'e-on the son of Jo'ash hath done this thing.

30 Then the men of the city said unto Jo'ash, Bring out thy son, that he may die: because he hath cast down the altar of Ba'al, and because he hath cut down the grove that *was* by it.

31 And Jo'ash said unto all that stood against him, Will ye plead for Ba'al? will ye save him? he that will plead for him, let him be put to death whilst *it is yet* morning: if he *be* a god, let him plead for himself, because *one* hath cast down his altar.

32 Therefore on that day he called him Je-rub'ba-al, saying, Let Ba'al plead against him, because he hath thrown down his altar.

33 ¶ Then all the Mid'i-an-ites and the Am'a-lek-ites and the children of the east were gathered together, and went over, and pitched in the valley of Jez're-el.

34 But the Spirit of the LORD came upon Gid'e-on, and he blew a trumpet; and A'bi-e'zer was gathered after him.

35 And he sent messengers throughout all Ma-nas'seh; who also was gathered after him: and he sent messengers unto Ash'er, and unto Zeb'u-lun, and unto Naph'ta-li; and they came up to meet them.

36 ¶ And Gid'e-on said unto God, If thou wilt save Is'ra-el by mine hand, as thou hast said,

37 Behold, I will put a fleece of wool in the floor; *and* if the dew be on the fleece only, and *it be* dry upon all the earth *beside*, then shall I know that thou wilt save Is'ra-el by mine hand, as thou hast said.

38 And it was so: for he rose up early on the morrow, and thrust the fleece together, and wringed the dew out of the fleece, a bowl full of water.

39 And Gid'e-on said unto God, Let not thine anger be hot against me, and I will speak but this once: let me prove, I pray thee, but this once with the fleece; let it now be dry only upon the fleece, and upon all the ground let there be dew.

40 And God did so that night: for it was dry upon the fleece only, and there was dew on all the ground.

7 THEN Je-rub'ba-al, who *is* Gid'e-on, and all the people that *were* with him, rose up early, and pitched beside the well of Ha'rod: so that the host of the Mid'i-an-ites were on the north side of them, by the hill of Mo'reh, in the valley.

2 And the LORD said unto Gid'e-on, The people that *are* with thee *are* too many for me to give the Mid'i-an-ites into their hands, lest Is'ra-el vaunt themselves against me, saying, Mine own hand hath saved me.

3 Now therefore go to, proclaim in the ears of the people, saying, Whosoever *is* fearful and afraid, let him return and depart early from mount Gil'e-ad. And there returned of the people twenty and two thousand; and there remained ten thousand.

4 And the LORD said unto Gid'e-on, The people *are* yet too many; bring them down unto the water, and I will try them for thee there: and it shall be, *that* of whom I say unto thee, This shall go with thee, the same shall go with thee; and of whomsoever I say unto thee, This shall not go with thee, the same shall not go.

5 So he brought down the people unto the water: and the LORD said unto Gid'e-on, Every one that lappeth of the water with his tongue, as a dog lappeth, him shalt thou set by himself;

likewise every one that boweth down upon his knees to drink.

6 And the number of them that lapped, *putting* their hand to their mouth, were three hundred men: but all the rest of the people bowed down upon their knees to drink water.

7 And the LORD said unto Gid'e-on, By the three hundred men that lapped will I save you, and deliver the Mid'i-an-ites into thine hand: and let all the *other* people go every man unto his place.

8 So the people took victuals in their hand, and their trumpets: and he sent all *the rest of* Is'ra-el every man unto his tent, and retained those three hundred men: and the host of Mid'i-an was beneath him in the valley.

9 ¶ And it came to pass the same night, that the LORD said unto him, Arise, get thee down unto the host; for I have delivered it into thine hand.

10 But if thou fear to go down, go thou with Phu'rah thy servant down to the host:

11 And thou shalt hear what they say; and afterward shall thine hands be strengthened to go down unto the host. Then went he down with Phu'rah his servant unto the outside of the armed men that *were* in the host.

12 And the Mid'i-an-ites and the Am'a-lek-ites and all the children of the east lay along in the valley like grasshoppers for multitude; and their camels *were* without number, as the sand by the sea side for multitude.

13 And when Gid'e-on was come, behold, *there was* a man that told a dream unto his fellow, and said, Behold, I dreamed a dream, and, lo, a cake of barley bread tumbled into the host of Mid'i-an, and came unto a tent, and smote it that it fell, and overturned it, that the tent lay along.

14 And his fellow answered and said, This *is* nothing else save the sword of Gid'e-on the son of Jo'ash, a man of Is'ra-el: *for* into his hand hath God delivered Mid'i-an, and all the host.

15 ¶ And it was so, when Gid'e-on heard the telling of the dream, and the interpretation thereof, that he worshipped, and returned into the host of Is'ra-el, and said, Arise; for the LORD hath delivered into your hand the host of Mid'i-an.

16 And he divided the three hundred men *into* three companies, and he put a trumpet in every man's hand, with empty pitchers, and lamps within the pitchers.

17 And he said unto them, Look on me, and do likewise: and, behold, when I come to the outside of the camp, it shall be *that*, as I do, so shall ye do.

18 When I blow with a trumpet, I and all that *are* with me, then blow ye the trumpets also on every side of all the camp, and say, The sword of the LORD, and of Gid'e-on.

19 ¶ So Gid'e-on, and the hundred men that *were* with him, came unto the outside of the camp in the beginning of the middle watch; and they had but newly set the watch: and they blew the trumpets, and brake the pitchers that *were* in their hands.

20 And the three companies blew the trumpets, and brake the pitchers, and held the lamps in their left hands, and the trumpets in their right hands to blow *withal*: and they cried, The sword of the LORD, and of Gid'e-on.

21 And they stood every man in his place round about the camp: and all the host ran, and cried, and fled.

22 And the three hundred blew the trumpets, and the LORD set every man's sword against his fellow, even throughout all the host: and the host fled to Beth-shit'tah in Zer'e-rath, *and* to the border of A'bel-me-ho'lah, unto Tab'bath.

23 And the men of Is'ra-el gathered themselves together out of Naph'ta-li, and out of Ash'er, and out of all Ma-nas'seh, and pursued after the Mid'i-an-ites.

24 ¶ And Gid'e-on sent messengers throughout all mount E'phra-im, saying, Come down against the Mid'i-an-ites, and take before them the waters unto Beth-ba'rah and Jor'dan. Then all the men of E'phra-im gathered themselves together, and took the waters unto Beth-ba'rah and Jor'dan.

25 And they took two princes of the Mid'i-an-ites, O'reb and Ze'eb; and they slew O'reb upon the rock O'reb, and Ze'eb they slew at the winepress of Ze'eb, and pursued Mid'i-an, and brought the heads of O'reb and Ze'eb to Gid'e-on on the other side Jor'dan.

8 AND the men of E'phra-im said unto him, Why hast thou served us thus, that thou calledst us not, when thou wentest to fight with the Mid'i-an-ites? And they did chide with him sharply.

2 And he said unto them, What have I done now in comparison of you? *Is* not the gleaning of the grapes of E'phra-im better than the vintage of A'bi-e'zer?

3 God hath delivered into your hands the princes of Mid'i-an, O'reb and Ze'eb: and what was I able to do in comparison of you? Then their anger was abated toward him, when he had said that.

4 ¶ And Gid'e-on came to Jor'dan, *and* passed over, he, and the three hundred men that *were* with him, faint, yet pursuing *them*.

5 And he said unto the men of Suc'coth, Give, I pray you, loaves of bread unto the people that follow me; for they *be* faint, and I am pursuing after Ze'bah and Zal-mun'na, kings of Mid'i-an.

6 ¶ And the princes of Suc'coth said, *Are* the hands of Ze'bah and Zal-mun'na now in thine hand, that we should give bread unto thine army?

7 And Gid'e-on said, Therefore when the LORD hath delivered Ze'bah and Zal-mun'na into mine hand, then I will tear your flesh with the thorns of the wilderness and with briers.

8 ¶ And he went up thence to Pe-nu'el, and spake unto them likewise: and the men of Pe-nu'el answered him as the men of Suc'coth had answered *him*.

9 And he spake also unto the men of Pe-nu'el, saying, When I come again in peace, I will break down this tower.

10 ¶ Now Ze'bah and Zal-mun'na *were* in Kar'kor, and their hosts with them, about fifteen thousand *men*, all that were left of all the hosts of the children of the east: for there fell an hundred and twenty thousand men that drew sword.

11 ¶ And Gid'e-on went up by the way of them that dwelt in tents on the east of No'bah and Jog'be-hah, and smote the host: for the host was secure.

12 And when Ze'bah and Zal-mun'na fled, he pursued after them, and took the two kings of Mid'i-an, Ze'bah and Zal-mun'na, and discomfited all the host.

13 ¶ And Gid'e-on the son of Jo'ash returned from battle before the sun *was up*,

14 And caught a young man of the men of Suc'coth, and enquired of him: and he de-

scribed unto him the princes of Suc'coth, and the elders thereof, *even* threescore and seventeen men.

15 And he came unto the men of Suc'coth, and said, Behold Ze'bah and Zal-mun'na, with whom ye did upbraid me, saying, *Are* the hands of Ze'bah and Zal-mun'na now in thine hand, that we should give bread unto thy men *that are* weary?

16 And he took the elders of the city, and thorns of the wilderness and briers, and with them he taught the men of Suc'coth.

17 And he beat down the tower of Pe-nu'el, and slew the men of the city.

18 ¶ Then said he unto Ze'bah and Zal-mun'na, What manner of men *were they* whom ye slew at Ta'bor? And they answered, As thou *art*, so *were* they; each one resembled the children of a king.

19 And he said, They *were* my brethren, *even* the sons of my mother: *as* the Lord liveth, if ye had saved them alive, I would not slay you.

20 And he said unto Je'ther his firstborn, Up, *and* slay them. But the youth drew not his sword: for he feared, because he *was* yet a youth.

21 Then Ze'bah and Zal-mun'na said, Rise thou, and fall upon us: for as the man *is, so is* his strength. And Gid'e-on arose, and slew Ze'bah and Zal-mun'na, and took away the ornaments that *were* on their camels' necks.

22 ¶ Then the men of Is'ra-el said unto Gid'e-on, Rule thou over us, both thou, and thy son, and thy son's son also: for thou hast delivered us from the hand of Mid'i-an.

23 And Gid'e-on said unto them, I will not rule over you, neither shall my son rule over you: the Lord shall rule over you.

24 ¶ And Gid'e-on said unto them, I would desire a request of you, that ye would give me every man the earrings of his prey. (For they had golden earrings, because they *were* Ish'ma-el-ites.)

25 And they answered, We will willingly give *them*. And they spread a garment, and did cast therein every man the earrings of his prey.

26 And the weight of the golden earrings that he requested was a thousand and seven hundred *shekels* of gold; beside ornaments, and collars, and purple raiment that *was* on the kings of Mid'i-an, and beside the chains that *were* about their camels' necks.

27 And Gid'e-on made an ephod thereof, and put it in his city, *even* in Oph'rah: and all Is'ra-el went thither a whoring after it: which thing became a snare unto Gid'e-on, and to his house.

28 ¶ Thus was Mid'i-an subdued before the children of Is'ra-el, so that they lifted up their heads no more. And the country was in quietness forty years in the days of Gid'e-on.

29 ¶ And Je-rub'ba-al the son of Jo'ash went and dwelt in his own house.

30 And Gid'e-on had threescore and ten sons of his body begotten: for he had many wives.

31 And his concubine that *was* in She'chem, she also bare him a son, whose name he called A-bim'e-lech.

32 ¶ And Gid'e-on the son of Jo'ash died in a good old age, and was buried in the sepulchre of Jo'ash his father, in Oph'rah of the A'bi-ez'-rites.

33 And it came to pass, as soon as Gid'e-on was dead, that the children of Is'ra-el turned again, and went a whoring after Ba'al-im, and made Ba'al-be'rith their god.

34 And the children of Is'ra-el remembered not the Lord their God, who had delivered

them out of the hands of all their enemies on every side:

35 Neither shewed they kindness to the house of Je-rub'ba-al, *namely*, Gid'e-on, according to all the goodness which he had shewed unto Is'ra-el.

9 AND A-bim'e-lech the son of Je-rub'ba-al went unto She'chem unto his mother's brethren, and communed with them, and with all the family of the house of his mother's father, saying,

2 Speak, I pray you, in the ears of all the men of She'chem, Whether *is* better for you, either that all the sons of Je-rub'ba-al, *which are* threescore and ten persons, reign over you, or that one reign over you? remember also that I *am* your bone and your flesh.

3 And his mother's brethren spake of him in the ears of all the men of She'chem all these words: and their hearts inclined to follow A-bim'e-lech; for they said, He *is* our brother.

4 And they gave him threescore and ten *pieces* of silver out of the house of Ba'al-be'rith, wherewith A-bim'e-lech hired vain and light persons, which followed him.

5 And he went unto his father's house at Oph'rah, and slew his brethren the sons of Je-rub'ba-al, *being* threescore and ten persons, upon one stone: notwithstanding yet Jo'tham the youngest son of Je-rub'ba-al was left; for he hid himself.

6 And all the men of She'chem gathered together, and all the house of Mil'lo, and went, and made A-bim'e-lech king, by the plain of the pillar that *was* in She'chem.

7 ¶ And when they told *it* to Jo'tham, he went and stood in the top of mount Ger'i-zim, and lifted up his voice, and cried, and said unto them, Hearken unto me, ye men of She'chem, that God may hearken unto you.

8 The trees went forth *on a time* to anoint a king over them; and they said unto the olive tree, Reign thou over us.

9 But the olive tree said unto them, Should I leave my fatness, wherewith by me they honour God and man, and go to be promoted over the trees?

10 And the trees said to the fig tree, Come thou, *and* reign over us.

11 But the fig tree said unto them, Should I forsake my sweetness, and my good fruit, and go to be promoted over the trees?

12 Then said the trees unto the vine, Come thou, *and* reign over us.

13 And the vine said unto them, Should I leave my wine, which cheereth God and man, and go to be promoted over the trees?

14 Then said all the trees unto the bramble, Come thou, *and* reign over us.

15 And the bramble said unto the trees, If in truth ye anoint me king over you, *then* come *and* put your trust in my shadow: and if not, let fire come out of the bramble, and devour the cedars of Leb'a-non.

16 Now therefore, if ye have done truly and sincerely, in that ye have made A-bim'e-lech king, and if ye have dealt well with Je-rub'ba-al and his house, and have done unto him according to the deserving of his hands;

17 (For my father fought for you, and adventured his life far, and delivered you out of the hand of Mid'i-an:

18 And ye are risen up against my father's house this day, and have slain his sons, threescore and ten persons, upon one stone, and have made A-bim'e-lech, the son of his maidser-

vant, king over the men of She'chem, because he *is* your brother;)

19 If ye then have dealt truly and sincerely with Je-rub'ba-al and with his house this day, *then* rejoice ye in A-bim'e-lech, and let him also rejoice in you:

20 But if not, let fire come out from A-bim'e-lech, and devour the men of She'chem, and the house of Mil'lo; and let fire come out from the men of She'chem, and from the house of Mil'lo, and devour A-bim'e-lech.

21 And Jo'tham ran away, and fled, and went to Be'er, and dwelt there, for fear of A-bim'e-lech his brother.

22 ¶ When A-bim'e-lech had reigned three years over Is'ra-el,

23 Then God sent an evil spirit between A-bim'e-lech and the men of She'chem; and the men of She'chem dealt treacherously with A-bim'e-lech:

24 That the cruelty *done* to the threescore and ten sons of Je-rub'ba-al might come, and their blood be laid upon A-bim'e-lech their brother, which slew them; and upon the men of She'chem, which aided him in the killing of his brethren.

25 And the men of She'chem set liers in wait for him in the top of the mountains, and they robbed all that came along that way by them: and it was told A-bim'e-lech.

26 And Ga'al the son of E'bed came with his brethren, and went over to She'chem: and the men of She'chem put their confidence in him.

27 And they went out into the fields, and gathered their vineyards, and trode *the grapes*, and made merry, and went into the house of their god, and did eat and drink, and cursed A-bim'e-lech.

28 And Ga'al the son of E'bed said, Who *is* A-bim'e-lech, and who *is* She'chem, that we should serve him? *is* not *he* the son of Je-rub'ba-al? and Ze'bul his officer? serve the men of Ha'mor the father of She'chem: for why should we serve him?

29 And would to God this people were under my hand! then would I remove A-bim'e-lech. And he said to A-bim'e-lech, Increase thine army, and come out.

30 ¶ And when Ze'bul the ruler of the city heard the words of Ga'al the son of E'bed, his anger was kindled.

31 And he sent messengers unto A-bim'e-lech privily, saying, Behold, Ga'al the son of E'-bed and his brethren be come to She'chem; and, behold, they fortify the city against thee.

32 Now therefore up by night, thou and the people that *is* with thee, and lie in wait in the field:

33 And it shall be, *that* in the morning, as soon as the sun is up, thou shalt rise early, and set upon the city: and, behold, *when* he and the people that *is* with him come out against thee, then mayest thou do to them as thou shalt find occasion.

34 ¶ And A-bim'e-lech rose up, and all the people that *were* with him, by night, and they laid wait against She'chem in four companies.

35 And Ga'al the son of E'bed went out, and stood in the entering of the gate of the city: and A-bim'e-lech rose up, and the people that *were* with him, from lying in wait.

36 And when Ga'al saw the people, he said to Ze'bul, Behold, there come people down from the top of the mountains. And Ze'bul said unto him, Thou seest the shadow of the mountains as *if they were* men.

37 And Ga'al spake again and said, See there come people down by the middle of the land, and another company come along by the plain of Me-on'e-nim.

38 Then said Ze'bul unto him, Where *is* now thy mouth, wherewith thou saidst, Who *is* A-bim'e-lech, that we should serve him? *is* not this the people that thou hast despised? go out, I pray now, and fight with them.

39 And Ga'al went out before the men of She'chem, and fought with A-bim'e-lech.

40 And A-bim'e-lech chased him, and he fled before him, and many were overthrown *and* wounded, *even* unto the entering of the gate.

41 And A-bim'e-lech dwelt at A-ru'mah: and Ze'bul thrust out Ga'al and his brethren, that they should not dwell in She'chem.

42 And it came to pass on the morrow, that the people went out into the field; and they told A-bim'e-lech.

43 And he took the people, and divided them into three companies, and laid wait in the field, and looked, and, behold, the people *were* come forth out of the city; and he rose up against them, and smote them.

44 And A-bim'e-lech, and the company that *was* with him, rushed forward, and stood in the entering of the gate of the city: and the two *oth-er* companies ran upon all *the people* that *were* in the fields, and slew them.

45 And A-bim'e-lech fought against the city all that day; and he took the city, and slew the people that *was* therein, and beat down the city, and sowed it with salt.

46 ¶ And when all the men of the tower of She'chem heard *that*, they entered into an hold of the house of the god Be'rith.

47 And it was told A-bim'e-lech, that all the men of the tower of She'chem were gathered together.

48 And A-bim'e-lech gat him up to mount Zal'mon, he and all the people that *were* with him; and A-bim'e-lech took an ax in his hand, and cut down a bough from the trees, and took it, and laid *it* on his shoulder, and said unto the people that *were* with him, What ye have seen me do, make haste, *and* do as I *have done*.

49 And all the people likewise cut down every man his bough, and followed A-bim'e-lech, and put *them* to the hold, and set the hold on fire upon them; so that all the men of the tower of She'chem died also, about a thousand men and women.

50 ¶ Then went A-bim'e-lech to The'bez, and encamped against The'bez, and took it.

51 But there was a strong tower within the city, and thither fled all the men and women, and all they of the city, and shut *it* to them, and gat them up to the top of the tower.

52 And A-bim'e-lech came unto the tower, and fought against it, and went hard unto the door of the tower to burn it with fire.

53 And a certain woman cast a piece of a millstone upon A-bim'e-lech's head, and all to brake his skull.

54 Then he called hastily unto the young man his armourbearer, and said unto him, Draw thy sword, and slay me, that men say not of me, A woman slew him. And his young man thrust him through, and he died.

55 And when the men of Is'ra-el saw that A-bim'e-lech was dead, they departed every man unto his place.

56 ¶ Thus God rendered the wickedness of A-bim'e-lech, which he did unto his father, in slaying his seventy brethren:

57 And all the evil of the men of She'chem did God render upon their heads: and upon

them came the curse of Jo'tham the son of Je-rub'ba-al.

10 AND after A-bim'e-lech there arose to defend Is'ra-el To'la the son of Pu'ah, the son of Do'do, a man of Is'sa-char; and he dwelt in Sha'mir in mount E'phra-im.

2 And he judged Is'ra-el twenty and three years, and died, and was buried in Sha'mir.

3 ¶ And after him arose Ja'ir, a Gil'e-ad-ite, and judged Is'ra-el twenty and two years.

4 And he had thirty sons that rode on thirty ass colts, and they had thirty cities, which are called Ha'voth-ja'ir unto this day, which are in the land of Gil'e-ad.

5 And Ja'ir died, and was buried in Ca'mon.

6 ¶ And the children of Is'ra-el did evil again in the sight of the LORD, and served Ba'al-im, and Ash'ta-roth, and the gods of Syr'i-a, and the gods of Zi'don, and the gods of Mo'ab, and the gods of the children of Am'mon, and the gods of the Phi-lis'tines, and forsook the LORD, and served not him.

7 And the anger of the LORD was hot against Is'ra-el, and he sold them into the hands of the Phi-lis'tines, and into the hands of the children of Am'mon.

8 And that year they vexed and oppressed the children of Is'ra-el: eighteen years, all the children of Is'ra-el that were on the other side Jor'dan in the land of the Am'or-ites, which is in Gil'e-ad.

9 Moreover the children of Am'mon passed over Jor'dan to fight also against Ju'dah, and against Ben'ja-min, and against the house of E'-phra-im; so that Is'ra-el was sore distressed.

10 ¶ And the children of Is'ra-el cried unto the LORD, saying, We have sinned against thee, both because we have forsaken our God, and also served Ba'al-im.

11 And the LORD said unto the children of Is'-ra-el, Did not I deliver you from the E-gyp'tians, and from the Am'or-ites, from the children of Am'mon, and from the Phi-lis'tines?

12 The Zi-do'ni-ans also, and the Am'a-lek-ites, and the Ma'on-ites, did oppress you; and ye cried to me, and I delivered you out of their hand.

13 Yet ye have forsaken me, and served oth-er gods: wherefore I will deliver you no more.

14 Go and cry unto the gods which ye have chosen; let them deliver you in the time of your tribulation.

15 ¶ And the children of Is'ra-el said unto the LORD, We have sinned: do thou unto us whatsoever seemeth good unto thee; deliver us only, we pray thee, this day.

16 And they put away the strange gods from among them, and served the LORD: and his soul was grieved for the misery of Is'ra-el.

17 Then the children of Am'mon were gath-ered together, and encamped in Gil'e-ad. And the children of Is'ra-el assembled themselves together, and encamped in Miz'peh.

18 And the people and princes of Gil'e-ad said one to another, What man is he that will begin to fight against the children of Am'mon? he shall be head over all the inhabitants of Gil'e-ad.

11 NOW Jeph'thah the Gil'e-ad-ite was a mighty man of valour, and he was the son of an harlot: and Gil'e-ad begat Jeph'thah.

2 And Gil'e-ad's wife bare him sons; and his wife's sons grew up, and they thrust out Jeph'-thah, and said unto him, Thou shalt not inherit

in our father's house; for thou art the son of a strange woman.

3 Then Jeph'thah fled from his brethren, and dwelt in the land of Tob: and there were gath-ered vain men to Jeph'thah, and went out with him.

4 ¶ And it came to pass in process of time, that the children of Am'mon made war against Is'ra-el.

5 And it was so, that when the children of Am'mon made war against Is'ra-el, the elders of Gil'e-ad went to fetch Jeph'thah out of the land of Tob:

6 And they said unto Jeph'thah, Come, and be our captain, that we may fight with the chil-dren of Am'mon.

7 And Jeph'thah said unto the elders of Gil'e-ad, Did not ye hate me, and expel me out of my father's house? and why are ye come unto me now when ye are in distress?

8 And the elders of Gil'e-ad said unto Jeph'-thah, Therefore we turn again to thee now, that thou mayest go with us, and fight against the children of Am'mon, and be our head over all the inhabitants of Gil'e-ad.

9 And Jeph'thah said unto the elders of Gil'e-ad, If ye bring me home again to fight against the children of Am'mon, and the LORD deliver them before me, shall I be your head?

10 And the elders of Gil'e-ad said unto Jeph'-thah, The LORD be witness between us, if we do not so according to thy words.

11 Then Jeph'thah went with the elders of Gil'e-ad, and the people made him head and captain over them: and Jeph'thah uttered all his words before the LORD in Miz'peh.

12 ¶ And Jeph'thah sent messengers unto the king of the children of Am'mon, saying, What hast thou to do with me, that thou art come against me to fight in my land?

13 And the king of the children of Am'mon answered unto the messengers of Jeph'thah, Because Is'ra-el took away my land, when they came up out of E'gypt, from Ar'non even unto Jab'bok, and unto Jor'dan: now therefore re-store those lands again peaceably.

14 And Jeph'thah sent messengers again unto the king of the children of Am'mon:

15 And said unto him, Thus saith Jeph'thah, Is'ra-el took not away the land of Mo'ab, nor the land of the children of Am'mon:

16 But when Is'ra-el came up from E'gypt, and walked through the wilderness unto the Red sea, and came to Ka'desh;

17 Then Is'ra-el sent messengers unto the king of E'dom, saying, Let me, I pray thee, pass through thy land: but the king of E'dom would not hearken thereto. And in like manner they sent unto the king of Mo'ab: but he would not consent: and Is'ra-el abode in Ka'desh.

18 Then they went along through the wilder-ness, and compassed the land of E'dom, and the land of Mo'ab, and came by the east side of the land of Mo'ab, and pitched on the other side of Ar'non, but came not within the border of Mo'-ab: for Ar'non was the border of Mo'ab.

19 And Is'ra-el sent messengers unto Si'hon king of the Am'or-ites, the king of Hesh'bon; and Is'ra-el said unto him, Let us pass, we pray thee, through thy land into my place.

20 But Si'hon trusted not Is'ra-el to pass through his coast: but Si'hon gathered all his people together, and pitched in Ja'haz, and fought against Is'ra-el.

21 And the LORD God of Is'ra-el delivered Si'-hon and all his people into the hand of Is'ra-el, and they smote them: so Is'ra-el possessed all

the land of the Am'or-ites, the inhabitants of that country.

22 And they possessed all the coasts of the Am'or-ites, from Ar'non even unto Jab'bok, and from the wilderness even unto Jor'dan.

23 So now the LORD God of Is'ra-el hath dispossessed the Am'or-ites from before his people Is'ra-el, and shouldest thou possess it?

24 Wilt not thou possess that which Che'-mosh thy god giveth thee to possess? So whomsoever the LORD our God shall drive out from before us, them will we possess.

25 And now art thou any thing better than Ba'lak the son of Zip'por, king of Mo'ab? did he ever strive against Is'ra-el, or did he ever fight against them,

26 While Is'ra-el dwelt in Hesh'bon and her towns, and in Ar'o-er and her towns, and in all the cities that be along by the coasts of Ar'non, three hundred years? why therefore did ye not recover them within that time?

27 Wherefore I have not sinned against thee, but thou doest me wrong to war against me: the LORD the Judge be judge this day between the children of Is'ra-el and the children of Am'mon.

28 Howbeit the king of the children of Am'-mon hearkened not unto the words of Jeph'thah which he sent him.

29 ¶ Then the Spirit of the LORD came upon Jeph'thah, and he passed over Gil'e-ad, and Ma-nas'seh, and passed over Miz'peh of Gil'e-ad, and from Miz'peh of Gil'e-ad he passed over unto the children of Am'mon.

30 And Jeph'thah vowed a vow unto the LORD, and said, If thou shalt without fail deliver the children of Am'mon into mine hands,

31 Then it shall be, that whatsoever cometh forth of the doors of my house to meet me, when I return in peace from the children of Am'mon, shall surely be the LORD'S, and I will offer it up for a burnt offering.

32 ¶ So Jeph'thah passed over unto the children of Am'mon to fight against them; and the LORD delivered them into his hands.

33 And he smote them from Ar'o-er, even till thou come to Min'nith, even twenty cities, and unto the plain of the vineyards, with a very great slaughter. Thus the children of Am'mon were subdued before the children of Is'ra-el.

34 ¶ And Jeph'thah came to Miz'peh unto his house, and, behold, his daughter came out to meet him with timbrels and with dances: and she was his only child; beside her he had neither son nor daughter.

35 And it came to pass, when he saw her, that he rent his clothes, and said, Alas, my daughter! thou hast brought me very low, and thou art one of them that trouble me: for I have opened my mouth unto the LORD, and I cannot go back.

36 And she said unto him, My father, if thou hast opened thy mouth unto the LORD, do to me according to that which hath proceeded out of thy mouth; forasmuch as the LORD hath taken vengeance for thee of thine enemies, even of the children of Am'mon.

37 And she said unto her father, Let this thing be done for me: let me alone two months, that I may go up and down upon the mountains, and bewail my virginity, I and my fellows.

38 And he said, Go. And he sent her away for two months: and she went with her companions, and bewailed her virginity upon the mountains.

39 And it came to pass at the end of two months, that she returned unto her father, who did with her according to his vow which he had vowed: and she knew no man. And it was a custom in Is'ra-el,

40 That the daughters of Is'ra-el went yearly to lament the daughter of Jeph'thah the Gil'e-ad-ite four days in a year.

12 AND the men of E'phra-im gathered themselves together, and went northward, and said unto Jeph'thah, Wherefore passedst thou over to fight against the children of Am'mon, and didst not call us to go with thee? we will burn thine house upon thee with fire.

2 And Jeph'thah said unto them, I and my people were at great strife with the children of Am'mon; and when I called you, ye delivered me not out of their hands.

3 And when I saw that ye delivered me not, I put my life in my hands, and passed over against the children of Am'mon, and the LORD delivered them into my hand: wherefore then are ye come up unto me this day, to fight against me?

4 Then Jeph'thah gathered together all the men of Gil'e-ad, and fought with E'phra-im: and the men of Gil'e-ad smote E'phra-im, because they said, Ye Gil'e-ad-ites are fugitives of E'-phra-im among the E'phra-im-ites, and among the Ma-nas'sites.

5 And the Gil'e-ad-ites took the passages of Jor'dan before the E'phra-im-ites: and it was so, that when those E'phra-im-ites which were escaped said, Let me go over; that the men of Gil'-e-ad said unto him, Art thou an E'phra-im-ite? If he said, Nay;

6 Then said they unto him, Say now Shib'bo-leth: and he said Sib'bo-leth: for he could not frame to pronounce it right. Then they took him, and slew him at the passages of Jor'dan: and there fell at that time of the E'phra-im-ites forty and two thousand.

7 And Jeph'thah judged Is'ra-el six years. Then died Jeph'thah the Gil'e-ad-ite, and was buried in one of the cities of Gil'e-ad.

8 ¶ And after him Ib'zan of Beth'-le-hem judged Is'ra-el.

9 And he had thirty sons, and thirty daughters, whom he sent abroad, and took in thirty daughters from abroad for his sons. And he judged Is'ra-el seven years.

10 Then died Ib'zan, and was buried at Beth'--le-hem.

11 ¶ And after him E'lon, a Zeb'u-lon-ite, judged Is'ra-el; and he judged Is'ra-el ten years.

12 And E'lon the Zeb'u-lon-ite died, and was buried in Aij'a-lon in the country of Zeb'u-lun.

13 ¶ And after him Ab'don the son of Hil'lel, a Pir'a-thon-ite, judged Is'ra-el.

14 And he had forty sons and thirty nephews, that rode on threescore and ten ass colts: and he judged Is'ra-el eight years.

15 And Ab'don the son of Hil'lel the Pir'a-thon-ite died, and was buried in Pir'a-thon in the land of E'phra-im, in the mount of the Am'a-lek-ites.

13 AND the children of Is'ra-el did evil again in the sight of the LORD; and the LORD delivered them into the hand of the Phi-lis'tines forty years.

2 ¶ And there was a certain man of Zo'rah, of the family of the Dan'ites, whose name was Ma-no'ah; and his wife was barren, and bare not.

3 And the angel of the LORD appeared unto the woman, and said unto her, Behold now,

thou *art* barren, and bearest not: but thou shalt conceive, and bear a son.

4 Now therefore beware, I pray thee, and drink not wine nor strong drink, and eat not any unclean *thing*:

5 For, lo, thou shalt conceive, and bear a son; and no razor shall come on his head: for the child shall be a Naz′a-rite unto God from the womb: and he shall begin to deliver Is′ra-el out of the hand of the Phi-lis′tines.

6 ¶ Then the woman came and told her husband, saying, A man of God came unto me, and his countenance *was* like the countenance of an angel of God, very terrible: but I asked him not whence he *was*, neither told he me his name:

7 But he said unto me, Behold, thou shalt conceive, and bear a son; and now drink no wine nor strong drink, neither eat any unclean *thing*: for the child shall be a Naz′a-rite to God from the womb to the day of his death.

8 ¶ Then Ma-no′ah intreated the LORD, and said, O my Lord, let the man of God which thou didst send come again unto us, and teach us what we shall do unto the child that shall be born.

9 And God hearkened to the voice of Ma-no′ah; and the angel of God came again unto the woman as she sat in the field: but Ma-no′ah her husband *was* not with her.

10 And the woman made haste, and ran, and shewed her husband, and said unto him, Behold, the man hath appeared unto me, that came unto me the *other* day.

11 And Ma-no′ah arose, and went after his wife, and came to the man, and said unto him, *Art* thou the man that spakest unto the woman? And he said, I *am*.

12 And Ma-no′ah said, Now let thy words come to pass. How shall we order the child, and *how* shall we do unto him?

13 And the angel of the LORD said unto Ma-no′ah, Of all that I said unto the woman let her beware.

14 She may not eat of any *thing* that cometh of the vine, neither let her drink wine or strong drink, nor eat any unclean *thing*: all that I commanded her let her observe.

15 ¶ And Ma-no′ah said unto the angel of the LORD, I pray thee, let us detain thee, until we shall have made ready a kid for thee.

16 And the angel of the LORD said unto Ma-no′ah, Though thou detain me, I will not eat of thy bread: and if thou wilt offer a burnt offering, thou must offer it unto the LORD. For Ma-no′ah knew not that he *was* an angel of the LORD.

17 And Ma-no′ah said unto the angel of the LORD, What *is* thy name, that when thy sayings come to pass we may do thee honour?

18 And the angel of the LORD said unto him, Why askest thou thus after my name, seeing it *is* secret?

19 So Ma-no′ah took a kid with a meat offering, and offered *it* upon a rock unto the LORD: and *the angel* did wonderously; and Ma-no′ah and his wife looked on.

20 For it came to pass, when the flame went up toward heaven from off the altar, that the angel of the LORD ascended in the flame of the altar. And Ma-no′ah and his wife looked on *it*, and fell on their faces to the ground.

21 But the angel of the LORD did no more appear to Ma-no′ah and to his wife. Then Ma-no′ah knew that he *was* an angel of the LORD.

22 And Ma-no′ah said unto his wife, We shall surely die, because we have seen God.

23 But his wife said unto him, If the LORD were pleased to kill us, he would not have received a burnt offering and a meat offering at our hands, neither would he have shewed us all these *things*, nor would as at this time have told us *such things* as these.

24 ¶ And the woman bare a son, and called his name Sam′son: and the child grew, and the LORD blessed him.

25 And the Spirit of the LORD began to move him at times in the camp of Dan between Zo′rah and Esh′ta-ol.

14 AND Sam′son went down to Tim′nath, and saw a woman in Tim′nath of the daughters of the Phi-lis′tines.

2 And he came up, and told his father and his mother, and said, I have seen a woman in Tim′-nath of the daughters of the Phi-lis′tines: now therefore get her for me to wife.

3 Then his father and his mother said unto him, *Is there* never a woman among the daughters of thy brethren, or among all my people, that thou goest to take a wife of the uncircumcised Phi-lis′tines? And Sam′son said unto his father, Get her for me; for she pleaseth me well.

4 But his father and his mother knew not that it *was* of the LORD, that he sought an occasion against the Phi-lis′tines: for at that time the Phi-lis′tines had dominion over Is′ra-el.

5 ¶ Then went Sam′son down, and his father and his mother, to Tim′nath, and came to the vineyards of Tim′nath: and, behold, a young lion roared against him.

6 And the Spirit of the LORD came mightily upon him, and he rent him as he would have rent a kid, and *he had* nothing in his hand: but he told not his father or his mother what he had done.

7 And he went down, and talked with the woman; and she pleased Sam′son well.

8 ¶ And after a time he returned to take her, and he turned aside to see the carcase of the lion: and, behold, *there was* a swarm of bees and honey in the carcase of the lion.

9 And he took thereof in his hands, and went on eating, and came to his father and mother, and he gave them, and they did eat: but he told not them that he had taken the honey out of the carcase of the lion.

10 ¶ So his father went down unto the woman: and Sam′son made there a feast; for so used the young men to do.

11 And it came to pass, when they saw him, that they brought thirty companions to be with him.

12 ¶ And Sam′son said unto them, I will now put forth a riddle unto you: if ye can certainly declare it me within the seven days of the feast, and find *it* out, then I will give you thirty sheets and thirty change of garments:

13 But if ye cannot declare *it* me, then shall ye give me thirty sheets and thirty change of garments. And they said unto him, Put forth thy riddle, that we may hear it.

14 And he said unto them, Out of the eater came forth meat, and out of the strong came forth sweetness. And they could not in three days expound the riddle.

15 And it came to pass on the seventh day, that they said unto Sam′son's wife, Entice thy husband, that he may declare unto us the riddle, lest we burn thee and thy father's house with fire: have ye called us to take that we have? *is it* not *so*?

16 And Sam′son's wife wept before him, and said, Thou dost but hate me, and lovest me not: thou hast put forth a riddle unto the children of my people, and hast not told *it* me. And he said

unto her, Behold, I have not told *it* my father nor my mother, and shall I tell *it* thee?

17 And she wept before him the seven days, while their feast lasted: and it came to pass on the seventh day, that he told her, because she lay sore upon him: and she told the riddle to the children of her people.

18 And the men of the city said unto him on the seventh day before the sun went down, What *is* sweeter than honey? and what *is* stronger than a lion? And he said unto them, If ye had not plowed with my heifer, ye had not found out my riddle.

19 ¶ And the Spirit of the LORD came upon him and he went down to Ash'ke-lon, and slew thirty men of them, and took their spoil, and gave change of garments unto them which expounded the riddle. And his anger was kindled, and he went up to his father's house.

20 But Sam'son's wife was *given* to his companion, whom he had used as his friend.

15 BUT it came to pass within a while after, in the time of wheat harvest, that Sam'son visited his wife with a kid; and he said, I will go in to my wife into the chamber. But her father would not suffer him to go in.

2 And her father said, I verily thought that thou hadst utterly hated her; therefore I gave her to thy companion: *is* not her younger sister fairer than she? take her, I pray thee, instead of her.

3 ¶ And Sam'son said concerning them, Now shall I be more blameless than the Phi-lis'tines, though I do them a displeasure.

4 And Sam'son went and caught three hundred foxes, and took firebrands, and turned tail to tail, and put a firebrand in the midst between two tails.

5 And when he had set the brands on fire, he let *them* go into the standing corn of the Phi-lis'tines, and burnt up both the shocks, and also the standing corn, with the vineyards *and* olives.

6 ¶ Then the Phi-lis'tines said, Who hath done this? And they answered, Sam'son, the son in law of the Tim'nite, because he had taken his wife, and given her to his companion. And the Phi-lis'tines came up, and burnt her and her father with fire.

7 ¶ And Sam'son said unto them, Though ye have done this, yet will I be avenged of you, and after that I will cease.

8 And he smote them hip and thigh with a great slaughter: and he went down and dwelt in the top of the rock E'tam.

9 ¶ Then the Phi-lis'tines went up, and pitched in Ju'dah, and spread themselves in Le'hi.

10 And the men of Ju'dah said, Why are ye come up against us? And they answered, To bind Sam'son are we come up, to do to him as he hath done to us.

11 Then three thousand men of Ju'dah went to the top of the rock E'tam, and said to Sam'son, Knowest thou not that the Phi-lis'tines *are* rulers over us? what *is* this *that* thou hast done unto us? And he said unto them, As they did unto me, so have I done unto them.

12 And they said unto him, We are come down to bind thee, that we may deliver thee into the hand of the Phi-lis'tines. And Sam'son said unto them, Swear unto me, that ye will not fall upon me yourselves.

13 And they spake unto him, saying, No; but we will bind thee fast, and deliver thee into their hand: but surely we will not kill thee. And they bound him with two new cords, and brought him up from the rock.

14 ¶ *And* when he came unto Le'hi, the Phi-lis'tines shouted against him: and the Spirit of the LORD came mightily upon him, and the cords that *were* upon his arms became as flax that was burnt with fire, and his bands loosed from off his hands.

15 And he found a new jawbone of an ass, and put forth his hand, and took it, and slew a thousand men therewith.

16 And Sam'son said, With the jawbone of an ass, heaps upon heaps, with the jaw of an ass have I slain a thousand men.

17 And it came to pass, when he had made an end of speaking, that he cast away the jawbone out of his hand, and called that place Ra'math-le'hi.

18 ¶ And he was sore athirst, and called on the LORD, and said, Thou hast given this great deliverance into the hand of thy servant: and now shall I die for thirst, and fall into the hand of the uncircumcised?

19 But God clave an hollow place that *was* in the jaw, and there came water thereout; and when he had drunk, his spirit came again, and he revived: wherefore he called the name thereof En-hak'ko-re, which *is* in Le'hi unto this day.

20 And he judged Is'ra-el in the days of the Phi-lis'tines twenty years.

16 THEN went Sam'son to Ga'za, and saw there an harlot, and went in unto her.

2 *And it was told* the Ga'zites, saying, Sam'son is come hither. And they compassed *him* in, and laid wait for him all night in the gate of the city, and were quiet all the night, saying, In the morning, when it is day, we shall kill him.

3 And Sam'son lay till midnight, and arose at midnight, and took the doors of the gate of the city, and the two posts, and went away with them, bar and all, and put *them* upon his shoulders, and carried them up to the top of an hill that *is* before He'bron.

4 ¶ And it came to pass afterward, that he loved a woman in the valley of So'rek, whose name *was* De-li'lah.

5 And the lords of the Phi-lis'tines came up unto her, and said unto her, Entice him, and see wherein his great strength *lieth*, and by what *means* we may prevail against him, that we may bind him to afflict him: and we will give thee every one of us eleven hundred *pieces* of silver.

6 ¶ And De-li'lah said to Sam'son, Tell me, I pray thee, wherein thy great strength *lieth*, and wherewith thou mightest be bound to afflict thee.

7 And Sam'son said unto her, If they bind me with seven green withs that were never dried, then shall I be weak, and be as another man.

8 Then the lords of the Phi-lis'tines brought up to her seven green withs which had not been dried, and she bound him with them.

9 Now *there were* men lying in wait, abiding with her in the chamber. And she said unto him, The Phi-lis'tines *be* upon thee, Sam'son. And he brake the withs, as a thread of tow is broken when it toucheth the fire. So his strength was not known.

10 And De-li'lah said unto Sam'son, Behold, thou hast mocked me, and told me lies: now tell me, I pray thee, wherewith thou mightest be bound.

11 And he said unto her, If they bind me fast

with new ropes that never were occupied, then shall I be weak, and be as another man.

12 De-li'lah therefore took new ropes, and bound him therewith, and said unto him, The Phi-lis'tines be upon thee, Sam'son. And there were liers in wait abiding in the chamber. And he brake them from off his arms like a thread.

13 And De-li'lah said unto Sam'son, Hitherto thou hast mocked me, and told me lies: tell me wherewith thou mightest be bound. And he said unto her, If thou weavest the seven locks of my head with the web.

14 And she fastened it with the pin, and said unto him, The Phi-lis'tines be upon thee, Sam'-son. And he awaked out of his sleep, and went away with the pin of the beam, and with the web.

15 ¶ And she said unto him, How canst thou say, I love thee, when thine heart is not with me? and hast not told me wherein thy great strength lieth.

16 And it came to pass, when she pressed him daily with her words, and urged him, so that his soul was vexed unto death;

17 That he told her all his heart, and said unto her, There hath not come a razor upon mine head; for I have been a Naz'a-rite unto God from my mother's womb: if I be shaven, then my strength will go from me, and I shall become weak, and be like any other man.

18 And when De-li'lah saw that he had told her all his heart, she sent and called for the lords of the Phi-lis'tines, saying, Come up this once, for he hath shewed me all his heart. Then the lords of the Phi-lis'tines came up unto her, and brought money in their hand.

19 And she made him sleep upon her knees; and she called for a man, and she caused him to shave off the seven locks of his head; and she began to afflict him, and his strength went from him.

20 And she said, The Phi-lis'tines be upon thee, Sam'son. And he awoke out of his sleep, and said, I will go out as at other times before, and shake myself. And he wist not that the LORD was departed from him.

21 ¶ But the Phi-lis'tines took him, and put out his eyes, and brought him down to Ga'za, and bound him with fetters of brass; and he did grind in the prison house.

22 Howbeit the hair of his head began to grow again after he was shaven.

23 Then the lords of the Phi-lis'tines gathered them together for to offer a great sacrifice unto Da'gon their god, and to rejoice: for they said, Our god hath delivered Sam'son our enemy into our hand.

24 And when the people saw him, they praised their god: for they said, Our god hath delivered into our hands our enemy, and the destroyer of our country, which slew many of us.

25 And it came to pass, when their hearts were merry, that they said, Call for Sam'son, that he may make us sport. And they called for Sam'son out of the prison house; and he made them sport: and they set him between the pillars.

26 And Sam'son said unto the lad that held him by the hand, Suffer me that I may feel the pillars whereupon the house standeth, that I may lean upon them.

27 Now the house was full of men and women; and all the lords of the Phi-lis'tines were there; and there were upon the roof about three thousand men and women, that beheld while Sam'son made sport.

28 And Sam'son called unto the LORD, and said, O Lord GOD, remember me, I pray thee, and strengthen me, I pray thee, only this once, O God, that I may be at once avenged of the Phi-lis'tines for my two eyes.

29 And Sam'son took hold of the two middle pillars upon which the house stood, and on which it was borne up, of the one with his right hand, and of the other with his left.

30 And Sam'son said, Let me die with the Phi-lis'tines. And he bowed himself with all his might; and the house fell upon the lords, and upon all the people that were therein. So the dead which he slew at his death were more than they which he slew in his life.

31 Then his brethren and all the house of his father came down, and took him, and brought him up, and buried him between Zo'rah and Esh'ta-ol in the buryingplace of Ma-no'ah his father. And he judged Is'ra-el twenty years.

17 AND there was a man of mount E'phra-im, whose name was Mi'cah.

2 And he said unto his mother, The eleven hundred shekels of silver that were taken from thee, about which thou cursedst, and spakest of also in mine ears, behold, the silver is with me; I took it. And his mother said, Blessed be thou of the LORD, my son.

3 And when he had restored the eleven hundred shekels of silver to his mother, his mother said, I had wholly dedicated the silver unto the LORD from my hand for my son, to make a graven image and a molten image: now therefore I will restore it unto thee.

4 Yet he restored the money unto his mother; and his mother took two hundred shekels of silver, and gave them to the founder, who made thereof a graven image and a molten image: and they were in the house of Mi'cah.

5 And the man Mi'cah had an house of gods, and made an ephod, and teraphim, and consecrated one of his sons, who became his priest.

6 In those days there was no king in Is'ra-el, but every man did that which was right in his own eyes.

7 ¶ And there was a young man out of Beth'-le-hem-ju'dah of the family of Ju'dah, who was a Le'vite, and he sojourned there.

8 And the man departed out of the city from Beth'-le-hem-ju'dah to sojourn where he could find a place: and he came to mount E'phra-im to the house of Mi'cah, as he journeyed.

9 And Mi'cah said unto him, Whence comest thou? And he said unto him, I am a Le'vite of Beth'-le-hem-ju'dah, and I go to sojourn where I may find a place.

10 And Mi'cah said unto him, Dwell with me, and be unto me a father and a priest, and I will give thee ten shekels of silver by the year, and a suit of apparel, and thy victuals. So the Le'vite went in.

11 And the Le'vite was content to dwell with the man; and the young man was unto him as one of his sons.

12 And Mi'cah consecrated the Le'vite; and the young man became his priest, and was in the house of Mi'cah.

13 Then said Mi'cah, Now know I that the LORD will do me good, seeing I have a Le'vite to my priest.

18 IN those days there was no king in Is'ra-el: and in those days the tribe of the Dan'ites sought them an inheritance to dwell in; for unto that day all their inheritance had not fallen unto them among the tribes of Is'ra-el.

2 And the children of Dan sent of their family five men from their coasts, men of valour, from Zo'rah, and from Esh'ta-ol, to spy out the land, and to search it; and they said unto them, Go, search the land: who when they came to mount E'phra-im to the house of Mi'cah, they lodged there.

3 When they *were* by the house of Mi'cah, they knew the voice of the young man the Le'vite: and they turned in thither, and said unto him, Who brought thee hither? and what makest thou in this *place?* and what hast thou here?

4 And he said unto them, Thus and thus dealeth Mi'cah with me, and hath hired me, and I am his priest.

5 And they said unto him, Ask counsel, we pray thee, of God, that we may know whether our way which we go shall be prosperous.

6 And the priest said unto them, Go in peace: before the LORD *is* your way wherein ye go.

7 ¶ Then the five men departed, and came to La'ish, and saw the people that *were* therein, how they dwelt careless, after the manner of the Zi-do'ni-ans, quiet and secure; and *there was* no magistrate in the land, that might put *them* to shame in *any* thing; and they *were* far from the Zi-do'ni-ans, and had no business with *any* man.

8 And they came unto their brethren to Zo'rah and Esh'ta-ol: and their brethren said unto them, What say ye?

9 And they said, Arise, that we may go up against them: for we have seen the land, and, behold, it *is* very good: and *are* ye still? be not slothful to go, *and* to enter to possess the land.

10 When ye go, ye shall come unto a people secure, and to a large land: for God hath given it into your hands; a place where *there is* no want of any thing that *is* in the earth.

11 ¶ And there went from thence of the family of the Dan'ites, out of Zo'rah and out of Esh'ta-ol, six hundred men appointed with weapons of war.

12 And they went up, and pitched in Kir'jath-je'a-rim, in Ju'dah: wherefore they called that place Ma'ha-neh-dan unto this day: behold, *it is* behind Kir'jath-je'a-rim.

13 And they passed thence unto mount E'phra-im, and came unto the house of Mi'cah.

14 ¶ Then answered the five men that went to spy out the country of La'ish, and said unto their brethren, Do ye know that there is in these houses an ephod, and teraphim, and a graven image, and a molten image? now therefore consider what ye have to do.

15 And they turned thitherward, and came to the house of the young man the Le'vite, *even* unto the house of Mi'cah, and saluted him.

16 And the six hundred men appointed with their weapons of war, which *were* of the children of Dan, stood by the entering of the gate.

17 And the five men that went to spy out the land went up, *and* came in thither, *and* took the graven image, and the ephod, and the teraphim, and the molten image: and the priest stood in the entering of the gate with the six hundred men *that were* appointed with weapons of war.

18 And these went into Mi'cah's house, and fetched the carved image, the ephod, and the teraphim, and the molten image. Then said the priest unto them, What do ye?

19 And they said unto him, Hold thy peace, lay thine hand upon thy mouth, and go with us, and be to us a father and a priest: *is it* better for thee to be a priest unto the house of one man, or that thou be a priest unto a tribe and a family in Is'ra-el?

20 And the priest's heart was glad, and he took the ephod, and the teraphim, and the graven image, and went in the midst of the people.

21 So they turned and departed, and put the little ones and the cattle and the carriage before them.

22 ¶ *And* when they were a good way from the house of Mi'cah, the men that *were* in the houses near to Mi'cah's house were gathered together, and overtook the children of Dan.

23 And they cried unto the children of Dan. And they turned their faces, and said unto Mi'cah, What aileth thee, that thou comest with such a company?

24 And he said, Ye have taken away my gods which I made, and the priest, and ye are gone away: and what have I more? and what *is* this *that* ye say unto me, What aileth thee?

25 And the children of Dan said unto him, Let not thy voice be heard among us, lest angry fellows run upon thee, and thou lose thy life, with the lives of thy household.

26 And the children of Dan went their way: and when Mi'cah saw that they *were* too strong for him, he turned and went back unto his house.

27 And they took the *things* which Mi'cah had made, and the priest which he had, and came unto La'ish, unto a people *that were* at quiet and secure: and they smote them with the edge of the sword, and burnt the city with fire.

28 And *there was* no deliverer, because it *was* far from Zi'don, and they had no business with *any* man; and it was in the valley that *lieth* by Beth-re'hob. And they built a city, and dwelt therein.

29 And they called the name of the city Dan, after the name of Dan their father, who was born unto Is'ra-el: howbeit the name of the city *was* La'ish at the first.

30 ¶ And the children of Dan set up the graven image: and Jon'a-than, the son of Ger'shom, the son of Ma-nas'seh, he and his sons were priests to the tribe of Dan until the day of the captivity of the land.

31 And they set them up Mi'cah's graven image, which he made, all the time that the house of God was in Shi'loh.

19 AND it came to pass in those days, when *there was* no king in Is'ra-el, that there was a certain Le'vite sojourning on the side of mount E'phra-im, who took to him a concubine out of Beth'-le-hem-ju'dah.

2 And his concubine played the whore against him, and went away from him unto her father's house to Beth'-le-hem-ju'dah, and was there four whole months.

3 And her husband arose, and went after her, to speak friendly unto her, *and* to bring her again, having his servant with him, and a couple of asses: and she brought him into her father's house: and when the father of the damsel saw him, he rejoiced to meet him.

4 And his father in law, the damsel's father, retained him; and he abode with him three days: so they did eat and drink, and lodged there.

5 ¶ And it came to pass on the fourth day, when they arose early in the morning, that he rose up to depart: and the damsel's father said unto his son in law, Comfort thine heart with a morsel of bread, and afterward go your way.

6 And they sat down, and did eat and drink both of them together: for the damsel's father

had said unto the man, Be content, I pray thee, and tarry all night, and let thine heart be merry.

7 And when the man rose up to depart, his father in law urged him: therefore he lodged there again.

8 And he arose early in the morning on the fifth day to depart: and the damsel's father said, Comfort thine heart, I pray thee. And they tarried until afternoon, and they did eat both of them.

9 And when the man rose up to depart, he, and his concubine, and his servant, his father in law, the damsel's father, said unto him, Behold, now the day draweth toward evening, I pray you tarry all night: behold, the day groweth to an end, lodge here, that thine heart may be merry; and to morrow get you early on your way, that thou mayest go home.

10 But the man would not tarry that night, but he rose up and departed, and came over against Je′bus, which is Je-ru′sa-lem; and there were with him two asses saddled, his concubine also was with him.

11 And when they were by Je′bus, the day was far spent; and the servant said unto his master, Come, I pray thee, and let us turn in into this city of the Jeb′u-sites, and lodge in it.

12 And his master said unto him, We will not turn aside hither into the city of a stranger, that is not of the children of Is′ra-el; we will pass over to Gib′e-ah.

13 And he said unto his servant, Come, and let us draw near to one of these places to lodge all night, in Gib′e-ah, or in Ra′mah.

14 And they passed on and went their way; and the sun went down upon them when they were by Gib′e-ah, which belongeth to Ben′ja-min.

15 And they turned aside thither, to go in and to lodge in Gib′e-ah: and when he went in, he sat him down in a street of the city: for there was no man that took them into his house to lodging.

16 ¶ And, behold, there came an old man from his work out of the field at even, which was also of mount E′phra-im; and he sojourned in Gib′e-ah: but the men of the place were Ben′ja-mites.

17 And when he had lifted up his eyes, he saw a wayfaring man in the street of the city: and the old man said, Whither goest thou? and whence comest thou?

18 And he said unto him, We are passing from Beth′-le-hem-ju′dah toward the side of mount E′phra-im; from thence am I: and I went to Beth′-le-hem-ju′dah, but I am now going to the house of the Lord; and there is no man that receiveth me to house.

19 Yet there is both straw and provender for our asses; and there is bread and wine also for me, and for thy handmaid, and for the young man which is with thy servants: there is no want of any thing.

20 And the old man said, Peace be with thee; howsoever let all thy wants lie upon me; only lodge not in the street.

21 So he brought him into his house, and gave provender unto the asses: and they washed their feet, and did eat and drink.

22 ¶ Now as they were making their hearts merry, behold, the men of the city, certain sons of Be′li-al, beset the house round about, and beat at the door, and spake to the master of the house, the old man, saying, Bring forth the man that came into thine house, that we may know him.

23 And the man, the master of the house, went out unto them, and said unto them, Nay, my brethren, nay, I pray you, do not so wickedly; seeing that this man is come into mine house, do not this folly.

24 Behold, here is my daughter a maiden, and his concubine; them I will bring out now, and humble ye them, and do with them what seemeth good unto you: but unto this man do not so vile a thing.

25 But the men would not hearken to him: so the man took his concubine, and brought her forth unto them; and they knew her, and abused her all the night until the morning: and when the day began to spring, they let her go.

26 Then came the woman in the dawning of the day, and fell down at the door of the man's house where her lord was, till it was light.

27 And her lord rose up in the morning, and opened the doors of the house, and went out to go his way: and, behold, the woman his concubine was fallen down at the door of the house, and her hands were upon the threshold.

28 And he said unto her, Up, and let us be going. But none answered. Then the man took her up upon an ass, and the man rose up, and gat him unto his place.

29 ¶ And when he was come into his house, he took a knife, and laid hold on his concubine, and divided her, together with her bones, into twelve pieces, and sent her into all the coasts of Is′ra-el.

30 And it was so, that all that saw it said, There was no such deed done nor seen from the day that the children of Is′ra-el came up out of the land of E′gypt unto this day: consider of it, take advice, and speak your minds.

20

THEN all the children of Is′ra-el went out, and the congregation was gathered together as one man, from Dan even to Be′er-she′ba, with the land of Gil′e-ad, unto the Lord in Miz′peh.

2 And the chief of all the people, even of all the tribes of Is′ra-el, presented themselves in the assembly of the people of God, four hundred thousand footmen that drew sword.

3 (Now the children of Ben′ja-min heard that the children of Is′ra-el were gone up to Miz′-peh.) Then said the children of Is′ra-el, Tell us, how was this wickedness?

4 And the Le′vite, the husband of the woman that was slain, answered and said, I came into Gib′e-ah that belongeth to Ben′ja-min, I and my concubine, to lodge.

5 And the men of Gib′e-ah rose against me, and beset the house round about upon me by night, and thought to have slain me: and my concubine have they forced, that she is dead.

6 And I took my concubine, and cut her in pieces, and sent her throughout all the country of the inheritance of Is′ra-el: for they have committed lewdness and folly in Is′ra-el.

7 Behold, ye are all children of Is′ra-el; give here your advice and counsel.

8 ¶ And all the people arose as one man, saying, We will not any of us go to his tent, neither will we any of us turn into his house.

9 But now this shall be the thing which we will do to Gib′e-ah; we will go up by lot against it;

10 And we will take ten men of an hundred throughout all the tribes of Is′ra-el, and an hundred of a thousand, and a thousand out of ten thousand, to fetch victual for the people, that they may do, when they come to Gib′e-ah of Ben′ja-min, according to all the folly that they have wrought in Is′ra-el.

11 So all the men of Is′ra-el were gathered against the city, knit together as one man.

12 ¶ And the tribes of Is′ra-el sent men through all the tribe of Ben′ja-min, saying, What wickedness is this that is done among you?

13 Now therefore, deliver us the men, the children of Be′li-al, which are in Gib′e-ah, that we may put them to death, and put away evil from Is′ra-el. But the children of Ben′ja-min would not hearken to the voice of their brethren the children of Is′ra-el:

14 But the children of Ben′ja-min gathered themselves together out of the cities unto Gib′e-ah, to go out to battle against the children of Is′ra-el.

15 And the children of Ben′ja-min were numbered at that time out of the cities twenty and six thousand men that drew sword, beside the inhabitants of Gib′e-ah, which were numbered seven hundred chosen men.

16 Among all this people there were seven hundred chosen men lefthanded; every one could sling stones at an hair breadth, and not miss.

17 And the men of Is′ra-el, beside Ben′ja-min, were numbered four hundred thousand men that drew sword: all these were men of war.

18 ¶ And the children of Is′ra-el arose, and went up to the house of God, and asked counsel of God, and said, Which of us shall go up first to the battle against the children of Ben′ja-min? And the LORD said, Ju′dah shall go up first.

19 And the children of Is′ra-el rose up in the morning, and encamped against Gib′e-ah.

20 And the men of Is′ra-el went out to battle against Ben′ja-min; and the men of Is′ra-el put themselves in array to fight against them at Gib′e-ah.

21 And the children of Ben′ja-min came forth out of Gib′e-ah, and destroyed down to the ground of the Is′ra-el-ites that day twenty and two thousand men.

22 And the people the men of Is′ra-el encouraged themselves, and set their battle again in array in the place where they put themselves in array the first day.

23 (And the children of Is′ra-el went up and wept before the LORD until even, and asked counsel of the LORD, saying, Shall I go up again to battle against the children of Ben′ja-min my brother? And the LORD said, Go up against him.)

24 And the children of Is′ra-el came near against the children of Ben′ja-min the second day.

25 And Ben′ja-min went forth against them out of Gib′e-ah the second day, and destroyed down to the ground of the children of Is′ra-el again eighteen thousand men; all these drew the sword.

26 ¶ Then all the children of Is′ra-el, and all the people, went up, and came unto the house of God, and wept, and sat there before the LORD, and fasted that day until even, and offered burnt offerings and peace offerings before the LORD.

27 And the children of Is′ra-el enquired of the LORD, (for the ark of the covenant of God was there in those days,

28 And Phin′e-has, the son of E-le-a′zar, the son of Aar′on, stood before it in those days,) saying, Shall I yet again go out to battle against the children of Ben′ja-min my brother, or shall I cease? And the LORD said, Go up; for to-morrow I will deliver them into thine hand.

29 And Is′ra-el set liers in wait round about Gib′e-ah.

30 And the children of Is′ra-el went up against the children of Ben′ja-min on the third day, and put themselves in array against Gib′e-ah, as at other times.

31 And the children of Ben′ja-min went out against the people, and were drawn away from the city; and they began to smite of the people, and kill, as at other times, in the highways, of which one goeth up to the house of God, and the other to Gib′e-ah in the field, about thirty men of Is′ra-el.

32 And the children of Ben′ja-min said, They are smitten down before us, as at the first. But the children of Is′ra-el said, Let us flee, and draw them from the city unto the highways.

33 And all the men of Is′ra-el rose up out of their place, and put themselves in array at Ba′-al-ta′mar: and the liers in wait of Is′ra-el came forth out of their places, even out of the meadows of Gib′e-ah.

34 And there came against Gib′e-ah ten thousand chosen men out of all Is′ra-el, and the battle was sore: but they knew not that evil was near them.

35 And the LORD smote Ben′ja-min before Is′ra-el: and the children of Is′ra-el destroyed of the Ben′ja-mites that day twenty and five thousand and an hundred men: all these drew the sword.

36 So the children of Ben′ja-min saw that they were smitten: for the men of Is′ra-el gave place to the Ben′ja-mites, because they trusted unto the liers in wait which they had set beside Gib′e-ah.

37 And the liers in wait hasted, and rushed upon Gib′e-ah; and the liers in wait drew themselves along, and smote all the city with the edge of the sword.

38 Now there was an appointed sign between the men of Is′ra-el and the liers in wait, that they should make a great flame with smoke rise up out of the city.

39 And when the men of Is′ra-el retired in the battle, Ben′ja-min began to smite and kill of the men of Is′ra-el about thirty persons: for they said, Surely they are smitten down before us, as in the first battle.

40 But when the flame began to arise up out of the city with a pillar of smoke, the Ben′ja-mites looked behind them, and, behold, the flame of the city ascended up to heaven.

41 And when the men of Is′ra-el turned again, the men of Ben′ja-min were amazed: for they saw that evil was come upon them.

42 Therefore they turned their backs before the men of Is′ra-el unto the way of the wilderness; but the battle overtook them; and them which came out of the cities they destroyed in the midst of them.

43 Thus they inclosed the Ben′ja-mites round about, and chased them, and trode them down with ease over against Gib′e-ah toward the sunrising.

44 And there fell of Ben′ja-min eighteen thousand men; all these were men of valour.

45 And they turned and fled toward the wilderness unto the rock of Rim′mon: and they gleaned of them in the highways five thousand men; and pursued hard after them unto Gi′dom, and slew two thousand men of them.

46 So that all which fell that day of Ben′ja-min were twenty and five thousand men that drew the sword; all these were men of valour.

47 But six hundred men turned and fled to

the wilderness unto the rock Rim′mon, and abode in the rock Rim′mon four months.

48 And the men of Is′ra-el turned again upon the children of Ben′ja-min, and smote them with the edge of the sword, as well the men of every city, as the beast, and all that came to hand: also they set on fire all the cities that they came to.

21 NOW the men of Is′ra-el had sworn in Miz′peh, saying, There shall not any of us give his daughter unto Ben′ja-min to wife.

2 And the people came to the house of God, and abode there till even before God, and lifted up their voices, and wept sore;

3 And said, O LORD God of Is′ra-el, why is this come to pass in Is′ra-el, that there should be to day one tribe lacking in Is′ra-el?

4 And it came to pass on the morrow, that the people rose early, and built there an altar, and offered burnt offerings and peace offerings.

5 And the children of Is′ra-el said, Who is there among all the tribes of Is′ra-el that came not up with the congregation unto the LORD? For they had made a great oath concerning him that came not up to the LORD to Miz′peh, saying, He shall surely be put to death.

6 And the children of Is′ra-el repented them for Ben′ja-min their brother, and said, There is one tribe cut off from Is′ra-el this day.

7 How shall we do for wives for them that remain, seeing we have sworn by the LORD that we will not give them of our daughters to wives?

8 ¶ And they said, What one is there of the tribes of Is′ra-el that came not up to Miz′peh to the LORD? And, behold, there came none to the camp from Ja′besh-gil′e-ad to the assembly.

9 For the people were numbered, and, behold, there were none of the inhabitants of Ja′-besh-gil′e-ad there.

10 And the congregation sent thither twelve thousand men of the valiantest, and commanded them, saying, Go and smite the inhabitants of Ja′besh-gil′e-ad with the edge of the sword, with the women and the children.

11 And this is the thing that ye shall do, Ye shall utterly destroy every male, and every woman that hath lain by man.

12 And they found among the inhabitants of Ja′besh-gil′e-ad four hundred young virgins, that had known no man by lying with any male: and they brought them unto the camp to Shi′-loh, which is in the land of Ca′naan.

13 And the whole congregation sent some to speak to the children of Ben′ja-min that were in the rock Rim′mon, and to call peaceably unto them.

14 And Ben′ja-min came again at that time; and they gave them wives which they had saved alive of the women of Ja′besh-gil′e-ad: and yet so they sufficed them not.

15 And the people repented them for Ben′ja-min, because that the LORD had made a breach in the tribes of Is′ra-el.

16 ¶ Then the elders of the congregation said, How shall we do for wives for them that remain, seeing the women are destroyed out of Ben′ja-min?

17 And they said, There must be an inheritance for them that be escaped of Ben′ja-min, that a tribe be not destroyed out of Is′ra-el.

18 Howbeit we may not give them wives of our daughters: for the children of Is′ra-el have sworn, saying, Cursed be he that giveth a wife to Ben′ja-min.

19 Then they said, Behold, there is a feast of the LORD in Shi′loh yearly in a place which is on the north side of Beth′-el, on the east side of the highway that goeth up from Beth′-el to She′-chem, and on the south of Le′bo-nah.

20 Therefore they commanded the children of Ben′ja-min, saying, Go and lie in wait in the vineyards;

21 And see, and, behold, if the daughters of Shi′loh come out to dance in dances, then come ye out of the vineyards, and catch you every man his wife of the daughters of Shi′loh, and go to the land of Ben′ja-min.

22 And it shall be, when their fathers or their brethren come unto us to complain, that we will say unto them, Be favourable unto them for our sakes: because we reserved not to each man his wife in the war: for ye did not give unto them at this time, that ye should be guilty.

23 And the children of Ben′ja-min did so, and took them wives, according to their number, of them that danced, whom they caught: and they went and returned unto their inheritance, and repaired the cities, and dwelt in them.

24 And the children of Is′ra-el departed thence at that time, every man to his tribe and to his family, and they went out from thence every man to his inheritance.

25 In those days there was no king in Is′ra-el: every man did that which was right in his own eyes.

THE BOOK OF

RUTH

1 NOW it came to pass in the days when the judges ruled, that there was a famine in the land. And a certain man of Beth′-le-hem-ju′dah went to sojourn in the country of Mo′ab, he, and his wife, and his two sons.

2 And the name of the man was E-lim′e-lech, and the name of his wife Na-o′mi, and the name of his two sons Mah′lon and Chil′i-on, Eph′rath-ites of Beth′-le-hem-ju′dah. And they came into the country of Mo′ab, and continued there.

3 And E-lim′e-lech Na-o′mi's husband died; and she was left, and her two sons.

4 And they took them wives of the women of Mo′ab; the name of the one was Or′pah, and the

name of the other Ruth: and they dwelled there about ten years.

5 And Mah′lon and Chil′i-on died also both of them; and the woman was left of her two sons and her husband.

6 ¶ Then she arose with her daughters in law, that she might return from the country of Mo′ab: for she had heard in the country of Mo′-ab how that the LORD had visited his people in giving them bread.

7 Wherefore she went forth out of the place where she was, and her two daughters in law with her; and they went on the way to return unto the land of Ju′dah.

8 And Na-o′mi said unto her two daughters

in law, Go, return each to her mother's house: the LORD deal kindly with you, as ye have dealt with the dead, and with me.

9 The LORD grant you that ye may find rest, each of you in the house of her husband. Then she kissed them; and they lifted up their voice, and wept.

10 And they said unto her, Surely we will return with thee unto thy people.

11 And Na-o'mi said, Turn again, my daughters: why will ye go with me? are there yet any more sons in my womb, that they may be your husbands?

12 Turn again, my daughters, go your way; for I am too old to have an husband. If I should say, I have hope, if I should have an husband also to night, and should also bear sons;

13 Would ye tarry for them till they were grown? would ye stay for them from having husbands? nay, my daughters; for it grieveth me much for your sakes that the hand of the LORD is gone out against me.

14 And they lifted up their voice, and wept again: and Or'pah kissed her mother in law; but Ruth clave unto her.

15 And she said, Behold, thy sister in law is gone back unto her people, and unto her gods: return thou after thy sister in law.

16 And Ruth said, Intreat me not to leave thee, or to return from following after thee: for whither thou goest, I will go; and where thou lodgest, I will lodge: thy people shall be my people, and thy God my God:

17 Where thou diest, will I die, and there will I be buried: the LORD do so to me, and more also, if ought but death part thee and me.

18 When she saw that she was stedfastly minded to go with her, then she left speaking unto her.

19 ¶ So they two went until they came to Beth'-le-hem. And it came to pass, when they were come to Beth'-le-hem, that all the city was moved about them, and they said, Is this Na-o'mi?

20 And she said unto them, Call me not Na-o'mi, call me Ma'ra: for the Almighty hath dealt very bitterly with me.

21 I went out full, and the LORD hath brought me home again empty: why then call ye me Na-o'mi, seeing the LORD hath testified against me, and the Almighty hath afflicted me?

22 So Na-o'mi returned, and Ruth the Mo'ab-it-ess, her daughter in law, with her, which returned out of the country of Mo'ab: and they came to Beth'-le-hem in the beginning of barley harvest.

2 AND Na-o'mi had a kinsman of her husband's, a mighty man of wealth, of the family of E-lim'e-lech; and his name was Bo'az.

2 And Ruth the Mo'ab-it-ess said unto Na-o'mi, Let me now go to the field, and glean ears of corn after him in whose sight I shall find grace. And she said unto her, Go, my daughter.

3 And she went, and came, and gleaned in the field after the reapers: and her hap was to light on a part of the field belonging unto Bo'az, who was of the kindred of E-lim'e-lech.

4 ¶ And, behold, Bo'az came from Beth'-le-hem, and said unto the reapers, The LORD be with you. And they answered him, The LORD bless thee.

5 Then said Bo'az unto his servant that was set over the reapers, Whose damsel is this?

6 And the servant that was set over the reapers answered and said, It is the Mo'ab-it-ish damsel that came back with Na-o'mi out of the country of Mo'ab:

7 And she said, I pray you, let me glean and gather after the reapers among the sheaves: so she came, and hath continued even from the morning until now, that she tarried a little in the house.

8 Then said Bo'az unto Ruth, Hearest thou not, my daughter? Go not to glean in another field, neither go from hence, but abide here fast by my maidens:

9 Let thine eyes be on the field that they do reap, and go thou after them: have I not charged the young men that they shall not touch thee? and when thou art athirst, go unto the vessels, and drink of that which the young men have drawn.

10 Then she fell on her face, and bowed herself to the ground, and said unto him, Why have I found grace in thine eyes, that thou shouldest take knowledge of me, seeing I am a stranger?

11 And Bo'az answered and said unto her, It hath fully been shewed me, all that thou hast done unto thy mother in law since the death of thine husband: and how thou hast left thy father and thy mother, and the land of thy nativity, and art come unto a people which thou knewest not heretofore.

12 The LORD recompense thy work, and a full reward be given thee of the LORD God of Is'ra-el, under whose wings thou art come to trust.

13 Then she said, Let me find favour in thy sight, my lord; for that thou hast comforted me, and for that thou hast spoken friendly unto thine handmaid, though I be not like unto one of thine handmaidens.

14 And Bo'az said unto her, At mealtime come thou hither, and eat of the bread, and dip thy morsel in the vinegar. And she sat beside the reapers: and he reached her parched corn, and she did eat, and was sufficed, and left.

15 And when she was risen up to glean, Bo'az commanded his young men, saying, Let her glean even among the sheaves, and reproach her not:

16 And let fall also some of the handfuls of purpose for her, and leave them, that she may glean them, and rebuke her not.

17 So she gleaned in the field until even, and beat out that she had gleaned: and it was about an ephah of barley.

18 ¶ And she took it up, and went into the city: and her mother in law saw what she had gleaned: and she brought forth, and gave to her that she had reserved after she was sufficed.

19 And her mother in law said unto her, Where hast thou gleaned to day? and where wroughtest thou? blessed be he that did take knowledge of thee. And she shewed her mother in law with whom she had wrought, and said, The man's name with whom I wrought to day is Bo'az.

20 And Na-o'mi said unto her daughter in law, Blessed be he of the LORD, who hath not left off his kindness to the living and to the dead. And Na-o'mi said unto her, The man is near of kin unto us, one of our next kinsmen.

21 And Ruth the Mo'ab-it-ess said, He said unto me also, Thou shalt keep fast by my young men, until they have ended all my harvest.

22 And Na-o'mi said unto Ruth her daughter in law, It is good, my daughter, that thou go out with his maidens, that they meet thee not in any other field.

23 So she kept fast by the maidens of Bo'az to glean unto the end of barley harvest and of

wheat harvest; and dwelt with her mother in law.

3 THEN Na-o'mi her mother in law said unto her, My daughter, shall I not seek rest for thee, that it may be well with thee?

2 And now is not Bo'az of our kindred, with whose maidens thou wast? Behold, he winnoweth barley to night in the threshingfloor.

3 Wash thyself therefore, and anoint thee, and put thy raiment upon thee, and get thee down to the floor: but make not thyself known unto the man, until he shall have done eating and drinking.

4 And it shall be, when he lieth down, that thou shalt mark the place where he shall lie, and thou shalt go in, and uncover his feet, and lay thee down; and he will tell thee what thou shalt do.

5 And she said unto her, All that thou sayest unto me I will do.

6 ¶ And she went down unto the floor, and did according to all that her mother in law bade her.

7 And when Bo'az had eaten and drunk, and his heart was merry, he went to lie down at the end of the heap of corn: and she came softly, and uncovered his feet, and laid her down.

8 ¶ And it came to pass at midnight, that the man was afraid, and turned himself: and, behold, a woman lay at his feet.

9 And he said, Who art thou? And she answered, I am Ruth thine handmaid: spread therefore thy skirt over thine handmaid; for thou art a near kinsman.

10 And he said, Blessed be thou of the LORD, my daughter: for thou hast shewed more kindness in the latter end than at the beginning, inasmuch as thou followedst not young men, whether poor or rich.

11 And now, my daughter, fear not; I will do to thee all that thou requirest: for all the city of my people doth know that thou art a virtuous woman.

12 And now it is true that I am thy near kinsman: howbeit there is a kinsman nearer than I.

13 Tarry this night, and it shall be in the morning, that if he will perform unto thee the part of a kinsman, well; let him do the kinsman's part: but if he will not do the part of a kinsman to thee, then will I do the part of a kinsman to thee, as the LORD liveth: lie down until the morning.

14 ¶ And she lay at his feet until the morning: and she rose up before one could know another. And he said, Let it not be known that a woman came into the floor.

15 Also he said, Bring the veil that thou hast upon thee, and hold it. And when she held it, he measured six measures of barley, and laid it on her: and she went into the city.

16 And when she came to her mother in law, she said, Who art thou, my daughter? And she told her all that the man had done to her.

17 And she said, These six measures of barley gave he me; for he said to me, Go not empty unto thy mother in law.

18 Then said she, Sit still, my daughter, until thou know how the matter will fall: for the man will not be in rest, until he have finished the thing this day.

4 THEN went Bo'az up to the gate, and sat him down there: and, behold, the kinsman of whom Bo'az spake came by; unto whom he said, Ho, such a one! turn aside, sit down here. And he turned aside, and sat down.

2 And he took ten men of the elders of the city, and said, Sit ye down here. And they sat down.

3 And he said unto the kinsman, Na-o'mi, that is come again out of the country of Mo'ab, selleth a parcel of land, which was our brother E-lim'e-lech's:

4 And I thought to advertise thee, saying, Buy it before the inhabitants, and before the elders of my people. If thou wilt redeem it, redeem it: but if thou wilt not redeem it, then tell me, that I may know: for there is none to redeem it beside thee; and I am after thee. And he said, I will redeem it.

5 Then said Bo'az, What day thou buyest the field of the hand of Na-o'mi, thou must buy it also of Ruth the Mo'ab-it-ess, the wife of the dead, to raise up the name of the dead upon his inheritance.

6 ¶ And the kinsman said, I cannot redeem it for myself, lest I mar mine own inheritance: redeem thou my right to thyself; for I cannot redeem it.

7 Now this was the manner in former time in Is'ra-el concerning redeeming and concerning changing, for to confirm all things; a man plucked off his shoe, and gave it to his neighbour: and this was a testimony in Is'ra-el.

8 Therefore the kinsman said unto Bo'az, Buy it for thee. So he drew off his shoe.

9 ¶ And Bo'az said unto the elders, and unto all the people, Ye are witnesses this day, that I have bought all that was E-lim'e-lech's, and all that was Chil'i-on's and Mah'lon's, of the hand of Na-o'mi.

10 Moreover Ruth the Mo'ab-it-ess, the wife of Mah'lon, have I purchased to be my wife, to raise up the name of the dead upon his inheritance, that the name of the dead be not cut off from among his brethren, and from the gate of his place: ye are witnesses this day.

11 And all the people that were in the gate, and the elders, said, We are witnesses. The LORD make the woman that is come into thine house like Ra'chel and like Le'ah, which two did build the house of Is'ra-el: and do thou worthily in Eph'ra-tah, and be famous in Beth'-le-hem:

12 And let thy house be like the house of Pha'rez, whom Ta'mar bare unto Ju'dah, of the seed which the LORD shall give thee of this young woman.

13 ¶ So Bo'az took Ruth, and she was his wife: and when he went in unto her, the LORD gave her conception, and she bare a son.

14 And the women said unto Na-o'mi, Blessed be the LORD, which hath not left thee this day without a kinsman, that his name may be famous in Is'ra-el.

15 And he shall be unto thee a restorer of thy life, and a nourisher of thine old age: for thy daughter in law, which loveth thee, which is better to thee than seven sons, hath born him.

16 And Na-o'mi took the child, and laid it in her bosom, and became nurse unto it.

17 And the women her neighbours gave it a name, saying, There is a son born to Na-o'mi; and they called his name O'bed: he is the father of Jes'se, the father of Da'vid.

18 ¶ Now these are the generations of Pha'rez: Pha'rez begat Hez'ron,

19 And Hez'ron begat Ram, and Ram begat Am-min'a-dab,

20 And Am-min'a-dab begat Nah'shon, and Nah'shon begat Sal'mon,

21 And Sal'mon begat Bo'az, and Bo'az begat O'bed,

22 And O'bed begat Jes'se, and Jes'se begat Da'vid.

SAMUEL

1 NOW there was a certain man of Ra-math-a'im-zo'phim, of mount E'phra-im, and his name was El'ka-nah, the son of Jer'o-ham, the son of E-li'hu, the son of To'hu, the son of Zuph, an Eph'rath-ite:

2 And he had two wives; the name of the one was Han'nah, and the name of the other Pe-nin'nah: and Pe-nin'nah had children, but Han'nah had no children.

3 And this man went up out of his city yearly to worship and to sacrifice unto the LORD of hosts in Shi'loh: And the two sons of E'li, Hoph'ni and Phin'e-has, the priests of the LORD, were there.

4 ¶ And when the time was that El'ka-nah offered, he gave to Pe-nin'nah his wife, and to all her sons and her daughters, portions:

5 But unto Han'nah he gave a worthy portion; for he loved Han'nah: but the LORD had shut up her womb.

6 And her adversary also provoked her sore, for to make her fret, because the LORD had shut up her womb.

7 And as he did so year by year, when she went up to the house of the LORD, so she provoked her; therefore she wept, and did not eat.

8 Then said El'ka-nah her husband to her, Han'nah, why weepest thou? and why eatest thou not? and why is thy heart grieved? am not I better to thee than ten sons?

9 ¶ So Han'nah rose up after they had eaten in Shi'loh, and after they had drunk. Now E'li the priest sat upon a seat by a post of the temple of the LORD.

10 And she was in bitterness of soul, and prayed unto the LORD, and wept sore.

11 And she vowed a vow, and said, O LORD of hosts, if thou wilt indeed look on the affliction of thine handmaid, and remember me, and not forget thine handmaid, but wilt give unto thine handmaid a man child, then I will give him unto the LORD all the days of his life, and there shall no razor come upon his head.

12 And it came to pass, as she continued praying before the LORD, that E'li marked her mouth.

13 Now Han'nah, she spake in her heart; only her lips moved, but her voice was not heard: therefore E'li thought she had been drunken.

14 And E'li said unto her, How long wilt thou be drunken? put away thy wine from thee.

15 And Han'nah answered and said, No, my lord, I am a woman of a sorrowful spirit: I have drunk neither wine nor strong drink, but have poured out my soul before the LORD.

16 Count not thine handmaid for a daughter of Be'li-al: for out of the abundance of my complaint and grief have I spoken hitherto.

17 Then E'li answered and said, Go in peace: and the God of Is'ra-el grant thee thy petition that thou hast asked of him.

18 And she said, Let thine handmaid find grace in thy sight. So the woman went her way, and did eat, and her countenance was no more sad.

19 ¶ And they rose up in the morning early, and worshipped before the LORD, and returned, and came to their house to Ra'mah: and El'ka-nah knew Han'nah his wife; and the LORD remembered her.

20 Wherefore it came to pass, when the time was come about after Han'nah had conceived, that she bare a son, and called his name Sam'u-el, saying, Because I have asked him of the LORD.

21 And the man El'ka-nah, and all his house, went up to offer unto the LORD the yearly sacrifice, and his vow.

22 But Han'nah went not up; for she said unto her husband, I will not go up until the child be weaned, and then I will bring him, that he may appear before the LORD, and there abide for ever.

23 And El'ka-nah her husband said unto her, Do what seemeth thee good; tarry until thou have weaned him; only the LORD establish his word. So the woman abode, and gave her son suck until she weaned him.

24 ¶ And when she had weaned him, she took him up with her, with three bullocks, and one ephah of flour, and a bottle of wine, and brought him unto the house of the LORD in Shi'loh: and the child was young.

25 And they slew a bullock, and brought the child to E'li.

26 And she said, Oh my lord, as thy soul liveth, my lord, I am the woman that stood by thee here, praying unto the LORD.

27 For this child I prayed; and the LORD hath given me my petition which I asked of him:

28 Therefore also I have lent him to the LORD; as long as he liveth he shall be lent to the LORD. And he worshipped the LORD there.

2 AND Han'nah prayed, and said, My heart rejoiceth in the LORD, mine horn is exalted in the LORD: my mouth is enlarged over mine enemies; because I rejoice in thy salvation.

2 There is none holy as the LORD: for there is none beside thee: neither is there any rock like our God.

3 Talk no more so exceeding proudly; let not arrogancy come out of your mouth: for the LORD is a God of knowledge, and by him actions are weighed.

4 The bows of the mighty men are broken, and they that stumbled are girded with strength.

5 They that were full have hired out themselves for bread; and they that were hungry ceased: so that the barren hath born seven; and she that hath many children is waxed feeble.

6 The LORD killeth, and maketh alive: he bringeth down to the grave, and bringeth up.

7 The LORD maketh poor, and maketh rich: he bringeth low, and lifteth up.

8 He raiseth up the poor out of the dust, and lifteth up the beggar from the dunghill, to set them among princes, and to make them inherit the throne of glory: for the pillars of the earth are the LORD's, and he hath set the world upon them.

9 He will keep the feet of his saints, and the wicked shall be silent in darkness; for by strength shall no man prevail.

10 The adversaries of the LORD shall be broken to pieces; out of heaven shall he thunder upon them: the LORD shall judge the ends of the earth; and he shall give strength unto his king, and exalt the horn of his anointed.

11 And El'ka-nah went to Ra'mah to his house. And the child did minister unto the LORD before E'li the priest.

12 ¶ Now the sons of E'li were sons of Be'li-al; they knew not the LORD.

13 And the priest's custom with the people was, that, when any man offered sacrifice, the priest's servant came, while the flesh was in seething, with a fleshhook of three teeth in his hand;

14 And he struck it into the pan, or kettle, or caldron, or pot; all that the fleshhook brought up the priest took for himself. So they did in Shi'loh unto all the Is'ra-el-ites that came thither.

15 Also before they burnt the fat, the priest's servant came, and said to the man that sacrificed, Give flesh to roast for the priest; for he will not have sodden flesh of thee, but raw.

16 And if any man said unto him, Let them not fail to burn the fat presently, and then take as much as thy soul desireth; then he would answer him, Nay; but thou shalt give it me now: and if not, I will take it by force.

17 Wherefore the sin of the young men was very great before the LORD: for men abhorred the offering of the LORD.

18 ¶ But Sam'u-el ministered before the LORD, being a child, girded with a linen ephod.

19 Moreover his mother made him a little coat, and brought it to him from year to year, when she came up with her husband to offer the yearly sacrifice.

20 ¶ And E'li blessed El'ka-nah and his wife, and said, The LORD give thee seed of this woman for the loan which is lent to the LORD. And they went unto their own home.

21 And the LORD visited Han'nah, so that she conceived, and bare three sons and two daughters. And the child Sam'u-el grew before the LORD.

22 ¶ Now E'li was very old, and heard all that his sons did unto all Is'ra-el; and how they lay with the women that assembled at the door of the tabernacle of the congregation.

23 And he said unto them, Why do ye such things? for I hear of your evil dealings by all this people.

24 Nay, my sons; for it is no good report that I hear: ye make the LORD's people to transgress.

25 If one man sin against another, the judge shall judge him: but if a man sin against the LORD, who shall intreat for him? Notwithstanding they hearkened not unto the voice of their father, because the LORD would slay them.

26 And the child Sam'u-el grew on, and was in favour both with the LORD, and also with men.

27 ¶ And there came a man of God unto E'li, and said unto him, Thus saith the LORD, Did I plainly appear unto the house of thy father, when they were in E'gypt in Pha'raoh's house?

28 And did I choose him out of all the tribes of Is'ra-el to be my priest, to offer upon mine altar, to burn incense, to wear an ephod before me? and did I give unto the house of thy father all the offerings made by fire of the children of Is'ra-el?

29 Wherefore kick ye at my sacrifice and at mine offering, which I have commanded in my habitation; and honourest thy sons above me, to make yourselves fat with the chiefest of all the offerings of Is'ra-el my people?

30 Wherefore the LORD God of Is'ra-el saith, I said indeed that thy house, and the house of thy father, should walk before me for ever: but now the LORD saith, Be it far from me; for them that honour me I will honour, and they that despise me shall be lightly esteemed.

31 Behold, the days come, that I will cut off

thine arm, and the arm of thy father's house, that there shall not be an old man in thine house.

32 And thou shalt see an enemy in my habitation, in all the wealth which God shall give Is'ra-el: and there shall not be an old man in thine house for ever.

33 And the man of thine, whom I shall not cut off from mine altar, shall be to consume thine eyes, and to grieve thine heart: and all the increase of thine house shall die in the flower of their age.

34 And this shall be a sign unto thee, that shall come upon thy sons, on Hoph'ni and Phin'-e-has; in one day they shall die both of them.

35 And I will raise me up a faithful priest, that shall do according to that which is in mine heart and in my mind: and I will build him a sure house; and he shall walk before mine anointed for ever.

36 And it shall come to pass, that every one that is left in thine house shall come and crouch to him for a piece of silver and a morsel of bread, and shall say, Put me, I pray thee, into one of the priests' offices, that I may eat a piece of bread.

3 AND the child Sam'u-el ministered unto the LORD before E'li. And the word of the LORD was precious in those days; there was no open vision.

2 And it came to pass at that time, when E'li was laid down in his place, and his eyes began to wax dim, that he could not see;

3 And ere the lamp of God went out in the temple of the LORD, where the ark of God was, and Sam'u-el was laid down to sleep;

4 That the LORD called Sam'u-el: and he answered, Here am I.

5 And he ran unto E'li, and said, Here am I; for thou calledst me. And he said, I called not; lie down again. And he went and lay down.

6 And the LORD called yet again, Sam'u-el. And Sam'u-el arose and went to E'li, and said, Here am I; for thou didst call me. And he answered, I called not, my son; lie down again.

7 Now Sam'u-el did not yet know the LORD, neither was the word of the LORD yet revealed unto him.

8 And the LORD called Sam'u-el again the third time. And he arose and went to E'li, and said, Here am I; for thou didst call me. And E'li perceived that the LORD had called the child.

9 Therefore E'li said unto Sam'u-el, Go, lie down: and it shall be, if he call thee, that thou shalt say, Speak, LORD; for thy servant heareth. So Sam'u-el went and lay down in his place.

10 And the LORD came, and stood, and called as at other times, Sam'u-el, Sam'u-el. Then Sam'u-el answered, Speak; for thy servant heareth.

11 ¶ And the LORD said to Sam'u-el, Behold, I will do a thing in Is'ra-el, at which both the ears of every one that heareth it shall tingle.

12 In that day I will perform against E'li all things which I have spoken concerning his house: when I begin, I will also make an end.

13 For I have told him that I will judge his house for ever for the iniquity which he knoweth; because his sons made themselves vile, and he restrained them not.

14 And therefore I have sworn unto the house of E'li, that the iniquity of E'li's house shall not be purged with sacrifice nor offering for ever.

15 ¶ And Sam'u-el lay until the morning, and

opened the doors of the house of the LORD. And Sam'u-el feared to shew E'li the vision.

16 Then E'li called Sam'u-el, and said, Sam'u-el, my son. And he answered, Here *am* I.

17 And he said, What *is* the thing that the LORD hath said unto thee? I pray thee hide *it* not from me: God do so to thee, and more also, if thou hide *any* thing from me of all the things that he said unto thee.

18 And Sam'u-el told him every whit, and hid nothing from him. And he said, It *is* the LORD: let him do what seemeth him good.

19 ¶ And Sam'u-el grew, and the LORD was with him, and did let none of his words fall to the ground.

20 And all Is'ra-el from Dan even to Be'er-she'ba knew that Sam'u-el *was* established to be a prophet of the LORD.

21 And the LORD appeared again in Shi'loh: for the LORD revealed himself to Sam'u-el in Shi'loh by the word of the LORD.

4 AND the word of Sam'u-el came to all Is'ra-el. Now Is'ra-el went out against the Phi-lis'tines to battle, and pitched beside Eb'en-e'zer: and the Phi-lis'tines pitched in A'phek.

2 And the Phi-lis'tines put themselves in array against Is'ra-el: and when they joined battle, Is'ra-el was smitten before the Phi-lis'tines: and they slew of the army in the field about four thousand men.

3 ¶ And when the people were come into the camp, the elders of Is'ra-el said, Wherefore hath the LORD smitten us to day before the Phi-lis'tines? Let us fetch the ark of the covenant of the LORD out of Shi'loh unto us, that, when it cometh among us, it may save us out of the hand of our enemies.

4 So the people sent to Shi'loh, that they might bring from thence the ark of the covenant of the LORD of hosts, which dwelleth *between* the cherubims: and the two sons of E'li, Hoph'ni and Phin'e-has, *were* there with the ark of the covenant of God.

5 And when the ark of the covenant of the LORD came into the camp, all Is'ra-el shouted with a great shout, so that the earth rang again.

6 And when the Phi-lis'tines heard the noise of the shout, they said, What *meaneth* the noise of this great shout in the camp of the He'brews? And they understood that the ark of the LORD was come into the camp.

7 And the Phi-lis'tines were afraid, for they said, God is come into the camp. And they said, Woe unto us! for there hath not been such a thing heretofore.

8 Woe unto us! who shall deliver us out of the hand of these mighty Gods? these *are* the Gods that smote the E-gyp'tians with all the plagues in the wilderness.

9 Be strong, and quit yourselves like men, O ye Phi-lis'tines, that ye be not servants unto the He'brews, as they have been to you: quit yourselves like men, and fight.

10 ¶ And the Phi-lis'tines fought, and Is'ra-el was smitten, and they fled every man into his tent: and there was a very great slaughter; for there fell of Is'ra-el thirty thousand footmen.

11 And the ark of God was taken; and the two sons of E'li, Hoph'ni and Phin'e-has, were slain.

12 ¶ And there ran a man of Ben'ja-min out of the army, and came to Shi'loh the same day with his clothes rent, and with earth upon his head.

13 And when he came, lo, E'li sat upon a seat by the wayside watching: for his heart trembled for the ark of God. And when the man came into the city, and told *it,* all the city cried out.

14 And when E'li heard the noise of the crying, he said, What *meaneth* the noise of this tumult? And the man came in hastily, and told E'li.

15 Now E'li was ninety and eight years old; and his eyes were dim, that he could not see.

16 And the man said unto E'li, I *am* he that came out of the army, and I fled to day out of the army. And he said, What is there done, my son?

17 And the messenger answered and said, Is'ra-el is fled before the Phi-lis'tines, and there hath been also a great slaughter among the people, and thy two sons also, Hoph'ni and Phin'e-has, are dead, and the ark of God is taken.

18 And it came to pass, when he made mention of the ark of God, that he fell from off the seat backward by the side of the gate, and his neck brake, and he died: for he was an old man, and heavy. And he had judged Is'ra-el forty years.

19 ¶ And his daughter in law, Phin'e-has' wife, was with child, *near* to be delivered: and when she heard the tidings that the ark of God was taken, and that her father in law and her husband were dead, she bowed herself and travailed; for her pains came upon her.

20 And about the time of her death the women that stood by her said unto her, Fear not; for thou hast born a son. But she answered not, neither did she regard *it.*

21 And she named the child I'-cha-bod, saying, The glory is departed from Is'ra-el: because the ark of God was taken, and because of her father in law and her husband.

22 And she said, The glory is departed from Is'ra-el: for the ark of God is taken.

5 AND the Phi-lis'tines took the ark of God, and brought it from Eb'en-e'zer unto Ash'-dod.

2 When the Phi-lis'tines took the ark of God, they brought it into the house of Da'gon, and set it by Da'gon.

3 ¶ And when they of Ash'dod arose early on the morrow, behold, Da'gon *was* fallen upon his face to the earth before the ark of the LORD. And they took Da'gon, and set him in his place again.

4 And when they arose early on the morrow morning, behold, Da'gon *was* fallen upon his face to the ground before the ark of the LORD; and the head of Da'gon and both the palms of his hands *were* cut off upon the threshold; only *the stump of* Da'gon was left to him.

5 Therefore neither the priests of Da'gon, nor any that come into Da'gon's house, tread on the threshold of Da'gon in Ash'dod unto this day.

6 But the hand of the LORD was heavy upon them of Ash'dod, and he destroyed them, and smote them with emerods, *even* Ash'dod and the coasts thereof.

7 And when the men of Ash'dod saw that *it was* so, they said, The ark of the God of Is'ra-el shall not abide with us: for his hand is sore upon us, and upon Da'gon our god.

8 They sent therefore and gathered all the lords of the Phi-lis'tines unto them, and said, What shall we do with the ark of the God of Is'ra-el? And they answered, Let the ark of the God of Is'ra-el be carried about unto Gath. And they carried the ark of the God of Is'ra-el about *thither.*

9 And it was *so,* that, after they had carried it about, the hand of the LORD was against the

city with a very great destruction: and he smote the men of the city, both small and great, and they had emerods in their secret parts.

10 ¶ Therefore they sent the ark of God to Ek'ron. And it came to pass, as the ark of God came to Ek'ron, that the Ek'ron-ites cried out, saying, They have brought about the ark of the God of Is'ra-el to us, to slay us and our people.

11 So they sent and gathered together all the lords of the Phi-lis'tines, and said, Send away the ark of the God of Is'ra-el, and let it go again to his own place, that it slay us not, and our people: for there was a deadly destruction throughout all the city; the hand of God was very heavy there.

12 And the men that died not were smitten with the emerods: and the cry of the city went up to heaven.

6 AND the ark of the LORD was in the country of the Phi-lis'tines seven months.

2 And the Phi-lis'tines called for the priests and the diviners, saying, What shall we do to the ark of the LORD? tell us wherewith we shall send it to his place.

3 And they said, If ye send away the ark of the God of Is'ra-el, send it not empty; but in any wise return him a trespass offering: then ye shall be healed, and it shall be known to you why his hand is not removed from you.

4 Then said they, What shall be the trespass offering which we shall return to him? They answered, Five golden emerods, and five golden mice, according to the number of the lords of the Phi-lis'tines: for one plague was on you all, and on your lords.

5 Wherefore ye shall make images of your emerods, and images of your mice that mar the land; and ye shall give glory unto the God of Is'ra-el: peradventure he will lighten his hand from off you, and from off your gods, and from off your land.

6 Wherefore then do ye harden your hearts, as the E-gyp'tians and Pha'raoh hardened their hearts? when he had wrought wonderfully among them, did they not let the people go, and they departed?

7 Now therefore make a new cart, and take two milch kine, on which there hath come no yoke, and tie the kine to the cart, and bring their calves home from them:

8 And take the ark of the LORD, and lay it upon the cart; and put the jewels of gold, which ye return him for a trespass offering, in a coffer by the side thereof; and send it away, that it may go.

9 And see, if it goeth up by the way of his own coast to Beth-she'mesh, then he hath done us this great evil: but if not, then we shall know that it is not his hand that smote us; it was a chance that happened to us.

10 ¶ And the men did so; and took two milch kine, and tied them to the cart, and shut up their calves at home:

11 And they laid the ark of the LORD upon the cart, and the coffer with the mice of gold and the images of their emerods.

12 And the kine took the straight way to the way of Beth-she'mesh, and went along the highway, lowing as they went, and turned not aside to the right hand or to the left; and the lords of the Phi-lis'tines went after them unto the border of Beth-she'mesh.

13 And they of Beth-she'mesh were reaping their wheat harvest in the valley: and they lifted up their eyes, and saw the ark, and rejoiced to see it.

14 And the cart came into the field of Josh'u-a, a Beth-she'mite, and stood there, where there was a great stone: and they clave the wood of the cart, and offered the kine a burnt offering unto the LORD.

15 And the Le'vites took down the ark of the LORD, and the coffer that was with it, wherein the jewels of gold were, and put them on the great stone: and the men of Beth-she'mesh offered burnt offerings and sacrificed sacrifices the same day unto the LORD.

16 And when the five lords of the Phi-lis'tines had seen it, they returned to Ek'ron the same day.

17 And these are the golden emerods which the Phi-lis'tines returned for a trespass offering unto the LORD; for Ash'dod one, for Ga'za one, for As'ke-lon one, for Gath one, for Ek'ron one;

18 And the golden mice, according to the number of all the cities of the Phi-lis'tines belonging to the five lords, both of fenced cities, and of country villages, even unto the great stone of A'bel, whereon they set down the ark of the LORD: which stone remaineth unto this day in the field of Josh'u-a, the Beth-she'mite.

19 ¶ And he smote the men of Beth-she'mesh, because they had looked into the ark of the LORD, even he smote of the people fifty thousand and threescore and ten men: and the people lamented, because the LORD had smitten many of the people with a great slaughter.

20 And the men of Beth-she'mesh said, Who is able to stand before this holy LORD God? and to whom shall he go up from us?

21 ¶ And they sent messengers to the inhabitants of Kir'jath-je'a-rim, saying, The Phi-lis'-tines have brought again the ark of the LORD; come ye down, and fetch it up to you.

7 AND the men of Kir'jath-je'a-rim came, and fetched up the ark of the LORD, and brought it into the house of A-bin'a-dab in the hill, and sanctified E-le-a'zar his son to keep the ark of the LORD.

2 And it came to pass, while the ark abode in Kir'jath-je'a-rim, that the time was long; for it was twenty years: and all the house of Is'ra-el lamented after the LORD.

3 ¶ And Sam'u-el spake unto all the house of Is'ra-el, saying, If ye do return unto the LORD with all your hearts, then put away the strange gods and Ash'ta-roth from among you, and prepare your hearts unto the LORD, and serve him only: and he will deliver you out of the hand of the Phi-lis'tines.

4 Then the children of Is'ra-el did put away Ba'al-im and Ash'ta-roth, and served the LORD only.

5 And Sam'u-el said, Gather all Is'ra-el to Miz'peh, and I will pray for you unto the LORD.

6 And they gathered together to Miz'peh, and drew water, and poured it out before the LORD, and fasted on that day, and said there, We have sinned against the LORD. And Sam'u-el judged the children of Is'ra-el in Miz'peh.

7 And when the Phi-lis'tines heard that the children of Is'ra-el were gathered together to Miz'peh, the lords of the Phi-lis'tines went up against Is'ra-el. And when the children of Is'ra-el heard it, they were afraid of the Phi-lis'tines.

8 And the children of Is'ra-el said to Sam'u-el, Cease not to cry unto the LORD our God for us, that he will save us out of the hand of the Phi-lis'tines.

9 ¶ And Sam'u-el took a sucking lamb, and offered it for a burnt offering wholly unto the

LORD: and Sam'u-el cried unto the LORD for Is'-ra-el; and the LORD heard him.

10 And as Sam'u-el was offering up the burnt offering, the Phi-lis'tines drew near to battle against Is'ra-el: but the LORD thundered with a great thunder on that day upon the Phi-lis'tines, and discomfited them; and they were smitten before Is'ra-el.

11 And the men of Is'ra-el went out of Miz'-peh, and pursued the Phi-lis'tines, and smote them, until they came under Beth'-car.

12 Then Sam'u-el took a stone, and set it between Miz'peh and Shen, and called the name of it Eb'en-e'zer, saying, Hitherto hath the LORD helped us.

13 ¶ So the Phi-lis'tines were subdued, and they came no more into the coast of Is'ra-el: and the hand of the LORD was against the Phi-lis'tines all the days of Sam'u-el.

14 And the cities which the Phi-lis'tines had taken from Is'ra-el were restored to Is'ra-el, from Ek'ron even unto Gath; and the coasts thereof did Is'ra-el deliver out of the hands of the Phi-lis'tines. And there was peace between Is'ra-el and the Am'or-ites.

15 And Sam'u-el judged Is'ra-el all the days of his life.

16 And he went from year to year in circuit to Beth'-el, and Gil'gal, and Miz'peh, and judged Is'ra-el in all those places.

17 And his return was to Ra'mah; for there was his house; and there he judged Is'ra-el; and there he built an altar unto the LORD.

8 AND it came to pass, when Sam'u-el was old, that he made his sons judges over Is'-ra-el.

2 Now the name of his firstborn was Jo'el; and the name of his second, A-bi'ah: they were judges in Be'er-she'ba.

3 And his sons walked not in his ways, but turned aside after lucre, and took bribes, and perverted judgment.

4 Then all the elders of Is'ra-el gathered themselves together, and came to Sam'u-el unto Ra'mah,

5 And said unto him, Behold, thou art old, and thy sons walk not in thy ways: now make us a king to judge us like all the nations.

6 ¶ But the thing displeased Sam'u-el, when they said, Give us a king to judge us. And Sam'-u-el prayed unto the LORD.

7 And the LORD said unto Sam'u-el, Hearken unto the voice of the people in all that they say unto thee: for they have not rejected thee, but they have rejected me, that I should not reign over them.

8 According to all the works which they have done since the day that I brought them up out of E'gypt even unto this day, wherewith they have forsaken me, and served other gods, so do they also unto thee.

9 Now therefore hearken unto their voice: howbeit yet protest solemnly unto them, and shew them the manner of the king that shall reign over them.

10 ¶ And Sam'u-el told all the words of the LORD unto the people that asked of him a king.

11 And he said, This will be the manner of the king that shall reign over you: He will take your sons, and appoint them for himself, for his chariots, and to be his horsemen; and some shall run before his chariots.

12 And he will appoint him captains over thousands, and captains over fifties; and will set them to ear his ground, and to reap his harvest, and to make his instruments of war, and instruments of his chariots.

13 And he will take your daughters to be confectionaries, and to be cooks, and to be bakers.

14 And he will take your fields, and your vineyards, and your oliveyards, even the best of them, and give them to his servants.

15 And he will take the tenth of your seed, and of your vineyards, and give to his officers, and to his servants.

16 And he will take your menservants, and your maidservants, and your goodliest young men, and your asses, and put them to his work.

17 He will take the tenth of your sheep: and ye shall be his servants.

18 And ye shall cry out in that day because of your king which ye shall have chosen you; and the LORD will not hear you in that day.

19 ¶ Nevertheless the people refused to obey the voice of Sam'u-el; and they said, Nay; but we will have a king over us;

20 That we also may be like all the nations; and that our king may judge us, and go out before us, and fight our battles.

21 And Sam'u-el heard all the words of the people, and he rehearsed them in the ears of the LORD.

22 And the LORD said to Sam'u-el, Hearken unto their voice, and make them a king. And Sam'u-el said unto the men of Is'ra-el, Go ye every man unto his city.

9 NOW there was a man of Ben'ja-min, whose name was Kish, the son of A-bi'el, the son of Ze'ror, the son of Be-cho'rath, the son of A-phi'ah, a Ben'ja-mite, a mighty man of power.

2 And he had a son, whose name was Saul, a choice young man, and a goodly: and there was not among the children of Is'ra-el a goodlier person than he: from his shoulders and upward he was higher than any of the people.

3 And the asses of Kish Saul's father were lost. And Kish said to Saul his son, Take now one of the servants with thee, and arise, go seek the asses.

4 And he passed through mount E'phra-im, and passed through the land of Shal'i-sha, but they found them not: then they passed through the land of Sha'lim, and there they were not: and he passed through the land of the Ben'ja-mites, but they found them not.

5 And when they were come to the land of Zuph, Saul said to his servant that was with him, Come, and let us return; lest my father leave caring for the asses, and take thought for us.

6 And he said unto him, Behold now, there is in this city a man of God, and he is an honourable man; all that he saith cometh surely to pass: now let us go thither; peradventure he can shew us our way that we should go.

7 Then said Saul to his servant, But, behold, if we go, what shall we bring the man? for the bread is spent in our vessels, and there is not a present to bring to the man of God: what have we?

8 And the servant answered Saul again, and said, Behold, I have here at hand the fourth part of a shekel of silver: that will I give to the man of God, to tell us our way.

9 (Beforetime in Is'ra-el, when a man went to enquire of God, thus he spake, Come, and let us go to the seer: for he that is now called a Prophet was beforetime called a Seer.)

10 Then said Saul to his servant, Well said;

come, let us go. So they went unto the city where the man of God *was*.

11 ¶ *And* as they went up the hill to the city, they found young maidens going out to draw water, and said unto them, Is the seer here?

12 And they answered them, and said, He is; behold, *he is* before you: make haste now, for he came to day to the city; for *there is* a sacrifice of the people to day in the high place:

13 As soon as ye be come into the city, ye shall straightway find him, before he go up to the high place to eat: for the people will not eat until he come, because he doth bless the sacrifice; *and* afterwards they eat that be bidden. Now therefore get you up; for about this time ye shall find him.

14 And they went up into the city: *and* when they were come into the city, behold, Sam'u-el came out against them, for to go up to the high place.

15 ¶ Now the LORD had told Sam'u-el in his ear a day before Saul came, saying,

16 To morrow about this time I will send thee a man out of the land of Ben'ja-min, and thou shalt anoint him *to be* captain over my people Is'ra-el, that he may save my people out of the hand of the Phi-lis'tines: for I have looked upon my people, because their cry is come unto me.

17 And when Sam'u-el saw Saul, the LORD said unto him, Behold the man whom I spake to thee of! this same shall reign over my people.

18 Then Saul drew near to Sam'u-el in the gate, and said, Tell me, I pray thee, where the seer's house *is*.

19 And Sam'u-el answered Saul, and said, I *am* the seer: go up before me unto the high place; for ye shall eat with me to day, and to morrow I will let thee go, and will tell thee all that *is* in thine heart.

20 And as for thine asses that were lost three days ago, set not thy mind on them; for they are found. And on whom *is* all the desire of Is'ra-el? *Is it* not on thee, and on all thy father's house?

21 And Saul answered and said, *Am* not I a Ben'ja-mite, of the smallest of the tribes of Is'ra-el? and my family the least of all the families of the tribe of Ben'ja-min? wherefore then speakest thou so to me?

22 And Sam'u-el took Saul and his servant, and brought them into the parlour, and made them sit in the chiefest place among them that were bidden, which *were* about thirty persons.

23 And Sam'u-el said unto the cook, Bring the portion which I gave thee, of which I said unto thee, Set it by thee.

24 And the cook took up the shoulder, and *that* which *was* upon it, and set *it* before Saul. And Sam'u-el said, Behold that which is left! set *it* before thee, *and* eat: for unto this time hath it been kept for thee since I said, I have invited the people. So Saul did eat with Sam'u-el that day.

25 ¶ And when they were come down from the high place into the city, Sam'u-el communed with Saul upon the top of the house.

26 And they arose early: and it came to pass about the spring of the day, that Sam'u-el called Saul to the top of the house, saying, Up, that I may send thee away. And Saul arose, and they went out both of them, he and Sam'u-el, abroad.

27 *And* as they were going down to the end of the city, Sam'u-el said to Saul, Bid the servant pass on before us, (and he passed on,) but stand thou still a while, that I may shew thee the word of God.

10

THEN Sam'u-el took a vial of oil, and poured *it* upon his head, and kissed him, and said, *Is it* not because the LORD hath anointed thee *to be* captain over his inheritance?

2 When thou art departed from me to day, then thou shalt find two men by Ra'chel's sepulchre in the border of Ben'ja-min at Zel'zah; and they will say unto thee, The asses which thou wentest to seek are found: and, lo, thy father hath left the care of the asses, and sorroweth for you, saying, What shall I do for my son?

3 Then shalt thou go on forward from thence, and thou shalt come to the plain of Ta'bor, and there shall meet thee three men going up to God to Beth'-el, one carrying three kids, and another carrying three loaves of bread, and another carrying a bottle of wine:

4 And they will salute thee, and give thee two *loaves* of bread; which thou shalt receive of their hands.

5 After that thou shalt come to the hill of God, where *is* the garrison of the Phi-lis'tines: and it shall come to pass, when thou art come thither to the city, that thou shalt meet a company of prophets coming down from the high place with a psaltery, and a tabret, and a pipe, and a harp, before them; and they shall prophesy:

6 And the Spirit of the LORD will come upon thee, and thou shalt prophesy with them, and shalt be turned into another man.

7 And let it be, when these signs are come unto thee, *that* thou do as occasion serve thee; for God *is* with thee.

8 And thou shalt go down before me to Gil'gal; and, behold, I will come down unto thee, to offer burnt offerings, *and* to sacrifice sacrifices of peace offerings: seven days shalt thou tarry, till I come to thee, and shew thee what thou shalt do.

9 ¶ And it was *so*, that when he had turned his back to go from Sam'u-el, God gave him another heart: and all those signs came to pass that day.

10 And when they came thither to the hill, behold, a company of prophets met him; and the Spirit of God came upon him, and he prophesied among them.

11 And it came to pass, when all that knew him beforetime saw that, behold, he prophesied among the prophets, then the people said one to another, What *is* this *that* is come unto the son of Kish? *Is* Saul also among the prophets?

12 And one of the same place answered and said, But who *is* their father? Therefore it became a proverb, *Is* Saul also among the prophets?

13 And when he had made an end of prophesying, he came to the high place.

14 ¶ And Saul's uncle said unto him and to his servant, Whither went ye? And he said, To seek the asses: and when we saw that *they were* no where, we came to Sam'u-el.

15 And Saul's uncle said, Tell me, I pray thee, what Sam'u-el said unto you.

16 And Saul said unto his uncle, He told us plainly that the asses were found. But of the matter of the kingdom, whereof Sam'u-el spake, he told him not.

17 ¶ And Sam'u-el called the people together unto the LORD to Miz'peh;

18 And said unto the children of Is'ra-el, Thus saith the LORD God of Is'ra-el, I brought up Is'ra-el out of E'gypt, and delivered you out of the hand of the E-gyp'tians, and out of the

hand of all kingdoms, *and* of them that oppressed you:

19 And ye have this day rejected your God, who himself saved you out of all your adversities and your tribulations; and ye have said unto him, Nay, but set a king over us. Now therefore present yourselves before the LORD by your tribes, and by your thousands.

20 And when Sam'u-el had caused all the tribes of Is'ra-el to come near, the tribe of Ben'-ja-min was taken.

21 When he had caused the tribe of Ben'ja-min to come near by their families, the family of Ma'tri was taken, and Saul the son of Kish was taken: and when they sought him, he could not be found.

22 Therefore they enquired of the LORD further, if the man should yet come thither. And the LORD answered, Behold, he hath hid himself among the stuff.

23 And they ran and fetched him thence: and when he stood among the people, he was higher than any of the people from his shoulders and upward.

24 And Sam'u-el said to all the people, See ye him whom the LORD hath chosen, that *there is* none like him among all the people? And all the people shouted, and said, God save the king.

25 Then Sam'u-el told the people the manner of the kingdom, and wrote *it* in a book, and laid *it* up before the LORD. And Sam'u-el sent all the people away, every man to his house.

26 ¶ And Saul also went home to Gib'e-ah; and there went with him a band of men, whose hearts God had touched.

27 But the children of Be'li-al said, How shall this man save us? And they despised him, and brought him no presents. But he held his peace.

11 THEN Na'hash the Am'mon-ite came up, and encamped against Ja'besh-gil'e-ad: and all the men of Ja'besh said unto Na'-hash, Make a covenant with us, and we will serve thee.

2 And Na'hash the Am'mon-ite answered them, On this *condition* will I make a *covenant* with you, that I may thrust out all your right eyes, and lay it *for* a reproach upon all Is'ra-el.

3 And the elders of Ja'besh said unto him, Give us seven days' respite, that we may send messengers unto all the coasts of Is'ra-el: and then, if *there be* no man to save us, we will come out to thee.

4 ¶ Then came the messengers to Gib'e-ah of Saul, and told the tidings in the ears of the people: and all the people lifted up their voices, and wept.

5 And, behold, Saul came after the herd out of the field; and Saul said, What *aileth* the people that they weep? And they told him the tidings of the men of Ja'besh.

6 And the Spirit of God came upon Saul when he heard those tidings, and his anger was kindled greatly.

7 And he took a yoke of oxen, and hewed them in pieces, and sent *them* throughout all the coasts of Is'ra-el by the hands of messengers, saying, Whosoever cometh not forth after Saul and after Sam'u-el, so shall it be done unto his oxen. And the fear of the LORD fell on the people, and they came out with one consent.

8 And when he numbered them in Be'zek, the children of Is'ra-el were three hundred thousand, and the men of Ju'dah thirty thousand.

9 And they said unto the messengers that came, Thus shall ye say unto the men of Ja'-besh-gil'e-ad, To morrow, by *that time* the sun be hot, ye shall have help. And the messengers came and shewed *it* to the men of Ja'besh; and they were glad.

10 Therefore the men of Ja'besh said, To morrow we will come out unto you, and ye shall do with us all that seemeth good unto you.

11 And it was *so* on the morrow, that Saul put the people in three companies; and they came into the midst of the host in the morning watch, and slew the Am'mon-ites until the heat of the day: and it came to pass, that they which remained were scattered, so that two of them were not left together.

12 ¶ And the people said unto Sam'u-el, Who *is* he that said, Shall Saul reign over us? bring the men, that we may put them to death.

13 And Saul said, There shall not a man be put to death this day: for to day the LORD hath wrought salvation in Is'ra-el.

14 Then said Sam'u-el to the people, Come, and let us go to Gil'gal, and renew the kingdom there.

15 And all the people went to Gil'gal; and there they made Saul king before the LORD in Gil'gal; and there they sacrificed sacrifices of peace offerings before the LORD; and there Saul and all the men of Is'ra-el rejoiced greatly.

12 AND Sam'u-el said unto all Is'ra-el, Behold, I have hearkened unto your voice in all that ye said unto me, and have made a king over you.

2 And now, behold, the king walketh before you: and I am old and grayheaded; and, behold, my sons *are* with you: and I have walked before you from my childhood unto this day.

3 Behold, here I *am:* witness against me before the LORD, and before his anointed: whose ox have I taken? or whose ass have I taken? or whom have I defrauded? whom have I oppressed? or of whose hand have I received *any* bribe to blind mine eyes therewith? and I will restore it you.

4 And they said, Thou hast not defrauded us, nor oppressed us, neither hast thou taken ought of any man's hand.

5 And he said unto them, The LORD *is* witness against you, and his anointed *is* witness this day, that ye have not found ought in my hand. And they answered, He *is* witness.

6 ¶ And Sam'u-el said unto the people, It *is* the LORD that advanced Mo'ses and Aar'on, and that brought your fathers up out of the land of E'gypt.

7 Now therefore stand still, that I may reason with you before the LORD of all the righteous acts of the LORD, which he did to you and to your fathers.

8 When Ja'cob was come into E'gypt, and your fathers cried unto the LORD, then the LORD sent Mo'ses and Aar'on, which brought forth your fathers out of E'gypt, and made them dwell in this place.

9 And when they forgat the LORD their God, he sold them into the hand of Sis'e-ra, captain of the host of Ha'zor, and into the hand of the Phi-lis'tines, and into the hand of the king of Mo'ab, and they fought against them.

10 And they cried unto the LORD, and said, We have sinned, because we have forsaken the LORD, and have served Ba'al-im and Ash'ta-roth: but now deliver us out of the hand of our enemies, and we will serve thee.

11 And the LORD sent Je-rub'ba-al, and Be'-dan, and Jeph'thah, and Sam'u-el, and delivered you out of the hand of your enemies on every side, and ye dwelled safe.

12 And when ye saw that Na'hash the king of the children of Am'mon came against you, ye said unto me, Nay; but a king shall reign over us: when the LORD your God *was* your king.

13 Now therefore behold the king whom ye have chosen, *and* whom ye have desired! and, behold, the LORD hath set a king over you.

14 If ye will fear the LORD, and serve him, and obey his voice, and not rebel against the commandment of the LORD, then shall both ye and also the king that reigneth over you continue following the LORD your God:

15 But if ye will not obey the voice of the LORD, but rebel against the commandment of the LORD, then shall the hand of the LORD be against you, as *it was* against your fathers.

16 ¶ Now therefore stand and see this great thing, which the LORD will do before your eyes.

17 *Is it* not wheat harvest to-day? I will call unto the LORD, and he shall send thunder and rain; that ye may perceive and see that your wickedness *is* great, which ye have done in the sight of the LORD, in asking you a king.

18 So Sam'u-el called unto the LORD; and the LORD sent thunder and rain that day: and all the people greatly feared the LORD and Sam'u-el.

19 And all the people said unto Sam'u-el, Pray for thy servants unto the LORD thy God, that we die not: for we have added unto all our sins *this* evil, to ask us a king.

20 ¶ And Sam'u-el said unto the people, Fear not: ye have done all this wickedness: yet turn not aside from following the LORD, but serve the LORD with all your heart;

21 And turn ye not aside: for *then should ye* go after vain *things*, which cannot profit nor deliver; for they *are* vain.

22 For the LORD will not forsake his people for his great name's sake: because it hath pleased the LORD to make you his people.

23 Moreover as for me, God forbid that I should sin against the LORD in ceasing to pray for you: but I will teach you the good and the right way:

24 Only fear the LORD, and serve him in truth with all your heart: for consider how great *things* he hath done for you.

25 But if ye shall still do wickedly, ye shall be consumed, both ye and your king.

13 SAUL reigned one year; and when he had reigned two years over Is'ra-el,

2 Saul chose him three thousand *men* of Is'ra-el; *whereof* two thousand were with Saul in Mich'mash and in mount Beth'-el, and a thousand were with Jon'a-than in Gib'e-ah of Ben'ja-min: and the rest of the people he sent every man to his tent.

3 And Jon'a-than smote the garrison of the Phi-lis'tines that *was* in Ge'ba, and the Phi-lis'tines heard *of it*. And Saul blew the trumpet throughout all the land, saying, Let the He'brews hear.

4 And all Is'ra-el heard say *that* Saul had smitten a garrison of the Phi-lis'tines, and *that* Is'ra-el also was had in abomination with the Phi-lis'tines. And the people were called together after Saul to Gil'gal.

5 ¶ And the Phi-lis'tines gathered themselves together to fight with Is'ra-el, thirty thousand chariots, and six thousand horsemen, and people as the sand which *is* on the sea shore in multitude: and they came up, and pitched in Mich'mash, eastward from Beth-a'ven.

6 When the men of Is'ra-el saw that they were in a strait, (for the people were distressed,) then the people did hide themselves in caves, and in thickets, and in rocks, and in high places, and in pits.

7 And *some of* the He'brews went over Jor'dan to the land of Gad and Gil'e-ad. As for Saul, he *was* yet in Gil'gal, and all the people followed him trembling.

8 ¶ And he tarried seven days, according to the set time that Sam'u-el *had* appointed: but Sam'u-el came not to Gil'gal; and the people were scattered from him.

9 And Saul said, Bring hither a burnt offering to me, and peace offerings. And he offered the burnt offering.

10 And it came to pass, that as soon as he had made an end of offering the burnt offering, behold, Sam'u-el came; and Saul went out to meet him, that he might salute him.

11 ¶ And Sam'u-el said, What hast thou done? And Saul said, Because I saw that the people were scattered from me, and *that* thou camest not within the days appointed, and *that* the Phi-lis'tines gathered themselves together at Mich'mash;

12 Therefore said I, The Phi-lis'tines will come down now upon me to Gil'gal, and I have not made supplication unto the LORD: I forced myself therefore, and offered a burnt offering.

13 And Sam'u-el said to Saul, Thou hast done foolishly: thou hast not kept the commandment of the LORD thy God, which he commanded thee: for now would the LORD have established thy kingdom upon Is'ra-el for ever.

14 But now thy kingdom shall not continue: the LORD hath sought him a man after his own heart, and the LORD hath commanded him *to be* captain over his people, because thou hast not kept *that* which the LORD commanded thee.

15 And Sam'u-el arose, and gat him up from Gil'gal unto Gib'e-ah of Ben'ja-min. And Saul numbered the people *that were* present with him, about six hundred men.

16 And Saul, and Jon'a-than his son, and the people *that were* present with them, abode in Gib'e-ah of Ben'ja-min: but the Phi-lis'tines encamped in Mich'mash.

17 ¶ And the spoilers came out of the camp of the Phi-lis'tines in three companies: one company turned unto the way *that leadeth to* Oph'rah, unto the land of Shu'al:

18 And another company turned the way *to* Beth-ho'ron: and another company turned *to* the way of the border that looketh to the valley of Ze-bo'im toward the wilderness.

19 ¶ Now there was no smith found throughout all the land of Is'ra-el: for the Phi-lis'tines said, Lest the He'brews make *them* swords or spears:

20 But all the Is'ra-el-ites went down to the Phi-lis'tines, to sharpen every man his share, and his coulter, and his ax, and his mattock.

21 Yet they had a file for the mattocks, and for the coulters, and for the forks, and for the axes, and to sharpen the goads.

22 So it came to pass in the day of battle, that there was neither sword nor spear found in the hand of any of the people that *were* with Saul and Jon'a-than: but with Saul and with Jon'a-than his son was there found.

23 And the garrison of the Phi-lis'tines went out to the passage of Mich'mash.

14 NOW it came to pass upon a day, that Jon'a-than the son of Saul said unto the young man that bare his armour, Come, and let us go over to the Phi-lis'tines' garrison, that *is* on the other side. But he told not his father.

2 And Saul tarried in the uttermost part of

Gib'e-ah under a pomegranate tree which *is* in Mig'ron: and the people that *were* with him *were* about six hundred men;

3 And A-hi'ah, the son of A-hi'tub, I-cha-bod's brother, the son of Phin'e-has, the son of E'li, the LORD's priest in Shi'loh, wearing an e-phod. And the people knew not that Jon'a-than was gone.

4 ¶ And between the passages, by which Jon'a-than sought to go over unto the Phi-lis'-tines' garrison, *there was* a sharp rock on the one side, and a sharp rock on the other side: and the name of one *was* Bo'zez, and the name of the other Se'neh.

5 The forefront of the one *was* situate north-ward over against Mich'mash, and the other southward over against Gib'e-ah.

6 And Jon'a-than said to the young man that bare his armour, Come, and let us go over unto the garrison of these uncircumcised: it may be that the LORD will work for us: for *there is* no restraint to the LORD to save by many or by few.

7 And his armourbearer said unto him, Do all that *is* in thine heart: turn thee; behold, I *am* with thee according to thy heart.

8 Then said Jon'a-than, Behold, we will pass over unto *these* men, and we will discover our-selves unto them.

9 If they say thus unto us, Tarry until we come to you; then we will stand still in our place, and will not go up unto them.

10 But if they say thus, Come up unto us; then we will go up: for the LORD hath delivered them into our hand: and this *shall be* a sign unto us.

11 And both of them discovered themselves unto the garrison of the Phi-lis'tines: and the Phi-lis'tines said, Behold, the He'brews come forth out of the holes where they had hid them-selves.

12 And the men of the garrison answered Jon'a-than and his armourbearer, and said, Come up to us, and we will shew you a thing. And Jon'a-than said unto his armourbearer, Come up after me: for the LORD hath delivered them into the hand of Is'ra-el.

13 And Jon'a-than climbed up upon his hands and upon his feet, and his armourbearer after him: and they fell before Jon'a-than; and his armourbearer slew after him.

14 And that first slaughter, which Jon'a-than and his armourbearer made, was about twenty men, within as it were an half acre of land, *which* a yoke of oxen *might* plow.

15 And there was trembling in the host, in the field, and among all the people: the garri-son, and the spoilers, they also trembled, and the earth quaked: so it was a very great trem-bling.

16 And the watchmen of Saul in Gib'e-ah of Ben'ja-min looked; and, behold, the multitude melted away, and they went on beating down *one another.*

17 Then said Saul unto the people that *were* with him, Number now, and see who is gone from us. And when they had numbered, behold, Jon'a-than and his armourbearer *were* not there.

18 And Saul said unto A-hi'ah, Bring hither the ark of God. For the ark of God was at that time with the children of Is'ra-el.

19 ¶ And it came to pass, while Saul talked unto the priest, that the noise that *was* in the host of the Phi-lis'tines went on and increased: and Saul said unto the priest, Withdraw thine hand.

20 And Saul and all the people that *were* with him, assembled themselves, and they came to the battle: and, behold, every man's sword was against his fellow, *and there was* a very great discomfiture.

21 Moreover the He'brews *that* were with the Phi-lis'tines before that time, which went up with them into the camp *from the country* round about, even they also *turned* to be with the Is'ra-el-ites that *were* with Saul and Jon'a-than.

22 Likewise all the men of Is'ra-el which had hid themselves in mount E'phra-im, *when* they heard that the Phi-lis'tines fled, even they also followed hard after them in the battle.

23 So the LORD saved Is'ra-el that day: and the battle passed over unto Beth-a'ven.

24 ¶ And the men of Is'ra-el were distressed that day: for Saul had adjured the people, say-ing, Cursed *be* the man that eateth *any* food un-til evening, that I may be avenged on mine en-emies. So none of the people tasted *any* food.

25 And all *they of* the land came to a wood; and there was honey upon the ground.

26 And when the people were come into the wood, behold, the honey dropped; but no man put his hand to his mouth: for the people feared the oath.

27 But Jon'a-than heard not when his father charged the people with the oath: wherefore he put forth the end of the rod that *was* in his hand, and dipped it in an honeycomb, and put his hand to his mouth; and his eyes were en-lightened.

28 Then answered one of the people, and said, Thy father straitly charged the people with an oath, saying, Cursed *be* the man that eateth *any* food this day. And the people were faint.

29 Then said Jon'a-than, My father hath trou-bled the land: see, I pray you, how mine eyes have been enlightened, because I tasted a little of this honey.

30 How much more, if haply the people had eaten freely to day of the spoil of their enemies which they found? for had there not been now a much greater slaughter among the Phi-lis'tines?

31 And they smote the Phi-lis'tines that day from Mich'mash to Aij'a-lon: and the people were very faint.

32 And the people flew upon the spoil, and took sheep, and oxen, and calves, and slew *them* on the ground: and the people did eat *them* with the blood.

33 ¶ Then they told Saul, saying, Behold, the people sin against the LORD, in that they eat with the blood. And he said, Ye have trans-gressed: roll a great stone unto me this day.

34 And Saul said, Disperse yourselves among the people, and say unto them, Bring me hither every man his ox, and every man his sheep, and slay *them* here, and eat; and sin not against the LORD in eating with the blood. And all the people brought every man his ox with him that night, and slew *them* there.

35 And Saul built an altar unto the LORD: the same was the first altar that he built unto the LORD.

36 ¶ And Saul said, Let us go down after the Phi-lis'tines by night, and spoil them until the morning light, and let us not leave a man of them. And they said, Do whatsoever seemeth good unto thee. Then said the priest, Let us draw near hither unto God.

37 And Saul asked counsel of God, Shall I go down after the Phi-lis'tines? wilt thou deliver them into the hand of Is'ra-el? But he answered him not that day.

38 And Saul said, Draw ye near hither, all the chief of the people: and know and see wherein this sin hath been this day.

39 For, *as* the LORD liveth, which saveth Is'-ra-el, though it be in Jon'a-than my son, he shall surely die. But *there was* not a man among all the people *that* answered him.

40 Then said he unto all Is'ra-el, Be ye on one side, and I and Jon'a-than my son will be on the other side. And the people said unto Saul, Do what seemeth good unto thee.

41 Therefore Saul said unto the LORD God of Is'ra-el, Give a perfect *lot.* And Saul and Jon'a-than were taken: but the people escaped.

42 And Saul said, Cast *lots* between me and Jon'a-than my son. And Jon'a-than was taken.

43 Then Saul said to Jon'a-than, Tell me what thou hast done. And Jon'a-than told him, and said, I did but taste a little honey with the end of the rod that *was* in mine hand, *and,* lo, I must die.

44 And Saul answered, God do so and more also: for thou shalt surely die, Jon'a-than.

45 And the people said unto Saul, Shall Jon'-a-than die, who hath wrought this great salvation in Is'ra-el? God forbid: *as* the LORD liveth, there shall not one hair of his head fall to the ground; for he hath wrought with God this day. So the people rescued Jon'a-than, that he died not.

46 Then Saul went up from following the Phi-lis'tines: and the Phi-lis'tines went to their own place.

47 ¶ So Saul took the kingdom over Is'ra-el, and fought against all his enemies on every side, against Mo'ab, and against the children of Am'mon, and against E'dom, and against the kings of Zo'bah, and against the Phi-lis'tines: and whithersoever he turned himself, he vexed *them.*

48 And he gathered an host, and smote the Am'a-lek-ites, and delivered Is'ra-el out of the hands of them that spoiled them.

49 Now the sons of Saul were Jon'a-than, and Ish'u-i, and Mel'chi-shu'a: and the names of his two daughters *were these;* the name of the firstborn Me'rab, and the name of the younger Mi'chal:

50 And the name of Saul's wife *was* A-hin'o-am, the daughter of A-him'a-az: and the name of the captain of his host *was* Ab'ner, the son of Ner, Saul's uncle.

51 And Kish *was* the father of Saul; and Ner the father of Ab'ner *was* the son of A-bi'el.

52 And there was sore war against the Phi-lis'tines all the days of Saul: and when Saul saw any strong man, or any valiant man, he took him unto him.

15 SAM'U-EL also said unto Saul, The LORD sent me to anoint thee *to be* king over his people, over Is'ra-el: now therefore hearken thou unto the voice of the words of the LORD.

2 Thus saith the LORD of hosts, I remember *that* which Am'a-lek did to Is'ra-el, how he laid *wait* for him in the way, when he came up from E'gypt.

3 Now go and smite Am'a-lek, and utterly destroy all that they have, and spare them not; but slay both man and woman, infant and suckling, ox and sheep, camel and ass.

4 And Saul gathered the people together, and numbered them in Tel'a-im, two hundred thousand footmen, and ten thousand men of Ju'dah.

5 And Saul came to a city of Am'a-lek, and laid wait in the valley.

6 ¶ And Saul said unto the Ken'ites, Go, depart, get you down from among the Am'a-lek-ites, lest I destroy you with them: for ye shewed kindness to all the children of Is'ra-el, when they came up out of E'gypt. So the Ken'ites departed from among the Am'a-lek-ites.

7 And Saul smote the Am'a-lek-ites from Hav'i-lah *until* thou comest to Shur, that *is* over against E'gypt.

8 And he took A'gag the king of the Am'a-lek-ites alive, and utterly destroyed all the people with the edge of the sword.

9 But Saul and the people spared A'gag, and the best of the sheep, and of the oxen, and of the fatlings, and the lambs, and all *that was* good, and would not utterly destroy them: but every thing *that was* vile and refuse, that they destroyed utterly.

10 ¶ Then came the word of the LORD unto Sam'u-el, saying,

11 It repenteth me that I have set up Saul *to be* king: for he is turned back from following me, and hath not performed my commandments. And it grieved Sam'u-el; and he cried unto the LORD all night.

12 And when Sam'u-el rose early to meet Saul in the morning, it was told Sam'u-el, saying, Saul came to Car'mel, and, behold, he set him up a place, and is gone about, and passed on, and gone down to Gil'gal.

13 And Sam'u-el came to Saul: and Saul said unto him, Blessed *be* thou of the LORD: I have performed the commandment of the LORD.

14 And Sam'u-el said, What *meaneth* then this bleating of the sheep in mine ears, and the lowing of the oxen which I hear?

15 And Saul said, They have brought them from the Am'a-lek-ites: for the people spared the best of the sheep and of the oxen, to sacrifice unto the LORD thy God; and the rest we have utterly destroyed.

16 Then Sam'u-el said unto Saul, Stay, and I will tell thee what the LORD hath said to me this night. And he said unto him, Say on.

17 And Sam'u-el said, When thou *wast* little in thine own sight, *wast* thou not *made* the head of the tribes of Is'ra-el, and the LORD anointed thee king over Is'ra-el?

18 And the LORD sent thee on a journey, and said, Go and utterly destroy the sinners the Am'a-lek-ites, and fight against them until they be consumed.

19 Wherefore then didst thou not obey the voice of the LORD, but didst fly upon the spoil, and didst evil in the sight of the LORD?

20 And Saul said unto Sam'u-el, Yea, I have obeyed the voice of the LORD, and have gone the way which the LORD sent me, and have brought A'gag the king of Am'a-lek, and have utterly destroyed the Am'a-lek-ites.

21 But the people took of the spoil, sheep and oxen, the chief of the things which should have been utterly destroyed, to sacrifice unto the LORD thy God in Gil'gal.

22 And Sam'u-el said, Hath the LORD *as great* delight in burnt offerings and sacrifices, as in obeying the voice of the LORD? Behold, to obey *is* better than sacrifice, *and* to hearken than the fat of rams.

23 For rebellion *is as* the sin of witchcraft, and stubbornness *is as* iniquity and idolatry. Because thou hast rejected the word of the LORD, he hath also rejected thee from *being* king.

24 ¶ And Saul said unto Sam'u-el, I have sinned: for I have transgressed the command-

ment of the LORD, and thy words: because I feared the people, and obeyed their voice.

25 Now therefore, I pray thee, pardon my sin, and turn again with me, that I may worship the LORD.

26 And Sam'u-el said unto Saul, I will not return with thee: for thou hast rejected the word of the LORD, and the LORD hath rejected thee from being king over Is'ra-el.

27 And as Sam'u-el turned about to go away, he laid hold upon the skirt of his mantle, and it rent.

28 And Sam'u-el said unto him, The LORD hath rent the kingdom of Is'ra-el from thee this day, and hath given it to a neighbour of thine, *that is* better than thou.

29 And also the Strength of Is'ra-el will not lie nor repent: for he *is* not a man, that he should repent.

30 Then he said, I have sinned: *yet* honour me now, I pray thee, before the elders of my people, and before Is'ra-el, and turn again with me, that I may worship the LORD thy God.

31 So Sam'u-el turned again after Saul; and Saul worshipped the LORD.

32 ¶ Then said Sam'u-el, Bring ye hither to me A'gag the king of the Am'a-lek-ites. And A'gag came unto him delicately. And A'gag said, Surely the bitterness of death is past.

33 And Sam'u-el said, As thy sword hath made women childless, so shall thy mother be childless among women. And Sam'u-el hewed A'gag in pieces before the LORD in Gil'gal.

34 ¶ Then Sam'u-el went to Ra'mah; and Saul went up to his house to Gib'e-ah of Saul.

35 And Sam'u-el came no more to see Saul until the day of his death: nevertheless Sam'u-el mourned for Saul: and the LORD repented that he had made Saul king over Is'ra-el.

16 AND the LORD said unto Sam'u-el, How long wilt thou mourn for Saul, seeing I have rejected him from reigning over Is'ra-el? fill thine horn with oil, and go, I will send thee to Jes'se the Beth'-le-hem-ite: for I have provided me a king among his sons.

2 And Sam'u-el said, How can I go? if Saul hear *it*, he will kill me. And the LORD said, Take an heifer with thee, and say, I am come to sacrifice to the LORD.

3 And call Jes'se to the sacrifice, and I will shew thee what thou shalt do: and thou shalt anoint unto me *him* whom I name unto thee.

4 And Sam'u-el did that which the LORD spake, and came to Beth'-le-hem. And the elders of the town trembled at his coming, and said, Comest thou peaceably?

5 And he said, Peaceably: I am come to sacrifice unto the LORD: sanctify yourselves, and come with me to the sacrifice. And he sanctified Jes'se and his sons, and called them to the sacrifice.

6 ¶ And it came to pass, when they were come, that he looked on E-li'ab, and said, Surely the LORD's anointed *is* before him.

7 But the LORD said unto Sam'u-el, Look not on his countenance, or on the height of his stature; because I have refused him: for *the LORD seeth* not as man seeth; for man looketh on the outward appearance, but the LORD looketh on the heart.

8 Then Jes'se called A-bin'a-dab, and made him pass before Sam'u-el. And he said, Neither hath the LORD chosen this.

9 Then Jes'se made Sham'mah to pass by. And he said, Neither hath the LORD chosen this.

10 Again, Jes'se made seven of his sons to pass before Sam'u-el. And Sam'u-el said unto Jes'se, The LORD hath not chosen these.

11 And Sam'u-el said unto Jes'se, Are here all *thy* children? And he said, There remaineth yet the youngest, and, behold, he keepeth the sheep. And Sam'u-el said unto Jes'se, Send and fetch him: for we will not sit down till he come hither.

12 And he sent, and brought him in. Now he *was* ruddy, *and* withal of a beautiful countenance, and goodly to look to. And the LORD said, Arise, anoint him: for this *is* he.

13 Then Sam'u-el took the horn of oil, and anointed him in the midst of his brethren: and the Spirit of the LORD came upon Da'vid from that day forward. So Sam'u-el rose up, and went to Ra'mah.

14 ¶ But the Spirit of the LORD departed from Saul, and an evil spirit from the LORD troubled him.

15 And Saul's servants said unto him, Behold now, an evil spirit from God troubleth thee.

16 Let our lord now command thy servants, *which are* before thee, to seek out a man, *who is* a cunning player on an harp: and it shall come to pass, when the evil spirit from God is upon thee, that he shall play with his hand, and thou shalt be well.

17 And Saul said unto his servants, Provide me now a man that can play well, and bring *him* to me.

18 Then answered one of the servants, and said, Behold, I have seen a son of Jes'se the Beth'-le-hem-ite, *that is* cunning in playing, and a mighty valiant man, and a man of war, and prudent in matters, and a comely person, and the LORD *is* with him.

19 ¶ Wherefore Saul sent messengers unto Jes'se, and said, Send me Da'vid thy son, which *is* with the sheep.

20 And Jes'se took an ass *laden* with bread, and a bottle of wine, and a kid, and sent *them* by Da'vid his son unto Saul.

21 And Da'vid came to Saul, and stood before him: and he loved him greatly; and he became his armourbearer.

22 And Saul sent to Jes'se, saying, Let Da'vid, I pray thee, stand before me; for he hath found favour in my sight.

23 And it came to pass, when the *evil* spirit from God was upon Saul, that Da'vid took an harp, and played with his hand: so Saul was refreshed, and was well, and the evil spirit departed from him.

17 NOW the Phi-lis'tines gathered together their armies to battle, and were gathered together at Sho'choh, which *belongeth* to Ju'dah, and pitched between Sho'choh and A-ze'kah, in E'phes–dam'mim.

2 And Saul and the men of Is'ra-el were gathered together, and pitched by the valley of E'lah, and set the battle in array against the Phi-lis'tines.

3 And the Phi-lis'tines stood on a mountain on the one side, and Is'ra-el stood on a mountain on the other side: and *there was* a valley between them.

4 ¶ And there went out a champion out of the camp of the Phi-lis'tines, named Go-li'ath, of Gath, whose height *was* six cubits and a span.

5 And *he had* an helmet of brass upon his head, and he *was* armed with a coat of mail; and the weight of the coat *was* five thousand shekels of brass.

6 And *he had* greaves of brass upon his legs, and a target of brass between his shoulders.

7 And the staff of his spear *was* like a weaver's beam; and his spear's head *weighed* six hundred shekels of iron: and one bearing a shield went before him.

8 And he stood and cried unto the armies of Is'ra-el, and said unto them, Why are ye come out to set *your* battle in array? *am* not I a Phi-lis'tine, and ye servants to Saul? choose you a man for you, and let him come down to me.

9 If he be able to fight with me, and to kill me, then will we be your servants: but if I prevail against him, and kill him, then shall ye be our servants, and serve us.

10 And the Phi-lis'tine said, I defy the armies of Is'ra-el this day; give me a man, that we may fight together.

11 When Saul and all Is'ra-el heard those words of the Phi-lis'tine, they were dismayed, and greatly afraid.

12 ¶ Now Da'vid *was* the son of that Eph'-rath-ite of Beth'-le-hem-ju'dah, whose name *was* Jes'se; and he had eight sons: and the man went among men *for* an old man in the days of Saul.

13 And the three eldest sons of Jes'se went *and* followed Saul to the battle: and the names of his three sons that went to the battle *were* E-li'ab the firstborn, and next unto him A-bin'a-dab, and the third Sham'mah.

14 And Da'vid *was* the youngest: and the three eldest followed Saul.

15 But Da'vid went and returned from Saul to feed his father's sheep at Beth'-le-hem.

16 And the Phi-lis'tine drew near morning and evening, and presented himself forty days.

17 And Jes'se said unto Da'vid his son, Take now for thy brethren an ephah of this parched *corn*, and these ten loaves, and run to the camp to thy brethren;

18 And carry these ten cheeses unto the captain of *their* thousand, and look how thy brethren fare, and take their pledge.

19 Now Saul, and they, and all the men of Is'ra-el, *were* in the valley of E'lah, fighting with the Phi-lis'tines.

20 ¶ And Da'vid rose up early in the morning, and left the sheep with a keeper, and took, and went, as Jes'se had commanded him; and he came to the trench, as the host was going forth to the fight, and shouted for the battle.

21 For Is'ra-el and the Phi-lis'tines had put the battle in array, army against army.

22 And Da'vid left his carriage in the hand of the keeper of the carriage, and ran into the army, and came and saluted his brethren.

23 And as he talked with them, behold, there came up the champion, the Phi-lis'tine of Gath, Go-li'ath by name, out of the armies of the Phi-lis'tines, and spake according to the same words: and Da'vid heard *them*.

24 And all the men of Is'ra-el, when they saw the man, fled from him, and were sore afraid.

25 And the men of Is'ra-el said, Have ye seen this man that is come up? surely to defy Is'ra-el is he come up: and it shall be, *that* the man who killeth him, the king will enrich him with great riches, and will give him his daughter, and make his father's house free in Is'ra-el.

26 And Da'vid spake to the men that stood by him, saying, What shall be done to the man that killeth this Phi-lis'tine, and taketh away the reproach from Is'ra-el? for who *is* this uncircumcised Phi-lis'tine, that he should defy the armies of the living God?

27 And the people answered him after this manner, saying, So shall it be done to the man that killeth him.

28 ¶ And E-li'ab his eldest brother heard when he spake unto the men; and E-li'ab's anger was kindled against Da'vid, and he said, Why camest thou down hither? and with whom hast thou left those few sheep in the wilderness? I know thy pride, and the naughtiness of thine heart; for thou art come down that thou mightest see the battle.

29 And Da'vid said, What have I now done? *Is there* not a cause?

30 ¶ And he turned from him toward another, and spake after the same manner: and the people answered him again after the former manner.

31 And when the words were heard which Da'vid spake, they rehearsed *them* before Saul: and he sent for him.

32 ¶ And Da'vid said to Saul, Let no man's heart fail because of him; thy servant will go and fight with this Phi-lis'tine.

33 And Saul said to Da'vid, Thou art not able to go against this Phi-lis'tine to fight with him: for thou *art but* a youth, and he a man of war from his youth.

34 And Da'vid said unto Saul, Thy servant kept his father's sheep, and there came a lion, and a bear, and took a lamb out of the flock:

35 And I went out after him, and smote him, and delivered *it* out of his mouth: and when he arose against me, I caught *him* by his beard, and smote him, and slew him.

36 Thy servant slew both the lion and the bear: and this uncircumcised Phi-lis'tine shall be as one of them, seeing he hath defied the armies of the living God.

37 Da'vid said moreover, The LORD that delivered me out of the paw of the lion, and out of the paw of the bear, he will deliver me out of the hand of this Phi-lis'tine. And Saul said unto Da'vid, Go, and the LORD be with thee.

38 ¶ And Saul armed Da'vid with his armour, and he put an helmet of brass upon his head; also he armed him with a coat of mail.

39 And Da'vid girded his sword upon his armour, and he assayed to go; for he had not proved *it*. And Da'vid said unto Saul, I cannot go with these; for I have not proved *them*. And Da'vid put them off him.

40 And he took his staff in his hand, and chose him five smooth stones out of the brook, and put them in a shepherd's bag which he had, even in a scrip; and his sling *was* in his hand: and he drew near to the Phi-lis'tine.

41 And the Phi-lis'tine came on and drew near unto Da'vid; and the man that bare the shield *went* before him.

42 And when the Phi-lis'tine looked about, and saw Da'vid, he disdained him: for he was *but* a youth, and ruddy, and of a fair countenance.

43 And the Phi-lis'tine said unto Da'vid, *Am* I a dog, that thou comest to me with staves? And the Phi-lis'tine cursed Da'vid by his gods.

44 And the Phi-lis'tine said to Da'vid, Come to me, and I will give thy flesh unto the fowls of the air, and to the beasts of the field.

45 Then said Da'vid to the Phi-lis'tine, Thou comest to me with a sword, and with a spear, and with a shield: but I come to thee in the name of the LORD of hosts, the God of the armies of Is'ra-el, whom thou hast defied.

46 This day will the LORD deliver thee into mine hand; and I will smite thee, and take thine head from thee; and I will give the carcases of the host of the Phi-lis'tines this day unto the

fowls of the air, and to the wild beasts of the earth; that all the earth may know that there is a God in Is′ra-el.

47 And all this assembly shall know that the LORD saveth not with sword and spear: for the battle is the LORD's, and he will give you into our hands.

48 And it came to pass, when the Phi-lis′tine arose, and came and drew nigh to meet Da′vid, that Da′vid hasted, and ran toward the army to meet the Phi-lis′tine.

49 And Da′vid put his hand in his bag, and took thence a stone, and slang it, and smote the Phi-lis′tine in his forehead, that the stone sunk into his forehead; and he fell upon his face to the earth.

50 So Da′vid prevailed over the Phi-lis′tine with a sling and with a stone, and smote the Phi-lis′tine, and slew him; but there was no sword in the hand of Da′vid.

51 Therefore Da′vid ran, and stood upon the Phi-lis′tine, and took his sword, and drew it out of the sheath thereof, and slew him, and cut off his head therewith. And when the Phi-lis′tines saw their champion was dead, they fled.

52 And the men of Is′ra-el and of Ju′dah arose, and shouted, and pursued the Phi-lis′-tines, until thou come to the valley, and to the gates of Ek′ron. And the wounded of the Phi-lis′tines fell down by the way to Sha-a-ra′im, even unto Gath, and unto Ek′ron.

53 And the children of Is′ra-el returned from chasing after the Phi-lis′tines, and they spoiled their tents.

54 And Da′vid took the head of the Phi-lis′-tine, and brought it to Je-ru′sa-lem; but he put his armour in his tent.

55 ¶ And when Saul saw Da′vid go forth against the Phi-lis′tine, he said unto Ab′ner, the captain of the host, Ab′ner, whose son is this youth? And Ab′ner said, As thy soul liveth, O king, I cannot tell.

56 And the king said, Enquire thou whose son the stripling is.

57 And as Da′vid returned from the slaughter of the Phi-lis′tine, Ab′ner took him, and brought him before Saul with the head of the Phi-lis′tine in his hand.

58 And Saul said to him, Whose son art thou, thou young man? And Da′vid answered, I am the son of thy servant Jes′se the Beth′-le-hem-ite.

18

AND it came to pass, when he had made an end of speaking unto Saul, that the soul of Jon′a-than was knit with the soul of Da′vid, and Jon′a-than loved him as his own soul.

2 And Saul took him that day, and would let him go no more home to his father's house.

3 Then Jon′a-than and Da′vid made a covenant, because he loved him as his own soul.

4 And Jon′a-than stripped himself of the robe that was upon him, and gave it to Da′vid, and his garments, even to his sword, and to his bow, and to his girdle.

5 ¶ And Da′vid went out whithersoever Saul sent him, and behaved himself wisely: and Saul set him over the men of war, and he was accepted in the sight of all the people, and also in the sight of Saul's servants.

6 And it came to pass as they came, when Da′vid was returned from the slaughter of the Phi-lis′tine, that the women came out of all cities of Is′ra-el, singing and dancing, to meet king Saul, with tabrets, with joy, and with instruments of musick.

7 And the women answered one another as they played, and said, Saul hath slain his thousands, and Da′vid his ten thousands.

8 And Saul was very wroth, and the saying displeased him; and he said, They have ascribed unto Da′vid ten thousands, and to me they have ascribed but thousands: and what can he have more but the kingdom?

9 And Saul eyed Da′vid from that day and forward.

10 ¶ And it came to pass on the morrow, that the evil spirit from God came upon Saul, and he prophesied in the midst of the house: and Da′vid played with his hand, as at other times: and there was a javelin in Saul's hand.

11 And Saul cast the javelin; for he said, I will smite Da′vid even to the wall with it. And Da′vid avoided out of his presence twice.

12 ¶ And Saul was afraid of Da′vid, because the LORD was with him, and was departed from Saul.

13 Therefore Saul removed him from him, and made him his captain over a thousand; and he went out and came in before the people.

14 And Da′vid behaved himself wisely in all his ways; and the LORD was with him.

15 Wherefore when Saul saw that he behaved himself very wisely, he was afraid of him.

16 But all Is′ra-el and Ju′dah loved Da′vid, because he went out and came in before them.

17 ¶ And Saul said to Da′vid, Behold my elder daughter Me′rab, her will I give thee to wife: only be thou valiant for me, and fight the LORD's battles. For Saul said, Let not mine hand be upon him, but let the hand of the Phi-lis′tines be upon him.

18 And Da′vid said unto Saul, Who am I? and what is my life, or my father's family in Is′ra-el, that I should be son in law to the king?

19 But it came to pass at the time when Me′-rab Saul's daughter should have been given to Da′vid, that she was given unto A′dri-el the Me-hol′ath-ite to wife.

20 And Mi′chal Saul's daughter loved Da′vid: and they told Saul, and the thing pleased him.

21 And Saul said, I will give him her, that she may be a snare to him, and that the hand of the Phi-lis′tines may be against him. Wherefore Saul said to Da′vid, Thou shalt this day be my son in law in the one of the twain.

22 ¶ And Saul commanded his servants, saying, Commune with Da′vid secretly, and say, Behold, the king hath delight in thee, and all his servants love thee: now therefore be the king's son in law.

23 And Saul's servants spake those words in the ears of Da′vid. And Da′vid said, Seemeth it to you a light thing to be a king's son in law, seeing that I am a poor man, and lightly esteemed?

24 And the servants of Saul told him, saying, On this manner spake Da′vid.

25 And Saul said, Thus shall ye say to Da′vid, The king desireth not any dowry, but an hundred foreskins of the Phi-lis′tines, to be avenged of the king's enemies. But Saul thought to make Da′vid fall by the hand of the Phi-lis′tines.

26 And when his servants told Da′vid these words, it pleased Da′vid well to be the king's son in law: and the days were not expired.

27 Wherefore Da′vid arose and went, he and his men, and slew of the Phi-lis′tines two hundred men; and Da′vid brought their foreskins, and they gave them in full tale to the king, that he might be the king's son in law. And Saul gave him Mi′chal his daughter to wife.

28 ¶ And Saul saw and knew that the LORD

was with Da'vid, and *that* Mi'chal Saul's daughter loved him.

29 And Saul was yet the more afraid of Da'vid; and Saul became Da'vid's enemy continually.

30 Then the princes of the Phi-lis'tines went forth: and it came to pass, after they went forth, *that* Da'vid behaved himself more wisely than all the servants of Saul; so that his name was much set by.

19 AND Saul spake to Jon'a-than his son, and to all his servants, that they should kill Da'vid.

2 But Jon'a-than Saul's son delighted much in Da'vid: and Jon'a-than told Da'vid, saying, Saul my father seeketh to kill thee: now therefore, I pray thee, take heed to thyself until the morning, and abide in a secret *place*, and hide thyself:

3 And I will go out and stand beside my father in the field where thou *art*, and I will commune with my father of thee; and what I see, that I will tell thee.

4 ¶ And Jon'a-than spake good of Da'vid unto Saul his father, and said unto him, Let not the king sin against his servant, against Da'vid; because he hath not sinned against thee, and because his works *have been* to thee-ward very good:

5 For he did put his life in his hand, and slew the Phi-lis'tine, and the LORD wrought a great salvation for all Is'ra-el: thou sawest *it*, and didst rejoice: wherefore then wilt thou sin against innocent blood, to slay Da'vid without a cause?

6 And Saul hearkened unto the voice of Jon'a-than: and Saul sware, *As* the LORD liveth, he shall not be slain.

7 And Jon'a-than called Da'vid, and Jon'a-than shewed him all those things. And Jon'a-than brought Da'vid to Saul, and he was in his presence, as in times past.

8 ¶ And there was war again: and Da'vid went out, and fought with the Phi-lis'tines, and slew them with a great slaughter; and they fled from him.

9 And the evil spirit from the LORD was upon Saul, as he sat in his house with his javelin in his hand: and Da'vid played with *his* hand.

10 And Saul sought to smite Da'vid even to the wall with the javelin; but he slipped away out of Saul's presence, and he smote the javelin into the wall: and Da'vid fled, and escaped that night.

11 Saul also sent messengers unto Da'vid's house, to watch him, and to slay him in the morning: and Mi'chal Da'vid's wife told him, saying, If thou save not thy life to night, to morrow thou shalt be slain.

12 ¶ So Mi'chal let Da'vid down through a window: and he went, and fled, and escaped.

13 And Mi'chal took an image, and laid *it* in the bed, and put a pillow of goats' hair for his bolster, and covered *it* with a cloth.

14 And when Saul sent messengers to take Da'vid, she said, He *is* sick.

15 And Saul sent the messengers *again* to see Da'vid, saying, Bring him up to me in the bed, that I may slay him.

16 And when the messengers were come in, behold, *there was* an image in the bed, with a pillow of goats' *hair* for his bolster.

17 And Saul said unto Mi'chal, Why hast thou deceived me so, and sent away mine enemy, that he is escaped? And Mi'chal answered Saul, He said unto me, Let me go; why should I kill thee?

18 ¶ So Da'vid fled, and escaped, and came to Sam'u-el to Ra'mah, and told him all that Saul had done to him. And he and Sam'u-el went and dwelt in Na'ioth.

19 And it was told Saul, saying, Behold, Da'vid *is* at Na'ioth in Ra'mah.

20 And Saul sent messengers to take Da'vid: and when they saw the company of the prophets prophesying, and Sam'u-el standing *as* appointed over them, the Spirit of God was upon the messengers of Saul, and they also prophesied.

21 And when it was told Saul, he sent other messengers, and they prophesied likewise. And Saul sent messengers again the third time, and they prophesied also.

22 Then went he also to Ra'mah, and came to a great well that *is* in Se'chu: and he asked and said, Where *are* Sam'u-el and Da'vid? And *one* said, Behold, *they be* at Na'ioth in Ra'mah.

23 And he went thither to Na'ioth in Ra'mah: and the Spirit of God was upon him also, and he went on, and prophesied, until he came to Na'ioth in Ra'mah.

24 And he stripped off his clothes also, and prophesied before Sam'u-el in like manner, and lay down naked all that day and all that night. Wherefore they say, *Is* Saul also among the prophets?

20 AND Da'vid fled from Na'ioth in Ra'mah, and came and said before Jon'a-than, What have I done? what *is* mine iniquity? and what *is* my sin before thy father, that he seeketh my life?

2 And he said unto him, God forbid; thou shalt not die: behold, my father will do nothing either great or small, but that he will shew it me: and why should my father hide this thing from me? it *is* not so.

3 And Da'vid sware moreover, and said, Thy father certainly knoweth that I have found grace in thine eyes; and he saith, Let not Jon'a-than know this, lest he be grieved: but truly *as* the LORD liveth, and *as* thy soul liveth, *there is* but a step between me and death.

4 Then said Jon'a-than unto Da'vid, Whatsoever thy soul desireth, I will even do *it* for thee.

5 And Da'vid said unto Jon'a-than, Behold, to morrow *is* the new moon, and I should not fail to sit with the king at meat: but let me go, that I may hide myself in the field unto the third *day* at even.

6 If thy father at all miss me, then say, Da'vid earnestly asked *leave* of me that he might run to Beth'-le-hem his city: for *there is* a yearly sacrifice there for all the family.

7 If he say thus, *It is* well; thy servant shall have peace: but if he be very wroth, *then* be sure that evil is determined by him.

8 Therefore thou shalt deal kindly with thy servant; for thou hast brought thy servant into a covenant of the LORD with thee: notwithstanding, if there be in me iniquity, slay me thyself; for why shouldest thou bring me to thy father?

9 And Jon'a-than said, Far be it from thee: for if I knew certainly that evil were determined by my father to come upon thee, then would not I tell it thee?

10 Then said Da'vid to Jon'a-than, Who shall tell me? or what *if* thy father answer thee roughly?

11 ¶ And Jon'a-than said unto Da'vid, Come, and let us go out into the field. And they went out both of them into the field.

12 And Jon'a-than said unto Da'vid, O LORD God of Is'ra-el, when I have sounded my father about to morrow any time, *or the third day,* and, behold, *if there be* good toward Da'vid, and I then send not unto thee, and shew it thee;

13 The LORD do so and much more to Jon'a-than: but if it please my father *to do* thee evil, then I will shew it thee, and send thee away, that thou mayest go in peace: and the LORD be with thee, as he hath been with my father.

14 And thou shalt not only while yet I live shew me the kindness of the LORD, that I die not:

15 But *also* thou shalt not cut off thy kindness from my house for ever: no, not when the LORD hath cut off the enemies of Da'vid every one from the face of the earth.

16 So Jon'a-than made *a* covenant with the house of Da'vid, *saying,* Let the LORD even require *it* at the hand of Da'vid's enemies.

17 And Jon'a-than caused Da'vid to swear again, because he loved him: for he loved him as he loved his own soul.

18 Then Jon'a-than said to Da'vid, To morrow *is* the new moon: and thou shalt be missed, because thy seat will be empty.

19 And *when* thou hast stayed three days, *then* thou shalt go down quickly, and come to the place where thou didst hide thyself when the business was *in hand,* and shalt remain by the stone E'zel.

20 And I will shoot three arrows on the side *thereof,* as though I shot at a mark.

21 And, behold, I will send a lad, *saying,* Go, find out the arrows. If I expressly say unto the lad, Behold, the arrows *are* on this side of thee, take them; then come thou: for *there is* peace to thee, and no hurt; *as* the LORD liveth.

22 But if I say thus unto the young man, Behold, the arrows *are* beyond thee; go thy way: for the LORD hath sent thee away.

23 And *as touching* the matter which thou and I have spoken of, behold, the LORD *be* between thee and me for ever.

24 ¶ So Da'vid hid himself in the field: and when the new moon was come, the king sat him down to eat meat.

25 And the king sat upon his seat, as at other times, *even* upon a seat by the wall: and Jon'a-than arose, and Ab'ner sat by Saul's side, and Da'vid's place was empty.

26 Nevertheless Saul spake not any thing that day: for he thought, Something hath befallen him, he *is* not clean; surely he *is* not clean.

27 And it came to pass on the morrow, *which was* the second *day* of the month, that Da'vid's place was empty: and Saul said unto Jon'a-than his son, Wherefore cometh not the son of Jes'se to meat, neither yesterday, nor to day?

28 And Jon'a-than answered Saul, Da'vid earnestly asked *leave* of me *to* go to Beth'-le-hem:

29 And he said, Let me go, I pray thee; for our family hath a sacrifice in the city; and my brother, he hath commanded me *to be there:* and now, if I have found favour in thine eyes, let me get away, I pray thee, and see my brethren. Therefore he cometh not unto the king's table.

30 Then Saul's anger was kindled against Jon'a-than, and he said unto him, Thou son of the perverse rebellious *woman,* do not I know that thou hast chosen the son of Jes'se to thine own confusion, and unto the confusion of thy mother's nakedness?

31 For as long as the son of Jes'se liveth upon the ground, thou shalt not be established, nor

thy kingdom. Wherefore now send and fetch him unto me, for he shall surely die.

32 And Jon'a-than answered Saul his father, and said unto him, Wherefore shall he be slain? what hath he done?

33 And Saul cast a javelin at him to smite him: whereby Jon'a-than knew that it was determined of his father to slay Da'vid.

34 So Jon'a-than arose from the table in fierce anger, and did eat no meat the second day of the month: for he was grieved for Da'vid, because his father had done him shame.

35 ¶ And it came to pass in the morning, that Jon'a-than went out into the field at the time appointed with Da'vid, and a little lad with him.

36 And he said unto his lad, Run, find out now the arrows which I shoot. *And* as the lad ran, he shot an arrow beyond him.

37 And when the lad was come to the place of the arrow which Jon'a-than had shot, Jon'a-than cried after the lad, and said, *Is* not the arrow beyond thee?

38 And Jon'a-than cried after the lad, Make speed, haste, stay not. And Jon'a-than's lad gathered up the arrows, and came to his master.

39 But the lad knew not any thing: only Jon'-a-than and Da'vid knew the matter.

40 And Jon'a-than gave his artillery unto his lad, and said unto him, Go, carry *them* to the city.

41 ¶ *And* as soon as the lad was gone, Da'vid arose out of *a* place toward the south, and fell on his face to the ground, and bowed himself three times: and they kissed one another, and wept one with another, until Da'vid exceeded.

42 And Jon'a-than said to Da'vid, Go in peace, forasmuch as we have sworn both of us in the name of the LORD, saying, The LORD be between me and thee, and between my seed and thy seed for ever. And he arose and departed: and Jon'a-than went into the city.

21 THEN came Da'vid to Nob to A-him'e-lech the priest: and A-him'e-lech was afraid at the meeting of Da'vid, and said unto him, Why *art* thou alone, and no man with thee?

2 And Da'vid said unto A-him'e-lech the priest, The king hath commanded me a business, and hath said unto me, Let no man know any thing of the business whereabout I send thee, and what I have commanded thee: and I have appointed *my* servants to such and such a place.

3 Now therefore what is under thine hand? give *me* five *loaves of* bread in mine hand, or what there is present.

4 And the priest answered Da'vid, and said, *There is* no common bread under mine hand, but there is hallowed bread; if the young men have kept themselves at least from women.

5 And Da'vid answered the priest, and said unto him, Of a truth women *have been* kept from us about these three days, since I came out, and the vessels of the young men are holy, and *the* bread *is* in a manner common, yea, though it were sanctified this day in the vessel.

6 So the priest gave him hallowed *bread:* for there was no bread there but the shewbread, that was taken from before the LORD, to put hot bread in the day when it was taken away.

7 Now a certain man of the servants of Saul *was* there that day, detained before the LORD; and his name *was* Do'eg, an E'dom-ite, the chiefest of the herdmen that *belonged* to Saul.

8 ¶ And Da'vid said unto A-him'e-lech, And

is there not here under thine hand spear or sword? for I have neither brought my sword nor my weapons with me, because the king's business required haste.

9 And the priest said, The sword of Go-li'ath the Phi-lis'tine, whom thou slewest in the valley of E'lah, behold, it *is here* wrapped in a cloth behind the ephod: if thou wilt take that, take *it:* for *there is* no other save that here. And Da'vid said, *There is* none like that; give it me.

10 ¶ And Da'vid arose, and fled that day for fear of Saul, and went to A'chish the king of Gath.

11 And the servants of A'chish said unto him, *Is* not this Da'vid the king of the land? did they not sing one to another of him in dances, saying, Saul hath slain his thousands, and Da'-vid his ten thousands?

12 And Da'vid laid up these words in his heart, and was sore afraid of A'chish the king of Gath.

13 And he changed his behaviour before them, and feigned himself mad in their hands, and scrabbled on the doors of the gate, and let his spittle fall down upon his beard.

14 Then said A'chish unto his servants, Lo, ye see the man is mad: wherefore *then* have ye brought him to me?

15 Have I need of mad men, that ye have brought this *fellow* to play the mad man in my presence? shall this *fellow* come into my house?

22 DA'VID therefore departed thence, and escaped to the cave A-dul'lam: and when his brethren and all his father's house heard *it*, they went down thither to him.

2 And every one *that was* in distress, and every one *that was* in debt, and every one *that was* discontented, gathered themselves unto him; and he became a captain over them: and there were with him about four hundred men.

3 ¶ And Da'vid went thence to Miz'peh of Mo'ab: and he said unto the king of Mo'ab, Let my father and my mother, I pray thee, come forth, *and be* with you, till I know what God will do for me.

4 And he brought them before the king of Mo'ab: and they dwelt with him all the while that Da'vid was in the hold.

5 ¶ And the prophet Gad said unto Da'vid, Abide not in the hold; depart, and get thee into the land of Ju'dah. Then Da'vid departed, and came into the forest of Ha'reth.

6 ¶ When Saul heard that Da'vid was discovered, and the men that *were* with him, (now Saul abode in Gib'e-ah under a tree in Ra'mah, having his spear in his hand, and all his servants *were* standing about him;)

7 Then Saul said unto his servants that stood about him, Hear now, ye Ben'ja-mites; will the son of Jes'se give every one of you fields and vineyards, *and* make you all captains of thousands, and captains of hundreds;

8 That all of you have conspired against me, and *there is* none that sheweth me that my son hath made a league with the son of Jes'se, and *there is* none of you that is sorry for me, or sheweth unto me that my son hath stirred up my servant against me, to lie in wait, as at this day?

9 ¶ Then answered Do'eg the E'dom-ite, which was set over the servants of Saul, and said, I saw the son of Jes'se coming to Nob, to A-him'e-lech the son of A-hi'tub.

10 And he enquired of the LORD for him, and gave him victuals, and gave him the sword of Go-li'ath the Phi-lis'tine.

11 Then the king sent to call A-him'e-lech the priest, the son of A-hi'tub, and all his father's house, the priests that *were* in Nob: and they came all of them to the king.

12 And Saul said, Hear now, thou son of A-hi'tub. And he answered, Here I *am*, my lord.

13 And Saul said unto him, Why have ye conspired against me, thou and the son of Jes'-se, in that thou hast given him bread, and a sword, and hast enquired of God for him, that he should rise against me, to lie in wait, as at this day?

14 Then A-him'e-lech answered the king, and said, And who *is* so faithful among all thy servants as Da'vid, which is the king's son in law, and goeth at thy bidding, and is honourable in thine house?

15 Did I then begin to enquire of God for him? be it far from me: let not the king impute *any* thing unto his servant, *nor* to all the house of my father: for thy servant knew nothing of all this, less or more.

16 And the king said, Thou shalt surely die, A-him'e-lech, thou, and all thy father's house.

17 ¶ And the king said unto the footmen that stood about him, Turn, and slay the priests of the LORD; because their hand also *is* with Da'-vid, and because they knew when he fled, and did not shew it to me. But the servants of the king would not put forth their hand to fall upon the priests of the LORD.

18 And the king said to Do'eg, Turn thou, and fall upon the priests. And Do'eg the E'dom-ite turned, and he fell upon the priests, and slew on that day fourscore and five persons that did wear a linen ephod.

19 And Nob, the city of the priests, smote he with the edge of the sword, both men and women, children and sucklings, and oxen, and asses, and sheep, with the edge of the sword.

20 ¶ And one of the sons of A-him'e-lech the son of A-hi'tub, named A-bi'a-thar, escaped, and fled after Da'vid.

21 And A-bi'a-thar shewed Da'vid that Saul had slain the LORD's priests.

22 And Da'vid said unto A-bi'a-thar, I knew *it* that day, when Do'eg the E'dom-ite *was* there, that he would surely tell Saul: I have occasioned *the death* of all the persons of thy father's house.

23 Abide thou with me, fear not: for he that seeketh my life seeketh thy life: but with me thou *shalt be* in safeguard.

23 THEN they told Da'vid, saying, Behold, the Phi-lis'tines fight against Kei'lah, and they rob the threshingfloors.

2 Therefore Da'vid enquired of the LORD, saying, Shall I go and smite these Phi-lis'tines? And the LORD said unto Da'vid, Go, and smite the Phi-lis'tines, and save Kei'lah.

3 And Da'vid's men said unto him, Behold, we be afraid here in Ju'dah: how much more then if we come to Kei'lah against the armies of the Phi-lis'tines?

4 Then Da'vid enquired of the LORD yet again. And the LORD answered him and said, Arise, go down to Kei'lah; for I will deliver the Phi-lis'tines into thine hand.

5 So Da'vid and his men went to Kei'lah, and fought with the Phi-lis'tines, and brought away their cattle, and smote them with a great slaughter. So Da'vid saved the inhabitants of Kei'lah.

6 And it came to pass, when A-bi'a-thar the son of A-him'e-lech fled to Da'vid to Kei'lah, *that* he came down *with* an ephod in his hand.

7 ¶ And it was told Saul that Da'vid was come to Kei'lah. And Saul said, God hath delivered him into mine hand; for he is shut in, by entering into a town that hath gates and bars.

8 And Saul called all the people together to war, to go down to Kei'lah, to besiege Da'vid and his men.

9 ¶ And Da'vid knew that Saul secretly practised mischief against him; and he said to A-bi'a-thar the priest, Bring hither the ephod.

10 Then said Da'vid, O LORD God of Is'ra-el, thy servant hath certainly heard that Saul seeketh to come to Kei'lah, to destroy the city for my sake.

11 Will the men of Kei'lah deliver me up into his hand? will Saul come down, as thy servant hath heard? O LORD God of Is'ra-el, I beseech thee, tell thy servant. And the LORD said, He will come down.

12 Then said Da'vid, Will the men of Kei'lah deliver me and my men into the hand of Saul? And the LORD said, They will deliver *thee* up.

13 ¶ Then Da'vid and his men, *which were* about six hundred, arose and departed out of Kei'lah, and went whithersoever they could go. And it was told Saul that Da'vid was escaped from Kei'lah; and he forbare to go forth.

14 And Da'vid abode in the wilderness in strong holds, and remained in a mountain in the wilderness of Ziph. And Saul sought him every day, but God delivered him not into his hand.

15 And Da'vid saw that Saul was come out to seek his life: and Da'vid *was* in the wilderness of Ziph in a wood.

16 ¶ And Jon'a-than Saul's son arose, and went to Da'vid into the wood, and strengthened his hand in God.

17 And he said unto him, Fear not: for the hand of Saul my father shall not find thee; and thou shalt be king over Is'ra-el, and I shall be next unto thee; and that also Saul my father knoweth.

18 And they two made a covenant before the LORD: and Da'vid abode in the wood, and Jon'a-than went to his house.

19 ¶ Then came up the Ziph'ites to Saul to Gib'e-ah, saying, Doth not Da'vid hide himself with us in strong holds in the wood, in the hill of Hach'i-lah, which *is* on the south of Jesh'i-mon?

20 Now therefore, O king, come down according to all the desire of thy soul to come down; and our part *shall be* to deliver him into the king's hand.

21 And Saul said, Blessed *be* ye of the LORD; for ye have compassion on me.

22 Go, I pray you, prepare yet, and know and see his place where his haunt is, *and* who hath seen him there: for it is told me *that* he dealeth very subtilly.

23 See therefore, and take knowledge of all the lurking places where he hideth himself, and come ye again to me with the certainty, and I will go with you: and it shall come to pass, if he be in the land, that I will search him out throughout all the thousands of Ju'dah.

24 And they arose, and went to Ziph before Saul: but Da'vid and his men *were* in the wilderness of Ma'on, in the plain on the south of Jesh'i-mon.

25 Saul also and his men went to seek *him.* And they told Da'vid: wherefore he came down into a rock, and abode in the wilderness of Ma'on. And when Saul heard *that,* he pursued after Da'vid in the wilderness of Ma'on.

26 And Saul went on this side of the mountain, and Da'vid and his men on that side of the mountain: and Da'vid made haste to get away

for fear of Saul; for Saul and his men compassed Da'vid and his men round about to take them.

27 ¶ But there came a messenger unto Saul, saying, Haste thee, and come; for the Phi-lis'-tines have invaded the land.

28 Wherefore Saul returned from pursuing after Da'vid, and went against the Phi-lis'tines: therefore they called that place Se'la–ham-mah-le'koth.

29 ¶ And Da'vid went up from thence, and dwelt in strong holds at En-ge'di.

24 AND it came to pass, when Saul was returned from following the Phi-lis'tines, that it was told him, saying, Behold, Da'vid *is* in the wilderness of En-ge'di.

2 Then Saul took three thousand chosen men out of all Is'ra-el, and went to seek Da'vid and his men upon the rocks of the wild goats.

3 And he came to the sheepcotes by the way, where *was* a cave; and Saul went in to cover his feet: and Da'vid and his men remained in the sides of the cave.

4 And the men of Da'vid said unto him, Behold the day of which the LORD said unto thee, Behold, I will deliver thine enemy into thine hand, that thou mayest do to him as it shall seem good unto thee. Then Da'vid arose, and cut off the skirt of Saul's robe privily.

5 And it came to pass afterward, that Da'-vid's heart smote him, because he had cut off Saul's skirt.

6 And he said unto his men, The LORD forbid that I should do this thing unto my master, the LORD's anointed, to stretch forth mine hand against him, seeing he *is* the anointed of the LORD.

7 So Da'vid stayed his servants with these words, and suffered them not to rise against Saul. But Saul rose up out of the cave, and went on *his* way.

8 Da'vid also arose afterward, and went out of the cave, and cried after Saul, saying, My lord the king. And when Saul looked behind him, Da'vid stooped with his face to the earth, and bowed himself.

9 ¶ And Da'vid said to Saul, Wherefore hearest thou men's words, saying, Behold, Da'vid seeketh thy hurt?

10 Behold, this day thine eyes have seen how that the LORD had delivered thee to day into mine hand in the cave: and *some* bade *me* kill thee: but *mine eye* spared thee; and I said, I will not put forth mine hand against my lord; for he *is* the LORD's anointed.

11 Moreover, my father, see, yea, see the skirt of thy robe in my hand: for in that I cut off the skirt of thy robe, and killed thee not, know thou and see that *there is* neither evil nor transgression in mine hand, and I have not sinned against thee; yet thou huntest my soul to take it.

12 The LORD judge between me and thee, and the LORD avenge me of thee: but mine hand shall not be upon thee.

13 As saith the proverb of the ancients, Wickedness proceedeth from the wicked: but mine hand shall not be upon thee.

14 After whom is the king of Is'ra-el come out? after whom dost thou pursue? after a dead dog, after a flea.

15 The LORD therefore be judge, and judge between me and thee, and see, and plead my cause, and deliver me out of thine hand.

16 ¶ And it came to pass, when Da'vid had made an end of speaking these words unto Saul, that Saul said, *Is* this thy voice, my son

Da'vid? And Saul lifted up his voice, and wept.

17 And he said to Da'vid, Thou *art* more righteous than I: for thou hast rewarded me good, whereas I have rewarded thee evil.

18 And thou hast shewed this day how that thou hast dealt well with me: forasmuch as when the LORD had delivered me into thine hand, thou killedst me not.

19 For if a man find his enemy, will he let him go well away? wherefore the LORD reward thee good for that thou hast done unto me this day.

20 And now, behold, I know well that thou shalt surely be king, and that the kingdom of Is'ra-el shall be established in thine hand.

21 Swear now therefore unto me by the LORD, that thou wilt not cut off my seed after me, and that thou wilt not destroy my name out of my father's house.

22 And Da'vid sware unto Saul. And Saul went home; but Da'vid and his men gat them up unto the hold.

25 AND Sam'u-el died; and all the Is'ra-elites were gathered together, and lamented him, and buried him in his house at Ra'-mah. And Da'vid arose, and went down to the wilderness of Pa'ran.

2 And *there was* a man in Ma'on, whose possessions *were* in Car'mel; and the man *was* very great, and he had three thousand sheep, and a thousand goats: and he was shearing his sheep in Car'mel.

3 Now the name of the man *was* Na'bal; and the name of his wife Ab'i-gail: and *she was* a woman of good understanding, and of a beautiful countenance: but the man *was* churlish and evil in his doings; and he *was* of the house of Ca'leb.

4 ¶ And Da'vid heard in the wilderness that Na'bal did shear his sheep.

5 And Da'vid sent out ten young men, and Da'vid said unto the young men, Get you up to Car'mel, and go to Na'bal, and greet him in my name:

6 And thus shall ye say to him that liveth *in* prosperity, Peace *be* both to thee, and peace *be* to thine house, and peace *be* unto all that thou hast.

7 And now I have heard that thou hast shearers: now thy shepherds which were with us, we hurt them not, neither was there ought missing unto them, all the while they were in Car'mel.

8 Ask thy young men, and they will shew thee. Wherefore let the young men find favour in thine eyes: for we come in a good day: give, I pray thee, whatsoever cometh to thine hand unto thy servants, and to thy son Da'vid.

9 And when Da'vid's young men came, they spake to Na'bal according to all those words in the name of Da'vid, and ceased.

10 ¶ And Na'bal answered Da'vid's servants, and said, Who *is* Da'vid? and who *is* the son of Jes'se? there be many servants now a days that break away every man from his master.

11 Shall I then take my bread, and my water, and my flesh that I have killed for my shearers, and give *it* unto men, whom I know not whence they *be*?

12 So Da'vid's young men turned their way, and went again, and came and told him all those sayings.

13 And Da'vid said unto his men, Gird ye on every man his sword. And they girded on every man his sword; and Da'vid also girded on his sword: and there went up after Da'vid about four hundred men; and two hundred abode by the stuff.

14 ¶ But one of the young men told Ab'i-gail, Na'bal's wife, saying, Behold, Da'vid sent messengers out of the wilderness to salute our master; and he railed on them.

15 But the men *were* very good unto us, and we were not hurt, neither missed we any thing, as long as we were conversant with them, when we were in the fields:

16 They were a wall unto us both by night and day, all the while we were with them keeping the sheep.

17 Now therefore know and consider what thou wilt do; for evil is determined against our master, and against all his household: for he *is* such a son of Be'li-al, that *a man* cannot speak to him.

18 ¶ Then Ab'i-gail made haste, and took two hundred loaves, and two bottles of wine, and five sheep ready dressed, and five measures of parched *corn*, and an hundred clusters of raisins, and two hundred cakes of figs, and laid *them* on asses.

19 And she said unto her servants, Go on before me; behold, I come after you. But she told not her husband Na'bal.

20 And it was so, *as* she rode on the ass, that she came down by the covert of the hill, and, behold, Da'vid and his men came down against her; and she met them.

21 Now Da'vid had said, Surely in vain have I kept all that this *fellow* hath in the wilderness, so that nothing was missed of all that *pertained* unto him: and he hath requited me evil for good.

22 So and more also do God unto the enemies of Da'vid, if I leave of all that *pertain* to him by the morning light any that pisseth against the wall.

23 And when Ab'i-gail saw Da'vid, she hasted, and lighted off the ass, and fell before Da'vid on her face, and bowed herself to the ground,

24 And fell at his feet, and said, Upon me, my lord, *upon* me *let this* iniquity *be*: and let thine handmaid, I pray thee, speak in thine audience, and hear the words of thine handmaid.

25 Let not my lord, I pray thee, regard this man of Be'li-al, *even* Na'bal: for as his name *is*, so *is* he; Na'bal *is* his name, and folly *is* with him: but I thine handmaid saw not the young men of my lord, whom thou didst send.

26 Now therefore, my lord, *as* the LORD liveth, and *as* thy soul liveth, seeing the LORD hath withholden thee from coming to *shed* blood, and from avenging thyself with thine own hand, now let thine enemies, and they that seek evil to my lord, be as Na'bal.

27 And now this blessing which thine handmaid hath brought unto my lord, let it even be given unto the young men that follow my lord.

28 I pray thee, forgive the trespass of thine handmaid: for the LORD will certainly make my lord a sure house; because my lord fighteth the battles of the LORD, and evil hath not been found in thee *all* thy days.

29 Yet a man is risen to pursue thee, and to seek thy soul: but the soul of my lord shall be bound in the bundle of life with the LORD thy God; and the souls of thine enemies, them shall he sling out, *as out* of the middle of a sling.

30 And it shall come to pass, when the LORD shall have done to my lord according to all the good that he hath spoken concerning thee, and shall have appointed thee ruler over Is'ra-el;

31 That this shall be no grief unto thee, nor

offence of heart unto my lord, either that thou hast shed blood causeless, or that my lord hath avenged himself: but when the LORD shall have dealt well with my lord, then remember thine handmaid.

32 ¶ And Da'vid said to Ab'i-gail, Blessed be the LORD God of Is'ra-el, which sent thee this day to meet me:

33 And blessed be thy advice, and blessed be thou, which hast kept me this day from coming to shed blood, and from avenging myself with mine own hand.

34 For in very deed, as the LORD God of Is'ra-el liveth, which hath kept me back from hurting thee, except thou hadst hasted and come to meet me, surely there had not been left unto Na'bal by the morning light any that pisseth against the wall.

35 So Da'vid received of her hand that which she had brought him, and said unto her, Go up in peace to thine house; see, I have hearkened to thy voice, and have accepted thy person.

36 ¶ And Ab'i-gail came to Na'bal; and, behold, he held a feast in his house, like the feast of a king; and Na'bal's heart was merry within him, for he was very drunken: wherefore she told him nothing, less or more, until the morning light.

37 But it came to pass in the morning, when the wine was gone out of Na'bal, and his wife had told him these things, that his heart died within him, and he became as a stone.

38 And it came to pass about ten days after, that the LORD smote Na'bal, that he died.

39 ¶ And when Da'vid heard that Na'bal was dead, he said, Blessed be the LORD, that hath pleaded the cause of my reproach from the hand of Na'bal, and hath kept his servant from evil: for the LORD hath returned the wickedness of Na'bal upon his own head. And Da'vid sent and communed with Ab'i-gail, to take her to him to wife.

40 And when the servants of Da'vid were come to Ab'i-gail to Car'mel, they spake unto her, saying, Da'vid sent us unto thee, to take thee to him to wife.

41 And she arose, and bowed herself on her face to the earth, and said, Behold, let thine handmaid be a servant to wash the feet of the servants of my lord.

42 And Ab'i-gail hasted, and arose, and rode upon an ass, with five damsels of hers that went after her; and she went after the messengers of Da'vid, and became his wife.

43 And Da'vid also took A-hin'o-am of Jez're-el; and they were also both of them his wives.

44 ¶ But Saul had given Mi'chal his daughter, Da'vid's wife, to Phal'ti the son of La'ish, which was of Gal'lim.

26
AND the Ziph'ites came unto Saul to Gib'e-ah, saying, Doth not Da'vid hide himself in the hill of Hach'i-lah, which is before Jesh'i-mon?

2 Then Saul arose, and went down to the wilderness of Ziph, having three thousand chosen men of Is'ra-el with him, to seek Da'vid in the wilderness of Ziph.

3 And Saul pitched in the hill of Hach'i-lah, which is before Jesh'i-mon, by the way. But Da'vid abode in the wilderness, and he saw that Saul came after him into the wilderness.

4 Da'vid therefore sent out spies, and understood that Saul was come in very deed.

5 ¶ And Da'vid arose, and came to the place where Saul had pitched: and Da'vid beheld the place where Saul lay, and Ab'ner the son of Ner, the captain of his host: and Saul lay in the trench, and the people pitched round about him.

6 Then answered Da'vid and said to A-him'e-lech the Hit'tite, and to A-bish'a-i the son of Zer-u-i'ah, brother to Jo'ab, saying, Who will go down with me to Saul to the camp? And A-bish'a-i said, I will go down with thee.

7 So Da'vid and A-bish'a-i came to the people by night: and, behold, Saul lay sleeping within the trench, and his spear stuck in the ground at his bolster: but Ab'ner and the people lay round about him.

8 Then said A-bish'a-i to Da'vid, God hath delivered thine enemy into thine hand this day: now therefore let me smite him, I pray thee, with the spear even to the earth at once, and I will not smite him the second time.

9 And Da'vid said to A-bish'a-i, Destroy him not: for who can stretch forth his hand against the LORD's anointed, and be guiltless?

10 Da'vid said furthermore, As the LORD liveth, the LORD shall smite him; or his day shall come to die; or he shall descend into battle, and perish.

11 The LORD forbid that I should stretch forth mine hand against the LORD's anointed: but, I pray thee, take thou now the spear that is at his bolster, and the cruse of water, and let us go.

12 So Da'vid took the spear and the cruse of water from Saul's bolster; and they gat them away, and no man saw it, nor knew it, neither awaked: for they were all asleep; because a deep sleep from the LORD was fallen upon them.

13 ¶ Then Da'vid went over to the other side, and stood on the top of an hill afar off; a great space being between them:

14 And Da'vid cried to the people, and to Ab'ner the son of Ner, saying, Answerest thou not, Ab'ner? Then Ab'ner answered and said, Who art thou that criest to the king?

15 And Da'vid said to Ab'ner, Art not thou a valiant man? and who is like to thee in Is'ra-el? wherefore then hast thou not kept thy lord the king? for there came one of the people in to destroy the king thy lord.

16 This thing is not good that thou hast done. As the LORD liveth, ye are worthy to die, because ye have not kept your master, the LORD's anointed. And now see where the king's spear is, and the cruse of water that was at his bolster.

17 And Saul knew Da'vid's voice, and said, Is this thy voice, my son Da'vid? And Da'vid said, It is my voice, my lord, O king.

18 And he said, Wherefore doth my lord thus pursue after his servant? for what have I done? or what evil is in mine hand?

19 Now therefore, I pray thee, let my lord the king hear the words of his servant. If the LORD have stirred thee up against me, let him accept an offering: but if they be the children of men, cursed be they before the LORD; for they have driven me out this day from abiding in the inheritance of the LORD, saying, Go, serve other gods.

20 Now therefore, let not my blood fall to the earth before the face of the LORD: for the king of Is'ra-el is come out to seek a flea, as when one doth hunt a partridge in the mountains.

21 ¶ Then said Saul, I have sinned: return, my son Da'vid: for I will no more do thee harm, because my soul was precious in thine eyes this day: behold, I have played the fool, and have erred exceedingly.

22 And Da'vid answered and said, Behold the

king's spear! and let one of the young men come over and fetch it.

23 The LORD render to every man his righteousness and his faithfulness: for the LORD delivered thee into *my* hand to day, but I would not stretch forth mine hand against the LORD's anointed.

24 And, behold, as thy life was much set by this day in mine eyes, so let my life be much set by in the eyes of the LORD, and let him deliver me out of all tribulation.

25 Then Saul said to Da'vid, Blessed *be* thou, my son Da'vid: thou shalt both do great *things*, and also shalt still prevail. So Da'vid went on his way, and Saul returned to his place.

27 AND Da'vid said in his heart, I shall now perish one day by the hand of Saul: *there is* nothing better for me than that I should speedily escape into the land of the Phi-lis'tines; and Saul shall despair of me, to seek me any more in any coast of Is'ra-el: so shall I escape out of his hand.

2 And Da'vid arose, and he passed over with the six hundred men that *were* with him unto A'chish, the son of Ma'och, king of Gath.

3 And Da'vid dwelt with A'chish at Gath, he and his men, every man with his household, *even* Da'vid with his two wives, A-hin'o-am the Jez're-it-ess, and Ab'i-gail the Car'mel-it-ess, Na'bal's wife.

4 And it was told Saul that Da'vid was fled to Gath: and he sought no more again for him.

5 ¶ And Da'vid said unto A'chish, If I have now found grace in thine eyes, let them give me a place in some town in the country, that I may dwell there: for why should thy servant dwell in the royal city with thee?

6 Then A'chish gave him Zik'lag that day: wherefore Zik'lag pertaineth unto the kings of Ju'dah unto this day.

7 And the time that Da'vid dwelt in the country of the Phi-lis'tines was a full year and four months.

8 ¶ And Da'vid and his men went up, and invaded the Gesh'u-rites, and the Gez'rites, and the Am'a-lek-ites: for those *nations were* of old the inhabitants of the land, as thou goest to Shur, even unto the land of E'gypt.

9 And Da'vid smote the land, and left neither man nor woman alive, and took away the sheep, and the oxen, and the asses, and the camels, and the apparel, and returned, and came to A'chish.

10 And A'chish said, Whither have ye made a road to day? And Da'vid said, Against the south of Ju'dah, and against the south of the Je-rah'me-el-ites, and against the south of the Ken'ites.

11 And Da'vid saved neither man nor woman alive, to bring *tidings* to Gath, saying, Lest they should tell on us, saying, So did Da'vid, and so *will be* his manner all the while he dwelleth in the country of the Phi-lis'tines.

12 And A'chish believed Da'vid, saying, He hath made his people Is'ra-el utterly to abhor him; therefore he shall be my servant for ever.

28 AND it came to pass in those days, that the Phi-lis'tines gathered their armies together for warfare, to fight with Is'ra-el. And A'chish said unto Da'vid, Know thou assuredly, that thou shalt go out with me to battle, thou and thy men.

2 And Da'vid said to A'chish, Surely thou shalt know what thy servant can do. And A'-chish said to Da'vid, Therefore will I make thee keeper of mine head for ever.

3 ¶ Now Sam'u-el was dead, and all Is'ra-el had lamented him, and buried him in Ra'mah, even in his own city. And Saul had put away those that had familiar spirits, and the wizards, out of the land.

4 And the Phi-lis'tines gathered themselves together, and came and pitched in Shu'nem: and Saul gathered all Is'ra-el together, and they pitched in Gil-bo'a.

5 And when Saul saw the host of the Phi-lis'-tines, he was afraid, and his heart greatly trembled.

6 And when Saul enquired of the LORD, the LORD answered him not, neither by dreams, nor by U'rim, nor by prophets.

7 ¶ Then said Saul unto his servants, Seek me a woman that hath a familiar spirit, that I may go to her, and enquire of her. And his servants said to him, Behold, *there is* a woman that hath a familiar spirit at En'-dor.

8 And Saul disguised himself, and put on other raiment, and he went, and two men with him, and they came to the woman by night: and he said, I pray thee, divine unto me by the familiar spirit, and bring me *him* up, whom I shall name unto thee.

9 And the woman said unto him, Behold, thou knowest what Saul hath done, how he hath cut off those that have familiar spirits, and the wizards, out of the land: wherefore then layest thou a snare for my life, to cause me to die?

10 And Saul sware to her by the LORD, saying, *As* the LORD liveth, there shall no punishment happen to thee for this thing.

11 Then said the woman, Whom shall I bring up unto thee? And he said, Bring me up Sam'u-el.

12 And when the woman saw Sam'u-el, she cried with a loud voice: and the woman spake to Saul, saying, Why hast thou deceived me? for thou *art* Saul.

13 And the king said unto her, Be not afraid: for what sawest thou? And the woman said unto Saul, I saw gods ascending out of the earth.

14 And he said unto her, What form *is* he of? And she said, An old man cometh up; and he *is* covered with a mantle. And Saul perceived that it *was* Sam'u-el, and he stooped with *his* face to the ground, and bowed himself.

15 ¶ And Sam'u-el said to Saul, Why hast thou disquieted me, to bring me up? And Saul answered, I am sore distressed; for the Phi-lis'-tines make war against me, and God is departed from me, and answereth me no more, neither by prophets, nor by dreams: therefore I have called thee, that thou mayest make known unto me what I shall do.

16 Then said Sam'u-el, Wherefore then dost thou ask of me, seeing the LORD is departed from thee, and is become thine enemy?

17 And the LORD hath done to him, as he spake by me: for the LORD hath rent the kingdom out of thine hand, and given it to thy neighbour, *even* to Da'vid:

18 Because thou obeyedst not the voice of the LORD, nor executedst his fierce wrath upon Am'a-lek, therefore hath the LORD done this thing unto thee this day.

19 Moreover the LORD will also deliver Is'ra-el with thee into the hand of the Phi-lis'tines: and to morrow *shalt* thou and thy sons *be* with me: the LORD also shall deliver the host of Is'ra-el into the hand of the Phi-lis'tines.

20 Then Saul fell straightway all along on the

earth, and was sore afraid, because of the words of Sam'u-el: and there was no strength in him; for he had eaten no bread all the day, nor all the night.

21 ¶ And the woman came unto Saul, and saw that he was sore troubled, and said unto him, Behold, thine handmaid hath obeyed thy voice, and I have put my life in my hand, and have hearkened unto thy words which thou spakest unto me.

22 Now therefore, I pray thee, hearken thou also unto the voice of thine handmaid, and let me set a morsel of bread before thee; and eat, that thou mayest have strength, when thou goest on thy way.

23 But he refused, and said, I will not eat. But his servants, together with the woman, compelled him; and he hearkened unto their voice. So he arose from the earth, and sat upon the bed.

24 And the woman had a fat calf in the house; and she hasted, and killed it, and took flour, and kneaded it, and did bake unleavened bread thereof:

25 And she brought it before Saul, and before his servants; and they did eat. Then they rose up, and went away that night.

29 NOW the Phi-lis'tines gathered together all their armies to A'phek: and the Is'ra-el-ites pitched by a fountain which is in Jez're-el.

2 And the lords of the Phi-lis'tines passed on by hundreds, and by thousands: but Da'vid and his men passed on in the rereward with A'chish.

3 Then said the princes of the Phi-lis'tines, What do these He'brews here? And A'chish said unto the princes of the Phi-lis'tines, Is not this Da'vid, the servant of Saul the king of Is'ra-el, which hath been with me these days, or these years, and I have found no fault in him since he fell unto me unto this day?

4 And the princes of the Phi-lis'tines were wroth with him; and the princes of the Phi-lis'-tines said unto him, Make this fellow return, that he may go again to his place which thou hast appointed him, and let him not go down with us to battle, lest in the battle he be an adversary to us: for wherewith should he reconcile himself unto his master? should it not be with the heads of these men?

5 Is not this Da'vid, of whom they sang one to another in dances, saying, Saul slew his thousands, and Da'vid his ten thousands?

6 ¶ Then A'chish called Da'vid, and said unto him, Surely, as the LORD liveth, thou hast been upright, and thy going out and thy coming in with me in the host is good in my sight: for I have not found evil in thee since the day of thy coming unto me unto this day: nevertheless the lords favour thee not.

7 Wherefore now return, and go in peace, that thou displease not the lords of the Phi-lis'-tines.

8 ¶ And Da'vid said unto A'chish, But what have I done? and what hast thou found in thy servant so long as I have been with thee unto this day, that I may not go fight against the enemies of my lord the king?

9 And A'chish answered and said to Da'vid, I know that thou art good in my sight, as an angel of God: notwithstanding the princes of the Phi-lis'tines have said, He shall not go up with us to the battle.

10 Wherefore now rise up early in the morning with thy master's servants that are come with thee: and as soon as ye be up early in the morning, and have light, depart.

11 So Da'vid and his men rose up early to depart in the morning, to return into the land of the Phi-lis'tines. And the Phi-lis'tines went up to Jez're-el.

30 AND it came to pass, when Da'vid and his men were come to Zik'lag on the third day, that the Am'a-lek-ites had invaded the south, and Zik'lag, and smitten Zik'lag, and burned it with fire;

2 And had taken the women captives, that were therein: they slew not any, either great or small, but carried them away, and went on their way.

3 ¶ So Da'vid and his men came to the city, and, behold, it was burned with fire; and their wives, and their sons, and their daughters, were taken captives.

4 Then Da'vid and the people that were with him lifted up their voice and wept, until they had no more power to weep.

5 And Da'vid's two wives were taken captives, A-hin'o-am the Jez're-el-it-ess, and Ab'i-gail the wife of Na'bal the Car'mel-ite.

6 And Da'vid was greatly distressed; for the people spake of stoning him, because the soul of all the people was grieved, every man for his sons and for his daughters: but Da'vid encouraged himself in the LORD his God.

7 And Da'vid said to A-bi'a-thar the priest, A-him'e-lech's son, I pray thee, bring me hither the ephod. And A-bi'a-thar brought thither the ephod to Da'vid.

8 And Da'vid enquired at the LORD, saying, Shall I pursue after this troop? shall I overtake them? And he answered him, Pursue: for thou shalt surely overtake them, and without fail recover all.

9 So Da'vid went, he and the six hundred men that were with him, and came to the brook Be'sor, where those that were left behind stayed.

10 But Da'vid pursued, he and four hundred men: for two hundred abode behind, which were so faint that they could not go over the brook Be'sor.

11 ¶ And they found an E-gyp'tian in the field, and brought him to Da'vid, and gave him bread, and he did eat; and they made him drink water;

12 And they gave him a piece of a cake of figs, and two clusters of raisins: and when he had eaten, his spirit came again to him: for he had eaten no bread, nor drunk any water, three days and three nights.

13 And Da'vid said unto him, To whom belongest thou? and whence art thou? And he said, I am a young man of E'gypt, servant to an Am'a-lek-ite; and my master left me, because three days agone I fell sick.

14 We made an invasion upon the south of the Cher'eth-ites, and upon the coast which belongeth to Ju'dah, and upon the south of Ca'leb; and we burned Zik'lag with fire.

15 And Da'vid said to him, Canst thou bring me down to this company? And he said, Swear unto me by God, that thou wilt neither kill me, nor deliver me into the hands of my master, and I will bring thee down to this company.

16 ¶ And when he had brought him down, behold, they were spread abroad upon all the earth, eating and drinking, and dancing, because of all the great spoil that they had taken out of the land of the Phi-lis'tines, and out of the land of Ju'dah.

17 And Da′vid smote them from the twilight even unto the evening of the next day: and there escaped not a man of them, save four hundred young men, which rode upon camels, and fled.

18 And Da′vid recovered all that the Am′a-lek-ites had carried away: and Da′vid rescued his two wives.

19 And there was nothing lacking to them, neither small nor great, neither sons nor daughters, neither spoil, nor any thing that they had taken to them: Da′vid recovered all.

20 And Da′vid took all the flocks and the herds, which they drave before those other cattle, and said, This is Da′vid's spoil.

21 ¶ And Da′vid came to the two hundred men, which were so faint that they could not follow Da′vid, whom they had made also to abide at the brook Be′sor: and they went forth to meet Da′vid, and to meet the people that were with him: and when Da′vid came near to the people, he saluted them.

22 Then answered all the wicked men and men of Be′li-al, of those that went with Da′vid, and said, Because they went not with us, we will not give them ought of the spoil that we have recovered, save to every man his wife and his children, that they may lead them away, and depart.

23 Then said Da′vid, Ye shall not do so, my brethren, with that which the LORD hath given us, who hath preserved us, and delivered the company that came against us into our hand.

24 For who will hearken unto you in this matter? but as his part is that goeth down to the battle, so shall his part be that tarrieth by the stuff: they shall part alike.

25 And it was so from that day forward, that he made it a statute and an ordinance for Is′ra-el unto this day.

26 ¶ And when Da′vid came to Zik′lag, he sent of the spoil unto the elders of Ju′dah, even to his friends, saying, Behold a present for you of the spoil of the enemies of the LORD;

27 To them which were in Beth′-el, and to them which were in south Ra′moth, and to them which were in Jat′tir,

28 And to them which were in Ar′o-er, and to them which were in Siph′moth, and to them which were in Esh-te-mo′a,

29 And to them which were in Ra′chal, and to them which were in the cities of the Je-rah′me-el-ites, and to them which were in the cities of the Ken′ites,

30 And to them which were in Hor′mah, and

to them which were in Chor-a′shan, and to them which were in A′thach,

31 And to them which were in He′bron, and to all the places where Da′vid himself and his men were wont to haunt.

31 NOW the Phi-lis′tines fought against Is′-ra-el: and the men of Is′ra-el fled from before the Phi-lis′tines, and fell down slain in mount Gil-bo′a.

2 And the Phi-lis′tines followed hard upon Saul and upon his sons; and the Phi-lis′tines slew Jon′a-than, and A-bin′a-dab, and Mel′chi-shu′a, Saul's sons.

3 And the battle went sore against Saul, and the archers hit him; and he was sore wounded of the archers.

4 Then said Saul unto his armourbearer, Draw thy sword, and thrust me through therewith; lest these uncircumcised come and thrust me through, and abuse me. But his armourbearer would not; for he was sore afraid. Therefore Saul took a sword, and fell upon it.

5 And when his armourbearer saw that Saul was dead, he fell likewise upon his sword, and died with him.

6 So Saul died, and his three sons, and his armourbearer, and all his men, that same day together.

7 ¶ And when the men of Is′ra-el that were on the other side of the valley, and they that were on the other side Jor′dan, saw that the men of Is′ra-el fled, and that Saul and his sons were dead, they forsook the cities, and fled; and the Phi-lis′tines came and dwelt in them.

8 And it came to pass on the morrow, when the Phi-lis′tines came to strip the slain, that they found Saul and his three sons fallen in mount Gil-bo′a.

9 And they cut off his head, and stripped off his armour, and sent into the land of the Phi-lis′tines round about, to publish it in the house of their idols, and among the people.

10 And they put his armour in the house of Ash′ta-roth: and they fastened his body to the wall of Beth′-shan.

11 ¶ And when the inhabitants of Ja′besh-gil′e-ad heard of that which the Phi-lis′tines had done to Saul;

12 All the valiant men arose, and went all night, and took the body of Saul and the bodies of his sons from the wall of Beth′-shan, and came to Ja′besh, and burnt them there.

13 And they took their bones, and buried them under a tree at Ja′besh, and fasted seven days.

THE SECOND BOOK OF

SAMUEL

1 NOW it came to pass after the death of Saul, when Da′vid was returned from the slaughter of the Am′a-lek-ites, and Da′vid had abode two days in Zik′lag;

2 It came even to pass on the third day, that, behold, a man came out of the camp from Saul with his clothes rent, and earth upon his head: and so it was, when he came to Da′vid, that he fell to the earth, and did obeisance.

3 And Da′vid said unto him, From whence comest thou? And he said unto him, Out of the camp of Is′ra-el am I escaped.

4 And Da′vid said unto him, How went the

matter? I pray thee, tell me. And he answered, That the people are fled from the battle, and many of the people also are fallen and dead; and Saul and Jon′a-than his son are dead also.

5 And Da′vid said unto the young man that told him, How knowest thou that Saul and Jon′-a-than his son be dead?

6 And the young man that told him said, As I happened by chance upon mount Gil-bo′a, behold, Saul leaned upon his spear; and, lo, the chariots and horsemen followed hard after him.

7 And when he looked behind him, he saw me, and called unto me. And I answered, Here am I.

8 And he said unto me, Who *art* thou? And I answered him, I *am* an Am′a-lek-ite.

9 He said unto me again, Stand, I pray thee, upon me, and slay me: for anguish is come upon me, because my life *is* yet whole in me.

10 So I stood upon him, and slew him, because I was sure that he could not live after that he was fallen: and I took the crown that *was* upon his head, and the bracelet that *was* on his arm, and have brought them hither unto my lord.

11 Then Da′vid took hold on his clothes, and rent them; and likewise all the men that *were* with him:

12 And they mourned, and wept, and fasted until even, for Saul, and for Jon′a-than his son, and for the people of the LORD, and for the house of Is′ra-el; because they were fallen by the sword.

13 ¶ And Da′vid said unto the young man that told him, Whence *art* thou? And he answered, I *am* the son of a stranger, an Am′a-lek-ite.

14 And Da′vid said unto him, How wast thou not afraid to stretch forth thine hand to destroy the LORD'S anointed?

15 And Da′vid called one of the young men, and said, Go near, *and* fall upon him. And he smote him that he died.

16 And Da′vid said unto him, Thy blood *be* upon thy head; for thy mouth hath testified against thee, saying, I have slain the LORD'S anointed.

17 ¶ And Da′vid lamented with this lamentation over Saul and over Jon′a-than his son:

18 (Also he bade them teach the children of Ju′dah *the use of* the bow: behold, *it is* written in the book of Ja′sher.)

19 The beauty of Is′ra-el is slain upon thy high places: how are the mighty fallen!

20 Tell *it* not in Gath, publish *it* not in the streets of As′ke-lon; lest the daughters of the Phi-lis′tines rejoice, lest the daughters of the uncircumcised triumph.

21 Ye mountains of Gil-bo′a, *let there be* no dew, neither *let there be* rain, upon you, nor fields of offerings: for there the shield of the mighty is vilely cast away, the shield of Saul, *as though he had* not *been* anointed with oil.

22 From the blood of the slain, from the fat of the mighty, the bow of Jon′a-than turned not back, and the sword of Saul returned not empty.

23 Saul and Jon′a-than *were* lovely and pleasant in their lives, and in their death they were not divided: they were swifter than eagles, they were stronger than lions.

24 Ye daughters of Is′ra-el, weep over Saul, who clothed you in scarlet, with *other* delights, who put on ornaments of gold upon your apparel.

25 How are the mighty fallen in the midst of the battle! O Jon′a-than, *thou wast* slain in thine high places.

26 I am distressed for thee, my brother Jon′a-than: very pleasant hast thou been unto me: thy love to me was wonderful, passing the love of women.

27 How are the mighty fallen, and the weapons of war perished!

2 AND it came to pass after this, that Da′vid enquired of the LORD, saying, Shall I go up into any of the cities of Ju′dah? And the LORD said unto him, Go up. And Da′vid said, Whither shall I go up? And he said, Unto He′bron.

2 So Da′vid went up thither, and his two wives also, A-hin′o-am the Jez′re-el-it-ess, and Ab′i-gail Na′bal's wife the Car′mel-ite.

3 And his men that *were* with him did Da′vid bring up, every man with his household: and they dwelt in the cities of He′bron.

4 And the men of Ju′dah came, and there they anointed Da′vid king over the house of Ju′dah. And they told Da′vid, saying, *That* the men of Ja′besh-gil′e-ad *were they* that buried Saul.

5 ¶ And Da′vid sent messengers unto the men of Ja′besh-gil′e-ad, and said unto them, Blessed *be* ye of the LORD, that ye have shewed this kindness unto your lord, *even* unto Saul, and have buried him.

6 And now the LORD shew kindness and truth unto you: and I also will requite you this kindness, because ye have done this thing.

7 Therefore now let your hands be strengthened, and be ye valiant: for your master Saul is dead, and also the house of Ju′dah have anointed me king over them.

8 ¶ But Ab′ner the son of Ner, captain of Saul's host, took Ish-bo′sheth the son of Saul, and brought him over to Ma-ha-na′im;

9 And made him king over Gil′e-ad, and over the Ash′ur-ites, and over Jez′re-el, and over E′-phra-im, and over Ben′ja-min, and over all Is′ra-el.

10 Ish-bo′sheth Saul's son *was* forty years old when he began to reign over Is′ra-el, and reigned two years. But the house of Ju′dah followed Da′vid.

11 And the time that Da′vid was king in He′-bron over the house of Ju′dah was seven years and six months.

12 ¶ And Ab′ner the son of Ner, and the servants of Ish-bo′sheth the son of Saul, went out from Ma-ha-na′im to Gib′e-on.

13 And Jo′ab the son of Zer-u-i′ah, and the servants of Da′vid, went out, and met together by the pool of Gib′e-on: and they sat down, the one on the one side of the pool, and the other on the other side of the pool.

14 And Ab′ner said to Jo′ab, Let the young men now arise, and play before us. And Jo′ab said, Let them arise.

15 Then there arose and went over by number twelve of Ben′ja-min, which *pertained* to Ish-bo′sheth the son of Saul, and twelve of the servants of Da′vid.

16 And they caught every one his fellow by the head, and *thrust* his sword in his fellow's side; so they fell down together: wherefore that place was called Hel′kath-haz′zu-rim, which *is* in Gib′e-on.

17 And there was a very sore battle that day; and Ab′ner was beaten, and the men of Is′ra-el, before the servants of Da′vid.

18 ¶ And there were three sons of Zer-u-i′ah there, Jo′ab, and A-bish′a-i, and A′sa-hel: and A′sa-hel *was as* light of foot as a wild roe.

19 And A′sa-hel pursued after Ab′ner; and in going he turned not to the right hand nor to the left from following Ab′ner.

20 Then Ab′ner looked behind him, and said, *Art* thou A′sa-hel? And he answered, I *am.*

21 And Ab′ner said to him, Turn thee aside to thy right hand or to thy left, and lay thee hold on one of the young men, and take thee his armour. But A′sa-hel would not turn aside from following of him.

22 And Ab′ner said again to A′sa-hel, Turn thee aside from following me: wherefore should I smite thee to the ground? how then should I hold up my face to Jo′ab thy brother?

23 Howbeit he refused to turn aside: wherefore Ab′ner with the hinder end of the spear

smote him under the fifth *rib*, that the spear came out behind him; and he fell down there, and died in the same place: and it came to pass, *that* as many as came to the place where A'sahel fell down and died stood still.

24 Jo'ab also and A-bish'a-i pursued after Ab'ner: and the sun went down when they were come to the hill of Am'mah, that *lieth* before Gi'ah by the way of the wilderness of Gib'e-on.

25 ¶ And the children of Ben'ja-min gathered themselves together after Ab'ner, and became one troop, and stood on the top of an hill.

26 Then Ab'ner called to Jo'ab, and said, Shall the sword devour for ever? knowest thou not that it will be bitterness in the latter end? how long shall it be then, ere thou bid the people return from following their brethren?

27 And Jo'ab said, *As* God liveth, unless thou hadst spoken, surely then in the morning the people had gone up every one from following his brother.

28 So Jo'ab blew a trumpet, and all the people stood still, and pursued after Is'ra-el no more, neither fought they any more.

29 And Ab'ner and his men walked all that night through the plain, and passed over Jor'dan, and went through all Bith'ron, and they came to Ma-ha-na'im.

30 And Jo'ab returned from following Ab'ner: and when he had gathered all the people together, there lacked of Da'vid's servants nineteen men and A'sa-hel.

31 But the servants of Da'vid had smitten of Ben'ja-min, and of Ab'ner's men, *so that* three hundred and threescore men died.

32 ¶ And they took up A'sa-hel, and buried him in the sepulchre of his father, which *was in* Beth'-le-hem. And Jo'ab and his men went all night, and they came to He'bron at break of day.

3 NOW there was long war between the house of Saul and the house of Da'vid: but Da'vid waxed stronger and stronger, and the house of Saul waxed weaker and weaker.

2 ¶ And unto Da'vid were sons born in He'bron: and his firstborn was Am'non, of A-hin'o-am the Jez're-el-it-ess;

3 And his second, Chil'e-ab, of Ab'i-gail the wife of Na'bal the Car'mel-ite; and the third, Ab'sa-lom the son of Ma'a-cah the daughter of Tal'mai king of Ge'shur;

4 And the fourth, Ad-o-ni'jah the son of Hag'gith; and the fifth, Sheph-a-ti'ah the son of Ab'i-tal;

5 And the sixth, Ith're-am, by Eg'lah Da'vid's wife. These were born to Da'vid in He'bron.

6 ¶ And it came to pass, while there was war between the house of Saul and the house of Da'vid, that Ab'ner made himself strong for the house of Saul.

7 And Saul had a concubine, whose name *was* Riz'pah, the daughter of A-i'ah: and Ish-bo'sheth said to Ab'ner, Wherefore hast thou gone in unto my father's concubine?

8 Then was Ab'ner very wroth for the words of Ish-bo'sheth, and said, *Am* I a dog's head, which against Ju'dah do shew kindness this day unto the house of Saul thy father, to his brethren, and to his friends, and have not delivered thee into the hand of Da'vid, that thou chargest me to day with a fault concerning this woman?

9 So do God to Ab'ner, and more also, except, as the LORD hath sworn to Da'vid, even so I do to him;

10 To translate the kingdom from the house of Saul, and to set up the throne of Da'vid over

Is'ra-el and over Ju'dah, from Dan even to Be'-er-she'ba.

11 And he could not answer Ab'ner a word again, because he feared him.

12 ¶ And Ab'ner sent messengers to Da'vid on his behalf, saying, Whose *is* the land? saying *also*, Make thy league with me, and, behold, my hand *shall be* with thee, to bring about all Is'ra-el unto thee.

13 ¶ And he said, Well; I will make a league with thee: but one thing I require of thee, that is, Thou shalt not see my face, except thou first bring Mi'chal Saul's daughter, when thou comest to see my face.

14 And Da'vid sent messengers to Ish-bo'-sheth Saul's son, saying, Deliver *me* my wife Mi'chal, which I espoused to me for an hundred foreskins of the Phi-lis'tines.

15 And Ish-bo'sheth sent, and took her from *her* husband, *even* from Phal'ti-el the son of La'-ish.

16 And her husband went with her along weeping behind her to Ba-hu'rim. Then said Ab'ner unto him, Go, return. And he returned.

17 ¶ And Ab'ner had communication with the elders of Is'ra-el, saying, Ye sought for Da'-vid in times past *to be* king over you:

18 Now then do *it*: for the LORD hath spoken of Da'vid, saying, By the hand of my servant Da'vid I will save my people Is'ra-el out of the hand of the Phi-lis'tines, and out of the hand of all their enemies.

19 And Ab'ner also spake in the ears of Ben'-ja-min: and Ab'ner went also to speak in the ears of Da'vid in He'bron all that seemed good to Is'ra-el, and that seemed good to the whole house of Ben'ja-min.

20 So Ab'ner came to Da'vid to He'bron, and twenty men with him. And Da'vid made Ab'ner and the men that *were* with him a feast.

21 And Ab'ner said unto Da'vid, I will arise and go, and will gather all Is'ra-el unto my lord the king, that they may make a league with thee, and that thou mayest reign over all that thine heart desireth. And Da'vid sent Ab'ner away; and he went in peace.

22 ¶ And, behold, the servants of Da'vid and Jo'ab came from *pursuing* a troop, and brought in a great spoil with them: but Ab'ner *was* not with Da'vid in He'bron; for he had sent him away, and he was gone in peace.

23 When Jo'ab and all the host that *was* with him were come, they told Jo'ab, saying, Ab'ner the son of Ner came to the king, and he hath sent him away, and he is gone in peace.

24 Then Jo'ab came to the king, and said, What hast thou done? behold, Ab'ner came unto thee; why *is* it *that* thou hast sent him away, and he is quite gone?

25 Thou knowest Ab'ner the son of Ner, that he came to deceive thee, and to know thy going out and thy coming in, and to know all that thou doest.

26 And when Jo'ab was come out from Da'-vid, he sent messengers after Ab'ner, which brought him again from the well of Si'rah: but Da'vid knew *it* not.

27 And when Ab'ner was returned to He'-bron, Jo'ab took him aside in the gate to speak with him quietly, and smote him there under the fifth *rib*, that he died, for the blood of A'sa-hel his brother.

28 ¶ And afterward when Da'vid heard *it*, he said, I and my kingdom *are* guiltless before the LORD for ever, from the blood of Ab'ner the son of Ner:

29 Let it rest on the head of Jo'ab, and on all

his father's house; and let there not fail from the house of Jo'ab one that hath an issue, or that is a leper, or that leaneth on a staff, or that falleth on the sword, or that lacketh bread.

30 So Jo'ab and A-bish'a-i his brother slew Ab'ner, because he had slain their brother A'sa-hel at Gib'e-on in the battle.

31 ¶ And Da'vid said to Jo'ab, and to all the people that were with him, Rend your clothes, and gird you with sackcloth, and mourn before Ab'ner. And king Da'vid himself followed the bier.

32 And they buried Ab'ner in He'bron: and the king lifted up his voice, and wept at the grave of Ab'ner; and all the people wept.

33 And the king lamented over Ab'ner, and said, Died Ab'ner as a fool dieth?

34 Thy hands were not bound, nor thy feet put into fetters: as a man falleth before wicked men, so fellest thou. And all the people wept again over him.

35 And when all the people came to cause Da'vid to eat meat while it was yet day, Da'vid sware, saying, So do God to me, and more also, if I taste bread, or ought else, till the sun be down.

36 And all the people took notice of it, and it pleased them: as whatsoever the king did pleased all the people.

37 For all the people and all Is'ra-el understood that day that it was not of the king to slay Ab'ner the son of Ner.

38 And the king said unto his servants, Know ye not that there is a prince and a great man fallen this day in Is'ra-el?

39 And I am this day weak, though anointed king; and these men the sons of Zer-u-i'ah be too hard for me: the LORD shall reward the doer of evil according to his wickedness.

4 AND when Saul's son heard that Ab'ner was dead in He'bron, his hands were feeble, and all the Is'ra-el-ites were troubled.

2 And Saul's son had two men that were captains of bands: the name of the one was Ba'a-nah, and the name of the other Re'chab, the sons of Rim'mon a Be-e'roth-ite, of the children of Ben'ja-min: (for Be-e'roth also was reckoned to Ben'ja-min.

3 And the Be-e'roth-ites fled to Git'ta-im, and were sojourners there until this day.)

4 And Jon'a-than, Saul's son, had a son that was lame of his feet. He was five years old when the tidings came of Saul and Jon'a-than out of Jez're-el, and his nurse took him up, and fled: and it came to pass, as she made haste to flee, that he fell, and became lame. And his name was Me-phib'o-sheth.

5 And the sons of Rim'mon the Be-e'roth-ite, Re'chab and Ba'a-nah, went, and came about the heat of the day to the house of Ish-bo'sheth, who lay on a bed at noon.

6 And they came thither into the midst of the house, as though they would have fetched wheat; and they smote him under the fifth rib: and Re'chab and Ba'a-nah his brother escaped.

7 For when they came into the house, he lay on his bed in his bedchamber, and they smote him, and slew him, and beheaded him, and took his head, and gat them away through the plain all night.

8 And they brought the head of Ish-bo'sheth unto Da'vid to He'bron, and said to the king, Behold the head of Ish-bo'sheth the son of Saul thine enemy, which sought thy life; and the LORD hath avenged my lord the king this day of Saul, and of his seed.

9 ¶ And Da'vid answered Re'chab and Ba'a-nah his brother, the sons of Rim'mon the Be-e'roth-ite, and said unto them, As the LORD liveth, who hath redeemed my soul out of all adversity,

10 When one told me, saying, Behold, Saul is dead, thinking to have brought good tidings, I took hold of him, and slew him in Zik'lag, who thought that I would have given him a reward for his tidings:

11 How much more, when wicked men have slain a righteous person in his own house upon his bed? shall I not therefore now require his blood of your hand, and take you away from the earth?

12 And Da'vid commanded his young men, and they slew them, and cut off their hands and their feet, and hanged them up over the pool in He'bron. But they took the head of Ish-bo'-sheth, and buried it in the sepulchre of Ab'ner in He'bron.

5 THEN came all the tribes of Is'ra-el to Da'-vid unto He'bron, and spake, saying, Behold, we are thy bone and thy flesh.

2 Also in time past, when Saul was king over us, thou wast he that leddest out and broughtest in Is'ra-el: and the LORD said to thee, Thou shalt feed my people Is'ra-el, and thou shalt be a captain over Is'ra-el.

3 So all the elders of Is'ra-el came to the king to He'bron; and king Da'vid made a league with them in He'bron before the LORD: and they anointed Da'vid king over Is'ra-el.

4 ¶ Da'vid was thirty years old when he began to reign, and he reigned forty years.

5 In He'bron he reigned over Ju'dah seven years and six months: and in Je-ru'sa-lem he reigned thirty and three years over all Is'ra-el and Ju'dah.

6 ¶ And the king and his men went to Je-ru'sa-lem unto the Jeb'u-sites, the inhabitants of the land: which spake unto Da'vid, saying, Except thou take away the blind and the lame, thou shalt not come in hither: thinking, Da'vid cannot come in hither.

7 Nevertheless Da'vid took the strong hold of Zi'on: the same is the city of Da'vid.

8 And Da'vid said on that day, Whosoever getteth up to the gutter, and smiteth the Jeb'u-sites, and the lame and the blind, that are hated of Da'vid's soul, he shall be chief and captain. Wherefore they said, The blind and the lame shall not come into the house.

9 So Da'vid dwelt in the fort, and called it the city of Da'vid. And Da'vid built round about from Mil'lo and inward.

10 And Da'vid went on, and grew great, and the LORD God of hosts was with him.

11 ¶ And Hi'ram king of Tyre sent messengers to Da'vid, and cedar trees, and carpenters, and masons: and they built Da'vid an house.

12 And Da'vid perceived that the LORD had established him king over Is'ra-el, and that he had exalted his kingdom for his people Is'ra-el's sake.

13 ¶ And Da'vid took him more concubines and wives out of Je-ru'sa-lem, after he was come from He'bron: and there were yet sons and daughters born to Da'vid.

14 And these be the names of those that were born unto him in Je-ru'sa-lem; Sham-mu'ah, and Sho'bab, and Na'than, and Sol'o-mon,

15 Ib'har also, and El-i-shu'a, and Ne'pheg, and Ja-phi'a,

16 And E-lish'a-ma, and E-li'a-da, and E-liph'a-let.

17 ¶ But when the Phi-lis′tines heard that they had anointed Da′vid king over Is′ra-el, all the Phi-lis′tines came up to seek Da′vid; and Da′vid heard of it, and went down to the hold.

18 The Phi-lis′tines also came and spread themselves in the valley of Reph′a-im.

19 And Da′vid enquired of the LORD, saying, Shall I go up to the Phi-lis′tines? wilt thou deliver them into mine hand? And the LORD said unto Da′vid, Go up: for I will doubtless deliver the Phi-lis′tines into thine hand.

20 And Da′vid came to Ba′al-per′a-zim, and Da′vid smote them there, and said, The LORD hath broken forth upon mine enemies before me, as the breach of waters. Therefore he called the name of that place Ba′al-per′a-zim.

21 And there they left their images, and Da′vid and his men burned them.

22 ¶ And the Phi-lis′tines came up yet again, and spread themselves in the valley of Reph′a-im.

23 And when Da′vid enquired of the LORD, he said, Thou shalt not go up; but fetch a compass behind them, and come upon them over against the mulberry trees.

24 And let it be, when thou hearest the sound of a going in the tops of the mulberry trees, that then thou shalt bestir thyself: for then shall the LORD go out before thee, to smite the host of the Phi-lis′tines.

25 And Da′vid did so, as the LORD had commanded him; and smote the Phi-lis′tines from Ge′ba until thou come to Ga′zer.

6 AGAIN, Da′vid gathered together all the chosen men of Is′ra-el, thirty thousand.

2 And Da′vid arose, and went with all the people that were with him from Ba′a-le of Ju′dah, to bring up from thence the ark of God, whose name is called by the name of the LORD of hosts that dwelleth between the cherubims.

3 And they set the ark of God upon a new cart, and brought it out of the house of A-bin′a-dab that was in Gib′e-ah: and Uz′zah and A-hi′o, the sons of A-bin′a-dab, drave the new cart.

4 And they brought it out of the house of A-bin′a-dab which was at Gib′e-ah, accompanying the ark of God: and A-hi′o went before the ark.

5 And Da′vid and all the house of Is′ra-el played before the LORD on all manner of instruments made of fir wood, even on harps, and on psalteries, and on timbrels, and on cornets, and on cymbals.

6 ¶ And when they came to Na′chon′s threshingfloor, Uz′zah put forth his hand to the ark of God, and took hold of it; for the oxen shook it.

7 And the anger of the LORD was kindled against Uz′zah; and God smote him there for his error; and there he died by the ark of God.

8 And Da′vid was displeased, because the LORD had made a breach upon Uz′zah: and he called the name of the place Pe′rez-uz′zah to this day.

9 And Da′vid was afraid of the LORD that day, and said, How shall the ark of the LORD come to me?

10 So Da′vid would not remove the ark of the LORD unto him into the city of Da′vid: but Da′vid carried it aside into the house of O′bed-e′dom the Git′tite.

11 And the ark of the LORD continued in the house of O′bed-e′dom the Git′tite three months: and the LORD blessed O′bed-e′dom, and all his household.

12 ¶ And it was told king Da′vid, saying, The LORD hath blessed the house of O′bed-e′dom, and all that pertaineth unto him, because of the ark of God. So Da′vid went and brought up the ark of God from the house of O′bed-e′dom into the city of Da′vid with gladness.

13 And it was so, that when they that bare the ark of the LORD had gone six paces, he sacrificed oxen and fatlings.

14 And Da′vid danced before the LORD with all his might; and Da′vid was girded with a linen ephod.

15 So Da′vid and all the house of Is′ra-el brought up the ark of the LORD with shouting, and with the sound of the trumpet.

16 And as the ark of the LORD came into the city of Da′vid, Mi′chal Saul′s daughter looked through a window, and saw king Da′vid leaping and dancing before the LORD; and she despised him in her heart.

17 ¶ And they brought in the ark of the LORD, and set it in his place, in the midst of the tabernacle that Da′vid had pitched for it: and Da′vid offered burnt offerings and peace offerings before the LORD.

18 And as soon as Da′vid had made an end of offering burnt offerings and peace offerings, he blessed the people in the name of the LORD of hosts.

19 And he dealt among all the people, even among the whole multitude of Is′ra-el, as well to the women as men, to every one a cake of bread, and a good piece of flesh, and a flagon of wine. So all the people departed every one to his house.

20 ¶ Then Da′vid returned to bless his household. And Mi′chal the daughter of Saul came out to meet Da′vid, and said, How glorious was the king of Is′ra-el to day, who uncovered himself to day in the eyes of the handmaids of his servants, as one of the vain fellows shamelessly uncovereth himself!

21 And Da′vid said unto Mi′chal, It was before the LORD, which chose me before thy father, and before all his house, to appoint me ruler over the people of the LORD, over Is′ra-el: therefore will I play before the LORD.

22 And I will yet be more vile than thus, and will be base in mine own sight: and of the maidservants which thou hast spoken of, of them shall I be had in honour.

23 Therefore Mi′chal the daughter of Saul had no child unto the day of her death.

7 AND it came to pass, when the king sat in his house, and the LORD had given him rest round about from all his enemies;

2 That the king said unto Na′than the prophet, See now, I dwell in an house of cedar, but the ark of God dwelleth within curtains.

3 And Na′than said to the king, Go, do all that is in thine heart; for the LORD is with thee.

4 ¶ And it came to pass that night, that the word of the LORD came unto Na′than, saying,

5 Go and tell my servant Da′vid, Thus saith the LORD, Shalt thou build me an house for me to dwell in?

6 Whereas I have not dwelt in any house since the time that I brought up the children of Is′ra-el out of E′gypt, even to this day, but have walked in a tent and in a tabernacle.

7 In all the places wherein I have walked with all the children of Is′ra-el spake I a word with any of the tribes of Is′ra-el, whom I commanded to feed my people Is′ra-el, saying, Why build ye not me an house of cedar?

8 Now therefore so shalt thou say unto my servant Da′vid, Thus saith the LORD of hosts, I

took thee from the sheepcote, from following the sheep, to be ruler over my people, over Is'-ra-el:

9 And I was with thee whithersoever thou wentest, and have cut off all thine enemies out of thy sight, and have made thee a great name, like unto the name of the great *men* that *are* in the earth.

10 Moreover I will appoint a place for my people Is'ra-el, and will plant them, that they may dwell in a place of their own, and move no more; neither shall the children of wickedness afflict them any more, as beforetime,

11 And as since the time that I commanded judges *to be* over my people Is'ra-el, and have caused thee to rest from all thine enemies. Also the LORD telleth thee that he will make thee an house.

12 ¶ And when thy days be fulfilled, and thou shalt sleep with thy fathers, I will set up thy seed after thee, which shall proceed out of thy bowels, and I will establish his kingdom.

13 He shall build an house for my name, and I will stablish the throne of his kingdom for ever.

14 I will be his father, and he shall be my son. If he commit iniquity, I will chasten him with the rod of men, and with the stripes of the children of men:

15 But my mercy shall not depart away from him, as I took *it* from Saul, whom I put away before thee.

16 And thine house and thy kingdom shall be established for ever before thee: thy throne shall be established for ever.

17 According to all these words, and according to all this vision, so did Na'than speak unto Da'vid.

18 ¶ Then went king Da'vid in, and sat before the LORD, and he said, Who *am* I, O Lord GOD? and what *is* my house, that thou hast brought me hitherto?

19 And this was yet a small thing in thy sight, O Lord GOD; but thou hast spoken also of thy servant's house for a great while to come. And *is* this the manner of man, O Lord GOD?

20 And what can Da'vid say more unto thee? for thou, Lord GOD, knowest thy servant.

21 For thy word's sake, and according to thine own heart, hast thou done all these great things, to make thy servant know *them*.

22 Wherefore thou art great, O LORD God: for *there* is none like thee, neither *is there any* God beside thee, according to all that we have heard with our ears.

23 And what one nation in the earth *is* like thy people, *even* like Is'ra-el, whom God went to redeem for a people to himself, and to make him a name, and to do for you great things and terrible, for thy land, before thy people, which thou redeemedst to thee from E'gypt, *from* the nations and their gods?

24 For thou hast confirmed to thyself thy people Is'ra-el *to be* a people unto thee for ever: and thou, LORD, art become their God.

25 And now, O LORD God, the word that thou hast spoken concerning thy servant, and concerning his house, establish *it* for ever, and do as thou hast said.

26 And let thy name be magnified for ever, saying, The LORD of hosts *is* the God over Is'ra-el: and let the house of thy servant Da'vid be established before thee.

27 For thou, O LORD of hosts, God of Is'ra-el, hast revealed to thy servant, saying, I will build thee an house: therefore hath thy servant found in his heart to pray this prayer unto thee.

28 And now, O Lord GOD, thou *art* that God, and thy words be true, and thou hast promised this goodness unto thy servant:

29 Therefore now let it please thee to bless the house of thy servant, that it may continue for ever before thee: for thou, O Lord GOD, hast spoken *it*: and with thy blessing let the house of thy servant be blessed for ever.

8 AND after this it came to pass, that Da'vid smote the Phi-lis'tines, and subdued them: and Da'vid took Me'theg–am'mah out of the hand of the Phi-lis'tines.

2 And he smote Mo'ab, and measured them with a line, casting them down to the ground; even with two lines measured he to put to death, and with one full line to keep alive. And so the Mo'ab-ites became Da'vid's servants, *and* brought gifts.

3 ¶ Da'vid smote also Had-ad-e'zer, the son of Re'hob, king of Zo'bah, as he went to recover his border at the river Eu-phra'tes.

4 And Da'vid took from him a thousand *chariots*, and seven hundred horsemen, and twenty thousand footmen: and Da'vid houghed all the chariot *horses*, but reserved of them *for* an hundred chariots.

5 And when the Syr'i-ans of Da-mas'cus came to succour Had-ad-e'zer king of Zo'bah, Da'vid slew of the Syr'i-ans two and twenty thousand men.

6 Then Da'vid put garrisons in Syr'i-a of Da-mas'cus: and the Syr'i-ans became servants to Da'vid, *and* brought gifts. And the LORD preserved Da'vid whithersoever he went.

7 And Da'vid took the shields of gold that were on the servants of Had-ad-e'zer, and brought them to Je-ru'sa-lem.

8 And from Be'tah, and from Ber'o-thai, cities of Had-ad-e'zer, king Da'vid took exceeding much brass.

9 ¶ When To'i king of Ha'math heard that Da'vid had smitten all the host of Had-ad-e'zer,

10 Then To'i sent Jo'ram his son unto king Da'vid, to salute him, and to bless him, because he had fought against Had-ad-e'zer, and smitten him: for Had-ad-e'zer had wars with To'i. And Jo'ram brought with him vessels of silver, and vessels of gold, and vessels of brass:

11 Which also king Da'vid did dedicate unto the LORD, with the silver and gold that he had dedicated of all nations which he subdued;

12 Of Syr'i-a, and of Mo'ab, and of the children of Am'mon, and of the Phi-lis'tines, and of Am'a-lek, and of the spoil of Had-ad-e'zer, son of Re'hob, king of Zo'bah.

13 And Da'vid gat *him* a name when he returned from smiting of the Syr'i-ans in the valley of salt, *being* eighteen thousand *men*.

14 ¶ And he put garrisons in E'dom; throughout all E'dom put he garrisons, and all they of E'dom became Da'vid's servants. And the LORD preserved Da'vid whithersoever he went.

15 And Da'vid reigned over all Is'ra-el; and Da'vid executed judgment and justice unto all his people.

16 And Jo'ab the son of Zer-u-i'ah *was* over the host; and Je-hosh'a-phat the son of A-hi'lud *was* recorder;

17 And Za'dok the son of A-hi'tub, and A-him'e-lech the son of A-bi'a-thar, *were* the priests; and Ser-a-i'ah *was* the scribe;

18 And Be-na'iah the son of Je-hoi'a-da *was* over both the Cher'eth-ites and the Pe'leth-ites; and Da'vid's sons were chief rulers.

9 AND Da'vid said, Is there yet any that is left of the house of Saul, that I may shew him kindness for Jon'a-than's sake?

2 And *there was* of the house of Saul a servant whose name *was* Zi'ba. And when they had called him unto Da'vid, the king said unto him, *Art* thou Zi'ba? And he said, Thy servant *is* he.

3 And the king said, *Is* there not yet any of the house of Saul, that I may shew the kindness of God unto him? And Zi'ba said unto the king, Jon'a-than hath yet a son, *which is* lame on *his* feet.

4 And the king said unto him, Where *is* he? And Zi'ba said unto the king, Behold, he *is* in the house of Ma'chir, the son of Am'mi-el, in Lo-de'bar.

5 ¶ Then king Da'vid sent, and fetched him out of the house of Ma'chir, the son of Am'mi-el, from Lo-de'bar.

6 Now when Me-phib'o-sheth, the son of Jon'a-than, the son of Saul, was come unto Da'-vid, he fell on his face, and did reverence. And Da'vid said, Me-phib'o-sheth. And he answered, Behold thy servant!

7 ¶ And Da'vid said unto him, Fear not: for I will surely shew thee kindness for Jon'a-than thy father's sake, and will restore thee all the land of Saul thy father; and thou shalt eat bread at my table continually.

8 And he bowed himself, and said, What *is* thy servant, that thou shouldest look upon such a dead dog as I *am?*

9 ¶ Then the king called to Zi'ba, Saul's servant, and said unto him, I have given unto thy master's son all that pertained to Saul and to all his house.

10 Thou therefore, and thy sons, and thy servants, shall till the land for him, and thou shalt bring in *the fruits,* that thy master's son may have food to eat: but Me-phib'o-sheth thy master's son shall eat bread alway at my table. Now Zi'ba had fifteen sons and twenty servants.

11 Then said Zi'ba unto the king, According to all that my lord the king hath commanded his servant, so shall thy servant do. As for Me-phib'o-sheth, *said the king,* he shall eat at my table, as one of the king's sons.

12 And Me-phib'o-sheth had a young son, whose name *was* Mi'cha. And all that dwelt in the house of Zi'ba *were* servants unto Me-phib'-o-sheth.

13 So Me-phib'o-sheth dwelt in Je-ru'sa-lem: for he did eat continually at the king's table; and was lame on both his feet.

10 AND it came to pass after this, that the king of the children of Am'mon died, and Ha'nun his son reigned in his stead.

2 Then said Da'vid, I will shew kindness unto Ha'nun the son of Na'hash, as his father shewed kindness unto me. And Da'vid sent to comfort him by the hand of his servants for his father. And Da'vid's servants came into the land of the children of Am'mon.

3 And the princes of the children of Am'mon said unto Ha'nun their lord, Thinkest thou that Da'vid doth honour thy father, that he hath sent comforters unto thee? hath not Da'vid *rather* sent his servants unto thee, to search the city, and to spy it out, and to overthrow it?

4 Wherefore Ha'nun took Da'vid's servants, and shaved off the one half of their beards, and cut off their garments in the middle, *even* to their buttocks, and sent them away.

5 When they told *it* unto Da'vid, he sent to meet them, because the men were greatly ashamed: and the king said, Tarry at Jer'i-cho until your beards be grown, and *then* return.

6 ¶ And when the children of Am'mon saw that they stank before Da'vid, the children of Am'mon sent and hired the Syr'i-ans of Beth-re'hob, and the Syr'i-ans of Zo'ba, twenty thousand footmen, and of king Ma'a-cah a thousand men, and of Ish'-tob twelve thousand men.

7 And when Da'vid heard of *it,* he sent Jo'ab, and all the host of the mighty men.

8 And the children of Am'mon came out, and put the battle in array at the entering in of the gate: and the Syr'i-ans of Zo'ba, and of Re'hob, and Ish'-tob, and Ma'a-cah, *were* by themselves in the field.

9 When Jo'ab saw that the front of the battle was against him before and behind, he chose of all the choice *men* of Is'ra-el, and put *them* in array against the Syr'i-ans:

10 And the rest of the people he delivered into the hand of A-bish'a-i his brother, that he might put *them* in array against the children of Am'mon.

11 And he said, If the Syr'i-ans be too strong for me, then thou shalt help me: but if the children of Am'mon be too strong for thee, then I will come and help thee.

12 Be of good courage, and let us play the men for our people, and for the cities of our God: and the LORD do that which seemeth him good.

13 And Jo'ab drew nigh, and the people that *were* with him, unto the battle against the Syr'i-ans: and they fled before him.

14 And when the children of Am'mon saw that the Syr'i-ans were fled, then fled they also before A-bish'a-i, and entered into the city. So Jo'ab returned from the children of Am'mon, and came to Je-ru'sa-lem.

15 ¶ And when the Syr'i-ans saw that they were smitten before Is'ra-el, they gathered themselves together.

16 And Had-ar-e'zer sent, and brought out the Syr'i-ans that *were* beyond the river: and they came to He'lam; and Sho'bach the captain of the host of Had-ar-e'zer *went* before them.

17 And when it was told Da'vid, he gathered all Is'ra-el together, and passed over Jor'dan, and came to He'lam. And the Syr'i-ans set themselves in array against Da'vid, and fought with him.

18 And the Syr'i-ans fled before Is'ra-el; and Da'vid slew *the men of* seven hundred chariots of the Syr'i-ans, and forty thousand horsemen, and smote Sho'bach the captain of their host, who died there.

19 And when all the kings *that were* servants to Had-ar-e'zer saw that they were smitten before Is'ra-el, they made peace with Is'ra-el, and served them. So the Syr'i-ans feared to help the children of Am'mon any more.

11 AND it came to pass, after the year was expired, at the time when kings go forth *to battle,* that Da'vid sent Jo'ab, and his servants with him, and all Is'ra-el; and they destroyed the children of Am'mon, and besieged Rab'bah. But Da'vid tarried still at Je-ru'sa-lem.

2 ¶ And it came to pass in an eveningtide, that Da'vid arose from off his bed, and walked upon the roof of the king's house: and from the roof he saw a woman washing herself; and the woman *was* very beautiful to look upon.

3 And Da'vid sent and enquired after the woman. And one said, *Is* not this Bath'-she-ba, the daughter of E-li'am, the wife of U-ri'ah the Hit'tite?

4 And Da'vid sent messengers, and took her; and she came in unto him, and he lay with her; for she was purified from her uncleanness: and she returned unto her house.

5 And the woman conceived, and sent and told Da'vid, and said, I *am* with child.

6 ¶ And Da'vid sent to Jo'ab, *saying,* Send me U-ri'ah the Hit'tite. And Jo'ab sent U-ri'ah to Da'vid.

7 And when U-ri'ah was come unto him, Da'-vid demanded *of him* how Jo'ab did, and how the people did, and how the war prospered.

8 And Da'vid said to U-ri'ah, Go down to thy house, and wash thy feet. And U-ri'ah departed out of the king's house, and there followed him a mess *of meat* from the king.

9 But U-ri'ah slept at the door of the king's house, with all the servants of his lord, and went not down to his house.

10 And when they had told Da'vid, saying, U-ri'ah went not down unto his house, Da'vid said unto U-ri'ah, Camest thou not from *thy* journey? why *then* didst thou not go down unto thine house?

11 And U-ri'ah said unto Da'vid, The ark, and Is'ra-el, and Ju'dah, abide in tents; and my lord Jo'ab, and the servants of my lord, are encamped in the open fields; shall I then go into mine house, to eat and to drink, and to lie with my wife? *as* thou livest, and *as* thy soul liveth, I will not do this thing.

12 And Da'vid said to U-ri'ah, Tarry here to day also, and to morrow I will let thee depart. So U-ri'ah abode in Je-ru'sa-lem that day, and the morrow.

13 And when Da'vid had called him, he did eat and drink before him; and he made him drunk: and at even he went out to lie on his bed with the servants of his lord, but went not down to his house.

14 ¶ And it came to pass in the morning, that Da'vid wrote a letter to Jo'ab, and sent *it* by the hand of U-ri'ah.

15 And he wrote in the letter, saying, Set ye U-ri'ah in the forefront of the hottest battle, and retire ye from him, that he may be smitten, and die.

16 And it came to pass, when Jo'ab observed the city, that he assigned U-ri'ah unto a place where he knew that valiant men *were.*

17 And the men of the city went out, and fought with Jo'ab: and there fell *some* of the people of the servants of Da'vid; and U-ri'ah the Hit'tite died also.

18 ¶ Then Jo'ab sent and told Da'vid all the things concerning the war;

19 And charged the messenger, saying, When thou hast made an end of telling the matters of the war unto the king,

20 And if so be that the king's wrath arise, and he say unto thee, Wherefore approached ye so nigh unto the city when ye did fight? knew ye not that they would shoot from the wall?

21 Who smote A-bim'e-lech the son of Je-rub'be-sheth? did not a woman cast a piece of a millstone upon him from the wall, that he died in The'bez? why went ye nigh the wall? then say thou, Thy servant U-ri'ah the Hit'tite is dead also.

22 ¶ So the messenger went, and came and shewed Da'vid all that Jo'ab had sent him for.

23 And the messenger said unto Da'vid, Surely the men prevailed against us, and came out unto us into the field, and we were upon them even unto the entering of the gate.

24 And the shooters shot from off the wall upon thy servants; and *some* of the king's ser-vants be dead, and thy servant U-ri'ah the Hit'-tite is dead also.

25 Then Da'vid said unto the messenger, Thus shalt thou say unto Jo'ab, Let not this thing displease thee, for the sword devoureth one as well as another: make thy battle more strong against the city, and overthrow it: and encourage thou him.

26 ¶ And when the wife of U-ri'ah heard that U-ri'ah her husband was dead, she mourned for her husband.

27 And when the mourning was past, Da'vid sent and fetched her to his house, and she became his wife, and bare him a son. But the thing that Da'vid had done displeased the LORD.

12 AND the LORD sent Na'than unto Da'-vid. And he came unto him, and said unto him, There were two men in one city; the one rich, and the other poor.

2 The rich *man* had exceeding many flocks and herds:

3 But the poor *man* had nothing, save one little ewe lamb, which he had bought and nourished up: and it grew up together with him, and with his children; it did eat of his own meat, and drank of his own cup, and lay in his bosom, and was unto him as a daughter.

4 And there came a traveller unto the rich man, and he spared to take of his own flock and of his own herd, to dress for the wayfaring man that was come unto him; but took the poor man's lamb, and dressed it for the man that was come to him.

5 And Da'vid's anger was greatly kindled against the man; and he said to Na'than, *As* the LORD liveth, the man that hath done this *thing* shall surely die:

6 And he shall restore the lamb fourfold, because he did this thing, and because he had no pity.

7 ¶ And Na'than said to Da'vid, Thou *art* the man. Thus saith the LORD God of Is'ra-el, I anointed thee king over Is'ra-el, and I delivered thee out of the hand of Saul;

8 And I gave thee thy master's house, and thy master's wives into thy bosom, and gave thee the house of Is'ra-el and of Ju'dah; and if *that had been* too little, I would moreover have given unto thee such and such things.

9 Wherefore hast thou despised the commandment of the LORD, to do evil in his sight? thou hast killed U-ri'ah the Hit'tite with the sword, and hast taken his wife *to be* thy wife, and hast slain him with the sword of the children of Am'mon.

10 Now therefore the sword shall never depart from thine house; because thou hast despised me, and hast taken the wife of U-ri'ah the Hit'tite to be thy wife.

11 Thus saith the LORD, Behold, I will raise up evil against thee out of thine own house, and I will take thy wives before thine eyes, and give *them* unto thy neighbour, and he shall lie with thy wives in the sight of this sun.

12 For thou didst *it* secretly: but I will do this thing before all Is'ra-el, and before the sun.

13 And Da'vid said unto Na'than, I have sinned against the LORD. And Na'than said unto Da'vid, The LORD also hath put away thy sin; thou shalt not die.

14 Howbeit, because by this deed thou hast given great occasion to the enemies of the LORD to blaspheme, the child also *that is* born unto thee shall surely die.

15 ¶ And Na'than departed unto his house.

And the LORD struck the child that U-ri'ah's wife bare unto Da'vid, and it was very sick.

16 Da'vid therefore besought God for the child; and Da'vid fasted, and went in, and lay all night upon the earth.

17 And the elders of his house arose, *and went* to him, to raise him up from the earth: but he would not, neither did he eat bread with them.

18 And it came to pass on the seventh day, that the child died. And the servants of Da'vid feared to tell him that the child was dead: for they said, Behold, while the child was yet alive, we spake unto him, and he would not hearken unto our voice: how will he then vex himself, if we tell him that the child is dead?

19 But when Da'vid saw that his servants whispered, Da'vid perceived that the child was dead: therefore Da'vid said unto his servants, Is the child dead? And they said, He is dead.

20 Then Da'vid arose from the earth, and washed, and anointed *himself,* and changed his apparel, and came into the house of the LORD, and worshipped: then he came to his own house; and when he required, they set bread before him, and he did eat.

21 Then said his servants unto him, What thing *is* this that thou hast done? thou didst fast and weep for the child, *while it was* alive; but when the child was dead, thou didst rise and eat bread.

22 And he said, While the child was yet alive, I fasted and wept: for I said, Who can tell *whether* GOD will be gracious to me, that the child may live?

23 But now he is dead, wherefore should I fast? can I bring him back again? I shall go to him, but he shall not return to me.

24 ¶ And Da'vid comforted Bath'-she-ba his wife, and went in unto her, and lay with her: and she bare a son, and he called his name Sol'-o-mon: and the LORD loved him.

25 And he sent by the hand of Na'than the prophet; and he called his name Jed-i-di'ah, because of the LORD.

26 ¶ And Jo'ab fought against Rab'bah of the children of Am'mon, and took the royal city.

27 And Jo'ab sent messengers to Da'vid, and said, I have fought against Rab'bah, and have taken the city of waters.

28 Now therefore gather the rest of the people together, and encamp against the city, and take it: lest I take the city, and it be called after my name.

29 And Da'vid gathered all the people together, and went to Rab'bah, and fought against it, and took it.

30 And he took their king's crown from off his head, the weight whereof *was* a talent of gold with the precious stones: and it was *set* on Da'vid's head. And he brought forth the spoil of the city in great abundance.

31 And he brought forth the people that *were* therein, and put *them* under saws, and under harrows of iron, and under axes of iron, and made them pass through the brickkiln: and thus did he unto all the cities of the children of Am'-mon. So Da'vid and all the people returned unto Je-ru'sa-lem.

13 AND it came to pass after this, that Ab'-sa-lom the son of Da'vid had a fair sister, whose name *was* Ta'mar; and Am'non the son of Da'vid loved her.

2 And Am'non was so vexed, that he fell sick for his sister Ta'mar; for she *was* a virgin; and

Am'non thought it hard for him to do any thing to her.

3 But Am'non had a friend, whose name *was* Jon'a-dab, the son of Shim'e-ah Da'vid's brother: and Jon'a-dab *was* a very subtil man.

4 And he said unto him, Why *art* thou, *being* the king's son, lean from day to day? wilt thou not tell me? And Am'non said unto him, I love Ta'mar, my brother Ab'sa-lom's sister.

5 And Jon'a-dab said unto him, Lay thee down on thy bed, and make thyself sick: and when thy father cometh to see thee, say unto him, I pray thee, Let my sister Ta'mar come, and give me meat, and dress the meat in my sight, that I may see *it,* and eat *it* at her hand.

6 ¶ So Am'non lay down, and made himself sick: and when the king was come to see him, Am'non said unto the king, I pray thee, let Ta'-mar my sister come, and make me a couple of cakes in my sight, that I may eat at her hand.

7 Then Da'vid sent home to Ta'mar, saying, Go now to thy brother Am'non's house, and dress him meat.

8 So Ta'mar went to her brother Am'non's house; and he was laid down. And she took flour, and kneaded *it,* and made cakes in his sight, and did bake the cakes.

9 And she took a pan, and poured *them* out before him; but he refused to eat. And Am'non said, Have out all men from me. And they went out every man from him.

10 And Am'non said unto Ta'mar, Bring the meat into the chamber, that I may eat of thine hand. And Ta'mar took the cakes which she had made, and brought *them* into the chamber to Am'non her brother.

11 And when she had brought *them* unto him to eat, he took hold of her, and said unto her, Come lie with me, my sister.

12 And she answered him, Nay, my brother, do not force me; for no such thing ought to be done in Is'ra-el: do not thou this folly.

13 And I, whither shall I cause my shame to go? and as for thee, thou shalt be as one of the fools in Is'ra-el. Now therefore, I pray thee, speak unto the king; for he will not withhold me from thee.

14 Howbeit he would not hearken unto her voice: but, being stronger than she, forced her, and lay with her.

15 ¶ Then Am'non hated her exceedingly; so that the hatred wherewith he hated her *was* greater than the love wherewith he had loved her. And Am'non said unto her, Arise, be gone.

16 And she said unto him, *There* is no cause: this evil in sending me away *is* greater than the other that thou didst unto me. But he would not hearken unto her.

17 Then he called his servant that ministered unto him, and said, Put now this *woman* out from me, and bolt the door after her.

18 And *she had* a garment of divers colours upon her: for with such robes were the king's daughters *that were* virgins apparelled. Then his servant brought her out, and bolted the door after her.

19 ¶ And Ta'mar put ashes on her head, and rent her garment of divers colours that *was* on her, and laid her hand on her head, and went on crying.

20 And Ab'sa-lom her brother said unto her, Hath Am'non thy brother been with thee? but hold now thy peace, my sister: he *is* thy brother; regard not this thing. So Ta'mar remained desolate in her brother Ab'sa-lom's house.

21 ¶ But when king Da'vid heard of all these things, he was very wroth.

22 And Ab'sa-lom spake unto his brother Am'non neither good nor bad: for Ab'sa-lom hated Am'non, because he had forced his sister Ta'mar.

23 ¶ And it came to pass after two full years, that Ab'sa-lom had sheepshearers in Ba'al-ha'-zor, which is beside E'phra-im: and Ab'sa-lom invited all the king's sons.

24 And Ab'sa-lom came to the king, and said, Behold now, thy servant hath sheepshearers; let the king, I beseech thee, and his servants go with thy servant.

25 And the king said to Ab'sa-lom, Nay, my son, let us not all now go, lest we be chargeable unto thee. And he pressed him: howbeit he would not go, but blessed him.

26 Then said Ab'sa-lom, If not, I pray thee, let my brother Am'non go with us. And the king said unto him, Why should he go with thee?

27 But Ab'sa-lom pressed him, that he let Am'non and all the king's sons go with him.

28 ¶ Now Ab'sa-lom had commanded his servants, saying, Mark ye now when Am'non's heart is merry with wine, and when I say unto you, Smite Am'non; then kill him, fear not: have not I commanded you? be courageous, and be valiant.

29 And the servants of Ab'sa-lom did unto Am'non as Ab'sa-lom had commanded. Then all the king's sons arose, and every man gat him up upon his mule, and fled.

30 ¶ And it came to pass, while they were in the way, that tidings came to Da'vid, saying, Ab'sa-lom hath slain all the king's sons, and there is not one of them left.

31 Then the king arose, and tare his garments, and lay on the earth; and all his servants stood by with their clothes rent.

32 And Jon'a-dab, the son of Shim'e-ah Da'-vid's brother, answered and said, Let not my lord suppose that they have slain all the young men the king's sons; for Am'non only is dead: for by the appointment of Ab'sa-lom this hath been determined from the day that he forced his sister Ta'mar.

33 Now therefore let not my lord the king take the thing to his heart, to think that all the king's sons are dead: for Am'non only is dead.

34 But Ab'sa-lom fled. And the young man that kept the watch lifted up his eyes, and looked, and, behold, there came much people by the way of the hill side behind him.

35 And Jon'a-dab said unto the king, Behold, the king's sons come: as thy servant said, so it is.

36 And it came to pass, as soon as he had made an end of speaking, that, behold, the king's sons came, and lifted up their voice and wept: and the king also and all his servants wept very sore.

37 ¶ But Ab'sa-lom fled, and went to Tal'-mai, the son of Am-mi'hud, king of Ge'shur. And Da'vid mourned for his son every day.

38 So Ab'sa-lom fled, and went to Ge'shur, and was there three years.

39 And the soul of king Da'vid longed to go forth unto Ab'sa-lom: for he was comforted concerning Am'non, seeing he was dead.

14 NOW Jo'ab the son of Zer-u-i'ah perceived that the king's heart was toward Ab'sa-lom.

2 And Jo'ab sent to Te-ko'ah, and fetched thence a wise woman, and said unto her, I pray thee, feign thyself to be a mourner, and put on now mourning apparel, and anoint not thyself with oil, but be as a woman that had a long time mourned for the dead:

3 And come to the king, and speak on this manner unto him. So Jo'ab put the words in her mouth.

4 ¶ And when the woman of Te-ko'ah spake to the king, she fell on her face to the ground, and did obeisance, and said, Help, O king.

5 And the king said unto her, What aileth thee? And she answered, I am indeed a widow woman, and mine husband is dead.

6 And thy handmaid had two sons, and they two strove together in the field, and there was none to part them, but the one smote the other, and slew him.

7 And, behold, the whole family is risen against thine handmaid, and they said, Deliver him that smote his brother, that we may kill him, for the life of his brother whom he slew; and we will destroy the heir also: and so they shall quench my coal which is left, and shall not leave to my husband neither name nor remainder upon the earth.

8 And the king said unto the woman, Go to thine house, and I will give charge concerning thee.

9 And the woman of Te-ko'ah said unto the king, My lord, O king, the iniquity be on me, and on my father's house: and the king and his throne be guiltless.

10 And the king said, Whosoever saith ought unto thee, bring him to me, and he shall not touch thee any more.

11 Then said she, I pray thee, let the king remember the LORD thy God, that thou wouldest not suffer the revengers of blood to destroy any more, lest they destroy my son. And he said, As the LORD liveth, there shall not one hair of thy son fall to the earth.

12 Then the woman said, Let thine handmaid, I pray thee, speak one word unto my lord the king. And he said, Say on.

13 And the woman said, Wherefore then hast thou thought such a thing against the people of God? for the king doth speak this thing as one which is faulty, in that the king doth not fetch home again his banished.

14 For we must needs die, and are as water spilt on the ground, which cannot be gathered up again; neither doth God respect any person: yet doth he devise means, that his banished be not expelled from him.

15 Now therefore that I am come to speak of this thing unto my lord the king, it is because the people have made me afraid: and thy handmaid said, I will now speak unto the king; it may be that the king will perform the request of his handmaid.

16 For the king will hear, to deliver his handmaid out of the hand of the man that would destroy me and my son together out of the inheritance of God.

17 Then thine handmaid said, The word of my lord the king shall now be comfortable: for as an angel of God, so is my lord the king to discern good and bad: therefore the LORD thy God will be with thee.

18 Then the king answered and said unto the woman, Hide not from me, I pray thee, the thing that I shall ask thee. And the woman said, Let my lord the king now speak.

19 And the king said, Is not the hand of Jo'ab with thee in all this? And the woman answered and said, As thy soul liveth, my lord the king, none can turn to the right hand or to the left from ought that my lord the king hath spoken: for thy servant Jo'ab, he bade me, and he put all

these words in the mouth of thine handmaid:

20 To fetch about this form of speech hath thy servant Jo'ab done this thing: and my lord *is* wise, according to the wisdom of an angel of God, to know all *things* that *are* in the earth.

21 ¶ And the king said unto Jo'ab, Behold now, I have done this thing: go therefore, bring the young man Ab'sa-lom again.

22 And Jo'ab fell to the ground on his face, and bowed himself, and thanked the king: and Jo'ab said, To day thy servant knoweth that I have found grace in thy sight, my lord, O king, in that the king hath fulfilled the request of his servant.

23 So Jo'ab arose and went to Ge'shur, and brought Ab'sa-lom to Je-ru'sa-lem.

24 And the king said, Let him turn to his own house, and let him not see my face. So Ab'sa-lom returned to his own house, and saw not the king's face.

25 ¶ But in all Is'ra-el there was none to be so much praised as Ab'sa-lom for his beauty: from the sole of his foot even to the crown of his head there was no blemish in him.

26 And when he polled his head, (for it was at every year's end that he polled *it*: because *the* hair was heavy on him, therefore he polled it:) he weighed the hair of his head at two hundred shekels after the king's weight.

27 And unto Ab'sa-lom there were born three sons, and one daughter, whose name *was* Ta'-mar: she was a woman of a fair countenance.

28 ¶ So Ab'sa-lom dwelt two full years in Je-ru'sa-lem, and saw not the king's face.

29 Therefore Ab'sa-lom sent for Jo'ab, to have sent him to the king; but he would not come to him: and when he sent again the second time, he would not come.

30 Therefore he said unto his servants, See, Jo'ab's field is near mine, and he hath barley there; go and set it on fire. And Ab'sa-lom's servants set the field on fire.

31 Then Jo'ab arose, and came to Ab'sa-lom unto *his* house, and said unto him, Wherefore have thy servants set my field on fire?

32 And Ab'sa-lom answered Jo'ab, Behold, I sent unto thee, saying, Come hither, that I may send thee to the king, to say, Wherefore am I come from Ge'shur? *it had been* good for me *to have been* there still: now therefore let me see the king's face; and if there be *any* iniquity in me, let him kill me.

33 So Jo'ab came to the king, and told him: and when he had called for Ab'sa-lom, he came to the king, and bowed himself on his face to the ground before the king: and the king kissed Ab'sa-lom.

15 AND it came to pass after this, that Ab'-sa-lom prepared him chariots and horses, and fifty men to run before him.

2 And Ab'sa-lom rose up early, and stood beside the way of the gate: and it was *so*, that when any man that had a controversy came to the king for judgment, then Ab'sa-lom called unto him, and said, Of what city *art* thou? And he said, Thy servant *is* of one of the tribes of Is'ra-el.

3 And Ab'sa-lom said unto him, See, thy matters *are* good and right; but *there is* no man *deputed* of the king to hear thee.

4 Ab'sa-lom said moreover, Oh that I were made judge in the land, that every man which hath any suit or cause might come unto me, and I would do him justice!

5 And it was *so*, that when any man came

nigh *to him* to do him obeisance, he put forth his hand, and took him, and kissed him.

6 And on this manner did Ab'sa-lom to all Is'ra-el that came to the king for judgment: so Ab'sa-lom stole the hearts of the men of Is'ra-el.

7 ¶ And it came to pass after forty years, that Ab'sa-lom said unto the king, I pray thee, let me go and pay my vow, which I have vowed unto the LORD, in He'bron.

8 For thy servant vowed a vow while I abode at Ge'shur in Syr'i-a, saying, If the LORD shall bring me again indeed to Je-ru'sa-lem, then I will serve the LORD.

9 And the king said unto him, Go in peace. So he arose, and went to He'bron.

10 ¶ But Ab'sa-lom sent spies throughout all the tribes of Is'ra-el, saying, As soon as ye hear the sound of the trumpet, then ye shall say, Ab'-sa-lom reigneth in He'bron.

11 And with Ab'sa-lom went two hundred men out of Je-ru'sa-lem, *that were* called; and they went in their simplicity, and they knew not any thing.

12 And Ab'sa-lom sent for A-hith'o-phel the Gi'lo-nite, Da'vid's counsellor, from his city, *even* from Gi'loh, while he offered sacrifices. And the conspiracy was strong; for the people increased continually with Ab'sa-lom.

13 ¶ And there came a messenger to Da'vid, saying, The hearts of the men of Is'ra-el are after Ab'sa-lom.

14 And Da'vid said unto all his servants that *were* with him at Je-ru'sa-lem, Arise, and let us flee; for we shall not *else* escape from Ab'sa-lom: make speed to depart, lest he overtake us suddenly, and bring evil upon us, and smite the city with the edge of the sword.

15 And the king's servants said unto the king, Behold, thy servants *are ready to do* whatsoever my lord the king shall appoint.

16 And the king went forth, and all his household after him. And the king left ten women, *which were* concubines, to keep the house.

17 And the king went forth, and all the people after him, and tarried in a place that was far off.

18 And all his servants passed on beside him; and all the Cher'eth-ites, and all the Pe'leth-ites, and all the Git'tites, six hundred men which came after him from Gath, passed on before the king.

19 ¶ Then said the king to It'ta-i the Git'tite, Wherefore goest thou also with us? return to thy place, and abide with the king: for thou *art* a stranger, and also an exile.

20 Whereas thou camest *but* yesterday, should I this day make thee go up and down with us? seeing I go whither I may, return thou, and take back thy brethren: mercy and truth *be* with thee.

21 And It'ta-i answered the king, and said, *As* the LORD liveth, and *as* my lord the king liveth, surely in what place my lord the king shall be, whether in death or life, even there also will thy servant be.

22 And Da'vid said to It'ta-i, Go and pass over. And It'ta-i the Git'tite passed over, and all his men, and all the little ones that *were* with him.

23 And all the country wept with a loud voice, and all the people passed over: the king also himself passed over the brook Kid'ron, and all the people passed over, toward the way of the wilderness.

24 ¶ And lo Za'dok also, and all the Le'vites *were* with him, bearing the ark of the covenant

of God: and they set down the ark of God; and A-bi'a-thar went up, until all the people had done passing out of the city.

25 And the king said unto Za'dok, Carry back the ark of God into the city: if I shall find favour in the eyes of the LORD, he will bring me again, and shew me *both* it, and his habitation:

26 But if he thus say, I have no delight in thee; behold, *here am* I, let him do to me as seemeth good unto him.

27 The king said also unto Za'dok the priest, *Art not* thou a seer? return into the city in peace, and your two sons with you, A-him'a-az thy son, and Jon'a-than the son of A-bi'a-thar.

28 See, I will tarry in the plain of the wilderness, until there come word from you to certify me.

29 Za'dok therefore and A-bi'a-thar carried the ark of God again to Je-ru'sa-lem: and they tarried there.

30 ¶ And Da'vid went up by the ascent of *mount* Ol'i-vet, and wept as he went up, and had his head covered, and he went barefoot: and all the people that *was* with him covered every man his head, and they went up, weeping as they went up.

31 And *one* told Da'vid, saying, A-hith'o-phel *is* among the conspirators with Ab'sa-lom. And Da'vid said, O LORD, I pray thee, turn the counsel of A-hith'o-phel into foolishness.

32 ¶ And it came to pass, that *when* Da'vid was come to the top *of the mount*, where he worshipped God, behold, Hu'shai the Ar'chite came to meet him with his coat rent, and earth upon his head.

33 Unto whom Da'vid said, If thou passest on with me, then thou shalt be a burden unto me:

34 But if thou return to the city, and say unto Ab'sa-lom, I will be thy servant, O king; *as I have been* thy father's servant hitherto, so *will* I now also *be* thy servant: then mayest thou for me defeat the counsel of A-hith'o-phel.

35 And *hast thou* not there with thee Za'dok and A-bi'a-thar the priests? therefore it shall be, *that* what thing soever thou shalt hear out of the king's house, thou shalt tell *it* to Za'dok and A-bi'a-thar the priests.

36 Behold, *they have* there with them their two sons, A-him'a-az Za'dok's *son*, and Jon'a-than A-bi'a-thar's *son;* and by them ye shall send unto me every thing that ye can hear.

37 So Hu'shai Da'vid's friend came into the city, and Ab'sa-lom came into Je-ru'sa-lem.

16 AND when Da'vid was a little past the top *of the hill*, behold, Zi'ba the servant of Me-phib'o-sheth met him, with a couple of asses saddled, and upon them two hundred *loaves* of bread, and an hundred bunches of raisins, and an hundred of summer fruits, and a bottle of wine.

2 And the king said unto Zi'ba, What meanest thou by these? And Zi'ba said, The asses *be* for the king's household to ride on; and the bread and summer fruit for the young men to eat; and the wine, that such as be faint in the wilderness may drink.

3 And the king said, And where *is* thy master's son? And Zi'ba said unto the king, Behold, he abideth at Je-ru'sa-lem: for he said, To day shall the house of Is'ra-el restore me the kingdom of my father.

4 Then said the king to Zi'ba, Behold, thine *are* all that *pertained* unto Me-phib'o-sheth. And Zi'ba said, I humbly beseech thee *that* I may find grace in thy sight, my lord, O king.

5 ¶ And when king Da'vid came to Ba-hu'-rim, behold, thence came out a man of the family of the house of Saul, whose name *was* Shim'-e-i, the son of Ge'ra: he came forth, and cursed still as he came.

6 And he cast stones at Da'vid, and at all the servants of king Da'vid: and all the people and all the mighty men *were* on his right hand and on his left.

7 And thus said Shim'e-i when he cursed, Come out, come out, thou bloody man, and thou man of Be'li-al:

8 The LORD hath returned upon thee all the blood of the house of Saul, in whose stead thou hast reigned; and the LORD hath delivered the kingdom into the hand of Ab'sa-lom thy son: and, behold, thou *art taken* in thy mischief, because thou *art* a bloody man.

9 ¶ Then said A-bish'a-i the son of Zer-u-i'ah unto the king, Why should this dead dog curse my lord the king? let me go over, I pray thee, and take off his head.

10 And the king said, What have I to do with you, ye sons of Zer-u-i'ah? so let him curse, because the LORD hath said unto him, Curse Da'-vid. Who shall then say, Wherefore hast thou done so?

11 And Da'vid said to A-bish'a-i, and to all his servants, Behold, my son, which came forth of my bowels, seeketh my life: how much more now *may this* Ben'ja-mite *do it?* let him alone, and let him curse; for the LORD hath bidden him.

12 It may be that the LORD will look on mine affliction, and that the LORD will requite me good for his cursing this day.

13 And as Da'vid and his men went by the way, Shim'e-i went along on the hill's side over against him, and cursed as he went, and threw stones at him, and cast dust.

14 And the king, and all the people that *were* with him, came weary, and refreshed themselves there.

15 ¶ And Ab'sa-lom, and all the people the men of Is'ra-el, came to Je-ru'sa-lem, and A-hith'o-phel with him.

16 And it came to pass, when Hu'shai the Ar'chite, Da'vid's friend, was come unto Ab'sa-lom, that Hu'shai said unto Ab'sa-lom, God save the king, God save the king.

17 And Ab'sa-lom said to Hu'shai, *Is* this thy kindness to thy friend? why wentest thou not with thy friend?

18 And Hu'shai said unto Ab'sa-lom, Nay; but whom the LORD, and this people, and all the men of Is'ra-el, choose, his will I be, and with him will I abide.

19 And again, whom should I serve? *should I* not *serve* in the presence of his son? as I have served in thy father's presence, so will I be in thy presence.

20 ¶ Then said Ab'sa-lom to A-hith'o-phel, Give counsel among you what we shall do.

21 And A-hith'o-phel said unto Ab'sa-lom, Go in unto thy father's concubines, which he hath left to keep the house; and all Is'ra-el shall hear that thou art abhorred of thy father: then shall the hands of all that *are* with thee be strong.

22 So they spread Ab'sa-lom a tent upon the top of the house; and Ab'sa-lom went in unto his father's concubines in the sight of all Is'ra-el.

23 And the counsel of A-hith'o-phel, which he counselled in those days, *was* as if a man had enquired at the oracle of God: so *was* all the counsel of A-hith'o-phel both with Da'vid and with Ab'sa-lom.

17 MOREOVER A-hith'o-phel said unto Ab'sa-lom, Let me now choose out twelve thousand men, and I will arise and pursue after Da'vid this night:

2 And I will come upon him while he *is* weary and weak handed, and will make him afraid: and all the people that *are* with him shall flee; and I will smite the king only:

3 And I will bring back all the people unto thee: the man whom thou seekest *is* as if all returned: *so* all the people shall be in peace.

4 And the saying pleased Ab'sa-lom well, and all the elders of Is'ra-el.

5 Then said Ab'sa-lom, Call now Hu'shai the Ar'chite also, and let us hear likewise what he saith.

6 And when Hu'shai was come to Ab'sa-lom, Ab'sa-lom spake unto him, saying, A-hith'o-phel hath spoken after this manner: shall we do *after* his saying? if not; speak thou.

7 And Hu'shai said unto Ab'sa-lom, The counsel that A-hith'o-phel hath given *is* not good at this time.

8 For, said Hu'shai, thou knowest thy father and his men, that they *be* mighty men, and they *be* chafed in their minds, as a bear robbed of her whelps in the field: and thy father *is* a man of war, and will not lodge with the people.

9 Behold, he is hid now in some pit, or in some *other* place: and it will come to pass, when some of them be overthrown at the first, that whosoever heareth it will say, There is a slaughter among the people that follow Ab'sa-lom.

10 And he also *that is* valiant, whose heart *is* as the heart of a lion, shall utterly melt: for all Is'ra-el knoweth that thy father *is* a mighty man, and *they* which *be* with him *are* valiant men.

11 Therefore I counsel that all Is'ra-el be generally gathered unto thee, from Dan even to Be'er-she'ba, as the sand that *is* by the sea for multitude; and that thou go to battle in thine own person.

12 So shall we come upon him in some place where he shall be found, and we will light upon him as the dew falleth on the ground: and of him and of all the men that *are* with him there shall not be left so much as one.

13 Moreover, if he be gotten into a city, then shall all Is'ra-el bring ropes to that city, and we will draw it into the river, until there be not one small stone found there.

14 And Ab'sa-lom and all the men of Is'ra-el said, The counsel of Hu'shai the Ar'chite *is* better than the counsel of A-hith'o-phel. For the LORD had appointed to defeat the good counsel of A-hith'o-phel, to the intent that the LORD might bring evil upon Ab'sa-lom.

15 ¶ Then said Hu'shai unto Za'dok and to A-bi'a-thar the priests, Thus and thus did A-hith'o-phel counsel Ab'sa-lom and the elders of Is'ra-el; and thus and thus have I counselled.

16 Now therefore send quickly, and tell Da'vid, saying, Lodge not this night in the plains of the wilderness, but speedily pass over; lest the king be swallowed up, and all the people that *are* with him.

17 Now Jon'a-than and A-him'a-az stayed by En-ro'gel; for they might not be seen to come into the city: and a wench went and told them; and they went and told king Da'vid.

18 Nevertheless a lad saw them, and told Ab'sa-lom: but they went both of them away quickly, and came to a man's house in Ba-hu'-rim, which had a well in his court; whither they went down.

19 And the woman took and spread a covering over the well's mouth, and spread ground corn thereon; and the thing was not known.

20 And when Ab'sa-lom's servants came to the woman to the house, they said, Where *is* A-him'a-az and Jon'a-than? And the woman said unto them, They be gone over the brook of water. And when they had sought and could not find *them,* they returned to Je-ru'sa-lem.

21 And it came to pass, after they were departed, that they came up out of the well, and went and told king Da'vid, and said unto Da'vid, Arise, and pass quickly over the water: for thus hath A-hith'o-phel counselled against you.

22 Then Da'vid arose, and all the people that *were* with him, and they passed over Jor'dan: by the morning light there lacked not one of them that was not gone over Jor'dan.

23 ¶ And when A-hith'o-phel saw that his counsel was not followed, he saddled *his* ass, and arose, and gat him home to his house, to his city, and put his household in order, and hanged himself, and died, and was buried in the sepulchre of his father.

24 Then Da'vid came to Ma-ha-na'im. And Ab'sa-lom passed over Jor'dan, he and all the men of Is'ra-el with him.

25 ¶ And Ab'sa-lom made Am'a-sa captain of the host instead of Jo'ab: which Am'a-sa *was* a man's son, whose name *was* Ith'ra an Is'ra-el-ite, that went in to Ab'i-gail the daughter of Na'-hash, sister to Zer-u-i'ah Jo'ab's mother.

26 So Is'ra-el and Ab'sa-lom pitched in the land of Gil'e-ad.

27 ¶ And it came to pass, when Da'vid was come to Ma-ha-na'im, that Sho'bi the son of Na'hash of Rab'bah of the children of Am'mon, and Ma'chir the son of Am'mi-el of Lo-de'bar, and Bar-zil'la-i the Gil'e-ad-ite of Ro-ge'lim,

28 Brought beds, and basons, and earthen vessels, and wheat, and barley, and flour, and parched *corn,* and beans, and lentiles, and parched *pulse,*

29 And honey, and butter, and sheep, and cheese of kine, for Da'vid, and for the people that *were* with him, to eat: for they said, The people *is* hungry, and weary, and thirsty, in the wilderness.

18 AND Da'vid numbered the people that *were* with him, and set captains of thousands and captains of hundreds over them.

2 And Da'vid sent forth a third part of the people under the hand of Jo'ab, and a third part under the hand of A-bish'a-i the son of Zer-u-i'ah, Jo'ab's brother, and a third part under the hand of It'ta-i the Git'tite. And the king said unto the people, I will surely go forth with you myself also.

3 But the people answered, Thou shalt not go forth: for if we flee away, they will not care for us; neither if half of us die, will they care for us: but now *thou art* worth ten thousand of us: therefore now *it is* better that thou succour us out of the city.

4 And the king said unto them, What seemeth you best I will do. And the king stood by the gate side, and all the people came out by hundreds and by thousands.

5 And the king commanded Jo'ab and A-bish'a-i and It'ta-i, saying, *Deal* gently for my sake with the young man, *even* with Ab'sa-lom. And all the people heard when the king gave all the captains charge concerning Ab'sa-lom.

6 ¶ So the people went out into the field against Is'ra-el: and the battle was in the wood of E'phra-im;

7 Where the people of Is'ra-el were slain before the servants of Da'vid, and there was there a great slaughter that day of twenty thousand men.

8 For the battle was there scattered over the face of all the country: and the wood devoured more people that day than the sword devoured.

9 ¶ And Ab'sa-lom met the servants of Da'-vid. And Ab'sa-lom rode upon a mule, and the mule went under the thick boughs of a great oak, and his head caught hold of the oak, and he was taken up between the heaven and the earth; and the mule that was under him went away.

10 And a certain man saw it, and told Jo'ab, and said, Behold, I saw Ab'sa-lom hanged in an oak.

11 And Jo'ab said unto the man that told him, And, behold, thou sawest him, and why didst thou not smite him there to the ground? and I would have given thee ten shekels of silver, and a girdle.

12 And the man said unto Jo'ab, Though I should receive a thousand shekels of silver in mine hand, yet would I not put forth mine hand against the king's son: for in our hearing the king charged thee and A-bish'a-i and It'ta-i, saying, Beware that none touch the young man Ab'sa-lom.

13 Otherwise I should have wrought falsehood against mine own life: for there is no matter hid from the king, and thou thyself wouldest have set thyself against me.

14 Then said Jo'ab, I may not tarry thus with thee. And he took three darts in his hand, and thrust them through the heart of Ab'sa-lom, while he was yet alive in the midst of the oak.

15 And ten young men that bare Jo'ab's armour compassed about and smote Ab'sa-lom, and slew him.

16 And Jo'ab blew the trumpet, and the people returned from pursuing after Is'ra-el: for Jo'ab held back the people.

17 And they took Ab'sa-lom, and cast him into a great pit in the wood, and laid a very great heap of stones upon him: and all Is'ra-el fled every one to his tent.

18 ¶ Now Ab'sa-lom in his lifetime had taken and reared up for himself a pillar, which is in the king's dale: for he said, I have no son to keep my name in remembrance: and he called the pillar after his own name: and it is called unto this day, Ab'sa-lom's place.

19 ¶ Then said A-him'a-az the son of Za'dok, Let me now run, and bear the king tidings, how that the LORD hath avenged him of his enemies.

20 And Jo'ab said unto him, Thou shalt not bear tidings this day, but thou shalt bear tidings another day: but this day thou shalt bear no tidings, because the king's son is dead.

21 Then said Jo'ab to Cu'shi, Go tell the king what thou hast seen. And Cu'shi bowed himself unto Jo'ab, and ran.

22 Then said A-him'a-az the son of Za'dok yet again to Jo'ab, But howsoever, let me, I pray thee, also run after Cu'shi. And Jo'ab said, Wherefore wilt thou run, my son, seeing that thou hast no tidings ready?

23 But howsoever, said he, let me run. And he said unto him, Run. Then A-him'a-az ran by the way of the plain, and overran Cu'shi.

24 And Da'vid sat between the two gates: and the watchman went up to the roof over the gate unto the wall, and lifted up his eyes, and looked, and behold a man running alone.

25 And the watchman cried, and told the king. And the king said, If he be alone, there is tidings in his mouth. And he came apace, and drew near.

26 And the watchman saw another man running: and the watchman called unto the porter, and said, Behold another man running alone. And the king said, He also bringeth tidings.

27 And the watchman said, Me thinketh the running of the foremost is like the running of A-him'a-az the son of Za'dok. And the king said, He is a good man, and cometh with good tidings.

28 And A-him'a-az called, and said unto the king, All is well. And he fell down to the earth upon his face before the king, and said, Blessed be the LORD thy God, which hath delivered up the men that lifted up their hand against my lord the king.

29 And the king said, Is the young man Ab'-sa-lom safe? And A-him'a-az answered, When Jo'ab sent the king's servant, and me thy servant, I saw a great tumult, but I knew not what it was.

30 And the king said unto him, Turn aside, and stand here. And he turned aside, and stood still.

31 And, behold, Cu'shi came; and Cu'shi said, Tidings, my lord the king: for the LORD hath avenged thee this day of all them that rose up against thee.

32 And the king said unto Cu'shi, Is the young man Ab'sa-lom safe? And Cu'shi answered, The enemies of my lord the king, and all that rise against thee to do thee hurt, be as that young man is.

33 ¶ And the king was much moved, and went up to the chamber over the gate, and wept: and as he went, thus he said, O my son Ab'sa-lom, my son, my son Ab'sa-lom! would God I had died for thee, O Ab'sa-lom, my son, my son!

19 AND it was told Jo'ab, Behold, the king weepeth and mourneth for Ab'sa-lom.

2 And the victory that day was turned into mourning unto all the people: for the people heard say that day how the king was grieved for his son.

3 And the people gat them by stealth that day into the city, as people being ashamed steal away when they flee in battle.

4 But the king covered his face, and the king cried with a loud voice, O my son Ab'sa-lom, O Ab'sa-lom, my son, my son!

5 And Jo'ab came into the house to the king, and said, Thou hast shamed this day the faces of all thy servants, which this day have saved thy life, and the lives of thy sons and of thy daughters, and the lives of thy wives, and the lives of thy concubines;

6 In that thou lovest thine enemies, and hatest thy friends. For thou hast declared this day, that thou regardest neither princes nor servants: for this day I perceive, that if Ab'sa-lom had lived, and all we had died this day, then it had pleased thee well.

7 Now therefore arise, go forth, and speak comfortably unto thy servants: for I swear by the LORD, if thou go not forth, there will not tarry one with thee this night: and that will be worse unto thee than all the evil that befell thee from thy youth until now.

8 Then the king arose, and sat in the gate. And they told unto all the people, saying, Behold, the king doth sit in the gate. And all the people came before the king: for Is'ra-el had fled every man to his tent.

9 ¶ And all the people were at strife through-

out all the tribes of Is'ra-el, saying, The king saved us out of the hand of our enemies, and he delivered us out of the hand of the Phi-lis'tines; and now he is fled out of the land for Ab'sa-lom.

10 And Ab'sa-lom, whom we anointed over us, is dead in battle. Now therefore why speak ye not a word of bringing the king back?

11 ¶ And king Da'vid sent to Za'dok and to A-bi'a-thar the priests, saying, Speak unto the elders of Ju'dah, saying, Why are ye the last to bring the king back to his house? seeing the speech of all Is'ra-el is come to the king, even to his house.

12 Ye are my brethren, ye are my bones and my flesh: wherefore then are ye the last to bring back the king?

13 And say ye to Am'a-sa, Art thou not of my bone, and of my flesh? God do so to me, and more also, if thou be not captain of the host before me continually in the room of Jo'ab.

14 And he bowed the heart of all the men of Ju'dah, even as the heart of one man; so that they sent this word unto the king, Return thou, and all thy servants.

15 So the king returned, and came to Jor'dan. And Ju'dah came to Gil'gal, to go to meet the king, to conduct the king over Jor'dan.

16 ¶ And Shim'e-i the son of Ge'ra, a Ben'ja-mite, which was of Ba-hu'rim, hasted and came down with the men of Ju'dah to meet king Da'-vid.

17 And there were a thousand men of Ben'ja-min with him, and Zi'ba the servant of the house of Saul, and his fifteen sons and his twenty servants with him; and they went over Jor'dan before the king.

18 And there went over a ferry boat to carry over the king's household, and to do what he thought good. And Shim'e-i the son of Ge'ra fell down before the king, as he was come over Jor'-dan;

19 And said unto the king, Let not my lord impute iniquity unto me, neither do thou remember that which thy servant did perversely the day that my lord the king went out of Je-ru'sa-lem, that the king should take it to his heart.

20 For thy servant doth know that I have sinned: therefore, behold, I am come the first this day of all the house of Jo'seph to go down to meet my lord the king.

21 But A-bish'a-i the son of Zer-u-i'ah answered and said, Shall not Shim'e-i be put to death for this, because he cursed the LORD's anointed?

22 And Da'vid said, What have I to do with you, ye sons of Zer-u-i'ah, that ye should this day be adversaries unto me? shall there any man be put to death this day in Is'ra-el? for do not I know that I am this day king over Is'ra-el?

23 Therefore the king said unto Shim'e-i, Thou shalt not die. And the king sware unto him.

24 ¶ And Me-phib'o-sheth the son of Saul came down to meet the king, and had neither dressed his feet, nor trimmed his beard, nor washed his clothes, from the day the king departed until the day he came again in peace.

25 And it came to pass, when he was come to Je-ru'sa-lem to meet the king, that the king said unto him, Wherefore wentest not thou with me, Me-phib'o-sheth?

26 And he answered, My lord, O king, my servant deceived me: for thy servant said, I will saddle me an ass, that I may ride thereon, and go to the king; because thy servant is lame.

27 And he hath slandered thy servant unto my lord the king; but my lord the king is as an angel of God: do therefore what is good in thine eyes.

28 For all of my father's house were but dead men before my lord the king: yet didst thou set thy servant among them that did eat at thine own table. What right therefore have I yet to cry any more unto the king?

29 And the king said unto him, Why speakest thou any more of thy matters? I have said, Thou and Zi'ba divide the land.

30 And Me-phib'o-sheth said unto the king, Yea, let him take all, forasmuch as my lord the king is come again in peace unto his own house.

31 ¶ And Bar-zil'la-i the Gil'e-ad-ite came down from Ro-ge'lim, and went over Jor'dan with the king, to conduct him over Jor'dan.

32 Now Bar-zil'la-i was a very aged man, even fourscore years old: and he had provided the king of sustenance while he lay at Ma-ha-na'im; for he was a very great man.

33 And the king said unto Bar-zil'la-i, Come thou over with me, and I will feed thee with me in Je-ru'sa-lem.

34 And Bar-zil'la-i said unto the king, How long have I to live, that I should go up with the king unto Je-ru'sa-lem?

35 I am this day fourscore years old: and can I discern between good and evil? can thy servant taste what I eat or what I drink? can I hear any more the voice of singing men and singing women? wherefore then should thy servant be yet a burden unto my lord the king?

36 Thy servant will go a little way over Jor'-dan with the king: and why should the king recompense it me with such a reward?

37 Let thy servant, I pray thee, turn back again, that I may die in mine own city, and be buried by the grave of my father and of my mother. But behold thy servant Chim'ham; let him go over with my lord the king; and do to him what shall seem good unto thee.

38 And the king answered, Chim'ham shall go over with me, and I will do to him that which shall seem good unto thee: and whatsoever thou shalt require of me, that will I do for thee.

39 And all the people went over Jor'dan. And when the king was come over, the king kissed Bar-zil'la-i, and blessed him; and he returned unto his own place.

40 Then the king went on to Gil'gal, and Chim'ham went on with him: and all the people of Ju'dah conducted the king, and also half the people of Is'ra-el.

41 ¶ And, behold, all the men of Is'ra-el came to the king, and said unto the king, Why have our brethren the men of Ju'dah stolen thee away, and have brought the king, and his household, and all Da'vid's men with him, over Jor'dan?

42 And all the men of Ju'dah answered the men of Is'ra-el, Because the king is near of kin to us: wherefore then be ye angry for this matter? have we eaten at all of the king's cost? or hath he given us any gift?

43 And the men of Is'ra-el answered the men of Ju'dah, and said, We have ten parts in the king, and we have also more right in Da'vid than ye: why then did ye despise us, that our advice should not be first had in bringing back our king? And the words of the men of Ju'dah were fiercer than the words of the men of Is'ra-el.

20 AND there happened to be there a man of Be'li-al, whose name was She'ba, the son of Bich'ri, a Ben'ja-mite: and he blew a trumpet, and said, We have no part in Da'vid, neither have we inheritance in the son of Jes'se: every man to his tents, O Is'ra-el.

2 So every man of Is'ra-el went up from after Da'vid, *and* followed She'ba the son of Bich'ri: but the men of Ju'dah clave unto their king, from Jor'dan even to Je-ru'sa-lem.

3 ¶ And Da'vid came to his house at Je-ru'sa-lem; and the king took the ten women *his* concubines, whom he had left to keep the house, and put them in ward, and fed them, but went not in unto them. So they were shut up unto the day of their death, living in widowhood.

4 ¶ Then said the king to Am'a-sa, Assemble me the men of Ju'dah within three days, and be thou here present.

5 So Am'a-sa went to assemble *the men of* Ju'dah: but he tarried longer than the set time which he had appointed him.

6 And Da'vid said to A-bish'a-i, Now shall She'ba the son of Bich'ri do us more harm than *did* Ab'sa-lom: take thou thy lord's servants, and pursue after him, lest he get him fenced cities, and escape us.

7 And there went out after him Jo'ab's men, and the Cher'eth-ites, and the Pe'leth-ites, and all the mighty men: and they went out of Je-ru'sa-lem, to pursue after She'ba the son of Bich'ri.

8 When they *were* at the great stone which *is* in Gib'e-on, Am'a-sa went before them. And Jo'ab's garment that he had put on was girded unto him, and upon it a girdle *with* a sword fastened upon his loins in the sheath thereof; and as he went forth it fell out.

9 And Jo'ab said to Am'a-sa, *Art* thou in health, my brother? And Jo'ab took Am'a-sa by the beard with the right hand to kiss him.

10 But Am'a-sa took no heed to the sword that *was* in Jo'ab's hand: so he smote him therewith in the fifth *rib*, and shed out his bowels to the ground, and struck him not again; and he died. So Jo'ab and A-bish'a-i his brother pursued after She'ba the son of Bich'ri.

11 And one of Jo'ab's men stood by him, and said, He that favoureth Jo'ab, and he that *is* for Da'vid, *let him go* after Jo'ab.

12 And Am'a-sa wallowed in blood in the midst of the highway. And when the man saw that all the people stood still, he removed Am'a-sa out of the highway into the field, and cast a cloth upon him, when he saw that every one that came by him stood still.

13 When he was removed out of the highway, all the people went on after Jo'ab, to pursue after She'ba the son of Bich'ri.

14 ¶ And he went through all the tribes of Is'ra-el unto A'bel, and to Beth-ma'a-chah, and all the Be'rites: and they were gathered together, and went also after him.

15 And they came and besieged him in A'bel of Beth-ma'a-chah, and they cast up a bank against the city, and it stood in the trench: and all the people that *were* with Jo'ab battered the wall, to throw it down.

16 ¶ Then cried a wise woman out of the city, Hear, hear; say, I pray you, unto Jo'ab, Come near hither, that I may speak with thee.

17 And when he was come near unto her, the woman said, *Art* thou Jo'ab? And he answered, I *am* he. Then she said unto him, Hear the words of thine handmaid. And he answered, I do hear.

18 Then she spake, saying, They were wont to speak in old time, saying, They shall surely

ask *counsel* at A'bel: and so they ended *the matter.*

19 I *am one of them that are* peaceable *and* faithful in Is'ra-el: thou seekest to destroy a city and a mother in Is'ra-el: why wilt thou swallow up the inheritance of the LORD?

20 And Jo'ab answered and said, Far be it, far be it from me, that I should swallow up or destroy.

21 The matter *is* not so: but a man of mount E'phra-im, She'ba the son of Bich'ri by name, hath lifted up his hand against the king, *even* against Da'vid: deliver him only, and I will depart from the city. And the woman said unto Jo'ab, Behold, his head shall be thrown to thee over the wall.

22 Then the woman went unto all the people in her wisdom. And they cut off the head of She'ba the son of Bich'ri, and cast *it* out to Jo'ab. And he blew a trumpet, and they retired from the city, every man to his tent. And Jo'ab returned to Je-ru'sa-lem unto the king.

23 ¶ Now Jo'ab *was* over all the host of Is'ra-el: and Be-na'iah the son of Je-hoi'a-da *was* over the Cher'eth-ites and over the Pe'leth-ites:

24 And A-do'ram *was* over the tribute: and Je-hosh'a-phat the son of A-hi'lud *was* recorder:

25 And She'va *was* scribe: and Za'dok and A-bi'a-thar *were* the priests:

26 And I'ra also the Ja'ir-ite was a chief ruler about Da'vid.

21 THEN there was a famine in the days of Da'vid three years, year after year; and Da'vid enquired of the LORD. And the LORD answered, *It is* for Saul, and for *his* bloody house, because he slew the Gib'e-on-ites.

2 And the king called the Gib'e-on-ites, and said unto them; (now the Gib'e-on-ites *were* not of the children of Is'ra-el, but of the remnant of the Am'or-ites; and the children of Is'ra-el had sworn unto them: and Saul sought to slay them in his zeal to the children of Is'ra-el and Ju'dah.)

3 Wherefore Da'vid said unto the Gib'e-on-ites, What shall I do for you? and wherewith shall I make the atonement, that ye may bless the inheritance of the LORD?

4 And the Gib'e-on-ites said unto him, We will have no silver nor gold of Saul, nor of his house; neither for us shalt thou kill any man in Is'ra-el. And he said, What ye shall say, *that* will I do for you.

5 And they answered the king, The man that consumed us, and that devised against us *that* we should be destroyed from remaining in any of the coasts of Is'ra-el,

6 Let seven men of his sons be delivered unto us, and we will hang them up unto the LORD in Gib'e-ah of Saul, *whom* the LORD did choose. And the king said, I will give *them.*

7 But the king spared Me-phib'o-sheth, the son of Jon'a-than the son of Saul, because of the LORD's oath that *was* between them, between Da'vid and Jon'a-than the son of Saul.

8 But the king took the two sons of Riz'pah the daughter of A-i'ah, whom she bare unto Saul, Ar-mo'ni and Me-phib'o-sheth; and the five sons of Mi'chal the daughter of Saul, whom she brought up for A'dri-el the son of Bar-zil'la-i the Me-hol'ath-ite:

9 And he delivered them into the hands of the Gib'e-on-ites, and they hanged them in the hill before the LORD: and they fell *all* seven together, and were put to death in the days of harvest, in the first *days*, in the beginning of barley harvest.

10 ¶ And Riz'pah the daughter of A-i'ah took

sackcloth, and spread it for her upon the rock, from the beginning of harvest until water dropped upon them out of heaven, and suffered neither the birds of the air to rest on them by day, nor the beasts of the field by night.

11 And it was told Da′vid what Riz′pah the daughter of A-i′ah, the concubine of Saul, had done.

12 ¶ And Da′vid went and took the bones of Saul and the bones of Jon′a-than his son from the men of Ja′besh-gil′e-ad, which had stolen them from the street of Beth′-shan, where the Phi-lis′tines had hanged them, when the Phi-lis′-tines had slain Saul in Gil-bo′a:

13 And he brought up from thence the bones of Saul and the bones of Jon′a-than his son; and they gathered the bones of them that were hanged.

14 And the bones of Saul and Jon′a-than his son buried they in the country of Ben′ja-min in Ze′lah, in the sepulchre of Kish his father: and they performed all that the king commanded. And after that God was intreated for the land.

15 ¶ Moreover the Phi-lis′tines had yet war again with Is′ra-el; and Da′vid went down, and his servants with him, and fought against the Phi-lis′tines: and Da′vid waxed faint.

16 And Ish′bi-be′nob, which was of the sons of the giant, the weight of whose spear weighed three hundred shekels of brass in weight, he being girded with a new sword, thought to have slain Da′vid.

17 But A-bish′a-i the son of Zer-u-i′ah succoured him, and smote the Phi-lis′tine, and killed him. Then the men of Da′vid sware unto him, saying, Thou shalt go no more out with us to battle, that thou quench not the light of Is′ra-el.

18 And it came to pass after this, that there was again a battle with the Phi-lis′tines at Gob: then Sib′be-chai the Hu′shath-ite slew Saph, which was of the sons of the giant.

19 And there was again a battle in Gob with the Phi-lis′tines, where El-ha′nan the son of Ja-ar′e-or′e-gim, a Beth′-le-hem-ite, slew the brother of Go-li′ath the Git′tite, the staff of whose spear was like a weaver's beam.

20 And there was yet a battle in Gath, where was a man of great stature, that had on every hand six fingers, and on every foot six toes, four and twenty in number; and he also was born to the giant.

21 And when he defied Is′ra-el, Jon′a-than the son of Shim′e-ah the brother of Da′vid slew him.

22 These four were born to the giant in Gath, and fell by the hand of Da′vid, and by the hand of his servants.

22 AND Da′vid spake unto the LORD the words of this song in the day that the LORD had delivered him out of the hand of all his enemies, and out of the hand of Saul:

2 And he said, The LORD is my rock, and my fortress, and my deliverer;

3 The God of my rock; in him will I trust: he is my shield, and the horn of my salvation, my high tower, and my refuge, my saviour; thou savest me from violence.

4 I will call on the LORD, who is worthy to be praised: so shall I be saved from mine enemies.

5 When the waves of death compassed me, the floods of ungodly men made me afraid;

6 The sorrows of hell compassed me about; the snares of death prevented me;

7 In my distress I called upon the LORD, and cried to my God: and he did hear my voice out of his temple, and my cry did enter into his ears.

8 Then the earth shook and trembled; the foundations of heaven moved and shook, because he was wroth.

9 There went up a smoke out of his nostrils, and fire out of his mouth devoured: coals were kindled by it.

10 He bowed the heavens also, and came down; and darkness was under his feet.

11 And he rode upon a cherub, and did fly: and he was seen upon the wings of the wind.

12 And he made darkness pavilions round about him, dark waters, and thick clouds of the skies.

13 Through the brightness before him were coals of fire kindled.

14 The LORD thundered from heaven, and the most High uttered his voice.

15 And he sent out arrows, and scattered them; lightning, and discomfited them.

16 And the channels of the sea appeared, the foundations of the world were discovered, at the rebuking of the LORD, at the blast of the breath of his nostrils.

17 He sent from above, he took me; he drew me out of many waters;

18 He delivered me from my strong enemy, and from them that hated me: for they were too strong for me.

19 They prevented me in the day of my calamity: but the LORD was my stay.

20 He brought me forth also into a large place: he delivered me, because he delighted in me.

21 The LORD rewarded me according to my righteousness: according to the cleanness of my hands hath he recompensed me.

22 For I have kept the ways of the LORD, and have not wickedly departed from my God.

23 For all his judgments were before me: and as for his statutes, I did not depart from them.

24 I was also upright before him, and have kept myself from mine iniquity.

25 Therefore the LORD hath recompensed me according to my righteousness; according to my cleanness in his eye sight.

26 With the merciful thou wilt shew thyself merciful, and with the upright man thou wilt shew thyself upright.

27 With the pure thou wilt shew thyself pure; and with the froward thou wilt shew thyself unsavoury.

28 And the afflicted people thou wilt save: but thine eyes are upon the haughty, that thou mayest bring them down.

29 For thou art my lamp, O LORD: and the LORD will lighten my darkness.

30 For by thee I have run through a troop: by my God have I leaped over a wall.

31 As for God, his way is perfect; the word of the LORD is tried: he is a buckler to all them that trust in him.

32 For who is God, save the LORD? and who is a rock, save our God?

33 God is my strength and power: and he maketh my way perfect.

34 He maketh my feet like hinds' feet: and setteth me upon my high places.

35 He teacheth my hands to war; so that a bow of steel is broken by mine arms.

36 Thou hast also given me the shield of thy salvation: and thy gentleness hath made me great.

37 Thou hast enlarged my steps under me; so that my feet did not slip.

38 I have pursued mine enemies, and de-

stroyed them; and turned not again until I had consumed them.

39 And I have consumed them, and wounded them, that they could not arise: yea, they are fallen under my feet.

40 For thou hast girded me with strength to battle: them that rose up against me hast thou subdued under me.

41 Thou hast also given me the necks of mine enemies, that I might destroy them that hate me.

42 They looked, but *there was* none to save; *even* unto the LORD, but he answered them not.

43 Then did I beat them as small as the dust of the earth, I did stamp them as the mire of the street, *and* did spread them abroad.

44 Thou also hast delivered me from the strivings of my people, thou hast kept me *to be* head of the heathen: a people *which* I knew not shall serve me.

45 Strangers shall submit themselves unto me: as soon as they hear, they shall be obedient unto me.

46 Strangers shall fade away, and they shall be afraid out of their close places.

47 The LORD liveth; and blessed *be* my rock; and exalted be the God of the rock of my salvation.

48 It *is* God that avengeth me, and that bringeth down the people under me,

49 And that bringeth me forth from mine enemies: thou also hast lifted me up on high above them that rose up against me: thou hast delivered me from the violent man.

50 Therefore I will give thanks unto thee, O LORD, among the heathen, and I will sing praises unto thy name.

51 *He is* the tower of salvation for his king: and sheweth mercy to his anointed, unto Da'-vid, and to his seed for evermore.

23 NOW these *be* the last words of Da'vid. Da'vid the son of Jes'se said, and the man *who was* raised up on high, the anointed of the God of Ja'cob, and the sweet psalmist of Is'ra-el, said,

2 The Spirit of the LORD spake by me, and his word *was* in my tongue.

3 The God of Is'ra-el said, the Rock of Is'ra-el spake to me, He that ruleth over men *must be* just, ruling in the fear of God.

4 And *he shall be* as the light of the morning, *when* the sun riseth, *even* a morning without clouds; *as* the tender grass *springing* out of the earth by clear shining after rain.

5 Although my house *be* not so with God; yet he hath made with me an everlasting covenant, ordered in all *things*, and sure: for *this is* all my salvation, and all *my* desire, although he make *it* not to grow.

6 ¶ But *the sons* of Be'li-al *shall be* all of them as thorns thrust away, because they cannot be taken with hands:

7 But the man *that* shall touch them must be fenced with iron and the staff of a spear; and they shall be utterly burned with fire in the *same* place.

8 ¶ These *be* the names of the mighty men whom Da'vid had: The Tach'mo-nite that sat in the seat, chief among the captains; the same *was* Ad'i-no the Ez'nite: *he lift up his spear* against eight hundred, whom he slew at one time.

9 And after him *was* E-le-a'zar the son of Do'do the A-ho'hite, *one* of the three mighty men with Da'vid, when they defied the Phi-lis'-

tines *that* were there gathered together to battle, and the men of Is'ra-el were gone away:

10 He arose, and smote the Phi-lis'tines until his hand was weary, and his hand clave unto the sword: and the LORD wrought a great victory that day; and the people returned after him only to spoil.

11 And after him *was* Sham'mah the son of Ag'e-e the Ha'ra-rite. And the Phi-lis'tines were gathered together into a troop, where was a piece of ground full of lentiles: and the people fled from the Phi-lis'tines.

12 But he stood in the midst of the ground, and defended it, and slew the Phi-lis'tines: and the LORD wrought a great victory.

13 And three of the thirty chief went down, and came to Da'vid in the harvest time unto the cave of A-dul'lam: and the troop of the Phi-lis'-tines pitched in the valley of Reph'a-im.

14 And Da'vid *was* then in an hold, and the garrison of the Phi-lis'tines *was* then *in* Beth'-le-hem.

15 And Da'vid longed, and said, Oh that one would give me drink of the water of the well of Beth'-le-hem, which *is* by the gate!

16 And the three mighty men brake through the host of the Phi-lis'tines, and drew water out of the well of Beth'-le-hem, that *was* by the gate, and took *it*, and brought *it* to Da'vid: nevertheless he would not drink thereof, but poured it out unto the LORD.

17 And he said, Be it far from me, O LORD, that I should do this: *is not this* the blood of the men that went in jeopardy of their lives? therefore he would not drink it. These things did these three mighty men.

18 And A-bish'a-i, the brother of Jo'ab, the son of Zer-u-i'ah, was chief among three. And he lifted up his spear against three hundred, *and* slew *them*, and had the name among three.

19 Was he not most honourable of three? therefore he was their captain: howbeit he attained not unto the *first* three.

20 And Be-na'iah the son of Je-hoi'a-da, the son of a valiant man, of Kab'ze-el, who had done many acts, he slew two lionlike men of Mo'ab: he went down also and slew a lion in the midst of a pit in time of snow:

21 And he slew an E-gyp'tian, a goodly man: and the E-gyp'tian had a spear in his hand; but he went down to him with a staff, and plucked the spear out of the E-gyp'tian's hand, and slew him with his own spear.

22 These *things* did Be-na'iah the son of Je-hoi'a-da, and had the name among three mighty men.

23 He was more honourable than the thirty, but he attained not to the *first* three. And Da'vid set him over his guard.

24 A'sa-hel the brother of Jo'ab *was* one of the thirty; El-ha'nan the son of Do'do of Beth'-le-hem,

25 Sham'mah the Ha'rod-ite, El'i-ka the Ha'-rod-ite,

26 He'lez the Pal'tite, I'ra the son of Ik'kesh the Te-ko'ite,

27 A-bi-e'zer the An'e-thoth-ite, Me-bun'nai the Hu'shath-ite,

28 Zal'mon the A-ho'hite, Ma-har'a-i the Ne-toph'a-thite,

29 He'leb the son of Ba'a-nah, a Ne-toph'a-thite, It'ta-i the son of Ri'bai out of Gib'e-ah of the children of Ben'ja-min,

30 Be-na'iah the Pir'a-thon-ite, Hid'da-i of the brooks of Ga'ash,

31 A'bi-al'bon the Ar'bath-ite, Az'ma-veth the Bar-hu'mite,

32 E-li′ah-ba the Sha-al′bo-nite, of the sons of Ja′shen, Jon′a-than,

33 Sham′mah the Ha′ra-rite, A-hi′am the son of Sha′rar the Ha′ra-rite,

34 E-liph′e-let the son of A-has′ba-i, the son of the Ma-ach′a-thite, E-li′am the son of A-hith′-o-phel the Gi′lo-nite,

35 Hez′ra-i the Car′mel-ite, Pa′a-rai the Ar′bite,

36 I′gal the son of Na′than of Zo′bah, Ba′ni the Gad′ite,

37 Ze′lek the Am′mon-ite, Na′ha-ri the Be-e′roth-ite, armourbearer to Jo′ab the son of Zer-u-i′ah,

38 I′ra an Ith′rite, Ga′reb an Ith′rite,

39 U-ri′ah the Hit′tite: thirty and seven in all.

24 AND again the anger of the LORD was kindled against Is′ra-el, and he moved Da′vid against them to say, Go, number Is′ra-el and Ju′dah.

2 For the king said to Jo′ab the captain of the host, which was with him, Go now through all the tribes of Is′ra-el, from Dan even to Be′er-she′ba, and number ye people, that I may know the number of the people.

3 And Jo′ab said unto the king, Now the LORD thy God add unto the people, how many soever they be, an hundredfold, and that the eyes of my lord the king may see it: but why doth my lord the king delight in this thing?

4 Notwithstanding the king's word prevailed against Jo′ab, and against the captains of the host. And Jo′ab and the captains of the host went out from the presence of the king, to number the people of Is′ra-el.

5 ¶ And they passed over Jor′dan, and pitched in Ar′o-er, on the right side of the city that lieth in the midst of the river of Gad, and toward Ja′zer:

6 Then they came to Gil′e-ad, and to the land of Tah′tim-hod′shi; and they came to Dan-ja′-an, and about to Zi′don,

7 And came to the strong hold of Tyre, and to all the cities of the Hi′vites, and of the Ca′naan-ites: and they went out to the south of Ju′dah, even to Be′er-she′ba.

8 So when they had gone through all the land, they came to Je-ru′sa-lem at the end of nine months and twenty days.

9 And Jo′ab gave up the sum of the number of the people unto the king: and there were in Is′ra-el eight hundred thousand vailant men that drew the sword; and the men of Ju′dah were five hundred thousand men.

10 ¶ And Da′vid's heart smote him after that he had numbered the people. And Da′vid said unto the LORD, I have sinned greatly in that I have done: and now, I beseech thee, O LORD, take away the iniquity of thy servant; for I have done very foolishly.

11 ¶ For when Da′vid was up in the morning, the word of the LORD came unto the prophet Gad, Da′vid's seer, saying,

12 Go and say unto Da′vid, Thus saith the LORD, I offer thee three things; choose thee one of them, that I may do it unto thee.

13 So Gad came to Da′vid, and told him, and said unto him, Shall seven years of famine come unto thee in thy land? or wilt thou flee three months before thine enemies, while they pursue thee? or that there be three days' pestilence in thy land? now advise, and see what answer I shall return to him that sent me.

14 And Da′vid said unto Gad, I am in a great strait: let us fall now into the hand of the LORD; for his mercies are great: and let me not fall into the hand of man.

15 ¶ So the LORD sent a pestilence upon Is′ra-el from the morning even to the time appointed: and there died of the people from Dan even to Be′er-she′ba seventy thousand men.

16 And when the angel stretched out his hand upon Je-ru′sa-lem to destroy it, the LORD repented him of the evil, and said to the angel that destroyed the people, It is enough: stay now thine hand. And the angel of the LORD was by the threshingplace of A-rau′nah the Jeb′u-site.

17 And Da′vid spake unto the LORD when he saw the angel that smote the people, and said, Lo, I have sinned, and I have done wickedly: but these sheep, what have they done? let thine hand, I pray thee, be against me, and against my father's house.

18 ¶ And Gad came that day to Da′vid, and said unto him, Go up, rear an altar unto the LORD in the threshingfloor of A-rau′nah the Jeb′u-site.

19 And Da′vid, according to the saying of Gad, went up as the LORD commanded.

20 And A-rau′nah looked, and saw the king and his servants coming on toward him: and A-rau′nah went out, and bowed himself before the king on his face upon the ground.

21 And A-rau′nah said, Wherefore is my lord the king come to his servant? And Da′vid said, To buy the threshingfloor of thee, to build an altar unto the LORD, that the plague may be stayed from the people.

22 And A-rau′nah said unto Da′vid, Let my lord the king take and offer up what seemeth good unto him: behold, here be oxen for burnt sacrifice, and threshing instruments and other instruments of the oxen for wood.

23 All these things did A-rau′nah, as a king, give unto the king. And A-rau′nah said unto the king, The LORD thy God accept thee.

24 And the king said unto A-rau′nah, Nay; but I will surely buy it of thee at a price: neither will I offer burnt offerings unto the LORD my God of that which doth cost me nothing. So Da′vid bought the threshingfloor and the oxen for fifty shekels of silver.

25 And Da′vid built there an altar unto the LORD, and offered burnt offerings and peace offerings. So the LORD was intreated for the land, and the plague was stayed from Is′ra-el.

THE FIRST BOOK OF THE

KINGS

1 NOW king Da′vid was old and stricken in years; and they covered him with clothes, but he gat no heat.

2 Wherefore his servants said unto him, Let there be sought for my lord the king a young virgin: and let her stand before the king, and let her cherish him, and let her lie in thy bosom, that my lord the king may get heat.

3 So they sought for a fair damsel throughout all the coasts of Is′ra-el, and found Ab′i-

shag a Shu'nam-mite, and brought her to the king.

4 And the damsel was very fair, and cherished the king, and ministered to him: but the king knew her not.

5 ¶ Then Ad-o-ni'jah the son of Hag'gith exalted himself, saying, I will be king: and he prepared him chariots and horsemen, and fifty men to run before him.

6 And his father had not displeased him at any time in saying, Why hast thou done so? and he also was a very goodly man; and his mother bare him after Ab'sa-lom.

7 And he conferred with Jo'ab the son of Zer-u-i'ah, and with A-bi'a-thar the priest: and they following Ad-o-ni'jah helped him.

8 But Za'dok the priest, and Be-na'iah the son of Je-hoi'a-da, and Na'than the prophet, and Shim'e-i, and Re'i, and the mighty men which belonged to Da'vid, were not with Ad-o-ni'jah.

9 And Ad-o-ni'jah slew sheep and oxen and fat cattle by the stone of Zo'he-leth, which is by En-ro'gel, and called all his brethren the king's sons, and all the men of Ju'dah the king's servants:

10 But Na'than the prophet, and Be-na'iah, and the mighty men, and Sol'o-mon his brother, he called not.

11 ¶ Wherefore Na'than spake unto Bath'-she-ba the mother of Sol'o-mon, saying, Hast thou not heard that Ad-o-ni'jah the son of Hag'-gith doth reign, and Da'vid our lord knoweth it not?

12 Now therefore come, let me, I pray thee, give thee counsel, that thou mayest save thine own life, and the life of thy son Sol'o-mon.

13 Go and get thee in unto king Da'vid, and say unto him, Didst not thou, my lord, O king, swear unto thine handmaid, saying, Assuredly Sol'o-mon thy son shall reign after me, and he shall sit upon my throne? why then doth Ad-o-ni'jah reign?

14 Behold, while thou yet talkest there with the king, I also will come in after thee, and confirm thy words.

15 ¶ And Bath'-she-ba went in unto the king into the chamber: and the king was very old; and Ab'i-shag the Shu'nam-mite ministered unto the king.

16 And Bath'-she-ba bowed, and did obeisance unto the king. And the king said, What wouldest thou?

17 And she said unto him, My lord, thou swarest by the LORD thy God unto thine handmaid, saying, Assuredly Sol'o-mon thy son shall reign after me, and he shall sit upon my throne.

18 And now, behold, Ad-o-ni'jah reigneth; and now, my lord the king, thou knowest it not:

19 And he hath slain oxen and fat cattle and sheep in abundance, and hath called all the sons of the king, and A-bi'a-thar the priest, and Jo'ab the captain of the host: but Sol'o-mon thy servant hath he not called.

20 And thou, my lord, O king, the eyes of all Is'ra-el are upon thee, that thou shouldest tell them who shall sit on the throne of my lord the king after him.

21 Otherwise it shall come to pass, when my lord the king shall sleep with his fathers, that I and my son Sol'o-mon shall be counted offenders.

22 ¶ And, lo, while she yet talked with the king, Na'than the prophet also came in.

23 And they told the king, saying, Behold Na'than the prophet. And when he was come in before the king, he bowed himself before the king with his face to the ground.

24 And Na'than said, My lord, O king, hast thou said, Ad-o-ni'jah shall reign after me, and he shall sit upon my throne?

25 For he is gone down this day, and hath slain oxen and fat cattle and sheep in abundance, and hath called all the king's sons, and the captains of the host, and A-bi'a-thar the priest; and, behold, they eat and drink before him, and say, God save king Ad-o-ni'jah.

26 But me, even me thy servant, and Za'dok the priest, and Be-na'iah the son of Je-hoi'a-da, and thy servant Sol'o-mon, hath he not called.

27 Is this thing done by my lord the king, and thou hast not shewed it unto thy servant, who should sit on the throne of my lord the king after him?

28 ¶ Then king Da'vid answered and said, Call me Bath'-she-ba. And she came into the king's presence, and stood before the king.

29 And the king sware, and said, As the LORD liveth, that hath redeemed my soul out of all distress,

30 Even as I sware unto thee by the LORD God of Is'ra-el, saying, Assuredly Sol'o-mon thy son shall reign after me, and he shall sit upon my throne in my stead; even so will I certainly do this day.

31 Then Bath'-she-ba bowed with her face to the earth, and did reverence to the king, and said, Let my lord king Da'vid live for ever.

32 ¶ And king Da'vid said, Call me Za'dok the priest, and Na'than the prophet, and Be-na'-iah the son of Je-hoi'a-da. And they came before the king.

33 The king also said unto them, Take with you the servants of your lord, and cause Sol'o-mon my son to ride upon mine own mule, and bring him down to Gi'hon:

34 And let Za'dok the priest and Na'than the prophet anoint him there king over Is'ra-el: and blow ye with the trumpet, and say, God save king Sol'o-mon.

35 Then ye shall come up after him, that he may come and sit upon my throne; for he shall be king in my stead: and I have appointed him to be ruler over Is'ra-el and over Ju'dah.

36 And Be-na'iah the son of Je-hoi'a-da answered the king, and said, Amen: the LORD God of my lord the king say so too.

37 As the LORD hath been with my lord the king even so be he with Sol'o-mon, and make his throne greater than the throne of my lord king Da'vid.

38 So Za'dok the priest, and Na'than the prophet, and Be-na'iah the son of Je-hoi'a-da, and the Cher'eth-ites, and the Pe'leth-ites, went down, and caused Sol'o-mon to ride upon king Da'vid's mule, and brought him to Gi'hon.

39 And Za'dok the priest took an horn of oil out of the tabernacle, and anointed Sol'o-mon. And they blew the trumpet; and all the people said, God save king Sol'o-mon.

40 And all the people came up after him, and the people piped with pipes, and rejoiced with great joy, so that the earth rent with the sound of them.

41 ¶ And Ad-o-ni'jah and all the guests that were with him heard it as they had made an end of eating. And when Jo'ab heard the sound of the trumpet, he said, Wherefore is this noise of the city being in an uproar?

42 And while he yet spake, behold, Jon'a-than the son of A-bi'a-thar the priest came: and Ad-o-ni'jah said unto him, Come in; for thou art a valiant man, and bringest good tidings.

43 And Jon'a-than answered and said to Ad-

o-ni′jah, Verily our lord king Da′vid hath made Sol′o-mon king.

44 And the king hath sent with him Za′dok the priest, and Na′than the prophet, and Be-na′-iah the son of Je-hoi′a-da, and the Cher′eth-ites, and the Pe′leth-ites, and they have caused him to ride upon the king's mule:

45 And Za′dok the priest and Na′than the prophet have anointed him king in Gi′hon: and they are come up from thence rejoicing, so that the city rang again. This is the noise that ye have heard.

46 And also Sol′o-mon sitteth on the throne of the kingdom.

47 And moreover the king's servants came to bless our lord king Da′vid, saying, God make the name of Sol′o-mon better than thy name, and make his throne greater than thy throne. And the king bowed himself upon the bed.

48 And also thus said the king, Blessed be the LORD God of Is′ra-el, which hath given one to sit on my throne this day, mine eyes even seeing it.

49 And all the guests that were with Ad-o-ni′jah were afraid, and rose up, and went every man his way.

50 ¶ And Ad-o-ni′jah feared because of Sol′-o-mon, and arose, and went, and caught hold on the horns of the altar.

51 And it was told Sol′o-mon, saying, Behold, Ad-o-ni′jah feareth king Sol′o-mon: for, lo, he hath caught hold on the horns of the altar, saying, Let king Sol′o-mon swear unto me to day that he will not slay his servant with the sword.

52 And Sol′o-mon said, If he will shew himself a worthy man, there shall not an hair of him fall to the earth: but if wickedness shall be found in him, he shall die.

53 So king Sol′o-mon sent, and they brought him down from the altar. And he came and bowed himself to king Sol′o-mon: and Sol′o-mon said unto him, Go to thine house.

2 NOW the days of Da′vid drew nigh that he should die; and he charged Sol′o-mon his son, saying,

2 I go the way of all the earth: be thou strong therefore, and shew thyself a man;

3 And keep the charge of the LORD thy God, to walk in his ways, to keep his statutes, and his commandments, and his judgments, and his testimonies, as it is written in the law of Mo′ses, that thou mayest prosper in all that thou doest, and whithersoever thou turnest thyself:

4 That the LORD may continue his word which he spake concerning me, saying, If thy children take heed to their way, to walk before me in truth with all their heart and with all their soul, there shall not fail thee (said he) a man on the throne of Is′ra-el.

5 Moreover thou knowest also what Jo′ab the son of Zer-u-i′ah did to me, and what he did to the two captains of the hosts of Is′ra-el, unto Ab′ner the son of Ner, and unto Am′a-sa the son of Je′ther, whom he slew, and shed the blood of war in peace, and put the blood of war upon his girdle that was about his loins, and in his shoes that were on his feet.

6 Do therefore according to thy wisdom, and let not his hoar head go down to the grave in peace.

7 But shew kindness unto the sons of Bar-zil′la-i the Gil′e-ad-ite, and let them be of those that eat at thy table: for so they came to me when I fled because of Ab′sa-lom thy brother.

8 And, behold, thou hast with thee Shim′e-i the son of Ge′ra, a Ben′ja-mite of Ba-hu′rim, which cursed me with a grievous curse in the

day when I went to Ma-ha-na′im: but he came down to meet me at Jor′dan, and I sware to him by the LORD, saying, I will not put thee to death with the sword.

9 Now therefore hold him not guiltless: for thou art a wise man, and knowest what thou oughtest to do unto him; but his hoar head bring thou down to the grave with blood.

10 So Da′vid slept with his fathers, and was buried in the city of Da′vid.

11 And the days that Da′vid reigned over Is′-ra-el were forty years: seven years reigned he in He′bron, and thirty and three years reigned he in Je-ru′sa-lem.

12 Then sat Sol′o-mon upon the throne of Da′vid his father; and his kingdom was established greatly.

13 ¶ And Ad-o-ni′jah the son of Hag′gith came to Bath′-she-ba the mother of Sol′o-mon. And she said, Comest thou peaceably? And he said, Peaceably.

14 He said moreover, I have somewhat to say unto thee. And she said, Say on.

15 And he said, Thou knowest that the kingdom was mine, and that all Is′ra-el set their faces on me, that I should reign: howbeit the kingdom is turned about, and is become my brother's: for it was his from the LORD.

16 And now I ask one petition of thee, deny me not. And she said unto him, Say on.

17 And he said, Speak, I pray thee, unto Sol′-o-mon the king, (for he will not say thee nay,) that he give me Ab′i-shag the Shu′nam-mite to wife.

18 And Bath′-she-ba said, Well; I will speak for thee unto the king.

19 ¶ Bath′-she-ba therefore went unto king Sol′o-mon, to speak unto him for Ad-o-ni′jah. And the king rose up to meet her, and bowed himself unto her, and sat down on his throne, and caused a seat to be set for the king's mother; and she sat on his right hand.

20 Then she said, I desire one small petition of thee; I pray thee, say me not nay. And the king said unto her, Ask on, my mother: for I will not say thee nay.

21 And she said, Let Ab′i-shag the Shu′nam-mite be given to Ad-o-ni′jah thy brother to wife.

22 And king Sol′o-mon answered and said unto his mother, And why dost thou ask Ab′i-shag the Shu′nam-mite for Ad-o-ni′jah? ask for him the kingdom also; for he is mine elder brother; even for him, and for A-bi′a-thar the priest, and for Jo′ab the son of Zer-u-i′ah.

23 Then king Sol′o-mon sware by the LORD, saying, God do so to me, and more also, if Ad-o-ni′jah have not spoken this word against his own life.

24 Now therefore, as the LORD liveth, which hath established me, and set me on the throne of Da′vid my father, and who hath made me an house, as he promised, Ad-o-ni′jah shall be put to death this day.

25 And king Sol′o-mon sent by the hand of Be-na′iah the son of Je-hoi′a-da; and he fell upon him that he died.

26 ¶ And unto A-bi′a-thar the priest said the king, Get thee to An′a-thoth, unto thine own fields; for thou art worthy of death: but I will not at this time put thee to death, because thou barest the ark of the Lord GOD before Da′vid my father, and because thou hast been afflicted in all wherein my father was afflicted.

27 So Sol′o-mon thrust out A-bi′a-thar from being priest unto the LORD; that he might fulfil the word of the LORD, which he spake concerning the house of E′li in Shi′loh.

28 ¶ Then tidings came to Jo'ab: for Jo'ab had turned after Ad-o-ni'jah, though he turned not after Ab'sa-lom. And Jo'ab fled unto the tabernacle of the LORD, and caught hold on the horns of the altar.

29 And it was told king Sol'o-mon that Jo'ab was fled unto the tabernacle of the LORD; and, behold, *he is* by the altar. Then Sol'o-mon sent Be-na'iah the son of Je-hoi'a-da, saying, Go, fall upon him.

30 And Be-na'iah came to the tabernacle of the LORD, and said unto him, Thus saith the king, Come forth. And he said, Nay: but I will die here. And Be-na'iah brought the king word again, saying, Thus said Jo'ab, and thus he answered me.

31 And the king said unto him, Do as he hath said, and fall upon him, and bury him; that thou mayest take away the innocent blood, which Jo'ab shed, from me, and from the house of my father.

32 And the LORD shall return his blood upon his own head, who fell upon two men more righteous and better than he, and slew them with the sword, my father Da'vid not knowing *thereof, to wit,* Ab'ner the son of Ner, captain of the host of Is'ra-el, and Am'a-sa the son of Je'-ther, captain of the host of Ju'dah.

33 Their blood shall therefore return upon the head of Jo'ab, and upon the head of his seed for ever: but upon Da'vid, and upon his seed, and upon his house, and upon his throne, shall there be peace for ever from the LORD.

34 So Be-na'iah the son of Je-hoi'a-da went up, and fell upon him, and slew him: and he was buried in his own house in the wilderness.

35 ¶ And the king put Be-na'iah the son of Je-hoi'a-da in his room over the host: and Za'-dok the priest did the king put in the room of A-bi'a-thar.

36 ¶ And the king sent and called for Shim'e-i, and said unto him, Build thee an house in Je-ru'sa-lem, and dwell there, and go not forth thence any whither.

37 For it shall be, *that* on the day thou goest out, and passest over the brook Kid'ron, thou shalt know for certain that thou shalt surely die: thy blood shall be upon thine own head.

38 And Shim'e-i said unto the king, The saying *is* good: as my lord the king hath said, so will thy servant do. And Shim'e-i dwelt in Je-ru'sa-lem many days.

39 And it came to pass at the end of three years, that two of the servants of Shim'e-i ran away unto A'chish son of Ma'a-chah king of Gath. And they told Shim'e-i, saying, Behold, thy servants *be* in Gath.

40 And Shim'e-i arose, and saddled his ass, and went to Gath to A'chish to seek his servants: and Shim'e-i went, and brought his servants from Gath.

41 And it was told Sol'o-mon that Shim'e-i had gone from Je-ru'sa-lem to Gath, and was come again.

42 And the king sent and called for Shim'e-i, and said unto him, Did I not make thee to swear by the LORD, and protested unto thee, saying, Know for a certain, on the day thou goest out, and walkest abroad any whither, that thou shalt surely die? and thou saidst unto me, The word *that* I have heard *is* good.

43 Why then hast thou not kept the oath of the LORD, and the commandment that I have charged thee with?

44 The king said moreover to Shim'e-i, Thou knowest all the wickedness which thine heart is privy to, that thou didst to Da'vid my father:

therefore the LORD shall return thy wickedness upon thine own head;

45 And king Sol'o-mon *shall be* blessed, and the throne of Da'vid shall be established before the LORD for ever.

46 So the king commanded Be-na'iah the son of Je-hoi'a-da; which went out, and fell upon him, that he died. And the kingdom was established in the hand of Sol'o-mon.

3 AND Sol'o-mon made affinity with Pha'-raoh king of E'gypt, and took Pha'raoh's daughter, and brought her into the city of Da'-vid, until he had made an end of building his own house, and the house of the LORD, and the wall of Je-ru'sa-lem round about.

2 Only the people sacrificed in high places, because there was no house built unto the name of the LORD, until those days.

3 And Sol'o-mon loved the LORD, walking in the statutes of Da'vid his father: only he sacrificed and burnt incense in high places.

4 And the king went to Gib'e-on to sacrifice there; for that *was* the great high place: a thousand burnt offerings did Sol'o-mon offer upon that altar.

5 ¶ In Gib'e-on the LORD appeared to Sol'o-mon in a dream by night: and God said, Ask what I shall give thee.

6 And Sol'o-mon said, Thou hast shewed unto thy servant Da'vid my father great mercy, according as he walked before thee in truth, and in righteousness, and in uprightness of heart with thee; and thou hast kept for him this great kindness, that thou hast given him a son to sit on his throne, as *it is* this day.

7 And now, O LORD my God, thou hast made thy servant king instead of Da'vid my father: and I *am but* a little child: I know not *how* to go out or come in.

8 And thy servant *is* in the midst of thy people which thou hast chosen, a great people, that cannot be numbered nor counted for multitude.

9 Give therefore thy servant an understanding heart to judge thy people, that I may discern between good and bad: for who is able to judge this thy so great a people?

10 And the speech pleased the LORD, that Sol'o-mon had asked this thing.

11 And God said unto him, Because thou hast asked this thing, and hast not asked for thyself long life; neither hast asked riches for thyself, nor hast asked the life of thine enemies; but hast asked for thyself understanding to discern judgment;

12 Behold, I have done according to thy words: lo, I have given thee a wise and an understanding heart; so that there was none like thee before thee, neither after thee shall any arise like unto thee.

13 And I have also given thee that which thou hast not asked, both riches, and honour: so that there shall not be any among the kings like unto thee all thy days.

14 And if thou wilt walk in my ways, to keep my statutes and my commandments, as thy father Da'vid did walk, then I will lengthen thy days.

15 And Sol'o-mon awoke; and, behold, *it was* a dream. And he came to Je-ru'sa-lem, and stood before the ark of the covenant of the LORD, and offered up burnt offerings, and offered peace offerings, and made a feast to all his servants.

16 ¶ Then came there two women, *that were* harlots, unto the king, and stood before him.

17 And the one woman said, O my lord, I and

this woman dwell in one house; and I was delivered of a child with her in the house.

18 And it came to pass the third day after that I was delivered, that this woman was delivered also: and we were together; there was no stranger with us in the house, save we two in the house.

19 And this woman's child died in the night; because she overlaid it.

20 And she arose at midnight, and took my son from beside me, while thine handmaid slept, and laid it in her bosom, and laid her dead child in my bosom.

21 And when I rose in the morning to give my child suck, behold, it was dead: but when I had considered it in the morning, behold, it was not my son, which I did bear.

22 And the other woman said, Nay; but the living is my son, and the dead is thy son. And this said, No; but the dead is thy son, and the living is my son. Thus they spake before the king.

23 Then said the king, The one saith, This is my son that liveth, and thy son is the dead: and the other saith, Nay; but thy son is the dead, and my son is the living.

24 And the king said, Bring me a sword. And they brought a sword before the king.

25 And the king said, Divide the living child in two, and give half to the one, and half to the other.

26 Then spake the woman whose the living child was unto the king, for her bowels yearned upon her son, and she said, O my lord, give her the living child, and in no wise slay it. But the other said, Let it be neither mine nor thine, but divide it.

27 Then the king answered and said, Give her the living child, and in no wise slay it: she is the mother thereof.

28 And all Is'ra-el heard of the judgment which the king had judged; and they feared the king: for they saw that the wisdom of God was in him, to do judgment.

4 SO king Sol'o-mon was king over all Is'ra-el.

2 And these were the princes which he had; Az-a-ri'ah the son of Za'dok the priest,

3 El-i-ho'reph and A-hi'ah, the sons of Shi'-sha, scribes; Je-hosh'a-phat the son of A-hi'lud, the recorder.

4 And Be-na'iah the son of Je-hoi'a-da was over the host: and Za'dok and A-bi'a-thar were the priests:

5 And Az-a-ri'ah the son of Na'than was over the officers: and Za'bud the son of Na'than was principal officer, and the king's friend:

6 And A-hi'shar was over the household: and Ad-o-ni'ram the son of Ab'da was over the tribute.

7 ¶ And Sol'o-mon had twelve officers over all Is'ra-el, which provided victuals for the king and his household: each man his month in a year made provision.

8 And these are their names: The son of Hur, in mount E'phra-im:

9 The son of De'kar, in Ma'kaz, and in Sha-al'bim, and Beth-she'mesh, and E'lon-beth-ha'-nan:

10 The son of He'sed, in Ar'u-both; to him pertained So'choh, and all the land of He'pher:

11 The son of A-bin'a-dab, in all the region of Dor; which had Ta'phath the daughter of Sol'o-mon to wife:

12 Ba'a-na the son of A-hi'lud; to him pertained Ta'a-nach and Me-gid'do, and all Beth-she'an, which is by Zar'ta-nah beneath Jez're-el, from Beth-she'an to A'bel-me-ho'lah, even unto the place that is beyond Jok'ne-am:

13 The son of Ge'ber, in Ra'moth-gil'e-ad; to him pertained the towns of Ja'ir the son of Ma-nas'seh, which are in Gil'e-ad; to him also pertained the region of Ar'gob, which is in Ba'shan, threescore great cities with walls and brasen bars:

14 A-hin'a-dab the son of Id'do had Ma-ha-na'im:

15 A-him'a-az was in Naph'ta-li; he also took Bas'math the daughter of Sol'o-mon to wife:

16 Ba'a-nah the son of Hu'shai was in Ash'er and in A'loth:

17 Je-hosh'a-phat the son of Par'u-ah, in Is'-sa-char:

18 Shim'e-i the son of E'lah, in Ben'ja-min:

19 Ge'ber the son of U'ri was in the country of Gil'e-ad, in the country of Si'hon king of the Am'or-ites, and of Og king of Ba'shan; and he was the only officer which was in the land.

20 ¶ Ju'dah and Is'ra-el were many, as the sand which is by the sea in multitude, eating and drinking, and making merry.

21 And Sol'o-mon reigned over all kingdoms from the river unto the land of the Phi-lis'tines, and unto the border of E'gypt: they brought presents, and served Sol'o-mon all the days of his life.

22 ¶ And Sol'o-mon's provision for one day was thirty measures of fine flour, and threescore measures of meal,

23 Ten fat oxen, and twenty oxen out of the pastures, and an hundred sheep, beside harts, and roebucks, and fallowdeer, and fatted fowl.

24 For he had dominion over all the region on this side the river, from Tiph'sah even to Az'-zah, over all the kings on this side the river: and he had peace on all sides round about him.

25 And Ju'dah and Is'ra-el dwelt safely, every man under his vine and under his fig tree, from Dan even to Be'er-she'ba, all the days of Sol'o-mon.

26 ¶ And Sol'o-mon had forty thousand stalls of horses for his chariots, and twelve thousand horsemen.

27 And those officers provided victual for king Sol'o-mon, and for all that came unto king Sol'o-mon's table, every man in his month: they lacked nothing.

28 Barley also and straw for the horses and dromedaries brought they unto the place where the officers were, every man according to his charge.

29 ¶ And God gave Sol'o-mon wisdom and understanding exceeding much, and largeness of heart, even as the sand that is on the sea shore.

30 And Sol'o-mon's wisdom excelled the wisdom of all the children of the east country, and all the wisdom of E'gypt.

31 For he was wiser than all men; than E'-than the Ez'ra-hite, and He'man, and Chal'col, and Dar'da, the sons of Ma'hol: and his fame was in all nations round about.

32 And he spake three thousand proverbs: and his songs were a thousand and five.

33 And he spake of trees, from the cedar tree that is in Leb'a-non even unto the hyssop that springeth out of the wall: he spake also of beasts, and of fowl, and of creeping things, and of fishes.

34 And there came of all people to hear the wisdom of Sol'o-mon, from all kings of the earth, which had heard of his wisdom.

5 AND Hi'ram king of Tyre sent his servants unto Sol'o-mon; for he had heard that they had anointed him king in the room of his father: for Hi'ram was ever a lover of Da'vid.

2 And Sol'o-mon sent to Hi'ram, saying,

3 Thou knowest how that Da'vid my father could not build an house unto the name of the LORD his God for the wars which were about him on every side, until the LORD put them under the soles of his feet.

4 But now the LORD my God hath given me rest on every side, so that there is neither adversary nor evil occurrent.

5 And, behold, I purpose to build an house unto the name of the LORD my God, as the LORD spake unto Da'vid my father, saying, Thy son, whom I will set upon thy throne in thy room, he shall build an house unto my name.

6 Now therefore command thou that they hew me cedar trees out of Leb'a-non; and my servants shall be with thy servants: and unto thee will I give hire for thy servants according to all that thou shalt appoint: for thou knowest that there is not among us any that can skill to hew timber like unto the Si-do'ni-ans.

7 ¶ And it came to pass, when Hi'ram heard the words of Sol'o-mon, that he rejoiced greatly, and said, Blessed be the LORD this day, which hath given unto Da'vid a wise son over this great people.

8 And Hi'ram sent to Sol'o-mon, saying, I have considered the things which thou sentest to me for: and I will do all thy desire concerning timber of cedar, and concerning timber of fir.

9 My servants shall bring them down from Leb'a-non unto the sea: and I will convey them by sea in floats unto the place that thou shalt appoint me, and will cause them to be discharged there, and thou shalt receive them: and thou shalt accomplish my desire, in giving food for my household.

10 So Hi'ram gave Sol'o-mon cedar trees and fir trees according to all his desire.

11 And Sol'o-mon gave Hi'ram twenty thousand measures of wheat for food to his household, and twenty measures of pure oil: thus gave Sol'o-mon to Hi'ram year by year.

12 And the LORD gave Sol'o-mon wisdom, as he promised him: and there was peace between Hi'ram and Sol'o-mon; and they two made a league together.

13 ¶ And king Sol'o-mon raised a levy out of all Is'ra-el; and the levy was thirty thousand men.

14 And he sent them to Leb'a-non, ten thousand a month by courses: a month they were in Leb'a-non, and two months at home: and Ad-o-ni'ram was over the levy.

15 And Sol'o-mon had threescore and ten thousand that bare burdens, and fourscore thousand hewers in the mountains;

16 Beside the chief of Sol'o-mon's officers which were over the work, three thousand and three hundred, which ruled over the people that wrought in the work.

17 And the king commanded, and they brought great stones, costly stones, and hewed stones to lay the foundation of the house.

18 And Sol'o-mon's builders and Hi'ram's builders did hew them, and the stonesquarers: so they prepared timber and stones to build the house.

6 AND it came to pass in the four hundred and eightieth year after the children of Is'ra-el were come out of the land of E'gypt, in the fourth year of Sol'o-mon's reign over Is'ra-el, in the month Zif, which is the second month, that he began to build the house of the LORD.

2 And the house which king Sol'o-mon built for the LORD, the length thereof was threescore cubits, and the breadth thereof twenty cubits, and the height thereof thirty cubits.

3 And the porch before the temple of the house, twenty cubits was the length thereof, according to the breadth of the house; and ten cubits was the breadth thereof before the house.

4 And for the house he made windows of narrow lights.

5 ¶ And against the wall of the house he built chambers round about, against the walls of the house round about, both of the temple and of the oracle: and he made chambers round about:

6 The nethermost chamber was five cubits broad, and the middle was six cubits broad, and the third was seven cubits broad: for without in the wall of the house he made narrowed rests round about, that the beams should not be fastened in the walls of the house.

7 And the house, when it was in building, was built of stone made ready before it was brought thither: so that there was neither hammer nor ax nor any tool of iron heard in the house, while it was in building.

8 The door for the middle chamber was in the right side of the house: and they went up with winding stairs into the middle chamber, and out of the middle into the third.

9 So he built the house, and finished it; and covered the house with beams and boards of cedar.

10 And then he built chambers against all the house, five cubits high: and they rested on the house with timber of cedar.

11 ¶ And the word of the LORD came to Sol'o-mon, saying,

12 Concerning this house which thou art in building, if thou wilt walk in my statutes, and execute my judgments, and keep all my commandments to walk in them; then will I perform my word with thee, which I spake unto Da'vid thy father:

13 And I will dwell among the children of Is'ra-el, and will not forsake my people Is'ra-el.

14 So Sol'o-mon built the house, and finished it.

15 And he built the walls of the house within with boards of cedar, both the floor of the house, and the walls of the ceiling: and he covered them on the inside with wood, and covered the floor of the house with planks of fir.

16 And he built twenty cubits on the sides of the house, both the floor and the walls with boards of cedar: he even built them for it within, even for the oracle, even for the most holy place.

17 And the house, that is, the temple before it, was forty cubits long.

18 And the cedar of the house within was carved with knops and open flowers: all was cedar; there was no stone seen.

19 And the oracle he prepared in the house within, to set there the ark of the covenant of the LORD.

20 And the oracle in the forepart was twenty cubits in length, and twenty cubits in breadth, and twenty cubits in the height thereof: and he overlaid it with pure gold; and so covered the altar which was of cedar.

21 So Sol'o-mon overlaid the house within with pure gold: and he made a partition by the chains of gold before the oracle; and he overlaid it with gold.

22 And the whole house he overlaid with gold, until he had finished all the house: also the whole altar that *was* by the oracle he overlaid with gold.

23 ¶ And within the oracle he made two cherubims *of* olive tree, *each* ten cubits high.

24 And five cubits *was* the one wing of the cherub, and five cubits the other wing of the cherub: from the uttermost part of the one wing unto the uttermost part of the other *were* ten cubits.

25 And the other cherub *was* ten cubits: both the cherubims *were* of one measure and one size.

26 The height of the one cherub *was* ten cubits, and so *was* it of the other cherub.

27 And he set the cherubims within the inner house: and they stretched forth the wings of the cherubims, so that the wing of the one touched the *one* wall, and the wing of the other cherub touched the other wall; and their wings touched one another in the midst of the house.

28 And he overlaid the cherubims with gold.

29 And he carved all the walls of the house round about with carved figures of cherubims and palm trees and open flowers, within and without.

30 And the floor of the house he overlaid with gold, within and without.

31 ¶ And for the entering of the oracle he made doors *of* olive tree: the lintel *and* side posts *were* a fifth part *of the wall.*

32 The two doors also *were of* olive tree; and he carved upon them carvings of cherubims and palm trees and open flowers, and overlaid *them* with gold, and spread gold upon the cherubims, and upon the palm trees.

33 So also made he for the door of the temple posts *of* olive tree, a fourth part *of the wall.*

34 And the two doors *were of* fir tree: the two leaves of the one door *were* folding, and the two leaves of the other door *were* folding.

35 And he carved *thereon* cherubims and palm trees and open flowers: and covered *them* with gold fitted upon the carved work.

36 ¶ And he built the inner court with three rows of hewed stone, and a row of cedar beams.

37 ¶ In the fourth year was the foundation of the house of the LORD laid, in the month Zif:

38 And in the eleventh year, in the month Bul, which *is* the eighth month, was the house finished throughout all the parts thereof, and according to all the fashion of it. So was he seven years in building it.

7 BUT Sol'o-mon was building his own house thirteen years, and he finished all his house.

2 ¶ He built also the house of the forest of Leb'a-non; the length thereof *was* an hundred cubits, and the breadth thereof fifty cubits, and the height thereof thirty cubits, upon four rows of cedar pillars, with cedar beams upon the pillars.

3 And *it was* covered with cedar above upon the beams, that *lay* on forty five pillars, fifteen in a row.

4 And *there were* windows *in* three rows, and light *was* against light *in* three ranks.

5 And all the doors and posts *were* square, with the windows: and light *was* against light *in* three ranks.

6 ¶ And he made a porch of pillars; the length thereof *was* fifty cubits, and the breadth thereof thirty cubits: and the porch *was* before them: and the *other* pillars and the thick beam *were* before them.

7 ¶ Then he made a porch for the throne where he might judge, *even* the porch of judgment: and *it was* covered with cedar from one side of the floor to the other.

8 ¶ And his house where he dwelt *had* another court within the porch, *which* was of the like work. Sol'o-mon made also an house for Pha'raoh's daughter, whom he had taken *to* wife, like unto this porch.

9 All these *were of* costly stones, according to the measures of hewed stones, sawed with saws, within and without, even from the foundation unto the coping, and *so* on the outside toward the great court.

10 And the foundation *was of* costly stones, even great stones, stones of ten cubits, and stones of eight cubits.

11 And above *were* costly stones, after the measures of hewed stones, and cedars.

12 And the great court round about *was* with three rows of hewed stones, and a row of cedar beams, both for the inner court of the house of the LORD, and for the porch of the house.

13 ¶ And king Sol'o-mon sent and fetched Hi'ram out of Tyre.

14 He *was* a widow's son of the tribe of Naph'ta-li, and his father *was* a man of Tyre, a worker in brass: and he was filled with wisdom, and understanding, and cunning to work all works in brass. And he came to king Sol'o-mon, and wrought all his work.

15 For he cast two pillars of brass, of eighteen cubits high apiece: and a line of twelve cubits did compass either of them about.

16 And he made two chapiters *of* molten brass, to set upon the tops of the pillars: the height of the one chapiter *was* five cubits, and the height of the other chapiter *was* five cubits:

17 *And* nets of checker work, and wreaths of chain work, for the chapiters which *were* upon the top of the pillars; seven for the one chapiter, and seven for the other chapiter.

18 And he made the pillars, and two rows round about upon the one network, to cover the chapiters that *were* upon the top, with pomegranates: and so did he for the other chapiter.

19 And the chapiters that *were* upon the top of the pillars *were* of lily work in the porch, four cubits.

20 And the chapiters upon the two pillars *had* pomegranates also above, over against the belly which *was* by the network: and the pomegranates *were* two hundred in rows round about upon the other chapiter.

21 And he set up the pillars in the porch of the temple: and he set up the right pillar, and called the name thereof Ja'chin: and he set up the left pillar, and called the name thereof Bo'-az.

22 And upon the top of the pillars *was* lily work: so was the work of the pillars finished.

23 ¶ And he made a molten şea, ten cubits from the one brim to the other: *it was* round all about, and his height *was* five cubits: and a line of thirty cubits did compass it round about.

24 And under the brim of it round about *there were* knops compassing it, ten in a cubit, compassing the sea round about: the knops *were* cast in two rows, when it was cast.

25 It stood upon twelve oxen, three looking toward the north, and three looking toward the west, and three looking toward the south, and three looking toward the east: and the sea *was set* above upon them, and all their hinder parts *were* inward.

26 And it *was* an hand breadth thick, and the brim thereof was wrought like the brim of a

cup, with flowers of lilies: it contained two thousand baths.

27 ¶ And he made ten bases of brass; four cubits was the length of one base, and four cubits the breadth thereof, and three cubits the height of it.

28 And the work of the bases was on this manner: they had borders, and the borders were between the ledges:

29 And on the borders that were between the ledges were lions, oxen, and cherubims: and upon the ledges there was a base above: and beneath the lions and oxen were certain additions made of thin work.

30 And every base had four brasen wheels, and plates of brass: and the four corners thereof had undersetters: under the laver were undersetters molten, at the side of every addition.

31 And the mouth of it within the chapiter and above was a cubit: but the mouth thereof was round after the work of the base, a cubit and an half: and also upon the mouth of it were gravings with their borders, foursquare, not round.

32 And under the borders were four wheels; and the axletrees of the wheels were joined to the base: and the height of a wheel was a cubit and half a cubit.

33 And the work of the wheels was like the work of a chariot wheel: their axletrees, and their naves, and their felloes, and their spokes, were all molten.

34 And there were four undersetters to the four corners of one base: and the undersetters were of the very base itself.

35 And in the top of the base was there a round compass of half a cubit high: and on the top of the base the ledges thereof and the borders thereof were of the same.

36 For on the plates of the ledges thereof, and on the borders thereof, he graved cherubims, lions, and palm trees, according to the proportion of every one, and additions round about.

37 After this manner he made the ten bases: all of them had one casting, one measure, and one size.

38 ¶ Then made he ten lavers of brass: one laver contained forty baths: and every laver was four cubits: and upon every one of the ten bases one laver.

39 And he put five bases on the right side of the house, and five on the left side of the house: and he set the sea on the right side of the house eastward over against the south.

40 ¶ And Hi'ram made the lavers, and the shovels, and the basons. So Hi'ram made an end of doing all the work that he made king Sol'o-mon for the house of the LORD.

41 The two pillars, and the two bowls of the chapiters that were on the top of the two pillars; and the two networks, to cover the two bowls of the chapiters which were upon the top of the pillars;

42 And four hundred pomegranates for the two networks, even two rows of pomegranates for one network, to cover the two bowls of the chapiters that were upon the pillars;

43 And the ten bases, and ten lavers on the bases;

44 And one sea, and twelve oxen under the sea;

45 And the pots, and the shovels, and the basons: and all these vessels, which Hi'ram made to king Sol'o-mon for the house of the LORD, were of bright brass.

46 In the plain of Jor'dan did the king cast them, in the clay ground between Suc'coth and Zar'than.

47 And Sol'o-mon left all the vessels unweighed, because they were exceeding many: neither was the weight of the brass found out.

48 And Sol'o-mon made all the vessels that pertained unto the house of the LORD: the altar of gold, and the table of gold, whereupon the shewbread was,

49 And the candlesticks of pure gold, five on the right side, and five on the left, before the oracle, with the flowers, and the lamps, and the tongs of gold,

50 And the bowls, and the snuffers, and the basons, and the spoons, and the censers of pure gold; and the hinges of gold, both for the doors of the inner house, the most holy place, and for the doors of the house, to wit, of the temple.

51 So was ended all the work that king Sol'o-mon made for the house of the LORD. And Sol'o-mon brought in the things which Da'vid his father had dedicated; even the silver, and the gold, and the vessels, did he put among the treasures of the house of the LORD.

8 THEN Sol'o-mon assembled the elders of Is'ra-el, and all the heads of the tribes, the chief of the fathers of the children of Is'ra-el, unto king Sol'o-mon in Je-ru'sa-lem, that they might bring up the ark of the covenant of the LORD out of the city of Da'vid, which is Zi'on.

2 And all the men of Is'ra-el assembled themselves unto king Sol'o-mon at the feast in the month Eth'a-nim, which is the seventh month.

3 And all the elders of Is'ra-el came, and the priests took up the ark.

4 And they brought up the ark of the LORD, and the tabernacle of the congregation, and all the holy vessels that were in the tabernacle, even those did the priests and the Le'vites bring up.

5 And king Sol'o-mon, and all the congregation of Is'ra-el, that were assembled unto him, were with him before the ark, sacrificing sheep and oxen, that could not be told nor numbered for multitude.

6 And the priests brought in the ark of the covenant of the LORD unto his place, into the oracle of the house, to the most holy place, even under the wings of the cherubims.

7 For the cherubims spread forth their two wings over the place of the ark, and the cherubims covered the ark and the staves thereof above.

8 And they drew out the staves, that the ends of the staves were seen out in the holy place before the oracle, and they were not seen without: and there they are unto this day.

9 There was nothing in the ark save the two tables of stone, which Mo'ses put there at Ho'reb, when the LORD made a covenant with the children of Is'ra-el, when they came out of the land of E'gypt.

10 And it came to pass, when the priests were come out of the holy place, that the cloud filled the house of the LORD,

11 So that the priests could not stand to minister because of the cloud: for the glory of the LORD had filled the house of the LORD.

12 ¶ Then spake Sol'o-mon, The LORD said that he would dwell in the thick darkness.

13 I have surely built thee an house to dwell in, a settled place for thee to abide in for ever.

14 And the king turned his face about, and blessed all the congregation of Is'ra-el: (and all the congregation of Is'ra-el stood;)

15 And he said, Blessed be the LORD God of

Is'ra-el, which spake with his mouth unto Da'-vid my father, and hath with his hand fulfilled *it*, saying,

16 Since the day that I brought forth my people Is'ra-el out of E'gypt, I chose no city out of all the tribes of Is'ra-el to build an house, that my name might be therein; but I chose Da'vid to be over my people Is'ra-el.

17 And it was in the heart of Da'vid my father to build an house for the name of the LORD God of Is'ra-el.

18 And the LORD said unto Da'vid my father, Whereas it was in thine heart to build an house unto my name, thou didst well that it was in thine heart.

19 Nevertheless thou shalt not build the house; but thy son that shall come forth out of thy loins, he shall build the house unto my name.

20 And the LORD hath performed his word that he spake, and I am risen up in the room of Da'vid my father, and sit on the throne of Is'ra-el, as the LORD promised, and have built an house for the name of the LORD God of Is'ra-el.

21 And I have set there a place for the ark, wherein *is* the covenant of the LORD, which he made with our fathers, when he brought them out of the land of E'gypt.

22 ¶ And Sol'o-mon stood before the altar of the LORD in the presence of all the congregation of Is'ra-el, and spread forth his hands toward heaven:

23 And he said, LORD God of Is'ra-el, *there is* no God like thee, in heaven above, or on earth beneath, who keepest covenant and mercy with thy servants that walk before thee with all their heart:

24 Who hast kept with thy servant Da'vid my father that thou promisedst him: thou spakest also with thy mouth, and has fulfilled *it* with thine hand, as *it is* this day.

25 Therefore now, LORD God of Is'ra-el, keep with thy servant Da'vid my father that thou promisedst him, saying, There shall not fail thee a man in my sight to sit on the throne of Is'ra-el; so that thy children take heed to their way, that they walk before me as thou hast walked before me.

26 And now, O God of Is'ra-el, let thy word, I pray thee, be verified, which thou spakest unto thy servant Da'vid my father.

27 But will God indeed dwell on the earth? behold, the heaven and heaven of heavens cannot contain thee; how much less this house that I have builded?

28 Yet have thou respect unto the prayer of thy servant, and to his supplication, O LORD my God, to hearken unto the cry and to the prayer, which thy servant prayeth before thee to day:

29 That thine eyes may be open toward this house night and day, *even* toward the place of which thou hast said, My name shall be there: that thou mayest hearken unto the prayer which thy servant shall make toward this place.

30 And hearken thou to the supplication of thy servant, and of thy people Is'ra-el, when they shall pray toward this place: and hear thou in heaven thy dwelling place: and when thou hearest, forgive.

31 ¶ If any man trespass against his neighbour, and an oath be laid upon him to cause him to swear, and the oath come before thine altar in this house:

32 Then hear thou in heaven, and do, and judge thy servants, condemning the wicked, to bring his way upon his head; and justifying the righteous, to give him according to his righteousness.

33 ¶ When thy people Is'ra-el be smitten down before the enemy, because they have sinned against thee, and shall turn again to thee, and confess thy name, and pray, and make supplication unto thee in this house:

34 Then hear thou in heaven, and forgive the sin of thy people Is'ra-el, and bring them again unto the land which thou gavest unto their fathers.

35 ¶ When heaven is shut up, and there is no rain, because they have sinned against thee; if they pray toward this place, and confess thy name, and turn from their sin, when thou afflictest them:

36 Then hear thou in heaven, and forgive the sin of thy servants, and of thy people Is'ra-el, that thou teach them the good way wherein they should walk, and give rain upon thy land, which thou hast given to thy people for an inheritance.

37 ¶ If there be in the land famine, if there be pestilence, blasting, mildew, locust, *or* if there be caterpiller; if their enemy besiege them in the land of their cities; whatsoever plague, whatsoever sickness *there be*;

38 What prayer and supplication soever be *made* by any man, *or* by all thy people Is'ra-el, which shall know every man the plague of his own heart, and spread forth his hands toward this house:

39 Then hear thou in heaven thy dwelling place, and forgive, and do, and give to every man according to his ways, whose heart thou knowest; (for thou, *even* thou only, knowest the hearts of all the children of men;)

40 That they may fear thee all the days that they live in the land which thou gavest unto our fathers.

41 Moreover concerning a stranger, that *is* not of thy people Is'ra-el, but cometh out of a far country for thy name's sake;

42 (For they shall hear of thy great name, and of thy strong hand, and of thy stretched out arm;) when he shall come and pray toward this house;

43 Hear thou in heaven thy dwelling place, and do according to all that the stranger calleth to thee for: that all people of the earth may know thy name, to fear thee, as *do* thy people Is'ra-el; and that they may know that this house, which I have builded, is called by thy name.

44 ¶ If thy people go out to battle against their enemy, whithersoever thou shalt send them, and shall pray unto the LORD toward the city which thou hast chosen, and *toward* the house that I have built for thy name:

45 Then hear thou in heaven their prayer and their supplication, and maintain their cause.

46 If they sin against thee, (for *there is* no man that sinneth not,) and thou be angry with them, and deliver them to the enemy, so that they carry them away captives unto the land of the enemy, far or near;

47 *Yet* if they shall bethink themselves in the land whither they were carried captives, and repent, and make supplication unto thee in the land of them that carried them captives, saying, We have sinned, and have done perversely, we have committed wickedness;

48 And *so* return unto thee with all their heart, and with all their soul, in the land of their enemies, which led them away captive, and pray unto thee toward their land, which thou gavest unto their fathers, the city which thou

hast chosen, and the house which I have built for thy name:

49 Then hear thou their prayer and their supplication in heaven thy dwelling place, and maintain their cause,

50 And forgive thy people that have sinned against thee, and all their transgressions wherein they have transgressed against thee, and give them compassion before them who carried them captive, that they may have compassion on them:

51 For they *be* thy people, and thine inheritance, which thou broughtest forth out of E'-gypt, from the midst of the furnace of iron:

52 That thine eyes may be open unto the supplication of thy servant, and unto the supplication of thy people Is'ra-el, to hearken unto them in all that they call for unto thee.

53 For thou didst separate them from among all the people of the earth, *to be* thine inheritance, as thou spakest by the hand of Mo'ses thy servant, when thou broughtest our fathers out of E'gypt, O Lord GOD.

54 And it was *so*, that when Sol'o-mon had made an end of praying all this prayer and supplication unto the LORD, he arose from before the altar of the LORD, from kneeling on his knees with his hands spread up to heaven.

55 And he stood, and blessed all the congregation of Is'ra-el with a loud voice, saying,

56 Blessed *be* the LORD, that hath given rest unto his people Is'ra-el, according to all that he promised: there hath not failed one word of all his good promise, which he promised by the hand of Mo'ses his servant.

57 The LORD our God be with us, as he was with our fathers: let him not leave us, nor forsake us:

58 That he may incline our hearts unto him, to walk in all his ways, and to keep his commandments, and his statutes, and his judgments, which he commanded our fathers.

59 And let these my words, wherewith I have made supplication before the LORD, be nigh unto the LORD our God day and night, that he maintain the cause of his servant, and the cause of his people Is'ra-el at all times, as the matter shall require:

60 That all the people of the earth may know that the LORD *is* God, *and that there is* none else.

61 Let your heart therefore be perfect with the LORD our God, to walk in his statutes, and to keep his commandments, as at this day.

62 ¶ And the king, and all Is'ra-el with him, offered sacrifice before the LORD.

63 And Sol'o-mon offered a sacrifice of peace offerings, which he offered unto the LORD, two and twenty thousand oxen, and an hundred and twenty thousand sheep. So the king and all the children of Is'ra-el dedicated the house of the LORD.

64 The same day did the king hallow the middle of the court that *was* before the house of the LORD: for there he offered burnt offerings, and meat offerings, and the fat of the peace offerings: because the brasen altar that *was* before the LORD *was* too little to receive the burnt offerings, and meat offerings, and the fat of the peace offerings.

65 And at that time Sol'o-mon held a feast, and all Is'ra-el with him, a great congregation, from the entering in of Ha'math unto the river of E'gypt, before the LORD our God, seven days and seven days, *even* fourteen days.

66 On the eighth day he sent the people away: and they blessed the king, and went unto their tents joyful and glad of heart for all the goodness that the LORD had done for Da'vid his servant, and for Is'ra-el his people.

9 AND it came to pass, when Sol'o-mon had finished the building of the house of the LORD, and the king's house, and all Sol'o-mon's desire which he was pleased to do,

2 That the LORD appeared to Sol'o-mon the second time, as he had appeared unto him at Gib'e-on.

3 And the LORD said unto him, I have heard thy prayer and thy supplication, that thou hast made before me: I have hallowed this house, which thou hast built, to put my name there for ever; and mine eyes and mine heart shall be there perpetually.

4 And if thou wilt walk before me, as Da'vid thy father walked, in integrity of heart, and in uprightness, to do according to all that I have commanded thee, *and* wilt keep my statutes and my judgments:

5 Then I will establish the throne of thy kingdom upon Is'ra-el for ever, as I promised to Da'-vid thy father, saying, There shall not fail thee a man upon the throne of Is'ra-el.

6 *But* if ye shall at all turn from following me, ye or your children, and will not keep my commandments *and* my statutes which I have set before you, but go and serve other gods, and worship them:

7 Then will I cut off Is'ra-el out of the land which I have given them; and this house, which I have hallowed for my name, will I cast out of my sight; and Is'ra-el shall be a proverb and a byword among all people:

8 And at this house, *which* is high, every one that passeth by it shall be astonished, and shall hiss; and they shall say, Why hath the LORD done thus unto this land, and to this house?

9 And they shall answer, Because they forsook the LORD their God, who brought forth their fathers out of the land of E'gypt, and have taken hold upon other gods, and have worshipped them, and served them: therefore hath the LORD brought upon them all this evil.

10 ¶ And it came to pass at the end of twenty years, when Sol'o-mon had built the two houses, the house of the LORD, and the king's house,

11 (*Now* Hi'ram the king of Tyre had furnished Sol'o-mon with cedar trees and fir trees, and with gold, according to all his desire,) that then king Sol'o-mon gave Hi'ram twenty cities in the land of Gal'i-lee.

12 And Hi'ram came out from Tyre to see the cities which Sol'o-mon had given him; and they pleased him not.

13 And he said, What cities *are* these which thou hast given me, my brother? And he called them the land of Ca'bul unto this day.

14 And Hi'ram sent to the king sixscore talents of gold.

15 ¶ And this *is* the reason of the levy which king Sol'o-mon raised; for to build the house of the LORD, and his own house, and Mil'lo, and the wall of Je-ru'sa-lem, and Ha'zor, and Me-gid'do, and Ge'zer.

16 *For* Pha'raoh king of E'gypt had gone up, and taken Ge'zer, and burnt it with fire, and slain the Ca'naan-ites that dwelt in the city, and given it *for* a present unto his daughter, Sol'o-mon's wife.

17 And Sol'o-mon built Ge'zer, and Beth-ho'-ron the nether,

18 And Ba'al-ath, and Tad'mor in the wilderness, in the land,

19 And all the cities of store that Sol′o-mon had, and cities for his chariots, and cities for his horsemen, and that which Sol′o-mon desired to build in Je-ru′sa-lem, and in Leb′a-non, and in all the land of his dominion.

20 And all the people *that were* left of the Am′or-ites, Hit′tites, Per′iz-zites, Hi′vites, and Jeb′u-sites, which *were* not of the children of Is′ra-el,

21 Their children that were left after them in the land, whom the children of Is′ra-el also were not able utterly to destroy, upon those did Solomon levy a tribute of bondservice unto this day.

22 But of the children of Is′ra-el did Sol′o-mon make no bondmen: but they *were* men of war, and his servants, and his princes, and his captains, and rulers of his chariots, and his horsemen.

23 These *were* the chief of the officers that *were* over Sol′o-mon′s work, five hundred and fifty, which bare rule over the people that wrought in the work.

24 ¶ But Pha′raoh′s daughter came up out of the city of Da′vid unto her house which Sol′o-mon had built for her: then did he build Mil′lo.

25 ¶ And three times in a year did Sol′o-mon offer burnt offerings and peace offerings upon the altar which he built unto the LORD, and he burnt incense upon the altar that *was* before the LORD. So he finished the house.

26 ¶ And king Sol′o-mon made a navy of ships in E′zi-on-ge′ber, which *is* beside E′loth, on the shore of the Red sea, in the land of E′-dom.

27 And Hi′ram sent in the navy his servants, shipmen that had knowledge of the sea, with the servants of Sol′o-mon.

28 And they came to O′phir, and fetched from thence gold, four hundred and twenty talents, and brought *it* to king Sol′o-mon.

10 AND when the queen of She′ba heard of the fame of Sol′o-mon concerning the name of the LORD, she came to prove him with hard questions.

2 And she came to Je-ru′sa-lem with a very great train, with camels that bare spices, and very much gold, and precious stones: and when she was come to Sol′o-mon, she communed with him of all that was in her heart.

3 And Sol′o-mon told her all her questions: there was not *any* thing hid from the king, which he told her not.

4 And when the queen of She′ba had seen all Sol′o-mon′s wisdom, and the house that he had built,

5 And the meat of his table, and the sitting of his servants, and the attendance of his ministers, and their apparel, and his cupbearers, and his ascent by which he went up unto the house of the LORD; there was no more spirit in her.

6 And she said to the king, It was a true report that I heard in mine own land of thy acts and of thy wisdom.

7 Howbeit I believed not the words, until I came, and mine eyes had seen *it*: and, behold, the half was not told me: thy wisdom and prosperity exceedeth the fame which I heard.

8 Happy *are* thy men, happy *are* these thy servants, which stand continually before thee, *and* that hear thy wisdom.

9 Blessed be the LORD thy God, which delighted in thee, to set thee on the throne of Is′ra-el: because the LORD loved Is′ra-el for ever, therefore made he thee king, to do judgment and justice.

10 And she gave the king an hundred and twenty talents of gold, and of spices very great store, and precious stones: there came no more such abundance of spices as these which the queen of She′ba gave to king Sol′o-mon.

11 And the navy also of Hi′ram, that brought gold from O′phir, brought in from O′phir great plenty of almug trees, and precious stones.

12 And the king made of the almug trees pillars for the house of the LORD, and for the king′s house, harps also and psalteries for singers: there came no such almug trees, nor were seen unto this day.

13 And king Sol′o-mon gave unto the queen of She′ba all her desire, whatsoever she asked, beside *that* which Sol′o-mon gave her of his royal bounty. So she turned and went to her own country, she and her servants.

14 ¶ Now the weight of gold that came to Sol′o-mon in one year was six hundred threescore and six talents of gold,

15 Beside *that he had* of the merchantmen, and of the traffick of the spice merchants, and of all the kings of A-ra′bi-a, and of the governors of the country.

16 ¶ And king Sol′o-mon made two hundred targets *of* beaten gold: six hundred *shekels* of gold went to one target.

17 And *he made* three hundred shields *of* beaten gold; three pound of gold went to one shield: and the king put them in the house of the forest of Leb′a-non.

18 ¶ Moreover the king made a great throne of ivory, and overlaid it with the best gold.

19 The throne had six steps, and the top of the throne *was* round behind: and *there were* stays on either side on the place of the seat, and two lions stood beside the stays.

20 And twelve lions stood there on the one side and on the other upon the six steps: there was not the like made in any kingdom.

21 ¶ And all king Sol′o-mon′s drinking vessels *were of* gold, and all the vessels of the house of the forest of Leb′a-non *were of* pure gold; none *were of* silver: it was nothing accounted of in the days of Sol′o-mon.

22 For the king had at sea a navy of Thar′-shish with the navy of Hi′ram: once in three years came the navy of Thar′shish, bringing gold, and silver, ivory, and apes, and peacocks.

23 So king Sol′o-mon exceeded all the kings of the earth for riches and for wisdom.

24 ¶ And all the earth sought to Sol′o-mon, to hear his wisdom, which God had put in his heart.

25 And they brought every man his present, vessels of silver, and vessels of gold, and garments, and armour, and spices, horses, and mules, a rate year by year.

26 ¶ And Sol′o-mon gathered together chariots and horsemen: and he had a thousand and four hundred chariots, and twelve thousand horsemen, whom he bestowed in the cities for chariots, and with the king at Je-ru′sa-lem.

27 And the king made silver *to be* in Je-ru′sa-lem as stones, and cedars made he *to be* as the sycomore trees that *are* in the vale, for abundance.

28 ¶ And Sol′o-mon had horses brought out of E′gypt, and linen yarn: the king′s merchants received the linen yarn at a price.

29 And a chariot came up and went out of E′gypt for six hundred *shekels* of silver, and an horse for an hundred and fifty: and so for all the kings of the Hit′tites, and for the kings of Syr′i-a, did they bring *them* out by their means.

11 BUT king Sol'o-mon loved many strange women, together with the daughter of Pha'raoh, women of the Mo'ab-ites, Am'mon-ites, E'dom-ites, Zi-do'ni-ans, *and* Hit'-tites;

2 Of the nations *concerning* which the LORD said unto the children of Is'ra-el, Ye shall not go in to them, neither shall they come in unto you: *for* surely they will turn away your heart after their gods: Sol'o-mon clave unto these in love.

3 And he had seven hundred wives, princesses, and three hundred concubines: and his wives turned away his heart.

4 For it came to pass, when Sol'o-mon was old, *that* his wives turned away his heart after other gods: and his heart was not perfect with the LORD his God, as *was* the heart of Da'vid his father.

5 For Sol'o-mon went after Ash'to-reth the goddess of the Zi-do'ni-ans, and after Mil'com the abomination of the Am'mon-ites.

6 And Sol'o-mon did evil in the sight of the LORD, and went not fully after the LORD, as *did* Da'vid his father.

7 Then did Sol'o-mon build an high place for Che'mosh, the abomination of Mo'ab, in the hill that *is* before Je-ru'sa-lem, and for Mo'lech, the abomination of the children of Am'mon.

8 And likewise did he for all his strange wives, which burnt incense and sacrificed unto their gods.

9 ¶ And the LORD was angry with Sol'o-mon, because his heart was turned from the LORD God of Is'ra-el, which had appeared unto him twice,

10 And had commanded him concerning this thing, that he should not go after other gods: but he kept not that which the LORD commanded.

11 Wherefore the LORD said unto Sol'o-mon, Forasmuch as this is done of thee, and thou hast not kept my covenant and my statutes, which I have commanded thee, I will surely rend the kingdom from thee, and will give it to thy servant.

12 Notwithstanding in thy days I will not do it for Da'vid thy father's sake: *but* I will rend it out of the hand of thy son.

13 Howbeit I will not rend away all the kingdom; *but* will give one tribe to thy son for Da'-vid my servant's sake, and for Je-ru'sa-lem's sake which I have chosen.

14 ¶ And the LORD stirred up an adversary unto Sol'o-mon, Ha'dad the E'dom-ite: he *was* of the king's seed in E'dom.

15 For it came to pass, when Da'vid was in E'dom, and Jo'ab the captain of the host was gone up to bury the slain, after he had smitten every male in E'dom;

16 (For six months did Jo'ab remain there with all Is'ra-el, until he had cut off every male in E'dom:)

17 That Ha'dad fled, he and certain E'dom-ites of his father's servants with him, to go into E'gypt; Ha'dad *being* yet a little child.

18 And they arose out of Mid'i-an, and came to Pa'ran: and they took men with them out of Pa'ran, and they came to E'gypt, unto Pha'raoh king of E'gypt; which gave him an house, and appointed him victuals, and gave him land.

19 And Ha'dad found great favour in the sight of Pha'raoh, so that he gave him to wife the sister of his own wife, the sister of Tah'pen-es the queen.

20 And the sister of Tah'pen-es bare him Ge-nu'bath his son, whom Tah'pen-es weaned in Pha'raoh's house: and Ge-nu'bath was in Pha'-

raoh's household among the sons of Pha'raoh.

21 And when Ha'dad heard in E'gypt that Da'vid slept with his fathers, and that Jo'ab the captain of the host was dead, Ha'dad said to Pha'raoh, Let me depart, that I may go to mine own country.

22 Then Pha'raoh said unto him, But what hast thou lacked with me, that, behold, thou seekest to go to thine own country? And he answered, Nothing: howbeit let me go in any wise.

23 ¶ And God stirred him up *another* adversary, Re'zon the son of E-li'a-dah, which fled from his lord Had-ad-e'zer king of Zo'bah:

24 And he gathered men unto him, and became captain over a band, when Da'vid slew them *of Zo'bah:* and they went to Da-mas'cus, and dwelt therein, and reigned in Da-mas'cus.

25 And he was an adversary to Is'ra-el all the days of Sol'o-mon, beside the mischief that Ha'-dad *did:* and he abhorred Is'ra-el, and reigned over Syr'i-a.

26 ¶ And Jer-o-bo'am the son of Ne'bat, an Eph'rath-ite of Zer'e-da, Sol'o-mon's servant, whose mother's name *was* Ze-ru'ah, a widow woman, even he lifted up *his* hand against the king.

27 And this *was* the cause that he lifted up *his* hand against the king: Sol'o-mon built Mil'-lo, *and* repaired the breaches of the city of Da'-vid his father.

28 And the man Jer-o-bo'am *was* a mighty man of valour: and Sol'o-mon seeing the young man that he was industrious, he made him ruler over all the charge of the house of Jo'seph.

29 And it came to pass at that time when Jer-o-bo'am went out of Je-ru'sa-lem, that the prophet A-hi'jah the Shi'lo-nite found him in the way; and he had clad himself with a new garment; and they two *were* alone in the field:

30 And A-hi'jah caught the new garment that *was* on him, and rent it *in* twelve pieces:

31 And he said to Jer-o-bo'am, Take thee ten pieces: for thus saith the LORD, the God of Is'ra-el, Behold, I will rend the kingdom out of the hand of Sol'o-mon, and will give ten tribes to thee:

32 (But he shall have one tribe for my servant Da'vid's sake, and for Je-ru'sa-lem's sake, the city which I have chosen out of all the tribes of Is'ra-el:)

33 Because that they have forsaken me, and have worshipped Ash'to-reth the goddess of the Zi-do'ni-ans, Che'mosh the god of the Mo'ab-ites, and Mil'com the god of the children of Am'mon, and have not walked in my ways, to do *that which is* right in mine eyes, and *to keep* my statutes and my judgments, as *did* Da'vid his father.

34 Howbeit I will not take the whole kingdom out of his hand: but I will make him prince all the days of his life for Da'vid my servant's sake, whom I chose, because he kept my commandments and my statutes:

35 But I will take the kingdom out of his son's hand, and will give it unto thee, *even* ten tribes.

36 And unto his son will I give one tribe, that Da'vid my servant may have a light alway before me in Je-ru'sa-lem, the city which I have chosen me to put my name there.

37 And I will take thee, and thou shalt reign according to all that thy soul desireth, and shalt be king over Is'ra-el.

38 And it shall be, if thou wilt hearken unto all that I command thee, and wilt walk in my ways, and do *that is* right in my sight, to keep my statutes and my commandments, as Da'vid

my servant did; that I will be with thee, and build thee a sure house, as I built for Da'vid, and will give Is'ra-el unto thee.

39 And I will for this afflict the seed of Da'-vid, but not for ever.

40 Sol'o-mon sought therefore to kill Jer-o-bo'am. And Jer-o-bo'am arose, and fled into E'-gypt, unto Shi'shak king of E'gypt, and was in E'gypt until the death of Sol'o-mon.

41 ¶ And the rest of the acts of Sol'o-mon, and all that he did, and his wisdom, are they not written in the book of the acts of Sol'o-mon?

42 And the time that Sol'o-mon reigned in Je-ru'sa-lem over all Is'ra-el was forty years.

43 And Sol'o-mon slept with his fathers, and was buried in the city of Da'vid his father: and Re-ho-bo'am his son reigned in his stead.

12 AND Re-ho-bo'am went to She'chem: for all Is'ra-el were come to She'chem to make him king.

2 And it came to pass, when Jer-o-bo'am the son of Ne'bat, who was yet in E'gypt, heard of it, (for he was fled from the presence of king Sol'o-mon, and Jer-o-bo'am dwelt in E'gypt;)

3 That they sent and called him. And Jer-o-bo'am and all the congregation of Is'ra-el came, and spake unto Re-ho-bo'am, saying,

4 Thy father made our yoke grievous: now therefore make thou the grievous service of thy father, and his heavy yoke which he put upon us, lighter, and we will serve thee.

5 And he said unto them, Depart yet for three days, then come again to me. And the people departed.

6 ¶ And king Re-ho-bo'am consulted with the old men, that stood before Sol'o-mon his father while he yet lived, and said, How do ye advise that I may answer this people?

7 And they spake unto him, saying, If thou wilt be a servant unto this people this day, and wilt serve them, and answer them, and speak good words to them, then they will be thy servants for ever.

8 But he forsook the counsel of the old men, which they had given him, and consulted with the young men that were grown up with him, and which stood before him:

9 And he said unto them, What counsel give ye that we may answer this people, who have spoken to me, saying, Make the yoke which thy father did put upon us lighter?

10 And the young men that were grown up with him spake unto him, saying, Thus shalt thou speak unto this people that spake unto thee, saying, Thy father made our yoke heavy, but make thou it lighter unto us; thus shalt thou say unto them, My little finger shall be thicker than my father's loins.

11 And now whereas my father did lade you with a heavy yoke, I will add to your yoke: my father hath chastised you with whips, but I will chastise you with scorpions.

12 ¶ So Jer-o-bo'am and all the people came to Re-ho-bo'am the third day, as the king had appointed, saying, Come to me again the third day.

13 And the king answered the people roughly, and forsook the old men's counsel that they gave him;

14 And spake to them after the counsel of the young men, saying, My father made your yoke heavy, and I will add to your yoke: my father also chastised you with whips, but I will chastise you with scorpions.

15 Wherefore the king hearkened not unto the people; for the cause was from the LORD, that he might perform his saying, which the LORD spake by A-hi'jah the Shi'lo-nite unto Jer-o-bo'am the son of Ne'bat.

16 ¶ So when all Is'ra-el saw that the king hearkened not unto them, the people answered the king, saying, What portion have we in Da'-vid? neither have we inheritance in the son of Jes'se: to your tents, O Is'ra-el: now see to thine own house, Da'vid. So Is'ra-el departed unto their tents.

17 But as for the children of Is'ra-el which dwelt in the cities of Ju'dah, Re-ho-bo'am reigned over them.

18 Then king Re-ho-bo'am sent A-do'ram, who was over the tribute; and all Is'ra-el stoned him with stones, that he died. Therefore king Re-ho-bo'am made speed to get him up to his chariot, to flee to Je-ru'sa-lem.

19 So Is'ra-el rebelled against the house of Da'vid unto this day.

20 And it came to pass, when all Is'ra-el heard that Jer-o-bo'am was come again, that they sent and called him unto the congregation, and made him king over all Is'ra-el: there was none that followed the house of Da'vid, but the tribe of Ju'dah only.

21 ¶ And when Re-ho-bo'am was come to Je-ru'sa-lem, he assembled all the house of Ju'dah, with the tribe of Ben'ja-min, an hundred and fourscore thousand chosen men, which were warriors, to fight against the house of Is'-ra-el, to bring the kingdom again to Re-ho-bo'-am the son of Sol'o-mon.

22 But the word of God came unto Shem-a-i'ah the man of God, saying,

23 Speak unto Re-ho-bo'am, the son of Sol'o-mon, king of Ju'dah, and unto all the house of Ju'dah and Ben'ja-min, and to the remnant of the people, saying,

24 Thus saith the LORD, Ye shall not go up, nor fight against your brethren the children of Is'ra-el: return every man to his house; for this thing is from me. They hearkened therefore to the word of the LORD, and returned to depart, according to the word of the LORD.

25 ¶ Then Jer-o-bo'am built She'chem in mount E'phra-im, and dwelt therein; and went out from thence, and built Pe-nu'el.

26 And Jer-o-bo'am said in his heart, Now shall the kingdom return to the house of Da'vid:

27 If this people go up to do sacrifice in the house of the LORD at Je-ru'sa-lem, then shall the heart of this people turn again unto their lord, even unto Re-ho-bo'am king of Ju'dah, and they shall kill me, and go again to Re-ho-bo'am king of Ju'dah.

28 Whereupon the king took counsel, and made two calves of gold, and said unto them, It is too much for you to go up to Je-ru'sa-lem: behold thy gods, O Is'ra-el, which brought thee up out of the land of E'gypt.

29 And he set the one in Beth'-el, and the other put he in Dan.

30 And this thing became a sin: for the people went to worship before the one, even unto Dan.

31 And he made an house of high places, and made priests of the lowest of the people, which were not of the sons of Le'vi.

32 And Jer-o-bo'am ordained a feast in the eighth month, on the fifteenth day of the month, like unto the feast that is in Ju'dah, and he offered upon the altar. So did he in Beth'-el, sacrificing unto the calves that he had made: and he placed in Beth'-el the priests of the high places which he had made.

33 So he offered upon the altar which he had

made in Beth'-el the fifteenth day of the eighth month, *even* in the month which he had devised of his own heart; and ordained a feast unto the children of Is'ra-el: and he offered upon the altar, and burnt incense.

13 AND, behold, there came a man of God out of Ju'dah by the word of the LORD unto Beth'-el: and Jer-o-bo'am stood by the altar to burn incense.

2 And he cried against the altar in the word of the LORD, and said, O altar, altar, thus saith the LORD; Behold, a child shall be born unto the house of Da'vid, Jo-si'ah by name; and upon thee shall he offer the priests of the high places that burn incense upon thee, and men's bones shall be burnt upon thee.

3 And he gave a sign the same day, saying, This *is* the sign which the LORD hath spoken; Behold, the altar shall be rent, and the ashes that *are* upon it shall be poured out.

4 And it came to pass, when king Jer-o-bo'-am heard the saying of the man of God, which had cried against the altar in Beth'-el, that he put forth his hand from the altar, saying, Lay hold on him. And his hand, which he put forth against him, dried up, so that he could not pull it in again to him.

5 The altar also was rent, and the ashes poured out from the altar, according to the sign which the man of God had given by the word of the LORD.

6 And the king answered and said unto the man of God, Intreat now the face of the LORD thy God, and pray for me, that my hand may be restored me again. And the man of God besought the LORD, and the king's hand was restored him again, and became as *it was* before.

7 And the king said unto the man of God, Come now with me, and refresh thyself, and I will give thee a reward.

8 And the man of God said unto the king, If thou wilt give me half thine house, I will not go in with thee, neither will I eat bread nor drink water in this place:

9 For so was it charged me by the word of the LORD, saying, Eat no bread, nor drink water, nor turn again by the same way that thou camest.

10 So he went another way, and returned not by the way that he came to Beth'-el.

11 ¶ Now there dwelt an old prophet in Beth'-el; and his sons came and told him all the works that the man of God had done that day in Beth'-el: the words which he had spoken unto the king, them they told also to their father.

12 And their father said unto them, What way went he? For his sons had seen what way the man of God went, which came from Ju'dah.

13 And he said unto his sons, Saddle me the ass. So they saddled him the ass: and he rode thereon,

14 And went after the man of God, and found him sitting under an oak: and he said unto him, Art thou the man of God that camest from Ju'-dah? And he said, I *am*.

15 Then he said unto him, Come home with me, and eat bread.

16 And he said, I may not return with thee, nor go in with thee: neither will I eat bread nor drink water with thee in this place:

17 For it was said to me by the word of the LORD, Thou shalt eat no bread nor drink water there, nor turn again to go by the way that thou camest.

18 He said unto him, I *am* a prophet also as thou *art;* and an angel spake unto me by the word of the LORD, saying, Bring him back with thee into thine house, that he may eat bread and drink water. *But* he lied unto him.

19 So he went back with him, and did eat bread in his house, and drank water.

20 ¶ And it came to pass, as they sat at the table, that the word of the LORD came unto the prophet that brought him back:

21 And he cried unto the man of God that came from Ju'dah, saying, Thus saith the LORD, Forasmuch as thou hast disobeyed the mouth of the LORD, and hast not kept the commandment which the LORD thy God commanded thee,

22 But camest back, and hast eaten bread and drunk water in the place, of the which *the* LORD did say to thee, Eat no bread, and drink no water; thy carcase shall not come unto the sepulchre of thy fathers.

23 ¶ And it came to pass, after he had eaten bread, and after he had drunk, that he saddled for him the ass, *to wit,* for the prophet whom he had brought back.

24 And when he was gone, a lion met him by the way, and slew him: and his carcase was cast in the way, and the ass stood by it, the lion also stood by the carcase.

25 And, behold, men passed by, and saw the carcase cast in the way, and the lion standing by the carcase: and they came and told *it* in the city where the old prophet dwelt.

26 And when the prophet that brought him back from the way heard *thereof,* he said, It *is* the man of God, who was disobedient unto the word of the LORD: therefore the LORD hath delivered him unto the lion, which hath torn him, and slain him, according to the word of the LORD, which he spake unto him.

27 And he spake to his sons, saying, Saddle me the ass. And they saddled *him.*

28 And he went and found his carcase cast in the way, and the ass and the lion standing by the carcase: the lion had not eaten the carcase, nor torn the ass.

29 And the prophet took up the carcase of the man of God, and laid it upon the ass, and brought it back: and the old prophet came to the city, to mourn and to bury him.

30 And he laid his carcase in his own grave; and they mourned over him, *saying,* Alas, my brother!

31 And it came to pass, after he had buried him, that he spake to his sons, saying, When I am dead, then bury me in the sepulchre wherein the man of God *is* buried; lay my bones beside his bones:

32 For the saying which he cried by the word of the LORD against the altar in Beth'-el, and against all the houses of the high places which *are* in the cities of Sa-ma'ri-a, shall surely come to pass.

33 ¶ After this thing Jer-o-bo'am returned not from his evil way, but made again of the lowest of the people priests of the high places: whosoever would, he consecrated him, and he became *one* of the priests of the high places.

34 And this thing became sin unto the house of Jer-o-bo'am, even to cut *it* off, and to destroy *it* from off the face of the earth.

14 AT that time A-bi'jah the son of Jer-o-bo'am fell sick.

2 And Jer-o-bo'am said to his wife, Arise, I pray thee, and disguise thyself, that thou be not known to be the wife of Jer-o-bo'am; and get thee to Shi'loh: behold, there *is* A-hi'jah the prophet, which told me that I *should be* king over this people.

3 And take with thee ten loaves, and crack-nels, and a cruse of honey, and go to him: he shall tell thee what shall become of the child.

4 And Jer-o-bo'am's wife did so, and arose, and went to Shi'loh, and came to the house of A-hi'jah. But A-hi'jah could not see; for his eyes were set by reason of his age.

5 ¶ And the LORD said unto A-hi'jah, Behold, the wife of Jer-o-bo'am cometh to ask a thing of thee for her son; for he is sick: thus and thus shalt thou say unto her: for it shall be, when she cometh in, that she shall feign herself to be another woman.

6 And it was so, when A-hi'jah heard the sound of her feet, as she came in at the door, that he said, Come in, thou wife of Jer-o-bo'am; why feignest thou thyself to be another? for I am sent to thee with heavy tidings.

7 Go, tell Jer-o-bo'am, Thus saith the LORD God of Is'ra-el, Forasmuch as I exalted thee from among the people, and made thee prince over my people Is'ra-el,

8 And rent the kingdom away from the house of Da'vid, and gave it thee: and yet thou hast not been as my servant Da'vid, who kept my commandments, and who followed me with all his heart, to do that only which was right in mine eyes;

9 But hast done evil above all that were before thee: for thou hast gone and made thee other gods, and molten images, to provoke me to anger, and hast cast me behind thy back:

10 Therefore, behold, I will bring evil upon the house of Jer-o-bo'am, and will cut off from Jer-o-bo'am him that pisseth against the wall, and him that is shut up and left in Is'ra-el, and will take away the remnant of the house of Jer-o-bo'am, as a man taketh away dung, till it be all gone.

11 Him that dieth of Jer-o-bo'am in the city shall the dogs eat; and him that dieth in the field shall the fowls of the air eat: for the LORD hath spoken it.

12 Arise thou therefore, get thee to thine own house: and when thy feet enter into the city, the child shall die.

13 And all Is'ra-el shall mourn for him, and bury him: for he only of Jer-o-bo'am shall come to the grave, because in him there is found some good thing toward the LORD God of Is'ra-el in the house of Jer-o-bo'am.

14 Moreover the LORD shall raise him up a king over Is'ra-el, who shall cut off the house of Jer-o-bo'am that day: but what? even now.

15 For the LORD shall smite Is'ra-el, as a reed is shaken in the water, and he shall root up Is'ra-el out of this good land, which he gave to their fathers, and shall scatter them beyond the river, because they have made their groves, provoking the LORD to anger.

16 And he shall give Is'ra-el up because of the sins of Jer-o-bo'am, who did sin, and who made Is'ra-el to sin.

17 ¶ And Jer-o-bo'am's wife arose, and departed, and came to Tir'zah: and when she came to the threshold of the door, the child died;

18 And they buried him; and all Is'ra-el mourned for him, according to the word of the LORD, which he spake by the hand of his servant A-hi'jah the prophet.

19 And the rest of the acts of Jer-o-bo'am, how he warred, and how he reigned, behold, they are written in the book of the chronicles of the kings of Is'ra-el.

20 And the days which Jer-o-bo'am reigned were two and twenty years: and he slept with his fathers, and Na'dab his son reigned in his stead.

21 ¶ And Re-ho-bo'am the son of Sol'o-mon reigned in Ju'dah. Re-ho-bo'am was forty and one years old when he began to reign, and he reigned seventeen years in Je-ru'sa-lem, the city which the LORD did choose out of all the tribes of Is'ra-el, to put his name there. And his mother's name was Na'a-mah an Am'mon-it-ess.

22 And Ju'dah did evil in the sight of the LORD, and they provoked him to jealousy with their sins which they had committed, above all that their fathers had done.

23 For they also built them high places, and images, and groves, on every high hill, and under every green tree.

24 And there were also sodomites in the land: and they did according to all the abominations of the nations which the LORD cast out before the children of Is'ra-el.

25 ¶ And it came to pass in the fifth year of king Re-ho-bo'am, that Shi'shak king of E'gypt came up against Je-ru'sa-lem:

26 And he took away the treasures of the house of the LORD, and the treasures of the king's house; he even took away all: and he took away all the shields of gold which Sol'o-mon had made.

27 And king Re-ho-bo'am made in their stead brasen shields, and committed them unto the hands of the chief of the guard, which kept the door of the king's house.

28 And it was so, when the king went into the house of the LORD, that the guard bare them, and brought them back into the guard chamber.

29 ¶ Now the rest of the acts of Re-ho-bo'am, and all that he did, are they not written in the book of the chronicles of the kings of Ju'dah?

30 And there was war between Re-ho-bo'am and Jer-o-bo'am all their days.

31 And Re-ho-bo'am slept with his fathers, and was buried with his fathers in the city of Da'vid. And his mother's name was Na'a-mah an Am'mon-it-ess. And A-bi'jam his son reigned in his stead.

15 NOW in the eighteenth year of king Jer-o-bo'am the son of Ne'bat reigned A-bi'jam over Ju'dah.

2 Three years reigned he in Je-ru'sa-lem. And his mother's name was Ma'a-chah, the daughter of A-bish'a-lom.

3 And he walked in all the sins of his father, which he had done before him: and his heart was not perfect with the LORD his God, as the heart of Da'vid his father.

4 Nevertheless for Da'vid's sake did the LORD his God give him a lamp in Je-ru'sa-lem, to set up his son after him, and to establish Je-ru'sa-lem:

5 Because Da'vid did that which was right in the eyes of the LORD, and turned not aside from any thing that he commanded him all the days of his life, save only in the matter of U-ri'ah the Hit'tite.

6 And there was war between Re-ho-bo'am and Jer-o-bo'am all the days of his life.

7 Now the rest of the acts of A-bi'jam, and all that he did, are they not written in the book of the chronicles of the kings of Ju'dah? And there was war between A-bi'jam and Jer-o-bo'am.

8 And A-bi'jam slept with his fathers; and they buried him in the city of Da'vid: and A'sa his son reigned in his stead.

9 ¶ And in the twentieth year of Jer-o-bo'am king of Is'ra-el reigned A'sa over Ju'dah.

10 And forty and one years reigned he in Je-ru'sa-lem. And his mother's name was Ma'a-chah, the daughter of A-bish'a-lom.

11 And A'sa did that which was right in the eyes of the LORD, as did Da'vid his father.

12 And he took away the sodomites out of the land, and removed all the idols that his fathers had made.

13 And also Ma'a-chah his mother, even her he removed from being queen, because she had made an idol in a grove; and A'sa destroyed her idol, and burnt it by the brook Kid'ron.

14 But the high places were not removed: nevertheless A'sa's heart was perfect with the LORD all his days.

15 And he brought in the things which his father had dedicated, and the things which himself had dedicated, into the house of the LORD, silver, and gold, and vessels.

16 ¶ And there was war between A'sa and Ba'a-sha king of Is'ra-el all their days.

17 And Ba'a-sha king of Is'ra-el went up against Ju'dah, and built Ra'mah, that he might not suffer any to go out or come in to A'sa king of Ju'dah.

18 Then A'sa took all the silver and the gold that were left in the treasures of the house of the LORD, and the treasures of the king's house, and delivered them into the hand of his servants: and king A'sa sent them to Ben-ha'dad, the son of Tab'ri-mon, the son of He'zi-on, king of Syr'i-a, that dwelt at Da-mas'cus, saying,

19 There is a league between me and thee, and between my father and thy father: behold, I have sent unto thee a present of silver and gold; come and break thy league with Ba'a-sha king of Is'ra-el, that he may depart from me.

20 So Ben-ha'dad hearkened unto king A'sa, and sent the captains of the hosts which he had against the cities of Is'ra-el, and smote I'jon, and Dan, and A'bel-beth-ma'a-chah, and all Cin'ne-roth, with all the land of Naph'ta-li.

21 And it came to pass, when Ba'a-sha heard thereof, that he left off building of Ra'mah, and dwelt in Tir'zah.

22 Then king A'sa made a proclamation throughout all Ju'dah; none was exempted: and they took away the stones of Ra'mah, and the timber thereof, wherewith Ba'a-sha had builded; and king A'sa built with them Ge'ba of Ben'ja-min, and Miz'pah.

23 The rest of all the acts of A'sa, and all his might, and all that he did, and the cities which he built, are they not written in the book of the chronicles of the kings of Ju'dah? Nevertheless in the time of his old age he was diseased in his feet.

24 And A'sa slept with his fathers, and was buried with his fathers in the city of Da'vid his father: and Je-hosh'a-phat his son reigned in his stead.

25 ¶ And Na'dab the son of Jer-o-bo'am began to reign over Is'ra-el in the second year of A'sa king of Ju'dah, and reigned over Is'ra-el two years.

26 And he did evil in the sight of the LORD, and walked in the way of his father, and in his sin wherewith he made Is'ra-el to sin.

27 ¶ And Ba'a-sha the son of A-hi'jah, of the house of Is'sa-char, conspired against him; and Ba'a-sha smote him at Gib'be-thon, which belonged to the Phi-lis'tines; for Na'dab and all Is'ra-el laid siege to Gib'be-thon.

28 Even in the third year of A'sa king of Ju'-dah did Ba'a-sha slay him, and reigned in his stead.

29 And it came to pass, when he reigned, that he smote all the house of Jer-o-bo'am; he left not to Jer-o-bo'am any that breathed, until he had destroyed him, according unto the saying of the LORD, which he spake by his servant A-hi'jah the Shi'lo-nite:

30 Because of the sins of Jer-o-bo'am which he sinned, and which he made Is'ra-el sin, by his provocation wherewith he provoked the LORD God of Is'ra-el to anger.

31 ¶ Now the rest of the acts of Na'dab, and all that he did, are they not written in the book of the chronicles of the kings of Is'ra-el?

32 And there was war between A'sa and Ba'-a-sha king of Is'ra-el all their days.

33 In the third year of A'sa king of Ju'dah began Ba'a-sha the son of A-hi'jah to reign over all Is'ra-el in Tir'zah, twenty and four years.

34 And he did evil in the sight of the LORD, and walked in the way of Jer-o-bo'am, and in his sin wherewith he made Is'ra-el to sin.

16 THEN the word of the LORD came to Je'-hu the son of Ha-na'ni against Ba'a-sha, saying,

2 Forasmuch as I exalted thee out of the dust, and made thee prince over my people Is'-ra-el; and thou hast walked in the way of Jer-o-bo'am, and hast made my people Is'ra-el to sin, to provoke me to anger with their sins;

3 Behold, I will take away the posterity of Ba'a-sha, and the posterity of his house; and will make thy house like the house of Jer-o-bo'-am the son of Ne'bat.

4 Him that dieth of Ba'a-sha in the city shall the dogs eat; and him that dieth of his in the fields shall the fowls of the air eat.

5 Now the rest of the acts of Ba'a-sha, and what he did, and his might, are they not written in the book of the chronicles of the kings of Is'-ra-el?

6 So Ba'a-sha slept with his fathers, and was buried in Tir'zah: and E'lah his son reigned in his stead.

7 And also by the hand of the prophet Je'hu the son of Ha-na'ni came the word of the LORD against Ba'a-sha, and against his house, even for all the evil that he did in the sight of the LORD, in provoking him to anger with the work of his hands, in being like the house of Jer-o-bo'am; and because he killed him.

8 ¶ In the twenty and sixth year of A'sa king of Ju'dah began E'lah the son of Ba'a-sha to reign over Is'ra-el in Tir'zah, two years.

9 And his servant Zim'ri, captain of half his chariots, conspired against him, as he was in Tir'zah, drinking himself drunk in the house of Ar'za steward of his house in Tir'zah.

10 And Zim'ri went in and smote him, and killed him, in the twenty and seventh year of A'sa king of Ju'dah, and reigned in his stead.

11 And it came to pass, when he began to reign, as soon as he sat on his throne, that he slew all the house of Ba'a-sha he left him not one that pisseth against a wall, neither of his kinsfolks, nor of his friends.

12 Thus did Zim'ri destroy all the house of Ba'a-sha, according to the word of the LORD, which he spake against Ba'a-sha by Je'hu the prophet,

13 For all the sins of Ba'a-sha, and the sins of E'lah his son, by which they sinned, and by which they made Is'ra-el to sin, in provoking the LORD God of Is'ra-el to anger with their vanities.

14 Now the rest of the acts of E'lah, and all that he did, *are* they not written in the book of the chronicles of the kings of Is'ra-el?

15 ¶ In the twenty and seventh year of A'sa king of Ju'dah did Zim'ri reign seven days in Tir'zah. And the people *were* encamped against Gib'be-thon, which *belonged* to the Phi-lis'tines.

16 And the people *that were* encamped heard say, Zim'ri hath conspired, and hath also slain the king: wherefore all Is'ra-el made Om'ri, the captain of the host, king over Is'ra-el that day in the camp.

17 And Om'ri went up from Gib'be-thon, and all Is'ra-el with him, and they besieged Tir'zah.

18 And it came to pass, when Zim'ri saw that the city was taken, that he went into the palace of the king's house, and burnt the king's house over him with fire, and died,

19 For his sins which he sinned in doing evil in the sight of the LORD, in walking in the way of Jer-o-bo'am, and in his sin which he did, to make Is'ra-el to sin.

20 Now the rest of the acts of Zim'ri, and his treason that he wrought, *are* they not written in the book of the chronicles of the kings of Is'ra-el?

21 ¶ Then were the people of Is'ra-el divided into two parts: half of the people followed Tib'-ni the son of Gi'nath, to make him king; and half followed Om'ri.

22 But the people that followed Om'ri prevailed against the people that followed Tib'ni the son of Gi'nath: so Tib'ni died, and Om'ri reigned.

23 ¶ In the thirty and first year of A'sa king of Ju'dah began Om'ri to reign over Is'ra-el, twelve years: six years reigned he in Tir'zah.

24 And he bought the hill Sa-ma'ri-a of She'-mer for two talents of silver, and built on the hill, and called the name of the city which he built, after the name of She'mer, owner of the hill, Sa-ma'ri-a.

25 ¶ But Om'ri wrought evil in the eyes of the LORD, and did worse than all that *were* before him.

26 For he walked in all the way of Jer-o-bo'-am the son of Ne'bat, and in his sin wherewith he made Is'ra-el to sin, to provoke the LORD God of Is'ra-el to anger with their vanities.

27 Now the rest of the acts of Om'ri which he did, and his might that he shewed, *are* they not written in the book of the chronicles of the kings of Is'ra-el?

28 So Om'ri slept with his fathers, and was buried in Sa-ma'ri-a: and A'hab his son reigned in his stead.

29 ¶ And in the thirty and eighth year of A'-sa king of Ju'dah began A'hab the son of Om'ri to reign over Is'ra-el: and A'hab the son of Om'-ri reigned over Is'ra-el in Sa-ma'ri-a twenty and two years.

30 And A'hab the son of Om'ri did evil in the sight of the LORD above all that *were* before him.

31 And it came to pass, as if it had been a light thing for him to walk in the sins of Jer-o-bo'am the son of Ne'bat, that he took to wife Jez'e-bel the daughter of Eth'ba-al king of the Zi-do'ni-ans, and went and served Ba'al, and worshipped him.

32 And he reared up an altar for Ba'al in the house of Ba'al, which he had built in Sa-ma'ri-a.

33 And A'hab made a grove; and A'hab did more to provoke the LORD God of Is'ra-el to anger than all the kings of Is'ra-el that were before him.

34 ¶ In his days did Hi'el the Beth'-el-ite build Jer'i-cho: he laid the foundation thereof in A-bi'ram his firstborn, and set up the gates thereof in his youngest *son* Se'gub, according to the word of the LORD, which he spake by Josh'-u-a the son of Nun.

17 AND E-li'jah the Tish'bite, *who was* of the inhabitants of Gil'e-ad, said unto A'-hab, *As* the LORD God of Is'ra-el liveth, before whom I stand, there shall not be dew nor rain these years, but according to my word.

2 And the word of the LORD came unto him, saying,

3 Get thee hence, and turn thee eastward, and hide thyself by the brook Che'rith, that *is* before Jor'dan.

4 And it shall be, *that* thou shalt drink of the brook; and I have commanded the ravens to feed thee there.

5 So he went and did according unto the word of the LORD: for he went and dwelt by the brook Che'rith, that *is* before Jor'dan.

6 And the ravens brought him bread and flesh in the morning, and bread and flesh in the evening; and he drank of the brook.

7 And it came to pass, after a while, that the brook dried up, because there had been no rain in the land.

8 ¶ And the word of the LORD came unto him, saying,

9 Arise, get thee to Zar'e-phath, which *be*-longeth to Zi'don, and dwell there: behold, I have commanded a widow woman there to sustain thee.

10 So he arose and went to Zar'e-phath. And when he came to the gate of the city, behold, the widow woman *was* there gathering of sticks: and he called to her, and said, Fetch me, I pray thee, a little water in a vessel, that I may drink.

11 And as she was going to fetch *it,* he called to her, and said, Bring me, I pray thee, a morsel of bread in thine hand.

12 And she said, *As* the LORD thy God liveth, I have not a cake, but an handful of meal in a barrel, and a little oil in a cruse: and, behold, I *am* gathering two sticks, that I may go in and dress it for me and my son, that we may eat it, and die.

13 And E-li'jah said unto her, Fear not; go *and* do as thou hast said: but make me thereof a little cake first, and bring *it* unto me, and after make for thee and for thy son.

14 For thus saith the LORD God of Is'ra-el, The barrel of meal shall not waste, neither shall the cruse of oil fail, until the day *that* the LORD sendeth rain upon the earth.

15 And she went and did according to the saying of E-li'jah: and she, and he, and her house, did eat *many* days.

16 *And* the barrel of meal wasted not, neither did the cruse of oil fail, according to the word of the LORD, which he spake by E-li'jah.

17 ¶ And it came to pass after these things, *that* the son of the woman, the mistress of the house, fell sick; and his sickness was so sore, that there was no breath left in him.

18 And she said unto E-li'jah, What have I to do with thee, O thou man of God? art thou come unto me to call my sin to remembrance, and to slay my son?

19 And he said unto her, Give me thy son. And he took him out of her bosom, and carried him up into a loft, where he abode, and laid him upon his own bed.

20 And he cried unto the LORD, and said, O LORD my God, hast thou also brought evil upon

the widow with whom I sojourn, by slaying her son?

21 And he stretched himself upon the child three times, and cried unto the LORD, and said, O LORD my God, I pray thee, let this child's soul come into him again.

22 And the LORD heard the voice of E-li'jah; and the soul of the child came into him again, and he revived.

23 And E-li'jah took the child, and brought him down out of the chamber into the house, and delivered him unto his mother: and E-li'jah said, See, thy son liveth.

24 ¶ And the woman said to E-li'jah, Now by this I know that thou art a man of God, and that the word of the LORD in thy mouth is truth.

18 AND it came to pass after many days, that the word of the LORD came to E-li'jah in the third year, saying, Go, shew thyself unto A'hab; and I will send rain upon the earth.

2 And E-li'jah went to shew himself unto A'-hab. And there was a sore famine in Sa-ma'ri-a.

3 And A'hab called O-ba-di'ah, which was the governor of his house. (Now O-ba-di'ah feared the LORD greatly:

4 For it was so, when Jez'e-bel cut off the prophets of the LORD, that O-ba-di'ah took an hundred prophets, and hid them by fifty in a cave, and fed them with bread and water.)

5 And A'hab said unto O-ba-di'ah, Go into the land, unto all fountains of water, and unto all brooks: peradventure we may find grass to save the horses and mules alive, that we lose not all the beasts.

6 So they divided the land between them to pass throughout it: A'hab went one way by himself, and O-ba-di'ah went another way by himself.

7 ¶ And as O-ba-di'ah was in the way, behold, E-li'jah met him: and he knew him, and fell on his face, and said, Art thou that my lord E-li'jah?

8 And he answered him, I am: go, tell thy lord, Behold, E-li'jah is here.

9 And he said, What have I sinned, that thou wouldest deliver thy servant into the hand of A'hab, to slay me?

10 As the LORD thy God liveth, there is no nation or kingdom, whither my lord hath not sent to seek thee: and when they said, He is not there; he took an oath of the kingdom and nation, that they found thee not.

11 And now thou sayest, Go, tell thy lord, Behold, E-li'jah is here.

12 And it shall come to pass, as soon as I am gone from thee, that the Spirit of the LORD shall carry thee whither I know not; and so when I come and tell A'hab, and he cannot find thee, he shall slay me: but I thy servant fear the LORD from my youth.

13 Was it not told my lord what I did when Jez'e-bel slew the prophets of the LORD, how I hid an hundred men of the LORD's prophets by fifty in a cave, and fed them with bread and water?

14 And now thou sayest, Go, tell thy lord, Behold, E-li'jah is here: and he shall slay me.

15 And E-li'jah said, As the LORD of hosts liveth, before whom I stand, I will surely shew myself unto him to day.

16 So O-ba-di'ah went to meet A'hab, and told him: and A'hab went to meet E-li'jah.

17 ¶ And it came to pass, when A'hab saw E-li'jah, that A'hab said unto him, Art thou he that troubleth Is'ra-el?

18 And he answered, I have not troubled Is'-ra-el; but thou, and thy father's house, in that ye have forsaken the commandments of the LORD, and thou hast followed Ba'al-im.

19 Now therefore send, and gather to me all Is'ra-el unto mount Car'mel, and the prophets of Ba'al four hundred and fifty, and the prophets of the groves four hundred, which eat at Jez'e-bel's table.

20 So A'hab sent unto all the children of Is'-ra-el, and gathered the prophets together unto mount Car'mel.

21 And E-li'jah came unto all the people, and said, How long halt ye between two opinions? if the LORD be God, follow him: but if Ba'al, then follow him. And the people answered him not a word.

22 Then said E-li'jah unto the people, I, even I only, remain a prophet of the LORD; but Ba'al's prophets are four hundred and fifty men.

23 Let them therefore give us two bullocks; and let them choose one bullock for themselves, and cut it in pieces, and lay it on wood, and put no fire under: and I will dress the other bullock, and lay it on wood, and put no fire under:

24 And call ye on the name of your gods, and I will call on the name of the LORD: and the God that answereth by fire, let him be God. And all the people answered and said, It is well spoken.

25 And E-li'jah said unto the prophets of Ba'-al, Choose you one bullock for yourselves, and dress it first; for ye are many; and call on the name of your gods, but put no fire under.

26 And they took the bullock which was given them, and they dressed it, and called on the name of Ba'al from morning even until noon, saying, O Ba'al, hear us. But there was no voice, nor any that answered. And they leaped upon the altar which was made.

27 And it came to pass at noon, that E-li'jah mocked them, and said, Cry aloud: for he is a god; either he is talking, or he is pursuing, or he is in a journey, or peradventure he sleepeth, and must be awaked.

28 And they cried aloud, and cut themselves after their manner with knives and lancets, till the blood gushed out upon them.

29 And it came to pass, when midday was past, and they prophesied until the time of the offering of the evening sacrifice, that there was neither voice, nor any to answer, nor any that regarded.

30 And E-li'jah said unto all the people, Come near unto me. And all the people came near unto him. And he repaired the altar of the LORD that was broken down.

31 And E-li'jah took twelve stones, according to the number of the tribes of the sons of Ja'-cob, unto whom the word of the LORD came, saying, Is'ra-el shall be thy name:

32 And with the stones he built an altar in the name of the LORD: and he made a trench about the altar, as great as would contain two measures of seed.

33 And he put the wood in order, and cut the bullock in pieces, and laid him on the wood, and said, Fill four barrels with water, and pour it on the burnt sacrifice, and on the wood.

34 And he said, Do it the second time. And they did it the second time. And he said, Do it the third time. And they did it the third time.

35 And the water ran round about the altar; and he filled the trench also with water.

36 And it came to pass at the time of the offering of the evening sacrifice, that E-li'jah the prophet came near, and said, LORD God of A'-bra-ham, I'saac, and of Is'ra-el, let it be known this day that thou art God in Is'ra-el, and that I

am thy servant, and *that* I have done all these things at thy word.

37 Hear me, O LORD, hear me, that this people may know that thou *art* the LORD God, and *that* thou hast turned their heart back again.

38 Then the fire of the LORD fell, and consumed the burnt sacrifice, and the wood, and the stones, and the dust, and licked up the water that *was* in the trench.

39 And when all the people saw *it,* they fell on their faces: and they said, The LORD, he *is* the God; the LORD, he *is* the God.

40 And E-li'jah said unto them, Take the prophets of Ba'al; let not one of them escape. And they took them: and E-li'jah brought them down to the brook Ki'shon, and slew them there.

41 ¶ And E-li'jah said unto A'hab, Get thee up, eat and drink; for *there is* a sound of abundance of rain.

42 So A'hab went up to eat and to drink. And E-li'jah went up to the top of Car'mel; and he cast himself down upon the earth, and put his face between his knees,

43 And said to his servant, Go up now, look toward the sea. And he went up, and looked, and said, *There is* nothing. And he said, Go again seven times.

44 And it came to pass at the seventh time, that he said, Behold, there ariseth a little cloud out of the sea, like a man's hand. And he said, Go up, say unto A'hab, Prepare *thy chariot,* and get thee down, that the rain stop thee not.

45 And it came to pass in the mean while, that the heaven was black with clouds and wind, and there was a great rain. And A'hab rode, and went to Jez're-el.

46 And the hand of the LORD was on E-li'jah; and he girded up his loins, and ran before A'hab to the entrance of Jez're-el.

19 AND A'hab told Jez'e-bel all that E-li'jah had done, and withal how he had slain all the prophets with the sword.

2 Then Jez'e-bel sent a messenger unto E-li'jah, saying, So let the gods do *to me,* and more also, if I make not thy life as the life of one of them by to morrow about this time.

3 And when he saw *that,* he arose, and went for his life, and came to Be'er-she'ba, which *belongeth* to Ju'dah, and left his servant there.

4 ¶ But he himself went a day's journey into the wilderness, and came and sat down under a juniper tree: and he requested for himself that he might die; and said, It is enough; now, O LORD, take away my life; for I *am* not better than my fathers.

5 And as he lay and slept under a juniper tree, behold, then an angel touched him, and said unto him, Arise *and* eat.

6 And he looked, and, behold, *there was* a cake baken on the coals, and a cruse of water at his head. And he did eat and drink, and laid him down again.

7 And the angel of the LORD came again the second time, and touched him, and said, Arise *and* eat; because the journey *is* too great for thee.

8 And he arose, and did eat and drink, and went in the strength of that meat forty days and forty nights unto Ho'reb the mount of God.

9 ¶ And he came thither unto a cave, and lodged there; and, behold, the word of the LORD *came* to him, and he said unto him, What doest thou here, E-li'jah?

10 And he said, I have been very jealous for the LORD God of hosts: for the children of Is'ra-

el have forsaken thy covenant, thrown down thine altars, and slain thy prophets with the sword; and I, *even* I only, am left; and they seek my life, to take it away.

11 And he said, Go forth, and stand upon the mount before the LORD. And, behold, the LORD passed by, and a great and strong wind rent the mountains, and brake in pieces the rocks before the LORD; *but* the LORD *was* not in the wind: and after the wind an earthquake; *but* the LORD *was* not in the earthquake:

12 And after the earthquake a fire; *but* the LORD *was* not in the fire: and after the fire a still small voice.

13 And it was *so,* when E-li'jah heard *it,* that he wrapped his face in his mantle, and went out, and stood in the entering in of the cave. And, behold, *there came* a voice unto him, and said, What doest thou here, E-li'jah?

14 And he said, I have been very jealous for the LORD God of hosts: because the children of Is'ra-el have forsaken thy covenant, thrown down thine altars, and slain thy prophets with the sword; and I, *even* I only, am left; and they seek my life, to take it away.

15 And the LORD said unto him, Go, return on thy way to the wilderness of Da-mas'cus: and when thou comest, anoint Haz'a-el *to be* king over Syr'i-a:

16 And Je'hu the son of Nim'shi shalt thou anoint *to be* king over Is'ra-el: and E-li'sha the son of Sha'phat of A'bel-me-ho'lah shalt thou anoint *to be* prophet in thy room.

17 And it shall come to pass, *that* him that escapeth the sword of Haz'a-el shall Je'hu slay: and him that escapeth from the sword of Je'hu shall E-li'sha slay.

18 Yet I have left *me* seven thousand in Is'ra-el, all the knees which have not bowed unto Ba'-al, and every mouth which hath not kissed him.

19 ¶ So he departed thence, and found E-li'sha the son of Sha'phat, who *was* plowing *with* twelve yoke *of* oxen before him, and he with the twelfth: and E-li'jah passed by him, and cast his mantle upon him.

20 And he left the oxen, and ran after E-li'jah, and said, Let me, I pray thee, kiss my father and my mother, and *then* I will follow thee. And he said unto him, Go back again: for what have I done to thee?

21 And he returned back from him, and took a yoke of oxen, and slew them, and boiled their flesh with the instruments of the oxen, and gave unto the people, and they did eat. Then he arose, and went after E-li'jah, and ministered unto him.

20 AND Ben-ha'dad the king of Syr'i-a gathered all his host together: and *there were* thirty and two kings with him, and horses, and chariots: and he went up and besieged Sa-ma'ri-a, and warred against it.

2 And he sent messengers to A'hab king of Is'ra-el into the city, and said unto him, Thus saith Ben-ha'dad,

3 Thy silver and thy gold *is* mine; thy wives also and thy children, *even* the goodliest, *are* mine.

4 And the king of Is'ra-el answered and said, My lord, O king, according to thy saying, I *am* thine, and all that I have.

5 And the messengers came again, and said, Thus speaketh Ben-ha'dad, saying, Although I have sent unto thee, saying, Thou shalt deliver me thy silver, and thy gold, and thy wives, and thy children;

6 Yet I will send my servants unto thee to

morrow about this time, and they shall search thine house, and the houses of thy servants; and it shall be, *that* whatsoever is pleasant in thine eyes, they shall put *it* in their hand, and take *it* away.

7 Then the king of Is'ra-el called all the elders of the land, and said, Mark, I pray you, and see how this *man* seeketh mischief: for he sent unto me for my wives, and for my children, and for my silver, and for my gold; and I denied him not.

8 And all the elders and all the people said unto him, Hearken not *unto him*, nor consent.

9 Wherefore he said unto the messengers of Ben-ha'dad, Tell my lord the king, All that thou didst send for to thy servant at the first I will do: but this thing I may not do. And the messengers departed, and brought him word again.

10 And Ben-ha'dad sent unto him, and said, The gods do unto me, and more also, if the dust of Sa-ma'ri-a shall suffice for handfuls for all the people that follow me.

11 And the king of Is'ra-el answered and said, Tell *him*, Let not him that girdeth on *his* harness boast himself as he that putteth it off.

12 And it came to pass, when *Ben-ha'dad* heard this message, as he *was* drinking, he and the kings in the pavilions, that he said unto his servants, Set *yourselves in array*. And they set *themselves in array* against the city.

13 ¶ And, behold, there came a prophet unto A'hab king of Is'ra-el, saying, Thus saith the LORD, Hast thou seen all this great multitude? behold, I will deliver it into thine hand this day; and thou shalt know that I *am* the LORD.

14 And A'hab said, By whom? And he said, Thus saith the LORD, *Even* by the young men of the princes of the provinces. Then he said, Who shall order the battle? And he answered, Thou.

15 Then he numbered the young men of the princes of the provinces, and they were two hundred and thirty two: and after them he numbered all the people, *even* all the children of Is'ra-el, *being* seven thousand.

16 And they went out at noon. But Ben-ha'-dad *was* drinking himself drunk in the pavilions, he and the kings, the thirty and two kings that helped him.

17 And the young men of the princes of the provinces went out first; and Ben-ha'dad sent out, and they told him, saying, There are men come out of Sa-ma'ri-a.

18 And he said, Whether they be come out for peace, take them alive; or whether they be come out for war, take them alive.

19 So these young men of the princes of the provinces came out of the city, and the army which followed them.

20 And they slew every one his man: and the Syr'i-ans fled; and Is'ra-el pursued them: and Ben-ha'dad the king of Syr'i-a escaped on an horse with the horsemen.

21 And the king of Is'ra-el went out, and smote the horses and chariots, and slew the Syr'i-ans with a great slaughter.

22 ¶ And the prophet came to the king of Is'-ra-el, and said unto him, Go, strengthen thyself, and mark, and see what thou doest: for at the return of the year the king of Syr'i-a will come up against thee.

23 And the servants of the king of Syr'i-a said unto him, Their gods *are* gods of the hills; therefore they were stronger than we; but let us fight against them in the plain, and surely we shall be stronger than they.

24 And do this thing, Take the kings away, every man out of his place, and put captains in their rooms:

25 And number thee an army, like the army that thou hast lost, horse for horse, and chariot for chariot: and we will fight against them in the plain, *and* surely we shall be stronger than they. And he hearkened unto their voice, and did so.

26 And it came to pass at the return of the year, that Ben-ha'dad numbered the Syr'i-ans, and went up to A'phek, to fight against Is'ra-el.

27 And the children of Is'ra-el were numbered, and were all present, and went against them: and the children of Is'ra-el pitched before them like two little flocks of kids; but the Syr'i-ans filled the country.

28 ¶ And there came a man of God, and spake unto the king of Is'ra-el, and said, Thus saith the LORD, Because the Syr'i-ans have said, The LORD *is* God of the hills, but he *is* not God of the valleys, therefore will I deliver all this great multitude into thine hand, and ye shall know that I *am* the LORD.

29 And they pitched one over against the other seven days. And *so* it was, that in the seventh day the battle was joined: and the children of Is'ra-el slew of the Syr'i-ans an hundred thousand footmen in one day.

30 But the rest fled to A'phek, into the city; and *there* a wall fell upon twenty and seven thousand of the men *that were* left. And Ben-ha'dad fled, and came into the city, into an inner chamber.

31 ¶ And his servants said unto him, Behold now, we have heard that the kings of the house of Is'ra-el *are* merciful kings: let us, I pray thee, put sackcloth on our loins, and ropes upon our heads, and go out to the king of Is'ra-el: peradventure he will save thy life.

32 So they girded sackcloth on their loins, and *put* ropes on their heads, and came to the king of Is'ra-el, and said, Thy servant Ben-ha'-dad saith, I pray thee, let me live. And he said, *Is* he yet alive? he *is* my brother.

33 Now the men did diligently observe whether *any thing would come* from him, and did hastily catch *it:* and they said, Thy brother Ben-ha'dad. Then he said, Go ye, bring him. Then Ben-ha'dad came forth to him; and he caused him to come up into the chariot.

34 And *Ben-ha'dad* said unto him, The cities, which my father took from thy father, I will restore; and thou shalt make streets for thee in Da-mas'cus, as my father made in Sa-ma'ri-a. Then *said A'hab*, I will send thee away with this covenant. So he made a covenant with him, and sent him away.

35 ¶ And a certain man of the sons of the prophets said unto his neighbour in the word of the LORD, Smite me, I pray thee. And the man refused to smite him.

36 Then said he unto him, Because thou hast not obeyed the voice of the LORD, behold, as soon as thou art departed from me, a lion shall slay thee. And as soon as he was departed from him, a lion found him, and slew him.

37 Then he found another man, and said, Smite me, I pray thee. And the man smote him, so that in smiting he wounded *him*.

38 So the prophet departed, and waited for the king by the way, and disguised himself with ashes upon his face.

39 And as the king passed by, he cried unto the king: and he said, Thy servant went out into the midst of the battle; and, behold, a man turned aside, and brought a man unto me, and said, Keep this man: if by any means he be miss-

ing, then shall thy life be for his life, or else thou shalt pay a talent of silver.

40 And as thy servant was busy here and there, he was gone. And the king of Is'ra-el said unto him, So *shall* thy judgment *be*: thyself hast decided *it*.

41 And he hasted, and took the ashes away from his face; and the king of Is'ra-el discerned him that he *was* of the prophets.

42 And he said unto him, Thus saith the LORD, Because thou hast let go out of *thy* hand a man whom I appointed to utter destruction, therefore thy life shall go for his life, and thy people for his people.

43 And the king of Is'ra-el went to his house heavy and displeased, and came to Sa-ma'ri-a.

21 AND it came to pass after these things, *that* Na'both the Jez're-el-ite had a vineyard, which *was* in Jez're-el, hard by the palace of A'hab king of Sa-ma'ri-a.

2 And A'hab spake unto Na'both, saying, Give me thy vineyard, that I may have it for a garden of herbs, because it *is* near unto my house: and I will give thee for it a better vineyard than it; *or*, if it seem good to thee, I will give thee the worth of it in money.

3 And Na'both said to A'hab, The LORD forbid it me, that I should give the inheritance of my fathers unto thee.

4 And A'hab came into his house heavy and displeased because of the word which Na'both the Jez're-el-ite had spoken to him: for he had said, I will not give thee the inheritance of my fathers. And he laid him down upon his bed, and turned away his face, and would eat no bread.

5 ¶ But Jez'e-bel his wife came to him, and said unto him, Why is thy spirit so sad, that thou eatest no bread?

6 And he said unto her, Because I spake unto Na'both the Jez're-el-ite, and said unto him, Give me thy vineyard for money; or else, if it please thee, I will give thee *another* vineyard for it: and he answered, I will not give thee my vineyard.

7 And Jez'e-bel his wife said unto him, Dost thou now govern the kingdom of Is'ra-el? arise, *and* eat bread, and let thine heart be merry: I will give thee the vineyard of Na'both the Jez'-re-el-ite.

8 So she wrote letters in A'hab's name, and sealed *them* with his seal, and sent the letters unto the elders and to the nobles that *were* in his city, dwelling with Na'both.

9 And she wrote in the letters, saying, Proclaim a fast, and set Na'both on high among the people:

10 And set two men, sons of Be'li-al, before him, to bear witness against him, saying, Thou didst blaspheme God and the king. And *then* carry him out, and stone him, that he may die.

11 And the men of his city, *even* the elders and the nobles who were the inhabitants in his city, did as Jez'e-bel had sent unto them, *and* as it *was* written in the letters which she had sent unto them.

12 They proclaimed a fast, and set Na'both on high among the people.

13 And there came in two men, children of Be'li-al, and sat before him: and the men of Be'-li-al witnessed against him, *even* against Na'-both, in the presence of the people, saying, Na'-both did blaspheme God and the king. Then they carried him forth out of the city, and stoned him with stones, that he died.

14 Then they sent to Jez'e-bel, saying, Na'-both is stoned, and is dead.

15 ¶ And it came to pass, when Jez'e-bel heard that Na'both was stoned, and was dead, that Jez'e-bel said to A'hab, Arise, take possession of the vineyard of Na'both the Jez're-el-ite, which he refused to give thee for money: for Na'both is not alive, but dead.

16 And it came to pass, when A'hab heard that Na'both was dead, that A'hab rose up to go down to the vineyard of Na'both the Jez're-el-ite, to take possession of it.

17 ¶ And the word of the LORD came to E-li'jah the Tish'bite, saying,

18 Arise, go down to meet A'hab king of Is'-ra-el, which *is* in Sa-ma'ri-a: behold, *he is* in the vineyard of Na'both, whither he is gone down to possess it.

19 And thou shalt speak unto him, saying, Thus saith the LORD, Hast thou killed, and also taken possession? And thou shalt speak unto him, saying, Thus saith the LORD, In the place where dogs licked the blood of Na'both shall dogs lick thy blood, even thine.

20 And A'hab said to E-li'jah, Hast thou found me, O mine enemy? And he answered, I have found *thee*: because thou hast sold thyself to work evil in the sight of the LORD.

21 Behold, I will bring evil upon thee, and will take away thy posterity, and will cut off from A'hab him that pisseth against the wall, and him that is shut up and left in Is'ra-el,

22 And will make thine house like the house of Jer-o-bo'am the son of Ne'bat, and like the house of Ba'a-sha the son of A-hi'jah, for the provocation wherewith thou hast provoked *me* to anger, and made Is'ra-el to sin.

23 And of Jez'e-bel also spake the LORD, saying, The dogs shall eat Jez'e-bel by the wall of Jez're-el.

24 Him that dieth of A'hab in the city the dogs shall eat; and him that dieth in the field shall the fowls of the air eat.

25 ¶ But there was none like unto A'hab, which did sell himself to work wickedness in the sight of the LORD, whom Jez'e-bel his wife stirred up.

26 And he did very abominably in following idols, according to all *things* as did the Am'or-ites, whom the LORD cast out before the children of Is'ra-el.

27 And it came to pass, when A'hab heard those words, that he rent his clothes, and put sackcloth upon his flesh, and fasted, and lay in sackcloth, and went softly.

28 And the word of the LORD came to E-li'jah the Tish'bite, saying,

29 Seest thou how A'hab humbleth himself before me? because he humbleth himself before me, I will not bring the evil in his days: *but* in his son's days will I bring the evil upon his house.

22 AND they continued three years without war between Syr'i-a and Is'ra-el.

2 And it came to pass in the third year, that Je-hosh'a-phat the king of Ju'dah came down to the king of Is'ra-el.

3 And the king of Is'ra-el said unto his servants, Know ye that Ra'moth in Gil'e-ad *is* ours, and we *be* still, *and* take it not out of the hand of the king of Syr'i-a?

4 And he said unto Je-hosh'a-phat, Wilt thou go with me to battle to Ra'moth–gil'e-ad? And Je-hosh'a-phat said to the king of Is'ra-el, I *am* as thou *art*, my people as thy people, my horses as thy horses.

5 And Je-hosh'a-phat said unto the king of Is'ra-el, Enquire, I pray thee, at the word of the LORD to day.

6 Then the king of Is'ra-el gathered the prophets together, about four hundred men, and said unto them, Shall I go against Ra'moth-gil'e-ad to battle, or shall I forbear? And they said, Go up; for the LORD shall deliver it into the hand of the king.

7 And Je-hosh'a-phat said, Is there not here a prophet of the LORD besides, that we might enquire of him?

8 And the king of Is'ra-el said unto Je-hosh'a-phat, There is yet one man, Mi-ca'iah the son of Im'lah, by whom we may enquire of the LORD: but I hate him; for he doth not prophesy good concerning me, but evil. And Je-hosh'a-phat said, Let not the king say so.

9 Then the king of Is'ra-el called an officer, and said, Hasten hither Mi-ca'iah the son of Im'lah.

10 And the king of Is'ra-el and Je-hosh'a-phat the king of Ju'dah sat each on his throne, having put on their robes, in a void place in the entrance of the gate of Sa-ma'ri-a; and all the prophets prophesied before them.

11 And Zed-e-ki'ah the son of Che-na'a-nah made him horns of iron: and he said, Thus saith the LORD, With these shalt thou push the Syr'i-ans, until thou have consumed them.

12 And all the prophets prophesied so, saying, Go up to Ra'moth-gil'e-ad, and prosper: for the LORD shall deliver it into the king's hand.

13 And the messenger that was gone to call Mi-ca'iah spake unto him, saying, Behold now, the words of the prophets declare good unto the king with one mouth: let thy word, I pray thee, be like the word of one of them, and speak that which is good.

14 And Mi-ca'iah said, As the LORD liveth, what the LORD saith unto me, that will I speak.

15 ¶ So he came to the king. And the king said unto him, Mi-ca'iah, shall we go against Ra'moth-gil'e-ad to battle, or shall we forbear? And he answered him, Go, and prosper: for the LORD shall deliver it into the hand of the king.

16 And the king said unto him, How many times shall I adjure thee that thou tell me nothing but that which is true in the name of the LORD?

17 And he said, I saw all Is'ra-el scattered upon the hills, as sheep that have not a shepherd: and the LORD said, These have no master: let them return every man to his house in peace.

18 And the king of Is'ra-el said unto Je-hosh'a-phat, Did I not tell thee that he would prophesy no good concerning me, but evil?

19 And he said, Hear thou therefore the word of the LORD: I saw the LORD sitting on his throne, and all the host of heaven standing by him on his right hand and on his left.

20 And the LORD said, Who shall persuade A'hab, that he may go up and fall at Ra'moth-gil'e-ad? And one said on this manner, and another said on that manner.

21 And there came forth a spirit, and stood before the LORD, and said, I will persuade him.

22 And the LORD said unto him, Wherewith? And he said, I will go forth, and I will be a lying spirit in the mouth of all his prophets. And he said, Thou shalt persuade him, and prevail also: go forth, and do so.

23 Now therefore, behold, the LORD hath put a lying spirit in the mouth of all these thy prophets, and the LORD hath spoken evil concerning thee.

24 But Zed-e-ki'ah the son of Che-na'a-nah went near, and smote Mi-ca'iah on the cheek, and said, Which way went the Spirit of the LORD from me to speak unto thee?

25 And Mi-ca'iah said, Behold, thou shalt see in that day, when thou shalt go into an inner chamber to hide thyself.

26 And the king of Is'ra-el said, Take Mi-ca'iah, and carry him back unto A'mon the governor of the city, and to Jo'ash the king's son;

27 And say, Thus saith the king, Put this fellow in the prison, and feed him with bread of affliction and with water of affliction, until I come in peace.

28 And Mi-ca'iah said, If thou return at all in peace, the LORD hath not spoken by me. And he said, Hearken, O people, every one of you.

29 So the king of Is'ra-el and Je-hosh'a-phat the king of Ju'dah went up to Ra'moth-gil'e-ad.

30 And the king of Is'ra-el said unto Je-hosh'a-phat, I will disguise myself, and enter into the battle; but put thou on thy robes. And the king of Is'ra-el disguised himself, and went into the battle.

31 But the king of Syr'i-a commanded his thirty and two captains that had rule over his chariots, saying, Fight neither with small nor great, save only with the king of Is'ra-el.

32 And it came to pass, when the captains of the chariots saw Je-hosh'a-phat, that they said, Surely it is the king of Is'ra-el. And they turned aside to fight against him: and Je-hosh'a-phat cried out.

33 And it came to pass, when the captains of the chariots perceived that it was not the king of Is'ra-el, that they turned back from pursuing him.

34 And a certain man drew a bow at a venture, and smote the king of Is'ra-el between the joints of the harness: wherefore he said unto the driver of his chariot, Turn thine hand, and carry me out of the host; for I am wounded.

35 And the battle increased that day: and the king was stayed up in his chariot against the Syr'i-ans, and died at even: and the blood ran out of the wound into the midst of the chariot.

36 And there went a proclamation throughout the host about the going down of the sun, saying, Every man to his city, and every man to his own country.

37 ¶ So the king died, and was brought to Sa-ma'ri-a; and they buried the king in Sa-ma'ri-a.

38 And one washed the chariot in the pool of Sa-ma'ri-a; and the dogs licked up his blood; and they washed his armour; according unto the word of the LORD which he spake.

39 Now the rest of the acts of A'hab, and all that he did, and the ivory house which he made, and all the cities that he built, are they not written in the book of the chronicles of the kings of Is'ra-el?

40 So A'hab slept with his fathers; and A-ha-zi'ah his son reigned in his stead.

41 ¶ And Je-hosh'a-phat the son of A'sa began to reign over Ju'dah in the fourth year of A'hab king of Is'ra-el.

42 Je-hosh'a-phat was thirty and five years old when he began to reign; and he reigned twenty and five years in Je-ru'sa-lem. And his mother's name was A-zu'bah the daughter of Shil'hi.

43 And he walked in all the ways of A'sa his father; he turned not aside from it, doing that which was right in the eyes of the LORD: nevertheless the high places were not taken away; for the people offered and burnt incense yet in the high places.

44 And Je-hosh′a-phat made peace with the king of Is′ra-el.

45 Now the rest of the acts of Je-hosh′a-phat, and his might that he shewed, and how he warred, *are* they not written in the book of the chronicles of the kings of Ju′dah?

46 And the remnant of the sodomites, which remained in the days of his father A′sa, he took out of the land.

47 *There was* then no king in E′dom: a deputy *was* king.

48 Je-hosh′a-phat made ships of Thar′shish to go to O′phir for gold: but they went not; for the ships were broken at E′zi-on-ge′ber.

49 Then said A-ha-zi′ah the son of A′hab unto Je-hosh′a-phat, Let my servants go with thy servants in the ships. But Je-hosh′a-phat would not.

50 ¶ And Je-hosh′a-phat slept with his fathers, and was buried with his fathers in the city of Da′vid his father: and Je-ho′ram his son reigned in his stead.

51 ¶ A-ha-zi′ah the son of A′hab began to reign over Is′ra-el in Sa-ma′ri-a the seventeenth year of Je-hosh′a-phat king of Ju′dah, and reigned two years over Is′ra-el.

52 And he did evil in the sight of the LORD, and walked in the way of his father, and in the way of his mother, and in the way of Jer-o-bo′am the son of Ne′bat, who made Is′ra-el to sin:

53 For he served Ba′al, and worshipped him, and provoked to anger the LORD God of Is′ra-el, according to all that his father had done.

THE SECOND BOOK OF THE

KINGS

1 THEN Mo′ab rebelled against Is′ra-el after the death of A′hab.

2 And A-ha-zi′ah fell down through a lattice in his upper chamber that *was* in Sa-ma′ri-a, and was sick: and he sent messengers, and said unto them, Go, enquire of Ba′al-ze′bub the god of Ek′ron whether I shall recover of this disease.

3 But the angel of the LORD said to E-li′jah the Tish′bite, Arise, go up to meet the messengers of the king of Sa-ma′ri-a, and say unto them, *Is it* not because *there is* not a God in Is′ra-el, *that* ye go to enquire of Ba′al-ze′bub the god of Ek′ron?

4 Now therefore thus saith the LORD, Thou shalt not come down from that bed on which thou art gone up, but shalt surely die. And E-li′jah departed.

5 ¶ And when the messengers turned back unto him, he said unto them, Why are ye now turned back?

6 And they said unto him, There came a man up to meet us, and said unto us, Go, turn again unto the king that sent you, and say unto him, Thus saith the LORD, *Is it* not because *there is* not a God in Is′ra-el, *that* thou sendest to enquire of Ba′al-ze′bub the god of Ek′ron? therefore thou shalt not come down from that bed on which thou art gone up, but shalt surely die.

7 And he said unto them, What manner of man *was he* which came up to meet you, and told you these words?

8 And they answered him, *He was* an hairy man, and girt with a girdle of leather about his loins. And he said, *It is* E-li′jah the Tish′bite.

9 Then the king sent unto him a captain of fifty with his fifty. And he went up to him: and, behold, he sat on the top of an hill. And he spake unto him, Thou man of God, the king hath said, Come down.

10 And E-li′jah answered and said to the captain of fifty, If I *be* a man of God, then let fire come down from heaven, and consume thee and thy fifty. And there came down fire from heaven, and consumed him and his fifty.

11 Again also he sent unto him another captain of fifty with his fifty. And he answered and said unto him, O man of God, thus hath the king said, Come down quickly.

12 And E-li′jah answered and said unto them, If I *be* a man of God, let fire come down from heaven, and consume thee and thy fifty. And the fire of God came down from heaven, and consumed him and his fifty.

13 ¶ And he sent again a captain of the third fifty with his fifty. And the third captain of fifty went up, and came and fell on his knees before E-li′jah, and besought him, and said unto him, O man of God, I pray thee, let my life, and the life of these fifty thy servants, be precious in thy sight.

14 Behold, there came fire down from heaven, and burnt up the two captains of the former fifties with their fifties: therefore let my life now be precious in thy sight.

15 And the angel of the LORD said unto E-li′jah, Go down with him: be not afraid of him. And he arose, and went down with him unto the king.

16 And he said unto him, Thus saith the LORD, Forasmuch as thou hast sent messengers to enquire of Ba′al-ze′bub the god of Ek′ron, *is it* not because *there is* no God in Is′ra-el to enquire of his word? therefore thou shalt not come down off that bed on which thou art gone up, but shalt surely die.

17 ¶ So he died according to the word of the LORD which E-li′jah had spoken. And Je-ho′ram reigned in his stead in the second year of Je-ho′ram the son of Je-hosh′a-phat king of Ju′dah; because he had no son.

18 Now the rest of the acts of A-ha-zi′ah which he did, *are* they not written in the book of the chronicles of the kings of Is′ra-el?

2 AND it came to pass, when the LORD would take up E-li′jah into heaven by a whirlwind, that E-li′jah went with E-li′sha from Gil′gal.

2 And E-li′jah said unto E-li′sha, Tarry here, I pray thee; for the LORD hath sent me to Beth′-el. And E-li′sha said *unto him,* As the LORD liv-eth, and *as* thy soul liveth, I will not leave thee. So they went down to Beth′-el.

3 And the sons of the prophets that *were* at Beth′-el came forth to E-li′sha, and said unto him, Knowest thou that the LORD will take away thy master from thy head to day? And he said, Yea, I know *it;* hold ye your peace.

4 And E-li′jah said unto him, E-li′sha, tarry here, I pray thee; for the LORD hath sent me to Jer′i-cho. And he said, *As* the LORD liveth, and *as* thy soul liveth, I will not leave thee. So they came to Jer′i-cho.

5 And the sons of the prophets that *were* at Jer'i-cho came to E-li'sha, and said unto him, Knowest thou that the LORD will take away thy master from thy head to day? And he answered, Yea, I know it: hold ye your peace.

6 And E-li'jah said unto him, Tarry, I pray thee, here; for the LORD hath sent me to Jor'dan. And he said, *As* the LORD liveth, and *as* thy soul liveth, I will not leave thee. And they two went on.

7 And fifty men of the sons of the prophets went, and stood to view afar off: and they two stood by Jor'dan.

8 And E-li'jah took his mantle, and wrapped *it* together, and smote the waters, and they were divided hither and thither, so that they two went over on dry ground.

9 ¶ And it came to pass, when they were gone over, that E-li'jah said unto E-li'sha, Ask what I shall do for thee, before I be taken away from thee. And E-li'sha said, I pray thee, let a double portion of thy spirit be upon me.

10 And he said, Thou hast asked a hard thing: *nevertheless*, if thou see me *when I am* taken from thee, it shall be so unto thee; but if not, it shall not be *so*.

11 And it came to pass, as they still went on, and talked, that, behold, *there appeared* a chariot of fire, and horses of fire, and parted them both asunder; and E-li'jah went up by a whirlwind into heaven.

12 ¶ And E-li'sha saw *it*, and he cried, My father, my father, the chariot of Is'ra-el, and the horsemen thereof. And he saw him no more: and he took hold of his own clothes, and rent them in two pieces.

13 He took up also the mantle of E-li'jah that fell from him, and went back and stood by the bank of Jor'dan;

14 And he took the mantle of E-li'jah that fell from him, and smote the waters, and said, Where *is* the LORD God of E-li'jah? and when he also had smitten the waters, they parted hither and thither: and E-li'sha went over.

15 And when the sons of the prophets which *were* to view at Jer'i-cho saw him, they said, The spirit of E-li'jah doth rest on E-li'sha. And they came to meet him, and bowed themselves to the ground before him.

16 ¶ And they said unto him, Behold now, there be with thy servants fifty strong men; let them go, we pray thee, and seek thy master: lest peradventure the Spirit of the LORD hath taken him up, and cast him upon some mountain, or into some valley. And he said, Ye shall not send.

17 And when they urged him till he was ashamed, he said, Send. They sent therefore fifty men; and they sought three days, but found him not.

18 And when they came again to him, (for he tarried at Jer'i-cho,) he said unto them, Did I not say unto you, Go not?

19 ¶ And the men of the city said unto E-li'sha, Behold, I pray thee, the situation of this city *is* pleasant, as my lord seeth: but the water *is* naught, and the ground barren.

20 And he said, Bring me a new cruse, and put salt therein. And they brought *it* to him.

21 And he went forth unto the spring of the waters, and cast the salt in there, and said, Thus saith the LORD, I have healed these waters; there shall not be from thence any more death or barren *land*.

22 So the waters were healed unto this day, according to the saying of E-li'sha which he spake.

23 ¶ And he went up from thence unto Beth'--el: and as he was going up by the way, there came forth little children out of the city, and mocked him, and said unto him, Go up, thou bald head; go up, thou bald head.

24 And he turned back, and looked on them, and cursed them in the name of the LORD. And there came forth two she bears out of the wood, and tare forty and two children of them.

25 And he went from thence to mount Car'-mel, and from thence he returned to Sa-ma'ri-a.

3 NOW Je-ho'ram the son of A'hab began to reign over Is'ra-el in Sa-ma'ri-a the eighteenth year of Je-hosh'a-phat king of Ju'dah, and reigned twelve years.

2 And he wrought evil in the sight of the LORD; but not like his father, and like his mother: for he put away the image of Ba'al that his father had made.

3 Nevertheless he cleaved unto the sins of Jer-o-bo'am the son of Ne'bat, which made Is'-ra-el to sin; he departed not therefrom.

4 ¶ And Me'sha king of Mo'ab was a sheepmaster, and rendered unto the king of Is'ra-el an hundred thousand lambs, and an hundred thousand rams, with the wool.

5 But it came to pass, when A'hab was dead, that the king of Mo'ab rebelled against the king of Is'ra-el.

6 ¶ And king Je-ho'ram went out of Sa-ma'-ri-a the same time, and numbered all Is'ra-el.

7 And he went and sent to Je-hosh'a-phat the king of Ju'dah, saying, The king of Mo'ab hath rebelled against me: wilt thou go with me against Mo'ab to battle? And he said, I will go up: I *am* as thou *art*, my people as thy people, *and* my horses as thy horses.

8 And he said, Which way shall we go up? And he answered, The way through the wilderness of E'dom.

9 So the king of Is'ra-el went, and the king of Ju'dah, and the king of E'dom: and they fetched a compass of seven days' journey: and there was no water for the host, and for the cattle that followed them.

10 And the king of Is'ra-el said, Alas! that the LORD hath called these three kings together, to deliver them into the hand of Mo'ab!

11 But Je-hosh'a-phat said, *Is there* not here a prophet of the LORD, that we may enquire of the LORD by him? And one of the king of Is'ra-el's servants answered and said, Here *is* E-li'sha the son of Sha'phat, which poured water on the hands of E-li'jah.

12 And Je-hosh'a-phat said, The word of the LORD is with him. So the king of Is'ra-el and Je-hosh'a-phat and the king of E'dom went down to him.

13 And E-li'sha said unto the king of Is'ra-el, What have I to do with thee? get thee to the prophets of thy father, and to the prophets of thy mother. And the king of Is'ra-el said unto him, Nay: for the LORD hath called these three kings together, to deliver them into the hand of Mo'ab.

14 And E-li'sha said, *As* the LORD of hosts liveth, before whom I stand, surely, were it not that I regard the presence of Je-hosh'a-phat the king of Ju'dah, I would not look toward thee, nor see thee.

15 But now bring me a minstrel. And it came to pass, when the minstrel played, that the hand of the LORD came upon him.

16 And he said, Thus saith the LORD, Make this valley full of ditches.

17 For thus saith the LORD, Ye shall not see

wind, neither shall ye see rain; yet that valley shall be filled with water, that ye may drink, both ye, and your cattle, and your beasts.

18 And this is *but* a light thing in the sight of the LORD: he will deliver the Mo'ab-ites also into your hand.

19 And ye shall smite every fenced city, and every choice city, and shall fell every good tree, and stop all wells of water, and mar every good piece of land with stones.

20 And it came to pass in the morning, when the meat offering was offered, that, behold, there came water by the way of E'dom, and the country was filled with water.

21 ¶ And when all the Mo'ab-ites heard that the kings were come up to fight against them, they gathered all that were able to put on armour, and upward, and stood in the border.

22 And they rose up early in the morning, and the sun shone upon the water, and the Mo'-ab-ites saw the water on the other side *as* red as blood:

23 And they said, This *is* blood: the kings are surely slain, and they have smitten one another: now therefore, Mo'ab, to the spoil.

24 And when they came to the camp of Is'ra-el, the Is'ra-el-ites rose up and smote the Mo'ab-ites, so that they fled before them: but they went forward smiting the Mo'ab-ites, even in *their* country.

25 And they beat down the cities, and on every good piece of land cast every man his stone, and filled it; and they stopped all the wells of water, and felled all the good trees: only in Kir-har-a-seth left they the stones thereof; howbeit the slingers went about *it*, and smote it.

26 ¶ And when the king of Mo'ab saw that the battle was too sore for him, he took with him seven hundred men that drew swords, to break through *even* unto the king of E'dom: but they could not.

27 Then he took his eldest son that should have reigned in his stead, and offered him *for* a burnt offering upon the wall. And there was great indignation against Is'ra-el: and they departed from him, and returned to *their own* land.

4 NOW there cried a certain woman of the wives of the sons of the prophets unto E-li'sha, saying, Thy servant my husband is dead; and thou knowest that thy servant did fear the LORD: and the creditor is come to take unto him my two sons to be bondmen.

2 And E-li'sha said unto her, What shall I do for thee? tell me, what hast thou in the house? And she said, Thine handmaid hath not any thing in the house, save a pot of oil.

3 Then he said, Go, borrow thee vessels abroad of all thy neighbours, *even* empty vessels; borrow not a few.

4 And when thou art come in, thou shalt shut the door upon thee and upon thy sons, and shalt pour out into all those vessels, and thou shalt set aside that which is full.

5 So she went from him, and shut the door upon her and upon her sons, who brought *the vessels* to her; and she poured out.

6 And it came to pass, when the vessels were full, that she said unto her son, Bring me yet a vessel. And he said unto her, *There is* not a vessel more. And the oil stayed.

7 Then she came and told the man of God. And he said, Go, sell the oil, and pay thy debt, and live thou and thy children of the rest.

8 ¶ And it fell on a day, that E-li'sha passed to Shu'nem, where *was* a great woman; and she constrained him to eat bread. And *so* it was, *that* as oft as he passed by, he turned in thither to eat bread.

9 And she said unto her husband, Behold now, I perceive that this *is* an holy man of God, which passeth by us continually.

10 Let us make a little chamber, I pray thee, on the wall; and let us set for him there a bed, and a table, and a stool, and a candlestick: and it shall be, when he cometh to us, that he shall turn in thither.

11 And it fell on a day, that he came thither, and he turned into the chamber, and lay there.

12 And he said to Ge-ha'zi his servant, Call this Shu'nam-mite. And when he had called her, she stood before him.

13 And he said unto him, Say now unto her, Behold, thou hast been careful for us with all this care; what *is* to be done for thee? wouldest thou be spoken for to the king, or to the captain of the host? And she answered, I dwell among mine own people.

14 And he said, What then *is* to be done for her? And Ge-ha'zi answered, Verily she hath no child, and her husband is old.

15 And he said, Call her. And when he had called her, she stood in the door.

16 And he said, About this season, according to the time of life, thou shalt embrace a son. And she said, Nay, my lord, *thou* man of God, do not lie unto thine handmaid.

17 And the woman conceived, and bare a son at that season that E-li'sha had said unto her, according to the time of life.

18 ¶ And when the child was grown, it fell on a day, that he went out to his father to the reapers.

19 And he said unto his father, My head, my head. And he said to a lad, Carry him to his mother.

20 And when he had taken him, and brought him to his mother, he sat on her knees till noon, and *then* died.

21 And she went up, and laid him on the bed of the man of God, and shut *the door* upon him, and went out.

22 And she called unto her husband, and said, Send me, I pray thee, one of the young men, and one of the asses, that I may run to the man of God, and come again.

23 And he said, Wherefore wilt thou go to him to day? *it is* neither new moon, nor sabbath. And she said, *It shall be* well.

24 Then she saddled an ass, and said to her servant, Drive, and go forward; slack not *thy* riding for me, except I bid thee.

25 So she went and came unto the man of God to mount Car'mel. And it came to pass, when the man of God saw her afar off, that he said to Ge-ha'zi his servant, Behold, *yonder is* that Shu'nam-mite:

26 Run now, I pray thee, to meet her, and say unto her, *Is it* well with thee? *is it* well with thy husband? *is it* well with the child? And she answered, *It is* well.

27 And when she came to the man of God to the hill, she caught him by the feet: but Ge-ha'zi came near to thrust her away. And the man of God said, Let her alone; for her soul *is* vexed within her: and the LORD hath hid *it* from me, and hath not told me.

28 Then she said, Did I desire a son of my lord? did I not say, Do not deceive me?

29 Then he said to Ge-ha'zi, Gird up thy loins, and take my staff in thine hand, and go thy way: if thou meet any man, salute him not;

and if any salute thee, answer him not again: and lay my staff upon the face of the child.

30 And the mother of the child said, As the LORD liveth, and as thy soul liveth, I will not leave thee. And he arose, and followed her.

31 And Ge-ha'zi passed on before them, and laid the staff upon the face of the child; but there was neither voice, nor hearing. Wherefore he went again to meet him, and told him, saying, The child is not awaked.

32 And when E-li'sha was come into the house, behold, the child was dead, and laid upon his bed.

33 He went in therefore, and shut the door upon them twain, and prayed unto the LORD.

34 And he went up, and lay upon the child, and put his mouth upon his mouth, and his eyes upon his eyes, and his hands upon his hands: and he stretched himself upon the child; and the flesh of the child waxed warm.

35 Then he returned, and walked in the house to and fro; and went up, and stretched himself upon him: and the child sneezed seven times, and the child opened his eyes.

36 And he called Ge-ha'zi, and said, Call this Shu'nam-mite. So he called her. And when she was come in unto him, he said, Take up thy son.

37 Then she went in, and fell at his feet, and bowed herself to the ground, and took up her son, and went out.

38 ¶ And E-li'sha came again to Gil'gal: and there was a dearth in the land; and the sons of the prophets were sitting before him: and he said unto his servant, Set on the great pot, and seethe pottage for the sons of the prophets.

39 And one went out into the field to gather herbs, and found a wild vine, and gathered thereof wild gourds his lap full, and came and shred them into the pot of pottage: for they knew them not.

40 So they poured out for the men to eat. And it came to pass, as they were eating of the pottage, that they cried out, and said, O thou man of God, there is death in the pot. And they could not eat thereof.

41 But he said, Then bring meal. And he cast it into the pot; and he said, Pour out for the people, that they may eat. And there was no harm in the pot.

42 ¶ And there came a man from Ba'al–shal'-i-sha, and brought the man of God bread of the first-fruits, twenty loaves of barley, and full ears of corn in the husk thereof. And he said, Give unto the people, that they may eat.

43 And his servitor said, What, should I set this before an hundred men? He said again, Give the people, that they may eat: for thus saith the LORD, They shall eat, and shall leave thereof.

44 So he set it before them, and they did eat, and left thereof, according to the word of the LORD.

5 NOW Na'a-man, captain of the host of the king of Syr'i-a, was a great man with his master, and honourable, because by him the LORD had given deliverance unto Syr'i-a: he was also a mighty man in valour, but he was a leper.

2 And the Syr'i-ans had gone out by companies, and had brought away captive out of the land of Is'ra-el a little maid; and she waited on Na'a-man's wife.

3 And she said unto her mistress, Would God my lord were with the prophet that is in Sa-ma'ri-a! for he would recover him of his leprosy.

4 And one went in, and told his lord, saying, Thus and thus said the maid that is of the land of Is'ra-el.

5 And the king of Syr'i-a said, Go to, go, and I will send a letter unto the king of Is'ra-el. And he departed, and took with him ten talents of silver, and six thousand pieces of gold, and ten changes of raiment.

6 And he brought the letter to the king of Is'-ra-el, saying, Now when this letter is come unto thee, behold, I have therewith sent Na'a-man my servant to thee, that thou mayest recover him of his leprosy.

7 And it came to pass, when the king of Is'ra-el had read the letter, that he rent his clothes, and said, Am I God, to kill and to make alive, that this man doth send unto me to recover a man of his leprosy? wherefore consider, I pray you, and see how he seeketh a quarrel against me.

8 ¶ And it was so, when E-li'sha the man of God had heard that the king of Is'ra-el had rent his clothes, that he sent to the king, saying, Wherefore hast thou rent thy clothes? let him come now to me, and he shall know that there is a prophet in Is'ra-el.

9 So Na'a-man came with his horses and with his chariot, and stood at the door of the house of E-li'sha.

10 And E-li'sha sent a messenger unto him, saying, Go and wash in Jor'dan seven times, and thy flesh shall come again to thee, and thou shalt be clean.

11 But Na'a-man was wroth, and went away, and said, Behold, I thought, He will surely come out to me, and stand, and call on the name of the LORD his God, and strike his hand over the place, and recover the leper.

12 Are not Ab'a-na and Phar'par, rivers of Da-mas'cus, better than all the waters of Is'ra-el? may I not wash in them, and be clean? So he turned and went away in a rage.

13 And his servants came near, and spake unto him, and said, My father, if the prophet had bid thee do some great thing, wouldest thou not have done it? how much rather then, when he saith to thee, Wash, and be clean?

14 Then went he down, and dipped himself seven times in Jor'dan, according to the saying of the man of God: and his flesh came again like unto the flesh of a little child, and he was clean.

15 ¶ And he returned to the man of God, he and all his company, and came, and stood before him: and he said, Behold, now I know that there is no God in all the earth, but in Is'ra-el: now therefore, I pray thee, take a blessing of thy servant.

16 But he said, As the LORD liveth, before whom I stand, I will receive none. And he urged him to take it; but he refused.

17 And Na'a-man said, Shall there not then, I pray thee, be given to thy servant two mules' burden of earth? for thy servant will henceforth offer neither burnt offering nor sacrifice unto other gods, but unto the LORD.

18 In this thing the LORD pardon thy servant, that when my master goeth into the house of Rim'mon to worship there, and he leaneth on my hand, and I bow myself in the house of Rim'mon: when I bow down myself in the house of Rim'mon, the LORD pardon thy servant in this thing.

19 And he said unto him, Go in peace. So he departed from him a little way.

20 ¶ But Ge-ha'zi, the servant of E-li'sha the man of God, said, Behold, my master hath spared Na'a-man this Syr'i-an, in not receiving at his hands that which he brought: but, as the

LORD liveth, I will run after him, and take somewhat of him.

21 So Ge-ha′zi followed after Na′a-man. And when Na′a-man saw *him* running after him, he lighted down from the chariot to meet him, and said, *Is* all well?

22 And he said, All *is* well. My master hath sent me, saying, Behold, even now there be come to me from mount E′phra-im two young men of the sons of the prophets: give them, I pray thee, a talent of silver, and two changes of garments.

23 And Na′a-man said, Be content, take two talents. And he urged him, and bound two talents of silver in two bags, with two changes of garments, and laid *them* upon two of his servants; and they bare *them* before him.

24 And when he came to the tower, he took *them* from their hand, and bestowed *them* in the house: and he let the men go, and they departed.

25 But he went in, and stood before his master. And E-li′sha said unto him, Whence *comest thou*, Ge-ha′zi? And he said, Thy servant went no whither.

26 And he said unto him, Went not mine heart *with thee*, when the man turned again from his chariot to meet thee? *Is it* a time to receive money, and to receive garments, and oliveyards, and vineyards, and sheep, and oxen, and menservants, and maidservants?

27 The leprosy therefore of Na′a-man shall cleave unto thee, and unto thy seed for ever. And he went out from his presence a leper *as white* as snow.

6 AND the sons of the prophets said unto E-li′sha, Behold now, the place where we dwell with thee is too strait for us.

2 Let us go, we pray thee, unto Jor′dan, and take thence every man a beam, and let us make us a place there, where we may dwell. And he answered, Go ye.

3 And one said, Be content, I pray thee, and go with thy servants. And he answered, I will go.

4 So he went with them. And when they came to Jor′dan, they cut down wood.

5 But as one was felling a beam, the ax head fell into the water: and he cried, and said, Alas, master! for it was borrowed.

6 And the man of God said, Where fell it? And he shewed him the place. And he cut down a stick, and cast *it* in thither; and the iron did swim.

7 Therefore said he, Take *it* up to thee. And he put out his hand, and took it.

8 ¶ Then the king of Syr′i-a warred against Is′ra-el, and took counsel with his servants, saying, In such and such a place *shall* be my camp.

9 And the man of God sent unto the king of Is′ra-el, saying, Beware that thou pass not such a place; for thither the Syr′i-ans are come down.

10 And the king of Is′ra-el sent to the place which the man of God told him and warned him of, and saved himself there, not once nor twice.

11 Therefore the heart of the king of Syr′i-a was sore troubled for this thing; and he called his servants, and said unto them, Will ye not shew me which of us *is* for the king of Is′ra-el?

12 And one of his servants said, None, my lord, O king: but E-li′sha, the prophet that *is* in Is′ra-el, telleth the king of Is′ra-el the words that thou speakest in thy bedchamber.

13 ¶ And he said, Go and spy where he *is*, that I may send and fetch him. And it was told him, saying, Behold, *he is* in Do′than.

14 Therefore sent he thither horses, and chariots, and a great host: and they came by night, and compassed the city about.

15 And when the servant of the man of God was risen early, and gone forth, behold, an host compassed the city both with horses and chariots. And his servant said unto him, Alas, my master! how shall we do?

16 And he answered, Fear not: for they that *be* with us *are* more than they that *be* with them.

17 And E-li′sha prayed, and said, LORD, I pray thee, open his eyes, that he may see. And the LORD opened the eyes of the young man; and he saw: and, behold, the mountain *was* full of horses and chariots of fire round about E-li′sha.

18 And when they came down to him, E-li′sha prayed unto the LORD, and said, Smite this people, I pray thee, with blindness. And he smote them with blindness according to the word of E-li′sha.

19 ¶ And E-li′sha said unto them, This *is* not the way, neither *is* this the city: follow me, and I will bring you to the man whom ye seek. But he led them to Sa-ma′ri-a.

20 And it came to pass, when they were come into Sa-ma′ri-a, that E-li′sha said, LORD, open the eyes of these *men*, that they may see. And the LORD opened their eyes, and they saw; and, behold, *they were* in the midst of Sa-ma′ri-a.

21 And the king of Is′ra-el said unto E-li′sha, when he saw them, My father, shall I smite *them*? shall I smite *them*?

22 And he answered, Thou shalt not smite *them*: wouldest thou smite those whom thou hast taken captive with thy sword and with thy bow? set bread and water before them, that they may eat and drink, and go to their master.

23 And he prepared great provision for them: and when they had eaten and drunk, he sent them away, and they went to their master. So the bands of Syr′i-a came no more into the land of Is′ra-el.

24 ¶ And it came to pass after this, that Ben-ha′dad king of Syr′i-a gathered all his host, and went up, and besieged Sa-ma′ri-a.

25 And there was a great famine in Sa-ma′ri-a: and, behold, they besieged it, until an ass′s head was *sold* for fourscore *pieces* of silver, and the fourth part of a cab of dove′s dung for five *pieces* of silver.

26 And as the king of Is′ra-el was passing by upon the wall, there cried a woman unto him, saying, Help, my lord, O king.

27 And he said, If the LORD do not help thee, whence shall I help thee? out of the barnfloor, or out of the winepress?

28 And the king said unto her, What aileth thee? And she answered, This woman said unto me, Give thy son, that we may eat him to day, and we will eat my son to morrow.

29 So we boiled my son, and did eat him: and I said unto her on the next day, Give thy son, that we may eat him: and she hath hid her son.

30 ¶ And it came to pass, when the king heard the words of the woman, that he rent his clothes; and he passed by upon the wall, and the people looked, and, behold, *he had* sackcloth within upon his flesh.

31 Then he said, God do so and more also to me, if the head of E-li′sha the son of Sha′phat shall stand on him this day.

32 But E-li′sha sat in his house, and the elders sat with him; and *the king* sent a man from before him: but ere the messenger came to him,

he said to the elders, See ye how this son of a murderer hath sent to take away mine head? look, when the messenger cometh, shut the door, and hold him fast at the door: is not the sound of his master's feet behind him?

33 And while he yet talked with them, behold, the messenger came down unto him: and he said, Behold, this evil is of the LORD; what should I wait for the LORD any longer?

7 THEN E-li'sha said, Hear ye the word of the LORD; Thus saith the LORD, To morrow about this time shall a measure of fine flour be sold for a shekel, and two measures of barley for a shekel, in the gate of Sa-ma'ri-a.

2 Then a lord on whose hand the king leaned answered the man of God, and said, Behold, if the LORD would make windows in heaven, might this thing be? And he said, Behold, thou shalt see it with thine eyes, but shalt not eat thereof.

3 ¶ And there were four leprous men at the entering in of the gate: and they said one to another, Why sit we here until we die?

4 If we say, We will enter into the city, then the famine is in the city, and we shall die there: and if we sit still here, we die also. Now therefore come, and let us fall unto the host of the Syr'i-ans: if they save us alive, we shall live; and if they kill us, we shall but die.

5 And they rose up in the twilight, to go unto the camp of the Syr'i-ans: and when they were come to the uttermost part of the camp of Syr'i-a, behold, there was no man there.

6 For the LORD had made the host of the Syr'-i-ans to hear a noise of chariots, and a noise of horses, even the noise of a great host: and they said one to another, Lo, the king of Is'ra-el hath hired against us the kings of the Hit'tites, and the kings of the E-gyp'tians, to come upon us.

7 Wherefore they arose and fled in the twilight, and left their tents, and their horses, and their asses, even the camp as it was, and fled for their life.

8 And when these lepers came to the uttermost part of the camp, they went into one tent, and did eat and drink, and carried thence silver, and gold, and raiment, and went and hid it; and came again, and entered into another tent, and carried thence also, and went and hid it.

9 Then they said one to another, We do not well: this day is a day of good tidings, and we hold our peace: if we tarry till the morning light, some mischief will come upon us: now therefore come, that we may go and tell the king's household.

10 So they came and called unto the porter of the city: and they told them, saying, We came to the camp of the Syr'i-ans, and, behold, there was no man there, neither voice of man, but horses tied, and asses tied, and the tents as they were.

11 And he called the porters; and they told it to the king's house within.

12 ¶ And the king arose in the night, and said unto his servants, I will now shew you what the Syr'i-ans have done to us. They know that we be hungry; therefore are they gone out of the camp to hide themselves in the field, saying, When they come out of the city, we shall catch them alive, and get into the city.

13 And one of his servants answered and said, Let some take, I pray thee, five of the horses that remain, which are left in the city, (behold, they are as all the multitude of Is'ra-el that are left in it: behold, I say, they are even as all the multitude of the Is-ra-el-ites that are consumed:) and let us send and see.

14 They took therefore two chariot horses; and the king sent after the host of the Syr'i-ans, saying, Go and see.

15 And they went after them unto Jor'dan: and, lo, all the way was full of garments and vessels, which the Syr'i-ans had cast away in their haste. And the messengers returned, and told the king.

16 And the people went out, and spoiled the tents of the Syr'i-ans. So a measure of fine flour was sold for a shekel, and two measures of barley for a shekel, according to the word of the LORD.

17 ¶ And the king appointed the lord on whose hand he leaned to have the charge of the gate: and the people trode upon him in the gate, and he died, as the man of God had said, who spake when the king came down to him.

18 And it came to pass as the man of God had spoken to the king, saying, Two measures of barley for a shekel, and a measure of fine flour for a shekel, shall be to morrow about this time in the gate of Sa-ma'ri-a:

19 And that lord answered the man of God, and said, Now, behold, if the LORD should make windows in heaven, might such a thing be? And he said, Behold, thou shalt see it with thine eyes, but shalt not eat thereof.

20 And so it fell out unto him: for the people trode upon him in the gate, and he died.

8 THEN spake E-li'sha unto the woman, whose son he had restored to life, saying, Arise, and go thou and thine household, and sojourn wheresoever thou canst sojourn: for the LORD hath called for a famine; and it shall also come upon the land seven years.

2 And the woman arose, and did after the saying of the man of God: and she went with her household, and sojourned in the land of the Phi-lis'tines seven years.

3 And it came to pass at the seven years' end, that the woman returned out of the land of the Phi-lis'tines: and she went forth to cry unto the king for her house and for her land.

4 And the king talked with Ge-ha'zi the servant of the man of God, saying, Tell me, I pray thee, all the great things that E-li'sha hath done.

5 And it came to pass, as he was telling the king how he had restored a dead body to life, that, behold, the woman, whose son he had restored to life, cried to the king for her house and for her land. And Ge-ha'zi said, My lord, O king, this is the woman, and this is her son, whom E-li'sha restored to life.

6 And when the king asked the woman, she told him. So the king appointed unto her a certain officer, saying, Restore all that was hers, and all the fruits of the field since the day that she left the land, even until now.

7 ¶ And E-li'sha came to Da-mas'cus; and Ben-ha'dad the king of Syr'i-a was sick; and it was told him, saying, The man of God is come hither.

8 And the king said unto Haz'a-el, Take a present in thine hand, and go, meet the man of God, and enquire of the LORD by him, saying, Shall I recover of this disease?

9 So Haz'a-el went to meet him, and took a present with him, even of every good thing of Da-mas'cus, forty camels' burden, and came and stood before him, and said, Thy son Ben-ha'dad king of Syr'i-a hath sent me to thee, saying, Shall I recover of this disease?

10 And E-li'sha said unto him, Go, say unto

him, Thou mayest certainly recover: howbeit the LORD hath shewed me that he shall surely die.

11 And he settled his countenance stedfastly, until he was ashamed: and the man of God wept.

12 And Haz'a-el said, Why weepeth my lord? And he answered, Because I know the evil that thou wilt do unto the children of Is'ra-el: their strong holds wilt thou set on fire, and their young men wilt thou slay with the sword, and wilt dash their children, and rip up their women with child.

13 And Haz'a-el said, But what, is thy servant a dog, that he should do this great thing? And E-li'sha answered, The LORD hath shewed me that thou shalt be king over Syr'i-a.

14 So he departed from E-li'sha, and came to his master; who said to him, What said E-li'sha to thee? And he answered, He told me that thou shouldest surely recover.

15 And it came to pass on the morrow, that he took a thick cloth, and dipped it in water, and spread it on his face, so that he died: and Haz'a-el reigned in his stead.

16 ¶ And in the fifth year of Jo'ram the son of A'hab king of Is'ra-el, Je-hosh'a-phat being then king of Ju'dah, Je-ho'ram the son of Je-hosh'a-phat king of Ju'dah began to reign.

17 Thirty and two years old was he when he began to reign; and he reigned eight years in Je-ru'sa-lem.

18 And he walked in the way of the kings of Is'ra-el, as did the house of A'hab: for the daughter of A'hab was his wife: and he did evil in the sight of the LORD.

19 Yet the LORD would not destroy Ju'dah for Da'vid his servant's sake, as he promised him to give him alway a light, and to his children.

20 ¶ In his days E'dom revolted from under the hand of Ju'dah, and made a king over themselves.

21 So Jo'ram went over to Za'ir, and all the chariots with him: and he rose by night, and smote the E'dom-ites which compassed him about, and the captains of the chariots: and the people fled into their tents.

22 Yet E'dom revolted from under the hand of Ju'dah unto this day. Then Lib'nah revolted at the same time.

23 And the rest of the acts of Jo'ram, and all that he did, are they not written in the book of the chronicles of the kings of Ju'dah?

24 And Jo'ram slept with his fathers, and was buried with his fathers in the city of Da'vid: and A-ha-zi'ah his son reigned in his stead.

25 ¶ In the twelfth year of Jo'ram the son of A'hab king of Is'ra-el did A-ha-zi'ah the son of Je-ho'ram king of Ju'dah begin to reign.

26 Two and twenty years old was A-ha-zi'ah when he began to reign; and he reigned one year in Je-ru'sa-lem. And his mother's name was Ath-a-li'ah, the daughter of Om'ri king of Is'ra-el.

27 And he walked in the way of the house of A'hab, and did evil in the sight of the LORD, as did the house of A'hab: for he was the son in law of the house of A'hab.

28 ¶ And he went with Jo'ram the son of A'-hab to the war against Haz'a-el king of Syr'i-a in Ra'moth-gil'e-ad; and the Syr'i-ans wounded Jo'ram.

29 And king Jo'ram went back to be healed in Jez're-el of the wounds which the Syr'i-ans had given him at Ra'mah, when he fought against Haz'a-el king of Syr'i-a. And A-ha-zi'ah the son of Je-ho'ram king of Ju'dah went down

to see Jo'ram the son of A'hab in Jez're-el, because he was sick.

9 AND E-li'sha the prophet called one of the children of the prophets, and said unto him, Gird up thy loins, and take this box of oil in thine hand, and go to Ra'moth-gil'e-ad:

2 And when thou comest thither, look out there Je'hu the son of Je-hosh'a-phat the son of Nim'shi, and go in, and make him arise up from among his brethren, and carry him to an inner chamber;

3 Then take the box of oil, and pour it on his head, and say, Thus saith the LORD, I have anointed thee king over Is'ra-el. Then open the door, and flee, and tarry not.

4 ¶ So the young man, even the young man the prophet, went to Ra'moth-gil'e-ad.

5 And when he came, behold, the captains of the host were sitting; and he said, I have an errand to thee, O captain. And Je'hu said, Unto which of all us? And he said, To thee, O captain.

6 And he arose, and went into the house; and he poured the oil on his head, and said unto him, Thus saith the LORD God of Is'ra-el, I have anointed thee king over the people of the LORD, even over Is'ra-el.

7 And thou shalt smite the house of A'hab thy master, that I may avenge the blood of my servants the prophets, and the blood of all the servants of the LORD, at the hand of Jez'e-bel.

8 For the whole house of A'hab shall perish: and I will cut off from A'hab him that pisseth against the wall, and him that is shut up and left in Is'ra-el:

9 And I will make the house of A'hab like the house of Jer-o-bo'am the son of Ne'bat, and like the house of Ba'a-sha the son of A-hi'jah:

10 And the dogs shall eat Jez'e-bel in the portion of Jez're-el, and there shall be none to bury her. And he opened the door, and fled.

11 ¶ Then Je'hu came forth to the servants of his lord: and one said unto him, Is all well? wherefore came this mad fellow to thee? And he said unto them, Ye know the man, and his communication.

12 And they said, It is false; tell us now. And he said, Thus and thus spake he to me, saying, Thus saith the LORD, I have anointed thee king over Is'ra-el.

13 Then they hasted, and took every man his garment, and put it under him on the top of the stairs, and blew with trumpets, saying, Je'hu is king.

14 So Je'hu the son of Je-hosh'a-phat the son of Nim'shi conspired against Jo'ram. (Now Jo'-ram had kept Ra'moth-gil'e-ad, he and all Is'ra-el, because of Haz'a-el king of Syr'i-a.

15 But king Jo'ram was returned to be healed in Jez're-el of the wounds which the Syr'i-ans had given him, when he fought with Haz'a-el king of Syr'i-a.) And Je'hu said, If it be your minds, then let none go forth nor escape out of the city to go to tell it in Jez're-el.

16 So Je'hu rode in a chariot, and went to Jez're-el; for Jo'ram lay there. And A-ha-zi'ah king of Ju'dah was come down to see Jo'ram.

17 And there stood a watchman on the tower in Jez're-el, and he spied the company of Je'hu as he came, and said, I see a company. And Jo'-ram said, Take an horseman, and send to meet them, and let him say, Is it peace?

18 So there went one on horseback to meet him, and said, Thus saith the king, Is it peace? And Je'hu said, What hast thou to do with peace? turn thee behind me. And the watchman

told, saying, The messenger came to them, but he cometh not again.

19 Then he sent out a second on horseback, which came to them, and said, Thus saith the king, Is it peace? And Je'hu answered, What hast thou to do with peace? turn thee behind me.

20 And the watchman told, saying, He came even unto them, and cometh not again: and the driving is like the driving of Je'hu the son of Nim'shi; for he driveth furiously.

21 And Jo'ram said, Make ready. And his chariot was made ready. And Jo'ram king of Is'ra-el and A-ha-zi'ah king of Ju'dah went out, each in his chariot, and they went out against Je'hu, and met him in the portion of Na'both the Jez're-el-ite.

22 And it came to pass, when Jo'ram saw Je'hu, that he said, Is it peace, Je'hu? And he answered, What peace, so long as the whoredoms of thy mother Jez'e-bel and her witchcrafts are so many?

23 And Jo'ram turned his hands, and fled, and said to A-ha-zi'ah, There is treachery, O A-ha-zi'ah.

24 And Je'hu drew a bow with his full strength, and smote Je-ho'ram between his arms, and the arrow went out at his heart, and he sunk down in his chariot.

25 Then said Je'hu to Bid'kar his captain, Take up, and cast him in the portion of the field of Na'both the Jez're-el-ite: for remember how that, when I and thou rode together after A'hab his father, the LORD laid this burden upon him;

26 Surely I have seen yesterday the blood of Na'both, and the blood of his sons, saith the LORD; and I will requite thee in this plat, saith the LORD. Now therefore take and cast him into the plat of ground, according to the word of the LORD.

27 ¶ But when A-ha-zi'ah the king of Ju'dah saw this, he fled by the way of the garden house. And Je'hu followed after him, and said, Smite him also in the chariot. And they did so at the going up to Gur, which is by Ib'le-am. And he fled to Me-gid'do, and died there.

28 And his servants carried him in a chariot to Je-ru'sa-lem, and buried him in his sepulchre with his fathers in the city of Da'vid.

29 And in the eleventh year of Jo'ram the son of A'hab began A-ha-zi'ah to reign over Ju'dah.

30 ¶ And when Je'hu was come to Jez're-el, Jez'e-bel heard of it; and she painted her face, and tired her head, and looked out at a window.

31 And as Je'hu entered in at the gate, she said, Had Zim'ri peace, who slew his master?

32 And he lifted up his face to the window, and said, Who is on my side? who? And there looked out to him two or three eunuchs.

33 And he said, Throw her down. So they threw her down: and some of her blood was sprinkled on the wall, and on the horses: and he trode her under foot.

34 And when he was come in, he did eat and drink, and said, Go, see now this cursed woman, and bury her: for she is a king's daughter.

35 And they went to bury her: but they found no more of her than the skull, and the feet, and the palms of her hands.

36 Wherefore they came again, and told him. And he said, This is the word of the LORD, which he spake by his servant E-li'jah the Tish'bite, saying, In the portion of Jez're-el shall dogs eat the flesh of Jez'e-bel:

37 And the carcase of Jez'e-bel shall be as dung upon the face of the field in the portion of Jez're-el; so that they shall not say, This is Jez'e-bel.

10 AND A'hab had seventy sons in Sa-ma'ri-a. And Je'hu wrote letters, and sent to Sa-ma'ri-a, unto the rulers of Jez're-el, to the elders, and to them that brought up A'hab's children, saying,

2 Now as soon as this letter cometh to you, seeing your master's sons are with you, and there are with you chariots and horses, a fenced city also, and armour;

3 Look even out the best and meetest of your master's sons, and set him on his father's throne, and fight for your master's house.

4 But they were exceedingly afraid, and said, Behold, two kings stood not before him: how then shall we stand?

5 And he that was over the house, and he that was over the city, the elders also, and the bringers up of the children, sent to Je'hu, saying, We are thy servants, and will do all that thou shalt bid us; we will not make any king: do thou that which is good in thine eyes.

6 Then he wrote a letter the second time to them, saying, If ye be mine, and if ye will hearken unto my voice, take ye the heads of the men your master's sons, and come to me to Jez're-el by to morrow this time. Now the king's sons, being seventy persons, were with the great men of the city, which brought them up.

7 And it came to pass, when the letter came to them, that they took the king's sons, and slew seventy persons, and put their heads in baskets, and sent him them to Jez're-el.

8 ¶ And there came a messenger, and told him, saying, They have brought the heads of the king's sons. And he said, Lay ye them in two heaps at the entering in of the gate until the morning.

9 And it came to pass in the morning, that he went out, and stood, and said to all the people, Ye be righteous: behold, I conspired against my master, and slew him: but who slew all these?

10 Know now that there shall fall unto the earth nothing of the word of the LORD, which the LORD spake concerning the house of A'hab: for the LORD hath done that which he spake by his servant E-li'jah.

11 So Je'hu slew all that remained of the house of A'hab in Jez're-el, and all his great men, and his kinsfolks, and his priests, until he left him none remaining.

12 ¶ And he arose and departed, and came to Sa-ma'ri-a. And as he was at the shearing house in the way,

13 Je'hu met with the brethren of A-ha-zi'ah king of Ju'dah, and said, Who are ye? And they answered, We are the brethren of A-ha-zi'ah; and we go down to salute the children of the king and the children of the queen.

14 And he said, Take them alive. And they took them alive, and slew them at the pit of the shearing house, even two and forty men; neither left he any of them.

15 ¶ And when he was departed thence, he lighted on Je-hon'a-dab the son of Re'chab coming to meet him: and he saluted him, and said to him, Is thine heart right, as my heart is with thy heart? And Je-hon'a-dab answered, It is. If it be, give me thine hand. And he gave him his hand; and he took him up to him into the chariot.

16 And he said, Come with me, and see my zeal for the LORD. So they made him ride in his chariot.

17 And when he came to Sa-ma'ri-a, he slew all that remained unto A'hab in Sa-ma'ri-a, till

he had destroyed him, according to the saying of the LORD, which he spake to E-li'jah.

18 ¶ And Je'hu gathered all the people together, and said unto them, A'hab served Ba'al a little; but Je'hu shall serve him much.

19 Now therefore call unto me all the prophets of Ba'al, all his servants, and all his priests; let none be wanting: for I have a great sacrifice to do to Ba'al; whosoever shall be wanting, he shall not live. But Je'hu did it in subtilty, to the intent that he might destroy the worshippers of Ba'al.

20 And Je'hu said, Proclaim a solemn assembly for Ba'al. And they proclaimed it.

21 And Je'hu sent through all Is'ra-el: and all the worshippers of Ba'al came, so that there was not a man left that came not. And they came into the house of Ba'al; and the house of Ba'al was full from one end to another.

22 And he said unto him that was over the vestry, Bring forth vestments for all the worshippers of Ba'al. And he brought them forth vestments.

23 And Je'hu went, and Je-hon'a-dab the son of Re'chab, into the house of Ba'al, and said unto the worshippers of Ba'al, Search, and look that there be here with you none of the servants of the LORD, but the worshippers of Ba'al only.

24 And when they went in to offer sacrifices and burnt offerings, Je'hu appointed fourscore men without, and said, If any of the men whom I have brought into your hands escape, he that letteth him go, his life shall be for the life of him.

25 And it came to pass, as soon as he had made an end of offering the burnt offering, that Je'hu said to the guard and to the captains, Go in, and slay them; let none come forth. And they smote them with the edge of the sword; and the guard and the captains cast them out, and went to the city of the house of Ba'al.

26 And they brought forth the images out of the house of Ba'al, and burned them.

27 And they brake down the image of Ba'al, and brake down the house of Ba'al, and made it a draught house unto this day.

28 Thus Je'hu destroyed Ba'al out of Is'ra-el.

29 ¶ Howbeit from the sins of Jer-o-bo'am the son of Ne'bat, who made Is'ra-el to sin, Je'-hu departed not from after them, to wit, the golden calves that were in Beth'-el, and that were in Dan.

30 And the LORD said unto Je'hu, Because thou hast done well in executing that which is right in mine eyes, and hast done unto the house of A'hab according to all that was in mine heart, thy children of the fourth generation shall sit on the throne of Is'ra-el.

31 But Je'hu took no heed to walk in the law of the LORD God of Is'ra-el with all his heart: for he departed not from the sins of Jer-o-bo'am, which made Is'ra-el to sin.

32 ¶ In those days the LORD began to cut Is'-ra-el short: and Haz'a-el smote them in all the coasts of Is'ra-el;

33 From Jor'dan eastward, all the land of Gil'e-ad, the Gad'ites, and the Reu'ben-ites, and the Ma-nas'sites, from Ar'o-er, which is by the river Ar'non, even Gil'e-ad and Ba'shan.

34 Now the rest of the acts of Je'hu, and all that he did, and all his might, are they not written in the book of the chronicles of the kings of Is'ra-el?

35 And Je'hu slept with his fathers: and they buried him in Sa-ma'ri-a. And Je-ho'a-haz his son reigned in his stead.

36 And the time that Je'hu reigned over Is'ra-el in Sa-ma'ri-a was twenty and eight years.

11 AND when Ath-a-li'ah the mother of A-ha-zi'ah saw that her son was dead, she arose and destroyed all the seed royal.

2 But Je-hosh'e-ba, the daughter of king Jo'ram, sister of A-ha-zi'ah, took Jo'ash the son of A-ha-zi'ah, and stole him from among the king's sons which were slain; and they hid him, even him and his nurse, in the bedchamber from Ath-a-li'ah, so that he was not slain.

3 And he was with her hid in the house of the LORD six years. And Ath-a-li'ah did reign over the land.

4 ¶ And the seventh year Je-hoi'a-da sent and fetched the rulers over hundreds, with the captains and the guard, and brought them to him into the house of the LORD, and made a covenant with them, and took an oath of them in the house of the LORD, and shewed them the king's son.

5 And he commanded them, saying, This is the thing that ye shall do; A third part of you that enter in on the sabbath shall even be keepers of the watch of the king's house;

6 And a third part shall be at the gate of Sur; and a third part at the gate behind the guard: so shall ye keep the watch of the house, that it be not broken down.

7 And two parts of all you that go forth on the sabbath, even they shall keep the watch of the house of the LORD about the king.

8 And ye shall compass the king round about, every man with his weapons in his hand: and he that cometh within the ranges, let him be slain: and be ye with the king as he goeth out and as he cometh in.

9 And the captains over the hundreds did according to all things that Je-hoi'a-da the priest commanded: and they took every man his men that were to come in on the sabbath, with them that should go out on the sabbath, and came to Je-hoi'a-da the priest.

10 And to the captains over hundreds did the priest give king Da'vid's spears and shields, that were in the temple of the LORD.

11 And the guard stood, every man with his weapons in his hand, round about the king, from the right corner of the temple to the left corner of the temple, along by the altar and the temple.

12 And he brought forth the king's son, and put the crown upon him, and gave him the testimony; and they made him king, and anointed him; and they clapped their hands, and said, God save the king.

13 ¶ And when Ath-a-li'ah heard the noise of the guard and of the people, she came to the people into the temple of the LORD.

14 And when she looked, behold, the king stood by a pillar, as the manner was, and the princes and the trumpeters by the king, and all the people of the land rejoiced, and blew with trumpets: and Ath-a-li'ah rent her clothes, and cried, Treason, Treason.

15 But Je-hoi'a-da the priest commanded the captains of the hundreds, the officers of the host, and said unto them, Have her forth without the ranges: and him that followeth her kill with the sword. For the priest had said, Let her not be slain in the house of the LORD.

16 And they laid hands on her; and she went by the way by the which the horses came into the king's house: and there was she slain.

17 ¶ And Je-hoi'a-da made a covenant between the LORD and the king and the people,

that they should be the LORD's people; between the king also and the people.

18 And all the people of the land went into the house of Ba'al, and brake it down; his altars and his images brake they in pieces thoroughly, and slew Mat'tan the priest of Ba'al before the altars. And the priest appointed officers over the house of the LORD.

19 And he took the rulers over hundreds, and the captains, and the guard, and all the people of the land; and they brought down the king from the house of the LORD, and came by the way of the gate of the guard to the king's house. And he sat on the throne of the kings.

20 And all the people of the land rejoiced, and the city was in quiet: and they slew Ath-a-li'ah with the sword *beside* the king's house.

21 Seven years old *was* Je-ho'ash when he began to reign.

12 IN the seventh year of Je'hu Je-ho'ash began to reign; and forty years reigned he in Je-ru'sa-lem. And his mother's name *was* Zib'i-ah of Be'er-she'ba.

2 And Je-ho'ash did *that which was* right in the sight of the LORD all his days wherein Je-hoi'a-da the priest instructed him.

3 But the high places were not taken away: the people still sacrificed and burnt incense in the high places.

4 ¶ And Je-ho'ash said to the priests, All the money of the dedicated things that is brought into the house of the LORD, *even* the money of every one that passeth *the account*, the money that every man is set at, *and* all the money that cometh into any man's heart to bring into the house of the LORD,

5 Let the priests take *it* to them, every man of his acquaintance: and let them repair the breaches of the house, wheresoever any breach shall be found.

6 But it was *so, that* in the three and twentieth year of king Je-ho'ash the priests had not repaired the breaches of the house.

7 Then king Je-ho'ash called for Je-hoi'a-da the priest, and the *other* priests, and said unto them, Why repair ye not the breaches of the house? now therefore receive no *more* money of your acquaintance, but deliver it for the breaches of the house.

8 And the priests consented to receive no *more* money of the people, neither to repair the breaches of the house.

9 But Je-hoi'a-da the priest took a chest, and bored a hole in the lid of it, and set it beside the altar, on the right side as one cometh into the house of the LORD: and the priests that kept the door put therein all the money *that was* brought into the house of the LORD.

10 And it was *so*, when they saw that *there was* much money in the chest, that the king's scribe and the high priest came up, and they put up in bags, and told the money that was found in the house of the LORD.

11 And they gave the money, being told, into the hands of them that did the work, that had the oversight of the house of the LORD: and they laid it out to the carpenters and builders, that wrought upon the house of the LORD,

12 And to masons, and hewers of stone, and to buy timber and hewed stone to repair the breaches of the house of the LORD, and for all that was laid out for the house to repair *it*.

13 Howbeit there were not made for the house of the LORD bowls of silver, snuffers, basons, trumpets, any vessels of gold, or vessels of silver, of the money *that was* brought into the house of the LORD:

14 But they gave that to the workmen, and repaired therewith the house of the LORD.

15 Moreover they reckoned not with the men, into whose hand they delivered the money to be bestowed on workmen: for they dealt faithfully.

16 The trespass money and sin money was not brought into the house of the LORD: it was the priests'.

17 ¶ Then Haz'a-el king of Syr'i-a went up, and fought against Gath, and took it: and Haz'a-el set his face to go up to Je-ru'sa-lem.

18 And Je-ho'ash king of Ju'dah took all the hallowed things that Je-hosh'a-phat, and Je-ho'-ram, and A-ha-zi'ah, his fathers, kings of Ju'-dah, had dedicated, and his own hallowed things, and all the gold *that was* found in the treasures of the house of the LORD, and in the king's house, and sent *it* to Haz'a-el king of Syr'i-a: and he went away from Je-ru'sa-lem.

19 ¶ And the rest of the acts of Jo'ash, and all that he did, *are* they not written in the book of the chronicles of the kings of Ju'dah?

20 And his servants arose, and made a conspiracy, and slew Jo'ash in the house of Mil'lo, which goeth down to Sil'la.

21 For Joz'a-char the son of Shim'e-ath, and Je-hoz'a-bad the son of Sho'mer, his servants, smote him, and he died; and they buried him with his fathers in the city of Da'vid: and Am-a-zi'ah his son reigned in his stead.

13 IN the three and twentieth year of Jo'-ash the son of A-ha-zi'ah king of Ju'dah Je-ho'a-haz the son of Je'hu began to reign over Is'ra-el in Sa-ma'ri-a, *and reigned* seventeen years.

2 And he did *that which was* evil in the sight of the LORD, and followed the sins of Jer-o-bo'-am the son of Ne'bat, which made Is'ra-el to sin; he departed not therefrom.

3 ¶ And the anger of the LORD was kindled against Is'ra-el, and he delivered them into the hand of Haz'a-el king of Syr'i-a, and into the hand of Ben-ha'dad the son of Haz'a-el, all *their* days.

4 And Je-ho'a-haz besought the LORD, and the LORD hearkened unto him: for he saw the oppression of Is'ra-el, because the king of Syr'i-a oppressed them.

5 (And the LORD gave Is'ra-el a saviour, so that they went out from under the hand of the Syr'i-ans: and the children of Is'ra-el dwelt in their tents, as beforetime.

6 Nevertheless they departed not from the sins of the house of Jer-o-bo'am, who made Is'-ra-el sin, *but* walked therein: and there remained the grove also in Sa-ma'ri-a.)

7 Neither did he leave of the people to Je-ho'a-haz but fifty horsemen, and ten chariots, and ten thousand footmen; for the king of Syr'i-a had destroyed them, and had made them like the dust by threshing.

8 ¶ Now the rest of the acts of Je-ho'a-haz, and all that he did, and his might, *are* they not written in the book of the chronicles of the kings of Is'ra-el?

9 And Je-ho'a-haz slept with his fathers; and they buried him in Sa-ma'ri-a: and Jo'ash his son reigned in his stead.

10 ¶ In the thirty and seventh year of Jo'ash king of Ju'dah began Je-ho'ash the son of Je-ho'a-haz to reign over Is'ra-el in Sa-ma'ri-a, *and reigned* sixteen years.

11 And he did *that which was* evil in the

sight of the LORD; he departed not from all the sins of Jer-o-bo'am the son of Ne'bat, who made Is'ra-el sin: but he walked therein.

12 And the rest of the acts of Jo'ash, and all that he did, and his might wherewith he fought against Am-a-zi'ah king of Ju'dah, are they not written in the book of the chronicles of the kings of Is'ra-el?

13 And Jo'ash slept with his fathers; and Jer-o-bo'am sat upon his throne: and Jo'ash was buried in Sa-ma'ri-a with the kings of Is'ra-el.

14 ¶ Now E-li'sha was fallen sick of his sickness whereof he died. And Jo'ash the king of Is'ra-el came down unto him, and wept over his face, and said, O my father, my father, the chariot of Is'ra-el, and the horsemen thereof.

15 And E-li'sha said unto him, Take bow and arrows. And he took unto him bow and arrows.

16 And he said to the king of Is'ra-el, Put thine hand upon the bow. And he put his hand upon it: and E-li'sha put his hands upon the king's hands.

17 And he said, Open the window eastward. And he opened it. Then E-li'sha said, Shoot. And he shot. And he said, The arrow of the LORD's deliverance, and the arrow of deliverance from Syr'i-a: for thou shalt smite the Syr'i-ans in A'phek, till thou have consumed them.

18 And he said, Take the arrows. And he took them. And he said unto the king of Is'ra-el, Smite upon the ground. And he smote thrice, and stayed.

19 And the man of God was wroth with him, and said, Thou shouldest have smitten five or six times; then hadst thou smitten Syr'i-a till thou hadst consumed it: whereas now thou shalt smite Syr'i-a but thrice.

20 ¶ And E-li'sha died, and they buried him. And the bands of the Mo'ab-ites invaded the land at the coming in of the year.

21 And it came to pass, as they were burying a man, that, behold, they spied a band of men; and they cast the man into the sepulchre of E-li'sha: and when the man was let down, and touched the bones of E-li'sha, he revived, and stood up on his feet.

22 ¶ But Haz'a-el king of Syr'i-a oppressed Is'ra-el all the days of Je-ho'a-haz.

23 And the LORD was gracious unto them, and had compassion on them, and had respect unto them, because of his covenant with A'bra-ham, I'saac, and Ja'cob, and would not destroy them, neither cast he them from his presence as yet.

24 So Haz'a-el king of Syr'i-a died; and Ben-ha'dad his son reigned in his stead.

25 And Je-ho'ash the son of Je-ho'a-haz took again out of the hand of Ben-ha'dad the son of Haz'a-el the cities, which he had taken out of the hand of Je-ho'a-haz his father by war. Three times did Jo'ash beat him, and recovered the cities of Is'ra-el.

14

IN the second year of Jo'ash son of Je-ho'a-haz king of Is'ra-el reigned Am-a-zi'ah the son of Jo'ash king of Ju'dah.

2 He was twenty and five years old when he began to reign, and reigned twenty and nine years in Je-ru'sa-lem. And his mother's name was Je-ho-ad'dan of Je-ru'sa-lem.

3 And he did that which was right in the sight of the LORD, yet not like Da'vid his father: he did according to all things as Jo'ash his father did.

4 Howbeit the high places were not taken away: as yet the people did sacrifice and burnt incense on the high places.

5 ¶ And it came to pass, as soon as the kingdom was confirmed in his hand, that he slew his servants which had slain the king his father.

6 But the children of the murderers he slew not: according to that which is written in the book of the law of Mo'ses, wherein the LORD commanded, saying, The fathers shall not be put to death for the children, nor the children be put to death for the fathers; but every man shall be put to death for his own sin.

7 He slew of E'dom in the valley of salt ten thousand, and took Se'lah by war, and called the name of it Jok'the-el unto this day.

8 ¶ Then Am-a-zi'ah sent messengers to Je-ho'ash, the son of Je-ho'a-haz son of Je'hu, king of Is'ra-el, saying, Come, let us look one another in the face.

9 And Je-ho'ash the king of Is'ra-el sent to Am-a-zi'ah king of Ju'dah, saying, The thistle that was in Leb'a-non sent to the cedar that was in Leb'a-non, saying, Give thy daughter to my son to wife: and there passed by a wild beast that was in Leb'a-non, and trode down the thistle.

10 Thou hast indeed smitten E'dom, and thine heart hath lifted thee up: glory of this, and tarry at home: for why shouldest thou meddle to thy hurt, that thou shouldest fall, even thou, and Ju'dah with thee?

11 But Am-a-zi'ah would not hear. Therefore Je-ho'ash king of Is'ra-el went up; and he and Am-a-zi'ah king of Ju'dah looked one another in the face at Beth–she'mesh, which belongeth to Ju'dah.

12 And Ju'dah was put to the worse before Is'ra-el; and they fled every man to their tents.

13 And Je-ho'ash king of Is'ra-el took Am-a-zi'ah king of Ju'dah, the son of Je-ho'ash the son of A-ha-zi'ah, at Beth–she'mesh, and came to Je-ru'sa-lem, and brake down the wall of Je-ru'-sa-lem from the gate of E'phra-im unto the corner gate, four hundred cubits.

14 And he took all the gold and silver, and all the vessels that were found in the house of the LORD, and in the treasures of the king's house, and hostages, and returned to Sa-ma'ri-a.

15 ¶ Now the rest of the acts of Je-ho'ash which he did, and his might, and how he fought with Am-a-zi'ah king of Ju'dah, are they not written in the book of the chronicles of the kings of Is'ra-el?

16 And Je-ho'ash slept with his fathers, and was buried in Sa-ma'ri-a with the kings of Is'ra-el; and Jer-o-bo'am his son reigned in his stead.

17 ¶ And Am-a-zi'ah the son of Jo'ash king of Ju'dah lived after the death of Je-ho'ash son of Je-ho'a-haz king of Is'ra-el fifteen years.

18 And the rest of the acts of Am-a-zi'ah, are they not written in the book of the chronicles of the kings of Ju'dah?

19 Now they made a conspiracy against him in Je-ru'sa-lem: and he fled to La'chish; but they sent after him to La'chish, and slew him there.

20 And they brought him on horses: and he was buried at Je-ru'sa-lem with his fathers in the city of Da'vid.

21 ¶ And all the people of Ju'dah took Az-a-ri'ah, which was sixteen years old, and made him king instead of his father Am-a-zi'ah.

22 He built E'lath, and restored it to Ju'dah, after that the king slept with his fathers.

23 ¶ In the fifteenth year of Am-a-zi'ah the son of Jo'ash king of Ju'dah Jer-o-bo'am the son of Jo'ash king of Is'ra-el began to reign in Sa-ma'ri-a, and reigned forty and one years.

24 And he did that which was evil in the sight of the LORD: he departed not from all the

sins of Jer-o-bo'am the son of Ne'bat, who made Is'ra-el to sin.

25 He restored the coast of Is'ra-el from the entering of Ha'math unto the sea of the plain, according to the word of the LORD God of Is'ra-el, which he spake by the hand of his servant Jo'nah, the son of A-mit'ta-i, the prophet, which was of Gath-he'pher.

26 For the LORD saw the affliction of Is'ra-el, that it was very bitter: for there was not any shut up, nor any left, nor any helper for Is'ra-el.

27 And the LORD said not that he would blot out the name of Is'ra-el from under heaven: but he saved them by the hand of Jer-o-bo'am the son of Jo'ash.

28 ¶ Now the rest of the acts of Jer-o-bo'am, and all that he did, and his might, how he warred, and how he recovered Da-mas'cus, and Ha'math, which belonged to Ju'dah, for Is'ra-el, are they not written in the book of the chronicles of the kings of Is'ra-el?

29 And Jer-o-bo'am slept with his fathers, even with the kings of Is'ra-el; and Zach-a-ri'ah his son reigned in his stead.

15 IN the twenty and seventh year of Jer-o-bo'am king of Is'ra-el began Az-a-ri'ah son of Am-a-zi'ah king of Ju'dah to reign.

2 Sixteen years old was he when he began to reign, and he reigned two and fifty years in Je-ru'sa-lem. And his mother's name was Jech-o-li'ah of Je-ru'sa-lem.

3 And he did that which was right in the sight of the LORD, according to all that his father Am-a-zi'ah had done;

4 Save that the high places were not removed: the people sacrificed and burnt incense still on the high places.

5 ¶ And the LORD smote the king, so that he was a leper unto the day of his death, and dwelt in a several house. And Jo'tham the king's son was over the house, judging the people of the land.

6 And the rest of the acts of Az-a-ri'ah, and all that he did, are they not written in the book of the chronicles of the kings of Ju'dah?

7 So Az-a-ri'ah slept with his fathers; and they buried him with his fathers in the city of Da'vid: and Jo'tham his son reigned in his stead.

8 ¶ In the thirty and eighth year of Az-a-ri'ah king of Ju'dah did Zach-a-ri'ah the son of Jer-o-bo'am reign over Is'ra-el in Sa-ma'ri-a six months.

9 And he did that which was evil in the sight of the LORD, as his fathers had done: he departed not from the sins of Jer-o-bo'am the son of Ne'bat, who made Is'ra-el to sin.

10 And Shal'lum the son of Ja'besh conspired against him, and smote him before the people, and slew him, and reigned in his stead.

11 And the rest of the acts of Zach-a-ri'ah, behold, they are written in the book of the chronicles of the kings of Is'ra-el.

12 This was the word of the LORD which he spake unto Je'hu, saying, Thy sons shall sit on the throne of Is'ra-el unto the fourth generation. And so it came to pass.

13 ¶ Shal'lum the son of Ja'besh began to reign in the nine and thirtieth year of Uz-zi'ah king of Ju'dah; and he reigned a full month in Sa-ma'ri-a.

14 For Men'a-hem the son of Ga'di went up from Tir'zah, and came to Sa-ma'ri-a, and smote Shal'lum the son of Ja'besh in Sa-ma'ri-a, and slew him, and reigned in his stead.

15 And the rest of the acts of Shal'lum, and his conspiracy which he made, behold, they are written in the book of the chronicles of the kings of Is'ra-el.

16 ¶ Then Men'a-hem smote Tiph'sah, and all that were therein, and the coasts thereof from Tir'zah: because they opened not to him, therefore he smote it: and all the women therein that were with child he ripped up.

17 In the nine and thirtieth year of Az-a-ri'ah king of Ju'dah began Men'a-hem the son of Ga'di to reign over Is'ra-el, and reigned ten years in Sa-ma'ri-a.

18 And he did that which was evil in the sight of the LORD: he departed not all his days from the sins of Jer-o-bo'am the son of Ne'bat, who made Is'ra-el to sin.

19 And Pul the king of As-syr'i-a came against the land: and Men'a-hem gave Pul a thousand talents of silver, that his hand might be with him to confirm the kingdom in his hand.

20 And Men'a-hem exacted the money of Is'-ra-el, even of all the mighty men of wealth, of each man fifty shekels of silver, to give to the king of As-syr'i-a. So the king of As-syr'i-a turned back, and stayed not there in the land.

21 ¶ And the rest of the acts of Men'a-hem, and all that he did, are they not written in the book of the chronicles of the kings of Is'ra-el?

22 And Men'a-hem slept with his fathers; and Pek-a-hi'ah his son reigned in his stead.

23 ¶ In the fiftieth year of Az-a-ri'ah king of Ju'dah Pek-a-hi'ah the son of Men'a-hem began to reign over Is'ra-el in Sa-ma'ri-a, and reigned two years.

24 And he did that which was evil in the sight of the LORD: he departed not from the sins of Jer-o-bo'am the son of Ne'bat, who made Is'-ra-el to sin.

25 But Pe'kah the son of Rem-a-li'ah, a captain of his, conspired against him, and smote him in Sa-ma'ri-a, in the palace of the king's house, with Ar'gob and A-ri'eh, and with him fifty men of the Gil'e-ad-ites: and he killed him, and reigned in his room.

26 And the rest of the acts of Pek-a-hi'ah, and all that he did, behold, they are written in the book of the chronicles of the kings of Is'ra-el.

27 ¶ In the two and fiftieth year of Az-a-ri'ah king of Ju'dah Pe'kah the son of Rem-a-li'ah began to reign over Is'ra-el in Sa-ma'ri-a, and reigned twenty years.

28 And he did that which was evil in the sight of the LORD: he departed not from the sins of Jer-o-bo'am the son of Ne'bat, who made Is'-ra-el to sin.

29 In the days of Pe'kah king of Is'ra-el came Tig'lath-pi-le'ser king of As-syr'i-a, and took I'-jon, and A'bel-beth-ma'a-chah, and Ja-no'ah, and Ke'desh, and Ha'zor, and Gil'e-ad, and Gal'-i-lee, all the land of Naph'ta-li, and carried them captive to As-syr'i-a.

30 And Ho-she'a the son of E'lah made a conspiracy against Pe'kah the son of Rem-a-li'ah, and smote him, and slew him, and reigned in his stead, in the twentieth year of Jo'tham the son of Uz-zi'ah.

31 And the rest of the acts of Pe'kah, and all that he did, behold, they are written in the book of the chronicles of the kings of Is'ra-el.

32 ¶ In the second year of Pe'kah the son of Rem-a-li'ah king of Is'ra-el began Jo'tham the son of Uz-zi'ah king of Ju'dah to reign.

33 Five and twenty years old was he when he began to reign, and he reigned sixteen years in Je-ru'sa-lem. And his mother's name was Je-ru'sha, the daughter of Za'dok.

34 And he did that which was right in the

sight of the LORD: he did according to all that his father Uz-zi′ah had done.

35 ¶ Howbeit the high places were not removed: the people sacrificed and burned incense still in the high places. He built the higher gate of the house of the LORD.

36 ¶ Now the rest of the acts of Jo′tham, and all that he did, *are* they not written in the book of the chronicles of the kings of Ju′dah?

37 In those days the LORD began to send against Ju′dah Re′zin the king of Syr′i-a, and Pe′kah the son of Rem-a-li′ah.

38 And Jo′tham slept with his fathers, and was buried with his fathers in the city of Da′vid his father: and A′haz his son reigned in his stead.

16 IN the seventeenth year of Pe′kah the son of Rem-a-li′ah A′haz the son of Jo′tham king of Ju′dah began to reign.

2 Twenty years old *was* A′haz when he began to reign, and reigned sixteen years in Je-ru′sa-lem, and did not *that which was* right in the sight of the LORD his God, like Da′vid his father.

3 But he walked in the way of the kings of Is′ra-el, yea, and made his son to pass through the fire, according to the abominations of the heathen, whom the LORD cast out from before the children of Is′ra-el.

4 And he sacrificed and burnt incense in the high places, and on the hills, and under every green tree.

5 ¶ Then Re′zin king of Syr′i-a and Pe′kah son of Rem-a-li′ah king of Is′ra-el came up to Je-ru′sa-lem to war: and they besieged A′haz, but could not overcome *him.*

6 At that time Re′zin king of Syr′i-a recovered E′lath to Syr′i-a, and drave the Jews from E′lath: and the Syr′i-ans came to E′lath, and dwelt there unto this day.

7 So A′haz sent messengers to Tig′lath-pi-le′ser king of As-syr′i-a, saying, I *am* thy servant and thy son: come up, and save me out of the hand of the king of Syr′i-a, and out of the hand of the king of Is′ra-el, which rise up against me.

8 And A′haz took the silver and gold that was found in the house of the LORD, and in the treasures of the king's house, and sent *it for* a present to the king of As-syr′i-a.

9 And the king of As-syr′i-a hearkened unto him: for the king of As-syr′i-a went up against Da-mas′cus, and took it, and carried *the people of* it captive to Kir, and slew Re′zin.

10 ¶ And king A′haz went to Da-mas′cus to meet Tig′lath-pi-le′ser king of As-syr′i-a, and saw an altar that *was* at Da-mas′cus: and king A′haz sent to U-ri′jah the priest the fashion of the altar, and the pattern of it, according to all the workmanship thereof.

11 And U-ri′jah the priest built an altar according to all that king A′haz had sent from Da-mas′cus: so U-ri′jah the priest made *it* against king A′haz came from Da-mas′cus.

12 And when the king was come from Da-mas′cus, the king saw the altar: and the king approached to the altar, and offered thereon.

13 And he burnt his burnt offering and his meat offering, and poured his drink offering, and sprinkled the blood of his peace offerings, upon the altar.

14 And he brought also the brasen altar, which *was* before the LORD, from the forefront of the house, from between the altar and the house of the LORD, and put it on the north side of the altar.

15 And king A′haz commanded U-ri′jah the priest, saying, Upon the great altar burn the morning burnt offering, and the evening meat offering, and the king's burnt sacrifice, and his meat offering, with the burnt offering of all the people of the land, and their meat offering, and their drink offerings; and sprinkle upon it all the blood of the burnt offering, and all the blood of the sacrifice: and the brasen altar shall be for me to enquire *by.*

16 Thus did U-ri′jah the priest, according to all that king A′haz commanded.

17 ¶ And king A′haz cut off the borders of the bases, and removed the laver from off them; and took down the sea from off the brasen oxen that *were* under it, and put it upon a pavement of stones.

18 And the covert for the sabbath that they had built in the house, and the king's entry without, turned he from the house of the LORD for the king of As-syr′i-a.

19 ¶ Now the rest of the acts of A′haz which he did, *are* they not written in the book of the chronicles of the kings of Ju′dah?

20 And A′haz slept with his fathers, and was buried with his fathers in the city of Da′vid: and Hez-e-ki′ah his son reigned in his stead.

17 IN the twelfth year of A′haz king of Ju′dah began Ho-she′a the son of E′lah to reign in Sa-ma′ri-a over Is′ra-el nine years.

2 And he did *that which was* evil in the sight of the LORD, but not as the kings of Is′ra-el that were before him.

3 ¶ Against him came up Shal-man-e′ser king of As-syr′i-a; and Ho-she′a became his servant, and gave him presents.

4 And the king of As-syr′i-a found conspiracy in Ho-she′a: for he had sent messengers to So king of E′gypt, and brought no present to the king of As-syr′i-a, as *he had done* year by year: therefore the king of As-syr′i-a shut him up, and bound him in prison.

5 ¶ Then the king of As-syr′i-a came up throughout all the land, and went up to Sa-ma′ri-a, and besieged it three years.

6 ¶ In the ninth year of Ho-she′a the king of As-syr′i-a took Sa-ma′ri-a, and carried Is′ra-el away into As-syr′i-a, and placed them in Ha′lah and in Ha′bor *by* the river of Go′zan, and in the cities of the Medes.

7 For *so* it was, that the children of Is′ra-el had sinned against the LORD their God, which had brought them up out of the land of E′gypt, from under the hand of Pha′raoh king of E′gypt, and had feared other gods,

8 And had walked in the statutes of the heathen, whom the LORD cast out from before the children of Is′ra-el, and of the kings of Is′ra-el, which they had made.

9 And the children of Is′ra-el did secretly *those* things that *were* not right against the LORD their God, and they built them high places in all their cities, from the tower of the watchmen to the fenced city.

10 And they set them up images and groves in every high hill, and under every green tree:

11 And there they burnt incense in all the high places, as *did* the heathen whom the LORD carried away before them; and wrought wicked things to provoke the LORD to anger:

12 For they served idols, whereof the LORD had said unto them, Ye shall not do this thing.

13 Yet the LORD testified against Is′ra-el, and against Ju′dah, by all the prophets, *and by* all the seers, saying, Turn ye from your evil ways, and keep my commandments *and* my statutes,

according to all the law which I commanded your fathers, and which I sent to you by my servants the prophets.

14 Notwithstanding they would not hear, but hardened their necks, like to the neck of their fathers, that did not believe in the LORD their God.

15 And they rejected his statutes, and his covenant that he made with their fathers, and his testimonies which he testified against them; and they followed vanity, and became vain, and went after the heathen that *were* round about them, *concerning* whom the LORD had charged them, that they should not do like them.

16 And they left all the commandments of the LORD their God, and made them molten images, *even* two calves, and made a grove, and worshipped all the host of heaven, and served Ba'al.

17 And they caused their sons and their daughters to pass through the fire, and used divination and enchantments, and sold themselves to do evil in the sight of the LORD, to provoke him to anger.

18 Therefore the LORD was very angry with Is'ra-el, and removed them out of his sight: there was none left but the tribe of Ju'dah only.

19 Also Ju'dah kept not the commandments of the LORD their God, but walked in the statutes of Is'ra-el which they made.

20 And the LORD rejected all the seed of Is'ra-el, and afflicted them, and delivered them into the hand of spoilers, until he had cast them out of his sight.

21 For he rent Is'ra-el from the house of Da'vid; and they made Jer-o-bo'am the son of Ne'bat king: and Jer-o-bo'am drave Is'ra-el from following the LORD, and made them sin a great sin.

22 For the children of Is'ra-el walked in all the sins of Jer-o-bo'am which he did; they departed not from them;

23 Until the LORD removed Is'ra-el out of his sight, as he had said by all his servants the prophets. So was Is'ra-el carried away out of their own land to As-syr'i-a unto this day.

24 ¶ And the king of As-syr'i-a brought *men* from Bab'y-lon, and from Cu'thah, and from A'va, and from Ha'math, and from Seph-ar-va'im, and placed *them* in the cities of Sa-ma'ri-a instead of the children of Is'ra-el: and they possessed Sa-ma'ri-a, and dwelt in the cities thereof.

25 And *so* it was at the beginning of their dwelling there, *that* they feared not the LORD: therefore the LORD sent lions among them, which slew *some* of them.

26 Wherefore they spake to the king of As-syr'i-a, saying, The nations which thou hast removed, and placed in the cities of Sa-ma'ri-a, know not the manner of the God of the land: therefore he hath sent lions among them, and, behold, they slay them, because they know not the manner of the God of the land.

27 Then the king of As-syr'i-a commanded, saying, Carry thither one of the priests whom ye brought from thence; and let them go and dwell there, and let him teach them the manner of the God of the land.

28 Then one of the priests whom they had carried away from Sa-ma'ri-a came and dwelt in Beth'-el, and taught them how they should fear the LORD.

29 Howbeit every nation made gods of their own, and put *them* in the houses of the high places which the Sa-mar'i-tans had made, every nation in their cities wherein they dwelt.

30 And the men of Bab'y-lon made Suc'coth-be'noth, and the men of Cuth made Ner'gal, and the men of Ha'math made Ash'i-ma,

31 And the A'vites made Nib'haz and Tar'tak, and the Seph'ar-vites burnt their children in fire to A-dram'me-lech and A-nam'me-lech, the gods of Seph-ar-va'im.

32 So they feared the LORD, and made unto themselves of the lowest of them priests of the high places, which sacrificed for them in the houses of the high places.

33 They feared the LORD, and served their own gods, after the manner of the nations whom they carried away from thence.

34 Unto this day they do after the former manners: they fear not the LORD, neither do they after their statutes, or after their ordinances, or after the law and commandment which the LORD commanded the children of Ja'cob, whom he named Is'ra-el;

35 With whom the LORD had made a covenant, and charged them, saying, Ye shall not fear other gods, nor bow yourselves to them, nor serve them, nor sacrifice to them:

36 But the LORD, who brought you up out of the land of E'gypt with great power and a stretched out arm, him shall ye fear, and him shall ye worship, and to him shall ye do sacrifice.

37 And the statutes, and the ordinances, and the law, and the commandment, which he wrote for you, ye shall observe to do for evermore; and ye shall not fear other gods.

38 And the covenant that I have made with you ye shall not forget; neither shall ye fear other gods.

39 But the LORD your God ye shall fear; and he shall deliver you out of the hand of all your enemies.

40 Howbeit they did not hearken, but they did after their former manner.

41 So these nations feared the LORD, and served their graven images, both their children, and their children's children: as did their fathers, so do they unto this day.

18 NOW it came to pass in the third year of Ho-she'a son of E'lah king of Is'ra-el, *that* Hez-e-ki'ah the son of A'haz king of Ju'dah began to reign.

2 Twenty and five years old was he when he began to reign; and he reigned twenty and nine years in Je-ru'sa-lem. His mother's name also *was* A'bi, the daughter of Zach-a-ri'ah.

3 And he did *that which was* right in the sight of the LORD, according to all that Da'vid his father did.

4 ¶ He removed the high places, and brake the images, and cut down the groves, and brake in pieces the brasen serpent that Mo'ses had made: for unto those days the children of Is'ra-el did burn incense to it: and he ·called it Ne-hush'tan.

5 He trusted in the LORD God of Is'ra-el; so that after him was none like him among all the kings of Ju'dah, nor *any* that were before him.

6 For he clave to the LORD, *and* departed not from following him, but kept his commandments, which the LORD commanded Mo'ses.

7 And the LORD was with him; *and* he prospered whithersoever he went forth: and he rebelled against the king of As-syr'i-a, and served him not.

8 He smote the Phi-lis'tines, *even* unto Ga'za, and the borders thereof, from the tower of the watchmen to the fenced city.

9 ¶ And it came to pass in the fourth year of

king Hez-e-ki'ah, which *was* the seventh year of Ho-she'a son of E'lah king of Is'ra-el, *that* Shal-man-e'ser king of As-syr'i-a came up against Sa-ma'ri-a, and besieged it.

10 And at the end of three years they took it: *even* in the sixth year of Hez-e-ki'ah, that *is* the ninth year of Ho-she'a king of Is'ra-el, Sa-ma'ri-a was taken.

11 And the king of As-syr'i-a did carry away Is'ra-el unto As-syr'i-a, and put them in Ha'lah and in Ha'bor *by* the river of Go'zan, and in the cities of the Medes:

12 Because they obeyed not the voice of the LORD their God, but transgressed his covenant, *and* all that Mo'ses the servant of the LORD commanded, and would not hear *them,* nor do *them.*

13 ¶ Now in the fourteenth year of king Hez-e-ki'ah did Sen-nach'e-rib king of As-syr'i-a come up against all the fenced cities of Ju'dah, and took them.

14 And Hez-e-ki'ah king of Ju'dah sent to the king of As-syr'i-a to La'chish, saying, I have offended; return from me: that which thou puttest on me will I bear. And the king of As-syr'i-a appointed unto Hez-e-ki'ah king of Ju'dah three hundred talents of silver and thirty talents of gold.

15 And Hez-e-ki'ah gave *him* all the silver that was found in the house of the LORD, and in the treasures of the king's house.

16 At that time did Hez-e-ki'ah cut off *the* gold *from* the doors of the temple of the LORD, and *from* the pillars which Hez-e-ki'ah king of Ju'dah had overlaid, and gave it to the king of As-syr'i-a.

17 ¶ And the king of As-syr'i-a sent Tar'tan and Rab'sa-ris and Rab'-sha-keh from La'chish to king Hez-e-ki'ah with a great host against Je-ru'sa-lem. And they went up and came to Je-ru'sa-lem. And when they were come up, they came and stood by the conduit of the upper pool, which *is* in the highway of the fuller's field.

18 And when they had called to the king, there came out to them E-li'a-kim the son of Hil-ki'ah, which *was* over the household, and Sheb'na the scribe, and Jo'ah the son of A'saph the recorder.

19 And Rab'-sha-keh said unto them, Speak ye now to Hez-e-ki'ah, Thus saith the great king, the king of As-syr'i-a, What confidence *is* this wherein thou trustest?

20 Thou sayest, (but *they are but* vain words,) *I have* counsel and strength for the war. Now on whom dost thou trust, that thou rebellest against me?

21 Now, behold, thou trustest upon the staff of this bruised reed, *even* upon E'gypt, on which if a man lean, it will go into his hand, and pierce it: so *is* Pha'raoh king of E'gypt unto all that trust on him.

22 But if ye say unto me, We trust in the LORD our God: *is* not that he, whose high places and whose altars Hez-e-ki'ah hath taken away, and hath said to Ju'dah and Je-ru'sa-lem, Ye shall worship before this altar in Je-ru'sa-lem?

23 Now therefore, I pray thee, give pledges to my lord the king of As-syr'i-a, and I will deliver thee two thousand horses, if thou be able on thy part to set riders upon them.

24 How then wilt thou turn away the face of one captain of the least of my master's servants, and put thy trust on E'gypt for chariots and for horsemen?

25 Am I now come up without the LORD against this place to destroy it? The LORD said

to me, Go up against this land, and destroy it.

26 Then said E-li'a-kim the son of Hil-ki'ah, and Sheb'na, and Jo'ah, unto Rab'-sha-keh, Speak, I pray thee, to thy servants in the Syr'i-an language; for we understand *it:* and talk not with us in the Jews' language in the ears of the people that *are* on the wall.

27 But Rab'-sha-keh said unto them, Hath my master sent me to thy master, and to thee, to speak these words? *hath he* not *sent me* to the men which sit on the wall, that they may eat their own dung, and drink their own piss with you?

28 Then Rab'-sha-keh stood and cried with a loud voice in the Jews' language, and spake, saying, Hear the word of the great king, the king of As-syr'i-a:

29 Thus saith the king, Let not Hez-e-ki'ah deceive you: for he shall not be able to deliver you out of his hand:

30 Neither let Hez-e-ki'ah make you trust in the LORD, saying, The LORD will surely deliver us, and this city shall not be delivered into the hand of the king of As-syr'i-a.

31 Hearken not to Hez-e-ki'ah: for thus saith the king of As-syr'i-a, Make *an agreement* with me by a present, and come out to me, and *then* eat ye every man of his own vine, and every one of his fig tree, and drink ye every one the waters of his cistern:

32 Until I come and take you away to a land like your own land, a land of corn and wine, a land of bread and vineyards, a land of oil olive and of honey, that ye may live, and not die: and hearken not unto Hez-e-ki'ah, when he persuadeth you, saying, The LORD will deliver us.

33 Hath any of the gods of the nations delivered at all his land out of the hand of the king of As-syr'i-a?

34 Where *are* the gods of Ha'math, and of Ar'pad? where *are* the gods of Seph-ar-va'im, He'na, and I'vah? have they delivered Sa-ma'ri-a out of mine hand?

35 Who *are* they among all the gods of the countries, that have delivered their country out of mine hand, that the LORD should deliver Je-ru'sa-lem out of mine hand?

36 But the people held their peace, and answered him not a word: for the king's commandment was, saying, Answer him not.

37 Then came E-li'a-kim the son of Hil-ki'ah, which *was* over the household, and Sheb'na the scribe, and Jo'ah the son of A'saph the recorder, to Hez-e-ki'ah with *their* clothes rent, and told him the words of Rab'-sha-keh.

19 AND it came to pass, when king Hez-e-ki'ah heard *it,* that he rent his clothes, and covered himself with sackcloth, and went into the house of the LORD.

2 And he sent E-li'a-kim, which *was* over the household, and Sheb'na the scribe, and the elders of the priests, covered with sackcloth, to I-sa'iah the prophet the son of A'moz.

3 And they said unto him, Thus saith Hez-e-ki'ah, This day *is* a day of trouble, and of rebuke, and blasphemy: for the children are come to the birth, and *there is* not strength to bring forth.

4 It may be the LORD thy God will hear all the words of Rab'-sha-keh, whom the king of As-syr'i-a his master hath sent to reproach the living God; and will reprove the words which the LORD thy God hath heard: wherefore lift up *thy* prayer for the remnant that are left.

5 So the servants of king Hez-e-ki'ah came to I-sa'iah.

6 ¶ And I-sa'iah said unto them, Thus shall ye say to your master, Thus saith the LORD, Be not afraid of the words which thou hast heard, with which the servants of the king of As-syr'i-a have blasphemed me.

7 Behold, I will send a blast upon him, and he shall hear a rumour, and shall return to his own land; and I will cause him to fall by the sword in his own land.

8 ¶ So Rab'-sha-keh returned, and found the king of As-syr'i-a warring against Lib'nah: for he had heard that he was departed from La'-chish.

9 And when he heard say of Tir'ha-kah king of E-thi-o'pi-a, Behold, he is come out to fight against thee: he sent messengers again unto Hez-e-ki'ah, saying,

10 Thus shall ye speak to Hez-e-ki'ah king of Ju'dah, saying, Let not thy God in whom thou trustest deceive thee, saying, Je-ru'sa-lem shall not be delivered into the hand of the king of As-syr'i-a.

11 Behold, thou hast heard what the kings of As-syr'i-a have done to all lands, by destroying them utterly: and shalt thou be delivered?

12 Have the gods of the nations delivered them which my fathers have destroyed; as Go'-zan, and Ha'ran, and Re'zeph, and the children of E'den which were in The-la'sar?

13 Where is the king of Ha'math, and the king of Ar'pad, and the king of the city of Seph-ar-va'im, of He'na, and I'vah?

14 ¶ And Hez-e-ki'ah received the letter of the hand of the messengers, and read it: and Hez-e-ki'ah went up into the house of the LORD, and spread it before the LORD.

15 And Hez-e-ki'ah prayed before the LORD, and said, O LORD God of Is'ra-el, which dwellest between the cherubims, thou art the God, even thou alone, of all the kingdoms of the earth; thou hast made heaven and earth.

16 LORD, bow down thine ear, and hear: open, LORD, thine eyes, and see: and hear the words of Sen-nach'e-rib, which hath sent him to reproach the living God.

17 Of a truth, LORD, the kings of As-syr'i-a have destroyed the nations and their lands,

18 And have cast their gods into the fire: for they were no gods, but the work of men's hands, wood and stone: therefore they have destroyed them.

19 Now therefore, O LORD our God, I beseech thee, save thou us out of his hand, that all the kingdoms of the earth may know that thou art the LORD God, even thou only.

20 ¶ Then I-sa'iah the son of A'moz sent to Hez-e-ki'ah, saying, Thus saith the LORD God of Is'ra-el, That which thou hast prayed to me against Sen-nach'e-rib king of As-syr'i-a I have heard.

21 This is the word that the LORD hath spoken concerning him; The virgin the daughter of Zi'on hath despised thee, and laughed thee to scorn; the daughter of Je-ru'sa-lem hath shaken her head at thee.

22 Whom hast thou reproached and blasphemed? and against whom hast thou exalted thy voice, and lifted up thine eyes on high? even against the Holy One of Is'ra-el.

23 By thy messengers thou hast reproached the LORD, and hast said, With the multitude of my chariots I am come up to the height of the mountains, to the sides of Leb'a-non, and will cut down the tall cedar trees thereof, and the choice fir trees thereof: and I will enter into the lodgings of his borders, and into the forest of his Car'mel.

24 I have digged and drunk strange waters, and with the sole of my feet have I dried up all the rivers of besieged places.

25 Hast thou not heard long ago how I have done it, and of ancient times that I have formed it? now have I brought it to pass, that thou shouldest be to lay waste fenced cities into ruinous heaps.

26 Therefore their inhabitants were of small power, they were dismayed and confounded; they were as the grass of the field, and as the green herb, as the grass on the house tops, and as corn blasted before it be grown up.

27 But I know thy abode, and thy going out, and thy coming in, and thy rage against me.

28 Because thy rage against me and thy tumult is come up into mine ears, therefore I will put my hook in thy nose, and my bridle in thy lips, and I will turn thee back by the way by which thou camest.

29 And this shall be a sign unto thee, Ye shall eat this year such things as grow of themselves, and in the second year that which springeth of the same; and in the third year sow ye, and reap, and plant vineyards, and eat the fruits thereof.

30 And the remnant that is escaped of the house of Ju'dah shall yet again take root downward, and bear fruit upward.

31 For out of Je-ru'sa-lem shall go forth a remnant, and they that escape out of mount Zi'-on: the zeal of the LORD of hosts shall do this.

32 Therefore thus saith the LORD concerning the king of As-syr'i-a, He shall not come into this city, nor shoot an arrow there, nor come before it with shield, nor cast a bank against it.

33 By the way that he came, by the same shall he return, and shall not come into this city, saith the LORD.

34 For I will defend this city, to save it, for mine own sake, and for my servant Da'vid's sake.

35 ¶ And it came to pass that night, that the angel of the LORD went out, and smote in the camp of the As-syr'i-ans an hundred fourscore and five thousand: and when they arose early in the morning, behold, they were all dead corpses.

36 So Sen-nach'e-rib king of As-syr'i-a departed, and went and returned, and dwelt at Nin'e-veh.

37 And it came to pass, as he was worshipping in the house of Nis'roch his god, that A-dram'me-lech and Sha-re'zer his sons smote him with the sword: and they escaped into the land of Ar-me'ni-a. And E'sar-had'don his son reigned in his stead.

20 IN those days was Hez-e-ki'ah sick unto death. And the prophet I-sa'iah the son of A'moz came to him, and said unto him, Thus saith the LORD, Set thine house in order; for thou shalt die, and not live.

2 Then he turned his face to the wall, and prayed unto the LORD, saying,

3 I beseech thee, O LORD, remember now how I have walked before thee in truth and with a perfect heart, and have done that which is good in thy sight. And Hez-e-ki'ah wept sore.

4 And it came to pass, afore I-sa'iah was gone out into the middle court, that the word of the LORD came to him, saying,

5 Turn again, and tell Hez-e-ki'ah the captain of my people, Thus saith the LORD, the God of Da'vid thy father, I have heard thy prayer, I have seen thy tears: behold, I will heal thee: on

the third day thou shalt go up unto the house of the LORD.

6 And I will add unto thy days fifteen years; and I will deliver thee and this city out of the hand of the king of As-syr'i-a; and I will defend this city for mine own sake, and for my servant Da'vid's sake.

7 And I-sa'iah said, Take a lump of figs. And they took and laid *it* on the boil, and he recovered.

8 ¶ And Hez-e-ki'ah said unto I-sa'iah, What *shall be* the sign that the LORD will heal me, and that I shall go up into the house of the LORD the third day?

9 And I-sa'iah said, This sign shalt thou have of the LORD, that the LORD will do the thing that he hath spoken: shall the shadow go forward ten degrees, or go back ten degrees?

10 And Hez-e-ki'ah answered, It is a light thing for the shadow to go down ten degrees: nay, but let the shadow return backward ten degrees.

11 And I-sa'iah the prophet cried unto the LORD: and he brought the shadow ten degrees backward, by which it had gone down in the dial of A'haz.

12 ¶ At that time Be-ro'dach–bal'a-dan, the son of Bal'a-dan, king of Bab'y-lon, sent letters and a present unto Hez-e-ki'ah: for he had heard that Hez-e-ki'ah had been sick.

13 And Hez-e-ki'ah hearkened unto them, and shewed them all the house of his precious things, the silver, and the gold, and the spices, and the precious ointment, and *all* the house of his armour, and all that was found in his treasures: there was nothing in his house, nor in all his dominion, that Hez-e-ki'ah shewed them not.

14 ¶ Then came I-sa'iah the prophet unto king Hez-e-ki'ah, and said unto him, What said these men? and from whence came they unto thee? And Hez-e-ki'ah said, They are come from a far country, *even* from Bab'y-lon.

15 And he said, What have they seen in thine house? And Hez-e-ki'ah answered, All *the things* that *are* in mine house have they seen: there is nothing among my treasures that I have not shewed them.

16 And I-sa'iah said unto Hez-e-ki'ah, Hear the word of the LORD.

17 Behold, the days come, that all that *is* in thine house, and that which thy fathers have laid up in store unto this day, shall be carried into Bab'y-lon: nothing shall be left, saith the LORD.

18 And of thy sons that shall issue from thee, which thou shalt beget, shall they take away; and they shall be eunuchs in the palace of the king of Bab'y-lon.

19 Then said Hez-e-ki'ah unto I-sa'iah, Good *is* the word of the LORD which thou hast spoken. And he said, *Is it* not good, if peace and truth be in my days?

20 ¶ And the rest of the acts of Hez-e-ki'ah, and all his might, and how he made a pool, and a conduit, and brought water into the city, *are* they not written in the book of the chronicles of the kings of Ju'dah?

21 And Hez-e-ki'ah slept with his fathers: and Ma-nas'seh his son reigned in his stead.

21 MA-NAS'SEH *was* twelve years old when he began to reign, and reigned fifty and five years in Je-ru'sa-lem. And his mother's name *was* Heph'zi-bah.

2 And he did *that which was* evil in the sight of the LORD, after the abominations of the hea-

then, whom the LORD cast out before the children of Is'ra-el.

3 For he built up again the high places which Hez-e-ki'ah his father had destroyed; and he reared up altars for Ba'al, and made a grove, as did A'hab king of Is'ra-el; and worshipped all the host of heaven, and served them.

4 And he built altars in the house of the LORD, of which the LORD said, In Je-ru'sa-lem will I put my name.

5 And he built altars for all the host of heaven in the two courts of the house of the LORD.

6 And he made his son pass through the fire, and observed times, and used enchantments, and dealt with familiar spirits and wizards: he wrought much wickedness in the sight of the LORD, to provoke *him* to anger.

7 And he set a graven image of the grove that he had made in the house, of which the LORD said to Da'vid, and to Sol'o-mon his son, In this house, and in Je-ru'sa-lem, which I have chosen out of all tribes of Is'ra-el, will I put my name for ever:

8 Neither will I make the feet of Is'ra-el move any more out of the land which I gave their fathers; only if they will observe to do according to all that I have commanded them, and according to all the law that my servant Mo'ses commanded them.

9 But they hearkened not: and Ma-nas'seh seduced them to do more evil than did the nations whom the LORD destroyed before the children of Is'ra-el.

10 ¶ And the LORD spake by his servants the prophets, saying,

11 Because Ma-nas'seh king of Ju'dah hath done these abominations, *and* hath done wickedly above all that the Am'or-ites did, which *were* before him, and hath made Ju'dah also to sin with his idols:

12 Therefore thus saith the LORD God of Is'ra-el, Behold, I *am* bringing *such* evil upon Je-ru'sa-lem and Ju'dah, that whosoever heareth of it, both his ears shall tingle.

13 And I will stretch over Je-ru'sa-lem the line of Sa-ma'ri-a, and the plummet of the house of A'hab: and I will wipe Je-ru'sa-lem as *a man* wipeth a dish, wiping *it*, and turning *it* upside down.

14 And I will forsake the remnant of mine inheritance, and deliver them into the hand of their enemies; and they shall become a prey and a spoil to all their enemies:

15 Because they have done *that which was* evil in my sight, and have provoked me to anger, since the day their fathers came forth out of E'gypt, even unto this day.

16 Moreover Ma-nas'seh shed innocent blood very much, till he had filled Je-ru'sa-lem from one end to another; beside his sin wherewith he made Ju'dah to sin, in doing *that which was* evil in the sight of the LORD.

17 ¶ Now the rest of the acts of Ma-nas'seh, and all that he did, and his sin that he sinned, *are* they not written in the book of the chronicles of the kings of Ju'dah?

18 And Ma-nas'seh slept with his fathers, and was buried in the garden of his own house, in the garden of Uz'za: and A'mon his son reigned in his stead.

19 ¶ A'mon *was* twenty and two years old when he began to reign, and he reigned two years in Je-ru'sa-lem. And his mother's name *was* Me-shul'le-meth, the daughter of Ha'ruz of Jot'bah.

20 And he did *that which was* evil in the sight of the LORD, as his father Ma-nas´seh did.

21 And he walked in all the way that his father walked in, and served the idols that his father served, and worshipped them:

22 And he forsook the LORD God of his fathers, and walked not in the way of the LORD.

23 ¶ And the servants of A´mon conspired against him, and slew the king in his own house.

24 And the people of the land slew all them that had conspired against king A´mon; and the people of the land made Jo-si´ah his son king in his stead.

25 Now the rest of the acts of A´mon which he did, *are* they not written in the book of the chronicles of the kings of Ju´dah?

26 And he was buried in his sepulchre in the garden of Uz´za: and Jo-si´ah his son reigned in his stead.

22 JO-SI´AH *was* eight years old when he began to reign, and he reigned thirty and one years in Je-ru´sa-lem. And his mother's name *was* Je-di´dah, the daughter of Ad-a-i´ah of Bos´cath.

2 And he did *that which was* right in the sight of the LORD, and walked in all the way of Da´vid his father, and turned not aside to the right hand or to the left.

3 ¶ And it came to pass in the eighteenth year of king Jo-si´ah, *that* the king sent Sha´-phan the son of Az-a-li´ah, the son of Me-shul´-lam, the scribe, to the house of the LORD, saying,

4 Go up to Hil-ki´ah the high priest, that he may sum the silver which is brought into the house of the LORD, which the keepers of the door have gathered of the people:

5 And let them deliver it into the hand of the doers of the work, that have the oversight of the house of the LORD: and let them give it to the doers of the work which *is* in the house of the LORD, to repair the breaches of the house,

6 Unto carpenters, and builders, and masons, and to buy timber and hewn stone to repair the house.

7 Howbeit there was no reckoning made with them of the money that was delivered into their hand, because they dealt faithfully.

8 ¶ And Hil-ki´ah the high priest said unto Sha´phan the scribe, I have found the book of the law in the house of the LORD. And Hil-ki´ah gave the book to Sha´phan, and he read it.

9 And Sha´phan the scribe came to the king, and brought the king word again, and said, Thy servants have gathered the money that was found in the house, and have delivered it into the hand of them that do the work, that have the oversight of the house of the LORD.

10 And Sha´phan the scribe shewed the king, saying, Hil-ki´ah the priest hath delivered me a book. And Sha´phan read it before the king.

11 And it came to pass, when the king had heard the words of the book of the law, that he rent his clothes.

12 And the king commanded Hil-ki´ah the priest, and A-hi´kam the son of Sha´phan, and Ach´bor the son of Mi-cha´iah, and Sha´phan the scribe, and A-sa-hi´ah a servant of the king's, saying,

13 Go ye, enquire of the LORD for me, and for the people, and for all Ju´dah, concerning the words of this book that is found: for great *is* the wrath of the LORD that is kindled against us, because our fathers have not hearkened unto the words of this book, to do according unto all that which is written concerning us.

14 So Hil-ki´ah the priest, and A-hi´kam, and Ach´bor, and Sha´phan, and A-sa-hi´ah, went unto Hul´dah the prophetess, the wife of Shal´-lum the son of Tik´vah, the son of Har´has, keeper of the wardrobe; (now she dwelt in Je-ru´sa-lem in the college;) and they communed with her.

15 ¶ And she said to them, Thus saith the LORD God of Is´ra-el, Tell the man that sent you to me,

16 Thus saith the LORD, Behold, I will bring evil upon this place, and upon the inhabitants thereof, *even* all the words of the book which the king of Ju´dah hath read:

17 Because they have forsaken me, and have burned incense unto other gods, that they might provoke me to anger with all the works of their hands; therefore my wrath shall be kindled against this place, and shall not be quenched.

18 But to the king of Ju´dah which sent you to enquire of the LORD, thus shall ye say to him, Thus saith the LORD God of Is´ra-el, *As touching* the words which thou hast heard;

19 Because thine heart was tender, and thou hast humbled thyself before the LORD, when thou heardest what I spake against this place, and against the inhabitants thereof, that they should become a desolation and a curse, and hast rent thy clothes, and wept before me; I also have heard *thee*, saith the LORD.

20 Behold therefore, I will gather thee unto thy fathers, and thou shalt be gathered into thy grave in peace; and thine eyes shall not see all the evil which I will bring upon this place. And they brought the king word again.

23 AND the king sent, and they gathered unto him all the elders of Ju´dah and of Je-ru´sa-lem.

2 And the king went up into the house of the LORD, and all the men of Ju´dah and all the inhabitants of Je-ru´sa-lem with him, and the priests, and the prophets, and all the people, both small and great: and he read in their ears all the words of the book of the covenant which was found in the house of the LORD.

3 ¶ And the king stood by a pillar, and made a covenant before the LORD, to walk after the LORD, and to keep his commandments and his testimonies and his statutes with all *their* heart and all *their* soul, to perform the words of this covenant that were written in this book. And all the people stood to the covenant.

4 And the king commanded Hil-ki´ah the high priest, and the priests of the second order, and the keepers of the door, to bring forth out of the temple of the LORD all the vessels that were made for Ba´al, and for the grove, and for all the host of heaven: and he burned them without Je-ru´sa-lem in the fields of Kid´ron, and carried the ashes of them unto Beth´-el.

5 And he put down the idolatrous priests, whom the kings of Ju´dah had ordained to burn incense in the high places in the cities of Ju´dah, and in the places round about Je-ru´sa-lem; them also that burned incense unto Ba´al, to the sun, and to the moon, and to the planets, and to all the host of heaven.

6 And he brought out the grove from the house of the LORD, without Je-ru´sa-lem, unto the brook Kid´ron, and burned it at the brook Kid´ron, and stamped *it* small to powder, and cast the powder thereof upon the graves of the children of the people.

7 And he brake down the houses of the sodomites, that *were* by the house of the LORD, where the women wove hangings for the grove.

8 And he brought all the priests out of the cities of Ju'dah, and defiled the high places where the priests had burned incense, from Ge'ba to Be'er-she'ba, and brake down the high places of the gates that *were* in the entering in of the gate of Josh'u-a the governor of the city, which *were* on a man's left hand at the gate of the city.

9 Nevertheless the priests of the high places came not up to the altar of the LORD in Je-ru'sa-lem, but they did eat of the unleavened bread among their brethren.

10 And he defiled To'pheth, which *is* in the valley of the children of Hin'nom, that no man might make his son or his daughter to pass through the fire to Mo'lech.

11 And he took away the horses that the kings of Ju'dah had given to the sun, at the entering in of the house of the LORD, by the chamber of Na'than-me'lech the chamberlain, which *was* in the suburbs, and burned the chariots of the sun with fire.

12 And the altars that *were* on the top of the upper chamber of A'haz, which the kings of Ju'dah had made, and the altars which Ma-nas'seh had made in the two courts of the house of the LORD, did the king beat down, and brake *them* down from thence, and cast the dust of them into the brook Kid'ron.

13 And the high places that *were* before Je-ru'sa-lem, which *were* on the right hand of the mount of corruption, which Sol'o-mon the king of Is'ra-el had builded for Ash'to-reth the abomination of the Zi-do'ni-ans, and for Che'mosh the abomination of the Mo'ab-ites, and for Mil'com the abomination of the children of Am'mon, did the king defile.

14 And he brake in pieces the images, and cut down the groves, and filled their places with the bones of men.

15 ¶ Moreover the altar that *was* at Beth'-el, *and* the high place which Jer-o-bo'am the son of Ne'bat, who made Is'ra-el to sin, had made, both that altar and the high place he brake down, and burned the high place, *and* stamped *it* small to powder, and burned the grove.

16 And as Jo-si'ah turned himself, he spied the sepulchres that *were* there in the mount, and sent, and took the bones out of the sepulchres, and burned *them* upon the altar, and polluted it, according to the word of the LORD which the man of God proclaimed, who proclaimed these words.

17 Then he said, What title *is* that that I see? And the men of the city told him, *It is* the sepulchre of the man of God, which came from Ju'dah, and proclaimed these things that thou hast done against the altar of Beth'-el.

18 And he said, Let him alone; let no man move his bones. So they let his bones alone, with the bones of the prophet that came out of Sa-ma'ri-a.

19 And all the houses also of the high places that *were* in the cities of Sa-ma'ri-a, which the kings of Is'ra-el had made to provoke the LORD to anger, Jo-si'ah took away, and did to them according to all the acts that he had done in Beth'-el.

20 And he slew all the priests of the high places that *were* there upon the altars, and burned men's bones upon them, and returned to Je-ru'sa-lem.

21 ¶ And the king commanded all the people, saying, Keep the passover unto the LORD your God, as *it is* written in the book of this covenant.

22 Surely there was not holden such a passover from the days of the judges that judged Is'ra-el, nor in all the days of the kings of Is'ra-el, nor of the kings of Ju'dah;

23 But in the eighteenth year of king Jo-si'ah, *wherein* this passover was holden to the LORD in Je-ru'sa-lem.

24 ¶ Moreover, the *workers with* familiar spirits, and the wizards, and the images, and the idols, and all the abominations that were spied in the land of Ju'dah and in Je-ru'sa-lem, did Jo-si'ah put away, that he might perform the words of the law which were written in the book that Hil-ki'ah the priest found in the house of the LORD.

25 And like unto him was there no king before him, that turned to the LORD with all his heart, and with all his soul, and with all his might, according to all the law of Mo'ses; neither after him arose there *any* like him.

26 ¶ Notwithstanding the LORD turned not from the fierceness of his great wrath, wherewith his anger was kindled against Ju'dah, because of all the provocations that Ma-nas'seh had provoked him withal.

27 And the LORD said, I will remove Ju'dah also out of my sight, as I have removed Is'ra-el, and will cast off this city Je-ru'sa-lem which I have chosen, and the house of which I said, My name shall be there.

28 Now the rest of the acts of Jo-si'ah, and all that he did, *are* they not written in the book of the chronicles of the kings of Ju'dah?

29 ¶ In his days Pha'raoh-ne'choh king of E'gypt went up against the king of As-syr'i-a to the river Eu-phra'tes: and king Jo-si'ah went against him; and he slew him at Me-gid'do, when he had seen him.

30 And his servants carried him in a chariot dead from Me-gid'do, and brought him to Je-ru'sa-lem, and buried him in his own sepulchre. And the people of the land took Je-ho'a-haz the son of Jo-si'ah, and anointed him, and made him king in his father's stead.

31 ¶ Je-ho'a-haz *was* twenty and three years old when he began to reign; and he reigned three months in Je-ru'sa-lem. And his mother's name *was* Ha-mu'tal, the daughter of Jer-e-mi'ah of Lib'nah.

32 And he did *that which was* evil in the sight of the LORD, according to all that his fathers had done.

33 And Pha'raoh-ne'choh put him in bands at Rib'lah in the land of Ha'math, that he might not reign in Je-ru'sa-lem; and put the land to a tribute of an hundred talents of silver, and a talent of gold.

34 And Pha'raoh-ne'choh made E-li'a-kim the son of Jo-si'ah king in the room of Jo-si'ah his father, and turned his name to Je-hoi'a-kim, and took Je-ho'a-haz away: and he came to E'gypt, and died there.

35 And Je-hoi'a-kim gave the silver and the gold to Pha'raoh; but he taxed the land to give the money according to the commandment of Pha'raoh: he exacted the silver and the gold of the people of the land, of every one according to his taxation, to give *it* unto Pha'raoh-ne'choh.

36 ¶ Je-hoi'a-kim *was* twenty and five years old when he began to reign; and he reigned eleven years in Je-ru'sa-lem. And his mother's name *was* Ze-bu'dah, the daughter of Pe-da'iah of Ru'mah.

37 And he did *that which was* evil in the

sight of the LORD, according to all that his fathers had done.

24 IN his days Neb-u-chad-nez′zar king of Bab′y-lon came up, and Je-hoi′a-kim became his servant three years: then he turned and rebelled against him.

2 And the LORD sent against him bands of the Chal′dees, and bands of the Syr′i-ans, and bands of the Mo′ab-ites, and bands of the children of Am′mon, and sent them against Ju′dah to destroy it, according to the word of the LORD, which he spake by his servants the prophets.

3 Surely at the commandment of the LORD came this upon Ju′dah, to remove them out of his sight, for the sins of Ma-nas′seh, according to all that he did;

4 And also for the innocent blood that he shed: for he filled Je-ru′sa-lem with innocent blood; which the LORD would not pardon.

5 ¶ Now the rest of the acts of Je-hoi′a-kim, and all that he did, are they not written in the book of the chronicles of the kings of Ju′dah?

6 So Je-hoi′a-kim slept with his fathers: and Je-hoi′a-chin his son reigned in his stead.

7 And the king of E′gypt came not again any more out of his land: for the king of Bab′y-lon had taken from the river of E′gypt unto the river Eu-phra′tes all that pertained to the king of E′gypt.

8 ¶ Je-hoi′a-chin was eighteen years old when he began to reign, and he reigned in Je-ru′sa-lem three months. And his mother's name was Ne-hush′ta, the daughter of El′na-than of Je-ru′sa-lem.

9 And he did that which was evil in the sight of the LORD, according to all that his father had done.

10 ¶ At that time the servants of Neb-u-chad-nez′zar king of Bab′y-lon came up against Je-ru′sa-lem, and the city was besieged.

11 And Neb-u-chad-nez′zar king of Bab′y-lon came against the city, and his servants did besiege it.

12 And Je-hoi′a-chin the king of Ju′dah went out to the king of Bab′y-lon, he, and his mother, and his servants, and his princes, and his officers: and the king of Bab′y-lon took him in the eighth year of his reign.

13 And he carried out thence all the treasures of the house of the LORD, and the treasures of the king's house, and cut in pieces all the vessels of gold which Sol′o-mon king of Is′ra-el had made in the temple of the LORD, as the LORD had said.

14 And he carried away all Je-ru′sa-lem, and all the princes, and all the mighty men of valour, even ten thousand captives, and all the craftsmen and smiths: none remained, save the poorest sort of the people of the land.

15 And he carried away Je-hoi′a-chin to Bab′y-lon, and the king's mother, and the king's wives, and his officers, and the mighty of the land, those carried he into captivity from Je-ru′sa-lem to Bab′y-lon.

16 And all the men of might, even seven thousand, and craftsmen and smiths a thousand, all that were strong and apt for war, even them the king of Bab′y-lon brought captive to Bab′y-lon.

17 ¶ And the king of Bab′y-lon made Mat-ta-ni′ah his father's brother king in his stead, and changed his name to Zed-e-ki′ah.

18 Zed-e-ki′ah was twenty and one years old when he began to reign, and he reigned eleven years in Je-ru′sa-lem. And his mother's name was Ha-mu′tal, the daughter of Jer-e-mi′ah of Lib′nah.

19 And he did that which was evil in the sight of the LORD, according to all that Je-hoi′a-kim had done.

20 For through the anger of the LORD it came to pass in Je-ru′sa-lem and Ju′dah, until he had cast them out from his presence, that Zed-e-ki′-ah rebelled against the king of Bab′y-lon.

25 AND it came to pass in the ninth year of his reign, in the tenth month, in the tenth day of the month, that Neb-u-chad-nez′-zar king of Bab′y-lon came, he, and all his host, against Je-ru′sa-lem, and pitched against it; and they built forts against it round about.

2 And the city was besieged unto the eleventh year of king Zed-e-ki′ah.

3 And on the ninth day of the fourth month the famine prevailed in the city, and there was no bread for the people of the land.

4 ¶ And the city was broken up, and all the men of war fled by night by the way of the gate between two walls, which is by the king's garden: (now the Chal′dees were against the city round about:) and the king went the way toward the plain.

5 And the army of the Chal′dees pursued after the king, and overtook him in the plains of Jer′i-cho: and all his army was scattered from him.

6 So they took the king, and brought him up to the king of Bab′y-lon to Rib′lah; and they gave judgment upon him.

7 And they slew the sons of Zed-e-ki′ah before his eyes, and put out the eyes of Zed-e-ki′ah, and bound him with fetters of brass, and carried him to Bab′y-lon.

8 ¶ And in the fifth month, on the seventh day of the month, which is the nineteenth year of king Neb-u-chad-nez′zar king of Bab′y-lon, came Neb′u-zar-a′dan, captain of the guard, a servant of the king of Bab′y-lon, unto Je-ru′sa-lem:

9 And he burnt the house of the LORD, and the king's house, and all the houses of Je-ru′sa-lem, and every great man's house burnt he with fire.

10 And all the army of the Chal′dees, that were with the captain of the guard, brake down the walls of Je-ru′sa-lem round about.

11 Now the rest of the people that were left in the city, and the fugitives that fell away to the king of Bab′y-lon, with the remnant of the multitude, did Neb′u-zar-a′dan the captain of the guard carry away.

12 But the captain of the guard left of the poor of the land to be vinedressers and husbandmen.

13 And the pillars of brass that were in the house of the LORD, and the bases, and the brasen sea that was in the house of the LORD, did the Chal′dees break in pieces, and carried the brass of them to Bab′y-lon.

14 And the pots, and the shovels, and the snuffers, and the spoons, and all the vessels of brass wherewith they ministered, took they away.

15 And the firepans, and the bowls, and such things as were of gold, in gold, and of silver, in silver, the captain of the guard took away.

16 The two pillars, one sea, and the bases which Sol′o-mon had made for the house of the LORD; the brass of all these vessels was without weight.

17 The height of the one pillar was eighteen

cubits, and the chapiter upon it *was* brass: and the height of the chapiter three cubits; and the wreathen work, and pomegranates upon the chapiter round about, all of brass: and like unto these had the second pillar with wreathen work.

18 ¶ And the captain of the guard took Ser-a-i'ah the chief priest, and Zeph-a-ni'ah the second priest, and the three keepers of the door:

19 And out of the city he took an officer that was set over the men of war, and five men of them that were in the king's presence, which were found in the city, and the principal scribe of the host, which mustered the people of the land, and threescore men of the people of the land *that were* found in the city:

20 And Neb'u-zar-a'dan captain of the guard took these, and brought them to the king of Bab'y-lon to Rib'lah:

21 And the king of Bab'y-lon smote them, and slew them at Rib'lah in the land of Ha'-math. So Ju'dah was carried away out of their land.

22 ¶ And *as for* the people that remained in the land of Ju'dah, whom Neb-u-chad-nez'zar king of Bab'y-lon had left, even over them he made Ged-a-li'ah the son of A-hi'kam, the son of Sha'phan, ruler.

23 And when all the captains of the armies, they and their men, heard that the king of Bab'-y-lon had made Ged-a-li'ah governor, there came to Ged-a-li'ah to Miz'pah, even Ish'ma-el the son of Neth-a-ni'ah, and Jo-ha'nan the son

of Ca-re'ah, and Ser-a-i'ah the son of Tan'hu-meth the Ne-toph'a-thite, and Ja-az-a-ni'ah the son of a Ma-ach'a-thite, they and their men.

24 And Ged-a-li'ah sware to them, and to their men, and said unto them, Fear not to be the servants of the Chal'dees: dwell in the land, and serve the king of Bab'y-lon; and it shall be well with you.

25 But it came to pass in the seventh month, that Ish'ma-el the son of Neth-a-ni'ah, the son of E-lish'a-ma, of the seed royal, came, and ten men with him, and smote Ged-a-li'ah, that he died, and the Jews and the Chal'dees that were with him at Miz'pah.

26 And all the people, both small and great, and the captains of the armies, arose, and came to E'gypt: for they were afraid of the Chal'dees.

27 ¶ And it came to pass in the seven and thirtieth year of the captivity of Je-hoi'a-chin king of Ju'dah, in the twelfth month, on the seven and twentieth *day* of the month, *that* E'-vil-me-ro'dach king of Bab'y-lon in the year that he began to reign did lift up the head of Je-hoi'a-chin king of Ju'dah out of prison;

28 And he spake kindly to him, and set his throne above the throne of the kings that *were* with him in Bab'y-lon:

29 And changed his prison garments: and he did eat bread continually before him all the days of his life.

30 And his allowance *was* a continual allowance given him of the king, a daily rate for every day, all the days of his life.

THE FIRST BOOK OF THE

CHRONICLES

1 AD'AM, Sheth, E'nosh,
2 Ke'nan, Ma-ha-la-le-el, Je'red,
3 He'noch, Me-thu'se-lah, La'mech,
4 No'ah, Shem, Ham, and Ja'pheth.
5 ¶ The sons of Ja'pheth; Go'mer, and Ma'-gog, and Mad'a-i, and Ja'van, and Tu'bal, and Me'shech, and Ti'ras.
6 And the sons of Go'mer; Ash'che-naz, and Ri'phath, and To-gar'mah.
7 And the sons of Ja'van; E-li'shah, and Tar'-shish, Kit'tim, and Dod'a-nim.
8 ¶ The sons of Ham; Cush, and Miz'ra-im, Put, and Ca'naan.
9 And the sons of Cush; Se'ba, and Hav'i-lah, and Sab'ta, and Ra'a-mah, and Sab'te-cha. And the sons of Ra'a-mah; She'ba, and De'dan.
10 And Cush begat Nim'rod: he began to be mighty upon the earth.
11 And Miz'ra-im begat Lu'dim, and An'a-mim, and Le'ha-bim, and Naph'tu-him,
12 And Path-ru'sim, and Cas'lu-him, (of whom came the Phi-lis'tines,) and Caph'tho-rim.
13 And Ca'naan begat Zi'don his firstborn, and Heth,
14 The Jeb'u-site also, and the Am'or-ite, and the Gir'ga-shite,
15 And the Hi'vite, and the Ark'ite, and the Sin'ite,
16 And the Ar'vad-ite, and the Zem'a-rite, and the Ha'math-ite.
17 ¶ The sons of Shem; E'lam, and Assh'ur, and Ar-phax'ad, and Lud, and A'ram, and Uz, and Hul, and Ge'ther, and Me'shech.
18 And Ar-phax'ad begat She'lah, and She'-lah begat E'ber.

19 And unto E'ber were born two sons: the name of the one *was* Pe'leg; because in his days the earth was divided: and his brother's name *was* Jok'tan.
20 And Jok'tan begat Al-mo'dad, and She'-leph, and Ha'zar-ma'veth, and Je'rah,
21 Ha-do'ram also, and U'zal, and Dik'lah,
22 And E'bal, and A-bim'a-el, and She'ba,
23 And O'phir, and Hav'i-lah, and Jo'bab. All these *were* the sons of Jok'tan.
24 ¶ Shem, Ar-phax'ad, She'lah,
25 E'ber, Pe'leg, Re'u,
26 Se'rug, Na'hor, Te'rah,
27 A'bram; the same *is* A'bra-ham.
28 The sons of A'bra-ham; I'saac, and Ish'-ma-el.
29 ¶ These *are* their generations: The first-born of Ish'ma-el, Ne-ba'ioth; then Ke'dar, and Ad'be-el, and Mib'sam,
30 Mish'ma, and Du'mah, Mas'sa, Ha'dad, and Te'ma,
31 Je'tur, Na'phish, and Ked'e-mah. These are the sons of Ish'ma-el.
32 ¶ Now the sons of Ke-tu'rah, A'bra-ham's concubine: she bare Zim'ran, and Jok'shan, and Me'dan, and Mid'i-an, and Ish'bak, and Shu'ah. And the sons of Jok'shan; She'ba, and De'dan.
33 And the sons of Mid'i-an; E'phah, and E'-pher, and He'noch, and A-bi'da, and El'da-ah. All these *are* the sons of Ke-tu'rah.
34 And A'bra-ham begat I'saac. The sons of I'saac; E'sau and Is'ra-el.
35 ¶ The son's of E'sau; El'i-phaz, Reu'el, and Je'ush, and Ja-a'lam, and Ko'rah.
36 The sons of El'i-phaz; Te'man, and O'mar,

Ze'phi, and Ga'tam, Ke'naz, and Tim'na, and Am'a-lek.

37 The sons of Reu'el; Na'hath, Ze'rah, Sham'mah, and Miz'zah.

38 And the sons of Se'ir; Lo'tan, and Sho'bal, and Zib'e-on, and A'nah, and Di'shon, and E'zar, and Di'shan.

39 And the sons of Lo'tan; Ho'ri, and Ho'mam: and Tim'na was Lo'tan's sister.

40 The sons of Sho'bal; A-li'an, and Man'a-hath, and E'bal, She'phi, and O'nam. And the sons of Zib'e-on; A-i'ah, and A'nah.

41 The sons of A'nah; Di'shon. And the sons of Di'shon; Am'ram, and Esh'ban, and Ith'ran, and Che'ran.

42 The sons of E'zer; Bil'han, and Za'van, and Ja'kan. The sons of Di'shan; Uz, and A'ran.

43 ¶ Now these are the kings that reigned in the land of E'dom before any king reigned over the children of Is'ra-el; Be'la the son of Be'or: and the name of his city was Din'ha-bah.

44 And when Be'la was dead, Jo'bab the son of Ze'rah of Boz'rah reigned in his stead.

45 And when Jo'bab was dead, Hu'sham of the land of the Te'man-ites reigned in his stead.

46 And when Hu'sham was dead, Ha'dad the son of Be'dad, which smote Mid'i-an in the field of Mo'ab, reigned in his stead: and the name of his city was A'vith.

47 And when Ha'dad was dead, Sam'lah of Mas're-kah reigned in his stead.

48 And when Sam'lah was dead, Sha'ul of Re-ho'both by the river reigned in his stead.

49 And when Sha'ul was dead, Ba'al-ha'nan the son of Ach'bor reigned in his stead.

50 And when Ba'al-ha'nan was dead, Ha'dad reigned in his stead: and the name of his city was Pa'i; and his wife's name was Me-het'a-bel, the daughter of Ma'tred, the daughter of Mez'a-hab.

51 ¶ Ha'dad died also. And the dukes of E'dom were; duke Tim'nah, duke A-li'ah, duke Je'theth,

52 Duke A-ho-lib'a-mah, duke E'lah, duke Pi'non,

53 Duke Ke'naz, duke Te'man, duke Mib'zar,

54 Duke Mag'di-el, duke I'ram. These are the dukes of E'dom.

2 THESE are the sons of Is'ra-el; Reu'ben, Sim'e-on, Le'vi, and Ju'dah, Is'sa-char, and Zeb'u-lun,

2 Dan, Jo'seph, and Ben'ja-min, Naph'ta-li, Gad, and Ash'er.

3 ¶ The sons of Ju'dah; Er, and O'nan, and She'lah: which three were born unto him of the daughter of Shu'a the Ca'naan-it-ess. And Er, the firstborn of Ju'dah, was evil in the sight of the LORD; and he slew him.

4 And Ta'mar his daughter in law bare him Pha'rez and Ze'rah. All the sons of Ju'dah were five.

5 The sons of Pha'rez; Hez'ron, and Ha'mul.

6 And the sons of Ze'rah; Zim'ri, and E'than, and He'man, and Cal'col, and Da'ra: five of them in all.

7 And the sons of Car'mi; A'char, the troubler of Is'ra-el, who transgressed in the thing accursed.

8 And the sons of E'than; Az-a-ri'ah.

9 The sons also of Hez'ron, that were born unto him; Je-rah'me-el, and Ram, and Che-lu'bai.

10 And Ram begat Am-min'a-dab; and Am-min'a-dab begat Nah'shon, prince of the children of Ju'dah;

11 And Nah'shon begat Sal'ma, and Sal'ma begat Bo'az,

12 And Bo'az begat O'bed, and O'bed begat Jes'se,

13 ¶ And Jes'se begat his firstborn E-li'ab, and A-bin'a-dab the second, and Shim'ma the third,

14 Ne-than'e-el the fourth, Rad'da-i the fifth,

15 O'zem the sixth, Da'vid the seventh:

16 Whose sisters were Zer-u-i'ah, and Ab'i-gail. And the sons of Zer-u-i'ah; A-bish'a-i, and Jo'ab, and A'sa-hel, three.

17 And Ab'i-gail bare Am'a-sa: and the father of Am'a-sa was Je'ther the Ish'me-el-ite.

18 ¶ And Ca'leb the son of Hez'ron begat children of A-zu'bah his wife, and of Je'ri-oth: her sons are these; Je'sher, and Sho'bab, and Ar'don.

19 And when A-zu'bah was dead, Ca'leb took unto him Eph'rath, which bare him Hur.

20 And Hur begat U'ri, and U'ri begat Be-zal'e-el.

21 ¶ And afterward Hez'ron went in to the daughter of Ma'chir the father of Gil'e-ad, whom he married when he was threescore years old; and she bare him Se'gub.

22 And Se'gub begat Ja'ir, who had three and twenty cities in the land of Gil'e-ad.

23 And he took Ge'shur, and A'ram, with the towns of Ja'ir, from them, with Ke'nath, and the towns thereof, even threescore cities. All these belonged to the sons of Ma'chir the father of Gil'e-ad.

24 And after that Hez'ron was dead in Ca'leb-eph'ra-tah, then A-bi'ah Hez'ron's wife bare him Ash'ur the father of Te-ko'a.

25 ¶ And the sons of Je-rah'me-el the firstborn of Hez'ron were, Ram the firstborn, and Bu'nah, and O'ren, and O'zem, and A-hi'jah.

26 Je-rah'me-el had also another wife, whose name was At'a-rah; she was the mother of O'nam.

27 And the sons of Ram the firstborn of Je-rah'me-el were, Ma'az, and Ja'min, and E'ker.

28 And the sons of O'nam were, Sham'ma-i, and Ja'da. And the sons of Sham'ma-i; Na'dab and Ab'i-shur.

29 And the name of the wife of Ab'i-shur was Ab-i-ha'il, and she bare him Ah'ban, and Mo'lid.

30 And the sons of Na'dab; Se'led, and Ap'pa-im: but Se'led died without children.

31 And the sons of Ap'pa-im; Ish'i. And the sons of Ish'i; She'shan. And the children of She'shan; Ah'lai.

32 And the sons of Ja'da the brother of Sham'ma-i; Je'ther, and Jon'a-than: and Je'ther died without children.

33 And the sons of Jon'a-than; Pe'leth, and Za'za. These were the sons of Je-rah'me-el.

34 ¶ Now She'shan had no sons, but daughters. And She'shan had a servant, an E-gyp'tian, whose name was Jar'ha.

35 And She'shan gave his daughter to Jar'ha his servant to wife; and she bare him At'tai.

36 And At'tai begat Na'than, and Na'than begat Za'bad,

37 And Za'bad begat Eph'lal, and Eph'lal begat O'bed,

38 And O'bed begat Je'hu, and Je'hu begat Az-a-ri'ah,

39 And Az-a-ri'ah begat He'lez, and He'lez begat E-le'a-sah,

40 And E-le'a-sah begat Si-sam'a-i, and Si-sam'a-i begat Shal'lum,

41 And Shal'lum begat Jek-a-mi'ah, and Jek-a-mi'ah begat E-lish'a-ma.

42 ¶ Now the sons of Ca'leb the brother of

Je-rah'me-el were, Me'sha his firstborn, which was the father of Ziph; and the sons of Ma-re'-shah the father of He'bron.

43 And the sons of He'bron; Ko'rah, and Tap'pu-ah, and Re'kem, and She'ma.

44 And She'ma begat Ra'ham, the father of Jor'ko-am: and Re'kem begat Sham'ma-i.

45 And the son of Sham'ma-i was Ma'on: and Ma'on was the father of Beth'-zur.

46 And E'phah, Ca'leb's concubine, bare Ha'-ran, and Mo'za, and Ga'zez: and Ha'ran begat Ga'zez.

47 And the sons of Jah'da-i; Re'gem, and Jo'-tham, and Ge'sham, and Pe'let, and E'phah, and Sha'aph.

48 Ma'a-chah, Ca'leb's concubine, bare She'-ber, and Tir'ha-nah.

49 She bare also Sha'aph the father of Mad-man'nah, She'va the father of Mach'be-nah, and the father of Gib'e-a: and the daughter of Ca'leb was Ach'sa.

50 ¶ These were the sons of Ca'leb the son of Hur, the firstborn of Eph'ra-tah; Sho'bal the father of Kir'jath-je'a-rim,

51 Sal'ma the father of Beth'-le-hem, Ha'-reph the father of Beth-ga'der.

52 And Sho'bal the father of Kir'jath-je'a-rim had sons; Har'o-eh, and half of the Ma-na'-heth-ites.

53 And the families of Kir'jath-je'a-rim; the Ithrites, and the Pu'hites, and the Shu'math-ites, and the Mish'ra-ites; of them came the Za'-re-ath-ites, and the Esh'ta-ul-ites.

54 The sons of Sal'ma; Beth'-le-hem, and the Ne-toph'a-thites, At'a-roth, the house of Jo'ab, and half of the Ma-na'heth-ites, the Zo'rites.

55 And the families of the scribes which dwelt at Ja'bez; the Ti'rath-ites, the Shim'e-ath-ites, and Su'chath-ites. These are the Ken'ites that came of He'math, the father of the house of Re'chab.

3 NOW these were the sons of Da'vid, which were born unto him in He'bron; the first-born Am'non, of A-hin'o-am the Jez're-el-it-ess; the second Dan'iel, of Ab'i-gail the Car'mel-it-ess:

2 The third, Ab'sa-lom the son of Ma'a-chah the daughter of Tal'mai king of Ge'shur; the fourth, Ad-o-ni'jah the son of Hag'gith:

3 The fifth, Sheph-a-ti'ah of Ab'i-tal: the sixth, Ith're-am by Eg'lah his wife.

4 These six were born unto him in He'bron; and there he reigned seven years and six months: and in Je-ru'sa-lem he reigned thirty and three years.

5 And these were born unto him in Je-ru'sa-lem; Shim'e-a, and Sho'bab, and Na'than, and Sol'o-mon, four, of Bath'-shu-a the daughter of Am'mi-el:

6 Ib'har also, and E-lish'a-ma, and E-liph'e-let,

7 And No'gah, and Ne'pheg, and Ja-phi'a,

8 And E-lish'a-ma, and E-li'a-da, and E-liph'-e-let, nine.

9 These were all the sons of Da'vid, beside the sons of the concubines, and Ta'mar their sister.

10 ¶ And Sol'o-mon's son was Re-ho-bo'am, A-bi'a his son, A'sa his son, Je-hosh'a-phat his son,

11 Jo'ram his son, A-ha-zi'ah his son, Jo'ash his son,

12 Am-a-zi'ah his son, Az-a-ri'ah his son, Jo'-tham his son,

13 A'haz his son, Hez-e-ki'ah his son, Ma-nas'seh his son,

14 A'mon his son, Jo-si'ah his son.

15 And the sons of Jo-si'ah were, the first-born Jo-ha'nan, the second Je-hoi'a-kim, the third Zed-e-ki'ah, the fourth Shal'lum.

16 And the sons of Je-hoi'a-kim: Jec-o-ni'ah his son, Zed-e-ki'ah his son.

17 ¶ And the sons of Jec-o-ni'ah; As'sir, Sa-la'-thi-el his son,

18 Mal-chi'ram also, and Pe-da'iah, and She-na'zar, Jec-a-mi'ah, Hosh'a-ma, and Ned-a-bi'-ah.

19 And the sons of Pe-da'iah were, Ze-rub'-ba-bel, and Shim'e-i: and the sons of Ze-rub'ba-bel; Me-shul'lam, and Han-a-ni'ah, and Shel'o-mith their sister:

20 And Ha-shu'bah, and O'hel, and Ber-e-chi'ah, and Has-a-di'ah, Ju'shab-he'sed, five.

21 And the sons of Han-a-ni'ah; Pel-a-ti'ah, and Je'sa'iah: the sons of Reph-a-i'ah, the sons of Ar'nan, the sons of O-ba-di'ah, the sons of Shech-a'ni'ah.

22 And the sons of Shech-a'ni'ah; Shem-a-i'-ah: and the sons of Shem-a-i'ah; Hat'tush, and Ig'e-al, and Ba-ri'ah, and Ne-a-ri'ah, and Sha'-phat, six.

23 And the sons of Ne-a-ri'ah; El-i-o-e'na-i, and Hez-e-ki'ah, and Az'ri-kam, three.

24 And the sons of El-i-o-e'na-i were, Hod-a-i'ah, and E-li'a-shib, and Pel-a-i'ah, and Ak'kub, and Jo-ha'nan, and Dal-a-i'ah, and An-a'ni, seven.

4 THE sons of Ju'dah; Pha'rez, Hez'ron, and Car'mi, and Hur, and Sho'bal.

2 And Re-a-i'ah the son of Sho'bal begat Ja'-hath; and Ja'hath begat A-hu'ma-i, and La'had. These are the families of the Zo'rath-ites.

3 And these were of the father of E'tam; Jez'-re-el, and Ish'ma, and Id'bash: and the name of their sister was Haz-e-lel-po'ni:

4 And Pe-nu'el the father of Ge'dor, and E'zer the father of Hu'shah. These are the sons of Hur, the firstborn of Eph'ra-tah, the father of Beth'-le-hem.

5 ¶ And Ash'ur the father of Te-ko'a had two wives, He'lah and Na'a-rah.

6 And Na'a-rah bare him A-hu'zam, and He'-pher, and Tem'e-ni, and Ha-a-hash'ta-ri. These were the sons of Na'a-rah.

7 And the sons of He'lah were, Ze'reth, and Jez'o-ar, and Eth-nan.

8 And Coz begat A'nub, and Zo-be'bah, and the families of A-har'hel the son of Ha'rum.

9 ¶ And Ja'bez was more honourable than his brethren: and his mother called his name Ja'bez, saying, Because I bare him with sorrow.

10 And Ja'bez called on the God of Is'ra-el, saying, Oh that thou wouldest bless me indeed, and enlarge my coast, and that thine hand might be with me, and that thou wouldest keep me from evil, that it may not grieve me! And God granted him that which he requested.

11 ¶ And Che'lub the brother of Shu'ah be-gat Me'hir, which was the father of Esh'ton.

12 And Esh'ton begat Beth-ra'pha, and Pa-se'ah, and Te-hin'nah the father of Ir-na'hash. These are the men of Re'chah.

13 And the sons of Ke'naz; Oth'ni-el, and Ser-a-i'ah: and the sons of Oth'ni-el; Ha'thath.

14 And Me-on'o-thai begat Oph'rah: and Ser-a-i'ah begat Jo'ab, the father of the valley of Char'a-shim; for they were craftsmen.

15 And the sons of Ca'leb the son of Je-phun'neh; I'ru, E'lah, and Na'am: and the sons of E'lah, even Ke'naz.

16 And the sons of Je-ha-le'le-el; Ziph, and Zi'phah, Tir'i-a, and A-sa're-el.

17 And the sons of Ez'ra were, Je'ther, and Me'red, and E'pher, and Ja'lon: and she bare Mir'i-am, and Sham'ma-i, and Ish'bah the father of Esh-te-mo'a.

18 And his wife Je-hu-di'jah bare Je'red the father of Ge'dor, and He'ber the father of So'cho, and Je-ku'thi-el the father of Za-no'ah. And these are the sons of Bith'i-ah the daughter of Pha'raoh, which Me'red took.

19 And the sons of his wife Ho-di'ah the sister of Na'ham, the father of Kei'lah the Gar'mite, and Esh-te-mo'a the Ma-ach'a-thite.

20 And the sons of Shi'mon were, Am'non, and Rin'nah, Ben-ha'nan, and Ti'lon. And the sons of Ish'i were, Zo'heth, and Ben-zo'heth.

21 ¶ The sons of She'lah the son of Ju'dah were, Er the father of Le'cah, and La'a-dah the father of Ma-re'shah, and the families of the house of them that wrought fine linen, of the house of Ash-be'a,

22 And Jo'kim, and the men of Cho'ze-ba, and Jo'ash, and Sa'raph, who had the dominion in Mo'ab, and Jash'u-bi-le'hem. And these are ancient things.

23 These were the potters, and those that dwelt among plants and hedges: there they dwelt with the king for his work.

24 ¶ The sons of Sim'e-on were, Ne-mu'el, and Ja'min, Ja'rib, Ze'rah, and Sha'ul:

25 Shal'lum his son, Mib'sam his son, Mish'ma his son.

26 And the sons of Mish'ma; Ha-mu'el his son, Zac'chur his son, Shim'e-i his son.

27 And Shim'e-i had sixteen sons and six daughters; but his brethren had not many children, neither did all their family multiply, like to the children of Ju'dah.

28 And they dwelt at Be'er-she'ba, and Mol'a-dah, and Ha'zar-shu'al,

29 And at Bil'hah, and at E'zem, and at To'-lad,

30 And at Beth-u'el, and at Hor'mah, and at Zik'lag,

31 And at Beth-mar'ca-both, and Ha'zar-su'-sim, and at Beth-bir'e-i, and at Sha-a-ra'im. These were their cities unto the reign of Da'vid.

32 And their villages were, E'tam, and A'in, Rim'mon, and To'chen, and A'shan, five cities:

33 And all their villages that were round about the same cities, unto Ba'al. These were their habitations, and their genealogy.

34 And Me-sho'bab, and Jam'lech, and Jo'shah the son of Am-a-zi'ah,

35 And Jo'el, and Je'hu the son of Jos-i-bi'ah, the son of Ser-a-i'ah, the son of A'si-el,

36 And El-i-o-e'na-i, and Ja-ak'o-bah, and Jesh-o-ha-i'ah, and A-sa-i'ah, and A-di'el, and Je-sim'i-el, and Be-na'iah,

37 And Zi'za the son of Shi'phi, the son of Al'lon, the son of Je-da'iah, the son of Shim'ri, the son of Shem-a-i'ah;

38 These mentioned by their names were princes in their families: and the house of their fathers increased greatly.

39 ¶ And they went to the entrance of Ge'-dor, even unto the east side of the valley, to seek pasture for their flocks.

40 And they found fat pasture and good, and the land was wide, and quiet, and peaceable; for they of Ham had dwelt there of old.

41 And these written by name came in the days of Hez-e-ki'ah king of Ju'dah, and smote their tents, and the habitations that were found there, and destroyed them utterly unto this day, and dwelt in their rooms: because there was pasture there for their flocks.

42 And some of them, even of the sons of Sim'e-on, five hundred men, went to mount Se'ir, having for their captains Pel-a-ti'ah, and Ne-a-ri'ah, and Reph-a-i'ah, and Uz'zi-el, the sons of Ish'i.

43 And they smote the rest of the Am'a-lek-ites that were escaped, and dwelt there unto this day.

5 NOW the sons of Reu'ben the firstborn of Is'ra-el, (for he was the firstborn; but, forasmuch as he defiled his father's bed, his birthright was given unto the sons of Jo'seph the son of Is'ra-el: and the genealogy is not to be reckoned after the birthright.

2 For Ju'dah prevailed above his brethren, and of him came the chief ruler; but the birthright was Jo'seph's:)

3 The sons, I say, of Reu'ben the firstborn of Is'ra-el were, Ha'noch, and Pal'lu, Hez'ron, and Car'mi.

4 The sons of Jo'el; Shem-a-i'ah his son, Gog his son, Shim'e-i his son,

5 Mi'cah his son, Re-a-i'a his son, Ba'al his son,

6 Be-e'rah his son, whom Til'gath-pil-ne'ser king of As-syr'i-a carried away captive: he was prince of the Reu'ben-ites.

7 And his brethren by their families, when the genealogy of their generations was reckoned, were the chief, Je-i'el, and Zech-a-ri'ah,

8 And Be'la the son of A'zaz, the son of She'ma, the son of Jo'el, who dwelt in Ar'o-er, even unto Ne'bo and Ba'al-me'on:

9 And eastward he inhabited unto the entering in of the wilderness from the river Eu-phra'tes: because their cattle were multiplied in the land of Gil'e-ad.

10 And in the days of Saul they made war with the Ha'gar-ites, who fell by their hand: and they dwelt in their tents throughout all the east land of Gil'e-ad.

11 ¶ And the children of Gad dwelt over against them, in the land of Ba'shan unto Sal'cah:

12 Jo'el the chief, and Sha'pham the next, and Ja-a'nai, and Sha'phat in Ba'shan.

13 And their brethren of the house of their fathers were, Mi'chael, and Me-shul'lam, and She'ba, and Jo'ra-i, and Ja'chan, and Zi'a, and He'ber, seven.

14 These are the children of Ab-i-ha'il the son of Hu'ri, the son of Ja-ro'ah, the son of Gil'e-ad, the son of Mi'chael, the son of Je-shish'a-i, the son of Jah'do, the son of Buz;

15 A'hi the son of Ab'di-el, the son of Gu'ni, chief of the house of their fathers.

16 And they dwelt in Gil'e-ad in Ba'shan, and in her towns, and in all the suburbs of Shar'on, upon their borders.

17 All these were reckoned by genealogies in the days of Jo'tham king of Ju'dah, and in the days of Jer-o-bo'am king of Is'ra-el.

18 ¶ The sons of Reu'ben, and the Gad'ites, and half the tribe of Ma-nas'seh, of valiant men, men able to bear buckler and sword, and to shoot with bow, and skilful in war, were four and forty thousand seven hundred and three-score, that went out to war.

19 And they made war with the Ha'gar-ites, with Je'tur, and Ne'phish, and No'dab.

20 And they were helped against them, and the Ha'gar-ites were delivered into their hand, and all that were with them: for they cried to God in the battle, and he was intreated of them; because they put their trust in him.

21 And they took away their cattle; of their camels fifty thousand, and of sheep two hun-

dred and fifty thousand, and of asses two thousand, and of men an hundred thousand.

22 For there fell down many slain, because the war *was* of God. And they dwelt in their steads until the captivity.

23 ¶ And the children of the half tribe of Manas'seh dwelt in the land: they increased from Ba'shan unto Ba'al-her'mon and Se'nir, and unto mount Her'mon.

24 And these *were* the heads of the house of their fathers, even E'pher, and Ish'i, and E-li'el, and Az'ri-el, and Jer-e-mi'ah, and Hod-a-vi'ah, and Jah'di-el, mighty men of valour, famous men, *and* heads of the house of their fathers.

25 ¶ And they transgressed against the God of their fathers, and went a whoring after the gods of the people of the land, whom God destroyed before them.

26 And the God of Is'ra-el stirred up the spirit of Pul king of As-syr'i-a, and the spirit of Til'gath-pil-ne'ser king of As-syr'i-a, and he carried them away, even the Reu'ben-ites, and the Gad'ites, and the half tribe of Ma-nas'seh, and brought them unto Ha'lah, and Ha'bor, and Ha'ra, and to the river Go'zan, unto this day.

6 THE sons of Le'vi; Ger'shon, Ko'hath, and Me-ra'ri.

2 And the sons of Ko'hath; Am'ram, Iz'har, and He'bron, and Uz'zi-el.

3 And the children of Am'ram; Aar'on, and Mo'ses, and Mir'i-am. The sons also of Aar'on; Na'dab, and A-bi'hu, E-le-a'zar, and Ith'a-mar.

4 ¶ E-le-a'zar begat Phin'e-has, Phin'e-has begat A-bish'u-a,

5 And A-bish'u-a begat Buk'ki, and Buk'ki begat Uz'zi,

6 And Uz'zi begat Zer-a-hi'ah, and Zer-a-hi'ah begat Me-ra'ioth,

7 Me-ra'ioth begat Am-a-ri'ah, and Am-a-ri'ah begat A-hi'tub,

8 And A-hi'tub begat Za'dok, and Za'dok begat A-him'a-az,

9 And A-him'a-az begat Az-a-ri'ah, and Az-a-ri'ah begat Jo-ha'nan,

10 And Jo-ha'nan begat Az-a-ri'ah, (he *it is* that executed the priest's office in the temple that Sol'o-mon built in Je-ru'sa-lem:)

11 And Az-a-ri'ah begat Am-a-ri'ah, and Am-a-ri'ah begat A-hi'tub,

12 And A-hi'tub begat Za'dok, and Za'dok begat Shal'lum,

13 And Shal'lum begat Hil-ki'ah, and Hil-ki'ah begat Az-a-ri'ah,

14 And Az-a-ri'ah begat Ser-a-i'ah, and Ser-a-i'ah begat Je-hoz'a-dak,

15 And Je-hoz'a-dak went *into captivity*, when the LORD carried away Ju'dah and Je-ru'sa-lem by the hand of Neb-u-chad-nez'zar.

16 ¶ The sons of Le'vi; Ger'shom, Ko'hath, and Me-ra'ri.

17 And these *be* the names of the sons of Ger'shom; Lib'ni, and Shim'e-i.

18 And the sons of Ko'hath *were*, Am'ram, and Iz'har, and He'bron, and Uz'zi-el.

19 The sons of Me-ra'ri; Mah'li, and Mu'shi. And these *are* the families of the Le'vites according to their fathers.

20 Of Ger'shom; Lib'ni his son, Ja'hath his son, Zim'mah his son,

21 Jo'ah his son, Id'do his son, Ze'rah his son, Je-at'e-rai his son.

22 The sons of Ko'hath; Am-min'a-dab his son, Ko'rah his son, As'sir his son,

23 El'ka-nah his son, and E-bi'a-saph his son, and As'sir his son,

24 Ta'hath his son, U'ri-el his son, Uz-zi'ah his son, and Sha'ul his son.

25 And the sons of El'ka-nah; A-mas'a-i, and A-hi'moth.

26 *As for* El'ka-nah: the sons of El'ka-nah; Zo'phai his son, and Na'hath his son,

27 E-li'ab his son, Jer'o-ham his son, El'ka-nah his son.

28 And the sons of Sam'u-el; the firstborn Vash'ni, and A-bi'ah.

29 The sons of Me-ra'ri; Mah'li, Lib'ni his son, Shim'e-i his son, Uz'za his son,

30 Shim'e-a his son, Hag-gi'ah his son, A-sai'ah his son.

31 And these *are they* whom Da'vid set over the service of song in the house of the LORD, after that the ark had rest.

32 And they ministered before the dwelling place of the tabernacle of the congregation with singing, until Sol'o-mon had built the house of the LORD in Je-ru'sa-lem: and *then* they waited on their office according to their order.

33 And these *are* they that waited with their children. Of the sons of the Ko'hath-ites: He'man a singer, the son of Jo'el, the son of She-mu'el,

34 The son of El'ka-nah, the son of Jer'o-ham, the son of E-li'el, the son of To'ah,

35 The son of Zuph, the son of El'ka-nah, the son of Ma'hath, the son of A-mas'a-i,

36 The son of El'ka-nah, the son of Jo'el, the son of Az-a-ri'ah, the son of Zeph-a-ni'ah,

37 The son of Ta'hath, the son of As'sir, the son of E-bi'a-saph, the son of Ko'rah,

38 The son of Iz'har, the son of Ko'hath, the son of Le'vi, the son of Is'ra-el.

39 And his brother A'saph, who stood on his right hand, *even* A'saph the son of Ber-a-chi'ah, the son of Shim'e-a,

40 The son of Mi'chael, the son of Ba-a-se'iah, the son of Mal-chi'ah,

41 The son of Eth'ni, the son of Ze'rah, the son of Ad-a-i'ah,

42 The son of E'than, the son of Zim'mah, the son of Shim'e-i,

43 The son of Ja'hath, the son of Ger'shom, the son of Le'vi.

44 And their brethren the sons of Me-ra'ri *stood* on the left hand: E'than the son of Kish'i, the son of Ab'di, the son of Mal'luch,

45 The son of Hash-a-bi'ah, the son of Am-a-zi'ah, the son of Hil-ki'ah,

46 The son of Am'zi, the son of Ba'ni, the son of Sha'mer,

47 The son of Mah'li, the son of Mu'shi, the son of Me-ra'ri, the son of Le'vi.

48 Their brethren also the Le'vites *were* appointed unto all manner of service of the tabernacle of the house of God.

49 ¶ But Aar'on and his sons offered upon the altar of the burnt offering, and on the altar of incense, *and were appointed* for all the work of the *place* most holy, and to make an atonement for Is'ra-el, according to all that Mo'ses the servant of God had commanded.

50 And these *are* the sons of Aar'on; E-le-a'zar his son, Phin'e-has his son, A-bish'u-a his son,

51 Buk'ki his son, Uz'zi his son, Zer-a-hi'ah his son,

52 Me-ra'ioth his son, Am-a-ri'ah his son, A-hi'tub his son,

53 Za'dok his son, A-him'a-az his son.

54 ¶ Now these *are* their dwelling places throughout their castles in their coasts, of the sons of Aar'on, of the families of the Ko'hath-ites: for theirs was the lot.

55 And they gave them He'bron in the land of Ju'dah, and the suburbs thereof round about it.

56 But the fields of the city, and the villages thereof, they gave to Ca'leb the son of Je-phun'-neh.

57 And to the sons of Aar'on they gave the cities of Ju'dah, namely, He'bron, the city of refuge, and Lib'nah with her suburbs, and Jat'-tir, and Esh-te-mo'a, with their suburbs,

58 And Hi'len with her suburbs, De'bir with her suburbs,

59 And A'shan with her suburbs, and Beth–she'mesh with her suburbs:

60 And out of the tribe of Ben'ja-min; Ge'ba with her suburbs, and Al'e-meth with her suburbs, and An'a-thoth with her suburbs. All their cities throughout their families were thirteen cities.

61 And unto the sons of Ko'hath, which were left of the family of that tribe, were cities given out of the half tribe, namely, out of the half tribe of Ma-nas'seh, by lot, ten cities.

62 And to the sons of Ger'shom throughout their families out of the tribe of Is'sa-char, and out of the tribe of Ash'er, and out of the tribe of Ma-nas'seh in Ba'shan, thirteen cities.

63 Unto the sons of Me-ra'ri were given by lot, throughout their families, out of the tribe of Reu'ben, and out of the tribe of Gad, and out of the tribe of Zeb'u-lun, twelve cities.

64 And the children of Is'ra-el gave to the Le'vites these cities with their suburbs.

65 And they gave by lot out of the tribe of the children of Ju'dah, and out of the tribe of the children of Sim'e-on, and out of the tribe of the children of Ben'ja-min, these cities, which are called by their names.

66 And the residue of the families of the sons of Ko'hath had cities of their coasts out of the tribe of E'phra-im.

67 And they gave unto them, of the cities of refuge, Shechem in mount E'phra-im with her suburbs; they gave also Ge'zer with her suburbs,

68 And Jok'me-am with her suburbs, and Beth-ho'ron with her suburbs,

69 And Aij'a-lon with her suburbs, and Gath-rim'mon with her suburbs:

70 And out of the half tribe of Ma-nas'seh; A'ner with her suburbs, and Bil'e-am with her suburbs, for the family of the remnant of the sons of Ko'hath.

71 Unto the sons of Ger'shom were given out of the family of the half tribe of Ma-nas'seh, Go'lan in Ba'shan with her suburbs, and Ash'ta-roth with her suburbs:

72 And out of the tribe of Is'sa-char; Ke'desh with her suburbs, Dab'e-rath with her suburbs,

73 And Ra'moth with her suburbs, and A'-nem with her suburbs:

74 And out of the tribe of Ash'er; Ma'shal with her suburbs, and Ab'don with her suburbs,

75 And Hu'kok with her suburbs, and Re'hob with her suburbs:

76 And out of the tribe of Naph'ta-li; Ke'desh in Gal'i-lee with her suburbs, and Ham'mon with her suburbs, and Kir-jath-a'im with her suburbs.

77 Unto the rest of the children of Me-ra'ri were given out of the tribe of Zeb'u-lun, Rim'-mon with her suburbs, Ta'bor with her suburbs:

78 And on the other side Jor'dan by Jer'i-cho, on the east side of Jor'dan, were given them out of the tribe of Reu'ben, Be'zer in the wilderness with her suburbs, and Jah'zah with her suburbs,

79 Ked'e-moth also with her suburbs, and Meph'a-ath with her suburbs:

80 And out of the tribe of Gad; Ra'moth in Gil'e-ad with her suburbs, and Ma-ha-na'im with her suburbs,

81 And Hesh'bon with her suburbs, and Ja'-zer with her suburbs.

7 NOW the sons of Is'sa-char were, To'la, and Pu'ah, Jash'ub, and Shim'rom, four.

2 And the sons of To'la; Uz'zi, and Reph-a-i'ah, and Je'ri-el, and Jah'ma-i, and Jib'sam, and She-mu'el, heads of their father's house, to wit, of To'la: they were valiant men of might in their generations; whose number was in the days of Da'vid two and twenty thousand and six hundred.

3 And the sons of Uz'zi; Iz-ra-hi'ah: and the sons of Iz-ra-hi'ah; Mi'chael, and O-ba-di'ah, and Jo'el, Ish-i'ah, five: all of them chief men.

4 And with them, by their generations, after the house of their fathers, were bands of soldiers for war, six and thirty thousand men: for they had many wives and sons.

5 And their brethren among all the families of Is'sa-char were valiant men of might, reckoned in all by their genealogies fourscore and seven thousand.

6 ¶ The sons of Ben'ja-min; Be'la, and Be'-cher, and Je-di'a-el, three.

7 And the sons of Be'la; Ez'bon, and Uz'zi, and Uz'zi-el, and Jer'i-moth, and I'ri, five; heads of the house of their fathers, mighty men of valour; and were reckoned by their genealogies twenty and two thousand and thirty and four.

8 And the sons of Be'cher; Ze-mi'ra, and Jo'-ash, and E-li-e'zer, and El-i-o-e'na-i, and Om'ri, and Jer'i-moth, and A-bi'ah, and An'a-thoth, and Al'a-meth. All these are the sons of Be'cher.

9 And the number of them, after their genealogy by their generations, heads of the house of their fathers, mighty men of valour, was twenty thousand and two hundred.

10 The sons also of Je-di'a-el; Bil'han: and the sons of Bil'han; Je'ush, and Ben'ja-min, and E'-hud, and Che-na'a-nah, and Ze'than, and Thar'-shish, and A-hish'a-har.

11 All these the sons of Je-di'a-el, by the heads of their fathers, mighty men of valour, were seventeen thousand and two hundred soldiers, fit to go out for war and battle.

12 Shup'pim also, and Hup'pim, the children of Ir, and Hu'shim, the sons of A'her.

13 ¶ The sons of Naph'ta-li; Jah'zi-el, and Gu'ni, and Je'zer, and Shal'lum, the sons of Bil'-hah.

14 ¶ The sons of Ma-nas'seh; Ash'ri-el, whom she bare: (but his concubine the A'ram-it-ess bare Ma'chir the father of Gil'e-ad:

15 And Ma'chir took to wife the sister of Hup'pim and Shup'pim, whose sister's name was Ma'a-chah;) and the name of the second was Ze-lo'phe-had: and Ze-lo'phe-had had daughters.

16 And Ma'a-chah the wife of Ma'chir bare a son, and she called his name Pe'resh; and the name of his brother was She'resh; and his sons were U'lam and Ra'kem.

17 And the sons of U'lam; Be'dan. These were the sons of Gil'e-ad, the son of Ma'chir, the son of Ma-nas'seh.

18 And his sister Ham-mol'e-keth bare I'-shod, and A-bi-e'zer, and Ma-ha'lah.

19 And the sons of She-mi'dah were, A-hi'an, and She'chem, and Lik'hi, and A'ni-am.

20 ¶ And the sons of E'phra-im; Shu'the-lah,

and Be'red his son, and Ta'hath his son, and El'-a-dah his son, and Ta'hath his son,

21 ¶ And Za'bad his son, and Shu'the-lah his son, and E'zer, and E'le-ad, whom the men of Gath *that were* born in *that* land slew, because they came down to take away their cattle.

22 And E'phra-im their father mourned many days, and his brethren came to comfort him.

23 ¶ And when he went in to his wife, she conceived, and bare a son, and he called his name Be-ri'ah, because it went evil with his house.

24 (And his daughter *was* She'rah, who built Beth-ho'ron the nether, and the upper, and Uz'-zen-she'rah.)

25 And Re'phah *was* his son, also Re'sheph, and Te'lah his son, and Ta'han his son,

26 La'a-dan his son, Am-mi'hud his son, E-lish'a-ma his son,

27 Non his son, Je-hosh'u-ah his son.

28 ¶ And their possessions and habitations *were*, Beth'-el and the towns thereof, and eastward Na'a-ran, and westward Ge'zer, with the towns thereof; She'chem also and the towns thereof, unto Ga'za and the towns thereof:

29 And by the borders of the children of Ma-nas'seh, Beth-she'an and her towns, Ta'a-nach and her towns, Me-gid'do and her towns, Dor and her towns. In these dwelt the children of Jo'seph the son of Is'ra-el.

30 ¶ The sons of Ash'er; Im'nah, and Is'u-ah, and Ish'u-ai, and Be-ri'ah, and Se'rah their sister.

31 And the sons of Be-ri'ah; He'ber, and Mal'-chi-el, who *is* the father of Bir'za-vith.

32 And He'ber begat Japh'let, and Sho'mer, and Ho'tham, and Shu'a their sister.

33 And the sons of Japh'let; Pa'sach, and Bim'hal, and Ash'vath. These *are* the children of Japh'let.

34 And the sons of Sha'mer; A'hi, and Roh'-gah, Je-hub'bah, and A'ram.

35 And the sons of his brother He'lem; Zo'-phah, and Im'na, and She'lesh, and A'mal.

36 The sons of Zo'phah; Su'ah, and Har'ne-pher, and Shu'al, and Be'ri, and Im'rah,

37 Be'zer, and Hod, and Sham'ma, and Shil'-shah, and Ith'ran, and Be-e'ra.

38 And the sons of Je'ther; Je-phun'neh, and Pis'pah, and A'ra.

39 And the sons of Ul'la; A'rah, and Han'i-el, and Re-zi'a.

40 All these *were* the children of Ash'er, heads of *their* father's house, choice *and* mighty men of valour, chief of the princes. And the number throughout the genealogy of them that were apt to the war *and* to battle *was* twenty and six thousand men.

8 NOW Ben'ja-min begat Be'la his firstborn, Ash'bel the second, and A-har'ah the third,

2 No'hah the fourth, and Ra'pha the fifth.

3 And the sons of Be'la were, Ad'dar, and Ge'ra, and A-bi'hud,

4 And A-bish'u-a, and Na'a-man, and A-ho'-ah,

5 And Ge'ra, and She-phu'phan, and Hu'ram.

6 And these *are* the sons of E'hud: these are the heads of the fathers of the inhabitants of Ge'ba, and they removed them to Man'a-hath:

7 And Na'a-man, and A-hi'ah, and Ge'ra, he removed them, and begat Uz'za, and A-hi'hud.

8 And Sha-ha-ra'im begat *children* in the country of Mo'ab, after he had sent them away; Hu'shim and Ba'a-ra *were* his wives.

9 And he begat of Ho'desh his wife, Jo'bab, and Zib'i-a, and Me'sha, and Mal'cham,

10 And Je'uz, and Shach-i'a and Mir'ma. These *were* his sons, heads of the fathers.

11 And of Hu'shim he begat Ab'i-tub, and El'-pa-al.

12 The sons of El'pa-al; E'ber, and Mi'sham, and Sha'med, who built O'no, and Lod, with the towns thereof:

13 Be-ri'ah also, and She'ma, who *were* heads of the fathers of the inhabitants of Aij'a-lon, who drove away the inhabitants of Gath:

14 And A-hi'o, Sha'shak, and Jer'e-moth,

15 And Zeb-a-di'ah, and A'rad, and A'der,

16 And Mi'chael, and Is'pah, and Jo'ha, the sons of Be-ri'ah;

17 And Zeb-a-di'ah, and Me-shul'lam, and Hez'e-ki, and He'ber,

18 And Ish'me-rai also, and Jez-li'ah, and Jo'bab, the sons of El'pa-al;

19 And Ja'kim, and Zich'ri, and Zab'di,

20 And E-li-e'na-i, and Zil'thai, and E-li'el,

21 And Ad-a-i'ah, and Ber-a-i'ah, and Shim'-rath, the sons of Shim'hi;

22 And Ish'pan, and He'ber, and E-li'el,

23 And Ab'don, and Zich'ri, and Ha'nan,

24 And Han-a-ni'ah, and E'lam, and An-to-thi'jah,

25 And Iph-e-de'iah, and Pe-nu'el, the sons of Sha'shak:

26 And Sham-she-ra'i, and She-ha-ri'ah, and Ath-a-li'ah,

27 And Jar'e-si'ah, and E-li'ah, and Zich'ri, the sons of Jer'o-ham.

28 These *were* heads of the fathers, by their generations, chief *men*. These dwelt in Je-ru'sa-lem.

29 And at Gib'e-on dwelt the father of Gib'e-on; whose wife's name *was* Ma'a-chah:

30 And his firstborn son Ab'don, and Zur, and Kish, and Ba'al, and Na'dab,

31 And Ge'dor, and A-hi'o, and Za'cher.

32 And Mik'loth begat Shim'e-ah. And these also dwelt with their brethren in Je-ru'sa-lem, over against them.

33 ¶ And Ner begat Kish, and Kish begat Saul, and Saul begat Jon'a-than, and Mal-chi-shu'a, and A-bin'a-dab, and Esh-ba'al.

34 And the son of Jon'a-than *was* Mer'ib-ba'-al: and Mer'ib-ba'al begat Mi'cah.

35 And the sons of Mi'cah *were*, Pi'thon, and Me'lech, and Ta're-a, and A'haz.

36 And A'haz begat Je-ho'a-dah; and Je-ho'a-dah begat Al'e-meth, and Az'ma-veth, and Zim'ri; and Zim'ri begat Mo'za,

37 And Mo'za begat Bin'e-a: Ra'pha *was* his son, E-le'a-sah his son, A'zel his son:

38 And A'zel had six sons, whose names *are* these, Az'ri-kam, Boch'e-ru, and Ish'ma-el, and She-a-ri'ah, and O-ba-di'ah, and Ha'nan. All these *were* the sons of A'zel.

39 And the sons of E'shek his brother *were*, U'lam his firstborn, Je'nush the second, and E-liph'e-let the third.

40 And the sons of U'lam were mighty men of valour, archers, and had many sons, and sons' sons, an hundred and fifty. All these *are* of the sons of Ben'ja-min.

9 SO all Is'ra-el were reckoned by geneal-ogies; and, behold, they *were* written in the book of the kings of Is'ra-el and Ju'dah, who were carried away to Bab'y-lon for their trans-gression.

2 ¶ Now the first inhabitants that *dwelt* in their possessions in their cities *were*, the Is'ra-el-ites, the priests, Le'vites, and the Neth'i-nims.

3 And in Je-ru'sa-lem dwelt of the children of

Ju'dah, and of the children of Ben'ja-min, and of the children of E'phra-im, and Ma-nas'seh;

4 U'tha-i the son of Am-mi'hud, the son of Om'ri, the son of Im'ri, the son of Ba'ni, of the children of Pha'rez the son of Ju'dah.

5 And of the Shi'lo-nites; A-sa-i'ah the firstborn, and his sons.

6 And of the sons of Ze'rah; Je-u'el, and their brethren, six hundred and ninety.

7 And of the sons of Ben'ja-min; Sal'lu the son of Me-shul'lam, the son of Hod-a-vi'ah, the son of Has-e-nu'ah,

8 And Ib-ne'iah the son of Jer'o-ham, and E'-lah the son of Uz'zi, the son of Mich'ri, and Me-shul'lam the son of Sheph-a-thi'ah, the son of Reu'el, the son of Ib-ni'jah;

9 And their brethren, according to their generations, nine hundred and fifty and six. All these men were chief of the fathers in the house of their fathers.

10 ¶ And of the priests; Je-da'iah, and Je-hoi'a-rib, and Ja'chin,

11 And Az-a-ri'ah the son of Hil-ki'ah, the son of Me-shul'lam, the son of Za'dok, the son of Me-ra'ioth, the son of A-hi'tub, the ruler of the house of God;

12 And Ad-a-i'ah the son of Jer'o-ham, the son of Pash'ur, the son of Mal-chi'jah, and Ma-as'i-ai the son of A-di'el, the son of Jah'ze-rah, the son of Me-shul'lam, the son of Me-shil'le-mith, the son of Im'mer;

13 And their brethren, heads of the house of their fathers, a thousand and seven hundred and threescore; very able men for the work of the service of the house of God.

14 And of the Le'vites; Shem-a-i'ah the son of Has'shub, the son of Az'ri-kam, the son of Hash-a-bi'ah, of the sons of Me-ra'ri;

15 And Bak-bak'kar, He'resh, and Gal'al, and Mat-ta-ni'ah, the son of Mi'cah, the son of Zich'-ri, the son of A'saph;

16 And O-ba-di'ah the son of Shem-a-i'ah, the son of Ga'lal, the son of Jed'u-thun, and Ber-e-chi'ah the son of A'sa, the son of El'ka-nah, that dwelt in the villages of the Ne-toph'a-thites.

17 And the porters were, Shal'lum, and Ak'-kub, and Tal'mon, and A-hi'man, and their brethren: Shal'lum was the chief;

18 Who hitherto waited in the king's gate eastward: they were porters in the companies of the children of Le'vi.

19 And Shal'lum the son of Ko're, the son of E-bi'a-saph, the son of Ko'rah, and his brethren, of the house of his father, the Ko'rah-ites, were over the work of the service, keepers of the gates of the tabernacle: and their fathers, being over the host of the LORD, were keepers of the entry.

20 And Phin'e-has the son of E-le-a'zar was the ruler over them in time past, and the LORD was with him.

21 And Zech-a-ri'ah the son of Me-shel-e-mi'-ah was porter of the door of the tabernacle of the congregation.

22 All these which were chosen to be porters in the gates were two hundred and twelve. These were reckoned by their genealogy in their villages, whom Da'vid and Sam'u-el the seer did ordain in their set office.

23 So they and their children had the oversight of the gates of the house of the LORD, namely, the house of the tabernacle, by wards.

24 In four quarters were the porters, toward the east, west, north, and south.

25 And their brethren, which were in their villages, were to come after seven days from time to time with them.

26 For these Le'vites, the four chief porters, were in their set office, and were over the chambers and treasuries of the house of God.

27 ¶ And they lodged round about the house of God, because the charge was upon them, and the opening thereof every morning pertained to them.

28 And certain of them had the charge of the ministering vessels, that they should bring them in and out by tale.

29 Some of them also were appointed to oversee the vessels, and all the instruments of the sanctuary, and the fine flour, and the wine, and the oil, and the frankincense, and the spices.

30 And some of the sons of the priests made the ointment of the spices.

31 And Mat-ti-thi'ah, one of the Le'vites, who was the firstborn of Shal'lum the Ko'rah-ite, had the set office over the things that were made in the pans.

32 And other of their brethren, of the sons of the Ko'hath-ites, were over the shewbread, to prepare it every sabbath.

33 And these are the singers, chief of the fathers of the Le'vites, who remaining in the chambers were free: for they were employed in that work day and night.

34 These chief fathers of the Le'vites were chief throughout their generations; these dwelt at Je-ru'sa-lem.

35 ¶ And in Gib'e-on dwelt the father of Gib'e-on, Je-hi'el, whose wife's name was Ma'a-chah:

36 And his firstborn son Ab'don, then Zur, and Kish, and Ba'al, and Ner, and Na'dab,

37 And Ge'dor, and A-hi'o, and Zech-a-ri'ah, and Mik'loth.

38 And Mik'loth begat Shim'e-am. And they also dwelt with their brethren at Je-ru'sa-lem, over against their brethren.

39 And Ner begat Kish; and Kish begat Saul; and Saul begat Jon'a-than, and Mal-chi-shu'a, and A-bin'a-dab, and Esh-ba'al.

40 And the son of Jon'a-than was Mer'ib-ba'-al: and Mer'ib-ba'al begat Mi'cah.

41 And the sons of Mi'cah were, Pi'thon, and Me'lech, and Tah-re'a, and A'haz.

42 And A'haz begat Ja'rah; and Ja'rah begat Al'e-meth, and Az'ma-veth, and Zim'ri; and Zim'ri begat Mo'za;

43 And Mo'za begat Bin'e-a; and Reph-a-i'ah his son, E-le'a-sah his son, A'zel his son.

44 And A'zel had six sons, whose names are these, Az'ri-kam, Boch'e-ru, and Ish'ma-el, and She-a-ri'ah, and O-ba-di'ah, and Ha'nan: these were the sons of A'zel.

10 NOW the Phi-lis'tines fought against Is'-ra-el; and the men of Is'ra-el fled from before the Phi-lis'tines, and fell down slain in mount Gil-bo'a.

2 And the Phi-lis'tines followed hard after Saul, and after his sons; and the Phi-lis'tines slew Jon'a-than, and A-bin'a-dab, and Mal-chi-shu'a, the sons of Saul.

3 And the battle went sore against Saul, and the archers hit him, and he was wounded of the archers.

4 Then said Saul to his armourbearer, Draw thy sword, and thrust me through therewith; lest these uncircumcised come and abuse me. But his armourbearer would not; for he was sore afraid. So Saul took a sword, and fell upon it.

5 And when his armourbearer saw that Saul was dead, he fell likewise on the sword, and died.

6 So Saul died, and his three sons, and all his house died together.

7 And when all the men of Is'ra-el that were in the valley saw that they fled, and that Saul and his sons were dead, then they forsook their cities, and fled: and the Phi-lis'tines came and dwelt in them.

8 ¶ And it came to pass on the morrow, when the Phi-lis'tines came to strip the slain, that they found Saul and his sons fallen in mount Gil-bo'a.

9 And when they had stripped him, they took his head, and his armour, and sent into the land of the Phi-lis'tines round about, to carry tidings unto their idols, and to the people.

10 And they put his armour in the house of their gods, and fastened his head in the temple of Da'gon.

11 ¶ And when all Ja'besh-gil'e-ad heard all that the Phi-lis'tines had done to Saul,

12 They arose, all the valiant men, and took away the body of Saul, and the bodies of his sons, and brought them to Ja'besh, and buried their bones under the oak in Ja'besh, and fasted seven days.

13 ¶ So Saul died for his transgression which he committed against the LORD, even against the word of the LORD, which he kept not, and also for asking counsel of one that had a familiar spirit, to enquire of it;

14 And enquired not of the LORD: therefore he slew him, and turned the kingdom unto Da'vid the son of Jes'se.

11 THEN all Is'ra-el gathered themselves to Da'vid unto He'bron, saying, Behold, we are thy bone and thy flesh.

2 And moreover in time past, even when Saul was king, thou wast he that leddest out and broughtest in Is'ra-el: and the LORD thy God said unto thee, Thou shalt feed my people Is'ra-el, and thou shalt be ruler over my people Is'ra-el.

3 Therefore came all the elders of Is'ra-el to the king to He'bron; and Da'vid made a covenant with them in He'bron before the LORD; and they anointed Da'vid king over Is'ra-el, according to the word of the LORD by Sam'u-el.

4 ¶ And Da'vid and all Is'ra-el went to Je-ru'sa-lem, which is Je'bus; where the Jeb'u-sites were, the inhabitants of the land.

5 And the inhabitants of Je'bus said to Da'-vid, Thou shalt not come hither. Nevertheless Da'vid took the castle of Zi'on, which is the city of Da'vid.

6 And Da'vid said, Whosoever smiteth the Jeb'u-sites first shall be chief and captain. So Jo'ab the son of Zer-u-i'ah went first up, and was chief.

7 And Da'vid dwelt in the castle; therefore they called it the city of Da'vid.

8 And he built the city round about, even from Mil'lo round about: and Jo'ab repaired the rest of the city.

9 So Da'vid waxed greater and greater: for the LORD of hosts was with him.

10 ¶ These also are the chief of the mighty men whom Da'vid had, who strengthened themselves with him in his kingdom, and with all Is'ra-el, to make him king, according to the word of the LORD concerning Is'ra-el.

11 And this is the number of the mighty men whom Da'vid had; Ja-sho'be-am, an Hach'mo-nite, the chief of the captains: he lifted up his spear against three hundred slain by him at one time.

12 And after him was E-le-a'zar the son of Do'do, the A-ho'hite, who was one of the three mighties.

13 He was with Da'vid at Pas-dam'mim, and there the Phi-lis'tines were gathered together to battle, where was a parcel of ground full of barley; and the people fled from before the Phi-lis'-tines.

14 And they set themselves in the midst of that parcel, and delivered it, and slew the Phi-lis'tines; and the LORD saved them by a great deliverance.

15 ¶ Now three of the thirty captains went down to the rock to Da'vid, into the cave of A-dul'lam; and the host of the Phi-lis'tines encamped in the valley of Reph'a-im.

16 And Da'vid was then in the hold, and the Phi-lis'tines' garrison was then at Beth'-le-hem.

17 And Da'vid longed, and said, Oh that one would give me drink of the water of the well of Beth'-le-hem, that is at the gate!

18 And the three brake through the host of the Phi-lis'tines, and drew water out of the well of Beth'-le-hem, that was by the gate, and took it, and brought it to Da'vid: but Da'vid would not drink of it, but poured it out to the LORD,

19 And said, My God forbid it me, that I should do this thing: shall I drink the blood of these men that have put their lives in jeopardy? for with the jeopardy of their lives they brought it. Therefore he would not drink it. These things did these three mightiest.

20 ¶ And A-bish'a-i the brother of Jo'ab, he was chief of the three: for lifting up his spear against three hundred, he slew them, and had a name among the three.

21 Of the three, he was more honourable than the two; for he was their captain: howbeit he attained not to the first three.

22 Be-na'iah the son of Je-hoi'a-da, the son of a valiant man of Kab'ze-el, who had done many acts; he slew two lionlike men of Mo'ab: also he went down and slew a lion in a pit in a snowy day.

23 And he slew an E-gyp'tian, a man of great stature, five cubits high; and in the E-gyp'tian's hand was a spear like a weaver's beam; and he went down to him with a staff, and plucked the spear out of the E-gyp'tian's hand, and slew him with his own spear.

24 These things did Be-na'iah the son of Je-hoi'a-da, and had the name among the three mighties.

25 Behold, he was honourable among the thirty, but attained not to the first three: and Da'vid set him over his guard.

26 ¶ Also the valiant men of the armies were, A'sa-hel the brother of Jo'ab, El-ha'nan the son of Do'do of Beth'-le-hem,

27 Sham'moth the Ha'ro-rite, He'lez the Pel'-o-nite,

28 I'ra the son of Ik'kesh the Te-ko'ite, A-bi-e'zer the An'toth-ite,

29 Sib'be-cai the Hu'shath-ite, I'lai the A-ho'-hite,

30 Ma-har'a-i the Ne-toph'a-thite, He'led the son of Ba'a-nah the Ne-toph'a-thite,

31 Ith'a-i the son of Ri'bai of Gib'e-ah, that pertained to the children of Ben'ja-min, Be-na'-iah the Pir'a-thon-ite,

32 Hu'rai of the brooks of Ga'ash, A-bi'el the Ar'bath-ite,

33 Az'ma-veth the Ba-ha'rum-ite, E-li'ah-ba the Sha-al'bo-nite,

34 The sons of Ha'shem the Gi'zo-nite, Jon'a-than the son of Sha'ge the Ha'ra-rite,

35 A-hi'am the son of Sa'car the Ha'ra-rite, El'i-phal the son of Ur,

36 He'pher the Mech'e-rath-ite, A-hi'jah the Pel'o-nite,

37 Hez'ro the Car'mel-ite, Na'a-rai the son of Ez'ba-i,

38 Jo'el the brother of Na'than, Mib'har the son of Hag-ge'ri,

39 Ze'lek the Am'mon-ite, Na-har'a-i the Be'-roth-ite, the armourbearer of Jo'ab the son of Zer-u-i'ah,

40 I'ra the Ith'rite, Ga'reb the Ith'rite,

41 U-ri'ah the Hit'tite, Za'bad the son of Ah'-lai,

42 Ad'i-na the son of Shi'za the Reu'ben-ite, a captain of the Reu'ben-ites, and thirty with him,

43 Ha'nan the son of Ma'a-chah, and Josh'a-phat the Mith'nite,

44 Uz-zi'a the Ash'te-rath-ite, Sha'ma and Je-hi'el the sons of Ho'than the Ar'o-er-ite,

45 Je-di'a-el the son of Shim'ri, and Jo'ha his brother, the Ti'zite,

46 E-li'el the Ma'ha-vite, and Jer'i-bai, and Josh-a-vi'ah, the sons of El'na-am, and Ith'mah the Mo'ab-ite,

47 E-li'el, and O'bed, and Ja'si-el the Mes'o-ba-ite.

12 NOW these are they that came to Da'-vid to Zik'lag, while he yet kept himself close because of Saul the son of Kish: and they were among the mighty men, helpers of the war.

2 They were armed with bows, and could use both the right hand and the left in hurling stones and shooting arrows out of a bow, even of Saul's brethren of Ben'ja-min.

3 The chief was A-hi-e'zer, then Jo'ash, the sons of She-ma'ah the Gib'e-ath-ite; and Je'zi-el, and Pe'let, the sons of Az'ma-veth; and Ber'a-chah, and Je'hu the An'toth-ite,

4 And Is-ma-i'ah the Gib'e-on-ite, a mighty man among the thirty, and over the thirty; and Jer-e-mi'ah, and Ja-ha'zi-el, and Jo-ha'nan, and Jos'a-bad the Ged'e-rath-ite,

5 E-lu'za-i, and Jer'i-moth, and Be-a-li'ah, and Shem-a-ri'ah, and Sheph-a-ti'ah the Har'u-phite,

6 El'ka-nah, and Je-si'ah, and A-zar'e-el, and Jo-e'zer, and Ja-sho'be-am, the Kor'hites,

7 And Jo-e'lah, and Zeb-a-di'ah, the sons of Jer'o-ham of Ge'dor.

8 And of the Gad'ites there separated themselves unto Da'vid into the hold to the wilderness men of might, and men of war fit for the battle, that could handle shield and buckler, whose faces were like the faces of lions, and were as swift as the roes upon the mountains;

9 E'zer the first, O-ba-di'ah the second, E-li'-ab the third,

10 Mish-man'nah the fourth, Jer-e-mi'ah the fifth,

11 At'tai the sixth, E-li'el the seventh,

12 Jo-ha'nan the eighth, El'za-bad the ninth,

13 Jer-e-mi'ah the tenth, Mach'ba-nai the eleventh.

14 These were of the sons of Gad, captains of the host: one of the least was over an hundred, and the greatest over a thousand.

15 These are they that went over Jor'dan in the first month, when it had overflown all his banks; and they put to flight all them of the valleys, both toward the east, and toward the west.

16 And there came of the children of Ben'ja-min and Ju'dah to the hold unto Da'vid.

17 And Da'vid went out to meet them, and answered and said unto them, If ye be come peaceably unto me to help me, mine heart shall be knit unto you: but if ye be come to betray me to mine enemies, seeing there is no wrong in mine hands, the God of our fathers look thereon, and rebuke it.

18 Then the spirit came upon A-mas'a-i, who was chief of the captains, and he said, Thine are we, Da'vid, and on thy side, thou son of Jes'se: peace, peace be unto thee, and peace be to thine helpers; for thy God helpeth thee. Then Da'vid received them, and made them captains of the band.

19 And there fell some of Ma-nas'seh to Da'-vid, when he came with the Phi-lis'tines against Saul to battle: but they helped them not: for the lords of the Phi-lis'tines upon advisement sent him away, saying, He will fall to his master Saul to the jeopardy of our heads.

20 As he went to Zik'lag, there fell to him of Ma-nas'seh, Ad'nah, and Joz'a-bad, and Je-di'a-el, and Mi'chael, and Joz'a-bad, and E-li'hu, and Zil'thai, captains of the thousands that were of Ma-nas'seh.

21 And they helped Da'vid against the band of the rovers: for they were all mighty men of valour, and were captains in the host.

22 For at that time day by day there came to Da'vid to help him, until it was a great host, like the host of God.

23 ¶ And these are the numbers of the bands that were ready armed to the war, and came to Da'vid to He'bron, to turn the kingdom of Saul to him, according to the word of the LORD.

24 The children of Ju'dah that bare shield and spear were six thousand and eight hundred, ready armed to the war.

25 Of the children of Sim'e-on, mighty men of valour for the war, seven thousand and one hundred.

26 Of the children of Le'vi four thousand and six hundred.

27 And Je-hoi'a-da was the leader of the Aar'on-ites, and with him were three thousand and seven hundred;

28 And Za'dok, a young man mighty of valour, and of his father's house twenty and two captains.

29 And of the children of Ben'ja-min, the kindred of Saul, three thousand: for hitherto the greatest part of them had kept the ward of the house of Saul.

30 And of the children of E'phra-im twenty thousand and eight hundred, mighty men of valour, famous throughout the house of their fathers.

31 And of the half tribe of Ma-nas'seh eighteen thousand, which were expressed by name, to come and make Da'vid king.

32 And of the children of Is'sa-char, which were men that had understanding of the times, to know what Is'ra-el ought to do; the heads of them were two hundred; and all their brethren were at their commandment.

33 Of Zeb'u-lun, such as went forth to battle, expert in war, with all instruments of war, fifty thousand, which could keep rank: they were not of double heart.

34 And of Naph'ta-li a thousand captains, and with them with shield and spear thirty and seven thousand.

35 And of the Dan'ites expert in war twenty and eight thousand and six hundred.

36 And of Ash'er, such as went forth to battle, expert in war, forty thousand.

37 And on the other side of Jor'dan, of the

Reu'ben-ites, and the Gad'ites, and of the half tribe of Ma-nas'seh, with all manner of instruments of war for the battle, an hundred and twenty thousand.

38 All these men of war, that could keep rank, came with a perfect heart to He'bron, to make Da'vid king over all Is'ra-el: and all the rest also of Is'ra-el were of one heart to make Da'vid king.

39 And there they were with Da'vid three days, eating and drinking: for their brethren had prepared for them.

40 Moreover they that were nigh them, even unto Is'sa-char and Zeb'u-lun and Naph'ta-li, brought bread on asses, and on camels, and on mules, and on oxen, and meat, meal, cakes of figs, and bunches of raisins, and wine, and oil, and oxen, and sheep abundantly: for there was joy in Is'ra-el.

13 AND Da'vid consulted with the captains of thousands and hundreds, and with every leader.

2 And Da'vid said unto all the congregation of Is'ra-el, If it seem good unto you, and that it be of the LORD our God, let us send abroad unto our brethren every where, that are left in all the land of Is'ra-el, and with them also to the priests and Le'vites which are in their cities and suburbs, that they may gather themselves unto us:

3 And let us bring again the ark of our God to us: for we enquired not at it in the days of Saul.

4 And all the congregation said that they would do so: for the thing was right in the eyes of all the people.

5 So Da'vid gathered all Is'ra-el together, from Shi'hor of E'gypt even unto the entering of He'math, to bring the ark of God from Kir'jath-je'a-rim.

6 And Da'vid went up, and all Is'ra-el, to Ba'-al-ah, that is, to Kir'jath-je'a-rim, which belonged to Ju'dah, to bring up thence the ark of God the LORD, that dwelleth between the cherubims, whose name is called on it.

7 And they carried the ark of God in a new cart out of the house of A-bin'a-dab: and Uz'za and A-hi'o drave the cart.

8 And Da'vid and all Is'ra-el played before God with all their might, and with singing, and with harps, and with psalteries, and with timbrels, and with cymbals, and with trumpets.

9 ¶ And when they came unto the threshingfloor of Chi'don, Uz'za put forth his hand to hold the ark; for the oxen stumbled.

10 And the anger of the LORD was kindled against Uz'za, and he smote him, because he put his hand to the ark: and there he died before God.

11 And Da'vid was displeased, because the LORD had made a breach upon Uz'za: wherefore that place is called Pe'rez-uz'za to this day.

12 And Da'vid was afraid of God that day, saying, How shall I bring the ark of God home to me?

13 So Da'vid brought not the ark home to himself to the city of Da'vid, but carried it aside into the house of O'bed-e'dom the Git'tite.

14 And the ark of God remained with the family of O'bed-e'dom in his house three months. And the LORD blessed the house of O'-bed-e'dom, and all that he had.

14 NOW Hi'ram king of Tyre sent messengers to Da'vid, and timber of cedars, with masons and carpenters, to build him an house.

2 And Da'vid perceived that the LORD had confirmed him king over Is'ra-el, for his kingdom was lifted up on high, because of his people Is'ra-el.

3 ¶ And Da'vid took more wives at Je-ru'sa-lem: and Da'vid begat more sons and daughters.

4 Now these are the names of his children which he had in Je-ru'sa-lem; Sham-mu'a, and Sho'bab, Na'than, and Sol'o-mon,

5 And Ib'har, and El-i-shu'a, and El'pa-let,

6 And No'gah, and Ne'pheg, and Ja-phi'a,

7 And E-lish'a-ma, and Be-el-i'a-da, and E-liph'a-let.

8 ¶ And when the Phi-lis'tines heard that Da'vid was anointed king over all Is'ra-el, all the Phi-lis'tines went up to seek Da'vid. And Da'vid heard of it, and went out against them.

9 And the Phi-lis'tines came and spread themselves in the valley of Reph'a-im.

10 And Da'vid enquired of God, saying, Shall I go up against the Phi-lis'tines? And wilt thou deliver them into mine hand? And the LORD said unto him, Go up; for I will deliver them into thine hand.

11 So they came up to Ba'al-per'a-zim; and Da'vid smote them there. Then Da'vid said, God hath broken in upon mine enemies by mine hand like the breaking forth of waters: therefore they called the name of that place Ba'al-per'a-zim.

12 And when they had left their gods there, Da'vid gave a commandment, and they were burned with fire.

13 And the Phi-lis'tines yet again spread themselves abroad in the valley.

14 Therefore Da'vid enquired again of God; and God said unto him, Go not up after them; turn away from them, and come upon them over against the mulberry trees.

15 And it shall be, when thou shalt hear a sound of going in the tops of the mulberry trees, that then thou shalt go out to battle: for God is gone forth before thee to smite the host of the Phi-lis'tines.

16 Da'vid therefore did as God commanded him: and they smote the host of the Phi-lis'tines from Gib'e-on even to Ga'zer.

17 And the fame of Da'vid went out into all lands; and the LORD brought the fear of him upon all nations.

15 AND Da'vid made him houses in the city of Da'vid, and prepared a place for the ark of God, and pitched for it a tent.

2 Then Da'vid said, None ought to carry the ark of God but the Le'vites: for them hath the LORD chosen to carry the ark of God, and to minister unto him for ever.

3 And Da'vid gathered all Is'ra-el together to Je-ru'sa-lem, to bring up the ark of the LORD unto his place, which he had prepared for it.

4 And Da'vid assembled the children of Aar'-on, and the Le'vites:

5 Of the sons of Ko'hath; U'ri-el the chief, and his brethren an hundred and twenty:

6 Of the sons of Me-ra'ri; A-sa-i'ah the chief, and his brethren two hundred and twenty:

7 Of the sons of Ger'shom; Jo'el the chief, and his brethren an hundred and thirty:

8 Of the sons of E-liz'a-phan; Shem-a-i'ah the chief, and his brethren two hundred:

9 Of the sons of He'bron; E-li'el the chief, and his brethren fourscore:

10 Of the sons of Uz'zi-el; Am-min'a-dab the chief, and his brethren an hundred and twelve:

11 And Da'vid called for Za'dok and A-bi'a-

thar the priests, and for the Le′vites, for U′ri-el, A-sa-i′ah, and Jo′el, Shem-a-i′ah, and E-li′el, and Am-min′a-dab,

12 And said unto them, Ye are the chief of the fathers of the Le′vites: sanctify yourselves, both ye and your brethren, that ye may bring up the ark of the LORD God of Is′ra-el unto the place that I have prepared for it.

13 For because ye did it not at the first, the LORD our God made a breach upon us, for that we sought him not after the due order.

14 So the priests and the Le′vites sanctified themselves to bring up the ark of the LORD God of Is′ra-el.

15 And the children of the Le′vites bare the ark of God upon their shoulders with the staves thereon, as Mo′ses commanded according to the word of the LORD.

16 And Da′vid spake to the chief of the Le′-vites to appoint their brethren to be the singers with instruments of musick, psalteries and harps and cymbals, sounding, by lifting up the voice with joy.

17 So the Le′vites appointed He′man the son of Jo′el; and of his brethren, A′saph the son of Ber-e-chi′ah; and of the sons of Me-ra′ri their brethren, E′than the son of Kush-a′iah;

18 And with them their brethren of the second degree, Zech-a-ri′ah, Ben, and Ja-a′zi-el, and She-mir′a-moth, and Je-hi′el, and Un′ni, E-li′ab, and Be-na′iah, and Ma-a-se′iah, and Mat-ti-thi′ah, and E-liph′e-leh, and Mik-ne′iah, and O′bed-e′dom, and Je-i′el, the porters.

19 So the singers, He′man, A′saph, and E′-than, were appointed to sound with cymbals of brass;

20 And Zech-a-ri′ah, and A′zi-el, and She-mir′a-moth, and Je-hi′el, and Un′ni, and E-li′ab, and Ma-a-se′iah, and Be-na′iah, with psalteries on Al′a-moth;

21 And Mat-ti-thi′ah, and E-liph′e-leh, and Mik-ne′iah, and O′bed-e′dom, and Je-i′el, and Az-a-zi′ah, with harps on the Shem′i-nith to excel.

22 And Chen-a-ni′ah, chief of the Le′vites, was for song: he instructed about the song, because he was skilful.

23 And Ber-e-chi′ah and El′ka-nah were doorkeepers for the ark.

24 And Sheb-a-ni′ah, and Je-hosh′a-phat, and Ne-than′e-el, and A-mas′a-i, and Zech-a-ri′ah, and Be-na′iah, and E-li-e′zer, the priests, did blow with the trumpets before the ark of God: and O′bed-e′dom and Je-hi′ah were doorkeepers for the ark.

25 ¶ So Da′vid, and the elders of Is′ra-el, and the captains over thousands, went to bring up the ark of the covenant of the LORD out of the house of O′bed-e′dom with joy.

26 And it came to pass, when God helped the Le′vites that bare the ark of the covenant of the LORD, that they offered seven bullocks and seven rams.

27 And Da′vid was clothed with a robe of fine linen, and all the Le′vites that bare the ark, and the singers, and Chen-a-ni′ah the master of the song with the singers: Da′vid also had upon him an ephod of linen.

28 Thus all Is′ra-el brought up the ark of the covenant of the LORD with shouting, and with sound of the cornet, and with trumpets, and with cymbals, making a noise with psalteries and harps.

29 ¶ And it came to pass, as the ark of the covenant of the LORD came to the city of Da′vid, that Mi′chal the daughter of Saul looking out at a window saw king Da′vid dancing and playing: and she despised him in her heart.

16 SO they brought the ark of God, and set it in the midst of the tent that Da′vid had pitched for it: and they offered burnt sacrifices and peace offerings before God.

2 And when Da′vid had made an end of offering the burnt offerings and the peace offerings, he blessed the people in the name of the LORD.

3 And he dealt to every one of Is′ra-el, both man and woman, to every one a loaf of bread, and a good piece of flesh, and a flagon of wine.

4 ¶ And he appointed certain of the Le′vites to minister before the ark of the LORD, and to record, and to thank and praise the LORD God of Is′ra-el:

5 A′saph the chief, and next to him Zech-a-ri′ah, Je-i′el, and She-mir′a-moth, and Je-hi′el, and Mat-ti-thi′ah, and E-li′ab, and Be-na′iah, and O′bed-e′dom: and Je-i′el with psalteries and with harps; but A′saph made a sound with cymbals;

6 Be-na′iah also and Ja-ha′zi-el the priests with trumpets continually before the ark of the covenant of God.

7 ¶ Then on that day Da′vid delivered first this psalm to thank the LORD into the hand of A′saph and his brethren.

8 Give thanks unto the LORD, call upon his name, make known his deeds among the people.

9 Sing unto him, sing psalms unto him, talk ye of all his wondrous works.

10 Glory ye in his holy name: let the heart of them rejoice that seek the LORD.

11 Seek the LORD and his strength, seek his face continually.

12 Remember his marvellous works that he hath done, his wonders, and the judgments of his mouth;

13 O ye seed of Is′ra-el his servant, ye children of Ja′cob, his chosen ones.

14 He is the LORD our God; his judgments are in all the earth.

15 Be ye mindful always of his covenant; the word which he commanded to a thousand generations;

16 Even of the covenant which he made with A′bra-ham, and of his oath unto I′saac;

17 And hath confirmed the same to Ja′cob for a law, and to Is′ra-el for an everlasting covenant,

18 Saying, Unto thee will I give the land of Ca′naan, the lot of your inheritance;

19 When ye were but few, even a few, and strangers in it.

20 And when they went from nation to nation, and from one kingdom to another people;

21 He suffered no man to do them wrong: yea, he reproved kings for their sakes,

22 Saying, Touch not mine anointed, and do my prophets no harm.

23 Sing unto the LORD, all the earth; shew forth from day to day his salvation.

24 Declare his glory among the heathen; his marvellous works among all nations.

25 For great is the LORD, and greatly to be praised: he also is to be feared above all gods.

26 For all the gods of the people are idols: but the LORD made the heavens.

27 Glory and honour are in his presence; strength and gladness are in his place.

28 Give unto the LORD, ye kindreds of the people, give unto the LORD glory and strength.

29 Give unto the LORD the glory due unto his

name: bring an offering, and come before him: worship the LORD in the beauty of holiness.

30 Fear before him, all the earth: the world also shall be stable, that it be not moved.

31 Let the heavens be glad, and let the earth rejoice: and let men say among the nations, The LORD reigneth.

32 Let the sea roar, and the fulness thereof: let the fields rejoice, and all that is therein.

33 Then shall the trees of the wood sing out at the presence of the LORD, because he cometh to judge the earth.

34 O give thanks unto the LORD; for he is good; for his mercy endureth for ever.

35 And say ye, Save us, O God of our salvation, and gather us together, and deliver us from the heathen, that we may give thanks to thy holy name, and glory in thy praise.

36 Blessed be the LORD God of Is′ra-el for ever and ever. And all the people said, Amen, and praised the LORD.

37 ¶ So he left there before the ark of the covenant of the LORD A′saph and his brethren, to minister before the ark continually, as every day's work required:

38 And O′bed-e′dom with their brethren, threescore and eight; O′bed-e′dom also the son of Jed′u-thun and Ho′sah to be porters:

39 And Za′dok the priest, and his brethren the priests, before the tabernacle of the LORD in the high place that was at Gib′e-on,

40 To offer burnt offerings unto the LORD upon the altar of the burnt offering continually morning and evening, and to do according to all that is written in the law of the LORD, which he commanded Is′ra-el;

41 And with them He′man and Jed′u-thun, and the rest that were chosen, who were expressed by name, to give thanks to the LORD, because his mercy endureth for ever;

42 And with them He′man and Jed′u-thun with trumpets and cymbals for those that should make a sound, and with musical instruments of God. And the sons of Jed′u-thun were porters.

43 And all the people departed every man to his house: and Da′vid returned to bless his house.

17 NOW it came to pass, as Da′vid sat in his house, that Da′vid said to Na′than the prophet, Lo, I dwell in an house of cedars, but the ark of the covenant of the LORD remaineth under curtains.

2 Then Na′than said unto Da′vid, Do all that is in thine heart; for God is with thee.

3 ¶ And it came to pass the same night, that the word of God came to Na′than, saying,

4 Go and tell Da′vid my servant, Thus saith the LORD, Thou shalt not build me an house to dwell in:

5 For I have not dwelt in an house since the day that I brought up Is′ra-el unto this day; but have gone from tent to tent, and from one tabernacle to another.

6 Wheresoever I have walked with all Is′ra-el, spake I a word to any of the judges of Is′ra-el, whom I commanded to feed my people, saying, Why have ye not built me an house of cedars?

7 Now therefore thus shalt thou say unto my servant Da′vid, Thus saith the LORD of hosts, I took thee from the sheepcote, even from following the sheep, that thou shouldest be ruler over my people Is′ra-el:

8 And I have been with thee whithersoever thou hast walked, and have cut off all thine enemies from before thee, and have made thee a name like the name of the great men that are in the earth.

9 Also I will ordain a place for my people Is′-ra-el, and will plant them, and they shall dwell in their place, and shall be moved no more; neither shall the children of wickedness waste them any more, as at the beginning,

10 And since the time that I commanded judges to be over my people Is′ra-el. Moreover I will subdue all thine enemies. Furthermore I tell thee that the LORD will build thee an house.

11 ¶ And it shall come to pass, when thy days be expired that thou must go to be with thy fathers, that I will raise up thy seed after thee, which shall be of thy sons; and I will establish his kingdom.

12 He shall build me an house, and I will stablish his throne for ever.

13 I will be his father, and he shall be my son: and I will not take my mercy away from him, as I took it from him that was before thee:

14 But I will settle him in mine house and in my kingdom for ever: and his throne shall be established for evermore.

15 According to all these words, and according to all this vision, so did Na′than speak unto Da′vid.

16 ¶ And Da′vid the king came and sat before the LORD, and said, Who am I, O LORD God, and what is mine house, that thou hast brought me hitherto?

17 And yet this was a small thing in thine eyes, O God; for thou hast also spoken of thy servant's house for a great while to come, and hast regarded me according to the estate of a man of high degree, O LORD God.

18 What can Da′vid speak more to thee for the honour of thy servant? for thou knowest thy servant.

19 O LORD, for thy servant's sake, and according to thine own heart, hast thou done all this greatness, in making known all these great things.

20 O LORD, there is, none like thee, neither is there any God beside thee, according to all that we have heard with our ears.

21 And what one nation in the earth is like thy people Is′ra-el, whom God went to redeem to be his own people, to make thee a name of greatness and terribleness, by driving out nations from before thy people, whom thou hast redeemed out of E′gypt?

22 For thy people Is′ra-el didst thou make thine own people for ever; and thou, LORD, becamest their God.

23 Therefore now, LORD, let the thing that thou hast spoken concerning thy servant and concerning his house be established for ever, and do as thou hast said.

24 Let it even be established, that thy name may be magnified for ever, saying, The LORD of hosts is the God of Is′ra-el, even a God to Is′ra-el: and let the house of Da′vid thy servant be established before thee.

25 For thou, O my God, hast told thy servant that thou wilt build him an house: therefore thy servant hath found in his heart to pray before thee.

26 And now, LORD, thou art God, and hast promised this goodness unto thy servant:

27 Now therefore let it please thee to bless the house of thy servant, that it may be before thee for ever: for thou blessest, O LORD, and it shall be blessed for ever.

18 NOW after this it came to pass, that Da'vid smote the Phi-lis'tines, and subdued them, and took Gath and her towns out of the hand of the Phi-lis'tines.

2 And he smote Mo'ab; and the Mo'ab-ites became Da'vid's servants, *and* brought gifts.

3 ¶ And Da'vid smote Had-ar-e'zer king of Zo'bah unto Ha'math, as he went to stablish his dominion by the river Eu-phra'tes.

4 And Da'vid took from him a thousand chariots, and seven thousand horsemen, and twenty thousand footmen: Da'vid also houghed all the chariot *horses*, but reserved of them an hundred chariots.

5 And when the Syr'i-ans of Da-mas'cus came to help Had-ar-e'zer king of Zo'bah, Da'vid slew of the Syr'i-ans two and twenty thousand men.

6 Then Da'vid put *garrisons* in Syr'i-a-da-mas'cus; and the Syr'i-ans became Da'vid's servants, *and* brought gifts. Thus the LORD preserved Da'vid whithersoever he went.

7 And Da'vid took the shields of gold that were on the servants of Had-ar-e'zer, and brought them to Je-ru'sa-lem.

8 Likewise from Tib'hath, and from Chun, cities of Had-ar-e'zer, brought Da'vid very much brass, wherewith Sol'o-mon made the brasen sea, and the pillars, and the vessels of brass.

9 ¶ Now when To'u king of Ha'math heard how Da'vid had smitten all the host of Had-ar-e'zer king of Zo'bah;

10 He sent Ha-do'ram his son to king Da'vid, to enquire of his welfare, and to congratulate him, because he had fought against Had-ar-e'zer, and smitten him; (for Had-ar-e'zer had war with To'u;) and *with him* all manner of vessels of gold and silver and brass.

11 ¶ Them also king Da'vid dedicated unto the LORD, with the silver and the gold that he brought from all *these* nations; from E'dom, and from Mo'ab, and from the children of Am'mon, and from the Phi-lis'tines, and from Am'a-lek.

12 Moreover A-bish'a-i the son of Zer-u-i'ah slew of the E'dom-ites in the valley of salt eighteen thousand.

13 ¶ And he put garrisons in E'dom; and all the E'dom-ites became Da'vid's servants. Thus the LORD preserved Da'vid whithersoever he went.

14 ¶ So Da'vid reigned over all Is'ra-el, and executed judgment and justice among all his people.

15 And Jo'ab the son of Zer-u-i'ah *was* over the host; and Je-hosh'a-phat the son of A-hi'lud, recorder.

16 And Za'dok the son of A-hi'tub, and A-bim'e-lech the son of A-bi'a-thar, *were* the priests; and Shav'sha was scribe;

17 And Be-na'iah the son of Je-hoi'a-da *was* over the Cher'eth-ites and the Pe'leth-ites; and the sons of Da'vid *were* chief about the king.

19 NOW it came to pass after this, that Na'hash the king of the children of Am'mon died, and his son reigned in his stead.

2 And Da'vid said, I will shew kindness unto Ha'nun the son of Na'hash, because his father shewed kindness to me. And Da'vid sent messengers to comfort him concerning his father. So the servants of Da'vid came into the land of the children of Am'mon to Ha'nun, to comfort him.

3 But the princes of the children of Am'mon said to Ha'nun, Thinkest thou that Da'vid doth honour thy father, that he hath sent comforters unto thee? are not his servants come unto thee for to search, and to overthrow, and to spy out the land?

4 Wherefore Ha'nun took Da'vid's servants, and shaved them, and cut off their garments in the midst hard by their buttocks, and sent them away.

5 Then there went *certain*, and told Da'vid how the men were served. And he sent to meet them: for the men were greatly ashamed. And the king said, Tarry at Jer'i-cho until your beards be grown, and *then* return.

6 ¶ And when the children of Am'mon saw that they had made themselves odious to Da'vid, Ha'nun and the children of Am'mon sent a thousand talents of silver to hire them chariots and horsemen out of Mes-o-po-ta'mi-a, and out of Syr'i-a-ma'a-chah, and out of Zo'bah.

7 So they hired thirty and two thousand chariots, and the king of Ma'a-chah and his people; who came and pitched before Med'e-ba. And the children of Am'mon gathered themselves together from their cities, and came to battle.

8 And when Da'vid heard *of it*, he sent Jo'ab, and all the host of the mighty men.

9 And the children of Am'mon came out, and put the battle in array before the gate of the city: and the kings that were come *were* by themselves in the field.

10 Now when Jo'ab saw that the battle was set against him before and behind, he chose out of all the choice of Is'ra-el, and put *them* in array against the Syr'i-ans.

11 And the rest of the people he delivered unto the hand of A-bish'a-i his brother, and they set *themselves* in array against the children of Am'mon.

12 And he said, If the Syr'i-ans be too strong for me, then thou shalt help me: but if the children of Am'mon be too strong for thee, then I will help thee.

13 Be of good courage, and let us behave ourselves valiantly for our people, and for the cities of our God: and let the LORD do *that which is* good in his sight.

14 So Jo'ab and the people that *were* with him drew nigh before the Syr'i-ans unto the battle; and they fled before him.

15 And when the children of Am'mon saw that the Syr'i-ans were fled, they likewise fled before A-bish'a-i his brother, and entered into the city. Then Jo'ab came to Je-ru'sa-lem.

16 ¶ And when the Syr'i-ans saw that they were put to the worse before Is'ra-el, they sent messengers, and drew forth the Syr'i-ans that *were* beyond the river: and Sho'phach the captain of the host of Had-ar-e'zer *went* before them.

17 And it was told Da'vid; and he gathered all Is'ra-el, and passed over Jor'dan, and came upon them, and set *the battle* in array against them. So when Da'vid had put the battle in array against the Syr'i-ans, they fought with him.

18 But the Syr'i-ans fled before Is'ra-el; and Da'vid slew of the Syr'i-ans seven thousand *men which fought* in chariots, and forty thousand footmen, and killed Sho'phach the captain of the host.

19 And when the servants of Had-ar-e'zer saw that they were put to the worse before Is'ra-el, they made peace with Da'vid, and became his servants: neither would the Syr'i-ans help the children of Am'mon any more.

20 AND it came to pass, that after the year was expired, at the time that kings go out *to battle*, Jo'ab led forth the power of the army, and wasted the country of the children of Am'mon, and came and besieged Rab'bah. But Da'vid tarried at Je-ru'sa-lem. And Jo'ab smote Rab'bah, and destroyed it.

2 And Da'vid took the crown of their king from off his head, and found it to weigh a talent of gold, and *there were* precious stones in it; and it was set upon Da'vid's head: and he brought also exceeding much spoil out of the city.

3 And he brought out the people that *were* in it, and cut *them* with saws, and with harrows of iron, and with axes. Even so dealt Da'vid with all the cities of the children of Am'mon. And Da'vid and all the people returned to Je-ru'sa-lem.

4 ¶ And it came to pass after this, that there arose war at Ge'zer with the Phi-lis'tines; at which time Sib'be-chai the Hu'shath-ite slew Sip'pai, *that was* of the children of the giant: and they were subdued.

5 And there was war again with the Phi-lis'-tines; and El-ha'nan the son of Ja'ir slew Lah'mi the brother of Go-li'ath the Git'tite, whose spear staff *was* like a weaver's beam.

6 And yet again there was war at Gath, where was a man of *great* stature, whose fingers and toes *were* four and twenty, six *on each hand*, and six *on each foot*: and he also was the son of the giant.

7 But when he defied Is'ra-el, Jon'a-than the son of Shim'e-a Da'vid's brother slew him.

8 These were born unto the giant in Gath; and they fell by the hand of Da'vid, and by the hand of his servants.

21 AND Sa'tan stood up against Is'ra-el, and provoked Da'vid to number Is'ra-el.

2 And Da'vid said to Jo'ab and to the rulers of the people, Go, number Is'ra-el from Be'er-she'ba even to Dan; and bring the number of them to me, that I may know *it*.

3 And Jo'ab answered, The LORD make his people an hundred times so many more as they *be*: but, my lord the king, *are* they not all my lord's servants? why then doth my lord require this thing? why will he be a cause of trespass to Is'ra-el?

4 Nevertheless the king's word prevailed against Jo'ab. Wherefore Jo'ab departed, and went throughout all Is'ra-el, and came to Je-ru'-sa-lem.

5 ¶ And Jo'ab gave the sum of the number of the people unto Da'vid. And all *they* of Is'ra-el were a thousand thousand and an hundred thousand men that drew sword: and Ju'dah *was* four hundred threescore and ten thousand men that drew sword.

6 But Le'vi and Ben'ja-min counted he not among them: for the king's word was abominable to Jo'ab.

7 And God was displeased with this thing; therefore he smote Is'ra-el.

8 And Da'vid said unto God, I have sinned greatly, because I have done this thing: but now, I beseech thee, do away the iniquity of thy servant; for I have done very foolishly.

9 ¶ And the LORD spake unto Gad, Da'vid's seer, saying,

10 Go and tell Da'vid, saying, Thus saith the LORD, I offer thee three *things*: choose thee one of them, that I may do *it* unto thee.

11 So Gad came to Da'vid, and said unto him, Thus saith the LORD, Choose thee

12 Either three years' famine; or three months to be destroyed before thy foes, while

that the sword of thine enemies overtaketh *thee*; or else three days the sword of the LORD, even the pestilence, in the land, and the angel of the LORD destroying throughout all the coasts of Is'ra-el. Now therefore advise thyself what word I shall bring again to him that sent me.

13 And Da'vid said unto Gad, I am in a great strait: let me fall now into the hand of the LORD; for very great *are* his mercies: but let me not fall into the hand of man.

14 ¶ So the LORD sent pestilence upon Is'ra-el: and there fell of Is'ra-el seventy thousand men.

15 And God sent an angel unto Je-ru'sa-lem to destroy it: and as he was destroying, the LORD beheld, and he repented him of the evil, and said to the angel that destroyed, It is enough, stay now thine hand. And the angel of the LORD stood by the threshingfloor of Or'nan the Jeb'u-site.

16 And Da'vid lifted up his eyes, and saw the angel of the LORD stand between the earth and the heaven, having a drawn sword in his hand stretched out over Je-ru'sa-lem. Then Da'vid and the elders *of Is'ra-el, who were* clothed in sackcloth, fell upon their faces.

17 And Da'vid said unto God, *Is it* not I *that* commanded the people to be numbered? even I it is that have sinned and done evil indeed; but *as for* these sheep, what have they done? let thine hand, I pray thee, O LORD my God, be on me, and on my father's house; but not on thy people, that they should be plagued.

18 ¶ Then the angel of the LORD commanded Gad to say to Da'vid, that Da'vid should go up, and set up an altar unto the LORD in the threshingfloor of Or'nan the Jeb'u-site.

19 And Da'vid went up at the saying of Gad, which he spake in the name of the LORD.

20 And Or'nan turned back, and saw the angel; and his four sons with him hid themselves. Now Or'nan was threshing wheat.

21 And as Da'vid came to Or'nan, Or'nan looked and saw Da'vid, and went out of the threshingfloor, and bowed himself to Da'vid with *his* face to the ground.

22 Then Da'vid said to Or'nan, Grant me the place of *this* threshingfloor, that I may build an altar therein unto the LORD: thou shalt grant it me for the full price: that the plague may be stayed from the people.

23 And Or'nan said unto Da'vid, Take *it* to thee, and let my lord the king do *that which is* good in his eyes: lo, I give *thee* the oxen *also* for burnt offerings, and the threshing instruments for wood, and the wheat for the meat offering; I give it all.

24 And king Da'vid said to Or'nan, Nay; but I will verily buy it for the full price: for I will not take *that* which *is* thine for the LORD, nor offer burnt offerings without cost.

25 So Da'vid gave to Or'nan for the place six hundred shekels of gold by weight.

26 And Da'vid built there an altar unto the LORD, and offered burnt offerings and peace-offerings, and called upon the LORD; and he answered him from heaven by fire upon the altar of burnt offering.

27 And the LORD commanded the angel; and he put up his sword again into the sheath thereof.

28 ¶ At that time when Da'vid saw that the LORD had answered him in the threshingfloor of Or'nan the Jeb'u-site, then he sacrificed there.

29 For the tabernacle of the LORD, which Mo'ses made in the wilderness, and the altar of

the burnt offering, were at that season in the high place at Gib'e-on.

30 But Da'vid could not go before it to enquire of God: for he was afraid because of the sword of the angel of the LORD.

22 THEN Da'vid said, This is the house of the LORD God, and this is the altar of the burnt offering for Is'ra-el.

2 And Da'vid commanded to gather together the strangers that were in the land of Is'ra-el; and he set masons to hew wrought stones to build the house of God.

3 And Da'vid prepared iron in abundance for the nails for the doors of the gates, and for the joinings; and brass in abundance without weight;

4 Also cedar trees in abundance: for the Zi-do'ni-ans and they of Tyre brought much cedar wood to Da'vid.

5 And Da'vid said, Sol'o-mon my son is young and tender, and the house that is to be builded for the LORD must be exceeding magnifical, of fame and of glory throughout all countries: I will therefore now make preparation for it. So Da'vid prepared abundantly before his death.

6 ¶ Then he called for Sol'o-mon his son, and charged him to build an house for the LORD God of Is'ra-el.

7 And Da'vid said to Sol'o-mon, My son, as for me, it was in my mind to build an house unto the name of the LORD my God:

8 But the word of the LORD came to me, saying, Thou hast shed blood abundantly, and hast made great wars: thou shalt not build an house unto my name, because thou hast shed much blood upon the earth in my sight.

9 Behold, a son shall be born to thee, who shall be a man of rest; and I will give him rest from all his enemies round about: for his name shall be Sol'o-mon, and I will give peace and quietness unto Is'ra-el in his days.

10 He shall build an house for my name; and he shall be my son, and I will be his father; and I will establish the throne of his kingdom over Is'ra-el for ever.

11 Now, my son, the LORD be with thee; and prosper thou, and build the house of the LORD thy God, as he hath said of thee.

12 Only the LORD give thee wisdom and understanding, and give thee charge concerning Is'ra-el, that thou mayest keep the law of the LORD thy God.

13 Then shalt thou prosper, if thou takest heed to fulfil the statutes and judgments which the LORD charged Mo'ses with concerning Is'ra-el: be strong, and of good courage; dread not, nor be dismayed.

14 Now, behold, in my trouble I have prepared for the house of the LORD an hundred thousand talents of gold, and a thousand thousand talents of silver; and of brass and iron without weight; for it is in abundance: timber also and stone have I prepared; and thou mayest add thereto.

15 Moreover there are workmen with thee in abundance, hewers and workers of stone and timber, and all manner of cunning men for every manner of work.

16 Of the gold, the silver, and the brass, and the iron, there is no number. Arise therefore, and be doing, and the LORD be with thee.

17 ¶ Da'vid also commanded all the princes of Is'ra-el to help Sol'o-mon his son, saying,

18 Is not the LORD your God with you? and hath he not given you rest on every side? for he hath given the inhabitants of the land into mine hand; and the land is subdued before the LORD, and before his people.

19 Now set your heart and your soul to seek the LORD your God; arise therefore, and build ye the sanctuary of the LORD God, to bring the ark of the covenant of the LORD, and the holy vessels of God, into the house that is to be built to the name of the LORD.

23 SO when Da'vid was old and full of days, he made Sol'o-mon his son king over Is'ra-el.

2 ¶ And he gathered together all the princes of Is'ra-el, with the priests and the Le'vites.

3 Now the Le'vites were numbered from the age of thirty years and upward: and their number by their polls, man by man, was thirty and eight thousand.

4 Of which, twenty and four thousand were to set forward the work of the house of the LORD; and six thousand were officers and judges:

5 Moreover four thousand were porters; and four thousand praised the LORD with the instruments which I made, said Da'vid, to praise therewith.

6 And Da'vid divided them into courses among the sons of Le'vi, namely, Ger'shon, Ko'-hath, and Me-ra'ri.

7 ¶ Of the Ger'shon-ites were, La'a-dan, and Shim'e-i.

8 The sons of La'a-dan; the chief was Je-hi'el, and Ze'tham, and Jo'el, three.

9 The sons of Shim'e-i; Shel'o-mith, and Ha'-zi-el, and Ha'ran, three. These were the chief of the fathers of La'a-dan.

10 And the sons of Shim'e-i were, Ja'hath, Zi'na, and Je'ush, and Be-ri'ah. These four were the sons of Shim'e-i.

11 And Ja'hath was the chief, and Zi'zah the second: but Je'ush and Be-ri'ah had not many sons; therefore they were in one reckoning, according to their father's house.

12 ¶ The sons of Ko'hath; Am'ram, Iz'har, He'bron, and Uz'zi-el, four.

13 The sons of Am'ram; Aar'on and Mo'ses: and Aar'on was separated, that he should sanctify the most holy things, he and his sons for ever, to burn incense before the LORD, to minister unto him, and to bless in his name for ever.

14 Now concerning Mo'ses the man of God, his sons were named of the tribe of Le'vi.

15 The sons of Mo'ses were, Ger'shom, and E-li-e'zer.

16 Of the sons of Ger'shom, Sheb'u-el was the chief.

17 And the sons of E-li-e'zer were, Re-ha-bi'-ah the chief. And E-li-e'zer had none other sons; but the sons of Re-ha-bi'ah were very many.

18 Of the sons of Iz'har; Shel'o-mith the chief.

19 Of the sons of He'bron; Je-ri'ah the first, Am-a-ri'ah the second, Ja-ha'zi-el the third, and Jek-a-me'am the fourth.

20 Of the sons of Uz'zi-el; Mi'cah the first, and Je-si'ah the second.

21 ¶ The sons of Me-ra'ri; Mah'li, and Mu'-shi. The sons of Mah'li; E-le-a'zar, and Kish.

22 And E-le-a'zar died, and had no sons, but daughters: and their brethren the sons of Kish took them.

23 The sons of Mu'shi; Mah'li, and E'der, and Jer'e-moth, three.

24 ¶ These were the sons of Le'vi after the house of their fathers; even the chief of the fathers, as they were counted by number of

names by their polls, that did the work for the service of the house of the LORD, from the age of twenty years and upward.

25 For Da'vid said, The LORD God of Is'ra-el hath given rest unto his people, that they may dwell in Je-ru'sa-lem for ever:

26 And also unto the Le'vites; they shall no more carry the tabernacle, nor any vessels of it for the service thereof.

27 For by the last words of Da'vid the Le'-vites were numbered from twenty years old and above:

28 Because their office was to wait on the sons of Aar'on for the service of the house of the LORD, in the courts, and in the chambers, and in the purifying of all holy things, and the work of the service of the house of God;

29 Both for the shewbread, and for the fine flour for meat offering, and for the unleavened cakes, and for that which is baked in the pan, and for that which is fried, and for all manner of measure and size;

30 And to stand every morning to thank and praise the LORD, and likewise at even;

31 And to offer all burnt sacrifices unto the LORD in the sabbaths, in the new moons, and on the set feasts, by number, according to the order commanded unto them, continually before the LORD:

32 And that they should keep the charge of the tabernacle of the congregation, and the charge of the holy place, and the charge of the sons of Aar'on their brethren, in the service of the house of the LORD.

24 NOW these are the divisions of the sons of Aar'on. The sons of Aar'on; Na'dab, and A-bi'hu, E-le-a'zar, and Ith'a-mar.

2 But Na'dab and A-bi'hu died before their father, and had no children: therefore E-le-a'zar and Ith'a-mar executed the priest's office.

3 And Da'vid distributed them, both Za'dok of the sons of E-le-a'zar, and A-him'e-lech of the sons of Ith'a-mar, according to their offices in their service.

4 And there were more chief men found of the sons of E-le-a'zar than of the sons of Ith'a-mar; and thus were they divided. Among the sons of E-le-a'zar there were sixteen chief men of the house of their fathers, and eight among the sons of Ith'a-mar according to the house of their fathers.

5 Thus were they divided by lot, one sort with another; for the governors of the sanctuary, and governors of the house of God, were of the sons of E-le-a'zar, and of the sons of Ith'a-mar.

6 And Shem-a-i'ah the son of Ne-than'e-el the scribe, one of the Le'vites, wrote them before the king, and the princes, and Za'dok the priest, and A-him'e-lech the son of A-bi'a-thar, and before the chief of the fathers of the priests and Le'vites: one principal household being taken for E-le-a'zar, and one taken for Ith'a-mar.

7 Now the first lot came forth to Je-hoi'a-rib, the second to Je-da'iah.

8 The third to Ha'rim, the fourth to Se-o'rim,

9 The fifth to Mal-chi'jah, the sixth to Mij'a-min,

10 The seventh to Hak'koz, the eighth to A-bi'jah,

11 The ninth to Jesh'u-ah, the tenth to Shech-a-ni'ah,

12 The eleventh to E-li'a-shib, the twelfth to Ja'kim,

13 The thirteenth to Hup'pah, the fourteenth to Je'sheb'e-ab,

14 The fifteenth to Bil'gah, the sixteenth to Im'mer,

15 The seventeenth to He'zir, the eighteenth to Aph'ses,

16 The nineteenth to Peth-a-hi'ah, the twentieth to Je-hez'e-kel,

17 The one and twentieth to Ja'chin, the two and twentieth to Ga'mul,

18 The three and twentieth to Del-a-i'ah, the four and twentieth to Ma-a-zi'ah.

19 These were the orderings of them in their service to come into the house of the LORD, according to their manner, under Aar'on their father, as the LORD God of Is'ra-el had commanded him.

20 ¶ And the rest of the sons of Le'vi were these: Of the sons of Am'ram; Shu'ba-el: of the sons of Shu'ba-el; Jeh-de'iah.

21 Concerning Re-ha-bi'ah: of the sons of Re-ha-bi'ah, the first was Issh-i'ah.

22 Of the Iz'har-ites; Shel'o-moth: of the sons of Shel'o-moth; Ja'hath.

23 And the sons of He'bron; Je-ri'ah the first, Am-a-ri'ah the second, Ja-ha'zi-el the third, Jek-a-me'am the fourth.

24 Of the sons of Uz'zi-el; Mi'chah: of the sons of Mi'chah; Sha'mir.

25 The brother of Mi'chah was Issh-i'ah: of the sons of Issh-i'ah; Zech-a-ri'ah.

26 The sons of Me-ra'ri were Mah'li and Mu'-shi: the sons of Ja-a-zi'ah; Be'no.

27 ¶ The sons of Me-ra'ri by Ja-a-zi'ah; Be'-no, and Sho'ham, and Zac'cur, and Ib'ri.

28 Of Mah'li came E-le-a'zar, who had no sons.

29 Concerning Kish: the son of Kish was Je-rah'me-el.

30 The sons also of Mu'shi; Mah'li, and E'der, and Jer'i-moth. These were the sons of the Le'-vites after the house of their fathers.

31 These likewise cast lots over against their brethren the sons of Aar'on in the presence of Da'vid the king, and Za'dok, and A-him'e-lech, and the chief of the fathers of the priests and Le'vites, even the principal fathers over against their younger brethren.

25 MOREOVER Da'vid and the captains of the host separated to the service of the sons of A'saph, and of He'man, and of Jed'u-thun, who should prophesy with harps, with psalteries, and with cymbals: and the number of the workmen according to their service was:

2 Of the sons of A'saph; Zac'cur, and Jo'seph, and Neth-a-ni'ah, and As-a-re'lah, the sons of A'saph under the hands of A'saph, which prophesied according to the order of the king.

3 Of Jed'u-thun: the sons of Jed'u-thun; Ged-a-li'ah, and Ze'ri, and Je-sha'iah, Hash-a-bi'ah, and Mat-ti-thi'ah, six, under the hands of their father Jed'u-thun, who prophesied with a harp, to give thanks and to praise the LORD.

4 Of He'man: the sons of He'man; Buk-ki'ah, Mat-ta-ni'ah, Uz'zi-el, Sheb'u-el, and Jer'i-moth, Han-a-ni'ah, Ha-na'ni, E-li'a-thah, Gid-dal'ti, and Ro-mam'ti-e'zer, Josh-bek'a-shah, Mal'lo-thi, Ho'thir, and Ma-ha'zi-oth:

5 All these were the sons of He'man the king's seer in the words of God, to lift up the horn. And God gave to He'man fourteen sons and three daughters.

6 All these were under the hands of their father for song in the house of the LORD, with cymbals, psalteries, and harps, for the service

of the house of God, according to the king's order to A'saph, Jed'u-thun, and He'man.

7 So the number of them, with their brethren that were instructed in the songs of the LORD, even all that were cunning, was two hundred fourscore and eight.

8 ¶ And they cast lots, ward against ward, as well the small as the great, the teacher as the scholar.

9 Now the first lot came forth for A'saph to Jo'seph: the second to Ged-a-li'ah, who with his brethren and sons were twelve:

10 The third to Zac'cur, he, his sons, and his brethren, were twelve:

11 The fourth to Iz'ri, he, his sons, and his brethren, were twelve:

12 The fifth to Neth-a-ni'ah, he, his sons, and his brethren, were twelve:

13 The sixth to Buk-ki'ah, he, his sons, and his brethren, were twelve:

14 The seventh to Je-shar'e-lah, he, his sons, and his brethren, were twelve:

15 The eighth to Je-sha'iah, he, his sons, and his brethren, were twelve:

16 The ninth to Mat-ta-ni'ah, he, his sons, and his brethren, were twelve:

17 The tenth to Shim'e-i, he, his sons, and his brethren, were twelve:

18 The eleventh to A-zar'e-el, he, his sons, and his brethren, were twelve:

19 The twelfth to Hash-a-bi'ah, he, his sons, and his brethren, were twelve:

20 The thirteenth to Shu'ba-el, he, his sons, and his brethren, were twelve:

21 The fourteenth to Mat-ti-thi'ah, he, his sons, and his brethren, were twelve:

22 The fifteenth to Jer'e-moth, he, his sons, and his brethren, were twelve:

23 The sixteenth to Han-a-ni'ah, he, his sons, and his brethren, were twelve:

24 The seventeenth to Josh-bek'a-shah, he, his sons, and his brethren, were twelve:

25 The eighteenth to Ha-na'ni, he, his sons, and his brethren, were twelve:

26 The nineteenth to Mal'lo-thi, he, his sons, and his brethren, were twelve:

27 The twentieth to E-li'a-thah, he, his sons, and his brethren, were twelve:

28 The one and twentieth to Ho'thir, he, his sons, and his brethren, were twelve:

29 The two and twentieth to Gid-dal'ti, he, his sons, and his brethren, were twelve:

30 The three and twentieth to Ma-ha'zi-oth, he, his sons, and his brethren, were twelve:

31 The four and twentieth to Ro-mam'ti-e'zer, he, his sons, and his brethren, were twelve.

26 CONCERNING the divisions of the porters: Of the Kor'hites was Me-shel-e-mi'ah the son of Ko're, of the sons of A'saph.

2 And the sons of Me-shel-e-mi'ah were, Zech-a-ri'ah the firstborn, Je-di'a-el the second, Zeb-a-di'ah the third, Jath'ni-el the fourth,

3 E'lam the fifth, Je-ho-ha'nan the sixth, El-i-o-e'na-i the seventh.

4 Moreover the sons of O'bed-e'dom were, Shem-a-i'ah the firstborn, Je-hoz'a-bad the second, Jo'ah the third, and Sa'car the fourth, and Ne-than'e-el the fifth,

5 Am'mi-el the sixth, Is'sa-char the seventh, Pe-ul'thai the eighth: for God blessed him.

6 Also unto Shem-a-i'ah his son were sons born, that ruled throughout the house of their father: for they were mighty men of valour.

7 The sons of Shem-a-i'ah; Oth'ni, and Re'pha-el, and O'bed, El'za-bad, whose brethren were strong men, E-li'hu, and Sem-a-chi'ah.

8 All these of the sons of O'bed-e'dom: they and their sons and their brethren, able men for strength for the service, were threescore and two of O'bed-e'dom.

9 And Me-shel-e-mi'ah had sons and brethren, strong men, eighteen.

10 Also Ho'sah, of the children of Me-ra'ri, had sons; Sim'ri the chief, (for though he was not the firstborn, yet his father made him the chief;)

11 Hil-ki'ah the second, Teb-a-li'ah the third, Zech-a-ri'ah the fourth: all the sons and brethren of Ho'sah were thirteen.

12 Among these were the divisions of the porters, even among the chief men, having wards one against another, to minister in the house of the LORD.

13 ¶ And they cast lots, as well the small as the great, according to the house of their fathers, for every gate.

14 And the lot eastward fell to Shel-e-mi'ah. Then for Zech-a-ri'ah his son, a wise counsellor, they cast lots; and his lot came out northward.

15 To O'bed-e'dom southward; and to his sons the house of A-sup'pim.

16 To Shup'pim and Ho'sah the lot came forth westward, with the gate Shal'le-cheth, by the causeway of the going up, ward against ward.

17 Eastward were six Le'vites, northward four a day, southward four a day, and toward A-sup'pim two and two.

18 At Par'bar westward, four at the causeway, and two at Par'bar.

19 These are the divisions of the porters among the sons of Ko're, and among the sons of Me-ra'ri.

20 ¶ And of the Le'vites, A-hi'jah was over the treasures of the house of God, and over the treasures of the dedicated things.

21 As concerning the sons of La'a-dan; the sons of the Ger'shon-ite La'a-dan, chief fathers, even of La'a-dan the Ger'shon-ite, were Je-hi'e-li.

22 The sons of Je-hi'e-li; Ze'tham, and Jo'el his brother, which were over the treasures of the house of the LORD.

23 Of the Am'ram-ites, and the Iz'har-ites, the He'bron-ites, and the Uz'zi-el-ites:

24 And Sheb'u-el the son of Ger'shom, the son of Mo'ses, was ruler of the treasures.

25 And his brethren by E-li-e'zer; Re-ha-bi'ah his son, and Je-sha'iah his son, and Jo'ram his son, and Zich'ri his son, and Shel'o-mith his son.

26 Which Shel'o-mith and his brethren were over all the treasures of the dedicated things, which Da'vid the king, and the chief fathers, the captains over thousands and hundreds, and the captains of the host, had dedicated.

27 Out of the spoils won in battles did they dedicate to maintain the house of the LORD.

28 And all that Sam'u-el the seer, and Saul the son of Kish, and Ab'ner the son of Ner, and Jo'ab the son of Zer-u-i'ah, had dedicated; and whosoever had dedicated any thing, it was under the hand of Shel'o-mith, and of his brethren.

29 ¶ Of the Iz'har-ites, Chen-a-ni'ah and his sons were for the outward business over Is'ra-el, for officers and judges.

30 And of the He'bron-ites, Hash-a-bi'ah and his brethren, men of valour, a thousand and seven hundred, were officers among them of Is'ra-el on this side Jor'dan westward in all the business of the LORD, and in the service of the king.

31 Among the He'bron-ites was Je-ri'jah the

chief, *even* among the He'bron-ites, according to the generations of his fathers. In the fortieth year of the reign of Da'vid they were sought for, and there were found among them mighty men of valour at Ja'zer of Gil'e-ad.

32 And his brethren, men of valour, *were* two thousand and seven hundred chief fathers, whom king Da'vid made rulers over the Reu'-ben-ites, the Gad'ites, and the half tribe of Ma-nas'seh, for every matter pertaining to God, and affairs of the king.

27 NOW the children of Is'ra-el after their number, *to wit,* the chief fathers and captains of thousands and hundreds, and their officers that served the king in any matter of the courses, which came in and went out month by month throughout all the months of the year, of every course *were* twenty and four thousand.

2 Over the first course for the first month *was* Ja-sho'be-am the son of Zab'di-el: and in his course *were* twenty and four thousand.

3 Of the children of Pe'rez *was* the chief of all the captains of the host for the first month.

4 And over the course of the second month *was* Dod'a-i an A-ho'hite, and of his course *was* Mik'loth also the ruler: in his course likewise *were* twenty and four thousand.

5 The third captain of the host for the third month *was* Be-na'iah the son of Je-hoi'a-da, a chief priest: and in his course *were* twenty and four thousand.

6 This *is that* Be-na'iah, who *was* mighty among the thirty, and above the thirty: and in his course *was* Am-miz'a-bad his son.

7 The fourth *captain* for the fourth month *was* A'sa-hel the brother of Jo'ab, and Zeb-a-di'ah his son after him: and in his course *were* twenty and four thousand.

8 The fifth captain for the fifth month *was* Sham'huth the Iz'ra-hite: and in his course *were* twenty and four thousand.

9 The sixth *captain* for the sixth month *was* I'ra the son of Ik'kesh the Te-ko'ite: and in his course *were* twenty and four thousand.

10 The seventh *captain* for the seventh month *was* He'lez the Pel'o-nite, of the children of E'phra-im: and in his course *were* twenty and four thousand.

11 The eighth *captain* for the eighth month *was* Sib'be-cai the Hu'shath-ite, of the Zar'-hites: and in his course *were* twenty and four thousand.

12 The ninth *captain* for the ninth month *was* A-bi-e'zer the An'e-toth-ite, of the Ben'ja-mites: and in his course *were* twenty and four thousand.

13 The tenth *captain* for the tenth month *was* Ma-har'a-i the Ne-toph'a-thite, of the Zar'-hites: and in his course *were* twenty and four thousand.

14 The eleventh *captain* for the eleventh month *was* Be-na'iah the Pir'a-thon-ite, of the children of E'phra-im: and in his course *were* twenty and four thousand.

15 The twelfth *captain* for the twelfth month *was* Hel'da-i the Ne-toph'a-thite, of Oth'ni-el: and in his course *were* twenty and four thousand.

16 ¶ Furthermore over the tribes of Is'ra-el: the ruler of the Reu'ben-ites *was* E-li-e'zer the son of Zich'ri: of the Sim'e-on-ites, Sheph-a-ti'-ah the son of Ma'a-chah:

17 Of the Le'vites, Hash-a-bi'ah the son of Ke-mu'el: of the Aar'on-ites, Za'dok:

18 Of Ju'dah, E-li'hu, *one* of the brethren of Da'vid: of Is'sa-char, Om'ri the son of Mi'chael:

19 Of Zeb'u-lun, Ish-ma-i'ah the son of O-ba-di'ah: of Naph'ta-li, Jer'i-moth the son of Az'ri-el:

20 Of the children of E'phra-im, Ho-she'a the son of Az-a-zi'ah: of the half tribe of Ma-nas'-seh, Jo'el the son of Pe-da'iah:

21 Of the half *tribe* of Ma-nas'seh in Gil'e-ad, Id'do the son of Zech-a-ri'ah: of Ben'ja-min, Ja-a'si-el the son of Ab'ner:

22 Of Dan, A-zar'e-el the son of Jer'o-ham. These *were* the princes of the tribes of Is'ra-el.

23 ¶ But Da'vid took not the number of them from twenty years old and under: because the LORD had said he would increase Is'ra-el like to the stars of the heavens.

24 Jo'ab the son of Zer-u-i'ah began to number, but he finished not, because there fell wrath for it against Is'ra-el; neither was the number put in the account of the chronicles of king Da'vid.

25 ¶ And over the king's treasures *was* Az'-ma-veth the son of A-di'el: and over the store-houses in the fields, in the cities, and in the villages, and in the castles, *was* Je-hon'a-than the son of Uz-zi'ah:

26 And over them that did the work of the field for tillage of the ground *was* Ez'ri the son of Che'lub:

27 And over the vineyards *was* Shim'e-i the Ra'math-ite: over the increase of the vineyards for the wine cellars *was* Zab'di the Shiph'mite:

28 And over the olive trees and the sycomore trees that *were* in the low plains *was* Ba'al–ha'-nan the Ged'e-rite: and over the cellars of oil *was* Jo'ash:

29 And over the herds that fed in Shar'on *was* Shit'ra-i the Shar'on-ite: and over the herds *that were* in the valleys *was* Sha'phat the son of Ad'la-i:

30 Over the camels also *was* O'bil the Ish'-ma-el-ite: and over the asses *was* Jeh-de'iah the Me-ron'-o-thite:

31 And over the flocks *was* Ja'ziz the Ha'ger-ite. All these *were* the rulers of the substance which *was* king Da'vid's.

32 Also Jon'a-than Da'vid's uncle was a counsellor, a wise man, and a scribe: and Je-hi'el the son of Hach'mo-ni *was* with the king's sons:

33 And A-hith'o-phel *was* the king's counsel-lor: and Hu'shai the Ar'chite *was* the king's companion:

34 And after A-hith'o-phel *was* Je-hoi'a-da the son of Be-na'iah, and A-bi'a-thar: and the general of the king's army *was* Jo'ab.

28 AND Da'vid assembled all the princes of Is'ra-el, the princes of the tribes, and the captains of the companies that ministered to the king by course, and the captains over the thousands, and captains over the hundreds, and the stewards over all the substance and posses-sion of the king, and of his sons, with the offi-cers, and with the mighty men, and with all the valiant men, unto Je-ru'sa-lem.

2 Then Da'vid the king stood up upon his feet, and said, Hear me, my brethren, and my people: *As for me,* I had in mine heart to build an house of rest for the ark of the covenant of the LORD, and for the footstool of our God, and had made ready for the building:

3 But God said unto me, Thou shalt not build an house for my name, because thou *hast been* a man of war, and hast shed blood.

4 Howbeit the LORD God of Is'ra-el chose me before all the house of my father to be king over Is'ra-el for ever: for he hath chosen Ju'dah *to be*

the ruler; and of the house of Ju'dah, the house of my father; and among the sons of my father he liked me to make *me* king over all Is'ra-el:

5 And of all my sons, (for the LORD hath given me many sons,) he hath chosen Sol'o-mon my son to sit upon the throne of the kingdom of the LORD over Is'ra-el.

6 And he said unto me, Sol'o-mon thy son, he shall build my house and my courts: for I have chosen him *to be* my son, and I will be his father.

7 Moreover I will establish his kingdom for ever, if he be constant to do my commandments and my judgments, as at this day.

8 Now therefore in the sight of all Is'ra-el the congregation of the LORD, and in the audience of our God, keep and seek for all the commandments of the LORD your God: that ye may possess this good land, and leave *it* for an inheritance for your children after you for ever.

9 ¶ And thou, Sol'o-mon my son, know thou the God of thy father, and serve him with a perfect heart and with a willing mind: for the LORD searcheth all hearts, and understandeth all the imaginations of the thoughts: if thou seek him, he will be found of thee; but if thou forsake him, he will cast thee off for ever.

10 Take heed now; for the LORD hath chosen thee to build an house for the sanctuary: be strong, and do *it*.

11 ¶ Then Da'vid gave to Sol'o-mon his son the pattern of the porch, and of the houses thereof, and of the treasuries thereof, and of the upper chambers thereof, and of the inner parlours thereof, and of the place of the mercy seat,

12 And the pattern of all that he had by the spirit, of the courts of the house of the LORD, and of all the chambers round about, of the treasuries of the house of God, and of the treasuries of the dedicated things:

13 Also for the courses of the priests and the Le'vites, and for all the work of the service of the house of the LORD, and for all the vessels of service in the house of the LORD.

14 *He gave* of gold by weight for *things* of gold, for all instruments of all manner of service; *silver also* for all instruments of silver by weight, for all instruments of every kind of service:

15 Even the weight for the candlesticks of gold, and for their lamps of gold, by weight for every candlestick, and for the lamps thereof: and for the candlesticks of silver by weight, *both* for the candlestick, and *also* for the lamps thereof, according to the use of every candlestick.

16 And by weight *he gave* gold for the tables of shewbread, for every table; and *likewise* silver for the tables of silver:

17 Also pure gold for the fleshhooks, and the bowls, and the cups: and for the golden basons *he gave gold* by weight for every bason; and *likewise silver* by weight for every bason of silver:

18 And for the altar of incense refined gold by weight; and gold for the pattern of the chariot of the cherubims, that spread out *their* wings, and covered the ark of the covenant of the LORD.

19 All *this, said* Da'vid, the LORD made me understand in writing by *his* hand upon me, *even* all the works of this pattern.

20 And Da'vid said to Sol'o-mon his son, Be strong and of good courage, and do *it*: fear not, nor be dismayed: for the LORD God, *even* my God, *will be* with thee; he will not fail thee, nor forsake thee, until thou hast finished all the work for the service of the house of the LORD.

21 And, behold, the courses of the priests and the Le'vites, *even they shall be with thee* for all the service of the house of God: and *there shall be* with thee for all manner of workmanship every willing skilful man, for any manner of service: also the princes and all the people *will be* wholly at thy commandment.

29 FURTHERMORE Da'vid the king said unto all the congregation, Sol'o-mon my son, whom alone God hath chosen, *is yet* young and tender, and the work *is* great: for the palace *is* not for man, but for the LORD God.

2 Now I have prepared with all my might for the house of my God the gold for *things to be made* of gold, and the silver for *things* of silver, and the brass for *things* of brass, the iron for *things* of iron, and wood for *things* of wood; onyx stones, and *stones* to be set, glistering stones, and of divers colours, and all manner of precious stones, and marble stones in abundance.

3 Moreover, because I have set my affection to the house of my God, I have of mine own proper good, of gold and silver, *which* I have given to the house of my God, over and above all that I have prepared for the holy house,

4 *Even* three thousand talents of gold, of the gold of O'phir, and seven thousand talents of refined silver, to overlay the walls of the houses *withal:*

5 The gold for *things* of gold, and the silver for *things* of silver, and for all manner of work *to be made* by the hands of artificers. And who *then* is willing to consecrate his service this day unto the LORD?

6 ¶ Then the chief of the fathers and princes of the tribes of Is'ra-el, and the captains of thousands and of hundreds, with the rulers of the king's work, offered willingly,

7 And gave for the service of the house of God of gold five thousand talents and ten thousand drams, and of silver ten thousand talents, and of brass eighteen thousand talents, and one hundred thousand talents of iron.

8 And they with whom *precious* stones were found gave *them* to the treasure of the house of the LORD, by the hand of Je-hi'el the Ger'shonite.

9 Then the people rejoiced, for that they offered willingly, because with perfect heart they offered willingly to the LORD: and Da'vid the king also rejoiced with great joy.

10 ¶ Wherefore Da'vid blessed the LORD before all the congregation: and Da'vid said, Blessed *be* thou, LORD God of Is'ra-el our father, for ever and ever.

11 Thine, O LORD, *is* the greatness, and the power, and the glory, and the victory, and the majesty: for all *that is* in the heaven and in the earth *is thine*; thine *is* the kingdom, O LORD, and thou art exalted as head above all.

12 Both riches and honour *come* of thee, and thou reignest over all; and in thine hand *is* power and might; and in thine hand *it is* to make great, and to give strength unto all.

13 Now therefore, our God, we thank thee, and praise thy glorious name.

14 But who *am* I, and what *is* my people, that we should be able to offer so willingly after this sort? for all things *come* of thee, and of thine own have we given thee.

15 For we *are* strangers before thee, and sojourners, as *were* all our fathers: our days on

the earth *are* as a shadow, and *there is* none abiding.

16 O LORD our God, all this store that we have prepared to build thee an house for thine holy name *cometh* of thine hand, and *is* all thine own.

17 I know also, my God, that thou triest the heart, and hast pleasure in uprightness. As for me, in the uprightness of mine heart I have willingly offered all these things: and now have I seen with joy thy people, which are present here, to offer willingly unto thee.

18 O LORD God of A′bra-ham, I′saac, and of Is′ra-el, our fathers, keep this for ever in the imagination of the thoughts of the heart of thy people, and prepare their heart unto thee:

19 And give unto Sol′o-mon my son a perfect heart, to keep thy commandments, thy testimonies, and thy statutes, and to do all *these things,* and to build the palace, *for* the which I have made provision.

20 ¶ And Da′vid said to all the congregation, Now bless the LORD your God. And all the congregation blessed the LORD God of their fathers, and bowed down their heads, and worshipped the LORD, and the king.

21 And they sacrificed sacrifices unto the LORD, and offered burnt offerings unto the LORD, on the morrow after that day, *even* a thousand bullocks, a thousand rams, *and* a thousand lambs, with their drink offerings, and sacrifices in abundance for all Is′ra-el:

22 And did eat and drink before the LORD on that day with great gladness. And they made Sol′o-mon the son of Da′vid king the second time, and anointed *him* unto the LORD *to be* the chief governor, and Za′dok *to be* priest.

23 Then Sol′o-mon sat on the throne of the LORD as king instead of Da′vid his father, and prospered; and all Is′ra-el obeyed him.

24 And all the princes, and the mighty men, and all the sons likewise of king Da′vid, submitted themselves unto Sol′o-mon the king.

25 And the LORD magnified Sol′o-mon exceedingly in the sight of all Is′ra-el, and bestowed upon him *such* royal majesty as had not been on any king before him in Is′ra-el.

26 ¶ Thus Da′vid the son of Jes′se reigned over all Is′ra-el.

27 And the time that he reigned over Is′ra-el *was* forty years; seven years reigned he in He′bron, and thirty and three *years* reigned he in Je-ru′sa-lem.

28 And he died in a good old age, full of days, riches, and honour: and Sol′o-mon his son reigned in his stead.

29 Now the acts of Da′vid the king, first and last, behold, they *are* written in the book of Sam′u-el the seer, and in the book of Na′than the prophet, and in the book of Gad the seer,

30 With all his reign and his might, and the times that went over him, and over Is′ra-el, and over all the kingdoms of the countries.

THE SECOND BOOK OF THE

CHRONICLES

1 AND Sol′o-mon the son of Da′vid was strengthened in his kingdom, and the LORD his God *was* with him, and magnified him exceedingly.

2 Then Sol′o-mon spake unto all Is′ra-el, to the captains of thousands and of hundreds, and to the judges, and to every governor in all Is′ra-el, the chief of the fathers.

3 So Sol′o-mon, and all the congregation with him, went to the high place that *was* at Gib′e-on; for there was the tabernacle of the congregation of God, which Mo′ses the servant of the LORD had made in the wilderness.

4 But the ark of God had Da′vid brought up from Kir′jath–je′a-rim to *the place which* Da′vid had prepared for it: for he had pitched a tent for it at Je-ru′sa-lem.

5 Moreover the brasen altar, that Be-zal′e-el the son of U′ri, the son of Hur had made, he put before the tabernacle of the LORD: and Sol′o-mon and the congregation sought unto it.

6 And Sol′o-mon went up thither to the brasen altar before the LORD, which *was* at the tabernacle of the congregation, and offered a thousand burnt offerings upon it.

7 ¶ In that night did God appear unto Sol′o-mon, and said unto him, Ask what I shall give thee.

8 And Sol′o-mon said unto God, Thou hast shewed great mercy unto Da′vid my father, and hast made me to reign in his stead.

9 Now, O LORD God, let thy promise unto Da′vid my father be established: for thou hast made me king over a people like the dust of the earth in multitude.

10 Give me now wisdom and knowledge, that I may go out and come in before this people: for who can judge this thy people, *that is so* great?

11 And God said to Sol′o-mon, Because this was in thine heart, and thou hast not asked riches, wealth, or honour, nor the life of thine enemies, neither yet hast asked long life; but hast asked wisdom and knowledge for thyself, that thou mayest judge my people, over whom I have made thee king:

12 Wisdom and knowledge *is* granted unto thee; and I will give thee riches, and wealth, and honour, such as none of the kings have had that *have been* before thee, neither shall there any after thee have the like.

13 ¶ Then Sol′o-mon came *from his journey* to the high place that *was* at Gib′e-on to Je-ru′sa-lem, from before the tabernacle of the congregation, and reigned over Is′ra-el.

14 And Sol′o-mon gathered chariots and horsemen: and he had a thousand and four hundred chariots, and twelve thousand horsemen, which he placed in the chariot cities, and with the king at Je-ru′sa-lem.

15 And the king made silver and gold at Je-ru′sa-lem *as* plenteous as stones, and cedar trees made he as the sycomore trees that *are* in the vale for abundance.

16 And Sol′o-mon had horses brought out of E′gypt, and linen yarn: the king's merchants received the linen yarn at a price.

17 And they fetched up, and brought forth out of E′gypt a chariot for six hundred *shekels* of silver, and an horse for an hundred and fifty: and so brought they out *horses* for all the kings of the Hit′tites, and for the kings of Syr′i-a, by their means.

2 AND Sol'o-mon determined to build an house for the name of the LORD, and an house for his kingdom.

2 And Sol'o-mon told out threescore and ten thousand men to bear burdens, and fourscore thousand to hew in the mountain, and three thousand and six hundred to oversee them.

3 ¶ And Sol'o-mon sent to Hu'ram the king of Tyre, saying, As thou didst deal with Da'vid my father, and didst send him cedars to build him an house to dwell therein, *even so deal with me.*

4 Behold, I build an house to the name of the LORD my God, to dedicate *it* to him, *and* to burn before him sweet incense, and for the continual shewbread, and for the burnt offerings morning and evening, on the sabbaths, and on the new moons, and on the solemn feasts of the LORD our God. This *is an ordinance* for ever to Is'ra-el.

5 And the house which I build *is* great: for great *is* our God above all gods.

6 But who is able to build him an house, seeing the heaven and heaven of heavens cannot contain him? who *am* I then, that I should build him an house, save only to burn sacrifice before him?

7 Send me now therefore a man cunning to work in gold, and in silver, and in brass, and in iron, and in purple, and crimson, and blue, and that can skill to grave with the cunning men that *are* with me in Ju'dah and in Je-ru'sa-lem, whom Da'vid my father did provide.

8 Send me also cedar trees, fir trees, and algum trees, out of Leb'a-non: for I know that thy servants can skill to cut timber in Leb'a-non; and, behold, my servants *shall be* with thy servants,

9 Even to prepare me timber in abundance: for the house which I am about to build *shall be* wonderful great.

10 And, behold, I will give to thy servants, the hewers that cut timber, twenty thousand measures of beaten wheat, and twenty thousand measures of barley, and twenty thousand baths of wine, and twenty thousand baths of oil.

11 ¶ Then Hu'ram the king of Tyre answered in writing, which he sent to Sol'o-mon, Because the LORD hath loved his people, he hath made thee king over them.

12 Hu'ram said moreover, Blessed *be* the LORD God of Is'ra-el, that made heaven and earth, who hath given to Da'vid the king a wise son, endued with prudence and understanding, that might build an house for the LORD, and an house for his kingdom.

13 And now I have sent a cunning man, endued with understanding, of Hu'ram my father's,

14 The son of a woman of the daughters of Dan, and his father *was* a man of Tyre, skilful to work in gold, and in silver, in brass, in iron, in stone, and in timber, in purple, in blue, and in fine linen, and in crimson; also to grave any manner of graving, and to find out every device which shall be put to him, with thy cunning men, and with the cunning men of my lord Da'vid thy father.

15 Now therefore the wheat, and the barley, the oil, and the wine, which my lord hath spoken of, let him send unto his servants:

16 And we will cut wood out of Leb'a-non, as much as thou shalt need: and we will bring it to thee in floats by sea to Jop'pa; and thou shalt carry it up to Je-ru'sa-lem.

17 ¶ And Sol'o-mon numbered all the strangers that *were* in the land of Is'ra-el, after the numbering wherewith Da'vid his father had numbered them; and they were found an hundred and fifty thousand and three thousand and six hundred.

18 And he set threescore and ten thousand of them *to be* bearers of burdens, and fourscore thousand *to be* hewers in the mountain, and three thousand and six hundred overseers to set the people a work.

3 THEN Sol'o-mon began to build the house of the LORD at Je-ru'sa-lem in mount Mo-ri'ah, where *the LORD* appeared unto Da'vid his father, in the place that Da'vid had prepared in the threshingfloor of Or'nan the Jeb'u-site.

2 And he began to build in the second *day* of the second month, in the fourth year of his reign.

3 ¶ Now these *are the things wherein* Sol'o-mon was instructed for the building of the house of God. The length by cubits after the first measure *was* threescore cubits, and the breadth twenty cubits.

4 And the porch that *was* in the front *of the house,* the length *of it was* according to the breadth of the house, twenty cubits, and the height *was* an hundred and twenty: and he overlaid it within with pure gold.

5 And the greater house he cieled with fir tree, which he overlaid with fine gold, and set thereon palm trees and chains.

6 And he garnished the house with precious stones for beauty: and the gold *was* gold of Par-va'im.

7 He overlaid also the house, the beams, the posts, and the walls thereof, and the doors thereof, with gold; and graved cherubims on the walls.

8 And he made the most holy house, the length whereof *was* according to the breadth of the house, twenty cubits, and the breadth thereof twenty cubits: and he overlaid it with fine gold, *amounting* to six hundred talents.

9 And the weight of the nails *was* fifty shekels of gold. And he overlaid the upper chambers with gold.

10 And in the most holy house he made two cherubims of image work, and overlaid them with gold.

11 ¶ And the wings of the cherubims *were* twenty cubits long: one wing *of the one cherub was* five cubits, reaching to the wall of the house: and the other wing *was likewise* five cubits, reaching to the wing of the other cherub.

12 And *one* wing of the other cherub *was* five cubits, reaching to the wall of the house: and the other wing *was* five cubits also, joining to the wing of the other cherub.

13 The wings of these cherubims spread themselves forth twenty cubits: and they stood on their feet, and their faces *were* inward.

14 ¶ And he made the veil *of* blue, and purple, and crimson, and fine linen, and wrought cherubims thereon.

15 Also he made before the house two pillars of thirty and five cubits high, and the chapiter that *was* on the top of each of them *was* five cubits.

16 And he made chains, *as* in the oracle, and put *them* on the heads of the pillars; and made an hundred pomegranates, and put *them* on the chains.

17 And he reared up the pillars before the temple, one on the right hand, and the other on the left; and called the name of that on the right hand Ja'chin, and the name of that on the left Bo'az.

4 MOREOVER he made an altar of brass, twenty cubits the length thereof, and twenty cubits the breadth thereof, and ten cubits the height thereof.

2 ¶ Also he made a molten sea of ten cubits from brim to brim, round in compass, and five cubits the height thereof; and a line of thirty cubits did compass it round about.

3 And under it was the similitude of oxen, which did compass it round about: ten in a cubit, compassing the sea round about. Two rows of oxen were cast, when it was cast.

4 It stood upon twelve oxen, three looking toward the north, and three looking toward the west, and three looking toward the south, and three looking toward the east: and the sea was set above upon them, and all their hinder parts were inward.

5 And the thickness of it was an handbreadth, and the brim of it like the work of the brim of a cup, with flowers of lilies; and it received and held three thousand baths.

6 ¶ He made also ten lavers, and put five on the right hand, and five on the left, to wash in them: such things as they offered for the burnt offering they washed in them; but the sea was for the priests to wash in.

7 And he made ten candlesticks of gold according to their form, and set them in the temple, five on the right hand, and five on the left.

8 He made also ten tables, and placed them in the temple, five on the right side, and five on the left. And he made an hundred basons of gold.

9 ¶ Furthermore he made the court of the priests, and the great court, and doors for the court, and overlaid the doors of them with brass.

10 And he set the sea on the right side of the east end, over against the south.

11 And Hu'ram made the pots, and the shovels, and the basons. And Hu'ram finished the work that he was to make for king Sol'o-mon for the house of God;

12 To wit, the two pillars, and the pommels, and the chapiters which were on the top of the two pillars, and the two wreaths to cover the two pommels of the chapiters which were on the top of the pillars;

13 And four hundred pomegranates on the two wreaths; two rows of pomegranates on each wreath, to cover the two pommels of the chapiters which were upon the pillars.

14 He made also bases, and lavers made he upon the bases;

15 One sea, and twelve oxen under it.

16 The pots also, and the shovels, and the fleshhooks, and all their instruments, did Hu'ram his father make to king Sol'o-mon for the house of the LORD of bright brass.

17 In the plain of Jor'dan did the king cast them, in the clay ground between Suc'coth and Ze-red'a-thah.

18 Thus Sol'o-mon made all these vessels in great abundance: for the weight of the brass could not be found out.

19 ¶ And Sol'o-mon made all the vessels that were for the house of God, the golden altar also, and the tables whereon the shewbread was set;

20 Moreover the candlesticks with their lamps, that they should burn after the manner before the oracle, of pure gold;

21 And the flowers, and the lamps, and the tongs, made he of gold, and that perfect gold;

22 And the snuffers, and the basons, and the spoons, and the censers, of pure gold: and the entry of the house, the inner doors thereof for the most holy place, and the doors of the house of the temple, were of gold.

5 THUS all the work that Sol'o-mon made for the house of the LORD was finished: and Sol'o-mon brought in all the things that Da'vid his father had dedicated; and the silver, and the gold, and all the instruments, put he among the treasures of the house of God.

2 ¶ Then Sol'o-mon assembled the elders of Is'ra-el, and all the heads of the tribes, the chief of the fathers of the children of Is'ra-el, unto Je-ru'sa-lem, to bring up the ark of the covenant of the LORD out of the city of Da'vid, which is Zi'on.

3 Wherefore all the men of Is'ra-el assembled themselves unto the king in the feast which was in the seventh month.

4 And all the elders of Is'ra-el came; and the Le'vites took up the ark.

5 And they brought up the ark, and the tabernacle of the congregation, and all the holy vessels that were in the tabernacle, these did the priests and the Le'vites bring up.

6 Also king Sol'o-mon, and all the congregation of Is'ra-el that were assembled unto him before the ark, sacrificed sheep and oxen, which could not be told nor numbered for multitude.

7 And the priests brought in the ark of the covenant of the LORD unto his place, to the oracle of the house, into the most holy place, even under the wings of the cherubims:

8 For the cherubims spread forth their wings over the place of the ark, and the cherubims covered the ark and the staves thereof above.

9 And they drew out the staves of the ark, that the ends of the staves were seen from the ark before the oracle; but they were not seen without. And there it is unto this day.

10 There was nothing in the ark save the two tables which Mo'ses put therein at Ho'reb, when the LORD made a covenant with the children of Is'ra-el, when they came out of E'gypt.

11 ¶ And it came to pass, when the priests were come out of the holy place: (for all the priests that were present were sanctified, and did not then wait by course:

12 Also the Le'vites which were the singers, all of them of A'saph, of He'man, of Jed'u-thun, with their sons and their brethren, being arrayed in white linen, having cymbals and psalteries and harps, stood at the east end of the altar, and with them an hundred and twenty priests sounding with trumpets:)

13 It came even to pass, as the trumpeters and singers were as one, to make one sound to be heard in praising and thanking the LORD; and when they lifted up their voice with the trumpets and cymbals and instruments of musick, and praised the LORD, saying, For he is good; for his mercy endureth for ever: that then the house was filled with a cloud, even the house of the LORD;

14 So that the priests could not stand to minister by reason of the cloud: for the glory of the LORD had filled the house of God.

6 THEN said Sol'o-mon, The LORD hath said that he would dwell in the thick darkness.

2 But I have built an house of habitation for thee, and a place for thy dwelling for ever.

3 And the king turned his face, and blessed the whole congregation of Is'ra-el: and all the congregation of Is'ra-el stood.

4 And he said, Blessed be the LORD God of Is'ra-el, who hath with his hands fulfilled that

which he spake with his mouth to my father Da'vid, saying,

5 Since the day that I brought forth my people out of the land of E'gypt I chose no city among all the tribes of Is'ra-el to build an house in, that my name might be there; neither chose I any man to be a ruler over my people Is'ra-el:

6 But I have chosen Je-ru'sa-lem, that my name might be there; and have chosen Da'vid to be over my people Is'ra-el.

7 Now it was in the heart of Da'vid my father to build an house for the name of the LORD God of Is'ra-el.

8 But the LORD said to Da'vid my father, Forasmuch as it was in thine heart to build an house for my name, thou didst well in that it was in thine heart:

9 Notwithstanding thou shalt not build the house; but thy son which shall come forth out of thy loins, he shall build the house for my name.

10 The LORD therefore hath performed his word that he hath spoken: for I am risen up in the room of Da'vid my father, and am set on the throne of Is'ra-el, as the LORD promised, and have built the house for the name of the LORD God of Is'ra-el.

11 And in it have I put the ark, wherein is the covenant of the LORD, that he made with the children of Is'ra-el.

12 ¶ And he stood before the altar of the LORD in the presence of all the congregation of Is'ra-el, and spread forth his hands:

13 For Sol'o-mon had made a brasen scaffold, of five cubits long, and five cubits broad, and three cubits high, and had set it in the midst of the court: and upon it he stood, and kneeled down upon his knees before all the congregation of Is'ra-el, and spread forth his hands toward heaven,

14 And said, O LORD God of Is'ra-el, there is no God like thee in the heaven, nor in the earth; which keepest covenant, and shewest mercy unto thy servants, that walk before thee with all their hearts:

15 Thou which hast kept with thy servant Da'vid my father that which thou hast promised him; and spakest with thy mouth, and hast fulfilled it with thine hand, as it is this day.

16 Now therefore, O LORD God of Is'ra-el, keep with thy servant Da'vid my father that which thou hast promised him, saying, There shall not fail thee a man in my sight to sit upon the throne of Is'ra-el; yet so that thy children take heed to their way to walk in my law, as thou hast walked before me.

17 Now then, O LORD God of Is'ra-el, let thy word be verified, which thou hast spoken unto thy servant Da'vid.

18 But will God in very deed dwell with men on the earth? behold, heaven and the heaven of heavens cannot contain thee; how much less this house which I have built!

19 Have respect therefore to the prayer of thy servant, and to his supplication, O LORD my God, to hearken unto the cry and the prayer which thy servant prayeth before thee:

20 That thine eyes may be open upon this house day and night, upon the place whereof thou hast said that thou wouldest put thy name there; to hearken unto the prayer which thy servant prayeth toward this place.

21 Hearken therefore unto the supplications of thy servant, and of thy people Is'ra-el, which they shall make toward this place: hear thou from thy dwelling place, even from heaven; and when thou hearest, forgive.

22 ¶ If a man sin against his neighbour, and an oath be laid upon him to make him swear, and the oath come before thine altar in this house;

23 Then hear thou from heaven, and do, and judge thy servants, by requiting the wicked, by recompensing his way upon his own head; and by justifying the righteous, by giving him according to his righteousness.

24 ¶ And if thy people Is'ra-el be put to the worse before the enemy, because they have sinned against thee; and shall return and confess thy name, and pray and make supplication before thee in this house;

25 Then hear thou from the heavens, and forgive the sin of thy people Is'ra-el, and bring them again unto the land which thou gavest to them and to their fathers.

26 ¶ When the heaven is shut up, and there is no rain, because they have sinned against thee; yet if they pray toward this place, and confess thy name, and turn from their sin, when thou dost afflict them;

27 Then hear thou from heaven, and forgive the sin of thy servants, and of thy people Is'ra-el, when thou hast taught them the good way, wherein they should walk; and send rain upon thy land, which thou hast given unto thy people for an inheritance.

28 ¶ If there be dearth in the land, if there be pestilence, if there be blasting, or mildew, locusts, or caterpillers; if their enemies besiege them in the cities of their land; whatsoever sore or whatsoever sickness there be:

29 Then what prayer or what supplication soever shall be made of any man, or of all thy people Is'ra-el, when every one shall know his own sore and his own grief, and shall spread forth his hands in this house:

30 Then hear thou from heaven thy dwelling place, and forgive, and render unto every man according unto all his ways, whose heart thou knowest; (for thou only knowest the hearts of the children of men:)

31 That they may fear thee, to walk in thy ways, so long as they live in the land which thou gavest unto our fathers.

32 ¶ Moreover concerning the stranger, which is not of thy people Is'ra-el, but is come from a far country for thy great name's sake, and thy mighty hand, and thy stretched out arm; if they come and pray in this house;

33 Then hear thou from the heavens, even from thy dwelling place, and do according to all that the stranger calleth to thee for; that all people of the earth may know thy name, and fear thee, as doth thy people Is'ra-el, and may know that this house which I have built is called by thy name.

34 If thy people go out to war against their enemies by the way that thou shalt send them, and they pray unto thee toward this city which thou hast chosen, and the house which I have built for thy name;

35 Then hear thou from the heavens their prayer and their supplication, and maintain their cause.

36 If they sin against thee, (for there is no man which sinneth not,) and thou be angry with them, and deliver them over before their enemies, and they carry them away captives unto a land far off or near;

37 Yet if they bethink themselves in the land whither they are carried captive, and turn and pray unto thee in the land of their captivity, saying, We have sinned, we have done amiss, and have dealt wickedly;

38 If they return to thee with all their heart and with all their soul in the land of their captivity, whither they have carried them captives, and pray toward their land, which thou gavest unto their fathers, and toward the city which thou hast chosen, and toward the house which I have built for thy name:

39 Then hear thou from the heavens, even from thy dwelling place, their prayer and their supplications, and maintain their cause, and forgive thy people which have sinned against thee.

40 Now, my God, let, I beseech thee, thine eyes be open, and let thine ears be attent unto the prayer that is made in this place.

41 Now therefore arise, O LORD God, into thy resting place, thou, and the ark of thy strength: let thy priests, O LORD God, be clothed with salvation, and let thy saints rejoice in goodness.

42 O LORD God, turn not away the face of thine anointed: remember the mercies of Da'vid thy servant.

7 NOW when Sol'o-mon had made an end of praying, the fire came down from heaven, and consumed the burnt offering and the sacrifices; and the glory of the LORD filled the house.

2 And the priests could not enter into the house of the LORD, because the glory of the LORD had filled the LORD's house.

3 And when all the children of Is'ra-el saw how the fire came down, and the glory of the LORD upon the house, they bowed themselves with their faces to the ground upon the pavement, and worshipped, and praised the LORD, saying, For he is good; for his mercy endureth for ever.

4 ¶ Then the king and all the people offered sacrifices before the LORD.

5 And king Sol'o-mon offered a sacrifice of twenty and two thousand oxen, and an hundred and twenty thousand sheep: so the king and all the people dedicated the house of God.

6 And the priests waited on their offices: the Le'vites also with instruments of musick of the LORD, which Da'vid the king had made to praise the LORD, because his mercy endureth for ever, when Da'vid praised by their ministry; and the priests sounded trumpets before them, and all Is'ra-el stood.

7 Moreover Sol'o-mon hallowed the middle of the court that was before the house of the LORD: for there he offered burnt offerings, and the fat of the peace offerings, because the brasen altar which Sol'o-mon had made was not able to receive the burnt offerings, and the meat offerings, and the fat.

8 ¶ Also at the same time Sol'o-mon kept the feast seven days, and all Is'ra-el with him, a very great congregation, from the entering in of Ha'math unto the river of E'gypt.

9 And in the eighth day they made a solemn assembly: for they kept the dedication of the altar seven days, and the feast seven days.

10 And on the three and twentieth day of the seventh month he sent the people away into their tents, glad and merry in heart for the goodness that the LORD had shewed unto Da'vid, and to Sol'o-mon, and to Is'ra-el his people.

11 Thus Sol'o-mon finished the house of the LORD, and the king's house: and all that came into Sol'o-mon's heart to make in the house of the LORD, and in his own house, he prosperously effected.

12 ¶ And the LORD appeared to Sol'o-mon by night, and said unto him, I have heard thy prayer, and have chosen this place to myself for an house of sacrifice.

13 If I shut up heaven that there be no rain, or if I command the locusts to devour the land, or if I send pestilence among my people;

14 If my people, which are called by my name, shall humble themselves, and pray, and seek my face, and turn from their wicked ways; then will I hear from heaven, and will forgive their sin, and will heal their land.

15 Now mine eyes shall be open, and mine ears attent unto the prayer that is made in this place.

16 For now have I chosen and sanctified this house, that my name may be there for ever: and mine eyes and mine heart shall be there perpetually.

17 And as for thee, if thou wilt walk before me, as Da'vid thy father walked, and do according to all that I have commanded thee, and shalt observe my statutes and my judgments;

18 Then will I stablish the throne of thy kingdom, according as I have covenanted with Da'vid thy father, saying, There shall not fail thee a man to be ruler in Is'ra-el.

19 But if ye turn away, and forsake my statutes and my commandments, which I have set before you, and shall go and serve other gods, and worship them;

20 Then will I pluck them up by the roots out of my land which I have given them; and this house, which I have sanctified for my name, will I cast out of my sight, and will make it to be a proverb and a byword among all nations.

21 And this house, which is high, shall be an astonishment to every one that passeth by it; so that he shall say, Why hath the LORD done thus unto this land, and unto this house?

22 And it shall be answered, Because they forsook the LORD God of their fathers, which brought them forth out of the land of E'gypt, and laid hold on other gods, and worshipped them, and served them: therefore hath he brought all this evil upon them.

8 AND it came to pass at the end of twenty years, wherein Sol'o-mon had built the house of the LORD, and his own house,

2 That the cities which Hu'ram had restored to Sol'o-mon, Sol'o-mon built them, and caused the children of Is'ra-el to dwell there.

3 And Sol'o-mon went to Ha'math-zo'bah, and prevailed against it.

4 And he built Tad'mor in the wilderness, and all the store cities, which he built in Ha'math.

5 Also he built Beth-ho'ron the upper, and Beth-ho'ron the nether, fenced cities, with walls, gates, and bars;

6 And Ba'al-ath, and all the store cities that Sol'o-mon had, and all the chariot cities, and the cities of the horsemen, and all that Sol'o-mon desired to build in Je-ru'sa-lem, and in Leb'a-non, and throughout all the land of his dominion.

7 ¶ As for all the people that were left of the Hit'tites, and the Am'or-ites, and the Per'izzites, and the Hi'vites, and the Jeb'u-sites, which were not of Is'ra-el,

8 But of their children, who were left after them in the land, whom the children of Is'ra-el consumed not, them did Sol'o-mon make to pay tribute until this day.

9 But of the children of Is'ra-el did Sol'o-mon make no servants for his work; but they were men of war, and chief of his captains, and captains of his chariots and horsemen.

10 And these *were* the chief of king Sol'o-mon's officers, *even* two hundred and fifty, that bare rule over the people.

11 ¶ And Sol'o-mon brought up the daughter of Pha'raoh out of the city of Da'vid unto the house that he had built for her: for he said, My wife shall not dwell in the house of Da'vid king of Is'ra-el, because *the places are* holy, whereunto the ark of the LORD hath come.

12 ¶ Then Sol'o-mon offered burnt offerings unto the LORD on the altar of the LORD, which he had built before the porch,

13 Even after a certain rate every day, offering according to the commandment of Mo'ses, on the sabbaths, and on the new moons, and on the solemn feasts, three times in the year, *even* in the feast of unleavened bread, and in the feast of weeks, and in the feast of tabernacles.

14 ¶ And he appointed, according to the order of Da'vid his father, the courses of the priests to their service, and the Le'vites to their charges, to praise and minister before the priests, as the duty of every day required: the porters also by their courses at every gate: for so had Da'vid the man of God commanded.

15 And they departed not from the commandment of the king unto the priests and Le'-vites concerning any matter, or concerning the treasures.

16 Now all the work of Sol'o-mon was prepared unto the day of the foundation of the house of the LORD, and until it was finished. So the house of the LORD was perfected.

17 ¶ Then went Sol'o-mon to E'zi-on-ge'ber, and to E'loth, at the sea side in the land of E'-dom.

18 And Hu'ram sent him by the hands of his servants ships, and servants that had knowledge of the sea; and they went with the servants of Sol'o-mon to O'phir, and took thence four hundred and fifty talents of gold, and brought *them* to king Sol'o-mon.

9 AND when the queen of She'ba heard of the fame of Sol'o-mon, she came to prove Sol'o-mon with hard questions at Je-ru'sa-lem, with a very great company, and camels that bare spices, and gold in abundance, and precious stones: and when she was come to Sol'o-mon, she communed with him of all that was in her heart.

2 And Sol'o-mon told her all her questions: and there was nothing hid from Sol'o-mon which he told her not.

3 And when the queen of She'ba had seen the wisdom of Sol'o-mon, and the house that he had built,

4 And the meat of his table, and the sitting of his servants, and the attendance of his ministers, and their apparel; his cupbearers also, and their apparel; and his ascent by which he went up into the house of the LORD; there was no more spirit in her.

5 And she said to the king, *It was* a true report which I heard in mine own land of thine acts, and of thy wisdom:

6 Howbeit I believed not their words, until I came, and mine eyes had seen *it*: and, behold, the one half of the greatness of thy wisdom was not told me: *for* thou exceedest the fame that I heard.

7 Happy *are* thy men, and happy *are* these thy servants, which stand continually before thee, and hear thy wisdom.

8 Blessed be the LORD thy God, which delighted in thee to set thee on his throne, *to be* king for the LORD thy God: because thy God loved Is'ra-el, to establish them for ever, therefore made he thee king over them, to do judgment and justice.

9 And she gave the king an hundred and twenty talents of gold, and of spices great abundance, and precious stones: neither was there any such spice as the queen of She'ba gave king Sol'o-mon.

10 And the servants also of Hu'ram, and the servants of Sol'o-mon, which brought gold from O'phir, brought algum trees and precious stones.

11 And the king made *of* the algum trees terraces to the house of the LORD, and to the king's palace, and harps and psalteries for singers: and there were none such seen before in the land of Ju'dah.

12 And king Sol'o-mon gave to the queen of She'ba all her desire, whatsoever she asked, beside *that* which she had brought unto the king. So she turned, and went away to her own land, she and her servants.

13 ¶ Now the weight of gold that came to Sol'o-mon in one year was six hundred and threescore and six talents of gold;

14 Beside *that which* chapmen and merchants brought. And all the kings of A-ra'bi-a and governors of the country brought gold and silver to Sol'o-mon.

15 ¶ And king Sol'o-mon made two hundred targets *of* beaten gold: six hundred *shekels* of beaten gold went to one target.

16 And three hundred shields made he *of* beaten gold: three hundred *shekels* of gold went to one shield. And the king put them in the house of the forest of Leb'a-non.

17 Moreover the king made a great throne of ivory, and overlaid it with pure gold.

18 And *there were* six steps to the throne, with a footstool of gold, *which were* fastened to the throne, and stays on each side of the sitting place, and two lions standing by the stays:

19 And twelve lions stood there on the one side and the other upon the six steps. There was not the like made in any kingdom.

20 ¶ And all the drinking vessels of king Sol'o-mon *were of* gold, and all the vessels of the house of the forest of Leb'a-non *were of* pure gold: none *were of* silver; it was *not* any thing accounted of in the days of Sol'o-mon.

21 For the king's ships went to Tar'shish with the servants of Hu'ram: every three years once came the ships of Tar'shish bringing gold, and silver, ivory, and apes, and peacocks.

22 And king Sol'o-mon passed all the kings of the earth in riches and wisdom.

23 ¶ And all the kings of the earth sought the presence of Sol'o-mon, to hear his wisdom, that God had put in his heart.

24 And they brought every man his present, vessels of silver, and vessels of gold, and raiment, harness, and spices, horses, and mules, a rate year by year.

25 ¶ And Sol'o-mon had four thousand stalls for horses and chariots, and twelve thousand horsemen; whom he bestowed in the chariot cities, and with the king at Je-ru'sa-lem.

26 ¶ And he reigned over all the kings from the river even unto the land of the Phi-lis'tines, and to the border of E'gypt.

27 And the king made silver in Je-ru'sa-lem as stones, and cedar trees made he as the sycomore trees that *are* in the low plains in abundance.

28 And they brought unto Sol'o-mon horses out of E'gypt, and out of all lands.

29 ¶ Now the rest of the acts of Sol'o-mon,

first and last, *are* they not written in the book of Na'than the prophet, and in the prophecy of A-hi'jah the Shi'lo-nite, and in the visions of Id'do the seer against Jer-o-bo'am the son of Ne'bat?

30 And Sol'o-mon reigned in Je-ru'sa-lem over all Is'ra-el forty years.

31 And Sol'o-mon slept with his fathers, and he was buried in the city of Da'vid his father: and Re-ho-bo'am his son reigned in his stead.

10 AND Re-ho-bo'am went to She'chem: for to She'chem were all Is'ra-el come to make him king.

2 And it came to pass, when Jer-o-bo'am the son of Ne'bat, who *was* in E'gypt, whither he had fled from the presence of Sol'o-mon the king, heard *it*, that Jer-o-bo'am returned out of E'gypt.

3 And they sent and called him. So Jer-o-bo'-am and all Is'ra-el came and spake to Re-ho-bo'am, saying,

4 Thy father made our yoke grievous: now therefore ease thou somewhat the grievous servitude of thy father, and his heavy yoke that he put upon us, and we will serve thee.

5 And he said unto them, Come again unto me after three days. And the people departed.

6 ¶ And king Re-ho-bo'am took counsel with the old men that had stood before Sol'o-mon his father while he yet lived, saying, What counsel give ye *me* to return answer to this people?

7 And they spake unto him, saying, If thou be kind to this people, and please them, and speak good words to them, they will be thy servants for ever.

8 But he forsook the counsel which the old men gave him, and took counsel with the young men that were brought up with him, that stood before him:

9 And he said unto them, What advice give ye that we may return answer to this people, which have spoken to me, saying, Ease somewhat the yoke that thy father did put upon us?

10 And the young men that were brought up with him spake unto him, saying, Thus shalt thou answer the people that spake unto thee, saying, Thy father made our yoke heavy, but make thou *it* somewhat lighter for us; thus shalt thou say unto them, My little *finger* shall be thicker than my father's loins.

11 For whereas my father put a heavy yoke upon you, I will put more to your yoke: my father chastised you with whips, but I *will chastise you* with scorpions.

12 So Jer-o-bo'am and all the people came to Re-ho-bo'am on the third day, as the king bade, saying, Come again to me on the third day.

13 And the king answered them roughly; and king Re-ho-bo'am forsook the counsel of the old men,

14 And answered them after the advice of the young men, saying, My father made your yoke heavy, but I will add thereto: my father chastised you with whips, but I *will chastise you* with scorpions.

15 So the king hearkened not unto the people: for the cause was of God, that the LORD might perform his word, which he spake by the hand of A-hi'jah the Shi'lo-nite to Jer-o-bo'am the son of Ne'bat.

16 ¶ And when all Is'ra-el *saw* that the king would not hearken unto them, the people answered the king, saying, What portion have we in Da'vid? and *we have* none inheritance in the son of Jes'se: every man to your tents, O Is'ra-el: *and* now, Da'vid, see to thine own house. So all Is'ra-el went to their tents.

17 But *as for* the children of Is'ra-el that dwelt in the cities of Ju'dah, Re-ho-bo'am reigned over them.

18 Then king Re-ho-bo'am sent Ha-do'ram that *was* over the tribute; and the children of Is'ra-el stoned him with stones, that he died. But king Re-ho-bo'am made speed to get him up to *his* chariot, to flee to Je-ru'sa-lem.

19 And Is'ra-el rebelled against the house of Da'vid unto this day.

11 AND when Re-ho-bo'am was come to Je-ru'sa-lem, he gathered of the house of Ju'dah and Ben'ja-min an hundred and four-score thousand chosen *men*, which were warriors, to fight against Is'ra-el, that he might bring the kingdom again to Re-ho-bo'am.

2 But the word of the LORD came to Shem-a-i'ah the man of God, saying,

3 Speak unto Re-ho-bo'am the son of Sol'o-mon, king of Ju'dah, and to all Is'ra-el in Ju'dah and Ben'ja-min, saying,

4 Thus saith the LORD, Ye shall not go up, nor fight against your brethren: return every man to his house: for this thing is done of me. And they obeyed the words of the LORD, and returned from going against Jer-o-bo'am.

5 ¶ And Re-ho-bo'am dwelt in Je-ru'sa-lem, and built cities for defence in Ju'dah.

6 He built even Beth'-le-hem, and E'tam, and Te-ko'a,

7 And Beth'-zur, and Sho'co, and A-dul'lam,

8 And Gath, and Ma-re'shah, and Ziph,

9 And Ad-o-ra'im, and La'chish, and A-ze'-kah,

10 And Zo'rah, and Aij'a-lon, and He'bron, which *are* in Ju'dah and in Ben'ja-min fenced cities.

11 And he fortified the strong holds, and put captains in them, and store of victual, and of oil and wine.

12 And in every several city *he put* shields and spears, and made them exceeding strong, having Ju'dah and Ben'ja-min on his side.

13 ¶ And the priests and the Le'vites that *were* in all Is'ra-el resorted to him out of all their coasts.

14 For the Le'vites left their suburbs and their possession, and came to Ju'dah and Je-ru'sa-lem: for Jer-o-bo'am and his sons had cast them off from executing the priest's office unto the LORD:

15 And he ordained him priests for the high places, and for the devils, and for the calves which he had made.

16 And after them out of all the tribes of Is'-ra-el such as set their hearts to seek the LORD God of Is'ra-el came to Je-ru'sa-lem, to sacrifice unto the LORD God of their fathers.

17 So they strengthened the kingdom of Ju'-dah, and made Re-ho-bo'am the son of Sol'o-mon strong, three years: for three years they walked in the way of Da'vid and Sol'o-mon.

18 ¶ And Re-ho-bo'am took him Ma'ha-lath the daughter of Jer'i-moth the son of Da'vid to wife, *and* Ab-i-ha'il the daughter of E-li'ab the son of Jes'se;

19 Which bare him children; Je'ush, and Sham-a-ri'ah, and Za'ham.

20 And after her he took Ma'a-chah the daughter of Ab'sa-lom; which bare him A-bi'-jah, and At'tai, and Zi'za, and Shel'o-mith.

21 And Re-ho-bo'am loved Ma'a-chah the daughter of Ab'sa-lom above all his wives and his concubines: (for he took eighteen wives, and threescore concubines; and begat twenty and eight sons, and threescore daughters.)

22 And Re-ho-bo'am made A-bi'jah the son of Ma'a-chah the chief, to be ruler among his brethren: for he thought to make him king.

23 And he dealt wisely, and dispersed of all his children throughout all the countries of Ju'dah and Ben'ja-min, unto every fenced city: and he gave them victual in abundance. And he desired many wives.

12 AND it came to pass, when Re-ho-bo'-am had established the kingdom, and had strengthened himself, he forsook the law of the LORD, and all Is'ra-el with him.

2 And it came to pass, that in the fifth year of king Re-ho-bo'am Shi'shak king of E'gypt came up against Je-ru'sa-lem, because they had transgressed against the LORD,

3 With twelve hundred chariots, and threescore thousand horsemen: and the people were without number that came with him out of E'-gypt; the Lu'bims, the Suk'ki-ims, and the E-thi-o'pi-ans.

4 And he took the fenced cities which pertained to Ju'dah, and came to Je-ru'sa-lem.

5 ¶ Then came Shem-a-i'ah the prophet to Re-ho-bo'am, and to the princes of Ju'dah, that were gathered together to Je-ru'sa-lem because of Shi'shak, and said unto them, Thus saith the LORD, Ye have forsaken me, and therefore have I also left you in the hand of Shi'shak.

6 Whereupon the princes of Is'ra-el and the king humbled themselves; and they said, The LORD is righteous.

7 And when the LORD saw that they humbled themselves, the word of the LORD came to Shem-a-i'ah, saying, They have humbled themselves; therefore I will not destroy them, but I will grant them some deliverance; and my wrath shall not be poured out upon Je-ru'sa-lem by the hand of Shi'shak.

8 Nevertheless they shall be his servants; that they may know my service, and the service of the kingdoms of the countries.

9 So Shi'shak king of E'gypt came up against Je-ru'sa-lem, and took away the treasures of the house of the LORD, and the treasures of the king's house; he took all: he carried away also the shields of gold which Sol'o-mon had made.

10 Instead of which king Re-ho-bo'am made shields of brass, and committed them to the hands of the chief of the guard, that kept the entrance of the king's house.

11 And when the king entered into the house of the LORD, the guard came and fetched them, and brought them again into the guard chamber.

12 And when he humbled himself, the wrath of the LORD turned from him, that he would not destroy him altogether: and also in Ju'dah things went well.

13 ¶ So king Re-ho-bo'am strengthened himself in Je-ru'sa-lem, and reigned: for Re'ho-bo'-am was one and forty years old when he began to reign, and he reigned seventeen years in Je-ru'sa-lem, the city which the LORD had chosen out of all the tribes of Is'ra-el, to put his name there. And his mother's name was Na'a-mah an Am'mon-it-ess.

14 And he did evil, because he prepared not his heart to seek the LORD.

15 Now the acts of Re-ho-bo'am, first and last, are they not written in the book of Shem-a-i'ah the prophet, and of Id'do the seer concerning genealogies? And there were wars between Re-ho-bo'am and Jer-o-bo'am continually.

16 And Re-ho-bo'am slept with his fathers, and was buried in the city of Da'vid: and A-bi'jah his son reigned in his stead.

13 NOW in the eighteenth year of king Jer-o-bo'am began A-bi'jah to reign over Ju'dah.

2 He reigned three years in Je-ru'sa-lem. His mother's name also was Mi-cha'iah the daughter of U'ri-el of Gib'e-ah. And there was war between A-bi'jah and Jer-o-bo'am.

3 And A-bi'jah set the battle in array with an army of valiant men of war, even four hundred thousand chosen men: Jer-o-bo'am also set the battle in array against him with eight hundred thousand chosen men, being mighty men of valour.

4 ¶ And A-bi'jah stood up upon mount Zem-a-ra'im, which is in mount E'phra-im, and said, Hear me, thou Jer-o-bo'am, and all Is'ra-el;

5 Ought ye not to know that the LORD God of Is'ra-el gave the kingdom over Is'ra-el to Da'vid for ever, even to him and to his sons by a covenant of salt?

6 Yet Jer-o-bo'am the son of Ne'bat, the servant of Sol'o-mon the son of Da'vid, is risen up, and hath rebelled against his lord.

7 And there are gathered unto him vain men, the children of Be'li-al, and have strengthened themselves against Re-ho-bo'am the son of Sol'-o-mon, when Re-ho-bo'am was young and tenderhearted, and could not withstand them.

8 And now ye think to withstand the kingdom of the LORD in the hand of the sons of Da'-vid; and ye be a great multitude, and there are with you golden calves, which Jer-o-bo'am made you for gods.

9 Have ye not cast out the priests of the LORD, the sons of Aar'on, and the Le'vites, and have made you priests after the manner of the nations of other lands? so that whosoever cometh to consecrate himself with a young bullock and seven rams, the same may be a priest of them that are no gods.

10 But as for us, the LORD is our God, and we have not forsaken him; and the priests, which minister unto the LORD, are the sons of Aar'on, and the Le'vites wait upon their business:

11 And they burn unto the LORD every morning and every evening burnt sacrifices and sweet incense: the shewbread also set they in order upon the pure table; and the candlestick of gold with the lamps thereof, to burn every evening: for we keep the charge of the LORD our God; but ye have forsaken him.

12 And, behold, God himself is with us for our captain, and his priests with sounding trumpets to cry alarm against you. O children of Is'ra-el, fight ye not against the LORD God of your fathers; for ye shall not prosper.

13 ¶ But Jer-o-bo'am caused an ambushment to come about behind them: so they were before Ju'dah, and the ambushment was behind them.

14 And when Ju'dah looked back, behold, the battle was before and behind: and they cried unto the LORD, and the priests sounded with the trumpets.

15 Then the men of Ju'dah gave a shout: and as the men of Ju'dah shouted, it came to pass, that God smote Jer-o-bo'am and all Is'ra-el before A-bi'jah and Ju'dah.

16 And the children of Is'ra-el fled before Ju'-dah: and God delivered them into their hand.

17 And A-bi'jah and his people slew them with a great slaughter: so there fell down slain of Is'ra-el five hundred thousand chosen men.

18 Thus the children of Is'ra-el were brought

under at that time, and the children of Ju'dah prevailed, because they relied upon the LORD God of their fathers.

19 And A-bi'jah pursued after Jer-o-bo'am, and took cities from him, Beth'-el with the towns thereof, and Jesh'a-nah with the towns thereof, and E'phra-in with the towns thereof.

20 Neither did Jer-o-bo'am recover strength again in the days of A-bi'jah: and the LORD struck him, and he died.

21 ¶ But A-bi'jah waxed mighty, and married fourteen wives, and begat twenty and two sons, and sixteen daughters.

22 And the rest of the acts of A-bi'jah, and his ways, and his sayings, are written in the story of the prophet Id'do.

14 SO A-bi'jah slept with his fathers, and they buried him in the city of Da'vid: and A'sa his son reigned in his stead. In his days the land was quiet ten years.

2 And A'sa did that which was good and right in the eyes of the LORD his God:

3 For he took away the altars of the strange gods, and the high places, and brake down the images, and cut down the groves:

4 And commanded Ju'dah to seek the LORD God of their fathers, and to do the law and the commandment.

5 Also he took away out of all the cities of Ju'dah the high places and the images: and the kingdom was quiet before him.

6 ¶ And he built fenced cities in Ju'dah: for the land had rest, and he had no war in those years; because the LORD had given him rest.

7 Therefore he said unto Ju'dah, Let us build these cities, and make about them walls, and towers, gates, and bars, while the land is yet before us; because we have sought the LORD our God, we have sought him, and he hath given us rest on every side. So they built and prospered.

8 And A'sa had an army of men that bare targets and spears, out of Ju'dah three hundred thousand; and out of Ben'ja-min, that bare shields and drew bows, two hundred and fourscore thousand: all these were mighty men of valour.

9 ¶ And there came out against them Ze'rah the E-thi-o'pi-an with an host of a thousand thousand, and three hundred chariots; and came unto Ma-re'shah.

10 Then A'sa went out against him, and they set the battle in array in the valley of Zeph'a-thah at Ma-re'shah.

11 And A'sa cried unto the LORD his God, and said, LORD, it is nothing with thee to help, whether with many, or with them that have no power: help us, O LORD our God; for we rest on thee, and in thy name we go against this multitude. O LORD, thou art our God; let not man prevail against thee.

12 So the LORD smote the E-thi-o'pi-ans before A'sa, and before Ju'dah; and the E-thi-o'pi-ans fled.

13 And A'sa and the people that were with him pursued them unto Ge'rar: and the E-thi-o'pi-ans were overthrown, that they could not recover themselves; for they were destroyed before the LORD, and before his host; and they carried away very much spoil.

14 And they smote all the cities round about Ge'rar; for the fear of the LORD came upon them: and they spoiled all the cities; for there was exceeding much spoil in them.

15 They smote also the tents of cattle, and carried away sheep and camels in abundance, and returned to Je-ru'sa-lem.

15 AND the Spirit of God came upon Az-a-ri'ah the son of O'ded:

2 And he went out to meet A'sa, and said unto him, Hear ye me, A'sa, and all Ju'dah and Ben'ja-min; The LORD is with you, while ye be with him; and if ye seek him, he will be found of you; but if ye forsake him, he will forsake you.

3 Now for a long season Is'ra-el hath been without the true God, and without a teaching priest, and without law.

4 But when in their trouble did turn unto the LORD God of Is'ra-el, and sought him, he was found of them.

5 And in those times there was no peace to him that went out, nor to him that came in, but great vexations were upon all the inhabitants of the countries.

6 And nation was destroyed of nation, and city of city: for God did vex them with all adversity.

7 Be ye strong therefore, and let not your hands be weak: for your work shall be rewarded.

8 And when A'sa heard these words, and the prophecy of O'ded the prophet, he took courage, and put away the abominable idols out of all the land of Ju'dah and Ben'ja-min, and out of the cities which he had taken from mount E'-phra-im, and renewed the altar of the LORD, that was before the porch of the LORD.

9 And he gathered all Ju'dah and Ben'ja-min, and the strangers with them out of E'phra-im and Ma-nas'seh, and out of Sim'e-on: for they fell to him out of Is'ra-el in abundance, when they saw that the LORD his God was with him.

10 So they gathered themselves together at Je-ru'sa-lem in the third month, in the fifteenth year of the reign of A'sa.

11 And they offered unto the LORD the same time, of the spoil which they had brought, seven hundred oxen and seven thousand sheep.

12 And they entered into a covenant to seek the LORD God of their fathers with all their heart and with all their soul;

13 That whosoever would not seek the LORD God of Is'ra-el should be put to death, whether small or great, whether man or woman.

14 And they sware unto the LORD with a loud voice, and with shouting, and with trumpets, and with cornets.

15 And all Ju'dah rejoiced at the oath: for they had sworn with all their heart, and sought him with their whole desire; and he was found of them: and the LORD gave them rest round about.

16 ¶ And also concerning Ma'a-chah the mother of A'sa the king, he removed her from being queen, because she had made an idol in a grove: and A'sa cut down her idol, and stamped it, and burnt it at the brook Kid'ron.

17 But the high places were not taken away out of Is'ra-el: nevertheless the heart of A'sa was perfect all his days.

18 ¶ And he brought into the house of God the things that his father had dedicated, and that he himself had dedicated, silver, and gold, and vessels.

19 And there was no more war unto the five and thirtieth year of the reign of A'sa.

16 IN the six and thirtieth year of the reign of A'sa Ba'a-sha king of Is'ra-el came up against Ju'dah, and built Ra'mah, to the intent

that he might let none go out or come in to A'sa king of Ju'dah.

2 Then A'sa brought out silver and gold out of the treasures of the house of the LORD and of the king's house, and sent to Ben-ha'dad king of Syr'i-a, that dwelt at Da-mas'cus, saying,

3 There is a league between me and thee, as there was between my father and thy father: behold, I have sent thee silver and gold; go, break thy league with Ba'a-sha king of Is'ra-el, that he may depart from me.

4 And Ben-ha'dad hearkened unto king A'sa, and sent the captains of his armies against the cities of Is'ra-el; and they smote I'jon, and Dan, and A'bel-ma'im, and all the store cities of Naph'ta-li.

5 And it came to pass, when Ba'a-sha heard it, that he left off building of Ra'mah, and let his work cease.

6 Then A'sa the king took all Ju'dah; and they carried away the stones of Ra'mah, and the timber thereof, wherewith Ba'a-sha was building; and he built therewith Ge'ba and Miz'-pah.

7 ¶ And at that time Ha-na'ni the seer came to A'sa king of Ju'dah, and said unto him, Because thou hast relied on the king of Syr'i-a, and not relied on the LORD thy God, therefore is the host of the king of Syr'i-a escaped out of thine hand.

8 Were not the E-thi-o'pi-ans and the Lu'-bims a huge host, with very many chariots and horsemen? yet, because thou didst rely on the LORD, he delivered them into thine hand.

9 For the eyes of the LORD run to and fro throughout the whole earth, to shew himself strong in the behalf of them whose heart is perfect toward him. Herein thou hast done foolishly: therefore from henceforth thou shalt have wars.

10 Then A'sa was wroth with the seer, and put him in a prison house; for he was in a rage with him because of this thing. And A'sa oppressed some of the people the same time.

11 ¶ And, behold, the acts of A'sa, first and last, lo, they are written in the book of the kings of Ju'dah and Is'ra-el.

12 And A'sa in the thirty and ninth year of his reign was diseased in his feet, until his disease was exceeding great: yet in his disease he sought not to the LORD, but to the physicians.

13 ¶ And A'sa slept with his fathers, and died in the one and fortieth year of his reign:

14 And they buried him in his own sepulchres, which he had made for himself in the city of Da'vid, and laid him in the bed which was filled with sweet odours and divers kinds of spices prepared by the apothecaries' art: and they made a very great burning for him.

17 AND Je-hosh'a-phat his son reigned in his stead, and strengthened himself against Is'ra-el.

2 And he placed forces in all the fenced cities of Ju'dah, and set garrisons in the land of Ju'-dah, and in the cities of E'phra-im, which A'sa his father had taken.

3 And the LORD was with Je-hosh'a-phat, because he walked in the first ways of his father Da'vid, and sought not unto Ba'al-im;

4 But sought to the LORD God of his father, and walked in his commandments, and not after the doings of Is'ra-el.

5 Therefore the LORD stablished the kingdom in his hand: and all Ju'dah brought to Je-hosh'a-phat presents; and he had riches and honour in abundance.

6 And his heart was lifted up in the ways of the LORD: moreover he took away the high places and groves out of Ju'dah.

7 ¶ Also in the third year of his reign he sent to his princes, even to Ben-ha'il, and to O-ba-di'ah, and to Zech-a-ri'ah, and to Ne-than'e-el, and to Mi-cha'iah, to teach in the cities of Ju'-dah.

8 And with them he sent Le'vites, even Shem-a-i'ah, and Neth-a-ni'ah, and Zeb-a-di'ah, and A'sa-hel, and She-mir'a-moth, and Je-hon'-a-than, and Ad-o-ni'jah, and To-bi'jah, and Tob-ad-o-ni'jah, Le'vites; and with them E-lish'a-ma and Je-ho'ram, priests.

9 And they taught in Ju'dah, and had the book of the law of the LORD with them, and went about throughout all the cities of Ju'dah, and taught the people.

10 ¶ And the fear of the LORD fell upon all the kingdoms of the lands that were round about Ju'dah, so that they made no war against Je-hosh'a-phat.

11 Also some of the Phi-lis'tines brought Je-hosh'a-phat presents, and tribute silver; and the A-ra'bi-ans brought him flocks, seven thousand and seven hundred rams, and seven thousand and seven hundred he goats.

12 ¶ And Je-hosh'a-phat waxed great exceedingly; and he built in Ju'dah castles, and cities of store.

13 And he had much business in the cities of Ju'dah: and the men of war, mighty men of valour, were in Je-ru'sa-lem.

14 And these are the numbers of them according to the house of their fathers: Of Ju'dah, the captains of thousands; Ad'nah the chief, and with him mighty men of valour three hundred thousand.

15 And next to him was Je-ho-ha'nan the captain, and with him two hundred and fourscore thousand.

16 And next him was Am-a-si'ah the son of Zich'ri, who willingly offered himself unto the LORD; and with him two hundred thousand mighty men of valour.

17 And of Ben'ja-min; E-li'a-da a mighty man of valour, and with him armed men with bow and shield two hundred thousand.

18 And next him was Je-hoz'a-bad, and with him an hundred and fourscore thousand ready prepared for the war.

19 These waited on the king, beside those whom the king put in the fenced cities throughout all Ju'dah.

18 NOW Je-hosh'a-phat had riches and honour in abundance, and joined affinity with A'hab.

2 And after certain years he went down to A'hab to Sa-ma'ri-a. And A'hab killed sheep and oxen for him in abundance, and for the people that he had with him, and persuaded him to go up with him to Ra'moth-gil'e-ad.

3 And A'hab king of Is'ra-el said unto Je-hosh'a-phat king of Ju'dah, Wilt thou go with me to Ra'moth-gil'e-ad? And he answered him, I am as thou art, and my people as thy people; and we will be with thee in the war.

4 ¶ And Je-hosh'a-phat said unto the king of Is'ra-el, Enquire, I pray thee, at the word of the LORD to day.

5 Therefore the king of Is'ra-el gathered together of prophets four hundred men, and said unto them, Shall we go to Ra'moth-gil'e-ad to battle, or shall I forbear? And they said, Go up; for God will deliver it into the king's hand.

6 But Je-hosh'a-phat said, Is there not here a

prophet of the LORD besides, that we might enquire of him?

7 And the king of Is'ra-el said unto Je-hosh'a-phat, *There* is yet one man, by whom we may enquire of the LORD: but I hate him; for he never prophesied good unto me, but always evil: the same is Mi-ca'iah the son of Im'la. And Je-hosh'a-phat said, Let not the king say so.

8 And the king of Is'ra-el called for one *of his* officers, and said, Fetch quickly Mi-ca'iah the son of Im'la.

9 And the king of Is'ra-el and Je-hosh'a-phat king of Ju'dah sat either of them on his throne, clothed in *their* robes, and they sat in a void place at the entering in of the gate of Sa-ma'ri-a; and all the prophets prophesied before them.

10 And Zed-e-ki'ah the son of Che-na'a-nah had made him horns of iron, and said, Thus saith the LORD, With these thou shalt push Syr'-i-a until they be consumed.

11 And all the prophets prophesied so, saying, Go up to Ra'moth-gil'e-ad, and prosper: for the LORD shall deliver *it* into the hand of the king.

12 And the messenger that went to call Mi-ca'iah spake to him, saying, Behold, the words of the prophets *declare* good to the king with one assent; let thy word therefore, I pray thee, be like one of theirs, and speak thou good.

13 And Mi-ca'iah said, *As* the LORD liveth, even what my God saith, that will I speak.

14 And when he was come to the king, the king said unto him, Mi-ca'iah, shall we go to Ra'-moth-gil'e-ad to battle, or shall I forbear? And he said, Go ye up, and prosper, and they shall be delivered into your hand.

15 And the king said to him, How many times shall I adjure thee that thou say nothing but the truth to me in the name of the LORD?

16 Then he said, I did see all Is'ra-el scattered upon the mountains, as sheep that have no shepherd: and the LORD said, These have no master; let them return *therefore* every man to his house in peace.

17 And the king of Is'ra-el said to Je-hosh'a-phat, Did I not tell thee *that* he would not prophesy good unto me, but evil?

18 Again he said, Therefore hear the word of the LORD; I saw the LORD sitting upon his throne, and all the host of heaven standing on his right hand and *on* his left.

19 And the LORD said, Who shall entice A'-hab king of Is'ra-el, that he may go up and fall at Ra'moth-gil'e-ad? And one spake saying after this manner, and another saying after that manner.

20 Then there came out a spirit, and stood before the LORD, and said, I will entice him. And the LORD said unto him, Wherewith?

21 And he said, I will go out, and be a lying spirit in the mouth of all his prophets. And *the LORD* said, Thou shalt entice *him,* and thou shalt also prevail: go out, and do *even* so.

22 Now therefore, behold, the LORD hath put a lying spirit in the mouth of these thy prophets, and the LORD hath spoken evil against thee.

23 Then Zed-e-ki'ah the son of Che-na'a-nah came near, and smote Mi-ca'iah upon the cheek, and said, Which way went the Spirit of the LORD from me to speak unto thee?

24 And Mi-ca'iah said, Behold, thou shalt see on that day when thou shalt go into an inner chamber to hide thyself.

25 Then the king of Is'ra-el said, Take ye Mi-ca'iah, and carry him back to A'mon the governor of the city, and to Jo'ash the king's son;

26 And say, Thus saith the king, Put this *fellow* in the prison, and feed him with bread of affliction and with water of affliction, until I return in peace.

27 And Mi-ca'iah said, If thou certainly return in peace, *then* hath not the LORD spoken by me. And he said, Hearken, all ye people.

28 So the king of Is'ra-el and Je-hosh'a-phat the king of Ju'dah went up to Ra'moth-gil'e-ad.

29 And the king of Is'ra-el said unto Je-hosh'-a-phat, I will disguise myself, and will go to the battle; but put thou on thy robes. So the king of Is'ra-el disguised himself; and they went to the battle.

30 Now the king of Syr'i-a had commanded the captains of the chariots that *were* with him, saying, Fight ye not with small or great, save only with the king of Is'ra-el.

31 And it came to pass, when the captains of the chariots saw Je-hosh'a-phat, that they said, It *is* the king of Is'ra-el. Therefore they compassed about him to fight: but Je-hosh'a-phat cried out, and the LORD helped him; and God moved them *to depart* from him.

32 For it came to pass, that, when the captains of the chariots perceived that it was not the king of Is'ra-el, they turned back again from pursuing him.

33 And a *certain* man drew a bow at a venture, and smote the king of Is'ra-el between the joints of the harness: therefore he said to his chariot man, Turn thine hand, that thou mayest carry me out of the host; for I am wounded.

34 And the battle increased that day: howbeit the king of Is'ra-el stayed *himself* up in *his* chariot against the Syr'i-ans until the even: and about the time of the sun going down he died.

19 AND Je-hosh'a-phat the king of Ju'dah returned to his house in peace to Je-ru'sa-lem.

2 And Je'hu the son of Ha-na'ni the seer went out to meet him, and said to king Je-hosh'a-phat, Shouldest thou help the ungodly, and love them that hate the LORD? therefore *is* wrath upon thee from before the LORD.

3 Nevertheless there are good things found in thee, in that thou hast taken away the groves out of the land, and hast prepared thine heart to seek God.

4 And Je-hosh'a-phat dwelt at Je-ru'sa-lem: and he went out again through the people from Be'er-she'ba to mount E'phra-im, and brought them back unto the LORD God of their fathers.

5 ¶ And he set judges in the land throughout all the fenced cities of Ju'dah, city by city,

6 And said to the judges, Take heed what ye do: for ye judge not for man, but for the LORD, who *is* with you in the judgment.

7 Wherefore now let the fear of the LORD be upon you; take heed and do *it:* for *there is* no iniquity with the LORD our God, nor respect of persons, nor taking of gifts.

8 ¶ Moreover in Je-ru'sa-lem did Je-hosh'a-phat set of the Le'vites, and *of* the priests, and of the chief of the fathers of Is'ra-el, for the judgment of the LORD, and for controversies, when they returned to Je-ru'sa-lem.

9 And he charged them, saying, Thus shall ye do in the fear of the LORD, faithfully, and with a perfect heart.

10 And what cause soever shall come to you of your brethren that dwell in their cities, between blood and blood, between law and commandment, statutes and judgments, ye shall even warn them that they trespass not against the LORD, and *so* wrath come upon you, and

upon your brethren: this do, and ye shall not trespass.

11 And, behold, Am-a-ri'ah the chief priest *is* over you in all matters of the LORD; and Zeb-a-di'ah the son of Ish'ma-el, the ruler of the house of Ju'dah, for all the king's matters: also the Le'vites *shall be* officers before you. Deal courageously, and the LORD shall be with the good.

20 IT came to pass after this also, *that* the children of Mo'ab, and the children of Am'mon, and with them *other* beside the Am'mon-ites, came against Je-hosh'a-phat to battle.

2 Then there came some that told Je-hosh'a-phat, saying, There cometh a great multitude against thee from beyond the sea on this side Syr'i-a; and, behold, they *be* in Haz'a-zon-ta'mar, which *is* En-ge'di.

3 And Je-hosh'a-phat feared, and set himself to seek the LORD, and proclaimed a fast throughout all Ju'dah.

4 And Ju'dah gathered themselves together, to ask *help* of the LORD: even out of all the cities of Ju'dah they came to seek the LORD.

5 ¶ And Je-hosh'a-phat stood in the congregation of Ju'dah and Je-ru'sa-lem, in the house of the LORD, before the new court,

6 And said, O LORD God of our fathers, *art* not thou God in heaven? and rulest *not* thou over all the kingdoms of the heathen? and in thine hand *is there not* power and might, so that none is able to withstand thee?

7 *Art* not thou our God, *who* didst drive out the inhabitants of this land before thy people Is'ra-el, and gavest it to the seed of A'bra-ham thy friend for ever?

8 And they dwelt therein, and have built thee a sanctuary therein for thy name, saying,

9 If, *when* evil cometh upon us, *as* the sword, judgment, or pestilence, or famine, we stand before this house, and in thy presence, (for thy name *is* in this house,) and cry unto thee in our affliction, then thou wilt hear and help.

10 And now, behold, the children of Am'mon and Mo'ab and mount Se'ir, whom thou wouldest not let Is'ra-el invade, when they came out of the land of E'gypt, but they turned from them, and destroyed them not;

11 Behold, *I* say, *how* they reward us, to come to cast us out of thy possession, which thou hast given us to inherit.

12 O our God, wilt thou not judge them? for we have no might against this great company that cometh against us; neither know we what to do: but our eyes *are* upon thee.

13 And all Ju'dah stood before the LORD, with their little ones, their wives, and their children.

14 ¶ Then upon Ja-ha'zi-el the son of Zech-a-ri'ah, the son of Be-na'iah, the son of Je-i'el, the son of Mat-ta-ni'ah, a Le'vite of the sons of A'saph, came the Spirit of the LORD in the midst of the congregation;

15 And he said, Hearken ye, all Ju'dah, and ye inhabitants of Je-ru'sa-lem, and thou king Je-hosh'a-phat, Thus saith the LORD unto you, Be not afraid nor dismayed by reason of this great multitude; for the battle *is* not yours, but God's.

16 To morrow go ye down against them: behold, they come up by the cliff of Ziz; and ye shall find them at the end of the brook, before the wilderness of Jer'u-el.

17 Ye shall not *need* to fight in this *battle:* set yourselves, stand ye *still,* and see the salvation of the LORD with you, O Ju'dah and Je-ru'sa-lem: fear not, nor be dismayed; to morrow go out against them: for the LORD *will be* with you.

18 And Je-hosh'a-phat bowed his head with *his* face to the ground: and all Ju'dah and the inhabitants of Je-ru'sa-lem fell before the LORD, worshipping the LORD.

19 And the Le'vites, of the children of the Ko'hath-ites, and of the children of the Kor'-hites, stood up to praise the LORD God of Is'ra-el with a loud voice on high.

20 ¶ And they rose early in the morning, and went forth into the wilderness of Te-ko'a: and as they went forth, Je-hosh'a-phat stood and said, Hear me, O Ju'dah, and ye inhabitants of Je-ru'sa-lem; Believe in the LORD your God, so shall ye be established; believe his prophets, so shall ye prosper.

21 And when he had consulted with the people, he appointed singers unto the LORD, and that should praise the beauty of holiness, as they went out before the army, and to say, Praise the LORD; for his mercy *endureth* for ever.

22 ¶ And when they began to sing and to praise, the LORD set ambushments against the children of Am'mon, Mo'ab, and mount Se'ir, which were come against Ju'dah; and they were smitten.

23 For the children of Am'mon and Mo'ab stood up against the inhabitants of mount Se'ir, utterly to slay and destroy *them:* and when they had made an end of the inhabitants of Se'ir, every one helped to destroy another.

24 And when Ju'dah came toward the watch tower in the wilderness, they looked unto the multitude, and, behold, they *were* dead bodies fallen to the earth, and none escaped.

25 And when Je-hosh'a-phat and his people came to take away the spoil of them, they found among them in abundance both riches with the dead bodies, and precious jewels, which they stripped off for themselves, more than they could carry away: and they were three days in gathering of the spoil, it was so much.

26 ¶ And on the fourth day they assembled themselves in the valley of Ber'a-chah; for there they blessed the LORD: therefore the name of the same place was called, The valley of Ber'a-chah, unto this day.

27 Then they returned, every man of Ju'dah and Je-ru'sa-lem, and Je-hosh'a-phat in the forefront of them, to go again to Je-ru'sa-lem with joy; for the LORD had made them to rejoice over their enemies.

28 And they came to Je-ru'sa-lem with psalteries and harps and trumpets unto the house of the LORD.

29 And the fear of God was on all the kingdoms of *those* countries, when they had heard that the LORD fought against the enemies of Is'ra-el.

30 So the realm of Je-hosh'a-phat was quiet: for his God gave him rest round about.

31 ¶ And Je-hosh'a-phat reigned over Ju'dah: *he was* thirty and five years old when he began to reign, and he reigned twenty and five years in Je-ru'sa-lem. And his mother's name *was* A-zu'bah the daughter of Shil'hi.

32 And he walked in the way of A'sa his father, and departed not from it, doing *that which was* right in the sight of the LORD.

33 Howbeit the high places were not taken away: for as yet the people had not prepared their hearts unto the God of their fathers.

34 Now the rest of the acts of Je-hosh'a-phat, first and last, behold, they *are* written in the book of Je'hu the son of Ha-na'ni, who *is* mentioned in the book of the kings of Is'ra-el.

35 ¶ And after this did Je-hosh'a-phat king

of Ju'dah join himself with A-ha-zi'ah king of Is'ra-el, who did very wickedly:

36 And he joined himself with him to make ships to go to Tar'shish: and they made the ships in E'zi-on-ga'ber.

37 Then E-li-e'zer the son of Dod'a-vah of Ma-re'shah prophesied against Je-hosh'a-phat, saying, Because thou hast joined thyself with A-ha-zi'ah, the LORD hath broken thy works. And the ships were broken, that they were not able to go to Tar'shish.

21 NOW Je-hosh'a-phat slept with his fathers, and was buried with his fathers in the city of Da'vid. And Je-ho'ram his son reigned in his stead.

2 And he had brethren the sons of Je-hosh'a-phat, Az-a-ri'ah, and Je-hi'el, and Zech-a-ri'ah, and Az-a-ri'ah, and Mi'chael, and Sheph-a-ti'ah: all these were the sons of Je-hosh'a-phat king of Is'ra-el.

3 And their father gave them great gifts of silver, and of gold, and of precious things, with fenced cities in Ju'dah: but the kingdom gave he to Je-ho'ram; because he was the firstborn.

4 Now when Je-ho'ram was risen up to the kingdom of his father, he strengthened himself, and slew all his brethren with the sword, and divers also of the princes of Is'ra-el.

5 ¶ Je-ho'ram was thirty and two years old when he began to reign, and he reigned eight years in Je-ru'sa-lem.

6 And he walked in the way of the kings of Is'ra-el, like as did the house of A'hab: for he had the daughter of A'hab to wife: and he wrought that which was evil in the eyes of the LORD.

7 Howbeit the LORD would not destroy the house of Da'vid, because of the covenant that he had made with Da'vid, and as he promised to give a light to him and to his sons for ever.

8 ¶ In his days the E'dom-ites revolted from under the dominion of Ju'dah, and made themselves a king.

9 Then Je-ho'ram went forth with his princes, and all his chariots with him: and he rose up by night, and smote the E'dom-ites which compassed him in, and the captains of the chariots.

10 So the E'dom-ites revolted from under the hand of Ju'dah unto this day. The same time also did Lib'nah revolt from under his hand; because he had forsaken the LORD God of his fathers.

11 Moreover he made high places in the mountains of Ju'dah, and caused the inhabitants of Je-ru'sa-lem to commit fornication, and compelled Ju'dah thereto.

12 ¶ And there came a writing to him from E-li'jah the prophet, saying, Thus saith the LORD God of Da'vid thy father, Because thou hast not walked in the ways of Je-hosh'a-phat thy father, nor in the ways of A'sa king of Ju'dah,

13 But hast walked in the way of the kings of Is'ra-el, and hast made Ju'dah and the inhabitants of Je-ru'sa-lem to go a whoring, like to the whoredoms of the house of A'hab, and also hast slain thy brethren of thy father's house, which were better than thyself:

14 Behold, with a great plague will the LORD smite thy people, and thy children, and thy wives, and all thy goods:

15 And thou shalt have great sickness by disease of thy bowels, until thy bowels fall out by reason of the sickness day by day.

16 ¶ Moreover the LORD stirred up against Je-ho'ram the spirit of the Phi-lis'tines, and of the A-ra'bi-ans, that were near the E-thi-o'pi-ans:

17 And they came up into Ju'dah, and brake into it, and carried away all the substance that was found in the king's house, and his sons also, and his wives; so that there was never a son left him, save Je-ho'a-haz, the youngest of his sons.

18 ¶ And after all this the LORD smote him in his bowels with an incurable disease.

19 And it came to pass, that in process of time, after the end of two years, his bowels fell out by reason of his sickness: so he died of sore diseases. And his people made no burning for him, like the burning of his fathers.

20 Thirty and two years old was he when he began to reign, and he reigned in Je-ru'sa-lem eight years, and departed without being desired. Howbeit they buried him in the city of Da'vid, but not in the sepulchres of the kings.

22 AND the inhabitants of Je-ru'sa-lem made A-ha-zi'ah his youngest son king in his stead: for the band of men that came with the A-ra'bi-ans to the camp had slain all the eldest. So A-ha-zi'ah the son of Je-ho'ram king of Ju'dah reigned.

2 Forty and two years old was A-ha-zi'ah when he began to reign, and he reigned one year in Je-ru'sa-lem. His mother's name also was Ath-a-li'ah the daughter of Om'ri.

3 He also walked in the ways of the house of A'hab: for his mother was his counsellor to do wickedly.

4 Wherefore he did evil in the sight of the LORD like the house of A'hab: for they were his counsellors after the death of his father to his destruction.

5 ¶ He walked also after their counsel, and went with Je-ho'ram the son of A'hab king of Is'ra-el to war against Haz'a-el king of Syr'i-a at Ra'moth–gil'e-ad: and the Syr'i-ans smote Jo'-ram.

6 And he returned to be healed in Jez're-el because of the wounds which were given him at Ra'mah, when he fought with Haz'a-el king of Syr'i-a. And Az-a-ri'ah the son of Je-ho'ram king of Ju'dah went down to see Je-ho'ram the son of A'hab at Jez're-el, because he was sick.

7 And the destruction of A-ha-zi'ah was of God by coming to Jo'ram: for when he was come, he went out with Je-ho'ram against Je'hu the son of Nim'shi, whom the LORD had anointed to cut off the house of A'hab.

8 And it came to pass, that, when Je'hu was executing judgment upon the house of A'hab, and found the princes of Ju'dah, and the sons of the brethren of A-ha-zi'ah, that ministered to A-ha-zi'ah, he slew them.

9 And he sought A-ha-zi'ah: and they caught him, (for he was hid in Sa-ma'ri-a,) and brought him to Je'hu: and when they had slain him, they buried him: Because, said they, he is the son of Je-hosh'a-phat, who sought the LORD with all his heart. So the house of A-ha-zi'ah had no power to keep still the kingdom.

10 ¶ But when Ath-a-li'ah the mother of A-ha-zi'ah saw that her son was dead, she arose and destroyed all the seed royal of the house of Ju'dah.

11 But Je-ho-shab'e-ath, the daughter of the king, took Jo'ash the son of A-ha-zi'ah, and stole him from among the king's sons that were slain, and put him and his nurse in a bedchamber. So Je-ho-shab'e-ath, the daughter of king Je-ho'ram, the wife of Je-hoi'a-da the priest, (for

she was the sister of A-ha-zi'ah,) hid him from Ath-a-li'ah, so that she slew him not.

12 And he was with them hid in the house of God six years: and Ath-a-li'ah reigned over the land.

23 AND in the seventh year Je-hoi'a-da strengthened himself, and took the captains of hundreds, Az-a-ri'ah the son of Jer'o-ham, and Ish'ma-el the son of Je-ho-ha'nan, and Az-a-ri'ah the son of O'bed, and Ma-a-se'iah the son of Ad-a-i'ah, and E-lish'a-phat the son of Zich'ri, into covenant with him.

2 And they went about in Ju'dah, and gathered the Le'vites out of all the cities of Ju'dah, and the chief of the fathers of Is'ra-el, and they came to Je-ru'sa-lem.

3 And all the congregation made a covenant with the king in the house of God. And he said unto him, Behold, the king's son shall reign, as the LORD hath said of the sons of Da'vid.

4 This is the thing that ye shall do; A third part of you entering on the sabbath, of the priests and of the Le'vites, shall be porters of the doors;

5 And a third part shall be at the king's house; and a third part at the gate of the foundation: and all the people shall be in the courts of the house of the LORD.

6 But let none come into the house of the LORD, save the priests, and they that minister of the Le'vites; they shall go in, for they are holy: but all the people shall keep the watch of the LORD.

7 And the Le'vites shall compass the king round about, every man with his weapons in his hand; and whosoever else cometh into the house, he shall be put to death: but be ye with the king when he cometh in, and when he goeth out.

8 So the Le'vites and all Ju'dah did according to all things that Je-hoi'a-da the priest had commanded, and took every man his men that were to come in on the sabbath: with them that were to go out on the sabbath: for Je-hoi'a-da the priest dismissed not the courses.

9 Moreover Je-hoi'a-da the priest delivered to the captains of hundreds spears, and bucklers, and shields, that had been king Da'vid's, which were in the house of God.

10 And he set all the people, every man having his weapon in his hand, from the right side of the temple to the left side of the temple, along by the altar and the temple, by the king round about.

11 Then they brought out the king's son, and put upon him the crown, and gave him the testimony, and made him king. And Je-hoi'a-da and his sons anointed him, and said, God save the king.

12 ¶ Now when Ath-a-li'ah heard the noise of the people running and praising the king, she came to the people into the house of the LORD:

13 And she looked, and, behold, the king stood at his pillar at the entering in, and the princes and the trumpets by the king: and all the people of the land rejoiced, and sounded with trumpets, also the singers with instruments of musick, and such as taught to sing praise. Then Ath-a-li'ah rent her clothes, and said, Treason, Treason.

14 Then Je-hoi'a-da the priest brought out the captains of hundreds that were set over the host, and said unto them, Have her forth of the ranges: and whoso followeth her, let him be slain with the sword. For the priest said, Slay her not in the house of the LORD.

15 So they laid hands on her; and when she was come to the entering of the horse gate by the king's house, they slew her there.

16 ¶ And Je-hoi'a-da made a covenant between him, and between all the people, and between the king, that they should be the LORD's people.

17 Then all the people went to the house of Ba'al, and brake it down, and brake his altars and his images in pieces, and slew Mat'tan the priest of Ba'al before the altars.

18 Also Je-hoi'a-da appointed the offices of the house of the LORD by the hand of the priests the Le'vites, whom Da'vid had distributed in the house of the LORD, to offer the burnt offerings of the LORD, as it is written in the law of Mo'ses, with rejoicing and with singing, as it was ordained by Da'vid.

19 And he set the porters at the gates of the house of the LORD, that none which was unclean in any thing should enter in.

20 And he took the captains of hundreds, and the nobles, and the governors of the people, and all the people of the land, and brought down the king from the house of the LORD: and they came through the high gate into the king's house, and set the king upon the throne of the kingdom.

21 And all the people of the land rejoiced: and the city was quiet, after that they had slain Ath-a-li'ah with the sword.

24 JO'ASH was seven years old when he began to reign, and he reigned forty years in Je-ru'sa-lem. His mother's name also was Zib'i-ah of Be'er-she'ba.

2 And Jo'ash did that which was right in the sight of the LORD all the days of Je-hoi'a-da the priest.

3 And Je-hoi'a-da took for him two wives; and he begat sons and daughters.

4 ¶ And it came to pass after this, that Jo'ash was minded to repair the house of the LORD.

5 And he gathered together the priests and the Le'vites, and said to them, Go out unto the cities of Ju'dah, and gather of all Is'ra-el money to repair the house of your God from year to year, and see that ye hasten the matter. Howbeit the Le'vites hastened it not.

6 And the king called for Je-hoi'a-da the chief, and said unto him, Why hast thou not required of the Le'vites to bring in out of Ju'dah and out of Je-ru'sa-lem the collection, according to the commandment of Mo'ses the servant of the LORD, and of the congregation of Is'ra-el, for the tabernacle of witness?

7 For the sons of Ath-a-li'ah, that wicked woman, had broken up the house of God; and also all the dedicated things of the house of the LORD did they bestow upon Ba'al-im.

8 And at the king's commandment they made a chest, and set it without at the gate of the house of the LORD.

9 And they made a proclamation through Ju'dah and Je-ru'sa-lem, to bring in to the LORD the collection that Mo'ses the servant of God laid upon Is'ra-el in the wilderness.

10 And all the princes and all the people rejoiced, and brought in, and cast into the chest, until they had made an end.

11 Now it came to pass, that at what time the chest was brought unto the king's office by the hand of the Le'vites, and when they saw that there was much money, the king's scribe and the high priest's officer came and emptied the chest, and took it, and carried it to his place again. Thus they did day by day, and gathered money in abundance.

12 And the king and Je-hoi'a-da gave it to such as did the work of the service of the house of the LORD, and hired masons and carpenters to repair the house of the LORD, and also such as wrought iron and brass to mend the house of the LORD.

13 So the workmen wrought, and the work was perfected by them, and they set the house of God in his state, and strengthened it.

14 And when they had finished it, they brought the rest of the money before the king and Je-hoi'a-da, whereof were made vessels for the house of the LORD, even vessels to minister, and to offer withal, and spoons, and vessels of gold and silver. And they offered burnt offerings in the house of the LORD continually all the days of Je-hoi'a-da.

15 ¶ But Je-hoi'a-da waxed old, and was full of days when he died; an hundred and thirty years old was he when he died.

16 And they buried him in the city of Da'vid among the kings, because he had done good in Is'ra-el, both toward God, and toward his house.

17 Now after the death of Je-hoi'a-da came the princes of Ju'dah, and made obeisance to the king. Then the king hearkened unto them.

18 And they left the house of the LORD God of their fathers, and served groves and idols: and wrath came upon Ju'dah and Je-ru'sa-lem for this their trespass.

19 Yet he sent prophets to them, to bring them again unto the LORD; and they testified against them: but they would not give ear.

20 And the Spirit of God came upon Zech-a-ri'ah the son of Je-hoi'a-da the priest, which stood above the people, and said unto them, Thus saith God, Why transgress ye the commandments of the LORD, that ye cannot prosper? because ye have forsaken the LORD, he hath also forsaken you.

21 And they conspired against him, and stoned him with stones at the commandment of the king in the court of the house of the LORD.

22 Thus Jo'ash the king remembered not the kindness which Je-hoi'a-da his father had done to him, but slew his son. And when he died, he said, The LORD look upon it, and require it.

23 ¶ And it came to pass at the end of the year, that the host of Syr'i-a came up against him: and they came to Ju'dah and Je-ru'sa-lem, and destroyed all the princes of the people from among the people, and sent all the spoil of them unto the king of Da-mas'cus.

24 For the army of the Syr'i-ans came with a small company of men, and the LORD delivered a very great host into their hand, because they had forsaken the LORD God of their fathers. So they executed judgment against Jo'ash.

25 And when they were departed from him, (for they left him in great diseases,) his own servants conspired against him for the blood of the sons of Je-hoi'a-da the priest, and slew him on his bed, and he died: and they buried him in the city of Da'vid, but they buried him not in the sepulchres of the kings.

26 And these are they that conspired against him; Za'bad the son of Shim'e-ath an Am'mon-it-ess, and Je-hoz'a-bad the son of Shim'rith a Mo'ab-it-ess.

27 ¶ Now concerning his sons, and the greatness of the burdens laid upon him, and the repairing of the house of God, behold, they are written in the story of the book of the kings. And Am-a-zi'ah his son reigned in his stead.

25 AM-A-ZI'AH was twenty and five years old when he began to reign, and he reigned twenty and nine years in Je-ru'sa-lem. And his mother's name was Je-ho-ad'dan of Je-ru'sa-lem.

2 And he did that which was right in the sight of the LORD, but not with a perfect heart.

3 ¶ Now it came to pass, when the kingdom was established to him, that he slew his servants that had killed the king his father.

4 But he slew not their children, but did as it is written in the law in the book of Mo'ses, where the LORD commanded, saying, The fathers shall not die for the children, neither shall the children die for the fathers, but every man shall die for his own sin.

5 ¶ Moreover Am-a-zi'ah gathered Ju'dah together, and made them captains over thousands, and captains over hundreds, according to the houses of their fathers, throughout all Ju'dah and Ben'ja-min: and he numbered them from twenty years old and above, and found them three hundred thousand choice men, able to go forth to war, that could handle spear and shield.

6 He hired also an hundred thousand mighty men of valour out of Is'ra-el for an hundred talents of silver.

7 But there came a man of God to him, saying, O king, let not the army of Is'ra-el go with thee; for the LORD is not with Is'ra-el, to wit, with all the children of E'phra-im.

8 But if thou wilt go, do it, be strong for the battle: God shall make thee fall before the enemy: for God hath power to help, and to cast down.

9 And Am-a-zi'ah said to the man of God, But what shall we do for the hundred talents which I have given to the army of Is'ra-el? And the man of God answered, The LORD is able to give thee much more than this.

10 Then Am-a-zi'ah separated them, to wit, the army that was come to him out of E'phra-im, to go home again: wherefore their anger was greatly kindled against Ju'dah, and they returned home in great anger.

11 ¶ And Am-a-zi'ah strengthened himself, and led forth his people, and went to the valley of salt, and smote of the children of Se'ir ten thousand.

12 And other ten thousand left alive did the children of Ju'dah carry away captive, and brought them unto the top of the rock, and cast them down from the top of the rock, that they all were broken in pieces.

13 ¶ But the soldiers of the army which Am-a-zi'ah sent back, that they should not go with him to battle, fell upon the cities of Ju'dah, from Sa-ma'ri-a even unto Beth-ho'ron, and smote three thousand of them, and took much spoil.

14 ¶ Now it came to pass, after that Am-a-zi'ah was come from the slaughter of the E'dom-ites, that he brought the gods of the children of Se'ir, and set them up to be his gods, and bowed down himself before them, and burned incense unto them.

15 Wherefore the anger of the LORD was kindled against Am-a-zi'ah, and he sent unto him a prophet, which said unto him, Why hast thou sought after the gods of the people, which could not deliver their own people out of thine hand?

16 And it came to pass, as he talked with him, that the king said unto him, Art thou made of the king's counsel? forbear; why shouldest thou be smitten? Then the prophet forbare, and said, I know that God hath determined to de-

stroy thee, because thou hast done this, and hast not hearkened unto my counsel.

17 ¶ Then Am-a-zi′ah king of Ju′dah took advice, and sent to Jo′ash, the son of Je-ho′a-haz, the son of Je′hu, king of Is′ra-el, saying, Come, let us see one another in the face.

18 And Jo′ash king of Is′ra-el sent to Am-a-zi′ah king of Ju′dah, saying, The thistle that *was* in Leb′a-non sent to the cedar that *was* in Leb′a-non, saying, Give thy daughter to my son to wife: and there passed by a wild beast that *was* in Leb′a-non, and trode down the thistle.

19 Thou sayest, Lo, thou hast smitten the E′-dom-ites; and thine heart lifteth thee up to boast: abide now at home; why shouldest thou meddle to *thine* hurt, that thou shouldest fall, *even* thou, and Ju′dah with thee?

20 But Am-a-zi′ah would not hear; for it *came* of God, that he might deliver them into the hand *of their enemies*, because they sought after the gods of E′dom.

21 So Jo′ash the king of Is′ra-el went up; and they saw one another in the face, *both* he and Am-a-zi′ah king of Ju′dah, at Beth-she′mesh, which *belongeth* to Ju′dah.

22 And Ju′dah was put to the worse before Is′ra-el, and they fled every man to his tent.

23 And Jo′ash the king of Is′ra-el took Am-a-zi′ah king of Ju′dah, the son of Jo′ash, the son of Je-ho′a-haz, at Beth-she′mesh, and brought him to Je-ru′sa-lem, and brake down the wall of Je-ru′sa-lem from the gate of E′phra-im to the corner gate, four hundred cubits.

24 And *he took* all the gold and the silver, and all the vessels that were found in the house of God with O′bed-e′dom, and the treasures of the king's house, the hostages also, and returned to Sa-ma′ri-a.

25 ¶ And Am-a-zi′ah the son of Jo′ash king of Ju′dah lived after the death of Jo′ash son of Je-ho′a-haz king of Is′ra-el fifteen years.

26 Now the rest of the acts of Am-a-zi′ah, first and last, behold, *are* they not written in the book of the kings of Ju′dah and Is′ra-el?

27 ¶ Now after the time that Am-a-zi′ah did turn away from following the LORD they made a conspiracy against him in Je-ru′sa-lem; and he fled to La′chish: but they sent to La′chish after him, and slew him there.

28 And they brought him upon horses, and buried him with his fathers in the city of Ju′dah.

26 THEN all the people of Ju′dah took Uz-zi′ah, who *was* sixteen years old, and made him king in the room of his father Am-a-zi′ah.

2 He built E′loth, and restored it to Ju′dah, after that the king slept with his fathers.

3 Sixteen years old *was* Uz-zi′ah when he began to reign, and he reigned fifty and two years in Je-ru′sa-lem. His mother's name also *was* Jec-o-li′ah of Je-ru′sa-lem.

4 And he did *that which was* right in the sight of the LORD, according to all that his father Am-a-zi′ah did.

5 And he sought God in the days of Zech-a-ri′ah, who had understanding in the visions of God: and as long as he sought the LORD, God made him to prosper.

6 And he went forth and warred against the Phi-lis′tines, and brake down the wall of Gath, and the wall of Jab′neh, and the wall of Ash′-dod, and built cities about Ash′dod, and among the Phi-lis′tines.

7 And God helped him against the Phi-lis′tines, and against the A-ra′bi-ans that dwelt in Gur-ba′al, and the Me-hu′nims.

8 And the Am′mon-ites gave gifts to Uz-zi′ah: and his name spread abroad *even* to the entering in of E′gypt; for he strengthened *himself* exceedingly.

9 Moreover Uz-zi′ah built towers in Je-ru′sa-lem at the corner gate, and at the valley gate, and at the turning *of the wall*, and fortified them.

10 Also he built towers in the desert, and digged many wells: for he had much cattle, both in the low country, and in the plains: husbandmen *also*, and vine dressers in the mountains, and in Car′mel: for he loved husbandry.

11 Moreover Uz-zi′ah had an host of fighting men, that went out to war by bands, according to the number of their account by the hand of Je-i′el the scribe and Ma-a-se′iah the ruler, under the hand of Han-a-ni′ah, *one* of the king's captains.

12 The whole number of the chief of the fathers of the mighty men of valour *were* two thousand and six hundred.

13 And under their hand *was* an army, three hundred thousand and seven thousand and five hundred, that made war with mighty power, to help the king against the enemy.

14 And Uz-zi′ah prepared for them throughout all the host shields, and spears, and helmets, and habergeons, and bows, and slings *to* cast stones.

15 And he made in Je-ru′sa-lem engines, invented by cunning men, to be on the towers and upon the bulwarks, to shoot arrows and great stones withal. And his name spread far abroad; for he was marvellously helped, till he was strong.

16 ¶ But when he was strong, his heart was lifted up to *his* destruction: for he transgressed against the LORD his God, and went into the temple of the LORD to burn incense upon the altar of incense.

17 And Az-a-ri′ah the priest went in after him, and with him fourscore priests of the LORD, *that were* valiant men:

18 And they withstood Uz-zi′ah the king, and said unto him, It *appertaineth* not unto thee, Uz-zi′ah, to burn incense unto the LORD, but to the priests the sons of Aar′on, that are consecrated to burn incense: go out of the sanctuary; for thou hast trespassed; neither *shall it be* for thine honour from the LORD God.

19 Then Uz-zi′ah was wroth, and *had* a censer in his hand to burn incense: and while he was wroth with the priests, the leprosy even rose up in his forehead before the priests in the house of the LORD, from beside the incense altar.

20 And Az-a-ri′ah the chief priest, and all the priests, looked upon him, and, behold, he *was* leprous in his forehead, and they thrust him out from thence; yea, himself hasted also to go out, because the LORD had smitten him.

21 And Uz-zi′ah the king was a leper unto the day of his death, and dwelt in a several house, *being* a leper; for he was cut off from the house of the LORD: and Jo′tham his son *was* over the king's house, judging the people of the land.

22 ¶ Now the rest of the acts of Uz-zi′ah, first and last, did I-sa′iah the prophet, the son of A′moz, write.

23 So Uz-zi′ah slept with his fathers, and they buried him with his fathers in the field of the burial which *belonged* to the kings; for they said, He *is* a leper: and Jo′tham his son reigned in his stead.

27 JO'THAM *was* twenty and five years old when he began to reign, and he reigned sixteen years in Je-ru'sa-lem. His mother's name also *was* Je-ru'-shah, the daughter of Za'-dok.

2 And he did *that which was* right in the sight of the LORD, according to all that his father Uz-zi'ah did: howbeit he entered not into the temple of the LORD. And the people did yet corruptly.

3 He built the high gate of the house of the LORD, and on the wall of O'phel he built much.

4 Moreover he built cities in the mountains of Ju'dah, and in the forests he built castles and towers.

5 ¶ He fought also with the king of the Am'-mon-ites, and prevailed against them. And the children of Am'mon gave him the same year an hundred talents of silver, and ten thousand measures of wheat, and ten thousand of barley. So much did the children of Am'mon pay unto him, both the second year, and the third.

6 So Jo'tham became mighty, because he prepared his ways before the LORD his God.

7 ¶ Now the rest of the acts of Jo'tham, and all his wars, and his ways, lo, they *are* written in the book of the kings of Is'ra-el and Ju'dah.

8 He was five and twenty years old when he began to reign, and reigned sixteen years in Je-ru'sa-lem.

9 ¶ And Jo'tham slept with his fathers, and they buried him in the city of Da'vid: and A'haz his son reigned in his stead.

28 AHAZ *was* twenty years old when he began to reign, and he reigned sixteen years in Je-ru'sa-lem: but he did not *that which was* right in the sight of the LORD, like Da'vid his father:

2 For he walked in the ways of the kings of Is'ra-el, and made also molten images for Ba'al-im.

3 Moreover he burnt incense in the valley of the son of Hin'nom, and burnt his children in the fire, after the abominations of the heathen whom the LORD had cast out before the children of Is'ra-el.

4 He sacrificed also and burnt incense in the high places, and on the hills, and under every green tree.

5 Wherefore the LORD his God delivered him into the hand of the king of Syr'i-a; and they smote him, and carried away a great multitude of them captives, and brought *them* to Da-mas'-cus. And he was also delivered into the hand of the king of Is'ra-el, who smote him with a great slaughter.

6 ¶ For Pe'kah the son of Rem-a-li'ah slew in Ju'dah an hundred and twenty thousand in one day, *which were* all valiant men; because they had forsaken the LORD God of their fathers.

7 And Zich'ri, a mighty man of E'phra-im, slew Ma-a-se'iah the king's son, and Az'ri-kam the governor of the house, and El'ka-nah *that was* next to the king.

8 And the children of Is'ra-el carried away captive of their brethren two hundred thousand, women, sons, and daughters, and took also away much spoil from them, and brought the spoil to Sa-ma'ri-a.

9 But a prophet of the LORD was there, whose name *was* O'ded: and he went out before the host that came to Sa-ma'ri-a, and said unto them, Behold, because the LORD God of your fathers was wroth with Ju'dah, he hath delivered them into your hand, and ye have slain them in a rage *that* reacheth up unto heaven.

10 And now ye purpose to keep under the children of Ju'dah and Je-ru'sa-lem for bondmen and bondwomen unto you: *but are there* not with you, even with you, sins against the LORD your God?

11 Now hear me therefore, and deliver the captives again, which ye have taken captive of your brethren: for the fierce wrath of the LORD *is* upon you.

12 Then certain of the heads of the children of E'phra-im, Az-a-ri'ah the son of Jo-ha'nan, Ber-e-chi'ah the son of Me-shil'le-moth, and Je-hiz-ki'ah the son of Shal'lum, and Am'a-sa the son of Had'la-i, stood up against them that came from the war,

13 And said unto them, Ye shall not bring in the captives hither: for whereas we have offended against the LORD *already,* ye intend to add *more* to our sins and to our trespass: for our trespass is great, and *there is* fierce wrath against Is'ra-el.

14 So the armed men left the captives and the spoil before the princes and all the congregation.

15 And the men which were expressed by name rose up, and took the captives, and with the spoil clothed all that were naked among them, and arrayed them, and shod them, and gave them to eat and to drink, and anointed them, and carried all the feeble of them upon asses, and brought them to Jer'i-cho, the city of palm trees, to their brethren: then they returned to Sa-ma'ri-a.

16 ¶ At that time did king A'haz send unto the kings of As-syr'i-a to help him.

17 For again the E'dom-ites had come and smitten Ju'dah, and carried away captives.

18 The Phi-lis'tines also had invaded the cities of the low country, and of the south of Ju'dah, and had taken Beth–she'mesh, and Aj'a-lon, and Ge-de'roth, and Sho'cho with the villages thereof, and Tim'nah with the villages thereof, Gim'zo also and the villages thereof: and they dwelt there.

19 For the LORD brought Ju'dah low because of A'haz king of Is'ra-el; for he made Ju'dah naked, and transgressed sore against the LORD.

20 And Til'gath–pil-ne'ser king of As-syr'i-a came unto him, and distressed him, but strengthened him not.

21 For A'haz took away a portion *out* of the house of the LORD, and *out* of the house of the king, and of the princes, and gave *it* unto the king of As-syr'i-a: but he helped him not.

22 ¶ And in the time of his distress did he trespass yet more against the LORD: this *is that* king A'haz.

23 For he sacrificed unto the gods of Da-mas'cus, which smote him: and he said, Because the gods of the kings of Syr'i-a help them, *therefore* will I sacrifice to them, that they may help me. But they were the ruin of him, and of all Is'ra-el.

24 And A'haz gathered together the vessels of the house of God, and cut in pieces the vessels of the house of God, and shut up the doors of the house of the LORD, and he made him altars in every corner of Je-ru'sa-lem.

25 And in every several city of Ju'dah he made high places to burn incense unto other gods, and provoked to anger the LORD God of his fathers.

26 ¶ Now the rest of his acts and of all his ways, first and last, behold, they *are* written in the book of the kings of Ju'dah and Is'ra-el.

27 And A'haz slept with his fathers, and they buried him in the city, *even* in Je-ru'sa-lem: but

they brought him not into the sepulchres of the kings of Is'ra-el: and Hez-e-ki'ah his son reigned in his stead.

29 HEZ-E-KI'AH began to reign *when he was* five and twenty years old, and he reigned nine and twenty years in Je-ru'sa-lem. And his mother's name *was* A-bi'jah, the daughter of Zech-a-ri'ah.

2 And he did *that which was* right in the sight of the LORD, according to all that Da'vid his father had done.

3 ¶ He in the first year of his reign, in the first month, opened the doors of the house of the LORD, and repaired them.

4 And he brought in the priests and the Le'vites, and gathered them together into the east street,

5 And said unto them, Hear me, ye Le'vites, sanctify now yourselves, and sanctify the house of the LORD God of your fathers, and carry forth the filthiness out of the holy *place.*

6 For our fathers have trespassed, and done *that which was* evil in the eyes of the LORD our God, and have forsaken him, and have turned away their faces from the habitation of the LORD, and turned *their* backs.

7 Also they have shut up the doors of the porch, and put out the lamps, and have not burned incense nor offered burnt offerings in the holy *place* unto the God of Is'ra-el.

8 Wherefore the wrath of the LORD was upon Ju'dah and Je-ru'sa-lem, and he hath delivered them to trouble, to astonishment, and to hissing, as ye see with your eyes.

9 For, lo, our fathers have fallen by the sword, and our sons and our daughters and our wives *are* in captivity for this.

10 Now *it is* in mine heart to make a covenant with the LORD God of Is'ra-el, that his fierce wrath may turn away from us.

11 My sons, be not now negligent: for the LORD hath chosen you to stand before him, to serve him, and that ye should minister unto him, and burn incense.

12 ¶ Then the Le'vites arose, Ma'hath the son of A-mas'a-i, and Jo'el the son of Az-a-ri'ah, of the sons of the Ko'hath-ites: and of the sons of Me-ra'ri, Kish the son of Ab'di, and Az-a-ri'ah the son of Je-hal'e-lel: and of the Ger'shon-ites; Jo'ah the son of Zim'mah, and E'den the son of Jo'ah:

13 And of the sons of El'za-phan; Shim'ri, and Je-i'el: and of the sons of A'saph; Zech-a-ri'ah, and Mat-ta-ni'ah:

14 And of the sons of He'man; Je-hi'el, and Shim'e-i: and of the sons of Jed'u-thun; Shem-a-i'ah, and Uz'zi-el.

15 And they gathered their brethren, and sanctified themselves, and came, according to the commandment of the king, by the words of the LORD, to cleanse the house of the LORD.

16 And the priests went into the inner part of the house of the LORD, to cleanse *it,* and brought out all the uncleanness that they found in the temple of the LORD into the court of the house of the LORD. And the Le'vites took *it,* to carry *it* out abroad into the brook Kid'ron.

17 Now they began on the first *day* of the first month to sanctify, and on the eighth day of the month came they to the porch of the LORD: so they sanctified the house of the LORD in eight days; and in the sixteenth day of the first month they made an end.

18 Then they went in to Hez-e-ki'ah the king, and said, We have cleansed all the house of the LORD, and the altar of burnt offering, with all

the vessels thereof, and the shewbread table, with all the vessels thereof.

19 Moreover all the vessels, which king A'-haz in his reign did cast away in his transgression, have we prepared and sanctified, and, behold, they *are* before the altar of the LORD.

20 ¶ Then Hez-e-ki'ah the king rose early, and gathered the rulers of the city, and went up to the house of the LORD.

21 And they brought seven bullocks, and seven rams, and seven lambs, and seven he goats, for a sin offering for the kingdom, and for the sanctuary, and for Ju'dah. And he commanded the priests the sons of Aar'on to offer *them* on the altar of the LORD.

22 So they killed the bullocks, and the priests received the blood, and sprinkled *it* on the altar: likewise, when they had killed the rams, they sprinkled the blood upon the altar: they killed also the lambs, and they sprinkled the blood upon the altar.

23 And they brought forth the he goats *for* the sin offering before the king and the congregation; and they laid their hands upon them:

24 And the priests killed them, and they made reconciliation with their blood upon the altar, to make an atonement for all Is'ra-el: for the king commanded *that* the burnt offering and the sin offering *should be made* for all Is'ra-el.

25 And he set the Le'vites in the house of the LORD with cymbals, with psalteries, and with harps, according to the commandment of Da'-vid, and of Gad the king's seer, and Na'than the prophet: for *so was* the commandment of the LORD by his prophets.

26 And the Le'vites stood with the instruments of Da'vid, and the priests with the trumpets.

27 And Hez-e-ki'ah commanded to offer the burnt offering upon the altar. And when the burnt offering began, the song of the LORD began *also* with the trumpets, and with the instruments *ordained* by Da'vid king of Is'ra-el.

28 And all the congregation worshipped, and the singers sang, and the trumpeters sounded: *and* all *this continued* until the burnt offering was finished.

29 And when they had made an end of offering, the king and all that were present with him bowed themselves, and worshipped.

30 Moreover Hez-e-ki'ah the king and the princes commanded the Le'vites to sing praise unto the LORD with the words of Da'vid, and of A'saph the seer. And they sang praises with gladness, and they bowed their heads and worshipped.

31 Then Hez-e-ki'ah answered and said, Now ye have consecrated yourselves unto the LORD, come near and bring sacrifices and thank offerings into the house of the LORD. And the congregation brought in sacrifices and thank offerings; and as many as were of a free heart burnt offerings.

32 And the number of the burnt offerings, which the congregation brought, was threescore and ten bullocks, an hundred rams, *and* two hundred lambs: all these *were* for a burnt offering to the LORD.

33 And the consecrated things *were* six hundred oxen and three thousand sheep.

34 But the priests were too few, so that they could not flay all the burnt offerings: wherefore their brethren the Le'vites did help them, till the work was ended, and until the *other* priests had sanctified themselves: for the Le'vites *were*

more upright in heart to sanctify themselves than the priests.

35 And also the burnt offerings *were* in abundance, with the fat of the peace offerings, and the drink offerings for *every* burnt offering. So the service of the house of the LORD was set in order.

36 And Hez-e-ki′ah rejoiced, and all the people, that God had prepared the people: for the thing was *done* suddenly.

30 AND Hez-e-ki′ah sent to all Is′ra-el and Ju′dah, and wrote letters also to E′phra-im and Ma-nas′seh, that they should come to the house of the LORD at Je-ru′sa-lem, to keep the passover unto the LORD God of Is′ra-el.

2 For the king had taken counsel, and his princes, and all the congregation in Je-ru′sa-lem, to keep the passover in the second month.

3 For they could not keep it at that time, because the priests had not sanctified themselves sufficiently, neither had the people gathered themselves together to Je-ru′sa-lem.

4 And the thing pleased the king and all the congregation.

5 So they established a decree to make proclamation throughout all Is′ra-el, from Be′er-she′ba even to Dan, that they should come to keep the passover unto the LORD God of Is′ra-el at Je-ru′sa-lem: for they had not done *it* of a long *time in such sort* as it was written.

6 So the posts went with the letters from the king and his princes throughout all Is′ra-el and Ju′dah, and according to the commandment of the king, saying, Ye children of Is′ra-el, turn again unto the LORD God of A′bra-ham, I′saac, and Is′ra-el, and he will return to the remnant of you, that are escaped out of the hand of the kings of As-syr′i-a.

7 And be not ye like your fathers, and like your brethren, which trespassed against the LORD God of their fathers, *who* therefore gave them up to desolation, as ye see.

8 Now be ye not stiffnecked, as your fathers *were*, *but* yield yourselves unto the LORD, and enter into his sanctuary, which he hath sanctified for ever: and serve the LORD your God, that the fierceness of his wrath may turn away from you.

9 For if ye turn again unto the LORD, your brethren and your children *shall find* compassion before them that lead them captive, so that they shall come again into this land: for the LORD your God *is* gracious and merciful, and will not turn away *his* face from you, if ye return unto him.

10 So the posts passed from city to city through the country of E′phra-im and Ma-nas′-seh even unto Zeb′u-lun: but they laughed them to scorn, and mocked them.

11 Nevertheless divers of Ash′er and Ma-nas′seh and of Zeb′u-lun humbled themselves, and came to Je-ru′sa-lem.

12 Also in Ju′dah the hand of God was to give them one heart to do the commandment of the king and of the princes, by the word of the LORD.

13 ¶ And there assembled at Je-ru′sa-lem much people to keep the feast of unleavened bread in the second month, a very great congregation.

14 And they arose and took away the altars that *were* in Je-ru′sa-lem, and all the altars for incense took they away, and cast *them* into the brook Kid′ron.

15 Then they killed the passover on the fourteenth *day* of the second month: and the priests

and the Le′vites were ashamed, and sanctified themselves, and brought in the burnt offerings into the house of the LORD.

16 And they stood in their place after their manner, according to the law of Mo′ses the man of God: the priests sprinkled the blood, *which they received* of the hand of the Le′vites.

17 For *there were* many in the congregation that were not sanctified: therefore the Le′vites had the charge of the killing of the passovers for every one *that was* not clean, to sanctify *them* unto the LORD.

18 For a multitude of the people, *even* many of E′phra-im, and Ma-nas′seh, Is′sa-char, and Zeb′u-lun, had not cleansed themselves, yet did they eat the passover otherwise than it was written. But Hez-e-ki′ah prayed for them, saying, The good LORD pardon every one

19 *That* prepareth his heart to seek God, the LORD God of his fathers, though *he be* not *cleansed* according to the purification of the sanctuary.

20 And the LORD hearkened to Hez-e-ki′ah, and healed the people.

21 And the children of Is′ra-el that were present at Je-ru′sa-lem, kept the feast of unleavened bread seven days with great gladness: and the Le′vites and the priests praised the LORD day by day, *singing* with loud instruments unto the LORD.

22 And Hez-e-ki′ah spake comfortably unto all the Le′vites that taught the good knowledge of the LORD: and they did eat throughout the feast seven days, offering peace offerings, and making confession to the LORD God of their fathers.

23 And the whole assembly took counsel to keep *other* seven days: and they kept *other* seven days with gladness.

24 For Hez-e-ki′ah king of Ju′dah did give to the congregation a thousand bullocks and seven thousand sheep; and the princes gave to the congregation a thousand bullocks and ten thousand sheep: and a great number of priests sanctified themselves.

25 And all the congregation of Ju′dah, with the priests and the Le′vites, and all the congregation that came out of Is′ra-el, and the strangers that came out of the land of Is′ra-el, and that dwelt in Ju′dah, rejoiced.

26 So there was great joy in Je-ru′sa-lem: for since the time of Sol′o-mon the son of Da′vid king of Is′ra-el *there was* not the like in Je-ru′sa-lem.

27 ¶ Then the priests the Le′vites arose and blessed the people: and their voice was heard, and their prayer came *up* to his holy dwelling place, *even* unto heaven.

31 NOW when all this was finished, all Is′-ra-el that were present went out to the cities of Ju′dah, and brake the images in pieces, and cut down the groves, and threw down the high places and the altars out of all Ju′dah and Ben′ja-min, in E′phra-im also and Ma-nas′seh, until they had utterly destroyed them all. Then all the children of Is′ra-el returned, every man to his possession, into their own cities.

2 ¶ And Hez-e-ki′ah appointed the courses of the priests and the Le′vites after their courses, every man according to his service, the priests and Le′vites for burnt offerings and for peace offerings, to minister, and to give thanks, and to praise in the gates of the tents of the LORD.

3 *He appointed* also the king's portion of his substance for the burnt offerings, *to wit*, for the

morning and evening burnt offerings, and the burnt offerings for the sabbaths, and for the new moons, and for the set feasts, as *it is* written in the law of the LORD.

4 Moreover he commanded the people that dwelt in Je-ru′sa-lem to give the portion of the priests and the Le′vites, that they might be encouraged in the law of the LORD.

5 ¶ And as soon as the commandment came abroad, the children of Is′ra-el brought in abundance the firstfruits of corn, wine, and oil, and honey, and of all the increase of the field; and the tithe of all *things* brought they in abundantly.

6 And *concerning* the children of Is′ra-el and Ju′dah, that dwelt in the cities of Ju′dah, they also brought in the tithe of oxen and sheep, and the tithe of holy things which were consecrated unto the LORD their God, and laid *them* by heaps.

7 In the third month they began to lay the foundation of the heaps, and finished *them* in the seventh month.

8 And when Hez-e-ki′ah and the princes came and saw the heaps, they blessed the LORD, and his people Is′ra-el.

9 Then Hez-e-ki′ah questioned with the priests and the Le′vites concerning the heaps.

10 And Az-a-ri′ah the chief priest of the house of Za′dok answered him, and said, Since *the people* began to bring the offerings into the house of the LORD, we have had enough to eat, and have left plenty: for the LORD hath blessed his people; and that which is left *is* this great store.

11 ¶ Then Hez-e-ki′ah commanded to prepare chambers in the house of the LORD; and they prepared *them*,

12 And brought in the offerings and the tithes and the dedicated *things* faithfully: over which Con-o-ni′ah the Le′vite *was* ruler, and Shim′e-i his brother *was* the next.

13 And Je-hi′el, and Az-a-zi′ah, and Na′hath, and A′sa-hel, and Jer′i-moth, and Joz′a-bad, and E-li′el, and Is-ma-chi′ah, and Ma′hath, and Be-na′iah, *were* overseers under the hand of Con-o-ni′ah and Shim′e-i his brother, at the commandment of Hez-e-ki′ah the king, and Az-a-ri′ah the ruler of the house of God.

14 And Ko′re the son of Im′nah the Le′vite, the porter toward the east, *was* over the freewill offerings of God, to distribute the oblations of the LORD, and the most holy things.

15 And next him *were* E′den, and Mi-ni′a-min, and Jesh′u-a, and Shem-a-i′ah, Am-a-ri′ah, and Shec-a-ni′ah, in the cities of the priests, in *their* set office, to give to their brethren by courses, as well to the great as to the small:

16 Beside their genealogy of males, from three years old and upward, *even* unto every one that entereth into the house of the LORD, his daily portion for their service in their charges according to their courses;

17 Both to the genealogy of the priests by the house of their fathers, and the Le′vites from twenty years old and upward, in their charges by their courses;

18 And to the genealogy of all their little ones, their wives, and their sons, and their daughters, through all the congregation: for in their set office they sanctified themselves in holiness:

19 Also of the sons of Aar′on the priests, which were in the fields of the suburbs of their cities, in every several city, the men that were expressed by name, to give portions to all the males among the priests, and to all that were reckoned by genealogies among the Le′vites.

20 ¶ And thus did Hez-e-ki′ah throughout all Ju′dah, and wrought *that which was* good and right and truth before the LORD his God.

21 And in every work that he began in the service of the house of God, and in the law, and in the commandments, to seek his God, he did *it* with all his heart, and prospered.

32 AFTER these things, and the establishment thereof, Sen-nach′e-rib king of As-syr′i-a came, and entered into Ju′dah, and encamped against the fenced cities, and thought to win them for himself.

2 And when Hez-e-ki′ah saw that Sen-nach′-e-rib was come, and that he was purposed to fight against Je-ru′sa-lem,

3 He took counsel with his princes and his mighty men to stop the waters of the fountains which *were* without the city: and they did help him.

4 So there was gathered much people together, who stopped all the fountains, and the brook that ran through the midst of the land, saying, Why should the kings of As-syr′i-a come, and find much water?

5 Also he strengthened himself, and built up all the wall that was broken, and raised *it* up to the towers, and another wall without, and repaired Mil′lo *in* the city of Da′vid, and made darts and shields in abundance.

6 And he set captains of war over the people, and gathered them together to him in the street of the gate of the city, and spake comfortably to them, saying,

7 Be strong and courageous, be not afraid nor dismayed for the king of As-syr′i-a, nor for all the multitude that *is* with him: for *there be* more with us than with him:

8 With him *is* an arm of flesh; but with us *is* the LORD our God to help us, and to fight our battles. And the people rested themselves upon the words of Hez-e-ki′ah king of Ju′dah.

9 ¶ After this did Sen-nach′e-rib king of As-syr′i-a send his servants to Je-ru′sa-lem, (but he *himself laid* siege against La′chish, and all his power with him,) unto Hez-e-ki′ah king of Ju′-dah, and unto all Ju′dah that *were* at Je-ru′sa-lem, saying,

10 Thus saith Sen-nach′e-rib king of As-syr′i-a, Whereon do ye trust, that ye abide in the siege in Je-ru′sa-lem?

11 Doth not Hez-e-ki′ah persuade you to give over yourselves to die by famine and by thirst, saying, The LORD our God shall deliver us out of the hand of the king of As-syr′i-a?

12 Hath not the same Hez-e-ki′ah taken away his high places and his altars, and commanded Ju′dah and Je-ru′sa-lem, saying, Ye shall worship before one altar, and burn incense upon it?

13 Know ye not what I and my fathers have done unto all the people of *other* lands? were the gods of the nations of those lands any ways able to deliver their lands out of mine hand?

14 Who *was there* among all the gods of those nations that my fathers utterly destroyed, that could deliver his people out of mine hand, that your God should be able to deliver you out of mine hand?

15 Now therefore let not Hez-e-ki′ah deceive you, nor persuade you on this manner, neither yet believe him: for no god of any nation or kingdom was able to deliver his people out of mine hand, and out of the hand of my fathers:

how much less shall your God deliver you out of mine hand?

16 And his servants spake yet *more* against the LORD God, and against his servant Hez-e-ki′ah.

17 He wrote also letters to rail on the LORD God of Is′ra-el, and to speak against him, saying, As the gods of the nations of *other* lands have not delivered their people out of mine hand, so shall not the God of Hez-e-ki′ah deliver his people out of mine hand.

18 Then they cried with a loud voice in the Jews′ speech unto the people of Je-ru′sa-lem that *were* on the wall, to affright them, and to trouble them; that they might take the city.

19 And they spake against the God of Je-ru′sa-lem, as against the gods of the people of the earth, *which were* the work of the hands of man.

20 And for this *cause* Hez-e-ki′ah the king, and the prophet I-sa′iah the son of A′moz, prayed and cried to heaven.

21 ¶ And the LORD sent an angel, which cut off all the mighty men of valour, and the leaders and captains in the camp of the king of As-syr′i-a. So he returned with shame of face to his own land. And when he was come into the house of his god, they that came forth of his own bowels slew him there with the sword.

22 Thus the LORD saved Hez-e-ki′ah and the inhabitants of Je-ru′sa-lem from the hand of Sen-nach′e-rib the king of As-syr′i-a, and from the hand of all *other,* and guided them on every side.

23 And many brought gifts unto the LORD to Je-ru′sa-lem, and presents to Hez-e-ki′ah king of Ju′dah: so that he was magnified in the sight of all nations from thenceforth.

24 ¶ In those days Hez-e-ki′ah was sick to the death, and prayed unto the LORD: and he spake unto him, and he gave him a sign.

25 But Hez-e-ki′ah rendered not again according to the benefit *done* unto him; for his heart was lifted up: therefore there was wrath upon him, and upon Ju′dah and Je-ru′sa-lem.

26 Notwithstanding Hez-e-ki′ah humbled himself for the pride of his heart, *both* he and the inhabitants of Je-ru′sa-lem, so that the wrath of the LORD came not upon them in the days of Hez-e-ki′ah.

27 ¶ And Hez-e-ki′ah had exceeding much riches and honour: and he made himself treasuries for silver, and for gold, and for precious stones, and for spices, and for shields, and for all manner of pleasant jewels;

28 Storehouses also for the increase of corn, and wine, and oil; and stalls for all manner of beasts, and cotes for flocks.

29 Moreover he provided him cities, and possessions of flocks and herds in abundance: for God had given him substance very much.

30 This same Hez-e-ki′ah also stopped the upper watercourse of Gi′hon, and brought it straight down to the west side of the city of Da′vid. And Hez-e-ki′ah prospered in all his works.

31 ¶ Howbeit in *the business of* the ambassadors of the princes of Bab′y-lon, who sent unto him to enquire of the wonder that was *done* in the land, God left him, to try him, that he might know all *that was* in his heart.

32 ¶ Now the rest of the acts of Hez-e-ki′ah, and his goodness, behold, they *are* written in the vision of I-sa′iah the prophet, the son of A′moz, *and* in the book of the kings of Ju′dah and Is′ra-el.

33 And Hez-e-ki′ah slept with his fathers, and they buried him in the chiefest of the sepulchres of the sons of Da′vid: and all Ju′dah and the inhabitants of Je-ru′sa-lem did him honour at his death. And Ma-nas′seh his son reigned in his stead.

33 MA-NAS′SEH *was* twelve years old when he began to reign, and he reigned fifty and five years in Je-ru′sa-lem:

2 But did *that which was* evil in the sight of the LORD, like unto the abominations of the heathen, whom the LORD had cast out before the children of Is′ra-el.

3 ¶ For he built again the high places which Hez-e-ki′ah his father had broken down, and he reared up altars for Ba′al-im, and made groves, and worshipped all the host of heaven, and served them.

4 Also he built altars in the house of the LORD, whereof the LORD had said, In Je-ru′sa-lem shall my name be for ever.

5 And he built altars for all the host of heaven in the two courts of the house of the LORD.

6 And he caused his children to pass through the fire in the valley of the son of Hin′nom: also he observed times, and used enchantments, and used witchcraft, and dealt with a familiar spirit, and with wizards: he wrought much evil in the sight of the LORD, to provoke him to anger.

7 And he set a carved image, the idol which he had made, in the house of God, of which God had said to Da′vid and to Sol′o-mon his son, In this house, and in Je-ru′sa-lem, which I have chosen before all the tribes of Is′ra-el, will I put my name for ever:

8 Neither will I any more remove the foot of Is′ra-el from out of the land which I have appointed for your fathers; so that they will take heed to do all that I have commanded them, according to the whole law and the statutes and the ordinances by the hand of Mo′ses.

9 So Ma-nas′seh made Ju′dah and the inhabitants of Je-ru′sa-lem to err, *and* to do worse than the heathen, whom the LORD had destroyed before the children of Is′ra-el.

10 And the LORD spake to Ma-nas′seh, and to his people: but they would not hearken.

11 ¶ Wherefore the LORD brought upon them the captains of the host of the king of As-syr′i-a, which took Ma-nas′seh among the thorns, and bound him with fetters, and carried him to Bab′y-lon.

12 And when he was in affliction, he besought the LORD his God, and humbled himself greatly before the God of his fathers,

13 And prayed unto him: and he was intreated of him, and heard his supplication, and brought him again to Je-ru′sa-lem into his kingdom. Then Ma-nas′seh knew that the LORD he *was* God.

14 Now after this he built a wall without the city of Da′vid, on the west side of Gi′hon, in the valley, even to the entering in at the fish gate, and compassed about O′phel, and raised it up a very great height, and put captains of war in all the fenced cities of Ju′dah.

15 And he took away the strange gods, and the idol out of the house of the LORD, and all the altars that he had built in the mount of the house of the LORD, and in Je-ru′sa-lem, and cast *them* out of the city.

16 And he repaired the altar of the LORD, and sacrificed thereon peace offerings and thank offerings, and commanded Ju′dah to serve the LORD God of Is′ra-el.

17 Nevertheless the people did sacrifice still

in the high places, *yet* unto the LORD their God only.

18 ¶ Now the rest of the acts of Ma-nas'seh, and his prayer unto his God, and the words of the seers that spake to him in the name of the LORD God of Is'ra-el, behold, they *are written* in the book of the kings of Is'ra-el.

19 His prayer also, and *how God was* intreated of him, and all his sins, and his trespass, and the places wherein he built high places, and set up groves and graven images, before he was humbled: behold, they *are* written among the sayings of the seers.

20 ¶ So Ma-nas'seh slept with his fathers, and they buried him in his own house: and A'-mon his son reigned in his stead.

21 ¶ A'mon *was* two and twenty years old when he began to reign, and reigned two years in Je-ru'sa-lem.

22 But he did *that which was* evil in the sight of the LORD, as did Ma-nas'seh his father: for A'mon sacrificed unto all the carved images which Ma-nas'seh his father had made, and served them;

23 And humbled not himself before the LORD, as Ma-nas'seh his father had humbled himself; but A'mon trespassed more and more.

24 And his servants conspired against him, and slew him in his own house.

25 ¶ But the people of the land slew all them that had conspired against king A'mon; and the people of the land made Jo-si'ah his son king in his stead.

34 JO-SI'AH *was* eight years old when he began to reign, and he reigned in Je-ru'-sa-lem one and thirty years.

2 And he did *that which was* right in the sight of the LORD, and walked in the ways of Da'vid his father, and declined *neither* to the right hand, nor to the left.

3 ¶ For in the eighth year of his reign, while he was yet young, he began to seek after the God of Da'vid his father: and in the twelfth year he began to purge Ju'dah and Je-ru'sa-lem from the high places, and the groves, and the carved images, and the molten images.

4 And they brake down the altars of Ba'al-im in his presence; and the images, that *were* on high above them, he cut down; and the groves, and the carved images, and the molten images, he brake in pieces, and made dust *of them,* and strowed *it* upon the graves of them that had sacrificed unto them.

5 And he burnt the bones of the priests upon their altars, and cleansed Ju'dah and Je-ru'sa-lem.

6 And *so did he* in the cities of Ma-nas'seh, and E'phra-im, and Sim'e-on, even unto Naph'-ta-li, with their mattocks round about.

7 And when he had broken down the altars and the groves, and had beaten the graven images into powder, and cut down all the idols throughout all the land of Is'ra-el, he returned to Je-ru'sa-lem.

8 ¶ Now in the eighteenth year of his reign, when he had purged the land, and the house, he sent Sha'phan the son of Az-a-li'ah, and Ma-a-se'iah the governor of the city, and Jo'ah the son of Jo'a-haz the recorder, to repair the house of the LORD his God.

9 And when they came to Hil-ki'ah the high priest, they delivered the money that was brought into the house of God, which the Le'-vites that kept the doors had gathered of the hand of Ma-nas'seh and E'phra-im, and of all the remnant of Is'ra-el, and of all Ju'dah and Ben'ja-min; and they returned to Je-ru'sa-lem.

10 And they put *it* in the hand of the workmen that had the oversight of the house of the LORD, and they gave it to the workmen that wrought in the house of the LORD, to repair and amend the house:

11 Even to the artificers and builders gave they *it,* to buy hewn stone, and timber for couplings, and to floor the houses which the kings of Ju'dah had destroyed.

12 And the men did the work faithfully: and the overseers of them *were* Ja'hath and O-ba-di'ah, the Le'vites, of the sons of Me-ra'ri; and Zech-a-ri'ah and Me-shul'lam, of the sons of the Ko'hath-ites, to set *it* forward; and *other of* the Le'vites, all that could skill of instruments of musick.

13 Also *they were* over the bearers of burdens, and *were* overseers of all that wrought the work in any manner of service: and of the Le'-vites *there were* scribes, and officers, and porters.

14 ¶ And when they brought out the money that was brought into the house of the LORD, Hil-ki'ah the priest found a book of the law of the LORD *given* by Mo'ses.

15 And Hil-ki'ah answered and said to Sha'-phan the scribe, I have found the book of the law in the house of the LORD. And Hil-ki'ah delivered the book to Sha'phan.

16 And Sha'phan carried the book to the king, and brought the king word back again, saying, All that was committed to thy servants, they do *it.*

17 And they have gathered together the money that was found in the house of the LORD, and have delivered it into the hand of the overseers, and to the hand of the workmen.

18 Then Sha'phan the scribe told the king, saying, Hil-ki'ah the priest hath given me a book. And Sha'phan read it before the king.

19 And it came to pass, when the king had heard the words of the law, that he rent his clothes.

20 And the king commanded Hil-ki'ah, and A-hi'kam the son of Sha'phan, and Ab'don the son of Mi'cah, and Sha'phan the scribe, and A-sa-i'ah a servant of the king's, saying,

21 Go, enquire of the LORD for me, and for them that are left in Is'ra-el and in Ju'dah, concerning the words of the book that is found: for great *is* the wrath of the LORD that is poured out upon us, because our fathers have not kept the word of the LORD, to do after all that is written in this book.

22 And Hil-ki'ah, and *they* that the king *had appointed,* went to Hul'dah the prophetess, the wife of Shal'lum the son of Tik'vath, the son of Has'rah, keeper of the wardrobe; (now she dwelt in Je-ru'sa-lem in the college:) and they spake to her to that *effect.*

23 ¶ And she answered them, Thus saith the LORD God of Is'ra-el, Tell ye the man that sent you to me,

24 Thus saith the LORD, Behold, I will bring evil upon this place, and upon the inhabitants thereof, *even* all the curses that are written in the book which they have read before the king of Ju'dah:

25 Because they have forsaken me, and have burned incense unto other gods, that they might provoke me to anger with all the works of their hands; therefore my wrath shall be poured out upon this place, and shall not be quenched.

26 And as for the king of Ju'dah, who sent you to enquire of the LORD, so shall ye say unto

him, Thus saith the LORD God of Is'ra-el con-cerning the words which thou hast heard;

27 Because thine heart was tender, and thou didst humble thyself before God, when thou heardest his words against this place, and against the inhabitants thereof, and humbledst thyself before me, and didst rend thy clothes, and weep before me; I have even heard thee also, saith the LORD.

28 Behold, I will gather thee to thy fathers, and thou shalt be gathered to thy grave in peace, neither shall thine eyes see all the evil that I will bring upon this place, and upon the inhabitants of the same. So they brought the king word again.

29 ¶ Then the king sent and gathered together all the elders of Ju'dah and Je-ru'sa-lem.

30 And the king went up into the house of the LORD, and all the men of Ju'dah, and the inhabitants of Je-ru'sa-lem, and the priests, and the Le'vites, and all the people, great and small: and he read in their ears all the words of the book of the covenant that was found in the house of the LORD.

31 And the king stood in his place, and made a covenant before the LORD, to walk after the LORD, and to keep his commandments, and his testimonies, and his statutes, with all his heart, and with all his soul, to perform the words of the covenant which are written in this book.

32 And he caused all that were present in Je-ru'sa-lem and Ben'ja-min to stand to it. And the inhabitants of Je-ru'sa-lem did according to the covenant of God, the God of their fathers.

33 And Jo-si'ah took away all the abominations out of all the countries that pertained to the children of Is'ra-el, and made all that were present in Is'ra-el to serve, even to serve the LORD their God. And all his days they departed not from following the LORD, the God of their fathers.

35 MOREOVER Jo-si'ah kept a passover unto the LORD in Je-ru'sa-lem: and they killed the passover on the fourteenth day of the first month.

2 And he set the priests in their charges, and encouraged them to the service of the house of the LORD,

3 And said unto the Le'vites that taught all Is'ra-el, which were holy unto the LORD, Put the holy ark in the house which Sol'o-mon the son of Da'vid king of Is'ra-el did build; it shall not be a burden upon your shoulders: serve now the LORD your God, and his people Is'ra-el,

4 And prepare yourselves by the houses of your fathers, after your courses, according to the writing of Da'vid king of Is'ra-el, and according to the writing of Sol'o-mon his son.

5 And stand in the holy place according to the divisions of the families of the fathers of your brethren the people, and after the division of the families of the Le'vites.

6 So kill the passover, and sanctify yourselves, and prepare your brethren, that they may do according to the word of the LORD by the hand of Mo'ses.

7 And Jo-si'ah gave to the people, of the flock, lambs and kids, all for the passover offerings, for all that were present, to the number of thirty thousand, and three thousand bullocks: these were of the king's substance.

8 And his princes gave willingly unto the people, to the priests, and to the Le'vites: Hil-ki'ah and Zech-a-ri'ah and Je-hi'el, rulers of the house of God, gave unto the priests for the passover offerings two thousand and six hundred small cattle, and three hundred oxen.

9 Con-a-ni'ah also, and Shem-a-i'ah and Ne-than'e-el, his brethren, and Hash-a-bi'ah and Je-i'el and Joz'a-bad, chief of the Le'vites, gave unto the Le'vites for passover offerings five thousand small cattle, and five hundred oxen.

10 So the service was prepared, and the priests stood in their place, and the Le'vites in their courses, according to the king's commandment.

11 And they killed the passover, and the priests sprinkled the blood from their hands, and the Le'vites flayed them.

12 And they removed the burnt offerings, that they might give according to the divisions of the families of the people, to offer unto the LORD, as it is written in the book of Mo'ses. And so did they with the oxen.

13 And they roasted the passover with fire according to the ordinance: but the other holy offerings sod they in pots, and in caldrons, and in pans, and divided them speedily among all the people.

14 And afterward they made ready for themselves, and for the priests: because the priests the sons of Aar'on were busied in offering of burnt offerings and the fat until night; therefore the Le'vites prepared for themselves, and for the priests the sons of Aar'on.

15 And the singers the sons of A'saph were in their place, according to the commandment of Da'vid, and A'saph, and He'man, and Jed'u-thun the king's seer; and the porters waited at every gate; they might not depart from their service; for their brethren the Le'vites prepared for them.

16 So all the service of the LORD was prepared the same day, to keep the passover, and to offer burnt offerings upon the altar of the LORD, according to the commandment of king Jo-si'ah.

17 And the children of Is'ra-el that were present kept the passover at that time, and the feast of unleavened bread seven days.

18 And there was no passover like to that kept in Is'ra-el from the days of Sam'u-el the prophet; neither did all the kings of Is'ra-el keep such a passover as Jo-si'ah kept, and the priests, and the Le'vites, and all Ju'dah and Is'ra-el that were present, and the inhabitants of Je-ru'sa-lem.

19 In the eighteenth year of the reign of Jo-si'ah was this passover kept.

20 ¶ After all this, when Jo-si'ah had prepared the temple, Ne'cho king of E'gypt came up to fight against Char'che-mish by Eu-phra'tes: and Jo-si'ah went out against him.

21 But he sent ambassadors to him, saying, What have I to do with thee, thou king of Ju'dah? I come not against thee this day, but against the house wherewith I have war: for God commanded me to make haste: forbear thee from meddling with God, who is with me, that he destroy thee not.

22 Nevertheless Jo-si'ah would not turn his face from him, but disguised himself, that he might fight with him, and hearkened not unto the words of Ne'cho from the mouth of God, and came to fight in the valley of Me-gid'do.

23 And the archers shot at king Jo-si'ah; and the king said to his servants, Have me away; for I am sore wounded.

24 His servants therefore took him out of that chariot, and put him in the second chariot that he had; and they brought him to Je-ru'sa-lem, and he died, and was buried in one of the

sepulchres of his fathers. And all Ju'dah and Je-ru'sa-lem mourned for Jo-si'ah.

25 ¶ And Jer-e-mi'ah lamented for Jo-si'ah: and all the singing men and the singing women spake of Jo-si'ah in their lamentations to this day, and made them an ordinance in Is'ra-el: and, behold, they are written in the lamentations.

26 Now the rest of the acts of Jo-si'ah, and his goodness, according to that which was written in the law of the LORD,

27 And his deeds, first and last, behold, they are written in the book of the kings of Is'ra-el and Ju'dah.

36 THEN the people of the land took Je-ho'a-haz the son of Jo-si'ah, and made him king in his father's stead in Je-ru'sa-lem.

2 Je-ho'a-haz was twenty and three years old when he began to reign, and he reigned three months in Je-ru'sa-lem.

3 And the king of E'gypt put him down at Je-ru'sa-lem, and condemned the land in an hundred talents of silver and a talent of gold.

4 And the king of E'gypt made E-li'a-kim his brother king over Ju'dah and Je-ru'sa-lem, and turned his name to Je-hoi'a-kim. And Ne'cho took Je-ho'a-haz his brother, and carried him to E'gypt.

5 ¶ Je-hoi'a-kim was twenty and five years old when he began to reign, and he reigned eleven years in Je-ru'sa-lem: and he did that which was evil in the sight of the LORD his God.

6 Against him came up Neb-u-chad-nez'zar king of Bab'y-lon, and bound him in fetters, to carry him to Bab'y-lon.

7 Neb-u-chad-nez'zar also carried of the vessels of the house of the LORD to Bab'y-lon, and put them in his temple at Bab'y-lon.

8 Now the rest of the acts of Je-hoi'a-kim, and his abominations which he did, and that which was found in him, behold, they are written in the book of the kings of Is'ra-el and Ju'-dah: and Je-hoi'a-chin his son reigned in his stead.

9 ¶ Je-hoi'a-chin was eight years old when he began to reign, and he reigned three months and ten days in Je-ru'sa-lem: and he did that which was evil in the sight of the LORD.

10 And when the year was expired, king Neb-u-chad-nez'zar sent, and brought him to Bab'y-lon, with the goodly vessels of the house of the LORD, and made Zed-e-ki'ah his brother king over Ju'dah and Je-ru'sa-lem.

11 ¶ Zed-e-ki'ah was one and twenty years old when he began to reign, and reigned eleven years in Je-ru'sa-lem.

12 And he did that which was evil in the sight of the LORD his God, and humbled not himself before Jer-e-mi'ah the prophet speaking from the mouth of the LORD.

13 And he also rebelled against king Neb-u-chad-nez'zar, who had made him swear by God: but he stiffened his neck, and hardened his heart from turning unto the LORD God of Is'ra-el.

14 ¶ Moreover all the chief of the priests, and the people, transgressed very much after all the abominations of the heathen; and polluted the house of the LORD which he had hallowed in Je-ru'sa-lem.

15 And the LORD God of their fathers sent to them by his messengers, rising up betimes, and sending; because he had compassion on his people, and on his dwelling place:

16 But they mocked the messengers of God, and despised his words, and misused his prophets, until the wrath of the LORD arose against his people, till there was no remedy.

17 Therefore he brought upon them the king of the Chal'dees, who slew their young men with the sword in the house of their sanctuary, and had no compassion upon young man or maiden, old man, or him that stooped for age: he gave them all into his hand.

18 And all the vessels of the house of God, great and small, and the treasures of the house of the LORD, and the treasures of the king, and of his princes; all these he brought to Bab'y-lon.

19 And they burnt the house of God, and brake down the wall of Je-ru'sa-lem, and burnt all the palaces thereof with fire, and destroyed all the goodly vessels thereof.

20 And them that had escaped from the sword carried he away to Bab'y-lon; where they were servants to him and his sons until the reign of the kingdom of Per'sia:

21 To fulfil the word of the LORD by the mouth of Jer-e-mi'ah, until the land had enjoyed her sabbaths: for as long as she lay desolate she kept sabbath, to fulfil threescore and ten years.

22 ¶ Now in the first year of Cy'rus king of Per'sia, that the word of the LORD spoken by the mouth of Jer-e-mi'ah might be accomplished, the LORD stirred up the spirit of Cy'rus king of Per'sia, that he made a proclamation throughout all his kingdom, and put it also in writing, saying,

23 Thus saith Cy'rus king of Per'sia, All the kingdoms of the earth hath the LORD God of heaven given me; and he hath charged me to build him an house in Je-ru'sa-lem, which is in Ju'dah. Who is there among you of all his people? The LORD his God be with him, and let him go up.

THE BOOK OF

EZRA

1 NOW in the first year of Cy'rus king of Per'sia, that the word of the LORD by the mouth of Jer-e-mi'ah might be fulfilled, the LORD stirred up the spirit of Cy'rus king of Per'sia, that he made a proclamation throughout all his kingdom, and put it also in writing, saying,

2 Thus saith Cy'rus king of Per'sia, The LORD God of heaven hath given me all the kingdoms of the earth; and he hath charged me to build him an house at Je-ru'sa-lem, which is in Ju'dah.

3 Who is there among you of all his people? his God be with him, and let him go up to Je-ru'sa-lem, which is in Ju'dah, and build the house of the LORD God of Is'ra-el, (he is the God,) which is in Je-ru'sa-lem.

4 And whosoever remaineth in any place where he sojourneth, let the men of his place help him with silver, and with gold, and with goods, and with beasts, beside the freewill offering for the house of God that is in Je-ru'sa-lem.

5 ¶ Then rose up the chief of the fathers of Ju'dah and Ben'ja-min, and the priests, and the Le'vites, with all *them* whose spirit God had raised, to go up to build the house of the LORD which *is* in Je-ru'sa-lem.

6 And all they that *were* about them strengthened their hands with vessels of silver, with gold, with goods, and with beasts, and with precious things, beside all *that* was willingly offered.

7 ¶ Also Cy'rus the king brought forth the vessels of the house of the LORD, which Neb-u-chad-nez'zar had brought forth out of Je-ru'sa-lem, and had put them in the house of his gods;

8 Even those did Cy'rus king of Per'sia bring forth by the hand of Mith're-dath the treasurer, and numbered them unto Shesh-baz'zar, the prince of Ju'dah.

9 And this *is* the number of them: thirty chargers of gold, a thousand chargers of silver, nine and twenty knives,

10 Thirty basons of gold, silver basons of a second *sort* four hundred and ten, *and* other vessels a thousand.

11 All the vessels of gold and of silver *were* five thousand and four hundred. All *these* did Shesh-baz'zar bring up with *them of* the captivity that were brought up from Bab'y-lon unto Je-ru'sa-lem.

2 NOW these *are* the children of the province that went up out of the captivity, of those which had been carried away, whom Neb-u-chad-nez'zar the king of Bab'y-lon had carried away unto Bab'y-lon, and came again unto Je-ru'sa-lem and Ju'dah, every one unto his city;

2 Which came with Ze-rub'ba-bel: Jesh'u-a, Ne-he-mi'ah, Ser-a-i'ah, Re-el-a'iah, Mor'de-cai, Bil'shan, Miz'par, Big'va-i, Re'hum, Ba'a-nah. The number of the men of the people of Is'ra-el:

3 The children of Pa'rosh, two thousand an hundred seventy and two.

4 The children of Sheph-a-ti'ah, three hundred seventy and two.

5 The children of A'rah, seven hundred seventy and five.

6 The children of Pa'hath–mo'ab, of the children of Jesh'u-a *and* Jo'ab, two thousand eight hundred and twelve.

7 The children of E'lam, a thousand two hundred fifty and four.

8 The children of Zat'tu, nine hundred forty and five.

9 The children of Zac'ca-i, seven hundred and threescore.

10 The children of Ba'ni, six hundred forty and two.

11 The children of Beb'a-i; six hundred twenty and three.

12 The children of Az'gad, a thousand two hundred twenty and two.

13 The children of A-don'i-kam, six hundred sixty and six.

14 The children of Big'va-i, two thousand fifty and six.

15 The children of A'din, four hundred fifty and four.

16 The children of A'ter of Hez-e-ki'ah, ninety and eight.

17 The children of Be'zai, three hundred twenty and three.

18 The children of Jo'rah, an hundred and twelve.

19 The children of Ha'shum, two hundred twenty and three.

20 The children of Gib'bar, ninety and five.

21 The children of Beth'-le-hem, an hundred twenty and three.

22 The men of Ne-to'phah, fifty and six.

23 The men of An'a-thoth, an hundred twenty and eight.

24 The children of Az'ma-veth, forty and two.

25 The children of Kir'jath–a'rim, Che-phi'-rah, and Be-e'roth, seven hundred and forty and three.

26 The children of Ra'mah and Ga'ba, six hundred twenty and one.

27 The men of Mich'mas, an hundred twenty and two.

28 The men of Beth'-el and A'i, two hundred twenty and three.

29 The children of Ne'bo, fifty and two.

30 The children of Mag'bish, an hundred fifty and six.

31 The children of the other E'lam, a thousand two hundred fifty and four.

32 The children of Ha'rim, three hundred and twenty.

33 The children of Lod, Ha'did, and O'no, seven hundred twenty and five.

34 The children of Jer'i-cho, three hundred forty and five.

35 The children of Se-na'ah, three thousand and six hundred and thirty.

36 ¶ The priests: the children of Je-da'iah, of the house of Jesh'u-a, nine hundred seventy and three.

37 The children of Im'mer, a thousand fifty and two.

38 The children of Pash'ur, a thousand two hundred forty and seven.

39 The children of Ha'rim, a thousand and seventeen.

40 ¶ The Le'vites: the children of Jesh'u-a and Kad'mi-el, of the children of Hod-a-vi'ah, seventy and four.

41 ¶ The singers: the children of A'saph, an hundred twenty and eight.

42 ¶ The children of the porters: the children of Shal'lum, the children of A'ter, the children of Tal'mon, the children of Ak'kub, the children of Hat'i-ta, the children of Sho'ba-i, *in* all an hundred thirty and nine.

43 ¶ The Neth'i-nims: the children of Zi'ha, the children of Ha-su'pha, the children of Tab'-ba-oth,

44 The children of Ke'ros, the children of Si'-a-ha, the children of Pa'don,

45 The children of Leb'a-nah, the children of Hag'a-bah, the children of Ak'kub,

46 The children of Ha'gab, the children of Shal'ma-i, the children of Ha'nan,

47 The children of Gid'del, the children of Ga'har, the children of Re-a-i'ah,

48 The children of Re'zin, the children of Ne-ko'da, the children of Gaz'zam,

49 The children of Uz'za, the children of Pa-se'ah, the children of Be'sai,

50 The children of As'nah, the children of Me-hu'nim, the children of Ne-phu'sim,

51 The children of Bak'buk, the children of Ha-ku'pha, the children of Har'hur,

52 The children of Baz'luth, the children of Me-hi'da, the children of Har'sha,

53 The children of Bar'kos, the children of Sis'e-ra, the children of Tha'mah,

54 The children of Ne-zi'ah, the children of Hat'i-pha.

55 ¶ The children of Sol'o-mon's servants: the children of So'ta-i, the children of Soph'e-reth, the children of Pe-ru'da,

56 The children of Ja-a'lah, the children of Dar'kon, the children of Gid'del,

57 The children of Sheph-a-ti'ah, the children of Hat'til, the children of Poch'e-reth of Ze-ba'-im, the children of A'mi.

58 All the Neth'i-nims, and the children of Sol'o-mon's servants, were three hundred ninety and two.

59 And these were they which went up from Tel-me'lah, Tel-har'sa, Che'rub, Ad'dan, and Im'mer: but they could not shew their father's house, and their seed, whether they were of Is'-ra-el:

60 The children of Del-a-i'ah, the children of To-bi'ah, the children of Ne-ko'da, six hundred fifty and two.

61 ¶ And of the children of the priests: the children of Ha-ba'iah, the children of Koz, the children of Bar-zil'la-i; which took a wife of the daughters of Bar-zil'la-i the Gil'e-ad-ite, and was called after their name:

62 These sought their register among those that were reckoned by genealogy, but they were not found: therefore were they, as polluted, put from the priesthood.

63 And the Tir'sha-tha said unto them, that they should not eat of the most holy things, till there stood up a priest with U'rim and with Thum'mim.

64 ¶ The whole congregation together was forty and two thousand three hundred and threescore,

65 Beside their servants and their maids, of whom there were seven thousand three hundred thirty and seven: and there were among them two hundred singing men and singing women.

66 Their horses were seven hundred thirty and six; their mules, two hundred forty and five;

67 Their camels, four hundred thirty and five; their asses, six thousand seven hundred and twenty.

68 ¶ And some of the chief of the fathers, when they came to the house of the LORD which is at Je-ru'sa-lem, offered freely for the house of God to set it up in his place:

69 They gave after their ability unto the treasure of the work threescore and one thousand drams of gold, and five thousand pound of silver, and one hundred priests' garments.

70 So the priests, and the Le'vites, and some of the people, and the singers, and the porters, and the Neth'i-nims, dwelt in their cities, and all Is'ra-el in their cities.

3 AND when the seventh month was come, and the children of Is'ra-el were in the cities, the people gathered themselves together as one man to Je-ru'sa-lem.

2 Then stood up Jesh'u-a the son of Joz'a-dak, and his brethren the priests, and Ze-rub'-ba-bel the son of She-al'ti-el, and his brethren, and builded the altar of the God of Is'ra-el, to offer burnt offerings thereon, as it is written in the law of Mo'ses the man of God.

3 And they set the altar upon his bases; for fear was upon them because of the people of those countries: and they offered burnt offerings thereon unto the LORD, even burnt offerings morning and evening.

4 They kept also the feast of tabernacles, as it is written, and offered the daily burnt offerings by number, according to the custom, as the duty of every day required;

5 And afterward offered the continual burnt offering, both of the new moons, and of all the set feasts of the LORD that were consecrated,

and of every one that willingly offered a freewill offering unto the LORD.

6 From the first day of the seventh month began they to offer burnt offerings unto the LORD. But the foundation of the temple of the LORD was not yet laid.

7 They gave money also unto the masons, and to the carpenters; and meat, and drink, and oil, unto them of Zi'don, and to them of Tyre, to bring cedar trees from Leb'a-non to the sea of Jop'pa, according to the grant that they had of Cy'rus king of Per'sia.

8 ¶ Now in the second year of their coming unto the house of God at Je-ru'sa-lem, in the second month, began Ze-rub'ba-bel the son of She-al'ti-el, and Jesh'u-a the son of Joz'a-dak, and the remnant of their brethren the priests and the Le'vites, and all they that were come out of the captivity unto Je-ru'sa-lem; and appointed the Le'vites, from twenty years old and upward, to set forward the work of the house of the LORD.

9 Then stood Jesh'u-a with his sons and his brethren, Kad'mi-el and his sons, the sons of Ju'dah, together, to set forward the workmen in the house of God: the sons of Hen'a-dad, with their sons and their brethren the Le'vites.

10 And when the builders laid the foundation of the temple of the LORD, they set the priests in their apparel with trumpets, and the Le'vites the sons of A'saph with cymbals, to praise the LORD, after the ordinance of Da'vid king of Is'-ra-el.

11 And they sang together by course in praising and giving thanks unto the LORD; because he is good, for his mercy endureth for ever toward Is'ra-el. And all the people shouted with a great shout, when they praised the LORD, because the foundation of the house of the LORD was laid.

12 But many of the priests and Le'vites and chief of the fathers, who were ancient men, that had seen the first house, when the foundation of this house was laid before their eyes, wept with a loud voice; and many shouted aloud for joy:

13 So that the people could not discern the noise of the shout of joy from the noise of the weeping of the people: for the people shouted with a loud shout, and the noise was heard afar off.

4 NOW when the adversaries of Ju'dah and Ben'ja-min heard that the children of the captivity builded the temple unto the LORD God of Is'ra-el;

2 Then they came to Ze-rub'ba-bel, and to the chief of the fathers, and said unto them, Let us build with you: for we seek your God, as ye do; and we do sacrifice unto him since the days of E'sar-had'don king of As'sur, which brought us up hither.

3 But Ze-rub'ba-bel, and Jesh'u-a, and the rest of the chief of the fathers of Is'ra-el, said unto them, Ye have nothing to do with us to build an house unto our God; but we ourselves together will build unto the LORD God of Is'ra-el, as king Cy'rus the king of Per'sia hath commanded us.

4 Then the people of the land weakened the hands of the people of Ju'dah, and troubled them in building,

5 And hired counsellors against them, to frustrate their purpose, all the days of Cy'rus king of Per'sia, even until the reign of Da-ri'us king of Per'sia.

6 And in the reign of A-has-u-e'rus, in the beginning of his reign, wrote they unto him an

accusation against the inhabitants of Ju'dah and Je-ru'sa-lem.

7 ¶ And in the days of Ar-tax-erx'es wrote Bish'lam, Mith're-dath, Ta'be-el, and the rest of their companions, unto Ar-tax-erx'es king of Per'sia; and the writing of the letter *was* written in the Syr'i-an tongue, and interpreted in the Syr'i-an tongue.

8 Re'hum the chancellor and Shim'shai the scribe wrote a letter against Je-ru'sa-lem to Ar-tax-erx'es the king in this sort:

9 Then *wrote* Re'hum the chancellor, and Shim'shai the scribe, and the rest of their companions; the Di'na-ites, the A-phar'sath-chites, the Tar'pel-ites, the A-phar'sites, the Ar'che-vites, the Bab-y-lo'ni-ans, the Su'san-chites, the De-ha'vites, *and* the E'lam-ites,

10 And the rest of the nations whom the great and noble As-nap'per brought over, and set in the cities of Sa-ma'ri-a, and the rest *that are* on this side the river, and at such a time.

11 ¶ This *is* the copy of the letter that they sent unto him, *even* unto Ar-tax-erx'es the king; Thy servants the men on this side the river, and at such a time.

12 Be it known unto the king, that the Jews which came up from thee to us are come unto Je-ru'sa-lem, building the rebellious and the bad city, and have set up the walls *thereof,* and joined the foundations.

13 Be it known now unto the king, that, if this city be builded, and the walls set up *again,* then will they not pay toll, tribute, and custom, and *so* thou shalt endamage the revenue of the kings.

14 Now because we have maintenance from *the king's* palace, and it was not meet for us to see the king's dishonour, therefore have we sent and certified the king;

15 That search may be made in the book of the records of thy fathers: so shalt thou find in the book of the records, and know that this city *is* a rebellious city, and hurtful unto kings and provinces, and that they have moved sedition within the same of old time: for which cause was this city destroyed.

16 We certify the king that, if this city be builded *again,* and the walls thereof set up, by this means thou shalt have no portion on this side the river.

17 ¶ *Then* sent the king an answer unto Re'-hum the chancellor, and *to* Shim'shai the scribe, and *to* the rest of their companions that dwell in Sa-ma'ri-a, and *unto* the rest beyond the river, Peace, and at such a time.

18 The letter which ye sent unto us hath been plainly read before me.

19 And I commanded, and search hath been made, and it is found that this city of old time hath made insurrection against kings, and *that* rebellion and sedition have been made therein.

20 There have been mighty kings also over Je-ru'sa-lem, which have ruled over all *countries* beyond the river; and toll, tribute, and custom, was paid unto them.

21 Give ye now commandment to cause these men to cease, and that this city be not builded, until *another* commandment shall be given from me.

22 Take heed now that ye fail not to do this: why should damage grow to the hurt of the kings?

23 ¶ Now when the copy of king Ar-tax-erx'es' letter *was* read before Re'hum, and Shim'shai the scribe, and their companions, they went up in haste to Je-ru'sa-lem unto the Jews, and made them to cease by force and power.

24 Then ceased the work of the house of God which *is* at Je-ru'sa-lem. So it ceased unto the second year of the reign of Da-ri'us king of Per'sia.

5 THEN the prophets, Hag'ga-i the prophet, and Zech-a-ri'ah the son of Id'do, prophesied unto the Jews that *were* in Ju'dah and Je-ru'sa-lem in the name of the God of Is'ra-el, *even* unto them.

2 Then rose up Ze-rub'ba-bel the son of She-al'ti-el, and Jesh'u-a the son of Joz'a-dak, and began to build the house of God which *is* at Je-ru'sa-lem: and with them *were* the prophets of God helping them.

3 ¶ At the same time came to them Tatnai, governor on this side the river, and She'thar-boz'na-i, and their companions, and said thus unto them, Who hath commanded you to build this house, and to make up this wall?

4 Then said we unto them after this manner, What are the names of the men that make this building?

5 But the eye of their God was upon the elders of the Jews, that they could not cause them to cease, till the matter came to Da-ri'us: and then they returned answer by letter concerning this *matter.*

6 ¶ The copy of the letter that Tat'na-i, governor on this side the river, and She'thar-boz'-na-i, and his companions the A-phar'sach-ites, which *were* on this side the river, sent unto Da-ri'us the king:

7 They sent a letter unto him, wherein was written thus; Unto Da-ri'us the king, all peace.

8 Be it known unto the king, that we went into the province of Ju-de'a, to the house of the great God, which is builded with great stones, and timber is laid in the walls, and this work goeth fast on, and prospereth in their hands.

9 Then asked we those elders, *and* said unto them thus, Who commanded you to build this house, and to make up these walls?

10 We asked their names also, to certify thee, that we might write the names of the men that *were* the chief of them.

11 And thus they returned us answer, saying, We are the servants of the God of heaven and earth, and build the house that was builded these many years ago, which a great king of Is'ra-el builded and set up.

12 But after that our fathers had provoked the God of heaven unto wrath, he gave them into the hand of Neb-u-chad-nez'zar the king of Bab'y-lon, the Chal-de'an, who destroyed this house, and carried the people away into Bab'y-lon.

13 But in the first year of Cy'rus the king of Bab'y-lon *the same* king Cy'rus made a decree to build this house of God.

14 And the vessels also of gold and silver of the house of God, which Neb-u-chad-nez'zar took out of the temple that *was* in Je-ru'sa-lem, and brought them into the temple of Bab'y-lon, those did Cy'rus the king take out of the temple of Bab'y-lon, and they were delivered unto *one,* whose name *was* Shesh-baz'zar, whom he had made governor;

15 And said unto him, Take these vessels, go, carry them into the temple that *is* in Je-ru'sa-lem, and let the house of God be builded in his place.

16 Then came the same Shesh-baz'zar, *and* laid the foundation of the house of God which *is* in Je-ru'sa-lem: and since that time even until now hath it been in building, and *yet* it is not finished.

17 Now therefore, if *it seem* good to the king, let there be search made in the king's treasure house, which *is* there at Bab'y-lon, whether it be *so,* that a decree was made of Cy'rus the king to build this house of God at Je-ru'sa-lem, and let the king send his pleasure to us concerning this matter.

6 THEN Da-ri'us the king made a decree, and search was made in the house of the rolls, where the treasures were laid up in Bab'y-lon.

2 And there was found at Ach'me-tha, in the palace that *is* in the province of the Medes, a roll, and therein *was* a record thus written:

3 In the first year of Cy'rus the king *the same* Cy'rus the king made a decree *concerning* the house of God at Je-ru'sa-lem, Let the house be builded, the place where they offered sacrifices, and let the foundations thereof be strongly laid; the height thereof threescore cubits, *and* the breadth thereof threescore cubits;

4 *With* three rows of great stones, and a row of new timber: and let the expenses be given out of the king's house:

5 And also let the golden and silver vessels of the house of God, which Neb-u-chad-nez'zar took forth out of the temple which *is* at Je-ru'-sa-lem, and brought unto Bab'y-lon, be restored, and brought again unto the temple which *is* at Je-ru'sa-lem, *every* one to his place, and place *them* in the house of God.

6 Now *therefore,* Tat'na-i, governor beyond the river, She'thar–boz'na-i, and your companions the A-phar'sach-ites, which *are* beyond the river, be ye far from thence:

7 Let the work of this house of God alone; let the governor of the Jews and the elders of the Jews build this house of God in his place.

8 Moreover I make a decree what ye shall do to the elders of these Jews for the building of this house of God: that of the king's goods, *even* of the tribute beyond the river, forthwith expenses be given unto these men, that they be not hindered.

9 And that which they have need of, both young bullocks, and rams, and lambs, for the burnt offerings of the God of heaven, wheat, salt, wine, and oil, according to the appointment of the priests which *are* at Je-ru'sa-lem, let it be given them day by day without fail:

10 That they may offer sacrifices of sweet savours unto the God of heaven, and pray for the life of the king, and of his sons.

11 Also I have made a decree, that whosoever shall alter this word, let timber be pulled down from his house, and being set up, let him be hanged thereon; and let his house be made a dunghill for this.

12 And the God that hath caused his name to dwell there destroy all kings and people, that shall put to their hand to alter *and* to destroy this house of God which *is* at Je-ru'sa-lem. I Da-ri'us have made a decree; let it be done with speed.

13 ¶ Then Tat'na-i, governor on this side the river, She'thar–boz'na-i, and their companions, according to that which Da-ri'us the king had sent, so they did speedily.

14 And the elders of the Jews builded, and they prospered through the prophesying of Hag'ga-i the prophet and Zech-a-ri'ah the son of Id'do. And they builded, and finished *it,* according to the commandment of the God of Is'ra-el, and according to the commandment of Cy'rus, and Da-ri'us, and Ar-tax-erx'es king of Per'sia.

15 And this house was finished on the third day of the month A'dar, which was in the sixth year of the reign of Da-ri'us the king.

16 ¶ And the children of Is'ra-el, the priests, and the Le'vites, and the rest of the children of the captivity, kept the dedication of this house of God with joy,

17 And offered at the dedication of this house of God an hundred bullocks, two hundred rams, four hundred lambs; and for a sin offering for all Is'ra-el, twelve he goats, according to the number of the tribes of Is'ra-el.

18 And they set the priests in their divisions, and the Le'vites in their courses, for the service of God, which *is* at Je-ru'sa-lem; as it is written in the book of Mo'ses.

19 And the children of the captivity kept the passover upon the fourteenth *day* of the first month.

20 For the priests and the Le'vites were purified together, all of them *were* pure, and killed the passover for all the children of the captivity, and for their brethren the priests, and for themselves.

21 And the children of Is'ra-el, which were come again out of captivity, and all such as had separated themselves unto them from the filthiness of the heathen of the land, to seek the Lord God of Is'ra-el, did eat,

22 And kept the feast of unleavened bread seven days with joy: for the Lord had made them joyful, and turned the heart of the king of As-syr'i-a unto them, to strengthen their hands in the work of the house of God, the God of Is'ra-el.

7 NOW after these things, in the reign of Ar-tax-erx'es king of Per'sia, Ez'ra the son of Ser-a-i'ah, the son of Az-a-ri'ah, the son of Hil-ki'ah,

2 The son of Shal'lum, the son of Za'dok, the son of A-hi'tub,

3 The son of Am-a-ri'ah, the son of Az-a-ri'-ah, the son of Me-ra'ioth,

4 The son of Zer-a-hi'ah, the son of Uz'zi, the son of Buk'ki,

5 The son of A-bish'u-a, the son of Phin'e-has, the son of E-le-a'zar, the son of Aar'on the chief priest:

6 This Ez'ra went up from Bab'y-lon; and he *was* a ready scribe in the law of Mo'ses, which the Lord God of Is'ra-el had given: and the king granted him all his request, according to the hand of the Lord his God upon him.

7 And there went up *some* of the children of Is'ra-el, and of the priests, and the Le'vites, and the singers, and the porters, and the Neth'i-nims, unto Je-ru'sa-lem, in the seventh year of Ar-tax-erx'es the king.

8 And he came to Je-ru'sa-lem in the fifth month, which *was* in the seventh year of the king.

9 For upon the first *day* of the first month began he to go up from Bab'y-lon, and on the first *day* of the fifth month came he to Je-ru'sa-lem, according to the good hand of his God upon him.

10 For Ez'ra had prepared his heart to seek the law of the Lord, and to do *it,* and to teach in Is'ra-el statutes and judgments.

11 ¶ Now this *is* the copy of the letter that the king Ar-tax-erx'es gave unto Ez'ra the priest, the scribe, *even* a scribe of the words of the commandments of the Lord, and of his statutes to Is'ra-el.

12 Ar-tax-erx'es, king of kings, unto Ez'ra the priest, a scribe of the law of the God of heaven, perfect *peace,* and at such a time.

13 I make a decree, that all they of the people of Is'ra-el, and of his priests and Le'vites, in my realm, which are minded of their own freewill to go up to Je-ru'sa-lem, go with thee.

14 Forasmuch as thou art sent of the king, and of his seven counsellors, to enquire concerning Ju'dah and Je-ru'sa-lem, according to the law of thy God which is in thine hand;

15 And to carry the silver and gold, which the king and his counsellors have freely offered unto the God of Is'ra-el, whose habitation is in Je-ru'sa-lem,

16 And all the silver and gold that thou canst find in all the province of Bab'y-lon, with the freewill offering of the people, and of the priests, offering willingly for the house of their God which is in Je-ru'sa-lem:

17 That thou mayest buy speedily with this money bullocks, rams, lambs, with their meat offerings and their drink offerings, and offer them upon the altar of the house of your God which is in Je-ru'sa-lem.

18 And whatsoever shall seem good to thee, and to thy brethren, to do with the rest of the silver and the gold, that do after the will of your God.

19 The vessels also that are given thee for the service of the house of thy God, those deliver thou before the God of Je-ru'sa-lem.

20 And whatsoever more shall be needful for the house of thy God, which thou shalt have occasion to bestow, bestow it out of the king's treasure house.

21 And I, even I Ar-tax-erx'es the king, do make a decree to all the treasurers which are beyond the river, that whatsoever Ez'ra the priest, the scribe of the law of the God of heaven, shall require of you, it be done speedily,

22 Unto an hundred talents of silver, and to an hundred measures of wheat, and to an hundred baths of wine, and to an hundred baths of oil, and salt without prescribing how much.

23 Whatsoever is commanded by the God of heaven, let it be diligently done for the house of the God of heaven: for why should there be wrath against the realm of the king and his sons?

24 Also we certify you, that touching any of the priests and Le'vites, singers, porters, Neth'i-nims, or ministers of this house of God, it shall not be lawful to impose toll, tribute, or custom, upon them.

25 And thou, Ez'ra, after the wisdom of thy God, that is in thine hand, set magistrates and judges, which may judge all the people that are beyond the river, all such as know the laws of thy God; and teach ye them that know them not.

26 And whosoever will not do the law of thy God, and the law of the king, let judgment be executed speedily upon him, whether it be unto death, or to banishment, or to confiscation of goods, or to imprisonment.

27 ¶ Blessed be the LORD God of our fathers, which hath put such a thing as this in the king's heart, to beautify the house of the LORD which is in Je-ru'sa-lem:

28 And hath extended mercy unto me before the king, and his counsellors, and before all the king's mighty princes. And I was strengthened as the hand of the LORD my God was upon me, and I gathered together out of Is'ra-el chief men to go up with me.

8 THESE are now the chief of their fathers, and this is the genealogy of them that went up with me from Bab'y-lon, in the reign of Ar-tax-erx'es the king.

2 Of the sons of Phin'e-has; Ger'shom: of the sons of Ith'a-mar; Dan'iel: of the sons of Da'vid; Hat'tush.

3 Of the sons of Shech-a-ni'ah, of the sons of Pha'rosh; Zech-a-ri'ah: and with him were reckoned by genealogy of the males an hundred and fifty.

4 Of the sons of Pa'hath-mo'ab; El-i-ho-e'na-i the son of Zer-a-hi'ah, and with him two hundred males.

5 Of the sons of Shech-a-ni'ah; the son of Ja-ha'zi-el, and with him three hundred males.

6 Of the sons also of A'din; E'bed the son of Jon'a-than, and with him fifty males.

7 And of the sons of E'lam; Je-sha'iah the son of Ath-a-li'ah, and with him seventy males.

8 And of the sons of Sheph-a-ti'ah; Zeb-a-di'-ah the son of Mi'chael, and with him fourscore males.

9 Of the sons of Jo'ab; O-ba-di'ah the son of Je-hi'el, and with him two hundred and eighteen males.

10 And of the sons of Shel'o-mith; the son of Jos-i-phi'ah, and with him an hundred and threescore males.

11 And of the sons of Beb'a-i; Zech-a-ri'ah the son of Beb'a-i, and with him twenty and eight males.

12 And of the sons of Az'gad; Jo-ha'nan the son of Hak'ka-tan, and with him an hundred and ten males.

13 And of the last sons of A-don'i-kam, whose names are these, E-liph'e-let, Je-i'el, and Shem-a-i'ah, and with them threescore males.

14 Of the sons also of Big'va-i; U'tha-i, and Zab'bud, and with them seventy males.

15 ¶ And I gathered them together to the river that runneth to A-ha'va; and there abode we in tents three days: and I viewed the people, and the priests, and found there none of the sons of Le'vi.

16 Then sent I for E-li-e'zer, for A'ri-el, for Shem-a-i'ah, and for El'na-than, and for Ja'rib, and for El'na-than, and for Na'than, and for Zech-a-ri'ah, and for Me-shul'lam, chief men; also for Joi'a-rib, and for El'na-than, men of understanding.

17 And I sent them with commandment unto Id'do the chief at the place Ca-siph'i-a, and I told them what they should say unto Id'do, and to his brethren the Neth'i-nims, at the place Ca-siph'i-a, that they should bring unto us ministers for the house of our God.

18 And by the good hand of our God upon us they brought us a man of understanding, of the sons of Mah'li, the son of Le'vi, the son of Is'ra-el; and Sher-e-bi'ah, with his sons and his brethren, eighteen;

19 And Hash-a-bi'ah, and with him Je-sha'-iah of the sons of Me-ra'ri, his brethren and their sons, twenty;

20 Also of the Neth'i-nims, whom Da'vid and the princes had appointed for the service of the Le'vites, two hundred and twenty Neth'i-nims: all of them were expressed by name.

21 ¶ Then I proclaimed a fast there, at the river of A-ha'va, that we might afflict ourselves before our God, to seek of him a right way for us, and for our little ones, and for all our substance.

22 For I was ashamed to require of the king a band of soldiers and horsemen to help us against the enemy in the way: because we had spoken unto the king, saying, The hand of our God is upon all them for good that seek him;

but his power and his wrath *is* against all them that forsake him.

23 So we fasted and besought our God for this: and he was intreated of us.

24 ¶ Then I separated twelve of the chief of the priests, Sher-e-bi'ah, Hash-a-bi'ah, and ten of their brethren with them,

25 And weighed unto them the silver, and the gold, and the vessels, *even* the offering of the house of our God, which the king, and his counsellors, and his lords, and all Is'ra-el *there* present, had offered:

26 I even weighed unto their hand six hundred and fifty talents of silver, and silver vessels an hundred talents, *and* of gold an hundred talents;

27 Also twenty basons of gold, of a thousand drams; and two vessels of fine copper, precious as gold.

28 And I said unto them, Ye *are* holy unto the LORD; the vessels *are* holy also; and the silver and the gold *are* a freewill offering unto the LORD God of your fathers.

29 Watch ye, and keep *them*, until ye weigh *them* before the chief of the priests and the Le'-vites, and chief of the fathers of Is'ra-el, at Je-ru'sa-lem, in the chambers of the house of the LORD.

30 So took the priests and the Le'vites the weight of the silver, and the gold, and the vessels, to bring *them* to Je-ru'sa-lem unto the house of our God.

31 ¶ Then we departed from the river of A-ha'va on the twelfth *day* of the first month, to go unto Je-ru'sa-lem: and the hand of our God was upon us, and he delivered us from the hand of the enemy, and of such as lay in wait by the way.

32 And we came to Je-ru'sa-lem, and abode there three days.

33 ¶ Now on the fourth day was the silver and the gold and the vessels weighed in the house of our God by the hand of Mer'e-moth the son of U-ri'ah the priest; and with him *was* E-le-a'zar the son of Phin'e-has; and with them *was* Joz'a-bad the son of Jesh'u-a, and No-a-di'ah the son of Bin'nu-i, Le'vites;

34 By number *and* by weight of every one: and all the weight was written at that time.

35 *Also* the children of those that had been carried away, which were come out of the captivity, offered burnt offerings unto the God of Is'ra-el, twelve bullocks for all Is'ra-el, ninety and six rams, seventy and seven lambs, twelve he goats *for* a sin offering: all *this was* a burnt offering unto the LORD.

36 ¶ And they delivered the king's commissions unto the king's lieutenants, and to the governors on this side the river: and they furthered the people, and the house of God.

9 NOW when these things were done, the princes came to me, saying, The people of Is'ra-el, and the priests, and the Le'vites, have not separated themselves from the people of the lands, *doing* according to their abominations, *even* of the Ca'naan-ites, the Hit'tites, the Per'iz-zites, the Jeb'u-sites, the Am'mon-ites, the Mo'ab-ites, the E-gyptians, and the Am'or-ites.

2 For they have taken of their daughters for themselves, and for their sons: so that the holy seed have mingled themselves with the people of *those* lands: yea, the hand of the princes and rulers hath been chief in this trespass.

3 And when I heard this thing, I rent my garment and my mantle, and plucked off the hair of my head and of my beard, and sat down astonied.

4 Then were assembled unto me every one that trembled at the words of the God of Is'ra-el, because of the transgression of those that had been carried away; and I sat astonied until the evening sacrifice.

5 ¶ And at the evening sacrifice I arose up from my heaviness; and having rent my garment and my mantle, I fell upon my knees, and spread out my hands unto the LORD my God,

6 And said, O my God, I am ashamed and blush to lift up my face to thee, my God: for our iniquities are increased over *our* head, and our trespass is grown up unto the heavens.

7 Since the days of our fathers have we *been* in a great trespass unto this day; and for our iniquities have we, our kings, *and* our priests, been delivered into the hand of the kings of the lands, to the sword, to captivity, and to a spoil, and to confusion of face, as *it is* this day.

8 And now for a little space grace hath been *shewed* from the LORD our God, to leave us a remnant to escape, and to give us a nail in his holy place, that our God may lighten our eyes, and give us a little reviving in our bondage.

9 For we *were* bondmen; yet our God hath not forsaken us in our bondage, but hath extended mercy unto us in the sight of the kings of Per'sia, to give us a reviving, to set up the house of our God, and to repair the desolations thereof, and to give us a wall in Ju'dah and in Je-ru'sa-lem.

10 And now, O our God, what shall we say after this? for we have forsaken thy commandments,

11 Which thou hast commanded by thy servants the prophets, saying, The land, unto which ye go to possess it, is an unclean land with the filthiness of the people of the lands, with their abominations, which have filled it from one end to another with their uncleanness.

12 Now therefore give not your daughters unto their sons, neither take their daughters unto your sons, nor seek their peace or their wealth for ever: that ye may be strong, and eat the good of the land, and leave *it* for an inheritance to your children for ever.

13 And after all that is come upon us for our evil deeds, and for our great trespass, seeing that thou our God hast punished us less than our iniquities *deserve*, and hast given us *such* deliverance as this;

14 Should we again break thy commandments, and join in affinity with the people of these abominations? wouldest not thou be angry with us till thou hadst consumed *us*, so that *there should be* no remnant nor escaping?

15 O LORD God of Is'ra-el, thou *art* righteous: for we remain yet escaped, as *it is* this day: behold, we *are* before thee in our trespasses: for we cannot stand before thee because of this.

10 NOW when Ez'ra had prayed, and when he had confessed, weeping and casting himself down before the house of God, there assembled unto him out of Is'ra-el a very great congregation of men and women and children: for the people wept very sore.

2 And Shech-a-ni'ah the son of Je-hi'el, *one* of the sons of E'lam, answered and said unto Ez'ra, We have trespassed against our God, and have taken strange wives of the people of the land: yet now there is hope in Is'ra-el concerning this thing.

3 Now therefore let us make a covenant with our God to put away all the wives, and such as

are born of them, according to the counsel of my lord, and of those that tremble at the commandment of our God; and let it be done according to the law.

4 Arise; for *this* matter *belongeth* unto thee: we also *will be* with thee: be of good courage, and do *it*.

5 Then arose Ez'ra, and made the chief priests, the Le'vites, and all Is'ra-el, to swear that they should do according to this word. And they sware.

6 ¶ Then Ez'ra rose up from before the house of God, and went into the chamber of Jo-ha'nan the son of E-li'a-shib: and *when* he came thither, he did eat no bread, nor drink water: for he mourned because of the transgression of them that had been carried away.

7 And they made proclamation throughout Ju'dah and Je-ru'sa-lem unto all the children of the captivity, that they should gather themselves together unto Je-ru'sa-lem;

8 And that whosoever would not come within three days, according to the counsel of the princes and the elders, all his substance should be forfeited, and himself separated from the congregation of those that had been carried away.

9 ¶ Then all the men of Ju'dah and Ben'ja-min gathered themselves together unto Je-ru'sa-lem within three days. It *was* the ninth month, on the twentieth *day* of the month; and all the people sat in the street of the house of God, trembling because of *this* matter, and for the great rain.

10 And Ez'ra the priest stood up, and said unto them, Ye have transgressed, and have taken strange wives, to increase the trespass of Is'ra-el.

11 Now therefore make confession unto the LORD God of your fathers, and do his pleasure: and separate yourselves from the people of the land, and from the strange wives.

12 Then all the congregation answered and said with a loud voice, As thou hast said, so must we do.

13 But the people *are* many, and *it is* a time of much rain, and we are not able to stand without, neither *is this* a work of one day or two: for we are many that have transgressed in this thing.

14 Let now our rulers of all the congregation stand, and let all them which have taken strange wives in our cities come at appointed times, and with them the elders of every city, and the judges thereof, until the fierce wrath of our God for this matter be turned from us.

15 ¶ Only Jon'a-than the son of A'sa-hel and Ja-ha-zi'ah the son of Tik'vah were employed about this *matter*: and Me-shul'lam and Shab-beth'a-i the Le'vite helped them.

16 And the children of the captivity did so. And Ez'ra the priest, *with* certain chief of the fathers, after the house of their fathers, and all of them by *their* names, were separated, and sat down in the first day of the tenth month to examine the matter.

17 And they made an end with all the men that had taken strange wives by the first day of the first month.

18 ¶ And among the sons of the priests there were found that had taken strange wives: *namely*, of the sons of Jesh'u-a the son of Joz'a-dak, and his brethren; Ma-a-se'iah, and E-li-e'-zer, and Ja'rib, and Ged-a-li'ah.

19 And they gave their hands that they would put away their wives; and *being* guilty, *they offered* a ram of the flock for their trespass.

20 And of the sons of Im'mer; Ha-na'ni, and Zeb-a-di'ah.

21 And of the sons of Ha'rim; Ma-a-se'iah, and E-li'jah, and Shem-a-i'ah, and Je-hi'el, and Uz-zi'ah.

22 And of the sons of Pash'ur; El-i-o-e'na-i, Ma-a-se'iah, Ish'ma-el, Ne-than'e-el, Joz'a-bad, and El'-a-sah.

23 Also of the Le'vites; Joz'a-bad, and Shim'-e-i, and Ke-la'iah, (the same *is* Kel'i-ta,) Peth-a-hi'ah, Ju'dah, and E-li-e'zer.

24 Of the singers also; E-li'a-shib: and of the porters; Shal'lum, and Te'lem, and U'ri.

25 Moreover of Is'ra-el: of the sons of Pa'-rosh; Ra-mi'ah, and Je-zi'ah, and Mal-chi'ah, and Mi'a-min, and E-le-a'zar, and Mal-chi'jah, and Be-na'iah.

26 And of the sons of E'lam; Mat-ta-ni'ah, Zech-a-ri'ah, and Je-hi'el, and Ab'di, and Jer'e-moth, and E-li'ah.

27 And of the sons of Zat'tu; El-i-o-e'na-i, E-li'a-shib, Mat-ta-ni'ah, and Jer'e-moth, and Za'-bad, and A-zi'za.

28 Of the sons of Beb'a-i; Je-ho-ha'nan, Han-a-ni'ah, Zab'bai, *and* Ath'lai.

29 And of the sons of Ba'ni; Me-shul'lam, Mal'luch, and Ad-a-i'ah, Jash'ub, and She'al, and Ra'moth.

30 And of the sons of Pa'hath-mo'ab; Ad'na, and Che'lal, Be-na'iah, Ma-a-se'iah, Mat-ta-ni'-ah, Be-zal'e-el, and Bin'nu-i, and Ma-nas'seh.

31 And of the sons of Ha'rim; E-li-e'zer, Ish-i'jah, Mal-chi'ah, Shem-a-i'ah, Shim'e-on,

32 Ben'ja-min, Mal'luch, *and* Shem-a-ri'ah.

33 Of the sons of Ha'shum; Mat-te-na'i, Mat'-ta-thah, Za'bad, E-liph'e-let, Jer'e-mai, Ma-nas'-seh, *and* Shim'e-i.

34 Of the sons of Ba'ni, Ma-ad'ai, Am'ram, and U'el,

35 Be-na'iah, Be-de'iah, Chel'luh,

36 Va-ni'ah, Mer'e-moth, E-li'a-shib,

37 Mat-ta-ni'ah, Mat-te-na'i, and Ja'a-sau,

38 And Ba'ni, and Bin'nu-i, Shim'e-i,

39 And Shel-e-mi'ah, and Na'than, and Ad-a-i'ah,

40 Mach-na-de'bai, Shash'a-i, Shar'a-i,

41 A-zar'e-el, and Shel-e-mi'ah, Shem-a-ri'-ah,

42 Shal'lum, Am-a-ri'ah, *and* Jo'seph.

43 Of the sons of Ne'bo; Je-i'el, Mat-ti-thi'ah, Za'bad, Ze-bi'na, Ja-da'u, and Jo'el, Be-na'iah.

44 All these had taken strange wives: and *some* of them had wives by whom they had children.

NEHEMIAH

1 THE words of Ne-he-mi'ah the son of Hach-a-li'ah. And it came to pass in the month Chis'leu, in the twentieth year, as I was in Shu'shan the palace,

2 That Ha-na'ni, one of my brethren, came, he and *certain* men of Ju'dah; and I asked them concerning the Jews that had escaped, which were left of the captivity, and concerning Je-ru'sa-lem.

3 And they said unto me, The remnant that are left of the captivity there in the province *are* in great affliction and reproach: the wall of Je-ru'sa-lem also *is* broken down, and the gates thereof are burned with fire.

4 ¶ And it came to pass, when I heard these words, that I sat down and wept, and mourned *certain* days, and fasted, and prayed before the God of heaven,

5 And said, I beseech thee, O LORD God of heaven, the great and terrible God, that keepeth covenant and mercy for them that love him and observe his commandments:

6 Let thine ear now be attentive, and thine eyes open, that thou mayest hear the prayer of thy servant, which I pray before thee now, day and night, for the children of Is'ra-el thy servants, and confess the sins of the children of Is'ra-el, which we have sinned against thee: both I and my father's house have sinned.

7 We have dealt very corruptly against thee, and have not kept the commandments, nor the statutes, nor the judgments, which thou commandedst thy servant Mo'ses.

8 Remember, I beseech thee, the word that thou commandedst thy servant Mo'ses, saying, *If* ye transgress, I will scatter you abroad among the nations:

9 But *if* ye turn unto me, and keep my commandments, and do them; though there were of you cast out unto the uttermost part of the heaven, *yet* will I gather them from thence, and will bring them unto the place that I have chosen to set my name there.

10 Now these *are* thy servants and thy people, whom thou hast redeemed by thy great power, and by thy strong hand.

11 O Lord, I beseech thee, let now thine ear be attentive to the prayer of thy servant, and to the prayer of thy servants, who desire to fear thy name: and prosper, I pray thee, thy servant this day, and grant him mercy in the sight of this man. For I was the king's cupbearer.

2 AND it came to pass in the month Ni'san, in the twentieth year of Ar-tax-erx'es the king, *that* wine *was* before him: and I took up the wine, and gave *it* unto the king. Now I had not been *beforetime* sad in his presence.

2 Wherefore the king said unto me, Why *is* thy countenance sad, seeing thou *art* not sick? this *is* nothing *else* but sorrow of heart. Then I was very sore afraid,

3 And said unto the king, Let the king live for ever: why should not my countenance be sad, when the city, the place of my fathers' sepulchres, *lieth* waste, and the gates thereof are consumed with fire?

4 Then the king said unto me, For what dost thou make request? So I prayed to the God of heaven.

5 And I said unto the king, If it please the king, and if thy servant have found favour in thy sight, that thou wouldest send me unto Ju'dah, unto the city of my fathers' sepulchres, that I may build it.

6 And the king said unto me, (the queen also sitting by him,) For how long shall thy journey be? and when wilt thou return? So it pleased the king to send me; and I set him a time.

7 Moreover I said unto the king, If it please the king, let letters be given me to the governors beyond the river, that they may convey me over till I come into Ju'dah;

8 And a letter unto A'saph the keeper of the king's forest, that he may give me timber to make beams for the gates of the palace which *appertained* to the house, and for the wall of the city, and for the house that I shall enter into. And the king granted me, according to the good hand of my God upon me.

9 ¶ Then I came to the governors beyond the river, and gave them the king's letters. Now the king had sent captains of the army and horsemen with me.

10 When San-bal'lat the Hor'o-nite, and To-bi'ah the servant, the Am'mon-ite, heard *of it*, it grieved them exceedingly that there was come a man to seek the welfare of the children of Is'ra-el.

11 So I came to Je-ru'sa-lem, and was there three days.

12 ¶ And I arose in the night, I and some few men with me; neither told I *any* man what my God had put in my heart to do at Je-ru'sa-lem: neither *was there any* beast with me, save the beast that I rode upon.

13 And I went out by night by the gate of the valley, even before the dragon well, and to the dung port, and viewed the walls of Je-ru'sa-lem, which were broken down, and the gates thereof were consumed with fire.

14 Then I went on to the gate of the fountain, and to the king's pool: but *there was* no place for the beast *that was* under me to pass.

15 Then went I up in the night by the brook, and viewed the wall, and turned back, and entered by the gate of the valley, and *so* returned.

16 And the rulers knew not whither I went, or what I did; neither had I as yet told *it* to the Jews, nor to the priests, nor to the nobles, nor to the rulers, nor to the rest that did the work.

17 ¶ Then said I unto them, Ye see the distress that we *are* in, how Je-ru'sa-lem *lieth* waste, and the gates thereof are burned with fire: come, and let us build up the wall of Je-ru'sa-lem, that we be no more a reproach.

18 Then I told them of the hand of my God which was good upon me; as also the king's words that he had spoken unto me. And they said, Let us rise up and build. So they strengthened their hands for *this* good *work*.

19 But when San-bal'lat the Hor'o-nite, and To-bi'ah the servant, the Am'mon-ite, and Ge'shem the A-ra'bi-an, heard *it*, they laughed us to scorn, and despised us, and said, What *is* this thing that ye do? will ye rebel against the king?

20 Then answered I them, and said unto them, The God of heaven, he will prosper us; therefore we his servants will arise and build: but ye have no portion, nor right, nor memorial, in Je-ru'sa-lem.

3 THEN E-li'a-shib the high priest rose up with his brethren the priests, and they builded the sheep gate; they sanctified it, and set up the doors of it; even unto the tower of Me'ah they sanctified it, unto the tower of Ha-nan'e-el.

2 And next unto him builded the men of Jer'i-cho. And next to them builded Zac'cur the son of Im'ri.

3 But the fish gate did the sons of Has-se-na'ah build, who *also* laid the beams thereof, and set up the doors thereof, the locks thereof, and the bars thereof.

4 And next unto them repaired Mer'e-moth the son of U-ri'jah, the son of Koz. And next unto them repaired Me-shul'lam the son of Ber-e-chi'ah, the son of Me-shez'a-be-el. And next unto them repaired Za'dok the son of Ba'a-na.

5 And next unto them the Te-ko'ites repaired; but their nobles put not their necks to the work of their Lord.

6 Moreover the old gate repaired Je-hoi'a-da the son of Pa-se'ah, and Me-shul'lam the son of Bes-o-de'iah; they laid the beams thereof, and set up the doors thereof, and the locks thereof, and the bars thereof.

7 And next unto them repaired Mel-a-ti'ah the Gib'e-on-ite, and Ja'don the Me-ron'o-thite, the men of Gib'e-on, and of Miz'pah, unto the throne of the governor on this side the river.

8 Next unto him repaired Uz'zi-el the son of Har-ha-i'ah, of the goldsmiths. Next unto him also repaired Han-a-ni'ah the son of *one of the* apothecaries, and they fortified Je-ru'sa-lem unto the broad wall.

9 And next unto them repaired Reph-a-i'ah the son of Hur, the ruler of the half part of Je-ru'sa-lem.

10 And next unto them repaired Je-da'iah the son of Ha-ru'maph, even over against his house. And next unto him repaired Hat'tush the son of Hash-ab-ni'ah.

11 Mal-chi'jah the son of Ha'rim, and Ha'-shub the son of Pa'hath-mo'ab, repaired the other piece, and the tower of the furnaces.

12 And next unto him repaired Shal'lum the son of Ha-lo'hesh, the ruler of the half part of Je-ru'sa-lem, he and his daughters.

13 The valley gate repaired Ha'nun, and the inhabitants of Za-no'ah; they built it, and set up the doors thereof, the locks thereof, and the bars thereof, and a thousand cubits on the wall unto the dung gate.

14 But the dung gate repaired Mal-chi'ah the son of Re'chab, the ruler of part of Beth-hac'ce-rem; he built it, and set up the doors thereof, the locks thereof, and the bars thereof.

15 But the gate of the fountain repaired Shal'lun the son of Col-ho'zeh, the ruler of part of Miz'pah; he built it, and covered it, and set up the doors thereof, the locks thereof, and the bars thereof, and the wall of the pool of Si-lo'ah by the king's garden, and unto the stairs that go down from the city of Da'vid.

16 After him repaired Ne-he-mi'ah the son of Az'buk, the ruler of the half part of Beth'-zur, unto *the place* over against the sepulchres of Da'vid, and to the pool that was made, and unto the house of the mighty.

17 After him repaired the Le'vites, Re'hum the son of Ba'ni. Next unto him repaired Hash-a-bi'ah, the ruler of the half part of Kei'lah, in his part.

18 After him repaired their brethren, Bav'a-i the son of Hen'a-dad, the ruler of the half part of Kei'lah.

19 And next to him repaired E'zer the son of Jesh'u-a, the ruler of Miz'pah, another piece over against the going up to the armoury at the turning *of the wall.*

20 After him Ba'ruch the son of Zab'bai earnestly repaired the other piece, from the turning *of the wall* unto the door of the house of E-li'a-shib the high priest.

21 After him repaired Mer'e-moth the son of U-ri'jah the son of Koz another piece, from the door of the house of E-li'a-shib even to the end of the house of E-li'a-shib.

22 And after him repaired the priests, the men of the plain.

23 After him repaired Ben'ja-min and Ha'-shub over against their house. After him repaired Az-a-ri'ah the son of Ma-a-se'iah the son of An-a-ni'ah by his house.

24 After him repaired Bin'nu-i the son of Hen'a-dad another piece, from the house of Az-a-ri'ah unto the turning *of the wall,* even unto the corner.

25 Pa'lal the son of U'za-i, over against the turning *of the wall,* and the tower which lieth out from the king's high house, that *was* by the court of the prison. After him Pe-da'iah the son of Pa'rosh.

26 Moreover the Neth'i-nims dwelt in O'phel, unto *the place* over against the water gate toward the east, and the tower that lieth out.

27 After them the Te-ko'ites repaired another piece, over against the great tower that lieth out, even unto the wall of O'phel.

28 From above the horse gate repaired the priests, every one over against his house.

29 After them repaired Za'dok the son of Im'-mer over against his house. After him repaired also Shem-a-i'ah the son of Shech-a-ni'ah, the keeper of the east gate.

30 After him repaired Han-a-ni'ah the son of Shel-e-mi'ah, and Ha'nun the sixth son of Za'-laph, another piece. After him repaired Me-shul'lam the son of Ber-e-chi'ah over against his chamber.

31 After him repaired Mal-chi'ah the goldsmith's son unto the place of the Neth'i-nims, and of the merchants, over against the gate Miph'kad, and to the going up of the corner.

32 And between the going up of the corner unto the sheep gate repaired the goldsmiths and the merchants.

4 BUT it came to pass, that when San-bal'lat heard that we builded the wall, he was wroth, and took great indignation, and mocked the Jews.

2 And he spake before his brethren and the army of Sa-ma'ri-a, and said, What do these feeble Jews? will they fortify themselves? will they sacrifice? will they make an end in a day? will they revive the stones out of the heaps of the rubbish which are burned?

3 Now To-bi'ah the Am'mon-ite *was* by him, and he said, Even that which they build, if a fox go up, he shall even break down their stone wall.

4 Hear, O our God; for we are despised: and turn their reproach upon their own head, and give them for a prey in the land of captivity:

5 And cover not their iniquity, and let not their sin be blotted out from before thee: for they have provoked *thee* to anger before the builders.

6 So built we the wall; and all the wall was joined together unto the half thereof: for the people had a mind to work.

7 ¶ But it came to pass, *that* when San-bal'-lat, and To-bi'ah, and the A-ra'bi-ans, and the Am'mon-ites, and the Ash'dod-ites, heard that

the walls of Je-ru'sa-lem were made up, *and* that the breaches began to be stopped, then they were very wroth,

8 And conspired all of them together to come *and* to fight against Je-ru'sa-lem, and to hinder it.

9 Nevertheless we made our prayer unto our God, and set a watch against them day and night, because of them.

10 And Ju'dah said, The strength of the bearers of burdens is decayed, and *there is* much rubbish; so that we are not able to build the wall.

11 And our adversaries said, They shall not know, neither see, till we come in the midst among them, and slay them, and cause the work to cease.

12 And it came to pass, that when the Jews which dwelt by them came, they said unto us ten times, From all places whence ye shall return unto us *they will be upon you.*

13 ¶ Therefore set I in the lower places behind the wall, *and* on the higher places, I even set the people after their families with their swords, their spears, and their bows.

14 And I looked, and rose up, and said unto the nobles, and to the rulers, and to the rest of the people, Be not ye afraid of them: remember the LORD, *which is* great and terrible, and fight for your brethren, your sons, and your daughters, your wives, and your houses.

15 And it came to pass, when our enemies heard that it was known unto us, and God had brought their counsel to nought, that we returned all of us to the wall, every one unto his work.

16 And it came to pass from that time forth, *that* the half of my servants wrought in the work, and the other half of them held both the spears, the shields, and the bows, and the habergeons; and the rulers *were* behind all the house of Ju'dah.

17 They which builded on the wall, and they that bare burdens, with those that laded, *every one* with one of his hands wrought in the work, and with the other *hand* held a weapon.

18 For the builders, every one had his sword girded by his side, and *so* builded. And he that sounded the trumpet *was* by me.

19 ¶ And I said unto the nobles, and to the rulers, and to the rest of the people, The work *is* great and large, and we are separated upon the wall, one far from another.

20 In what place *therefore* ye hear the sound of the trumpet, resort ye thither unto us: our God shall fight for us.

21 So we laboured in the work: and half of them held the spears from the rising of the morning till the stars appeared.

22 Likewise at the same time said I unto the people, Let every one with his servant lodge within Je-ru'sa-lem, that in the night they may be a guard to us, and labour on the day.

23 So neither I, nor my brethren, nor my servants, nor the men of the guard which followed me, none of us put off our clothes, *saving that* every one put them off for washing.

5 AND there was a great cry of the people and of their wives against their brethren the Jews.

2 For there were that said, We, our sons, and our daughters, *are* many: therefore we take up corn *for them,* that we may eat, and live.

3 *Some* also there were that said, We have mortgaged our lands, vineyards, and houses, that we might buy corn, because of the dearth.

4 There were also that said, We have borrowed money for the king's tribute, *and that* upon our lands and vineyards.

5 Yet now our flesh *is* as the flesh of our brethren, our children as their children: and, lo, we bring into bondage our sons and our daughters to be servants, and *some* of our daughters are brought unto bondage *already:* neither *is it* in our power *to* redeem *them;* for other men have our lands and vineyards.

6 ¶ And I was very angry when I heard their cry and these words.

7 Then I consulted with myself, and I rebuked the nobles, and the rulers, and said unto them, Ye exact usury, every one of his brother. And I set a great assembly against them.

8 And I said unto them, We after our ability have redeemed our brethren the Jews, which were sold unto the heathen; and will ye even sell your brethren? or shall they be sold unto us? Then held they their peace, and found nothing *to answer.*

9 Also I said, It *is* not good that ye do: ought ye not to walk in the fear of our God because of the reproach of the heathen our enemies?

10 I likewise, *and* my brethren, and my servants, might exact of them money and corn: I pray you, let us leave off this usury.

11 Restore, I pray you, to them, even this day, their lands, their vineyards, their oliveyards, and their houses, also the hundredth *part* of the money, and of the corn, the wine, and the oil, that ye exact of them.

12 Then said they, We will restore *them,* and will require nothing of them; so will we do as thou sayest. Then I called the priests, and took an oath of them, that they should do according to this promise.

13 Also I shook my lap, and said, So God shake out every man from his house, and from his labour, that performeth not this promise, even thus be he shaken out, and emptied. And all the congregation said, Amen, and praised the LORD. And the people did according to this promise.

14 ¶ Moreover from the time that I was appointed to be their governor in the land of Ju'-dah, from the twentieth year even unto the two and thirtieth year of Ar-tax-erx'es the king, *that is,* twelve years, I and my brethren have not eaten the bread of the governor.

15 But the former governors that *had been* before me were chargeable unto the people, and had taken of them bread and wine, beside forty shekels of silver; yea, even their servants bare rule over the people: but so did not I, because of the fear of God.

16 Yea, also I continued in the work of this wall, neither bought we any land: and all my servants *were* gathered thither unto the work.

17 Moreover *there were* at my table an hundred and fifty of the Jews and rulers, beside those that came unto us from among the heathen that *are* about us.

18 Now *that* which was prepared *for me* daily *was* one ox *and* six choice sheep; also fowls were prepared for me, and once in ten days store of all sorts of wine: yet for all this required not I the bread of the governor, because the bondage was heavy upon this people.

19 Think upon me, my God, for good, *according* to all that I have done for this people.

6 NOW it came to pass, when San-bal'lat, and To-bi'ah, and Ge'shem the A-ra'bi-an, and the rest of our enemies, heard that I had builded the wall, and *that* there was no breach

left therein; (though at that time I had not set up the doors upon the gates;)

2 That San-bal'lat and Ge'shem sent unto me, saying, Come, let us meet together in *some one of* the villages in the plain of O'no. But they thought to do me mischief.

3 And I sent messengers unto them, saying, I *am* doing a great work, so that I cannot come down: why should the work cease, whilst I leave it, and come down to you?

4 Yet they sent unto me four times after this sort; and I answered them after the same manner.

5 Then sent San-bal'lat his servant unto me in like manner the fifth time with an open letter in his hand;

6 Wherein *was* written, It is reported among the heathen, and Gash'mu saith *it, that* thou and the Jews think to rebel: for which cause thou buildest the wall, that thou mayest be their king, according to these words.

7 And thou hast also appointed prophets to preach of thee at Je-ru'sa-lem, saying, *There is* a king in Ju'dah: and now shall it be reported to the king according to these words. Come now therefore, and let us take counsel together.

8 Then I sent unto him, saying, There are no such things done as thou sayest, but thou feignest them out of thine own heart.

9 For they all made us afraid, saying, Their hands shall be weakened from the work, that it be not done. Now therefore, O God, strengthen my hands.

10 Afterward I came unto the house of Shem-a-i'ah the son of Del-a-i'ah the son of Me-het'a-beel, who *was* shut up; and he said, Let us meet together in the house of God, within the temple, and let us shut the doors of the temple: for they will come to slay thee; yea, in the night will they come to slay thee.

11 And I said, Should such a man as I flee? and who *is there,* that, *being* as I *am,* would go into the temple to save his life? I will not go in.

12 And, lo, I perceived that God had not sent him; but that he pronounced this prophecy against me: for To-bi'ah and San-bal'lat had hired him.

13 Therefore *was* he hired, that I should be afraid, and do so, and sin, and *that* they might have *matter* for an evil report, that they might reproach me.

14 My God, think thou upon To-bi'ah and San-bal'lat according to these their works, and on the prophetess No-a-di'ah, and the rest of the prophets, that would have put me in fear.

15 ¶ So the wall was finished in the twenty and fifth *day* of the month E'lul, in fifty and two days.

16 And it came to pass, that when all our enemies heard *thereof,* and all the heathen that *were* about us saw *these things,* they were much cast down in their own eyes: for they perceived that this work was wrought of our God.

17 ¶ Moreover in those days the nobles of Ju'dah sent many letters unto To-bi'ah, and *the letters* of To-bi'ah came unto them.

18 For *there were* many in Ju'dah sworn unto him, because he *was* the son in law of Shech-a-ni'ah the son of A'rah; and his son Jo-ha'nan had taken the daughter of Me-shul'lam the son of Ber-e-chi'ah.

19 Also they reported his good deeds before me, and uttered my words to him. *And* To-bi'ah sent letters to put me in fear.

7 NOW it came to pass, when the wall was built, and I had set up the doors, and the porters and the singers and the Le'vites were appointed,

2 That I gave my brother Ha-na'ni, and Han-a-ni'ah the ruler of the palace, charge over Je-ru'sa-lem: for he *was* a faithful man, and feared God above many.

3 And I said unto them, Let not the gates of Je-ru'sa-lem be opened until the sun be hot; and while they stand by, let them shut the doors, and bar *them:* and appoint watches of the inhabitants of Je-ru'sa-lem, every one in his watch, and every one *to be* over against his house.

4 Now the city *was* large and great: but the people *were* few therein, and the houses *were* not builded.

5 ¶ And my God put into mine heart to gather together the nobles, and the rulers, and the people, that they might be reckoned by genealogy. And I found a register of the genealogy of them which came up at the first, and found written therein,

6 These *are* the children of the province, that went up out of the captivity, of those that had been carried away, whom Neb-u-chad-nez'zar the king of Bab'y-lon had carried away, and came again to Je-ru'sa-lem and to Ju'dah, every one unto his city;

7 Who came with Ze-rub'ba-bel, Jesh'u-a, Ne-he-mi'ah, Az-a-ri'ah, Ra-a-mi'ah, Na-ham'a-ni, Mor'de-cai, Bil'shan, Mis'pe-reth, Big'va-i, Ne'hum, Ba'a-nah. The number, *I say,* of the men of the people of Is'ra-el *was this;*

8 The children of Pa'rosh, two thousand an hundred seventy and two.

9 The children of Sheph-a-ti'ah, three hundred seventy and two.

10 The children of A'rah, six hundred fifty and two.

11 The children of Pa'hath-mo'ab, of the children of Jesh'u-a and Jo'ab, two thousand and eight hundred *and* eighteen.

12 The children of E'lam, a thousand two hundred fifty and four.

13 The children of Zat'tu, eight hundred forty and five.

14 The children of Zac'ca-i, seven hundred and threescore.

15 The children of Bin'nu-i, six hundred forty and eight.

16 The children of Beb'a-i, six hundred twenty and eight.

17 The children of Az'gad, two thousand three hundred twenty and two.

18 The children of A-don'i-kam, six hundred threescore and seven.

19 The children of Big'va-i, two thousand threescore and seven.

20 The children of A'din, six hundred fifty and five.

21 The children of A'ter of Hez-e-ki'ah, ninety and eight.

22 The children of Ha'shum, three hundred twenty and eight.

23 The children of Be'zai, three hundred twenty and four.

24 The children of Ha'riph, an hundred and twelve.

25 The children of Gib'e-on, ninety and five.

26 The men of Beth'-le-hem and Ne-to'phah, an hundred fourscore and eight.

27 The men of An'a-thoth, an hundred twenty and eight.

28 The men of Beth-az'ma-veth, forty and two.

29 The men of Kir'jath-je'a-rim, Che-phi'rah, and Be-e'roth, seven hundred forty and three.

30 The men of Ra'mah and Ga'ba, six hundred twenty and one.

31 The men of Mich'mas, an hundred and twenty and two.

32 The men of Beth'-el and A'i, an hundred twenty and three.

33 The men of the other Ne'bo, fifty and two.

34 The children of the other E'lam, a thousand two hundred fifty and four.

35 The children of Ha'rim, three hundred and twenty.

36 The children of Jer'i-cho, three hundred forty and five.

37 The children of Lod, Ha'did, and O'no, seven hundred twenty and one.

38 The children of Se-na'ah, three thousand nine hundred and thirty.

39 ¶ The priests: the children of Je-da'iah, of the house of Jesh'u-a, nine hundred seventy and three.

40 The children of Im'mer, a thousand fifty and two.

41 The children of Pash'ur, a thousand two hundred forty and seven.

42 The children of Ha'rim, a thousand and seventeen.

43 ¶ The Le'vites: the children of Jesh'u-a, of Kad'mi-el, and of the children of Ho-de'vah, seventy and four.

44 ¶ The singers: the children of A'saph, an hundred forty and eight.

45 ¶ The porters: the children of Shal'lum, the children of A'ter, the children of Tal'mon, the children of Ak'kub, the children of Hat'i-ta, the children of Sho'ba-i, an hundred thirty and eight.

46 ¶ The Neth'i-nims: the children of Zi'ha, the children of Ha-su'pha, the children of Tab'-ba-oth,

47 The children of Ke'ros, the children of Si'-a, the children of Pa'don,

48 The children of Leb'a-na, the children of Hag'a-ba, the children of Shal'ma-i,

49 The children of Ha'nan, the children of Gid'del, the children of Ga'har,

50 The children of Re-a-i'ah, the children of Re'zin, the children of Ne-ko'da,

51 The children of Gaz'zam, the children of Uz'za, the children of Pha-se'ah,

52 The children of Be'sai, the children of Me-u'nim, the children of Ne-phish'e-sim,

53 The children of Bak'buk, the children of Ha-ku'pha, the children of Har'hur,

54 The children of Baz'lith, the children of Me-hi'da, the children of Har'sha,

55 The children of Bar'kos, the children of Sis'e-ra, the children of Ta'mah,

56 The children of Ne-zi'ah, the children of Hat'i-pha.

57 ¶ The children of Sol'o-mon's servants: the children of So'ta-i, the children of Soph'e-reth, the children of Pe-ri'da,

58 The children of Ja-a'la, the children of Dar'kon, the children of Gid'del,

59 The children of Sheph-a-ti'ah, the children of Hat'til, the children of Poch'e-reth of Ze-ba'-im, the children of A'mon.

60 All the Neth'i-nims, and the children of Sol'o-mon's servants, were three hundred ninety and two.

61 And these were they which went up also from Tel-me'lah, Tel-ha-re'sha, Che'rub, Ad'don, and Im'mer: but they could not shew their father's house, nor their seed, whether they were of Is'ra-el.

62 The children of Del-a-i'ah, the children of

To-bi'ah, the children of Ne-ko'da, six hundred forty and two.

63 ¶ And of the priests: the children of Ha-ba'iah, the children of Koz, the children of Bar-zil'la-i, which took one of the daughters of Bar-zil'la-i the Gil'e-ad-ite to wife, and was called after their name.

64 These sought their register among those that were reckoned by genealogy, but it was not found: therefore were they, as polluted, put from the priesthood.

65 And the Tir'sha-tha said unto them, that they should not eat of the most holy things, till there stood up a priest with U'rim and Thum'-mim.

66 ¶ The whole congregation together was forty and two thousand three hundred and threescore,

67 Beside their manservants and their maid-servants, of whom there were seven thousand three hundred thirty and seven: and they had two hundred forty and five singing men and singing women.

68 Their horses, seven hundred thirty and six: their mules, two hundred forty and five:

69 Their camels, four hundred thirty and five: six thousand seven hundred and twenty asses.

70 ¶ And some of the chief of the fathers gave unto the work. The Tir'sha-tha gave to the treasure a thousand drams of gold, fifty basons, five hundred and thirty priests' garments.

71 And some of the chief of the fathers gave to the treasure of the work twenty thousand drams of gold, and two thousand and two hundred pound of silver.

72 And that which the rest of the people gave was twenty thousand drams of gold, and two thousand pound of silver, and threescore and seven priests' garments.

73 So the priests, and the Le'vites, and the porters, and the singers, and some of the people, and the Neth'i-nims, and all Is'ra-el, dwelt in their cities; and when the seventh month came, the children of Is'ra-el were in their cities.

8 AND all the people gathered themselves together as one man into the street that was before the water gate; and they spake unto Ez'ra the scribe to bring the book of the law of Mo'ses, which the LORD had commanded to Is'-ra-el.

2 And Ez'ra the priest brought the law before the congregation both of men and women, and all that could hear with understanding, upon the first day of the seventh month.

3 And he read therein before the street that was before the water gate from the morning until midday, before the men and the women, and those that could understand; and the ears of all the people were attentive unto the book of the law.

4 And Ez'ra the scribe stood upon a pulpit of wood, which they had made for the purpose; and beside him stood Mat-ti-thi'ah, and She'ma, and An-a-i'ah, and U-ri'jah, and Hil-ki'ah, and Ma-a-se'iah, on his right hand; and on his left hand, Pe-da'iah, and Mish'a-el, and Mal-chi'ah, and Ha'shum, and Hash-bad'a-na, Zech-a-ri'ah, and Me-shul'lam.

5 And Ez'ra opened the book in the sight of all the people; (for he was above all the people;) and when he opened it, all the people stood up:

6 And Ez'ra blessed the LORD, the great God. And all the people answered, Amen, Amen, with lifting up their hands: and they bowed

their heads, and worshipped the LORD with *their* faces to the ground.

7 Also Jesh'u-a, and Ba'ni, and Sher-e-bi'ah, Ja'min, Ak'kub, Shab-beth'a-i, Ho-di'jah, Ma-a-se'iah, Kel'i-ta, Az-a-ri'ah, Joz'a-bad, Ha'nan, Pel-a-i'ah, and the Le'vites, caused the people to understand the law: and the people *stood* in their place.

8 So they read in the book in the law of God distinctly, and gave the sense, and caused *them* to understand the reading.

9 ¶ And Ne-he-mi'ah, which *is* the Tir'sha-tha, and Ez'ra the priest the scribe, and the Le'-vites that taught the people, said unto all the people, This day *is* holy unto the LORD your God; mourn not, nor weep. For all the people wept, when they heard the words of the law.

10 Then he said unto them, Go your way, eat the fat, and drink the sweet, and send portions unto them for whom nothing is prepared: for *this* day *is* holy unto our Lord: neither be ye sorry; for the joy of the LORD is your strength.

11 So the Le'vites stilled all the people, say-ing, Hold your peace, for the day *is* holy; neither be ye grieved.

12 And all the people went their way to eat, and to drink, and to send portions, and to make great mirth, because they had understood the words that were declared unto them.

13 ¶ And on the second day were gathered together the chief of the fathers of all the peo-ple, the priests, and the Le'vites, unto Ez'ra the scribe, even to understand the words of the law.

14 And they found written in the law which the LORD had commanded by Mo'ses, that the children of Is'ra-el should dwell in booths in the feast of the seventh month:

15 And that they should publish and pro-claim in all their cities, and in Je-ru'sa-lem, say-ing, Go forth unto the mount, and fetch olive branches, and pine branches, and myrtle branches, and palm branches, and branches of thick trees, to make booths, as *it is* written.

16 ¶ So the people went forth, and brought *them*, and made themselves booths, every one upon the roof of his house, and in their courts, and in the courts of the house of God, and in the street of the water gate, and in the street of the gate of E'phra-im.

17 And all the congregation of them that were come again out of the captivity made booths, and sat under the booths: for since the days of Jesh'u-a the son of Nun unto that day had not the children of Is'ra-el done so. And there was very great gladness.

18 Also day by day, from the first day unto the last day, he read in the book of the law of God. And they kept the feast seven days; and on the eighth day *was* a solemn assembly, ac-cording unto the manner.

9 NOW in the twenty and fourth day of this month the children of Is'ra-el were assem-bled with fasting, and with sackclothes, and earth upon them.

2 And the seed of Is'ra-el separated them-selves from all strangers, and stood and con-fessed their sins, and the iniquities of their fa-thers.

3 And they stood up in their place, and read in the book of the law of the LORD their God one fourth part of the day; and *another* fourth part they confessed, and worshipped the LORD their God.

4 ¶ Then stood up upon the stairs, of the Le'-vites, Jesh'u-a, and Ba'ni, Kad'mi-el, Sheb-a-ni'-ah, Bun'ni, Sher-e-bi'ah, Ba'ni, *and* Chen'a-ni,

and cried with a loud voice unto the LORD their God.

5 Then the Le'vites, Jesh'u-a, and Kad'mi-el, Ba'ni, Hash-ab-ni'ah, Sher-e-bi'ah, Ho-di'jah, Sheb-a-ni'ah, *and* Peth-a-hi'ah, said, Stand up *and* bless the LORD your God for ever and ever: and blessed be thy glorious name, which is ex-alted above all blessing and praise.

6 Thou, *even* thou, *art* LORD alone; thou hast made heaven, the heaven of heavens, with all their host, the earth, and all *things* that *are* therein, the seas, and all that *is* therein, and thou preservest them all; and the host of heaven worshippeth thee.

7 Thou *art* the LORD the God, who didst choose A'bram, and broughtest him forth out of Ur of the Chal'dees, and gavest him the name of A'bra-ham;

8 And foundest his heart faithful before thee, and madest a covenant with him to give the land of the Ca'naan-ites, the Hit'tites, the Am'-or-ites, and the Per'iz-zites, and the Jeb'u-sites, and the Gir'ga-shites, to give *it*, *I say*, to his seed, and hast performed thy words; for thou *art* righteous:

9 And didst see the affliction of our fathers in E'gypt, and heardest their cry by the Red sea;

10 And shewedst signs and wonders upon Pha'raoh, and on all his servants, and on all the people of his land: for thou knewest that they dealt proudly against them. So didst thou get thee a name, as *it is* this day.

11 And thou didst divide the sea before them, so that they went through the midst of the sea on the dry land; and their persecutors thou threwest into the deeps, as a stone into the mighty waters.

12 Moreover thou leddest them in the day by a cloudy pillar; and in the night by a pillar of fire, to give them light in the way wherein they should go.

13 Thou camest down also upon mount Si'-nai, and spakest with them from heaven, and gavest them right judgments, and true laws, good statutes and commandments:

14 And madest known unto them thy holy sabbath, and commandedst them precepts, statutes, and laws, by the hand of Mo'ses thy servant:

15 And gavest them bread from heaven for their hunger, and broughtest forth water for them out of the rock for their thirst, and prom-isedst them that they should go in to possess the land which thou hadst sworn to give them.

16 But they and our fathers dealt proudly, and hardened their necks, and hearkened not to thy commandments,

17 And refused to obey, neither were mindful of thy wonders that thou didst among them; but hardened their necks, and in their rebellion ap-pointed a captain to return to their bondage: but thou *art* a God ready to pardon, gracious and merciful, slow to anger, and of great kind-ness, and forsookest them not.

18 Yea, when they had made them a molten calf, and said, This *is* thy God that brought thee up out of E'gypt, and had wrought great provo-cations;

19 Yet thou in thy manifold mercies forsook-est them not in the wilderness: the pillar of the cloud departed not from them by day, to lead them in the way; neither the pillar of fire by night, to shew them light, and the way wherein they should go.

20 Thou gavest also thy good spirit to in-struct them, and withheldest not thy manna

from their mouth, and gavest them water for their thirst.

21 Yea, forty years didst thou sustain them in the wilderness, so that they lacked nothing; their clothes waxed not old, and their feet swelled not.

22 Moreover thou gavest them kingdoms and nations, and didst divide them into corners: so they possessed the land of Si'hon, and the land of the king of Hesh'bon, and the land of Og king of Ba'shan.

23 Their children also multipliedst thou as the stars of heaven, and broughtest them into the land, concerning which thou hadst promised to their fathers, that they should go in to possess it.

24 So the children went in and possessed the land, and thou subduedst before them the inhabitants of the land, the Ca'naan-ites, and gavest them into their hands, with their kings, and the people of the land, that they might do with them as they would.

25 And they took strong cities, and a fat land, and possessed houses full of all goods, wells digged, vineyards, and oliveyards, and fruit trees in abundance: so they did eat, and were filled, and became fat, and delighted themselves in thy great goodness.

26 Nevertheless they were disobedient, and rebelled against thee, and cast thy law behind their backs, and slew thy prophets which testified against them to turn them to thee, and they wrought great provocations.

27 Therefore thou deliveredst them into the hand of their enemies, who vexed them: and in the time of their trouble, when they cried unto thee, thou heardest them from heaven; and according to thy manifold mercies thou gavest them saviours, who saved them out of the hand of their enemies.

28 But after they had rest, they did evil again before thee: therefore leftest thou them in the hand of their enemies, so that they had the dominion over them: yet when they returned, and cried unto thee, thou heardest them from heaven; and many times didst thou deliver them according to thy mercies;

29 And testifiedst against them, that thou mightest bring them again unto thy law: yet they dealt proudly, and hearkened not unto thy commandments, but sinned against thy judgments, (which if a man do, he shall live in them;) and withdrew the shoulder, and hardened their neck, and would not hear.

30 Yet many years didst thou forbear them, and testifiedst against them by thy spirit in thy prophets: yet would they not give ear: therefore gavest thou them into the hand of the people of the lands.

31 Nevertheless for thy great mercies' sake thou didst not utterly consume them, nor forsake them; for thou art a gracious and merciful God.

32 Now therefore, our God, the great, the mighty, and the terrible God, who keepest covenant and mercy, let not all the trouble seem little before thee, that hath come upon us, on our kings, on our princes, and on our priests, and on our prophets, and on our fathers, and on all thy people, since the time of the kings of As-syr'i-a unto this day.

33 Howbeit thou art just in all that is brought upon us; for thou hast done right, but we have done wickedly:

34 Neither have our kings, our princes, our priests, nor our fathers, kept thy law, nor heark-ened unto thy commandments and thy testimonies, wherewith thou didst testify against them.

35 For they have not served thee in their kingdom, and in thy great goodness that thou gavest them, and in the large and fat land which thou gavest before them, neither turned they from their wicked works.

36 Behold, we are servants this day, and for the land that thou gavest unto our fathers to eat the fruit thereof and the good thereof, behold, we are servants in it:

37 And it yieldeth much increase unto the kings whom thou hast set over us because of our sins: also they have dominion over our bodies, and over our cattle, at their pleasure, and we are in great distress.

38 And because of all this we make a sure covenant, and write it; and our princes, Le'-vites, and priests, seal unto it.

10 NOW those that sealed were, Ne-he-mi'-ah, the Tir'sha-tha, the son of Hach-a-li'ah, and Zid-ki'jah,

2 Ser-a-i'ah, Az-a-ri'ah, Jer-e-mi'ah,

3 Pash'ur, Am-a-ri'ah, Mal-chi'jah,

4 Hat'tush, Sheb-a-ni'ah, Mal'luch,

5 Ha'rim, Mer'e-moth, O-ba-di'ah,

6 Dan'iel, Gin'ne-thon, Ba'ruch,

7 Me-shul'lam, A-bi'jah, Mij'a-min,

8 Ma-a-zi'ah, Bil'ga-i, Shem-a-i'ah: these were the priests.

9 And the Le'vites: both Jesh'u-a the son of Az-a-ni'ah, Bin'nu-i of the sons of Hen'a-dad, Kad'mi-el;

10 And their brethren, Sheb-a-ni'ah, Ho-di'-jah, Kel'i-ta, Pel-a-i'ah, Ha'nan,

11 Mi'cha, Re'hob, Hash-a-bi'ah,

12 Zac'cur, Sher-e-bi'ah, Sheb-a-ni'ah,

13 Ho-di'jah, Ba'ni, Ben'i-nu.

14 The chief of the people; Pa'rosh, Pa'hath-mo'ab, E'lam, Zat'thu, Ba'ni,

15 Bun'ni, Az'gad, Beb'a-i,

16 Ad-o-ni'jah, Big'va-i, A'din,

17 A'ter, Hiz-ki'jah, Az'zur,

18 Ho-di'jah, Ha'shum, Be'zai,

19 Ha'riph, An'a-thoth, Neb'a-i,

20 Mag'pi-ash, Me-shul'lam, He'zir,

21 Me-shez'a-be-el, Za'dok, Jad-du'a,

22 Pel-a-ti'ah, Ha'nan, An-a-i'ah,

23 Ho-she'a, Han-a-ni'ah, Ha'shub,

24 Hal-lo'hesh, Pil'e-ha, Sho'bek,

25 Re'hum, Ha-shab'nah, Ma-a-se'iah,

26 And A-hi'jah, Ha'nan, A'nan,

27 Mal'luch, Ha'rim, Ba'a-nah.

28 ¶ And the rest of the people, the priests, the Le'vites, the porters, the singers, the Neth'i-nims, and all they that had separated themselves from the people of the lands unto the law of God, their wives, their sons, and their daughters, every one having knowledge, and having understanding;

29 They clave to their brethren, their nobles, and entered into a curse, and into an oath, to walk in God's law, which was given by Mo'ses the servant of God, and to observe and do all the commandments of the LORD our Lord, and his judgments and his statutes;

30 And that we would not give our daughters unto the people of the land, nor take their daughters for our sons:

31 And if the people of the land bring ware or any victuals on the sabbath day to sell, that we would not buy it of them on the sabbath, or on the holy day: and that we would leave the seventh year, and the exaction of every debt.

32 Also we made ordinances for us, to

charge ourselves yearly with the third part of a shekel for the service of the house of our God;

33 For the shewbread, and for the continual meat offering, and for the continual burnt offering, of the sabbaths, of the new moons, for the set feasts, and for the holy things, and for the sin offerings to make an atonement for Is'ra-el, and for all the work of the house of our God.

34 And we cast the lots among the priests, the Le'vites, and the people, for the wood offering, to bring it into the house of our God, after the houses of our fathers, at times appointed year by year, to burn upon the altar of the LORD our God, as it is written in the law:

35 And to bring the firstfruits of our ground, and the firstfruits of all fruit of all trees, year by year, unto the house of the LORD:

36 Also the firstborn of our sons, and of our cattle, as it is written in the law, and the firstlings of our herds and of our flocks, to bring to the house of our God, unto the priests that minister in the house of our God:

37 And that we should bring the firstfruits of our dough, and our offerings, and the fruit of all manner of trees, of wine and of oil, unto the priests, to the chambers of the house of our God; and the tithes of our ground unto the Le'-vites, that the same Le'vites might have the tithes in all the cities of our tillage.

38 And the priest the son of Aar'on shall be with the Le'vites, when the Le'vites take tithes: and the Le'vites shall bring up the tithe of the tithes unto the house of our God, to the chambers, into the treasure house.

39 For the children of Is'ra-el and the children of Le'vi shall bring the offering of the corn, of the new wine, and the oil, unto the chambers, where are the vessels of the sanctuary, and the priests that minister, and the porters, and the singers: and we will not forsake the house of our God.

11 AND the rulers of the people dwelt at Je-ru'sa-lem: the rest of the people also cast lots, to bring one of ten to dwell in Je-ru'sa-lem the holy city, and nine parts to dwell in other cities.

2 And the people blessed all the men, that willingly offered themselves to dwell at Je-ru'-sa-lem.

3 ¶ Now these are the chief of the province that dwelt in Je-ru'sa-lem: but in the cities of Ju'dah dwelt every one in his possession in their cities, to wit, Is'ra-el, the priests, and the Le'-vites, and the Neth'i-nims, and the children of Sol'o-mon's servants.

4 And at Je-ru'sa-lem dwelt certain of the children of Ju'dah, and of the children of Ben'ja-min. Of the children of Ju'dah; Ath-a-i'ah the son of Uz-zi'ah, the son of Zech-a-ri'ah, the son of Am-a-ri'ah, the son of Sheph-a-ti'ah, the son of Ma-ha'la-le-el, of the children of Pe'rez;

5 And Ma-a-se'iah the son of Ba'ruch, the son of Col-ho'zeh, the son of Ha-za'iah, the son of Ad-a-i'ah, the son of Joi'a-rib, the son of Zech-a-ri'ah, the son of Shi-lo'ni.

6 All the sons of Pe'rez that dwelt at Je-ru'sa-lem were four hundred threescore and eight valiant men.

7 And these are the sons of Ben'ja-min; Sal'lu the son of Me-shul'lam, the son of Jo'ed, the son of Pe-da'iah, the son of Kol-a-i'ah, the son of Ma-a-se'iah, the son of Ith'i-el, the son of Je'sa'-iah.

8 And after him Gab'ba-i, Sal'la-i, nine hundred twenty and eight.

9 And Jo'el the son of Zich'ri was their over-

seer: and Ju'dah the son of Se-nu'ah was second over the city.

10 Of the priests: Je-da'iah the son of Joi'a-rib, Ja'chin.

11 Ser-a-i'ah the son of Hil-ki'ah, the son of Me-shul'lam, the son of Za'dok, the son of Me-ra'ioth, the son of A-hi'tub, was the ruler of the house of God.

12 And their brethren that did the work of the house were eight hundred twenty and two: and Ad-a-i'ah the son of Jer'o-ham, the son of Pel-a-li'ah, the son of Am'zi, the son of Zech-a-ri'ah, the son of Pash'ur, the son of Mal-chi'ah,

13 And his brethren, chief of the fathers, two hundred forty and two: and A-mash'a-i the son of A-zar'e-el, the son of A-has'a-i, the son of Me-shil'le-moth, the son of Im'mer,

14 And their brethren, mighty men of valour, an hundred twenty and eight: and their overseer was Zab'di-el, the son of one of the great men.

15 Also of the Le'vites: Shem-a-i'ah the son of Ha'shub, the son of Az'ri-kam, the son of Hash-a-bi'ah, the son of Bun'ni;

16 And Shab-beth'a-i and Joz'a-bad, of the chief of the Le'vites, had the oversight of the outward business of the house of God.

17 And Mat-ta-ni'ah the son of Mi'cha, the son of Zab'di, the son of A'saph, was the principal to begin the thanksgiving in prayer: and Bak-buk-i'ah the second among his brethren, and Ab'da the son of Sham-mu'a, the son of Ga'lal, the son of Jed'u-thun.

18 All the Le'vites in the holy city were two hundred fourscore and four.

19 Moreover the porters, Ak'kub, Tal'mon, and their brethren that kept the gates, were an hundred seventy and two.

20 ¶ And the residue of Is'ra-el, of the priests, and the Le'vites, were in all the cities of Ju'dah, every one in his inheritance.

21 But the Neth'i-nims dwelt in O'phel: and Zi'ha and Gis'pa were over the Neth'i-nims.

22 The overseer also of the Le'vites at Je-ru'-sa-lem was Uz'zi the son of Ba'ni, the son of Hash-a-bi'ah, the son of Mat-ta-ni'ah, the son of Mi'cha. Of the sons of A'saph, the singers were over the business of the house of God.

23 For it was the king's commandment concerning them, that a certain portion should be for the singers, due for every day.

24 And Peth-a-hi'ah the son of Me-shez'a-be-el, of the children of Ze'rah the son of Ju'dah, was at the king's hand in all matters concerning the people.

25 And for the villages, with their fields, some of the children of Ju'dah dwelt at Kir'-jath-ar'ba, and in the villages thereof, and at Di'bon, and in the villages thereof, and at Je-kab'ze-el, and in the villages thereof,

26 And at Jesh'u-a, and at Mol'a-dah, and at Beth-phe'let,

27 And at Ha'zar-shu'al, and at Be'er-she'ba, and in the villages thereof,

28 And at Zik'lag, and at Mek'o-nah, and in the villages thereof,

29 And at En-rim'mon, and at Za're-ah, and at Jar'muth,

30 Za-no'ah, A-dul'lam, and in their villages, at La'chish, and the fields thereof, at A-ze'kah, and in the villages thereof. And they dwelt from Be'er-she'ba unto the valley of Hin'nom.

31 The children also of Ben'ja-min from Ge'-ba dwelt at Mich'mash, and A-i'ja, and Beth'-el, and in their villages,

32 And at An'a-thoth, Nob, An-a-ni'ah,

33 Ha'zor, Ra'mah, Git'ta-im,

34 Ha'did, Ze-bo'im, Ne-bal'lat,

35 Lod, and O'no, the valley of craftsmen.

36 And of the Le'vites *were* divisions in Ju'-dah, *and* in Ben'ja-min.

12 NOW these *are* the priests and the Le'-vites that went up with Ze-rub'ba-bel the son of She-al'ti-el, and Jesh'u-a: Ser-a-i'ah, Jer-e-mi'ah, Ez'ra,

2 Am-a-ri'ah, Mal'luch, Hat'tush,

3 Shech-a-ni'ah, Re'hum, Mer'e-moth,

4 Id'do, Gin'ne-tho, A-bi'jah,

5 Mi'a-min, Ma-a-di'ah, Bil'gah,

6 Shem-a-i'ah, and Joi'a-rib, Je-da'iah,

7 Sal'lu, A'mok, Hil-ki'ah, Je-da'iah. These *were* the chief of the priests and of their brethren in the days of Jesh'u-a.

8 Moreover the Le'vites: Jesh'u-a, Bin'nu-i, Kad'mi-el, Sher-e-bi'ah, Ju'dah, *and* Mat-ta-ni'-ah, *which was* over the thanksgiving, he and his brethren.

9 Also Bak-buk-i'ah and Un'ni, their brethren, *were* over against them in the watches.

10 ¶ And Jesh'u-a begat Joi'a-kim, Joi'a-kim also begat E-li'a-shib, and E-li'a-shib begat Joi'-a-da,

11 And Joi'a-da begat Jon'a-than, and Jon'a-than begat Jad-du'a.

12 And in the days of Joi'a-kim were priests, the chief of the fathers: of Ser-a-i'ah, Mer-a-i'-ah; of Jer-e-mi'ah, Han-a-ni'ah;

13 Of Ez'ra, Me-shul'lam; of Am-a-ri'ah, Je-ho-ha'nan;

14 Of Mel'i-cu, Jon'a-than; of Sheb-a-ni'ah, Jo'seph;

15 Of Ha'rim, Ad'na; of Me-ra'ioth, Hel'ka-i;

16 Of Id'do, Zech-a-ri'ah; of Gin'ne-thon, Me-shul'lam;

17 Of A-bi'jah, Zich'ri; of Mi-ni'a-min, of Mo-a-di'ah, Pil'tai;

18 Of Bil'gah, Sham-mu'a; of Shem-a-i'ah, Je-hon'a-than;

19 And of Joi'a-rib, Mat-te-na'i; of Je-da'iah, Uz'zi;

20 Of Sal'la-i, Kal'la-i; of A'mok, E'ber;

21 Of Hil-ki'ah, Hash-a-bi'ah; of Je-da'iah, Ne-than'e-el.

22 ¶ The Le'vites in the days of E-li'a-shib, Joi'a-da, and Jo-ha'nan, and Jad-du'a, *were* recorded chief of the fathers: also the priests, to the reign of Da-ri'us the Per'sian.

23 The sons of Le'vi, the chief of the fathers, *were* written in the book of the chronicles, even until the days of Jo-ha'nan the son of E-li'a-shib.

24 And the chief of the Le'vites: Hash-a-bi'-ah, Sher-e-bi'ah, and Jesh'u-a the son of Kad'-mi-el, with their brethren over against them, to praise *and* to give thanks, according to the commandment of Da'vid the man of God, ward over against ward.

25 Mat-ta-ni'ah, and Bak-buk-i'ah, O-ba-di'-ah, Me-shul'lam, Tal'mon, Ak'kub, *were* porters keeping the ward at the thresholds of the gates.

26 These *were* in the days of Joi'a-kim the son of Jesh'u-a, the son of Joz'a-dak, and in the days of Ne-he-mi'ah the governor, and of Ez'ra the priest, the scribe.

27 ¶ And at the dedication of the wall of Je-ru'sa-lem they sought the Le'vites out of all their places, to bring them to Je-ru'sa-lem, to keep the dedication with gladness, both with thanksgivings, and with singing, *with* cymbals, psalteries, and with harps.

28 And the sons of the singers gathered themselves together, both out of the plain country round about Je-ru'sa-lem, and from the villages of Ne-toph'a-thi;

29 Also from the house of Gil'gal, and out of the fields of Ge'ba and Az'ma-veth: for the singers had builded them villages round about Je-ru'sa-lem.

30 And the priests and the Le'vites purified themselves, and purified the people, and the gates, and the wall.

31 Then I brought up the princes of Ju'dah upon the wall, and appointed two great *companies of them that* gave thanks, whereof one went on the right hand upon the wall toward the dung gate:

32 And after them went Hosh-a-i'ah, and half of the princes of Ju'dah,

33 And Az-a-ri'ah, Ez'ra, and Me-shul'lam,

34 Ju'dah, and Ben'ja-min, and Shem-a-i'ah, and Jer-e-mi'ah,

35 And *certain* of the priests' sons with trumpets; *namely,* Zech-a-ri'ah the son of Jon'a-than, the son of Shem-a-i'ah, the son of Mat-ta-ni'ah, the son of Mi-cha'iah, the son of Zac'cur, the son of A'saph:

36 And his brethren, Shem-a-i'ah, and A-zar'-a-el, Mil-a-la'i, Gil'a-lai, Ma-a'i, Ne-than'e-el, and Ju'dah, Ha-na'ni, with the musical instruments of Da'vid the man of God, and Ez'ra the scribe before them.

37 And at the fountain gate, which was over against them, they went up by the stairs of the city of Da'vid, at the going up of the wall, above the house of Da'vid, even unto the water gate eastward.

38 And the other *company of them that gave* thanks went over against *them,* and I after them, and the half of the people upon the wall, from beyond the tower of the furnaces even unto the broad wall;

39 And from above the gate of E'phra-im, and above the old gate, and above the fish gate, and the tower of Ha-nan'e-el, and the tower of Me'ah, even unto the sheep gate: and they stood still in the prison gate.

40 So stood the two *companies of them that gave* thanks in the house of God, and I, and the half of the rulers with me:

41 And the priests; E-li'a-kim, Ma-a-se'iah, Mi-ni'a-min, Mi-cha'iah, El-i-o-e'na-i, Zech-a-ri'-ah, *and* Han-a-ni'ah, with trumpets;

42 And Ma-a-se'iah, and Shem-a-i'ah, and E-le-a'zar, and Uz'zi, and Je-ho-ha'nan, and Mal-chi'jah, and E'lam, and E'zer. And the singers sang loud, with Jez-ra-hi'ah *their* overseer.

43 Also that day they offered great sacrifices, and rejoiced: for God had made them rejoice with great joy: the wives also and the children rejoiced: so that the joy of Je-ru'sa-lem was heard even afar off.

44 ¶ And at that time were some appointed over the chambers for the treasures, for the offerings, for the firstfruits, and for the tithes, to gather into them out of the fields of the cities the portions of the law for the priests and Le'-vites: for Ju'dah rejoiced for the priests and for the Le'vites that waited.

45 And both the singers and the porters kept the ward of their God, and the ward of the purification, according to the commandment of Da'-vid, *and* of Sol'o-mon his son.

46 For in the days of Da'vid and A'saph of old *there were* chief of the singers, and songs of praise and thanksgiving unto God.

47 And all Is'ra-el in the days of Ze-rub'ba-bel, and in the days of Ne-he-mi'ah, gave the portions of the singers and the porters, every day his portion: and they sanctified *holy things* unto the Le'vites; and the Le'vites sanctified *them* unto the children of Aar'on.

13 ON that day they read in the book of Mo'-ses in the audience of the people; and therein was found written, that the Am'mon-ite and the Mo'ab-ite should not come into the congregation of God for ever;

2 Because they met not the children of Is'ra-el with bread and with water, but hired Ba'laam against them, that he should curse them: howbeit our God turned the curse into a blessing.

3 Now it came to pass, when they had heard the law, that they separated from Is'ra-el all the mixed multitude.

4 ¶ And before this, E-li'a-shib the priest, having the oversight of the chamber of the house of our God, was allied unto To-bi'ah:

5 And he had prepared for him a great chamber, where aforetime they laid the meat offerings, the frankincense, and the vessels, and the tithes of the corn, the new wine, and the oil, which was commanded to be given to the Le'-vites, and the singers, and the porters; and the offerings of the priests.

6 But in all this time was not I at Je-ru'sa-lem: for in the two and thirtieth year of Ar-tax-erx'es king of Bab'y-lon came I unto the king, and after certain days obtained I leave of the king:

7 And I came to Je-ru'sa-lem, and understood of the evil that E-li'a-shib did for To-bi'ah, in preparing him a chamber in the courts of the house of God.

8 And it grieved me sore: therefore I cast forth all the household stuff of To-bi'ah out of the chamber.

9 Then I commanded, and they cleansed the chambers: and thither brought I again the vessels of the house of God, with the meat offering and the frankincense.

10 ¶ And I perceived that the portions of the Le'vites had not been given them: for the Le'-vites and the singers, that did the work, were fled every one to his field.

11 Then contended I with the rulers, and said, Why is the house of God forsaken? And I gathered them together, and set them in their place.

12 Then brought all Ju'dah the tithe of the corn and the new wine and the oil unto the treasuries.

13 And I made treasurers over the treasuries, Shel-e-mi'ah the priest, and Za'dok the scribe, and of the Le'vites, Pe-da'iah: and next to them was Ha'nan the son of Zac'cur, the son of Mat-ta-ni'ah: for they were counted faithful, and their office was to distribute unto their brethren.

14 Remember me, O my God, concerning this, and wipe not out my good deeds that I have done for the house of my God, and for the offices thereof.

15 ¶ In those days saw I in Ju'dah some treading wine presses on the sabbath, and bringing in sheaves, and lading asses; as also wine, grapes, and figs, and all manner of burdens, which they brought into Je-ru'sa-lem on the sabbath day: and I testified against them in the day wherein they sold victuals.

16 There dwelt men of Tyre also therein, which brought fish, and all manner of ware, and sold on the sabbath unto the children of Ju'dah, and in Je-ru'sa-lem.

17 Then I contended with the nobles of Ju'-dah, and said unto them, What evil thing is this that ye do, and profane the sabbath day?

18 Did not your fathers thus, and did not our God bring all this evil upon us, and upon this city? yet ye bring more wrath upon Is'ra-el by profaning the sabbath.

19 And it came to pass, that when the gates of Je-ru'sa-lem began to be dark before the sabbath, I commanded that the gates should be shut, and charged that they should not be opened till after the sabbath: and some of my servants set I at the gates, that there should no burden be brought in on the sabbath day.

20 So the merchants and sellers of all kind of ware lodged without Je-ru'sa-lem once or twice.

21 Then I testified against them, and said unto them, Why lodge ye about the wall? if ye do so again, I will lay hands on you. From that time forth came they no more on the sabbath.

22 And I commanded the Le'vites that they should cleanse themselves, and that they should come and keep the gates, to sanctify the sabbath day. Remember me, O my God, concerning this also, and spare me according to the greatness of thy mercy.

23 ¶ In those days also saw I Jews that had married wives of Ash'dod, of Am'mon, and of Mo'ab:

24 And their children spake half in the speech of Ash'dod, and could not speak in the Jews' language, but according to the language of each people.

25 And I contended with them, and cursed them, and smote certain of them, and plucked off their hair, and made them swear by God, saying, Ye shall not give your daughters unto their sons, nor take their daughters unto your sons, or for yourselves.

26 Did not Sol'o-mon king of Is'ra-el sin by these things? yet among many nations was there no king like him, who was beloved of his God, and God made him king over all Is'ra-el: nevertheless even him did outlandish women cause to sin.

27 Shall we then hearken unto you to do all this great evil, to transgress against our God in marrying strange wives?

28 And one of the sons of Joi'a-da, the son of E-li'a-shib the high priest, was son in law to San-bal'lat the Hor'o-nite: therefore I chased him from me.

29 Remember them, O my God, because they have defiled the priesthood, and the covenant of the priesthood, and of the Le'vites.

30 Thus cleansed I them from all strangers, and appointed the wards of the priests and the Le'vites, every one in his business;

31 And for the wood offering, at times appointed, and for the firstfruits. Remember me, O my God, for good.

THE BOOK OF

ESTHER

1 NOW it came to pass in the days of A-has-u-e′rus, (this is A-has-u-e′rus which reigned, from Ind′ia even unto E-thi-o′pi-a, over an hundred and seven and twenty provinces:)

2 That in those days, when the king A-has-u-e′rus sat on the throne of his kingdom, which was in Shu′shan the palace,

3 In the third year of his reign, he made a feast unto all his princes and his servants; the power of Per′sia and Me′di-a, the nobles and princes of the provinces, being before him:

4 When he shewed the riches of his glorious kingdom and the honour of his excellent majesty many days, even an hundred and fourscore days.

5 And when these days were expired, the king made a feast unto all the people that were present in Shu′shan the palace, both unto great and small, seven days, in the court of the garden of the king's palace;

6 Where were white, green, and blue, hangings, fastened with cords of fine linen and purple to silver rings and pillars of marble: the beds were of gold and silver, upon a pavement of red, and blue, and white, and black, marble.

7 And they gave them drink in vessels of gold, (the vessels being diverse one from another,) and royal wine in abundance, according to the state of the king.

8 And the drinking was according to the law; none did compel: for so the king had appointed to all the officers of his house, that they should do according to every man's pleasure.

9 Also Vash′ti the queen made a feast for the women in the royal house which belonged to king A-has-u-e′rus.

10 ¶ On the seventh day, when the heart of the king was merry with wine, he commanded Me-hu′man, Biz′tha, Har-bo′na, Big′tha, and A-bag′tha, Ze′thar, and Car′cas, the seven chamberlains that served in the presence of A-has-u-e′rus the king,

11 To bring Vash′ti the queen before the king with the crown royal, to shew the people and the princes her beauty: for she was fair to look on.

12 But the queen Vash′ti refused to come at the king's commandment by his chamberlains: therefore was the king very wroth, and his anger burned in him.

13 ¶ Then the king said to the wise men, which knew the times, (for so was the king's manner toward all that knew law and judgment:

14 And the next unto him was Car-she′na, She′thar, Ad′ma-tha, Tar′shish, Me′res, Mar′se-na, and Me-mu′can, the seven princes of Per′sia and Me′di-a, which saw the king's face, and which sat the first in the kingdom;)

15 What shall we do unto the queen Vash′ti according to law, because she hath not performed the commandment of the king A-has-u-e′rus by the chamberlains?

16 And Me-mu′can answered before the king and the princes, Vash′ti the queen hath not done wrong to the king only, but also to all the princes, and to all the people that are in all the provinces of the king A-has-u-e′rus.

17 For this deed of the queen shall come abroad unto all women, so that they shall despise their husbands in their eyes, when it shall

be reported, The king A-has-u-e′rus commanded Vash′ti the queen to be brought in before him, but she came not.

18 Likewise shall the ladies of Per′sia and Me′di-a say this day unto all the king's princes, which have heard of the deed of the queen. Thus shall there arise too much contempt and wrath.

19 If it please the king, let there go a royal commandment from him, and let it be written among the laws of the Per′sians and the Medes, that it be not altered, That Vash′ti come no more before king A-has-u-e′rus; and let the king give her royal estate unto another that is better than she.

20 And when the king's decree which he shall make shall be published throughout all his empire, (for it is great,) all the wives shall give to their husbands honour, both to great and small.

21 And the saying pleased the king and the princes; and the king did according to the word of Me-mu′can:

22 For he sent letters into all the king's provinces, into every province according to the writing thereof, and to every people after their language, that every man should bear rule in his own house, and that it should be published according to the language of every people.

2 AFTER these things, when the wrath of king A-has-u-e′rus was appeased, he remembered Vash′ti, and what she had done, and what was decreed against her.

2 Then said the king's servants that ministered unto him, Let there be fair young virgins sought for the king:

3 And let the king appoint officers in all the provinces of his kingdom, that they may gather together all the fair young virgins unto Shu′-shan the palace, to the house of the women, unto the custody of He′ge the king's chamberlain, keeper of the women; and let their things for purification be given them:

4 And let the maiden which pleaseth the king be queen instead of Vash′ti. And the thing pleased the king; and he did so.

5 ¶ Now in Shu′shan the palace there was a certain Jew, whose name was Mor′de-cai, the son of Ja′ir, the son of Shim′e-i, the son of Kish, a Ben′ja-mite;

6 Who had been carried away from Je-ru′sa-lem with the captivity which had been carried away with Jec-o-ni′ah king of Ju′dah, whom Neb-u-chad-nez′zar the king of Bab′y-lon had carried away.

7 And he brought up Ha-das′sah, that is, Es′ther, his uncle's daughter: for she had neither father nor mother, and the maid was fair and beautiful; whom Mor′de-cai, when her father and mother were dead, took for his own daughter.

8 ¶ So it came to pass, when the king's commandment and his decree was heard, and when many maidens were gathered together unto Shu′shan the palace, to the custody of Heg′a-i, that Es′ther was brought also unto the king's house, to the custody of Heg′a-i, keeper of the women.

9 And the maiden pleased him, and she obtained kindness of him; and he speedily gave her her things for purification, with such things

as belonged to her, and seven maidens, *which were* meet to be given her, out of the king's house: and he preferred her and her maids unto the best *place* of the house of the women.

10 Es'ther had not shewed her people nor her kindred: for Mor'de-cai had charged her that she should not shew *it*.

11 And Mor'de-cai walked every day before the court of the women's house, to know how Es'ther did, and what should become of her.

12 ¶ Now when every maid's turn was come to go in to king A-has-u-e'rus, after that she had been twelve months, according to the manner of the women, (for so were the days of their purifications accomplished, *to wit*, six months with oil of myrrh, and six months with sweet odours, and with *other* things for the purifying of the women;)

13 Then thus came *every* maiden unto the king; whatsoever she desired was given her to go with her out of the house of the women unto the king's house.

14 In the evening she went, and on the morrow she returned into the second house of the women, to the custody of Sha-ash'gaz, the king's chamberlain, which kept the concubines: she came in unto the king no more, except the king delighted in her, and that she were called by name.

15 ¶ Now when the turn of Es'ther, the daughter of Ab-i-ha'il the uncle of Mor'de-cai, who had taken her for his daughter, was come to go in unto the king, she required nothing but what Heg'a-i the king's chamberlain, the keeper of the women, appointed. And Es'ther obtained favour in the sight of all them that looked upon her.

16 So Es'ther was taken unto king A-has-u-e'rus into his house royal in the tenth month, which *is* the month Te'beth, in the seventh year of his reign.

17 And the king loved Es'ther above all the women, and she obtained grace and favour in his sight more than all the virgins; so that he set the royal crown upon her head, and made her queen instead of Vash'ti.

18 Then the king made a great feast unto all his princes and his servants, *even* Es'ther's feast; and he made a release to the provinces, and gave gifts, according to the state of the king.

19 And when the virgins were gathered together the second time, then Mor'de-cai sat in the king's gate.

20 Es'ther had not *yet* shewed her kindred nor her people; as Mor'de-cai had charged her: for Es'ther did the commandment of Mor'de-cai, like as when she was brought up with him.

21 ¶ In those days, while Mor'de-cai sat in the king's gate, two of the king's chamberlains, Big'than and Te'resh, of those which kept the door, were wroth, and sought to lay hand on the king A-has-u-e'rus.

22 And the thing was known to Mor'de-cai, who told *it* unto Es'ther the queen; and Es'ther certified the king *thereof* in Mor'de-cai's name.

23 And when inquisition was made of the matter, it was found out; therefore they were both hanged on a tree: and it was written in the book of the chronicles before the king.

3 AFTER these things did king A-has-u-e'rus promote Ha'man the son of Ham-med'a-tha the A'gag-ite, and advanced him, and set his seat above all the princes that *were* with him.

2 And all the king's servants, that *were* in the king's gate, bowed, and reverenced Ha'man: for

the king had so commanded concerning him. But Mor'de-cai bowed not, nor did *him* reverence.

3 Then the king's servants, which *were* in the king's gate, said unto Mor'de-cai, Why transgressest thou the king's commandment?

4 Now it came to pass, when they spake daily unto him, and he hearkened not unto them, that they told Ha'man, to see whether Mor'de-cai's matters would stand: for he had told them that he *was* a Jew.

5 And when Ha'man saw that Mor'de-cai bowed not, nor did him reverence, then was Ha'man full of wrath.

6 And he thought scorn to lay hands on Mor'-de-cai alone; for they had shewed him the people of Mor'de-cai: wherefore Ha'man sought to destroy all the Jews that *were* throughout the whole kingdom of A-has-u-e'rus, *even* the people of Mor'de-cai.

7 ¶ In the first month, that *is*, the month Ni'-san, in the twelfth year of king A-has-u-e'rus, they cast Pur, that *is*, the lot, before Ha'man from day to day, and from month to month, *to* the twelfth *month*, that *is*, the month A'dar.

8 ¶ And Ha'man said unto king A-has-u-e'rus, There is a certain people scattered abroad and dispersed among the people in all the provinces of thy kingdom; and their laws *are* diverse from all people; neither keep they the king's laws: therefore it *is* not for the king's profit to suffer them.

9 If it please the king, let it be written that they may be destroyed: and I will pay ten thousand talents of silver to the hands of those that have the charge of the business, to bring *it* into the king's treasuries.

10 And the king took his ring from his hand, and gave it unto Ha'man the son of Ham-med'a-tha the A'gag-ite, the Jews' enemy.

11 And the king said unto Ha'man, The silver *is* given to thee, the people also, to do with them as it seemeth good to thee.

12 Then were the king's scribes called on the thirteenth day of the first month, and there was written according to all that Ha'man had commanded unto the king's lieutenants, and to the governors that *were* over every province, and to the rulers of every people of every province according to the writing thereof, and *to* every people after their language; in the name of king A-has-u-e'rus was it written, and sealed with the king's ring.

13 And the letters were sent by posts into all the king's provinces, to destroy, to kill, and to cause to perish, all Jews, both young and old, little children and women, in one day, *even* upon the thirteenth *day* of the twelfth month, which *is* the month A'dar, and *to take* the spoil of them for a prey.

14 The copy of the writing for a commandment to be given in every province was published unto all people, that they should be ready against that day.

15 The posts went out, being hastened by the king's commandment, and the decree was given in Shu'shan the palace. And the king and Ha'-man sat down to drink; but the city Shu'shan was perplexed.

4 WHEN Mor'de-cai perceived all that was done, Mor'de-cai rent his clothes, and put on sackcloth with ashes, and went out into the midst of the city, and cried with a loud and a bitter cry;

2 And came even before the king's gate: for

none *might* enter into the king's gate clothed with sackcloth.

3 And in every province, whithersoever the king's commandment and his decree came, *there was* great mourning among the Jews, and fasting, and weeping, and wailing; and many lay in sackcloth and ashes.

4 ¶ So Es'ther's maids and her chamberlains came and told *it* her. Then was the queen exceedingly grieved; and she sent raiment to clothe Mor'de-cai, and to take away his sackcloth from him: but he received *it* not.

5 Then called Es'ther for Ha'tach, *one* of the king's chamberlains, whom he had appointed to attend upon her, and gave him a commandment to Mor'de-cai, to know what it *was*, and why it *was*.

6 So Ha'tach went forth to Mor'de-cai unto the street of the city, which *was* before the king's gate.

7 And Mor'de-cai told him of all that had happened unto him, and of the sum of the money that Ha'man had promised to pay to the king's treasuries for the Jews, to destroy them.

8 Also he gave him the copy of the writing of the decree that was given at Shu'shan to destroy them, to shew *it* unto Es'ther, and to declare *it* unto her, and to charge her that she should go in unto the king, to make supplication unto him, and to make request before him for her people.

9 And Ha'tach came and told Es'ther the words of Mor'de-cai.

10 Again Es'ther spake unto Ha'tach, and gave him commandment unto Mor'de-cai;

11 All the king's servants, and the people of the king's provinces, do know, that whosoever, whether man or woman, shall come unto the king into the inner court, who is not called, *there is* one law of his to put *him* to death, except such to whom the king shall hold out the golden sceptre, that he may live: but I have not been called to come in unto the king these thirty days.

12 And they told to Mor'de-cai Es'ther's words.

13 Then Mor'de-cai commanded to answer Es'ther, Think not with thyself that thou shalt escape in the king's house, more than all the Jews.

14 For if thou altogether holdest thy peace at this time, *then* shall there enlargement and deliverance arise to the Jews from another place; but thou and thy father's house shall be destroyed: and who knoweth whether thou art come to the kingdom for *such* a time as this?

15 ¶ Then Es'ther bade *them* return Mor'de-cai *this* answer,

16 Go, gather together all the Jews that are present in Shu'shan, and fast ye for me, and neither eat nor drink three days, night or day: I also and my maidens will fast likewise; and so will I go in unto the king, which *is* not according to the law: and if I perish, I perish.

17 So Mor'de-cai went his way, and did according to all that Es'ther had commanded him.

5 NOW it came to pass on the third day, that Es'ther put on *her* royal *apparel*, and stood in the inner court of the king's house, over against the king's house: and the king sat upon his royal throne in the royal house, over against the gate of the house.

2 And it was so, when the king saw Es'ther the queen standing in the court, *that* she obtained favour in his sight: and the king held out to Es'ther the golden sceptre that *was* in his hand. So Es'ther drew near, and touched the top of the sceptre.

3 Then said the king unto her, What wilt thou, queen Es'ther? and what *is* thy request? it shall be even given thee to the half of the kingdom.

4 And Es'ther answered, If *it seem* good unto the king, let the king and Ha'man come this day unto the banquet that I have prepared for him.

5 Then the king said, Cause Ha'man to make haste, that he may do as Es'ther hath said. So the king and Ha'man came to the banquet that Es'ther had prepared.

6 ¶ And the king said unto Es'ther at the banquet of wine, What *is* thy petition? and it shall be granted thee: and what *is* thy request? even to the half of the kingdom it shall be performed.

7 Then answered Es'ther, and said, My petition and my request *is*;

8 If I have found favour in the sight of the king, and if it please the king to grant my petition, and to perform my request, let the king and Ha'man come to the banquet that I shall prepare for them, and I will do to morrow as the king hath said.

9 ¶ Then went Ha'man forth that day joyful and with a glad heart: but when Ha'man saw Mor'de-cai in the king's gate, that he stood not up, nor moved for him, he was full of indignation against Mor'de-cai.

10 Nevertheless Ha'man refrained himself: and when he came home, he sent and called for his friends, and Ze'resh his wife.

11 And Ha'man told them of the glory of his riches, and the multitude of his children, and all *the things* wherein the king had promoted him, and how he had advanced him above the princes and servants of the king.

12 Ha'man said moreover, Yea, Es'ther the queen did let no man come in with the king unto the banquet that she had prepared but myself; and to morrow am I invited unto her also with the king.

13 Yet all this availeth me nothing, so long as I see Mor'de-cai the Jew sitting at the king's gate.

14 ¶ Then said Ze'resh his wife and all his friends unto him, Let a gallows be made of fifty cubits high, and to morrow speak thou unto the king that Mor'de-cai may be hanged thereon: then go thou in merrily with the king unto the banquet. And the thing pleased Ha'man; and he caused the gallows to be made.

6 ON that night could not the king sleep, and he commanded to bring the book of records of the chronicles; and they were read before the king.

2 And it was found written, that Mor'de-cai had told of Big'tha-na and Te'resh, two of the king's chamberlains, the keepers of the door, who sought to lay hand on the king A-has-u-e'rus.

3 And the king said, What honour and dignity hath been done to Mor'de-cai for this? Then said the king's servants that ministered unto him, There is nothing done for him.

4 ¶ And the king said, Who *is* in the court? Now Ha'man was come into the outward court of the king's house, to speak unto the king to hang Mor'de-cai on the gallows that he had prepared for him.

5 And the king's servants said unto him, Behold, Ha'man standeth in the court. And the king said, Let him come in.

6 So Ha'man came in. And the king said unto

him, What shall be done unto the man whom the king delighteth to honour? Now Ha'man thought in his heart, To whom would the king delight to do honour more than to myself?

7 And Ha'man answered the king, For the man whom the king delighteth to honour,

8 Let the royal apparel be brought which the king *useth* to wear, and the horse that the king rideth upon, and the crown royal which is set upon his head:

9 And let this apparel and horse be delivered to the hand of one of the king's most noble princes, that they may array the man *withal* whom the king delighteth to honour, and bring him on horseback through the street of the city, and proclaim before him, Thus shall it be done to the man whom the king delighteth to honour.

10 Then the king said to Ha'man, Make haste, *and* take the apparel and the horse, as thou hast said, and do even so to Mor'de-cai the Jew, that sitteth at the king's gate: let nothing fail of all that thou hast spoken.

11 Then took Ha'man the apparel and the horse, and arrayed Mor'de-cai, and brought him on horseback through the street of the city, and proclaimed before him, Thus shall it be done unto the man whom the king delighteth to honour.

12 ¶ And Mor'de-cai came again to the king's gate. But Ha'man hasted to his house mourning, and having his head covered.

13 And Ha'man told Ze'resh his wife and all his friends every *thing* that had befallen him. Then said his wise men and Ze'resh his wife unto him, If Mor'de-cai *be* of the seed of the Jews, before whom thou hast begun to fall, thou shalt not prevail against him, but shalt surely fall before him.

14 And while they *were* yet talking with him, came the king's chamberlains, and hasted to bring Ha'man unto the banquet that Es'ther had prepared.

7 SO the king and Ha'man came to banquet with Es'ther the queen.

2 And the king said again unto Es'ther on the second day at the banquet of wine, What *is* thy petition, queen Es'ther? and it shall be granted thee: and what *is* thy request? and it shall be performed, *even* to the half of the kingdom.

3 Then Es'ther the queen answered and said, If I have found favour in thy sight, O king, and if it please the king, let my life be given me at my petition, and my people at my request:

4 For we are sold, I and my people, to be destroyed, to be slain, and to perish. But if we had been sold for bondmen and bondwomen, I had held my tongue, although the enemy could not countervail the king's damage.

5 ¶ Then the king A-has-u-e'rus answered and said unto Es'ther the queen, Who is he, and where is he, that durst presume in his heart to do so?

6 And Es'ther said, The adversary and enemy *is* this wicked Ha'man. Then Ha'man was afraid before the king and the queen.

7 ¶ And the king arising from the banquet of wine in his wrath *went* into the palace garden: and Ha'man stood up to make request for his life to Es'ther the queen; for he saw that there was evil determined against him by the king.

8 Then the king returned out of the palace garden into the place of the banquet of wine; and Ha'man was fallen upon the bed whereon Es'ther *was*. Then said the king, Will he force the queen also before me in the house? As the

word went out of the king's mouth, they covered Ha'man's face.

9 And Har-bo'nah, one of the chamberlains, said before the king, Behold also, the gallows fifty cubits high, which Ha'man had made for Mor'de-cai, who had spoken good for the king, standeth in the house of Ha'man. Then the king said, Hang him thereon.

10 So they hanged Ha'man on the gallows that he had prepared for Mor'de-cai. Then was the king's wrath pacified.

8 ON that day did the king A-has-u-e'rus give the house of Ha'man the Jews' enemy unto Es'ther the queen. And Mor'de-cai came before the king; for Es'ther had told what he *was* unto her.

2 And the king took off his ring, which he had taken from Ha'man, and gave it unto Mor'-de-cai. And Es'ther set Mor'de-cai over the house of Ha'man.

3 ¶ And Es'ther spake yet again before the king, and fell down at his feet, and besought him with tears to put away the mischief of Ha'-man the A'gag-ite, and his device that he had devised against the Jews.

4 Then the king held out the golden sceptre toward Es'ther. So Es'ther arose, and stood before the king,

5 And said, If it please the king, and if I have found favour in his sight, and the thing *seem* right before the king, and I *be* pleasing in his eyes, let it be written to reverse the letters devised by Ha'man the son of Ham-med'a-tha the A'gag-ite, which he wrote to destroy the Jews which *are* in all the king's provinces:

6 For how can I endure to see the evil that shall come unto my people? or how can I endure to see the destruction of my kindred?

7 ¶ Then the king A-has-u-e'rus said unto Es'ther the queen and to Mor'de-cai the Jew, Behold, I have given Es'ther the house of Ha'-man, and him they have hanged upon the gallows, because he laid his hand upon the Jews.

8 Write ye also for the Jews, as it liketh you, in the king's name, and seal *it* with the king's ring: for the writing which is written in the king's name, and sealed with the king's ring, may no man reverse.

9 Then were the king's scribes called at that time in the third month, that *is*, the month Si'-van, on the three and twentieth *day* thereof; and it was written according to all that Mor'de-cai commanded unto the Jews, and to the lieutenants, and the deputies and rulers of the provinces which *are* from Ind'ia unto E-thi-o'pi-a, an hundred twenty and seven provinces, unto every province according to the writing thereof, and unto every people after their language, and to the Jews according to their writing, and according to their language.

10 And he wrote in the king A-has-u-e'rus' name, and sealed *it* with the king's ring, and sent letters by posts on horseback, *and* riders on mules, camels, *and* young dromedaries:

11 Wherein the king granted the Jews which *were* in every city to gather themselves together, and to stand for their life, to destroy, to slay, and to cause to perish, all the power of the people and province that would assault them, *both* little ones and women, and *to* take the spoil of them for a prey,

12 Upon one day in all the provinces of king A-has-u-e'rus, *namely*, upon the thirteenth *day* of the twelfth month, which *is* the month A'dar.

13 The copy of the writing for a commandment to be given in every province *was* pub-

lished unto all people, and that the Jews should be ready against that day to avenge themselves on their enemies.

14 So the posts that rode upon mules and camels went out, being hastened and pressed on by the king's commandment. And the decree was given at Shu'shan the palace.

15 ¶ And Mor'de-cai went out from the presence of the king in royal apparel of blue and white, and with a great crown of gold, and with a garment of fine linen and purple: and the city of Shu'shan rejoiced and was glad.

16 The Jews had light, and gladness, and joy, and honour.

17 And in every province, and in every city, whithersoever the king's commandment and his decree came, the Jews had joy and gladness, a feast and a good day. And many of the people of the land became Jews; for the fear of the Jews fell upon them.

9 NOW in the twelfth month, that is, the month A'dar, on the thirteenth day of the same, when the king's commandment and his decree drew near to be put in execution, in the day that the enemies of the Jews hoped to have power over them, (though it was turned to the contrary, that the Jews had rule over them that hated them;)

2 The Jews gathered themselves together in their cities throughout all the provinces of the king A-has-u-e'rus, to lay hand on such as sought their hurt: and no man could withstand them; for the fear of them fell upon all people.

3 And all the rulers of the provinces, and the lieutenants, and the deputies, and officers of the king, helped the Jews; because the fear of Mor'-de-cai fell upon them.

4 For Mor'de-cai was great in the king's house, and his fame went out throughout all the provinces: for this man Mor'de-cai waxed greater and greater.

5 Thus the Jews smote all their enemies with the stroke of the sword, and slaughter, and destruction, and did what they would unto those that hated them.

6 And in Shu'shan the palace the Jews slew and destroyed five hundred men.

7 And Par-shan'da-tha, and Dal'phon and As'pa-tha,

8 And Por'a-tha, and Ad-a-li'a, and A-rid'a-tha,

9 And Par-mash'ta, and A-ris'a-i, and A-rid'a-i, and Va-jez'a-tha,

10 The ten sons of Ha'man the son of Hammed'a-tha, the enemy of the Jews, slew they; but on the spoil laid they not their hand.

11 On that day the number of those that were slain in Shu'shan the palace was brought before the king.

12 ¶ And the king said unto Es'ther the queen, The Jews have slain and destroyed five hundred men in Shu'shan the palace, and the ten sons of Ha'man; what have they done in the rest of the king's provinces? now what is thy petition? and it shall be granted thee: or what is thy request further? and it shall be done.

13 Then said Es'ther, If it please the king, let it be granted to the Jews which are in Shu'shan to do to morrow also according unto this day's decree, and let Ha'man's ten sons be hanged upon the gallows.

14 And the king commanded it so to be done: and the decree was given at Shu'shan; and they hanged Ha'man's ten sons.

15 For the Jews that were in Shu'shan gathered themselves together on the fourteenth day also of the month A'dar, and slew three hundred men at Shu'shan; but on the prey they laid not their hand.

16 But the other Jews that were in the king's provinces gathered themselves together, and stood for their lives, and had rest from their enemies, and slew of their foes seventy and five thousand, but they laid not their hands on the prey,

17 On the thirteenth day of the month A'dar; and on the fourteenth day of the same rested they, and made it a day of feasting and gladness.

18 But the Jews that were at Shu'shan assembled together on the thirteenth day thereof, and on the fourteenth thereof; and on the fifteenth day of the same they rested, and made it a day of feasting and gladness.

19 Therefore the Jews of the villages, that dwelt in the unwalled towns, made the fourteenth day of the month A'dar a day of gladness and feasting, and a good day, and of sending portions one to another.

20 ¶ And Mor'de-cai wrote these things, and sent letters unto all the Jews that were in all the provinces of the king A-has-u-e'rus, both nigh and far,

21 To stablish this among them, that they should keep the fourteenth day of the month A'dar, and the fifteenth day of the same, yearly,

22 As the days wherein the Jews rested from their enemies, and the month which was turned unto them from sorrow to joy, and from mourning into a good day: that they should make them days of feasting and joy, and of sending portions one to another, and gifts to the poor.

23 And the Jews undertook to do as they had begun, and as Mor'de-cai had written unto them;

24 Because Ha'man the son of Ham-med'a-tha, the A'gag-ite, the enemy of all the Jews, had devised against the Jews to destroy them, and had cast Pur, that is, the lot, to consume them, and to destroy them;

25 But when Es'ther came before the king, he commanded by letters that his wicked device, which he devised against the Jews, should return upon his own head, and that he and his sons should be hanged on the gallows.

26 Wherefore they called these days Pu'rim after the name of Pur. Therefore for all the words of this letter, and of that which they had seen concerning this matter, and which had come unto them,

27 The Jews ordained, and took upon them, and upon their seed, and upon all such as joined themselves unto them, so as it should not fail, that they would keep these two days according to their writing, and according to their appointed time every year;

28 And that these days should be remembered and kept throughout every generation, every family, every province, and every city; and that these days of Pu'rim should not fail from among the Jews, nor the memorial of them perish from their seed.

29 Then Es'ther the queen, the daughter of Ab-i-ha'il, and Mor'de-cai the Jew, wrote with all authority, to confirm this second letter of Pu'rim.

30 And he sent the letters unto all the Jews, to the hundred twenty and seven provinces of the kingdom of A-has-u-e'rus, with words of peace and truth,

31 To confirm these days of Pu'rim in their times appointed, according as Mor'de-cai the Jew and Es'ther the queen had enjoined them,

and as they had decreed for themselves and for their seed, the matters of the fastings and their cry.

32 And the decree of Es′ther confirmed these matters of Pu′rim; and it was written in the book.

10 AND the king A-has-u-e′rus laid a tribute upon the land, and *upon* the isles of the sea.

2 And all the acts of his power and of his might, and the declaration of the greatness of Mor′de-cai, whereunto the king advanced him, *are* they not written in the book of the chronicles of the kings of Me′di-a and Per′sia?

3 For Mor′de-cai the Jew *was* next unto king A-has-u-e′rus, and great among the Jews, and accepted of the multitude of his brethren, seeking the wealth of his people, and speaking peace to all his seed.

THE BOOK OF

JOB

1 THERE was a man in the land of Uz, whose name *was* Job: and that man was perfect and upright, and one that feared God, and eschewed evil.

2 And there were born unto him seven sons and three daughters.

3 His substance also was seven thousand sheep, and three thousand camels, and five hundred yoke of oxen, and five hundred she asses, and a very great household; so that this man was the greatest of all the men of the east.

4 And his sons went and feasted *in their* houses, every one his day; and sent and called for their three sisters to eat and to drink with them.

5 And it was so, when the days of *their* feasting were gone about, that Job sent and sanctified them, and rose up early in the morning, and offered burnt offerings *according* to the number of them all: for Job said, It may be that my sons have sinned, and cursed God in their hearts. Thus did Job continually.

6 ¶ Now there was a day when the sons of God came to present themselves before the LORD, and Sa′tan came also among them.

7 And the LORD said unto Sa′tan, Whence comest thou? Then Sa′tan answered the LORD, and said, From going to and fro in the earth, and from walking up and down in it.

8 And the LORD said unto Sa′tan, Hast thou considered my servant Job, that *there is* none like him in the earth, a perfect and an upright man, one that feareth God, and escheweth evil?

9 Then Sa′tan answered the LORD, and said, Doth Job fear God for nought?

10 Hast not thou made an hedge about him, and about his house, and about all that he hath on every side? thou hast blessed the work of his hands, and his substance is increased in the land.

11 But put forth thine hand now, and touch all that he hath, and he will curse thee to thy face.

12 And the LORD said unto Sa′tan, Behold, all that he hath *is* in thy power; only upon himself put not forth thine hand. So Sa′tan went forth from the presence of the LORD.

13 ¶ And there was a day when his sons and his daughters *were* eating and drinking wine in their eldest brother's house:

14 And there came a messenger unto Job, and said, The oxen were plowing, and the asses feeding beside them:

15 And the Sa-be′ans fell *upon them,* and took them away; yea, they have slain the servants with the edge of the sword; and I only am escaped alone to tell thee.

16 While he *was* yet speaking, there came also another, and said, The fire of God is fallen from heaven, and hath burned up the sheep, and the servants, and consumed them; and I only am escaped alone to tell thee.

17 While he *was* yet speaking, there came also another, and said, The Chal-de′ans made out three bands, and fell upon the camels, and have carried them away, yea, and slain the servants with the edge of the sword; and I only am escaped alone to tell thee.

18 While he *was* yet speaking, there came also another, and said, Thy sons and thy daughters *were* eating and drinking wine in their eldest brother's house:

19 And, behold, there came a great wind from the wilderness, and smote the four corners of the house, and it fell upon the young men, and they are dead; and I only am escaped alone to tell thee.

20 Then Job arose, and rent his mantle, and shaved his head, and fell down upon the ground, and worshipped,

21 And said, Naked came I out of my mother's womb, and naked shall I return thither: the LORD gave, and the LORD hath taken away; blessed be the name of the LORD.

22 In all this Job sinned not, nor charged God foolishly.

2 AGAIN there was a day when the sons of God came to present themselves before the LORD, and Sa′tan came also among them to present himself before the LORD.

2 And the LORD said unto Sa′tan, From whence comest thou? And Sa′tan answered the LORD, and said, From going to and fro in the earth, and from walking up and down in it.

3 And the LORD said unto Sa′tan, Hast thou considered my servant Job, that *there is* none like him in the earth, a perfect and an upright man, one that feareth God, and escheweth evil? and still he holdeth fast his integrity, although thou movedst me against him, to destroy him without cause.

4 And Sa′tan answered the LORD, and said, Skin for skin, yea, all that a man hath will he give for his life.

5 But put forth thine hand now, and touch his bone and his flesh, and he will curse thee to thy face.

6 And the LORD said unto Sa′tan, Behold, he *is* in thine hand; but save his life.

7 ¶ So went Sa′tan forth from the presence of the LORD, and smote Job with sore boils from the sole of his foot unto his crown.

8 And he took him a potsherd to scrape himself withal; and he sat down among the ashes.

9 ¶ Then said his wife unto him, Dost thou still retain thine integrity? curse God, and die.

10 But he said unto her, Thou speakest as

one of the foolish women speaketh. What? shall we receive good at the hand of God, and shall we not receive evil? In all this did not Job sin with his lips.

11 ¶ Now when Job's three friends heard of all this evil that was come upon him, they came every one from his own place; El'i-phaz the Te'man-ite, and Bil'dad the Shu'hite, and Zo'phar the Na'a-math-ite: for they had made an appointment together to come to mourn with him and to comfort him.

12 And when they lifted up their eyes afar off, and knew him not, they lifted up their voice, and wept; and they rent every one his mantle, and sprinkled dust upon their heads toward heaven.

13 So they sat down with him upon the ground seven days and seven nights, and none spake a word unto him: for they saw that *his* grief was very great.

3 AFTER this opened Job his mouth, and cursed his day.

2 And Job spake, and said,

3 Let the day perish wherein I was born, and the night *in* which it was said, There is a man child conceived.

4 Let that day be darkness; let not God regard it from above, neither let the light shine upon it.

5 Let darkness and the shadow of death stain it; let a cloud dwell upon it; let the blackness of the day terrify it.

6 *As for* that night, let darkness seize upon it; let it not be joined unto the days of the year, let it not come into the number of the months.

7 Lo, let that night be solitary, let no joyful voice come therein.

8 Let them curse it that curse the day, who are ready to raise up their mourning.

9 Let the stars of the twilight thereof be dark; let it look for light, but *have* none; neither let it see the dawning of the day:

10 Because it shut not up the doors of my *mother's* womb, nor hid sorrow from mine eyes.

11 Why died I not from the womb? *why* did I *not* give up the ghost when I came out of the belly?

12 Why did the knees prevent me? or why the breasts that I should suck?

13 For now should I have lain still and been quiet, I should have slept: then had I been at rest,

14 With kings and counsellors of the earth, which built desolate places for themselves;

15 Or with princes that had gold, who filled their houses with silver:

16 Or as an hidden untimely birth I had not been; as infants *which* never saw light.

17 There the wicked cease *from* troubling; and there the weary be at rest.

18 *There* the prisoners rest together; they hear not the voice of the oppressor.

19 The small and great are there; and the servant *is* free from his master.

20 Wherefore is light given to him that is in misery, and life unto the bitter *in* soul;

21 Which long for death, but it *cometh* not; and dig for it more than for hid treasures;

22 Which rejoice exceedingly, *and* are glad, when they can find the grave?

23 *Why is* light *given* to a man whose way is hid, and whom God hath hedged in?

24 For my sighing cometh before I eat, and my roarings are poured out like the waters.

25 For the thing which I greatly feared is come upon me, and that which I was afraid of is come unto me.

26 I was not in safety, neither had I rest, neither was I quiet; yet trouble came.

4 THEN El'i-phaz the Te'man-ite answered and said,

2 *If* we assay to commune with thee, wilt thou be grieved? but who can withhold himself from speaking?

3 Behold, thou hast instructed many, and thou hast strengthened the weak hands.

4 Thy words have upholden him that was falling, and thou hast strengthened the feeble knees.

5 But now it is come upon thee, and thou faintest; it toucheth thee, and thou art troubled.

6 *Is* not *this* thy fear, thy confidence, thy hope, and the uprightness of thy ways?

7 Remember, I pray thee, who *ever* perished, being innocent? or where were the righteous cut off?

8 Even as I have seen, they that plow iniquity, and sow wickedness, reap the same.

9 By the blast of God they perish, and by the breath of his nostrils are they consumed.

10 The roaring of the lion, and the voice of the fierce lion, and the teeth of the young lions, are broken.

11 The old lion perisheth for lack of prey, and the stout lion's whelps are scattered abroad.

12 Now a thing was secretly brought to me, and mine ear received a little thereof.

13 In thoughts from the visions of the night, when deep sleep falleth on men,

14 Fear came upon me, and trembling, which made all my bones to shake.

15 Then a spirit passed before my face; the hair of my flesh stood up:

16 It stood still, but I could not discern the form thereof: an image *was* before mine eyes, *there was* silence, and I heard a voice, *saying,*

17 Shall mortal man be more just than God? shall a man be more pure than his maker?

18 Behold, he put no trust in his servants; and his angels he charged with folly:

19 How much less *in* them that dwell in houses of clay, whose foundation *is* in the dust, *which* are crushed before the moth?

20 They are destroyed from morning to evening: they perish for ever without any regarding *it.*

21 Doth not their excellency *which is* in them go away? they die, even without wisdom.

5 CALL now, if there be any that will answer thee; and to which of the saints wilt thou turn?

2 For wrath killeth the foolish man, and envy slayeth the silly one.

3 I have seen the foolish taking root: but suddenly I cursed his habitation.

4 His children are far from safety, and they are crushed in the gate, neither *is there* any to deliver *them.*

5 Whose harvest the hungry eateth up, and taketh it even out of the thorns, and the robber swalloweth up their substance.

6 Although affliction cometh not forth of the dust, neither doth trouble spring out of the ground;

7 Yet man is born unto trouble, as the sparks fly upward.

8 I would seek unto God, and unto God would I commit my cause:

9 Which doeth great things and unsearchable; marvellous things without number:

10 Who giveth rain upon the earth, and sendeth waters upon the fields:

11 To set up on high those that be low; that those which mourn may be exalted to safety.

12 He disappointeth the devices of the crafty, so that their hands cannot perform *their* enterprise.

13 He taketh the wise in their own craftiness: and the counsel of the froward is carried headlong.

14 They meet with darkness in the daytime, and grope in the noonday as in the night.

15 But he saveth the poor from the sword, from their mouth, and from the hand of the mighty.

16 So the poor hath hope, and iniquity stoppeth her mouth.

17 Behold, happy *is* the man whom God correcteth: therefore despise not thou the chastening of the Almighty:

18 For he maketh sore, and bindeth up: he woundeth, and his hands make whole.

19 He shall deliver thee in six troubles: yea, in seven there shall no evil touch thee.

20 In famine he shall redeem thee from death: and in war from the power of the sword.

21 Thou shalt be hid from the scourge of the tongue: neither shalt thou be afraid of destruction when it cometh.

22 At destruction and famine thou shalt laugh: neither shalt thou be afraid of the beasts of the earth.

23 For thou shalt be in league with the stones of the field: and the beasts of the field shall be at peace with thee.

24 And thou shalt know that thy tabernacle *shall be* in peace; and thou shalt visit thy habitation, and shalt not sin.

25 Thou shalt know also that thy seed *shall be* great, and thine offspring as the grass of the earth.

26 Thou shalt come to *thy* grave in a full age, like as a shock of corn cometh in in his season.

27 Lo this, we have searched it, so it *is;* hear it, and know thou *it* for thy good.

6 BUT Job answered and said,

2 Oh that my grief were throughly weighed, and my calamity laid in the balances together!

3 For now it would be heavier than the sand of the sea: therefore my words are swallowed up.

4 For the arrows of the Almighty *are* within me, the poison whereof drinketh up my spirit: the terrors of God do set themselves in array against me.

5 Doth the wild ass bray when he hath grass? or loweth the ox over his fodder?

6 Can that which is unsavoury be eaten without salt? or is there *any* taste in the white of an egg?

7 The things *that* my soul refused to touch *are* as my sorrowful meat.

8 Oh that I might have my request; and that God would grant *me* the thing that I long for!

9 Even that it would please God to destroy me; that he would let loose his hand, and cut me off!

10 Then should I yet have comfort; yea, I would harden myself in sorrow: let him not spare; for I have not concealed the words of the Holy One.

11 What *is* my strength, that I should hope? and what *is* mine end, that I should prolong my life?

12 *Is* my strength the strength of stones? or *is* my flesh of brass?

13 *Is* not my help in me? and is wisdom driven quite from me?

14 To him that is afflicted pity *should be* shewed from his friend; but he forsaketh the fear of the Almighty.

15 My brethren have dealt deceitfully as a brook, *and* as the stream of brooks they pass away;

16 Which are blackish by reason of the ice, *and* wherein the snow is hid:

17 What time they wax warm, they vanish: when it is hot, they are consumed out of their place.

18 The paths of their way are turned aside; they go to nothing, and perish.

19 The troops of Te′ma looked, the companies of She′ba waited for them.

20 They were confounded because they had hoped; they came thither, and were ashamed.

21 For now ye are nothing; ye see *my* casting down, and are afraid.

22 Did I say, Bring unto me? or, Give a reward for me of your substance?

23 Or, Deliver me from the enemy's hand? or, Redeem me from the hand of the mighty?

24 Teach me, and I will hold my tongue: and cause me to understand wherein I have erred.

25 How forcible are right words! but what doth your arguing reprove?

26 Do ye imagine to reprove words, and the speeches of one that is desperate, *which are* as wind?

27 Yea, ye overwhelm the fatherless, and ye dig *a pit* for your friend.

28 Now therefore be content, look upon me; for *it is* evident unto you if I lie.

29 Return, I pray you, let it not be iniquity; yea, return again, my righteousness *is* in it.

30 Is there iniquity in my tongue? cannot my taste discern perverse things?

7 IS there not an appointed time to man upon earth? *are not* his days also like the days of an hireling?

2 As a servant earnestly desireth the shadow, and as an hireling looketh for *the reward of* his work:

3 So am I made to possess months of vanity, and wearisome nights are appointed to me.

4 When I lie down, I say, When shall I arise, and the night be gone? and I am full of tossings to and fro unto the dawning of the day.

5 My flesh is clothed with worms and clods of dust; my skin is broken, and become loathsome.

6 My days are swifter than a weaver's shuttle, and are spent without hope.

7 O remember that my life *is* wind: mine eye shall no more see good.

8 The eye of him that hath seen me shall see me no *more:* thine eyes *are* upon me, and I *am* not.

9 *As* the cloud is consumed and vanisheth away: so he that goeth down to the grave shall come up no more.

10 He shall return no more to his house, neither shall his place know him any more.

11 Therefore I will not refrain my mouth; I will speak in the anguish of my spirit; I will complain in the bitterness of my soul.

12 *Am* I a sea, or a whale, that thou settest a watch over me?

13 When I say, My bed shall comfort me, my couch shall ease my complaint;

14 Then thou scarest me with dreams, and terrifiest me through visions:

15 So that my soul chooseth strangling, *and* death rather than my life.

16 I loathe *it*: I would not live alway: let me alone; for my days *are* vanity.

17 What *is* man, that thou shouldest magnify him? and that thou shouldest set thine heart upon him?

18 And *that* thou shouldest visit him every morning, *and* try him every moment?

19 How long wilt thou not depart from me, nor let me alone till I swallow down my spittle?

20 I have sinned; what shall I do unto thee, O thou preserver of men? why hast thou set me as a mark against thee, so that I am a burden to myself?

21 And why dost thou not pardon my transgression, and take away mine iniquity? for now shall I sleep in the dust; and thou shalt seek me in the morning, but I *shall* not *be*.

8 THEN answered Bil'dad the Shu'hite, and said,

2 How long wilt thou speak these *things*? and *how long shall* the words of thy mouth *be like* a strong wind?

3 Doth God pervert judgment? or doth the Almighty pervert justice?

4 If thy children have sinned against him, and he have cast them away for their transgression;

5 If thou wouldest seek unto God betimes, and make thy supplication to the Almighty;

6 If thou *wert* pure and upright; surely now he would awake for thee, and make the habitation of thy righteousness prosperous.

7 Though thy beginning was small, yet thy latter end should greatly increase.

8 For enquire, I pray thee, of the former age, and prepare thyself to the search of their fathers:

9 (For we *are but of* yesterday, and know nothing, because our days upon earth *are* a shadow:)

10 Shall not they teach thee, *and* tell thee, and utter words out of their heart?

11 Can the rush grow up without mire? can the flag grow without water?

12 Whilst it *is* yet in his greenness, *and* not cut down, it withereth before any *other* herb.

13 So *are* the paths of all that forget God; and the hypocrite's hope shall perish:

14 Whose hope shall be cut off, and whose trust *shall be* a spider's web.

15 He shall lean upon his house, but it shall not stand: he shall hold it fast, but it shall not endure.

16 He *is* green before the sun, and his branch shooteth forth in his garden.

17 His roots are wrapped about the heap, *and* seeth the place of stones.

18 If he destroy him from his place, then *it* shall deny him, *saying*, I have not seen thee.

19 Behold, this *is* the joy of his way, and out of the earth shall others grow.

20 Behold, God will not cast away a perfect *man*, neither will he help the evildoers:

21 Till he fill thy mouth with laughing, and thy lips with rejoicing.

22 They that hate thee shall be clothed with shame; and the dwelling place of the wicked shall come to nought.

9 THEN Job answered and said,

2 I know *it is* so of a truth: but how should man be just with God?

3 If he will contend with him, he cannot answer him one of a thousand.

4 *He is* wise in heart, and mighty in strength: who hath hardened *himself* against him, and hath prospered?

5 Which removeth the mountains, and they know not: which overturneth them in his anger.

6 Which shaketh the earth out of her place, and the pillars thereof tremble.

7 Which commandeth the sun, and it riseth not; and sealeth up the stars.

8 Which alone spreadeth out the heavens, and treadeth upon the waves of the sea.

9 Which maketh Arc-tu'rus, O-ri'on, and Ple'-ia-des, and the chambers of the south.

10 Which doeth great things past finding out; yea, and wonders without number.

11 Lo, he goeth by me, and I see *him* not: he passeth on also, but I perceive him not.

12 Behold, he taketh away, who can hinder him? who will say unto him, What doest thou?

13 *If* God will not withdraw his anger, the proud helpers do stoop under him.

14 How much less shall I answer him, *and* choose out my words *to reason* with him?

15 Whom, though I were righteous, *yet* would I not answer, *but* I would make supplication to my judge.

16 If I had called, and he had answered me; *yet* would I not believe that he had hearkened unto my voice.

17 For he breaketh me with a tempest, and multiplieth my wounds without cause.

18 He will not suffer me to take my breath, but filleth me with bitterness.

19 If *I speak* of strength, lo, *he is* strong: and if of judgment, who shall set me a time *to* plead?

20 If I justify myself, mine own mouth shall condemn me: *if I say*, I *am* perfect, it shall also prove me perverse.

21 *Though* I *were* perfect, *yet* would I not know my soul: I would despise my life.

22 This *is* one *thing*, therefore I said *it*, He destroyeth the perfect and the wicked.

23 If the scourge slay suddenly, he will laugh at the trial of the innocent.

24 The earth is given into the hand of the wicked: he covereth the faces of the judges thereof; if not, where, *and* who *is* he?

25 Now my days are swifter than a post: they flee away, they see no good.

26 They are passed away as the swift ships: as the eagle *that* hasteth to the prey.

27 If I say, I will forget my complaint, I will leave off my heaviness, and comfort *myself*:

28 I am afraid of all my sorrows, I know that thou wilt not hold me innocent.

29 *If* I be wicked, why then labour I in vain?

30 If I wash myself with snow water, and make my hands never so clean;

31 Yet shalt thou plunge me in the ditch, and mine own clothes shall abhor me.

32 For *he is* not a man, as I *am, that* I should answer him, *and* we should come together in judgment.

33 Neither is there any daysman betwixt us, *that* might lay his hand upon us both.

34 Let him take his rod away from me, and let not his fear terrify me:

35 *Then* would I speak, and not fear him; but *it is* not so with me.

10 MY soul is weary of my life; I will leave my complaint upon myself; I will speak in the bitterness of my soul.

2 I will say unto God, Do not condemn me; shew me wherefore thou contendest with me.

3 Is it good unto thee that thou shouldest oppress, that thou shouldest despise the work of thine hands, and shine upon the counsel of the wicked?

4 Hast thou eyes of flesh? or seest thou as man seeth?

5 Are thy days as the days of man? are thy years as man's days,

6 That thou enquirest after mine iniquity, and searchest after my sin?

7 Thou knowest that I am not wicked; and there is none that can deliver out of thine hand.

8 Thine hands have made me and fashioned me together round about; yet thou dost destroy me.

9 Remember, I beseech thee, that thou hast made me as the clay; and wilt thou bring me into dust again?

10 Hast thou not poured me out as milk, and curdled me like cheese?

11 Thou hast clothed me with skin and flesh, and hast fenced me with bones and sinews.

12 Thou hast granted me life and favour, and thy visitation hath preserved my spirit.

13 And these things hast thou hid in thine heart: I know that this is with thee.

14 If I sin, then thou markest me, and thou wilt not acquit me from mine iniquity.

15 If I be wicked, woe unto me; and if I be righteous, yet will I not lift up my head. I am full of confusion; therefore see thou mine affliction;

16 For it increaseth. Thou huntest me as a fierce lion: and again thou shewest thyself marvellous upon me.

17 Thou renewest thy witnesses against me, and increasest thine indignation upon me; changes and war are against me.

18 Wherefore then hast thou brought me forth out of the womb? Oh that I had given up the ghost, and no eye had seen me!

19 I should have been as though I had not been; I should have been carried from the womb to the grave.

20 Are not my days few? cease then, and let me alone, that I may take comfort a little,

21 Before I go whence I shall not return, even to the land of darkness and the shadow of death;

22 A land of darkness, as darkness itself; and of the shadow of death, without any order, and where the light is as darkness.

11 THEN answered Zo'phar the Na'amath-ite, and said,

2 Should not the multitude of words be answered? and should a man full of talk be justified?

3 Should thy lies make men hold their peace? and when thou mockest, shall no man make thee ashamed?

4 For thou hast said, My doctrine is pure, and I am clean in thine eyes.

5 But oh that God would speak, and open his lips against thee;

6 And that he would shew thee the secrets of wisdom, that they are double to that which is! Know therefore that God exacteth of thee less than thine iniquity deserveth.

7 Canst thou by searching find out God? canst thou find out the Almighty unto perfection?

8 It is as high as heaven; what canst thou do? deeper than hell; what canst thou know?

9 The measure thereof is longer than the earth, and broader than the sea.

10 If he cut off, and shut up, or gather together, then who can hinder him?

11 For he knoweth vain men: he seeth wickedness also; will he not then consider it?

12 For vain man would be wise, though man be born like a wild ass's colt.

13 If thou prepare thine heart, and stretch out thine hands toward him;

14 If iniquity be in thine hand, put it far away, and let not wickedness dwell in thy tabernacles.

15 For then shalt thou lift up thy face without spot; yea, thou shalt be stedfast, and shalt not fear:

16 Because thou shalt forget thy misery, and remember it as waters that pass away:

17 And thine age shall be clearer than the noonday; thou shalt shine forth, thou shalt be as the morning.

18 And thou shalt be secure, because there is hope; yea, thou shalt dig about thee, and thou shalt take thy rest in safety.

19 Also thou shalt lie down, and none shall make thee afraid; yea, many shall make suit unto thee.

20 But the eyes of the wicked shall fail, and they shall not escape, and their hope shall be as the giving up of the ghost.

12 AND Job answered and said,

2 No doubt but ye are the people, and wisdom shall die with you.

3 But I have understanding as well as you; I am not inferior to you: yea, who knoweth not such things as these?

4 I am as one mocked of his neighbour, who calleth upon God, and he answereth him: the just upright man is laughed to scorn.

5 He that is ready to slip with his feet is as a lamp despised in the thought of him that is at ease.

6 The tabernacles of robbers prosper, and they that provoke God are secure; into whose hand God bringeth abundantly.

7 But ask now the beasts, and they shall teach thee; and the fowls of the air, and they shall tell thee:

8 Or speak to the earth, and it shall teach thee: and the fishes of the sea shall declare unto thee.

9 Who knoweth not in all these that the hand of the LORD hath wrought this?

10 In whose hand is the soul of every living thing, and the breath of all mankind.

11 Doth not the ear try words? and the mouth taste his meat?

12 With the ancient is wisdom; and in length of days understanding.

13 With him is wisdom and strength, he hath counsel and understanding.

14 Behold, he breaketh down, and it cannot be built again: he shutteth up a man, and there can be no opening.

15 Behold, he withholdeth the waters, and they dry up: also he sendeth them out, and they overturn the earth.

16 With him is strength and wisdom: the deceived and the deceiver are his.

17 He leadeth counsellors away spoiled, and maketh the judges fools.

18 He looseth the bond of kings, and girdeth their loins with a girdle.

19 He leadeth princes away spoiled, and overthroweth the mighty.

20 He removeth away the speech of the

trusty, and taketh away the understanding of the aged.

21 He poureth contempt upon princes, and weakeneth the strength of the mighty.

22 He discovereth deep things out of darkness, and bringeth out to light the shadow of death.

23 He increaseth the nations, and destroyeth them: he enlargeth the nations, and straiteneth them *again*.

24 He taketh away the heart of the chief of the people of the earth, and causeth them to wander in a wilderness *where there is* no way.

25 They grope in the dark without light, and he maketh them to stagger like *a* drunken *man*.

13 LO, mine eye hath seen all *this*, mine ear hath heard and understood it.

2 What ye know, *the same* do I know also: I *am* not inferior unto you.

3 Surely I would speak to the Almighty, and I desire to reason with God.

4 But ye *are* forgers of lies, ye *are* all physicians of no value.

5 O that ye would altogether hold your peace! and it should be your wisdom.

6 Hear now my reasoning, and hearken to the pleadings of my lips.

7 Will ye speak wickedly for God? and talk deceitfully for him?

8 Will ye accept his person? will ye contend for God?

9 Is it good that he should search you out? or as one man mocketh another, do ye *so* mock him?

10 He will surely reprove you, if ye do secretly accept persons.

11 Shall not his excellency make you afraid? and his dread fall upon you?

12 Your remembrances *are* like unto ashes, your bodies to bodies of clay.

13 Hold your peace, let me alone, that I may speak, and let come on me what *will*.

14 Wherefore do I take my flesh in my teeth, and put my life in mine hand?

15 Though he slay me, yet will I trust in him: but I will maintain mine own ways before him.

16 He also *shall be* my salvation: for an hypocrite shall not come before him.

17 Hear diligently my speech, and my declaration with your ears.

18 Behold now, I have ordered *my* cause; I know that I shall be justified.

19 Who *is* he *that* will plead with me? for now, if I hold my tongue, I shall give up the ghost.

20 Only do not two *things* unto me: then will I not hide myself from thee.

21 Withdraw thine hand far from me: and let not thy dread make me afraid.

22 Then call thou, and I will answer: or let me speak, and answer thou me.

23 How many *are* mine iniquities and sins? make me to know my transgression and my sin.

24 Wherefore hidest thou thy face, and holdest me for thine enemy?

25 Wilt thou break a leaf driven to and fro? and wilt thou pursue the dry stubble?

26 For thou writest bitter things against me, and makest me to possess the iniquities of my youth.

27 Thou puttest my feet also in the stocks, and lookest narrowly unto all my paths; thou settest a print upon the heels of my feet.

28 And he, as a rotten thing, consumeth, as a garment that is moth eaten.

14 MAN *that is* born of a woman *is* of few days, and full of trouble.

2 He cometh forth like a flower, and is cut down: he fleeth also as a shadow, and continueth not.

3 And dost thou open thine eyes upon such an one, and bringest me into judgment with thee?

4 Who can bring a clean *thing* out of an unclean? not one.

5 Seeing his days *are* determined, the number of his months *are* with thee, thou hast appointed his bounds that he cannot pass:

6 Turn from him, that he may rest, till he shall accomplish, as an hireling, his day.

7 For there is hope of a tree, if it be cut down, that it will sprout again, and that the tender branch thereof will not cease.

8 Though the root thereof wax old in the earth, and the stock thereof die in the ground;

9 *Yet* through the scent of water it will bud, and bring forth boughs like a plant.

10 But man dieth, and wasteth away: yea, man giveth up the ghost, and where *is* he?

11 *As* the waters fail from the sea, and the flood decayeth and drieth up:

12 So man lieth down, and riseth not: till the heavens *be* no more, they shall not awake, nor be raised out of their sleep.

13 O that thou wouldest hide me in the grave, that thou wouldest keep me secret, until thy wrath be past, that thou wouldest appoint me a set time, and remember me!

14 If a man die, shall he live *again*? all the days of my appointed time will I wait, till my change come.

15 Thou shalt call, and I will answer thee: thou wilt have a desire to the work of thine hands.

16 For now thou numberest my steps: dost thou not watch over my sin?

17 My transgression *is* sealed up in a bag, and thou sewest up mine iniquity.

18 And surely the mountain falling cometh to nought, and the rock is removed out of his place.

19 The waters wear the stones: thou washest away the things which grow *out* of the dust of the earth; and thou destroyest the hope of man.

20 Thou prevailest for ever against him, and he passeth: thou changest his countenance, and sendest him away.

21 His sons come to honour, and he knoweth *it* not; and they are brought low, but he perceiveth *it* not of them.

22 But his flesh upon him shall have pain, and his soul within him shall mourn.

15 THEN answered El'i-phaz the Te'manite, and said,

2 Should a wise man utter vain knowledge, and fill his belly with the east wind?

3 Should he reason with unprofitable talk? or with speeches wherewith he can do no good?

4 Yea, thou castest off fear, and restrainest prayer before God.

5 For thy mouth uttereth thine iniquity, and thou choosest the tongue of the crafty.

6 Thine own mouth condemneth thee, and not I; yea, thine own lips testify against thee.

7 *Art* thou the first man *that* was born? or wast thou made before the hills?

8 Hast thou heard the secret of God? and dost thou restrain wisdom to thyself?

9 What knowest thou, that we know not? *what* understandest thou, which *is* not in us?

10 With us *are* both the grayheaded and very aged men, much elder than thy father.

11 *Are* the consolations of God small with thee? is there any secret thing with thee?

12 Why doth thine heart carry thee away? and what do thy eyes wink at,

13 That thou turnest thy spirit against God, and lettest *such* words go out of thy mouth?

14 What *is* man, that he should be clean? and *he which is* born of a woman, that he should be righteous?

15 Behold, he putteth no trust in his saints; yea, the heavens are not clean in his sight.

16 How much more abominable and filthy *is* man, which drinketh iniquity like water?

17 I will shew thee, hear me; and that *which* I have seen I will declare;

18 Which wise men have told from their fathers, and have not hid *it*:

19 Unto whom alone the earth was given, and no stranger passed among them.

20 The wicked man travaileth with pain all *his* days, and the number of years is hidden to the oppressor.

21 A dreadful sound *is* in his ears: in prosperity the destroyer shall come upon him.

22 He believeth not that he shall return out of darkness, and he is waited for of the sword.

23 He wandereth abroad for bread, *saying*, Where *is it?* he knoweth that the day of darkness is ready at his hand.

24 Trouble and anguish shall make him afraid; they shall prevail against him, as a king ready to the battle.

25 For he stretcheth out his hand against God, and strengtheneth himself against the Almighty.

26 He runneth upon him, *even* on *his* neck, upon the thick bosses of his bucklers:

27 Because he covereth his face with his fatness, and maketh collops of fat on *his* flanks.

28 And he dwelleth in desolate cities, *and* in houses which no man inhabiteth, which are ready to become heaps.

29 He shall not be rich, neither shall his substance continue, neither shall he prolong the perfection thereof upon the earth.

30 He shall not depart out of darkness; the flame shall dry up his branches, and by the breath of his mouth shall he go away.

31 Let not him that is deceived trust in vanity: for vanity shall be his recompence.

32 It shall be accomplished before his time, and his branch shall not be green.

33 He shall shake off his unripe grape as the vine, and shall cast off his flower as the olive.

34 For the congregation of hypocrites *shall* be desolate, and fire shall consume the tabernacles of bribery.

35 They conceive mischief, and bring forth vanity, and their belly prepareth deceit.

16 THEN Job answered and said,
2 I have heard many such things: miserable comforters *are* ye all.

3 Shall vain words have an end? or what emboldeneth thee that thou answerest?

4 I also could speak as ye *do*: if your soul were in my soul's stead, I could heap up words against you, and shake mine head at you.

5 *But* I would strengthen you with my mouth, and the moving of my lips should asswage *your* grief.

6 Though I speak, my grief is not asswaged: and *though* I forbear, what am I eased?

7 But now he hath made me weary: thou hast made desolate all my company.

8 And thou hast filled me with wrinkles, *which* is a witness *against me:* and my leanness rising up in me beareth witness to my face.

9 He teareth *me* in his wrath, who hateth me: he gnasheth upon me with his teeth; mine enemy sharpeneth his eyes upon me.

10 They have gaped upon me with their mouth; they have smitten me upon the cheek reproachfully; they have gathered themselves together against me.

11 God hath delivered me to the ungodly, and turned me over into the hands of the wicked.

12 I was at ease, but he hath broken me asunder: he hath also taken *me* by my neck, and shaken me to pieces, and set me up for his mark.

13 His archers compass me round about, he cleaveth my reins asunder, and doth not spare; he poureth out my gall upon the ground.

14 He breaketh me with breach upon breach, he runneth upon me like a giant.

15 I have sewed sackcloth upon my skin, and defiled my horn in the dust.

16 My face is foul with weeping, and on my eyelids *is* the shadow of death;

17 Not for *any* injustice in mine hands: also my prayer *is* pure.

18 O earth, cover not thou my blood, and let my cry have no place.

19 Also now, behold, my witness *is* in heaven, and my record *is* on high.

20 My friends scorn me: *but* mine eye poureth out *tears* unto God.

21 O that one might plead for a man with God, as a man *pleadeth* for his neighbour!

22 When a few years are come, then I shall go the way *whence* I shall not return.

17 MY breath is corrupt, my days are extinct, the graves *are* ready for me.

2 *Are there* not mockers with me? and doth not mine eye continue in their provocation?

3 Lay down now, put me in a surety with thee; who *is* he *that* will strike hands with me?

4 For thou hast hid their heart from understanding: therefore shalt thou not exalt *them*.

5 He that speaketh flattery to *his* friends, even the eyes of his children shall fail.

6 He hath made me also a byword of the people; and aforetime I was as a tabret.

7 Mine eye also is dim by reason of sorrow, and all my members *are* as a shadow.

8 Upright *men* shall be astonied at this, and the innocent shall stir up himself against the hypocrite.

9 The righteous also shall hold on his way, and he that hath clean hands shall be stronger and stronger.

10 But as for you all, do ye return, and come now: for I cannot find *one* wise *man* among you.

11 My days are past, my purposes are broken off, *even* the thoughts of my heart.

12 They change the night into day: the light *is* short because of darkness.

13 If I wait, the grave *is* mine house: I have made my bed in the darkness.

14 I have said to corruption, Thou *art* my father: to the worm, *Thou art* my mother, and my sister.

15 And where *is* now my hope? as for my hope, who shall see it?

16 They shall go down to the bars of the pit, when *our* rest together *is* in the dust.

18 THEN answered Bil'dad the Shu'hite, and said,

2 How long *will it be ere* ye make an end of words? mark, and afterwards we will speak.

3 Wherefore are we counted as beasts, *and* reputed vile in your sight?

4 He teareth himself in his anger: shall the earth be forsaken for thee? and shall the rock be removed out of his place?

5 Yea, the light of the wicked shall be put out, and the spark of his fire shall not shine.

6 The light shall be dark in his tabernacle, and his candle shall be put out with him.

7 The steps of his strength shall be straitened, and his own counsel shall cast him down.

8 For he is cast into a net by his own feet, and he walketh upon a snare.

9 The gin shall take *him* by the heel, *and* the robber shall prevail against him.

10 The snare *is* laid for him in the ground, and a trap for him in the way.

11 Terrors shall make him afraid on every side, and shall drive him to his feet.

12 His strength shall be hungerbitten, and destruction *shall be* ready at his side.

13 It shall devour the strength of his skin: *even* the firstborn of death shall devour his strength.

14 His confidence shall be rooted out of his tabernacle, and it shall bring him to the king of terrors.

15 It shall dwell in his tabernacle, because *it is* none of his: brimstone shall be scattered upon his habitation.

16 His roots shall be dried up beneath, and above shall his branch be cut off.

17 His remembrance shall perish from the earth, and he shall have no name in the street.

18 He shall be driven from light into darkness, and chased out of the world.

19 He shall neither have son nor nephew among his people, nor any remaining in his dwellings.

20 They that come after *him* shall be astonied at his day, as they that went before were affrighted.

21 Surely such *are* the dwellings of the wicked, and this *is* the place *of him that* knoweth not God.

19 THEN Job answered and said,

2 How long will ye vex my soul, and break me in pieces with words?

3 These ten times have ye reproached me: ye are not ashamed *that* ye make yourselves strange to me.

4 And be it indeed *that* I have erred, mine error remaineth with myself.

5 If indeed ye will magnify *yourselves* against me, and plead against me my reproach:

6 Know now that God hath overthrown me, and hath compassed me with his net.

7 Behold, I cry out of wrong, but I am not heard: I cry aloud, but *there is* no judgment.

8 He hath fenced up my way that I cannot pass, and he hath set darkness in my paths.

9 He hath stripped me of my glory, and taken the crown *from* my head.

10 He hath destroyed me on every side, and I am gone: and mine hope hath he removed like a tree.

11 He hath also kindled his wrath against me, and he counteth me unto him as *one of* his enemies.

12 His troops come together, and raise up their way against me, and encamp round about my tabernacle.

13 He hath put my brethren far from me, and mine acquaintance are verily estranged from me.

14 My kinsfolk have failed, and my familiar friends have forgotten me.

15 They that dwell in mine house, and my maids, count me for a stranger: I am an alien in their sight.

16 I called my servant, and he gave *me* no answer; I intreated him with my mouth.

17 My breath is strange to my wife, though I intreated for the children's *sake* of mine own body.

18 Yea, young children despised me; I arose, and they spake against me.

19 All my inward friends abhorred me: and they whom I loved are turned against me.

20 My bone cleaveth to my skin and to my flesh, and I am escaped with the skin of my teeth.

21 Have pity upon me, have pity upon me, O ye my friends; for the hand of God hath touched me.

22 Why do ye persecute me as God, and are not satisfied with my flesh?

23 Oh that my words were now written! oh that they were printed in a book!

24 That they were graven with an iron pen and lead in the rock for ever!

25 For I know *that* my redeemer liveth, and *that* he shall stand at the latter *day* upon the earth:

26 And *though* after my skin *worms* destroy this *body*, yet in my flesh shall I see God:

27 Whom I shall see for myself, and mine eyes shall behold, and not another; *though* my reins be consumed within me.

28 But ye should say, Why persecute we him, seeing the root of the matter is found in me?

29 Be ye afraid of the sword: for wrath *bringeth* the punishments of the sword, that ye may know *there* is a judgment.

20 THEN answered Zo'phar the Na'a-math-ite, and said,

2 Therefore do my thoughts cause me to answer, and for *this* I make haste.

3 I have heard the check of my reproach, and the spirit of my understanding causeth me to answer.

4 Knowest thou *not* this of old, since man was placed upon earth,

5 That the triumphing of the wicked *is* short, and the joy of the hypocrite *but* for a moment?

6 Though his excellency mount up to the heavens, and his head reach unto the clouds;

7 *Yet* he shall perish for ever like his own dung: they which have seen him shall say, Where *is* he?

8 He shall fly away as a dream, and shall not be found: yea, he shall be chased away as a vision of the night.

9 The eye also *which* saw him shall *see him* no more; neither shall his place any more behold him.

10 His children shall seek to please the poor, and his hands shall restore their goods.

11 His bones are full *of the sin* of his youth, which shall lie down with him in the dust.

12 Though wickedness be sweet in his mouth, *though* he hide it under his tongue;

13 *Though* he spare it, and forsake it not; but keep it still within his mouth:

14 *Yet* his meat in his bowels is turned, *it is* the gall of asps within him.

15 He hath swallowed down riches, and he

shall vomit them up again: God shall cast them out of his belly.

16 He shall suck the poison of asps: the viper's tongue shall slay him.

17 He shall not see the rivers, the floods, the brooks of honey and butter.

18 That which he laboured for shall he restore, and shall not swallow *it* down: according to *his* substance *shall* the restitution *be*, and he shall not rejoice *therein*.

19 Because he hath oppressed *and* hath forsaken the poor; *because* he hath violently taken away an house which he builded not;

20 Surely he shall not feel quietness in his belly, he shall not save of that which he desired.

21 There shall none of his meat be left; therefore shall no man look for his goods.

22 In the fulness of his sufficiency he shall be in straits: every hand of the wicked shall come upon him.

23 *When* he is about to fill his belly, God shall cast the fury of his wrath upon him, and shall rain *it* upon him while he is eating.

24 He shall flee from the iron weapon, *and* the bow of steel shall strike him through.

25 It is drawn, and cometh out of the body; yea, the glittering sword cometh out of his gall: terrors *are* upon him.

26 All darkness *shall be* hid in his secret places: a fire not blown shall consume him; it shall go ill with him that is left in his tabernacle.

27 The heaven shall reveal his iniquity; and the earth shall rise up against him.

28 The increase of his house shall depart, *and his goods* shall flow away in the day of his wrath.

29 This *is* the portion of a wicked man from God, and the heritage appointed unto him by God.

21 BUT Job answered and said,
2 Hear diligently my speech, and let this be your consolations.

3 Suffer me that I may speak; and after that I have spoken, mock on.

4 As for me, *is* my complaint to man? and if *it were so*, why should not my spirit be troubled?

5 Mark me, and be astonished, and lay *your* hand upon *your* mouth.

6 Even when I remember I am afraid, and trembling taketh hold on my flesh.

7 Wherefore do the wicked live, become old, yea, are mighty in power?

8 Their seed is established in their sight with them, and their offspring before their eyes.

9 Their houses *are* safe from fear, neither *is* the rod of God upon them.

10 Their bull gendereth, and faileth not; their cow calveth, and casteth not her calf.

11 They send forth their little ones like a flock, and their children dance.

12 They take the timbrel and harp, and rejoice at the sound of the organ.

13 They spend their days in wealth, and in a moment go down to the grave.

14 Therefore they say unto God, Depart from us; for we desire not the knowledge of thy ways.

15 What *is* the Almighty, that we should serve him? and what profit should we have, if we pray unto him?

16 Lo, their good *is* not in their hand: the counsel of the wicked is far from me.

17 How oft is the candle of the wicked put out! and how oft cometh their destruction upon them! *God* distributeth sorrows in his anger.

18 They are as stubble before the wind, and as chaff that the storm carrieth away.

19 God layeth up his iniquity for his children: he rewardeth him, and he shall know *it*.

20 His eyes shall see his destruction, and he shall drink of the wrath of the Almighty.

21 For what pleasure *hath* he in his house after him, when the number of his months is cut off in the midst?

22 Shall *any* teach God knowledge? seeing he judgeth those that are high.

23 One dieth in his full strength, being wholly at ease and quiet.

24 His breasts are full of milk, and his bones are moistened with marrow.

25 And another dieth in the bitterness of his soul, and never eateth with pleasure.

26 They shall lie down alike in the dust, and the worms shall cover them.

27 Behold, I know your thoughts, and the devices *which* ye wrongfully imagine against me.

28 For ye say, Where *is* the house of the prince? and where *are* the dwelling places of the wicked?

29 Have ye not asked them that go by the way? and do ye not know their tokens,

30 That the wicked is reserved to the day of destruction? they shall be brought forth to the day of wrath.

31 Who shall declare his way to his face? and who shall repay him *what* he hath done?

32 Yet shall he be brought to the grave, and shall remain in the tomb.

33 The clods of the valley shall be sweet unto him, and every man shall draw after him, as *there are* innumerable before him.

34 How then comfort ye me in vain, seeing in your answers there remaineth falsehood?

22 THEN El'i-phaz the Te'man-ite answered and said,
2 Can a man be profitable unto God, as he that is wise may be profitable unto himself?

3 *Is it* any pleasure to the Almighty, that thou are righteous? or *is it* gain *to him*, that thou makest thy ways perfect?

4 Will he reprove thee for fear of thee? will he enter with thee into judgment?

5 *Is* not thy wickedness great? and thine iniquities infinite?

6 For thou hast taken a pledge from thy brother for nought, and stripped the naked of their clothing.

7 Thou hast not given water to the weary to drink, and thou hast withholden bread from the hungry.

8 But *as for* the mighty man, he had the earth; and the honourable man dwelt in it.

9 Thou hast sent widows away empty, and the arms of the fatherless have been broken.

10 Therefore snares *are* round about thee, and sudden fear troubleth thee;

11 Or darkness, *that* thou canst not see; and abundance of waters cover thee.

12 *Is* not God in the height of heaven? and behold the height of the stars, how high they are!

13 And thou sayest, How doth God know? can he judge through the dark cloud?

14 Thick clouds *are* a covering to him, that he seeth not; and he walketh in the circuit of heaven.

15 Hast thou marked the old way which wicked men have trodden?

16 Which were cut down out of time, whose foundation was overflown with a flood:

17 Which said unto God, Depart from us: and what can the Almighty do for them?

18 Yet he filled their houses with good *things:* but the counsel of the wicked is far from me.

19 The righteous see *it,* and are glad: and the innocent laugh them to scorn.

20 Whereas our substance is not cut down, but the remnant of them the fire consumeth.

21 Acquaint now thyself with him, and be at peace: thereby good shall come unto thee.

22 Receive, I pray thee, the law from his mouth, and lay up his words in thine heart.

23 If thou return to the Almighty, thou shalt be built up, thou shalt put away iniquity far from thy tabernacles.

24 Then shalt thou lay up gold as dust, and the gold of O'phir as the stones of the brooks.

25 Yea, the Almighty shall be thy defence, and thou shalt have plenty of silver.

26 For then shalt thou have thy delight in the Almighty, and shalt lift up thy face unto God.

27 Thou shalt make thy prayer unto him, and he shall hear thee, and thou shalt pay thy vows.

28 Thou shalt also decree a thing, and it shall be established unto thee: and the light shall shine upon thy ways.

29 When *men* are cast down, then thou shalt say, *There is* lifting up; and he shall save the humble person.

30 He shall deliver the island of the innocent: and it is delivered by the pureness of thine hands.

23 THEN Job answered and said,
2 Even to day *is* my complaint bitter: my stroke is heavier than my groaning.

3 Oh that I knew where I might find him! *that* I might come *even* to his seat!

4 I would order *my* cause before him, and fill my mouth with arguments.

5 I would know the words *which* he would answer me, and understand what he would say unto me.

6 Will he plead against me with *his* great power? No; but he would put *strength* in me.

7 There the righteous might dispute with him; so should I be delivered for ever from my judge.

8 Behold, I go forward, but he *is* not *there:* and backward, but I cannot perceive him:

9 On the left hand, where he doth work, but I cannot behold *him:* he hideth himself on the right hand, that I cannot see *him:*

10 But he knoweth the way that I take: *when* he hath tried me, I shall come forth as gold.

11 My foot hath held his steps, his way have I kept, and not declined.

12 Neither have I gone back from the commandment of his lips; I have esteemed the words of his mouth more than my necessary food.

13 But he *is* in one *mind,* and who can turn him? and *what* his soul desireth, even *that* he doeth.

14 For he performeth the thing that is appointed for me: and many such *things are* with him.

15 Therefore am I troubled at his presence: when I consider, I am afraid of him.

16 For God maketh my heart soft and the Almighty troubleth me:

17 Because I was not cut off before the darkness, *neither* hath he covered the darkness from my face.

24 WHY, seeing times are not hidden from the Almighty, do they that know him not see his days?

2 *Some* remove the landmarks; they violently take away flocks, and feed *thereof.*

3 They drive away the ass of the fatherless, they take the widow's ox for a pledge.

4 They turn the needy out of the way: the poor of the earth hide themselves together.

5 Behold, *as* wild asses in the desert, go they forth to their work; rising betimes for a prey: the wilderness *yieldeth* food for them *and* for *their* children.

6 They reap *every one* his corn in the field: and they gather the vintage of the wicked.

7 They cause the naked to lodge without clothing, that *they have* no covering in the cold.

8 They are wet with the showers of the mountains, and embrace the rock for want of a shelter.

9 They pluck the fatherless from the breast, and take a pledge of the poor.

10 They cause *him* to go naked without clothing, and they take away the sheaf *from* the hungry;

11 *Which* make oil within their walls, *and* tread *their* winepresses, and suffer thirst.

12 Men groan from out of the city, and the soul of the wounded crieth out: yet God layeth not folly *to* them.

13 They are of those that rebel against the light; they know not the ways thereof, nor abide in the paths thereof.

14 The murderer rising with the light killeth the poor and needy, and in the night is as a thief.

15 The eye also of the adulterer waiteth for the twilight, saying, No eye shall see me: and disguiseth *his* face.

16 In the dark they dig through houses, *which* they had marked for themselves in the daytime: they know not the light.

17 For the morning *is* to them even as the shadow of death: if *one* know *them, they are in* the terrors of the shadow of death.

18 He *is* swift as the waters; their portion is cursed in the earth: he beholdeth not the way of the vineyards.

19 Drought and heat consume the snow waters: *so doth* the grave *those which* have sinned.

20 The womb shall forget him; the worm shall feed sweetly on him; he shall be no more remembered; and wickedness shall be broken as a tree.

21 He evil entreateth the barren *that* beareth not: and doeth not good to the widow.

22 He draweth also the mighty with his power: he riseth up, and no *man* is sure of life.

23 *Though* it be given him *to be* in safety, whereon he resteth; yet his eyes *are* upon their ways.

24 They are exalted for a little while, but are gone and brought low, they are taken out of the way as all *other,* and cut off as the tops of the ears of corn.

25 And if *it* be not *so* now, who will make me a liar, and make my speech nothing worth?

25 THEN answered Bil'dad the Shu'hite, and said,
2 Dominion and fear *are* with him, he maketh peace in his high places.

3 Is there any number of his armies? and upon whom doth not his light arise?

4 How then can man be justified with God? or how can he be clean *that is* born of a woman?

5 Behold even to the moon, and it shineth not; yea, the stars are not pure in his sight.

6 How much less man, *that is* a worm? and the son of man, *which is* a worm?

26

BUT Job answered and said,

2 How hast thou helped *him that is* without power? *how* savest thou the arm *that hath* no strength?

3 How hast thou counselled *him that hath* no wisdom? and *how* hast thou plentifully declared the thing as it is?

4 To whom hast thou uttered words? and whose spirit came from thee?

5 Dead *things* are formed from under the waters, and the inhabitants thereof.

6 Hell *is* naked before him, and destruction hath no covering.

7 He stretcheth out the north over the empty place, *and* hangeth the earth upon nothing.

8 He bindeth up the waters in his thick clouds; and the cloud is not rent under them.

9 He holdeth back the face of his throne, *and* spreadeth his cloud upon it.

10 He hath compassed the waters with bounds, until the day and night come to an end.

11 The pillars of heaven tremble and are astonished at his reproof.

12 He divideth the sea with his power, and by his understanding he smiteth through the proud.

13 By his spirit he hath garnished the heavens; his hand hath formed the crooked serpent.

14 Lo, these *are* parts of his ways: but how little a portion is heard of him? but the thunder of his power who can understand?

27

MOREOVER Job continued his parable, and said,

2 *As* God liveth, *who* hath taken away my judgment; and the Almighty, *who* hath vexed my soul;

3 All the while my breath *is* in me, and the spirit of God *is* in my nostrils;

4 My lips shall not speak wickedness, nor my tongue utter deceit.

5 God forbid that I should justify you: till I die I will not remove mine integrity from me.

6 My righteousness I hold fast, and will not let it go: my heart shall not reproach *me* so long as I live.

7 Let mine enemy be as the wicked, and he that riseth up against me as the unrighteous.

8 For what *is* the hope of the hypocrite, though he hath gained, when God taketh away his soul?

9 Will God hear his cry when trouble cometh upon him?

10 Will he delight himself in the Almighty? will he always call upon God?

11 I will teach you by the hand of God: *that* which *is* with the Almighty will I not conceal.

12 Behold, all ye yourselves have seen *it*; why then are ye thus altogether vain?

13 This *is* the portion of a wicked man with God, and the heritage of oppressors, *which* they shall receive of the Almighty.

14 If his children be multiplied, *it is* for the sword: and his offspring shall not be satisfied with bread.

15 Those that remain of him shall be buried in death: and his widows shall not weep.

16 Though he heap up silver as the dust, and prepare raiment as the clay;

17 He may prepare *it*, but the just shall put *it* on, and the innocent shall divide the silver.

18 He buildeth his house as a moth, and as a booth *that* the keeper maketh.

19 The rich man shall lie down, but he shall not be gathered: he openeth his eyes, and he *is* not.

20 Terrors take hold on him as waters, a tempest stealeth him away in the night.

21 The east wind carrieth him away, and he departeth: and as a storm hurleth him out of his place.

22 For *God* shall cast upon him, and not spare: he would fain flee out of his hand.

23 *Men* shall clap their hands at him, and shall hiss him out of his place.

28

SURELY there is a vein for the silver, and a place for gold *where* they fine *it*.

2 Iron is taken out of the earth, and brass *is* molten *out of* the stone.

3 He setteth an end to darkness, and searcheth out all perfection: the stones of darkness, and the shadow of death.

4 The flood breaketh out from the inhabitant; *even the waters* forgotten of the foot: they are dried up, they are gone away from men.

5 *As for* the earth, out of it cometh bread: and under it is turned up as it were fire.

6 The stones of it *are* the place of sapphires: and it hath dust of gold.

7 *There is* a path which no fowl knoweth, and which the vulture's eye hath not seen:

8 The lion's whelps have not trodden it, nor the fierce lion passed by it.

9 He putteth forth his hand upon the rock; he overturneth the mountains by the roots.

10 He cutteth out rivers among the rocks; and his eye seeth every precious thing.

11 He bindeth the floods from overflowing; and *the thing that is* hid bringeth he forth to light.

12 But where shall wisdom be found? and where *is* the place of understanding?

13 Man knoweth not the price thereof; neither is it found in the land of the living.

14 The depth saith, It *is* not in me: and the sea saith, *It is* not with me.

15 It cannot be gotten for gold, neither shall silver be weighed *for* the price thereof.

16 It cannot be valued with the gold of O'-phir, with the precious onyx, or the sapphire.

17 The gold and the crystal cannot equal it: and the exchange of it *shall not be for* jewels of fine gold.

18 No mention shall be made of coral, or of pearls: for the price of wisdom *is* above rubies.

19 The topaz of E-thi-o'pi-a shall not equal it, neither shall it be valued with pure gold.

20 Whence then cometh wisdom? and where *is* the place of understanding?

21 Seeing it is hid from the eyes of all living, and kept close from the fowls of the air.

22 Destruction and death say, We have heard the fame thereof with our ears.

23 God understandeth the way thereof, and he knoweth the place thereof.

24 For he looketh to the ends of the earth, *and* seeth under the whole heaven;

25 To make the weight for the winds; and he weigheth the waters by measure.

26 When he made a decree for the rain, and a way for the lightning of the thunder:

27 Then did he see it, and declare it; he prepared it, yea, and searched it out.

28 And unto man he said, Behold, the fear of the LORD, that *is* wisdom; and to depart from evil *is* understanding.

29 MOREOVER Job continued his parable, and said,

2 Oh that I were as *in* months past, as *in* the days *when* God preserved me;

3 When his candle shined upon my head, *and when* by his light I walked *through* darkness;

4 As I was in the days of my youth, when the secret of God *was* upon my tabernacle;

5 When the Almighty *was* yet with me, *when* my children *were* about me;

6 When I washed my steps with butter, and the rock poured me out rivers of oil;

7 When I went out to the gate through the city, *when* I prepared my seat in the street!

8 The young men saw me, and hid themselves: and the aged arose, *and* stood up.

9 The princes refrained talking, and laid *their* hand on their mouth.

10 The nobles held their peace, and their tongue cleaved to the roof of their mouth.

11 When the ear heard *me*, then it blessed me; and when the eye saw *me*, it gave witness to me:

12 Because I delivered the poor that cried, and the fatherless, and *him that had* none to help him.

13 The blessing of him that was ready to perish came upon me: and I caused the widow's heart to sing for joy.

14 I put on righteousness, and it clothed me: my judgment *was* as a robe and a diadem.

15 I was eyes to the blind, and feet *was* I to the lame.

16 I *was* a father to the poor: and the cause *which* I knew not I searched out.

17 And I brake the jaws of the wicked, and plucked the spoil out of his teeth.

18 Then I said, I shall die in my nest, and I shall multiply *my* days as the sand.

19 My root *was* spread out by the waters, and the dew lay all night upon my branch.

20 My glory *was* fresh in me, and my bow was renewed in my hand.

21 Unto me *men* gave ear, and waited, and kept silence at my counsel.

22 After my words they spake not again; and my speech dropped upon them.

23 And they waited for me as for the rain; and they opened their mouth wide *as* for the latter rain.

24 *If* I laughed on them, they believed *it* not; and the light of my countenance they cast not down.

25 I chose out their way, and sat chief, and dwelt as a king in the army, as one *that* comforteth the mourners.

30 BUT now *they that are* younger than I have me in derision, whose fathers I would have disdained to have set with the dogs of my flock.

2 Yea, whereto *might* the strength of their hands *profit* me, in whom old age was perished?

3 For want and famine *they were* solitary; fleeing into the wilderness in former time desolate and waste.

4 Who cut up mallows by the bushes, and juniper roots *for* their meat.

5 They were driven forth from among *men*, (they cried after them as *after* a thief;)

6 To dwell in the cliffs of the valleys, *in* caves of the earth, and *in* the rocks.

7 Among the bushes they brayed; under the nettles they were gathered together.

8 *They were* children of fools, yea, children of base men: they were viler than the earth.

9 And now am I their song, yea, I am their byword.

10 They abhor me, they flee far from me, and spare not to spit in my face.

11 Because he hath loosed my cord, and afflicted me, they have also let loose the bridle before me.

12 Upon *my* right *hand* rise the youth; they push away my feet, and they raise up against me the ways of their destruction.

13 They mar my path, they set forward my calamity, they have no helper.

14 They came *upon me* as a wide breaking in *of waters*: in the desolation they rolled themselves *upon me*.

15 Terrors are turned upon me: they pursue my soul as the wind: and my welfare passeth away as a cloud.

16 And now my soul is poured out upon me; the days of affliction have taken hold upon me.

17 My bones are pierced in me in the night season: and my sinews take no rest.

18 By the great force *of my disease* is my garment changed: it bindeth me about as the collar of my coat.

19 He hath cast me into the mire, and I am become like dust and ashes.

20 I cry unto thee, and thou dost not hear me: I stand up, and thou regardest me *not*.

21 Thou art become cruel to me: with thy strong hand thou opposest thyself against me.

22 Thou liftest me up to the wind; thou causest me to ride *upon it*, and dissolvest my substance.

23 For I know *that* thou wilt bring me *to* death, and *to* the house appointed for all living.

24 Howbeit he will not stretch out *his* hand to the grave, though they cry in his destruction.

25 Did not I weep for him that was in trouble? was *not* my soul grieved for the poor?

26 When I looked for good, then evil came *unto me*: and when I waited for light, there came darkness.

27 My bowels boiled, and rested not: the days of affliction prevented me.

28 I went mourning without the sun: I stood up, *and* I cried in the congregation.

29 I am a brother to dragons, and a companion to owls.

30 My skin is black upon me, and my bones are burned with heat.

31 My harp also is *turned* to mourning, and my organ into the voice of them that weep.

31 I MADE a covenant with mine eyes; why then should I think upon a maid?

2 For what portion of God *is there* from above? and *what* inheritance of the Almighty from on high?

3 *Is* not destruction to the wicked? and a strange *punishment* to the workers of iniquity?

4 Doth not he see my ways, and count all my steps?

5 If I have walked with vanity, or if my foot hath hasted to deceit;

6 Let me be weighed in an even balance, that God may know mine integrity.

7 If my step hath turned out of the way, and mine heart walked after mine eyes, and if any blot hath cleaved to mine hands;

8 *Then* let me sow, and let another eat; yea, let my offspring be rooted out.

9 If mine heart have been deceived by a woman, or *if* I have laid wait at my neighbour's door;

10 *Then* let my wife grind unto another, and let others bow down upon her.

11 For this *is* an heinous crime; yea, it *is* an iniquity *to be punished by* the judges.

12 For it *is* a fire *that* consumeth to destruction, and would root out all mine increase.

13 If I did despise the cause of my manservant or of my maidservant, when they contended with me;

14 What then shall I do when God riseth up? and when he visiteth, what shall I answer him?

15 Did not he that made me in the womb make him? and did not one fashion us in the womb?

16 If I have withheld the poor from *their* desire, or have caused the eyes of the widow to fail;

17 Or have eaten my morsel myself alone, and the fatherless hath not eaten thereof;

18 (For from my youth he was brought up with me, as *with* a father, and I have guided her from my mother's womb;)

19 If I have seen any perish for want of clothing, or any poor without covering;

20 If his loins have not blessed me, and *if* he were *not* warmed with the fleece of my sheep;

21 If I have lifted up my hand against the fatherless, when I saw my help in the gate:

22 *Then* let mine arm fall from my shoulder blade, and mine arm be broken from the bone.

23 For destruction *from* God *was* a terror to me, and by reason of his highness I could not endure.

24 If I have made gold my hope, or have said to the fine gold, *Thou art* my confidence;

25 If I rejoiced because my wealth *was* great, and because mine hand had gotten much;

26 If I beheld the sun when it shined, or the moon walking *in* brightness;

27 And my heart hath been secretly enticed, or my mouth hath kissed my hand:

28 This also *were* an iniquity *to be punished by* the judge: for I should have denied the God *that is* above.

29 If I rejoiced at the destruction of him that hated me, or lifted up myself when evil found him:

30 Neither have I suffered my mouth to sin by wishing a curse to his soul.

31 If the men of my tabernacle said not, Oh that we had of his flesh! we cannot be satisfied.

32 The stranger did not lodge in the street: *but* I opened my doors to the traveller.

33 If I covered my transgressions as Ad'am, by hiding mine iniquity in my bosom:

34 Did I fear a great multitude, or did the contempt of families terrify me, that I kept silence, *and* went not out of the door?

35 Oh that one would hear me! behold, my desire *is, that* the Almighty would answer me, and *that* mine adversary had written a book.

36 Surely I would take it upon my shoulder, *and* bind it *as* a crown to me.

37 I would declare unto him the number of my steps; as a prince would I go near unto him.

38 If my land cry against me, or that the furrows likewise thereof complain;

39 If I have eaten the fruits thereof without money, or have caused the owners therof to lose their life:

40 Let thistles grow instead of wheat, and cockle instead of barley. The words of Job are ended.

32 SO these three men ceased to answer Job, because he *was* righteous in his own eyes.

2 Then was kindled the wrath of E-li'hu the son of Bar'a-chel the Bu'zite, of the kindred of Ram: against Job was his wrath kindled, because he justified himself rather than God.

3 Also against his three friends was his wrath kindled, because they had found no answer, and *yet* had condemned Job.

4 Now E-li'hu had waited till Job had spoken, because they *were* elder than he.

5 When E-li'hu saw that *there was* no answer in the mouth of *these* three men, then his wrath was kindled.

6 And E-li'hu the son of Bar'a-chel the Bu'zite answered and said, I *am* young, and ye *are* very old; wherefore I was afraid, and durst not shew you mine opinion.

7 I said, Days should speak, and multitude of years should teach wisdom.

8 But *there is* a spirit in man: and the inspiration of the Almighty giveth them understanding.

9 Great men are not *always* wise: neither do the aged understand judgment.

10 Therefore I said, Hearken to me; I also will shew mine opinion.

11 Behold, I waited for your words; I gave ear to your reasons, whilst ye searched out what to say.

12 Yea, I attended unto you, and, behold, *there was* none of you that convinced Job, *or* that answered his words:

13 Lest ye should say, We have found out wisdom: God thrusteth him down, not man.

14 Now he hath not directed *his* words against me: neither will I answer him with your speeches.

15 They were amazed, they answered no more: they left off speaking.

16 When I had waited, (for they spake not, but stood still, *and* answered no more;)

17 *I said*, I will answer also my part, I also will shew mine opinion.

18 For I am full of matter, the spirit within me constraineth me.

19 Behold, my belly *is* as wine *which* hath no vent; it is ready to burst like new bottles.

20 I will speak, that I may be refreshed: I will open my lips and answer.

21 Let me not, I pray you, accept any man's person, neither let me give flattering titles unto man.

22 For I know not to give flattering titles; *in* so doing my maker would soon take me away.

33 WHEREFORE, Job, I pray thee, hear my speeches, and hearken to all my words.

2 Behold, now I have opened my mouth, my tongue hath spoken in my mouth.

3 My words *shall be of* the uprightness of my heart: and my lips shall utter knowledge clearly.

4 The spirit of God hath made me, and the breath of the Almighty hath given me life.

5 If thou canst answer me, set *thy words* in order before me, stand up.

6 Behold, I *am* according to thy wish in God's stead: I also am formed out of the clay.

7 Behold, my terror shall not make thee afraid, neither shall my hand be heavy upon thee.

8 Surely thou hast spoken in mine hearing, and I have heard the voice of *thy* words, *saying,*

9 I am clean without transgression, I *am* innocent; neither *is there* iniquity in me.

10 Behold, he findeth occasions against me, he counteth me for his enemy.

11 He putteth my feet in the stocks, he marketh all my paths.

12 Behold, in this thou art not just: I will answer thee, that God is greater than man.

13 Why dost thou strive against him? for he giveth not account of any of his matters.

14 For God speaketh once, yea twice, yet man perceiveth it not.

15 In a dream, in a vision of the night, when deep sleep falleth upon men, in slumberings upon the bed;

16 Then he openeth the ears of men, and sealeth their instruction,

17 That he may withdraw man from his purpose, and hide pride from man.

18 He keepeth back his soul from the pit, and his life from perishing by the sword.

19 He is chastened also with pain upon his bed, and the multitude of his bones with strong pain:

20 So that his life abhorreth bread, and his soul dainty meat.

21 His flesh is consumed away, that it cannnot be seen; and his bones that were not seen stick out.

22 Yea, his soul draweth near unto the grave, and his life to the destroyers.

23 If there be a messenger with him, an interpreter, one among a thousand, to shew unto man his uprightness:

24 Then he is gracious unto him, and saith, Deliver him from going down to the pit: I have found a ransom.

25 His flesh shall be fresher than a child's: he shall return to the days of his youth:

26 He shall pray unto God, and he will be favourable unto him: and he shall see his face with joy: for he will render unto man his righteousness.

27 He looketh upon men, and if any say, I have sinned, and perverted that which was right, and it profited me not:

28 He will deliver his soul from going into the pit, and his life shall see the light.

29 Lo, all these things worketh God oftentimes with man,

30 To bring back his soul from the pit, to be enlightened with the light of the living.

31 Mark well, O Job, hearken unto me: hold thy peace, and I will speak.

32 If thou hast any thing to say, answer me: speak, for I desire to justify thee.

33 If not, hearken unto me: hold thy peace, and I shall teach thee wisdom.

34 FURTHERMORE E-li′hu answered and said,

2 Hear my words, O ye wise men; and give ear unto me, ye that have knowledge.

3 For the ear trieth words, as the mouth tasteth meat.

4 Let us choose to us judgment: let us know among ourselves what is good.

5 For Job hath said, I am righteous: and God hath taken away my judgment.

6 Should I lie against my right? my wound is incurable without transgression.

7 What man is like Job, who drinketh up scorning like water?

8 Which goeth in company with the workers of iniquity, and walketh with wicked men.

9 For he hath said, It profiteth a man nothing that he should delight himself with God.

10 Therefore hearken unto me, ye men of understanding: far be it from God, that he should do wickedness; and from the Almighty, that he should commit iniquity.

11 For the work of a man shall he render unto him, and cause every man to find according to his ways.

12 Yea, surely God will not do wickedly, neither will the Almighty pervert judgment.

13 Who hath given him a charge over the earth? or who hath disposed the whole world?

14 If he set his heart upon man, if he gather unto himself his spirit and his breath;

15 All flesh shall perish together, and man shall turn again unto dust.

16 If now thou hast understanding, hear this: hearken to the voice of my words.

17 Shall even he that hateth right govern? and wilt thou condemn him that is most just?

18 Is it fit to say to a king, Thou art wicked? and to princes, Ye are ungodly?

19 How much less to him that accepteth not the persons of princes, nor regardeth the rich more than the poor? for they all are the work of his hands.

20 In a moment shall they die, and the people shall be troubled at midnight, and pass away: and the mighty shall be taken away without hand.

21 For his eyes are upon the ways of man, and he seeth all his goings.

22 There is no darkness, nor shadow of death, where the workers of iniquity may hide themselves.

23 For he will not lay upon man more than right; that he should enter into judgment with God.

24 He shall break in pieces mighty men without number, and set others in their stead.

25 Therefore he knoweth their works, and he overturneth them in the night, so that they are destroyed.

26 He striketh them as wicked men in the open sight of others;

27 Because they turned back from him, and would not consider any of his ways:

28 So that they cause the cry of the poor to come unto him, and he heareth the cry of the afflicted.

29 When he giveth quietness, who then can make trouble? and when he hideth his face, who then can behold him? whether it be done against a nation, or against a man only:

30 That the hypocrite reign not, lest the people be ensnared.

31 Surely it is meet to be said unto God, I have borne chastisement, I will not offend any more:

32 That which I see not teach thou me: if I have done iniquity, I will do no more.

33 Should it be according to thy mind? he will recompense it, whether thou refuse, or whether thou choose; and not I: therefore speak what thou knowest.

34 Let men of understanding tell me, and let a wise man hearken unto me.

35 Job hath spoken without knowledge, and his words were without wisdom.

36 My desire is that Job may be tried unto the end because of his answers for wicked men.

37 For he addeth rebellion unto his sin, he clappeth his hands among us, and multiplieth his words against God.

35 E-LI′HU spake moreover, and said,

2 Thinkest thou this to be right, that thou saidst, My righteousness is more than God's?

3 For thou saidst, What advantage will it be unto thee? and, What profit shall I have, if I be cleansed from my sin?

4 I will answer thee, and thy companions with thee.

5 Look unto the heavens, and see; and behold the clouds *which* are higher than thou.

6 If thou sinnest, what doest thou against him? or *if* thy transgressions be multiplied, what doest thou unto him?

7 If thou be righteous, what givest thou him? or what receiveth he of thine hand?

8 Thy wickedness *may hurt* a man as thou *art;* and thy righteousness *may profit* the son of man.

9 By reason of the multitude of oppressions they make *the oppressed* to cry: they cry out by reason of the arm of the mighty.

10 But none saith, Where *is* God my maker, who giveth songs in the night;

11 Who teacheth us more than the beasts of the earth, and maketh us wiser than the fowls of heaven?

12 There they cry, but none giveth answer, because of the pride of evil men.

13 Surely God will not hear vanity, neither will the Almighty regard it.

14 Although thou sayest thou shalt not see him, *yet* judgment *is* before him; therefore trust thou in him.

15 But now, because *it is* not *so,* he hath visited in his anger; yet he knoweth *it* not in great extremity:

16 Therefore doth Job open his mouth in vain; he multiplieth words without knowledge.

36 E-LI'HU also proceeded, and said,
2 Suffer me a little, and I will shew thee that *I have* yet to speak on God's behalf.

3 I will fetch my knowledge from afar, and will ascribe righteousness to my Maker.

4 For truly my words *shall* not *be* false: he that is perfect in knowledge *is* with thee.

5 Behold, God *is* mighty, and despiseth not *any: he is* mighty in strength *and* wisdom.

6 He preserveth not the life of the wicked: but giveth right to the poor.

7 He withdraweth not his eyes from the righteous: but with kings *are they* on the throne; yea, he doth establish them for ever, and they are exalted.

8 And if *they be* bound in fetters, *and* be holden in cords of affliction;

9 Then he sheweth them their work, and their transgressions that they have exceeded.

10 He openeth also their ear to discipline, and commandeth that they return from iniquity.

11 If they obey and serve *him,* they shall spend their days in prosperity, and their years in pleasures.

12 But if they obey not, they shall perish by the sword, and they shall die without knowledge.

13 But the hypocrites in heart heap up wrath: they cry not when he bindeth them.

14 They die in youth, and their life *is* among the unclean.

15 He delivereth the poor in his affliction, and openeth their ears in oppression.

16 Even so would he have removed thee out of the strait *into* a broad place, where *there is* no straitness; and that which should be set on thy table *should* be full of fatness.

17 But thou hast fulfilled the judgment of the wicked: judgment and justice take hold *on thee.*

18 Because *there is* wrath, *beware* lest he take thee away with *his* stroke: then a great ransom cannot deliver thee.

19 Will he esteem thy riches? *no,* not gold, nor all the forces of strength.

20 Desire not the night, when people are cut off in their place.

21 Take heed, regard not iniquity: for this hast thou chosen rather than affliction.

22 Behold, God exalteth by his power: who teacheth like him?

23 Who hath enjoined him his way? or who can say, Thou hast wrought iniquity?

24 Remember that thou magnify his work, which men behold.

25 Every man may see it; man may behold *it* afar off.

26 Behold, God *is* great, and we know *him* not, neither can the number of his years be searched out.

27 For he maketh small the drops of water: they pour down rain according to the vapour thereof:

28 Which the clouds do drop *and* distil upon man abundantly.

29 Also can *any* understand the spreadings of the clouds, *or* the noise of his tabernacle?

30 Behold, he spreadeth his light upon it, and covereth the bottom of the sea.

31 For by them judgeth he the people; he giveth meat in abundance.

32 With clouds he covereth the light; and commandeth it *not to shine* by *the* cloud that cometh betwixt.

33 The noise thereof sheweth concerning it, the cattle also concerning the vapour.

37 AT this also my heart trembleth, and is moved out of his place.

2 Hear attentively the noise of his voice, and the sound *that* goeth out of his mouth.

3 He directeth it under the whole heaven, and his lightning unto the ends of the earth.

4 After it a voice roareth: he thundereth with the voice of his excellency; and he will not stay them when his voice is heard.

5 God thundereth marvellously with his voice; great things doeth he, which we cannot comprehend.

6 For he saith to the snow, Be thou *on* the earth; likewise to the small rain, and to the great rain of his strength.

7 He sealeth up the hand of every man; that all men may know his work.

8 Then the beasts go into dens, and remain in their places.

9 Out of the south cometh the whirlwind: and cold out of the north.

10 By the breath of God frost is given: and the breadth of the waters is straitened.

11 Also by watering he wearieth the thick cloud: he scattereth his bright cloud:

12 And it is turned round about by his counsels: that they may do whatsoever he commandeth them upon the face of the world in the earth.

13 He causeth it to come, whether for correction, or for his land, or for mercy.

14 Hearken unto this, O Job: stand still, and consider the wondrous works of God.

15 Dost thou know when God disposed them, and caused the light of his cloud to shine?

16 Dost thou know the balancings of the clouds, the wondrous works of him which is perfect in knowledge?

17 How thy garments *are* warm, when he quieteth the earth by the south *wind?*

18 Hast thou with him spread out the sky, *which is* strong, *and* as a molten looking glass?

19 Teach us what we shall say unto him; *for*

we cannot order *our speech* by reason of darkness.

20 Shall it be told him that I speak? if a man speak, surely he shall be swallowed up.

21 And now *men* see not the bright light which *is* in the clouds: but the wind passeth, and cleanseth them.

22 Fair weather cometh out of the north: with God *is* terrible majesty.

23 *Touching* the Almighty, we cannot find him out: *he is* excellent in power, and in judgment, and in plenty of justice: he will not afflict.

24 Men do therefore fear him: he respecteth not any *that are* wise of heart.

38 THEN the LORD answered Job out of the whirlwind, and said,

2 Who *is* this that darkeneth counsel by words without knowledge?

3 Gird up now thy loins like a man; for I will demand of thee, and answer thou me.

4 Where wast thou when I laid the foundations of the earth? declare, if thou hast understanding.

5 Who hath laid the measures thereof, if thou knowest? or who hath stretched the line upon it?

6 Whereupon are the foundations thereof fastened? or who laid the corner stone thereof;

7 When the morning stars sang together, and all the sons of God shouted for joy?

8 Or *who* shut up the sea with doors, when it brake forth, *as if* it had issued out of the womb?

9 When I made the cloud the garment thereof, and thick darkness a swaddlingband for it,

10 And brake up for it my decreed *place*, and set bars and doors,

11 And said, Hitherto shalt thou come, but no further: and here shall thy proud waves be stayed?

12 Hast thou commanded the morning since thy days; *and* caused the dayspring to know his place;

13 That it might take hold of the ends of the earth, that the wicked might be shaken out of it?

14 It is turned as clay *to* the seal; and they stand as a garment.

15 And from the wicked their light is withholden, and the high arm shall be broken.

16 Hast thou entered into the springs of the sea? or hast thou walked in the search of the depth?

17 Have the gates of death been opened unto thee? or hast thou seen the doors of the shadow of death?

18 Hast thou perceived the breadth of the earth? declare if thou knowest it all.

19 Where *is* the way *where* light dwelleth? and *as for* darkness, where *is* the place thereof,

20 That thou shouldest take it to the bound thereof, and that thou shouldest know the paths *to* the house thereof?

21 Knowest thou *it*, because thou wast then born? or *because* the number of thy days *is* great?

22 Hast thou entered into the treasures of the snow? or hast thou seen the treasures of the hail,

23 Which I have reserved against the time of trouble, against the day of battle and war?

24 By what way is the light parted, *which* scattereth the east wind upon the earth?

25 Who hath divided a watercourse for the overflowing of waters, or a way for the lightning of thunder;

26 To cause it to rain on the earth, *where* no man *is; on* the wilderness, wherein *there is* no man;

27 To satisfy the desolate and waste *ground;* and to cause the bud of the tender herb to spring forth?

28 Hath the rain a father? or who hath begotten the drops of dew?

29 Out of whose womb came the ice? and the hoary frost of heaven, who hath gendered it?

30 The waters are hid as *with* a stone, and the face of the deep is frozen.

31 Canst thou bind the sweet influences of Ple'ia-des, or loose the bands of O-ri'on?

32 Canst thou bring forth Maz'za-roth in his season? or canst thou guide Arc-tu'rus with his sons?

33 Knowest thou the ordinances of heaven? canst thou set the dominion thereof in the earth?

34 Canst thou lift up thy voice to the clouds, that abundance of waters may cover thee?

35 Canst thou send lightnings, that they may go, and say unto thee, Here we *are?*

36 Who hath put wisdom in the inward parts? or who hath given understanding to the heart?

37 Who can number the clouds in wisdom? or who can stay the bottles of heaven,

38 When the dust groweth into hardness, and the clods cleave fast together?

39 Wilt thou hunt the prey for the lion? or fill the appetite of the young lions,

40 When they couch in *their* dens, *and* abide in the covert to lie in wait?

41 Who provideth for the raven his food? when his young ones cry unto God, they wander for lack of meat.

39 KNOWEST thou the time when the wild goats of the rock bring forth? *or* canst thou mark when the hinds do calve?

2 Canst thou number the months *that* they fulfil? or knowest thou the time when they bring forth?

3 They bow themselves, they bring forth their young ones, they cast out their sorrows.

4 Their young ones are in good liking, they grow up with corn; they go forth, and return not unto them.

5 Who hath sent out the wild ass free? or who hath loosed the bands of the wild ass?

6 Whose house I have made the wilderness, and the barren land his dwellings.

7 He scorneth the multitude of the city, neither regardeth he the crying of the driver.

8 The range of the mountains *is* his pasture, and he searcheth after every green thing.

9 Will the unicorn be willing to serve thee, or abide by thy crib?

10 Canst thou bind the unicorn with his band in the furrow? or will he harrow the valleys after thee?

11 Wilt thou trust him, because his strength *is* great? or wilt thou leave thy labour to him?

12 Wilt thou believe him, that he will bring home thy seed, and gather *it into* thy barn?

13 *Gavest thou* the goodly wings unto the peacocks? or wings and feathers unto the ostrich?

14 Which leaveth her eggs in the earth, and warmeth them in dust,

15 And forgetteth that the foot may crush them, or that the wild beast may break them.

16 She is hardened against her young ones, as though *they were* not hers: her labour is in vain without fear;

17 Because God hath deprived her of wisdom, neither hath he imparted to her understanding.

18 What time she lifteth up herself on high, she scorneth the horse and his rider.

19 Hast thou given the horse strength? hast thou clothed his neck with thunder?

20 Canst thou make him afraid as a grasshopper? the glory of his nostrils *is* terrible.

21 He paweth in the valley, and rejoiceth in *his* strength: he goeth on to meet the armed men.

22 He mocketh at fear, and is not affrighted; neither turneth he back from the sword.

23 The quiver rattleth against him, the glittering spear and the shield.

24 He swalloweth the ground with fierceness and rage: neither believeth he that *it is* the sound of the trumpet.

25 He saith among the trumpets, Ha, ha; and he smelleth the battle afar off, the thunder of the captains, and the shouting.

26 Doth the hawk fly by thy wisdom, *and* stretch her wings toward the south?

27 Doth the eagle mount up at thy command, and make her nest on high?

28 She dwelleth and abideth on the rock, upon the crag of the rock, and the strong place.

29 From thence she seeketh the prey, *and* her eyes behold afar off.

30 Her young ones also suck up blood: and where the slain *are*, there *is* she.

40 MOREOVER the LORD answered Job, and said,

2 Shall he that contendeth with the Almighty instruct *him*? he that reproveth God, let him answer it.

3 ¶ Then Job answered the LORD, and said,

4 Behold, I am vile; what shall I answer thee? I will lay mine hand upon my mouth.

5 Once have I spoken; but I will not answer: yea, twice; but I will proceed no further.

6 ¶ Then answered the LORD unto Job out of the whirlwind, and said,

7 Gird up thy loins now like a man: I will demand of thee, and declare thou unto me.

8 Wilt thou also disannul my judgment? wilt thou condemn me, that thou mayest be righteous?

9 Hast thou an arm like God? or canst thou thunder with a voice like him?

10 Deck thyself now *with* majesty and excellency; and array thyself with glory and beauty.

11 Cast abroad the rage of thy wrath: and behold every one *that is* proud, and abase him.

12 Look on every one *that is* proud, *and* bring him low; and tread down the wicked in their place.

13 Hide them in the dust together; *and* bind their faces in secret.

14 Then will I also confess unto thee that thine own right hand can save thee.

15 ¶ Behold now behemoth, which I made with thee; he eateth grass as an ox.

16 Lo now, his strength *is* in his loins, and his force *is* in the navel of his belly.

17 He moveth his tail like a cedar: the sinews of his stones are wrapped together.

18 His bones *are as* strong pieces of brass; his bones *are* like bars of iron.

19 He *is* the chief of the ways of God: he that made him can make his sword to approach *unto* him.

20 Surely the mountains bring him forth food, where all the beasts of the field play.

21 He lieth under the shady trees, in the covert of the reed, and fens.

22 The shady trees cover him *with* their shadow; the willows of the brook compass him about.

23 Behold, he drinketh up a river, *and* hasteth not: he trusteth that he can draw up Jor'dan into his mouth.

24 He taketh it with his eyes: *his* nose pierceth through snares.

41 CANST thou draw out leviathan with an hook? or his tongue with a cord *which* thou lettest down?

2 Canst thou put an hook into his nose? or bore his jaw through with a thorn?

3 Will he make many supplications unto thee? will he speak soft *words* unto thee?

4 Will he make a covenant with thee? wilt thou take him for a servant for ever?

5 Wilt thou play with him as *with* a bird? or wilt thou bind him for thy maidens?

6 Shall the companions make a banquet of him? shall they part him among the merchants?

7 Canst thou fill his skin with barbed irons? or his head with fish spears?

8 Lay thine hand upon him, remember the battle, do no more.

9 Behold, the hope of him is in vain: shall not *one* be cast down even at the sight of him?

10 None *is so* fierce that dare stir him up: who then is able to stand before me?

11 Who hath prevented me, that I should repay *him*? *whatsoever is* under the whole heaven is mine.

12 I will not conceal his parts, nor his power, nor his comely proportion.

13 Who can discover the face of his garment? *or* who can come *to him* with his double bridle?

14 Who can open the doors of his face? his teeth *are* terrible round about.

15 *His* scales *are his* pride, shut up together *as with* a close seal.

16 One is so near to another, that no air can come between them.

17 They are joined one to another, they stick together, that they cannot be sundered.

18 By his neesings a light doth shine, and his eyes *are* like the eyelids of the morning.

19 Out of his mouth go burning lamps, *and* sparks of fire leap out.

20 Out of his nostrils goeth smoke, as *out of* a seething pot or caldron.

21 His breath kindleth coals, and a flame goeth out of his mouth.

22 In his neck remaineth strength, and sorrow is turned into joy before him.

23 The flakes of his flesh are joined together: they are firm in themselves; they cannot be moved.

24 His heart is as firm as a stone; yea, as hard as a piece of the nether *millstone*.

25 When he raiseth up himself, the mighty are afraid: by reason of breakings they purify themselves.

26 The sword of him that layeth at him cannot hold: the spear, the dart, nor the habergeon.

27 He esteemeth iron as straw, *and* brass as rotten wood.

28 The arrow cannot make him flee: slingstones are turned with him into stubble.

29 Darts are counted as stubble: he laugheth at the shaking of a spear.

30 Sharp stones *are* under him: he spreadeth sharp pointed things upon the mire.

31 He maketh the deep to boil like a pot: he maketh the sea like a pot of ointment.

32 He maketh a path to shine after him; *one* would think the deep *to be* hoary.

33 Upon earth there is not his like, who is made without fear.

34 He beholdeth all high *things*: he *is* a king over all the children of pride.

42 THEN Job answered the LORD, and said,
2 I know that thou canst do every *thing*, and *that* no thought can be withholden from thee.

3 Who *is* he that hideth counsel without knowledge? therefore have I uttered that I understood not; things too wonderful for me, which I knew not.

4 Hear, I beseech thee, and I will speak: I will demand of thee, and declare thou unto me.

5 I have heard of thee by the hearing of the ear: but now mine eye seeth thee.

6 Wherefore I abhor *myself*, and repent in dust and ashes.

7 ¶ And it was *so*, that after the LORD had spoken these words unto Job, the LORD said to El´i-phaz the Te´man-ite, My wrath is kindled against thee, and against thy two friends: for ye have not spoken of me *the thing that is* right, as my servant Job *hath*.

8 Therefore take unto you now seven bullocks and seven rams, and go to my servant Job, and offer up for yourselves a burnt offering; and my servant Job shall pray for you: for him will I accept: lest I deal with you *after your* folly, in that ye have not spoken of me *the thing which is* right, like my servant Job.

9 So El´i-phaz the Te´man-ite and Bil´dad the Shu´hite *and* Zo´phar the Na´a-math-ite went, and did according as the LORD commanded them: the LORD also accepted Job.

10 And the LORD turned the captivity of Job, when he prayed for his friends: also the LORD gave Job twice as much as he had before.

11 Then came there unto him all his brethren, and all his sisters, and all they that had been of his acquaintance before, and did eat bread with him in his house: and they bemoaned him, and comforted him over all the evil that the LORD had brought upon him: every man also gave him a piece of money, and every one an earring of gold.

12 So the LORD blessed the latter end of Job more than his beginning: for he had fourteen thousand sheep, and six thousand camels, and a thousand yoke of oxen, and a thousand she asses.

13 He had also seven sons and three daughters.

14 And he called the name of the first, Je-mi´ma; and the name of the second, Ke-zi´a; and the name of the third, Ker´en-hap´puch.

15 And in all the land were no women found *so* fair as the daughters of Job: and their father gave them inheritance among their brethren.

16 After this lived Job an hundred and forty years, and saw his sons, and his sons' sons, *even* four generations.

17 So Job died, *being* old and full of days.

THE PSALMS

1 BLESSED *is* the man that walketh not in the counsel of the ungodly, nor standeth in the way of sinners, nor sitteth in the seat of the scornful.

2 But his delight *is* in the law of the LORD; and in his law doth he meditate day and night.

3 And he shall be like a tree planted by the rivers of water, that bringeth forth his fruit in his season; his leaf also shall not wither; and whatsoever he doeth shall prosper.

4 The ungodly *are* not so: but *are* like the chaff which the wind driveth away.

5 Therefore the ungodly shall not stand in the judgment, nor sinners in the congregation of the righteous.

6 For the LORD knoweth the way of the righteous: but the way of the ungodly shall perish.

2 WHY do the heathen rage, and the people imagine a vain thing?

2 The kings of the earth set themselves, and the rulers take counsel together, against the LORD, and against his anointed, *saying*,

3 Let us break their bands asunder, and cast away their cords from us.

4 He that sitteth in the heavens shall laugh: the LORD shall have them in derision.

5 Then shall he speak unto them in his wrath, and vex them in his sore displeasure.

6 Yet have I set my king upon my holy hill of Zi´on.

7 I will declare the decree: the LORD hath said unto me, Thou *art* my Son; this day have I begotten thee.

8 Ask of me, and I shall give *thee* the heathen *for* thine inheritance, and the uttermost parts of the earth *for* thy possession.

9 Thou shalt break them with a rod of iron; thou shalt dash them in pieces like a potter's vessel.

10 Be wise now therefore, O ye kings: be instructed, ye judges of the earth.

11 Serve the LORD with fear, and rejoice with trembling.

12 Kiss the Son, lest he be angry, and ye perish *from* the way, when his wrath is kindled but a little. Blessed *are* all they that put their trust in him.

A Psalm of David, when he fled from Absalom his son.

3 LORD, how are they increased that trouble me! many *are* they that rise up against me.

2 Many *there be* which say of my soul, *There is* no help for him in God. Se´lah.

3 But thou, O LORD, *art* a shield for me; my glory, and the lifter up of mine head.

4 I cried unto the LORD with my voice, and he heard me out of his holy hill. Se´lah.

5 I laid me down and slept; I awaked; for the LORD sustained me.

6 I will not be afraid of ten thousands of people, that have set *themselves* against me round about.

7 Arise, O LORD; save me, O my God: for thou hast smitten all mine enemies *upon* the cheek bone; thou hast broken the teeth of the ungodly.

8 Salvation *belongeth* unto the LORD: thy blessing *is* upon thy people. Se´lah.

To the chief Musician on Neginoth. A Psalm of David.

4 HEAR me when I call, O God of my righteousness: thou hast enlarged me *when I was* in distress; have mercy upon me, and hear my prayer.

2 O ye sons of men, how long *will ye turn* my glory into shame? *how long* will ye love vanity, *and* seek after leasing? Se'lah.

3 But know that the LORD hath set apart him that is godly for himself: the LORD will hear when I call unto him.

4 Stand in awe, and sin not: commune with your own heart upon your bed, and be still. Se'-lah.

5 Offer the sacrifices of righteousness, and put your trust in the LORD.

6 *There be* many that say, Who will shew us *any* good? LORD, lift thou up the light of thy countenance upon us.

7 Thou hast put gladness in my heart, more than in the time *that* their corn and their wine increased.

8 I will both lay me down in peace, and sleep: for thou, LORD, only makest me dwell in safety.

To the chief Musician upon Nehiloth, A Psalm of David.

5 GIVE ear to my words, O LORD, consider my meditation.

2 Hearken unto the voice of my cry, my King, and my God: for unto thee will I pray.

3 My voice shalt thou hear in the morning, O LORD; in the morning will I direct *my prayer* unto thee, and will look up.

4 For thou *art* not a God that hath pleasure in wickedness: neither shall evil dwell with thee.

5 The foolish shall not stand in thy sight: thou hatest all workers of iniquity.

6 Thou shalt destroy them that speak leasing: the LORD will abhor the bloody and deceitful man.

7 But as for me, I will come *into* thy house in the multitude of thy mercy: *and* in thy fear will I worship toward thy holy temple.

8 Lead me, O LORD, in thy righteousness because of mine enemies; make thy way straight before my face.

9 For *there is* no faithfulness in their mouth; their inward part *is* very wickedness; their throat *is* an open sepulchre; they flatter with their tongue.

10 Destroy thou them, O God; let them fall by their own counsels; cast them out in the multitude of their transgressions; for they have rebelled against thee.

11 But let all those that put their trust in thee rejoice: let them ever shout for joy, because thou defendest them: let them also that love thy name be joyful in thee.

12 For thou, LORD, wilt bless the righteous; with favour wilt thou compass him as *with* a shield.

To the chief Musician on Neginoth upon Sheminith, A Psalm of David.

6 O LORD, rebuke me not in thine anger, neither chasten me in thy hot displeasure.

2 Have mercy upon me, O LORD; for I *am* weak: O LORD, heal me; for my bones are vexed.

3 My soul is also sore vexed: but thou, O LORD, how long?

4 Return, O LORD, deliver my soul: oh save me for thy mercies' sake.

5 For in death *there is* no remembrance of thee: in the grave who shall give thee thanks?

6 I am weary with my groaning; all the night make I my bed to swim; I water my couch with my tears.

7 Mine eye is consumed because of grief; it waxeth old because of all mine enemies.

8 Depart from me, all ye workers of iniquity; for the LORD hath heard the voice of my weeping.

9 The LORD hath heard my supplication; the LORD will receive my prayer.

10 Let all mine enemies be ashamed and sore vexed: let them return *and* be ashamed suddenly.

Shiggaion of David, which he sang unto the LORD, concerning the words of Cush the Benjamite.

7 O LORD my God, in thee do I put my trust: save me from all them that persecute me, and deliver me:

2 Lest he tear my soul like a lion, rending *it* in pieces, while *there is* none to deliver.

3 O LORD my God, if I have done this; if there be iniquity in my hands;

4 If I have rewarded evil unto him that was at peace with me; (yea, I have delivered him that without cause is mine enemy:)

5 Let the enemy persecute my soul, and take *it;* yea, let him tread down my life upon the earth, and lay mine honour in the dust. Se'lah.

6 Arise, O LORD, in thine anger, lift up thyself because of the rage of mine enemies: and awake for me *to* the judgment *that* thou hast commanded.

7 So shall the congregation of the people compass thee about: for their sakes therefore return thou on high.

8 The LORD shall judge the people: judge me, O LORD, according to my righteousness, and according to mine integrity *that is* in me.

9 Oh let the wickedness of the wicked come to an end; but establish the just: for the righteous God trieth the hearts and reins.

10 My defence *is* of God, which saveth the upright in heart.

11 God judgeth the righteous, and God is angry *with the wicked* every day.

12 If he turn not, he will whet his sword; he hath bent his bow, and made it ready.

13 He hath also prepared for him the instruments of death; he ordaineth his arrows against the persecutors.

14 Behold, he travaileth with iniquity, and hath conceived mischief, and brought forth falsehood.

15 He made a pit, and digged it, and is fallen into the ditch *which* he made.

16 His mischief shall return upon his own head, and his violent dealing shall come down upon his own pate.

17 I will praise the LORD according to his righteousness: and will sing praise to the name of the LORD most high.

To the chief Musician upon Gittith, A Psalm of David.

8 O LORD our Lord, how excellent *is* thy name in all the earth! who hast set thy glory above the heavens.

2 Out of the mouth of babes and sucklings hast thou ordained strength because of thine enemies, that thou mightest still the enemy and the avenger.

3 When I consider thy heavens, the work of thy fingers, the moon and the stars, which thou hast ordained;

4 What is man, that thou art mindful of him? and the son of man, that thou visitest him?

5 For thou hast made him a little lower than the angels, and hast crowned him with glory and honour.

6 Thou madest him to have dominion over the works of thy hands; thou hast put all *things* under his feet;

7 All sheep and oxen, yea, and the beasts of the field;

8 The fowl of the air, and the fish of the sea, *and whatsoever* passeth through the paths of the seas.

9 O LORD our Lord, how excellent *is* thy name in all the earth!

To the chief Musician upon Muth-labben, A Psalm of David.

9 I WILL praise *thee*, O LORD, with my whole heart; I will shew forth all thy marvellous works.

2 I will be glad and rejoice in thee: I will sing praise to thy name, O thou most High.

3 When mine enemies are turned back, they shall fall and perish at thy presence.

4 For thou hast maintained my right and my cause; thou satest in the throne judging right.

5 Thou hast rebuked the heathen, thou hast destroyed the wicked, thou hast put out their name for ever and ever.

6 O thou enemy, destructions are come to a perpetual end: and thou hast destroyed cities; their memorial is perished with them.

7 But the LORD shall endure for ever: he hath prepared his throne for judgment.

8 And he shall judge the world in righteousness, he shall minister judgment to the people in uprightness.

9 The LORD also will be a refuge for the oppressed, a refuge in times of trouble.

10 And they that know thy name will put their trust in thee: for thou, LORD, hast not forsaken them that seek thee.

11 Sing praises to the LORD, which dwelleth in Zi'on: declare among the people his doings.

12 When he maketh inquisition for blood, he remembereth them: he forgetteth not the cry of the humble.

13 Have mercy upon me, O LORD; consider my trouble *which I suffer* of them that hate me, thou that liftest me up from the gates of death:

14 That I may shew forth all thy praise in the gates of the daughter of Zi'on: I will rejoice in thy salvation.

15 The heathen are sunk down in the pit *that* they made: in the net which they hid is their own foot taken.

16 The LORD is known *by* the judgment *which* he executeth: the wicked is snared in the work of his own hands. Hig-ga'ion. Se'lah.

17 The wicked shall be turned into hell, *and* all the nations that forget God.

18 For the needy shall not always be forgotten: the expectation of the poor shall *not* perish for ever.

19 Arise, O LORD; let not man prevail: let the heathen be judged in thy sight.

20 Put them in fear, O LORD: *that* the nations may know themselves *to be but* men. Se'lah.

10 WHY standest thou afar off, O LORD? *why* hidest thou *thyself* in times of trouble?

2 The wicked in *his* pride doth persecute the poor: let them be taken in the devices that they have imagined.

3 For the wicked boasteth of his heart's desire, and blesseth the covetous, *whom* the LORD abhorreth.

4 The wicked through the pride of his countenance, will not seek *after God*: God *is* not in all his thoughts.

5 His ways are always grievous; thy judgments *are* far above out of his sight: *as for* all his enemies, he puffeth at them.

6 He hath said in his heart, I shall not be moved: for *I shall* never *be* in adversity.

7 His mouth is full of cursing and deceit and fraud: under his tongue *is* mischief and vanity.

8 He sitteth in the lurking places of the villages: in the secret places doth he murder the innocent: his eyes are privily set against the poor.

9 He lieth in wait secretly as a lion in his den: he lieth in wait to catch the poor: he doth catch the poor, when he draweth him into his net.

10 He croucheth, *and* humbleth himself, that the poor may fall by his strong ones.

11 He hath said in his heart, God hath forgotten: he hideth his face; he will never see *it*.

12 Arise, O LORD; O God, lift up thine hand: forget not the humble.

13 Wherefore doth the wicked contemn God? he hath said in his heart, Thou wilt not require *it*.

14 Thou hast seen *it*; for thou beholdest mischief and spite, to requite *it* with thy hand: the poor committeth himself unto thee; thou art the helper of the fatherless.

15 Break thou the arm of the wicked and the evil *man*: seek out his wickedness *till* thou find none.

16 The LORD *is* King for ever and ever: the heathen are perished out of his land.

17 LORD, thou hast heard the desire of the humble: thou wilt prepare their hearts, thou wilt cause thine ear to hear:

18 To judge the fatherless and the oppressed, that the man of the earth may no more oppress.

To the chief Musician, *A Psalm* of David.

11 IN the LORD put I my trust: how say ye to my soul, Flee *as* a bird to your mountain?

2 For, lo, the wicked bend *their* bow, they make ready their arrow upon the string, that they may privily shoot at the upright in heart.

3 If the foundations be destroyed, what can the righteous do?

4 The LORD *is* in his holy temple, the LORD's throne *is* in heaven: his eyes behold, his eyelids try, the children of men.

5 The LORD trieth the righteous: but the wicked and him that loveth violence his soul hateth.

6 Upon the wicked he shall rain snares, fire and brimstone, and an horrible tempest: *this shall be* the portion of their cup.

7 For the righteous LORD loveth righteousness; his countenance doth behold the upright.

To the chief Musician upon Sheminith, A Psalm of David.

12 HELP, LORD; for the godly man ceaseth; for the faithful fail from among the children of men.

2 They speak vanity every one with his neighbour: *with* flattering lips *and* with a double heart do they speak.

3 The LORD shall cut off all flattering lips, *and* the tongue that speaketh proud things:

4 Who have said, With our tongue will we prevail; our lips *are* our own: who *is* lord over us?

5 For the oppression of the poor, for the sighing of the needy, now will I arise, saith the LORD; I will set *him* in safety *from him that* puffeth at him.

6 The words of the LORD *are* pure words: *as* silver tried in a furnace of earth, purified seven times.

7 Thou shalt keep them, O LORD, thou shalt preserve them from this generation for ever.

8 The wicked walk on every side, when the vilest men are exalted.

To the chief Musician, A Psalm of David.

13 HOW long wilt thou forget me, O LORD? for ever? how long wilt thou hide thy face from me?

2 How long shall I take counsel in my soul, *having* sorrow in my heart daily? how long shall mine enemy be exalted over me?

3 Consider *and* hear me, O LORD my God: lighten mine eyes, lest I sleep the *sleep of* death;

4 Lest mine enemy say, I have prevailed against him; *and* those that trouble me rejoice when I am moved.

5 But I have trusted in thy mercy; my heart shall rejoice in thy salvation.

6 I will sing unto the LORD, because he hath dealt bountifully with me.

To the chief Musician, *A Psalm* of David.

14 THE fool hath said in his heart, *There is* no God. They are corrupt, they have done abominable works, *there is* none that doeth good.

2 The LORD looked down from heaven upon the children of men, to see if there were any that did understand, *and* seek God.

3 They are all gone aside, they are *all* together become filthy: *there is* none that doeth good, no, not one.

4 Have all the workers of iniquity no knowledge? who eat up my people *as* they eat bread, and call not upon the LORD.

5 There were they in great fear: for God *is* in the generation of the righteous.

6 Ye have shamed the counsel of the poor, because the LORD *is* his refuge.

7 Oh that the salvation of Is'ra-el *were* come out of Zi'on! when the LORD bringeth back the captivity of his people, Ja'cob shall rejoice, *and* Is'ra-el shall be glad.

A Psalm of David.

15 LORD, who shall abide in thy tabernacle? who shall dwell in thy holy hill?

2 He that walketh uprightly, and worketh righteousness, and speaketh the truth in his heart.

3 *He that* backbiteth not with his tongue, nor doeth evil to his neighbour, nor taketh up a reproach against his neighbour.

4 In whose eyes a vile person is contemned; but he honoureth them that fear the LORD. He *that* sweareth to *his own* hurt, and changeth not.

5 *He that* putteth not out his money to usury, nor taketh reward against the innocent. He that doeth these *things* shall never be moved.

Michtam of David.

16 PRESERVE me, O God: for in thee do I put my trust.

2 *O my soul*, thou hast said unto the LORD, Thou *art* my LORD: my goodness *extendeth* not to thee;

3 *But* to the saints that *are* in the earth, and to the excellent, in whom *is* all my delight.

4 Their sorrows shall be multiplied *that* hasten *after* another god: their drink offerings of blood will I not offer, nor take up their names into my lips.

5 The LORD *is* the portion of mine inheritance and of my cup: thou maintainest my lot.

6 The lines are fallen unto me in pleasant *places;* yea, I have a goodly heritage.

7 I will bless the LORD, who hath given me counsel: my reins also instruct me in the night seasons.

8 I have set the LORD always before me: because *he is* at my right hand, I shall not be moved.

9 Therefore my heart is glad, and my glory rejoiceth: my flesh also shall rest in hope.

10 For thou wilt not leave my soul in hell; neither wilt thou suffer thine Holy One to see corruption.

11 Thou wilt shew me the path of life: in thy presence *is* fulness of joy; at thy right hand *there are* pleasures for evermore.

A Prayer of David.

17 HEAR the right, O LORD, attend unto my cry, give ear unto my prayer, *that* goeth not out of feigned lips.

2 Let my sentence come forth from thy presence; let thine eyes behold the things that are equal.

3 Thou hast proved mine heart; thou hast visited *me* in the night; thou hast tried me, *and* shalt find nothing; I am purposed *that* my mouth shall not transgress.

4 Concerning the works of men, by the word of thy lips I have kept *me from* the paths of the destroyer.

5 Hold up my goings in thy paths, *that* my footsteps slip not.

6 I have called upon thee, for thou wilt hear me, O God: incline thine ear unto me, *and hear* my speech.

7 Shew thy marvellous lovingkindness, O thou that savest by thy right hand them which put their trust *in thee* from those that rise up *against them.*

8 Keep me as the apple of the eye, hide me under the shadow of thy wings,

9 From the wicked that oppress me, *from* my deadly enemies, *who* compass me about.

10 They are inclosed in their own fat: with their mouth they speak proudly.

11 They have now compassed us in our steps: they have set their eyes bowing down to the earth;

12 Like as a lion *that is* greedy of his prey, and as it were a young lion lurking in secret places.

13 Arise, O LORD, disappoint him, cast him down: deliver my soul from the wicked, *which is* thy sword:

14 From men *which are* thy hand, O LORD, from men of the world, *which have* their portion in *this* life, and whose belly thou fillest with thy hid *treasure:* they are full of children, and leave the rest of their *substance* to their babes.

15 As for me, I will behold thy face in righteousness: I shall be satisfied, when I awake, with thy likeness.

To the chief Musician, *A Psalm* of David, the servant of the LORD, who spake unto the LORD the words of this song in the day *that* the LORD delivered him from the hand of all his enemies, and from the hand of Saul: And he said.

18 I WILL love thee, O LORD, my strength.

2 The LORD *is* my rock, and my fortress, and my deliverer; my God, my strength, in whom I will trust; my buckler, and the horn of my salvation, *and* my high tower.

3 I will call upon the LORD, *who is worthy* to be praised: so shall I be saved from mine enemies.

4 The sorrows of death compassed me, and the floods of ungodly men made me afraid.

5 The sorrows of hell compassed me about: the snares of death prevented me.

6 In my distress I called upon the LORD, and cried unto my God: he heard my voice out of his temple, and my cry came before him, *even* into his ears.

7 Then the earth shook and trembled; the foundations also of the hills moved and were shaken, because he was wroth.

8 There went up a smoke out of his nostrils, and fire out of his mouth devoured: coals were kindled by it.

9 He bowed the heavens also, and came down: and darkness *was* under his feet.

10 And he rode upon a cherub, and did fly: yea, he did fly upon the wings of the wind.

11 He made darkness his secret place; his pavilion round about him *were* dark waters *and* thick clouds of the skies.

12 At the brightness *that was* before him his thick clouds passed, hail *stones* and coals of fire.

13 The LORD also thundered in the heavens, and the Highest gave his voice; hail *stones* and coals of fire.

14 Yea, he sent out his arrows, and scattered them; and he shot out lightnings, and discomfited them.

15 Then the channels of waters were seen, and the foundations of the world were discovered at thy rebuke, O LORD, at the blast of the breath of thy nostrils.

16 He sent from above, he took me, he drew me out of many waters.

17 He delivered me from my strong enemy, and from them which hated me: for they were too strong for me.

18 They prevented me in the day of my calamity: but the LORD was my stay.

19 He brought me forth also into a large place; he delivered me, because he delighted in me.

20 The LORD rewarded me according to my righteousness; according to the cleanness of my hands hath he recompensed me.

21 For I have kept the ways of the LORD, and have not wickedly departed from my God.

22 For all his judgments *were* before me, and I did not put away his statutes from me.

23 I was also upright before him, and I kept myself from mine iniquity.

24 Therefore hath the LORD recompensed me according to my righteousness, according to the cleanness of my hands in his eyesight.

25 With the merciful thou wilt shew thyself merciful; with an upright man thou wilt shew thyself upright;

26 With the pure thou wilt shew thyself pure; and with the froward thou wilt shew thyself froward.

27 For thou wilt save the afflicted people; but wilt bring down high looks.

28 For thou wilt light my candle: the LORD my God will enlighten my darkness.

29 For by thee I have run through a troop; and by my God have I leaped over a wall.

30 *As for* God, his way *is* perfect: the word of the LORD is tried: he *is* a buckler to all those that trust in him.

31 For who *is* God save the LORD? or who *is* a rock save our God?

32 *It is* God that girdeth me with strength, and maketh my way perfect.

33 He maketh my feet like hinds' *feet*, and setteth me upon my high places.

34 He teacheth my hands to war, so that a bow of steel is broken by mine arms.

35 Thou hast also given me the shield of thy salvation: and thy right hand hath holden me up, and thy gentleness hath made me great.

36 Thou hast enlarged my steps under me, that my feet did not slip.

37 I have pursued mine enemies, and overtaken them: neither did I turn again till they were consumed.

38 I have wounded them that they were not able to rise: they are fallen under my feet.

39 For thou hast girded me with strength unto the battle: thou hast subdued under me those that rose up against me.

40 Thou hast also given me the necks of mine enemies; that I might destroy them that hate me.

41 They cried, but *there was* none to save *them: even* unto the LORD, but he answered them not.

42 Then did I beat them small as the dust before the wind: I did cast them out as the dirt in the streets.

43 Thou hast delivered me from the strivings of the people; *and* thou hast made me the head of the heathen: a people *whom* I have not known shall serve me.

44 As soon as they hear of me, they shall obey me: the strangers shall submit themselves unto me.

45 The strangers shall fade away, and be afraid out of their close places.

46 The LORD liveth; and blessed *be* my rock; and let the God of my salvation be exalted.

47 *It is* God that avengeth me, and subdueth the people under me.

48 He delivereth me from mine enemies: yea, thou liftest me up above those that rise up against me: thou hast delivered me from the violent man.

49 Therefore will I give thanks unto thee, O LORD, among the heathen, and sing praises unto thy name.

50 Great deliverance giveth he to his king; and sheweth mercy to his anointed, to Da'vid, and to his seed for evermore.

To the chief Musician, A Psalm of David.

19 THE heavens declare the glory of God; and the firmament sheweth his handywork.

2 Day unto day uttereth speech, and night unto night sheweth knowledge.

3 *There is* no speech nor language, *where* their voice is not heard.

4 Their line is gone out through all the earth, and their words to the end of the world. In them hath he set a tabernacle for the sun,

5 Which *is* as a bridegroom coming out of his chamber, *and* rejoiceth as a strong man to run a race.

6 His going forth *is* from the end of the heaven, and his circuit unto the ends of it: and there is nothing hid from the heat thereof.

7 The law of the LORD *is* perfect, converting the soul: the testimony of the LORD *is* sure, making wise the simple.

8 The statutes of the LORD *are* right, rejoicing the heart: the commandment of the LORD *is* pure, enlightening the eyes.

9 The fear of the LORD *is* clean, enduring for ever: the judgments of the LORD *are* true *and* righteous altogether.

10 More to be desired *are they* than gold, yea, than much fine gold: sweeter also than honey and the honeycomb.

11 Moreover by them is thy servant warned: *and* in keeping of them *there is* great reward.

12 Who can understand *his* errors? cleanse thou me from secret *faults*.

13 Keep back thy servant also from presumptuous *sins;* let them not have dominion over me: then shall I be upright, and I shall be innocent from the great transgression.

14 Let the words of my mouth, and the meditation of my heart, be acceptable in thy sight, O LORD, my strength, and my redeemer.

To the chief Musician, A Psalm of David.

20 THE LORD hear thee in the day of trouble; the name of the God of Ja'cob defend thee;

2 Send thee help from the sanctuary, and strengthen thee out of Zi'on;

3 Remember all thy offerings, and accept thy burnt sacrifice; Se'lah.

4 Grant thee according to thine own heart, and fulfil all thy counsel.

5 We will rejoice in thy salvation, and in the name of our God we will set up *our* banners: the LORD fulfil all thy petitions.

6 Now know I that the LORD saveth his anointed; he will hear him from his holy heaven with the saving strength of his right hand.

7 Some *trust* in chariots, and some in horses: but we will remember the name of the LORD our God.

8 They are brought down and fallen: but we are risen, and stand upright.

9 Save, LORD: let the king hear us when we call.

To the chief Musician, A Psalm of David.

21 THE king shall joy in thy strength, O LORD; and in thy salvation how greatly shall he rejoice!

2 Thou hast given him his heart's desire, and hast not withholden the request of his lips. Se'-lah.

3 For thou preventest him with the blessings of goodness: thou settest a crown of pure gold on his head.

4 He asked life of thee, *and* thou gavest *it* him, *even* length of days for ever and ever.

5 His glory *is* great in thy salvation: honour and majesty hast thou laid upon him.

6 For thou hast made him most blessed for ever: thou hast made him exceeding glad with thy countenance.

7 For the king trusteth in the LORD, and through the mercy of the most High he shall not be moved.

8 Thine hand shall find out all thine enemies: thy right hand shall find out those that hate thee.

9 Thou shalt make them as a fiery oven in the time of thine anger: the LORD shall swallow them up in his wrath, and the fire shall devour them.

10 Their fruit shalt thou destroy from the earth, and their seed from among the children of men.

11 For they intended evil against thee: they imagined a mischievous device, *which* they are not able *to perform*.

12 Therefore shalt thou make them turn their back, *when* thou shalt make ready *thine arrows* upon thy strings against the face of them.

13 Be thou exalted, LORD, in thine own strength: *so* will we sing and praise thy power.

To the chief Musician upon Aijeleth Shahar, A Psalm of David.

22 MY God, my God, why hast thou forsaken me? *why art thou so* far from helping me, *and from* the words of my roaring?

2 O my God, I cry in the daytime, but thou hearest not; and in the night season, and am not silent.

3 But thou *art* holy, O *thou* that inhabitest the praises of Is'ra-el.

4 Our fathers trusted in thee: they trusted, and thou didst deliver them.

5 They cried unto thee, and were delivered: they trusted in thee, and were not confounded.

6 But I *am* a worm, and no man; a reproach of men, and despised of the people.

7 All they that see me laugh me to scorn: they shoot out the lip, they shake the head, *saying*,

8 He trusted on the LORD *that* he would deliver him: let him deliver him, seeing he delighted in him.

9 But thou *art* he that took me out of the womb: thou didst make me hope *when I was* upon my mother's breasts.

10 I was cast upon thee from the womb: thou *art* my God from my mother's belly.

11 Be not far from me; for trouble *is* near; for *there is* none to help.

12 Many bulls have compassed me: strong *bulls* of Ba'shan have beset me round.

13 They gaped upon me *with* their mouths, *as* a ravening and a roaring lion.

14 I am poured out like water, and all my bones are out of joint: my heart is like wax; it is melted in the midst of my bowels.

15 My strength is dried up like a potsherd; and my tongue cleaveth to my jaws; and thou hast brought me into the dust of death.

16 For dogs have compassed me: the assembly of the wicked have inclosed me: they pierced my hands and my feet.

17 I may tell all my bones: they look *and* stare upon me.

18 They part my garments among them, and cast lots upon my vesture.

19 But be not far from me, O LORD: O my strength, haste thee to help me.

20 Deliver my soul from the sword; my darling from the power of the dog.

21 Save me from the lion's mouth: for thou hast heard me from the horns of the unicorns.

22 I will declare thy name unto my brethren: in the midst of the congregation will I praise thee.

23 Ye that fear the LORD, praise him; all ye the seed of Ja'cob, glorify him; and fear him, all ye the seed of Is'ra-el.

24 For he hath not despised nor abhorred the affliction of the afflicted; neither hath he hid his face from him; but when he cried unto him, he heard.

25 My praise *shall be* of thee in the great congregation: I will pay my vows before them that fear him.

26 The meek shall eat and be satisfied: they shall praise the LORD that seek him: your heart shall live for ever.

27 All the ends of the world shall remember and turn unto the LORD: and all the kindreds of the nations shall worship before thee.

28 For the kingdom *is* the LORD'S: and he *is* the governor among the nations.

29 All *they that be* fat upon earth shall eat and worship: all they that go down to the dust shall bow before him: and none can keep alive his own soul.

30 A seed shall serve him; it shall be accounted to the Lord for a generation.

31 They shall come, and shall declare his righteousness unto a people that shall be born, that he hath done *this*.

A Psalm of David.

23 THE LORD *is* my shepherd; I shall not want.

2 He maketh me to lie down in green pastures: he leadeth me beside the still waters.

3 He restoreth my soul: he leadeth me in the paths of righteousness for his name's sake.

4 Yea, though I walk through the valley of the shadow of death, I will fear no evil: for thou *art* with me; thy rod and thy staff they comfort me.

5 Thou preparest a table before me in the presence of mine enemies: thou anointest my head with oil; my cup runneth over.

6 Surely goodness and mercy shall follow me all the days of my life: and I will dwell in the house of the LORD for ever.

A Psalm of David.

24 THE earth *is* the LORD'S, and the fulness thereof; the world, and they that dwell therein.

2 For he hath founded it upon the seas, and established it upon the floods.

3 Who shall ascend into the hill of the LORD? or who shall stand in his holy place?

4 He that hath clean hands, and a pure heart; who hath not lifted up his soul unto vanity, nor sworn deceitfully.

5 He shall receive the blessing from the LORD, and righteousness from the God of his salvation.

6 This *is* the generation of them that seek him, that seek thy face, O Ja'cob. Se'lah.

7 Lift up your heads, O ye gates; and be ye lift up, ye everlasting doors; and the King of glory shall come in.

8 Who *is* this King of glory? The LORD strong and mighty, the LORD mighty in battle.

9 Lift up your heads, O ye gates; even lift *them* up, ye everlasting doors; and the King of glory shall come in.

10 Who is this King of glory? The LORD of hosts, he *is* the King of glory. Se'lah.

A Psalm of David.

25 UNTO thee, O LORD, do I lift up my soul.
2 O my God, I trust in thee: let me not be ashamed, let not mine enemies triumph over me.

3 Yea, let none that wait on thee be ashamed: let them be ashamed which transgress without cause.

4 Shew me thy ways, O LORD; teach me thy paths.

5 Lead me in thy truth, and teach me: for thou *art* the God of my salvation; on thee do I wait all the day.

6 Remember, O LORD, thy tender mercies and thy lovingkindnesses; for they *have been* ever of old.

7 Remember not the sins of my youth, nor my transgressions: according to thy mercy remember thou me for thy goodness' sake, O LORD.

8 Good and upright *is* the LORD: therefore will he teach sinners in the way.

9 The meek will he guide in judgment: and the meek will he teach his way.

10 All the paths of the LORD *are* mercy and truth unto such as keep his covenant and his testimonies.

11 For thy name's sake, O LORD, pardon mine iniquity; for it *is* great.

12 What man *is* he that feareth the LORD? him shall he teach in the way *that* he shall choose.

13 His soul shall dwell at ease; and his seed shall inherit the earth.

14 The secret of the LORD *is* with them that fear him; and he will shew them his covenant.

15 Mine eyes *are* ever toward the LORD; for he shall pluck my feet out of the net.

16 Turn thee unto me, and have mercy upon me; for I *am* desolate and afflicted.

17 The troubles of my heart are enlarged: O bring thou me out of my distresses.

18 Look upon mine affliction and my pain; and forgive all my sins.

19 Consider mine enemies; for they are many; and they hate me with cruel hatred.

20 O keep my soul, and deliver me: let me not be ashamed; for I put my trust in thee.

21 Let integrity and uprightness preserve me; for I wait on thee.

22 Redeem Is'ra-el, O God, out of all his troubles.

A Psalm of David.

26 JUDGE me, O LORD; for I have walked in mine integrity: I have trusted also in the LORD; *therefore* I shall not slide.

2 Examine me, O LORD, and prove me; try my reins and my heart.

3 For thy lovingkindness *is* before mine eyes: and I have walked in thy truth.

4 I have not sat with vain persons, neither will I go in with dissemblers.

5 I have hated the congregation of evildoers; and will not sit with the wicked.

6 I will wash mine hands in innocency: so will I compass thine altar, O LORD:

7 That I may publish with the voice of thanksgiving, and tell of all thy wondrous works.

8 LORD, I have loved the habitation of thy house, and the place where thine honour dwelleth.

9 Gather not my soul with sinners, nor my life with bloody men:

10 In whose hands *is* mischief, and their right hand is full of bribes.

11 But as for me, I will walk in mine integrity: redeem me, and be merciful unto me.

12 My foot standeth in an even place: in the congregations will I bless the LORD.

A Psalm of David.

27 THE LORD *is* my light and my salvation; whom shall I fear? the LORD *is* the strength of my life; of whom shall I be afraid?

2 When the wicked, *even* mine enemies and my foes, came upon me to eat up my flesh, they stumbled and fell.

3 Though an host should encamp against me, my heart shall not fear: though war should rise against me, in this *will* I *be* confident.

4 One *thing* have I desired of the LORD, that will I seek after; that I may dwell in the house of the LORD all the days of my life, to behold the beauty of the LORD, and to enquire in his temple.

5 For in the time of trouble he shall hide me in his pavilion: in the secret of his tabernacle shall he hide me; he shall set me up upon a rock.

6 And now shall mine head be lifted up above mine enemies round about me: therefore will I offer in his tabernacle sacrifices of joy; I will sing, yea, I will sing praises unto the LORD.

7 Hear, O LORD, *when* I cry with my voice: have mercy also upon me, and answer me.

8 *When thou saidst,* Seek ye my face; my heart said unto thee, Thy face, LORD, will I seek.

9 Hide not thy face *far* from me; put not thy servant away in anger: thou hast been my help; leave me not, neither forsake me, O God of my salvation.

10 When my father and my mother forsake me, then the LORD will take me up.

11 Teach me thy way, O LORD, and lead me in a plain path, because of mine enemies.

12 Deliver me not over unto the will of mine enemies: for false witnesses are risen up against me, and such as breathe out cruelty.

13 *I had fainted,* unless I had believed to see the goodness of the LORD in the land of the living.

14 Wait on the LORD: be of good courage, and he shall strengthen thine heart: wait, I say, on the LORD.

A Psalm of David.

28 UNTO thee will I cry, O LORD my rock; be not silent to me: lest, *if* thou be silent to me, I become like them that go down into the pit.

2 Hear the voice of my supplications, when I cry unto thee, when I lift up my hands toward thy holy oracle.

3 Draw me not away with the wicked, and with the workers of iniquity, which speak peace to their neighbours, but mischief *is* in their hearts.

4 Give them according to their deeds, and according to the wickedness of their endeavours: give them after the work of their hands; render to them their desert.

5 Because they regard not the works of the LORD, nor the operation of his hands, he shall destroy them, and not build them up.

6 Blessed *be* the LORD, because he hath heard the voice of my supplications.

7 The LORD *is* my strength and my shield; my heart trusted in him, and I am helped: therefore my heart greatly rejoiceth; and with my song will I praise him.

8 The LORD *is* their strength, and he *is* the saving strength of his anointed.

9 Save thy people, and bless thine inheritance: feed them also, and lift them up for ever.

A Psalm of David.

29 GIVE unto the LORD, O ye mighty, give unto the LORD glory and strength.

2 Give unto the LORD the glory due unto his name; worship the LORD in the beauty of holiness.

3 The voice of the LORD *is* upon the waters: the God of glory thundereth: the LORD *is* upon many waters.

4 The voice of the LORD *is* powerful; the voice of the LORD *is* full of majesty.

5 The voice of the LORD breaketh the cedars; yea, the LORD breaketh the cedars of Leb'a-non.

6 He maketh them also to skip like a calf; Leb'a-non and Sir'i-on like a young unicorn.

7 The voice of the LORD divideth the flames of fire.

8 The voice of the LORD shaketh the wilderness; the LORD shaketh the wilderness of Ka'-desh.

9 The voice of the LORD maketh the hinds to calve, and discovereth the forests: and in his temple doth every one speak of *his* glory.

10 The LORD sitteth upon the flood; yea, the LORD sitteth King for ever.

11 The LORD will give strength unto his people; the LORD will bless his people with peace.

A Psalm and Song at the dedication of the house of David.

30 I WILL extol thee, O LORD; for thou hast lifted me up, and hast not made my foes to rejoice over me.

2 O LORD my God, I cried unto thee, and thou hast healed me.

3 O LORD, thou hast brought up my soul from the grave: thou hast kept me alive, that I should not go down to the pit.

4 Sing unto the LORD, O ye saints of his, and give thanks at the remembrance of his holiness.

5 For his anger *endureth but* a moment; in his favour *is* life: weeping may endure for a night, but joy *cometh* in the morning.

6 And in my prosperity I said, I shall never be moved.

7 LORD, by thy favour thou hast made my mountain to stand strong: thou didst hide thy face, *and* I was troubled.

8 I cried to thee, O LORD; and unto the LORD I made supplication.

9 What profit *is there* in my blood, when I go down to the pit? Shall the dust praise thee? shall it declare thy truth?

10 Hear, O LORD, and have mercy upon me: LORD, be thou my helper.

11 Thou hast turned for me my mourning into dancing: thou hast put off my sackcloth, and girded me with gladness;

12 To the end that *my* glory may sing praise to thee, and not be silent. O LORD my God, I will give thanks unto thee for ever.

To the chief Musician, A Psalm of David.

31 IN thee, O LORD, do I put my trust; let me never be ashamed: deliver me in thy righteousness.

2 Bow down thine ear to me; deliver me speedily: be thou my strong rock, for an house of defence to save me.

3 For thou *art* my rock and my fortress; therefore for thy name's sake lead me, and guide me.

4 Pull me out of the net that they have laid privily for me: for thou *art* my strength.

5 Into thine hand I commit my spirit: thou hast redeemed me, O LORD God of truth.

6 I have hated them that regard lying vanities: but I trust in the LORD.

7 I will be glad and rejoice in thy mercy: for thou hast considered my trouble; thou hast known my soul in adversities;

8 And hast not shut me up into the hand of the enemy: thou hast set my feet in a large room.

9 Have mercy upon me, O LORD, for I am in trouble: mine eye is consumed with grief, *yea*, my soul and my belly.

10 For my life is spent with grief, and my years with sighing: my strength faileth because of mine iniquity, and my bones are consumed.

11 I was a reproach among all mine enemies, but especially among my neighbours, and a fear to mine acquaintance: they that did see me without fled from me.

12 I am forgotten as a dead man out of mind: I am like a broken vessel.

13 For I have heard the slander of many: fear *was* on every side: while they took counsel together against me, they devised to take away my life.

14 But I trusted in thee, O LORD: I said, Thou *art* my God.

15 My times *are* in thy hand: deliver me from the hands of mine enemies, and from them that persecute me.

16 Make thy face to shine upon thy servant: save me for thy mercies' sake.

17 Let me not be ashamed, O LORD; for I have called upon thee: let the wicked be ashamed, *and* let them be silent in the grave.

18 Let the lying lips be put to silence; which speak grievous things proudly and contemptuously against the righteous.

19 *Oh* how great *is* thy goodness, which thou hast laid up for them that fear thee; *which* thou hast wrought for them that trust in thee before the sons of men!

20 Thou shalt hide them in the secret of thy presence from the pride of man: thou shalt keep them secretly in a pavilion from the strife of tongues.

21 Blessed *be* the LORD: for he hath shewed me his marvellous kindness in a strong city.

22 For I said in my haste, I am cut off from before thine eyes: nevertheless thou heardest the voice of my supplications when I cried unto thee.

23 O love the LORD, all ye his saints: *for* the LORD preserveth the faithful, and plentifully rewardeth the proud doer.

24 Be of good courage, and he shall strengthen your heart, all ye that hope in the LORD.

A Psalm of David, Maschil.

32 BLESSED *is* he whose transgression *is* forgiven, *whose* sin *is* covered.

2 Blessed *is* the man unto whom the LORD imputeth not iniquity, and in whose spirit *there is* no guile.

3 When I kept silence, my bones waxed old through my roaring all the day long.

4 For day and night thy hand was heavy upon me: my moisture is turned into the drought of summer. Se'lah.

5 I acknowledged my sin unto thee, and mine iniquity have I not hid. I said, I will confess my transgressions unto the LORD; and thou forgavest the iniquity of my sin. Se'lah.

6 For this shall every one that is godly pray unto thee in a time when thou mayest be found: surely in the floods of great waters they shall not come nigh unto him.

7 Thou *art* my hiding place; thou shalt preserve me from trouble; thou shalt compass me about with songs of deliverance. Se'lah.

8 I will instruct thee and teach thee in the way which thou shalt go: I will guide thee with mine eye.

9 Be ye not as the horse, *or* as the mule, *which* have no understanding: whose mouth must be held in with bit and bridle, lest they come near unto thee.

10 Many sorrows *shall be* to the wicked: but he that trusteth in the LORD, mercy shall compass him about.

11 Be glad in the LORD, and rejoice, ye righteous: and shout for joy, all *ye that are* upright in heart.

33 REJOICE in the LORD, O ye righteous: *for* praise is comely for the upright.

2 Praise the LORD with harp: sing unto him with the psaltery *and* an instrument of ten strings.

3 Sing unto him a new song; play skilfully with a loud noise.

4 For the word of the LORD *is* right; and all his works *are done* in truth.

5 He loveth righteousness and judgment: the earth is full of the goodness of the LORD.

6 By the word of the LORD were the heavens made; and all the host of them by the breath of his mouth.

7 He gathereth the waters of the sea together as an heap: he layeth up the depth in storehouses.

8 Let all the earth fear the LORD: let all the inhabitants of the world stand in awe of him.

9 For he spake, and it was *done*; he commanded, and it stood fast.

10 The LORD bringeth the counsel of the heathen to nought: he maketh the devices of the people of none effect.

11 The counsel of the LORD standeth for ever, the thoughts of his heart to all generations.

12 Blessed *is* the nation whose God *is* the LORD; *and* the people *whom* he hath chosen for his own inheritance.

13 The LORD looketh from heaven; he beholdeth all the sons of men.

14 From the place of his habitation he looketh upon all the inhabitants of the earth.

15 He fashioneth their hearts alike; he considereth all their works.

16 There is no king saved by the multitude of an host: a mighty man is not delivered by much strength.

17 An horse *is* a vain thing for safety: neither shall he deliver *any* by his great strength.

18 Behold, the eye of the LORD *is* upon them that fear him, upon them that hope in his mercy;

19 To deliver their soul from death, and to keep them alive in famine.

20 Our soul waiteth for the LORD: he *is* our help and our shield.

21 For our heart shall rejoice in him, because we have trusted in his holy name.

22 Let thy mercy, O LORD, be upon us, according as we hope in thee.

A Psalm of David, when he changed his behaviour before Abimelech, who drove him away, and he departed.

34 I WILL bless the LORD at all times: his praise *shall* continually *be* in my mouth.

2 My soul shall make her boast in the LORD: the humble shall hear *thereof*, and be glad.

3 O magnify the LORD with me, and let us exalt his name together.

4 I sought the LORD, and he heard me, and delivered me from all my fears.

5 They looked unto him, and were lightened: and their faces were not ashamed.

6 This poor man cried, and the LORD heard *him*, and saved him out of all his troubles.

7 The angel of the LORD encampeth round about them that fear him, and delivereth them.

8 O taste and see that the LORD *is* good: blessed *is* the man *that* trusteth in him.

9 O fear the LORD, ye his saints: for *there is* no want to them that fear him.

10 The young lions do lack, and suffer hunger: but they that seek the LORD shall not want any good *thing*.

11 Come, ye children, hearken unto me: I will teach you the fear of the LORD.

12 What man *is he that* desireth life, *and* loveth *many* days, that he may see good?

13 Keep thy tongue from evil, and thy lips from speaking guile.

14 Depart from evil, and do good; seek peace, and pursue it.

15 The eyes of the LORD *are* upon the righteous, and his ears *are* open unto their cry.

16 The face of the LORD *is* against them that do evil, to cut off the remembrance of them from the earth.

17 *The righteous* cry, and the LORD heareth, and delivereth them out of all their troubles.

18 The LORD *is* nigh unto them that are of a broken heart; and saveth such as be of a contrite spirit.

19 Many *are* the afflictions of the righteous: but the LORD delivereth him out of them all.

20 He keepeth all his bones: not one of them is broken.

21 Evil shall slay the wicked: and they that hate the righteous shall be desolate.

22 The LORD redeemeth the soul of his servants: and none of them that trust in him shall be desolate.

A Psalm of David.

35 PLEAD *my cause*, O LORD, with them that strive with me: fight against them that fight against me.

2 Take hold of shield and buckler, and stand up for mine help.

3 Draw out also the spear, and stop *the way* against them that persecute me: say unto my soul, I *am* thy salvation.

4 Let them be confounded and put to shame that seek after my soul: let them be turned back and brought to confusion that devise my hurt.

5 Let them be as chaff before the wind: and let the angel of the LORD chase *them*.

6 Let their way be dark and slippery: and let the angel of the LORD persecute them.

7 For without cause have they hid for me their net *in* a pit, *which* without cause they have digged for my soul.

8 Let destruction come upon him at unawares; and let his net that he hath hid catch himself: into that very destruction let him fall.

9 And my soul shall be joyful in the LORD: it shall rejoice in his salvation.

10 All my bones shall say, LORD, who *is* like unto thee, which deliverest the poor from him that is too strong for him, yea, the poor and the needy from him that spoileth him?

11 False witnesses did rise up; they laid to my charge *things* that I knew not.

12 They rewarded me evil for good *to* the spoiling of my soul.

13 But as for me, when they were sick, my clothing *was* sackcloth: I humbled my soul with fasting; and my prayer returned into mine own bosom.

14 I behaved myself as though *he had been* my friend *or* brother: I bowed down heavily, as one that mourneth *for his* mother.

15 But in mine adversity they rejoiced, and gathered themselves together: *yea,* the abjects gathered themselves together against me, and I knew *it* not; they did tear *me,* and ceased not:

16 With hypocritical mockers in feasts, they gnashed upon me with their teeth.

17 Lord, how long wilt thou look on? rescue my soul from their destructions, my darling from the lions.

18 I will give thee thanks in the great congregation: *i* will praise thee among much people.

19 Let not them that are mine enemies wrongfully rejoice over me: *neither* let them wink with the eye that hate me without a cause.

20 For they speak not peace: but they devise deceitful matters against *them that are* quiet in the land.

21 Yea, they opened their mouth wide against me, *and* said, Aha, aha, our eye hath seen *it.*

22 *This* thou hast seen, O LORD: keep not silence: O Lord, be not far from me.

23 Stir up thyself, and awake to my judgment, *even* unto my cause, my God and my Lord.

24 Judge me, O LORD my God, according to thy righteousness; and let them not rejoice over me.

25 Let them not say in their hearts, Ah, so would we have it: let them not say, We have swallowed him up.

26 Let them be ashamed and brought to confusion together that rejoice at mine hurt: let them be clothed with shame and dishonour that magnify *themselves* against me.

27 Let them shout for joy, and be glad, that favour my righteous cause: yea, let them say continually, Let the LORD be magnified, which hath pleasure in the prosperity of his servant.

28 And my tongue shall speak of thy righteousness *and* of thy praise all the day long.

To the chief Musician, *A Psalm* of David the servant of the LORD.

36 THE transgression of the wicked saith within my heart, *that there is* no fear of God before his eyes.

2 For he flattereth himself in his own eyes, until his iniquity be found to be hateful.

3 The words of his mouth *are* iniquity and deceit: he hath left off to be wise, *and* to do good.

4 He deviseth mischief upon his bed; he setteth himself in a way *that is* not good; he abhorreth not evil.

5 Thy mercy, O LORD, *is* in the heavens; *and* thy faithfulness *reacheth* unto the clouds.

6 Thy righteousness *is* like the great mountains; thy judgments *are* a great deep: O LORD, thou preservest man and beast.

7 How excellent *is* thy lovingkindness, O God! therefore the children of men put their trust under the shadow of thy wings.

8 They shall be abundantly satisfied with the fatness of thy house; and thou shalt make them drink of the river of thy pleasures.

9 For with thee *is* the fountain of life: in thy light shall we see light.

10 O continue thy lovingkindness unto them that know thee; and thy righteousness to the upright in heart.

11 Let not the foot of pride come against me, and let not the hand of the wicked remove me.

12 There are the workers of iniquity fallen: they are cast down, and shall not be able to rise.

A Psalm of David.

37 FRET not thyself because of evildoers, neither be thou envious against the workers of iniquity.

2 For they shall soon be cut down like the grass, and wither as the green herb.

3 Trust in the LORD, and do good; *so* shalt thou dwell in the land, and verily thou shalt be fed.

4 Delight thyself also in the LORD; and he shall give thee the desires of thine heart.

5 Commit thy way unto the LORD; trust also in him; and he shall bring *it* to pass.

6 And he shall bring forth thy righteousness as the light, and thy judgment as the noonday.

7 Rest in the LORD, and wait patiently for him: fret not thyself because of him who prospereth in his way, because of the man who bringeth wicked devices to pass.

8 Cease from anger, and forsake wrath: fret not thyself in any wise to do evil.

9 For evildoers shall be cut off: but those that wait upon the LORD, they shall inherit the earth.

10 For yet a little while, and the wicked *shall* not *be*: yea, thou shalt diligently consider his place, and it *shall* not *be*.

11 But the meek shall inherit the earth; and shall delight themselves in the abundance of peace.

12 The wicked plotteth against the just, and gnasheth upon him with his teeth.

13 The Lord shall laugh at him: for he seeth that his day is coming.

14 The wicked have drawn out the sword, and have bent their bow, to cast down the poor and needy, *and* to slay such as be of upright conversation.

15 Their sword shall enter into their own heart, and their bows shall be broken.

16 A little that a righteous man hath *is* better than the riches of many wicked.

17 For the arms of the wicked shall be broken: but the LORD upholdeth the righteous.

18 The LORD knoweth the days of the upright: and their inheritance shall be for ever.

19 They shall not be ashamed in the evil time: and in the days of famine they shall be satisfied.

20 But the wicked shall perish, and the enemies of the LORD *shall be* as the fat of lambs: they shall consume; into smoke shall they consume away.

21 The wicked borroweth, and payeth not again: but the righteous sheweth mercy, and giveth.

22 For *such as be* blessed of him shall inherit the earth; and *they that be* cursed of him shall be cut off.

23 The steps of a *good* man are ordered by the LORD: and he delighteth in his way.

24 Though he fall, he shall not be utterly cast down: for the LORD upholdeth *him with* his hand.

25 I have been young, and *now* am old; yet have I not seen the righteous forsaken, nor his seed begging bread.

26 *He is* ever merciful, and lendeth; and his seed *is* blessed.

27 Depart from evil, and do good; and dwell for evermore.

28 For the LORD loveth judgment, and forsaketh not his saints; they are preserved for ever: but the seed of the wicked shall be cut off.

29 The righteous shall inherit the land, and dwell therein for ever.

30 The mouth of the righteous speaketh wisdom, and his tongue talketh of judgment.

31 The law of his God *is* in his heart; none of his steps shall slide.

32 The wicked watcheth the righteous, and seeketh to slay him.

33 The LORD will not leave him in his hand, nor condemn him when he is judged.

34 Wait on the LORD, and keep his way, and he shall exalt thee to inherit the land: when the wicked are cut off, thou shalt see *it.*

35 I have seen the wicked in great power, and spreading himself like a green bay tree.

36 Yet he passed away, and, lo, he *was* not: yea, I sought him, but he could not be found.

37 Mark the perfect *man*, and behold the upright: for the end of *that* man *is* peace.

38 But the transgressors shall be destroyed together: the end of the wicked shall be cut off.

39 But the salvation of the righteous *is* of the LORD: *he is* their strength in the time of trouble.

40 And the LORD shall help them, and deliver them: he shall deliver them from the wicked, and save them, because they trust in him.

A Psalm of David, to bring to remembrance.

38 O LORD, rebuke me not in thy wrath: neither chasten me in thy hot displeasure.

2 For thine arrows stick fast in me, and thy hand presseth me sore.

3 *There is* no soundness in my flesh because of thine anger; neither *is there any* rest in my bones because of my sin.

4 For mine iniquities are gone over mine head: as an heavy burden they are too heavy for me.

5 My wounds stink *and* are corrupt because of my foolishness.

6 I am troubled; I am bowed down greatly; I go mourning all the day long.

7 For my loins are filled with a loathsome *disease:* and *there is* no soundness in my flesh.

8 I am feeble and sore broken: I have roared by reason of the disquietness of my heart.

9 Lord, all my desire *is* before thee; and my groaning is not hid from thee.

10 My heart panteth, my strength faileth me: as for the light of mine eyes, it also is gone from me.

11 My lovers and my friends stand aloof from my sore; and my kinsmen stand afar off.

12 They also that seek after my life lay snares *for me:* and they that seek my hurt speak mischievous things, and imagine deceits all the day long.

13 But I, as a deaf *man*, heard not; and *I was* as a dumb man *that* openeth not his mouth.

14 Thus I was as a man that heareth not, and in whose mouth *are* no reproofs.

15 For in thee, O LORD, do I hope: thou wilt hear, O Lord my God.

16 For I said, *Hear me*, lest *otherwise* they should rejoice over me: when my foot slippeth, they magnify *themselves* against me.

17 For I *am* ready to halt, and my sorrow *is* continually before me.

18 For I will declare mine iniquity; I will be sorry for my sin.

19 But mine enemies *are* lively, *and* they are strong: and they that hate me wrongfully are multiplied.

20 They also that render evil for good are mine adversaries; because I follow *the thing that* good *is*.

21 Forsake me not, O LORD: O my God, be not far from me.

22 Make haste to help me, O Lord my salvation.

To the chief Musician, *even* to Jeduthun, A Psalm of David.

39 I SAID, I will take heed to my ways, that I sin not with my tongue: I will keep my mouth with a bridle, while the wicked is before me.

2 I was dumb with silence, I held my peace, *even* from good; and my sorrow was stirred.

3 My heart was hot within me; while I was musing the fire burned: *then* spake I with my tongue,

4 LORD, make me to know mine end, and the measure of my days, what it *is; that* I may know how frail I *am*.

5 Behold, thou hast made my days *as* an handbreadth; and mine age *is* as nothing before thee: verily every man at his best state *is* altogether vanity. Se'lah.

6 Surely every man walketh in a vain shew: surely they are disquieted in vain: he heapeth up *riches*, and knoweth not who shall gather them.

7 And now, Lord, what wait I for? my hope *is* in thee.

8 Deliver me from all my transgressions: make me not the reproach of the foolish.

9 I was dumb, I opened not my mouth; because thou didst *it*.

10 Remove thy stroke away from me: I am consumed by the blow of thine hand.

11 When thou with rebukes dost correct man for iniquity, thou makest his beauty to consume away like a moth: surely every man *is* vanity. Se'lah.

12 Hear my prayer, O LORD, and give ear unto my cry; hold not thy peace at my tears: for I *am* a stranger with thee, *and* a sojourner, as all my fathers *were*.

13 O spare me, that I may recover strength, before I go hence, and be no more.

To the chief Musician, A Psalm of David.

40 I WAITED patiently for the LORD; and he inclined unto me, and heard my cry.

2 He brought me up also out of an horrible pit, out of the miry clay, and set my feet upon a rock, *and* established my goings.

3 And he hath put a new song in my mouth, *even* praise unto our God: many shall see *it*, and fear, and shall trust in the LORD.

4 Blessed *is* that man that maketh the LORD his trust, and respecteth not the proud, nor such as turn aside to lies.

5 Many, O LORD my God, *are* thy wonderful works *which* thou hast done, and thy thoughts *which are* to us-ward: they cannot be reckoned up in order unto thee: *if* I would declare and speak *of them*, they are more than can be numbered.

6 Sacrifice and offering thou didst not desire; mine ears hast thou opened: burnt offering and sin offering hast thou not required.

7 Then said I, Lo, I come: in the volume of the book *it is* written of me,

8 I delight to do thy will, O my God: yea, thy law *is* within my heart.

9 I have preached righteousness in the great congregation: lo, I have not refrained my lips, O LORD, thou knowest.

10 I have not hid thy righteousness within my heart; I have declared thy faithfulness and thy salvation: I have not concealed thy lovingkindness and thy truth from the great congregation.

11 Withhold not thou thy tender mercies from me, O LORD: let thy lovingkindness and thy truth continually preserve me.

12 For innumerable evils have compassed me about: mine iniquities have taken hold upon me, so that I am not able to look up; they are more than the hairs of mine head: therefore my heart faileth me.

13 Be pleased, O LORD, to deliver me: O LORD, make haste to help me.

14 Let them be ashamed and confounded together that seek after my soul to destroy it; let them be driven backward and put to shame that wish me evil.

15 Let them be desolate for a reward of their shame that say unto me, Aha, aha.

16 Let all those that seek thee rejoice and be glad in thee: let such as love thy salvation say continually, The LORD be magnified.

17 But I *am* poor and needy; *yet* the Lord thinketh upon me: thou *art* my help and my deliverer; make no tarrying, O my God.

To the chief Musician, A Psalm of David.

41 BLESSED *is* he that considereth the poor: the LORD will deliver him in time of trouble.

2 The LORD will preserve him, and keep him alive; *and* he shall be blessed upon the earth: and thou wilt not deliver him unto the will of his enemies.

3 The LORD will strengthen him upon the bed of languishing: thou wilt make all his bed in his sickness.

4 I said, LORD, be merciful unto me: heal my soul; for I have sinned against thee.

5 Mine enemies speak evil of me, When shall he die, and his name perish?

6 And if he come to see *me*, he speaketh vanity: his heart gathereth iniquity to itself; *when* he goeth abroad, he telleth *it*.

7 All that hate me whisper together against me: against me do they devise my hurt.

8 An evil disease, *say they*, cleaveth fast unto him: and *now* that he lieth he shall rise up no more.

9 Yea, mine own familiar friend, in whom I trusted, which did eat of my bread, hath lifted up *his* heel against me.

10 But thou, O LORD, be merciful unto me, and raise me up, that I may requite them.

11 By this I know that thou favourest me, because mine enemy doth not triumph over me.

12 And as for me, thou upholdest me in mine integrity, and settest me before thy face for ever.

13 Blessed *be* the LORD God of Is'ra-el from everlasting, and to everlasting. Amen, and Amen.

To the chief Musician, Maschil, for the sons of Korah.

42 AS the hart panteth after the water brooks, so panteth my soul after thee, O God.

2 My soul thirsteth for God, for the living God: when shall I come and appear before God?

3 My tears have been my meat day and night, while they continually say unto me, Where *is* thy God?

4 When I remember these *things,* I pour out my soul in me: for I had gone with the multitude, I went with them to the house of God, with the voice of joy and praise, with a multitude that kept holyday.

5 Why art thou cast down, O my soul? and *why* art thou disquieted in me? hope thou in God: for I shall yet praise him *for* the help of his countenance.

6 O my God, my soul is cast down within me: therefore will I remember thee from the land of Jor'dan, and of the Her'mon-ites, from the hill Mi'zar.

7 Deep calleth unto deep at the noise of thy waterspouts: all thy waves and thy billows are gone over me.

8 *Yet* the LORD will command his lovingkindness in the daytime, and in the night his song *shall be* with me, *and* my prayer unto the God of my life.

9 I will say unto God my rock, Why hast thou forgotten me? why go I mourning because of the oppression of the enemy?

10 *As* with a sword in my bones, mine enemies reproach me; while they say daily unto me, Where *is* thy God?

11 Why art thou cast down, O my soul? and why art thou disquieted within me? hope thou in God: for I shall yet praise him, *who is* the health of my countenance, and my God.

43 JUDGE me, O God, and plead my cause against an ungodly nation: O deliver me from the deceitful and unjust man.

2 For thou *art* the God of my strength: why dost thou cast me off? why go I mourning because of the oppression of the enemy?

3 O send out thy light and thy truth: let them lead me; let them bring me unto thy holy hill, and to thy tabernacles.

4 Then will I go unto the altar of God, unto God my exceeding joy: yea, upon the harp will I praise thee, O God my God.

5 Why art thou cast down, O my soul? and why art thou disquieted within me? hope in God: for I shall yet praise him, *who is* the health of my countenance, and my God.

To the chief Musician for the sons of Korah, Maschil.

44 WE have heard with our ears, O God, our fathers have told us, *what* work thou didst in their days, in the times of old.

2 *How* thou didst drive out the heathen with thy hand, and plantedst them; *how* thou didst afflict the people, and cast them out.

3 For they got not the land in possession by their own sword, neither did their own arm save them: but thy right hand, and thine arm, and the light of thy countenance, because thou hadst a favour unto them.

4 Thou art my King, O God: command deliverances for Ja'cob.

5 Through thee will we push down our enemies: through thy name will we tread them under that rise up against us.

6 For I will not trust in my bow, neither shall my sword save me.

7 But thou hast saved us from our enemies, and hast put them to shame that hated us.

8 In God we boast all the day long, and praise thy name for ever. Se'lah.

9 But thou hast cast off, and put us to shame; and goest not forth with our armies.

10 Thou makest us to turn back from the enemy: and they which hate us spoil for themselves.

11 Thou hast given us like sheep *appointed* for meat; and hast scattered us among the heathen.

12 Thou sellest thy people for nought, and dost not increase *thy wealth* by their price.

13 Thou makest us a reproach to our neighbours, a scorn and a derision to them that are round about us.

14 Thou makest us a byword among the heathen, a shaking of the head among the people.

15 My confusion *is* continually before me, and the shame of my face hath covered me,

16 For the voice of him that reproacheth and blasphemeth; by reason of the enemy and avenger.

17 All this is come upon us; yet have we not forgotten thee, neither have we dealt falsely in thy covenant.

18 Our heart is not turned back, neither have our steps declined from thy way;

19 Though thou hast sore broken us in the place of dragons, and covered us with the shadow of death.

20 If we have forgotten the name of our God, or stretched out our hands to a strange god;

21 Shall not God search this out? for he knoweth the secrets of the heart.

22 Yea, for thy sake are we killed all the day long; we are counted as sheep for the slaughter.

23 Awake, why sleepest thou, O Lord? arise, cast *us* not off for ever.

24 Wherefore hidest thou thy face, *and* forgettest our affliction and our oppression?

25 For our soul is bowed down to the dust: our belly cleaveth unto the earth.

26 Arise for our help, and redeem us for thy mercies' sake.

To the chief Musician upon Shoshannim, for the sons of Korah, Maschil, A Song of loves.

45 MY heart is inditing a good matter: I speak of the things which I have made touching the king: my tongue *is* the pen of a ready writer.

2 Thou art fairer than the children of men: grace is poured into thy lips: therefore God hath blessed thee for ever.

3 Gird thy sword upon *thy* thigh, O *most* mighty, with thy glory and thy majesty.

4 And in thy majesty ride prosperously because of truth and meekness *and* righteousness; and thy right hand shall teach thee terrible things.

5 Thine arrows *are* sharp in the heart of the king's enemies; *whereby* the people fall under thee.

6 Thy throne, O God, *is* for ever and ever: the sceptre of thy kingdom *is* a right sceptre.

7 Thou lovest righteousness, and hatest wickedness: therefore God, thy God, hath anointed thee with the oil of gladness above thy fellows.

8 All thy garments *smell* of myrrh, and aloes, *and* cassia, out of the ivory palaces, whereby they have made thee glad.

9 Kings' daughters *were* among thy honourable women: upon thy right hand did stand the queen in gold of O'phir.

10 Hearken, O daughter, and consider, and incline thine ear; forget also thine own people, and thy father's house;

11 So shall the king greatly desire thy beauty: for he *is* thy LORD; and worship thou him.

12 And the daughter of Tyre *shall be there* with a gift; *even* the rich among the people shall intreat thy favour.

13 The king's daughter *is* all glorious within: her clothing *is* of wrought gold.

14 She shall be brought unto the king in raiment of needlework: the virgins her companions that follow her shall be brought unto thee.

15 With gladness and rejoicing shall they be brought: they shall enter into the king's palace.

16 Instead of thy fathers shall be thy children, whom thou mayest make princes in all the earth.

17 I will make thy name to be remembered in all generations: therefore shall the people praise thee for ever and ever.

To the chief Musician for the sons of Korah, A Song upon Alamoth.

46 GOD *is* our refuge and strength, a very present help in trouble.

2 Therefore will not we fear, though the earth be removed, and though the mountains be carried into the midst of the sea;

3 *Though* the waters thereof roar *and* be troubled, *though* the mountains shake with the swelling thereof. Se'lah.

4 *There is* a river, the streams whereof shall make glad the city of God, the holy *place* of the tabernacles of the most High.

5 God *is* in the midst of her; she shall not be moved: God shall help her, *and that* right early.

6 The heathen raged, the kingdoms were moved: he uttered his voice, the earth melted.

7 The LORD of hosts *is* with us; the God of Ja'cob *is* our refuge. Se'lah.

8 Come, behold the works of the LORD, what desolations he hath made in the earth.

9 He maketh wars to cease unto the end of the earth; he breaketh the bow, and cutteth the spear in sunder; he burneth the chariot in the fire.

10 Be still, and know that I *am* God: I will be exalted among the heathen, I will be exalted in the earth.

11 The LORD of hosts *is* with us; the God of Ja'cob *is* our refuge. Se'lah.

To the chief Musician, A Psalm for the sons of Korah.

47 O CLAP your hands, all ye people; shout unto God with the voice of triumph.

2 For the LORD most high *is* terrible; *he is* a great King over all the earth.

3 He shall subdue the people under us, and the nations under our feet.

4 He shall choose our inheritance for us, the excellency of Ja'cob whom he loved. Se'lah.

5 God is gone up with a shout, the LORD with the sound of a trumpet.

6 Sing praises to God, sing praises: sing praises unto our King, sing praises.

7 For God *is* the King of all the earth: sing ye praises with understanding.

8 God reigneth over the heathen: God sitteth upon the throne of his holiness.

9 The princes of the people are gathered together, *even* the people of the God of A'braham: for the shields of the earth *belong* unto God: he is greatly exalted.

A Song *and* Psalm for the sons of Korah.

48 GREAT *is* the LORD, and greatly to be praised in the city of our God, *in* the mountain of his holiness.

2 Beautiful for situation, the joy of the whole earth, *is* mount Zi'on, *on* the sides of the north, the city of the great King.

3 God is known in her palaces for a refuge.

4 For, lo, the kings were assembled, they passed by together.

5 They saw *it, and* so they marvelled; they were troubled, *and* hasted away.

6 Fear took hold upon them there, *and* pain, as of a woman in travail.

7 Thou breakest the ships of Tar'shish with an east wind.

8 As we have heard, so have we seen in the city of the LORD of hosts, in the city of our God: God will establish it for ever. Se'lah.

9 We have thought of thy lovingkindness, O God, in the midst of thy temple.

10 According to thy name, O God, so *is* thy praise unto the ends of the earth: thy right hand is full of righteousness.

11 Let mount Zi'on rejoice, let the daughters of Ju'dah be glad, because of thy judgments.

12 Walk about Zi'on, and go round about her: tell the towers thereof.

13 Mark ye well her bulwarks, consider her palaces; that ye may tell *it* to the generation following.

14 For this God *is* our God for ever and ever: he will be our guide *even* unto death.

To the chief Musician, A Psalm for the sons of Korah.

49 HEAR this, all *ye* people; give ear, all *ye* inhabitants of the world:

2 Both low and high, rich and poor, together.

3 My mouth shall speak of wisdom; and the meditation of my heart *shall be* of understanding.

4 I will incline mine ear to a parable: I will open my dark saying upon the harp.

5 Wherefore should I fear in the days of evil, *when* the iniquity of my heels shall compass me about?

6 They that trust in their wealth, and boast themselves in the multitude of their riches;

7 None *of them* can by any means redeem his brother, nor give to God a ransom for him:

8 (For the redemption of their soul *is* precious, and it ceaseth for ever:)

9 That he should still live for ever, *and* not see corruption.

10 For he seeth *that* wise men die, likewise the fool and the brutish person perish, and leave their wealth to others.

11 Their inward thought *is, that* their houses *shall continue* for ever, *and* their dwelling places to all generations; they call *their* lands after their own names.

12 Nevertheless man *being* in honour abideth not: he is like the beasts *that* perish.

13 This their way *is* their folly: yet their posterity approve their sayings. Se'lah.

14 Like sheep they are laid in the grave; death shall feed on them; and the upright shall have dominion over them in the morning; and their beauty shall consume in the grave from their dwelling.

15 But God will redeem my soul from the power of the grave: for he shall receive me. Se'lah.

16 Be not thou afraid when one is made rich, when the glory of his house is increased;

17 For when he dieth he shall carry nothing away: his glory shall not descend after him.

18 Though while he lived he blessed his soul: and *men* will praise thee, when thou doest well to thyself.

19 He shall go to the generation of his fathers; they shall never see light.

20 Man *that is* in honour, and understandeth not, is like the beasts *that* perish.

A Psalm of Asaph.

50 THE mighty God, *even* the LORD, hath spoken, and called the earth from the rising of the sun unto the going down thereof.

2 Out of Zi'on, the perfection of beauty, God hath shined.

3 Our God shall come, and shall not keep silence: a fire shall devour before him, and it shall be very tempestuous round about him.

4 He shall call to the heavens from above, and to the earth, that he may judge his people.

5 Gather my saints together unto me; those that have made a covenant with me by sacrifice.

6 And the heavens shall declare his righteousness: for God *is* judge himself. Se'lah.

7 Hear, O my people, and I will speak; O Is'-ra-el, and I will testify against thee: I *am* God, *even* thy God.

8 I will not reprove thee for thy sacrifices or thy burnt offerings, *to have been* continually before me.

9 I will take no bullock out of thy house, *nor* he goats out of thy folds.

10 For every beast of the forest *is* mine, *and* the cattle upon a thousand hills.

11 I know all the fowls of the mountains: and the wild beasts of the field *are* mine.

12 If I were hungry, I would not tell thee: for the world *is* mine, and the fulness thereof.

13 Will I eat the flesh of bulls, or drink the blood of goats?

14 Offer unto God thanksgiving; and pay thy vows unto the most High:

15 And call upon me in the day of trouble: I will deliver thee, and thou shalt glorify me.

16 But unto the wicked God saith, What hast thou to do to declare my statutes, or *that* thou shouldest take my covenant in thy mouth?

17 Seeing thou hatest instruction, and castest my words behind thee.

18 When thou sawest a thief, then thou consentedst with him, and hast been partaker with adulterers.

19 Thou givest thy mouth to evil, and thy tongue frameth deceit.

20 Thou sittest *and* speakest against thy brother; thou slanderest thine own mother's son.

21 These *things* hast thou done, and I kept silence; thou thoughtest that I was altogether *such an one* as thyself: *but* I will reprove thee, and set *them* in order before thine eyes.

22 Now consider this, ye that forget God, lest I tear *you* in pieces, and *there be* none to deliver.

23 Whoso offereth praise glorifieth me: and to him that ordereth *his* conversation *aright* will I shew the salvation of God.

To the chief Musician, A Psalm of David, when Nathan the prophet came unto him, after he had gone in to Bath-sheba.

51 HAVE mercy upon me, O God, according to thy lovingkindness: according unto the multitude of thy tender mercies blot out my transgressions.

2 Wash me throughly from mine iniquity, and cleanse me from my sin.

3 For I acknowledge my transgressions: and my sin *is* ever before me.

4 Against thee, thee only, have I sinned, and done *this* evil in thy sight: that thou mightest be justified when thou speakest, *and* be clear when thou judgest.

5 Behold, I was shapen in iniquity; and in sin did my mother conceive me.

6 Behold, thou desirest truth in the inward parts: and in the hidden *part* thou shalt make me to know wisdom.

7 Purge me with hyssop, and I shall be clean: wash me, and I shall be whiter than snow.

8 Make me to hear joy and gladness; *that* the bones *which* thou hast broken may rejoice.

9 Hide thy face from my sins, and blot out all mine iniquities.

10 Create in me a clean heart, O God; and renew a right spirit within me.

11 Cast me not away from thy presence; and take not thy holy spirit from me.

12 Restore unto me the joy of thy salvation; and uphold me *with thy* free spirit.

13 *Then* will I teach transgressors thy ways; and sinners shall be converted unto thee.

14 Deliver me from bloodguiltiness, O God, thou God of my salvation: *and* my tongue shall sing aloud of thy righteousness.

15 O Lord, open thou my lips; and my mouth shall shew forth thy praise.

16 For thou desirest not sacrifice; else would I give *it:* thou delightest not in burnt offering.

17 The sacrifices of God *are* a broken spirit: a broken and a contrite heart, O God, thou wilt not despise.

18 Do good in thy good pleasure unto Zi'on: build thou the walls of Je-ru'sa-lem.

19 Then shalt thou be pleased with the sacrifices of righteousness, with burnt offering and whole burnt offering: then shall they offer bullocks upon thine altar.

To the chief Musician, Maschil, *A Psalm* of David, when Doeg the Edomite came and told Saul, and said unto him, David is come to the house of Ahimelech.

52 WHY boastest thou thyself in mischief, O mighty man? the goodness of God *endureth* continually.

2 Thy tongue deviseth mischiefs; like a sharp razor, working deceitfully.

3 Thou lovest evil more than good; *and* lying rather than to speak righteousness. Se'lah.

4 Thou lovest all devouring words, O *thou* deceitful tongue.

5 God shall likewise destroy thee for ever, he shall take thee away, and pluck thee out of *thy* dwelling place, and root thee out of the land of the living. Se'lah.

6 The righteous also shall see, and fear, and shall laugh at him:

7 Lo, *this is* the man *that* made not God his strength; but trusted in the abundance of his riches, *and* strengthened himself in his wickedness.

8 But I *am* like a green olive tree in the house of God: I trust in the mercy of God for ever and ever.

9 I will praise thee for ever, because thou hast done *it:* and I will wait on thy name; for *it is* good before thy saints.

To the chief Musician, upon Mahalath, Maschil, *A Psalm* of David.

53 THE fool hath said in his heart, *There is* no God. Corrupt are they, and have done abominable iniquity: *there is* none that doeth good.

2 God looked down from heaven upon the children of men, to see if there were *any* that did understand, that did seek God.

3 Every one of them is gone back: they are altogether become filthy; *there is* none that doeth good, no, not one.

4 Have the workers of iniquity no knowledge? who eat up my people *as* they eat bread: they have not called upon God.

5 There were they in great fear, *where* no fear was: for God hath scattered the bones of him that encampeth *against* thee: thou hast put *them* to shame, because God hath despised them.

6 Oh that the salvation of Is'ra-el *were come* out of Zi'on! When God bringeth back the captivity of his people, Ja'cob shall rejoice *and* Is'-ra-el shall be glad.

To the chief Musician on Neginoth, Maschil, *A Psalm* of David, when the Ziphims came and said to Saul, Doth not David hide himself with us?

54 SAVE me, O God, by thy name, and judge me by thy strength.

2 Hear my prayer, O God; give ear to the words of my mouth.

3 For strangers are risen up against me, and oppressors seek after my soul: they have not set God before them. Se'lah.

4 Behold, God *is* mine helper: the Lord *is* with them that uphold my soul.

5 He shall reward evil unto mine enemies: cut them off in thy truth.

6 I will freely sacrifice unto thee: I will praise thy name, O LORD; for *it is* good.

7 For he hath delivered me out of all trouble: and mine eye hath seen *his desire* upon mine enemies.

To the chief Musician on Neginoth, Maschil, *A Psalm* of David.

55 GIVE ear to my prayer, O God; and hide not thyself from my supplication.

2 Attend unto me, and hear me: I mourn in my complaint, and make a noise;

3 Because of the voice of the enemy, because of the oppression of the wicked: for they cast iniquity upon me, and in wrath they hate me.

4 My heart is sore pained within me: and the terrors of death are fallen upon me.

5 Fearfulness and trembling are come upon me, and horror hath overwhelmed me.

6 And I said, Oh that I had wings like a dove! *for then* would I fly away, and be at rest.

7 Lo, *then* would I wander far off, *and* remain in the wilderness. Se'lah.

8 I would hasten my escape from the windy storm and tempest.

9 Destroy, O Lord, *and* divide their tongues: for I have seen violence and strife in the city.

10 Day and night they go about it upon the walls thereof: mischief also and sorrow *are* in the midst of it.

11 Wickedness *is* in the midst thereof: deceit and guile depart not from her streets.

12 For *it was* not an enemy *that* reproached me; then I could have borne *it*: neither *was it* he that hated me *that* did magnify *himself* against me; then I would have hid myself from him:

13 But *it was* thou, a man mine equal, my guide, and mine acquaintance.

14 We took sweet counsel together, *and* walked unto the house of God in company.

15 Let death seize upon them, *and* let them go down quick into hell: for wickedness *is* in their dwellings, *and* among them.

16 As for me, I will call upon God; and the LORD shall save me.

17 Evening, and morning, and at noon, will I pray, and cry aloud: and he shall hear my voice.

18 He hath delivered my soul in peace from the battle *that was* against me: for there were many with me.

19 God shall hear, and afflict them, even he that abideth of old. Se'lah. Because they have no changes, therefore they fear not God.

20 He hath put forth his hands against such as be at peace with him: he hath broken his covenant.

21 *The words* of his mouth were smoother than butter, but war *was* in his heart: his words were softer than oil, yet *were* they drawn swords.

22 Cast thy burden upon the LORD, and he shall sustain thee: he shall never suffer the righteous to be moved.

23 But thou, O God, shalt bring them down into the pit of destruction: bloody and deceitful men shall not live out half their days; but I will trust in thee.

To the chief Musician upon Jonath-elem-rechokim, Michtam of David, when the Philistines took him in Gath.

56 BE merciful unto me, O God: for man would swallow me up; he fighting daily oppresseth me.

2 Mine enemies would daily swallow *me* up: for *they* be many that fight against me, O thou most High.

3 What time I am afraid, I will trust in thee.

4 In God I will praise his word, in God I have put my trust; I will not fear what flesh can do unto me.

5 Every day they wrest my words: all their thoughts *are* against me for evil.

6 They gather themselves together, they hide themselves, they mark my steps, when they wait for my soul.

7 Shall they escape by iniquity? in *thine* anger cast down the people, O God.

8 Thou tellest my wanderings: put thou my tears into thy bottle: *are they* not in thy book?

9 When I cry *unto thee*, then shall mine enemies turn back: this I know; for God *is* for me.

10 In God will I praise *his* word: in the LORD will I praise *his* word.

11 In God have I put my trust: I will not be afraid what man can do unto me.

12 Thy vows *are* upon me, O God: I will render praises unto thee.

13 For thou hast delivered my soul from death: *wilt* not *thou deliver* my feet from falling, that I may walk before God in the light of the living?

To the chief Musician, Al-taschith, Michtam of David, when he fled from Saul in the cave.

57 BE merciful unto me, O God, be merciful unto me: for my soul trusteth in thee: yea, in the shadow of thy wings will I make my refuge, until *these* calamities be overpast.

2 I will cry unto God most high; unto God that performeth *all things* for me.

3 He shall send from heaven, and save me *from* the reproach of him that would swallow me up. Se'lah. God shall send forth his mercy and his truth.

4 My soul *is* among lions: *and* I lie *even among* them that are set on fire, *even* the sons of men, whose teeth *are* spears and arrows, and their tongue a sharp sword.

5 Be thou exalted, O God, above the heavens; *let* thy glory *be* above all the earth.

6 They have prepared a net for my steps; my soul is bowed down: they have digged a pit before me, into the midst whereof they are fallen *themselves*. Se'lah.

7 My heart is fixed, O God, my heart is fixed: I will sing and give praise.

8 Awake up, my glory; awake, psaltery and harp: I *myself* will awake early.

9 I will praise thee, O Lord, among the people: I will sing unto thee among the nations.

10 For thy mercy *is* great unto the heavens, and thy truth unto the clouds.

11 Be thou exalted, O God, above the heavens: *let* thy glory *be* above all the earth.

To the chief Musician, Al-taschith, Michtam of David.

58 DO ye indeed speak righteousness, O congregation? do ye judge uprightly, O ye sons of men?

2 Yea, in heart ye work wickedness; ye weigh the violence of your hands in the earth.

3 The wicked are estranged from the womb: they go astray as soon as they be born, speaking lies.

4 Their poison *is* like the poison of a serpent: *they are* like the deaf adder *that* stoppeth her ear;

5 Which will not hearken to the voice of charmers, charming never so wisely.

6 Break their teeth, O God, in their mouth: break out the great teeth of the young lions, O LORD.

7 Let them melt away as waters *which* run continually: *when* he bendeth *his* bow *to shoot* his arrows, let them be as cut in pieces.

8 As a snail *which* melteth, let *every one of them* pass away: *like* the untimely birth of a woman, *that* they may not see the sun.

9 Before your pots can feel the thorns, he shall take them away as with a whirlwind, both living, and in *his* wrath.

10 The righteous shall rejoice when he seeth the vengeance: he shall wash his feet in the blood of the wicked.

11 So that a man shall say, Verily *there is* a reward for the righteous: verily he *is* a God that judgeth in the earth.

To the chief Musician, Al-taschith, Michtam of David, when Saul sent, and they watched the house to kill him.

59 DELIVER me from mine enemies, O my God: defend me from them that rise up against me.

2 Deliver me from the workers of iniquity, and save me from bloody men.

3 For, lo, they lie in wait for my soul: the mighty are gathered against me; not *for* my transgression, nor *for* my sin, O LORD.

4 They run and prepare themselves without *my* fault: awake to help me, and behold.

5 Thou therefore, O LORD God of hosts, the God of Is'ra-el, awake to visit all the heathen: be not merciful to any wicked transgressors. Se'lah.

6 They return at evening: they make a noise like a dog, and go round about the city.

7 Behold, they belch out with their mouth: swords *are* in their lips: for who, *say they,* doth hear?

8 But thou, O LORD, shalt laugh at them; thou shalt have all the heathen in derision.

9 *Because of* his strength will I wait upon thee: for God *is* my defence.

10 The God of my mercy shall prevent me: God shall let me see *my desire* upon mine enemies.

11 Slay them not, lest my people forget: scatter them by thy power; and bring them down, O Lord our shield.

12 *For* the sin of their mouth *and* the words of their lips let them even be taken in their pride: and for cursing and lying *which* they speak.

13 Consume *them* in wrath, consume *them,* that they *may* not *be:* and let them know that God ruleth in Ja'cob unto the ends of the earth. Se'lah.

14 And at evening let them return; *and* let them make a noise like a dog, and go round about the city.

15 Let them wander up and down for meat, and grudge if they be not satisfied.

16 But I will sing of thy power; yea, I will sing aloud of thy mercy in the morning: for thou hast been my defence and refuge in the day of my trouble.

17 Unto thee, O my strength, will I sing: for God *is* my defence, *and* the God of my mercy.

To the chief Musician upon Shushan-eduth, Michtam of David, to teach; when he strove with Aram-naharaim, and with Aram-zobah, when Joab returned, and smote of Edom in the valley of Salt twelve thousand.

60 O GOD, thou hast cast us off, thou hast scattered us, thou hast been displeased; O turn thyself to us again.

2 Thou hast made the earth to tremble; thou hast broken it: heal the breaches thereof; for it shaketh.

3 Thou hast shewed thy people hard things: thou hast made us to drink the wine of astonishment.

4 Thou hast given a banner to them that fear thee, that it may be displayed because of the truth. Se'lah.

5 That thy beloved may be delivered; save *with* thy right hand, and hear me.

6 God hath spoken in his holiness; I will rejoice, I will divide She'chem, and mete out the valley of Suc'coth.

7 Gil'e-ad *is* mine, and Ma-nas'seh *is* mine; E'phra-im also *is* the strength of mine head; Ju'-dah *is* my lawgiver;

8 Mo'ab *is* my washpot; over E'dom will I cast out my shoe: Phi-lis'tia, triumph thou because of me.

9 Who will bring me *into* the strong city? who will lead me into E'dom?

10 *Wilt* not thou, O God, *which* hadst cast us off? and thou, O God, *which* didst not go out with our armies?

11 Give us help from trouble: for vain *is* the help of man.

12 Through God we shall do valiantly: for he *it is that* shall tread down our enemies.

To the chief Musician upon Neginah, *A Psalm* of David.

61 HEAR my cry, O God; attend unto my prayer.

2 From the end of the earth will I cry unto thee, when my heart is overwhelmed: lead me to the rock *that* is higher than I.

3 For thou hast been a shelter for me, *and a* strong tower from the enemy.

4 I will abide in thy tabernacle for ever: I will trust in the covert of thy wings. Se'lah.

5 For thou, O God, hast heard my vows: thou hast given *me* the heritage of those that fear thy name.

6 Thou wilt prolong the king's life: *and* his years as many generations.

7 He shall abide before God for ever: O prepare mercy and truth, *which* may preserve him.

8 So will I sing praise unto thy name for ever, that I may daily perform my vows.

To the chief Musician, to Jeduthun, A Psalm of David.

62 TRULY my soul waiteth upon God: from him *cometh* my salvation.

2 He only *is* my rock and my salvation; *he is* my defence; I shall not be greatly moved.

3 How long will ye imagine mischief against a man? ye shall be slain all of you: as a bowing wall *shall ye be, and as* a tottering fence.

4 They only consult to cast *him* down from his excellency: they delight in lies: they bless with their mouth, but they curse inwardly. Se'lah.

5 My soul, wait thou only upon God; for my expectation *is* from him.

6 He only *is* my rock and my salvation: *he is* my defence; I shall not be moved.

7 In God *is* my salvation and my glory: the rock of my strength, *and* my refuge, *is* in God.

8 Trust in him at all times; ye people, pour out your heart before him: God *is* a refuge for us. Se'lah.

9 Surely men of low degree *are* vanity, *and* men of high degree *are* a lie: to be laid in the balance, they *are* altogether *lighter* than vanity.

10 Trust not in oppression, and become not vain in robbery: if riches increase, set not your heart *upon them.*

11 God hath spoken once; twice have I heard this; that power *belongeth* unto God.

12 Also unto thee, O Lord, *belongeth* mercy: for thou renderest to every man according to his work.

A Psalm of David, when he was in the wilderness of Judah.

63 O GOD, thou *art* my God; early will I seek thee: my soul thirsteth for thee, my flesh longeth for thee in a dry and thirsty land, where no water is;

2 To see thy power and thy glory, so *as* I have seen thee in the sanctuary.

3 Because thy lovingkindness *is* better than life, my lips shall praise thee.

4 Thus will I bless thee while I live: I will lift up my hands in thy name.

5 My soul shall be satisfied as *with* marrow and fatness; and my mouth shall praise *thee* with joyful lips:

6 When I remember thee upon my bed, *and* meditate on thee in the *night* watches.

7 Because thou hast been my help, therefore in the shadow of thy wings will I rejoice.

8 My soul followeth hard after thee: thy right hand upholdeth me.

9 But those *that* seek my soul, to destroy *it,* shall go into the lower parts of the earth.

10 They shall fall by the sword: they shall be a portion for foxes.

11 But the king shall rejoice in God; every one that sweareth by him shall glory: but the mouth of them that speak lies shall be stopped.

To the chief Musician, A Psalm of David.

64 HEAR my voice, O God, in my prayer: preserve my life from fear of the enemy.

2 Hide me from the secret counsel of the wicked; from the insurrection of the workers of iniquity:

3 Who whet their tongue like a sword, *and* bend *their bows to shoot* their arrows, *even* bitter words:

4 That they may shoot in secret at the perfect: suddenly do they shoot at him, and fear not.

5 They encourage themselves *in* an evil matter: they commune of laying snares privily; they say, Who shall see them?

6 They search out iniquities; they accomplish a diligent search: both the inward *thought* of every one *of them,* and the heart, *is* deep.

7 But God shall shoot at them *with* an arrow; suddenly shall they be wounded.

8 So they shall make their own tongue to fall upon themselves: all that see them shall flee away.

9 And all men shall fear, and shall declare the work of God; for they shall wisely consider of his doing.

10 The righteous shall be glad in the LORD, and shall trust in him; and all the upright in heart shall glory.

To the chief Musician, A Psalm *and* Song of David.

65 PRAISE waiteth for thee, O God, in Si'on: and unto thee shall the vow be performed:

2 O thou that hearest prayer, unto thee shall all flesh come.

3 Iniquities prevail against me: *as for* our transgressions, thou shalt purge them away.

4 Blessed *is the* man *whom* thou choosest, and causest to approach *unto thee, that* he may dwell in thy courts: we shall be satisfied with the goodness of thy house, *even* of thy holy temple.

5 *By* terrible things in righteousness wilt thou answer us, O God of our salvation; *who art* the confidence of all the ends of the earth, and of them that are afar off *upon* the sea:

6 Which by his strength setteth fast the mountains; *being* girded with power:

7 Which stilleth the noise of the seas, the noise of their waves, and the tumult of the people.

8 They also that dwell in the uttermost parts are afraid at thy tokens: thou makest the outgoings of the morning and evening to rejoice.

9 Thou visitest the earth, and waterest it: thou greatly enrichest it with the river of God, *which* is full of water: thou preparest them corn, when thou hast so provided for it.

10 Thou waterest the ridges thereof abundantly: thou settlest the furrows thereof: thou makest it soft with showers: thou blessest the springing thereof.

11 Thou crownest the year with thy goodness; and thy paths drop fatness.

12 They drop *upon* the pastures of the wilderness: and the little hills rejoice on every side.

13 The pastures are clothed with flocks; the valleys also are covered over with corn; they shout for joy, they also sing.

To the chief Musician, A Song *or* Psalm.

66 MAKE a joyful noise unto God, all ye lands:

2 Sing forth the honour of his name: make his praise glorious.

3 Say unto God, How terrible *art thou in* thy works! through the greatness of thy power shall thine enemies submit themselves unto thee.

4 All the earth shall worship thee, and shall sing unto thee; they shall sing *to* thy name. Se'-lah.

5 Come and see the works of God: *he is* terrible *in his* doing toward the children of men.

6 He turned the sea into dry land: they went through the flood on foot: there did we rejoice in him.

7 He ruleth by his power for ever; his eyes behold the nations: let not the rebellious exalt themselves. Se'lah.

8 O bless our God, ye people, and make the voice of his praise to be heard:

9 Which holdeth our soul in life, and suffereth not our feet to be moved.

10 For thou, O God, hast proved us: thou hast tried us, as silver is tried.

11 Thou broughtest us into the net; thou laidst affliction upon our loins.

12 Thou hast caused men to ride over our heads; we went through fire and through water: but thou broughtest us out into a wealthy *place.*

13 I will go into thy house with burnt offerings: I will pay thee my vows,

14 Which my lips have uttered, and my mouth hath spoken, when I was in trouble.

15 I will offer unto thee burnt sacrifices of fatlings, with the incense of rams; I will offer bullocks with goats. Se'lah.

16 Come *and* hear, all ye that fear God, and I will declare what he hath done for my soul.

17 I cried unto him with my mouth, and he was extolled with my tongue.

18 If I regard iniquity in my heart, the Lord will not hear *me:*

19 *But* verily God hath heard *me;* he hath attended to the voice of my prayer.

20 Blessed *be* God, which hath not turned away my prayer, nor his mercy from me.

To the chief Musician on Neginoth, A Psalm *or* Song.

67 GOD be merciful unto us, and bless us; *and* cause his face to shine upon us; Se'-lah.

2 That thy way may be known upon earth, thy saving health among all nations.

3 Let the people praise thee, O God; let all the people praise thee.

4 O let the nations be glad and sing for joy: for thou shalt judge the people righteously, and govern the nations upon earth. Se'lah

5 Let the people praise thee, O God; let all the people praise thee.

6 *Then* shall the earth yield her increase; *and* God, *even* our own God, shall bless us.

7 God shall bless us; and all the ends of the earth shall fear him.

To the chief Musician, A Psalm *or* Song of David.

68 LET God arise, let his enemies be scattered: let them also that hate him flee before him.

2 As smoke is driven away, *so* drive *them* away: as wax melteth before the fire, *so* let the wicked perish at the presence of God.

3 But let the righteous be glad; let them rejoice before God: yea, let them exceedingly rejoice.

4 Sing unto God, sing praises to his name: extol him that rideth upon the heavens by his name JAH, and rejoice before him.

5 A father of the fatherless, and a judge of the widows, *is* God in his holy habitation.

6 God setteth the solitary in families: he bringeth out those which are bound with chains: but the rebellious dwell in a dry *land.*

7 O God, when thou wentest forth before thy people, when thou didst march through the wilderness; Se'lah:

8 The earth shook, the heavens also dropped at the presence of God: *even* Si'nai itself *was moved* at the presence of God, the God of Is'ra-el.

9 Thou, O God, didst send a plentiful rain, whereby thou didst confirm thine inheritance, when it was weary.

10 Thy congregation hath dwelt therein: thou, O God, hast prepared of thy goodness for the poor.

11 The Lord gave the word: great *was* the company of those that published *it.*

12 Kings of armies did flee apace: and she that tarried at home divided the spoil.

13 Though ye have lien among the pots, *yet shall ye be as* the wings of a dove covered with silver, and her feathers with yellow gold.

14 When the Almighty scattered kings in it, it was *white* as snow in Sal'mon.

15 The hill of God *is as* the hill of Ba'shan; an high hill *as* the hill of Ba'shan.

16 Why leap ye, ye high hills? *this is* the hill *which* God desireth to dwell in; yea, the LORD will dwell *in it* for ever.

17 The chariots of God *are* twenty thousand, *even* thousands of angels: the Lord *is* among them, *as in* Si'nai, in the holy *place.*

18 Thou hast ascended on high, thou hast led captivity captive: thou hast received gifts for men; yea, *for* the rebellious also, that the LORD God might dwell *among them.*

19 Blessed *be* the Lord, *who* daily loadeth us *with benefits, even* the God of our salvation. Se'lah.

20 *He that is* our God *is* the God of salvation; and unto GOD the Lord *belong* the issues from death.

21 But God shall wound the head of his enemies, *and* the hairy scalp of such an one as goeth on still in his trespasses.

22 The Lord said, I will bring again from Ba'-shan, I will bring *my people* again from the depths of the sea:

23 That thy foot may be dipped in the blood of *thine* enemies, *and* the tongue of thy dogs in the same.

24 They have seen thy goings, O God; *even* the goings of my God, my King, in the sanctuary.

25 The singers went before, the players on instruments *followed* after; among *them were* the damsels playing with timbrels.

26 Bless ye God in the congregations, *even* the Lord, from the fountain of Is'ra-el.

27 There is little Ben′ja-min with their ruler, the princes of Ju′dah and their council, the princes of Zeb′u-lun, and the princes of Naph′-ta-li.

28 Thy God hath commanded thy strength: strengthen, O God, that which thou hast wrought for us.

29 Because of thy temple at Je-ru′sa-lem shall kings bring presents unto thee.

30 Rebuke the company of spearmen, the multitude of the bulls, with the calves of the people, till every one submit himself with pieces of silver: scatter thou the people that delight in war.

31 Princes shall come out of E′gypt; E-thi-o′-pi-a shall soon stretch out her hands unto God.

32 Sing unto God, ye kingdoms of the earth; O sing praises unto the Lord; Se′lah:

33 To him that rideth upon the heavens of heavens, which were of old; lo, he doth send out his voice, and that a mighty voice.

34 Ascribe ye strength unto God: his excellency is over Is′ra-el, and his strength is in the clouds.

35 O God, thou art terrible out of thy holy places: the God of Is′ra-el is he that giveth strength and power unto his people. Blessed be God.

To the chief Musician upon Shoshannim, A Psalm of David.

69 SAVE me, O God; for the waters are come in unto my soul.

2 I sink in deep mire, where there is no standing: I am come into deep waters, where the floods overflow me.

3 I am weary of my crying: my throat is dried: mine eyes fail while I wait for my God.

4 They that hate me without a cause are more than the hairs of mine head: they that would destroy me, being mine enemies wrongfully, are mighty: then I restored that which I took not away.

5 O God, thou knowest my foolishness; and my sins are not hid from thee.

6 Let not them that wait on thee, O Lord GOD of hosts, be ashamed for my sake: let not those that seek thee be confounded for my sake, O God of Is′ra-el.

7 Because for thy sake I have borne reproach; shame hath covered my face.

8 I am become a stranger unto my brethren, and an alien unto my mother's children.

9 For the zeal of thine house hath eaten me up; and the reproaches of them that reproached thee are fallen upon me.

10 When I wept, and chastened my soul with fasting, that was to my reproach.

11 I made sackcloth also my garment; and I became a proverb to them.

12 They that sit in the gate speak against me; and I was the song of the drunkards.

13 But as for me, my prayer is unto thee, O Lord, in an acceptable time: O God, in the multitude of thy mercy hear me, in the truth of thy salvation.

14 Deliver me out of the mire, and let me not sink: let me be delivered from them that hate me, and out of the deep waters.

15 Let not the waterflood overflow me, neither let the deep swallow me up, and let not the pit shut her mouth upon me.

16 Hear me, O Lord; for thy lovingkindness is good: turn unto me according to the multitude of thy tender mercies.

17 And hide not thy face from thy servant; for I am in trouble: hear me speedily.

18 Draw nigh unto my soul, and redeem it: deliver me because of mine enemies.

19 Thou hast known my reproach, and my shame, and my dishonour: mine adversaries are all before thee.

20 Reproach hath broken my heart; and I am full of heaviness: and I looked for some to take pity, but there was none; and for comforters, but I found none.

21 They gave me also gall for my meat; and in my thirst they gave me vinegar to drink.

22 Let their table become a snare before them: and that which should have been for their welfare, let it become a trap.

23 Let their eyes be darkened, that they see not; and make their loins continually to shake.

24 Pour out thine indignation upon them, and let thy wrathful anger take hold of them.

25 Let their habitation be desolate; and let none dwell in their tents.

26 For they persecute him whom thou hast smitten; and they talk to the grief of those whom thou hast wounded.

27 Add iniquity unto their iniquity: and let them not come into thy righteousness.

28 Let them be blotted out of the book of the living, and not be written with the righteous.

29 But I am poor and sorrowful: let thy salvation, O God, set me up on high.

30 I will praise the name of God with a song, and will magnify him with thanksgiving.

31 This also shall please the LORD better than an ox or bullock that hath horns and hoofs.

32 The humble shall see this, and be glad: and your heart shall live that seek God.

33 For the LORD heareth the poor, and despiseth not his prisoners.

34 Let the heaven and earth praise him, the seas, and every thing that moveth therein.

35 For God will save Zi′on, and will build the cities of Ju′dah: that they may dwell there, and have it in possession.

36 The seed also of his servants shall inherit it: and they that love his name shall dwell therein.

To the chief Musician, A Psalm of David, to bring to remembrance.

70 MAKE haste, O God, to deliver me; make haste to help me, O LORD.

2 Let them be ashamed and confounded that seek after my soul: let them be turned backward, and put to confusion, that desire my hurt.

3 Let them be turned back for a reward of their shame that say, Aha, aha.

4 Let all those that seek thee rejoice and be glad in thee: and let such as love thy salvation say continually, Let God be magnified.

5 But I am poor and needy: make haste unto me, O God, thou art my help and my deliverer; O LORD, make no tarrying.

71 IN thee, O LORD, do I put my trust: let me never be put to confusion.

2 Deliver me in thy righteousness, and cause me to escape: incline thine ear unto me, and save me.

3 Be thou my strong habitation, whereunto I may continually resort: thou hast given commandment to save me; for thou art my rock and my fortress.

4 Deliver me, O my God, out of the hand of the wicked, out of the hand of the unrighteous and cruel man.

5 For thou *art* my hope, O Lord God: *thou art* my trust from my youth.

6 By thee have I been holden up from the womb: thou art he that took me out of my mother's bowels: my praise *shall be* continually of thee.

7 I am as a wonder unto many; but thou *art* my strong refuge.

8 Let my mouth be filled *with* thy praise *and* with thy honour all the day.

9 Cast me not off in the time of old age; forsake me not when my strength faileth.

10 For mine enemies speak against me; and they that lay wait for my soul take counsel together.

11 Saying, God hath forsaken him: persecute and take him; for *there is* none to deliver *him.*

12 O God, be not far from me: O my God, make haste for my help.

13 Let them be confounded *and* consumed that are adversaries to my soul; let them be covered *with* reproach and dishonour that seek my hurt.

14 But I will hope continually, and will yet praise thee more and more.

15 My mouth shall shew forth thy righteousness *and* thy salvation all the day; for I know not the numbers *thereof.*

16 I will go in the strength of the Lord God: I will make mention of thy righteousness, *even* of thine only.

17 O God, thou hast taught me from my youth: and hitherto have I declared thy wondrous works.

18 Now also when I am old and grayheaded, O God, forsake me not; until I have shewed thy strength unto *this* generation, *and* thy power to every one *that* is to come.

19 Thy righteousness also, O God, *is* very high, who hast done great things: O God, who *is* like unto thee!

20 *Thou,* which hast shewed me great and sore troubles, shalt quicken me again, and shalt bring me up again from the depths of the earth.

21 Thou shalt increase my greatness, and comfort me on every side.

22 I will also praise thee with the psaltery, *even* thy truth, O my God: unto thee will I sing with the harp, O thou Holy One of Is'ra-el.

23 My lips shall greatly rejoice when I sing unto thee; and my soul, which thou hast redeemed.

24 My tongue also shall talk of thy righteousness all the day long: for they are confounded, for they are brought unto shame, that seek my hurt.

A Psalm for Solomon.

72 GIVE the king thy judgments, O God, and thy righteousness unto the king's son.

2 He shall judge thy people with righteousness, and thy poor with judgment.

3 The mountains shall bring peace to the people, and the little hills, by righteousness.

4 He shall judge the poor of the people, he shall save the children of the needy, and shall break in pieces the oppressor.

5 They shall fear thee as long as the sun and moon endure, throughout all generations.

6 He shall come down like rain upon the mown grass: as showers *that* water the earth.

7 In his days shall the righteous flourish; and abundance of peace so long as the moon endureth.

8 He shall have dominion also from sea to sea, and from the river unto the ends of the earth.

9 They that dwell in the wilderness shall bow before him; and his enemies shall lick the dust.

10 The kings of Tar'shish and of the isles shall bring presents: the kings of She'ba and Se'ba shall offer gifts.

11 Yea, all kings shall fall down before him: all nations shall serve him.

12 For he shall deliver the needy when he crieth; the poor also, and *him* that hath no helper.

13 He shall spare the poor and needy, and shall save the souls of the needy.

14 He shall redeem their soul from deceit and violence: and precious shall their blood be in his sight.

15 And he shall live, and to him shall be given of the gold of She'ba: prayer also shall be made for him continually; *and* daily shall he be praised.

16 There shall be an handful of corn in the earth upon the top of the mountains; the fruit thereof shall shake like Leb'a-non: and *they* of the city shall flourish like grass of the earth.

17 His name shall endure for ever: his name shall be continued as long as the sun: and *men* shall be blessed in him: all nations shall call him blessed.

18 Blessed *be* the Lord God, the God of Is'ra-el, who only doeth wondrous things.

19 And blessed *be* his glorious name for ever: and let the whole earth be filled *with* his glory; Amen, and Amen.

20 The prayers of Da'vid the son of Jes'se are ended.

A Psalm of Asaph.

73 TRULY God *is* good to Is'ra-el, *even* to such as are of a clean heart.

2 But as for me, my feet were almost gone; my steps had well nigh slipped.

3 For I was envious at the foolish, *when* I saw the prosperity of the wicked.

4 For *there are* no bands in their death: but their strength *is* firm.

5 They *are* not in trouble *as other* men; neither are they plagued like *other* men.

6 Therefore pride compasseth them about as a chain; violence covereth them *as* a garment.

7 Their eyes stand out with fatness: they have more than heart could wish.

8 They are corrupt, and speak wickedly concerning oppression: they speak loftily.

9 They set their mouth against the heavens, and their tongue walketh through the earth.

10 Therefore his people return hither: and waters of a full *cup* are wrung out to them.

11 And they say, How doth God know? and is there knowledge in the most High?

12 Behold, these *are* the ungodly, who prosper in the world; they increase in riches.

13 Verily I have cleansed my heart *in* vain, and washed my hands in innocency.

14 For all the day long have I been plagued, and chastened every morning.

15 If I say, I will speak thus; behold, I should offend *against* the generation of thy children.

16 When I thought to know this, it *was* too painful for me;

17 Until I went into the sanctuary of God; *then* understood I their end.

18 Surely thou didst set them in slippery places: thou castedst them down into destruction.

19 How are they *brought* into desolation, as

in a moment! they are utterly consumed with terrors.

20 As a dream when *one* awaketh; *so*, O Lord, when thou awakest, thou shalt despise their image.

21 Thus my heart was grieved, and I was pricked in my reins.

22 So foolish *was* I, and ignorant: I was *as* a beast before thee.

23 Nevertheless I *am* continually with thee: thou hast holden *me* by my right hand.

24 Thou shalt guide me with thy counsel, and afterward receive me *to* glory.

25 Whom have I in heaven *but thee?* and *there is* none upon earth *that* I desire beside thee.

26 My flesh and my heart faileth: *but* God *is* the strength of my heart, and my portion for ever.

27 For, lo, they that are far from thee shall perish: thou hast destroyed all them that go a whoring from thee.

28 But *it is* good for me to draw near to God: I have put my trust in the Lord GOD, that I may declare all thy works.

Maschil of Asaph.

74 O GOD, why hast thou cast *us* off for ever? *why* doth thine anger smoke against the sheep of thy pasture?

2 Remember thy congregation, *which* thou hast purchased of old; the rod of thine inheritance, *which* thou hast redeemed; this mount Zi'on, wherein thou hast dwelt.

3 Lift up thy feet unto the perpetual desolations; *even all that* the enemy hath done wickedly in the sanctuary.

4 Thine enemies roar in the midst of thy congregations; they set up their ensigns *for* signs.

5 *A man* was famous according as he had lifted up axes upon the thick trees.

6 But now they break down the carved work thereof at once with axes and hammers.

7 They have cast fire into thy sanctuary, they have defiled *by casting down* the dwelling place of thy name to the ground.

8 They said in their hearts, Let us destroy them together: they have burned up all the synagogues of God in the land.

9 We see not our signs: *there is* no more any prophet: neither *is there* among us any that knoweth how long.

10 O God, how long shall the adversary reproach? shall the enemy blaspheme thy name for ever?

11 Why withdrawest thou thy hand, even thy right hand? pluck *it* out of thy bosom.

12 For God *is* my King of old, working salvation in the midst of the earth.

13 Thou didst divide the sea by thy strength: thou brakest the heads of the dragons in the waters.

14 Thou brakest the heads of leviathan in pieces, *and* gavest him *to be* meat to the people inhabiting the wilderness.

15 Thou didst cleave the fountain and the flood: thou driedst up mighty rivers.

16 The day *is* thine, the night also *is* thine: thou hast prepared the light and the sun.

17 Thou hast set all the borders of the earth: thou hast made summer and winter.

18 Remember this, *that* the enemy hath reproached, O LORD, and *that* the foolish people have blasphemed thy name.

19 O deliver not the soul of thy turtledove unto the multitude *of the wicked:* forget not the congregation of thy poor for ever.

20 Have respect unto the covenant: for the dark places of the earth are full of the habitations of cruelty.

21 O let not the oppressed return ashamed: let the poor and needy praise thy name.

22 Arise, O God, plead thine own cause: remember how the foolish man reproacheth thee daily.

23 Forget not the voice of thine enemies: the tumult of those that rise up against thee increaseth continually.

To the chief Musician, Al-taschith, A Psalm *or* Song of Asaph.

75 UNTO thee, O God, do we give thanks, *unto thee* do we give thanks: for *that* thy name is near thy wondrous works declare.

2 When I shall receive the congregation I will judge uprightly.

3 The earth and all the inhabitants thereof are dissolved: I bear up the pillars of it. Se'lah.

4 I said unto the fools, Deal not foolishly: and to the wicked, Lift not up the horn:

5 Lift not up your horn on high: speak *not* with a stiff neck.

6 For promotion *cometh* neither from the east, nor from the west, nor from the south.

7 But God *is* the judge: he putteth down one, and setteth up another.

8 For in the hand of the LORD *there is* a cup, and the wine is red; it is full of mixture; and he poureth out of the same: but the dregs thereof, all the wicked of the earth shall wring *them* out, *and* drink *them.*

9 But I will declare for ever; I will sing praises to the God of Ja'cob.

10 All the horns of the wicked also will I cut off; *but* the horns of the righteous shall be exalted.

To the chief Musician on Neginoth, A Psalm *or* Song of Asaph.

76 IN Ju'dah *is* God known: his name *is* great in Is'ra-el.

2 In Sa'lem also is his tabernacle, and his dwelling place in Zi'on.

3 There brake he the arrows of the bow, the shield, and the sword, and the battle. Se'lah.

4 Thou *art* more glorious *and* excellent than the mountains of prey.

5 The stouthearted are spoiled, they have slept their sleep: and none of the men of might have found their hands.

6 At thy rebuke, O God of Ja'cob, both the chariot and horse are cast into a dead sleep.

7 Thou, *even* thou, *art* to be feared: and who may stand in thy sight when once thou art angry?

8 Thou didst cause judgment to be heard from heaven; the earth feared, and was still,

9 When God arose to judgment, to save all the meek of the earth. Se'lah.

10 Surely the wrath of man shall praise thee: the remainder of wrath shalt thou restrain.

11 Vow, and pay unto the LORD your God: let all that be round about him bring presents unto him that ought to be feared.

12 He shall cut off the spirit of princes: *he is* terrible to the kings of the earth.

To the chief Musician, to Jeduthun, A Psalm of Asaph.

77 I CRIED unto God with my voice, *even* unto God with my voice; and he gave ear unto me.

2 In the day of my trouble I sought the Lord: my sore ran in the night, and ceased not: my soul refused to be comforted.

3 I remembered God, and was troubled: I complained, and my spirit was overwhelmed. Se'lah.

4 Thou holdest mine eyes waking: I am so troubled that I cannot speak.

5 I have considered the days of old, the years of ancient times.

6 I call to remembrance my song in the night: I commune with mine own heart: and my spirit made diligent search.

7 Will the Lord cast off for ever? and will he be favourable no more?

8 Is his mercy clean gone for ever? doth *his* promise fail for evermore?

9 Hath God forgotten to be gracious? hath he in anger shut up his tender mercies? Se'lah.

10 And I said, This *is* my infirmity: *but I will remember* the years of the right hand of the most High.

11 I will remember the works of the LORD: surely I will remember thy wonders of old.

12 I will meditate also of all thy work, and talk of thy doings.

13 Thy way, O God, *is* in the sanctuary: who *is so* great a God as *our* God?

14 Thou *art* the God that doest wonders: thou hast declared thy strength among the people.

15 Thou hast with *thine* arm redeemed thy people, the sons of Ja'cob and Jo'seph. Se'lah.

16 The waters saw thee, O God, the waters saw thee; they were afraid: the depths also were troubled.

17 The clouds poured out water: the skies sent out a sound: thine arrows also went abroad.

18 The voice of thy thunder *was* in the heaven: the lightnings lightened the world: the earth trembled and shook.

19 Thy way *is* in the sea, and thy path in the great waters, and thy footsteps are not known.

20 Thou leddest thy people like a flock by the hand of Mo'ses and Aar'on.

Maschil of Asaph.

78 GIVE ear, O my people, *to* my law: incline your ears to the words of my mouth.

2 I will open my mouth in a parable: I will utter dark sayings of old:

3 Which we have heard and known, and our fathers have told us.

4 We will not hide *them* from their children, shewing to the generation to come the praises of the LORD, and his strength, and his wonderful works that he hath done.

5 For he established a testimony in Ja'cob, and appointed a law in Is'ra-el, which he commanded our fathers, that they should make them known to their children:

6 That the generation to come might know *them, even* the children *which* should be born; *who* should arise and declare *them* to their children:

7 That they might set their hope in God, and not forget the works of God, but keep his commandments:

8 And might not be as their fathers, a stubborn and rebellious generation; a generation *that* set not their heart aright, and whose spirit was not stedfast with God.

9 The children of E'phra-im, *being* armed, *and* carrying bows, turned back in the day of battle.

10 They kept not the covenant of God, and refused to walk in his law;

11 And forgat his works, and his wonders that he had shewed them.

12 Marvellous things did he in the sight of their fathers, in the land of E'gypt, *in* the field of Zo'an.

13 He divided the sea, and caused them to pass through; and he made the waters to stand as an heap.

14 In the daytime also he led them with a cloud, and all the night with a light of fire.

15 He clave the rocks in the wilderness, and gave *them* drink as *out of* the great depths.

16 He brought streams also out of the rock, and caused waters to run down like rivers.

17 And they sinned yet more against him by provoking the most High in the wilderness.

18 And they tempted God in their heart by asking meat for their lust.

19 Yea, they spake against God; they said, Can God furnish a table in the wilderness?

20 Behold, he smote the rock, that the waters gushed out, and the streams overflowed; can he give bread also? can he provide flesh for his people?

21 Therefore the LORD heard *this,* and was wroth: so a fire was kindled against Ja'cob, and anger also came up against Is'ra-el;

22 Because they believed not in God, and trusted not in his salvation:

23 Though he had commanded the clouds from above, and opened the doors of heaven,

24 And had rained down manna upon them to eat, and had given them of the corn of heaven.

25 Man did eat angels' food: he sent them meat to the full.

26 He caused an east wind to blow in the heaven: and by his power he brought in the south wind.

27 He rained flesh also upon them as dust, and feathered fowls like as the sand of the sea:

28 And he let *it* fall in the midst of their camp, round about their habitations.

29 So they did eat, and were well filled: for he gave them their own desire;

30 They were not estranged from their lust. But while their meat *was* yet in their mouths,

31 The wrath of God came upon them, and slew the fattest of them, and smote down the chosen *men* of Is'ra-el.

32 For all this they sinned still, and believed not for his wondrous works.

33 Therefore their days did he consume in vanity, and their years in trouble.

34 When he slew them, then they sought him: and they returned and enquired early after God.

35 And they remembered that God *was* their rock, and the high God their redeemer.

36 Nevertheless they did flatter him with their mouth, and they lied unto him with their tongues.

37 For their heart was not right with him, neither were they stedfast in his covenant.

38 But he, *being* full of compassion, forgave *their* iniquity, and destroyed *them* not: yea, many a time turned he his anger away, and did not stir up all his wrath.

39 For he remembered that they *were but* flesh; a wind that passeth away, and cometh not again.

40 How oft did they provoke him in the wilderness, *and* grieve him in the desert!

41 Yea, they turned back and tempted God, and limited the Holy One of Is'ra-el.

42 They remembered not his hand, *nor* the day when he delivered them from the enemy.

43 How he had wrought his signs in E'gypt, and his wonders in the field of Zo'an:

44 And had turned their rivers into blood; and their floods, that they could not drink.

45 He sent divers sorts of flies among them, which devoured them; and frogs, which destroyed them.

46 He gave also their increase unto the caterpiller, and their labour unto the locust.

47 He destroyed their vines with hail, and their sycomore trees with frost.

48 He gave up their cattle also to the hail, and their flocks to hot thunderbolts.

49 He cast upon them the fierceness of his anger, wrath, and indignation, and trouble, by sending evil angels *among* them.

50 He made a way to his anger; he spared not their soul from death, but gave their life over to the pestilence;

51 And smote all the firstborn in E'gypt; the chief of *their* strength in the tabernacles of Ham:

52 But made his own people to go forth like sheep, and guided them in the wilderness like a flock.

53 And he led them on safely, so that they feared not: but the sea overwhelmed their enemies.

54 And he brought them to the border of his sanctuary, *even to* this mountain, *which* his right hand had purchased.

55 He cast out the heathen also before them, and divided them an inheritance by line, and made the tribes of Is'ra-el to dwell in their tents.

56 Yet they tempted and provoked the most high God, and kept not his testimonies:

57 But turned back, and dealt unfaithfully like their fathers: they were turned aside like a deceitful bow.

58 For they provoked him to anger with their high places, and moved him to jealousy with their graven images.

59 When God heard *this,* he was wroth, and greatly abhorred Is'ra-el:

60 So that he forsook the tabernacle of Shi'-loh, the tent *which* he placed among men;

61 And delivered his strength into captivity, and his glory into the enemy's hand.

62 He gave his people over also unto the sword; and was wroth with his inheritance.

63 The fire consumed their young men; and their maidens were not given to marriage.

64 Their priests fell by the sword; and their widows made no lamentation.

65 Then the Lord awaked as one out of sleep, *and* like a mighty man that shouteth by reason of wine.

66 And he smote his enemies in the hinder parts: he put them to a perpetual reproach.

67 Moreover he refused the tabernacle of Jo'-seph, and chose not the tribe of E'phra-im:

68 But chose the tribe of Ju'dah, the mount Zi'on which he loved.

69 And he built his sanctuary like high *palaces,* like the earth which he hath established for ever.

70 He chose Da'vid also his servant, and took him from the sheepfolds:

71 From following the ewes great with young he brought him to feed Ja'cob his people, and Is'ra-el his inheritance.

72 So he fed them according to the integrity of his heart; and guided them by the skilfulness of his hands.

A Psalm of Asaph.

79 O GOD, the heathen are come into thine inheritance; thy holy temple have they defiled; they have laid Je-ru'sa-lem on heaps.

2 The dead bodies of thy servants have they given *to be* meat unto the fowls of the heaven, the flesh of thy saints unto the beasts of the earth.

3 Their blood have they shed like water round about Je-ru'sa-lem; and *there was* none to bury *them.*

4 We are become a reproach to our neighbours, a scorn and derision to them that are round about us.

5 How long, LORD? wilt thou be angry for ever? shall thy jealousy burn like fire?

6 Pour out thy wrath upon the heathen that have not known thee, and upon the kingdoms that have not called upon thy name.

7 For they have devoured Ja'cob, and laid waste his dwelling place.

8 O remember not against us former iniquities: let thy tender mercies speedily prevent us: for we are brought very low.

9 Help us, O God of our salvation, for the glory of thy name: and deliver us, and purge away our sins, for thy name's sake.

10 Wherefore should the heathen say, Where *is* their God? let him be known among the heathen in our sight *by* the revenging of the blood of thy servants *which is* shed.

11 Let the sighing of the prisoner come before thee; according to the greatness of thy power preserve thou those that are appointed to die;

12 And render unto our neighbours sevenfold into their bosom their reproach, wherewith they have reproached thee, O Lord.

13 So we thy people and sheep of thy pasture will give thee thanks for ever: we will shew forth thy praise to all generations.

To the chief Musician upon Shoshannimeduth, A Psalm of Asaph.

80 GIVE ear, O Shepherd of Is'ra-el, thou that leadest Jo'seph like a flock; thou that dwellest *between* the cherubims, shine forth.

2 Before E'phra-im and Ben'ja-min and Manas'seh stir up thy strength, and come *and* save us.

3 Turn us again, O God, and cause thy face to shine; and we shall be saved.

4 O LORD God of hosts, how long wilt thou be angry against the prayer of thy people?

5 Thou feedest them with the bread of tears; and givest them tears to drink in great measure.

6 Thou makest us a strife unto our neighbours: and our enemies laugh among themselves.

7 Turn us again, O God of hosts, and cause thy face to shine; and we shall be saved.

8 Thou hast brought a vine out of E'gypt: thou hast cast out the heathen, and planted it.

9 Thou preparedst *room* before it, and didst cause it to take deep root, and it filled the land.

10 The hills were covered with the shadow of it, and the boughs thereof *were like* the goodly cedars.

11 She sent out her boughs unto the sea, and her branches unto the river.

12 Why hast thou *then* broken down her

hedges, so that all they which pass by the way do pluck her?

13 The boar out of the wood doth waste it, and the wild beast of the field doth devour it.

14 Return, we beseech thee, O God of hosts: look down from heaven, and behold, and visit this vine;

15 And the vineyard which thy right hand hath planted, and the branch *that* thou madest strong for thyself.

16 *It is* burned with fire, *it is* cut down: they perish at the rebuke of thy countenance.

17 Let thy hand be upon the man of thy right hand, upon the son of man *whom* thou madest strong for thyself.

18 So will not we go back from thee: quicken us, and we will call upon thy name.

19 Turn us again, O LORD God of hosts, cause thy face to shine; and we shall be saved.

To the chief Musician upon Gittith, *A Psalm* of Asaph.

81 SING aloud unto God our strength: make a joyful noise unto the God of Ja'-cob.

2 Take a psalm, and bring hither the timbrel, the pleasant harp with the psaltery.

3 Blow up the trumpet in the new moon, in the time appointed, on our solemn feast day.

4 For this *was* a statute for Is'ra-el, *and* a law of the God of Ja'cob.

5 This he ordained in Jo'seph *for* a testimony, when he went out through the land of E'gypt: *where* I heard a language *that* I understood not.

6 I removed his shoulder from the burden: his hands were delivered from the pots.

7 Thou calledst in trouble, and I delivered thee; I answered thee in the secret place of thunder: I proved thee at the waters of Meribah. Se'lah.

8 Hear, O my people, and I will testify unto thee: O Is'ra-el, if thou wilt hearken unto me;

9 There shall no strange god be in thee; neither shalt thou worship any strange god.

10 I *am* the LORD thy God, which brought thee out of the land of E'gypt: open thy mouth wide, and I will fill it.

11 But my people would not hearken to my voice; and Is'ra-el would none of me.

12 So I gave them up unto their own hearts' lust: *and* they walked in their own counsels.

13 Oh that my people had hearkened unto me, *and* Is'ra-el had walked in my ways!

14 I should soon have subdued their enemies, and turned my hand against their adversaries.

15 The haters of the LORD should have submitted themselves unto him: but their time should have endured for ever.

16 He should have fed them also with the finest of the wheat: and with honey out of the rock should I have satisfied thee.

A Psalm of Asaph.

82 GOD standeth in the congregation of the mighty; he judgeth among the gods.

2 How long will ye judge unjustly, and accept the persons of the wicked? Se'lah.

3 Defend the poor and fatherless: do justice to the afflicted and needy.

4 Deliver the poor and needy: rid *them* out of the hand of the wicked.

5 They know not, neither will they understand; they walk on in darkness: all the foundations of the earth are out of course.

6 I have said, Ye *are* gods; and all of you *are* children of the most High.

7 But ye shall die like men, and fall like one of the princes.

8 Arise, O God, judge the earth: for thou shalt inherit all nations.

A Song *or* Psalm of Asaph.

83 KEEP not thou silence, O God: hold not thy peace, and be not still, O God.

2 For, lo, thine enemies make a tumult: and they that hate thee have lifted up the head.

3 They have taken crafty counsel against thy people, and consulted against thy hidden ones.

4 They have said, Come, and let us cut them off from *being* a nation; that the name of Is'ra-el may be no more in remembrance.

5 For they have consulted together with one consent: they are confederate against thee:

6 The tabernacles of E'dom, and the Ish'ma-el-ites; of Mo'ab, and the Ha'gar-enes;

7 Ge'bal, and Am'mon, and Am'a-lek; the Phi-lis'tines with the inhabitants of Tyre;

8 As'sur also is joined with them: they have holpen the children of Lot. Se'lah.

9 Do unto them as *unto* the Mid'i-an-ites; as *to* Sis'e-ra, as *to* Ja'bin, at the brook of Ki'son:

10 *Which* perished at En'–dor: they became *as* dung for the earth.

11 Make their nobles like O'reb, and like Ze'-eb: yea, all their princes as Ze'bah, and as Zal-mun'na:

12 Who said, Let us take to ourselves the houses of God in possession.

13 O my God, make them like a wheel; as the stubble before the wind.

14 As the fire burneth a wood, and as the flame setteth the mountains on fire;

15 So persecute them with thy tempest, and make them afraid with thy storm.

16 Fill their faces with shame; that they may seek thy name, O LORD.

17 Let them be confounded and troubled for ever; yea, let them be put to shame, and perish:

18 That *men* may know that thou, whose name alone *is* JE-HO'VAH, *art* the most high over all the earth.

To the chief Musician upon Gittith, A Psalm for the sons of Korah.

84 HOW amiable *are* thy tabernacles, O LORD of hosts!

2 My soul longeth, yea, even fainteth for the courts of the LORD: my heart and my flesh crieth out for the living God.

3 Yea, the sparrow hath found an house, and the swallow a nest for herself, where she may lay her young, *even* thine altars, O LORD of hosts, my King, and my God.

4 Blessed *are* they that dwell in thy house: they will be still praising thee. Se'lah.

5 Blessed *is* the man whose strength *is* in thee; in whose heart *are* the ways *of them.*

6 *Who* passing through the valley of Ba'ca make it a well; the rain also filleth the pools.

7 They go from strength to strength, *every* one of them in Zi'on appeareth before God.

8 O LORD God of hosts, hear my prayer: give ear, O God of Ja'cob. Se'lah.

9 Behold, O God our shield, and look upon the face of thine anointed.

10 For a day in thy courts *is* better than a thousand. I had rather be a doorkeeper in the house of my God, than to dwell in the tents of wickedness.

11 For the LORD God *is* a sun and shield: the LORD will give grace and glory: no good *thing*

will he withhold from them that walk uprightly.

12 O LORD of hosts, blessed *is* the man that trusteth in thee.

To the chief Musician, A Psalm for the sons of Korah.

85 LORD, thou hast been favourable unto thy land: thou hast brought back the captivity of Ja′cob.

2 Thou hast forgiven the iniquity of thy people, thou hast covered all their sin. Se′lah.

3 Thou hast taken away all thy wrath: thou hast turned *thyself* from the fierceness of thine anger.

4 Turn us, O God of our salvation, and cause thine anger toward us to cease.

5 Wilt thou be angry with us for ever? wilt thou draw out thine anger to all generations?

6 Wilt thou not revive us again: that thy people may rejoice in thee?

7 Shew us thy mercy, O LORD, and grant us thy salvation.

8 I will hear what God the LORD will speak: for he will speak peace unto his people, and to his saints: but let them not turn again to folly.

9 Surely his salvation *is* nigh them that fear him; that glory may dwell in our land.

10 Mercy and truth are met together; righteousness and peace have kissed *each other*.

11 Truth shall spring out of the earth; and righteousness shall look down from heaven.

12 Yea, the LORD shall give *that which is* good; and our land shall yield her increase.

13 Righteousness shall go before him; and shall set *us* in the way of his steps.

A Prayer of David.

86 BOW down thine ear, O LORD, hear me: for I *am* poor and needy.

2 Preserve my soul; for I *am* holy: O thou my God, save thy servant that trusteth in thee.

3 Be merciful unto me, O Lord: for I cry unto thee daily.

4 Rejoice the soul of thy servant: for unto thee, O Lord, do I lift up my soul.

5 For thou, Lord, *art* good, and ready to forgive; and plenteous in mercy unto all them that call upon thee.

6 Give ear, O LORD, unto my prayer; and attend to the voice of my supplications.

7 In the day of my trouble I will call upon thee: for thou wilt answer me.

8 Among the gods *there is* none like unto thee, O Lord; neither *are there any* works like unto thy works.

9 All nations whom thou hast made shall come and worship before thee, O Lord; and shall glorify thy name.

10 For thou *art* great, and doest wondrous things: thou *art* God alone.

11 Teach me thy way, O LORD; I will walk in thy truth: unite my heart to fear thy name.

12 I will praise thee, O Lord my God, with all my heart: and I will glorify thy name for evermore.

13 For great *is* thy mercy toward me: and thou hast delivered my soul from the lowest hell.

14 O God, the proud are risen against me, and the assemblies of violent *men* have sought after my soul; and have not set thee before them.

15 But thou, O Lord, *art* a God full of compassion, and gracious, longsuffering, and plenteous in mercy and truth.

16 O turn unto me, and have mercy upon me;

give thy strength unto thy servant, and save the son of thine handmaid.

17 Shew me a token for good; that they which hate me may see *it*, and be ashamed: because thou, LORD, hast holpen me, and comforted me.

A Psalm *or* Song for the sons of Korah.

87 HIS foundation *is* in the holy mountains.

2 The LORD loveth the gates of Zi′on more than all the dwellings of Ja′cob.

3 Glorious things are spoken of thee, O city of God. Se′lah.

4 I will make mention of Ra′hab and Bab′ylon to them that know me: behold Phi-lis′ti-a, and Tyre, with E-thi-o′pi-a; this *man* was born there.

5 And of Zi′on it shall be said, This and that man was born in her: and the highest himself shall establish her.

6 The LORD shall count, when he writeth up the people, *that* this *man* was born there. Se′lah.

7 As well the singers as the players on instruments *shall be there*: all my springs *are* in thee.

A Song *or* Psalm for the sons of Korah, to the chief Musician upon Mahalath Leannoth, Maschil of Heman the Ezrahite.

88 O LORD God of my salvation, I have cried day *and* night before thee:

2 Let my prayer come before thee: incline thine ear unto my cry;

3 For my soul is full of troubles: and my life draweth nigh unto the grave.

4 I am counted with them that go down into the pit: I am as a man *that hath* no strength:

5 Free among the dead, like the slain that lie in the grave, whom thou rememberest no more: and they are cut off from thy hand.

6 Thou hast laid me in the lowest pit, in darkness, in the deeps.

7 Thy wrath lieth hard upon me, and thou hast afflicted *me* with all thy waves. Se′lah.

8 Thou hast put away mine acquaintance far from me; thou hast made me an abomination unto them: *I am* shut up, and I cannot come forth.

9 Mine eye mourneth by reason of affliction: LORD, I have called daily upon thee, I have stretched out my hands unto thee.

10 Wilt thou shew wonders to the dead? shall the dead arise *and* praise thee? Se′lah.

11 Shall thy lovingkindness be declared in the grave? *or* thy faithfulness in destruction?

12 Shall thy wonders be known in the dark? and thy righteousness in the land of forgetfulness?

13 But unto thee have I cried, O LORD; and in the morning shall my prayer prevent thee.

14 LORD, why castest thou off my soul? *why* hidest thou thy face from me?

15 I *am* afflicted and ready to die from *my* youth up: *while* I suffer thy terrors I am distracted.

16 Thy fierce wrath goeth over me; thy terrors have cut me off.

17 They came round about me daily like water; they compassed me about together.

18 Lover and friend hast thou put far from me, *and* mine acquaintance into darkness.

Maschil of Ethan the Ezrahite.

89 I WILL sing of the mercies of the LORD for ever: with my mouth will I make known thy faithfulness to all generations.

2 For I have said, Mercy shall be built up for ever; thy faithfulness shalt thou establish in the very heavens.

3 I have made a covenant with my chosen, I have sworn unto Da′vid my servant,

4 Thy seed will I establish for ever, and build up thy throne to all generations. Se′lah.

5 And the heavens shall praise thy wonders, O Lord: thy faithfulness also in the congregation of the saints.

6 For who in the heaven can be compared unto the Lord? who among the sons of the mighty can be likened unto the Lord?

7 God is greatly to be feared in the assembly of the saints, and to be had in reverence of all them that are about him.

8 O Lord God of hosts, who is a strong Lord like unto thee? or to thy faithfulness round about thee?

9 Thou rulest the raging of the sea: when the waves thereof arise, thou stillest them.

10 Thou hast broken Ra′hab in pieces, as one that is slain; thou hast scattered thine enemies with thy strong arm.

11 The heavens are thine, the earth also is thine: as for the world and the fulness thereof, thou hast founded them.

12 The north and the south thou hast created them: Ta′bor and Her′mon shall rejoice in thy name.

13 Thou hast a mighty arm: strong is thy hand, and high is thy right hand.

14 Justice and judgment are the habitation of thy throne: mercy and truth shall go before thy face.

15 Blessed is the people that know the joyful sound: they shall walk, O Lord, in the light of thy countenance.

16 In thy name shall they rejoice all the day: and in thy righteousness shall they be exalted.

17 For thou art the glory of their strength: and in thy favour our horn shall be exalted.

18 For the Lord is our defence; and the Holy One of Is′ra-el is our king.

19 Then thou spakest in vision to thy holy one, and saidst, I have laid help upon one that is mighty; I have exalted one chosen out of the people.

20 I have found Da′vid my servant; with my holy oil have I anointed him:

21 With whom my hand shall be established: mine arm also shall strengthen him.

22 The enemy shall not exact upon him; nor the son of wickedness afflict him.

23 And I will beat down his foes before his face, and plague them that hate him.

24 But my faithfulness and my mercy shall be with him: and in my name shall his horn be exalted.

25 I will set his hand also in the sea, and his right hand in the rivers.

26 He shall cry unto me, Thou art my father, my God, and the rock of my salvation.

27 Also I will make him my firstborn, higher than the kings of the earth.

28 My mercy will I keep for him for evermore, and my covenant shall stand fast with him.

29 His seed also will I make to endure for ever, and his throne as the days of heaven.

30 If his children forsake my law, and walk not in my judgments;

31 If they break my statutes, and keep not my commandments;

32 Then will I visit their transgression with the rod, and their iniquity with stripes.

33 Nevertheless my lovingkindness will I not utterly take from him, nor suffer my faithfulness to fail.

34 My covenant will I not break, nor alter the thing that is gone out of my lips.

35 Once have I sworn by my holiness that I will not lie unto Da′vid.

36 His seed shall endure for ever, and his throne as the sun before me.

37 It shall be established for ever as the moon, and as a faithful witness in heaven. Se′-lah.

38 But thou hast cast off and abhorred, thou hast been wroth with thine anointed.

39 Thou hast made void the covenant of thy servant: thou hast profaned his crown by casting it to the ground.

40 Thou hast broken down all his hedges; thou hast brought his strong holds to ruin.

41 All that pass by the way spoil him: he is a reproach to his neighbours.

42 Thou hast set up the right hand of his adversaries; thou hast made all his enemies to rejoice.

43 Thou hast also turned the edge of his sword, and hast not made him to stand in the battle.

44 Thou hast made his glory to cease, and cast his throne down to the ground.

45 The days of his youth hast thou shortened: thou hast covered him with shame. Se′-lah.

46 How long, Lord? wilt thou hide thyself for ever? shall thy wrath burn like fire?

47 Remember how short my time is: wherefore hast thou made all men in vain?

48 What man is he that liveth, and shall not see death? shall he deliver his soul from the hand of the grave? Se′lah.

49 Lord, where are thy former lovingkindnesses, which thou swarest unto Da′vid in thy truth?

50 Remember, Lord, the reproach of thy servants; how I do bear in my bosom the reproach of all the mighty people;

51 Wherewith thine enemies have reproached, O Lord; wherewith they have reproached the footsteps of thine anointed.

52 Blessed be the Lord for evermore. Amen, and Amen.

A Prayer of Moses the man of God.

90 LORD, thou hast been our dwelling place in all generations.

2 Before the mountains were brought forth, or ever thou hadst formed the earth and the world, even from everlasting to everlasting, thou art God.

3 Thou turnest man to destruction; and sayest, Return, ye children of men.

4 For a thousand years in thy sight are but as yesterday when it is past, and as a watch in the night.

5 Thou carriest them away as with a flood; they are as a sleep: in the morning they are like grass which groweth up.

6 In the morning it flourisheth, and groweth up; in the evening it is cut down, and withereth.

7 For we are consumed by thine anger, and by thy wrath are we troubled.

8 Thou hast set our iniquities before thee, our secret sins in the light of thy countenance.

9 For all our days are passed away in thy wrath: we spend our years as a tale that is told.

10 The days of our years are threescore years and ten; and if by reason of strength they be

fourscore years, yet *is* their strength labour and sorrow; for it is soon cut off, and we fly away.

11 Who knoweth the power of thine anger? even according to thy fear, *so is* thy wrath.

12 So teach *us* to number our days, that we may apply *our* hearts unto wisdom.

13 Return, O LORD, how long? and let it repent thee concerning thy servants.

14 O satisfy us early with thy mercy; that we may rejoice and be glad all our days.

15 Make us glad according to the days *wherein* thou hast afflicted us, *and* the years *wherein* we have seen evil.

16 Let thy work appear unto thy servants, and thy glory unto their children.

17 And let the beauty of the LORD our God be upon us: and establish thou the work of our hands upon us; yea, the work of our hands establish thou it.

91 HE that dwelleth in the secret place of the most High shall abide under the shadow of the Almighty.

2 I will say of the LORD, *He is* my refuge and my fortress: my God; in him will I trust.

3 Surely he shall deliver thee from the snare of the fowler, *and* from the noisome pestilence.

4 He shall cover thee with his feathers, and under his wings shalt thou trust: his truth *shall be thy* shield and buckler.

5 Thou shalt not be afraid for the terror by night; *nor* for the arrow *that* flieth by day;

6 *Nor* for the pestilence *that* walketh in darkness; *nor* for the destruction *that* wasteth at noonday.

7 A thousand shall fall at thy side, and ten thousand at thy right hand; *but* it shall not come nigh thee.

8 Only with thine eyes shalt thou behold and see the reward of the wicked.

9 Because thou hast made the LORD, *which is* my refuge, *even* the most High, thy habitation;

10 There shall no evil befall thee, neither shall any plague come nigh thy dwelling.

11 For he shall give his angels charge over thee, to keep thee in all thy ways.

12 They shall bear thee up in *their* hands, lest thou dash thy foot against a stone.

13 Thou shalt tread upon the lion and adder: the young lion and the dragon shalt thou trample under feet.

14 Because he hath set his love upon me, therefore will I deliver him: I will set him on high, because he hath known my name.

15 He shall call upon me, and I will answer him: I *will* be with him in trouble; I will deliver him, and honour him.

16 With long life will I satisfy him, and shew him my salvation.

A Psalm *or* Song for the sabbath day.

92 IT *is* a good *thing* to give thanks unto the LORD, and to sing praises unto thy name, O most High:

2 To shew forth thy lovingkindness in the morning, and thy faithfulness every night,

3 Upon an instrument of ten strings, and upon the psaltery; upon the harp with a solemn sound.

4 For thou, Lord, hast made me glad through thy work: I will triumph in the works of thy hands.

5 O LORD, how great are thy works! *and* thy thoughts are very deep.

6 A brutish man knoweth not; neither doth a fool understand this.

7 When the wicked spring as the grass, and when all the workers of iniquity do flourish; *it is* that they shall be destroyed for ever:

8 But thou, LORD, *art most* high for evermore.

9 For, lo, thine enemies, O LORD, for, lo, thine enemies shall perish; all the workers of iniquity shall be scattered.

10 But my horn shalt thou exalt like *the horn of* an unicorn: I shall be anointed with fresh oil.

11 Mine eye also shall see *my desire* on mine enemies, *and* mine ears shall hear *my desire* of the wicked that rise up against me.

12 The righteous shall flourish like the palm tree: he shall grow like a cedar in Leb'a-non.

13 Those that be planted in the house of the LORD shall flourish in the courts of our God.

14 They shall still bring forth fruit in old age; they shall be fat and flourishing;

15 To shew that the LORD *is* upright: *he is* my rock, and *there is* no unrighteousness in him.

93 THE LORD reigneth, he is clothed with majesty; the LORD is clothed with strength, *wherewith* he hath girded himself: the world also is stablished, that it cannot be moved.

2 Thy throne *is* established of old: thou *art* from everlasting.

3 The floods have lifted up, O LORD, the floods have lifted up their voice; the floods lift up their waves.

4 The LORD on high *is* mightier than the noise of many waters, *yea, than* the mighty waves of the sea.

5 Thy testimonies are very sure: holiness becometh thine house, O LORD, for ever.

94 O LORD God, to whom vengeance belongeth; O God, to whom vengeance belongeth, shew thyself.

2 Lift up thyself, thou judge of the earth: render a reward to the proud.

3 LORD, how long shall the wicked, how long shall the wicked triumph?

4 *How long* shall they utter *and* speak hard things? *and* all the workers of iniquity boast themselves?

5 They break in pieces thy people, O LORD, and afflict thine heritage.

6 They slay the widow and the stranger, and murder the fatherless.

7 Yet they say, The LORD shall not see, neither shall the God of Ja'cob regard *it*.

8 Understand, ye brutish among the people: and ye fools, when will ye be wise?

9 He that planted the ear, shall he not hear? he that formed the eye, shall he not see?

10 He that chastiseth the heathen, shall not he correct? he that teacheth man knowledge, *shall not he know?*

11 The LORD knoweth the thoughts of man, that they *are* vanity.

12 Blessed *is* the man whom thou chastenest, O LORD, and teachest him out of thy law;

13 That thou mayest give him rest from the days of adversity, until the pit be digged for the wicked.

14 For the LORD will not cast off his people, neither will he forsake his inheritance.

15 But judgment shall return unto righteousness: and all the upright in heart shall follow it.

16 Who will rise up for me against the evildoers? or who will stand up for me against the workers of iniquity?

17 Unless the LORD *had been* my help, my soul had almost dwelt in silence.

18 When I said, My foot slippeth; thy mercy, O Lᴏʀᴅ, held me up.

19 In the multitude of my thoughts within me thy comforts delight my soul.

20 Shall the throne of iniquity have fellowship with thee, which frameth mischief by a law?

21 They gather themselves together against the soul of the righteous, and condemn the innocent blood.

22 But the Lᴏʀᴅ is my defence; and my God is the rock of my refuge.

23 And he shall bring upon them their own iniquity, and shall cut them off in their own wickedness; yea, the Lᴏʀᴅ our God shall cut them off.

95 O COME, let us sing unto the Lᴏʀᴅ: let us make a joyful noise to the rock of our salvation.

2 Let us come before his presence with thanksgiving, and make a joyful noise unto him with psalms.

3 For the Lᴏʀᴅ is a great God, and a great King above all gods.

4 In his hand are the deep places of the earth: the strength of the hills is his also.

5 The sea is his, and he made it: and his hands formed the dry land.

6 O come, let us worship and bow down: let us kneel before the Lᴏʀᴅ our maker.

7 For he is our God; and we are the people of his pasture, and the sheep of his hand. To day if ye will hear his voice,

8 Harden not your heart, as in the provocation, and as in the day of temptation in the wilderness:

9 When your fathers tempted me, proved me, and saw my work.

10 Forty years long was I grieved with this generation, and said, It is a people that do err in their heart, and they have not known my ways:

11 Unto whom I sware in my wrath that they should not enter into my rest.

96 O SING unto the Lᴏʀᴅ a new song: sing unto the Lᴏʀᴅ, all the earth.

2 Sing unto the Lᴏʀᴅ, bless his name; shew forth his salvation from day to day.

3 Declare his glory among the heathen, his wonders among all people.

4 For the Lᴏʀᴅ is great, and greatly to be praised: he is to be feared above all gods.

5 For all the gods of the nations are idols: but the Lᴏʀᴅ made the heavens.

6 Honour and majesty are before him: strength and beauty are in his sanctuary.

7 Give unto the Lᴏʀᴅ, O ye kindreds of the people, give unto the Lᴏʀᴅ glory and strength.

8 Give unto the Lᴏʀᴅ the glory due unto his name: bring an offering, and come into his courts.

9 O worship the Lᴏʀᴅ in the beauty of holiness: fear before him, all the earth.

10 Say among the heathen that the Lᴏʀᴅ reigneth: the world also shall be established that it shall not be moved: he shall judge the people righteously.

11 Let the heavens rejoice, and let the earth be glad; let the sea roar, and the fulness thereof.

12 Let the field be joyful, and all that is therein: then shall all the trees of the wood rejoice

13 Before the Lᴏʀᴅ: for he cometh, for he cometh to judge the earth: he shall judge the world with righteousness, and the people with his truth.

97 THE Lᴏʀᴅ reigneth; let the earth rejoice; let the multitude of isles be glad thereof.

2 Clouds and darkness are round about him: righteousness and judgment are the habitation of his throne.

3 A fire goeth before him, and burneth up his enemies round about.

4 His lightnings enlightened the world: the earth saw, and trembled.

5 The hills melted like wax at the presence of the Lᴏʀᴅ, at the presence of the Lᴏʀᴅ of the whole earth.

6 The heavens declare his righteousness, and all the people see his glory.

7 Confounded be all they that serve graven images, that boast themselves of idols: worship him, all ye gods.

8 Zi'on heard, and was glad; and the daughters of Ju'dah rejoiced because of thy judgments, O Lᴏʀᴅ.

9 For thou, Lᴏʀᴅ, art high above all the earth: thou art exalted far above all gods.

10 Ye that love the Lᴏʀᴅ, hate evil: he preserveth the souls of his saints; he delivereth them out of the hand of the wicked.

11 Light is sown for the righteous, and gladness for the upright in heart.

12 Rejoice in the Lᴏʀᴅ, ye righteous; and give thanks at the remembrance of his holiness.

A Psalm.

98 O SING unto the Lᴏʀᴅ a new song; for he hath done marvellous things: his right hand, and his holy arm, hath gotten him the victory.

2 The Lᴏʀᴅ hath made known his salvation: his righteousness hath he openly shewed in the sight of the heathen.

3 He hath remembered his mercy and his truth toward the house of Is'ra-el: all the ends of the earth have seen the salvation of our God.

4 Make a joyful noise unto the Lᴏʀᴅ, all the earth: make a loud noise, and rejoice, and sing praise.

5 Sing unto the Lᴏʀᴅ with the harp; with the harp, and the voice of a psalm.

6 With trumpets and sound of cornet make a joyful noise before the Lᴏʀᴅ, the King.

7 Let the sea roar, and the fulness thereof; the world, and they that dwell therein.

8 Let the floods clap their hands: let the hills be joyful together

9 Before the Lᴏʀᴅ; for he cometh to judge the earth: with righteousness shall he judge the world, and the people with equity.

99 THE Lᴏʀᴅ reigneth; let the people tremble: he sitteth between the cherubims; let the earth be moved.

2 The Lᴏʀᴅ is great in Zi'on; and he is high above all the people.

3 Let them praise thy great and terrible name; for it is holy.

4 The king's strength also loveth judgment; thou dost establish equity, thou executest judgment and righteousness in Ja'cob.

5 Exalt ye the Lᴏʀᴅ our God, and worship at his footstool; for he is holy.

6 Mo'ses and Aar'on among his priests, and Sam'u-el among them that call upon his name; they called upon the Lᴏʀᴅ, and he answered them.

7 He spake unto them in the cloudy pillar: they kept his testimonies, and the ordinance that he gave them.

8 Thou answeredst them, O Lᴏʀᴅ our God:

thou wast a God that forgavest them, though thou tookest vengeance of their inventions.

9 Exalt the LORD our God, and worship at his holy hill; for the LORD our God is holy.

A Psalm of praise.

100 MAKE a joyful noise unto the LORD, all ye lands.

2 Serve the LORD with gladness: come before his presence with singing.

3 Know ye that the LORD he is God: it is he that hath made us, and not we ourselves; we are his people, and the sheep of his pasture.

4 Enter into his gates with thanksgiving, and into his courts with praise: be thankful unto him, and bless his name.

5 For the LORD is good; his mercy is everlasting; and his truth endureth to all generations.

A Psalm of David.

101 I WILL sing of mercy and judgment: unto thee, O LORD, will I sing.

2 I will behave myself wisely in a perfect way. O when wilt thou come unto me? I will walk within my house with a perfect heart.

3 I will set no wicked thing before mine eyes: I hate the work of them that turn aside; it shall not cleave to me.

4 A froward heart shall depart from me: I will not know a wicked person.

5 Whoso privily slandereth his neighbour, him will I cut off: him that hath an high look and a proud heart will not I suffer.

6 Mine eyes shall be upon the faithful of the land, that they may dwell with me: he that walketh in a perfect way, he shall serve me.

7 He that worketh deceit shall not dwell within my house: he that telleth lies shall not tarry in my sight.

8 I will early destroy all the wicked of the land; that I may cut off all wicked doers from the city of the LORD.

A Prayer of the afflicted, when he is overwhelmed, and poureth out his complaint before the LORD.

102 HEAR my prayer, O LORD, and let my cry come unto thee.

2 Hide not thy face from me in the day when I am in trouble; incline thine ear unto me: in the day when I call answer me speedily.

3 For my days are consumed like smoke, and my bones are burned as an hearth.

4 My heart is smitten, and withered like grass; so that I forget to eat my bread.

5 By reason of the voice of my groaning my bones cleave to my skin.

6 I am like a pelican of the wilderness: I am like an owl of the desert.

7 I watch, and am as a sparrow alone upon the house top.

8 Mine enemies reproach me all the day; and they that are mad against me are sworn against me.

9 For I have eaten ashes like bread, and mingled my drink with weeping,

10 Because of thine indignation and thy wrath: for thou hast lifted me up, and cast me down.

11 My days are like a shadow that declineth; and I am withered like grass.

12 But thou, O LORD, shalt endure for ever; and thy remembrance unto all generations.

13 Thou shalt arise, and have mercy upon Zi'on: for the time to favour her, yea, the set time, is come.

14 For thy servants take pleasure in her stones, and favour the dust thereof.

15 So the heathen shall fear the name of the LORD, and all the kings of the earth thy glory.

16 When the LORD shall build up Zi'on, he shall appear in his glory.

17 He will regard the prayer of the destitute, and not despise their prayer.

18 This shall be written for the generation to come: and the people which shall be created shall praise the LORD.

19 For he hath looked down from the height of his sanctuary; from heaven did the LORD behold the earth;

20 To hear the groaning of the prisoner; to loose those that are appointed to death;

21 To declare the name of the LORD in Zi'on, and his praise in Je-ru'sa-lem;

22 When the people are gathered together, and the kingdoms, to serve the LORD.

23 He weakened my strength in the way; he shortened my days.

24 I said, O my God, take me not away in the midst of my days: thy years are throughout all generations.

25 Of old hast thou laid the foundation of the earth: and the heavens are the work of thy hands.

26 They shall perish, but thou shalt endure: yea, all of them shall wax old like a garment; as a vesture shalt thou change them, and they shall be changed:

27 But thou art the same, and thy years shall have no end.

28 The children of thy servants shall continue, and their seed shall be established before thee.

A Psalm of David.

103 BLESS the LORD, O my soul: and all that is within me, bless his holy name.

2 Bless the LORD, O my soul, and forget not all his benefits:

3 Who forgiveth all thine iniquities; who healeth all thy diseases;

4 Who redeemeth thy life from destruction; who crowneth thee with lovingkindness and tender mercies;

5 Who satisfieth thy mouth with good things; so that thy youth is renewed like the eagle's.

6 The LORD executeth righteousness and judgment for all that are oppressed.

7 He made known his ways unto Mo'ses, his acts unto the children of Is'ra-el.

8 The LORD is merciful and gracious, slow to anger, and plenteous in mercy.

9 He will not always chide: neither will he keep his anger for ever.

10 He hath not dealt with us after our sins; nor rewarded us according to our iniquities.

11 For as the heaven is high above the earth, so great is his mercy toward them that fear him.

12 As far as the east is from the west, so far hath he removed our transgressions from us.

13 Like as a father pitieth his children, so the LORD pitieth them that fear him.

14 For he knoweth our frame; he remembereth that we are dust.

15 As for man, his days are as grass: as a flower of the field, so he flourisheth.

16 For the wind passeth over it, and it is

gone; and the place thereof shall know it no more.

17 But the mercy of the LORD is from everlasting to everlasting upon them that fear him, and his righteousness unto children's children;

18 To such as keep his covenant, and to those that remember his commandments to do them.

19 The LORD hath prepared his throne in the heavens; and his kingdom ruleth over all.

20 Bless the LORD, ye his angels, that excel in strength, that do his commandments, hearkening unto the voice of his word.

21 Bless ye the LORD, all ye his hosts; ye ministers of his, that do his pleasure.

22 Bless the LORD, all his works in all places of his dominion: bless the LORD, O my soul.

104 BLESS the LORD, O my soul. O LORD my God, thou art very great; thou art clothed with honour and majesty.

2 Who coverest thyself with light as with a garment: who stretchest out the heavens like a curtain:

3 Who layeth the beams of his chambers in the waters: who maketh the clouds his chariot: who walketh upon the wings of the wind:

4 Who maketh his angels spirits; his ministers a flaming fire:

5 Who laid the foundations of the earth, that it should not be removed for ever.

6 Thou coveredst it with the deep as with a garment: the waters stood above the mountains.

7 At thy rebuke they fled; at the voice of thy thunder they hasted away.

8 They go up by the mountains; they go down by the valleys unto the place which thou hast founded for them.

9 Thou hast set a bound that they may not pass over; that they turn not again to cover the earth.

10 He sendeth the springs into the valleys, which run among the hills.

11 They give drink to every beast of the field: the wild asses quench their thirst.

12 By them shall the fowls of the heaven have their habitation, which sing among the branches.

13 He watereth the hills from his chambers: the earth is satisfied with the fruit of thy works.

14 He causeth the grass to grow for the cattle, and herb for the service of man: that he may bring forth food out of the earth;

15 And wine that maketh glad the heart of man, and oil to make his face to shine, and bread which strengtheneth man's heart.

16 The trees of the LORD are full of sap; the cedars of Leb'a-non, which he hath planted;

17 Where the birds make their nests: as for the stork, the fir trees are her house.

18 The high hills are a refuge for the wild goats; and the rocks for the conies.

19 He appointed the moon for seasons: the sun knoweth his going down.

20 Thou makest darkness, and it is night: wherein all the beasts of the forest do creep forth.

21 The young lions roar after their prey, and seek their meat from God.

22 The sun ariseth, they gather themselves together, and lay them down in their dens.

23 Man goeth forth unto his work and to his labour until the evening.

24 O LORD, how manifold are thy works! in wisdom hast thou made them all: the earth is full of thy riches.

25 So is this great and wide sea, wherein are things creeping innumerable, both small and great beasts.

26 There go the ships: there is that leviathan, whom thou hast made to play therein.

27 These wait all upon thee; that thou mayest give them their meat in due season.

28 That thou givest them they gather: thou openest thine hand, they are filled with good.

29 Thou hidest thy face, they are troubled: thou takest away their breath, they die, and return to their dust.

30 Thou sendest forth thy spirit, they are created: and thou renewest the face of the earth.

31 The glory of the LORD shall endure for ever: the LORD shall rejoice in his works.

32 He looketh on the earth, and it trembleth: he toucheth the hills, and they smoke.

33 I will sing unto the LORD as long as I live: I will sing praise to my God while I have my being.

34 My meditation of him shall be sweet: I will be glad in the LORD.

35 Let the sinners be consumed out of the earth, and let the wicked be no more. Bless thou the LORD, O my soul. Praise ye the LORD.

105 O GIVE thanks unto the LORD; call upon his name: make known his deeds among the people.

2 Sing unto him, sing psalms unto him: talk ye of all his wondrous works.

3 Glory ye in his holy name: let the heart of them rejoice that seek the LORD.

4 Seek the LORD, and his strength: seek his face evermore.

5 Remember his marvellous works that he hath done; his wonders, and the judgments of his mouth;

6 O ye seed of A'bra-ham his servant, ye children of Ja'cob his chosen.

7 He is the LORD our God: his judgments are in all the earth.

8 He hath remembered his covenant for ever, the word which he commanded to a thousand generations.

9 Which covenant he made with A'bra-ham, and his oath unto I'saac;

10 And confirmed the same unto Ja'cob for a law, and to Is'ra-el for an everlasting covenant:

11 Saying, Unto thee will I give the land of Ca'naan the lot of your inheritance:

12 When they were but a few men in number; yea, very few, and strangers in it.

13 When they went from one nation to another, from one kingdom to another people;

14 He suffered no man to do them wrong: yea, he reproved kings for their sakes;

15 Saying, Touch not mine anointed, and do my prophets no harm.

16 Moreover he called for a famine upon the land: he brake the whole staff of bread.

17 He sent a man before them, even Jo'seph, who was sold for a servant:

18 Whose feet they hurt with fetters: he was laid in iron:

19 Until the time that his word came: the word of the LORD tried him.

20 The king sent and loosed him; even the ruler of the people, and let him go free.

21 He made him lord of his house, and ruler of all his substance:

22 To bind his princes at his pleasure; and teach his senators wisdom.

23 Is'ra-el also came into E'gypt; and Ja'cob sojourned in the land of Ham.

24 And he increased his people greatly; and made them stronger than their enemies.

25 He turned their heart to hate his people, to deal subtilly with his servants.

26 He sent Mo'ses his servant; *and* Aar'on whom he had chosen.

27 They shewed his signs among them, and wonders in the land of Ham.

28 He sent darkness, and made it dark; and they rebelled not against his word.

29 He turned their waters into blood, and slew their fish.

30 Their land brought forth frogs in abundance, in the chambers of their kings.

31 He spake, and there came divers sorts of flies, *and* lice in all their coasts.

32 He gave them hail for rain, *and* flaming fire in their land.

33 He smote their vines also and their fig trees; and brake the trees of their coasts.

34 He spake, and the locusts came, and caterpillers, and that without number,

35 And did eat up all the herbs in their land, and devoured the fruit of their ground.

36 He smote also all the firstborn in their land, the chief of all their strength.

37 He brought them forth also with silver and gold: and *there was* not one feeble *person* among their tribes.

38 E'gypt was glad when they departed: for the fear of them fell upon them.

39 He spread a cloud for a covering; and fire to give light in the night.

40 *The* people asked, and he brought quails, and satisfied them with the bread of heaven.

41 He opened the rock, and the waters gushed out; they ran in the dry places *like* a river.

42 For he remembered his holy promise, *and* A'bra-ham his servant.

43 And he brought forth his people with joy, *and* his chosen with gladness:

44 And gave them the lands of the heathen: and they inherited the labour of the people;

45 That they might observe his statutes, and keep his laws. Praise ye the LORD.

106

PRAISE ye the LORD. O give thanks unto the LORD; for *he is* good: for his mercy *endureth* for ever.

2 Who can utter the mighty acts of the LORD? *who* can shew forth all his praise?

3 Blessed *are* they that keep judgment, *and* he that doeth righteousness at all times.

4 Remember me, O LORD, with the favour *that* thou bearest unto thy people: O visit me with thy salvation;

5 That I may see the good of thy chosen, that I may rejoice in the gladness of thy nation, that I may glory with thine inheritance.

6 We have sinned with our fathers, we have committed iniquity, we have done wickedly.

7 Our fathers understood not thy wonders in E'gypt; they remembered not the multitude of thy mercies; but provoked *him* at the sea, *even* at the Red sea.

8 Nevertheless he saved them for his name's sake, that he might make his mighty power to be known.

9 He rebuked the Red sea also, and it was dried up: so he led them through the depths, as through the wilderness.

10 And he saved them from the hand of him that hated *them*, and redeemed them from the hand of the enemy.

11 And the waters covered their enemies: there was not one of them left.

12 Then believed they his words; they sang his praise.

13 They soon forgat his works; they waited not for his counsel.

14 But lusted exceedingly in the wilderness, and tempted God in the desert.

15 And he gave them their request; but sent leanness into their soul.

16 They envied Mo'ses also in the camp, *and* Aar'on the saint of the LORD.

17 The earth opened and swallowed up Da'-than, and covered the company of A-bi'ram.

18 And a fire was kindled in their company; the flame burned up the wicked.

19 They made a calf in Ho'reb, and worshipped the molten image.

20 Thus they changed their glory into the similitude of an ox that eateth grass.

21 They forgat God their saviour, which had done great things in E'gypt;

22 Wondrous works in the land of Ham, *and* terrible things by the Red sea.

23 Therefore he said that he would destroy them, had not Mo'ses his chosen stood before him in the breach, to turn away his wrath, lest he should destroy *them.*

24 Yea, they despised the pleasant land, they believed not his word:

25 But murmured in their tents, *and* hearkened not unto the voice of the LORD.

26 Therefore he lifted up his hand against them, to overthrow them in the wilderness:

27 To overthrow their seed also among the nations, and to scatter them in the lands.

28 They joined themselves also unto Ba'al-pe'or, and ate the sacrifices of the dead.

29 Thus they provoked *him* to anger with their inventions: and the plague brake in upon them.

30 Then stood up Phin'e-has, and executed judgment: and so the plague was stayed.

31 And that was counted unto him for righteousness unto all generations for evermore.

32 They angered *him* also at the waters of strife, so that it went ill with Mo'ses for their sakes:

33 Because they provoked his spirit, so that he spake unadvisedly with his lips.

34 They did not destroy the nations, concerning whom the LORD commanded them:

35 But were mingled among the heathen, and learned their works.

36 And they served their idols: which were a snare unto them.

37 Yea, they sacrificed their sons and their daughters unto devils,

38 And shed innocent blood, *even* the blood of their sons and of their daughters, whom they sacrificed unto the idols of Ca'naan: and the land was polluted with blood.

39 Thus were they defiled with their own works, and went a whoring with their own inventions.

40 Therefore was the wrath of the LORD kindled against his people, insomuch that he abhorred his own inheritance.

41 And he gave them into the hand of the heathen; and they that hated them ruled over them.

42 Their enemies also oppressed them, and they were brought into subjection under their hand.

43 Many times did he deliver them; but they provoked *him* with their counsel, and were brought low for their iniquity.

44 Nevertheless he regarded their affliction, when he heard their cry:

45 And he remembered for them his covenant, and repented according to the multitude of his mercies.

46 He made them also to be pitied of all those that carried them captives.

47 Save us, O LORD our God, and gather us from among the heathen, to give thanks unto thy holy name, *and* to triumph in thy praise.

48 Blessed *be* the LORD God of Is'ra-el from everlasting to everlasting: and let all the people say. Amen. Praise ye the LORD.

107 O GIVE thanks unto the LORD, for *he is* good: for his mercy *endureth* for ever.

2 Let the redeemed of the LORD say *so,* whom he hath redeemed from the hand of the enemy;

3 And gathered them out of the lands, from the east, and from the west, from the north, and from the south.

4 They wandered in the wilderness in a solitary way; they found no city to dwell in.

5 Hungry and thirsty, their soul fainted in them.

6 Then they cried unto the LORD in their trouble, *and* he delivered them out of their distresses.

7 And he led them forth by the right way, that they might go to a city of habitation.

8 Oh that *men* would praise the LORD *for* his goodness, and *for* his wonderful works to the children of men!

9 For he satisfieth the longing soul, and filleth the hungry soul with goodness.

10 Such as sit in darkness and in the shadow of death, *being* bound in affliction and iron;

11 Because they rebelled against the words of God, and contemned the counsel of the most High:

12 Therefore he brought down their heart with labour; they fell down, and *there was* none to help.

13 Then they cried unto the LORD in their trouble, *and* he saved them out of their distresses.

14 He brought them out of darkness and the shadow of death, and brake their bands in sunder.

15 Oh that *men* would praise the LORD *for* his goodness, and *for* his wonderful works to the children of men!

16 For he hath broken the gates of brass, and cut the bars of iron in sunder.

17 Fools because of their transgression, and because of their iniquities, are afflicted.

18 Their soul abhorreth all manner of meat; and they draw near unto the gates of death.

19 Then they cry unto the LORD in their trouble, *and* he saveth them out of their distresses.

20 He sent his word, and healed them, and delivered *them* from their destructions.

21 Oh that *men* would praise the LORD *for* his goodness, and *for* his wonderful works to the children of men!

22 And let them sacrifice the sacrifices of thanksgiving, and declare his works with rejoicing.

23 They that go down to the sea in ships, that do business in great waters;

24 These see the works of the LORD, and his wonders in the deep.

25 For he commandeth, and raiseth the stormy wind, which lifteth up the waves thereof.

26 They mount up to the heaven, they go down again to the depths: their soul is melted because of trouble.

27 They reel to and fro, and stagger like a drunken man, and are at their wit's end.

28 Then they cry unto the LORD in their trouble, and he bringeth them out of their distresses.

29 He maketh the storm a calm, so that the waves thereof are still.

30 Then are they glad because they be quiet; so he bringeth them unto their desired haven.

31 Oh that *men* would praise the LORD *for* his goodness, and *for* his wonderful works to the children of men!

32 Let them exalt him also in the congregation of the people, and praise him in the assembly of the elders.

33 He turneth rivers into a wilderness, and the watersprings into dry ground;

34 A fruitful land into barrenness, for the wickedness of them that dwell therein.

35 He turneth the wilderness into a standing water, and dry ground into watersprings.

36 And there he maketh the hungry to dwell, that they may prepare a city for habitation;

37 And sow the fields, and plant vineyards, which may yield fruits of increase.

38 He blesseth them also, so that they are multiplied greatly; and suffereth not their cattle to decrease.

39 Again, they are minished and brought low through oppression, affliction, and sorrow.

40 He poureth contempt upon princes, and causeth them to wander in the wilderness, *where there is* no way.

41 Yet setteth he the poor on high from affliction, and maketh *him* families like a flock.

42 The righteous shall see *it,* and rejoice: and all iniquity shall stop her mouth.

43 Whoso *is* wise, and will observe these *things,* even they shall understand the lovingkindness of the LORD.

A Song *or* Psalm of David.

108 O GOD, my heart is fixed; I will sing and give praise, even with my glory.

2 Awake, psaltery and harp: I *myself* will awake early.

3 I will praise thee, O LORD, among the people: and I will sing praises unto thee among the nations.

4 For thy mercy *is* great above the heavens: and thy truth *reacheth* unto the clouds.

5 Be thou exalted, O God, above the heavens: and thy glory above all the earth;

6 That thy beloved may be delivered: save *with* thy right hand, and answer me.

7 God hath spoken in his holiness; I will rejoice, I will divide She'chem, and mete out the valley of Suc'coth.

8 Gil'e-ad *is* mine; Ma-nas'seh *is* mine; E'phra-im also *is* the strength of mine head; Ju'dah *is* my lawgiver;

9 Mo'ab *is* my washpot: over E'dom will I cast out my shoe; over Phi-lis'tia will I triumph.

10 Who will bring me into the strong city? who will lead me into E'dom?

11 *Wilt* not *thou,* O God, *who* hast cast us off? and wilt not thou, O God, go forth with our hosts?

12 Give us help from trouble: for vain *is* the help of man.

13 Through God we shall do valiantly: for he *it is that* shall tread down our enemies.

To the chief Musician, A Psalm of David.

109 HOLD not thy peace, O God of my praise;

2 For the mouth of the wicked and the mouth of the deceitful are opened against me: they have spoken against me with a lying tongue.

3 They compassed me about also with words of hatred; and fought against me without a cause.

4 For my love they are my adversaries: but I *give myself unto* prayer.

5 And they have rewarded me evil for good, and hatred for my love.

6 Set thou a wicked man over him: and let Sa'tan stand at his right hand.

7 When he shall be judged, let him be condemned: and let his prayer become sin.

8 Let his days be few; *and* let another take his office.

9 Let his children be fatherless, and his wife a widow.

10 Let his children be continually vagabonds, and beg: let them seek *their bread* also out of their desolate places.

11 Let the extortioner catch all that he hath; and let the strangers spoil his labour.

12 Let there be none to extend mercy unto him: neither let there be any to favour his fatherless children.

13 Let his posterity be cut off; *and* in the generation following let their name be blotted out.

14 Let the iniquity of his fathers be remembered with the LORD; and let not the sin of his mother be blotted out.

15 Let them be before the LORD continually, that he may cut off the memory of them from the earth.

16 Because that he remembered not to shew mercy, but persecuted the poor and needy man, that he might even slay the broken in heart.

17 As he loved cursing, so let it come unto him: as he delighted not in blessing, so let it be far from him.

18 As he clothed himself with cursing like as with his garment, so let it come into his bowels like water, and like oil into his bones.

19 Let it be unto him as the garment *which* covereth him, and for a girdle wherewith he is girded continually.

20 *Let* this *be* the reward of mine adversaries from the LORD, and of them that speak evil against my soul.

21 But do thou for me, O GOD the Lord, for thy name's sake: because thy mercy *is* good, deliver thou me.

22 For I *am* poor and needy, and my heart is wounded within me.

23 I am gone like the shadow when it declineth: I am tossed up and down as the locust.

24 My knees are weak through fasting; and my flesh faileth of fatness.

25 I became also a reproach unto them: *when* they looked upon me they shaked their heads.

26 Help me, O LORD my God: O save me according to thy mercy:

27 That they may know that this *is* thy hand; *that* thou, LORD, hast done it.

28 Let them curse, but bless thou: when they arise, let them be ashamed; but let thy servant rejoice.

29 Let mine adversaries be clothed with shame, and let them cover themselves with their own confusion, as with a mantle.

30 I will greatly praise the LORD with my mouth; yea, I will praise him among the multitude.

31 For he shall stand at the right hand of the poor, to save *him* from those that condemn his soul.

A Psalm of David.

110 THE LORD said unto my Lord, Sit thou at my right hand, until I make thine enemies thy footstool.

2 The LORD shall send the rod of thy strength out of Zi'on: rule thou in the midst of thine enemies.

3 Thy people *shall be* willing in the day of thy power, in the beauties of holiness from the womb of the morning: thou hast the dew of thy youth.

4 The LORD hath sworn, and will not repent, Thou *art* a priest for ever after the order of Melchiz'e-dek.

5 The Lord at thy right hand shall strike through kings in the day of his wrath.

6 He shall judge among the heathen, he shall fill *the places* with the dead bodies; he shall wound the heads over many countries.

7 He shall drink of the brook in the way: therefore shall he lift up the head.

111 PRAISE ye the LORD. I will praise the LORD with *my* whole heart, in the assembly of the upright, and *in* the congregation.

2 The works of the LORD *are* great, sought out of all them that have pleasure therein.

3 His work *is* honourable and glorious: and his righteousness endureth for ever.

4 He hath made his wonderful works to be remembered: the LORD *is* gracious and full of compassion.

5 He hath given meat unto them that fear him: he will ever be mindful of his covenant.

6 He hath shewed his people the power of his works, that he may give them the heritage of the heathen.

7 The works of his hands *are* verity and judgment; all his commandments *are* sure.

8 They stand fast for ever and ever, *and are* done in truth and uprightness.

9 He sent redemption unto his people: he hath commanded his covenant for ever: holy and reverend *is* his name.

10 The fear of the LORD *is* the beginning of wisdom: a good understanding have all they that do *his commandments:* his praise endureth for ever.

112 PRAISE ye the LORD. Blessed *is* the man *that* feareth the LORD, *that* delighteth greatly in his commandments.

2 His seed shall be mighty upon earth: the generation of the upright shall be blessed.

3 Wealth and riches *shall be* in his house: and his righteousness endureth for ever.

4 Unto the upright there ariseth light in the darkness: *he is* gracious, and full of compassion, and righteous.

5 A good man sheweth favour, and lendeth: he will guide his affairs with discretion.

6 Surely he shall not be moved for ever: the righteous shall be in everlasting remembrance.

7 He shall not be afraid of evil tidings: his heart is fixed, trusting in the LORD.

8 His heart *is* established, he shall not be afraid, until he see *his desire* upon his enemies.

9 He hath dispersed, he hath given to the poor; his righteousness endureth for ever; his horn shall be exalted with honour.

10 The wicked shall see *it*, and be grieved; he

shall gnash with his teeth, and melt away: the desire of the wicked shall perish.

113 PRAISE ye the LORD. Praise, O ye servants of the LORD, praise the name of the LORD.

2 Blessed be the name of the LORD from this time forth and for evermore.

3 From the rising of the sun unto the going down of the same the LORD's name *is* to be praised.

4 The LORD *is* high above all nations, *and* his glory above the heavens.

5 Who *is* like unto the LORD our God, who dwelleth on high,

6 Who humbleth *himself* to behold *the things that are* in heaven, and in the earth!

7 He raiseth up the poor out of the dust, *and* lifteth the needy out of the dunghill;

8 That he may set *him* with princes, *even* with the princes of his people.

9 He maketh the barren woman to keep house, *and to be* a joyful mother of children. Praise ye the LORD.

114 WHEN Is'ra-el went out of E'gypt, the house of Ja'cob from a people of strange language;

2 Ju'dah was his sanctuary, *and* Is'ra-el his dominion.

3 The sea saw *it,* and fled: Jor'dan was driven back.

4 The mountains skipped like rams, *and* the little hills like lambs.

5 What *ailed* thee, O thou sea, that thou fleddest? thou Jor'dan, *that* thou wast driven back?

6 Ye mountains, *that* ye skipped like rams; *and* ye little hills, like lambs?

7 Tremble, thou earth, at the presence of the Lord, at the presence of the God of Ja'cob;

8 Which turned the rock *into* a standing water, the flint into a fountain of waters.

115 NOT unto us, O LORD, not unto us, but unto thy name give glory, for thy mercy, *and* for thy truth's sake.

2 Wherefore should the heathen say, Where *is* now their God?

3 But our God *is* in the heavens: he hath done whatsoever he hath pleased.

4 Their idols *are* silver and gold, the work of men's hands.

5 They have mouths, but they speak not: eyes have they, but they see not:

6 They have ears, but they hear not: noses have they, but they smell not:

7 They have hands, but they handle not: feet have they, but they walk not: neither speak they through their throat.

8 They that make them are like unto them; *so is* every one that trusteth in them.

9 O Is'ra-el, trust thou in the LORD: he *is* their help and their shield.

10 O house of Aar'on, trust in the LORD: he *is* their help and their shield.

11 Ye that fear the LORD, trust in the LORD: he *is* their help and their shield.

12 The LORD hath been mindful of us: he will bless *us;* he will bless the house of Is'ra-el; he will bless the house of Aar'on.

13 He will bless them that fear the LORD, *both* small and great.

14 The LORD shall increase you more and more, you and your children.

15 Ye *are* blessed of the LORD which made heaven and earth.

16 The heaven, *even* the heavens, *are* the

LORD's: but the earth hath he given to the children of men.

17 The dead praise not the LORD, neither any that go down into silence.

18 But we will bless the LORD from this time forth and for evermore. Praise the LORD.

116 I LOVE the LORD, because he hath heard my voice *and* my supplications.

2 Because he hath inclined his ear unto me, therefore will I call upon *him* as long as I live.

3 The sorrows of death compassed me, and the pains of hell gat hold upon me: I found trouble and sorrow.

4 Then called I upon the name of the LORD; O LORD, I beseech thee, deliver my soul.

5 Gracious *is* the LORD, and righteous; yea, our God *is* merciful.

6 The LORD preserveth the simple: I was brought low, and he helped me.

7 Return unto thy rest, O my soul; for the LORD hath dealt bountifully with thee.

8 For thou hast delivered my soul from death, mine eyes from tears, *and* my feet from falling.

9 I will walk before the LORD in the land of the living.

10 I believed, therefore have I spoken: I was greatly afflicted:

11 I said in my haste, All men *are* liars.

12 What shall I render unto the LORD *for* all his benefits toward me?

13 I will take the cup of salvation, and call upon the name of the LORD.

14 I will pay my vows unto the LORD now in the presence of all his people.

15 Precious *is* in the sight of the LORD *is* the death of his saints.

16 O LORD, truly I *am* thy servant; I *am* thy servant, *and* the son of thine handmaid: thou hast loosed my bonds.

17 I will offer to thee the sacrifice of thanksgiving, and will call upon the name of the LORD.

18 I will pay my vows unto the LORD now in the presence of all his people,

19 In the courts of the LORD's house, in the midst of thee, O Je-ru'sa-lem. Praise ye the LORD.

117 O PRAISE the LORD, all ye nations: praise him, all ye people.

2 For his merciful kindness is great toward us: and the truth of the LORD *endureth* for ever. Praise ye the LORD.

118 O GIVE thanks unto the LORD; for *he is* good: because his mercy *endureth* for ever.

2 Let Is'ra-el now say, that his mercy *endureth* for ever.

3 Let the house of Aar'on now say, that his mercy *endureth* for ever.

4 Let them now that fear the LORD say, that his mercy *endureth* for ever.

5 I called upon the LORD in distress: the LORD answered me, *and set me* in a large place.

6 The LORD *is* on my side; I will not fear: what can man do unto me?

7 The LORD taketh my part with them that help me: therefore shall I see *my desire* upon them that hate me.

8 *It is* better to trust in the LORD than to put confidence in man.

9 *It is* better to trust in the LORD than to put confidence in princes.

10 All nations compassed me about: but in the name of the LORD will I destroy them.

11 They compassed me about; yea, they compassed me about: but in the name of the LORD I will destroy them.

12 They compassed me about like bees; they are quenched as the fire of thorns: for in the name of the LORD I will destroy them.

13 Thou hast thrust sore at me that I might fall: but the LORD helped me.

14 The LORD is my strength and song, and is become my salvation.

15 The voice of rejoicing and salvation is in the tabernacles of the righteous: the right hand of the LORD doeth valiantly.

16 The right hand of the LORD is exalted: the right hand of the LORD doeth valiantly.

17 I shall not die, but live, and declare the works of the LORD.

18 The LORD hath chastened me sore: but he hath not given me over unto death.

19 Open to me the gates of righteousness: I will go into them, and I will praise the LORD:

20 This gate of the LORD, into which the righteous shall enter.

21 I will praise thee: for thou hast heard me, and art become my salvation.

22 The stone which the builders refused is become the head stone of the corner.

23 This is the LORD's doing; it is marvellous in our eyes.

24 This is the day which the LORD hath made; we will rejoice and be glad in it.

25 Save now, I beseech thee, O LORD: O LORD, I beseech thee, send now prosperity.

26 Blessed be he that cometh in the name of the LORD: we have blessed you out of the house of the LORD.

27 God is the LORD, which hath shewed us light: bind the sacrifice with cords, even unto the horns of the altar.

28 Thou art my God, and I will praise thee: thou art my God, I will exalt thee.

29 O give thanks unto the LORD; for he is good: for his mercy endureth for ever.

ALEPH.

119 BLESSED are the undefiled in the way, who walk in the law of the LORD.

2 Blessed are they that keep his testimonies, and that seek him with the whole heart.

3 They also do no iniquity: they walk in his ways.

4 Thou hast commanded us to keep thy precepts diligently.

5 O that my ways were directed to keep thy statutes!

6 Then shall I not be ashamed, when I have respect unto all thy commandments.

7 I will praise thee with uprightness of heart, when I shall have learned thy righteous judgments.

8 I will keep thy statutes: O forsake me not utterly.

BETH.

9 Wherewithal shall a young man cleanse his way? by taking heed thereto according to thy word.

10 With my whole heart have I sought thee: O let me not wander from thy commandments.

11 Thy word have I hid in mine heart, that I might not sin against thee.

12 Blessed art thou, O LORD: teach me thy statutes.

13 With my lips have I declared all the judgments of thy mouth.

14 I have rejoiced in the way of thy testimonies, as much as in all riches.

15 I will meditate in thy precepts, and have respect unto thy ways.

16 I will delight myself in thy statutes: I will not forget thy word.

GIMEL.

17 Deal bountifully with thy servant, that I may live, and keep thy word.

18 Open thou mine eyes, that I may behold wondrous things out of thy law.

19 I am a stranger in the earth: hide not thy commandments from me.

20 My soul breaketh for the longing that it hath unto thy judgments at all times.

21 Thou hast rebuked the proud that are cursed, which do err from thy commandments.

22 Remove from me reproach and contempt; for I have kept thy testimonies.

23 Princes also did sit and speak against me: but thy servant did meditate in thy statutes.

24 Thy testimonies also are my delight and my counsellors.

DALETH.

25 My soul cleaveth unto the dust: quicken thou me according to thy word.

26 I have declared my ways, and thou heardest me: teach me thy statutes.

27 Make me to understand the way of thy precepts: so shall I talk of thy wondrous works.

28 My soul melteth for heaviness: strengthen thou me according unto thy word.

29 Remove from me the way of lying: and grant me thy law graciously.

30 I have chosen the way of truth: thy judgments have I laid before me.

31 I have stuck unto thy testimonies: O LORD, put me not to shame.

32 I will run the way of thy commandments, when thou shalt enlarge my heart.

HE.

33 Teach me, O LORD, the way of thy statutes; and I shall keep it unto the end.

34 Give me understanding, and I shall keep thy law; yea, I shall observe it with my whole heart.

35 Make me to go in the path of thy commandments; for therein do I delight.

36 Incline my heart unto thy testimonies, and not to covetousness.

37 Turn away mine eyes from beholding vanity; and quicken thou me in thy way.

38 Stablish thy word unto thy servant, who is devoted to thy fear.

39 Turn away my reproach which I fear: for thy judgments are good.

40 Behold, I have longed after thy precepts: quicken me in thy righteousness.

VAU.

41 Let thy mercies come also unto me, O LORD, even thy salvation, according to thy word.

42 So shall I have wherewith to answer him that reproacheth me: for I trust in thy word.

43 And take not the word of truth utterly out of my mouth; for I have hoped in thy judgments.

44 So shall I keep thy law continually for ever and ever.

45 And I will walk at liberty: for I seek thy precepts.

46 I will speak of thy testimonies also before kings, and will not be ashamed.

47 And I will delight myself in thy commandments, which I have loved.

48 My hands also will I lift up unto thy commandments, which I have loved; and I will meditate in thy statutes.

ZAIN.

49 Remember the word unto thy servant, upon which thou hast caused me to hope.

50 This is my comfort in my affliction: for thy word hath quickened me.

51 The proud have had me greatly in derision: yet have I not declined from thy law.

52 I remembered thy judgments of old, O LORD; and have comforted myself.

53 Horror hath taken hold upon me because of the wicked that forsake thy law.

54 Thy statutes have been my songs in the house of my pilgrimage.

55 I have remembered thy name, O LORD, in the night, and have kept thy law.

56 This I had, because I kept thy precepts.

CHETH.

57 Thou art my portion, O LORD: I have said that I would keep thy words.

58 I intreated thy favour with my whole heart: be merciful unto me according to thy word.

59 I thought on my ways, and turned my feet unto thy testimonies.

60 I made haste, and delayed not to keep thy commandments.

61 The bands of the wicked have robbed me: but I have not forgotten thy law.

62 At midnight I will rise to give thanks unto thee because of thy righteous judgments.

63 I am a companion of all them that fear thee, and of them that keep thy precepts.

64 The earth, O LORD, is full of thy mercy: teach me thy statutes.

TETH.

65 Thou hast dealt well with thy servant, O LORD, according unto thy word.

66 Teach me good judgment and knowledge: for I have believed thy commandments.

67 Before I was afflicted I went astray: but now have I kept thy word.

68 Thou art good, and doest good; teach me thy statutes.

69 The proud have forged a lie against me: but I will keep thy precepts with my whole heart.

70 Their heart is as fat as grease; but I delight in thy law.

71 It is good for me that I have been afflicted; that I might learn thy statutes.

72 The law of thy mouth is better unto me than thousands of gold and silver.

JOD.

73 Thy hands have made me and fashioned me: give me understanding, that I may learn thy commandments.

74 They that fear thee will be glad when they see me; because I have hoped in thy word.

75 I know, O LORD, that thy judgments are right, and that thou in faithfulness hast afflicted me.

76 Let, I pray thee, thy merciful kindness be for my comfort, according to thy word unto thy servant.

77 Let thy tender mercies come unto me, that I may live: for thy law is my delight.

78 Let the proud be ashamed; for they dealt perversely with me without a cause: but I will meditate in thy precepts.

79 Let those that fear thee turn unto me, and those that have known thy testimonies.

80 Let my heart be sound in thy statutes; that I be not ashamed.

CAPH.

81 My soul fainteth for thy salvation: but I hope in thy word.

82 Mine eyes fail for thy word, saying, When wilt thou comfort me?

83 For I am become like a bottle in the smoke; yet do I not forget thy statutes.

84 How many are the days of thy servant? when wilt thou execute judgment on them that persecute me?

85 The proud have digged pits for me, which are not after thy law.

86 All thy commandments are faithful: they persecute me wrongfully; help thou me.

87 They had almost consumed me upon earth; but I forsook not thy precepts.

88 Quicken me after thy lovingkindness; so shall I keep the testimony of thy mouth.

LAMED.

89 For ever, O LORD, thy word is settled in heaven.

90 Thy faithfulness is unto all generations: thou hast established the earth, and it abideth.

91 They continue this day according to thine ordinances: for all are thy servants.

92 Unless thy law had been my delights, I should then have perished in mine affliction.

93 I will never forget thy precepts: for with them thou hast quickened me.

94 I am thine, save me; for I have sought thy precepts.

95 The wicked have waited for me to destroy me: but I will consider thy testimonies.

96 I have seen an end of all perfection: but thy commandment is exceeding broad.

MEM.

97 O how love I thy law! it is my meditation all the day.

98 Thou through thy commandments hast made me wiser than mine enemies: for they are ever with me.

99 I have more understanding than all my teachers: for thy testimonies are my meditation.

100 I understand more than the ancients, because I keep thy precepts.

101 I have refrained my feet from every evil way, that I might keep thy word.

102 I have not departed from thy judgments: for thou hast taught me.

103 How sweet are thy words unto my taste! yea, sweeter than honey to my mouth!

104 Through thy precepts I get understanding: therefore I hate every false way.

NUN.

105 Thy word is a lamp unto my feet, and a light unto my path.

106 I have sworn, and I will perform it, that I will keep thy righteous judgments.

107 I am afflicted very much: quicken me, O LORD, according unto thy word.

108 Accept, I beseech thee, the freewill offerings of my mouth, O LORD, and teach me thy judgments.

109 My soul is continually in my hand: yet do I not forget thy law.

110 The wicked have laid a snare for me: yet I erred not from thy precepts.

111 Thy testimonies have I taken as an heritage for ever: for they *are* the rejoicing of my heart.

112 I have inclined mine heart to perform thy statutes alway, *even unto* the end.

SAMECH.

113 I hate *vain* thoughts: but thy law do I love.

114 Thou *art* my hiding place and my shield: I hope in thy word.

115 Depart from me, ye evildoers: for I will keep the commandments of my God.

116 Uphold me according unto thy word, that I may live: and let me not be ashamed of my hope.

117 Hold thou me up, and I shall be safe: and I will have respect unto thy statutes continually.

118 Thou hast trodden down all them that err from thy statutes: for their deceit *is* falsehood.

119 Thou puttest away all the wicked of the earth *like* dross: therefore I love thy testimonies.

120 My flesh trembleth for fear of thee; and I am afraid of thy judgments.

AIN.

121 I have done judgment and justice: leave me not to mine oppressors.

122 Be surety for thy servant for good: let not the proud oppress me.

123 Mine eyes fail for thy salvation, and for the word of thy righteousness.

124 Deal with thy servant according unto thy mercy, and teach me thy statutes.

125 I *am* thy servant; give me understanding, that I may know thy testimonies.

126 *It is* time for *thee*, LORD, to work: *for* they have made void thy law.

127 Therefore I love thy commandments above gold; yea, above fine gold.

128 Therefore I esteem all *thy* precepts *concerning* all *things to be* right; *and* I hate every false way.

PE.

129 Thy testimonies *are* wonderful: therefore doth my soul keep them.

130 The entrance of thy words giveth light; it giveth understanding unto the simple.

131 I opened my mouth, and panted: for I longed for thy commandments.

132 Look thou upon me, and be merciful unto me, as thou usest to do unto those that love thy name.

133 Order my steps in thy word: and let not any iniquity have dominion over me.

134 Deliver me from the oppression of man: so will I keep thy precepts.

135 Make thy face to shine upon thy servant; and teach me thy statutes.

136 Rivers of waters run down mine eyes, because they keep not thy law.

TZADDI.

137 Righteous *art* thou, O LORD, and upright *are* thy judgments.

138 Thy testimonies *that* thou hast commanded *are* righteous and very faithful.

139 My zeal hath consumed me, because mine enemies have forgotten thy words.

140 Thy word *is* very pure: therefore thy servant loveth it.

141 I *am* small and despised: *yet* do not I forget thy precepts.

142 Thy righteousness *is* an everlasting righteousness, and thy law *is* the truth.

143 Trouble and anguish have taken hold on me: *yet* thy commandments *are* my delights.

144 The righteousness of thy testimonies *is* everlasting: give me understanding, and I shall live.

KOPH.

145 I cried with *my* whole heart; hear me, O LORD: I will keep thy statutes.

146 I cried unto thee; save me, and I shall keep thy testimonies.

147 I prevented the dawning of the morning, and cried: I hoped in thy word.

148 Mine eyes prevent the *night* watches, that I might meditate in thy word.

149 Hear my voice according unto thy lovingkindness: O LORD, quicken me according to thy judgment.

150 They draw nigh that follow after mischief: they are far from thy law.

151 Thou *art* near, O LORD; and all thy commandments *are* truth.

152 Concerning thy testimonies, I have known of old that thou hast founded them for ever.

RESH.

153 Consider mine affliction, and deliver me: for I do not forget thy law.

154 Plead my cause, and deliver me: quicken me according to thy word.

155 Salvation *is* far from the wicked: for they seek not thy statutes.

156 Great *are* thy tender mercies, O LORD: quicken me according to thy judgments.

157 Many *are* my persecutors and mine enemies; *yet* do I not decline from thy testimonies.

158 I beheld the transgressors, and was grieved; because they kept not thy word.

159 Consider how I love thy precepts: quicken me, O LORD, according to thy lovingkindness.

160 Thy word *is* true *from* the beginning: and every one of thy righteous judgments *endureth* for ever.

SCHIN.

161 Princes have persecuted me without a cause: but my heart standeth in awe of thy word.

162 I rejoice at thy word, as one that findeth great spoil.

163 I hate and abhor lying: *but* thy law do I love.

164 Seven times a day do I praise thee because of thy righteous judgments.

165 Great peace have they which love thy law: and nothing shall offend them.

166 LORD, I have hoped for thy salvation, and done thy commandments.

167 My soul hath kept thy testimonies; and I love them exceedingly.

168 I have kept thy precepts and thy testimonies: for all my ways *are* before thee.

TAU.

169 Let my cry come near before thee, O LORD: give me understanding according to thy word.

170 Let my supplication come before thee: deliver me according to thy word.

171 My lips shall utter praise, when thou hast taught me thy statutes.

172 My tongue shall speak of thy word: for all thy commandments *are* righteousness.
173 Let thine hand help me; for I have chosen thy precepts.
174 I have longed for thy salvation, O LORD; and thy law *is* my delight.
175 Let my soul live, and it shall praise thee; and let thy judgments help me.
176 I have gone astray like a lost sheep; seek thy servant; for I do not forget thy commandments.

A Song of degrees.

120 IN my distress I cried unto the LORD, and he heard me.
2 Deliver my soul, O LORD, from lying lips, *and* from a deceitful tongue.
3 What shall be given unto thee? or what shall be done unto thee, thou false tongue?
4 Sharp arrows of the mighty, with coals of juniper.
5 Woe is me, that I sojourn in Me'sech, *that* I dwell in the tents of Ke'dar!
6 My soul hath long dwelt with him that hateth peace.
7 I *am for* peace: but when I speak, they *are* for war.

A Song of degrees.

121 I WILL lift up mine eyes unto the hills, from whence cometh my help.
2 My help *cometh* from the LORD, which made heaven and earth.
3 He will not suffer thy foot to be moved: he that keepeth thee will not slumber.
4 Behold, he that keepeth Is'ra-el shall neither slumber nor sleep.
5 The LORD *is* thy keeper: the LORD *is* thy shade upon thy right hand.
6 The sun shall not smite thee by day, nor the moon by night.
7 The LORD shall preserve thee from all evil: he shall preserve thy soul.
8 The LORD shall preserve thy going out and thy coming in from this time forth, and even for evermore.

A Song of degrees of David.

122 I WAS glad when they said unto me, Let us go into the house of the LORD.
2 Our feet shall stand within thy gates, O Je-ru'sa-lem.
3 Je-ru'sa-lem is builded as a city that is compact together:
4 Whither the tribes go up, the tribes of the LORD, unto the testimony of Is'ra-el, to give thanks unto the name of the LORD.
5 For there are set thrones of judgment, the thrones of the house of Da'vid.
6 Pray for the peace of Je-ru'sa-lem: they shall prosper that love thee.
7 Peace be within thy walls, *and* prosperity within thy palaces.
8 For my brethren and companions' sakes, I will now say, Peace *be* within thee.
9 Because of the house of the LORD our God I will seek thy good.

A Song of degrees.

123 UNTO thee lift I up mine eyes, O thou that dwellest in the heavens.
2 Behold, as the eyes of servants *look* unto the hand of their masters, *and* as the eyes of a maiden unto the hand of her mistress; so our eyes *wait* upon the LORD our God, until that he have mercy upon us.
3 Have mercy upon us, O LORD, have mercy upon us: for we are exceedingly filled with contempt.
4 Our soul is exceedingly filled with the scorning of those that are at ease, *and* with the contempt of the proud.

A Song of degrees of David.

124 IF *it had not been* the LORD who was on our side, now may Is'ra-el say;
2 If *it had not been* the LORD who was on our side, when men rose up against us:
3 Then they had swallowed us up quick, when their wrath was kindled against us:
4 Then the waters had overwhelmed us, the stream had gone over our soul:
5 Then the proud waters had gone over our soul.
6 Blessed *be* the LORD, who hath not given us *as* a prey to their teeth.
7 Our soul is escaped as a bird out of the snare of the fowlers: the snare is broken, and we are escaped.
8 Our help *is* in the name of the LORD, who made heaven and earth.

A Song of degrees.

125 THEY that trust in the LORD *shall be* as mount Zi'on, *which* cannot be removed, *but* abideth for ever.
2 *As* the mountains *are* round about Je-ru'sa-lem, so the LORD *is* round about his people from henceforth even for ever.
3 For the rod of the wicked shall not rest upon the lot of the righteous; lest the righteous put forth their hands unto iniquity.
4 Do good, O LORD, unto *those that be* good, and to *them that are* upright in their hearts.
5 As for such as turn aside unto their crooked ways, the LORD shall lead them forth with the workers of iniquity: *but* peace *shall be* upon Is'ra-el.

A Song of degrees.

126 WHEN the LORD turned again the captivity of Zi'on, we were like them that dream.
2 Then was our mouth filled with laughter, and our tongue with singing: then said they among the heathen, The LORD hath done great things for them.
3 The LORD hath done great things for us; *whereof* we are glad.
4 Turn again our captivity, O LORD, as the streams in the south.
5 They that sow in tears shall reap in joy.
6 He that goeth forth and weepeth, bearing precious seed, shall doubtless come again with rejoicing, bringing his sheaves *with him.*

A Song of degrees *for Solomon.

127 EXCEPT the LORD build the house, they labour in vain that build it: except the LORD keep the city, the watchman waketh *but* in vain.
2 *It is* vain for you to rise up early, to sit up late, to eat the bread of sorrows: *for so* he giveth his beloved sleep.
3 Lo, children *are* an heritage of the LORD: *and* the fruit of the womb *is his* reward.

4 As arrows *are* in the hand of a mighty man; so *are* children of the youth.

5 Happy *is* the man that hath his quiver full of them: they shall not be ashamed, but they shall speak with the enemies in the gate.

A Song of degrees.

128 BLESSED *is* every one that feareth the LORD; that walketh in his ways.

2 For thou shalt eat the labour of thine hands: happy *shalt* thou *be*, and *it shall be* well with thee.

3 Thy wife *shall be* as a fruitful vine by the sides of thine house: thy children like olive plants round about thy table.

4 Behold, that thus shall the man be blessed that feareth the LORD.

5 The LORD shall bless thee out of Zi'on: and thou shalt see the good of Je-ru'sa-lem all the days of thy life.

6 Yea, thou shalt see thy children's children, *and* peace upon Is'ra-el.

A Song of degrees.

129 MANY a time have they afflicted me from my youth, may Is'ra-el now say:

2 Many a time have they afflicted me from my youth: yet they have not prevailed against me.

3 The plowers plowed upon my back: they made long their furrows.

4 The LORD *is* righteous: he hath cut asunder the cords of the wicked.

5 Let them all be confounded and turned back that hate Zi'on.

6 Let them be as the grass *upon* the house tops, which withereth afore it groweth up:

7 Wherewith the mower filleth not his hand; nor he that bindeth sheaves his bosom.

8 Neither do they which go by say, The blessing of the LORD *be* upon you: we bless you in the name of the LORD.

A Song of degrees.

130 OUT of the depths have I cried unto thee, O LORD.

2 Lord, hear my voice: let thine ears be attentive to the voice of my supplications.

3 If thou, LORD, shouldest mark iniquities, O Lord, who shall stand?

4 But *there is* forgiveness with thee, that thou mayest be feared.

5 I wait for the LORD, my soul doth wait, and in his word do I hope.

6 My soul *waiteth* for the Lord more than they that watch for the morning: *I say, more than* they that watch for the morning.

7 Let Is'ra-el hope in the LORD: for with the LORD *there is* mercy, and with him *is* plenteous redemption.

8 And he shall redeem Is'ra-el from all his iniquities.

A Song of degrees of David.

131 LORD, my heart is not haughty, nor mine eyes lofty: neither do I exercise myself in great matters, or in things too high for me.

2 Surely I have behaved and quieted myself, as a child that is weaned of his mother: my soul *is* even as a weaned child.

3 Let Is'ra-el hope in the LORD from henceforth and for ever.

A Song of degrees.

132 LORD, remember Da'vid, *and* all his afflictions:

2 How he sware unto the LORD, *and* vowed unto the mighty *God* of Ja'cob;

3 Surely I will not come into the tabernacle of my house, nor go up into my bed;

4 I will not give sleep to mine eyes, *or* slumber to mine eyelids,

5 Until I find out a place for the LORD, an habitation for the mighty *God* of Ja'cob.

6 Lo, we heard of it at Eph'ra-tah: we found it in the fields of the wood.

7 We will go into his tabernacles: we will worship at his footstool.

8 Arise, O LORD, into thy rest; thou, and the ark of thy strength.

9 Let thy priests be clothed with righteousness; and let thy saints shout for joy.

10 For thy servant Da'vid's sake turn not away the face of thine anointed.

11 The LORD hath sworn *in* truth unto Da'vid; he will not turn from it; Of the fruit of thy body will I set upon thy throne.

12 If thy children will keep my covenant and my testimony that I shall teach them, their children shall also sit upon thy throne for evermore.

13 For the LORD hath chosen Zi'on; he hath desired *it* for his habitation.

14 This *is* my rest for ever: here will I dwell; for I have desired it.

15 I will abundantly bless her provision: I will satisfy her poor with bread.

16 I will also clothe her priests with salvation: and her saints shall shout aloud for joy.

17 There will I make the horn of Da'vid to bud: I have ordained a lamp for mine anointed.

18 His enemies will I clothe with shame: but upon himself shall his crown flourish.

A Song of degrees of David.

133 BEHOLD, how good and how pleasant *it is* for brethren to dwell together in unity!

2 *It is* like the precious ointment upon the head, that ran down upon the beard, *even* Aar'-on's beard: that went down to the skirts of his garments;

3 As the dew of Her'mon, *and as the dew* that descended upon the mountains of Zi'on: for there the LORD commanded the blessing, *even* life for evermore.

A Song of degrees.

134 BEHOLD, bless ye the LORD, all ye servants of the LORD, which by night stand in the house of the LORD.

2 Lift up your hands *in* the sanctuary, and bless the LORD.

3 The LORD that made heaven and earth bless thee out of Zi'on.

135 PRAISE ye the LORD. Praise ye the name of the LORD; praise *him*, O ye servants of the LORD.

2 Ye that stand in the house of the LORD, in the courts of the house of our God,

3 Praise the LORD; for the LORD *is* good: sing praises unto his name; for *it is* pleasant.

4 For the LORD hath chosen Ja'cob unto himself, *and* Is'ra-el for his peculiar treasure.

5 For I know that the LORD *is* great, and *that* our Lord *is* above all gods.

6 Whatsoever the LORD pleased, *that* did he in heaven, and in earth, in the seas, and all deep places.

7 He causeth the vapours to ascend from the ends of the earth; he maketh lightnings for the rain; he bringeth the wind out of his treasuries.

8 Who smote the firstborn of E'gypt, both of man and beast.

9 *Who* sent tokens and wonders into the midst of thee, O E'gypt, upon Pha'raoh, and upon all his servants.

10 Who smote great nations, and slew mighty kings;

11 Si'hon king of the Am'or-ites, and Og king of Ba'shan, and all the kingdoms of Ca'naan:

12 And gave their land *for* an heritage, an heritage unto Is'ra-el his people.

13 Thy name, O LORD, *endureth* for ever; *and* thy memorial, O LORD, throughout all generations.

14 For the LORD will judge his people, and he will repent himself concerning his servants.

15 The idols of the heathen *are* silver and gold, the work of men's hands.

16 They have mouths, but they speak not; eyes have they, but they see not;

17 They have ears, but they hear not; neither is there *any* breath in their mouths.

18 They that make them are like unto them: *so is* every one that trusteth in them.

19 Bless the LORD, O house of Is'ra-el: bless the LORD, O house of Aar'on:

20 Bless the LORD, O house of Le'vi: ye that fear the LORD, bless the LORD.

21 Blessed be the LORD out of Zi'on, which dwelleth at Je-ru'sa-lem. Praise ye the LORD.

136

O GIVE thanks unto the LORD; for *he* is good: for his mercy *endureth* for ever.

2 O give thanks unto the God of gods: for his mercy *endureth* for ever.

3 O give thanks to the Lord of lords: for his mercy *endureth* for ever.

4 To him who alone doeth great wonders: for his mercy *endureth* for ever.

5 To him that by wisdom made the heavens: for his mercy *endureth* for ever.

6 To him that stretched out the earth above the waters: for his mercy *endureth* for ever.

7 To him that made great lights: for his mercy *endureth* for ever:

8 The sun to rule by day: for his mercy *endureth* for ever:

9 The moon and stars to rule by night: for his mercy *endureth* for ever.

10 To him that smote E'gypt in their firstborn: for his mercy *endureth* for ever:

11 And brought out Is'ra-el from among them: for his mercy *endureth* for ever.

12 With a strong hand, and with a stretched out arm: for his mercy *endureth* for ever.

13 To him which divided the Red sea into parts: for his mercy *endureth* for ever:

14 And made Is'ra-el to pass through the midst of it: for his mercy *endureth* for ever:

15 But overthrew Pha'raoh and his host in the Red sea: for his mercy *endureth* for ever.

16 To him which led his people through the wilderness: for his mercy *endureth* for ever.

17 To him which smote great kings: for his mercy *endureth* for ever:

18 And slew famous kings: for his mercy *endureth* for ever:

19 Si'hon king of the Am'or-ites: for his mercy *endureth* for ever:

20 And Og the king of Ba'shan: for his mercy *endureth* for ever:

21 And gave their land for an heritage: for his mercy *endureth* for ever:

22 *Even* an heritage unto Is'ra-el his servant: for his mercy *endureth* for ever.

23 Who remembered us in our low estate: for his mercy *endureth* for ever.

24 And hath redeemed us from our enemies: for his mercy *endureth* for ever.

25 Who giveth food to all flesh: for his mercy *endureth* for ever.

26 O give thanks unto the God of heaven: for his mercy *endureth* for ever.

137

BY the rivers of Bab'y-lon, there we sat down, yea, we wept, when we remembered Zi'on.

2 We hanged our harps upon the willows in the midst thereof.

3 For there they that carried us away captive required of us a song; and they that wasted us *required of us* mirth, *saying,* Sing us *one* of the songs of Zi'on.

4 How shall we sing the LORD'S song in a strange land?

5 If I forget thee, O Je-ru'sa-lem, let my right hand forget *her cunning.*

6 If I do not remember thee, let my tongue cleave to the roof of my mouth; if I prefer not Je-ru'sa-lem above my chief joy.

7 Remember, O LORD, the children of E'dom in the day of Je-ru'sa-lem; who said, Rase *it,* rase *it, even* to the foundation thereof.

8 O daughter of Bab'y-lon, who art to be destroyed; happy *shall he be,* that rewardeth thee as thou hast served us.

9 Happy *shall he be,* that taketh and dasheth thy little ones against the stones.

A Psalm of David.

138

I WILL praise thee with my whole heart: before the gods will I sing praise unto thee.

2 I will worship toward thy holy temple, and praise thy name for thy lovingkindness and for thy truth: for thou hast magnified thy word above all thy name.

3 In the day when I cried thou answeredst me, *and* strengthenedst me *with* strength in my soul.

4 All the kings of the earth shall praise thee, O LORD, when they hear the words of thy mouth.

5 Yea, they shall sing in the ways of the LORD: for great *is* the glory of the LORD.

6 Though the LORD *be* high, yet hath he respect unto the lowly: but the proud he knoweth afar off.

7 Though I walk in the midst of trouble, thou wilt revive me: thou shalt stretch forth thine hand against the wrath of mine enemies, and thy right hand shall save me.

8 The LORD will perfect *that which* concerneth me: thy mercy, O LORD, *endureth* for ever: forsake not the works of thine own hands.

To the chief Musician, A Psalm of David.

139

O LORD, thou hast searched me, and known *me.*

2 Thou knowest my downsitting and mine uprising, thou understandest my thought afar off.

3 Thou compassest my path and my lying down, and art acquainted *with* all my ways.

4 For *there is* not a word in my tongue, *but,* lo, O LORD, thou knowest it altogether.

5 Thou hast beset me behind and before, and laid thine hand upon me.

6 *Such* knowledge *is* too wonderful for me; it is high, I cannot *attain* unto it.

7 Whither shall I go from thy spirit? or whither shall I flee from thy presence?

8 If I ascend up into heaven, thou *art* there: if I make my bed in hell, behold, thou *art there.*

9 *If* I take the wings of the morning, *and* dwell in the uttermost parts of the sea;

10 Even there shall thy hand lead me, and thy right hand shall hold me.

11 If I say, Surely the darkness shall cover me; even the night shall be light about me.

12 Yea, the darkness hideth not from thee; but the night shineth as the day: the darkness and the light *are* both alike *to thee.*

13 For thou hast possessed my reins: thou hast covered me in my mother's womb.

14 I will praise thee; for I am fearfully *and* wonderfully made: marvellous *are* thy works; and *that* my soul knoweth right well.

15 My substance was not hid from thee, when I was made in secret, *and* curiously wrought in the lowest parts of the earth.

16 Thine eyes did see my substance, yet being unperfect; and in thy book all *my members* were written, *which* in continuance were fashioned, when *as yet there was* none of them.

17 How precious also are thy thoughts unto me, O God! how great is the sum of them!

18 *If* I should count them, they are more in number than the sand: when I awake, I am still with thee.

19 Surely thou wilt slay the wicked, O God: depart from me therefore, ye bloody men.

20 For they speak against thee wickedly, *and* thine enemies take *thy name* in vain.

21 Do not I hate them, O LORD, that hate thee? and am not I grieved with those that rise up against thee?

22 I hate them with perfect hatred: I count them mine enemies.

23 Search me, O God, and know my heart: try me, and know my thoughts:

24 And see if *there be any* wicked way in me, and lead me in the way everlasting.

To the chief Musician, A Psalm of David.

140 DELIVER me, O LORD from the evil man: preserve me from the violent man;

2 Which imagine mischiefs in *their* heart; continually are they gathered together *for* war.

3 They have sharpened their tongues like a serpent; adders' poison *is* under their lips. Se'lah.

4 Keep me, O LORD, from the hands of the wicked; preserve me from the violent man; who have purposed to overthrow my goings.

5 The proud have hid a snare for me, and cords; they have spread a net by the wayside; they have set gins for me. Se'lah.

6 I said unto the LORD, Thou *art* my God: hear the voice of my supplications, O LORD.

7 O GOD the Lord, the strength of my salvation, thou hast covered my head in the day of battle.

8 Grant not, O LORD, the desires of the wicked: further not his wicked device; *lest* they exalt themselves. Se'lah.

9 *As for* the head of those that compass me about, let the mischief of their own lips cover them.

10 Let burning coals fall upon them: let them be cast into the fire; into deep pits, that they rise not up again.

11 Let not an evil speaker be established in the earth: evil shall hunt the violent man to overthrow *him.*

12 I know that the LORD will maintain the cause of the afflicted, *and* the right of the poor.

13 Surely the righteous shall give thanks unto thy name: the upright shall dwell in thy presence.

A Psalm of David.

141 LORD, I cry unto thee: make haste unto me; give ear unto my voice, when I cry unto thee.

2 Let my prayer be set forth before thee *as* incense; *and* the lifting up of my hands *as* the evening sacrifice.

3 Set a watch, O LORD, before my mouth; keep the door of my lips.

4 Incline not my heart to *any* evil thing, to practise wicked works with men that work iniquity: and let me not eat of their dainties.

5 Let the righteous smite me; *it shall be* a kindness: and let him reprove me; *it shall be* an excellent oil, *which* shall not break my head: for yet my prayer also *shall be* in their calamities.

6 When their judges are overthrown in stony places, they shall hear my words; for they are sweet.

7 Our bones are scattered at the grave's mouth, as when one cutteth and cleaveth *wood* upon the earth.

8 But mine eyes *are* unto thee, O GOD the Lord: in thee is my trust; leave not my soul destitute.

9 Keep me from the snares *which* they have laid for me, and the gins of the workers of iniquity.

10 Let the wicked fall into their own nets, whilst that I withal escape.

* Maschil of David; A Prayer when he was in the cave.

142 I CRIED unto the LORD with my voice; with my voice unto the LORD did I make my supplication.

2 I poured out my complaint before him; I shewed before him my trouble.

3 When my spirit was overwhelmed within me, then thou knewest my path. In the way wherein I walked have they privily laid a snare for me.

4 I looked on *my* right hand, and beheld, but *there was* no man that would know me: refuge failed me; no man cared for my soul.

5 I cried unto thee, O LORD: I said, Thou *art* my refuge *and* my portion in the land of the living.

6 Attend unto my cry; for I am brought very low: deliver me from my persecutors; for they are stronger than I.

7 Bring my soul out of prison, that I may praise thy name: the righteous shall compass me about; for thou shalt deal bountifully with me.

A Psalm of David.

143 HEAR my prayer, O LORD, give ear to my supplications: in thy faithfulness answer me, *and* in thy righteousness.

2 And enter not into judgment with thy servant: for in thy sight shall no man living be justified.

3 For the enemy hath persecuted my soul; he hath smitten my life down to the ground; he hath made me to dwell in darkness, as those that have been long dead.

4 Therefore is my spirit overwhelmed within me; my heart within me is desolate.

5 I remember the days of old; I meditate on all thy works; I muse on the work of thy hands.

6 I stretch forth my hands unto thee: my soul *thirsteth* after thee, as a thirsty land. Se'lah.

7 Hear me speedily, O Lord: my spirit faileth: hide not thy face from me, lest I be like unto them that go down into the pit.

8 Cause me to hear thy lovingkindness in the morning; for in thee do I trust: cause me to know the way wherein I should walk; for I lift up my soul unto thee.

9 Deliver me, O Lord, from mine enemies: I flee unto thee to hide me.

10 Teach me to do thy will; for thou *art* my God: thy spirit *is* good; lead me into the land of uprightness.

11 Quicken me, O Lord, for thy name's sake: for thy righteousness' sake bring my soul out of trouble.

12 And of thy mercy cut off mine enemies, and destroy all them that afflict my soul: for I *am* thy servant.

A Psalm of David.

144 BLESSED *be* the Lord my strength, which teacheth my hands to war, *and* my fingers to fight:

2 My goodness, and my fortress; my high tower, and my deliverer; my shield, and *he* in whom I trust; who subdueth my people under me.

3 Lord, what *is* man, that thou takest knowledge of him! *or* the son of man, that thou makest account of him!

4 Man is like to vanity: his days *are* as a shadow that passeth away.

5 Bow thy heavens, O Lord, and come down: touch the mountains, and they shall smoke.

6 Cast forth lightning, and scatter them: shoot out thine arrows, and destroy them.

7 Send thine hand from above; rid me, and deliver me out of great waters, from the hand of strange children;

8 Whose mouth speaketh vanity, and their right hand *is* a right hand of falsehood.

9 I will sing a new song unto thee, O God: upon a psaltery *and* an instrument of ten strings will I sing praises unto thee.

10 *It is* he that giveth salvation unto kings: who delivereth Da'vid his servant from the hurtful sword.

11 Rid me, and deliver me from the hand of strange children, whose mouth speaketh vanity, and their right hand *is* a right hand of falsehood:

12 That our sons *may be* as plants grown up in their youth; *that* our daughters *may be* as corner stones, polished *after* the similitude of a palace:

13 *That* our garners *may be* full, affording all manner of store: *that* our sheep may bring forth thousands and ten thousands in our streets:

14 *That* our oxen *may be* strong to labour; *that there be* no breaking in, nor going out; that *there be* no complaining in our streets.

15 Happy *is that* people, that is in such a case: yea, happy *is that* people, whose God *is* the Lord.

David's Psalm of praise.

145 I WILL extol thee, my God, O king; and I will bless thy name for ever and ever.

2 Every day will I bless thee; and I will praise thy name for ever and ever.

3 Great *is* the Lord, and greatly to be praised; and his greatness *is* unsearchable.

4 One generation shall praise thy works to another, and shall declare thy mighty acts.

5 I will speak of the glorious honour of thy majesty, and of thy wondrous works.

6 And *men* shall speak of the might of thy terrible acts: and I will declare thy greatness.

7 They shall abundantly utter the memory of thy great goodness, and shall sing of thy righteousness.

8 The Lord *is* gracious, and full of compassion; slow to anger, and of great mercy.

9 The Lord *is* good to all: and his tender mercies *are* over all his works.

10 All thy works shall praise thee, O Lord; and thy saints shall bless thee.

11 They shall speak of the glory of thy kingdom, and talk of thy power;

12 To make known to the sons of men his mighty acts, and the glorious majesty of his kingdom.

13 Thy kingdom *is* an everlasting kingdom, and thy dominion *endureth* throughout all generations.

14 The Lord upholdeth all that fall, and raiseth up all *those that be* bowed down.

15 The eyes of all wait upon thee; and thou givest them their meat in due season.

16 Thou openest thine hand, and satisfiest the desire of every living thing.

17 The Lord *is* righteous in all his ways, and holy in all his works.

18 The Lord *is* nigh unto all them that call upon him, to all that call upon him in truth.

19 He will fulfil the desire of them that fear him: he also will hear their cry, and will save them.

20 The Lord preserveth all them that love him: but all the wicked will he destroy.

21 My mouth shall speak the praise of the Lord: and let all flesh bless his holy name for ever and ever.

146 PRAISE ye the Lord. Praise the Lord, O my soul.

2 While I live will I praise the Lord: I will sing praises unto my God while I have any being.

3 Put not your trust in princes, *nor* in the son of man, in whom *there is* no help.

4 His breath goeth forth, he returneth to his earth; in that very day his thoughts perish.

5 Happy *is* he that *hath* the God of Ja'cob for his help, whose hope *is* in the Lord his God:

6 Which made heaven, and earth, the sea, and all that therein *is*: which keepeth truth for ever:

7 Which executeth judgment for the oppressed: which giveth food to the hungry. The Lord looseth the prisoners:

8 The Lord openeth *the eyes of* the blind: the Lord raiseth them that are bowed down: the Lord loveth the righteous.

9 The Lord preserveth the strangers; he relieveth the fatherless and widow: but the way of the wicked he turneth upside down.

10 The Lord shall reign for ever, *even* thy God, O Zi'on, unto all generations. Praise ye the Lord.

147 PRAISE ye the Lord: for *it is* good to sing praises unto our God; for *it is* pleasant; *and* praise is comely.

2 The Lord doth build up Je-ru'sa-lem: he gathereth together the outcasts of Is'ra-el.

3 He healeth the broken in heart, and bindeth up their wounds.

4 He telleth the number of the stars; he calleth them all by *their* names.

5 Great *is* our Lord, and of great power: his understanding *is* infinite.

6 The Lord lifteth up the meek: he casteth the wicked down to the ground.

7 Sing unto the Lord with thanksgiving; sing praise upon the harp unto our God:

8 Who covereth the heaven with clouds, who prepareth rain for the earth, who maketh grass to grow upon the mountains.

9 He giveth to the beast his food, *and* to the young ravens which cry.

10 He delighteth not in the strength of the horse: he taketh not pleasure in the legs of a man.

11 The Lord taketh pleasure in them that fear him, in those that hope in his mercy.

12 Praise the Lord, O Je-ru'sa-lem; praise thy God, O Zi'on.

13 For he hath strengthened the bars of thy gates; he hath blessed thy children within thee.

14 He maketh peace *in* thy borders, *and* filleth thee with the finest of the wheat.

15 He sendeth forth his commandment *upon* earth: his word runneth very swiftly.

16 He giveth snow like wool: he scattereth the hoarfrost like ashes.

17 He casteth forth his ice like morsels: who can stand before his cold?

18 He sendeth out his word, and melteth them: he causeth his wind to blow, *and* the waters flow.

19 He sheweth his word unto Ja'cob, his statutes and his judgments unto Is'ra-el.

20 He hath not dealt so with any nation: and *as for his* judgments, they have not known them. Praise ye the Lord.

148 PRAISE ye the Lord. Praise ye the Lord from the heavens: praise him in the heights.

2 Praise ye him, all his angels: praise ye him, all his hosts.

3 Praise ye him, sun and moon: praise him, all ye stars of light.

4 Praise him, ye heavens of heavens, and ye waters that *be* above the heavens.

5 Let them praise the name of the Lord: for he commanded, and they were created.

6 He hath also stablished them for ever and ever: he hath made a decree which shall not pass.

7 Praise the Lord from the earth, ye dragons, and all deeps:

8 Fire, and hail; snow, and vapours; stormy wind fulfilling his word:

9 Mountains, and all hills; fruitful trees, and all cedars:

10 Beasts, and all cattle; creeping things, and flying fowl:

11 Kings of the earth, and all people; princes, and all judges of the earth:

12 Both young men, and maidens; old men, and children:

13 Let them praise the name of the Lord: for his name alone is excellent; his glory *is* above the earth and heaven.

14 He also exalteth the horn of his people, the praise of all his saints; *even* of the children of Is'ra-el, a people near unto him. Praise ye the Lord.

149 PRAISE ye the Lord. Sing unto the Lord a new song, *and* his praise in the congregation of saints.

2 Let Is'ra-el rejoice in him that made him: let the children of Zi'on be joyful in their King.

3 Let them praise his name in the dance: let them sing praises unto him with the timbrel and harp.

4 For the Lord taketh pleasure in his people: he will beautify the meek with salvation.

5 Let the saints be joyful in glory: let them sing aloud upon their beds.

6 *Let* the high *praises* of God *be* in their mouth, and a twoedged sword in their hand;

7 To execute vengeance upon the heathen, *and* punishments upon the people;

8 To bind their kings with chains, and their nobles with fetters of iron;

9 To execute upon them the judgment written: this honour have all his saints. Praise ye the Lord.

150 PRAISE ye the Lord. Praise God in his sanctuary: praise him in the firmament of his power.

2 Praise him for his mighty acts: praise him according to his excellent greatness.

3 Praise him with the sound of the trumpet: praise him with the psaltery and harp.

4 Praise him with the timbrel and dance: praise him with stringed instruments and organs.

5 Praise him upon the loud cymbals: praise him upon the high sounding cymbals.

6 Let every thing that hath breath praise the Lord. Praise ye the Lord.

THE PROVERBS

1 THE proverbs of Sol'o-mon the son of Da'vid, king of Is'ra-el;

2 To know wisdom and instruction; to perceive the words of understanding;

3 To receive the instruction of wisdom, justice, and judgment, and equity;

4 To give subtilty to the simple, to the young man knowledge and discretion.

5 A wise *man* will hear, and will increase learning; and a man of understanding shall attain unto wise counsels:

6 To understand a proverb, and the interpretation; the words of the wise, and their dark sayings.

7 ¶ The fear of the Lord *is* the beginning of knowledge: *but* fools despise wisdom and instruction.

8 My son, hear the instruction of thy father, and forsake not the law of thy mother:

9 For they *shall be* an ornament of grace unto thy head, and chains about thy neck.

10 ¶ My son, if sinners entice thee, consent thou not.

11 If they say, Come with us, let us lay wait

for blood, let us lurk privily for the innocent without cause:

12 Let us swallow them up alive as the grave; and whole, as those that go down into the pit:

13 We shall find all precious substance, we shall fill our houses with spoil:

14 Cast in thy lot among us; let us all have one purse:

15 My son, walk not thou in the way with them; refrain thy foot from their path:

16 For their feet run to evil, and make haste to shed blood.

17 Surely in vain the net is spread in the sight of any bird.

18 And they lay wait for their *own* blood; they lurk privily for their *own* lives.

19 So *are* the ways of every one that is greedy of gain; *which* taketh away the life of the owners thereof.

20 ¶ Wisdom crieth without; she uttereth her voice in the streets:

21 She crieth in the chief place of concourse, in the openings of the gates: in the city she uttereth her words, *saying*,

22 How long, ye simple ones, will ye love simplicity? and the scorners delight in their scorning, and fools hate knowledge?

23 Turn you at my reproof: behold, I will pour out my spirit unto you, I will make known my words unto you.

24 ¶ Because I have called, and ye refused; I have stretched out my hand, and no man regarded;

25 But ye have set at nought all my counsel, and would none of my reproof:

26 I also will laugh at your calamity; I will mock when your fear cometh;

27 When your fear cometh as desolation, and your destruction cometh as a whirlwind; when distress and anguish cometh upon you.

28 Then shall they call upon me, but I will not answer; they shall seek me early, but they shall not find me:

29 For that they hated knowledge, and did not choose the fear of the LORD:

30 They would none of my counsel: they despised all my reproof.

31 Therefore shall they eat of the fruit of their own way, and be filled with their own devices.

32 For the turning away of the simple shall slay them, and the prosperity of fools shall destroy them.

33 But whoso hearkeneth unto me shall dwell safely, and shall be quiet from fear of evil.

2 MY son, if thou wilt receive my words, and hide my commandments with thee;

2 So that thou incline thine ear unto wisdom, *and* apply thine heart to understanding;

3 Yea, if thou criest after knowledge, *and* liftest up thy voice for understanding;

4 If thou seekest her as silver, and searchest for her as *for* hid treasures;

5 Then shalt thou understand the fear of the LORD, and find the knowledge of God.

6 For the LORD giveth wisdom: out of his mouth *cometh* knowledge and understanding.

7 He layeth up sound wisdom for the righteous: *he is* a buckler to them that walk uprightly.

8 He keepeth the paths of judgment, and preserveth the way of his saints.

9 Then shalt thou understand righteousness, and judgment, and equity; *yea*, every good path.

10 ¶ When wisdom entereth into thine heart, and knowledge is pleasant unto thy soul;

11 Discretion shall preserve thee, understanding shall keep thee:

12 To deliver thee from the way of the evil *man*, from the man that speaketh froward things;

13 Who leave the paths of uprightness, to walk in the ways of darkness;

14 Who rejoice to do evil, *and* delight in the frowardness of the wicked;

15 Whose ways *are* crooked, and *they* froward in their paths:

16 To deliver thee from the strange woman, *even* from the stranger *which* flattereth with her words;

17 Which forsaketh the guide of her youth, and forgetteth the covenant of her God.

18 For her house inclineth unto death, and her paths unto the dead.

19 None that go unto her return again, neither take they hold of the paths of life.

20 That thou mayest walk in the way of good *men*, and keep the paths of the righteous.

21 For the upright shall dwell in the land, and the perfect shall remain in it.

22 But the wicked shall be cut off from the earth, and the transgressors shall be rooted out of it.

3 MY son, forget not my law; but let thine heart keep my commandments:

2 For length of days, and long life, and peace, shall they add to thee.

3 Let not mercy and truth forsake thee: bind them about thy neck; write them upon the table of thine heart:

4 So shalt thou find favour and good understanding in the sight of God and man.

5 ¶ Trust in the LORD with all thine heart; and lean not unto thine own understanding.

6 In all thy ways acknowledge him, and he shall direct thy paths.

7 ¶ Be not wise in thine own eyes: fear the LORD, and depart from evil.

8 It shall be health to thy navel, and marrow to thy bones.

9 Honour the LORD with thy substance, and with the firstfruits of all thine increase:

10 So shall thy barns be filled with plenty, and thy presses shall burst out with new wine.

11 ¶ My son, despise not the chastening of the LORD; neither be weary of his correction:

12 For whom the LORD loveth he correcteth; even as a father the son *in whom* he delighteth.

13 ¶ Happy *is* the man *that* findeth wisdom, and the man *that* getteth understanding.

14 For the merchandise of it *is* better than the merchandise of silver, and the gain thereof than fine gold.

15 She *is* more precious than rubies: and all the things thou canst desire are not to be compared unto her.

16 Length of days *is* in her right hand; *and* in her left hand riches and honour.

17 Her ways *are* ways of pleasantness, and all her paths *are* peace.

18 She *is* a tree of life to them that lay hold upon her: and happy *is every one* that retaineth her.

19 The LORD by wisdom hath founded the earth; by understanding hath he established the heavens.

20 By his knowledge the depths are broken up, and the clouds drop down the dew.

21 ¶ My son, let not them depart from thine eyes: keep sound wisdom and discretion:

22 So shall they be life unto thy soul, and grace to thy neck.

23 Then shalt thou walk in thy way safely, and thy foot shall not stumble.

24 When thou liest down, thou shalt not be afraid: yea, thou shalt lie down, and thy sleep shall be sweet.

25 Be not afraid of sudden fear, neither of the desolation of the wicked, when it cometh.

26 For the LORD shall be thy confidence, and shall keep thy foot from being taken.

27 ¶ Withhold not good from them to whom it is due, when it is in the power of thine hand to do it.

28 Say not unto thy neighbour, Go, and come again, and to morrow I will give; when thou hast it by thee.

29 Devise not evil against thy neighbour, seeing he dwelleth securely by thee.

30 ¶ Strive not with a man without cause, if he have done thee no harm.

31 ¶ Envy thou not the oppressor, and choose none of his ways.

32 For the froward is abomination to the LORD: but his secret is with the righteous.

33 ¶ The curse of the LORD is in the house of the wicked: but he blesseth the habitation of the just.

34 Surely he scorneth the scorners: but he giveth grace unto the lowly.

35 The wise shall inherit glory: but shame shall be the promotion of fools.

4 HEAR, ye children, the instruction of a father, and attend to know understanding.

2 For I give you good doctrine, forsake ye not my law.

3 For I was my father's son, tender and only beloved in the sight of my mother.

4 He taught me also, and said unto me, Let thine heart retain my words: keep my commandments, and live.

5 Get wisdom, get understanding: forget it not; neither decline from the words of my mouth.

6 Forsake her not, and she shall preserve thee: love her, and she shall keep thee.

7 Wisdom is the principal thing; therefore get wisdom: and with all thy getting get understanding.

8 Exalt her, and she shall promote thee: she shall bring thee to honour, when thou dost embrace her.

9 She shall give to thine head an ornament of grace: a crown of glory shall she deliver to thee.

10 Hear, O my son, and receive my sayings; and the years of thy life shall be many.

11 I have taught thee in the way of wisdom; I have led thee in right paths.

12 When thou goest, thy steps shall not be straitened; and when thou runnest, thou shalt not stumble.

13 Take fast hold of instruction; let her not go: keep her; for she is thy life.

14 ¶ Enter not into the path of the wicked, and go not in the way of evil men.

15 Avoid it, pass not by it, turn from it, and pass away.

16 For they sleep not, except they have done mischief; and their sleep is taken away, unless they cause some to fall.

17 For they eat the bread of wickedness, and drink the wine of violence.

18 But the path of the just is as the shining light, that shineth more and more unto the perfect day.

19 The way of the wicked is as darkness: they know not at what they stumble.

20 ¶ My son, attend to my words; incline thine ear unto my sayings.

21 Let them not depart from thine eyes; keep them in the midst of thine heart.

22 For they are life unto those that find them, and health to all their flesh.

23 ¶ Keep thy heart with all diligence; for out of it are the issues of life.

24 Put away from thee a froward mouth, and perverse lips put far from thee.

25 Let thine eyes look right on, and let thine eyelids look straight before thee.

26 Ponder the path of thy feet, and let all thy ways be established.

27 Turn not to the right hand nor to the left: remove thy foot from evil.

5 MY son, attend unto my wisdom, and bow thine ear to my understanding:

2 That thou mayest regard discretion, and that thy lips may keep knowledge.

3 ¶ For the lips of a strange woman drop as an honeycomb, and her mouth is smoother than oil:

4 But her end is bitter as wormwood, sharp as a twoedged sword.

5 Her feet go down to death; her steps take hold on hell.

6 Lest thou shouldest ponder the path of life, her ways are moveable, that thou canst not know them.

7 Hear me now therefore, O ye children, and depart not from the words of my mouth.

8 Remove thy way far from her, and come not nigh the door of her house:

9 Lest thou give thine honour unto others, and thy years unto the cruel:

10 Lest strangers be filled with thy wealth; and thy labours be in the house of a stranger;

11 And thou mourn at the last, when thy flesh and thy body are consumed,

12 And say, How have I hated instruction, and my heart despised reproof;

13 And have not obeyed the voice of my teachers, nor inclined mine ear to them that instructed me!

14 I was almost in all evil in the midst of the congregation and assembly.

15 ¶ Drink waters out of thine own cistern, and running waters out of thine own well.

16 Let thy fountains be dispersed abroad, and rivers of waters in the streets.

17 Let them be only thine own, and not strangers' with thee.

18 Let thy fountain be blessed: and rejoice with the wife of thy youth.

19 Let her be as the loving hind and pleasant roe; let her breasts satisfy thee at all times; and be thou ravished always with her love.

20 And why wilt thou, my son, be ravished with a strange woman, and embrace the bosom of a stranger?

21 For the ways of man are before the eyes of the LORD, and he pondereth all his goings.

22 ¶ His own iniquities shall take the wicked himself, and he shall be holden with the cords of his sins.

23 He shall die without instruction; and in the greatness of his folly he shall go astray.

6 MY son, if thou be surety for thy friend, if thou hast stricken thy hand with a stranger,

2 Thou art snared with the words of thy

mouth, thou art taken with the words of thy mouth.

3 Do this now, my son, and deliver thyself, when thou art come into the hand of thy friend; go, humble thyself, and make sure thy friend.

4 Give not sleep to thine eyes, nor slumber to thine eyelids.

5 Deliver thyself as a roe from the hand *of the hunter*, and as a bird from the hand of the fowler.

6 ¶ Go to the ant, thou sluggard; consider her ways, and be wise:

7 Which having no guide, overseer, or ruler,

8 Provideth her meat in the summer, *and* gathereth her food in the harvest.

9 How long wilt thou sleep, O sluggard? when wilt thou arise out of thy sleep?

10 *Yet* a little sleep, a little slumber, a little folding of the hands to sleep:

11 So shall thy poverty come as one that travelleth, and thy want as an armed man.

12 ¶ A naughty person, a wicked man, walketh with a froward mouth.

13 He winketh with his eyes, he speaketh with his feet, he teacheth with his fingers;

14 Frowardness *is* in his heart, he deviseth mischief continually; he soweth discord.

15 Therefore shall his calamity come suddenly; suddenly shall he be broken without remedy.

16 ¶ These six *things* doth the LORD hate: yea, seven *are* an abomination unto him:

17 A proud look, a lying tongue, and hands that shed innocent blood,

18 An heart that deviseth wicked imaginations, feet that be swift in running to mischief,

19 A false witness *that* speaketh lies, and he that soweth discord among brethren.

20 ¶ My son, keep thy father's commandment, and forsake not the law of thy mother:

21 Bind them continually upon thine heart, *and* tie them about thy neck.

22 When thou goest, it shall lead thee; when thou sleepest, it shall keep thee; and *when* thou awakest, it shall talk with thee.

23 For the commandment *is* a lamp; and the law *is* light; and reproofs of instruction *are* the way of life:

24 To keep thee from the evil woman, from the flattery of the tongue of a strange woman.

25 Lust not after her beauty in thine heart; neither let her take thee with her eyelids.

26 For by means of a whorish woman *a man is brought* to a piece of bread: and the adulteress will hunt for the precious life.

27 Can a man take fire in his bosom, and his clothes not be burned?

28 Can one go upon hot coals, and his feet not be burned?

29 So he that goeth in to his neighbour's wife; whosoever toucheth her shall not be innocent.

30 *Men* do not despise a thief, if he steal to satisfy his soul when he is hungry;

31 But *if* he be found, he shall restore sevenfold; he shall give all the substance of his house.

32 *But* whoso committeth adultery with a woman lacketh understanding: he *that* doeth it destroyeth his own soul.

33 A wound and dishonour shall he get; and his reproach shall not be wiped away.

34 For jealousy *is* the rage of a man: therefore he will not spare in the day of vengeance.

35 He will not regard any ransom; neither will he rest content, though thou givest many gifts.

7 MY son, keep my words, and lay up my commandments with thee.

2 Keep my commandments, and live; and my law as the apple of thine eye.

3 Bind them upon thy fingers, write them upon the table of thine heart.

4 Say unto wisdom, Thou *art* my sister; and call understanding *thy* kinswoman:

5 That they may keep thee from the strange woman, from the stranger *which* flattereth with her words.

6 ¶ For at the window of my house I looked through my casement,

7 And beheld among the simple ones, I discerned among the youths, a young man void of understanding,

8 Passing through the street near her corner; and he went the way to her house,

9 In the twilight, in the evening, in the black and dark night:

10 And, behold, there met him a woman *with* the attire of an harlot, and subtil of heart.

11 (She *is* loud and stubborn; her feet abide not in her house:

12 Now *is she* without, now in the streets, and lieth in wait at every corner.)

13 So she caught him, and kissed him, *and* with an impudent face said unto him,

14 *I have* peace offerings with me; this day have I payed my vows.

15 Therefore came I forth to meet thee, diligently to seek thy face, and I have found thee.

16 I have decked my bed with coverings of tapestry, with carved *works*, with fine linen of E'gypt.

17 I have perfumed my bed with myrrh, aloes, and cinnamon.

18 Come, let us take our fill of love until the morning: let us solace ourselves with loves.

19 For the goodman *is* not at home, he is gone a long journey:

20 He hath taken a bag of money with him, *and* will come home at the day appointed.

21 With her much fair speech she caused him to yield, with the flattering of her lips she forced him.

22 He goeth after her straightway, as an ox goeth to the slaughter, or as a fool to the correction of the stocks;

23 Till a dart strike through his liver; as a bird hasteth to the snare, and knoweth not that it *is* for his life.

24 ¶ Hearken unto me now therefore, O ye children, and attend to the words of my mouth.

25 Let not thine heart decline to her ways, go not astray in her paths.

26 For she hath cast down many wounded: yea, many strong *men* have been slain by her.

27 Her house *is* the way to hell, going down to the chambers of death.

8 DOTH not wisdom cry? and understanding put forth her voice?

2 She standeth in the top of high places, by the way in the places of the paths.

3 She crieth at the gates, at the entry of the city, at the coming in at the doors.

4 Unto you, O men, I call; and my voice *is* to the sons of man.

5 O ye simple, understand wisdom: and, ye fools, be ye of an understanding heart.

6 Hear; for I will speak of excellent things; and the opening of my lips *shall be* right things.

7 For my mouth shall speak truth; and wickedness *is* an abomination to my lips.

8 All the words of my mouth *are* in right-

eousness; *there is* nothing froward or perverse in them.

9 They *are* all plain to him that understandeth, and right to them that find knowledge.

10 Receive my instruction, and not silver; and knowledge rather than choice gold.

11 For wisdom *is* better than rubies; and all the things that may be desired are not to be compared to it.

12 I wisdom dwell with prudence, and find out knowledge of witty inventions.

13 The fear of the LORD *is* to hate evil: pride, and arrogancy, and the evil way, and the froward mouth, do I hate.

14 Counsel *is* mine, and sound wisdom: I *am* understanding; I have strength.

15 By me kings reign, and princes decree justice.

16 By me princes rule, and nobles, *even* all the judges of the earth.

17 I love them that love me; and those that seek me early shall find me.

18 Riches and honour *are* with me; *yea,* durable riches and righteousness.

19 My fruit *is* better than gold, yea, than fine gold; and my revenue than choice silver.

20 I lead in the way of righteousness, in the midst of the paths of judgment:

21 That I may cause those that love me to inherit substance; and I will fill their treasures.

22 The LORD possessed me in the beginning of his way, before his works of old.

23 I was set up from everlasting, from the beginning, or ever the earth was.

24 When *there were* no depths, I was brought forth; when *there were* no fountains abounding with water.

25 Before the mountains were settled, before the hills was I brought forth:

26 While as yet he had not made the earth, nor the fields, nor the highest part of the dust of the world.

27 When he prepared the heavens, I *was* there: when he set a compass upon the face of the depth:

28 When he established the clouds above: when he strengthened the fountains of the deep:

29 When he gave to the sea his decree, that the waters should not pass his commandment: when he appointed the foundations of the earth:

30 Then I was by him, *as* one brought up *with him:* and I was daily *his* delight, rejoicing always before him;

31 Rejoicing in the habitable part of his earth; and my delights *were* with the sons of men.

32 Now therefore hearken unto me, O ye children: for blessed *are they that* keep my ways.

33 Hear instruction, and be wise, and refuse it not.

34 Blessed *is* the man that heareth me, watching daily at my gates, waiting at the posts of my doors.

35 For whoso findeth me findeth life, and shall obtain favour of the LORD.

36 But he that sinneth against me wrongeth his own soul: all they that hate me love death.

9 WISDOM hath builded her house, she hath hewn out her seven pillars:

2 She hath killed her beasts; she hath mingled her wine; she hath also furnished her table.

3 She hath sent forth her maidens: she crieth upon the highest places of the city,

4 Whoso *is* simple, let him turn in hither: as

for him that wanteth understanding, she saith to him,

5 Come, eat of my bread, and drink of the wine *which* I have mingled.

6 Forsake the foolish, and live; and go in the way of understanding.

7 He that reproveth a scorner getteth to himself shame: and he that rebuketh a wicked *man getteth* himself a blot.

8 Reprove not a scorner, lest he hate thee: rebuke a wise man, and he will love thee.

9 Give *instruction* to a wise *man,* and he will be yet wiser: teach a just *man,* and he will increase in learning.

10 The fear of the LORD *is* the beginning of wisdom: and the knowledge of the holy *is* understanding.

11 For by me thy days shall be multiplied, and the years of thy life shall be increased.

12 If thou be wise, thou shalt be wise for thyself: but *if* thou scornest, thou alone shalt bear *it.*

13 ¶ A foolish woman *is* clamorous: *she is* simple, and knoweth nothing.

14 For she sitteth at the door of her house, on a seat in the high places of the city,

15 To call passengers who go right on their ways:

16 Whoso *is* simple, let him turn in hither: and *as for* him that wanteth understanding, she saith to him,

17 Stolen waters are sweet, and bread *eaten* in secret is pleasant.

18 But he knoweth not that the dead *are* there; *and that* her guests *are* in the depths of hell.

10 THE proverbs of Sol′o-mon. A wise son maketh a glad father: but a foolish son *is* the heaviness of his mother.

2 Treasures of wickedness profit nothing: but righteousness delivereth from death.

3 The LORD will not suffer the soul of the righteous to famish: but he casteth away the substance of the wicked.

4 He becometh poor that dealeth *with* a slack hand: but the hand of the diligent maketh rich.

5 He that gathereth in summer *is* a wise son: *but* he that sleepeth in harvest *is* a son that causeth shame.

6 Blessings *are* upon the head of the just: but violence covereth the mouth of the wicked.

7 The memory of the just *is* blessed: but the name of the wicked shall rot.

8 The wise in heart will receive commandments: but a prating fool shall fall.

9 He that walketh uprightly walketh surely: but he that perverteth his ways shall be known.

10 He that winketh with the eye causeth sorrow: but a prating fool shall fall.

11 The mouth of a righteous *man* is a well of life: but violence covereth the mouth of the wicked.

12 Hatred stirreth up strifes: but love covereth all sins.

13 In the lips of him that hath understanding wisdom is found: but a rod *is* for the back of him that is void of understanding.

14 Wise *men* lay up knowledge: but the mouth of the foolish *is* near destruction.

15 The rich man's wealth *is* his strong city: the destruction of the poor *is* their poverty.

16 The labour of the righteous *tendeth* to life: the fruit of the wicked to sin.

17 He *is in* the way of life that keepeth instruction: but he that refuseth reproof erreth.

18 He that hideth hatred *with* lying lips, and he that uttereth a slander, *is* a fool.

19 In the multitude of words there wanteth not sin: but he that refraineth his lips *is* wise.

20 The tongue of the just *is as* choice silver: the heart of the wicked *is* little worth.

21 The lips of the righteous feed many: but fools die for want of wisdom.

22 The blessing of the LORD, it maketh rich, and he addeth no sorrow with it.

23 *It is* as sport to a fool to do mischief: but a man of understanding hath wisdom.

24 The fear of the wicked, it shall come upon him: but the desire of the righteous shall be granted.

25 As the whirlwind passeth, so *is* the wicked no *more:* but the righteous *is* an everlasting foundation.

26 As vinegar to the teeth, and as smoke to the eyes, so *is* the sluggard to them that send him.

27 The fear of the LORD prolongeth days: but the years of the wicked shall be shortened.

28 The hope of the righteous *shall be* gladness: but the expectation of the wicked shall perish.

29 The way of the LORD *is* strength to the upright: but destruction *shall be* to the workers of iniquity.

30 The righteous shall never be removed: but the wicked shall not inhabit the earth.

31 The mouth of the just bringeth forth wisdom: but the froward tongue shall be cut out.

32 The lips of the righteous know what is acceptable: but the mouth of the wicked *speaketh* frowardness.

11 A FALSE balance *is* abomination to the LORD: but a just weight *is* his delight.

2 *When* pride cometh, then cometh shame: but with the lowly *is* wisdom.

3 The integrity of the upright shall guide them: but the perverseness of transgressors shall destroy them.

4 Riches profit not in the day of wrath: but righteousness delivereth from death.

5 The righteousness of the perfect shall direct his way: but the wicked shall fall by his own wickedness.

6 The righteousness of the upright shall deliver them: but transgressors shall be taken in *their* own naughtiness.

7 When a wicked man dieth, *his* expectation shall perish: and the hope of unjust *men* perisheth.

8 The righteous is delivered out of trouble, and the wicked cometh in his stead.

9 An hypocrite with *his* mouth destroyeth his neighbour: but through knowledge shall the just be delivered.

10 When it goeth well with the righteous, the city rejoiceth: and when the wicked perish, *there is* shouting.

11 By the blessing of the upright the city is exalted: but it is overthrown by the mouth of the wicked.

12 He that is void of wisdom despiseth his neighbour: but a man of understanding holdeth his peace.

13 A talebearer revealeth secrets: but he that is of a faithful spirit concealeth the matter.

14 Where no counsel *is*, the people fall: but in the multitude of counsellors *there is* safety.

15 He that is surety for a stranger shall smart *for it:* and he that hateth suretiship is sure.

16 A gracious woman retaineth honour: and strong *men* retain riches.

17 The merciful man doeth good to his own soul: but *he that is* cruel troubleth his own flesh.

18 The wicked worketh a deceitful work: but to him that soweth righteousness *shall be* a sure reward.

19 As righteousness *tendeth* to life: so he that pursueth evil *pursueth it* to his own death.

20 They that are of a froward heart *are* abomination to the LORD: but *such as are* upright in *their* way *are* his delight.

21 *Though* hand *join* in hand, the wicked shall not be unpunished: but the seed of the righteous shall be delivered.

22 *As* a jewel of gold in a swine's snout, *so is* a fair woman which is without discretion.

23 The desire of the righteous *is* only good: *but* the expectation of the wicked *is* wrath.

24 There is that scattereth, and yet increaseth; and *there is* that withholdeth more than is meet, but *it tendeth* to poverty.

25 The liberal soul shall be made fat: and he that watereth shall be watered also himself.

26 He that withholdeth corn, the people shall curse him: but blessing *shall be* upon the head of him that selleth *it*.

27 He that diligently seeketh good procureth favour: but he that seeketh mischief, it shall come unto him.

28 He that trusteth in his riches shall fall: but the righteous shall flourish as a branch.

29 He that troubleth his own house shall inherit the wind: and the fool *shall be* servant to the wise of heart.

30 The fruit of the righteous *is* a tree of life; and he that winneth souls *is* wise.

31 Behold, the righteous shall be recompensed in the earth: much more the wicked and the sinner.

12 WHOSO loveth instruction loveth knowledge: but he that hateth reproof *is* brutish.

2 A good *man* obtaineth favour of the LORD: but a man of wicked devices will he condemn.

3 A man shall not be established by wickedness: but the root of the righteous shall not be moved.

4 A virtuous woman *is* a crown to her husband: but she that maketh ashamed *is* as rottenness in his bones.

5 The thoughts of the righteous *are* right: *but* the counsels of the wicked *are* deceit.

6 The words of the wicked *are* to lie in wait for blood: but the mouth of the upright shall deliver them.

7 The wicked are overthrown, and *are* not: but the house of the righteous shall stand.

8 A man shall be commended according to his wisdom: but he that is of a perverse heart shall be despised.

9 *He that is* despised, and hath a servant, *is* better than he that honoureth himself, and lacketh bread.

10 A righteous *man* regardeth the life of his beast: but the tender mercies of the wicked *are* cruel.

11 He that tilleth his land shall be satisfied with bread: but he that followeth vain *persons is* void of understanding.

12 The wicked desireth the net of evil *men:* but the root of the righteous yieldeth *fruit.*

13 The wicked is snared by the transgression of *his* lips: but the just shall come out of trouble.

14 A man shall be satisfied with good by the fruit of *his* mouth: and the recompence of a man's hands shall be rendered unto him.

15 The way of a fool *is* right in his own eyes: but he that hearkeneth unto counsel *is* wise.

16 A fool's wrath is presently known: but a prudent *man* covereth shame.

17 *He that* speaketh truth sheweth forth righteousness: but a false witness deceit.

18 There is that speaketh like the piercings of a sword: but the tongue of the wise *is* health.

19 The lip of truth shall be established for ever: but a lying tongue *is* but for a moment.

20 Deceit *is* in the heart of them that imagine evil: but to the counsellors of peace *is* joy.

21 There shall no evil happen to the just: but the wicked shall be filled with mischief.

22 Lying lips *are* abomination to the LORD: but they that deal truly *are* his delight.

23 A prudent man concealeth knowledge: but the heart of fools proclaimeth foolishness.

24 The hand of the diligent shall bear rule: but the slothful shall be under tribute.

25 Heaviness in the heart of man maketh it stoop: but a good word maketh it glad.

26 The righteous *is* more excellent than his neighbour: but the way of the wicked seduceth them.

27 The slothful *man* roasteth not that which he took in hunting: but the substance of a diligent man *is* precious.

28 In the way of righteousness *is* life; and *in* the pathway *thereof there is* no death.

13 A WISE son *heareth* his father's instruction: but a scorner heareth not rebuke.

2 A man shall eat good by the fruit of *his* mouth: but the soul of the transgressors *shall eat* violence.

3 He that keepeth his mouth keepeth his life: *but* he that openeth wide his lips shall have destruction.

4 The soul of the sluggard desireth, and *hath* nothing: but the soul of the diligent shall be made fat.

5 A righteous *man* hateth lying: but a wicked *man* is loathsome, and cometh to shame.

6 Righteousness keepeth *him that is* upright in the way: but wickedness overthroweth the sinner.

7 There is that maketh himself rich, yet *hath* nothing: *there is* that maketh himself poor, yet *hath* great riches.

8 The ransom of a man's life *are* his riches: but the poor heareth not rebuke.

9 The light of the righteous rejoiceth: but the lamp of the wicked shall be put out.

10 Only by pride cometh contention: but with the well advised *is* wisdom.

11 Wealth *gotten* by vanity shall be diminished: but he that gathereth by labour shall increase.

12 Hope deferred maketh the heart sick: but *when* the desire cometh, *it is* a tree of life.

13 Whoso despiseth the word shall be destroyed: but he that feareth the commandment shall be rewarded.

14 The law of the wise *is* a fountain of life, to depart from the snares of death.

15 Good understanding giveth favour: but the way of transgressors *is* hard.

16 Every prudent *man* dealeth with knowledge: but a fool layeth open *his* folly.

17 A wicked messenger falleth into mischief: but a faithful ambassador *is* health.

18 Poverty and shame *shall be to* him that refuseth instruction: but he that regardeth reproof shall be honoured.

19 The desire accomplished is sweet to the soul: but *it is* abomination to fools to depart from evil.

20 He that walketh with wise *men* shall be wise: but a companion of fools shall be destroyed.

21 Evil pursueth sinners: but to the righteous good shall be repayed.

22 A good *man* leaveth an inheritance to his children's children: and the wealth of the sinner *is* laid up for the just.

23 Much food *is in* the tillage of the poor: but there is *that is* destroyed for want of judgment.

24 He that spareth his rod hateth his son: but he that loveth him chasteneth him betimes.

25 The righteous eateth to the satisfying of his soul: but the belly of the wicked shall want.

14 EVERY wise woman buildeth her house: but the foolish plucketh it down with her hands.

2 He that walketh in his uprightness feareth the LORD: but *he that is* perverse in his ways despiseth him.

3 In the mouth of the foolish *is* a rod of pride: but the lips of the wise shall preserve them.

4 Where no oxen *are*, the crib *is* clean: but much increase *is* by the strength of the ox.

5 A faithful witness will not lie: but a false witness will utter lies.

6 A scorner seeketh wisdom, and *findeth it* not: but knowledge *is* easy unto him that understandeth.

7 Go from the presence of a foolish man, when thou perceivest not *in him* the lips of knowledge.

8 The wisdom of the prudent is to understand his way: but the folly of fools *is* deceit.

9 Fools make a mock at sin: but among the righteous *there is* favour.

10 The heart knoweth his own bitterness; and a stranger doth not intermeddle with his joy.

11 The house of the wicked shall be overthrown: but the tabernacle of the upright shall flourish.

12 There is a way which seemeth right unto a man, but the end thereof *are* the ways of death.

13 Even in laughter the heart is sorrowful; and the end of that mirth *is* heaviness.

14 The backslider in heart shall be filled with his own ways: and a good man *shall be satisfied* from himself.

15 The simple believeth every word: but the prudent *man* looketh well to his going.

16 A wise *man* feareth, and departeth from evil: but the fool rageth, and is confident.

17 *He that is* soon angry dealeth foolishly: and a man of wicked devices is hated.

18 The simple inherit folly: but the prudent are crowned with knowledge.

19 The evil bow before the good; and the wicked at the gates of the righteous.

20 The poor is hated even of his own neighbour: but the rich *hath* many friends.

21 He that despiseth his neighbour sinneth: but he that hath mercy on the poor, happy *is* he.

22 Do they not err that devise evil? but mercy and truth *shall be* to them that devise good.

23 In all labour there is profit: but the talk of the lips *tendeth* only to penury.

24 The crown of the wise *is* their riches: *but* the foolishness of fools *is* folly.

25 A true witness delivereth souls: but a deceitful *witness* speaketh lies.

26 In the fear of the LORD *is* strong confidence: and his children shall have a place of refuge.

27 The fear of the LORD is a fountain of life, to depart from the snares of death.

28 In the multitude of people is the king's honour: but in the want of people is the destruction of the prince.

29 He that is slow to wrath is of great understanding: but he that is hasty of spirit exalteth folly.

30 A sound heart is the life of the flesh: but envy the rottenness of the bones.

31 He that oppresseth the poor reproacheth his Maker: but he that honoureth him hath mercy on the poor.

32 The wicked is driven away in his wickedness: but the righteous hath hope in his death.

33 Wisdom resteth in the heart of him that hath understanding: but that which is in the midst of fools is made known.

34 Righteousness exalteth a nation: but sin is a reproach to any people.

35 The king's favour is toward a wise servant: but his wrath is against him that causeth shame.

15 A SOFT answer turneth away wrath: but grievous words stir up anger.

2 The tongue of the wise useth knowledge aright: but the mouth of fools poureth out foolishness.

3 The eyes of the LORD are in every place, beholding the evil and the good.

4 A wholesome tongue is a tree of life: but perverseness therein is a breach in the spirit.

5 A fool despiseth his father's instruction: but he that regardeth reproof is prudent.

6 In the house of the righteous is much treasure: but in the revenues of the wicked is trouble.

7 The lips of the wise disperse knowledge: but the heart of the foolish doeth not so.

8 The sacrifice of the wicked is an abomination to the LORD: but the prayer of the upright is his delight.

9 The way of the wicked is an abomination unto the LORD: but he loveth him that followeth after righteousness.

10 Correction is grievous unto him that forsaketh the way: and he that hateth reproof shall die.

11 Hell and destruction are before the LORD: how much more then the hearts of the children of men?

12 A scorner loveth not one that reproveth him: neither will he go unto the wise.

13 A merry heart maketh a cheerful countenance: but by sorrow of the heart the spirit is broken.

14 The heart of him that hath understanding seeketh knowledge: but the mouth of fools feedeth on foolishness.

15 All the days of the afflicted are evil: but he that is of a merry heart hath a continual feast.

16 Better is little with the fear of the LORD than great treasure and trouble therewith.

17 Better is a dinner of herbs where love is, than a stalled ox and hatred therewith.

18 A wrathful man stirreth up strife: but he that is slow to anger appeaseth strife.

19 The way of the slothful man is as an hedge of thorns: but the way of the righteous is made plain.

20 A wise son maketh a glad father: but a foolish man despiseth his mother.

21 Folly is joy to him that is destitute of wisdom: but a man of understanding walketh uprightly.

22 Without counsel purposes are disappointed: but in the multitude of counsellors they are established.

23 A man hath joy by the answer of his mouth: and a word spoken in due season, how good is it!

24 The way of life is above to the wise, that he may depart from hell beneath.

25 The LORD will destroy the house of the proud: but he will establish the border of the widow.

26 The thoughts of the wicked are an abomination to the LORD: but the words of the pure are pleasant words.

27 He that is greedy of gain troubleth his own house; but he that hateth gifts shall live.

28 The heart of the righteous studieth to answer: but the mouth of the wicked poureth out evil things.

29 The LORD is far from the wicked: but he heareth the prayer of the righteous.

30 The light of the eyes rejoiceth the heart: and a good report maketh the bones fat.

31 The ear that heareth the reproof of life abideth among the wise.

32 He that refuseth instruction despiseth his own soul: but he that heareth reproof getteth understanding.

33 The fear of the LORD is the instruction of wisdom; and before honour is humility.

16 THE preparations of the heart in man, and the answer of the tongue, is from the LORD.

2 All the ways of a man are clean in his own eyes; but the LORD weigheth the spirits.

3 Commit thy works unto the LORD, and thy thoughts shall be established.

4 The LORD hath made all things for himself: yea, even the wicked for the day of evil.

5 Every one that is proud in heart is an abomination to the LORD: though hand join in hand, he shall not be unpunished.

6 By mercy and truth iniquity is purged: and by the fear of the LORD men depart from evil.

7 When a man's ways please the LORD, he maketh even his enemies to be at peace with him.

8 Better is a little with righteousness than great revenues without right.

9 A man's heart deviseth his way: but the LORD directeth his steps.

10 A divine sentence is in the lips of the king: his mouth transgresseth not in judgment.

11 A just weight and balance are the LORD'S: all the weights of the bag are his work.

12 It is an abomination to kings to commit wickedness: for the throne is established by righteousness.

13 Righteous lips are the delight of kings; and they love him that speaketh right.

14 The wrath of a king is as messengers of death: but a wise man will pacify it.

15 In the light of the king's countenance is life; and his favour is as a cloud of the latter rain.

16 How much better is it to get wisdom than gold! and to get understanding rather to be chosen than silver!

17 The highway of the upright is to depart from evil: he that keepeth his way preserveth his soul.

18 Pride goeth before destruction, and an haughty spirit before a fall.

19 Better it is to be of an humble spirit with the lowly, than to divide the spoil with the proud.

20 He that handleth a matter wisely shall

find good: and whoso trusteth in the LORD, happy *is* he.

21 The wise in heart shall be called prudent: and the sweetness of the lips increaseth learning.

22 Understanding *is* a wellspring of life unto him that hath it: but the instruction of fools *is* folly.

23 The heart of the wise teacheth his mouth, and addeth learning to his lips.

24 Pleasant words *are as* an honeycomb, sweet to the soul, and health to the bones.

25 There is a way that seemeth right unto a man, but the end thereof *are* the ways of death.

26 He that laboureth laboureth for himself; for his mouth craveth it of him.

27 An ungodly man diggeth up evil: and in his lips *there is* as a burning fire.

28 A froward man soweth strife: and a whisperer separateth chief friends.

29 A violent man enticeth his neighbour, and leadeth him into the way *that is* not good.

30 He shutteth his eyes to devise froward things: moving his lips he bringeth evil to pass.

31 The hoary head *is* a crown of glory, *if* it be found in the way of righteousness.

32 *He that is* slow to anger *is* better than the mighty; and he that ruleth his spirit than he that taketh a city.

33 The lot is cast into the lap; but the whole disposing thereof *is* of the LORD.

17 BETTER *is* a dry morsel, and quietness therewith, than an house full of sacrifices *with* strife.

2 A wise servant shall have rule over a son that causeth shame, and shall have part of the inheritance among the brethren.

3 The fining pot *is* for silver, and the furnace for gold: but the LORD trieth the hearts.

4 A wicked doer giveth heed to false lips; *and* a liar giveth ear to a naughty tongue.

5 Whoso mocketh the poor reproacheth his Maker: *and* he that is glad at calamities shall not be unpunished.

6 Children's children *are* the crown of old men; and the glory of children *are* their fathers.

7 Excellent speech becometh not a fool: much less do lying lips a prince.

8 A gift *is as* a precious stone in the eyes of him that hath it: whithersoever it turneth, it prospereth.

9 He that covereth a transgression seeketh love; but he that repeateth a matter separateth *very* friends.

10 A reproof entereth more into a wise man than an hundred stripes into a fool.

11 An evil *man* seeketh only rebellion: therefore a cruel messenger shall be sent against him.

12 Let a bear robbed of her whelps meet a man, rather than a fool in his folly.

13 Whoso rewardeth evil for good, evil shall not depart from his house.

14 The beginning of strife *is as* when one letteth out water: therefore leave off contention, before it be meddled with.

15 He that justifieth the wicked, and he that condemneth the just, even they both *are* abomination to the LORD.

16 Wherefore *is there* a price in the hand of a fool to get wisdom, seeing *he hath* no heart to it?

17 A friend loveth at all times, and a brother is born for adversity.

18 A man void of understanding striketh hands, *and* becometh surety in the presence of his friend.

19 He loveth transgression that loveth strife: *and* he that exalteth his gate seeketh destruction.

20 He that hath a froward heart findeth no good: and he that hath a perverse tongue falleth into mischief.

21 He that begetteth a fool *doeth it* to his sorrow: and the father of a fool hath no joy.

22 A merry heart doeth good *like* a medicine: but a broken spirit drieth the bones.

23 A wicked *man* taketh a gift out of the bosom to pervert the ways of judgment.

24 Wisdom *is* before him that hath understanding; but the eyes of a fool *are* in the ends of the earth.

25 A foolish son *is* a grief to his father, and bitterness to her that bare him.

26 Also to punish the just *is* not good, *nor* to strike princes for equity.

27 He that hath knowledge spareth his words: *and* a man of understanding is of an excellent spirit.

28 Even a fool, when he holdeth his peace, is counted wise: *and* he that shutteth his lips *is esteemed* a man of understanding.

18 THROUGH desire a man, having separated himself, seeketh *and* intermeddleth with all wisdom.

2 A fool hath no delight in understanding, but that his heart may discover itself.

3 When the wicked cometh, *then* cometh also contempt, and with ignominy reproach.

4 The words of a man's mouth *are as* deep waters, *and* the wellspring of wisdom *as* a flowing brook.

5 *It is* not good to accept the person of the wicked, to overthrow the righteous in judgment.

6 A fool's lips enter into contention, and his mouth calleth for strokes.

7 A fool's mouth *is* his destruction, and his lips *are* the snare of his soul.

8 The words of a talebearer *are* as wounds, and they go down into the innermost parts of the belly.

9 He also that is slothful in his work is brother to him that is a great waster.

10 The name of the LORD *is* a strong tower: the righteous runneth into it, and is safe.

11 The rich man's wealth *is* his strong city, and as an high wall in his own conceit.

12 Before destruction the heart of man is haughty, and before honour *is* humility.

13 He that answereth a matter before he heareth *it*, it *is* folly and shame unto him.

14 The spirit of a man will sustain his infirmity; but a wounded spirit who can bear?

15 The heart of the prudent getteth knowledge; and the ear of the wise seeketh knowledge.

16 A man's gift maketh room for him, and bringeth him before great men.

17 *He that is* first in his own cause *seemeth* just; but his neighbour cometh and searcheth him.

18 The lot causeth contentions to cease, and parteth between the mighty.

19 A brother offended *is harder to be* won than a strong city: and *their* contentions *are* like the bars of a castle.

20 A man's belly shall be satisfied with the fruit of his mouth; *and* with the increase of his lips shall he be filled.

21 Death and life *are* in the power of the

tongue: and they that love it shall eat the fruit thereof.

22 *Whoso* findeth a wife findeth a good *thing*, and obtaineth favour of the LORD.

23 The poor useth intreaties; but the rich answereth roughly.

24 A man *that hath* friends must shew himself friendly: and there is a friend *that* sticketh closer than a brother.

19 BETTER *is* the poor that walketh in his integrity, than *he that is* perverse in his lips, and is a fool.

2 Also, *that* the soul *be* without knowledge, *it is* not good; and he that hasteth with *his* feet sinneth.

3 The foolishness of man perverteth his way: and his heart fretteth against the LORD.

4 Wealth maketh many friends; but the poor is separated from his neighbour.

5 A false witness shall not be unpunished, and he *that* speaketh lies shall not escape.

6 Many will intreat the favour of the prince: and every man *is* a friend to him that giveth gifts.

7 All the brethren of the poor do hate him: how much more do his friends go far from him? he pursueth *them with* words, *yet* they *are* wanting *to him*.

8 He that getteth wisdom loveth his own soul: he that keepeth understanding shall find good.

9 A false witness shall not be unpunished, and *he that* speaketh lies shall perish.

10 Delight is not seemly for a fool; much less for a servant to have rule over princes.

11 The discretion of a man deferreth his anger; and *it is* his glory to pass over a transgression.

12 The king's wrath *is* as the roaring of a lion; but his favour *is* as dew upon the grass.

13 A foolish son *is* the calamity of his father: and the contentions of a wife *are* a continual dropping.

14 House and riches *are* the inheritance of fathers: and a prudent wife *is* from the LORD.

15 Slothfulness casteth into a deep sleep; and an idle soul shall suffer hunger.

16 He that keepeth the commandment keepeth his own soul; *but* he that despiseth his ways shall die.

17 He that hath pity upon the poor lendeth unto the LORD; and that which he hath given will he pay him again.

18 Chasten thy son while there is hope, and let not thy soul spare for his crying.

19 A man of great wrath shall suffer punishment: for if thou deliver *him*, yet thou must do it again.

20 Hear counsel, and receive instruction, that thou mayest be wise in thy latter end.

21 *There are* many devices in a man's heart; nevertheless the counsel of the LORD, that shall stand.

22 The desire of a man *is* his kindness: and a poor man *is* better than a liar.

23 The fear of the LORD *tendeth* to life: and *he that hath it* shall abide satisfied; he shall not be visited with evil.

24 A slothful *man* hideth his hand in *his* bosom, and will not so much as bring it to his mouth again.

25 Smite a scorner, and the simple will beware: and reprove one that hath understanding, *and* he will understand knowledge.

26 He that wasteth *his* father, *and* chaseth away *his* mother, *is* a son that causeth shame, and bringeth reproach.

27 Cease, my son, to hear the instruction *that causeth* to err from the words of knowledge.

28 An ungodly witness scorneth judgment: and the mouth of the wicked devoureth iniquity.

29 Judgments are prepared for scorners, and stripes for the back of fools.

20 WINE *is* a mocker, strong drink *is* raging: and whosoever is deceived thereby is not wise.

2 The fear of a king *is* as the roaring of a lion: *whoso* provoketh him to anger sinneth *against* his own soul.

3 *It is* an honour for a man to cease from strife: but every fool will be meddling.

4 The sluggard will not plow by reason of the cold; *therefore* shall he beg in harvest, and *have* nothing.

5 Counsel in the heart of man *is like* deep water; but a man of understanding will draw it out.

6 Most men will proclaim every one his own goodness: but a faithful man who can find?

7 The just *man* walketh in his integrity: his children *are* blessed after him.

8 A king that sitteth in the throne of judgment scattereth away all evil with his eyes.

9 Who can say, I have made my heart clean, I am pure from my sin?

10 Divers weights, *and* divers measures, both of them *are* alike abomination to the LORD.

11 Even a child is known by his doings, whether his work *be* pure, and whether *it be* right.

12 The hearing ear, and the seeing eye, the LORD hath made even both of them.

13 Love not sleep, lest thou come to poverty; open thine eyes, *and* thou shalt be satisfied with bread.

14 *It is* naught, *it is* naught, saith the buyer: but when he is gone his way, then he boasteth.

15 There is gold, and a multitude of rubies: but the lips of knowledge *are* a precious jewel.

16 Take his garment that is surety for a stranger: and take a pledge of him for a strange woman.

17 Bread of deceit *is* sweet to a man; but afterwards his mouth shall be filled with gravel.

18 *Every* purpose is established by counsel: and with good advice make war.

19 He that goeth about *as* a talebearer revealeth secrets: therefore meddle not with him that flattereth with his lips.

20 Whoso curseth his father or his mother, his lamp shall be put out in obscure darkness.

21 An inheritance *may be* gotten hastily at the beginning; but the end thereof shall not be blessed.

22 Say not thou, I will recompense evil; *but* wait on the LORD, and he shall save thee.

23 Divers weights *are* an abomination unto the LORD; and a false balance *is* not good.

24 Man's goings *are* of the LORD; how can a man then understand his own way?

25 *It is* a snare to the man *who* devoureth *that* which is holy, and after vows to make enquiry.

26 A wise king scattereth the wicked, and bringeth the wheel over them.

27 The spirit of man *is* the candle of the LORD, searching all the inward parts of the belly.

28 Mercy and truth preserve the king: and his throne is upholden by mercy.

29 The glory of young men is their strength: and the beauty of old men is the gray head.

30 The blueness of a wound cleanseth away evil: so do stripes the inward parts of the belly.

21 THE king's heart is in the hand of the LORD, as the rivers of water: he turneth it whithersoever he will.

2 Every way of a man is right in his own eyes: but the LORD pondereth the hearts.

3 To do justice and judgment is more acceptable to the LORD than sacrifice.

4 An high look, and a proud heart, and the plowing of the wicked, is sin.

5 The thoughts of the diligent tend only to plenteousness; but of every one that is hasty only to want.

6 The getting of treasures by a lying tongue is a vanity tossed to and fro of them that seek death.

7 The robbery of the wicked shall destroy them; because they refuse to do judgment.

8 The way of man is froward and strange: but as for the pure, his work is right.

9 It is better to dwell in a corner of the house top, than with a brawling woman in a wide house.

10 The soul of the wicked desireth evil: his neighbour findeth no favour in his eyes.

11 When the scorner is punished, the simple is made wise: and when the wise is instructed, he receiveth knowledge.

12 The righteous man wisely considereth the house of the wicked: but God overthroweth the wicked for their wickedness.

13 Whoso stoppeth his ears at the cry of the poor, he also shall cry himself, but shall not be heard.

14 A gift in secret pacifieth anger: and a reward in the bosom strong wrath.

15 It is joy to the just to do judgment: but destruction shall be to the workers of iniquity.

16 The man that wandereth out of the way of understanding shall remain in the congregation of the dead.

17 He that loveth pleasure shall be a poor man: he that loveth wine and oil shall not be rich.

18 The wicked shall be a ransom for the righteous, and the transgressor for the upright.

19 It is better to dwell in the wilderness, than with a contentious and an angry woman.

20 There is treasure to be desired and oil in the dwelling of the wise; but a foolish man spendeth it up.

21 He that followeth after righteousness and mercy findeth life, righteousness, and honour.

22 A wise man scaleth the city of the mighty, and casteth down the strength of the confidence thereof.

23 Whoso keepeth his mouth and his tongue keepeth his soul from troubles.

24 Proud and haughty scorner is his name, who dealeth in proud wrath.

25 The desire of the slothful killeth him; for his hands refuse to labour.

26 He coveteth greedily all the day long: but the righteous giveth and spareth not.

27 The sacrifice of the wicked is abomination: how much more, when he bringeth it with a wicked mind?

28 A false witness shall perish: but the man that heareth speaketh constantly.

29 A wicked man hardeneth his face: but as for the upright, he directeth his way.

30 There is no wisdom nor understanding nor counsel against the LORD.

31 The horse is prepared against the day of battle: but safety is of the LORD.

22 A GOOD name is rather to be chosen than great riches, and loving favour rather than silver and gold.

2 The rich and poor meet together: the LORD is the maker of them all.

3 A prudent man forseeth the evil, and hideth himself: but the simple pass on, and are punished.

4 By humility and the fear of the LORD are riches, and honour, and life.

5 Thorns and snares are in the way of the froward: he that doth keep his soul shall be far from them.

6 Train up a child in the way he should go: and when he is old, he will not depart from it.

7 The rich ruleth over the poor, and the borrower is servant to the lender.

8 He that soweth iniquity shall reap vanity: and the rod of his anger shall fail.

9 He that hath a bountiful eye shall be blessed; for he giveth of his bread to the poor.

10 Cast out the scorner, and contention shall go out; yea, strife and reproach shall cease.

11 He that loveth pureness of heart, for the grace of his lips the king shall be his friend.

12 The eyes of the LORD preserve knowledge, and he overthroweth the words of the transgressor.

13 The slothful man saith, There is a lion without, I shall be slain in the streets.

14 The mouth of strange women is a deep pit: he that is abhorred of the LORD shall fall therein.

15 Foolishness is bound in the heart of a child; but the rod of correction shall drive it far from him.

16 He that oppresseth the poor to increase his riches, and he that giveth to the rich, shall surely come to want.

17 Bow down thine ear, and hear the words of the wise, and apply thine heart unto my knowledge.

18 For it is a pleasant thing if thou keep them within thee; they shall withal be fitted in thy lips.

19 That thy trust may be in the LORD, I have made known to thee this day, even to thee.

20 Have not I written to thee excellent things in counsels and knowledge,

21 That I might make thee know the certainty of the words of truth; that thou mightest answer the words of truth to them that send unto thee?

22 Rob not the poor, because he is poor: neither oppress the afflicted in the gate:

23 For the LORD will plead their cause, and spoil the soul of those that spoiled them.

24 Make no friendship with an angry man; and with a furious man thou shalt not go:

25 Lest thou learn his ways, and get a snare to thy soul.

26 Be not thou one of them that strike hands, or of them that are sureties for debts.

27 If thou hast nothing to pay, why should he take away thy bed from under thee?

28 Remove not the ancient landmark, which thy fathers have set.

29 Seest thou a man diligent in his business? he shall stand before kings; he shall not stand before mean men.

23 WHEN thou sittest to eat with a ruler, consider diligently what is before thee:

2 And put a knife to thy throat, if thou be a man given to appetite.

3 Be not desirous of his dainties: for they are deceitful meat.

4 Labour not to be rich: cease from thine own wisdom.

5 Wilt thou set thine eyes upon that which is not? for riches certainly make themselves wings; they fly away as an eagle toward heaven.

6 Eat thou not the bread of him that hath an evil eye, neither desire thou his dainty meats:

7 For as he thinketh in his heart, so is he: Eat and drink, saith he to thee; but his heart is not with thee.

8 The morsel which thou hast eaten shalt thou vomit up, and lose thy sweet words.

9 Speak not in the ears of a fool: for he will despise the wisdom of thy words.

10 Remove not the old landmark; and enter not into the fields of the fatherless:

11 For their redeemer is mighty; he shall plead their cause with thee.

12 Apply thine heart unto instruction, and thine ears to the words of knowledge.

13 Withhold not correction from the child: for if thou beatest him with the rod, he shall not die.

14 Thou shalt beat him with the rod, and shalt deliver his soul from hell.

15 My son, if thine heart be wise, my heart shall rejoice, even mine.

16 Yea, my reins shall rejoice, when thy lips speak right things.

17 Let not thine heart envy sinners: but be thou in the fear of the LORD all the day long.

18 For surely there is an end; and thine expectation shall not be cut off.

19 Hear thou, my son, and be wise, and guide thine heart in the way.

20 Be not among winebibbers; among riotous eaters of flesh:

21 For the drunkard and the glutton shall come to poverty: and drowsiness shall clothe a man with rags.

22 Hearken unto thy father that begat thee, and despise not thy mother when she is old.

23 Buy the truth, and sell it not; also wisdom, and instruction, and understanding.

24 The father of the righteous shall greatly rejoice: and he that begetteth a wise child shall have joy of him.

25 Thy father and thy mother shall be glad, and she that bare thee shall rejoice.

26 My son, give me thine heart, and let thine eyes observe my ways.

27 For a whore is a deep ditch; and a strange woman is a narrow pit.

28 She also lieth in wait as for a prey, and increaseth the transgressors among men.

29 Who hath woe? who hath sorrow? who hath contentions? who hath babbling? who hath wounds without cause? who hath redness of eyes?

30 They that tarry long at the wine; they that go to seek mixed wine.

31 Look not thou upon the wine when it is red, when it giveth his colour in the cup, when it moveth itself aright.

32 At the last it biteth like a serpent, and stingeth like an adder.

33 Thine eyes shall behold strange women, and thine heart shall utter perverse things.

34 Yea, thou shalt be as he that lieth down in the midst of the sea, or as he that lieth upon the top of a mast.

35 They have stricken me, shalt thou say, and I was not sick; they have beaten me, and I felt it not: when shall I awake? I will seek it yet again.

24 BE not thou envious against evil men, neither desire to be with them.

2 For their heart studieth destruction, and their lips talk of mischief.

3 Through wisdom is an house builded; and by understanding it is established:

4 And by knowledge shall the chambers be filled with all precious and pleasant riches.

5 A wise man is strong; yea, a man of knowledge increaseth strength.

6 For by wise counsel thou shalt make thy war: and in multitude of counsellors there is safety.

7 Wisdom is too high for a fool: he openeth not his mouth in the gate.

8 He that deviseth to do evil shall be called a mischievous person.

9 The thought of foolishness is sin: and the scorner is an abomination to men.

10 If thou faint in the day of adversity, thy strength is small.

11 If thou forbear to deliver them that are drawn unto death, and those that are ready to be slain;

12 If thou sayest, Behold, we knew it not; doth not he that pondereth the heart consider it? and he that keepeth thy soul, doth not he know it? and shall not he render to every man according to his works?

13 My son, eat thou honey, because it is good; and the honeycomb, which is sweet to thy taste:

14 So shall the knowledge of wisdom be unto thy soul: when thou hast found it, then there shall be a reward, and thy expectation shall not be cut off.

15 Lay not wait, O wicked man, against the dwelling of the righteous; spoil not his resting place:

16 For a just man falleth seven times, and riseth up again: but the wicked shall fall into mischief.

17 Rejoice not when thine enemy falleth, and let not thine heart be glad when he stumbleth:

18 Lest the LORD see it, and it displease him, and he turn away his wrath from him.

19 Fret not thyself because of evil men, neither be thou envious at the wicked;

20 For there shall be no reward to the evil man; the candle of the wicked shall be put out.

21 My son, fear thou the LORD and the king: and meddle not with them that are given to change:

22 For their calamity shall rise suddenly; and who knoweth the ruin of them both?

23 These things also belong to the wise. It is not good to have respect of persons in judgment.

24 He that saith unto the wicked, Thou art righteous; him shall the people curse, nations shall abhor him:

25 But to them that rebuke him shall be delight, and a good blessing shall come upon them.

26 Every man shall kiss his lips that giveth a right answer.

27 Prepare thy work without, and make it fit for thyself in the field; and afterwards build thine house.

28 Be not a witness against thy neighbour without cause; and deceive not with thy lips.

29 Say not, I will do so to him as he hath

done to me: I will render to the man according to his work.

30 I went by the field of the slothful, and by the vineyard of the man void of understanding;

31 And, lo, it was all grown over with thorns, *and* nettles had covered the face thereof, and the stone wall thereof was broken down.

32 Then I saw, *and* considered *it* well: I looked upon *it, and* received instruction.

33 *Yet* a little sleep, a little slumber, a little folding of the hands to sleep:

34 So shall thy poverty come *as* one that travelleth; and thy want as an armed man.

25

THESE *are* also proverbs of Sol'o-mon, which the men of Hez-e-ki'ah king of Ju'dah copied out.

2 *It is* the glory of God to conceal a thing: but the honour of kings *is* to search out a matter.

3 The heaven for height, and the earth for depth, and the heart of kings is unsearchable.

4 Take away the dross from the silver, and there shall come forth a vessel for the finer.

5 Take away the wicked *from* before the king, and his throne shall be established in righteousness.

6 Put not forth thyself in the presence of the king, and stand not in the place of great *men*:

7 For better *it is* that it be said unto thee, Come up hither; than that thou shouldest be put lower in the presence of the prince whom thine eyes have seen.

8 Go not forth hastily to strive, lest *thou know not* what to do in the end thereof, when thy neighbour hath put thee to shame.

9 Debate thy cause with thy neighbour *himself;* and discover not a secret to another:

10 Lest he that heareth *it* put thee to shame, and thine infamy turn not away.

11 A word fitly spoken *is like* apples of gold in pictures of silver.

12 *As* an earring of gold, and an ornament of fine gold, *so is* a wise reprover upon an obedient ear.

13 As the cold of snow in the time of harvest, *so is* a faithful messenger to them that send him: for he refresheth the soul of his masters.

14 Whoso boasteth himself of a false gift *is like* clouds and wind without rain.

15 By long forbearing is a prince persuaded, and a soft tongue breaketh the bone.

16 Hast thou found honey? eat so much as is sufficient for thee, lest thou be filled therewith, and vomit it.

17 Withdraw thy foot from thy neighbour's house; lest he be weary of thee, and *so* hate thee.

18 A man that beareth false witness against his neighbour *is* a maul, and a sword, and a sharp arrow.

19 Confidence in an unfaithful man in time of trouble *is like* a broken tooth, and a foot out of joint.

20 *As* he that taketh away a garment in cold weather, *and as* vinegar upon nitre, *so is* he that singeth songs to an heavy heart.

21 If thine enemy be hungry, give him bread to eat; and if he be thirsty, give him water to drink:

22 For thou shalt heap coals of fire upon his head, and the LORD shall reward thee.

23 The north wind driveth away rain: so *doth* an angry countenance a backbiting tongue.

24 *It is* better to dwell in the corner of the house top, than with a brawling woman and in a wide house.

25 *As* cold waters to a thirsty soul, so *is* good news from a far country.

26 A righteous man falling down before the wicked *is as* a troubled fountain, and a corrupt spring.

27 *It is* not good to eat much honey: so *for men* to search their own glory *is not* glory.

28 He that *hath* no rule over his own spirit *is like* a city *that is* broken down, *and* without walls.

26

AS snow in summer, and as rain in harvest, so honour is not seemly for a fool.

2 As the bird by wandering, as the swallow by flying, so the curse causeless shall not come.

3 A whip for the horse, a bridle for the ass, and a rod for the fool's back.

4 Answer not a fool according to his folly, lest thou also be like unto him.

5 Answer a fool according to his folly, lest he be wise in his own conceit.

6 He that sendeth a message by the hand of a fool cutteth off the feet, *and* drinketh damage.

7 The legs of the lame are not equal: so *is* a parable in the mouth of fools.

8 As he that bindeth a stone in a sling, so *is* he that giveth honour to a fool.

9 *As* a thorn goeth up into the hand of a drunkard, so *is* a parable in the mouth of fools.

10 The great *God* that formed all *things* rewardeth the fool, and rewardeth transgressors.

11 As a dog returneth to his vomit, *so* a fool returneth to his folly.

12 Seest thou a man wise in his own conceit? *there is* more hope of a fool than of him.

13 The slothful *man* saith, *There is* a lion in the way; a lion *is* in the streets.

14 *As* the door turneth upon his hinges, so *doth* the slothful upon his bed.

15 The slothful hideth his hand in *his* bosom; it grieveth him to bring it again to his mouth.

16 The sluggard *is* wiser in his own conceit than seven men that can render a reason.

17 He that passeth by, *and* meddleth with strife *belonging* not to him, *is like* one that taketh a dog by the ears.

18 As a mad *man* who casteth firebrands, arrows, and death,

19 So *is* the man *that* deceiveth his neighbour, and saith, Am not I in sport?

20 Where no wood is, *there* the fire goeth out: so where *there is* no talebearer, the strife ceaseth.

21 *As* coals *are* to burning coals, and wood to fire; so *is* a contentious man to kindle strife.

22 The words of a talebearer *are* as wounds, and they go down into the innermost parts of the belly.

23 Burning lips and a wicked heart *are like* a potsherd covered with silver dross.

24 He that hateth dissembleth with his lips, and layeth up deceit within him;

25 When he speaketh fair, believe him not: for *there are* seven abominations in his heart.

26 *Whose* hatred is covered by deceit, his wickedness shall be shewed before the *whole* congregation.

27 Whoso diggeth a pit shall fall therein: and he that rolleth a stone, it will return upon him.

28 A lying tongue hateth *those that are* afflicted by it; and a flattering mouth worketh ruin.

27

BOAST not thyself of to morrow; for thou knowest not what a day may bring forth.

2 Let another man praise thee, and not thine own mouth; a stranger, and not thine own lips.

3 A stone is heavy, and the sand weighty; but a fool's wrath is heavier than them both.

4 Wrath is cruel, and anger is outrageous; but who is able to stand before envy?

5 Open rebuke is better than secret love.

6 Faithful are the wounds of a friend; but the kisses of an enemy are deceitful.

7 The full soul loatheth an honeycomb; but to the hungry soul every bitter thing is sweet.

8 As a bird that wandereth from her nest, so is a man that wandereth from his place.

9 Ointment and perfume rejoice the heart: so doth the sweetness of a man's friend by hearty counsel.

10 Thine own friend, and thy father's friend, forsake not; neither go into thy brother's house in the day of thy calamity: for better is a neighbour that is near than a brother far off.

11 My son, be wise, and make my heart glad, that I may answer him that reproacheth me.

12 A prudent man foreseeth the evil, and hideth himself; but the simple pass on, and are punished.

13 Take his garment that is surety for a stranger, and take a pledge of him for a strange woman.

14 He that blesseth his friend with a loud voice, rising early in the morning, it shall be counted a curse to him.

15 A continual dropping in a very rainy day and a contentious woman are alike.

16 Whosoever hideth her hideth the wind, and the ointment of his right hand, which bewrayeth itself.

17 Iron sharpeneth iron; so a man sharpeneth the countenance of his friend.

18 Whoso keepeth the fig tree shall eat the fruit thereof: so he that waiteth on his master shall be honoured.

19 As in water face answereth to face, so the heart of man to man.

20 Hell and destruction are never full; so the eyes of man are never satisfied.

21 As the fining pot for silver, and the furnace for gold; so is a man to his praise.

22 Though thou shouldest bray a fool in a mortar among wheat with a pestle, yet will not his foolishness depart from him.

23 Be thou diligent to know the state of thy flocks, and look well to thy herds.

24 For riches are not for ever: and doth the crown endure to every generation?

25 The hay appeareth, and the tender grass sheweth itself, and herbs of the mountains are gathered.

26 The lambs are for thy clothing, and the goats are the price of the field.

27 And thou shalt have goats' milk enough for thy food, for the food of thy household, and for the maintenance for thy maidens.

28

THE wicked flee when no man pursueth: but the righteous are bold as a lion.

2 For the transgression of a land many are the princes thereof: but by a man of understanding and knowledge the state thereof shall be prolonged.

3 A poor man that oppresseth the poor is like a sweeping rain which leaveth no food.

4 They that forsake the law praise the wicked: but such as keep the law contend with them.

5 Evil men understand not judgment: but they that seek the LORD understand all things.

6 Better is the poor that walketh in his uprightness, than he that is perverse in his ways, though he be rich.

7 Whoso keepeth the law is a wise son: but he that is a companion of riotous men shameth his father.

8 He that by usury and unjust gain increaseth his substance, he shall gather it for him that will pity the poor.

9 He that turneth away his ear from hearing the law, even his prayer shall be abomination.

10 Whoso causeth the righteous to go astray in an evil way, he shall fall himself into his own pit: but the upright shall have good things in possession.

11 The rich man is wise in his own conceit; but the poor that hath understanding searcheth him out.

12 When righteous men do rejoice, there is great glory: but when the wicked rise, a man is hidden.

13 He that covereth his sins shall not prosper: but whoso confesseth and forsaketh them shall have mercy.

14 Happy is the man that feareth alway: but he that hardeneth his heart shall fall into mischief.

15 As a roaring lion, and a ranging bear; so is a wicked ruler over the poor people.

16 The prince that wanteth understanding is also a great oppressor: but he that hateth covetousness shall prolong his days.

17 A man that doeth violence to the blood of any person shall flee to the pit; let no man stay him.

18 Whoso walketh uprightly shall be saved: but he that is perverse in his ways shall fall at once.

19 He that tilleth his land shall have plenty of bread: but he that followeth after vain persons shall have poverty enough.

20 A faithful man shall abound with blessings: but he that maketh haste to be rich shall not be innocent.

21 To have respect of persons is not good: for for a piece of bread that man will transgress.

22 He that hasteth to be rich hath an evil eye, and considereth not that poverty shall come upon him.

23 He that rebuketh a man afterwards shall find more favour than he that flattereth with the tongue.

24 Whoso robbeth his father or his mother, and saith, It is no transgression: the same is the companion of a destroyer.

25 He that is of a proud heart stirreth up strife: but he that putteth his trust in the LORD shall be made fat.

26 He that trusteth in his own heart is a fool: but whoso walketh wisely, he shall be delivered.

27 He that giveth unto the poor shall not lack: but he that hideth his eyes shall have many a curse.

28 When the wicked rise, men hide themselves: but when they perish, the righteous increase.

29

HE, that being often reproved hardeneth his neck, shall suddenly be destroyed, and that without remedy.

2 When the righteous are in authority, the people rejoice: but when the wicked beareth rule, the people mourn.

3 Whoso loveth wisdom rejoiceth his father: but he that keepeth company with harlots spendeth his substance.

4 The king by judgment establisheth the land: but he that receiveth gifts overthroweth it.

5 A man that flattereth his neighbour spreadeth a net for his feet.

6 In the transgression of an evil man *there is* a snare: but the righteous doth sing and rejoice.

7 The righteous considereth the cause of the poor: *but* the wicked regardeth not to know *it*.

8 Scornful men bring a city into a snare: but wise *men* turn away wrath.

9 *If* a wise man contendeth with a foolish man, whether he rage or laugh, *there is* no rest.

10 The bloodthirsty hate the upright: but the just seek his soul.

11 A fool uttereth all his mind: but a wise *man* keepeth it in till afterwards.

12 If a ruler hearken to lies, all his servants *are* wicked.

13 The poor and the deceitful man meet together: the LORD lighteneth both their eyes.

14 The king that faithfully judgeth the poor, his throne shall be established for ever.

15 The rod and reproof give wisdom: but a child left *to himself* bringeth his mother to shame.

16 When the wicked are multiplied, transgression increaseth: but the righteous shall see their fall.

17 Correct thy son, and he shall give thee rest; yea, he shall give delight unto thy soul.

18 Where *there is* no vision, the people perish: but he that keepeth the law, happy *is* he.

19 A servant will not be corrected by words: for though he understand he will not answer.

20 Seest thou a man *that is* hasty in his words? *there is* more hope of a fool than of him.

21 He that delicately bringeth up his servant from a child shall have him become *his* son at the length.

22 An angry man stirreth up strife, and a furious man aboundeth in transgression.

23 A man's pride shall bring him low: but honour shall uphold the humble in spirit.

24 Whoso is partner with a thief hateth his own soul: he heareth cursing, and bewrayeth *it* not.

25 The fear of man bringeth a snare: but whoso putteth his trust in the LORD shall be safe.

26 Many seek the ruler's favour; but *every* man's judgment *cometh* from the LORD.

27 An unjust man *is* an abomination to the just: and *he that is* upright in the way *is* abomination to the wicked.

30 THE words of A′gur the son of Ja′keh, *even* the prophecy: the man spake unto Ith′i-el, even unto Ith′i-el and U′cal,

2 Surely I *am* more brutish than *any* man, and have not the understanding of a man.

3 I neither learned wisdom, nor have the knowledge of the holy.

4 Who hath ascended up into heaven, or descended? who hath gathered the wind in his fists? who hath bound the waters in a garment? who hath established all the ends of the earth? what *is* his name, and what *is* his son's name, if thou canst tell?

5 Every word of God *is* pure: he *is* a shield unto them that put their trust in him.

6 Add thou not unto his words, lest he reprove thee, and thou be found a liar.

7 Two *things* have I required of thee; deny me *them* not before I die:

8 Remove far from me vanity and lies: give me neither poverty nor riches; feed me with food convenient for me:

9 Lest I be full, and deny *thee,* and say, Who *is* the LORD? or lest I be poor, and steal, and take the name of my God *in* vain.

10 Accuse not a servant unto his master, lest he curse thee, and thou be found guilty.

11 *There is* a generation *that* curseth their father, and doth not bless their mother.

12 *There is* a generation *that are* pure in their own eyes, and *yet* is not washed from their filthiness.

13 *There is* a generation, O how lofty are their eyes! and their eyelids are lifted up.

14 *There is* a generation, whose teeth *are as* swords, and their jaw teeth *as* knives, to devour the poor from off the earth, and the needy from among men.

15 The horseleach hath two daughters, *crying,* Give, give. There are three *things that* are never satisfied, *yea,* four *things* say not, It is enough:

16 The grave; and the barren womb; the earth *that* is not filled with water; and the fire *that* saith not, It is enough.

17 The eye *that* mocketh at *his* father, and despiseth to obey *his* mother, the ravens of the valley shall pick it out, and the young eagles shall eat it.

18 There be three *things which* are too wonderful for me, yea, four which I know not:

19 The way of an eagle in the air; the way of a serpent upon a rock; the way of a ship in the midst of the sea; and the way of a man with a maid.

20 Such *is* the way of an adulterous woman; she eateth, and wipeth her mouth, and saith, I have done no wickedness.

21 For three *things* the earth is disquieted, and for four *which* it cannot bear:

22 For a servant when he reigneth; and a fool when he is filled with meat;

23 For an odious *woman* when she is married; and an handmaid that is heir to her mistress.

24 There be four *things which are* little upon the earth, but they *are* exceeding wise:

25 The ants *are* a people not strong, yet they prepare their meat in the summer;

26 The conies *are but* a feeble folk, yet make they their houses in the rocks;

27 The locusts have no king, yet go they forth all of them by bands;

28 The spider taketh hold with her hands, and is in kings' palaces.

29 There be three *things* which go well, yea, four are comely in going:

30 A lion *which is* strongest among beasts, and turneth not away for any;

31 A greyhound; an he goat also; and a king, against whom *there is* no rising up.

32 If thou hast done foolishly in lifting up thyself, or if thou hast thought evil, *lay* thine hand upon thy mouth.

33 Surely the churning of milk bringeth forth butter, and the wringing of the nose bringeth forth blood: so the forcing of wrath bringeth forth strife.

31 THE words of king Lem′u-el, the prophecy that his mother taught him.

2 What, my son? and what, the son of my womb? and what, the son of my vows?

3 Give not thy strength unto women, nor thy ways to that which destroyeth kings.

4 *It is* not for kings, O Lem′u-el, *it is* not for kings to drink wine; nor for princes strong drink:

5 Lest they drink, and forget the law, and pervert the judgment of any of the afflicted.

6 Give strong drink unto him that is ready to perish, and wine unto those that be of heavy hearts.

7 Let him drink, and forget his poverty, and remember his misery no more.

8 Open thy mouth for the dumb in the cause of all such as are appointed to destruction.

9 Open thy mouth, judge righteously, and plead the cause of the poor and needy.

10 ¶ Who can find a virtuous woman? for her price *is* far above rubies.

11 The heart of her husband doth safely trust in her, so that he shall have no need of spoil.

12 She will do him good and not evil all the days of her life.

13 She seeketh wool, and flax, and worketh willingly with her hands.

14 She is like the merchants' ships; she bringeth her food from afar.

15 She riseth also while it is yet night, and giveth meat to her household, and a portion to her maidens.

16 She considereth a field, and buyeth it: with the fruit of her hands she planteth a vineyard.

17 She girdeth her loins with strength, and strengtheneth her arms.

18 She perceiveth that her merchandise *is* good: her candle goeth not out by night.

19 She layeth her hands to the spindle, and her hands hold the distaff.

20 She stretcheth out her hand to the poor; yea, she reacheth forth her hands to the needy.

21 She is not afraid of the snow for her household: for all her household *are* clothed with scarlet.

22 She maketh herself coverings of tapestry; her clothing *is* silk and purple.

23 Her husband is known in the gates, when he sitteth among the elders of the land.

24 She maketh fine linen, and selleth *it;* and delivereth girdles unto the merchant.

25 Strength and honour *are* her clothing; and she shall rejoice in time to come.

26 She openeth her mouth with wisdom: and in her tongue *is* the law of kindness.

27 She looketh well to the ways of her household, and eateth not the bread of idleness.

28 Her children arise up, and call her blessed; her husband *also,* and he praiseth her.

29 Many daughters have done virtuously, but thou excellest them all.

30 Favour *is* deceitful, and beauty *is* vain: *but* a woman *that* feareth the LORD, she shall be praised.

31 Give her of the fruit of her hands; and let her own works praise her in the gates.

ECCLESIASTES

OR, THE PREACHER

1 THE words of the Preacher, the son of Da'-vid, king in Je-ru'sa-lem.

2 Vanity of vanities, saith the Preacher, vanity of vanities; all *is* vanity.

3 What profit hath a man of all his labour which he taketh under the sun?

4 *One* generation passeth away, and *another* generation cometh: but the earth abideth for ever.

5 The sun also ariseth, and the sun goeth down, and hasteth to his place where he arose.

6 The wind goeth toward the south, and turneth about unto the north; it whirleth about continually, and the wind returneth again according to his circuits.

7 All the rivers run into the sea; yet the sea *is* not full; unto the place from whence the rivers come, thither they return again.

8 All things *are* full of labour; man cannot utter *it:* the eye is not satisfied with seeing, nor the ear filled with hearing.

9 The thing that hath been, it *is that* which shall be; and that which is done *is* that which shall be done: and *there is* no new *thing* under the sun.

10 Is there *any* thing whereof it may be said, See, this *is* new? it hath been already of old time, which was before us.

11 *There is* no remembrance of former *things;* neither shall there be *any* remembrance of *things* that are to come with *those* that shall come after.

12 ¶ I the Preacher was king over Is'ra-el in Je-ru'sa-lem.

13 And I gave my heart to seek and search out by wisdom concerning all *things* that are done under heaven: this sore travail hath God given to the sons of man to be exercised therewith.

14 I have seen all the works that are done under the sun; and, behold, all *is* vanity and vexation of spirit.

15 *That which is* crooked cannot be made straight: and that which is wanting cannot be numbered.

16 I communed with mine own heart, saying, Lo, I am come to great estate, and have gotten more wisdom than all *they* that have been before me in Je-ru'sa-lem: yea, my heart had great experience of wisdom and knowledge.

17 And I gave my heart to know wisdom, and to know madness and folly: I perceived that this also is vexation of spirit.

18 For in much wisdom *is* much grief: and he that increaseth knowledge increaseth sorrow.

2 I SAID in mine heart, Go to now, I will prove thee with mirth, therefore enjoy pleasure: and, behold, this also *is* vanity.

2 I said of laughter, It *is* mad: and of mirth, What doeth it?

3 I sought in mine heart to give myself unto wine, yet acquainting mine heart with wisdom; and to lay hold on folly, till I might see what *was* that good for the sons of men, which they should do under the heaven all the days of their life.

4 I made me great works; I builded me houses; I planted me vineyards:

5 I made me gardens and orchards, and I planted trees in them of all *kind of* fruits:

6 I made me pools of water, to water therewith the wood that bringeth forth trees:

7 I got *me* servants and maidens, and had servants born in my house; also I had great possessions of great and small cattle above all that were in Je-ru'sa-lem before me:

8 I gathered me also silver and gold, and the

peculiar treasure of kings and of the provinces: I gat me men singers and women singers, and the delights of the sons of men, *as* musical instruments, and that of all sorts.

9 So I was great, and increased more than all that were before me in Je-ru'sa-lem: also my wisdom remained with me.

10 And whatsoever mine eyes desired I kept not from them, I withheld not my heart from any joy; for my heart rejoiced in all my labour: and this was my portion of all my labour.

11 Then I looked on all the works that my hands had wrought, and on the labour that I had laboured to do: and, behold, all *was* vanity and vexation of spirit, and *there was* no profit under the sun.

12 ¶ And I turned myself to behold wisdom, and madness, and folly: for what *can* the man *do* that cometh after the king? *even* that which hath been already done.

13 Then I saw that wisdom excelleth folly, as far as light excelleth darkness.

14 The wise man's eyes *are* in his head; but the fool walketh in darkness: and I myself perceived also that one event happeneth to them all.

15 Then said I in my heart, As it happeneth to the fool, so it happeneth even to me; and why was I then more wise? Then I said in my heart, that this also *is* vanity.

16 For *there is* no remembrance of the wise more than of the fool for ever; seeing that which now *is* in the days to come shall all be forgotten. And how dieth the wise *man*? as the fool.

17 Therefore I hated life; because the work that is wrought under the sun *is* grievous unto me: for all *is* vanity and vexation of spirit.

18 ¶ Yea, I hated all my labour which I had taken under the sun: because I should leave it unto the man that shall be after me.

19 And who knoweth whether he shall be a wise *man* or a fool? yet shall he have rule over all my labour wherein I have laboured, and wherein I have shewed myself wise under the sun. This *is* also vanity.

20 Therefore I went about to cause my heart to despair of all the labour which I took under the sun.

21 For there is a man whose labour *is* in wisdom, and in knowledge, and in equity; yet to a man that hath not laboured therein shall he leave it *for* his portion. This also *is* vanity and a great evil.

22 For what hath man of all his labour, and of the vexation of his heart, wherein he hath laboured under the sun?

23 For all his days *are* sorrows, and his travail grief; yea, his heart taketh not rest in the night. This also *is* vanity.

24 ¶ *There is* nothing better for a man, *than* that he should eat and drink, and *that* he should make his soul enjoy good in his labour. This also I saw, that it *was* from the hand of God.

25 For who can eat, or who else can hasten *hereunto*, more than I?

26 For God giveth to a man that *is* good in his sight wisdom, and knowledge, and joy: but to the sinner he giveth travail, to gather and to heap up, that he may give to *him that is* good before God. This also *is* vanity and vexation of spirit.

3 TO every *thing there is* a season, and a time to every purpose under the heaven:

2 A time to be born, and a time to die; a time to plant, and a time to pluck up *that which is* planted;

3 A time to kill, and a time to heal; a time to break down, and a time to build up;

4 A time to weep, and a time to laugh; a time to mourn, and a time to dance;

5 A time to cast away stones, and a time to gather stones together; a time to embrace, and a time to refrain from embracing;

6 A time to get, and a time to lose; a time to keep, and a time to cast away;

7 A time to rend, and a time to sew; a time to keep silence, and a time to speak;

8 A time to love, and a time to hate; a time of war, and a time of peace.

9 What profit hath he that worketh in that wherein he laboureth?

10 I have seen the travail, which God hath given to the sons of men to be exercised in it.

11 He hath made every *thing* beautiful in his time: also he hath set the world in their heart, so that no man can find out the work that God maketh from the beginning to the end.

12 I know that *there is* no good in them, but for *a man* to rejoice, and to do good in his life.

13 And also that every man should eat and drink, and enjoy the good of all his labour, it *is* the gift of God.

14 I know that, whatsoever God doeth, it shall be for ever: nothing can be put to it, nor any thing taken from it: and God doeth *it*, that *men* should fear before him.

15 That which hath been is now; and that which is to be hath already been; and God requireth that which is past.

16 ¶ And moreover I saw under the sun the place of judgment, *that* wickedness *was* there; and the place of righteousness, *that* iniquity *was* there.

17 I said in mine heart, God shall judge the righteous and the wicked: for *there is* a time there for every purpose and for every work.

18 I said in mine heart concerning the estate of the sons of men, that God might manifest them, and that they might see that they themselves are beasts.

19 For that which befalleth the sons of men befalleth beasts; even one thing befalleth them: as the one dieth, so dieth the other; yea, they have all one breath; so that a man hath no preeminence above a beast: for all *is* vanity.

20 All go unto one place; all are of the dust, and all turn to dust again.

21 Who knoweth the spirit of man that goeth upward, and the spirit of the beast that goeth downward to the earth?

22 Wherefore I perceive that *there is* nothing better, than that a man should rejoice in his own works; for that *is* his portion: for who shall bring him to see what shall be after him?

4 SO I returned, and considered all the oppressions that are done under the sun: and behold the tears of *such as were* oppressed, and they had no comforter; and on the side of their oppressors *there was* power; but they had no comforter.

2 Wherefore I praised the dead which are already dead more than the living which are yet alive.

3 Yea, better *is* he than both they, which hath not yet been, who hath not seen the evil work that is done under the sun.

4 ¶ Again, I considered all travail, and every right work, that for this a man is envied of his neighbour. This *is* also vanity and vexation of spirit.

5 The fool foldeth his hands together, and eateth his own flesh.

6 Better *is* an handful *with* quietness, than both the hands full *with* travail and vexation of spirit.

7 ¶ Then I returned, and I saw vanity under the sun.

8 There is one *alone*, and *there* is not a second; yea, he hath neither child nor brother: yet *is there* no end of all his labour; neither is his eye satisfied with riches; neither *saith he*, For whom do I labour, and bereave my soul of good? This *is* also vanity, yea, it *is* a sore travail.

9 ¶ Two *are* better than one; because they have a good reward for their labour.

10 For if they fall, the one will lift up his fellow: but woe to him *that is* alone when he falleth; for *he hath* not another to help him up.

11 Again, if two lie together, then they have heat: but how can one be warm *alone*?

12 And if one prevail against him, two shall withstand him; and a threefold cord is not quickly broken.

13 ¶ Better *is* a poor and a wise child than an old and foolish king, who will no more be admonished.

14 For out of prison he cometh to reign; whereas also *he that is* born in his kingdom becometh poor.

15 I considered all the living which walk under the sun, with the second child that shall stand up in his stead.

16 *There* is no end of all the people, *even* of all that have been before them: they also that come after shall not rejoice in him. Surely this also *is* vanity and vexation of spirit.

5 KEEP thy foot when thou goest to the house of God, and be more ready to hear, than to give the sacrifice of fools: for they consider not that they do evil.

2 Be not rash with thy mouth, and let not thine heart be hasty to utter *any* thing before God: for God *is* in heaven, and thou upon earth: therefore let thy words be few.

3 For a dream cometh through the multitude of business; and a fool's voice *is known* by multitude of words.

4 When thou vowest a vow unto God, defer not to pay it; for *he hath* no pleasure in fools: pay that which thou hast vowed.

5 Better *is* it that thou shouldest not vow, than that thou shouldest vow and not pay.

6 Suffer not thy mouth to cause thy flesh to sin; neither say thou before the angel, that it *was* an error: wherefore should God be angry at thy voice, and destroy the work of thine hands?

7 For in the multitude of dreams and many words *there are* also *divers* vanities: but fear thou God.

8 ¶ If thou seest the oppression of the poor, and violent perverting of judgment and justice in a province, marvel not at the matter: for *he that is* higher than the highest regardeth; and *there be* higher than they.

9 ¶ Moreover the profit of the earth is for all: the king *himself* is served by the field.

10 He that loveth silver shall not be satisfied with silver; nor he that loveth abundance with increase: this *is* also vanity.

11 When goods increase, they are increased that eat them: and what good *is there* to the owners thereof, saving the beholding *of them* with their eyes?

12 The sleep of a labouring man *is* sweet, whether he eat little or much: but the abundance of the rich will not suffer him to sleep.

13 There is a sore evil *which* I have seen under the sun, *namely*, riches kept for the owners thereof to their hurt.

14 But those riches perish by evil travail: and he begetteth a son, and *there is* nothing in his hand.

15 As he came forth of his mother's womb, naked shall he return to go as he came, and shall take nothing of his labour, which he may carry away in his hand.

16 And this also *is* a sore evil, *that* in all points as he came, so shall he go: and what profit hath he that hath laboured for the wind?

17 All his days also he eateth in darkness, and *he hath* much sorrow and wrath with his sickness.

18 ¶ Behold *that* which I have seen: *it is* good and comely *for one* to eat and to drink, and to enjoy the good of all his labour that he taketh under the sun all the days of his life, which God giveth him: for it *is* his portion.

19 Every man also to whom God hath given riches and wealth, and hath given him power to eat thereof, and to take his portion, and to rejoice in his labour; this *is* the gift of God.

20 For he shall not much remember the days of his life; because God answereth *him* in the joy of his heart.

6 THERE is an evil which I have seen under the sun, and it *is* common among men:

2 A man to whom God hath given riches, wealth, and honour, so that he wanteth nothing for his soul of all that he desireth, yet God giveth him not power to eat thereof, but a stranger eateth it: this *is* vanity, and it *is* an evil disease.

3 ¶ If a man beget an hundred *children*, and live many years, so that the days of his years be many, and his soul be not filled with good, and also *that* he have no burial; I say, *that* an untimely birth *is* better than he.

4 For he cometh in with vanity, and departeth in darkness, and his name shall be covered with darkness.

5 Moreover he hath not seen the sun, nor known *any* thing: this hath more rest than the other.

6 ¶ Yea, though he live a thousand years twice *told*, yet hath he seen no good: do not all go to one place?

7 All the labour of man *is* for his mouth, and yet the appetite is not filled.

8 For what hath the wise more than the fool? what hath the poor, that knoweth to walk before the living?

9 ¶ Better *is* the sight of the eyes than the wandering of the desire: this *is* also vanity and vexation of spirit.

10 That which hath been is named already, and it is known that it *is* man: neither may he contend with him that is mightier than he.

11 ¶ Seeing there be many things that increase vanity, what *is* man the better?

12 For who knoweth what *is* good for man in *this* life, all the days of his vain life which he spendeth as a shadow? for who can tell a man what shall be after him under the sun?

7 A GOOD name *is* better than precious ointment; and the day of death than the day of one's birth.

2 ¶ *It is* better to go to the house of mourning, than to go to the house of feasting: for that *is* the end of all men; and the living will lay *it* to his heart.

3 Sorrow *is* better than laughter: for by the

sadness of the countenance the heart is made better.

4 The heart of the wise *is* in the house of mourning; but the heart of fools *is* in the house of mirth.

5 *It is* better to hear the rebuke of the wise, than for a man to hear the song of fools.

6 For as the crackling of thorns under a pot, so *is* the laughter of the fool: this also *is* vanity.

7 ¶ Surely oppression maketh a wise man mad; and a gift destroyeth the heart.

8 Better *is* the end of a thing than the beginning thereof: *and* the patient in spirit *is* better than the proud in spirit.

9 Be not hasty in thy spirit to be angry: for anger resteth in the bosom of fools.

10 Say not thou, What is *the cause* that the former days were better than these? for thou dost not enquire wisely concerning this.

11 ¶ Wisdom *is* good with an inheritance: and *by it there is* profit to them that see the sun.

12 For wisdom *is* a defence, *and* money *is* a defence: but the excellency of knowledge *is, that* wisdom giveth life to them that have it.

13 Consider the work of God: for who can make *that* straight, which he hath made crooked?

14 In the day of prosperity be joyful, but in the day of adversity consider: God also hath set the one over against the other, to the end that man should find nothing after him.

15 All *things* have I seen in the days of my vanity: there is a just *man* that perisheth in his righteousness, and there is a wicked *man* that prolongeth *his* life in his wickedness.

16 Be not righteous over much; neither make thyself over wise: why shouldest thou destroy thyself?

17 Be not over much wicked, neither be thou foolish: why shouldest thou die before thy time?

18 *It is* good that thou shouldest take hold of this; yea, also from this withdraw not thine hand: for he that feareth God shall come forth of them all.

19 Wisdom strengtheneth the wise more than ten mighty *men* which are in the city.

20 For *there is* not a just man upon earth, that doeth good, and sinneth not.

21 Also take no heed unto all words that are spoken; lest thou hear thy servant curse thee:

22 For oftentimes also thine own heart knoweth that thou thyself likewise hast cursed others.

23 ¶ All this have I proved by wisdom: I said, I will be wise; but it *was* far from me.

24 That which is far off, and exceeding deep, who can find it out?

25 I applied mine heart to know, and to search, and to seek out wisdom, and the reason *of things*, and to know the wickedness of folly, even of foolishness *and* madness:

26 And I find more bitter than death the woman, whose heart *is* snares and nets, *and* her hands *as* bands: whoso pleaseth God shall escape from her; but the sinner shall be taken by her.

27 Behold, this have I found, saith the preacher, *counting* one by one, to find out the account:

28 Which yet my soul seeketh, but I find not: one man among a thousand have I found; but a woman among all those have I not found.

29 Lo, this only have I found, that God hath made man upright; but they have sought out many inventions.

8 WHO *is* as the wise *man*? and who knoweth the interpretation of a thing? a man's wisdom maketh his face to shine, and the boldness of his face shall be changed.

2 I *counsel thee* to keep the king's commandment, and *that* in regard of the oath of God.

3 Be not hasty to go out of his sight: stand not in an evil thing; for he doeth whatsoever pleaseth him.

4 Where the word of a king *is, there is* power: and who may say unto him, What doest thou?

5 Whoso keepeth the commandment shall feel no evil thing: and a wise man's heart discerneth both time and judgment.

6 ¶ Because to every purpose there is time and judgment, therefore the misery of man *is* great upon him.

7 For he knoweth not that which shall be: for who can tell him when it shall be?

8 *There is* no man that hath power over the spirit to retain the spirit; neither *hath he* power in the day of death: and *there is* no discharge in *that* war; neither shall wickedness deliver those that are given to it.

9 All this have I seen, and applied my heart unto every work that is done under the sun: *there is* a time wherein one man ruleth over another to his own hurt.

10 And so I saw the wicked buried, who had come and gone from the place of the holy, and they were forgotten in the city where they had so done: this *is* also vanity.

11 Because sentence against an evil work is not executed speedily, therefore the heart of the sons of men is fully set in them to do evil.

12 ¶ Though a sinner do evil an hundred times, and his *days* be prolonged, yet surely I know that it shall be well with them that fear God, which fear before him:

13 But it shall not be well with the wicked, neither shall he prolong *his* days, *which are* as a shadow; because he feareth not before God.

14 There is a vanity which is done upon the earth; that there be just *men*, unto whom it happeneth according to the work of the wicked; again, there be wicked *men*, to whom it happeneth according to the work of the righteous: I said that this also *is* vanity.

15 Then I commended mirth, because a man hath no better thing under the sun, than to eat, and to drink, and to be merry: for that shall abide with him of his labour the days of his life, which God giveth him under the sun.

16 ¶ When I applied mine heart to know wisdom, and to see the business that is done upon the earth: (for also *there is* that neither day nor night seeth sleep with his eyes:)

17 Then I beheld all the work of God, that a man cannot find out the work that is done under the sun: because though a man labour to seek *it* out, yet he shall not find *it*: yea farther; though a wise *man* think to know *it*, yet shall he not be able to find *it*.

9 FOR all this I considered in my heart even to declare all this, that the righteous, and the wise, and their works, *are* in the hand of God: no man knoweth either love or hatred *by* all *that is* before them.

2 All *things* come alike to all: *there is* one event to the righteous, and to the wicked; to the good and to the clean, and to the unclean; to him that sacrificeth, and to him that sacrificeth not: as *is* the good, so *is* the sinner; *and* he that sweareth, as *he* that feareth an oath.

3 This *is* an evil among all *things* that are

done under the sun, that *there is* one event unto all: yea, also the heart of the sons of men is full of evil, and madness *is* in their heart while they live, and after that *they* go to the dead.

4 ¶ For to him that is joined to all the living there is hope: for a living dog is better than a dead lion.

5 For the living know that they shall die: but the dead know not any thing, neither have they any more a reward; for the memory of them is forgotten.

6 Also their love, and their hatred, and their envy, is now perished; neither have they any more a portion for ever in any *thing* that is done under the sun.

7 ¶ Go thy way, eat thy bread with joy, and drink thy wine with a merry heart; for God now accepteth thy works.

8 Let thy garments be always white; and let thy head lack no ointment.

9 Live joyfully with the wife whom thou lovest all the days of the life of thy vanity, which he hath given thee under the sun, all the days of thy vanity: for that *is* thy portion in *this* life, and in thy labour which thou takest under the sun.

10 Whatsoever thy hand findeth to do, do *it* with thy might; for *there is* no work, nor device, nor knowledge, nor wisdom, in the grave, whither thou goest.

11 ¶ I returned, and saw under the sun, that the race *is* not to the swift, nor the battle to the strong, neither yet bread to the wise, nor yet riches to men of understanding, nor yet favour to men of skill; but time and chance happeneth to them all.

12 For man also knoweth not his time: as the fishes that are taken in an evil net, and as the birds that are caught in the snare; so *are* the sons of men snared in an evil time, when it falleth suddenly upon them.

13 ¶ This wisdom have I seen also under the sun, and it *seemed* great unto me:

14 *There was* a little city, and few men within it; and there came a great king against it, and besieged it, and built great bulwarks against it:

15 Now there was found in it a poor wise man, and he by his wisdom delivered the city; yet no man remembered that same poor man.

16 Then said I, Wisdom *is* better than strength: nevertheless the poor man's wisdom *is* despised, and his words are not heard.

17 The words of wise *men are* heard in quiet more than the cry of him that ruleth among fools.

18 Wisdom *is* better than weapons of war: but one sinner destroyeth much good.

10 DEAD flies cause the ointment of the apothecary to send forth a stinking savour: *so doth* a little folly him that is in reputation for wisdom *and* honour.

2 A wise man's heart *is* at his right hand; but a fool's heart at his left.

3 Yea also, when he that is a fool walketh by the way, his wisdom faileth *him*, and he saith to every one *that* he *is* a fool.

4 If the spirit of the ruler rise up against thee, leave not thy place; for yielding pacifieth great offences.

5 There is an evil *which* I have seen under the sun, as an error *which* proceedeth from the ruler:

6 Folly is set in great dignity, and the rich sit in low place.

7 I have seen servants upon horses, and princes walking as servants upon the earth.

8 He that diggeth a pit shall fall into it; and

whoso breaketh an hedge, a serpent shall bite him.

9 Whoso removeth stones shall be hurt therewith; *and* he that cleaveth wood shall be endangered thereby.

10 If the iron be blunt, and he do not whet the edge, then must he put to more strength: but wisdom *is* profitable to direct.

11 Surely the serpent will bite without enchantment; and a babbler is no better.

12 The words of a wise man's mouth *are* gracious; but the lips of a fool will swallow up himself.

13 The beginning of the words of his mouth *is* foolishness: and the end of his talk *is* mischievous madness.

14 A fool also is full of words: a man cannot tell what shall be; and what shall be after him, who can tell him?

15 The labour of the foolish wearieth every one of them, because he knoweth not how to go to the city.

16 Woe to thee, O land, when thy king *is* a child, and thy princes eat in the morning!

17 Blessed *art* thou, O land, when thy king *is* the son of nobles, and thy princes eat in due season, for strength, and not for drunkenness!

18 ¶ By much slothfulness the building decayeth; and through idleness of the hands the house droppeth through.

19 ¶ A feast is made for laughter, and wine maketh merry: but money answereth all *things*.

20 ¶ Curse not the king, no not in thy thought; and curse not the rich in thy bedchamber: for a bird of the air shall carry the voice, and that which hath wings shall tell the matter.

11 CAST thy bread upon the waters: for thou shalt find it after many days.

2 Give a portion to seven, and also to eight; for thou knowest not what evil shall be upon the earth.

3 If the clouds be full of rain, they empty *themselves* upon the earth: and if the tree fall toward the south, or toward the north, in the place where the tree falleth, there it shall be.

4 He that observeth the wind shall not sow; and he that regardeth the clouds shall not reap.

5 As thou knowest not what *is* the way of the spirit, *nor* how the bones *do* grow in the womb of her that is with child: even so thou knowest not the works of God who maketh all.

6 In the morning sow thy seed, and in the evening withhold not thine hand: for thou knowest not whether shall prosper, either this or that, or whether they both *shall be* alike good.

7 ¶ Truly the light *is* sweet, and a pleasant *thing it is* for the eyes to behold the sun:

8 But if a man live many years, *and* rejoice in them all; yet let him remember the days of darkness; for they shall be many. All that cometh *is* vanity.

9 ¶ Rejoice, O young man, in thy youth; and let thy heart cheer thee in the days of thy youth, and walk in the ways of thine heart, and in the sight of thine eyes: but know thou, that for all these *things* God will bring thee into judgment.

10 Therefore remove sorrow from thy heart, and put away evil from thy flesh: for childhood and youth *are* vanity.

12 REMEMBER now thy Creator in the days of thy youth, while the evil days come not, nor the years draw nigh, when thou shalt say, I have no pleasure in them;

2 While the sun, or the light, or the moon, or the stars, be not darkened, nor the clouds return after the rain:

3 In the day when the keepers of the house shall tremble, and the strong men shall bow themselves, and the grinders cease because they are few, and those that look out of the windows be darkened,

4 And the doors shall be shut in the streets, when the sound of the grinding is low, and he shall rise up at the voice of the bird, and all the daughters of musick shall be brought low;

5 Also *when* they shall be afraid of *that which is* high, and fears *shall be* in the way, and the almond tree shall flourish, and the grasshopper shall be a burden, and desire shall fail: because man goeth to his long home, and the mourners go about the streets:

6 Or ever the silver cord be loosed, or the golden bowl be broken, or the pitcher be broken at the fountain, or the wheel broken at the cistern.

7 Then shall the dust return to the earth as it was: and the spirit shall return unto God who gave it.

8 ¶ Vanity of vanities, saith the preacher; all *is* vanity.

9 And moreover, because the preacher was wise, he still taught the people knowledge; yea, he gave good heed, and sought out, *and* set in order many proverbs.

10 The preacher sought to find out acceptable words: and *that which was* written *was* upright, *even* words of truth.

11 The words of the wise *are* as goads, and as nails fastened *by* the masters of assemblies, *which* are given from one shepherd.

12 And further, by these, my son, be admonished: of making many books *there is* no end; and much study *is* a weariness of the flesh.

13 ¶ Let us hear the conclusion of the whole matter: Fear God, and keep his commandments: for this *is* the whole *duty* of man.

14 For God shall bring every work into judgment, with every secret thing, whether *it be* good, or whether *it be* evil.

THE SONG OF SOLOMON

1 THE song of songs, which *is* Sol'o-mon's.

2 Let him kiss me with the kisses of his mouth: for thy love *is* better than wine.

3 Because of the savour of thy good ointments thy name *is as* ointment poured forth, therefore do the virgins love thee.

4 Draw me, we will run after thee: the king hath brought me into his chambers: we will be glad and rejoice in thee, we will remember thy love more than wine: the upright love thee.

5 I *am* black, but comely, O ye daughters of Je-ru'sa-lem, as the tents of Ke'dar, as the curtains of Sol'o-mon.

6 Look not upon me, because I *am* black, because the sun hath looked upon me: my mother's children were angry with me; they made me the keeper of the vineyards; *but* mine own vineyard have I not kept.

7 Tell me, O thou whom my soul loveth, where thou feedest, where thou makest *thy flock* to rest at noon: for why should I be as one that turneth aside by the flocks of thy companions?

8 ¶ If thou know not, O thou fairest among women, go thy way forth by the footsteps of the flock, and feed thy kids beside the shepherds' tents.

9 I have compared thee, O my love, to a company of horses in Pha'raoh's chariots.

10 Thy cheeks are comely with rows *of jewels,* thy neck with chains *of gold.*

11 We will make thee borders of gold with studs of silver.

12 ¶ While the king *sitteth* at his table, my spikenard sendeth forth the smell thereof.

13 A bundle of myrrh *is* my wellbeloved unto me; he shall lie all night betwixt my breasts.

14 My beloved *is* unto me *as* a cluster of camphire in the vineyards of En-ge'di.

15 Behold, thou *art* fair, my love; behold, thou *art* fair; thou *hast* doves' eyes.

16 Behold, thou *art* fair, my beloved, yea, pleasant: also our bed *is* green.

17 The beams of our house *are* cedar, *and* our rafters of fir.

2 I AM the rose of Shar'on, *and* the lily of the valleys.

2 As the lily among thorns, so *is* my love among the daughters.

3 As the apple tree among the trees of the wood, so *is* my beloved among the sons. I sat down under his shadow with great delight, and his fruit *was* sweet to my taste.

4 He brought me to the banqueting house, and his banner over me *was* love.

5 Stay me with flagons, comfort me with apples: for I *am* sick of love.

6 His left hand *is* under my head, and his right hand doth embrace me.

7 I charge you, O ye daughters of Je-ru'salem, by the roes, and by the hinds of the field, that ye stir not up, nor awake *my* love, till he please.

8 ¶ The voice of my beloved! behold, he cometh leaping upon the mountains, skipping upon the hills.

9 My beloved is like a roe or a young hart: behold, he standeth behind our wall, he looketh forth at the windows, shewing himself through the lattice.

10 My beloved spake, and said unto me, Rise up, my love, my fair one, and come away.

11 For, lo, the winter is past, the rain is over *and* gone;

12 The flowers appear on the earth; the time of the singing *of birds* is come, and the voice of the turtle is heard in our land;

13 The fig tree putteth forth her green figs, and the vines *with* the tender grape give a *good* smell. Arise, my love, my fair one, and come away.

14 ¶ O my dove, *that art* in the clefts of the rock, in the secret *places* of the stairs, let me see thy countenance, let me hear thy voice; for sweet *is* thy voice, and thy countenance *is* comely.

15 Take us the foxes, the little foxes, that spoil the vines: for our vines *have* tender grapes.

16 ¶ My beloved *is* mine, and I *am* his: he feedeth among the lilies.

17 Until the day break, and the shadows flee away, turn, my beloved, and be thou like a roe or a young hart upon the mountains of Be'ther.

3 BY night on my bed I sought him whom my soul loveth: I sought him, but I found him not.

2 I will rise now, and go about the city in the streets, and in the broad ways I will seek him whom my soul loveth: I sought him, but I found him not.

3 The watchmen that go about the city found me: to whom I said, Saw ye him whom my soul loveth?

4 It was but a little that I passed from them, but I found him whom my soul loveth: I held him, and would not let him go, until I had brought him into my mother's house, and into the chamber of her that conceived me.

5 I charge you, O ye daughters of Je-ru'sa-lem, by the roes, and by the hinds of the field, that ye stir not up, nor awake my love, till he please.

6 ¶ Who is this that cometh out of the wilderness like pillars of smoke, perfumed with myrrh and frankincense, with all powders of the merchant?

7 Behold his bed, which is Sol'o-mon's; threescore valiant men are about it, of the valiant of Is'ra-el.

8 They all hold swords, being expert in war: every man hath his sword upon his thigh because of fear in the night.

9 King Sol'o-mon made himself a chariot of the wood of Leb'a-non.

10 He made the pillars thereof of silver, the bottom thereof of gold, the covering of it of purple, the midst thereof being paved with love, for the daughters of Je-ru'sa-lem.

11 Go forth, O ye daughters of Zi'on, and behold king Sol'o-mon with the crown wherewith his mother crowned him in the day of his espousals, and in the day of the gladness of his heart.

4 BEHOLD, thou art fair, my love; behold, thou art fair; thou hast doves' eyes within thy locks: thy hair is as a flock of goats, that appear from mount Gil'e-ad.

2 Thy teeth are like a flock of sheep that are even shorn, which came up from the washing; whereof every one bear twins, and none is barren among them.

3 Thy lips are like a thread of scarlet, and thy speech is comely: thy temples are like a piece of a pomegranate within thy locks.

4 Thy neck is like the tower of Da'vid builded for an armoury, whereon there hang a thousand bucklers, all shields of mighty men.

5 Thy two breasts are like two young roes that are twins, which feed among the lilies.

6 Until the day break, and the shadows flee away, I will get me to the mountain of myrrh, and to the hill of frankincense.

7 Thou art all fair, my love; there is no spot in thee.

8 ¶ Come with me from Leb'a-non, my spouse, with me from Leb'a-non: look from the top of Am'a-na, from the top of She'nir and Her'mon, from the lions' dens, from the mountains of the leopards.

9 Thou hast ravished my heart, my sister, my spouse; thou hast ravished my heart with one of thine eyes, with one chain of thy neck.

10 How fair is thy love, my sister, my spouse! how much better is thy love than wine! and the smell of thine ointments than all spices!

11 Thy lips, O my spouse, drop as the honeycomb: honey and milk are under thy tongue; and the smell of thy garments is like the smell of Leb'a-non.

12 A garden inclosed is my sister, my spouse; a spring shut up, a fountain sealed.

13 Thy plants are an orchard of pomegranates, with pleasant fruits; camphire, with spikenard,

14 Spikenard and saffron; calamus and cinnamon, with all trees of frankincense; myrrh and aloes, with all the chief spices:

15 A fountain of gardens, a well of living waters, and streams from Leb'a-non.

16 ¶ Awake, O north wind; and come, thou south; blow upon my garden, that the spices thereof may flow out. Let my beloved come into his garden, and eat his pleasant fruits.

5 I AM come into my garden, my sister, my spouse: I have gathered my myrrh with my spice; I have eaten my honeycomb with my honey; I have drunk my wine with my milk: eat, O friends; drink, yea, drink abundantly, O beloved.

2 ¶ I sleep, but my heart waketh: it is the voice of my beloved that knocketh, saying, Open to me, my sister, my love, my dove, my undefiled: for my head is filled with dew, and my locks with the drops of the night.

3 I have put off my coat; how shall I put it on? I have washed my feet; how shall I defile them?

4 My beloved put in his hand by the hole of the door, and my bowels were moved for him.

5 I rose up to open to my beloved; and my hands dropped with myrrh, and my fingers with sweet smelling myrrh, upon the handles of the lock.

6 I opened to my beloved; but my beloved had withdrawn himself, and was gone: my soul failed when he spake: I sought him, but I could not find him; I called him, but he gave me no answer.

7 The watchmen that went about the city found me, they smote me, they wounded me; the keepers of the walls took away my veil from me.

8 I charge you, O daughters of Je-ru'sa-lem, if ye find my beloved, that ye tell him, that I am sick of love.

9 ¶ What is thy beloved more than another beloved, O thou fairest among women? what is thy beloved more than another beloved, that thou dost so charge us?

10 My beloved is white and ruddy, the chiefest among ten thousand.

11 His head is as the most fine gold, his locks are bushy, and black as a raven.

12 His eyes are as the eyes of doves by the rivers of waters, washed with milk, and fitly set.

13 His cheeks are as a bed of spices, as sweet flowers: his lips like lilies, dropping sweet smelling myrrh.

14 His hands are as gold rings set with the beryl: his belly is as bright ivory overlaid with sapphires.

15 His legs are as pillars of marble, set upon sockets of fine gold: his countenance is as Leb'-a-non, excellent as the cedars.

16 His mouth is most sweet: yea, he is altogether lovely. This is my beloved, and this is my friend, O daughters of Je-ru'sa-lem.

6 WHITHER is thy beloved gone, O thou fairest among women? whither is thy beloved turned aside? that we may seek him with thee.

2 My beloved is gone down into his garden,

to the beds of spices, to feed in the gardens, and to gather lilies.

3 I *am* my beloved's, and my beloved *is* mine: he feedeth among the lilies.

4 ¶ Thou *art* beautiful, O my love, as Tir′zah, comely as Je-ru′sa-lem, terrible as *an army* with banners.

5 Turn away thine eyes from me, for they have overcome me: thy hair *is* as a flock of goats that appear from Gil′e-ad.

6 Thy teeth *are* as a flock of sheep which go up from the washing, whereof every one beareth twins, and *there is* not one barren among them.

7 As a piece of a pomegranate *are* thy temples within thy locks.

8 There are threescore queens, and fourscore concubines, and virgins without number.

9 My dove, my undefiled is *but* one; she *is* the *only* one of her mother, she *is* the choice *one* of her that bare her. The daughters saw her, and blessed her; *yea*, the queens and the concubines, and they praised her.

10 ¶ Who *is* she *that* looketh forth as the morning, fair as the moon, clear as the sun, *and* terrible as *an army* with banners?

11 I went down into the garden of nuts to see the fruits of the valley, *and* to see whether the vine flourished, *and* the pomegranates budded.

12 Or ever I was aware, my soul made me *like* the chariots of Am-mi′-na-dib.

13 Return, return, O Shu′lam-ite; return, return, that we may look upon thee. What will ye see in the Shu′lam-ite? As it were the company of two armies.

7 HOW beautiful are thy feet with shoes, O prince's daughter! the joints of thy thighs *are* like jewels, the work of the hands of a cunning workman.

2 Thy navel *is like* a round goblet, *which* wanteth not liquor: thy belly *is like* an heap of wheat set about with lilies.

3 Thy two breasts *are* like two young roes *that are* twins.

4 Thy neck *is* as a tower of ivory; thine eyes *like* the fishpools in Hesh′bon, by the gate of Bath-rab′bim: thy nose *is* as the tower of Leb′a-non which looketh toward Da-mas′cus.

5 Thine head upon thee *is* like Car′mel, and the hair of thine head like purple; the king *is* held in the galleries.

6 How fair and how pleasant art thou, O love, for delights!

7 This thy stature is like to a palm tree, and thy breasts to clusters *of grapes.*

8 I said, I will go up to the palm tree, I will take hold of the boughs thereof: now also thy breasts shall be as clusters of the vine, and the smell of thy nose like apples;

9 And the roof of thy mouth like the best wine for my beloved, that goeth *down* sweetly,

causing the lips of those that are asleep to speak.

10 ¶ I *am* my beloved's, and his desire *is* toward me.

11 Come, my beloved, let us go forth into the field; let us lodge in the villages.

12 Let us get up early to the vineyards; let us see if the vine flourish, *whether* the tender grape appear, *and* the pomegranates bud forth: there will I give thee my loves.

13 The mandrakes give a smell, and at our gates *are* all manner of pleasant *fruits,* new and old, *which* I have laid up for thee, O my beloved.

8 O THAT thou *wert* as my brother, that sucked the breasts of my mother! *when* I should find thee without, I would kiss thee; yea, I should not be despised.

2 I would lead thee, *and* bring thee into my mother's house, *who* would instruct me: I would cause thee to drink of spiced wine of the juice of my pomegranate.

3 His left hand *should be* under my head, and his right hand should embrace me.

4 I charge you, O daughters of Je-ru′sa-lem, that ye stir not up, nor awake *my* love, until he please.

5 Who *is* this that cometh up from the wilderness, leaning upon her beloved? I raised thee up under the apple tree: there thy mother brought thee forth: there she brought thee forth *that* bare thee.

6 ¶ Set me as a seal upon thine heart, as a seal upon thine arm: for love *is* strong as death; jealousy *is* cruel as the grave: the coals thereof *are* coals of fire, *which hath* a most vehement flame.

7 Many waters cannot quench love, neither can the floods drown it: if a man would give all the substance of his house for love, it would utterly be contemned.

8 ¶ We have a little sister, and she hath no breasts: what shall we do for our sister in the day when she shall be spoken for?

9 If *she be* a wall, we will build upon her a palace of silver: and if *she be* a door, we will inclose her with boards of cedar.

10 I *am* a wall, and my breasts like towers: then was I in his eyes as one that found favour.

11 Sol′o-mon had a vineyard at Ba′al-ha′-mon; he let out the vineyard unto keepers; every one for the fruit thereof was to bring a thousand *pieces* of silver.

12 My vineyard, which *is* mine, *is* before me: thou, O Sol′o-mon, *must have* a thousand, and those that keep the fruit thereof two hundred.

13 Thou that dwellest in the gardens, the companions hearken to thy voice: cause me to hear *it.*

14 ¶ Make haste, my beloved, and be thou like to a roe or to a young hart upon the mountains of spices.

THE BOOK OF

ISAIAH

1 THE vision of I-sa′iah the son of A′moz, which he saw concerning Ju′dah and Je-ru′sa-lem in the days of Uz-zi′ah, Jo′tham, A′-haz, *and* Hez-e-ki′ah, kings of Ju′dah.

2 Hear, O heavens, and give ear, O earth: for the LORD hath spoken, I have nourished and

brought up children, and they have rebelled against me.

3 The ox knoweth his owner, and the ass his master's crib: *but* Is′ra-el doth not know, my people doth not consider.

4 Ah sinful nation, a people laden with iniq-

uity, a seed of evildoers, children that are corrupters: they have forsaken the LORD, they have provoked the Holy One of Is'ra-el unto anger, they are gone away backward.

5 ¶ Why should ye be stricken any more? ye will revolt more and more: the whole head is sick, and the whole heart faint.

6 From the sole of the foot even unto the head *there is* no soundness in it; *but* wounds, and bruises, and putrifying sores: they have not been closed, neither bound up, neither mollified with ointment.

7 Your country *is* desolate, your cities *are* burned with fire: your land, strangers devour it in your presence, and *it is* desolate, as overthrown by strangers.

8 And the daughter of Zi'on is left as a cottage in a vineyard, as a lodge in a garden of cucumbers, as a besieged city.

9 Except the LORD of hosts had left unto us a very small remnant, we should have been as Sod'om, *and* we should have been like unto Go-mor'rah.

10 ¶ Hear the word of the LORD, ye rulers of Sod'om; give ear unto the law of our God, ye people of Go-mor'rah.

11 To what purpose *is* the multitude of your sacrifices unto me? saith the LORD: I am full of the burnt offerings of rams, and the fat of fed beasts; and I delight not in the blood of bullocks, or of lambs, or of he goats.

12 When ye come to appear before me, who hath required this at your hand, to tread my courts?

13 Bring no more vain oblations; incense is an abomination unto me; the new moons and sabbaths, the calling of assemblies, I cannot away with; *it is* iniquity, even the solemn meeting.

14 Your new moons and your appointed feasts my soul hateth: they are a trouble unto me; I am weary to bear *them*.

15 And when ye spread forth your hands, I will hide mine eyes from you: yea, when ye make many prayers, I will not hear: your hands are full of blood.

16 ¶ Wash you, make you clean; put away the evil of your doings from before mine eyes; cease to do evil;

17 Learn to do well; seek judgment, relieve the oppressed, judge the fatherless, plead for the widow.

18 Come now, and let us reason together, saith the LORD: though your sins be as scarlet, they shall be as white as snow; though they be red like crimson, they shall be as wool.

19 If ye be willing and obedient, ye shall eat the good of the land:

20 But if ye refuse and rebel, ye shall be devoured with the sword: for the mouth of the LORD hath spoken *it*.

21 ¶ How is the faithful city become an harlot! it was full of judgment; righteousness lodged in it; but now murderers.

22 Thy silver is become dross, thy wine mixed with water:

23 Thy princes *are* rebellious, and companions of thieves: every one loveth gifts, and followeth after rewards: they judge not the fatherless, neither doth the cause of the widow come unto them.

24 Therefore saith the Lord, the LORD of hosts, the mighty One of Is'ra-el, Ah, I will ease me of mine adversaries, and avenge me of mine enemies:

25 ¶ And I will turn my hand upon thee, and purely purge away thy dross, and take away all thy tin:

26 And I will restore thy judges as at the first, and thy counsellors as at the beginning: afterward thou shalt be called, The city of righteousness, the faithful city.

27 Zi'on shall be redeemed with judgment, and her converts with righteousness.

28 ¶ And the destruction of the transgressors and of the sinners *shall be* together, and they that forsake the LORD shall be consumed.

29 For they shall be ashamed of the oaks which ye have desired, and ye shall be confounded for the gardens that ye have chosen.

30 For ye shall be as an oak whose leaf fadeth, and as a garden that hath no water.

31 And the strong shall be as tow, and the maker of it as a spark, and they shall both burn together, and none shall quench *them*.

2 THE word that I-sa'iah the son of A'moz saw concerning Ju'dah and Je-ru'sa-lem.

2 And it shall come to pass in the last days, *that* the mountain of the LORD's house shall be established in the top of the mountains, and shall be exalted above the hills; and all nations shall flow unto it.

3 And many people shall go and say, Come ye, and let us go up to the mountain of the LORD, to the house of the God of Ja'cob; and he will teach us of his ways, and we will walk in his paths: for out of Zi'on shall go forth the law, and the word of the LORD from Je-ru'sa-lem.

4 And he shall judge among the nations, and shall rebuke many people: and they shall beat their swords into plowshares, and their spears into pruninghooks: nation shall not lift up sword against nation, neither shall they learn war any more.

5 O house of Ja'cob, come ye, and let us walk in the light of the LORD.

6 ¶ Therefore thou hast forsaken thy people the house of Ja'cob, because they be replenished from the east, and *are* soothsayers like the Phi-lis'tines, and they please themselves in the children of strangers.

7 Their land also is full of silver and gold, neither *is there any* end of their treasures; their land is also full of horses, neither *is there any* end of their chariots:

8 Their land also is full of idols; they worship the work of their own hands, that which their own fingers have made:

9 And the mean man boweth down, and the great man humbleth himself: therefore forgive them not.

10 ¶ Enter into the rock, and hide thee in the dust, for fear of the LORD, and for the glory of his majesty.

11 The lofty looks of man shall be humbled, and the haughtiness of men shall be bowed down, and the LORD alone shall be exalted in that day.

12 For the day of the LORD of hosts *shall be* upon every *one that is* proud and lofty, and upon every *one that is* lifted up; and he shall be brought low:

13 And upon all the cedars of Leb'a-non, *that are* high and lifted up, and upon all the oaks of Ba'shan,

14 And upon all the high mountains, and upon all the hills *that are* lifted up,

15 And upon every high tower, and upon every fenced wall,

16 And upon all the ships of Tar'shish, and upon all pleasant pictures.

17 And the loftiness of man shall be bowed

down, and the haughtiness of men shall be made low: and the LORD alone shall be exalted in that day.

18 And the idols he shall utterly abolish.

19 And they shall go into the holes of the rocks, and into the caves of the earth, for fear of the LORD, and for the glory of his majesty, when he ariseth to shake terribly the earth.

20 In that day a man shall cast his idols of silver, and his idols of gold, which they made *each one* for himself to worship, to the moles and to the bats;

21 To go into the clefts of the rocks, and into the tops of the ragged rocks, for fear of the LORD, and for the glory of his majesty, when he ariseth to shake terribly the earth.

22 Cease ye from man, whose breath *is* in his nostrils: for wherein is he to be accounted of?

3 FOR, behold, the Lord, the LORD of hosts, doth take away from Je-ru'sa-lem and from Ju'dah the stay and the staff, the whole stay of bread, and the whole stay of water,

2 The mighty man, and the man of war, the judge, and the prophet, and the prudent, and the ancient,

3 The captain of fifty, and the honourable man, and the counsellor, and the cunning artificer, and the eloquent orator.

4 And I will give children *to be* their princes, and babes shall rule over them.

5 And the people shall be oppressed, every one by another, and every one by his neighbour: the child shall behave himself proudly against the ancient, and the base against the honourable.

6 When a man shall take hold of his brother of the house of his father, *saying*, Thou hast clothing, be thou our ruler, and *let* this ruin *be* under thy hand:

7 In that day shall he swear, saying, I will not be an healer; for in my house *is* neither bread nor clothing: make me not a ruler of the people.

8 For Je-ru'sa-lem is ruined, and Ju'dah is fallen: because their tongue and their doings *are* against the LORD, to provoke the eyes of his glory.

9 ¶ The shew of their countenance doth witness against them; and they declare their sin as Sod'om, they hide *it* not. Woe unto their soul! for they have rewarded evil unto themselves.

10 Say ye to the righteous, that *it shall be* well *with him*: for they shall eat the fruit of their doings.

11 Woe unto the wicked! *it shall be* ill *with him*: for the reward of his hands shall be given him.

12 ¶ *As for* my people, children *are* their oppressors, and women rule over them. O my people, they which lead thee cause *thee* to err, and destroy the way of thy paths.

13 The LORD standeth up to plead, and standeth to judge the people.

14 The LORD will enter into judgment with the ancients of his people, and the princes thereof: for ye have eaten up the vineyard; the spoil of the poor *is* in your houses.

15 What mean ye *that* ye beat my people to pieces, and grind the faces of the poor? saith the Lord GOD of hosts.

16 ¶ Moreover the LORD saith, Because the daughters of Zi'on are haughty, and walk with stretched forth necks and wanton eyes, walking and mincing *as* they go, and making a tinkling with their feet:

17 Therefore the Lord will smite with a scab the crown of the head of the daughters of Zi'on,

and the LORD will discover their secret parts.

18 In that day the Lord will take away the bravery of *their* tinkling ornaments *about their feet*, and *their* cauls, and *their* round tires like the moon,

19 The chains, and the bracelets, and the mufflers,

20 The bonnets, and the ornaments of the legs, and the headbands, and the tablets, and the earrings,

21 The rings, and nose jewels,

22 The changeable suits of apparel, and the mantles, and the wimples, and the crisping pins,

23 The glasses, and the fine linen, and the hoods, and the vails.

24 And it shall come to pass, *that* instead of sweet smell there shall be stink; and instead of a girdle a rent; and instead of well set hair baldness; and instead of a stomacher a girding of sackcloth; *and* burning instead of beauty.

25 Thy men shall fall by the sword, and thy mighty in the war.

26 And her gates shall lament and mourn; and she *being* desolate shall sit upon the ground.

4 AND in that day seven women shall take hold of one man, saying, We will eat our own bread, and wear our own apparel: only let us be called by thy name, to take away our reproach.

2 In that day shall the branch of the LORD be beautiful and glorious, and the fruit of the earth *shall be* excellent and comely for them that are escaped of Is'ra-el.

3 And it shall come to pass, *that he that is* left in Zi'on, and *he that* remaineth in Je-ru'sa-lem, shall be called holy, *even* every one that is written among the living in Je-ru'sa-lem:

4 When the Lord shall have washed away the filth of the daughters of Zi'on, and shall have purged the blood of Je-ru'sa-lem from the midst thereof by the spirit of judgment, and by the spirit of burning.

5 And the LORD will create upon every dwelling place of mount Zi'on, and upon her assemblies, a cloud and smoke by day, and the shining of a flaming fire by night: for upon all the glory *shall be* a defence.

6 And there shall be a tabernacle for a shadow in the daytime from the heat, and for a place of refuge, and for a covert from storm and from rain.

5 NOW will I sing to my wellbeloved a song of my beloved touching his vineyard. My wellbeloved hath a vineyard in a very fruitful hill:

2 And he fenced it, and gathered out the stones thereof, and planted it with the choicest vine, and built a tower in the midst of it, and also made a winepress therein: and he looked that it should bring forth grapes, and it brought forth wild grapes.

3 And now, O inhabitants of Je-ru'sa-lem, and men of Ju'dah, judge, I pray you, betwixt me and my vineyard.

4 What could have been done more to my vineyard, that I have not done in it? wherefore, when I looked that it should bring forth grapes, brought it forth wild grapes?

5 And now go to; I will tell you what I will do to my vineyard: I will take away the hedge thereof, and it shall be eaten up; *and* break down the wall thereof, and it shall be trodden down:

6 And I will lay it waste: it shall not be pruned, nor digged; but there shall come up briers and thorns: I will also command the clouds that they rain no rain upon it.

7 For the vineyard of the LORD of hosts *is* the house of Is'ra-el, and the men of Ju'dah his pleasant plant: and he looked for judgment, but behold oppression; for righteousness, but behold a cry.

8 ¶ Woe unto them that join house to house, *that* lay field to field, till *there be* no place, that they may be placed alone in the midst of the earth!

9 In mine ears *said* the LORD of hosts, Of a truth many houses shall be desolate, *even* great and fair, without inhabitant.

10 Yea, ten acres of vineyard shall yield one bath, and the seed of an homer shall yield an ephah.

11 ¶ Woe unto them that rise up early in the morning, *that* they may follow strong drink; that continue until night, *till* wine inflame them!

12 And the harp, and the viol, the tabret, and pipe, and wine, are in their feasts: but they regard not the work of the LORD, neither consider the operation of his hands.

13 ¶ Therefore my people are gone into captivity, because *they have* no knowledge: and their honourable men *are* famished, and their multitude dried up with thirst.

14 Therefore hell hath enlarged herself, and opened her mouth without measure: and their glory, and their multitude, and their pomp, and he that rejoiceth, shall descend into it.

15 And the mean man shall be brought down, and the mighty man shall be humbled, and the eyes of the lofty shall be humbled:

16 But the LORD of hosts shall be exalted in judgment, and God that is holy shall be sanctified in righteousness.

17 Then shall the lambs feed after their manner, and the waste places of the fat ones shall strangers eat.

18 Woe unto them that draw iniquity with cords of vanity, and sin as it were with a cart rope:

19 That say, Let him make speed, *and* hasten his work, that we may see *it:* and let the counsel of the Holy One of Is'ra-el draw nigh and come, that we may know *it!*

20 ¶ Woe unto them that call evil good, and good evil; that put darkness for light, and light for darkness; that put bitter for sweet, and sweet for bitter!

21 Woe unto *them that are* wise in their own eyes, and prudent in their own sight!

22 Woe unto *them that are* mighty to drink wine, and men of strength to mingle strong drink:

23 Which justify the wicked for reward, and take away the righteousness of the righteous from him!

24 Therefore as the fire devoureth the stubble, and the flame consumeth the chaff, *so* their root shall be as rottenness, and their blossom shall go up as dust: because they have cast away the law of the LORD of hosts, and despised the word of the Holy One of Is'ra-el.

25 Therefore is the anger of the LORD kindled against his people, and he hath stretched forth his hand against them, and hath smitten them: and the hills did tremble, and their carcases *were* torn in the midst of the streets. For all this his anger is not turned away, but his hand *is* stretched out still.

26 ¶ And he will lift up an ensign to the nations from far, and will hiss unto them from the end of the earth: and, behold, they shall come with speed swiftly:

27 None shall be weary nor stumble among them; none shall slumber nor sleep; neither shall the girdle of their loins be loosed, nor the latchet of their shoes be broken:

28 Whose arrows *are* sharp, and all their bows bent, their horses' hoofs shall be counted like flint, and their wheels like a whirlwind:

29 Their roaring *shall be* like a lion, they shall roar like young lions: yea, they shall roar, and lay hold of the prey, and shall carry *it* away safe, and none shall deliver *it.*

30 And in that day they shall roar against them like the roaring of the sea: and if *one* look unto the land, behold darkness *and* sorrow, and the light is darkened in the heavens thereof.

6 IN the year that king Uz-zi'ah died I saw also the Lord sitting upon a throne, high and lifted up, and his train filled the temple.

2 Above it stood the seraphims: each one had six wings; with twain he covered his face, and with twain he covered his feet, and with twain he did fly.

3 And one cried unto another, and said, Holy, holy, holy, *is* the LORD of hosts: the whole earth *is* full of his glory.

4 And the posts of the door moved at the voice of him that cried, and the house was filled with smoke.

5 ¶ Then said I, Woe *is* me! for I am undone; because I *am* a man of unclean lips, and I dwell in the midst of a people of unclean lips: for mine eyes have seen the King, the LORD of hosts.

6 Then flew one of the seraphims unto me, having a live coal in his hand, *which* he had taken with the tongs from off the altar:

7 And he laid *it* upon my mouth, and said, Lo, this hath touched thy lips; and thine iniquity is taken away, and thy sin purged.

8 Also I heard the voice of the Lord, saying, Whom shall I send, and who will go for us? Then said I, Here *am* I; send me.

9 ¶ And he said, Go, and tell this people, Hear ye indeed, but understand not; and see ye indeed, but perceive not.

10 Make the heart of this people fat, and make their ears heavy, and shut their eyes; lest they see with their eyes, and hear with their ears, and understand with their heart, and convert, and be healed.

11 Then said I, Lord, how long? And he answered, Until the cities be wasted without inhabitant, and the houses without man, and the land be utterly desolate,

12 And the LORD have removed men far away, and *there be* a great forsaking in the midst of the land.

13 ¶ But yet in it *shall be* a tenth, and *it* shall return, and shall be eaten: as a teil tree, and as an oak, whose substance *is* in them, when they cast *their leaves: so* the holy seed *shall be* the substance thereof.

7 AND it came to pass in the days of A'haz the son of Jo'tham, the son of Uz-zi'ah, king of Ju'dah, *that* Re'zin the king of Syr'i-a, and Pe'kah the son of Rem-a-li'ah, king of Is'ra-el, went up toward Je-ru'sa-lem to war against it, but could not prevail against it.

2 And it was told the house of Da'vid, saying, Syr'i-a is confederate with E'phra-im. And his heart was moved, and the heart of his people, as the trees of the wood are moved with the wind.

3 Then said the LORD unto I-sa'iah, Go forth now to meet A'haz, thou, and She'ar-ja'shub

thy son, at the end of the conduit of the upper pool in the highway of the fuller's field;

4 And say unto him, Take heed, and be quiet; fear not, neither be fainthearted for the two tails of these smoking firebrands, for the fierce anger of Re′zin with Syr′i-a, and of the son of Rem-a-li′ah.

5 Because Syr′i-a, E′phra-im, and the son of Rem-a-li′ah, have taken evil counsel against thee, saying,

6 Let us go up against Ju′dah, and vex it, and let us make a breach therein for us, and set a king in the midst of it, even the son of Ta′be-al:

7 Thus saith the Lord God, It shall not stand, neither shall it come to pass.

8 For the head of Syr′i-a is Da-mas′cus, and the head of Da-mas′cus is Re′zin; and within threescore and five years shall E′phra-im be broken, that it be not a people.

9 And the head of E′phra-im is Sa-ma′ri-a, and the head of Sa-ma′ri-a is Rem-a-li′ah's son. If ye will not believe, surely ye shall not be established.

10 ¶ Moreover the Lord spake again unto A′haz, saying,

11 Ask thee a sign of the Lord thy God; ask it either in the depth, or in the height above.

12 But A′haz said, I will not ask, neither will I tempt the Lord.

13 And he said, Hear ye now, O house of Da′-vid; Is it a small thing for you to weary men, but will ye weary my God also?

14 Therefore the Lord himself shall give you a sign; Behold, a virgin shall conceive, and bear a son, and shall call his name Im-man′u-el.

15 Butter and honey shall he eat, that he may know to refuse the evil, and choose the good.

16 For before the child shall know to refuse the evil, and choose the good, the land that thou abhorrest shall be forsaken of both her kings.

17 ¶ The Lord shall bring upon thee, and upon thy people, and upon thy father's house, days that have not come, from the day that E′-phra-im departed from Ju′dah; even the king of As-syr′i-a.

18 And it shall come to pass in that day, that the Lord shall hiss for the fly that is in the uttermost part of the rivers of E′gypt, and for the bee that is in the land of As-syr′i-a.

19 And they shall come, and shall rest all of them in the desolate valleys, and in the holes of the rocks, and upon all thorns, and upon all bushes.

20 In the same day shall the Lord shave with a razor that is hired, namely, by them beyond the river, by the king of As-syr′i-a, the head, and the hair of the feet: and it shall also consume the beard.

21 And it shall come to pass in that day, that a man shall nourish a young cow, and two sheep;

22 And it shall come to pass, for the abundance of milk that they shall give he shall eat butter: for butter and honey shall every one eat that is left in the land.

23 And it shall come to pass in that day, that every place shall be, where there were a thousand vines at a thousand silverlings, it shall even be for briers and thorns.

24 With arrows and with bows shall men come thither; because all the land shall become briers and thorns.

25 And on all hills that shall be digged with the mattock, there shall not come thither the fear of briers and thorns: but it shall be for the sending forth of oxen, and for the treading of lesser cattle.

8 MOREOVER the Lord said unto me, Take thee a great roll, and write in it with a man's pen concerning Ma′her-shal′al-hash′-baz.

2 And I took unto me faithful witnesses to record, U-ri′ah the priest, and Zech-a-ri′ah the son of Je-ber-e-chi′ah.

3 And I went unto the prophetess; and she conceived, and bare a son. Then said the Lord to me, Call his name Ma′her-shal′al-hash′-baz.

4 For before the child shall have knowledge to cry, My father, and my mother, the riches of Da-mas′cus and the spoil of Sa-ma′ri-a shall be taken away before the king of As-syr′i-a.

5 ¶ The Lord spake also unto me again, saying,

6 Forasmuch as this people refuseth the waters of Shi-lo′ah that go softly, and rejoice in Re′zin and Rem-a-li′ah's son;

7 Now therefore, behold, the Lord bringeth up upon them the waters of the river, strong and many, even the king of As-syr′i-a, and all his glory: and he shall come up over all his channels, and go over all his banks:

8 And he shall pass through Ju′dah; he shall overflow and go over, he shall reach even to the neck; and the stretching out of his wings shall fill the breadth of thy land, O Im-man′u-el.

9 ¶ Associate yourselves, O ye people, and ye shall be broken in pieces; and give ear, all ye of far countries: gird yourselves, and ye shall be broken in pieces; gird yourselves, and ye shall be broken in pieces.

10 Take counsel together, and it shall come to nought; speak the word, and it shall not stand: for God is with us.

11 ¶ For the Lord spake thus to me with a strong hand, and instructed me that I should not walk in the way of this people, saying,

12 Say ye not, A confederacy, to all them to whom this people shall say, A confederacy; neither fear ye their fear, nor be afraid.

13 Sanctify the Lord of hosts himself; and let him be your fear, and let him be your dread.

14 And he shall be for a sanctuary; but for a stone of stumbling and for a rock of offence to both the houses of Is′ra-el, for a gin and for a snare to the inhabitants of Je-ru′sa-lem.

15 And many among them shall stumble, and fall, and be broken, and be snared, and be taken.

16 Bind up the testimony, seal the law among my disciples.

17 And I will wait upon the Lord, that hideth his face from the house of Ja′cob, and I will look for him.

18 Behold, I and the children whom the Lord hath given me are for signs and for wonders in Is′ra-el from the Lord of hosts, which dwelleth in mount Zi′on.

19 ¶ And when they shall say unto you, Seek unto them that have familiar spirits, and unto wizards that peep, and that mutter: should not a people seek unto their God? for the living to the dead?

20 To the law and to the testimony: if they speak not according to this word, it is because there is no light in them.

21 And they shall pass through it, hardly bestead and hungry: and it shall come to pass, that when they shall be hungry, they shall fret themselves, and curse their king and their God, and look upward.

22 And they shall look unto the earth; and behold trouble and darkness, dimness of anguish; and they shall be driven to darkness.

9 NEVERTHELESS the dimness *shall* not *be* such as *was* in her vexation, when at the first he lightly afflicted the land of Zeb'u-lun and the land of Naph'ta-li, and afterward did more grievously afflict *her by* the way of the sea, beyond Jor'dan, in Gal'i-lee of the nations.

2 The people that walked in darkness have seen a great light: they that dwell in the land of the shadow of death, upon them hath the light shined.

3 Thou hast multiplied the nation, *and* not increased the joy: they joy before thee according to the joy in harvest, *and* as *men* rejoice when they divide the spoil.

4 For thou hast broken the yoke of his burden, and the staff of his shoulder, the rod of his oppressor, as in the day of Mid'i-an.

5 For every battle of the warrior *is* with confused noise, and garments rolled in blood; but *this* shall be with burning *and* fuel of fire.

6 For unto us a child is born, unto us a son is given: and the government shall be upon his shoulder: and his name shall be called Wonderful, Counsellor, The mighty God, The everlasting Father, The Prince of Peace.

7 Of the increase of *his* government and peace *there shall be* no end, upon the throne of Da'vid, and upon his kingdom, to order it, and to establish it with judgment and with justice from henceforth even for ever. The zeal of the LORD of hosts will perform this.

8 ¶ The Lord sent a word into Ja'cob, and it hath lighted upon Is'ra-el.

9 And all the people shall know, *even* E'phra-im and the inhabitant of Sa-ma'ri-a, that say in the pride and stoutness of heart,

10 The bricks are fallen down, but we will build with hewn stones: the sycomores are cut down, but we will change *them* into cedars.

11 Therefore the LORD shall set up the adversaries of Re'zin against him, and join his enemies together;

12 The Syr'i-ans before, and the Phi-lis'tines behind; and they shall devour Is'ra-el with open mouth. For all this his anger is not turned away, but his hand *is* stretched out still.

13 ¶ For the people turneth not unto him that smiteth them, neither do they seek the LORD of hosts.

14 Therefore the LORD will cut off from Is'ra-el head and tail, branch and rush, in one day.

15 The ancient and honourable, he *is* the head; and the prophet that teacheth lies, he *is* the tail.

16 For the leaders of this people cause *them* to err; and *they that are* led of them *are* destroyed.

17 Therefore the Lord shall have no joy in their young men, neither shall have mercy on their fatherless and widows: for every one *is* an hypocrite and an evildoer, and every mouth speaketh folly. For all this his anger is not turned away, but his hand *is* stretched out still.

18 ¶ For wickedness burneth as the fire: it shall devour the briers and thorns, and shall kindle in the thickets of the forest, and they shall mount up *like* the lifting up of smoke.

19 Through the wrath of the LORD of hosts is the land darkened, and the people shall be as the fuel of the fire: no man shall spare his brother.

20 And he shall snatch on the right hand, and be hungry; and he shall eat on the left hand, and they shall not be satisfied: they shall eat every man the flesh of his own arm:

21 Ma-nas'seh, E'phra-im; and E'phra-im, Ma-nas'seh: *and* they together *shall be* against Ju'dah. For all this his anger is not turned away, but his hand *is* stretched out still.

10 WOE unto them that decree unrighteous decrees, and that write grievousness *which* they have prescribed:

2 To turn aside the needy from judgment, and to take away the right from the poor of my people, that widows may be their prey, and *that* they may rob the fatherless!

3 And what will ye do in the day of visitation, and in the desolation *which* shall come from far? to whom will ye flee for help? and where will ye leave your glory?

4 Without me they shall bow down under the prisoners, and they shall fall under the slain. For all this his anger is not turned away, but his hand *is* stretched out still.

5 ¶ O As-syr'i-an, the rod of mine anger, and the staff in their hand is mine indignation.

6 I will send him against an hypocritical nation, and against the people of my wrath will I give him a charge, to take the spoil, and to take the prey, and to tread them down like the mire of the streets.

7 Howbeit he meaneth not so, neither doth his heart think so; but *it is* in his heart to destroy and cut off nations not a few.

8 For he saith, *Are* not my princes altogether kings?

9 *Is* not Cal'no as Car'che-mish? *is* not Ha'math as Ar'pad? *is* not Sa-ma'ri-a as Da-mas'-cus?

10 As my hand hath found the kingdoms of the idols, and whose graven images did excel them of Je-ru'sa-lem and of Sa-ma'ri-a;

11 Shall I not, as I have done unto Sa-ma'ri-a and her idols, so do to Je-ru'sa-lem and her idols?

12 Wherefore it shall come to pass, *that* when the Lord hath performed his whole work upon mount Zi'on and on Je-ru'sa-lem, I will punish the fruit of the stout heart of the king of As-syr'i-a, and the glory of his high looks.

13 For he saith, By the strength of my hand I have done *it*, and by my wisdom; for I am prudent: and I have removed the bounds of the people, and have robbed their treasures, and I have put down the inhabitants like a valiant *man*:

14 And my hand hath found as a nest the riches of the people: and as one gathereth eggs *that are* left, have I gathered all the earth; and there was none that moved the wing, or opened the mouth, or peeped.

15 Shall the ax boast itself against him that heweth therewith? *or* shall the saw magnify itself against him that shaketh it? as if the rod should shake *itself* against them that lift it up, *or* as if the staff should lift up *itself, as if it were* no wood.

16 Therefore shall the Lord, the Lord of hosts, send among his fat ones leanness; and under his glory he shall kindle a burning like the burning of a fire.

17 And the light of Is'ra-el shall be for a fire, and his Holy One for a flame: and it shall burn and devour his thorns and his briers in one day;

18 And shall consume the glory of his forest, and of his fruitful field, both soul and body: and they shall be as when a standardbearer fainteth.

19 And the rest of the trees of his forest shall be few, that a child may write them.

20 ¶ And it shall come to pass in that day, *that* the remnant of Is'ra-el, and such as are escaped of the house of Ja'cob, shall no more again stay upon him that smote them; but shall

stay upon the LORD, the Holy One of Is'ra-el, in truth.

21 The remnant shall return, *even* the remnant of Ja'cob, unto the mighty God.

22 For though thy people Is'ra-el be as the sand of the sea, *yet* a remnant of them shall return: the consumption decreed shall overflow with righteousness.

23 For the Lord GOD of hosts shall make a consumption, even determined, in the midst of all the land.

24 ¶ Therefore thus saith the Lord GOD of hosts, O my people that dwellest in Zi'on, be not afraid of the As-syr'i-an: he shall smite thee with a rod, and shall lift up his staff against thee, after the manner of E'gypt.

25 For yet a very little while, and the indignation shall cease, and mine anger in their destruction.

26 And the LORD of hosts shall stir up a scourge for him according to the slaughter of Mid'i-an at the rock of O'reb: and *as* his rod *was* upon the sea, so shall he lift it up after the manner of E'gypt.

27 And it shall come to pass in that day, *that* his burden shall be taken away from off thy shoulder, and his yoke from off thy neck, and the yoke shall be destroyed because of the anointing.

28 He is come to A-i'ath, he is passed to Mig'-ron; at Mich'mash he hath laid up his carriages.

29 They are gone over the passage: they have taken up their lodging at Ge'ba; Ra'mah is afraid; Gib'e-ah of Saul is fled.

30 Lift up thy voice, O daughter of Gal'lim: cause it to be heard unto La'ish, O poor An'a-thoth.

31 Mad-me'nah is removed; the inhabitants of Ge'bim gather themselves to flee.

32 As yet shall he remain at Nob that day: he shall shake his hand *against* the mount of the daughter of Zi'on, the hill of Je-ru'sa-lem.

33 Behold, the Lord, the LORD of hosts, shall lop the bough with terror: and the high ones of stature *shall be* hewn down, and the haughty shall be humbled.

34 And he shall cut down the thickets of the forest with iron, and Leb'a-non shall fall by a mighty one.

11 AND there shall come forth a rod out of the stem of Jes'se, and a Branch shall grow out of his roots:

2 And the spirit of the LORD shall rest upon him, the spirit of wisdom and understanding, the spirit of counsel and might, the spirit of knowledge and of the fear of the LORD;

3 And shall make him of quick understanding in the fear of the LORD: and he shall not judge after the sight of his eyes, neither reprove after the hearing of his ears:

4 But with righteousness shall he judge the poor, and reprove with equity for the meek of the earth: and he shall smite the earth with the rod of his mouth, and with the breath of his lips shall he slay the wicked.

5 And righteousness shall be the girdle of his loins, and faithfulness the girdle of his reins.

6 The wolf also shall dwell with the lamb, and the leopard shall lie down with the kid; and the calf and the young lion and the fatling together; and a little child shall lead them.

7 And the cow and the bear shall feed; their young ones shall lie down together: and the lion shall eat straw like the ox.

8 And the sucking child shall play on the hole of the asp, and the weaned child shall put his hand on the cockatrice' den.

9 They shall not hurt nor destroy in all my holy mountain: for the earth shall be full of the knowledge of the LORD, as the waters cover the sea.

10 ¶ And in that day there shall be a root of Jes'se, which shall stand for an ensign of the people; to it shall the Gen-tiles seek: and his rest shall be glorious.

11 And it shall come to pass in that day, *that* the Lord shall set his hand again the second time to recover the remnant of his people, which shall be left, from As-syr'i-a, and from E'gypt, and from Path'ros, and from Cush, and from E'lam, and from Shi'nar, and from Ha'-math, and from the islands of the sea.

12 And he shall set up an ensign for the nations, and shall assemble the outcasts of Is'ra-el, and gather together the dispersed of Ju'dah from the four corners of the earth.

13 The envy also of E'phra-im shall depart, and the adversaries of Ju'dah shall be cut off: E'phra-im shall not envy Ju'dah, and Ju'dah shall not vex E'phra-im.

14 But they shall fly upon the shoulders of the Phi-lis'tines toward the west; they shall spoil them of the east together: they shall lay their hand upon E'dom and Mo'ab; and the children of Am'mon shall obey them.

15 And the LORD shall utterly destroy the tongue of the E-gyp'tian sea; and with his mighty wind shall he shake his hand over the river, and shall smite it in the seven streams, and make *men* go over dryshod.

16 And there shall be an highway for the remnant of his people, which shall be left, from As-syr'i-a; like as it was to Is'ra-el in the day that he came up out of the land of E'gypt.

12 AND in that day thou shalt say, O LORD, I will praise thee: though thou wast angry with me, thine anger is turned away, and thou comfortedst me.

2 Behold, God *is* my salvation; I will trust, and not be afraid: for the LORD JE-HO'VAH *is* my strength and *my* song; he also is become my salvation.

3 Therefore with joy shall ye draw water out of the wells of salvation.

4 And in that day shall ye say, Praise the LORD, call upon his name, declare his doings among the people, make mention that his name is exalted.

5 Sing unto the LORD; for he hath done excellent things: this *is* known in all the earth.

6 Cry out and shout, thou inhabitant of Zi'on: for great *is* the Holy One of Is'ra-el in the midst of thee.

13 THE burden of Bab'y-lon, which I-sa'iah the son of A'moz did see.

2 Lift ye up a banner upon the high mountain, exalt the voice unto them, shake the hand, that they may go into the gates of the nobles.

3 I have commanded my sanctified ones, I have also called my mighty ones for mine anger, *even* them that rejoice in my highness.

4 The noise of a multitude in the mountains, like as of a great people; a tumultuous noise of the kingdoms of nations gathered together: the LORD of hosts mustereth the host of the battle.

5 They come from a far country, from the end of heaven, *even* the LORD, and the weapons of his indignation, to destroy the whole land.

6 ¶ Howl ye; for the day of the LORD *is* at

hand; it shall come as a destruction from the Almighty.

7 Therefore shall all hands be faint, and every man's heart shall melt:

8 And they shall be afraid: pangs and sorrows shall take hold of them; they shall be in pain as a woman that travaileth: they shall be amazed one at another; their faces *shall be as* flames.

9 Behold, the day of the LORD cometh, cruel both with wrath and fierce anger, to lay the land desolate: and he shall destroy the sinners thereof out of it.

10 For the stars of heaven and the constellations thereof shall not give their light: the sun shall be darkened in his going forth, and the moon shall not cause her light to shine.

11 And I will punish the world for *their* evil, and the wicked for their iniquity; and I will cause the arrogancy of the proud to cease, and will lay low the haughtiness of the terrible.

12 I will make a man more precious than fine gold; even a man than the golden wedge of O'-phir.

13 Therefore I will shake the heavens, and the earth shall remove out of her place, in the wrath of the LORD of hosts, and in the day of his fierce anger.

14 And it shall be as the chased roe, and as a sheep that no man taketh up: they shall every man turn to his own people, and flee every one into his own land.

15 Every one that is found shall be thrust through; and every one that is joined *unto them* shall fall by the sword.

16 Their children also shall be dashed to pieces before their eyes; their houses shall be spoiled, and their wives ravished.

17 Behold, I will stir up the Medes against them, which shall not regard silver; and *as for* gold, they shall not delight in it.

18 *Their* bows also shall dash the young men to pieces; and they shall have no pity on the fruit of the womb; their eye shall not spare children.

19 ¶ And Bab'y-lon, the glory of kingdoms, the beauty of the Chal'dees' excellency, shall be as when God overthrew Sod'om and Go-mor'-rah.

20 It shall never be inhabited, neither shall it be dwelt in from generation to generation: neither shall the A-ra'bi-an pitch tent there; neither shall the shepherds make their fold there.

21 But wild beasts of the desert shall lie there; and their houses shall be full of doleful creatures; and owls shall dwell there, and satyrs shall dance there.

22 And the wild beasts of the islands shall cry in their desolate houses, and dragons in *their* pleasant palaces: and her time *is* near to come, and her days shall not be prolonged.

14 FOR the LORD will have mercy on Ja'-cob, and will yet choose Is'ra-el, and set them in their own land: and the strangers shall be joined with them, and they shall cleave to the house of Ja'cob.

2 And the people shall take them, and bring them to their place: and the house of Is'ra-el shall possess them in the land of the LORD for servants and handmaids: and they shall take them captives, whose captives they were; and they shall rule over their oppressors.

3 And it shall come to pass in the day that the LORD shall give thee rest from thy sorrow, and from thy fear, and from the hard bondage wherein thou wast made to serve,

4 ¶ That thou shalt take up this proverb against the king of Bab'y-lon, and say, How hath the oppressor ceased! the golden city ceased!

5 The LORD hath broken the staff of the wicked, *and* the sceptre of the rulers.

6 He who smote the people in wrath with a continual stroke, he that ruled the nations in anger, is persecuted, *and* none hindereth.

7 The whole earth is at rest, *and* is quiet: they break forth into singing.

8 Yea, the fir trees rejoice at thee, *and* the cedars of Leb'a-non, *saying,* Since thou art laid down, no feller is come up against us.

9 Hell from beneath is moved for thee to meet *thee* at thy coming: it stirreth up the dead for thee, *even* all the chief ones of the earth; it hath raised up from their thrones all the kings of the nations.

10 All they shall speak and say unto thee, Art thou also become weak as we? art thou become like unto us?

11 Thy pomp is brought down to the grave, *and* the noise of thy viols: the worm is spread under thee, and the worms cover thee.

12 How art thou fallen from heaven, O Lu'ci-fer, son of the morning! *how* art thou cut down to the ground, which didst weaken the nations!

13 For thou hast said in thine heart, I will ascend into heaven, I will exalt my throne above the stars of God: I will sit also upon the mount of the congregation, in the sides of the north:

14 I will ascend above the heights of the clouds; I will be like the most High.

15 Yet thou shalt be brought down to hell, to the sides of the pit.

16 They that see thee shall narrowly look upon thee, *and* consider thee, *saying, Is* this the man that made the earth to tremble, that did shake kingdoms;

17 *That* made the world as a wilderness, and destroyed the cities thereof; *that* opened not the house of his prisoners?

18 All the kings of the nations, *even* all of them, lie in glory, every one in his own house.

19 But thou art cast out of thy grave like an abominable branch, *and as* the raiment of those that are slain, thrust through with a sword, that go down to the stones of the pit; as a carcase trodden under feet.

20 Thou shalt not be joined with them in burial, because thou hast destroyed thy land, *and* slain thy people: the seed of evildoers shall never be renowned.

21 Prepare slaughter for his children for the iniquity of their fathers; that they do not rise, nor possess the land, nor fill the face of the world with cities.

22 For I will rise up against them, saith the LORD of hosts, and cut off from Bab'y-lon the name, and remnant, and son, and nephew, saith the LORD.

23 I will also make it a possession for the bittern, and pools of water: and I will sweep it with the besom of destruction, saith the LORD of hosts.

24 ¶ The LORD of hosts hath sworn, saying, Surely as I have thought, so shall it come to pass; and as I have purposed, *so* shall it stand:

25 That I will break the As-syr'i-an in my land, and upon my mountains tread him under foot: then shall his yoke depart from off them, and his burden depart from off their shoulders.

26 This *is* the purpose that is purposed upon the whole earth: and this *is* the hand that is stretched out upon all the nations.

27 For the LORD of hosts hath purposed, and

who shall disannul *it*? and his hand *is* stretched out, and who shall turn it back?

28 In the year that king A'haz died was this burden.

29 ¶ Rejoice not thou, whole Pal-es-ti'na, because the rod of him that smote thee is broken: for out of the serpent's root shall come forth a cockatrice, and his fruit *shall be* a fiery flying serpent.

30 And the firstborn of the poor shall feed, and the needy shall lie down in safety: and I will kill thy root with famine, and he shall slay thy remnant.

31 Howl, O gate; cry, O city; thou, whole Pal-es-ti'na, *art* dissolved: for there shall come from the north a smoke, and none *shall be* alone in his appointed times.

32 What shall *one* then answer the messengers of the nation? That the LORD hath founded Zi'on, and the poor of his people shall trust in it.

15 THE burden of Mo'ab. Because in the night Ar of Mo'ab is laid waste, *and* brought to silence; because in the night Kir of Mo'ab is laid waste, *and* brought to silence;

2 He is gone up to Ba'jith, and to Di'bon, the high places, to weep: Mo'ab shall howl over Ne'bo, and over Med'e-ba: on all their heads *shall be* baldness, *and* every beard cut off.

3 In their streets they shall gird themselves with sackcloth: on the tops of their houses, and in their streets, every one shall howl, weeping abundantly.

4 And Hesh'bon shall cry, and E-le-a'leh: their voice shall be heard *even* unto Ja'haz: therefore the armed soldiers of Mo'ab shall cry out; his life shall be grievous unto him.

5 My heart shall cry out for Mo'ab; his fugitives *shall flee* unto Zo'ar, a heifer of three years old: for by the mounting up of Lu'hith with weeping shall they go it up; for in the way of Hor-o-na'im they shall raise up a cry of destruction.

6 For the waters of Nim'rim shall be desolate: for the hay is withered away, the grass faileth, there is no green thing.

7 Therefore the abundance they have gotten, and that which they have laid up, shall they carry away to the brook of the willows.

8 For the cry is gone round about the borders of Mo'ab; the howling thereof unto Eg'la-im, and the howling thereof unto Be'er-e'lim.

9 For the waters of Di'mon shall be full of blood: for I will bring more upon Di'mon, lions upon him that escapeth of Mo'ab, and upon the remnant of the land.

16 SEND ye the lamb to the ruler of the land from Se'la to the wilderness, unto the mount of the daughter of Zi'on.

2 For it shall be, *that*, as a wandering bird cast out of the nest, *so* the daughters of Mo'ab shall be at the fords of Ar'non.

3 Take counsel, execute judgment; make thy shadow as the night in the midst of the noonday; hide the outcasts; bewray not him that wandereth.

4 Let mine outcasts dwell with thee, Mo'ab; be thou a covert to them from the face of the spoiler: for the extortioner is at an end, the spoiler ceaseth, the oppressors are consumed out of the land.

5 And in mercy shall the throne be established: and he shall sit upon it in truth in the tabernacle of Da'vid, judging, and seeking judgment, and hasting righteousness.

6 ¶ We have heard of the pride of Mo'ab; he

is very proud: *even* of his haughtiness, and his pride, and his wrath: *but* his lies *shall* not *be* so.

7 Therefore shall Mo'ab howl for Mo'ab, every one shall howl: for the foundations of Kir-har'e-seth shall ye mourn; surely *they are* stricken.

8 For the fields of Hesh'bon languish, *and* the vine of Sib'mah: the lords of the heathen have broken down the principal plants thereof, they are come *even* unto Ja'zer, they wandered *through* the wilderness: her branches are stretched out, they are gone over the sea.

9 ¶ Therefore I will bewail with the weeping of Ja'zer the vine of Sib'mah: I will water thee with my tears, O Hesh'bon, and E-le-a'leh: for the shouting for thy summer fruits and for thy harvest is fallen.

10 And gladness is taken away, and joy out of the plentiful field; and in the vineyards there shall be no singing, neither shall there be shouting: the treaders shall tread out no wine in *their* presses; I have made *their* vintage shouting to cease.

11 Wherefore my bowels shall sound like an harp for Mo'ab, and mine inward parts for Kir-ha'resh.

12 ¶ And it shall come to pass, when it is seen that Mo'ab is weary on the high place, that he shall come to his sanctuary to pray; but he shall not prevail.

13 This *is* the word that the LORD hath spoken concerning Mo'ab since that time.

14 But now the LORD hath spoken, saying, Within three years, as the years of an hireling, and the glory of Mo'ab shall be contemned, with all that great multitude; and the remnant *shall be* very small *and* feeble.

17 THE burden of Da-mas'cus. Behold, Da-mas'cus is taken away from *being* a city, and it shall be a ruinous heap.

2 The cities of Ar'o-er *are* forsaken: they shall be for flocks, which shall lie down, and none shall make *them* afraid.

3 The fortress also shall cease from E'phra-im, and the kingdom from Da-mas'cus, and the remnant of Syr'i-a: they shall be as the glory of the children of Is'ra-el, saith the LORD of hosts.

4 And in that day it shall come to pass, *that* the glory of Ja'cob shall be made thin, and the fatness of his flesh shall wax lean.

5 And it shall be as when the harvestman gathereth the corn, and reapeth the ears with his arm; and it shall be as he that gathereth ears in the valley of Reph'a-im.

6 ¶ Yet gleaning grapes shall be left in it, as the shaking of an olive tree, two *or* three berries in the top of the uppermost bough, four *or* five in the outmost fruitful branches thereof, saith the LORD God of Is'ra-el.

7 At that day shall a man look to his Maker, and his eyes shall have respect to the Holy One of Is'ra-el.

8 And he shall not look to the altars, the work of his hands, neither shall respect *that* which his fingers have made, either the groves, or the images.

9 ¶ In that day shall his strong cities be as a forsaken bough, and an uppermost branch, which they left because of the children of Is'ra-el: and there shall be desolation.

10 Because thou hast forgotten the God of thy salvation, and hast not been mindful of the rock of thy strength, therefore shalt thou plant pleasant plants, and shalt set it with strange slips:

11 In the day shalt thou make thy plant to

grow, and in the morning shalt thou make thy seed to flourish: *but* the harvest *shall be* a heap in the day of grief and of desperate sorrow.

12 ¶ Woe to the multitude of many people, *which* make a noise like the noise of the seas; and to the rushing of nations, *that* make a rushing like the rushing of mighty waters!

13 The nations shall rush like the rushing of many waters: but God shall rebuke them, and they shall flee far off, and shall be chased as the chaff of the mountains before the wind, and like a rolling thing before the whirlwind.

14 And behold at eveningtide trouble; *and* before the morning he *is* not. This *is* the portion of them that spoil us, and the lot of them that rob us.

18 WOE to the land shadowing with wings, which *is* beyond the rivers of E-thi-o'pi-a:

2 That sendeth ambassadors by the sea, even in vessels of bulrushes upon the waters, *saying,* Go, ye swift messengers, to a nation scattered and peeled, to a people terrible from their beginning hitherto; a nation meted out and trodden down, whose land the rivers have spoiled!

3 All ye inhabitants of the world, and dwellers on the earth, see ye, when he lifteth up an ensign on the mountains; and when he bloweth a trumpet, hear ye.

4 For so the LORD said unto me, I will take my rest, and I will consider in my dwelling place like a clear heat upon herbs, *and* like a cloud of dew in the heat of harvest.

5 For afore the harvest, when the bud is perfect, and the sour grape is ripening in the flower, he shall both cut off the sprigs with pruning hooks, and take away *and* cut down the branches.

6 They shall be left together unto the fowls of the mountains, and to the beasts of the earth: and the fowls shall summer upon them, and all the beasts of the earth shall winter upon them.

7 ¶ In that time shall the present be brought unto the LORD of hosts of a people scattered and peeled, and from a people terrible from their beginning hitherto; a nation meted out and trodden under foot, whose land the rivers have spoiled, to the place of the name of the LORD of hosts, the mount Zi'on.

19 THE burden of E'gypt. Behold, the LORD rideth upon a swift cloud, and shall come into E'gypt: and the idols of E'gypt shall be moved at his presence, and the heart of E'-gypt shall melt in the midst of it.

2 And I will set the E-gyp'tians against the E-gyp'tians: and they shall fight every one against his brother, and every one against his neighbour; city against city, *and* kingdom against kingdom.

3 And the spirit of E'gypt shall fail in the midst thereof; and I will destroy the counsel thereof: and they shall seek to the idols, and to the charmers, and to them that have familiar spirits, and to the wizards.

4 And the E-gyp'tians will I give over into the hand of a cruel lord; and a fierce king shall rule over them, saith the Lord, the LORD of hosts.

5 And the waters shall fail from the sea, and the river shall be wasted and dried up.

6 And they shall turn the rivers far away; *and* the brooks of defence shall be emptied and dried up: the reeds and flags shall wither.

7 The paper reeds by the brooks, by the mouth of the brooks, and every thing sown by

the brooks, shall wither, be driven away, and be no *more.*

8 The fishers also shall mourn, and all they that cast angle into the brooks shall lament, and they that spread nets upon the waters shall languish.

9 Moreover they that work in fine flax, and they that weave networks, shall be confounded.

10 And they shall be broken in the purposes thereof, all that make sluices *and* ponds for fish.

11 ¶ Surely the princes of Zo'an *are* fools, the counsel of the wise counsellors of Pha'raoh is become brutish: how say ye unto Pha'raoh, I *am* the son of the wise, the son of ancient kings?

12 Where *are* they? where *are* thy wise *men?* and let them tell thee now, and let them know what the LORD of hosts hath purposed upon E'-gypt.

13 The princes of Zo'an are become fools, the princes of Noph are deceived; they have also seduced E'gypt, *even they that are* the stay of the tribes thereof.

14 The LORD hath mingled a perverse spirit in the midst thereof: and they have caused E'-gypt to err in every work thereof, as a drunken *man* staggereth in his vomit.

15 Neither shall there be *any* work for E'-gypt, which the head or tail, branch or rush, may do.

16 In that day shall E'gypt be like unto women: and it shall be afraid and fear because of the shaking of the hand of the LORD of hosts, which he shaketh over it.

17 And the land of Ju'dah shall be a terror unto E'gypt, every one that maketh mention thereof shall be afraid in himself, because of the counsel of the LORD of hosts, which he hath determined against it.

18 ¶ In that day shall five cities in the land of E'gypt speak the language of Ca'naan, and swear to the LORD of hosts; one shall be called, The city of destruction.

19 In that day shall there be an altar to the LORD in the midst of the land of E'gypt, and a pillar at the border thereof to the LORD.

20 And it shall be for a sign and for a witness unto the LORD of hosts in the land of E'gypt: for they shall cry unto the LORD because of the oppressors, and he shall send them a saviour, and a great one, and he shall deliver them.

21 And the LORD shall be known to E'gypt, and the E-gyp'tians shall know the LORD in that day, and shall do sacrifice and oblation; yea, they shall vow a vow unto the LORD, and perform *it.*

22 And the LORD shall smite E'gypt: he shall smite and heal *it:* and they shall return *even* to the LORD, and he shall be intreated of them, and shall heal them.

23 ¶ In that day shall there be a highway out of E'gypt to As-syr'i-a, and the As-syr'i-an shall come into E'gypt, and the E-gyp'tian into As-syr'i-a, and the E-gyp'tians shall serve with the As-syr'i-ans.

24 In that day shall Is'ra-el be the third with E'gypt and with As-syr'i-a, *even* a blessing in the midst of the land:

25 Whom the LORD of hosts shall bless, saying, Blessed *be* E'gypt my people, and As-syr'i-a the work of my hands, and Is'ra-el mine inheritance.

20 IN the year that Tar'tan came unto Ash'-dod, (when Sar'gon the king of As-syr'i-a sent him,) and fought against Ash'dod, and took it;

2 At the same time spake the LORD by I-sa'-iah the son of A'moz, saying, Go and loose the sackcloth from off thy loins, and put off thy shoe from thy foot. And he did so, walking naked and barefoot.

3 And the LORD said, Like as my servant I-sa'iah hath walked naked and barefoot three years *for* a sign and wonder upon E'gypt and upon E-thi-o'pi-a;

4 So shall the king of As-syr'i-a lead away the E-gyp'tians prisoners, and the E-thi-o'pi-ans captives, young and old, naked and barefoot, even with *their* buttocks uncovered, to the shame of E'gypt.

5 And they shall be afraid and ashamed of E-thi-o'pi-a their expectation, and of E'gypt their glory.

6 And the inhabitant of this isle shall say in that day, Behold, such *is* our expectation, whither we flee for help to be delivered from the king of As-syr'i-a: and how shall we escape?

21 THE burden of the desert of the sea. As whirlwinds in the south pass through; *so* it cometh from the desert, from a terrible land.

2 A grievous vision is declared unto me; the treacherous dealer dealeth treacherously, and the spoiler spoileth. Go up, O E'lam: besiege, O Me'di-a; all the sighing thereof have I made to cease.

3 Therefore are my loins filled with pain: pangs have taken hold upon me, as the pangs of a woman that travaileth: I was bowed down at the hearing *of it;* I was dismayed at the seeing *of it.*

4 My heart panted, fearfulness affrighted me: the night of my pleasure hath he turned into fear unto me.

5 Prepare the table, watch in the watchtower, eat, drink: arise, ye princes, *and* anoint the shield.

6 For thus hath the Lord said unto me, Go, set a watchman, let him declare what he seeth.

7 And he saw a chariot *with* a couple of horsemen, a chariot of asses, *and* a chariot of camels; and he hearkened diligently with much heed:

8 And he cried, A lion: My lord, I stand continually upon the watchtower in the daytime, and I am set in my ward whole nights:

9 And, behold, here cometh a chariot of men, *with* a couple of horsemen. And he answered and said, Bab'y-lon is fallen, is fallen; and all the graven images of her gods he hath broken unto the ground.

10 O my threshing, and the corn of my floor: that which I have heard of the LORD of hosts, the God of Is'ra-el, have I declared unto you.

11 ¶ The burden of Du'mah. He calleth to me out of Se'ir, Watchman, what of the night? Watchman, what of the night?

12 The watchman said, The morning cometh, and also the night: if ye will enquire, enquire ye: return, come.

13 ¶ The burden upon A-ra'bi-a. In the forest in A-ra'bi-a shall ye lodge, O ye travelling companies of Ded'a-nim.

14 The inhabitants of the land of Tema brought water to him that was thirsty, they prevented with their bread him that fled.

15 For they fled from the swords, from the drawn sword, and from the bent bow, and from the grievousness of war.

16 For thus hath the Lord said unto me, Within a year, according to the years of an hireling, and all the glory of Ke'dar shall fail:

17 And the residue of the number of archers, the mighty men of the children of Ke'dar, shall be diminished: for the LORD God of Is'ra-el hath spoken *it.*

22 THE burden of the valley of vision. What aileth thee now, that thou art wholly gone up to the house tops?

2 Thou that art full of stirs, a tumultuous city, a joyous city: thy slain *men are* not slain with the sword, nor dead in battle.

3 All thy rulers are fled together, they are bound by the archers: all that are found in thee are bound together, *which* have fled from far.

4 Therefore said I, Look away from me; I will weep bitterly, labour not to comfort me, because of the spoiling of the daughter of my people.

5 For *it is* a day of trouble, and of treading down, and of perplexity by the Lord GOD of hosts in the valley of vision, breaking down the walls, and of crying to the mountains.

6 And E'lam bare the quiver with chariots of men *and* horsemen, and Kir uncovered the shield.

7 And it shall come to pass, *that* thy choicest valleys shall be full of chariots, and the horsemen shall set themselves in array at the gate.

8 ¶ And he discovered the covering of Ju'-dah, and thou didst look in that day to the armour of the house of the forest.

9 Ye have seen also the breaches of the city of Da'vid, that they are many: and ye gathered together the waters of the lower pool.

10 And ye have numbered the houses of Je-ru'sa-lem, and the houses have ye broken down to fortify the wall.

11 Ye made also a ditch between the two walls for the water of the old pool: but ye have not looked unto the maker thereof, neither had respect unto him that fashioned it long ago.

12 And in that day did the Lord GOD of hosts call to weeping, and to mourning, and to baldness, and to girding with sackcloth:

13 And behold joy and gladness, slaying oxen, and killing sheep, eating flesh, and drinking wine: let us eat and drink; for to morrow we shall die.

14 And it was revealed in mine ears by the LORD of hosts, Surely this iniquity shall not be purged from you till ye die, saith the Lord GOD of hosts.

15 ¶ Thus saith the Lord GOD of hosts, Go, get thee unto this treasurer, *even* unto Sheb'na, which *is* over the house, *and say,*

16 What hast thou here? and whom hast thou here, that thou hast hewed thee out a sepulchre here, *as* he that heweth him out a sepulchre on high, *and* that graveth an habitation for himself in a rock?

17 Behold, the LORD will carry thee away with a mighty captivity, and will surely cover thee.

18 He will surely violently turn and toss thee *like* a ball into a large country: there shalt thou die, and there the chariots of thy glory *shall be* the shame of thy lord's house.

19 And I will drive thee from thy station, and from thy state shall he pull thee down.

20 ¶ And it shall come to pass in that day, that I will call my servant E-li'a-kim the son of Hil-ki'ah:

21 And I will clothe him with thy robe, and strengthen him with thy girdle, and I will commit thy government into his hand: and he shall be a father to the inhabitants of Je-ru'sa-lem, and to the house of Ju'dah.

22 And the key of the house of Da'vid will I

lay upon his shoulder; so he shall open, and none shall shut; and he shall shut, and none shall open.

23 And I will fasten him as a nail in a sure place; and he shall be for a glorious throne to his father's house.

24 And they shall hang upon him all the glory of his father's house, the offspring and the issue, all vessels of small quantity, from the vessels of cups, even to all the vessels of flagons.

25 In that day, saith the LORD of hosts, shall the nail that is fastened in the sure place be removed, and be cut down, and fall; and the burden that *was* upon it shall be cut off: for the LORD hath spoken *it*.

23 THE burden of Tyre. Howl, ye ships of Tar'shish; for it is laid waste, so that there is no house, no entering in: from the land of Chit'tim it is revealed to them.

2 Be still, ye inhabitants of the isle; thou whom the merchants of Zi'don, that pass over the sea, have replenished.

3 And by great waters the seed of Si'hor, the harvest of the river, *is* her revenue; and she is a mart of nations.

4 Be thou ashamed, O Zi'don: for the sea hath spoken, *even* the strength of the sea, saying, I travail not, nor bring forth children, neither do I nourish up young men, *nor* bring up virgins.

5 As at the report concerning E'gypt, *so* shall they be sorely pained at the report of Tyre.

6 Pass ye over to Tar'shish; howl, ye inhabitants of the isle.

7 *Is* this your joyous *city*, whose antiquity *is* of ancient days? her own feet shall carry her afar off to sojourn.

8 Who hath taken this counsel against Tyre, the crowning *city*, whose merchants *are* princes, whose traffickers *are* the honourable of the earth?

9 The LORD of hosts hath purposed it, to stain the pride of all glory, *and* to bring into contempt all the honourable of the earth.

10 Pass through thy land as a river, O daughter of Tar'shish: *there is* no more strength.

11 He stretched out his hand over the sea, he shook the kingdoms: the LORD hath given a commandment against the merchant *city*, to destroy the strong holds thereof.

12 And he said, Thou shalt no more rejoice, O thou oppressed virgin, daughter of Zi'don: arise, pass over to Chit'tim; there also shalt thou have no rest.

13 Behold the land of the Chal-de'ans; this people was not, *till* the As-syr'i-an founded it for them that dwell in the wilderness: they set up the towers thereof, they raised up the palaces thereof; *and* he brought it to ruin.

14 Howl, ye ships of Tar'shish: for your strength is laid waste.

15 And it shall come to pass in that day, that Tyre shall be forgotten seventy years, according to the days of one king: after the end of seventy years shall Tyre sing as an harlot.

16 Take an harp, go about the city, thou harlot that hast been forgotten; make sweet melody, sing many songs, that thou mayest be remembered.

17 ¶ And it shall come to pass after the end of seventy years, that the LORD will visit Tyre, and she shall turn to her hire, and shall commit fornication with all the kingdoms of the world upon the face of the earth.

18 And her merchandise and her hire shall be holiness to the LORD: it shall not be treasured nor laid up; for her merchandise shall be for them that dwell before the LORD, to eat sufficiently, and for durable clothing.

24 BEHOLD, the LORD maketh the earth empty, and maketh it waste, and turneth it upside down, and scattereth abroad the inhabitants thereof.

2 And it shall be, as with the people, so with the priest; as with the servant, so with his master; as with the maid, so with her mistress; as with the buyer, so with the seller; as with the lender, so with the borrower; as with the taker of usury, so with the giver of usury to him.

3 The land shall be utterly emptied, and utterly spoiled: for the LORD hath spoken this word.

4 The earth mourneth *and* fadeth away, the world languisheth *and* fadeth away, the haughty people of the earth do languish.

5 The earth also is defiled under the inhabitants thereof; because they have transgressed the laws, changed the ordinance, broken the everlasting covenant.

6 Therefore hath the curse devoured the earth, and they that dwell therein are desolate: therefore the inhabitants of the earth are burned, and few men left.

7 The new wine mourneth, the vine languisheth, all the merryhearted do sigh.

8 The mirth of tabrets ceaseth, the noise of them that rejoice endeth, the joy of the harp ceaseth.

9 They shall not drink wine with a song; strong drink shall be bitter to them that drink it.

10 The city of confusion is broken down: every house is shut up, that no man may come in.

11 *There is* a crying for wine in the streets; all joy is darkened, the mirth of the land is gone.

12 In the city is left desolation, and the gate is smitten with destruction.

13 ¶ When thus it shall be in the midst of the land among the people, *there shall be* as the shaking of an olive tree, *and* as the gleaning grapes when the vintage is done.

14 They shall lift up their voice, they shall sing for the majesty of the LORD, they shall cry aloud from the sea.

15 Wherefore glorify ye the LORD in the fires, *even* the name of the LORD God of Is'ra-el in the isles of the sea.

16 ¶ From the uttermost part of the earth have we heard songs, *even* glory to the righteous. But I said, My leanness, my leanness, woe unto me! the treacherous dealers have dealt treacherously; yea, the treacherous dealers have dealt very treacherously.

17 Fear, and the pit, and the snare, *are* upon thee, O inhabitant of the earth.

18 And it shall come to pass, *that* he who fleeth from the noise of the fear shall fall into the pit; and he that cometh up out of the midst of the pit shall be taken in the snare: for the windows from on high are open, and the foundations of the earth do shake.

19 The earth is utterly broken down, the earth is clean dissolved, the earth is moved exceedingly.

20 The earth shall reel to and fro like a drunkard, and shall be removed like a cottage; and the transgression thereof shall be heavy upon it; and it shall fall, and not rise again.

21 And it shall come to pass in that day, *that* the LORD shall punish the host of the high ones *that are* on high, and the kings of the earth upon the earth.

22 And they shall be gathered together, *as* prisoners are gathered in the pit, and shall be shut up in the prison, and after many days shall they be visited.

23 Then the moon shall be confounded, and the sun ashamed, when the LORD of hosts shall reign in mount Zi'on, and in Je-ru'sa-lem, and before his ancients gloriously.

25 O LORD, thou *art* my God; I will exalt thee, I will praise thy name; for thou hast done wonderful *things; thy* counsels of old *are* faithfulness *and* truth.

2 For thou hast made of a city an heap; *of a* defenced city a ruin: a palace of strangers to be no city; it shall never be built.

3 Therefore shall the strong people glorify thee, the city of the terrible nations shall fear thee.

4 For thou hast been a strength to the poor, a strength to the needy in his distress, a refuge from the storm, a shadow from the heat, when the blast of the terrible ones *is* as a storm *against* the wall.

5 Thou shalt bring down the noise of strangers, as the heat in a dry place; *even* the heat with the shadow of a cloud: the branch of the terrible ones shall be brought low.

6 ¶ And in this mountain shall the LORD of hosts make unto all people a feast of fat things, a feast of wines on the lees, of fat things full of marrow, of wines on the lees well refined.

7 And he will destroy in this mountain the face of the covering cast over all people, and the veil that is spread over all nations.

8 He will swallow up death in victory; and the Lord GOD will wipe away tears from off all faces; and the rebuke of his people shall he take away from off all the earth: for the LORD hath spoken *it.*

9 ¶ And it shall be said in that day, Lo, this *is* our God; we have waited for him, and he will save us: this *is* the LORD; we have waited for him, we will be glad and rejoice in his salvation.

10 For in this mountain shall the hand of the LORD rest, and Mo'ab shall be trodden down under him, even as straw is trodden down for the dunghill.

11 And he shall spread forth his hands in the midst of them, as he that swimmeth spreadeth forth *his hands* to swim: and he shall bring down their pride together with the spoils of their hands.

12 And the fortress of the high fort of thy walls shall he bring down, lay low, *and* bring to the ground, *even* to the dust.

26 IN that day shall this song be sung in the land of Ju'dah; We have a strong city; salvation will *God* appoint *for* walls and bulwarks.

2 Open ye the gates, that the righteous nation which keepeth the truth may enter in.

3 Thou wilt keep *him* in perfect peace, *whose* mind *is* stayed *on thee:* because he trusteth in thee.

4 Trust ye in the LORD for ever: for in the LORD JE-HO'VAH *is* everlasting strength:

5 ¶ For he bringeth down them that dwell on high; the lofty city, he layeth it low; he layeth it low, *even* to the ground; he bringeth it *even* to the dust.

6 The foot shall tread it down, *even* the feet of the poor, *and* the steps of the needy.

7 The way of the just *is* uprightness: thou, most upright, dost weigh the path of the just.

8 Yea, in the way of thy judgments, O LORD,

have we waited for thee; the desire of *our* soul *is* to thy name, and to the remembrance of thee.

9 With my soul have I desired thee in the night; yea, with my spirit within me will I seek thee early: for when thy judgments *are* in the earth, the inhabitants of the world will learn righteousness.

10 Let favour be shewed to the wicked, *yet* will he not learn righteousness; in the land of uprightness will he deal unjustly, and will not behold the majesty of the LORD.

11 LORD, *when* thy hand is lifted up, they will not see: *but* they shall see, and be ashamed for *their* envy at the people; yea, the fire of thine enemies shall devour them.

12 ¶ LORD, thou wilt ordain peace for us: for thou also hast wrought all our works in us.

13 O LORD our God, *other* lords beside thee have had dominion over us: *but* by thee only will we make mention of thy name.

14 *They are* dead, they shall not live; *they are* deceased, they shall not rise: therefore hast thou visited and destroyed them, and made all their memory to perish.

15 Thou hast increased the nation, O LORD, thou hast increased the nation: thou art glorified: thou hadst removed *it* far *unto* all the ends of the earth.

16 LORD, in trouble have they visited thee, they poured out a prayer *when* thy chastening *was* upon them.

17 Like as a woman with child, *that* draweth near the time of her delivery, is in pain, *and* crieth out in her pangs; so have we been in thy sight, O LORD.

18 We have been with child, we have been in pain, we have as it were brought forth wind; we have not wrought any deliverance in the earth; neither have the inhabitants of the world fallen.

19 Thy dead *men* shall live, *together with* my dead body shall they arise. Awake and sing, ye that dwell in dust: for thy dew *is as* the dew of herbs, and the earth shall cast out the dead.

20 ¶ Come, my people, enter thou into thy chambers, and shut thy doors about thee: hide thyself as it were for a little moment, until the indignation be overpast.

21 For, behold, the LORD cometh out of his place to punish the inhabitants of the earth for their iniquity: the earth also shall disclose her blood, and shall no more cover her slain.

27 IN that day the LORD with his sore and great and strong sword shall punish leviathan the piercing serpent, even leviathan that crooked serpent; and he shall slay the dragon that *is* in the sea.

2 In that day sing ye unto her, A vineyard of red wine.

3 I the LORD do keep it; I will water it every moment: lest *any* hurt it, I will keep it night and day.

4 Fury *is* not in me: who would set the briers *and* thorns against me in battle? I would go through them, I would burn them together.

5 Or let him take hold of my strength, *that* he may make peace with me; *and* he shall make peace with me.

6 He shall cause them that come of Ja'cob to take root: Is'ra-el shall blossom and bud, and fill the face of the world with fruit.

7 ¶ Hath he smitten him, as he smote those that smote him? *or* is he slain according to the slaughter of them that are slain by him?

8 In measure, when it shooteth forth, thou wilt debate with it: he stayeth his rough wind in the day of the east wind.

9 By this therefore shall the iniquity of Ja′cob be purged; and this *is* all the fruit to take away his sin; when he maketh all the stones of the altar as chalkstones that are beaten in sunder, the groves and images shall not stand up.

10 Yet the defenced city *shall be* desolate, *and* the habitation forsaken, and left like a wilderness: there shall the calf feed, and there shall he lie down, and consume the branches thereof.

11 When the boughs thereof are withered, they shall be broken off: the women come, *and* set them on fire: for it *is* a people of no understanding: therefore he that made them will not have mercy on them, and he that formed them will shew them no favour.

12 ¶ And it shall come to pass in that day, *that* the LORD shall beat off from the channel of the river unto the stream of E′gypt, and ye shall be gathered one by one, O ye children of Is′ra-el.

13 And it shall come to pass in that day, *that* the great trumpet shall be blown, and they shall come which were ready to perish in the land of As-syr′i-a, and the outcasts in the land of E′-gypt, and shall worship the LORD in the holy mount at Je-ru′sa-lem.

28 WOE to the crown of pride, to the drunkards of E′phra-im, whose glorious beauty *is* a fading flower, which *are* on the head of the fat valleys of them that are overcome with wine!

2 Behold, the Lord hath a mighty and strong one, *which* as a tempest of hail *and* a destroying storm, as a flood of mighty waters overflowing, shall cast down to the earth with the hand.

3 The crown of pride, the drunkards of E′-phra-im, shall be trodden under feet:

4 And the glorious beauty, which *is* on the head of the fat valley, shall be a fading flower, *and* as the hasty fruit before the summer; which *when* he that looketh upon it seeth, while it is yet in his hand he eateth it up.

5 ¶ In that day shall the LORD of hosts be for a crown of glory, and for a diadem of beauty, unto the residue of his people,

6 And for a spirit of judgment to him that sitteth in judgment, and for strength to them that turn the battle to the gate.

7 ¶ But they also have erred through wine, and through strong drink are out of the way; the priest and the prophet have erred through strong drink, they are swallowed up of wine, they are out of the way through strong drink; they err in vision, they stumble in judgment.

8 For all tables are full of vomit *and* filthiness, *so that there is* no place clean.

9 ¶ Whom shall he teach knowledge? and whom shall he make to understand doctrine? *them that are* weaned from the milk, *and* drawn from the breasts.

10 For precept *must be* upon precept, precept upon precept; line upon line, line upon line; here a little *and* there a little:

11 For with stammering lips and another tongue will he speak to this people.

12 To whom he said, This *is* the rest *wherewith* ye may cause the weary to rest; and this *is* the refreshing: yet they would not hear.

13 But the word of the LORD was unto them precept upon precept, precept upon precept; line upon line, line upon line; here a little, *and* there a little; that they might go, and fall backward, and be broken, and snared, and taken.

14 ¶ Wherefore hear the word of the LORD, ye scornful men, that rule this people which *is* in Je-ru′sa-lem.

15 Because ye have said, We have made a covenant with death, and with hell are we at agreement; when the overflowing scourge shall pass through, it shall not come unto us: for we have made lies our refuge, and under falsehood have we hid ourselves:

16 ¶ Therefore thus saith the Lord GOD, Behold, I lay in Zi′on for a foundation a stone, a tried stone, a precious corner *stone*, a sure foundation: he that believeth shall not make haste.

17 Judgment also will I lay to the line, and righteousness to the plummet: and the hail shall sweep away the refuge of lies, and the waters shall overflow the hiding place.

18 ¶ And your covenant with death shall be disannulled, and your agreement with hell shall not stand; when the overflowing scourge shall pass through, then ye shall be trodden down by it.

19 From the time that it goeth forth it shall take you: for morning by morning shall it pass over, by day and by night: and it shall be a vexation only *to* understand the report.

20 For the bed is shorter than that *a man* can stretch himself *on it*: and the covering narrower than that he can wrap himself *in it*.

21 For the LORD shall rise up as *in* mount Per′a-zim, he shall be wroth as *in* the valley of Gib′e-on, that he may do his work, his strange work; and bring to pass his act, his strange act.

22 Now therefore be ye not mockers, lest your bands be made strong: for I have heard from the Lord GOD of hosts a consumption, even determined upon the whole earth.

23 ¶ Give ye ear, and hear my voice; hearken, and hear my speech.

24 Doth the plowman plow all day to sow? doth he open and break the clods of his ground?

25 When he hath made plain the face thereof, doth he not cast abroad the fitches, and scatter the cummin, and cast in the principal wheat and the appointed barley and the rie in their place?

26 For his God doth instruct him to discretion, *and* doth teach him.

27 For the fitches are not threshed with a threshing instrument, neither is a cart wheel turned about upon the cummin; but the fitches are beaten out with a staff, and the cummin with a rod.

28 Bread *corn* is bruised; because he will not ever be threshing it, nor break *it* with the wheel of his cart, nor bruise it *with* his horsemen.

29 This also cometh forth from the LORD of hosts, *which* is wonderful in counsel, *and* excellent in working.

29 WOE to A′ri-el, to A′ri-el, the city *where* Da′vid dwelt! add ye year to year; let them kill sacrifices.

2 Yet I will distress A′ri-el, and there shall be heaviness and sorrow: and it shall be unto me as A′ri-el.

3 And I will camp against thee round about, and will lay siege against thee with a mount, and I will raise forts against thee.

4 And thou shalt be brought down, *and* shalt speak out of the ground, and thy speech shall be low out of the dust, and thy voice shall be, as of one that hath a familiar spirit, out of the ground, and thy speech shall whisper out of the dust.

5 Moreover the multitude of thy strangers shall be like small dust, and the multitude of the

terrible ones *shall be* as chaff that passeth away: yea, it shall be at an instant suddenly.

6 Thou shalt be visited of the LORD of hosts with thunder, and with earthquake, and great noise, with storm and tempest, and the flame of devouring fire.

7 ¶ And the multitude of all the nations that fight against A'ri-el, even all that fight against her and her munition, and that distress her, shall be as a dream of a night vision.

8 It shall even be as when an hungry *man* dreameth, and, behold, he eateth; but he awaketh, and his soul is empty: or as when a thirsty man dreameth, and, behold, he drinketh; but he awaketh, and, behold, *he is* faint, and his soul hath appetite: so shall the multitude of all the nations be, that fight against mount Zi'on.

9 ¶ Stay yourselves, and wonder; cry ye out, and cry: they are drunken, but not with wine; they stagger, but not with strong drink.

10 For the LORD hath poured out upon you the spirit of deep sleep, and hath closed your eyes: the prophets and your rulers, the seers hath he covered.

11 And the vision of all is become unto you as the words of a book that is sealed, which *men* deliver to one that is learned, saying, Read this, I pray thee: and he saith, I cannot; for it *is* sealed:

12 And the book is delivered to him that is not learned, saying, Read this, I pray thee: and he saith, I am not learned.

13 ¶ Wherefore the Lord said, Forasmuch as this people draw near *me* with their mouth, and with their lips do honour me, but have removed their heart far from me, and their fear toward me is taught by the precept of men:

14 Therefore, behold, I will proceed to do a marvellous work among this people, *even* a marvellous work and a wonder: for the wisdom of their wise *men* shall perish, and the understanding of their prudent *men* shall be hid.

15 Woe unto them that seek deep to hide their counsel from the LORD, and their works are in the dark, and they say, Who seeth us? and who knoweth us?

16 Surely your turning of things upside down shall be esteemed as the potter's clay: for shall the work say of him that made it, He made me not? or shall the thing framed say of him that framed it, He had no understanding?

17 *Is* it not yet a very little while, and Leb'a-non shall be turned into a fruitful field, and the fruitful field shall be esteemed as a forest?

18 ¶ And in that day shall the deaf hear the words of the book, and the eyes of the blind shall see out of obscurity, and out of darkness.

19 The meek also shall increase *their* joy in the LORD, and the poor among men shall rejoice in the Holy One of Is'ra-el.

20 For the terrible one is brought to nought, and the scorner is consumed, and all that watch for iniquity are cut off:

21 That make a man an offender for a word, and lay a snare for him that reproveth in the gate, and turn aside the just for a thing of nought.

22 Therefore thus saith the LORD, who redeemed A'bra-ham, concerning the house of Ja'cob, Ja'cob shall not now be ashamed, neither shall his face now wax pale.

23 But when he seeth his children, the work of mine hands, in the midst of him, they shall sanctify my name, and sanctify the Holy One of Ja'cob, and shall fear the God of Is'ra-el.

24 They also that erred in spirit shall come to understanding, and they that murmured shall learn doctrine.

30 WOE to the rebellious children, saith the LORD, that take counsel, but not of me; and that cover with a covering, but not of my spirit, that they may add sin to sin:

2 That walk to go down into E'gypt, and have not asked at my mouth; to strengthen themselves in the strength of Pha'raoh, and to trust in the shadow of E'gypt!

3 Therefore shall the strength of Pha'raoh be your shame, and the trust in the shadow of E'gypt *your* confusion.

4 For his princes were at Zo'an, and his ambassadors came to Ha'nes.

5 They were all ashamed of a people *that* could not profit them, nor be an help nor profit, but a shame, and also a reproach.

6 The burden of the beasts of the south: into the land of trouble and anguish, from whence *come* the young and old lion, the viper and fiery flying serpent, they will carry their riches upon the shoulders of young asses, and their treasures upon the bunches of camels, to a people *that* shall not profit *them.*

7 For the E-gyp'tians shall help in vain, and to no purpose: therefore have I cried concerning this, Their strength *is* to sit still.

8 ¶ Now go, write it before them in a table, and note it in a book, that it may be for the time to come for ever and ever:

9 That this *is* a rebellious people, lying children, children *that* will not hear the law of the LORD:

10 Which say to the seers, See not; and to the prophets, Prophesy not unto us right things, speak unto us smooth things, prophesy deceits:

11 Get you out of the way, turn aside out of the path, cause the Holy One of Is'ra-el to cease from before us.

12 Wherefore thus saith the Holy One of Is'ra-el, Because ye despise this word, and trust in oppression and perverseness, and stay thereon:

13 Therefore this iniquity shall be to you as a breach ready to fall, swelling out in a high wall, whose breaking cometh suddenly at an instant.

14 And he shall break it as the breaking of the potters' vessel that is broken in pieces; he shall not spare: so that there shall not be found in the bursting of it a sherd to take fire from the hearth, or to take water *withal* out of the pit.

15 For thus saith the Lord GOD, the Holy One of Is'ra-el; In returning and rest shall ye be saved; in quietness and in confidence shall be your strength: and ye would not.

16 But ye said, No; for we will flee upon horses; therefore shall ye flee: and, We will ride upon the swift; therefore shall they that pursue you be swift.

17 One thousand *shall flee* at the rebuke of one; at the rebuke of five shall ye flee: till ye be left as a beacon upon the top of a mountain, and as an ensign on an hill.

18 ¶ And therefore will the LORD wait, that he may be gracious unto you, and therefore will he be exalted, that he may have mercy upon you: for the LORD *is* a God of judgment: blessed *are* all they that wait for him.

19 For the people shall dwell in Zi'on at Je-ru'sa-lem: thou shalt weep no more: he will be very gracious unto thee at the voice of thy cry; when he shall hear it, he will answer thee.

20 And *though* the LORD give you the bread of adversity, and the water of affliction, yet shall not thy teachers be removed into a corner any more, but thine eyes shall see thy teachers:

21 And thine ears shall hear a word behind thee, saying, This is the way, walk ye in it, when ye turn to the right hand, and when ye turn to the left.

22 Ye shall defile also the covering of thy graven images of silver, and the ornament of thy molten images of gold: thou shalt cast them away as a menstruous cloth; thou shalt say unto it, Get thee hence.

23 Then shall he give the rain of thy seed, that thou shalt sow the ground withal; and bread of the increase of the earth, and it shall be fat and plenteous: in that day shall thy cattle feed in large pastures.

24 The oxen likewise and the young asses that ear the ground shall eat clean provender, which hath been winnowed with the shovel and with the fan.

25 And there shall be upon every high mountain, and upon every high hill, rivers and streams of waters in the day of the great slaughter, when the towers fall.

26 Moreover the light of the moon shall be as the light of the sun, and the light of the sun shall be sevenfold, as the light of seven days, in the day that the LORD bindeth up the breach of his people, and healeth the stroke of their wound.

27 ¶ Behold, the name of the LORD cometh from far, burning with his anger, and the burden therof is heavy: his lips are full of indignation, and his tongue as a devouring fire:

28 And his breath, as an overflowing stream, shall reach to the midst of the neck, to sift the nations with the sieve of vanity: and there shall be a bridle in the jaws of the people, causing them to err.

29 Ye shall have a song, as in the night when a holy solemnity is kept; and gladness of heart, as when one goeth with a pipe to come into the mountain of the LORD, to the mighty One of Is'-ra-el.

30 And the LORD shall cause his glorious voice to be heard, and shall shew the lighting down of his arm, with the indignation of his anger, and with the flame of a devouring fire, with scattering, and tempest, and hailstones.

31 For through the voice of the LORD shalt the As-syr'i-an be beaten down, which smote with a rod.

32 And in every place where the grounded staff shall pass, which the LORD shall lay upon him, it shall be with tabrets and harps: and in battles of shaking will he fight with it.

33 For To'phet is ordained of old; yea, for the king it is prepared; he hath made it deep and large: the pile thereof is fire and much wood; the breath of the LORD, like a stream of brimstone, doth kindle it.

31 WOE to them that go down to E'gypt for help; and stay on horses, and trust in chariots, because they are many; and in horsemen, because they are very strong; but they look not unto the Holy One of Is'ra-el, neither seek the LORD!

2 Yet he also is wise, and will bring evil, and will not call back his words: but will arise against the house of the evildoers, and against the help of them that work iniquity.

3 Now the E-gyp'tians are men, and not God; and their horses flesh, and not spirit. When the LORD shall stretch out his hand, both he that helpeth shall fall, and he that is holpen shall fall down, and they all shall fail together.

4 For thus hath the LORD spoken unto me, Like as the lion and the young lion roaring on his prey, when a multitude of shepherds is called forth against him, he will not be afraid of their voice, nor abase himself for the noise of them: so shall the LORD of hosts come down to fight for mount Zi'on, and for the hill thereof.

5 As birds flying, so will the LORD of hosts defend Je-ru'sa-lem; defending also he will deliver it; and passing over he will preserve it.

6 ¶ Turn ye unto him from whom the children of Is'ra-el have deeply revolted.

7 For in that day every man shall cast away his idols of silver, and his idols of gold, which your own hands have made unto you for a sin.

8 ¶ Then shall the As-syr'i-an fall with the sword, not of a mighty man; and the sword, not of a mean man, shall devour him: but he shall flee from the sword, and his young men shall be discomfited.

9 And he shall pass over to his strong hold for fear, and his princes shall be afraid of the ensign, saith the LORD, whose fire is in Zi'on, and his furnace in Je-ru'sa-lem.

32 BEHOLD, a king shall reign in righteousness, and princes shall rule in judgment.

2 And a man shall be as an hiding place from the wind, and a covert from the tempest; as rivers of water in a dry place, as the shadow of a great rock in a weary land.

3 And the eyes of them that see shall not be dim, and the ears of them that hear shall hearken.

4 The heart also of the rash shall understand knowledge, and the tongue of the stammerers shall be ready to speak plainly.

5 The vile person shall be no more called liberal, nor the churl said to be bountiful.

6 For the vile person will speak villany, and his heart will work iniquity, to practise hypocrisy, and to utter error against the LORD, to make empty the soul of the hungry, and he will cause the drink of the thirsty to fail.

7 The instruments also of the churl are evil: he deviseth wicked devices to destroy the poor with lying words, even when the needy speaketh right.

8 But the liberal deviseth liberal things; and by liberal things shall he stand.

9 ¶ Rise up, ye women that are at ease; hear my voice, ye careless daughters; give ear unto my speech.

10 Many days and years shall ye be troubled, ye careless women: for the vintage shall fail, the gathering shall not come.

11 Tremble, ye women that are at ease; be troubled, ye careless ones: strip you, and make you bare, and gird sackcloth upon your loins.

12 They shall lament for the teats, for the pleasant fields, for the fruitful vine.

13 Upon the land of my people shall come up thorns and briers; yea, upon all the houses of joy in the joyous city:

14 Because the palaces shall be forsaken; the multitude of the city shall be left; the forts and towers shall be for dens for ever, a joy of wild asses, a pasture of flocks;

15 Until the spirit be poured upon us from on high, and the wilderness be a fruitful field, and the fruitful field be counted for a forest.

16 Then judgment shall dwell in the wilderness, and righteousness remain in the fruitful field.

17 And the work of righteousness shall be peace; and the effect of righteousness quietness and assurance for ever.

18 And my people shall dwell in a peaceable

habitation, and in sure dwellings, and in quiet resting places;

19 When it shall hail, coming down on the forest; and the city shall be low in a low place.

20 Blessed *are* ye that sow beside all waters, that send forth *thither* the feet of the ox and the ass.

33 WOE to thee that spoilest, and thou *wast* not spoiled; and dealest treacherously, and they dealt not treacherously with thee! when thou shalt cease to spoil, thou shalt be spoiled; *and* when thou shalt make an end to deal treacherously, they shall deal treacherously with thee.

2 O LORD, be gracious unto us; we have waited for thee: be thou their arm every morning, our salvation also in the time of trouble.

3 At the noise of the tumult the people fled; at the lifting up of thyself the nations were scattered.

4 And your spoil shall be gathered *like* the gathering of the caterpiller: as the running to and fro of locusts shall he run upon them.

5 The LORD is exalted; for he dwelleth on high: he hath filled Zi'on with judgment and righteousness.

6 And wisdom and knowledge shall be the stability of thy times, *and* strength of salvation: the fear of the LORD *is* his treasure.

7 Behold, their valiant ones shall cry without: the ambassadors of peace shall weep bitterly.

8 The highways lie waste, the wayfaring man ceaseth: he hath broken the covenant, he hath despised the cities, he regardeth no man.

9 The earth mourneth *and* languisheth: Leb'a-non is ashamed *and* hewn down: Shar'on is like a wilderness; and Ba'shan and Car'mel shake off *their fruits.*

10 Now will I rise, saith the LORD; now will I be exalted; now will I lift up myself.

11 Ye shall conceive chaff, ye shall bring forth stubble: your breath, *as* fire, shall devour you.

12 And the people shall be *as* the burnings of lime: *as* thorns cut up shall they be burned in the fire.

13 ¶ Hear, ye *that are* far off, what I have done; and, ye *that are* near, acknowledge my might.

14 The sinners in Zi'on are afraid; fearfulness hath surprised the hypocrites. Who among us shall dwell with the devouring fire? who among us shall dwell with everlasting burnings?

15 He that walketh righteously, and speaketh uprightly; he that despiseth the gain of oppressions, that shaketh his hands from holding of bribes, that stoppeth his ears from hearing of blood, and shutteth his eyes from seeing evil;

16 He shall dwell on high: his place of defence *shall be* the munitions of rocks: bread shall be given him; his waters *shall be* sure.

17 Thine eyes shall see the king in his beauty: they shall behold the land that is very far off.

18 Thine heart shall meditate terror. Where *is* the scribe? where *is* the receiver? where *is* he that counted the towers?

19 Thou shalt not see a fierce people, a people of a deeper speech than thou canst perceive; of a stammering tongue, *that thou canst* not understand.

20 Look upon Zi'on, the city of our solemnities: thine eyes shall see Je-ru'sa-lem a quiet habitation, a tabernacle *that* shall not be taken down; not one of the stakes thereof shall ever be removed, neither shall any of the cords thereof be broken.

21 But there the glorious LORD *will be* unto us a place of broad rivers *and* streams; wherein shall go no galley with oars, neither shall gallant ship pass thereby.

22 For the LORD is our judge, the LORD *is* our lawgiver, the LORD *is* our king; he will save us.

23 Thy tacklings are loosed; they could not well strengthen their mast, they could not spread the sail: then is the prey of a great spoil divided; the lame take the prey.

24 And the inhabitant shall not say, I am sick: the people that dwell therein *shall be* forgiven *their* iniquity.

34 COME near, ye nations, to hear; and hearken, ye people: let the earth hear, and all that is therein; the world, and all things that come forth of it.

2 For the indignation of the LORD *is* upon all nations, and *his* fury upon all their armies: he hath utterly destroyed them, he hath delivered them to the slaughter.

3 Their slain also shall be cast out, and their stink shall come up out of their carcases, and the mountains shall be melted with their blood.

4 And all the host of heaven shall be dissolved, and the heavens shall be rolled together as a scroll: and all their host shall fall down, as the leaf falleth off from the vine, and as a falling *fig* from the fig tree.

5 For my sword shall be bathed in heaven: behold, it shall come down upon I-du-me'a, and upon the people of my curse, to judgment.

6 The sword of the LORD is filled with blood, it is made fat with fatness, *and* with the blood of lambs and goats, with the fat of the kidneys of rams: for the LORD hath a sacrifice in Boz'-rah, and a great slaughter in the land of I-du-me'a.

7 And the unicorns shall come down with them, and the bullocks with the bulls; and their land shall be soaked with blood, and their dust made fat with fatness.

8 For *it is* the day of the LORD's vengeance, *and* the year of recompences for the controversy of Zi'on.

9 And the streams thereof shall be turned into pitch, and the dust thereof into brimstone, and the land thereof shall become burning pitch.

10 It shall not be quenched night nor day; the smoke thereof shall go up for ever: from generation to generation it shall lie waste; none shall pass through it for ever and ever.

11 ¶ But the cormorant and the bittern shall possess it; the owl also and the raven shall dwell in it: and he shall stretch out upon it the line of confusion, and the stones of emptiness.

12 They shall call the nobles thereof to the kingdom, but none *shall be* there, and all her princes shall be nothing.

13 And thorns shall come up in her palaces, nettles and brambles in the fortresses thereof: and it shall be an habitation of dragons, *and* a court for owls.

14 The wild beasts of the desert shall also meet with the wild beasts of the island, and the satyr shall cry to his fellow; the screech owl also shall rest there, and find for herself a place of rest.

15 There shall the great owl make her nest, and lay, and hatch, and gather under her shadow: there shall the vultures also be gathered, every one with her mate.

16 ¶ Seek ye out of the book of the LORD, and read: no one of these shall fail, none shall want her mate: for my mouth it hath com-

manded, and his spirit it hath gathered them.

17 And he hath cast the lot for them, and his hand hath divided it unto them by line: they shall possess it for ever, from generation to generation shall they dwell therein.

35 THE wilderness and the solitary place shall be glad for them; and the desert shall rejoice, and blossom as the rose.

2 It shall blossom abundantly, and rejoice even with joy and singing: the glory of Leb'a-non shall be given unto it, the excellency of Car'mel and Shar'on, they shall see the glory of the LORD, *and* the excellency of our God.

3 ¶ Strengthen ye the weak hands, and confirm the feeble knees.

4 Say to them *that are* of a fearful heart, Be strong, fear not: behold, your God will come *with* vengeance, *even* God *with* a recompence; he will come and save you.

5 Then the eyes of the blind shall be opened, and the ears of the deaf shall be unstopped.

6 Then shall the lame *man* leap as an hart, and the tongue of the dumb sing: for in the wilderness shall waters break out, and streams in the desert.

7 And the parched ground shall become a pool, and the thirsty land springs of water: in the habitation of dragons, where each lay, *shall be* grass with reeds and rushes.

8 And an highway shall be there, and a way, and it shall be called The way of holiness; the unclean shall not pass over it; but it *shall be* for those: the wayfaring men, though fools, shall not err *therein.*

9 No lion shall be there, nor *any* ravenous beast shall go up thereon, it shall not be found there; but the redeemed shall walk *there:*

10 And the ransomed of the LORD shall return, and come to Zi'on with songs and everlasting joy upon their heads: they shall obtain joy and gladness, and sorrow and sighing shall flee away.

36 NOW it came to pass in the fourteenth year of king Hez-e-ki'ah, *that* Sen-nach'-e-rib king of As-syr'i-a came up against all the defenced cities of Ju'dah, and took them.

2 And the king of As-syr'i-a sent Rab'sha-keh from La'chish to Je-ru'sa-lem unto king Hez-e-ki'ah with a great army. And he stood by the conduit of the upper pool in the highway of the fuller's field.

3 Then came forth unto him E-li'a-kim, Hil-ki'ah's son, which was over the house, and Sheb'na the scribe, and Jo'ah, A'saph's son, the recorder.

4 ¶ And Rab'sha-keh said unto them, Say ye now to Hez-e-ki'ah, Thus saith the great king, the king of As-syr'i-a, What confidence *is* this wherein thou trustest?

5 I say, *sayest thou,* (but *they are but* vain words) *I have* counsel and strength for war: now on whom dost thou trust, that thou rebellest against me?

6 Lo, thou trustest in the staff of this broken reed, on E'gypt; whereon if a man lean, it will go into his hand, and pierce it: so *is* Pha'raoh king of E'gypt to all that trust in him.

7 But if thou say to me, We trust in the LORD our God: *is it* not he, whose high places and whose altars Hez-e-ki'ah hath taken away, and said to Ju'dah and to Je-ru'sa-lem, Ye shall worship before this altar?

8 Now therefore give pledges, I pray thee, to my master the king of As-syr'i-a, and I will give thee two thousand horses, if thou be able on thy part to set riders upon them.

9 How then wilt thou turn away the face of one captain of the least of my master's servants, and put thy trust on E'gypt for chariots and for horsemen?

10 And am I now come up without the LORD against this land to destroy it? the LORD said unto me, Go up against this land, and destroy it.

11 ¶ Then said E-li'a-ki'm and Sheb'na and Jo'ah unto Rab'sha-keh, Speak, I pray thee, unto thy servants in the Syr'i-an language; for we understand *it:* and speak not to us in the Jews' language, in the ears of the people that *are* on the wall.

12 ¶ But Rab'sha-keh said, Hath my master sent me to thy master and to thee to speak these words? *hath he* not *sent me* to the men that sit upon the wall, that they may eat their own dung, and drink their own piss with you?

13 Then Rab'sha-keh stood, and cried with a loud voice in the Jews' language, and said, Hear ye the words of the great king, the king of As-syr'i-a.

14 Thus saith the LORD, Let not Hez-e-ki'ah deceive you: for he shall not be able to deliver you.

15 Neither let Hez-e-ki'ah make you trust in the LORD, saying, The LORD will surely deliver us: this city shall not be delivered into the hand of the king of As-syr'i-a.

16 Hearken not to Hez-e-ki'ah: for thus saith the king of As-syr'i-a, Make *an agreement* with me *by* a present, and come out to me: and eat ye every one of his vine, and every one of his fig tree, and drink ye every one the waters of his own cistern;

17 Until I come and take you away to a land like your own land, a land of corn and wine, a land of bread and vineyards.

18 *Beware* lest Hez-e-ki'ah persuade you, saying, The LORD will deliver us. Hath any of the gods of the nations delivered his land out of the hand of the king of As-syr'i-a?

19 Where *are* the gods of Ha'math and Ar-phad? where *are* the gods of Seph-ar-va'im? and have they delivered Sa-ma'ri-a out of my hand?

20 Who *are they* among all the gods of these lands, that have delivered their land out of my hand, that the LORD should deliver Je-ru'sa-lem out of my hand?

21 But they held their peace, and answered him not a word: for the king's commandment was, saying, Answer him not.

22 ¶ Then came E-li'a-kim, the son of Hil-ki'-ah, that *was* over the household, and Sheb'na the scribe, and Jo'ah, the son of A'saph, the recorder to Hez-e-ki'ah with *their* clothes rent, and told him the words of Rab'sha-keh.

37 AND it came to pass, when king Hez-e-ki'ah heard *it*, that he rent his clothes, and covered himself with sackcloth, and went into the house of the LORD.

2 And he sent E-li'a-kim, who *was* over the household, and Sheb'na the scribe, and the elders of the priests covered with sackcloth, unto I-sa'iah the prophet the son of A'moz.

3 And they said unto him, Thus saith Hez-e-ki'ah, This day *is* a day of trouble, and of rebuke, and of blasphemy: for the children are come to the birth, and *there is* not strength to bring forth.

4 It may be the LORD thy God will hear the words of Rab'sha-keh, whom the king of As-syr'i-a his master hath sent to reproach the living God, and will reprove the words which the

LORD thy God hath heard: wherefore lift up *thy* prayer for the remnant that is left.

5 So the servants of king Hez-e-ki'ah came to I-sa'iah.

6 ¶ And I-sa'iah said unto them, Thus shall ye say unto your master, Thus saith the LORD, Be not afraid of the words that thou hast heard, wherewith the servants of the king of As-syr'i-a have blasphemed me.

7 Behold, I will send a blast upon him, and he shall hear a rumour, and return to his own land; and I will cause him to fall by the sword in his own land.

8 ¶ So Rab'sha-keh returned, and found the king of As-syr'i-a warring against Lib'nah: for he had heard that he was departed from La'-chish.

9 And he heard say concerning Tir'ha-kah king of E-thi-o'pi-a, He is come forth to make war with thee. And when he heard *it*, he sent messengers to Hez-e-ki'ah, saying,

10 Thus shall ye speak to Hez-e-ki'ah king of Ju'dah, saying, Let not thy God, in whom thou trustest, deceive thee, saying, Je-ru'sa-lem shall not be given into the hand of the king of As-syr'i-a.

11 Behold, thou hast heard what the kings of As-syr'i-a have done to all lands by destroying them utterly; and shalt thou be delivered?

12 Have the gods of the nations delivered them which my fathers have destroyed, *as* Go'-zan, and Ha'ran, and Re'zeph, and the children of E'den which *were* in Te-las'sar?

13 Where *is* the king of Ha'math, and the king of Ar'phad, and the king of the city of Seph-ar-va'im, He'na, and I'vah?

14 ¶ And Hez-e-ki'ah received the letter from the hand of the messengers, and read it: and Hez-e-ki'ah went up unto the house of the LORD, and spread it before the LORD.

15 And Hez-e-ki'ah prayed unto the LORD, saying,

16 O LORD of hosts, God of Is'ra-el, that dwellest *between* the cherubims, thou *art* the God, *even* thou alone, of all the kingdoms of the earth: thou hast made heaven and earth.

17 Incline thine ear, O LORD, and hear; open thine eyes, O LORD, and see: and hear all the words of Sen-nach'e-rib, which hath sent to reproach the living God.

18 Of a truth, LORD, the kings of As-syr'i-a have laid waste all the nations, and their countries,

19 And have cast their gods into the fire: for they *were* no gods, but the work of men's hands, wood and stone: therefore they have destroyed them.

20 Now therefore, O LORD our God, save us from his hand, that all the kingdoms of the earth may know that thou *art* the LORD, *even* thou only.

21 ¶ Then I-sa'iah the son of A'moz sent unto Hez-e-ki'ah, saying, Thus saith the LORD God of Is'ra-el, Whereas thou hast prayed to me against Sen-nach'e-rib king of As-syr'i-a:

22 This *is* the word which the LORD hath spoken concerning him; The virgin, the daughter of Zi'on, hath despised thee, *and* laughed thee to scorn; the daughter of Je-ru'sa-lem hath shaken her head at thee.

23 Whom hast thou reproached and blasphemed? and against whom hast thou exalted *thy* voice, and lifted up thine eyes on high? *even* against the Holy One of Is'ra-el.

24 By thy servants hast thou reproached the Lord, and hast said, By the multitude of my chariots am I come up to the height of the mountains, to the sides of Leb'a-non; and I will cut down the tall cedars thereof, *and* the choice fir trees thereof: and I will enter into the height of his border, *and* the forest of his Car'mel.

25 I have digged, and drunk water; and with the sole of my feet have I dried up all the rivers of the besieged places.

26 Hast thou not heard long ago, *how* I have done it; *and* of ancient times, that I have formed it? now have I brought it to pass, that thou shouldest be to lay waste defenced cities *into* ruinous heaps.

27 Therefore their inhabitants *were* of small power, they were dismayed and confounded: they were *as* the grass of the field, and *as* the green herb, *as* the grass on the house tops, and *as corn* blasted before it be grown up.

28 But I know thy abode, and thy going out, and thy coming in, and thy rage against me.

29 Because thy rage against me, and thy tumult, is come up into mine ears, therefore will I put my hook in thy nose, and my bridle in thy lips, and I will turn thee back by the way by which thou camest.

30 And this *shall be* a sign unto thee, Ye shall eat *this* year such as groweth of itself; and the second year that which springeth of the same: and in the third year sow ye, and reap, and plant vineyards, and eat the fruit thereof.

31 And the remnant that is escaped of the house of Ju'dah shall again take root downward, and bear fruit upward:

32 For out of Je-ru'sa-lem shall go forth a remnant, and they that escape out of mount Zi'-on: the zeal of the LORD of hosts shall do this.

33 Therefore thus saith the LORD concerning the king of As-syr'i-a, He shall not come into this city, nor shoot an arrow there, nor come before it with shields, nor cast a bank against it.

34 By the way that he came, by the same shall he return, and shall not come into this city, saith the LORD.

35 For I will defend this city to save it for mine own sake, and for my servant Da'vid's sake.

36 Then the angel of the LORD went forth, and smote in the camp of the As-syr'i-ans a hundred and fourscore and five thousand: and when they arose early in the morning, behold, they *were* all dead corpses.

37 ¶ So Sen-nach'e-rib king of As-syr'i-a departed, and went and returned, and dwelt at Nin'e-veh.

38 And it came to pass, as he was worshipping in the house of Nis'roch his god, that A-dram'me-lech and Sha-re'zer his sons smote him with the sword; and they escaped into the land of Ar-me'ni-a: and E'sar-had'don his son reigned in his stead.

38 IN those days was Hez-e-ki'ah sick unto death. And I-sa'iah the prophet the son of A'moz came unto him, and said unto him, Thus saith the LORD, Set thine house in order: for thou shalt die, and not live.

2 Then Hez-e-ki'ah turned his face toward the wall, and prayed unto the LORD,

3 And said, Remember now, O LORD, I beseech thee, how I have walked before thee in truth and with a perfect heart, and have done *that which is* good in thy sight. And Hez-e-ki'ah wept sore.

4 ¶ Then came the word of the LORD to I-sa'iah, saying,

5 Go, and say to Hez-e-ki'ah, Thus saith the LORD, the God of Da'vid thy father, I have heard

thy prayer, I have seen thy tears: behold, I will add unto thy days fifteen years.

6 And I will deliver thee and this city out of the hand of the king of As-syr'i-a: and I will defend this city.

7 And this *shall be* a sign unto thee from the LORD, that the LORD will do this thing that he hath spoken;

8 Behold, I will bring again the shadow of the degrees, which is gone down in the sun dial of A'haz, ten degrees backward. So the sun returned ten degrees, by which degrees it was gone down.

9 ¶ The writing of Hez-e-ki'ah king of Ju'dah, when he had been sick, and was recovered of his sickness:

10 I said in the cutting off of my days, I shall go to the gates of the grave: I am deprived of the residue of my years.

11 I said, I shall not see the LORD, *even* the LORD, in the land of the living: I shall behold man no more with the inhabitants of the world.

12 Mine age is departed, and is removed from me as a shepherd's tent: I have cut off like a weaver my life: he will cut me off with pining sickness: from day *even* to night wilt thou make an end of me.

13 I reckoned till morning, *that,* as a lion, so will he break all my bones: from day *even* to night wilt thou make an end of me.

14 Like a crane *or* a swallow, so did I chatter: I did mourn as a dove: mine eyes fail *with looking* upward: O LORD, I am oppressed; undertake for me.

15 What shall I say? he hath both spoken unto me, and himself hath done *it;* I shall go softly all my years in the bitterness of my soul.

16 O Lord, by these *things men* live, and in all these *things is* the life of my spirit: so wilt thou recover me, and make me to live.

17 Behold, for peace I had great bitterness: but thou hast in love to my soul *delivered it* from the pit of corruption: for thou hast cast all my sins behind thy back.

18 For the grave cannot praise thee, death can *not* celebrate thee: they that go down into the pit cannot hope for thy truth.

19 The living, the living, he shall praise thee, as I *do* this day: the father to the children shall make known thy truth.

20 The LORD *was ready* to save me: therefore we will sing my songs to the stringed instruments all the days of our life in the house of the LORD.

21 For I-sa'iah had said, Let them take a lump of figs, and lay *it* for a plaister upon the boil, and he shall recover.

22 Hez-e-ki'ah also had said What *is* the sign that I shall go up to the house of the LORD?

39 AT that time Me-ro'dach-bal'a-dan, the son of Bal'a-dan, king of Bab'y-lon, sent letters and a present to Hez-e-ki'ah: for he had heard that he had been sick, and was recovered.

2 And Hez-e-ki'ah was glad of them, and shewed them the house of his precious things, the silver, and the gold, and the spices, and the precious ointment, and all the house of his armour, and all that was found in his treasures: there was nothing in his house, nor in all his dominion, that Hez-e-ki'ah shewed them not.

3 ¶ Then came I-sa'iah the prophet unto king Hez-e-ki'ah, and said unto him, What said these men? and from whence came they unto thee? And Hez-e-ki'ah said, They are come from a far country unto me, *even* from Bab'y-lon.

4 Then said he, What have they seen in thine house? And Hez-e-ki'ah answered, All that *is* in mine house have they seen: there is nothing among my treasures that I have not shewed them.

5 Then said I-sa'iah to Hez-e-ki'ah, Hear the word of the LORD of hosts:

6 Behold, the days come, that all that *is* in thine house, and *that* which thy fathers have laid up in store until this day, shall be carried to Bab'y-lon: nothing shall be left, saith the LORD.

7 And of thy sons that shall issue from thee, which thou shalt beget, shall they take away; and they shall be eunuchs in the palace of the king of Bab'y-lon.

8 Then said Hez-e-ki'ah to I-sa'iah, Good *is* the word of the LORD which thou hast spoken. He said moreover, For there shall be peace and truth in my days.

40 COMFORT ye, comfort ye my people, saith your God.

2 Speak ye comfortably to Je-ru'sa-lem, and cry unto her, that her warfare is accomplished, that her iniquity is pardoned: for she hath received of the LORD's hand double for all her sins.

3 ¶ The voice of him that crieth in the wilderness, Prepare ye the way of the LORD, make straight in the desert a highway for our God.

4 Every valley shall be exalted, and every mountain and hill shall be made low: and the crooked shall be made straight, and the rough places plain:

5 And the glory of the LORD shall be revealed, and all flesh shall see *it* together: for the mouth of the LORD hath spoken *it.*

6 The voice said, Cry. And he said, What shall I cry? All flesh *is* grass, and all the goodliness thereof *is* as the flower of the field:

7 The grass withereth, the flower fadeth: because the spirit of the LORD bloweth upon it: surely the people *is* grass.

8 The grass withereth, the flower fadeth: but the word of our God shall stand for ever.

9 ¶ O Zi'on, that bringest good tidings, get thee up into the high mountain; O Je-ru'sa-lem, that bringest good tidings, lift up thy voice with strength; lift *it* up, be not afraid; say unto the cities of Ju'dah, Behold your God!

10 Behold, the Lord GOD will come with strong *hand,* and his arm shall rule for him: behold, his reward *is* with him, and his work before him.

11 He shall feed his flock like a shepherd: he shall gather the lambs with his arm, and carry *them* in his bosom, *and* shall gently lead those that are with young.

12 ¶ Who hath measured the waters in the hollow of his hand, and meted out heaven with the span, and comprehended the dust of the earth in a measure, and weighed the mountains in scales, and the hills in a balance?

13 Who hath directed the Spirit of the LORD, or *being* his counsellor hath taught him?

14 With whom took he counsel, and *who* instructed him, and taught him in the path of judgment, and taught him knowledge, and shewed to him the way of understanding?

15 Behold, the nations *are* as a drop of a bucket, and are counted as the small dust of the balance: behold, he taketh up the isles as a very little thing.

16 And Leb'a-non *is* not sufficient to burn, nor the beasts thereof sufficient for a burnt offering.

17 All nations before him *are* as nothing; and

they are counted to him less than nothing, and vanity.

18 ¶ To whom then will ye liken God? or what likeness will ye compare unto him?

19 The workman melteth a graven image, and the goldsmith spreadeth it over with gold, and casteth silver chains.

20 He that *is* so impoverished that he hath no oblation chooseth a tree *that* will not rot; he seeketh unto him a cunning workman to prepare a graven image, *that* shall not be moved.

21 Have ye not known? have ye not heard? hath it not been told you from the beginning? have ye not understood from the foundations of the earth?

22 *It is* he that sitteth upon the circle of the earth, and the inhabitants thereof *are* as grasshoppers; that stretcheth out the heavens as a curtain, and spreadeth them out as a tent to dwell in:

23 That bringeth the princes to nothing; he maketh the judges of the earth as vanity.

24 Yea, they shall not be planted; yea, they shall not be sown: yea, their stock shall not take root in the earth: and he shall also blow upon them, and they shall wither, and the whirlwind shall take them away as stubble.

25 To whom then will ye liken me, or shall I be equal? saith the Holy One.

26 Lift up your eyes on high, and behold who hath created these *things*, that bringeth out their host by number: he calleth them all by names by the greatness of his might, for that *he is* strong in power; not one faileth.

27 Why sayest thou, O Ja′cob, and speakest, O Is′ra-el, My way is hid from the LORD, and my judgment is passed over from my God?

28 ¶ Hast thou not known? hast thou not heard, *that* the everlasting God, the LORD, the Creator of the ends of the earth, fainteth not, neither is weary? *there is* no searching of his understanding.

29 He giveth power to the faint; and to *them that have* no might he increaseth strength.

30 Even the youths shall faint and be weary, and the young men shall utterly fall:

31 But they that wait upon the LORD shall renew *their* strength; they shall mount up with wings as eagles; they shall run, and not be weary; *and* they shall walk, and not faint.

41 KEEP silence before me, O islands; and let the people renew *their* strength: let them come near; then let them speak: let us come near together to judgment.

2 Who raised up the righteous *man* from the east, called him to his foot, gave the nations before him, and made *him* rule over kings? he gave *them* as the dust to his sword, *and* as driven stubble to his bow.

3 He pursued them, *and* passed safely; *even* by the way *that* he had not gone with his feet.

4 Who hath wrought and done *it*, calling the generations from the beginning? I the LORD, the first, and with the last; I *am* he.

5 The isles saw *it*, and feared; the ends of the earth were afraid, drew near, and came.

6 They helped every one his neighbour; and *every one* said to his brother, Be of good courage.

7 So the carpenter encouraged the goldsmith, *and* he that smootheth *with* the hammer him that smote the anvil, saying, It *is* ready for the sodering: and he fastened it with nails, *that* it should not be moved.

8 But thou, Is′ra-el, *art* my servant, Ja′cob

whom I have chosen, the seed of A′bra-ham my friend.

9 *Thou* whom I have taken from the ends of the earth, and called thee from the chief men thereof, and said unto thee, Thou *art* my servant; I have chosen thee, and not cast thee away.

10 ¶ Fear thou not; for I *am* with thee: be not dismayed; for I *am* thy God: I will strengthen thee; yea, I will help thee; yea, I will uphold thee with the right hand of my righteousness.

11 Behold, all they that were incensed against thee shall be ashamed and confounded: they shall be as nothing; and they that strive with thee shall perish.

12 Thou shalt seek them, and shalt not find them, *even* them that contended with thee: they that war against thee shall be as nothing, and as a thing of nought.

13 For I the LORD thy God will hold thy right hand, saying unto thee, Fear not; I will help thee.

14 Fear not, thou worm Ja′cob, *and* ye men of Is′ra-el; I will help thee, saith the LORD, and thy redeemer, the Holy One of Is′ra-el.

15 Behold, I will make thee a new sharp threshing instrument having teeth: thou shalt thresh the mountains, and beat *them* small, and shalt make the hills as chaff.

16 Thou shalt fan them, and the wind shall carry them away, and the whirlwind shall scatter them: and thou shalt rejoice in the LORD, *and* shalt glory in the Holy One of Is′ra-el.

17 *When* the poor and needy seek water, and *there is* none, *and* their tongue faileth for thirst, I the LORD will hear them, *I* the God of Is′ra-el will not forsake them.

18 I will open rivers in high places, and fountains in the midst of the valleys: I will make the wilderness a pool of water, and the dry land springs of water.

19 I will plant in the wilderness the cedar, the shittah tree, and the myrtle, and the oil tree; I will set in the desert the fir tree, *and* the pine, and the box tree together:

20 That they may see, and know, and consider, and understand together, that the hand of the LORD hath done this, and the Holy One of Is′ra-el hath created it.

21 Produce your cause, saith the LORD; bring forth your strong *reasons*, saith the King of Ja′-cob.

22 Let them bring *them* forth, and shew us what shall happen: let them shew the former things, what they *be*, that we may consider them, and know the latter end of them; or declare us things for to come.

23 Shew the things that are to come hereafter, that we may know that ye *are* gods; yea, do good, or do evil, that we may be dismayed, and behold *it* together.

24 Behold, ye *are* of nothing, and your work of nought: an abomination *is he that* chooseth you.

25 I have raised up *one* from the north, and he shall come: from the rising of the sun shall he call upon my name: and he shall come upon princes as *upon* morter, and as the potter treadeth clay.

26 Who hath declared from the beginning, that we may know? and beforetime, that we may say, He *is* righteous? yea, *there is* none that sheweth, yea, *there is* none that declareth, yea, *there is* none that heareth your words.

27 The first *shall say* to Zi′on, Behold, behold them: and I will give to Je-ru′sa-lem one that bringeth good tidings.

28 For I beheld, and *there was* no man; even among them, and *there was* no counsellor, that, when I asked of them, could answer a word.

29 Behold, they *are* all vanity; their works *are* nothing: their molten images *are* wind and confusion.

42 BEHOLD my servant, whom I uphold; mine elect, *in whom* my soul delighteth; I have put my spirit upon him: he shall bring forth judgment to the Gen'tiles.

2 He shall not cry, nor lift up, nor cause his voice to be heard in the street.

3 A bruised reed shall he not break, and the smoking flax shall he not quench: he shall bring forth judgment unto truth.

4 He shall not fail nor be discouraged, till he have set judgment in the earth: and the isles shall wait for his law.

5 ¶ Thus saith God the LORD, he that created the heavens, and stretched them out; he that spread forth the earth, and that which cometh out of it; he that giveth breath unto the people upon it, and spirit to them that walk therein:

6 I the LORD have called thee in righteousness, and will hold thine hand, and will keep thee, and give thee for a covenant of the people, for a light of the Gen'tiles;

7 To open the blind eyes, to bring out the prisoners from the prison, *and* them that sit in darkness out of the prison house.

8 I *am* the LORD: that *is* my name: and my glory will I not give to another, neither my praise to graven images.

9 Behold, the former things are come to pass, and new things do I declare: before they spring forth I tell you of them.

10 Sing unto the LORD a new song, *and* his praise from the end of the earth, ye that go down to the sea, and all that is therein; the isles, and the inhabitants thereof.

11 Let the wilderness and the cities thereof lift up *their voice*, the villages *that* Ke'dar doth inhabit: let the inhabitants of the rock sing, let them shout from the top of the mountains.

12 Let them give glory unto the LORD, and declare his praise in the islands.

13 The LORD shall go forth as a mighty man, he shall stir up jealousy like a man of war: he shall cry, yea, roar; he shall prevail against his enemies.

14 I have long time holden my peace; I have been still, *and* refrained myself: *now* will I cry like a travailing woman; I will destroy and devour at once.

15 I will make waste mountains and hills, and dry up all their herbs; and I will make the rivers islands, and I will dry up the pools.

16 And I will bring the blind by a way *that* they knew not; I will lead them in paths *that* they have not known: I will make darkness light before them, and crooked things straight. These things will I do unto them, and not forsake them.

17 ¶ They shall be turned back, they shall be greatly ashamed, that trust in graven images, that say to the molten images, Ye *are* our gods.

18 Hear, ye deaf; and look, ye blind, that ye may see.

19 Who *is* blind, but my servant? or deaf, as my messenger *that* I sent? who *is* blind as he *that is* perfect, and blind as the LORD's servant?

20 Seeing many things, but thou observest not; opening the ears, but he heareth not.

21 The LORD is well pleased for his righteousness' sake; he will magnify the law, and make *it* honourable.

22 But this *is* a people robbed and spoiled; *they are* all of them snared in holes, and they are hid in prison houses: they are for a prey, and none delivereth; for a spoil, and none saith, Restore.

23 Who among you will give ear to this? *who* will hearken and hear for the time to come?

24 Who gave Ja'cob for a spoil, and Is'ra-el to the robbers? did not the LORD, he against whom we have sinned? for they would not walk in his ways, neither were they obedient unto his law.

25 Therefore he hath poured upon him the fury of his anger, and the strength of battle: and it hath set him on fire round about, yet he knew not; and it burned him, yet he laid *it* not to heart.

43 BUT now thus saith the LORD that created thee, O Ja'cob, and he that formed thee, O Is'ra-el, Fear not: for I have redeemed thee, I have called *thee* by thy name; thou *art* mine.

2 When thou passest through the waters, I *will be* with thee; and through the rivers, they shall not overflow thee: when thou walkest through the fire, thou shalt not be burned; neither shall the flame kindle upon thee.

3 For I *am* the LORD thy God, the Holy One of Is'ra-el, thy Saviour: I gave E'gypt *for* thy ransom, E-thi-o'pi-a and Se'ba for thee.

4 Since thou wast precious in my sight, thou hast been honourable, and I have loved thee: therefore will I give men for thee, and people for thy life.

5 Fear not: for I *am* with thee: I will bring thy seed from the east, and gather thee from the west;

6 I will say to the north, Give up; and to the south, Keep not back: bring my sons from far, and my daughters from the ends of the earth;

7 *Even* every one that is called by my name: for I have created him for my glory, I have formed him; yea, I have made him.

8 ¶ Bring forth the blind people that have eyes, and the deaf that have ears.

9 Let all the nations be gathered together, and let the people be assembled: who among them can declare this, and shew us former things? let them bring forth their witnesses, that they may be justified: or let them hear, and say, It *is* truth.

10 Ye *are* my witnesses, saith the LORD, and my servant whom I have chosen: that ye may know and believe me, and understand that I *am* he: before me there was no God formed, neither shall there be after me.

11 I, *even* I, *am* the LORD; and beside me *there is* no saviour.

12 I have declared, and have saved, and I have shewed, when *there was* no strange god among you: therefore ye *are* my witnesses, saith the LORD, that I *am* God.

13 Yea, before the day *was* I *am* he; and *there is* none that can deliver out of my hand: I will work, and who shall let it?

14 ¶ Thus saith the LORD, your redeemer, the Holy One of Is'ra-el; For your sake I have sent to Bab'y-lon, and have brought down all their nobles, and the Chal-de'ans, whose cry *is* in the ships.

15 I *am* the LORD, your Holy One, the creator of Is'ra-el, your King.

16 Thus saith the LORD, which maketh a way in the sea, and a path in the mighty waters;

17 Which bringeth forth the chariot and horse, the army and the power; they shall lie

down together, they shall not rise: they are extinct, they are quenched as tow.

18 ¶ Remember ye not the former things, neither consider the things of old.

19 Behold, I will do a new thing; now it shall spring forth; shall ye not know it? I will even make a way in the wilderness, *and* rivers in the desert.

20 The beast of the field shall honour me, the dragons and the owls: because I give waters in the wilderness, *and* rivers in the desert, to give drink to my people, my chosen.

21 This people have I formed for myself; they shall shew forth my praise.

22 ¶ But thou hast not called upon me, O Ja'cob; but thou hast been weary of me, O Is'ra-el.

23 Thou hast not brought me the small cattle of thy burnt offerings; neither hast thou honoured me with thy sacrifices. I have not caused thee to serve with an offering, nor wearied thee with incense.

24 Thou hast bought me no sweet cane with money, neither hast thou filled me with the fat of thy sacrifices: but thou hast made me to serve with thy sins, thou hast wearied me with thine iniquities.

25 I, *even* I, *am* he that blotteth out thy transgressions for mine own sake, and will not remember thy sins.

26 Put me in remembrance: let us plead together: declare thou, that thou mayest be justified.

27 Thy first father hath sinned, and thy teachers have transgressed against me.

28 Therefore I have profaned the princes of the sanctuary, and have given Ja'cob to the curse, and Is'ra-el to reproaches.

44 YET now hear, O Ja'cob my servant; and Is'ra-el, whom I have chosen:

2 Thus saith the LORD that made thee, and formed thee from the womb, *which* will help thee; Fear not, O Ja'cob, my servant; and thou, Jes'u-run, whom I have chosen.

3 For I will pour water upon him that is thirsty, and floods upon the dry ground: I will pour my spirit upon thy seed, and my blessing upon thine offspring:

4 And they shall spring up *as* among the grass, as willows by the water courses.

5 One shall say, I *am* the LORD'S; and another shall call *himself* by the name of Ja'cob; and another shall subscribe *with* his hand unto the LORD, and surname *himself* by the name of Is'ra-el.

6 Thus saith the LORD the King of Is'ra-el, and his redeemer the LORD of hosts; I *am* the first, and I *am* the last; and beside me *there is* no God.

7 And who, as I, shall call, and shall declare it, and set it in order for me, since I appointed the ancient people? and the things that are coming, and shall come, let them shew unto them.

8 Fear ye not, neither be afraid: have not I told thee from that time, and have declared *it?* ye *are* even my witnesses. Is there a God beside me? yea, *there is* no God; I know not *any.*

9 ¶ They that make a graven image *are* all of them vanity; and their delectable things shall not profit; and they *are* their own witnesses; they see not, nor know; that they may be ashamed.

10 Who hath formed a god, or molten a graven image *that* is profitable for nothing?

11 Behold, all his fellows shall be ashamed: and the workmen, they *are* of men: let them all be gathered together, let them stand up; yet

they shall fear, *and* they shall be ashamed together.

12 The smith with the tongs both worketh in the coals, and fashioneth it with hammers, and worketh it with the strength of his arms: yea, he is hungry, and his strength faileth: he drinketh no water, and is faint.

13 The carpenter stretcheth out *his* rule; he marketh it out with a line; he fitteth it with planes, and he marketh it out with the compass, and maketh it after the figure of a man, according to the beauty of a man; that it may remain in the house.

14 He heweth him down cedars, and taketh the cypress and the oak, which he strengtheneth for himself among the trees of the forest: he planteth an ash, and the rain doth nourish *it.*

15 Then shall it be for a man to burn: for he will take thereof, and warm himself; yea, he kindleth *it,* and baketh bread; yea, he maketh a god, and worshippeth *it;* he maketh it a graven image, and falleth down thereto.

16 He burneth part thereof in the fire; with part thereof he eateth flesh; he roasteth roast, and is satisfied: yea, he warmeth *himself,* and saith, Aha, I am warm, I have seen the fire:

17 And the residue thereof he maketh a god, *even* his graven image: he falleth down unto it, and worshippeth *it,* and prayeth unto it, and saith, Deliver me; for thou *art* my god.

18 They have not known nor understood: for he hath shut their eyes, that they cannot see; *and* their hearts, that they cannot understand.

19 And none considereth in his heart, neither *is there* knowledge nor understanding to say, I have burned part of it in the fire; yea, also I have baked bread upon the coals thereof; I have roasted flesh, and eaten *it:* and shall I make the residue thereof an abomination? shall I fall down to the stock of a tree?

20 He feedeth on ashes: a deceived heart hath turned him aside, that he cannot deliver his soul, nor say, *Is there* not a lie in my right hand?

21 ¶ Remember these, O Ja'cob and Is'ra-el; for thou *art* my servant: I have formed thee; thou *art* my servant: O Is'ra-el, thou shalt not be forgotten of me.

22 I have blotted out, as a thick cloud, thy transgressions, and, as a cloud, thy sins: return unto me; for I have redeemed thee.

23 Sing, O ye heavens; for the LORD hath done *it:* shout, ye lower parts of the earth: break forth into singing, ye mountains, O forest, and every tree therein: for the LORD hath redeemed Ja'cob, and glorified himself in Is'ra-el.

24 Thus saith the LORD, thy redeemer, and he that formed thee from the womb, I *am* the LORD that maketh all *things;* that stretcheth forth the heavens alone; that spreadeth abroad the earth by myself;

25 That frustrateth the tokens of the liars, and maketh diviners mad; that turneth wise *men* backward, and maketh their knowledge foolish;

26 That confirmeth the word of his servant, and performeth the counsel of his messengers; that saith to Je-ru'sa-lem, Thou shalt be inhabited; and to the cities of Ju'dah, Ye shall be built, and I will raise up the decayed places thereof:

27 That saith to the deep, Be dry, and I will dry up thy rivers:

28 That saith of Cy'rus, *He is* my shepherd, and shall perform all my pleasure: even saying to Je-ru'sa-lem, Thou shalt be built; and to the temple, Thy foundation shall be laid.

45

THUS saith the LORD to his anointed, to Cy'rus, whose right hand I have holden, to subdue nations before him; and I will loose the loins of kings, to open before him the two leaved gates; and the gates shall not be shut;

2 I will go before thee, and make the crooked places straight: I will break in pieces the gates of brass, and cut in sunder the bars of iron:

3 And I will give thee the treasures of darkness, and hidden riches of secret places, that thou mayest know that I, the LORD which call thee by thy name, am the God of Is'ra-el.

4 For Ja'cob my servant's sake, and Is'ra-el mine elect, I have even called thee by thy name: I have surnamed thee, though thou hast not known me.

5 ¶ I am the LORD, and there is none else, there is no God beside me: I girded thee, though thou hast not known me:

6 That they may know from the rising of the sun, and from the west, that there is none beside me. I am the LORD, and there is none else.

7 I form the light, and create darkness: I make peace, and create evil: I the LORD do all these things.

8 Drop down, ye heavens, from above, and let the skies pour down righteousness: let the earth open, and let them bring forth salvation, and let righteousness spring up together; I the LORD have created it.

9 Woe unto him that striveth with his Maker! Let the potsherd strive with the potsherds of the earth. Shall the clay say to him that fashioneth it, What makest thou? or thy work, He hath no hands?

10 Woe unto him that saith unto his father, What begettest thou? or to the woman, What hast thou brought forth?

11 Thus saith the LORD, the Holy One of Is'ra-el, and his Maker, Ask me of things to come concerning my sons, and concerning the work of my hands command ye me.

12 I have made the earth, and created man upon it: I, even my hands, have stretched out the heavens, and all their host have I commanded.

13 I have raised him up in righteousness, and I will direct all his ways: he shall build my city, and he shall let go my captives, not for price nor reward, saith the LORD of hosts.

14 Thus saith the LORD, The labour of E'gypt, and merchandise of E-thi-o'pi-a and of the Sa-be'ans, men of stature, shall come over unto thee, and they shall be thine: they shall come after thee; in chains they shall come over, and they shall fall down unto thee, they shall make supplication unto thee, saying, Surely God is in thee; and there is none else, there is no God.

15 Verily thou art a God that hidest thyself, O God of Is'ra-el, the Saviour.

16 They shall be ashamed, and also confounded, all of them: they shall go to confusion together that are makers of idols.

17 But Is'ra-el shall be saved in the LORD with an everlasting salvation: ye shall not be ashamed nor confounded world without end.

18 For thus saith the LORD that created the heavens; God himself that formed the earth and made it; he hath established it, he created it not in vain, he formed it to be inhabited: I am the LORD; and there is none else.

19 I have not spoken in secret, in a dark place of the earth: I said not unto the seed of Ja'cob, Seek ye me in vain: I the LORD speak righteousness, I declare things that are right.

20 ¶ Assemble yourselves and come; draw near together, ye that are escaped of the nations: they have no knowledge that set up the wood of their graven image, and pray unto a god that cannot save.

21 Tell ye, and bring them near; yea, let them take counsel together: who hath declared this from ancient time? who hath told it from that time? have not I the LORD? and there is no God else beside me; a just God and a Saviour; there is none beside me.

22 Look unto me, and be ye saved, all the ends of the earth: for I am God, and there is none else.

23 I have sworn by myself, the word is gone out of my mouth in righteousness, and shall not return, That unto me every knee shall bow, every tongue shall swear.

24 Surely, shall one say, in the LORD have I righteousness and strength: even to him shall men come; and all that are incensed against him shall be ashamed.

25 In the LORD shall all the seed of Is'ra-el be justified, and shall glory.

46

BEL boweth down, Ne'bo stoopeth, their idols were upon the beasts, and upon the cattle: your carriages were heavy loaden; they are a burden to the weary beast.

2 They stoop, they bow down together; they could not deliver the burden, but themselves are gone into captivity.

3 ¶ Hearken unto me, O house of Ja'cob, and all the remnant of the house of Is'ra-el, which are borne by me from the belly, which are carried from the womb:

4 And even to your old age I am he; and even to hoar hairs will I carry you: I have made, and I will bear; even I will carry, and will deliver you.

5 ¶ To whom will ye liken me, and make me equal, and compare me, that we may be like?

6 They lavish gold out of the bag, and weigh silver in the balance, and hire a goldsmith; and he maketh it a god: they fall down, yea, they worship.

7 They bear him upon the shoulder, they carry him, and set him in his place, and he standeth; from his place shall he not remove: yea, one shall cry unto him, yet can he not answer, nor save him out of his trouble.

8 Remember this, and shew yourselves men: bring it again to mind, O ye transgressors.

9 Remember the former things of old: for I am God, and there is none else; I am God, and there is none like me,

10 Declaring the end from the beginning, and from ancient times the things that are not yet done, saying, My counsel shall stand, and I will do all my pleasure:

11 Calling a ravenous bird from the east, the man that executeth my counsel from a far country: yea, I have spoken it, I will also bring it to pass; I have purposed it, I will also do it.

12 ¶ Hearken unto me, ye stouthearted, that are far from righteousness:

13 I bring near my righteousness; it shall not be far off, and my salvation shall not tarry: and I will place salvation in Zi'on for Is'ra-el my glory.

47

COME down, and sit in the dust, O virgin daughter of Bab'y-lon, sit on the ground: there is no throne, O daughter of the Chal-de'ans: for thou shalt no more be called tender and delicate.

2 Take the millstones, and grind meal: uncover thy locks, make bare the leg, uncover the thigh, pass over the rivers.

3 Thy nakedness shall be uncovered, yea, thy shame shall be seen: I will take vengeance, and I will not meet *thee as* a man.

4 *As for* our redeemer, the LORD of hosts *is* his name, the Holy One of Is'ra-el.

5 Sit thou silent, and get thee into darkness, O daughter of the Chal-de'ans: for thou shalt no more be called, The lady of kingdoms.

6 ¶ I was wroth with my people, I have polluted mine inheritance, and given them into thine hand: thou didst shew them no mercy; upon the ancient hast thou very heavily laid thy yoke.

7 ¶ And thou saidst, I shall be a lady for ever: *so* that thou didst not lay these *things* to thy heart, neither didst remember the latter end of it.

8 Therefore hear now this, *thou that art* given to pleasures, that dwellest carelessly, that sayest in thine heart, I *am*, and none else beside me; I shall not sit *as* a widow, neither shall I know the loss of children:

9 But these two *things* shall come to thee in a moment in one day, the loss of children, and widowhood: they shall come upon thee in their perfection for the multitude of thy sorceries, *and* for the great abundance of thine enchantments.

10 ¶ For thou hast trusted in thy wickedness: thou hast said, None seeth me. Thy wisdom and thy knowledge, it hath perverted thee; and thou hast said in thine heart, I *am*, and none else beside me.

11 ¶ Therefore shall evil come upon thee; thou shalt not know from whence it riseth: and mischief shall fall upon thee; thou shalt not be able to put it off: and desolation shall come upon thee suddenly, *which* thou shalt not know.

12 Stand now with thine enchantments, and with the multitude of thy sorceries, wherein thou hast laboured from thy youth; if so be thou shalt be able to profit, if so be thou mayest prevail.

13 Thou art wearied in the multitude of thy counsels. Let now the astrologers, the stargazers, the monthly prognosticators, stand up, and save thee from *these things* that shall come upon thee.

14 Behold, they shall be as stubble; the fire shall burn them; they shall not deliver themselves from the power of the flame: *there shall* not *be* a coal to warm at, *nor* fire to sit before it.

15 Thus shall they be unto thee with whom thou hast laboured, *even* thy merchants, from thy youth: they shall wander every one to his quarter; none shall save thee.

48 HEAR ye this, O house of Ja'cob, which are called by the name of Is'ra-el, and are come forth out of the waters of Ju'dah, which swear by the name of the LORD, and make mention of the God of Is'ra-el, *but* not in truth, nor in righteousness.

2 For they call themselves of the holy city, and stay themselves upon the God of Is'ra-el; The LORD of hosts *is* his name.

3 I have declared the former things from the beginning; and they went forth out of my mouth, and I shewed them; I did *them* suddenly, and they came to pass.

4 Because I knew that thou *art* obstinate, and thy neck *is* an iron sinew, and thy brow brass;

5 I have even from the beginning declared *it* to thee; before it came to pass I shewed *it* thee: lest thou shouldest say, Mine idol hath done them, and my graven image, and my molten image, hath commanded them.

6 Thou hast heard, see all this; and will not ye declare *it?* I have shewed thee new things from this time, even hidden things, and thou didst not know them.

7 They are created now, and not from the beginning; even before the day when thou heardest them not; lest thou shouldest say, Behold, I knew them.

8 Yea, thou heardest not; yea, thou knewest not; yea, from that time *that* thine ear was not opened: for I knew that thou wouldest deal very treacherously, and wast called a transgressor from the womb.

9 ¶ For my name's sake will I defer mine anger, and for my praise will I refrain for thee, that I cut thee not off.

10 Behold, I have refined thee, but not with silver; I have chosen thee in the furnace of affliction.

11 For mine own sake, *even* for mine own sake, will I do *it:* for how should *my name* be polluted? and I will not give my glory unto another.

12 ¶ Hearken unto me, O Ja'cob and Is'ra-el, my called; I *am* he; I *am* the first, I also *am* the last.

13 Mine hand also hath laid the foundation of the earth, and my right hand hath spanned the heavens: *when* I call unto them, they stand up together.

14 All ye, assemble yourselves, and hear; which among them hath declared these *things?* The LORD hath loved him: he will do his pleasure on Bab'y-lon, and his arm *shall be on* the Chal-de'ans.

15 I, *even* I, have spoken; yea, I have called him: I have brought him, and he shall make his way prosperous.

16 ¶ Come ye near unto me, hear ye this; I have not spoken in secret from the beginning; from the time that it was, there *am* I: and now the Lord GOD, and his Spirit, hath sent me.

17 Thus saith the LORD, thy redeemer, the Holy One of Is'ra-el; I *am* the LORD thy God which teacheth thee to profit, which leadeth thee by the way *that* thou shouldest go.

18 O that thou hadst hearkened to my commandments! then had thy peace been as a river, and thy righteousness as the waves of the sea:

19 Thy seed also had been as the sand, and the offspring of thy bowels like the gravel thereof; his name should not have been cut off nor destroyed from before me.

20 ¶ Go ye forth of Bab'y-lon, flee ye from the Chal-de'ans, with a voice of singing declare ye, tell this, utter it *even* to the end of the earth; say ye, The LORD hath redeemed his servant Ja'cob.

21 And they thirsted not *when* he led them through the deserts: he caused the waters to flow out of the rock for them: he clave the rock also, and the waters gushed out.

22 *There is* no peace, saith the LORD, unto the wicked.

49 LISTEN O isles, unto me; and hearken, ye people, from far; The LORD hath called me from the womb; from the bowels of my mother hath he made mention of my name.

2 And he hath made my mouth like a sharp sword; in the shadow of his hand hath he hid me, and made me a polished shaft; in his quiver hath he hid me;

3 And said unto me, Thou *art* my servant, O Is'ra-el, in whom I will be glorified.

4 Then I said, I have laboured in vain, I have spent my strength for nought, and in vain: yet

surely my judgment is with the LORD, and my work with my God.

5 ¶ And now, saith the LORD that formed me from the womb his servant, to bring Ja'-cob again to him, Though Is'ra-el be not gathered, yet shall I be glorious in the eyes of the LORD, and my God shall be my strength.

6 And he said, It is a light thing that thou shouldest be my servant to raise up the tribes of Ja'cob, and to restore the preserved of Is'ra-el: I will also give thee for a light to the Gen'tiles, that thou mayest be my salvation unto the end of the earth.

7 Thus saith the LORD, the Redeemer of Is'ra-el, and his Holy One, to him whom man despiseth, to him whom the nation abhorreth, to a servant of rulers, Kings shall see and arise, princes also shall worship, because of the LORD that is faithful, and the Holy One of Is'ra-el, and he shall choose thee.

8 Thus saith the LORD, In an acceptable time have I heard thee, and in a day of salvation have I helped thee: and I will preserve thee, and give thee for a covenant of the people, to establish the earth, to cause to inherit the desolate heritages;

9 That thou mayest say to the prisoners, Go forth; to them that are in darkness, Shew yourselves. They shall feed in the ways, and their pastures shall be in all high places.

10 They shall not hunger nor thirst; neither shall the heat nor sun smite them: for he that hath mercy on them shall lead them, even by the springs of water shall he guide them.

11 And I will make all my mountains a way, and my highways shall be exalted.

12 Behold, these shall come from far: and, lo, these from the north and from the west; and these from the land of Si'nim.

13 ¶ Sing, O heavens; and be joyful, O earth; and break forth into singing, O mountains: for the LORD hath comforted his people, and will have mercy upon his afflicted.

14 But Zi'on said, The LORD hath forsaken me, and my Lord hath forgotten me.

15 Can a woman forget her sucking child, that she should not have compassion on the son of her womb? yea, they may forget, yet will I not forget thee.

16 Behold, I have graven thee upon the palms of my hands; thy walls are continually before me.

17 Thy children shall make haste; thy destroyers and they that made thee waste shall go forth of thee.

18 ¶ Lift up thine eyes round about, and behold: all these gather themselves together, and come to thee. As I live, saith the LORD, thou shalt surely clothe thee with them all, as with an ornament, and bind them on thee, as a bride doeth.

19 For thy waste and thy desolate places, and the land of thy destruction, shall even now be too narrow by reason of the inhabitants, and they that swallowed thee up shall be far away.

20 The children which thou shalt have, after thou hast lost the other, shall say again in thine ears, The place is too strait for me: give place to me that I may dwell.

21 Then shalt thou say in thine heart, Who hath begotten me these, seeing I have lost my children, and am desolate, a captive, and removing to and fro? and who hath brought up these? Behold, I was left alone; these, where had they been?

22 Thus saith the Lord GOD, Behold, I will lift up mine hand to the Gen'tiles, and set up my standard to the people: and they shall bring thy sons in their arms, and thy daughters shall be carried upon their shoulders.

23 And kings shall be thy nursing fathers, and their queens thy nursing mothers: they shall bow down to thee with their face toward the earth, and lick up the dust of thy feet; and thou shalt know that I am the LORD: for they shall not be ashamed that wait for me.

24 ¶ Shall the prey be taken from the mighty, or the lawful captive delivered?

25 But thus saith the LORD, Even the captives of the mighty shall be taken away, and the prey of the terrible shall be delivered: for I will contend with him that contendeth with thee, and I will save thy children.

26 And I will feed them that oppress thee with their own flesh; and they shall be drunken with their own blood, as with sweet wine: and all flesh shall know that I the LORD am thy Saviour and thy Redeemer, the mighty One of Ja'-cob.

50 THUS saith the LORD, Where is the bill of your mother's divorcement, whom I have put away? or which of my creditors is it to whom I have sold you? Behold, for your iniquities have ye sold yourselves, and for your transgressions is your mother put away.

2 Wherefore, when I came, was there no man? when I called, was there none to answer? Is my hand shortened at all, that it cannot redeem? or have I no power to deliver? behold, at my rebuke I dry up the sea, I make the rivers a wilderness: their fish stinketh, because there is no water, and dieth for thirst.

3 I clothe the heavens with blackness, and I make sackcloth their covering.

4 The Lord GOD hath given me the tongue of the learned, that I should know how to speak a word in season to him that is weary: he wakeneth morning by morning, he wakeneth mine ear to hear as the learned.

5 ¶ The Lord GOD hath opened mine ear, and I was not rebellious, neither turned away back.

6 I gave my back to the smiters, and my cheeks to them that plucked off the hair: I hid not my face from shame and spitting.

7 ¶ For the Lord GOD will help me; therefore shall I not be confounded: therefore have I set my face like a flint, and I know that I shall not be ashamed.

8 He is near that justifieth me; who will contend with me? let us stand together: who is mine adversary? let him come near to me.

9 Behold, the Lord GOD will help me; who is he that shall condemn me? lo, they all shall wax old as a garment; the moth shall eat them up.

10 ¶ Who is among you that feareth the LORD, that obeyeth the voice of his servant, that walketh in darkness, and hath no light? let him trust in the name of the LORD, and stay upon his God.

11 Behold, all ye that kindle a fire, that compass yourselves about with sparks: walk in the light of your fire, and in the sparks that ye have kindled. This shall ye have of mine hand; ye shall lie down in sorrow.

51 HEARKEN to me, ye that follow after righteousness, ye that seek the LORD: look unto the rock whence ye are hewn, and to the hole of the pit whence ye are digged.

2 Look unto A'bra-ham your father, and unto Sa'rah that bare you: for I called him alone, and blessed him, and increased him.

3 For the LORD shall comfort Zi'on: he will

comfort all her waste places; and he will make her wilderness like E′den, and her desert like the garden of the LORD; joy and gladness shall be found therein, thanksgiving, and the voice of melody.

4 ¶ Hearken unto me, my people; and give ear unto me, O my nation: for a law shall proceed from me, and I will make my judgment to rest for a light of the people.

5 My righteousness *is* near; my salvation is gone forth, and mine arms shall judge the people; the isles shall wait upon me, and on mine arm shall they trust.

6 Lift up your eyes to the heavens, and look upon the earth beneath: for the heavens shall vanish away like smoke, and the earth shall wax old like a garment, and they that dwell therein shall die in like manner: but my salvation shall be for ever, and my righteousness shall not be abolished.

7 ¶ Hearken unto me, ye that know righteousness, the people in whose heart *is* my law; fear ye not the reproach of men, neither be ye afraid of their revilings.

8 For the moth shall eat them up like a garment, and the worm shall eat them like wool: but my righteousness shall be for ever, and my salvation from generation to generation.

9 ¶ Awake, awake, put on strength, O arm of the LORD; awake, as in the ancient days, in the generations of old. *Art* thou not it that hath cut Ra′hab, *and* wounded the dragon?

10 *Art* thou not it which hath dried the sea, the waters of the great deep; that hath made the depths of the sea a way for the ransomed to pass over?

11 Therefore the redeemed of the LORD shall return, and come with singing unto Zi′on; and everlasting joy *shall be* upon their head: they shall obtain gladness and joy; *and* sorrow and mourning shall flee away.

12 I, *even* I, *am* he that comforteth you: who *art* thou, that thou shouldest be afraid of a man *that* shall die, and of the son of man *which* shall be made *as* grass;

13 And forgettest the LORD thy maker, that hath stretched forth the heavens, and laid the foundations of the earth; and hast feared continually every day because of the fury of the oppressor, as if he were ready to destroy? and where *is* the fury of the oppressor?

14 The captive exile hasteneth that he may be loosed, and that he should not die in the pit, nor that his bread should fail.

15 But I *am* the LORD thy God, that divided the sea, whose waves roared: The LORD of hosts *is* his name.

16 And I have put my words in thy mouth, and I have covered thee in the shadow of mine hand, that I may plant the heavens, and lay the foundations of the earth, and say unto Zi′on, Thou *art* my people.

17 ¶ Awake, awake, stand up, O Je-ru′sa-lem, which hast drunk at the hand of the LORD the cup of his fury; thou hast drunken the dregs of the cup of trembling, *and* wrung *them* out.

18 *There is* none to guide her among all the sons *whom* she hath brought forth; neither *is there any* that taketh her by the hand of all the sons *that* she hath brought up.

19 These two *things* are come unto thee; who shall be sorry for thee? desolation, and destruction, and the famine, and the sword: by whom shall I comfort thee?

20 Thy sons have fainted, they lie at the head of all the streets, as a wild bull in a net: they are full of the fury of the LORD, the rebuke of thy God.

21 ¶ Therefore hear now this, thou afflicted, and drunken, but not with wine:

22 Thus saith thy Lord the LORD, and thy God *that* pleadeth the cause of his people, Behold, I have taken out of thine hand the cup of trembling, *even* the dregs of the cup of my fury; thou shalt no more drink it again:

23 But I will put it into the hand of them that afflict thee; which have said to thy soul, Bow down, that we may go over: and thou hast laid thy body as the ground, and as the street, to them that went over.

52 AWAKE, awake; put on thy strength, O Zi′on; put on thy beautiful garments, O Je-ru′sa-lem, the holy city: for henceforth there shall no more come into thee the uncircumcised and the unclean.

2 Shake thyself from the dust; arise, *and* sit down, O Je-ru′sa-lem: loose thyself from the bands of thy neck, O captive daughter of Zi′on.

3 For thus saith the LORD, Ye have sold yourselves for nought; and ye shall be redeemed without money.

4 For thus saith the Lord GOD, My people went down aforetime into E′gypt to sojourn there; and the As-syr′i-an oppressed them without cause.

5 Now therefore, what have I here, saith the LORD, that my people is taken away for nought? they that rule over them make them to howl, saith the LORD; and my name continually every day *is* blasphemed.

6 Therefore my people shall know my name: therefore *they shall know* in that day that I *am* he that doth speak: behold, *it is* I.

7 ¶ How beautiful upon the mountains are the feet of him that bringeth good tidings, that publisheth peace; that bringeth good tidings of good, that publisheth salvation; that saith unto Zi′on, Thy God reigneth!

8 Thy watchmen shall lift up the voice; with the voice together shall they sing: for they shall see eye to eye, when the LORD shall bring again Zi′on.

9 ¶ Break forth into joy, sing together, ye waste places of Je-ru′sa-lem: for the LORD hath comforted his people, he hath redeemed Je-ru′sa-lem.

10 The LORD hath made bare his holy arm in the eyes of all the nations; and all the ends of the earth shall see the salvation of our God.

11 ¶ Depart ye, depart ye, go ye out from thence, touch no unclean *thing*; go ye out of the midst of her; be ye clean, that bear the vessels of the LORD.

12 For ye shall not go out with haste, nor go by flight: for the LORD will go before you; and the God of Is′ra-el *will be* your rereward.

13 ¶ Behold, my servant shall deal prudently, he shall be exalted and extolled, and be very high.

14 As many were astonied at thee; his visage was so marred more than any man, and his form more than the sons of men:

15 So shall he sprinkle many nations; the kings shall shut their mouths at him: for *that* which had not been told them shall they see; and *that* which they had not heard shall they consider.

53 WHO hath believed our report? and to whom is the arm of the LORD revealed?

2 For he shall grow up before him as a tender plant, and as a root out of a dry ground: he hath

no form nor comeliness; and when we shall see him, *there is* no beauty that we should desire him.

3 He is despised and rejected of men; a man of sorrows, and acquainted with grief: and we hid as it were *our* faces from him; he was despised, and we esteemed him not.

4 ¶ Surely he hath borne our griefs, and carried our sorrows: yet we did esteem him stricken, smitten of God, and afflicted.

5 But he *was* wounded for our transgressions, *he was* bruised for our iniquities: the chastisement of our peace *was* upon him; and with his stripes we are healed.

6 All we like sheep have gone astray; we have turned every one to his own way; and the Lord hath laid on him the iniquity of us all.

7 He was oppressed, and he was afflicted, yet he opened not his mouth: he is brought as a lamb to the slaughter, and as a sheep before her shearers is dumb, so he openeth not his mouth.

8 He was taken from prison and from judgment: and who shall declare his generation? for he was cut off out of the land of the living: for the transgression of my people was he stricken.

9 And he made his grave with the wicked, and with the rich in his death; because he had done no violence, neither *was any* deceit in his mouth.

10 ¶ Yet it pleased the Lord to bruise him; he hath put *him* to grief: when thou shalt make his soul an offering for sin, he shall see *his* seed, he shall prolong *his* days, and the pleasure of the Lord shall prosper in his hand.

11 He shall see of the travail of his soul, *and* shall be satisfied: by his knowledge shall my righteous servant justify many; for he shall bear their iniquities.

12 Therefore will I divide him *a portion* with the great, and he shall divide the spoil with the strong; because he hath poured out his soul unto death: and he was numbered with the transgressors; and he bare the sin of many, and made intercession for the transgressors.

54

SING, O barren, thou *that* didst not bear; break forth into singing, and cry aloud, thou *that* didst not travail with child: for more *are* the children of the desolate than the children of the married wife, saith the Lord.

2 Enlarge the place of thy tent, and let them stretch forth the curtains of thine habitations: spare not, lengthen thy cords, and strengthen thy stakes;

3 For thou shalt break forth on the right hand and on the left; and thy seed shall inherit the Gen'tiles, and make the desolate cities to be inhabited.

4 Fear not; for thou shalt not be ashamed: neither be thou confounded; for thou shalt not be put to shame: for thou shalt forget the shame of thy youth, and shalt not remember the reproach of thy widowhood any more.

5 For thy Maker *is* thine husband; the Lord of hosts *is* his name; and thy Redeemer the Holy One of Is'ra-el; The God of the whole earth shall he be called.

6 For the Lord hath called thee as a woman forsaken and grieved in spirit, and a wife of youth, when thou wast refused, saith thy God.

7 For a small moment have I forsaken thee; but with great mercies will I gather thee.

8 In a little wrath I hid my face from thee for a moment; but with everlasting kindness will I have mercy on thee, saith the Lord thy Redeemer.

9 For this *is as* the waters of No'ah unto me: for *as* I have sworn that the waters of No'ah should no more go over the earth; so have I sworn that I would not be wroth with thee, nor rebuke thee.

10 For the mountains shall depart, and the hills be removed; but my kindness shall not depart from thee, neither shall the covenant of my peace be removed, saith the Lord that hath mercy on thee.

11 ¶ O thou afflicted, tossed with tempest, *and* not comforted, behold, I will lay thy stones with fair colours, and lay thy foundations with sapphires.

12 And I will make thy windows of agates, and thy gates of carbuncles, and all thy borders of pleasant stones.

13 And all thy children *shall be* taught of the Lord; and great *shall be* the peace of thy children.

14 In righteousness shalt thou be established: thou shalt be far from oppression; for thou shalt not fear: and from terror; for it shall not come near thee.

15 Behold, they shall surely gather together, *but* not by me: whosoever shall gather together against thee shall fall for thy sake.

16 Behold, I have created the smith that bloweth the coals in the fire, and that bringeth forth an instrument for his work; and I have created the waster to destroy.

17 ¶ No weapon that is formed against thee shall prosper; and every tongue *that* shall rise against thee in judgment thou shalt condemn. This *is* the heritage of the servants of the Lord, and their righteousness *is* of me, saith the Lord.

55

HO, every one that thirsteth, come ye to the waters, and he that hath no money; come ye, buy, and eat; yea, come, buy wine and milk without money and without price.

2 Wherefore do ye spend money for *that* which *is* not bread? and your labour for *that* which satisfieth not? hearken diligently unto me, and eat ye *that which is* good, and let your soul delight itself in fatness.

3 Incline your ear, and come unto me: hear, and your soul shall live; and I will make an everlasting covenant with you, *even* the sure mercies of Da'vid.

4 Behold, I have given him *for* a witness to the people, a leader and commander to the people.

5 Behold, thou shalt call a nation *that* thou knowest not, and nations *that* knew not thee shall run unto thee because of the Lord thy God, and for the Holy One of Is'ra-el; for he hath glorified thee.

6 ¶ Seek ye the Lord while he may be found, call ye upon him while he is near:

7 Let the wicked forsake his way, and the unrighteous man his thoughts: and let him return unto the Lord, and he will have mercy upon him; and to our God, for he will abundantly pardon.

8 ¶ For my thoughts *are* not your thoughts, neither *are* your ways my ways, saith the Lord.

9 For *as* the heavens are higher than the earth, so are my ways higher than your ways, and my thoughts than your thoughts.

10 For as the rain cometh down, and the snow from heaven, and returneth not thither, but watereth the earth, and maketh it bring forth and bud, that it may give seed to the sower, and bread to the eater:

11 So shall my word be that goeth forth out of my mouth: it shall not return unto me void, but it shall accomplish that which I please, and

it shall prosper *in the thing* whereto I sent it.

12 For ye shall go out with joy, and be led forth with peace: the mountains and the hills shall break forth before you into singing, and all the trees of the field shall clap *their* hands.

13 Instead of the thorn shall come up the fir tree, and instead of the brier shall come up the myrtle tree: and it shall be to the LORD for a name, for an everlasting sign *that* shall not be cut off.

56 THUS saith the LORD, Keep ye judgment, and do justice: for my salvation *is* near to come, and my righteousness to be revealed.

2 Blessed *is* the man *that* doeth this, and the son of man *that* layeth hold on it; that keepeth the sabbath from polluting it, and keepeth his hand from doing any evil.

3 ¶ Neither let the son of the stranger, that hath joined himself to the LORD, speak, saying, The LORD hath utterly separated me from his people: neither let the eunuch say, Behold, I *am* a dry tree.

4 For thus saith the LORD unto the eunuchs that keep my sabbaths, and choose *the things* that please me, and take hold of my covenant;

5 Even unto them will I give in mine house and within my walls a place and a name better than of sons and of daughters: I will give them an everlasting name, that shall not be cut off.

6 Also the sons of the stranger, that join themselves to the LORD, to serve him, and to love the name of the LORD, to be his servants, every one that keepeth the sabbath from polluting it, and taketh hold of my covenant;

7 Even them will I bring to my holy mountain, and make them joyful in my house of prayer: their burnt offerings and their sacrifices *shall be* accepted upon mine altar; for mine house shall be called an house of prayer for all people.

8 The Lord GOD which gathereth the outcasts of Is'ra-el saith, Yet will I gather *others* to him, beside those that are gathered unto him.

9 ¶ All ye beasts of the field, come to devour, *yea,* all ye beasts in the forest.

10 His watchmen *are* blind: they are all ignorant, they *are* all dumb dogs, they cannot bark; sleeping, lying down, loving to slumber.

11 Yea, *they are* greedy dogs *which* can never have enough, and they *are* shepherds *that* cannot understand: they all look to their own way, every one for his gain, from his quarter.

12 Come ye, *say they,* I will fetch wine, and we will fill ourselves with strong drink; and to morrow shall be as this day, *and* much more abundant.

57 THE righteous perisheth, and no man layeth *it* to heart: and merciful men *are* taken away, none considering that the righteous is taken away from the evil *to come.*

2 He shall enter into peace: they shall rest in their beds, *each one* walking *in* his uprightness.

3 ¶ But draw near hither, ye sons of the sorceress, the seed of the adulterer and the whore.

4 Against whom do ye sport yourselves? against whom make ye a wide mouth, *and* draw out the tongue? *are* ye not children of transgression, a seed of falsehood,

5 Enflaming yourselves with idols under every green tree, slaying the children in the valleys under the clifts of the rocks?

6 Among the smooth *stones* of the stream *is* thy portion; they, they *are* thy lot: even to them hast thou poured a drink offering, thou hast of-

fered a meat offering. Should I receive comfort in these?

7 Upon a lofty and high mountain hast thou set thy bed: even thither wentest thou up to offer sacrifice.

8 Behind the doors also and the posts hast thou set up thy remembrance: for thou hast discovered *thyself to another* than me, and art gone up; thou hast enlarged thy bed, and made thee *a covenant* with them; thou lovedst their bed where thou sawest *it.*

9 And thou wentest to the king with ointment, and didst increase thy perfumes, and didst send thy messengers far off, and didst debase *thyself even* unto hell.

10 Thou art wearied in the greatness of thy way; *yet* saidst thou not, There is no hope: thou hast found the life of thine hand; therefore thou wast not grieved.

11 And of whom hast thou been afraid or feared, that thou hast lied, and hast not remembered me, nor laid *it* to thy heart? have not I held my peace even of old, and thou fearest me not?

12 I will declare thy righteousness, and thy works; for they shall not profit thee.

13 ¶ When thou criest, let thy companies deliver thee; but the wind shall carry them all away; vanity shall take *them:* but he that putteth his trust in me shall possess the land, and shall inherit my holy mountain;

14 And shall say, Cast ye up, cast ye up, prepare the way, take up the stumblingblock out of the way of my people.

15 For thus saith the high and lofty One that inhabiteth eternity, whose name *is* Holy; I dwell in the high and holy *place,* with him also *that is* of a contrite and humble spirit, to revive the spirit of the humble, and to revive the heart of the contrite ones.

16 For I will not contend for ever, neither will I be always wroth: for the spirit should fail before me, and the souls *which* I have made.

17 For the iniquity of his covetousness was I wroth, and smote him: I hid me, and was wroth, and he went on frowardly in the way of his heart.

18 I have seen his ways, and will heal him: I will lead him also, and restore comforts unto him and to his mourners.

19 I create the fruit of the lips; Peace, peace to *him that* is far off, and to *him that is* near, saith the LORD; and I will heal him.

20 But the wicked *are* like the troubled sea, when it cannot rest, whose waters cast up mire and dirt.

21 *There is* no peace, saith my God, to the wicked.

58 CRY aloud, spare not, lift up thy voice like a trumpet, and shew my people their transgression, and the house of Ja'cob their sins.

2 Yet they seek me daily, and delight to know my ways, as a nation that did righteousness, and forsook not the ordinance of their God: they ask of me the ordinances of justice; they take delight in approaching to God.

3 ¶ Wherefore have we fasted, *say they,* and thou seest not? *wherefore* have we afflicted our soul, and thou takest no knowledge? Behold, in the day of your fast ye find pleasure, and exact all your labours.

4 Behold, ye fast for strife and debate, and to smite with the fist of wickedness: ye shall not fast as *ye do this* day, to make your voice to be heard on high.

5 Is it such a fast that I have chosen? a day for a man to afflict his soul? *is it* to bow down his head as a bulrush, and to spread sackcloth and ashes *under him?* wilt thou call this a fast, and an acceptable day to the LORD?

6 *Is* not this the fast that I have chosen? to loose the bands of wickedness, to undo the heavy burdens, and to let the oppressed go free, and that ye break every yoke?

7 *Is it* not to deal thy bread to the hungry, and that thou bring the poor that are cast out to thy house? when thou seest the naked, that thou cover him; and that thou hide not thyself from thine own flesh?

8 ¶ Then shall thy light break forth as the morning, and thine health shall spring forth speedily: and thy righteousness shall go before thee: the glory of the LORD shall be thy rereward.

9 Then shalt thou call, and the LORD shall answer; thou shalt cry, and he shall say, Here I *am.* If thou take away from the midst of thee the yoke, the putting forth of the finger, and speaking vanity;

10 And *if* thou draw out thy soul to the hungry, and satisfy the afflicted soul; then shall thy light rise in obscurity, and thy darkness *be* as the noon day:

11 And the LORD shall guide thee continually, and satisfy thy soul in drought, and make fat thy bones: and thou shalt be like a watered garden, and like a spring of water, whose waters fail not.

12 And *they that shall be* of thee shall build the old waste places: thou shalt raise up the foundations of many generations; and thou shalt be called, The repairer of the breach, The restorer of paths to dwell in.

13 ¶ If thou turn away thy foot from the sabbath, *from* doing thy pleasure on my holy day; and call the sabbath a delight, the holy of the LORD, honourable; and shalt honour him, not doing thine own ways, nor finding thine own pleasure, nor speaking *thine own* words:

14 Then shalt thou delight thyself in the LORD; and I will cause thee to ride upon the high places of the earth, and feed thee with the heritage of Ja′cob thy father: for the mouth of the LORD hath spoken *it.*

59 BEHOLD, the LORD's hand is not shortened, that it cannot save; neither his ear heavy, that it cannot hear:

2 But your iniquities have separated between you and your God, and your sins have hid *his* face from you, that he will not hear.

3 For your hands are defiled with blood, and your fingers with iniquity; your lips have spoken lies, your tongue hath muttered perverseness.

4 None calleth for justice, nor *any* pleadeth for truth: they trust in vanity, and speak lies; they conceive mischief, and bring forth iniquity.

5 They hatch cockatrice′ eggs, and weave the spider's web: he that eateth of their eggs dieth, and that which is crushed breaketh out into a viper.

6 Their webs shall not become garments, neither shall they cover themselves with their works: their works *are* works of iniquity, and the act of violence *is* in their hands.

7 Their feet run to evil, and they make haste to shed innocent blood: their thoughts *are* thoughts of iniquity; wasting and destruction *are* in their paths.

8 The way of peace they know not; and *there is* no judgment in their goings: they have made them crooked paths: whosoever goeth therein shall not know peace.

9 ¶ Therefore is judgment far from us, neither doth justice overtake us: we wait for light, but behold obscurity; for brightness, *but* we walk in darkness.

10 We grope for the wall like the blind, and we grope as if *we had* no eyes: we stumble at noon day as in the night; *we are* in desolate places as dead *men.*

11 We roar all like bears, and mourn sore like doves: we look for judgment, but *there is* none; for salvation, *but* it is far off from us.

12 For our transgressions are multiplied before thee, and our sins testify against us: for our transgressions *are* with us; and *as for* our iniquities, we know them;

13 In transgressing and lying against the LORD, and departing away from our God, speaking oppression and revolt, conceiving and uttering from the heart words of falsehood.

14 And judgment is turned away backward, and justice standeth afar off: for truth is fallen in the street, and equity cannot enter.

15 Yea, truth faileth; and he *that* departeth from evil maketh himself a prey: and the LORD saw *it,* and it displeased him that *there was* no judgment.

16 ¶ And he saw that *there was* no man, and wondered that *there was* no intercessor: therefore his arm brought salvation unto him; and his righteousness, it sustained him.

17 For he put on righteousness as a breastplate, and an helmet of salvation upon his head; and he put on the garments of vengeance *for* clothing, and was clad with zeal as a cloke.

18 According to *their* deeds, accordingly he will repay, fury to his adversaries, recompence to his enemies; to the islands he will repay recompence.

19 So shall they fear the name of the LORD from the west, and his glory from the rising of the sun. When the enemy shall come in like a flood, the Spirit of the LORD shall lift up a standard against him.

20 ¶ And the Redeemer shall come to Zi′on, and unto them that turn from transgression in Ja′cob, saith the LORD.

21 As for me, this *is* my covenant with them, saith the LORD; My spirit that *is* upon thee, and my words which I have put in thy mouth, shall not depart out of thy mouth, nor out of the mouth of thy seed, nor out of the mouth of thy seed's seed, saith the LORD, from henceforth and for ever.

60 ARISE, shine; for thy light is come, and the glory of the LORD is risen upon thee.

2 For, behold, the darkness shall cover the earth, and gross darkness the people: but the LORD shall arise upon thee, and his glory shall be seen upon thee.

3 And the Gen′tiles shall come to thy light, and kings to the brightness of thy rising.

4 Lift up thine eyes round about, and see: all they gather themselves together, they come to thee: thy sons shall come from far, and thy daughters shall be nursed at *thy* side.

5 Then thou shalt see, and flow together, and thine heart shall fear, and be enlarged; because the abundance of the sea shall be converted unto thee, the forces of the Gen′tiles shall come unto thee.

6 The multitude of camels shall cover thee, the dromedaries of Mid′i-an and E′phah; all they from She′ba shall come: they shall bring

gold and incense; and they shall shew forth the praises of the LORD.

7 All the flocks of Ke'dar shall be gathered together unto thee, the rams of Ne-ba'ioth shall minister unto thee: they shall come up with acceptance on mine altar, and I will glorify the house of my glory.

8 Who *are* these *that* fly as a cloud, and as the doves to their windows?

9 Surely the isles shall wait for me, and the ships of Tar'shish first, to bring thy sons from far, their silver and their gold with them, unto the name of the LORD thy God, and to the Holy One of Is'ra-el, because he hath glorified thee.

10 And the sons of strangers shall build up thy walls, and their kings shall minister unto thee: for in my wrath I smote thee, but in my favour have I had mercy on thee.

11 Therefore thy gates shall be open continually; they shall not be shut day nor night; that *men* may bring unto thee the forces of the Gen'-tiles, and *that* their kings *may be* brought.

12 For the nation and kingdom that will not serve thee shall perish; yea, *those* nations shall be utterly wasted.

13 The glory of Leb'a-non shall come unto thee, the fir tree, the pine tree, and the box together, to beautify the place of my sanctuary; and I will make the place of my feet glorious.

14 The sons also of them that afflicted thee shall come bending unto thee; and all they that despised thee shall bow themselves down at the soles of thy feet; and they shall call thee, The city of the LORD, The Zi'on of the Holy One of Is'ra-el.

15 Whereas thou hast been forsaken and hated, so that no man went through *thee*, I will make thee an eternal excellency, a joy of many generations.

16 Thou shalt also suck the milk of the Gen'-tiles, and shalt suck the breast of kings: and thou shalt know that I the LORD *am* thy Saviour and thy Redeemer, the mighty One of Ja'cob.

17 For brass I will bring gold, and for iron I will bring silver, and for wood brass, and for stones iron: I will also make thy officers peace, and thine exactors righteousness.

18 Violence shall no more be heard in thy land, wasting nor destruction within thy borders; but thou shalt call thy walls Salvation, and thy gates Praise.

19 The sun shall be no more thy light by day; neither for brightness shall the moon give light unto thee: but the LORD shall be unto thee an everlasting light, and thy God thy glory.

20 Thy sun shall no more go down; neither shall thy moon withdraw itself: for the LORD shall be thine everlasting light, and the days of thy mourning shall be ended.

21 Thy people also *shall be* all righteous: they shall inherit the land for ever, the branch of my planting, the work of my hands, that I may be glorified.

22 A little one shall become a thousand, and a small one a strong nation: I the LORD will hasten it in his time.

61 THE Spirit of the Lord GOD *is* upon me; because the LORD hath anointed me to preach good tidings unto the meek; he hath sent me to bind up the brokenhearted, to proclaim liberty to the captives, and the opening of the prison to *them that are* bound;

2 To proclaim the acceptable year of the LORD, and the day of vengeance of our God; to comfort all that mourn;

3 To appoint unto them that mourn in Zi'on,

to give unto them beauty for ashes, the oil of joy for mourning, the garment of praise for the spirit of heaviness; that they might be called trees of righteousness, the planting of the LORD, that he might be glorified.

4 ¶ And they shall build the old wastes, they shall raise up the former desolations, and they shall repair the waste cities, the desolations of many generations.

5 And strangers shall stand and feed your flocks, and the sons of the alien *shall be* your plowmen and your vinedressers.

6 But ye shall be named the Priests of the LORD: *men* shall call you the Ministers of our God: ye shall eat the riches of the Gen'tiles, and in their glory shall ye boast yourselves.

7 ¶ For your shame *ye shall have* double; and *for* confusion they shall rejoice in their portion: therefore in their land they shall possess the double: everlasting joy shall be unto them.

8 For I the LORD love judgment, I hate robbery for burnt offering; and I will direct their work in truth, and I will make an everlasting covenant with them.

9 And their seed shall be known among the Gen'tiles, and their offspring among the people: all that see them shall acknowledge them, that they *are* the seed *which* the LORD hath blessed.

10 I will greatly rejoice in the LORD, my soul shall be joyful in my God; for he hath clothed me with the garments of salvation, he hath covered me with the robe of righteousness, as a bridegroom decketh *himself* with ornaments, and as a bride adorneth *herself* with her jewels.

11 For as the earth bringeth forth her bud, and as the garden causeth the things that are sown in it to spring forth; so the Lord GOD will cause righteousness and praise to spring forth before all the nations.

62 FOR Zi'on's sake will I not hold my peace, and for Je-ru'sa-lem's sake I will not rest, until the righteousness thereof go forth as brightness, and the salvation thereof as a lamp *that* burneth.

2 And the Gen'tiles shall see thy righteousness, and all kings thy glory: and thou shalt be called by a new name, which the mouth of the LORD shall name.

3 Thou shalt also be a crown of glory in the hand of the LORD, and a royal diadem in the hand of thy God.

4 Thou shalt no more be termed Forsaken; neither shall thy land any more be termed Desolate: but thou shalt be called Heph'zi-bah, and thy land Beu'lah: for the LORD delighteth in thee, and thy land shall be married.

5 ¶ For *as* a young man marrieth a virgin, *so* shall thy sons marry thee: and *as* the bridegroom rejoiceth over the bride, *so* shall thy God rejoice over thee.

6 I have set watchmen upon thy walls, O Je-ru'sa-lem, *which* shall never hold their peace day nor night: ye that make mention of the LORD, keep not silence,

7 And give him no rest, till he establish, and till he make Je-ru'sa-lem a praise in the earth.

8 The LORD hath sworn by his right hand, and by the arm of his strength, Surely I will no more give thy corn *to be* meat for thine enemies; and the sons of the stranger shall not drink thy wine, for the which thou hast laboured:

9 But they that have gathered it shall eat it, and praise the LORD; and they that have brought it together shall drink it in the courts of my holiness.

10 ¶ Go through, go through the gates; prepare ye the way of the people; cast up, cast up the highway; gather out the stones; lift up a standard for the people.

11 Behold, the LORD hath proclaimed unto the end of the world, Say ye to the daughter of Zi'on, Behold, thy salvation cometh; behold, his reward *is* with him, and his work before him.

12 And they shall call them, The holy people, The redeemed of the LORD: and thou shalt be called, Sought out, A city not forsaken.

63 WHO *is* this that cometh from E'dom, with dyed garments from Boz'rah? this *that is* glorious in his apparel, travelling in the greatness of his strength? I that speak in righteousness, mighty to save.

2 Wherefore *art thou* red in thine apparel, and thy garments like him that treadeth in the winefat?

3 I have trodden the winepress alone; and of the people *there was* none with me: for I will tread them in mine anger, and trample them in my fury; and their blood shall be sprinkled upon my garments, and I will stain all my raiment.

4 For the day of vengeance *is* in mine heart, and the year of my redeemed is come.

5 And I looked, and *there was* none to help; and I wondered that *there was* none to uphold: therefore mine own arm brought salvation unto me; and my fury, it upheld me.

6 And I will tread down the people in mine anger, and make them drunk in my fury, and I will bring down their strength to the earth.

7 ¶ I will mention the lovingkindnesses of the LORD, *and* the praises of the LORD, according to all that the LORD hath bestowed on us, and the great goodness toward the house of Is'-ra-el, which he hath bestowed on them according to his mercies, and according to the multitude of his lovingkindnesses.

8 For he said, Surely they *are* my people, children *that* will not lie: so he was their Saviour.

9 In all their affliction he was afflicted, and the angel of his presence saved them: in his love and in his pity he redeemed them; and he bare them, and carried them all the days of old.

10 ¶ But they rebelled, and vexed his holy Spirit: therefore he was turned to be their enemy, *and* he fought against them.

11 Then he remembered the days of old, Mo'-ses, *and* his people, *saying*, Where *is* he that brought them up out of the sea with the shepherd of his flock? where *is* he that put his holy Spirit within him?

12 That led *them* by the right hand of Mo'ses with his glorious arm, dividing the water before them, to make himself an everlasting name?

13 That led them through the deep, as an horse in the wilderness, *that* they should not stumble?

14 As a beast goeth down into the valley, the Spirit of the LORD caused him to rest: so didst thou lead thy people, to make thyself a glorious name.

15 ¶ Look down from heaven, and behold from the habitation of thy holiness and of thy glory: where *is* thy zeal and thy strength, the sounding of thy bowels and of thy mercies toward me? are they restrained?

16 Doubtless thou *art* our father, though A'-bra-ham be ignorant of us, and Is'ra-el acknowledge us not: thou, O LORD, *art* our father, our redeemer; thy name *is* from everlasting.

17 ¶ O LORD, why hast thou made us to err from thy ways, *and* hardened our hearts from thy fear? Return for thy servants' sake, the tribes of thine inheritance.

18 The people of thy holiness have possessed *it* but a little while: our adversaries have trodden down thy sanctuary.

19 We are *thine:* thou never barest rule over them; they were not called by thy name.

64 OH that thou wouldest rend the heavens, that thou wouldest come down, that the mountains might flow down at thy presence,

2 As *when* the melting fire burneth, the fire causeth the waters to boil, to make thy name known to thine adversaries, *that* the nations may tremble at thy presence!

3 When thou didst terrible things *which* we looked not for, thou camest down, the mountains flowed down at thy presence.

4 For since the beginning of the world *men* have not heard, nor perceived by the ear, neither hath the eye seen, O God, beside thee, *what* he hath prepared for him that waiteth for him.

5 Thou meetest him that rejoiceth and worketh righteousness, *those that* remember thee in thy ways: behold, thou art wroth; for we have sinned: in those is continuance, and we shall be saved.

6 But we are all as an unclean *thing,* and all our righteousnesses *are* as filthy rags; and we all do fade as a leaf; and our iniquities, like the wind, have taken us away.

7 And *there is* none that calleth upon thy name, that stirreth up himself to take hold of thee: for thou hast hid thy face from us, and hast consumed us, because of our iniquities.

8 But now, O LORD, thou *art* our father; we *are* the clay, and thou our potter; and we all *are* the work of thy hand.

9 ¶ Be not wroth very sore, O LORD, neither remember iniquity for ever: behold, see, we beseech thee, we *are* all thy people.

10 Thy holy cities are a wilderness, Zi'on is a wilderness, Je-ru'sa-lem a desolation.

11 Our holy and our beautiful house, where our fathers praised thee, is burned up with fire: and all our pleasant things are laid waste.

12 Wilt thou refrain thyself for these *things,* O LORD? wilt thou hold thy peace, and afflict us very sore?

65 I AM sought of *them that* asked not *for me;* I am found of *them that* sought me not: I said, Behold me, behold me, unto a nation *that* was not called by my name.

2 I have spread out my hands all the day unto a rebellious people, which walketh in a way *that was* not good, after their own thoughts;

3 A people that provoketh me to anger continually to my face; that sacrificeth in gardens, and burneth incense upon altars of brick;

4 Which remain among the graves, and lodge in the monuments, which eat swine's flesh, and broth of abominable *things is* in their vessels;

5 Which say, Stand by thyself, come not near to me; for I am holier than thou. These *are* a smoke in my nose, a fire that burneth all the day.

6 Behold, *it is* written before me: I will not keep silence, but will recompense, even recompense into their bosom,

7 Your iniquities, and the iniquities of your fathers together, saith the LORD, which have burned incense upon the mountains, and blasphemed me upon the hills: therefore will I measure their former work into their bosom.

8 ¶ Thus saith the LORD, As the new wine is found in the cluster, and one saith, Destroy it not; for a blessing is in it: so will I do for my servants' sakes, that I may not destroy them all.

9 And I will bring forth a seed out of Ja'cob, and out of Ju'dah an inheritor of my mountains: and mine elect shall inherit it, and my servants shall dwell there.

10 And Shar'on shall be a fold of flocks, and the valley of A'chor a place for the herds to lie down in, for my people that have sought me.

11 ¶ But ye are they that forsake the LORD, that forget my holy mountain, that prepare a table for that troop, and that furnish the drink offering unto that number.

12 Therefore will I number you to the sword, and ye shall all bow down to the slaughter: because when I called, ye did not answer; when I spake, ye did not hear; but did evil before mine eyes, and did choose that wherein I delighted not.

13 Therefore thus saith the Lord GOD, Behold, my servants shall eat, but ye shall be hungry: behold, my servants shall drink, but ye shall be thirsty: behold, my servants shall rejoice, but ye shall be ashamed:

14 Behold, my servants shall sing for joy of heart, but ye shall cry for sorrow of heart, and shall howl for vexation of spirit.

15 And ye shall leave your name for a curse unto my chosen: for the Lord GOD shall slay thee, and call his servants by another name:

16 That he who blesseth himself in the earth shall bless himself in the God of truth; and he that sweareth in the earth shall swear by the God of truth; because the former troubles are forgotten, and because they are hid from mine eyes.

17 ¶ For, behold, I create new heavens and a new earth: and the former shall not be remembered, nor come into mind.

18 But be ye glad and rejoice for ever in that which I create: for, behold, I create Je-ru'sa-lem a rejoicing, and her people a joy.

19 And I will rejoice in Je-ru'sa-lem, and joy in my people: and the voice of weeping shall be no more heard in her, nor the voice of crying.

20 There shall be no more thence an infant of days, nor an old man that hath not filled his days: for the child shall die an hundred years old; but the sinner being an hundred years old shall be accursed.

21 And they shall build houses, and inhabit them; and they shall plant vineyards, and eat the fruit of them.

22 They shall not build, and another inhabit; they shall not plant, and another eat: for as the days of a tree are the days of my people, and mine elect shall long enjoy the work of their hands.

23 They shall not labour in vain, nor bring forth for trouble; for they are the seed of the blessed of the LORD, and their offspring with them.

24 And it shall come to pass, that before they call, I will answer; and while they are yet speaking, I will hear.

25 The wolf and the lamb shall feed together, and the lion shall eat straw like the bullock: and dust shall be the serpent's meat. They shall not hurt nor destroy in all my holy mountain, saith the LORD.

66 THUS saith the LORD, The heaven is my throne, and the earth is my footstool: where is the house that ye build unto me? and where is the place of my rest?

2 For all those things hath mine hand made, and all those things have been, saith the LORD: but to this man will I look, even to him that is poor and of a contrite spirit, and trembleth at my word.

3 He that killeth an ox is as if he slew a man; he that sacrificeth a lamb, as if he cut off a dog's neck; he that offereth an oblation, as if he offered swine's blood; he that burneth incense, as if he blessed an idol. Yea, they have chosen their own ways, and their soul delighteth in their abominations.

4 I also will choose their delusions, and will bring their fears upon them; because when I called, none did answer; when I spake, they did not hear: but they did evil before mine eyes, and chose that in which I delighted not.

5 ¶ Hear the word of the LORD, ye that tremble at his word; Your brethren that hated you, that cast you out for my name's sake, said, Let the LORD be glorified: but he shall appear to your joy, and they shall be ashamed.

6 A voice of noise from the city, a voice from the temple, a voice of the LORD that rendereth recompence to his enemies.

7 Before she travailed, she brought forth; before her pain came, she was delivered of a man child.

8 Who hath heard such a thing? who hath seen such things? Shall the earth be made to bring forth in one day? or shall a nation be born at once? for as soon as Zi'on travailed, she brought forth her children.

9 Shall I bring to the birth, and not cause to bring forth? saith the LORD: shall I cause to bring forth, and shut the womb? saith my God.

10 Rejoice ye with Je-ru'sa-lem, and be glad with her, all ye that love her: rejoice for joy with her, all ye that mourn for her:

11 That ye may suck, and be satisfied with the breasts of her consolations; that ye may milk out, and be delighted with the abundance of her glory.

12 For thus saith the LORD, Behold I will extend peace to her like a river, and the glory of the Gen'tiles like a flowing stream: then shall ye suck, ye shall be borne upon her sides, and be dandled upon her knees.

13 As one whom his mother comforteth, so will I comfort you; and ye shall be comforted in Je-ru'sa-lem.

14 And when ye see this, your heart shall rejoice, and your bones shall flourish like an herb: and the hand of the LORD shall be known toward his servants, and his indignation toward his enemies.

15 For, behold, the LORD will come with fire, and with his chariots like a whirlwind, to render his anger with fury, and his rebuke with flames of fire.

16 For by fire and by his sword will the LORD plead with all flesh: and the slain of the LORD shall be many.

17 They that sanctify themselves, and purify themselves in the gardens, behind one tree in the midst, eating swine's flesh, and the abomination, and the mouse, shall be consumed together, saith the LORD.

18 For I know their works and their thoughts: it shall come, that I will gather all nations and tongues; and they shall come, and see my glory.

19 And I will set a sign among them, and I will send those that escape of them unto the nations, to Tar'shish, Pul, and Lud, that draw the bow, to Tu'bal, and Ja'van, to the isles afar off, that have not heard my fame, neither have

seen my glory; and they shall declare my glory among the Gen'tiles.

20 And they shall bring all your brethren *for* an offering unto the LORD out of all nations upon horses, and in chariots, and in litters, and upon mules, and upon swift beasts, to my holy mountain Je-ru'sa-lem, saith the LORD, as the children of Is'ra-el bring an offering in a clean vessel into the house of the LORD.

21 And I will also take of them for priests *and* for Le'vites, saith the LORD.

22 For as the new heavens and the new earth, which I will make, shall remain before me, saith the LORD, so shall your seed and your name remain.

23 And it shall come to pass, *that* from one new moon to another, and from one sabbath to another, shall all flesh come to worship before me, saith the LORD.

24 And they shall go forth, and look upon the carcases of the men that have transgressed against me: for their worm shall not die, neither shall their fire be quenched; and they shall be an abhorring unto all flesh.

THE BOOK OF

JEREMIAH

1 THE words of Jer-e-mi'ah the son of Hil-ki'ah, of the priests that *were* in An'a-thoth in the land of Ben'ja-min:

2 To whom the word of the LORD came in the days of Jo-si'ah the son of A'mon king of Ju'-dah, in the thirteenth year of his reign.

3 It came also in the days of Je-hoi'a-kim the son of Jo-si'ah king of Ju'dah, unto the end of the eleventh year of Zed-e-ki'ah the son of Jo-si'ah king of Ju'dah, unto the carrying away of Je-ru'sa-lem captive in the fifth month.

4 Then the word of the LORD came unto me, saying,

5 Before I formed thee in the belly I knew thee; and before thou camest forth out of the womb I sanctified thee, *and* I ordained thee a prophet unto the nations.

6 Then said I, Ah, Lord GOD! behold, I cannot speak: for I *am* a child.

7 ¶ But the LORD said unto me, Say not, I *am* a child: for thou shalt go to all that I shall send thee, and whatsoever I command thee thou shalt speak.

8 Be not afraid of their faces: for I *am* with thee to deliver thee, saith the LORD.

9 Then the LORD put forth his hand, and touched my mouth. And the LORD said unto me, Behold, I have put my words in thy mouth.

10 See, I have this day set thee over the nations and over the kingdoms, to root out, and to pull down, and to destroy, and to throw down, to build, and to plant.

11 ¶ Moreover the word of the LORD came unto me, saying, Jer-e-mi'ah, what seest thou? And I said, I see a rod of an almond tree.

12 Then said the LORD unto me, Thou hast well seen: for I will hasten my word to perform it.

13 And the word of the LORD came unto me the second time, saying, What seest thou? And I said, I see a seething pot; and the face thereof *is* toward the north.

14 Then the LORD said unto me, Out of the north an evil shall break forth upon all the inhabitants of the land.

15 For, lo, I will call all the families of the kingdoms of the north, saith the LORD; and they shall come, and they shall set every one his throne at the entering of the gates of Je-ru'sa-lem, and against all the walls thereof round about, and against all the cities of Ju'dah.

16 And I will utter my judgments against them touching all their wickedness, who have forsaken me, and have burned incense unto other gods, and worshipped the works of their own hands.

17 ¶ Thou therefore gird up thy loins, and arise, and speak unto them all that I command thee: be not dismayed at their faces, lest I confound thee before them.

18 For, behold, I have made thee this day a defenced city, and an iron pillar, and brasen walls against the whole land, against the kings of Ju'dah, against the princes thereof, against the priests thereof, and against the people of the land.

19 And they shall fight against thee; but they shall not prevail against thee; for I *am* with thee, saith the LORD, to deliver thee.

2 MOREOVER the word of the LORD came to me, saying,

2 Go and cry in the ears of Je-ru'sa-lem, saying, Thus saith the LORD; I remember thee, the kindness of thy youth, the love of thine espousals, when thou wentest after me in the wilderness, in a land *that was* not sown.

3 Is'ra-el *was* holiness unto the LORD, *and* the firstfruits of his increase: all that devour him shall offend; evil shall come upon them, saith the LORD.

4 Hear ye the word of the LORD, O house of Ja'cob, and all the families of the house of Is'ra-el:

5 ¶ Thus saith the LORD, What iniquity have your fathers found in me, that they are gone far from me, and have walked after vanity, and are become vain?

6 Neither said they, Where *is* the LORD that brought us up out of the land of E'gypt, that led us through the wilderness, through a land of deserts and of pits, through a land of drought, and of the shadow of death, through a land that no man passed through, and where no man dwelt?

7 And I brought you into a plentiful country, to eat the fruit thereof and the goodness thereof; but when ye entered, ye defiled my land, and made mine heritage an abomination.

8 The priests said not, Where *is* the LORD? and they that handle the law knew me not: the pastors also transgressed against me, and the prophets prophesied by Ba'al, and walked after *things that* do not profit.

9 ¶ Wherefore I will yet plead with you, saith the LORD, and with your children's children will I plead.

10 For pass over the isles of Chit'tim, and see; and send unto Ke'dar, and consider diligently, and see if there be such a thing.

11 Hath a nation changed *their* gods, which *are* yet no gods? but my people have changed their glory for *that which* doth not profit.

12 Be astonished, O ye heavens, at this, and be horribly afraid, be ye very desolate, saith the LORD.

13 For my people have committed two evils; they have forsaken me the fountain of living waters, *and* hewed them out cisterns, broken cisterns, that can hold no water.

14 ¶ *Is* Is'ra-el a servant? *is* he a homeborn *slave*? why is he spoiled?

15 The young lions roared upon him, *and* yelled, and they made his land waste: his cities are burned without inhabitant.

16 Also the children of Noph and Ta'hap'a-nes have broken the crown of thy head.

17 Hast thou not procured this unto thyself, in that thou hast forsaken the LORD thy God, when he led thee by the way?

18 And now what hast thou to do in the way of E'gypt, to drink the waters of Si'hor? or what hast thou to do in the way of As-syr'i-a, to drink the waters of the river?

19 Thine own wickedness shall correct thee, and thy backslidings shall reprove thee: know therefore and see that *it is* an evil *thing* and bitter, that thou hast forsaken the LORD thy God, and that my fear *is* not in thee, saith the Lord GOD of hosts.

20 ¶ For of old time I have broken thy yoke, *and* burst thy bands; and thou saidst, I will not transgress; when upon every high hill and under every green tree thou wanderest, playing the harlot.

21 Yet I had planted thee a noble vine, wholly a right seed: how then art thou turned into the degenerate plant of a strange vine unto me?

22 For though thou wash thee with nitre, and take thee much sope, *yet* thine iniquity is marked before me, saith the Lord GOD.

23 How canst thou say, I am not polluted, I have not gone after Ba'al-im? see thy way in the valley, know what thou hast done: *thou art* a swift dromedary traversing her ways;

24 A wild ass used to the wilderness, *that* snuffeth up the wind at her pleasure; in her occasion who can turn her away? all they that seek her will not weary themselves; in her month they shall find her.

25 Withhold thy foot from being unshod, and thy throat from thirst: but thou saidst, There is no hope: no; for I have loved strangers, and after them will I go.

26 As the thief is ashamed when he is found, so is the house of Is'ra-el ashamed; they, their kings, their princes, and their priests, and their prophets,

27 Saying to a stock, Thou *art* my father; and to a stone, Thou hast brought me forth: for they have turned *their* back unto me, and not *their* face: but in the time of their trouble they will say, Arise, and save us.

28 But where *are* thy gods that thou hast made thee? let them arise, if they can save thee in the time of their trouble: for *according to* the number of thy cities are thy gods, O Ju'dah.

29 Wherefore will ye plead with me? ye all have transgressed against me, saith the LORD.

30 In vain have I smitten your children; they received no correction: your own sword hath devoured your prophets, like a destroying lion.

31 ¶ O generation, see ye the word of the LORD. Have I been a wilderness unto Is'ra-el? a land of darkness? wherefore say my people, We are lords; we will come no more unto thee?

32 Can a maid forget her ornaments, *or* a bride her attire? yet my people have forgotten me days without number.

33 Why trimmest thou thy way to seek love? therefore hast thou also taught the wicked ones thy ways.

34 Also in thy skirts is found the blood of the souls of the poor innocents: I have not found it by secret search, but upon all these.

35 Yet thou sayest, Because I am innocent, surely his anger shall turn from me. Behold, I will plead with thee, because thou sayest, I have not sinned.

36 Why gaddest thou about so much to change thy way? thou also shalt be ashamed of E'gypt, as thou wast ashamed of As-syr'i-a.

37 Yea, thou shalt go forth from him, and thine hands upon thine head: for the LORD hath rejected thy confidences, and thou shalt not prosper in them.

3 THEY say, If a man put away his wife, and she go from him, and become another man's, shall he return unto her again? shall not that land be greatly polluted? but thou hast played the harlot with many lovers; yet return again to me, saith the LORD.

2 Lift up thine eyes unto the high places, and see where thou hast not been lien with. In the ways hast thou sat for them, as the A-ra'bi-an in the wilderness; and thou hast polluted the land with thy whoredoms and with thy wickedness.

3 Therefore the showers have been withholden, and there hath been no latter rain; and thou hadst a whore's forehead, thou refusedst to be ashamed.

4 Wilt thou not from this time cry unto me, My father, thou *art* the guide of my youth?

5 Will he reserve *his anger* for ever? will he keep *it* to the end? Behold, thou hast spoken and done evil things as thou couldest.

6 ¶ The LORD said also unto me in the days of Jo-si'ah the king, Hast thou seen *that* which backsliding Is'ra-el hath done? she is gone up upon every high mountain and under every green tree, and there hath played the harlot.

7 And I said after she had done all these *things*, Turn thou unto me. But she returned not. And her treacherous sister Ju'dah saw *it*.

8 And I saw, when for all the causes whereby backsliding Is'ra-el committed adultery I had put her away, and given her a bill of divorce; yet her treacherous sister Ju'dah feared not, but went and played the harlot also.

9 And it came to pass through the lightness of her whoredom, that she defiled the land, and committed adultery with stones and with stocks.

10 And yet for all this her treacherous sister Ju'dah hath not turned unto me with her whole heart, but feignedly, saith the LORD.

11 And the LORD said unto me, The backsliding Is'ra-el hath justified herself more than treacherous Ju'dah.

12 ¶ Go and proclaim these words toward the north, and say, Return, thou backsliding Is'-ra-el, saith the LORD; *and* I will not cause mine anger to fall upon you: for I *am* merciful, saith the LORD, *and* I will not keep *anger* for ever.

13 Only acknowledge thine iniquity, that thou hast transgressed against the LORD thy God, and hast scattered thy ways to the strangers under every green tree, and ye have not obeyed my voice, saith the LORD.

14 Turn, O backsliding children, saith the LORD; for I am married unto you: and I will take you one of a city, and two of a family, and I will bring you to Zi'on:

15 And I will give you pastors according to

mine heart, which shall feed you with knowledge and understanding.

16 And it shall come to pass, when ye be multiplied and increased in the land, in those days, saith the LORD, they shall say no more, The ark of the covenant of the LORD: neither shall it come to mind: neither shall they remember it; neither shall they visit *it;* neither shall *that* be done any more.

17 At that time they shall call Je-ru'sa-lem the throne of the LORD; and all the nations shall be gathered unto it, to the name of the LORD, to Je-ru'sa-lem: neither shall they walk any more after the imagination of their evil heart.

18 In those days the house of Ju'dah shall walk with the house of Is'ra-el, and they shall come together out of the land of the north to the land that I have given for an inheritance unto your fathers.

19 But I said, How shall I put thee among the children, and give thee a pleasant land, a goodly heritage of the hosts of nations? and I said, Thou shalt call me, My father; and shalt not turn away from me.

20 ¶ Surely *as* a wife treacherously departeth from her husband, so have ye dealt treacherously with me, O house of Is'ra-el, saith the LORD.

21 A voice was heard upon the high places, weeping *and* supplications of the children of Is'-ra-el: for they have perverted their way, *and* they have forgotten the LORD their God.

22 Return, ye backsliding children, *and* I will heal your backslidings. Behold, we come unto thee; for thou *art* the LORD our God.

23 Truly in vain *is salvation hoped for* from the hills, *and from* the multitude of mountains: truly in the LORD our God *is* the salvation of Is'ra-el.

24 For shame hath devoured the labour of our fathers from our youth; their flocks and their herds, their sons and their daughters.

25 We lie down in our shame, and our confusion covereth us: for we have sinned against the LORD our God, we and our fathers, from our youth even unto this day, and have not obeyed the voice of the LORD our God.

4 IF thou wilt return, O Is'ra-el, saith the LORD, return unto me: and if thou wilt put away thine abominations out of my sight, then shalt thou not remove.

2 And thou shalt swear, The LORD liveth, in truth, in judgment, and in righteousness; and the nations shall bless themselves in him, and in him shall they glory.

3 ¶ For thus saith the LORD to the men of Ju'dah and Je-ru'sa-lem, Break up your fallow ground, and sow not among thorns.

4 Circumcise yourselves to the LORD, and take away the foreskins of your heart, ye men of Ju'dah and inhabitants of Je-ru'sa-lem: lest my fury come forth like fire, and burn that none can quench *it,* because of the evil of your doings.

5 Declare ye in Ju'dah, and publish in Je-ru'-sa-lem; and say, Blow ye the trumpet in the land: cry, gather together, and say, Assemble yourselves, and let us go into the defenced cities.

6 Set up the standard toward Zi'on: retire, stay not: for I will bring evil from the north, and a great destruction.

7 The lion is come up from his thicket, and the destroyer of the Gen-tiles is on his way; he is gone forth from his place to make thy land desolate; *and* thy cities shall be laid waste, without an inhabitant.

8 For this gird you with sackcloth, lament and howl: for the fierce anger of the LORD is not turned back from us.

9 And it shall come to pass at that day, saith the LORD, *that* the heart of the king shall perish, and the heart of the princes; and the priests shall be astonished, and the prophets shall wonder.

10 Then said I, Ah, Lord GOD! surely thou hast greatly deceived this people and Je-ru'sa-lem, saying, Ye shall have peace; whereas the sword reacheth unto the soul.

11 At that time shall it be said to this people and to Je-ru'sa-lem, A dry wind of the high places in the wilderness toward the daughter of my people, not to fan, nor to cleanse,

12 *Even* a full wind from those *places* shall come unto me: now also will I give sentence against them.

13 Behold, he shall come up as clouds, and his chariots *shall be* as a whirlwind: his horses are swifter than eagles. Woe unto us! for we are spoiled.

14 O Je-ru'sa-lem, wash thine heart from wickedness, that thou mayest be saved. How long shall thy vain thoughts lodge within thee?

15 For a voice declareth from Dan, and publisheth affliction from mount E'phra-im.

16 Make ye mention to the nations; behold, publish against Je-ru'sa-lem, *that* watchers come from a far country, and give out their voice against the cities of Ju'dah.

17 As keepers of a field, are they against her round about; because she hath been rebellious against me, saith the LORD.

18 Thy way and thy doings have procured these *things* unto thee; this *is* thy wickedness, because it is bitter, because it reacheth unto thine heart.

19 ¶ My bowels, my bowels! I am pained at my very heart; my heart maketh a noise in me; I cannot hold my peace, because thou hast heard, O my soul, the sound of the trumpet, the alarm of war.

20 Destruction upon destruction is cried; for the whole land is spoiled: suddenly are my tents spoiled, *and* my curtains in a moment.

21 How long shall I see the standard, *and* hear the sound of the trumpet?

22 For my people *is* foolish, they have not known me; they *are* sottish children, and they have none understanding: they *are* wise to do evil, but to do good they have no knowledge.

23 I beheld the earth, and, lo, *it was* without form, and void; and the heavens, and they *had* no light.

24 I beheld the mountains, and, lo, they trembled, and all the hills moved lightly.

25 I beheld, and, lo, *there was* no man, and all the birds of the heavens were fled.

26 I beheld, and, lo, the fruitful place *was* a wilderness, and all the cities thereof were broken down at the presence of the LORD, *and* by his fierce anger.

27 For thus hath the LORD said, The whole land shall be desolate; yet will I not make a full end.

28 For this shall the earth mourn, and the heavens above be black: because I have spoken *it,* I have purposed *it,* and will not repent, neither will I turn back from it.

29 The whole city shall flee for the noise of the horsemen and bowmen; they shall go into thickets, and climb up upon the rocks: every

city *shall be* forsaken, and not a man dwell therein.

30 And *when* thou *art* spoiled, what wilt thou do? Though thou clothest thyself with crimson, though thou deckest thee with ornaments of gold, though thou rentest thy face with painting, in vain shalt thou make thyself fair; *thy* lovers will despise thee, they will seek thy life.

31 For I have heard a voice as of a woman in travail, *and* the anguish as of her that bringeth forth her first child, the voice of the daughter of Zi'on, *that* bewaileth herself, *that* spreadeth her hands, *saying,* Woe *is* me now! for my soul is wearied because of murderers.

5 RUN ye to and fro through the streets of Je-ru'sa-lem, and see now, and know, and seek in the broad places thereof, if ye can find a man, if there be *any* that executeth judgment, that seeketh the truth; and I will pardon it.

2 And though they say, The LORD liveth; surely they swear falsely.

3 O LORD, *are* not thine eyes upon the truth? thou hast stricken them, but they have not grieved; thou hast consumed them, *but* they have refused to receive correction: they have made their faces harder than a rock; they have refused to return.

4 Therefore I said, Surely these *are* poor; they are foolish: for they know not the way of the LORD, *nor* the judgment of their God.

5 I will get me unto the great men, and will speak unto them; for they have known the way of the LORD, *and* the judgment of their God: but these have altogether broken the yoke, *and* burst the bonds.

6 Wherefore a lion out of the forest shall slay them, *and* a wolf of the evenings shall spoil them, a leopard shall watch over their cities: every one that goeth out thence shall be torn in pieces: because their transgressions are many, *and* their backslidings are increased.

7 ¶ How shall I pardon thee for this? thy children have forsaken me, and sworn by *them that are* no gods: when I had fed them to the full, they then committed adultery, and assembled themselves by troops in the harlots' houses.

8 They were *as* fed horses in the morning: every one neighed after his neighbour's wife.

9 Shall I not visit for these *things?* saith the LORD: and shall not my soul be avenged on such a nation as this?

10 ¶ Go ye up upon her walls, and destroy; but make not a full end: take away her battlements; for they *are* not the LORD's.

11 For the house of Is'ra-el and the house of Ju'dah have dealt very treacherously against me, saith the LORD.

12 They have belied the LORD, and said, *It is* not he; neither shall evil come upon us; neither shall we see sword nor famine:

13 And the prophets shall become wind, and the word *is* not in them: thus shall it be done unto them.

14 Wherefore thus saith the LORD God of hosts, Because ye speak this word, behold, I will make my words in thy mouth fire, and this people wood, and it shall devour them.

15 Lo, I will bring a nation upon you from far, O house of Is'ra-el, saith the LORD: it *is* a mighty nation, it *is* an ancient nation, a nation whose language thou knowest not, neither understandest what they say.

16 Their quiver *is* as an open sepulchre, they *are* all mighty men.

17 And they shall eat up thine harvest, and thy bread, *which* thy sons and thy daughters should eat: they shall eat up thy flocks and thine herds: they shall eat up thy vines and thy fig trees: they shall impoverish thy fenced cities, wherein thou trustedst, with the sword.

18 Nevertheless in those days, saith the LORD, I will not make a full end with you.

19 ¶ And it shall come to pass, when ye shall say, Wherefore doeth the LORD our God all these *things* unto us? then shalt thou answer them, Like as ye have forsaken me, and served strange gods in your land, so shall ye serve strangers in a land *that is* not yours.

20 Declare this in the house of Ja'cob, and publish it in Ju'dah, saying,

21 Hear now this, O foolish people, and without understanding; which have eyes, and see not; which have ears, and hear not:

22 Fear ye not me? saith the LORD: will ye not tremble at my presence, which have placed the sand *for* the bound of the sea by a perpetual decree, that it cannot pass it: and though the waves thereof toss themselves, yet can they not prevail; though they roar, yet can they not pass over it?

23 But this people hath a revolting and a rebellious heart; they are revolted and gone.

24 Neither say they in their heart, Let us now fear the LORD our God, that giveth rain, both the former and the latter, in his season: he reserveth unto us the appointed weeks of the harvest.

25 ¶ Your iniquities have turned away these *things,* and your sins have withholden good *things* from you.

26 For among my people are found wicked *men:* they lay wait, as he that setteth snares; they set a trap, they catch men.

27 As a cage is full of birds, so *are* their houses full of deceit: therefore they are become great, and waxen rich.

28 They are waxen fat, they shine: yea, they overpass the deeds of the wicked: they judge not the cause, the cause of the fatherless, yet they prosper; and the right of the needy do they not judge.

29 Shall I not visit for these *things?* saith the LORD: shall not my soul be avenged on such a nation as this?

30 ¶ A wonderful and horrible thing is committed in the land;

31 The prophets prophesy falsely, and the priests bear rule by their means; and my people love to have it so: and what will ye do in the end thereof?

6 O YE children of Ben'ja-min, gather yourselves to flee out of the midst of Je-ru'sa-lem, and blow the trumpet in Te-ko'a, and set up a sign of fire in Beth-hac'ce-rem: for evil appeareth out of the north, and great destruction.

2 I have likened the daughter of Zi'on to a comely and delicate *woman.*

3 The shepherds with their flocks shall come unto her; they shall pitch *their* tents against her round about; they shall feed every one in his place.

4 Prepare ye war against her; arise, and let us go up at noon. Woe unto us! for the day goeth away, for the shadows of the evening are stretched out.

5 Arise, and let us go by night, and let us destroy her palaces.

6 ¶ For thus hath the LORD of hosts said, Hew ye down trees, and cast a mount against Je-ru'sa-lem: this *is* the city to be visited; she *is* wholly oppression in the midst of her.

7 As a fountain casteth out her waters, so she casteth out her wickedness: violence and spoil is heard in her; before me continually *is* grief and wounds.

8 Be thou instructed, O Je-ru′sa-lem, lest my soul depart from thee; lest I make thee desolate, a land not inhabited.

9 ¶ Thus saith the LORD of hosts, They shall throughly glean the remnant of Is′ra-el as a vine: turn back thine hand as a grapegatherer into the baskets.

10 To whom shall I speak, and give warning, that they may hear? behold, their ear *is* uncircumcised, and they cannot hearken: behold, the word of the LORD is unto them a reproach; they have no delight in it.

11 Therefore I am full of the fury of the LORD; I am weary with holding in: I will pour it out upon the children abroad, and upon the assembly of young men together: for even the husband with the wife shall be taken, the aged with *him that is* full of days.

12 And their houses shall be turned unto others, *with their* fields and wives together: for I will stretch out my hand upon the inhabitants of the land, saith the LORD.

13 For from the least of them even unto the greatest of them every one *is* given to covetousness; and from the prophet even unto the priest every one dealeth falsely.

14 They have healed also the hurt *of the daughter* of my people slightly, saying, Peace, peace; when *there is* no peace.

15 Were they ashamed when they had committed abomination? nay, they were not at all ashamed, neither could they blush: therefore they shall fall among them that fall: at the time *that* I visit them they shall be cast down, saith the LORD.

16 Thus saith the LORD, Stand ye in the ways, and see, and ask for the old paths, where *is* the good way, and walk therein, and ye shall find rest for your souls. But they said, We will not walk *therein.*

17 Also I set watchmen over you, *saying,* Hearken to the sound of the trumpet. But they said, We will not hearken.

18 ¶ Therefore hear, ye nations, and know, O congregation, what *is* among them.

19 Hear, O earth: behold, I will bring evil upon this people, *even* the fruit of their thoughts, because they have not hearkened unto my words, nor to my law, but rejected it.

20 To what purpose cometh there to me incense from She′ba, and the sweet cane from a far country? your burnt offerings *are* not acceptable, nor your sacrifices sweet unto me.

21 Therefore thus saith the LORD, Behold, I will lay stumblingblocks before this people, and the fathers and the sons together shall fall upon them; the neighbour and his friend shall perish.

22 Thus saith the LORD, Behold, a people cometh from the north country, and a great nation shall be raised from the sides of the earth.

23 They shall lay hold on bow and spear; they *are* cruel, and have no mercy; their voice roareth like the sea; and they ride upon horses, set in array as men for war against thee, O daughter of Zi′on.

24 We have heard the fame thereof: our hands wax feeble: anguish hath taken hold of us, *and* pain, as of a woman in travail.

25 Go not forth into the field, nor walk by the way; for the sword of the enemy *and* fear *is* on every side.

26 ¶ O daughter of my people, gird *thee* with sackcloth, and wallow thyself in ashes: make thee mourning, *as for* an only son, most bitter lamentation: for the spoiler shall suddenly come upon us.

27 I have set thee *for* a tower *and* a fortress among my people, that thou mayest know and try their way.

28 They *are* all grievous revolters, walking with slanders: *they are* brass and iron; they *are* all corrupters.

29 The bellows are burned, the lead is consumed of the fire; the founder melteth in vain: for the wicked are not plucked away.

30 Reprobate silver shall *men* call them, because the LORD hath rejected them.

7 THE word that came to Jer-e-mi′ah from the LORD, saying,

2 Stand in the gate of the LORD'S house, and proclaim there this word, and say, Hear the word of the LORD, all ye of Ju′dah, that enter in at these gates to worship the LORD.

3 Thus saith the LORD of hosts, the God of Is′ra-el, Amend your ways and your doings, and I will cause you to dwell in this place.

4 Trust ye not in lying words, saying, The temple of the LORD, The temple of the LORD, The temple of the LORD, *are* these.

5 For if ye throughly amend your ways and your doings; if ye throughly execute judgment between a man and his neighbour;

6 *If* ye oppress not the stranger, the fatherless, and the widow, and shed not innocent blood in this place, neither walk after other gods to your hurt:

7 Then will I cause you to dwell in this place, in the land that I gave to your fathers, for ever and ever.

8 ¶ Behold, ye trust in lying words, that cannot profit.

9 Will ye steal, murder, and commit adultery, and swear falsely, and burn incense unto Ba′al, and walk after other gods whom ye know not;

10 And come and stand before me in this house, which is called by my name, and say, We are delivered to do all these abominations?

11 Is this house, which is called by my name, become a den of robbers in your eyes? Behold, even I have seen *it,* saith the LORD.

12 But go ye now unto my place which *was* in Shi′loh, where I set my name at the first, and see what I did to it for the wickedness of my people Is′ra-el.

13 And now, because ye have done all these works, saith the LORD, and I spake unto you, rising up early and speaking, but ye heard not; and I called you, but ye answered not;

14 Therefore will I do unto *this* house, which is called by my name, wherein ye trust, and unto the place which I gave to you and to your fathers, as I have done to Shi′loh.

15 And I will cast you out of my sight, as I have cast out all your brethren, *even* the whole seed of E′phra-im.

16 Therefore pray not thou for this people, neither lift up cry nor prayer for them, neither make intercession to me: for I will not hear thee.

17 ¶ Seest thou not what they do in the cities of Ju′dah and in the streets of Je-ru′sa-lem?

18 The children gather wood, and the fathers kindle the fire, and the women knead *their* dough, to make cakes to the queen of heaven, and to pour out drink offerings unto other gods, that they may provoke me to anger.

19 Do they provoke me to anger? saith the

LORD: *do they* not *provoke* themselves to the confusion of their own faces?

20 Therefore thus saith the Lord GOD; Behold, mine anger and my fury shall be poured out upon this place, upon man, and upon beast, and upon the trees of the field, and upon the fruit of the ground; and it shall burn, and shall not be quenched.

21 ¶ Thus saith the LORD of hosts, the God of Is'ra-el; Put your burnt offerings unto your sacrifices, and eat flesh.

22 For I spake not unto your fathers, nor commanded them in the day that I brought them out of the land of E'gypt, concerning burnt offerings or sacrifices:

23 But this thing commanded I them, saying, Obey my voice, and I will be your God, and ye shall be my people: and walk ye in all the ways that I have commanded you, that it may be well unto you.

24 But they hearkened not, nor inclined their ear, but walked in the counsels *and* in the imagination of their evil heart, and went backward, and not forward.

25 Since the day that your fathers came forth out of the land of E'gypt unto this day I have even sent unto you all my servants the prophets, daily rising up early and sending *them:*

26 Yet they hearkened not unto me, nor inclined their ear, but hardened their neck: they did worse than their fathers.

27 Therefore thou shalt speak all these words unto them; but they will not hearken to thee: thou shalt also call unto them; but they will not answer thee.

28 But thou shalt say unto them, This *is* a nation that obeyeth not the voice of the LORD their God, nor receiveth correction: truth is perished, and is cut off from their mouth.

29 ¶ Cut off thine hair, *O Je-ru'sa-lem,* and cast *it* away, and take up a lamentation on high places; for the LORD hath rejected and forsaken the generation of his wrath.

30 For the children of Ju'dah have done evil in my sight, saith the LORD: they have set their abominations in the house which is called by my name, to pollute it.

31 And they have built the high places of To'-phet, which *is* in the valley of the son of Hin'-nom, to burn their sons and their daughters in the fire; which I commanded *them* not, neither came it into my heart.

32 ¶ Therefore, behold, the days come, saith the LORD, that it shall no more be called To'-phet, nor the valley of the son of Hin'nom, but the valley of slaughter: for they shall bury in To'phet, till there be no place.

33 And the carcases of this people shall be meat for the fowls of the heaven, and for the beasts of the earth; and none shall fray *them* away.

34 Then will I cause to cease from the cities of Ju'dah, and from the streets of Je-ru'sa-lem, the voice of mirth, and the voice of gladness, the voice of the bridegroom, and the voice of the bride: for the land shall be desolate.

8 AT that time, saith the LORD, they shall bring out the bones of the kings of Ju'dah, and the bones of his princes, and the bones of the priests, and the bones of the prophets, and the bones of the inhabitants of Je-ru'sa-lem, out of their graves:

2 And they shall spread them before the sun, and the moon, and all the host of heaven, whom they have loved, and whom they have served, and after whom they have walked, and whom

they have sought, and whom they have worshipped: they shall not be gathered, nor be buried; they shall be for dung upon the face of the earth.

3 And death shall be chosen rather than life by all the residue of them that remain of this evil family, which remain in all the places whither I have driven them, saith the LORD of hosts.

4 ¶ Moreover thou shalt say unto them, Thus saith the LORD; Shall they fall, and not arise? shall he turn away, and not return?

5 Why *then* is this people of Je-ru'sa-lem slidden back by a perpetual backsliding? they hold fast deceit, they refuse to return.

6 I hearkened and heard, *but* they spake not aright: no man repented him of his wickedness, saying, What have I done? every one turned to his course, as the horse rusheth into the battle.

7 Yea, the stork in the heaven knoweth her appointed times; and the turtle and the crane and the swallow observe the time of their coming; but my people know not the judgment of the LORD.

8 How do ye say, We *are* wise, and the law of the LORD *is* with us? Lo, certainly in vain made he *it;* the pen of the scribes *is* in vain.

9 The wise *men* are ashamed, they are dismayed and taken: lo, they have rejected the word of the LORD; and what wisdom *is* in them?

10 Therefore will I give their wives unto others, *and* their fields to them that shall inherit *them:* for every one from the least even unto the greatest is given to covetousness, from the prophet even unto the priest every one dealeth falsely.

11 For they have healed the hurt of the daughter of my people slightly, saying, Peace, peace; when *there is* no peace.

12 Were they ashamed when they had committed abomination? nay, they were not at all ashamed, neither could they blush: therefore shall they fall among them that fall: in the time of their visitation they shall be cast down, saith the LORD.

13 ¶ I will surely consume them, saith the LORD: *there shall be* no grapes on the vine, nor figs on the fig tree, and the leaf shall fade; and *the things that* I have given them shall pass away from them.

14 Why do we sit still? assemble yourselves, and let us enter into the defenced cities, and let us be silent there: for the LORD our God hath put us to silence, and given us water of gall to drink, because we have sinned against the LORD.

15 We looked for peace, but no good *came; and* for a time of health, and behold trouble!

16 The snorting of his horses was heard from Dan: the whole land trembled at the sound of the neighing of his strong ones; for they are come, and have devoured the land, and all that is in it; the city, and those that dwell therein.

17 For, behold, I will send serpents, cockatrices, among you, which *will* not *be* charmed, and they shall bite you, saith the LORD.

18 ¶ *When* I would comfort myself against sorrow, my heart *is* faint in me.

19 Behold the voice of the cry of the daughter of my people because of them that dwell in a far country: *Is* not the LORD in Zi'on? *is* not her king in her? Why have they provoked me to anger with their graven images, *and* with strange vanities?

20 The harvest is past, the summer is ended, and we are not saved.

21 For the hurt of the daughter of my people

am I hurt; I am black; astonishment hath taken hold on me.

22 Is there no balm in Gil'e-ad; is there no physician there? why then is not the health of the daughter of my people recovered?

9 OH that my head were waters, and mine eyes a fountain of tears, that I might weep day and night for the slain of the daughter of my people!

2 Oh that I had in the wilderness a lodging place of wayfaring men; that I might leave my people, and go from them! for they be all adulterers, an assembly of treacherous men.

3 And they bend their tongues like their bow for lies: but they are not valiant for the truth upon the earth; for they proceed from evil to evil, and they know not me, saith the LORD.

4 Take ye heed every one of his neighbour, and trust ye not in any brother: for every brother will utterly supplant, and every neighbour will walk with slanders.

5 And they will deceive every one his neighbour, and will not speak the truth: they have taught their tongue to speak lies, and weary themselves to commit iniquity.

6 Thine habitation is in the midst of deceit; through deceit they refuse to know me, saith the LORD.

7 Therefore thus saith the LORD of hosts, Behold, I will melt them, and try them; for how shall I do for the daughter of my people?

8 Their tongue is as an arrow shot out; it speaketh deceit: one speaketh peaceably to his neighbour with his mouth, but in heart he layeth his wait.

9 ¶ Shall I not visit them for these things? saith the LORD: shall not my soul be avenged on such a nation as this?

10 For the mountains will I take up a weeping and wailing, and for the habitations of the wilderness a lamentation, because they are burned up, so that none can pass through them; neither can men hear the voice of the cattle; both the fowl of the heavens and the beast are fled; they are gone.

11 And I will make Je-ru'sa-lem heaps, and a den of dragons; and I will make the cities of Ju'dah desolate, without an inhabitant.

12 ¶ Who is the wise man, that may understand this? and who is he to whom the mouth of the LORD hath spoken, that he may declare it, for what the land perisheth and is burned up like a wilderness, that none passeth through?

13 And the LORD saith, Because they have forsaken my law which I set before them, and have not obeyed my voice, neither walked therein;

14 But have walked after the imagination of their own heart, and after Ba'al-im, which their fathers taught them:

15 Therefore thus saith the LORD of hosts, the God of Is'ra-el; Behold, I will feed them, even this people, with wormwood, and give them water of gall to drink.

16 I will scatter them also among the heathen, whom neither they nor their fathers have known: and I will send a sword after them, till I have consumed them.

17 ¶ Thus saith the LORD of hosts, Consider ye, and call for the mourning women, that they may come; and send for cunning women, that they may come:

18 And let them make haste, and take up a wailing for us, that our eyes may run down with tears, and our eyelids gush out with waters.

19 For a voice of wailing is heard out of Zi'-on, How are we spoiled! we are greatly confounded, because we have forsaken the land, because our dwellings have cast us out.

20 Yet hear the word of the LORD, O ye women, and let your ear receive the word of his mouth, and teach your daughters wailing, and every one her neighbour lamentation.

21 For death is come up into our windows, and is entered into our palaces, to cut off the children from without, and the young men from the streets.

22 Speak, Thus saith the LORD, Even the carcases of men shall fall as dung upon the open field, and as the handful after the harvestman, and none shall gather them.

23 ¶ Thus saith the LORD, Let not the wise man glory in his wisdom, neither let the mighty man glory in his might, let not the rich man glory in his riches:

24 But let him that glorieth glory in this, that he understandeth and knoweth me, that I am the LORD which exercise lovingkindness, judgment, and righteousness, in the earth: for in these things I delight, saith the LORD.

25 ¶ Behold, the days come, saith the LORD, that I will punish all them which are circumcised with the uncircumcised;

26 E'gypt, and Ju'dah, and E'dom, and the children of Am'mon, and Mo'ab, and all that are in the utmost corners, that dwell in the wilderness: for all these nations are uncircumcised, and all the house of Is'ra-el are uncircumcised in the heart.

10 HEAR ye the word which the LORD speaketh unto you, O house of Is'ra-el:

2 Thus saith the LORD, Learn not the way of the heathen, and be not dismayed at the signs of heaven, for the heathen are dismayed at them.

3 For the customs of the people are vain: for one cutteth a tree out of the forest, the work of the hands of the workman, with the ax.

4 They deck it with silver and with gold; they fasten it with nails and with hammers, that it move not.

5 They are upright as the palm tree, but speak not: they must needs be borne, because they cannot go. Be not afraid of them; for they cannot do evil, neither also is it in them to do good.

6 Forasmuch as there is none like unto thee, O LORD; thou art great, and thy name is great in might.

7 Who would not fear thee, O King of nations? for to thee doth it appertain: forasmuch as among all the wise men of the nations, and in all their kingdoms, there is none like unto thee.

8 But they are altogether brutish and foolish: the stock is a doctrine of vanities.

9 Silver spread into plates is brought from Tar'shish, and gold from U'phaz, the work of the workman, and of the hands of the founder: blue and purple is their clothing: they are all the work of cunning men.

10 But the LORD is the true God, he is the living God, and an everlasting king: at his wrath the earth shall tremble, and the nations shall not be able to abide his indignation.

11 Thus shall ye say unto them, The gods that have not made the heavens and the earth, even they shall perish from the earth, and from under these heavens.

12 He hath made the earth by his power, he hath established the world by his wisdom, and hath stretched out the heavens by his discretion.

13 When he uttereth his voice, *there is* a multitude of waters in the heavens, and he causeth the vapours to ascend from the ends of the earth; he maketh lightnings with rain, and bringeth forth the wind out of his treasures.

14 Every man is brutish in *his* knowledge: every founder is confounded by the graven image: for his molten image *is* falsehood, and *there is* no breath in them.

15 They *are* vanity, *and* the work of errors: in the time of their visitation they shall perish.

16 The portion of Ja'cob *is* not like them: for he *is* the former of all *things*; and Is'ra-el *is* the rod of his inheritance: The LORD of hosts *is* his name.

17 ¶ Gather up thy wares out of the land, O inhabitant of the fortress.

18 For thus saith the LORD, Behold, I will sling out the inhabitants of the land at this once, and will distress them, that they may find *it* so.

19 ¶ Woe is me for my hurt! my wound is grievous: but I said, Truly this *is* a grief, and I must bear it.

20 My tabernacle is spoiled, and all my cords are broken: my children are gone forth of me, and they *are* not: *there is* none to stretch forth my tent any more, and to set up my curtains.

21 For the pastors are become brutish, and have not sought the LORD: therefore they shall not prosper, and all their flocks shall be scattered.

22 Behold, the noise of the bruit is come, and a great commotion out of the north country, to make the cities of Ju'dah desolate, *and* a den of dragons.

23 ¶ O LORD, I know that the way of man *is* not in himself: *it is* not in man that walketh to direct his steps.

24 O LORD, correct me, but with judgment; not in thine anger, lest thou bring me to nothing.

25 Pour out thy fury upon the heathen that know thee not, and upon the families that call not on thy name: for they have eaten up Ja'cob, and devoured him, and consumed him, and have made his habitation desolate.

11 THE word that came to Jer-e-mi'ah from the LORD, saying,

2 Hear ye the words of this covenant, and speak unto the men of Ju'dah, and to the inhabitants of Je-ru'sa-lem;

3 And say thou unto them, Thus saith the LORD God of Is'ra-el; Cursed *be* the man that obeyeth not the words of this covenant,

4 Which I commanded your fathers in the day *that* I brought them forth out of the land of E'gypt, from the iron furnace, saying, Obey my voice, and do them, according to all which I command you: so shall ye be my people, and I will be your God:

5 That I may perform the oath which I have sworn unto your fathers, to give them a land flowing with milk and honey, as *it is* this day. Then answered I, and said, So be it, O LORD.

6 Then the LORD said unto me, Proclaim all these words in the cities of Ju'dah, and in the streets of Je-ru'sa-lem, saying, Hear ye the words of this covenant, and do them.

7 For I earnestly protested unto your fathers in the day *that* I brought them up out of the land of E'gypt, *even* unto this day, rising early and protesting, saying, Obey my voice.

8 Yet they obeyed not, nor inclined their ear, but walked every one in the imagination of their evil heart: therefore I will bring upon them all the words of this covenant, which I commanded *them* to do; but they did *them* not.

9 And the LORD said unto me, A conspiracy is found among the men of Ju'dah, and among the inhabitants of Je-ru'sa-lem.

10 They are turned back to the iniquities of their forefathers, which refused to hear my words; and they went after other gods to serve them: the house of Is'ra-el and the house of Ju'dah have broken my covenant which I made with their fathers.

11 ¶ Therefore thus saith the LORD, Behold, I will bring evil upon them, which they shall not be able to escape; and though they shall cry unto me, I will not hearken unto them.

12 Then shall the cities of Ju'dah and inhabitants of Je-ru'sa-lem go, and cry unto the gods unto whom they offer incense: but they shall not save them at all in the time of their trouble.

13 For *according to* the number of thy cities were thy gods, O Ju'dah; and *according to* the number of the streets of Je-ru'sa-lem have ye set up altars to *that* shameful thing, *even* altars to burn incense unto Ba'al.

14 Therefore pray not thou for this people, neither lift up a cry or prayer for them: for I will not hear *them* in the time that they cry unto me for their trouble.

15 What hath my beloved to do in mine house, *seeing* she hath wrought lewdness with many, and the holy flesh is passed from thee? when thou doest evil, then thou rejoicest.

16 The LORD called thy name, A green olive tree, fair, *and* of goodly fruit: with the noise of a great tumult he hath kindled fire upon it, and the branches of it are broken.

17 For the LORD of hosts, that planted thee, hath pronounced evil against thee, for the evil of the house of Is'ra-el and of the house of Ju'dah, which they have done against themselves to provoke me to anger in offering incense unto Ba'al.

18 ¶ And the LORD hath given me knowledge *of it*, and I know *it*: then thou shewedst me their doings.

19 But I *was* like a lamb *or* an ox *that* is brought to the slaughter; and I knew not that they had devised devices against me, *saying*, Let us destroy the tree with the fruit thereof, and let us cut him off from the land of the living, that his name may be no more remembered.

20 But, O LORD of hosts, that judgest righteously, that triest the reins and the heart, let me see thy vengeance on them: for unto thee have I revealed my cause.

21 Therefore thus saith the LORD of the men of An'a-thoth, that seek thy life, saying, Prophesy not in the name of the LORD, that thou die not by our hand:

22 Therefore thus saith the LORD of hosts, Behold, I will punish them: the young men shall die by the sword; their sons and their daughters shall die by famine:

23 And there shall be no remnant of them: for I will bring evil upon the men of An'a-thoth, *even* the year of their visitation.

12 RIGHTEOUS *art* thou, O LORD, when I plead with thee: yet let me talk with thee of *thy* judgments: Wherefore doth the way of the wicked prosper? *wherefore* are all they happy that deal very treacherously?

2 Thou hast planted them, yea, they have taken root: they grow, yea, they bring forth fruit: thou *art* near in their mouth, and far from their reins.

3 But thou, O LORD, knowest me: thou hast seen me, and tried mine heart toward thee: pull them out like sheep for the slaughter, and prepare them for the day of slaughter.

4 How long shall the land mourn, and the herbs of every field wither, for the wickedness of them that dwell therein? the beasts are consumed, and the birds; because they said, He shall not see our last end.

5 ¶ If thou hast run with the footmen, and they have wearied thee, then how canst thou contend with horses? and *if* in the land of peace, *wherein* thou trustedst, *they wearied thee,* then how wilt thou do in the swelling of Jor'dan?

6 For even thy brethren, and the house of thy father, even they have dealt treacherously with thee; yea, they have called a multitude after thee: believe them not, though they speak fair words unto thee.

7 ¶ I have forsaken mine house, I have left mine heritage; I have given the dearly beloved of my soul into the hand of her enemies.

8 Mine heritage is unto me as a lion in the forest; it crieth out against me: therefore have I hated it.

9 Mine heritage *is* unto me *as* a speckled bird, the birds round about *are* against her; come ye, assemble all the beasts of the field, come to devour.

10 Many pastors have destroyed my vineyard, they have trodden my portion under foot, they have made my pleasant portion a desolate wilderness.

11 They have made it desolate, *and being* desolate it mourneth unto me; the whole land is made desolate, because no man layeth *it* to heart.

12 The spoilers are come upon all high places through the wilderness: for the sword of the LORD shall devour from the *one* end of the land even to the *other* end of the land: no flesh shall have peace.

13 They have sown wheat, but shall reap thorns: they have put themselves to pain, *but* shall not profit: and they shall be ashamed of your revenues because of the fierce anger of the LORD.

14 ¶ Thus saith the LORD against all mine evil neighbours, that touch the inheritance which I have caused my people Is'ra-el to inherit; Behold, I will pluck them out of their land, and pluck out the house of Ju'dah from among them.

15 And it shall come to pass, after that I have plucked them out I will return, and have compassion on them, and will bring them again, every man to his heritage, and every man to his land.

16 And it shall come to pass, if they will diligently learn the ways of my people, to swear by my name, The LORD liveth; as they taught my people to swear by Ba'al; then shall they be built in the midst of my people.

17 But if they will not obey, I will utterly pluck up and destroy that nation, saith the LORD.

13 THUS saith the LORD unto me, Go and get thee a linen girdle, and put it upon thy loins, and put it not in water.

2 So I got a girdle according to the word of the LORD, and put *it* on my loins.

3 And the word of the LORD came unto me the second time, saying,

4 Take the girdle that thou hast got, which *is* upon thy loins, and arise, go to Eu-phra'tes, and hide it there in a hole of the rock.

5 So I went, and hid it by Eu-phra'tes, as the LORD commanded me.

6 And it came to pass after many days, that the LORD said unto me, Arise, go to Eu-phra'tes, and take the girdle from thence, which I commanded thee to hide there.

7 Then I went to Eu-phra'tes, and digged, and took the girdle from the place where I had hid it: and, behold, the girdle was marred, it was profitable for nothing.

8 Then the word of the LORD came unto me, saying,

9 Thus saith the LORD, After this manner will I mar the pride of Ju'dah, and the great pride of Je-ru'sa-lem.

10 This evil people, which refuse to hear my words, which walk in the imagination of their heart, and walk after other gods, to serve them, and to worship them, shall even be as this girdle, which is good for nothing.

11 For as the girdle cleaveth to the loins of a man, so have I caused to cleave unto me the whole house of Is'ra-el and the whole house of Ju'dah, saith the LORD; that they might be unto me for a people, and for a name, and for a praise, and for a glory: but they would not hear.

12 ¶ Therefore thou shalt speak unto them this word; Thus saith the LORD God of Is'ra-el, Every bottle shall be filled with wine: and they shall say unto thee, Do we not certainly know that every bottle shall be filled with wine?

13 Then shalt thou say unto them, Thus saith the LORD, Behold, I will fill all the inhabitants of this land, even the kings that sit upon Da'vid's throne, and the priests, and the prophets, and all the inhabitants of Je-ru'sa-lem, with drunkenness.

14 And I will dash them one against another, even the fathers and the sons together, saith the LORD: I will not pity, nor spare, nor have mercy, but destroy them.

15 ¶ Hear ye, and give ear; be not proud: for the LORD hath spoken.

16 Give glory to the LORD your God, before he cause darkness, and before your feet stumble upon the dark mountains, and, while ye look for light, he turn it into the shadow of death, *and* make *it* gross darkness.

17 But if ye will not hear it, my soul shall weep in secret places for *your* pride; and mine eye shall weep sore, and run down with tears, because the LORD's flock is carried away captive.

18 Say unto the king and to the queen, Humble yourselves, sit down: for your principalities shall come down, *even* the crown of your glory.

19 The cities of the south shall be shut up, and none shall open *them:* Ju'dah shall be carried away captive all of it, it shall be wholly carried away captive.

20 Lift up your eyes, and behold them that come from the north: where *is* the flock *that* was given thee, thy beautiful flock?

21 What wilt thou say when he shall punish thee? for thou hast taught them *to be* captains, *and* as chief over thee: shall not sorrows take thee, as a woman in travail?

22 ¶ And if thou say in thine heart, Wherefore come these things upon me? For the greatness of thine iniquity are thy skirts discovered, *and* thy heels made bare.

23 Can the E-thi-o'pi-an change his skin, or the leopard his spots? *then* may ye also do good, that are accustomed to do evil.

24 Therefore will I scatter them as the stub-

ble that passeth away by the wind of the wilderness.

25 This is thy lot, the portion of thy measures from me, saith the LORD; because thou hast forgotten me, and trusted in falsehood.

26 Therefore will I discover thy skirts upon thy face, that thy shame may appear.

27 I have seen thine adulteries, and thy neighings, the lewdness of thy whoredom, and thine abominations on the hills in the fields. Woe unto thee, O Je-ru'sa-lem! wilt thou not be made clean? when shall it once be?

14 THE word of the LORD that came to Jer-e-mi'ah concerning the dearth.

2 Ju'dah mourneth, and the gates thereof languish; they are black unto the ground; and the cry of Je-ru'sa-lem is gone up.

3 And their nobles have sent their little ones to the waters: they came to the pits, and found no water; they returned with their vessels empty; they were ashamed and confounded, and covered their heads.

4 Because the ground is chapt, for there was no rain in the earth, the plowmen were ashamed, they covered their heads.

5 Yea, the hind also calved in the field, and forsook it, because there was no grass.

6 And the wild asses did stand in the high places, they snuffed up the wind like dragons; their eyes did fail, because there was no grass.

7 ¶ O LORD, though our iniquities testify against us, do thou it for thy name's sake: for our backslidings are many; we have sinned against thee.

8 O the hope of Is'ra-el, the saviour thereof in time of trouble, why shouldest thou be as a stranger in the land, and as a wayfaring man that turneth aside to tarry for a night?

9 Why shouldest thou be as a man astonied, as a mighty man that cannot save? yet thou, O LORD, art in the midst of us, and we are called by thy name; leave us not.

10 ¶ Thus saith the LORD unto this people, Thus have they loved to wander, they have not refrained their feet, therefore the LORD doth not accept them; he will now remember their iniquity, and visit their sins.

11 Then said the LORD unto me, Pray not for this people for their good.

12 When they fast, I will not hear their cry; and when they offer burnt offering and an oblation, I will not accept them: but I will consume them by the sword, and by the famine, and by the pestilence.

13 ¶ Then said I, Ah, Lord GOD! behold, the prophets say unto them, Ye shall not see the sword, neither shall ye have famine; but I will give you assured peace in this place.

14 Then the LORD said unto me, The prophets prophesy lies in my name: I sent them not, neither have I commanded them, neither spake unto them: they prophesy unto you a false vision and divination, and a thing of nought, and the deceit of their heart.

15 Therefore thus saith the LORD concerning the prophets that prophesy in my name, and I sent them not, yet they say, Sword and famine shall not be in this land; By sword and famine shall those prophets be consumed.

16 And the people to whom they prophesy shall be cast out in the streets of Je-ru'sa-lem because of the famine and the sword; and they shall have none to bury them, them, their wives, nor their sons, nor their daughters: for I will pour their wickedness upon them.

17 ¶ Therefore thou shalt say this word unto

them; Let mine eyes run down with tears night and day, and let them not cease: for the virgin daughter of my people is broken with a great breach, with a very grievous blow.

18 If I go forth into the field, then behold the slain with the sword! and if I enter into the city, then behold them that are sick with famine! yea, both the prophet and the priest go about into a land that they know not.

19 Hast thou utterly rejected Ju'dah? hath thy soul loathed Zi'on? why hast thou smitten us, and there is no healing for us? we looked for peace, and there is no good; and for the time of healing, and behold trouble!

20 We acknowledge, O LORD, our wickedness, and the iniquity of our fathers: for we have sinned against thee.

21 Do not abhor us, for thy name's sake, do not disgrace the throne of thy glory: remember, break not thy covenant with us.

22 Are there any among the vanities of the Gen'tiles that can cause rain? or can the heavens give showers? art not thou he, O LORD our God? therefore we will wait upon thee: for thou hast made all these things.

15 THEN said the LORD unto me, Though Mo'ses and Sam'u-el stood before me, yet my mind could not be toward this people: cast them out of my sight, and let them go forth.

2 And it shall come to pass, if they say unto thee, Whither shall we go forth? then thou shalt tell them, Thus saith the LORD; Such as are for death, to death; and such as are for the sword, to the sword; and such as are for the famine, to the famine; and such as are for the captivity, to the captivity.

3 And I will appoint over them four kinds, saith the LORD: the sword to slay, and the dogs to tear, and the fowls of the heaven, and the beasts of the earth, to devour and destroy.

4 And I will cause them to be removed into all kingdoms of the earth, because of Ma-nas'-seh the son of Hez-e-ki'ah king of Ju'dah, for that which he did in Je-ru'sa-lem.

5 For who shall have pity upon thee, O Je-ru'sa-lem? or who shall bemoan thee? or who shall go aside to ask how thou doest?

6 Thou hast forsaken me, saith the LORD, thou art gone backward: therefore will I stretch out my hand against thee, and destroy thee; I am weary with repenting.

7 And I will fan them with a fan in the gates of the land; I will bereave them of children, I will destroy my people, since they return not from their ways.

8 Their widows are increased to me above the sand of the seas: I have brought upon them against the mother of the young men a spoiler at noonday: I have caused him to fall upon it suddenly, and terrors upon the city.

9 She that hath borne seven languisheth: she hath given up the ghost; her sun is gone down while it was yet day: she hath been ashamed and confounded: and the residue of them will I deliver to the sword before their enemies, saith the LORD.

10 ¶ Woe is me, my mother, that thou hast borne me a man of strife and a man of contention to the whole earth! I have neither lent on usury, nor men have lent to me on usury; yet every one of them doth curse me.

11 The LORD said, Verily it shall be well with thy remnant; verily I will cause the enemy tô entreat thee well in the time of evil and in the time of affliction.

12 Shall iron break the northern iron and the steel?

13 Thy substance and thy treasures will I give to the spoil without price, and that for all thy sins, even in all thy borders.

14 And I will make thee to pass with thine enemies into a land which thou knowest not: for a fire is kindled in mine anger, which shall burn upon you.

15 ¶ O LORD, thou knowest: remember me, and visit me, and revenge me of my persecutors; take me not away in thy longsuffering: know that for thy sake I have suffered rebuke.

16 Thy words were found, and I did eat them; and thy word was unto me the joy and rejoicing of mine heart: for I am called by thy name, O LORD God of hosts.

17 I sat not in the assembly of the mockers, nor rejoiced; I sat alone because of thy hand: for thou hast filled me with indignation.

18 Why is my pain perpetual, and my wound incurable, which refuseth to be healed? wilt thou be altogether unto me as a liar, and as waters that fail?

19 ¶ Therefore thus saith the LORD, If thou return, then will I bring thee again, and thou shalt stand before me: and if thou take forth the precious from the vile, thou shalt be as my mouth: let them return unto thee; but return not thou unto them.

20 And I will make thee unto this people a fenced brasen wall: and they shall fight against thee, but they shall not prevail against thee: for I am with thee to save thee and to deliver thee, saith the LORD.

21 And I will deliver thee out of the hand of the wicked, and I will redeem thee out of the hand of the terrible.

16 THE word of the LORD came also unto me, saying,

2 Thou shalt not take thee a wife, neither shalt thou have sons or daughters in this place.

3 For thus saith the LORD concerning the sons and concerning the daughters that are born in this place, and concerning their mothers that bare them, and concerning their fathers that begat them in this land;

4 They shall die of grievous deaths; they shall not be lamented; neither shall they be buried; but they shall be as dung upon the face of the earth: and they shall be consumed by the sword, and by famine; and their carcases shall be meat for the fowls of heaven, and for the beasts of the earth.

5 For thus saith the LORD, Enter not into the house of mourning, neither go to lament nor bemoan them: for I have taken away my peace from this people, saith the LORD, even lovingkindness and mercies.

6 Both the great and the small shall die in this land: they shall not be buried, neither shall men lament for them, nor cut themselves, nor make themselves bald for them:

7 Neither shall men tear themselves for them in mourning, to comfort them for the dead; neither shall men give them the cup of consolation to drink for their father or for their mother.

8 Thou shalt not also go into the house of feasting, to sit with them to eat and to drink.

9 For thus saith the LORD of hosts, the God of Is'ra-el; Behold, I will cause to cease out of this place in your eyes, and in your days, the voice of mirth, and the voice of gladness, the voice of the bridegroom, and the voice of the bride.

10 ¶ And it shall come to pass, when thou shalt shew this people all these words, and they shall say unto thee, Wherefore hath the LORD pronounced all this great evil against us? or what is our iniquity? or what is our sin that we have committed against the LORD our God?

11 Then shalt thou say unto them, Because your fathers have forsaken me, saith the LORD, and have walked after other gods, and have served them, and have worshipped them, and have forsaken me, and have not kept my law;

12 And ye have done worse than your fathers; for, behold, ye walk every one after the imagination of his evil heart, that they may not hearken unto me:

13 Therefore will I cast you out of this land into a land that ye know not, neither ye nor your fathers; and there shall ye serve other gods day and night; where I will not shew you favour.

14 ¶ Therefore, behold, the days come, saith the LORD, that it shall no more be said, The LORD liveth, that brought up the children of Is'-ra-el out of the land of E'gypt;

15 But, The LORD liveth, that brought up the children of Is'ra-el from the land of the north, and from all the lands whither he had driven them: and I will bring them again into their land that I gave unto their fathers.

16 ¶ Behold, I will send for many fishers, saith the LORD, and they shall fish them; and after will I send for many hunters, and they shall hunt them from every mountain, and from every hill, and out of the holes of the rocks.

17 For mine eyes are upon all their ways: they are not hid from my face, neither is their iniquity hid from mine eyes.

18 And first I will recompense their iniquity and their sin double; because they have defiled my land, they have filled mine inheritance with the carcases of their detestable and abominable things.

19 O LORD, my strength, and my fortress, and my refuge in the day of affliction, the Gen'-tiles shall come unto thee from the ends of the earth, and shall say, Surely our fathers have inherited lies, vanity, and things wherein there is no profit.

20 Shall a man make gods unto himself, and they are no gods?

21 Therefore, behold, I will this once cause them to know, I will cause them to know mine hand and my might; and they shall know that my name is The LORD.

17 THE sin of Ju'dah is written with a pen of iron, and with the point of a diamond: it is graven upon the table of their heart, and upon the horns of your altars;

2 Whilst their children remember their altars and their groves by the green trees upon the high hills.

3 O my mountain in the field, I will give thy substance and all thy treasures to the spoil, and thy high places for sin, throughout all thy borders.

4 And thou, even thyself, shalt discontinue from thine heritage that I gave thee; and I will cause thee to serve thine enemies in the land which thou knowest not: for ye have kindled a fire in mine anger, which shall burn for ever.

5 ¶ Thus saith the LORD; Cursed be the man that trusteth in man, and maketh flesh his arm, and whose heart departeth from the LORD.

6 For he shall be like the heath in the desert, and shall not see when good cometh; but shall inhabit the parched places in the wilderness, in a salt land and not inhabited.

7 Blessed *is* the man that trusteth in the LORD, and whose hope the LORD is.

8 For he shall be as a tree planted by the waters, and *that* spreadeth out her roots by the river, and shall not see when heat cometh, but her leaf shall be green; and shall not be careful in the year of drought, neither shall cease from yielding fruit.

9 ¶ The heart *is* deceitful above all *things*, and desperately wicked: who can know it?

10 I the LORD search the heart, *I* try the reins, even to give every man according to his ways, *and* according to the fruit of his doings.

11 *As* the partridge sitteth *on eggs*, and hatcheth *them* not; *so* he that getteth riches, and not by right, shall leave them in the midst of his days, and at his end shall be a fool.

12 ¶ A glorious high throne from the beginning *is* the place of our sanctuary.

13 O LOᴿD, the hope of Is'ra-el, all that forsake thee shall be ashamed, *and* they that depart from me shall be written in the earth, because they have forsaken the LORD, the fountain of living waters.

14 Heal me, O LORD, and I shall be healed; save me, and I shall be saved: for thou *art* my praise.

15 ¶ Behold, they say unto me, Where *is* the word of the LORD? let it come now.

16 As for me, I have not hastened from *being* a pastor to follow thee: neither have I desired the woeful day; thou knowest: that which came out of my lips was *right* before thee.

17 Be not a terror unto me: thou *art* my hope in the day of evil.

18 Let them be confounded that persecute me, but let not me be confounded: let them be dismayed, but let not me be dismayed: bring upon them the day of evil, and destroy them with double destruction.

19 ¶ Thus said the LORD unto me; Go and stand in the gate of the children of the people, whereby the kings of Ju'dah come in, and by the which they go out, and in all the gates of Je-ru'sa-lem;

20 And say unto them, Hear ye the word of the LORD, ye kings of Ju'dah, and all Ju'dah, and all the inhabitants of Je-ru'sa-lem, that enter in by these gates:

21 Thus saith the LORD; Take heed to yourselves, and bear no burden on the sabbath day, nor bring *it* in by the gates of Je-ru'sa-lem;

22 Neither carry forth a burden out of your houses on the sabbath day, neither do ye any work, but hallow ye the sabbath day, as I commanded your fathers.

23 But they obeyed not, neither inclined their ear, but made their neck stiff, that they might not hear, nor receive instruction.

24 And it shall come to pass, if ye diligently hearken unto me, saith the LORD, to bring in no burden through the gates of this city on the sabbath day, but hallow the sabbath day, to do no work therein;

25 Then shall there enter into the gates of this city kings and princes sitting upon the throne of Da'vid, riding in chariots and on horses, they, and their princes, the men of Ju'dah, and the inhabitants of Je-ru'sa-lem: and this city shall remain for ever.

26 And they shall come from the cities of Ju'dah, and from the places about Je-ru'sa-lem, and from the land of Ben'ja-min, and from the plain, and from the mountains, and from the south, bringing burnt offerings, and sacrifices, and meat offerings, and incense, and bringing sacrifices of praise, unto the house of the LORD.

27 But if ye will not hearken unto me to hallow the sabbath day, and not to bear a burden, even entering in at the gates of Je-ru'sa-lem on the sabbath day; then will I kindle a fire in the gates thereof, and it shall devour the palaces of Je-ru'sa-lem, and it shall not be quenched.

18 THE word which came to Jer-e-mi'ah from the LORD, saying,

2 Arise, and go down to the potter's house, and there I will cause thee to hear my words.

3 Then I went down to the potter's house, and, behold, he wrought a work on the wheels.

4 And the vessel that he made of clay was marred in the hand of the potter: so he made it again another vessel, as seemed good to the potter to make *it*.

5 Then the word of the LORD came to me, saying,

6 O house of Is'ra-el, cannot I do with you as this potter? saith the LORD. Behold, as the clay *is* in the potter's hand, so *are* ye in mine hand, O house of Is'ra-el.

7 At *what* instant I shall speak concerning a nation, and concerning a kingdom, to pluck up, and to pull down, and to destroy *it;*

8 If that nation, against whom I have pronounced, turn from their evil, I will repent of the evil that I thought to do unto them.

9 And at *what* instant I shall speak concerning a nation, and concerning a kingdom, to build and to plant *it;*

10 If it do evil in my sight, that it obey not my voice, then I will repent of the good, wherewith I said I would benefit them.

11 ¶ Now therefore go to, speak to the men of Ju'dah, and to the inhabitants of Je-ru'sa-lem, saying, Thus saith the LORD; Behold, I frame evil against you, and devise a device against you: return ye now every one from his evil way, and make your ways and your doings good.

12 And they said, There is no hope: but we will walk after our own devices, and we will every one do the imagination of his evil heart.

13 Therefore thus saith the LORD; Ask ye now among the heathen, who hath heard such things: the virgin of Is'ra-el hath done a very horrible thing.

14 Will *a man* leave the snow of Leb'a-non *which cometh* from the rock of the field? or shall the cold flowing waters that come from another place be forsaken?

15 Because my people hath forgotten me, they have burned incense to vanity, and they have caused them to stumble in their ways *from* the ancient paths, to walk in paths, *in* a way not cast up;

16 To make their land desolate, *and* a perpetual hissing; every one that passeth thereby shall be astonished, and wag his head.

17 I will scatter them as with an east wind, before the enemy; I will shew them the back, and not the face, in the day of their calamity.

18 ¶ Then said they, Come, and let us devise devices against Jer-e-mi'ah; for the law shall not perish from the priest, nor counsel from the wise, nor the word from the prophet. Come, and let us smite him with the tongue, and let us not give heed to any of his words.

19 Give heed to me, O LORD, and hearken to the voice of them that contend with me.

20 Shall evil be recompensed for good? for they have digged a pit for my soul. Remember that I stood before thee to speak good for them, *and* to turn away thy wrath from them.

21 Therefore deliver up their children to the

famine, and pour out their *blood* by the force of the sword; and let their wives be bereaved of their children, and *be* widows; and let their men be put to death; *let* their young men *be* slain by the sword in battle.

22 Let a cry be heard from their houses, when thou shalt bring a troop suddenly upon them: for they have digged a pit to take me, and hid snares for my feet.

23 Yet, Lord, thou knowest all their counsel against me to slay *me:* forgive not their iniquity, neither blot out their sin from thy sight, but let them be overthrown before thee; deal *thus* with them in the time of thine anger.

19 THUS saith the Lord, Go and get a potter's earthen bottle, and *take* of the ancients of the people, and of the ancients of the priests;

2 And go forth unto the valley of the son of Hin'nom, which *is* by the entry of the east gate, and proclaim there the words that I shall tell thee,

3 And say, Hear ye the word of the Lord, O kings of Ju'dah, and inhabitants of Je-ru'sa-lem; Thus saith the Lord of hosts, the God of Is'ra-el; Behold, I will bring evil upon this place, the which whosoever heareth, his ears shall tingle.

4 Because they have forsaken me, and have estranged this place, and have burned incense in it unto other gods, whom neither they nor their fathers have known, nor the kings of Ju'dah, and have filled this place with the blood of innocents;

5 They have built also the high places of Ba'-al, to burn their sons with fire *for* burnt offerings unto Ba'al, which I commanded not, nor spake *it,* neither came *it* into my mind:

6 Therefore, behold, the days come, saith the Lord, that this place shall no more be called To'phet, nor The valley of the son of Hin'nom, but The valley of slaughter.

7 And I will make void the counsel of Ju'dah and Je-ru'sa-lem in this place; and I will cause them to fall by the sword before their enemies, and by the hands of them that seek their lives: and their carcases will I give to be meat for the fowls of the heaven, and for the beasts of the earth.

8 And I will make this city desolate, and an hissing; every one that passeth thereby shall be astonished and hiss because of all the plagues thereof.

9 And I will cause them to eat the flesh of their sons and the flesh of their daughters, and they shall eat every one the flesh of his friend in the siege and straitness, wherewith their enemies, and they that seek their lives, shall straiten them.

10 Then shalt thou break the bottle in the sight of the men that go with thee,

11 And shalt say unto them, Thus saith the Lord of hosts; Even so will I break this people and this city as *one* breaketh a potter's vessel, that cannot be made whole again: and they shall bury *them* in To'phet, till *there be* no place to bury.

12 Thus will I do unto this place, saith the Lord, and to the inhabitants thereof, and *even* make this city as To'phet:

13 And the houses of Je-ru'sa-lem, and the houses of the kings of Ju'dah, shall be defiled as the place of To'phet, because of all the houses upon whose roofs they have burned incense unto all the host of heaven, and have poured out drink offerings unto other gods.

14 Then came Jer-e-mi'ah from To'phet, whither the Lord had sent him to prophesy; and he stood in the court of the Lord's house; and said to all the people,

15 Thus saith the Lord of hosts, the God of Is'ra-el; Behold, I will bring upon this city and upon all her towns all the evil that I have pronounced against it, because they have hardened their necks, that they might not hear my words.

20 NOW Pash'ur the son of Im'mer the priest, who *was* also chief governor in the house of the Lord, heard that Jer-e-mi'ah prophesied these things.

2 Then Pash'ur smote Jer-e-mi'ah the prophet, and put him in the stocks that *were* in the high gate of Ben'ja-min, which *was* by the house of the Lord.

3 And it came to pass on the morrow, that Pash'ur brought forth Jer-e-mi'ah out of the stocks. Then said Jer-e-mi'ah unto him, The Lord hath not called thy name Pash'ur, but Ma'gor-mis'sa-bib.

4 For thus saith the Lord, Behold, I will make thee a terror to thyself, and to all thy friends: and they shall fall by the sword of their enemies, and thine eyes shall behold *it:* and I will give all Ju'dah into the hand of the king of Bab'y-lon, and he shall carry them captive into Bab'y-lon, and shall slay them with the sword.

5 Moreover I will deliver all the strength of this city, and all the labours thereof, and all the precious things thereof, and all the treasures of the kings of Ju'dah will I give into the hand of their enemies, which shall spoil them, and take them, and carry them to Bab'y-lon.

6 And thou, Pash'ur, and all that dwell in thine house shall go into captivity: and thou shalt come to Bab'y-lon, and there thou shalt die, and shalt be buried there, thou, and all thy friends, to whom thou hast prophesied lies.

7 ¶ O Lord, thou hast deceived me, and I was deceived: thou art stronger than I, and hast prevailed: I am in derision daily, every one mocketh me.

8 For since I spake, I cried out, I cried violence and spoil; because the word of the Lord was made a reproach unto me, and a derision, daily.

9 Then I said, I will not make mention of him, nor speak any more in his name. But *his word* was in mine heart as a burning fire shut up in my bones, and I was weary with forbearing, and I could not *stay.*

10 ¶ For I heard the defaming of many, fear on every side. Report, *say they,* and we will report it. All my familiars watched for my halting, *saying,* Peradventure he will be enticed, and we shall prevail against him, and we shall take our revenge on him.

11 But the Lord *is* with me as a mighty terrible one: therefore my persecutors shall stumble, and they shall not prevail: they shall be greatly ashamed; for they shall not prosper: *their* everlasting confusion shall never be forgotten.

12 But, O Lord of hosts, that triest the righteous, *and* seest the reins and the heart, let me see thy vengeance on them: for unto thee have I opened my cause.

13 Sing unto the Lord, praise ye the Lord: for he hath delivered the soul of the poor from the hand of evildoers.

14 ¶ Cursed *be* the day wherein I was born: let not the day wherein my mother bare me be blessed.

15 Cursed *be* the man who brought tidings to

my father, saying, A man child is born unto thee; making him very glad.

16 And let that man be as the cities which the LORD overthrew, and repented not: and let him hear the cry in the morning, and the shouting at noontide;

17 Because he slew me not from the womb; or that my mother might have been my grave, and her womb to be always great with me.

18 Wherefore came I forth out of the womb to see labour and sorrow, that my days should be consumed with shame?

21 THE word which came unto Jer-e-mi′ah from the LORD, when king Zed-e-ki′ah sent unto him Pash′ur the son of Mel-chi′ah, and Zeph-a-ni′ah the son of Ma-a-se′iah the priest, saying,

2 Enquire, I pray thee, of the LORD for us; for Neb-u-chad-rez′zar king of Bab′y-lon maketh war against us; if so be that the LORD will deal with us according to all his wondrous works, that he may go up from us.

3 ¶ Then said Jer-e-mi′ah unto them, Thus shall ye say to Zed-e-ki′ah:

4 Thus saith the LORD God of Is′ra-el; Behold, I will turn back the weapons of war that are in your hands, wherewith ye fight against the king of Bab′y-lon, and against the Chal-de′ans, which besiege you without the walls, and I will assemble them into the midst of this city.

5 And I myself will fight against you with an outstretched hand and with a strong arm, even in anger, and in fury, and in great wrath.

6 And I will smite the inhabitants of this city, both man and beast: they shall die of a great pestilence.

7 And afterward, saith the LORD, I will deliver Zed-e-ki′ah king of Ju′dah, and his servants, and the people, and such as are left in this city from the pestilence, from the sword, and from the famine, into the hand of Neb-u-chad-rez′zar king of Bab′y-lon, and into the hand of their enemies, and into the hand of those that seek their life: and he shall smite them with the edge of the sword; he shall not spare them, neither have pity, nor have mercy.

8 ¶ And unto this people thou shalt say, Thus saith the LORD; Behold, I set before you the way of life, and the way of death.

9 He that abideth in this city shall die by the sword, and by the famine, and by the pestilence: but he that goeth out, and falleth to the Chal-de′ans that besiege you, he shall live, and his life shall be unto him for a prey.

10 For I have set my face against this city for evil, and not for good, saith the LORD: it shall be given into the hand of the king of Bab′y-lon, and he shall burn it with fire.

11 ¶ And touching the house of the king of Ju′dah, say, Hear ye the word of the LORD;

12 O house of Da′vid, thus saith the LORD; Execute judgment in the morning, and deliver him that is spoiled out of the hand of the oppressor, lest my fury go out like fire, and burn that none can quench it, because of the evil of your doings.

13 Behold, I am against thee, O inhabitant of the valley, and rock of the plain, saith the LORD; which say, Who shall come down against us? or who shall enter into our habitations?

14 But I will punish you according to the fruit of your doings, saith the LORD: and I will kindle a fire in the forest thereof, and it shall devour all things round about it.

22 THUS saith the LORD; Go down to the house of the king of Ju′dah, and speak there this word,

2 And say, Hear the word of the LORD, O king of Ju′dah, that sittest upon the throne of Da′vid, thou, and thy servants, and thy people that enter in by these gates:

3 Thus saith the LORD; Execute ye judgment and righteousness, and deliver the spoiled out of the hand of the oppressor: and do no wrong, do no violence to the stranger, the fatherless, nor the widow, neither shed innocent blood in this place.

4 For if ye do this thing indeed, then shall there enter in by the gates of this house kings sitting upon the throne of Da′vid, riding in chariots and on horses, he, and his servants, and his people.

5 But if ye will not hear these words, I swear by myself, saith the LORD, that this house shall become a desolation.

6 For thus saith the LORD unto the king's house of Ju′dah; Thou art Gil′e-ad unto me, and the head of Leb′a-non: yet surely I will make thee a wilderness, and cities which are not inhabited.

7 And I will prepare destroyers against thee, every one with his weapons: and they shall cut down thy choice cedars, and cast them into the fire.

8 And many nations shall pass by this city, and they shall say every man to his neighbour, Wherefore hath the LORD done thus unto this great city?

9 Then they shall answer, Because they have forsaken the covenant of the LORD their God, and worshipped other gods, and served them.

10 ¶ Weep ye not for the dead, neither bemoan him: but weep sore for him that goeth away: for he shall return no more, nor see his native country.

11 For thus saith the LORD touching Shal′lum the son of Jo-si′ah king of Ju′dah, which reigned instead of Jo-si′ah his father, which went forth out of this place; He shall not return thither any more:

12 But he shall die in the place whither they have led him captive, and shall see this land no more.

13 ¶ Woe unto him that buildeth his house by unrighteousness, and his chambers by wrong; that useth his neighbour's service without wages, and giveth him not for his work;

14 That saith, I will build me a wide house and large chambers, and cutteth him out windows; and it is cieled with cedar, and painted with vermilion.

15 Shalt thou reign, because thou closest thyself in cedar? did not thy father eat and drink, and do judgment and justice, and then it was well with him?

16 He judged the cause of the poor and needy; then it was well with him: was not this to know me? saith the LORD.

17 But thine eyes and thine heart are not but for thy covetousness, and for to shed innocent blood, and for oppression, and for violence, to do it.

18 Therefore thus saith the LORD concerning Je-hoi′a-kim the son of Jo-si′ah king of Ju′dah; They shall not lament for him, saying, Ah my brother! or, Ah sister! they shall not lament for him, saying, Ah lord! or, Ah his glory!

19 He shall be buried with the burial of an ass, drawn and cast forth beyond the gates of Je-ru′sa-lem.

20 ¶ Go up to Leb′a-non, and cry; and lift up

thy voice in Ba'shan, and cry from the passages: for all thy lovers are destroyed.

21 I spake unto thee in thy prosperity; *but* thou saidst, I will not hear. This *hath been* thy manner from thy youth, that thou obeyedst not my voice.

22 The wind shall eat up all thy pastors, and thy lovers shall go into captivity: surely then shalt thou be ashamed and confounded for all thy wickedness.

23 O inhabitant of Leb'a-non, that makest thy nest in the cedars, how gracious shalt thou be when pangs come upon thee, the pain as of a woman in travail!

24 *As* I live, saith the LORD, though Co-ni'ah the son of Je-hoi'a-kim king of Ju'dah were the signet upon my right hand, yet would I pluck thee thence;

25 And I will give thee into the hand of them that seek thy life, and into the hand *of them* whose face thou fearest, even into the hand of Neb-u-chad-rez'zar king of Bab'y-lon, and into the hand of the Chal-de'ans.

26 And I will cast thee out, and thy mother that bare thee, into another country, where ye were not born; and there shall ye die.

27 But to the land whereunto they desire to return, thither shall they not return.

28 *Is* this man Co-ni'ah a despised broken idol? *is he* a vessel wherein *is* no pleasure? wherefore are they cast out, he and his seed, and are cast into a land which they know not?

29 O earth, earth, earth, hear the word of the LORD.

30 Thus saith the LORD, Write ye this man childless, a man *that* shall not prosper in his days: for no man of his seed shall prosper, sitting upon the throne of Da'vid, and ruling any more in Ju'dah.

23 WOE be unto the pastors that destroy and scatter the sheep of my pasture! saith the LORD.

2 Therefore thus saith the LORD God of Is'ra-el against the pastors that feed my people; Ye have scattered my flock, and driven them away, and have not visited them: behold, I will visit upon you the evil of your doings, saith the LORD.

3 And I will gather the remnant of my flock out of all countries whither I have driven them, and will bring them again to their folds; and they shall be fruitful and increase.

4 And I will set up shepherds over them which shall feed them: and they shall fear no more, nor be dismayed, neither shall they be lacking, saith the LORD.

5 ¶ Behold, the days come, saith the LORD, that I will raise unto Da'vid a righteous Branch, and a King shall reign and prosper, and shall execute judgment and justice in the earth.

6 In his days Ju'dah shall be saved, and Is'ra-el shall dwell safely: and this *is* his name whereby he shall be called, THE LORD OUR RIGHTEOUSNESS.

7 Therefore, behold, the days come, saith the LORD, that they shall no more say, The LORD liveth, which brought up the children of Is'ra-el out of the land of E'gypt;

8 But, The LORD liveth, which brought up and which led the seed of the house of Is'ra-el out of the north country, and from all countries whither I had driven them; and they shall dwell in their own land.

9 ¶ Mine heart within me is broken because of the prophets; all my bones shake; I am like a drunken man, and like a man whom wine hath overcome, because of the LORD, and because of the words of his holiness.

10 For the land is full of adulterers; for because of swearing the land mourneth; the pleasant places of the wilderness are dried up, and their course is evil, and their force *is* not right.

11 For both prophet and priest are profane; yea, in my house have I found their wickedness, saith the LORD.

12 Wherefore their way shall be unto them as slippery *ways* in the darkness: they shall be driven on, and fall therein: for I will bring evil upon them, *even* the year of their visitation, saith the LORD.

13 And I have seen folly in the prophets of Sa-ma'ri-a; they prophesied in Ba'al, and caused my people Is'ra-el to err.

14 I have seen also in the prophets of Je-ru'sa-lem an horrible thing: they commit adultery, and walk in lies: they strengthen also the hands of evildoers, that none doth return from his wickedness: they are all of them unto me as Sod'om, and the inhabitants thereof as Go-mor'rah.

15 Therefore thus saith the LORD of hosts concerning the prophets; Behold, I will feed them with wormwood, and make them drink the water of gall: for from the prophets of Je-ru'sa-lem is profaneness gone forth into all the land.

16 Thus saith the LORD of hosts, Hearken not unto the words of the prophets that prophesy unto you: they make you vain: they speak a vision of their own heart, *and* not out of the mouth of the LORD.

17 They say still unto them that despise me, The LORD hath said, Ye shall have peace; and they say unto every one that walketh after the imagination of his own heart, No evil shall come upon you.

18 For who hath stood in the counsel of the LORD, and hath perceived and heard his word? who hath marked his word, and heard *it?*

19 Behold, a whirlwind of the LORD is gone forth in fury, even a grievous whirlwind: it shall fall grievously upon the head of the wicked.

20 The anger of the LORD shall not return, until he have executed, and till he have performed the thoughts of his heart: in the latter days ye shall consider it perfectly.

21 I have not sent these prophets, yet they ran: I have not spoken to them, yet they prophesied.

22 But if they had stood in my counsel, and had caused my people to hear my words, then they should have turned them from their evil way, and from the evil of their doings.

23 *Am* I a God at hand, saith the LORD, and not a God afar off?

24 Can any hide himself in secret places that I shall not see him? saith the LORD. Do not I fill heaven and earth? saith the LORD.

25 I have heard what the prophets said, that prophesy lies in my name, saying, I have dreamed, I have dreamed.

26 How long shall *this* be in the heart of the prophets that prophesy lies? yea, *they are* prophets of the deceit of their own heart;

27 Which think to cause my people to forget my name by their dreams which they tell every man to his neighbour, as their fathers have forgotten my name for Ba'al.

28 The prophet that hath a dream, let him tell a dream; and he that hath my word, let him speak my word faithfully. What *is* the chaff to the wheat? saith the LORD.

29 *Is* not my word like as a fire? saith the

LORD; and like a hammer *that* breaketh the rock in pieces?

30 Therefore, behold, I *am* against the prophets, saith the LORD, that steal my words every one from his neighbour.

31 Behold, I *am* against the prophets, saith the LORD, that use their tongues, and say, He saith.

32 Behold, I *am* against them that prophesy false dreams, saith the LORD, and do tell them, and cause my people to err by their lies, and by their lightness; yet I sent them not, nor commanded them: therefore they shall not profit this people at all, saith the LORD.

33 ¶ And when this people, or the prophet, or a priest, shall ask thee, saying, What *is* the burden of the LORD? thou shalt then say unto them, What burden? I will even forsake you, saith the LORD.

34 And *as for* the prophet, and the priest, and the people, that shall say, The burden of the LORD, I will even punish that man and his house.

35 Thus shall ye say every one to his neighbour, and every one to his brother, What hath the LORD answered? and, What hath the LORD spoken?

36 And the burden of the LORD shall ye mention no more: for every man's word shall be his burden; for ye have perverted the words of the living God, of the LORD of hosts our God.

37 Thus shalt thou say to the prophet, What hath the LORD answered thee? and, What hath the LORD spoken?

38 But since ye say, The burden of the LORD; therefore thus saith the LORD; Because ye say this word, The burden of the LORD, and I have sent unto you, saying, Ye shall not say, The burden of the LORD;

39 Therefore, behold, I, even I, will utterly forget you, and I will forsake you, and the city that I gave you and your fathers, *and cast you* out of my presence:

40 And I will bring an everlasting reproach upon you, and a perpetual shame, which shall not be forgotten.

24 THE LORD shewed me, and, behold, two baskets of figs *were* set before the temple of the LORD, after that Neb-u-chad-rez'zar king of Bab'y-lon had carried away captive Jec-o-ni'ah the son of Je-hoi'a-kim king of Ju'dah, and the princes of Ju'dah, with the carpenters and smiths, from Je-ru'sa-lem, and had brought them to Bab'y-lon.

2 One basket *had* very good figs, *even* like the figs *that are* first ripe: and the other basket *had* very naughty figs, which could not be eaten, they were so bad.

3 Then said the LORD unto me, What seest thou, Jer-e-mi'ah? And I said, Figs; the good figs, very good; and the evil, very evil, that cannot be eaten, they are so evil.

4 ¶ Again the word of the LORD came unto me, saying,

5 Thus saith the LORD, the God of Is'ra-el; Like these good figs, so will I acknowledge them that are carried away captive of Ju'dah, whom I have sent out of this place into the land of the Chal-de'ans for *their* good.

6 For I will set mine eyes upon them for good, and I will bring them again to this land: and I will build them, and not pull *them* down; and I will plant them, and not pluck *them* up.

7 And I will give them an heart to know me, that I *am* the LORD: and they shall be my people, and I will be their God: for they shall return unto me with their whole heart.

8 ¶ And as the evil figs, which cannot be eaten, they are so evil; surely thus saith the LORD, So will I give Zed-e-ki'ah the king of Ju'dah, and his princes, and the residue of Je-ru'sa-lem, that remain in this land, and them that dwell in the land of E'gypt:

9 And I will deliver them to be removed into all the kingdoms of the earth for *their* hurt, *to be* a reproach and a proverb, a taunt and a curse, in all places whither I shall drive them.

10 And I will send the sword, the famine, and the pestilence, among them, till they be consumed from off the land that I gave unto them and to their fathers.

25 THE word that came to Jer-e-mi'ah concerning all the people of Ju'dah in the fourth year of Je-hoi'a-kim the son of Jo-si'ah king of Ju'dah, that *was* the first year of Neb-u-chad-rez'zar king of Bab'y-lon;

2 The which Jer-e-mi'ah the prophet spake unto all the people of Ju'dah, and to all the inhabitants of Je-ru'sa-lem, saying,

3 From the thirteenth year of Jo-si'ah the son of A'mon king of Ju'dah, even unto this day, that *is* the three and twentieth year, the word of the LORD hath come unto me, and I have spoken unto you, rising early and speaking; but ye have not hearkened.

4 And the LORD hath sent unto you all his servants the prophets, rising early and sending *them*; but ye have not hearkened, nor inclined your ear to hear.

5 They said, Turn ye again now every one from his evil way, and from the evil of your doings, and dwell in the land that the LORD hath given unto you and to your fathers for ever and ever:

6 And go not after other gods to serve them, and to worship them, and provoke me not to anger with the works of your hands; and I will do you no hurt.

7 Yet ye have not hearkened unto me, saith the LORD; that ye might provoke me to anger with the works of your hands to your own hurt.

8 ¶ Therefore thus saith the LORD of hosts; Because ye have not heard my words,

9 Behold, I will send and take all the families of the north, saith the LORD, and Neb-u-chad-rez'zar the king of Bab'y-lon, my servant, and will bring them against this land, and against the inhabitants thereof, and against all these nations round about, and will utterly destroy them, and make them an astonishment, and an hissing, and perpetual desolations.

10 Moreover I will take from them the voice of mirth, and the voice of gladness, the voice of the bridegroom, and the voice of the bride, the sound of the millstones, and the light of the candle.

11 And this whole land shall be a desolation, *and* an astonishment; and these nations shall serve the king of Bab'y-lon seventy years.

12 ¶ And it shall come to pass, when seventy years are accomplished, *that* I will punish the king of Bab'y-lon, and that nation, saith the LORD, for their iniquity, and the land of the Chal-de'ans, and will make it perpetual desolations.

13 And I will bring upon that land all my words which I have pronounced against it, *even* all that is written in this book, which Jer-e-mi'-ah hath prophesied against all the nations.

14 For many nations and great kings shall serve themselves of them also: and I will rec-

ompense them according to their deeds, and according to the works of their own hands.

15 ¶ For thus saith the LORD God of Is'ra-el unto me; Take the wine cup of this fury at my hand, and cause all the nations, to whom I send thee, to drink it.

16 And they shall drink, and be moved, and be mad, because of the sword that I will send among them.

17 Then took I the cup at the LORD's hand, and made all the nations to drink, unto whom the LORD had sent me:

18 To wit, Je-ru'sa-lem, and the cities of Ju'-dah, and the kings thereof, and the princes thereof, to make them a desolation, an astonishment, an hissing, and a curse; as it is this day;

19 Pha'raoh king of E'gypt, and his servants, and his princes, and all his people;

20 And all the mingled people, and all the kings of the land of Uz, and all the kings of the land of the Phi-lis'tines, and Ash'ke-lon, and Az'zah, and Ek'ron, and the remnant of Ash'-dod,

21 E'dom, and Mo'ab, and the children of Am'mon,

22 And all the kings of Ty'rus, and all the kings of Zi'don, and the kings of the isles which are beyond the sea,

23 De'dan, and Te'ma, and Buz, and all that are in the utmost corners,

24 And all the kings of A-ra'bi-a, and all the kings of the mingled people that dwell in the desert,

25 And all the kings of Zim'ri, and all the kings of E'lam, and all the kings of the Medes,

26 And all the kings of the north, far and near, one with another, and all the kingdoms of the world, which are upon the face of the earth: and the king of She'shach shall drink after them.

27 Therefore thou shalt say unto them, Thus saith the LORD of hosts, the God of Is'ra-el; Drink ye, and be drunken, and spue, and fall, and rise no more, because of the sword which I will send among you.

28 And it shall be, if they refuse to take the cup at thine hand to drink, then shalt thou say unto them, Thus saith the LORD of hosts; Ye shall certainly drink.

29 For, lo, I begin to bring evil on the city which is called by my name, and should ye be utterly unpunished? Ye shall not be unpunished: for I will call for a sword upon all the inhabitants of the earth, saith the LORD of hosts.

30 Therefore prophesy thou against them all these words, and say unto them, The LORD shall roar from on high, and utter his voice from his holy habitation; he shall mightily roar upon his habitation; he shall give a shout, as they that tread the grapes, against all the inhabitants of the earth.

31 A noise shall come even to the ends of the earth; for the LORD hath a controversy with the nations, he will plead with all flesh; he will give them that are wicked to the sword, saith the LORD.

32 Thus saith the LORD of hosts, Behold, evil shall go forth from nation to nation, and a great whirlwind shall be raised up from the coasts of the earth.

33 And the slain of the LORD shall be at that day from one end of the earth even unto the other end of the earth: they shall not be lamented, neither gathered, nor buried; they shall be dung upon the ground.

34 ¶ Howl, ye shepherds, and cry; and wallow yourselves in the ashes, ye principal of the flock: for the days of your slaughter and of your dispersions are accomplished; and ye shall fall like a pleasant vessel.

35 And the shepherds shall have no way to flee, nor the principal of the flock to escape.

36 A voice of the cry of the shepherds, and an howling of the principal of the flock, shall be heard: for the LORD hath spoiled their pasture.

37 And the peaceable habitations are cut down because of the fierce anger of the LORD.

38 He hath forsaken his covert, as the lion: for their land is desolate because of the fierceness of the oppressor, and because of his fierce anger.

26 IN the beginning of the reign of Je-hoi'a-kim the son of Jo-si'ah king of Ju'dah came this word from the LORD, saying,

2 Thus saith the LORD; Stand in the court of the LORD's house, and speak unto all the cities of Ju'dah, which come to worship in the LORD's house, all the words that I command thee to speak unto them; diminish not a word:

3 If so be they will hearken, and turn every man from his evil way, that I may repent me of the evil, which I purpose to do unto them because of the evil of their doings.

4 And thou shalt say unto them, Thus saith the LORD; If ye will not hearken to me, to walk in my law, which I have set before you,

5 To hearken to the words of my servants the prophets, whom I sent unto you, both rising up early, and sending them, but ye have not hearkened;

6 Then will I make this house like Shi'loh, and will make this city a curse to all the nations of the earth.

7 So the priests and the prophets and all the people heard Jer-e-mi'ah speaking these words in the house of the LORD.

8 ¶ Now it came to pass, when Jer-e-mi'ah had made an end of speaking all that the LORD had commanded him to speak unto all the people, that the priests and the prophets and all the people took him, saying, Thou shalt surely die.

9 Why hast thou prophesied in the name of the LORD, saying, This house shall be like Shi'-loh, and this city shall be desolate without an inhabitant? And all the people were gathered against Jer-e-mi'ah in the house of the LORD.

10 ¶ When the princes of Ju'dah heard these things, then they came up from the king's house unto the house of the LORD, and sat down in the entry of the new gate of the LORD's house.

11 Then spake the priests and the prophets unto the princes and to all the people, saying, This man is worthy to die; for he hath prophesied against this city, as ye have heard with your ears.

12 ¶ Then spake Jer-e-mi'ah unto all the princes and to all the people, saying, The LORD sent me to prophesy against this house and against this city all the words that ye have heard.

13 Therefore now amend your ways and your doings, and obey the voice of the LORD your God; and the LORD will repent him of the evil that he hath pronounced against you.

14 As for me, behold, I am in your hand: do with me as seemeth good and meet unto you.

15 But know ye for certain, that if ye put me to death, ye shall surely bring innocent blood upon yourselves, and upon this city, and upon the inhabitants thereof: for of a truth the LORD hath sent me unto you to speak all these words in your ears.

16 ¶ Then said the princes and all the people

unto the priests and to the prophets; This man *is* not worthy to die: for he hath spoken to us in the name of the LORD our God.

17 Then rose up certain of the elders of the land, and spake to all the assembly of the people, saying,

18 Mi'cah the Mo'ras-thite prophesied in the days of Hez-e-ki'ah king of Ju'dah, and spake to all the people of Ju'dah, saying, Thus saith the LORD of hosts; Zi'on shall be plowed *like* a field, and Je-ru'sa-lem shall become heaps, and the mountain of the house as the high places of a forest.

19 Did Hez-e-ki'ah king of Ju'dah and all Ju'dah put him at all to death? did he not fear the LORD, and besought the LORD, and the LORD repented him of the evil which he had pronounced against them? Thus might we procure great evil against our souls.

20 And there was also a man that prophesied in the name of the LORD, U-ri'jah the son of Shem-a-i'ah of Kir'jath-je'a-rim, who prophesied against this city and against this land according to all the words of Jer-e-mi'ah:

21 And when Je-hoi'a-kim the king, with all his mighty men, and all the princes, heard his words, the king sought to put him to death: but when U-ri'jah heard it, he was afraid, and fled, and went into E'gypt;

22 And Je-hoi'a-kim the king sent men into E'gypt, *namely*, El'na-than the son of Ach'bor, and *certain* men with him into E'gypt.

23 And they fetched forth U-ri'jah out of E'gypt, and brought him unto Je-hoi'a-kim the king; who slew him with the sword, and cast his dead body into the graves of the common people.

24 Nevertheless the hand of A-hi'kam the son of Sha'phan was with Jer-e-mi'ah, that they should not give him into the hand of the people to put him to death.

27 IN the beginning of the reign of Je-hoi'a-kim the son of Jo-si'ah king of Ju'dah came this word unto Jer-e-mi'ah from the LORD, saying,

2 Thus saith the LORD to me; Make thee bonds and yokes, and put them upon thy neck,

3 And send them to the king of E'dom, and to the king of Mo'ab, and to the king of the Am'-mon-ites, and to the king of Ty'rus, and to the king of Zi'don, by the hand of the messengers which come to Je-ru'sa-lem unto Zed-e-ki'ah king of Ju'dah;

4 And command them to say unto their masters, Thus saith the LORD of hosts, the God of Is'ra-el; Thus shall ye say unto your masters;

5 I have made the earth, the man and the beast that *are* upon the ground, by my great power and by my outstretched arm, and have given it unto whom it seemed meet unto me.

6 And now have I given all these lands into the hand of Neb-u-chad-nez'zar the king of Bab'y-lon, my servant; and the beasts of the field have I given him also to serve him.

7 And all nations shall serve him, and his son, and his son's son, until the very time of his land come: and then many nations and great kings shall serve themselves of him.

8 And it shall come to pass, *that* the nation and kingdom which will not serve the same Neb-u-chad-nez'zar the king of Bab'y-lon, and that will not put their neck under the yoke of the king of Bab'y-lon, that nation will I punish, saith the LORD, with the sword, and with the famine, and with the pestilence, until I have consumed them by his hand.

9 Therefore hearken not ye to your prophets, nor to your diviners, nor to your dreamers, nor to your enchanters, nor to your sorcerers, which speak unto you, saying, Ye shall not serve the king of Bab'y-lon:

10 For they prophesy a lie unto you, to remove you far from your land; and that I should drive you out, and ye should perish.

11 But the nations that bring their neck under the yoke of the king of Bab'y-lon, and serve him, those will I let remain still in their own land, saith the LORD; and they shall till it, and dwell therein.

12 ¶ I spake also to Zed-e-ki'ah king of Ju'dah according to all these words, saying, Bring your necks under the yoke of the king of Bab'y-lon, and serve him and his people, and live.

13 Why will ye die, thou and thy people, by the sword, by the famine, and by the pestilence, as the LORD hath spoken against the nation that will not serve the king of Bab'y-lon?

14 Therefore hearken not unto the words of the prophets that speak unto you, saying, Ye shall not serve the king of Bab'y-lon: for they prophesy a lie unto you.

15 For I have not sent them, saith the LORD, yet they prophesy a lie in my name; that I might drive you out, and that ye might perish, ye, and the prophets that prophesy unto you.

16 Also I spake to the priests and to all this people, saying, Thus saith the LORD; Hearken not to the words of your prophets that prophesy unto you, saying, Behold, the vessels of the LORD'S house shall now shortly be brought again from Bab'y-lon: for they prophesy a lie unto you.

17 Hearken not unto them; serve the king of Bab'y-lon, and live: wherefore should this city be laid waste?

18 But if they *be* prophets, and if the word of the LORD be with them, let them now make intercession to the LORD of hosts, that the vessels which are left in the house of the LORD, and in the house of the king of Ju'dah, and at Je-ru'sa-lem, go not to Bab'y-lon.

19 ¶ For thus saith the LORD of hosts concerning the pillars, and concerning the sea, and concerning the bases, and concerning the residue of the vessels that remain in this city,

20 Which Neb-u-chad-nez'zar king of Bab'y-lon took not, when he carried away captive Jec-o-ni'ah the son of Je-hoi'a-kim king of Ju'dah from Je-ru'sa-lem to Bab'y-lon, and all the nobles of Ju'dah and Je-ru'sa-lem;

21 Yea, thus saith the LORD of hosts, the God of Is'ra-el, concerning the vessels that remain *in* the house of the LORD, and *in* the house of the king of Ju'dah and of Je-ru'sa-lem;

22 They shall be carried to Bab'y-lon, and there shall they be until the day that I visit them, saith the LORD; then will I bring them up, and restore them to this place.

28 AND it came to pass the same year, in the beginning of the reign of Zed-e-ki'ah king of Ju'dah, in the fourth year, *and* in the fifth month, *that* Han-a-ni'ah the son of A'zur the prophet, which *was* of Gib'e-on, spake unto me in the house of the LORD, in the presence of the priests and of all the people, saying,

2 Thus speaketh the LORD of hosts, the God of Is'ra-el, saying, I have broken the yoke of the king of Bab'y-lon.

3 Within two full years will I bring again into this place all the vessels of the LORD'S house, that Neb-u-chad-nez'zar king of Bab'y-lon took

away from this place, and carried them to Bab'-y-lon:

4 And I will bring again to this place Jec-o-ni'ah the son of Je-hoi'a-kim king of Ju'dah, with all the captives of Ju'dah, that went into Bab'y-lon, saith the LORD: for I will break the yoke of the king of Bab'y-lon.

5 ¶ Then the prophet Jer-e-mi'ah said unto the prophet Han-a-ni'ah in the presence of the priests, and in the presence of all the people that stood in the house of the LORD,

6 Even the prophet Jer-e-mi'ah said, Amen: the LORD do so: the LORD perform thy words which thou hast prophesied, to bring again the vessels of the LORD's house, and all that is carried away captive, from Bab'y-lon into this place.

7 Nevertheless hear thou now this word that I speak in thine ears, and in the ears of all the people;

8 The prophets that have been before me and before thee of old prophesied both against many countries, and against great kingdoms, of war, and of evil, and of pestilence.

9 The prophet which prophesieth of peace, when the word of the prophet shall come to pass, then shall the prophet be known, that the LORD hath truly sent him.

10 ¶ Then Han-a-ni'ah the prophet took the yoke from off the prophet Jer-e-mi'ah's neck, and brake it.

11 And Han-a-ni'ah spake in the presence of all the people, saying, Thus saith the LORD; Even so will I break the yoke of Neb-u-chad-nez'zar king of Bab'y-lon from the neck of all nations within the space of two full years. And the prophet Jer-e-mi'ah went his way.

12 ¶ Then the word of the LORD came unto Jer-e-mi'ah the prophet, after that Han-a-ni'ah the prophet had broken the yoke from off the neck of the prophet Jer-e-mi'ah, saying,

13 Go and tell Han-a-ni'ah, saying, Thus saith the LORD; Thou hast broken the yokes of wood; but thou shalt make for them yokes of iron.

14 For thus saith the LORD of hosts, the God of Is'ra-el; I have put a yoke of iron upon the neck of all these nations, that they may serve Neb-u-chad-nez'zar king of Bab'y-lon; and they shall serve him: and I have given him the beasts of the field also.

15 ¶ Then said the prophet Jer-e-mi'ah unto Han-a-ni'ah the prophet, Hear now, Han-a-ni'-ah; The LORD hath not sent thee; but thou makest this people to trust in a lie.

16 Therefore thus saith the LORD; Behold, I will cast thee from off the face of the earth: this year thou shalt die, because thou hast taught rebellion against the LORD.

17 So Han-a-ni'ah the prophet died the same year in the seventh month.

29 NOW these are the words of the letter that Jer-e-mi'ah the prophet sent from Je-ru'sa-lem unto the residue of the elders which were carried away captives, and to the priests, and to the prophets, and to all the people whom Neb-u-chad-nez'zar had carried away captive from Je-ru'sa-lem to Bab'y-lon;

2 (After that Jec-o-ni'ah the king, and the queen, and the eunuchs, the princes of Ju'dah and Je-ru'sa-lem, and the carpenters, and the smiths, were departed from Je-ru'sa-lem;)

3 By the hand of El'-a-sah the son of Sha'-phan, and Gem-a-ri'ah the son of Hil-ki'ah, (whom Zed-e-ki'ah king of Ju'dah sent unto Bab'y-lon to Neb-u-chad-nez'zar king of Bab'y-lon) saying,

4 Thus saith the LORD of hosts, the God of Is'ra-el, unto all that are carried away captives, whom I have caused to be carried away from Je-ru'sa-lem unto Bab'y-lon;

5 Build ye houses, and dwell in them; and plant gardens, and eat the fruit of them;

6 Take ye wives, and beget sons and daughters; and take wives for your sons, and give your daughters to husbands, that they may bear sons and daughters; that ye may be increased there, and not diminished.

7 And seek the peace of the city whither I have caused you to be carried away captives, and pray unto the LORD for it: for in the peace thereof shall ye have peace.

8 ¶ For thus saith the LORD of hosts, the God of Is'ra-el; Let not your prophets and your diviners, that be in the midst of you, deceive you, neither hearken to your dreams which ye cause to be dreamed.

9 For they prophesy falsely unto you in my name: I have not sent them, saith the LORD.

10 ¶ For thus saith the LORD, That after seventy years be accomplished at Bab'y-lon I will visit you, and perform my good word toward you, in causing you to return to this place.

11 For I know the thoughts that I think toward you, saith the LORD, thoughts of peace, and not of evil, to give you an expected end.

12 Then shall ye call upon me, and ye shall go and pray unto me, and I will hearken unto you.

13 And ye shall seek me, and find me, when ye shall search for me with all your heart.

14 And I will be found of you, saith the LORD: and I will turn away your captivity, and I will gather you from all the nations, and from all the places whither I have driven you, saith the LORD; and I will bring you again into the place whence I caused you to be carried away captive.

15 ¶ Because ye have said, The LORD hath raised us up prophets in Bab'y-lon;

16 Know that thus saith the LORD of the king that sitteth upon the throne of Da'vid, and of all the people that dwelleth in this city, and of your brethren that are not gone forth with you into captivity;

17 Thus saith the LORD of hosts; Behold, I will send upon them the sword, the famine, and the pestilence, and will make them like vile figs, that cannot be eaten, they are so evil.

18 And I will persecute them with the sword, with the famine, and with the pestilence, and will deliver them to be removed to all the kingdoms of the earth, to be a curse, and an astonishment, and an hissing, and a reproach, among all the nations whither I have driven them:

19 Because they have not hearkened to my words, saith the LORD, which I sent unto them by my servants the prophets, rising up early and sending them; but ye would not hear, saith the LORD.

20 ¶ Hear ye therefore the word of the LORD, all ye of the captivity, whom I have sent from Je-ru'sa-lem to Bab'y-lon:

21 Thus saith the LORD of hosts, the God of Is'ra-el, of A'hab the son of Kol-a-i'ah, and of Zed-e-ki'ah the son of Ma-a-se'iah, which prophesy a lie unto you in my name; Behold, I will deliver them into the hand of Neb-u-chad-rez'zar king of Bab'y-lon; and he shall slay them before your eyes;

22 And of them shall be taken up a curse by all the captivity of Ju'dah which are in Bab'y-lon, saying, The LORD make thee like Zed-e-ki'-

ah and like A'hab, whom the king of Bab'y-lon roasted in the fire;

23 Because they have committed villany in Is'ra-el, and have committed adultery with their neighbours' wives, and have spoken lying words in my name, which I have not commanded them; even I know, and *am* a witness, saith the LORD.

24 ¶ *Thus* shalt thou also speak to Shem-a-i'ah the Ne-hel'a-mite, saying,

25 Thus speaketh the LORD of hosts, the God of Is'ra-el, saying, Because thou hast sent letters in thy name unto all the people that *are* at Je-ru'sa-lem, and to Zeph-a-ni'ah the son of Ma-a-se'iah the priest, and to all the priests, saying,

26 The LORD hath made thee priest in the stead of Je-hoi'a-da the priest, that ye should be officers in the house of the LORD, for every man *that is* mad, and maketh himself a prophet, that thou shouldest put him in prison, and in the stocks.

27 Now therefore why hast thou not reproved Jer-e-mi'ah of An'a-thoth, which maketh himself a prophet to you?

28 For therefore he sent unto us *in* Bab'y-lon, saying, This *captivity is* long: build ye houses, and dwell *in them;* and plant gardens, and eat the fruit of them.

29 And Zeph-a-ni'ah the priest read this letter in the ears of Jer-e-mi'ah the prophet.

30 ¶ Then came the word of the LORD unto Jer-e-mi'ah, saying,

31 Send to all them of the captivity, saying, Thus saith the LORD concerning Shem-a-i'ah the Ne-hel'a-mite; Because that Shem-a-i'ah hath prophesied unto you, and I sent him not, and he caused you to trust in a lie:

32 Therefore thus saith the LORD; Behold, I will punish Shem-a-i'ah the Ne-hel'a-mite, and his seed: he shall not have a man to dwell among this people; neither shall he behold the good that I will do for my people, saith the LORD; because he hath taught rebellion against the LORD.

30 THE word that came to Jer-e-mi'ah from the LORD, saying,

2 Thus speaketh the LORD God of Is'ra-el, saying, Write thee all the words that I have spoken unto thee in a book.

3 For, lo, the days come, saith the LORD, that I will bring again the captivity of my people Is'ra-el and Ju'dah, saith the LORD: and I will cause them to return to the land that I gave to their fathers, and they shall possess it.

4 ¶ And these *are* the words that the LORD spake concerning Is'ra-el and concerning Ju'dah.

5 For thus saith the LORD; We have heard a voice of trembling, of fear, and not of peace.

6 Ask ye now, and see whether a man doth travail with child? wherefore do I see every man with his hands on his loins, as a woman in travail, and all faces are turned into paleness?

7 Alas! for that day *is* great, so that none *is* like it: *it is* even the time of Ja'cob's trouble; but he shall be saved out of it.

8 For it shall come to pass in that day, saith the LORD of hosts, *that* I will break his yoke from off thy neck, and will burst thy bonds, and strangers shall no more serve themselves of him:

9 But they shall serve the LORD their God, and Da'vid their king, whom I will raise up unto them.

10 ¶ Therefore fear thou not, O my servant Ja'cob, saith the LORD; neither be dismayed, O Is'ra-el: for, lo, I will save thee from afar, and thy seed from the land of their captivity; and Ja'cob shall return, and shall be in rest, and quiet, and none shall make *him* afraid.

11 For I *am* with thee, saith the LORD, to save thee: though I make a full end of all nations whither I have scattered thee, yet will I not make a full end of thee: but I will correct thee in measure, and will not leave thee altogether unpunished.

12 For thus saith the LORD, Thy bruise *is* incurable, *and* thy wound *is* grievous.

13 *There is* none to plead thy cause, that thou mayest be bound up: thou hast no healing medicines.

14 All thy lovers have forgotten thee; they seek thee not; for I have wounded thee with the wound of an enemy, with the chastisement of a cruel one, for the multitude of thine iniquity; *because* thy sins were increased.

15 Why criest thou for thine affliction? thy sorrow *is* incurable for the multitude of thine iniquity: *because* thy sins were increased, I have done these things unto thee.

16 Therefore all they that devour thee shall be devoured; and all thine adversaries, every one of them, shall go into captivity; and they that spoil thee shall be a spoil, and all that prey upon thee will I give for a prey.

17 For I will restore health unto thee, and I will heal thee of thy wounds, saith the LORD; because they called thee an Outcast, *saying*, This *is* Zi'on, whom no man seeketh after.

18 ¶ Thus saith the LORD; Behold, I will bring again the captivity of Ja'cob's tents, and have mercy on his dwellingplaces; and the city shall be builded upon her own heap, and the palace shall remain after the manner thereof.

19 And out of them shall proceed thanksgiving and the voice of them that make merry: and I will multiply them, and they shall not be few; I will also glorify them, and they shall not be small.

20 Their children also shall be as aforetime, and their congregation shall be established before me, and I will punish all that oppress them.

21 And their nobles shall be of themselves, and their governor shall proceed from the midst of them; and I will cause him to draw near, and he shall approach unto me: for who *is* this that engaged his heart to approach unto me? saith the LORD.

22 And ye shall be my people, and I will be your God.

23 Behold, the whirlwind of the LORD goeth forth with fury, a continuing whirlwind: it shall fall with pain upon the head of the wicked.

24 The fierce anger of the LORD shall not return, until he have done *it,* and until he have performed the intents of his heart: in the latter days ye shall consider it.

31 AT the same time, saith the LORD, will I be the God of all the families of Is'ra-el, and they shall be my people.

2 Thus saith the LORD, The people *which were* left of the sword found grace in the wilderness; *even* Is'ra-el, when I went to cause him to rest.

3 The LORD hath appeared of old unto me, *saying,* Yea, I have loved thee with an everlasting love: therefore with lovingkindness have I drawn thee.

4 Again I will build thee, and thou shalt be built, O virgin of Is'ra-el: thou shalt again be adorned with thy tabrets, and shalt go forth in the dances of them that make merry.

5 Thou shalt yet plant vines upon the mountains of Sa-ma'ri-a: the planters shall plant, and shall eat *them* as common things.

6 For there shall be a day, *that* the watchmen upon the mount E'phra-im shall cry, Arise ye, and let us go up to Zi'on unto the LORD our God.

7 For thus saith the LORD; Sing with gladness for Ja'cob, and shout among the chief of the nations: publish ye, praise ye, and say, O LORD, save thy people, the remnant of Is'ra-el.

8 Behold, I will bring them from the north country, and gather them from the coasts of the earth, *and* with them the blind and the lame, the woman with child and her that travaileth with child together: a great company shall return thither.

9 They shall come with weeping, and with supplications will I lead them: I will cause them to walk by the rivers of waters in a straight way, wherein they shall not stumble: for I am a father to Is'ra-el, and E'phra-im *is* my firstborn.

10 ¶ Hear the word of the LORD, O ye nations, and declare *it* in the isles afar off, and say, He that scattered Is'ra-el will gather him, and keep him, as a shepherd *doth* his flock.

11 For the LORD hath redeemed Ja'cob, and ransomed him from the hand of *him that was* stronger than he.

12 Therefore they shall come and sing in the height of Zi'on, and shall flow together to the goodness of the LORD, for wheat, and for wine, and for oil, and for the young of the flock and of the herd: and their soul shall be as a watered garden; and they shall not sorrow any more at all.

13 Then shall the virgin rejoice in the dance, both young men and old together: for I will turn their mourning into joy, and will comfort them, and make them rejoice from their sorrow.

14 And I will satiate the soul of the priests with fatness, and my people shall be satisfied with my goodness, saith the LORD.

15 ¶ Thus saith the LORD; A voice was heard in Ra'mah, lamentation, *and* bitter weeping; Ra'hel weeping for her children refused to be comforted for her children, because they *were* not.

16 Thus saith the LORD; Refrain thy voice from weeping, and thine eyes from tears: for thy work shall be rewarded, saith the LORD; and they shall come again from the land of the enemy.

17 And there is hope in thine end, saith the LORD, that thy children shall come again to their own border.

18 ¶ I have surely heard E'phra-im bemoaning himself *thus;* Thou hast chastised me, and I was chastised, as a bullock unaccustomed *to the yoke:* turn thou me, and I shall be turned; for thou *art* the LORD my God.

19 Surely after that I was turned, I repented; and after that I was instructed, I smote upon *my* thigh: I was ashamed, yea, even confounded, because I did bear the reproach of my youth.

20 *Is* E'phra-im my dear son? *is he* a pleasant child? for since I spake against him, I do earnestly remember him still: therefore my bowels are troubled for him; I will surely have mercy upon him, saith the LORD.

21 Set thee up waymarks, make thee high heaps: set thine heart toward the highway, *even* the way *which* thou wentest: turn again, O virgin of Is'ra-el, turn again to these thy cities.

22 ¶ How long wilt thou go about, O thou backsliding daughter? for the LORD hath created a new thing in the earth, A woman shall compass a man.

23 Thus saith the LORD of hosts, the God of Is'ra-el; As yet they shall use this speech in the land of Ju'dah and in the cities thereof, when I shall bring again their captivity; The LORD bless thee, O habitation of justice, *and* mountain of holiness.

24 And there shall dwell in Ju'dah itself, and in all the cities thereof together, husbandmen, and they *that* go forth with flocks.

25 For I have satiated the weary soul, and I have replenished every sorrowful soul.

26 Upon this I awaked, and beheld; and my sleep was sweet unto me.

27 ¶ Behold, the days come, saith the LORD, that I will sow the house of Is'ra-el and the house of Ju'dah with the seed of man, and with the seed of beast.

28 And it shall come to pass, *that* like as I have watched over them, to pluck up, and to break down, and to throw down, and to destroy, and to afflict; so will I watch over them, to build, and to plant, saith the LORD.

29 In those days they shall say no more, The fathers have eaten a sour grape, and the children's teeth are set on edge.

30 But every one shall die for his own iniquity: every man that eateth the sour grape, his teeth shall be set on edge.

31 ¶ Behold, the days come, saith the LORD, that I will make a new covenant with the house of Is'ra-el, and with the house of Ju'dah:

32 Not according to the covenant that I made with their fathers in the day *that* I took them by the hand to bring them out of the land of E'gypt; which my covenant they brake, although I was an husband unto them, saith the LORD:

33 But this *shall be* the covenant that I will make with the house of Is'ra-el; After those days, saith the LORD, I will put my law in their inward parts, and write it in their hearts; and will be their God, and they shall be my people.

34 And they shall teach no more every man his neighbour, and every man his brother, saying, Know the LORD: for they shall all know me, from the least of them unto the greatest of them, saith the LORD: for I will forgive their iniquity, and I will remember their sin no more.

35 ¶ Thus saith the LORD, which giveth the sun for a light by day, *and* the ordinances of the moon and of the stars for a light by night, which divideth the sea when the waves thereof roar; The LORD of hosts *is* his name:

36 If those ordinances depart from before me, saith the LORD, *then* the seed of Is'ra-el also shall cease from being a nation before me for ever.

37 Thus saith the LORD; If heaven above can be measured, and the foundations of the earth searched out beneath, I will also cast off all the seed of Is'ra-el for all that they have done, saith the LORD.

38 ¶ Behold, the days come, saith the LORD, that the city shall be built to the LORD from the tower of Ha-nan'e-el unto the gate of the corner.

39 And the measuring line shall yet go forth over against it upon the hill Ga'reb, and shall compass about to Go'ath.

40 And the whole valley of the dead bodies, and of the ashes, and all the fields unto the brook of Kid'ron, unto the corner of the horse gate toward the east, *shall be* holy unto the LORD; it shall not be plucked up, nor thrown down any more for ever.

32 THE word that came to Jer-e-mi′ah from the LORD in the tenth year of Zed-e-ki′ah king of Ju′dah, which was the eighteenth year of Neb-u-chad-rez′zar.

2 For then the king of Bab′y-lon's army besieged Je-ru′sa-lem: and Jer-e-mi′ah the prophet was shut up in the court of the prison, which was in the king of Ju′dah's house.

3 For Zed-e-ki′ah king of Ju′dah had shut him up, saying, Wherefore dost thou prophesy, and say, Thus saith the LORD, Behold, I will give this city into the hand of the king of Bab′y-lon, and he shall take it;

4 And Zed-e-ki′ah king of Ju′dah shall not escape out of the hand of the Chal-de′ans, but shall surely be delivered into the hand of the king of Bab′y-lon, and shall speak with him mouth to mouth, and his eyes shall behold his eyes;

5 And he shall lead Zed-e-ki′ah to Bab′y-lon, and there shall he be until I visit him, saith the LORD: though ye fight with the Chal-de′ans, ye shall not prosper.

6 ¶ And Jer-e-mi′ah said, The word of the LORD came unto me, saying,

7 Behold, Ha-nam′e-el the son of Shal′lum thine uncle shall come unto thee, saying, Buy thee my field that is in An′a-thoth: for the right of redemption is thine to buy it.

8 So Ha-nam′e-el mine uncle's son came to me in the court of the prison according to the word of the LORD, and said unto me, Buy my field, I pray thee, that is in An′a-thoth, which is in the country of Ben′ja-min: for the right of inheritance is thine, and the redemption is thine; buy it for thyself. Then I knew that this was the word of the LORD.

9 And I bought the field of Ha-nam′e-el my uncle's son, that was in An′a-thoth, and weighed him the money, even seventeen shekels of silver.

10 And I subscribed the evidence, and sealed it, and took witnesses, and weighed him the money in the balances.

11 So I took the evidence of the purchase, both that which was sealed according to the law and custom, and that which was open:

12 And I gave the evidence of the purchase unto Ba′ruch the son of Ne-ri′ah, the son of Ma-a-se′iah, in the sight of Ha-nam′e-el mine uncle's son, and in the presence of the witnesses that subscribed the book of the purchase, before all the Jews that sat in the court of the prison.

13 ¶ And I charged Ba′ruch before them, saying,

14 Thus saith the LORD of hosts, the God of Is′ra-el; Take these evidences, this evidence of the purchase, both which is sealed, and this evidence which is open; and put them in an earthen vessel, that they may continue many days.

15 For thus saith the LORD of hosts, the God of Is′ra-el; Houses and fields and vineyards shall be possessed again in this land.

16 ¶ Now when I had delivered the evidence of the purchase unto Ba′ruch the son of Ne-ri′ah, I prayed unto the LORD, saying,

17 Ah Lord GOD! behold, thou hast made the heaven and the earth by thy great power and stretched out arm, and there is nothing too hard for thee:

18 Thou shewest lovingkindness unto thousands, and recompensest the iniquity of the fathers into the bosom of their children after them: the Great, the Mighty God, the LORD of hosts, is his name,

19 Great in counsel, and mighty in work: for thine eyes are open upon all the ways of the sons of men: to give every one according to his ways, and according to the fruit of his doings:

20 Which hast set signs and wonders in the land of E′gypt, even unto this day, and in Is′ra-el, and among other men; and hast made thee a name, as at this day;

21 And hast brought forth thy people Is′ra-el out of the land of E′gypt with signs, and with wonders, and with a strong hand, and with a stretched out arm, and with great terror;

22 And hast given them this land, which thou didst swear to their fathers to give them, a land flowing with milk and honey;

23 And they came in, and possessed it; but they obeyed not thy voice, neither walked in thy law; they have done nothing of all that thou commandedst them to do: therefore thou hast caused all this evil to come upon them:

24 Behold the mounts, they are come unto the city to take it; and the city is given into the hand of the Chal-de′ans, that fight against it, because of the sword, and of the famine, and of the pestilence: and what thou hast spoken is come to pass; and, behold, thou seest it.

25 And thou hast said unto me, O Lord GOD, Buy thee the field for money, and take witnesses; for the city is given into the hand of the Chal-de′ans.

26 ¶ Then came the word of the LORD unto Jer-e-mi′ah, saying,

27 Behold, I am the LORD, the God of all flesh: is there any thing too hard for me?

28 Therefore thus saith the LORD; Behold, I will give this city into the hand of the Chal-de′-ans, and into the hand of Neb-u-chad-rez′zar king of Bab′y-lon, and he shall take it:

29 And the Chal-de′ans, that fight against this city, shall come and set fire on this city, and burn it with the houses, upon whose roofs they have offered incense unto Ba′al, and poured out drink offerings unto other gods, to provoke me to anger.

30 For the children of Is′ra-el and the children of Ju′dah have only done evil before me from their youth: for the children of Is′ra-el have only provoked me to anger with the work of their hands, saith the LORD.

31 For this city hath been to me as a provocation of mine anger and of my fury from the day that they built it even unto this day; that I should remove it from before my face,

32 Because of all the evil of the children of Is′ra-el and of the children of Ju′dah, which they have done to provoke me to anger, they, their kings, their princes, their priests, and their prophets, and the men of Ju′dah, and the inhabitants of Je-ru′sa-lem.

33 And they have turned unto me the back, and not the face: though I taught them, rising up early and teaching them, yet they have not hearkened to receive instruction.

34 But they set their abominations in the house, which is called by my name, to defile it.

35 And they built the high places of Ba′al, which are in the valley of the son of Hin′nom, to cause their sons and their daughters to pass through the fire unto Mo′lech; which I commanded them not, neither came it into my mind, that they should do this abomination, to cause Ju′dah to sin.

36 ¶ And now therefore thus saith the LORD, the God of Is′ra-el, concerning this city, whereof ye say, It shall be delivered into the hand of the king of Bab′y-lon by the sword, and by the famine, and by the pestilence;

37 Behold, I will gather them out of all countries, whither I have driven them in mine anger, and in my fury, and in great wrath; and I will bring them again unto this place, and I will cause them to dwell safely:

38 And they shall be my people, and I will be their God:

39 And I will give them one heart, and one way, that they may fear me for ever, for the good of them, and of their children after them:

40 And I will make an everlasting covenant with them, that I will not turn away from them, to do them good; but I will put my fear in their hearts, that they shall not depart from me.

41 Yea, I will rejoice over them to do them good, and I will plant them in this land assuredly with my whole heart and with my whole soul.

42 For thus saith the LORD; Like as I have brought all this great evil upon this people, so will I bring upon them all the good that I have promised them.

43 And fields shall be bought in this land, whereof ye say, It is desolate without man or beast; it is given into the hand of the Chal-de′-ans.

44 Men shall buy fields for money, and subscribe evidences, and seal them, and take witnesses in the land of Ben′ja-min, and in the places about Je-ru′sa-lem, and in the cities of Ju′dah, and in the cities of the mountains, and in the cities of the valley, and in the cities of the south: for I will cause their captivity to return, saith the LORD.

33 MOREOVER the word of the LORD came unto Jer-e-mi′ah the second time, while he was yet shut up in the court of the prison, saying,

2 Thus saith the LORD the maker thereof, the LORD that formed it, to establish it; the LORD is his name;

3 Call unto me, and I will answer thee, and shew thee great and mighty things, which thou knowest not.

4 For thus saith the LORD, the God of Is′ra-el, concerning the houses of this city, and concerning the houses of the kings of Ju′dah, which are thrown down by the mounts, and by the sword;

5 They come to fight with the Chal-de′ans, but it is to fill them with the dead bodies of men, whom I have slain in mine anger and in my fury, and for all whose wickedness I have hid my face from this city.

6 Behold, I will bring it health and cure, and I will cure them, and will reveal unto them the abundance of peace and truth.

7 And I will cause the captivity of Ju′dah and the captivity of Is′ra-el to return, and will build them, as at the first.

8 And I will cleanse them from all their iniquity, whereby they have sinned against me; and I will pardon all their iniquities, whereby they have sinned, and whereby they have transgressed against me.

9 ¶ And it shall be to me a name of joy, a praise and an honour before all the nations of the earth, which shall hear all the good that I do unto them: and they shall fear and tremble for all the goodness and for all the prosperity that I procure unto it.

10 Thus saith the LORD; Again there shall be heard in this place, which ye say shall be desolate without man and without beast, even in the cities of Ju′dah, and in the streets of Je-ru′sa-lem, that are desolate, without man, and without inhabitant, and without beast,

11 The voice of joy, and the voice of gladness, the voice of the bridegroom, and the voice of the bride, the voice of them that shall say, Praise the LORD of hosts: for the LORD is good; for his mercy endureth for ever: and of them that shall bring the sacrifice of praise into the house of the LORD. For I will cause to return the captivity of the land, as at the first, saith the LORD.

12 Thus saith the LORD of hosts; Again in this place, which is desolate without man and without beast, and in all the cities thereof, shall be an habitation of shepherds causing their flocks to lie down.

13 In the cities of the mountains, in the cities of the vale, and in the cities of the south, and in the land of Ben′ja-min, and in the places about Je-ru′sa-lem, and in the cities of Ju′dah, shall the flocks pass again under the hands of him that telleth them, saith the LORD.

14 Behold, the days come, saith the LORD, that I will perform that good thing which I have promised unto the house of Is′ra-el and to the house of Ju′dah.

15 ¶ In those days, and at that time, will I cause the Branch of righteousness to grow up unto Da′vid; and he shall execute judgment and righteousness in the land.

16 In those days shall Ju′dah be saved, and Je-ru′sa-lem shall dwell safely: and this is the name wherewith she shall be called, The LORD our righteousness.

17 ¶ For thus saith the LORD; Da′vid shall never want a man to sit upon the throne of the house of Is′ra-el;

18 Neither shall the priests the Le′vites want a man before me to offer burnt offerings, and to kindle meat offerings, and to do sacrifice continually.

19 ¶ And the word of the LORD came unto Jer-e-mi′ah, saying,

20 Thus saith the LORD; If ye can break my covenant of the day, and my covenant of the night, and that there should not be day and night in their season;

21 Then may also my covenant be broken with Da′vid my servant, that he should not have a son to reign upon his throne; and with the Le′vites the priests, my ministers.

22 As the host of heaven cannot be numbered, neither the sand of the sea measured: so will I multiply the seed of Da′vid my servant, and the Le′vites that minister unto me.

23 Moreover the word of the LORD came to Jer-e-mi′ah, saying,

24 Considerest thou not what this people have spoken, saying, The two families which the LORD hath chosen, he hath even cast them off? thus they have despised my people, that they should be no more a nation before them.

25 Thus saith the LORD; If my covenant be not with day and night, and if I have not appointed the ordinances of heaven and earth;

26 Then will I cast away the seed of Ja′cob, and Da′vid my servant, so that I will not take any of his seed to be rulers over the seed of A′bra-ham, I′saac, and Ja′cob: for I will cause their captivity to return, and have mercy on them.

34 THE word which came unto Jer-e-mi′ah from the LORD, when Neb-u-chad-nez′-zar king of Bab′y-lon, and all his army, and all the kingdoms of the earth of his dominion, and all the people, fought against Je-ru′sa-lem, and against all the cities thereof, saying,

2 Thus saith the LORD, the God of Is′ra-el; Go

and speak to Zed-e-ki'ah king of Ju'dah, and tell him, Thus saith the LORD; Behold, I will give this city into the hand of the king of Bab'y-lon, and he shall burn it with fire:

3 And thou shalt not escape out of his hand, but shalt surely be taken, and delivered into his hand; and thine eyes shall behold the eyes of the king of Bab'y-lon, and he shall speak with thee mouth to mouth, and thou shalt go to Bab'-y-lon.

4 Yet hear the word of the LORD, O Zed-e-ki'ah king of Ju'dah; Thus saith the LORD of thee, Thou shalt not die by the sword:

5 *But* thou shalt die in peace: and with the burnings of thy fathers, the former kings which were before thee, so shall they burn *odours* for thee; and they will lament thee, *saying*, Ah lord! for I have pronounced the word, saith the LORD.

6 Then Jer-e-mi'ah the prophet spake all these words unto Zed-e-ki'ah king of Ju'dah in Je-ru'sa-lem,

7 When the king of Bab'y-lon's army fought against Je-ru'sa-lem, and against all the cities of Ju'dah that were left, against La'chish, and against A-ze'kah: for these defenced cities remained of the cities of Ju'dah.

8 ¶ *This is* the word that came unto Jer-e-mi'ah from the LORD, after that the king Zed-e-ki'ah had made a covenant with all the people which *were* at Je-ru'sa-lem, to proclaim liberty unto them;

9 That every man should let his manservant, and every man his maidservant, *being* an He'-brew or an He'brew-ess, go free; that none should serve himself of them, *to wit*, of a Jew his brother.

10 Now when all the princes, and all the people, which had entered into the covenant, heard that every one should let his manservant, and every one his maidservant, go free, that none should serve themselves of them any more, then they obeyed, and let *them* go.

11 But afterward they turned, and caused the servants and the handmaids, whom they had let go free, to return, and brought them into subjection for servants and for handmaids.

12 ¶ Therefore the word of the LORD came to Jer-e-mi'ah from the LORD, saying,

13 Thus saith the LORD, the God of Is'ra-el; I made a covenant with your fathers in the day that I brought them forth out of the land of E'-gypt, out of the house of bondmen, saying,

14 At the end of seven years let ye go every man his brother an He'brew, which hath been sold unto thee; and when he hath served thee six years, thou shalt let him go free from thee: but your fathers hearkened not unto me, neither inclined their ear.

15 And ye were now turned, and had done right in my sight, in proclaiming liberty every man to his neighbour; and ye had made a covenant before me in the house which is called by my name:

16 But ye turned and polluted my name, and caused every man his servant, and every man his handmaid, whom he had set at liberty at their pleasure, to return, and brought them into subjection, to be unto you for servants and for handmaids.

17 Therefore thus saith the LORD; Ye have not hearkened unto me, in proclaiming liberty, every one to his brother, and every man to his neighbour: behold, I proclaim a liberty for you, saith the LORD, to the sword, to the pestilence, and to the famine; and I will make you to be removed into all the kingdoms of the earth.

18 And I will give the men that have transgressed my covenant, which have not performed the words of the covenant which they had made before me, when they cut the calf in twain, and passed between the parts thereof,

19 The princes of Ju'dah, and the princes of Je-ru'sa-lem, the eunuchs, and the priests, and all the people of the land, which passed between the parts of the calf;

20 I will even give them into the hand of their enemies, and into the hand of them that seek their life: and their dead bodies shall be for meat unto the fowls of the heaven, and to the beasts of the earth.

21 And Zed-e-ki'ah king of Ju'dah and his princes will I give into the hand of their enemies, and into the hand of them that seek their life, and into the hand of the king of Bab'y-lon's army, which are gone up from you.

22 Behold, I will command, saith the LORD, and cause them to return to this city; and they shall fight against it, and take it, and burn it with fire: and I will make the cities of Ju'dah a desolation without an inhabitant.

35 THE word which came unto Jer-e-mi'ah from the LORD in the days of Je-hoi'a-kim the son of Jo-si'ah king of Ju'dah, saying,

2 Go unto the house of the Re'chab-ites, and speak unto them, and bring them into the house of the LORD, into one of the chambers, and give them wine to drink.

3 Then I took Ja-az-a-ni'ah the son of Jer-e-mi'ah, the son of Hab-a-zi-ni'ah, and his brethren, and all his sons, and the whole house of the Re'chab-ites;

4 And I brought them into the house of the LORD, into the chamber of the sons of Ha'nan, the son of Ig-da-li'ah, a man of God, which *was* by the chamber of the princes, which *was* above the chamber of Ma-a-se'iah the son of Shal'lum, the keeper of the door:

5 And I set before the sons of the house of the Re'chab-ites pots full of wine, and cups, and I said unto them, Drink ye wine.

6 But they said, We will drink no wine: for Jon'a-dab the son of Re'chab our father commanded us, saying, Ye shall drink no wine, *neither* ye, nor your sons for ever:

7 Neither shall ye build house, nor sow seed, nor plant vineyard, nor have *any*: but all your days ye shall dwell in tents; that ye may live many days in the land where ye *be* strangers.

8 Thus have we obeyed the voice of Jon'a-dab the son of Re'chab our father in all that he hath charged us, to drink no wine all our days, we, our wives, our sons, nor our daughters;

9 Nor to build houses for us to dwell in: neither have we vineyard, nor field, nor seed:

10 But we have dwelt in tents, and have obeyed, and done according to all that Jon'a-dab our father commanded us.

11 But it came to pass, when Neb-u-chad-rez'zar king of Bab'y-lon came up into the land, that we said, Come, and let us go to Je-ru'sa-lem for fear of the army of the Chal-de'ans, and for fear of the army of the Syr'i-ans: so we dwell at Je-ru'sa-lem.

12 ¶ Then came the word of the LORD unto Jer-e-mi'ah, saying,

13 Thus saith the LORD of hosts, the God of Is'ra-el; Go and tell the men of Ju'dah and the inhabitants of Je-ru'sa-lem, Will ye not receive instruction to hearken to my words? saith the LORD.

14 The words of Jon'a-dab the son of Re'-chab, that he commanded his sons not to drink wine, are performed; for unto this day they

drink none, but obey their father's commandment: notwithstanding I have spoken unto you, rising early and speaking; but ye hearkened not unto me.

15 I have sent also unto you all my servants the prophets, rising up early and sending *them*, saying, Return ye now every man from his evil way, and amend your doings, and go not after other gods to serve them, and ye shall dwell in the land which I have given to you and to your fathers: but ye have not inclined your ear, nor hearkened unto me.

16 Because the sons of Jon'a-dab the son of Re'chab have performed the commandment of their father, which he commanded them; but this people hath not hearkened unto me:

17 Therefore thus saith the LORD God of hosts, the God of Is'ra-el; Behold, I will bring upon Ju'dah and upon all the inhabitants of Je-ru'sa-lem all the evil that I have pronounced against them: because I have spoken unto them, but they have not heard; and I have called unto them, but they have not answered.

18 ¶ And Jer-e-mi'ah said unto the house of the Re'chab-ites, Thus saith the LORD of hosts, the God of Is'ra-el; Because ye have obeyed the commandment of Jon'a-dab your father, and kept all his precepts, and done according unto all that he hath commanded you:

19 Therefore thus saith the LORD of hosts, the God of Is'ra-el; Jon'a-dab the son of Re'chab shall not want a man to stand before me for ever.

36 AND it came to pass in the fourth year of Je-hoi'a-kim the son of Jo-si'ah king of Ju'dah, *that* this word came unto Jer-e-mi'ah from the LORD, saying,

2 Take thee a roll of a book, and write therein all the words that I have spoken unto thee against Is'ra-el, and against Ju'dah, and against all the nations, from the day I spake unto thee, from the days of Jo-si'ah, even unto this day.

3 It may be that the house of Ju'dah will hear all the evil which I purpose to do unto them; that they may return every man from his evil way; that I may forgive their iniquity and their sin.

4 Then Jer-e-mi'ah called Ba'ruch the son of Ne-ri'ah: and Ba'ruch wrote from the mouth of Jer-e-mi'ah all the words of the LORD, which he had spoken unto him, upon a roll of a book.

5 And Jer-e-mi'ah commanded Ba'ruch, saying, I *am* shut up; I cannot go into the house of the LORD:

6 Therefore go thou, and read in the roll, which thou hast written from my mouth, the words of the LORD in the ears of the people in the LORD's house upon the fasting day: and also thou shalt read them in the ears of all Ju'dah that come out of their cities.

7 It may be they will present their supplication before the LORD, and will return every one from his evil way: for great *is* the anger and the fury that the LORD hath pronounced against this people.

8 And Ba'ruch the son of Ne-ri'ah did according to all that Jer-e-mi'ah the prophet commanded him, reading in the book the words of the LORD in the LORD's house.

9 And it came to pass in the fifth year of Je-hoi'a-kim the son of Jo-si'ah king of Ju'dah, in the ninth month, *that* they proclaimed a fast before the LORD to all the people in Je-ru'sa-lem, and to all the people that came from the cities of Ju'dah unto Je-ru'sa-lem.

10 Then read Ba'ruch in the book the words of Jer-e-mi'ah in the house of the LORD, in the chamber of Gem-a-ri'ah the son of Sha'phan the scribe, in the higher court, at the entry of the new gate of the LORD's house, in the ears of all the people.

11 ¶ When Mi-cha'iah the son of Gem-a-ri'-ah, the son of Sha'phan, had heard out of the book all the words of the LORD,

12 Then he went down into the king's house, into the scribe's chamber: and, lo, all the princes sat there, *even* E-lish'a-ma the scribe, and Del-a-i'ah the son of Shem-a-i'ah, and El'-na-than the son of Ach'bor, and Gem-a-ri'ah the son of Sha'phan, and Zed-e-ki'ah the son of Han-a-ni'ah, and all the princes.

13 Then Mi-cha'iah declared unto them all the words that he had heard, when Ba'ruch read the book in the ears of the people.

14 Therefore all the princes sent Je-hu'di the son of Neth-a-ni'ah, the son of Shel-e-mi'ah, the son of Cu'shi, unto Ba'ruch, saying, Take in thine hand the roll wherein thou hast read in the ears of the people, and come. So Ba'ruch the son of Ne-ri'ah took the roll in his hand, and came unto them.

15 And they said unto him, Sit down now, and read it in our ears. So Ba'ruch read *it* in their ears.

16 Now it came to pass, when they had heard all the words, they were afraid both one and other, and said unto Ba'ruch, We will surely tell the king of all these words.

17 And they asked Ba'ruch, saying, Tell us now, How didst thou write all these words at his mouth?

18 Then Ba'ruch answered them, He pronounced all these words unto me with his mouth, and I wrote *them* with ink in the book.

19 Then said the princes unto Ba'ruch, Go, hide thee, thou and Jer-e-mi'ah; and let no man know where ye be.

20 ¶ And they went in to the king into the court, but they laid up the roll in the chamber of E-lish'a-ma the scribe, and told all the words in the ears of the king.

21 So the king sent Je-hu'di to fetch the roll: and he took it out of E-lish'a-ma the scribe's chamber. And Je-hu'di read it in the ears of the king, and in the ears of all the princes which stood beside the king.

22 Now the king sat in the winterhouse in the ninth month: and *there was a fire* on the hearth burning before him.

23 And it came to pass, *that* when Je-hu'di had read three or four leaves, he cut it with the penknife, and cast *it* into the fire that *was* on the hearth, until all the roll was consumed in the fire that *was* on the hearth.

24 Yet they were not afraid, nor rent their garments, *neither* the king, nor any of his servants that heard all these words.

25 Nevertheless El'na-than and Del-a-i'ah and Gem-a-ri'ah had made intercession to the king that he would not burn the roll: but he would not hear them.

26 But the king commanded Je-rah'me-el the son of Ham'me-lech, and Ser-a-i'ah the son of Az'ri-el, and Shel-e-mi'ah the son of Ab'de-el, to take Ba'ruch the scribe and Jer-e-mi'ah the prophet: but the LORD hid them.

27 ¶ Then the word of the LORD came to Jer-e-mi'ah, after that the king had burned the roll, and the words which Ba'ruch wrote at the mouth of Jer-e-mi'ah, saying,

28 Take thee again another roll, and write in it all the former words that were in the first roll,

which Je-hoi'a-kim the king of Ju'dah hath burned.

29 And thou shalt say to Je-hoi'a-kim king of Ju'dah, Thus saith the LORD; Thou hast burned this roll, saying, Why hast thou written therein, saying, The king of Bab'y-lon shall certainly come and destroy this land, and shall cause to cease from thence man and beast?

30 Therefore thus saith the LORD of Je-hoi'a-kim king of Ju'dah; He shall have none to sit upon the throne of Da'vid: and his dead body shall be cast out in the day to the heat, and in the night to the frost.

31 And I will punish him and his seed and his servants for their iniquity; and I will bring upon them, and upon the inhabitants of Je-ru'sa-lem, and upon the men of Ju'dah, all the evil that I have pronounced against them; but they hearkened not.

32 ¶ Then took Jer-e-mi'ah another roll, and gave it to Ba'ruch the scribe, the son of Ne-ri'ah; who wrote therein from the mouth of Jer-e-mi'ah all the words of the book which Je-hoi'a-kim king of Ju'dah had burned in the fire: and there were added besides unto them many like words.

37 AND king Zed-e-ki'ah the son of Jo-si'-ah reigned instead of Co-ni'ah the son of Je-hoi'a-kim, whom Neb-u-chad-rez'zar king of Bab'y-lon made king in the land of Ju'dah.

2 But neither he, nor his servants, nor the people of the land, did hearken unto the words of the LORD, which he spake by the prophet Jer-e-mi'ah.

3 And Zed-e-ki'ah the king sent Je'hu-cal the son of Shel-e-mi'ah and Zeph-a-ni'ah the son of Ma-a-se'iah the priest to the prophet Jer-e-mi'-ah, saying, Pray now unto the LORD our God for us.

4 Now Jer-e-mi'ah came in and went out among the people: for they had not put him into prison.

5 Then Pha'raoh's army was come forth out of E'gypt: and when the Chal-de'ans that besieged Je-ru'sa-lem heard tidings of them, they departed from Je-ru'sa-lem.

6 ¶ Then came the word of the LORD unto the prophet Jer-e-mi'ah, saying,

7 Thus saith the LORD, the God of Is'ra-el; Thus shall ye say to the king of Ju'dah, that sent you unto me to enquire of me; Behold, Pha'-raoh's army, which is come forth to help you, shall return to E'gypt into their own land.

8 And the Chal-de'ans shall come again, and fight against this city, and take it, and burn it with fire.

9 Thus saith the LORD; Deceive not yourselves, saying, The Chal-de'ans shall surely depart from us: for they shall not depart.

10 For though ye had smitten the whole army of the Chal-de'ans that fight against you, and there remained but wounded men among them, yet should they rise up every man in his tent, and burn this city with fire.

11 ¶ And it came to pass, that when the army of the Chal-de'ans was broken up from Je-ru'sa-lem for fear of Pha'raoh's army,

12 Then Jer-e-mi'ah went forth out of Je-ru'-sa-lem to go into the land of Ben'ja-min, to separate himself thence in the midst of the people.

13 And when he was in the gate of Ben'ja-min, a captain of the ward was there, whose name was I-ri'jah, the son of Shel-e-mi'ah, the son of Han-a-ni'ah; and he took Jer-e-mi'ah the

prophet, saying, Thou fallest away to the Chal-de'ans.

14 Then said Jer-e-mi'ah, It is false; I fall not away to the Chal-de'ans. But he hearkened not to him: so I-ri'jah took Jer-e-mi'ah, and brought him to the princes.

15 Wherefore the princes were wroth with Jer-e-mi'ah, and smote him, and put him in prison in the house of Jon'a-than the scribe: for they had made that his prison.

16 ¶ When Jer-e-mi'ah was entered into the dungeon, and into the cabins, and Jer-e-mi'ah had remained there many days;

17 Then Zed-e-ki'ah the king sent, and took him out: and the king asked him secretly in his house, and said, Is there any word from the LORD? And Jer-e-mi'ah said, There is: for, said he, thou shalt be delivered into the hand of the king of Bab'y-lon.

18 Moreover Jer-e-mi'ah said unto king Zed-e-ki'ah, What have I offended against thee, or against thy servants, or against this people, that ye have put me in prison?

19 Where are now your prophets which prophesied unto you, saying, The king of Bab'y-lon shall not come against you, nor against this land?

20 Therefore hear now, I pray thee, O my lord the king: let my supplication, I pray thee, be accepted before thee; that thou cause me not to return to the house of Jon'a-than the scribe, lest I die there.

21 Then Zed-e-ki'ah the king commanded that they should commit Jer-e-mi'ah into the court of the prison, and that they should give him daily a piece of bread out of the bakers' street, until all the bread in the city were spent. Thus Jer-e-mi'ah remained in the court of the prison.

38 THEN Sheph-a-ti'ah the son of Mat'tan, and Ged-a-li'ah the son of Pash'ur, and Ju'cal the son of Shel-e-mi'ah, and Pash'ur the son of Mal-chi'ah, heard the words that Jer-e-mi'ah had spoken unto all the people, saying,

2 Thus saith the LORD, He that remaineth in this city shall die by the sword, by the famine, and by the pestilence: but he that goeth forth to the Chal-de'ans shall live; for he shall have his life for a prey, and shall live.

3 Thus saith the LORD, This city shall surely be given into the hand of the king of Bab'y-lon's army, which shall take it.

4 Therefore the princes said unto the king, We beseech thee, let this man be put to death: for thus he weakeneth the hands of the men of war that remain in this city, and the hands of all the people, in speaking such words unto them: for this man seeketh not the welfare of this people, but the hurt.

5 Then Zed-e-ki'ah the king said, Behold, he is in your hand: for the king is not he that can do any thing against you.

6 Then took they Jer-e-mi'ah, and cast him into the dungeon of Mal-chi'ah the son of Ham'-me-lech, that was in the court of the prison: and they let down Jer-e-mi'ah with cords. And in the dungeon there was no water, but mire: so Jer-e-mi'ah sunk in the mire.

7 ¶ Now when E'bed-me'lech the E-thi-o'pi-an, one of the eunuchs which was in the king's house, heard that they had put Jer-e-mi'ah in the dungeon; the king then sitting in the gate of Ben'ja-min;

8 E'bed-me'lech went forth out of the king's house, and spake to the king, saying,

9 My lord the king, these men have done evil

in all that they have done to Jer-e-mi'ah the prophet, whom they have cast into the dungeon; and he is like to die for hunger in the place where he is: for *there is* no more bread in the city.

10 Then the king commanded E'bed-me'lech the E-thi-o'pi-an, saying, Take from hence thirty men with thee, and take up Jer-e-mi'ah the prophet out of the dungeon, before he die.

11 So E'bed-me'lech took the men with him, and went into the house of the king under the treasury, and took thence old cast clouts and old rotten rags, and let them down by cords into the dungeon to Jer-e-mi'ah.

12 And E'bed-me'lech the E-thi-o'pi-an said unto Jer-e-mi'ah, Put now *these* old cast clouts and rotten rags under thine armholes under the cords. And Jer-e-mi'ah did so.

13 So they drew up Jer-e-mi'ah with cords, and took him up out of the dungeon: and Jer-e-mi'ah remained in the court of the prison.

14 ¶ Then Zed-e-ki'ah the king sent, and took Jer-e-mi'ah the prophet unto him into the third entry that *is* in the house of the LORD: and the king said unto Jer-e-mi'ah, I will ask thee a thing; hide nothing from me.

15 Then Jer-e-mi'ah said unto Zed-e-ki'ah, If I declare *it* unto thee, wilt thou not surely put me to death? and if I give thee counsel, wilt thou not hearken unto me?

16 So Zed-e-ki'ah the king sware secretly unto Jer-e-mi'ah, saying, *As* the LORD liveth, that made us this soul, I will not put thee to death, neither will I give thee into the hand of these men that seek thy life.

17 Then said Jer-e-mi'ah unto Zed-e-ki'ah, Thus saith the LORD, the God of hosts, the God of Is'ra-el; If thou wilt assuredly go forth unto the king of Bab'y-lon's princes, then thy soul shall live, and this city shall not be burned with fire; and thou shalt live, and thine house:

18 But if thou wilt not go forth to the king of Bab'y-lon's princes, then shall this city be given into the hand of the Chal-de'ans, and they shall burn it with fire, and thou shalt not escape out of their hand.

19 And Zed-e-ki'ah the king said unto Jer-e-mi'ah, I am afraid of the Jews that are fallen to the Chal-de'ans, lest they deliver me into their hand, and they mock me.

20 But Jer-e-mi'ah said, They shall not deliver *thee.* Obey, I beseech thee, the voice of the LORD, which I speak unto thee: so it shall be well unto thee, and thy soul shall live.

21 But if thou refuse to go forth, this *is* the word that the LORD hath shewed me:

22 And, behold, all the women that are left in the king of Ju'dah's house *shall be* brought forth to the king of Bab'y-lon's princes, and those *women* shall say, Thy friends have set thee on, and have prevailed against thee: thy feet are sunk in the mire, *and* they are turned away back.

23 So they shall bring out all thy wives and thy children to the Chal-de'ans: and thou shalt not escape out of their hand, but shalt be taken by the hand of the king of Bab'y-lon: and thou shalt cause this city to be burned with fire.

24 ¶ Then said Zed-e-ki'ah unto Jer-e-mi'ah, Let no man know of these words, and thou shalt not die.

25 But if the princes hear that I have talked with thee, and they come unto thee, and say unto thee, Declare unto us now what thou hast said unto the king, hide it not from us, and we will not put thee to death; also what the king said unto thee:

26 Then thou shalt say unto them, I presented my supplication before the king, that he would not cause me to return to Jon'a-than's house, to die there.

27 Then came all the princes unto Jer-e-mi'-ah, and asked him: and he told them according to all these words that the king had commanded. So they left off speaking with him; for the matter was not perceived.

28 So Jer-e-mi'ah abode in the court of the prison until the day that Je-ru'sa-lem was taken: and he was *there* when Je-ru'sa-lem was taken.

39 IN the ninth year of Zed-e-ki'ah king of Ju'dah, in the tenth month, came Neb-u-chad-rez'zar king of Bab'y-lon and all his army against Je-ru'sa-lem, and they besieged it.

2 *And* in the eleventh year of Zed-e-ki'ah, in the fourth month, the ninth *day* of the month, the city was broken up.

3 And all the princes of the king of Bab'y-lon came in, and sat in the middle gate, *even* Ner'-gal-sha-re'zer, Sam'gar-ne'bo, Sar-se'chim, Rab'-sa-ris, Ner'gal-sha-re'zer, Rab'-mag, with all the residue of the princes of the king of Bab'-y-lon.

4 ¶ And it came to pass, *that* when Zed-e-ki'ah the king of Ju'dah saw them, and all the men of war, then they fled, and went forth out of the city by night, by the way of the king's garden, by the gate betwixt the two walls: and he went out the way of the plain.

5 But the Chal-de'ans' army pursued after them, and overtook Zed-e-ki'ah in the plains of Jer'i-cho: and when they had taken him, they brought him up to Neb-u-chad-nez'zar king of Bab'y-lon to Rib'lah in the land of Ha'math, where he gave judgment upon him.

6 Then the king of Bab'y-lon slew the sons of Zed-e-ki'ah in Rib'lah before his eyes: also the king of Bab'y-lon slew all the nobles of Ju'dah.

7 Moreover he put out Zed-e-ki'ah's eyes, and bound him with chains, to carry him to Bab'y-lon.

8 ¶ And the Chal-de'ans burned the king's house, and the houses of the people, with fire, and brake down the walls of Je-ru'sa-lem.

9 Then Neb'u-zar-a'dan the captain of the guard carried away captive into Bab'y-lon the remnant of the people that remained in the city, and those that fell away, that fell to him, with the rest of the people that remained.

10 But Neb'u-zar-a'dan the captain of the guard left of the poor of the people, which had nothing, in the land of Ju'dah, and gave them vineyards and fields at the same time.

11 ¶ Now Neb-u-chad-rez'zar king of Bab'y-lon gave charge concerning Jer-e-mi'ah to Neb'-u-zar-a'dan the captain of the guard, saying,

12 Take him, and look well to him, and do him no harm; but do unto him even as he shall say unto thee.

13 So Neb'u-zar-a'dan the captain of the guard sent, and Neb-u-shas'ban, Rab'-sa-ris, and Ner'gal-sha-re'zer, Rab'-mag, and all the king of Bab'y-lon's princes;

14 Even they sent, and took Jer-e-mi'ah out of the court of the prison, and committed him unto Ged-a-li'ah the son of A-hi'kam the son of Sha'phan, that he should carry him home: so he dwelt among the people.

15 ¶ Now the word of the LORD came unto Jer-e-mi'ah, while he was shut up in the court of the prison, saying,

16 Go and speak to E'bed-me'lech the E-thi-o'pi-an, saying, Thus saith the LORD of hosts,

the God of Is'ra-el; Behold, I will bring my words upon this city for evil, and not for good; and they shall be *accomplished* in that day before thee.

17 But I will deliver thee in that day, saith the LORD: and thou shalt not be given into the hand of the men of whom thou *art* afraid.

18 For I will surely deliver thee, and thou shalt not fall by the sword, but thy life shall be for a prey unto thee: because thou hast put thy trust in me, saith the LORD.

40 THE word that came to Jer-e-mi'ah from the LORD, after that Neb'u-zar-a'-dan the captain of the guard had let him go from Ra'mah, when he had taken him being bound in chains among all that were carried away captive of Je-ru'sa-lem and Ju'dah, which were carried away captive unto Bab'y-lon.

2 And the captain of the guard took Jer-e-mi'ah, and said unto him, The LORD thy God hath pronounced this evil upon this place.

3 Now the LORD hath brought *it*, and done according as he hath said: because ye have sinned against the LORD, and have not obeyed his voice, therefore this thing is come upon you.

4 And now, behold, I loose thee this day from the chains which *were* upon thine hand. If it seem good unto thee to come with me into Bab'y-lon, come; and I will look well unto thee: but if it seem ill unto thee to come with me into Bab'y-lon, forbear: behold, all the land *is* before thee: whither it seemeth good and convenient for thee to go, thither go.

5 Now while he was not yet gone back, he *said*, Go back also to Ged-a-li'ah the son of A-hi'kam the son of Sha'phan, whom the king of Bab'y-lon hath made governor over the cities of Ju'dah, and dwell with him among the people: or go wheresoever it seemeth convenient unto thee to go. So the captain of the guard gave him victuals and a reward, and let him go.

6 Then went Jer-e-mi'ah unto Ged-a-li'ah the son of A-hi'kam to Miz'pah; and dwelt with him among the people that were left in the land.

7 ¶ Now when all the captains of the forces which *were* in the fields, *even* they and their men, heard that the king of Bab'y-lon had made Ged-a-li'ah the son of A-hi'kam governor in the land, and had committed unto him men, and women, and children, and of the poor of the land, of them that were not carried away captive to Bab'y-lon;

8 Then they came to Ged-a-li'ah to Miz'pah, even Ish'ma-el the son of Neth-a-ni'ah, and Jo-ha'nan and Jon'a-than the sons of Ka-re'ah, and Ser-a-i'ah the son of Tan'hu-meth, and the sons of E'phai the Ne-toph'a-thite, and Jez-a-ni'ah the son of a Ma-ach'a-thite, they and their men.

9 And Ged-a-li'ah the son of A-hi'kam the son of Sha'phan sware unto them and to their men, saying, Fear not to serve the Chal-de'ans: dwell in the land, and serve the king of Bab'y-lon, and it shall be well with you.

10 As for me, behold, I will dwell at Miz'pah, to serve the Chal-de'ans, which will come unto us: but ye, gather ye wine, and summer fruits, and oil, and put *them* in your vessels, and dwell in your cities that ye have taken.

11 Likewise when all the Jews that *were* in Mo'ab, and among the Am'mon-ites, and in E'-dom, and *that were* in all the countries, heard that the king of Bab'y-lon had left a remnant of Ju'dah, and that he had set over them Ged-a-li'ah the son of A-hi'kam the son of Sha'phan;

12 Even all the Jews returned out of all places whither they were driven, and came to the land of Ju'dah, to Ged-a-li'ah, unto Miz'pah, and gathered wine and summer fruits very much.

13 ¶ Moreover Jo-ha'nan the son of Ka-re'-ah, and all the captains of the forces that *were* in the fields, came to Ged-a-li'ah to Miz'pah,

14 And said unto him, Dost thou certainly know that Ba'a-lis the king of the Am'mon-ites hath sent Ish'ma-el the son of Neth-a-ni'ah to slay thee? But Ged-a-li'ah the son of A-hi'kam believed them not.

15 Then Jo-ha'nan the son of Ka-re'ah spake to Ged-a-li'ah in Miz'pah secretly, saying, Let me go, I pray thee, and I will slay Ish'ma-el the son of Neth-a-ni'ah, and no man shall know *it*: wherefore should he slay thee, that all the Jews which are gathered unto thee should be scattered, and the remnant in Ju'dah perish?

16 But Ged-a-li'ah the son of A-hi'kam said unto Jo-ha'nan the son of Ka-re'ah, Thou shalt not do this thing: for thou speakest falsely of Ish'ma-el.

41 NOW it came to pass in the seventh month, *that* Ish'ma-el the son of Neth-a-ni'ah the son of E-lish'a-ma, of the seed royal, and the princes of the king, even ten men with him, came unto Ged-a-li'ah the son of A-hi'kam to Miz'pah; and there they did eat bread together in Miz'pah.

2 Then arose Ish'ma-el the son of Neth-a-ni'-ah, and the ten men that were with him, and smote Ged-a-li'ah the son of A-hi'kam the son of Sha'phan with the sword, and slew him, whom the king of Bab'y-lon had made governor over the land.

3 Ish'ma-el also slew all the Jews that were with him, *even* with Ged-a-li'ah, at Miz'pah, and the Chal-de'ans that were found there, *and* the men of war.

4 And it came to pass the second day after he had slain Ged-a-li'ah, and no man knew *it*,

5 That there came certain from She'chem, from Shi'loh, and from Sa-ma'ri-a, *even* fourscore men, having their beards shaven, and their clothes rent, and having cut themselves, with offerings and incense in their hand, to bring *them* to the house of the LORD.

6 And Ish'ma-el the son of Neth-a-ni'ah went forth from Miz'pah to meet them, weeping all along as he went: and it came to pass, as he met them, he said unto them, Come to Ged-a-li'ah the son of A-hi'kam.

7 And it was *so*, when they came into the midst of the city, that Ish'ma-el the son of Neth-a-ni'ah slew them, *and cast them* into the midst of the pit, he, and the men that *were* with him.

8 But ten men were found among them that said unto Ish'ma-el, Slay us not: for we have treasures in the field, of wheat, and of barley, and of oil, and of honey. So he forbare, and slew them not among their brethren.

9 Now the pit wherein Ish'ma-el had cast all the dead bodies of the men, whom he had slain because of Ged-a-li'ah, *was* it which A'sa the king had made for fear of Ba'a-sha king of Is'ra-el: *and* Ish'ma-el the son of Neth-a-ni'ah filled it with *them that were* slain.

10 Then Ish'ma-el carried away captive all the residue of the people that *were* in Miz'pah, *even* the king's daughters, and all the people that remained in Miz'pah, whom Neb'u-zar-a'-dan the captain of the guard had committed to Ged-a-li'ah the son of A-hi'kam: and Ish'ma-el the son of Neth-a-ni'ah carried them away captive, and departed to go over to the Am'mon-ites.

11 ¶ But when Jo-ha'nan the son of Ka-re'ah, and all the captains of the forces that were with him, heard of all the evil that Ish'ma-el the son of Neth-a-ni'ah had done,

12 Then they took all the men, and went to fight with Ish'ma-el the son of Neth-a-ni'ah, and found him by the great waters that are in Gib'e-on.

13 Now it came to pass, that when all the people which were with Ish'ma-el saw Jo-ha'-nan the son of Ka-re'ah, and all the captains of the forces that were with him, then they were glad.

14 So all the people that Ish'ma-el had carried away captive from Miz'pah cast about and returned, and went unto Jo-ha'nan the son of Ka-re'ah.

15 But Ish'ma-el the son of Neth-a-ni'ah escaped from Jo-ha'nan with eight men, and went to the Am'mon-ites.

16 Then took Jo-ha'nan the son of Ka-re'ah, and all the captains of the forces that were with him, all the remnant of the people whom he had recovered from Ish'ma-el the son of Neth-a-ni'-ah, from Miz'pah, after that he had slain Ged-a-li'ah the son of A-hi'kam, even mighty men of war, and the women, and the children, and the eunuchs, whom he had brought again from Gib'e-on:

17 And they departed, and dwelt in the habitation of Chim'ham, which is by Beth'-le-hem, to go to enter into E'gypt,

18 Because of the Chal-de'ans: for they were afraid of them, because Ish'ma-el the son of Neth-a-ni'ah had slain Ged-a-li'ah the son of A-hi'kam, whom the king of Bab'y-lon made governor in the land.

42 THEN all the captains of the forces, and Jo-ha'nan the son of Ka-re'ah, and Jez-a-ni'ah the son of Hosh-a-i'ah, and all the people from the least even unto the greatest, came near,

2 And said unto Jer-e-mi'ah the prophet, Let, we beseech thee, our supplication be accepted before thee, and pray for us unto the LORD thy God, even for all this remnant; (for we are left but a few of many, as thine eyes do behold us:)

3 That the LORD thy God may shew us the way wherein we may walk, and the thing that we may do.

4 Then Jer-e-mi'ah the prophet said unto them, I have heard you; behold, I will pray unto the LORD your God according to your words; and it shall come to pass, that whatsoever thing the LORD shall answer you, I will declare it unto you; I will keep nothing back from you.

5 Then they said to Jer-e-mi'ah, The LORD be a true and faithful witness between us, if we do not even according to all things for the which the LORD thy God shall send thee to us.

6 Whether it be good, or whether it be evil, we will obey the voice of the LORD our God, to whom we send thee; that it may be well with us, when we obey the voice of the LORD our God.

7 ¶ And it came to pass after ten days, that the word of the LORD came unto Jer-e-mi'ah.

8 Then called he Jo-ha'nan the son of Ka-re'-ah, and all the captains of the forces which were with him, and all the people from the least even to the greatest,

9 And said unto them, Thus saith the LORD, the God of Is'ra-el, unto whom ye sent me to present your supplication before him;

10 If ye will still abide in this land, then will I build you, and not pull you down, and I will plant you, and not pluck you up: for I repent me of the evil that I have done unto you.

11 Be not afraid of the king of Bab'y-lon, of whom ye are afraid; be not afraid of him, saith the LORD: for I am with you to save you, and to deliver you from his hand.

12 And I will shew mercies unto you, that he may have mercy upon you, and cause you to return to your own land.

13 ¶ But if ye say, We will not dwell in this land, neither obey the voice of the LORD your God,

14 Saying, No; but we will go into the land of E'gypt, where we shall see no war, nor hear the sound of the trumpet, nor have hunger of bread; and there will we dwell:

15 And now therefore hear the word of the LORD, ye remnant of Ju'dah; Thus saith the LORD of hosts, the God of Is'ra-el; If ye wholly set your faces to enter into E'gypt, and go to sojourn there;

16 Then it shall come to pass, that the sword, which ye feared, shall overtake you there in the land of E'gypt, and the famine, whereof ye were afraid, shall follow close after you there in E'-gypt; and there ye shall die.

17 So shall it be with all the men that set their faces to go into E'gypt to sojourn there; they shall die by the sword, by the famine, and by the pestilence: and none of them shall remain or escape from the evil that I will bring upon them.

18 For thus saith the LORD of hosts, the God of Is'ra-el; As mine anger and my fury hath been poured forth upon the inhabitants of Je-ru'sa-lem; so shall my fury be poured forth upon you, when ye shall enter into E'gypt: and ye shall be an execration, and an astonishment, and a curse, and a reproach; and ye shall see this place no more.

19 ¶ The LORD hath said concerning you, O ye remnant of Ju'dah; Go ye not into E'gypt: know certainly that I have admonished you this day.

20 For ye dissembled in your hearts, when ye sent me unto the LORD your God, saying, Pray for us unto the LORD our God; and according unto all that the LORD our God shall say, so declare unto us, and we will do it.

21 And now I have this day declared it to you; but ye have not obeyed the voice of the LORD your God, nor any thing for the which he hath sent me unto you.

22 Now therefore know certainly that ye shall die by the sword, by the famine, and by the pestilence, in the place whither ye desire to go and to sojourn.

43 AND it came to pass, that when Jer-e-mi'ah had made an end of speaking unto all the people all the words of the LORD their God, for which the LORD their God had sent him to them, even all these words,

2 Then spake Az-a-ri'ah the son of Hosh-a-i'ah, and Jo-ha'nan the son of Ka-re'ah, and all the proud men, saying unto Jer-e-mi'ah, Thou speakest falsely: the LORD our God hath not sent thee to say, Go not into E'gypt to sojourn there:

3 But Ba'ruch the son of Ne-ri'ah setteth thee on against us, for to deliver us into the hand of the Chal-de'ans, that they might put us to death, and carry us away captives into Bab'y-lon.

4 So Jo-ha'nan the son of Ka-re'ah, and all the captains of the forces, and all the people,

obeyed not the voice of the LORD, to dwell in the land of Ju'dah.

5 But Jo-ha'nan the son of Ka-re'ah, and all the captains of the forces, took all the remnant of Ju'dah; that were returned from all nations, whither they had been driven, to dwell in the land of Ju'dah;

6 *Even* men, and women, and children, and the king's daughters, and every person that Neb'u-zar-a'dan the captain of the guard had left with Ged-a-li'ah the son of A-hi'kam the son of Sha'phan, and Jer-e-mi'ah the prophet, and Ba'ruch the son of Ne-ri'ah.

7 So they came into the land of E'gypt: for they obeyed not the voice of the LORD: thus came they *even* to Tah'pan-hes.

8 ¶ Then came the word of the LORD unto Jer-e-mi'ah in Tah'pan-hes, saying,

9 Take great stones in thine hand, and hide them in the clay in the brickkiln, which *is* at the entry of Pha'raoh's house in Tah'pan-hes, in the sight of the men of Ju'dah;

10 And say unto them, Thus saith the LORD of hosts, the God of Is'ra-el; Behold, I will send and take Neb-u-chad-rez'zar the king of Bab'y-lon, my servant, and will set his throne upon these stones that I have hid; and he shall spread his royal pavilion over them.

11 And when he cometh, he shall smite the land of E'gypt, *and deliver* such *as are* for death to death; and such *as are* for captivity to captivity; and such *as are* for the sword to the sword.

12 And I will kindle a fire in the houses of the gods of E'gypt; and he shall burn them, and carry them away captives: and he shall array himself with the land of E'gypt, as a shepherd putteth on his garment; and he shall go forth from thence in peace.

13 He shall break also the images of Beth-she'mesh, that *is* in the land of E'gypt; and the houses of the gods of the E-gyp'tians shall he burn with fire.

44 THE word that came to Jer-e-mi'ah concerning all the Jews which dwell in the land of E'gypt, which dwell at Mig'dol, and at Tah'pan-hes, and at Noph, and in the country of Path'ros, saying,

2 Thus saith the LORD of hosts, the God of Is'ra-el; Ye have seen all the evil that I have brought upon Je-ru'sa-lem, and upon all the cities of Ju'dah; and, behold, this day they *are* a desolation, and no man dwelleth therein,

3 Because of their wickedness which they have committed to provoke me to anger, in that they went to burn incense, *and* to serve other gods, whom they knew not, *neither* they, ye, nor your fathers.

4 Howbeit I sent unto you all my servants the prophets, rising early and sending *them*, saying, Oh, do not this abominable thing that I hate.

5 But they hearkened not, nor inclined their ear to turn from their wickedness, to burn no incense unto other gods.

6 Wherefore my fury and mine anger was poured forth, and was kindled in the cities of Ju'dah and in the streets of Je-ru'sa-lem; and they are wasted *and* desolate, as at this day.

7 Therefore now thus saith the LORD, the God of hosts, the God of Is'ra-el; Wherefore commit ye *this* great evil against your souls, to cut off from you man and woman, child and suckling, out of Ju'dah, to leave you none to remain;

8 In that ye provoke me unto wrath with the works of your hands, burning incense unto other gods in the land of E'gypt, whither ye be gone to dwell, that ye might cut yourselves off, and that ye might be a curse and a reproach among all the nations of the earth?

9 Have ye forgotten the wickedness of your fathers, and the wickedness of the kings of Ju'-dah, and the wickedness of their wives, and your own wickedness, and the wickedness of your wives, which they have committed in the land of Ju'dah, and in the streets of Je-ru'sa-lem?

10 They are not humbled *even* unto this day, neither have they feared, nor walked in my law, nor in my statutes, that I set before you and before your fathers.

11 ¶ Therefore thus saith the LORD of hosts, the God of Is'ra-el; Behold, I will set my face against you for evil, and to cut off all Ju'dah.

12 And I will take the remnant of Ju'dah, that have set their faces to go into the land of E'gypt to sojourn there, and they shall all be consumed, *and* fall in the land of E'gypt; they shall *even* be consumed by the sword *and* by the famine: they shall die, from the least even unto the greatest, by the sword and by the famine: and they shall be an execration, *and* an astonishment, and a curse, and a reproach.

13 For I will punish them that dwell in the land of E'gypt, as I have punished Je-ru'sa-lem, by the sword, by the famine, and by the pestilence:

14 So that none of the remnant of Ju'dah, which are gone into the land of E'gypt to sojourn there, shall escape or remain, that they should return into the land of Ju'dah, to the which they have a desire to return to dwell there: for none shall return but such as shall escape.

15 ¶ Then all the men which knew that their wives had burned incense unto other gods, and all the women that stood by, a great multitude, even all the people that dwelt in the land of E'-gypt, in Path'ros, answered Jer-e-mi'ah, saying,

16 *As for* the word that thou hast spoken unto us in the name of the LORD, we will not hearken unto thee.

17 But we will certainly do whatsoever thing goeth forth out of our own mouth, to burn incense unto the queen of heaven, and to pour out drink offerings unto her, as we have done, we and our fathers, our kings, and our princes, in the cities of Ju'dah, and in the streets of Je-ru'-sa-lem: for *then* had we plenty of victuals, and were well, and saw no evil.

18 But since we left off to burn incense to the queen of heaven, and to pour out drink offerings unto her, we have wanted all *things*, and have been consumed by the sword and by the famine.

19 And when we burned incense to the queen of heaven, and poured out drink offerings unto her, did we make her cakes to worship her, and pour out drink offerings unto her, without our men?

20 ¶ Then Jer-e-mi'ah said unto all the people, to the men, and to the women, and to all the people which had given him *that* answer, saying,

21 The incense that ye burned in the cities of Ju'dah, and in the streets of Je-ru'sa-lem, ye, and your fathers, your kings, and your princes, and the people of the land, did not the LORD remember them, and came it *not* into his mind?

22 So that the LORD could no longer bear, because of the evil of your doings, *and* because of the abominations which ye have committed; therefore is your land a desolation, and an as-

tonishment, and a curse, without an inhabitant, as at this day.

23 Because ye have burned incense, and because ye have sinned against the LORD, and have not obeyed the voice of the LORD, nor walked in his law, nor in his statutes, nor in his testimonies; therefore this evil is happened unto you, as at this day.

24 Moreover Jer-e-mi′ah said unto all the people, and to all the women, Hear the word of the LORD, all Ju′dah that are in the land of E′-gypt:

25 Thus saith the LORD of hosts, the God of Is′ra-el, saying; Ye and your wives have both spoken with your mouths, and fulfilled with your hand, saying, We will surely perform our vows that we have vowed, to burn incense to the queen of heaven, and to pour out drink offerings unto her: ye will surely accomplish your vows, and surely perform your vows.

26 Therefore hear ye the word of the LORD, all Ju′dah that dwell in the land of E′gypt; Behold, I have sworn by my great name, saith the LORD, that my name shall no more be named in the mouth of any man of Ju′dah in all the land of E′gypt, saying, The Lord GOD liveth.

27 Behold, I will watch over them for evil, and not for good: and all the men of Ju′dah that are in the land of E′gypt shall be consumed by the sword and by the famine, until there be an end of them.

28 Yet a small number that escape the sword shall return out of the land of E′gypt into the land of Ju′dah, and all the remnant of Ju′dah, that are gone into the land of E′gypt to sojourn there, shall know whose words shall stand, mine, or theirs.

29 ¶ And this shall be a sign unto you, saith the LORD, that I will punish you in this place, that ye may know that my words shall surely stand against you for evil:

30 Thus saith the LORD; Behold, I will give Pha′raoh-hoph′ra king of E′gypt into the hand of his enemies, and into the hand of them that seek his life; as I gave Zed-e-ki′ah king of Ju′-dah into the hand of Neb-u-chad-rez′zar king of Bab′y-lon, his enemy, and that sought his life.

45 THE word that Jer-e-mi′ah the prophet spake unto Ba′ruch the son of Ne-ri′ah, when he had written these words in a book at the mouth of Jer-e-mi′ah, in the fourth year of Je-hoi′a-kim the son of Jo-si′ah king of Ju′dah, saying,

2 Thus saith the LORD, the God of Is′ra-el, unto thee, O Ba′ruch;

3 Thou didst say, Woe is me now! for the LORD hath added grief to my sorrow; I fainted in my sighing, and I find no rest.

4 ¶ Thus shalt thou say unto him, The LORD saith thus; Behold, that which I have built will I break down, and that which I have planted I will pluck up, even this whole land.

5 And seekest thou great things for thyself? seek them not: for, behold, I will bring evil upon all flesh, saith the LORD: but thy life will I give unto thee for a prey in all places whither thou goest.

46 THE word of the LORD which came to Jer-e-mi′ah the prophet against the Gen′tiles;

2 Against E′gypt, against the army of Pha′-raoh-ne′cho king of E′gypt, which was by the river Eu-phra′tes in Car′che-mish, which Neb′u-chad-rez′zar king of Bab′y-lon smote in the fourth year of Je-hoi′a-kim the son of Jo-si′ah king of Ju′dah.

3 Order ye the buckler and shield, and draw near to battle.

4 Harness the horses; and get up, ye horsemen, and stand forth with your helmets; furbish the spears, and put on the brigandines.

5 Wherefore have I seen them dismayed and turned away back? and their mighty ones are beaten down, and are fled apace, and look not back: for fear was round about, saith the LORD.

6 Let not the swift flee away, nor the mighty man escape; they shall stumble, and fall toward the north by the river Eu-phra′tes.

7 Who is this that cometh up as a flood, whose waters are moved as the rivers?

8 E′gypt riseth up like a flood, and his waters are moved like the rivers; and he saith, I will go up, and will cover the earth; I will destroy the city and the inhabitants thereof.

9 Come up, ye horses; and rage, ye chariots; and let the mighty men come forth; the E-thi-o′pi-ans and the Lib′y-ans, that handle the shield; and the Lyd′i-ans, that handle and bend the bow.

10 For this is the day of the Lord GOD of hosts, a day of vengeance, that he may avenge him of his adversaries: and the sword shall devour, and it shall be satiate and made drunk with their blood: for the Lord GOD of hosts hath a sacrifice in the north country by the river Eu-phra′tes.

11 Go up into Gil′e-ad, and take balm, O virgin, the daughter of E′gypt: in vain shalt thou use many medicines; for thou shalt not be cured.

12 The nations have heard of thy shame, and thy cry hath filled the land: for the mighty man hath stumbled against the mighty, and they are fallen both together.

13 ¶ The word that the LORD spake to Jer-e-mi′ah the prophet, how Neb-u-chad-rez′zar king of Bab′y-lon should come and smite the land of E′gypt.

14 Declare ye in E′gypt, and publish in Mig′-dol, and publish in Noph and in Tah′pan-hes: say ye, Stand fast, and prepare thee; for the sword shall devour round about thee.

15 Why are thy valiant men swept away? they stood not, because the LORD did drive them.

16 He made many to fall, yea, one fell upon another: and they said, Arise, and let us go again to our own people, and to the land of our nativity, from the oppressing sword.

17 They did cry there, Pha′raoh king of E′-gypt is but a noise; he hath passed the time appointed.

18 As I live, saith the King, whose name is the LORD of hosts, Surely as Ta′bor is among the mountains, and as Car′mel by the sea, so shall he come.

19 O thou daughter dwelling in E′gypt, furnish thyself to go into captivity: for Noph shall be waste and desolate without an inhabitant.

20 E′gypt is like a very fair heifer, but destruction cometh; it cometh out of the north.

21 Also her hired men are in the midst of her like fatted bullocks; for they also are turned back, and are fled away together: they did not stand, because the day of their calamity was come upon them, and the time of their visitation.

22 The voice thereof shall go like a serpent; for they shall march with an army, and come against her with axes, as hewers of wood.

23 They shall cut down her forest, saith the

LORD, though it cannot be searched; because they are more than the grasshoppers, and *are* innumerable.

24 The daughter of E'gypt shall be confounded; she shall be delivered into the hand of the people of the north.

25 The LORD of hosts, the God of Is'ra-el, saith; Behold, I will punish the multitude of No, and Pha'raoh, and E'gypt, with their gods, and their kings; even Pha'raoh, and *all* them that trust in him:

26 And I will deliver them into the hand of those that seek their lives, and into the hand of Neb-u-chad-rez'zar king of Bab'y-lon, and into the hand of his servants: and afterward it shall be inhabited, as in the days of old, saith the LORD.

27 ¶ But fear not thou, O my servant Ja'cob, and be not dismayed, O Is'ra-el: for, behold, I will save thee from afar off, and thy seed from the land of their captivity; and Ja'cob shall return, and be in rest and at ease, and none shall make *him* afraid.

28 Fear thou not, O Ja'cob my servant, saith the LORD: for I *am* with thee; for I will make a full end of all the nations whither I have driven thee: but I will not make a full end of thee, but correct thee in measure; yet will I not leave thee wholly unpunished.

47 THE word of the LORD that came to Jer-e-mi'ah the prophet against the Phi-lis'-tines, before that Pha'raoh smote Ga'za.

2 Thus saith the LORD; Behold, waters rise up out of the north, and shall be an overflowing flood, and shall overflow the land, and all that is therein; the city, and them that dwell therein: then the men shall cry, and all the inhabitants of the land shall howl.

3 At the noise of the stamping of the hoofs of his strong *horses*, at the rushing of his chariots, *and* at the rumbling of his wheels, the fathers shall not look back to *their* children for feebleness of hands;

4 Because of the day that cometh to spoil all the Phi-lis'tines, *and* to cut off from Ty'rus and Zi'don every helper that remaineth: for the LORD will spoil the Phi-lis'tines, the remnant of the country of Caph'tor.

5 Baldness is come upon Ga'za; Ash'ke-lon is cut off *with* the remnant of their valley: how long wilt thou cut thyself?

6 O thou sword of the LORD, how long *will it be* ere thou be quiet? put up thyself into thy scabbard, rest, and be still.

7 How can it be quiet, seeing the LORD hath given it a charge against Ash'ke-lon, and against the sea shore? there hath he appointed it.

48 AGAINST Mo'ab thus saith the LORD of hosts, the God of Is'ra-el; Woe unto Ne'-bo! for it is spoiled: Kir-i-a-tha'im is confounded *and* taken: Mis'gab is confounded and dismayed.

2 *There shall be* no more praise of Mo'ab: in Hesh'bon they have devised evil against it; come, and let us cut it off from *being* a nation. Also thou shalt be cut down, O Mad'men; the sword shall pursue thee.

3 A voice of crying *shall be* from Hor-o-na'-im, spoiling and great destruction.

4 Mo'ab is destroyed; her little ones have caused a cry to be heard.

5 For in the going up of Lu'hith continual weeping shall go up; for in the going down of Hor-o-na'im the enemies have heard a cry of destruction.

6 Flee, save your lives, and be like the heath in the wilderness.

7 ¶ For because thou hast trusted in thy works and in thy treasures, thou shalt also be taken: and Che'mosh shall go forth into captivity *with* his priests and his princes together.

8 And the spoiler shall come upon every city, and no city shall escape: the valley also shall perish, and the plain shall be destroyed, as the LORD hath spoken.

9 Give wings unto Mo'ab, that it may flee and get away: for the cities thereof shall be desolate, without any to dwell therein.

10 Cursed *be* he that doeth the work of the LORD deceitfully, and cursed *be* he that keepeth back his sword from blood.

11 ¶ Mo'ab hath been at ease from his youth, and he hath settled on his lees, and hath not been emptied from vessel to vessel, neither hath he gone into captivity: therefore his taste remained in him, and his scent is not changed.

12 Therefore, behold, the days come, saith the LORD, that I will send unto him wanderers, that shall cause him to wander, and shall empty his vessels, and break their bottles.

13 And Mo'ab shall be ashamed of Che'-mosh, as the house of Is'ra-el was ashamed of Beth'-el their confidence.

14 ¶ How say ye, We *are* mighty and strong men for the war?

15 Mo'ab is spoiled, and gone up *out of* her cities, and his chosen young men are gone down to the slaughter, saith the King, whose name *is* the LORD of hosts.

16 The calamity of Mo'ab *is* near to come, and his affliction hasteth fast.

17 All ye that are about him, bemoan him; and all ye that know his name, say, How is the strong staff broken, *and* the beautiful rod!

18 Thou daughter that dost inhabit Di'bon, come down from *thy* glory, and sit in thirst; for the spoiler of Mo'ab shall come upon thee, *and* he shall destroy thy strong holds.

19 O inhabitant of Ar'o-er, stand by the way, and espy; ask him that fleeth, and her that escapeth, *and* say, What is done?

20 Mo'ab is confounded; for it is broken down: howl and cry; tell ye it in Ar'non, that Mo'ab is spoiled,

21 And judgment is come upon the plain country; upon Ho'lon, and upon Ja-ha'zah, and upon Meph'a-ath,

22 And upon Di'bon, and upon Ne'bo, and upon Beth–dib-la-tha'im,

23 And upon Kir-i-a-tha'im, and upon Beth-ga'mul, and upon Beth-me'on,

24 And upon Ke'ri-oth, and upon Boz'rah, and upon all the cities of the land of Mo'ab, far or near.

25 The horn of Mo'ab is cut off, and his arm is broken, saith the LORD.

26 ¶ Make ye him drunken: for he magnified *himself* against the LORD: Mo'ab also shall wallow in his vomit, and he also shall be in derision.

27 For was not Is'ra-el a derision unto thee? was he found among thieves? for since thou spakest of him, thou skippedst for joy.

28 O ye that dwell in Mo'ab, leave the cities, and dwell in the rock, and be like the dove *that* maketh her nest in the sides of the hole's mouth.

29 We have heard the pride of Mo'ab, (he is exceeding proud) his loftiness, and his arro-

gancy, and his pride, and the haughtiness of his heart.

30 I know his wrath, saith the LORD; but *it shall* not *be* so; his lies shall not so effect *it*.

31 Therefore will I howl for Mo'ab, and I will cry out for all Mo'ab; *mine heart* shall mourn for the men of Kir–he'res.

32 O vine of Sib'mah, I will weep for thee with the weeping of Ja'zer: thy plants are gone over the sea, they reach *even* to the sea of Ja'zer: the spoiler is fallen upon thy summer fruits and upon thy vintage.

33 And joy and gladness is taken from the plentiful field, and from the land of Mo'ab; and I have caused wine to fail from the winepresses: none shall tread with shouting; *their* shouting *shall be* no shouting.

34 From the cry of Hesh'bon *even* unto E-le-a'leh, *and even* unto Ja'haz, have they uttered their voice, from Zo'ar *even* unto Hor-o-na'im, *as* an heifer of three years old: for the waters also of Nim'rim shall be desolate.

35 Moreover I will cause to cease in Mo'ab, saith the LORD, him that offereth in the high places, and him that burneth incense to his gods.

36 Therefore mine heart shall sound for Mo'ab like pipes, and mine heart shall sound like pipes for the men of Kir–he'res: because the riches *that* he hath gotten are perished.

37 For every head *shall be* bald, and every beard clipped: upon all the hands *shall be* cuttings, and upon the loins sackcloth.

38 *There shall be* lamentation generally upon all the house tops of Mo'ab and in the streets thereof: for I have broken Mo'ab like a vessel wherein *is* no pleasure, saith the LORD.

39 They shall howl, *saying*, How is it broken down! how hath Mo'ab turned the back with shame! so shall Mo'ab be a derision and a dismaying to all them about him.

40 For thus saith the LORD; Behold, he shall fly as an eagle, and shall spread his wings over Mo'ab.

41 Ke'ri-oth is taken, and the strong holds are surprised, and the mighty men's hearts in Mo'ab at that day shall be as the heart of a woman in her pangs.

42 And Mo'ab shall be destroyed from *being* a people, because he hath magnified *himself* against the LORD.

43 Fear, and the pit, and the snare, *shall be* upon thee, O inhabitant of Mo'ab, saith the LORD.

44 He that fleeth from the fear shall fall into the pit; and he that getteth up out of the pit shall be taken in the snare: for I will bring upon it, *even* upon Mo'ab, the year of their visitation, saith the LORD.

45 They that fled stood under the shadow of Hesh'bon because of the force: but a fire shall come forth out of Hesh'bon, and a flame from the midst of Si'hon, and shall devour the corner of Mo'ab, and the crown of the head of the tumultuous ones.

46 Woe be unto thee, O Mo'ab! the people of Che'mosh perisheth: for thy sons are taken captives, and thy daughters captives.

47 ¶ Yet will I bring again the captivity of Mo'ab in the latter days, saith the LORD. Thus far *is* the judgment of Mo'ab.

49

CONCERNING the Am'mon-ites, thus saith the LORD; Hath Is'ra-el no sons? hath he no heir? why *then* doth their king inherit Gad, and his people dwell in his cities?

2 Therefore, behold, the days come, saith the LORD, that I will cause an alarm of war to be heard in Rab'bah of the Am'mon-ites; and it shall be a desolate heap, and her daughters shall be burned with fire: then shall Is'ra-el be heir unto them that were his heirs, saith the LORD.

3 Howl, O Hesh'bon, for A'i is spoiled: cry, ye daughters of Rab'bah, gird you with sackcloth; lament, and run to and fro by the hedges; for their king shall go into captivity, *and* his priests and his princes together.

4 Wherefore gloriest thou in the valleys, thy flowing valley, O backsliding daughter? that trusted in her treasures, *saying*, Who shall come unto me?

5 Behold, I will bring a fear upon thee, saith the Lord GOD of hosts, from all those that be about thee; and ye shall be driven out every man right forth; and none shall gather up him that wandereth.

6 And afterward I will bring again the captivity of the children of Am'mon, saith the LORD.

7 ¶ Concerning E'dom, thus saith the LORD of hosts; *Is* wisdom no more in Te'man? is counsel perished from the prudent? is their wisdom vanished?

8 Flee ye, turn back, dwell deep, O inhabitants of De'dan; for I will bring the calamity of E'sau upon him, the time *that* I will visit him.

9 If grapegatherers come to thee, would they not leave *some* gleaning grapes? if thieves by night, they will destroy till they have enough.

10 But I have made E'sau bare, I have uncovered his secret places, and he shall not be able to hide himself: his seed is spoiled, and his brethren, and his neighbours, and he *is* not.

11 Leave thy fatherless children, I will preserve *them* alive; and let thy widows trust in me.

12 For thus saith the LORD; Behold, they whose judgment *was* not to drink of the cup have assuredly drunken; and *art* thou he *that* shall altogether go unpunished? thou shalt not go unpunished, but thou shalt surely drink *of it.*

13 For I have sworn by myself, saith the LORD, that Boz'rah shall become a desolation, a reproach, a waste, and a curse; and all the cities thereof shall be perpetual wastes.

14 I have heard a rumour from the LORD, and an ambassador is sent unto the heathen, *saying*, Gather ye together, and come against her, and rise up to the battle.

15 For, lo, I will make thee small among the heathen, *and* despised among men.

16 Thy terribleness hath deceived thee, *and* the pride of thine heart, O thou that dwellest in the clefts of the rock, that holdest the height of the hill: though thou shouldest make thy nest as high as the eagle, I will bring thee down from thence, saith the LORD.

17 Also E'dom shall be a desolation: every one that goeth by it shall be astonished, and shall hiss at all the plagues thereof.

18 As in the overthrow of Sod'om and Gomor'rah and the neighbour *cities* thereof, saith the LORD, no man shall abide there, neither shall a son of man dwell in it.

19 Behold, he shall come up like a lion from the swelling of Jor'dan against the habitation of the strong: but I will suddenly make him run away from her: and who *is* a chosen *man, that* I may appoint over her? for who *is* like me? and who will appoint me the time? and who *is* that shepherd that will stand before me?

20 Therefore hear the counsel of the LORD, that he hath taken against E'dom; and his purposes, that he hath purposed against the inhabi-

tants of Te'man: Surely the least of the flock shall draw them out: surely he shall make their habitations desolate with them.

21 The earth is moved at the noise of their fall, at the cry the noise thereof was heard in the Red sea.

22 Behold, he shall come up and fly as the eagle, and spread his wings over Boz'rah: and at that day shall the heart of the mighty men of E'dom be as the heart of a woman in her pangs.

23 ¶ Concerning Da-mas'cus. Ha'math is confounded, and Ar'pad: for they have heard evil tidings: they are fainthearted; there is sorrow on the sea; it cannot be quiet.

24 Da-mas'cus is waxed feeble, and turneth herself to flee, and fear hath seized on her: anguish and sorrows have taken her, as a woman in travail.

25 How is the city of praise not left, the city of my joy!

26 Therefore her young men shall fall in her streets, and all the men of war shall be cut off in that day, saith the LORD of hosts.

27 And I will kindle a fire in the wall of Da-mas'cus, and it shall consume the palaces of Ben-ha'dad.

28 ¶ Concerning Ke'dar, and concerning the kingdoms of Ha'zor, which Neb-u-chad-rez'zar king of Bab'y-lon shall smite, thus saith the LORD; Arise ye, go up to Ke'dar, and spoil the men of the east.

29 Their tents and their flocks shall they take away: they shall take to themselves their curtains, and all their vessels, and their camels; and they shall cry unto them, Fear is on every side.

30 ¶ Flee, get you far off, dwell deep, O ye inhabitants of Ha'zor, saith the LORD; for Neb-u-chad-rez'zar king of Bab'y-lon hath taken counsel against you, and hath conceived a purpose against you.

31 Arise, get you up unto the wealthy nation, that dwelleth without care, saith the LORD, which have neither gates nor bars, which dwell alone.

32 And their camels shall be a booty, and the multitude of their cattle a spoil: and I will scatter into all winds them that are in the utmost corners; and I will bring their calamity from all sides thereof, saith the LORD.

33 And Ha'zor shall be a dwelling for dragons, and a desolation for ever: there shall no man abide there, nor any son of man dwell in it.

34 ¶ The word of the LORD that came to Jer-e-mi'ah the prophet against E'lam in the beginning of the reign of Zed-e-ki'ah king of Ju'dah, saying,

35 Thus saith the LORD of hosts; Behold, I will break the bow of E'lam, the chief of their might.

36 And upon E'lam will I bring the four winds from the four quarters of heaven, and will scatter them toward all those winds; and there shall be no nation whither the outcasts of E'lam shall not come.

37 For I will cause E'lam to be dismayed before their enemies, and before them that seek their life: and I will bring evil upon them, even my fierce anger, saith the LORD; and I will send the sword after them, till I have consumed them:

38 And I will set my throne in E'lam, and will destroy from thence the king and the princes, saith the LORD.

39 ¶ But it shall come to pass in the latter days, that I will bring again the captivity of E'-lam, saith the LORD.

50 THE word that the LORD spake against Bab'y-lon and against the land of the Chal-de'ans by Jer-e-mi'ah the prophet.

2 Declare ye among the nations, and publish, and set up a standard; publish, and conceal not: say, Bab'y-lon is taken, Bel is confounded, Me-ro'dach is broken in pieces; her idols are confounded, her images are broken in pieces.

3 For out of the north there cometh up a nation against her, which shall make her land desolate, and none shall dwell therein: they shall remove, they shall depart, both man and beast.

4 ¶ In those days, and in that time, saith the LORD, the children of Is'ra-el shall come, they and the children of Ju'dah together, going and weeping: they shall go, and seek the LORD their God.

5 They shall ask the way to Zi'on with their faces thitherward, saying, Come, and let us join ourselves to the LORD in a perpetual covenant that shall not be forgotten.

6 My people hath been lost sheep: their shepherds have caused them to go astray, they have turned them away on the mountains: they have gone from mountain to hill, they have forgotten their restingplace.

7 All that found them have devoured them: and their adversaries said, We offend not, because they have sinned against the LORD, the habitation of justice, even the LORD, the hope of their fathers.

8 Remove out of the midst of Bab'y-lon, and go forth out of the land of the Chal-de'ans, and be as the he goats before the flocks.

9 ¶ For, lo, I will raise and cause to come up against Bab'y-lon an assembly of great nations from the north country: and they shall set themselves in array against her; from thence she shall be taken: their arrows shall be as of a mighty expert man; none shall return in vain.

10 And Chal-de'a shall be a spoil: all that spoil her shall be satisfied, saith the LORD.

11 Because ye were glad, because ye rejoiced, O ye destroyers of mine heritage, because ye are grown fat as the heifer at grass, and bellow as bulls;

12 Your mother shall be sore confounded; she that bare you shall be ashamed: behold, the hindermost of the nations shall be a wilderness, a dry land, and a desert.

13 Because of the wrath of the LORD it shall not be inhabited, but it shall be wholly desolate: every one that goeth by Bab'y-lon shall be astonished, and hiss at all her plagues.

14 Put yourselves in array against Bab'y-lon round about: all ye that bend the bow, shoot at her, spare no arrows: for she hath sinned against the LORD.

15 Shout against her round about: she hath given her hand: her foundations are fallen, her walls are thrown down: for it is the vengeance of the LORD: take vengeance upon her; as she hath done, do unto her.

16 Cut off the sower from Bab'y-lon, and him that handleth the sickle in the time of harvest: for fear of the oppressing sword they shall turn every one to his people, and they shall flee every one to his own land.

17 ¶ Israel is a scattered sheep; the lions have driven him away: first the king of As-syr'i-a hath devoured him; and last this Neb-u-chad-rez'zar king of Bab'y-lon hath broken his bones.

18 Therefore thus saith the LORD of hosts, the God of Is'ra-el; Behold, I will punish the king of Bab'y-lon and his land, as I have punished the king of As-syr'i-a.

19 And I will bring Is'ra-el again to his habitation, and he shall feed on Car'mel and Ba'shan, and his soul shall be satisfied upon mount E'phra-im and Gil'e-ad.

20 In those days, and in that time, saith the LORD, the iniquity of Is'ra-el shall be sought for, and *there shall be* none; and the sins of Ju'dah, and they shall not be found: for I will pardon them whom I reserve.

21 ¶ Go up against the land of Mer-a-tha'im, *even* against it, and against the inhabitants of Pe'kod: waste and utterly destroy after them, saith the LORD, and do according to all that I have commanded thee.

22 A sound of battle *is* in the land, and of great destruction.

23 How is the hammer of the whole earth cut asunder and broken! how is Bab'y-lon become a desolation among the nations!

24 I have laid a snare for thee, and thou art also taken, O Bab'y-lon, and thou wast not aware: thou art found, and also caught, because thou hast striven against the LORD.

25 The LORD hath opened his armoury, and hath brought forth the weapons of his indignation: for this *is* the work of the Lord GOD of hosts in the land of the Chal-de'ans.

26 Come against her from the utmost border, open her storehouses: cast her up as heaps, and destroy her utterly: let nothing of her be left.

27 Slay all her bullocks; let them go down to the slaughter: woe unto them! for their day is come, the time of their visitation.

28 The voice of them that flee and escape out of the land of Bab'y-lon, to declare in Zi'on the vengeance of the LORD our God, the vengeance of his temple.

29 Call together the archers against Bab'y-lon: all ye that bend the bow, camp against it round about; let none thereof escape: recompense her according to her work; according to all that she hath done, do unto her: for she hath been proud against the LORD, against the Holy One of Is'ra-el.

30 Therefore shall her young men fall in the streets, and all her men of war shall be cut off in that day, saith the LORD.

31 Behold, I *am* against thee, O *thou* most proud, saith the Lord GOD of hosts: for thy day is come, the time *that* I will visit thee.

32 And the most proud shall stumble and fall, and none shall raise him up: and I will kindle a fire in his cities, and it shall devour all round about him.

33 ¶ Thus saith the LORD of hosts; The children of Is'ra-el and the children of Ju'dah *were* oppressed together: and all that took them captives held them fast; they refused to let them go.

34 Their Redeemer *is* strong; the LORD of hosts *is* his name: he shall throughly plead their cause, that he may give rest to the land, and disquiet the inhabitants of Bab'y-lon.

35 ¶ A sword *is* upon the Chal-de'ans, saith the LORD, and upon the inhabitants of Bab'y-lon, and upon her princes, and upon her wise *men.*

36 A sword *is* upon the liars; and they shall dote: a sword *is* upon her mighty men; and they shall be dismayed.

37 A sword *is* upon their horses, and upon their chariots, and upon all the mingled people that *are* in the midst of her; and they shall become as women: a sword *is* upon her treasures; and they shall be robbed.

38 A drought *is* upon her waters; and they shall be dried up: for it *is* the land of graven images, and they are mad upon *their* idols.

39 Therefore the wild beasts of the desert with the wild beasts of the islands shall dwell *there,* and the owls shall dwell therein: and it shall be no more inhabited for ever; neither shall it be dwelt in from generation to generation.

40 As God overthrew Sod'om and Go-mor'-rah and the neighbour *cities* thereof, saith the LORD; *so* shall no man abide there, neither shall any son of man dwell therein.

41 Behold, a people shall come from the north, and a great nation, and many kings shall be raised up from the coasts of the earth.

42 They shall hold the bow and the lance: they *are* cruel, and will not shew mercy: their voice shall roar like the sea, and they shall ride upon horses, *every one* put in array, like a man to the battle, against thee, O daughter of Bab'y-lon.

43 The king of Bab'y-lon hath heard the report of them, and his hands waxed feeble: anguish took hold of him, *and* pangs as of a woman in travail.

44 Behold, he shall come up like a lion from the swelling of Jor'dan unto the habitation of the strong: but I will make them suddenly run away from her: and who *is* a chosen *man, that* I may appoint over her? for who *is* like me? and who will appoint me the time? and who *is* that shepherd that will stand before me?

45 Therefore hear ye the counsel of the LORD, that he hath taken against Bab'y-lon; and his purposes, that he hath purposed against the land of the Chal-de'ans: Surely the least of the flock shall draw them out: surely he shall make *their* habitation desolate with them.

46 At the noise of the taking of Bab'y-lon the earth is moved, and the cry is heard among the nations.

51 THUS saith the LORD; Behold, I will raise up against Bab'y-lon, and against them that dwell in the midst of them that rise up against me, a destroying wind;

2 And will send unto Bab'y-lon fanners, that shall fan her, and shall empty her land: for in the day of trouble they shall be against her round about.

3 Against *him that* bendeth let the archer bend his bow, and against *him that* lifteth himself up in his brigandine: and spare ye not her young men; destroy ye utterly all her host.

4 Thus the slain shall fall in the land of the Chal-de'ans, and *they that are* thrust through in her streets.

5 For Is'ra-el *hath* not *been* forsaken, nor Ju'-dah of his God, of the LORD of hosts; though their land was filled with sin against the Holy One of Is'ra-el.

6 Flee out of the midst of Bab'y-lon, and deliver every man his soul: be not cut off in her iniquity; for this *is* the time of the LORD's vengeance; he will render unto her a recompence.

7 Bab'y-lon *hath been* a golden cup in the LORD's hand, that made all the earth drunken: the nations have drunken of her wine; therefore the nations are mad.

8 Bab'y-lon is suddenly fallen and destroyed: howl for her; take balm for her pain, if so be she may be healed.

9 We would have healed Bab'y-lon, but she is not healed: forsake her, and let us go every one into his own country: for her judgment reacheth unto heaven, and is lifted up *even* to the skies.

10 The LORD hath brought forth our righteousness: come, and let us declare in Zi'on the work of the LORD our God.

11 Make bright the arrows; gather the shields: the LORD hath raised up the spirit of the kings of the Medes: for his device is against Bab'y-lon, to destroy it; because it is the vengeance of the LORD, the vengeance of his temple.

12 Set up the standard upon the walls of Bab'y-lon, make the watch strong, set up the watchmen, prepare the ambushes: for the LORD hath both devised and done that which he spake against the inhabitants of Bab'y-lon.

13 O thou that dwellest upon many waters, abundant in treasures, thine end is come, and the measure of thy covetousness.

14 The LORD of hosts hath sworn by himself, saying, Surely I will fill thee with men, as with caterpillers; and they shall lift up a shout against thee.

15 He hath made the earth by his power, he hath established the world by his wisdom, and hath stretched out the heaven by his understanding.

16 When he uttereth his voice, there is a multitude of waters in the heavens; and he causeth the vapours to ascend from the ends of the earth: he maketh lightnings with rain, and bringeth forth the wind out of his treasures.

17 Every man is brutish by his knowledge; every founder is confounded by the graven image: for his molten image is falsehood, and there is no breath in them.

18 They are vanity, the work of errors: in the time of their visitation they shall perish.

19 The portion of Ja'cob is not like them; for he is the former of all things: and Is'ra-el is the rod of his inheritance: the LORD of hosts is his name.

20 Thou art my battle ax and weapons of war: for with thee will I break in pieces the nations, and with thee will I destroy kingdoms;

21 And with thee will I break in pieces the horse and his rider; and with thee will I break in pieces the chariot and his rider;

22 With thee also will I break in pieces man and woman; and with thee will I break in pieces old and young; and with thee will I break in pieces the young man and the maid;

23 I will also break in pieces with thee the shepherd and his flock; and with thee will I break in pieces the husbandman and his yoke of oxen; and with thee will I break in pieces captains and rulers.

24 And I will render unto Bab'y-lon and to all the inhabitants of Chal-de'a all their evil that they have done in Zi'on in your sight, saith the LORD.

25 Behold, I am against thee, O destroying mountain, saith the LORD, which destroyest all the earth: and I will stretch out mine hand upon thee, and roll thee down from the rocks, and will make thee a burnt mountain.

26 And they shall not take of thee a stone for a corner, nor a stone for foundations; but thou shalt be desolate for ever, saith the LORD.

27 Set ye up a standard in the land, blow the trumpet among the nations, prepare the nations against her, call together against her the kingdoms of Ar'a-rat, Min'ni, and Ash'che-naz; appoint a captain against her; cause the horses to come up as the rough caterpillers.

28 Prepare against her the nations with the kings of the Medes, the captains thereof, and all the rulers thereof, and all the land of his dominion.

29 And the land shall tremble and sorrow: for every purpose of the LORD shall be performed against Bab'y-lon, to make the land of Bab'y-lon a desolation without an inhabitant.

30 The mighty men of Bab'y-lon have forborn to fight, they have remained in their holds: their might hath failed; they became as women: they have burned her dwellingplaces; her bars are broken.

31 One post shall run to meet another, and one messenger to meet another, to shew the king of Bab'y-lon that his city is taken at one end,

32 And that the passages are stopped, and the reeds they have burned with fire, and the men of war are affrighted.

33 For thus saith the LORD of hosts, the God of Is'ra-el; The daughter of Bab'y-lon is like a threshingfloor, it is time to thresh her: yet a little while, and the time of her harvest shall come.

34 Neb-u-chad-rez'zar the king of Bab'y-lon hath devoured me, he hath crushed me, he hath made me an empty vessel, he hath swallowed me up like a dragon, he hath filled his belly with my delicates, he hath cast me out.

35 The violence done to me and to my flesh be upon Bab'y-lon, shall the inhabitant of Zi'on say; and my blood upon the inhabitants of Chalde'a, shall Je-ru'sa-lem say.

36 Therefore thus saith the LORD; Behold, I will plead thy cause, and take vengeance for thee; and I will dry up her sea, and make her springs dry.

37 And Bab'y-lon shall become heaps, a dwellingplace for dragons, an astonishment, and an hissing, without an inhabitant.

38 They shall roar together like lions: they shall yell as lions' whelps.

39 In their heat I will make their feasts, and I will make them drunken, that they may rejoice, and sleep a perpetual sleep, and not wake, saith the LORD.

40 I will bring them down like lambs to the slaughter, like rams with he goats.

41 How is She'shach taken! and how is the praise of the whole earth surprised! how is Bab'y-lon become an astonishment among the nations!

42 The sea is come up upon Bab'y-lon: she is covered with the multitude of the waves thereof.

43 Her cities are a desolation, a dry land, and a wilderness, a land wherein no man dwelleth, neither doth any son of man pass thereby.

44 And I will punish Bel in Bab'y-lon, and I will bring forth out of his mouth that which he hath swallowed up: and the nations shall not flow together any more unto him: yea, the wall of Bab'y-lon shall fall.

45 My people, go ye out of the midst of her, and deliver ye every man his soul from the fierce anger of the LORD.

46 And lest your heart faint, and ye fear for the rumour that shall be heard in the land; a rumour shall both come one year, and after that in another year shall come a rumour, and violence in the land, ruler against ruler.

47 Therefore, behold, the days come, that I will do judgment upon the graven images of Bab'y-lon: and her whole land shall be confounded, and all her slain shall fall in the midst of her.

48 Then the heaven and the earth, and all that is therein, shall sing for Bab'y-lon: for the spoilers shall come unto her from the north, saith the LORD.

49 As Bab'y-lon *hath caused* the slain of Is'-ra-el to fall, so at Bab'y-lon shall fall the slain of all the earth.

50 Ye that have escaped the sword, go away, stand not still: remember the LORD afar off, and let Je-ru'sa-lem come into your mind.

51 We are confounded, because we have heard reproach: shame hath covered our faces: for strangers are come into the sanctuaries of the LORD's house.

52 Wherefore, behold, the days come, saith the LORD, that I will do judgment upon her graven images: and through all her land the wounded shall groan.

53 Though Bab'y-lon should mount up to heaven, and though she should fortify the height of her strength, *yet* from me shall spoilers come unto her, saith the LORD.

54 A sound of a cry *cometh* from Bab'y-lon, and great destruction from the land of the Chal-de'ans:

55 Because the LORD hath spoiled Bab'y-lon, and destroyed out of her the great voice; when her waves do roar like great waters, a noise of their voice is uttered:

56 Because the spoiler is come upon her, *even* upon Bab'y-lon, and her mighty men are taken, every one of their bows is broken: for the LORD God of recompences shall surely requite.

57 And I will make drunk her princes, and her wise *men*, her captains, and her rulers, and her mighty men: and they shall sleep a perpetual sleep, and not wake, saith the King, whose name *is* the LORD of hosts.

58 Thus saith the LORD of hosts; The broad walls of Bab'y-lon shall be utterly broken, and her high gates shall be burned with fire; and the people shall labour in vain, and the folk in the fire, and they shall be weary.

59 ¶ The word which Jer-e-mi'ah the prophet commanded Ser-a-i'ah the son of Ne-ri'ah, the son of Ma-a-se'iah, when he went with Zed-e-ki'ah the king of Ju'dah into Bab'y-lon in the fourth year of his reign. And *this* Ser-a-i'ah *was* a quiet prince.

60 So Jer-e-mi'ah wrote in a book all the evil that should come upon Bab'y-lon, *even* all these words that are written against Bab'y-lon.

61 And Jer-e-mi'ah said to Ser-a-i'ah, When thou comest to Bab'y-lon, and shalt see, and shalt read all these words;

62 Then shalt thou say, O LORD, thou hast spoken against this place, to cut it off, that none shall remain in it, neither man nor beast, but that it shall be desolate for ever.

63 And it shall be, when thou hast made an end of reading this book, *that* thou shalt bind a stone to it, and cast it into the midst of Eu-phra'tes:

64 And thou shalt say, Thus shall Bab'y-lon sink, and shall not rise from the evil that I will bring upon her: and they shall be weary. Thus far *are* the words of Jer-e-mi'ah.

52 ZED-E-KI'AH *was* one and twenty years old when he began to reign, and he reigned eleven years in Je-ru'sa-lem. And his mother's name *was* Ha-mu'tal the daughter of Jer-e-mi'ah of Lib'nah.

2 And he did *that which was* evil in the eyes of the LORD, according to all that Je-hoi'a-kim had done.

3 For through the anger of the LORD it came to pass in Je-ru'sa-lem and Ju'dah, till he had cast them out from his presence, that Zed-e-ki'-ah rebelled against the king of Bab'y-lon.

4 ¶ And it came to pass in the ninth year of his reign, in the tenth month, in the tenth *day* of the month, *that* Neb-u-chad-rez'zar king of Bab'y-lon came, he and all his army, against Je-ru'sa-lem, and pitched against it, and built forts against it round about.

5 So the city was besieged unto the eleventh year of king Zed-e-ki'ah.

6 And in the fourth month, in the ninth *day* of the month, the famine was sore in the city, so that there was no bread for the people of the land.

7 Then the city was broken up and all the men of war fled, and went forth out of the city by night by the way of the gate between the two walls, which *was* by the king's garden; (now the Chal-de'ans *were* by the city round about:) and they went by the way of the plain.

8 ¶ But the army of the Chal-de'ans pursued after the king, and overtook Zed-e-ki'ah in the plains of Jer'i-cho; and all his army was scattered from him.

9 Then they took the king, and carried him up unto the king of Bab'y-lon to Rib'lah in the land of Ha'math; where he gave judgment upon him.

10 And the king of Bab'y-lon slew the sons of Zed-e-ki'ah before his eyes: he slew also all the princes of Ju'dah in Rib'lah.

11 Then he put out the eyes of Zed-e-ki'ah; and the king of Bab'y-lon bound him in chains, and carried him to Bab'y-lon, and put him in prison till the day of his death.

12 ¶ Now in the fifth month, in the tenth *day* of the month, which *was* the nineteenth year of Neb-u-chad-rez'zar king of Bab'y-lon, came Neb'u-zar-a'dan, captain of the guard, *which* served the king of Bab'y-lon, into Je-ru'sa-lem,

13 And burned the house of the LORD, and the king's house; and all the houses of Je-ru'sa-lem, and all the houses of the great *men*, burned he with fire:

14 And all the army of the Chal-de'ans, that *were* with the captain of the guard, brake down all the walls of Je-ru'sa-lem round about.

15 Then Neb'u-zar-a'dan the captain of the guard carried away captive *certain* of the poor of the people, and the residue of the people that remained in the city, and those that fell away, that fell to the king of Bab'y-lon, and the rest of the multitude.

16 But Neb'u-zar-a'dan the captain of the guard left *certain* of the poor of the land for vinedressers and for husbandmen.

17 Also the pillars of brass that *were* in the house of the LORD, and the bases, and the brasen sea that *was* in the house of the LORD, the Chal-de'ans brake, and carried all the brass of them to Bab'y-lon.

18 The caldrons also, and the shovels, and the snuffers, and the bowls, and the spoons, and all the vessels of brass wherewith they ministered, took they away.

19 And the basons, and the firepans, and the bowls, and the caldrons, and the candlesticks, and the spoons, and the cups; *that* which *was* of gold *in* gold, and *that* which *was* of silver *in* silver, took the captain of the guard away.

20 The two pillars, one sea, and twelve brasen bulls that *were* under the bases, which king Sol'o-mon had made in the house of the LORD: the brass of all these vessels was without weight.

21 And *concerning* the pillars, the height of one pillar *was* eighteen cubits; and a fillet of twelve cubits did compass it; and the thickness thereof *was* four fingers: *it was* hollow.

22 And a chapter of brass *was* upon it; and the height of one chapter *was* five cubits, with network and pomegranates upon the chapiters round about, all *of* brass. The second pillar also and the pomegranates *were* like unto these.

23 And there were ninety and six pomegranates on a side; *and* all the pomegranates upon the network *were* an hundred round about.

24 ¶ And the captain of the guard took Ser-a-i′ah the chief priest, and Zeph-a-ni′ah the second priest, and the three keepers of the door:

25 He took also out of the city an eunuch, which had the charge of the men of war; and seven men of them that were near the king's person, which were found in the city; and the principal scribe of the host, who mustered the people of the land; and threescore men of the people of the land, that were found in the midst of the city.

26 So Neb′u-zar-a′dan the captain of the guard took them, and brought them to the king of Bab′y-lon to Rib′lah.

27 And the king of Bab′y-lon smote them, and put them to death in Rib′lah in the land of Ha′math. Thus Ju′dah was carried away captive out of his own land.

28 This *is* the people whom Neb-u-chad-rez′-zar carried away captive: in the seventh year three thousand Jews and three and twenty:

29 In the eighteenth year of Neb-u-chad-rez′-zar he carried away captive from Je-ru′sa-lem eight hundred thirty and two persons:

30 In the three and twentieth year of Neb-u-chad-rez′zar Neb′u-zar-a′dan the captain of the guard carried away captive of the Jews seven hundred forty and five persons: all the persons *were* four thousand and six hundred.

31 ¶ And it came to pass in the seven and thirtieth year of the captivity of Je-hoi′a-chin king of Ju′dah, in the twelfth month, in the five and twentieth *day* of the month, *that* E′vil-me-ro′dach king of Bab′y-lon in the *first* year of his reign lifted up the head of Je-hoi′a-chin king of Ju′dah, and brought him forth out of prison,

32 And spake kindly unto him, and set his throne above the throne of the kings that *were* with him in Bab′y-lon,

33 And changed his prison garments: and he did continually eat bread before him all the days of his life.

34 And *for* his diet, there was a continual diet given him of the king of Bab′y-lon, every day a portion until the day of his death, all the days of his life.

THE LAMENTATIONS

OF JEREMIAH

1 HOW doth the city sit solitary, *that was* full of people! *how* is she become as a widow! she *that was* great among the nations, *and* princess among the provinces, *how* is she become tributary!

2 She weepeth sore in the night, and her tears *are* on her cheeks: among all her lovers she hath none to comfort *her:* all her friends have dealt treacherously with her, they are become her enemies.

3 Ju′dah is gone into captivity because of affliction, and because of great servitude: she dwelleth among the heathen, she findeth no rest: all her persecutors overtook her between the straits.

4 The ways of Zi′on do mourn, because none come to the solemn feasts: all her gates are desolate: her priests sigh, her virgins are afflicted, and she *is* in bitterness.

5 Her adversaries are the chief, her enemies prosper; for the LORD hath afflicted her for the multitude of her transgressions: her children are gone into captivity before the enemy.

6 And from the daughter of Zi′on all her beauty is departed: her princes are become like harts *that* find no pasture, and they are gone without strength before the pursuer.

7 Je-ru′sa-lem remembered in the days of her affliction and of her miseries all her pleasant things that she had in the days of old, when her people fell into the hand of the enemy, and none did help her: the adversaries saw her, *and* did mock at her sabbaths.

8 Je-ru′sa-lem hath grievously sinned; therefore she is removed: all that honoured her despise her, because they have seen her nakedness: yea, she sigheth, and turneth backward.

9 Her filthiness *is* in her skirts; she remembereth not her last end; therefore she came down wonderfully: she had no comforter. O LORD, behold my affliction: for the enemy hath magnified *himself.*

10 The adversary hath spread out his hand upon all her pleasant things: for she hath seen *that* the heathen entered into her sanctuary, whom thou didst command *that* they should not enter into thy congregation.

11 All her people sigh, they seek bread; they have given their pleasant things for meat to relieve the soul: see, O LORD, and consider; for I am become vile.

12 ¶ *Is it* nothing to you, all ye that pass by? behold, and see if there be any sorrow like unto my sorrow, which is done unto me, wherewith the LORD hath afflicted *me* in the day of his fierce anger.

13 From above hath he sent fire into my bones, and it prevaileth against them: he hath spread a net for my feet, he hath turned me back: he hath made me desolate *and* faint all the day.

14 The yoke of my transgressions is bound by his hand: they are wreathed, *and* come up upon my neck: he hath made my strength to fall, the Lord hath delivered me into *their* hands, *from whom* I am not able to rise up.

15 The Lord hath trodden under foot all my mighty *men* in the midst of me: he hath called an assembly against me to crush my young men: the Lord hath trodden the virgin, the daughter of Ju′dah, *as* in a winepress.

16 For these *things* I weep; mine eye, mine eye runneth down with water, because the comforter that should relieve my soul is far from me: my children are desolate, because the enemy prevailed.

17 Zi′on spreadeth forth her hands, *and there is* none to comfort her: the LORD hath commanded concerning Ja′cob, *that* his adversaries *should be* round about him: Je-ru′sa-lem is as a menstruous woman among them.

18 ¶ The LORD is righteous; for I have rebelled against his commandment: hear, I pray

you, all people, and behold my sorrow: my virgins and my young men are gone into captivity.

19 I called for my lovers, *but* they deceived me: my priests and mine elders gave up the ghost in the city, while they sought their meat to relieve their souls.

20 Behold, O LORD; for I *am* in distress: my bowels are troubled; mine heart is turned within me; for I have grievously rebelled: abroad the sword bereaveth, at home *there is* as death.

21 They have heard that I sigh: *there is* none to comfort me: all mine enemies have heard of my trouble; they are glad that thou hast done *it:* thou wilt bring the day *that* thou hast called, and they shall be like unto me.

22 Let all their wickedness come before thee; and do unto them, as thou hast done unto me for all my transgressions: for my sighs *are* many, and my heart *is* faint.

2 HOW hath the Lord covered the daughter of Zi'on with a cloud in his anger, *and* cast down from heaven unto the earth the beauty of Is'ra-el, and remembered not his footstool in the day of his anger!

2 The Lord hath swallowed up all the habitations of Ja'cob, and hath not pitied: he hath thrown down in his wrath the strong holds of the daughter of Ju'dah; he hath brought *them* down to the ground: he hath polluted the kingdom and the princes thereof.

3 He hath cut off in *his* fierce anger all the horn of Is'ra-el: he hath drawn back his right hand from before the enemy, and he burned against Ja'cob like a flaming fire, *which* devoureth round about.

4 He hath bent his bow like an enemy: he stood with his right hand as an adversary, and slew all *that were* pleasant to the eye in the tabernacle of the daughter of Zi'on: he poured out his fury like fire.

5 The Lord was as an enemy: he hath swallowed up Is'ra-el, he hath swallowed up all her palaces: he hath destroyed his strong holds, and hath increased in the daughter of Ju'dah mourning and lamentation.

6 And he hath violently taken away his tabernacle, as *if it were of* a garden: he hath destroyed his places of the assembly: the LORD hath caused the solemn feasts and sabbaths to be forgotten in Zi'on, and hath despised in the indignation of his anger the king and the priest.

7 The Lord hath cast off his altar, he hath abhorred his sanctuary, he hath given up into the hand of the enemy the walls of her palaces; they have made a noise in the house of the LORD, as in the day of a solemn feast.

8 The LORD hath purposed to destroy the wall of the daughter of Zi'on: he hath stretched out a line, he hath not withdrawn his hand from destroying: therefore he made the rampart and the wall to lament; they languished together.

9 Her gates are sunk into the ground; he hath destroyed and broken her bars: her king and her princes *are* among the Gen'tiles: the law *is* no *more;* her prophets also find no vision from the LORD.

10 The elders of the daughter of Zi'on sit upon the ground, *and* keep silence: they have cast up dust upon their heads; they have girded themselves with sackcloth: the virgins of Je-ru'sa-lem hang down their heads to the ground.

11 Mine eyes do fail with tears, my bowels are troubled, my liver is poured upon the earth, for the destruction of the daughter of my people; because the children and the sucklings swoon in the streets of the city.

12 They say to their mothers, Where *is* corn and wine? when they swooned as the wounded in the streets of the city, when their soul was poured out into their mothers' bosom.

13 What thing shall I take to witness for thee? what thing shall I liken to thee, O daughter of Je-ru'sa-lem? what shall I equal to thee, that I may comfort thee, O virgin daughter of Zi'on? for thy breach *is* great like the sea: who can heal thee?

14 Thy prophets have seen vain and foolish things for thee: and they have not discovered thine iniquity, to turn away thy captivity; but have seen for thee false burdens and causes of banishment.

15 All that pass by clap *their* hands at thee; they hiss and wag their head at the daughter of Je-ru'sa-lem, *saying, Is* this the city that *men* call The perfection of beauty, The joy of the whole earth?

16 All thine enemies have opened their mouth against thee: they hiss and gnash the teeth: they say, We have swallowed *her* up: certainly this *is* the day that we looked for; we have found, we have seen *it.*

17 The LORD hath done *that* which he had devised; he hath fulfilled his word that he had commanded in the days of old: he hath thrown down, and hath not pitied: and he hath caused *thine* enemy to rejoice over thee, he hath set up the horn of thine adversaries.

18 Their heart cried unto the Lord, O wall of the daughter of Zi'on, let tears run down like a river day and night: give thyself no rest; let not the apple of thine eye cease.

19 Arise, cry out in the night: in the beginning of the watches pour out thine heart like water before the face of the Lord: lift up thy hands toward him for the life of thy young children, that faint for hunger in the top of every street.

20 ¶ Behold, O LORD, and consider to whom thou hast done this. Shall the women eat their fruit, *and* children of a span long? shall the priest and the prophet be slain in the sanctuary of the Lord?

21 The young and the old lie on the ground in the streets: my virgins and my young men are fallen by the sword; thou hast slain *them* in the day of thine anger; thou hast killed, *and* not pitied.

22 Thou hast called as in a solemn day my terrors round about, so that in the day of the LORD'S anger none escaped nor remained: those that I have swaddled and brought up hath mine enemy consumed.

3 I AM the man *that* hath seen affliction by the rod of his wrath.

2 He hath led me, and brought *me into* darkness, but not *into* light.

3 Surely against me is he turned; he turneth his hand *against me* all the day.

4 My flesh and my skin hath he made old; he hath broken my bones.

5 He hath builded against me, and compassed *me* with gall and travail.

6 He hath set me in dark places, as *they that* be dead of old.

7 He hath hedged me about, that I cannot get out: he hath made my chain heavy.

8 Also when I cry and shout, he shutteth out my prayer.

9 He hath inclosed my ways with hewn stone, he hath made my paths crooked.

10 He *was* unto me *as* a bear lying in wait, *and as* a lion in secret places.

11 He hath turned aside my ways, and pulled me in pieces: he hath made me desolate.

12 He hath bent his bow, and set me as a mark for the arrow.

13 He hath caused the arrows of his quiver to enter into my reins.

14 I was a derision to all my people; *and* their song all the day.

15 He hath filled me with bitterness, he hath made me drunken with wormwood.

16 He hath also broken my teeth with gravel stones, he hath covered me with ashes.

17 And thou hast removed my soul far off from peace: I forgat prosperity.

18 And I said, My strength and my hope is perished from the LORD:

19 Remembering mine affliction and my misery, the wormwood and the gall.

20 My soul hath *them* still in remembrance, and is humbled in me.

21 This I recall to my mind, therefore have I hope.

22 ¶ *It is of* the LORD'S mercies that we are not consumed, because his compassions fail not.

23 *They are* new every morning: great *is* thy faithfulness.

24 The LORD *is* my portion, saith my soul; therefore will I hope in him.

25 The LORD *is* good unto them that wait for him, to the soul *that* seeketh him.

26 *It is* good that *a* man should both hope and quietly wait for the salvation of the LORD.

27 *It is* good for a man that he bear the yoke in his youth.

28 He sitteth alone and keepeth silence, because he hath borne *it* upon him.

29 He putteth his mouth in the dust; if so be there may be hope.

30 He giveth *his* cheek to him that smiteth him: he is filled full with reproach.

31 For the Lord will not cast off for ever:

32 But though he cause grief, yet will he have compassion according to the multitude of his mercies.

33 For he doth not afflict willingly nor grieve the children of men.

34 To crush under his feet all the prisoners of the earth,

35 To turn aside the right of a man before the face of the most High,

36 To subvert a man in his cause, the Lord approveth not.

37 ¶ Who *is* he *that* saith, and it cometh to pass, *when* the Lord commandeth *it* not?

38 Out of the mouth of the most High proceedeth not evil and good?

39 Wherefore doth a living man complain, a man for the punishment of his sins?

40 Let us search and try our ways, and turn again to the LORD.

41 Let us lift up our heart with *our* hands unto God in the heavens.

42 We have transgressed and have rebelled: thou hast not pardoned.

43 Thou hast covered with anger, and persecuted us: thou hast slain, thou hast not pitied.

44 Thou hast covered thyself with a cloud, that *our* prayer should not pass through.

45 Thou hast made us *as* the offscouring and refuse in the midst of the people.

46 All our enemies have opened their mouths against us.

47 Fear and a snare is come upon us, desolation and destruction.

48 Mine eye runneth down with rivers of water for the destruction of the daughter of my people.

49 Mine eye trickleth down, and ceaseth not, without any intermission,

50 Till the LORD look down, and behold from heaven.

51 Mine eye affecteth mine heart because of all the daughters of my city.

52 Mine enemies chased me sore, like a bird, without cause.

53 They have cut off my life in the dungeon, and cast a stone upon me.

54 Waters flowed over mine head; *then* I said, I am cut off.

55 ¶ I called upon thy name, O LORD, out of the low dungeon.

56 Thou hast heard my voice: hide not thine ear at my breathing, at my cry.

57 Thou drewest near in the day *that* I called upon thee: thou saidst, Fear not.

58 O Lord, thou hast pleaded the causes of my soul; thou hast redeemed my life.

59 O LORD, thou hast seen my wrong: judge thou my cause.

60 Thou hast seen all their vengeance *and* all their imaginations against me.

61 Thou hast heard their reproach, O LORD, *and* all their imaginations against me;

62 The lips of those that rose up against me, and their device against me all the day.

63 Behold their sitting down, and their rising up; I *am* their musick.

64 ¶ Render unto them a recompence, O LORD, according to the work of their hands.

65 Give them sorrow of heart, thy curse unto them.

66 Persecute and destroy them in anger from under the heavens of the LORD.

4 HOW is the gold become dim! *how* is the most fine gold changed! the stones of the sanctuary are poured out in the top of every street.

2 The precious sons of Zi'on, comparable to fine gold, how are they esteemed as earthen pitchers, the work of the hands of the potter!

3 Even the sea monsters draw out the breast, they give suck to their young ones: the daughter of my people *is become* cruel, like the ostriches in the wilderness.

4 The tongue of the sucking child cleaveth to the roof of his mouth for thirst: the young children ask bread, *and* no man breaketh *it* unto them.

5 They that did feed delicately are desolate in the streets: they that were brought up in scarlet embrace dunghills.

6 For the punishment of the iniquity of the daughter of my people is greater than the punishment of the sin of Sod'om, that was overthrown as in a moment, and no hands stayed on her.

7 Her Naz'a-rites were purer than snow, they were whiter than milk, they were more ruddy in body than rubies, their polishing *was* of sapphire:

8 Their visage is blacker than a coal; they are not known in the streets: their skin cleaveth to their bones; it is withered, it is become like a stick.

9 *They that be* slain with the sword are better than *they that be* slain with hunger: for these pine away, stricken through for *want of* the fruits of the field.

10 The hands of the pitiful women have sodden their own children: they were their meat in the destruction of the daughter of my people.

11 The LORD hath accomplished his fury; he hath poured out his fierce anger, and hath kindled a fire in Zi'on, and it hath devoured the foundations thereof.

12 The kings of the earth, and all the inhabitants of the world, would not have believed that the adversary and the enemy should have entered into the gates of Je-ru'sa-lem.

13 ¶ For the sins of her prophets, *and* the iniquities of her priests, that have shed the blood of the just in the midst of her,

14 They have wandered *as* blind *men* in the streets, they have polluted themselves with blood, so that men could not touch their garments.

15 They cried unto them, Depart ye; *it is* unclean; depart, depart, touch not: when they fled away and wandered, they said among the heathen, They shall no more sojourn *there*.

16 The anger of the LORD hath divided them; he will no more regard them: they respected not the persons of the priests, they favoured not the elders.

17 As for us, our eyes as yet failed for our vain help: in our watching we have watched for a nation *that* could not save *us*.

18 They hunt our steps, that we cannot go in our streets: our end is near, our days are fulfilled; for our end is come.

19 Our persecutors are swifter than the eagles of the heaven: they pursued us upon the mountains, they laid wait for us in the wilderness.

20 The breath of our nostrils, the anointed of the LORD, was taken in their pits, of whom we said, Under his shadow we shall live among the heathen.

21 ¶ Rejoice and be glad, O daughter of E'dom, that dwellest in the land of Uz; the cup also shall pass through unto thee: thou shalt be drunken, and shalt make thyself naked.

22 ¶ The punishment of thine iniquity is accomplished, O daughter of Zi'on; he will no more carry thee away into captivity: he will visit thine iniquity, O daughter of E'dom; he will discover thy sins.

5 REMEMBER, O LORD, what is come upon us: consider, and behold our reproach.

2 Our inheritance is turned to strangers, our houses to aliens.

3 We are orphans and fatherless, our mothers *are* as widows.

4 We have drunken our water for money; our wood is sold unto us.

5 Our necks *are* under persecution: we labour, *and* have no rest.

6 We have given the hand to the E-gyp'tians, *and* to the As-syr'i-ans, to be satisfied with bread.

7 Our fathers have sinned, *and are* not; and we have borne their iniquities.

8 Servants have ruled over us: *there is* none that doth deliver *us* out of their hand.

9 We gat our bread with *the* peril *of* our lives because of the sword of the wilderness.

10 Our skin was black like an oven because of the terrible famine.

11 They ravished the women in Zi'on, *and* the maids in the cities of Ju'dah.

12 Princes are hanged up by their hand: the faces of elders were not honoured.

13 They took the young men to grind, and the children fell under the wood.

14 The elders have ceased from the gate, the young men from their musick.

15 The joy of our heart is ceased; our dance is turned into mourning.

16 The crown is fallen *from* our head: woe unto us, that we have sinned!

17 For this our heart is faint; for these *things* our eyes are dim.

18 Because of the mountain of Zi'on, which is desolate, the foxes walk upon it.

19 Thou, O LORD, remainest for ever; thy throne from generation to generation.

20 Wherefore dost thou forget us for ever, *and* forsake us so long time?

21 Turn thou us unto thee, O LORD, and we shall be turned; renew our days as of old.

22 But thou hast utterly rejected us; thou art very wroth against us.

THE BOOK OF

EZEKIEL

1 NOW it came to pass in the thirtieth year, in the fourth *month*, in the fifth *day* of the month, as I *was* among the captives by the river of Che'bar, *that* the heavens were opened, and I saw visions of God.

2 In the fifth *day* of the month, which *was* the fifth year of king Je-hoi'a-chin's captivity,

3 The word of the LORD came expressly unto E-ze'ki-el the priest, the son of Bu'zi, in the land of the Chal-de'ans by the river Che'bar; and the hand of the LORD was there upon him.

4 ¶ And I looked, and, behold, a whirlwind came out of the north, a great cloud, and a fire infolding itself, and a brightness *was* about it, and out of the midst thereof as the colour of amber, out of the midst of the fire.

5 Also out of the midst thereof *came* the likeness of four living creatures. And this *was* their appearance; they had the likeness of a man.

6 And every one had four faces, and every one had four wings.

7 And their feet *were* straight feet; and the sole of their feet *was* like the sole of a calf's foot: and they sparkled like the colour of burnished brass.

8 And *they had* the hands of a man under their wings on their four sides; and they four had their faces and their wings.

9 Their wings *were* joined one to another; they turned not when they went; they went every one straight forward.

10 As for the likeness of their faces, they four had the face of a man, and the face of a lion, on the right side: and they four had the face of an ox on the left side; they four also had the face of an eagle.

11 Thus *were* their faces: and their wings *were* stretched upward; two *wings* of every one *were* joined one to another, and two covered their bodies.

12 And they went every one straight forward: whither the spirit was to go, they went; *and* they turned not when they went.

13 As for the likeness of the living creatures,

their appearance *was* like burning coals of fire, *and* like the appearance of lamps: it went up and down among the living creatures; and the fire was bright, and out of the fire went forth lightning.

14 And the living creatures ran and returned as the appearance of a flash of lightning.

15 ¶ Now as I beheld the living creatures, behold one wheel upon the earth by the living creatures, with his four faces.

16 The appearance of the wheels and their work *was* like unto the colour of a beryl: and they four had one likeness: and their appearance and their work *was* as it were a wheel in the middle of a wheel.

17 When they went, they went upon their four sides: *and* they turned not when they went.

18 As for their rings, they were so high that they were dreadful; and their rings *were* full of eyes round about them four.

19 And when the living creatures went, the wheels went by them: and when the living creatures were lifted up from the earth, the wheels were lifted up.

20 Whithersoever the spirit was to go, they went, thither *was their* spirit to go; and the wheels were lifted up over against them: for the spirit of the living creature *was* in the wheels.

21 When those went, *these* went; and when those stood, *these* stood; and when those were lifted up from the earth, the wheels were lifted up over against them: for the spirit of the living creature *was* in the wheels.

22 And the likeness of the firmament upon the heads of the living creature *was* as the colour of the terrible crystal, stretched forth over their heads above.

23 And under the firmament *were* their wings straight, the one toward the other: every one had two, which covered on this side, and every one had two, which covered on that side, their bodies.

24 And when they went, I heard the noise of their wings, like the noise of great waters, as the voice of the Almighty, the voice of speech, as the noise of an host: when they stood, they let down their wings.

25 And there was a voice from the firmament that *was* over their heads, when they stood, *and* had let down their wings.

26 ¶ And above the firmament that *was* over their heads *was* the likeness of a throne, as the appearance of a sapphire stone: and upon the likeness of the throne *was* the likeness as the appearance of a man above upon it.

27 And I saw as the colour of amber, as the appearance of fire round about within it, from the appearance of his loins even upward, and from the appearance of his loins even downward, I saw as it were the appearance of fire, and it had brightness round about.

28 As the appearance of the bow that is in the cloud in the day of rain, so *was* the appearance of the brightness round about. This *was* the appearance of the likeness of the glory of the LORD. And when I saw *it,* I fell upon my face, and I heard a voice of one that spake.

2 AND he said unto me, Son of man, stand upon thy feet, and I will speak unto thee.

2 And the spirit entered into me when he spake unto me, and set me upon my feet, that I heard him that spake unto me.

3 And he said unto me, Son of man, I send thee to the children of Is′ra-el, to a rebellious nation that hath rebelled against me: they and

their fathers have transgressed against me, *even* unto this very day.

4 For *they are* impudent children and stiff-hearted. I do send thee unto them; and thou shalt say unto them, Thus saith the Lord GOD.

5 And they, whether they will hear, or whether they will forbear, (for they *are* a rebellious house,) yet shall know that there hath been a prophet among them.

6 ¶ And thou, son of man, be not afraid of them, neither be afraid of their words, though briers and thorns *be* with thee, and thou dost dwell among scorpions: be not afraid of their words, nor be dismayed at their looks, though they *be* a rebellious house.

7 And thou shalt speak my words unto them, whether they will hear, or whether they will forbear: for they *are* most rebellious.

8 But thou, son of man, hear what I say unto thee; Be not thou rebellious like that rebellious house: open thy mouth, and eat that I give thee.

9 ¶ And when I looked, behold, an hand *was* sent unto me; and, lo, a roll of a book *was* therein;

10 And he spread it before me; and it *was* written within and without: and *there was* written therein lamentations, and mourning, and woe.

3 MOREOVER he said unto me, Son of man, eat that thou findest; eat this roll, and go speak unto the house of Is′ra-el.

2 So I opened my mouth, and he caused me to eat that roll.

3 And he said unto me, Son of man, cause thy belly to eat, and fill thy bowels with this roll that I give thee. Then did I eat *it;* and it was in my mouth as honey for sweetness.

4 ¶ And he said unto me, Son of man, go, get thee unto the house of Is′ra-el, and speak with my words unto them.

5 For thou *art* not sent to a people of a strange speech and of an hard language, *but* to the house of Is′ra-el;

6 Not to many people of a strange speech and of an hard language, whose words thou canst not understand. Surely, had I sent thee to them, they would have hearkened unto thee.

7 But the house of Is′ra-el will not hearken unto thee; for they will not hearken unto me: for all the house of Is′ra-el *are* impudent and hard-hearted.

8 Behold, I have made thy face strong against their faces, and thy forehead strong against their foreheads.

9 As an adamant harder than flint have I made thy forehead: fear them not, neither be dismayed at their looks, though they *be* a rebellious house.

10 Moreover he said unto me, Son of man, all my words that I shall speak unto thee receive in thine heart, and hear with thine ears.

11 And go, get thee to them of the captivity, unto the children of thy people, and speak unto them, and tell them, Thus saith the Lord GOD; whether they will hear, or whether they will forbear.

12 Then the spirit took me up, and I heard behind me a voice of a great rushing, *saying,* Blessed *be* the glory of the LORD from his place.

13 *I heard* also the noise of the wings of the living creatures that touched one another, and the noise of the wheels over against them, and a noise of a great rushing.

14 So the spirit lifted me up, and took me away, and I went in bitterness, in the heat of my

spirit; but the hand of the LORD was strong upon me.

15 ¶ Then I came to them of the captivity at Tel-a'bib, that dwelt by the river of Che'bar, and I sat where they sat, and remained there astonished among them seven days.

16 And it came to pass at the end of seven days, that the word of the LORD came unto me, saying,

17 Son of man, I have made thee a watchman unto the house of Is'ra-el: therefore hear the word at my mouth, and give them warning from me.

18 When I say unto the wicked, Thou shalt surely die; and thou givest him not warning, nor speakest to warn the wicked from his wicked way, to save his life; the same wicked *man* shall die in his iniquity; but his blood will I require at thine hand.

19 Yet if thou warn the wicked, and he turn not from his wickedness, nor from his wicked way, he shall die in his iniquity; but thou hast delivered thy soul.

20 Again, When a righteous *man* doth turn from his righteousness, and commit iniquity, and I lay a stumblingblock before him, he shall die: because thou hast not given him warning, he shall die in his sin, and his righteousness which he hath done shall not be remembered; but his blood will I require at thine hand.

21 Nevertheless if thou warn the righteous *man*, that the righteous sin not, and he doth not sin, he shall surely live, because he is warned; also thou hast delivered thy soul.

22 ¶ And the hand of the LORD was there upon me; and he said unto me, Arise, go forth into the plain, and I will there talk with thee.

23 Then I arose, and went forth into the plain: and, behold, the glory of the LORD stood there, as the glory which I saw by the river of Che'bar: and I fell on my face.

24 Then the spirit entered into me, and set me upon my feet, and spake with me, and said unto me, Go, shut thyself within thine house.

25 But thou, O son of man, behold, they shall put bands upon thee, and shall bind thee with them, and thou shalt not go out among them:

26 And I will make thy tongue cleave to the roof of thy mouth, that thou shalt be dumb, and shalt not be to them a reprover: for they *are* a rebellious house.

27 But when I speak with thee, I will open thy mouth, and thou shalt say unto them, Thus saith the Lord GOD; He that heareth, let him hear; and he that forbeareth, let him forbear: for they *are* a rebellious house.

4 THOU also, son of man, take thee a tile, and lay it before thee, and pourtray upon it the city, *even* Je-ru'sa-lem:

2 And lay siege against it, and build a fort against it, and cast a mount against it; set the camp also against it, and set *battering* rams against it round about.

3 Moreover take thou unto thee an iron pan, and set it *for* a wall of iron between thee and the city: and set thy face against it, and it shall be besieged, and thou shalt lay siege against it. This *shall be* a sign to the house of Is'ra-el.

4 Lie thou also upon thy left side, and lay the iniquity of the house of Is'ra-el upon it: *according* to the number of the days that thou shalt lie upon it thou shalt bear their iniquity.

5 For I have laid upon thee the years of their iniquity, according to the number of the days, three hundred and ninety days: so shalt thou bear the iniquity of the house of Is'ra-el.

6 And when thou hast accomplished them, lie again on thy right side, and thou shalt bear the iniquity of the house of Ju'dah forty days: I have appointed thee each day for a year.

7 Therefore thou shalt set thy face toward the siege of Je-ru'sa-lem, and thine arm *shall be* uncovered, and thou shalt prophesy against it.

8 And, behold, I will lay bands upon thee, and thou shalt not turn thee from one side to another, till thou hast ended the days of thy siege.

9 ¶ Take thou also unto thee wheat, and barley, and beans, and lentiles, and millet, and fitches, and put them in one vessel, and make thee bread thereof, *according* to the number of the days that thou shalt lie upon thy side, three hundred and ninety days shalt thou eat thereof.

10 And thy meat which thou shalt eat *shall be* by weight, twenty shekels a day: from time to time shalt thou eat it.

11 Thou shalt drink also water by measure, the sixth part of an hin: from time to time shalt thou drink.

12 And thou shalt eat it *as* barley cakes, and thou shalt bake it with dung that cometh out of man, in their sight.

13 And the LORD said, Even thus shall the children of Is'ra-el eat their defiled bread among the Gen'tiles, whither I will drive them.

14 Then said I, Ah Lord GOD! behold, my soul hath not been polluted: for from my youth up even till now have I not eaten of that which dieth of itself, or is torn in pieces; neither came there abominable flesh into my mouth.

15 Then he said unto me, Lo, I have given thee cow's dung for man's dung, and thou shalt prepare thy bread therewith.

16 Moreover he said unto me, Son of man, behold, I will break the staff of bread in Je-ru'-sa-lem: and they shall eat bread by weight, and with care; and they shall drink water by measure, and with astonishment:

17 That they may want bread and water, and be astonied one with another, and consume away for their iniquity.

5 AND thou, son of man, take thee a sharp knife, take thee a barber's razor, and cause *it* to pass upon thine head and upon thy beard: then take thee balances to weigh, and divide the *hair*.

2 Thou shalt burn with fire a third part in the midst of the city, when the days of the siege are fulfilled: and thou shalt take a third part, *and* smite about it with a knife: and a third part thou shalt scatter in the wind; and I will draw out a sword after them.

3 Thou shalt also take thereof a few in number, and bind them in thy skirts.

4 Then take of them again, and cast them into the midst of the fire, and burn them in the fire; *for* thereof shall a fire come forth into all the house of Is'ra-el.

5 ¶ Thus saith the Lord GOD; This *is* Je-ru'sa-lem: I have set it in the midst of the nations and countries *that are* round about her.

6 And she hath changed my judgments into wickedness more than the nations, and my statutes more than the countries that *are* round about her: for they have refused my judgments and my statutes, they have not walked in them.

7 Therefore thus saith the Lord GOD; Because ye multiplied more than the nations that *are* round about you, *and* have not walked in my statutes, neither have kept my judgments, neither have done according to the judgments of the nations *that are* round about you;

8 Therefore thus saith the Lord God; Behold, I, even I, *am* against thee, and will execute judgments in the midst of thee in the sight of the nations.

9 And I will do in thee that which I have not done, and whereunto I will not do any more the like, because of all thine abominations.

10 Therefore the fathers shall eat the sons in the midst of thee, and the sons shall eat their fathers; and I will execute judgments in thee, and the whole remnant of thee will I scatter into all the winds.

11 Wherefore, *as* I live, saith the Lord God; Surely, because thou hast defiled my sanctuary with all thy detestable things, and with all thine abominations, therefore will I also diminish *thee;* neither shall mine eye spare, neither will I have any pity.

12 ¶ A third part of thee shall die with the pestilence, and with famine shall they be consumed in the midst of thee: and a third part shall fall by the sword round about thee; and I will scatter a third part into all the winds, and I will draw out a sword after them.

13 Thus shall mine anger be accomplished, and I will cause my fury to rest upon them, and I will be comforted: and they shall know that I the Lord have spoken *it* in my zeal, when I have accomplished my fury in them.

14 Moreover I will make thee waste, and a reproach among the nations that *are* round about thee, in the sight of all that pass by.

15 So it shall be a reproach and a taunt, an instruction and an astonishment unto the nations that *are* round about thee, when I shall execute judgments in thee in anger and in fury and in furious rebukes. I the Lord have spoken *it.*

16 When I shall send upon them the evil arrows of famine, which shall be for *their* destruction, *and* which I will send to destroy you: and I will increase the famine upon you, and will break your staff of bread:

17 So will I send upon you famine and evil beasts, and they shall bereave thee; and pestilence and blood shall pass through thee; and I will bring the sword upon thee. I the Lord have spoken *it.*

6 AND the word of the Lord came unto me, saying,

2 Son of man, set thy face toward the mountains of Is'ra-el, and prophesy against them,

3 And say, Ye mountains of Is'ra-el, hear the word of the Lord God; Thus saith the Lord God to the mountains, and to the hills, to the rivers, and to the valleys; Behold, I, *even* I, will bring a sword upon you, and I will destroy your high places.

4 And your altars shall be desolate, and your images shall be broken: and I will cast down your slain *men* before your idols.

5 And I will lay the dead carcases of the children of Is'ra-el before their idols; and I will scatter your bones round about your altars.

6 In all your dwellingplaces the cities shall be laid waste, and the high places shall be desolate; that your altars may be laid waste and made desolate, and your idols may be broken and cease, and your images may be cut down, and your works may be abolished.

7 And the slain shall fall in the midst of you, and ye shall know that I *am* the Lord.

8 ¶ Yet will I leave a remnant, that ye may have *some* that shall escape the sword among the nations, when ye shall be scattered through the countries.

9 And they that escape of you shall remember me among the nations whither they shall be carried captives, because I am broken with their whorish heart, which hath departed from me, and with their eyes, which go a whoring after their idols: and they shall loathe themselves for the evils which they have committed in all their abominations.

10 And they shall know that I *am* the Lord, *and that* I have not said in vain that I would do this evil unto them.

11 ¶ Thus saith the Lord God; Smite with thine hand, and stamp with thy foot, and say, Alas for all the evil abominations of the house of Is'ra-el! for they shall fall by the sword, by the famine, and by the pestilence.

12 He that is far off shall die of the pestilence; and he that is near shall fall by the sword; and he that remaineth and is besieged shall die by the famine: thus will I accomplish my fury upon them.

13 Then shall ye know that I *am* the Lord, when their slain *men* shall be among their idols round about their altars, upon every high hill, in all the tops of the mountains, and under every green tree, and under every thick oak, the place where they did offer sweet savour to all their idols.

14 So will I stretch out my hand upon them, and make the land desolate, yea, more desolate than the wilderness toward Dib'lath, in all their habitations: and they shall know that I *am* the Lord.

7 MOREOVER the word of the Lord came unto me, saying,

2 Also, thou son of man, thus saith the Lord God unto the land of Is'ra-el; An end, the end is come upon the four corners of the land.

3 Now *is* the end *come* upon thee, and I will send mine anger upon thee, and will judge thee according to thy ways, and will recompense upon thee all thine abominations.

4 And mine eye shall not spare thee, neither will I have pity: but I will recompense thy ways upon thee, and thine abominations shall be in the midst of thee: and ye shall know that I *am* the Lord.

5 Thus saith the Lord God; An evil, an only evil, behold, is come.

6 An end is come, the end is come: it watcheth for thee; behold, it is come.

7 The morning is come unto thee, O thou that dwellest in the land: the time is come, the day of trouble *is* near, and not the sounding again of the mountains.

8 Now will I shortly pour out my fury upon thee, and accomplish mine anger upon thee: and I will judge thee according to thy ways, and will recompense thee for all thine abominations.

9 And mine eye shall not spare, neither will I have pity: I will recompense thee according to thy ways and thine abominations *that* are in the midst of thee; and ye shall know that I *am* the Lord that smiteth.

10 Behold the day, behold, it is come: the morning is gone forth; the rod hath blossomed, pride hath budded.

11 Violence is risen up into a rod of wickedness: none of them *shall remain,* nor of their multitude, nor of any of theirs: neither *shall there be* wailing for them.

12 The time is come, the day draweth near: let not the buyer rejoice, nor the seller mourn: for wrath *is* upon all the multitude thereof.

13 For the seller shall not return to that

which is sold, although they were yet alive: for the vision *is* touching the whole multitude thereof, *which* shall not return; neither shall any strengthen himself in the iniquity of his life.

14 They have blown the trumpet, even to make all ready; but none goeth to the battle: for my wrath *is* upon all the multitude thereof.

15 The sword *is* without, and the pestilence and the famine within: he that *is* in the field shall die with the sword; and he that *is* in the city, famine and pestilence shall devour him.

16 ¶ But they that escape of them shall escape, and shall be on the mountains like doves of the valleys, all of them mourning, every one for his iniquity.

17 All hands shall be feeble, and all knees shall be weak *as* water.

18 They shall also gird *themselves* with sackcloth, and horror shall cover them; and shame *shall be* upon all faces, and baldness upon all their heads.

19 They shall cast their silver in the streets, and their gold shall be removed: their silver and their gold shall not be able to deliver them in the day of the wrath of the LORD: they shall not satisfy their souls, neither fill their bowels: because it is the stumblingblock of their iniquity.

20 ¶ As for the beauty of his ornament, he set it in majesty: but they made the images of their abominations *and* of their detestable things therein: therefore have I set it far from them.

21 And I will give it into the hands of the strangers for a prey, and to the wicked of the earth for a spoil; and they shall pollute it.

22 My face will I turn also from them, and they shall pollute my secret *place:* for the robbers shall enter into it, and defile it.

23 ¶ Make a chain: for the land is full of bloody crimes, and the city is full of violence.

24 Wherefore I will bring the worst of the heathen, and they shall possess their houses: I will also make the pomp of the strong to cease; and their holy places shall be defiled.

25 Destruction cometh; and they shall seek peace, and *there shall be* none.

26 Mischief shall come upon mischief, and rumour shall be upon rumour; then shall they seek a vision of the prophet; but the law shall perish from the priest, and counsel from the ancients.

27 The king shall mourn, and the prince shall be clothed with desolation, and the hands of the people of the land shall be troubled: I will do unto them after their way, and according to their deserts will I judge them; and they shall know that I *am* the LORD.

8 AND it came to pass in the sixth year, in the sixth *month,* in the fifth *day* of the month, *as* I sat in mine house, and the elders of Ju'dah sat before me, that the hand of the Lord GOD fell there upon me.

2 Then I beheld, and lo a likeness as the appearance of fire: from the appearance of his loins even downward, fire; and from his loins even upward, as the appearance of brightness, as the colour of amber.

3 And he put forth the form of an hand, and took me by a lock of mine head; and the spirit lifted me up between the earth and the heaven, and brought me in the visions of God to Je-ru'-sa-lem, to the door of the inner gate that looketh toward the north; where *was* the seat of the image of jealousy, which provoketh to jealousy.

4 And, behold, the glory of the God of Is'ra-el *was* there, according to the vision that I saw in the plain.

5 ¶ Then said he unto me, Son of man, lift up thine eyes now the way toward the north. So I lifted up mine eyes the way toward the north, and behold northward at the gate of the altar this image of jealousy in the entry.

6 He said furthermore unto me, Son of man, seest thou what they do? *even* the great abominations that the house of Is'ra-el committeth here, that I should go far off from my sanctuary? but turn thee yet again, *and* thou shalt see greater abominations.

7 ¶ And he brought me to the door of the court; and when I looked, behold a hole in the wall.

8 Then said he unto me, Son of man, dig now in the wall: and when I had digged in the wall, behold a door.

9 And he said unto me, Go in, and behold the wicked abominations that they do here.

10 So I went in and saw; and behold every form of creeping things, and abominable beasts, and all the idols of the house of Is'ra-el, pourtrayed upon the wall round about.

11 And there stood before them seventy men of the ancients of the house of Is'ra-el, and in the midst of them stood Ja-az-a-ni'ah the son of Sha'phan, with every man his censer in his hand; and a thick cloud of incense went up.

12 Then said he unto me, Son of man, hast thou seen what the ancients of the house of Is'-ra-el do in the dark, every man in the chambers of his imagery? for they say, The LORD seeth us not; the LORD hath forsaken the earth.

13 ¶ He said also unto me, Turn thee yet again, *and* thou shalt see greater abominations that they do.

14 Then he brought me to the door of the gate of the LORD's house which *was* toward the north; and, behold, there sat women weeping for Tam'muz.

15 ¶ Then said he unto me, Hast thou seen *this,* O son of man? turn thee yet again, *and* thou shalt see greater abominations than these.

16 And he brought me into the inner court of the LORD's house, and, behold, at the door of the temple of the LORD, between the porch and the altar, *were* about five and twenty men, with their backs toward the temple of the LORD, and their faces toward the east; and they worshipped the sun toward the east.

17 ¶ Then he said unto me, Hast thou seen *this,* O son of man? Is it a light thing to the house of Ju'dah that they commit the abominations which they commit here? for they have filled the land with violence, and have returned to provoke me to anger: and, lo, they put the branch to their nose.

18 Therefore will I also deal in fury: mine eye shall not spare, neither will I have pity: and though they cry in mine ears with a loud voice, *yet* will I not hear them.

9 HE cried also in mine ears with a loud voice, saying, Cause them that have charge over the city to draw near, even every man *with* his destroying weapon in his hand.

2 And, behold, six men came from the way of the higher gate, which lieth toward the north, and every man a slaughter weapon in his hand; and one man among them *was* clothed with linen, with a writer's inkhorn by his side: and they went in, and stood beside the brasen altar.

3 And the glory of the God of Is'ra-el was gone up from the cherub, whereupon he was, to the threshold of the house. And he called to the

man clothed with linen, which *had* the writer's inkhorn by his side;

4 And the LORD said unto him, Go through the midst of the city, through the midst of Je-ru'sa-lem, and set a mark upon the foreheads of the men that sigh and that cry for all the abominations that be done in the midst thereof.

5 ¶ And to the others he said in mine hearing, Go ye after him through the city, and smite: let not your eye spare, neither have ye pity:

6 Slay utterly old *and* young, both maids, and little children, and women: but come not near any man upon whom *is* the mark; and begin at my sanctuary. Then they began at the ancient men which *were* before the house.

7 And he said unto them, Defile the house, and fill the courts with the slain: go ye forth. And they went forth, and slew in the city.

8 ¶ And it came to pass, while they were slaying them, and I was left, that I fell upon my face, and cried, and said, Ah Lord GOD! wilt thou destroy all the residue of Is'ra-el in thy pouring out of thy fury upon Je-ru'sa-lem?

9 Then said he unto me, The iniquity of the house of Is'ra-el and Ju'dah *is* exceeding great, and the land is full of blood, and the city full of perverseness: for they say, The LORD hath forsaken the earth, and the LORD seeth not.

10 And as for me also, mine eye shall not spare, neither will I have pity, *but* I will recompense their way upon their head.

11 And, behold, the man clothed with linen, which *had* the inkhorn by his side, reported the matter, saying, I have done as thou hast commanded me.

10 THEN I looked, and, behold, in the firmament that was above the head of the cherubims there appeared over them as it were a sapphire stone, as the appearance of the likeness of a throne.

2 And he spake unto the man clothed with linen, and said, Go in between the wheels, *even* under the cherub, and fill thine hand with coals of fire from between the cherubims, and scatter *them* over the city. And he went in in my sight.

3 Now the cherubims stood on the right side of the house, when the man went in; and the cloud filled the inner court.

4 Then the glory of the LORD went up from the cherub, *and* stood over the threshold of the house; and the house was filled with the cloud, and the court was full of the brightness of the LORD's glory.

5 And the sound of the cherubims' wings was heard *even* to the outer court, as the voice of the Almighty God when he speaketh.

6 And it came to pass, *that* when he had commanded the man clothed with linen, saying, Take fire from between the wheels, from between the cherubims; then he went in, and stood beside the wheels.

7 And *one* cherub stretched forth his hand from between the cherubims unto the fire that *was* between the cherubims, and took *thereof*, and put *it* into the hands of *him that was* clothed with linen: who took *it*, and went out.

8 ¶ And there appeared in the cherubims the form of a man's hand under their wings.

9 And when I looked, behold the four wheels by the cherubims, one wheel by one cherub, and another wheel by another cherub: and the appearance of the wheels *was* as the colour of a beryl stone.

10 And *as for* their appearances, they four had one likeness, as if a wheel had been in the midst of a wheel.

11 When they went, they went upon their four sides; they turned not as they went, but to the place whither the head looked they followed it; they turned not as they went.

12 And their whole body, and their backs, and their hands, and their wings, and the wheels, *were* full of eyes round about, *even* the wheels that they four had.

13 As for the wheels, it was cried unto them in my hearing, O wheel.

14 And every one had four faces: the first face *was* the face of a cherub, and the second face *was* the face of a man, and the third the face of a lion, and the fourth the face of an eagle.

15 And the cherubims were lifted up. This *is* the living creature that I saw by the river of Che'bar.

16 And when the cherubims went, the wheels went by them: and when the cherubims lifted up their wings to mount up from the earth, the same wheels also turned not from beside them.

17 When they stood, *these* stood; and when they were lifted up, *these* lifted up themselves *also*: for the spirit of the living creature *was* in them.

18 Then the glory of the LORD departed from off the threshold of the house, and stood over the cherubims.

19 And the cherubims lifted up their wings, and mounted up from the earth in my sight: when they went out, the wheels also *were* beside them, and *every* one stood at the door of the east gate of the LORD's house; and the glory of the God of Is'ra-el *was* over them above.

20 This *is* the living creature that I saw under the God of Is'ra-el by the river of Che'bar; and I knew that they *were* the cherubims.

21 Every one had four faces apiece, and every one four wings; and the likeness of the hands of a man *was* under their wings.

22 And the likeness of their faces *was* the same faces which I saw by the river of Che'bar, their appearances and themselves: they went every one straight forward.

11 MOREOVER the spirit lifted me up, and brought me unto the east gate of the LORD's house, which looketh eastward: and behold at the door of the gate five and twenty men; among whom I saw Ja-az-a-ni'ah the son of A'zur, and Pel-a-ti'ah the son of Be-na'iah, princes of the people.

2 Then said he unto me, Son of man, these *are* the men that devise mischief, and give wicked counsel in this city:

3 Which say, *It is* not near; let us build houses: this *city is* the caldron, and we *be* the flesh.

4 ¶ Therefore prophesy against them, prophesy, O son of man.

5 And the Spirit of the LORD fell upon me, and said unto me, Speak; Thus saith the LORD; Thus have ye said, O house of Is'ra-el: for I know the things that come into your mind, *every* one of them.

6 Ye have multiplied your slain in this city, and ye have filled the streets thereof with the slain.

7 Therefore thus saith the Lord GOD; Your slain whom ye have laid in the midst of it, they *are* the flesh, and this *city is* the caldron: but I will bring you forth out of the midst of it.

8 Ye have feared the sword; and I will bring a sword upon you, saith the Lord GOD.

9 And I will bring you out of the midst

thereof, and deliver you into the hands of strangers, and will execute judgments among you.

10 Ye shall fall by the sword; I will judge you in the border of Is'ra-el; and ye shall know that I am the LORD.

11 This city shall not be your caldron, neither shall ye be the flesh in the midst thereof; but I will judge you in the border of Is'ra-el:

12 And ye shall know that I am the LORD: for ye have not walked in my statutes, neither executed my judgments, but have done after the manners of the heathen that are round about you.

13 ¶ And it came to pass, when I prophesied, that Pel-a-ti'ah the son of Be-na'iah died. Then fell I down upon my face, and cried with a loud voice, and said, Ah Lord God! wilt thou make a full end of the remnant of Is'ra-el?

14 Again the word of the LORD came unto me, saying,

15 Son of man, thy brethren, even thy brethren, the men of thy kindred, and all the house of Is'ra-el wholly, are they unto whom the inhabitants of Je-ru'sa-lem have said, Get you far from the LORD: unto us is this land given in possession.

16 Therefore say, Thus saith the Lord GOD; Although I have cast them far off among the heathen, and although I have scattered them among the countries, yet will I be to them as a little sanctuary in the countries where they shall come.

17 Therefore say, Thus saith the Lord GOD; I will even gather you from the people, and assemble you out of the countries where ye have been scattered, and I will give you the land of Is'ra-el.

18 And they shall come thither, and they shall take away all the detestable things thereof and all the abominations thereof from thence.

19 And I will give them one heart, and I will put a new spirit within you; and I will take the stony heart out of their flesh, and will give them an heart of flesh:

20 That they may walk in my statutes, and keep mine ordinances, and do them: and they shall be my people, and I will be their God.

21 But as for them whose heart walketh after the heart of their detestable things and their abominations, I will recompense their way upon their own heads, saith the Lord GOD.

22 ¶ Then did the cherubims lift up their wings, and the wheels beside them; and the glory of the God of Is'ra-el was over them above.

23 And the glory of the LORD went up from the midst of the city, and stood upon the mountain which is on the east side of the city.

24 ¶ Afterwards the spirit took me up, and brought me in a vision by the Spirit of God into Chal-de'a, to them of the captivity. So the vision that I had seen went up from me.

25 Then I spake unto them of the captivity all the things that the LORD had shewed me.

12 THE word of the LORD also came unto me, saying,

2 Son of man, thou dwellest in the midst of a rebellious house, which have eyes to see, and see not; they have ears to hear, and hear not: for they are a rebellious house.

3 Therefore, thou son of man, prepare thee stuff for removing, and remove by day in their sight; and thou shalt remove from thy place to another place in their sight: it may be they will consider, though they be a rebellious house.

4 Then shalt thou bring forth thy stuff by day

in their sight, as stuff for removing: and thou shalt go forth at even in their sight, as they that go forth into captivity.

5 Dig thou through the wall in their sight, and carry out thereby.

6 In their sight shalt thou bear it upon thy shoulders, and carry it forth in the twilight: thou shalt cover thy face, that thou see not the ground: for I have set thee for a sign unto the house of Is'ra-el.

7 And I did so as I was commanded: I brought forth my stuff by day, as stuff for captivity, and in the even I digged through the wall with mine hand; I brought it forth in the twilight, and I bare it upon my shoulder in their sight.

8 ¶ And in the morning came the word of the LORD unto me, saying,

9 Son of man, hath not the house of Is'ra-el, the rebellious house, said unto thee, What doest thou?

10 Say thou unto them, Thus saith the Lord GOD; This burden concerneth the prince in Je-ru'sa-lem, and all the house of Is'ra-el that are among them.

11 Say, I am your sign: like as I have done, so shall it be done unto them: they shall remove and go into captivity.

12 And the prince that is among them shall bear upon his shoulder in the twilight, and shall go forth: they shall dig through the wall to carry out thereby: he shall cover his face, that he see not the ground with his eyes.

13 My net also will I spread upon him, and he shall be taken in my snare: and I will bring him to Bab'y-lon to the land of the Chal-de'ans; yet shall he not see it, though he shall die there.

14 And I will scatter toward every wind all that are about him to help him, and all his bands; and I will draw out the sword after them.

15 And they shall know that I am the LORD, when I shall scatter them among the nations, and disperse them in the countries.

16 But I will leave a few men of them from the sword, from the famine, and from the pestilence; that they may declare all their abominations among the heathen whither they come; and they shall know that I am the LORD.

17 ¶ Moreover the word of the LORD came to me, saying,

18 Son of man, eat thy bread with quaking, and drink thy water with trembling and with carefulness;

19 And say unto the people of the land, Thus saith the Lord GOD of the inhabitants of Je-ru'sa-lem, and of the land of Is'ra-el; They shall eat their bread with carefulness, and drink their water with astonishment, that her land may be desolate from all that is therein, because of the violence of all them that dwell therein.

20 And the cities that are inhabited shall be laid waste, and the land shall be desolate; and ye shall know that I am the LORD.

21 ¶ And the word of the LORD came unto me, saying,

22 Son of man, what is that proverb that ye have in the land of Is'ra-el, saying, The days are prolonged, and every vision faileth?

23 Tell them therefore, Thus saith the Lord GOD; I will make this proverb to cease, and they shall no more use it as a proverb in Is'ra-el; but say unto them, The days are at hand, and the effect of every vision.

24 For there shall be no more any vain vision nor flattering divination within the house of Is'ra-el.

25 For I *am* the LORD: I will speak, and the word that I shall speak shall come to pass; it shall be no more prolonged: for in your days, O rebellious house, will I say the word, and will perform it, saith the Lord GOD.

26 ¶ Again the word of the LORD came to me, saying,

27 Son of man, behold, *they of* the house of Is'ra-el say, The vision that he seeth *is* for many days *to come,* and he prophesieth of the times *that are* far off.

28 Therefore say unto them, Thus saith the Lord GOD; There shall none of my words be prolonged any more, but the word which I have spoken shall be done, saith the Lord GOD.

13 AND the word of the LORD came unto me, saying,

2 Son of man, prophesy against the prophets of Is'ra-el that prophesy, and say thou unto them that prophesy out of their own hearts, Hear ye the word of the LORD;

3 Thus saith the Lord GOD; Woe unto the foolish prophets, that follow their own spirit, and have seen nothing!

4 O Is'ra-el, thy prophets are like the foxes in the deserts.

5 Ye have not gone up into the gaps, neither made up the hedge for the house of Is'ra-el to stand in the battle in the day of the LORD.

6 They have seen vanity and lying divination, saying, The LORD saith: and the LORD hath not sent them: and they have made *others* to hope that they would confirm the word.

7 Have ye not seen a vain vision, and have ye not spoken a lying divination, whereas ye say, The LORD saith *it:* albeit I have not spoken?

8 Therefore thus saith the Lord GOD; Because ye have spoken vanity, and seen lies, therefore, behold, I *am* against you, saith the Lord GOD.

9 And mine hand shall be upon the prophets that see vanity, and that divine lies: they shall not be in the assembly of my people, neither shall they be written in the writing of the house of Is'ra-el, neither shall they enter into the land of Is'ra-el; and ye shall know that I *am* the Lord GOD.

10 ¶ Because, even because they have seduced my people, saying, Peace; and *there was* no peace; and one built up a wall, and, lo, others daubed it with untempered *morter:*

11 Say unto them which daub *it* with untempered *morter,* that it shall fall: there shall be an overflowing shower; and ye, O great hailstones, shall fall; and a stormy wind shall rend *it.*

12 Lo, when the wall is fallen, shall it not be said unto you, Where *is* the daubing wherewith ye have daubed *it?*

13 Therefore thus saith the Lord GOD; I will even rend *it* with a stormy wind in my fury; and there shall be an overflowing shower in mine anger, and great hailstones in *my* fury to consume *it.*

14 So will I break down the wall that ye have daubed with untempered *morter,* and bring it down to the ground, so that the foundation thereof shall be discovered, and it shall fall, and ye shall be consumed in the midst thereof: and ye shall know that I *am* the LORD.

15 Thus will I accomplish my wrath upon the wall, and upon them that have daubed it with untempered *morter,* and will say unto you, The wall *is* no *more,* neither they that daubed it;

16 *To wit,* the prophets of Is'ra-el which prophesy concerning Je-ru'sa-lem, and which see visions of peace for her, and *there is* no peace, saith the Lord GOD.

17 ¶ Likewise, thou son of man, set thy face against the daughters of thy people, which prophesy out of their own heart; and prophesy thou against them,

18 And say, Thus saith the Lord GOD; Woe to the *women* that sew pillows to all armholes, and make kerchiefs upon the head of every stature to hunt souls! Will ye hunt the souls of my people, and will ye save the souls alive *that* come unto you?

19 And will ye pollute me among my people for handfuls of barley and for pieces of bread, to slay the souls that should not die, and to save the souls alive that should not live, by your lying to my people that hear *your* lies?

20 Wherefore thus saith the Lord GOD; Behold, I *am* against your pillows, wherewith ye there hunt the souls to make *them* fly, and I will tear them from your arms, and will let the souls go, *even* the souls that ye hunt to make *them* fly.

21 Your kerchiefs also will I tear, and deliver my people out of your hand, and they shall be no more in your hand to be hunted; and ye shall know that I *am* the LORD.

22 Because with lies ye have made the heart of the righteous sad, whom I have not made sad; and strengthened the hands of the wicked, that he should not return from his wicked way, by promising him life:

23 Therefore ye shall see no more vanity, nor divine divinations: for I will deliver my people out of your hand: and ye shall know that I *am* the LORD.

14 THEN came certain of the elders of Is'-ra-el unto me, and sat before me.

2 And the word of the LORD came unto me, saying,

3 Son of man, these men have set up their idols in their heart, and put the stumblingblock of their iniquity before their face: should I be enquired of at all by them?

4 Therefore speak unto them, and say unto them, Thus saith the Lord GOD; Every man of the house of Is'ra-el that setteth up his idols in his heart, and putteth the stumblingblock of his iniquity before his face, and cometh to the prophet; I the LORD will answer him that cometh according to the multitude of his idols;

5 That I may take the house of Is'ra-el in their own heart, because they are all estranged from me through their idols.

6 ¶ Therefore say unto the house of Is'ra-el, Thus saith the Lord GOD; Repent, and turn *yourselves* from your idols; and turn away your faces from all your abominations.

7 For every one of the house of Is'ra-el, or of the stranger that sojourneth in Is'ra-el, which separateth himself from me, and setteth up his idols in his heart, and putteth the stumblingblock of his iniquity before his face, and cometh to a prophet to enquire of him concerning me; I the LORD will answer him by myself:

8 And I will set my face against that man, and will make him a sign and a proverb, and I will cut him off from the midst of my people; and ye shall know that I *am* the LORD.

9 And if the prophet be deceived when he hath spoken a thing, I the LORD have deceived that prophet, and I will stretch out my hand upon him, and will destroy him from the midst of my people Is'ra-el.

10 And they shall bear the punishment of their iniquity: the punishment of the prophet shall be even as the punishment of him that seeketh *unto him;*

11 That the house of Is'ra-el may go no more astray from me, neither be polluted any more with all their transgressions; but that they may be my people, and I may be their God, saith the Lord GOD.

12 ¶ The word of the LORD came again to me, saying,

13 Son of man, when the land sinneth against me by trespassing grievously, then will I stretch out mine hand upon it, and will break the staff of the bread thereof, and will send famine upon it, and will cut off man and beast from it:

14 Though these three men, No'ah, Dan'iel, and Job, were in it, they should deliver but their own souls by their righteousness, saith the Lord GOD.

15 ¶ If I cause noisome beasts to pass through the land, and they spoil it, so that it be desolate, that no man may pass through because of the beasts:

16 Though these three men were in it, as I live, saith the Lord GOD, they shall deliver neither sons nor daughters; they only shall be delivered, but the land shall be desolate.

17 ¶ Or if I bring a sword upon that land, and say, Sword, go through the land; so that I cut off man and beast from it:

18 Though these three men were in it, as I live, saith the Lord GOD, they shall deliver neither sons nor daughters, but they only shall be delivered themselves.

19 ¶ Or if I send a pestilence into that land, and pour out my fury upon it in blood, to cut off from it man and beast:

20 Though No'ah, Dan'iel, and Job, were in it, as I live, saith the Lord GOD, they shall deliver neither son nor daughter; they shall but deliver their own souls by their righteousness.

21 For thus saith the Lord GOD; How much more when I send my four sore judgments upon Je-ru'sa-lem, the sword, and the famine, and the noisome beast, and the pestilence, to cut off from it man and beast?

22 ¶ Yet, behold, therein shall be left a remnant that shall be brought forth, both sons and daughters: behold, they shall come forth unto you, and ye shall see their way and their doings: and ye shall be comforted concerning the evil that I have brought upon Je-ru'sa-lem, even concerning all that I have brought upon it.

23 And they shall comfort you, when ye see their ways and their doings: and ye shall know that I have not done without cause all that I have done in it, saith the Lord GOD.

15 AND the word of the LORD came unto me, saying,

2 Son of man, What is the vine tree more than any tree, or than a branch which is among the trees of the forest?

3 Shall wood be taken thereof to do any work? or will men take a pin of it to hang any vessel thereon?

4 Behold, it is cast into the fire for fuel; the fire devoureth both the ends of it, and the midst of it is burned. Is it meet for any work?

5 Behold, when it was whole, it was meet for no work: how much less shall it be meet yet for any work, when the fire hath devoured it, and it is burned?

6 ¶ Therefore thus saith the Lord GOD; As the vine tree among the trees of the forest, which I have given to the fire for fuel, so will I give the inhabitants of Je-ru'sa-lem.

7 And I will set my face against them; they shall go out from one fire, and another fire shall devour them; and ye shall know that I am the LORD, when I set my face against them.

8 And I will make the land desolate, because they have committed a trespass, saith the Lord GOD.

16 AGAIN the word of the LORD came unto me, saying,

2 Son of man, cause Je-ru'sa-lem to know her abominations,

3 And say, Thus saith the Lord GOD unto Je-ru'sa-lem; Thy birth and thy nativity is of the land of Ca'naan; thy father was an Am'or-ite, and thy mother an Hit'tite.

4 And as for thy nativity, in the day thou wast born thy navel was not cut, neither wast thou washed in water to supple thee; thou wast not salted at all, nor swaddled at all.

5 None eye pitied thee, to do any of these unto thee, to have compassion upon thee; but thou wast cast out in the open field, to the loathing of thy person, in the day that thou wast born.

6 ¶ And when I passed by thee, and saw thee polluted in thine own blood, I said unto thee when thou wast in thy blood, Live; yea, I said unto thee when thou wast in thy blood, Live.

7 I have caused thee to multiply as the bud of the field, and thou hast increased and waxen great, and thou art come to excellent ornaments: thy breasts are fashioned, and thine hair is grown, whereas thou wast naked and bare.

8 Now when I passed by thee, and looked upon thee, behold, thy time was the time of love; and I spread my skirt over thee, and covered thy nakedness: yea, I sware unto thee, and entered into a covenant with thee, saith the Lord GOD, and thou becamest mine.

9 Then washed I thee with water; yea, I throughly washed away thy blood from thee, and I anointed thee with oil.

10 I clothed thee also with broidered work, and shod thee with badgers' skin, and I girded thee about with fine linen, and I covered thee with silk.

11 I decked thee also with ornaments, and I put bracelets upon thy hands, and a chain on thy neck.

12 And I put a jewel on thy forehead, and earrings in thine ears, and a beautiful crown upon thine head.

13 Thus wast thou decked with gold and silver; and thy raiment was of fine linen, and silk, and broidered work; thou didst eat fine flour, and honey, and oil: and thou wast exceeding beautiful, and thou didst prosper into a kingdom.

14 And thy renown went forth among the heathen for thy beauty: for it was perfect through my comeliness, which I had put upon thee, saith the Lord GOD.

15 ¶ But thou didst trust in thine own beauty, and playedst the harlot because of thy renown, and pouredst out thy fornications on every one that passed by; his it was.

16 And of thy garments thou didst take, and deckedst thy high places with divers colours, and playedst the harlot thereupon: the like things shall not come, neither shall it be so.

17 Thou hast also taken thy fair jewels of my gold and of my silver, which I had given thee, and madest to thyself images of men, and didst commit whoredom with them,

18 And tookest thy broidered garments, and coveredst them: and thou hast set mine oil and mine incense before them.

19 My meat also which I gave thee, fine flour,

and oil, and honey, *wherewith* I fed thee, thou hast even set it before them for a sweet savour: and *thus* it was, saith the Lord GOD.

20 Moreover thou hast taken thy sons and thy daughters, whom thou hast borne unto me, and these hast thou sacrificed unto them to be devoured. *Is this* of thy whoredoms a small matter,

21 That thou hast slain my children, and delivered them to cause them to pass through *the fire* for them?

22 And in all thine abominations and thy whoredoms thou hast not remembered the days of thy youth, when thou wast naked and bare, *and* wast polluted in thy blood.

23 And it came to pass after all thy wickedness, (woe, woe unto thee! saith the Lord GOD;)

24 *That* thou hast also built unto thee an eminent place, and hast made thee an high place in every street.

25 Thou hast built thy high place at every head of the way, and hast made thy beauty to be abhorred, and hast opened thy feet to every one that passed by, and multiplied thy whoredoms.

26 Thou hast also committed fornication with the E-gyp′tians thy neighbours, great of flesh; and hast increased thy whoredoms, to provoke me to anger.

27 Behold, therefore I have stretched out my hand over thee, and have diminished thine ordinary *food*, and delivered thee unto the will of them that hate thee, the daughters of the Phi-lis′tines, which are ashamed of thy lewd way.

28 Thou hast played the whore also with the As-syr′i-ans, because thou wast unsatiable; yea, thou hast played the harlot with them, and yet couldest not be satisfied.

29 Thou hast moreover multiplied thy fornication in the land of Ca′naan unto Chal-de′a; and yet thou wast not satisfied herewith.

30 How weak is thine heart, saith the Lord GOD, seeing thou doest all these *things,* the work of an imperious whorish woman;

31 In that thou buildest thine eminent place in the head of every way, and makest thine high place in every street; and hast not been as an harlot, in that thou scornest hire;

32 *But as* a wife that committeth adultery, *which* taketh strangers instead of her husband!

33 They give gifts to all whores: but thou givest thy gifts to all thy lovers, and hirest them, that they may come unto thee on every side for thy whoredom.

34 And the contrary is in thee from *other* women in thy whoredoms, whereas none followeth thee to commit whoredoms: and in that thou givest a reward, and no reward is given unto thee, therefore thou art contrary.

35 ¶ Wherefore, O harlot, hear the word of the LORD:

36 Thus saith the Lord GOD; Because thy filthiness was poured out, and thy nakedness discovered through thy whoredoms with thy lovers, and with all the idols of thy abominations, and by the blood of thy children, which thou didst give unto them;

37 Behold, therefore I will gather all thy lovers, with whom thou hast taken pleasure, and all *them* that thou hast loved, with all *them* that thou hast hated; I will even gather them round about against thee, and will discover thy nakedness unto them, that they may see all thy nakedness.

38 And I will judge thee, as women that break wedlock and shed blood are judged; and I will give thee blood in fury and jealousy.

39 And I will also give thee into their hand, and they shall throw down thine eminent place, and shall break down thy high places; they shall strip thee also of thy clothes, and shall take thy fair jewels, and leave thee naked and bare.

40 They shall also bring up a company against thee, and they shall stone thee with stones, and thrust thee through with their swords.

41 And they shall burn thine houses with fire, and execute judgments upon thee in the sight of many women: and I will cause thee to cease from playing the harlot, and thou also shalt give no hire any more.

42 So will I make my fury toward thee to rest, and my jealousy shall depart from thee, and I will be quiet, and will be no more angry.

43 Because thou hast not remembered the days of thy youth, but hast fretted me in all these *things;* behold, therefore I also will recompense thy way upon *thine* head, saith the Lord GOD: and thou shalt not commit this lewdness above all thine abominations.

44 ¶ Behold, every one that useth proverbs shall use *this* proverb against thee, saying, As *is* the mother, *so is* her daughter.

45 Thou *art* thy mother's daughter, that loatheth her husband and her children; and thou *art* the sister of thy sisters, which loathed their husbands and their children: your mother *was* an Hit′tite, and your father an Am′or-ite.

46 And thine elder sister *is* Sa-ma′ri-a, she and her daughters that dwell at thy left hand: and thy younger sister, that dwelleth at thy right hand, *is* Sod′om and her daughters.

47 Yet hast thou not walked after their ways, nor done after their abominations: but, as *if that were* a very little *thing*, thou wast corrupted more than they in all thy ways.

48 *As* I live, saith the Lord GOD, Sod′om thy sister hath not done, she nor her daughters, as thou hast done, thou and thy daughters.

49 Behold, this was the iniquity of thy sister Sod′om, pride, fulness of bread, and abundance of idleness was in her and in her daughters, neither did she strengthen the hand of the poor and needy.

50 And they were haughty, and committed abomination before me: therefore I took them away as I saw *good*.

51 Neither hath Sa-ma′ri-a committed half of thy sins; but thou hast multiplied thine abominations more than they, and hast justified thy sisters in all thine abominations which thou hast done.

52 Thou also, which hast judged thy sisters, bear thine own shame for thy sins that thou hast committed more abominable than they: they are more righteous than thou: yea, be thou confounded also, and bear thy shame, in that thou hast justified thy sisters.

53 When I shall bring again their captivity, the captivity of Sod′om and her daughters, and the captivity of Sa-ma′ri-a and her daughters, then *will I bring again* the captivity of thy captives in the midst of them:

54 That thou mayest bear thine own shame, and mayest be confounded in all that thou hast done, in that thou art a comfort unto them.

55 When thy sisters, Sod′om and her daughters, shall return to their former estate, and Sa-ma′ri-a and her daughters shall return to their former estate, then thou and thy daughters shall return to your former estate.

56 For thy sister Sod′om was not mentioned by thy mouth in the day of thy pride,

57 Before thy wickedness was discovered, as

at the time of *thy* reproach of the daughters of Syr'i-a, and all *that are* round about her, the daughters of the Phi-lis'tines, which despise thee round about.

58 Thou hast borne thy lewdness and thine abominations, saith the LORD.

59 For thus saith the Lord GOD; I will even deal with thee as thou hast done, which hast despised the oath in breaking the covenant.

60 ¶ Nevertheless I will remember my covenant with thee in the days of thy youth, and I will establish unto thee an everlasting covenant.

61 Then thou shalt remember thy ways, and be ashamed, when thou shalt receive thy sisters, thine elder and thy younger: and I will give them unto thee for daughters, but not by thy covenant.

62 And I will establish my covenant with thee; and thou shalt know that I *am* the LORD:

63 That thou mayest remember, and be confounded, and never open thy mouth any more because of thy shame, when I am pacified toward thee for all that thou hast done, saith the Lord GOD.

17 AND the word of the LORD came unto me, saying,

2 Son of man, put forth a riddle, and speak a parable unto the house of Is'ra-el;

3 And say, Thus saith the Lord GOD; A great eagle with great wings, longwinged, full of feathers, which had divers colours, came unto Leb'a-non, and took the highest branch of the cedar:

4 He cropped off the top of his young twigs, and carried it into a land of traffick; he set it in a city of merchants.

5 He took also of the seed of the land, and planted it in a fruitful field; he placed *it* by great waters, *and* set it *as* a willow tree.

6 And it grew, and became a spreading vine of low stature, whose branches turned toward him, and the roots thereof were under him: so it became a vine, and brought forth branches, and shot forth sprigs.

7 There was also another great eagle with great wings and many feathers: and, behold, this vine did bend her roots toward him, and shot forth her branches toward him, that he might water it by the furrows of her plantation.

8 It was planted in a good soil by great waters, that it might bring forth branches, and that it might bear fruit, that it might be a goodly vine.

9 Say thou, Thus saith the Lord GOD; Shall it prosper? shall he not pull up the roots thereof, and cut off the fruit thereof, that it wither? it shall wither in all the leaves of her spring, even without great power or many people to pluck it up by the roots thereof.

10 Yea, behold, *being* planted, shall it prosper? shall it not utterly wither, when the east wind toucheth it? it shall wither in the furrows where it grew.

11 ¶ Moreover the word of the LORD came unto me, saying,

12 Say now to the rebellious house, Know ye not what these *things mean?* tell *them*, Behold, the king of Bab'y-lon is come to Je-ru'sa-lem, and hath taken the king thereof, and the princes thereof, and led them with him to Bab'y-lon;

13 And hath taken of the king's seed, and made a covenant with him, and hath taken an oath of him: he hath also taken the mighty of the land:

14 That the kingdom might be base, that it might not lift itself up, *but* that by keeping of his covenant it might stand.

15 But he rebelled against him in sending his ambassadors into E'gypt, that they might give him horses and much people. Shall he prosper? shall he escape that doeth such *things?* or shall he break the covenant, and be delivered?

16 *As* I live, saith the Lord GOD, surely in the place *where* the king *dwelleth* that made him king, whose oath he despised, and whose covenant he brake, *even* with him in the midst of Bab'y-lon he shall die.

17 Neither shall Pha'raoh with *his* mighty army and great company make for him in the war, by casting up mounts, and building forts, to cut off many persons:

18 Seeing he despised the oath by breaking the covenant, when, lo, he had given his hand, and hath done all these *things*, he shall not escape.

19 Therefore thus saith the Lord GOD; *As* I live, surely mine oath that he hath despised, and my covenant that he hath broken, even it will I recompense upon his own head.

20 And I will spread my net upon him, and he shall be taken in my snare, and I will bring him to Bab'y-lon, and will plead with him there for his trespass that he hath trespassed against me.

21 And all his fugitives with all his bands shall fall by the sword, and they that remain shall be scattered toward all winds: and ye shall know that I the LORD have spoken *it*.

22 ¶ Thus saith the Lord GOD; I will also take of the highest branch of the high cedar, and will set *it*: I will crop off from the top of his young twigs a tender one, and will plant *it* upon an high mountain and eminent:

23 In the mountain of the height of Is'ra-el will I plant it; and it shall bring forth boughs, and bear fruit, and be a goodly cedar: and under it shall dwell all fowl of every wing; in the shadow of the branches thereof shall they dwell.

24 And all the trees of the field shall know that I the LORD have brought down the high tree, have exalted the low tree, have dried up the green tree, and have made the dry tree to flourish: I the LORD have spoken and have done *it*.

18 THE word of the LORD came unto me again, saying,

2 What mean ye, that ye use this proverb concerning the land of Is'ra-el, saying, The fathers have eaten sour grapes, and the children's teeth are set on edge?

3 *As* I live, saith the Lord GOD, ye shall not have *occasion* any more to use this proverb in Is'ra-el.

4 Behold, all souls are mine; as the soul of the father, so also the soul of the son is mine: the soul that sinneth, it shall die.

5 ¶ But if a man be just, and do that which is lawful and right,

6 *And* hath not eaten upon the mountains, neither hath lifted up his eyes to the idols of the house of Is'ra-el, neither hath defiled his neighbour's wife, neither hath come near to a menstruous woman,

7 And hath not oppressed any, *but* hath restored to the debtor his pledge, hath spoiled none by violence, hath given his bread to the hungry, and hath covered the naked with a garment;

8 He *that* hath not given forth upon usury, neither hath taken any increase, *that* hath with-

drawn his hand from iniquity, hath executed true judgment between man and man,

9 Hath walked in my statutes, and hath kept my judgments, to deal truly; he *is* just, he shall surely live, saith the Lord GOD.

10 ¶ If he beget a son *that is* a robber, a shedder of blood, and *that* doeth the like to *any* one of these *things*,

11 And that doeth not any of those *duties*, but even hath eaten upon the mountains, and defiled his neighbour's wife,

12 Hath oppressed the poor and needy, hath spoiled by violence, hath not restored the pledge, and hath lifted up his eyes to the idols, hath committed abomination.

13 Hath given forth upon usury, and hath taken increase: shall he then live? he shall not live: he hath done all these abominations; he shall surely die; his blood shall be upon him.

14 Now, lo, *if* he beget a son, that seeth all his father's sins which he hath done, and considereth, and doeth not such like,

15 *That* hath not eaten upon the mountains, neither hath lifted up his eyes to the idols of the house of Is'ra-el, hath not defiled his neighbour's wife,

16 Neither hath oppressed any, hath not withholden the pledge, neither hath spoiled by violence, *but* hath given his bread to the hungry, and hath covered the naked with a garment,

17 *That* hath taken off his hand from the poor, *that* hath not received usury nor increase, hath executed my judgments, hath walked in my statutes; he shall not die for the iniquity of his father, he shall surely live.

18 *As for* his father, because he cruelly oppressed, spoiled his brother by violence, and did *that* which *is* not good among his people, lo, even he shall die in his iniquity.

19 Yet say ye, Why? doth not the son bear the iniquity of the father? When the son hath done that which is lawful and right, *and* hath kept all my statutes, and hath done them, he shall surely live.

20 The soul that sinneth, it shall die. The son shall not bear the iniquity of the father, neither shall the father bear the iniquity of the son: the righteousness of the righteous shall be upon him, and the wickedness of the wicked shall be upon him.

21 But if the wicked will turn from all his sins that he hath committed, and keep all my statutes, and do that which is lawful and right, he shall surely live, he shall not die.

22 All his transgressions that he hath committed, they shall not be mentioned unto him: in his righteousness that he hath done he shall live.

23 Have I any pleasure at all that the wicked should die? saith the Lord GOD: *and* not that he should return from his ways, and live?

24 ¶ But when the righteous turneth away from his righteousness, and committeth iniquity, *and* doeth according to all the abominations that the wicked *man* doeth, shall he live? All his righteousness that he hath done shall not be mentioned: in his trespass that he hath trespassed, and in his sin that he hath sinned, in them shall he die.

25 ¶ Yet ye say, The way of the Lord is not equal. Hear now, O house of Is'ra-el; Is not my way equal? are not your ways unequal?

26 When a righteous *man* turneth away from his righteousness, and committeth iniquity, and dieth in them; for his iniquity that he hath done shall he die.

27 Again, when the wicked *man* turneth away from his wickedness that he hath committed, and doeth that which is lawful and right, he shall save his soul alive.

28 Because he considereth, and turneth away from all his transgressions that he hath committed, he shall surely live, he shall not die.

29 Yet saith the house of Is'ra-el, The way of the Lord is not equal. O house of Is'ra-el, are not my ways equal? are not your ways unequal?

30 Therefore I will judge you, O house of Is'-ra-el, every one according to his ways, saith the Lord GOD. Repent, and turn *yourselves* from all your transgressions; so iniquity shall not be your ruin.

31 ¶ Cast away from you all your transgressions, whereby ye have transgressed; and make you a new heart and a new spirit: for why will ye die, O house of Is'ra-el?

32 For I have no pleasure in the death of him that dieth, saith the Lord GOD: wherefore turn *yourselves*, and live ye.

19 MOREOVER take thou up a lamentation for the princes of Is'ra-el,

2 And say, What *is* thy mother? A lioness: she lay down among lions, she nourished her whelps among young lions.

3 And she brought up one of her whelps: it became a young lion, and it learned to catch the prey; it devoured men.

4 The nations also heard of him; he was taken in their pit, and they brought him with chains unto the land of E'gypt.

5 Now when she saw that she had waited, *and* her hope was lost, then she took another of her whelps, *and* made him a young lion.

6 And he went up and down among the lions, he became a young lion, and learned to catch the prey, *and* devoured men.

7 And he knew their desolate palaces, and he laid waste their cities; and the land was desolate, and the fulness thereof, by the noise of his roaring.

8 Then the nations set against him on every side from the provinces, and spread their net over him: he was taken in their pit.

9 And they put him in ward in chains, and brought him to the king of Bab'y-lon: they brought him into holds, that his voice should no more be heard upon the mountains of Is'ra-el.

10 ¶ Thy mother *is* like a vine in thy blood, planted by the waters: she was fruitful and full of branches by reason of many waters.

11 And she had strong rods for the sceptres of them that bare rule, and her stature was exalted among the thick branches, and she appeared in her height with the multitude of her branches.

12 But she was plucked up in fury, she was cast down to the ground, and the east wind dried up her fruit: her strong rods were broken and withered; the fire consumed them.

13 And now she *is* planted in the wilderness, in a dry and thirsty ground.

14 And fire is gone out of a rod of her branches, *which* hath devoured her fruit, so that she hath no strong rod *to be* a sceptre to rule. This *is* a lamentation, and shall be for a lamentation.

20 AND it came to pass in the seventh year, in the fifth *month*, the tenth *day* of the month, *that* certain of the elders of Is'ra-el came to enquire of the LORD, and sat before me.

2 Then came the word of the LORD unto me, saying,

3 Son of man, speak unto the elders of Is'ra-el, and say unto them, Thus saith the Lord GOD; Are ye come to enquire of me? As I live, saith the Lord GOD, I will not be enquired of by you.

4 Wilt thou judge them, son of man, wilt thou judge them? cause them to know the abominations of their fathers:

5 ¶ And say unto them, Thus saith the Lord GOD; In the day when I chose Is'ra-el, and lifted up mine hand unto the seed of the house of Ja'-cob, and made myself known unto them in the land of E'gypt, when I lifted up mine hand unto them, saying, I am the LORD your God;

6 In the day that I lifted up mine hand unto them, to bring them forth of the land of E'gypt into a land that I had espied for them, flowing with milk and honey, which is the glory of all lands:

7 Then said I unto them, Cast ye away every man the abominations of his eyes, and defile not yourselves with the idols of E'gypt: I am the LORD your God.

8 But they rebelled against me, and would not hearken unto me: they did not every man cast away the abominations of their eyes, neither did they forsake the idols of E'gypt: then I said, I will pour out my fury upon them, to accomplish my anger against them in the midst of the land of E'gypt.

9 But I wrought for my name's sake, that it should not be polluted before the heathen, among whom they were, in whose sight I made myself known unto them, in bringing them forth out of the land of E'gypt.

10 ¶ Wherefore I caused them to go forth out of the land of E'gypt, and brought them into the wilderness.

11 And I gave them my statutes, and shewed them my judgments, which if a man do, he shall even live in them.

12 Moreover also I gave them my sabbaths, to be a sign between me and them, that they might know that I am the LORD that sanctify them.

13 But the house of Is'ra-el rebelled against me in the wilderness: they walked not in my statutes, and they despised my judgments, which if a man do, he shall even live in them; and my sabbaths they greatly polluted: then I said, I would pour out my fury upon them in the wilderness, to consume them.

14 But I wrought for my name's sake, that it should not be polluted before the heathen, in whose sight I brought them out.

15 Yet also I lifted up my hand unto them in the wilderness, that I would not bring them into the land which I had given them, flowing with milk and honey, which is the glory of all lands;

16 Because they despised my judgments, and walked not in my statutes, but polluted my sabbaths: for their heart went after their idols.

17 Nevertheless mine eye spared them from destroying them, neither did I make an end of them in the wilderness.

18 But I said unto their children in the wilderness, Walk ye not in the statutes of your fathers, neither observe their judgments, nor defile yourselves with their idols:

19 I am the LORD your God; walk in my statutes, and keep my judgments, and do them;

20 And hallow my sabbaths; and they shall be a sign between me and you, that ye may know that I am the LORD your God.

21 Notwithstanding the children rebelled against me: they walked not in my statutes, neither kept my judgments to do them, which if a man do, he shall even live in them; they pol-

luted my sabbaths: then I said, I would pour out my fury upon them, to accomplish my anger against them in the wilderness.

22 Nevertheless I withdrew mine hand, and wrought for my name's sake, that it should not be polluted in the sight of the heathen, in whose sight I brought them forth.

23 I lifted up mine hand unto them also in the wilderness, that I would scatter them among the heathen, and disperse them through the countries;

24 Because they had not executed my judgments, but had despised my statutes, and had polluted my sabbaths, and their eyes were after their fathers' idols.

25 Wherefore I gave them also statutes that were not good, and judgments whereby they should not live;

26 And I polluted them in their own gifts, in that they caused to pass through the fire all that openeth the womb, that I might make them desolate, to the end that they might know that I am the LORD.

27 ¶ Therefore, son of man, speak unto the house of Is'ra-el, and say unto them, Thus saith the Lord GOD; Yet in this your fathers have blasphemed me, in that they have committed a trespass against me.

28 For when I had brought them into the land, for the which I lifted up mine hand to give it to them, then they saw every high hill, and all the thick trees, and they offered there their sacrifices, and there they presented the provocation of their offering: there also they made their sweet savour, and poured out there their drink offerings.

29 Then I said unto them, What is the high place whereunto ye go? And the name thereof is called Ba'mah unto this day.

30 Wherefore say unto the house of Is'ra-el, Thus saith the Lord GOD; Are ye polluted after the manner of your fathers? and commit ye whoredom after their abominations?

31 For when ye offer your gifts, when ye make your sons to pass through the fire, ye pollute yourselves with all your idols, even unto this day: and shall I be enquired of by you, O house of Is'ra-el? As I live, saith the Lord GOD, I will not be enquired of by you.

32 And that which cometh into your mind shall not be at all, that ye say, We will be as the heathen, as the families of the countries, to serve wood and stone.

33 ¶ As I live, saith the Lord GOD, surely with a mighty hand, and with a stretched out arm, and with fury poured out, will I rule over you:

34 And I will bring you out from the people, and will gather you out of the countries wherein ye are scattered, with a mighty hand, and with a stretched out arm, and with fury poured out.

35 And I will bring you into the wilderness of the people, and there will I plead with you face to face.

36 Like as I pleaded with your fathers in the wilderness of the land of E'gypt, so will I plead with you, saith the Lord GOD.

37 And I will cause you to pass under the rod, and I will bring you into the bond of the covenant:

38 And I will purge out from among you the rebels, and them that transgress against me: I will bring them forth out of the country where they sojourn, and they shall not enter into the land of Is'ra-el: and ye shall know that I am the LORD.

39 As for you, O house of Is'ra-el, thus saith

the Lord God; Go ye, serve ye every one his idols, and hereafter *also*, if ye will not hearken unto me: but pollute ye my holy name no more with your gifts, and with your idols.

40 For in mine holy mountain, in the mountain of the height of Is'ra-el, saith the Lord God, there shall all the house of Is'ra-el, all of them in the land, serve me: there will I accept them, and there will I require your offerings, and the firstfruits of your oblations, with all your holy things.

41 I will accept you with your sweet savour, when I bring you out from the people, and gather you out of the countries wherein ye have been scattered; and I will be sanctified in you before the heathen.

42 And ye shall know that I *am* the LORD, when I shall bring you into the land of Is'ra-el, into the country *for* the which I lifted up mine hand to give it to your fathers.

43 And there shall ye remember your ways, and all your doings, wherein ye have been defiled; and ye shall loathe yourselves in your own sight for all your evils that ye have committed.

44 And ye shall know that I *am* the LORD, when I have wrought with you for my name's sake, not according to your wicked ways, nor according to your corrupt doings, O ye house of Is'ra-el, saith the Lord God.

45 ¶ Moreover the word of the LORD came unto me, saying,

46 Son of man, set thy face toward the south, and drop *thy word* toward the south, and prophesy against the forest of the south field;

47 And say to the forest of the south, Hear the word of the LORD; Thus saith the Lord God; Behold, I will kindle a fire in thee, and it shall devour every green tree in thee, and every dry tree: the flaming flame shall not be quenched, and all faces from the south to the north shall be burned therein.

48 And all flesh shall see that I the LORD have kindled it: it shall not be quenched.

49 Then said I, Ah Lord God! they say of me, Doth he not speak parables?

21 AND the word of the LORD came unto me, saying,

2 Son of man, set thy face toward Je-ru'sa-lem, and drop *thy word* toward the holy places, and prophesy against the land of Is'ra-el,

3 And say to the land of Is'ra-el, Thus saith the LORD; Behold, I *am* against thee, and will draw forth my sword out of his sheath, and will cut off from thee the righteous and the wicked.

4 Seeing then that I will cut off from thee the righteous and the wicked, therefore shall my sword go forth out of his sheath against all flesh from the south to the north:

5 That all flesh may know that I the LORD have drawn forth my sword out of his sheath: it shall not return any more.

6 Sigh therefore, thou son of man, with the breaking of *thy* loins; and with bitterness sigh before their eyes.

7 And it shall be, when they say unto thee, Wherefore sighest thou? that thou shalt answer, For the tidings; because it cometh: and every heart shall melt, and all hands shall be feeble, and every spirit shall faint, and all knees shall be weak *as* water: behold, it cometh, and shall be brought to pass, saith the Lord God.

8 ¶ Again the word of the LORD came unto me, saying,

9 Son of man, prophesy, and say, Thus saith the LORD; Say, A sword, a sword is sharpened, and also furbished:

10 It is sharpened to make a sore slaughter; it is furbished that it may glitter: should we then make mirth? it contemneth the rod of my son, *as* every tree.

11 And he hath given it to be furbished, that it may be handled: this sword is sharpened, and it is furbished, to give it into the hand of the slayer.

12 Cry and howl, son of man: for it shall be upon my people, it *shall be* upon all the princes of Is'ra-el: terrors by reason of the sword shall be upon my people: smite therefore upon *thy* thigh.

13 Because *it is* a trial, and what if *the sword* contemn even the rod? it shall be no *more*, saith the LORD God.

14 Thou therefore, son of man, prophesy, and smite *thine* hands together, and let the sword be doubled the third time, the sword of the slain: it *is* the sword of the great *men that are* slain, which entereth into their privy chambers.

15 I have set the point of the sword against all their gates, that *their* heart may faint, and *their* ruins be multiplied: ah! *it is* made bright, *it* is wrapped up for the slaughter.

16 Go thee one way or other, *either* on the right hand, *or* on the left, whithersoever thy face *is* set.

17 I will also smite mine hands together, and I will cause my fury to rest: I the LORD have said *it*.

18 ¶ The word of the LORD came unto me again, saying,

19 Also, thou son of man, appoint thee two ways, that the sword of the king of Bab'y-lon may come: both twain shall come forth out of one land: and choose thou a place, choose *it* at the head of the way to the city.

20 Appoint a way, that the sword may come to Rab'bath of the Am'mon-ites, and to Ju'dah in Je-ru'sa-lem the defenced.

21 For the king of Bab'y-lon stood at the parting of the way, at the head of the two ways, to use divination: he made *his* arrows bright, he consulted with images, he looked in the liver.

22 At his right hand was the divination for Je-ru'sa-lem, to appoint captains, to open the mouth in the slaughter, to lift up the voice with shouting, to appoint *battering* rams against the gates, to cast a mount, *and* to build a fort.

23 And it shall be unto them as a false divination in their sight, to them that have sworn oaths: but he will call to remembrance the iniquity, that they may be taken.

24 Therefore thus saith the Lord God; Because ye have made your iniquity to be remembered, in that your transgressions are discovered, so that in all your doings your sins do appear; because, *I say*, that ye are come to remembrance, ye shall be taken with the hand.

25 ¶ And thou, profane wicked prince of Is'-ra-el, whose day is come, when iniquity *shall have* an end,

26 Thus saith the Lord God; Remove the diadem, and take off the crown: this *shall* not *be* the same: exalt *him that is* low, and abase *him that is* high.

27 I will overturn, overturn, overturn, it: and it shall be no *more*, until he come whose right it is; and I will give it *him*.

28 ¶ And thou, son of man, prophesy and say, Thus saith the Lord God concerning the Am'mon-ites, and concerning their reproach; even say thou, The sword, the sword *is* drawn: for the slaughter *it is* furbished, to consume because of the glittering:

29 Whiles they see vanity unto thee, whiles

they divine a lie unto thee, to bring thee upon the necks of *them that are* slain, of the wicked, whose day is come, when their iniquity *shall have* an end.

30 Shall I cause *it* to return into his sheath? I will judge thee in the place where thou wast created, in the land of thy nativity.

31 And I will pour out mine indignation upon thee, I will blow against thee in the fire of my wrath, and deliver thee into the hand of brutish men, *and* skilful to destroy.

32 Thou shalt be for fuel to the fire; thy blood shall be in the midst of the land; thou shalt be no *more* remembered: for I the LORD have spoken *it.*

22 MOREOVER the word of the LORD came unto me, saying,

2 Now, thou son of man, wilt thou judge, wilt thou judge the bloody city? yea, thou shalt shew her all her abominations.

3 Then say thou, Thus saith the Lord GOD, The city sheddeth blood in the midst of it, that her time may come, and maketh idols against herself to defile herself.

4 Thou art become guilty in thy blood that thou hast shed; and hast defiled thyself in thine idols which thou hast made; and thou hast caused thy days to draw near, and art come *even* unto thy years: therefore have I made thee a reproach unto the heathen, and a mocking to all countries.

5 *Those that be* near, and *those that be* far from thee, shall mock thee, *which art* infamous *and* much vexed.

6 Behold, the princes of Is'ra-el, every one were in thee to their power to shed blood.

7 In thee have they set light by father and mother: in the midst of thee have they dealt by oppression with the stranger: in thee have they vexed the fatherless and the widow.

8 Thou hast despised mine holy things, and hast profaned my sabbaths.

9 In thee are men that carry tales to shed blood: and in thee they eat upon the mountains: in the midst of thee they commit lewdness.

10 In thee have they discovered their fathers' nakedness: in thee have they humbled her that was set apart for pollution.

11 And one hath committed abomination with his neighbour's wife; and another hath lewdly defiled his daughter in law; and another in thee hath humbled his sister, his father's daughter.

12 In thee have they taken gifts to shed blood; thou hast taken usury and increase, and thou hast greedily gained of thy neighbours by extortion, and hast forgotten me, saith the Lord GOD.

13 ¶ Behold, therefore I have smitten mine hand at thy dishonest gain which thou hast made, and at thy blood which hath been in the midst of thee.

14 Can thine heart endure, or can thine hands be strong, in the days that I shall deal with thee? I the LORD have spoken *it,* and will do *it.*

15 And I will scatter thee among the heathen, and disperse thee in the countries, and will consume thy filthiness out of thee.

16 And thou shalt take thine inheritance in thyself in the sight of the heathen, and thou shalt know that I *am* the LORD.

17 And the word of the LORD came unto me, saying,

18 Son of man, the house of Is'ra-el is to me become dross: all they *are* brass, and tin, and iron, and lead, in the midst of the furnace; they are *even* the dross of silver.

19 Therefore thus saith the Lord GOD; Because ye are all become dross, behold, therefore I will gather you into the midst of Je-ru'sa-lem.

20 *As* they gather silver, and brass, and iron, and lead, and tin, into the midst of the furnace, to blow the fire upon it, to melt *it;* so will I gather *you* in mine anger and in my fury, and I will leave *you* there, and melt you.

21 Yea, I will gather you, and blow upon you in the fire of my wrath, and ye shall be melted in the midst thereof.

22 As silver is melted in the midst of the furnace, so shall ye be melted in the midst thereof; and ye shall know that I the LORD have poured out my fury upon you.

23 ¶ And the word of the LORD came unto me, saying,

24 Son of man, say unto her, Thou *art* the land that is not cleansed, nor rained upon in the day of indignation.

25 *There is* a conspiracy of her prophets in the midst thereof, like a roaring lion ravening the prey; they have devoured souls; they have taken the treasure and precious things; they have made her many widows in the midst thereof.

26 Her priests have violated my law, and have profaned mine holy things: they have put no difference between the holy and profane, neither have they shewed *difference* between the unclean and the clean, and have hid their eyes from my sabbaths, and I am profaned among them.

27 Her princes in the midst thereof *are* like wolves ravening the prey, to shed blood, *and* to destroy souls, to get dishonest gain.

28 And her prophets have daubed them with untempered *morter,* seeing vanity, and divining lies unto them, saying, Thus saith the Lord GOD, when the LORD hath not spoken.

29 The people of the land have used oppression, and exercised robbery, and have vexed the poor and needy: yea, they have oppressed the stranger wrongfully.

30 And I sought for a man among them, that should make up the hedge, and stand in the gap before me for the land, that I should not destroy it: but I found none.

31 Therefore have I poured out mine indignation upon them; I have consumed them with the fire of my wrath: their own way have I recompensed upon their heads, saith the Lord GOD.

23 THE word of the LORD came again unto me, saying,

2 Son of man, there were two women, the daughters of one mother:

3 And they committed whoredoms in E'gypt; they committed whoredoms in their youth: there were their breasts pressed, and there they bruised the teats of their virginity.

4 And the names of them *were* A-ho'lah the elder, and A-hol'i-bah her sister: and they were mine, and they bare sons and daughters. Thus *were* their names; Sa-ma'ri-a *is* A-ho'lah, and Je-ru'sa-lem A-hol'i-bah.

5 And A-ho'lah played the harlot when she was mine; and she doted on her lovers, on the As-syr'i-ans *her* neighbours,

6 *Which were* clothed with blue, captains and rulers, all of them desirable young men, horsemen riding upon horses.

7 Thus she committed her whoredoms with them, with all them *that were* the chosen men

of As-syr'i-a, and with all on whom she doted: with all their idols she defiled herself.

8 Neither left she her whoredoms *brought* from E'gypt: for in her youth they lay with her, and they bruised the breasts of her virginity, and poured their whoredom upon her.

9 Wherefore I have delivered her into the hand of her lovers, into the hand of the As-syr'i-ans, upon whom she doted.

10 These discovered her nakedness: they took her sons and her daughters, and slew her with the sword: and she became famous among women; for they had executed judgment upon her.

11 And when her sister A-hol'i-bah saw *this*, she was more corrupt in her inordinate love than she, and in her whoredoms more than her sister in *her* whoredoms.

12 She doted upon the As-syr'i-ans *her* neighbours, captains and rulers clothed most gorgeously, horsemen riding upon horses, all of them desirable young men.

13 Then I saw that she was defiled, *that* they *took* both one way,

14 And *that* she increased her whoredoms: for when she saw men pourtrayed upon the wall, the images of the Chal-de'ans pourtrayed with vermilion,

15 Girded with girdles upon their loins, exceeding in dyed attire upon their heads, all of them princes to look to, after the manner of the Bab-y-lo'ni-ans of Chal-de'a, the land of their nativity:

16 And as soon as she saw them with her eyes, she doted upon them, and sent messengers unto them into Chal-de'a.

17 And the Bab-y-lo'ni-ans came to her into the bed of love, and they defiled her with their whoredom, and she was polluted with them, and her mind was alienated from them.

18 So she discovered her whoredoms, and discovered her nakedness: then my mind was alienated from her, like as my mind was alienated from her sister.

19 Yet she multiplied her whoredoms, in calling to remembrance the days of her youth, wherein she had played the harlot in the land of E'gypt.

20 For she doted upon their paramours, whose flesh *is as* the flesh of asses, and whose issue *is like* the issue of horses.

21 Thus thou calledst to remembrance the lewdness of thy youth, in bruising thy teats by the E-gyp'tians for the paps of thy youth.

22 ¶ Therefore, O A-hol'i-bah, thus saith the Lord GOD; Behold, I will raise up thy lovers against thee, from whom thy mind is alienated, and I will bring them against thee on every side;

23 The Bab-y-lo'ni-ans, and all the Chal-de'-ans, Pe'kod, and Sho'a, and Ko'a, *and* all the As-syr'i-ans with them: all of them desirable young men, captains and rulers, great lords and renowned, all of them riding upon horses.

24 And they shall come against thee with chariots, wagons, and wheels, and with an assembly of people, *which* shall set against thee the buckler and shield and helmet round about: and I will set judgment before them, and they shall judge thee according to their judgments.

25 And I will set my jealousy against thee, and they shall deal furiously with thee: they shall take away thy nose and thine ears; and thy remnant shall fall by the sword: they shall take thy sons and thy daughters; and thy residue shall be devoured by the fire.

26 They shall also strip thee out of thy clothes, and take away thy fair jewels.

27 Thus will I make thy lewdness to cease from thee, and thy whoredom *brought* from the land of E'gypt: so that thou shalt not lift up thine eyes unto them, nor remember E'gypt any more.

28 For thus saith the Lord GOD; Behold, I will deliver thee into the hand *of them* whom thou hatest, into the hand *of them* from whom thy mind is alienated:

29 And they shall deal with thee hatefully, and shall take away all thy labour, and shall leave thee naked and bare: and the nakedness of thy whoredoms shall be discovered, both thy lewdness and thy whoredoms.

30 I will do these *things* unto thee, because thou hast gone a whoring after the heathen, *and* because thou art polluted with their idols.

31 Thou hast walked in the way of thy sister; therefore will I give her cup into thine hand.

32 Thus saith the Lord GOD; Thou shalt drink of thy sister's cup deep and large: thou shalt be laughed to scorn and had in derision; it containeth much.

33 Thou shalt be filled with drunkenness and sorrow, with the cup of astonishment and desolation, with the cup of thy sister Sa-ma'ri-a.

34 Thou shalt even drink it and suck *it* out, and thou shalt break the sherds thereof, and pluck off thine own breasts: for I have spoken *it*, saith the Lord GOD.

35 Therefore thus saith the Lord GOD; Because thou hast forgotten me, and cast me behind thy back, therefore bear thou also thy lewdness and thy whoredoms.

36 ¶ The LORD said moreover unto me; Son of man, wilt thou judge A-ho'lah and A-hol'i-bah? yea, declare unto them their abominations;

37 That they have committed adultery, and blood *is* in their hands, and with their idols have they committed adultery, and have also caused their sons, whom they bare unto me, to pass for them through *the fire*, to devour *them*.

38 Moreover this they have done unto me: they have defiled my sanctuary in the same day, and have profaned my sabbaths.

39 For when they had slain their children to their idols, then they came the same day into my sanctuary to profane it; and, lo, thus have they done in the midst of mine house.

40 And furthermore, that ye have sent for men to come from far, unto whom a messenger *was* sent; and, lo, they came: for whom thou didst wash thyself, paintedst thy eyes, and deckedst thyself with ornaments,

41 And satest upon a stately bed, and a table prepared before it, whereupon thou hast set mine incense and mine oil.

42 And a voice of a multitude being at ease *was* with her: and with the men of the common sort *were* brought Sa-be'ans from the wilderness, which put bracelets upon their hands, and beautiful crowns upon their heads.

43 Then said I unto *her that was* old in adulteries, Will they now commit whoredoms with her, and she *with them*?

44 Yet they went in unto her, as they go in unto a woman that playeth the harlot: so went they in unto A-ho'lah and unto A-hol'i-bah, the lewd women.

45 ¶ And the righteous men, they shall judge them after the manner of adulteresses, and after the manner of women that shed blood; because they *are* adulteresses, and blood *is* in their hands.

46 For thus saith the Lord GOD; I will bring

up a company upon them, and will give them to be removed and spoiled.

47 And the company shall stone them with stones, and dispatch them with their swords; they shall slay their sons and their daughters, and burn up their houses with fire.

48 Thus will I cause lewdness to cease out of the land, that all women may be taught not to do after your lewdness.

49 And they shall recompense your lewdness upon you, and ye shall bear the sins of your idols: and ye shall know that I am the Lord GOD.

24 AGAIN in the ninth year, in the tenth month, in the tenth day of the month, the word of the LORD came unto me, saying,

2 Son of man, write thee the name of the day, even of this same day: the king of Bab'y-lon set himself against Je-ru'sa-lem this same day.

3 And utter a parable unto the rebellious house, and say unto them, Thus saith the Lord GOD; Set on a pot, set it on, and also pour water into it:

4 Gather the pieces thereof into it, even every good piece, the thigh, and the shoulder; fill it with the choice bones.

5 Take the choice of the flock, and burn also the bones under it, and make it boil well, and let them seethe the bones of it therein.

6 ¶ Wherefore thus saith the Lord GOD; Woe to the bloody city, to the pot whose scum is therein, and whose scum is not gone out of it! bring it out piece by piece; let no lot fall upon it.

7 For her blood is in the midst of her; she set it upon the top of a rock; she poured it not upon the ground, to cover it with dust;

8 That it might cause fury to come up to take vengeance; I have set her blood upon the top of a rock, that it should not be covered.

9 Therefore thus saith the Lord GOD; Woe to the bloody city! I will even make the pile for fire great.

10 Heap on wood, kindle the fire, consume the flesh, and spice it well, and let the bones be burned.

11 Then set it empty upon the coals thereof, that the brass of it may be hot, and may burn, and that the filthiness of it may be molten in it, that the scum of it may be consumed.

12 She hath wearied herself with lies, and her great scum went not forth out of her: her scum shall be in the fire.

13 In thy filthiness is lewdness: because I have purged thee, and thou wast not purged, thou shalt not be purged from thy filthiness any more, till I have caused my fury to rest upon thee.

14 I the LORD have spoken it: it shall come to pass, and I will do it; I will not go back, neither will I spare, neither will I repent; according to thy ways, and according to thy doings, shall they judge thee, saith the Lord GOD.

15 ¶ Also the word of the LORD came unto me, saying,

16 Son of man, behold, I take away from thee the desire of thine eyes with a stroke: yet neither shalt thou mourn nor weep, neither shall thy tears run down.

17 Forbear to cry, make no mourning for the dead, bind the tire of thine head upon thee, and put on thy shoes upon thy feet, and cover not thy lips, and eat not the bread of men.

18 So I spake unto the people in the morning: and at even my wife died; and I did in the morning as I was commanded.

19 ¶ And the people said unto me, Wilt thou

not tell us what these things are to us, that thou doest so?

20 Then I answered them, The word of the LORD came unto me, saying,

21 Speak unto the house of Is'ra-el, Thus saith the Lord GOD; Behold, I will profane my sanctuary, the excellency of your strength, the desire of your eyes, and that which your soul pitieth; and your sons and your daughters whom ye have left shall fall by the sword.

22 And ye shall do as I have done: ye shall not cover your lips, nor eat the bread of men.

23 And your tires shall be upon your heads, and your shoes upon your feet: ye shall not mourn nor weep; but ye shall pine away for your iniquities, and mourn one toward another.

24 Thus E-ze'ki-el is unto you a sign: according to all that he hath done shall ye do: and when this cometh, ye shall know that I am the Lord GOD.

25 Also, thou son of man, shall it not be in the day when I take from them their strength, the joy of their glory, the desire of their eyes, and that whereupon they set their minds, their sons and their daughters,

26 That he that escapeth in that day shall come unto thee, to cause thee to hear it with thine ears?

27 In that day shall thy mouth be opened to him which is escaped, and thou shalt speak, and be no more dumb: and thou shalt be a sign unto them; and they shall know that I am the LORD.

25 THE word of the LORD came again unto me, saying,

2 Son of man, set thy face against the Am'mon-ites, and prophesy against them;

3 And say unto the Am'mon-ites, Hear the word of the Lord GOD; Thus saith the Lord GOD; Because thou saidst, Aha, against my sanctuary, when it was profaned; and against the land of Is'ra-el, when it was desolate; and against the house of Ju'dah, when they went into captivity;

4 Behold, therefore I will deliver thee to the men of the east for a possession, and they shall set their palaces in thee, and make their dwellings in thee: they shall eat thy fruit, and they shall drink thy milk.

5 And I will make Rab'bah a stable for camels, and the Am'mon-ites a couching place for flocks: and ye shall know that I am the LORD.

6 For thus saith the Lord GOD; Because thou hast clapped thine hands, and stamped with the feet, and rejoiced in heart with all thy despite against the land of Is'ra-el;

7 Behold, therefore I will stretch out mine hand upon thee, and will deliver thee for a spoil to the heathen; and I will cut thee off from the people, and I will cause thee to perish out of the countries: I will destroy thee; and thou shalt know that I am the LORD.

8 ¶ Thus saith the Lord GOD; Because that Mo'ab and Se'ir do say, Behold, the house of Ju'dah is like unto all the heathen;

9 Therefore, behold, I will open the side of Mo'ab from the cities, from his cities which are on his frontiers, the glory of the country, Beth-jesh'i-moth, Ba'al-me'on, and Kir-i-a-tha'im,

10 Unto the men of the east with the Am'mon-ites, and will give them in possession, that the Am'mon-ites may not be remembered among the nations.

11 And I will execute judgments upon Mo'ab; and they shall know that I am the LORD.

12 ¶ Thus saith the Lord GOD; Because that E'dom hath dealt against the house of Ju'dah by

taking vengeance, and hath greatly offended, and revenged himself upon them;

13 Therefore thus saith the Lord GOD; I will also stretch out mine hand upon E'dom, and will cut off man and beast from it; and I will make it desolate from Te'man; and they of De'-dan shall fall by the sword.

14 And I will lay my vengeance upon E'dom by the hand of my people Is'ra-el: and they shall do in E'dom according to mine anger and according to my fury; and they shall know my vengeance, saith the Lord GOD.

15 ¶ Thus saith the Lord GOD; Because the Phi-lis'tines have dealt by revenge, and have taken vengeance with a despiteful heart, to destroy it for the old hatred;

16 Therefore thus saith the Lord GOD; Behold, I will stretch out mine hand upon the Phi-lis'tines, and I will cut off the Cher'eth-ims, and destroy the remnant of the sea coast.

17 And I will execute great vengeance upon them with furious rebukes; and they shall know that I am the LORD, when I shall lay my vengeance upon them.

26 AND it came to pass in the eleventh year, in the first day of the month, that the word of the LORD came unto me, saying,

2 Son of man, because that Ty'rus hath said against Je-ru'sa-lem, Aha, she is broken that was the gates of the people: she is turned unto me: I shall be replenished, now she is laid waste:

3 Therefore thus saith the Lord GOD; Behold, I am against thee, O Ty'rus, and will cause many nations to come up against thee, as the sea causeth his waves to come up.

4 And they shall destroy the walls of Ty'rus, and break down her towers: I will also scrape her dust from her, and make her like the top of a rock.

5 It shall be a place for the spreading of nets in the midst of the sea: for I have spoken it, saith the Lord GOD: and it shall become a spoil to the nations.

6 And her daughters which are in the field shall be slain by the sword; and they shall know that I am the LORD.

7 ¶ For thus saith the Lord GOD; Behold, I will bring upon Ty'rus Neb-u-chad-rez'zar king of Bab'y-lon, a king of kings, from the north, with horses, and with chariots, and with horsemen, and companies, and much people.

8 He shall slay with the sword thy daughters in the field: and he shall make a fort against thee, and cast a mount against thee, and lift up the buckler against thee.

9 And he shall set engines of war against thy walls, and with his axes he shall break down thy towers.

10 By reason of the abundance of his horses their dust shall cover thee: thy walls shall shake at the noise of the horsemen, and of the wheels, and of the chariots, when he shall enter into thy gates, as men enter into a city wherein is made a breach.

11 With the hoofs of his horses shall he tread down all thy streets: he shall slay thy people by the sword, and thy strong garrisons shall go down to the ground.

12 And they shall make a spoil of thy riches, and make a prey of thy merchandise: and they shall break down thy walls, and destroy thy pleasant houses: and they shall lay thy stones and thy timber and thy dust in the midst of the water.

13 And I will cause the noise of thy songs to cease; and the sound of thy harps shall be no more heard.

14 And I will make thee like the top of a rock: thou shalt be a place to spread nets upon; thou shalt be built no more: for I the LORD have spoken it, saith the Lord GOD.

15 ¶ Thus saith the Lord GOD to Ty'rus; Shall not the isles shake at the sound of thy fall, when the wounded cry, when the slaughter is made in the midst of thee?

16 Then all the princes of the sea shall come down from their thrones, and lay away their robes, and put off their broidered garments: they shall clothe themselves with trembling; they shall sit upon the ground, and shall tremble at every moment, and be astonished at thee.

17 And they shall take up a lamentation for thee, and say to thee, How art thou destroyed, that wast inhabited of seafaring men, the renowned city, which wast strong in the sea, she and her inhabitants, which cause their terror to be on all that haunt it!

18 Now shall the isles tremble in the day of thy fall; yea, the isles that are in the sea shall be troubled at thy departure.

19 For thus saith the Lord GOD; When I shall make thee a desolate city, like the cities that are not inhabited; when I shall bring up the deep upon thee, and great waters shall cover thee;

20 When I shall bring thee down with them that descend into the pit, with the people of old time, and shall set thee in the low parts of the earth, in places desolate of old, with them that go down to the pit, that thou be not inhabited; and I shall set glory in the land of the living;

21 I will make thee a terror, and thou shalt be no more: though thou be sought for, yet shalt thou never be found again, saith the Lord GOD.

27 THE word of the LORD came again unto me, saying,

2 Now, thou son of man, take up a lamentation for Ty'rus;

3 And say unto Ty'rus, O thou that art situate at the entry of the sea, which art a merchant of the people for many isles, Thus saith the Lord GOD; O Ty'rus, thou hast said, I am of perfect beauty.

4 Thy borders are in the midst of the seas, thy builders have perfected thy beauty.

5 They have made all thy ship boards of fir trees of Se'nir: they have taken cedars from Leb'a-non to make masts for thee.

6 Of the oaks of Ba'shan have they made thine oars; the company of the Ash'ur-ites have made thy benches of ivory, brought out of the isles of Chit'tim.

7 Fine linen with broidered work from E'gypt was that which thou spreadest forth to be thy sail; blue and purple from the isles of E-li'shah was that which covered thee.

8 The inhabitants of Zi'don and Ar'vad were thy mariners: thy wise men, O Ty'rus, that were in thee, were thy pilots.

9 The ancients of Ge'bal and the wise men thereof were in thee thy calkers: all the ships of the sea with their mariners were in thee to occupy thy merchandise.

10 They of Per'sia and of Lud and of Phut were in thine army, thy men of war: they hanged the shield and helmet in thee; they set forth thy comeliness.

11 The men of Ar'vad with thine army were upon thy walls round about, and the Gam'ma-dims were in thy towers: they hanged their shields upon thy walls round about; they have made thy beauty perfect.

12 Tar'shish *was* thy merchant by reason of the multitude of all *kind* of riches; with silver, iron, tin, and lead, they traded in thy fairs.

13 Ja'van, Tu'bal, and Me'shech, they *were* thy merchants: they traded the persons of men and vessels of brass in thy market.

14 They of the house of To-gar'mah traded in thy fairs with horses and horsemen and mules.

15 The men of De'dan *were* thy merchants; many isles *were* the merchandise of thine hand: they brought thee *for* a present horns of ivory and ebony.

16 Syr'i-a *was* thy merchant by reason of the multitude of the wares of thy making: they occupied in thy fairs with emeralds, purple, and broidered work, and fine linen, and coral, and agate.

17 Ju'dah, and the land of Is'ra-el, they *were* thy merchants: they traded in thy market wheat of Min'nith, and Pan'nag, and honey, and oil, and balm.

18 Da-mas'cus *was* thy merchant in the multitude of the wares of thy making, for the multitude of all riches; in the wine of Hel'bon, and white wool.

19 Dan also and Ja'van going to and fro occupied in thy fairs: bright iron, cassia, and calamus, were in thy market.

20 De'dan *was* thy merchant in precious clothes for chariots.

21 A-ra'bi-a, and all the princes of Ke'dar, they occupied with thee in lambs, and rams, and goats: in these *were* they thy merchants.

22 The merchants of She'ba and Ra'a-mah, they *were* thy merchants: they occupied in thy fairs with chief of all spices, and with all precious stones, and gold.

23 Ha'ran, and Can'neh, and E'den, the merchants of She'ba, Assh'ur, *and* Chil'mad, *were* thy merchants.

24 These *were* thy merchants in all sorts *of things*, in blue clothes, and broidered work, and in chests of rich apparel, bound with cords, and made of cedar, among thy merchandise.

25 The ships of Tar'shish did sing of thee in thy market: and thou wast replenished, and made very glorious in the midst of the seas.

26 ¶ Thy rowers have brought thee into great waters: the east wind hath broken thee in the midst of the seas.

27 Thy riches, and thy fairs, thy merchandise, thy mariners, and thy pilots, thy calkers, and the occupiers of thy merchandise, and all thy men of war, that *are* in thee, and in all thy company which *is* in the midst of thee, shall fall into the midst of the seas in the day of thy ruin.

28 The suburbs shall shake at the sound of the cry of thy pilots.

29 And all that handle the oar, the mariners, *and* all the pilots of the sea, shall come down from their ships, they shall stand upon the land;

30 And shall cause their voice to be heard against thee, and shall cry bitterly, and shall cast up dust upon their heads, they shall wallow themselves in the ashes:

31 And they shall make themselves utterly bald for thee, and gird them with sackcloth, and they shall weep for thee with bitterness of heart *and* bitter wailing.

32 And in their wailing they shall take up a lamentation for thee, and lament over thee, *saying*, What *city is* like Ty'rus, like the destroyed in the midst of the sea?

33 When thy wares went forth out of the seas, thou filledst many people; thou didst enrich the kings of the earth with the multitude of thy riches and of thy merchandise.

34 In the time *when* thou shalt be broken by the seas in the depths of the waters thy merchandise and all thy company in the midst of thee shall fall.

35 All the inhabitants of the isles shall be astonished at thee, and their kings shall be sore afraid, they shall be troubled in *their* countenance.

36 The merchants among the people shall hiss at thee; thou shalt be a terror, and never *shalt be* any more.

28 THE word of the LORD came again unto me, saying,

2 Son of man, say unto the prince of Ty'rus, Thus saith the Lord GOD; Because thine heart *is* lifted up, and thou hast said, I *am* a God, I sit *in* the seat of God, in the midst of the seas; yet thou *art* a man, and not God, though thou set thine heart as the heart of God:

3 Behold, thou *art* wiser than Dan'iel; there is no secret that they can hide from thee:

4 With thy wisdom and with thine understanding thou hast gotten thee riches, and hast gotten gold and silver into thy treasures:

5 By thy great wisdom *and* by thy traffick hast thou increased thy riches, and thine heart is lifted up because of thy riches:

6 Therefore thus saith the Lord GOD; Because thou hast set thine heart as the heart of God;

7 Behold, therefore I will bring strangers upon thee, the terrible of the nations: and they shall draw their swords against the beauty of thy wisdom, and they shall defile thy brightness.

8 They shall bring thee down to the pit, and thou shalt die the deaths of *them that are* slain in the midst of the seas.

9 Wilt thou yet say before him that slayeth thee, I *am* God? but thou *shalt be* a man, and no God, in the hand of him that slayeth thee.

10 Thou shalt die the deaths of the uncircumcised by the hand of strangers: for I have spoken *it*, saith the Lord GOD.

11 ¶ Moreover the word of the LORD came unto me, saying,

12 Son of man, take up a lamentation upon the king of Ty'rus, and say unto him, Thus saith the Lord GOD; Thou sealest up the sum, full of wisdom, and perfect in beauty.

13 Thou hast been in E'den the garden of God; every precious stone *was* thy covering, the sardius, topaz, and the diamond, the beryl, the onyx, and the jasper, the sapphire, the emerald, and the carbuncle, and gold: the workmanship of thy tabrets and of thy pipes was prepared in thee in the day that thou wast created.

14 Thou *art* the anointed cherub that covereth; and I have set thee *so:* thou wast upon the holy mountain of God; thou hast walked up and down in the midst of the stones of fire.

15 Thou *wast* perfect in thy ways from the day that thou wast created, till iniquity was found in thee.

16 By the multitude of thy merchandise they have filled the midst of thee with violence, and thou hast sinned: therefore I will cast thee as profane out of the mountain of God: and I will destroy thee, O covering cherub, from the midst of the stones of fire.

17 Thine heart was lifted up because of thy beauty, thou hast corrupted thy wisdom by reason of thy brightness: I will cast thee to the ground, I will lay thee before kings, that they may behold thee.

18 Thou hast defiled thy sanctuaries by the multitude of thine iniquities, by the iniquity of

thy traffick; therefore will I bring forth a fire from the midst of thee, it shall devour thee, and I will bring thee to ashes upon the earth in the sight of all them that behold thee.

19 All they that know thee among the people shall be astonished at thee: thou shalt be a terror, and never *shalt* thou *be* any more.

20 ¶ Again the word of the LORD came unto me, saying,

21 Son of man, set thy face against Zi′don, and prophesy against it,

22 And say, Thus saith the Lord GOD; Behold, I *am* against thee, O Zi′don; and I will be glorified in the midst of thee: and they shall know that I *am* the LORD, when I shall have executed judgments in her, and shall be sanctified in her.

23 For I will send into her pestilence, and blood into her streets; and the wounded shall be judged in the midst of her by the sword upon her on every side; and they shall know that I *am* the LORD.

24 ¶ And there shall be no more a pricking brier unto the house of Is′ra-el, nor *any* grieving thorn of all *that are* round about them, that despised them; and they shall know that I *am* the Lord GOD.

25 Thus saith the Lord GOD; When I shall have gathered the house of Is′ra-el from the people among whom they are scattered, and shall be sanctified in them in the sight of the heathen, then shall they dwell in their land that I have given to my servant Ja′cob.

26 And they shall dwell safely therein, and shall build houses, and plant vineyards; yea, they shall dwell with confidence, when I have executed judgments upon all those that despise them round about them; and they shall know that I *am* the LORD their God.

29 IN the tenth year, in the tenth *month*, in the twelfth *day* of the month, the word of the LORD came unto me, saying,

2 Son of man, set thy face against Pha′raoh king of E′gypt, and prophesy against him, and against all E′gypt:

3 Speak, and say, Thus saith the Lord GOD; Behold, I *am* against thee, Pha′raoh king of E′-gypt, the great dragon that lieth in the midst of his rivers, which hath said, My river *is* mine own, and I have made *it* for myself.

4 But I will put hooks in thy jaws, and I will cause the fish of thy rivers to stick unto thy scales, and I will bring thee up out of the midst of thy rivers, and all the fish of thy rivers shall stick unto thy scales.

5 And I will leave thee *thrown* into the wilderness, thee and all the fish of thy rivers: thou shalt fall upon the open fields; thou shalt not be brought together, nor gathered: I have given thee for meat to the beasts of the field and to the fowls of the heaven.

6 And all the inhabitants of E′gypt shall know that I *am* the LORD, because they have been a staff of reed to the house of Is′ra-el.

7 When they took hold of thee by thy hand, thou didst break, and rend all their shoulder: and when they leaned upon thee, thou brakest, and madest all their loins to be at a stand.

8 ¶ Therefore thus saith the Lord GOD; Behold, I will bring a sword upon thee, and cut off man and beast out of thee.

9 And the land of E′gypt shall be desolate and waste; and they shall know that I *am* the LORD: because he hath said, The river *is* mine, and I have made *it.*

10 Behold, therefore I *am* against thee, and against thy rivers, and I will make the land of E′gypt utterly waste *and* desolate, from the tower of Sy-e′ne even unto the border of E-thi-o′pi-a.

11 No foot of man shall pass through it, nor foot of beast shall pass through it, neither shall it be inhabited forty years.

12 And I will make the land of E′gypt desolate in the midst of the countries *that are* desolate, and her cities among the cities *that are* laid waste shall be desolate forty years: and I will scatter the E-gyp′tians among the nations, and will disperse them through the countries.

13 ¶ Yet thus saith the Lord GOD; At the end of forty years will I gather the E-gyp′tians from the people whither they were scattered:

14 And I will bring again the captivity of E′-gypt, and will cause them to return *into* the land of Path′ros, into the land of their habitation; and they shall be there a base kingdom.

15 It shall be the basest of the kingdoms; neither shall it exalt itself any more above the nations: for I will diminish them, that they shall no more rule over the nations.

16 And it shall be no more the confidence of the house of Is′ra-el, which bringeth *their* iniquity to remembrance, when they shall look after them: but they shall know that I *am* the Lord GOD.

17 ¶ And it came to pass in the seven and twentieth year, in the first *month*, in the first *day* of the month, the word of the LORD came unto me, saying,

18 Son of man, Neb-u-chad-rez′zar king of Bab′y-lon caused his army to serve a great service against Ty′rus: every head *was* made bald, and every shoulder *was* peeled: yet had he no wages, nor his army, for Ty′rus, for the service that he had served against it:

19 Therefore thus saith the Lord GOD; Behold, I will give the land of E′gypt unto Neb-u-chad-rez′zar king of Bab′y-lon; and he shall take her multitude, and take her spoil, and take her prey; and it shall be the wages for his army.

20 I have given him the land of E′gypt *for* his labour wherewith he served against it, because they wrought for me, saith the Lord GOD.

21 ¶ In that day will I cause the horn of the house of Is′ra-el to bud forth, and I will give thee the opening of the mouth in the midst of them; and they shall know that I *am* the LORD.

30 THE word of the LORD came again unto me, saying,

2 Son of man, prophesy and say, Thus saith the Lord GOD; Howl ye, Woe worth the day!

3 For the day *is* near, even the day of the LORD *is* near, a cloudy day; it shall be the time of the heathen.

4 And the sword shall come upon E′gypt, and great pain shall be in E-thi-o′pi-a, when the slain shall fall in E′gypt, and they shall take away her multitude, and her foundations shall be broken down.

5 E-thi-o′pi-a, and Lib′y-a, and Lyd′i-a, and all the mingled people, and Chub, and the men of the land that is in league, shall fall with them by the sword.

6 Thus saith the LORD; They also that uphold E′gypt shall fall; and the pride of her power shall come down: from the tower of Sy-e′ne shall they fall in it by the sword, saith the Lord GOD.

7 And they shall be desolate in the midst of the countries *that are* desolate, and her cities shall be in the midst of the cities *that are* wasted.

8 And they shall know that I *am* the LORD,

when I have set a fire in E'gypt, and *when* all her helpers shall be destroyed.

9 In that day shall messengers go forth from me in ships to make the careless E-thi-o'pi-ans afraid, and great pain shall come upon them, as in the day of E'gypt: for, lo, it cometh.

10 Thus saith the Lord GOD; I will also make the multitude of E'gypt to cease by the hand of Neb-u-chad-rez'zar king of Bab'y-lon.

11 He and his people with him, the terrible of the nations, shall be brought to destroy the land: and they shall draw their swords against E'gypt, and fill the land with the slain.

12 And I will make the rivers dry, and sell the land into the hand of the wicked: and I will make the land waste, and all that is therein, by the hand of strangers: I the LORD have spoken *it.*

13 Thus saith the Lord GOD; I will also destroy the idols, and I will cause *their* images to cease out of Noph; and there shall be no more a prince of the land of E'gypt: and I will put a fear in the land of E'gypt.

14 And I will make Path'ros desolate, and will set fire in Zo'an, and will execute judgments in No.

15 And I will pour my fury upon Sin, the strength of E'gypt; and I will cut off the multitude of No.

16 And I will set fire in E'gypt: Sin shall have great pain, and No shall be rent asunder, and Noph *shall have* distresses daily.

17 The young men of A'ven and of Pi-be'seth shall fall by the sword: and these *cities* shall go into captivity.

18 At Te-haph'ne-hes also the day shall be darkened, when I shall break there the yokes of E'gypt: and the pomp of her strength shall cease in her: as for her, a cloud shall cover her, and her daughters shall go into captivity.

19 Thus will I execute judgments in E'gypt: and they shall know that I *am* the LORD.

20 ¶ And it came to pass in the eleventh year, in the first *month*, in the seventh *day* of the month, *that* the word of the LORD came unto me, saying,

21 Son of man, I have broken the arm of Pha'raoh king of E'gypt; and, lo, it shall not be bound up to be healed, to put a roller to bind it, to make it strong to hold the sword.

22 Therefore thus saith the Lord GOD; Behold, I *am* against Pha'raoh king of E'gypt, and will break his arms, the strong, and that which was broken; and I will cause the sword to fall out of his hand.

23 And I will scatter the E-gyp'tians among the nations, and will disperse them through the countries.

24 And I will strengthen the arms of the king of Bab'y-lon, and put my sword in his hand: but I will break Pha'raoh's arms, and he shall groan before him with the groanings of a deadly wounded *man.*

25 But I will strengthen the arms of the king of Bab'y-lon, and the arms of Pha'raoh shall fall down; and they shall know that I *am* the LORD, when I shall put my sword into the hand of the king of Bab'y-lon, and he shall stretch it out upon the land of E'gypt.

26 And I will scatter the E-gyp'tians among the nations, and disperse them among the countries; and they shall know that I *am* the LORD.

31 AND it came to pass in the eleventh year, in the third *month*, in the first *day* of the month, *that* the word of the LORD came unto me, saying,

2 Son of man, speak unto Pha'raoh king of E'gypt, and to his multitude; Whom art thou like in thy greatness?

3 ¶ Behold, the As-syr'i-an *was* a cedar in Leb'a-non with fair branches, and with a shadowing shroud, and of an high stature; and his top was among the thick boughs.

4 The waters made him great, the deep set him up on high with her rivers running round about his plants, and sent out her little rivers unto all the trees of the field.

5 Therefore his height was exalted above all the trees of the field, and his boughs were multiplied, and his branches became long because of the multitude of waters, when he shot forth.

6 All the fowls of heaven made their nests in his boughs, and under his branches did all the beasts of the field bring forth their young, and under his shadow dwelt all great nations.

7 Thus was he fair in his greatness, in the length of his branches: for his root was by great waters.

8 The cedars in the garden of God could not hide him: the fir trees were not like his boughs, and the chesnut trees were not like his branches; nor any tree in the garden of God was like unto him in his beauty.

9 I have made him fair by the multitude of his branches: so that all the trees of E'den, that *were* in the garden of God, envied him.

10 ¶ Therefore thus saith the Lord GOD; Because thou hast lifted up thyself in height, and he hath shot up his top among the thick boughs, and his heart is lifted up in his height;

11 I have therefore delivered him into the hand of the mighty one of the heathen; he shall surely deal with him: I have driven him out for his wickedness.

12 And strangers, the terrible of the nations, have cut him off, and have left him: upon the mountains and in all the valleys his branches are fallen, and his boughs are broken by all the rivers of the land; and all the people of the earth are gone down from his shadow, and have left him.

13 Upon his ruin shall all the fowls of the heaven remain, and all the beasts of the field shall be upon his branches:

14 To the end that none of all the trees by the waters exalt themselves for their height, neither shoot up their top among the thick boughs, neither their trees stand up in their height, all that drink water: for they are all delivered unto death, to the nether parts of the earth, in the midst of the children of men, with them that go down to the pit.

15 Thus saith the Lord GOD; In the day when he went down to the grave I caused a mourning: I covered the deep for him, and I restrained the floods thereof, and the great waters were stayed: and I caused Leb'a-non to mourn for him, and all the trees of the field fainted for him.

16 I made the nations to shake at the sound of his fall, when I cast him down to hell with them that descend into the pit: and all the trees of E'den, the choice and best of Leb'a-non, all that drink water, shall be comforted in the nether parts of the earth.

17 They also went down into hell with him unto *them that be* slain with the sword; and *they that were* his arm, *that* dwelt under his shadow in the midst of the heathen.

18 ¶ To whom art thou thus like in glory and in greatness among the trees of E'den? yet shalt thou be brought down with the trees of E'den unto the nether parts of the earth: thou shalt lie

in the midst of the uncircumcised with *them that be* slain by the sword. This is Pha'raoh and all his multitude, saith the Lord GOD.

32 AND it came to pass in the twelfth year, in the twelfth month, in the first *day* of the month, *that* the word of the LORD came unto me, saying,

2 Son of man, take up a lamentation for Pha'-raoh king of E'gypt, and say unto him, Thou art like a young lion of the nations, and thou *art* as a whale in the seas: and thou camest forth with thy rivers, and troubledst the waters with thy feet, and fouledst their rivers.

3 Thus saith the Lord GOD; I will therefore spread out my net over thee with a company of many people; and they shall bring thee up in my net.

4 Then will I leave thee upon the land, I will cast thee forth upon the open field, and will cause all the fowls of the heaven to remain upon thee, and I will fill the beasts of the whole earth with thee.

5 And I will lay thy flesh upon the mountains, and fill the valleys with thy height.

6 I will also water with thy blood the land wherein thou swimmest, *even* to the mountains; and the rivers shall be full of thee.

7 And when I shall put thee out, I will cover the heaven, and make the stars thereof dark; I will cover the sun with a cloud, and the moon shall not give her light.

8 All the bright lights of heaven will I make dark over thee, and set darkness upon thy land, saith the Lord GOD.

9 I will also vex the hearts of many people, when I shall bring thy destruction among the nations, into the countries which thou hast not known.

10 Yea, I will make many people amazed at thee, and their kings shall be horribly afraid for thee, when I shall brandish my sword before them; and they shall tremble at *every* moment, every man for his own life, in the day of thy fall.

11 ¶ For thus saith the Lord GOD; The sword of the king of Bab'y-lon shall come upon thee.

12 By the swords of the mighty will I cause thy multitude to fall, the terrible of the nations, all of them: and they shall spoil the pomp of E'gypt, and all the multitude thereof shall be destroyed.

13 I will destroy also all the beasts thereof from beside the great waters; neither shall the foot of man trouble them any more, nor the hoofs of beasts trouble them.

14 Then will I make their waters deep, and cause their rivers to run like oil, saith the Lord GOD.

15 When I shall make the land of E'gypt desolate, and the country shall be destitute of that whereof it was full, when I shall smite all them that dwell therein, then shall they know that I *am* the LORD.

16 This *is* the lamentation wherewith they shall lament her: the daughters of the nations shall lament her: they shall lament for her, *even* for E'gypt, and for all her multitude, saith the Lord GOD.

17 ¶ It came to pass also in the twelfth year, in the fifteenth *day* of the month, *that* the word of the LORD came unto me, saying,

18 Son of man, wail for the multitude of E'-gypt, and cast them down, *even* her, and the daughters of the famous nations, unto the nether parts of the earth, with them that go down into the pit.

19 Whom dost thou pass in beauty? go down, and be thou laid with the uncircumcised.

20 They shall fall in the midst of *them that are* slain by the sword: she is delivered to the sword: draw her and all her multitudes.

21 The strong among the mighty shall speak to him out of the midst of hell with them that help him: they are gone down, they lie uncir-cumcised, slain by the sword.

22 Assh'ur *is* there and all her company: his graves *are* about him: all of them slain, fallen by the sword:

23 Whose graves are set in the sides of the pit, and her company is round about her grave: all of them slain, fallen by the sword, which caused terror in the land of the living.

24 There *is* E'lam and all her multitude round about her grave, all of them slain, fallen by the sword, which are gone down uncircumcised into the nether parts of the earth, which caused their terror in the land of the living; yet have they borne their shame with them that go down to the pit.

25 They have set her a bed in the midst of the slain with all her multitude: her graves *are* round about him: all of them uncircumcised, slain by the sword: though their terror was caused in the land of the living, yet have they borne their shame with them that go down to the pit: he is put in the midst of *them that be* slain.

26 There *is* Me'shech, Tu'bal, and all her mul-titude: her graves *are* round about him: all of them uncircumcised, slain by the sword, though they caused their terror in the land of the living.

27 And they shall not lie with the mighty *that are* fallen of the uncircumcised, which are gone down to hell with their weapons of war: and they have laid their swords under their heads, but their iniquities shall be upon their bones, though *they were* the terror of the mighty in the land of the living.

28 Yea, thou shalt be broken in the midst of the uncircumcised, and shalt lie with *them that are* slain with the sword.

29 There *is* E'dom, her kings, and all her princes, which with their might are laid by *them that were* slain by the sword: they shall lie with the uncircumcised, and with them that go down to the pit.

30 There *be* the princes of the north, all of them, and all the Zi-do'ni-ans, which are gone down with the slain; with their terror they are ashamed of their might; and they lie uncircum-cised with *them that be* slain by the sword, and bear their shame with them that go down to the pit.

31 Pha'raoh shall see them, and shall be com-forted over all his multitude, *even* Pha'raoh and all his army slain by the sword, saith the Lord GOD.

32 For I have caused my terror in the land of the living: and he shall be laid in the midst of the uncircumcised with *them that are* slain with the sword, *even* Pha'raoh and all his multitude, saith the Lord GOD.

33 AGAIN the word of the LORD came unto me, saying,

2 Son of man, speak to the children of thy people, and say unto them, When I bring the sword upon a land, if the people of the land take a man of their coasts, and set him for their watchman:

3 If when he seeth the sword come upon the land, he blow the trumpet, and warn the people;

4 Then whosoever heareth the sound of the

trumpet, and taketh not warning; if the sword come, and take him away, his blood shall be upon his own head.

5 He heard the sound of the trumpet, and took not warning; his blood shall be upon him. But he that taketh warning shall deliver his soul.

6 But if the watchman see the sword come, and blow not the trumpet, and the people be not warned; if the sword come, and take any person from among them, he is taken away in his iniquity; but his blood will I require at the watchman's hand.

7 ¶ So thou, O son of man, I have set thee a watchman unto the house of Is'ra-el; therefore thou shalt hear the word at my mouth, and warn them from me.

8 When I say unto the wicked, O wicked man, thou shalt surely die; if thou dost not speak to warn the wicked from his way, that wicked man shall die in his iniquity; but his blood will I require at thine hand.

9 Nevertheless, if thou warn the wicked of his way to turn from it; if he do not turn from his way, he shall die in his iniquity; but thou hast delivered thy soul.

10 Therefore, O thou son of man, speak unto the house of Is'ra-el; Thus ye speak, saying, If our transgressions and our sins be upon us, and we pine away in them, how should we then live?

11 Say unto them, As I live, saith the Lord GOD, I have no pleasure in the death of the wicked; but that the wicked turn from his way and live: turn ye, turn ye from your evil ways; for why will ye die, O house of Is'ra-el?

12 Therefore, thou son of man, say unto the children of thy people, The righteousness of the righteous shall not deliver him in the day of his transgression: as for the wickedness of the wicked, he shall not fall thereby in the day that he turneth from his wickedness; neither shall the righteous be able to live for his righteousness in the day that he sinneth.

13 When I shall say to the righteous, that he shall surely live; if he trust to his own righteousness, and commit iniquity, all his righteousnesses shall not be remembered; but for his iniquity that he hath committed, he shall die for it.

14 Again, when I say unto the wicked, Thou shalt surely die; if he turn from his sin, and do that which is lawful and right;

15 If the wicked restore the pledge, give again that he had robbed, walk in the statutes of life, without committing iniquity; he shall surely live, he shall not die.

16 None of his sins that he hath committed shall be mentioned unto him: he hath done that which is lawful and right; he shall surely live.

17 ¶ Yet the children of thy people say, The way of the Lord is not equal: but as for them, their way is not equal.

18 When the righteous turneth from his righteousness, and committeth iniquity, he shall even die thereby.

19 But if the wicked turn from his wickedness, and do that which is lawful and right, he shall live thereby.

20 ¶ Yet ye say, The way of the Lord is not equal. O ye house of Is'ra-el, I will judge you every one after his ways.

21 ¶ And it came to pass in the twelfth year of our captivity, in the tenth month, in the fifth day of the month, that one that had escaped out of Je-ru'sa-lem came unto me, saying, The city is smitten.

22 Now the hand of the LORD was upon me in the evening, afore he that was escaped came; and had opened my mouth, until he came to me in the morning; and my mouth was opened, and I was no more dumb.

23 Then the word of the LORD came unto me, saying,

24 Son of man, they that inhabit those wastes of the land of Is'ra-el speak, saying, A'-bra-ham was one, and he inherited the land: but we are many; the land is given us for inheritance.

25 Wherefore say unto them, Thus saith the Lord GOD; Ye eat with the blood, and lift up your eyes toward your idols, and shed blood: and shall ye possess the land?

26 Ye stand upon your sword, ye work abomination, and ye defile every one his neighbour's wife: and shall ye possess the land?

27 Say thou thus unto them, Thus saith the Lord GOD; As I live, surely they that are in the wastes shall fall by the sword, and him that is in the open field will I give to the beasts to be devoured, and they that be in the forts and in the caves shall die of the pestilence.

28 For I will lay the land most desolate, and the pomp of her strength shall cease; and the mountains of Is'ra-el shall be desolate, that none shall pass through.

29 Then shall they know that I am the LORD, when I have laid the land most desolate because of all their abominations which they have committed.

30 ¶ Also, thou son of man, the children of thy people still are talking against thee by the walls and in the doors of the houses, and speak one to another, every one to his brother, saying, Come, I pray you, and hear what is the word that cometh forth from the LORD.

31 And they come unto thee as the people cometh, and they sit before thee as my people, and they hear thy words, but they will not do them: for with their mouth they shew much love, but their heart goeth after their covetousness.

32 And, lo, thou art unto them as a very lovely song of one that hath a pleasant voice, and can play well on an instrument: for they hear thy words, but they do them not.

33 And when this cometh to pass, (lo, it will come,) then shall they know that a prophet hath been among them.

34 AND the word of the LORD came unto me, saying,

2 Son of man, prophesy against the shepherds of Is'ra-el, prophesy, and say unto them, Thus saith the Lord GOD unto the shepherds; Woe be to the shepherds of Is'ra-el that do feed themselves! should not the shepherds feed the flocks?

3 Ye eat the fat, and ye clothe you with the wool, ye kill them that are fed: but ye feed not the flock.

4 The diseased have ye not strengthened, neither have ye healed that which was sick, neither have ye bound up that which was broken, neither have ye brought again that which was driven away, neither have ye sought that which was lost; but with force and with cruelty have ye ruled them.

5 And they were scattered, because there is no shepherd: and they became meat to all the beasts of the field, when they were scattered.

6 My sheep wandered through all the mountains, and upon every high hill: yea, my flock

was scattered upon all the face of the earth, and none did search or seek *after them.*

7 ¶ Therefore, ye shepherds, hear the word of the LORD;

8 *As* I live, saith the Lord GOD, surely because my flock became a prey, and my flock became meat to every beast of the field, because *there was* no shepherd, neither did my shepherds search for my flock, but the shepherds fed themselves, and fed not my flock;

9 Therefore, O ye shepherds, hear the word of the LORD;

10 Thus saith the Lord GOD; Behold, I *am* against the shepherds; and I will require my flock at their hand, and cause them to cease from feeding the flock; neither shall the shepherds feed themselves any more; for I will deliver my flock from their mouth, that they may not be meat for them.

11 ¶ For thus saith the Lord GOD; Behold, I, *even* I, will both search my sheep, and seek them out.

12 As a shepherd seeketh out his flock in the day that he is among his sheep *that are* scattered; so will I seek out my sheep, and will deliver them out of all places where they have been scattered in the cloudy and dark day.

13 And I will bring them out from the people, and gather them from the countries, and will bring them to their own land, and feed them upon the mountains of Is'ra-el by the rivers, and in all the inhabited places of the country.

14 I will feed them in a good pasture, and upon the high mountains of Is'ra-el shall their fold be: there shall they lie in a good fold, and *in* a fat pasture shall they feed upon the mountains of Is'ra-el.

15 I will feed my flock, and I will cause them to lie down, saith the Lord GOD.

16 I will seek that which was lost, and bring again that which was driven away, and will bind up *that which was* broken, and will strengthen that which was sick: but I will destroy the fat and the strong; I will feed them with judgment.

17 And *as for* you, O my flock, thus saith the Lord GOD; Behold, I judge between cattle and cattle, between the rams and the he goats.

18 *Seemeth it* a small thing unto you to have eaten up the good pasture, but ye must tread down with your feet the residue of your pastures? and to have drunk of the deep waters, but ye must foul the residue with your feet?

19 And *as for* my flock, they eat that which ye have trodden with your feet; and they drink that which ye have fouled with your feet.

20 ¶ Therefore thus saith the Lord GOD unto them; Behold, I, *even* I, will judge between the fat cattle and between the lean cattle.

21 Because ye have thrust with side and with shoulder, and pushed all the diseased with your horns, till ye have scattered them abroad;

22 Therefore will I save my flock, and they shall no more be a prey; and I will judge between cattle and cattle.

23 And I will set up one shepherd over them, and he shall feed them, *even* my servant Da'vid; he shall feed them, and he shall be their shepherd.

24 And I the LORD will be their God, and my servant Da'vid a prince among them; I the LORD have spoken *it.*

25 And I will make with them a covenant of peace, and will cause the evil beasts to cease out of the land: and they shall dwell safely in the wilderness, and sleep in the woods.

26 And I will make them and the places round about my hill a blessing; and I will cause the shower to come down in his season; there shall be showers of blessing.

27 And the tree of the field shall yield her fruit, and the earth shall yield her increase, and they shall be safe in their land, and shall know that I *am* the LORD, when I have broken the bands of their yoke, and delivered them out of the hand of those that served themselves of them.

28 And they shall no more be a prey to the heathen, neither shall the beast of the land devour them; but they shall dwell safely, and none shall make *them* afraid.

29 And I will raise up for them a plant of renown, and they shall be no more consumed with hunger in the land, neither bear the shame of the heathen any more.

30 Thus shall they know that I the LORD their God *am* with them, and *that* they, *even* the house of Is'ra-el, *are* my people, saith the Lord GOD.

31 And ye my flock, the flock of my pasture, *are* men, *and* I *am* your God, saith the Lord GOD.

35

MOREOVER the word of the LORD came unto me, saying,

2 Son of man, set thy face against mount Se'-ir, and prophesy against it,

3 And say unto it, Thus saith the Lord GOD; Behold, O mount Se'ir, I *am* against thee, and I will stretch out mine hand against thee, and I will make thee most desolate.

4 I will lay thy cities waste, and thou shalt be desolate, and thou shalt know that I *am* the LORD.

5 Because thou hast had a perpetual hatred, and hast shed *the blood of* the children of Is'ra-el by the force of the sword in the time of their calamity, in the time *that their* iniquity *had* an end:

6 Therefore, *as* I live, saith the Lord GOD, I will prepare thee unto blood, and blood shall pursue thee: sith thou hast not hated blood, even blood shall pursue thee.

7 Thus will I make mount Se'ir most desolate, and cut off from it him that passeth out and him that returneth.

8 And I will fill his mountains with his slain *men:* in thy hills, and in thy valleys, and in all thy rivers, shall they fall that are slain with the sword.

9 I will make thee perpetual desolations, and thy cities shall not return: and ye shall know that I *am* the LORD.

10 Because thou hast said, These two nations and these two countries shall be mine, and we will possess it; whereas the LORD was there:

11 Therefore, *as* I live, saith the Lord GOD, I will even do according to thine anger, and according to thine envy which thou hast used out of thy hatred against them; and I will make myself known among them, when I have judged thee.

12 And thou shalt know that I *am* the LORD, *and that* I have heard all thy blasphemies which thou hast spoken against the mountains of Is'-ra-el, saying, They are laid desolate, they are given us to consume.

13 Thus with your mouth ye have boasted against me, and have multiplied your words against me: I have heard *them.*

14 Thus saith the Lord GOD; When the whole earth rejoiceth, I will make thee desolate.

15 As thou didst rejoice at the inheritance of the house of Is'ra-el, because it was desolate, so

will I do unto thee: thou shalt be desolate, O mount Se′ir, and all I-du-me′a, *even* all of it: and they shall know that I *am* the LORD.

36 ALSO, thou son of man, prophesy unto the mountains of Is′ra-el, and say, Ye mountains of Is′ra-el, hear the word of the LORD:

2 Thus saith the Lord GOD; Because the enemy hath said against you, Aha, even the ancient high places are ours in possession:

3 Therefore prophesy and say, Thus saith the Lord GOD; Because they have made *you* desolate, and swallowed you up on every side, that ye might be a possession unto the residue of the heathen, and ye are taken up in the lips of talkers, and *are* an infamy of the people:

4 Therefore, ye mountains of Is′ra-el, hear the word of the Lord GOD; Thus saith the Lord GOD to the mountains, and to the hills, to the rivers, and to the valleys, to the desolate wastes, and to the cities that are forsaken, which became a prey and derision to the residue of the heathen that *are* round about;

5 Therefore thus saith the Lord GOD; Surely in the fire of my jealousy have I spoken against the residue of the heathen, and against all I-du-me′a, which have appointed my land into their possession with the joy of all *their* heart, with despiteful minds, to cast it out for a prey.

6 Prophesy therefore concerning the land of Is′ra-el, and say unto the mountains, and to the hills, to the rivers, and to the valleys, Thus saith the Lord GOD; Behold, I have spoken in my jealousy and in my fury, because ye have borne the shame of the heathen:

7 Therefore thus saith the Lord GOD; I have lifted up mine hand, Surely the heathen that *are* about you, they shall bear their shame.

8 ¶ But ye, O mountains of Is′ra-el, ye shall shoot forth your branches, and yield your fruit to my people of Is′ra-el: for they are at hand to come.

9 For, behold, I *am* for you, and I will turn unto you, and ye shall be tilled and sown:

10 And I will multiply men upon you, all the house of Is′ra-el, *even* all of it: and the cities shall be inhabited, and the wastes shall be builded:

11 And I will multiply upon you man and beast; and they shall increase and bring fruit: and I will settle you after your old estates, and will do better *unto* you than at your beginnings: and ye shall know that I *am* the LORD.

12 Yea, I will cause men to walk upon you, *even* my people Is′ra-el; and they shall possess thee, and thou shalt be their inheritance, and thou shalt no more henceforth bereave them *of* men.

13 Thus saith the Lord GOD; Because they say unto you, Thou *land* devourest up men, and hast bereaved thy nations;

14 Therefore thou shalt devour men no more, neither bereave thy nations any more, saith the Lord GOD.

15 Neither will I cause *men* to hear in thee the shame of the heathen any more, neither shalt thou bear the reproach of the people any more, neither shalt thou cause thy nations to fall any more, saith the Lord GOD.

16 ¶ Moreover the word of the LORD came unto me, saying,

17 Son of man, when the house of Is′ra-el dwelt in their own land, they defiled it by their own way and by their doings: their way was before me as the uncleanness of a removed woman.

18 Wherefore I poured my fury upon them for the blood that they had shed upon the land, and for their idols *wherewith* they had polluted it:

19 And I scattered them among the heathen, and they were dispersed through the countries: according to their way and according to their doings I judged them.

20 And when they entered unto the heathen, whither they went, they profaned my holy name, when they said to them, These *are* the people of the LORD, and are gone forth out of his land.

21 ¶ But I had pity for mine holy name, which the house of Is′ra-el had profaned among the heathen, whither they went.

22 Therefore say unto the house of Is′ra-el, Thus saith the Lord GOD; I do not *this* for your sakes, O house of Is′ra-el, but for mine holy name′s sake, which ye have profaned among the heathen, whither ye went.

23 And I will sanctify my great name, which was profaned among the heathen, which ye have profaned in the midst of them; and the heathen shall know that I *am* the LORD, saith the Lord GOD, when I shall be sanctified in you before their eyes.

24 For I will take you from among the heathen, and gather you out of all countries, and will bring you into your own land.

25 ¶ Then will I sprinkle clean water upon you, and ye shall be clean: from all your filthiness, and from all your idols, will I cleanse you.

26 A new heart also will I give you, and a new spirit will I put within you: and I will take away the stony heart out of your flesh, and I will give you an heart of flesh.

27 And I will put my spirit within you, and cause you to walk in my statutes, and ye shall keep my judgments, and do *them*.

28 And ye shall dwell in the land that I gave to your fathers; and ye shall be my people, and I will be your God.

29 I will also save you from all your uncleannesses: and I will call for the corn, and will increase it, and lay no famine upon you.

30 And I will multiply the fruit of the tree, and the increase of the field, that ye shall receive no more reproach of famine among the heathen.

31 Then shall ye remember your own evil ways, and your doings that *were* not good, and shall loathe yourselves in your own sight for your iniquities and for your abominations.

32 Not for your sakes do I *this*, saith the Lord GOD, be it known unto you: be ashamed and confounded for your own ways, O house of Is′-ra-el.

33 Thus saith the Lord GOD; In the day that I shall have cleansed you from all your iniquities I will also cause *you* to dwell in the cities, and the wastes shall be builded.

34 And the desolate land shall be tilled, whereas it lay desolate in the sight of all that passed by.

35 And they shall say, This land that was desolate is become like the garden of E′den; and the waste and desolate and ruined cities *are* become fenced, *and* are inhabited.

36 Then the heathen that are left round about you shall know that I the LORD build the ruined *places, and* plant that that was desolate: I the LORD have spoken *it*, and I will do *it*.

37 Thus saith the Lord GOD; I will yet *for* this be enquired of by the house of Is′ra-el, to do *it* for them; I will increase them with men like a flock.

38 As the holy flock, as the flock of Je-ru'sa-lem in her solemn feasts; so shall the waste cities be filled with flocks of men: and they shall know that I *am* the LORD.

37 THE hand of the LORD was upon me, and carried me out in the spirit of the LORD, and set me down in the midst of the valley which *was* full of bones,

2 And caused me to pass by them round about: and, behold, *there were* very many in the open valley; and, lo, *they were* very dry.

3 And he said unto me, Son of man, can these bones live? And I answered, O Lord GOD, thou knowest.

4 Again he said unto me, Prophesy upon these bones, and say unto them, O ye dry bones, hear the word of the LORD.

5 Thus saith the Lord GOD unto these bones; Behold, I will cause breath to enter into you, and ye shall live:

6 And I will lay sinews upon you, and will bring up flesh upon you, and cover you with skin, and put breath in you, and ye shall live; and ye shall know that I *am* the LORD.

7 So I prophesied as I was commanded: and as I prophesied, there was a noise, and behold a shaking, and the bones came together, bone to his bone.

8 And when I beheld, lo, the sinews and the flesh came up upon them, and the skin covered them above: but *there was* no breath in them.

9 Then said he unto me, Prophesy unto the wind, prophesy, son of man, and say to the wind, Thus saith the Lord GOD; Come from the four winds, O breath, and breathe upon these slain, that they may live.

10 So I prophesied as he commanded me, and the breath came into them, and they lived, and stood up upon their feet, an exceeding great army.

11 ¶ Then he said unto me, Son of man, these bones are the whole house of Is'ra-el: behold, they say, Our bones are dried, and our hope is lost: we are cut off for our parts.

12 Therefore prophesy and say unto them, Thus saith the Lord GOD; Behold, O my people, I will open your graves, and cause you to come up out of your graves, and bring you into the land of Is'ra-el.

13 And ye shall know that I *am* the LORD, when I have opened your graves, O my people, and brought you up out of your graves,

14 And shall put my spirit in you, and ye shall live, and I shall place you in your own land: then shall ye know that I the LORD have spoken *it*, and performed *it*, saith the LORD.

15 ¶ The word of the LORD came again unto me, saying,

16 Moreover, thou son of man, take thee one stick, and write upon it, For Ju'dah, and for the children of Is'ra-el his companions: then take another stick, and write upon it, For Jo'seph, the stick of E'phra-im, and *for* all the house of Is'ra-el his companions:

17 And join them one to another into one stick; and they shall become one in thine hand.

18 ¶ And when the children of thy people shall speak unto thee, saying, Wilt thou not shew us what thou *meanest* by these?

19 Say unto them, Thus saith the Lord GOD; Behold, I will take the stick of Jo'seph, which *is* in the hand of E'phra-im, and the tribes of Is'ra-el his fellows, and will put them with him, *even* with the stick of Ju'dah, and make them one stick, and they shall be one in mine hand.

20 ¶ And the sticks whereon thou writest shall be in thine hand before their eyes.

21 And say unto them, Thus saith the Lord GOD; Behold, I will take the children of Is'ra-el from among the heathen, whither they be gone, and will gather them on every side, and bring them into their own land:

22 And I will make them one nation in the land upon the mountains of Is'ra-el; and one king shall be king to them all: and they shall be no more two nations, neither shall they be divided into two kingdoms any more at all:

23 Neither shall they defile themselves any more with their idols, nor with their detestable things, nor with any of their transgressions: but I will save them out of all their dwellingplaces, wherein they have sinned, and will cleanse them: so shall they be my people, and I will be their God.

24 And Da'vid my servant *shall be* king over them; and they all shall have one shepherd: they shall also walk in my judgments, and observe my statutes, and do them.

25 And they shall dwell in the land that I have given unto Ja'cob my servant, wherein your fathers have dwelt; and they shall dwell therein, *even* they, and their children, and their children's children for ever: and my servant Da'vid *shall be* their prince for ever.

26 Moreover I will make a covenant of peace with them; it shall be an everlasting covenant with them: and I will place them, and multiply them, and will set my sanctuary in the midst of them for evermore.

27 My tabernacle also shall be with them: yea, I will be their God, and they shall be my people.

28 And the heathen shall know that I the LORD do sanctify Is'ra-el, when my sanctuary shall be in the midst of them for evermore.

38 AND the word of the LORD came unto me, saying,

2 Son of man, set thy face against Gog, the land of Ma'gog, the chief prince of Me'shech and Tu'bal, and prophesy against him,

3 And say, Thus saith the Lord GOD; Behold, I *am* against thee, O Gog, the chief prince of Me'shech and Tu'bal:

4 And I will turn thee back, and put hooks into thy jaws, and I will bring thee forth, and all thine army, horses and horsemen, all of them clothed with all sorts *of armour, even* a great company *with* bucklers and shields, all of them handling swords:

5 Per'sia, E-thi-o'pi-a, and Lib'y-a with them; all of them with shield and helmet:

6 Go'mer, and all his bands; the house of To-gar'mah of the north quarters, and all his bands: *and* many people with thee.

7 Be thou prepared, and prepare for thyself, thou, and all thy company that are assembled unto thee, and be thou a guard unto them.

8 ¶ After many days thou shalt be visited: in the latter years thou shalt come into the land *that is* brought back from the sword, *and is* gathered out of many people, against the mountains of Is'ra-el, which have been always waste: but it is brought forth out of the nations, and they shall dwell safely all of them.

9 Thou shalt ascend and come like a storm, thou shalt be like a cloud to cover the land, thou, and all thy bands, and many people with thee.

10 Thus saith the Lord GOD; It shall also come to pass, *that* at the same time shall things

come into thy mind, and thou shalt think an evil thought:

11 And thou shalt say, I will go up to the land of unwalled villages; I will go to them that are at rest, that dwell safely, all of them dwelling without walls, and having neither bars nor gates,

12 To take a spoil, and to take a prey; to turn thine hand upon the desolate places *that are now* inhabited, and upon the people *that are* gathered out of the nations, which have gotten cattle and goods, that dwell in the midst of the land.

13 She′ba, and De′dan, and the merchants of Tar′shish, with all the young lions thereof, shall say unto thee, Art thou come to take a spoil? hast thou gathered thy company to take a prey? to carry away silver and gold, to take away cattle and goods, to take a great spoil?

14 ¶ Therefore, son of man, prophesy and say unto Gog, Thus saith the Lord GOD; In that day when my people of Is′ra-el dwelleth safely, shalt thou not know *it?*

15 And thou shalt come from thy place out of the north parts, thou, and many people with thee, all of them riding upon horses, a great company, and a mighty army:

16 And thou shalt come up against my people of Is′ra-el, as a cloud to cover the land; it shall be in the latter days, and I will bring thee against my land, that the heathen may know me, when I shall be sanctified in thee, O Gog, before their eyes.

17 Thus saith the Lord GOD; *Art* thou he of whom I have spoken in old time by my servants the prophets of Is′ra-el, which prophesied in those days *many* years that I would bring thee against them?

18 And it shall come to pass at the same time when Gog shall come against the land of Is′ra-el, saith the Lord GOD, *that* my fury shall come up in my face.

19 For in my jealousy *and* in the fire of my wrath have I spoken, Surely in that day there shall be a great shaking in the land of Is′ra-el;

20 So that the fishes of the sea, and the fowls of the heaven, and the beasts of the field, and all creeping things that creep upon the earth, and all the men that *are* upon the face of the earth, shall shake at my presence, and the mountains shall be thrown down, and the steep places shall fall, and every wall shall fall to the ground.

21 And I will call for a sword against him throughout all my mountains, saith the Lord GOD: every man′s sword shall be against his brother.

22 And I will plead against him with pestilence and with blood; and I will rain upon him, and upon his bands, and upon the many people that *are* with him, an overflowing rain, and great hailstones, fire, and brimstone.

23 Thus will I magnify myself, and sanctify myself; and I will be known in the eyes of many nations, and they shall know that I *am* the LORD.

39 THEREFORE, thou son of man, prophesy against Gog, and say, Thus saith the Lord GOD; Behold, I *am* against thee, O Gog, the chief prince of Me′shech and Tu′bal:

2 And I will turn thee back, and leave but the sixth part of thee, and will cause thee to come up from the north parts, and will bring thee upon the mountains of Is′ra-el:

3 And I will smite thy bow out of thy left hand, and will cause thine arrows to fall out of thy right hand.

4 Thou shalt fall upon the mountains of Is′ra-el, thou, and all thy bands, and the people that *is* with thee: I will give thee unto the ravenous birds of every sort, and *to* the beasts of the field to be devoured.

5 Thou shalt fall upon the open field: for I have spoken *it,* saith the Lord GOD.

6 And I will send a fire on Ma′gog, and among them that dwell carelessly in the isles: and they shall know that I *am* the LORD.

7 So will I make my holy name known in the midst of my people Is′ra-el; and I will not *let them* pollute my holy name any more: and the heathen shall know that I *am* the LORD, the Holy One in Is′ra-el.

8 ¶ Behold, it is come, and it is done, saith the Lord GOD; this *is* the day whereof I have spoken.

9 And they that dwell in the cities of Is′ra-el shall go forth, and shall set on fire and burn the weapons, both the shields and the bucklers, the bows and the arrows, and the handstaves, and the spears, and they shall burn them with fire seven years:

10 So that they shall take no wood out of the field, neither cut down any out of the forests; for they shall burn the weapons with fire: and they shall spoil those that spoiled them, and rob those that robbed them, saith the Lord GOD.

11 ¶ And it shall come to pass in that day, *that* I will give unto Gog a place there of graves in Is′ra-el, the valley of the passengers on the east of the sea: and it shall stop the *noses* of the passengers: and there shall they bury Gog and all his multitude: and they shall call *it* The valley of Ha′mon-gog.

12 And seven months shall the house of Is′ra-el be burying of them, that they may cleanse the land.

13 Yea, all the people of the land shall bury *them;* and it shall be to them a renown the day that I shall be glorified, saith the Lord GOD.

14 And they shall sever out men of continual employment, passing through the land to bury with the passengers those that remain upon the face of the earth, to cleanse it: after the end of seven months shall they search.

15 And the passengers *that* pass through the land, when *any* seeth a man′s bone, then shall he set up a sign by it, till the buriers have buried it in the valley of Ha′mon-gog.

16 And also the name of the city *shall be* Ha-mo′nah. Thus shall they cleanse the land.

17 ¶ And, thou son of man, thus saith the Lord GOD; Speak unto every feathered fowl, and to every beast of the field, Assemble yourselves, and come; gather yourselves on every side to my sacrifice that I do sacrifice for you, *even* a great sacrifice upon the mountains of Is′ra-el, that ye may eat flesh, and drink blood.

18 Ye shall eat the flesh of the mighty, and drink the blood of the princes of the earth, of rams, of lambs, and of goats, of bullocks, all of them fatlings of Ba′shan.

19 And ye shall eat fat till ye be full, and drink blood till ye be drunken, of my sacrifice which I have sacrificed for you.

20 Thus ye shall be filled at my table with horses and chariots, with mighty men, and with all men of war, saith the Lord GOD.

21 And I will set my glory among the heathen, and all the heathen shall see my judgment that I have executed, and my hand that I have laid upon them.

22 So the house of Is′ra-el shall know that I *am* the LORD their God from that day and forward.

23 ¶ And the heathen shall know that the house of Is'ra-el went into captivity for their iniquity: because they trespassed against me, therefore hid I my face from them, and gave them into the hand of their enemies: so fell they all by the sword.

24 According to their uncleanness and according to their transgressions have I done unto them, and hid my face from them.

25 Therefore thus saith the Lord GOD; Now will I bring again the captivity of Ja'cob, and have mercy upon the whole house of Is'ra-el, and will be jealous for my holy name;

26 After that they have borne their shame, and all their trespasses whereby they have trespassed against me, when they dwelt safely in their land, and none made them afraid.

27 When I have brought them again from the people, and gathered them out of their enemies' lands, and am sanctified in them in the sight of many nations;

28 Then shall they know that I am the LORD their God, which caused them to be led into captivity among the heathen: but I have gathered them unto their own land, and have left none of them any more there.

29 Neither will I hide my face any more from them: for I have poured out my spirit upon the house of Is'ra-el, saith the Lord GOD.

40 IN the five and twentieth year of our captivity, in the beginning of the year, in the tenth day of the month, in the fourteenth year after that the city was smitten, in the selfsame day the hand of the LORD was upon me, and brought me thither.

2 In the visions of God brought he me into the land of Is'ra-el, and set me upon a very high mountain, by which was as the frame of a city on the south.

3 And he brought me thither, and, behold, there was a man, whose appearance was like the appearance of brass, with a line of flax in his hand, and a measuring reed; and he stood in the gate.

4 And the man said unto me, Son of man, behold with thine eyes, and hear with thine ears, and set thine heart upon all that I shall shew thee; for to the intent that I might shew them unto thee art thou brought hither: declare all that thou seest to the house of Is'ra-el.

5 And behold a wall on the outside of the house round about, and in the man's hand a measuring reed of six cubits long by the cubit and an hand breadth: so he measured the breadth of the building, one reed; and the height, one reed.

6 ¶ Then came he unto the gate which looketh toward the east, and went up the stairs thereof, and measured the threshold of the gate, which was one reed broad; and the other threshold of the gate, which was one reed broad.

7 And every little chamber was one reed long, and one reed broad; and between the little chambers were five cubits; and the threshold of the gate by the porch of the gate within was one reed.

8 He measured also the porch of the gate within, one reed.

9 Then measured he the porch of the gate, eight cubits; and the posts thereof, two cubits; and the porch of the gate was inward.

10 And the little chambers of the gate eastward were three on this side, and three on that side; they three were of one measure: and the posts had one measure on this side and on that side.

11 And he measured the breadth of the entry of the gate, ten cubits; and the length of the gate, thirteen cubits.

12 The space also before the little chambers was one cubit on this side, and the space was one cubit on that side: and the little chambers were six cubits on this side, and six cubits on that side.

13 He measured then the gate from the roof of one little chamber to the roof of another: the breadth was five and twenty cubits, door against door.

14 He made also posts of threescore cubits, even unto the post of the court round about the gate.

15 And from the face of the gate of the entrance unto the face of the porch of the inner gate were fifty cubits.

16 And there were narrow windows to the little chambers, and to their posts within the gate round about, and likewise to the arches: and windows were round about inward: and upon each post were palm trees.

17 Then brought he me into the outward court, and, lo, there were chambers, and a pavement made for the court round about: thirty chambers were upon the pavement.

18 And the pavement by the side of the gates over against the length of the gates was the lower pavement.

19 Then he measured the breadth from the forefront of the lower gate unto the forefront of the inner court without, an hundred cubits eastward and northward.

20 ¶ And the gate of the outward court that looked toward the north, he measured the length thereof, and the breadth thereof.

21 And the little chambers thereof were three on this side and three on that side; and the posts thereof and the arches thereof were after the measure of the first gate: the length thereof was fifty cubits, and the breadth five and twenty cubits.

22 And their windows, and their arches, and their palm trees, were after the measure of the gate that looketh toward the east; and they went up unto it by seven steps; and the arches thereof were before them.

23 And the gate of the inner court was over against the gate toward the north, and toward the east; and he measured from gate to gate an hundred cubits.

24 ¶ After that he brought me toward the south, and behold a gate toward the south: and he measured the posts thereof and the arches thereof according to these measures.

25 And there were windows in it and in the arches thereof round about, like those windows: the length was fifty cubits, and the breadth five and twenty cubits.

26 And there were seven steps to go up to it, and the arches thereof were before them: and it had palm trees, one on this side, and another on that side, upon the posts thereof.

27 And there was a gate in the inner court toward the south: and he measured from gate to gate toward the south an hundred cubits.

28 And he brought me to the inner court by the south gate: and he measured the south gate according to these measures;

29 And the little chambers thereof, and the posts thereof, and the arches thereof, according to these measures: and there were windows in it and in the arches thereof round about: it was

fifty cubits long, and five and twenty cubits broad.

30 And the arches round about *were* five and twenty cubits long, and five cubits broad.

31 And the arches thereof *were* toward the utter court; and palm trees *were* upon the posts thereof: and the going up to it *had* eight steps.

32 ¶ And he brought me into the inner court toward the east: and he measured the gate according to these measures.

33 And the little chambers thereof, and the posts thereof, and the arches thereof, *were* according to these measures: and *there were* windows therein and in the arches thereof round about: it was fifty cubits long, and five and twenty cubits broad.

34 And the arches thereof *were* toward the outward court; and palm trees *were* upon the posts thereof, on this side, and on that side: and the going up to it *had* eight steps.

35 ¶ And he brought me to the north gate, and measured *it* according to these measures;

36 The little chambers thereof, the posts thereof, and the arches thereof, and the windows to it round about: the length *was* fifty cubits, and the breadth five and twenty cubits.

37 And the posts thereof *were* toward the utter court; and palm trees *were* upon the posts thereof, on this side, and on that side: and the going up to it *had* eight steps.

38 And the chambers and the entries thereof *were* by the posts of the gates, where they washed the burnt offering.

39 ¶ And in the porch of the gate *were* two tables on this side, and two tables on that side, to slay thereon the burnt offering and the sin offering and the trespass offering.

40 And at the side without, as one goeth up to the entry of the north gate, *were* two tables; and on the other side, which *was* at the porch of the gate, *were* two tables.

41 Four tables *were* on this side, and four tables on that side, by the side of the gate; eight tables, whereupon they slew *their sacrifices*.

42 And the four tables *were* of hewn stone for the burnt offering, of a cubit and an half long, and a cubit and an half broad, and one cubit high: whereupon also they laid the instruments wherewith they slew the burnt offering and the sacrifice.

43 And within *were* hooks, an hand broad, fastened round about: and upon the tables *was* the flesh of the offering.

44 ¶ And without the inner gate *were* the chambers of the singers in the inner court, which *was* at the side of the north gate; and their prospect *was* toward the south: one at the side of the east gate *having* the prospect toward the north.

45 And he said unto me, This chamber, whose prospect *is* toward the south, *is* for the priests, the keepers of the charge of the house.

46 And the chamber whose prospect *is* toward the north *is* for the priests, the keepers of the charge of the altar: these *are* the sons of Za'dok among the sons of Le'vi, which come near to the Lord to minister unto him.

47 So he measured the court, an hundred cubits long, and an hundred cubits broad, foursquare; and the altar *that was* before the house.

48 ¶ And he brought me to the porch of the house, and measured *each* post of the porch, five cubits on this side, and five cubits on that side: and the breadth of the gate *was* three cubits on this side, and three cubits on that side.

49 The length of the porch *was* twenty cubits, and the breadth eleven cubits; and *he*

brought me by the steps whereby they went up to it: and *there were* pillars by the posts, one on this side, and another on that side.

41 AFTERWARD he brought me to the temple, and measured the posts, six cubits broad on the one side, and six cubits broad on the other side, *which was* the breadth of the tabernacle.

2 And the breadth of the door *was* ten cubits; and the sides of the door *were* five cubits on the one side, and five cubits on the other side: and he measured the length thereof, forty cubits: and the breadth, twenty cubits.

3 Then went he inward, and measured the post of the door, two cubits; and the door, six cubits; and the breadth of the door, seven cubits.

4 So he measured the length thereof, twenty cubits; and the breadth, twenty cubits, before the temple: and he said unto me, This *is* the most holy *place*.

5 After he measured the wall of the house, six cubits; and the breadth of *every* side chamber, four cubits, round about the house on every side.

6 And the side chambers *were* three, one over another, and thirty in order; and they entered into the wall which *was* of the house for the side chambers round about, that they might have hold, but they had not hold in the wall of the house.

7 And *there was* an enlarging, and a winding about still upward to the side chambers: for the winding about of the house went still upward round about the house: therefore the breadth of the house *was still* upward, and so increased *from* the lowest *chamber* to the highest by the midst.

8 I saw also the height of the house round about: the foundations of the side chambers *were* a full reed of six great cubits.

9 The thickness of the wall, which *was* for the side chamber without, *was* five cubits: and *that* which *was* left *was* the place of the side chambers that *were* within.

10 And between the chambers *was* the wideness of twenty cubits round about the house on every side.

11 And the doors of the side chambers *were* toward *the place that was* left, one door toward the north, and another door toward the south: and the breadth of the place that was left *was* five cubits round about.

12 Now the building that *was* before the separate place at the end toward the west *was* seventy cubits broad; and the wall of the building *was* five cubits thick round about, and the length thereof ninety cubits.

13 So he measured the house, an hundred cubits long; and the separate place, and the building, with the walls thereof, an hundred cubits long;

14 Also the breadth of the face of the house, and of the separate place toward the east, an hundred cubits.

15 And he measured the length of the building over against the separate place which *was* behind it, and the galleries thereof on the one side and on the other side, an hundred cubits, with the inner temple, and the porches of the court;

16 The door posts, and the narrow windows, and the galleries round about on their three stories, over against the door, cieled with wood round about, and from the ground up to the windows, and the windows *were* covered;

17 To that above the door, even unto the inner house, and without, and by all the wall round about within and without, by measure.

18 And *it was* made with cherubims and palm trees, so that a palm tree *was* between a cherub and a cherub; and *every* cherub had two faces;

19 So that the face of a man *was* toward the palm tree on the one side, and the face of a young lion toward the palm tree on the other side: *it was* made through all the house round about.

20 From the ground unto above the door *were* cherubims and palm trees made, and *on* the wall of the temple.

21 The posts of the temple *were* squared, *and* the face of the sanctuary; the appearance *of the one* as the appearance *of the other.*

22 The altar of wood *was* three cubits high, and the length thereof two cubits; and the corners thereof, and the length thereof, and the walls thereof, *were* of wood: and he said unto me, This *is* the table that *is* before the LORD.

23 And the temple and the sanctuary had two doors.

24 And the doors had two leaves *apiece,* two turning leaves; two *leaves* for the one door, and two leaves for the other *door.*

25 And *there were* made on them, on the doors of the temple, cherubims and palm trees, like as *were* made upon the walls; and *there were* thick planks upon the face of the porch without.

26 And *there were* narrow windows and palm trees on the one side and on the other side, on the sides of the porch, and *upon* the side chambers of the house, and thick planks.

42 THEN he brought me forth into the utter court, the way toward the north: and he brought me into the chamber that *was* over against the separate place, and which *was* before the building toward the north.

2 Before the length of an hundred cubits *was* the north door, and the breadth *was* fifty cubits.

3 Over against the twenty *cubits* which *were* for the inner court, and over against the pavement which *was* for the utter court, *was* gallery against gallery in three *stories.*

4 And before the chambers *was* a walk of ten cubits breadth inward, a way of one cubit; and their doors toward the north.

5 Now the upper chambers *were* shorter: for the galleries were higher than these, than the lower, and than the middlemost of the building.

6 For they *were* in three *stories,* but had not pillars as the pillars of the courts: therefore *the building* was straitened more than the lowest and the middlemost from the ground.

7 And the wall that *was* without over against the chambers, toward the utter court on the forepart of the chambers, the length thereof *was* fifty cubits.

8 For the length of the chambers that *were* in the utter court *was* fifty cubits: and, lo, before the temple *were* an hundred cubits.

9 And from under these chambers *was* the entry on the east side, as one goeth into them from the utter court.

10 The chambers *were* in the thickness of the wall of the court toward the east, over against the separate place, and over against the building.

11 And the way before them *was* like the appearance of the chambers which *were* toward the north, as long as they, *and* as broad as they:

and all their goings out *were* both according to their fashions, and according to their doors.

12 And according to the doors of the chambers that *were* toward the south *was* a door in the head of the way, *even* the way directly before the wall toward the east, as one entereth into them.

13 ¶ Then said he unto me, The north chambers *and* the south chambers, which *are* before the separate place, they *be* holy chambers, where the priests that approach unto the LORD shall eat the most holy things: there shall they lay the most holy things, and the meat offering, and the sin offering, and the trespass offering; for the place *is* holy.

14 When the priests enter therein, then shall they not go out of the holy *place* into the utter court, but there they shall lay their garments wherein they minister; for they *are* holy; and shall put on other garments, and shall approach to *those things* which *are* for the people.

15 Now when he had made an end of measuring the inner house, he brought me forth toward the gate whose prospect *is* toward the east, and measured it round about.

16 He measured the east side with the measuring reed, five hundred reeds, with the measuring reed round about.

17 He measured the north side, five hundred reeds, with the measuring reed round about.

18 He measured the south side, five hundred reeds, with the measuring reed.

19 ¶ He turned about to the west side, *and* measured five hundred reeds with the measuring reed.

20 He measured it by the four sides: it had a wall round about, five hundred *reeds* long, and five hundred broad, to make a separation between the sanctuary and the profane place.

43 AFTERWARD he brought me to the gate, *even* the gate that looketh toward the east:

2 And, behold, the glory of the God of Is'ra-el came from the way of the east: and his voice *was* like a noise of many waters: and the earth shined with his glory.

3 And *it was* according to the appearance of the vision which I saw, *even* according to the vision that I saw when I came to destroy the city: and the visions *were* like the vision that I saw by the river Che'bar; and I fell upon my face.

4 And the glory of the LORD came into the house by the way of the gate whose prospect *is* toward the east.

5 So the spirit took me up, and brought me into the inner court; and, behold, the glory of the LORD filled the house.

6 And I heard *him* speaking unto me out of the house; and the man stood by me.

7 ¶ And he said unto me, Son of man, the place of my throne, and the place of the soles of my feet, where I will dwell in the midst of the children of Is'ra-el for ever, and my holy name, shall the house of Is'ra-el no more defile, *neither* they, nor their kings, by their whoredom, nor by the carcases of their kings in their high places.

8 In their setting of their threshold by my thresholds, and their post by my posts, and the wall between me and them, they have even defiled my holy name by their abominations that they have committed: wherefore I have consumed them in mine anger.

9 Now let them put away their whoredom, and the carcases of their kings, far from me, and I will dwell in the midst of them for ever.

10 ¶ Thou son of man, shew the house to the house of Is′ra-el, that they may be ashamed of their iniquities: and let them measure the pattern.

11 And if they be ashamed of all that they have done, shew them the form of the house, and the fashion thereof, and the goings out thereof, and the comings in thereof, and all the forms thereof, and all the ordinances thereof, and all the forms thereof, and all the laws thereof: and write it in their sight, that they may keep the whole form thereof, and all the ordinances thereof, and do them.

12 This is the law of the house; Upon the top of the mountain the whole limit thereof round about shall be most holy. Behold, this is the law of the house.

13 ¶ And these are the measures of the altar after the cubits: The cubit is a cubit and an hand breadth; even the bottom shall be a cubit, and the breadth a cubit, and the border thereof by the edge thereof round about shall be a span: and this shall be the higher place of the altar.

14 And from the bottom upon the ground even to the lower settle shall be two cubits, and the breadth one cubit; and from the lesser settle even to the greater settle shall be four cubits, and the breadth one cubit.

15 So the altar shall be four cubits; and from the altar and upward shall be four horns.

16 And the altar shall be twelve cubits long, twelve broad, square in the four squares thereof.

17 And the settle shall be fourteen cubits long and fourteen broad in the four squares thereof; and the border about it shall be half a cubit; and the bottom thereof shall be a cubit about; and his stairs shall look toward the east.

18 ¶ And he said unto me, Son of man, thus saith the Lord GOD; These are the ordinances of the altar in the day when they shall make it, to offer burnt offerings thereon, and to sprinkle blood thereon.

19 And thou shalt give to the priests the Le′-vites that be of the seed of Za′dok, which approach unto me, to minister unto me, saith the Lord GOD, a young bullock for a sin offering.

20 And thou shalt take of the blood thereof, and put it on the four horns of it, and on the four corners of the settle, and upon the border round about: thus shalt thou cleanse and purge it.

21 Thou shalt take the bullock also of the sin offering, and he shall burn it in the appointed place of the house, without the sanctuary.

22 And on the second day thou shalt offer a kid of the goats without blemish for a sin offering; and they shall cleanse the altar, as they did cleanse it with the bullock.

23 When thou hast made an end of cleansing it, thou shalt offer a young bullock without blemish, and a ram out of the flock without blemish.

24 And thou shalt offer them before the LORD, and the priests shall cast salt upon them, and they shall offer them up for a burnt offering unto the LORD.

25 Seven days shalt thou prepare every day a goat for a sin offering: they shall also prepare a young bullock, and a ram out of the flock, without blemish.

26 Seven days shall they purge the altar and purify it; and they shall consecrate themselves.

27 And when these days are expired, it shall be, that upon the eighth day, and so forward, the priests shall make your burnt offerings upon the altar, and your peace offerings; and I will accept you, saith the Lord GOD.

44 THEN he brought me back the way of the gate of the outward sanctuary which looketh toward the east; and it was shut.

2 Then said the LORD unto me; This gate shall be shut, it shall not be opened, and no man shall enter in by it; because the LORD, the God of Is′-ra-el, hath entered in by it, therefore it shall be shut.

3 It is for the prince; the prince, he shall sit in it to eat bread before the LORD; he shall enter by the way of the porch of that gate, and shall go out by the way of the same.

4 ¶ Then brought he me the way of the north gate before the house: and I looked, and, behold, the glory of the LORD filled the house of the LORD: and I fell upon my face.

5 And the LORD said unto me, Son of man, mark well, and behold with thine eyes, and hear with thine ears all that I say unto thee concerning all the ordinances of the house of the LORD, and all the laws thereof; and mark well the entering in of the house, with every going forth of the sanctuary.

6 And thou shalt say to the rebellious, even to the house of Is′ra-el, Thus saith the Lord GOD; O ye house of Is′ra-el, let it suffice you of all your abominations,

7 In that ye have brought into my sanctuary strangers, uncircumcised in heart, and uncircumcised in flesh, to be in my sanctuary, to pollute it, even my house, when ye offer my bread, the fat and the blood, and they have broken my covenant because of all your abominations.

8 And ye have not kept the charge of mine holy things: but ye have set keepers of my charge in my sanctuary for yourselves.

9 ¶ Thus saith the Lord GOD; No stranger, uncircumcised in heart, nor uncircumcised in flesh, shall enter into my sanctuary, of any stranger that is among the children of Is′ra-el.

10 And the Le′vites that are gone away far from me, when Is′ra-el went astray, which went astray away from me after their idols; they shall even bear their iniquity.

11 Yet they shall be ministers in my sanctuary, having charge at the gates of the house, and ministering to the house: they shall slay the burnt offering and the sacrifice for the people, and they shall stand before them to minister unto them.

12 Because they ministered unto them before their idols, and caused the house of Is′ra-el to fall into iniquity; therefore have I lifted up mine hand against them, saith the Lord GOD, and they shall bear their iniquity.

13 And they shall not come near unto me, to do the office of a priest unto me, nor to come near to any of my holy things, in the most holy place: but they shall bear their shame, and their abominations which they have committed.

14 But I will make them keepers of the charge of the house, for all the service thereof, and for all that shall be done therein.

15 ¶ But the priests the Le′vites, the sons of Za′dok, that kept the charge of my sanctuary when the children of Is′ra-el went astray from me, they shall come near to me to minister unto me, and they shall stand before me to offer unto me the fat and the blood, saith the Lord GOD:

16 They shall enter into my sanctuary, and they shall come near to my table, to minister unto me, and they shall keep my charge.

17 ¶ And it shall come to pass, that when they enter in at the gates of the inner court,

they shall be clothed with linen garments; and
no wool shall come upon them, whiles they
minister in the gates of the inner court, and
within.

18 They shall have linen bonnets upon their
heads, and shall have linen breeches upon their
loins; they shall not gird *themselves* with any
thing that causeth sweat.

19 And when they go forth into the utter
court, *even* into the utter court to the people,
they shall put off their garments wherein they
ministered, and lay them in the holy chambers,
and they shall put on other garments; and they
shall not sanctify the people with their garments.

20 Neither shall they shave their heads, nor
suffer their locks to grow long; they shall only
poll their heads.

21 Neither shall any priest drink wine, when
they enter into the inner court.

22 Neither shall they take for their wives a
widow, nor her that is put away: but they shall
take maidens of the seed of the house of Is'ra-el,
or a widow that had a priest before.

23 And they shall teach my people *the difference* between the holy and profane, and cause
them to discern between the unclean and the
clean.

24 And in controversy they shall stand in
judgment; *and* they shall judge it according to
my judgments: and they shall keep my laws and
my statutes in all mine assemblies; and they
shall hallow my sabbaths.

25 And they shall come at no dead person to
defile themselves: but for father, or for mother,
or for son, or for daughter, for brother, or for
sister that hath had no husband, they may defile
themselves.

26 And after he is cleansed, they shall reckon
unto him seven days.

27 And in the day that he goeth into the sanctuary, unto the inner court, to minister in the
sanctuary, he shall offer his sin offering, saith
the Lord GOD.

28 And it shall be unto them for an inheritance: I *am* their inheritance: and ye shall give
them no possession in Is'ra-el: I *am* their possession.

29 They shall eat the meat offering, and the
sin offering, and the trespass offering; and every dedicated thing in Is'ra-el shall be theirs.

30 And the first of all the firstfruits of all
things, and every oblation of all, of every *sort* of
your oblations, shall be the priest's: ye shall
also give unto the priest the first of your dough,
that he may cause the blessing to rest in thine
house.

31 The priests shall not eat of any thing that
is dead of itself, or torn, whether it be fowl or
beast.

45 MOREOVER, when ye shall divide by
lot the land for inheritance, ye shall offer an oblation unto the LORD, an holy portion
of the land: the length *shall be* the length of five
and twenty thousand *reeds,* and the breadth
shall be ten thousand. This *shall be* holy in all
the borders thereof round about.

2 Of this there shall be for the sanctuary five
hundred *in* length, with five hundred *in*
breadth, square round about; and fifty cubits
round about for the suburbs thereof.

3 And of this measure shalt thou measure the
length of five and twenty thousand, and the
breadth of ten thousand: and in it shall be the
sanctuary *and* the most holy *place.*

4 The holy *portion* of the land shall be for the

priests the ministers of the sanctuary, which
shall come near to minister unto the LORD: and
it shall be a place for their houses, and an holy
place for the sanctuary.

5 And the five and twenty thousand of
length, and the ten thousand of breadth, shall
also the Le'vites, the ministers of the house,
have for themselves, for a possession for
twenty chambers.

6 ¶ And ye shall appoint the possession of
the city five thousand broad, and five and
twenty thousand long, over against the oblation
of the holy *portion:* it shall be for the whole
house of Is'ra-el.

7 ¶ And a *portion shall be* for the prince on
the one side and on the other side of the oblation of the holy *portion,* and of the possession
of the city, before the oblation of the holy *portion,* and before the possession of the city, from
the west side westward, and from the east side
eastward: and the length *shall be* over against
one of the portions, from the west border unto
the east border.

8 In the land shall be his possession in Is'ra-
el: and my princes shall no more oppress my
people; and *the rest* of the land shall they give
to the house of Is'ra-el according to their tribes.

9 ¶ Thus saith the Lord GOD; Let it suffice
you, O princes of Is'ra-el: remove violence and
spoil, and execute judgment and justice, take
away your exactions from my people, saith the
Lord GOD.

10 Ye shall have just balances, and a just e-
phah, and a just bath.

11 The ephah and the bath shall be of one
measure, that the bath may contain the tenth
part of an homer, and the ephah the tenth part
of an homer: the measure thereof shall be after
the homer.

12 And the shekel *shall be* twenty gerahs:
twenty shekels, five and twenty shekels, fifteen
shekels, shall be your maneh.

13 This *is* the oblation that ye shall offer; the
sixth part of an ephah of an homer of wheat,
and ye shall give the sixth part of an ephah of
an homer of barley:

14 Concerning the ordinance of oil, the bath
of oil, *ye shall offer* the tenth part of a bath out
of the cor, *which is* an homer of ten baths; for
ten baths *are* an homer:

15 And one lamb out of the flock, out of two
hundred, out of the fat pastures of Is'ra-el; for a
meat offering, and for a burnt offering, and for
peace offerings, to make reconciliation for
them, saith the Lord GOD.

16 All the people of the land shall give this
oblation for the prince in Is'ra-el.

17 And it shall be the prince's part *to give*
burnt offerings, and meat offerings, and drink
offerings, in the feasts, and in the new moons,
and in the sabbaths, in all solemnities of the
house of Is'ra-el: he shall prepare the sin offering, and the meat offering, and the burnt offering, and the peace offerings, to make reconciliation for the house of Is'ra-el.

18 Thus saith the Lord GOD; In the first
month, in the first *day* of the month, thou shalt
take a young bullock without blemish, and
cleanse the sanctuary:

19 And the priest shall take of the blood of
the sin offering, and put *it* upon the posts of the
house, and upon the four corners of the settle of
the altar, and upon the posts of the gate of the
inner court.

20 And so thou shalt do the seventh *day* of
the month for every one that erreth, and for *him
that is* simple: so shall ye reconcile the house.

21 In the first *month*, in the fourteenth day of the month, ye shall have the passover, a feast of seven days; unleavened bread shall be eaten.

22 And upon that day shall the prince prepare for himself and for all the people of the land a bullock *for* a sin offering.

23 And seven days of the feast he shall prepare a burnt offering to the LORD, seven bullocks and seven rams without blemish daily the seven days; and a kid of the goats daily *for* a sin offering.

24 And he shall prepare a meat offering of an ephah for a bullock, and an ephah for a ram, and an hin of oil for an ephah.

25 In the seventh *month*, in the fifteenth day of the month, shall he do the like in the feast of the seven days, according to the sin offering, according to the burnt offering, and according to the meat offering, and according to the oil.

46 THUS saith the Lord GOD; The gate of the inner court that looketh toward the east shall be shut the six working days; but on the sabbath it shall be opened, and in the day of the new moon it shall be opened.

2 And the prince shall enter by the way of the porch of *that* gate without, and shall stand by the post of the gate, and the priests shall prepare his burnt offering and his peace offerings, and he shall worship at the threshold of the gate: then he shall go forth; but the gate shall not be shut until the evening.

3 Likewise the people of the land shall worship at the door of this gate before the LORD in the sabbaths and in the new moons.

4 And the burnt offering that the prince shall offer unto the LORD in the sabbath day *shall be* six lambs without blemish, and a ram without blemish.

5 And the meat offering *shall be* an ephah for a ram, and the meat offering for the lambs as he shall be able to give, and an hin of oil to an ephah.

6 And in the day of the new moon *it shall be* a young bullock without blemish, and six lambs, and a ram: they shall be without blemish.

7 And he shall prepare a meat offering, an ephah for a bullock, and an ephah for a ram, and for the lambs according as his hand shall attain unto, and an hin of oil to an ephah.

8 And when the prince shall enter, he shall go in by the way of the porch of *that* gate, and he shall go forth by the way thereof.

9 ¶ But when the people of the land shall come before the LORD in the solemn feasts, he that entereth in by the way of the north gate to worship shall go out by the way of the south gate; and he that entereth in by the way of the south gate shall go forth by the way of the north gate: he shall not return by the way of the gate whereby he came in, but shall go forth over against it.

10 And the prince in the midst of them, when they go in, shall go in; and when they go forth, shall go forth.

11 And in the feasts and in the solemnities the meat offering shall be an ephah to a bullock, and an ephah to a ram, and to the lambs as he is able to give, and an hin of oil to an ephah.

12 Now when the prince shall prepare a voluntary burnt offering or peace offerings voluntarily unto the LORD, *one* shall then open him the gate that looketh toward the east, and he shall prepare his burnt offering and his peace offerings, as he did on the sabbath day: then he

shall go forth; and after his going forth *one* shall shut the gate.

13 Thou shalt daily prepare a burnt offering unto the LORD *of* a lamb of the first year without blemish: thou shalt prepare it every morning.

14 And thou shalt prepare a meat offering for it every morning, the sixth part of an ephah, and the third part of an hin of oil, to temper with the fine flour; a meat offering continually by a perpetual ordinance unto the LORD.

15 Thus shall they prepare the lamb, and the meat offering, and the oil, every morning *for* a continual burnt offering.

16 ¶ Thus saith the Lord GOD; If the prince give a gift unto any of his sons, the inheritance thereof shall be his sons'; it *shall be* their possession by inheritance.

17 But if he give a gift of his inheritance to one of his servants, then it shall be his to the year of liberty; after it shall return to the prince: but his inheritance shall be his sons' for them.

18 Moreover the prince shall not take of the people's inheritance by oppression, to thrust them out of their possession; *but* he shall give his sons inheritance out of his own possession: that my people be not scattered every man from his possession.

19 ¶ After he brought me through the entry, which *was* at the side of the gate, into the holy chambers of the priests, which looked toward the north: and, behold, there *was* a place on the two sides westward.

20 Then said he unto me, This *is* the place where the priests shall boil the trespass offering and the sin offering, where they shall bake the meat offering; that they bear *them* not out into the utter court, to sanctify the people.

21 Then he brought me forth into the utter court, and caused me to pass by the four corners of the court; and, behold, in every corner of the court *there was* a court.

22 In the four corners of the court *there were* courts joined of forty *cubits* long and thirty broad: these four corners *were* of one measure.

23 And *there was* a row of building round about in them, round about them four, and *it was* made with boiling places under the rows round about.

24 Then said he unto me, These *are* the places of them that boil, where the ministers of the house shall boil the sacrifice of the people.

47 AFTERWARD he brought me again unto the door of the house; and, behold, waters issued out from under the threshold of the house eastward: for the forefront of the house *stood toward* the east, and the waters came down from under from the right side of the house, at the south *side* of the altar.

2 Then brought he me out of the way of the gate northward, and led me about the way without unto the utter gate by the way that looketh eastward; and, behold, there ran out waters on the right side.

3 And when the man that had the line in his hand went forth eastward, he measured a thousand cubits, and he brought me through the waters; the waters *were* to the ancles.

4 Again he measured a thousand, and brought me through the waters; the waters *were* to the knees. Again he measured a thousand, and brought me through; the waters *were* to the loins.

5 Afterward he measured a thousand; *and it was* a river that I could not pass over: for the

waters were risen, waters to swim in, a river that could not be passed over.

6 ¶ And he said unto me, Son of man, hast thou seen *this?* Then he brought me, and caused me to return to the brink of the river.

7 Now when I had returned, behold, at the bank of the river *were* very many trees on the one side and on the other.

8 Then said he unto me, These waters issue out toward the east country, and go down into the desert, and go into the sea: *which being* brought forth into the sea, the waters shall be healed.

9 And it shall come to pass, *that* every thing that liveth, which moveth, whithersoever the rivers shall come, shall live: and there shall be a very great multitude of fish, because these waters shall come thither: for they shall be healed; and every thing shall live whither the river cometh.

10 And it shall come to pass, *that* the fishers shall stand upon it from En-ge'di even unto En-eg'la-im; they shall be a *place* to spread forth nets; their fish shall be according to their kinds, as the fish of the great sea, exceeding many.

11 But the miry places thereof and the marishes thereof shall not be healed; they shall be given to salt.

12 And by the river upon the bank thereof, on this side and on that side, shall grow all trees for meat, whose leaf shall not fade, neither shall the fruit thereof be consumed: it shall bring forth new fruit according to his months, because their waters they issued out of the sanctuary: and the fruit thereof shall be for meat, and the leaf thereof for medicine.

13 ¶ Thus saith the Lord God; This *shall be* the border, whereby ye shall inherit the land according to the twelve tribes of Is'ra-el: Jo'seph *shall have* two portions.

14 And ye shall inherit it, one as well as another: *concerning* the which I lifted up mine hand to give it unto your fathers: and this land shall fall unto you for inheritance.

15 And this *shall be* the border of the land toward the north side, from the great sea, the way of Heth'lon, as men go to Ze'dad;

16 Ha'math, Be-ro'thah, Sib'ra-im, which *is* between the border of Da-mas'cus and the border of Ha'math; Ha'zar-hat'ti-con, which *is* by the coast of Hau'ran.

17 And the border from the sea shall be Ha'-zar-e'nan, the border of Da-mas'cus, and the north northward, and the border of Ha'math. And *this is* the north side.

18 And the east side ye shall measure from Hau'ran, and from Da-mas'cus, and from Gil'e-ad, and from the land of Is'ra-el by Jor'dan, from the border unto the east sea. And *this is* the east side.

19 And the south side southward, from Ta'-mar *even* to the waters of strife in Ka'desh, the river to the great sea. And *this is* the south side southward.

20 The west side also *shall be* the great sea from the border, till a man come over against Ha'math. This *is* the west side.

21 So shall ye divide this land unto you according to the tribes of Is'ra-el.

22 ¶ And it shall come to pass, *that* ye shall divide it by lot for an inheritance unto you, and to the strangers that sojourn among you, which shall beget children among you: and they shall be unto you as born in the country among the children of Is'ra-el; they shall have inheritance with you among the tribes of Is'ra-el.

23 And it shall come to pass, *that* in what tribe the stranger sojourneth, there shall ye give *him* his inheritance, saith the Lord God.

48

NOW these *are* the names of the tribes. From the north to the coast of the way of Heth'lon, as one goeth to Ha'math, Ha'-zar-e'nan, the border of Da-mas'cus northward, to the coast of Ha'math; for these are his sides east *and* west; a *portion for* Dan.

2 And by the border of Dan, from the east side unto the west side, a *portion for* Ash'er.

3 And by the border of Ash'er, from the east side even unto the west side, a *portion for* Naph'ta-li.

4 And by the border of Naph'ta-li, from the east side unto the west side, a *portion for* Ma-nas'seh.

5 And by the border of Ma-nas'seh, from the east side unto the west side, a *portion for* E'-phra-im.

6 And by the border of E'phra-im, from the east side even unto the west side, a *portion for* Reu'ben.

7 And by the border of Reu'ben, from the east side unto the west side, a *portion for* Ju'-dah.

8 ¶ And by the border of Ju'dah, from the east side unto the west side, shall be the offering which ye shall offer of five and twenty thousand *reeds in* breadth, and *in* length as one of the *other* parts, from the east side unto the west side: and the sanctuary shall be in the midst of it.

9 The oblation that ye shall offer unto the Lord *shall be* of five and twenty thousand in length, and of ten thousand in breadth.

10 And for them, *even* for the priests, shall be *this* holy oblation; toward the north five and twenty thousand *in length,* and toward the west ten thousand in breadth, and toward the east ten thousand in breadth, and toward the south five and twenty thousand in length: and the sanctuary of the Lord shall be in the midst thereof.

11 *It shall be* for the priests that are sanctified of the sons of Za'dok; which have kept my charge, which went not astray when the children of Is'ra-el went astray, as the Le'vites went astray.

12 And *this* oblation of the land that is offered shall be unto them a thing most holy by the border of the Le'vites.

13 And over against the border of the priests the Le'vites *shall have* five and twenty thousand in length, and ten thousand in breadth: all the length *shall be* five and twenty thousand, and the breadth ten thousand.

14 And they shall not sell of it, neither exchange, nor alienate the firstfruits of the land: for *it is* holy unto the Lord.

15 ¶ And the five thousand, that are left in the breadth over against the five and twenty thousand, shall be a profane *place* for the city, for dwelling, and for suburbs: and the city shall be in the midst thereof.

16 And these *shall be* the measures thereof; the north side four thousand and five hundred, and the south side four thousand and five hundred, and on the east side four thousand and five hundred, and the west side four thousand and five hundred.

17 And the suburbs of the city shall be toward the north two hundred and fifty, and toward the south two hundred and fifty, and toward the east two hundred and fifty, and toward the west two hundred and fifty.

18 And the residue in length over against the oblation of the holy *portion shall be* ten thousand eastward, and ten thousand westward: and it shall be over against the oblation of the holy *portion*; and the increase thereof shall be for food unto them that serve the city.

19 And they that serve the city shall serve it out of all the tribes of Is'ra-el.

20 All the oblation *shall be* five and twenty thousand by five and twenty thousand: ye shall offer the holy oblation foursquare, with the possession of the city.

21 ¶ And the residue *shall be* for the prince, on the one side and on the other of the holy oblation, and of the possession of the city, over against the five and twenty thousand of the oblation toward the east border, and westward over against the five and twenty thousand toward the west border, over against the portions for the prince: and it shall be the holy oblation; and the sanctuary of the house *shall be* in the midst thereof.

22 Moreover from the possession of the Le'-vites, and from the possession of the city, *being* in the midst *of that* which is the prince's, between the border of Ju'dah and the border of Ben'ja-min, shall be for the prince.

23 As for the rest of the tribes, from the east side unto the west side, Ben'ja-min *shall have* a *portion*.

24 And by the border of Ben'ja-min, from the east side unto the west side, Sim'e-on *shall have* a portion.

25 And by the border of Sim'e-on, from the east side unto the west side, Is'sa-char a *portion*.

26 And by the border of Is'sa-char, from the east side unto the west side, Zeb'u-lun a *portion*.

27 And by the border of Zeb'u-lun, from the east side unto the west side, Gad a *portion*.

28 And by the border of Gad at the south side southward, the border shall be even from Ta'mar *unto* the waters of strife *in* Ka'desh, *and* to the river toward the great sea.

29 This *is* the land which ye shall divide by lot unto the tribes of Is'ra-el for inheritance, and these *are* their portions, saith the Lord God.

30 ¶ And these *are* the goings out of the city on the north side, four thousand and five hundred measures.

31 And the gates of the city *shall be* after the names of the tribes of Is'ra-el: three gates northward; one gate of Reu'ben, one gate of Ju'-dah, one gate of Le'vi.

32 And at the east side four thousand and five hundred: and three gates; and one gate of Jo'seph, one gate of Ben'ja-min, one gate of Dan.

33 And at the south side four thousand and five hundred measures: and three gates; one gate of Sim'e-on, one gate of Is'sa-char, one gate of Zeb'u-lun.

34 At the west side four thousand and five hundred, *with* their three gates; one gate of Gad, one gate of Ash'er, one gate of Naph'ta-li.

35 *It was* round about eighteen thousand *measures*: and the name of the city from *that* day *shall be*, The LORD *is* there.

THE BOOK OF

DANIEL

1 IN the third year of the reign of Je-hoi'a-kim king of Ju'dah came Neb-u-chad-nez'-zar king of Bab'y-lon unto Je-ru'sa-lem, and besieged it.

2 And the Lord gave Je-hoi'a-kim king of Ju'-dah into his hand, with part of the vessels of the house of God: which he carried into the land of Shi'nar to the house of his god; and he brought the vessels into the treasure house of his god.

3 ¶ And the king spake unto Ash'pe-naz the master of his eunuchs, that he should bring *certain* of the children of Is'ra-el, and of the king's seed, and of the princes;

4 Children in whom *was* no blemish, but well favoured, and skilful in all wisdom, and cunning in knowledge, and understanding science, and such as *had* ability in them to stand in the king's palace, and whom they might teach the learning and the tongue of the Chal-de'ans.

5 And the king appointed them a daily provision of the king's meat, and of the wine which he drank: so nourishing them three years, that at the end thereof they might stand before the king.

6 Now among these were of the children of Ju'dah, Dan'iel, Han-a-ni'ah, Mish'a-el, and Az-a-ri'ah:

7 Unto whom the prince of the eunuchs gave names: for he gave unto Dan'iel *the name* of Bel-te-shaz'zar; and to Han-a-ni'ah, of Sha'-drach; and to Mish'a-el, of Me'shach; and to Az-a-ri'ah, of A-bed'-ne-go.

8 ¶ But Dan'iel purposed in his heart that he would not defile himself with the portion of the king's meat, nor with the wine which he drank: therefore he requested of the prince of the eunuchs that he might not defile himself.

9 Now God had brought Dan'iel into favour and tender love with the prince of the eunuchs.

10 And the prince of the eunuchs said unto Dan'iel, I fear my lord the king, who hath appointed your meat and your drink: for why should he see your faces worse liking than the children which *are* of your sort? then shall ye make *me* endanger my head to the king.

11 Then said Dan'iel to Mel'zar, whom the prince of the eunuchs had set over Dan'iel, Han-a-ni'ah, Mish'a-el, and Az-a-ri'ah,

12 Prove thy servants, I beseech thee, ten days; and let them give us pulse to eat, and water to drink.

13 Then let our countenances be looked upon before thee, and the countenance of the children that eat of the portion of the king's meat: and as thou seest, deal with thy servants.

14 So he consented to them in this matter, and proved them ten days.

15 And at the end of ten days their countenances appeared fairer and fatter in flesh than all the children which did eat the portion of the king's meat.

16 Thus Mel'zar took away the portion of their meat, and the wine that they should drink; and gave them pulse.

17 ¶ As for these four children, God gave them knowledge and skill in all learning and wisdom: and Dan'iel had understanding in all visions and dreams.

18 Now at the end of the days that the king had said he should bring them in, then the prince of the eunuchs brought them in before Neb-u-chad-nez'zar.

19 And the king communed with them; and among them all was found none like Dan'iel, Han-a-ni'ah, Mish'a-el, and Az-a-ri'ah: therefore stood they before the king.

20 And in all matters of wisdom *and* understanding, that the king enquired of them, he found them ten times better than all the magicians *and* astrologers that *were* in all his realm.

21 And Dan'iel continued *even* unto the first year of king Cy'rus.

2 AND in the second year of the reign of Neb-u-chad-nez'zar Neb-u-chad-nez'zar dreamed dreams, wherewith his spirit was troubled, and his sleep brake from him.

2 Then the king commanded to call the magicians, and the astrologers, and the sorcerers, and the Chal-de'ans, for to shew the king his dreams. So they came and stood before the king.

3 And the king said unto them, I have dreamed a dream, and my spirit was troubled to know the dream.

4 Then spake the Chal-de'ans to the king in Syr'i-ack, O king, live for ever: tell thy servants the dream, and we will shew the interpretation.

5 The king answered and said to the Chal-de'ans, The thing is gone from me: if ye will not make known unto me the dream, with the interpretation thereof, ye shall be cut in pieces, and your houses shall be made a dunghill.

6 But if ye shew the dream, and the interpretation thereof, ye shall receive of me gifts and rewards and great honour: therefore shew me the dream, and the interpretation thereof.

7 They answered again and said, Let the king tell his servants the dream, and we will shew the interpretation of it.

8 The king answered and said, I know of certainty that ye would gain the time, because ye see the thing is gone from me.

9 But if ye will not make known unto me the dream, *there is but* one decree for you: for ye have prepared lying and corrupt words to speak before me, till the time be changed: therefore tell me the dream, and I shall know that ye can shew me the interpretation thereof.

10 ¶ The Chal-de'ans answered before the king, and said, There is not a man upon the earth that can shew the king's matter: therefore *there is* no king, lord, nor ruler, *that* asked such things at any magician, or astrologer, or Chal-de'an.

11 And *it is* a rare thing that the king requireth, and there is none other that can shew it before the king, except the gods, whose dwelling is not with flesh.

12 For this cause the king was angry and very furious, and commanded to destroy all the wise *men* of Bab'y-lon.

13 And the decree went forth that the wise *men* should be slain; and they sought Dan'iel and his fellows to be slain.

14 ¶ Then Dan'iel answered with counsel and wisdom to A'ri-och the captain of the king's guard, which was gone forth to slay the wise *men* of Bab'y-lon:

15 He answered and said to A'ri-och the king's captain, Why *is* the decree *so* hasty from the king? Then A'ri-och made the thing known to Dan'iel.

16 Then Dan'iel went in, and desired of the king that he would give him time, and that he would shew the king the interpretation.

17 Then Dan'iel went to his house, and made the thing known to Han-a-ni'ah, Mish'a-el, and Az-a-ri'ah, his companions:

18 That they would desire mercies of the God of heaven concerning this secret; that Dan'iel and his fellows should not perish with the rest of the wise *men* of Bab'y-lon.

19 ¶ Then was the secret revealed unto Dan'iel in a night vision. Then Dan'iel blessed the God of heaven.

20 Dan'iel answered and said, Blessed be the name of God for ever and ever: for wisdom and might are his:

21 And he changeth the times and the seasons: he removeth kings, and setteth up kings: he giveth wisdom unto the wise, and knowledge to them that know understanding:

22 He revealeth the deep and secret things: he knoweth what *is* in the darkness, and the light dwelleth with him.

23 I thank thee, and praise thee, O thou God of my fathers, who hast given me wisdom and might, and hast made known unto me now what we desired of thee: for thou hast *now* made known unto us the king's matter.

24 ¶ Therefore Dan'iel went in unto A'ri-och, whom the king had ordained to destroy the wise *men* of Bab'y-lon: he went and said thus unto him; Destroy not the wise *men* of Bab'y-lon: bring me in before the king, and I will shew unto the king the interpretation.

25 Then A'ri-och brought in Dan'iel before the king in haste, and said thus unto him, I have found a man of the captives of Ju'dah, that will make known unto the king the interpretation.

26 The king answered and said to Dan'iel, whose name *was* Bel-te-shaz'zar, Art thou able to make known unto me the dream which I have seen, and the interpretation thereof?

27 Dan'iel answered in the presence of the king, and said, The secret which the king hath demanded cannot the wise *men*, the astrologers, the magicians, the soothsayers, shew unto the king;

28 But there is a God in heaven that revealeth secrets, and maketh known to the king Neb-u-chad-nez'zar what shall be in the latter days. Thy dream, and the visions of thy head upon thy bed, are these;

29 As for thee, O king, thy thoughts came *into thy mind* upon thy bed, what should come to pass hereafter: and he that revealeth secrets maketh known to thee what shall come to pass.

30 But as for me, this secret is not revealed to me for *any* wisdom that I have more than any living, but for *their* sakes that shall make known the interpretation to the king, and that thou mightest know the thoughts of thy heart.

31 ¶ Thou, O king, sawest, and behold a great image. This great image, whose brightness *was* excellent, stood before thee; and the form thereof *was* terrible.

32 This image's head *was* of fine gold, his breast and his arms of silver, his belly and his thighs of brass,

33 His legs of iron, his feet part of iron and part of clay.

34 Thou sawest till that a stone was cut out without hands, which smote the image upon his feet *that were* of iron and clay, and brake them to pieces.

35 Then was the iron, the clay, the brass, the silver, and the gold, broken to pieces together, and became like the chaff of the summer threshingfloors; and the wind carried them

away, that no place was found for them: and the stone that smote the image became a great mountain, and filled the whole earth.

36 ¶ This is the dream; and we will tell the interpretation thereof before the king.

37 Thou, O king, art a king of kings: for the God of heaven hath given thee a kingdom, power, and strength, and glory.

38 And wheresoever the children of men dwell, the beasts of the field and the fowls of the heaven hath he given into thine hand, and hath made thee ruler over them all. Thou art this head of gold.

39 And after thee shall arise another kingdom inferior to thee, and another third kingdom of brass, which shall bear rule over all the earth.

40 And the fourth kingdom shall be strong as iron: forasmuch as iron breaketh in pieces and subdueth all things: and as iron that breaketh all these, shall it break in pieces and bruise.

41 And whereas thou sawest the feet and toes, part of potters' clay, and part of iron, the kingdom shall be divided; but there shall be in it of the strength of the iron, forasmuch as thou sawest the iron mixed with miry clay.

42 And as the toes of the feet were part of iron, and part of clay, so the kingdom shall be partly strong, and partly broken.

43 And whereas thou sawest iron mixed with miry clay, they shall mingle themselves with the seed of men: but they shall not cleave one to another, even as iron is not mixed with clay.

44 And in the days of these kings shall the God of heaven set up a kingdom, which shall never be destroyed: and the kingdom shall not be left to other people, but it shall break in pieces and consume all these kingdoms, and it shall stand for ever.

45 Forasmuch as thou sawest that the stone was cut out of the mountain without hands, and that it brake in pieces the iron, the brass, the clay, the silver, and the gold; the great God hath made known to the king what shall come to pass hereafter: and the dream is certain, and the interpretation thereof sure.

46 ¶ Then the king Neb-u-chad-nez'zar fell upon his face, and worshipped Dan'iel, and commanded that they should offer an oblation and sweet odours unto him.

47 The king answered unto Dan'iel, and said, Of a truth it is, that your God is a God of gods, and a Lord of kings, and a revealer of secrets, seeing thou couldest reveal this secret.

48 Then the king made Dan'iel a great man, and gave him many great gifts, and made him ruler over the whole province of Bab'y-lon, and chief of the governors over all the wise men of Bab'y-lon.

49 Then Dan'iel requested of the king, and he set Sha'drach, Me'shach, and A-bed'-ne-go, over the affairs of the province of Bab'y-lon: but Dan'iel sat in the gate of the king.

3 NEB-CHAD-NEZ'ZAR the king made an image of gold, whose height was threescore cubits, and the breadth thereof six cubits: he set it up in the plain of Du'ra, in the province of Bab'y-lon.

2 Then Neb-u-chad-nez'zar the king sent to gather together the princes, the governors, and the captains, the judges, the treasurers, the counsellors, the sheriffs, and all the rulers of the provinces, to come to the dedication of the image which Neb-u-chad-nez'zar the king had set up.

3 Then the princes, the governors, and captains, the judges, the treasurers, the counsellors, the sheriffs, and all the rulers of the provinces, were gathered together unto the dedication of the image that Neb-u-chad-nez'zar the king had set up; and they stood before the image that Neb-u-chad-nez'zar had set up.

4 Then an herald cried aloud, To you it is commanded, O people, nations, and languages,

5 That at what time ye hear the sound of the cornet, flute, harp, sackbut, psaltery, dulcimer, and all kinds of musick, ye fall down and worship the golden image that Neb-u-chad-nez'zar the king hath set up:

6 And whoso falleth not down and worshippeth shall the same hour be cast into the midst of a burning fiery furnace.

7 Therefore at that time, when all the people heard the sound of the cornet, flute, harp, sackbut, psaltery, and all kinds of musick, all the people, the nations, and the languages, fell down and worshipped the golden image that Neb-u-chad-nez'zar the king had set up.

8 ¶ Wherefore at that time certain Chal-de'-ans came near, and accused the Jews.

9 They spake and said to the king Neb-u-chad-nez'zar, O king, live for ever.

10 Thou, O king, hast made a decree, that every man that shall hear the sound of the cornet, flute, harp, sackbut, psaltery, and dulcimer, and all kinds of musick, shall fall down and worship the golden image:

11 And whoso falleth not down and worshippeth, that he should be cast into the midst of a burning fiery furnace.

12 There are certain Jews whom thou hast set over the affairs of the province of Bab'y-lon, Sha'drach, Me'shach, and A-bed'-ne-go; these men, O king, have not regarded thee: they serve not thy gods, nor worship the golden image which thou hast set up.

13 ¶ Then Neb-u-chad-nez'zar in his rage and fury commanded to bring Sha'drach, Me'-shach, and A-bed'-ne-go. Then they brought these men before the king.

14 Neb-u-chad-nez'zar spake and said unto them, Is it true, O Sha'drach, Me'shach, and A-bed'-nego, do not ye serve my gods, nor worship the golden image which I have set up?

15 Now if ye be ready that at what time ye hear the sound of the cornet, flute, harp, sackbut, psaltery, and dulcimer, and all kinds of musick, ye fall down and worship the image which I have made; well: but if ye worship not, ye shall be cast the same hour into the midst of a burning fiery furnace; and who is that God that shall deliver you out of my hands?

16 Sha'drach, Me'shach, and A-bed'-ne-go, answered and said to the king, O Neb-u-chad-nez'zar, we are not careful to answer thee in this matter.

17 If it be so, our God whom we serve is able to deliver us from the burning fiery furnace, and he will deliver us out of thine hand, O king.

18 But if not, be it known unto thee, O king, that we will not serve thy gods, nor worship the golden image which thou hast set up.

19 ¶ Then was Neb-u-chad-nez'zar full of fury, and the form of his visage was changed against Sha'drach, Me'shach, and A-bed'-ne-go: therefore he spake, and commanded that they should heat the furnace one seven times more than it was wont to be heated.

20 And he commanded the most mighty men that were in his army to bind Sha'drach, Me'-shach, and A-bed'-ne-go, and to cast them into the burning fiery furnace.

21 Then these men were bound in their coats, their hosen, and their hats, and their other gar-

ments, and were cast into the midst of the burning fiery furnace.

22 Therefore because the king's commandment was urgent, and the furnace exceeding hot, the flame of the fire slew those men that took up Sha'drach, Me'shach, and A-bed'-nego.

23 And these three men, Sha'drach, Me'shach, and A-bed'-ne-go, fell down bound into the midst of the burning fiery furnace.

24 Then Neb-u-chad-nez'zar the king was astonied, and rose up in haste, *and* spake, and said unto his counsellors, Did not we cast three men bound into the midst of the fire? They answered and said unto the king, True, O king.

25 He answered and said, Lo, I see four men loose, walking in the midst of the fire, and they have no hurt; and the form of the fourth is like the Son of God.

26 ¶ Then Neb-u-chad-nez'zar came near to the mouth of the burning fiery furnace, *and* spake, and said, Sha'drach, Me'shach, and A-bed'-ne-go, ye servants of the most high God, come forth, and come *hither*. Then Sha'drach, Me'shach, and A-bed'-ne-go, came forth of the midst of the fire.

27 And the princes, governors, and captains, and the king's counsellors, being gathered together saw these men, upon whose bodies the fire had no power, nor was an hair of their head singed, neither were their coats changed, nor the smell of fire had passed on them.

28 *Then* Neb-u-chad-nez'zar spake, and said, Blessed *be* the God of Sha'drach, Me'shach, and A-bed'-ne-go, who hath sent his angel, and delivered his servants that trusted in him, and have changed the king's word, and yielded their bodies, that they might not serve nor worship any god, except their own God.

29 Therefore I make a decree, That every people, nation, and language, which speak any thing amiss against the God of Sha'drach, Me'shach, and A-bed'-ne-go, shall be cut in pieces, and their houses shall be made a dunghill: because there is no other God that can deliver after this sort.

30 Then the king promoted Sha'drach, Me'shach, and A-bed'-ne-go, in the province of Bab'y-lon.

4 NEB-CHAD-NEZ'ZAR the king, unto all people, nations, and languages, that dwell in all the earth; Peace be multiplied unto you.

2 I thought it good to shew the signs and wonders that the high God hath wrought toward me.

3 How great *are* his signs! and how mighty *are* his wonders! his kingdom *is* an everlasting kingdom, and his dominion *is* from generation to generation.

4 ¶ I Neb-u-chad-nez'zar was at rest in mine house, and flourishing in my palace:

5 I saw a dream which made me afraid, and the thoughts upon my bed and the visions of my head troubled me.

6 Therefore made I a decree to bring in all the wise *men* of Bab'y-lon before me, that they might make known unto me the interpretation of the dream.

7 Then came in the magicians, the astrologers, the Chal-de'ans, and the soothsayers: and I told the dream before them; but they did not make known unto me the interpretation thereof.

8 ¶ But at the last Dan'iel came in before me, whose name *was* Bel-te-shaz'zar, according to the name of my god, and in whom *is* the spirit of the holy gods: and before him I told the dream, *saying*,

9 O Bel-te-shaz'zar, master of the magicians, because I know that the spirit of the holy gods *is* in thee, and no secret troubleth thee, tell me the visions of my dream that I have seen, and the interpretation thereof.

10 Thus *were* the visions of mine head in my bed; I saw, and behold a tree in the midst of the earth, and the height thereof *was* great.

11 The tree grew, and was strong, and the height thereof reached unto heaven, and the sight thereof to the end of all the earth:

12 The leaves thereof *were* fair, and the fruit thereof much, and in it *was* meat for all: the beasts of the field had shadow under it, and the fowls of the heaven dwelt in the boughs thereof, and all flesh was fed of it.

13 I saw in the visions of my head upon my bed, and, behold, a watcher and an holy one came down from heaven;

14 He cried aloud, and said thus, Hew down the tree, and cut off his branches, shake off his leaves, and scatter his fruit: let the beasts get away from under it, and the fowls from his branches:

15 Nevertheless leave the stump of his roots in the earth, even with a band of iron and brass, in the tender grass of the field; and let it be wet with the dew of heaven, and *let* his portion *be* with the beasts in the grass of the earth:

16 Let his heart be changed from man's, and let a beast's heart be given unto him; and let seven times pass over him.

17 This matter *is* by the decree of the watchers, and the demand by the word of the holy ones: to the intent that the living may know that the most High ruleth in the kingdom of men, and giveth it to whomsoever he will, and setteth up over it the basest of men.

18 This dream I king Neb-u-chad-nez'zar have seen. Now thou, O Bel-te-shaz'zar, declare the interpretation thereof, forasmuch as all the wise *men* of my kingdom are not able to make known unto me the interpretation: but thou *art* able; for the spirit of the holy gods *is* in thee.

19 ¶ Then Dan'iel, whose name *was* Bel-te-shaz'zar, was astonied for one hour, and his thoughts troubled him. The king spake, and said, Bel-te-shaz'zar, let not the dream, or the interpretation thereof, trouble thee. Bel-te-shaz'zar answered and said, My lord, the dream *be* to them that hate thee, and the interpretation thereof to thine enemies.

20 The tree that thou sawest, which grew, and was strong, whose height reached unto the heaven, and the sight thereof to all the earth;

21 Whose leaves *were* fair, and the fruit thereof much, and in it *was* meat for all; under which the beasts of the field dwelt, and upon whose branches the fowls of the heaven had their habitation:

22 It *is* thou, O king, that art grown and become strong: for thy greatness is grown, and reacheth unto heaven, and thy dominion to the end of the earth.

23 And whereas the king saw a watcher and an holy one coming down from heaven, and saying, Hew the tree down, and destroy it; yet leave the stump of the roots thereof in the earth, even with a band of iron and brass, in the tender grass of the field; and let it be wet with the dew of heaven, and *let* his portion *be* with the beasts of the field, till seven times pass over him;

24 This *is* the interpretation, O king, and this

is the decree of the most High, which is come upon my lord the king:

25 That they shall drive thee from men, and thy dwelling shall be with the beasts of the field, and they shall make thee to eat grass as oxen, and they shall wet thee with the dew of heaven, and seven times shall pass over thee, till thou know that the most High ruleth in the kingdom of men, and giveth it to whomsoever he will.

26 And whereas they commanded to leave the stump of the tree roots; thy kingdom shall be sure unto thee, after that thou shalt have known that the heavens do rule.

27 Wherefore, O king, let my counsel be acceptable unto thee, and break off thy sins by righteousness, and thine iniquities by shewing mercy to the poor; if it may be a lengthening of thy tranquillity.

28 ¶ All this came upon the king Neb-u-chad-nez'zar.

29 At the end of twelve months he walked in the palace of the kingdom of Bab'y-lon.

30 The king spake, and said, Is not this great Bab'y-lon, that I have built for the house of the kingdom by the might of my power, and for the honour of my majesty?

31 While the word *was* in the king's mouth, there fell a voice from heaven, *saying*, O king Neb-u-chad-nez'zar, to thee it is spoken; The kingdom is departed from thee.

32 And they shall drive thee from men, and thy dwelling *shall be* with the beasts of the field: they shall make thee to eat grass as oxen, and seven times shall pass over thee, until thou know that the most High ruleth in the kingdom of men, and giveth it to whomsoever he will.

33 The same hour was the thing fulfilled upon Neb-u-chad-nez'zar: and he was driven from men, and did eat grass as oxen, and his body was wet with the dew of heaven, till his hairs were grown like eagles' *feathers*, and his nails like birds' *claws*.

34 And at the end of the days I Neb-u-chad-nez'zar lifted up mine eyes unto heaven, and mine understanding returned unto me, and I blessed the most High, and I praised and honoured him that liveth for ever, whose dominion *is* an everlasting dominion, and his kingdom *is* from generation to generation:

35 And all the inhabitants of the earth *are* reputed as nothing: and he doeth according to his will in the army of heaven, and *among* the inhabitants of the earth: and none can stay his hand, or say unto him, What doest thou?

36 At the same time my reason returned unto me; and for the glory of my kingdom, mine honour and brightness returned unto me; and my counsellors and my lords sought unto me; and I was established in my kingdom, and excellent majesty was added unto me.

37 Now I Neb-u-chad-nez'zar praise and extol and honour the King of heaven, all whose works *are* truth, and his ways judgment: and those that walk in pride he is able to abase.

5 BEL-SHAZ'ZAR the king made a great feast to a thousand of his lords, and drank wine before the thousand.

2 Bel-shaz'zar, whiles he tasted the wine, commanded to bring the golden and silver vessels which his father Neb-u-chad-nez'zar had taken out of the temple which *was* in Je-ru'sa-lem; that the king, and his princes, his wives, and his concubines, might drink therein.

3 Then they brought the golden vessels that were taken out of the temple of the house of God which *was* at Je-ru'sa-lem; and the king, and his princes, his wives, and his concubines, drank in them.

4 They drank wine, and praised the gods of gold, and of silver, of brass, of iron, of wood, and of stone.

5 ¶ In the same hour came forth fingers of a man's hand, and wrote over against the candlestick upon the plaister of the wall of the king's palace: and the king saw the part of the hand that wrote.

6 Then the king's countenance was changed, and his thoughts troubled him, so that the joints of his loins were loosed, and his knees smote one against another.

7 The king cried aloud to bring in the astrologers, the Chal-de'ans, and the soothsayers. *And* the king spake, and said to the wise *men* of Bab'y-lon, Whosoever shall read this writing, and shew me the interpretation thereof, shall be clothed with scarlet, and *have* a chain of gold about his neck, and shall be the third ruler in the kingdom.

8 Then came in all the king's wise *men:* but they could not read the writing, nor make known to the king the interpretation thereof.

9 Then was king Bel-shaz'zar greatly troubled, and his countenance was changed in him, and his lords were astonied.

10 ¶ *Now* the queen by reason of the words of the king and his lords came into the banquet house: *and* the queen spake and said, O king, live for ever: let not thy thoughts trouble thee, nor let thy countenance be changed:

11 There is a man in thy kingdom, in whom *is* the spirit of the holy gods; and in the days of thy father light and understanding and wisdom, like the wisdom of the gods, was found in him; whom the king Neb-u-chad-nez'zar thy father, the king, *I say*, thy father, made master of the magicians, astrologers, Chal-de'ans, *and* soothsayers;

12 Forasmuch as an excellent spirit, and knowledge, and understanding, interpreting of dreams, and shewing of hard sentences, and dissolving of doubts, were found in the same Dan'iel, whom the king named Bel-te-shaz'zar: now let Dan'iel be called, and he will shew the interpretation.

13 Then was Dan'iel brought in before the king. *And* the king spake and said unto Dan'iel, *Art* thou that Dan'iel, which *art* of the children of the captivity of Ju'dah, whom the king my father brought out of Jew'ry?

14 I have even heard of thee, that the spirit of the gods *is* in thee, and *that* light and understanding and excellent wisdom is found in thee.

15 And now the wise *men*, the astrologers, have been brought in before me, that they should read this writing, and make known unto me the interpretation thereof: but they could not shew the interpretation of the thing:

16 And I have heard of thee, that thou canst make interpretations, and dissolve doubts: now if thou canst read the writing, and make known to me the interpretation thereof, thou shalt be clothed with scarlet, and *have* a chain of gold about thy neck, and shalt be the third ruler in the kingdom.

17 ¶ Then Dan'iel answered and said before the king, Let thy gifts be to thyself, and give thy rewards to another; yet I will read the writing unto the king, and make known to him the interpretation.

18 O thou king, the most high God gave Neb-u-chad-nez'zar thy father a kingdom, and majesty, and glory, and honour:

19 And for the majesty that he gave him, all people, nations, and languages, trembled and feared before him: whom he would he slew; and whom he would he kept alive; and whom he would he set up; and whom he would he put down.

20 But when his heart was lifted up, and his mind hardened in pride, he was deposed from his kingly throne, and they took his glory from him:

21 And he was driven from the sons of men; and his heart was made like the beasts, and his dwelling *was* with the wild asses: they fed him with grass like oxen, and his body was wet with the dew of heaven; till he knew that the most high God ruled in the kingdom of men, and *that* he appointeth over it whomsoever he will.

22 And thou his son, O Bel-shaz'zar, hast not humbled thine heart, though thou knewest all this;

23 But hast lifted up thyself against the Lord of heaven; and they have brought the vessels of his house before thee, and thou, and thy lords, thy wives, and thy concubines, have drunk wine in them; and thou hast praised the gods of silver, and gold, of brass, iron, wood, and stone, which see not, nor hear, nor know: and the God in whose hand thy breath *is*, and whose *are* all thy ways, hast thou not glorified:

24 Then was the part of the hand sent from him; and this writing was written.

25 ¶ And this *is* the writing that was written, ME'NE, ME'NE, TE'KEL, U-PHAR'SIN.

26 This *is* the interpretation of the thing: ME'NE; God hath numbered thy kingdom, and finished it.

27 TE'KEL; Thou art weighed in the balances, and art found wanting.

28 PE'RES; Thy kingdom is divided, and given to the Medes and Per'sians.

29 Then commanded Bel-shaz'zar, and they clothed Dan'iel with scarlet, and *put* a chain of gold about his neck, and made a proclamation concerning him, that he should be the third ruler in the kingdom.

30 ¶ In that night was Bel-shaz'zar the king of the Chal-de'ans slain.

31 And Da-ri'us the Me'di-an took the kingdom, *being* about threescore and two years old.

6 IT pleased Da-ri'us to set over the kingdom an hundred and twenty princes, which should be over the whole kingdom;

2 And over these three presidents; of whom Dan'iel *was* first: that the princes might give accounts unto them, and the king should have no damage.

3 Then this Dan'iel was preferred above the presidents and princes, because an excellent spirit *was* in him; and the king thought to set him over the whole realm.

4 ¶ Then the presidents and princes sought to find occasion against Dan'iel concerning the kingdom; but they could find none occasion nor fault; forasmuch as he *was* faithful, neither was there any error or fault found in him.

5 Then said these men, We shall not find any occasion against this Dan'iel, except we find *it* against him concerning the law of his God.

6 Then these presidents and princes assembled together to the king, and said thus unto him, King Da-ri'us, live for ever.

7 All the presidents of the kingdom, the governors, and the princes, the counsellors, and the captains, have consulted together to establish a royal statute, and to make a firm decree, that whosoever shall ask a petition of any God or man for thirty days, save of thee, O king, he shall be cast into the den of lions.

8 Now, O king, establish the decree, and sign the writing, that it be not changed, according to the law of the Medes and Per'sians, which altereth not.

9 Wherefore king Da-ri'us signed the writing and the decree.

10 ¶ Now when Dan'iel knew that the writing was signed, he went into his house; and his windows being open in his chamber toward Je-ru'sa-lem, he kneeled upon his knees three times a day, and prayed, and gave thanks before his God, as he did aforetime.

11 Then these men assembled, and found Dan'iel praying and making supplication before his God.

12 Then they came near, and spake before the king concerning the king's decree; Hast thou not signed a decree, that every man that shall ask *a petition* of any God or man within thirty days, save of thee, O king, shall be cast into the den of lions? The king answered and said, The thing *is* true, according to the law of the Medes and Per'sians, which altereth not.

13 Then answered they and said before the king, That Dan'iel, which *is* of the children of the captivity of Ju'dah, regardeth not thee, O king, nor the decree that thou hast signed, but maketh his petition three times a day.

14 Then the king, when he heard *these* words, was sore displeased with himself, and set *his* heart on Dan'iel to deliver him: and he laboured till the going down of the sun to deliver him.

15 Then these men assembled unto the king, and said unto the king, Know, O king, that the law of the Medes and Per'sians *is*, That no decree nor statute which the king establisheth may be changed.

16 Then the king commanded, and they brought Dan'iel, and cast *him* into the den of lions. *Now* the king spake and said unto Dan'iel, Thy God whom thou servest continually, he will deliver thee.

17 And a stone was brought, and laid upon the mouth of the den; and the king sealed it with his own signet, and with the signet of his lords; that the purpose might not be changed concerning Dan'iel.

18 ¶ Then the king went to his palace, and passed the night fasting: neither were instruments of musick brought before him: and his sleep went from him.

19 Then the king arose very early in the morning, and went in haste unto the den of lions.

20 And when he came to the den, he cried with a lamentable voice unto Dan'iel: *and* the king spake and said to Dan'iel, O Dan'iel, servant of the living God, is thy God, whom thou servest continually, able to deliver thee from the lions?

21 Then said Dan'iel unto the king, O king, live for ever.

22 My God hath sent his angel, and hath shut the lions' mouths, that they have not hurt me: forasmuch as before him innocency was found in me; and also before thee, O king, have I done no hurt.

23 Then was the king exceeding glad for him, and commanded that they should take Dan'iel up out of the den. So Dan'iel was taken up out of the den, and no manner of hurt was found upon him, because he believed in his God.

24 ¶ And the king commanded, and they brought those men which had accused Dan'iel,

and they cast *them* into the den of lions, them, their children, and their wives; and the lions had the mastery of them, and brake all their bones in pieces or ever they came at the bottom of the den.

25 ¶ Then king Da-ri′us wrote unto all people, nations, and languages, that dwell in all the earth; Peace be multiplied unto you.

26 I make a decree, That in every dominion of my kingdom men tremble and fear before the God of Dan′iel: for he *is* the living God, and stedfast for ever, and his kingdom *that* which shall not be destroyed, and his dominion *shall be even* unto the end.

27 He delivereth and rescueth, and he worketh signs and wonders in heaven and in earth, who hath delivered Dan′iel from the power of the lions.

28 So this Dan′iel prospered in the reign of Da-ri′us, and in the reign of Cy′rus the Per′sian.

7 IN the first year of Bel-shaz′zar king of Bab′y-lon Dan′iel had a dream and visions of his head upon his bed: then he wrote the dream, *and* told the sum of the matters.

2 Dan′iel spake and said, I saw in my vision by night, and, behold, the four winds of the heaven strove upon the great sea.

3 And four great beasts came up from the sea, diverse one from another.

4 The first *was* like a lion, and had eagle's wings: I beheld till the wings thereof were plucked, and it was lifted up from the earth, and made stand upon the feet as a man, and a man's heart was given to it.

5 And behold another beast, a second, like to a bear, and it raised up itself on one side, and *it had* three ribs in the mouth of it between the teeth of it: and they said thus unto it, Arise, devour much flesh.

6 After this I beheld, and lo another, like a leopard, which had upon the back of it four wings of a fowl; the beast had also four heads; and dominion was given to it.

7 After this I saw in the night visions, and behold a fourth beast, dreadful and terrible, and strong exceedingly; and it had great iron teeth: it devoured and brake in pieces, and stamped the residue with the feet of it: and it *was* diverse from all the beasts that *were* before it; and it had ten horns.

8 I considered the horns, and, behold, there came up among them another little horn, before whom there were three of the first horns plucked up by the roots: and, behold, in this horn *were* eyes like the eyes of man, and a mouth speaking great things.

9 ¶ I beheld till the thrones were cast down, and the Ancient of days did sit, whose garment *was* white as snow, and the hair of his head like the pure wool: his throne *was like* the fiery flame, *and* his wheels *as* burning fire.

10 A fiery stream issued and came forth from before him: thousand thousands ministered unto him, and ten thousand times ten thousand stood before him: the judgment was set, and the books were opened.

11 I beheld then because of the voice of the great words which the horn spake: I beheld *even* till the beast was slain, and his body destroyed, and given to the burning flame.

12 As concerning the rest of the beasts, they had their dominion taken away: yet their lives were prolonged for a season and time.

13 I saw in the night visions, and, behold, *one* like the Son of man came with the clouds of heaven, and came to the Ancient of days, and they brought him near before him.

14 And there was given him dominion, and glory, and a kingdom, that all people, nations, and languages, should serve him: his dominion *is* an everlasting dominion, which shall not pass away, and his kingdom *that* which shall not be destroyed.

15 ¶ I Dan′iel was grieved in my spirit in the midst of *my* body, and the visions of my head troubled me.

16 I came near unto one of them that stood by, and asked him the truth of all this. So he told me, and made me know the interpretation of the things.

17 These great beasts, which are four, *are* four kings, *which* shall arise out of the earth.

18 But the saints of the most High shall take the kingdom, and possess the kingdom for ever, even for ever and ever.

19 Then I would know the truth of the fourth beast, which was diverse from all the others, exceeding dreadful, whose teeth *were of* iron, and his nails *of* brass; *which* devoured, brake in pieces, and stamped the residue with his feet;

20 And of the ten horns that *were* in his head, and *of* the other which came up, and before whom three fell; even *of* that horn that had eyes, and a mouth that spake very great things, whose look *was* more stout than his fellows.

21 I beheld, and the same horn made war with the saints, and prevailed against them;

22 Until the Ancient of days came, and judgment was given to the saints of the most High; and the time came that the saints possessed the kingdom.

23 Thus he said, The fourth beast shall be the fourth kingdom upon earth, which shall be diverse from all kingdoms, and shall devour the whole earth, and shall tread it down, and break it in pieces.

24 And the ten horns out of this kingdom *are* ten kings *that* shall arise: and another shall rise after them; and he shall be diverse from the first, and he shall subdue three kings.

25 And he shall speak *great* words against the most High, and shall wear out the saints of the most High, and think to change times and laws: and they shall be given into his hand until a time and times and the dividing of time.

26 But the judgment shall sit, and they shall take away his dominion, to consume and to destroy *it* unto the end.

27 And the kingdom and dominion, and the greatness of the kingdom under the whole heaven, shall be given to the people of the saints of the most High, whose kingdom *is* an everlasting kingdom, and all dominions shall serve and obey him.

28 Hitherto *is* the end of the matter. As for me Dan′iel, my cogitations much troubled me, and my countenance changed in me: but I kept the matter in my heart.

8 IN the third year of the reign of king Belshaz′zar a vision appeared unto me, *even unto* me Dan′iel, after that which appeared unto me at the first.

2 And I saw in a vision; and it came to pass, when I saw, that I *was* at Shu′shan *in* the palace, which *is* in the province of E′lam; and I saw in a vision, and I was by the river of U′la-i.

3 Then I lifted up mine eyes, and saw, and, behold, there stood before the river a ram which had *two* horns: and the *two* horns *were* high; but one *was* higher than the other, and the higher came up last.

4 I saw the ram pushing westward, and northward, and southward; so that no beasts might stand before him, neither *was there any* that could deliver out of his hand; but he did according to his will, and became great.

5 And as I was considering, behold, an he goat came from the west on the face of the whole earth, and touched not the ground: and the goat *had* a notable horn between his eyes.

6 And he came to the ram that had *two* horns, which I had seen standing before the river, and ran unto him in the fury of his power.

7 And I saw him come close unto the ram, and he was moved with choler against him, and smote the ram, and brake his two horns: and there was no power in the ram to stand before him, but he cast him down to the ground, and stamped upon him: and there was none that could deliver the ram out of his hand.

8 Therefore the he goat waxed very great: and when he was strong, the great horn was broken; and for it came up four notable ones toward the four winds of heaven.

9 And out of one of them came forth a little horn, which waxed exceeding great, toward the south, and toward the east, and toward ·the pleasant *land.*

10 And it waxed great, *even* to the host of heaven; and it cast down *some* of the host and of the stars to the ground, and stamped upon them.

11 Yea, he magnified *himself* even to the prince of the host, and by him the daily *sacrifice* was taken away, and the place of his sanctuary was cast down.

12 And an host was given *him* against the daily *sacrifice* by reason of transgression, and it cast down the truth to the ground; and it practised, and prospered.

13 ¶ Then I heard one saint speaking, and another saint said unto that certain *saint* which spake, How long *shall be* the vision *concerning* the daily *sacrifice,* and the transgression of desolation, to give both the sanctuary and the host to be trodden under foot?

14 And he said unto me, Unto two thousand and three hundred days; then shall the sanctuary be cleansed.

15 ¶ And it came to pass, when I, *even* I Dan′iel, had seen the vision, and sought for the meaning, then, behold, there stood before me as the appearance of a man.

16 And I heard a man's voice between *the banks of* U′la-i, which called, and said, Ga′bri-el, make this *man* to understand the vision.

17 So he came near where I stood: and when he came, I was afraid, and fell upon my face: but he said unto me, Understand, O son of man: for at the time of the end *shall be* the vision.

18 Now as he was speaking with me, I was in a deep sleep on my face toward the ground: but he touched me, and set me upright.

19 And he said, Behold, I will make thee know what shall be in the last end of the indignation: for at the time appointed the end *shall be.*

20 The ram which thou sawest having *two* horns *are* the kings of Me′di-a and Per′sia.

21 And the rough goat *is* the king of Gre′cia: and the great horn that *is* between his eyes *is* the first king.

22 Now that being broken, whereas four stood up for it, four kingdoms shall stand up out of the nation, but not in his power.

23 And in the latter time of their kingdom, when the transgressors are come to the full, a king of fierce countenance, and understanding dark sentences, shall stand up.

24 And his power shall be mighty, but not by his own power: and he shall destroy wonderfully, and shall prosper, and practise, and shall destroy the mighty and the holy people.

25 And through his policy also he shall cause craft to prosper in his hand; and he shall magnify *himself* in his heart, and by peace shall destroy many: he shall also stand up against the Prince of princes; but he shall be broken without hand.

26 And the vision of the evening and the morning which was told *is* true: wherefore shut thou up the vision; for it *shall be* for many days.

27 And I Dan′iel fainted, and was sick *certain* days; afterward I rose up, and did the king's business; and I was astonished at the vision, but none understood *it.*

9 IN the first year of Da-ri′us the son of A-has-u-e′rus, of the seed of the Medes, which was made king over the realm of the Chal-de′ans;

2 In the first year of his reign I Dan′iel understood by books the number of the years, whereof the word of the LORD came to Jer-e-mi′ah the prophet, that he would accomplish seventy years in the desolations of Je-ru′sa-lem.

3 ¶ And I set my face unto the Lord God, to seek by prayer and supplications, with fasting, and sackcloth, and ashes:

4 And I prayed unto the LORD my God, and made my confession, and said, O Lord, the great and dreadful God, keeping the covenant and mercy to them that love him, and to them that keep his commandments;

5 We have sinned, and have committed iniquity, and have done wickedly, and have rebelled, even by departing from thy precepts and from thy judgments:

6 Neither have we hearkened unto thy servants the prophets, which spake in thy name to our kings, our princes, and our fathers, and to all the people of the land.

7 O Lord, righteousness *belongeth* unto thee, but unto us confusion of faces, as at this day; to the men of Ju′dah, and to the inhabitants of Je-ru′sa-lem, and unto all Is′ra-el, *that are* near, and *that are* far off, through all the countries whither thou hast driven them, because of their trespass that they have trespassed against thee.

8 O Lord, to us *belongeth* confusion of face, to our kings, to our princes, and to our fathers, because we have sinned against thee.

9 To the Lord our God *belong* mercies and forgivenesses, though we have rebelled against him;

10 Neither have we obeyed the voice of the LORD our God, to walk in his laws, which he set before us by his servants the prophets.

11 Yea, all Is′ra-el have transgressed thy law, even by departing, that they might not obey thy voice; therefore the curse is poured upon us, and the oath that *is* written in the law of Mo′ses the servant of God, because we have sinned against him.

12 And he hath confirmed his words, which he spake against us, and against our judges that judged us, by bringing upon us a great evil: for under the whole heaven hath not been done as hath been done upon Je-ru′sa-lem.

13 As *it is* written in the law of Mo′ses, all this evil is come upon us: yet made we not our prayer before the LORD our God, that we might turn from our iniquities, and understand thy truth.

14 Therefore hath the LORD watched upon the evil, and brought it upon us: for the LORD our God is righteous in all his works which he doeth: for we obeyed not his voice.

15 And now, O Lord our God, that hast brought thy people forth out of the land of E'-gypt with a mighty hand, and hast gotten thee renown, as at this day; we have sinned, we have done wickedly.

16 ¶ O Lord, according to all thy righteousness, I beseech thee, let thine anger and thy fury be turned away from thy city Je-ru'sa-lem, thy holy mountain: because for our sins, and for the iniquities of our fathers, Je-ru'sa-lem and thy people are become a reproach to all that are about us.

17 Now therefore, O our God, hear the prayer of thy servant, and his supplications, and cause thy face to shine upon thy sanctuary that is desolate, for the Lord's sake.

18 O my God, incline thine ear, and hear; open thine eyes, and behold our desolations, and the city which is called by thy name: for we do not present our supplications before thee for our righteousnesses, but for thy great mercies.

19 O Lord, hear; O Lord, forgive; O Lord, hearken and do; defer not, for thine own sake, O my God: for thy city and thy people are called by thy name.

20 ¶ And whiles I was speaking, and praying, and confessing my sin and the sin of my people Is'ra-el, and presenting my supplication before the LORD my God for the holy mountain of my God;

21 Yea, whiles I was speaking in prayer, even the man Ga'bri-el, whom I had seen in the vision at the beginning, being caused to fly swiftly, touched me about the time of the evening oblation.

22 And he informed me, and talked with me, and said, O Dan'iel, I am now come forth to give thee skill and understanding.

23 At the beginning of thy supplications the commandment came forth, and I am come to shew thee; for thou art greatly beloved: therefore understand the matter, and consider the vision.

24 Seventy weeks are determined upon thy people and upon thy holy city, to finish the transgression, and to make an end of sins, and to make reconciliation for iniquity, and to bring in everlasting righteousness, and to seal up the vision and prophecy, and to anoint the most Holy.

25 Know therefore and understand, that from the going forth of the commandment to restore and to build Je-ru'sa-lem unto the Mes-si'ah the Prince shall be seven weeks, and threescore and two weeks: the street shall be built again, and the wall, even in troublous times.

26 And after threescore and two weeks shall Mes-si'ah be cut off, but not for himself: and the people of the prince that shall come shall destroy the city and the sanctuary; and the end thereof shall be with a flood, and unto the end of the war desolations are determined.

27 And he shall confirm the covenant with many for one week: and in the midst of the week he shall cause the sacrifice and the oblation to cease, and for the overspreading of abominations he shall make it desolate, even until the consummation, and that determined shall be poured upon the desolate.

10 IN the third year of Cy'rus king of Per'-sia a thing was revealed unto Dan'iel, whose name was called Bel-te-shaz'zar; and the thing was true, but the time appointed was long: and he understood the thing, and had understanding of the vision.

2 In those days I Dan'iel was mourning three full weeks.

3 I ate no pleasant bread, neither came flesh nor wine in my mouth, neither did I anoint myself at all, till three whole weeks were fulfilled.

4 And in the four and twentieth day of the first month, as I was by the side of the great river, which is Hid'de-kel;

5 Then I lifted up mine eyes, and looked, and behold a certain man clothed in linen, whose loins were girded with fine gold of U'phaz:

6 His body also was like the beryl, and his face as the appearance of lightning, and his eyes as lamps of fire, and his arms and his feet like in colour to polished brass, and the voice of his words like the voice of a multitude.

7 And I Dan'iel alone saw the vision: for the men that were with me saw not the vision; but a great quaking fell upon them, so that they fled to hide themselves.

8 Therefore I was left alone, and saw this great vision, and there remained no strength in me: for my comeliness was turned in me into corruption, and I retained no strength.

9 Yet heard I the voice of his words: and when I heard the voice of his words, then was I in a deep sleep on my face, and my face toward the ground.

10 ¶ And, behold, an hand touched me, which set me upon my knees and upon the palms of my hands.

11 And he said unto me, O Dan'iel, a man greatly beloved, understand the words that I speak unto thee, and stand upright: for unto thee am I now sent. And when he had spoken this word unto me, I stood trembling.

12 Then said he unto me, Fear not, Dan'iel: for from the first day that thou didst set thine heart to understand, and to chasten thyself before thy God, thy words were heard, and I am come for thy words.

13 But the prince of the kingdom of Per'sia withstood me one and twenty days: but, lo, Mi'-chael, one of the chief princes, came to help me; and I remained there with the kings of Per'sia.

14 Now I am come to make thee understand what shall befall thy people in the latter days: for yet the vision is for many days.

15 And when he had spoken such words unto me, I set my face toward the ground, and I became dumb.

16 And, behold, one like the similitude of the sons of men touched my lips: then I opened my mouth, and spake, and said unto him that stood before me, O my lord, by the vision my sorrows are turned upon me, and I have retained no strength.

17 For how can the servant of this my lord talk with this my lord? for as for me, straightway there remained no strength in me, neither is there breath left in me.

18 Then there came again and touched me one like the appearance of a man, and he strengthened me,

19 And said, O man greatly beloved, fear not: peace be unto thee, be strong, yea, be strong. And when he had spoken unto me, I was strengthened, and said, Let my lord speak; for thou hast strengthened me.

20 Then said he, Knowest thou wherefore I come unto thee? and now will I return to fight with the prince of Per'sia: and when I am gone forth, lo, the prince of Gre'cia shall come.

21 But I will shew thee that which is noted in the scripture of truth: and *there is* none that holdeth with me in these things, but Mi′chael your prince.

11 ALSO I in the first year of Da-ri′us the Mede, *even* I, stood to confirm and to strengthen him.

2 And now will I shew thee the truth. Behold, there shall stand up yet three kings in Per′sia; and the fourth shall be far richer than *they* all: and by his strength through his riches he shall stir up all against the realm of Gre′cia.

3 And a mighty king shall stand up, that shall rule with great dominion, and do according to his will.

4 And when he shall stand up, his kingdom shall be broken, and shall be divided toward the four winds of heaven; and not to his posterity, nor according to his dominion which he ruled: for his kingdom shall be plucked up, even for others beside those.

5 ¶ And the king of the south shall be strong, and *one* of his princes; and he shall be strong above him, and have dominion; his dominion *shall be* a great dominion.

6 And in the end of years they shall join themselves together; for the king's daughter of the south shall come to the king of the north to make an agreement: but she shall not retain the power of the arm; neither shall he stand, nor his arm: but she shall be given up, and they that brought her, and he that begat her, and he that strengthened her in *these* times.

7 But out of a branch of her roots shall *one* stand up in his estate, which shall come with an army, and shall enter into the fortress of the king of the north, and shall deal against them, and shall prevail:

8 And shall also carry captives into E′gypt their gods, with their princes, *and* with their precious vessels of silver and of gold; and he shall continue *more* years than the king of the north.

9 So the king of the south shall come into *his* kingdom, and shall return into his own land.

10 But his sons shall be stirred up, and shall assemble a multitude of great forces: and *one* shall certainly come, and overflow, and pass through: then shall he return, and be stirred up, *even* to his fortress.

11 And the king of the south shall be moved with choler, and shall come forth and fight with him, *even* with the king of the north: and he shall set forth a great multitude; but the multitude shall be given into his hand.

12 *And* when he hath taken away the multitude, his heart shall be lifted up; and he shall cast down *many* ten thousands: but he shall not be strengthened *by it.*

13 For the king of the north shall return, and shall set forth a multitude greater than the former, and shall certainly come after certain years with a great army and with much riches.

14 And in those times there shall many stand up against the king of the south: also the robbers of thy people shall exalt themselves to establish the vision; but they shall fall.

15 So the king of the north shall come, and cast up a mount, and take the most fenced cities: and the arms of the south shall not withstand, neither his chosen people, neither *shall there be any* strength to withstand.

16 But he that cometh against him shall do according to his own will, and none shall stand before him: and he shall stand in the glorious land, which by his hand shall be consumed.

17 He shall also set his face to enter with the strength of his whole kingdom, and upright ones with him; thus shall he do: and he shall give him the daughter of women, corrupting her: but she shall not stand *on his side,* neither be for him.

18 After this shall he turn his face unto the isles, and shall take many: but a prince for his own behalf shall cause the reproach offered by him to cease; without his own reproach he shall cause *it* to turn upon him.

19 Then he shall turn his face toward the fort of his own land: but he shall stumble and fall, and not be found.

20 Then shall stand up in his estate a raiser of taxes *in* the glory of the kingdom: but within few days he shall be destroyed, neither in anger, nor in battle.

21 And in his estate shall stand up a vile person, to whom they shall not give the honour of the kingdom: but he shall come in peaceably, and obtain the kingdom by flatteries.

22 And with the arms of a flood shall they be overflown from before him, and shall be broken; yea, also the prince of the covenant.

23 And after the league *made* with him he shall work deceitfully: for he shall come up, and shall become strong with a small people.

24 He shall enter peaceably even upon the fattest places of the province; and he shall do *that* which his fathers have not done, nor his fathers' fathers; he shall scatter among them the prey, and spoil, and riches: *yea,* and he shall forecast his devices against the strong holds, even for a time.

25 And he shall stir up his power and his courage against the king of the south with a great army; and the king of the south shall be stirred up to battle with a very great and mighty army; but he shall not stand: for they shall forecast devices against him.

26 Yea, they that feed of the portion of his meat shall destroy him, and his army shall overflow: and many shall fall down slain.

27 And both these kings' hearts *shall be* to do mischief, and they shall speak lies at one table; but it shall not prosper: for yet the end *shall be* at the time appointed.

28 Then shall he return into his land with great riches; and his heart *shall be* against the holy covenant; and he shall do *exploits,* and return to his own land.

29 At the time appointed he shall return, and come toward the south; but it shall not be as the former, or as the latter.

30 ¶ For the ships of Chit′tim shall come against him: therefore he shall be grieved, and return, and have indignation against the holy covenant: so shall he do; he shall even return, and have intelligence with them that forsake the holy covenant.

31 And arms shall stand on his part, and they shall pollute the sanctuary of strength, and shall take away the daily *sacrifice,* and they shall place the abomination that maketh desolate.

32 And such as do wickedly against the covenant shall he corrupt by flatteries: but the people that do know their God shall be strong, and do *exploits.*

33 And they that understand among the people shall instruct many : yet they shall fall by the sword, and by flame, by captivity, and by spoil, *many* days.

34 Now when they shall fall, they shall be holpen with a little help: but many shall cleave to them with flatteries.

35 And *some* of them of understanding shall fall, to try them, and to purge, and to make *them* white, *even* to the time of the end: because *it is* yet for a time appointed.

36 And the king shall do according to his will; and he shall exalt himself, and magnify himself above every god, and shall speak marvellous things against the God of gods, and shall prosper till the indignation be accomplished: for that that is determined shall be done.

37 Neither shall he regard the God of his fathers, nor the desire of women, nor regard any god: for he shall magnify himself above all.

38 But in his estate shall he honour the God of forces: and a god whom his fathers knew not shall he honour with gold, and silver, and with precious stones, and pleasant things.

39 Thus shall he do in the most strong holds with a strange god, whom he shall acknowledge *and* increase with glory: and he shall cause them to rule over many, and shall divide the land for gain.

40 And at the time of the end shall the king of the south push at him: and the king of the north shall come against him like a whirlwind, with chariots, and with horsemen, and with many ships; and he shall enter into the countries, and shall overflow and pass over.

41 He shall enter also into the glorious land, and many *countries* shall be overthrown: but these shall escape out of his hand, *even* E'dom, and Mo'ab, and the chief of the children of Am'-mon.

42 He shall stretch forth his hand also upon the countries: and the land of E'gypt shall not escape.

43 But he shall have power over the treasures of gold and of silver, and over all the precious things of E'gypt: and the Lib'y-ans and the E-thi-o'pi-ans *shall be* at his steps.

44 But tidings out of the east and out of the north shall trouble him: therefore he shall go forth with great fury to destroy, and utterly to make away many.

45 And he shall plant the tabernacles of his palace between the seas in the glorious holy mountain; yet he shall come to his end, and none shall help him.

12 AND at that time shall Mi'chael stand up, the great prince which standeth for the children of thy people: and there shall be a time of trouble, such as never was since there was a nation *even* to that same time: and at that time thy people shall be delivered, every one that shall be found written in the book.

2 And many of them that sleep in the dust of the earth shall awake, some to everlasting life, and some to shame *and* everlasting contempt.

3 And they that be wise shall shine as the brightness of the firmament; and they that turn many to righteousness as the stars for ever and ever.

4 But thou, O Dan'iel, shut up the words, and seal the book, *even* to the time of the end: many shall run to and fro, and knowledge shall be increased.

5 ¶ Then I Dan'iel looked, and, behold, there stood other two, the one on this side of the bank of the river, and the other on that side of the bank of the river.

6 And *one* said to the man clothed in linen, which *was* upon the waters of the river, How long *shall it be to* the end of these wonders?

7 And I heard the man clothed in linen, which *was* upon the waters of the river, when he held up his right hand and his left hand unto heaven, and sware by him that liveth for ever that *it shall be* for a time, times, and an half; and when he shall have accomplished to scatter the power of the holy people, all these *things* shall be finished.

8 And I heard, but I understood not : then said I, O my Lord, what *shall be* the end of these *things?*

9 And he said, Go thy way, Dan'iel: for the words *are* closed up and sealed till the time of the end.

10 Many shall be purified, and made white, and tried; but the wicked shall do wickedly: and none of the wicked shall understand; but the wise shall understand.

11 And from the time *that* the daily *sacrifice* shall be taken away, and the abomination that maketh desolate set up, *there shall be* a thousand two hundred and ninety days.

12 Blessed *is* he that waiteth, and cometh to the thousand three hundred and five and thirty days.

13 But go thou thy way till the end *be:* for thou shalt rest, and stand in thy lot at the end of the days.

THE BOOK OF

HOSEA

1 THE word of the Lord that came unto Ho-se'a, the son of Be-e'ri, in the days of Uz-zi'ah, Jo'tham, A'haz, *and* Hez-e-ki'ah, kings of Ju'dah, and in the days of Jer-o-bo'am the son of Jo'ash, king of Is'ra-el.

2 The beginning of the word of the Lord by Ho-se'a. And the Lord said to Ho-se'a, Go, take unto thee a wife of whoredoms and children of whoredoms: for the land hath committed great whoredom, *departing* from the Lord.

3 So he went and took Go'mer the daughter of Dib'la-im; which conceived, and bare him a son.

4 And the Lord said unto him, Call his name Jez're-el; for yet a little *while,* and I will avenge the blood of Jez're-el upon the house of Je'hu, and will cause to cease the kingdom of the house of Is'ra-el.

5 And it shall come to pass at that day, that I will break the bow of Is'ra-el in the valley of Jez're-el.

6 ¶ And she conceived again, and bare a daughter. And God said unto him, Call her name Lo-ru'ha-mah: for I will no more have mercy upon the house of Is'ra-el; but I will utterly take them away.

7 But I will have mercy upon the house of Ju'dah, and will save them by the Lord their God, and will not save them by bow, nor by sword, nor by battle, by horses, nor by horsemen.

8 ¶ Now when she had weaned Lo-ru'ha-mah, she conceived, and bare a son.

9 Then said God, Call his name Lo-am'mi: for ye *are* not my people, and I will not be your God.

10 ¶ Yet the number of the children of Is'ra-el shall be as the sand of the sea, which cannot be measured nor numbered; and it shall come to pass, *that* in the place where it was said unto them, Ye *are* not my people, *there* it shall be said unto them, Ye *are* the sons of the living God.

11 Then shall the children of Ju'dah and the children of Is'ra-el be gathered together, and appoint themselves one head, and they shall come up out of the land: for great *shall be* the day of Jez're-el.

2 SAY ye unto your brethren, Am'mi; and to your sisters, Ru'ha-mah.

2 Plead with your mother, plead: for she *is* not my wife, neither *am* I her husband: let her therefore put away her whoredoms out of her sight, and her adulteries from between her breasts;

3 Lest I strip her naked, and set her as in the day that she was born, and make her as a wilderness, and set her like a dry land, and slay her with thirst.

4 And I will not have mercy upon her children; for they *be* the children of whoredoms.

5 For their mother hath played the harlot: she that conceived them hath done shamefully: for she said, I will go after my lovers, that give *me* my bread and my water, my wool and my flax, mine oil and my drink.

6 ¶ Therefore, behold, I will hedge up thy way with thorns, and make a wall, that she shall not find her paths.

7 And she shall follow after her lovers, but she shall not overtake them; and she shall seek them, but shall not find *them:* then shall she say, I will go and return to my first husband; for then *was it* better with me than now.

8 For she did not know that I gave her corn, and wine, and oil, and multiplied her silver and gold, *which* they prepared for Ba'al.

9 Therefore will I return, and take away my corn in the time thereof, and my wine in the season thereof, and will recover my wool and my flax *given* to cover her nakedness.

10 And now will I discover her lewdness in the sight of her lovers, and none shall deliver her out of mine hand.

11 I will also cause all her mirth to cease, her feast days, her new moons, and her sabbaths, and all her solemn feasts.

12 And I will destroy her vines and her fig trees, whereof she hath said, These *are* my rewards that my lovers have given me: and I will make them a forest, and the beasts of the field shall eat them.

13 And I will visit upon her the days of Ba'al-im, wherein she burned incense to them, and she decked herself with her earrings and her jewels, and she went after her lovers, and forgat me, saith the LORD.

14 ¶ Therefore, behold, I will allure her, and bring her into the wilderness, and speak comfortably unto her.

15 And I will give her her vineyards from thence, and the valley of A'chor for a door of hope: and she shall sing there, as in the days of her youth, and as in the day when she came up out of the land of E'gypt.

16 And it shall be at that day, saith the LORD, *that* thou shalt call me Ish'i; and shalt call me no more Ba'al-i.

17 For I will take away the names of Ba'al-im out of her mouth, and they shall no more be remembered by their name.

18 And in that day will I make a covenant for them with the beasts of the field, and with the fowls of heaven, and *with* the creeping things of the ground: and I will break the bow and the sword and the battle out of the earth, and will make them to lie down safely.

19 And I will betroth thee unto me for ever; yea, I will betroth thee unto me in righteousness, and in judgment, and in lovingkindness, and in mercies.

20 I will even betroth thee unto me in faithfulness: and thou shalt know the LORD.

21 And it shall come to pass in that day, I will hear, saith the LORD, I will hear the heavens, and they shall hear the earth;

22 And the earth shall hear the corn, and the wine, and the oil; and they shall hear Jez're-el.

23 And I will sow her unto me in the earth; and I will have mercy upon her that had not obtained mercy; and I will say to *them which were* not my people, Thou *art* my people; and they shall say, *Thou art* my God.

3 THEN said the LORD unto me, Go yet, love a woman beloved of *her* friend, yet an adulteress, according to the love of the LORD toward the children of Is'ra-el, who look to other gods, and love flagons of wine.

2 So I bought her to me for fifteen *pieces* of silver, and *for* an homer of barley, and an half homer of barley:

3 And I said unto her, Thou shalt abide for me many days; thou shalt not play the harlot, and thou shalt not be for *another* man: so *will* I also *be* for thee.

4 For the children of Is'ra-el shall abide many days without a king, and without a prince, and without a sacrifice, and without an image, and without an ephod, and *without* teraphim:

5 Afterward shall the children of Is'ra-el return, and seek the LORD their God, and Da'vid their king; and shall fear the LORD and his goodness in the latter days.

4 HEAR the word of the LORD, ye children of Is'ra-el: for the LORD hath a controversy with the inhabitants of the land, because *there is* no truth, nor mercy, nor knowledge of God in the land.

2 By swearing, and lying, and killing, and stealing, and committing adultery, they break out, and blood toucheth blood.

3 Therefore shall the land mourn, and every one that dwelleth therein shall languish, with the beasts of the field, and with the fowls of heaven; yea, the fishes of the sea also shall be taken away.

4 Yet let no man strive, nor reprove another: for thy people *are* as they that strive with the priest.

5 Therefore shalt thou fall in the day, and the prophet also shall fall with thee in the night, and I will destroy thy mother.

6 ¶ My people are destroyed for lack of knowledge: because thou hast rejected knowledge, I will also reject thee, that thou shalt be no priest to me: seeing thou hast forgotten the law of thy God, I will also forget thy children.

7 As they were increased, so they sinned against me: *therefore* will I change their glory into shame.

8 They eat up the sin of my people, and they set their heart on their iniquity.

9 And there shall be, like people, like priest: and I will punish them for their ways, and reward them their doings.

10 For they shall eat, and not have enough: they shall commit whoredom, and shall not in-

crease: because they have left off to take heed to the LORD.

11 Whoredom and wine and new wine take away the heart.

12 ¶ My people ask counsel at their stocks, and their staff declareth unto them: for the spirit of whoredoms hath caused *them* to err, and they have gone a whoring from under their God.

13 They sacrifice upon the tops of the mountains, and burn incense upon the hills, under oaks and poplars and elms, because the shadow thereof *is* good: therefore your daughters shall commit whoredom, and your spouses shall commit adultery.

14 I will not punish your daughters when they commit whoredom, nor your spouses when they commit adultery: for themselves are separated with whores, and they sacrifice with harlots: therefore the people *that* doth not understand shall fall.

15 ¶ Though thou, Is'ra-el, play the harlot, *yet* let not Ju'dah offend; and come not ye unto Gil'gal, neither go ye up to Beth-a'ven, nor swear, The LORD liveth.

16 For Is'ra-el slideth back as a backsliding heifer: now the LORD will feed them as a lamb in a large place.

17 E'phra-im *is* joined to idols: let him alone.

18 Their drink is sour: they have committed whoredom continually: her rulers *with* shame do love, Give ye.

19 The wind hath bound her up in her wings, and they shall be ashamed because of their sacrifices.

5 HEAR ye this, O priests; and hearken, ye house of Is'ra-el; and give ye ear, O house of the king; for judgment *is* toward you, because ye have been a snare on Miz'pah, and a net spread upon Ta'bor.

2 And the revolters are profound to make slaughter, though I *have been* a rebuker of them all.

3 I know E'phra-im, and Is'ra-el is not hid from me: for now, O E'phra-im, thou committest whoredom, *and* Is'ra-el is defiled.

4 They will not frame their doings to turn unto their God: for the spirit of whoredoms *is* in the midst of them, and they have not known the LORD.

5 And the pride of Is'ra-el doth testify to his face: therefore shall Is'ra-el and E'phra-im fall in their iniquity; Ju'dah also shall fall with them.

6 They shall go with their flocks and with their herds to seek the LORD; but they shall not find *him;* he hath withdrawn himself from them.

7 They have dealt treacherously against the LORD: for they have begotten strange children: now shall a month devour them with their portions.

8 Blow ye the cornet in Gib'e-ah, *and* the trumpet in Ra'mah: cry aloud *at* Beth-a'ven, after thee, O Ben'ja-min.

9 E'phra-im shall be desolate in the day of rebuke: among the tribes of Is'ra-el have I made known that which shall surely be.

10 The princes of Ju'dah were like them that remove the bound: *therefore* I will pour out my wrath upon them like water.

11 E'phra-im *is* oppressed *and* broken in judgment, because he willingly walked after the commandment.

12 Therefore *will* I *be* unto E'phra-im as a moth, and to the house of Ju'dah as rottenness.

13 When E'phra-im saw his sickness, and Ju'dah *saw* his wound, then went E'phra-im to the As-syr'i-an, and sent to king Ja'reb: yet could he not heal you, nor cure you of your wound.

14 For I *will be* unto E'phra-im as a lion, and as a young lion to the house of Ju'dah: I, *even* I, will tear and go away; I will take away, and none shall rescue *him.*

15 ¶ I will go *and* return to my place, till they acknowledge their offence, and seek my face: in their affliction they will seek me early.

6 COME, and let us return unto the LORD: for he hath torn, and he will heal us; he hath smitten, and he will bind us up.

2 After two days will he revive us: in the third day he will raise us up, and we shall live in his sight.

3 Then shall we know, *if* we follow on to know the LORD: his going forth is prepared as the morning; and he shall come unto us as the rain, as the latter *and* former rain unto the earth.

4 ¶ O E'phra-im, what shall I do unto thee? O Ju'dah, what shall I do unto thee? for your goodness *is* as a morning cloud, and as the early dew it goeth away.

5 Therefore have I hewed *them* by the prophets; I have slain them by the words of my mouth: and thy judgments *are as* the light *that* goeth forth.

6 For I desired mercy, and not sacrifice; and the knowledge of God more than burnt offerings.

7 But they like men have transgressed the covenant: there have they dealt treacherously against me.

8 Gil'e-ad *is* a city of them that work iniquity, *and* is polluted with blood.

9 And as troops of robbers wait for a man, *so* the company of priests murder in the way by consent: for they commit lewdness.

10 I have seen an horrible thing in the house of Is'ra-el: there *is* the whoredom of E'phra-im, Is'ra-el is defiled.

11 Also, O Ju'dah, he hath set an harvest for thee, when I returned the captivity of my people.

7 WHEN I would have healed Is'ra-el, then the iniquity of E'phra-im was discovered, and the wickedness of Sa-ma'ri-a: for they commit falsehood; and the thief cometh in, *and* the troop of robbers spoileth without.

2 And they consider not in their hearts *that* I remember all their wickedness: now their own doings have beset them about; they are before my face.

3 They make the king glad with their wickedness, and the princes with their lies.

4 They *are* all adulterers, as an oven heated by the baker, *who* ceaseth from raising after he hath kneaded the dough, until it be leavened.

5 In the day of our king the princes have made *him* sick with bottles of wine; he stretched out his hand with scorners.

6 For they have made ready their heart like an oven, whiles they lie in wait: their baker sleepeth all the night; in the morning it burneth as a flaming fire.

7 They are all hot as an oven, and have devoured their judges; all their kings are fallen: *there is* none among them that calleth unto me.

8 E'phra-im, he hath mixed himself among the people; E'phra-im is a cake not turned.

9 Strangers have devoured his strength, and he knoweth it not: yea, gray hairs are here and there upon him, yet he knoweth not.

10 And the pride of Is'ra-el testifieth to his face: and they do not return to the LORD their God, nor seek him for all this.

11 ¶ E'phra-im also is like a silly dove without heart: they call to E'gypt, they go to As-syr'i-a.

12 When they shall go, I will spread my net upon them; I will bring them down as the fowls of the heaven; I will chastise them, as their congregation hath heard.

13 Woe unto them! for they have fled from me: destruction unto them! because they have transgressed against me: though I have redeemed them, yet they have spoken lies against me.

14 And they have not cried unto me with their heart, when they howled upon their beds: they assemble themselves for corn and wine, and they rebel against me.

15 Though I have bound and strengthened their arms, yet do they imagine mischief against me.

16 They return, but not to the most High: they are like a deceitful bow: their princes shall fall by the sword for the rage of their tongue: this shall be their derision in the land of E'gypt.

8 SET the trumpet to thy mouth. He shall come as an eagle against the house of the LORD, because they have transgressed my covenant, and trespassed against my law.

2 Is'ra-el shall cry unto me, My God, we know thee.

3 Is'ra-el hath cast off the thing that is good: the enemy shall pursue him.

4 They have set up kings, but not by me: they have made princes, and I knew it not: of their silver and their gold have they made them idols, that they may be cut off.

5 ¶ Thy calf, O Sa-ma'ri-a, hath cast thee off; mine anger is kindled against them: how long will it be ere they attain to innocency?

6 For from Is'ra-el was it also: the workman made it; therefore it is not God: but the calf of Sa-ma'ri-a shall be broken in pieces.

7 For they have sown the wind, and they shall reap the whirlwind: it hath no stalk: the bud shall yield no meal: if so be it yield, the strangers shall swallow it up.

8 Is'ra-el is swallowed up: now shall they be among the Gen'tiles as a vessel wherein is no pleasure.

9 For they are gone up to As-syr'i-a, a wild ass alone by himself: E'phra-im hath hired lovers.

10 Yea, though they have hired among the nations, now will I gather them, and they shall sorrow a little for the burden of the king of princes.

11 Because E'phra-im hath made many altars to sin, altars shall be unto him to sin.

12 I have written to him the great things of my law, but they were counted as a strange thing.

13 They sacrifice flesh for the sacrifices of mine offerings, and eat it; but the LORD accepteth them not; now will he remember their iniquity, and visit their sins: they shall return to E'-gypt.

14 For Is'ra-el hath forgotten his Maker, and buildeth temples; and Ju'dah hath multiplied fenced cities: but I will send a fire upon his cities, and it shall devour the palaces thereof.

9 REJOICE not, O Is'ra-el, for joy, as other people: for thou hast gone a whoring from thy God, thou hast loved a reward upon every cornfloor.

2 The floor and the winepress shall not feed them, and the new wine shall fail in her.

3 They shall not dwell in the LORD's land; but E'phra-im shall return to E'gypt, and they shall eat unclean things in As-syr'i-a.

4 They shall not offer wine offerings to the LORD, neither shall they be pleasing unto him: their sacrifices shall be unto them as the bread of mourners; all that eat thereof shall be polluted: for their bread for their soul shall not come into the house of the LORD.

5 What will ye do in the solemn day, and in the day of the feast of the LORD?

6 For, lo, they are gone because of destruction: E'gypt shall gather them up, Mem'phis shall bury them: the pleasant places for their silver, nettles shall possess them: thorns shall be in their tabernacles.

7 The days of visitation are come, the days of recompence are come; Is'ra-el shall know it: the prophet is a fool, the spiritual man is mad, for the multitude of thine iniquity, and the great hatred.

8 The watchman of E'phra-im was with my God: but the prophet is a snare of a fowler in all his ways, and hatred in the house of his God.

9 They have deeply corrupted themselves, as in the days of Gib'e-ah: therefore he will remember their iniquity, he will visit their sins.

10 I found Is'ra-el like grapes in the wilderness; I saw your fathers as the firstripe in the fig tree at her first time: but they went to Ba'al-pe'-or, and separated themselves unto that shame; and their abominations were according as they loved.

11 As for E'phra-im, their glory shall fly away like a bird, from the birth, and from the womb, and from the conception.

12 Though they bring up their children, yet will I bereave them, that there shall not be a man left: yea, woe also to them when I depart from them!

13 E'phra-im, as I saw Ty'rus, is planted in a pleasant place: but E'phra-im shall bring forth his children to the murderer.

14 Give them, O LORD: what wilt thou give? give them a miscarrying womb and dry breasts.

15 All their wickedness is in Gil'gal: for there I hated them: for the wickedness of their doings I will drive them out of mine house, I will love them no more: all their princes are revolters.

16 E'phra-im is smitten, their root is dried up, they shall bear no fruit: yea, though they bring forth, yet will I slay even the beloved fruit of their womb.

17 My God will cast them away, because they did not hearken unto him: and they shall be wanderers among the nations.

10 IS'RA-EL is an empty vine, he bringeth forth fruit unto himself: according to the multitude of his fruit he hath increased the altars; according to the goodness of his land they have made goodly images.

2 Their heart is divided; now shall they be found faulty: he shall break down their altars, he shall spoil their images.

3 For now they shall say, We have no king, because we feared not the LORD; what then should a king do to us?

4 They have spoken words, swearing falsely in making a covenant: thus judgment springeth up as hemlock in the furrows of the field.

5 The inhabitants of Sa-ma'ri-a shall fear because of the calves of Beth-a'ven: for the people thereof shall mourn over it, and the priests thereof *that* rejoiced on it, for the glory thereof, because it is departed from it.

6 It shall be also carried unto As-syr'i-a *for a* present to king Ja'reb: E'phra-im shall receive shame, and Is'ra-el shall be ashamed of his own counsel.

7 *As for* Sa-ma'ri-a, her king is cut off as the foam upon the water.

8 The high places also of A'ven, the sin of Is'ra-el, shall be destroyed: the thorn and the thistle shall come up on their altars; and they shall say to the mountains, Cover us; and to the hills, Fall on us.

9 O Is'ra-el, thou hast sinned from the days of Gib'e-ah: there they stood: the battle in Gib'-e-ah against the children of iniquity did not overtake them.

10 *It is* in my desire that I should chastise them; and the people shall be gathered against them, when they shall bind themselves in their two furrows.

11 And E'phra-im *is as* an heifer *that is* taught, *and* loveth to tread out *the corn;* but I passed over upon her fair neck: I will make E'phra-im to ride; Ju'dah shall plow, *and* Ja'cob shall break his clods.

12 Sow to yourselves in righteousness, reap in mercy; break up your fallow ground: for *it is* time to seek the LORD, till he come and rain righteousness upon you.

13 Ye have plowed wickedness, ye have reaped iniquity; ye have eaten the fruit of lies: because thou didst trust in thy way, in the multitude of thy mighty men.

14 Therefore shall a tumult arise among thy people, and all thy fortresses shall be spoiled, as Shal'man spoiled Beth-ar'bel in the day of battle: the mother was dashed in pieces upon *her* children.

15 So shall Beth'-el do unto you because of your great wickedness: in a morning shall the king of Is'ra-el utterly be cut off.

11 WHEN Is'ra-el *was* a child, then I loved him, and called my son out of E'gypt.

2 *As* they called them, so they went from them: they sacrificed unto Ba'al-im, and burned incense to graven images.

3 I taught E'phra-im also to go, taking them by their arms; but they knew not that I healed them.

4 I drew them with cords of a man, with bands of love: and I was to them as they that take off the yoke on their jaws, and I laid meat unto them.

5 ¶ He shall not return into the land of E'-gypt, but the As-syr'i-an shall be his king, because they refused to return.

6 And the sword shall abide on his cities, and shall consume his branches, and devour *them,* because of their own counsels.

7 And my people are bent to backsliding from me: though they called them to the most High, none at all would exalt *him.*

8 How shall I give thee up, E'phra-im? how shall I deliver thee, Is'ra-el? how shall I make thee as Ad'-mah? how shall I set thee as Ze-bo'im? mine heart is turned within me, my repentings are kindled together.

9 I will not execute the fierceness of mine anger, I will not return to destroy E'phra-im: for I *am* God, and not man; the Holy One in the midst of thee: and I will not enter into the city.

10 They shall walk after the LORD: he shall roar like a lion: when he shall roar, then the children shall tremble from the west.

11 They shall tremble as a bird out of E'gypt, and as a dove out of the land of As-syr'i-a: and I will place them in their houses, saith the LORD.

12 E'phra-im compasseth me about with lies, and the house of Is'ra-el with deceit: but Ju'dah yet ruleth with God, and is faithful with the saints.

12 E'PHRA-IM feedeth on wind, and followeth after the east wind: he daily increaseth lies and desolation; and they do make a covenant with the As-syr'i-ans, and oil is carried into E'gypt.

2 The LORD hath also a controversy with Ju'-dah, and will punish Ja'cob according to his ways; according to his doings will he recompense him.

3 ¶ He took his brother by the heel in the womb, and by his strength he had power with God:

4 Yea, he had power over the angel, and prevailed: he wept, and made supplication unto him: he found him *in* Beth'-el, and there he spake with us;

5 Even the LORD God of hosts; the LORD *is* his memorial.

6 Therefore turn thou to thy God: keep mercy and judgment, and wait on thy God continually.

7 ¶ *He is* a merchant, the balances of deceit *are* in his hand: he loveth to oppress.

8 And E'phra-im said, Yet I am become rich, I have found me out substance: *in* all my labours they shall find none iniquity in me that *were* sin.

9 And I *that am* the LORD thy God from the land of E'gypt will yet make thee to dwell in tabernacles, as in the days of the solemn feast.

10 I have also spoken by the prophets, and I have multiplied visions, and used similitudes, by the ministry of the prophets.

11 *Is there* iniquity in Gil'e-ad? surely they are vanity: they sacrifice bullocks in Gil'gal; yea, their altars *are* as heaps in the furrows of the fields.

12 And Ja'cob fled into the country of Syr'i-a, and Is'ra-el served for a wife, and for a wife he kept *sheep.*

13 And by a prophet the LORD brought Is'ra-el out of E'gypt, and by a prophet was he preserved.

14 E'phra-im provoked *him* to anger most bitterly: therefore shall he leave his blood upon him, and his reproach shall his LORD return unto him.

13 WHEN E'phra-im spake trembling, he exalted himself in Is'ra-el; but when he offended in Ba'al, he died.

2 And now they sin more and more, and have made them molten images of their silver, *and* idols according to their own understanding, all of it the work of the craftsmen: they say of them, Let the men that sacrifice kiss the calves.

3 Therefore they shall be as the morning cloud, and as the early dew that passeth away, as the chaff *that* is driven with the whirlwind out of the floor, and as the smoke out of the chimney.

4 Yet I *am* the LORD thy God from the land of E'gypt and thou shalt know no god but me: for *there is* no saviour beside me.

5 ¶ I did know thee in the wilderness, in the land of great drought.

6 According to their pasture, so were they

filled; they were filled, and their heart was exalted; therefore have they forgotten me.

7 Therefore I will be unto them as a lion: as a leopard by the way will I observe *them:*

8 I will meet them as a bear *that is* bereaved *of her whelps,* and will rend the caul of their heart, and there will I devour them like a lion: the wild beast shall tear them.

9 ¶ O Is'ra-el, thou hast destroyed thyself; but in me *is* thine help.

10 I will be thy king: where *is any other* that may save thee in all thy cities? and thy judges of whom thou saidst, Give me a king and princes?

11 I gave thee a king in mine anger, and took *him* away in my wrath.

12 The iniquity of E'phra-im *is* bound up; his sin *is* hid.

13 The sorrows of a travailing woman shall come upon him: he *is* an unwise son; for he should not stay long in *the place of* the breaking forth of children.

14 I will ransom them from the power of the grave; I will redeem them from death: O death, I will be thy plagues; O grave, I will be thy destruction: repentance shall be hid from mine eyes.

15 ¶ Though he be fruitful among *his* brethren, an east wind shall come, the wind of the LORD shall come up from the wilderness, and his spring shall become dry, and his fountain shall be dried up: he shall spoil the treasure of all pleasant vessels.

16 Sa-ma'ri-a shall become desolate; for she hath rebelled against her God: they shall fall by the sword: their infants shall be dashed in pieces, and their women with child shall be ripped up.

14 O IS'RA-EL, return unto the LORD thy God; for thou hast fallen by thine iniquity.

2 Take with you words, and turn to the LORD: say unto him, Take away all iniquity, and receive *us* graciously: so will we render the calves of our lips.

3 Assh'ur shall not save us; we will not ride upon horses: neither will we say any more to the work of our hands, Ye are our gods: for in thee the fatherless findeth mercy.

4 ¶ I will heal their backsliding, I will love them freely: for mine anger is turned away from him.

5 I will be as the dew unto Is'ra-el: he shall grow as the lily, and cast forth his roots as Leb'a-non.

6 His branches shall spread, and his beauty shall be as the olive tree, and his smell as Leb'a-non.

7 They that dwell under his shadow shall return; they shall revive *as* the corn, and grow as the vine: the scent thereof *shall be* as the wine of Leb'a-non.

8 E'phra-im *shall say,* What have I to do any more with idols? I have heard *him,* and observed him: I *am* like a green fir tree. From me is thy fruit found.

9 Who *is* wise, and he shall understand these *things?* prudent, and he shall know them? for the ways of the LORD *are* right, and the just shall walk in them: but the transgressors shall fall therein.

THE BOOK OF

JOEL

1 THE word of the LORD that came to Jo'el the son of Pe-thu'el.

2 Hear this, ye old men, and give ear, all ye inhabitants of the land. Hath this been in your days, or even in the days of your fathers?

3 Tell ye your children of it, and *let* your children *tell* their children, and their children another generation.

4 That which the palmerworm hath left hath the locust eaten; and that which the locust hath left hath the cankerworm eaten; and that which the cankerworm hath left hath the caterpiller eaten.

5 Awake, ye drunkards, and weep; and howl, all ye drinkers of wine, because of the new wine; for it is cut off from your mouth.

6 For a nation is come up upon my land, strong, and without number, whose teeth *are* the teeth of a lion, and he hath the cheek teeth of a great lion.

7 He hath laid my vine waste, and barked my fig tree: he hath made it clean bare, and cast *it* away; the branches thereof are made white.

8 ¶ Lament like a virgin girded with sackcloth for the husband of her youth.

9 The meat offering and the drink offering is cut off from the house of the LORD; the priests, the LORD's ministers, mourn.

10 The field is wasted, the land mourneth; for the corn is wasted: the new wine is dried up, the oil languisheth.

11 Be ye ashamed, O ye husbandmen; howl, O ye vinedressers, for the wheat and for the barley; because the harvest of the field is perished.

12 The vine is dried up, and the fig tree languisheth; the pomegranate tree, the palm tree also, and the apple tree, *even* all the trees of the field, are withered: because joy is withered away from the sons of men.

13 Gird yourselves, and lament, ye priests: howl, ye ministers of the altar: come, lie all night in sackcloth, ye ministers of my God: for the meat offering and the drink offering is withholden from the house of your God.

14 ¶ Sanctify ye a fast, call a solemn assembly, gather the elders *and* all the inhabitants of the land *into* the house of the LORD your God, and cry unto the LORD.

15 Alas for the day! for the day of the LORD *is* at hand, and as a destruction from the Almighty shall it come.

16 Is not the meat cut off before our eyes, *yea,* joy and gladness from the house of our God?

17 The seed is rotten under their clods, the garners are laid desolate, the barns are broken down; for the corn is withered.

18 How do the beasts groan! the herds of cattle are perplexed, because they have no pasture; yea, the flocks of sheep are made desolate.

19 O LORD, to thee will I cry: for the fire hath devoured the pastures of the wilderness, and the flame hath burned all the trees of the field.

20 The beasts of the field cry also unto thee: for the rivers of waters are dried up, and the fire hath devoured the pastures of the wilderness.

2 BLOW ye the trumpet in Zi'on, and sound an alarm in my holy mountain: let all the inhabitants of the land tremble: for the day of the LORD cometh, for *it is* nigh at hand;

2 A day of darkness and of gloominess, a day of clouds and of thick darkness, as the morning spread upon the mountains: a great people and a strong; there hath not been ever the like, neither shall be any more.after it, *even* to the years of many generations.

3 A fire devoureth before them; and behind them a flame burneth: the land *is* as the garden of E'den before them, and behind them a desolate wilderness; yea, and nothing shall escape them.

4 The appearance of them *is* as the appearance of horses; and as horsemen, so shall they run.

5 Like the noise of chariots on the tops of mountains shall they leap, like the noise of a flame of fire that devoureth the stubble, as a strong people set in battle array.

6 Before their face the people shall be much pained: all faces shall gather blackness.

7 They shall run like mighty men; they shall climb the wall like men of war; and they shall march every one on his ways, and they shall not break their ranks:

8 Neither shall one thrust another; they shall walk every one in his path: and *when* they fall upon the sword, they shall not be wounded.

9 They shall run to and fro in the city; they shall run upon the wall, they shall climb up upon the houses; they shall enter in at the windows like a thief.

10 The earth shall quake before them; the heavens shall tremble: the sun and the moon shall be dark, and the stars shall withdraw their shining:

11 And the LORD shall utter his voice before his army: for his camp *is* very great: for *he is* strong that executeth his word: for the day of the LORD *is* great and very terrible; and who can abide it?

12 ¶ Therefore also now, saith the LORD, turn ye *even* to me with all your heart, and with fasting, and with weeping, and with mourning:

13 And rend your heart, and not your garments, and turn unto the LORD your God: for he *is* gracious and merciful, slow to anger, and of great kindness, and repenteth him of the evil.

14 Who knoweth *if* he will return and repent, and leave a blessing behind him; *even* a meat offering and a drink offering unto the LORD your God?

15 ¶ Blow the trumpet in Zi'on, sanctify a fast, call a solemn assembly:

16 Gather the people, sanctify the congregation, assemble the elders, gather the children, and those that suck the breasts: let the bridegroom go forth of his chamber, and the bride out of her closet.

17 Let the priests, the ministers of the LORD, weep between the porch and the altar, and let them say, Spare thy people, O LORD, and give not thine heritage to reproach, that the heathen should rule over them: wherefore should they say among the people, Where *is* their God?

18 ¶ Then will the LORD be jealous for his land, and pity his people.

19 Yea, the LORD will answer and say unto his people, Behold, I will send you corn, and wine, and oil, and ye shall be satisfied therewith: and I will no more make you a reproach among the heathen:

20 But I will remove far off from you the northern *army,* and will drive him into a land barren and desolate, with his face toward the east sea, and his hinder part toward the utmost sea, and his stink shall come up, and his ill savour shall come up, because he hath done great things.

21 ¶ Fear not, O land; be glad and rejoice: for the LORD will do great things.

22 Be not afraid, ye beasts of the field: for the pastures of the wilderness do spring, for the tree beareth her fruit, the fig tree and the vine do yield their strength.

23 Be glad then, ye children of Zi'on, and rejoice in the LORD your God: for he hath given you the former rain moderately, and he will cause to come down for you the rain, the former rain, and the latter rain in the first *month.*

24 And the floors shall be full of wheat, and the fats shall overflow with wine and oil.

25 And I will restore to you the years that the locust hath eaten, the cankerworm, and the caterpiller, and the palmerworm, my great army which I sent among you.

26 And ye shall eat in plenty, and be satisfied, and praise the name of the LORD your God, that hath dealt wondrously with you: and my people shall never be ashamed.

27 And ye shall know that I *am* in the midst of Is'ra-el, and that I *am* the LORD your God, and none else: and my people shall never be ashamed.

28 ¶ And it shall come to pass afterward, *that* I will pour out my spirit upon all flesh; and your sons and your daughters shall prophesy, your old men shall dream dreams, your young men shall see visions:

29 And also upon the servants and upon the handmaids in those days will I pour out my spirit.

30 And I will shew wonders in the heavens and in the earth, blood, and fire, and pillars of smoke.

31 The sun shall be turned into darkness, and the moon into blood, before the great and the terrible day of the LORD come.

32 And it shall come to pass, *that* whosoever shall call on the name of the LORD shall be delivered: for in mount Zi'on and in Je-ru'sa-lem shall be deliverance, as the LORD hath said, and in the remnant whom the LORD shall call.

3 FOR, behold, in those days, and in that time, when I shall bring again the captivity of Ju'dah and Je-ru'sa-lem,

2 I will also gather all nations, and will bring them down into the valley of Je-hosh'a-phat, and will plead with them there for my people and *for* my heritage Is'ra-el, whom they have scattered among the nations, and parted my land.

3 And they have cast lots for my people; and have given a boy for an harlot, and sold a girl for wine, that they might drink.

4 Yea, and what have ye to do with me, O Tyre, and Zi'don, and all the coasts of Pal'es-tine? will ye render me a recompence? and if ye recompense me, swiftly *and* speedily will I return your recompence upon your own head;

5 Because ye have taken my silver and my gold, and have carried into your temples my goodly pleasant things:

6 The children also of Ju'dah and the chil-

dren of Je-ru'sa-lem have ye sold unto the Gre'-cians, that ye might remove them far from their border.

7 Behold, I will raise them out of the place whither ye have sold them, and will return your recompence upon your own head;

8 And I will sell your sons and your daughters into the hand of the children of Ju'dah, and they shall sell them to the Sa-be'ans, to a people far off: for the LORD hath spoken it.

9 ¶ Proclaim ye this among the Gen'tiles; Prepare war, wake up the mighty men, let all the men of war draw near; let them come up:

10 Beat your plowshares into swords, and your pruninghooks into spears: let the weak say, I am strong.

11 Assemble yourselves, and come, all ye heathen, and gather yourselves together round about: thither cause thy mighty ones to come down, O LORD.

12 Let the heathen be wakened, and come up to the valley of Je-hosh'a-phat: for there will I sit to judge all the heathen round about.

13 Put ye in the sickle, for the harvest is ripe: come, get you down; for the press is full, the fats overflow; for their wickedness is great.

14 Multitudes, multitudes in the valley of de-cision: for the day of the LORD is near in the valley of decision.

15 The sun and the moon shall be darkened, and the stars shall withdraw their shining.

16 The LORD also shall roar out of Zi'on, and utter his voice from Je-ru'sa-lem; and the heavens and the earth shall shake: but the LORD will be the hope of his people, and the strength of the children of Is'ra-el.

17 So shall ye know that I am the LORD your God dwelling in Zi'on, my holy mountain: then shall Je-ru'sa-lem be holy, and there shall no strangers pass through her any more.

18 ¶ And it shall come to pass in that day, that the mountains shall drop down new wine, and the hills shall flow with milk, and all the rivers of Ju'dah shall flow with waters, and a fountain shall come forth of the house of the LORD, and shall water the valley of Shit'tim.

19 E'gypt shall be a desolation, and E'dom shall be a desolate wilderness, for the violence against the children of Ju'dah, because they have shed innocent blood in their land.

20 But Ju'dah shall dwell for ever, and Je-ru'sa-lem from generation to generation.

21 For I will cleanse their blood that I have not cleansed: for the LORD dwelleth in Zi'on.

THE BOOK OF

AMOS

1 THE words of A'mos, who was among the herdmen of Te-ko'a, which he saw concerning Is'ra-el in the days of Uz-zi'ah king of Ju'dah, and in the days of Jer-o-bo'am the son of Jo'ash king of Is'ra-el, two years before the earthquake.

2 And he said, The LORD will roar from Zi'on, and utter his voice from Je-ru'sa-lem; and the habitations of the shepherds shall mourn, and the top of Car'mel shall wither.

3 Thus saith the LORD; For three transgressions of Da-mas'cus, and for four, I will not turn away the punishment thereof; because they have threshed Gil'e-ad with threshing instruments of iron:

4 But I will send a fire into the house of Haz'-a-el, which shall devour the palaces of Ben-ha'-dad.

5 I will break also the bar of Da-mas'cus, and cut off the inhabitant from the plain of A'ven, and him that holdeth the sceptre from the house of E'den: and the people of Syr'i-a shall go into captivity unto Kir, saith the LORD.

6 ¶ Thus saith the LORD; For three transgressions of Ga'za, and for four, I will not turn away the punishment thereof; because they carried away captive the whole captivity, to deliver them up to E'dom:

7 But I will send a fire on the wall of Ga'za, which shall devour the palaces thereof:

8 And I will cut off the inhabitant from Ash'-dod, and him that holdeth the sceptre from Ash'ke-lon, and I will turn mine hand against Ek'ron: and the remnant of the Phi-lis'tines shall perish, saith the Lord GOD.

9 ¶ Thus saith the LORD; For three transgressions of Ty'rus, and for four, I will not turn away the punishment thereof; because they delivered up the whole captivity to E'dom, and remembered not the brotherly covenant:

10 But I will send a fire on the wall of Ty'rus, which shall devour the palaces thereof.

11 ¶ Thus saith the LORD; For three transgressions of E'dom, and for four, I will not turn away the punishment thereof; because he did pursue his brother with the sword, and did cast off all pity, and his anger did tear perpetually, and he kept his wrath for ever:

12 But I will send a fire upon Te'man, which shall devour the palaces of Boz'rah.

13 ¶ Thus saith the LORD; For three transgressions of the children of Am'mon, and for four, I will not turn away the punishment thereof; because they have ripped up the women with child of Gil'e-ad, that they might enlarge their border:

14 But I will kindle a fire in the wall of Rab'-bah, and it shall devour the palaces thereof, with shouting in the day of battle, with a tempest in the day of the whirlwind:

15 And their king shall go into captivity, he and his princes together, saith the LORD.

2 THUS saith the LORD; For three transgressions of Mo'ab, and for four, I will not turn away the punishment thereof; because he burned the bones of the king of E'dom into lime:

2 But I will send a fire upon Mo'ab, and it shall devour the palaces of Kir'i-oth: and Mo'ab shall die with tumult, with shouting, and with the sound of the trumpet:

3 And I will cut off the judge from the midst thereof, and will slay all the princes thereof with him, saith the LORD.

4 ¶ Thus saith the LORD; For three transgressions of Ju'dah, and for four, I will not turn away the punishment thereof; because they have despised the law of the LORD, and have not kept his commandments, and their lies caused them to err, after the which their fathers have walked:

5 But I will send a fire upon Ju'dah, and it shall devour the palaces of Je-ru'sa-lem.

6 ¶ Thus saith the LORD; For three transgressions of Is-ra-el, and for four, I will not turn away *the punishment* thereof; because they sold the righteous for silver, and the poor for a pair of shoes;

7 That pant after the dust of the earth on the head of the poor, and turn aside the way of the meek: and a man and his father will go in unto the *same* maid, to profane my holy name:

8 And they lay *themselves* down upon clothes laid to pledge by every altar, and they drink the wine of the condemned *in* the house of their god.

9 ¶ Yet destroyed I the Am'or-ite before them, whose height *was* like the height of the cedars, and he *was* strong as the oaks; yet I destroyed his fruit from above, and his roots from beneath.

10 Also I brought you up from the land of E'gypt, and led you forty years through the wilderness, to possess the land of the Am'or-ite.

11 And I raised up of your sons for prophets, and of your young men for Naz'a-rites. *Is it* not even thus, O ye children of Is'ra-el? saith the LORD.

12 But ye gave the Naz'a-rites wine to drink; and commanded the prophets, saying, Prophesy not.

13 Behold, I am pressed under you, as a cart is pressed *that is* full of sheaves.

14 Therefore the flight shall perish from the swift, and the strong shall not strengthen his force, neither shall the mighty deliver himself:

15 Neither shall he stand that handleth the bow; and *he that* is swift of foot shall not deliver *himself*: neither shall he that rideth the horse deliver himself.

16 And *he that* is courageous among the mighty shall flee away naked in that day, saith the LORD.

3 HEAR this word that the LORD hath spoken against you, O children of Is'ra-el, against the whole family which I brought up from the land of E'gypt, saying,

2 You only have I known of all the families of the earth: therefore I will punish you for all your iniquities.

3 Can two walk together, except they be agreed?

4 Will a lion roar in the forest, when he hath no prey? will a young lion cry out of his den, if he have taken nothing?

5 Can a bird fall in a snare upon the earth, where no gin *is* for him? shall *one* take up a snare from the earth, and have taken nothing at all?

6 Shall a trumpet be blown in the city, and the people not be afraid? shall there be evil in a city, and the LORD hath not done *it*?

7 Surely the Lord GOD will do nothing, but he revealeth his secret unto his servants the prophets.

8 The lion hath roared, who will not fear? the Lord GOD hath spoken, who can but prophesy?

9 ¶ Publish in the palaces of Ash'dod, and in the palaces in the land of E'gypt, and say, Assemble yourselves upon the mountains of Sa-ma'ri-a, and behold the great tumults in the midst thereof, and the oppressed in the midst thereof.

10 For they know not to do right, saith the LORD, who store up violence and robbery in their palaces.

11 Therefore thus saith the Lord GOD; An adversary *there shall be* even round about the land; and he shall bring down thy strength from thee, and thy palaces shall be spoiled.

12 Thus saith the LORD; As the shepherd taketh out of the mouth of the lion two legs, or a piece of an ear; so shall the children of Is'ra-el be taken out that dwell in Sa-ma'ri-a in the corner of a bed, and in Da-mas'cus *in* a couch.

13 Hear ye, and testify in the house of Ja'cob, saith the Lord GOD, the God of hosts,

14 That in the day that I shall visit the transgressions of Is'ra-el upon him I will also visit the altars of Beth'-el: and the horns of the altar shall be cut off, and fall to the ground.

15 And I will smite the winter house with the summer house; and the houses of ivory shall perish, and the great houses shall have an end, saith the LORD.

4 HEAR this word, ye kine of Ba'shan, that *are* in the mountain of Sa-ma'ri-a, which oppress the poor, which crush the needy, which say to their masters, Bring, and let us drink.

2 The Lord GOD hath sworn by his holiness, that, lo, the days shall come upon you, that he will take you away with hooks, and your posterity with fishhooks.

3 And ye shall go out at the breaches, every *cow at that which is* before her; and ye shall cast *them* into the palace, saith the LORD.

4 ¶ Come to Beth'-el, and transgress; at Gil'gal multiply transgression; and bring your sacrifices every morning, *and* your tithes after three years:

5 And offer a sacrifice of thanksgiving with leaven, and proclaim *and* publish the free offerings: for this liketh you, O ye children of Is'ra-el, saith the Lord GOD.

6 ¶ And I also have given you cleanness of teeth in all your cities, and want of bread in all your places: yet have ye not returned unto me, saith the LORD.

7 And also I have withholden the rain from you, when *there were* yet three months to the harvest: and I caused it to rain upon one city, and caused it not to rain upon another city: one piece was rained upon, and the piece whereupon it rained not withered.

8 So two *or* three cities wandered unto one city, to drink water; but they were not satisfied: yet have ye not returned unto me, saith the LORD.

9 I have smitten you with blasting and mildew: when your gardens and your vineyards and your fig trees and your olive trees increased, the palmerworm devoured *them*: yet have ye not returned unto me, saith the LORD.

10 I have sent among you the pestilence after the manner of E'gypt: your young men have I slain with the sword, and have taken away your horses; and I have made the stink of your camps to come up unto your nostrils: yet have ye not returned unto me, saith the LORD.

11 I have overthrown *some* of you, as God overthrew Sod'om and Go-mor'rah, and ye were as a firebrand plucked out of the burning: yet have ye not returned unto me, saith the LORD.

12 Therefore thus will I do unto thee, O Is'ra-el: *and* because I will do this unto thee, prepare to meet thy God, O Is'ra-el.

13 For, lo, he that formeth the mountains, and createth the wind, and declareth unto man what *is* his thought, that maketh the morning darkness, and treadeth upon the high places of the earth, The LORD, The God of hosts, *is* his name.

5 HEAR ye this word which I take up against you, *even* a lamentation, O house of Is'ra-el.

2 The virgin of Is'ra-el is fallen; she shall no more rise: she is forsaken upon her land; *there is* none to raise her up.

3 For thus saith the Lord GOD; The city that went out *by* a thousand shall leave an hundred, and that which went forth *by* an hundred shall leave ten, to the house of Is'ra-el.

4 ¶ For thus saith the LORD unto the house of Is'ra-el, Seek ye me, and ye shall live:

5 But seek not Beth'-el, nor enter into Gil'gal, and pass not to Be'er–she'ba: for Gil'gal shall surely go into captivity, and Beth'-el shall come to nought.

6 Seek the LORD, and ye shall live; lest he break out like fire in the house of Jo'seph, and devour *it*, and *there be* none to quench *it* in Beth'-el.

7 Ye who turn judgment to wormwood, and leave off righteousness in the earth,

8 *Seek him* that maketh the seven stars and O-ri'on, and turneth the shadow of death into the morning, and maketh the day dark with night: that calleth for the waters of the sea, and poureth them out upon the face of the earth: The LORD *is* his name:

9 That strengtheneth the spoiled against the strong, so that the spoiled shall come against the fortress.

10 They hate him that rebuketh in the gate, and they abhor him that speaketh uprightly.

11 Forasmuch therefore as your treading *is* upon the poor, and ye take from him burdens of wheat: ye have built houses of hewn stone, but ye shall not dwell in them; ye have planted pleasant vineyards, but ye shall not drink wine of them.

12 For I know your manifold transgressions and your mighty sins: they afflict the just, they take a bribe, and they turn aside the poor in the gate *from their right.*

13 Therefore the prudent shall keep silence in that time; for it *is* an evil time.

14 Seek good, and not evil, that ye may live: and so the LORD, the God of hosts, shall be with you, as ye have spoken.

15 Hate the evil, and love the good, and establish judgment in the gate: it may be that the LORD God of hosts will be gracious unto the remnant of Jo'seph.

16 Therefore the LORD, the God of hosts, the Lord, saith thus; Wailing *shall be* in all streets; and they shall say in all the highways, Alas! alas! and they shall call the husbandman to mourning, and such as are skilful of lamentation to wailing.

17 And in all vineyards *shall be* wailing: for I will pass through thee, saith the LORD.

18 Woe unto you that desire the day of the LORD! to what end *is* it for you? the day of the LORD *is* darkness, and not light.

19 As if a man did flee from a lion, and a bear met him; or went into the house, and leaned his hand on the wall, and a serpent bit him.

20 *Shall* not the day of the LORD *be* darkness, and not light? even very dark, and no brightness in it?

21 ¶ I hate, I despise your feast days, and I will not smell in your solemn assemblies.

22 Though ye offer me burnt offerings and your meat offerings, I will not accept *them:* neither will I regard the peace offerings of your fat beasts.

23 Take thou away from me the noise of thy songs; for I will not hear the melody of thy viols.

24 But let judgment run down as waters, and righteousness as a mighty stream.

25 Have ye offered unto me sacrifices and offerings in the wilderness forty years, O house of Is'ra-el?

26 But ye have borne the tabernacle of your Mo'loch and Chi'un your images, the star of your god, which ye made to yourselves.

27 Therefore will I cause you to go into captivity beyond Da-mas'cus, saith the LORD, whose name *is* The God of hosts.

6 WOE to them *that are* at ease in Zi'on, and trust in the mountain of Sa-ma'ri-a, *which are* named chief of the nations, to whom the house of Is'ra-el came!

2 Pass ye unto Cal'neh, and see; and from thence go ye to Ha'math the great: then go down to Gath of the Phi-lis'tines: *be they* better than these kingdoms? or their border greater than your border?

3 Ye that put far away the evil day, and cause the seat of violence to come near;

4 That lie upon beds of ivory, and stretch themselves upon their couches, and eat the lambs out of the flock, and the calves out of the midst of the stall;

5 That chant to the sound of the viol, *and* invent to themselves instruments of musick like Da'vid;

6 That drink wine in bowls, and anoint themselves with the chief ointments: but they are not grieved for the affliction of Jo'seph.

7 ¶ Therefore now shall they go captive with the first that go captive, and the banquet of them that stretched themselves shall be removed.

8 The Lord GOD hath sworn by himself, saith the LORD the God of hosts, I abhor the excellency of Ja'cob, and hate his palaces: therefore will I deliver up the city with all that is therein.

9 And it shall come to pass, if there remain ten men in one house, that they shall die.

10 And a man's uncle shall take him up, and he that burneth him, to bring out the bones out of the house, and shall say unto him that *is* by the sides of the house, Is there yet *any* with thee? and he shall say, No. Then shall he say, Hold thy tongue: for we may not make mention of the name of the LORD.

11 For, behold, the LORD commandeth, and he will smite the great house with breaches, and the little house with clefts.

12 ¶ Shall horses run upon the rock? will *one* plow *there* with oxen? for ye have turned judgment into gall, and the fruit of righteousness into hemlock:

13 Ye which rejoice in a thing of nought, which say, Have we not taken to us horns by our own strength?

14 But, behold, I will raise up against you a nation, O house of Is'ra-el, saith the LORD God of hosts; and they shall afflict you from the entering in of He'math unto the river of the wilderness.

7 THUS hath the Lord GOD shewed unto me; and, behold, he formed grasshoppers in the beginning of the shooting up of the latter growth; and, lo, *it was* the latter growth after the king's mowings.

2 And it came to pass, *that* when they had made an end of eating the grass of the land, then I said, O Lord GOD, forgive, I beseech thee: by whom shall Ja'cob arise? for he *is* small.

3 The LORD repented for this: It shall not be, saith the LORD.

4 ¶ Thus hath the Lord GOD shewed unto me: and, behold, the Lord GOD called to contend by fire, and it devoured the great deep, and did eat up a part.

5 Then said I, O Lord GOD, cease, I beseech thee: by whom shall Ja'cob arise? for he *is* small.

6 The LORD repented for this: This also shall not be, saith the Lord GOD.

7 ¶ Thus he shewed me: and, behold, the Lord stood upon a wall *made* by a plumbline, with a plumbline in his hand.

8 And the LORD said unto me, A'mos, what seest thou? And I said, A plumbline. Then said the Lord, Behold, I will set a plumbline in the midst of my people Is'ra-el: I will not again pass by them any more:

9 And the high places of I'saac shall be desolate, and the sanctuaries of Is'ra-el shall be laid waste; and I will rise against the house of Jer-o-bo'am with the sword.

10 ¶ Then Am-a-zi'ah the priest of Beth'-el sent to Jer-o-bo'am king of Is'ra-el, saying, A'-mos hath conspired against thee in the midst of the house of Is'ra-el: the land is not able to bear all his words.

11 For thus A'mos saith, Jer-o-bo'am shall die by the sword, and Is'ra-el shall surely be led away captive out of their own land.

12 Also Am-a-zi'ah said unto A'mos, O thou seer, go, flee thee away into the land of Ju'dah, and there eat bread, and prophesy there:

13 But prophesy not again any more at Beth'--el: for it *is* the king's chapel, and it *is* the king's court.

14 ¶ Then answered A'mos, and said to Am-a-zi'ah, I *was* no prophet, neither *was* I a prophet's son; but I *was* an herdman, and a gatherer of sycomore fruit:

15 And the LORD took me as I followed the flock, and the LORD said unto me, Go, prophesy unto my people Is'ra-el.

16 ¶ Now therefore hear thou the word of the LORD: Thou sayest, Prophesy not against Is'-ra-el, and drop not *thy word* against the house of I'saac.

17 Therefore thus saith the LORD; Thy wife shall be an harlot in the city, and thy sons and thy daughters shall fall by the sword, and thy land shall be divided by line; and thou shalt die in a polluted land: and Is'ra-el shall surely go into captivity forth of his land.

8 THUS hath the Lord GOD shewed unto me: and behold a basket of summer fruit.

2 And he said, A'mos, what seest thou? And I said, A basket of summer fruit. Then said the LORD unto me, The end is come upon my people of Is'ra-el; I will not again pass by them any more.

3 And the songs of the temple shall be howlings in that day, saith the Lord GOD: *there shall be* many dead bodies in every place; they shall cast *them* forth with silence.

4 ¶ Hear this, O ye that swallow up the needy, even to make the poor of the land to fail,

5 Saying, When will the new moon be gone, that we may sell corn? and the sabbath, that we may set forth wheat, making the ephah small, and the shekel great, and falsifying the balances by deceit?

6 That we may buy the poor for silver, and the needy for a pair of shoes; *yea*, and sell the refuse of the wheat?

7 The LORD hath sworn by the excellency of Ja'cob, Surely I will never forget any of their works.

8 Shall not the land tremble for this, and every one mourn that dwelleth therein? and it shall rise up wholly as a flood; and it shall be cast out and drowned, as *by* the flood of E'gypt.

9 And it shall come to pass in that day, saith the Lord GOD, that I will cause the sun to go down at noon, and I will darken the earth in the clear day:

10 And I will turn your feasts into mourning, and all your songs into lamentation; and I will bring up sackcloth upon all loins, and baldness upon every head; and I will make it as the mourning of an only *son*, and the end thereof as a bitter day.

11 ¶ Behold, the days come, saith the Lord GOD, that I will send a famine in the land, not a famine of bread, nor a thirst for water, but of hearing the words of the LORD:

12 And they shall wander from sea to sea, and from the north even to the east, they shall run to and fro to seek the word of the LORD, and shall not find *it*.

13 In that day shall the fair virgins and young men faint for thirst.

14 They that swear by the sin of Sa-ma'ri-a, and say, Thy god, O Dan, liveth; and, The manner of Be'er-she'ba liveth; even they shall fall, and never rise up again.

9 I SAW the Lord standing upon the altar: and he said, Smite the lintel of the door, that the posts may shake: and cut them in the head, all of them; and I will slay the last of them with the sword: he that fleeth of them shall not flee away, and he that escapeth of them shall not be delivered.

2 Though they dig into hell, thence shall mine hand take them; though they climb up to heaven, thence will I bring them down:

3 And though they hide themselves in the top of Car'mel, I will search and take them out thence; and though they be hid from my sight in the bottom of the sea, thence will I command the serpent, and he shall bite them:

4 And though they go into captivity before their enemies, thence will I command the sword, and it shall slay them: and I will set mine eyes upon them for evil, and not for good.

5 And the Lord GOD of hosts *is* he that toucheth the land, and it shall melt, and all that dwell therein shall mourn: and it shall rise up wholly like a flood; and shall be drowned, as *by* the flood of E'gypt.

6 *It is* he that buildeth his stories in the heaven, and hath founded his troop in the earth; he that calleth for the waters of the sea, and poureth them out upon the face of the earth: The LORD *is* his name.

7 *Are* ye not as children of the E-thi-o'pi-ans unto me, O children of Is'ra-el? saith the LORD. Have not I brought up Is'ra-el out of the land of E'gypt? and the Phi-lis'tines from Caph'tor, and the Syr'i-ans from Kir?

8 Behold, the eyes of the Lord GOD *are* upon the sinful kingdom, and I will destroy it from off the face of the earth; saving that I will not utterly destroy the house of Ja'cob, saith the LORD.

9 For, lo, I will command, and I will sift the house of Is'ra-el among all nations, like as *corn* is sifted in a sieve, yet shall not the least grain fall upon the earth.

10 All the sinners of my people shall die by the sword, which say, The evil shall not overtake nor prevent us.

11 ¶ In that day will I raise up the tabernacle

of Da'vid that is fallen, and close up the breaches thereof; and I will raise up his ruins, and I will build it as in the days of old:

12 That they may possess the remnant of E'-dom, and of all the heathen, which are called by my name, saith the LORD that doeth this.

13 Behold, the days come, saith the LORD, that the plowman shall overtake the reaper, and the treader of grapes him that soweth seed; and the mountains shall drop sweet wine, and all the hills shall melt.

14 And I will bring again the captivity of my people of Is'ra-el, and they shall build the waste cities, and inhabit *them;* and they shall plant vineyards, and drink the wine thereof; they shall also make gardens, and eat the fruit of them.

15 And I will plant them upon their land, and they shall no more be pulled up out of their land which I have given them, saith the LORD thy God.

THE BOOK OF

OBADIAH

THE vision of O-ba-di'ah. Thus saith the Lord GOD concerning E'dom; We have heard a rumour from the LORD, and an ambassador is sent among the heathen, Arise ye, and let us rise up against her in battle.

2 Behold, I have made thee small among the heathen: thou art greatly despised.

3 ¶ The pride of thine heart hath deceived thee, thou that dwellest in the clefts of the rock, whose habitation *is* high; that saith in his heart, Who shall bring me down to the ground?

4 Though thou exalt *thyself* as the eagle, and though thou set thy nest among the stars, thence will I bring thee down, saith the LORD.

5 If thieves came to thee, if robbers by night, (how art thou cut off!) would they not have stolen till they had enough? if the grapegatherers came to thee, would they not leave *some* grapes?

6 How are *the things* of E'sau searched out! *how* are his hidden things sought up!

7 All the men of thy confederacy have brought thee *even* to the border: the men that were at peace with thee have deceived thee, *and* prevailed against thee; *they that eat* thy bread have laid a wound under thee: *there is* none understanding in him.

8 Shall I not in that day, saith the LORD, even destroy the wise *men* out of E'dom, and understanding out of the mount of E'sau?

9 And thy mighty *men,* O Te'man, shall be dismayed, to the end that every one of the mount of E'sau may be cut off by slaughter.

10 ¶ For *thy* violence against thy brother Ja'-cob shame shall cover thee, and thou shalt be cut off for ever.

11 In the day that thou stoodest on the other side, in the day that the strangers carried away captive his forces, and foreigners entered into his gates, and cast lots upon Je-ru'sa-lem, even thou *wast* as one of them.

12 But thou shouldest not have looked on the day of thy brother in the day that he became a stranger; neither shouldest thou have rejoiced over the children of Ju'dah in the day of their destruction; neither shouldest thou have spoken proudly in the day of distress.

13 Thou shouldest not have entered into the gate of my people in the day of their calamity; yea, thou shouldest not have looked on their affliction in the day of their calamity, nor have laid *hands* on their substance in the day of their calamity;

14 Neither shouldest thou have stood in the crossway, to cut off those of his that did escape; neither shouldest thou have delivered up those of his that did remain in the day of distress.

15 For the day of the LORD *is* near upon all the heathen: as thou hast done, it shall be done unto thee: thy reward shall return upon thine own head.

16 For as ye have drunk upon my holy mountain, *so* shall all the heathen drink continually, yea, they shall drink, and they shall swallow down, and they shall be as though they had not been.

17 ¶ But upon mount Zi'on shall be deliverance, and there shall be holiness; and the house of Ja'cob shall possess their possessions.

18 And the house of Ja'cob shall be a fire, and the house of Jo'seph a flame, and the house of E'sau for stubble, and they shall kindle in them, and devour them; and there shall not be *any* remaining of the house of E'sau; for the LORD hath spoken *it.*

19 And *they of* the south shall possess the mount of E'sau; and *they of* the plain the Phi-lis'tines: and they shall possess the fields of E'-phra-im, and the fields of Sa-ma'ri-a: and Ben'-ja-min *shall possess* Gil'e-ad.

20 And the captivity of this host of the children of Is'ra-el *shall possess* that of the Ca'-naan-ites, *even* unto Zar'e-phath; and the captivity of Je-ru'sa-lem, which *is* in Seph'a-rad, shall possess the cities of the south.

21 And saviours shall come up on mount Zi'-on to judge the mount of E'sau; and the kingdom shall be the LORD'S.

THE BOOK OF

JONAH

1 NOW the word of the LORD came unto Jo'-nah the son of A-mit'ta-i, saying,

2 Arise, go to Nin'e-veh, that great city, and cry against it; for their wickedness is come up before me.

3 But Jo'nah rose up to flee unto Tar'shish from the presence of the LORD, and went down to Jop'pa; and he found a ship going to Tar'-shish: so he paid the fare thereof, and went down into it, to go with them unto Tar'shish from the presence of the LORD.

4 ¶ But the LORD sent out a great wind into the sea, and there was a mighty tempest in the sea, so that the ship was like to be broken.

5 Then the mariners were afraid, and cried every man unto his god, and cast forth the wares that were in the ship into the sea, to lighten it of them. But Jo'nah was gone down into the sides of the ship; and he lay, and was fast asleep.

6 So the shipmaster came to him, and said unto him, What meanest thou, O sleeper? arise, call upon thy God, if so be that God will think upon us, that we perish not.

7 And they said every one to his fellow, Come, and let us cast lots, that we may know for whose cause this evil is upon us. So they cast lots, and the lot fell upon Jo'nah.

8 Then said they unto him, Tell us, we pray thee, for whose cause this evil is upon us; What is thine occupation? and whence comest thou? what is thy country? and of what people art thou?

9 And he said unto them, I am an He'brew; and I fear the Lord, the God of heaven, which hath made the sea and the dry land.

10 Then were the men exceedingly afraid, and said unto him, Why hast thou done this? For the men knew that he fled from the presence of the Lord, because he had told them.

11 ¶ Then said they unto him, What shall we do unto thee, that the sea may be calm unto us? for the sea wrought, and was tempestuous.

12 And he said unto them, Take me up, and cast me forth into the sea; so shall the sea be calm unto you: for I know that for my sake this great tempest is upon you.

13 Nevertheless the men rowed hard to bring it to the land; but they could not: for the sea wrought, and was tempestuous against them.

14 Wherefore they cried unto the Lord, and said, We beseech thee, O Lord, we beseech thee, let us not perish for this man's life, and lay not upon us innocent blood: for thou, O Lord, hast done as it pleased thee.

15 So they took up Jo'nah, and cast him forth into the sea: and the sea ceased from her raging.

16 Then the men feared the Lord exceedingly, and offered a sacrifice unto the Lord, and made vows.

17 ¶ Now the Lord had prepared a great fish to swallow up Jo'nah. And Jo'nah was in the belly of the fish three days and three nights.

2 THEN Jo'nah prayed unto the Lord his God out of the fish's belly,

2 And said, I cried by reason of mine affliction unto the Lord, and he heard me; out of the belly of hell cried I, and thou heardest my voice.

3 For thou hadst cast me into the deep, in the midst of the seas; and the floods compassed me about: all thy billows and thy waves passed over me.

4 Then I said, I am cast out of thy sight; yet I will look again toward thy holy temple.

5 The waters compassed me about, even to the soul: the depth closed me round about, the weeds were wrapped about my head.

6 I went down to the bottoms of the mountains; the earth with her bars was about me for ever: yet hast thou brought up my life from corruption, O Lord my God.

7 When my soul fainted within me I remembered the Lord: and my prayer came in unto thee, into thine holy temple.

8 They that observe lying vanities forsake their own mercy.

9 But I will sacrifice unto thee with the voice of thanksgiving; I will pay that that I have vowed. Salvation is of the Lord.

10 ¶ And the Lord spake unto the fish, and it vomited out Jo'nah upon the dry land.

3 AND the word of the Lord came unto Jo'-nah the second time, saying,

2 Arise, go unto Nin'e-veh, that great city, and preach unto it the preaching that I bid thee.

3 So Jo'nah arose, and went unto Nin'e-veh, according to the word of the Lord. Now Nin'e-veh was an exceeding great city of three days' journey.

4 And Jo'nah began to enter into the city a day's journey, and he cried, and said, Yet forty days, and Nin'e-veh shall be overthrown.

5 ¶ So the people of Nin'e-veh believed God, and proclaimed a fast, and put on sackcloth, from the greatest of them even to the least of them.

6 For word came unto the king of Nin'e-veh, and he arose from his throne, and he laid his robe from him, and covered him with sackcloth, and sat in ashes.

7 And he caused it to be proclaimed and published through Nin'e-veh by the decree of the king and his nobles, saying, Let neither man nor beast, herd nor flock, taste any thing: let them not feed, nor drink water:

8 But let man and beast be covered with sackcloth, and cry mightily unto God: yea, let them turn every one from his evil way, and from the violence that is in their hands.

9 Who can tell if God will turn and repent, and turn away from his fierce anger, that we perish not?

10 ¶ And God saw their works, that they turned from their evil way; and God repented of the evil, that he had said that he would do unto them; and he did it not.

4 BUT it displeased Jo'nah exceedingly, and he was very angry.

2 And he prayed unto the Lord, and said, I pray thee, O Lord, was not this my saying, when I was yet in my country? Therefore I fled before unto Tar'shish: for I knew that thou art a gracious God, and merciful, slow to anger, and of great kindness, and repentest thee of the evil.

3 Therefore now, O Lord, take, I beseech thee, my life from me; for it is better for me to die than to live.

4 ¶ Then said the Lord, Doest thou well to be angry?

5 So Jo'nah went out of the city, and sat on the east side of the city, and there made him a booth, and sat under it in the shadow, till he might see what would become of the city.

6 And the Lord God prepared a gourd, and made it to come up over Jo'nah, that it might be a shadow over his head, to deliver him from his grief. So Jo'nah was exceeding glad of the gourd.

7 But God prepared a worm when the morning rose the next day, and it smote the gourd that it withered.

8 And it came to pass, when the sun did arise, that God prepared a vehement east wind; and the sun beat upon the head of Jo'nah, that he fainted, and wished in himself to die, and said, It is better for me to die than to live.

9 And God said to Jo'nah, Doest thou well to be angry for the gourd? And he said, I do well to be angry, even unto death.

10 Then said the Lord, Thou hast had pity on

the gourd, for the which thou hast not laboured, neither madest it grow; which came up in a night, and perished in a night:

11 And should not I spare Nin'e-veh, that great city, wherein are more than sixscore thousand persons that cannot discern between their right hand and their left hand; and *also* much cattle?

THE BOOK OF

MICAH

1 THE word of the LORD that came to Mi'cah the Mo'ras-thite in the days of Jo'tham, A'-haz, *and* Hez-e-ki'ah, kings of Ju'dah, which he saw concerning Sa-ma'ri-a and Je-ru'sa-lem.

2 Hear, all ye people; hearken, O earth, and all that therein is: and let the Lord GOD be witness against you, the Lord from his holy temple.

3 For, behold, the LORD cometh forth out of his place, and will come down, and tread upon the high places of the earth.

4 And the mountains shall be molten under him, and the valleys shall be cleft, as wax before the fire, *and* as the waters *that are* poured down a steep place.

5 For the transgression of Ja'cob *is* all this, and for the sins of the house of Is'ra-el. What *is* the transgression of Ja'cob? *is it* not Sa-ma'ri-a? and what *are* the high places of Ju'dah? *are they* not Je-ru'sa-lem?

6 Therefore I will make Sa-ma'ri-a as an heap of the field, *and* as plantings of a vineyard: and I will pour down the stones thereof into the valley, and I will discover the foundations thereof.

7 And all the graven images thereof shall be beaten to pieces, and all the hires thereof shall be burned with the fire, and all the idols thereof will I lay desolate: for she gathered *it* of the hire of an harlot, and they shall return to the hire of an harlot.

8 Therefore I will wail and howl, I will go stripped and naked: I will make a wailing like the dragons, and mourning as the owls.

9 For her wound *is* incurable; for it is come unto Ju'dah; he is come unto the gate of my people, *even* to Je-ru'sa-lem.

10 ¶ Declare ye *it* not at Gath, weep ye not at all: in the house of Aph'rah roll thyself in the dust.

11 Pass ye away, thou inhabitant of Saph'ir, having thy shame naked: the inhabitant of Za'a-nan came not forth in the mourning of Beth-e'-zel; he shall receive of you his standing.

12 For the inhabitant of Ma'roth waited carefully for good: but evil came down from the LORD unto the gate of Je-ru'sa-lem.

13 O thou inhabitant of La'chish, bind the chariot to the swift beast: she *is* the beginning of the sin to the daughter of Zi'on: for the transgressions of Is'ra-el were found in thee.

14 Therefore shalt thou give presents to Mor'esh-eth-gath: the houses of Ach'zib *shall be* a lie to the kings of Is'ra-el.

15 Yet will I bring an heir unto thee, O inhabitant of Ma-re'shah: he shall come unto A-dul'lam the glory of Is'ra-el.

16 Make thee bald, and poll thee for thy delicate children; enlarge thy baldness as the eagle; for they are gone into captivity from thee.

2 WOE to them that devise iniquity, and work evil upon their beds! when the morning is light, they practise it, because it is in the power of their hand.

2 And they covet fields, and take *them* by violence; and houses, and take *them* away: so they oppress a man and his house, even a man and his heritage.

3 Therefore thus saith the LORD; Behold, against this family do I devise an evil, from which ye shall not remove your necks; neither shall ye go haughtily: for this time *is* evil.

4 ¶ In that day shall *one* take up a parable against you, and lament with a doleful lamentation, *and* say, We be utterly spoiled: he hath changed the portion of my people: how hath he removed *it* from me! turning away he hath divided our fields.

5 Therefore thou shalt have none that shall cast a cord by lot in the congregation of the LORD.

6 Prophesy ye not, *say they to them that* prophesy: they shall not prophesy to them, *that* they shall not take shame.

7 ¶ O *thou that art* named the house of Ja'-cob, is the spirit of the LORD straitened? *are* these his doings? do not my words do good to him that walketh uprightly?

8 Even of late my people is risen up as an enemy: ye pull off the robe with the garment from them that pass by securely as men averse from war.

9 The women of my people have ye cast out from their pleasant houses; from their children have ye taken away my glory for ever.

10 Arise ye, and depart; for this *is* not *your* rest: because it is polluted, it shall destroy *you*, even with a sore destruction.

11 If a man walking in the spirit and falsehood do lie, *saying*, I will prophesy unto thee of wine and of strong drink; he shall even be the prophet of this people.

12 ¶ I will surely assemble, O Ja'cob, all of thee; I will surely gather the remnant of Is'ra-el; I will put them together as the sheep of Boz'rah, as the flock in the midst of their fold: they shall make great noise by reason of *the multitude of* men.

13 The breaker is come up before them: they have broken up, and have passed through the gate, and are gone out by it: and their king shall pass before them, and the LORD on the head of them.

3 AND I said, Hear, I pray you, O heads of Ja'cob, and ye princes of the house of Is'ra-el; *Is it* not for you to know judgment?

2 Who hate the good, and love the evil; who pluck off their skin from off them, and their flesh from off their bones;

3 Who also eat the flesh of my people, and flay their skin from off them; and they break their bones, and chop them in pieces, as for the pot, and as flesh within the caldron.

4 Then shall they cry unto the LORD, but he will not hear them: he will even hide his face from them at that time, as they have behaved themselves ill in their doings.

5 ¶ Thus saith the LORD concerning the prophets that make my people err, that bite with their teeth, and cry, Peace; and he that

putteth not into their mouths, they even prepare war against him.

6 Therefore night *shall be* unto you, that ye shall not have a vision; and it shall be dark unto you, that ye shall not divine; and the sun shall go down over the prophets, and the day shall be dark over them.

7 Then shall the seers be ashamed, and the diviners confounded: yea, they shall all cover their lips; for *there is* no answer of God.

8 ¶ But truly I am full of power by the spirit of the LORD, and of judgment, and of might, to declare unto Ja'cob his transgression, and to Is'-ra-el his sin.

9 Hear this, I pray you, ye heads of the house of Ja'cob, and princes of the house of Is'ra-el, that abhor judgment, and pervert all equity.

10 They build up Zi'on with blood, and Je-ru'sa-lem with iniquity.

11 The heads thereof judge for reward, and the priests thereof teach for hire, and the prophets thereof divine for money: yet will they lean upon the LORD, and say, *Is* not the LORD among us? none evil can come upon us.

12 Therefore shall Zi'on for your sake be plowed *as* a field, and Je-ru'sa-lem shall become heaps, and the mountain of the house as the high places of the forest.

4 BUT in the last days it shall come to pass, *that* the mountain of the house of the LORD shall be established in the top of the mountains, and it shall be exalted above the hills; and people shall flow unto it.

2 And many nations shall come, and say, Come, and let us go up to the mountain of the LORD, and to the house of the God of Ja'cob; and he will teach us of his ways, and we will walk in his paths: for the law shall go forth of Zi'on, and the word of the LORD from Je-ru'sa-lem.

3 ¶ And he shall judge among many people, and rebuke strong nations afar off; and they shall beat their swords into plowshares, and their spears into pruninghooks: nation shall not lift up a sword against nation, neither shall they learn war any more.

4 But they shall sit every man under his vine and under his fig tree; and none shall make *them* afraid: for the mouth of the LORD of hosts hath spoken *it*.

5 For all people will walk every one in the name of his god, and we will walk in the name of the LORD our God for ever and ever.

6 In that day, saith the LORD, will I assemble her that halteth, and I will gather her that is driven out, and her that I have afflicted;

7 And I will make her that halted a remnant, and her that was cast far off a strong nation: and the LORD shall reign over them in mount Zi'on from henceforth, even for ever.

8 ¶ And thou, O tower of the flock, the strong hold of the daughter of Zi'on, unto thee shall it come, even the first dominion; the kingdom shall come to the daughter of Je-ru'sa-lem.

9 Now why dost thou cry out aloud? *is there* no king in thee? is thy counsellor perished? for pangs have taken thee as a woman in travail.

10 Be in pain, and labour to bring forth, O daughter of Zi'on, like a woman in travail: for now shalt thou go forth out of the city, and thou shalt dwell in the field, and thou shalt go *even* to Bab'y-lon; there shalt thou be delivered; there the LORD shall redeem thee from the hand of thine enemies.

11 ¶ Now also many nations are gathered against thee, that say, Let her be defiled, and let our eye look upon Zi'on.

12 But they know not the thoughts of the LORD, neither understand they his counsel: for he shall gather them as the sheaves into the floor.

13 Arise and thresh, O daughter of Zi'on: for I will make thine horn iron, and I will make thy hoofs brass: and thou shalt beat in pieces many people: and I will consecrate their gain unto the LORD, and their substance unto the Lord of the whole earth.

5 NOW gather thyself in troops, O daughter of troops: he hath laid siege against us: they shall smite the judge of Is'ra-el with a rod upon the cheek.

2 But thou, Beth'-le-hem Eph'ra-tah, *though* thou be little among the thousands of Ju'dah, *yet* out of thee shall he come forth unto me *that is* to be ruler in Is'ra-el; whose goings forth *have been* from of old, from everlasting.

3 Therefore will he give them up, until the time *that* she which travaileth hath brought forth: then the remnant of his brethren shall return unto the children of Is'ra-el.

4 ¶ And he shall stand and feed in the strength of the LORD, in the majesty of the name of the LORD his God; and they shall abide: for now shall he be great unto the ends of the earth.

5 And this *man* shall be the peace, when the As-syr'i-an shall come into our land: and when he shall tread in our palaces, then shall we raise against him seven shepherds, and eight principal men.

6 And they shall waste the land of As-syr'i-a with the sword, and the land of Nim'rod in the entrances thereof: thus shall he deliver *us* from the As-syr'i-an, when he cometh into our land, and when he treadeth within our borders.

7 And the remnant of Ja'cob shall be in the midst of many people as a dew from the LORD, as the showers upon the grass, that tarrieth not for man, nor waiteth for the sons of men.

8 ¶ And the remnant of Ja'cob shall be among the Gen'tiles in the midst of many people as a lion among the beasts of the forest, as a young lion among the flocks of sheep: who, if he go through, both treadeth down, and teareth in pieces, and none can deliver.

9 Thine hand shall be lifted up upon thine adversaries, and all thine enemies shall be cut off.

10 And it shall come to pass in that day, saith the LORD, that I will cut off thy horses out of the midst of thee, and I will destroy thy chariots:

11 And I will cut off the cities of thy land, and throw down all thy strong holds:

12 And I will cut off witchcrafts out of thine hand; and thou shalt have no *more* soothsayers:

13 Thy graven images also will I cut off, and thy standing images out of the midst of thee; and thou shalt no more worship the work of thine hands.

14 And I will pluck up thy groves out of the midst of thee: so will I destroy thy cities.

15 And I will execute vengeance in anger and fury upon the heathen, such as they have not heard.

6 HEAR ye now what the LORD saith; Arise, contend thou before the mountains, and let the hills hear thy voice.

2 Hear ye, O mountains, the LORD's controversy, and ye strong foundations of the earth: for the LORD hath a controversy with his people, and he will plead with Is'ra-el.

3 O my people, what have I done unto thee? and wherein have I wearied thee? testify against me.

4 For I brought thee up out of the land of E'gypt, and redeemed thee out of the house of servants; and I sent before thee Mo'ses, Aar'on, and Mir'i-am.

5 O my people, remember now what Ba'lak king of Mo'ab consulted, and what Ba'laam the son of Be'or answered him from Shit'tim unto Gil'gal; that ye may know the righteousness of the LORD.

6 ¶ Wherewith shall I come before the LORD, and bow myself before the high God? shall I come before him with burnt offerings, with calves of a year old?

7 Will the LORD be pleased with thousands of rams, or with ten thousands of rivers of oil? shall I give my firstborn for my transgression, the fruit of my body for the sin of my soul?

8 He hath shewed thee, O man, what is good; and what doth the LORD require of thee, but to do justly, and to love mercy, and to walk humbly with thy God?

9 The LORD'S voice crieth unto the city, and the man of wisdom shall see thy name: hear ye the rod, and who hath appointed it.

10 ¶ Are there yet the treasures of wickedness in the house of the wicked, and the scant measure that is abominable?

11 Shall I count them pure with the wicked balances, and with the bag of deceitful weights?

12 For the rich men thereof are full of violence, and the inhabitants thereof have spoken lies, and their tongue is deceitful in their mouth.

13 Therefore also will I make thee sick in smiting thee, in making thee desolate because of thy sins.

14 Thou shalt eat, but not be satisfied; and thy casting down shall be in the midst of thee; and thou shalt take hold, but shalt not deliver; and that which thou deliverest will I give up to the sword.

15 Thou shalt sow, but thou shalt not reap; thou shalt tread the olives, but thou shalt not anoint thee with oil; and sweet wine, but shalt not drink wine.

16 ¶ For the statutes of Om'ri are kept, and all the works of the house of A'hab, and ye walk in their counsels; that I should make thee a desolation, and the inhabitants thereof an hissing: therefore ye shall bear the reproach of my people.

7 WOE is me! for I am as when they have gathered the summer fruits, as the grape-gleanings of the vintage: there is no cluster to eat: my soul desired the firstripe fruit.

2 The good man is perished out of the earth: and there is none upright among men: they all lie in wait for blood; they hunt every man his brother with a net.

3 ¶ That they may do evil with both hands earnestly, the prince asketh, and the judge ask-eth for a reward; and the great man, he uttereth his mischievous desire: so they wrap it up.

4 The best of them is as a brier: the most upright is sharper than a thorn hedge: the day of thy watchmen and thy visitation cometh; now shall be their perplexity.

5 ¶ Trust ye not in a friend, put ye not confidence in a guide: keep the doors of thy mouth from her that lieth in thy bosom.

6 For the son dishonoureth the father, the daughter riseth up against her mother, the daughter in law against her mother in law; a man's enemies are the men of his own house.

7 Therefore I will look unto the LORD; I will wait for the God of my salvation: my God will hear me.

8 ¶ Rejoice not against me, O mine enemy: when I fall, I shall arise; when I sit in darkness, the LORD shall be a light unto me.

9 I will bear the indignation of the LORD, because I have sinned against him, until he plead my cause, and execute judgment for me: he will bring me forth to the light, and I shall behold his righteousness.

10 Then she that is mine enemy shall see it, and shame shall cover her which said unto me, Where is the LORD thy God? mine eyes shall behold her: now shall she be trodden down as the mire of the streets.

11 In the day that thy walls are to be built, in that day shall the decree be far removed.

12 In that day also he shall come even to thee from As-syr'i-a, and from the fortified cities, and from the fortress even to the river, and from sea to sea, and from mountain to mountain.

13 Notwithstanding the land shall be desolate because of them that dwell therein, for the fruit of their doings.

14 ¶ Feed thy people with thy rod, the flock of thine heritage, which dwell solitarily in the wood, in the midst of Car'mel: let them feed in Ba'shan and Gil'e-ad, as in the days of old.

15 According to the days of thy coming out of the land of E'gypt will I shew unto him marvellous things.

16 ¶ The nations shall see and be confounded at all their might: they shall lay their hand upon their mouth, their ears shall be deaf.

17 They shall lick the dust like a serpent, they shall move out of their holes like worms of the earth: they shall be afraid of the LORD our God, and shall fear because of thee.

18 Who is a God like unto thee, that pardoneth iniquity, and passeth by the transgression of the remnant of his heritage? he retaineth not his anger for ever, because he delighteth in mercy.

19 He will turn again, he will have compassion upon us; he will subdue our iniquities; and thou wilt cast all their sins into the depths of the sea.

20 Thou wilt perform the truth to Ja'cob, and the mercy to A'bra-ham, which thou hast sworn unto our fathers from the days of old.

THE BOOK OF

NAHUM

1 THE burden of Nin′e-veh. The book of the vision of Na′hum the El′kosh-ite.
2 God *is* jealous, and the LORD revengeth; the LORD revengeth, and *is* furious; the LORD will take vengeance on his adversaries, and he reserveth *wrath* for his enemies.
3 The LORD *is* slow to anger, and great in power, and will not at all acquit *the wicked:* the LORD *hath* his way in the whirlwind and in the storm, and the clouds *are* the dust of his feet.
4 He rebuketh the sea, and maketh it dry, and drieth up all the rivers: Ba′shan languisheth, and Car′mel, and the flower of Leb′a-non languisheth.
5 The mountains quake at him, and the hills melt, and the earth is burned at his presence, yea, the world, and all that dwell therein.
6 Who can stand before his indignation? and who can abide in the fierceness of his anger? his fury is poured out like fire, and the rocks are thrown down by him.
7 The LORD *is* good, a strong hold in the day of trouble; and he knoweth them that trust in him.
8 But with an overrunning flood he will make an utter end of the place thereof, and darkness shall pursue his enemies.
9 What do ye imagine against the LORD? he will make an utter end: affliction shall not rise up the second time.
10 For while *they* be folden together *as* thorns, and while they are drunken *as* drunkards, they shall be devoured as stubble fully dry.
11 There is *one* come out of thee, that imagineth evil against the LORD, a wicked counsellor.
12 Thus saith the LORD; Though *they be* quiet, and likewise many, yet thus shall they be cut down, when he shall pass through. Though I have afflicted thee, I will afflict thee no more.
13 For now will I break his yoke from off thee and will burst thy bonds in sunder.
14 And the LORD hath given a commandment concerning thee, *that* no more of thy name be sown: out of the house of thy gods will I cut off the graven image and the molten image: I will make thy grave; for thou art vile.
15 Behold upon the mountains the feet of him that bringeth good tidings, that publisheth peace! O Ju′dah, keep thy solemn feasts, perform thy vows: for the wicked shall no more pass through thee; he is utterly cut off.

2 HE that dasheth in pieces is come up before thy face: keep the munition, watch the way, make *thy* loins strong, fortify *thy* power mightily.
2 For the LORD hath turned away the excellency of Ja′cob, as the excellency of Is′ra-el: for the emptiers have emptied them out, and marred their vine branches.
3 The shield of his mighty men is made red, the valiant men *are* in scarlet: the chariots *shall be* with flaming torches in the day of his preparation, and the fir trees shall be terribly shaken.
4 The chariots shall rage in the streets, they shall justle one against another in the broad ways: they shall seem like torches, they shall run like the lightnings.
5 He shall recount his worthies: they shall stumble in their walk; they shall make haste to

the wall thereof, and the defence shall be prepared.
6 The gates of the rivers shall be opened, and the palace shall be dissolved.
7 And Huz′zab shall be led away captive, she shall be brought up, and her maids shall lead *her* as with the voice of doves, tabering upon their breasts.
8 But Nin′e-veh *is* of old like a pool of water: yet they shall flee away. Stand, stand, *shall they* cry; but none shall look back.
9 Take ye the spoil of silver, take the spoil of gold: for *there is* none end of the store *and* glory out of all the pleasant furniture.
10 She is empty, and void, and waste: and the heart melteth, and the knees smite together, and much pain *is* in all loins, and the faces of them all gather blackness.
11 Where *is* the dwelling of the lions, and the feedingplace of the young lions, where the lion, *even* the old lion, walked, *and* the lion's whelp, and none made *them* afraid?
12 The lion did tear in pieces enough for his whelps, and strangled for his lionesses, and filled his holes with prey, and his dens with ravin.
13 Behold, I *am* against thee, saith the LORD of hosts, and I will burn her chariots in the smoke, and the sword shall devour thy young lions: and I will cut off thy prey from the earth, and the voice of thy messengers shall no more be heard.

3 WOE to the bloody city! it *is* all full of lies *and* robbery, the prey departeth not;
2 The noise of a whip, and the noise of the rattling of the wheels, and of the pransing horses, and of the jumping chariots.
3 The horseman lifteth up both the bright sword and the glittering spear: and *there is* a multitude of slain, and a great number of carcases; and *there is* none end of *their* corpses; they stumble upon their corpses:
4 Because of the multitude of the whoredoms of the wellfavoured harlot, the mistress of witchcrafts, that selleth nations through her whoredoms, and families through her witchcrafts.
5 Behold, I *am* against thee, saith the LORD of hosts; and I will discover thy skirts upon thy face, and I will shew the nations thy nakedness, and the kingdoms thy shame.
6 And I will cast abominable filth upon thee, and make thee vile, and will set thee as a gazingstock.
7 And it shall come to pass, *that* all they that look upon thee shall flee from thee, and say, Nin′e-veh is laid waste: who will bemoan her? whence shall I seek comforters for thee?
8 Art thou better than populous No, that was situate among the rivers, *that had* the waters round about it, whose rampart *was* the sea, *and* her wall *was* from the sea?
9 E-thi-o′pi-a and E′gypt *were* her strength, and *it was* infinite; Put and Lu′bim were thy helpers.
10 Yet *was* she carried away, she went into captivity: her young children also were dashed in pieces at the top of all the streets: and they cast lots for her honourable men, and all her great men were bound in chains.
11 Thou also shalt be drunken: thou shalt be

hid, thou also shalt seek strength because of the enemy.

12 All thy strong holds *shall be like* fig trees with the firstripe figs: if they be shaken, they shall even fall into the mouth of the eater.

13 Behold, thy people in the midst of thee *are* women: the gates of thy land shall be set wide open unto thine enemies: the fire shall devour thy bars.

14 Draw thee waters for the siege, fortify thy strong holds: go into clay, and tread the morter, make strong the brickkiln.

15 There shall the fire devour thee; the sword shall cut thee off, it shall eat thee up like the cankerworm: make thyself many as the cankerworm, make thyself many as the locusts.

16 Thou hast multiplied thy merchants above the stars of heaven: the cankerworm spoileth, and fleeth away.

17 Thy crowned *are* as the locusts, and thy captains as the great grasshoppers, which camp in the hedges in the cold day, *but* when the sun ariseth they flee away, and their place is not known where they *are.*

18 Thy shepherds slumber, O king of As-syr'-i-a: thy nobles shall dwell *in the dust:* thy people is scattered upon the mountains, and no man gathereth *them.*

19 *There is* no healing of thy bruise; thy wound is grievous: all that hear the bruit of thee shall clap the hands over thee: for upon whom hath not thy wickedness passed continually?

THE BOOK OF

HABAKKUK

1 THE burden which Ha-bak'kuk the prophet did see.

2 O LORD, how long shall I cry, and thou wilt not hear! *even* cry out unto thee *of* violence, and thou wilt not save!

3 Why dost thou shew me iniquity, and cause *me* to behold grievance? for spoiling and violence *are* before me: and there are *that* raise up strife and contention.

4 Therefore the law is slacked, and judgment doth never go forth: for the wicked doth compass about the righteous; therefore wrong judgment proceedeth.

5 ¶ Behold ye among the heathen, and regard, and wonder marvellously: for I will work a work in your days, *which* ye will not believe, though it be told *you.*

6 For, lo, I raise up the Chal-de'ans, *that* bitter and hasty nation, which shall march through the breadth of the land, to possess the dwellingplaces *that are* not theirs.

7 They *are* terrible and dreadful: their judgment and their dignity shall proceed of themselves.

8 Their horses also are swifter than the leopards, and are more fierce than the evening wolves: and their horsemen shall spread themselves, and their horsemen shall come from far; they shall fly as the eagle *that* hasteth to eat.

9 They shall come all for violence: their faces shall sup up *as* the east wind, and they shall gather the captivity as the sand.

10 And they shall scoff at the kings, and the princes shall be a scorn unto them: they shall deride every strong hold; for they shall heap dust, and take it.

11 Then shall *his* mind change, and he shall pass over, and offend, *imputing* this his power unto his god.

12 ¶ *Art* thou not from everlasting, O LORD my God, mine Holy One? we shall not die. O LORD, thou hast ordained them for judgment; and, O mighty God, thou hast established them for correction.

13 *Thou art* of purer eyes than to behold evil, and canst not look on iniquity: wherefore lookest thou upon them that deal treacherously, *and* holdest thy tongue when the wicked devoureth *the man that is* more righteous than he?

14 And makest men as the fishes of the sea, as the creeping things, *that have* no ruler over them?

15 They take up all of them with the angle, they catch them in their net, and gather them in their drag: therefore they rejoice and are glad.

16 Therefore they sacrifice unto their net, and burn incense unto their drag; because by them their portion *is* fat, and their meat plenteous.

17 Shall they therefore empty their net, and not spare continually to slay the nations?

2 I WILL stand upon my watch, and set me upon the tower, and will watch to see what he will say unto me, and what I shall answer when I am reproved.

2 And the LORD answered me, and said, Write the vision, and make *it* plain upon tables, that he may run that readeth it.

3 For the vision *is* yet for an appointed time, but at the end it shall speak, and not lie: though it tarry, wait for it; because it will surely come, it will not tarry.

4 Behold, his soul *which* is lifted up is not upright in him: but the just shall live by his faith.

5 ¶ Yea also, because he transgresseth by wine, *he is* a proud man, neither keepeth at home, who enlargeth his desire as hell, and *is* as death, and cannot be satisfied, but gathereth unto him all nations, and heapeth unto him all people:

6 Shall not all these take up a parable against him, and a taunting proverb against him, and say, Woe to him that increaseth *that which is* not his! how long? and to him that ladeth himself with thick clay!

7 Shall they not rise up suddenly that shall bite thee, and awake that shall vex thee, and thou shalt be for booties unto them?

8 Because thou hast spoiled many nations, all the remnant of the people shall spoil thee; because of men's blood, and *for* the violence of the land, of the city, and of all that dwell therein.

9 ¶ Woe to him that coveteth an evil covetousness to his house, that he may set his nest on high, that he may be delivered from the power of evil!

10 Thou hast consulted shame to thy house by cutting off many people, and hast sinned *against* thy soul.

11 For the stone shall cry out of the wall, and the beam out of the timber shall answer it.

12 ¶ Woe to him that buildeth a town with blood, and stablisheth a city by iniquity!

13 Behold, *is it* not of the LORD of hosts that the people shall labour in the very fire, and the people shall weary themselves for very vanity?

14 For the earth shall be filled with the knowledge of the glory of the LORD, as the waters cover the sea.

15 ¶ Woe unto him that giveth his neighbour drink, that puttest thy bottle to *him*, and makest *him* drunken also, that thou mayest look on their nakedness!

16 Thou art filled with shame for glory: drink thou also, and let thy foreskin be uncovered: the cup of the LORD's right hand shall be turned unto thee, and shameful spewing *shall be* on thy glory.

17 For the violence of Leb'a-non shall cover thee, and the spoil of beasts, *which* made them afraid, because of men's blood, and for the violence of the land, of the city, and of all that dwell therein.

18 ¶ What profiteth the graven image that the maker thereof hath graven it; the molten image, and a teacher of lies, that the maker of his work trusteth therein, to make dumb idols?

19 Woe unto him that saith to the wood, Awake; to the dumb stone, Arise, it shall teach! Behold, it *is* laid over with gold and silver, and *there is* no breath at all in the midst of it.

20 But the LORD *is* in his holy temple: let all the earth keep silence before him.

3 A PRAYER of Ha-bak'kuk the prophet upon Shi-gi'o-noth.

2 O LORD, I have heard thy speech, *and* was afraid: O LORD, revive thy work in the midst of the years, in the midst of the years make known; in wrath remember mercy.

3 God came from Te'man, and the Holy One from mount Pa'ran. Se'lah. His glory covered the heavens, and the earth was full of his praise.

4 And *his* brightness was as the light; he had horns *coming* out of his hand: and there *was* the hiding of his power.

5 Before him went the pestilence, and burning coals went forth at his feet.

6 He stood, and measured the earth: he beheld, and drove asunder the nations; and the everlasting mountains were scattered, the perpetual hills did bow: his ways *are* everlasting.

7 I saw the tents of Cu'shan in affliction: *and* the curtains of the land of Mid'i-an did tremble.

8 Was the LORD displeased against the rivers? *was* thine anger against the rivers? *was* thy wrath against the sea, that thou didst ride upon thine horses *and* thy chariots of salvation?

9 Thy bow was made quite naked, *according* to the oaths of the tribes, *even thy* word. Se'lah. Thou didst cleave the earth with rivers.

10 The mountains saw thee, *and* they trembled: the overflowing of the water passed by: the deep uttered his voice, *and* lifted up his hands on high.

11 The sun *and* moon stood still in their habitation: at the light of thine arrows they went, *and* at the shining of thy glittering spear.

12 Thou didst march through the land in indignation, thou didst thresh the heathen in anger.

13 Thou wentest forth for the salvation of thy people, *even* for salvation with thine anointed; thou woundedst the head out of the house of the wicked, by discovering the foundation unto the neck. Se'lah.

14 Thou didst strike through with his staves the head of his villages: they came out as a whirlwind to scatter me: their rejoicing *was* as to devour the poor secretly.

15 Thou didst walk through the sea with thine horses, *through* the heap of great waters.

16 When I heard, my belly trembled; my lips quivered at the voice: rottenness entered into my bones, and I trembled in myself, that I might rest in the day of trouble: when he cometh up unto the people, he will invade them with his troops.

17 ¶ Although the fig tree shall not blossom, neither *shall* fruit *be* in the vines; the labour of the olive shall fail, and the fields shall yield no meat; the flock shall be cut off from the fold, and *there shall be* no herd in the stalls:

18 Yet I will rejoice in the LORD, I will joy in the God of my salvation.

19 The LORD God *is* my strength, and he will make my feet like hinds' *feet*, and he will make me to walk upon mine high places. To the chief singer on my stringed instruments.

THE BOOK OF

ZEPHANIAH

1 THE word of the LORD which came unto Zeph-a-ni'ah the son of Cu'shi, the son of Ged-a-li'ah, the son of Am-a-ri'ah, the son of Hiz-ki'ah, in the days of Jo-si'ah the son of A'-mon, king of Ju'dah.

2 I will utterly consume all *things* from off the land, saith the LORD.

3 I will consume man and beast; I will consume the fowls of the heaven, and the fishes of the sea, and the stumblingblocks with the wicked; and I will cut off man from off the land, saith the LORD.

4 I will also stretch out mine hand upon Ju'-dah, and upon all the inhabitants of Je-ru'sa-lem; and I will cut off the remnant of Ba'al from this place, *and* the name of the Chem'a-rims with the priests;

5 And them that worship the host of heaven upon the house tops; and them that worship *and* that swear by the LORD, and that swear by Mal'cham;

6 And them that are turned back from the LORD; and *those* that have not sought the LORD, nor enquired for him.

7 Hold thy peace at the presence of the Lord GOD: for the day of the LORD *is* at hand: for the LORD hath prepared a sacrifice, he hath bid his guests.

8 And it shall come to pass in the day of the LORD'S sacrifice, that I will punish the princes, and the king's children, and all such as are clothed with strange apparel.

9 In the same day also will I punish all those that leap on the threshold, which fill their masters' houses with violence and deceit.

10 And it shall come to pass in that day, saith the LORD, *that there shall be* the noise of a cry from the fish gate, and an howling from the second, and a great crashing from the hills.

11 Howl, ye inhabitants of Mak'tesh, for all the merchant people are cut down; all they that bear silver are cut off.

541

ZEPHANIAH 3

12 And it shall come to pass at that time, *that* I will search Je-ru'sa-lem with candles, and punish the men that are settled on their lees: that say in their heart, The LORD will not do good, neither will he do evil.

13 Therefore their goods shall become a booty, and their houses a desolation: they shall also build houses, but not inhabit *them*; and they shall plant vineyards, but not drink the wine thereof.

14 The great day of the LORD *is* near, *it is* near, and hasteth greatly, *even* the voice of the day of the LORD: the mighty man shall cry there bitterly.

15 That day *is* a day of wrath, a day of trouble and distress, a day of wasteness and desolation, a day of darkness and gloominess, a day of clouds and thick darkness,

16 A day of the trumpet and alarm against the fenced cities, and against the high towers.

17 And I will bring distress upon men, that they shall walk like blind men, because they have sinned against the LORD: and their blood shall be poured out as dust, and their flesh as the dung.

18 Neither their silver nor their gold shall be able to deliver them in the day of the LORD's wrath; but the whole land shall be devoured by the fire of his jealousy: for he shall make even a speedy riddance of all them that dwell in the land.

2 GATHER yourselves together, yea, gather together, O nation not desired;

2 Before the decree bring forth, *before* the day pass as the chaff, before the fierce anger of the LORD come upon you, before the day of the LORD's anger come upon you.

3 Seek ye the LORD, all ye meek of the earth, which have wrought his judgment; seek righteousness, seek meekness: it may be ye shall be hid in the day of the LORD's anger.

4 ¶ For Ga'za shall be forsaken, and Ash'ke-lon a desolation: they shall drive out Ash'dod at the noon day, and Ek'ron shall be rooted up.

5 Woe unto the inhabitants of the sea coast, the nation of the Cher'eth-ites! the word of the LORD *is* against you; O Ca'naan, the land of the Phi-lis'tines, I will even destroy thee, that there shall be no inhabitant.

6 And the sea coast shall be dwellings *and* cottages for shepherds, and folds for flocks.

7 And the coast shall be for the remnant of the house of Ju'dah; they shall feed thereupon: in the houses of Ash'ke-lon shall they lie down in the evening: for the LORD their God shall visit them, and turn away their captivity.

8 ¶ I have heard the reproach of Mo'ab, and the revilings of the children of Am'mon, whereby they have reproached my people, and magnified *themselves* against their border.

9 Therefore *as* I live, saith the LORD of hosts, the God of Is'ra-el, Surely Mo'ab shall be as Sod'om, and the children of Am'mon as Go-mor'rah, *even* the breeding of nettles, and salt-pits, and a perpetual desolation: the residue of my people shall spoil them, and the remnant of my people shall possess them.

10 This shall they have for their pride, because they have reproached and magnified *themselves* against the people of the LORD of hosts.

11 The LORD *will be* terrible unto them: for he will famish all the gods of the earth; and *men* shall worship him, every one from his place, *even* all the isles of the heathen.

12 ¶ Ye E-thi-o'pi-ans also, ye *shall be* slain by my sword.

13 And he will stretch out his hand against the north, and destroy As-syr'i-a; and will make Nin'e-veh a desolation, *and* dry like a wilderness.

14 And flocks shall lie down in the midst of her, all the beasts of the nations: both the cormorant and the bittern shall lodge in the upper lintels of it; *their* voice shall sing in the windows; desolation *shall be* in the thresholds: for he shall uncover the cedar work.

15 This *is* the rejoicing city that dwelt carelessly, that said in her heart, I *am*, and *there is* none beside me: how is she become a desolation, a place for beasts to lie down in! every one that passeth by her shall hiss, *and* wag his hand.

3 WOE to her that is filthy and polluted, to the oppressing city!

2 She obeyed not the voice; she received not correction; she trusted not in the LORD; she drew not near to her God.

3 Her princes within her *are* roaring lions; her judges *are* evening wolves; they gnaw not the bones till the morrow.

4 Her prophets *are* light *and* treacherous persons: her priests have polluted the sanctuary, they have done violence to the law.

5 The just LORD *is* in the midst thereof; he will not do iniquity: every morning doth he bring his judgment to light, he faileth not; but the unjust knoweth no shame.

6 I have cut off the nations: their towers are desolate; I made their streets waste, that none passeth by: their cities are destroyed, so that there is no man, that there is none inhabitant.

7 I said, Surely thou wilt fear me, thou wilt receive instruction; so their dwelling should not be cut off, howsoever I punished them: but they rose early, *and* corrupted all their doings.

8 ¶ Therefore wait ye upon me, saith the LORD, until the day that I rise up to the prey: for my determination *is* to gather the nations, that I may assemble the kingdoms, to pour upon them mine indignation, *even* all my fierce anger: for all the earth shall be devoured with the fire of my jealousy.

9 For then will I turn to the people a pure language, that they may all call upon the name of the LORD, to serve him with one consent.

10 From beyond the rivers of E-thi-o'pi-a my suppliants, *even* the daughter of my dispersed, shall bring mine offering.

11 In that day shalt thou not be ashamed for all thy doings, wherein thou hast transgressed against me: for then I will take away out of the midst of thee them that rejoice in thy pride, and thou shalt no more be haughty because of my holy mountain.

12 I will also leave in the midst of thee an afflicted and poor people, and they shall trust in the name of the LORD.

13 The remnant of Is'ra-el shall not do iniquity, nor speak lies; neither shall a deceitful tongue be found in their mouth: for they shall feed and lie down, and none shall make *them* afraid.

14 ¶ Sing, O daughter of Zi'on; shout, O Is'ra-el; be glad and rejoice with all the heart, O daughter of Je-ru'sa-lem.

15 The LORD hath taken away thy judgments, he hath cast out thine enemy: the king of Is'ra-el, *even* the LORD, *is* in the midst of thee: thou shalt not see evil any more.

16 In that day it shall be said to Je-ru'sa-lem, Fear thou not: *and to* Zi'on, Let not thine hands be slack.

17 The LORD thy God in the midst of thee *is* mighty; he will save, he will rejoice over thee with joy; he will rest in his love, he will joy over thee with singing.

18 I will gather *them that are* sorrowful for the solemn assembly, *who* are of thee, *to whom* the reproach of it *was* a burden.

19 Behold, at that time I will undo all that afflict thee: and I will save her that halteth, and gather her that was driven out; and I will get them praise and fame in every land where they have been put to shame.

20 At that time will I bring you *again*, even in the time that I gather you: for I will make you a name and a praise among all people of the earth, when I turn back your captivity before your eyes, saith the LORD.

THE BOOK OF

HAGGAI

1 IN the second year of Da-ri'us the king, in the sixth month, in the first day of the month, came the word of the LORD by Hag'ga-i the prophet unto Ze-rub'ba-bel the son of She-al'ti-el, governor of Ju'dah, and to Josh'u-a the son of Jos'e-dech, the high priest, saying,

2 Thus speaketh the LORD of hosts, saying, This people say, The time is not come, the time that the LORD's house should be built.

3 Then came the word of the LORD by Hag'-ga-i the prophet, saying,

4 *Is it* time for you, O ye, to dwell in your cieled houses, and this house *lie* waste?

5 Now therefore thus saith the LORD of hosts; Consider your ways.

6 Ye have sown much, and bring in little; ye eat, but ye have not enough; ye drink, but ye are not filled with drink; ye clothe you, but there is none warm; and he that earneth wages earneth wages *to put it* into a bag with holes.

7 ¶ Thus saith the LORD of hosts; Consider your ways.

8 Go up to the mountain, and bring wood, and build the house; and I will take pleasure in it, and I will be glorified, saith the LORD.

9 Ye looked for much, and, lo, *it came* to little; and when ye brought *it* home, I did blow upon it. Why? saith the LORD of hosts. Because of mine house that *is* waste, and ye run every man unto his own house.

10 Therefore the heaven over you is stayed from dew, and the earth is stayed *from* her fruit.

11 And I called for a drought upon the land, and upon the mountains, and upon the corn, and upon the new wine, and upon the oil, and upon *that* which the ground bringeth forth, and upon men, and upon cattle, and upon all the labour of the hands.

12 ¶ Then Ze-rub'ba-bel the son of She-al'ti-el, and Josh'u-a the son of Jos'e-dech, the high priest, with all the remnant of the people, obeyed the voice of the LORD their God, and the words of Hag'ga-i the prophet, as the LORD their God had sent him, and the people did fear before the LORD.

13 Then spake Hag'ga-i the LORD's messenger in the LORD's message unto the people, saying, I *am* with you, saith the LORD.

14 And the LORD stirred up the spirit of Ze-rub'ba-bel the son of She-al'ti-el, governor of Ju'dah, and the spirit of Josh'u-a the son of Jos'-e-dech, the high priest, and the spirit of all the remnant of the people; and they came and did work in the house of the LORD of hosts, their God,

15 In the four and twentieth day of the sixth month, in the second year of Da-ri'us the king.

2 IN the seventh *month*, in the one and twentieth *day* of the month, came the word of the LORD by the prophet Hag'ga-i, saying,

2 Speak now to Ze-rub'ba-bel the son of She-al'ti-el, governor of Ju'dah, and to Josh'u-a the son of Jos'e-dech, the high priest, and to the residue of the people, saying,

3 Who *is* left among you that saw this house in her first glory? and how do ye see it now? *is it* not in your eyes in comparison of it as nothing?

4 Yet now be strong, O Ze-rub'ba-bel, saith the LORD; and be strong, O Josh'u-a, son of Jos'-e-dech, the high priest; and be strong, all ye people of the land, saith the LORD, and work: for I *am* with you, saith the LORD of hosts:

5 *According to* the word that I covenanted with you when ye came out of E'gypt, so my spirit remaineth among you: fear ye not.

6 For thus saith the LORD of hosts; Yet once, it *is* a little while, and I will shake the heavens, and the earth, and the sea, and the dry *land;*

7 And I will shake all nations, and the desire of all nations shall come: and I will fill this house with glory, saith the LORD of hosts.

8 The silver *is* mine, and the gold *is* mine, saith the LORD of hosts.

9 The glory of this latter house shall be greater than of the former, saith the LORD of hosts: and in this place will I give peace, saith the LORD of hosts.

10 ¶ In the four and twentieth *day* of the ninth *month*, in the second year of Da-ri'us, came the word of the LORD by Hag'ga-i the prophet, saying,

11 Thus saith the LORD of hosts; Ask now the priests *concerning* the law, saying,

12 If one bear holy flesh in the skirt of his garment, and with his skirt do touch bread, or pottage, or wine, or oil, or any meat, shall it be holy? And the priests answered and said, No.

13 Then said Hag'ga-i, If *one that is* unclean by a dead body touch any of these, shall it be unclean? And the priests answered and said, It shall be unclean.

14 Then answered Hag'ga-i, and said, So *is* this people, and so *is* this nation before me, saith the LORD; and so *is* every work of their hands; and that which they offer there *is* unclean.

15 And now, I pray you, consider from this day and upward, from before a stone was laid upon a stone in the temple of the LORD:

16 Since those *days* were, when *one* came to an heap of twenty *measures*, there were *but* ten: when *one* came to the pressfat for to draw out fifty *vessels* out of the press, there were *but* twenty

17 I smote you with blasting and with mildew and with hail in all the labours of your hands; yet ye *turned* not to me, saith the LORD.

18 Consider now from this day and upward, from the four and twentieth day of the ninth *month, even* from the day that the foundation of the LORD's temple was laid, consider *it.*

19 Is the seed yet in the barn? yea, as yet the vine, and the fig tree, and the pomegranate, and the olive tree, hath not brought forth: from this day will I bless *you.*

20 ¶ And again the word of the LORD came unto Hag'ga-i in the four and twentieth *day* of the month, saying,

21 Speak to Ze-rub'ba-bel, governor of Ju'dah, saying, I will shake the heavens and the earth;

22 And I will overthrow the throne of kingdoms, and I will destroy the strength of the kingdoms of the heathen; and I will overthrow the chariots, and those that ride in them; and the horses and their riders shall come down, every one by the sword of his brother.

23 In that day, saith the LORD of hosts, will I take thee, O Ze-rub'ba-bel, my servant, the son of She-al'ti-el, saith the LORD, and will make thee as a signet: for I have chosen thee, saith the LORD of hosts.

THE BOOK OF

ZECHARIAH

1 IN the eighth month, in the second year of Da-ri'us, came the word of the LORD unto Zech-a-ri'ah, the son of Ber-e-chi'ah, the son of Id'do the prophet, saying,

2 The LORD hath been sore displeased with your fathers.

3 Therefore say thou unto them, Thus saith the LORD of hosts; Turn ye unto me, saith the LORD of hosts, and I will turn unto you, saith the LORD of hosts.

4 Be ye not as your fathers, unto whom the former prophets have cried, saying, Thus saith the LORD of hosts; Turn ye now from your evil ways, and *from* your evil doings: but they did not hear, nor hearken unto me, saith the LORD.

5 Your fathers, where *are* they? and the prophets, do they live for ever?

6 But my words and my statutes, which I commanded my servants the prophets, did they not take hold of your fathers? and they returned and said, Like as the LORD of hosts thought to do unto us, according to our ways, and according to our doings, so hath he dealt with us.

7 ¶ Upon the four and twentieth day of the eleventh month, which *is* the month Se'bat, in the second year of Da-ri'us, came the word of the LORD unto Zech-a-ri'ah, the son of Ber-e-chi'ah, the son of Id'do the prophet, saying,

8 I saw by night, and behold a man riding upon a red horse, and he stood among the myrtle trees that *were* in the bottom; and behind him *were there* red horses, speckled, and white.

9 Then said I, O my lord, what *are* these? And the angel that talked with me said unto me, I will shew thee what these *be.*

10 And the man that stood among the myrtle trees answered and said, These *are* they whom the LORD hath sent to walk to and fro through the earth.

11 And they answered the angel of the LORD that stood among the myrtle trees, and said, We have walked to and fro through the earth, and, behold, all the earth sitteth still, and is at rest.

12 ¶ Then the angel of the LORD answered and said, O LORD of hosts, how long wilt thou not have mercy on Je-ru'sa-lem and on the cities of Ju'dah, against which thou hast had indignation these threescore and ten years?

13 And the LORD answered the angel that talked with me *with* good words *and* comfortable words.

14 So the angel that communed with me said unto me, Cry thou, saying, Thus saith the LORD of hosts; I am jealous for Je-ru'sa-lem and for Zi'on with a great jealousy.

15 And I am very sore displeased with the heathen *that are* at ease: for I was but a little displeased, and they helped forward the affliction.

16 Therefore thus saith the LORD; I am returned to Je-ru'sa-lem with mercies: my house shall be built in it, saith the LORD of hosts, and a line shall be stretched forth upon Je-ru'sa-lem.

17 Cry yet, saying, Thus saith the LORD of hosts; My cities through prosperity shall yet be spread abroad; and the LORD shall yet comfort Zi'on, and shall yet choose Je-ru'sa-lem.

18 ¶ Then lifted I up mine eyes, and saw, and behold four horns.

19 And I said unto the angel that talked with me, What *be* these? And he answered me, These *are* the horns which have scattered Ju'dah, Is'ra-el, and Je-ru'sa-lem.

20 And the LORD shewed me four carpenters.

21 Then said I, What come these to do? And he spake, saying, These *are* the horns which have scattered Ju'dah, so that no man did lift up his head: but these are come to fray them, to cast out the horns of the Gen'tiles, which lifted up *their* horn over the land of Ju'dah to scatter it.

2 I LIFTED up mine eyes again, and looked, and behold a man with a measuring line in his hand.

2 Then said I, Whither goest thou? And he said unto me, To measure Je-ru'sa-lem, to see what *is* the breadth thereof, and what *is* the length thereof.

3 And, behold, the angel that talked with me went forth, and another angel went out to meet him,

4 And said unto him, Run, speak to this young man, saying, Je-ru'sa-lem shall be inhabited *as* towns without walls for the multitude of men and cattle therein:

5 For I, saith the LORD, will be unto her a wall of fire round about, and will be the glory in the midst of her.

6 ¶ Ho, ho, *come forth,* and flee from the land of the north, saith the LORD: for I have spread you abroad as the four winds of the heaven, saith the LORD.

7 Deliver thyself, O Zi'on, that dwellest *with* the daughter of Bab'y-lon.

8 For thus saith the LORD of hosts; After the glory hath he sent me unto the nations which spoiled you: for he that toucheth you toucheth the apple of his eye.

9 For, behold, I will shake mine hand upon them, and they shall be a spoil to their servants:

and ye shall know that the LORD of hosts hath sent me.

10 ¶ Sing and rejoice, O daughter of Zi'on: for, lo, I come, and I will dwell in the midst of thee, saith the LORD.

11 And many nations shall be joined to the LORD in that day, and shall be my people: and I will dwell in the midst of thee, and thou shalt know that the LORD of hosts hath sent me unto thee.

12 And the LORD shall inherit Ju'dah his portion in the holy land, and shall choose Je-ru'sa-lem again.

13 Be silent, O all flesh, before the LORD: for he is raised up out of his holy habitation.

3 AND he shewed me Josh'u-a the high priest standing before the angel of the LORD, and Sa'tan standing at his right hand to resist him.

2 And the LORD said unto Sa'tan, The LORD rebuke thee, O Sa'tan; even the LORD that hath chosen Je-ru'sa-lem rebuke thee: is not this a brand plucked out of the fire?

3 Now Josh'u-a was clothed with filthy garments, and stood before the angel.

4 And he answered and spake unto those that stood before him, saying, Take away the filthy garments from him. And unto him he said, Behold, I have caused thine iniquity to pass from thee, and I will clothe thee with change of raiment.

5 And I said, Let them set a fair mitre upon his head. So they set a fair mitre upon his head, and clothed him with garments. And the angel of the LORD stood by.

6 And the angel of the LORD protested unto Josh'u-a, saying,

7 Thus saith the LORD of hosts; If thou wilt walk in my ways, and if thou wilt keep my charge, then thou shalt also judge my house, and shalt also keep my courts, and I will give thee places to walk among these that stand by.

8 Hear now, O Josh'u-a the high priest, thou, and thy fellows that sit before thee: for they are men wondered at: for, behold, I will bring forth my servant the BRANCH.

9 For behold the stone that I have laid before Josh'u-a; upon one stone shall be seven eyes: behold, I will engrave the graving thereof, saith the LORD of hosts, and I will remove the iniquity of that land in one day.

10 In that day, saith the LORD of hosts, shall ye call every man his neighbour under the vine and under the fig tree.

4 AND the angel that talked with me came again, and waked me, as a man that is wakened out of his sleep,

2 And said unto me, What seest thou? And I said, I have looked, and behold a candlestick all of gold, with a bowl upon the top of it, and his seven lamps thereon, and seven pipes to the seven lamps, which are upon the top thereof:

3 And two olive trees by it, one upon the right side of the bowl, and the other upon the left side thereof.

4 So I answered and spake to the angel that talked with me, saying, What are these, my lord?

5 Then the angel that talked with me answered and said unto me, Knowest thou not what these be? And I said, No, my lord.

6 Then he answered and spake unto me, saying, This is the word of the LORD unto Ze-rub'-ba-bel, saying, Not by might, nor by power, but by my spirit, saith the LORD of hosts.

7 Who art thou, O great mountain? before Ze-rub'ba-bel thou shalt become a plain: and he shall bring forth the headstone thereof with shoutings, crying, Grace, grace unto it.

8 Moreover the word of the LORD came unto me, saying,

9 The hands of Ze-rub'ba-bel have laid the foundation of this house; his hands shall also finish it; and thou shalt know that the LORD of hosts hath sent me unto you.

10 For who hath despised the day of small things? for they shall rejoice, and shall see the plummet in the hand of Ze-rub'ba-bel with those seven; they are the eyes of the LORD, which run to and fro through the whole earth.

11 ¶ Then answered I, and said unto him, What are these two olive trees upon the right side of the candlestick and upon the left side thereof?

12 And I answered again, and said unto him, What be these two olive branches which through the two golden pipes empty the golden oil out of themselves?

13 And he answered me and said, Knowest thou not what these be? And I said, No, my lord.

14 Then said he, These are the two anointed ones, that stand by the Lord of the whole earth.

5 THEN I turned, and lifted up mine eyes, and looked, and behold a flying roll.

2 And he said unto me, What seest thou? And I answered, I see a flying roll; the length thereof is twenty cubits, and the breadth thereof ten cubits.

3 Then said he unto me, This is the curse that goeth forth over the face of the whole earth: for every one that stealeth shall be cut off as on this side according to it; and every one that sweareth shall be cut off as on that side according to it.

4 I will bring it forth, saith the LORD of hosts, and it shall enter into the house of the thief, and into the house of him that sweareth falsely by my name, and it shall remain in the midst of his house, and shall consume it with the timber thereof and the stones thereof.

5 ¶ Then the angel that talked with me went forth, and said unto me, Lift up now thine eyes, and see what is this that goeth forth.

6 And I said, What is it? And he said, This is an ephah that goeth forth. He said moreover, This is their resemblance through all the earth.

7 And, behold, there was lifted up a talent of lead: and this is a woman that sitteth in the midst of the ephah.

8 And he said, This is wickedness. And he cast it into the midst of the ephah; and he cast the weight of lead upon the mouth thereof.

9 Then lifted I up mine eyes, and looked, and, behold, there came out two women, and the wind was in their wings; for they had wings like the wings of a stork: and they lifted up the e-phah between the earth and the heaven.

10 Then said I to the angel that talked with me, Whither do these bear the ephah?

11 And he said unto me, To build it an house in the land of Shi'nar: and it shall be established, and set there upon her own base.

6 AND I turned, and lifted up mine eyes, and looked, and, behold, there came four chariots out from between two mountains; and the mountains were mountains of brass.

2 In the first chariot were red horses; and in the second chariot black horses;

3 And in the third chariot white horses; and in the fourth chariot grisled and bay horses.

4 Then I answered and said unto the angel that talked with me, What *are* these, my lord?

5 And the angel answered and said unto me, These *are* the four spirits of the heavens, which go forth from standing before the Lord of all the earth.

6 The black horses which *are* therein go forth into the north country; and the white go forth after them; and the grisled go forth toward the south country.

7 And the bay went forth, and sought to go that they might walk to and fro through the earth: and he said, Get you hence, walk to and fro through the earth. So they walked to and fro through the earth.

8 Then cried he upon me, and spake unto me, saying, Behold, these that go toward the north country have quieted my spirit in the north country.

9 ¶ And the word of the LORD came unto me, saying,

10 Take of *them of* the captivity, *even of* Hel′da-i, of To-bi′jah, and of Je-da′iah, which are come from Bab′y-lon, and come thou the same day, and go into the house of Jo-si′ah the son of Zeph-a-ni′ah;

11 Then take silver and gold, and make crowns, and set *them* upon the head of Josh′u-a the son of Jos′e-dech, the high priest;

12 And speak unto him, saying, Thus speaketh the LORD of hosts, saying, Behold the man whose name *is* The BRANCH; and he shall grow up out of his place, and he shall build the temple of the LORD:

13 Even he shall build the temple of the LORD; and he shall bear the glory, and shall sit and rule upon his throne; and he shall be a priest upon his throne: and the counsel of peace shall be between them both.

14 And the crowns shall be to He′lem, and to To-bi′jah, and to Je-da′iah, and to Hen the son of Zeph-a-ni′ah, for a memorial in the temple of the LORD.

15 And they *that are* far off shall come and build in the temple of the LORD, and ye shall know that the LORD of hosts hath sent me unto you. And *this* shall come to pass, if ye will diligently obey the voice of the LORD your God.

7 AND it came to pass in the fourth year of king Da-ri′us, *that* the word of the LORD came unto Zech-a-ri′ah in the fourth *day* of the ninth month, *even* in Chis′leu;

2 When they had sent unto the house of God She-re′zer and Re′gem-me′lech, and their men, to pray before the LORD,

3 *And* to speak unto the priests which *were* in the house of the LORD of hosts, and to the prophets, saying, Should I weep in the fifth month, separating myself, as I have done these so many years?

4 ¶ Then came the word of the LORD of hosts unto me, saying,

5 Speak unto all the people of the land, and to the priests, saying, When ye fasted and mourned in the fifth and seventh *month*, even those seventy years, did ye at all fast unto me, *even* to me?

6 And when ye did eat, and when ye did drink, did not ye eat *for yourselves*, and drink *for yourselves*?

7 *Should* ye not *hear* the words which the LORD hath cried by the former prophets, when Je-ru′sa-lem was inhabited and in prosperity, and the cities thereof round about her, when *men* inhabited the south and the plain?

8 ¶ And the word of the LORD came unto Zech-a-ri′ah, saying,

9 Thus speaketh the LORD of hosts, saying, Execute true judgment, and shew mercy and compassions every man to his brother:

10 And oppress not the widow, nor the fatherless, the stranger, nor the poor; and let none of you imagine evil against his brother in your heart.

11 But they refused to hearken, and pulled away the shoulder, and stopped their ears, that they should not hear.

12 Yea, they made their hearts *as* an adamant stone, lest they should hear the law, and the words which the LORD of hosts hath sent in his spirit by the former prophets: therefore came a great wrath from the LORD of hosts.

13 Therefore it is come to pass, *that* as he cried, and they would not hear; so they cried, and I would not hear, saith the LORD of hosts:

14 But I scattered them with a whirlwind among all the nations whom they knew not. Thus the land was desolate after them, that no man passed through nor returned: for they laid the pleasant land desolate.

8 AGAIN the word of the LORD of hosts came *to me*, saying,

2 Thus saith the LORD of hosts; I was jealous for Zi′on with great jealousy, and I was jealous for her with great fury.

3 Thus saith the LORD; I am returned unto Zi′on, and will dwell in the midst of Je-ru′sa-lem: and Je-ru′sa-lem shall be called a city of truth; and the mountain of the LORD of hosts the holy mountain.

4 Thus saith the LORD of hosts; There shall yet old men and old women dwell in the streets of Je-ru′sa-lem, and every man with his staff in his hand for very age.

5 And the streets of the city shall be full of boys and girls playing in the streets thereof.

6 Thus saith the LORD of hosts; If it be marvellous in the eyes of the remnant of this people in these days, should it also be marvellous in mine eyes? saith the LORD of hosts.

7 Thus saith the LORD of hosts; Behold, I will save my people from the east country, and from the west country;

8 And I will bring them, and they shall dwell in the midst of Je-ru′sa-lem: and they shall be my people, and I will be their God, in truth and in righteousness.

9 ¶ Thus saith the LORD of hosts; Let your hands be strong, ye *that* hear in these days these words by the mouth of the prophets, which *were* in the day *that* the foundation of the house of the LORD of hosts was laid, that the temple might be built.

10 For before these days there was no hire for man, nor any hire for beast; neither *was there any* peace to him that went out or came in because of the affliction: for I set all men every one against his neighbour.

11 But now I *will* not *be* unto the residue of this people as in the former days, saith the LORD of hosts.

12 For the seed *shall be* prosperous; the vine shall give her fruit, and the ground shall give her increase, and the heavens shall give their dew; and I will cause the remnant of this people to possess all these *things*.

13 And it shall come to pass, *that* as ye were a curse among the heathen, O house of Ju′dah, and house of Is′ra-el; so will I save you, and ye shall be a blessing: fear not, *but* let your hands be strong.

14 For thus saith the LORD of hosts; As I thought to punish you, when your fathers provoked me to wrath, saith the LORD of hosts, and I repented not:

15 So again have I thought in these days to do well unto Je-ru'sa-lem and to the house of Ju'dah: fear ye not.

16 ¶ These are the things that ye shall do; Speak ye every man the truth to his neighbour; execute the judgment of truth and peace in your gates:

17 And let none of you imagine evil in your hearts against his neighbour; and love no false oath: for all these are things that I hate, saith the LORD.

18 ¶ And the word of the LORD of hosts came unto me, saying,

19 Thus saith the LORD of hosts; The fast of the fourth month, and the fast of the fifth, and the fast of the seventh, and the fast of the tenth, shall be to the house of Ju'dah joy and gladness, and cheerful feasts; therefore love the truth and peace.

20 Thus saith the LORD of hosts; It shall yet come to pass, that there shall come people, and the inhabitants of many cities:

21 And the inhabitants of one city shall go to another, saying, Let us go speedily to pray before the LORD, and to seek the LORD of hosts: I will go also.

22 Yea, many people and strong nations shall come to seek the LORD of hosts in Je-ru'sa-lem, and to pray before the LORD.

23 Thus saith the LORD of hosts; In those days it shall come to pass, that ten men shall take hold out of all languages of the nations, even shall take hold of the skirt of him that is a Jew, saying, We will go with you: for we have heard that God is with you.

9 THE burden of the word of the LORD in the land of Ha'drach, and Da-mas'cus shall be the rest thereof: when the eyes of man, as of all the tribes of Is'ra-el, shall be toward the LORD.

2 And Ha'math also shall border thereby; Ty'rus, and Zi'don, though it be very wise.

3 And Ty'rus did build herself a strong hold, and heaped up silver as the dust, and fine gold as the mire of the streets.

4 Behold, the Lord will cast her out, and he will smite her power in the sea; and she shall be devoured with fire.

5 Ash'ke-lon shall see it, and fear; Ga'za also shall see it, and be very sorrowful, and Ek'ron; for her expectation shall be ashamed; and the king shall perish from Ga'za, and Ash'ke-lon shall not be inhabited.

6 And a bastard shall dwell in Ash'dod, and I will cut off the pride of the Phi-lis'tines.

7 And I will take away his blood out of his mouth, and his abominations from between his teeth: but he that remaineth, even he, shall be for our God, and he shall be as a governor in Ju'dah, and Ek'ron as a Jeb'u-site.

8 And I will encamp about mine house because of the army, because of him that passeth by, and because of him that returneth: and no oppressor shall pass through them any more: for now have I seen with mine eyes.

9 ¶ Rejoice greatly, O daughter of Zi'on; shout, O daughter of Je-ru'sa-lem: behold, thy King cometh unto thee: he is just, and having salvation; lowly, and riding upon an ass, and upon a colt the foal of an ass.

10 And I will cut off the chariot from E'phra-im, and the horse from Je-ru'sa-lem, and the battle bow shall be cut off: and he shall speak peace unto the heathen: and his dominion shall be from sea even to sea, and from the river even to the ends of the earth.

11 As for thee also, by the blood of thy covenant I have sent forth thy prisoners out of the pit wherein is no water.

12 ¶ Turn you to the strong hold, ye prisoners of hope: even to day do I declare that I will render double unto thee;

13 When I have bent Ju'dah for me, filled the bow with E'phra-im, and raised up thy sons, O Zi'on, against thy sons, O Greece, and made thee as the sword of a mighty man.

14 And the LORD shall be seen over them, and his arrow shall go forth as the lightning: and the Lord GOD shall blow the trumpet, and shall go with whirlwinds of the south.

15 The LORD of hosts shall defend them; and they shall devour, and subdue with sling stones; and they shall drink, and make a noise as through wine; and they shall be filled like bowls, and as the corners of the altar.

16 And the LORD their God shall save them in that day as the flock of his people: for they shall be as the stones of a crown, lifted up as an ensign upon his land.

17 For how great is his goodness, and how great is his beauty! corn shall make the young men cheerful, and new wine the maids.

10 ASK ye of the LORD rain in the time of the latter rain; so the LORD shall make bright clouds, and give them showers of rain, to every one grass in the field.

2 For the idols have spoken vanity, and the diviners have seen a lie, and have told false dreams; they comfort in vain: therefore they went their way as a flock, they were troubled, because there was no shepherd.

3 Mine anger was kindled against the shepherds, and I punished the goats: for the LORD of hosts hath visited his flock the house of Ju'dah, and hath made them as his goodly horse in the battle.

4 Out of him came forth the corner, out of him the nail, out of him the battle bow, out of him every oppressor together.

5 ¶ And they shall be as mighty men, which tread down their enemies in the mire of the streets in the battle: and they shall fight, because the LORD is with them, and the riders on horses shall be confounded.

6 And I will strengthen the house of Ju'dah, and I will save the house of Jo'seph, and I will bring them again to place them; for I have mercy upon them: and they shall be as though I had not cast them off: for I am the LORD their God, and will hear them.

7 And they of E'phra-im shall be like a mighty man, and their heart shall rejoice as through wine: yea, their children shall see it, and be glad; their heart shall rejoice in the LORD.

8 I will hiss for them, and gather them; for I have redeemed them: and they shall increase as they have increased.

9 And I will sow them among the people: and they shall remember me in far countries; and they shall live with their children, and turn again.

10 I will bring them again also out of the land of E'gypt, and gather them out of As-syr'i-a; and I will bring them into the land of Gil'e-ad and Leb'a-non; and place shall not be found for them.

11 And he shall pass through the sea with affliction, and shall smite the waves in the sea,

and all the deeps of the river shall dry up: and the pride of As-syr'i-a shall be brought down, and the sceptre of E'gypt shall depart away.

12 And I will strengthen them in the LORD; and they shall walk up and down in his name, saith the LORD.

11 OPEN thy doors, O Leb'a-non, that the fire may devour thy cedars.

2 Howl, fir tree; for the cedar is fallen; because the mighty are spoiled: howl, O ye oaks of Ba'shan; for the forest of the vintage is come down.

3 ¶ There is a voice of the howling of the shepherds; for their glory is spoiled: a voice of the roaring of young lions; for the pride of Jor'-dan is spoiled.

4 Thus saith the LORD my God; Feed the flock of the slaughter;

5 Whose possessors slay them, and hold themselves not guilty: and they that sell them say, Blessed be the LORD; for I am rich: and their own shepherds pity them not.

6 For I will no more pity the inhabitants of the land, saith the LORD: but, lo, I will deliver the men every one into his neighbour's hand, and into the hand of his king: and they shall smite the land, and out of their hand I will not deliver them.

7 And I will feed the flock of slaughter, even you, O poor of the flock. And I took unto me two staves; the one I called Beauty, and the other I called Bands; and I fed the flock.

8 Three shepherds also I cut off in one month; and my soul loathed them, and their soul also abhorred me.

9 Then said I, I will not feed you: that that dieth, let it die; and that that is to be cut off, let it be cut off; and let the rest eat every one the flesh of another.

10 ¶ And I took my staff, even Beauty, and cut it asunder, that I might break my covenant which I had made with all the people.

11 And it was broken in that day: and so the poor of the flock that waited upon me knew that it was the word of the LORD.

12 And I said unto them, If ye think good, give me my price; and if not, forbear. So they weighed for my price thirty pieces of silver.

13 And the LORD said unto me, Cast it unto the potter: a goodly price that I was prised at of them. And I took the thirty pieces of silver, and cast them to the potter in the house of the LORD.

14 Then I cut asunder mine other staff, even Bands, that I might break the brotherhood between Ju'dah and Is'ra-el.

15 ¶ And the LORD said unto me, Take unto thee yet the instruments of a foolish shepherd.

16 For, lo, I will raise up a shepherd in the land, which shall not visit those that be cut off, neither shall seek the young one, nor heal that that is broken, nor feed that that standeth still: but he shall eat the flesh of the fat, and tear their claws in pieces.

17 Woe to the idol shepherd that leaveth the flock! the sword shall be upon his arm, and upon his right eye: his arm shall be clean dried up, and his right eye shall be utterly darkened.

12 THE burden of the word of the LORD for Is'ra-el, saith the LORD, which stretcheth forth the heavens, and layeth the foundation of the earth, and formeth the spirit of man within him.

2 Behold, I will make Je-ru'sa-lem a cup of trembling unto all the people round about, when they shall be in the siege both against Ju'-dah and against Je-ru'sa-lem.

3 ¶ And in that day will I make Je-ru'sa-lem a burdensome stone for all people: all that burden themselves with it shall be cut in pieces, though all the people of the earth be gathered together against it.

4 In that day, saith the LORD, I will smite every horse with astonishment, and his rider with madness: and I will open mine eyes upon the house of Ju'dah, and will smite every horse of the people with blindness.

5 And the governors of Ju'dah shall say in their heart, The inhabitants of Je-ru'sa-lem shall be my strength in the LORD of hosts their God.

6 ¶ In that day will I make the governors of Ju'dah like an hearth of fire among the wood, and like a torch of fire in a sheaf; and they shall devour all the people round about, on the right hand and on the left: and Je-ru'sa-lem shall be inhabited again in her own place, even in Je-ru'sa-lem.

7 The LORD also shall save the tents of Ju'dah first, that the glory of the house of Da'vid and the glory of the inhabitants of Je-ru'sa-lem do not magnify themselves against Ju'dah.

8 In that day shall the LORD defend the inhabitants of Je-ru'sa-lem; and he that is feeble among them at that day shall be as Da'vid; and the house of Da'vid shall be as God, as the angel of the LORD before them.

9 ¶ And it shall come to pass in that day, that I will seek to destroy all the nations that come against Je-ru'sa-lem.

10 And I will pour upon the house of Da'vid, and upon the inhabitants of Je-ru'sa-lem, the spirit of grace and of supplications: and they shall look upon me whom they have pierced, and they shall mourn for him, as one mourneth for his only son, and shall be in bitterness for him, as one that is in bitterness for his firstborn.

11 In that day shall there be a great mourning in Je-ru'sa-lem, as the mourning of Ha-dad-rim'mon in the valley of Me-gid'don.

12 And the land shall mourn, every family apart; the family of the house of Da'vid apart, and their wives apart; the family of the house of Na'than apart, and their wives apart;

13 The family of the house of Le'vi apart, and their wives apart; the family of Shim'e-i apart, and their wives apart;

14 All the families that remain, every family apart, and their wives apart.

13 IN that day there shall be a fountain opened to the house of Da'vid and to the inhabitants of Je-ru'sa-lem for sin and for uncleanness.

2 ¶ And it shall come to pass in that day, saith the LORD of hosts, that I will cut off the names of the idols out of the land, and they shall no more be remembered: and also I will cause the prophets and the unclean spirit to pass out of the land.

3 And it shall come to pass, that when any shall yet prophesy, then his father and his mother that begat him shall say unto him, Thou shalt not live; for thou speakest lies in the name of the LORD: and his father and his mother that begat him shall thrust him through when he prophesieth.

4 And it shall come to pass in that day, that the prophets shall be ashamed every one of his vision, when he hath prophesied; neither shall they wear a rough garment to deceive:

5 But he shall say, I *am* no prophet, I *am* an husbandman; for man taught me to keep cattle from my youth.

6 And *one* shall say unto him, What *are* these wounds in thine hands? Then he shall answer, *Those* with which I was wounded *in* the house of my friends.

7 ¶ Awake, O sword, against my shepherd, and against the man *that is* my fellow, saith the LORD of hosts: smite the shepherd, and the sheep shall be scattered: and I will turn mine hand upon the little ones.

8 And it shall come to pass, *that* in all the land, saith the LORD, two parts therein shall be cut off *and* die; but the third shall be left therein.

9 And I will bring the third part through the fire, and will refine them as silver is refined, and will try them as gold is tried: they shall call on my name, and I will hear them: I will say, It *is* my people: and they shall say, The LORD *is* my God.

14 BEHOLD, the day of the LORD cometh, and thy spoil shall be divided in the midst of thee.

2 For I will gather all nations against Je-ru'-sa-lem to battle; and the city shall be taken, and the houses rifled, and the women ravished; and half of the city shall go forth into captivity, and the residue of the people shall not be cut off from the city.

3 Then shall the LORD go forth, and fight against those nations, as when he fought in the day of battle.

4 ¶ And his feet shall stand in that day upon the mount of Ol'ives, which *is* before Je-ru'sa-lem on the east, and the mount of Ol'ives shall cleave in the midst thereof toward the east and toward the west, *and there shall be* a very great valley; and half of the mountain shall remove toward the north, and half of it toward the south.

5 And ye shall flee *to* the valley of the mountains; for the valley of the mountains shall reach unto A'zal: yea, ye shall flee, like as ye fled from before the earthquake in the days of Uz-zi'ah king of Ju'dah: and the LORD my God shall come, *and* all the saints with thee.

6 And it shall come to pass in that day, *that* the light shall not be clear, *nor* dark:

7 But it shall be one day which shall be known to the LORD, not day, nor night: but it shall come to pass, *that* at evening time it shall be light.

8 And it shall be in that day, *that* living waters shall go out from Je-ru'sa-lem; half of them toward the former sea, and half of them toward the hinder sea: in summer and in winter shall it be.

9 And the LORD shall be king over all the earth: in that day shall there be one LORD, and his name one.

10 All the land shall be turned as a plain from Ge'ba to Rim'mon south of Je-ru'sa-lem: and it shall be lifted up, and inhabited in her place, from Ben'ja-min's gate unto the place of the first gate, unto the corner gate, and *from* the tower of Ha-nan'e-el unto the king's winepresses.

11 And *men* shall dwell in it, and there shall be no more utter destruction; but Je-ru'sa-lem shall be safely inhabited.

12 ¶ And this shall be the plague wherewith the LORD will smite all the people that have fought against Je-ru'sa-lem; Their flesh shall consume away while they stand upon their feet, and their eyes shall consume away in their holes, and their tongue shall consume away in their mouth.

13 And it shall come to pass in that day, *that* a great tumult from the LORD shall be among them; and they shall lay hold every one on the hand of his neighbour, and his hand shall rise up against the hand of his neighbour.

14 And Ju'dah also shall fight at Je-ru'sa-lem; and the wealth of all the heathen round about shall be gathered together, gold, and silver, and apparel, in great abundance.

15 And so shall be the plague of the horse, of the mule, of the camel, and of the ass, and of all the beasts that shall be in these tents, as this plague.

16 ¶ And it shall come to pass, *that* every one that is left of all the nations which came against Je-ru'sa-lem shall even go up from year to year to worship the King, the LORD of hosts, and to keep the feast of tabernacles.

17 And it shall be, *that* whoso will not come up of *all* the families of the earth unto Je-ru'sa-lem to worship the King, the LORD of hosts, even upon them shall be no rain.

18 And if the family of E'gypt go not up, and come not, that *have* no *rain*; there shall be the plague, wherewith the LORD will smite the heathen that come not up to keep the feast of tabernacles.

19 This shall be the punishment of E'gypt, and the punishment of all nations that come not up to keep the feast of tabernacles.

20 ¶ In that day shall there be upon the bells of the horses, HOLINESS UNTO THE LORD; and the pots in the LORD's house shall be like the bowls before the altar.

21 Yea, every pot in Je-ru'sa-lem and in Ju'dah shall be holiness unto the LORD of hosts: and all they that sacrifice shall come and take of them, and seethe therein: and in that day there shall be no more the Ca'naan-ite in the house of the LORD of hosts.

THE BOOK OF

MALACHI

1 THE burden of the word of the LORD to Is'-ra-el by Mal'a-chi.

2 I have loved you, saith the LORD. Yet ye say, Wherein hast thou loved us? *Was* not E'sau Ja'cob's brother? saith the LORD: yet I loved Ja'cob,

3 And I hated E'sau, and laid his mountains and his heritage waste for the dragons of the wilderness.

4 Whereas E'dom saith, We are impover-ished, but we will return and build the desolate places; thus saith the LORD of hosts, They shall build, but I will throw down; and they shall call them, The border of wickedness, and, The people against whom the LORD hath indignation for ever.

5 And your eyes shall see, and ye shall say, The LORD will be magnified from the border of Is'ra-el.

6 ¶ A son honoureth *his* father, and a ser-

vant his master: if then I *be* a father, where *is* mine honour? and if I *be* a master, where *is* my fear? saith the LORD of hosts unto you, O priests, that despise my name. And ye say, Wherein have we despised thy name?

7 Ye offer polluted bread upon mine altar; and ye say, Wherein have we polluted thee? In that ye say, The table of the LORD *is* contemptible.

8 And if ye offer the blind for sacrifice, *is it* not evil? and if ye offer the lame and sick, *is it* not evil? offer it now unto thy governor; will he be pleased with thee, or accept thy person? saith the LORD of hosts.

9 And now, I pray you, beseech God that he will be gracious unto us: this hath been by your means: will he regard your persons? saith the LORD of hosts.

10 Who *is there* even among you that would shut the doors *for nought?* neither do ye kindle *fire* on mine altar for nought. I have no pleasure in you, saith the LORD of hosts, neither will I accept an offering at your hand.

11 For from the rising of the sun even unto the going down of the same my name *shall be* great among the Gen'tiles; and in every place incense *shall be* offered unto my name, and a pure offering: for my name *shall be* great among the heathen, saith the LORD of hosts.

12 ¶ But ye have profaned it, in that ye say, The table of the LORD *is* polluted; and the fruit thereof, *even* his meat, *is* contemptible.

13 Ye said also, Behold, what a weariness *is it!* and ye have snuffed at it, saith the LORD of hosts; and ye brought *that which was* torn, and the lame, and the sick; thus ye brought an offering: should I accept this of your hand? saith the LORD.

14 But cursed *be* the deceiver, which hath in his flock a male, and voweth, and sacrificeth unto the Lord a corrupt thing: for I *am* a great King, saith the LORD of hosts, and my name *is* dreadful among the heathen.

2

AND now, O ye priests, this commandment *is* for you.

2 If ye will not hear, and if ye will not lay *it* to heart, to give glory unto my name, saith the LORD of hosts, I will even send a curse upon you, and I will curse your blessings: yea, I have cursed them already, because ye do not lay *it* to heart.

3 Behold, I will corrupt your seed, and spread dung upon your faces, *even* the dung of your solemn feasts; and *one* shall take you away with it.

4 And ye shall know that I have sent this commandment unto you, that my covenant might be with Le'vi, saith the LORD of hosts.

5 My covenant was with him of life and peace; and I gave them to him *for* the fear wherewith he feared me, and was afraid before my name.

6 The law of truth was in his mouth, and iniquity was not found in his lips: he walked with me in peace and equity, and did turn many away from iniquity.

7 For the priest's lips should keep knowledge, and they should seek the law at his mouth: for he *is* the messenger of the LORD of hosts.

8 But ye are departed out of the way; ye have caused many to stumble at the law; ye have corrupted the covenant of Le'vi, saith the LORD of hosts.

9 Therefore have I also made you contemptible and base before all the people, according as

ye have not kept my ways, but have been partial in the law.

10 Have we not all one father? hath not one God created us? why do we deal treacherously every man against his brother, by profaning the covenant of our fathers?

11 ¶ Ju'dah hath dealt treacherously, and an abomination is committed in Is'ra-el and in Je-ru'sa-lem; for Ju'dah hath profaned the holiness of the LORD which he loved, and hath married the daughter of a strange god.

12 The LORD will cut off the man that doeth this, the master and the scholar, out of the tabernacles of Ja'cob, and him that offereth an offering unto the LORD of hosts.

13 And this have ye done again, covering the altar of the LORD with tears, with weeping, and with crying out, insomuch that he regardeth not the offering any more, or receiveth *it* with good will at your hand.

14 ¶ Yet ye say, Wherefore? Because the LORD hath been witness between thee and the wife of thy youth, against whom thou hast dealt treacherously: yet *is* she thy companion, and the wife of thy covenant.

15 And did not he make one? Yet had he the residue of the spirit. And wherefore one? That he might seek a godly seed. Therefore take heed to your spirit, and let none deal treacherously against the wife of his youth.

16 For the LORD, the God of Is'ra-el, saith that he hateth putting away: for *one* covereth violence with his garment, saith the LORD of hosts: therefore take heed to your spirit, that ye deal not treacherously.

17 ¶ Ye have wearied the LORD with your words. Yet ye say, Wherein have we wearied *him?* When ye say, Every one that doeth evil *is* good in the sight of the LORD, and he delighteth in them; or, Where *is* the God of judgment?

3

BEHOLD, I will send my messenger, and he shall prepare the way before me: and the Lord, whom ye seek, shall suddenly come to his temple, even the messenger of the covenant, whom ye delight in: behold, he shall come, saith the LORD of hosts.

2 But who may abide the day of his coming? and who shall stand when he appeareth? for he *is* like a refiner's fire, and like fullers' sope:

3 And he shall sit *as* a refiner and purifier of silver: and he shall purify the sons of Le'vi, and purge them as gold and silver, that they may offer unto the LORD an offering in righteousness.

4 Then shall the offering of Ju'dah and Je-ru'sa-lem be pleasant unto the LORD, as in the days of old, and as in former years.

5 And I will come near to you to judgment; and I will be a swift witness against the sorcerers, and against the adulterers, and against false swearers, and against those that oppress the hireling in *his* wages, the widow, and the fatherless, and that turn aside the stranger *from his* right, and fear not me, saith the LORD of hosts.

6 For I *am* the LORD, I change not; therefore ye sons of Ja'cob are not consumed.

7 ¶ Even from the days of your fathers ye are gone away from mine ordinances, and have not kept *them*. Return unto me, and I will return unto you, saith the LORD of hosts. But ye said, Wherein shall we return?

8 ¶ Will a man rob God? Yet ye have robbed me. But ye say, Wherein have we robbed thee? In tithes and offerings.

9 Ye *are* cursed with a curse: for ye have robbed me, *even* this whole nation.

10 Bring ye all the tithes into the storehouse, that there may be meat in mine house, and prove me now herewith, saith the LORD of hosts, if I will not open you the windows of heaven, and pour you out a blessing, that *there* shall not *be room* enough *to receive it.*

11 And I will rebuke the devourer for your sakes, and he shall not destroy the fruits of your ground; neither shall your vine cast her fruit before the time in the field, saith the LORD of hosts.

12 And all nations shall call you blessed: for ye shall be a delightsome land, saith the LORD of hosts.

13 ¶ Your words have been stout against me, saith the LORD. Yet ye say, What have we spoken *so much* against thee?

14 Ye have said, It *is* vain to serve God: and what profit *is it* that we have kept his ordinance, and that we have walked mournfully before the LORD of hosts?

15 And now we call the proud happy; yea, they that work wickedness are set up; yea, *they that* tempt God are even delivered.

16 ¶ Then they that feared the LORD spake often one to another: and the LORD hearkened, and heard *it,* and a book of remembrance was written before him for them that feared the LORD, and that thought upon his name.

17 And they shall be mine, saith the LORD of hosts, in that day when I make up my jewels; and I will spare them, as a man spareth his own son that serveth him.

18 Then shall ye return, and discern between the righteous and the wicked, between him that serveth God and him that serveth him not.

4 FOR, behold, the day cometh, that shall burn as an oven; and all the proud, yea, and all that do wickedly, shall be stubble: and the day that cometh shall burn them up, saith the LORD of hosts, that it shall leave them neither root nor branch.

2 ¶ But unto you that fear my name shall the Sun of righteousness arise with healing in his wings; and ye shall go forth, and grow up as calves of the stall.

3 And ye shall tread down the wicked; for they shall be ashes under the soles of your feet in the day that I shall do *this,* saith the LORD of hosts.

4 ¶ Remember ye the law of Mo'ses my servant, which I commanded unto him in Ho'reb for all Is'ra-el, *with* the statutes and judgments.

5 ¶ Behold, I will send you E-li'jah the prophet before the coming of the great and dreadful day of the LORD:

6 And he shall turn the heart of the fathers to the children, and the heart of the children to their fathers, lest I come and smite the earth with a curse.

THE END OF THE OLD TESTAMENT.

THE
NEW TESTAMENT

MATTHEW

1 THE book of the generation of Je′sus Christ, the son of Da′vid, the son of A′bra-ham.

2 A′bra-ham begat I′saac; and I′saac begat Ja′cob; and Ja′cob begat Ju′das and his brethren;

3 And Ju′das begat Pha′res and Za′ra of Tha′mar; and Pha′res, begat Es′rom; and Es′rom begat A′ram;

4 And A′ram begat A-min′a-dab; and A-min′a-dab begat Na-as′son; and Na-as′son begat Sal′mon;

5 And Sal′mon begat Bo′oz of Ra′chab; and Bo′oz begat O′bed of Ruth; and O′bed begat Jes′se;

6 And Jes′se begat Da′vid the king; and Da′vid the king begat Sol′o-mon of her *that had been the wife* of U-ri′as;

7 And Sol′o-mon begat Ro-bo′am; and Ro-bo′am begat A-bi′a; and A-bi′a begat A′sa;

8 And A′sa begat Jos′a-phat; and Jos′a-phat begat Jo′ram; and Jo′ram begat O-zi′as;

9 And O-zi′as begat Jo′a-tham; and Jo′a-tham begat A′chaz; and A′chaz begat Ez-e-ki′as;

10 And Ez-e-ki′as begat Ma-nas′ses; and Ma-nas′ses begat A′mon; and A′mon begat Jo-si′as;

11 And Jo-si′as begat Jech-o-ni′as and his brethren, about the time they were carried away to Bab′y-lon:

12 And after they were brought to Bab′y-lon, Jech-o-ni′as begat Sa-la′thi-el; and Sa-la′thi-el begat Zo-rob′a-bel;

13 And Zo-rob′a-bel begat A-bi′ud; and A-bi′ud begat E-li′a-kim; and E-li′a-kim begat A′zor;

14 And A′zor begat Sa′doc; and Sa′doc begat A′chim; and A′chim begat E-li′ud;

15 And E-li′ud begat E-le-a′zar; and E-le-a′zar begat Mat′than; and Mat′than begat Ja′cob;

16 And Ja′cob begat Jo′seph the husband of Ma′ry, of whom was born Je′sus, who is called Christ.

17 So all the generations from A′bra-ham to Da′vid *are* fourteen generations; and from Da′vid until the carrying away into Bab′y-lon *are* fourteen generations; and from the carrying away into Bab′y-lon unto Christ *are* fourteen generations.

18 ¶ Now the birth of Je′sus Christ was on this wise: When as his mother Ma′ry was espoused to Jo′seph, before they came together, she was found with child of the Ho′ly Ghost.

19 Then Jo′seph her husband, being a just *man*, and not willing to make her a publick example, was minded to put her away privily.

20 But while he thought on these things, behold, the angel of the Lord appeared unto him in a dream, saying, Jo′seph, thou son of Da′vid, fear not to take unto thee Ma′ry thy wife: for that which is conceived in her is of the Ho′ly Ghost.

21 And she shall bring forth a son, and thou shalt call his name JE′SUS: for he shall save his people from their sins.

22 Now all this was done, that it might be fulfilled which was spoken of the Lord by the prophet, saying,

23 Behold, a virgin shall be with child, and shall bring forth a son, and they shall call his name Em-man′u-el, which being interpreted is, God with us.

24 Then Jo′seph being raised from sleep did as the angel of the Lord had bidden him, and took unto him his wife:

25 And knew her not till she had brought forth her firstborn son: and he called his name JE′SUS.

2 NOW when Je′sus was born in Beth′le-hem of Ju-dæ′a in the days of Her′od the king, behold, there came wise men from the east to Je-ru′sa-lem,

2 Saying, Where is he that is born King of the Jews? for we have seen his star in the east, and are come to worship him.

3 When Her′od the king had heard *these things,* he was troubled, and all Je-ru′sa-lem with him.

4 And when he had gathered all the chief priests and scribes of the people together, he demanded of them where Christ should be born.

5 And they said unto him, In Beth′le-hem of Ju-dæ′a: for thus it is written by the prophet,

6 And thou Beth′le-hem, *in* the land of Ju′da, art not the least among the princes of Ju′da: for out of thee shall come a Governor, that shall rule my people Is′ra-el.

7 Then Her′od, when he had privily called the wise men, enquired of them diligently what time the star appeared.

8 And he sent them to Beth′le-hem, and said, Go and search diligently for the young child; and when ye have found *him,* bring me word again, that I may come and worship him also.

9 When they had heard the king, they departed; and, lo, the star, which they saw in the east, went before them, till it came and stood over where the young child was.

10 When they saw the star, they rejoiced with exceeding great joy.

11 ¶ And when they were come into the house, they saw the young child with Ma′ry his mother, and fell down, and worshipped him: and when they had opened their treasures, they presented unto him gifts; gold, frankincense, and myrrh.

12 And being warned of God in a dream that they should not return to Her′od, they departed into their own country another way.

13 And when they were departed, behold, the angel of the Lord appeareth to Jo′seph in a dream, saying, Arise, and take the young child and his mother, and flee into E′gypt; and be thou there until I bring thee word: for Her′od will seek the young child to destroy him.

14 When he arose, he took the young child and his mother by night, and departed into E′gypt:

15 And was there until the death of Her′od: that it might be fulfilled which was spoken of the Lord by the prophet, saying, Out of E′gypt have I called my son.

16 ¶ Then Her′od, when he saw that he was mocked of the wise men, was exceeding wroth, and sent forth, and slew all the children that were in Beth′le-hem, and in all the coasts thereof, from two years old and under, according to the time which he had diligently enquired of the wise men.

17 Then was fulfilled that which was spoken by Jer′e-my the prophet, saying,

18 In Ra′ma was there a voice heard, lamentation, and weeping, and great mourning, Ra′-

chel weeping *for* her children, and would not be comforted, because they are not.

19 ¶ But when Her'od was dead, behold, an angel of the Lord appeareth in a dream to Jo'-seph in E'gypt,

20 Saying, Arise, and take the young child and his mother, and go into the land of Is'ra-el: for they are dead which sought the young child's life.

21 And he arose, and took the young child and his mother, and came into the land of Is'ra-el.

22 But when he heard that Ar-che-la'us did reign in Ju-dæ'a in the room of his father Her'-od, he was afraid to go thither: notwithstand-ing, being warned of God in a dream, he turned aside into the parts of Gal'i-lee:

23 And he came and dwelt in a city called Naz'a-reth: that it might be fulfilled which was spoken by the prophets, He shall be called a Naz'a-rene.

3 IN those days came John the Bap'tist, preaching in the wilderness of Ju-dæ'a,

2 And saying, Repent ye: for the kingdom of heaven is at hand.

3 For this is he that was spoken of by the prophet E-sa'ias, saying, The voice of one cry-ing in the wilderness, Prepare ye the way of the Lord, make his paths straight.

4 And the same John had his raiment of cam-el's hair, and a leathern girdle about his loins; and his meat was locusts and wild honey.

5 Then went out to him Je-ru'sa-lem, and all Ju-dæ'a, and all the region round about Jor'dan,

6 And were baptized of him in Jor'dan, con-fessing their sins.

7 ¶ But when he saw many of the Phar'i-sees and Sad'du-cees come to his baptism, he said unto them, O generation of vipers, who hath warned you to flee from the wrath to come?

8 Bring forth therefore fruits meet for repen-tance:

9 And think not to say within yourselves, We have A'bra-ham to *our* father: for I say unto you, that God is able of these stones to raise up children unto A'bra-ham.

10 And now also the ax is laid unto the root of the trees: therefore every tree which bringeth not forth good fruit is hewn down, and cast into the fire.

11 I indeed baptize you with water unto re-pentance: but he that cometh after me is might-ier than I, whose shoes I am not worthy to bear: he shall baptize you with the Ho'ly Ghost, and *with* fire:

12 Whose fan *is* in his hand, and he will throughly purge his floor, and gather his wheat into the garner; but he will burn up the chaff with unquenchable fire.

13 ¶ Then cometh Je'sus from Gal'i-lee to Jor'dan unto John, to be baptized of him.

14 But John forbad him, saying, I have need to be baptized of thee, and comest thou to me?

15 And Je'sus answering said unto him, Suf-fer *it to be so* now: for thus it becometh us to fulfill all righteousness. Then he suffered him.

16 And Je'sus, when he was baptized, went up straightway out of the water: and, lo, the heavens were opened unto him, and he saw the Spirit of God descending like a dove, and light-ing upon him:

17 And lo a voice from heaven, saying, This is my beloved Son, in whom I am well pleased.

4 THEN was Je'sus led up of the spirit into the wilderness to be tempted of the devil.

2 And when he had fasted forty days and forty nights, he was afterward an hungred.

3 And when the tempter came to him, he said, If thou be the Son of God, command that these stones be made bread.

4 But he answered and said, It is written, Man shall not live by bread alone, but by every word that proceedeth out of the mouth of God.

5 Then the devil taketh him up into the holy city, and setteth him on a pinnacle of the tem-ple,

6 And saith unto him, If thou be the Son of God, cast thyself down: for it is written, He shall give his angels charge concerning thee: and in *their* hands they shall bear thee up, lest at any time thou dash thy foot against a stone.

7 Je'sus said unto him, It is written again, Thou shalt not tempt the Lord thy God.

8 Again, the devil taketh him up into an ex-ceeding high mountain, and sheweth him all the kingdoms of the world, and the glory of them;

9 And saith unto him, All these things will I give thee, if thou wilt fall down and worship me.

10 Then saith Je'sus unto him, Get thee hence, Sa'tan: for it is written, Thou shalt wor-ship the Lord thy God, and him only shalt thou serve.

11 Then the devil leaveth him, and, behold, angels came and ministered unto him.

12 ¶ Now when Je'sus had heard that John was cast into prison, he departed into Gal'i-lee;

13 And leaving Naz'a-reth, he came and dwelt in Ca-per'na-um, which is upon the sea coast, in the borders of Zab'u-lon and Neph'tha-lim:

14 That it might be fulfilled which was spo-ken by E-sa'ias the prophet, saying,

15 The land of Zab'u-lon, and the land of Neph'tha-lim, by the way of the sea, beyond Jor'dan, Gal'i-lee of the Gen'tiles;

16 The people which sat in darkness saw great light; and to them which sat in the region and shadow of death light is sprung up.

17 ¶ From that time Je'sus began to preach, and to say, Repent: for the kingdom of heaven is at hand.

18 ¶ And Je'sus, walking by the sea of Gal'i-lee, saw two brethren, Si'mon called Pe'ter, and Andrew his brother, casting a net into the sea: for they were fishers.

19 And he saith unto them, Follow me, and I will make you fishers of men.

20 And they straightway left *their* nets, and followed him.

21 And going on from thence, he saw other two brethren, James *the son* of Zeb'e-dee, and John his brother, in a ship with Zeb'e-dee their father, mending their nets; and he called them.

22 And they immediately left the ship and their father, and followed him.

23 ¶ And Je'sus went about all Gal'i-lee, teaching in their synagogues, and preaching the gospel of the kingdom, and healing all manner of sickness and all manner of disease among the people.

24 And his fame went throughout all Syr'i-a: and they brought unto him all sick people that were taken with divers diseases and torments, and those which were possessed with devils, and those which were lunatick, and those that had the palsy; and he healed them.

25 And there followed him great multitudes of people from Gal'i-lee, and *from* De-cap'o-lis, and *from* Je-ru'sa-lem, and *from* Ju-dæ'a, and *from* beyond Jor'dan.

5 AND seeing the multitudes, he went up into a mountain: and when he was set, his disciples came unto him:

2 And he opened his mouth, and taught them, saying,

3 Blessed *are* the poor in spirit: for theirs is the kingdom of heaven.

4 Blessed *are* they that mourn: for they shall be comforted.

5 Blessed *are* the meek: for they shall inherit the earth.

6 Blessed *are* they which do hunger and thirst after righteousness: for they shall be filled.

7 Blessed *are* the merciful: for they shall obtain mercy.

8 Blessed *are* the pure in heart: for they shall see God.

9 Blessed *are* the peacemakers: for they shall be called the children of God.

10 Blessed *are* they which are persecuted for righteousness' sake: for theirs is the kingdom of heaven.

11 Blessed are ye, when *men* shall revile you, and persecute *you*, and shall say all manner of evil against you falsely, for my sake.

12 Rejoice, and be exceeding glad: for great *is* your reward in heaven: for so persecuted they the prophets which were before you.

13 ¶ Ye are the salt of the earth: but if the salt have lost his savour, wherewith shall it be salted? it is thenceforth good for nothing, but to be cast out, and to be trodden under foot of men.

14 Ye are the light of the world. A city that is set on an hill cannot be hid.

15 Neither do men light a candle, and put it under a bushel, but on a candlestick; and it giveth light unto all that are in the house.

16 Let your light so shine before men, that they may see your good works, and glorify your Father which is in heaven.

17 ¶ Think not that I am come to destroy the law, or the prophets: I am not come to destroy, but to fulfil.

18 For verily I say unto you, Till heaven and earth pass, one jot or one tittle shall in no wise pass from the law, till all be fulfilled.

19 Whosoever therefore shall break one of these least commandments, and shall teach men so, he shall be called the least in the kingdom of heaven: but whosoever shall do and teach *them*, the same shall be called great in the kingdom of heaven.

20 For I say unto you, That except your righteousness shall exceed *the righteousness* of the scribes and Phar'i-sees, ye shall in no case enter into the kingdom of heaven.

21 ¶ Ye have heard that it was said by them of old time, Thou shalt not kill; and whosoever shall kill shall be in danger of the judgment:

22 But I say unto you, That whosoever is angry with his brother without a cause shall be in danger of the judgment: and whosoever shall say to his brother, Raca, shall be in danger of the council: but whosoever shall say, Thou fool, shall be in danger of hell fire.

23 Therefore if thou bring thy gift to the altar, and there rememberest that thy brother hath ought against thee;

24 Leave there thy gift before the altar, and go thy way; first be reconciled to thy brother, and then come and offer thy gift.

25 Agree with thine adversary quickly, whiles thou art in the way with him; lest at any time the adversary deliver thee to the judge, and the judge deliver thee to the officer, and thou be cast into prison.

26 Verily I say unto thee, Thou shalt by no means come out thence, till thou hast paid the uttermost farthing.

27 ¶ Ye have heard that it was said by them of old time, Thou shalt not commit adultery:

28 But I say unto you, That whosoever looketh on a woman to lust after her hath committed adultery with her already in his heart.

29 And if thy right eye offend thee, pluck it out, and cast *it* from thee: for it is profitable for thee that one of thy members should perish, and not *that* thy whole body should be cast into hell.

30 And if thy right hand offend thee, cut it off, and cast *it* from thee: for it is profitable for thee that one of thy members should perish, and not *that* thy whole body should be cast into hell.

31 It hath been said, Whosoever shall put away his wife, let him give her a writing of divorcement:

32 But I say unto you, That whosoever shall put away his wife, saving for the cause of fornication, causeth her to commit adultery: and whosoever shall marry her that is divorced committeth adultery.

33 ¶ Again, ye have heard that it hath been said by them of old time, Thou shalt not forswear thyself, but shalt perform unto the Lord thine oaths:

34 But I say unto you, Swear not at all; neither by heaven; for it is God's throne:

35 Nor by the earth; for it is his footstool: neither by Je-ru'sa-lem; for it is the city of the great King.

36 Neither shalt thou swear by thy head, because thou canst not make one hair white or black.

37 But let your communication be, Yea, yea; Nay, nay: for whatsoever is more than these cometh of evil.

38 ¶ Ye have heard that it hath been said, An eye for an eye, and a tooth for a tooth:

39 But I say unto you, That ye resist not evil: but whosoever shall smite thee on thy right cheek, turn to him the other also.

40 And if any man will sue thee at the law, and take away thy coat, let him have *thy* cloke also.

41 And whosoever shall compel thee to go a mile, go with him twain.

42 Give to him that asketh thee, and from him that would borrow of thee turn not thou away.

43 ¶ Ye have heard that it hath been said, Thou shalt love thy neighbour, and hate thine enemy.

44 But I say unto you, Love your enemies, bless them that curse you, do good to them that hate you, and pray for them which despitefully use you, and persecute you;

45 That ye may be the children of your Father which is in heaven: for he maketh his sun to rise on the evil and on the good, and sendeth rain on the just and on the unjust.

46 For if ye love them which love you, what reward have ye? do not even the publicans so?

47 And if ye salute your brethren only, what do ye more *than others?* do not even the publicans so?

48 Be ye therefore perfect, even as your Father which is in heaven is perfect.

6 TAKE heed that ye do not your alms before men, to be seen of them: otherwise ye have no reward of your Father which is in heaven.

2 Therefore when thou doest *thine* alms, do not sound a trumpet before thee, as the hypocrites do in the synagogues and in the streets, that they may have glory of men. Verily I say unto you, They have their reward.

3 But when thou doest alms, let not thy left hand know what thy right hand doeth:

4 That thine alms may be in secret: and thy Father which seeth in secret himself shall reward thee openly.

5 ¶ And when thou prayest, thou shalt not be as the hypocrites *are*: for they love to pray standing in the synagogues and in the corners of the streets, that they may be seen of men. Verily I say unto you, They have their reward.

6 But thou, when thou prayest, enter into thy closet, and when thou hast shut thy door, pray to thy Father which is in secret; and thy Father which seeth in secret shall reward thee openly.

7 But when ye pray, use not vain repetitions, as the heathen *do*: for they think that they shall be heard for their much speaking.

8 Be not ye therefore like unto them: for your Father knoweth what things ye have need of, before ye ask him.

9 After this manner therefore pray ye: Our Father which art in heaven, Hallowed be thy name.

10 Thy kingdom come. Thy will be done in earth, as *it is* in heaven.

11 Give us this day our daily bread.

12 And forgive us our debts, as we forgive our debtors.

13 And lead us not into temptation, but deliver us from evil: For thine is the kingdom, and the power, and the glory, for ever. Amen.

14 For if ye forgive men their trespasses, your heavenly Father will also forgive you:

15 But if ye forgive not men their trespasses, neither will your Father forgive your trespasses.

16 ¶ Moreover when ye fast, be not, as the hypocrites, of a sad countenance: for they disfigure their faces, that they may appear unto men to fast. Verily I say unto you, They have their reward.

17 But thou, when thou fastest, anoint thine head, and wash thy face;

18 That thou appear not unto men to fast, but unto thy Father which is in secret: and thy Father, which seeth in secret, shall reward thee openly.

19 ¶ Lay not up for yourselves treasures upon earth, where moth and rust doth corrupt, and where thieves break through and steal:

20 But lay up for yourselves treasures in heaven, where neither moth nor rust doth corrupt, and where thieves do not break through nor steal:

21 For where your treasure is, there will your heart be also.

22 The light of the body is the eye: if therefore thine eye be single, thy whole body shall be full of light.

23 But if thine eye be evil, thy whole body shall be full of darkness. If therefore the light that is in thee be darkness, how great *is* that darkness!

24 ¶ No man can serve two masters: for either he will hate the one, and love the other; or else he will hold to the one, and despise the other. Ye cannot serve God and mammon.

25 Therefore I say unto you, Take no thought for your life, what ye shall eat, or what ye shall drink; nor yet for your body, what ye shall put on. Is not the life more than meat, and the body than raiment?

26 Behold the fowls of the air: for they sow not, neither do they reap, nor gather into barns; yet your heavenly Father feedeth them. Are ye not much better than they?

27 Which of you by taking thought can add one cubit unto his stature?

28 And why take ye thought for raiment? Consider the lilies of the field, how they grow; they toil not, neither do they spin:

29 And yet I say unto you, That even Sol'o-mon in all his glory was not arrayed like one of these.

30 Wherefore, if God so clothe the grass of the field, which to day is, and to morrow is cast into the oven, *shall he* not much more *clothe* you, O ye of little faith?

31 Therefore take no thought, saying, What shall we eat? or, What shall we drink? or, Wherewithal shall we be clothed?

32 (For after all these things do the Gen'tiles seek:) for your heavenly Father knoweth that ye have need of all these things.

33 But seek ye first the kingdom of God, and his righteousness; and all these things shall be added unto you.

34 Take therefore no thought for the morrow: for the morrow shall take thought for the things of itself. Sufficient unto the day *is* the evil thereof.

7 JUDGE not, that ye be not judged.
2 For with what judgment ye judge, ye shall be judged: and with what measure ye mete, it shall be measured to you again.

3 And why beholdest thou the mote that is in thy brother's eye, but considerest not the beam that is in thine own eye?

4 Or how wilt thou say to thy brother, Let me pull out the mote out of thine eye; and, behold, a beam *is* in thine own eye?

5 Thou hypocrite, first cast out the beam out of thine own eye; and then shalt thou see clearly to cast out the mote out of thy brother's eye.

6 ¶ Give not that which is holy unto the dogs, neither cast ye your pearls before swine, lest they trample them under their feet, and turn again and rend you.

7 ¶ Ask, and it shall be given you; seek, and ye shall find; knock, and it shall be opened unto you:

8 For every one that asketh receiveth; and he that seeketh findeth; and to him that knocketh it shall be opened.

9 Or what man is there of you, whom if his son ask bread, will he give him a stone?

10 Or if he ask a fish, will he give him a serpent?

11 If ye then, being evil, know how to give good gifts unto your children, how much more shall your Father which is in heaven give good things to them that ask him?

12 Therefore all things whatsoever ye would that men should do to you, do ye even so to them: for this is the law and the prophets.

13 ¶ Enter ye in at the strait gate: for wide *is* the gate, and broad *is* the way, that leadeth to destruction, and many there be which go in thereat:

14 Because strait *is* the gate, and narrow *is* the way, which leadeth unto life, and few there be that find it.

15 ¶ Beware of false prophets, which come

to you in sheep's clothing, but inwardly they are ravening wolves.

16 Ye shall know them by their fruits. Do men gather grapes of thorns, or figs of thistles?

17 Even so every good tree bringeth forth good fruit; but a corrupt tree bringeth forth evil fruit.

18 A good tree cannot bring forth evil fruit, neither *can* a corrupt tree bring forth good fruit.

19 Every tree that bringeth not forth good fruit is hewn down, and cast into the fire.

20 Wherefore by their fruits ye shall know them.

21 ¶ Not every one that saith unto me, Lord, Lord, shall enter into the kingdom of heaven; but he that doeth the will of my Father which is in heaven.

22 Many will say to me in that day, Lord, Lord, have we not prophesied in thy name? and in thy name have cast out devils? and in thy name done many wonderful works?

23 And then will I profess unto them, I never knew you: depart from me, ye that work iniquity.

24 ¶ Therefore whosoever heareth these sayings of mine, and doeth them, I will liken him unto a wise man, which built his house upon a rock:

25 And the rain descended, and the floods came, and the winds blew, and beat upon that house; and it fell not: for it was founded upon a rock.

26 And every one that heareth these sayings of mine, and doeth them not, shall be likened unto a foolish man, which built his house upon the sand:

27 And the rain descended, and the floods came, and the winds blew, and beat upon that house; and it fell and great was the fall of it.

28 And it came to pass, when Je′sus had ended these sayings, the people were astonished at his doctrine:

29 For he taught them as *one* having authority, and not as the scribes.

8 WHEN he was come down from the mountain, great multitudes followed him.

2 And, behold, there came a leper and worshipped him, saying, Lord, if thou wilt, thou canst make me clean.

3 And Je′sus put forth *his* hand, and touched him, saying, I will; be thou clean. And immediately his leprosy was cleansed.

4 And Je′sus saith unto him, See thou tell no man; but go thy way, shew thyself to the priest, and offer the gift that Mo′ses commanded, for a testimony unto them.

5 ¶ And when Je′sus was entered into Ca-per′na-um, there came unto him a centurion, beseeching him,

6 And saying, Lord, my servant lieth at home sick of the palsy, grievously tormented.

7 And Je′sus saith unto him, I will come and heal him.

8 The centurion answered and said, Lord, I am not worthy that thou shouldest come under my roof: but speak the word only, and my servant shall be healed.

9 For I am a man under authority, having soldiers under me; and I say to this *man*, Go, and he goeth; and to another, Come, and he cometh; and to my servant, Do this, and he doeth *it.*

10 When Je′sus heard *it,* he marvelled, and said to them that followed, Verily I say unto you, I have not found so great faith, no, not in Is′ra-el.

11 And I say unto you, That many shall come from the east and west, and shall sit down with A′bra-ham, and I′saac, and Ja′cob, in the kingdom of heaven.

12 But the children of the kingdom shall be cast out into outer darkness: there shall be weeping and gnashing of teeth.

13 And Je′sus said unto the centurion, Go thy way; and as thou hast believed, *so* be it done unto thee. And his servant was healed in the selfsame hour.

14 ¶ And when Je′sus was come into Pe′ter's house, he saw his wife's mother laid, and sick of a fever.

15 And he touched her hand, and the fever left her: and she arose, and ministered unto them.

16 ¶ When the even was come, they brought unto him many that were possessed with devils: and he cast out the spirits with *his* word, and healed all that were sick:

17 That it might be fulfilled which was spoken by E-sa′ias the prophet, saying, Himself took our infirmities, and bare *our* sicknesses.

18 ¶ Now when Je′sus saw great multitudes about him, he gave commandment to depart unto the other side.

19 And a certain scribe came, and said unto him, Master, I will follow thee whithersoever thou goest.

20 And Je′sus saith unto him, The foxes have holes, and the birds of the air *have* nests; but the Son of man hath not where to lay *his* head.

21 And another of his disciples said unto him, Lord, suffer me first to go and bury my father.

22 But Je′sus said unto him, Follow me; and let the dead bury their dead.

23 ¶ And when he was entered into a ship, his disciples followed him.

24 And, behold, there arose a great tempest in the sea, insomuch that the ship was covered with the waves: but he was asleep.

25 And his disciples came to *him,* and awoke him, saying, Lord, save us: we perish.

26 And he saith unto them, Why are ye fearful, O ye of little faith? Then he arose, and rebuked the winds and the sea; and there was a great calm.

27 But the men marvelled, saying, What manner of man is this, that even the winds and the sea obey him!

28 ¶ And when he was come to the other side into the country of the Ger′ge-senes, there met him two possessed with devils, coming out of the tombs, exceeding fierce, so that no man might pass by that way.

29 And, behold, they cried out, saying, What have we to do with thee, Je′sus, thou Son of God? art thou come hither to torment us before the time?

30 And there was a good way off from them an herd of many swine feeding.

31 So the devils besought him, saying, If thou cast us out, suffer us to go away into the herd of swine.

32 And he said unto them, Go. And when they were come out, they went into the herd of swine: and, behold, the whole herd of swine ran violently down a steep place into the sea, and perished in the waters.

33 And they that kept them fled, and went their ways into the city, and told every thing, and what was befallen to the possessed of the devils.

34 And, behold, the whole city came out to meet Je′sus: and when they saw him, they be-

sought *him* that he would depart out of their coasts.

9 AND he entered into a ship, and passed over, and came into his own city.

2 And, behold, they brought to him a man sick of the palsy, lying on a bed: and Je'sus seeing their faith said unto the sick of the palsy, Son, be of good cheer; thy sins be forgiven thee.

3 And, behold, certain of the scribes said within themselves, This *man* blasphemeth.

4 And Je'sus knowing their thoughts said, Wherefore think ye evil in your hearts?

5 For whether is easier, to say, *Thy* sins be forgiven thee; or to say, Arise, and walk?

6 But that ye may know that the Son of man hath power on earth to forgive sins, (then saith he to the sick of the palsy,) Arise, take up thy bed, and go unto thine house.

7 And he arose, and departed to his house.

8 But when the multitudes saw *it,* they marvelled, and glorified God, which had given such power unto men.

9 ¶ And as Je'sus passed forth from thence, he saw a man, named Mat'thew, sitting at the receipt of custom: and he saith unto him, Follow me. And he arose, and followed him.

10 ¶ And it came to pass, as Je'sus sat at meat in the house, behold, many publicans and sinners came and sat down with him and his disciples.

11 And when the Phar'i-sees saw *it,* they said unto his disciples, Why eateth your Master with publicans and sinners?

12 But when Je'sus heard *that,* he said unto them, They that be whole need not a physician, but they that are sick.

13 But go ye and learn what *that* meaneth, I will have mercy, and not sacrifice: for I am not come to call the righteous, but sinners to repentance.

14 ¶ Then came to him the disciples of John, saying, Why do we and the Phar'i-sees fast oft, but thy disciples fast not?

15 And Je'sus said unto them, Can the children of the bridechamber mourn, as long as the bridegroom is with them? but the days will come, when the bridegroom shall be taken from them, and then shall they fast.

16 No man putteth a piece of new cloth unto an old garment, for that which is put in to fill it up taketh from the garment, and the rent is made worse.

17 Neither do men put new wine into old bottles: else the bottles break, and the wine runneth out, and the bottles perish: but they put new wine into new bottles, and both are preserved.

18 ¶ While he spake these things unto them, behold, there came a certain ruler, and worshipped him, saying, My daughter is even now dead: but come and lay thy hand upon her, and she shall live.

19 And Je'sus arose, and followed him, and *so did* his disciples.

20 ¶ And, behold, a woman, which was diseased with an issue of blood twelve years, came behind *him,* and touched the hem of his garment:

21 For she said within herself, If I may but touch his garment, I shall be whole.

22 But Je'sus turned him about, and when he saw her, he said, Daughter, be of good comfort; thy faith hath made thee whole. And the woman was made whole from that hour.

23 And when Je'sus came into the ruler's house, and saw the minstrels and the people making a noise,

24 He said unto them, Give place: for the maid is not dead, but sleepeth. And they laughed him to scorn.

25 But when the people were put forth, he went in, and took her by the hand, and the maid arose.

26 And the fame hereof went abroad into all that land.

27 ¶ And when Je'sus departed thence, two blind men followed him, crying, and saying, *Thou* son of Da'vid, have mercy on us.

28 And when he was come into the house, the blind men came to him: and Je'sus saith unto them, Believe ye that I am able to do this? They said unto him, Yea, Lord.

29 Then touched he their eyes, saying, According to your faith be it unto you.

30 And their eyes were opened; and Je'sus straitly charged them, saying, See *that* no man know *it.*

31 But they, when they were departed, spread abroad his fame in all that country.

32 ¶ As they went out, behold, they brought to him a dumb man possessed with a devil.

33 And when the devil was cast out, the dumb spake: and the multitudes marvelled, saying, It was never so seen in Is'ra-el.

34 But the Phar'i-sees said, He casteth out devils through the prince of the devils.

35 And Je'sus went about all the cities and villages, teaching in their synagogues, and preaching the gospel of the kingdom, and healing every sickness and every disease among the people.

36 ¶ But when he saw the multitudes, he was moved with compassion on them, because they fainted, and were scattered abroad, as sheep having no shepherd.

37 Then saith he unto his disciples, The harvest truly *is* plenteous, but the labourers *are* few;

38 Pray ye therefore the Lord of the harvest, that he will send forth labourers into his harvest.

10 AND when he had called unto *him* his twelve disciples, he gave them power *against* unclean spirits, to cast them out, and to heal all manner of sickness and all manner of disease.

2 Now the names of the twelve apostles are these; The first, Si'mon, who is called Pe'ter, and Andrew his brother; James *the son* of Zeb'e-dee, and John his brother;

3 Phil'ip, and Bar-thol'o-mew; Thom'as, and Mat'thew the publican; James *the son* of Al-phæ'us, and Leb-bæ'us, whose surname was Thad-dæ'us;

4 Si'mon the Ca'naan-ite, and Ju'das Is-car'i-ot, who also betrayed him.

5 These twelve Je'sus sent forth, and commanded them, saying, Go not into the way of the Gen'tiles, and into *any* city of the Sa-mar'i-tans enter ye not:

6 But go rather to the lost sheep of the house of Is'ra-el.

7 And as ye go, preach, saying, The kingdom of heaven is at hand.

8 Heal the sick, cleanse the lepers, raise the dead, cast out devils: freely ye have received, freely give.

9 Provide neither gold, nor silver, nor brass in your purses,

10 Nor scrip for *your* journey, neither two

coats, neither shoes, nor yet staves: for the workman is worthy of his meat.

11 And into whatsoever city or town ye shall enter, enquire who in it is worthy; and there abide till ye go thence.

12 And when ye come into an house, salute it.

13 And if the house be worthy, let your peace come upon it: but if it be not worthy, let your peace return to you.

14 And whosoever shall not receive you, nor hear your words, when ye depart out of that house or city, shake off the dust of your feet.

15 Verily I say unto you, It shall be more tolerable for the land of Sod'om and Go-mor'rha in the day of judgment, than for that city.

16 ¶ Behold, I send you forth as sheep in the midst of wolves: be ye therefore wise as serpents, and harmless as doves.

17 But beware of men: for they will deliver you up to the councils, and they will scourge you in their synagogues;

18 And ye shall be brought before governors and kings for my sake, for a testimony against them and the Gen'tiles.

19 But when they deliver you up, take no thought how or what ye shall speak: for it shall be given you in that same hour what ye shall speak.

20 For it is not ye that speak, but the Spirit of your Father which speaketh in you.

21 And the brother shall deliver up the brother to death, and the father the child: and the children shall rise up against *their* parents, and cause them to be put to death.

22 And ye shall be hated of all *men* for my name's sake: but he that endureth to the end shall be saved.

23 But when they persecute you in this city, flee ye into another: for verily I say unto you, Ye shall not have gone over the cities of Is'ra-el, till the Son of man be come.

24 The disciple is not above *his* master, nor the servant above his lord.

25 It is enough for the disciple that he be as his master, and the servant as his lord. If they have called the master of the house Be-el'ze-bub, how much more *shall they call* them of his household?

26 Fear them not therefore: for there is nothing covered, that shall not be revealed; and hid, that shall not be known.

27 What I tell you in darkness, *that* speak ye in light: and what ye hear in the ear, *that* preach ye upon the house tops.

28 And fear not them which kill the body, but are not able to kill the soul: but rather fear him which is able to destroy both soul and body in hell.

29 Are not two sparrows sold for a farthing? and one of them shall not fall on the ground without your Father.

30 But the very hairs of your head are all numbered.

31 Fear ye not therefore, ye are of more value than many sparrows.

32 Whosoever therefore shall confess me before men, him will I confess also before my Father which is in heaven.

33 But whosoever shall deny me before men, him will I also deny before my Father which is in heaven.

34 Think not that I am come to send peace on earth: I came not to send peace, but a sword.

35 For I am come to set a man at variance against his father, and the daughter against her mother, and the daughter in law against her mother in law.

36 And a man's foes *shall be* they of his own household.

37 He that loveth father or mother more than me is not worthy of me: and he that loveth son or daughter more than me is not worthy of me.

38 And he that taketh not his cross, and followeth after me, is not worthy of me.

39 He that findeth his life shall lose it: and he that loseth his life for my sake shall find it.

40 ¶ He that receiveth you receiveth me, and he that receiveth me receiveth him that sent me.

41 He that receiveth a prophet in the name of a prophet shall receive a prophet's reward; and he that receiveth a righteous man in the name of a righteous man shall receive a righteous man's reward.

42 And whosoever shall give to drink unto one of these little ones a cup of cold *water* only in the name of a disciple, verily I say unto you, he shall in no wise lose his reward.

11 AND it came to pass, when Je'sus had made an end of commanding his twelve disciples, he departed thence to teach and to preach in their cities.

2 Now when John had heard in the prison the works of Christ, he sent two of his disciples,

3 And said unto him, Art thou he that should come, or do we look for another?

4 Je'sus answered and said unto them, Go and shew John again those things which ye do hear and see:

5 The blind receive their sight, and the lame walk, the lepers are cleansed, and the deaf hear, the dead are raised up, and the poor have the gospel preached to them.

6 And blessed is *he*, whosoever shall not be offended in me.

7 ¶ And as they departed, Je'sus began to say unto the multitudes concerning John, What went ye out into the wilderness to see? A reed shaken with the wind?

8 But what went ye out for to see? A man clothed in soft raiment? behold, they that wear soft *clothing* are in kings' houses.

9 But what went ye out for to see? A prophet? yea, I say unto you, and more than a prophet.

10 For this is *he*, of whom it is written, Behold, I send my messenger before thy face, which shall prepare thy way before thee.

11 Verily I say unto you, Among them that are born of women there hath not risen a greater than John the Bap'tist: notwithstanding he that is least in the kingdom of heaven is greater than he.

12 And from the days of John the Bap'tist until now the kingdom of heaven suffereth violence, and the violent take it by force.

13 For all the prophets and the law prophesied until John.

14 And if ye will receive *it*, this is E-li'as, which was for to come.

15 He that hath ears to hear, let him hear.

16 ¶ But whereunto shall I liken this generation? It is like unto children sitting in the markets, and calling unto their fellows,

17 And saying, We have piped unto you, and ye have not danced; we have mourned unto you, and ye have not lamented.

18 For John came neither eating nor drinking, and they say, He hath a devil.

19 The Son of man came eating and drinking, and they say, Behold a man gluttonous, and a

winebibber, a friend of publicans and sinners. But wisdom is justified of her children.

20 ¶ Then began he to upbraid the cities wherein most of his mighty works were done, because they repented not:

21 Woe unto thee, Cho-ra'zin! woe unto thee, Beth-sa'i-da! for if the mighty works, which were done in you, had been done in Tyre and Si'don, they would have repented long ago in sackcloth and ashes.

22 But I say unto you, It shall be more tolerable for Tyre and Si'don at the day of judgment, than for you.

23 And thou, Ca-per'na-um, which art exalted unto heaven, shalt be brought down to hell: for if the mighty works, which have been done in thee, had been done in Sod'om, it would have remained until this day.

24 But I say unto you, That it shall be more tolerable for the land of Sod'om in the day of judgment, than for thee.

25 ¶ At that time Je'sus answered and said, I thank thee, O Father, Lord of heaven and earth, because thou hast hid these things from the wise and prudent, and hast revealed them unto babes.

26 Even so, Father: for so it seemed good in thy sight.

27 All things are delivered unto me of my Father: and no man knoweth the Son, but the Father; neither knoweth any man the Father, save the Son, and *he* to whomsoever the Son will reveal *him*.

28 ¶ Come unto me, all ye that labour and are heavy laden, and I will give you rest.

29 Take my yoke upon you, and learn of me; for I am meek and lowly in heart: and ye shall find rest unto your souls.

30 For my yoke *is* easy, and my burden is light.

12 AT that time Je'sus went on the sabbath day through the corn; and his disciples were an hungred, and began to pluck the ears of corn, and to eat.

2 But when the Phar'i-sees saw *it,* they said unto him, Behold, thy disciples do that which is not lawful to do upon the sabbath day.

3 But he said unto them, Have ye not read what Da'vid did, when he was an hungred, and they that were with him;

4 How he entered into the house of God, and did eat the shewbread, which was not lawful for him to eat, neither for them which were with him, but only for the priests?

5 Or have ye not read in the law, how that on the sabbath days the priests in the temple profane the sabbath, and are blameless?

6 But I say unto you, That in this place is *one* greater than the temple.

7 But if ye had known what *this* meaneth, I will have mercy, and not sacrifice, ye would not have condemned the guiltless.

8 For the Son of man is Lord even of the sabbath day.

9 And when he was departed thence, he went into their synagogue:

10 ¶ And, behold, there was a man which had *his* hand withered. And they asked him, saying, Is it lawful to heal on the sabbath days? that they might accuse him.

11 And he said unto them, What man shall there be among you, that shall have one sheep, and if it fall into a pit on the sabbath day, will he not lay hold on it, and lift *it* out?

12 How much then is a man better than a sheep? Wherefore it is lawful to do well on the sabbath days.

13 Then saith he to the man, Stretch forth thine hand. And he stretched *it* forth; and it was restored whole, like as the other.

14 ¶ Then the Phar'i-sees went out, and held a council against him, how they might destroy him.

15 But when Je'sus knew *it,* he withdrew himself from thence: and great multitudes followed him, and he healed them all;

16 And charged them that they should not make him known:

17 That it might be fulfilled which was spoken by E-sa'ias the prophet, saying,

18 Behold my servant, whom I have chosen; my beloved, in whom my soul is well pleased: I will put my spirit upon him, and he shall shew judgment to the Gen'tiles.

19 He shall not strive, nor cry; neither shall any man hear his voice in the streets.

20 A bruised reed shall he not break, and smoking flax shall he not quench, till he send forth judgment unto victory.

21 And in his name shall the Gen'tiles trust.

22 ¶ Then was brought unto him one possessed with a devil, blind, and dumb: and he healed him, insomuch that the blind and dumb both spake and saw.

23 And all the people were amazed, and said, Is not this the son of Da'vid?

24 But when the Phar'i-sees heard *it,* they said, This *fellow* doth not cast out devils, but by Be'el'ze-bub the prince of the devils.

25 And Je'sus knew their thoughts, and said unto them, Every kingdom divided against itself is brought to desolation; and every city or house divided against itself shall not stand:

26 And if Sa'tan cast out Sa'tan, he is divided against himself; how shall then his kingdom stand?

27 And if I by Be'el'ze-bub cast out devils, by whom do your children cast *them* out? therefore they shall be your judges.

28 But if I cast out devils by the Spirit of God, then the kingdom of God is come unto you.

29 Or else how can one enter into a strong man's house, and spoil his goods, except he first bind the strong man? and then he will spoil his house.

30 He that is not with me is against me; and he that gathereth not with me scattereth abroad.

31 ¶ Wherefore I say unto you, All manner of sin and blasphemy shall be forgiven unto men: but the blasphemy *against* the Ho'ly Ghost shall not be forgiven unto men.

32 And whosoever speaketh a word against the Son of man, it shall be forgiven him: but whosoever speaketh against the Ho'ly Ghost, it shall not be forgiven him, neither in this world, neither in the *world* to come.

33 Either make the tree good, and his fruit good; or else make the tree corrupt, and his fruit corrupt: for the tree is known by *his* fruit.

34 O generation of vipers, how can ye, being evil, speak good things? for out of the abundance of the heart the mouth speaketh.

35 A good man out of the good treasure of the heart bringeth forth good things: and an evil man out of the evil treasure bringeth forth evil things.

36 But I say unto you, That every idle word that men shall speak, they shall give account thereof in the day of judgment.

37 For by thy words thou shalt be justified, and by thy words thou shalt be condemned.

38 ¶ Then certain of the scribes and of the Phar'i-sees answered, saying, Master, we would see a sign from thee.

39 But he answered and said unto them, An evil and adulterous generation seeketh after a sign; and there shall no sign be given to it, but the sign of the prophet Jo'nas:

40 For as Jo'nas was three days and three nights in the whale's belly; so shall the Son of man be three days and three nights in the heart of the earth.

41 The men of Nin'e-veh shall rise in judgment with this generation, and shall condemn it: because they repented at the preaching of Jo'nas; and, behold, a greater than Jo'nas is here.

42 The queen of the south shall rise up in the judgment with this generation, and shall condemn it: for she came from the uttermost parts of the earth to hear the wisdom of Sol'o-mon; and, behold, a greater than Sol'o-mon is here.

43 When the unclean spirit is gone out of a man, he walketh through dry places, seeking rest, and findeth none.

44 Then he saith, I will return into my house from whence I came out; and when he is come, he findeth it empty, swept, and garnished.

45 Then goeth he, and taketh with himself seven other spirits more wicked than himself, and they enter in and dwell there: and the last state of that man is worse than the first. Even so shall it be also unto this wicked generation.

46 ¶ While he yet talked to the people, behold, his mother and his brethren stood without, desiring to speak with him.

47 Then one said unto him, Behold, thy mother and thy brethren stand without, desiring to speak with thee.

48 But he answered and said unto him that told him, Who is my mother? and who are my brethren?

49 And he stretched forth his hand toward his disciples, and said, Behold my mother and my brethren!

50 For whosoever shall do the will of my Father which is in heaven, the same is my brother, and sister, and mother.

13 THE same day went Je'sus out of the house, and sat by the sea side.

2 And great multitudes were gathered together unto him, so that he went into a ship, and sat; and the whole multitude stood on the shore.

3 And he spake many things unto them in parables, saying, Behold, a sower went forth to sow;

4 And when he sowed, some seeds fell by the way side, and the fowls came and devoured them up:

5 Some fell upon stony places, where they had not much earth: and forthwith they sprung up, because they had no deepness of earth:

6 And when the sun was up, they were scorched; and because they had no root, they withered away.

7 And some fell among thorns; and the thorns sprung up, and choked them:

8 But other fell into good ground, and brought forth fruit, some an hundredfold, some sixtyfold, some thirtyfold.

9 Who hath ears to hear, let him hear.

10 And the disciples came, and said unto him, Why speakest thou unto them in parables?

11 He answered and said unto them, Because

it is given unto you to know the mysteries of the kingdom of heaven, but to them it is not given.

12 For whosoever hath, to him shall be given, and he shall have more abundance: but whosoever hath not, from him shall be taken away even that he hath.

13 Therefore speak I to them in parables: because they seeing see not; and hearing they hear not, neither do they understand.

14 And in them is fulfilled the prophecy of E-sa'ias, which saith, By hearing ye shall hear, and shall not understand; and seeing ye shall see, and shall not perceive:

15 For this people's heart is waxed gross, and their ears are dull of hearing, and their eyes they have closed; lest at any time they should see with their eyes, and hear with their ears, and should understand with their heart, and should be converted, and I should heal them.

16 But blessed are your eyes, for they see: and your ears, for they hear.

17 For verily I say unto you, That many prophets and righteous men have desired to see those things which ye see, and have not seen them; and to hear those things which ye hear, and have not heard them.

18 ¶ Hear ye therefore the parable of the sower.

19 When any one heareth the word of the kingdom, and understandeth it not, then cometh the wicked one, and catcheth away that which was sown in his heart. This is he which received seed by the way side.

20 But he that received the seed into stony places, the same is he that heareth the word, and anon with joy receiveth it;

21 Yet hath he not root in himself, but dureth for a while: for when tribulation or persecution ariseth because of the word, by and by he is offended.

22 He also that received seed among the thorns is he that heareth the word; and the care of this world, and the deceitfulness of riches, choke the word, and he becometh unfruitful.

23 But he that received seed into the good ground is he that heareth the word, and understandeth it; which also beareth fruit, and bringeth forth, some an hundredfold, some sixty, some thirty.

24 ¶ Another parable put he forth unto them, saying, The kingdom of heaven is likened unto a man which sowed good seed in his field:

25 But while men slept, his enemy came and sowed tares among the wheat, and went his way.

26 But when the blade was sprung up, and brought forth fruit, then appeared the tares also.

27 So the servants of the householder came and said unto him, Sir, didst not thou sow good seed in thy field? from whence then hath it tares?

28 He said unto them, An enemy hath done this. The servants said unto him, Wilt thou then that we go and gather them up?

29 But he said, Nay; lest while ye gather up the tares, ye root up also the wheat with them.

30 Let both grow together until the harvest: and in the time of harvest I will say to the reapers, Gather ye together first the tares, and bind them in bundles to burn them: but gather the wheat into my barn.

31 ¶ Another parable put he forth unto them, saying, The kingdom of heaven is like a grain of mustard seed, which a man took, and sowed in his field:

32 Which indeed is the least of all seeds: but

when it is grown, it is the greatest among herbs, and becometh a tree, so that the birds of the air come and lodge in the branches thereof.

33 ¶ Another parable spake he unto them; The kingdom of heaven is like unto leaven, which a woman took, and hid in three measures of meal, till the whole was leavened.

34 All these things spake Je′sus unto the multitude in parables; and without a parable spake he not unto them:

35 That it might be fulfilled which was spoken by the prophet, saying, I will open my mouth in parables; I will utter things which have been kept secret from the foundation of the world.

36 Then Je′sus sent the multitude away, and went into the house: and his disciples came unto him, saying, Declare unto us the parable of the tares of the field.

37 He answered and said unto them, He that soweth the good seed is the Son of man;

38 The field is the world; the good seed are the children of the kingdom; but the tares are the children of the wicked *one*;

39 The enemy that sowed them is the devil; the harvest is the end of the world; and the reapers are the angels.

40 As therefore the tares are gathered and burned in the fire; so shall it be in the end of this world.

41 The Son of man shall send forth his angels, and they shall gather out of his kingdom all things that offend, and them which do iniquity;

42 And shall cast them into a furnace of fire: there shall be wailing and gnashing of teeth.

43 Then shall the righteous shine forth as the sun in the kingdom of their Father. Who hath ears to hear, let him hear.

44 ¶ Again, the kingdom of heaven is like unto treasure hid in a field; the which when a man hath found, he hideth, and for joy thereof goeth and selleth all that he hath, and buyeth that field.

45 ¶ Again, the kingdom of heaven is like unto a merchant man, seeking goodly pearls:

46 Who, when he had found one pearl of great price, went and sold all that he had, and bought it.

47 ¶ Again, the kingdom of heaven is like unto a net, that was cast into the sea, and gathered of every kind:

48 Which, when it was full, they drew to shore, and sat down, and gathered the good into vessels, but cast the bad away.

49 So shall it be at the end of the world: the angels shall come forth, and sever the wicked from among the just,

50 And shall cast them into the furnace of fire: there shall be wailing and gnashing of teeth.

51 Je′sus saith unto them, Have ye understood all these things? They say unto him, Yea, Lord.

52 Then said he unto them, Therefore every scribe *which is* instructed unto the kingdom of heaven is like unto a man *that is* an householder, which bringeth forth out of his treasure *things* new and old.

53 ¶ And it came to pass, *that* when Je′sus had finished these parables, he departed thence.

54 And when he was come into his own country, he taught them in their synagogue, insomuch that they were astonished, and said, Whence hath this *man* this wisdom, and *these* mighty works?

55 Is not this the carpenter's son? is not his mother called Ma′ry? and his brethren, James, and Jo′ses, and Si′mon, and Ju′das?

56 And his sisters, are they not all with us? Whence then hath this *man* all these things?

57 And they were offended in him. But Je′sus said unto them, A prophet is not without honour, save in his own country, and in his own house.

58 And he did not many mighty works there because of their unbelief.

14 AT that time Her′od the tetrarch heard of the fame of Je′sus,

2 And said unto his servants, This is John the Bap′tist; he is risen from the dead; and therefore mighty works do shew forth themselves in him.

3 ¶ For Her′od had laid hold on John, and bound him, and put *him* in prison for He-ro′di-as′ sake, his brother Phil′ip's wife.

4 For John said unto him, It is not lawful for thee to have her.

5 And when he would have put him to death, he feared the multitude, because they counted him as a prophet.

6 But when Her′od's birthday was kept, the daughter of He-ro′di-as danced before them, and pleased Her′od.

7 Whereupon he promised with an oath to give her whatsoever she would ask.

8 And she, being before instructed of her mother, said, Give me here John Bap′tist's head in a charger.

9 And the king was sorry: nevertheless for the oath's sake, and them which sat with him at meat, he commanded *it* to be given *her*.

10 And he sent, and beheaded John in the prison.

11 And his head was brought in a charger, and given to the damsel: and she brought *it* to her mother.

12 And his disciples came, and took up the body, and buried it, and went and told Je′sus.

13 ¶ When Je′sus heard *of it*, he departed thence by ship into a desert place apart: and when the people had heard *thereof*, they followed him on foot out of the cities.

14 And Je′sus went forth, and saw a great multitude, and was moved with compassion toward them, and he healed their sick.

15 ¶ And when it was evening, his disciples came to him, saying, This is a desert place, and the time is now past; send the multitude away, that they may go into the villages, and buy themselves victuals.

16 But Je′sus said unto them, They need not depart; give ye them to eat.

17 And they say unto him, We have here but five loaves, and two fishes.

18 He said, Bring them hither to me.

19 And he commanded the multitude to sit down on the grass, and took the five loaves, and the two fishes, and looking up to heaven, he blessed, and brake, and gave the loaves to *his* disciples, and the disciples to the multitude.

20 And they did all eat, and were filled: and they took up of the fragments that remained twelve baskets full.

21 And they that had eaten were about five thousand men, beside women and children.

22 ¶ And straightway Je′sus constrained his disciples to get into a ship, and to go before him unto the other side, while he sent the multitudes away.

23 And when he had sent the multitudes away, he went up into a mountain apart to pray:

and when the evening was come, he was there alone.

24 But the ship was now in the midst of the sea, tossed with waves: for the wind was contrary.

25 And in the fourth watch of the night Je'sus went unto them, walking on the sea.

26 And when the disciples saw him walking on the sea, they were troubled, saying, It is a spirit; and they cried out for fear.

27 But straightway Je'sus spake unto them, saying, Be of good cheer; it is I; be not afraid.

28 And Pe'ter answered him and said, Lord, if it be thou, bid me come unto thee on the water.

29 And he said, Come. And when Pe'ter was come down out of the ship, he walked on the water, to go to Je'sus.

30 But when he saw the wind boisterous, he was afraid; and beginning to sink, he cried, saying, Lord, save me.

31 And immediately Je'sus stretched forth *his* hand, and caught him, and said unto him, O thou of little faith, wherefore didst thou doubt?

32 And when they were come into the ship, the wind ceased.

33 Then they that were in the ship came and worshipped him, saying, Of a truth thou art the Son of God.

34 ¶ And when they were gone over, they came into the land of Gen-nes'a-ret.

35 And when the men of that place had knowledge of him, they sent out into all that country round about, and brought unto him all that were diseased;

36 And besought him that they might only touch the hem of his garment: and as many as touched were made perfectly whole.

15 THEN came to Je'sus scribes and Phar'i-sees, which were of Je-ru'sa-lem, saying,

2 Why do thy disciples transgress the tradition of the elders? for they wash not their hands when they eat bread.

3 But he answered and said unto them, Why do ye also transgress the commandment of God by your tradition?

4 For God commanded, saying, Honour thy father and mother: and, He that curseth father or mother, let him die the death.

5 But ye say, Whosoever shall say to *his* father or *his* mother, It is a gift, by whatsoever thou mightest be profited by me;

6 And honour not his father or his mother, *he shall be free.* Thus have ye made the commandment of God of none effect by your tradition.

7 *Ye* hypocrites, well did E-sa'ias prophesy of you, saying,

8 This people draweth nigh unto me with their mouth, and honoureth me with *their* lips; but their heart is far from me.

9 But in vain they do worship me, teaching *for* doctrines the commandments of men.

10 ¶ And he called the multitude, and said unto them, Hear, and understand:

11 Not that which goeth into the mouth defileth a man; but that which cometh out of the mouth, this defileth a man.

12 Then came his disciples, and said unto him, Knowest thou that the Phar'i-sees were offended, after they heard this saying?

13 But he answered and said, Every plant, which my heavenly Father hath not planted, shall be rooted up.

14 Let them alone: they be blind leaders of the blind. And if the blind lead the blind, both shall fall into the ditch.

15 Then answered Pe'ter and said unto him, Declare unto us this parable.

16 And Je'sus said, Are ye also yet without understanding?

17 Do not ye yet understand, that whatsoever entereth in at the mouth goeth into the belly, and is cast out into the draught?

18 But those things which proceed out of the mouth come forth from the heart; and they defile the man.

19 For out of the heart proceed evil thoughts, murders, adulteries, fornications, thefts, false witness, blasphemies:

20 These are *the things* which defile a man: but to eat with unwashen hands defileth not a man.

21 ¶ Then Je'sus went thence, and departed into the coasts of Tyre and Si'don.

22 And, behold, a woman of Ca'naan came out of the same coasts, and cried unto him, saying, Have mercy on me, O Lord, *thou* son of Da'vid; my daughter is grievously vexed with a devil.

23 But he answered her not a word. And his disciples came and besought him, saying, Send her away; for she crieth after us.

24 But he answered and said, I am not sent but unto the lost sheep of the house of Is'ra-el.

25 Then came she and worshipped him, saying Lord, help me.

26 But he answered and said, It is not meet to take the children's bread, and to cast *it* to dogs.

27 And she said, Truth, Lord: yet the dogs eat of the crumbs which fall from their masters' table.

28 Then Je'sus answered and said unto her, O woman, great *is* thy faith: be it unto thee even as thou wilt. And her daughter was made whole from that very hour.

29 And Je'sus departed from thence, and came nigh unto the sea of Gal'i-lee; and went up into a mountain, and sat down there.

30 And great multitudes came unto him, having with them *those that were* lame, blind, dumb, maimed, and many others, and cast them down at Je'sus' feet; and he healed them:

31 Insomuch that the multitude wondered, when they saw the dumb to speak, the maimed to be whole, the lame to walk, and the blind to see: and they glorified the God of Is'ra-el.

32 ¶ Then Je'sus called his disciples *unto him,* and said, I have compassion on the multitude, because they continue with me now three days, and have nothing to eat: and I will not send them away fasting, lest they faint in the way.

33 And his disciples say unto him, Whence should we have so much bread in the wilderness, as to fill so great a multitude?

34 And Je'sus saith unto them, How many loaves have ye? And they said, Seven, and a few little fishes.

35 And he commanded the multitude to sit down on the ground.

36 And he took the seven loaves and the fishes, and gave thanks, and brake *them,* and gave to his disciples, and the disciples to the multitude.

37 And they did all eat, and were filled: and they took up of the broken *meat* that was left seven baskets full.

38 And they that did eat were four thousand men, beside women and children.

39 And he sent away the multitude, and took ship, and came into the coasts of Mag'da-la.

16 THE Phar'i-sees also with the Sad'du-cees came, and tempting desired him that he would shew them a sign from heaven.

2 He answered and said unto them, When it is evening, ye say, It will be fair weather: for the sky is red.

3 And in the morning, It will be foul weather to day: for the sky is red and lowring. O ye hypocrites, ye can discern the face of the sky; but can ye not discern the signs of the times?

4 A wicked and adulterous generation seeketh after a sign; and there shall no sign be given unto it, but the sign of the prophet Jo'nas. And he left them, and departed.

5 And when his disciples were come to the other side, they had forgotten to take bread.

6 ¶ Then Je'sus said unto them, Take heed and beware of the leaven of the Phar'i-sees and of the Sad'du-cees.

7 And they reasoned among themselves, saying, It is because we have taken no bread.

8 Which when Je'sus perceived, he said unto them, O ye of little faith, why reason ye among yourselves, because ye have brought no bread?

9 Do ye not yet understand, neither remember the five loaves of the five thousand, and how many baskets ye took up?

10 Neither the seven loaves of the four thousand, and how many baskets ye took up?

11 How is it that ye do not undertand that I spake it not to you concerning bread, that ye should beware of the leaven of the Phar'i-sees and of the Sad'du-cees?

12 Then understood they how that he bade them not beware of the leaven of bread, but of the doctrine of the Phar'i-sees and of the Sad'-du-cees.

13 ¶ When Je'sus came into the coasts of Cæs-a-re'a Phi-lip'pi, he asked his disciples, saying, Whom do men say that I the Son of man am?

14 And they said, Some say that thou art John the Bap'tist: some, E-li'as; and others, Jer-e-mi'as, or one of the prophets.

15 He saith unto them, But whom say ye that I am?

16 And Si'mon Pe'ter answered and said, Thou art the Christ, the Son of the living God.

17 And Je'sus answered and said unto him, Blessed art thou, Si'mon Bar-jo'na: for flesh and blood hath not revealed it unto thee, but my Father which is in heaven.

18 And I say also unto thee, That thou art Pe'ter, and upon this rock I will build my church; and the gates of hell shall not prevail against it.

19 And I will give unto thee the keys of the kingdom of heaven: and whatsoever thou shalt bind on earth shall be bound in heaven: and whatsoever thou shalt loose on earth shall be loosed in heaven.

20 Then charged he his disciples that they should tell no man that he was Je'sus the Christ.

21 ¶ From that time forth began Je'sus to shew unto his disciples, how that he must go unto Je-ru'sa-lem, and suffer many things of the elders and chief priests and scribes, and be killed, and be raised again the third day.

22 Then Pe'ter took him, and began to rebuke him, saying, Be it far from thee, Lord: this shall not be unto thee.

23 But he turned, and said unto Pe'ter, Get thee behind me, Sa'tan: thou art an offence unto me: for thou savourest not the things that be of God, but those that be of men.

24 ¶ Then said Je'sus unto his disciples, If any man will come after me, let him deny himself, and take up his cross, and follow me.

25 For whosoever will save his life shall lose it: and whosoever will lose his life for my sake shall find it.

26 For what is a man profited, if he shall gain the whole world, and lose his own soul? or what shall a man give in exchange for his soul?

27 For the Son of man shall come in the glory of his Father with his angels; and then he shall reward every man according to his works.

28 Verily I say unto you, There be some standing here, which shall not taste of death, till they see the Son of man coming in his kingdom.

17 AND after six days Je'sus taketh Pe'ter, James, and John his brother, and bringeth them up into an high mountain apart,

2 And was transfigured before them: and his face did shine as the sun, and his raiment was white as the light.

3 And, behold, there appeared unto them Mo'ses and E-li'as talking with him.

4 Then answered Pe'ter, and said unto Je'sus, Lord, it is good for us to be here: if thou wilt, let us make here three tabernacles; one for thee, and one for Mo'ses, and one for E-li'as.

5 While he yet spake, behold, a bright cloud overshadowed them: and behold a voice out of the cloud, which said, This is my beloved Son, in whom I am well pleased; hear ye him.

6 And when the disciples heard it, they fell on their face, and were sore afraid.

7 And Je'sus came and touched them, and said, Arise, and be not afraid.

8 And when they had lifted up their eyes, they saw no man, save Je'sus only.

9 And as they came down from the mountain, Je'sus charged them, saying, Tell the vision to no man, until the Son of man be risen again from the dead.

10 And his disciples asked him, saying, Why then say the scribes that E-li'as must first come?

11 And Je'sus answered and said unto them, E-li'as truly shall first come, and restore all things.

12 But I say unto you, That E-li'as is come already, and they knew him not, but have done unto him whatsoever they listed. Likewise shall also the Son of man suffer of them.

13 Then the disciples understood that he spake unto them of John the Bap'tist.

14 ¶ And when they were come to the multitude, there came to him a certain man, kneeling down to him, and saying,

15 Lord, have mercy on my son: for he is lunatick, and sore vexed: for ofttimes he falleth into the fire, and oft into the water.

16 And I brought him to thy disciples, and they could not cure him.

17 Then Je'sus answered and said, O faithless and perverse generation, how long shall I be with you? how long shall I suffer you? bring him hither to me.

18 And Je'sus rebuked the devil; and he departed out of him: and the child was cured from that very hour.

19 Then came the disciples to Je'sus apart, and said, Why could not we cast him out?

20 And Je'sus said unto them, Because of your unbelief: for verily I say unto you, If ye have faith as a grain of mustard seed, ye shall say unto this mountain, Remove hence to yon-

der place; and it shall remove; and nothing shall be impossible unto you.

21 Howbeit this kind goeth not out but by prayer and fasting.

22 ¶ And while they abode in Gal'i-lee, Je'sus said unto them, The Son of man shall be betrayed into the hands of men:

23 And they shall kill him, and the third day he shall be raised again. And they were exceeding sorry.

24 ¶ And when they were come to Ca-per'-na-um, they that received tribute *money* came to Pe'ter, and said, Doth not your master pay tribute?

25 He saith, Yes. And when he was come into the house, Je'sus prevented him, saying, What thinkest thou, Si'mon? of whom do the kings of the earth take custom or tribute? of their own children, or of strangers?

26 Pe'ter saith unto him, Of strangers. Je'sus saith unto him, Then are the children free.

27 Notwithstanding, lest we should offend them, go thou to the sea, and cast an hook, and take up the fish that first cometh up; and when thou hast opened his mouth, thou shalt find a piece of money: that take, and give unto them for me and thee.

18 AT the same time came the disciples unto Je'sus, saying, Who is the greatest in the kingdom of heaven?

2 And Je'sus called a little child unto him, and set him in the midst of them,

3 And said, Verily I say unto you, Except ye be converted, and become as little children, ye shall not enter into the kingdom of heaven.

4 Whosoever therefore shall humble himself as this little child, the same is greatest in the kingdom of heaven.

5 And whoso shall receive one such little child in my name receiveth me.

6 But whoso shall offend one of these little ones which believe in me, it were better for him that a millstone were hanged about his neck, and *that* he were drowned in the depth of the sea.

7 ¶ Woe unto the world because of offences! for it must needs be that offences come; but woe to that man by whom the offence cometh!

8 Wherefore if thy hand or thy foot offend thee, cut them off, and cast *them* from thee: it is better for thee to enter into life halt or maimed, rather than having two hands or two feet to be cast into everlasting fire.

9 And if thine eye offend thee, pluck it out, and cast *it* from thee: it is better for thee to enter into life with one eye, rather than having two eyes to be cast into hell fire.

10 Take heed that ye despise not one of these little ones; for I say unto you, That in heaven their angels do always behold the face of my Father which is in heaven.

11 For the Son of man is come to save that which was lost.

12 How think ye? if a man have an hundred sheep, and one of them be gone astray, doth he not leave the ninety and nine, and goeth into the mountains, and seeketh that which is gone astray?

13 And if so be that he find it, verily I say unto you, he rejoiceth more of that *sheep*, than of the ninety and nine which went not astray.

14 Even so it is not the will of your Father which is in heaven, that one of these little ones should perish.

15 ¶ Moreover if thy brother shall trespass against thee, go and tell him his fault between thee and him alone: if he shall hear thee, thou hast gained thy brother.

16 But if he will not hear *thee, then* take with thee one or two more, that in the mouth of two or three witnesses every word may be established.

17 And if he shall neglect to hear them, tell *it* unto the church: but if he neglect to hear the church, let him be unto thee as an heathen man and a publican.

18 Verily I say unto you, Whatsoever ye shall bind on earth shall be bound in heaven: and whatsoever ye shall loose on earth shall be loosed in heaven.

19 Again I say unto you, That if two of you shall agree on earth as touching any thing that they shall ask, it shall be done for them of my Father which is in heaven.

20 For where two or three are gathered together in my name, there am I in the midst of them.

21 ¶ Then came Pe'ter to him, and said, Lord, how oft shall my brother sin against me, and I forgive him? till seven times?

22 Je'sus saith unto him, I say not unto thee, Until seven times: but, Until seventy times seven.

23 ¶ Therefore is the kingdom of heaven likened unto a certain king, which would take account of his servants.

24 And when he had begun to reckon, one was brought unto him, which owed him ten thousand talents.

25 But forasmuch as he had not to pay, his lord commanded him to be sold, and his wife, and children, and all that he had, and payment to be made.

26 The servant therefore fell down, and worshipped him, saying, Lord, have patience with me, and I will pay thee all.

27 Then the lord of that servant was moved with compassion, and loosed him, and forgave him the debt.

28 But the same servant went out, and found one of his fellowservants, which owed him an hundred pence: and he laid hands on him, and took *him* by the throat, saying, Pay me that thou owest.

29 And his fellowservant fell down at his feet, and besought him, saying, Have patience with me, and I will pay thee all.

30 And he would not: but went and cast him into prison, till he should pay the debt.

31 So when his fellowservants saw what was done, they were very sorry, and came and told unto their lord all that was done.

32 Then his lord, after that he had called him, said unto him, O thou wicked servant, I forgave thee all that debt, because thou desiredst me:

33 Shouldest not thou also have had compassion on thy fellowservant, even as I had pity on thee?

34 And his lord was wroth, and delivered him to the tormentors, till he should pay all that was due unto him.

35 So likewise shall my heavenly Father do also unto you, if ye from your hearts forgive not every one his brother their trespasses.

19 AND it came to pass, *that* when Je'sus had finished these sayings, he departed from Gal'i-lee, and came into the coasts of Ju-dæ'a beyond Jor'dan;

2 And great multitudes followed him; and he healed them there.

3 ¶ The Phar'i-sees also came unto him, tempting him, and saying unto him, Is it lawful

for a man to put away his wife for every cause?

4 And he answered and said unto them, Have ye not read, that he which made *them* at the beginning made them male and female,

5 And said, For this cause shall a man leave father and mother, and shall cleave to his wife: and they twain shall be one flesh?

6 Wherefore they are no more twain, but one flesh. What therefore God hath joined together, let not man put asunder.

7 They say unto him, Why did Mo'ses then command to give a writing of divorcement, and to put her away?

8 He saith unto them, Mo'ses because of the hardness of your hearts suffered you to put away your wives: but from the beginning it was not so.

9 And I say unto you, Whosoever shall put away his wife, except *it be* for fornication, and shall marry another, committeth adultery: and whoso marrieth her which is put away doth commit adultery.

10 ¶ His disciples say unto him, If the case of the man be so with *his* wife, it is not good to marry.

11 But he said unto them, All *men* cannot receive this saying, save *they* to whom it is given.

12 For there are some eunuchs, which were so born from *their* mother's womb: and there are some eunuchs, which were made eunuchs of men: and there be eunuchs, which have made themselves eunuchs for the kingdom of heaven's sake. He that is able to receive *it,* let him receive *it.*

13 ¶ Then were there brought unto him little children, that he should put *his* hands on them, and pray: and the disciples rebuked them.

14 But Je'sus said, Suffer little children, and forbid them not, to come unto me: for of such is the kingdom of heaven.

15 And he laid *his* hands on them, and departed thence.

16 ¶ And, behold, one came and said unto him, Good Master, what good thing shall I do, that I may have eternal life?

17 And he said unto him, Why callest thou me good? *there is* none good but one, *that is,* God: but if thou wilt enter into life, keep the commandments.

18 He saith unto him, Which? Je'sus said, Thou shalt do no murder, Thou shalt not commit adultery, Thou shalt not steal, Thou shalt not bear false witness,

19 Honour thy father and *thy* mother: and, Thou shalt love thy neighbour as thyself.

20 The young man saith unto him, All these things have I kept from my youth up: what lack I yet?

21 Je'sus said unto him, If thou wilt be perfect, go *and* sell that thou hast, and give to the poor, and thou shalt have treasure in heaven: and come *and* follow me.

22 But when the young man heard that saying, he went away sorrowful: for he had great possessions.

23 ¶ Then said Je'sus unto his disciples, Verily I say unto you, That a rich man shall hardly enter into the kingdom of heaven.

24 And again I say unto you, It is easier for a camel to go through the eye of a needle, than for a rich man to enter into the kingdom of God.

25 When his disciples heard *it,* they were exceedingly amazed, saying, Who then can be saved?

26 But Je'sus beheld *them,* and said unto them, With men this is impossible; but with God all things are possible.

27 ¶ Then answered Pe'ter and said unto him, Behold, we have forsaken all, and followed thee; what shall we have therefore?

28 And Je'sus said unto them, Verily I say unto you, That ye which have followed me, in the regeneration when the Son of man shall sit in the throne of his glory, ye also shall sit upon twelve thrones, judging the twelve tribes of Is'-ra-el.

29 And every one that hath forsaken houses, or brethren, or sisters, or father, or mother, or wife, or children, or lands, for my name's sake, shall receive an hundredfold, and shall inherit everlasting life.

30 But many *that are* first shall be last; and the last *shall be* first.

20 FOR the kingdom of heaven is like unto a man *that is* an householder, which went out early in the morning to hire labourers into his vineyard.

2 And when he had agreed with the labourers for a penny a day, he sent them into his vineyard.

3 And he went out about the third hour, and saw others standing idle in the marketplace,

4 And said unto them; Go ye also into the vineyard, and whatsoever is right I will give you. And they went their way.

5 Again he went out about the sixth and ninth hour, and did likewise.

6 And about the eleventh hour he went out, and found others standing idle, and saith unto them, Why stand ye here all the day idle?

7 They say unto him, Because no man hath hired us. He saith unto them, Go ye also into the vineyard; and whatsoever is right, *that* shall ye receive.

8 So when even was come, the lord of the vineyard saith unto his steward, Call the labourers, and give them *their* hire, beginning from the last unto the first.

9 And when they came that *were hired* about the eleventh hour, they received every man a penny.

10 But when the first came, they supposed that they should have received more; and they likewise received every man a penny.

11 And when they had received *it,* they murmured against the goodman of the house,

12 Saying, These last have wrought *but* one hour, and thou hast made them equal unto us, which have borne the burden and heat of the day.

13 But he answered one of them, and said, Friend, I do thee no wrong: didst not thou agree with me for a penny?

14 Take *that* thine *is,* and go thy way: I will give unto this last, even as unto thee.

15 Is it not lawful for me to do what I will with mine own? Is thine eye evil, because I am good?

16 So the last shall be first, and the first last: for many be called, but few chosen.

17 ¶ And Je'sus going up to Je-ru'sa-lem took the twelve disciples apart in the way, and said unto them,

18 Behold, we go up to Je-ru'sa-lem; and the Son of man shall be betrayed unto the chief priests and unto the scribes, and they shall condemn him to death,

19 And shall deliver him to the Gen'tiles to mock, and to scourge, and to crucify *him:* and the third day he shall rise again.

20 ¶ Then came to him the mother of Zeb'e-dee's children with her sons, worshipping *him,* and desiring a certain thing of him.

21 And he said unto her, What wilt thou? She saith unto him, Grant that these my two sons may sit, the one on thy right hand, and the other on the left in thy kingdom.

22 But Je′sus answered and said, Ye know not what ye ask. Are ye able to drink of the cup that I shall drink of, and to be baptized with the baptism that I am baptized with? They say unto him, We are able.

23 And he saith unto them, Ye shall drink indeed of my cup, and be baptized with the baptism that I am baptized with: but to sit on my right hand, and on my left, is not mine to give, but it shall be given to them for whom it is prepared of my Father.

24 And when the ten heard it, they were moved with indignation against the two brethren.

25 But Je′sus called them unto him, and said, Ye know that the princes of the Gen′tiles exercise dominion over them, and they that are great exercise authority upon them.

26 But it shall not be so among you: but whosoever will be great among you, let him be your minister;

27 And whosoever will be chief among you, let him be your servant:

28 Even as the Son of man came not to be ministered unto, but to minister, and to give his life a ransom for many.

29 And as they departed from Jer′i-cho, a great multitude followed him.

30 ¶ And, behold, two blind men sitting by the way side, when they heard that Je′sus passed by, cried out, saying, Have mercy on us, O Lord, thou son of Da′vid.

31 And the multitude rebuked them, because they should hold their peace: but they cried the more, saying, Have mercy on us, O Lord, thou son of Da′vid.

32 And Je′sus stood still, and called them, and said, What will ye that I shall do unto you?

33 They say unto him, Lord, that our eyes may be opened.

34 So Je′sus had compassion on them, and touched their eyes: and immediately their eyes received sight, and they followed him.

21 AND when they drew nigh unto Je-ru′sa-lem, and were come to Beth′pha-ge, unto the mount of Ol′ives, then sent Je′sus two disciples,

2 Saying unto them, Go into the village over against you, and straightway ye shall find an ass tied, and a colt with her: loose them, and bring them unto me.

3 And if any man say ought unto you, ye shall say, The Lord hath need of them; and straightway he will send them.

4 All this was done, that it might be fulfilled which was spoken by the prophet, saying,

5 Tell ye the daughter of Si′on, Behold, thy King cometh unto thee, meek, and sitting upon an ass, and a colt the foal of an ass.

6 And the disciples went, and did as Je′sus commanded them,

7 And brought the ass, and the colt, and put on them their clothes, and they set him thereon.

8 And a very great multitude spread their garments in the way; others cut down branches from the trees, and strawed them in the way.

9 And the multitudes that went before, and that followed, cried, saying, Ho-san′na to the son of Da′vid: Blessed is he that cometh in the name of the Lord; Ho-san′na in the highest.

10 And when he was come into Je-ru′sa-lem, all the city was moved, saying, Who is this?

11 And the multitude said, This is Je′sus the prophet of Naz′a-reth of Gal′i-lee.

12 ¶ And Je′sus went into the temple of God, and cast out all them that sold and bought in the temple, and overthrew the tables of the moneychangers, and the seats of them that sold doves,

13 And said unto them, It is written, My house shall be called the house of prayer; but ye have made it a den of thieves.

14 And the blind and the lame came to him in the temple; and he healed them.

15 And when the chief priests and scribes saw the wonderful things that he did, and the children crying in the temple, and saying, Ho-san′na to the son of Da′vid; they were sore displeased,

16 And said unto him, Hearest thou what these say? And Je′sus saith unto them, Yea; have ye never read, Out of the mouth of babes and sucklings thou hast perfected praise?

17 ¶ And he left them, and went out of the city into Beth′a-ny; and he lodged there.

18 Now in the morning as he returned into the city, he hungered.

19 And when he saw a fig tree in the way, he came to it, and found nothing thereon, but leaves only, and said unto it, Let no fruit grow on thee henceforward for ever. And presently the fig tree withered away.

20 And when the disciples saw it, they marvelled, saying, How soon is the fig tree withered away!

21 Je′sus answered and said unto them, Verily I say unto you, If ye have faith, and doubt not, ye shall not only do this which is done to the fig tree, but also if ye shall say unto this mountain, Be thou removed, and be thou cast into the sea; it shall be done.

22 And all things, whatsoever ye shall ask in prayer, believing, ye shall receive.

23 ¶ And when he was come into the temple, the chief priests and the elders of the people came unto him as he was teaching, and said, By what authority doest thou these things? and who gave thee this authority?

24 And Je′sus answered and said unto them, I also will ask you one thing, which if ye tell me, I in like wise will tell you by what authority I do these things.

25 The baptism of John, whence was it? from heaven, or of men? And they reasoned with themselves, saying, If we shall say, From heaven; he will say unto us, Why did ye not then believe him?

26 But if we shall say, Of men; we fear the people; for all hold John as a prophet.

27 And they answered Je′sus, and said, We cannot tell. And he said unto them, Neither tell I you by what authority I do these things.

28 ¶ But what think ye? A certain man had two sons; and he came to the first, and said, Son, go work to day in my vineyard.

29 He answered and said, I will not: but afterward he repented, and went.

30 And he came to the second, and said likewise. And he answered and said, I go, sir: and went not.

31 Whether of them twain did the will of his father? They say unto him, The first. Je′sus saith unto them, Verily I say unto you, That the publicans and the harlots go into the kingdom of God before you.

32 For John came unto you in the way of righteousness, and ye believed him not: but the publicans and the harlots believed him: and ye,

when ye had seen *it*, repented not afterward, that ye might believe him.

33 ¶ Hear another parable: There was a certain householder, which planted a vineyard, and hedged it round about, and digged a winepress in it, and built a tower, and let it out to husbandmen, and went into a far country:

34 And when the time of the fruit drew near, he sent his servants to the husbandmen, that they might receive the fruits of it.

35 And the husbandmen took his servants, and beat one, and killed another, and stoned another.

36 Again, he sent other servants more than the first: and they did unto them likewise.

37 But last of all he sent unto them his son, saying, They will reverence my son.

38 But when the husbandmen saw the son, they said among themselves, This is the heir; come, let us kill him, and let us seize on his inheritance.

39 And they caught him, and cast *him* out of the vineyard, and slew *him*.

40 When the lord therefore of the vineyard cometh, what will he do unto those husbandmen?

41 They say unto him, He will miserably destroy those wicked men, and will let out *his* vineyard unto other husbandmen, which shall render him the fruits in their seasons.

42 Je'sus saith unto them, Did ye never read in the scriptures, The stone which the builders rejected, the same is become the head of the corner: this is the Lord's doing, and it is marvellous in our eyes?

43 Therefore say I unto you, The kingdom of God shall be taken from you, and given to a nation bringing forth the fruits thereof.

44 And whosoever shall fall on this stone shall be broken: but on whomsoever it shall fall, it will grind him to powder.

45 And when the chief priests and Phar'i-sees had heard his parables, they perceived that he spake of them.

46 But when they sought to lay hands on him, they feared the multitude, because they took him for a prophet.

22 AND Je'sus answered and spake unto them again by parables, and said,

2 The kingdom of heaven is like unto a certain king, which made a marriage for his son,

3 And sent forth his servants to call them that were bidden to the wedding: and they would not come.

4 Again, he sent forth other servants, saying, Tell them which are bidden, Behold, I have prepared my dinner: my oxen and *my* fatlings *are* killed, and all things *are* ready: come unto the marriage.

5 But they made light of *it*, and went their ways, one to his farm, another to his merchandise:

6 And the remnant took his servants, and entreated *them* spitefully, and slew *them*.

7 But when the king heard *thereof*, he was wroth: and he sent forth his armies, and destroyed those murderers, and burned up their city.

8 Then saith he to his servants, The wedding is ready, but they which were bidden were not worthy.

9 Go ye therefore into the highways, and as many as ye shall find, bid to the marriage.

10 So those servants went out into the highways, and gathered together all as many as they found, both bad and good: and the wedding was furnished with guests.

11 ¶ And when the king came in to see the guests, he saw there a man which had not on a wedding garment:

12 And he saith unto him, Friend, how camest thou in hither not having a wedding garment? And he was speechless.

13 Then said the king to the servants, Bind him hand and foot, and take him away, and cast *him* into outer darkness; there shall be weeping and gnashing of teeth.

14 For many are called, but few *are* chosen.

15 ¶ Then went the Phar'i-sees, and took counsel how they might entangle him in *his* talk.

16 And they sent out unto him their disciples with the He-ro'di-ans, saying, Master, we know that thou art true, and teachest the way of God in truth, neither carest thou for any *man*: for thou regardest not the person of men.

17 Tell us therefore, What thinkest thou? Is it lawful to give tribute unto Cæ'sar, or not?

18 But Je'sus perceived their wickedness, and said, Why tempt ye me, *ye* hypocrites?

19 Shew me the tribute money. And they brought unto him a penny.

20 And he saith unto them, Whose *is* this image and superscription?

21 They say unto him, Cæ'sar's. Then saith he unto them, Render therefore unto Cæ'sar the things which are Cæ'sar's; and unto God the things that are God's.

22 When they had heard *these words*, they marvelled, and left him, and went their way.

23 ¶ The same day came to him the Sad'du-cees, which say that there is no resurrection, and asked him,

24 Saying, Master, Mo'ses said, If a man die, having no children, his brother shall marry his wife, and raise up seed unto his brother.

25 Now there were with us seven brethren: and the first, when he had married a wife, deceased, and, having no issue, left his wife unto his brother:

26 Likewise the second also, and the third, unto the seventh.

27 And last of all the woman died also.

28 Therefore in the resurrection whose wife shall she be of the seven? for they all had her.

29 Je'sus answered and said unto them, Ye do err, not knowing the scriptures, nor the power of God.

30 For in the resurrection they neither marry, nor are given in marriage, but are as the angels of God in heaven.

31 But as touching the resurrection of the dead, have ye not read that which was spoken unto you by God, saying,

32 I am the God of A'bra-ham, and the God of I'saac, and the God of Ja'cob? God is not the God of the dead, but of the living.

33 And when the multitude heard *this*, they were astonished at his doctrine.

34 ¶ But when the Phar'i-sees had heard that he had put the Sad'du-cees to silence, they were gathered together.

35 Then one of them, *which was* a lawyer, asked *him a question*, tempting him, and saying,

36 Master, which *is* the great commandment in the law?

37 Je'sus said unto him, Thou shalt love the Lord thy God with all thy heart, and with all thy soul, and with all thy mind.

38 This is the first and great commandment.

39 And the second *is* like unto it, Thou shalt love thy neighbour as thyself.

40 On these two commandments hang all the law and the prophets.

41 ¶ While the Phar'i-sees were gathered together, Je'sus asked them.

42 Saying, What think ye of Christ? whose son is he? They say unto him, *The son* of Da'vid.

43 He saith unto them, How then doth Da'vid in spirit call him Lord, saying,

44 The LORD said unto my Lord, Sit thou on my right hand, till I make thine enemies thy footstool?

45 If Da'vid then call him Lord, how is he his son?

46 And no man was able to answer him a word, neither durst any *man* from that day forth ask him any more *questions*.

23 THEN spake Je'sus to the multitude, and to his disciples,

2 Saying, The scribes and the Phar'i-sees sit in Mo'ses' seat:

3 All therefore whatsoever they bid you observe, *that* observe and do; but do not ye after their works: for they say, and do not.

4 For they bind heavy burdens and grievous to be borne, and lay *them* on men's shoulders; but they *themselves* will not move them with one of their fingers.

5 But all their works they do for to be seen of men: they make broad their phylacteries, and enlarge the borders of their garments,

6 And love the uppermost rooms at feasts, and the chief seats in the synagogues,

7 And greetings in the markets, and to be called of men, Rab'bi, Rab'bi.

8 But be not ye called Rab'bi: for one is your Master, *even* Christ; and all ye are brethren.

9 And call no *man* your father upon the earth: for one is your Father, which is in heaven.

10 Neither be ye called masters: for one is your Master, *even* Christ.

11 But he that is greatest among you shall be your servant.

12 And whosoever shall exalt himself shall be abased; and he that shall humble himself shall be exalted.

13 ¶ But woe unto you, scribes and Phar'i-sees, hypocrites! for ye shut up the kingdom of heaven against men: for ye neither go in *yourselves*, neither suffer ye them that are entering to go in.

14 Woe unto you, scribes and Phar'i-sees, hypocrites! for ye devour widows' houses, and for a pretence make long prayer: therefore ye shall receive the greater damnation.

15 Woe unto you, scribes and Phar'i-sees, hypocrites! for ye compass sea and land to make one proselyte, and when he is made, ye make him twofold more the child of hell than yourselves.

16 Woe unto you, ye blind guides, which say, Whosoever shall swear by the temple, it is nothing; but whosoever shall swear by the gold of the temple, he is a debtor!

17 Ye fools and blind: for whether is greater, the gold, or the temple that sanctifieth the gold?

18 And, Whosoever shall swear by the altar, it is nothing; but whosoever sweareth by the gift that is upon it, he is guilty.

19 Ye fools and blind: for whether is greater, the gift, or the altar that sanctifieth the gift?

20 Whoso therefore shall swear by the altar, sweareth by it, and by all things thereon.

21 And whoso shall swear by the temple, sweareth by it, and by him that dwelleth therein.

22 And he that shall swear by heaven, sweareth by the throne of God, and by him that sitteth thereon.

23 Woe unto you, scribes and Phar'i-sees, hypocrites! for ye pay tithe of mint and anise and cummin, and have omitted the weightier *matters* of the law, judgment, mercy, and faith: these ought ye to have done, and not to leave the other undone.

24 Ye blind guides, which strain at a gnat, and swallow a camel.

25 Woe unto you, scribes and Phar'i-sees, hypocrites! for ye make clean the outside of the cup and of the platter, but within they are full of extortion and excess.

26 *Thou* blind Phar'i-see, cleanse first that *which* is within the cup and platter, that the outside of them may be clean also.

27 Woe unto you, scribes and Phar'i-sees, hypocrites! for ye are like unto whited sepulchres, which indeed appear beautiful outward, but are within full of dead *men's* bones, and of all uncleanness.

28 Even so ye also outwardly appear righteous unto men, but within ye are full of hypocrisy and iniquity.

29 Woe unto you, scribes and Phar'i-sees, hypocrites! because ye build the tombs of the prophets, and garnish the sepulchres of the righteous,

30 And say, If we had been in the days of our fathers, we would not have been partakers with them in the blood of the prophets.

31 Wherefore ye be witnesses unto yourselves, that ye are the children of them which killed the prophets.

32 Fill ye up then the measure of your fathers.

33 Ye serpents, ye generation of vipers, how can ye escape the damnation of hell?

34 ¶ Wherefore, behold, I send unto you prophets, and wise men, and scribes: and *some* of them ye shall kill and crucify; and *some* of them shall ye scourge in your synagogues, and persecute *them* from city to city:

35 That upon you may come all the righteous blood shed upon the earth, from the blood of righteous A'bel unto the blood of Zach-a-ri'as son of Bar-a-chi'as, whom ye slew between the temple and the altar.

36 Verily I say unto you, All these things shall come upon this generation.

37 O Je-ru'sa-lem, Je-ru'sa-lem, *thou* that killest the prophets, and stonest them which are sent unto thee, how often would I have gathered thy children together, even as a hen gathereth her chickens under *her* wings, and ye would not!

38 Behold, your house is left unto you desolate.

39 For I say unto you, Ye shall not see me henceforth, till ye shall say, Blessed *is* he that cometh in the name of the Lord.

24 AND Je'sus went out, and departed from the temple: and his disciples came to *him* for to shew him the buildings of the temple.

2 And Je'sus said unto them, See ye not all these things? verily I say unto you, There shall not be left here one stone upon another, that shall not be thrown down.

3 ¶ And as he sat upon the mount of Ol'ives, the disciples came unto him privately, saying, Tell us, when shall these things be? and what

shall be the sign of thy coming, and of the end of the world?

4 And Je´sus answered and said unto them, Take heed that no man deceive you.

5 For many shall come in my name, saying, I am Christ; and shall deceive many.

6 And ye shall hear of wars and rumours of wars: see that ye be not troubled: for all *these things* must come to pass, but the end is not yet.

7 For nation shall rise against nation, and kingdom against kingdom: and there shall be famines, and pestilences, and earthquakes, in divers places.

8 All these *are* the beginning of sorrows.

9 Then shall they deliver you up to be afflicted, and shall kill you: and ye shall be hated of all nations for my name's sake.

10 And then shall many be offended, and shall betray one another, and shall hate one another.

11 And many false prophets shall rise, and shall deceive many.

12 And because iniquity shall abound, the love of many shall wax cold.

13 But he that shall endure unto the end, the same shall be saved.

14 And this gospel of the kingdom shall be preached in all the world for a witness unto all nations; and then shall the end come.

15 When ye therefore shall see the abomination of desolation, spoken of by Dan´iel the prophet, stand in the holy place, (whoso readeth, let him understand:)

16 Then let them which be in Ju-dæ´a flee into the mountains:

17 Let him which is on the house top not come down to take any thing out of his house:

18 Neither let him which is in the field return back to take his clothes.

19 And woe unto them that are with child, and to them that give suck in those days!

20 But pray ye that your flight be not in the winter, neither on the sabbath day:

21 For then shall be great tribulation, such as was not since the beginning of the world to this time, no, nor ever shall be.

22 And except those days should be shortened, there should no flesh be saved: but for the elect's sake those days shall be shortened.

23 Then if any man shall say unto you, Lo, here *is* Christ, or there; believe *it* not.

24 For there shall arise false Christs, and false prophets, and shall shew great signs and wonders; insomuch that, if *it were* possible, they shall deceive the very elect.

25 Behold, I have told you before.

26 Wherefore if they shall say unto you, Behold, he is in the desert; go not forth: behold, *he is* in the secret chambers; believe *it* not.

27 For as the lightning cometh out of the east, and shineth even unto the west; so shall also the coming of the Son of man be.

28 For wheresoever the carcase is, there will the eagles be gathered together.

29 ¶ Immediately after the tribulation of those days shall the sun be darkened, and the moon shall not give her light, and the stars shall fall from heaven, and the powers of the heavens shall be shaken:

30 And then shall appear the sign of the Son of man in heaven: and then shall all the tribes of the earth mourn, and they shall see the Son of man coming in the clouds of heaven with power and great glory.

31 And he shall send his angels with a great sound of a trumpet, and they shall gather together his elect from the four winds, from one end of heaven to the other.

32 Now learn a parable of the fig tree; When his branch is yet tender, and putteth forth leaves, ye know that summer *is* nigh:

33 So likewise ye, when ye shall see all these things, know that it is near, *even* at the doors.

34 Verily I say unto you, This generation shall not pass, till all these things be fulfilled.

35 Heaven and earth shall pass away, but my words shall not pass away.

36 ¶ But of that day and hour knoweth no *man*, no, not the angels of heaven, but my Father only.

37 But as the days of No´e *were*, so shall also the coming of the Son of man be.

38 For as in the days that were before the flood they were eating and drinking, marrying and giving in marriage, until the day that No´e entered into the ark,

39 And knew not until the flood came, and took them all away; so shall also the coming of the Son of man be.

40 Then shall two be in the field; the one shall be taken, and the other left.

41 Two *women shall* be grinding at the mill; the one shall be taken, and the other left.

42 ¶ Watch therefore: for ye know not what hour your Lord doth come.

43 But know this, that if the goodman of the house had known in what watch the thief would come, he would have watched, and would not have suffered his house to be broken up.

44 Therefore be ye also ready: for in such an hour as ye think not the Son of man cometh.

45 Who then is a faithful and wise servant, whom his lord hath made ruler over his household, to give them meat in due season?

46 Blessed *is* that servant, whom his lord when he cometh shall find so doing.

47 Verily I say unto you, That he shall make him ruler over all his goods.

48 But and if that evil servant shall say in his heart, My lord delayeth his coming;

49 And shall begin to smite *his* fellowservants, and to eat and drink with the drunken;

50 The lord of that servant shall come in a day when he looketh not for *him*, and in an hour that he is not aware of,

51 And shall cut him asunder, and appoint *him* his portion with the hypocrites: there shall be weeping and gnashing of teeth.

25

THEN shall the kingdom of heaven be likened unto ten virgins, which took their lamps, and went forth to meet the bridegroom.

2 And five of them were wise, and five *were* foolish.

3 They that *were* foolish took their lamps, and took no oil with them:

4 But the wise took oil in their vessels with their lamps.

5 While the bridegroom tarried, they all slumbered and slept.

6 And at midnight there was a cry made, Behold, the bridegroom cometh; go ye out to meet him.

7 Then all those virgins arose, and trimmed their lamps.

8 And the foolish said unto the wise, Give us of your oil; for our lamps are gone out.

9 But the wise answered, saying, Not so; lest there be not enough for us and you: but go ye rather to them that sell, and buy for yourselves.

10 And while they went to buy, the bridegroom came; and they that were ready went in

with him to the marriage: and the door was shut.

11 Afterward came also the other virgins, saying, Lord, Lord, open to us.

12 But he answered and said, Verily I say unto you, I know you not.

13 Watch therefore, for ye know neither the day nor the hour wherein the Son of man cometh.

14 ¶ For *the kingdom of heaven is* as a man travelling into a far country, *who* called his own servants, and delivered unto them his goods.

15 And unto one he gave five talents, to another two, and to another one; to every man according to his several ability; and straightway took his journey.

16 Then he that had received the five talents went and traded with the same, and made *them* other five talents.

17 And likewise he that *had received* two, he also gained other two.

18 But he that had received one went and digged in the earth, and hid his lord's money.

19 After a long time the lord of those servants cometh, and reckoneth with them.

20 And so he that had received five talents came and brought other five talents, saying, Lord, thou deliveredst unto me five talents: behold, I have gained beside them five talents more.

21 His lord said unto him, Well done, *thou* good and faithful servant: thou hast been faithful over a few things, I will make thee ruler over many things: enter thou into the joy of thy lord.

22 He also that had received two talents came and said, Lord, thou deliveredst unto me two talents: behold, I have gained two other talents beside them.

23 His lord said unto him, Well done, good and faithful servant; thou hast been faithful over a few things, I will make thee ruler over many things: enter thou into the joy of thy lord.

24 Then he which had received the one talent came and said, Lord, I knew thee that thou art an hard man, reaping where thou hast not sown, and gathering where thou hast not strawed:

25 And I was afraid, and went and hid thy talent in the earth: lo, *there* thou hast *that is* thine.

26 His lord answered and said unto him, *Thou* wicked and slothful servant, thou knewest that I reap where I sowed not, and gather where I have not strawed:

27 Thou oughtest therefore to have put my money to the exchangers, and *then* at my coming I should have received mine own with usury.

28 Take therefore the talent from him, and give *it* unto him which hath ten talents.

29 For unto every one that hath shall be given, and he shall have abundance: but from him that hath not shall be taken away even that which he hath.

30 And cast ye the unprofitable servant into outer darkness: there shall be weeping and gnashing of teeth.

31 ¶ When the Son of man shall come in his glory, and all the holy angels with him, then shall he sit upon the throne of his glory:

32 And before him shall be gathered all nations: and he shall separate them one from another, as a shepherd divideth *his* sheep from the goats:

33 And he shall set the sheep on his right hand, but the goats on the left.

34 Then shall the King say unto them on his right hand, Come, ye blessed of my Father, inherit the kingdom prepared for you from the foundation of the world:

35 For I was an hungred, and ye gave me meat: I was thirsty, and ye gave me drink: I was a stranger, and ye took me in:

36 Naked, and ye clothed me: I was sick, and ye visited me: I was in prison, and ye came unto me.

37 Then shall the righteous answer him, saying, Lord, when saw we thee an hungred, and fed *thee*? or thirsty, and gave *thee* drink?

38 When saw we thee a stranger, and took *thee* in? or naked, and clothed *thee*?

39 Or when saw we thee sick, or in prison, and came unto thee?

40 And the King shall answer and say unto them, Verily I say unto you, Inasmuch as ye have done *it* unto one of the least of these my brethren, ye have done *it* unto me.

41 Then shall he say also unto them on the left hand, Depart from me, ye cursed, into everlasting fire, prepared for the devil and his angels:

42 For I was an hungred, and ye gave me no meat: I was thirsty, and ye gave me no drink:

43 I was a stranger, and ye took me not in: naked, and ye clothed me not: sick, and in prison, and ye visited me not.

44 Then shall they also answer him, saying, Lord, when saw we thee an hungred, or athirst, or a stranger, or naked, or sick, or in prison, and did not minister unto thee?

45 Then shall he answer them, saying, Verily I say unto you, Inasmuch as ye did *it* not to one of the least of these, ye did *it* not to me.

46 And these shall go away into everlasting punishment: but the righteous into life eternal.

26 AND it came to pass, when Je'sus had finished all these sayings, he said unto his disciples,

2 Ye know that after two days is *the feast of* the passover, and the Son of man is betrayed to be crucified.

3 Then assembled together the chief priests, and the scribes, and the elders of the people, unto the palace of the high priest, who was called Ca'ia-phas,

4 And consulted that they might take Je'sus by subtilty, and kill *him*.

5 But they said, Not on the feast *day*, lest there be an uproar among the people.

6 ¶ Now when Je'sus was in Beth'a-ny, in the house of Si'mon the leper,

7 There came unto him a woman having an alabaster box of very precious ointment, and poured it on his head, as he sat *at meat*.

8 But when his disciples saw *it*, they had indignation, saying, To what purpose *is* this waste?

9 For this ointment might have been sold for much, and given to the poor.

10 When Je'sus understood *it*, he said unto them, Why trouble ye the woman? for she hath wrought a good work upon me.

11 For ye have the poor always with you; but me ye have not always.

12 For in that she hath poured this ointment on my body, she did *it* for my burial.

13 Verily I say unto you, Wheresoever this gospel shall be preached in the whole world, *there* shall also this, that this woman hath done, be told for a memorial of her.

14 ¶ Then one of the twelve, called Ju'das Is-car'i-ot, went unto the chief priests,

15 And said *unto them*, What will ye give

me, and I will deliver him unto you? And they covenanted with him for thirty pieces of silver.

16 And from that time he sought opportunity to betray him.

17 ¶ Now the first *day* of the *feast of* unleavened bread the disciples came to Je′sus, saying unto him, Where wilt thou that we prepare for thee to eat the passover?

18 And he said, Go into the city to such a man, and say unto him, The Master saith, My time is at hand; I will keep the passover at thy house with my disciples.

19 And the disciples did as Je′sus had appointed them; and they made ready the passover.

20 Now when the even was come, he sat down with the twelve.

21 And as they did eat, he said, Verily I say unto you, that one of you shall betray me.

22 And they were exceeding sorrowful, and began every one of them to say unto him, Lord, is it I?

23 And he answered and said, He that dippeth *his* hand with me in the dish, the same shall betray me.

24 The Son of man goeth as it is written of him: but woe unto that man by whom the Son of man is betrayed! it had been good for that man if he had not been born.

25 Then Ju′das, which betrayed him, answered and said, Master, is it I? He said unto him, Thou hast said.

26 ¶ And as they were eating, Je′sus took bread, and blessed *it,* and brake *it,* and gave *it* to the disciples, and said, Take, eat; this is my body.

27 And he took the cup, and gave thanks, and gave *it* to them, saying, Drink ye all of it;

28 For this is my blood of the new testament, which is shed for many for the remission of sins.

29 But I say unto you, I will not drink henceforth of this fruit of the vine, until that day when I drink it new with you in my Father's kingdom.

30 And when they had sung an hymn, they went out into the mount of Ol′ives.

31 Then saith Je′sus unto them, All ye shall be offended because of me this night: for it is written, I will smite the shepherd, and the sheep of the flock shall be scattered abroad.

32 But after I am risen again, I will go before you into Gal′i-lee.

33 Pe′ter answered and said unto him, Though all *men* shall be offended because of thee, *yet* will I never be offended.

34 Je′sus said unto him, Verily I say unto thee, That this night, before the cock crow, thou shalt deny me thrice.

35 Pe′ter said unto him, Though I should die with thee, yet will I not deny thee. Likewise also said all the disciples.

36 ¶ Then cometh Je′sus with them unto a place called Geth-sem′a-ne, and saith unto the disciples, Sit ye here, while I go and pray yonder.

37 And he took with him Pe′ter and the two sons of Zeb′e-dee, and began to be sorrowful and very heavy.

38 Then saith he unto them, My soul is exceeding sorrowful, even unto death: tarry ye here, and watch with me.

39 And he went a little farther, and fell on his face, and prayed, saying, O my Father, if it be possible, let this cup pass from me: nevertheless not as I will, but as thou *wilt.*

40 And he cometh unto the disciples, and findeth them asleep, and saith unto Pe′ter, What, could ye not watch with me one hour?

41 Watch and pray, that ye enter not into temptation: the spirit indeed *is* willing, but the flesh *is* weak.

42 He went away again the second time, and prayed, saying, O my Father, if this cup may not pass away from me, except I drink it, thy will be done.

43 And he came and found them asleep again: for their eyes were heavy.

44 And he left them, and went away again, and prayed the third time, saying the same words.

45 Then cometh he to his disciples, and saith unto them, Sleep on now, and take *your* rest: behold, the hour is at hand, and the Son of man is betrayed into the hands of sinners.

46 Rise, let us be going: behold, he is at hand that doth betray me.

47 ¶ And while he yet spake, lo, Ju′das, one of the twelve, came, and with him a great multitude with swords and staves, from the chief priests and elders of the people.

48 Now he that betrayed him gave them a sign, saying, Whomsoever I shall kiss, that same is he: hold him fast.

49 And forthwith he came to Je′sus, and said, Hail, master; and kissed him.

50 And Je′sus said unto him, Friend, wherefore art thou come? Then came they, and laid hands on Je′sus, and took him.

51 And, behold, one of them which were with Je′sus stretched out *his* hand, and drew his sword, and struck a servant of the high priest's, and smote off his ear.

52 Then said Je′sus unto him, Put up again thy sword into his place: for all they that take the sword shall perish with the sword.

53 Thinkest thou that I cannot now pray to my Father, and he shall presently give me more than twelve legions of angels?

54 But how then shall the scriptures be fulfilled, that thus it must be?

55 In that same hour said Je′sus to the multitudes, Are ye come out as against a thief with swords and staves for to take me? I sat daily with you teaching in the temple, and ye laid no hold on me.

56 But all this was done, that the scriptures of the prophets might be fulfilled. Then all the disciples forsook him, and fled.

57 ¶ And they that had laid hold on Je′sus led *him* away to Ca′ia-phas the high priest, where the scribes and the elders were assembled.

58 But Pe′ter followed him afar off unto the high priest's palace, and went in, and sat with the servants, to see the end.

59 Now the chief priests, and elders, and all the council, sought false witness against Je′sus, to put him to death;

60 But found none: yea, though many false witnesses came, *yet* found they none. At the last came two false witnesses,

61 And said, This *fellow* said, I am able to destroy the temple of God, and to build it in three days.

62 And the high priest arose, and said unto him, Answerest thou nothing? what *is it* which these witness against thee?

63 But Je′sus held his peace. And the high priest answered and said unto him, I adjure thee by the living God, that thou tell us whether thou be the Christ, the Son of God.

64 Je′sus saith unto him, Thou hast said: nevertheless I say unto you, Hereafter shall ye see

the Son of man sitting on the right hand of power, and coming in the clouds of heaven.

65 Then the high priest rent his clothes, saying, He hath spoken blasphemy; what further need have we of witnesses? behold, now ye have heard his blasphemy.

66 What think ye? They answered and said, He is guilty of death.

67 Then did they spit in his face, and buffeted him; and others smote *him* with the palms of their hands,

68 Saying, Prophesy unto us, thou Christ, Who is he that smote thee?

69 ¶ Now Pe′ter sat without in the palace: and a damsel came unto him, saying, Thou also wast with Je′sus of Gal′i-lee.

70 But he denied before *them* all, saying, I know not what thou sayest.

71 And when he was gone out into the porch, another *maid* saw him, and said unto them that were there, This *fellow* was also with Je′sus of Naz′a-reth.

72 And again he denied with an oath, I do not know the man.

73 And after a while came unto *him* they that stood by, and said to Pe′ter, Surely thou also art *one* of them; for thy speech bewrayeth thee.

74 Then began he to curse and to swear, *saying*, I know not the man. And immediately the cock crew.

75 And Pe′ter remembered the word of Je′sus, which said unto him, Before the cock crow, thou shalt deny me thrice. And he went out, and wept bitterly.

27 WHEN the morning was come, all the chief priests and elders of the people took counsel against Je′sus to put him to death:

2 And when they had bound him, they led *him* away, and delivered him to Pon′ti-us Pi′late the governor.

3 ¶ Then Ju′das, which had betrayed him, when he saw that he was condemned, repented himself, and brought again the thirty pieces of silver to the chief priests and elders,

4 Saying, I have sinned in that I have betrayed the innocent blood. And they said, What *is that* to us? see thou *to that*.

5 And he cast down the pieces of silver in the temple, and departed, and went and hanged himself.

6 And the chief priests took the silver pieces, and said, It is not lawful for to put them into the treasury, because it is the price of blood.

7 And they took counsel, and bought with them the potter's field, to bury strangers in.

8 Wherefore that field was called, The field of blood, unto this day.

9 Then was fulfilled that which was spoken by Jer′e-my the prophet, saying, And they took the thirty pieces of silver, the price of him that was valued, whom they of the children of Is′ra-el did value;

10 And gave them for the potter's field, as the Lord appointed me.

11 And Je′sus stood before the governor: and the governor asked him, saying, Art thou the King of the Jews? And Je′sus said unto him, Thou sayest.

12 And when he was accused of the chief priests and elders, he answered nothing.

13 Then said Pi′late unto him, Hearest thou not how many things they witness against thee?

14 And he answered him to never a word; insomuch that the governor marvelled greatly.

15 Now at *that* feast the governor was wont to release unto the people a prisoner, whom they would.

16 And they had then a notable prisoner, called Ba-rab′bas.

17 Therefore when they were gathered together, Pi′late said unto them, Whom will ye that I release unto you? Ba-rab′bas, or Je′sus which is called Christ?

18 For he knew that for envy they had delivered him.

19 ¶ When he was set down on the judgment seat, his wife sent unto him, saying, Have thou nothing to do with that just man: for I have suffered many things this day in a dream because of him,

20 But the chief priests and elders persuaded the multitude that they should ask Ba-rab′bas, and destroy Je′sus.

21 The governor answered and said unto them, Whether of the twain will ye that I release unto you? They said, Ba-rab′bas.

22 Pi′late saith unto them, What shall I do then with Je′sus which is called Christ? *They* all say unto him, Let him be crucified.

23 And the governor said, Why, what evil hath he done? But they cried out the more, saying, Let him be crucified.

24 ¶ When Pi′late saw that he could prevail nothing, but *that* rather a tumult was made, he took water, and washed *his* hands before the multitude, saying, I am innocent of the blood of this just person: see ye *to it*.

25 Then answered all the people, and said, His blood *be* on us, and on our children.

26 ¶ Then released he Ba-rab′bas unto them: and when he had scourged Je′sus, he delivered *him* to be crucified.

27 Then the soldiers of the governor took Je′-sus into the common hall, and gathered unto him the whole band *of soldiers*.

28 And they stripped him, and put on him a scarlet robe.

29 ¶ And when they had platted a crown of thorns, they put *it* upon his head, and a reed in his right hand: and they bowed the knee before him, and mocked him, saying, Hail, King of the Jews!

30 And they spit upon him, and took the reed, and smote him on the head.

31 And after that they had mocked him, they took the robe off from him, and put his own raiment on him, and led him away to crucify *him*.

32 And as they came out, they found a man of Cy-re′ne, Si′mon by name: him they compelled to bear his cross.

33 And when they were come unto a place called Gol′go-tha, that is to say, a place of a skull,

34 ¶ They gave him vinegar to drink mingled with gall: and when he had tasted *thereof*, he would not drink.

35 And they crucified him, and parted his garments, casting lots: that it might be fulfilled which was spoken by the prophet, They parted my garments among them, and upon my vesture did they cast lots.

36 And sitting down they watched him there;

37 And set up over his head his accusation written, THIS IS JE′SUS THE KING OF THE JEWS.

38 Then were there two thieves crucified with him, one on the right hand, and another on the left.

39 ¶ And they that passed by reviled him, wagging their heads,

40 And saying, Thou that destroyest the tem-

ple, and buildest *it* in three days, save thyself. If thou be the Son of God, come down from the cross.

41 Likewise also the chief priests mocking *him*, with the scribes and elders, said,

42 He saved others; himself he cannot save. If he be the King of Is'ra-el, let him now come down from the cross, and we will believe him.

43 He trusted in God; let him deliver him now, if he will have him: for he said, I am the Son of God.

44 The thieves also, which were crucified with him, cast the same in his teeth.

45 Now from the sixth hour there was darkness over all the land unto the ninth hour.

46 And about the ninth hour Je'sus cried with a loud voice, saying, E'li, E'li, la'ma sa-bach-tha'ni? that is to say, My God, my God, why hast thou forsaken me?

47 Some of them that stood there, when they heard *that*, said, This *man* calleth for E-li'as.

48 And straightway one of them ran, and took a spunge, and filled *it* with vinegar, and put *it* on a reed, and gave him to drink.

49 The rest said, Let be, let us see whether E-li'as will come to save him.

50 ¶ Je'sus, when he had cried again with a loud voice, yielded up the ghost.

51 And, behold, the veil of the temple was rent in twain from the top to the bottom; and the earth did quake, and the rocks rent;

52 And the graves were opened; and many bodies of the saints which slept arose,

53 And came out of the graves after his resurrection, and went into the holy city, and appeared unto many.

54 Now when the centurion, and they that were with him, watching Je'sus, saw the earthquake, and those things that were done, they feared greatly, saying, Truly this was the Son of God.

55 And many women were there beholding afar off, which followed Je'sus from Gal'i-lee, ministering unto him:

56 Among which was Ma'ry Mag-da-le'ne, and Ma'ry the mother of James and Jo'ses, and the mother of Zeb'e-dee's children.

57 When the even was come, there came a rich man of Ar-i-ma-thæ'a, named Jo'seph, who also himself was Je'sus' disciple:

58 He went to Pi'late, and begged the body of Je'sus. Then Pi'late commanded the body to be delivered.

59 And when Jo'seph had taken the body, he wrapped it in a clean linen cloth,

60 And laid it in his own new tomb, which he had hewn out in the rock: and he rolled a great stone to the door of the sepulchre, and departed.

61 And there was Ma'ry Mag-da-le'ne, and the other Ma'ry, sitting over against the sepulchre.

62 ¶ Now the next day, that followed the day of the preparation, the chief priests and Phar'i-sees came together unto Pi'late,

63 Saying, Sir, we remember that that deceiver said, while he was yet alive, After three days I will rise again.

64 Command therefore that the sepulchre be made sure until the third day, lest his disciples come by night, and steal him away, and say unto the people, He is risen from the dead: so the last error shall be worse than the first.

65 Pi'late said unto them, Ye have a watch: go your way, make *it* as sure as ye can.

66 So they went, and made the sepulchre sure, sealing the stone, and setting a watch.

28 IN the end of the sabbath, as it began to dawn toward the first *day* of the week, came Ma'ry Mag-da-le'ne and the other Ma'ry to see the sepulchre.

2 And, behold, there was a great earthquake: for the angel of the Lord descended from heaven, and came and rolled back the stone from the door, and sat upon it.

3 His countenance was like lightning, and his raiment white as snow:

4 And for fear of him the keepers did shake, and became as dead *men*,

5 And the angel answered and said unto the women, Fear not ye: for I know that ye seek Je'sus, which was crucified.

6 He is not here: for he is risen, as he said. Come, see the place where the Lord lay.

7 And go quickly, and tell his disciples that he is risen from the dead; and, behold, he goeth before you into Gal'i-lee; there shall ye see him: lo, I have told you.

8 And they departed quickly from the sepulchre with fear and great joy; and did run to bring his disciples word.

9 ¶ And as they went to tell his disciples, behold, Je'sus met them, saying All hail. And they came and held him by the feet, and worshipped him.

10 Then said Je'sus unto them, Be not afraid: go tell my brethren that they go into Gal'i-lee, and there shall they see me.

11 ¶ Now when they were going, behold, some of the watch came into the city, and shewed unto the chief priests all the things that were done.

12 And when they were assembled with the elders, and had taken counsel, they gave large money unto the soldiers,

13 Saying, Say ye, His disciples came by night, and stole him *away* while we slept.

14 And if this come to the governor's ears, we will persuade him, and secure you.

15 So they took the money, and did as they were taught: and this saying is commonly reported among the Jews until this day.

16 ¶ Then the eleven disciples went away into Gal'i-lee, into a mountain where Je'sus had appointed them.

17 And when they saw him, they worshipped him: but some doubted.

18 And Je'sus came and spake unto them, saying, All power is given unto me in heaven and in earth.

19 Go ye therefore, and teach all nations, baptizing them in the name of the Father, and of the Son, and of the Ho'ly Ghost:

20 Teaching them to observe all things whatsoever I have commanded you: and, lo, I am with you alway, *even* unto the end of the world. Amen.

MARK

1 THE beginning of the gospel of Je′sus Christ, the Son of God;

2 As it is written in the prophets, Behold, I send my messenger before thy face, which shall prepare thy way before thee.

3 The voice of one crying in the wilderness, Prepare ye the way of the Lord, make his paths straight.

4 John did baptize in the wilderness, and preach the baptism of repentance for the remission of sins.

5 And there went out unto him all the land of Ju-dæ′a, and they of Je-ru′sa-lem, and were all baptized of him in the river of Jor′dan, confessing their sins.

6 And John was clothed with camel's hair, and with a girdle of a skin about his loins; and he did eat locusts and wild honey;

7 And preached, saying, There cometh one mightier than I after me, the latchet of whose shoes I am not worthy to stoop down and unloose.

8 I indeed have baptized you with water: but he shall baptize you with the Ho′ly Ghost.

9 And it came to pass in those days, that Je′sus came from Naz′a-reth of Gal′i-lee, and was baptized of John in Jor′dan.

10 And straightway coming up out of the water, he saw the heavens opened, and the Spirit like a dove descending upon him:

11 And there came a voice from heaven, saying, Thou art my beloved Son, in whom I am well pleased.

12 And immediately the spirit driveth him into the wilderness.

13 And he was there in the wilderness forty days, tempted of Sa′tan; and was with the wild beasts; and the angels ministered unto him.

14 Now after that John was put in prison, Je′sus came into Gal′i-lee, preaching the gospel of the kingdom of God,

15 And saying, The time is fulfilled, and the kingdom of God is at hand: repent ye, and believe the gospel.

16 Now as he walked by the sea of Gal′i-lee, he saw Si′mon and Andrew his brother casting a net into the sea: for they were fishers.

17 And Je′sus said unto them, Come ye after me, and I will make you to become fishers of men.

18 And straightway they forsook their nets, and followed him.

19 And when he had gone a little farther thence, he saw James the son of Zeb′e-dee, and John his brother, who also were in the ship mending their nets.

20 And straightway he called them: and they left their father Zeb′e-dee in the ship with the hired servants, and went after him.

21 And they went into Ca-per′na-um; and straightway on the sabbath day he entered into the synagogue, and taught.

22 And they were astonished at his doctrine: for he taught them as one that had authority, and not as the scribes.

23 And there was in their synagogue a man with an unclean spirit; and he cried out,

24 Saying, Let us alone; what have we to do with thee, thou Je′sus of Naz′a-reth? art thou come to destroy us? I know thee who thou art, the Holy One of God.

25 And Je′sus rebuked him, saying, Hold thy peace, and come out of him.

26 And when the unclean spirit had torn him, and cried with a loud voice, he came out of him.

27 And they were all amazed, insomuch that they questioned among themselves, saying, What thing is this? what new doctrine is this? for with authority commandeth he even the unclean spirits, and they do obey him.

28 And immediately his fame spread abroad throughout all the region round about Gal′i-lee.

29 And forthwith, when they were come out of the synagogue, they entered into the house of Si′mon and Andrew, with James and John.

30 But Si′mon's wife's mother lay sick of a fever, and anon they tell him of her.

31 And he came and took her by the hand, and lifted her up; and immediately the fever left her, and she ministered unto them.

32 And at even, when the sun did set, they brought unto him all that were diseased, and them that were possessed with devils.

33 And all the city was gathered together at the door.

34 And he healed many that were sick of divers diseases, and cast out many devils; and suffered not the devils to speak, because they knew him.

35 And in the morning, rising up a great while before day, he went out, and departed into a solitary place, and there prayed.

36 And Si′mon and they that were with him followed after him.

37 And when they had found him, they said unto him, All men seek for thee.

38 And he said unto them, Let us go into the next towns, that I may preach there also: for therefore came I forth.

39 And he preached in their synagogues throughout all Gal′i-lee, and cast out devils.

40 And there came a leper to him, beseeching him, and kneeling down to him, and saying unto him, If thou wilt, thou canst make me clean.

41 And Je′sus, moved with compassion, put forth his hand, and touched him, and saith unto him, I will; be thou clean.

42 And as soon as he had spoken, immediately the leprosy departed from him, and he was cleansed.

43 And he straitly charged him, and forthwith sent him away;

44 And saith unto him, See thou say nothing to any man: but go thy way, shew thyself to the priest, and offer for thy cleansing those things which Mo′ses commanded, for a testimony unto them.

45 But he went out, and began to publish it much, and to blaze abroad the matter, insomuch that Je′sus could no more openly enter into the city, but was without in desert places: and they came to him from every quarter.

2 AND again he entered into Ca-per′na-um after some days; and it was noised that he was in the house.

2 And straightway many were gathered together, insomuch that there was no room to receive them, no, not so much as about the door: and he preached the word unto them.

3 And they come unto him, bringing one sick of the palsy, which was borne of four.

4 And when they could not come nigh unto him for the press, they uncovered the roof where he was: and when they had broken *it* up, they let down the bed wherein the sick of the palsy lay.

5 When Je'sus saw their faith, he said unto the sick of the palsy, Son, thy sins be forgiven thee.

6 But there were certain of the scribes sitting there, and reasoning in their hearts,

7 Why doth this *man* thus speak blasphemies? who can forgive sins but God only?

8 And immediately Je'sus perceived in his spirit that they so reasoned within themselves, he said unto them, Why reason ye these things in your hearts?

9 Whether is it easier to say to the sick of the palsy, *Thy* sins be forgiven thee; or to say, Arise, and take up thy bed, and walk?

10 But that ye may know that the Son of man hath power on earth to forgive sins, (he saith to the sick of the palsy,)

11 I say unto thee, Arise, and take up thy bed, and go thy way into thine house.

12 And immediately he arose, took up the bed, and went forth before them all; insomuch that they were all amazed, and glorified God, saying, We never saw it on this fashion.

13 And he went forth again by the sea side; and all the multitude resorted unto him, and he taught them.

14 And as he passed by, he saw Le'vi the *son* of Al-phæ'us sitting at the receipt of custom, and said unto him, Follow me. And he arose and followed him.

15 And it came to pass, that, as Je'sus sat at meat in his house, many publicans and sinners sat also together with Je'sus and his disciples: for there were many, and they followed him.

16 And when the scribes and Phar'i-sees saw him eat with publicans and sinners, they said unto his disciples, How is it that he eateth and drinketh with publicans and sinners?

17 When Je'sus heard *it*, he saith unto them, They that are whole have no need of the physician, but they that are sick: I came not to call the righteous, but sinners to repentance.

18 And the disciples of John and of the Phar'-i-sees used to fast: and they come and say unto him, Why do the disciples of John and of the Phar'i-sees fast, but thy disciples fast not?

19 And Je'sus said unto them, Can the children of the bridechamber fast, while the bridegroom is with them? as long as they have the bridegroom with them, they cannot fast.

20 But the days will come, when the bridegroom shall be taken away from them, and then shall they fast in those days.

21 No man also seweth a piece of new cloth on an old garment: else the new piece that filled it up taketh away from the old, and the rent is made worse.

22 And no man putteth new wine into old bottles: else the new wine doth burst the bottles, and the wine is spilled, and the bottles will be marred: but new wine must be put into new bottles.

23 And it came to pass, that he went through the corn fields on the sabbath day; and his disciples began, as they went, to pluck the ears of corn.

24 And the Phar'i-sees said unto him, Behold, why do they on the sabbath day that which is not lawful?

25 And he said unto them, Have ye never read what Da'vid did, when he had need, and was an hungred, he, and they that were with him?

26 How he went into the house of God in the days of A-bi'a-thar the high priest, and did eat the shewbread, which is not lawful to eat but for the priests, and gave also to them which were with him?

27 And he said unto them, The sabbath was made for man, and not man for the sabbath:

28 Therefore the Son of man is Lord also of the sabbath.

3 AND he entered again into the synagogue; and there was a man there which had a withered hand.

2 And they watched him, whether he would heal him on the sabbath day; that they might accuse him.

3 And he saith unto the man which had the withered hand, Stand forth.

4 And he saith unto them, Is it lawful to do good on the sabbath days, or to do evil? to save life, or to kill? But they held their peace.

5 And when he had looked round about on them with anger, being grieved for the hardness of their hearts, he saith unto the man, Stretch forth thine hand. And he stretched *it* out: and his hand was restored whole as the other.

6 And the Phar'i-sees went forth, and straightway took counsel with the He-ro'di-ans against him, how they might destroy him.

7 But Je'sus withdrew himself with his disciples to the sea: and a great multitude from Gal'-i-lee followed him, and from Ju-dæ'a,

8 And from Je-ru'sa-lem, and from I-du-mæ'-a, and *from* beyond Jor'dan; and they about Tyre and Si'don, a great multitude, when they had heard what great things he did, came unto him.

9 And he spake to his disciples, that a small ship should wait on him because of the multitude, lest they should throng him.

10 For he had healed many; insomuch that they pressed upon him for to touch him, as many as had plagues.

11 And unclean spirits, when they saw him, fell down before him, and cried, saying, Thou art the Son of God.

12 And he straitly charged them that they should not make him known.

13 And he goeth up into a mountain, and calleth *unto him* whom he would: and they came unto him.

14 And he ordained twelve, that they should be with him, and that he might send them forth to preach,

15 And to have power to heal sicknesses, and to cast out devils:

16 And Si'mon he surnamed Pe'ter;

17 And James the *son* of Zeb'e-dee, and John the brother of James; and he surnamed them Bo-an-er'ges, which is, The sons of thunder:

18 And Andrew, and Phil'ip, and Bar-thol'o-mew, and Mat'thew, and Thom'as, and James the *son* of Al-phæ'us, and Thad-dæ'us, and Si'-mon the Ca'naan-ite,

19 And Ju'das Is-car'i-ot, which also betrayed him: and they went into an house.

20 And the multitude cometh together again, so that they could not so much as eat bread.

21 And when his friends heard *of it*, they went out to lay hold on him: for they said, He is beside himself.

22 ¶ And the scribes which came down from Je-ru'sa-lem said, He hath Beel'ze-bub, and by the prince of the devils casteth he out devils.

23 And he called them *unto him*, and said

unto them in parables, How can Sa'tan cast out Sa'tan?

24 And if a kingdom be divided against itself, that kingdom cannot stand.

25 And if a house be divided against itself, that house cannot stand.

26 And if Sa'tan rise up against himself, and be divided, he cannot stand, but hath an end.

27 No man can enter into a strong man's house, and spoil his goods, except he will first bind the strong man; and then he will spoil his house.

28 Verily I say unto you, All sins shall be forgiven unto the sons of men, and blasphemies wherewith soever they shall blaspheme:

29 But he that shall blaspheme againt the Ho'ly Ghost hath never forgiveness, but is in danger of eternal damnation:

30 Because they said, He hath an unclean spirit.

31 ¶ There came then his brethren and his mother, and, standing without, sent unto him, calling him.

32 And the multitude sat about him, and they said unto him, Behold, thy mother and thy brethren without seek for thee.

33 And he answered them, saying, Who is my mother, or my brethren?

34 And he looked round about on them which sat about him, and said, Behold my mother and my brethren!

35 For whosoever shall do the will of God, the same is my brother, and my sister, and mother.

4 AND he began again to teach by the sea side: and there was gathered unto him a great multitude, so that he entered into a ship, and sat in the sea; and the whole multitude was by the sea on the land.

2 And he taught them many things by parables, and said unto them in his doctrine,

3 Hearken; Behold, there went out a sower to sow:

4 And it came to pass, as he sowed, some fell by the way side, and the fowls of the air came and devoured it up.

5 And some fell on stony ground, where it had not much earth; and immediately it sprang up, because it had no depth of earth:

6 But when the sun was up, it was scorched; and because it had no root, it withered away.

7 And some fell among thorns, and the thorns grew up, and choked it, and it yielded no fruit.

8 And other fell on good ground, and did yield fruit that sprang up and increased; and brought forth, some thirty, and some sixty, and some an hundred.

9 And he said unto them, He that hath ears to hear, let him hear.

10 And when he was alone, they that were about him with the twelve asked of him the parable.

11 And he said unto them, Unto you it is given to know the mystery of the kingdom of God: but unto them that are without, all *these* things are done in parables:

12 That seeing they may see, and not perceive; and hearing they may hear, and not understand; lest at any time they should be converted, and *their* sins should be forgiven them.

13 And he said unto them, Know ye not this parable? and how then will ye know all parables?

14 ¶ The sower soweth the word.

15 And these are they by the way side, where the word is sown; but when they have heard, Sa'tan cometh immediately, and taketh away the word that was sown in their hearts.

16 And these are they likewise which are sown on stony ground; who, when they have heard the word, immediately receive it with gladness;

17 And have no root in themselves, and so endure but for a time: afterward, when affliction or persecution ariseth for the word's sake, immediately they are offended.

18 And these are they which are sown among thorns; such as hear the word,

19 And the cares of this world, and the deceitfulness of riches, and the lusts of other things entering in, choke the word, and it becometh unfruitful.

20 And these are they which are sown on good ground; such as hear the word, and receive *it*, and bring forth fruit, some thirtyfold, some sixty, and some an hundred.

21 ¶ And he said unto them, Is a candle brought to be put under a bushel, or under a bed? and not to set on a candlestick?

22 For there is nothing hid, which shall not be manifested; neither was anything kept secret, but that it should come abroad.

23 If any man have ears to hear, let him hear.

24 And he said unto them, Take heed what ye hear: with what measure ye mete, it shall be measured to you: and unto you that hear shall more be given.

25 For he that hath, to him shall be given: and he that hath not, from him shall be taken even that which he hath.

26 ¶ And he said, So is the kingdom of God, as if a man should cast seed into the ground;

27 And should sleep, and rise night and day, and the seed should spring and grow up, he knoweth not how.

28 For the earth bringeth forth fruit of herself; first the blade, then the ear, after that the full corn in the ear.

29 But when the fruit is brought forth, immediately he putteth in the sickle, because the harvest is come.

30 ¶ And he said, Whereunto shall we liken the kingdom of God? or with what comparison shall we compare it?

31 *It is* like a grain of mustard seed, which, when it is sown in the earth, is less than all the seeds that be in the earth:

32 But when it is sown, it groweth up, and becometh greater than all herbs, and shooteth out great branches; so that the fowls of the air may lodge under the shadow of it.

33 And with many such parables spake he the word unto them, as they were able to hear it.

34 But without a parable spake he not unto them: and when they were alone, he expounded all things to his disciples.

35 And the same day, when the even was come, he saith unto them, Let us pass over unto the other side.

36 And when they had sent away the multitude, they took him even as he was in the ship. And there were also with him other little ships.

37 And there arose a great storm of wind, and the waves beat into the ship, so that it was now full.

38 And he was in the hinder part of the ship, asleep on a pillow: and they awake him, and say unto him, Master, carest thou not that we perish?

39 And he arose, and rebuked the wind, and

said unto the sea, Peace, be still. And the wind ceased, and there was a great calm.

40 And he said unto them, Why are ye so fearful? how is it that ye have no faith?

41 And they feared exceedingly, and said one to another, What manner of man is this, that even the wind and the sea obey him?

5 AND they came over unto the other side of the sea, into the country of the Gad′a-renes.

2 And when he was come out of the ship, immediately there met him out of the tombs a man with an unclean spirit,

3 Who had *his* dwelling among the tombs; and no man could bind him, no, not with chains:

4 Because that he had been often bound with fetters and chains, and the chains had been plucked asunder by him, and the fetters broken in pieces: neither could any *man* tame him.

5 And always, night and day, he was in the mountains, and in the tombs, crying, and cutting himself with stones.

6 But when he saw Je′sus afar off, he ran and worshipped him,

7 And cried with a loud voice, and said, What have I to do with thee, Je′sus, *thou* Son of the most high God? I adjure thee by God, that thou torment me not.

8 For he said unto him, Come out of the man, *thou* unclean spirit.

9 And he asked him, What *is* thy name? And he answered, saying, My name *is* Legion: for we are many.

10 And he besought him much that he would not send them away out of the country.

11 Now there was there nigh unto the mountains a great herd of swine feeding.

12 And all the devils besought him, saying, Send us into the swine, that we may enter into them.

13 And forthwith Je′sus gave them leave. And the unclean spirits went out, and entered into the swine: and the herd ran violently down a steep place into the sea, (they were about two thousand;) and were choked in the sea.

14 And they that fed the swine fled, and told *it* in the city, and in the country. And they went out to see what it was that was done.

15 And they come to Je′sus, and see him that was possessed with the devil, and had the legion, sitting, and clothed, and in his right mind: and they were afraid.

16 And they that saw *it* told them how it befell to him that was possessed with the devil, and *also* concerning the swine.

17 And they began to pray him to depart out of their coasts.

18 And when he was come into the ship, he that had been possessed with the devil prayed him that he might be with him.

19 Howbeit Je′sus suffered him not, but saith unto him, Go home to thy friends, and tell them how great things the Lord hath done for thee, and hath had compassion on thee.

20 And he departed, and began to publish in De-cap′o-lis how great things Je′sus had done for him: and all *men* did marvel.

21 And when Je′sus was passed over again by ship unto the other side, much people gathered unto him: and he was nigh unto the sea.

22 And, behold, there cometh one of the rulers of the synagogue, Ja-i′rus by name; and when he saw him, he fell at his feet,

23 And besought him greatly, saying, My little daughter lieth at the point of death: *I pray* thee, come and lay thy hands on her, that she may be healed; and she shall live.

24 And *Jesus* went with him; and much people followed him, and thronged him.

25 And a certain woman, which had an issue of blood twelve years,

26 And had suffered many things of many physicians, and had spent all that she had, and was nothing bettered, but rather grew worse,

27 When she had heard of Je′sus, came in the press behind, and touched his garment.

28 For she said, If I may touch but his clothes, I shall be whole.

29 And straightway the fountain of her blood was dried up; and she felt in *her* body that she was healed of that plague.

30 And Je′sus, immediately knowing in himself that virtue had gone out of him, turned him about in the press, and said, Who touched my clothes?

31 And his disciples said unto him, Thou seest the multitude thronging thee, and sayest thou, Who touched me?

32 And he looked round about to see her that had done this thing.

33 But the woman fearing and trembling, knowing what was done in her, came and fell down before him, and told him all the truth.

34 And he said unto her, Daughter, thy faith hath made thee whole; go in peace, and be whole of thy plague.

35 While he yet spake, there came from the ruler of the synagogue′s *house certain* which said, Thy daughter is dead: why troublest thou the Master any further?

36 As soon as Je′sus heard the word that was spoken, he saith unto the ruler of the synagogue, Be not afraid, only believe.

37 And he suffered no man to follow him, save Pe′ter, and James, and John the brother of James.

38 And he cometh to the house of the ruler of the synagogue, and seeth the tumult, and them that wept and wailed greatly.

39 And when he was come in, he saith unto them, Why make ye this ado, and weep? the damsel is not dead, but sleepeth.

40 And they laughed him to scorn. But when he had put them all out, he taketh the father and the mother of the damsel, and them that were with him, and entereth in where the damsel was lying.

41 And he took the damsel by the hand, and said unto her, Tal′i-tha cu′mi; which is, being interpreted, Damsel, I say unto thee, arise.

42 And straightway the damsel arose, and walked; for she was *of the age* of twelve years. And they were astonished with a great astonishment.

43 And he charged them straitly that no man should know it; and commanded that something should be given her to eat.

6 AND he went out from thence, and came into his own country; and his disciples follow him.

2 And when the sabbath day was come, he began to teach in the synagogue: and many hearing *him* were astonished, saying, From whence hath this *man* these things? and what wisdom *is* this which is given unto him, that even such mighty works are wrought by his hands?

3 Is not this the carpenter, the son of Ma′ry, the brother of James, and Jo′ses, and of Ju′da, and Si′mon? and are not his sisters here with us? And they were offended at him.

4 But Je'sus said unto them, A prophet is not without honour, but in his own country, and among his own kin, and in his own house.

5 And he could there do no mighty work, save that he laid his hands upon a few sick folk, and healed *them*.

6 And he marvelled because of their unbelief. And he went round about the villages, teaching.

7 ¶ And he called *unto him* the twelve, and began to send them forth by two and two; and gave them power over unclean spirits;

8 And commanded them that they should take nothing for *their* journey, save a staff only; no scrip, no bread, no money in *their* purse:

9 But *be* shod with sandals; and not put on two coats.

10 And he said unto them, In what place soever ye enter into an house, there abide till ye depart from that place.

11 And whosoever shall not receive you, nor hear you, when ye depart thence, shake off the dust under your feet for a testimony against them. Verily I say unto you, It shall be more tolerable for Sod'om and Go-mor'rha in the day of judgment, than for that city.

12 And they went out, and preached that men should repent.

13 And they cast out many devils, and anointed with oil many that were sick, and healed *them*.

14 And king Her'od heard *of him;* (for his name was spread abroad:) and he said, That John the Bap'tist was risen from the dead, and therefore mighty works do shew forth themselves in him.

15 Others said, That it is E-li'as. And others said, That it is a prophet, or as one of the prophets.

16 But when Her'od heard *thereof,* he said, It is John, whom I beheaded: he is risen from the dead.

17 For Her'od himself had sent forth and laid hold upon John, and bound him in prison for He-ro'di-as' sake, his brother Phil'ip's wife: for he had married her.

18 For John had said unto Her'od, It is not lawful for thee to have thy brother's wife.

19 Therefore He-ro'di-as had a quarrel against him, and would have killed him; but she could not:

20 For Her'od feared John, knowing that he was a just man and an holy, and observed him; and when he heard him, he did many things, and heard him gladly.

21 And when a convenient day was come, that Her'od on his birthday made a supper to his lords, high captains, and chief *estates* of Gal'i-lee;

22 And when the daughter of the said He-ro'-di-as came in, and danced, and pleased Her'od and them that sat with him, the king said unto the damsel, Ask of me whatsoever thou wilt, and I will give *it* thee.

23 And he sware unto her, Whatsoever thou shalt ask of me, I will give *it* thee, unto the half of my kingdom.

24 And she went forth, and said unto her mother, What shall I ask? And she said, The head of John the Bap'tist.

25 And she came in straightway with haste unto the king, and asked, saying, I will that thou give me by and by in a charger the head of John the Bap'tist.

26 And the king was exceeding sorry; *yet* for his oath's sake, and for their sakes which sat with him, he would not reject her.

27 And immediately the king sent an execu-tioner, and commanded his head to be brought: and he went and beheaded him in the prison,

28 And brought his head in a charger, and gave it to the damsel: and the damsel gave it to her mother.

29 And when his disciples heard *of it,* they came and took up his corpse, and laid it in a tomb.

30 And the apostles gathered themselves together unto Je'sus, and told him all things, both what they had done, and what they had taught.

31 And he said unto them, Come ye yourselves apart into a desert place, and rest a while: for there were many coming and going, and they had no leisure so much as to eat.

32 And they departed into a desert place by ship privately.

33 And the people saw them departing, and many knew him, and ran afoot thither out of all cities, and outwent them, and came together unto him.

34 And Je'sus, when he came out, saw much people, and was moved with compassion toward them, because they were as sheep not having a shepherd: and he began to teach them many things.

35 And when the day was now far spent, his disciples came unto him, and said, This is a desert place, and now the time *is* far passed:

36 Send them away, that they may go into the country round about, and into the villages, and buy themselves bread: for they have nothing to eat.

37 He answered and said unto them, Give ye them to eat. And they say unto him, Shall we go and buy two hundred pennyworth of bread, and give them to eat?

38 He saith unto them, How many loaves have ye? go and see. And when they knew, they say, Five, and two fishes.

39 And he commanded them to make all sit down by companies upon the green grass.

40 And they sat down in ranks, by hundreds, and by fifties.

41 And when he had taken the five loaves and the two fishes, he looked up to heaven, and blessed, and brake the loaves, and gave *them* to his disciples to set before them; and the two fishes divided he among them all.

42 And they did all eat, and were filled.

43 And they took up twelve baskets full of the fragments, and of the fishes.

44 And they that did eat of the loaves were about five thousand men.

45 And straightway he constrained his disciples to get into the ship, and to go to the other side before unto Beth-sa'i-da, while he sent away the people.

46 And when he had sent them away, he departed into a mountain to pray.

47 And when even was come, the ship was in the midst of the sea, and he alone on the land.

48 And he saw them toiling in rowing; for the wind was contrary unto them: and about the fourth watch of the night he cometh unto them, walking upon the sea, and would have passed by them.

49 But when they saw him walking upon the sea, they supposed it had been a spirit, and cried out:

50 For they all saw him, and were troubled. And immediately he talked with them, and saith unto them, Be of good cheer: it is I; be not afraid.

51 And he went up unto them into the ship; and the wind ceased: and they were sore

amazed in themselves beyond measure, and wondered.

52 For they considered not *the miracle* of the loaves: for their heart was hardened.

53 And when they had passed over, they came into the land of Gen-nes′a-ret, and drew to the shore.

54 And when they were come out of the ship, straightway they knew him,

55 And ran through that whole region round about, and began to carry about in beds those that were sick, where they heard he was.

56 And whithersoever he entered, into villages, or cities, or country, they laid the sick in the streets, and besought him that they might touch if it were but the border of his garment: and as many as touched him were made whole.

7 THEN came together unto him the Phar′i-sees, and certain of the scribes, which came from Je-ru′sa-lem.

2 And when they saw some of his disciples eat bread with defiled, that is to say, with unwashen, hands, they found fault.

3 For the Phar′i-sees, and all the Jews, except they wash *their* hands oft, eat not, holding the tradition of the elders.

4 And *when they come* from the market, except they wash, they eat not. And many other things there be, which they have received to hold, *as* the washing of cups, and pots, brasen vessels, and of tables.

5 Then the Phar′i-sees and scribes asked him, Why walk not thy disciples according to the tradition of the elders, but eat bread with unwashen hands?

6 He answered and said unto them, Well hath E-sa′ias prophesied of you hypocrites, as it is written, This people honoureth me with *their* lips, but their heart is far from me.

7 Howbeit in vain do they worship me, teaching *for* doctrines the commandments of men.

8 For laying aside the commandment of God, ye hold the tradition of men, *as* the washing of pots and cups: and many other such like things ye do.

9 And he said unto them, Full well ye reject the commandment of God, that ye may keep your own tradition.

10 For Mo′ses said, Honour thy father and thy mother; and, Whoso curseth father or mother, let him die the death:

11 But ye say, If a man shall say to his father or mother, It is Corban, that is to say, a gift, by whatsoever thou mightest be profited by me; *he shall be free.*

12 And ye suffer him no more to do ought for his father or his mother;

13 Making the word of God of none effect through your tradition, which ye have delivered: and many such like things do ye.

14 ¶ And when he had called all the people unto him, he said unto them, Hearken unto me every one *of you*, and understand:

15 There is nothing from without a man, that entering into him can defile him: but the things which come out of him, those are they that defile the man.

16 If any man have ears to hear, let him hear.

17 And when he was entered into the house from the people, his disciples asked him concerning the parable.

18 And he saith unto them, Are ye so without understanding also? Do ye not perceive, that whatsoever thing from without entereth into the man, *it* cannot defile him;

19 Because it entereth not into his heart, but into the belly, and goeth out into the draught, purging all meats?

20 And he said, That which cometh out of the man, that defileth the man.

21 For from within, out of the heart of men, proceed evil thoughts, adulteries, fornications, murders,

22 Thefts, covetousness, wickedness, deceit, lasciviousness, an evil eye, blasphemy, pride, foolishness:

23 All these evil things come from within, and defile the man.

24 ¶ And from thence he arose, and went into the borders of Tyre and Si′don, and entered into an house, and would have no man know *it*: but he could not be hid.

25 For a *certain* woman, whose young daughter had an unclean spirit, heard of him, and came and fell at his feet:

26 The women was a Greek, a Sy-ro-phe-ni′-cian by nation; and she besought him that he would cast forth the devil out of her daughter.

27 But Je′sus said unto her, Let the children first be filled: for it is not meet to take the children's bread, and to cast *it* unto the dogs.

28 And she answered and said unto him, Yes, Lord: yet the dogs under the table eat of the children's crumbs.

29 And he said unto her, For this saying go thy way; the devil is gone out of thy daughter.

30 And when she was come to her house, she found the devil gone out, and her daughter laid upon the bed.

31 ¶ And again, departing from the coasts of Tyre and Si′don, he came unto the sea of Gal′i-lee, through the midst of the coasts of De-cap′o-lis.

32 And they bring unto him one that was deaf, and had an impediment in his speech; and they beseech him to put his hand upon him.

33 And he took him aside from the multitude, and put his fingers into his ears, and he spit, and touched his tongue;

34 And looking up to heaven, he sighed, and saith unto him, Eph′pha-tha, that is, Be opened.

35 And straightway his ears were opened, and the string of his tongue was loosed, and he spake plain.

36 And he charged them that they should tell no man: but the more a great deal they published *it*;

37 And were beyond measure astonished, saying, He hath done all things well: he maketh both the deaf to hear, and the dumb to speak.

8 IN those days the multitude being very great, and having nothing to eat, Je′sus called his disciples *unto him*, and saith unto them,

2 I have compassion on the multitude, because they have now been with me three days, and have nothing to eat:

3 And if I send them away fasting to their own houses, they will faint by the way: for divers of them came from far.

4 And his disciples answered him, From whence can a man satisfy these *men* with bread here in the wilderness?

5 And he asked them, How many loaves have ye? And they said, Seven.

6 And he commanded the people to sit down on the ground: and he took the seven loaves, and gave thanks, and brake, and gave to his disciples to set before *them*; and they did set *them* before the people.

7 And they had a few small fishes: and he

blessed, and commanded to set them also before *them*.

8 So they did eat, and were filled: and they took up of the broken *meat* that was left seven baskets.

9 And they that had eaten were about four thousand: and he sent them away.

10 ¶ And straightway he entered into a ship with his disciples, and came into the parts of Dal-ma-nu'tha.

11 And the Phar'i-sees came forth, and began to question with him, seeking of him a sign from heaven, tempting him.

12 And he sighed deeply in his spirit, and saith, Why doth this generation seek after a sign? verily I say unto you, There shall no sign be given unto this generation.

13 And he left them, and entering into the ship again departed to the other side.

14 ¶ Now *the disciples* had forgotten to take bread, neither had they in the ship with them more than one loaf.

15 And he charged them, saying, Take heed, beware of the leaven of the Phar'i-sees, and *of* the leaven of Her'od.

16 And they reasoned among themselves, saying, *It is* because we have no bread.

17 And when Je'sus knew *it*, he saith unto them, Why reason ye, because ye have no bread? perceive ye not yet, neither understand? have ye your heart yet hardened?

18 Having eyes, see ye not? and having ears, hear ye not? and do ye not remember?

19 When I brake the five loaves among five thousand, how many baskets full of fragments took ye up? They say unto him, Twelve.

20 And when the seven among four thousand, how many baskets full of fragments took ye up? And they said, Seven.

21 And he said unto them, How is it that ye do not understand?

22 ¶ And he cometh to Beth-sa'i-da; and they bring a blind man unto him, and besought him to touch him.

23 And he took the blind man by the hand, and led him out of the town; and when he had spit on his eyes, and put his hands upon him, he asked him if he saw ought.

24 And he looked up, and said, I see men as trees, walking.

25 After that he put *his* hands again upon his eyes, and made him look up: and he was restored, and saw every man clearly.

26 And he sent him away to his house, saying, Neither go into the town, nor tell *it* to any in the town.

27 ¶ And Je'sus went out, and his disciples, into the towns of Cæs-a-re'a Phi-lip'pi: and by the way he asked his disciples, saying unto them, Whom do men say that I am?

28 And they answered, John the Bap'tist: but some *say*, E-li'as; and others, One of the prophets.

29 And he saith unto them, But whom say ye that I am? And Pe'ter answereth and saith unto him, Thou art the Christ.

30 And he charged them that they should tell no man of him.

31 And he began to teach them, that the Son of man must suffer many things, and be rejected of the elders, and *of* the chief priests, and scribes, and be killed, and after three days rise again.

32 And he spake that saying openly. And Pe'ter took him, and began to rebuke him.

33 But when he had turned about and looked on his disciples, he rebuked Pe'ter, saying, Get

thee behind me, Sa'tan: for thou savourest not the things that be of God, but the things that be of men.

34 ¶ And when he had called the people *unto him* with his disciples also, he said unto them, Whosoever will come after me, let him deny himself, and take up his cross, and follow me.

35 For whosoever will save his life shall lose it; but whosoever shall lose his life for my sake and the gospel's, the same shall save it.

36 For what shall it profit a man, if he shall gain the whole world, and lose his own soul?

37 Or what shall a man give in exchange for his soul?

38 Whosoever therefore shall be ashamed of me and of my words in this adulterous and sinful generation; of him also shall the Son of man be ashamed, when he cometh in the glory of his Father with the holy angels.

9 AND he said unto them, Verily I say unto you, That there be some of them that stand here, which shall not taste of death, till they have seen the kingdom of God come with power.

2 ¶ And after six days Je'sus taketh *with him* Pe'ter, and James, and John, and leadeth them up into an high mountain apart by themselves: and he was transfigured before them.

3 And his raiment became shining, exceeding white as snow; so as no fuller on earth can white them.

4 And there appeared unto them E-li'as with Mo'ses: and they were talking with Je'sus.

5 And Pe'ter answered and said to Je'sus, Master, it is good for us to be here: and let us make three tabernacles; one for thee, and one for Mo'ses, and one for E-li'as.

6 For he wist not what to say; for they were sore afraid.

7 And there was a cloud that overshadowed them: and a voice came out of the cloud, saying, This is my beloved Son: hear him.

8 And suddenly, when they had looked round about, they saw no man any more, save Je'sus only with themselves.

9 And as they came down from the mountain, he charged them that they should tell no man what things they had seen, till the Son of man were risen from the dead.

10 And they kept that saying with themselves, questioning one with another what the rising from the dead should mean.

11 ¶ And they asked him, saying, Why say the scribes that E-li'as must first come?

12 And he answered and told them, E-li'as verily cometh first, and restoreth all things; and how it is written of the Son of man, that he must suffer many things, and be set at nought.

13 But I say unto you, That E-li'as is indeed come, and they have done unto him whatsoever they listed, as it is written of him.

14 ¶ And when he came to *his* disciples, he saw a great multitude about them, and the scribes questioning with them.

15 And straightway all the people, when they beheld him, were greatly amazed, and running to *him* saluted him.

16 And he asked the scribes, What question ye with them?

17 And one of the multitude answered and said, Master, I have brought unto thee my son, which hath a dumb spirit;

18 And wheresoever he taketh him, he teareth him: and he foameth, and gnasheth with his teeth, and pineth away: and I spake to thy disci-

ples that they should cast him out; and they could not.

19 He answereth him, and saith, O faithless generation, how long shall I be with you? how long shall I suffer you? bring him unto me.

20 And they brought him unto him: and when he saw him, straightway the spirit tare him; and he fell on the ground, and wallowed foaming.

21 And he asked his father, How long is it ago since this came unto him? And he said, Of a child.

22 And ofttimes it hath cast him into the fire, and into the waters, to destroy him: but if thou canst do any thing, have compassion on us, and help us.

23 Je'sus said unto him, If thou canst believe, all things *are* possible to him that believeth.

24 And straightway the father of the child cried out, and said with tears, Lord, I believe; help thou mine unbelief.

25 When Je'sus saw that the people came running together, he rebuked the foul spirit, saying unto him, *Thou* dumb and deaf spirit, I charge thee, come out of him, and enter no more into him.

26 And *the spirit* cried, and rent him sore, and came out of him: and he was as one dead; insomuch that many said, He is dead.

27 But Je'sus took him by the hand, and lifted him up; and he arose.

28 And when he was come into the house, his disciples asked him privately, Why could not we cast him out?

29 And he said unto them, This kind can come forth by nothing, but by prayer and fasting.

30 ¶ And they departed thence, and passed through Gal'i-lee; and he would not that any man should know *it.*

31 For he taught his disciples, and said unto them, The Son of man is delivered into the hands of men, and they shall kill him; and after that he is killed, he shall rise the third day.

32 But they understood not that saying, and were afraid to ask him.

33 ¶ And he came to Ca-per'na-um: and being in the house he asked them, What was it that ye disputed among yourselves by the way?

34 But they held their peace: for by the way they had disputed among themselves, who *should be* the greatest.

35 And he sat down, and called the twelve, and saith unto them, If any man desire to be first, *the same* shall be last of all, and servant of all.

36 And he took a child, and set him in the midst of them: and when he had taken him in his arms, he said unto them,

37 Whosoever shall receive one of such children in my name, receiveth me: and whosoever shall receive me, receiveth not me, but him that sent me.

38 ¶ And John answered him, saying, Master, we saw one casting out devils in thy name, and he followeth not us: and we forbad him, because he followeth not us.

39 But Je'sus said, Forbid him not: for there is no man which shall do a miracle in my name, that can lightly speak evil of me.

40 For he that is not against us is on our part.

41 For whosoever shall give you a cup of water to drink in my name, because ye belong to Christ, verily I say unto you, he shall not lose his reward.

42 And whosoever shall offend one of *these* little ones that believe in me, it is better for him

that a millstone were hanged about his neck, and he were cast into the sea.

43 And if thy hand offend thee, cut it off: it is better for thee to enter into life maimed, than having two hands to go into hell, into the fire that never shall be quenched:

44 Where their worm dieth not, and the fire is not quenched.

45 And if thy foot offend thee, cut it off: it is better for thee to enter halt into life, than having two feet to be cast into hell, into the fire that never shall be quenched:

46 Where their worm dieth not, and the fire is not quenched.

47 And if thine eye offend thee, pluck it out: it is better for thee to enter into the kingdom of God with one eye, than having two eyes to be cast into hell fire:

48 Where their worm dieth not, and the fire is not quenched.

49 For every one shall be salted with fire, and every sacrifice shall be salted with salt.

50 Salt *is* good: but if the salt have lost his saltness, wherewith will ye season it? Have salt in yourselves, and have peace one with another.

10 AND he arose from thence, and cometh into the coasts of Ju-dæ'a by the farther side of Jor'dan: and the people resort unto him again; and, as he was wont, he taught them again.

2 ¶ And the Phar'i-sees came to him, and asked him, Is it lawful for a man to put away *his* wife? tempting him.

3 And he answered and said unto them, What did Mo'ses command you?

4 And they said, Mo'ses suffered to write a bill of divorcement, and to put *her* away.

5 And Je'sus answered and said unto them, For the hardness of your heart he wrote you this precept.

6 But from the beginning of the creation God made them male and female.

7 For this cause shall a man leave his father and mother, and cleave to his wife;

8 And they twain shall be one flesh: so then they are no more twain, but one flesh.

9 What therefore God hath joined together, let not man put asunder.

10 And in the house his disciples asked him again of the same *matter.*

11 And he saith unto them, Whosoever shall put away his wife, and marry another, committeth adultery against her.

12 And if a woman shall put away her husband, and be married to another, she committeth adultery.

13 ¶ And they brought young children to him, that he should touch them: and *his* disciples rebuked those that brought *them.*

14 But when Je'sus saw *it,* he was much displeased, and said unto them, Suffer the little children to come unto me, and forbid them not: for of such is the kingdom of God.

15 Verily I say unto you, Whosoever shall not receive the kingdom of God as a little child, he shall not enter therein.

16 And he took them up in his arms, put *his* hands upon them, and blessed them.

17 ¶ And when he was gone forth into the way, there came one running, and kneeled to him, and asked him, Good Master, what shall I do that I may inherit eternal life?

18 And Je'sus said unto him, Why callest thou me good? *there is* none good but one, *that is,* God.

19 Thou knowest the commandments, Do

not commit adultery, Do not kill, Do not steal, Do not bear false witness, Defraud not, Honour thy father and mother.

20 And he answered and said unto him, Master, all these have I observed from my youth.

21 Then Je′sus beholding him loved him, and said unto him, One thing thou lackest: go thy way, sell whatsoever thou hast, and give to the poor, and thou shalt have treasure in heaven: and come, take up the cross, and follow me.

22 And he was sad at that saying, and went away grieved: for he had great possessions.

23 ¶ And Je′sus looked round about, and saith unto his disciples, How hardly shall they that have riches enter into the kingdom of God!

24 And the disciples were astonished at his words. But Je′sus answereth again, and saith unto them, Children, how hard is it for them that trust in riches to enter into the kingdom of God!

25 It is easier for a camel to go through the eye of a needle, than for a rich man to enter into the kingdom of God.

26 And they were astonished out of measure, saying among themselves, Who then can be saved?

27 And Je′sus looking upon them saith, With men it is impossible, but not with God: for with God all things are possible.

28 ¶ Then Pe′ter began to say unto him, Lo, we have left all, and have followed thee.

29 And Je′sus answered and said, Verily I say unto you, There is no man that hath left house, or brethren, or sisters, or father, or mother, or wife, or children, or lands, for my sake, and the gospel's,

30 But he shall receive an hundredfold now in this time, houses, and brethren, and sisters, and mothers, and children, and lands, with persecutions; and in the world to come eternal life.

31 But many that are first shall be last; and the last first.

32 ¶ And they were in the way going up to Je′ru′sa-lem; and Je′sus went before them: and they were amazed; and as they followed, they were afraid. And he took again the twelve, and began to tell them what things should happen unto him,

33 Saying, Behold, we go up to Je-ru′sa-lem; and the Son of man shall be delivered unto the chief priests, and unto the scribes; and they shall condemn him to death, and shall deliver him to the Gen′tiles:

34 And they shall mock him, and shall scourge him, and shall spit upon him, and shall kill him: and the third day he shall rise again.

35 ¶ And James and John, the sons of Zeb′e-dee, come unto him, saying, Master, we would that thou shouldest do for us whatsoever we shall desire.

36 And he said unto them, What would ye that I should do for you?

37 They said unto him, Grant unto us that we may sit, one on thy right hand, and the other on thy left hand, in thy glory.

38 But Je′sus said unto them, Ye know not what ye ask: can ye drink of the cup that I drink of? and be baptized with the baptism that I am baptized with?

39 And they said unto him, We can. And Je′sus said unto them, Ye shall indeed drink of the cup that I drink of; and with the baptism that I am baptized withal shall ye be baptized:

40 But to sit on my right hand and on my left hand is not mine to give; but it shall be given to them for whom it is prepared.

41 And when the ten heard it, they began to be much displeased with James and John.

42 But Je′sus called them to him, and saith unto them, Ye know that they which are accounted to rule over the Gen′tiles exercise lordship over them; and their great ones exercise authority upon them.

43 But so shall it not be among you: but whosoever will be great among you, shall be your minister:

44 And whosoever of you will be the chiefest, shall be servant of all.

45 For even the Son of man came not to be ministered unto, but to minister, and to give his life a ransom for many.

46 ¶ And they came to Jer′i-cho: and as he went out of Jer′i-cho with his disciples and a great number of people, blind Bar-ti-mæ′us, the son of Ti-mæ′us, sat by the highway side begging.

47 And when he heard that it was Je′sus of Naz′a-reth, he began to cry out, and say, Je′sus, thou son of Da′vid, have mercy on me.

48 And many charged him that he should hold his peace: but he cried the more a great deal, Thou son of Da′vid, have mercy on me.

49 And Je′sus stood still, and commanded him to be called. And they call the blind man, saying unto him, Be of good comfort, rise; he calleth thee.

50 And he, casting away his garment, rose, and came to Je′sus.

51 And Je′sus answered and said unto him, What wilt thou that I should do unto thee? The blind man said unto him, Lord, that I might receive my sight.

52 And Je′sus said unto him, Go thy way; thy faith hath made thee whole. And immediately he received his sight, and followed Je′sus in the way.

11 AND when they came nigh to Je-ru′sa-lem, unto Beth′pha-ge and Beth′a-ny, at the mount of Ol′ives, he sendeth forth two of his disciples,

2 And saith unto them, Go your way into the village over against you: and as soon as ye be entered into it, ye shall find a colt tied, whereon never man sat; loose him, and bring him.

3 And if any man say unto you, Why do ye this? say ye that the Lord hath need of him; and straightway he will send him hither.

4 And they went their way, and found the colt tied by the door without in a place where two ways met; and they loose him.

5 And certain of them that stood there said unto them, What do ye, loosing the colt?

6 And they said unto them even as Je′sus had commanded: and they let them go.

7 And they brought the colt to Je′sus, and cast their garments on him; and he sat upon him.

8 And many spread their garments in the way: and others cut down branches off the trees, and strawed them in the way.

9 And they that went before, and they that followed, cried, saying, Ho-san′na; Blessed is he that cometh in the name of the Lord:

10 Blessed be the kingdom of our father Da′vid, that cometh in the name of the Lord: Ho-san′na in the highest.

11 And Je′sus entered into Je-ru′sa-lem, and into the temple: and when he had looked round about upon all things, and now the eventide was come, he went out unto Beth′a-ny with the twelve.

12 ¶ And on the morrow, when they were come from Beth′a-ny, he was hungry:

13 And seeing a fig tree afar off having leaves, he came, if haply he might find any thing thereon: and when he came to it, he found nothing but leaves; for the time of figs was not yet.

14 And Je′sus answered and said unto it, No man eat fruit of thee hereafter for ever. And his disciples heard it.

15 ¶ And they come to Je-ru′sa-lem: and Je′sus went into the temple, and began to cast out them that sold and bought in the temple, and overthrew the tables of the moneychangers, and the seats of them that sold doves;

16 And would not suffer that any man should carry any vessel through the temple.

17 And he taught, saying unto them, Is it not written, My house shall be called of all nations the house of prayer? but ye have made it a den of thieves.

18 And the scribes and chief priests heard it, and sought how they might destroy him: for they feared him, because all the people was astonished at his doctrine.

19 And when even was come, he went out of the city.

20 ¶ And in the morning, as they passed by, they saw the fig tree dried up from the roots.

21 And Pe′ter calling to remembrance saith unto him, Master, behold, the fig tree which thou cursedst is withered away.

22 And Je′sus answering saith unto them, Have faith in God.

23 For verily I say unto you, That whosoever shall say unto this mountain, Be thou removed, and be thou cast into the sea; and shall not doubt in his heart, but shall believe that those things which he saith shall come to pass; he shall have whatsoever he saith.

24 Therefore I say unto you, What things soever ye desire, when ye pray, believe that ye receive them, and ye shall have them.

25 And when ye stand praying, forgive, if ye have ought against any: that your Father also which is in heaven may forgive you your trespasses.

26 But if ye do not forgive, neither will your Father which is in heaven forgive your trespasses.

27 ¶ And they come again to Je-ru′sa-lem: and as he was walking in the temple, there come to him the chief priests, and the scribes, and the elders,

28 And say unto him, By what authority doest thou these things? and who gave thee this authority to do these things?

29 And Je′sus answered and said unto them, I will also ask of you one question, and answer me, and I will tell you by what authority I do these things.

30 The baptism of John, was it from heaven, or of men? answer me.

31 And they reasoned with themselves, saying, If we shall say, From heaven; he will say, Why then did ye not believe him?

32 But if we shall say, Of men; they feared the people: for all men counted John, that he was a prophet indeed.

33 And they answered and said unto Je′sus, We cannot tell. And Je′sus answering saith unto them, Neither do I tell you by what authority I do these things.

12 AND he began to speak unto them by parables. A certain man planted a vineyard, and set an hedge about it, and digged a place for the winefat, and built a tower, and let it out to husbandmen, and went into a far country.

2 And at the season he sent to the husbandmen a servant, that he might receive from the husbandmen of the fruit of the vineyard.

3 And they caught him, and beat him, and sent him away empty.

4 And again he sent unto them another servant; and at him they cast stones, and wounded him in the head, and sent him away shamefully handled.

5 And again he sent another; and him they killed, and many others; beating some, and killing some.

6 Having yet therefore one son, his wellbeloved, he sent him also last unto them, saying, They will reverence my son.

7 But those husbandmen said among themselves, This is the heir; come, let us kill him, and the inheritance shall be ours.

8 And they took him, and killed him, and cast him out of the vineyard.

9 What shall therefore the lord of the vineyard do? he will come and destroy the husbandmen, and will give the vineyard unto others.

10 And have ye not read this scripture; The stone which the builders rejected is become the head of the corner:

11 This was the Lord's doing, and it is marvellous in our eyes?

12 And they sought to lay hold on him, but feared the people: for they knew that he had spoken the parable against them: and they left him, and went their way.

13 ¶ And they send unto him certain of the Phar′i-sees and of the He-ro′di-ans, to catch him in his words.

14 And when they were come, they say unto him, Master, we know that thou art true, and carest for no man: for thou regardest not the person of men, but teachest the way of God in truth: Is it lawful to give tribute to Cæ′sar, or not?

15 Shall we give, or shall we not give? But he, knowing their hypocrisy, said unto them, Why tempt ye me? bring me a penny, that I may see it.

16 And they brought it. And he saith unto them, Whose is this image and superscription? And they said unto him, Cæ′sar's.

17 And Je′sus answering said unto them, Render to Cæ′sar the things that are Cæ′sar's, and to God the things that are God's. And they marvelled at him.

18 ¶ Then come unto him the Sad′du-cees, which say there is no resurrection; and they asked him, saying,

19 Master, Mo′ses wrote unto us, If a man's brother die, and leave his wife behind him, and leave no children, that his brother should take his wife, and raise up seed unto his brother.

20 Now there were seven brethren: and the first took a wife, and dying left no seed.

21 And the second took her, and died, neither left he any seed: and the third likewise.

22 And the seven had her, and left no seed: last of all the woman died also.

23 In the resurrection therefore, when they shall rise, whose wife shall she be of them? for the seven had her to wife.

24 And Je′sus answering said unto them, Do ye not therefore err, because ye know not the scriptures, neither the power of God?

25 For when they shall rise from the dead, they neither marry, nor are given in marriage; but are as the angels which are in heaven.

26 And as touching the dead, that they rise: have ye not read in the book of Mo'ses, how in the bush God spake unto him, saying, I *am* the God of A'bra-ham, and the God of I'saac, and the God of Ja'cob?

27 He is not the God of the dead, but the God of the living: ye therefore do greatly err.

28 ¶ And one of the scribes came, and having heard them reasoning together, and perceiving that he had answered them well, asked him, Which is the first commandment of all?

29 And Je'sus answered him, The first of all the commandments *is*, Hear, O Is'ra-el; the Lord our God is one Lord:

30 And thou shalt love the Lord thy God with all thy heart, and with all thy soul, and with all thy mind, and with all thy strength: this *is* the first commandment.

31 And the second *is* like, *namely* this, Thou shalt love thy neighbour as thyself. There is none other commandment greater than these.

32 And the scribe said unto him, Well, Master, thou hast said the truth: for there is one God; and there is none other but he:

33 And to love him with all the heart, and with all the understanding, and with all the soul, and with all the strength, and to love *his* neighbour as himself, is more than all whole burnt offerings and sacrifices.

34 And when Je'sus saw that he answered discreetly, he said unto him, Thou art not far from the kingdom of God. And no man after that durst ask him *any question.*

35 ¶ And Je'sus answered and said, while he taught in the temple, How say the scribes that Christ is the son of Da'vid?

36 For Da'vid himself said by the Ho'ly Ghost, The Lord said to my Lord, Sit thou on my right hand, till I make thine enemies thy footstool.

37 Da'vid therefore himself calleth him Lord; and whence is he *then* his son? And the common people heard him gladly.

38 ¶ And he said unto them in his doctrine, Beware of the scribes, which love to go in long clothing, and *love* salutations in the marketplaces,

39 And the chief seats in the synagogues, and the uppermost rooms at feasts:

40 Which devour widows' houses, and for a pretence make long prayers: these shall receive greater damnation.

41 ¶ And Je'sus sat over against the treasury, and beheld how the people cast money into the treasury: and many that were rich cast in much.

42 And there came a certain poor widow, and she threw in two mites, which make a farthing.

43 And he called *unto him* his disciples, and saith unto them, Verily I say unto you, That this poor widow hath cast more in, than all they which have cast into the treasury:

44 For all *they* did cast in of their abundance; but she of her want did cast in all that she had, *even* all her living.

13 AND as he went out of the temple, one of his disciples saith unto him, Master, see what manner of stones and what buildings *are here!*

2 And Je'sus answering said unto him, Seest thou these great buildings? there shall not be left one stone upon another, that shall not be thrown down.

3 And as he sat upon the mount of Ol'ives over against the temple, Pe'ter and James and John and An'drew asked him privately,

4 Tell us, when shall these things be? and what *shall be* the sign when all these things shall be fulfilled?

5 And Je'sus answering them began to say, Take heed lest any *man* deceive you:

6 For many shall come in my name, saying, I am *Christ;* and shall deceive many.

7 And when ye shall hear of wars and rumours of wars, be ye not troubled: for *such things* must needs be; but the end *shall* not *be* yet.

8 For nation shall rise against nation, and kingdom against kingdom: and there shall be earthquakes in divers places, and there shall be famines and troubles: these *are* the beginnings of sorrows.

9 ¶ But take heed to yourselves: for they shall deliver you up to councils; and in the synagogues ye shall be beaten: and ye shall be brought before rulers and kings for my sake, for a testimony against them.

10 And the gospel must first be published among all nations.

11 But when they shall lead *you,* and deliver you up, take no thought beforehand what ye shall speak, neither do ye premeditate: but whatsoever shall be given you in that hour, that speak ye: for it is not ye that speak, but the Ho'ly Ghost.

12 Now the brother shall betray the brother to death, and the father the son; and children shall rise up against *their* parents, and shall cause them to be put to death.

13 And ye shall be hated of all *men* for my name's sake: but he that shall endure unto the end, the same shall be saved.

14 ¶ But when ye shall see the abomination of desolation, spoken of by Dan'iel the prophet, standing where it ought not, (let him that readeth understand,) then let them that be in Ju-dæ'a flee to the mountains:

15 And let him that is on the house top not go down into the house, neither enter *therein,* to take any thing out of his house:

16 And let him that is in the field not turn back again for to take up his garment.

17 But woe to them that are with child, and to them that give suck in those days!

18 And pray ye that your flight be not in the winter.

19 For *in* those days shall be affliction, such as was not from the beginning of the creation which God created unto this time, neither shall be.

20 And except that the Lord had shortened those days, no flesh should be saved: but for the elect's sake, whom he hath chosen, he hath shortened the days.

21 And then if any man shall say to you, Lo, here *is* Christ; or, lo, *he is* there; believe *him* not:

22 For false Christs and false prophets shall rise, and shall shew signs and wonders, to seduce, if *it were* possible, even the elect.

23 But take ye heed: behold, I have foretold you all things.

24 ¶ But in those days, after that tribulation, the sun shall be darkened, and the moon shall not give her light,

25 And the stars of heaven shall fall, and the powers that are in heaven shall be shaken.

26 And then shall they see the Son of man coming in the clouds with great power and glory.

27 And then shall he send his angels, and

shall gather together his elect from the four winds, from the uttermost part of the earth to the uttermost part of heaven.

28 Now learn a parable of the fig tree; When her branch is yet tender, and putteth forth leaves, ye know that summer is near:

29 So ye in like manner, when ye shall see these things come to pass, know that it is nigh, *even* at the doors.

30 Verily I say unto you, that this generation shall not pass, till all these things be done.

31 Heaven and earth shall pass away: but my words shall not pass away.

32 ¶ But of that day and *that* hour knoweth no man, no, not the angels which are in heaven, neither the Son, but the Father.

33 Take ye heed, watch and pray: for ye know not when the time is.

34 *For the Son of man is* as a man taking a far journey, who left his house, and gave authority to his servants, and to every man his work, and commanded the porter to watch.

35 Watch ye therefore: for ye know not when the master of the house cometh, at even, or at midnight, or at the cockcrowing, or in the morning:

36 Lest coming suddenly he find you sleeping.

37 And what I say unto you I say unto all, Watch.

14 AFTER two days was *the feast of* the passover, and of unleavened bread: and the chief priests and the scribes sought how they might take him by craft, and put *him* to death.

2 But they said, Not on the feast *day*, lest there be an uproar of the people.

3 ¶ And being in Beth'a-ny in the house of Si'mon the leper, as he sat at meat, there came a woman having an alabaster box of ointment of spikenard very precious; and she brake the box, and poured *it* on his head.

4 And there were some that had indignation within themselves, and said, Why was this waste of the ointment made?

5 For it might have been sold for more than three hundred pence, and have been given to the poor. And they murmured against her.

6 And Je'sus said, Let her alone; why trouble ye her? she hath wrought a good work on me.

7 For ye have the poor with you always, and whensoever ye will ye may do them good: but me ye have not always.

8 She hath done what she could: she is come aforehand to anoint my body to the burying.

9 Verily I say unto you, Wheresoever this gospel shall be preached throughout the whole world, *this* also that she hath done shall be spoken of for a memorial of her.

10 ¶ And Ju'das Is-car'i-ot, one of the twelve, went unto the chief priests, to betray him unto them.

11 And when they heard *it*, they were glad, and promised to give him money. And he sought how he might conveniently betray him.

12 ¶ And the first day of unleavened bread, when they killed the passover, his disciples said unto him, Where wilt thou that we go and prepare that thou mayest eat the passover?

13 And he sendeth forth two of his disciples, and saith unto them, Go ye into the city, and there shall meet you a man bearing a pitcher of water: follow him.

14 And wheresoever he shall go in, say ye to the goodman of the house, The Master saith, Where is the guestchamber, where I shall eat the passover with my disciples?

15 And he will shew you a large upper room furnished *and* prepared: there make ready for us.

16 And his disciples went forth, and came into the city, and found as he had said unto them: and they made ready the passover.

17 And in the evening he cometh with the twelve.

18 And as they sat and did eat, Je'sus said, Verily I say unto you, One of you which eateth with me shall betray me.

19 And they began to be sorrowful, and to say unto him one by one, *Is* it I? and another said, *Is* it I?

20 And he answered and said unto them, *It is* one of the twelve, that dippeth with me in the dish.

21 The Son of man indeed goeth, as it is written of him: but woe to that man by whom the Son of man is betrayed! good were it for that man if he had never been born.

22 ¶ And as they did eat, Je'sus took bread, and blessed, and brake *it*, and gave to them, and said, Take, eat: this is my body.

23 And he took the cup, and when he had given thanks, he gave *it* to them: and they all drank of it.

24 And he said unto them, This is my blood of the new testament, which is shed for many.

25 Verily I say unto you, I will drink no more of the fruit of the vine, until that day that I drink it new in the kingdom of God.

26 ¶ And when they had sung an hymn, they went out into the mount of Ol'ives.

27 And Je'sus saith unto them, All ye shall be offended because of me this night: for it is written, I will smite the shepherd, and the sheep shall be scattered.

28 But after that I am risen, I will go before you into Gal'i-lee.

29 But Pe'ter said unto him, Although all shall be offended, yet *will* not I.

30 And Je'sus saith unto him, Verily I say unto thee, That this day, *even* in this night, before the cock crow twice, thou shalt deny me thrice.

31 But he spake the more vehemently, If I should die with thee, I will not deny thee in any wise. Likewise also said they all.

32 And they came to a place which was named Geth-sem'a-ne: and he saith to his disciples, Sit ye here, while I shall pray.

33 And he taketh with him Pe'ter and James and John, and began to be sore amazed, and to be very heavy;

34 And saith unto them, My soul is exceeding sorrowful unto death: tarry ye here, and watch.

35 And he went forward a little, and fell on the ground, and prayed that, if it were possible, the hour might pass from him.

36 And he said, Ab'ba, Father, all things *are* possible unto thee; take away this cup from me: nevertheless not what I will, but what thou wilt.

37 And he cometh, and findeth them sleeping, and saith unto Pe'ter, Si'mon, sleepest thou? couldest not thou watch one hour?

38 Watch ye and pray, lest ye enter into temptation. The spirit truly *is* ready, but the flesh *is* weak.

39 And again he went away, and prayed, and spake the same words.

40 And when he returned, he found them asleep again, (for their eyes were heavy,) neither wist they what to answer him.

41 And he cometh the third time, and saith unto them, Sleep on now, and take *your* rest: it is enough, the hour is come; behold, the Son of man is betrayed into the hands of sinners.

42 Rise up, let us go; lo, he that betrayeth me is at hand.

43 ¶ And immediately, while he yet spake, cometh Ju′das, one of the twelve, and with him a great mulitude with swords and staves, from the chief priests and the scribes and the elders.

44 And he that betrayed him had given them a token, saying, Whomsoever I shall kiss, that same is he; take him, and lead *him* away safely.

45 And as soon as he was come, he goeth straightway to him, and saith, Master, master; and kissed him.

46 ¶ And they laid their hands on him, and took him.

47 And one of them that stood by drew a sword, and smote a servant of the high priest, and cut off his ear.

48 And Je′sus answered and said unto them, Are ye come out, as against a thief, with swords and *with* staves to take me?

49 I was daily with you in the temple teaching, and ye took me not: but the scriptures must be fulfilled.

50 And they all forsook him, and fled.

51 And there followed him a certain young man, having a linen cloth cast about *his* naked *body;* and the young men laid hold on him:

52 And he left the linen cloth, and fled from them naked.

53 ¶ And they led Je′sus away to the high priest: and with him were assembled all the chief priests and the elders and the scribes.

54 And Pe′ter followed him afar off, even into the palace of the high priest: and he sat with the servants, and warmed himself at the fire.

55 And the chief priests and all the council sought for witness against Je′sus to put him to death; and found none.

56 For many bare false witness against him, but their witness agreed not together.

57 And there arose certain, and bare false witness against him, saying,

58 We heard him say, I will destroy this temple that is made with hands, and within three days I will build another made without hands.

59 But neither so did their witness agree together.

60 And the high priest stood up in the midst, and asked Je′sus, saying, Answerest thou nothing? what *is it which* these witness against thee?

61 But he held his peace, and answered nothing. Again the high priest asked him, and said unto him, Art thou the Christ, the Son of the Blessed?

62 And Je′sus said, I am: and ye shall see the Son of man sitting on the right hand of power, and coming in the clouds of heaven.

63 Then the high priest rent his clothes, and saith, What need we any further witnesses?

64 Ye have heard the blasphemy: what think ye? And they all condemned him to be guilty of death.

65 And some began to spit on him, and to cover his face, and to buffet him, and to say unto him, Prophesy: and the servants did strike him with the palms of their hands.

66 ¶ And as Pe′ter was beneath in the palace, there cometh one of the maids of the high priest:

67 And when she saw Pe′ter warming himself, she looked upon him, and said, And thou also wast with Je′sus of Naz′a-reth.

68 But he denied, saying, I know not, neither understand I what thou sayest. And he went out into the porch; and the cock crew.

69 And a maid saw him again, and began to say to them that stood by, This is *one* of them.

70 And he denied it again. And a little after, they that stood by said again to Pe′ter, Surely thou art *one* of them: for thou art a Gal-i-læ′an, and thy speech agreeth *thereto.*

71 But he began to curse and to swear, *saying,* I know not this man of whom ye speak.

72 And the second time the cock crew. And Pe′ter called to mind the word that Je′sus said unto him, Before the cock crow twice, thou shalt deny me thrice. And when he thought thereon, he wept.

15

AND straightway in the morning the chief priests held a consultation with the elders and scribes and the whole council, and bound Je′sus, and carried *him* away, and delivered *him* to Pi′late.

2 And Pi′late asked him, Art thou the King of the Jews? And he answering said unto him, Thou sayest *it.*

3 And the chief priests accused him of many things: but he answered nothing.

4 And Pi′late asked him again, saying, Answerest thou nothing? behold how many things they witness against thee.

5 But Je′sus yet answered nothing; so that Pi′late marvelled.

6 Now at *that* feast he released unto them one prisoner, whomsoever they desired.

7 And there was *one* named Ba-rab′bas, *which lay* bound with them that had made insurrection with him, who had committed murder in the insurrection.

8 And the multitude crying aloud began to desire *him to do* as he had ever done unto them.

9 But Pi′late answered them, saying, Will ye that I release unto you the King of the Jews?

10 For he knew that the chief priests had delivered him for envy.

11 But the chief priests moved the people, that he should rather release Ba-rab′bas unto them.

12 And Pi′late answered and said again unto them, What will ye then that I shall do *unto him* whom ye call the King of the Jews?

13 And they cried out again, Crucify him.

14 Then Pi′late said unto them, Why, what evil hath he done? And they cried out the more exceedingly, Crucify him.

15 ¶ And *so* Pi′late, willing to content the people, released Ba-rab′bas unto them, and delivered Je′sus, when he had scourged *him,* to be crucified.

16 And the soldiers led him away into the hall, called Præ-to′ri-um; and they call together the whole band.

17 And they clothed him with purple, and platted a crown of thorns, and put it about his *head,*

18 And began to salute him, Hail, King of the Jews!

19 And they smote him on the head with a reed, and did spit upon him, and bowing *their* knees worshipped him.

20 And when they had mocked him, they took off the purple from him, and put his own clothes on him, and led him out to crucify him.

21 And they compel one Si′mon a Cy-re′ni-an, who passed by, coming out of the country,

the father of Al-ex-an'der and Ru'fus, to bear his cross.

22 And they bring him unto the place Gol'go-tha, which is, being interpreted, The place of a skull.

23 And they gave him to drink wine mingled with myrrh: but he received it not.

24 And when they had crucified him, they parted his garments, casting lots upon them, what every man should take.

25 And it was the third hour, and they crucified him.

26 And the superscription of his accusation was written over, THE KING OF THE JEWS.

27 And with him they crucify two thieves; the one on his right hand, and the other on his left.

28 And the scripture was fulfilled, which saith, And he was numbered with the transgressors.

29 And they that passed by railed on him, wagging their heads, and saying, Ah, thou that destroyest the temple, and buildest it in three days,

30 Save thyself, and come down from the cross.

31 Likewise also the chief priests mocking said among themselves with the scribes, He saved others; himself he cannot save.

32 Let Christ the King of Is'ra-el descend now from the cross, that we may see and believe. And they that were crucified with him reviled him.

33 And when the sixth hour was come, there was darkness over the whole land until the ninth hour.

34 And at the ninth hour Je'sus cried with a loud voice, saying, E-lo'i, E-lo'i, la'ma sa-bach-tha'ni? which is, being interpreted, My God, my God, why hast thou forsaken me?

35 And some of them that stood by, when they heard it, said, Behold, he calleth E-li'as.

36 And one ran and filled a spunge full of vinegar, and put it on a reed, and gave him to drink, saying, Let alone; let us see whether E-li'as will come to take him down.

37 And Je'sus cried with a loud voice, and gave up the ghost.

38 And the veil of the temple was rent in twain from the top to the bottom.

39 ¶ And when the centurion, which stood over against him, saw that he so cried out, and gave up the ghost, he said, Truly this man was the Son of God.

40 There were also women looking on afar off: among whom was Ma'ry Mag-da-le'ne, and Ma'ry the mother of James the less and of Jo'-ses, and Sa-lo'me;

41 (Who also, when he was in Gal'i-lee, followed him, and ministered unto him;) and many other women which came up with him unto Je-ru'sa-lem.

42 ¶ And now when the even was come, because it was the preparation, that is, the day before the sabbath,

43 Jo'seph of Ar-i-ma-thæ'a, an honourable counsellor, which also waited for the kingdom of God, came, and went in boldly unto Pi'late, and craved the body of Je'sus.

44 And Pi'late marvelled if he were already dead: and calling unto him the centurion, he asked him whether he had been any while dead.

45 And when he knew it of the centurion, he gave the body to Jo'seph.

46 And he bought fine linen, and took him down, and wrapped him in the linen, and laid him in a sepulchre which was hewn out of a rock, and rolled a stone unto the door of the sepulchre.

47 And Ma'ry Mag-da-le'ne and Ma'ry the mother of Jo'ses beheld where he was laid.

16 AND when the sabbath was past, Ma'ry Mag-da-le'ne, and Ma'ry the mother of James, and Sa-lo'me, had bought sweet spices, that they might come and anoint him.

2 And very early in the morning the first day of the week, they came unto the sepulchre at the rising of the sun.

3 And they said among themselves, Who shall roll away the stone from the door of the sepulchre?

4 And when they looked, they saw that the stone was rolled away: for it was very great.

5 And entering into the sepulchre, they saw a young man sitting on the right side, clothed in a long white garment; and they were affrighted.

6 And he saith unto them, Be not affrighted: Ye seek Je'sus of Naz'a-reth, which was crucified: he is risen; he is not here: behold the place where they laid him.

7 But go your way, tell his disciples and Pe'ter that he goeth before you into Gal'i-lee: there shall ye see him, as he said unto you.

8 And they went out quickly, and fled from the sepulchre; for they trembled and were amazed: neither said they any thing to any man; for they were afraid.

9 ¶ Now when Jesus was risen early the first day of the week, he appeared first to Ma'ry Mag-da-le'ne, out of whom he had cast seven devils.

10 And she went and told them that had been with him, as they mourned and wept.

11 And they, when they had heard that he was alive, and had been seen of her, believed not.

12 ¶ After that he appeared in another form unto two of them, as they walked, and went into the country.

13 And they went and told it unto the residue: neither believed they them.

14 ¶ Afterward he appeared unto the eleven as they sat at meat, and upbraided them with their unbelief and hardness of heart, because they believed not them which had seen him after he was risen.

15 And he said unto them, Go ye into all the world, and preach the gospel to every creature.

16 He that believeth and is baptized shall be saved: but he that believeth not shall be damned.

17 And these signs shall follow them that believe; In my name shall they cast out devils; they shall speak with new tongues;

18 They shall take up serpents; and if they drink any deadly thing, it shall not hurt them; they shall lay hands on the sick, and they shall recover.

19 ¶ So then after the Lord had spoken unto them, he was received up into heaven, and sat on the right hand of God.

20 And they went forth, and preached every where, the Lord working with them, and confirming the word with signs following. Amen.

LUKE

1 FORASMUCH as many have taken in hand to set forth in order a declaration of those things which are most surely believed among us,

2 Even as they delivered them unto us, which from the beginning were eyewitnesses, and ministers of the word;

3 It seemed good to me also, having had perfect understanding of all things from the very first, to write unto thee in order, most excellent The-oph'i-lus,

4 That thou mightest know the certainty of those things, wherein thou hast been instructed.

5 ¶ THERE was in the days of Her'od, the king of Ju-dæ'a, a certain priest named Zach-a-ri'as, of the course of A-bi'a: and his wife was of the daughters of Aar'on, and her name was E-lis'a-beth.

6 And they were both righteous before God, walking in all the commandments and ordinances of the Lord blameless.

7 And they had no child, because that E-lis'a-beth was barren, and they both were now well stricken in years.

8 And it came to pass, that while he executed the priest's office before God in the order of his course,

9 According to the custom of the priest's office, his lot was to burn incense when he went into the temple of the Lord.

10 And the whole multitude of the people were praying without at the time of incense.

11 And there appeared unto him an angel of the Lord standing on the right side of the altar of incense.

12 And when Zach-a-ri'as saw him, he was troubled, and fear fell upon him.

13 But the angel said unto him, Fear not, Zach-a-ri'as: for thy prayer is heard; and thy wife E-lis'a-beth shall bear thee a son, and thou shalt call his name John.

14 And thou shalt have joy and gladness; and many shall rejoice at his birth.

15 For he shall be great in the sight of the Lord, and shall drink neither wine nor strong drink; and he shall be filled with the Ho'ly Ghost, even from his mother's womb.

16 And many of the children of Is'ra-el shall he turn to the Lord their God.

17 And he shall go before him in the spirit and power of E-li'as, to turn the hearts of the fathers to the children, and the disobedient to the wisdom of the just; to make ready a people prepared for the Lord.

18 And Zach-a-ri'as said unto the angel, Whereby shall I know this? for I am an old man, and my wife well stricken in years.

19 And the angel answering said unto him, I am Ga'bri-el, that stand in the presence of God; and am sent to speak unto thee, and to shew thee these glad tidings.

20 And, behold, thou shalt be dumb, and not able to speak, until the day that these things shall be performed, because thou believest not my words, which shall be fulfilled in their season.

21 And the people waited for Zach-a-ri'as, and marvelled that he tarried so long in the temple.

22 And when he came out, he could not speak unto them: and they perceived that he had seen a vision in the temple: for he beckoned unto them, and remained speechless.

23 And it came to pass, that, as soon as the days of his ministration were accomplished, he departed to his own house.

24 And after those days his wife E-lis'a-beth conceived, and hid herself five months, saying,

25 Thus hath the LORD dealt with me in the days wherein he looked on me, to take away my reproach among men.

26 And in the sixth month the angel Ga'bri-el was sent from God unto a city of Gal'i-lee, named Naz'a-reth,

27 To a virgin espoused to a man whose name was Jo'seph, of the house of Da'vid; and the virgin's name was Mary.

28 And the angel came in unto her, and said, Hail, thou that art highly favoured, the Lord is with thee: blessed art thou among women.

29 And when she saw him, she was troubled at his saying, and cast in her mind what manner of salutation this should be.

30 And the angel said unto her, Fear not, Ma'ry: for thou hast found favour with God.

31 And, behold, thou shalt conceive in thy womb, and bring forth a son, and shalt call his name JE'SUS.

32 He shall be great, and shall be called the Son of the Highest: and the Lord God shall give unto him the throne of his father Da'vid:

33 And he shall reign over the house of Ja'cob for ever; and of his kingdom there shall be no end.

34 Then said Ma'ry unto the angel, How shall this be, seeing I know not a man?

35 And the angel answered and said unto her, The Ho'ly Ghost shall come upon thee, and the power of the Highest shall overshadow thee: therefore also that holy thing which shall be born of thee shall be called the Son of God.

36 And, behold, thy cousin E-lis'a-beth, she hath also conceived a son in her old age: and this is the sixth month with her, who was called barren.

37 For with God nothing shall be impossible.

38 And Ma'ry said, Behold the handmaid of the Lord; be it unto me according to thy word. And the angel departed from her.

39 And Ma'ry arose in those days, and went into the hill country with haste, into a city of Ju'da;

40 And entered into the house of Zach-a-ri'as, and saluted E-lis'a-beth.

41 And it came to pass, that, when E-lis'a-beth heard the salutation of Ma'ry, the babe leaped in her womb; and E-lis'a-beth was filled with the Ho'ly Ghost:

42 And she spake out with a loud voice, and said, Blessed art thou among women, and blessed is the fruit of thy womb.

43 And whence is this to me, that the mother of my Lord should come to me?

44 For, lo, as soon as the voice of thy salutation sounded in mine ears, the babe leaped in my womb for joy.

45 And blessed is she that believed: for there shall be a performance of those things which were told her from the Lord.

46 And Ma'ry said, My soul doth magnify the Lord,

47 And my spirit hath rejoiced in God my Saviour.

48 For he hath regarded the low estate of his handmaiden: for, behold, from henceforth all generations shall call me blessed.

49 For he that is mighty hath done to me great things; and holy is his name.

50 And his mercy is on them that fear him from generation to generation.

51 He hath shewed strength with his arm; he hath scattered the proud in the imagination of their hearts.

52 He hath put down the mighty from their seats, and exalted them of low degree.

53 He hath filled the hungry with good things; and the rich he hath sent empty away.

54 He hath holpen his servant Is'ra-el, in remembrance of his mercy;

55 As he spake to our fathers, to A'bra-ham, and to his seed for ever.

56 And Ma'ry abode with her about three months, and returned to her own house.

57 Now E-lis'a-beth's full time came that she should be delivered; and she brought forth a son.

58 And her neighbours and her cousins heard how the Lord had shewed great mercy upon her; and they rejoiced with her.

59 And it came to pass, that on the eighth day they came to circumcise the child; and they called him Zach-a-ri'as, after the name of his father.

60 And his mother answered and said, Not so; but he shall be called John.

61 And they said unto her, There is none of thy kindred that is called by this name.

62 And they made signs to his father, how he would have him called.

63 And he asked for a writing table, and wrote, saying, His name is John. And they marvelled all.

64 And his mouth was opened immediately, and his tongue loosed, and he spake, and praised God.

65 And fear came on all that dwelt round about them: and all these sayings were noised abroad throughout all the hill country of Ju-dæ'a.

66 And all they that heard them laid them up in their hearts, saying, What manner of child shall this be! And the hand of the Lord was with him.

67 And his father Zach-a-ri'as was filled with the Ho'ly Ghost, and prophesied, saying,

68 Blessed be the Lord God of Is'ra-el; for he hath visited and redeemed his people,

69 And hath raised up an horn of salvation for us in the house of his servant Da'vid;

70 As he spake by the mouth of his holy prophets, which have been since the world began:

71 That we should be saved from our enemies, and from the hand of all that hate us;

72 To perform the mercy promised to our fathers, and to remember his holy covenant;

73 The oath which he sware to our father A'-bra-ham,

74 That he would grant unto us, that we being delivered out of the hand of our enemies might serve him without fear,

75 In holiness and righteousness before him, all the days of our life.

76 And thou, child, shalt be called the prophet of the Highest: for thou shalt go before the face of the Lord to prepare his ways;

77 To give knowledge of salvation unto his people by the remission of their sins,

78 Through the tender mercy of our God; whereby the dayspring from on high hath visited us,

79 To give light to them that sit in darkness and in the shadow of death, to guide our feet into the way of peace.

80 And the child grew, and waxed strong in spirit, and was in the deserts till the day of his shewing unto Is'ra-el.

2 AND it came to pass in those days, that there went out a decree from Cæ'sar Au-gus'tus, that all the world should be taxed.

2 (And this taxing was first made when Cy-re'ni-us was governor of Syr'i-a.)

3 And all went to be taxed, every one into his own city.

4 And Jo'seph also went up from Gal'i-lee, out of the city of Naz'a-reth, into Ju-dæ'a, unto the city of Da'vid, which is called Beth'le-hem; (because he was of the house and lineage of Da'vid:)

5 To be taxed with Ma'ry his espoused wife, being great with child.

6 And so it was, that, while they were there, the days were accomplished that she should be delivered.

7 And she brought forth her firstborn son, and wrapped him in swaddling clothes, and laid him in a manger; because there was no room for them in the inn.

8 And there were in the same country shepherds abiding in the field, keeping watch over their flock by night.

9 And, lo, the angel of the Lord came upon them, and the glory of the Lord shone round about them: and they were sore afraid.

10 And the angel said unto them, Fear not: for, behold, I bring you good tidings of great joy, which shall be to all people.

11 For unto you is born this day in the city of Da'vid a Saviour, which is Christ the Lord.

12 And this shall be a sign unto you; Ye shall find the babe wrapped in swaddling clothes, lying in a manger.

13 And suddenly there was with the angel a multitude of the heavenly host praising God, and saying,

14 Glory to God in the highest, and on earth peace, good will toward men.

15 And it came to pass, as the angels were gone away from them into heaven, the shepherds said one to another, Let us now go even unto Beth'le-hem, and see this thing which is come to pass, which the Lord hath made known unto us.

16 And they came with haste, and found Ma'-ry, and Jo'seph, and the babe lying in a manger.

17 And when they had seen it, they made known abroad the saying which was told them concerning this child.

18 And all they that heard it wondered at those things which were told them by the shepherds.

19 But Ma'ry kept all these things, and pondered them in her heart.

20 And the shepherds returned, glorifying and praising God for all the things that they had heard and seen, as it was told unto them.

21 And when eight days were accomplished for the circumcising of the child, his name was called JE'SUS, which was so named of the angel before he was conceived in the womb.

22 And when the days of her purification according to the law of Mo'ses were accomplished, they brought him to Je-ru'sa-lem, to present him to the Lord;

23 (As it is written in the law of the Lord,

Every male that openeth the womb shall be called holy to the Lord;)

24 And to offer a sacrifice according to that which is said in the law of the Lord, A pair of turtledoves, or two young pigeons.

25 And, behold, there was a man in Je-ru'sa-lem, whose name *was* Sim'e-on: and the same man *was* just and devout, waiting for the consolation of Is'ra-el: and the Ho'ly Ghost was upon him.

26 And it was revealed unto him by the Ho'ly Ghost, that he should not see death, before he had seen the Lord's Christ.

27 And he came by the Spirit into the temple: and when the parents brought in the child Je'sus, to do for him after the custom of the law,

28 Then took he him up in his arms, and blessed God, and said,

29 Lord, now lettest thou thy servant depart in peace, according to thy word:

30 For mine eyes have seen thy salvation,

31 Which thou hast prepared before the face of all people;

32 A light to lighten the Gen'tiles, and the glory of thy people Is'ra-el.

33 And Jo'seph and his mother marvelled at those things which were spoken of him.

34 And Sim'e-on blessed them, and said unto Ma'ry his mother, Behold, this *child* is set for the fall and rising again of many in Is'ra-el; and for a sign which shall be spoken against;

35 (Yea, a sword shall pierce through thy own soul also,) that the thoughts of many hearts may be revealed.

36 And there was one An'na, a prophetess, the daughter of Phan-u'el, of the tribe of A'ser: she was of a great age, and had lived with an husband seven years from her virginity;

37 And she *was* a widow of about fourscore and four years, which departed not from the temple, but served God with fastings and prayers night and day.

38 And she coming in that instant gave thanks likewise unto the Lord, and spake of him to all them that looked for redemption in Je-ru'sa-lem.

39 And when they had performed all things according to the law of the Lord, they returned into Gal'i-lee, to their own city Naz'a-reth.

40 And the child grew, and waxed strong in spirit, filled with wisdom: and the grace of God was upon him.

41 Now his parents went to Je-ru'sa-lem every year at the feast of the passover.

42 And when he was twelve years old, they went up to Je-ru'sa-lem after the custom of the feast.

43 And when they had fulfilled the days, as they returned, the child Je'sus tarried behind in Je-ru'sa-lem; and Jo'seph and his mother knew not *of* it.

44 But they, supposing him to have been in the company, went a day's journey; and they sought him among *their* kinsfolk and acquaintance.

45 And when they found him not, they turned back again to Je-ru'sa-lem, seeking him.

46 And it came to pass, that after three days they found him in the temple, sitting in the midst of the doctors, both hearing them, and asking them questions.

47 And all that heard him were astonished at his understanding and answers.

48 And when they saw him, they were amazed: and his mother said unto him, Son, why hast thou thus dealt with us? behold, thy father and I have sought thee sorrowing.

49 And he said unto them, How is it that ye sought me? wist ye not that I must be about my Father's business?

50 And they understood not the saying which he spake unto them.

51 And he went down with them, and came to Naz'a-reth, and was subject unto them: but his mother kept all these sayings in her heart.

52 And Je'sus increased in wisdom and stature, and in favour with God and man.

3 NOW in the fifteenth year of the reign of Ti-be'ri-us Cæ'sar, Pon'ti-us Pi'late being governor of Ju-dæ'a, and Her'od being tetrarch of Gal'i-lee, and his brother Phil'ip tetrarch of I-tu-ræ'a and of the region of Trach-o-ni'tis, and Ly-sa'ni-as the tetrarch of Ab-i-le'ne,

2 An'nas and Ca'ia-phas being the high priests, the word of God came unto John the son of Zach-a-ri'as in the wilderness.

3 And he came into all the country about Jor'dan, preaching the baptism of repentance for the remission of sins;

4 As it is written in the book of the words of E-sa'ias the prophet, saying, The voice of one crying in the wilderness, Prepare ye the way of the Lord, make his paths straight.

5 Every valley shall be filled, and every mountain and hill shall be brought low; and the crooked shall be made straight, and the rough ways *shall be* made smooth;

6 And all flesh shall see the salvation of God.

7 Then said he to the multitude that came forth to be baptized of him, O generation of vipers, who hath warned you to flee from the wrath to come?

8 Bring forth therefore fruits worthy of repentance, and begin not to say within yourselves, We have A'bra-ham to *our* father: for I say unto you, That God is able of these stones to raise up children unto A'bra-ham.

9 And now also the ax is laid unto the root of the trees: every tree therefore which bringeth not forth good fruit is hewn down, and cast into the fire.

10 And the people asked him, saying, What shall we do then?

11 He answereth and saith unto them, He that hath two coats, let him impart to him that hath none; and he that hath meat, let him do likewise.

12 Then came also publicans to be baptized, and said unto him, Master, what shall we do?

13 And he said unto them, Exact no more than that which is appointed you.

14 And the soldiers likewise demanded of him, saying, And what shall we do? And he said unto them, Do violence to no man, neither accuse *any* falsely; and be content with your wages.

15 And as the people were in expectation, and all men mused in their hearts of John, whether he were the Christ, or not;

16 John answered, saying unto *them* all, I indeed baptize you with water; but one mightier than I cometh, the latchet of whose shoes I am not worthy to unloose: he shall baptize you with the Ho'ly Ghost and with fire:

17 Whose fan *is* in his hand, and he will throughly purge his floor, and will gather the wheat into his garner; but the chaff he will burn with fire unquenchable.

18 And many other things in his exhortation preached he unto the people.

19 But Her'od the tetrarch, being reproved by him for He-ro'di-as his brother Phil'ip's wife, and for all the evils which Her'od had done,

20 Added yet this above all, that he shut up John in prison.

21 Now when all the people were baptized, it came to pass, that Je'sus also being baptized, and praying, the heaven was opened,

22 And the Ho'ly Ghost descended in a bodily shape like a dove upon him, and a voice came from heaven, which said, Thou art my beloved Son; in thee I am well pleased.

23 And Je'sus himself began to be about thirty years of age, being (as was supposed) the son of Jo'seph, which was *the son* of He'li,

24 Which was *the son* of Mat'that, which was *the son* of Le'vi, which was *the son* of Mel'chi, which was *the son* of Jan'na, which was *the son* of Jo'seph,

25 Which was *the son* of Mat-ta-thi'as, which was *the son* of A'mos, which was *the son* of Na'um, which was *the son* of Es'li, which was *the son* of Nag'ge,

26 Which was *the son* of Ma'ath, which was *the son* of Mat-ta-thi'as, which was *the son* of Sem'e-i, which was *the son* of Jo'seph, which was *the son* of Ju'da,

27 Which was *the son* of Jo-an'na, which was *the son* of Rhe'sa, which was *the son* of Zo-rob'-a-bel, which was *the son* of Sa-la'thi-el, which was *the son* of Ne'ri,

28 Which was *the son* of Mel'chi, which was *the son* of Ad'di, which was *the son* of Co'sam, which was *the son* of El-mo'dam, which was *the son* of Er,

29 Which was *the son* of Jo'se, which was *the son* of E-li-e'zer, which was *the son* of Jo'rim, which was *the son* of Mat'that, which was *the son* of Le'vi,

30 Which was *the son* of Sim'e-on, which was *the son* of Ju'da, which was *the son* of Jo'-seph, which was *the son* of Jo'nan, which was *the son* of E-li'a-kim,

31 Which was *the son* of Me'le-a, which was *the son* of Me'nan, which was *the son* of Mat'ta-tha, which was *the son* of Na'than, which was *the son* of Da'vid,

32 Which was *the son* of Jes'se, which was *the son* of O'bed, which was *the son* of Bo'oz, which was *the son* of Sal'mon, which was *the son* of Na-as'son,

33 Which was *the son* of A-min'a-dab, which was *the son* of A'ram, which was *the son* of Es'-rom, which was *the son* of Pha'res, which was *the son* of Ju'da,

34 Which was *the son* of Ja'cob, which was *the son* of I'saac, which was *the son* of A'bra-ham, which was *the son* of Tha'ra, which was *the son* of Na'chor,

35 Which was *the son* of Sa'ruch, which was *the son* of Ra'gau, which was *the son* of Pha'lec, which was *the son* of He'ber, which was *the son* of Sa'la,

36 Which was *the son* of Ca-i'nan, which was *the son* of Ar-phax'ad, which was *the son* of Sem, which was *the son* of No'e, which was *the son* of La'mech,

37 Which was *the son* of Ma-thu'sa-la, which was *the son* of E'noch, which was *the son* of Ja'red, which was *the son* of Ma-le'le-el, which was *the son* of Ca-i'nan,

38 Which was *the son* of E'nos, which was *the son* of Seth, which was *the son* of Ad'am, which was *the son* of God.

4 AND Je'sus being full of the Ho'ly Ghost returned from Jor'dan, and was led by the Spirit into the wilderness,

2 Being forty days tempted of the devil. And in those days he did eat nothing: and when they were ended, he afterward hungered.

3 And the devil said unto him, If thou be the Son of God, command this stone that it be made bread.

4 And Je'sus answered him, saying, It is written, That man shall not live by bread alone, but by every word of God.

5 And the devil taking him up into an high mountain, shewed unto him all the kingdoms of the world in a moment of time.

6 And the devil said unto him, All this power will I give thee, and the glory of them: for that is delivered unto me; and to whomsoever I will I give it.

7 If thou therefore wilt worship me, all shall be thine.

8 And Je'sus answered and said unto him, Get thee behind me, Sa'tan: for it is written, Thou shalt worship the Lord thy God, and him only shalt thou serve.

9 And he brought him to Je-ru'sa-lem, and set him on a pinnacle of the temple, and said unto him, If thou be the Son of God, cast thyself down from hence:

10 For it is written, He shall give his angels charge over thee, to keep thee:

11 And in *their* hands they shall bear thee up, lest at any time thou dash thy foot against a stone.

12 And Je'sus answering said unto him, It is said, Thou shalt not tempt the Lord thy God.

13 And when the devil had ended all the temptation, he departed from him for a season.

14 ¶ And Je'sus returned in the power of the Spirit into Gal'i-lee: and there went out a fame of him through all the region round about.

15 And he taught in their synagogues, being glorified of all.

16 ¶ And he came to Naz'a-reth, where he had been brought up: and, as his custom was, he went into the synagogue on the sabbath day, and stood up for to read.

17 And there was delivered unto him the book of the prophet E-sa'ias. And when he had opened the book he found the place where it was written,

18 The Spirit of the Lord *is* upon me, because he hath anointed me to preach the gospel to the poor; he hath sent me to heal the brokenheart-ed, to preach deliverance to the captives, and recovering of sight to the blind, to set at liberty them that are bruised,

19 To preach the acceptable year of the Lord.

20 And he closed the book, and he gave *it* again to the minister, and sat down. And the eyes of all them that were in the synagogue were fastened on him.

21 And he began to say unto them, This day is this scripture fulfilled in your ears.

22 And all bare him witness, and wondered at the gracious words which proceeded out of his mouth. And they said, Is not this Jo'seph's son?

23 And he said unto them, Ye will surely say unto me this proverb, Physician, heal thyself: whatsoever we have heard done in Ca-per'na-um, do also here in thy country.

24 And he said, Verily I say unto you, No prophet is accepted in his own country.

25 But I tell you of a truth, many widows were in Is'ra-el in the days of E-li'as, when the heaven was shut up three years and six months, when great famine was throughout all the land;

26 But unto none of them was E-li'as sent, save unto Sa-rep'ta, *a city* of Si'don, unto a woman *that was* a widow.

27 And many lepers were in Is'ra-el in the time of El-i-se'us the prophet; and none of them was cleansed, saving Na'a-man the Syr'i-an.

28 And all they in the synagogue, when they heard these things, were filled with wrath,

29 And rose up, and thrust him out of the city, and led him unto the brow of the hill whereon their city was built, that they might cast him down headlong.

30 But he passing through the midst of them went his way,

31 And came down to Ca-per'na-um, a city of Gal'i-lee, and taught them on the sabbath days.

32 And they were astonished at his doctrine: for his word was with power.

33 ¶ And in the synagogue there was a man, which had a spirit of an unclean devil, and cried out with a loud voice,

34 Saying, Let us alone; what have we to do with thee, thou Je'sus of Naz'a-reth? art thou come to destroy us? I know thee who thou art; the Holy One of God.

35 And Je'sus rebuked him, saying, Hold thy peace, and come out of him. And when the devil had thrown him in the midst, he came out of him, and hurt him not.

36 And they were all amazed, and spake among themselves, saying, What a word is this! for with authority and power he commandeth the unclean spirits, and they come out.

37 And the fame of him went out into every place of the country round about.

38 ¶ And he arose out of the synagogue, and entered into Si'mon's house. And Si'mon's wife's mother was taken with a great fever; and they besought him for her.

39 And he stood over her, and rebuked the fever; and it left her: and immediately she arose and ministered unto them.

40 ¶ Now when the sun was setting, all they that had any sick with divers diseases brought them unto him; and he laid his hands on every one of them, and healed them.

41 And devils also came out of many, crying out, and saying, Thou art Christ the Son of God. And he rebuking them suffered them not to speak: for they knew that he was Christ.

42 And when it was day, he departed and went into a desert place: and the people sought him, and came unto him, and stayed him, that he should not depart from them.

43 And he said unto them, I must preach the kingdom of God to other cities also: for therefore am I sent.

44 And he preached in the synagogues of Gal'i-lee.

5 AND it came to pass, that, as the people pressed upon him to hear the word of God, he stood by the lake of Gen-nes'a-ret,

2 And saw two ships standing by the lake: but the fishermen were gone out of them, and were washing their nets.

3 And he entered into one of the ships, which was Si'mon's, and prayed him that he would thrust out a little from the land. And he sat down, and taught the people out of the ship.

4 Now when he had left speaking, he said unto Si'mon, Launch out into the deep, and let down your nets for a draught.

5 And Si'mon answering said unto him, Master, we have toiled all the night, and have taken nothing: nevertheless at thy word I will let down the net.

6 And when they had this done, they inclosed a great multitude of fishes: and their net brake.

7 And they beckoned unto their partners, which were in the other ship, that they should come and help them. And they came, and filled both the ships, so that they began to sink.

8 When Si'mon Pe'ter saw it, he fell down at Je'sus' knees, saying, Depart from me; for I am a sinful man, O Lord.

9 For he was astonished, and all that were with him, at the draught of the fishes which they had taken:

10 And so was also James, and John, the sons of Zeb'e-dee, which were partners with Si'mon. And Je'sus said unto Si'mon, Fear not; from henceforth thou shalt catch men.

11 And when they had brought their ships to land, they forsook all, and followed him.

12 ¶ And it came to pass, when he was in a certain city, behold a man full of leprosy: who seeing Je'sus fell on his face, and besought him, saying, Lord, if thou wilt, thou canst make me clean.

13 And he put forth his hand, and touched him, saying, I will: be thou clean. And immediately the leprosy departed from him.

14 And he charged him to tell no man: but go, and shew thyself to the priest, and offer for thy cleansing, according as Mo'ses commanded, for a testimony unto them.

15 But so much the more went there a fame abroad of him: and great multitudes came together to hear, and to be healed by him of their infirmities.

16 ¶ And he withdrew himself into the wilderness, and prayed.

17 And it came to pass on a certain day, as he was teaching, that there were Phar'i-sees and doctors of the law sitting by, which were come out of every town of Gal'i-lee, and Ju-dæ'-a, and Je-ru'sa-lem: and the power of the Lord was present to heal them.

18 ¶ And, behold, men brought in a bed a man which was taken with a palsy: and they sought means to bring him in, and to lay him before him.

19 And when they could not find by what way they might bring him in because of the multitude, they went upon the house top, and let him down through the tiling with his couch into the midst before Je'sus.

20 And when he saw their faith, he said unto him, Man, thy sins are forgiven thee.

21 And the scribes and the Phar'i-sees began to reason, saying, Who is this which speaketh blasphemies? Who can forgive sins, but God alone?

22 But when Je'sus perceived their thoughts, he answering said unto them, What reason ye in your hearts?

23 Whether is easier, to say, Thy sins be forgiven thee; or to say, Rise up and walk?

24 But that ye may know that the Son of man hath power upon earth to forgive sins, (he said unto the sick of the palsy,) I say unto thee, Arise, and take up thy couch, and go into thine house.

25 And immediately he rose up before them, and took up that whereon he lay, and departed to his own house, glorifying God.

26 And they were all amazed, and they glorified God, and were filled with fear, saying, We have seen strange things to day.

27 ¶ And after these things he went forth, and saw a publican, named Le'vi, sitting at the receipt of custom: and he said unto him, Follow me.

28 And he left all, rose up, and followed him.

29 And Le'vi made him a great feast in his own house: and there was a great company of

publicans and of others that sat down with them.

30 But their scribes and Phar'i-sees murmured against his disciples, saying, Why do ye eat and drink with publicans and sinners?

31 And Je'sus answering said unto them, They that are whole need not a physician; but they that are sick.

32 I came not to call the righteous, but sinners to repentance.

33 ¶ And they said unto him, Why do the disciples of John fast often, and make prayers, and likewise *the disciples* of the Phar'i-sees; but thine eat and drink?

34 And he said unto them, Can ye make the children of the bridechamber fast, while the bridegroom is with them?

35 But the days will come, when the bridegroom shall be taken away from them, and then shall they fast in those days.

36 ¶ And he spake also a parable unto them; No man putteth a piece of a new garment upon an old; if otherwise, then both the new maketh a rent, and the piece that was *taken* out of the new agreeth not with the old.

37 And no man putteth new wine into old bottles; else the new wine will burst the bottles, and be spilled, and the bottles shall perish.

38 But new wine must be put into new bottles; and both are preserved.

39 No man also having drunk old *wine* straightway desireth new: for he saith, The old is better.

6 AND it came to pass on the second sabbath after the first, that he went through the corn fields; and his disciples plucked the ears of corn, and did eat rubbing *them* in *their* hands.

2 And certain of the Phar'i-sees said unto them, Why do ye that which is not lawful to do on the sabbath days?

3 And Je'sus answering them said, Have ye not read so much as this, what Da'vid did, when himself was an hungred, and they which were with him;

4 How he went into the house of God, and did take and eat the shewbread, and gave also to them that were with him; which it is not lawful to eat but for the priests alone?

5 And he said unto them, That the Son of man is Lord also of the sabbath.

6 And it came to pass also on another sabbath, that he entered into the synagogue and taught: and there was a man whose right hand was withered.

7 And the scribes and Phar'i-sees watched him, whether he would heal on the sabbath day; that they might find an accusation against him.

8 But he knew their thoughts, and said unto the man which had the withered hand, Rise up, and stand forth in the midst. And he arose and stood forth.

9 Then said Je'sus unto them, I will ask you one thing; Is it lawful on the sabbath days to do good, or to do evil? to save life, or to destroy *it?*

10 And looking round about upon them all, he said unto the man, Stretch forth thy hand. And he did so: and his hand was restored whole as the other.

11 And they were filled with madness; and communed one with another what they might do to Je'sus.

12 And it came to pass in those days, that he went out into a mountain to pray, and continued all night in prayer to God.

13 ¶ And when it was day, he called *unto* him his disciples: and of them he chose twelve, whom also he named apostles;

14 Si'mon, (whom he also named Pe'ter,) and Andrew his brother, James and John, Phil'ip and Bar-thol'o-mew,

15 Mat'thew and Thom'as, James the *son of* Al-phæ'us, and Si'mon called Ze-lo'tes,

16 And Ju'das *the brother* of James, and Ju'das Is-car'i-ot, which also was the traitor.

17 ¶ And he came down with them, and stood in the plain, and the company of his disciples, and a great multitude of people out of all Ju-dæ'a and Je-ru'sa-lem, and from the sea coast of Tyre and Si'don, which came to hear him, and to be healed of their diseases;

18 And they that were vexed with unclean spirits: and they were healed.

19 And the whole multitude sought to touch him: for there went virtue out of him, and healed *them* all.

20 ¶ And he lifted up his eyes on his disciples, and said, Blessed *be ye* poor: for yours is the kingdom of God.

21 Blessed *are ye* that hunger now: for ye shall be filled. Blessed *are ye* that weep now: for ye shall laugh.

22 Blessed are ye, when men shall hate you, and when they shall separate you *from their* company, and shall reproach *you,* and cast out your name as evil, for the Son of man's sake.

23 Rejoice ye in that day, and leap for joy: for, behold, your reward *is* great in heaven: for in the like manner did their fathers unto the prophets.

24 But woe unto you that are rich! for ye have received your consolation.

25 Woe unto you that are full! for ye shall hunger. Woe unto you that laugh now! for ye shall mourn and weep.

26 Woe unto you, when all men shall speak well of you! for so did their fathers to the false prophets.

27 ¶ But I say unto you which hear, Love your enemies, do good to them which hate you,

28 Bless them that curse you, and pray for them which despitefully use you.

29 And unto him that smiteth thee on the *one* cheek offer also the other; and him that taketh away thy cloke forbid not *to take thy* coat also.

30 Give to every man that asketh of thee; and of him that taketh away thy goods ask *them* not again.

31 And as ye would that men should do to you, do ye also to them likewise.

32 For if ye love them which love you, what thank have ye? for sinners also love those that love them.

33 And if ye do good to them which do good to you, what thank have ye? for sinners also do even the same.

34 And if ye lend *to them* of whom ye hope to receive, what thank have ye? for sinners also lend to sinners, to receive as much again.

35 But love ye your enemies, and do good, and lend, hoping for nothing again; and your reward shall be great, and ye shall be the children of the Highest: for he is kind unto the unthankful and *to* the evil.

36 Be ye therefore merciful, as your Father also is merciful.

37 Judge not, and ye shall not be judged: condemn not, and ye shall not be condemned: forgive, and ye shall be forgiven:

38 Give, and it shall be given unto you; good measure, pressed down, and shaken together, and running over, shall men give into your bos-

om. For with the same measure that ye mete withal it shall be measured to you again.

39 And he spake a parable unto them, Can the blind lead the blind: shall they not both fall into the ditch?

40 The disciple is not above his master: but every one that is perfect shall be as his master.

41 And why beholdest thou the mote that is in thy brother's eye, but perceivest not the beam that is in thine own eye?

42 Either how canst thou say to thy brother, Brother, let me pull out the mote that is in thine eye, when thou thyself beholdest not the beam that is in thine own eye? Thou hypocrite, cast out first the beam out of thine own eye, and then shalt thou see clearly to pull out the mote that is in thy brother's eye.

43 For a good tree bringeth not forth corrupt fruit; neither doth a corrupt tree bring forth good fruit.

44 For every tree is known by his own fruit. For of thorns men do not gather figs, nor of a bramble bush gather they grapes.

45 A good man out of the good treasure of his heart bringeth forth that which is good; and an evil man out of the evil treasure of his heart bringeth forth that which is evil: for of the abundance of the heart his mouth speaketh.

46 ¶ And why call ye me, Lord, Lord, and do not the things which I say?

47 Whosoever cometh to me, and heareth my sayings, and doeth them, I will shew you to whom he is like:

48 He is like a man which built an house, and digged deep, and laid the foundation on a rock: and when the flood arose, the stream beat vehemently upon that house, and could not shake it: for it was founded upon a rock.

49 But he that heareth, and doeth not, is like a man that without a foundation built an house upon the earth; against which the stream did beat vehemently, and immediately it fell; and the ruin of that house was great.

7 NOW when he had ended all his sayings in the audience of the people, he entered into Ca·per′na·um.

2 And a certain centurion's servant, who was dear unto him, was sick, and ready to die.

3 And when he heard of Je′sus, he sent unto him the elders of the Jews, beseeching him that he would come and heal his servant.

4 And when they came to Je′sus, they besought him instantly, saying, That he was worthy for whom he should do this:

5 For he loveth our nation, and he hath built us a synagogue.

6 Then Je′sus went with them. And when he was now not far from the house, the centurion sent friends to him, saying unto him, Lord, trouble not thyself: for I am not worthy that thou shouldest enter under my roof:

7 Wherefore neither thought I myself worthy to come unto thee: but say in a word, and my servant shall be healed.

8 For I also am a man set under authority, having under me soldiers, and I say unto one, Go, and he goeth; and to another, Come, and he cometh; and to my servant, Do this, and he doeth it.

9 When Je′sus heard these things, he marvelled at him, and turned him about, and said unto the people that followed him, I say unto you, I have not found so great faith, no, not in Is′ra-el.

10 And they that were sent, returning to the house, found the servant whole that had been sick.

11 ¶ And it came to pass the day after, that he went into a city called Na′in; and many of his disciples went with him, and much people.

12 Now when he came nigh to the gate of the city, behold, there was a dead man carried out, the only son of his mother, and she was a widow: and much people of the city was with her.

13 And when the Lord saw her, he had compassion on her, and said unto her, Weep not.

14 And he came and touched the bier: and they that bare him stood still. And he said, Young man, I say unto thee, Arise.

15 And he that was dead sat up, and began to speak. And he delivered him to his mother.

16 And there came a fear on all: and they glorified God, saying, That a great prophet is risen up among us; and, That God hath visited his people.

17 And this rumour of him went forth throughout all Ju-dæ′a, and throughout all the region round about.

18 And the disciples of John shewed him of all these things.

19 ¶ And John calling unto him two of his disciples sent them to Je′sus, saying, Art thou he that should come? or look we for another?

20 When the men were come unto him, they said, John Bap′tist hath sent us unto thee, saying, Art thou he that should come? or look we for another?

21 And in that same hour he cured many of their infirmities and plagues, and of evil spirits; and unto many that were blind he gave sight.

22 Then Je′sus answering said unto them, Go your way, and tell John what things ye have seen and heard; how that the blind see, the lame walk, the lepers are cleansed, the deaf hear, the dead are raised, to the poor the gospel is preached.

23 And blessed is he, whosoever shall not be offended in me.

24 ¶ And when the messengers of John were departed, he began to speak unto the people concerning John, What went ye out into the wilderness for to see? A reed shaken with the wind?

25 But what went ye out for to see? A man clothed in soft raiment? Behold, they which are gorgeously apparelled, and live delicately, are in kings' courts.

26 But what went ye out for to see? A prophet? Yea, I say unto you, and much more than a prophet.

27 This is he, of whom it is written, Behold, I send my messenger before thy face, which shall prepare thy way before thee.

28 For I say unto you, Among those that are born of women there is not a greater prophet than John the Bap′tist: but he that is least in the kingdom of God is greater than he.

29 And all the people that heard him, and the publicans, justified God, being baptized with the baptism of John.

30 But the Phar′i-sees and lawyers rejected the counsel of God against themselves, being not baptized of him.

31 ¶ And the Lord said, Whereunto then shall I liken the men of this generation? and to what are they like?

32 They are like unto children sitting in the marketplace, and calling one to another, and saying, We have piped unto you, and ye have not danced; we have mourned to you, and ye have not wept.

33 For John the Bap'tist came neither eating bread nor drinking wine; and ye say, He hath a devil.

34 The Son of man is come eating and drinking; and ye say, Behold a gluttonous man, and a winebibber, a friend of publicans and sinners!

35 But wisdom is justified of all her children.

36 ¶ And one of the Phar'i-sees desired him that he would eat with him. And he went into the Phar'i-see's house, and sat down to meat.

37 And, behold, a woman in the city, which was a sinner, when she knew that Je'sus sat at meat in the Phar'i-see's house, brought an alabaster box of ointment,

38 And stood at his feet behind *him* weeping, and began to wash his feet with tears, and did wipe *them* with the hairs of her head, and kissed his feet, and anointed *them* with the ointment.

39 Now when the Phar'i-see which had bidden him saw *it*, he spake within himself, saying, This man, if he were a prophet, would have known who and what manner of woman *this is* that toucheth him: for she is a sinner.

40 And Je'sus answering said unto him, Si'mon, I have somewhat to say unto thee. And he saith, Master, say on.

41 There was a certain creditor which had two debtors: the one owed five hundred pence, and the other fifty.

42 And when they had nothing to pay, he frankly forgave them both. Tell me therefore, which of them will love him most?

43 Si'mon answered and said, I suppose that *he*, to whom he forgave most. And he said unto him, Thou hast rightly judged.

44 And he turned to the woman, and said unto Si'mon, Seest thou this woman? I entered into thine house, thou gavest me no water for my feet: but she hath washed my feet with tears, and wiped *them* with the hairs of her head.

45 Thou gavest me no kiss: but this woman since the time I came in hath not ceased to kiss my feet.

46 My head with oil thou didst not anoint: but this woman hath anointed my feet with ointment.

47 Wherefore I say unto thee, Her sins, which are many, are forgiven; for she loved much: but to whom little is forgiven, *the same* loveth little.

48 And he said unto her, Thy sins are forgiven.

49 And they that sat at meat with him began to say within themselves, Who is this that forgiveth sins also?

50 And he said to the woman, Thy faith hath saved thee; go in peace.

8 AND it came to pass afterward, that he went throughout every city and village, preaching and shewing the glad tidings of the kingdom of God: and the twelve *were* with him,

2 And certain women, which had been healed of evil spirits and infirmities, Ma'ry called Mag-da-le'ne, out of whom went seven devils,

3 And Jo-an'na the wife of Chu'za Her'od's steward, and Su-san'na, and many others, which ministered unto him of their substance.

4 ¶ And when much people were gathered together, and were come to him out of every city, he spake by a parable:

5 A sower went out to sow his seed: and as he sowed, some fell by the way side; and it was trodden down, and the fowls of the air devoured it.

6 And some fell upon a rock; and as soon as it was sprung up, it withered away, because it lacked moisture.

7 And some fell among thorns; and the thorns sprang up with it, and choked it.

8 And other fell on good ground, and sprang up, and bare fruit a hundredfold. And when he had said these things, he cried, He that hath ears to hear, let him hear.

9 And his disciples asked him, saying, What might this parable be?

10 And he said, Unto you it is given to know the mysteries of the kingdom of God: but to others in parables; that seeing they might not see, and hearing they might not understand.

11 Now the parable is this: The seed is the word of God.

12 Those by the way side are they that hear; then cometh the devil, and taketh away the word out of their hearts, lest they should believe and be saved.

13 They on the rock *are they*, which, when they hear, receive the word with joy; and these have no root, which for a while believe, and in time of temptation fall away.

14 And that which fell among thorns are they, which, when they have heard, go forth, and are choked with cares and riches and pleasures of *this* life, and bring no fruit to perfection.

15 But that on the good ground are they, which in an honest and good heart, having heard the word, keep *it*, and bring forth fruit with patience.

16 ¶ No man, when he hath lighted a candle, covereth it with a vessel, or putteth *it* under a bed; but setteth *it* on a candlestick, that they which enter in may see the light.

17 For nothing is secret, that shall not be made manifest; neither *any thing* hid, that shall not be known and come abroad.

18 Take heed therefore how ye hear: for whosoever hath, to him shall be given; and whosoever hath not, from him shall be taken even that which he seemeth to have.

19 ¶ Then came to him *his* mother and his brethren, and could not come at him for the press.

20 And it was told him *by certain* which said, Thy mother and thy brethren stand without, desiring to see thee.

21 And he answered and said unto them, My mother and my brethren are these which hear the word of God, and do it.

22 ¶ Now it came to pass on a certain day, that he went into a ship with his disciples: and he said unto them, Let us go over unto the other side of the lake. And they launched forth.

23 But as they sailed he fell asleep: and there came down a storm of wind on the lake; and they were filled *with water*, and were in jeopardy.

24 And they came to him, and awoke him, saying, Master, master, we perish. Then he arose, and rebuked the wind and the raging of the water: and they ceased, and there was a calm.

25 And he said unto them, Where is your faith? And they being afraid wondered, saying one to another, What manner of man is this! for he commandeth even the winds and water, and they obey him.

26 ¶ And they arrived at the country of the Gad'a-renes, which is over against Gal'i-lee.

27 And when he went forth to land, there

met him out of the city a certain man, which had devils long time, and ware no clothes, neither abode in *any* house, but in the tombs.

28 When he saw Je′sus, he cried out, and fell down before him, and with a loud voice said, What have I to do with thee, Je′sus, *thou* Son of God most high? I beseech thee, torment me not.

29 (For he had commanded the unclean spirit to come out of the man. For oftentimes it had caught him: and he was kept bound with chains and in fetters; and he brake the bands, and was driven of the devil into the wilderness.)

30 And Je′sus asked him, saying, What is thy name? And he said, Legion: because many devils were entered into him.

31 And they besought him that he would not command them to go out into the deep.

32 And there was there an herd of many swine feeding on the mountain: and they besought him that he would suffer them to enter into them. And he suffered them.

33 Then went the devils out of the man, and entered into the swine: and the herd ran violently down a steep place into the lake, and were choked.

34 When they that fed *them* saw what was done, they fled, and went and told *it* in the city and in the country.

35 Then they went out to see what was done; and came to Je′sus, and found the man, out of whom the devils departed, sitting at the feet of Je′sus, clothed, and in his right mind: and they were afraid.

36 They also which saw *it* told them by what means he that was possessed of the devils was healed.

37 ¶ Then the whole multitude of the country of the Gad′a-renes round about besought him to depart from them; for they were taken with great fear: and he went up into the ship, and returned back again.

38 Now the man out of whom the devils were departed besought him that he might be with him: but Je′sus sent him away, saying,

39 Return to thine own house, and shew how great things God hath done unto thee. And he went his way, and published throughout the whole city how great things Je′sus had done unto him.

40 And it came to pass, that, when Je′sus was returned, the people gladly received him: for they were all waiting for him.

41 ¶ And, behold, there came a man named Ja-i′rus, and he was a ruler of the synagogue: and he fell down at Je′sus' feet, and besought him that he would come into his house:

42 For he had one only daughter, about twelve years of age, and she lay a dying. But as he went the people thronged him.

43 ¶ And a woman having an issue of blood twelve years, which had spent all her living upon physicians, neither could be healed of any,

44 Came behind *him*, and touched the border of his garment: and immediately her issue of blood stanched.

45 And Je′sus said, Who touched me? When all denied, Pe′ter and they that were with him said, Master, the multitude throng thee and press *thee*, and sayest thou, Who touched me?

46 And Je′sus said, Somebody hath touched me: for I perceive that virtue is gone out of me.

47 And when the woman saw that she was not hid, she came trembling, and falling down before him, she declared unto him before all the people for what cause she had touched him, and how she was healed immediately.

48 And he said unto her, Daughter, be of good comfort: thy faith hath made thee whole; go in peace.

49 ¶ While he yet spake, there cometh one from the ruler of the synagogue's *house*, saying to him, Thy daughter is dead; trouble not the Master.

50 But when Je′sus heard *it*, he answered him, saying, Fear not: believe only, and she shall be made whole.

51 And when he came into the house, he suffered no man to go in, save Pe′ter, and James, and John, and the father and the mother of the maiden.

52 And all wept, and bewailed her: but he said, Weep not; she is not dead, but sleepeth.

53 And they laughed him to scorn, knowing that she was dead.

54 And he put them all out, and took her by the hand, and called, saying, Maid, arise.

55 And her spirit came again, and she arose straightway: and he commanded to give her meat.

56 And her parents were astonished: but he charged them that they should tell no man what was done.

9 THEN he called his twelve disciples together, and gave them power and authority over all devils, and to cure diseases.

2 And he sent them to preach the kingdom of God, and to heal the sick.

3 And he said unto them, Take nothing for *your* journey, neither staves, nor scrip, neither bread, neither money; neither have two coats apiece.

4 And whatsoever house ye enter into, there abide, and thence depart.

5 And whosoever will not receive you, when ye go out of that city, shake off the very dust from your feet for a testimony against them.

6 And they departed, and went through the towns, preaching the gospel, and healing every where.

7 ¶ Now Her′od the tetrarch heard of all that was done by him: and he was perplexed, because that it was said of some, that John was risen from the dead;

8 And of some, that E-li′as had appeared; and of others, that one of the old prophets was risen again.

9 And Her′od said, John have I beheaded: but who is this, of whom I hear such things? And he desired to see him.

10 ¶ And the apostles, when they were returned, told him all that they had done. And he took them, and went aside privately into a desert place belonging to the city called Beth-sa′i-da.

11 And the people, when they knew *it*, followed him: and he received them, and spake unto them of the kingdom of God, and healed them that had need of healing.

12 And when the day began to wear away, then came the twelve, and said unto him, Send the multitude away, that they may go into the towns and country round about, and lodge, and get victuals: for we are here in a desert place.

13 But he said unto them, Give ye them to eat. And they said, We have no more but five loaves and two fishes; except we should go and buy meat for all this people.

14 For they were about five thousand men. And he said to his disciples, Make them sit down by fifties in a company.

15 And they did so, and made them all sit down.

16 Then he took the five loaves and the two

fishes, and looking up to heaven, he blessed them, and brake, and gave to the disciples to set before the multitude.

17 And they did eat, and were all filled: and there was taken up of fragments that remained to them twelve baskets.

18 ¶ And it came to pass, as he was alone praying, his disciples were with him: and he asked them, saying, Whom say the people that I am?

19 They answering said, John the Bap'tist; but some say, E-li'as; and others say, that one of the old prophets is risen again.

20 He said unto them, But whom say ye that I am? Pe'ter answering said, The Christ of God.

21 And he straitly charged them, and commanded them to tell no man that thing;

22 Saying, The Son of man must suffer many things, and be rejected of the elders and chief priests and scribes, and be slain, and be raised the third day.

23 ¶ And he said to them all, If any man will come after me, let him deny himself, and take up his cross daily, and follow me.

24 For whosoever will save his life shall lose it: but whosoever will lose his life for my sake, the same shall save it.

25 For what is a man advantaged, if he gain the whole world, and lose himself, or be cast away?

26 For whosoever shall be ashamed of me and of my words, of him shall the Son of man be ashamed, when he shall come in his own glory, and in his Father's, and of the holy angels.

27 But I tell you of a truth, there be some standing here, which shall not taste of death, till they see the kingdom of God.

28 ¶ And it came to pass about an eight days after these sayings, he took Pe'ter and John and James, and went up into a mountain to pray.

29 And as he prayed, the fashion of his countenance was altered, and his raiment was white and glistering.

30 And, behold, there talked with him two men, which were Mo'ses and E-li'as:

31 Who appeared in glory, and spake of his decease which he should accomplish at Je-ru'sa-lem.

32 But Pe'ter and they that were with him were heavy with sleep: and when they were awake, they saw his glory, and the two men that stood with him.

33 And it came to pass, as they departed from him, Pe'ter said unto Je'sus, Master, it is good for us to be here: and let us make three tabernacles; one for thee, and one for Mo'ses, and one for E-li'as: not knowing what he said.

34 While he thus spake, there came a cloud, and overshadowed them: and they feared as they entered into the cloud.

35 And there came a voice out of the cloud, saying, This is my beloved Son: hear him.

36 And when the voice was past, Je'sus was found alone. And they kept it close, and told no man in those days any of those things which they had seen.

37 ¶ And it came to pass, that on the next day, when they were come down from the hill, much people met him.

38 And, behold, a man of the company cried out, saying, Master, I beseech thee, look upon my son: for he is mine only child.

39 And, lo, a spirit taketh him, and he suddenly crieth out; and it teareth him that he foameth again, and bruising him hardly departeth from him.

40 And I besought thy disciples to cast him out; and they could not.

41 And Je'sus answering said, O faithless and perverse generation, how long shall I be with you, and suffer you? Bring thy son hither.

42 And as he was yet a coming, the devil threw him down, and tare him. And Je'sus rebuked the unclean spirit, and healed the child, and delivered him again to his father.

43 ¶ And they were all amazed at the mighty power of God. But while they wondered every one at all things which Je'sus did, he said unto his disciples,

44 Let these sayings sink down into your ears: for the Son of man shall be delivered into the hands of men.

45 But they understood not this saying, and it was hid from them, that they perceived it not: and they feared to ask him of that saying.

46 ¶ Then there arose a reasoning among them, which of them should be greatest.

47 And Je'sus, perceiving the thought of their heart, took a child, and set him by him,

48 And said unto them, Whosoever shall receive this child in my name receiveth me: and whosoever shall receive me receiveth him that sent me: for he that is least among you all, the same shall be great.

49 ¶ And John answered and said, Master, we saw one casting out devils in thy name; and we forbad him, because he followeth not with us.

50 And Je'sus said unto him, Forbid him not: for he that is not against us is for us.

51 ¶ And it came to pass, when the time was come that he should be received up, he stedfastly set his face to go to Je-ru'sa-lem,

52 And sent messengers before his face: and they went, and entered into a village of the Sa-mar'i-tans, to make ready for him.

53 And they did not receive him, because his face was as though he would go to Je-ru'sa-lem.

54 And when his disciples James and John saw this, they said, Lord, wilt thou that we command fire to come down from heaven, and consume them, even as E-li'as did?

55 But he turned, and rebuked them, and said, Ye know not what manner of spirit ye are of.

56 For the Son of man is not come to destroy men's lives, but to save them. And they went to another village.

57 ¶ And it came to pass, that, as they went in the way, a certain man said unto him, Lord, I will follow thee whithersoever thou goest.

58 And Je'sus said unto him, Foxes have holes, and birds of the air have nests; but the Son of man hath not where to lay his head.

59 And he said unto another, Follow me. But he said, Lord, suffer me first to go and bury my father.

60 Je'sus said unto him, Let the dead bury their dead: but go thou and preach the kingdom of God.

61 And another also said, LORD, I will follow thee; but let me first go bid them farewell, which are at home at my house.

62 And Je'sus said unto him, No man, having put his hand to the plow, and looking back, is fit for the kingdom of God.

10 AFTER these things the Lord appointed other seventy also, and sent them two and two before his face into every city and place, whither he himself would come.

2 Therefore said he unto them, The harvest truly is great, but the labourers are few: pray ye

therefore the Lord of the harvest, that he would send forth labourers into his harvest.

3 Go your ways: behold, I send you forth as lambs among wolves.

4 Carry neither purse, nor scrip, nor shoes: and salute no man by the way.

5 And into whatsoever house ye enter, first say, Peace be to this house.

6 And if the son of peace be there, your peace shall rest upon it: if not, it shall turn to you again.

7 And in the same house remain, eating and drinking such things as they give: for the labourer is worthy of his hire. Go not from house to house.

8 And into whatsoever city ye enter, and they receive you, eat such things as are set before you:

9 And heal the sick that are therein, and say unto them, The kingdom of God is come nigh unto you.

10 But into whatsoever city ye enter, and they receive you not, go your ways out into the streets of the same, and say,

11 Even the very dust of your city, which cleaveth on us, we do wipe off against you: notwithstanding be ye sure of this, that the kingdom of God is come nigh unto you.

12 But I say unto you, that it shall be more tolerable in that day for Sod'om, than for that city.

13 Woe unto thee, Cho-ra'zin! woe unto thee, Beth-sa'i-da! for if the mighty works had been done in Tyre and Si'don, which have been done in you, they had a great while ago repented, sitting in sackcloth and ashes.

14 But it shall be more tolerable for Tyre and Si'don at the judgment, than for you.

15 And thou Ca-per'na-um, which art exalted to heaven, shalt be thrust down to hell.

16 He that heareth you heareth me; and he that despiseth you despiseth me; and he that despiseth me despiseth him that sent me.

17 ¶ And the seventy returned again with joy, saying, Lord, even the devils are subject unto us through thy name.

18 And he said unto them, I beheld Sa'tan as lightning fall from heaven.

19 Behold, I give unto you power to tread on serpents and scorpions, and over all the power of the enemy: and nothing shall by any means hurt you.

20 Notwithstanding in this rejoice not, that the spirits are subject unto you; but rather rejoice, because your names are written in heaven.

21 ¶ In that hour Je'sus rejoiced in spirit, and said, I thank thee, O Father, Lord of heaven and earth, that thou hast hid these things from the wise and prudent, and hast revealed them unto babes: even so, Father; for so it seemed good in thy sight.

22 All things are delivered to me of my Father: and no man knoweth who the Son is, but the Father; and who the Father is, but the Son, and he to whom the Son will reveal him.

23 ¶ And he turned him unto his disciples, and said privately, Blessed are the eyes which see the things that ye see:

24 For I tell you, that many prophets and kings have desired to see those things which ye see, and have not seen them; and to hear those things which ye hear, and have not heard them.

25 ¶ And, behold, a certain lawyer stood up, and tempted him, saying, Master, what shall I do to inherit eternal life?

26 He said unto him, What is written in the law? how readest thou?

27 And he answering said, Thou shalt love the Lord thy God will all thy heart, and with all thy soul, and with all thy strength, and with all thy mind; and thy neighbour as thyself.

28 And he said unto him, Thou hast answered right; this do, and thou shalt live.

29 But he, willing to justify himself, said unto Je'sus, And who is my neighbour?

30 And Je'sus answering said, A certain man went down from Je-ru'sa-lem to Jer'i-cho, and fell among thieves, which stripped him of his raiment, and wounded him, and departed, leaving him half dead.

31 And by chance there came down a certain priest that way: and when he saw him, he passed by on the other side.

32 And likewise a Le'vite, when he was at the place, came and looked on him, and passed by on the other side.

33 But a certain Sa-mar'i-tan, as he journeyed, came where he was: and when he saw him, he had compassion on him.

34 And went to him, and bound up his wounds, pouring in oil and wine, and set him on his own beast, and brought him to an inn, and took care of him.

35 And on the morrow when he departed, he took out two pence, and gave them to the host, and said unto him, Take care of him; and whatsoever thou spendest more, when I come again, I will repay thee.

36 Which now of these three, thinkest thou, was neighbour unto him that fell among the thieves?

37 And he said, He that shewed mercy on him. Then said Je'sus unto him, Go, and do thou likewise.

38 ¶ Now it came to pass, as they went, that he entered into a certain village: and a certain woman named Mar'tha received him into her house.

39 And she had a sister called Ma'ry, which also sat at Je'sus' feet, and heard his word.

40 But Mar'tha was cumbered about much serving, and came to him, and said, Lord, dost thou not care that my sister hath left me to serve alone? bid her therefore that she help me.

41 And Je'sus answered and said unto her, Mar'tha, Mar'tha, thou art careful and troubled about many things:

42 But one thing is needful: and Ma'ry hath chosen that good part, which shall not be taken away from her.

11 AND it came to pass, that, as he was praying in a certain place, when he ceased, one of his disciples said unto him, Lord, teach us to pray, as John also taught his disciples.

2 And he said unto them, When ye pray, say, Our Father which art in heaven, Hallowed be thy name. Thy kingdom come. Thy will be done, as in heaven, so in earth.

3 Give us day by day our daily bread.

4 And forgive us our sins; for we also forgive every one that is indebted to us. And lead us not into temptation; but deliver us from evil.

5 And he said unto them, Which of you shall have a friend, and shall go unto him at midnight, and say unto him, Friend, lend me three loaves;

6 For a friend of mine in his journey is come to me, and I have nothing to set before him?

7 And he from within shall answer and say, Trouble me not: the door is now shut, and my

children are with me in bed; I cannot rise and give thee.

8 I say unto you, Though he will not rise and give him, because he is his friend, yet because of his importunity he will rise and give him as many as he needeth.

9 And I say unto you, Ask, and it shall be given you; seek, and ye shall find; knock, and it shall be opened unto you.

10 For every one that asketh receiveth; and he that seeketh findeth; and to him that knocketh it shall be opened.

11 If a son shall ask bread of any of you that is a father, will he give him a stone? or if *he ask* a fish, will he for a fish give him a serpent?

12 Or if he shall ask an egg, will he offer him a scorpion?

13 If ye then, being evil, know how to give good gifts unto your children: how much more shall *your* heavenly Father give the Ho'ly Spir'it to them that ask him?

14 ¶ And he was casting out a devil, and it was dumb. And it came to pass, when the devil was gone out, the dumb spake; and the people wondered.

15 But some of them said, He casteth out devils through Be'el'ze-bub the chief of the devils.

16 And others, tempting *him*, sought of him a sign from heaven.

17 But he, knowing their thoughts, said unto them, Every kingdom divided against itself is brought to desolation; and a house *divided* against a house falleth.

18 If Sa'tan also be divided against himself, how shall his kingdom stand? because ye say that I cast out devils through Be'el'ze-bub.

19 And if I by Be'el'ze-bub cast out devils, by whom do your sons cast *them* out? therefore shall they be your judges.

20 But if I with the finger of God cast out devils, no doubt the kingdom of God is come upon you.

21 When a strong man armed keepeth his palace, his goods are in peace:

22 But when a stronger than he shall come upon him, and overcome him, he taketh from him all his armour wherein he trusted, and divideth his spoils.

23 He that is not with me is against me: and he that gathereth not with me scattereth.

24 When the unclean spirit is gone out of a man, he walketh through dry places, seeking rest; and finding none, he saith, I will return unto my house whence I came out.

25 And when he cometh, he findeth *it* swept and garnished.

26 Then goeth he, and taketh *to him* seven other spirits more wicked than himself; and they enter in, and dwell there: and the last *state* of that man is worse than the first.

27 ¶ And it came to pass, as he spake these things, a certain woman of the company lifted up her voice, and said unto him, Blessed *is* the womb that bare thee, and the paps which thou hast sucked.

28 But he said, Yea rather, blessed *are* they that hear the word of God, and keep it.

29 ¶ And when the people were gathered thick together, he began to say, This is an evil generation: they seek a sign; and there shall no sign be given it, but the sign of Jo'nas the prophet.

30 For as Jo'nas was a sign unto the Nin'e-vites, so shall also the Son of man be to this generation.

31 The queen of the south shall rise up in the judgment with the men of this generation, and condemn them: for she came from the utmost parts of the earth to hear the wisdom of Sol'o-mon; and, behold, a greater than Sol'o-mon *is* here.

32 The men of Nin'e-ve shall rise up in the judgment with this generation, and shall condemn it: for they repented at the preaching of Jo'nas; and, behold, a greater than Jo'nas *is* here.

33 No man, when he hath lighted a candle, putteth *it* in a secret place, neither under a bushel, but on a candlestick, that they which come in may see the light.

34 The light of the body is the eye: therefore when thine eye is single, thy whole body also is full of light; but when *thine eye* is evil, thy body also *is* full of darkness.

35 Take heed therefore that the light which is in thee be not darkness.

36 If thy whole body therefore *be* full of light, having no part dark, the whole shall be full of light, as when the bright shining of a candle doth give thee light.

37 ¶ And as he spake, a certain Phar'i-see besought him to dine with him: and he went in, and sat down to meat.

38 And when the Phar'i-see saw *it*, he marvelled that he had not first washed before dinner.

39 And the Lord said unto him, Now do ye Phar'i-sees make clean the outside of the cup and the platter; but your inward part is full of ravening and wickedness.

40 *Ye* fools, did not he that made that which is without make that which is within also?

41 But rather give alms of such things as ye have; and, behold, all things are clean unto you.

42 But woe unto you, Phar'i-sees! for ye tithe mint and rue and all manner of herbs, and pass over judgment and the love of God: these ought ye to have done, and not to leave the other undone.

43 Woe unto you, Phar'i-sees! for ye love the uppermost seats in the synagogues, and greetings in the markets.

44 Woe unto you, scribes and Phar'i-sees, hypocrites! for ye are as graves which appear not, and the men that walk over *them* are not aware *of them*.

45 ¶ Then answered one of the lawyers, and said unto him, Master, thus saying thou reproachest us also.

46 And he said, Woe unto you also, *ye* lawyers! for ye lade men with burdens grievous to be borne, and ye yourselves touch not the burdens with one of your fingers.

47 Woe unto you! for ye build the sepulchres of the prophets, and your fathers killed them.

48 Truly ye bear witness that ye allow the deeds of your fathers: for they indeed killed them, and ye build their sepulchres.

49 Therefore also said the wisdom of God, I will send them prophets and apostles, and *some* of them they shall slay and persecute:

50 That the blood of all the prophets, which was shed from the foundation of the world, may be required of this generation;

51 From the blood of A'bel unto the blood of Zach-a-ri'as, which perished between the altar and the temple: verily I say unto you, It shall be required of this generation.

52 Woe unto you, lawyers! for ye have taken away the key of knowledge: ye entered not in yourselves, and them that were entering in ye hindered.

53 And as he said these things unto them, the

scribes and the Phar'i-sees began to urge *him* vehemently, and to provoke him to speak of many things:

54 Laying wait for him, and seeking to catch something out of his mouth, that they might accuse him.

12 IN the mean time, when there were gathered together an innumerable multitude of people, insomuch that they trode one upon another, he began to say unto his disciples first of all, Beware ye of the leaven of the Phar'i-sees, which is hypocrisy.

2 For there is nothing covered, that shall not be revealed; neither hid, that shall not be known.

3 Therefore whatsoever ye have spoken in darkness shall be heard in the light; and that which ye have spoken in the ear in closets shall be proclaimed upon the house tops.

4 And I say unto you my friends, Be not afraid of them that kill the body, and after that have no more that they can do.

5 But I will forewarn you whom ye shall fear: Fear him, which after he hath killed hath power to cast into hell; yea, I say unto you, Fear him.

6 Are not five sparrows sold for two farthings, and not one of them is forgotten before God?

7 But even the very hairs of your head are all numbered. Fear not therefore: ye are of more value than many sparrows.

8 Also I say unto you, Whosoever shall confess me before men, him shall the Son of man also confess before the angels of God:

9 But he that denieth me before men shall be denied before the angels of God.

10 And whosoever shall speak a word against the Son of man, it shall be forgiven him: but unto him that blasphemeth against the Ho'ly Ghost it shall not be forgiven.

11 And when they bring you unto the synagogues, and *unto* magistrates, and powers, take ye no thought how or what thing ye shall answer, or what ye shall say:

12 For the Ho'ly Ghost shall teach you in the same hour what ye ought to say.

13 ¶ And one of the company said unto him, Master, speak to my brother, that he divide the inheritance with me.

14 And he said unto him, Man, who made me a judge or a divider over you?

15 And he said unto them, Take heed, and beware of covetousness: for a man's life consisteth not in the abundance of the things which he possesseth.

16 And he spake a parable unto them, saying, The ground of a certain rich man brought forth plentifully:

17 And he thought within himself, saying, What shall I do, because I have no room where to bestow my fruits?

18 And he said, This will I do: I' will pull down my barns, and build greater; and there will I bestow all my fruits and my goods.

19 And I will say to my soul; Soul, thou hast much goods laid up for many years; take thine ease, eat, drink, *and* be merry.

20 But God said unto him, *Thou* fool, this night thy soul shall be required of thee: then whose shall those things be, which thou hast provided?

21 So *is* he that layeth up treasure for himself, and is not rich toward God.

22 ¶ And he said unto his disciples, Therefore I say unto you, Take no thought for your life, what

ye shall eat; neither for the body, what ye shall put on.

23 The life is more than meat, and the body *is more* than raiment.

24 Consider the ravens: for they neither sow nor reap; which neither have storehouse nor barn; and God feedeth them: how much more are ye better than the fowls?

25 And which of you with taking thought can add to his stature one cubit?

26 If ye then be not able to do that thing which is least, why take ye thought for the rest?

27 Consider the lilies how they grow: they toil not, they spin not; and yet I say unto you, that Sol'o-mon in all his glory was not arrayed like one of these.

28 If then God so clothe the grass, which is to day in the field, and to morrow is cast into the oven; how much more *will he clothe* you, O ye of little faith?

29 And seek not ye what ye shall eat, or what ye shall drink, neither be ye of doubtful mind.

30 For all these things do the nations of the world seek after: and your Father knoweth that ye have need of these things.

31 ¶ But rather seek ye the kingdom of God; and all these things shall be added unto you.

32 Fear not, little flock; for it is your Father's good pleasure to give you the kingdom.

33 Sell that ye have, and give alms; provide yourselves bags which wax not old, a treasure in the heavens that faileth not, where no thief approacheth, neither moth corrupteth.

34 For where your treasure is, there will your heart be also.

35 Let your loins be girded about, and *your* lights burning;

36 And ye yourselves like unto men that wait for their lord, when he will return from the wedding; that when he cometh and knocketh, they may open unto him immediately.

37 Blessed *are* those servants, whom the lord when he cometh shall find watching: verily I say unto you, that he shall gird himself, and make them to sit down to meat, and will come forth and serve them.

38 And if he shall come in the second watch, or come in the third watch, and find *them* so, blessed are those servants.

39 And this know, that if the goodman of the house had known what hour the thief would come, he would have watched, and not have suffered his house to be broken through.

40 Be ye therefore ready also: for the Son of man cometh at an hour when ye think not.

41 ¶ Then Pe'ter said unto him, Lord, speakest thou this parable unto us, or even to all?

42 And the Lord said, Who then is that faithful and wise steward, whom *his* lord shall make ruler over his household, to give *them* their portion of meat in due season?

43 Blessed *is* that servant, whom his lord when he cometh shall find so doing.

44 Of a truth I say unto you, that he will make him ruler over all that he hath.

45 But and if that servant say in his heart, My lord delayeth his coming; and shall begin to beat the menservants and maidens, and to eat and drink, and to be drunken;

46 The lord of that servant will come in a day when he looketh not for *him*, and at an hour when he is not aware, and will cut him in sunder, and will appoint him his portion with the unbelievers.

47 And that servant, which knew his lord's will, and prepared not *himself*, neither did ac-

cording to his will, shall be beaten with many *stripes*.

48 But he that knew not, and did commit things worthy of stripes, shall be beaten with few *stripes*. For unto whomsoever much is given, of him shall be much required: and to whom men have committed much, of them they will ask the more.

49 ¶ I am come to send fire on the earth; and what will I, if it be already kindled?

50 But I have a baptism to be baptized with; and how am I straitened till it be accomplished!

51 Suppose ye that I am come to give peace on earth? I tell you, Nay; but rather division:

52 For from henceforth there shall be five in one house divided, three against two, and two against three.

53 The father shall be divided against the son, and the son against the father; the mother against the daughter, and the daughter against the mother; the mother in law against her daughter in law, and the daughter in law against the mother in law.

54 ¶ And he said also to the people, When ye see a cloud rise out of the west, straightway ye say, There cometh a shower; and so it is.

55 And when *ye see* the south wind blow, ye say, There will be heat; and it cometh to pass.

56 *Ye* hypocrites, ye can discern the face of the sky and of the earth; but how is it that ye do not discern this time?

57 Yea, and why even of yourselves judge ye not what is right?

58 ¶ When thou goest with thine adversary to the magistrate, *as thou art* in the way, give diligence that thou mayest be delivered from him; lest he hale thee to the judge, and the judge deliver thee to the officer, and the officer cast thee into prison.

59 I tell thee, thou shalt not depart thence, till thou hast paid the very last mite.

13 THERE were present at that season some that told him of the Gal-i-læ′ans, whose blood Pi′late had mingled with their sacrifices.

2 And Je′sus answering said unto them, Suppose ye that these Gal-i-læ′ans were sinners above all the Gal-i-læ′ans, because they suffered such things?

3 I tell you, Nay: but, except ye repent, ye shall all likewise perish.

4 Or those eighteen, upon whom the tower in Si-lo′am fell, and slew them, think ye that they were sinners above all men that dwelt in Je-ru′sa-lem?

5 I tell you, Nay: but, except ye repent, ye shall all likewise perish.

6 ¶ He spake also this parable; A certain *man* had a fig tree planted in his vineyard; and he came and sought fruit thereon, and found none.

7 Then said he unto the dresser of his vineyard, Behold, these three years I come seeking fruit on this fig tree, and find none: cut it down; why cumbereth it the ground?

8 And he answering said unto him, Lord, let it alone this year also, till I shall dig about it, and dung *it*:

9 And if it bear fruit, *well*: and if not, *then* after that thou shalt cut it down.

10 And he was teaching in one of the synagogues on the sabbath.

11 ¶ And, behold, there was a woman which had a spirit of infirmity eighteen years, and was bowed together, and could in no wise lift up *herself*.

12 And when Je′sus saw her, he called *her to him*, and said unto her, Woman, thou art loosed from thine infirmity.

13 And he laid *his* hands on her: and immediately she was made straight, and glorified God.

14 And the ruler of the synagogue answered with indignation, because that Je′sus had healed on the sabbath day, and said unto the people, There are six days in which men ought to work: in them therefore come and be healed, and not on the sabbath day.

15 The Lord then answered him, and said, *Thou* hypocrite, doth not each one of you on the sabbath loose his ox or *his* ass from the stall, and lead *him* away to watering?

16 And ought not this woman, being a daughter of A′bra-ham, whom Sa′tan hath bound, lo, these eighteen years, be loosed from this bond on the sabbath day?

17 And when he had said these things, all his adversaries were ashamed: and all the people rejoiced for all the glorious things that were done by him.

18 ¶ Then said he, Unto what is the kingdom of God like? and whereunto shall I resemble it?

19 It is like a grain of mustard seed, which a man took, and cast into his garden; and it grew, and waxed a great tree; and the fowls of the air lodged in the branches of it.

20 And again he said, Whereunto shall I liken the kingdom of God?

21 It is like leaven, which a woman took and hid in three measures of meal, till the whole was leavened.

22 And he went through the cities and villages, teaching, and journeying toward Je-ru′sa-lem.

23 Then said one unto him, Lord, are there few that be saved? And he said unto them,

24 ¶ Strive to enter in at the strait gate: for many, I say unto you, will seek to enter in, and shall not be able.

25 When once the master of the house is risen up, and hath shut to the door, and ye begin to stand without, and to knock at the door, saying, Lord, Lord, open unto us; and he shall answer and say unto you, I know you not whence ye are:

26 Then shall ye begin to say, We have eaten and drunk in thy presence, and thou hast taught in our streets.

27 But he shall say, I tell you, I know you not whence ye are; depart from me, all *ye* workers of iniquity.

28 There shall be weeping and gnashing of teeth, when ye shall see A′bra-ham, and I′saac, and Ja′cob, and all the prophets, in the kingdom of God, and you *yourselves* thrust out.

29 And they shall come from the east, and *from* the west, and from the north, and *from* the south, and shall sit down in the kingdom of God.

30 And, behold, there are last which shall be first, and there are first which shall be last.

31 ¶ The same day there came certain of the Phar′i-sees, saying unto him, Get thee out, and depart hence: for Her′od will kill thee.

32 And he said unto them, Go ye, and tell that fox, Behold, I cast out devils, and I do cures to day and to morrow, and the third *day* I shall be perfected.

33 Nevertheless I must walk to day, and to morrow, and the *day* following: for it cannot be that a prophet perish out of Je-ru′sa-lem.

34 O Je-ru′sa-lem, Je-ru′sa-lem, which killest the prophets, and stonest them that are sent unto thee; how often would I have gathered thy

children together, as a hen *doth gather* her brood under *her* wings, and ye would not!

35 Behold, your house is left unto you desolate: and verily I say unto you, Ye shall not see me, until *the time* come when ye shall say, Blessed *is* he that cometh in the name of the Lord.

14 AND it came to pass, as he went into the house of one of the chief Phar'i-sees to eat bread on the sabbath day, that they watched him.

2 And, behold, there was a certain man before him which had the dropsy.

3 And Je'sus answering spake unto the lawyers and Phar'i-sees, saying, Is it lawful to heal on the sabbath day?

4 And they held their peace. And he took *him*, and healed him, and let him go;

5 And answered them, saying, Which of you shall have an ass or an ox fallen into a pit, and will not straightway pull him out on the sabbath day?

6 And they could not answer him again to these things.

7 ¶ And he put forth a parable to those which were bidden, when he marked how they chose out the chief rooms; saying unto them,

8 When thou art bidden of any *man* to a wedding, sit not down in the highest room; lest a more honourable man than thou be bidden of him;

9 And he that bade thee and him come and say to thee, Give this man place; and thou begin with shame to take the lowest room.

10 But when thou art bidden, go and sit down in the lowest room; that when he that bade thee cometh, he may say unto thee, Friend, go up higher: then shalt thou have worship in the presence of them that sit at meat with thee.

11 For whosoever exalteth himself shall be abased; and he that humbleth himself shall be exalted.

12 ¶ Then said he also to him that bade him, When thou makest a dinner or a supper, call not thy friends, nor thy brethren, neither thy kinsmen, nor *thy* rich neighbours, lest they also bid thee again, and a recompence be made thee.

13 But when thou makest a feast, call the poor, the maimed, the lame, the blind:

14 And thou shalt be blessed; for they cannot recompense thee: for thou shalt be recompensed at the resurrection of the just.

15 ¶ And when one of them that sat at meat with him heard these things, he said unto him, Blessed *is* he that shall eat bread in the kingdom of God.

16 Then said he unto him, A certain man made a great supper, and bade many:

17 And sent his servant at supper time to say to them that were bidden, Come; for all things are now ready.

18 And they all with one *consent* began to make excuse. The first said unto him, I have bought a piece of ground, and I must needs go and see it: I pray thee have me excused.

19 And another said, I have bought five yoke of oxen, and I go to prove them: I pray thee have me excused.

20 And another said, I have married a wife, and therefore I cannot come.

21 So that servant came, and shewed his lord these things. Then the master of the house being angry said to his servant, Go out quickly into the streets and lanes of the city, and bring in hither the poor, and the maimed, and the halt, and the blind.

22 And the servant said, Lord, it is done as thou hast commanded, and yet there is room.

23 And the lord said unto the servant, Go out into the highways and hedges, and compel *them* to come in, that my house may be filled.

24 For I say unto you, That none of those men which were bidden shall taste of my supper.

25 ¶ And there went great multitudes with him: and he turned, and said unto them,

26 If any *man* come to me, and hate not his father, and mother, and wife, and children, and brethren, and sisters, yea, and his own life also, he cannot be my disciple.

27 And whosoever doth not bear his cross, and come after me, cannot be my disciple.

28 For which of you, intending to build a tower, sitteth not down first, and counteth the cost, whether he have *sufficient* to finish it?

29 Lest haply, after he hath laid the foundation, and is not able to finish *it*, all that behold *it* begin to mock him,

30 Saying, This man began to build, and was not able to finish.

31 Or what king, going to make war against another king, sitteth not down first, and consulteth whether he be able with ten thousand to meet him that cometh against him with twenty thousand?

32 Or else, while the other is yet a great way off, he sendeth an ambassage, and desireth conditions of peace.

33 So likewise, whosoever he be of you that forsaketh not all that he hath, he cannot be my disciple.

34 ¶ Salt *is* good: but if the salt have lost his savour, wherewith shall it be seasoned?

35 It is neither fit for the land, nor yet for the dunghill; *but* men cast it out. He that hath ears to hear, let him hear.

15 THEN drew near unto him all the publicans and sinners for to hear him.

2 And the Phar'i-sees and scribes murmured, saying, This man receiveth sinners, and eateth with them.

3 ¶ And he spake this parable unto them, saying,

4 What man of you, having an hundred sheep, if he lose one of them, doth not leave the ninety and nine in the wilderness, and go after that which is lost, until he find it?

5 And when he hath found *it*, he layeth *it* on his shoulders, rejoicing.

6 And when he cometh home, he calleth together *his* friends and neighbours, saying unto them, Rejoice with me; for I have found my sheep which was lost.

7 I say unto you, that likewise joy shall be in heaven over one sinner that repenteth, more than over ninety and nine just persons, which need no repentance.

8 ¶ Either what woman having ten pieces of silver, if she lose one piece, doth not light a candle, and sweep the house, and seek diligently till she find *it*?

9 And when she hath found *it*, she calleth *her* friends and *her* neighbours together, saying, Rejoice with me; for I have found the piece which I had lost.

10 Likewise, I say unto you, there is joy in the presence of the angels of God over one sinner that repenteth.

11 ¶ And he said, A certain man had two sons:

12 And the younger of them said to *his* father, Father, give me the portion of goods that falleth *to me.* And he divided unto them *his* living.

13 And not many days after the younger son gathered all together, and took his journey into a far country, and there wasted his substance with riotous living.

14 And when he had spent all, there arose a mighty famine in that land; and he began to be in want.

15 And he went and joined himself to a citizen of that country; and he sent him into his fields to feed swine.

16 And he would fain have filled his belly with the husks that the swine did eat: and no man gave unto him.

17 And when he came to himself, he said, How many hired servants of my father's have bread enough and to spare, and I perish with hunger!

18 I will arise and go to my father, and will say unto him, Father, I have sinned against heaven, and before thee.

19 And am no more worthy to be called thy son: make me as one of thy hired servants.

20 And he arose, and came to his father. But when he was yet a great way off, his father saw him, and had compassion, and ran, and fell on his neck, and kissed him.

21 And the son said unto him, Father, I have sinned against heaven, and in thy sight, and am no more worthy to be called thy son.

22 But the father said to his servants, Bring forth the best robe, and put *it* on him; and put a ring on his hand, and shoes on *his* feet:

23 And bring hither the fatted calf, and kill *it;* and let us eat, and be merry:

24 For this my son was dead, and is alive again; he was lost, and is found. And they began to be merry.

25 Now his elder son was in the field: and as he came and drew nigh to the house, he heard musick and dancing.

26 And he called one of the servants, and asked what these things meant.

27 And he said unto him, Thy brother is come; and thy father hath killed the fatted calf, because he hath received him safe and sound.

28 And he was angry, and would not go in: therefore came his father out, and intreated him.

29 And he answering said to *his* father, Lo, these many years do I serve thee, neither transgressed I at any time thy commandment: and yet thou never gavest me a kid, that I might make merry with my friends:

30 But as soon as this thy son was come, which hath devoured thy living with harlots, thou hast killed for him the fatted calf.

31 And he said unto him, Son, thou art ever with me, and all that I have is thine.

32 It was meet that we should make merry, and be glad: for this thy brother was dead, and is alive again; and was lost, and is found.

16

AND he said also unto his disciples, There was a certain rich man, which had a steward; and the same was accused unto him that he had wasted his goods.

2 And he called him, and said unto him, How is it that I hear this of thee? give an account of thy stewardship; for thou mayest be no longer steward.

3 Then the steward said within himself, What shall I do? for my lord taketh away from me the stewardship: I cannot dig; to beg I am ashamed.

4 I am resolved what to do, that, when I am put out of the stewardship, they may receive me into their houses.

5 So he called every one of his lord's debtors *unto him,* and said unto the first, How much owest thou unto my lord?

6 And he said, An hundred measures of oil. And he said unto him, Take thy bill, and sit down quickly, and write fifty.

7 Then said he to another, And how much owest thou? And he said, An hundred measures of wheat. And he said unto him, Take thy bill, and write fourscore.

8 And the lord commended the unjust steward, because he had done wisely: for the children of this world are in their generation wiser than the children of light.

9 And I say unto you, Make to yourselves friends of the mammon of unrighteousness; that, when ye fail, they may receive you into everlasting habitations.

10 He that is faithful in that which is least is faithful also in much: and he that is unjust in the least is unjust also in much.

11 If therefore ye have not been faithful in the unrighteous mammon, who will commit to your trust the true *riches?*

12 And if ye have not been faithful in that which is another man's, who shall give you that which is your own?

13 ¶ No servant can serve two masters: for either he will hate the one, and love the other; or else he will hold to the one, and despise the other. Ye cannot serve God and mammon.

14 And the Phar'i-sees also, who were covetous, heard all these things: and they derided him.

15 And he said unto them, Ye are they which justify yourselves before men; but God knoweth your hearts: for that which is highly esteemed among men is abomination in the sight of God.

16 The law and the prophets *were* until John: since that time the kingdom of God is preached, and every man presseth into it.

17 And it is easier for heaven and earth to pass, than one tittle of the law to fail.

18 Whosoever putteth away his wife, and marrieth another, committeth adultery: and whosoever marrieth her that is put away from *her* husband committeth adultery.

19 ¶ There was a certain rich man, which was clothed in purple and fine linen, and fared sumptuously every day:

20 And there was a certain beggar named Laz'a-rus, which was laid at his gate, full of sores,

21 And desiring to be fed with the crumbs which fell from the rich man's table: moreover the dogs came and licked his sores.

22 And it came to pass, that the beggar died, and was carried by the angels into A'bra-ham's bosom: the rich man also died, and was buried;

23 And in hell he lift up his eyes, being in torments, and seeth A'bra-ham afar off, and Laz'a-rus in his bosom.

24 And he cried and said, Father A'bra-ham, have mercy on me, and send Laz'a-rus, that he may dip the tip of his finger in water, and cool my tongue; for I am tormented in this flame.

25 But A'bra-ham said, Son, remember that thou in thy lifetime receivedst thy good things, and likewise Laz'a-rus evil things: but now he is comforted, and thou art tormented.

26 And beside all this, between us and you

there is a great gulf fixed: so that they which would pass from hence to you cannot; neither can they pass to us, that *would come* from thence.

27 Then he said, I pray thee therefore, father, that thou wouldest send him to my father's house:

28 For I have five brethren; that he may testify unto them, lest they also come into this place of torment.

29 A'bra-ham saith unto him, They have Mo'-ses and the prophets; let them hear them.

30 And he said, Nay, father A'bra-ham: but if one went unto them from the dead, they will repent.

31 And he said unto him, If they hear not Mo'ses and the prophets, neither will they be persuaded, though one rose from the dead.

17 THEN said he unto the disciples, It is impossible but that offences will come: but woe *unto him,* through whom they come!

2 It were better for him that a millstone were hanged about his neck, and he cast into the sea, than that he should offend one of these little ones.

3 ¶ Take heed to yourselves: If thy brother trespass against thee, rebuke him; and if he repent, forgive him.

4 And if he trespass against thee seven times in a day, and seven times in a day turn again to thee, saying, I repent; thou shalt forgive him.

5 And the apostles said unto the Lord, Increase our faith.

6 And the Lord said, If ye had faith as a grain of mustard seed, ye might say unto this syca-mine tree, Be thou plucked up by the root, and be thou planted in the sea; and it should obey you.

7 But which of you, having a servant plowing or feeding cattle, will say unto him by and by, when he is come from the field, Go and sit down to meat?

8 And will not rather say unto him, Make ready wherewith I may sup, and gird thyself, and serve me, till I have eaten and drunken; and afterward thou shalt eat and drink?

9 Doth he thank that servant because he did the things that were commanded him? I trow not.

10 So likewise ye, when ye shall have done all those things which are commanded you, say, We are unprofitable servants: we have done that which was our duty to do.

11 ¶ And it came to pass, as he went to Je-ru'sa-lem, that he passed through the midst of Sa-ma'ri-a and Gal'i-lee.

12 And as he entered into a certain village, there met him ten men that were lepers, which stood afar off:

13 And they lifted up *their* voices, and said, Je'sus, Master, have mercy on us.

14 And when he saw *them,* he said unto them, Go shew yourselves unto the priests. And it came to pass, that, as they went, they were cleansed.

15 And one of them, when he saw that he was healed, turned back, and with a loud voice glorified God,

16 And fell down on *his* face at his feet, giving him thanks: and he was a Sa-mar'i-tan.

17 And Je'sus answering said, Were there not ten cleansed? but where *are* the nine?

18 There are not found that returned to give glory to God, save this stranger.

19 And he said unto him, Arise, go thy way: thy faith hath made thee whole.

20 ¶ And when he was demanded of the Phar'i-sees, when the kingdom of God should come, he answered them and said, The kingdom of God cometh not with observation:

21 Neither shall they say, Lo here! or, lo there! for, behold, the kingdom of God is within you.

22 And he said unto the disciples, The days will come, when ye shall desire to see one of the days of the Son of man, and ye shall not see *it.*

23 And they shall say to you, See here; or, see there: go not after *them,* nor follow *them.*

24 For as the lightning, that lighteneth out of the one *part* under heaven, shineth unto the other *part* under heaven; so shall also the Son of man be in his day.

25 But first must he suffer many things, and be rejected of this generation.

26 And as it was in the days of No'e, so shall it be also in the days of the Son of man.

27 They did eat, they drank, they married wives, they were given in marriage, until the day that No'e entered into the ark, and the flood came, and destroyed them all.

28 Likewise also as it was in the days of Lot; they did eat, they drank, they bought, they sold, they planted, they builded;

29 But the same day that Lot went out of Sod'om it rained fire and brimstone from heaven, and destroyed *them* all.

30 Even thus shall it be in the day when the Son of man is revealed.

31 In that day, he which shall be upon the house top, and his stuff in the house, let him not come down to take it away: and he that is in the field, let him likewise not return back.

32 Remember Lot's wife.

33 Whosoever shall seek to save his life shall lose it; and whosoever shall lose his life shall preserve it.

34 I tell you, in that night there shall be two *men* in one bed; the one shall be taken, and the other shall be left.

35 Two *women* shall be grinding together; the one shall be taken, and the other left.

36 Two *men* shall be in the field; the one shall be taken, and the other left.

37 And they answered and said unto him, Where, Lord? And he said unto them, Wheresoever the body *is,* thither will the eagles be gathered together.

18 AND he spake a parable unto them *to this end,* that men ought always to pray, and not to faint;

2 Saying, There was in a city a judge, which feared not God, neither regarded man:

3 And there was a widow in that city; and she came unto him, saying, Avenge me of mine adversary.

4 And he would not for a while: but afterward he said within himself, Though I fear not God, nor regard man;

5 Yet because this widow troubleth me, I will avenge her, lest by her continual coming she weary me.

6 And the Lord said, Hear what the unjust judge saith.

7 And shall not God avenge his own elect, which cry day and night unto him, though he bear long with them?

8 I tell you that he will avenge them speedily. Nevertheless when the Son of man cometh, shall he find faith on the earth?

9 And he spake this parable unto certain which trusted in themselves that they were righteous, and despised others:

10 Two men went up into the temple to pray; the one a Phar'i-see, and the other a publican.

11 The Phar'i-see stood and prayed thus with himself, God, I thank thee, that I am not as other men *are*, extortioners, unjust, adulterers, or even as this publican.

12 I fast twice in the week, I give tithes of all that I possess.

13 And the publican, standing afar off, would not lift up so much as *his* eyes unto heaven, but smote upon his breast, saying, God be merciful to me a sinner.

14 I tell you, this man went down to his house justified *rather* than the other: for every one that exalteth himself shall be abased; and he that humbleth himself shall be exalted.

15 And they brought unto him also infants, that he would touch them: but when *his* disciples saw *it*, they rebuked them.

16 But Je'sus called them *unto him*, and said, Suffer little children to come unto me, and forbid them not: for of such is the kingdom of God.

17 Verily I say unto you, Whosoever shall not receive the kingdom of God as a little child shall in no wise enter therein.

18 And a certain ruler asked him, saying, Good Master, what shall I do to inherit eternal life?

19 And Je'sus said unto him, Why callest thou me good? none *is* good, save one, *that is*, God.

20 Thou knowest the commandments, Do not commit adultery, Do not kill, Do not steal, Do not bear false witness, Honour thy father and thy mother.

21 And he said, All these have I kept from my youth up.

22 Now when Je'sus heard these things, he said unto him, Yet lackest thou one thing: sell all that thou hast, and distribute unto the poor, and thou shalt have treasure in heaven: and come follow me.

23 And when he heard this, he was very sorrowful: for he was very rich.

24 And when Je'sus saw that he was very sorrowful, he said, How hardly shall they that have riches enter into the kingdom of God!

25 For it is easier for a camel to go through a needle's eye, than for a rich man to enter into the kingdom of God.

26 And they that heard *it* said, Who then can be saved?

27 And he said, The things which are impossible with men are possible with God.

28 Then Pe'ter said, Lo, we have left all, and followed thee.

29 And he said unto them, Verily I say unto you, There is no man that hath left house, or parents, or brethren, or wife, or children, for the kingdom of God's sake,

30 Who shall not receive manifold more in this present time, and in the world to come life everlasting.

31 ¶ Then he took *unto him* the twelve, and said unto them, Behold, we go up to Je-ru'sa-lem, and all things that are written by the prophets concerning the Son of man shall be accomplished.

32 For he shall be delivered unto the Gen'-tiles, and shall be mocked, and spitefully entreated, and spitted on:

33 And they shall scourge *him*, and put him to death: and the third day he shall rise again.

34 And they understood none of these things: and this saying was hid from them, neither knew they the things which were spoken.

35 ¶ And it came to pass, that as he was come nigh unto Jer'i-cho, a certain blind man sat by the way side begging:

36 And hearing the multitude pass by, he asked what it meant.

37 And they told him, that Je'sus of Naz'a-reth passeth by.

38 And he cried, saying, Je'sus, *thou* son of Da'vid, have mercy on me.

39 And they which went before rebuked him, that he should hold his peace: but he cried so much the more, Thou son of Da'vid, have mercy on me.

40 And Je'sus stood, and commanded him to be brought unto him: and when he was come near, he asked him,

41 Saying, What wilt thou that I shall do unto thee? And he said, Lord, that I may receive my sight.

42 And Je'sus said unto him, Receive thy sight: thy faith hath saved thee.

43 And immediately he received his sight, and followed him, glorifying God: and all the people when they saw *it*, gave praise unto God.

19 AND Je'sus entered and passed through Jer'i-cho.

2 And, behold, *there was* a man named Zac-chæ'us, which was the chief among the publicans, and he was rich.

3 And he sought to see Je'sus who he was; and could not for the press, because he was little of stature.

4 And he ran before, and climbed up into a sycomore tree to see him: for he was to pass that *way*.

5 And when Je'sus came to the place, he looked up, and saw him, and said unto him, Zac-chæ'us, make haste, and come down; for to day I must abide at thy house.

6 And he made haste, and came down, and received him joyfully.

7 And when they saw *it*, they all murmured, saying, That he was gone to be guest with a man that is a sinner.

8 And Zac-chæ'us stood, and said unto the Lord; Behold, Lord, the half of my goods I give to the poor; and if I have taken any thing from any man by false accusation, I restore *him* fourfold.

9 And Je'sus said unto him, This day is salvation come to this house, forsomuch as he also is a son of A'bra-ham.

10 For the Son of man is come to seek and to save that which was lost.

11 And as they heard these things, he added and spake a parable, because he was nigh to Je-ru'sa-lem, and because they thought that the kingdom of God should immediately appear.

12 He said therefore, A certain nobleman went into a far country to receive for himself a kingdom, and to return.

13 And he called his ten servants, and delivered them ten pounds, and said unto them, Occupy till I come.

14 But his citizens hated him, and sent a message after him, saying, We will not have this *man* to reign over us.

15 And it came to pass, that when he was returned, having received the kingdom, then he commanded these servants to be called unto him, to whom he had given the money, that he might know how much every man had gained by trading.

16 Then came the first, saying, Lord, thy pound hath gained ten pounds.

17 And he said unto him, Well, thou good servant: because thou hast been faithful in a

very little, have thou authority over ten cities.

18 And the second came, saying, Lord, thy pound hath gained five pounds.

19 And he said likewise to him, Be thou also over five cities.

20 And another came, saying, Lord, behold, here is thy pound, which I have kept laid up in a napkin:

21 For I feared thee, because thou art an austere man: thou takest up that thou layedst not down, and reapest that thou didst not sow.

22 And he saith unto him, Out of thine own mouth will I judge thee, thou wicked servant. Thou knewest that I was an austere man, taking up that I laid not down, and reaping that I did not sow:

23 Wherefore then gavest not thou my money into the bank, that at my coming I might have required mine own with usury?

24 And he said unto them that stood by, Take from him the pound, and give it to him that hath ten pounds.

25 (And they said unto him, Lord, he hath ten pounds.)

26 For I say unto you, That unto every one which hath shall be given; and from him that hath not, even that he hath shall be taken away from him.

27 But those mine enemies, which would not that I should reign over them, bring hither, and slay them before me.

28 ¶ And when he had thus spoken, he went before, ascending up to Je·ru'sa·lem.

29 And it came to pass, when he was come nigh to Beth'pha·ge and Beth'a·ny, at the mount called the mount of Ol'ives, he sent two of his disciples,

30 Saying, Go ye into the village over against you; in the which at your entering ye shall find a colt tied, whereon yet never man sat: loose him, and bring him hither.

31 And if any man ask you, Why do ye loose him? thus shall ye say unto him, Because the Lord hath need of him.

32 And they that were sent went their way, and found even as he had said unto them.

33 And as they were loosing the colt, the owners thereof said unto them, Why loose ye the colt?

34 And they said, The Lord hath need of him.

35 And they brought him to Je'sus: and they cast their garments upon the colt, and they set Je'sus thereon.

36 And as he went, they spread their clothes in the way.

37 And when he was come nigh, even now at the descent of the mount of Ol'ives, the whole multitude of the disciples began to rejoice and praise God with a loud voice for all the mighty works that they had seen;

38 Saying, Blessed be the King that cometh in the name of the Lord: peace in heaven, and glory in the highest.

39 And some of the Phar'i·sees from among the multitude said unto him, Master, rebuke thy disciples.

40 And he answered and said unto them, I tell you that, if these should hold their peace, the stones would immediately cry out.

41 ¶ And when he was come near, he beheld the city, and wept over it,

42 Saying, If thou hadst known, even thou, at least in this thy day, the things which belong unto thy peace! but now they are hid from thine eyes.

43 For the days shall come upon thee, that thine enemies shall cast a trench about thee,

and compass thee round, and keep thee in on every side,

44 And shall lay thee even with the ground, and thy children within thee; and they shall not leave in thee one stone upon another; because thou knewest not the time of thy visitation.

45 And he went into the temple, and began to cast out them that sold therein, and them that bought;

46 Saying unto them, It is written, My house is the house of prayer: but ye have made it a den of thieves.

47 And he taught daily in the temple. But the chief priests and the scribes and the chief of the people sought to destroy him,

48 And could not find what they might do: for all the people were very attentive to hear him.

20 AND it came to pass, that on one of those days, as he taught the people in the temple, and preached the gospel, the chief priests and the scribes came upon him with the elders,

2 And spake unto him, saying, Tell us, by what authority doest thou these things? or who is he that gave thee this authority?

3 And he answered and said unto them, I will also ask you one thing; and answer me:

4 The baptism of John, was it from heaven, or of men?

5 And they reasoned with themselves, saying, If we shall say, From heaven; he will say, Why then believed ye him not?

6 But and if we say, Of men; all the people will stone us: for they be persuaded that John was a prophet.

7 And they answered, that they could not tell whence it was.

8 And Je'sus said unto them, Neither tell I you by what authority I do these things.

9 Then began he to speak to the people this parable; A certain man planted a vineyard, and let it forth to husbandmen, and went into a far country for a long time.

10 And at the season he sent a servant to the husbandmen, that they should give him of the fruit of the vineyard: but the husbandmen beat him, and sent him away empty.

11 And again he sent another servant: and they beat him also, and entreated him shamefully, and sent him away empty.

12 And again he sent a third: and they wounded him also, and cast him out.

13 Then said the lord of the vineyard, What shall I do? I will send my beloved son: it may be they will reverence him when they see him.

14 But when the husbandmen saw him, they reasoned among themselves, saying, This is the heir: come, let us kill him, that the inheritance may be ours.

15 So they cast him out of the vineyard, and killed him. What therefore shall the lord of the vineyard do unto them?

16 He shall come and destroy these husbandmen, and shall give the vineyard to others. And when they heard it, they said, God forbid.

17 And he beheld them, and said, What is this then that is written, The stone which the builders rejected, the same is become the head of the corner?

18 Whosoever shall fall upon that stone shall be broken; but on whomsoever it shall fall, it will grind him to powder.

19 ¶ And the chief priests and the scribes the same hour sought to lay hands on him; and they

feared the people: for they perceived that he had spoken this parable against them.

20 And they watched *him*, and sent forth spies, which should feign themselves just men, that they might take hold of his words, that so they might deliver him unto the power and authority of the governor.

21 And they asked him, saying, Master, we know that thou sayest and teachest rightly, neither acceptest thou the person of *any*, but teachest the way of God truly:

22 Is it lawful for us to give tribute unto Cæ'sar, or no?

23 But he perceived their craftiness, and said unto them, Why tempt ye me?

24 Shew me a penny. Whose image and superscription hath it? They answered and said, Cæ'sar's.

25 And he said unto them, Render therefore unto Cæ'sar the things which be Cæ'sar's, and unto God the things which be God's.

26 And they could not take hold of his words before the people: and they marvelled at his answer, and held their peace.

27 ¶ Then came to *him* certain of the Sad'ducees, which deny that there is any resurrection; and they asked him,

28 Saying, Master, Mo'ses wrote unto us, If any man's brother die, having a wife, and he die without children, that his brother should take his wife, and raise up seed unto his brother.

29 There were therefore seven brethren: and the first took a wife, and died without children.

30 And the second took her to wife, and he died childless.

31 And the third took her; and in like manner the seven also: and they left no children, and died.

32 Last of all the woman died also.

33 Therefore in the resurrection whose wife of them is she? for seven had her to wife.

34 And Je'sus answering said unto them, The children of this world marry, and are given in marriage:

35 But they which shall be accounted worthy to obtain that world, and the resurrection from the dead, neither marry, nor are given in marriage:

36 Neither can they die any more: for they are equal unto the angels; and are the children of God, being the children of the resurrection.

37 Now that the dead are raised, even Mo'ses shewed at the bush, when he calleth the Lord the God of A'bra-ham, and the God of I'saac, and the God of Ja'cob.

38 For he is not a God of the dead, but of the living: for all live unto him.

39 ¶ Then certain of the scribes answering said, Master, thou hast well said.

40 And after that they durst not ask him any *question at all*.

41 And he said unto them, How say they that Christ is Da'vid's son?

42 And Da'vid himself saith in the book of Psalms, The Lord said unto my Lord, Sit thou on my right hand,

43 Till I make thine enemies thy footstool.

44 Da'vid therefore calleth him Lord, how is he then his son?

45 ¶ Then in the audience of all the people he said unto his disciples,

46 Beware of the scribes, which desire to walk in long robes, and love greetings in the markets, and the highest seats in the synagogues, and the chief rooms at feasts;

47 Which devour widows' houses, and for a shew make long prayers: the same shall receive greater damnation.

21 AND he looked up, and saw the rich men casting their gifts into the treasury.

2 And he saw also a certain poor widow casting in thither two mites.

3 And he said, Of a truth I say unto you, that this poor widow hath cast in more than they all:

4 For all these have of their abundance cast in unto the offerings of God· but she of her penury hath cast in all the living that she had.

5 ¶ And as some spake of the temple, how it was adorned with goodly stones and gifts, he said,

6 *As for* these things which ye behold, the days will come, in the which there shall not be left one stone upon another, that shall not be thrown down.

7 And they asked him, saying, Master, but when shall these things be? and what sign *will there be* when these things shall come to pass?

8 And he said, Take heed that ye be not deceived: for many shall come in my name, saying, I am *Christ*; and the time draweth near: go ye not therefore after them.

9 But when ye shall hear of wars and commotions, be not terrified: for these things must first come to pass; but the end *is* not by and by.

10 Then said he unto them, Nation shall rise against nation, and kingdom against kingdom:

11 And great earthquakes shall be in divers places, and famines, and pestilences; and fearful sights and great signs shall there be from heaven.

12 But before all these, they shall lay their hands on you, and persecute *you*, delivering *you* up to the synagogues, and into prisons, being brought before kings and rulers for my name's sake.

13 And it shall turn to you for a testimony.

14 Settle *it* therefore in your hearts, not to meditate before what ye shall answer:

15 For I will give you a mouth and wisdom, which all your adversaries shall not be able to gainsay nor resist.

16 And ye shall be betrayed both by parents, and brethren, and kinsfolks, and friends; and *some* of you shall they cause to be put to death.

17 And ye shall be hated of all *men* for my name's sake.

18 But there shall not an hair of your head perish.

19 In your patience possess ye your souls.

20 And when ye shall see Je-ru'sa-lem compassed with armies, then know that the desolation thereof is nigh.

21 Then let them which are in Ju-dæ'a flee to the mountains; and let them which are in the midst of it depart out; and let not them that are in the countries enter thereinto.

22 For these be the days of vengeance, that all things which are written may be fulfilled.

23 But woe unto them that are with child, and to them that give suck, in those days! for there shall be great distress in the land, and wrath upon this people.

24 And they shall fall by the edge of the sword, and shall be led away captive into all nations: and Je-ru'sa-lem shall be trodden down of the Gen'tiles, until the times of the Gen'tiles be fulfilled.

25 ¶ And there shall be signs in the sun, and in the moon, and in the stars; and upon the earth distress of nations, with perplexity; the sea and the waves roaring;

26 Men's hearts failing them for fear, and for

looking after those things which are coming on the earth: for the powers of heaven shall be shaken.

27 And then shall they see the Son of man coming in a cloud with power and great glory.

28 And when these things begin to come to pass, then look up, and lift up your heads; for your redemption draweth nigh.

29 And he spake to them a parable; Behold the fig tree, and all the trees;

30 When they now shoot forth, ye see and know of your own selves that summer is now nigh at hand.

31 So likewise ye, when ye see these things come to pass, know ye that the kingdom of God is nigh at hand.

32 Verily I say unto you, This generation shall not pass away, till all be fulfilled.

33 Heaven and earth shall pass away: but my words shall not pass away.

34 ¶ And take heed to yourselves, lest at any time your hearts be overcharged with surfeiting, and drunkenness, and cares of this life, and so that day come upon you unawares.

35 For as a snare shall it come on all them that dwell on the face of the whole earth.

36 Watch ye therefore, and pray always, that ye may be accounted worthy to escape all these things that shall come to pass, and to stand before the Son of man.

37 And in the day time he was teaching in the temple; and at night he went out, and abode in the mount that is called the mount of Ol'ives.

38 And all the people came early in the morning to him in the temple, for to hear him.

22 NOW the feast of unleavened bread drew nigh, which is called the Passover.

2 And the chief priests and scribes sought how they might kill him; for they feared the people.

3 ¶ Then entered Sa'tan into Ju'das surnamed Is-car'i-ot, being of the number of the twelve.

4 And he went his way, and communed with the chief priests and captains, how he might betray him unto them.

5 And they were glad, and covenanted to give him money.

6 And he promised, and sought opportunity to betray him unto them in the absence of the multitude.

7 ¶ Then came the day of unleavened bread, when the passover must be killed.

8 And he sent Pe'ter and John, saying, Go and prepare us the passover, that we may eat.

9 And they said unto him, Where wilt thou that we prepare?

10 And he said unto them, Behold, when ye are entered into the city, there shall a man meet you, bearing a pitcher of water; follow him into the house where he entereth in.

11 And ye shall say unto the goodman of the house, The Master saith unto thee, Where is the guestchamber, where I shall eat the passover with my disciples?

12 And he shall shew you a large upper room furnished: there make ready.

13 And they went, and found as he had said unto them: and they made ready the passover.

14 And when the hour was come, he sat down, and the twelve apostles with him.

15 And he said unto them, With desire I have desired to eat this passover with you before I suffer:

16 For I say unto you, I will not any more eat

thereof, until it be fulfilled in the kingdom of God.

17 And he took the cup, and gave thanks, and said, Take this, and divide it among yourselves:

18 For I say unto you, I will not drink of the fruit of the vine, until the kingdom of God shall come.

19 ¶ And he took bread, and gave thanks, and brake it, and gave unto them, saying, This is my body which is given for you: this do in remembrance of me.

20 Likewise also the cup after supper, saying, This cup is the new testament in my blood, which is shed for you.

21 ¶ But, behold, the hand of him that betrayeth me is with me on the table.

22 And truly the Son of man goeth, as it was determined: but woe unto that man by whom he is betrayed!

23 And they began to enquire among themselves, which of them it was that should do this thing.

24 ¶ And there was also a strife among them, which of them should be accounted the greatest.

25 And he said unto them, The kings of the Gen'tiles exercise lordship over them; and they that exercise authority upon them are called benefactors.

26 But ye shall not be so: but he that is greatest among you, let him be as the younger; and he that is chief, as he that doth serve.

27 For whether is greater, he that sitteth at meat, or he that serveth? is not he that sitteth at meat? but I am among you as he that serveth.

28 Ye are they which have continued with me in my temptations.

29 And I appoint unto you a kingdom, as my Father hath appointed unto me;

30 That ye may eat and drink at my table in my kingdom, and sit on thrones judging the twelve tribes of Is'ra-el.

31 ¶ And the Lord said, Si'mon, Si'mon, behold, Sa'tan hath desired to have you, that he may sift you as wheat:

32 But I have prayed for thee, that thy faith fail not: and when thou art converted, strengthen thy brethren.

33 And he said unto him, Lord, I am ready to go with thee, both into prison, and to death.

34 And he said, I tell thee, Pe'ter, the cock shall not crow this day, before that thou shalt thrice deny that thou knowest me.

35 And he said unto them, When I sent you without purse, and scrip, and shoes, lacked ye any thing? And they said, Nothing.

36 Then said he unto them, But now, he that hath a purse, let him take it, and likewise his scrip: and he that hath no sword, let him sell his garment, and buy one.

37 For I say unto you, that this that is written must yet be accomplished in me, And he was reckoned among the transgressors: for the things concerning me have an end.

38 And they said, Lord, behold, here are two swords. And he said unto them, It is enough.

39 ¶ And he came out, and went, as he was wont, to the mount of Ol'ives; and his disciples also followed him.

40 And when he was at the place, he said unto them, Pray that ye enter not into temptation.

41 And he was withdrawn from them about a stone's cast, and kneeled down, and prayed,

42 Saying, Father, if thou be willing, remove

this cup from me: nevertheless not my will, but thine, be done.

43 And there appeared an angel unto him from heaven, strengthening him.

44 And being in an agony he prayed more earnestly: and his sweat was as it were great drops of blood falling down to the ground.

45 And when he rose up from prayer, and was come to his disciples, he found them sleeping for sorrow,

46 And said unto them, Why sleep ye? rise and pray, lest ye enter into temptation.

47 ¶ And while he yet spake, behold a multitude, and he that was called Ju'das, one of the twelve, went before them, and drew near unto Je'sus to kiss him.

48 But Je'sus said unto him, Ju'das, betrayest thou the Son of man with a kiss?

49 When they which were about him saw what would follow, they said unto him, Lord, shall we smite with the sword?

50 ¶ And one of them smote the servant of the high priest, and cut off his right ear.

51 And Je'sus answered and said, Suffer ye thus far. And he touched his ear, and healed him.

52 Then Je'sus said unto the chief priests, and captains of the temple, and the elders, which were come to him, Be ye come out, as against a thief, with swords and staves?

53 When I was daily with you in the temple, ye stretched forth no hands against me: but this is your hour, and the power of darkness.

54 ¶ Then took they him, and led *him*, and brought him into the high priest's house. And Pe'ter followed afar off.

55 And when they had kindled a fire in the midst of the hall, and were set down together, Pe'ter sat down among them.

56 But a certain maid beheld him as he sat by the fire, and earnestly looked upon him, and said, This man was also with him.

57 And he denied him, saying, Woman, I know him not.

58 And after a little while another saw him, and said, Thou art also of them. And Pe'ter said, Man, I am not.

59 And about the space of one hour after another confidently affirmed, saying, Of a truth this *fellow* also was with him: for he is a Gal-i-læ'an.

60 And Pe'ter said, Man, I know not what thou sayest. And immediately, while he yet spake, the cock crew.

61 And the Lord turned, and looked upon Pe'ter. And Pe'ter remembered the word of the Lord, how he had said unto him, Before the cock crow, thou shalt deny me thrice.

62 And Pe'ter went out, and wept bitterly.

63 ¶ And the men that held Je'sus mocked him, and smote *him*.

64 And when they had blindfolded him, they struck him on the face, and asked him, saying, Prophesy, who is it that smote thee?

65 And many other things blasphemously spake they against him.

66 ¶ And as soon as it was day, the elders of the people and the chief priests and the scribes came together, and led him into their council, saying,

67 Art thou the Christ? tell us. And he said unto them, If I tell you, ye will not believe:

68 And if I also ask *you*, ye will not answer me, nor let *me* go.

69 Hereafter shall the Son of man sit on the right hand of the power of God.

70 Then said they all, Art thou then the Son of God? And he said unto them, Ye say that I am.

71 And they said, What need we any further witness? for we ourselves have heard of his own mouth.

23

AND the whole multitude of them arose, and led him unto Pi'late.

2 And they began to accuse him, saying, We found this *fellow* perverting the nation, and forbidding to give tribute to Cæ'sar, saying that he himself is Christ a King.

3 And Pi'late asked him, saying, Art thou the King of the Jews? And he answered him and said, Thou sayest *it*.

4 Then said Pi'late to the chief priests and *to* the people, I find no fault in this man.

5 And they were the more fierce, saying, He stirreth up the people, teaching throughout all Jew'ry, beginning from Gal'i-lee to this place.

6 When Pi'late heard of Gal'i-lee, he asked whether the man were a Gal-i-læ'an.

7 And as soon as he knew that he belonged unto Her'od's jurisdiction, he sent him to Her'od, who himself also was at Je-ru'sa-lem at that time.

8 ¶ And when Her'od saw Je'sus, he was exceeding glad: for he was desirous to see him of a long *season*, because he had heard many things of him; and he hoped to have seen some miracle done by him.

9 Then he questioned with him in many words; but he answered him nothing.

10 And the chief priests and scribes stood and vehemently accused him.

11 And Her'od with his men of war set him at nought, and mocked *him*, and arrayed him in a gorgeous robe, and sent him again to Pi'late.

12 ¶ And the same day Pi'late and Her'od were made friends together: for before they were at enmity between themselves.

13 ¶ And Pi'late, when he had called together the chief priests and the rulers and the people,

14 Said unto them, Ye have brought this man unto me, as one that perverteth the people: and, behold, I, having examined *him* before you, have found no fault in this man touching those things whereof ye accuse him:

15 No, nor yet Her'od: for I sent you to him; and, lo, nothing worthy of death is done unto him.

16 I will therefore chastise him, and release *him*.

17 (For of necessity he must release one unto them at the feast.)

18 And they cried out all at once, saying, Away with this *man*, and release unto us Ba-rab'bas:

19 (Who for a certain sedition made in the city, and for murder, was cast into prison.)

20 Pi'late therefore, willing to release Je'sus, spake again to them.

21 But they cried, saying, Crucify *him*, crucify him.

22 And he said unto them the third time, Why, what evil hath he done? I have found no cause of death in him: I will therefore chastise him, and let *him* go.

23 And they were instant with loud voices, requiring that he might be crucified. And the voices of them and of the chief priests prevailed.

24 And Pi'late gave sentence that it should be as they required.

25 And he released unto them him that for sedition and murder was cast into prison,

whom they had desired; but he delivered Je′sus to their will.

26 And as they led him away, they laid hold upon one Si′mon, a Cy-re′ni-an, coming out of the country, and on him they laid the cross, that he might bear it after Je′sus.

27 ¶ And there followed him a great company of people, and of women, which also bewailed and lamented him.

28 But Je′sus turning unto them said, Daughters of Je-ru′sa-lem, weep not for me, but weep for yourselves, and for your children.

29 For, behold, the days are coming, in the which they shall say, Blessed are the barren, and the wombs that never bare, and the paps which never gave suck.

30 Then shall they begin to say to the mountains, Fall on us; and to the hills, Cover us.

31 For if they do these things in a green tree, what shall be done in the dry?

32 And there were also two other, malefactors, led with him to be put to death.

33 And when they were come to the place, which is called Cal′va-ry, there they crucified him, and the malefactors, one on the right hand, and the other on the left.

34 ¶ Then said Je′sus, Father, forgive them; for they know not what they do. And they parted his raiment, and cast lots.

35 And the people stood beholding. And the rulers also with them derided him, saying, He saved others; let him save himself, if he be Christ, the chosen of God.

36 And the soldiers also mocked him, coming to him, and offering him vinegar,

37 And saying, If thou be the king of the Jews, save thyself.

38 And a superscription also was written over him in letters of Greek, and Lat′in, and He′brew, THIS IS THE KING OF THE JEWS.

39 ¶ And one of the malefactors which were hanged railed on him, saying, If thou be Christ, save thyself and us.

40 But the other answering rebuked him, saying, Dost not thou fear God, seeing thou art in the same condemnation?

41 And we indeed justly; for we receive the due reward of our deeds: but this man hath done nothing amiss.

42 And he said unto Je′sus, Lord, remember me when thou comest into thy kingdom.

43 And Je′sus said unto him, Verily I say unto thee, To day shalt thou be with me in paradise.

44 And it was about the sixth hour, and there was a darkness over all the earth until the ninth hour.

45 And the sun was darkened, and the veil of the temple was rent in the midst.

46 ¶ And when Je′sus had cried with a loud voice, he said, Father, into thy hands I commend my spirit: and having said thus, he gave up the ghost.

47 Now when the centurion saw what was done, he glorified God, saying, Certainly this was a righteous man.

48 And all the people that came together to that sight, beholding the things which were done, smote their breasts, and returned.

49 And all his acquaintance, and the women that followed him from Gal′i-lee, stood afar off, beholding these things.

50 ¶ And, behold, there was a man named Jo′seph, a counsellor; and he was a good man, and a just:

51 (The same had not consented to the counsel and deed of them;) he was of Ar-i-ma-thæ′a,

a city of the Jews: who also himself waited for the kingdom of God.

52 This man went unto Pi′late, and begged the body of Je′sus.

53 And he took it down, and wrapped it in linen, and laid it in a sepulchre that was hewn in stone, wherein never man before was laid.

54 And that day was the preparation, and the sabbath drew on.

55 And the women also, which came with him from Gal′i-lee, followed after, and beheld the sepulchre, and how his body was laid.

56 And they returned, and prepared spices and ointments; and rested the sabbath day according to the commandment.

24 NOW upon the first day of the week, very early in the morning, they came unto the sepulchre, bringing the spices which they had prepared, and certain others with them.

2 And they found the stone rolled away from the sepulchre.

3 And they entered in, and found not the body of the Lord Je′sus.

4 And it came to pass, as they were much perplexed thereabout, behold, two men stood by them in shining garments:

5 And as they were afraid, and bowed down their faces to the earth, they said unto them, Why seek ye the living among the dead?

6 He is not here, but is risen: remember how he spake unto you when he was yet in Gal′i-lee,

7 Saying, The Son of man must be delivered into the hands of sinful men, and be crucified, and the third day rise again.

8 And they remembered his words,

9 And returned from the sepulchre, and told all these things unto the eleven, and to all the rest.

10 It was Ma′ry Mag-da-le′ne, and Jo-an′na, and Ma′ry the mother of James, and other women that were with them, which told these things unto the apostles.

11 And their words seemed to them as idle tales, and they believed them not.

12 Then arose Pe′ter, and ran unto the sepulchre; and stooping down, he beheld the linen clothes laid by themselves, and departed, wondering in himself at that which was come to pass.

13 ¶ And, behold, two of them went that same day to a village called Em′ma-us, which was from Je-ru′sa-lem about threescore furlongs.

14 And they talked together of all these things which had happened.

15 And it came to pass, that, while they communed together and reasoned, Je′sus himself drew near, and went with them.

16 But their eyes were holden that they should not know him.

17 And he said unto them, What manner of communications are these that ye have one to another, as ye walk, and are sad?

18 And the one of them, whose name was Cle′-o-pas, answering said unto him, Art thou only a stranger in Je-ru′sa-lem, and hast not known the things which are come to pass there in these days?

19 And he said unto them, What things? And they said unto him, Concerning Je′sus of Naz′a-reth, which was a prophet mighty in deed and word before God and all the people:

20 And how the chief priests and our rulers delivered him to be condemned to death, and have crucified him.

21 But we trusted that it had been he which should have redeemed Is′ra-el: and beside all this, to day is the third day since these things were done.

22 Yea, and certain women also of our company made us astonished, which were early at the sepulchre;

23 And when they found not his body, they came, saying, that they had also seen a vision of angels, which said that he was alive.

24 And certain of them which were with us went to the sepulchre, and found it even so as the women had said: but him they saw not.

25 Then he said unto them, O fools, and slow of heart to believe all that the prophets have spoken:

26 Ought not Christ to have suffered these things, and to enter into his glory?

27 And beginning at Mo′ses and all the prophets, he expounded unto them in all the scriptures the things concerning himself.

28 And they drew nigh unto the village, whither they went: and he made as though he would have gone further.

29 But they constrained him, saying, Abide with us: for it is toward evening, and the day is far spent. And he went in to tarry with them.

30 And it came to pass, as he sat at meat with them, he took bread, and blessed it, and brake, and gave to them.

31 And their eyes were opened, and they knew him; and he vanished out of their sight.

32 And they said one to another, Did not our heart burn within us, while he talked with us by the way, and while he opened to us the scriptures?

33 And they rose up the same hour, and returned to Je-ru′sa-lem, and found the eleven gathered together, and them that were with them,

34 Saying, The Lord is risen indeed, and hath appeared to Si′mon.

35 And they told what things were done in the way, and how he was known of them in breaking of bread.

36 ¶ And as they thus spake, Je′sus himself stood in the midst of them, and saith unto them, Peace be unto you.

37 But they were terrified and affrighted, and supposed that they had seen a spirit.

38 And he said unto them, Why are ye troubled? and why do thoughts arise in your hearts?

39 Behold my hands and my feet, that it is I myself: handle me, and see; for a spirit hath not flesh and bones, as ye see me have.

40 And when he had thus spoken, he shewed them his hands and his feet.

41 And while they yet believed not for joy, and wondered, he said unto them, Have ye here any meat?

42 And they gave him a piece of a broiled fish, and of an honeycomb.

43 And he took it, and did eat before them.

44 And he said unto them, These are the words which I spake unto you, while I was yet with you, that all things must be fulfilled, which were written in the law of Mo′ses, and in the prophets, and in the psalms, concerning me.

45 Then opened he their understanding, that they might understand the scriptures,

46 And said unto them, Thus it is written, and thus it behoved Christ to suffer, and to rise from the dead the third day:

47 And that repentance and remission of sins should be preached in his name among all nations, beginning at Je-ru′sa-lem.

48 And ye are witnesses of these things.

49 ¶ And, behold, I send the promise of my Father upon you: but tarry ye in the city of Je-ru′sa-lem, until ye be endued with power from on high.

50 ¶ And he led them out as far as to Beth′a-ny, and he lifted up his hands, and blessed them.

51 And it came to pass, while he blessed them, he was parted from them, and carried up into heaven.

52 And they worshipped him, and returned to Je-ru′sa-lem with great joy:

53 And were continually in the temple, praising and blessing God. Amen.

THE GOSPEL ACCORDING TO

JOHN

1 IN the beginning was the Word, and the Word was with God, and the Word was God.

2 The same was in the beginning with God.

3 All things were made by him; and without him was not any thing made that was made.

4 In him was life; and the life was the light of men.

5 And the light shineth in darkness; and the darkness comprehended it not.

6 ¶ There was a man sent from God, whose name was John.

7 The same came for a witness, to bear witness of the Light, that all men through him might believe.

8 He was not that Light, but was sent to bear witness of that Light.

9 That was the true Light, which lighteth every man that cometh into the world.

10 He was in the world, and the world was made by him, and the world knew him not.

11 He came unto his own, and his own received him not.

12 But as many as received him, to them gave he power to become the sons of GOD, even to them that believe on his name:

13 Which were born, not of blood, nor of the will of the flesh, nor of the will of man, but of God.

14 And the Word was made flesh, and dwelt among us, (and we beheld his glory, the glory as of the only begotten of the Father,) full of grace and truth.

15 ¶ John bare witness of him, and cried, saying, This was he of whom I spake, He that cometh after me is preferred before me: for he was before me.

16 And of his fulness have all we received, and grace for grace.

17 For the law was given by Mo′ses, but grace and truth came by Je′sus Christ.

18 No man hath seen God at any time; the only begotten Son, which is in the bosom of the Father, he hath declared him.

19 ¶ And this is the record of John, when the

Jews sent priests and Le'vites from Je-ru'sa-lem to ask him, Who art thou?

20 And he confessed, and denied not; but confessed, I am not the Christ.

21 And they asked him, What then? Art thou E-li'as? And he saith, I am not. Art thou that prophet? And he answered, No.

22 Then said they unto him, Who art thou? that we may give an answer to them that sent us. What sayest thou of thyself?

23 He said, I *am* the voice of one crying in the wilderness, Make straight the way of the LORD, as said the prophet E-sa'ias.

24 And they which were sent were of the Phar'i-sees.

25 And they asked him, and said unto him, Why baptizest thou then, if thou be not that Christ, nor E-li'as, neither that prophet?

26 John answered them, saying, I baptize with water: but there standeth one among you, whom ye know not;

27 He it is, who coming after me is preferred before me, whose shoe's latchet I am not worthy to unloose.

28 These things were done in Beth-ab'a-ra beyond Jor'dan, where John was baptizing.

29 ¶ The next day John seeth Je'sus coming unto him, and saith, Behold the Lamb of God, which taketh away the sin of the world.

30 This is he of whom I said, After me cometh a man which is preferred before me: for he was before me.

31 And I knew him not: but that he should be made manifest to Is'ra-el, therefore am I come baptizing with water.

32 And John bare record, saying, I saw the Spirit descending from heaven like a dove, and it abode upon him.

33 And I knew him not: but he that sent me to baptize with water, the same said unto me, Upon whom thou shalt see the Spirit descending, and remaining on him, the same is he which baptizeth with the Ho'ly Ghost.

34 And I saw, and bare record that this is the Son of God.

35 ¶ Again the next day after John stood, and two of his disciples;

36 And looking upon Je'sus as he walked, he saith, Behold the Lamb of God!

37 And the two disciples heard him speak, and they followed Je'sus.

38 Then Je'sus turned, and saw them following, and saith unto them, What seek ye? They said unto him, Rab'bi, (which is to say, being interpreted, Master,) where dwellest thou?

39 He saith unto them, Come and see. They came and saw where he dwelt, and abode with him that day: for it was about the tenth hour.

40 One of the two which heard John *speak*, and followed him, was Andrew, Si'mon Pe'ter's brother.

41 He first findeth his own brother Si'mon, and saith unto him, We have found the Mes-si'as, which is, being interpreted, the Christ.

42 And he brought him to Je'sus. And when Je'sus beheld him, he said, Thou art Si'mon the son of Jo'na: thou shalt be called Ce'phas, which is by interpretation, A stone.

43 ¶ The day following Je'sus would go forth into Gal'i-lee, and findeth Phil'ip, and saith unto him, Follow me.

44 Now Phil'ip was of Beth-sa'i-da, the city of Andrew and Pe'ter.

45 Phil'ip findeth Na-than'a-el, and saith unto him, We have found him, of whom Mo'ses in the law, and the prophets, did write, Je'sus of Naz'a-reth, the son of Jo'seph.

46 And Na-than'a-el said unto him, Can there any good thing come out of Naz'a-reth? Phil'ip saith unto him, Come and see.

47 Je'sus saw Na-than'a-el coming to him, and saith of him, Behold an Is'ra-el-ite indeed, in whom is no guile!

48 Na-than'a-el saith unto him, Whence knowest thou me? Je'sus answered and said unto him, Before that Phil'ip called thee, when thou wast under the fig tree, I saw thee.

49 Na-than'a-el answered and saith unto him, Rab'bi, thou art the Son of God; thou art the King of Is'ra-el.

50 Je'sus answered and said unto him, Because I said unto thee, I saw thee under the fig tree, believest thou? thou shalt see greater things than these.

51 And he saith unto him, Verily, verily, I say unto you, Hereafter ye shall see heaven open, and the angels of God ascending and descending upon the Son of man.

2 AND the third day there was a marriage in Ca'na of Gal'i-lee; and the mother of Je'sus was there:

2 And both Je'sus was called, and his disciples, to the marriage.

3 And when they wanted wine, the mother of Je'sus saith unto him, They have no wine.

4 Je'sus saith unto her, Woman, what have I to do with thee? mine hour is not yet come.

5 His mother saith unto the servants, Whatsoever he saith unto you, do *it*.

6 And there were set there six waterpots of stone, after the manner of the purifying of the Jews, containing two or three firkins apiece.

7 Je'sus saith unto them, Fill the waterpots with water. And they filled them up to the brim.

8 And he saith unto them, Draw out now, and bear unto the governor of the feast. And they bare *it*.

9 When the ruler of the feast had tasted the water that was made wine, and knew not whence it was: (but the servants which drew the water knew;) the governor of the feast called the bridegroom,

10 And saith unto him, Every man at the beginning doth set forth good wine; and when men have well drunk, then that which is worse: *but* thou hast kept the good wine until now.

11 This beginning of miracles did Je'sus in Ca'na of Gal'i-lee, and manifested forth his glory; and his disciples believed on him.

12 ¶ After this he went down to Ca-per'na-um, he, and his mother, and his brethren, and his disciples: and they continued there not many days.

13 ¶ And the Jews' passover was at hand, and Je'sus went up to Je-ru'sa-lem,

14 And found in the temple those that sold oxen and sheep and doves, and the changers of money sitting:

15 And when he had made a scourge of small cords, he drove them all out of the temple, and the sheep, and the oxen; and poured out the changers' money, and overthrew the tables;

16 And said unto them that sold doves, Take these things hence; make not my Father's house an house of merchandise.

17 And his disciples remembered that it was written, The zeal of thine house hath eaten me up.

18 ¶ Then answered the Jews and said unto him, What sign shewest thou unto us, seeing that thou doest these things?

19 Je'sus answered and said unto them, De-

stroy this temple, and in three days I will raise it up.

20 Then said the Jews, Forty and six years was this temple in building, and wilt thou rear it up in three days?

21 But he spake of the temple of his body.

22 When therefore he was risen from the dead, his disciples remembered that he had said this unto them; and they believed the scripture, and the word which Je′sus had said.

23 ¶ Now when he was in Je-ru′sa-lem at the passover, in the feast *day*, many believed in his name, when they saw the miracles which he did.

24 But Je′sus did not commit himself unto them, because he knew all *men*,

25 And needed not that any should testify of man: for he knew what was in man.

3 THERE was a man of the Phar′i-sees, named Nic-o-de′mus, a ruler of the Jews:

2 The same came to Je′sus by night, and said unto him, Rab′bi, we know that thou art a teacher come from God: for no man can do these miracles that thou doest, except God be with him.

3 Je′sus answered and said unto him, Verily, verily, I say unto thee, Except a man be born again, he cannot see the kingdom of God.

4 Nic-o-de′mus saith unto him, How can a man be born when he is old? can he enter the second time into his mother's womb, and be born?

5 Je′sus answered, Verily, verily, I say unto thee, Except a man be born of water and *of* the Spirit, he cannot enter into the kingdom of God.

6 That which is born of the flesh is flesh; and that which is born of the Spirit is spirit.

7 Marvel not that I said unto thee, Ye must be born again.

8 The wind bloweth where it listeth, and thou hearest the sound thereof, but canst not tell whence it cometh, and whither it goeth: so is every one that is born of the Spirit.

9 Nic-o-de′mus answered and said unto him, How can these things be?

10 Je′sus answered and said unto him, Art thou a master of Is′ra-el, and knowest not these things?

11 Verily, verily, I say unto thee, We speak that we do know, and testify that we have seen; and ye receive not our witness.

12 If I have told you earthly things, and ye believe not, how shall ye believe, if I tell you *of* heavenly things?

13 And no man hath ascended up to heaven, but he that came down from heaven, *even* the Son of man which is in heaven.

14 ¶ And as Mo′ses lifted up the serpent in the wilderness, even so must the Son of man be lifted up:

15 That whosoever believeth in him should not perish, but have eternal life.

16 ¶ For God so loved the world, that he gave his only begotten Son, that whosoever believeth in him should not perish, but have everlasting life.

17 For God sent not his Son into the world to condemn the world; but that the world through him might be saved.

18 ¶ He that believeth on him is not condemned: but he that believeth not is condemned already, because he hath not believed in the name of the only begotten Son of God.

19 And this is the condemnation, that light is come into the world, and men loved darkness rather than light, because their deeds were evil.

20 For every one that doeth evil hateth the light, neither cometh to the light, lest his deeds should be reproved.

21 But he that doeth truth cometh to the light, that his deeds may be made manifest, that they are wrought in God.

22 ¶ After these things came Je′sus and his disciples into the land of Ju-dæ′a; and there he tarried with them, and baptized.

23 ¶ And John also was baptizing in Æ′non near to Sa′lim, because there was much water there: and they came, and were baptized.

24 For John was not yet cast into prison.

25 ¶ Then there arose a question between *some* of John's disciples and the Jews about purifying.

26 And they came unto John, and said unto him, Rab′bi, he that was with thee beyond Jor′dan, to whom thou barest witness, behold, the same baptizeth, and all *men* come to him.

27 John answered and said, A man can receive nothing, except it be given him from heaven.

28 Ye yourselves bear me witness, that I said, I am not the Christ, but that I am sent before him.

29 He that hath the bride is the bridegroom: but the friend of the bridegroom, which standeth and heareth him, rejoiceth greatly because of the bridegroom's voice: this my joy therefore is fulfilled.

30 He must increase, but I *must* decrease.

31 He that cometh from above is above all: he that is of the earth is earthly, and speaketh of the earth: he that cometh from heaven is above all.

32 And what he hath seen and heard, that he testifieth; and no man receiveth his testimony.

33 He that hath received his testimony hath set to his seal that God is true.

34 For he whom God hath sent speaketh the words of God: for God giveth not the Spirit by measure *unto him.*

35 The Father loveth the Son, and hath given all things into his hand.

36 He that believeth on the Son hath everlasting life: and he that believeth not the Son shall not see life; but the wrath of God abideth on him.

4 WHEN therefore the Lord knew how the Phar′i-sees had heard that Je′sus made and baptized more disciples than John,

2 (Though Je′sus himself baptized not, but his disciples,)

3 He left Ju-dæ′a, and departed again into Gal′i-lee.

4 And he must needs go through Sa-ma′ri-a.

5 Then cometh he to a city of Sa-ma′ri-a, which is called Sy′char, near to the parcel of ground that Ja′cob gave to his son Jo′seph.

6 Now Ja′cob's well was there. Je′sus therefore, being wearied with *his* journey, sat thus on the well: *and* it was about the sixth hour.

7 There cometh a woman of Sa-ma′ri-a to draw water: Je′sus saith unto her, Give me to drink.

8 (For his disciples were gone away unto the city to buy meat.)

9 Then saith the woman of Sa-ma′ri-a unto him, How is it that thou, being a Jew, askest drink of me, which am a woman of Sa-ma′ri-a? for the Jews have no dealings with the Sa-mar′i-tans.

10 Je′sus answered and said unto her, If thou knewest the gift of God, and who it is that saith to thee, Give me to drink; thou wouldest have

asked of him, and he would have given thee living water.

11 The woman saith unto him, Sir, thou hast nothing to draw with, and the well is deep: from whence then hast thou that living water?

12 Art thou greater than our father Ja'cob, which gave us the well, and drank thereof himself, and his children, and his cattle?

13 Je'sus answered and said unto her, Whosoever drinketh of this water shall thirst again:

14 But whosoever drinketh of the water that I shall give him shall never thirst; but the water that I shall give him shall be in him a well of water springing up into everlasting life.

15 The woman saith unto him, Sir, give me this water, that I thirst not, neither come hither to draw.

16 Je'sus saith unto her, Go, call thy husband, and come hither.

17 The woman answered and said, I have no husband. Je'sus said unto her, Thou hast well said, I have no husband:

18 For thou hast had five husbands; and he whom thou now hast is not thy husband: in that saidst thou truly.

19 The woman saith unto him, Sir, I perceive that thou art a prophet.

20 Our fathers worshipped in this mountain; and ye say, that in Je-ru'sa-lem is the place where men ought to worship.

21 Je'sus saith unto her, Woman, believe me, the hour cometh, when ye shall neither in this mountain, nor yet at Je-ru'sa-lem, worship the Father.

22 Ye worship ye know not what: we know what we worship: for salvation is of the Jews.

23 But the hour cometh, and now is, when the true worshippers shall worship the Father in spirit and in truth: for the Father seeketh such to worship him.

24 God *is* a Spirit: and they that worship him must worship *him* in spirit and in truth.

25 The woman saith unto him, I know that Mes-si'as cometh, which is called Christ: when he is come, he will tell us all things.

26 Je'sus saith unto her, I that speak unto thee am *he.*

27 ¶ And upon this came his disciples, and marvelled that he talked with the woman: yet no man said, What seekest thou? or, Why talkest thou with her?

28 The woman then left her waterpot, and went her way into the city, and saith to the men,

29 Come, see a man, which told me all things that ever I did: is not this the Christ?

30 Then they went out of the city, and came unto him.

31 ¶ In the mean while his disciples prayed him, saying, Master, eat.

32 But he said unto them, I have meat to eat that ye know not of.

33 Therefore said the disciples one to another, Hath any man brought him *ought* to eat?

34 Je'sus saith unto them, My meat is to do the will of him that sent me, and to finish his work.

35 Say not ye, There are yet four months, and *then* cometh harvest? behold, I say unto you, Lift up your eyes, and look on the fields; for they are white already to harvest.

36 And he that reapeth receiveth wages, and gathereth fruit unto life eternal: that both he that soweth and he that reapeth may rejoice together.

37 And herein is that saying true, One soweth, and another reapeth.

38 I sent you to reap that whereon ye bestowed no labour: other men laboured, and ye are entered into their labours.

39 ¶ And many of the Sa-mar'i-tans of that city believed on him for the saying of the woman, which testified, He told me all that ever I did.

40 So when the Sa-mar'i-tans were come unto him, they besought him that he would tarry with them: and he abode there two days.

41 And many more believed because of his own word;

42 And said unto the woman, Now we believe, not because of thy saying: for we have heard *him* ourselves, and know that this is indeed the Christ, the Saviour of the world.

43 ¶ Now after two days he departed thence, and went into Gal'i-lee.

44 For Je'sus himself testified, that a prophet hath no honour in his own country.

45 Then when he was come into Gal'i-lee, the Gal-i-læ'ans received him, having seen all the things that he did at Je-ru'sa-lem at the feast: for they also went unto the feast.

46 So Je'sus came again into Ca'na of Gal'i-lee, where he made the water wine. And there was a certain nobleman, whose son was sick at Ca-per'na-um.

47 When he heard that Je'sus was come out of Ju-dæ'a into Gal'i-lee, he went unto him, and besought him that he would come down, and heal his son: for he was at the point of death.

48 Then said Je'sus unto him, Except ye see signs and wonders, ye will not believe.

49 The nobleman saith unto him, Sir, come down ere my child die.

50 Je'sus saith unto him, Go thy way; thy son liveth. And the man believed the word that Je'sus had spoken unto him, and he went his way.

51 And as he was now going down, his servants met him, and told *him,* saying, Thy son liveth.

52 Then enquired he of them the hour when he began to amend. And they said unto him, Yesterday at the seventh hour the fever left him.

53 So the father knew that *it was* at the same hour, in the which Je'sus said unto him, Thy son liveth: and himself believed, and his whole house.

54 This *is* again the second miracle *that* Je'sus did, when he was come out of Ju-dæ'a into Gal'i-lee.

5 AFTER this there was a feast of the Jews; and Je'sus went up to Je-ru'sa-lem.

2 Now there is at Je-ru'sa-lem by the sheep *market* a pool, which is called in the He'brew tongue Be-thes'da, having five porches.

3 In these lay a great multitude of impotent folk, of blind, halt, withered, waiting for the moving of the water.

4 For an angel went down at a certain season into the pool, and troubled the water: whosoever then first after the troubling of the water stepped in was made whole of whatsoever disease he had.

5 And a certain man was there, which had an infirmity thirty and eight years.

6 When Je'sus saw him lie, and knew that he had been now a long time *in that case,* he saith unto him, Wilt thou be made whole?

7 The impotent man answered him, Sir, I have no man, when the water is troubled, to put me into the pool: but while I am coming, another steppeth down before me.

8 Je'sus saith unto him, Rise, take up thy bed, and walk.

9 And immediately the man was made whole, and took up his bed, and walked: and on the same day was the sabbath.

10 ¶ The Jews therefore said unto him that was cured, It is the sabbath day: it is not lawful for thee to carry *thy* bed.

11 He answered them, He that made me whole, the same said unto me, Take up thy bed, and walk.

12 Then asked they him, What man is that which said unto thee, Take up thy bed, and walk?

13 And he that was healed wist not who it was: for Je'sus had conveyed himself away, a multitude being in *that* place.

14 Afterward Je'sus findeth him in the temple, and said unto him, Behold, thou art made whole: sin no more, lest a worse thing come unto thee.

15 The man departed, and told the Jews that it was Je'sus, which had made him whole.

16 And therefore did the Jews persecute Je'-sus, and sought to slay him, because he had done these things on the sabbath day.

17 ¶ But Je'sus answered them, My Father worketh hitherto, and I work.

18 Therefore the Jews sought the more to kill him, because he not only had broken the sabbath, but said also that God was his Father, making himself equal with God.

19 Then answered Je'sus and said unto them, Verily, verily, I say unto you, The Son can do nothing of himself, but what he seeth the Father do: for what things soever he doeth, these also doeth the Son likewise.

20 For the Father loveth the Son, and sheweth him all things that himself doeth: and he will shew him greater works than these, that ye may marvel.

21 For as the Father raiseth up the dead, and quickeneth *them;* even so the Son quickeneth whom he will.

22 For the Father judgeth no man, but hath committed all judgment unto the Son:

23 That all *men* should honour the Son, even as they honour the Father. He that honoureth not the Son honoureth not the Father which hath sent him.

24 Verily, verily, I say unto you, He that heareth my word, and believeth on him that sent me, hath everlasting life, and shall not come into condemnation; but is passed from death unto life.

25 Verily, verily, I say unto you, The hour is coming, and now is, when the dead shall hear the voice of the Son of God: and they that hear shall live.

26 For as the Father hath life in himself; so hath he given to the Son to have life in himself;

27 And hath given him authority to execute judgment also, because he is the Son of man.

28 Marvel not at this: for the hour is coming, in the which all that are in the graves shall hear his voice,

29 And shall come forth; they that have done good, unto the resurrection of life; and they that have done evil, unto the resurrection of damnation.

30 I can of mine own self do nothing: as I hear, I judge: and my judgment is just; because I seek not mine own will, but the will of the Father which hath sent me.

31 If I bear witness of myself, my witness is not true.

32 ¶ There is another that beareth witness of me; and I know that the witness which he witnesseth of me is true.

33 Ye sent unto John, and he bare witness unto the truth.

34 But I receive not testimony from man: but these things I say, that ye might be saved.

35 He was a burning and a shining light: and ye were willing for a season to rejoice in his light.

36 ¶ But I have greater witness than *that* of John: for the works which the Father hath given me to finish, the same works that I do, bear witness of me, that the Father hath sent me.

37 And the Father himself, which hath sent me, hath borne witness of me. Ye have neither heard his voice at any time, nor seen his shape.

38 And ye have not his word abiding in you: for whom he hath sent, him ye believe not.

39 ¶ Search the scriptures; for in them ye think ye have eternal life: and they are they which testify of me.

40 And ye will not come to me, that ye might have life.

41 I receive not honour from men.

42 But I know you, that ye have not the love of God in you.

43 I am come in my Father's name, and ye receive me not: if another shall come in his own name, him ye will receive.

44 How can ye believe, which receive honour one of another, and seek not the honour that *cometh* from God only?

45 Do not think that I will accuse you to the Father: there is *one* that accuseth you, *even* Mo'ses, in whom ye trust.

46 For had ye believed Mo'ses, ye would have believed me: for he wrote of me.

47 But if ye believe not his writings, how shall ye believe my words?

6 AFTER these things Je'sus went over the sea of Gal'i-lee, which is *the sea* of Ti-be'ri-as.

2 And a great multitude followed him, because they saw his miracles which he did on them that were diseased.

3 And Je'sus went up into a mountain, and there he sat with his disciples.

4 And the passover, a feast of the Jews, was nigh.

5 ¶ When Je'sus then lifted up *his* eyes, and saw a great company come unto him, he saith unto Phil'ip, Whence shall we buy bread, that these may eat?

6 And this he said to prove him: for he himself knew what he would do.

7 Phil'ip answered him, Two hundred pennyworth of bread is not sufficient for them, that every one of them may take a little.

8 One of his disciples, Andrew, Si'mon Pe'-ter's brother, saith unto him,

9 There is a lad here, which hath five barley loaves, and two small fishes: but what are they among so many?

10 And Je'sus said, Make the men sit down. Now there was much grass in the place. So the men sat down, in number about five thousand.

11 And Je'sus took the loaves; and when he had given thanks, he distributed to the disciples, and the disciples to them that were set down; and likewise of the fishes as much as they would.

12 When they were filled, he said unto his disciples, Gather up the fragments that remain, that nothing be lost.

13 Therefore they gathered *them* together, and filled twelve baskets with the fragments of

the five barley loaves, which remained over and above unto them that had eaten.

14 Then those men, when they had seen the miracle that Je'sus did, said, This is of a truth that prophet that should come into the world.

15 ¶ When Je'sus therefore perceived that they would come and take him by force, to make him a king, he departed again into a mountain himself alone.

16 And when even was *now* come, his disciples went down unto the sea,

17 And entered into a ship, and went over the sea toward Ca-per'na-um. And it was now dark, and Je'sus was not come to them.

18 And the sea arose by reason of a great wind that blew.

19 So when they had rowed about five and twenty or thirty furlongs, they see Je'sus walking on the sea, and drawing nigh unto the ship: and they were afraid.

20 But he saith unto them, It is I; be not afraid.

21 Then they willingly received him into the ship: and immediately the ship was at the land whither they went.

22 ¶ The day following, when the people which stood on the other side of the sea saw that there was none other boat there, save that one whereinto his disciples were entered, and that Je'sus went not with his disciples into the boat, but *that* his disciples were gone away alone;

23 (Howbeit there came other boats from Ti-be'ri-as nigh unto the place where they did eat bread, after that the Lord had given thanks:)

24 When the people therefore saw that Je'sus was not there, neither his disciples, they also took shipping, and came to Ca-per'na-um, seeking for Je'sus.

25 And when they had found him on the other side of the sea, they said unto him, Rab'bi, when camest thou hither?

26 Je'sus answered them and said, Verily, verily, I say unto you, Ye seek me, not because ye saw the miracles, but because ye did eat of the loaves, and were filled.

27 Labour not for the meat which perisheth, but for that meat which endureth unto everlasting life, which the Son of man shall give unto you: for him hath God the Father sealed.

28 Then said they unto him, What shall we do, that we might work the works of God?

29 Je'sus answered and said unto them, This is the work of God, that ye believe on him whom he hath sent.

30 They said therefore unto him, What sign shewest thou then, that we may see, and believe thee? what dost thou work?

31 Our fathers did eat manna in the desert; as it is written, He gave them bread from heaven to eat.

32 Then Je'sus said unto them, Verily, verily, I say unto you, Mo'ses gave you not that bread from heaven; but my Father giveth you the true bread from heaven.

33 For the bread of God is he which cometh down from heaven, and giveth life unto the world.

34 Then said they unto him, Lord, evermore give us this bread.

35 And Je'sus said unto them, I am the bread of life: he that cometh to me shall never hunger; and he that believeth on me shall never thirst.

36 But I said unto you, That ye also have seen me, and believe not.

37 All that the Father giveth me shall come to me; and him that cometh to me I will in no wise cast out.

38 For I came down from heaven, not to do mine own will, but the will of him that sent me.

39 And this is the Father's will which hath sent me, that of all which he hath given me I should lose nothing, but should raise it up again at the last day.

40 And this is the will of him that sent me, that every one which seeth the Son, and believeth on him, may have everlasting life: and I will raise him up at the last day.

41 The Jews then murmured at him, because he said, I am the bread which came down from heaven.

42 And they said, Is not this Je'sus, the son of Jo'seph, whose father and mother we know? how is it then that he saith, I came down from heaven?

43 Je'sus therefore answered and said unto them, Murmur not among yourselves.

44 No man can come to me, except the Father which hath sent me draw him: and I will raise him up at the last day.

45 It is written in the prophets, And they shall be all taught of God. Every man therefore that hath heard, and hath learned of the Father, cometh unto me.

46 Not that any man hath seen the Father, save he which is of God, he hath seen the Father.

47 Verily, verily, I say unto you, He that believeth on me hath everlasting life.

48 I am that bread of life.

49 Your fathers did eat manna in the wilderness, and are dead.

50 This is the bread which cometh down from heaven, that a man may eat thereof, and not die.

51 I am the living bread which came down from heaven: if any man eat of this bread, he shall live for ever: and the bread that I will give is my flesh, which I will give for the life of the world.

52 The Jews therefore strove among themselves, saying, How can this man give us *his* flesh to eat?

53 Then Je'sus said unto them, Verily, verily, I say unto you, Except ye eat the flesh of the Son of man, and drink his blood, ye have no life in you.

54 Whoso eateth my flesh, and drinketh my blood, hath eternal life; and I will raise him up at the last day.

55 For my flesh is meat indeed, and my blood is drink indeed.

56 He that eateth my flesh, and drinketh my blood, dwelleth in me, and I in him.

57 As the living Father hath sent me, and I live by the Father: so he that eateth me, even he shall live by me.

58 This is that bread which came down from heaven: not as your fathers did eat manna, and are dead: he that eateth of this bread shall live for ever.

59 These things said he in the synagogue, as he taught in Ca-per'na-um.

60 Many therefore of his disciples, when they had heard *this*, said, This is an hard saying; who can hear it?

61 When Je'sus knew in himself that his disciples murmured at it, he said unto them, Doth this offend you?

62 *What* and if ye shall see the Son of man ascend up where he was before?

63 It is the spirit that quickeneth; the flesh

profiteth nothing: the words that I speak unto you, *they* are spirit, and *they* are life.

64 But there are some of you that believe not. For Je'sus knew from the beginning who they were that believed not, and who should betray him.

65 And he said, Therefore said I unto you, that no man can come unto me, except it were given unto him of my Father.

66 ¶ From that *time* many of his disciples went back, and walked no more with him.

67 Then said Je'sus unto the twelve, Will ye also go away?

68 Then Si'mon Pe'ter answered him, Lord, to whom shall we go? thou hast the words of eternal life.

69 And we believe and are sure that thou art that Christ, the Son of the living God.

70 Je'sus answered them, Have not I chosen you twelve, and one of you is a devil?

71 He spake of Ju'das Is-car'i-ot *the son* of Si'mon: for he it was that should betray him, being one of the twelve.

7 AFTER these things Je'sus walked in Gal'i-lee: for he would not walk in Jew'ry, because the Jews sought to kill him.

2 Now the Jews' feast of tabernacles was at hand.

3 His brethren therefore said unto him, Depart hence, and go into Ju-dæ'a, that thy disciples also may see the works that thou doest.

4 For *there is* no man *that* doeth any thing in secret, and he himself seeketh to be known openly. If thou do these things, shew thyself to the world.

5 For neither did his brethren believe in him.

6 Then Je'sus said unto them, My time is not yet come: but your time is alway ready.

7 The world cannot hate you; but me it hateth, because I testify of it, that the works thereof are evil.

8 Go ye up unto this feast: I go not up yet unto this feast; for my time is not yet full come.

9 When he had said these words unto them, he abode *still* in Gal'i-lee.

10 ¶ But when his brethren were gone up, then went he also up unto the feast, not openly, but as it were in secret.

11 Then the Jews sought him at the feast, and said, Where is he?

12 And there was much murmuring among the people concerning him: for some said, He is a good man: others said, Nay; but he deceiveth the people.

13 Howbeit no man spake openly of him for fear of the Jews.

14 ¶ Now about the midst of the feast Je'sus went up into the temple, and taught.

15 And the Jews marvelled, saying, How knoweth this man letters, having never learned?

16 Je'sus answered them, and said, My doctrine is not mine, but his that sent me.

17 If any man will do his will, he shall know of the doctrine, whether it be of God, or *whether* I speak of myself.

18 He that speaketh of himself seeketh his own glory: but he that seeketh his glory that sent him, the same is true, and no unrighteousness is in him.

19 Did not Mo'ses give you the law, and *yet* none of you keepeth the law? Why go ye about to kill me?

20 The people answered and said, Thou hast a devil: who goeth about to kill thee?

21 Je'sus answered and said unto them, I have done one work, and ye all marvel.

22 Mo'ses therefore gave unto you circumcision; (not because it is of Mo'ses, but of the fathers;) and ye on the sabbath day circumcise a man.

23 If a man on the sabbath day receive circumcision, that the law of Mo'ses should not be broken; are ye angry at me, because I have made a man every whit whole on the sabbath day?

24 Judge not according to the appearance, but judge righteous judgment.

25 Then said some of them of Je-ru'sa-lem, Is not this he, whom they seek to kill?

26 But, lo, he speaketh boldly, and they say nothing unto him. Do the rulers know indeed that this is the very Christ?

27 Howbeit we know this man whence he is: but when Christ cometh, no man knoweth whence he is.

28 Then cried Je'sus in the temple as he taught, saying, Ye both know me, and ye know whence I am: and I am not come of myself, but he that sent me is true, whom ye know not.

29 But I know him: for I am from him, and he hath sent me.

30 Then they sought to take him: but no man laid hands on him, because his hour was not yet come.

31 And many of the people believed on him, and said, When Christ cometh, will he do more miracles than these which this *man* hath done?

32 ¶ The Phar'i-sees heard that the people murmured such things concerning him; and the Phar'i-sees and the chief priests sent officers to take him.

33 Then said Je'sus unto them, Yet a little while am I with you, and *then* I go unto him that sent me.

34 Ye shall seek me, and shall not find *me*: and where I am, *thither* ye cannot come.

35 Then said the Jews among themselves, Whither will he go, that we shall not find him? will he go unto the dispersed among the Gen'tiles, and teach the Gen'tiles?

36 What *manner of* saying is this that he said, Ye shall seek me, and shall not find *me*: and where I am, *thither* ye cannot come?

37 In the last day, that great *day* of the feast, Je'sus stood and cried, saying, If any man thirst, let him come unto me, and drink.

38 He that believeth on me, as the scripture hath said, out of his belly shall flow rivers of living water.

39 (But this spake he of the Spirit, which they that believe on him should receive: for the Ho'ly Ghost was not yet *given*: because that Je'sus was not yet glorified.)

40 ¶ Many of the people therefore, when they heard this saying, said, Of a truth this is the Prophet.

41 Others said, This is the Christ. But some said, Shall Christ come out of Gal'i-lee?

42 Hath not the scripture said, That Christ cometh of the seed of Da'vid, and out of the town of Beth'le-hem, where Da'vid was?

43 So there was a division among the people because of him.

44 And some of them would have taken him; but no man laid hands on him.

45 ¶ Then came the officers to the chief priests and Phar'i-sees; and they said unto them, Why have ye not brought him?

46 The officers answered, Never man spake like this man.

47 Then answered them the Phar'i-sees, Are ye also deceived?

48 Have any of the rulers or of the Phar'i-sees believed on him?

49 But this people who knoweth not the law are cursed.

50 Nic-o-de'mus saith unto them, (he that came to Je'sus by night, being one of them,)

51 Doth our law judge *any* man, before it hear him, and know what he doeth?

52 They answered and said unto him, Art thou also of Gal'i-lee? Search, and look: for out of Gal'i-lee ariseth no prophet.

53 And every man went unto his own house.

8 JE'SUS went unto the mount of Ol'ives.

2 And early in the morning he came again into the temple, and all the people came unto him; and he sat down, and taught them.

3 And the scribes and Phar'i-sees brought unto him a woman taken in adultery; and when they had set her in the midst,

4 They say unto him, Master, this woman was taken in adultery, in the very act.

5 Now Mo'ses in the law commanded us, that such should be stoned: but what sayest thou?

6 This they said, tempting him, that they might have to accuse him. But Je'sus stooped down, and with *his* finger wrote on the ground, *as though he heard them not.*

7 So when they continued asking him, he lifted up himself, and said unto them, He that is without sin among you, let him first cast a stone at her.

8 And again he stooped down, and wrote on the ground.

9 And they which heard *it*, being convicted by *their* own conscience, went out one by one, beginning at the eldest, *even* unto the last: and Je'sus was left alone, and the woman standing in the midst.

10 When Je'sus had lifted up himself, and saw none but the woman, he said unto her, Woman, where are those thine accusers? hath no man condemned thee?

11 She said, No man, Lord. And Je'sus said unto her, Neither do I condemn thee: go, and sin no more.

12 ¶ Then spake Je'sus again unto them, saying, I am the light of the world: he that followeth me shall not walk in darkness, but shall have the light of life.

13 The Phar'i-sees therefore said unto him, Thou bearest record of thyself; thy record is not true.

14 Je'sus answered and said unto them, Though I bear record of myself, *yet* my record is true: for I know whence I came, and whither I go; but ye cannot tell whence I come, and whither I go.

15 Ye judge after the flesh; I judge no man.

16 And yet if I judge, my judgment is true: for I am not alone, but I and the Father that sent me.

17 It is also written in your law, that the testimony of two men is true.

18 I am one that bear witness of myself, and the Father that sent me beareth witness of me.

19 Then said they unto him, Where is thy Father? Je'sus answered, Ye neither know me, nor my Father: if ye had known me, ye should have known my Father also.

20 These words spake Je'sus in the treasury, as he taught in the temple: and no man laid hands on him; for his hour was not yet come.

21 Then said Je'sus again unto them, I go my way, and ye shall seek me, and shall die in your sins: whither I go, ye cannot come.

22 Then said the Jews, Will he kill himself?

because he saith, Whither I go, ye cannot come.

23 And he said unto them, Ye are from beneath; I am from above: ye are of this world; I am not of this world.

24 I said therefore unto you, that ye shall die in your sins: for if ye believe not that I am *he*, ye shall die in your sins.

25 Then said they unto him, Who art thou? And Je'sus saith unto them, Even *the same* that I said unto you from the beginning.

26 I have many things to say and to judge of you: but he that sent me is true; and I speak to the world those things which I have heard of him.

27 They understood not that he spake to them of the Father.

28 Then said Je'sus unto them, When ye have lifted up the Son of man, then shall ye know that I am *he*, and *that* I do nothing of myself; but as my Father hath taught me, I speak these things.

29 And he that sent me is with me: the Father hath not left me alone; for I do always those things that please him.

30 As he spake these words, many believed on him.

31 Then said Je'sus to those Jews which believed on him, If ye continue in my word, *then* are ye my disciples indeed;

32 And ye shall know the truth, and the truth shall make you free.

33 ¶ They answered him, We be A'bra-ham's seed, and were never in bondage to any man: how sayest thou, Ye shall be made free?

34 Je'sus answered them, Verily, verily, I say unto you, Whosoever committeth sin is the servant of sin.

35 And the servant abideth not in the house for ever: *but* the Son abideth ever.

36 If the Son therefore shall make you free, ye shall be free indeed.

37 I know that ye are A'bra-ham's seed; but ye seek to kill me, because my word hath no place in you.

38 I speak that which I have seen with my Father: and ye do that which ye have seen with your father.

39 They answered and said unto him, A'bra-ham is our father. Je'sus saith unto them, If ye were A'bra-ham's children, ye would do the works of A'bra-ham.

40 But now ye seek to kill me, a man that hath told you the truth, which I have heard of God: this did not A'bra-ham.

41 Ye do the deeds of your father. Then said they to him, We be not born of fornication; we have one Father, *even* God.

42 Je'sus said unto them, If God were your Father, ye would love me: for I proceeded forth and came from God; neither came I of myself, but he sent me.

43 Why do ye not understand my speech? *even* because ye cannot hear my word.

44 Ye are of *your* father the devil, and the lusts of your father ye will do. He was a murderer from the beginning, and abode not in the truth, because there is no truth in him. When he speaketh a lie, he speaketh of his own: for he is a liar, and the father of it.

45 And because I tell *you* the truth, ye believe me not.

46 Which of you convinceth me of sin? And if I say the truth, why do ye not believe me?

47 He that is of God heareth God's words: ye therefore hear *them* not, because ye are not of God.

48 Then answered the Jews, and said unto

him, Say we not well that thou art a Sa-mar′i-tan, and hast a devil?

49 Je′sus answered, I have not a devil; but I honour my Father, and ye do dishonour me.

50 And I seek not mine own glory: there is one that seeketh and judgeth.

51 Verily, verily, I say unto you, If a man keep my saying, he shall never see death.

52 Then said the Jews unto him, Now we know that thou hast a devil. A′bra-ham is dead, and the prophets; and thou sayest, If a man keep my saying, he shall never taste of death.

53 Art thou greater than our father A′bra-ham, which is dead? and the prophets are dead: whom makest thou thyself?

54 Je′sus answered, If I honour myself, my honour is nothing: it is my Father that honour-eth me; of whom ye say, that he is your God:

55 Yet ye have not known him; but I know him: and if I should say, I know him not, I shall be a liar like unto you: but I know him, and keep his saying.

56 Your father A′bra-ham rejoiced to see my day; and he saw it, and was glad.

57 Then said the Jews unto him, Thou art not yet fifty years old, and hast thou seen A′bra-ham?

58 Je′sus said unto them, Verily, verily, I say unto you, Before A′bra-ham was, I am.

59 Then took they up stones to cast at him: but Je′sus hid himself, and went out of the temple, going through the midst of them, and so passed by.

9 AND as Je′sus passed by, he saw a man which was blind from his birth.

2 And his disciples asked him, saying, Master, who did sin, this man, or his parents, that he was born blind?

3 Je′sus answered, Neither hath this man sinned, nor his parents: but that the works of God should be made manifest in him.

4 I must work the works of him that sent me, while it is day: the night cometh, when no man can work.

5 As long as I am in the world, I am the light of the world.

6 When he had thus spoken, he spat on the ground, and made clay of the spittle, and he anointed the eyes of the blind man with the clay,

7 And said unto him, Go wash in the pool of Si-lo′am, (which is by interpretation, Sent.) He went his way therefore, and washed, and came seeing.

8 ¶ The neighbours therefore, and they which before had seen him that he was blind, said, Is not this he that sat and begged?

9 Some said, This is he: others said, He is like him: but he said, I am he.

10 Therefore said they unto him, How were thine eyes opened?

11 He answered and said, A man that is called Je′sus made clay, and anointed mine eyes, and said unto me, Go to the pool of Si-lo′am, and wash: and I went and washed, and I received sight.

12 Then said they unto him, Where is he? He said, I know not.

13 ¶ They brought to the Phar′i-sees him that aforetime was blind.

14 And it was the sabbath day when Je′sus made the clay, and opened his eyes.

15 Then again the Phar′i-sees also asked him how he had received his sight. He said unto them, He put clay upon mine eyes, and I washed, and do see.

16 Therefore said some of the Phar′i-sees, This man is not of God, because he keepeth not the sabbath day. Others said, How can a man that is a sinner do such miracles? And there was a division among them.

17 They say unto the blind man again, What sayest thou of him, that he hath opened thine eyes? He said, He is a prophet.

18 But the Jews did not believe concerning him, that he had been blind, and received his sight, until they called the parents of him that had received his sight.

19 And they asked them, saying, Is this your son, who ye say was born blind? how then doth he now see?

20 His parents answered them and said, We know that this is our son, and that he was born blind:

21 But by what means he now seeth, we know not; or who hath opened his eyes, we know not: he is of age; ask him: he shall speak for himself.

22 These words spake his parents, because they feared the Jews: for the Jews had agreed already, that if any man did confess that he was Christ, he should be put out of the synagogue.

23 Therefore said his parents, He is of age; ask him.

24 Then again called they the man that was blind, and said unto him, Give God the praise: we know that this man is a sinner.

25 He answered and said, Whether he be a sinner or no, I know not: one thing I know, that, whereas I was blind, now I see.

26 Then said they to him again, What did he to thee? how opened he thine eyes?

27 He answered them, I have told you already, and ye did not hear: wherefore would ye hear it again? will ye also be his disciples?

28 Then they reviled him, and said, Thou art his disciple; but we are Mo′ses' disciples.

29 We know that God spake unto Mo′ses: as for this fellow, we know not from whence he is.

30 The man answered and said unto them, Why herein is a marvellous thing, that ye know not from whence he is, and yet he hath opened mine eyes.

31 Now we know that God heareth not sinners: but if any man be a worshippper of God, and doeth his will, him he heareth.

32 Since the world began was it not heard that any man opened the eyes of one that was born blind.

33 If this man were not of God, he could do nothing.

34 They answered and said unto him, Thou wast altogether born in sins, and dost thou teach us? And they cast him out.

35 Je′sus heard that they had cast him out; and when he had found him, he said unto him, Dost thou believe on the Son of God?

36 He answered and said, Who is he, Lord, that I might believe on him?

37 And Je′sus said unto him, Thou hast both seen him, and it is he, that talketh with thee.

38 And he said, Lord, I believe. And he worshipped him.

39 ¶ And Je′sus said, For judgment I am come into this world, that they which see not might see; and that they which see might be made blind.

40 And some of the Phar′i-sees which were with him heard these words, and said unto him, Are we blind also?

41 Je′sus said unto them, If ye were blind, ye should have no sin: but now ye say, We see; therefore your sin remaineth.

10 VERILY, verily, I say unto you, He that entereth not by the door into the sheepfold, but climbeth up some other way, the same is a thief and a robber.

2 But he that entereth in by the door is the shepherd of the sheep.

3 To him the porter openeth; and the sheep hear his voice: and he calleth his own sheep by name, and leadeth them out.

4 And when he putteth forth his own sheep, he goeth before them, and the sheep follow him: for they know his voice.

5 And a stranger will they not follow, but will flee from him: for they know not the voice of strangers.

6 This parable spake Je′sus unto them: but they understood not what things they were which he spake unto them.

7 Then said Je′sus unto them again, Verily, verily, I say unto you, I am the door of the sheep.

8 All that ever came before me are thieves and robbers: but the sheep did not hear them.

9 I am the door: by me if any man enter in, he shall be saved, and shall go in and out, and find pasture.

10 The thief cometh not, but for to steal, and to kill, and to destroy: I am come that they might have life, and that they might have *it* more abundantly.

11 I am the good shepherd: the good shepherd giveth his life for the sheep.

12 But he that is an hireling, and not the shepherd, whose own the sheep are not, seeth the wolf coming, and leaveth the sheep, and fleeth: and the wolf catcheth them, and scattereth the sheep.

13 The hireling fleeth, because he is an hireling, and careth not for the sheep.

14 I am the good shepherd, and know my *sheep,* and am known of mine.

15 As the Father knoweth me, even so know I the Father: and I lay down my life for the sheep.

16 And other sheep I have, which are not of this fold: them also I must bring, and they shall hear my voice; and there shall be one fold, *and* one shepherd.

17 Therefore doth my Father love me, because I lay down my life, that I might take it again.

18 No man taketh it from me, but I lay it down of myself. I have power to lay it down, and I have power to take it again. This commandment have I received of my Father.

19 ¶ There was a division therefore again among the Jews for these sayings.

20 And many of them said, He hath a devil, and is mad; why hear ye him?

21 Others said, These are not the words of him that hath a devil. Can a devil open the eyes of the blind?

22 ¶ And it was at Je-ru′sa-lem the feast of the dedication, and it was winter.

23 And Je′sus walked in the temple in Sol′o-mon's porch.

24 Then came the Jews round about him, and said unto him, How long dost thou make us to doubt? If thou be the Christ, tell us plainly.

25 Je′sus answered them, I told you, and ye believed not: the works that I do in my Father's name, they bear witness of me.

26 But ye believe not, because ye are not of my sheep, as I said unto you.

27 My sheep hear my voice, and I know them, and they follow me:

28 And I give unto them eternal life; and they shall never perish, neither shall any *man* pluck them out of my hand.

29 My Father, which gave *them* me, is greater than all; and no *man* is able to pluck *them* out of my Father's hand.

30 I and *my* Father are one.

31 Then the Jews took up stones again to stone him.

32 Je′sus answered them, Many good works have I shewed you from my Father; for which of those works do ye stone me?

33 The Jews answered him, saying, For a good work we stone thee not; but for blasphemy; and because that thou, being a man, makest thyself God.

34 Je′sus answered them, Is it not written in your law, I said, Ye are gods?

35 If he called them gods, unto whom the word of God came, and the scripture cannot be broken;

36 Say ye of him, whom the Father hath sanctified, and sent into the world, Thou blasphemest; because I said, I am the Son of God?

37 If I do not the works of my Father, believe me not.

38 But if I do, though ye believe not me, believe the works: that ye may know, and believe, that the Father *is* in me, and I in him.

39 Therefore they sought again to take him: but he escaped out of their hand,

40 And went away again beyond Jor′dan into the place where John at first baptized; and there he abode.

41 And many resorted unto him, and said, John did no miracle: but all things that John spake of this man were true.

42 And many believed on him there.

11 NOW a certain *man* was sick, *named* Laz′a-rus, of Beth′a-ny, the town of Ma′-ry and her sister Mar′tha.

2 (It was *that* Ma′ry which anointed the Lord with ointment, and wiped his feet with her hair, whose brother Laz′a-rus was sick.)

3 Therefore his sisters sent unto him, saying, Lord, behold, he whom thou lovest is sick.

4 When Je′sus heard *that,* he said, This sickness is not unto death, but for the glory of God, that the Son of God might be glorified thereby.

5 Now Je′sus loved Mar′tha, and her sister, and Laz′a-rus.

6 When he had heard therefore that he was sick, he abode two days still in the same place where he was.

7 Then after that saith he to *his* disciples, Let us go into Ju-dæ′a again.

8 *His* disciples say unto him, Master, the Jews of late sought to stone thee; and goest thou thither again?

9 Je′sus answered, Are there not twelve hours in the day? If any man walk in the day, he stumbleth not, because he seeth the light of this world.

10 But if a man walk in the night, he stumbleth, because there is no light in him.

11 These things said he: and after that he saith unto them, Our friend Laz′a-rus sleepeth; but I go, that I may awake him out of sleep.

12 Then said his disciples, Lord, if he sleep, he shall do well.

13 Howbeit Je′sus spake of his death: but they thought that he had spoken of taking of rest in sleep.

14 Then said Je′sus unto them plainly, Laz′a-rus is dead.

15 And I am glad for your sakes that I was

not there, to the intent ye may believe; nevertheless let us go unto him.

16 Then said Thom'as, which is called Did'ymus, unto his fellowdisciples, Let us also go, that we may die with him.

17 Then when Je'sus came, he found that he had *lain* in the grave four days already.

18 Now Beth'a-ny was nigh unto Je-ru'salem, about fifteen furlongs off:

19 And many of the Jews came to Mar'tha and Ma'ry, to comfort them concerning their brother.

20 Then Mar'tha, as soon as she heard that Je'sus was coming, went and met him: but Ma'ry sat *still* in the house.

21 Then said Mar'tha unto Je'sus, Lord, if thou hadst been here, my brother had not died.

22 But I know, that even now, whatsoever thou wilt ask of God, God will give *it* thee.

23 Je'sus saith unto her, Thy brother shall rise again.

24 Mar'tha saith unto him, I know that he shall rise again in the resurrection at the last day.

25 Je'sus said unto her, I am the resurrection, and the life: he that believeth in me, though he were dead, yet shall he live:

26 And whosoever liveth and believeth in me shall never die. Believest thou this?

27 She saith unto him, Yea, Lord: I believe that thou art the Christ, the Son of God, which should come into the world.

28 And when she had so said, she went her way, and called Ma'ry her sister secretly, saying, The Master is come, and calleth for thee.

29 As soon as she heard *that*, she arose quickly, and came unto him.

30 Now Je'sus was not yet come into the town, but was in that place where Mar'tha met him.

31 The Jews then which were with her in the house, and comforted her, when they saw Ma'ry, that she rose up hastily and went out, followed her, saying, She goeth unto the grave to weep there.

32 Then when Ma'ry was come where Je'sus was, and saw him, she fell down at his feet, saying unto him, Lord, if thou hadst been here, my brother had not died.

33 When Je'sus therefore saw her weeping, and the Jews also weeping which came with her, he groaned in the spirit, and was troubled,

34 And said, Where have ye laid him? They said unto him, Lord, come and see.

35 Je'sus wept.

36 Then said the Jews, Behold how he loved him!

37 And some of them said, Could not this man, which opened the eyes of the blind, have caused that even this man should not have died?

38 Je'sus therefore again groaning in himself cometh to the grave. It was a cave, and a stone lay upon it.

39 Je'sus said, Take ye away the stone. Mar'tha, the sister of him that was dead, saith unto him, Lord, by this time he stinketh: for he hath been *dead* four days.

40 Je'sus saith unto her, Said I not unto thee, that, if thou wouldest believe, thou shouldest see the glory of God?

41 Then they took away the stone *from the place* where the dead was laid. And Je'sus lifted up *his* eyes, and said, Father, I thank thee that thou hast heard me.

42 And I knew that thou hearest me always: but because of the people which stand by I said *it*, that they may believe that thou hast sent me.

43 And when he thus had spoken, he cried with a loud voice, Laz'a-rus, come forth.

44 And he that was dead came forth, bound hand and foot with graveclothes: and his face was bound about with a napkin. Je'sus saith unto them, Loose him, and let him go.

45 Then many of the Jews which came to Ma'ry, and had seen the things which Je'sus did, believed on him.

46 But some of them went their ways to the Phar'i-sees, and told them what things Je'sus had done.

47 ¶ Then gathered the chief priests and the Phar'i-sees a council, and said, What do we? for this man doeth many miracles.

48 If we let him thus alone, all *men* will believe on him: and the Ro'mans shall come and take away both our place and nation.

49 And one of them, *named* Ca'ia-phas, being the high priest that same year, said unto them, Ye know nothing at all,

50 Nor consider that it is expedient for us, that one man should die for the people, and that the whole nation perish not.

51 And this spake he not of himself: but being high priest that year, he prophesied that Je'sus should die for that nation;

52 And not for that nation only, but that also he should gather together in one the children of God that were scattered abroad.

53 Then from that day forth they took counsel together for to put him to death.

54 Je'sus therefore walked no more openly among the Jews; but went thence unto a country near to the wilderness, into a city called E'-phra-im, and there continued with his disciples.

55 ¶ And the Jews' passover was nigh at hand: and many went out of the country up to Je-ru'sa-lem before the passover, to purify themselves.

56 Then sought they for Je'sus, and spake among themselves, as they stood in the temple, What think ye, that he will not come to the feast?

57 Now both the chief priests and the Phar'i-sees had given a commandment, that, if any man knew where he were, he should shew *it*, that they might take him.

12 THEN Je'sus six days before the passover came to Beth'a-ny, where Laz'a-rus was which had been dead, whom he raised from the dead.

2 There they made him a supper; and Mar'tha served: but Laz'a-rus was one of them that sat at the table with him.

3 Then took Ma'ry a pound of ointment of spikenard, very costly, and anointed the feet of Je'sus, and wiped his feet with her hair: and the house was filled with the odour of the ointment.

4 Then saith one of his disciples, Ju'das Is-car'i-ot, Si'mon's *son*, which should betray him,

5 Why was not this ointment sold for three hundred pence, and given to the poor?

6 This he said, not that he cared for the poor; but because he was a thief, and had the bag, and bare what was put therein.

7 Then said Je'sus, Let her alone: against the day of my burying hath she kept this.

8 For the poor always ye have with you; but me ye have not always.

9 Much people of the Jews therefore knew that he was there: and they came not for Je'sus' sake only, but that they might see Laz'a-rus also, whom he had raised from the dead.

10 ¶ But the chief priests consulted that they might put Laz'a-rus also to death:

11 Because that by reason of him many of the Jews went away, and believed on Je'sus.

12 ¶ On the next day much people that were come to the feast, when they heard that Je'sus was coming to Je-ru'sa-lem,

13 Took branches of palm trees, and went forth to meet him, and cried, Ho-san'na: Blessed *is* the King of Is'ra-el that cometh in the name of the Lord.

14 And Je'sus, when he had found a young ass, sat thereon; as it is written,

15 Fear not, daughter of Si'on: behold, thy King cometh, sitting on an ass's colt.

16 These things understood not his disciples at the first: but when Je'sus was glorified, then remembered they that these things were written of him, and *that* they had done these things unto him.

17 The people therefore that was with him when he called Laz'a-rus out of his grave, and raised him from the dead, bare record.

18 For this cause the people also met him, for that they heard that he had done this miracle.

19 The Phar'i-sees therefore said among themselves, Perceive ye how ye prevail nothing? behold, the world is gone after him.

20 ¶ And there were certain Greeks among them, that came up to worship at the feast:

21 The same came therefore to Phil'ip, which was of Beth-sa'i-da of Gal'i-lee, and desired him, saying, Sir, we would see Je'sus.

22 Phil'ip cometh and telleth An'drew: and again An'drew and Phil'ip tell Je'sus.

23 ¶ And Je'sus answered them, saying, The hour is come, that the Son of man should be glorified.

24 Verily, verily, I say unto you, Except a corn of wheat fall into the ground and die, it abideth alone: but if it die, it bringeth forth much fruit.

25 He that loveth his life shall lose it; and he that hateth his life in this world shall keep it unto life eternal.

26 If any man serve me, let him follow me; and where I am, there shall also my servant be: if any man serve me, him will *my* Father honour.

27 Now is my soul troubled; and what shall I say? Father, save me from this hour: but for this cause came I unto this hour.

28 Father, glorify thy name. Then came there a voice from heaven, *saying,* I have both glorified *it,* and will glorify *it* again.

29 The people therefore, that stood by, and heard *it,* said that it thundered: others said, An angel spake to him.

30 Je'sus answered and said, This voice came not because of me, but for your sakes.

31 Now is the judgment of this world: now shall the prince of this world be cast out.

32 And I, if I be lifted up from the earth, will draw all *men* unto me.

33 This he said, signifying what death he should die.

34 The people answered him, We have heard out of the law that Christ abideth for ever: and how sayest thou, The Son of man must be lifted up? who is this Son of man?

35 Then Je'sus said unto them, Yet a little while is the light with you. Walk while ye have the light, lest darkness come upon you: for he that walketh in darkness knoweth not whither he goeth.

36 While ye have light, believe in the light, that ye may be the children of light. These

things spake Je'sus, and departed, and did hide himself from them.

37 ¶ But though he had done so many miracles before them, yet they believed not on him:

38 That the saying of E-sa'ias the prophet might be fulfilled, which he spake, Lord, who hath believed our report? and to whom hath the arm of the Lord been revealed?

39 Therefore they could not believe, because that E-sa'ias said again,

40 He hath blinded their eyes, and hardened their heart; that they should not see with *their* eyes, nor understand with *their* heart, and be converted, and I should heal them.

41 These things said E-sa'ias, when he saw his glory, and spake of him.

42 ¶ Nevertheless among the chief rulers also many believed on him; but because of the Phar'i-sees they did not confess *him,* lest they should be put out of the synagogue:

43 For they loved the praise of men more than the praise of God.

44 ¶ Je'sus cried and said, He that believeth on me, believeth not on me, but on him that sent me.

45 And he that seeth me seeth him that sent me.

46 I am come a light into the world, that whosoever believeth on me should not abide in darkness.

47 And if any man hear my words, and believe not, I judge him not: for I came not to judge the world, but to save the world.

48 He that rejecteth me, and receiveth not my words, hath one that judgeth him: the word that I have spoken, the same shall judge him in the last day.

49 For I have not spoken of myself; but the Father which sent me, he gave me a commandment, what I should say, and what I should speak.

50 And I know that his commandment is life everlasting: whatsoever I speak therefore, even as the Father said unto me, so I speak.

13 NOW before the feast of the passover, when Je'sus knew that his hour was come that he should depart out of this world unto the Father, having loved his own which were in the world, he loved them unto the end.

2 And supper being ended, the devil having now put into the heart of Ju'das Is-car'i-ot, Si'mon's *son,* to betray him;

3 Je'sus knowing that the Father had given all things into his hands, and that he was come from God, and went to God;

4 He riseth from supper, and laid aside his garments; and took a towel, and girded himself.

5 After that he poureth water into a bason, and began to wash the disciples' feet, and to wipe *them* with the towel wherewith he was girded.

6 Then cometh he to Si'mon Pe'ter: and Pe'ter saith unto him, Lord, dost thou wash my feet?

7 Je'sus answered and said unto him, What I do thou knowest not now; but thou shalt know hereafter.

8 Pe'ter saith unto him, Thou shalt never wash my feet. Je'sus answered him, If I wash thee not, thou hast no part with me.

9 Si'mon Pe'ter saith unto him, Lord, not my feet only, but also *my* hands and *my* head.

10 Je'sus saith to him, He that is washed needeth not save to wash *his* feet, but is clean every whit: and ye are clean, but not all.

11 For he knew who should betray him; therefore said he, Ye are not all clean.

12 So after he had washed their feet, and had taken his garments, and was set down again, he said unto them, Know ye what I have done to you?

13 Ye call me Master and Lord: and ye say well; for so I am.

14 If I then, *your* Lord and Master, have washed your feet; ye also ought to wash one another's feet.

15 For I have given you an example, that ye should do as I have done to you.

16 Verily, verily, I say unto you, The servant is not greater than his lord; neither he that is sent greater than he that sent him.

17 If ye know these things, happy are ye if ye do them.

18 ¶ I speak not of you all: I know whom I have chosen: but that the scripture may be fulfilled, He that eateth bread with me hath lifted up his heel against me.

19 Now I tell you before it come, that, when it is come to pass, ye may believe that I am *he*.

20 Verily, verily, I say unto you, He that receiveth whomsoever I send receiveth me; and he that receiveth me receiveth him that sent me.

21 When Je'sus had thus said, he was troubled in spirit, and testified, and said, Verily, verily, I say unto you, that one of you shall betray me.

22 Then the disciples looked one on another, doubting of whom he spake.

23 Now there was leaning on Je'sus' bosom one of his disciples, whom Je'sus loved.

24 Si'mon Pe'ter therefore beckoned to him, that he should ask who it should be of whom he spake.

25 He then lying on Je'sus' breast saith unto him, Lord, who is it?

26 Je'sus answered, He it is, to whom I shall give a sop, when I have dipped *it*. And when he had dipped the sop, he gave *it* to Ju'das Is-car'i-ot, *the son* of Si'mon.

27 And after the sop Sa'tan entered into him. Then said Je'sus unto him, That thou doest, do quickly.

28 Now no man at the table knew for what intent he spake this unto him.

29 For some of *them* thought, because Ju'das had the bag, that Je'sus had said unto him, Buy *those things* that we have need of against the feast; or, that he should give something to the poor.

30 He then having received the sop went immediately out: and it was night.

31 ¶ Therefore, when he was gone out, Je'sus said, Now is the Son of man glorified, and God is glorified in him.

32 If God be glorified in him, God shall also glorify him in himself, and shall straightway glorify him.

33 Little children, yet a little while I am with you. Ye shall seek me: and as I said unto the Jews, Whither I go, ye cannot come; so now I say to you.

34 A new commandment I give unto you, That ye love one another; as I have loved you, that ye also love one another.

35 By this shall all *men* know that ye are my disciples, if ye have love one to another.

36 ¶ Si'mon Pe'ter said unto him, Lord, whither goest thou? Je'sus answered him, Whither I go, thou canst not follow me now; but thou shalt follow me afterwards.

37 Pe'ter said unto him, Lord, why cannot I follow thee now? I will lay down my life for thy sake.

38 Je'sus answered him, Wilt thou lay down thy life for my sake? Verily, verily, I say unto thee, The cock shall not crow, till thou hast denied me thrice.

14 LET not your heart be troubled: ye believe in God, believe also in me.

2 In my Father's house are many mansions: if *it were* not so, I would have told you. I go to prepare a place for you.

3 And if I go and prepare a place for you, I will come again, and receive you unto myself; that where I am, *there* ye may be also.

4 And whither I go ye know, and the way ye know.

5 Thom'as saith unto him, Lord, we know not whither thou goest; and how can we know the way?

6 Je'sus saith unto him, I am the way, the truth, and the life: no man cometh unto the Father, but by me.

7 If ye had known me, ye should have known my Father also: and from henceforth ye know him, and have seen him.

8 Phil'ip saith unto him, Lord, shew us the Father, and it sufficeth us.

9 Je'sus saith unto him, Have I been so long time with you, and yet hast thou not known me, Phil'ip? he that hath seen me hath seen the Father; and how sayest thou *then*, Shew us the Father?

10 Believest thou not that I am in the Father, and the Father in me? the words that I speak unto you I speak not of myself: but the Father that dwelleth in me, he doeth the works.

11 Believe me that I *am* in the Father, and the Father in me: or else believe me for the very works' sake.

12 Verily, verily, I say unto you, He that believeth on me, the works that I do shall he do also; and greater *works* than these shall he do; because I go unto my Father.

13 And whatsoever ye shall ask in my name, that will I do, that the Father may be glorified in the Son.

14 If ye shall ask any thing in my name, I will do *it*.

15 ¶ If ye love me, keep my commandments.

16 And I will pray the Father, and he shall give you another Comforter, that he may abide with you for ever;

17 *Even* the Spirit of truth; whom the world cannot receive, because it seeth him not, neither knoweth him: but ye know him; for he dwelleth with you, and shall be in you.

18 I will not leave you comfortless: I will come to you.

19 Yet a little while, and the world seeth me no more; but ye see me: because I live, ye shall live also.

20 At that day ye shall know that I *am* in my Father, and ye in me, and I in you.

21 He that hath my commandments, and keepeth them, he it is that loveth me: and he that loveth me shall be loved of my Father, and I will love him, and will manifest myself to him.

22 Ju'das saith unto him, not Is-car'i-ot, Lord, how is it that thou wilt manifest thyself unto us, and not unto the world?

23 Je'sus answered and said unto him, If a man love me, he will keep my words: and my Father will love him, and we will come unto him, and make our abode with him.

24 He that loveth me not keepeth not my

sayings: and the word which ye hear is not mine, but the Father's which sent me.

25 These things have I spoken unto you, being *yet* present with you.

26 But the Comforter, *which is* the Ho'ly Ghost, whom the Father will send in my name, he shall teach you all things, and bring all things to your remembrance, whatsoever I have said unto you.

27 Peace I leave with you, my peace I give unto you: not as the world giveth, give I unto you. Let not your heart be troubled, neither let it be afraid.

28 Ye have heard how I said unto you, I go away, and come *again* unto you. If ye loved me, ye would rejoice, because I said, I go unto the Father: for my Father is greater than I.

29 And now I have told you before it come to pass, that, when it is come to pass, ye might believe.

30 Hereafter I will not talk much with you: for the prince of this world cometh, and hath nothing in me.

31 But that the world may know that I love the Father; and as the Father gave me commandment, even so I do. Arise, let us go hence.

15 I AM the true vine, and my Father is the husbandman.

2 Every branch in me that beareth not fruit he taketh away: and every *branch* that beareth fruit, he purgeth it, that it may bring forth more fruit.

3 Now ye are clean through the word which I have spoken unto you.

4 Abide in me, and I in you. As the branch cannot bear fruit of itself, except it abide in the vine; no more can ye, except ye abide in me.

5 I am the vine, ye *are* the branches: He that abideth in me, and I in him, the same bringeth forth much fruit: for without me ye can do nothing.

6 If a man abide not in me, he is cast forth as a branch, and is withered; and men gather them, and cast *them* into the fire, and they are burned.

7 If ye abide in me, and my words abide in you, ye shall ask what ye will, and it shall be done unto you.

8 Herein is my Father glorified, that ye bear much fruit; so shall ye be my disciples.

9 As the Father hath loved me, so have I loved you: continue ye in my love.

10 If ye keep my commandments, ye shall abide in my love; even as I have kept my Father's commandments, and abide in his love.

11 These things have I spoken unto you, that my joy might remain in you, and *that* your joy might be full.

12 This is my commandment, That ye love one another, as I have loved you.

13 Greater love hath no man than this, that a man lay down his life for his friends.

14 Ye are my friends, if ye do whatsoever I command you.

15 Henceforth I call you not servants; for the servant knoweth not what his lord doeth: but I have called you friends; for all things that I have heard of my Father I have made known unto you.

16 Ye have not chosen me, but I have chosen you, and ordained you, that ye should go and bring forth fruit, and *that* your fruit should remain: that whatsoever ye shall ask of the Father in my name, he may give it you.

17 These things I command you, that ye love one another.

18 If the world hate you, ye know that it hated me before *it hated* you.

19 If ye were of the world, the world would love his own: but because ye are not of the world, but I have chosen you out of the world, therefore the world hateth you.

20 Remember the word that I said unto you, The servant is not greater than his lord. If they have persecuted me, they will also persecute you; if they have kept my saying, they will keep yours also.

21 But all these things will they do unto you for my name's sake, because they know not him that sent me.

22 If I had not come and spoken unto them, they had not had sin: but now they have no cloke for their sin.

23 He that hateth me hateth my Father also.

24 If I had not done among them the works which none other man did, they had not had sin: but now have they both seen and hated both me and my Father.

25 But *this cometh to pass*, that the word might be fulfilled that is written in their law, They hated me without a cause.

26 But when the Comforter is come, whom I will send unto you from the Father, *even* the Spirit of truth, which proceedeth from the Father, he shall testify of me:

27 And ye also shall bear witness, because ye have been with me from the beginning.

16 THESE things have I spoken unto you, that ye should not be offended.

2 They shall put you out of the synagogues: yea, the time cometh, that whosoever killeth you will think that he doeth God service.

3 And these things will they do unto you, because they have not known the Father, nor me.

4 But these things have I told you, that when the time shall come, ye may remember that I told you of them. And these things I said not unto you at the beginning, because I was with you.

5 But now I go my way to him that sent me; and none of you asketh me, Whither goest thou?

6 But because I have said these things unto you, sorrow hath filled your heart.

7 Nevertheless I tell you the truth; It is expedient for you that I go away: for if I go not away, the Comforter will not come unto you; but if I depart, I will send him unto you.

8 And when he is come, he will reprove the world of sin, and of righteousness, and of judgment:

9 Of sin, because they believe not on me;

10 Of righteousness, because I go to my Father, and ye see me no more;

11 Of judgment, because the prince of this world is judged.

12 I have yet many things to say unto you, but ye cannot bear them now.

13 Howbeit when he, the Spirit of truth, is come, he will guide you into all truth: for he shall not speak of himself; but whatsoever he shall hear, *that* shall he speak: and he will shew you things to come.

14 He shall glorify me: for he shall receive of mine, and shall shew *it* unto you.

15 All things that the Father hath are mine: therefore said I, that he shall take of mine, and shall shew *it* unto you.

16 A little while, and ye shall not see me: and again, a little while, and ye shall see me, because I go to the Father.

17 Then said *some* of his disciples among

themselves, What is this that he saith unto us, A little while, and ye shall not see me: and again, a little while, and ye shall see me: and, Because I go to the Father?

18 They said therefore, What is this that he saith, A little while? we cannot tell what he saith.

19 Now Je'sus knew that they were desirous to ask him, and said unto them, Do ye enquire among yourselves of that I said, A little while, and ye shall not see me: and again, a little while, and ye shall see me?

20 Verily, verily, I say unto you, That ye shall weep and lament, but the world shall rejoice: and ye shall be sorrowful, but your sorrow shall be turned into joy.

21 A woman when she is in travail hath sorrow, because her hour is come: but as soon as she is delivered of the child, she remembereth no more the anguish, for joy that a man is born into the world.

22 And ye now therefore have sorrow: but I will see you again, and your heart shall rejoice, and your joy no man taketh from you.

23 And in that day ye shall ask me nothing. Verily, verily, I say unto you, Whatsoever ye shall ask the Father in my name, he will give it you.

24 Hitherto have ye asked nothing in my name: ask, and ye shall receive, that your joy may be full.

25 These things have I spoken unto you in proverbs: but the time cometh, when I shall no more speak unto you in proverbs, but I shall shew you plainly of the Father.

26 At that day ye shall ask in my name: and I say not unto you, that I will pray the Father for you:

27 For the Father himself loveth you, because ye have loved me, and have believed that I came out from God.

28 I came forth from the Father, and am come into the world: again, I leave the world, and go to the Father.

29 His disciples said unto him, Lo, now speakest thou plainly, and speakest no proverb.

30 Now are we sure that thou knowest all things, and needest not that any man should ask thee: by this we believe that thou camest forth from God.

31 Je'sus answered them, Do ye now believe?

32 Behold, the hour cometh, yea, is now come, that ye shall be scattered, every man to his own, and shall leave me alone: and yet I am not alone, because the Father is with me.

33 These things I have spoken unto you, that in me ye might have peace. In the world ye shall have tribulation: but be of good cheer; I have overcome the world.

17 THESE words spake Je'sus, and lifted up his eyes to heaven, and said, Father, the hour is come; glorify thy Son, that thy Son also may glorify thee:

2 As thou hast given him power over all flesh, that he should give eternal life to as many as thou hast given him.

3 And this is life eternal, that they might know thee the only true God, and Je'sus Christ whom thou hast sent.

4 I have glorified thee on the earth: I have finished the work which thou gavest me to do.

5 And now, O Father, glorify thou me with thine own self with the glory which I had with thee before the world was.

6 I have manifested thy name unto the men which thou gavest me out of the world: thine

they were, and thou gavest me them; and they have kept thy word.

7 Now they have known that all things whatsoever thou hast given me are of thee.

8 For I have given unto them the words which thou gavest me; and they have received them, and have known surely that I came out from thee, and they have believed that thou didst send me.

9 I pray for them: I pray not for the world, but for them which thou hast given me; for they are thine.

10 And all mine are thine, and thine are mine; and I am glorified in them.

11 And now I am no more in the world, but these are in the world, and I come to thee. Holy Father, keep through thine own name those whom thou hast given me, that they may be one, as we are.

12 While I was with them in the world, I kept them in thy name: those that thou gavest me I have kept, and none of them is lost, but the son of perdition; that the scripture might be fulfilled.

13 And now come I to thee; and these things I speak in the world, that they might have my joy fulfilled in themselves.

14 I have given them thy word; and the world hath hated them, because they are not of the world, even as I am not of the world.

15 I pray not that thou shouldest take them out of the world, but that thou shouldest keep them from the evil.

16 They are not of the world, even as I am not of the world.

17 Sanctify them through thy truth: thy word is truth.

18 As thou hast sent me into the world, even so have I also sent them into the world.

19 And for their sakes I sanctify myself, that they also might be sanctified through the truth.

20 Neither pray I for these alone, but for them also which shall believe on me through their word;

21 That they all may be one; as thou, Father, art in me, and I in thee, that they also may be one in us: that the world may believe that thou hast sent me.

22 And the glory which thou gavest me I have given them; that they may be one, even as we are one:

23 I in them, and thou in me, that they may be made perfect in one; and that the world may know that thou hast sent me, and hast loved them, as thou hast loved me.

24 Father, I will that they also, whom thou hast given me, be with me where I am; that they may behold my glory, which thou hast given me: for thou lovedst me before the foundation of the world.

25 O righteous Father, the world hath not known thee: but I have known thee, and these have known that thou hast sent me.

26 And I have declared unto them thy name, and will declare it: that the love wherewith thou hast loved me may be in them, and I in them.

18 WHEN Je'sus had spoken these words, he went forth with his disciples over the brook Ce'dron, where was a garden, into the which he entered, and his disciples.

2 And Ju'das also, which betrayed him, knew the place: for Je'sus ofttimes resorted thither with his disciples.

3 Ju'das then, having received a band of men and officers from the chief priests and Phar'i-

sees, cometh thither with lanterns and torches and weapons.

4 Je'sus therefore, knowing all things that should come upon him, went forth, and said unto them, Whom seek ye?

5 They answered him, Je'sus of Naz'a-reth. Je'sus saith unto them, I am he. And Ju'das also, which betrayed him, stood with them.

6 As soon then as he had said unto them, I am he, they went backward, and fell to the ground.

7 Then asked he them again, Whom seek ye? And they said, Je'sus of Naz'a-reth.

8 Je'sus answered, I have told you that I am he: if therefore ye seek me, let these go their way:

9 That the saying might be fulfilled, which he spake, Of them which thou gavest me have I lost none.

10 Then Si'mon Pe'ter having a sword drew it, and smote the high priest's servant, and cut off his right ear. The servant's name was Mal'chus.

11 Then said Je'sus unto Pe'ter, Put up thy sword into the sheath: the cup which my Father hath given me, shall I not drink it?

12 Then the band and the captain and officers of the Jews took Je'sus, and bound him,

13 And led him away to An'nas first; for he was father in law to Ca'ia-phas, which was the high priest that same year.

14 Now Ca'ia-phas was he, which gave counsel to the Jews, that it was expedient that one man should die for the people.

15 ¶ And Si'mon Pe'ter followed Je'sus, and so did another disciple: that disciple was known unto the high priest, and went in with Je'sus into the palace of the high priest.

16 But Pe'ter stood at the door without. Then went out that other disciple, which was known unto the high priest, and spake unto her that kept the door, and brought in Pe'ter.

17 Then saith the damsel that kept the door unto Pe'ter, Art not thou also one of this man's disciples? He saith, I am not.

18 And the servants and officers stood there, who had made a fire of coals; for it was cold: and they warmed themselves: and Pe'ter stood with them, and warmed himself.

19 ¶ The high priest then asked Je'sus of his disciples, and of his doctrine.

20 Je'sus answered him, I spake openly to the world; I ever taught in the synagogue, and in the temple, whither the Jews always resort; and in secret have I said nothing.

21 Why askest thou me? ask them which heard me, what I have said unto them: behold, they know what I said.

22 And when he had thus spoken, one of the officers which stood by struck Je'sus with the palm of his hand, saying, Answerest thou the high priest so?

23 Je'sus answered him, If I have spoken evil, bear witness of the evil: but if well, why smitest thou me?

24 Now An'nas had sent him bound unto Ca'ia-phas the high priest.

25 And Si'mon Pe'ter stood and warmed himself. They said therefore unto him, Art not thou also one of his disciples? He denied it, and said, I am not.

26 One of the servants of the high priest, being his kinsman whose ear Pe'ter cut off, saith, Did not I see thee in the garden with him?

27 Pe'ter then denied again: and immediately the cock crew.

28 ¶ Then led they Je'sus from Ca'ia-phas unto the hall of judgment: and it was early; and they themselves went not into the judgment hall, lest they should be defiled; but that they might eat the passover.

29 Pi'late then went out unto them, and said, What accusation bring ye against this man?

30 They answered and said unto him, If he were not a malefactor, we would not have delivered him up unto thee.

31 Then said Pi'late unto them, Take ye him, and judge him according to your law. The Jews therefore said unto him, It is not lawful for us to put any man to death:

32 That the saying of Je'sus might be fulfilled, which he spake, signifying what death he should die.

33 Then Pi'late entered into the judgment hall again, and called Je'sus, and said unto him, Art thou the King of the Jews?

34 Je'sus answered him, Sayest thou this thing of thyself, or did others tell it thee of me?

35 Pi'late answered, Am I a Jew? Thine own nation and the chief priests have delivered thee unto me: what hast thou done?

36 Je'sus answered, My kingdom is not of this world: if my kingdom were of this world, then would my servants fight, that I should not be delivered to the Jews: but now is my kingdom not from hence.

37 Pi'late therefore said unto him, Art thou a king then? Je'sus answered, Thou sayest that I am a king. To this end was I born, and for this cause came I into the world, that I should bear witness unto the truth. Every one that is of the truth heareth my voice.

38 Pi'late saith unto him, What is truth? And when he had said this, he went out again unto the Jews, and saith unto them, I find in him no fault at all.

39 But ye have a custom, that I should release unto you one at the passover: will ye therefore that I release unto you the King of the Jews?

40 Then cried they all again, saying, Not this man, but Ba-rab'bas. Now Ba-rab'bas was a robber.

19 THEN Pi'late therefore took Je'sus, and scourged him.

2 And the soldiers platted a crown of thorns, and put it on his head, and they put on him a purple robe,

3 And said, Hail, King of the Jews! and they smote him with their hands.

4 Pi'late therefore went forth again, and saith unto them, Behold, I bring him forth to you, that ye may know that I find no fault in him.

5 Then came Je'sus forth, wearing the crown of thorns, and the purple robe. And Pi'late saith unto them, Behold the man!

6 When the chief priests therefore and officers saw him, they cried out, saying, Crucify him, crucify him. Pi'late saith unto them, Take ye him, and crucify him: for I find no fault in him.

7 The Jews answered him, We have a law, and by our law he ought to die, because he made himself the Son of God.

8 ¶ When Pi'late therefore heard that saying, he was the more afraid;

9 And went again into the judgment hall, and saith unto Je'sus, Whence art thou? But Je'sus gave him no answer.

10 Then saith Pi'late unto him, Speakest thou not unto me? knowest thou not that I have power to crucify thee, and have power to release thee?

11 Je'sus answered, Thou couldest have no power at all against me, except it were given thee from above: therefore he that delivered me unto thee hath the greater sin.

12 And from thenceforth Pi'late sought to release him: but the Jews cried out, saying, If thou let this man go, thou art not Cæ'sar's friend: whosoever maketh himself a king speaketh against Cæ'sar.

13 ¶ When Pi'late therefore heard that saying, he brought Je'sus forth, and sat down in the judgment seat in a place that is called the Pavement, but in the He'brew, Gab'ba-tha.

14 And it was the preparation of the passover, and about the sixth hour: and he saith unto the Jews, Behold your King!

15 But they cried out, Away with him, away with him, crucify him. Pi'late saith unto them, Shall I crucify your King? The chief priests answered, We have no king but Cæ'sar.

16 Then delivered he him therefore unto them to be crucified. And they took Je'sus, and led him away.

17 And he bearing his cross went forth into a place called the place of a skull, which is called in the He'brew Gol'go-tha:

18 Where they crucified him, and two other with him, on either side one, and Je'sus in the midst.

19 ¶ And Pi'late wrote a title, and put it on the cross. And the writing was, JE'SUS OF NAZ'A-RETH THE KING OF THE JEWS.

20 This title then read many of the Jews: for the place where Je'sus was crucified was nigh to the city: and it was written in He'brew, and Greek, and Lat'in.

21 Then said the chief priests of the Jews to Pi'late, Write not, The King of the Jews; but that he said, I am King of the Jews.

22 Pi'late answered, What I have written I have written.

23 ¶ Then the soldiers, when they had crucified Je'sus, took his garments, and made four parts, to every soldier a part; and also his coat: now the coat was without seam, woven from the top throughout.

24 They said therefore among themselves, Let us not rend it, but cast lots for it, whose it shall be: that the scripture might be fulfilled, which saith, They parted my raiment among them, and for my vesture they did cast lots. These things therefore the soldiers did.

25 ¶ Now there stood by the cross of Je'sus his mother, and his mother's sister, Ma'ry the wife of Cle'o-phas, and Ma'ry Mag-da-le'ne.

26 When Je'sus therefore saw his mother, and the disciple standing by, whom he loved, he saith unto his mother, Woman, behold thy son!

27 Then saith he to the disciple, Behold thy mother! And from that hour that disciple took her unto his own home.

28 ¶ After this, Je'sus knowing that all things were now accomplished, that the scripture might be fulfilled, saith, I thirst.

29 Now there was set a vessel full of vinegar: and they filled a spunge with vinegar, and put it upon hyssop, and put it to his mouth.

30 When Je'sus therefore had received the vinegar, he said, It is finished: and he bowed his head, and gave up the ghost.

31 The Jews therefore, because it was the preparation, that the bodies should not remain upon the cross on the sabbath day, (for that sabbath day was an high day,) besought Pi'late that their legs might be broken, and that they might be taken away.

32 Then came the soldiers, and brake the legs of the first, and of the other which was crucified with him.

33 But when they came to Je'sus, and saw that he was dead already, they brake not his legs:

34 But one of the soldiers with a spear pierced his side, and forthwith came there out blood and water.

35 And he that saw it bare record, and his record is true: and he knoweth that he saith true, that ye might believe.

36 For these things were done, that the scripture should be fulfilled, A bone of him shall not be broken.

37 And again another scripture saith, They shall look on him whom they pierced.

38 ¶ And after this Jo'seph of Ar-i-ma-thæ'a, being a disciple of Je'sus, but secretly for fear of the Jews, besought Pi'late that he might take away the body of Je'sus: and Pi'late gave him leave. He came therefore, and took the body of Je'sus.

39 And there came also Nic-o-de'mus, which at the first came to Je'sus by night, and brought a mixture of myrrh and aloes, about an hundred pound weight.

40 Then took they the body of Je'sus, and wound it in linen clothes with the spices, as the manner of the Jews is to bury.

41 Now in the place where he was crucified there was a garden; and in the garden a new sepulchre, wherein was never man yet laid.

42 There laid they Je'sus therefore because of the Jews' preparation day; for the sepulchre was nigh at hand.

20

THE first day of the week cometh Ma'ry Mag-da-le'ne early, when it was yet dark, unto the sepulchre, and seeth the stone taken away from the sepulchre.

2 Then she runneth, and cometh to Si'mon Pe'ter, and to the other disciple, whom Je'sus loved, and saith unto them, They have taken away the Lord out of the sepulchre, and we know not where they have laid him.

3 Pe'ter therefore went forth, and that other disciple, and came to the sepulchre.

4 So they ran both together: and the other disciple did outrun Pe'ter, and came first to the sepulchre.

5 And he stooping down, and looking in, saw the linen clothes lying; yet went he not in.

6 Then cometh Si'mon Pe'ter following him, and went into the sepulchre, and seeth the linen clothes lie,

7 And the napkin, that was about his head, not lying with the linen clothes, but wrapped together in a place by itself.

8 Then went in also that other disciple, which came first to the sepulchre, and he saw, and believed.

9 For as yet they knew not the scripture, that he must rise again from the dead.

10 Then the disciples went away again unto their own home.

11 ¶ But Ma'ry stood without at the sepulchre weeping: and as she wept, she stooped down, and looked into the sepulchre,

12 And seeth two angels in white sitting, the one at the head, and the other at the feet, where the body of Je'sus had lain.

13 And they say unto her, Woman, why weepest thou? She saith unto them, Because they have taken away my Lord, and I know not where they have laid him.

14 And when she had thus said, she turned herself back, and saw Je'sus standing, and knew not that it was Je'sus.

15 Je´sus saith unto her, Woman, why weepest thou? whom seekest thou? She, supposing him to be the gardener, saith unto him, Sir, if thou have borne him hence, tell me where thou hast laid him, and I will take him away.

16 Je´sus saith unto her, Ma´ry. She turned herself, and saith unto him, Rab-bo´ni; which is to say, Master.

17 Je´sus saith unto her, Touch me not; for I am not yet ascended to my Father: but go to my brethren, and say unto them, I ascend unto my Father, and your Father; and to my God, and your God.

18 Ma´ry Mag-da-le´ne came and told the disciples that she had seen the Lord, and that he had spoken these things unto her.

19 ¶ Then the same day at evening, being the first day of the week, when the doors were shut where the disciples were assembled for fear of the Jews, came Je´sus and stood in the midst, and saith unto them Peace be unto you.

20 And when he had so said, he shewed unto them his hands and his side. Then were the disciples glad, when they saw the Lord.

21 Then said Je´sus to them again, Peace be unto you: as my Father hath sent me, even so send I you.

22 And when he had said this, he breathed on them, and saith unto them, Receive ye the Ho´ly Ghost:

23 Whose soever sins ye remit, they are remitted unto them; and whose soever sins ye retain, they are retained.

24 ¶ But Thom´as, one of the twelve, called Did´y-mus, was not with them when Je´sus came.

25 The other disciples therefore said unto him, We have seen the Lord. But he said unto them, Except I shall see in his hands the print of the nails, and put my finger into the print of the nails, and thrust my hand into his side, I will not believe.

26 ¶ And after eight days again his disciples were within, and Thom´as with them: then came Je´sus, the doors being shut, and stood in the midst, and said, Peace be unto you.

27 Then saith he to Thom´as, Reach hither thy finger, and behold my hands; and reach hither thy hand, and thrust it into my side: and be not faithless, but believing.

28 And Thom´as answered and said unto him, My Lord and my God.

29 Je´sus saith unto him, Thom´as, because thou hast seen me, thou hast believed: blessed are they that have not seen, and yet have believed.

30 ¶ And many other signs truly did Je´sus in the presence of his disciples, which are not written in this book:

31 But these are written, that ye might believe that Je´sus is the Christ, the Son of God; and that believing ye might have life through his name.

21 AFTER these things Je´sus shewed himself again to the disciples at the sea of Ti-be´ri-as; and on this wise shewed he himself.

2 There were together Si´mon Pe´ter, and Thom´as called Did´y-mus, and Na-than´a-el of Ca´na in Gal´i-lee, and the sons of Zeb´e-dee, and two other of his disciples.

3 Si´mon Pe´ter saith unto them, I go a fishing. They say unto him, We also go with thee. They went forth, and entered into a ship immediately; and that night they caught nothing.

4 But when the morning was now come, Je´sus stood on the shore: but the disciples knew not that it was Je´sus.

5 Then Je´sus saith unto them, Children, have ye any meat? They answered him, No.

6 And he said unto them, Cast the net on the right side of the ship, and ye shall find. They cast therefore, and now they were not able to draw it for the multitude of fishes.

7 Therefore that disciple whom Je´sus loved saith unto Pe´ter, It is the Lord. Now when Si´mon Pe´ter heard that it was the Lord, he girt his fisher's coat unto him, (for he was naked,) and did cast himself into the sea.

8 And the other disciples came in a little ship; (for they were not far from land, but as it were two hundred cubits,) dragging the net with fishes.

9 As soon then as they were come to land, they saw a fire of coals there, and fish laid thereon, and bread.

10 Je´sus saith unto them, Bring of the fish which ye have now caught.

11 Si´mon Pe´ter went up, and drew the net to land full of great fishes, an hundred and fifty and three: and for all there were so many, yet was not the net broken.

12 Je´sus saith unto them, Come and dine. And none of the disciples durst ask him, Who art thou? knowing that it was the Lord.

13 Je´sus then cometh, and taketh bread, and giveth them, and fish likewise.

14 This is now the third time that Je´sus shewed himself to his disciples, after that he was risen from the dead.

15 ¶ So when they had dined, Je´sus saith to Si´mon Pe´ter, Si´mon, son of Jo´nas, lovest thou me more than these? He saith unto him, Yea, Lord; thou knowest that I love thee. He saith unto him, Feed my lambs.

16 He saith to him again the second time, Si´mon, son of Jo´nas, lovest thou me? He saith unto him, Yea, Lord; thou knowest that I love thee. He saith unto him, Feed my sheep.

17 He saith unto him the third time, Si´mon, son of Jo´nas, lovest thou me? Pe´ter was grieved because he said unto him the third time, Lovest thou me? And he said unto him, Lord, thou knowest all things; thou knowest that I love thee. Je´sus saith unto him, Feed my sheep.

18 Verily, verily, I say unto thee, When thou wast young, thou girdedst thyself, and walkedst whither thou wouldest: but when thou shalt be old, thou shalt stretch forth thy hands, and another shall gird thee, and carry thee whither thou wouldest not.

19 This spake he, signifying by what death he should glorify God. And when he had spoken this, he saith unto him, Follow me.

20 And Pe´ter, turning about, seeth the disciple whom Je´sus loved following; which also leaned on his breast at supper, and said, Lord, which is he that betrayeth thee?

21 Pe´ter seeing him saith to Je´sus, Lord, and what shall this man do?

22 Je´sus saith unto him, If I will that he tarry till I come, what is that to thee? follow thou me.

23 Then went this saying abroad among the brethren, that that disciple should not die: yet Je´sus said not unto him, He shall not die; but, If I will that he tarry till I come, what is that to thee?

24 This is the disciple which testifieth of these things, and wrote these things: and we know that his testimony is true.

25 And there are also many other things which Je´sus did, the which, if they should be written every one, I suppose that even the world itself could not contain the books that should be written. Amen.

ACTS OF THE APOSTLES

1 THE former treatise have I made, O The-oph'i-lus, of all that Je'sus began both to do and teach,

2 Until the day in which he was taken up, after that he through the Ho'ly Ghost had given commandments unto the apostles whom he had chosen:

3 To whom also he shewed himself alive after his passion by many infallible proofs, being seen of them forty days, and speaking of the things pertaining to the kingdom of God:

4 And, being assembled together with *them*, commanded them that they should not depart from Je-ru'sa-lem, but wait for the promise of the Father, which, *saith he*, ye have heard of me.

5 For John truly baptized with water; but ye shall be baptized with the Ho'ly Ghost not many days hence.

6 When they therefore were come together, they asked of him, saying, Lord, wilt thou at this time restore again the kingdom to Is'ra-el?

7 And he said unto them, It is not for you to know the times or the seasons, which the Father hath put in his own power.

8 But ye shall receive power, after that the Ho'ly Ghost is come upon you: and ye shall be witnesses unto me both in Je-ru'sa-lem, and in all Ju-dæ'a, and in Sa-ma'ri-a, and unto the uttermost part of the earth.

9 And when he had spoken these things, while they beheld, he was taken up; and a cloud received him out of their sight.

10 And while they looked stedfastly toward heaven as he went up, behold, two men stood by them in white apparel;

11 Which also said, Ye men of Gal'i-lee, why stand ye gazing up into heaven? this same Je'sus, which is taken up from you into heaven, shall so come in like manner as ye have seen him go into heaven.

12 Then returned they unto Je-ru'sa-lem from the mount called Ol'i-vet, which is from Je-ru'sa-lem a sabbath day's journey.

13 And when they were come in, they went up into an upper room, where abode both Pe'ter, and James, and John, and Andrew, Phil'ip, and Thom'as, Bar-thol'o-mew, and Mat'thew, James *the son* of Al-phæ'us, and Si'mon Ze-lo'tes, and Ju'das *the brother* of James.

14 These all continued with one accord in prayer and supplication, with the women, and Ma'ry the mother of Je'sus, and with his brethren.

15 ¶ And in those days Pe'ter stood up in the midst of the disciples, and said, (the number of names together were about an hundred and twenty,)

16 Men *and* brethren, this scripture must needs have been fulfilled, which the Ho'ly Ghost by the mouth of Da'vid spake before concerning Ju'das, which was guide to them that took Je'sus.

17 For he was numbered with us, and had obtained part of this ministry.

18 Now this man purchased a field with the reward of iniquity; and falling headlong, he burst asunder in the midst, and all his bowels gushed out.

19 And it was known unto all the dwellers at Je-ru'sa-lem; insomuch as that field is called in their proper tongue, A-cel'da-ma, that is to say, The field of blood.

20 For it is written in the book of Psalms, Let his habitation be desolate, and let no man dwell therein: and his bishoprick let another take.

21 Wherefore of these men which have companied with us all the time that the Lord Je'sus went in and out among us,

22 Beginning from the baptism of John, unto that same day that he was taken up from us, must one be ordained to be a witness with us of his resurrection.

23 And they appointed two, Jo'seph called Bar'sa-bas, who was surnamed Jus'tus, and Mat-thi'as.

24 And they prayed, and said, Thou, Lord, which knowest the hearts of all *men*, shew whether of these two thou hast chosen,

25 That he may take part of this ministry and apostleship, from which Ju'das by transgression fell, that he might go to his own place.

26 And they gave forth their lots; and the lot fell upon Mat-thi'as; and he was numbered with the eleven apostles.

2 AND when the day of Pen'te-cost was fully come, they were all with one accord in one place.

2 And suddenly there came a sound from heaven as of a rushing mighty wind, and it filled all the house where they were sitting.

3 And there appeared unto them cloven tongues like as of fire, and it sat upon each of them.

4 And they were all filled with the Ho'ly Ghost, and began to speak with other tongues, as the Spirit gave them utterance.

5 And there were dwelling at Je-ru'sa-lem Jews, devout men, out of every nation under heaven.

6 Now when this was noised abroad, the multitude came together, and were confounded, because that every man heard them speak in his own language.

7 And they were all amazed and marvelled, saying one to another, Behold, are not all these which speak Gal-i-læ'ans?

8 And how hear we every man in our own tongue, wherein we were born?

9 Par'thi-ans, and Medes, and E'lam-ites, and the dwellers in Mes-o-po-ta'mi-a, and in Ju-dæ'a, and Cap-pa-do'ci-a, in Pon'tus, and A'sia,

10 Phryg'i-a, and Pam-phyl'i-a, in E'gypt, and in the parts of Lib'y-a about Cy-re'ne, and strangers of Rome, Jews and proselytes,

11 Cretes and A-ra'bi-ans, we do hear them speak in our tongues the wonderful works of God.

12 And they were all amazed, and were in doubt, saying one to another, What meaneth this?

13 Others mocking said, These men are full of new wine.

14 ¶ But Pe'ter, standing up with the eleven, lifted up his voice, and said unto them, Ye men of Ju-dæ'a, and all ye that dwell at Je-ru'sa-lem, be this known unto you, and hearken to my words:

15 For these are not drunken, as ye suppose, seeing it is *but* the third hour of the day.

16 But this is that which was spoken by the prophet Jo'el;

17 And it shall come to pass in the last days, saith God, I will pour out of my Spirit upon all flesh: and your sons and your daughters shall prophesy, and your young men shall see visions, and your old men shall dream dreams:

18 And on my servants and on my handmaidens I will pour out in those days of my Spirit; and they shall prophesy:

19 And I will shew wonders in heaven above, and signs in the earth beneath; blood, and fire, and vapour of smoke:

20 The sun shall be turned into darkness, and the moon into blood, before that great and notable day of the Lord come:

21 And it shall come to pass, *that* whosoever shall call on the name of the Lord shall be saved.

22 Ye men of Is'ra-el, hear these words; Je'sus of Naz'a-reth, a man approved of God among you by miracles and wonders and signs, which God did by him in the midst of you, as ye yourselves also know:

23 Him, being delivered by the determinate counsel and foreknowledge of God, ye have taken, and by wicked hands have crucified and slain:

24 Whom God hath raised up, having loosed the pains of death: because it was not possible that he should be holden of it.

25 For Da'vid speaketh concerning him, I foresaw the Lord always before my face, for he is on my right hand, that I should not be moved:

26 Therefore did my heart rejoice, and my tongue was glad; moreover also my flesh shall rest in hope:

27 Because thou wilt not leave my soul in hell, neither wilt thou suffer thine Holy One to see corruption.

28 Thou hast made known to me the ways of life; thou shalt make me full of joy with thy countenance.

29 Men *and* brethren, let me freely speak unto you of the patriarch Da'vid, that he is both dead and buried, and his sepulchre is with us unto this day.

30 Therefore being a prophet, and knowing that God had sworn with an oath to him, that of the fruit of his loins, according to the flesh, he would raise up Christ to sit on his throne;

31 He seeing this before spake of the resurrection of Christ, that his soul was not left in hell, neither his flesh did see corruption.

32 This Je'sus hath God raised up, whereof we all are witnesses.

33 Therefore being by the right hand of God exalted, and having received of the Father the promise of the Ho'ly Ghost, he hath shed forth this, which ye now see and hear.

34 For Da'vid is not ascended into the heavens: but he saith himself, The LORD said unto my Lord, Sit thou on my right hand,

35 Until I make thy foes thy footstool.

36 Therefore let all the house of Is'ra-el know assuredly, that God hath made that same Je'sus, whom ye have crucified, both Lord and Christ.

37 ¶ Now when they heard *this,* they were pricked in their heart, and said unto Pe'ter and to the rest of the apostles, Men *and* brethren, what shall we do?

38 Then Pe'ter said unto them, Repent, and be baptized every one of you in the name of Je'sus Christ for the remission of sins, and ye shall receive the gift of the Ho'ly Ghost.

39 For the promise is unto you, and to your children, and to all that are afar off, *even* as many as the Lord our God shall call.

40 And with many other words did he testify and exhort, saying, Save yourselves from this untoward generation.

41 ¶ Then they that gladly received his word were baptized: and the same day there were added *unto them* about three thousand souls.

42 And they continued stedfastly in the apostles' doctrine and fellowship, and in breaking of bread, and in prayers.

43 And fear came upon every soul: and many wonders and signs were done by the apostles.

44 And all that believed were together, and had all things common;

45 And sold their possessions and goods, and parted them to all *men,* as every man had need.

46 And they, continuing daily with one accord in the temple, and breaking bread from house to house, did eat their meat with gladness and singleness of heart,

47 Praising God, and having favour with all the people. And the Lord added to the church daily such as should be saved.

3 NOW Pe'ter and John went up together into the temple at the hour of prayer, *being* the ninth *hour.*

2 And a certain man lame from his mother's womb was carried, whom they laid daily at the gate of the temple which is called Beautiful, to ask alms of them that entered into the temple;

3 Who seeing Pe'ter and John about to go into the temple asked an alms.

4 And Pe'ter, fastening his eyes upon him with John, said, Look on us.

5 And he gave heed unto them, expecting to receive something of them.

6 Then Pe'ter said, Silver and gold have I none; but such as I have give I thee: In the name of Je'sus Christ of Naz'a-reth rise up and walk.

7 And he took him by the right hand, and lifted *him* up: and immediately his feet and ancle bones received strength.

8 And he leaping up stood, and walked, and entered with them into the temple, walking, and leaping, and praising God.

9 And all the people saw him walking and praising God:

10 And they knew that it was he which sat for alms at the Beautiful gate of the temple: and they were filled with wonder and amazement at that which had happened unto him.

11 And as the lame man which was healed held Pe'ter and John, all the people ran together unto them in the porch that is called Sol'o-mon's, greatly wondering.

12 ¶ And when Pe'ter saw *it,* he answered unto the people, Ye men of Is'ra-el, why marvel ye at this? or why look ye so earnestly on us, as though by our own power or holiness we had made this man to walk?

13 The God of A'bra-ham, and of I'saac, and of Ja'cob, the God of our fathers, hath glorified his Son Je'sus; whom ye delivered up, and denied him in the presence of Pi'late, when he was determined to let *him* go.

14 But ye denied the Holy One and the Just, and desired a murderer to be granted unto you;

15 And killed the Prince of life, whom God hath raised from the dead; whereof we are witnesses.

16 And his name through faith in his name hath made this man strong, whom ye see and know: yea, the faith which is by him hath given him this perfect soundness in the presence of you all.

17 And now, brethren, I wot that through ignorance ye did *it,* as *did* also your rulers.

18 But those things, which God before had shewed by the mouth of all his prophets, that Christ should suffer, he hath so fulfilled.

19 ¶ Repent ye therefore, and be converted, that your sins may be blotted out, when the times of refreshing shall come from the presence of the Lord;

20 And he shall send Je'sus Christ, which before was preached unto you:

21 Whom the heaven must receive until the times of restitution of all things, which God hath spoken by the mouth of all his holy prophets since the world began.

22 For Mo'ses truly said unto the fathers, A prophet shall the Lord your God raise up unto you of your brethren, like unto me; him shall ye hear in all things whatsoever he shall say unto you.

23 And it shall come to pass, *that* every soul, which will not hear that prophet, shall be destroyed from among the people.

24 Yea, and all the prophets from Sam'u-el and those that follow after, as many as have spoken, have likewise foretold of these days.

25 Ye are the children of the prophets, and of the covenant which God made with our fathers, saying unto A'bra-ham, And in thy seed shall all the kindreds of the earth be blessed.

26 Unto you first God, having raised up his Son Je'sus, sent him to bless you, in turning away every one of you from his iniquities.

4 AND as they spake unto the people, the priests, and the captain of the temple, and the Sad'du-cees, came upon them,

2 Being grieved that they taught the people, and preached through Je'sus the resurrection from the dead.

3 And they laid hands on them, and put *them* in hold unto the next day: for it was now eventide.

4 Howbeit many of them which heard the word believed; and the number of the men was about five thousand.

5 ¶ And it came to pass on the morrow, that their rulers, and elders, and scribes,

6 And An'nas the high priest, and Ca'ia-phas, and John, and Al-ex-an'der, and as many as were of the kindred of the high priest, were gathered together at Je-ru'sa-lem.

7 And when they had set them in the midst, they asked, By what power, or by what name, have ye done this?

8 Then Pe'ter, filled with the Ho'ly Ghost, said unto them, Ye rulers of the people, and elders of Is'ra-el,

9 If we this day be examined of the good deed done to the impotent man, by what means he is made whole;

10 Be it known unto you all, and to all the people of Is'ra-el, that by the name of Je'sus Christ of Naz'a-reth, whom ye crucified, whom God raised from the dead, *even* by him doth this man stand here before you whole.

11 This is the stone which was set at nought of you builders, which is become the head of the corner.

12 Neither is there salvation in any other: for there is none other name under heaven given among men, whereby we must be saved.

13 ¶ Now when they saw the boldness of Pe'ter and John, and perceived that they were unlearned and ignorant men, they marvelled; and they took knowledge of them, that they had been with Je'sus.

14 And beholding the man which was healed standing with them, they could say nothing against it.

15 But when they had commanded them to go aside out of the council, they conferred among themselves,

16 Saying, What shall we do to these men? for that indeed a notable miracle hath been done by them is manifest to all them that dwell in Je-ru'sa-lem; and we cannot deny *it.*

17 But that it spread no further among the people, let us straitly threaten them, that they speak henceforth to no man in this name.

18 And they called them, and commanded them not to speak at all nor teach in the name of Je'sus.

19 But Pe'ter and John answered and said unto them, Whether it be right in the sight of God to hearken unto you more than unto God, judge ye.

20 For we cannot but speak the things which we have seen and heard.

21 So when they had further threatened them, they let them go, finding nothing how they might punish them, because of the people: for all *men* glorified God for that which was done.

22 For the man was above forty years old, on whom this miracle of healing was shewed.

23 ¶ And being let go, they went to their own company, and reported all that the chief priests and elders had said unto them.

24 And when they heard that, they lifted up their voice to God with one accord, and said, Lord, thou *art* God, which hast made heaven, and earth, and the sea, and all that in them is:

25 Who by the mouth of thy servant Da'vid hast said, Why did the heathen rage, and the people imagine vain things?

26 The kings of the earth stood up, and the rulers were gathered together against the Lord, and against his Christ.

27 For of a truth against thy holy child Je'sus, whom thou hast anointed, both Her'od, and Pon'ti-us Pi'late, with the Gen'tiles, and the people of Is'ra-el, were gathered together,

28 For to do whatsoever thy hand and thy counsel determined before to be done.

29 And now, Lord, behold their threatenings: and grant unto thy servants, that with all boldness they may speak thy word,

30 By stretching forth thine hand to heal; and that signs and wonders may be done by the name of thy holy child Je'sus.

31 ¶ And when they had prayed, the place was shaken where they were assembled together; and they were all filled with the Ho'ly Ghost, and they spake the word of God with boldness.

32 And the multitude of them that believed were of one heart and of one soul: neither said any *of them* that ought of the things which he possessed was his own; but they had all things common.

33 And with great power gave the apostles witness of the resurrection of the Lord Je'sus: and great grace was upon them all.

34 Neither was there any among them that lacked: for as many as were possessors of lands or houses sold them, and brought the prices of the things that were sold,

35 And laid *them* down at the apostles' feet: and distribution was made unto every man according as he had need.

36 And Jo'ses, who by the apostles was surnamed Bar'na-bas, (which is, being interpreted, The son of consolation,) a Le'vite, *and* of the country of Cy'prus,

37 Having land, sold it, and brought the money, and laid it at the apostles' feet.

5 BUT a certain man named An-a-ni'as, with Sap-phi'ra his wife, sold a possession,

2 And kept back part of the price, his wife also being privy to it, and brought a certain part, and laid it at the apostles' feet.

3 But Pe'ter said, An-a-ni'as, why hath Sa'tan filled thine heart to lie to the Ho'ly Ghost, and to keep back part of the price of the land?

4 Whiles it remained, was it not thine own? and after it was sold, was it not in thine own power? why hast thou conceived this thing in thine heart? thou hast not lied unto men, but unto God.

5 And An-a-ni'as hearing these words fell down, and gave up the ghost: and great fear came on all them that heard these things.

6 And the young men arose, wound him up, and carried him out, and buried him.

7 And it was about the space of three hours after, when his wife, not knowing what was done, came in.

8 And Pe'ter answered unto her, Tell me whether ye sold the land for so much? And she said, Yea, for so much.

9 Then Pe'ter said unto her, How is it that ye have agreed together to tempt the Spirit of the Lord? behold, the feet of them which have buried thy husband are at the door, and shall carry thee out.

10 Then fell she down straightway at his feet, and yielded up the ghost: and the young men came in, and found her dead, and, carrying her forth, buried her by her husband.

11 And great fear came upon all the church, and upon as many as heard these things.

12 ¶ And by the hands of the apostles were many signs and wonders wrought among the people; (and they were all with one accord in Sol'o-mon's porch.

13 And of the rest durst no man join himself to them: but the people magnified them.

14 And believers were the more added to the Lord, multitudes both of men and women.)

15 Insomuch that they brought forth the sick into the streets, and laid them on beds of couches, that at the least the shadow of Pe'ter passing by might overshadow some of them.

16 There came also a multitude out of the cities round about unto Je-ru'sa-lem, bringing sick folks, and them which were vexed with unclean spirits: and they were healed every one.

17 ¶ Then the high priest rose up, and all they that were with him, (which is the sect of the Sad'du-cees,) and were filled with indignation,

18 And laid their hands on the apostles, and put them in the common prison.

19 But the angel of the Lord by night opened the prison doors, and brought them forth, and said,

20 Go, stand and speak in the temple to the people all the words of this life.

21 And when they heard that, they entered into the temple early in the morning, and taught. But the high priest came, and they that were with him, and called the council together, and all the senate of the children of Is'ra-el, and sent to the prison to have them brought.

22 But when the officers came, and found them not in the prison, they returned, and told,

23 Saying, The prison truly found we shut with all safety, and the keepers standing without before the doors: but when we had opened, we found no man within.

24 Now when the high priest and the captain of the temple and the chief priests heard these things, they doubted of them whereunto this would grow.

25 Then came one and told them, saying, Behold, the men whom ye put in prison are standing in the temple, and teaching the people.

26 Then went the captain with the officers, and brought them without violence: for they feared the people, lest they should have been stoned.

27 And when they had brought them, they set them before the council: and the high priest asked them,

28 Saying, Did not we straitly command you that ye should not teach in this name? and, behold, ye have filled Je-ru'sa-lem with your doctrine, and intend to bring this man's blood upon us.

29 ¶ Then Pe'ter and the other apostles answered and said, We ought to obey God rather than men.

30 The God of our fathers raised up Je'sus, whom ye slew and hanged on a tree.

31 Him hath God exalted with his right hand to be a Prince and a Saviour, for to give repentance to Is'ra-el, and forgiveness of sins.

32 And we are his witnesses of these things; and so is also the Ho'ly Ghost, whom God hath given to them that obey him.

33 ¶ When they heard that, they were cut to the heart, and took counsel to slay them.

34 Then stood there up one in the council, a Phar'i-see, named Ga-ma'li-el, a doctor of the law, had in reputation among all the people, and commanded to put the apostles forth a little space;

35 And said unto them, Ye men of Is'ra-el, take heed to yourselves what ye intend to do as touching these men.

36 For before these days rose up Theu'das, boasting himself to be somebody; to whom a number of men, about four hundred, joined themselves: who was slain; and all, as many as obeyed him, were scattered, and brought to nought.

37 After this man rose up Ju'das of Gal'i-lee in the days of the taxing, and drew away much people after him: he also perished; and all, even as many as obeyed him, were dispersed.

38 And now I say unto you, Refrain from these men, and let them alone: for if this counsel or this work be of men, it will come to nought:

39 But if it be of God, ye cannot overthrow it; lest haply ye be found even to fight against God.

40 And to him they agreed: and when they had called the apostles, and beaten them, they commanded that they should not speak in the name of Je'sus, and let them go.

41 ¶ And they departed from the presence of the council, rejoicing that they were counted worthy to suffer shame for his name.

42 And daily in the temple, and in every house, they ceased not to teach and preach Je'sus Christ.

6 AND in those days, when the number of the disciples was multiplied, there arose a murmuring of the Gre'cians against the He'brews, because their widows were neglected in the daily ministration.

2 Then the twelve called the multitude of the disciples unto them, and said, It is not reason that we should leave the word of God, and serve tables.

3 Wherefore, brethren, look ye out among

you seven men of honest report, full of the Ho'-
ly Ghost and wisdom, whom we may appoint
over this business.

4 But we will give ourselves continually to
prayer, and to the ministry of the word.

5 ¶ And the saying pleased the whole multitude: and they chose Ste'phen, a man full of
faith and of the Ho'ly Ghost, and Phil'ip, and
Proch'o-rus, and Ni-ca'nor, and Ti'mon, and
Par'me-nas, and Nic'o-las a proselyte of An'ti-
och:

6 Whom they set before the apostles: and
when they had prayed, they laid their hands on
them.

7 And the word of God increased; and the
number of the disciples multiplied in Je-ru'sa-
lem greatly; and a great company of the priests
were obedient to the faith.

8 And Ste'phen, full of faith and power, did
great wonders and miracles among the people.

9 ¶ Then there arose certain of the synagogue, which is called the synagogue of the
Lib'er-tines, and Cy-re'ni-ans, and Al-ex-an'dri-
ans, and of them of Ci-li'cia and of A'sia, disputing with Ste'phen.

10 And they were not able to resist the wisdom and the spirit by which he spake.

11 Then they suborned men, which said, We
have heard him speak blasphemous words
against Mo'ses, and against God.

12 And they stirred up the people, and the
elders, and the scribes, and came upon him, and
caught him, and brought him to the council,

13 And set up false witnesses, which said,
This man ceaseth not to speak blasphemous
words against this holy place, and the law:

14 For we have heard him say, that this Je'-
sus of Naz'a-reth shall destroy this place, and
shall change the customs which Mo'ses delivered us.

15 And all that sat in the council, looking
stedfastly on him, saw his face as it had been
the face of an angel.

7 THEN said the high priest, Are these
things so?

2 And he said, Men, brethren, and fathers,
hearken; The God of glory appeared unto our
father A'bra-ham, when he was in Mes-o-po-ta'-
mi-a, before he dwelt in Char'ran,

3 And said unto him, Get thee out of thy
country, and from thy kindred, and come into
the land which I shall shew thee.

4 Then came he out of the land of the Chal-
dæ'ans, and dwelt in Char'ran: and from thence,
when his father was dead, he removed him into
this land, wherein ye now dwell.

5 And he gave him none inheritance in it, no,
not so much as to set his foot on: yet he promised that he would give it to him for a possession, and to his seed after him, when as yet he
had no child.

6 And God spake on this wise, That his seed
should sojourn in a strange land; and that they
should bring them into bondage, and entreat
them evil four hundred years.

7 And the nation to whom they shall be in
bondage will I judge, said God: and after that
shall they come forth, and serve me in this
place.

8 And he gave him the covenant of circumcision: and so A'bra-ham begat I'saac, and circumcised him the eighth day; and I'saac begat
Ja'cob; and Ja'cob begat the twelve patriarchs.

9 And the patriarchs, moved with envy, sold
Jo'seph into E'gypt: but God was with him,

10 And delivered him out of all afflictions,

and gave him favour and wisdom in the sight of
Pha'raoh king of E'gypt; and he made him governor over E'gypt and all his house.

11 Now there came a dearth over all the land
of E'gypt and Cha'naan, and great affliction:
and our fathers found no sustenance.

12 But when Ja'cob heard that there was
corn in E'gypt, he sent out our fathers first.

13 And at the second time Jo'seph was made
known to his brethren; and Jo'seph's kindred
was made known unto Pha'raoh.

14 Then sent Jo'seph, and called his father
Ja'cob to him, and all his kindred, threescore
and fifteen souls.

15 So Ja'cob went down into E'gypt, and
died, he, and our fathers,

16 And were carried over into Sy'chem, and
laid in the sepulchre that A'bra-ham bought for
a sum of money of the sons of Em'mor the father of Sy'chem.

17 But when the time of the promise drew
nigh, which God had sworn to A'bra-ham, the
people grew and multiplied in E'gypt,

18 Till another king arose, which knew not
Jo'seph.

19 The same dealt subtilly with our kindred,
and evil entreated our fathers, so that they cast
out their young children, to the end they might
not live.

20 In which time Mo'ses was born, and was
exceeding fair, and nourished up in his father's
house three months:

21 And when he was cast out, Pha'raoh's
daughter took him up, and nourished him for
her own son.

22 And Mo'ses was learned in all the wisdom
of the E-gyp'tians, and was mighty in words
and in deeds.

23 And when he was full forty years old, it
came into his heart to visit his brethren the children of Is'ra-el.

24 And seeing one of them suffer wrong, he
defended him, and avenged him that was oppressed, and smote the E-gyp'tian:

25 For he supposed his brethren would have
understood how that God by his hand would
deliver them: but they understood not.

26 And the next day he shewed himself unto
them as they strove, and would have set them
at one again, saying, Sirs, ye are brethren; why
do ye wrong one to another?

27 But he that did his neighbour wrong
thrust him away, saying, Who made thee a ruler
and a judge over us?

28 Wilt thou kill me, as thou diddest the E-
gyp'tian yesterday?

29 Then fled Mo'ses at this saying, and was a
stranger in the land of Ma'di-an, where he begat
two sons.

30 And when forty years were expired, there
appeared to him in the wilderness of mount Si'-
na an angel of the Lord in a flame of fire in a
bush.

31 When Mo'ses saw it, he wondered at the
sight: and as he drew near to behold it, the
voice of the Lord came unto him,

32 Saying, I am the God of thy fathers, the
God of A'bra-ham, and the God of I'saac, and
the God of Ja'cob. Then Mo'ses trembled, and
durst not behold.

33 Then said the Lord to him, Put off thy
shoes from thy feet: for the place where thou
standest is holy ground.

34 I have seen, I have seen the affliction of
my people which is in E'gypt, and I have heard
their groaning, and am come down to deliver

them. And now come, I will send thee into E'-gypt.

35 This Mo'ses whom they refused, saying, Who made thee a ruler and a judge? the same did God send to be a ruler and a deliverer by the hand of the angel which appeared to him in the bush.

36 He brought them out, after that he had shewed wonders and signs in the land of E'gypt, and in the Red sea, and in the wilderness forty years.

37 ¶ This is that Mo'ses, which said unto the children of Is'ra-el, A prophet shall the Lord your God raise up unto you of your brethren, like unto me; him shall ye hear.

38 This is he, that was in the church in the wilderness with the angel which spake to him in the mount Si'na, and with our fathers: who received the lively oracles to give unto us:

39 To whom our fathers would not obey, but thrust him from them, and in their hearts turned back again into E'gypt,

40 Saying unto Aar'on, Make us gods to go before us: for as for this Mo'ses, which brought us out of the land of E'gypt, we wot not what is become of him.

41 And they made a calf in those days, and offered sacrifice unto the idol, and rejoiced in the works of their own hands.

42 Then God turned, and gave them up to worship the host of heaven; as it is written in the book of the prophets, O ye house of Is'ra-el, have ye offered to me slain beasts and sacrifices by the space of forty years in the wilderness?

43 Yea, ye took up the tabernacle of Mo'loch, and the star of your god Rem'phan, figures which ye made to worship them: and I will carry you away beyond Bab'y-lon.

44 Our fathers had the tabernacle of witness in the wilderness, as he had appointed, speaking unto Mo'ses, that he should make it according to the fashion that he had seen.

45 Which also our fathers that came after brought in with Je'sus into the possession of the Gen'tiles, whom God drave out before the face of our fathers, unto the days of Da'vid;

46 Who found favour before God, and desired to find a tabernacle for the God of Ja'cob.

47 But Sol'o-mon built him an house.

48 Howbeit the most High dwelleth not in temples made with hands; as saith the prophet,

49 Heaven is my throne, and earth is my footstool: what house will ye build me? saith the Lord: or what is the place of my rest?

50 Hath not my hand made all these things?

51 ¶ Ye stiffnecked and uncircumcised in heart and ears, ye do always resist the Ho'ly Ghost: as your fathers did, so do ye.

52 Which of the prophets have not your fathers persecuted? and they have slain them which shewed before of the coming of the Just One; of whom ye have been now the betrayers and murderers:

53 Who have received the law by the disposition of angels, and have not kept it.

54 ¶ When they heard these things, they were cut to the heart, and they gnashed on him with their teeth.

55 But he, being full of the Ho'ly Ghost, looked up stedfastly into heaven, and saw the glory of God, and Je'sus standing on the right hand of God,

56 And said, Behold, I see the heavens opened, and the Son of man standing on the right hand of God.

57 Then they cried out with a loud voice, and stopped their ears, and ran upon him with one accord,

58 And cast him out of the city, and stoned him: and the witnesses laid down their clothes at a young man's feet, whose name was Saul.

59 And they stoned Ste'phen, calling upon God, and saying, Lord Je'sus, receive my spirit.

60 And he kneeled down, and cried with a loud voice, Lord, lay not this sin to their charge. And when he had said this, he fell asleep.

8 AND Saul was consenting unto his death. And at that time there was a great persecution against the church which was at Je-ru'-sa-lem; and they were all scattered abroad throughout the regions of Ju-dæ'a and Sa-ma'ri-a, except the apostles.

2 And devout men carried Ste'phen to his burial, and made great lamentation over him.

3 As for Saul, he made havock of the church, entering into every house, and haling men and women committed them to prison.

4 Therefore they that were scattered abroad went every where preaching the word.

5 Then Phil'ip went down to the city of Sa-ma'ri-a, and preached Christ unto them.

6 And the people with one accord gave heed unto those things which Phil'ip spake, hearing and seeing the miracles which he did.

7 For unclean spirits, crying with loud voice, came out of many that were possessed with them: and many taken with palsies, and that were lame, were healed.

8 And there was great joy in that city.

9 But there was a certain man, called Si'mon, which beforetime in the same city used sorcery, and bewitched the people of Sa-ma'ri-a, giving out that himself was some great one:

10 To whom they all gave heed, from the least to the greatest, saying, This man is the great power of God.

11 And to him they had regard, because that of long time he had bewitched them with sorceries.

12 But when they believed Phil'ip preaching the things concerning the kingdom of God, and the name of Je'sus Christ, they were baptized, both men and women.

13 Then Si'mon himself believed also: and when he was baptized, he continued with Phil'-ip, and wondered, beholding the miracles and signs which were done.

14 Now when the apostles which were at Je-ru'sa-lem heard that Sa-ma'ri-a had received the word of God, they sent unto them Pe'ter and John:

15 Who, when they were come down, prayed for them, that they might receive the Ho'ly Ghost:

16 (For as yet he was fallen upon none of them: only they were baptized in the name of the Lord Je'sus.)

17 Then laid they their hands on them, and they received the Ho'ly Ghost.

18 And when Si'mon saw that through laying on of the apostles' hands the Ho'ly Ghost was given, he offered them money,

19 Saying, Give me also this power, that on whomsoever I lay hands, he may receive the Ho'ly Ghost.

20 But Pe'ter said unto him, Thy money perish with thee, because thou hast thought that the gift of God may be purchased with money.

21 Thou hast neither part nor lot in this matter: for thy heart is not right in the sight of God.

22 Repent therefore of this thy wickedness,

and pray God, if perhaps the thought of thine heart may be forgiven thee.

23 For I perceive that thou art in the gall of bitterness, and in the bond of iniquity.

24 Then answered Si'mon, and said, Pray ye to the Lord for me, that none of these things which ye have spoken come upon me.

25 And they, when they had testified and preached the word of the Lord, returned to Je-ru'sa-lem, and preached the gospel in many villages of the Sa-mar'i-tans.

26 And the angel of the Lord spake unto Phil'ip, saying, Arise, and go toward the south unto the way that goeth down from Je-ru'sa-lem unto Ga'za, which is desert.

27 And he rose and went: and, behold, a man of E-thi-o'pi-a, an eunuch of great authority under Can'da-ce queen of the E-thi-o'pi-ans, who had the charge of all her treasure, and had come to Je-ru'sa-lem for to worship,

28 Was returning, and sitting in his chariot read E-sa'ias the prophet.

29 Then the Spirit said unto Phil'ip, Go near, and join thyself to this chariot.

30 And Phil'ip ran thither to him, and heard him read the prophet E-sa'ias, and said, Understandest thou what thou readest?

31 And he said, How can I, except some man should guide me? And he desired Phil'ip that he would come up and sit with him.

32 The place of the scripture which he read was this, He was led as a sheep to the slaughter; and like a lamb dumb before his shearer, so opened he not his mouth:

33 In his humiliation his judgment was taken away: and who shall declare his generation? for his life is taken from the earth.

34 And the eunuch answered Phil'ip, and said, I pray thee, of whom speaketh the prophet this? of himself, or of some other man?

35 Then Phil'ip opened his mouth, and began at the same scripture, and preached unto him Je'sus.

36 And as they went on their way, they came unto a certain water: and the eunuch said, See, here is water; what doth hinder me to be baptized?

37 And Phil'ip said, If thou believest with all thine heart, thou mayest. And he answered and said, I believe that Je'sus Christ is the Son of God.

38 And he commanded the chariot to stand still: and they went down both into the water, both Phil'ip and the eunuch; and he baptized him.

39 And when they were come up out of the water, the Spirit of the Lord caught away Phil'-ip, that the eunuch saw him no more: and he went on his way rejoicing.

40 But Phil'ip was found at A-zo'tus: and passing through he preached in all the cities, till he came to Cæs-a-re'a.

9 AND Saul, yet breathing out threatenings and slaughter against the disciples of the Lord, went unto the high priest,

2 And desired of him letters to Da-mas'cus to the synagogues, that if he found any of this way, whether they were men or women, he might bring them bound unto Je-ru'sa-lem.

3 And as he journeyed, he came near Da-mas'cus: and suddenly there shined round about him a light from heaven:

4 And he fell to the earth, and heard a voice saying unto him, Saul, Saul, why persecutest thou me?

5 And he said, Who art thou, Lord? And the Lord said, I am Je'sus whom thou persecutest: it is hard for thee to kick against the pricks.

6 And he trembling and astonished said, Lord, what wilt thou have me to do? And the Lord said unto him, Arise, and go into the city, and it shall be told thee what thou must do.

7 And the men which journeyed with him stood speechless, hearing a voice, but seeing no man.

8 And Saul arose from the earth; and when his eyes were opened, he saw no man: but they led him by the hand, and brought him into Da-mas'cus.

9 And he was three days without sight, and neither did eat nor drink.

10 ¶ And there was a certain disciple at Da-mas'cus, named An-a-ni'as; and to him said the Lord in a vision, An-a-ni'as. And he said, Behold, I am here, Lord.

11 And the Lord said unto him, Arise, and go into the street which is called Straight, and enquire in the house of Ju'das for one called Saul, of Tar'sus: for, behold, he prayeth,

12 And hath seen in a vision a man named An-a-ni'as coming in, and putting his hand on him, that he might receive his sight.

13 Then An-a-ni'as answered, Lord, I have heard by many of this man, how much evil he hath done to thy saints at Je-ru'sa-lem:

14 And here he hath authority from the chief priests to bind all that call on thy name.

15 But the Lord said unto him, Go thy way: for he is a chosen vessel unto me, to bear my name before the Gen'tiles, and kings, and the children of Is'ra-el:

16 For I will shew him how great things he must suffer for my name's sake.

17 And An-a-ni'as went his way, and entered into the house; and putting his hands on him said, Brother Saul, the Lord, even Je'sus, that appeared unto thee in the way as thou camest, hath sent me, that thou mightest receive thy sight, and be filled with the Ho'ly Ghost.

18 And immediately there fell from his eyes as it had been scales: and he received sight forthwith, and arose, and was baptized.

19 And when he had received meat, he was strengthened. Then was Saul certain days with the disciples which were at Da-mas'cus.

20 And straightway he preached Christ in the synagogues, that he is the Son of God.

21 But all that heard him were amazed, and said; Is not this he that destroyed them which called on this name in Je-ru'sa-lem, and came hither for that intent, that he might bring them bound unto the chief priests?

22 But Saul increased the more in strength, and confounded the Jews which dwelt at Da-mas'cus, proving that this is very Christ.

23 ¶ And after that many days were fulfilled, the Jews took counsel to kill him:

24 But their laying await was known of Saul. And they watched the gates day and night to kill him.

25 Then the disciples took him by night, and let him down by the wall in a basket.

26 And when Saul was come to Je-ru'sa-lem, he assayed to join himself to the disciples: but they were all afraid of him, and believed not that he was a disciple.

27 But Bar'na-bas took him, and brought him to the apostles, and declared unto them how he had seen the Lord in the way, and that he had spoken to him, and how he had preached boldly at Da-mas'cus in the name of Je'sus.

28 And he was with them coming in and going out at Je-ru'sa-lem.

29 And he spake boldly in the name of the Lord Je'sus, and disputed against the Gre'cians: but they went about to slay him.

30 *Which* when the brethren knew, they brought him down to Caes-a-re'a, and sent him forth to Tar'sus.

31 Then had the churches rest throughout all Ju-dæ'a and Gal'i-lee and Sa-ma'ri-a, and were edified; and walking in the fear of the Lord, and in the comfort of the Ho'ly Ghost, were multiplied.

32 ¶ And it came to pass, as Pe'ter passed throughout all *quarters,* he came down also to the saints which dwelt at Lyd'da.

33 And there he found a certain man named Æ'ne-as, which had kept his bed eight years, and was sick of the palsy.

34 And Pe'ter said unto him, Æ'ne-as, Je'sus Christ maketh thee whole: arise, and make thy bed. And h ɔ arose immediately.

35 And all that dwelt at Lyd'da and Sa'ron saw him, and turned to the Lord.

36 ¶ Now there was at Jop'pa a certain disciple named Tab'i-tha, which by interpretation is called Dor'cas: this woman was full of good works and almsdeeds which she did.

37 And it came to pass in those days, that she was sick, and died: whom when they had washed, they laid *her* in an upper chamber.

38 And forasmuch as Lyd'da was nigh to Jop'pa, and the disciples had heard that Pe'ter was there, they sent unto him two men, desiring *him* that he would not delay to come to them.

39 Then Pe'ter arose and went with them. When he was come, they brought him into the upper chamber: and all the widows stood by him weeping, and shewing the coats and garments which Dor'cas made, while she was with them.

40 But Pe'ter put them all forth, and kneeled down, and prayed; and turning *him* to the body said, Tab'i-tha, arise. And she opened her eyes: and when she saw Pe'ter, she sat up.

41 And he gave her *his* hand, and lifted her up, and when he had called the saints and widows, presented her alive.

42 And it was known throughout all Jop'pa; and many believed in the Lord.

43 And it came to pass, that he tarried many days in Jop'pa with one Si'mon a tanner.

10 THERE was a certain man in Cæs-a-re'a called Cor-ne'lius, a centurion of the band called the Ital'ian *band,*

2 A devout *man,* and one that feared God with all his house, which gave much alms to the people, and prayed to God alway.

3 He saw in a vision evidently about the ninth hour of the day an angel of God coming in to him, and saying unto him, Cor-ne'lius.

4 And when he looked on him, he was afraid, and said, What is it, Lord? And he said unto him, Thy prayers and thine alms are come up for a memorial before God.

5 And now send men to Jop'pa, and call for one Si'mon, whose surname is Pe'ter:

6 He lodgeth with one Si'mon a tanner, whose house is by the sea side: he shall tell thee what thou oughtest to do.

7 And when the angel which spake unto Cor-ne'lius was departed, he called two of his household servants, and a devout soldier of them that waited on him continually;

8 And when he had declared all *these* things unto them, he sent them to Jop'pa.

9 ¶ On the morrow, as they went on their journey, and drew nigh unto the city, Pe'ter

went up upon the house top to pray about the sixth hour:

10 And he became very hungry, and would have eaten: but while they made ready, he fell into a trance,

11 And saw heaven opened, and a certain vessel descending unto him, as it had been a great sheet knit at the four corners, and let down to the earth:

12 Wherein were all manner of fourfooted beasts of the earth, and wild beasts, and creeping things, and fowls of the air.

13 And there came a voice to him, Rise, Pe'ter; kill, and eat.

14 But Pe'ter said, Not so, Lord; for I have never eaten any thing that is common or unclean.

15 And the voice *spake* unto him again the second time, What God hath cleansed, *that* call not thou common.

16 This was done thrice: and the vessel was received up again into heaven.

17 Now while Pe'ter doubted in himself what this vision which he had seen should mean, behold, the men which were sent from Cor-ne'lius had made enquiry for Si'mon's house, and stood before the gate,

18 And called, and asked whether Si'mon, which was surnamed Pe'ter, were lodged there.

19 ¶ While Pe'ter thought on the vision, the Spirit said unto him, Behold, three men seek thee.

20 Arise therefore, and get thee down, and go with them, doubting nothing: for I have sent them.

21 Then Pe'ter went down to the men which were sent unto him from Cor-ne'lius; and said, Behold, I am he whom ye seek: what *is* the cause wherefore ye are come?

22 And they said, Cor-ne'lius the centurion, a just man, and one that feareth God, and of good report among all the nation of the Jews, was warned from God by an holy angel to send for thee into his house, and to hear words of thee.

23 Then called he them in, and lodged *them.* And on the morrow Pe'ter went away with them, and certain brethren from Jop'pa accompanied him.

24 And the morrow after they entered into Cæs-a-re'a. And Cor-ne'lius waited for them, and had called together his kinsmen and near friends.

25 And as Pe'ter was coming in, Cor-ne'lius met him, and fell down at his feet, and worshipped *him.*

26 But Pe'ter took him up, saying, Stand up; I myself also am a man.

27 And as he talked with him, he went in, and found many that were come together.

28 And he said unto them, Ye know how that it is an unlawful thing for a man that is a Jew to keep company, or come unto one of another nation; but God hath shewed me that I should not call any man common or unclean.

29 Therefore came I *unto you* without gainsaying, as soon as I was sent for: I ask therefore for what intent ye have sent for me?

30 And Cor-ne'lius said, Four days ago I was fasting until this hour; and at the ninth hour I prayed in my house, and behold, a man stood before me in bright clothing,

31 And said, Cor-ne'lius, thy prayer is heard, and thine alms are had in remembrance in the sight of God.

32 Send therefore to Jop'pa, and call hither Si'mon, whose surname is Pe'ter; he is lodged in the house of *one* Si'mon a tanner by the sea

side: who, when he cometh, shall speak unto
thee.

33 Immediately therefore I sent to thee; and
thou hast well done that thou art come. Now
therefore are we all here present before God, to
hear all things that are commanded thee of
God.

34 ¶ Then Pe'ter opened *his* mouth, and said,
Of a truth I perceive that God is no respecter of
persons:

35 But in every nation he that feareth him,
and worketh righteousness, is accepted with
him.

36 The word which God sent unto the children of Is'ra-el, preaching peace by Je'sus
Christ: (he is Lord of all:)

37 That word, *I say*, ye know, which was
published throughout all Ju-dæ'a, and began
from Gal'i-lee, after the baptism which John
preached;

38 How God anointed Je'sus of Naz'a-reth
with the Ho'ly Ghost and with power: who went
about doing good, and healing all that were oppressed of the devil; for God was with him.

39 And we are witnesses of all things which
he did both in the land of the Jews, and in Je-
ru'sa-lem; whom they slew and hanged on a
tree:

40 Him God raised up the third day, and
shewed him openly;

41 Not to all the people, but unto witnesses
chosen before of God, *even* to us, who did eat
and drink with him after he rose from the dead.

42 And he commanded us to preach unto the
people, and to testify that it is he which was
ordained of God *to be* the Judge of quick and
dead.

43 To him give all the prophets witness, that
through his name whosoever believeth in him
shall receive remission of sins.

44 ¶ While Pe'ter yet spake these words, the
Ho'ly Ghost fell on all them which heard the
word.

45 And they of the circumcision which believed were astonished, as many as came with
Pe'ter, because that on the Gen'tiles also was
poured out the gift of the Ho'ly Ghost.

46 For they heard them speak with tongues,
and magnify God. Then answered Pe'ter,

47 Can any man forbid water, that these
should not be baptized, which have received the
Ho'ly Ghost as well as we?

48 And he commanded them to be baptized
in the name of the Lord. Then prayed they him
to tarry certain days.

11 AND the apostles and brethren that
were in Ju-dæ'a heard that the Gen'tiles
had also received the word of God.

2 And when Pe'ter was come up to Je-ru'sa-
lem, they that were of the circumcision contended with him,

3 Saying, Thou wentest in to men uncircumcised, and didst eat with them.

4 But Pe'ter rehearsed *the matter* from the
beginning, and expounded *it* by order unto
them, saying,

5 I was in the city of Jop'pa praying: and in a
trance I saw a vision, A certain vessel descend,
as it had been a great sheet, let down from
heaven by four corners; and it came even to me:

6 Upon the which when I had fastened mine
eyes, I considered, and saw fourfooted beasts of
the earth, and wild beasts, and creeping things,
and fowls of the air.

7 And I heard a voice saying unto me, Arise,
Pe'ter; slay and eat.

8 But I said, Not so, Lord: for nothing common or unclean hath at any time entered into
my mouth.

9 But the voice answered me again from
heaven, What God hath cleansed, *that* call not
thou common.

10 And this was done three times: and all
were drawn up again into heaven.

11 And, behold, immediately there were
three men already come unto the house where I
was, sent from Cæs-a-re'a unto me.

12 And the spirit bade me go with them,
nothing doubting. Moreover these six brethren
accompanied me, and we entered into the
man's house:

13 And he shewed us how he had seen an
angel in his house, which stood and said unto
him, Send men to Jop'pa, and call for Si'mon,
whose surname is Pe'ter;

14 Who shall tell thee words, whereby thou
and all thy house shall be saved.

15 And as I began to speak, the Ho'ly Ghost
fell on them, as on us at the beginning.

16 Then remembered I the word of the Lord,
how that he said, John indeed baptized with
water; but ye shall be baptized with the Ho'ly
Ghost.

17 Forasmuch then as God gave them the
like gift as *he did* unto us, who believed on the
Lord Je'sus Christ; what was I, that I could
withstand God?

18 When they heard these things, they held
their peace, and glorified God, saying, Then
hath God also to the Gen'tiles granted repentance unto life.

19 ¶ Now they which were scattered abroad
upon the persecution that arose about Ste'phen
travelled as far as Phe-ni'ce, and Cy'prus, and
An'ti-och, preaching the word to none but unto
the Jews only.

20 And some of them were men of Cy'prus
and Cy-re'ne, which, when they were come to
An'ti-och, spake unto the Gre'cians, preaching
the Lord Je'sus.

21 And the hand of the Lord was with them:
and a great number believed, and turned unto
the Lord.

22 ¶ Then tidings of these things came unto
the ears of the church which was in Je-ru'sa-
lem: and they sent forth Bar'na-bas, that he
should go as far as An'ti-och.

23 Who, when he came, and had seen the
grace of God, was glad, and exhorted them all,
that with purpose of heart they would cleave
unto the Lord.

24 For he was a good man, and full of the
Ho'ly Ghost and of faith: and much people was
added unto the Lord.

25 Then departed Bar'na-bas to Tar'sus, for
to seek Saul:

26 And when he had found him, he brought
him unto An'ti-och. And it came to pass, that a
whole year they assembled themselves with the
church, and taught much people. And the disciples were called Chris'tians first in An'ti-och.

27 ¶ And in these days came prophets from
Je-ru'sa-lem unto An'ti-och.

28 And there stood up one of them named
Ag'a-bus, and signified by the spirit that there
should be great dearth throughout all the world:
which came to pass in the days of Clau'di-us
Cæ'sar.

29 Then the disciples, every man according
to his ability, determined to send relief unto the
brethren which dwelt in Ju-dæ'a:

30 Which also they did, and sent it to the elders by the hands of Bar'na-bas and Saul.

12 NOW about that time Her'od the king stretched forth *his* hands to vex certain of the church.

2 And he killed James the brother of John with the sword.

3 And because he saw it pleased the Jews, he proceeded further to take Pe'ter also. (Then were the days of unleavened bread.)

4 And when he had apprehended him, he put *him* in prison, and delivered *him* to four quaternions of soldiers to keep him; intending after Easter to bring him forth to the people.

5 Pe'ter therefore was kept in prison: but prayer was made without ceasing of the church unto God for him.

6 And when Her'od would have brought him forth, the same night Pe'ter was sleeping between two soldiers, bound with two chains: and the keepers before the door kept the prison.

7 And, behold, the angel of the Lord came upon *him*, and a light shined in the prison: and he smote Pe'ter on the side, and raised him up, saying, Arise up quickly. And his chains fell off from *his* hands.

8 And the angel said unto him, Gird thyself, and bind on *thy* sandals. And so he did. And he saith unto him, Cast thy garment about thee, and follow me.

9 And he went out, and followed him; and wist not that it was true which was done by the angel; but thought he saw a vision.

10 When they were past the first and the second ward, they came unto the iron gate that leadeth unto the city; which opened to them of his own accord: and they went out, and passed on through one street; and forthwith the angel departed from him.

11 And when Pe'ter was come to himself, he said, Now I know of a surety, that the Lord hath sent his angel, and hath delivered me out of the hand of Her'od, and *from* all the expectation of the people of the Jews.

12 And when he had considered *the thing*, he came to the house of Ma'ry the mother of John, whose surname was Mark; where many were gathered together praying.

13 And as Pe'ter knocked at the door of the gate, a damsel came to hearken, named Rho'da.

14 And when she knew Pe'ter's voice, she opened not the gate for gladness, but ran in, and told how Pe'ter stood before the gate.

15 And they said unto her, Thou art mad. But she constantly affirmed that it was even so. Then said they, It is his angel.

16 But Pe'ter continued knocking: and when they had opened *the door*, and saw him, they were astonished.

17 But he, beckoning unto them with the hand to hold their peace, declared unto them how the Lord had brought him out of the prison. And he said, Go shew these things unto James, and to the brethren. And he departed, and went into another place.

18 Now as soon as it was day, there was no small stir among the soldiers, what was become of Pe'ter.

19 And when Her'od had sought for him, and found him not, he examined the keepers, and commanded that *they* should be put to death. And he went down from Ju-dæ'a to Cæs-a-re'a, and *there* abode.

20 ¶ And Her'od was highly displeased with them of Tyre and Si'don: but they came with one accord to him, and, having made Blas'tus the king's chamberlain their friend, desired peace; because their country was nourished by the king's *country*.

21 And upon a set day Her'od, arrayed in royal apparel, sat upon his throne, and made an oration unto them.

22 And the people gave a shout, *saying, It is* the voice of a god, and not of a man.

23 And immediately the angel of the Lord smote him, because he gave not God the glory: and he was eaten of worms, and gave up the ghost.

24 ¶ But the word of God grew and multiplied.

25 And Bar'na-bas and Saul returned from Je-ru'sa-lem, when they had fulfilled *their* ministry, and took with them John, whose surname was Mark.

13 NOW there were in the church that was at An'ti-och certain prophets and teachers; as Bar'na-bas, and Sim'e-on that was called Ni'ger, and Lu'cius of Cy-re'ne, and Man'a-en, which had been brought up with Her'od the tetrarch, and Saul.

2 As they ministered to the Lord, and fasted, the Ho'ly Ghost said, Separate me Bar'na-bas and Saul for the work whereunto I have called them.

3 And when they had fasted and prayed, and laid *their* hands on them, they sent *them* away.

4 ¶ So they, being sent forth by the Ho'ly Ghost, departed unto Se-leu'ci-a; and from thence they sailed to Cy'prus.

5 And when they were at Sal'a-mis, they preached the word of God in the synagogues of the Jews: and they had also John to *their* minister.

6 And when they had gone through the isle unto Pa'phos, they found a certain sorcerer, a false prophet, a Jew, whose name *was* Bar-je'-sus:

7 Which was with the deputy of the country, Ser'gi-us Pau'lus, a prudent man; who called for Bar'na-bas and Saul, and desired to hear the word of God.

8 But El'y-mas the sorcerer (for so is his name by interpretation) withstood them, seeking to turn away the deputy from the faith.

9 Then Saul, (who also *is called* Paul,) filled with the Ho'ly Ghost, set his eyes on him,

10 And said, O full of all subtilty and all mischief, *thou* child of the devil, *thou* enemy of all righteousness, wilt thou not cease to pervert the right ways of the Lord?

11 And now, behold, the hand of the Lord *is* upon thee, and thou shalt be blind, not seeing the sun for a season. And immediately there fell on him a mist and a darkness; and he went about seeking some to lead him by the hand.

12 Then the deputy, when he saw what was done, believed, being astonished at the doctrine of the Lord.

13 Now when Paul and his company loosed from Pa'phos, they came to Per'ga in Pamphyl'i-a: and John departing from them returned to Je-ru'sa-lem.

14 ¶ But when they departed from Per'ga, they came to An'ti-och in Pi-sid'i-a, and went into the synagogue on the sabbath day, and sat down.

15 And after the reading of the law and the prophets the rulers of the synagogue sent unto them, saying, *Ye* men *and* brethren, if ye have any word of exhortation for the people, say on.

16 Then Paul stood up, and beckoning with *his* hand said, Men of Is'ra-el, ye that fear God, give audience.

17 The God of this people of Is'ra-el chose our fathers, and exalted the people when they

dwelt as strangers in the land of E'gypt, and with an high arm brought he them out of it.

18 And about the time of forty years suffered he their manners in the wilderness.

19 And when he had destroyed seven nations in the land of Cha'naan, he divided their land to them by lot.

20 And after that he gave *unto them* judges about the space of four hundred and fifty years, until Sam'u-el the prophet.

21 And afterward they desired a king: and God gave unto them Saul the son of Cis, a man of the tribe of Ben'ja-min, by the space of forty years.

22 And when he had removed him, he raised up unto them Da'vid to be their king; to whom also he gave testimony, and said, I have found Da'vid the *son* of Jes'se, a man after mine own heart, which shall fulfill all my will.

23 Of this man's seed hath God according to *his* promise raised unto Is'ra-el a Saviour, Je'sus:

24 When John had first preached before his coming the baptism of repentance to all the people of Is'ra-el.

25 And as John fulfilled his course, he said, Whom think ye that I am? I am not *he.* But, behold, there cometh one after me, whose shoes of *his* feet I am not worthy to loose.

26 Men *and* brethren, children of the stock of A'bra-ham, and whosoever among you feareth God, to you is the word of this salvation sent.

27 For they that dwell at Je-ru'sa-lem, and their rulers, because they knew him not, nor yet the voices of the prophets which are read every sabbath day, they have fulfilled *them* in condemning him.

28 And though they found no cause of death *in him*, yet desired they Pi'late that he should be slain.

29 And when they had fulfilled all that was written of him, they took *him* down from the tree, and laid *him* in a sepulchre.

30 But God raised him from the dead:

31 And he was seen many days of them which came up with him from Gal'i-lee to Je-ru'sa-lem, who are his witnesses unto the people.

32 And we declare unto you glad tidings, how that the promise which was made unto the fathers,

33 God hath fulfilled the same unto us their children, in that he hath raised up Je'sus again; as it is also written in the second psalm, Thou art my Son, this day have I begotten thee.

34 And as concerning that he raised him up from the dead, *now* no more to return to corruption, he said on this wise, I will give you the sure mercies of Da'vid.

35 Wherefore he saith also in another *psalm*, Thou shalt not suffer thine Holy One to see corruption.

36 For Da'vid, after he had served his own generation by the will of God, fell on sleep, and was laid unto his fathers, and saw corruption:

37 But he, whom God raised again, saw no corruption.

38 ¶ Be it known unto you therefore, men *and* brethren, that through this man is preached unto you the forgiveness of sins:

39 And by him all that believe are justified from all things, from which ye could not be justified by the law of Mo'ses.

40 Beware therefore, lest that come upon you, which is spoken of in the prophets;

41 Behold, ye despisers, and wonder, and perish: for I work a work in your days, a work which ye shall in no wise believe, though a man declare it unto you.

42 And when the Jews were gone out of the synagogue, the Gen'tiles besought that these words might be preached to them the next sabbath.

43 Now when the congregation was broken up, many of the Jews and religious proselytes followed Paul and Bar'na-bas: who, speaking to them, persuaded them to continue in the grace of God.

44 ¶ And the next sabbath day came almost the whole city together to hear the word of God.

45 But when the Jews saw the multitudes, they were filled with envy, and spake against those things which were spoken by Paul, contradicting and blaspheming.

46 Then Paul and Bar'na-bas waxed bold, and said, It was necessary that the word of God should first have been spoken to you: but seeing ye put it from you, and judge yourselves unworthy of everlasting life, lo, we turn to the Gen'tiles.

47 For so hath the Lord commanded us, *saying*, I have set thee to be a light of the Gen'tiles, that thou shouldest be for salvation unto the ends of the earth.

48 And when the Gen'tiles heard this, they were glad, and glorified the word of the Lord: and as many as were ordained to eternal life believed.

49 And the word of the Lord was published throughout all the region.

50 But the Jews stirred up the devout and honourable women, and the chief men of the city, and raised persecution against Paul and Bar'na-bas, and expelled them out of their coasts.

51 But they shook off the dust of their feet against them, and came unto I-co'ni-um.

52 And the disciples were filled with joy, and with the Ho'ly Ghost.

14 AND it came to pass in I-co'ni-um, that they went both together into the synagogue of the Jews, and so spake, that a great multitude both of the Jews and also of the Greeks believed.

2 But the unbelieving Jews stirred up the Gen'tiles, and made their minds evil affected against the brethren.

3 Long time therefore abode they speaking boldly in the Lord, which gave testimony unto the word of his grace, and granted signs and wonders to be done by their hands.

4 But the multitude of the city was divided: and part held with the Jews, and part with the apostles.

5 And when there was an assault made both of the Gen'tiles, and also of the Jews with their rulers, to use *them* despitefully, and to stone them,

6 They were ware of *it*, and fled unto Lys'tra and Der'be, cities of Lyc-a-o'ni-a, and unto the region that lieth round about:

7 And there they preached the gospel.

8 ¶ And there sat a certain man at Lys'tra, impotent in his feet, being a cripple from his mother's womb, who never had walked:

9 The same heard Paul speak: who stedfastly beholding him, and perceiving that he had faith to be healed,

10 Said with a loud voice, Stand upright on thy feet. And he leaped and walked.

11 And when the people saw what Paul had done, they lifted up their voices, saying in the

speech of Lyc-a-o'ni-a, The gods are come down to us in the likeness of men.

12 And they called Bar'na-bas, Ju'pi-ter; and Paul, Mer-cu'ri-us, because he was the chief speaker.

13 Then the priest of Ju'pi-ter, which was before their city, brought oxen and garlands unto the gates, and would have done sacrifice with the people.

14 *Which* when the apostles, Bar'na-bas and Paul, heard *of*, they rent their clothes, and ran in among the people, crying out,

15 And saying, Sirs, why do ye these things? We also are men of like passions with you, and preach unto you that ye should turn from these vanities unto the living God, which made heaven, and earth, and the sea, and all things that are therein:

16 Who in times past suffered all nations to walk in the'r own ways.

17 Nevertheless he left not himself without witness, in that he did good, and gave us rain from heaven, and fruitful seasons, filling our hearts with food and gladness.

18 And with these sayings scarce restrained they the people, that they had not done sacrifice unto them.

19 ¶ And there came thither *certain* Jews from An'ti-och and I-co'ni-um, who persuaded the people, and, having stoned Paul, drew *him* out of the city, supposing he had been dead.

20 Howbeit, as the disciples stood round about him, he rose up, and came into the city: and the next day he departed with Bar'na-bas to Der'be.

21 And when they had preached the gospel to that city, and had taught many, they returned again to Lys'tra, and *to* I-co'ni-um, and An'ti-och,

22 Confirming the souls of the disciples, *and* exhorting them to continue in the faith, and that we must through much tribulation enter into the kingdom of God.

23 And when they had ordained them elders in every church, and had prayed with fasting, they commended them to the Lord, on whom they believed.

24 And after they had passed throughout Pi-sid'i-a, they came to Pam-phyl'i-a.

25 And when they had preached the word in Per'ga, they went down into At'ta'li-a:

26 And thence sailed to An'ti-och, from whence they had been recommended to the grace of God for the work which they fulfilled.

27 And when they were come, and had gathered the church together, they rehearsed all that God had done with them, and how he had opened the door of faith unto the Gen'tiles.

28 And there they abode long time with the disciples.

15 AND certain men which came down from Ju-dæ'a taught the brethren, *and said*, Except ye be circumcised after the manner of Mo'ses, ye cannot be saved.

2 When therefore Paul and Bar'na-bas had no small dissension and disputation with them, they determined that Paul and Bar'na-bas, and certain other of them, should go up to Je-ru'sa-lem unto the apostles and elders about this question.

3 And being brought on their way by the church, they passed through Phe-ni'ce and Sa-ma'ri-a, declaring the conversion of the Gen'-tiles: and they caused great joy unto all the brethren.

4 And when they were come to Je-ru'sa-lem,

they were received of the church, and *of* the apostles and elders, and they declared all things that God had done with them.

5 But there rose up certain of the sect of the Phar'i-sees which believed, saying, That it was needful to circumcise them, and to command *them* to keep the law of Mo'ses.

6 ¶ And the apostles and elders came together for to consider of this matter.

7 And when there had been much disputing, Pe'ter rose up, and said unto them, Men *and* brethren, ye know how that a good while ago God made choice among us, that the Gen'tiles by my mouth should hear the word of the gospel, and believe.

8 And God, which knoweth the hearts, bare them witness, giving them the Ho'ly Ghost, even as *he did* unto us;

9 And put no difference between us and them, purifying their hearts by faith.

10 Now therefore why tempt ye God, to put a yoke upon the neck of the disciples, which neither our fathers nor we were able to bear?

11 But we believe that through the grace of the Lord Je'sus Christ we shall be saved, even as they.

12 ¶ Then all the multitude kept silence, and gave audience to Bar'na-bas and Paul, declaring what miracles and wonders God had wrought among the Gen'tiles by them.

13 ¶ And after they had held their peace, James answered, saying, Men *and* brethren, hearken unto me:

14 Sim'e-on hath declared how God at the first did visit the Gen'tiles, to take out of them a people for his name.

15 And to this agree the words of the prophets; as it is written,

16 After this I will return, and will build again the tabernacle of Da'vid, which is fallen down; and I will build again the ruins thereof, and I will set it up:

17 That the residue of men might seek after the Lord, and all the Gen'tiles, upon whom my name is called, saith the Lord, who doeth all these things.

18 Known unto God are all his works from the beginning of the world.

19 Wherefore my sentence is, that we trouble not them, which from among the Gen'tiles are turned to God:

20 But that we write unto them, that they abstain from pollutions of idols, and *from* fornication, and *from* things strangled, and *from* blood.

21 For Mo'ses of old time hath in every city them that preach him, being read in the synagogues every sabbath day.

22 Then pleased it the apostles and elders, with the whole church, to send chosen men of their own company to An'ti-och with Paul and Bar'na-bas; *namely*, Ju'das surnamed Bar'sa-bas, and Si'las, chief men among the brethren:

23 And they wrote *letters* by them after this manner; The apostles and elders and brethren *send* greeting unto the brethren which are of the Gen'tiles in An'ti-och and Syr'i-a and Ci-li'-cia:

24 Forasmuch as we have heard, that certain which went out from us have troubled you with words, subverting your souls, saying, Ye *must* be circumcised, and keep the law: to whom we gave no *such* commandment:

25 It seemed good unto us, being assembled with one accord, to send chosen men unto you with our beloved Bar'na-bas and Paul,

26 Men that have hazarded their lives for the name of our Lord Je′sus Christ.

27 We have sent therefore Ju′das and Si′las, who shall also tell you the same things by mouth.

28 For it seemed good to the Ho′ly Ghost, and to us, to lay upon you no greater burden than these necessary things;

29 That ye abstain from meats offered to idols, and from blood, and from things strangled, and from fornication: from which if ye keep yourselves, ye shall do well. Fare ye well.

30 So when they were dismissed, they came to An′ti-och: and when they had gathered the multitude together, they delivered the epistle:

31 Which when they had read, they rejoiced for the consolation.

32 And Ju′das and Si′las, being prophets also themselves, exhorted the brethren with many words, and confirmed them.

33 And after they had tarried there a space, they were let go in peace from the brethren unto the apostles.

34 Notwithstanding it pleased Si′las to abide there still.

35 Paul also and Bar′na-bas continued in An′ti-och, teaching and preaching the word of the Lord, with many others also.

36 ¶ And some days after Paul said unto Bar′na-bas, Let us go again and visit our brethren in every city where we have preached the word of the Lord, and see how they do.

37 And Bar′na-bas determined to take with them John, whose surname was Mark.

38 But Paul thought not good to take him with them, who departed from them from Pamphyl′i-a, and went not with them to the work.

39 And the contention was so sharp between them, that they departed asunder one from the other: and so Bar′na-bas took Mark, and sailed unto Cy′prus;

40 And Paul chose Si′las, and departed, being recommended by the brethren unto the grace of God.

41 And he went through Syr′i-a and Ci-li′cia, confirming the churches.

16 THEN came he to Der′be and Lys′tra: and, behold, a certain disciple was there, named Ti-mo′the-us, the son of a certain woman, which was a Jew′ess, and believed; but his father was a Greek:

2 Which was well reported of by the brethren that were at Lys′tra and I-co′ni-um.

3 Him would Paul have to go forth with him; and took and circumcised him because of the Jews which were in those quarters: for they knew all that his father was a Greek.

4 And as they went through the cities, they delivered them the decrees for to keep, that were ordained of the apostles and elders which were at Je-ru′sa-lem.

5 And so were the churches established in the faith, and increased in number daily.

6 Now when they had gone throughout Phryg′i-a and the region of Ga-la′tia, and were forbidden of the Ho′ly Ghost to preach the word in A′sia,

7 After they were come to Mys′ia, they assayed to go into Bi-thyn′i-a: but the Spirit suffered them not.

8 And they passing by Mys′ia came down to Tro′as.

9 And a vision appeared to Paul in the night; There stood a man of Mac-e-do′ni-a, and prayed him, saying, Come over into Mac-e-do′ni-a, and help us.

10 And after he had seen the vision, immediately we endeavoured to go into Mac-e-do′ni-a, assuredly gathering that the Lord had called us for to preach the gospel unto them.

11 Therefore loosing from Tro′as, we came with a straight course to Sam-o-thra′cia, and the next day to Ne-ap′o-lis;

12 And from thence to Phi-lip′pi, which is the chief city of that part of Mac-e-do′ni-a, and a colony: and we were in that city abiding certain days.

13 And on the sabbath we went out of the city by a river side, where prayer was wont to be made; and we sat down, and spake unto the women which resorted thither.

14 ¶ And a certain woman named Lyd′i-a, a seller of purple, of the city of Thy-a-ti′ra, which worshipped God, heard us: whose heart the Lord opened, that she attended unto the things which were spoken of Paul.

15 And when she was baptized, and her household, she besought us, saying, If ye have judged me to be faithful to the Lord, come into my house, and abide there. And she constrained us.

16 ¶ And it came to pass, as we went to prayer, a certain damsel possessed with a spirit of divination met us, which brought her masters much gain by soothsaying:

17 The same followed Paul and us, and cried, saying, These men are the servants of the most high God, which shew unto us the way of salvation.

18 And this did she many days. But Paul, being grieved, turned and said to the spirit, I command thee in the name of Je′sus Christ to come out of her. And he came out the same hour.

19 ¶ And when her masters saw that the hope of their gains was gone, they caught Paul and Si′las, and drew them into the marketplace unto the rulers,

20 And brought them to the magistrates, saying, These men, being Jews, do exceedingly trouble our city,

21 And teach customs, which are not lawful for us to receive, neither to observe, being Ro′mans.

22 And the multitude rose up together against them: and the magistrates rent off their clothes, and commanded to beat them.

23 And when they had laid many stripes upon them, they cast them into prison, charging the jailor to keep them safely:

24 Who, having received such a charge, thrust them into the inner prison, and made their feet fast in the stocks.

25 ¶ And at midnight Paul and Si′las prayed, and sang praises unto God: and the prisoners heard them.

26 And suddenly there was a great earthquake, so that the foundations of the prison were shaken: and immediately all the doors were opened, and every one's bands were loosed.

27 And the keeper of the prison awaking out of his sleep, and seeing the prison doors open, he drew out his sword, and would have killed himself, supposing that the prisoners had been fled.

28 But Paul cried with a loud voice, saying, Do thyself no harm: for we are all here.

29 Then he called for a light, and sprang in, and came trembling, and fell down before Paul and Si′las,

30 And brought them out, and said, Sirs, what must I do to be saved?

31 And they said, Believe on the Lord Je'sus Christ, and thou shalt be saved, and thy house.

32 And they spake unto him the word of the Lord, and to all that were in his house.

33 And he took them the same hour of the night, and washed *their* stripes; and was baptized, he and all his, straightway.

34 And when he had brought them into his house, he set meat before them, and rejoiced, believing in God with all his house.

35 And when it was day, the magistrates sent the serjeants, saying, Let those men go.

36 And the keeper of the prison told this saying to Paul, The magistrates have sent to let you go: now therefore depart, and go in peace.

37 But Paul said unto them, They have beaten us openly uncondemned, being Ro'mans, and have cast *us* into prison; and now do they thrust us out privily? nay verily; but let them come themselves and fetch us out.

38 And the serjeants told these words unto the magistrates: and they feared, when they heard that they were Ro'mans.

39 And they came and besought them, and brought *them* out, and desired *them* to depart out of the city.

40 And they went out of the prison, and entered into *the house of* Lyd'i-a: and when they had seen the brethren, they comforted them, and departed.

17 NOW when they had passed through Am-phip'o-lis and Ap-ol-lo'ni-a, they came to Thes-sa-lo-ni'ca, where was a synagogue of the Jews:

2 And Paul, as his manner was, went in unto them, and three sabbath days reasoned with them out of the scriptures,

3 Opening and alleging, that Christ must needs have suffered, and risen again from the dead; and that this Je'sus, whom I preach unto you, is Christ.

4 And some of them believed, and consorted with Paul and Si'las; and of the devout Greeks a great multitude, and of the chief women not a few.

5 ¶ But the Jews which believed not, moved with envy, took unto them certain lewd fellows of the baser sort, and gathered a company, and set all the city on an uproar, and assaulted the house of Ja'son, and sought to bring them out to the people.

6 And when they found them not, they drew Ja'son and certain brethren unto the rulers of the city, crying, These that have turned the world upside down are come hither also;

7 Whom Ja'son hath received: and these all do contrary to the decrees of Cæ'sar, saying that there is another king, one Je'sus.

8 And they troubled the people and the rulers of the city, when they heard these things.

9 And when they had taken security of Ja'son, and of the other, they let them go.

10 ¶ And the brethren immediately sent away Paul and Si'las by night unto Be-re'a: who coming *thither* went into the synagogue of the Jews.

11 These were more noble than those in Thes-sa-lo-ni'ca, in that they received the word with all readiness of mind, and searched the scriptures daily, whether those things were so.

12 Therefore many of them believed; also of honourable women which were Greeks, and of men, not a few.

13 But when the Jews of Thes-sa-lo-ni'ca had knowledge that the word of God was preached

of Paul at Be-re'a, they came thither also, and stirred up the people.

14 And then immediately the brethren sent away Paul to go as it were to the sea: but Si'las and Ti-mo'the-us abode there still.

15 And they that conducted Paul brought him unto Ath'ens: and receiving a commandment unto Si'las and Ti-mo'the-us for to come to him with all speed, they departed.

16 ¶ Now while Paul waited for them at Ath'ens, his spirit was stirred in him, when he saw the city wholly given to idolatry.

17 Therefore disputed he in the synagogue with the Jews, and with the devout persons, and in the market daily with them that met with him.

18 Then certain philosophers of the Ep-i-cu-re'ans, and of the Sto'icks, encountered him. And some said, What will this babbler say? other some, He seemeth to be a setter forth of strange gods: because he preached unto them Je'sus, and the resurrection.

19 And they took him, and brought him unto Ar-e-op'a-gus, saying, May we know what this new doctrine, whereof thou speakest, *is?*

20 For thou bringest certain strange things to our ears: we would know therefore what these things mean.

21 (For all the Ath-e'ni-ans and strangers which were there spent their time in nothing else, but either to tell, or to hear some new thing.)

22 ¶ Then Paul stood in the midst of Mars' hill, and said, *Ye* men of Ath'ens, I perceive that in all things ye are too superstitious.

23 For as I passed by, and beheld your devotions, I found an altar with this inscription, TO THE UNKNOWN GOD. Whom therefore ye ignorantly worship, him declare I unto you.

24 God that made the world and all things therein, seeing that he is Lord of heaven and earth, dwelleth not in temples made with hands;

25 Neither is worshipped with men's hands, as though he needed any thing, seeing he giveth to all life and breath, and all things;

26 And hath made of one blood all nations of men for to dwell on all the face of the earth, and hath determined the times before appointed, and the bounds of their habitation;

27 That they should seek the Lord, if haply they might feel after him, and find him, though he be not far from every one of us:

28 For in him we live, and move, and have our being; as certain also of your own poets have said, For we are also his offspring.

29 Forasmuch then as we are the offspring of God, we ought not to think that the Godhead is like unto gold, or silver, or stone, graven by art and man's device.

30 And the times of this ignorance God winked at; but now commandeth all men every where to repent:

31 Because he hath appointed a day, in the which he will judge the world in righteousness by *that* man whom he hath ordained; *whereof* he hath given assurance unto all *men*, in that he hath raised him from the dead.

32 ¶ And when they heard of the resurrection of the dead, some mocked: and others said, We will hear thee again of this *matter*.

33 So Paul departed from among them.

34 Howbeit certain men clave unto him, and believed: among the which *was* Di-o-nys'ius the Ar-e-op'a-gite, and a woman named Dam'a-ris, and others with them.

18 AFTER these things Paul departed from Ath'ens, and came to Cor'inth;

2 And found a certain Jew named A'qui-la, born in Pon'tus, lately come from It'a-ly, with his wife Pris-cil'la; (because that Clau'di-us had commanded all Jews to depart from Rome:) and came unto them.

3 And because he was of the same craft, he abode with them, and wrought: for by their occupation they were tentmakers.

4 And he reasoned in the synagogue every sabbath, and persuaded the Jews and the Greeks.

5 And when Si'las and Ti-mo'the-us were come from Mac-e-do'ni-a, Paul was pressed in the spirit, and testified to the Jews that Je'sus was Christ.

6 And when they opposed themselves, and blasphemed, he shook his raiment, and said unto them, Your blood be upon your own heads; I am clean: from henceforth I will go unto the Gen'tiles.

7 ¶ And he departed thence, and entered into a certain man's house, named Jus'tus, one that worshipped God, whose house joined hard to the synagogue.

8 And Cris'pus, the chief ruler of the synagogue, believed on the Lord with all his house; and many of the Co-rin'thi-ans hearing believed, and were baptized.

9 Then spake the Lord to Paul in the night by a vision, Be not afraid, but speak, and hold not thy peace:

10 For I am with thee, and no man shall set on thee to hurt thee: for I have much people in this city.

11 And he continued there a year and six months, teaching the word of God among them.

12 ¶ And when Gal'li-o was the deputy of A-cha'ia, the Jews made insurrection with one accord against Paul, and brought him to the judgment seat,

13 Saying, This fellow persuadeth men to worship God contrary to the law.

14 And when Paul was now about to open his mouth, Gal'li-o said unto the Jews, If it were a matter of wrong or wicked lewdness, O ye Jews, reason would that I should bear with you:

15 But if it be a question of words and names, and of your law, look ye to it; for I will be no judge of such matters.

16 And he drave them from the judgment seat.

17 Then all the Greeks took Sos'the-nes, the chief ruler of the synagogue, and beat him before the judgment seat. And Gal'li-o cared for none of those things.

18 ¶ And Paul after this tarried there yet a good while, and then took his leave of the brethren, and sailed thence into Syr'i-a, and with him Pris-cil'la and A'qui-la; having shorn his head in Cen'-chre-a: for he had a vow.

19 And he came to Eph'e-sus, and left them there: but he himself entered into the synagogue, and reasoned with the Jews.

20 When they desired him to tarry longer time with them, he consented not;

21 But bade them farewell, saying, I must by all means keep this feast that cometh in Je-ru'-sa-lem: but I will return again unto you, if God will. And he sailed from Eph'e-sus.

22 And when he had landed at Cæs-a-re'a, and gone up, and saluted the church, he went down to An'ti-och.

23 And after he had spent some time there, he departed, and went over all the country of Ga-la'tia and Phryg'i-a in order, strengthening all the disciples.

24 ¶ And a certain Jew named A-pol'los, born at Al-ex-an'dri-a, an eloquent man, and mighty in the scriptures, came to Eph'e-sus.

25 This man was instructed in the way of the Lord; and being fervent in the spirit, he spake and taught diligently the things of the Lord, knowing only the baptism of John.

26 And he began to speak boldly in the synagogue: whom when A'qui-la and Pris-cil'la had heard, they took him unto them, and expounded unto him the way of God more perfectly.

27 And when he was disposed to pass into A-cha'ia, the brethren wrote, exhorting the disciples to receive him: who, when he was come, helped them much which had believed through grace:

28 For he mightily convinced the Jews, and that publickly, shewing by the scriptures that Je'sus was Christ.

19 AND it came to pass, that, while A-pol'-los was at Cor'inth, Paul having passed through the upper coasts came to Eph'e-sus: and finding certain disciples,

2 He said unto them, Have ye received the Ho'ly Ghost since ye believed? And they said unto him, We have not so much as heard whether there be any Ho'ly Ghost.

3 And he said unto them, Unto what then were ye baptized? And they said, Unto John's baptism.

4 Then said Paul, John verily baptized with the baptism of repentance, saying unto the people, that they should believe on him which should come after him, that is, on Christ Je'sus.

5 When they heard this, they were baptized in the name of the Lord Je'sus.

6 And when Paul had laid his hands upon them, the Ho'ly Ghost came on them; and they spake with tongues, and prophesied.

7 And all the men were about twelve.

8 And he went into the synagogue, and spake boldly for the space of three months, disputing and persuading the things concerning the kingdom of God.

9 But when divers were hardened, and believed not, but spake evil of that way before the multitude, he departed from them, and separated the disciples, disputing daily in the school of one Ty-ran'nus.

10 And this continued by the space of two years; so that all they which dwelt in A'sia heard the word of the Lord Je'sus, both Jews and Greeks.

11 And God wrought special miracles by the hands of Paul:

12 So that from his body were brought unto the sick handkerchiefs or aprons, and the diseases departed from them, and the evil spirits went out of them.

13 ¶ Then certain of the vagabond Jews, exorcists, took upon them to call over them which had evil spirits the name of the Lord Je'sus, saying, We adjure you by Je'sus whom Paul preacheth.

14 And there were seven sons of one Sce'va, a Jew, and chief of the priests, which did so.

15 And the evil spirit answered and said, Je'-sus I know, and Paul I know; but who are ye?

16 And the man in whom the evil spirit was leaped on them, and overcame them, and prevailed against them, so that they fled out of that house naked and wounded.

17 And this was known to all the Jews and Greeks also dwelling at Eph'e-sus; and fear fell

on them all, and the name of the Lord Je′sus was magnified.

18 And many that believed came, and confessed, and shewed their deeds.

19 Many of them also which used curious arts brought their books together, and burned them before all *men:* and they counted the price of them, and found *it* fifty thousand *pieces* of silver.

20 So mightily grew the word of God and prevailed.

21 ¶ After these things were ended, Paul purposed in the spirit, when he had passed through Mac-e-do′ni-a and A-cha′ia, to go to Je-ru′sa-lem, saying, After I have been there, I must also see Rome.

22 So he sent into Mac-e-do′ni-a two of them that ministered unto him, Ti-mo′the-us and E-ras′tus; but he himself stayed in A′sia for a season.

23 And the same time there arose no small stir about that way.

24 For a certain *man* named De-me′tri-us, a silversmith, which made silver shrines for Di-an′a, brought no small gain unto the craftsmen;

25 Whom he called together with the workmen of like occupation, and said, Sirs, ye know that by this craft we have our wealth.

26 Moreover ye see and hear, that not alone at Eph′e-sus, but almost throughout all A′sia, this Paul hath persuaded and turned away much people, saying that they be no gods, which are made with hands:

27 So that not only this our craft is in danger to be set at nought; but also that the temple of the great goddess Di-an′a should be despised, and her magnificence should be destroyed, whom all A′sia and the world worshippeth.

28 And when they heard *these sayings,* they were full of wrath, and cried out, saying, Great *is* Di-an′a of the E-phe′sians.

29 And the whole city was filled with confusion: and having caught Ga′ius and Ar-is-tar′-chus, men of Mac-e-do′ni-a, Paul's companions in travel, they rushed with one accord into the theatre.

30 And when Paul would have entered in unto the people, the disciples suffered him not.

31 And certain of the chief of A′sia, which were his friends, sent unto him, desiring *him* that he would not adventure himself into the theatre.

32 Some therefore cried one thing, and some another: for the assembly was confused; and the more part knew not wherefore they were come together.

33 And they drew Al-ex-an′der out of the multitude, the Jews putting him forward. And Al-ex-an′der beckoned with the hand, and would have made his defence unto the people.

34 But when they knew that he was a Jew, all with one voice about the space of two hours cried out, Great *is* Di-an′a of the E-phe′sians.

35 And when the townclerk had appeased the people, he said, Ye men of Eph′e-sus, what man is there that knoweth not how that the city of the E-phe′sians is a worshipper of the great goddess Di-an′a, and of the *image* which fell down from Ju′pi-ter?

36 Seeing then that these things cannot be spoken against, ye ought to be quiet, and to do nothing rashly.

37 For ye have brought hither these men, which are neither robbers of churches, nor yet blasphemers of your goddess.

38 Wherefore if De-me′tri-us, and the craftsmen which are with him, have a matter against any man, the law is open, and there are deputies: let them implead one another.

39 But if ye enquire any thing concerning other matters, it shall be determined in a lawful assembly.

40 For we are in danger to be called in question for this day's uproar, there being no cause whereby we may give an account of this concourse.

41 And when he had thus spoken, he dismissed the assembly.

20 AND after the uproar was ceased, Paul called unto *him* the disciples, and embraced *them,* and departed for to go into Mac-e-do′ni-a.

2 And when he had gone over those parts, and had given them much exhortation, he came into Greece,

3 And *there* abode three months. And when the Jews laid wait for him, as he was about to sail into Syr′i-a, he purposed to return through Mac-e-do′ni-a.

4 And there accompanied him into A′sia Sop′a-ter of Be-re′a; and of the Thes-sa-lo′ni-ans, Ar-is-tar′chus and Se-cun′dus; and Ga′ius of Der′be, and Ti-mo′the-us; and of A′sia, Tych′-i-cus and Troph′i-mus.

5 These going before tarried for us at Tro′as.

6 And we sailed away from Phi-lip′pi after the days of unleavened bread, and came unto them to Tro′as in five days; where we abode seven days.

7 And upon the first *day* of the week, when the disciples came together to break bread, Paul preached unto them, ready to depart on the morrow; and continued his speech until midnight.

8 And there were many lights in the upper chamber, where they were gathered together.

9 And there sat in a window a certain young man named Eu′ty-chus, being fallen into a deep sleep: and as Paul was long preaching, he sunk down with sleep, and fell down from the third loft, and was taken up dead.

10 And Paul went down, and fell on him, and embracing *him* said, Trouble not yourselves; for his life is in him.

11 When he therefore was come up again, and had broken bread, and eaten, and talked a long while, even till break of day, so he departed.

12 And they brought the young man alive, and were not a little comforted.

13 ¶ And we went before to ship, and sailed unto As′sos, there intending to take in Paul: for so had he appointed, minding himself to go afoot.

14 And when he met with us at As′sos, we took him in, and came to Mit-y-le′ne.

15 And we sailed thence, and came the next *day* over against Chi′os: and the next *day* we arrived at Sa′mos, and tarried at Tro-gyl′li-um; and the next *day* we came to Mi-le′tus.

16 For Paul had determined to sail by Eph′e-sus, because he would not spend the time in A′sia: for he hasted, if it were possible for him, to be at Je-ru′sa-lem the day of Pen′te-cost.

17 ¶ And from Mi-le′tus he sent to Eph′e-sus, and called the elders of the church.

18 And when they were come to him, he said unto them, Ye know, from the first day that I came into A′sia, after what manner I have been with you at all seasons,

19 Serving the Lord with all humility of mind, and with many tears, and temptations, which befell me by the lying in wait of the Jews:

20 *And* how I kept back nothing that was profitable *unto you,* but have shewed you, and have taught you publickly, and from house to house,

21 Testifying both to the Jews, and also to the Greeks, repentance toward God, and faith toward our Lord Je′sus Christ.

22 And now, behold, I go bound in the spirit unto Je-ru′sa-lem, not knowing the things that shall befall me there:

23 Save that the Ho′ly Ghost witnesseth in every city, saying that bonds and afflictions abide me.

24 But none of these things move me, neither count I my life dear unto myself, so that I might finish my course with joy, and the ministry, which I have received of the Lord Je′sus, to testify the gospel of the grace of God.

25 And now, behold, I know that ye all, among whom I have gone preaching the kingdom of God, shall see my face no more.

26 Wherefore I take you to record this day, that I *am* pure from the blood of all *men.*

27 For I have not shunned to declare unto you all the counsel of God.

28 ¶ Take heed therefore unto yourselves, and to all the flock, over the which the Ho′ly Ghost hath made you overseers, to feed the church of God, which he hath purchased with his own blood.

29 For I know this, that after my departing shall grievous wolves enter in among you, not sparing the flock.

30 Also of your own selves shall men arise, speaking perverse things, to draw away disciples after them.

31 Therefore watch, and remember, that by the space of three years I ceased not to warn every one night and day with tears.

32 And now, brethren, I commend you to God, and to the word of his grace, which is able to build you up, and to give you an inheritance among all them which are sanctified.

33 I have coveted no man's silver, or gold, or apparel.

34 Yea, ye yourselves know, that these hands have ministered unto my necessities, and to them that were with me.

35 I have shewed you all things, how that so labouring ye ought to support the weak, and to remember the words of the Lord Je′sus, how he said, It is more blessed to give than to receive.

36 ¶ And when he had thus spoken, he kneeled down, and prayed with them all.

37 And they all wept sore, and fell on Paul's neck, and kissed him,

38 Sorrowing most of all for the words which he spake, that they should see his face no more. And they accompanied him unto the ship.

21 AND it came to pass, that after we were gotten from them, and had launched, we came with a straight course unto Co′os, and the *day* following unto Rhodes, and from thence unto Pat′a-ra:

2 And finding a ship sailing over unto Phe-ni′cia, we went aboard, and set forth.

3 Now when we had discovered Cy′prus, we left it on the left hand, and sailed into Syr′i-a, and landed at Tyre: for there the ship was to unlade her burden.

4 And finding disciples, we tarried there seven days: who said to Paul through the Spirit, that he should not go up to Je-ru′sa-lem.

5 And when we had accomplished those days, we departed and went our way; and they all brought us on our way, with wives and chil-

dren, till *we were* out of the city: and we kneeled down on the shore, and prayed.

6 And when we had taken our leave one of another, we took ship; and they returned home again.

7 And when we had finished *our* course from Tyre, we came to Ptol-e-ma′is, and saluted the brethren, and abode with them one day.

8 And the next *day* we that were of Paul's company departed, and came unto Cæs-a-re′a: and we entered into the house of Phil′ip the evangelist, which was *one* of the seven; and abode with him.

9 And the same man had four daughters, virgins, which did prophesy.

10 And as we tarried *there* many days, there came down from Ju-dæ′a a certain prophet, named Ag′a-bus.

11 And when he was come unto us, he took Paul's girdle, and bound his own hands and feet, and said, Thus saith the Ho′ly Ghost, So shall the Jews at Je-ru′sa-lem bind the man that owneth this girdle, and shall deliver *him* into the hands of the Gen′tiles.

12 And when we heard these things, both we, and they of that place, besought him not to go up to Je-ru′sa-lem.

13 Then Paul answered, What mean ye to weep and to break mine heart? for I am ready not to be bound only, but also to die at Je-ru′sa-lem for the name of the Lord Je′sus.

14 And when he would not be persuaded, we ceased, saying, The will of the Lord be done.

15 And after those days we took up our carriages, and went up to Je-ru′sa-lem.

16 There went with us also *certain* of the disciples of Cæs-a-re-a, and brought with them one Mna′son of Cy′prus, an old disciple, with whom we should lodge.

17 And when we were come to Je-ru′sa-lem, the brethren received us gladly.

18 And the *day* following Paul went in with us unto James; and all the elders were present.

19 And when he had saluted them, he declared particularly what things God had wrought among the Gen′tiles by his ministry.

20 And when they heard *it,* they glorified the Lord, and said unto him, Thou seest, brother, how many thousands of Jews there are which believe; and they are all zealous of the law:

21 And they are informed of thee, that thou teachest all the Jews which are among the Gen′tiles to forsake Mo′ses, saying that they ought not to circumcise *their* children, neither to walk after the customs.

22 What is it therefore? the multitude must needs come together: for they will hear that thou art come.

23 Do therefore this that we say to thee: We have four men which have a vow on them;

24 Them take, and purify thyself with them, and be at charges with them, that they may shave *their* heads: and all may know that those things, whereof they were informed concerning thee, are nothing; but *that* thou thyself also walkest orderly, and keepest the law.

25 As touching the Gen′tiles which believe, we have written *and* concluded that they observe no such thing, save only that they keep themselves from *things* offered to idols, and from blood, and from strangled, and from fornication.

26 Then Paul took the men, and the next day purifying himself with them entered into the temple, to signify the accomplishment of the days of purification, until that an offering should be offered for every one of them.

27 And when the seven days were almost ended, the Jews which were of A'sia, when they saw him in the temple, stirred up all the people, and laid hands on him,

28 Crying out, Men of Is'ra-el, help: This is the man, that teacheth all *men* every where against the people, and the law, and this place: and further brought Greeks also into the temple, and hath polluted this holy place.

29 (For they had seen before with him in the city Troph'i-mus an E-phe'sian, whom they supposed that Paul had brought into the temple.)

30 And all the city was moved, and the people ran together: and they took Paul, and drew him out of the temple: and forthwith the doors were shut.

31 And as they went about to kill him, tidings came unto the chief captain of the band, that all Je-ru'sa-lem was in an uproar.

32 Who immediately took soldiers and centurions, and ran down unto them: and when they saw the chief captain and the soldiers, they left beating of Paul.

33 Then the chief captain came near, and took him, and commanded *him* to be bound with two chains; and demanded who he was, and what he had done.

34 And some cried one thing, some another, among the multitude: and when he could not know the certainty for the tumult, he commanded him to be carried into the castle.

35 And when he came upon the stairs, so it was, that he was borne of the soldiers for the violence of the people.

36 For the multitude of the people followed after, crying, Away with him.

37 And as Paul was to be led into the castle, he said unto the chief captain, May I speak unto thee? Who said, Canst thou speak Greek?

38 Art not thou that E-gyp'tian, which before these days madest an uproar, and leddest out into the wilderness four thousand men that were murderers?

39 But Paul said, I am a man *which am* a Jew of Tar'sus, *a city* in Ci-li'cia, a citizen of no mean city: and, I beseech thee, suffer me to speak unto the people.

40 And when he had given him licence, Paul stood on the stairs, and beckoned with the hand unto the people. And when there was made a great silence, he spake unto *them* in the He'-brew tongue, saying,

22 MEN, brethren, and fathers, hear ye my defence *which I make* now unto you.

2 (And when they heard that he spake in the He'brew tongue to them, they kept the more silence: and he saith,)

3 I am verily a man *which am* a Jew, born in Tar'sus, *a city* in Ci-li'cia, yet brought up in this city at the feet of Ga-ma'li-el, *and* taught according to the perfect manner of the law of the fathers, and was zealous toward God, as ye all are this day.

4 And I persecuted this way unto the death, binding and delivering into prisons both men and women.

5 As also the high priest doth bear me witness, and all the estate of the elders: from whom also I received letters unto the brethren, and went to Da-mas'cus, to bring them which were there bound unto Je-ru'sa-lem, for to be punished.

6 And it came to pass, that, as I made my journey, and was come nigh unto Da-mas'cus about noon, suddenly there shone from heaven a great light round about me.

7 And I fell unto the ground, and heard a voice saying unto me, Saul, Saul, why persecutest thou me?

8 And I answered, Who art thou, Lord? And he said unto me, I am Je'sus of Naz'a-reth, whom thou persecutest.

9 And they that were with me saw indeed the light, and were afraid; but they heard not the voice of him that spake to me.

10 And I said, What shall I do, Lord? And the Lord said unto me, Arise, and go into Da-mas'-cus; and there it shall be told thee of all things which are appointed for thee to do.

11 And when I could not see for the glory of that light, being led by the hand of them that were with me, I came into Da-mas'cus.

12 And one An-a-ni'as, a devout man according to the law, having a good report of all the Jews which dwelt *there*,

13 Came unto me, and stood, and said unto me, Brother Saul, receive thy sight. And the same hour I looked up upon him.

14 And he said, The God of our fathers hath chosen thee, that thou shouldest know his will, and see that Just One, and shouldest hear the voice of his mouth.

15 For thou shalt be his witness unto all men of what thou hast seen and heard.

16 And now why tarriest thou? arise, and be baptized, and wash away thy sins, calling on the name of the Lord.

17 And it came to pass, that, when I was come again to Je-ru'sa-lem, even while I prayed in the temple, I was in a trance;

18 And saw him saying unto me, Make haste, and get thee quickly out of Je-ru'sa-lem: for they will not receive thy testimony concerning me.

19 And I said, Lord, they know that I imprisoned and beat in every synagogue them that believed on thee:

20 And when the blood of thy martyr Ste'-phen was shed, I also was standing by, and consenting unto his death, and kept the raiment of them that slew him.

21 And he said unto me, Depart: for I will send thee far hence unto the Gen'tiles.

22 And they gave him audience unto this word, and *then* lifted up their voices, and said, Away with such a *fellow* from the earth: for it is not fit that he should live.

23 And as they cried out, and cast off *their* clothes, and threw dust into the air,

24 The chief captain commanded him to be brought into the castle, and bade that he should be examined by scourging; that he might know wherefore they cried so against him.

25 And as they bound him with thongs, Paul said unto the centurion that stood by, Is it lawful for you to scourge a man that is a Ro'man, and uncondemned?

26 When the centurion heard *that*, he went and told the chief captain, saying, Take heed what thou doest: for this man is a Ro'man.

27 Then the chief captain came, and said unto him, Tell me, art thou a Ro'man? He said, Yea.

28 And the chief captain answered, With a great sum obtained I this freedom. And Paul said, But I was *free* born.

29 Then straightway they departed from him which should have examined him: and the chief captain also was afraid, after he knew that he was a Ro'man, and because he had bound him.

30 On the morrow, because he would have known the certainty wherefore he was accused of the Jews, he loosed him from *his* bands, and

commanded the chief priests and all their council to appear, and brought Paul down, and set him before them.

23 AND Paul, earnestly beholding the council, said, Men *and* brethren, I have lived in all good conscience before God until this day.

2 And the high priest An-a-ni'as commanded them that stood by him to smite him on the mouth.

3 Then said Paul unto him, God shall smite thee, *thou* whited wall: for sittest thou to judge me after the law, and commandest me to be smitten contrary to the law?

4 And they that stood by said, Revilest thou God's high priest?

5 Then said Paul, I wist not, brethren, that he was the high priest: for it is written, Thou shalt not speak evil of the ruler of thy people.

6 But when Paul perceived that the one part were Sad'du-cees, and the other Phar'i-sees, he cried out in the council, Men *and* brethren, I am a Phar'i-see, the son of a Phar'i-see: of the hope and resurrection of the dead I am called in question.

7 And when he had so said, there arose a dissension between the Phar'i-sees and the Sad'du-cees: and the multitude was divided.

8 For the Sad'du-cees say that there is no resurrection, neither angel, nor spirit: but the Phar'i-sees confess both.

9 And there arose a great cry: and the scribes *that were* of the Phar'i-sees' part arose, and strove, saying, We find no evil in this man: but if a spirit or an angel hath spoken to him, let us not fight against God.

10 And when there arose a great dissension, the chief captain, fearing lest Paul should have been pulled in pieces of them, commanded the soldiers to go down, and to take him by force from among them, and to bring *him* into the castle.

11 And the night following the Lord stood by him, and said, Be of good cheer, Paul: for as thou hast testified of me in Je-ru'sa-lem, so must thou bear witness also at Rome.

12 And when it was day, certain of the Jews banded together, and bound themselves under a curse, saying that they would neither eat nor drink till they had killed Paul.

13 And they were more than forty which had made this conspiracy.

14 And they came to the chief priests and elders, and said, We have bound ourselves under a great curse, that we will eat nothing until we have slain Paul.

15 Now therefore ye with the council signify to the chief captain that he bring him down unto you to morrow, as though ye would enquire something more perfectly concerning him: and we, or ever he come near, are ready to kill him.

16 And when Paul's sister's son heard of their lying in wait, he went and entered into the castle, and told Paul.

17 Then Paul called one of the centurions unto *him*, and said, Bring this young man unto the chief captain: for he hath a certain thing to tell him.

18 So he took him, and brought *him* to the chief captain, and said, Paul the prisoner called me unto *him*, and prayed me to bring this young man unto thee, who hath something to say unto thee.

19 Then the chief captain took him by the hand, and went *with him* aside privately, and asked *him*, What is that thou hast to tell me?

20 And he said, The Jews have agreed to desire thee that thou wouldest bring down Paul to morrow into the council, as though they would enquire somewhat of him more perfectly.

21 But do not thou yield unto them: for there lie in wait for him of them more than forty men, which have bound themselves with an oath, that they will neither eat nor drink till they have killed him: and now are they ready, looking for a promise from thee.

22 So the chief captain *then* let the young man depart, and charged *him*, See *thou* tell no man that thou hast shewed these things to me.

23 And he called unto *him* two centurions, saying, Make ready two hundred soldiers to go to Cæs-a-re'a, and horsemen threescore and ten, and spearmen two hundred, at the third hour of the night;

24 And provide *them* beasts, that they may set Paul on, and bring *him* safe unto Fe'lix the governor.

25 And he wrote a letter after this manner:

26 Clau'di-us Lys'ias unto the most excellent governor Fe'lix *sendeth* greeting.

27 This man was taken of the Jews, and should have been killed of them: then came I with an army, and rescued him, having understood that he was a Ro'man.

28 And when I would have known the cause wherefore they accused him, I brought him forth into their council:

29 Whom I perceived to be accused of questions of their law, but to have nothing laid to his charge worthy of death or of bonds.

30 And when it was told me how that the Jews laid wait for the man, I sent straightway to thee, and gave commandment to his accusers also to say before thee what *they had* against him. Farewell.

31 Then the soldiers, as it was commanded them, took Paul, and brought *him* by night to An-tip'a-tris.

32 On the morrow they left the horsemen to go with him, and returned to the castle:

33 Who, when they came to Cæs-a-re'a, and delivered the epistle to the governor, presented Paul also before him.

34 And when the governor had read *the letter*, he asked of what province he was. And when he understood that *he was* of Ci-li'cia;

35 I will hear thee, said he, when thine accusers are also come. And he commanded him to be kept in Her'od's judgment hall.

24 AND after five days An-a-ni'as the high priest descended with the elders, and *with* a certain orator *named* Ter-tul'lus, who informed the governor against Paul.

2 And when he was called forth, Ter-tul'lus began to accuse *him*, saying, Seeing that by thee we enjoy great quietness, and that very worthy deeds are done unto this nation by thy providence,

3 We accept *it* always, and in all places, most noble Fe'lix, with all thankfulness.

4 Notwithstanding, that I be not further tedious unto thee, I pray thee that thou wouldest hear us of thy clemency a few words.

5 For we have found this man *a* pestilent *fellow*, and a mover of sedition among all the Jews throughout the world, and a ringleader of the sect of the Naz'a-renes:

6 Who also hath gone about to profane the temple: whom we took, and would have judged according to our law.

7 But the chief captain Lys'ias came *upon us*,

and with great violence took *him* away out of our hands,

8 Commanding his accusers to come unto thee: by examining of whom thyself mayest take knowledge of all these things, whereof we accuse him.

9 And the Jews also assented, saying that these things were so.

10 Then Paul, after that the governor had beckoned unto him to speak, answered, Forasmuch as I know that thou hast been of many years a judge unto this nation, I do the more cheerfully answer for myself:

11 Because that thou mayest understand, that there are yet but twelve days since I went up to Je-ru′sa-lem for to worship.

12 And they neither found me in the temple disputing with any man, neither raising up the people, neither in the synagogues, nor in the city:

13 Neither can they prove the things whereof they now accuse me.

14 But this I confess unto thee, that after the way which they call heresy, so worship I the God of my fathers, believing all things which are written in the law and in the prophets:

15 And have hope toward God, which they themselves also allow, that there shall be a resurrection of the dead, both of the just and unjust.

16 And herein do I exercise myself, to have always a conscience void of offence toward God, and *toward* men.

17 Now after many years I came to bring alms to my nation, and offerings.

18 Whereupon certain Jews from A′sia found me purified in the temple, neither with multitude, nor with tumult.

19 Who ought to have been here before thee, and object, if they had ought against me.

20 Or else let these same *here* say, if they have found any evil doing in me, while I stood before the council,

21 Except it be for this one voice, that I cried standing among them, Touching the resurrection of the dead I am called in question by you this day.

22 And when Fe′lix heard these things, having more perfect knowledge of *that* way, he deferred them, and said, When Lys′ias the chief captain shall come down, I will know the uttermost of your matter.

23 And he commanded a centurion to keep Paul, and to let *him* have liberty, and that he should forbid none of his acquaintance to minister or come unto him.

24 And after certain days, when Fe′lix came with his wife Dru-sil′la, which was a Jew′ess, he sent for Paul, and heard him concerning the faith in Christ.

25 And as he reasoned of righteousness, temperance, and judgment to come, Fe′lix trembled, and answered, Go thy way for this time; when I have a convenient season, I will call for thee.

26 He hoped also that money should have been given him of Paul, that he might loose him: wherefore he sent for him the oftener, and communed with him.

27 But after two years Por′ci-us Fes′tus came into Fe′lix′ room: and Fe′lix, willing to shew the Jews a pleasure, left Paul bound.

25 NOW when Fes′tus was come into the province, after three days he ascended from Cæs-a-re′a to Je-ru′sa-lem.

2 Then the high priest and the chief of the Jews informed him against Paul, and besought him,

3 And desired favour against him, that he would send for him to Je-ru′sa-lem, laying wait in the way to kill him.

4 But Fes′tus answered, that Paul should be kept at Cæs-a-re′a, and that he himself would depart shortly *thither.*

5 Let them therefore, said he, which among you are able, go down with *me,* and accuse this man, if there be any wickedness in him.

6 And when he had tarried among them more than ten days, he went down unto Cæs-a-re′a; and the next day sitting on the judgment seat commanded Paul to be brought.

7 And when he was come, the Jews which came down from Je-ru′sa-lem stood round about, and laid many and grievous complaints against Paul, which they could not prove.

8 While he answered for himself, Neither against the law of the Jews, neither against the temple, nor yet against Caesar, have I offended any thing at all.

9 But Fes′tus, willing to do the Jews a pleasure, answered Paul, and said, Wilt thou go up to Je-ru′sa-lem, and there be judged of these things before me?

10 Then said Paul, I stand at Cæ′sar's judgment seat, where I ought to be judged: to the Jews have I done no wrong, as thou very well knowest.

11 For if I be an offender, or have committed any thing worthy of death, I refuse not to die: but if there be none of these things whereof these accuse me, no man may deliver me unto them. I appeal unto Cæ′sar.

12 Then Fes′tus, when he had conferred with the council, answered, Hast thou appealed unto Cæ′sar? unto Cæ′sar shalt thou go.

13 And after certain days king A-grip′pa and Ber-ni′ce came unto Cæs-a-re′a to salute Fes′-tus.

14 And when they had been there many days, Fes′tus declared Paul's cause unto the king, saying, There is a certain man left in bonds by Fe′lix:

15 About whom, when I was at Je-ru′sa-lem, the chief priests and the elders of the Jews informed *me,* desiring *to have* judgment against him.

16 To whom I answered, It is not the manner of the Ro′mans to deliver any man to die, before that he which is accused have the accusers face to face, and have licence to answer for himself concerning the crime laid against him.

17 Therefore, when they were come hither, without any delay on the morrow I sat on the judgment seat, and commanded the man to be brought forth.

18 Against whom when the accusers stood up, they brought none accusation of such things as I supposed:

19 But had certain questions against him of their own superstition, and of one Je′sus, which was dead, whom Paul affirmed to be alive.

20 And because I doubted of such manner of questions, I asked *him* whether he would go to Je-ru′sa-lem, and there be judged of these matters.

21 But when Paul had appealed to be reserved unto the hearing of Au-gus′tus, I commanded him to be kept till I might send him to Cæ′sar.

22 Then A-grip′pa said unto Fes′tus, I would also hear the man myself. To morrow, said he, thou shalt hear him.

23 And on the morrow, when A-grip′pa was

come, and Ber-ni'ce, with great pomp, and was entered into the place of hearing, with the chief captains, and principal men of the city, at Fes'-tus' commandment Paul was brought forth.

24 And Fes'tus said, King A-grip'pa, and all men which are here present with us, ye see this man, about whom all the multitude of the Jews have dealt with me, both at Je-ru'sa-lem, and also here, crying that he ought not to live any longer.

25 But when I found that he had committed nothing worthy of death, and that he himself hath appealed to Au-gus'tus, I have determined to send him.

26 Of whom I have no certain thing to write unto my lord. Wherefore I have brought him forth before you, and specially before thee, O king A-grip'pa, that, after examination had, I might have somewhat to write.

27 For it seemeth to me unreasonable to send a prisoner, and not withal to signify the crimes laid against him.

26 THEN A-grip'pa said unto Paul, Thou art permitted to speak for thyself. Then Paul stretched forth the hand, and answered for himself:

2 I think myself happy, king A-grip'pa, because I shall answer for myself this day before thee touching all the things whereof I am accused of the Jews:

3 Especially because I know thee to be expert in all customs and questions which are among the Jews: wherefore I beseech thee to hear me patiently.

4 My manner of life from my youth, which was at the first among mine own nation at Je-ru'sa-lem, know all the Jews;

5 Which knew me from the beginning, if they would testify, that after the most straitest sect of our religion I lived a Phar'i-see.

6 And now I stand and am judged for the hope of the promise made of God unto our fathers:

7 Unto which promise our twelve tribes, instantly serving God day and night, hope to come. For which hope's sake, king A-grip'pa, I am accused of the Jews.

8 Why should it be thought a thing incredible with you, that God should raise the dead?

9 I verily thought with myself, that I ought to do many things contrary to the name of Je'sus of Naz'a-reth.

10 Which thing I also did in Je-ru'sa-lem: and many of the saints did I shut up in prison, having received authority from the chief priests; and when they were put to death, I gave my voice against them.

11 And I punished them oft in every synagogue, and compelled them to blaspheme; and being exceedingly mad against them, I persecuted them even unto strange cities.

12 Whereupon as I went to Da-mas'cus with authority and commission from the chief priests,

13 At midday, O king, I saw in the way a light from heaven, above the brightness of the sun, shining round about me and them which journeyed with me.

14 And when we were all fallen to the earth, I heard a voice speaking unto me, and saying in the He'brew tongue, Saul, Saul, why persecutest thou me? it is hard for thee to kick against the pricks.

15 And I said, Who art thou, Lord? And he said, I am Je'sus whom thou persecutest.

16 But rise, and stand upon thy feet: for I

have appeared unto thee for this purpose, to make thee a minister and a witness both of these things which thou hast seen, and of those things in the which I will appear unto thee;

17 Delivering thee from the people, and from the Gen'tiles, unto whom now I send thee,

18 To open their eyes, and to turn them from darkness to light, and from the power of Sa'tan unto God, that they may receive forgiveness of sins, and inheritance among them which are sanctified by faith that is in me.

19 Whereupon, O king A-grip'pa, I was not disobedient unto the heavenly vision:

20 But shewed first unto them of Da-mas'-cus, and at Je-ru'sa-lem, and throughout all the coasts of Ju-dæ'a, and then to the Gen'tiles, that they should repent and turn to God, and do works meet for repentance.

21 For these causes the Jews caught me in the temple, and went about to kill me.

22 Having therefore obtained help of God, I continue unto this day, witnessing both to small and great, saying none other things than those which the prophets and Mo'ses did say should come:

23 That Christ should suffer, and that he should be the first that should rise from the dead, and should shew light unto the people, and to the Gen'tiles.

24 And as he thus spake for himself, Fes'tus said with a loud voice, Paul thou art beside thyself; much learning doth make thee mad.

25 But he said, I am not mad, most noble Fes'tus; but speak forth the words of truth and soberness.

26 For the king knoweth of these things, before whom also I speak freely: for I am persuaded that none of these things are hidden from him; for this thing was not done in a corner.

27 King A-grip'pa, believest thou the prophets? I know that thou believest.

28 Then A-grip'pa said unto Paul, Almost thou persuadest me to be a Chris'tian.

29 And Paul said, I would to God, that not only thou, but also all that hear me this day, were both almost, and altogether such as I am, except these bonds.

30 And when he had thus spoken, the king rose up, and the governor, and Ber-ni'ce, and they that sat with them:

31 And when they were gone aside, they talked between themselves, saying, This man doeth nothing worthy of death or of bonds.

32 Then said A-grip'pa unto Fes'tus, This man might have been set at liberty, if he had not appealed unto Cæ'sar.

27 AND when it was determined that we should sail into It'a-ly, they delivered Paul and certain other prisoners unto one named Ju'li-us, a centurion of Au-gus'tus' band.

2 And entering into a ship of Ad-ra-myt'ti-um, we launched, meaning to sail by the coasts of A'si-a; one Ar-is-tar'chus, a Mac-e-do'ni-an of Thes-sa-lo-ni'ca, being with us.

3 And the next day we touched at Si'don. And Ju'li-us courteously entreated Paul, and gave him liberty to go unto his friends to refresh himself.

4 And when we had launched from thence, we sailed under Cy'prus, because the winds were contrary.

5 And when we had sailed over the sea of Ci-li'ci-a and Pam-phyl'i-a, we came to My'ra, a city of Ly'ci-a.

6 And there the centurion found a ship of Al-

ex-an'dri-a sailing into It'a-ly; and he put us therein.

7 And when we had sailed slowly many days, and scarce were come over against Cni'dus, the wind not suffering us, we sailed under Crete, over against Sal-mo'ne;

8 And, hardly passing it, came unto a place which is called The fair havens; nigh whereunto was the city of La-se'a.

9 Now when much time was spent, and when sailing was now dangerous, because the fast was now already past, Paul admonished them,

10 And said unto them, Sirs, I perceive that this voyage will be with hurt and much damage, not only of the lading and ship, but also of our lives.

11 Nevertheless the centurion believed the master and the owner of the ship, more than those things which were spoken by Paul.

12 And because the haven was not commodious to winter in, the more part advised to depart thence also, if by any means they might attain to Phe-ni'ce, and there to winter; which is an haven of Crete, and lieth toward the south west and north west.

13 And when the south wind blew softly, supposing that they had obtained their purpose, loosing thence, they sailed close by Crete.

14 But not long after there arose against it a tempestuous wind, called Eu-roc'ly-don.

15 And when the ship was caught, and could not bear up into the wind, we let her drive.

16 And running under a certain island which is called Clau'da, we had much work to come by the boat:

17 Which when they had taken up, they used helps, undergirding the ship; and, fearing lest they should fall into the quicksands, strake sail, and so were driven.

18 And we being exceedingly tossed with a tempest, the next day they lightened the ship;

19 And the third day we cast out with our own hands the tackling of the ship.

20 And when neither sun nor stars in many days appeared, and no small tempest lay on us, all hope that we should be saved was then taken away.

21 But after long abstinence Paul stood forth in the midst of them, and said, Sirs, ye should have hearkened unto me, and not have loosed from Crete, and to have gained this harm and loss.

22 And now I exhort you to be of good cheer: for there shall be no loss of any man's life among you, but of the ship.

23 For there stood by me this night the angel of God, whose I am, and whom I serve,

24 Saying, Fear not, Paul; thou must be brought before Cæ'sar: and, lo, God hath given thee all them that sail with thee.

25 Wherefore, sirs, be of good cheer: for I believe God, that it shall be even as it was told me.

26 Howbeit we must be cast upon a certain island.

27 But when the fourteenth night was come, as we were driven up and down in A'dri-a, about midnight the shipmen deemed that they drew near to some country;

28 And sounded, and found it twenty fathoms: and when they had gone a little further, they sounded again, and found it fifteen fathoms.

29 Then fearing lest we should have fallen upon rocks, they cast four anchors out of the stern, and wished for the day.

30 And as the shipmen were about to flee out of the ship, when they had let down the boat

into the sea, under colour as though they would have cast anchors out of the foreship,

31 Paul said to the centurion and to the soldiers, Except these abide in the ship, ye cannot be saved.

32 Then the soldiers cut off the ropes of the boat, and let her fall off.

33 And while the day was coming on, Paul besought them all to take meat, saying, This day is the fourteenth day that ye have tarried and continued fasting, having taken nothing.

34 Wherefore I pray you to take some meat: for this is for your health: for there shall not an hair fall from the head of any of you.

35 And when he had thus spoken, he took bread, and gave thanks to God in presence of them all: and when he had broken it, he began to eat.

36 Then were they all of good cheer, and they also took some meat.

37 And we were in all in the ship two hundred threescore and sixteen souls.

38 And when they had eaten enough, they lightened the ship, and cast out the wheat into the sea.

39 And when it was day, they knew not the land: but they discovered a certain creek with a shore, into the which they were minded, if it were possible, to thrust in the ship.

40 And when they had taken up the anchors, they committed themselves unto the sea, and loosed the rudder bands, and hoised up the mainsail to the wind, and made toward shore.

41 And falling into a place where two seas met, they ran the ship aground; and the forepart stuck fast, and remained unmoveable, but the hinder part was broken with the violence of the waves.

42 And the soldiers' counsel was to kill the prisoners, lest any of them should swim out, and escape.

43 But the centurion, willing to save Paul, kept them from their purpose; and commanded that they which could swim should cast themselves first into the sea, and get to land:

44 And the rest, some on boards, and some on broken pieces of the ship. And so it came to pass, that they escaped all safe to land.

28 AND when they were escaped, then they knew that the island was called Mel'i-ta.

2 And the barbarous people shewed us no little kindness: for they kindled a fire, and received us every one, because of the present rain, and because of the cold.

3 And when Paul had gathered a bundle of sticks, and laid them on the fire, there came a viper out of the heat, and fastened on his hand.

4 And when the barbarians saw the venomous beast hang on his hand, they said among themselves, No doubt this man is a murderer, whom, though he hath escaped the sea, yet vengeance suffereth not to live.

5 And he shook off the beast into the fire, and felt no harm.

6 Howbeit they looked when he should have swollen, or fallen down dead suddenly: but after they had looked a great while, and saw no harm come to him, they changed their minds, and said that he was a god.

7 In the same quarters were possessions of the chief man of the island, whose name was Pub'li-us; who received us, and lodged us three days courteously.

8 And it came to pass, that the father of Pub'-li-us lay sick of a fever and of a bloody flux: to

whom Paul entered in, and prayed, and laid his hands on him, and healed him.

9 So when this was done, others also, which had diseases in the island, came, and were healed:

10 Who also honoured us with many honours; and when we departed, they laded us with such things as were necessary.

11 And after three months we departed in a ship of Al-ex-an′dri-a, which had wintered in the isle, whose sign was Cas′tor and Pol′lux.

12 And landing at Syr′a-cuse, we tarried there three days.

13 And from thence we fetched a compass, and came to Rhe′gi-um: and after one day the south wind blew, and we came the next day to Pu-te′o-li:

14 Where we found brethren, and were desired to tarry with them seven days: and so we went toward Rome.

15 And from thence, when the brethren heard of us, they came to meet us as far as Ap′-pi-i forum, and The three taverns: whom when Paul saw, he thanked God, and took courage.

16 And when we came to Rome, the centurion delivered the prisoners to the captain of the guard: but Paul was suffered to dwell by himself with a soldier that kept him.

17 And it came to pass, that after three days Paul called the chief of the Jews together: and when they were come together, he said unto them, Men and brethren, though I have committed nothing against the people, or customs of our fathers, yet was I delivered prisoner from Je-ru′sa-lem into the hands of the Ro′mans.

18 Who, when they had examined me, would have let me go, because there was no cause of death in me.

19 But when the Jews spake against it, I constrained to appeal unto Cæ′sar; not that I had ought to accuse my nation of.

20 For this cause therefore have I called for you, to see you, and to speak with you: because that for the hope of Is′ra-el I am bound with this chain.

21 And they said unto him, We neither received letters out of Ju-dæ′a concerning thee, neither any of the brethren that came shewed or spake any harm of thee.

22 But we desire to hear of thee what thou thinkest: for as concerning this sect, we know that every where it is spoken against.

23 And when they had appointed him a day, there came many to him into his lodging; to whom he expounded and testified the kingdom of God, persuading them concerning Je′sus, both out of the law of Mo′ses, and out of the prophets, from morning till evening.

24 And some believed the things which were spoken, and some believed not.

25 And when they agreed not among themselves, they departed, after that Paul had spoken one word, Well spake the Ho′ly Ghost by E-sa′ias the prophet unto our fathers,

26 Saying, Go unto this people, and say, Hearing ye shall hear, and shall not understand; and seeing ye shall see, and not perceive:

27 For the heart of this people is waxed gross, and their ears are dull of hearing, and their eyes have they closed; lest they should see with their eyes, and hear with their ears, and understand with their heart, and should be converted, and I should heal them.

28 Be it known therefore unto you, that the salvation of God is sent unto the Gen′tiles, and that they will hear it.

29 And when he had said these words, the Jews departed, and had great reasoning among themselves.

30 And Paul dwelt two whole years in his own hired house, and received all that came in unto him,

31 Preaching the kingdom of God, and teaching those things which concern the Lord Je′sus Christ, with all confidence, no man forbidding him.

THE LETTER OF PAUL TO THE

ROMANS

1 PAUL, a servant of Je′sus Christ, called to be an apostle, separated unto the gospel of God,

2 (Which he had promised afore by his prophets in the holy scriptures,)

3 Concerning his Son Je′sus Christ our Lord, which was made of the seed of Da′vid according to the flesh;

4 And declared to be the Son of God with power, according to the spirit of holiness, by the resurrection from the dead:

5 By whom we have received grace and apostleship, for obedience to the faith among all nations, for his name:

6 Among whom are ye also the called of Je′-sus Christ:

7 To all that be in Rome, beloved of God, called to be saints: Grace to you and peace from God our Father, and the Lord Je′sus Christ.

8 First, I thank my God through Je′sus Christ for you all, that your faith is spoken of throughout the whole world.

9 For God is my witness, whom I serve with my spirit in the gospel of his Son, that without ceasing I make mention of you always in my prayers;

10 Making request, if by any means now at length I might have a prosperous journey by the will of God to come unto you.

11 For I long to see you, that I may impart unto you some spiritual gift, to the end ye may be established;

12 That is, that I may be comforted together with you by the mutual faith both of you and me.

13 Now I would not have you ignorant, brethren, that oftentimes I purposed to come unto you, (but was let hitherto,) that I might have some fruit among you also, even as among other Gen′tiles.

14 I am debtor both to the Greeks, and to the Bar-ba′ri-ans; both to the wise, and to the unwise.

15 So, as much as in me is, I am ready to preach the gospel to you that are at Rome also.

16 For I am not ashamed of the gospel of Christ: for it is the power of God unto salvation to every one that believeth; to the Jew first, and also to the Greek.

17 For therein is the righteousness of God revealed from faith to faith: as it is written, The just shall live by faith.

18 For the wrath of God is revealed from

heaven against all ungodliness and unrighteousness of men, who hold the truth in unrighteousness;

19 Because that which may be known of God is manifest in them; for God hath shewed *it* unto them.

20 For the invisible things of him from the creation of the world are clearly seen, being understood by the things that are made, *even* his eternal power and Godhead; so that they are without excuse:

21 Because that, when they knew God, they glorified *him* not as God, neither were thankful; but became vain in their imaginations, and their foolish heart was darkened.

22 Professing themselves to be wise, they became fools,

23 And changed the glory of the uncorruptible God into an image made like to corruptible man, and to birds, and fourfooted beasts, and creeping things.

24 Wherefore God also gave them up to uncleanness through the lusts of their own hearts, to dishonour their own bodies between themselves:

25 Who changed the truth of God into a lie, and worshipped and served the creature more than the Creator, who is blessed for ever. Amen.

26 For this cause God gave them up into vile affections: for even their women did change the natural use into that which is against nature:

27 And likewise also the men, leaving the natural use of the woman, burned in their lust one toward another; men with men working that which is unseemly, and receiving in themselves that recompence of their error which was meet.

28 And even as they did not like to retain God in *their* knowledge, God gave them over to a reprobate mind, to do those things which are not convenient;

29 Being filled with all unrighteousness, fornication, wickedness, covetousness, maliciousness; full of envy, murder, debate, deceit, malignity; whisperers,

30 Backbiters, haters of God, despiteful, proud, boasters, inventors of evil things, disobedient to parents,

31 Without understanding, covenantbreakers, without natural affection, implacable, unmerciful:

32 Who knowing the judgment of God, that they which commit such things are worthy of death, not only do the same, but have pleasure in them that do them.

2 THEREFORE thou art inexcusable, O man, whosoever thou art that judgest: for wherein thou judgest another, thou condemnest thyself; for thou that judgest doest the same things.

2 But we are sure that the judgment of God is according to truth against them which commit such things.

3 And thinkest thou this, O man, that judgest them which do such things, and doest the same, that thou shalt escape the judgment of God?

4 Or despisest thou the riches of his goodness and forbearance and longsuffering; not knowing that the goodness of God leadeth thee to repentance?

5 But after thy hardness and impenitent heart treasurest up unto thyself wrath against the day of wrath and revelation of the righteous judgment of God;

6 Who will render to every man according to his deeds:

7 To them who by patient continuance in well doing seek for glory and honour and immortality, eternal life:

8 But unto them that are contentious, and do not obey the truth, but obey unrighteousness, indignation and wrath,

9 Tribulation and anguish, upon every soul of man that doeth evil, of the Jew first, and also of the Gen'tile;

10 But glory, honour, and peace, to every man that worketh good, to the Jew first, and also to the Gentile:

11 For there is no respect of persons with God.

12 For as many as have sinned without law shall also perish without law: and as many as have sinned in the law shall be judged by the law;

13 (For not the hearers of the law *are* just before God, but the doers of the law shall be justified.

14 For when the Gen'tiles, which have not the law, do by nature the things contained in the law, these, having not the law, are a law unto themselves:

15 Which shew the work of the law written in their hearts, their conscience also bearing witness, and *their* thoughts the mean while accusing or else excusing one another;)

16 In the day when God shall judge the secrets of men by Je'sus Christ according to my gospel.

17 Behold, thou art called a Jew, and restest in the law, and makest thy boast of God,

18 And knowest *his* will, and approvest the things that are more excellent, being instructed out of the law;

19 And art confident that thou thyself art a guide of the blind, a light of them which are in darkness,

20 An instructor of the foolish, a teacher of babes, which hast the form of knowledge and of the truth in the law.

21 Thou therefore which teachest another, teachest thou not thyself? thou that preachest a man should not steal, dost thou steal?

22 Thou that sayest a man should not commit adultery, dost thou commit adultery? thou that abhorrest idols, dost thou commit sacrilege?

23 Thou that makest thy boast of the law, through breaking the law dishonourest thou God?

24 For the name of God is blasphemed among the Gen'tiles through you, as it is written.

25 For circumcision verily profiteth, if thou keep the law: but if thou be a breaker of the law, thy circumcision is made uncircumcision.

26 Therefore if the uncircumcision keep the righteousness of the law, shall not his uncircumcision be counted for circumcision?

27 And shall not uncircumcision which is by nature, if it fulfil the law, judge thee, who by the letter and circumcision dost transgress the law?

28 For he is not a Jew, which is one outwardly; neither *is that* circumcision, which is outward in the flesh:

29 But he *is* a Jew, which is one inwardly; and circumcision *is that* of the heart, in the spirit, *and* not in the letter; whose praise *is* not of men, but of God.

3 WHAT advantage then hath the Jew? or what profit *is there* of circumcision?

2 Much every way: chiefly, because that unto them were committed the oracles of God.

3 For what if some did not believe? shall their unbelief make the faith of God without effect?

4 God forbid: yea, let God be true, but every man a liar; as it is written, That thou mightest be justified in thy sayings, and mightest overcome when thou art judged.

5 But if our unrighteousness commend the righteousness of God, what shall we say? *Is* God unrighteous who taketh vengeance? (I speak as a man)

6 God forbid: for then how shall God judge the world?

7 For if the truth of God hath more abounded through my lie unto his glory; why yet am I also judged as a sinner?

8 And not *rather*, (as we be slanderously reported, and as some affirm that we say,) Let us do evil, that good may come? whose damnation is just.

9 What then? are we better *than they?* No, in no wise: for we have before proved both Jews and Gen'tiles, that they are all under sin;

10 As it is written, There is none righteous, no, not one:

11 There is none that understandeth, there is none that seeketh after God.

12 They are all gone out of the way, they are together become unprofitable: there is none that doeth good, no, not one.

13 Their throat *is* an open sepulchre; with their tongues they have used deceit; the poison of asps *is* under their lips:

14 Whose mouth *is* full of cursing and bitterness:

15 Their feet *are* swift to shed blood:

16 Destruction and misery *are* in their ways:

17 And the way of peace have they not known:

18 There is no fear of God before their eyes.

19 Now we know that what things soever the law saith, it saith to them who are under the law: that every mouth may be stopped, and all the world may become guilty before God.

20 Therefore by the deeds of the law there shall no flesh be justified in his sight: for by the law *is* the knowledge of sin.

21 But now the righteousness of God without the law is manifested, being witnessed by the law and the prophets;

22 Even the righteousness of God *which is* by faith of Je'sus Christ unto all and upon all them that believe: for there is no difference:

23 For all have sinned, and come short of the glory of God;

24 Being justified freely by his grace through the redemption that is in Christ Je'sus:

25 Whom God hath set forth *to be* a propitiation through faith in his blood, to declare his righteousness for the remission of sins that are past, through the forbearance of God;

26 To declare, *I say*, at this time his righteousness: that he might be just, and the justifier of him which believeth in Je'sus.

27 Where *is* boasting then? It is excluded. By what law? of works? Nay: but by the law of faith.

28 Therefore we conclude that a man is justified by faith without the deeds of the law.

29 *Is he* the God of the Jews only? *is he* not also of the Gen'tiles? Yes, of the Gen'tiles also:

30 Seeing *it is* one God, which shall justify the circumcision by faith, and uncircumcision through faith.

31 Do we then make void the law through faith? God forbid: yea, we establish the law.

4 WHAT shall we say then that A'bra-ham our father, as pertaining to the flesh, hath found?

2 For if A'bra-ham were justified by works, he hath *whereof* to glory; but not before God.

3 For what saith the scripture? A'bra-ham believed God, and it was counted unto him for righteousness.

4 Now to him that worketh is the reward not reckoned of grace, but of debt.

5 But to him that worketh not, but believeth on him that justifieth the ungodly, his faith is counted for righteousness.

6 Even as Da'vid also describeth the blessedness of the man, unto whom God imputeth righteousness without works,

7 *Saying,* Blessed *are* they whose iniquities are forgiven, and whose sins are covered.

8 Blessed *is* the man to whom the Lord will not impute sin.

9 *Cometh* this blessedness then upon the circumcision *only,* or upon the uncircumcision also? for we say that faith was reckoned to A'bra-ham for righteousness.

10 How was it then reckoned? when he was in circumcision, or in uncircumcision? Not in circumcision, but in uncircumcision.

11 And he received the sign of circumcision, a seal of the righteousness of faith which *he had yet* being uncircumcised: that he might be the father of all them that believe, though they be not circumcised; that righteousness might be imputed unto them also:

12 And the father of circumcision to them who are not of the circumcision only, but who also walk in the steps of that faith of our father A'bra-ham, which *he had* being *yet* uncircumcised.

13 For the promise, that he should be the heir of the world, *was* not to A'bra-ham, or to his seed, through the law, but through the righteousness of faith.

14 For if they which are of the law *be* heirs, faith is made void, and the promise of none effect:

15 Because the law worketh wrath: for where no law is, *there is* no transgression.

16 Therefore *it is* of faith, that *it might be* by grace; to the end the promise might be sure to all the seed; not to that only which is of the law, but to that also which is of the faith of A'bra-ham; who is the father of us all,

17 (As it is written, I have made thee a father of many nations,) before him whom he believed, *even* God, who quickeneth the dead, and calleth those things which be not as though they were.

18 Who against hope believed in hope, that he might become the father of many nations, according to that which was spoken, So shall thy seed be.

19 And being not weak in faith, he considered not his own body now dead, when he was about an hundred years old, neither yet the deadness of Sa'-rah's womb:

20 He staggered not at the promise of God through unbelief; but was strong in faith, giving glory to God;

21 And being fully persuaded that, what he had promised, he was able also to perform.

22 And therefore it was imputed to him for righteousness.

23 Now it was not written for his sake alone, that it was imputed to him;

24 But for us also, to whom it shall be imputed, if we believe on him that raised up Je'sus our Lord from the dead;

25 Who was delivered for our offences, and was raised again for our justification.

5 THEREFORE being justified by faith, we have peace with God through our Lord Je'sus Christ:

2 By whom also we have access by faith into this grace wherein we stand, and rejoice in hope of the glory of God.

3 And not only so, but we glory in tribulations also: knowing that tribulation worketh patience;

4 And patience, experience; and experience, hope:

5 And hope maketh not ashamed; because the love of God is shed abroad in our hearts by the Ho'ly Ghost which is given unto us.

6 For when we were yet without strength, in due time Christ died for the ungodly.

7 For scarcely for a righteous man will one die: yet peradventure for a good man some would even dare to die.

8 But God commendeth his love toward us, in that, while we were yet sinners, Christ died for us.

9 Much more then, being now justified by his blood, we shall be saved from wrath through him.

10 For if, when we were enemies, we were reconciled to God by the death of his Son, much more, being reconciled, we shall be saved by his life.

11 And not only so, but we also joy in God through our Lord Je'sus Christ, by whom we have now received the atonement.

12 Wherefore, as by one man sin entered into the world, and death by sin; and so death passed upon all men, for that all have sinned:

13 (For until the law sin was in the world: but sin is not imputed when there is no law.

14 Nevertheless death reigned from Ad'am to Mo'ses, even over them that had not sinned after the similitude of Ad'am's transgression, who is the figure of him that was to come.

15 But not as the offence, so also is the free gift. For if through the offence of one many be dead, much more the grace of God, and the gift by grace, which is by one man, Je'sus Christ, hath abounded unto many.

16 And not as it was by one that sinned, so is the gift: for the judgment was by one to condemnation, but the free gift is of many offences unto justification.

17 For if by one man's offence death reigned by one; much more they which receive abundance of grace and of the gift of righteousness shall reign in life by one, Je'sus Christ.)

18 Therefore as by the offence of one judgment came upon all men to condemnation; even so by the righteousness of one the free gift came upon all men unto justification of life.

19 For as by one man's disobedience many were made sinners, so by the obedience of one shall many be made righteous.

20 Moreover the law entered, that the offence might abound. But where sin abounded, grace did much more abound:

21 That as sin hath reigned unto death, even so might grace reign through righteousness unto eternal life by Je'sus Christ our Lord.

6 WHAT shall we say then? Shall we continue in sin, that grace may abound?

2 God forbid. How shall we, that are dead to sin, live any longer therein?

3 Know ye not, that so many of us as were baptized into Je'sus Christ were baptized into his death?

4 Therefore we are buried with him by baptism into death: that like as Christ was raised up from the dead by the glory of the Father, even so we also should walk in newness of life.

5 For if we have been planted together in the likeness of his death, we shall be also in the likeness of his resurrection:

6 Knowing this, that our old man is crucified with him, that the body of sin might be destroyed, that henceforth we should not serve sin.

7 For he that is dead is freed from sin.

8 Now if we be dead with Christ, we believe that we shall also live with him:

9 Knowing that Christ being raised from the dead dieth no more; death hath no more dominion over him.

10 For in that he died, he died unto sin once: but in that he liveth, he liveth unto God.

11 Likewise reckon ye also yourselves to be dead indeed unto sin, but alive unto God through Je'sus Christ our Lord.

12 Let not sin therefore reign in your mortal body, that ye should obey it in the lusts thereof.

13 Neither yield ye your members as instruments of unrighteousness unto sin: but yield yourselves unto God, as those that are alive from the dead, and your members as instruments of righteousness unto God.

14 For sin shall not have dominion over you: for ye are not under the law, but under grace.

15 What then? shall we sin, because we are not under the law, but under grace? God forbid.

16 Know ye not, that to whom ye yield yourselves servants to obey, his servants ye are to whom ye obey; whether of sin unto death, or of obedience unto righteousness?

17 But God be thanked, that ye were the servants of sin, but ye have obeyed from the heart that form of doctrine which was delivered you.

18 Being then made free from sin, ye became the servants of righteousness.

19 I speak after the manner of men because of the infirmity of your flesh: for as ye have yielded your members servants to uncleanness and to iniquity unto iniquity; even so now yield your members servants to righteousness unto holiness.

20 For when ye were the servants of sin, ye were free from righteousness.

21 What fruit had ye then in those things whereof ye are now ashamed? for the end of those things is death.

22 But now being made free from sin, and become servants to God, ye have your fruit unto holiness, and the end everlasting life.

23 For the wages of sin is death; but the gift of God is eternal life through Je'sus Christ our Lord.

7 KNOW ye not, brethren, (for I speak to them that know the law,) how that the law hath dominion over a man as long as he liveth?

2 For the woman which hath an husband is bound by the law to her husband so long as he liveth; but if the husband be dead, she is loosed from the law of her husband.

3 So then if, while her husband liveth, she be married to another man, she shall be called an adulteress: but if her husband be dead, she is free from that law; so that she is no adulteress, though she be married to another man.

4 Wherefore, my brethren, ye also are become dead to the law by the body of Christ; that ye should be married to another, even to him who is raised from the dead, that we should bring forth fruit unto God.

5 For when we were in the flesh, the motions of sins, which were by the law, did work in our members to bring forth fruit unto death.

6 But now we are delivered from the law, that being dead wherein we were held; that we should serve in newness of spirit, and not in the oldness of the letter.

7 What shall we say then? Is the law sin? God forbid. Nay, I had not known sin, but by the law: for I had not known lust, except the law had said, Thou shalt not covet.

8 But sin, taking occasion by the commandment, wrought in me all manner of concupiscence. For without the law sin was dead.

9 For I was alive without the law once: but when the commandment came, sin revived, and I died.

10 And the commandment, which was ordained to life, I found to be unto death.

11 For sin, taking occasion by the commandment, deceived me, and by it slew me.

12 Wherefore the law is holy, and the commandment holy, and just, and good.

13 Was then that which is good made death unto me? God forbid. But sin, that it might appear sin, working death in me by that which is good; that sin by the commandment might become exceeding sinful.

14 For we know that the law is spiritual: but I am carnal, sold under sin.

15 For that which I do I allow not: for what I would, that do I not; but what I hate, that do I.

16 If then I do that which I would not, I consent unto the law that it is good.

17 Now then it is no more I that do it, but sin that dwelleth in me.

18 For I know that in me (that is, in my flesh,) dwelleth no good thing: for to will is present with me; but how to perform that which is good I find not.

19 For the good that I would I do not: but the evil which I would not, that I do.

20 Now if I do that I would not, it is no more I that do it, but sin that dwelleth in me.

21 I find then a law, that, when I would do good, evil is present with me.

22 For I delight in the law of God after the inward man:

23 But I see another law in my members, warring against the law of my mind, and bringing me into captivity to the law of sin which is in my members.

24 O wretched man that I am! who shall deliver me from the body of this death?

25 I thank God through Je'sus Christ our Lord. So then with the mind I myself serve the law of God; but with the flesh the law of sin.

8 THERE is therefore now no condemnation to them which are in Christ Je'sus, who walk not after the flesh, but after the Spirit.

2 For the law of the Spirit of life in Christ Je'sus hath made me free from the law of sin and death.

3 For what the law could not do, in that it was weak through the flesh, God sending his own Son in the likeness of sinful flesh, and for sin, condemned sin in the flesh:

4 That the righteousness of the law might be fulfilled in us, who walk not after the flesh, but after the Spirit.

5 For they that are after the flesh do mind the things of the flesh; but they that are after the Spirit the things of the Spirit.

6 For to be carnally minded is death; but to be spiritually minded is life and peace.

7 Because the carnal mind is enmity against God: for it is not subject to the law of God, neither indeed can be.

8 So then they that are in the flesh cannot please God.

9 But ye are not in the flesh, but in the Spirit, if so be that the Spirit of God dwell in you. Now if any man have not the Spirit of Christ, he is none of his.

10 And if Christ be in you, the body is dead because of sin; but the Spirit is life because of righteousness.

11 But if the Spirit of him that raised up Je'sus from the dead dwell in you, he that raised up Christ from the dead shall also quicken your mortal bodies by his Spirit that dwelleth in you.

12 Therefore, brethren, we are debtors, not to the flesh, to live after the flesh.

13 For if ye live after the flesh, ye shall die: but if ye through the Spirit do mortify the deeds of the body, ye shall live.

14 For as many as are led by the Spirit of God, they are the sons of God.

15 For ye have not received the spirit of bondage again to fear; but ye have received the Spirit of adoption, whereby we cry, Ab'ba, Father.

16 The Spirit itself beareth witness with our spirit, that we are the children of God:

17 And if children, then heirs; heirs of God, and joint-heirs with Christ; if so be that we suffer with him, that we may be also glorified together.

18 For I reckon that the sufferings of this present time are not worthy to be compared with the glory which shall be revealed in us.

19 For the earnest expectation of the creature waiteth for the manifestation of the sons of God.

20 For the creature was made subject to vanity, not willingly, but by reason of him who hath subjected the same in hope,

21 Because the creature itself also shall be delivered from the bondage of corruption into the glorious liberty of the children of God.

22 For we know that the whole creation groaneth and travaileth in pain together until now.

23 And not only they, but ourselves also, which have the firstfruits of the Spirit, even we ourselves groan within ourselves, waiting for the adoption, to wit, the redemption of our body.

24 For we are saved by hope: but hope that is seen is not hope: for what a man seeth, why doth he yet hope for?

25 But if we hope for that we see not, then do we with patience wait for it.

26 Likewise the Spirit also helpeth our infirmities: for we know not what we should pray for as we ought: but the Spirit itself maketh intercession for us with groanings which cannot be uttered.

27 And he that searcheth the hearts knoweth what is the mind of the Spirit, because he maketh intercession for the saints according to the will of God.

28 And we know that all things work together for good to them that love God, to them who are the called according to his purpose.

29 For whom he did foreknow, he also did predestinate to be conformed to the image of

his Son, that he might be the firstborn among many brethren.

30 Moreover whom he did predestinate, them he also called: and whom he called, them he also justified: and whom he justified, them he also glorified.

31 What shall we then say to these things? If God *be* for us, who *can be* against us?

32 He that spared not his own Son, but delivered him up for us all, how shall he not with him also freely give us all things?

33 Who shall lay any thing to the charge of God's elect? *It is* God that justifieth.

34 Who *is* he that condemneth? *It is* Christ that died, yea rather, that is risen again, who is even at the right hand of God, who also maketh intercession for us.

35 Who shall separate us from the love of Christ? *shall* tribulation, or distress, or persecution, or famine, or nakedness, or peril, or sword?

36 As it is written, For thy sake we are killed all the day long; we are accounted as sheep for the slaughter.

37 Nay, in all these things we are more than conquerors through him that loved us.

38 For I am persuaded, that neither death, nor life, nor angels, nor principalities, nor powers, nor things present, nor things to come,

39 Nor height, nor depth, nor any other creature, shall be able to separate us from the love of God, which is in Christ Je′sus our Lord.

9 I SAY the truth in Christ, I lie not, my conscience also bearing me witness in the Ho′ly Ghost,

2 That I have great heaviness and continual sorrow in my heart.

3 For I could wish that myself were accursed from Christ for my brethren, my kinsmen according to the flesh:

4 Who are Is′ra-el-ites; to whom *pertaineth* the adoption, and the glory, and the covenants, and the giving of the law, and the service *of God*, and the promises;

5 Whose *are* the fathers, and of whom as concerning the flesh Christ *came*, who is over all, God blessed for ever. Amen.

6 Not as though the word of God hath taken none effect. For they *are* not all Is′ra-el, which are of Is′ra-el:

7 Neither, because they are the seed of A′-bra-ham, *are they* all children: but, In I′saac shall thy seed be called.

8 That is, They which are the children of the flesh, these *are* not the children of God: but the children of the promise are counted for the seed.

9 For this *is* the word of promise, At this time will I come, and Sa′rah shall have a son.

10 And not only *this;* but when Re-bec′ca also had conceived by one, *even* by our father I′saac;

11 (For *the children* being not yet born, neither having done any good or evil, that the purpose of God according to election might stand, not of works, but of him that calleth;)

12 It was said unto her, The elder shall serve the younger.

13 As it is written, Ja′cob have I loved, but E′sau have I hated.

14 What shall we say then? *Is there* unrighteousness with God? God forbid.

15 For he saith to Mo′ses, I will have mercy on whom I will have mercy, and I will have compassion on whom I will have compassion.

16 So then *it is* not of him that willeth, nor of

him that runneth, but of God that sheweth mercy.

17 For the scripture saith unto Pha′raoh, Even for this same purpose have I raised thee up, that I might shew my power in thee, and that my name might be declared throughout all the earth.

18 Therefore hath he mercy on whom he will *have mercy*, and whom he will he hardeneth.

19 Thou wilt say then unto me, Why doth he yet find fault? For who hath resisted his will?

20 Nay but, O man, who art thou that repliest against God? Shall the thing formed say to him that formed *it*, Why hast thou made me thus?

21 Hath not the potter power over the clay; of the same lump to make one vessel unto honour, and another unto dishonour?

22 *What* if God, willing to shew *his* wrath, and to make his power known, endured with much longsuffering the vessels of wrath fitted to destruction:

23 And that he might make known the riches of his glory on the vessels of mercy, which he had afore prepared unto glory,

24 Even us, whom he hath called, not of the Jews only, but also of the Gen′tiles?

25 As he saith also in O′see, I will call them my people, which were not my people; and her beloved, which was not beloved.

26 And it shall come to pass, *that* in the place where it was said unto them, Ye *are* not my people; there shall they be called the children of the living God.

27 E-sa′ias also crieth concerning Is′ra-el, Though the number of the children of Is′ra-el be as the sand of the sea, a remnant shall be saved:

28 For he will finish the work, and cut *it* short in righteousness: because a short work will the Lord make upon the earth.

29 And as E-sa′ias said before, Except the Lord of Sab′a-oth had left us a seed, we had been as Sod′om-a, and been made like unto Go-mor′rha.

30 What shall we say then? That the Gen′-tiles, which followed not after righteousness, have attained to righteousness, even the righteousness which is of faith.

31 But Is′ra-el, which followed after the law of righteousness, hath not attained to the law of righteousness.

32 Wherefore? Because *they sought it* not by faith, but as it were by the works of the law. For they stumbled at that stumblingstone;

33 As it is written, Behold, I lay in Si′on a stumblingstone and rock of offence: and whosoever believeth on him shall not be ashamed.

10 BRETHREN, my heart's desire and prayer to God for Is′ra-el is, that they might be saved.

2 For I bear them record that they have a zeal of God, but not according to knowledge.

3 For they being ignorant of God's righteousness, and going about to establish their own righteousness, have not submitted themselves unto the righteousness of God.

4 For Christ *is* the end of the law for righteousness to every one that believeth.

5 For Mo′ses describeth the righteousness which is of the law, That the man which doeth those things shall live by them.

6 But the righteousness which is of faith speaketh on this wise, Say not in thine heart, Who shall ascend into heaven? (that is, to bring Christ down *from above:*)

7 Or, Who shall descend into the deep? (that is, to bring up Christ again from the dead.)

8 But what saith it? The word is nigh thee, *even* in thy mouth, and in thy heart: that is, the word of faith, which we preach;

9 That if thou shalt confess with thy mouth the Lord Je′sus, and shalt believe in thine heart that God hath raised him from the dead, thou shalt be saved.

10 For with the heart man believeth unto righteousness; and with the mouth confession is made unto salvation.

11 For the scripture saith, Whosoever believeth on him shall not be ashamed.

12 For there is no difference between the Jew and the Greek: for the same Lord over all is rich unto all that call upon him.

13 For whosoever shall call upon the name of the Lord shall be saved.

14 How then shall they call on him in whom they have not believed? and how shall they believe in him of whom they have not heard? and how shall they hear without a preacher?

15 And how shall they preach, except they be sent? as it is written, How beautiful are the feet of them that preach the gospel of peace, and bring glad tidings of good things!

16 But they have not all obeyed the gospel. For E-sa′ias saith, Lord, who hath believed our report?

17 So then faith *cometh* by hearing, and hearing by the word of God.

18 But I say, Have they not heard? Yes verily, their sound went into all the earth, and their words unto the ends of the world.

19 But I say, Did not Is′ra-el know? First Mo′ses saith, I will provoke you to jealousy by *them that are* no people, *and* by a foolish nation I will anger you.

20 But E-sa′ias is very bold, and saith, I was found of them that sought me not; I was made manifest unto them that asked not after me.

21 But to Is′ra-el he saith, All day long I have stretched forth my hands unto a disobedient and gainsaying people.

11 I SAY then, Hath God cast away his people? God forbid. For I also am an Is′ra-el-ite, of the seed of A′bra-ham, *of* the tribe of Ben′ja-min.

2 God hath not cast away his people which he foreknew. Wot ye not what the scripture saith of E-li′as? how he maketh intercession to God against Is′ra-el, saying,

3 Lord, they have killed thy prophets, and digged down thine altars; and I am left alone, and they seek my life.

4 But what saith the answer of God unto him? I have reserved to myself seven thousand men, who have not bowed the knee to *the image of* Ba′al.

5 Even so then at this present time also there is a remnant according to the election of grace.

6 And if by grace, then *is* it no more of works: otherwise grace is no more grace. But if *it be* of works, then is it no more grace: otherwise work is no more work.

7 What then? Is′ra-el hath not obtained that which he seeketh for; but the election hath obtained it, and the rest were blinded

8 (According as it is written, God hath given them the spirit of slumber, eyes that they should not see, and ears that they should not hear;) unto this day.

9 And Da′vid saith, Let their table be made a snare, and a trap, and a stumblingblock, and a recompence unto them:

10 Let their eyes be darkened, that they may not see, and bow down their back alway.

11 I say then, Have they stumbled that they should fall? God forbid: but *rather* through their fall salvation *is come* unto the Gen′tiles, for to provoke them to jealousy.

12 Now if the fall of them *be* the riches of the world, and the diminishing of them the riches of the Gen′tiles; how much more their fulness?

13 For I speak to you Gen′tiles, inasmuch as I am the apostle of the Gen′tiles, I magnify mine office:

14 If by any means I may provoke to emulation *them which are* my flesh, and might save some of them.

15 For if the casting away of them *be* the reconciling of the world, what *shall* the receiving *of them be,* but life from the dead?

16 For if the firstfruit *be* holy, the lump *is* also *holy:* and if the root *be* holy, so *are* the branches.

17 And if some of the branches be broken off, and thou, being a wild olive tree, wert graffed in among them, and with them partakest of the root and fatness of the olive tree;

18 Boast not against the branches. But if thou boast, thou bearest not the root, but the root thee.

19 Thou wilt say then, The branches were broken off, that I might be graffed in.

20 Well; because of unbelief they were broken off, and thou standest by faith. Be not highminded, but fear:

21 For if God spared not the natural branches, *take heed* lest he also spare not thee.

22 Behold therefore the goodness and severity of God: on them which fell, severity; but toward thee, goodness, if thou continue in *his* goodness: otherwise thou also shalt be cut off.

23 And they also, if they abide not still in unbelief, shall be graffed in: for God is able to graff them in again.

24 For if thou wert cut out of the olive tree which is wild by nature, and wert graffed contrary to nature into a good olive tree: how much more shall these, which be the natural *branches,* be graffed into their own olive tree?

25 For I would not, brethren, that ye should be ignorant of this mystery, lest ye should be wise in your own conceits; that blindness in part is happened to Is′ra-el, until the fulness of the Gen′tiles be come in.

26 And so all Is′ra-el shall be saved: as it is written, There shall come out of Si′on the Deliverer, and shall turn away ungodliness from Ja′cob:

27 For this *is* my covenant unto them, when I shall take away their sins.

28 As concerning the gospel, *they are* enemies for your sakes: but as touching the election, *they are* beloved for the fathers' sakes.

29 For the gifts and calling of God *are* without repentance.

30 For as ye in times past have not believed God, yet have now obtained mercy through their unbelief:

31 Even so have these also now not believed, that through your mercy they also may obtain mercy.

32 For God hath concluded them all in unbelief, that he might have mercy upon all.

33 O the depth of the riches both of the wisdom and knowledge of God! how unsearchable *are* his judgments, and his ways past finding out!

34 For who hath known the mind of the Lord? or who hath been his counsellor?

35 Or who hath first given to him, and it shall be recompensed unto him again?

36 For of him, and through him, and to him, *are* all things: to whom *be* glory for ever. Amen.

12 I BESEECH you therefore, brethren, by the mercies of God, that ye present your bodies a living sacrifice, holy, acceptable unto God, *which is* your reasonable service.

2 And be not conformed to this world: but be ye transformed by the renewing of your mind, that ye may prove what *is* that good, and acceptable, and perfect, will of God.

3 For I say, through the grace given unto me, to every man that is among you, not to think *of himself* more highly than he ought to think; but to think soberly, according as God hath dealt to every man the measure of faith.

4 For as we have many members in one body, and all members have not the same office:

5 So we, *being* many, are one body in Christ, and every one members one of another.

6 Having then gifts differing according to the grace that is given to us, whether prophecy, *let us prophesy* according to the proportion of faith;

7 Or ministry, *let us wait* on *our* ministering: or he that teacheth, on teaching;

8 Or he that exhorteth, on exhortation: he that giveth, *let him do it* with simplicity; he that ruleth, with diligence; he that sheweth mercy, with cheerfulness.

9 *Let* love be without dissimulation. Abhor that which is evil; cleave to that which is good.

10 *Be* kindly affectioned one to another with brotherly love; in honour preferring one another;

11 Not slothful in business; fervent in spirit; serving the Lord;

12 Rejoicing in hope; patient in tribulation; continuing instant in prayer;

13 Distributing to the necessity of saints; given to hospitality.

14 Bless them which persecute you: bless, and curse not.

15 Rejoice with them that do rejoice, and weep with them that weep.

16 *Be* of the same mind one toward another. Mind not high things, but condescend to men of low estate. Be not wise in your own conceits.

17 Recompense to no man evil for evil. Provide things honest in the sight of all men.

18 If it be possible, as much as lieth in you, live peaceably with all men.

19 Dearly beloved, avenge not yourselves, but *rather* give place unto wrath: for it is written, Vengeance *is* mine; I will repay, saith the Lord.

20 Therefore if thine enemy hunger, feed him; if he thirst, give him drink: for in so doing thou shalt heap coals of fire on his head.

21 Be not overcome of evil, but overcome evil with good.

13 LET every soul be subject unto the higher powers. For there is no power but of God: the powers that be are ordained of God.

2 Whosoever therefore resisteth the power, resisteth the ordinance of God: and they that resist shall receive to themselves damnation.

3 For rulers are not a terror to good works, but to the evil. Wilt thou then not be afraid of the power? do that which is good, and thou shalt have praise of the same:

4 For he is the minister of God to thee for good. But if thou do that which is evil, be afraid; for he beareth not the sword in vain: for he is the minister of God, a revenger to *execute* wrath upon him that doeth evil.

5 Wherefore *ye* must needs be subject, not only for wrath, but also for conscience sake.

6 For for this cause pay ye tribute also: for they are God's ministers, attending continually upon this very thing.

7 Render therefore to all their dues: tribute to whom tribute *is due*; custom to whom custom; fear to whom fear; honour to whom honour.

8 Owe no man any thing, but to love one another: for he that loveth another hath fulfilled the law.

9 For this, Thou shalt not commit adultery, Thou shalt not kill, Thou shalt not steal, Thou shalt not bear false witness, Thou shalt not covet; and if *there be* any other commandment, it is briefly comprehended in this saying, namely, Thou shalt love thy neighbour as thyself.

10 Love worketh no ill to his neighbour: therefore love *is* the fulfilling of the law.

11 And that, knowing the time, that now *it is* high time to awake out of sleep: for now *is* our salvation nearer than when we believed.

12 The night is far spent, the day is at hand: let us therefore cast off the works of darkness, and let us put on the armour of light.

13 Let us walk honestly, as in the day; not in rioting and drunkenness, not in chambering and wantonness, not in strife and envying.

14 But put ye on the Lord Je'sus Christ, and make not provision for the flesh, to *fulfil* the lusts *thereof*.

14 HIM that is weak in the faith receive ye, *but* not to doubtful disputations.

2 For one believeth that he may eat all things: another, who is weak, eateth herbs.

3 Let not him that eateth despise him that eateth not; and let not him which eateth not judge him that eateth: for God hath received him.

4 Who art thou that judgest another man's servant? to his own master he standeth or falleth. Yea, he shall be holden up: for God is able to make him stand.

5 One man esteemeth one day above another: another esteemeth every day *alike*. Let every man be fully persuaded in his own mind.

6 He that regardeth the day, regardeth *it* unto the Lord; and he that regardeth not the day, to the Lord he doth not regard *it*. He that eateth, eateth to the Lord, for he giveth God thanks; and he that eateth not, to the Lord he eateth not, and giveth God thanks.

7 For none of us liveth to himself, and no man dieth to himself.

8 For whether we live, we live unto the Lord; and whether we die, we die unto the Lord: whether we live therefore, or die, we are the Lord's.

9 For to this end Christ both died, and rose, and revived, that he might be Lord both of the dead and living.

10 But why dost thou judge thy brother? or why dost thou set at nought thy brother? for we shall all stand before the judgment seat of Christ.

11 For it is written, *As* I live, saith the Lord, every knee shall bow to me, and every tongue shall confess to God.

12 So then every one of us shall give account of himself to God.

13 Let us not therefore judge one another any more: but judge this rather, that no man

put a stumblingblock or an occasion to fall in his brother's way.

14 I know, and am persuaded by the Lord Je'sus, that there is nothing unclean of itself: but to him that esteemeth any thing to be unclean, to him it is unclean.

15 But if thy brother be grieved with thy meat, now walkest thou not charitably. Destroy not him with thy meat, for whom Christ died.

16 Let not then your good be evil spoken of:

17 For the kingdom of God is not meat and drink; but righteousness, and peace, and joy in the Ho'ly Ghost.

18 For he that in these things serveth Christ is acceptable to God, and approved of men.

19 Let us therefore follow after the things which make for peace, and things wherewith one may edify another.

20 For meat destroy not the work of God. All things indeed are pure; but it is evil for that man who eateth with offence.

21 It is good neither to eat flesh, nor to drink wine, nor any thing whereby thy brother stumbleth, or is offended, or is made weak.

22 Hast thou faith? have it to thyself before God. Happy is he that condemneth not himself in that thing which he alloweth.

23 And he that doubteth is damned if he eat, because he eateth not of faith: for whatsoever is not of faith is sin.

15 WE then that are strong ought to bear the infirmities of the weak, and not to please ourselves.

2 Let every one of us please his neighbour for his good to edification.

3 For even Christ pleased not himself; but, as it is written, The reproaches of them that reproached thee fell on me.

4 For whatsoever things were written aforetime were written for our learning, that we through patience and comfort of the scriptures might have hope.

5 Now the God of patience and consolation grant you to be likeminded one toward another according to Christ Je'sus:

6 That ye may with one mind and one mouth glorify God, even the Father of our Lord Je'sus Christ.

7 Wherefore receive ye one another, as Christ also received us to the glory of God.

8 Now I say that Je'sus Christ was a minister of the circumcision for the truth of God, to confirm the promises made unto the fathers:

9 And that the Gen'tiles might glorify God for his mercy; as it is written, For this cause I will confess to thee among the Gen'tiles, and sing unto thy name.

10 And again he saith, Rejoice, ye Gen'tiles, with his people.

11 And again, Praise the Lord, all ye Gen'tiles; and laud him, all ye people.

12 And again, E-sa'ias saith, There shall be a root of Jes'se, and he that shall rise to reign over the Gen'tiles; in him shall the Gen'tiles trust.

13 Now the God of hope fill you with all joy and peace in believing, that ye may abound in hope, through the power of the Ho'ly Ghost.

14 And I myself also am persuaded of you, my brethren, that ye also are full of goodness, filled with all knowledge, able also to admonish one another.

15 Nevertheless, brethren, I have written the more boldly unto you in some sort, as putting you in mind, because of the grace that is given to me of God,

16 That I should be the minister of Je'sus Christ to the Gen'tiles, ministering the gospel of God, that the offering up of the Gen'tiles might be acceptable, being sanctified by the Ho'ly Ghost.

17 I have therefore whereof I may glory through Je'sus Christ in those things which pertain to God.

18 For I will not dare to speak of any of those things which Christ hath not wrought by me, to make the Gen'tiles obedient, by word and deed,

19 Through mighty signs and wonders, by the power of the Spirit of God; so that from Je-ru'sa-lem, and round about unto Il-lyr'i-cum, I have fully preached the gospel of Christ.

20 Yea, so have I strived to preach the gospel, not where Christ was named, lest I should build upon another man's foundation:

21 But as it is written, To whom he was not spoken of, they shall see: and they that have not heard shall understand.

22 For which cause also I have been much hindered from coming to you.

23 But now having no more place in these parts, and having a great desire these many years to come unto you;

24 Whensoever I take my journey into Spain, I will come to you: for I trust to see you in my journey, and to be brought on my way thitherward by you, if first I be somewhat filled with your company.

25 But now I go unto Je-ru'sa-lem to minister unto the saints.

26 For it hath pleased them of Mac-e-do'ni-a and A-cha'ia to make a certain contribution for the poor saints which are at Je-ru'sa-lem.

27 It hath pleased them verily; and their debtors they are. For if the Gen'tiles have been made partakers of their spiritual things, their duty is also to minister unto them in carnal things.

28 When therefore I have performed this, and have sealed to them this fruit, I will come by you into Spain.

29 And I am sure that, when I come unto you, I shall come in the fulness of the blessing of the gospel of Christ.

30 Now I beseech you, brethren, for the Lord Je'sus Christ's sake, and for the love of the Spirit, that ye strive together with me in your prayers to God for me;

31 That I may be delivered from them that do not believe in Ju-dæ'a; and that my service which I have for Je-ru'sa-lem may be accepted of the saints;

32 That I may come unto you with joy by the will of God, and may with you be refreshed.

33 Now the God of peace be with you all. Amen.

16 I COMMEND unto you Phe'be our sister, which is a servant of the church which is at Cenchre-a:

2 That ye receive her in the Lord, as becometh saints, and that ye assist her in whatsoever business she hath need of you: for she hath been a succourer of many, and of myself also.

3 Greet Pris-cil'la and A'qui-la my helpers in Christ Je'sus:

4 Who have for my life laid down their own necks: unto whom not only I give thanks, but also all the churches of the Gen'tiles.

5 Likewise greet the church that is in their house. Salute my wellbeloved E-pæn'e-tus, who is the firstfruits of A-cha'ia unto Christ.

6 Greet Ma'ry, who bestowed much labour on us.

7 Salute An-dro-ni'cus and Ju'nia, my kinsmen, and my fellowprisoners, who are of note among the apostles, who also were in Christ before me.

8 Greet Am'pli-as my beloved in the Lord.

9 Salute Ur'bane, our helper in Christ, and Sta'chys my beloved.

10 Salute A-pelles approved in Christ. Salute them which are of Ar-is-to-bu'lus' *household.*

11 Salute He-ro'di-on my kinsman. Greet them that be of the *household* of Nar-cis'sus, which are in the Lord.

12 Salute Try-phe'na and Try-pho'sa, who labour in the Lord. Salute the beloved Per'sis, which laboured much in the Lord.

13 Salute Ru'fus chosen in the Lord, and his mother and mine.

14 Salute A-syn'cri-tus, Phle'gon, Her'mas, Pat'ro-bas, Her'mes, and the brethren which are with them.

15 Salute Phi-lolo'-gus, and Ju'lia, Ne're-us, and his sister, and O-lym'pas, and all the saints which are with them.

16 Salute one another with an holy kiss. The churches of Christ salute you.

17 Now I beseech you, brethren, mark them which cause divisions and offences contrary to the doctrine which ye have learned; and avoid them.

18 For they that are such serve not our Lord Je'sus Christ, but their own belly; and by good words and fair speeches deceive the hearts of the simple.

19 For your obedience is come abroad unto all *men.* I am glad therefore on your behalf: but yet I would have you wise unto that which is good, and simple concerning evil.

20 And the God of peace shall bruise Sa'tan under your feet shortly. The grace of our Lord Je'sus Christ *be* with you. Amen.

21 Ti-mo'the-us my workfellow, and Lu'cius, and Ja'son, and So-sip'a-ter, my kinsmen, salute you.

22 I Ter'tius, who wrote *this* epistle, salute you in the Lord.

23 Ga'ius mine host, and of the whole church, saluteth you. E-ras'tus the chamberlain of the city saluteth you, and Quar'tus a brother.

24 The grace of our Lord Je'sus Christ *be* with you all. Amen.

25 Now to him that is of power to stablish you according to my gospel, and the preaching of Je'sus Christ, according to the revelation of the mystery, which was kept secret since the world began,

26 But now is made manifest, and by the scriptures of the prophets, according to the commandment of the everlasting God, made known to all nations for the obedience of faith:

27 To God only wise, *be* glory through Je'sus Christ for ever. Amen.

Written to the Ro'mans from Co-rin'thus, *and sent* by Phe'be servant of the church at Cen'chre-a.

THE FIRST LETTER OF PAUL TO THE

CORINTHIANS

1 PAUL, called *to be* an apostle of Je'sus Christ through the will of God, and Sos'-the-nes *our* brother,

2 Unto the church of God which is at Cor'-inth, to them that are sanctified in Christ Je'sus, called *to be* saints, with all that in every place call upon the name of Je'sus Christ our Lord, both theirs and ours:

3 Grace *be* unto you, and peace, from God our Father, and *from* the Lord Je'sus Christ.

4 I thank my God always on your behalf, for the grace of God which is given you by Je'sus Christ;

5 That in every thing ye are enriched by him, in all utterance, and *in* all knowledge;

6 Even as the testimony of Christ was confirmed in you:

7 So that ye come behind in no gift; waiting for the coming of our Lord Je'sus Christ:

8 Who shall also confirm you unto the end, *that ye may be* blameless in the day of our Lord Je'sus Christ.

9 God *is* faithful, by whom ye were called unto the fellowship of his Son Je'sus Christ our Lord.

10 Now I beseech you, brethren, by the name of our Lord Je'sus Christ, that ye all speak the same thing, and *that* there be no divisions among you; but *that* ye be perfectly joined together in the same mind and in the same judgment.

11 For it hath been declared unto me of you, my brethren, by them *which are of the house* of Chlo'e, that there are contentions among you.

12 Now this I say, that every one of you saith, I am of Paul; and I of A-pol'los; and I of Ce'phas; and I of Christ.

13 Is Christ divided? was Paul crucified for you? or were ye baptized in the name of Paul?

14 I thank God that I baptized none of you, but Cris'pus and Ga'ius;

15 Lest any should say that I had baptized in mine own name.

16 And I baptized also the household of Steph'a-nas: besides, I know not whether I baptized any other.

17 For Christ sent me not to baptize, but to preach the gospel: not with wisdom of words, lest the cross of Christ should be made of none effect.

18 For the preaching of the cross is to them that perish foolishness; but unto us which are saved it is the power of God.

19 For it is written, I will destroy the wisdom of the wise, and will bring to nothing the understanding of the prudent.

20 Where *is* the wise? where *is* the scribe? where *is* the disputer of this world? hath not God made foolish the wisdom of this world?

21 For after that in the wisdom of God the world by wisdom knew not God, it pleased God by the foolishness of preaching to save them that believe.

22 For the Jews require a sign, and the Greeks seek after wisdom:

23 But we preach Christ crucified, unto the Jews a stumblingblock, and unto the Greeks foolishness;

24 But unto them which are called, both Jews and Greeks, Christ the power of God, and the wisdom of God.

25 Because the foolishness of God is wiser than men; and the weakness of God is stronger than men.

26 For ye see your calling, brethren, how that not many wise men after the flesh, not many mighty, not many noble, *are called*:

27 But God hath chosen the foolish things of the world to confound the wise; and God hath chosen the weak things of the world to confound the things which are mighty;

28 And base things of the world, and things which are despised, hath God chosen, *yea,* and things which are not, to bring to nought things that are:

29 That no flesh should glory in his presence.

30 But of him are ye in Christ Je′sus, who of God is made unto us wisdom, and righteousness, and sanctification, and redemption:

31 That, according as it is written, He that glorieth, let him glory in the Lord.

2 AND I, brethren, when I came to you, came not with excellency of speech or of wisdom, declaring unto you the testimony of God.

2 For I determined not to know any thing among you, save Je′sus Christ, and him crucified.

3 And I was with you in weakness, and in fear, and in much trembling.

4 And my speech and my preaching *was* not with enticing words of man's wisdom, but in demonstration of the Spirit and of power:

5 That your faith should not stand in the wisdom of men, but in the power of God.

6 Howbeit we speak wisdom among them that are perfect: yet not the wisdom of this world, nor of the princes of this world, that come to nought:

7 But we speak the wisdom of God in a mystery, *even* the hidden *wisdom,* which God ordained before the world unto our glory:

8 Which none of the princes of this world knew: for had they known *it,* they would not have crucified the Lord of glory.

9 But as it is written, Eye hath not seen, nor ear heard, neither have entered into the heart of man, the things which God hath prepared for them that love him.

10 But God hath revealed *them* unto us by his Spirit: for the Spirit searcheth all things, yea, the deep things of God.

11 For what man knoweth the things of a man, save the spirit of man which is in him? even so the things of God knoweth no man, but the Spirit of God.

12 Now we have received, not the spirit of the world, but the spirit which is of God; that we might know the things that are freely given to us of God.

13 Which things also we speak, not in the words which man's wisdom teacheth, but which the Ho′ly Ghost teacheth; comparing spiritual things with spiritual.

14 But the natural man receiveth not the things of the Spirit of God: for they are foolishness unto him: neither can he know *them,* because they are spiritually discerned.

15 But he that is spiritual judgeth all things, yet he himself is judged of no man.

16 For who hath known the mind of the Lord, that he may instruct him? But we have the mind of Christ.

3 AND I, brethren, could not speak unto you as unto spiritual, but as unto carnal, *even* as unto babes in Christ.

2 I have fed you with milk, and not with meat: for hitherto ye were not able *to bear it,* neither yet now are ye able.

3 For ye are yet carnal: for whereas *there is* among you envying, and strife, and divisions, are ye not carnal, and walk as men?

4 For while one saith, I am of Paul; and another, I *am* of A-pol′los; are ye not carnal?

5 Who then is Paul, and who *is* A-pol′los, but ministers by whom ye believed, even as the Lord gave to every man?

6 I have planted, A-pol′los watered; but God gave the increase.

7 So then neither is he that planteth any thing, neither he that watereth; but God that giveth the increase.

8 Now he that planteth and he that watereth are one: and every man shall receive his own reward according to his own labour.

9 For we are labourers together with God: ye are God's husbandry, *ye are* God's building.

10 According to the grace of God which is given unto me, as a wise masterbuilder, I have laid the foundation, and another buildeth thereon. But let every man take heed how he buildeth thereupon.

11 For other foundation can no man lay than that is laid, which is Je′sus Christ.

12 Now if any man build upon this foundation gold, silver, precious stones, wood, hay, stubble;

13 Every man's work shall be made manifest: for the day shall declare it, because it shall be revealed by fire; and the fire shall try every man's work of what sort it is.

14 If any man's work abide which he hath built thereupon, he shall receive a reward.

15 If any man's work shall be burned, he shall suffer loss: but he himself shall be saved; yet so as by fire.

16 Know ye not that ye are the temple of God, *that* the Spirit of God dwelleth in you?

17 If any man defile the temple of God, him shall God destroy; for the temple of God is holy, which *temple* ye are.

18 Let no man deceive himself. If any man among you seemeth to be wise in this world, let him become a fool, that he may be wise.

19 For the wisdom of this world is foolishness with God. For it is written, He taketh the wise in their own craftiness.

20 And again, The Lord knoweth the thoughts of the wise, that they are vain.

21 Therefore let no man glory in men. For all things are yours;

22 Whether Paul or A-pol′los, or Ce′phas, or the world, or life, or death, or things present, or things to come; all are yours;

23 And ye are Christ's; and Christ *is* God's.

4 LET a man so account of us, as of the ministers of Christ, and stewards of the mysteries of God.

2 Moreover it is required in stewards, that a man be found faithful.

3 But with me it is a very small thing that I should be judged of you, or of man's judgment: yea, I judge not mine own self.

4 For I know nothing by myself; yet am I not hereby justified: but he that judgeth me is the Lord.

5 Therefore judge nothing before the time, until the Lord come, who both will bring to light the hidden things of darkness, and will make manifest the counsels of the hearts: and then shall every man have praise of God.

6 And these things, brethren, I have in a fig-

ure transferred to myself and *to* A-pol'los for your sakes; that ye might learn in us not to think *of men* above that which is written, that no one of you be puffed up one against another.

7 For who maketh thee to differ *from another?* and what hast thou that thou didst not receive? now if thou didst receive *it,* why dost thou glory, as if thou hadst not received *it?*

8 Now ye are full, now ye are rich, ye have reigned as kings without us: and I would to God ye did reign, that we also might reign with you.

9 For I think that God hath set forth us the apostles last, as it were appointed to death: for we are made a spectacle unto the world, and to angels, and to men.

10 We *are* fools for Christ's sake, but ye *are* wise in Christ; we *are* weak, but ye *are* strong; ye *are* honourable, but we *are* despised.

11 Even unto this present hour we both hunger, and thirst, and are naked, and are buffeted, and have no certain dwellingplace;

12 And labour, working with our own hands: being reviled, we bless; being persecuted, we suffer it:

13 Being defamed, we intreat: we are made as the filth of the world, *and are* the offscouring of all things unto this day.

14 I write not these things to shame you, but as my beloved sons I warn *you.*

15 For though ye have ten thousand instructors in Christ, yet *have ye* not many fathers: for in Christ Je'sus I have begotten you through the gospel.

16 Wherefore I beseech you, be ye followers of me.

17 For this cause have I sent unto you Ti-mo'the-us, who is my beloved son, and faithful in the Lord, who shall bring you into remembrance of my ways which be in Christ, as I teach every where in every church.

18 Now some are puffed up, as though I would not come to you.

19 But I will come to you shortly, if the Lord will, and will know, not the speech of them which are puffed up, but the power.

20 For the kingdom of God *is* not in word, but in power.

21 What will ye? shall I come unto you with a rod, or in love, and *in* the spirit of meekness?

5 IT is reported commonly *that there is* fornication among you, and such fornication as is not so much as named among the Gen'-tiles, that one should have his father's wife.

2 And ye are puffed up, and have not rather mourned, that he that hath done this deed might be taken away from among you.

3 For I verily, as absent in body, but present in spirit, have judged already, as though I were present, *concerning* him that hath so done this deed,

4 In the name of our Lord Je'sus Christ, when ye are gathered together, and my spirit, with the power of our Lord Je'sus Christ,

5 To deliver such an one unto Sa'tan for the destruction of the flesh, that the spirit may be saved in the day of the Lord Je'sus.

6 Your glorying *is* not good. Know ye not that a little leaven leaveneth the whole lump?

7 Purge out therefore the old leaven, that ye may be a new lump, as ye are unleavened. For even Christ our passover is sacrificed for us:

8 Therefore let us keep the feast, not with old leaven, neither with the leaven of malice and wickedness; but with the unleavened *bread* of sincerity and truth.

9 I wrote unto you in an epistle not to company with fornicators:

10 Yet not altogether with the fornicators of this world, or with the covetous, or extortioners, or with idolaters; for then must ye needs go out of the world.

11 But now I have written unto you not to keep company, if any man that is called a brother be a fornicator, or covetous, or an idolater, or a railer, or a drunkard, or an extortioner; with such an one no no not to eat.

12 For what have I to do to judge them also that are without? do not ye judge them that are within?

13 But them that are without God judgeth. Therefore put away from among yourselves that wicked person.

6 DARE any of you, having a matter against another, go to law before the unjust, and not before the saints?

2 Do ye not know that the saints shall judge the world? and if the world shall be judged by you, are ye unworthy to judge the smallest matters?

3 Know ye not that we shall judge angels? how much more things that pertain to this life?

4 If then ye have judgments of things pertaining to this life, set them to judge who are least esteemed in the church.

5 I speak to your shame. Is it so, that there is not a wise man among you? no, not one that shall be able to judge between his brethren?

6 But brother goeth to law with brother, and that before the unbelievers.

7 Now therefore there is utterly a fault among you, because ye go to law one with another. Why do ye not rather take wrong? why do ye not rather *suffer yourselves to* be defrauded?

8 Nay, ye do wrong, and defraud, and that *your* brethren.

9 Know ye not that the unrighteous shall not inherit the kingdom of God? Be not deceived: neither fornicators, nor idolaters, nor adulterers, nor effeminate, nor abusers of themselves with mankind,

10 Nor thieves, nor covetous, nor drunkards, nor revilers, nor extortioners, shall inherit the kingdom of God.

11 And such were some of you: but ye are washed, but ye are sanctified, but ye are justified in the name of the Lord Je'sus, and by the Spirit of our God.

12 All things are lawful unto me, but all things are not expedient: all things are lawful for me, but I will not be brought under the power of any.

13 Meats for the belly, and the belly for meats: but God shall destroy both it and them. Now the body *is* not for fornication, but for the Lord; and the Lord for the body.

14 And God hath both raised up the Lord, and will also raise up us by his own power.

15 Know ye not that your bodies are the members of Christ? shall I then take the members of Christ, and make *them* the members of an harlot? God forbid.

16 What? know ye not that he which is joined to an harlot is one body? for two, saith he, shall be one flesh.

17 But he that is joined unto the Lord is one spirit.

18 Flee fornication. Every sin that a man doeth is without the body; but he that committeth fornication sinneth against his own body.

19 What? know ye not that your body is the

temple of the Ho'ly Ghost *which is* in you, which ye have of God, and ye are not your own?

20 For ye are bought with a price: therefore glorify God in your body, and in your spirit, which are God's.

7 NOW concerning the things whereof ye wrote unto me: *It is* good for a man not to touch a woman.

2 Nevertheless, *to avoid* fornication, let every man have his own wife, and let every woman have her own husband.

3 Let the husband render unto the wife due benevolence: and likewise also the wife unto the husband.

4 The wife hath not power of her own body, but the husband: and likewise also the husband hath not power of his own body, but the wife.

5 Defraud ye not one the other, except *it be* with consent for a time, that ye may give yourselves to fasting and prayer; and come together again, that Sa'tan tempt you not for your incontinency.

6 But I speak this by permission, *and* not of commandment.

7 For I would that all men were even as I myself. But every man hath his proper gift of God, one after this manner, and another after that.

8 I say therefore to the unmarried and widows, It is good for them if they abide even as I.

9 But if they cannot contain, let them marry: for it is better to marry than to burn.

10 And unto the married I command, *yet* not I, but the Lord, Let not the wife depart from *her* husband:

11 But and if she depart, let her remain unmarried, or be reconciled to *her* husband: and let not the husband put away *his* wife.

12 But to the rest speak I, not the Lord: If any brother hath a wife that believeth not, and she be pleased to dwell with him, let him not put her away.

13 And the woman which hath an husband that believeth not, and if he be pleased to dwell with her, let her not leave him.

14 For the unbelieving husband is sanctified by the wife, and the unbelieving wife is sanctified by the husband: else were your children unclean; but now are they holy.

15 But if the unbelieving depart, let him depart. A brother or a sister is not under bondage in such *cases:* but God hath called us to peace.

16 For what knowest thou, O wife, whether thou shalt save *thy* husband? or how knowest thou, O man, whether thou shalt save *thy* wife?

17 But as God hath distributed to every man, as the Lord hath called every one, so let him walk. And so ordain I in all churches.

18 Is any man called being circumcised? let him not become uncircumcised. Is any called in uncircumcision? let him not be circumcised.

19 Circumcision is nothing, and uncircumcision is nothing, but the keeping of the commandments of God.

20 Let every man abide in the same calling wherein he was called.

21 Art thou called *being* a servant? care not for it: but if thou mayest be made free, use *it* rather.

22 For he that is called in the Lord, *being* a servant, is the Lord's freeman: likewise also he that is called, *being* free, is Christ's servant.

23 Ye are bought with a price; be not ye the servants of men.

24 Brethren, let every man, wherein he is called, therein abide with God.

25 Now concerning virgins I have no commandment of the Lord: yet I give my judgment, as one that hath obtained mercy of the Lord to be faithful.

26 I suppose therefore that this is good for the present distress, *I say,* that *it is* good for a man so to be.

27 Art thou bound unto a wife? seek not to be loosed. Art thou loosed from a wife? seek not a wife.

28 But and if thou marry, thou hast not sinned; and if a virgin marry, she hath not sinned. Nevertheless such shall have trouble in the flesh: but I spare you.

29 But this I say, brethren, the time *is* short: it remaineth, that both they that have wives be as though they had none;

30 And they that weep, as though they wept not; and they that rejoice, as though they rejoiced not; and they that buy, as though they possessed not;

31 And they that use this world, as not abusing *it:* for the fashion of this world passeth away.

32 But I would have you without carefulness. He that is unmarried careth for the things that belong to the Lord, how he may please the Lord:

33 But he that is married careth for the things that are of the world, how he may please *his* wife.

34 There is difference *also* between a wife and a virgin. The unmarried woman careth for the things of the Lord, that she may be holy both in body and in spirit: but she that is married careth for the things of the world, how she may please *her* husband.

35 And this I speak for your own profit; not that I may cast a snare upon you, but for that which is comely, and that ye may attend upon the Lord without distraction.

36 But if any man think that he behaveth himself uncomely toward his virgin, if she pass the flower of *her* age, and need so require, let him do what he will, he sinneth not: let them marry.

37 Nevertheless he that standeth stedfast in his heart, having no necessity, but hath power over his own will, and hath so decreed in his heart that he will keep his virgin, doeth well.

38 So then he that giveth *her* in marriage doeth well; but he that giveth *her* not in marriage doeth better.

39 The wife is bound by the law as long as her husband liveth; but if her husband be dead, she is at liberty to be married to whom she will; only in the Lord.

40 But she is happier if she so abide, after my judgment: and I think also that I have the Spirit of God.

8 NOW as touching things offered unto idols, we know that we all have knowledge. Knowledge puffeth up, but charity edifieth.

2 And if any man think that he knoweth any thing, he knoweth nothing yet as he ought to know.

3 But if any man love God, the same is known of him.

4 As concerning therefore the eating of those things that are offered in sacrifice unto idols, we know that an idol *is* nothing in the world, and that *there is* none other God but one.

5 For though there be that are called gods, whether in heaven or in earth, (as there be gods many, and lords many,)

6 But to us *there is but* one God, the Father, of whom *are* all things, and we in him; and one Lord Je'sus Christ, by whom *are* all things, and we by him.

7 Howbeit *there is* not in every man that knowledge: for some with conscience of the idol unto this hour eat *it* as a thing offered unto an idol; and their conscience being weak is defiled.

8 But meat commmendeth us not to God: for neither, if we eat, are we the better; neither, if we eat not, are we the worse.

9 But take heed lest by any means this liberty of yours become a stumblingblock to them that are weak.

10 For if any man see thee which hast knowledge sit at meat in the idol's temple, shall not the conscience of him which is weak be emboldened to eat those things which are offered to idols;

11 And through thy knowledge shall the weak brother perish, for whom Christ died?

12 But when ye sin so against the brethren, and wound their weak conscience, ye sin against Christ.

13 Wherefore, if meat make my brother to offend, I will eat no flesh while the world standeth, lest I make my brother to offend.

9 AM I not an apostle? am I not free? have I not seen Je'sus Christ our Lord? are not ye my work in the Lord?

2 If I be not an apostle unto others, yet doubtless I am to you: for the seal of mine apostleship are ye in the Lord.

3 Mine answer to them that do examine me is this,

4 Have we not power to eat and to drink?

5 Have we not power to lead about a sister, a wife, as well as other apostles, and *as* the brethren of the Lord, and Ce'phas?

6 Or I only and Bar'na-bas, have not we power to forbear working?

7 Who goeth a warfare any time at his own charges? who planteth a vineyard, and eateth not of the fruit thereof? or who feedeth a flock, and eateth not of the milk of the flock?

8 Say I these things as a man? or saith not the law the same also?

9 For it is written in the law of Mo'ses, Thou shalt not muzzle the mouth of the ox that treadeth out the corn. Doth God take care for oxen?

10 Or saith he *it* altogether for our sakes? For our sakes, no doubt, *this* is written: that he that ploweth should plow in hope; and that he that thresheth in hope should be partaker of his hope.

11 If we have sown unto you spiritual things, *is it* a great thing if we shall reap your carnal things?

12 If others be partakers of *this* power over you, *are* not we rather? Nevertheless we have not used this power; but suffer all things, lest we should hinder the gospel of Christ.

13 Do ye not know that they which minister about holy things live *of the things* of the temple? and they which wait at the altar are partakers with the altar?

14 Even so hath the Lord ordained that they which preach the gospel should live of the gospel.

15 But I have used none of these things: neither have I written these things, that it should be so done unto me: for *it were* better for me to die, than that any man should make my glorying void.

16 For though I preach the gospel, I have nothing to glory of: for necessity is laid upon me; yea, woe is unto me, if I preach not the gospel!

17 For if I do this thing willingly, I have a reward: but if against my will, a dispensation *of the gospel* is committed unto me.

18 What is my reward then? *Verily* that, when I preach the gospel, I may make the gospel of Christ without charge, that I abuse not my power in the gospel.

19 For though I be free from all *men*, yet have I made myself servant unto all, that I might gain the more.

20 And unto the Jews I became as a Jew, that I might gain the Jews; to them that are under the law, as under the law, that I might gain them that are under the law;

21 To them that are without law, as without law, (being not without law to God, but under the law to Christ,) that I might gain them that are without law;

22 To the weak became I as weak, that I might gain the weak: I am made all things to all *men*, that I might by all means save some.

23 And this I do for the gospel's sake, that I might be partaker thereof with *you*.

24 Know ye not that they which run in a race run all, but one receiveth the prize? So run, that ye may obtain.

25 And every man that striveth for the mastery is temperate in all things. Now they *do it* to obtain a corruptible crown; but we an incorruptible.

26 I therefore so run, not as uncertainly; so fight I, not as one that beateth the air:

27 But I keep under my body, and bring *it* into subjection: lest that by any means, when I have preached to others, I myself should be a castaway.

10 MOREOVER, brethren, I would not that ye should be ignorant, how that all our fathers were under the cloud, and all passed through the sea;

2 And were all baptized unto Mo'ses in the cloud and in the sea;

3 And did all eat the same spiritual meat;

4 And did all drink the same spiritual drink: for they drank of that spiritual Rock that followed them: and that Rock was Christ.

5 But with many of them God was not well pleased: for they were overthrown in the wilderness.

6 Now these things were our examples, to the intent we should not lust after evil things, as they also lusted.

7 Neither be ye idolaters, as *were* some of them; as it is written, The people sat down to eat and drink, and rose up to play.

8 Neither let us commit fornication, as some of them committed, and fell in one day three and twenty thousand.

9 Neither let us tempt Christ, as some of them also tempted, and were destroyed of serpents.

10 Neither murmur ye, as some of them also murmured, and were destroyed of the destroyer.

11 Now all these things happened unto them for ensamples: and they are written for our admonition, upon whom the ends of the world are come.

12 Wherefore let him that thinketh he standeth take heed lest he fall.

13 There hath no temptation taken you but such as is common to man: but God *is* faithful, who will not suffer you to be tempted above

that ye are able; but will with the temptation also make a way to escape, that ye may be able to bear it.

14 Wherefore, my dearly beloved, flee from idolatry.

15 I speak as to wise men; judge ye what I say.

16 The cup of blessing which we bless, is it not the communion of the blood of Christ? The bread which we break, is it not the communion of the body of Christ?

17 For we being many are one bread, and one body: for we are all partakers of that one bread.

18 Behold Is'ra-el after the flesh: are not they which eat of the sacrifices partakers of the altar?

19 What say I then? that the idol is any thing, or that which is offered in sacrifice to idols is any thing?

20 But I say, that the things which the Gen'-tiles sacrifice, they sacrifice to devils, and not to God: and I would not that ye should have fellowship with devils.

21 Ye cannot drink the cup of the Lord, and the cup of devils: ye cannot be partakers of the Lord's table, and of the table of devils.

22 Do we provoke the Lord to jealousy? are we stronger than he?

23 All things are lawful for me, but all things are not expedient: all things are lawful for me, but all things edify not.

24 Let no man seek his own, but every man another's wealth.

25 Whatsoever is sold in the shambles, that eat, asking no question for conscience sake:

26 For the earth is the Lord's, and the fulness thereof.

27 If any of them that believe not bid you to a feast, and ye be disposed to go; whatsoever is set before you, eat, asking no question for conscience sake.

28 But if any man say unto you, This is offered in sacrifice unto idols, eat not for his sake that shewed it, and for conscience sake: for the earth is the Lord's, and the fulness thereof:

29 Conscience, I say, not thine own, but of the other: for why is my liberty judged of another man's conscience?

30 For if I by grace be a partaker, why am I evil spoken of for that for which I give thanks?

31 Whether therefore ye eat, or drink, or whatsoever ye do, do all to the glory of God.

32 Give none offence, neither to the Jews, nor to the Gen'tiles, nor to the church of God:

33 Even as I please all men in all things, not seeking mine own profit, but the profit of many, that they may be saved.

11

BE ye followers of me, even as I also am of Christ.

2 Now I praise you, brethren, that ye remember me in all things, and keep the ordinances, as I delivered them to you.

3 But I would have you know, that the head of every man is Christ; and the head of the woman is the man; and the head of Christ is God.

4 Every man praying or prophesying, having his head covered, dishonoureth his head.

5 But every woman that prayeth or prophesieth with her head uncovered dishonoureth her head: for that is even all one as if she were shaven.

6 For if the woman be not covered, let her also be shorn: but if it be a shame for a woman to be shorn or shaven, let her be covered.

7 For a man indeed ought not to cover his head, forasmuch as he is the image and glory of God: but the woman is the glory of the man.

8 For the man is not of the woman; but the woman of the man.

9 Neither was the man created for the woman; but the woman for the man.

10 For this cause ought the woman to have power on her head because of the angels.

11 Nevertheless neither is the man without the woman, neither the woman without the man, in the Lord.

12 For as the woman is of the man, even so is the man also by the woman; but all things of God.

13 Judge in yourselves: is it comely that a woman pray unto God uncovered?

14 Doth not even nature itself teach you, that, if a man have long hair, it is a shame unto him?

15 But if a woman have long hair, it is a glory to her: for her hair is given her for a covering.

16 But if any man seem to be contentious, we have no such custom, neither the churches of God.

17 Now in this that I declare unto you I praise you not, that ye come together not for the better, but for the worse.

18 For first of all, when ye come together in the church, I hear that there be divisions among you; and I partly believe it.

19 For there must be also heresies among you, that they which are approved may be made manifest among you.

20 When ye come together therefore into one place, this is not to eat the Lord's supper.

21 For in eating every one taketh before other his own supper: and one is hungry, and another is drunken.

22 What? have ye not houses to eat and to drink in? or despise ye the church of God, and shame them that have not? What shall I say to you? shall I praise you in this? I praise you not.

23 For I have received of the Lord that which also I delivered unto you, That the Lord Je'sus the same night in which he was betrayed took bread:

24 And when he had given thanks, he brake it, and said, Take, eat: this is my body, which is broken for you: this do in remembrance of me.

25 After the same manner also he took the cup, when he had supped, saying, This cup is the new testament in my blood: this do ye, as oft as ye drink it, in remembrance of me.

26 For as often as ye eat this bread, and drink this cup, ye do shew the Lord's death till he come.

27 Wherefore whosoever shall eat this bread, and drink this cup of the Lord, unworthily, shall be guilty of the body and blood of the Lord.

28 But let a man examine himself, and so let him eat of that bread, and drink of that cup.

29 For he that eateth and drinketh unworthily, eateth and drinketh damnation to himself, not discerning the Lord's body.

30 For this cause many are weak and sickly among you, and many sleep.

31 For if we would judge ourselves, we should not be judged.

32 But when we are judged we are chastened of the Lord, that we should not be condemned with the world.

33 Wherefore, my brethren, when ye come together to eat, tarry one for another.

34 And if any man hunger, let him eat at home; that ye come not together unto condem-

nation. And the rest will I set in order when I come.

12 NOW concerning spiritual *gifts*, brethren, I would not have you ignorant.

2 Ye know that ye were Gen'tiles, carried away unto these dumb idols, even as ye were led.

3 Wherefore I give you to understand, that no man speaking by the Spirit of God calleth Je'sus accursed: and *that* no man can say that Je'sus is the Lord but by the Ho'ly Ghost.

4 Now there are diversities of gifts, but the same Spirit.

5 And there are differences of administrations, but the same Lord.

6 And there are diversities of operations, but it is the same God which worketh all in all.

7 But the manifestation of the Spirit is given to every man to profit withal.

8 For to one is given by the Spirit the word of wisdom; to another the word of knowledge by the same Spirit;

9 To another faith by the same Spirit; to another the gifts of healing by the same Spirit;

10 To another the working of miracles; to another prophecy; to another discerning of spirits; to another *divers* kinds of tongues; to another the interpretation of tongues:

11 But all these worketh that one and the selfsame Spirit, dividing to every man severally as he will.

12 For as the body is one, and hath many members, and all the members of that one body, being many, are one body: so also *is* Christ.

13 For by one Spirit are we all baptized into one body, whether *we be* Jews or Gen'tiles, whether *we be* bond or free; and have been all made to drink into one Spirit.

14 For the body is not one member, but many.

15 If the foot shall say, Because I am not the hand, I am not of the body; is it therefore not of the body?

16 And if the ear shall say, Because I am not the eye, I am not of the body; is it therefore not of the body?

17 If the whole body *were* an eye, where *were* the hearing? If the whole *were* hearing, where *were* the smelling?

18 But now hath God set the members every one of them in the body, as it hath pleased him.

19 And if they were all one member, where *were* the body?

20 But now *are they* many members, yet but one body.

21 And the eye cannot say unto the hand, I have no need of thee: nor again the head to the feet, I have no need of you.

22 Nay, much more those members of the body, which seem to be more feeble, are necessary:

23 And those *members* of the body, which we think to be less honourable, upon these we bestow more abundant honour; and our uncomely *parts* have more abundant comeliness.

24 For our comely *parts* have no need: but God hath tempered the body together, having given more abundant honour to that *part* which lacked:

25 That there should be no schism in the body; but *that* the members should have the same care one for another.

26 And whether one member suffer, all the members suffer with it; or one member be honoured, all the members rejoice with it.

27 Now ye are the body of Christ, and members in particular.

28 And God hath set some in the church, first apostles, secondarily prophets, thirdly teachers, after that miracles, then gifts of healings, helps, governments, diversities of tongues.

29 *Are* all apostles? *are* all prophets? *are* all teachers? *are* all workers of miracles?

30 Have all the gifts of healing? do all speak with tongues? do all interpret?

31 But covet earnestly the best gifts: and yet shew I unto you a more excellent way.

13 THOUGH I speak with the tongues of men and of angels, and have not charity, I am become *as* sounding brass, or a tinkling cymbal.

2 And though I have *the gift of* prophecy, and understand all mysteries, and all knowledge; and though I have all faith, so that I could remove mountains, and have not charity, I am nothing.

3 And though I bestow all my goods to feed *the poor*, and though I give my body to be burned, and have not charity, it profiteth me nothing.

4 Charity suffereth long, *and* is kind; charity envieth not; charity vaunteth not itself, is not puffed up,

5 Doth not behave itself unseemly, seeketh not her own, is not easily provoked, thinketh no evil;

6 Rejoiceth not in iniquity, but rejoiceth in the truth;

7 Beareth all things, believeth all things, hopeth all things, endureth all things.

8 Charity never faileth: but whether *there be* prophecies, they shall fail; whether *there be* tongues, they shall cease; whether *there be* knowledge, it shall vanish away.

9 For we know in part, and we prophesy in part.

10 But when that which is perfect is come, then that which is in part shall be done away.

11 When I was a child, I spake as a child, I understood as a child, I thought as a child: but when I became a man, I put away childish things.

12 For now we see through a glass, darkly; but then face to face: now I know in part; but then shall I know even as also I am known.

13 And now abideth faith, hope, charity, these three; but the greatest of these *is* charity.

14 FOLLOW after charity, and desire spiritual *gifts*, but rather that ye may prophesy.

2 For he that speaketh in an *unknown* tongue speaketh not unto men, but unto God: for no man understandeth *him*; howbeit in the spirit he speaketh mysteries.

3 But he that prophesieth speaketh unto men *to* edification, and exhortation, and comfort.

4 He that speaketh in an *unknown* tongue edifieth himself; but he that prophesieth edifieth the church.

5 I would that ye all spake with tongues, but rather that ye prophesied: for greater *is* he that prophesieth than he that speaketh with tongues, except he interpret, that the church may receive edifying.

6 Now, brethren, if I come unto you speaking with tongues, what shall I profit you, except I shall speak to you either by revelation, or by knowledge, or by prophesying, or by doctrine?

7 And even things without life giving sound, whether pipe or harp, except they give a dis-

tinction in the sounds, how shall it be known what is piped or harped?

8 For if the trumpet give an uncertain sound, who shall prepare himself to the battle?

9 So likewise ye, except ye utter by the tongue words easy to be understood, how shall it be known what is spoken? for ye shall speak into the air.

10 There are, it may be, so many kinds of voices in the world, and none of them *is* without signification.

11 Therefore if I know not the meaning of the voice, I shall be unto him that speaketh a barbarian, and he that speaketh *shall be* a barbarian unto me.

12 Even so ye, forasmuch as ye are zealous of spiritual *gifts*, seek that ye may excel to the edifying of the church.

13 Wherefore let him that speaketh in an *unknown* tongue pray that he may interpret.

14 For if I pray in an *unknown* tongue, my spirit prayeth, but my understanding is unfruitful.

15 What is it then? I will pray with the spirit, and I will pray with the understanding also: I will sing with the spirit, and I will sing with the understanding also.

16 Else when thou shalt bless with the spirit, how shall he that occupieth the room of the unlearned say Amen at thy giving of thanks, seeing he understandeth not what thou sayest?

17 For thou verily givest thanks well, but the other is not edified.

18 I thank my God, I speak with tongues more than ye all:

19 Yet in the church I had rather speak five words with my understanding, that *by my voice* I might teach others also, than ten thousand words in an *unknown* tongue.

20 Brethren, be not children in understanding: howbeit in malice be ye children, but in understanding be men.

21 In the law it is written, With *men of* other tongues and other lips will I speak unto this people; and yet for all that will they not hear me, saith the Lord.

22 Wherefore tongues are for a sign, not to them that believe, but to them that believe not: but prophesying *serveth* not for them that believe not, but for them which believe.

23 If therefore the whole church be come together into one place, and all speak with tongues, and there come in *those that are* unlearned, or unbelievers, will they not say that ye are mad?

24 But if all prophesy, and there come in one that believeth not, or *one* unlearned, he is convinced of all, he is judged of all:

25 And thus are the secrets of his heart made manifest; and so falling down on *his* face he will worship God, and report that God is in you of a truth.

26 How is it then, brethren? when ye come together, every one of you hath a psalm, hath a doctrine, hath a tongue, hath a revelation, hath an interpretation. Let all things be done unto edifying.

27 If any man speak in an *unknown* tongue, *let it be* by two, or at the most *by* three, and *that* by course; and let one interpret.

28 But if there be no interpreter, let him keep silence in the church; and let him speak to himself, and to God.

29 Let the prophets speak two or three, and let the other judge.

30 If *any thing* be revealed to another that sitteth by, let the first hold his peace.

31 For ye may all prophesy one by one, that all may learn, and all may be comforted.

32 And the spirits of the prophets are subject to the prophets.

33 For God is not *the author* of confusion, but of peace, as in all churches of the saints.

34 Let your women keep silence in the churches: for it is not permitted unto them to speak; but *they are commanded* to be under obedience, as also saith the law.

35 And if they will learn any thing, let them ask their husbands at home: for it is a shame for women to speak in the church.

36 What? came the word of God out from you? or came it unto you only?

37 If any man think himself to be a prophet, or spiritual, let him acknowledge that the things that I write unto you are the commandments of the Lord.

38 But if any man be ignorant, let him be ignorant.

39 Wherefore, brethren, covet to prophesy, and forbid not to speak with tongues.

40 Let all things be done decently and in order.

15 MOREOVER, brethren, I declare unto you the gospel which I preached unto you, which also ye have received, and wherein ye stand;

2 By which also ye are saved, if ye keep in memory what I preached unto you, unless ye have believed in vain.

3 For I delivered unto you first of all that which I also received, how that Christ died for our sins according to the scriptures;

4 And that he was buried, and that he rose again the third day according to the scriptures:

5 And that he was seen of Ce′phas, then of the twelve:

6 After that, he was seen of above five hundred brethren at once; of whom the greater part remain unto this present, but some are fallen asleep.

7 After that, he was seen of James; then of all the apostles.

8 And last of all he was seen of me also, as of one born out of due time.

9 For I am the least of the apostles, that am not meet to be called an apostle, because I persecuted the church of God.

10 But by the grace of God I am what I am: and his grace which *was bestowed* upon me was not in vain; but I laboured more abundantly than they all: yet not I, but the grace of God which was with me.

11 Therefore whether *it were* I or they, so we preach, and so ye believed.

12 Now if Christ be preached that he rose from the dead, how say some among you that there is no resurrection of the dead?

13 But if there be no resurrection of the dead, then is Christ not risen:

14 And if Christ be not risen, then *is* our preaching vain, and your faith *is* also vain.

15 Yea, and we are found false witnesses of God; because we have testified of God that he raised up Christ: whom he raised not up, if so be that the dead rise not.

16 For if the dead rise not, then is not Christ raised:

17 And if Christ be not raised, your faith *is* vain; ye are yet in your sins.

18 Then they also which are fallen asleep in Christ are perished.

19 If in this life only we have hope in Christ, we are of all men most miserable.

20 But now is Christ risen from the dead, *and* become the firstfruits of them that slept.

21 For since by man *came* death, by man *came* also the resurrection of the dead.

22 For as in Ad'am all die, even so in Christ shall all be made alive.

23 But every man in his own order: Christ the firstfruits; afterward they that are Christ's at his coming.

24 Then *cometh* the end, when he shall have delivered up the kingdom to God, even the Father; when he shall have put down all rule and all authority and power.

25 For he must reign, till he hath put all enemies under his feet.

26 The last enemy *that* shall be destroyed *is* death.

27 For he hath put all things under his feet. But when he saith all things are put under *him,* it is manifest that he is excepted, which did put all things under him.

28 And when all things shall be subdued unto him, then shall the Son also himself be subject unto him that put all things under him, that God may be all in all.

29 Else what shall they do which are baptized for the dead, if the dead rise not at all? why are they then baptized for the dead?

30 And why stand we in jeopardy every hour?

31 I protest by your rejoicing which I have in Christ Je'sus our Lord, I die daily.

32 If after the manner of men I have fought with beasts at Eph'e-sus, what advantageth it me, if the dead rise not? let us eat and drink; for to morrow we die.

33 Be not deceived: evil communications corrupt good manners.

34 Awake to righteousness, and sin not; for some have not the knowledge of God: I speak *this* to your shame.

35 But some *man* will say, How are the dead raised up? and with what body do they come?

36 *Thou* fool, that which thou sowest is not quickened, except it die:

37 And that which thou sowest, thou sowest not that body that shall be, but bare grain, it may chance of wheat, or of some other *grain:*

38 But God giveth it a body as it hath pleased him, and to every seed his own body.

39 All flesh *is* not the same flesh: but *there is* one *kind* of flesh of men, another flesh of beasts, another of fishes, *and* another of birds.

40 *There are* also celestial bodies, and bodies terrestrial: but the glory of the celestial *is* one, and the *glory* of the terrestrial *is* another.

41 *There is* one glory of the sun, and another glory of the moon, and another glory of the stars: for *one* star differeth from *another* star in glory.

42 So also *is* the resurrection of the dead. It is sown in corruption: it is raised in incorruption:

43 It is sown in dishonour; it is raised in glory: it is sown in weakness; it is raised in power:

44 It is sown a natural body; it is raised a spiritual body. There is a natural body, and there is a spiritual body.

45 And so it is written, The first man Ad'am was made a living soul; the last Ad'am *was made* a quickening spirit.

46 Howbeit that *was* not first which is spiritual, but that which is natural; and afterward that which is spiritual.

47 The first man *is* of the earth, earthy: the second man *is* the Lord from heaven.

48 As *is* the earthy, such *are* they also that are earthy: and as *is* the heavenly, such *are* they also that are heavenly.

49 And as we have borne the image of the earthy, we shall also bear the image of the heavenly.

50 Now this I say, brethren, that flesh and blood cannot inherit the kingdom of God; neither doth corruption inherit incorruption.

51 Behold, I shew you a mystery; We shall not all sleep, but we shall all be changed,

52 In a moment, in the twinkling of an eye, at the last trump: for the trumpet shall sound, and the dead shall be raised incorruptible, and we shall be changed.

53 For this corruptible must put on incorruption, and this mortal *must* put on immortality.

54 So when this corruptible shall have put on incorruption, and this mortal shall have put on immortality, then shall be brought to pass the saying that is written, Death is swallowed up in victory.

55 O death, where *is* thy sting? O grave, where *is* thy victory?

56 The sting of death *is* sin; and the strength of sin *is* the law.

57 But thanks *be* to God, which giveth us the victory through our Lord Je'sus Christ.

58 Therefore, my beloved brethren, be ye stedfast, unmoveable, always abounding in the work of the Lord, forasmuch as ye know that your labour is not in vain in the Lord.

16 NOW concerning the collection for the saints, as I have given order to the churches of Ga-la'tia, even so do ye.

2 Upon the first *day* of the week let every one of you lay by him in store, as *God* hath prospered him, that there be no gatherings when I come.

3 And when I come, whomsoever ye shall approve by *your* letters, them will I send to bring your liberality unto Je-ru'sa-lem.

4 And if it be meet that I go also, they shall go with me.

5 Now I will come unto you, when I shall pass through Mac-e-do'ni-a: for I do pass through Mac-e-do'ni-a.

6 And it may be that I will abide, yea, and winter with you, that ye may bring me on my journey whithersoever I go.

7 For I will not see you now by the way; but I trust to tarry a while with you, if the Lord permit.

8 But I will tarry at Eph'e-sus until Pen'te-cost.

9 For a great door and effectual is opened unto me, and *there are* many adversaries.

10 Now if Ti-mo'the-us come, see that he may be with you without fear: for he worketh the work of the Lord, as I also *do.*

11 Let no man therefore despise him: but conduct him forth in peace, that he may come unto me: for I look for him with the brethren.

12 As touching *our* brother A-pol'los, I greatly desired him to come unto you with the brethren: but his will was not at all to come at this time; but he will come when he shall have convenient time.

13 Watch ye, stand fast in the faith, quit you like men, be strong.

14 Let all your things be done with charity.

15 I beseech you, brethren, (ye know the house of Steph'a-nas, that it is the firstfruits of A-cha'ia, and *that* they have addicted themselves to the ministry of the saints,)

16 That ye submit yourselves unto such, and to every one that helpeth with *us*, and laboureth.

17 I am glad of the coming of Steph'a-nas and For-tu-na'tus and A-cha'i-cus: for that which was lacking on your part they have supplied.

18 For they have refreshed my spirit and yours: therefore acknowledge ye them that are such.

19 The churches of A'sia salute you. A'qui-la and Pris-cil'la salute you much in the Lord, with the church that is in their house.

20 All the brethren greet you. Greet ye one another with an holy kiss.

21 The salutation of *me* Paul with mine own hand.

22 If any man love not the Lord Je'sus Christ, let him be An-ath'e-ma Mar-an-a'tha.

23 The grace of our Lord Je'sus Christ *be* with you.

24 My love *be* with you all in Christ Je'sus. Amen.

The first *epistle* to the Co-rin'thi-ans was written from Phi-lip'pi by Steph'a-nas, and For-tu-na'tus, and A-cha'-i-cus, and Ti-mo'the-us.

THE SECOND LETTER OF PAUL TO THE

CORINTHIANS

1 PAUL, an apostle of Je'sus Christ by the will of God, and Tim'o-thy *our* brother, unto the church of God which is at Cor'inth, with all the saints which are in all A-cha'ia:

2 Grace *be* to you and peace from God our Father, and *from* the Lord Je'sus Christ.

3 Blessed *be* God, even the Father of our Lord Je'sus Christ, the Father of mercies, and the God of all comfort;

4 Who comforteth us in all our tribulation, that we may be able to comfort them which are in any trouble, by the comfort wherewith we ourselves are comforted of God.

5 For as the sufferings of Christ abound in us, so our consolation also aboundeth by Christ.

6 And whether we be afflicted, *it is* for your consolation and salvation, which is effectual in the enduring of the same sufferings which we also suffer: or whether we be comforted, *it is* for your consolation and salvation.

7 And our hope of you *is* stedfast, knowing, that as ye are partakers of the sufferings, so *shall ye be* also of the consolation.

8 For we would not, brethren, have you ignorant of our trouble which came to us in A'sia, that we were pressed out of measure, above strength, insomuch that we despaired even of life:

9 But we had the sentence of death in ourselves, that we should not trust in ourselves, but in God which raiseth the dead:

10 Who delivered us from so great a death, and doth deliver: in whom we trust that he will yet deliver *us*;

11 Ye also helping together by prayer for us, that for the gift *bestowed* upon us by the means of many persons thanks may be given by many on our behalf.

12 For our rejoicing is this, the testimony of our conscience, that in simplicity and godly sincerity, not with fleshly wisdom, but by the grace of God, we have had our conversation in the world, and more abundantly to you-ward.

13 For we write none other things unto you, than what ye read or acknowledge; and I trust ye shall acknowledge even to the end;

14 As also ye have acknowledged us in part, that we are your rejoicing, even as ye also *are* ours in the day of the Lord Je'sus.

15 And in this confidence I was minded to come unto you before, that ye might have a second benefit;

16 And to pass by you into Mac-e-do'ni-a, and to come again out of Mac-e-do'ni-a unto you, and of you to be brought on my way toward Ju-dæ'a.

17 When I therefore was thus minded, did I use lightness? or the things that I purpose, do I purpose according to the flesh, that with me there should be yea yea, and nay nay?

18 But *as* God *is* true, our word toward you was not yea and nay.

19 For the Son of God, Je'sus Christ, who was preached among you by us, *even* by me and Sil-va'nus and Ti-mo'the-us, was not yea and nay, but in him was yea.

20 For all the promises of God in him *are* yea, and in him Amen, unto the glory of God by us.

21 Now he which stablisheth us with you in Christ, and hath anointed us, *is* God;

22 Who hath also sealed us, and given the earnest of the Spirit in our hearts.

23 Moreover I call God for a record upon my soul, that to spare you I came not as yet unto Cor'inth.

24 Not for that we have dominion over your faith, but are helpers of your joy: for by faith ye stand.

2 BUT I determined this with myself, that I would not come again to you in heaviness.

2 For if I make you sorry, who is he then that maketh me glad, but the same which is made sorry by me?

3 And I wrote this same unto you, lest, when I came, I should have sorrow from them of whom I ought to rejoice; having confidence in you all, that my joy is *the joy* of you all.

4 For out of much affliction and anguish of heart I wrote unto you with many tears; not that ye should be grieved, but that ye might know the love which I have more abundantly unto you.

5 But if any have caused grief, he hath not grieved me, but in part: that I may not overcharge you all.

6 Sufficient to such a man *is* this punishment, which *was inflicted* of many.

7 So that contrariwise ye *ought* rather to forgive *him*, and comfort *him*, lest perhaps such a one should be swallowed up with overmuch sorrow.

8 Wherefore I beseech you that ye would confirm *your* love toward him.

9 For to this end also did I write, that I might know the proof of you, whether ye be obedient in all things.

10 To whom ye forgive any thing, I *forgive* also: for if I forgave any thing, to whom I for-

gave it, for your sakes forgave I it in the person of Christ;

11 Lest Sa'tan should get an advantage of us: for we are not ignorant of his devices.

12 Furthermore, when I came to Tro'as to preach Christ's gospel, and a door was opened unto me of the Lord,

13 I had no rest in my spirit, because I found not Ti'tus my brother: but taking my leave of them, I went from thence into Mac-e-do'ni-a.

14 Now thanks be unto God, which always causeth us to triumph in Christ, and maketh manifest the savour of his knowledge by us in every place.

15 For we are unto God a sweet savour of Christ, in them that are saved, and in them that perish:

16 To the one we are the savour of death unto death; and to the other the savour of life unto life. And who is sufficient for these things?

17 For we are not as many, which corrupt the word of God: but as of sincerity, but as of God, in the sight of God speak we in Christ.

3 DO we begin again to commend ourselves? or need we, as some others, epistles of commendation to you, or letters of commendation from you?

2 Ye are our epistle written in our hearts, known and read of all men:

3 Forasmuch as ye are manifestly declared to be the epistle of Christ ministered by us, written not with ink, but with the Spirit of the living God; not in tables of stone, but in fleshy tables of the heart.

4 And such trust have we through Christ to Godward:

5 Not that we are sufficient of ourselves to think any thing as of ourselves; but our sufficiency is of God;

6 Who also hath made us able ministers of the new testament; not of the letter, but of the spirit: for the letter killeth, but the spirit giveth life.

7 But if the ministration of death, written and engraven in stones, was glorious, so that the children of Is'ra-el could not stedfastly behold the face of Mo'ses for the glory of his countenance; which glory was to be done away:

8 How shall not the ministration of the spirit be rather glorious?

9 For if the ministration of condemnation be glory, much more doth the ministration of righteousness exceed in glory.

10 For even that which was made glorious had no glory in this respect, by reason of the glory that excelleth.

11 For if that which is done away was glorious, much more that which remaineth is glorious.

12 Seeing then that we have such hope, we use great plainness of speech:

13 And not as Mo'ses, which put a veil over his face, that the children of Is'ra-el could not stedfastly look to the end of that which is abolished:

14 But their minds were blinded: for until this day remaineth the same veil untaken away in the reading of the old testament; which veil is done away in Christ.

15 But even unto this day, when Mo'ses is read, the veil is upon their heart.

16 Nevertheless when it shall turn to the Lord, the veil shall be taken away.

17 Now the Lord is that Spirit: and where the Spirit of the Lord is, there is liberty.

18 But we all, with open face beholding as in a glass the glory of the Lord, are changed into the same image from glory to glory, even as by the Spirit of the Lord.

4 THEREFORE seeing we have this ministry, as we have received mercy, we faint not;

2 But have renounced the hidden things of dishonesty, not walking in craftiness, nor handling the word of God deceitfully; but by manifestation of the truth commending ourselves to every man's conscience in the sight of God.

3 But if our gospel be hid, it is hid to them that are lost:

4 In whom the god of this world hath blinded the minds of them which believe not, lest the light of the glorious gospel of Christ, who is the image of God, should shine unto them.

5 For we preach not ourselves, but Christ Je'sus the Lord; and ourselves your servants for Je'sus' sake.

6 For God, who commanded the light to shine out of darkness, hath shined in our hearts, to give the light of the knowledge of the glory of God in the face of Je'sus Christ.

7 But we have this treasure in earthen vessels, that the excellency of the power may be of God, and not of us.

8 We are troubled on every side, yet not distressed; we are perplexed, but not in despair;

9 Persecuted, but not forsaken; cast down, but not destroyed;

10 Always bearing about in the body the dying of the Lord Je'sus, that the life also of Je'sus might be made manifest in our body.

11 For we which live are alway delivered unto death for Je'sus' sake, that the life also of Je'sus might be made manifest in our mortal flesh.

12 So then death worketh in us, but life in you.

13 We having the same spirit of faith, according as it is written, I believed, and therefore have I spoken; we also believe, and therefore speak;

14 Knowing that he which raised up the Lord Je'sus shall raise up us also by Je'sus, and shall present us with you.

15 For all things are for your sakes, that the abundant grace might through the thanksgiving of many redound to the glory of God.

16 For which cause we faint not; but though our outward man perish, yet the inward man is renewed day by day.

17 For our light affliction, which is but for a moment, worketh for us a far more exceeding and eternal weight of glory;

18 While we look not at the things which are seen, but at the things which are not seen: for the things which are seen are temporal; but the things which are not seen are eternal.

5 FOR we know that if our earthly house of this tabernacle were dissolved, we have a building of God, an house not made with hands, eternal in the heavens.

2 For in this we groan, earnestly desiring to be clothed upon with our house which is from heaven:

3 If so be that being clothed we shall not be found naked.

4 For we that are in this tabernacle do groan, being burdened: not for that we would be unclothed, but clothed upon, that mortality might be swallowed up of life.

5 Now he that hath wrought us for the self-

same thing is God, who also hath given unto us the earnest of the Spirit.

6 Therefore we are always confident, knowing that, whilst we are at home in the body, we are absent from the Lord:

7 (For we walk by faith, not by sight:)

8 We are confident, I say, and willing rather to be absent from the body, and to be present with the Lord.

9 Wherefore we labour, that, whether present or absent, we may be accepted of him.

10 For we must all appear before the judgment seat of Christ; that every one may receive the things done in his body, according to that he hath done, whether it be good or bad.

11 Knowing therefore the terror of the Lord, we persuade men; but we are made manifest unto God; and I trust also are made manifest in your consciences.

12 For we commend not ourselves again unto you, but give you occasion to glory on our behalf, that ye may have somewhat to answer them which glory in appearance, and not in heart.

13 For whether we be beside ourselves, it is to God: or whether we be sober, it is for your cause.

14 For the love of Christ constraineth us; because we thus judge, that if one died for all, then were all dead:

15 And that he died for all, that they which live should not henceforth live unto themselves, but unto him which died for them, and rose again.

16 Wherefore henceforth know we no man after the flesh: yea, though we have known Christ after the flesh, yet now henceforth know we him no more.

17 Therefore if any man be in Christ, he is a new creature: old things are passed away; behold, all things are become new.

18 And all things are of God, who hath reconciled us to himself by Je'sus Christ, and hath given to us the ministry of reconciliation;

19 To wit, that God was in Christ, reconciling the world unto himself, not imputing their trespasses unto them; and hath committed unto us the word of reconciliation.

20 Now then we are ambassadors for Christ, as though God did beseech you by us: we pray you in Christ's stead, be ye reconciled to God.

21 For he hath made him to be sin for us, who knew no sin; that we might be made the righteousness of God in him.

6 WE then, as workers together with him, beseech you also that ye receive not the grace of God in vain.

2 (For he saith, I have heard thee in a time accepted, and in the day of salvation have I succoured thee: behold, now is the accepted time; behold, now is the day of salvation.)

3 Giving no offence in any thing, that the ministry be not blamed:

4 But in all things approving ourselves as the ministers of God, in much patience, in afflictions, in necessities, in distresses,

5 In stripes, in imprisonments, in tumults, in labours, in watchings, in fastings;

6 By pureness, by knowledge, by longsuffering, by kindness, by the Ho'ly Ghost, by love unfeigned,

7 By the word of truth, by the power of God, by the armour of righteousness on the right hand and on the left,

8 By honour and dishonour, by evil report and good report: as deceivers, and yet true;

9 As unknown, and yet well known; as dying, and, behold, we live; as chastened, and not killed;

10 As sorrowful, yet alway rejoicing; as poor, yet making many rich; as having nothing, and yet possessing all things.

11 O ye Co-rin'thi-ans, our mouth is open unto you, our heart is enlarged.

12 Ye are not straitened in us, but ye are straitened in your own bowels.

13 Now for a recompence in the same, (I speak as unto my children,) be ye also enlarged.

14 Be ye not unequally yoked together with unbelievers: for what fellowship hath righteousness with unrighteousness? and what communion hath light with darkness?

15 And what concord hath Christ with Be'li-al? or what part hath he that believeth with an infidel?

16 And what agreement hath the temple of God with idols? for ye are the temple of the living God; as God hath said, I will dwell in them, and walk in them; and I will be their God, and they shall be my people.

17 Wherefore come out from among them, and be ye separate, saith the Lord, and touch not the unclean thing: and I will receive you,

18 And will be a Father unto you, and ye shall be my sons and daughters, saith the Lord Almighty.

7 HAVING therefore these promises, dearly beloved, let us cleanse ourselves from all filthiness of the flesh and spirit, perfecting holiness in the fear of God.

2 Receive us; we have wronged no man, we have corrupted no man, we have defrauded no man.

3 I speak not this to condemn you: for I have said before, that ye are in our hearts to die and live with you.

4 Great is my boldness of speech toward you, great is my glorying of you: I am filled with comfort, I am exceeding joyful in all our tribulation.

5 For, when we were come into Mac-e-do'ni-a, our flesh had no rest, but we were troubled on every side; without were fightings, within were fears.

6 Nevertheless God, that comforteth those that are cast down, comforted us by the coming of Ti'tus;

7 And not by his coming only, but by the consolation wherewith he was comforted in you, when he told us your earnest desire, your mourning, your fervent mind toward me; so that I rejoiced the more.

8 For though I made you sorry with a letter, I do not repent, though I did repent: for I perceive that the same epistle hath made you sorry, though it were but for a season.

9 Now I rejoice, not that ye were made sorry, but that ye sorrowed to repentance: for ye were made sorry after a godly manner, that ye might receive damage by us in nothing.

10 For godly sorrow worketh repentance to salvation not to be repented of: but the sorrow of the world worketh death.

11 For behold this selfsame thing, that ye sorrowed after a godly sort, what carefulness it wrought in you, yea, what clearing of yourselves, yea, what indignation, yea, what fear, yea, what vehement desire, yea, what zeal, yea, what revenge! In all things ye have approved yourselves to be clear in this matter.

12 Wherefore, though I wrote unto you, I did it not for his cause that had done the wrong, nor

for his cause that suffered wrong, but that our care for you in the sight of God might appear unto you.

13 Therefore we were comforted in your comfort: yea, and exceedingly the more joyed we for the joy of Ti'tus, because his spirit was refreshed by you all.

14 For if I have boasted any thing to him of you, I am not ashamed; but as we spake all things to you in truth, even so our boasting, which *I made* before Ti'tus, is found a truth.

15 And his inward affection is more abundant toward you, whilst he remembereth the obedience of you all, how with fear and trembling ye received him.

16 I rejoice therefore that I have confidence in you in all *things.*

8 MOREOVER, brethren, we do you to wit of the grace of God bestowed on the churches of Mac-e-do'ni-a;

2 How that in a great trial of affliction the abundance of their joy and their deep poverty abounded unto the riches of their liberality.

3 For to *their* power, I bear record, yea, and beyond *their* power *they were* willing of themselves;

4 Praying us with much intreaty that we would receive the gift, and *take upon us* the fellowship of the ministering to the saints.

5 And *this they did,* not as we hoped, but first gave their own selves to the Lord, and unto us by the will of God.

6 Insomuch that we desired Ti'tus, that as he had begun, so he would also finish in you the same grace also.

7 Therefore, as ye abound in every *thing, in* faith, and utterance, and knowledge, and *in* all diligence, and *in* your love to us, *see* that ye abound in this grace also.

8 I speak not by commandment, but by occasion of the forwardness of others, and to prove the sincerity of your love.

9 For ye know the grace of our Lord Je'sus Christ, that, though he was rich, yet for your sakes he became poor, that ye through his poverty might be rich.

10 And herein I give *my* advice: for this is expedient for you, who have begun before, not only to do, but also to be forward a year ago.

11 Now therefore perform the doing *of it;* that as *there was* a readiness to will, so *there may be* a performance also out of that which ye have.

12 For if there be first a willing mind, *it is* accepted according to that a man hath, *and* not according to that he hath not.

13 For *I mean* not that other men be eased, and ye burdened:

14 But by an equality, *that* now at this time your abundance *may be a supply* for their want, that their abundance also may be *a supply* for your want: that there may be equality:

15 As it is written, He that *had gathered* much had nothing over; and he that *had gathered* little had no lack.

16 But thanks *be* to God, which put the same earnest care into the heart of Ti'tus for you.

17 For indeed he accepted the exhortation; but being more forward, of his own accord he went unto you.

18 And we have sent with him the brother, whose praise *is* in the gospel throughout all the churches;

19 And not *that* only, but who was also chosen of the churches to travel with us with this grace, which is administered by us to the glory

of the same Lord, and *declaration of* your ready mind:

20 Avoiding this, that no man should blame us in this abundance which is administered by us:

21 Providing for honest things, not only in the sight of the Lord, but also in the sight of men.

22 And we have sent with them our brother, whom we have oftentimes proved diligent in many things, but now much more diligent, upon the great confidence which *I have* in you.

23 Whether *any do enquire* of Ti'tus, *he is* my partner and fellowhelper concerning you: or our brethren *be enquired of, they are* the messengers of the churches, *and* the glory of Christ.

24 Wherefore shew ye to them, and before the churches, the proof of your love, and of our boasting on your behalf.

9 FOR as touching the ministering to the saints, it is superfluous for me to write to you:

2 For I know the forwardness of your mind, for which I boast of you to them of Mac-e-do'ni-a, that A-cha'ia was ready a year ago; and your zeal hath provoked very many.

3 Yet have I sent the brethren, lest our boasting of you should be in vain in this behalf; that, as I said, ye may be ready:

4 Lest haply if they of Mac-e-do'ni-a come with me, and find you unprepared, we (that we say not, ye) should be ashamed in this same confident boasting.

5 Therefore I thought it necessary to exhort the brethren, that they would go before unto you, and make up beforehand your bounty, whereof ye had notice before, that the same might be ready, as *a matter of* bounty, and not as *of* covetousness.

6 But this *I say,* He which soweth sparingly shall reap also sparingly; and he which soweth bountifully shall reap also bountifully.

7 Every man according as he purposeth in his heart, *so let him give;* not grudgingly, or of necessity: for God loveth a cheerful giver.

8 And God *is* able to make all grace abound toward you; that ye, always having all sufficiency in all *things,* may abound to every good work:

9 (As it is written, He hath dispersed abroad; he hath given to the poor: his righteousness remaineth for ever.

10 Now he that ministereth seed to the sower both minister bread for *your* food, and multiply your seed sown, and increase the fruits of your righteousness;)

11 Being enriched in every thing to all bountifulness, which causeth through us thanksgiving to God.

12 For the administration of this service not only supplieth the want of the saints, but is abundant also by many thanksgivings unto God;

13 Whiles by the experiment of this ministration they glorify God for your professed subjection unto the gospel of Christ, and for *your* liberal distribution unto them, and unto all *men;*

14 And by their prayer for you, which long after you for the exceeding grace of God in you.

15 Thanks *be* unto God for his unspeakable gift.

10 NOW I Paul myself beseech you by the meekness and gentleness of Christ, who in presence *am* base among you, but being absent am bold toward you:

2 But I beseech *you*, that I may not be bold when I am present with that confidence, wherewith I think to be bold against some, which think of us as if we walked according to the flesh.

3 For though we walk in the flesh, we do not war after the flesh:

4 (For the weapons of our warfare *are* not carnal, but mighty through God to the pulling down of strong holds;)

5 Casting down imaginations, and every high thing that exalteth itself against the knowledge of God, and bringing into captivity every thought to the obedience of Christ;

6 And having in a readiness to revenge all disobedience, when your obedience is fulfilled.

7 Do ye look on things after the outward appearance? If any man trust to himself that he is Christ's, let him of himself think this again, that, as he *is* Christ's, even so *are* we Christ's.

8 For though I should boast somewhat more of our authority, which the Lord hath given us for edification, and not for your destruction, I should not be ashamed:

9 That I may not seem as if I would terrify you by letters.

10 For *his* letters, say they, *are* weighty and powerful; but *his* bodily presence *is* weak, and *his* speech contemptible.

11 Let such an one think this, that, such as we are in word by letters when we are absent, such *will we be* also in deed when we are present.

12 For we dare not make ourselves of the number, or compare ourselves with some that commend themselves; but they measuring themselves by themselves, and comparing themselves among themselves, are not wise.

13 But we will not boast of things without *our* measure, but according to the measure of the rule which God hath distributed to us, a measure to reach even unto you.

14 For we stretch not ourselves beyond *our measure*, as though we reached not unto you: for we are come as far as to you also in *preaching* the gospel of Christ:

15 Not boasting of things without *our* measure, *that is*, of other men's labours; but having hope, when your faith is increased, that we shall be enlarged by you according to our rule abundantly,

16 To preach the gospel in the *regions* beyond you, *and* not to boast in another man's line of things made ready to our hand.

17 But he that glorieth, let him glory in the Lord.

18 For not he that commendeth himself is approved, but whom the Lord commendeth.

11 WOULD to God ye could bear with me a little in *my* folly: and indeed bear with me.

2 For I am jealous over you with godly jealousy: for I have espoused you to one husband, that I may present *you as* a chaste virgin to Christ.

3 But I fear, lest by any means, as the serpent beguiled Eve through his subtilty, so your minds should be corrupted from the simplicity that is in Christ.

4 For if he that cometh preacheth another Je'sus, whom we have not preached, or *if* ye receive another spirit, which ye have not received, or another gospel, which ye have not accepted, ye might well bear with *him*.

5 For I suppose I was not a whit behind the very chiefest apostles.

6 But though *I be* rude in speech, yet not in knowledge; but we have been throughly made manifest among you in all things.

7 Have I committed an offence in abasing myself that ye might be exalted, because I have preached to you the gospel of God freely?

8 I robbed other churches, taking wages *of them*, to do you service.

9 And when I was present with you, and wanted, I was chargeable to no man: for that which was lacking to me the brethren which came from Mac-e-do'ni-a supplied: and in all *things* I have kept myself from being burdensome unto you, and *so* will I keep *myself*.

10 As the truth of Christ is in me, no man shall stop me of this boasting in the regions of A-cha'ia.

11 Wherefore? because I love you not? God knoweth.

12 But what I do, that I will do, that I may cut off occasion from them which desire occasion; that wherein they glory, they may be found even as we.

13 For such *are* false apostles, deceitful workers, transforming themselves into the apostles of Christ.

14 And no marvel; for Sa'tan himself is transformed into an angel of light.

15 Therefore *it is* no great thing if his ministers also be transformed as the ministers of righteousness; whose end shall be according to their works.

16 I say again, Let no man think me a fool; if otherwise, yet as a fool receive me, that I may boast myself a little.

17 That which I speak, I speak *it* not after the Lord, but as it were foolishly, in this confidence of boasting.

18 Seeing that many glory after the flesh, I will glory also.

19 For ye suffer fools gladly, seeing ye *yourselves* are wise.

20 For ye suffer, if a man bring you into bondage, if a man devour *you*, if a man take *of you*, if a man exalt himself, if a man smite you on the face.

21 I speak as concerning reproach, as though we had been weak. Howbeit whereinsoever any is bold, (I speak foolishly,) I am bold also.

22 Are they He'brews? so *am* I. Are they Is'-ra-el-ites? so *am* I. Are they the seed of A'braham? so *am* I.

23 Are they ministers of Christ? (I speak as a fool) I *am* more; in labours more abundant, in stripes above measure, in prisons more frequent, in deaths oft.

24 Of the Jews five times received I forty *stripes* save one.

25 Thrice was I beaten with rods, once was I stoned, thrice I suffered shipwreck, a night and a day I have been in the deep;

26 *In* journeyings often, *in* perils of waters, *in* perils of robbers, *in* perils by mine own countrymen, *in* perils by the heathen, *in* perils in the city, *in* perils in the wilderness, *in* perils in the sea, *in* perils among false brethren;

27 In weariness and painfulness, in watchings often, in hunger and thirst, in fastings often, in cold and nakedness.

28 Beside those things that are without, that which cometh upon me daily, the care of all the churches.

29 Who is weak, and I am not weak? who is offended, and I burn not?

30 If I must needs glory, I will glory of the things which concern mine infirmities.

31 The God and Father of our Lord Je'sus

Christ, which is blessed for evermore, knoweth that I lie not.

32 In Da-mas'cus the governor under Ar'e-tas the king kept the city of the Dam'as-cenes with a garrison, desirous to apprehend me:

33 And through a window in a basket was I let down by the wall, and escaped his hands.

12 IT is not expedient for me doubtless to glory. I will come to visions and revelations of the Lord.

2 I knew a man in Christ above fourteen years ago, (whether in the body, I cannot tell; or whether out of the body, I cannot tell: God knoweth;) such an one caught up to the third heaven.

3 And I knew such a man, (whether in the body, or out of the body, I cannot tell: God knoweth;)

4 How that he was caught up into paradise, and heard unspeakable words, which it is not lawful for a man to utter.

5 Of such an one will I glory: yet of myself I will not glory, but in mine infirmities.

6 For though I would desire to glory, I shall not be a fool; for I will say the truth: but now I forbear, lest any man should think of me above that which he seeth me to be, or that he heareth of me.

7 And lest I should be exalted above measure through the abundance of the revelations, there was given to me a thorn in the flesh, the messenger of Sa'tan to buffet me, lest I should be exalted above measure.

8 For this thing I besought the Lord thrice, that it might depart from me.

9 And he said unto me, My grace is sufficient for thee: for my strength is made perfect in weakness. Most gladly therefore will I rather glory in my infirmities, that the power of Christ may rest upon me.

10 Therefore I take pleasure in infirmities, in reproaches, in necessities, in persecutions, in distresses for Christ's sake: for when I am weak, then am I strong.

11 I am become a fool in glorying; ye have compelled me: for I ought to have been commended of you: for in nothing am I behind the very chiefest apostles, though I be nothing.

12 Truly the signs of an apostle were wrought among you in all patience, in signs, and wonders, and mighty deeds.

13 For what is it wherein ye were inferior to other churches, except it be that I myself was not burdensome to you? forgive me this wrong.

14 Behold, the third time I am ready to come to you; and I will not be burdensome to you: for I seek not yours, but you: for the children ought not to lay up for the parents, but the parents for the children.

15 And I will very gladly spend and be spent for you; though the more abundantly I love you, the less I be loved.

16 But be it so, I did not burden you: nevertheless, being crafty, I caught you with guile.

17 Did I make a gain of you by any of them whom I sent unto you?

18 I desired Ti'tus, and with him I sent a brother. Did Ti'tus make a gain of you? walked we not in the same spirit? walked we not in the same steps?

19 Again, think ye that we excuse ourselves unto you? we speak before God in Christ: but we do all things, dearly beloved, for your edifying.

20 For I fear, lest, when I come, I shall not find you such as I would, and that I shall be found unto you such as ye would not: lest there be debates, envyings, wraths, strifes, backbitings, whisperings, swellings, tumults:

21 And lest, when I come again, my God will humble me among you, and that I shall bewail many which have sinned already, and have not repented of the uncleanness and fornication and lasciviousness which they have committed.

13 THIS is the third time I am coming to you. In the mouth of two or three witnesses shall every word be established.

2 I told you before, and foretell you, as if I were present, the second time; and being absent now I write to them which heretofore have sinned, and to all other, that, if I come again, I will not spare:

3 Since ye seek a proof of Christ speaking in me, which to you-ward is not weak, but is mighty in you.

4 For though he was crucified through weakness, yet he liveth by the power of God. For we also are weak in him, but we shall live with him by the power of God toward you.

5 Examine yourselves, whether ye be in the faith; prove your own selves. Know ye not your own selves, how that Je'sus Christ is in you, except ye be reprobates?

6 But I trust that ye shall know that we are not reprobates.

7 Now I pray to God that ye do no evil; not that we should appear approved, but that ye should do that which is honest, though we be as reprobates.

8 For we can do nothing against the truth, but for the truth.

9 For we are glad, when we are weak, and ye are strong: and this also we wish, even your perfection.

10 Therefore I write these things being absent, lest being present I should use sharpness, according to the power which the Lord hath given me to edification, and not to destruction.

11 Finally, brethren, farewell. Be perfect, be of good comfort, be of one mind, live in peace; and the God of love and peace shall be with you.

12 Greet one another with an holy kiss.

13 All the saints salute you.

14 The grace of the Lord Je'sus Christ, and the love of God, and the communion of the Ho'-ly Ghost, be with you all. Amen.

The second epistle to the Co-rin'thi-ans was written from Phi-lip'pi, a city of Mac-e-do'ni-a, by Ti'tus and Lu'cas.

1 PAUL, an apostle, (not of men, neither by man, but by Je′sus Christ, and God the Father, who raised him from the dead;)

2 And all the brethren which are with me, unto the churches of Ga-la′tia:

3 Grace be to you and peace from God the Father, and from our Lord Je′sus Christ,

4 Who gave himself for our sins, that he might deliver us from this present evil world, according to the will of God and our Father:

5 To whom be glory for ever and ever. Amen.

6 I marvel that ye are so soon removed from him that called you into the grace of Christ unto another gospel:

7 Which is not another; but there be some that trouble you, and would pervert the gospel of Christ.

8 But though we, or an angel from heaven, preach any other gospel unto you than that which we have preached unto you, let him be accursed.

9 As we said before, so say I now again, If any man preach any other gospel unto you than that ye have received, let him be accursed.

10 For do I now persuade men, or God? or do I seek to please men? for if I yet pleased men, I should not be the servant of Christ.

11 But I certify you, brethren, that the gospel which was preached of me is not after man.

12 For I neither received it of man, neither was I taught it, but by the revelation of Je′sus Christ.

13 For ye have heard of my conversation in time past in the Jews' religion, how that beyond measure I persecuted the church of God, and wasted it:

14 And profited in the Jews' religion above many my equals in mine own nation, being more exceedingly zealous of the traditions of my fathers.

15 But when it pleased God, who separated me from my mother's womb, and called me by his grace,

16 To reveal his Son in me, that I might preach him among the heathen; immediately I conferred not with flesh and blood:

17 Neither went I up to Je-ru′sa-lem to them which were apostles before me; but I went into A-ra′bi-a, and returned again unto Da-mas′cus.

18 Then after three years I went up to Je-ru′sa-lem to see Pe′ter, and abode with him fifteen days.

19 But other of the apostles saw I none, save James the Lord's brother.

20 Now the things which I write unto you, behold, before God, I lie not.

21 Afterwards I came into the regions of Syr′i-a and Ci-li′cia;

22 And was unknown by face unto the churches of Ju-dæ′a which were in Christ:

23 But they had heard only, That he which persecuted us in times past now preacheth the faith which once he destroyed.

24 And they glorified God in me.

2 THEN fourteen years after I went up again to Je-ru′sa-lem with Bar′na-bas, and took Ti′tus with me also.

2 And I went up by revelation, and communicated unto them that gospel which I preach among the Gen′tiles, but privately to them which were of reputation, lest by any means I should run, or had run, in vain.

3 But neither Ti′tus, who was with me, being a Greek, was compelled to be circumcised:

4 And that because of false brethren unawares brought in, who came in privily to spy out our liberty which we have in Christ Je′sus, that they might bring us into bondage:

5 To whom we gave place by subjection, no, not for an hour; that the truth of the gospel might continue with you.

6 But of these who seemed to be somewhat, (whatsoever they were, it maketh no matter to me: God accepteth no man's person:) for they who seemed to be somewhat in conference added nothing to me:

7 But contrariwise, when they saw that the gospel of the uncircumcision was committed unto me, as the gospel of the circumcision was unto Pe′ter;

8 (For he that wrought effectually in Pe′ter to the apostleship of the circumcision, the same was mighty in me toward the Gen′tiles:)

9 And when James, Ce′phas, and John, who seemed to be pillars, perceived the grace that was given unto me, they gave to me and Bar′na-bas the right hands of fellowship; that we should go unto the heathen, and they unto the circumcision.

10 Only they would that we should remember the poor; the same which I also was forward to do.

11 But when Pe′ter was come to An′ti-och, I withstood him to the face, because he was to be blamed.

12 For before that certain came from James, he did eat with the Gen′tiles: but when they were come, he withdrew and separated himself, fearing them which were of the circumcision.

13 And the other Jews dissembled likewise with him; insomuch that Bar′na-bas also was carried away with their dissimulation.

14 But when I saw that they walked not uprightly according to the truth of the gospel, I said unto Pe′ter before them all, If thou, being a Jew, livest after the manner of Gen′tiles, and not as do the Jews, why compellest thou the Gen′tiles to live as do the Jews?

15 We who are Jews by nature, and not sinners of the Gen′tiles,

16 Knowing that a man is not justified by the works of the law, but by the faith of Je′sus Christ, even we have believed in Je′sus Christ, that we might be justified by the faith of Christ, and not by the works of the law: for by the works of the law shall no flesh be justified.

17 But if, while we seek to be justified by Christ, we ourselves also are found sinners, is therefore Christ the minister of sin? God forbid.

18 For if I build again the things which I destroyed, I make myself a transgressor.

19 For I through the law am dead to the law, that I might live unto God.

20 I am crucified with Christ: nevertheless I live; yet not I, but Christ liveth in me: and the life which I now live in the flesh I live by the faith of the Son of God, who loved me, and gave himself for me.

21 I do not frustrate the grace of God: for if righteousness come by the law, then Christ is dead in vain.

3 O FOOLISH Ga-la'tians, who hath bewitched you, that ye should not obey the truth, before whose eyes Je'sus Christ hath been evidently set forth, crucified among you?

2 This only would I learn of you, Received ye the Spirit by the works of the law, or by the hearing of faith?

3 Are ye so foolish? having begun in the Spirit, are ye now made perfect by the flesh?

4 Have ye suffered so many things in vain? if *it be* yet in vain.

5 He therefore that ministereth to you the Spirit, and worketh miracles among you, *doeth he it* by the works of the law, or by the hearing of faith?

6 Even as A'bra-ham believed God, and it was accounted to him for righteousness.

7 Know ye therefore that they which are of faith, the same are the children of A'bra-ham.

8 And the scripture, foreseeing that God would justify the heathen through faith, preached before the gospel unto A'bra-ham, *saying,* In thee shall all nations be blessed.

9 So then they which be of faith are blessed with faithful A'bra-ham.

10 For as many as are of the works of the law are under the curse: for it is written, Cursed *is* every one that continueth not in all things which are written in the book of the law to do them.

11 But that no man is justified by the law in the sight of God, *it is* evident: for, The just shall live by faith.

12 And the law is not of faith: but, The man that doeth them shall live in them.

13 Christ hath redeemed us from the curse of the law, being made a curse for us: for it is written, Cursed *is* every one that hangeth on a tree:

14 That the blessing of A'bra-ham might come on the Gen'tiles through Je'sus Christ; that we might receive the promise of the Spirit through faith.

15 Brethren, I speak after the manner of men; Though *it be* but a man's covenant, yet *if it be* confirmed, no man disannulleth, or addeth thereto.

16 Now to A'bra-ham and his seed were the promises made. He saith not, And to seeds, as of many; but as of one, And to thy seed, which is Christ.

17 And this I say, *that* the covenant, that was confirmed before of God in Christ, the law, which was four hundred and thirty years after, cannot disannul, that it should make the promise of none effect.

18 For if the inheritance *be* of the law, *it is* no more of promise: but God gave *it* to A'bra-ham by promise.

19 Wherefore then *serveth* the law? It was added because of transgressions, till the seed should come to whom the promise was made; *and it was* ordained by angels in the hand of a mediator.

20 Now a mediator is not *a mediator* of one, but God is one.

21 *Is* the law then against the promises of God? God forbid: for if there had been a law given which could have given life, verily righteousness should have been by the law.

22 But the scripture hath concluded all under sin, that the promise by faith of Je'sus Christ might be given to them that believe.

23 But before faith came, we were kept under the law, shut up unto the faith which should afterwards be revealed.

24 Wherefore the law was our schoolmaster

to bring us unto Christ, that we might be justified by faith.

25 But after that faith is come, we are no longer under a schoolmaster.

26 For ye are all the children of God by faith in Christ Je'sus.

27 For as many of you as have been baptized into Christ have put on Christ.

28 There is neither Jew nor Greek, there is neither bond nor free, there is neither male nor female: for ye are all one in Christ Je'sus.

29 And if ye *be* Christ's, then are ye A'braham's seed, and heirs according to the promise.

4 NOW I say, *That* the heir, as long as he is a child, differeth nothing from a servant, though he be lord of all;

2 But is under tutors and governors until the time appointed of the father.

3 Even so we, when we were children, were in bondage under the elements of the world:

4 But when the fulness of the time was come, God sent forth his Son, made of a woman, made under the law,

5 To redeem them that were under the law, that we might receive the adoption of sons.

6 And because ye are sons, God hath sent forth the Spirit of his Son into your hearts, crying, Ab'ba, Father.

7 Wherefore thou art no more a servant, but a son; and if a son, then an heir of God through Christ.

8 Howbeit then, when ye knew not God, ye did service unto them which by nature are no gods.

9 But now, after that ye have known God, or rather are known of God, how turn ye again to the weak and beggarly elements, whereunto ye desire again to be in bondage?

10 Ye observe days, and months, and times, and years.

11 I am afraid of you, lest I have bestowed upon you labour in vain.

12 Brethren, I beseech you, be as I *am*; for I *am* as ye *are*: ye have not injured me at all.

13 Ye know how through infirmity of the flesh I preached the gospel unto you at the first.

14 And my temptation which was in my flesh ye despised not, nor rejected; but received me as an angel of God, *even* as Christ Je'sus.

15 Where is then the blessedness ye spake of? for I bear you record, that, if *it had been* possible, ye would have plucked out your own eyes, and have given them to me.

16 Am I therefore become your enemy, because I tell you the truth?

17 They zealously affect you, *but* not well; yea, they would exclude you, that ye might affect them.

18 But *it is* good to be zealously affected always in *a* good *thing,* and not only when I am present with you.

19 My little children, of whom I travail in birth again until Christ be formed in you,

20 I desire to be present with you now, and to change my voice; for I stand in doubt of you.

21 Tell me, ye that desire to be under the law, do ye not hear the law?

22 For it is written, that A'bra-ham had two sons, the one by a bondmaid, the other by a freewoman.

23 But he *who was* of the bondwoman was born after the flesh; but he of the freewoman *was* by promise.

24 Which things are an allegory: for these are the two covenants; the one from the mount

Si'nai, which gendereth to bondage, which is A'gar.

25 For this A'gar is mount Si'nai in A-ra'bi-a, and answereth to Je-ru'sa-lem which now is, and is in bondage with her children.

26 But Je-ru'sa-lem which is above is free, which is the mother of us all.

27 For it is written, Rejoice, *thou* barren that bearest not; break forth and cry, thou that travailest not: for the desolate hath many more children than she which hath an husband.

28 Now we, brethren, as I'saac was, are the children of promise.

29 But as then he that was born after the flesh persecuted him *that was born* after the Spirit, even so *it is* now.

30 Nevertheless what saith the scripture? Cast out the bondwoman and her son: for the son of the bondwoman shall not be heir with the son of the freewoman.

31 So then, brethren, we are not children of the bondwoman, but of the free.

5 STAND fast therefore in the liberty wherewith Christ hath made us free, and be not entangled again with the yoke of bondage.

2 Behold, I Paul say unto you, that if ye be circumcised, Christ shall profit you nothing.

3 For I testify again to every man that is circumcised, that he is a debtor to do the whole law.

4 Christ is become of no effect unto you, whosoever of you are justified by the law; ye are fallen from grace.

5 For we through the Spirit wait for the hope of righteousness by faith.

6 For in Je'sus Christ neither circumcision availeth any thing, nor uncircumcision; but faith which worketh by love.

7 Ye did run well; who did hinder you that ye should not obey the truth?

8 This persuasion *cometh* not of him that calleth you.

9 A little leaven leaveneth the whole lump.

10 I have confidence in you through the Lord, that ye will be none otherwise minded: but he that troubleth you shall bear his judgment, whosoever he be.

11 And I, brethren, if I yet preach circumcision, why do I yet suffer persecution? then is the offence of the cross ceased.

12 I would they were even cut off which trouble you.

13 For, brethren, ye have been called unto liberty; only *use* not liberty for an occasion to the flesh, but by love serve one another.

14 For all the law is fulfilled in one word, *even* in this; Thou shalt love thy neighbour as thyself.

15 But if ye bite and devour one another, take heed that ye be not consumed one of another.

16 *This* I say then, Walk in the Spirit, and ye shall not fulfil the lust of the flesh.

17 For the flesh lusteth against the Spirit, and the Spirit against the flesh: and these are contrary the one to the other: so that ye cannot do the things that ye would.

18 But if ye be led of the Spirit, ye are not under the law.

19 Now the works of the flesh are manifest, which are *these*; Adultery, fornication, uncleanness, lasciviousness,

20 Idolatry, witchcraft, hatred, variance, emulations, wrath, strife, seditions, heresies,

21 Envyings, murders, drunkenness, revellings, and such like: of the which I tell you before, as I have also told *you* in time past, that they which do such things shall not inherit the kingdom of God.

22 But the fruit of the Spirit is love, joy, peace, longsuffering, gentleness, goodness, faith,

23 Meekness, temperance: against such there is no law.

24 And they that are Christ's have crucified the flesh with the affections and lusts.

25 If we live in the Spirit, let us also walk in the Spirit.

26 Let us not be desirous of vain glory, provoking one another, envying one another.

6 BRETHREN, if a man be overtaken in a fault, ye which are spiritual, restore such an one in the spirit of meekness; considering thyself, lest thou also be tempted.

2 Bear ye one another's burdens, and so fulfil the law of Christ.

3 For if a man think himself to be something, when he is nothing, he deceiveth himself.

4 But let every man prove his own work, and then shall he have rejoicing in himself alone, and not in another.

5 For every man shall bear his own burden.

6 Let him that is taught in the word communicate unto him that teacheth in all good things.

7 Be not deceived; God is not mocked: for whatsoever a man soweth, that shall he also reap.

8 For he that soweth to his flesh shall of the flesh reap corruption; but he that soweth to the Spirit shall of the Spirit reap life everlasting.

9 And let us not be weary in well doing: for in due season we shall reap, if we faint not.

10 As we have therefore opportunity, let us do good unto all *men*, especially unto them who are of the household of faith.

11 Ye see how large a letter I have written unto you with mine own hand.

12 As many as desire to make a fair shew in the flesh, they constrain you to be circumcised; only lest they should suffer persecution for the cross of Christ.

13 For neither they themselves who are circumcised keep the law; but desire to have you circumcised, that they may glory in your flesh.

14 But God forbid that I should glory, save in the cross of our Lord Je'sus Christ, by whom the world is crucified unto me, and I unto the world.

15 For in Christ Je'sus neither circumcision availeth any thing, nor uncircumcision, but a new creature.

16 And as many as walk according to this rule, peace *be* on them, and mercy, and upon the Is'ra-el of God.

17 From henceforth let no man trouble me: for I bear in my body the marks of the Lord Je'sus.

18 Brethren, the grace of our Lord Je'sus Christ *be* with your spirit. Amen.

Unto the Ga-la'tians written from Rome.

1 PAUL, an apostle of Je′sus Christ by the will of God, to the saints which are at Eph′-e-sus, and to the faithful in Christ Je′sus:

2 Grace be to you, and peace, from God our Father, and from the Lord Je′sus Christ.

3 Blessed be the God and Father of our Lord Je′sus Christ, who hath blessed us with all spiritual blessings in heavenly places in Christ:

4 According as he hath chosen us in him before the foundation of the world, that we should be holy and without blame before him in love:

5 Having predestinated us unto the adoption of children by Je′sus Christ to himself, according to the good pleasure of his will,

6 To the praise of the glory of his grace, wherein he hath made us accepted in the beloved.

7 In whom we have redemption through his blood, the forgiveness of sins, according to the riches of his grace;

8 Wherein he hath abounded toward us in all wisdom and prudence;

9 Having made known unto us the mystery of his will, according to his good pleasure which he hath purposed in himself:

10 That in the dispensation of the fulness of times he might gather together in one all things in Christ, both which are in heaven, and which are on earth; even in him:

11 In whom also we have obtained an inheritance, being predestinated according to the purpose of him who worketh all things after the counsel of his own will:

12 That we should be to the praise of his glory, who first trusted in Christ.

13 In whom ye also trusted, after that ye heard the word of truth, the gospel of your salvation: in whom also after that ye believed, ye were sealed with that holy Spirit of promise,

14 Which is the earnest of our inheritance until the redemption of the purchased possession, unto the praise of his glory.

15 Wherefore I also, after I heard of your faith in the Lord Je′sus, and love unto all the saints,

16 Cease not to give thanks for you, making mention of you in my prayers;

17 That the God of our Lord Je′sus Christ, the Father of glory, may give unto you the spirit of wisdom and revelation in the knowledge of him:

18 The eyes of your understanding being enlightened; that ye may know what is the hope of his calling, and what the riches of the glory of his inheritance in the saints,

19 And what is the exceeding greatness of his power to us-ward who believe, according to the working of his mighty power,

20 Which he wrought in Christ, when he raised him from the dead, and set him at his own right hand in the heavenly places,

21 Far above all principality, and power, and might, and dominion, and every name that is named, not only in this world, but also in that which is to come:

22 And hath put all things under his feet, and gave him to be the head over all things to the church,

23 Which is his body, the fulness of him that filleth all in all.

2 AND you hath he quickened, who were dead in trespasses and sins;

2 Wherein in time past ye walked according to the course of this world, according to the prince of the power of the air, the spirit that now worketh in the children of disobedience:

3 Among whom also we all had our conversation in times past in the lusts of our flesh, fulfilling the desires of the flesh and of the mind; and were by nature the children of wrath, even as others.

4 But God, who is rich in mercy, for his great love wherewith he loved us,

5 Even when we were dead in sins, hath quickened us together with Christ, (by grace ye are saved;)

6 And hath raised us up together, and made us sit together in heavenly places in Christ Je′sus:

7 That in the ages to come he might shew the exceeding riches of his grace in his kindness toward us through Christ Je′sus.

8 For by grace are ye saved through faith; and that not of yourselves: it is the gift of God:

9 Not of works, lest any man should boast.

10 For we are his workmanship, created in Christ Je′sus unto good works, which God hath before ordained that we should walk in them.

11 Wherefore remember, that ye being in time past Gen′tiles in the flesh, who are called Uncircumcision by that which is called the Circumcision in the flesh made by hands;

12 That at that time ye were without Christ, being aliens from the commonwealth of Is′ra-el, and strangers from the covenants of promise, having no hope, and without God in the world:

13 But now in Christ Je′sus ye who sometimes were far off are made nigh by the blood of Christ.

14 For he is our peace, who hath made both one, and hath broken down the middle wall of partition between us;

15 Having abolished in his flesh the enmity, even the law of commandments contained in ordinances; for to make in himself of twain one new man, so making peace;

16 And that he might reconcile both unto God in one body by the cross, having slain the enmity thereby:

17 And came and preached peace to you which were afar off, and to them that were nigh.

18 For through him we both have access by one Spirit unto the Father.

19 Now therefore ye are no more strangers and foreigners, but fellowcitizens with the saints, and of the household of God;

20 And are built upon the foundation of the apostles and prophets, Je′sus Christ himself being the chief corner stone;

21 In whom all the building fitly framed together groweth unto an holy temple in the Lord:

22 In whom ye also are builded together for an habitation of God through the Spirit.

3 FOR this cause I Paul, the prisoner of Je′-sus Christ for you Gen′tiles,

2 If ye have heard of the dispensation of the grace of God which is given me to you-ward:

3 How that by revelation he made known

unto me the mystery; (as I wrote afore in few words,

4 Whereby, when ye read, ye may understand my knowledge in the mystery of Christ)

5 Which in other ages was not made known unto the sons of men, as it is now revealed unto his holy apostles and prophets by the Spirit;

6 That the Gen'tiles should be fellowheirs, and of the same body, and partakers of his promise in Christ by the gospel:

7 Whereof I was made a minister, according to the gift of the grace of God given unto me by the effectual working of his power.

8 Unto me, who am less than the least of all saints, is this grace given, that I should preach among the Gen'tiles the unsearchable riches of Christ;

9 And to make all *men* see what *is* the fellowship of the mystery, which from the beginning of the world hath been hid in God, who created all things by Je'sus Christ:

10 To the intent that now unto the principalities and powers in heavenly *places* might be known by the church the manifold wisdom of God,

11 According to the eternal purpose which he purposed in Christ Je'sus our Lord:

12 In whom we have boldness and access with confidence by the faith of him.

13 Wherefore I desire that ye faint not at my tribulations for you, which is your glory.

14 For this cause I bow my knees unto the Father of our Lord Je'sus Christ,

15 Of whom the whole family in heaven and earth is named,

16 That he would grant you, according to the riches of his glory, to be strengthened with might by his Spirit in the inner man;

17 That Christ may dwell in your hearts by faith; that ye, being rooted and grounded in love,

18 May be able to comprehend with all saints what *is* the breadth, and length, and depth, and height;

19 And to know the love of Christ, which passeth knowledge, that ye might be filled with all the fulness of God.

20 Now unto him that is able to do exceeding abundantly above all that we ask or think, according to the power that worketh in us,

21 Unto him *be* glory in the church by Christ Je'sus throughout all ages, world without end. Amen.

4 I THEREFORE, the prisoner of the Lord, beseech you that ye walk worthy of the vocation wherewith ye are called,

2 With all lowliness and meekness, with longsuffering, forbearing one another in love;

3 Endeavouring to keep the unity of the Spirit in the bond of peace.

4 *There is* one body, and one Spirit, even as ye are called in one hope of your calling;

5 One Lord, one faith, one baptism,

6 One God and Father of all, who *is* above all, and through all, and in you all.

7 But unto every one of us is given grace according to the measure of the gift of Christ.

8 Wherefore he saith, When he ascended up on high, he led captivity captive, and gave gifts unto men.

9 (Now that he ascended, what is it but that he also descended first into the lower parts of the earth?

10 He that descended is the same also that ascended up far above all heavens, that he might fill all things.)

11 And he gave some, apostles; and some, prophets; and some, evangelists; and some, pastors and teachers;

12 For the perfecting of the saints, for the work of the ministry, for the edifying of the body of Christ:

13 Till we all come in the unity of the faith, and of the knowledge of the Son of God, unto a perfect man, unto the measure of the stature of the fulness of Christ:

14 That we *henceforth* be no more children, tossed to and fro, and carried about with every wind of doctrine, by the sleight of men, *and* cunning craftiness, whereby they lie in wait to deceive;

15 But speaking the truth in love, may grow up into him in all things, which is the head, *even* Christ:

16 From whom the whole body fitly joined together and compacted by that which every joint supplieth, according to the effectual working in the measure of every part, maketh increase of the body unto the edifying of itself in love.

17 This I say therefore, and testify in the Lord, that ye henceforth walk not as other Gen'tiles walk, in the vanity of their mind,

18 Having the understanding darkened, being alienated from the life of God through the ignorance that is in them, because of the blindness of their heart:

19 Who being past feeling have given themselves over unto lasciviousness, to work all uncleanness with greediness.

20 But ye have not so learned Christ;

21 If so be that ye have heard him, and have been taught by him, as the truth is in Je'sus:

22 That ye put off concerning the former conversation the old man, which is corrupt according to the deceitful lusts;

23 And be renewed in the spirit of your mind;

24 And that ye put on the new man, which after God is created in righteousness and true holiness.

25 Wherefore putting away lying, speak every man truth with his neighbour: for we are members one of another.

26 Be ye angry, and sin not: let not the sun go down upon your wrath:

27 Neither give place to the devil.

28 Let him that stole steal no more: but rather let him labour, working with *his* hands the thing which is good, that he may have to give to him that needeth.

29 Let no corrupt communication proceed out of your mouth, but that which is good to the use of edifying, that it may minister grace unto the hearers.

30 And grieve not the holy Spirit of God, whereby ye are sealed unto the day of redemption.

31 Let all bitterness, and wrath, and anger, and clamour, and evil speaking, be put away from you, with all malice:

32 And be ye kind one to another, tenderhearted, forgiving one another, even as God for Christ's sake hath forgiven you.

5 BE ye therefore followers of God, as dear children;

2 And walk in love, as Christ also hath loved us, and hath given himself for us an offering and a sacrifice to God for a sweetsmelling savour.

3 But fornication, and all uncleanness, or covetousness, let it not be once named among you, as becometh saints;

4 Neither filthiness, nor foolish talking, nor jesting, which are not convenient: but rather giving of thanks.

5 For this ye know, that no whoremonger, nor unclean person, nor covetous man, who is an idolater, hath any inheritance in the kingdom of Christ and of God.

6 Let no man deceive you with vain words: for because of these things cometh the wrath of God upon the children of disobedience.

7 Be not ye therefore partakers with them.

8 For ye were sometimes darkness, but now *are ye* light in the Lord: walk as children of light:

9 (For the fruit of the Spirit *is* in all goodness and righteousness and truth;)

10 Proving what is acceptable unto the Lord.

11 And have no fellowship with the unfruitful works of darkness, but rather reprove *them*.

12 For it is a shame even to speak of those things which are done of them in secret.

13 But all things that are reproved are made manifest by the light: for whatsoever doth make manifest is light.

14 Wherefore he saith, Awake thou that sleepest, and arise from the dead, and Christ shall give thee light.

15 See then that ye walk circumspectly, not as fools, but as wise,

16 Redeeming the time, because the days are evil.

17 Wherefore be ye not unwise, but understanding what the will of the Lord *is*.

18 And be not drunk with wine, wherein is excess; but be filled with the Spirit;

19 Speaking to yourselves in psalms and hymns and spiritual songs, singing and making melody in your heart to the Lord;

20 Giving thanks always for all things unto God and the Father in the name of our Lord Je'sus Christ;

21 Submitting yourselves one to another in the fear of God.

22 Wives, submit yourselves unto your own husbands, as unto the Lord.

23 For the husband is the head of the wife, even as Christ is the head of the church: and he is the saviour of the body.

24 Therefore as the church is subject unto Christ, so *let* the wives *be* to their own husbands in every thing.

25 Husbands, love your wives, even as Christ also loved the church, and gave himself for it;

26 That he might sanctify and cleanse it with the washing of water by the word,

27 That he might present it to himself a glorious church, not having spot, or wrinkle, or any such thing; but that it should be holy and without blemish.

28 So ought men to love their wives as their own bodies. He that loveth his wife loveth himself.

29 For no man ever yet hated his own flesh; but nourisheth and cherisheth it, even as the Lord the church:

30 For we are members of his body, of his flesh, and of his bones.

31 For this cause shall a man leave his father and mother, and shall be joined unto his wife, and they two shall be one flesh.

32 This is a great mystery: but I speak concerning Christ and the church.

33 Nevertheless let every one of you in particular so love his wife even as himself; and the wife *see* that she reverence *her* husband.

6 CHILDREN, obey your parents in the Lord: for this is right.

2 Honour thy father and mother; which is the first commandment with promise;

3 That it may be well with thee, and thou mayest live long on the earth.

4 And, ye fathers, provoke not your children to wrath: but bring them up in the nurture and admonition of the Lord.

5 Servants, be obedient to them that are *your* masters according to the flesh, with fear and trembling, in singleness of your heart, as unto Christ;

6 Not with eyeservice, as menpleasers; but as the servants of Christ, doing the will of God from the heart;

7 With good will doing service, as to the Lord, and not to men:

8 Knowing that whatsoever good thing any man doeth, the same shall he receive of the Lord, whether *he be* bond or free.

9 And, ye masters, do the same things unto them, forbearing threatening: knowing that your Master also is in heaven; neither is there respect of persons with him.

10 Finally, my brethren, be strong in the Lord, and in the power of his might.

11 Put on the whole armour of God, that ye may be able to stand against the wiles of the devil.

12 For we wrestle not against flesh and blood, but against principalities, against powers, against the rulers of the darkness of this world, against spiritual wickedness in high *places*.

13 Wherefore take unto you the whole armour of God, that ye may be able to withstand in the evil day, and having done all, to stand.

14 Stand therefore, having your loins girt about with truth, and having on the breastplate of righteousness;

15 And your feet shod with the preparation of the gospel of peace;

16 Above all, taking the shield of faith, wherewith ye shall be able to quench all the fiery darts of the wicked.

17 And take the helmet of salvation, and the sword of the Spirit, which is the word of God:

18 Praying always with all prayer and supplication in the Spirit, and watching thereunto with all perseverance and supplication for all saints;

19 And for me, that utterance may be given unto me, that I may open my mouth boldly, to make known the mystery of the gospel,

20 For which I am an ambassador in bonds: that therein I may speak boldly, as I ought to speak.

21 But that ye also may know my affairs, *and* how I do, Tych'i-cus, a beloved brother and faithful minister in the Lord, shall make known to you all things:

22 Whom I have sent unto you for the same purpose, that ye might know our affairs, and *that* he might comfort your hearts.

23 Peace *be* to the brethren, and love with faith, from God the Father and the Lord Je'sus Christ.

24 Grace *be* with all them that love our Lord Je'sus Christ in sincerity. Amen.

Written from Rome unto the E-phe'sians by Tych'i-cus.

1 PAUL and Ti-mo'the-us, the servants of Je'sus Christ, to all the saints in Christ Je'sus which are at Phi-lip'pi, with the bishops and deacons:

2 Grace *be* unto you, and peace, from God our Father, and *from* the Lord Je'sus Christ.

3 I thank my God upon every remembrance of you,

4 Always in every prayer of mine for you all making request with joy,

5 For your fellowship in the gospel from the first day until now;

6 Being confident of this very thing, that he which hath begun a good work in you will perform *it* until the day of Je'sus Christ:

7 Even as it is meet for me to think this of you all, because I have you in my heart; inasmuch as both in my bonds, and in the defence and confirmation of the gospel, ye all are partakers of my grace.

8 For God is my record, how greatly I long after you all in the bowels of Je'sus Christ.

9 And this I pray, that your love may abound yet more and more in knowledge and *in* all judgment;

10 That ye may approve things that are excellent; that ye may be sincere and without offence till the day of Christ;

11 Being filled with the fruits of righteousness, which are by Je'sus Christ, unto the glory and praise of God.

12 But I would ye should understand, brethren, that the things *which happened* unto me have fallen out rather unto the furtherance of the gospel;

13 So that my bonds in Christ are manifest in all the palace, and in all other *places*;

14 And many of the brethren in the Lord, waxing confident by my bonds, are much more bold to speak the word without fear.

15 Some indeed preach Christ even of envy and strife; and some also of good will:

16 The one preach Christ of contention, not sincerely, supposing to add affliction to my bonds:

17 But the other of love, knowing that I am set for the defence of the gospel.

18 What then? notwithstanding, every way, whether in pretence, or in truth, Christ is preached; and I therein do rejoice, yea, and will rejoice.

19 For I know that this shall turn to my salvation through your prayer, and the supply of the Spirit of Je'sus Christ,

20 According to my earnest expectation and *my* hope, that in nothing I shall be ashamed, but *that* with all boldness, as always, *so* now also Christ shall be magnified in my body, whether *it be* by life, or by death.

21 For to me to live *is* Christ, and to die *is* gain.

22 But if I live in the flesh, this *is* the fruit of my labour: yet what I shall choose I wot not.

23 For I am in a strait betwixt two, having a desire to depart, and to be with Christ; which is far better:

24 Nevertheless to abide in the flesh *is* more needful for you.

25 And having this confidence, I know that I shall abide and continue with you all for your furtherance and joy of faith;

26 That your rejoicing may be more abundant in Je'sus Christ for me by my coming to you again.

27 Only let your conversation be as it becometh the gospel of Christ: that whether I come and see you, or else be absent, I may hear of your affairs, that ye stand fast in one spirit, with one mind striving together for the faith of the gospel;

28 And in nothing terrified by your adversaries: which is to them an evident token of perdition, but to you of salvation, and that of God.

29 For unto you it is given in the behalf of Christ, not only to believe on him, but also to suffer for his sake;

30 Having the same conflict which ye saw in me, and now hear *to be* in me.

2 IF *there be* therefore any consolation in Christ, if any comfort of love, if any fellowship of the Spirit, if any bowels and mercies,

2 Fulfil ye my joy, that ye be likeminded, having the same love, *being* of one accord, of one mind.

3 *Let* nothing *be done* through strife or vainglory; but in lowliness of mind let each esteem other better than themselves.

4 Look not every man on his own things, but every man also on the things of others.

5 Let this mind be in you, which was also in Christ Je'sus:

6 Who, being in the form of God, thought it not robbery to be equal with God:

7 But made himself of no reputation, and took upon him the form of a servant, and was made in the likeness of men:

8 And being found in fashion as a man, he humbled himself, and became obedient unto death, even the death of the cross.

9 Wherefore God also hath highly exalted him, and given him a name which is above every name:

10 That at the name of Je'sus every knee should bow, of *things* in heaven, and *things* in earth, and *things* under the earth;

11 And *that* every tongue should confess that Je'sus Christ *is* Lord, to the glory of God the Father.

12 Wherefore, my beloved, as ye have always obeyed, not as in my presence only, but now much more in my absence, work out your own salvation with fear and trembling.

13 For it is God which worketh in you both to will and to do of *his* good pleasure.

14 Do all things without murmurings and disputings:

15 That ye may be blameless and harmless, the sons of God, without rebuke, in the midst of a crooked and perverse nation, among whom ye shine as lights in the world;

16 Holding forth the word of life; that I may rejoice in the day of Christ, that I have not run in vain, neither laboured in vain.

17 Yea, and if I be offered upon the sacrifice and service of your faith, I joy, and rejoice with you all.

18 For the same cause also do ye joy, and rejoice with me.

19 But I trust in the Lord Je'sus to send Ti-mo'the-us shortly unto you, that I also may be of good comfort, when I know your state.

20 For I have no man likeminded, who will naturally care for your state.

21 For all seek their own, not the things which are Je'sus Christ's.

22 But ye know the proof of him, that, as a son with the father, he hath served with me in the gospel.

23 Him therefore I hope to send presently, so soon as I shall see how it will go with me.

24 But I trust in the Lord that I also myself shall come shortly.

25 Yet I supposed it necessary to send to you E-paph-ro-di'tus, my brother, and companion in labour, and fellowsoldier, but your messenger, and he that ministered to my wants.

26 For he longed after you all, and was full of heaviness, because that ye had heard that he had been sick.

27 For indeed he was sick nigh unto death: but God had mercy on him; and not on him only, but on me also, lest I should have sorrow upon sorrow.

28 I sent him therefore the more carefully, that, when ye see him again, ye may rejoice, and that I may be the less sorrowful.

29 Receive him therefore in the Lord with all gladness; and hold such in reputation:

30 Because for the work of Christ he was nigh unto death, not regarding his life, to supply your lack of service toward me.

3 FINALLY, my brethren, rejoice in the Lord. To write the same things to you, to me indeed *is* not grievous, but for you *it is* safe.

2 Beware of dogs, beware of evil workers, beware of the concision.

3 For we are the circumcision, which worship God in the spirit, and rejoice in Christ Je'sus, and have no confidence in the flesh.

4 Though I might also have confidence in the flesh. If any other man thinketh that he hath whereof he might trust in the flesh, I more:

5 Circumcised the eighth day, of the stock of Is'ra-el, *of* the tribe of Ben'ja-min, an He'brew of the He'brews; as touching the law, a Phar'i-see;

6 Concerning zeal, persecuting the church; touching the righteousness which is in the law, blameless.

7 But what things were gain to me, those I counted loss for Christ.

8 Yea doubtless, and I count all things *but* loss for the excellency of the knowledge of Christ Je'sus my Lord: for whom I have suffered the loss of all things, and do count them *but* dung, that I may win Christ.

9 And be found in him, not having mine own righteousness, which is of the law, but that which is through the faith of Christ, the righteousness which is of God by faith:

10 That I may know him, and the power of his resurrection, and the fellowship of his sufferings, being made conformable unto his death;

11 If by any means I might attain unto the resurrection of the dead.

12 Not as though I had already attained, either were already perfect: but I follow after, if that I may apprehend that for which also I am apprehended of Christ Je'sus.

13 Brethren, I count not myself to have apprehended: but *this* one thing *I do,* forgetting those things which are behind, and reaching forth unto those things which are before,

14 I press toward the mark for the prize of the high calling of God in Christ Je'sus.

15 Let us therefore, as many as be perfect, be thus minded: and if in any thing ye be otherwise minded, God shall reveal even this unto you.

16 Nevertheless, whereto we have already attained, let us walk by the same rule, let us mind the same thing.

17 Brethren, be followers together of me, and mark them which walk so as ye have us for an ensample.

18 (For many walk, of whom I have told you often, and now tell you even weeping, *that they are* the enemies of the cross of Christ:

19 Whose end *is* destruction, whose God *is their* belly, and *whose* glory *is* in their shame, who mind earthly things.)

20 For our conversation is in heaven; from whence also we look for the Saviour, the Lord Je'sus Christ:

21 Who shall change our vile body, that it may be fashioned like unto his glorious body, according to the working whereby he is able even to subdue all things unto himself.

4 THEREFORE, my brethren dearly beloved and longed for, my joy and crown, so stand fast in the Lord, *my* dearly beloved.

2 I beseech Eu-o'di-as, and beseech Syn'ty-che, that they be of the same mind in the Lord.

3 And I intreat thee also, true yokefellow, help those women which laboured with me in the gospel, with Clem'ent also, and *with* other my fellowlabourers, whose names *are* in the book of life.

4 Rejoice in the Lord alway: *and* again I say, Rejoice.

5 Let your moderation be known unto all men. The Lord *is* at hand.

6 Be careful for nothing; but in every thing by prayer and supplication with thanksgiving let your requests be made known unto God.

7 And the peace of God, which passeth all understanding, shall keep your hearts and minds through Christ Je'sus.

8 Finally, brethren, whatsoever things are true, whatsoever things *are* honest, whatsoever things *are* just, whatsoever things *are* pure, whatsoever things *are* lovely, whatsoever things *are* of good report; if *there be* any virtue, and if *there be* any praise, think on these things.

9 Those things, which ye have both learned, and received, and heard, and seen in me, do: and the God of peace shall be with you.

10 But I rejoiced in the Lord greatly, that now at the last your care of me hath flourished again; wherein ye were also careful, but ye lacked opportunity.

11 Not that I speak in respect of want: for I have learned, in whatsoever state I am, *there-with* to be content.

12 I know both how to be abased, and I know how to abound: every where and in all things I am instructed both to be full and to be hungry, both to abound and to suffer need.

13 I can do all things through Christ which strengtheneth me.

14 Notwithstanding ye have well done, that ye did communicate with my affliction.

15 Now ye Phi-lip'pi-ans know also, that in the beginning of the gospel, when I departed from Mac-e-do'ni-a, no church communicated with me as concerning giving and receiving, but ye only.

16 For even in Thes-sa-lo-ni'ca ye sent once and again unto my necessity.

17 Not because I desire a gift: but I desire fruit that may abound to your account.

18 But I have all, and abound: I am full, having received of E-paph-ro-di'tus the things

which were sent from you, an odour of a sweet smell, a sacrifice acceptable, well pleasing to God.

19 But my God shall supply all your need according to his riches in glory by Christ Je′sus.

20 Now unto God and our Father *be* glory for ever and ever. Amen.

21 Salute every saint in Christ Je′sus. The brethren which are with me greet you.

22 All the saints salute you, chiefly they that are of Cæ′sar's household.

23 The grace of our Lord Je′sus Christ *be* with you all. Amen.

It was written to the Phi-lip′pi-ans from Rome by E-paph-ro-di′tus.

THE LETTER OF PAUL TO THE

COLOSSIANS

1 PAUL, an apostle of Je′sus Christ by the will of God, and Ti-mo′the-us *our* brother,

2 To the saints and faithful brethren in Christ which are at Co-los′se: Grace *be* unto you, and peace, from God our Father and the Lord Je′sus Christ.

3 We give thanks to God and the Father of our Lord Je′sus Christ, praying always for you,

4 Since we heard of your faith in Christ Je′-sus, and of the love *which ye have* to all the saints,

5 For the hope which is laid up for you in heaven, whereof ye heard before in the word of the truth of the gospel;

6 Which is come unto you, as *it is* in all the world; and bringeth forth fruit, as *it doth* also in you, since the day ye heard *of it,* and knew the grace of God in truth:

7 As ye also learned of Ep′a-phras our dear fellowservant, who is for you a faithful minister of Christ;

8 Who also declared unto us your love in the Spirit.

9 For this cause we also, since the day we heard *it,* do not cease to pray for you, and to desire that ye might be filled with the knowledge of his will in all wisdom and spiritual understanding;

10 That ye might walk worthy of the Lord unto all pleasing, being fruitful in every good work, and increasing in the knowledge of God;

11 Strengthened with all might, according to his glorious power, unto all patience and longsuffering with joyfulness;

12 Giving thanks unto the Father, which hath made us meet to be partakers of the inheritance of the saints in light:

13 Who hath delivered us from the power of darkness, and hath translated *us* into the kingdom of his dear Son:

14 In whom we have redemption through his blood, *even* the forgiveness of sins:

15 Who is the image of the invisible God, the firstborn of every creature:

16 For by him were all things created, that are in heaven, and that are in earth, visible and invisible, whether *they be* thrones, or dominions, or principalities, or powers: all things were created by him, and for him:

17 And he is before all things, and by him all things consist.

18 And he is the head of the body, the church: who is the beginning, the firstborn from the dead; that in all *things* he might have the preeminence.

19 For it pleased *the Father* that in him should all fulness dwell;

20 And, having made peace through the blood of his cross, by him to reconcile all things

unto himself; by him, *I say,* whether *they be* things in earth, or things in heaven.

21 And you, that were sometime alienated and enemies in *your* mind by wicked works, yet now hath he reconciled

22 In the body of his flesh through death, to present you holy and unblameable and unreproveable in his sight:

23 If ye continue in the faith grounded and settled, and *be* not moved away from the hope of the gospel, which ye have heard, *and* which was preached to every creature which is under heaven; whereof I Paul am made a minister;

24 Who now rejoice in my sufferings for you, and fill up that which is behind of the afflictions of Christ in my flesh for his body's sake, which is the church:

25 Whereof I am made a minister, according to the dispensation of God which is given to me for you, to fulfil the word of God;

26 *Even* the mystery which hath been hid from ages and from generations, but now is made manifest to his saints:

27 To whom God would make known what *is* the riches of the glory of this mystery among the Gen′tiles; which is Christ in you, the hope of glory:

28 Whom we preach, warning every man, and teaching every man in all wisdom; that we may present every man perfect in Christ Je′sus:

29 Whereunto I also labour, striving according to his working, which worketh in me mightily.

2 FOR I would that ye knew what great conflict I have for you, and *for* them at La-od-i-ce′a, and *for* as many as have not seen my face in the flesh;

2 That their hearts might be comforted, being knit together in love, and unto all riches of the full assurance of understanding, to the acknowledgement of the mystery of God, and of the Father, and of Christ;

3 In whom are hid all the treasures of wisdom and knowledge.

4 And this I say, lest any man should beguile you with enticing words.

5 For though I be absent in the flesh, yet am I with you in the spirit, joying and beholding your order, and the stedfastness of your faith in Christ.

6 As ye have therefore received Christ Je′sus the Lord, *so* walk ye in him:

7 Rooted and built up in him, and stablished in the faith, as ye have been taught, abounding therein with thanksgiving.

8 Beware lest any man spoil you through philosophy and vain deceit, after the tradition of men, after the rudiments of the world, and not after Christ.

9 For in him dwelleth all the fulness of the Godhead bodily.

10 And ye are complete in him, which is the head of all principality and power:

11 In whom also ye are circumcised with the circumcision made without hands, in putting off the body of the sins of the flesh by the circumcision of Christ:

12 Buried with him in baptism, wherein also ye are risen with *him* through the faith of the operation of God, who hath raised him from the dead.

13 And you, being dead in your sins and the uncircumcision of your flesh, hath he quickened together with him, having forgiven you all trespasses;

14 Blotting out the handwriting of ordinances that was against us, which was contrary to us, and took it out of the way, nailing it to his cross;

15 *And* having spoiled principalities and powers, he made a shew of them openly, triumphing over them in it.

16 Let no man therefore judge you in meat, or in drink, or in respect of an holyday, or of the new moon, or of the sabbath *days:*

17 Which are a shadow of things to come; but the body *is* of Christ.

18 Let no man beguile you of your reward in a voluntary humility and worshipping of angels, intruding into those things which he hath not seen, vainly puffed up by his fleshly mind,

19 And not holding the Head, from which all the body by joints and bands having nourishment ministered, and knit together, increaseth with the increase of God.

20 Wherefore if ye be dead with Christ from the rudiments of the world, why, as though living in the world, are ye subject to ordinances,

21 (Touch not; taste not; handle not;

22 Which all are to perish with the using;) after the commandments and doctrines of men?

23 Which things have indeed a shew of wisdom in will worship, and humility, and neglecting of the body; not in any honour to the satisfying of the flesh.

3 IF ye then be risen with Christ, seek those things which are above, where Christ sitteth on the right hand of God.

2 Set your affection on things above, not on things on the earth.

3 For ye are dead, and your life is hid with Christ in God.

4 When Christ, *who is* our life, shall appear, then shall ye also appear with him in glory.

5 Mortify therefore your members which are upon the earth; fornication, uncleanness, inordinate affection, evil concupiscence, and covetousness, which is idolatry:

6 For which things' sake the wrath of God cometh on the children of disobedience:'

7 In the which ye also walked some time, when ye lived in them.

8 But now ye also put off all these; anger, wrath, malice, blasphemy, filthy communication out of your mouth.

9 Lie not one to another, seeing that ye have put off the old man with his deeds;

10 And have put on the new *man,* which is renewed in knowledge after the image of him that created him:

11 Where there is neither Greek nor Jew, circumcision nor uncircumcision, Bar-ba'ri-an, Scyth'i-an, bond *nor* free: but Christ *is* all, and in all.

12 Put on therefore, as the elect of God, holy and beloved, bowels of mercies, kindness, humbleness of mind, meekness, longsuffering;

13 Forbearing one another, and forgiving one another, if any man have a quarrel against any: even as Christ forgave you, so also *do* ye.

14 And above all these things *put on* charity, which is the bond of perfectness.

15 And let the peace of God rule in your hearts, to the which also ye are called in one body; and be ye thankful.

16 Let the word of Christ dwell in you richly in all wisdom; teaching and admonishing one another in psalms and hymns and spiritual songs, singing with grace in your hearts to the Lord.

17 And whatsoever ye do in word or deed, *do* all in the name of the Lord Je'sus, giving thanks to God and the Father by him.

18 Wives, submit yourselves unto your own husbands, as it is fit in the Lord.

19 Husbands, love *your* wives, and be not bitter against them.

20 Children, obey *your* parents in all things: for this is well pleasing unto the Lord.

21 Fathers, provoke not your children *to anger,* lest they be discouraged.

22 Servants, obey in all things *your* masters according to the flesh; not with eyeservice, as menpleasers; but in singleness of heart, fearing God:

23 And whatsoever ye do, do *it* heartily, as to the Lord, and not unto men;

24 Knowing that of the Lord ye shall receive the reward of the inheritance: for ye serve the Lord Christ.

25 But he that doeth wrong shall receive for the wrong which he hath done: and there is no respect of persons.

4 MASTERS, give unto *your* servants that which is just and equal; knowing that ye also have a Master in heaven.

2 Continue in prayer, and watch in the same with thanksgiving;

3 Withal praying also for us, that God would open unto us a door of utterance, to speak the mystery of Christ, for which I am also in bonds:

4 That I may make it manifest, as I ought to speak.

5 Walk in wisdom toward them that are without, redeeming the time.

6 Let your speech *be* alway with grace, seasoned with salt, that ye may know how ye ought to answer every man.

7 All my state shall Tych'i-cus declare unto you, *who is* a beloved brother, and a faithful minister and fellowservant in the Lord:

8 Whom I have sent unto you for the same purpose, that he might know your estate, and comfort your hearts;

9 With O'nes'i-mus, a faithful and beloved brother, who is *one* of you. They shall make known unto you all things which *are* done here.

10 Ar-is-tar'chus my fellowprisoner saluteth you, and Mar'cus, sister's son to Bar'na-bas, (touching whom ye received commandments: if he come unto you, receive him;)

11 And Je'sus, which is called Jus'tus, who are of the circumcision. These only *are my* fellowworkers unto the kingdom of God, which have been a comfort unto me.

12 Ep'a-phras, who is *one* of you, a servant of Christ, saluteth you, always labouring fervently for you in prayers, that ye may stand perfect and complete in all the will of God.

13 For I bear him record, that he hath a great

zeal for you, and them *that are* in La-od-i-ce′a, and them in Hi-e-rap′o-lis.

14 Luke, the beloved physician, and De′mas, greet you.

15 Salute the brethren which are in La-od-i-ce′a, and Nym′phas, and the church which is in his house.

16 And when this epistle is read among you, cause that it be read also in the church of the La-od-i-ce′ans; and that ye likewise read the *epistle* from La-od-i-ce′a.

17 And say to Ar-chip′pus, Take heed to the ministry which thou hast received in the Lord, that thou fulfil it.

18 The salutation by the hand of me Paul. Remember my bonds. Grace *be* with you. Amen.

Written from Rome to the Co-los′si-ans by Tych′i-cus and O′nes′i-mus.

THE FIRST LETTER OF PAUL TO THE

THESSALONIANS

1 PAUL, and Sil-va′nus, and Ti-mo′the-us, unto the church of the Thes-sa-lo′ni-ans *which is* in God the Father and *in* the Lord Je′sus Christ: Grace *be* with you, and peace, from God our Father, and the Lord Je′sus Christ.

2 We give thanks to God always for you all, making mention of you in our prayers;

3 Remembering without ceasing your work of faith, and labour of love, and patience of hope in our Lord Je′sus Christ, in the sight of God and our Father;

4 Knowing, brethren beloved, your election of God.

5 For our gospel came not unto you in word only, but also in power, and in the Ho′ly Ghost, and in much assurance; as ye know what manner of men we were among you for your sake.

6 And ye became followers of us, and of the Lord, having received the word in much affliction, with joy of the Ho′ly Ghost:

7 So that ye were ensamples to all that believe in Mac-e-do′ni-a and A-cha′ia.

8 For from you sounded out the word of the Lord not only in Mac-e-do′ni-a and A-cha′ia, but also in every place your faith to God-ward is spread abroad; so that we need not to speak any thing.

9 For they themselves shew of us what manner of entering in we had unto you, and how ye turned to God from idols to serve the living and true God;

10 And to wait for his Son from heaven, whom he raised from the dead, *even* Je′sus, which delivered us from the wrath to come.

2 FOR yourselves, brethren, know our entrance in unto you, that it was not in vain:

2 But even after that we had suffered before, and were shamefully entreated, as ye know, at Phi-lip′pi, we were bold in our God to speak unto you the gospel of God with much contention.

3 For our exhortation *was* not of deceit, nor of uncleanness, nor in guile:

4 But as we were allowed of God to be put in trust with the gospel, even so we speak; not as pleasing men, but God, which trieth our hearts.

5 For neither at any time used we flattering words, as ye know, nor a cloke of covetousness; God *is* witness:

6 Nor of men sought we glory, neither of you, nor *yet* of others, when we might have been burdensome, as the apostles of Christ.

7 But we were gentle among you, even as a nurse cherisheth her children:

8 So being affectionately desirous of you, we were willing to have imparted unto you, not the gospel of God only, but also our own souls, because ye were dear unto us.

9 For ye remember, brethren, our labour and travail: for labouring night and day, because we would not be chargeable unto any of you, we preached unto you the gospel of God.

10 Ye *are* witnesses, and God *also*, how holily and justly and unblameably we behaved ourselves among you that believe:

11 As ye know how we exhorted and comforted and charged every one of you, as a father *doth* his children,

12 That ye would walk worthy of God, who hath called you unto his kingdom and glory.

13 For this cause also thank we God without ceasing, because, when ye received the word of God which ye heard of us, ye received *it* not *as* the word of men, but as it is in truth, the word of God, which effectually worketh also in you that believe.

14 For ye, brethren, became followers of the churches of God which in Ju-dæ′a are in Christ Je′sus: for ye also have suffered like things of your own countrymen, even as they *have of* the Jews:

15 Who both killed the Lord Je′sus, and their own prophets, and have persecuted us; and they please not God, and are contrary to all men:

16 Forbidding us to speak to the Gen′tiles that they might be saved, to fill up their sins alway: for the wrath is come upon them to the uttermost.

17 But we, brethren, being taken from you for a short time in presence, not in heart, endeavoured the more abundantly to see your face with great desire.

18 Wherefore we would have come unto you, even I Paul, once and again; but Sa′tan hindered us.

19 For what *is* our hope, or joy, or crown of rejoicing? *Are* not even ye in the presence of our Lord Je′sus Christ at his coming?

20 For ye are our glory and joy.

3 WHEREFORE when we could no longer forbear, we thought it good to be left at Ath′ens alone;

2 And sent Ti-mo′the-us, our brother, and minister of God, and our fellowlabourer in the gospel of Christ, to establish you, and to comfort you concerning your faith:

3 That no man should be moved by these afflictions: for yourselves know that we are appointed thereunto.

4 For verily, when we were with you, we told you before that we should suffer tribulation; even as it came to pass, and ye know.

5 For this cause, when I could no longer forbear, I sent to know your faith, lest by some

means the tempter have tempted you, and our labour be in vain.

6 But now when Ti-mo'the-us came from you unto us, and brought us good tidings of your faith and charity, and that ye have good remembrance of us always, desiring greatly to see us, as we also to see you:

7 Therefore, brethren, we were comforted over you in all our affliction and distress by your faith:

8 For now we live, if ye stand fast in the Lord.

9 For what thanks can we render to God again for you, for all the joy wherewith we joy for your sakes before our God;

10 Night and day praying exceedingly that we might see your face, and might perfect that which is lacking in your faith?

11 Now God himself and our Father, and our Lord Je'sus Christ, direct our way unto you.

12 And the Lord make you to increase and abound in love one toward another, and toward all men, even as we do toward you:

13 To the end he may stablish your hearts unblameable in holiness before God, even our Father, at the coming of our Lord Je'sus Christ with all his saints.

4 FURTHERMORE then we beseech you, brethren, and exhort you by the Lord Je'-sus, that as ye have received of us how ye ought to walk and to please God, so ye would abound more and more.

2 For ye know what commandments we gave you by the Lord Je'sus.

3 For this is the will of God, even your sanctification, that ye should abstain from fornication:

4 That every one of you should know how to possess his vessel in sanctification and honour;

5 Not in the lust of concupiscence, even as the Gen'tiles which know not God:

6 That no man go beyond and defraud his brother in any matter: because that the Lord is the avenger of all such, as we also have forewarned you and testified.

7 For God hath not called us unto uncleanness, but unto holiness.

8 He therefore that despiseth, despiseth not man, but God, who hath also given unto us his holy Spirit.

9 But as touching brotherly love ye need not that I write unto you: for ye yourselves are taught of God to love one another.

10 And indeed ye do it toward all the brethren which are in all Mac-e-do'ni-a: but we beseech you, brethren, that ye increase more and more;

11 And that ye study to be quiet, and to do your own business, and to work with your own hands, as we commanded you;

12 That ye may walk honestly toward them that are without, and that ye may have lack of nothing.

13 But I would not have you to be ignorant, brethren, concerning them which are asleep, that ye sorrow not, even as others which have no hope.

14 For if we believe that Je'sus died and rose again, even so them also which sleep in Je'sus will God bring with him.

15 For this we say unto you by the word of the Lord, that we which are alive and remain unto the coming of the Lord shall not prevent them which are asleep.

16 For the Lord himself shall descend from heaven with a shout, with the voice of the archangel, and with the trump of God: and the dead in Christ shall rise first:

17 Then we which are alive and remain shall be caught up together with them in the clouds, to meet the Lord in the air: and so shall we ever be with the Lord.

18 Wherefore comfort one another with these words.

5 BUT of the times and the seasons, brethren, ye have no need that I write unto you.

2 For yourselves know perfectly that the day of the Lord so cometh as a thief in the night.

3 For when they shall say, Peace and safety; then sudden destruction cometh upon them, as travail upon a woman with child; and they shall not escape.

4 But ye, brethren, are not in darkness, that that day should overtake you as a thief.

5 Ye are all the children of light, and the children of the day: we are not of the night, nor of darkness.

6 Therefore let us not sleep, as do others; but let us watch and be sober.

7 For they that sleep sleep in the night; and they that be drunken are drunken in the night.

8 But let us, who are of the day, be sober, putting on the breastplate of faith and love; and for an helmet, the hope of salvation.

9 For God hath not appointed us to wrath, but to obtain salvation by our Lord Je'sus Christ,

10 Who died for us, that, whether we wake or sleep, we should live together with him.

11 Wherefore comfort yourselves together, and edify one another, even as also ye do.

12 And we beseech you, brethren, to know them which labour among you, and are over you in the Lord, and admonish you;

13 And to esteem them very highly in love for their work's sake. And be at peace among yourselves.

14 Now we exhort you, brethren, warn them that are unruly, comfort the feebleminded, support the weak, be patient toward all men.

15 See that none render evil for evil unto any man; but ever follow that which is good, both among yourselves, and to all men.

16 Rejoice evermore.

17 Pray without ceasing.

18 In every thing give thanks: for this is the will of God in Christ Je'sus concerning you.

19 Quench not the Spirit.

20 Despise not prophesyings.

21 Prove all things; hold fast that which is good.

22 Abstain from all appearance of evil.

23 And the very God of peace sanctify you wholly; and I pray God your whole spirit and soul and body be preserved blameless unto the coming of our Lord Je'sus Christ.

24 Faithful is he that calleth you, who also will do it.

25 Brethren, pray for us.

26 Greet all the brethren with an holy kiss.

27 I charge you by the Lord that this epistle be read unto all the holy brethren.

28 The grace of our Lord Je'sus Christ be with you. Amen.

The first epistle unto the Thes-sa-lo'ni-ans was written from Ath'ens.

THESSALONIANS

1 PAUL, and Sil-va′nus, and Ti-mo′the-us, unto the church of the Thes-sa-lo′ni-ans in God our Father and the Lord Je′sus Christ:

2 Grace unto you, and peace, from God our Father and the Lord Je′sus Christ.

3 We are bound to thank God always for you, brethren, as it is meet, because that your faith groweth exceedingly, and the charity of every one of you all toward each other aboundeth;

4 So that we ourselves glory in you in the churches of God for your patience and faith in all your persecutions and tribulations that ye endure:

5 *Which is* a manifest token of the righteous judgment of God, that ye may be counted worthy of the kingdom of God, for which ye also suffer:

6 Seeing *it is* a righteous thing with God to recompense tribulation to them that trouble you;

7 And to you who are troubled rest with us, when the Lord Je′sus shall be revealed from heaven with his mighty angels,

8 In flaming fire taking vengeance on them that know not God, and that obey not the gospel of our Lord Je′sus Christ:

9 Who shall be punished with everlasting destruction from the presence of the Lord, and from the glory of his power;

10 When he shall come to be glorified in his saints, and to be admired in all them that believe (because our testimony among you was believed) in that day.

11 Wherefore also we pray always for you, that our God would count you worthy of *this* calling, and fulfil all the good pleasure of *his* goodness, and the work of faith with power:

12 That the name of our Lord Je′sus Christ may be glorified in you, and ye in him, according to the grace of our God and the Lord Je′sus Christ.

2 NOW we beseech you, brethren, by the coming of our Lord Je′sus Christ, and *by* our gathering together unto him,

2 That ye be not soon shaken in mind, or be troubled, neither by spirit, nor by word, nor by letter as from us, as that the day of Christ is at hand.

3 Let no man deceive you by any means: for *that day shall not come,* except there come a falling away first, and that man of sin be revealed, the son of perdition;

4 Who opposeth and exalteth himself above all that is called God, or that is worshipped; so that he as God sitteth in the temple of God, shewing himself that he is God.

5 Remember ye not, that, when I was yet with you, I told you these things?

6 And now ye know what withholdeth that he might be revealed in his time.

7 For the mystery of iniquity doth already work: only he who now letteth *will let,* until he be taken out of the way.

8 And then shall that Wicked be revealed, whom the Lord shall consume with the spirit of his mouth, and shall destroy with the brightness of his coming:

9 *Even him,* whose coming is after the working of Sa′tan with all power and signs and lying wonders,

10 And with all deceivableness of unright-

eousness in them that perish; because they received not the love of the truth, that they might be saved.

11 And for this cause God shall send them strong delusion, that they should believe a lie:

12 That they all might be damned who believed not the truth, but had pleasure in unrighteousness.

13 But we are bound to give thanks alway to God for you, brethren beloved of the Lord, because God hath from the beginning chosen you to salvation through sanctification of the Spirit and belief of the truth:

14 Whereunto he called you by our gospel, to the obtaining of the glory of our Lord Je′sus Christ.

15 Therefore, brethren, stand fast, and hold the traditions which ye have been taught, whether by word, or our epistle.

16 Now our Lord Je′sus Christ himself, and God, even our Father, which hath loved us, and hath given *us* everlasting consolation and good hope through grace,

17 Comfort your hearts, and stablish you in every good word and work.

3 FINALLY, brethren, pray for us, that the word of the Lord may have *free* course, and be glorified, even as *it is* with you:

2 And that we may be delivered from unreasonable and wicked men: for all *men* have not faith.

3 But the Lord is faithful, who shall stablish you, and keep *you* from evil.

4 And we have confidence in the Lord touching you, that ye both do and will do the things which we command you.

5 And the Lord direct your hearts into the love of God, and into the patient waiting for Christ.

6 Now we command you, brethren, in the name of our Lord Je′sus Christ, that ye withdraw yourselves from every brother that walketh disorderly, and not after the tradition which he received of us.

7 For yourselves know how ye ought to follow us: for we behaved not ourselves disorderly among you;

8 Neither did we eat any man's bread for nought; but wrought with labour and travail night and day, that we might not be chargeable to any of you:

9 Not because we have not power, but to make ourselves an ensample unto you to follow us.

10 For even when we were with you, this we commanded you, that if any would not work, neither should he eat.

11 For we hear that there are some which walk among you disorderly, working not at all, but are busybodies.

12 Now them that are such we command and exhort by our Lord Je′sus Christ, that with quietness they work, and eat their own bread.

13 But ye, brethren, be not weary in well doing.

14 And if any man obey not our word by this epistle, note that man, and have no company with him, that he may be ashamed.

15 Yet count *him* not as an enemy, but admonish *him* as a brother.

16 Now the Lord of peace himself give you peace always by all means. The Lord *be* with you all.

17 The salutation of Paul with mine own hand, which is the token in every epistle: so I write.

18 The grace of our Lord Je'sus Christ *be* with you all. Amen.

The second *epistle* to the Thes-sa-lo'ni-ans was written from Ath'ens.

THE FIRST LETTER OF PAUL TO

TIMOTHY

1 PAUL, an apostle of Je'sus Christ by the commandment of God our Saviour, and Lord Je'sus Christ, *which is* our hope;

2 Unto Tim'o-thy, *my* own son in the faith: Grace, mercy, *and* peace, from God our Father and Je'sus Christ our Lord.

3 As I besought thee to abide still at Eph'e-sus, when I went into Mac-e-do'ni-a, that thou mightest charge some that they teach no other doctrine,

4 Neither give heed to fables and endless genealogies, which minister questions, rather than godly edifying which is in faith: *so do.*

5 Now the end of the commandment is charity out of a pure heart, and *of* a good conscience, and *of* faith unfeigned:

6 From which some having swerved have turned aside unto vain jangling;

7 Desiring to be teachers of the law; understanding neither what they say, nor whereof they affirm.

8 But we know that the law *is* good, if a man use it lawfully;

9 Knowing this, that the law is not made for a righteous man, but for the lawless and disobedient, for the ungodly and for sinners, for unholy and profane, for murderers of fathers and murderers of mothers, for manslayers,

10 For whoremongers, for them that defile themselves with mankind, for menstealers, for liars, for perjured persons, and if there be any other thing that is contrary to sound doctrine;

11 According to the glorious gospel of the blessed God, which was committed to my trust.

12 And I thank Christ Je'sus our Lord, who hath enabled me, for that he counted me faithful, putting me into the ministry;

13 Who was before a blasphemer, and a persecutor, and injurious: but I obtained mercy, because I did *it* ignorantly in unbelief.

14 And the grace of our Lord was exceeding abundant with faith and love which is in Christ Je'sus.

15 This *is* a faithful saying, and worthy of all acceptation, that Christ Je'sus came into the world to save sinners; of whom I am chief.

16 Howbeit for this cause I obtained mercy, that in me first Je'sus Christ might shew forth all longsuffering, for a pattern to them which should hereafter believe on him to life everlasting.

17 Now unto the King eternal, immortal, invisible, the only wise God, *be* honour and glory for ever and ever. Amen.

18 This charge I commit unto thee, son Tim'o-thy, according to the prophecies which went before on thee, that thou by them mightest war a good warfare;

19 Holding faith, and a good conscience; which some having put away concerning faith have made shipwreck:

20 Of whom is Hy-me-næ'us and Al-ex-an'-der; whom I have delivered unto Sa'tan, that they may learn not to blaspheme.

2 I EXHORT therefore, that, first of all, supplications, prayers, intercessions, *and* giving of thanks, be made for all men;

2 For kings, and *for* all that are in authority; that we may lead a quiet and peaceable life in all godliness and honesty.

3 For this *is* good and acceptable in the sight of God our Saviour;

4 Who will have all men to be saved, and to come unto the knowledge of the truth.

5 For *there is* one God, and one mediator between God and men, the man Christ Je'sus;

6 Who gave himself a ransom for all, to be testified in due time.

7 Whereunto I am ordained a preacher, and an apostle, (I speak the truth in Christ, *and* lie not;) a teacher of the Gen'tiles in faith and verity.

8 I will therefore that men pray every where, lifting up holy hands, without wrath and doubting.

9 In like manner also, that women adorn themselves in modest apparel, with shamefacedness and sobriety; not with broided hair, or gold, or pearls, or costly array;

10 But (which becometh women professing godliness) with good works.

11 Let the woman learn in silence with all subjection.

12 But I suffer not a woman to teach, nor to usurp authority over the man, but to be in silence.

13 For Ad'am was first formed, then Eve.

14 And Ad'am was not deceived, but the woman being deceived was in the transgression.

15 Notwithstanding she shall be saved in childbearing, if they continue in faith and charity and holiness with sobriety.

3 THIS *is* a true saying, If a man desire the office of a bishop, he desireth a good work.

2 A bishop then must be blameless, the husband of one wife, vigilant, sober, of good behaviour, given to hospitality, apt to teach;

3 Not given to wine, no striker, not greedy of filthy lucre; but patient, not a brawler, not covetous;

4 One that ruleth well his own house, having his children in subjection with all gravity;

5 (For if a man know not how to rule his own house, how shall he take care of the church of God?)

6 Not a novice, lest being lifted up with pride he fall into the condemnation of the devil.

7 Moreover he must have a good report of them which are without; lest he fall into reproach and the snare of the devil.

8 Likewise *must* the deacons *be* grave, not

doubletongued, not given to much wine, not greedy of filthy lucre;

9 Holding the mystery of the faith in a pure conscience.

10 And let these also first be proved; then let them use the office of a deacon, being *found* blameless.

11 Even so *must their* wives *be* grave, not slanderers, sober, faithful in all things.

12 Let the deacons be the husbands of one wife, ruling their children and their own houses well.

13 For they that have used the office of a deacon well purchase to themselves a good degree, and great boldness in the faith which is in Christ Je′sus.

14 These things write I unto thee, hoping to come unto thee shortly:

15 But if I tarry long, that thou mayest know how thou oughtest to behave thyself in the house of God, which is the church of the living God, the pillar and ground of the truth.

16 And without controversy great is the mystery of godliness: God was manifest in the flesh, justified in the Spirit, seen of angels, preached unto the Gen′tiles, believed on in the world, received up into glory.

4 NOW the Spirit speaketh expressly, that in the latter times some shall depart from the faith, giving heed to seducing spirits, and doctrines of devils;

2 Speaking lies in hypocrisy; having their conscience seared with a hot iron;

3 Forbidding to marry, *and commanding* to abstain from meats, which God hath created to be received with thanksgiving of them which believe and know the truth.

4 For every creature of God *is* good, and nothing to be refused, if it be received with thanksgiving:

5 For it is sanctified by the word of God and prayer.

6 If thou put the brethren in remembrance of these things, thou shalt be a good minister of Je′sus Christ, nourished up in the words of faith and of good doctrine, whereunto thou hast attained.

7 But refuse profane and old wives' fables, and exercise thyself *rather* unto godliness.

8 For bodily exercise profiteth little: but godliness is profitable unto all things, having promise of the life that now is, and of that which is to come.

9 This *is* a faithful saying and worthy of all acceptation.

10 For therefore we both labour and suffer reproach, because we trust in the living God, who is the Saviour of all men, specially of those that believe.

11 These things command and teach.

12 Let no man despise thy youth; but be thou an example of the believers, in word, in conversation, in charity, in spirit, in faith, in purity.

13 Till I come, give attendance to reading, to exhortation, to doctrine.

14 Neglect not the gift that is in thee, which was given thee by prophecy, with the laying on of the hands of the presbytery.

15 Meditate upon these things; give thyself wholly to them; that thy profiting may appear to all.

16 Take heed unto thyself, and unto the doctrine; continue in them: for in doing this thou shalt both save thyself, and them that hear thee.

5 REBUKE not an elder, but intreat *him* as a father; *and* the younger men as brethren;

2 The elder women as mothers; the younger as sisters, with all purity.

3 Honour widows that are widows indeed.

4 But if any widow have children or nephews, let them learn first to shew piety at home, and to requite their parents: for that is good and acceptable before God.

5 Now she that is a widow indeed, and desolate, trusteth in God, and continueth in supplications and prayers night and day.

6 But she that liveth in pleasure is dead while she liveth.

7 And these things give in charge, that they may be blameless.

8 But if any provide not for his own, and specially for those of his own house, he hath denied the faith, and is worse than an infidel.

9 Let not a widow be taken into the number under threescore years old, having been the wife of one man,

10 Well reported of for good works; if she have brought up children, if she have lodged strangers, if she have washed the saints' feet, if she have relieved the afflicted, if she have diligently followed every good work.

11 But the younger widows refuse: for when they have begun to wax wanton against Christ, they will marry;

12 Having damnation, because they have cast off their first faith.

13 And withal they learn *to be* idle, wandering about from house to house; and not only idle, but tattlers also and busybodies, speaking things which they ought not.

14 I will therefore that the younger women marry, bear children, guide the house, give none occasion to the adversary to speak reproachfully.

15 For some are already turned aside after Sa′tan.

16 If any man or woman that believeth have widows, let them relieve them, and let not the church be charged; that it may relieve them that are widows indeed.

17 Let the elders that rule well be counted worthy of double honour, especially they who labour in the word and doctrine.

18 For the scripture saith, Thou shalt not muzzle the ox that treadeth out the corn. And, The labourer *is* worthy of his reward.

19 Against an elder receive not an accusation, but before two or three witnesses.

20 Them that sin rebuke before all, that others also may fear.

21 I charge *thee* before God, and the Lord Je′sus Christ, and the elect angels, that thou observe these things without preferring one before another, doing nothing by partiality.

22 Lay hands suddenly on no man, neither be partaker of other men's sins: keep thyself pure.

23 Drink no longer water, but use a little wine for thy stomach's sake and thine often infirmities.

24 Some men's sins are open beforehand, going before to judgment; and some *men* they follow after.

25 Likewise also the good works *of some* are manifest beforehand; and they that are otherwise cannot be hid.

6 LET as many servants as are under the yoke count their own masters worthy of all honour, that the name of God and *his* doctrine be not blasphemed.

2 And they that have believing masters, let them not despise *them*, because they are brethren; but rather do *them* service, because they

are faithful and beloved, partakers of the benefit. These things teach and exhort.

3 If any man teach otherwise, and consent not to wholesome words, *even* the words of our Lord Je′sus Christ, and to the doctrine which is according to godliness;

4 He is proud, knowing nothing, but doting about questions and strifes of words, whereof cometh envy, strife, railings, evil surmisings,

5 Perverse disputings of men of corrupt minds, and destitute of the truth, supposing that gain is godliness: from such withdraw thyself.

6 But godliness with contentment is great gain.

7 For we brought nothing into *this* world, *and it is* certain we can carry nothing out.

8 And having food and raiment let us be therewith content.

9 But they that will be rich fall into temptation and a snare, and *into* many foolish and hurtful lusts, which drown men in destruction and perdition.

10 For the love of money is the root of all evil: which while some coveted after, they have erred from the faith, and pierced themselves through with many sorrows.

11 But thou, O man of God, flee these things; and follow after righteousness, godliness, faith, love, patience, meekness.

12 Fight the good fight of faith, lay hold on eternal life, whereunto thou art also called, and hast professed a good profession before many witnesses.

13 I give thee charge in the sight of God, who quickeneth all things, and *before* Christ Je′sus, who before Pon′ti-us Pi′late witnessed a good confession;

14 That thou keep *this* commandment without spot, unrebukeable, until the appearing of our Lord Je′sus Christ:

15 Which in his times he shall shew, *who is* the blessed and only Potentate, the King of kings, and Lord of lords;

16 Who only hath immortality, dwelling in the light which no man can approach unto; whom no man hath seen, nor can see: to whom *be* honour and power everlasting. Amen.

17 Charge them that are rich in this world, that they be not highminded, nor trust in uncertain riches, but in the living God, who giveth us richly all things to enjoy;

18 That they do good, that they be rich in good works, ready to distribute, willing to communicate;

19 Laying up in store for themselves a good foundation against the time to come, that they may lay hold on eternal life.

20 O Tim′o-thy, keep that which is committed to thy trust, avoiding profane *and* vain babblings, and oppositions of science falsely so called:

21 Which some professing have erred concerning the faith. Grace *be* with thee. Amen.

The first to Tim′o-thy was written from La-od-i-ce′a, which is the chiefest city of Phryg′i-a Pa-ca-ti-a′na.

THE SECOND LETTER OF PAUL TO

TIMOTHY

1 PAUL, an apostle of Je′sus Christ by the will of God, according to the promise of life which is in Christ Je′sus,

2 To Tim′o-thy, *my* dearly beloved son: Grace, mercy, *and* peace, from God the Father and Christ Je′sus our Lord.

3 I thank God, whom I serve from *my* forefathers with pure conscience, that without ceasing I have remembrance of thee in my prayers night and day;

4 Greatly desiring to see thee, being mindful of thy tears, that I may be filled with joy;

5 When I call to remembrance the unfeigned faith that is in thee, which dwelt first in thy grandmother Lo′is, and thy mother Eu′nice; and I am persuaded that in thee also.

6 Wherefore I put thee in remembrance that thou stir up the gift of God, which is in thee by the putting on of my hands.

7 For God hath not given us the spirit of fear; but of power, and of love, and of a sound mind.

8 Be not thou therefore ashamed of the testimony of our Lord, nor of me his prisoner: but be thou partaker of the afflictions of the gospel according to the power of God;

9 Who hath saved us, and called *us* with an holy calling, not according to our works, but according to his own purpose and grace, which was given us in Christ Je′sus before the world began,

10 But is now made manifest by the appearing of our Saviour Je′sus Christ, who hath abolished death, and hath brought life and immortality to light through the gospel:

11 Whereunto I am appointed a preacher, and an apostle, and a teacher of the Gen′tiles.

12 For the which cause I also suffer these things: nevertheless I am not ashamed: for I know whom I have believed, and am persuaded that he is able to keep that which I have committed unto him against that day.

13 Hold fast the form of sound words, which thou hast heard of me, in faith and love which is in Christ Je′sus.

14 That good thing which was committed unto thee keep by the Ho′ly Ghost which dwelleth in us.

15 This thou knowest, that all they which are in A′sia be turned away from me; of whom are Phy-gel′lus and Her-mog′e-nes.

16 The Lord give mercy unto the house of On-e-siph′o-rus; for he oft refreshed me, and was not ashamed of my chain:

17 But, when he was in Rome, he sought me out very diligently, and found *me*.

18 The Lord grant unto him that he may find mercy of the Lord in that day: and in how many things he ministered unto me at Eph′e-sus, thou knowest very well.

2 THOU therefore, my son, be strong in the grace that is in Christ Je′sus.

2 And the things that thou hast heard of me among many witnesses, the same commit thou to faithful men, who shall be able to teach others also.

3 Thou therefore endure hardness, as a good soldier of Je′sus Christ.

4 No man that warreth entangleth himself

with the affairs of *this* life; that he may please him who hath chosen him to be a soldier.

5 And if a man also strive for masteries, *yet* is he not crowned, except he strive lawfully.

6 The husbandman that laboureth must be first partaker of the fruits.

7 Consider what I say; and the Lord give thee understanding in all things.

8 Remember that Je'sus Christ of the seed of Da'vid was raised from the dead according to my gospel:

9 Wherein I suffer trouble, as an evil doer, *even* unto bonds; but the word of God is not bound.

10 Therefore I endure all things for the elect's sakes, that they may also obtain the salvation which is in Christ Je'sus with eternal glory.

11 *It is* a faithful saying: For if we be dead with *him*, we shall also live with *him*:

12 If we suffer, we shall also reign with *him*: if we deny *him*, he also will deny us:

13 If we believe not, *yet* he abideth faithful: he cannot deny himself.

14 Of these things put *them* in remembrance, charging *them* before the Lord that they strive not about words to no profit, *but* to the subverting of the hearers.

15 Study to shew thyself approved unto God, a workman that needeth not to be ashamed, rightly dividing the word of truth.

16 But shun profane *and* vain babblings: for they will increase unto more ungodliness.

17 And their word will eat as doth a canker: of whom is Hy-me-næ'us and Phi-le'tus;

18 Who concerning the truth have erred, saying that the resurrection is past already; and overthrow the faith of some.

19 Nevertheless the foundation of God standeth sure, having this seal, The Lord knoweth them that are his. And, Let every one that nameth the name of Christ depart from iniquity.

20 But in a great house there are not only vessels of gold and of silver, but also of wood and of earth; and some to honour, and some to dishonour.

21 If a man therefore purge himself from these, he shall be a vessel unto honour, sanctified, and meet for the master's use, *and* prepared unto every good work.

22 Flee also youthful lusts: but follow righteousness, faith, charity, peace, with them that call on the Lord out of a pure heart.

23 But foolish and unlearned questions avoid, knowing that they do gender strifes.

24 And the servant of the Lord must not strive; but be gentle unto all *men*, apt to teach, patient,

25 In meekness instructing those that oppose themselves; if God peradventure will give them repentance to the acknowledging of the truth;

26 And *that* they may recover themselves out of the snare of the devil, who are taken captive by him at his will.

3 THIS know also, that in the last days perilous times shall come.

2 For men shall be lovers of their own selves, covetous, boasters, proud, blasphemers, disobedient to parents, unthankful, unholy,

3 Without natural affection, trucebreakers, false accusers, incontinent, fierce, despisers of those that are good,

4 Traitors, heady, highminded, lovers of pleasures more than lovers of God;

5 Having a form of godliness, but denying the power thereof: from such turn away.

6 For of this sort are they which creep into houses, and lead captive silly women laden with sins, led away with divers lusts,

7 Ever learning, and never able to come to the knowledge of the truth.

8 Now as Jan'nes and Jam'bres withstood Mo'ses, so do these also resist the truth: men of corrupt minds, reprobate concerning the faith.

9 But they shall proceed no further: for their folly shall be manifest unto all *men*, as theirs also was.

10 But thou hast fully known my doctrine, manner of life, purpose, faith, longsuffering, charity, patience,

11 Persecutions, afflictions, which came unto me at An'ti-och, at I-co'ni-um, at Lys'tra; what persecutions I endured: but out of *them* all the Lord delivered me.

12 Yea, and all that will live godly in Christ Je'sus shall suffer persecution.

13 But evil men and seducers shall wax worse and worse, deceiving, and being deceived.

14 But continue thou in the things which thou hast learned and hast been assured of, knowing of whom thou hast learned *them;*

15 And that from a child thou hast known the holy scriptures, which are able to make thee wise unto salvation through faith which is in Christ Je'sus.

16 All scripture *is* given by inspiration of God, and *is* profitable for doctrine, for reproof, for correction, for instruction in righteousness:

17 That the man of God may be perfect, throughly furnished unto all good works.

4 I CHARGE *thee* therefore before God, and the Lord Je'sus Christ, who shall judge the quick and the dead at his appearing and his kingdom;

2 Preach the word; be instant in season, out of season; reprove, rebuke, exhort with all longsuffering and doctrine.

3 For the time will come when they will not endure sound doctrine; but after their own lusts shall they heap to themselves teachers, having itching ears;

4 And they shall turn away *their* ears from the truth, and shall be turned unto fables.

5 But watch thou in all things, endure afflictions, do the work of an evangelist, make full proof of thy ministry.

6 For I am now ready to be offered, and the time of my departure is at hand.

7 I have fought a good fight, I have finished *my* course, I have kept the faith:

8 Henceforth there is laid up for me a crown of righteousness, which the Lord, the righteous judge, shall give me at that day: and not to me only, but unto all them also that love his appearing.

9 Do thy diligence to come shortly unto me:

10 For De'mas hath forsaken me, having loved this present world, and is departed unto Thes-sa-lo-ni'ca; Cres'cens to Ga-la'tia, Ti'tus unto Dal-ma'ti-a.

11 Only Luke is with me. Take Mark, and bring him with thee: for he is profitable to me for the ministry.

12 And Tych'i-cus have I sent to Eph'e-sus.

13 The cloke that I left at Tro'as with Car'pus, when thou comest, bring *with thee*, and the books, *but* especially the parchments.

14 Al-ex-an'der the coppersmith did me much evil: the Lord reward him according to his works:

15 Of whom be thou ware also; for he hath greatly withstood our words.

16 At my first answer no man stood with me, but all *men* forsook me: I pray God that it may not be laid to their charge.

17 Notwithstanding the Lord stood with me, and strengthened me; that by me the preaching might be fully known, and *that* all the Gen'tiles might hear: and I was delivered out of the mouth of the lion.

18 And the Lord shall deliver me from every evil work, and will preserve *me* unto his heavenly kingdom: to whom *be* glory for ever and ever. Amen.

19 Salute Pris'ca and A'qui-la, and the household of On-e-siph'o-rus.

20 E-ras'tus abode at Cor'inth: but Troph'i-mus have I left at Mi-le'tum sick.

21 Do thy diligence to come before winter. Eu-bu'lus greeteth thee, and Pu'dens, and Li'nus, and Clau'di-a, and all the brethren.

22 The Lord Je'sus Christ *be* with thy spirit. Grace *be* with you. Amen.

The second *epistle* unto Ti-mo'the-us, ordained the first bishop of the church of the E-phe'sians, was written from Rome, when Paul was brought before Ne'ro the second time.

THE LETTER OF PAUL TO

TITUS

1 PAUL, a servant of God, and an apostle of Je'sus Christ, according to the faith of God's elect, and the acknowledging of the truth which is after godliness;

2 In hope of eternal life, which God, that cannot lie, promised before the world began;

3 But hath in due times manifested his word through preaching, which is committed unto me according to the commandment of God our Saviour;

4 To Ti'tus, *mine* own son after the common faith: Grace, mercy, *and* peace, from God the Father and the Lord Je'sus Christ our Saviour.

5 For this cause left I thee in Crete, that thou shouldest set in order the things that are wanting, and ordain elders in every city, as I had appointed thee:

6 If any be blameless, the husband of one wife, having faithful children not accused of riot or unruly.

7 For a bishop must be blameless, as the steward of God; not selfwilled, not soon angry, not given to wine, no striker, not given to filthy lucre;

8 But a lover of hospitality, a lover of good men, sober, just, holy, temperate;

9 Holding fast the faithful word as he hath been taught, that he may be able by sound doctrine both to exhort and to convince the gainsayers.

10 For there are many unruly and vain talkers and deceivers, specially they of the circumcision:

11 Whose mouths must be stopped, who subvert whole houses, teaching things which they ought not, for filthy lucre's sake.

12 One of themselves, *even* a prophet of their own, said, The Cre'ti-ans *are* alway liars, evil beasts, slow bellies.

13 This witness is true. Wherefore rebuke them sharply, that they may be sound in the faith;

14 Not giving heed to Jew'ish fables, and commandments of men, that turn from the truth.

15 Unto the pure all things *are* pure: but unto them that are defiled and unbelieving *is* nothing pure; but even their mind and conscience is defiled.

16 They profess that they know God; but in works they deny *him*, being abominable, and disobedient, and unto every good work reprobate.

2 BUT speak thou the things which become sound doctrine:

2 That the aged men be sober, grave, temperate, sound in faith, in charity, in patience.

3 The aged women likewise, that *they be* in behaviour as becometh holiness, not false accusers, not given to much wine, teachers of good things;

4 That they may teach the young women to be sober, to love their husbands, to love their children,

5 *To be* discreet, chaste, keepers at home, good, obedient to their own husbands, that the word of God be not blasphemed.

6 Young men likewise exhort to be sober minded.

7 In all things shewing thyself a pattern of good works: in doctrine *shewing* uncorruptness, gravity, sincerity,

8 Sound speech, that cannot be condemned; that he that is of the contrary part may be ashamed, having no evil thing to say of you.

9 *Exhort* servants to be obedient unto their own masters, *and* to please *them* well in all things; not answering again;

10 Not purloining, but shewing all good fidelity; that they may adorn the doctrine of God our Saviour in all things.

11 For the grace of God that bringeth salvation hath appeared to all men,

12 Teaching us that, denying ungodliness and worldly lusts, we should live soberly, righteously, and godly, in this present world;

13 Looking for that blessed hope, and the glorious appearing of the great God and our Saviour Jesus Christ;

14 Who gave himself for us, that he might redeem us from all iniquity, and purify unto himself a peculiar people, zealous of good works.

15 These things speak, and exhort, and rebuke with all authority. Let no man despise thee.

3 PUT them in mind to be subject to principalities and powers, to obey magistrates, to be ready to every good work,

2 To speak evil of no man, to be no brawlers, *but* gentle, shewing all meekness unto all men.

3 For we ourselves also were sometimes foolish, disobedient, deceived, serving divers lusts and pleasures, living in malice and envy, hateful, *and* hating one another.

4 But after that the kindness and love of God our Saviour toward man appeared,

5 Not by works of righteousness which we have done, but according to his mercy he saved us, by the washing of regeneration, and renewing of the Ho′ly Ghost;

6 Which he shed on us abundantly through Je′sus Christ our Saviour;

7 That being justified by his grace, we should be made heirs according to the hope of eternal life.

8 *This is* a faithful saying, and these things I will that thou affirm constantly, that they which have believed in God might be careful to maintain good works. These things are good and profitable unto men.

9 But avoid foolish questions, and genealogies, and contentions, and strivings about the law; for they are unprofitable and vain.

10 A man that is an heretick after the first and second admonition reject;

11 Knowing that he that is such is subverted, and sinneth, being condemned of himself.

12 When I shall send Ar′te-mas unto thee, or Tych′i-cus, be diligent to come unto me to Ni-cop′o-lis: for I have determined there to winter.

13 Bring Ze′nas the lawyer and A-pol′los on their journey diligently, that nothing be wanting unto them.

14 And let ours also learn to maintain good works for necessary uses, that they be not unfruitful.

15 All that are with me salute thee. Greet them that love us in the faith. Grace *be* with you all. Amen.

It was written to Ti′tus, ordained the first bishop of the church of the Cre′ti-ans, from Ni-cop′o-lis of Mac-e-do′-ni-a.

THE LETTER OF PAUL TO

PHILEMON

PAUL, a prisoner of Je′sus Christ, and Tim′o-thy *our* brother, unto Phi-le′mon our dearly beloved, and fellowlabourer,

2 And to *our* beloved Apph′i-a, and Ar-chip′-pus our fellowsoldier, and to the church in thy house:

3 Grace to you, and peace, from God our Father and the Lord Je′sus Christ.

4 I thank my God, making mention of thee always in my prayers,

5 Hearing of thy love and faith, which thou hast toward the Lord Je′sus, and toward all saints;

6 That the communication of thy faith may become effectual by the acknowledging of every good thing which is in you in Christ Je′sus.

7 For we have great joy and consolation in thy love, because the bowels of the saints are refreshed by thee, brother.

8 Wherefore, though I might be much bold in Christ to enjoin thee that which is convenient,

9 Yet for love's sake I rather beseech *thee*, being such an one as Paul the aged, and now also a prisoner of Je′sus Christ.

10 I beseech thee for my son O′nes′i-mus, whom I have begotten in my bonds:

11 Which in time past was to thee unprofitable, but now profitable to thee and to me:

12 Whom I have sent again: thou therefore receive him, that is, mine own bowels:

13 Whom I would have retained with me, that in thy stead he might have ministered unto me in the bonds of the gospel:

14 But without thy mind would I do nothing; that thy benefit should not be as it were of necessity, but willingly.

15 For perhaps he therefore departed for a season, that thou shouldest receive him for ever;

16 Not now as a servant, but above a servant, a brother beloved, specially to me, but how much more unto thee, both in the flesh, and in the Lord?

17 If thou count me therefore a partner, receive him as myself.

18 If he hath wronged thee, or oweth *thee* ought, put that on mine account;

19 I Paul have written *it* with mine own hand, I will repay *it*: albeit I do not say to thee how thou owest unto me even thine own self besides.

20 Yea, brother, let me have joy of thee in the Lord: refresh my bowels in the Lord.

21 Having confidence in thy obedience I wrote unto thee, knowing that thou wilt also do more than I say.

22 But withal prepare me also a lodging: for I trust that through your prayers I shall be given unto you.

23 There salute thee Ep′a-phras, my fellowprisoner in Christ Je′sus;

24 Mar′cus, Ar-is-tar′chus, De′mas, Lu′cas, my fellowlabourers.

25 The grace of our Lord Je′sus Christ *be* with your spirit. Amen.

Written from Rome to Phi-le′mon, by O′nes′i-mus, a servant.

THE LETTER TO THE

HEBREWS

1 GOD, who at sundry times and in divers manners spake in time past unto the fathers by the prophets,

2 Hath in these last days spoken unto us by *his* Son, whom he hath appointed heir of all things, by whom also he made the worlds;

3 Who being the brightness of *his* glory, and the express image of his person, and upholding all things by the word of his power, when he had by himself purged our sins, sat down on the right hand of the Majesty on high;

4 Being made so much better than the an-

gels, as he hath by inheritance obtained a more excellent name than they.

5 For unto which of the angels said he at any time, Thou art my son, this day have I begotten thee? And again, I will be to him a Father, and he shall be to me a Son?

6 And again, when he bringeth in the firstbegotten into the world, he saith, And let all the angels of God worship him.

7 And of the angels he saith, Who maketh his angels spirits, and his ministers a flame of fire.

8 But unto the Son *he saith,* Thy throne, O God, *is* for ever and ever: a sceptre of righteousness *is* the sceptre of thy kingdom.

9 Thou hast loved righteousness, and hated iniquity; therefore God, *even* thy God, hath anointed thee with the oil of gladness above thy fellows.

10 And, Thou, Lord, in the beginning hast laid the foundation of the earth; and the heavens are the works of thine hands:

11 They shall perish; but thou remainest; and they all shall wax old as doth a garment;

12 And as a vesture shalt thou fold them up, and they shall be changed: but thou art the same, and thy years shall not fail.

13 But to which of the angels said he at any time, Sit on my right hand, until I make thine enemies thy footstool?

14 Are they not all ministering spirits, sent forth to minister for them who shall be heirs of salvation?

2 THEREFORE we ought to give the more earnest heed to the things which we have heard, lest at any time we should let *them* slip.

2 For if the word spoken by angels was stedfast, and every transgression and disobedience received a just recompence of reward;

3 How shall we escape, if we neglect so great salvation; which at the first began to be spoken by the Lord, and was confirmed unto us by them that heard *him;*

4 God also bearing *them* witness, both with signs and wonders, and with divers miracles, and gifts of the Ho'ly Ghost, according to his own will?

5 For unto the angels hath he not put in subjection the world to come, whereof we speak.

6 But one in a certain place testified, saying, What is man, that thou art mindful of him? or the son of man, that thou visitest him?

7 Thou madest him a little lower than the angels; thou crownedst him with glory and honour, and didst set him over the works of thy hands:

8 Thou hast put all things in subjection under his feet. For in that he put all in subjection under him, he left nothing *that is* not put under him. But now we see not yet all things put under him.

9 But we see Je'sus, who was made a little lower than the angels for the suffering of death, crowned with glory and honour; that he by the grace of God should taste death for every man.

10 For it became him, for whom *are* all things, and by whom *are* all things, in bringing many sons unto glory, to make the captain of their salvation perfect through sufferings.

11 For both he that sanctifieth and they who are sanctified *are* all of one: for which cause he is not ashamed to call them brethren,

12 Saying, I will declare thy name unto my brethren, in the midst of the church will I sing praise unto thee.

13 And again, I will put my trust in him. And again, Behold I and the children which God hath given me.

14 Forasmuch then as the children are partakers of flesh and blood, he also himself likewise took part of the same; that through death he might destroy him that had the power of death, that is, the devil;

15 And deliver them who through fear of death were all their lifetime subject to bondage.

16 For verily he took not on *him the nature of* angels; but he took on *him* the seed of A'braham.

17 Wherefore in all things it behoved him to be made like unto *his* brethren, that he might be a merciful and faithful high priest in things *pertaining* to God, to make reconciliation for the sins of the people.

18 For in that he himself hath suffered being tempted, he is able to succour them that are tempted.

3 WHEREFORE, holy brethren, partakers of the heavenly calling, consider the Apostle and High Priest of our profession, Christ Je'sus;

2 Who was faithful to him that appointed him, as also Mo'ses *was faithful* in all his house.

3 For this *man* was counted worthy of more glory than Mo'ses, inasmuch as he who hath builded the house hath more honour than the house.

4 For every house is builded by some *man;* but he that built all things *is* God.

5 And Mo'ses verily *was* faithful in all his house, as a servant, for a testimony of those things which were to be spoken after;

6 But Christ as a son over his own house; whose house are we, if we hold fast the confidence and the rejoicing of the hope firm unto the end.

7 Wherefore (as the Ho'ly Ghost saith, To day if ye will hear his voice,

8 Harden not your hearts, as in the provocation, in the day of temptation in the wilderness:

9 When your fathers tempted me, proved me, and saw my works forty years.

10 Wherefore I was grieved with that generation, and said, They do alway err in *their* heart; and they have not known my ways.

11 So I sware in my wrath, They shall not enter into my rest.)

12 Take heed, brethren, lest there be in any of you an evil heart of unbelief, in departing from the living God.

13 But exhort one another daily, while it is called To day; lest any of you be hardened through the deceitfulness of sin.

14 For we are made partakers of Christ, if we hold the beginning of our confidence stedfast unto the end;

15 While it is said, To day if ye will hear his voice, harden not your hearts, as in the provocation.

16 For some, when they had heard, did provoke: howbeit not all that came out of E'gypt by Mo'ses.

17 But with whom was he grieved forty years? *was it* not with them that had sinned, whose carcases fell in the wilderness?

18 And to whom sware he that they should not enter into his rest, but to them that believed not?

19 So we see that they could not enter in because of unbelief.

4 LET us therefore fear, lest, a promise being left *us* of entering into his rest, any of you should seem to come short of it.

2 For unto us was the gospel preached, as well as unto them: but the word preached did not profit them, not being mixed with faith in them that heard *it.*

3 For we which have believed do enter into rest, as he said, As I have sworn in my wrath, if they shall enter into my rest: although the works were finished from the foundation of the world.

4 For he spake in a certain place of the seventh *day* on this wise, And God did rest the seventh day from all his works.

5 And in this *place* again, If they shall enter into my rest.

6 Seeing therefore it remaineth that some must enter therein, and they to whom it was first preached entered not in because of unbelief:

7 Again, he limiteth a certain day, saying in Da'vid, To day, after so long a time; as it is said, To day if ye will hear his voice, harden not your hearts.

8 For if Je'sus had given them rest, then would he not afterward have spoken of another day.

9 There remaineth therefore a rest to the people of God.

10 For he that is entered into his rest, he also hath ceased from his own works, as God *did* from his.

11 Let us labour therefore to enter into that rest, lest any man fall after the same example of unbelief.

12 For the word of God *is* quick, and powerful, and sharper than any twoedged sword, piercing even to the dividing asunder of soul and spirit, and of the joints and marrow, and *is* a discerner of the thoughts and intents of the heart.

13 Neither is there any creature that is not manifest in his sight: but all things *are* naked and opened unto the eyes of him with whom we have to do.

14 Seeing then that we have a great high priest, that is passed into the heavens, Je'sus the Son of God, let us hold fast *our* profession.

15 For we have not an high priest which cannot be touched with the feeling of our infirmities; but was in all points tempted like as *we are, yet* without sin.

16 Let us therefore come boldly unto the throne of grace, that we may obtain mercy, and find grace to help in time of need.

5 FOR every high priest taken from among men is ordained for men in things *pertaining* to God, that he may offer both gifts and sacrifices for sins:

2 Who can have compassion on the ignorant, and on them that are out of the way; for that he himself also is compassed with infirmity.

3 And by reason hereof he ought, as for the people, so also for himself, to offer for sins.

4 And no man taketh this honour unto himself, but he that is called of God, as *was* Aar'on.

5 So also Christ glorified not himself to be made an high priest; but he that said unto him, Thou art my Son, to day have I begotten thee.

6 As he saith also in another *place,* Thou *art* a priest for ever after the order of Mel-chis'e-dec.

7 Who in the days of his flesh, when he had offered up prayers and supplications with strong crying and tears unto him that was able to save him from death, and was heard in that he feared;

8 Though he were a Son, yet learned he obedience by the things which he suffered;

9 And being made perfect, he became the author of eternal salvation unto all them that obey him;

10 Called of God an high priest after the order of Mel-chis'e-dec.

11 Of whom we have many things to say, and hard to be uttered, seeing ye are dull of hearing.

12 For when for the time ye ought to be teachers, ye have need that one teach you again which *be* the first principles of the oracles of God; and are become such as have need of milk, and not of strong meat.

13 For every one that useth milk is unskilful in the word of righteousness: for he is a babe.

14 But strong meat belongeth to them that are of full age, *even* those who by reason of use have their senses exercised to discern both good and evil.

6 THEREFORE leaving the principles of the doctrine of Christ, let us go on unto perfection; not laying again the foundation of repentance from dead works, and of faith toward God,

2 Of the doctrine of baptisms, and of laying on of hands, and of resurrection of the dead, and of eternal judgment.

3 And this will we do, if God permit.

4 For *it is* impossible for those who were once enlightened, and have tasted of the heavenly gift, and were made partakers of the Ho'ly Ghost,

5 And have tasted the good word of God, and the powers of the world to come,

6 If they shall fall away, to renew them again unto repentance; seeing they crucify to themselves the Son of God afresh, and put *him* to an open shame.

7 For the earth which drinketh in the rain that cometh oft upon it, and bringeth forth herbs meet for them by whom it is dressed, receiveth blessing from God:

8 But that which beareth thorns and briers *is* rejected, and *is* nigh unto cursing; whose end *is* to be burned.

9 But, beloved, we are persuaded better things of you, and things that accompany salvation, though we thus speak.

10 For God *is* not unrighteous to forget your work and labour of love, which ye have shewed toward his name, in that ye have ministered to the saints, and do minister.

11 And we desire that every one of you do shew the same diligence to the full assurance of hope unto the end:

12 That ye be not slothful, but followers of them who through faith and patience inherit the promises.

13 For when God made promise to A'braham, because he could swear by no greater, he sware by himself,

14 Saying, Surely blessing I will bless thee, and multiplying I will multiply thee.

15 And so, after he had patiently endured, he obtained the promise.

16 For men verily swear by the greater: and an oath for confirmation *is* to them an end of all strife.

17 Wherein God, willing more abundantly to shew unto the heirs of promise the immutability of his counsel, confirmed *it* by an oath:

18 That by two immutable things, in which *it was* impossible for God to lie, we might have a strong consolation, who have fled for refuge to lay hold upon the hope set before us:

19 Which *hope* we have as an anchor of the soul, both sure and stedfast, and which entereth into that within the veil;

20 Whither the forerunner is for us entered, *even* Je′sus, made an high priest for ever after the order of Mel-chis′e-dec.

7 FOR this Mel-chis′e-dec, king of Sa′lem, priest of the most high God, who met A′-bra-ham returning from the slaughter of the kings, and blessed him;

2 To whom also A′bra-ham gave a tenth part of all; first being by interpretation King of righteousness, and after that also King of Sa′lem, which is, King of peace;

3 Without father, without mother, without descent, having neither beginning of days, nor end of life; but made like unto the Son of God; abideth a priest continually.

4 Now consider how great this man *was*, unto whom even the patriarch A′bra-ham gave the tenth of the spoils.

5 And verily they that are of the sons of Le′-vi, who receive the office of the priesthood, have a commandment to take tithes of the people according to the law, that is, of their brethren, though they come out of the loins of A′bra-ham:

6 But he whose descent is not counted from them received tithes of A′bra-ham, and blessed him that had the promises.

7 And without all contradiction the less is blessed of the better.

8 And here men that die receive tithes; but there he *receiveth them*, of whom it is witnessed that he liveth.

9 And as I may so say, Le′vi also, who receiveth tithes, payed tithes in A′bra-ham.

10 For he was yet in the loins of his father, when Mel-chis′e-dec met him.

11 If therefore perfection were by the Le-vit′-i-cal priesthood, (for under it the people received the law,) what further need *was there* that another priest should rise after the order of Mel-chis′e-dec, and not be called after the order of Aar′on?

12 For the priesthood being changed, there is made of necessity a change also of the law.

13 For he of whom these things are spoken pertaineth to another tribe, of which no man gave attendance at the altar.

14 For *it is* evident that our Lord sprang out of Ju′da; of which tribe Mo′ses spake nothing concerning priesthood.

15 And it is yet far more evident: for that after the similitude of Mel-chis′e-dec there ariseth another priest,

16 Who is made, not after the law of a carnal commandment, but after the power of an endless life.

17 For he testifieth, Thou *art* a priest for ever after the order of Mel-chis′e-dec.

18 For there is verily a disannulling of the commandment going before for the weakness and unprofitableness thereof.

19 For the law made nothing perfect, but the bringing in of a better hope *did*; by the which we draw nigh unto God.

20 And inasmuch as not without an oath *he was made priest*:

21 (For those priests were made without an oath; but this with an oath by him that said unto him, The Lord sware and will not repent, Thou *art* a priest for ever after the order of Mel-chis′-e-dec:)

22 By so much was Je′sus made a surety of a better testament.

23 And they truly were many priests, because they were not suffered to continue by reason of death:

24 But this *man*, because he continueth ever, hath an unchangeable priesthood.

25 Wherefore he is able also to save them to the uttermost that come unto God by him, seeing he ever liveth to make intercession for them.

26 For such an high priest became us, *who is* holy, harmless, undefiled, separate from sinners, and made higher than the heavens;

27 Who needeth not daily, as those high priests, to offer up sacrifice, first for his own sins, and then for the people′s: for this he did once, when he offered up himself.

28 For the law maketh men high priests which have infirmity; but the word of the oath, which was since the law, *maketh* the Son, who is consecrated for evermore.

8 NOW of the things which we have spoken *this is* the sum: We have such an high priest, who is set on the right hand of the throne of the Majesty in the heavens;

2 A minister of the sanctuary, and of the true tabernacle, which the Lord pitched, and not man.

3 For every high priest is ordained to offer gifts and sacrifices: wherefore *it is* of necessity that this man have somewhat also to offer.

4 For if he were on earth, he should not be a priest, seeing that there are priests that offer gifts according to the law:

5 Who serve unto the example and shadow of heavenly things, as Mo′ses was admonished of God when he was about to make the tabernacle: for, See, saith he, *that* thou make all things according to the pattern shewed to thee in the mount.

6 But now hath he obtained a more excellent ministry, by how much also he is the mediator of a better covenant, which was established upon better promises.

7 For if that first *covenant* had been faultless, then should no place have been sought for the second.

8 For finding fault with them, he saith, Behold, the days come, saith the Lord, when I will make a new covenant with the house of Is′ra-el and with the house of Ju′dah:

9 Not according to the covenant that I made with their fathers in the day when I took them by the hand to lead them out of the land of E′-gypt; because they continued not in my covenant, and I regarded them not, saith the Lord.

10 For this *is* the covenant that I will make with the house of Is′ra-el after those days, saith the Lord; I will put my laws into their mind, and write them in their hearts: and I will be to them a God, and they shall be to me a people:

11 And they shall not teach every man his neighbour, and every man his brother, saying, Know the Lord: for all shall know me, from the least to the greatest.

12 For I will be merciful to their unrighteousness, and their sins and their iniquities will I remember no more.

13 In that he saith, A new *covenant*, he hath made the first old. Now that which decayeth and waxeth old *is* ready to vanish away.

9 THEN verily the first *covenant* had also ordinances of divine service, and a worldly sanctuary.

2 For there was a tabernacle made; the first,

wherein *was* the candlestick, and the table, and the shewbread; which is called the sanctuary.

3 And after the second veil, the tabernacle which is called the Holiest of all;

4 Which had the golden censer, and the ark of the covenant overlaid round about with gold, wherein *was* the golden pot that had manna, and Aar′on's rod that budded, and the tables of the covenant;

5 And over it the cherubims of glory shadowing the mercyseat; of which we cannot now speak particularly.

6 Now when these things were thus ordained, the priests went always into the first tabernacle, accomplishing the service *of* God.

7 But into the second *went* the high priest alone once every year, not without blood, which he offered for himself, and *for* the errors of the people:

8 The Ho′ly Ghost this signifying, that the way into the holiest of all was not yet made manifest, while as the first tabernacle was yet standing:

9 Which *was* a figure for the time then present, in which were offered both gifts, and sacrifices, that could not make him that did the service perfect, as pertaining to the conscience;

10 Which stood only in meats and drinks, and divers washings, and carnal ordinances, imposed *on them* until the time of reformation.

11 But Christ being come an high priest of good things to come, by a greater and more perfect tabernacle, not made with hands, that is to say, not of this building;

12 Neither by the blood of goats and calves, but by his own blood he entered in once into the holy place, having obtained eternal redemption *for us.*

13 For if the blood of bulls and of goats, and the ashes of an heifer sprinkling the unclean, sanctifieth to the purifying of the flesh:

14 How much more shall the blood of Christ, who through the eternal Spirit offered himself without spot to God, purge your conscience from dead works to serve the living God?

15 And for this cause he is the mediator of the new testament, that by means of death, for the redemption of the transgressions *that were* under the first testament, they which are called might receive the promise of eternal inheritance.

16 For where a testament *is,* there must also of necessity be the death of the testator.

17 For a testament *is* of force after men are dead: otherwise it is of no strength at all while the testator liveth.

18 Whereupon neither the first *testament* was dedicated without blood.

19 For when Mo′ses had spoken every precept to all the people according to the law, he took the blood of calves and of goats, with water, and scarlet wool, and hyssop, and sprinkled both the book, and all the people,

20 Saying, This *is* the blood of the testament which God hath enjoined unto you.

21 Moreover he sprinkled with blood both the tabernacle, and all the vessels of the ministry.

22 And almost all things are by the law purged with blood; and without shedding of blood is no remission.

23 *It was* therefore necessary that the patterns of things in the heavens should be purified with these; but the heavenly things themselves with better sacrifices than these.

24 For Christ is not entered into the holy places made with hands, *which are* the figures of the true; but into heaven itself, now to appear in the presence of God for us:

25 Nor yet that he should offer himself often, as the high priest entereth into the holy place every year with blood of others;

26 For then must he often have suffered since the foundation of the world: but now once in the end of the world hath he appeared to put away sin by the sacrifice of himself.

27 And as it is appointed unto men once to die, but after this the judgment:

28 So Christ was once offered to bear the sins of many; and unto them that look for him shall he appear the second time without sin unto salvation.

10 FOR the law having a shadow of good things to come, *and* not the very image of the things, can never with those sacrifices which they offered year by year continually make the comers thereunto perfect.

2 For then would they not have ceased to be offered? because that the worshippers once purged should have had no more conscience of sins.

3 But in those *sacrifices there is* a remembrance again *made* of sins every year.

4 For *it is* not possible that the blood of bulls and of goats should take away sins.

5 Wherefore when he cometh into the world, he saith, Sacrifice and offering thou wouldest not, but a body hast thou prepared me:

6 In burnt offerings and *sacrifices* for sin thou hast had no pleasure.

7 Then said I, Lo, I come (in the volume of the book it is written of me,) to do thy will, O God.

8 Above when he said, Sacrifice and offering and burnt offerings and *offering* for sin thou wouldest not, neither hadst pleasure *therein;* which are offered by the law;

9 Then said he, Lo, I come to do thy will, O God. He taketh away the first, that he may establish the second.

10 By the which will we are sanctified through the offering of the body of Je′sus Christ once *for all.*

11 And every priest standeth daily ministering and offering oftentimes the same sacrifices, which can never take away sins:

12 But this man, after he had offered one sacrifice for sins for ever, sat down on the right hand of God;

13 From henceforth expecting till his enemies be made his footstool.

14 For by one offering he hath perfected for ever them that are sanctified.

15 *Whereof* the Ho′ly Ghost also is a witness to us: for after that he had said before,

16 This *is* the covenant that I will make with them after those days, saith the Lord, I will put my laws into their hearts, and in their minds will I write them;

17 And their sins and iniquities will I remember no more.

18 Now where remission of these *is, there is* no more offering for sin.

19 Having therefore, brethren, boldness to enter into the holiest by the blood of Je′sus,

20 By a new and living way, which he hath consecrated for us, through the veil, that is to say, his flesh;

21 And *having* an high priest over the house of God;

22 Let us draw near with a true heart in full assurance of faith, having our hearts sprinkled

from an evil conscience, and our bodies washed with pure water.

23 Let us hold fast the profession of *our* faith without wavering; (for he *is* faithful that promised;)

24 And let us consider one another to provoke unto love and to good works:

25 Not forsaking the assembling of ourselves together, as the manner of some *is*; but exhorting *one another*: and so much the more, as ye see the day approaching.

26 For if we sin wilfully after that we have received the knowledge of the truth, there remaineth no more sacrifice for sins,

27 But a certain fearful looking for of judgment and fiery indignation, which shall devour the adversaries.

28 He that despised Mo'ses' law died without mercy under two or three witnesses:

29 Of how much sorer punishment, suppose ye, shall he be thought worthy, who hath trodden under foot the Son of God, and hath counted the blood of the covenant, wherewith he was sanctified, an unholy thing, and hath done despite unto the Spirit of grace?

30 For we know him that hath said, Vengeance *belongeth* unto me, I will recompense, saith the Lord. And again, The Lord shall judge his people.

31 *It is* a fearful thing to fall into the hands of the living God.

32 But call to remembrance the former days, in which, after ye were illuminated, ye endured a great fight of afflictions;

33 Partly, whilst ye were made a gazingstock both by reproaches and afflictions; and partly, whilst ye became companions of them that were so used.

34 For ye had compassion of me in my bonds, and took joyfully the spoiling of your goods, knowing in yourselves that ye have in heaven a better and an enduring substance.

35 Cast not away therefore your confidence, which hath great recompence of reward.

36 For ye have need of patience, that, after ye have done the will of God, ye might receive the promise.

37 For yet a little while, and he that shall come will come, and will not tarry.

38 Now the just shall live by faith: but if *any* man draw back, my soul shall have no pleasure in him.

39 But we are not of them who draw back unto perdition; but of them that believe to the saving of the soul.

11 NOW faith is the substance of things hoped for, the evidence of things not seen.

2 For by it the elders obtained a good report.

3 Through faith we understand that the worlds were framed by the word of God, so that things which are seen were not made of things which do appear.

4 By faith A'bel offered unto God a more excellent sacrifice than Cain, by which he obtained witness that he was righteous, God testifying of his gifts: and by it he being dead yet speaketh.

5 By faith E'noch was translated that he should not see death; and was not found, because God had translated him: for before his translation he had this testimony, that he pleased God.

6 But without faith *it is* impossible to please *him*: for he that cometh to God must believe

that he is, and *that* he is a rewarder of them that diligently seek him.

7 By faith No'ah, being warned of God of things not seen as yet, moved with fear, prepared an ark to the saving of his house; by the which he condemned the world, and became heir of the righteousness which is by faith.

8 By faith A'bra-ham, when he was called to go out into a place which he should after receive for an inheritance, obeyed; and he went out, not knowing whither he went.

9 By faith he sojourned in the land of promise, as *in* a strange country, dwelling in tabernacles with I'saac and Ja'cob, the heirs with him of the same promise:

10 For he looked for a city which hath foundations, whose builder and maker *is* God.

11 Through faith also Sa'ra herself received strength to conceive seed, and was delivered of a child when she was past age, because she judged him faithful who had promised.

12 Therefore sprang there even of one, and him as good as dead, so *many* as the stars of the sky in multitude, and as the sand which is by the sea shore innumerable.

13 These all died in faith, not having received the promises, but having seen them afar off, and were persuaded of *them*, and embraced *them*, and confessed that they were strangers and pilgrims on the earth.

14 For they that say such things declare plainly that they seek a country.

15 And truly, if they had been mindful of that *country* from whence they came out, they might have had opportunity to have returned.

16 But now they desire a better *country*, that is, an heavenly: wherefore God is not ashamed to be called their God: for he hath prepared for them a city.

17 By faith A'bra-ham, when he was tried, offered up I'saac: and he that had received the promises offered up his only begotten *son*,

18 Of whom it was said, That in I'saac shall thy seed be called:

19 Accounting that God *was* able to raise *him* up, even from the dead; from whence also he received him in a figure.

20 By faith I'saac blessed Ja'cob and E'sau concerning things to come.

21 By faith Ja'cob, when he was a dying, blessed both the sons of Jo'seph; and worshipped, *leaning* upon the top of his staff.

22 By faith Jo'seph, when he died, made mention of the departing of the children of Is'-ra-el; and gave commandment concerning his bones.

23 By faith Mo'ses, when he was born, was hid three months of his parents, because they saw *he was* a proper child; and they were not afraid of the king's commandment.

24 By faith Mo'ses, when he was come to years, refused to be called the son of Pha'raoh's daughter;

25 Choosing rather to suffer affliction with the people of God, than to enjoy the pleasures of sin for a season;

26 Esteeming the reproach of Christ greater riches than the treasures in E'gypt: for he had respect unto the recompence of the reward.

27 By faith he forsook E'gypt, not fearing the wrath of the king: for he endured, as seeing him who is invisible.

28 Through faith he kept the passover, and the sprinkling of blood, lest he that destroyed the firstborn should touch them.

29 By faith they passed through the Red sea

as by dry *land:* which the E-gyp'tians assaying to do were drowned.

30 By faith the walls of Jer'i-cho fell down, after they were compassed about seven days.

31 By faith the harlot Ra'hab perished not with them that believed not, when she had received the spies with peace.

32 And what shall I more say? for the time would fail me to tell of Ged'e-on, and of Ba'rak, and of Sam'son, and of Jeph'tha-e; of Da'vid also and Sam'u-el, and of the prophets:

33 Who through faith subdued kingdoms, wrought righteousness, obtained promises, stopped the mouths of lions,

34 Quenched the violence of fire, escaped the edge of the sword, out of weakness were made strong, waxed valiant in fight, turned to flight the armies of the aliens.

35 Women received their dead raised to life again: and others were tortured, not accepting deliverance; that they might obtain a better resurrection:

36 And others had trial of *cruel* mockings and scourgings, yea, moreover of bonds and imprisonment:

37 They were stoned, they were sawn asunder, were tempted, were slain with the sword: they wandered about in sheepskins and goatskins; being destitute, afflicted, tormented;

38 (Of whom the world was not worthy:) they wandered in deserts, and *in* mountains, and *in* dens and caves of the earth.

39 And these all, having obtained a good report through faith, received not the promise:

40 God having provided some better thing for us, that they without us should not be made perfect.

12 WHEREFORE seeing we also are compassed about with so great a cloud of witnesses, let us lay aside every weight, and the sin which doth so easily beset *us*, and let us run with patience the race that is set before us,

2 Looking unto Je'sus the author and finisher of *our* faith; who for the joy that was set before him endured the cross, despising the shame, and is set down at the right hand of the throne of God.

3 For consider him that endured such contradiction of sinners against himself, lest ye be wearied and faint in your minds.

4 Ye have not yet resisted unto blood, striving against sin.

5 And ye have forgotten the exhortation which speaketh unto you as unto children, My son, despise not thou the chastening of the Lord, nor faint when thou art rebuked of him:

6 For whom the Lord loveth he chasteneth, and scourgeth every son whom he receiveth.

7 If ye endure chastening, God dealeth with you as with sons; for what son is he whom the father chasteneth not?

8 But if ye be without chastisement, whereof all are partakers, then are ye bastards, and not sons.

9 Furthermore we have had fathers of our flesh which corrected *us*, and we gave *them* reverence: shall we not much rather be in subjection unto the Father of spirits, and live?

10 For they verily for a few days chastened *us* after their own pleasure; but he for *our* profit, that *we* might be partakers of his holiness.

11 Now no chastening for the present seemeth to be joyous, but grievous: nevertheless afterward it yieldeth the peaceable fruit of righteousness unto them which are exercised thereby.

12 Wherefore lift up the hands which hang down, and the feeble knees;

13 And make straight paths for your feet, lest that which is lame be turned out of the way; but let it rather be healed.

14 Follow peace with all *men*, and holiness, without which no man shall see the Lord:

15 Looking diligently lest any man fail of the grace of God; lest any root of bitterness springing up trouble *you*, and thereby many be defiled;

16 Lest there *be* any fornicator, or profane person, as E'sau, who for one morsel of meat sold his birthright.

17 For ye know how that afterward, when he would have inherited the blessing, he was rejected: for he found no place of repentance, though he sought it carefully with tears.

18 For ye are not come unto the mount that might be touched, and that burned with fire, nor unto blackness, and darkness, and tempest,

19 And the sound of a trumpet, and the voice of words; which *voice* they that heard intreated that the word should not be spoken to them any more:

20 (For they could not endure that which was commanded, And if so much as a beast touch the mountain, it shall be stoned, or thrust through with a dart:

21 And so terrible was the sight, *that* Mo'ses said, I exceedingly fear and quake:)

22 But ye are come unto mount Si'on, and unto the city of the living God, the heavenly Je-ru'sa-lem, and to an innumerable company of angels,

23 To the general assembly and church of the firstborn, which are written in heaven, and to God the Judge of all, and to the spirits of just men made perfect,

24 And to Je'sus the mediator of the new covenant, and to the blood of sprinkling, that speaketh better things than *that of* A'bel.

25 See that ye refuse not him that speaketh. For if they escaped not who refused him that spake on earth, much more *shall not* we *escape*, if we turn away from him that *speaketh* from heaven:

26 Whose voice then shook the earth: but now he hath promised, saying, Yet once more I shake not the earth only, but also heaven.

27 And this *word*, Yet once more, signifieth the removing of those things that are shaken, as of things that are made, that those things which cannot be shaken may remain.

28 Wherefore we receiving a kingdom which cannot be moved, let us have grace, whereby we may serve God acceptably with reverence and godly fear:

29 For our God *is* a consuming fire.

13 LET brotherly love continue.
2 Be not forgetful to entertain strangers: for thereby some have entertained angels unawares.

3 Remember them that are in bonds, as bound with them; *and* them which suffer adversity, as being yourselves also in the body.

4 Marriage *is* honourable in all, and the bed undefiled: but whoremongers and adulterers God will judge.

5 *Let your* conversation *be* without covetousness; *and be* content with such things as ye have: for he hath said, I will never leave thee, nor forsake thee.

6 So that we may boldly say, The Lord *is* my

helper, and I will not fear what man shall do unto me.

7 Remember them which have the rule over you, who have spoken unto you the word of God: whose faith follow, considering the end of *their* conversation.

8 Je´sus Christ the same yesterday, and to day, and for ever.

9 Be not carried about with divers and strange doctrines. For *it is* a good thing that the heart be established with grace; not with meats, which have not profited them that have been occupied therein.

10 We have an altar, whereof they have no right to eat which serve the tabernacle.

11 For the bodies of those beasts, whose blood is brought into the sanctuary by the high priest for sin, are burned without the camp.

12 Wherefore Je´sus also, that he might sanctify the people with his own blood, suffered without the gate.

13 Let us go forth therefore unto him without the camp, bearing his reproach.

14 For here have we no continuing city, but we seek one to come.

15 By him therefore let us offer the sacrifice of praise to God continually, that is, the fruit of *our* lips giving thanks to his name.

16 But to do good and to communicate forget not: for with such sacrifices God is well pleased.

17 Obey them that have the rule over you, and submit yourselves: for they watch for your souls, as they that must give account, that they may do it with joy, and not with grief: for that *is* unprofitable for you.

18 Pray for us: for we trust we have a good conscience, in all things willing to live honestly.

19 But I beseech *you* the rather to do this, that I may be restored to you the sooner.

20 Now the God of peace, that brought again from the dead our Lord Je´sus, that great shepherd of the sheep, through the blood of the everlasting covenant,

21 Make you perfect in every good work to do his will, working in you that which is well-pleasing in his sight, through Je´sus Christ; to whom *be* glory for ever and ever. Amen.

22 And I beseech you, brethren, suffer the word of exhortation: for I have written a letter unto you in few words.

23 Know ye that *our* brother Tim´o-thy is set at liberty; with whom, if he come shortly, I will see you.

24 Salute all them that have the rule over you, and all the saints. They of It´a-ly salute you.

25 Grace *be* with you all. Amen.

Written to the He´brews from It´a-ly by Tim´o-thy.

THE LETTER OF

JAMES

1 JAMES, a servant of God and of the Lord Je´sus Christ, to the twelve tribes which are scattered abroad, greeting.

2 My brethren, count it all joy when ye fall into divers temptations;

3 Knowing *this,* that the trying of your faith worketh patience.

4 But let patience have *her* perfect work, that ye may be perfect and entire, wanting nothing.

5 If any of you lack wisdom, let him ask of God, that giveth to all *men* liberally, and upbraideth not; and it shall be given him.

6 But let him ask in faith, nothing wavering. For he that wavereth is like a wave of the sea driven with the wind and tossed.

7 For let not that man think that he shall receive any thing of the Lord.

8 A double minded man *is* unstable in all his ways.

9 Let the brother of low degree rejoice in that he is exalted:

10 But the rich, in that he is made low: because as the flower of the grass he shall pass away.

11 For the sun is no sooner risen with a burning heat, but it withereth the grass, and the flower thereof falleth, and the grace of the fashion of it perisheth: so also shall the rich man fade away in his ways.

12 Blessed *is* the man that endureth temptation: for when he is tried, he shall receive the crown of life, which the Lord hath promised to them that love him.

13 Let no man say when he is tempted, I am tempted of God: for God cannot be tempted with evil, neither tempteth he any man:

14 But every man is tempted, when he is drawn away of his own lust, and enticed.

15 Then when lust hath conceived, it bringeth forth sin: and sin, when it is finished, bringeth forth death.

16 Do not err, my beloved brethren.

17 Every good gift and every perfect gift is from above, and cometh down from the Father of lights, with whom is no variableness, neither shadow of turning.

18 Of his own will begat he us with the word of truth, that we should be a kind of firstfruits of his creatures.

19 Wherefore, my beloved brethren, let every man be swift to hear, slow to speak, slow to wrath:

20 For the wrath of man worketh not the righteousness of God.

21 Wherefore lay apart all filthiness and superfluity of naughtiness, and receive with meekness the engrafted word, which is able to save your souls.

22 But be ye doers of the word, and not hearers only, deceiving your own selves.

23 For if any be a hearer of the word, and not a doer, he is like unto a man beholding his natural face in a glass:

24 For he beholdeth himself, and goeth his way, and straightway forgetteth what manner of man he was.

25 But whoso looketh into the perfect law of liberty, and continueth *therein,* he being not a forgetful hearer, but a doer of the work, this man shall be blessed in his deed.

26 If any man among you seem to be religious, and bridleth not his tongue, but deceiveth his own heart, this man's religion *is* vain.

27 Pure religion and undefiled before God and the Father is this, To visit the fatherless and widows in their affliction, *and* to keep himself unspotted from the world.

2 MY brethren, have not the faith of our Lord Je'sus Christ, *the Lord* of glory, with respect of persons.

2 For if there come unto your assembly a man with a gold ring, in goodly apparel, and there come in also a poor man in vile raiment;

3 And ye have respect to him that weareth the gay clothing, and say unto him, Sit thou here in a good place; and say to the poor, Stand thou there, or sit here under my footstool:

4 Are ye not then partial in yourselves, and are become judges of evil thoughts?

5 Hearken, my beloved brethren, Hath not God chosen the poor of this world rich in faith, and heirs of the kingdom which he hath promised to them that love him?

6 But ye have despised the poor. Do not rich men oppress you, and draw you before the judgment seats?

7 Do not they blaspheme that worthy name by the which ye are called?

8 If ye fulfil the royal law according to the scripture, Thou shalt love thy neighbour as thyself, ye do well:

9 But if ye have respect to persons, ye commit sin, and are convinced of the law as transgressors.

10 For whosoever shall keep the whole law, and yet offend in one *point*, he is guilty of all.

11 For he that said, Do not commit adultery, said also, Do not kill. Now if thou commit no adultery, yet if thou kill, thou art become a transgressor of the law.

12 So speak ye, and so do, as they that shall be judged by the law of liberty.

13 For he shall have judgment without mercy, that hath shewed no mercy; and mercy rejoiceth against judgment.

14 What *doth it* profit, my brethren, though a man say he hath faith, and have not works? can faith save him?

15 If a brother or sister be naked, and destitute of daily food,

16 And one of you say unto them, Depart in peace, be ye warmed and filled; notwithstanding ye give them not those things which are needful to the body; what *doth it* profit?

17 Even so faith, if it hath not works, is dead, being alone.

18 Yea, a man may say, Thou hast faith, and I have works: shew me thy faith without thy works, and I will shew thee my faith by my works.

19 Thou believest that there is one God; thou doest well: the devils also believe, and tremble.

20 But wilt thou know, O vain man, that faith without works is dead?

21 Was not A'bra-ham our father justified by works, when he had offered I'saac his son upon the altar?

22 Seest thou how faith wrought with his works, and by works was faith made perfect?

23 And the scripture was fulfilled which saith, A'bra-ham believed God, and it was imputed unto him for righteousness: and he was called the Friend of God.

24 Ye see then how that by works a man is justified, and not by faith only.

25 Likewise also was not Ra'hab the harlot justified by works, when she had received the messengers, and had sent *them* out another way?

26 For as the body without the spirit is dead, so faith without works is dead also.

3 MY brethren, be not many masters, knowing that we shall receive the greater condemnation.

2 For in many things we offend all. If any man offend not in word, the same *is* a perfect man, *and* able also to bridle the whole body.

3 Behold, we put bits in the horses' mouths, that they may obey us; and we turn about their whole body.

4 Behold also the ships, which though *they* be so great, and *are* driven of fierce winds, yet are they turned about with a very small helm, whithersoever the governor listeth.

5 Even so the tongue is a little member, and boasteth great things. Behold, how great a matter a little fire kindleth!

6 And the tongue *is* a fire, a world of iniquity: so is the tongue among our members, that it defileth the whole body, and setteth on fire the course of nature; and it is set on fire of hell.

7 For every kind of beasts, and of birds, and of serpents, and of things in the sea, is tamed, and hath been tamed of mankind:

8 But the tongue can no man tame; *it is* an unruly evil, full of deadly poison.

9 Therewith bless we God, even the Father; and therewith curse we men, which are made after the similitude of God.

10 Out of the same mouth proceedeth blessing and cursing. My brethren, these things ought not so to be.

11 Doth a fountain send forth at the same place sweet *water* and bitter?

12 Can the fig tree, my brethren, bear olive berries? either a vine, figs? so *can* no fountain both yield salt water and fresh.

13 Who *is* a wise man and endued with knowledge among you? let him shew out of a good conversation his works with meekness of wisdom.

14 But if ye have bitter envying and strife in your hearts, glory not, and lie not against the truth.

15 This wisdom descendeth not from above, but *is* earthly, sensual, devilish.

16 For where envying and strife *is*, there *is* confusion and every evil work.

17 But the wisdom that is from above is first pure, then peaceable, gentle, *and* easy to be intreated, full of mercy and good fruits, without partiality, and without hypocrisy.

18 And the fruit of righteousness is sown in peace of them that make peace.

4 FROM whence *come* wars and fightings among you? *come they* not hence, *even of* your lusts that war in your members?

2 Ye lust, and have not: ye kill, and desire to have, and cannot obtain: ye fight and war, yet ye have not, because ye ask not.

3 Ye ask, and receive not, because ye ask amiss, that ye may consume *it* upon your lusts.

4 Ye adulterers and adulteresses, know ye not that the friendship of the world is enmity with God? whosoever therefore will be a friend of the world is the enemy of God.

5 Do ye think that the scripture saith in vain, The spirit that dwelleth in us lusteth to envy?

6 But he giveth more grace. Wherefore he saith, God resisteth the proud, but giveth grace unto the humble.

7 Submit yourselves therefore to God. Resist the devil, and he will flee from you.

8 Draw nigh to God, and he will draw nigh to you. Cleanse *your* hands, *ye* sinners; and purify *your* hearts, *ye* double minded.

9 Be afflicted, and mourn, and weep: let your laughter be turned to mourning, and your joy to heaviness.

10 Humble yourselves in the sight of the Lord, and he shall lift you up.

11 Speak not evil one of another, brethren. He that speaketh evil of his brother, and judgeth his brother, speaketh evil of the law, and judgeth the law: but if thou judge the law, thou art not a doer of the law, but a judge.

12 There is one lawgiver, who is able to save and to destroy: who art thou that judgest another?

13 Go to now, ye that say, To day or to morrow we will go into such a city, and continue there a year, and buy and sell, and get gain:

14 Whereas ye know not what shall be on the morrow. For what is your life? It is even a vapour, that appeareth for a little time, and then vanisheth away.

15 For that ye ought to say, If the Lord will, we shall live, and do this, or that.

16 But now ye rejoice in your boastings: all such rejoicing is evil.

17 Therefore to him that knoweth to do good, and doeth it not, to him it is sin.

5 GO to now, ye rich men, weep and howl for your miseries that shall come upon you.

2 Your riches are corrupted, and your garments are motheaten.

3 Your gold and silver is cankered; and the rust of them shall be a witness against you, and shall eat your flesh as it were fire. Ye have heaped treasure together for the last days.

4 Behold, the hire of the labourers who have reaped down your fields, which is of you kept back by fraud, crieth: and the cries of them which have reaped are entered into the ears of the Lord of sab'a-oth.

5 Ye have lived in pleasure on the earth, and been wanton; ye have nourished your hearts, as in a day of slaughter.

6 Ye have condemned and killed the just; and he doth not resist you.

7 Be patient therefore, brethren, unto the coming of the Lord. Behold, the husbandman waiteth for the precious fruit of the earth, and hath long patience for it, until he receive the early and latter rain.

8 Be ye also patient; stablish your hearts: for the coming of the Lord draweth nigh.

9 Grudge not one against another, brethren, lest ye be condemned: behold, the judge standeth before the door.

10 Take, my brethren, the prophets, who have spoken in the name of the Lord, for an example of suffering affliction, and of patience.

11 Behold, we count them happy which endure. Ye have heard of the patience of Job, and have seen the end of the Lord; that the Lord is very pitiful, and of tender mercy.

12 But above all things, my brethren, swear not, neither by heaven, neither by the earth, neither by any other oath: but let your yea be yea; and your nay, nay; lest ye fall into condemnation.

13 Is any among you afflicted? let him pray. Is any merry? let him sing psalms.

14 Is any sick among you? let him call for the elders of the church; and let them pray over him, anointing him with oil in the name of the Lord:

15 And the prayer of faith shall save the sick, and the Lord shall raise him up; and if he have committed sins, they shall be forgiven him.

16 Confess your faults one to another, and pray one for another, that ye may be healed. The effectual fervent prayer of a righteous man availeth much.

17 E-li'as was a man subject to like passions as we are, and he prayed earnestly that it might not rain: and it rained not on the earth by the space of three years and six months.

18 And he prayed again, and the heaven gave rain, and the earth brought forth her fruit.

19 Brethren, if any of you do err from the truth, and one convert him;

20 Let him know, that he which converteth the sinner from the error of his way shall save a soul from death, and shall hide a multitude of sins.

THE FIRST LETTER OF

PETER

1 PE'TER, an apostle of Je'sus Christ, to the strangers scattered throughout Pon'tus, Ga-la'tia, Cap-pa-do'ci-a, A'sia, and Bi-thyn'i-a,

2 Elect according to the foreknowledge of God the Father, through sanctification of the Spirit, unto obedience and sprinkling of the blood of Je'sus Christ: Grace unto you, and peace, be multiplied.

3 Blessed be the God and Father of our Lord Je'sus Christ, which according to his abundant mercy hath begotten us again unto a lively hope by the resurrection of Je'sus Christ from the dead,

4 To an inheritance incorruptible, and undefiled, and that fadeth not away, reserved in heaven for you,

5 Who are kept by the power of God through faith unto salvation ready to be revealed in the last time.

6 Wherein ye greatly rejoice, though now for a season, if need be, ye are in heaviness through manifold temptations:

7 That the trial of your faith, being much more precious than of gold that perisheth, though it be tried with fire, might be found unto praise and honour and glory at the appearing of Je'sus Christ:

8 Whom having not seen, ye love; in whom, though now ye see him not, yet believing, ye rejoice with joy unspeakable and full of glory:

9 Receiving the end of your faith, even the salvation of your souls.

10 Of which salvation the prophets have enquired and searched diligently, who prophesied of the grace that should come unto you:

11 Searching what, or what manner of time the Spirit of Christ which was in them did signify, when it testified beforehand the sufferings of Christ, and the glory that should follow.

12 Unto whom it was revealed, that not unto themselves, but unto us they did minister the things, which are now reported unto you by them that have preached the gospel unto you with the Ho'ly Ghost sent down from heaven; which things the angels desire to look into.

13 Wherefore gird up the loins of your mind,

be sober, and hope to the end for the grace that is to be brought unto you at the revelation of Je'sus Christ;

14 As obedient children, not fashioning yourselves according to the former lusts in your ignorance:

15 But as he which hath called you is holy, so be ye holy in all manner of conversation;

16 Because it is written, Be ye holy; for I am holy.

17 And if ye call on the Father, who without respect of persons judgeth according to every man's work, pass the time of your sojourning *here* in fear:

18 Forasmuch as ye know that ye were not redeemed with corruptible things, *as* silver and gold, from your vain conversation *received* by tradition from your fathers;

19 But with the precious blood of Christ, as of a lamb without blemish and without spot:

20 Who verily was foreordained before the foundation of the world, but was manifest in these last times for you,

21 Who by him do believe in God, that raised him up from the dead, and gave him glory; that your faith and hope might be in God.

22 Seeing ye have purified your souls in obeying the truth through the Spirit unto unfeigned love of the brethren, *see that* ye love one another with a pure heart fervently:

23 Being born again, not of corruptible seed, but of incorruptible, by the word of God, which liveth and abideth for ever.

24 For all flesh *is* as grass, and all the glory of man as the flower of grass. The grass withereth, and the flower thereof falleth away:

25 But the word of the Lord endureth for ever. And this is the word which by the gospel is preached unto you.

2 WHEREFORE laying aside all malice, and all guile, and hypocrisies, and envies, and all evil speakings,

2 As newborn babes, desire the sincere milk of the word, that ye may grow thereby:

3 If so be ye have tasted that the Lord *is* gracious.

4 To whom coming, *as unto* a living stone, disallowed indeed of men, but chosen of God, *and* precious,

5 Ye also, as lively stones, are built up a spiritual house, an holy priesthood, to offer up spiritual sacrifices, acceptable to God by Je'sus Christ.

6 Wherefore also it is contained in the scripture, Behold, I lay in Si'on a chief corner stone, elect, precious: and he that believeth on him shall not be confounded.

7 Unto you therefore which believe *he is* precious: but unto them which be disobedient, the stone which the builders disallowed, the same is made the head of the corner,

8 And a stone of stumbling, and a rock of offence, *even to them* which stumble at the word, being disobedient: whereunto also they were appointed.

9 But ye *are* a chosen generation, a royal priesthood, an holy nation, a peculiar people; that ye should shew forth the praises of him who hath called you out of darkness into his marvellous light:

10 Which in time past *were* not a people, but *are* now the people of God: which had not obtained mercy, but now have obtained mercy.

11 Dearly beloved, I beseech *you* as strangers and pilgrims, abstain from fleshly lusts, which war against the soul;

12 Having your conversation honest among the Gen'tiles: that, whereas they speak against you as evildoers, they may by *your* good works, which they shall behold, glorify God in the day of visitation.

13 Submit yourselves to every ordinance of man for the Lord's sake: whether it be to the king, as supreme;

14 Or unto governors, as unto them that are sent by him for the punishment of evildoers, and for the praise of them that do well.

15 For so is the will of God, that with well doing ye may put to silence the ignorance of foolish men:

16 As free, and not using *your* liberty for a cloke of maliciousness, but as the servants of God.

17 Honour all *men*. Love the brotherhood. Fear God. Honour the king.

18 Servants, *be* subject to *your* masters with all fear; not only to the good and gentle, but also to the froward.

19 For this *is* thankworthy, if a man for conscience toward God endure grief, suffering wrongfully.

20 For what glory *is it*, if, when ye be buffeted for your faults, ye shall take it patiently? but if, when ye do well, and suffer *for it*, ye take it patiently, this *is* acceptable with God.

21 For even hereunto were ye called: because Christ also suffered for us, leaving us an example, that ye should follow his steps:

22 Who did no sin, neither was guile found in his mouth:

23 Who, when he was reviled, reviled not again; when he suffered, he threatened not; but committed *himself* to him that judgeth righteously:

24 Who his own self bare our sins in his own body on the tree, that we, being dead to sins, should live unto righteousness: by whose stripes ye were healed.

25 For ye were as sheep going astray; but are now returned unto the Shepherd and Bishop of your souls.

3 LIKEWISE ye wives, *be* in subjection to your own husbands; that, if any obey not the word, they also may without the word be won by the conversation of the wives;

2 While they behold your chaste conversation *coupled* with fear.

3 Whose adorning let it not be that outward *adorning* of plaiting the hair, and of wearing of gold, or of putting on of apparel;

4 But *let it be* the hidden man of the heart, in that which is not corruptible, *even the ornament* of a meek and quiet spirit, which is in the sight of God of great price.

5 For after this manner in the old time the holy women also, who trusted in God, adorned themselves, being in subjection unto their own husbands:

6 Even as Sa'ra obeyed A'bra-ham, calling him lord: whose daughters ye are, as long as ye do well, and are not afraid with any amazement.

7 Likewise, ye husbands, dwell with *them* according to knowledge, giving honour unto the wife, as unto the weaker vessel, and as being heirs together of the grace of life; that your prayers be not hindered.

8 Finally, *be ye* all of one mind, having compassion one of another, love as brethren, *be* pitiful, *be* courteous:

9 Not rendering evil for evil, or railing for railing: but contrariwise blessing; knowing that

ye are thereunto called, that ye should inherit a blessing.

10 For he that will love life, and see good days, let him refrain his tongue from evil, and his lips that they speak no guile:

11 Let him eschew evil, and do good; let him seek peace, and ensue it.

12 For the eyes of the Lord *are* over the righteous, and his ears *are open* unto their prayers: but the face of the Lord *is* against them that do evil.

13 And who *is* he that will harm you, if ye be followers of that which is good?

14 But and if ye suffer for righteousness' sake, happy *are ye:* and be not afraid of their terror, neither be troubled;

15 But sanctify the Lord God in your hearts: and *be* ready always to *give* an answer to every man that asketh you a reason of the hope that is in you with meekness and fear:

16 Having a good conscience; that, whereas they speak evil of you, as of evildoers, they may be ashamed that falsely accuse your good conversation in Christ.

17 For *it is* better, if the will of God be so, that ye suffer for well doing, than for evil doing.

18 For Christ also hath once suffered for sins, the just for the unjust, that he might bring us to God, being put to death in the flesh, but quickened by the Spirit:

19 By which also he went and preached unto the spirits in prison;

20 Which sometime were disobedient, when once the longsuffering of God waited in the days of No'ah, while the ark was a preparing, wherein few, that is, eight souls were saved by water.

21 The like figure whereunto *even* baptism doth also now save us (not the putting away of the filth of the flesh, but the answer of a good conscience toward God,) by the resurrection of Je'sus Christ:

22 Who is gone into heaven, and is on the right hand of God; angels and authorities and powers being made subject unto him.

4 FORASMUCH then as Christ hath suffered for us in the flesh, arm yourselves likewise with the same mind: for he that hath suffered in the flesh hath ceased from sin;

2 That he no longer should live the rest of *his* time in the flesh to the lusts of men, but to the will of God.

3 For the time past of *our* life may suffice us to have wrought the will of the Gen'tiles, when we walked in lasciviousness, lusts, excess of wine, revellings, banquetings, and abominable idolatries:

4 Wherein they think it strange that ye run not with *them* to the same excess of riot, speaking evil of *you:*

5 Who shall give account to him that is ready to judge the quick and the dead.

6 For for this cause was the gospel preached also to them that are dead, that they might be judged according to men in the flesh, but live according to God in the spirit.

7 But the end of all things is at hand: be ye therefore sober, and watch unto prayer.

8 And above all things have fervent charity among yourselves: for charity shall cover the multitude of sins.

9 Use hospitality one to another without grudging.

10 As every man hath received the gift, *even*

so minister the same one to another, as good stewards of the manifold grace of God.

11 If any man speak, *let him speak* as the oracles of God; if any man minister, *let him do it* as of the ability which God giveth: that God in all things may be glorified through Je'sus Christ, to whom be praise and dominion for ever and ever. Amen.

12 Beloved, think it not strange concerning the fiery trial which is to try you, as though some strange thing happened unto you:

13 But rejoice, inasmuch as ye are partakers of Christ's sufferings; that, when his glory shall be revealed, ye may be glad also with exceeding joy.

14 If ye be reproached for the name of Christ, happy *are ye;* for the spirit of glory and of God resteth upon you: on their part he is evil spoken of, but on your part he is glorified.

15 But let none of you suffer as a murderer, or *as* a thief, or *as* an evildoer, or as a busybody in other men's matters.

16 Yet if *any man suffer* as a Chris'tian, let him not be ashamed; but let him glorify God on this behalf.

17 For the time *is come* that judgment must begin at the house of God: and if *it* first *begin* at us, what shall the end *be* of them that obey not the gospel of God?

18 And if the righteous scarcely be saved, where shall the ungodly and the sinner appear?

19 Wherefore let them that suffer according to the will of God commit the keeping of their souls *to him* in well doing, as unto a faithful Creator.

5 THE elders which are among you I exhort, who am also an elder, and a witness of the sufferings of Christ, and also a partaker of the glory that shall be revealed:

2 Feed the flock of God which is among you, taking the oversight *thereof,* not by constraint, but willingly; not for filthy lucre, but of a ready mind;

3 Neither as being lords over *God's* heritage, but being ensamples to the flock.

4 And when the chief Shepherd shall appear, ye shall receive a crown of glory that fadeth not away.

5 Likewise, ye younger, submit yourselves unto the elder. Yea, all *of you* be subject one to another, and be clothed with humility: for God resisteth the proud, and giveth grace to the humble.

6 Humble yourselves therefore under the mighty hand of God, that he may exalt you in due time:

7 Casting all your care upon him; for he careth for you.

8 Be sober, be vigilant; because your adversary the devil, as a roaring lion, walketh about, seeking whom he may devour:

9 Whom resist stedfast in the faith, knowing that the same afflictions are accomplished in your brethren that are in the world.

10 But the God of all grace, who hath called us unto his eternal glory by Christ Je'sus, after that ye have suffered a while, make you perfect, stablish, strengthen, settle *you.*

11 To him *be* glory and dominion for ever and ever. Amen.

12 By Sil-va'nus, a faithful brother unto you, as I suppose, I have written briefly, exhorting, and testifying that this is the true grace of God wherein ye stand.

13 The *church that is* at Bab′y-lon, elected together with *you*, saluteth you; and *so doth* Mar′cus my son.

14 Greet ye one another with a kiss of charity. Peace *be* with you all that are in Christ Je′sus. Amen.

THE SECOND LETTER OF

PETER

1 SI′MON Pe′ter, a servant and an apostle of Je′sus Christ, to them that have obtained like precious faith with us through the righteousness of God and our Saviour Je′sus Christ:

2 Grace and peace be multiplied unto you through the knowledge of God, and of Je′sus our Lord,

3 According as his divine power hath given unto us all things that *pertain* unto life and godliness, through the knowledge of him that hath called us to glory and virtue:

4 Whereby are given unto us exceeding great and precious promises: that by these ye might be partakers of the divine nature, having escaped the corruption that is in the world through lust.

5 And beside this, giving all diligence, add to your faith virtue; and to virtue knowledge;

6 And to knowledge temperance; and to temperance patience; and to patience godliness;

7 And to godliness brotherly kindness; and to brotherly kindness charity.

8 For if these things be in you, and abound, they make *you that ye shall* neither *be* barren nor unfruitful in the knowledge of our Lord Je′sus Christ.

9 But he that lacketh these things is blind, and cannot see afar off, and hath forgotten that he was purged from his old sins.

10 Wherefore the rather, brethren, give diligence to make your calling and election sure: for if ye do these things, ye shall never fall:

11 For so an entrance shall be ministered unto you abundantly into the everlasting kingdom of our Lord and Saviour Je′sus Christ.

12 Wherefore I will not be negligent to put you always in remembrance of these things, though ye know *them*, and be established in the present truth.

13 Yea, I think it meet, as long as I am in this tabernacle, to stir you up by putting *you* in remembrance;

14 Knowing that shortly I must put off *this* my tabernacle, even as our Lord Je′sus Christ hath shewed me.

15 Moreover I will endeavor that ye may be able after my decease to have these things always in remembrance.

16 For we have not followed cunningly devised fables, when we made known unto you the power and coming of our Lord Je′sus Christ, but were eyewitnesses of his majesty.

17 For he received from God the Father honour and glory, when there came such a voice to him from the excellent glory, This is my beloved Son, in whom I am well pleased.

18 And this voice which came from heaven we heard, when we were with him in the holy mount.

19 We have also a more sure word of prophecy; whereunto ye do well that ye take heed, as unto a light that shineth in a dark place, until the day dawn, and the day star arise in your hearts:

20 Knowing this first, that no prophecy of the scripture is of any private interpretation.

21 For the prophecy came not in old time by the will of man: but holy men of God spake *as they were* moved by the Ho′ly Ghost.

2 BUT there were false prophets also among the people, even as there shall be false teachers among you, who privily shall bring in damnable heresies, even denying the Lord that bought them, and bring upon themselves swift destruction.

2 And many shall follow their pernicious ways; by reason of whom the way of truth shall be evil spoken of.

3 And through covetousness shall they with feigned words make merchandise of you: whose judgment now of a long time lingereth not, and their damnation slumbereth not.

4 For if God spared not the angels that sinned, but cast *them* down to hell, and delivered *them* into chains of darkness, to be reserved unto judgment;

5 And spared not the old world, but saved No′ah the eighth *person*, a preacher of righteousness, bringing in the flood upon the world of the ungodly;

6 And turning the cities of Sod′om and Gomor′rha into ashes condemned *them* with an overthrow, making *them* an ensample unto those that after should live ungodly;

7 And delivered just Lot, vexed with the filthy conversation of the wicked:

8 (For that righteous man dwelling among them, in seeing and hearing, vexed *his* righteous soul from day to day with *their* unlawful deeds;)

9 The Lord knoweth how to deliver the godly out of temptations, and to reserve the unjust unto the day of judgment to be punished:

10 But chiefly them that walk after the flesh in the lust of uncleanness, and despise government. Presumptuous *are they*, selfwilled, they are not afraid to speak evil of dignities.

11 Whereas angels, which are greater in power and might, bring not railing accusation against them before the Lord.

12 But these, as natural brute beasts, made to be taken and destroyed, speak evil of the things that they understand not; and shall utterly perish in their own corruption;

13 And shall receive the reward of unrighteousness, *as* they that count it pleasure to riot in the day time. Spots *they are* and blemishes, sporting themselves with their own deceivings while they feast with you;

14 Having eyes full of adultery, and that cannot cease from sin; beguiling unstable souls: an heart they have exercised with covetous practices; cursed children:

15 Which have forsaken the right way, and are gone astray, following the way of Ba′laam *the son* of Bo′sor, who loved the wages of unrighteousness;

16 But was rebuked for his iniquity: the dumb ass speaking with man's voice forbad the madness of the prophet.

17 These are wells without water, clouds that

are carried with a tempest; to whom the mist of darkness is reserved for ever.

18 For when they speak great swelling *words* of vanity, they allure through the lusts of the flesh, *through much* wantonness, those that were clean escaped from them who live in error.

19 While they promise them liberty, they themselves are the servants of corruption: for of whom a man is overcome, of the same is he brought in bondage.

20 For if after they have escaped the pollutions of the world through the knowledge of the Lord and Saviour Je′sus Christ, they are again entangled therein, and overcome, the latter end is worse with them than the beginning.

21 For it had been better for them not to have known the way of righteousness, than, after they have known *it*, to turn from the holy commandment delivered unto them.

22 But it is happened unto them according to the true proverb, The dog *is* turned to his own vomit again; and the sow that was washed to her wallowing in the mire.

3 THIS second epistle, beloved, I now write unto you; in *both* which I stir up your pure minds by way of remembrance:

2 That ye may be mindful of the words which were spoken before by the holy prophets, and of the commandment of us the apostles of the Lord and Saviour:

3 Knowing this first, that there shall come in the last days scoffers, walking after their own lusts,

4 And saying, Where is the promise of his coming? for since the fathers fell asleep, all things continue as *they were* from the beginning of the creation.

5 For this they willingly are ignorant of, that by the word of God the heavens were of old, and the earth standing out of the water and in the water:

6 Whereby the world that then was, being overflowed with water, perished:

7 But the heavens and the earth, which are now, by the same word are kept in store, reserved unto fire against the day of judgment and perdition of ungodly men.

8 But, beloved, be not ignorant of this one thing, that one day *is* with the Lord as a thousand years, and a thousand years as one day.

9 The Lord is not slack concerning his promise, as some men count slackness; but is longsuffering to us-ward, not willing that any should perish, but that all should come to repentance.

10 But the day of the Lord will come as a thief in the night; in the which the heavens shall pass away with a great noise, and the elements shall melt with fervent heat, the earth also and the works that are therein shall be burned up.

11 *Seeing* then *that* all these things shall be dissolved, what manner *of persons* ought ye to be in *all* holy conversation and godliness,

12 Looking for and hasting unto the coming of the day of God, wherein the heavens being on fire shall be dissolved, and the elements shall melt with fervent heat?

13 Nevertheless we, according to his promise, look for new heavens and a new earth, wherein dwelleth righteousness.

14 Wherefore, beloved, seeing that ye look for such things, be diligent that ye may be found of him in peace, without spot, and blameless.

15 And account *that* the longsuffering of our Lord *is* salvation; even as our beloved brother Paul also according to the wisdom given unto him hath written unto you;

16 As also in all *his* epistles, speaking in them of these things; in which are some things hard to be understood, which they that are unlearned and unstable wrest, as *they do* also the other scriptures, unto their own destruction.

17 Ye therefore, beloved, seeing ye know *these things* before, beware lest ye also, being led away with the error of the wicked, fall from your own stedfastness.

18 But grow in grace, and *in* the knowledge of our Lord and Saviour Je′sus Christ. To him *be* glory both now and for ever. Amen.

THE FIRST LETTER OF

JOHN

1 THAT which was from the beginning, which we have heard, which we have seen with our eyes, which we have looked upon, and our hands have handled, of the Word of life;

2 (For the life was manifested, and we have seen *it*, and bear witness, and shew unto you that eternal life, which was with the Father, and was manifested unto us;)

3 That which we have seen and heard declare we unto you, that ye also may have fellowship with us: and truly our fellowship *is* with the Father, and with his Son Je′sus Christ.

4 And these things write we unto you, that your joy may be full.

5 This then is the message which we have heard of him, and declare unto you, that God is light, and in him is no darkness at all.

6 If we say that we have fellowship with him, and walk in darkness, we lie, and do not the truth:

7 But if we walk in the light, as he is in the light, we have fellowship one with another, and the blood of Je′sus Christ his Son cleanseth us from all sin.

8 If we say that we have no sin, we deceive ourselves, and the truth is not in us.

9 If we confess our sins, he is faithful and just to forgive us *our* sins, and to cleanse us from all unrighteousness.

10 If we say that we have not sinned, we make him a liar, and his word is not in us.

2 MY little children, these things write I unto you, that ye sin not. And if any man sin, we have an advocate with the Father, Je′sus Christ the righteous:

2 And he is the propitiation for our sins: and not for ours only, but also for *the sins of* the whole world.

3 And hereby we do know that we know him, if we keep his commandments.

4 He that saith, I know him, and keepeth not his commandments, is a liar, and the truth is not in him.

5 But whoso keepeth his word, in him verily is the love of God perfected: hereby know we that we are in him.

6 He that saith he abideth in him ought himself also so to walk, even as he walked.

7 Brethren, I write no new commandment unto you, but an old commandment which ye had from the beginning. The old commandment is the word which ye have heard from the beginning.

8 Again, a new commandment I write unto you, which thing is true in him and in you: because the darkness is past, and the true light now shineth.

9 He that saith he is in the light, and hateth his brother, is in darkness even until now.

10 He that loveth his brother abideth in the light, and there is none occasion of stumbling in him.

11 But he that hateth his brother is in darkness, and walketh in darkness, and knoweth not whither he goeth, because that darkness hath blinded his eyes.

12 I write unto you, little children, because your sins are forgiven you for his name's sake.

13 I write unto you, fathers, because ye have known him *that is* from the beginning. I write unto you, young men, because ye have overcome the wicked one. I write unto you, little children, because ye have known the Father.

14 I have written unto you, fathers, because ye have known him *that is* from the beginning. I have written unto you, young men, because ye are strong, and the word of God abideth in you, and ye have overcome the wicked one.

15 Love not the world, neither the things *that are* in the world. If any man love the world, the love of the Father is not in him.

16 For all that *is* in the world, the lust of the flesh, and the lust of the eyes, and the pride of life, is not of the Father, but is of the world.

17 And the world passeth away, and the lust thereof: but he that doeth the will of God abideth for ever.

18 Little children, it is the last time: and as ye have heard that antichrist shall come, even now are there many antichrists; whereby we know that it is the last time.

19 They went out from us, but they were not of us; for if they had been of us, they would *no doubt* have continued with us: but *they went out,* that they might be made manifest that they were not all of us.

20 But ye have an unction from the Holy One, and ye know all things.

21 I have not written unto you because ye know not the truth, but because ye know it, and that no lie is of the truth.

22 Who is a liar but he that denieth that Je'-sus is the Christ? He is antichrist, that denieth the Father and the Son.

23 Whosoever denieth the Son, the same hath not the Father: [but] *he that acknowledgeth the Son hath the Father also.*

24 Let that therefore abide in you, which ye have heard from the beginning. If that which ye have heard from the beginning shall remain in you, ye also shall continue in the Son, and in the Father.

25 And this is the promise that he hath promised us, *even* eternal life.

26 These *things* have I written unto you concerning them that seduce you.

27 But the anointing which ye have received of him abideth in you, and ye need not that any man teach you: but as the same anointing teacheth you of all things, and is truth, and is no lie, and even as it hath taught you, ye shall abide in him.

28 And now, little children, abide in him; that, when he shall appear, we may have confidence, and not be ashamed before him at his coming.

29 If ye know that he is righteous, ye know that every one that doeth righteousness is born of him.

3 BEHOLD, what manner of love the Father hath bestowed upon us, that we should be called the sons of God: therefore the world knoweth us not, because it knew him not.

2 Beloved, now are we the sons of God, and it doth not yet appear what we shall be: but we know that, when he shall appear, we shall be like him; for we shall see him as he is.

3 And every man that hath this hope in him purifieth himself, even as he is pure.

4 Whosoever committeth sin transgresseth also the law: for sin is the transgression of the law.

5 And ye know that he was manifested to take away our sins; and in him is no sin.

6 Whosoever abideth in him sinneth not: whosoever sinneth hath not seen him, neither known him.

7 Little children, let no man deceive you: he that doeth righteousness is righteous, even as he is righteous.

8 He that committeth sin is of the devil; for the devil sinneth from the beginning. For this purpose the Son of God was manifested, that he might destroy the works of the devil.

9 Whosoever is born of God doth not commit sin; for his seed remaineth in him: and he cannot sin, because he is born of God.

10 In this the children of God are manifest, and the children of the devil: whosoever doeth not righteousness is not of God, neither he that loveth not his brother.

11 For this is the message that ye heard from the beginning, that we should love one another.

12 Not as Cain, *who* was of that wicked one, and slew his brother. And wherefore slew he him? Because his own works were evil, and his brother's righteous.

13 Marvel not, my brethren, if the world hate you.

14 We know that we have passed from death unto life, because we love the brethren. He that loveth not *his* brother abideth in death.

15 Whosoever hateth his brother is a murderer: and ye know that no murderer hath eternal life abiding in him.

16 Hereby perceive we the love of God, because he laid down his life for us: and we ought to lay down *our* lives for the brethren.

17 But whoso hath this world's good, and seeth his brother have need, and shutteth up his bowels of compassion from him, how dwelleth the love of God in him?

18 My little children, let us not love in word, neither in tongue; but in deed and in truth.

19 And hereby we know that we are of the truth, and shall assure our hearts before him.

20 For if our heart condemn us, God is greater than our heart, and knoweth all things.

21 Beloved, if our heart condemn us not, *then* have we confidence toward God.

22 And whatsoever we ask, we receive of him, because we keep his commandments, and do those things that are pleasing in his sight.

23 And this is his commandment, That we should believe on the name of his Son Je'sus

Christ, and love one another, as he gave us commandment.

24 And he that keepeth his commandments dwelleth in him, and he in him. And hereby we know that he abideth in us, by the Spirit which he hath given us.

4 BELOVED, believe not every spirit, but try the spirits whether they are of God: because many false prophets are gone out into the world.

2 Hereby know ye the Spirit of God: Every spirit that confesseth that Je'sus Christ is come in the flesh is of God:

3 And every spirit that confesseth not that Je'sus Christ is come in the flesh is not of God: and this is that *spirit* of antichrist, whereof ye have heard that it should come; and even now already is it in the world.

4 Ye are of God, little children, and have overcome them: because greater is he that is in you, than he that is in the world.

5 They are of the world: therefore speak they of the world, and the world heareth them.

6 We are of God: he that knoweth God heareth us; he that is not of God heareth not us. Hereby know we the spirit of truth, and the spirit of error.

7 Beloved, let us love one another: for love is of God; and every one that loveth is born of God, and knoweth God.

8 He that loveth not knoweth not God; for God is love.

9 In this was manifested the love of God toward us, because that God sent his only begotten Son into the world, that we might live through him.

10 Herein is love, not that we loved God, but that he loved us, and sent his Son *to be* the propitiation for our sins.

11 Beloved, if God so loved us, we ought also to love one another.

12 No man hath seen God at any time. If we love one another, God dwelleth in us, and his love is perfected in us.

13 Hereby know we that we dwell in him, and he in us, because he hath given us of his Spirit.

14 And we have seen and do testify that the Father sent the Son *to be* the Saviour of the world.

15 Whosoever shall confess that Je'sus is the Son of God, God dwelleth in him, and he in God.

16 And we have known and believed the love that God hath to us. God is love; and he that dwelleth in love dwelleth in God, and God in him.

17 Herein is our love made perfect, that we may have boldness in the day of judgment: because as he is, so are we in this world.

18 There is no fear in love; but perfect love casteth out fear: because fear hath torment. He that feareth is not made perfect in love.

19 We love him, because he first loved us.

20 If a man say, I love God, and hateth his brother, he is a liar: for he that loveth not his brother whom he hath seen, how can he love God whom he hath not seen?

21 And this commandment have we from him, That he who loveth God love his brother also.

5 WHOSOEVER believeth that Je'sus is the Christ is born of God: and every one that loveth him that begat loveth him also that is begotten of him.

2 By this we know that we love the children of God, when we love God, and keep his commandments.

3 For this is the love of God, that we keep his commandments: and his commandments are not grievous.

4 For whatsoever is born of God overcometh the world: and this is the victory that overcometh the world, *even* our faith.

5 Who is he that overcometh the world, but he that believeth that Je'sus is the Son of God?

6 This is he that came by water and blood, *even* Je'sus Christ; not by water only, but by water and blood. And it is the Spirit that beareth witness, because the Spirit is truth.

7 For there are three that bear record in heaven, the Father, the Word, and the Ho'ly Ghost: and these three are one.

8 And there are three that bear witness in earth, the spirit, and the water, and the blood: and these three agree in one.

9 If we receive the witness of men, the witness of God is greater: for this is the witness of God which he hath testified of his Son.

10 He that believeth on the Son of God hath the witness in himself: he that believeth not God hath made him a liar; because he believeth not the record that God gave of his Son.

11 And this is the record, that God hath given to us eternal life, and this life is in his Son.

12 He that hath the Son hath life; *and* he that hath not the Son of God hath not life.

13 These things have I written unto you that believe on the name of the Son of God; that ye may know that ye have eternal life, and that ye may believe on the name of the Son of God.

14 And this is the confidence that we have in him, that, if we ask any thing according to his will, he heareth us:

15 And if we know that he hear us, whatsoever we ask, we know that we have the petitions that we desired of him.

16 If any man see his brother sin a sin *which is* not unto death, he shall ask, and he shall give him life for them that sin not unto death. There is a sin unto death: I do not say that he shall pray for it.

17 All unrighteousness is sin: and there is a sin not unto death.

18 We know that whosoever is born of God sinneth not; but he that is begotten of God keepeth himself, and that wicked one toucheth him not.

19 *And* we know that we are of God, and the whole world lieth in wickedness.

20 And we know that the Son of God is come, and hath given us an understanding, that we may know him that is true, and we are in him that is true, *even* in his Son Je'sus Christ. This is the true God, and eternal life.

21 Little children, keep yourselves from idols. Amen.

JOHN

THE elder unto the elect lady and her children, whom I love in the truth; and not I only, but also all they that have known the truth;

2 For the truth's sake, which dwelleth in us, and shall be with us for ever.

3 Grace be with you, mercy, *and* peace, from God the Father, and from the Lord Je'sus Christ, the Son of the Father, in truth and love.

4 I rejoiced greatly that I found of thy children walking in truth, as we have received a commandment from the Father.

5 And now I beseech thee, lady, not as though I wrote a new commandment unto thee, but that which we had from the beginning, that we love one another.

6 And this is love, that we walk after his commandments. This is the commandment, That, as ye have heard from the beginning, ye should walk in it.

7 For many deceivers are entered into the world, who confess not that Je'sus Christ is come in the flesh. This is a deceiver and an antichrist.

8 Look to yourselves, that we lose not those things which we have wrought, but that we receive a full reward.

9 Whosoever transgresseth, and abideth not in the doctrine of Christ, hath not God. He that abideth in the doctrine of Christ, he hath both the Father and the Son.

10 If there come any unto you, and bring not this doctrine, receive him not into *your* house, neither bid him God speed:

11 For he that biddeth him God speed is partaker of his evil deeds.

12 Having many things to write unto you, I would not *write* with paper and ink: but I trust to come unto you, and speak face to face, that our joy may be full.

13 The children of thy elect sister greet thee. Amen.

JOHN

THE elder unto the wellbeloved Ga'ius, whom I love in the truth.

2 Beloved, I wish above all things that thou mayest prosper and be in health, even as thy soul prospereth.

3 For I rejoiced greatly, when the brethren came and testified of the truth that is in thee, even as thou walkest in the truth.

4 I have no greater joy than to hear that my children walk in truth.

5 Beloved, thou doest faithfully whatsoever thou doest to the brethren, and to strangers;

6 Which have borne witness of thy charity before the church: whom if thou bring forward on their journey after a godly sort, thou shalt do well:

7 Because that for his name's sake they went forth, taking nothing of the Gen'tiles.

8 We therefore ought to receive such, that we might be fellowhelpers to the truth.

9 I wrote unto the church: but Di-ot're-phes, who loveth to have the preeminence among them, receiveth us not.

10 Wherefore, if I come, I will remember his deeds which he doeth, prating against us with malicious words: and not content therewith, neither doth he himself receive the brethren, and forbiddeth them that would, and casteth *them* out of the church.

11 Beloved, follow not that which is evil, but that which is good. He that doeth good is of God: but he that doeth evil hath not seen God.

12 De-me'tri-us hath good report of all *men*, and of the truth itself: yea, and we *also* bear record; and ye know that our record is true.

13 I had many things to write, but I will not with ink and pen write unto thee:

14 But I trust I shall shortly see thee, and we shall speak face to face. Peace *be* to thee. *Our* friends salute thee. Greet the friends by name.

JUDE

JUDE, the servant of Je'sus Christ, and brother of James, to them that are sanctified by God the Father, and preserved in Je'sus Christ, *and* called:

2 Mercy unto you, and peace, and love, be multiplied.

3 Beloved, when I gave all diligence to write unto you of the common salvation, it was needful for me to write unto you, and exhort *you* that ye should earnestly contend for the faith which was once delivered unto the saints.

4 For there are certain men crept in unawares, who were before of old ordained to this condemnation, ungodly men, turning the grace of our God into lasciviousness, and denying the only Lord God, and our Lord Je'sus Christ.

5 I will therefore put you in remembrance, though ye once knew this, how that the Lord, having saved the people out of the land of E'-gypt, afterward destroyed them that believed not.

6 And the angels which kept not their first estate, but left their own habitation, he hath reserved in everlasting chains under darkness unto the judgment of the great day.

7 Even as Sod'om and Go-mor'rha, and the cities about them in like manner, giving themselves over to fornication, and going after

strange flesh, are set forth for an example, suffering the vengeance of eternal fire.

8 Likewise also these *filthy* dreamers defile the flesh, despise dominion, and speak evil of dignities.

9 Yet Mi'chael the archangel, when contending with the devil he disputed about the body of Mo'ses, durst not bring against him a railing accusation, but said, The Lord rebuke thee.

10 But these speak evil of those things which they know not: but what they know naturally, as brute beasts, in those things they corrupt themselves.

11 Woe unto them! for they have gone in the way of Cain, and ran greedily after the error of Ba'laam for reward, and perished in the gainsaying of Co're.

12 These are spots in your feasts of charity, when they feast with you, feeding themselves without fear: clouds *they are* without water, carried about of winds; trees whose fruit withereth, without fruit, twice dead, plucked up by the roots;

13 Raging waves of the sea, foaming out their own shame; wandering stars, to whom is reserved the blackness of darkness for ever.

14 And E'noch also, the seventh from Ad'am, prophesied of these, saying, Behold, the Lord cometh with ten thousands of his saints,

15 To execute judgment upon all, and to convince all that are ungodly among them of all their ungodly deeds which they have ungodly committed, and of all their hard *speeches* which ungodly sinners have spoken against him.

16 These are murmurers, complainers, walking after their own lusts; and their mouth speaketh great swelling *words*, having men's persons in admiration because of advantage.

17 But, beloved, remember ye the words which were spoken before of the apostles of our Lord Je'sus Christ;

18 How that they told you there should be mockers in the last time, who should walk after their own ungodly lusts.

19 These be they who separate themselves, sensual, having not the Spirit.

20 But ye, beloved, building up yourselves on your most holy faith, praying in the Ho'ly Ghost,

21 Keep yourselves in the love of God, looking for the mercy of our Lord Je'sus Christ unto eternal life.

22 And of some have compassion, making a difference:

23 And others save with fear, pulling *them* out of the fire; hating even the garment spotted by the flesh.

24 Now unto him that is able to keep you from falling, and to present *you* faultless before the presence of his glory with exceeding joy,

25 To the only wise God our Saviour, *be* glory and majesty, dominion and power, both now and ever. Amen.

THE

REVELATION TO JOHN
(The Apocalypse)

1 THE Revelation of Je'sus Christ, which God gave unto him, to shew unto his servants things which must shortly come to pass; and he sent and signified *it* by his angel unto his servant John:

2 Who bare record of the word of God, and of the testimony of Je'sus Christ, and of all things that he saw.

3 Blessed *is* he that readeth, and they that hear the words of this prophecy, and keep those things which are written therein for the time *is* at hand.

4 JOHN to the seven churches which are in A'sia: Grace *be* unto you, and peace, from him which is, and which was, and which is to come; and from the seven Spirits which are before his throne;

5 And from Je'sus Christ, *who is* the faithful witness, *and* the first begotten of the dead, and the prince of the kings of the earth. Unto him that loved us, and washed us from our sins in his own blood,

6 And hath made us kings and priests unto God and his Father; to him *be* glory and dominion for ever and ever. Amen.

7 Behold, he cometh with clouds; and every eye shall see him, and they *also* which pierced him: and all kindreds of the earth shall wail because of him. Even so, Amen.

8 I am Al'pha and O'me-ga, the beginning and the ending, saith the Lord, which is, and which was, and which is to come, the Almighty.

9 I John, who also am your brother, and companion in tribulation, and in the kingdom and patience of Je'sus Christ, was in the isle that is called Pat'mos, for the word of God, and for the testimony of Je'sus Christ.

10 I was in the Spirit on the Lord's day, and heard behind me a great voice, as of a trumpet,

11 Saying, I am Al'pha and O'me-ga, the first and the last: and, What thou seest, write in a book, and send *it* unto the seven churches which are in A'sia; unto Eph'e-sus, and unto Smyr'na, and unto Per'ga-mos, and unto Thy-a-ti'ra, and unto Sar'dis, and unto Phil-a-del'phi-a, and unto La-od-i-ce'a.

12 And I turned to see the voice that spake with me. And being turned, I saw seven golden candlesticks;

13 And in the midst of the seven candlesticks *one* like unto the Son of man, clothed with a garment down to the foot, and girt about the paps with a golden girdle.

14 His head and *his* hairs *were* white like wool, as white as snow; and his eyes *were* as a flame of fire;

15 And his feet like unto fine brass, as if they burned in a furnace; and his voice as the sound of many waters,

16 And he had in his right hand seven stars: and out of his mouth went a sharp twoedged sword: and his countenance *was* as the sun shineth in his strength.

17 And when I saw him, I fell at his feet as dead. And he laid his right hand upon me, saying unto me, Fear not; I am the first and the last:

18 *I am* he that liveth, and was dead; and, behold, I am alive for evermore, Amen; and have the keys of hell and of death.

19 Write the things which thou hast seen,

and the things which are, and the things which shall be hereafter;

20 The mystery of the seven stars which thou sawest in my right hand, and the seven golden candlesticks. The seven stars are the angels of the seven churches: and the seven candlesticks which thou sawest are the seven churches.

2 UNTO the angel of the church of Eph'e-sus write; These things saith he that holdeth the seven stars in his right hand, who walketh in the midst of the seven golden candlesticks;

2 I know thy works, and thy labour, and thy patience, and how thou canst not bear them which are evil: and thou hast tried them which say they are apostles, and are not, and hast found them liars:

3 And hast borne, and hast patience, and for my name's sake hast laboured, and hast not fainted.

4 Nevertheless I have *somewhat* against thee, because thou hast left thy first love.

5 Remember therefore from whence thou art fallen, and repent, and do the first works; or else I will come unto thee quickly, and will remove thy candlestick out of his place, except thou repent.

6 But this thou hast, that thou hatest the deeds of the Nic-o-la'i-tanes, which I also hate.

7 He that hath an ear, let him hear what the Spirit saith unto the churches; To him that overcometh will I give to eat of the tree of life, which is in the midst of the paradise of God.

8 And unto the angel of the church in Smyr'na write; These things saith the first and the last, which was dead, and is alive;

9 I know thy works, and tribulation, and poverty, (but thou art rich) and *I know* the blasphemy of them which say they are Jews, and are not, but *are* the synagogue of Sa'tan.

10 Fear none of those things which thou shalt suffer: behold, the devil shall cast *some* of you into prison, that ye may be tried; and ye shall have tribulation ten days: be thou faithful unto death, and I will give thee a crown of life.

11 He that hath an ear, let him hear what the Spirit saith unto the churches; He that overcometh shall not be hurt of the second death.

12 And to the angel of the church in Per'gamos write; These things saith he which hath the sharp sword with two edges;

13 I know thy works, and where thou dwellest, *even* where Sa'tan's seat *is*: and thou holdest fast my name, and hast not denied my faith, even in those days wherein An'ti-pas *was* my faithful martyr, who was slain among you, where Sa'tan dwelleth.

14 But I have a few things against thee, because thou hast there them that hold the doctrine of Ba'laam, who taught Ba'lac to cast a stumbling block before the children of Is'ra-el, to eat things sacrificed unto idols, and to commit fornication.

15 So hast thou also them that hold the doctrine of the Nic-o-la'i-tanes, which thing I hate.

16 Repent; or else I will come unto thee quickly, and will fight against them with the sword of my mouth.

17 He that hath an ear, let him hear what the Spirit saith unto the churches; To him that overcometh will I give to eat of the hidden manna, and will give him a white stone, and in the stone a new name written, which no man knoweth saving he that receiveth *it*.

18 And unto the angel of the church in Thy-a-ti'ra write; These things saith the Son of God, who hath his eyes like unto a flame of fire, and his feet *are* like fine brass;

19 I know thy works, and charity, and service, and faith, and thy patience, and thy works; and the last *to be* more than the first.

20 Notwithstanding I have a few things against thee, because thou sufferest that woman Jez'e-bel, which calleth herself a prophetess, to teach and to seduce my servants to commit fornication, and to eat things sacrificed unto idols.

21 And I gave her space to repent of her fornication; and she repented not.

22 Behold, I will cast her into a bed, and them that commit adultery with her into great tribulation, except they repent of their deeds.

23 And I will kill her children with death; and all the churches shall know that I am he which searcheth the reins and hearts: and I will give unto every one of you according to your works.

24 But unto you I say, and unto the rest in Thy-a-ti'ra, as many as have not this doctrine, and which have not known the depths of Sa'tan, as they speak; I will put upon you none other burden.

25 But that which ye have *already* hold fast till I come.

26 And he that overcometh, and keepeth my works unto the end, to him will I give power over the nations:

27 And he shall rule them with a rod of iron; as the vessels of a potter shall they be broken to shivers: even as I received of my Father.

28 And I will give him the morning star.

29 He that hath an ear, let him hear what the Spirit saith unto the churches.

3 AND unto the angel of the church in Sar'dis write; These things saith he that hath the seven Spirits of God, and the seven stars; I know thy works, that thou hast a name, that thou livest, and art dead.

2 Be watchful, and strengthen the things which remain, that are ready to die: for I have not found thy works perfect before God.

3 Remember therefore how thou hast received and heard, and hold fast, and repent. If therefore thou shalt not watch, I will come on thee as a thief, and thou shalt not know what hour I will come upon thee.

4 Thou hast a few names even in Sar'dis which have not defiled their garments; and they shall walk with me in white: for they are worthy.

5 He that overcometh, the same shall be clothed in white raiment; and I will not blot out his name out of the book of life, but I will confess his name before my Father, and before his angels.

6 He that hath an ear, let him hear what the Spirit saith unto the churches.

7 And to the angel of the church in Phil-a-del'phi-a write; These things saith he that is holy, he that is true, he that hath the key of Da'vid, he that openeth, and no man shutteth; and shutteth, and no man openeth;

8 I know thy works: behold, I have set before thee an open door, and no man can shut it: for thou hast a little strength, and hast kept my word, and hast not denied my name.

9 Behold, I will make them of the synagogue of Sa'tan, which say they are Jews, and are not, but do lie; behold, I will make them to come and worship before thy feet, and to know that I have loved thee.

10 Because thou hast kept the word of my patience, I also will keep thee from the hour of

temptation, which shall come upon all the world, to try them that dwell upon the earth.

11 Behold, I come quickly: hold that fast which thou hast, that no man take thy crown.

12 Him that overcometh will I make a pillar in the temple of my God, and he shall go no more out: and I will write upon him the name of my God, and the name of the city of my God, *which is* new Je-ru′sa-lem, which cometh down out of heaven from my God: and *I will write upon him* my new name.

13 He that hath an ear, let him hear what the Spirit saith unto the churches.

14 And unto the angel of the church of the La-od-i-ce′ans write; These things saith the Amen, the faithful and true witness, the beginning of the creation of God;

15 I know thy works, that thou art neither cold nor hot: I would thou wert cold or hot.

16 So then because thou art lukewarm, and neither cold nor hot, I will spue thee out of my mouth.

17 Because thou sayest, I am rich, and increased with goods, and have need of nothing; and knowest not that thou art wretched, and miserable, and poor, and blind, and naked:

18 I counsel thee to buy of me gold tried in the fire, that thou mayest be rich; and white raiment, that thou mayest be clothed, and *that* the shame of thy nakedness do not appear; and anoint thine eyes with eyesalve, that thou mayest see.

19 As many as I love, I rebuke and chasten: be zealous therefore, and repent.

20 Behold, I stand at the door, and knock: if any man hear my voice, and open the door, I will come in to him, and will sup with him, and he with me.

21 To him that overcometh will I grant to sit with me in my throne, even as I also overcame, and am set down with my Father in his throne.

22 He that hath an ear, let him hear what the Spirit saith unto the churches.

4 AFTER this I looked, and, behold, a door *was* opened in heaven: and the first voice which I heard *was* as it were of a trumpet talking with me; which said, Come up hither, and I will shew thee things which must be hereafter.

2 And immediately I was in the spirit: and, behold, a throne was set in heaven, and *one* sat on the throne.

3 And he that sat was to look upon like a jasper and a sardine stone: and *there was* a rainbow round about the throne, in sight like unto an emerald.

4 And round about the throne *were* four and twenty seats: and upon the seats I saw four and twenty elders sitting, clothed in white raiment; and they had on their heads crowns of gold.

5 And out of the throne proceeded lightnings and thunderings and voices: and *there were* seven lamps of fire burning before the throne, which are the seven Spirits of God.

6 And before the throne *there was* a sea of glass like unto crystal: and in the midst of the throne, and round about the throne, *were* four beasts full of eyes before and behind.

7 And the first beast *was* like a lion, and the second beast like a calf, and the third beast had a face as a man, and the fourth beast *was* like a flying eagle.

8 And the four beasts had each of them six wings about *him;* and *they were* full of eyes within: and they rest not day and night, saying, Holy, holy, holy, Lord God Almighty, which was, and is, and is to come.

9 And when those beasts give glory and honour and thanks to him that sat on the throne, who liveth for ever and ever,

10 The four and twenty elders fall down before him that sat on the throne, and worship him that liveth for ever and ever, and cast their crowns before the throne, saying,

11 Thou art worthy, O Lord, to receive glory and honour and power: for thou hast created all things, and for thy pleasure they are and were created.

5 AND I saw in the right hand of him that sat on the throne a book written within and on the backside, sealed with seven seals.

2 And I saw a strong angel proclaiming with a loud voice, Who is worthy to open the book, and to loose the seals thereof?

3 And no man in heaven, nor in earth, neither under the earth, was able to open the book, neither to look thereon.

4 And I wept much, because no man was found worthy to open and to read the book, neither to look thereon.

5 And one of the elders saith unto me, Weep not: behold, the Lion of the tribe of Ju′da, the Root of Da′vid, hath prevailed to open the book, and to loose the seven seals thereof.

6 And I beheld, and, lo, in the midst of the throne, and of the four beasts, and in the midst of the elders, stood a Lamb as it had been slain, having seven horns and seven eyes, which are the seven Spirits of God sent forth into all the earth.

7 And he came and took the book out of the right hand of him that sat upon the throne.

8 And when he had taken the book, the four beasts and four *and* twenty elders fell down before the Lamb, having every one of them harps, and golden vials full of odours, which are the prayers of saints.

9 And they sung a new song, saying, Thou art worthy to take the book, and to open the seals thereof: for thou wast slain, and hast redeemed us to God by thy blood out of every kindred, and tongue, and people, and nation;

10 And hast made us unto our God kings and priests: and we shall reign on the earth.

11 And I beheld, and I heard the voice of many angels round about the throne and the beasts and the elders: and the number of them was ten thousand times ten thousand, and thousands of thousands;

12 Saying with a loud voice, Worthy is the Lamb that was slain to receive power, and riches, and wisdom, and strength, and honour, and glory, and blessing.

13 And every creature which is in heaven, and on the earth, and under the earth, and such as are in the sea, and all that are in them, heard I saying, Blessing, and honour, and glory, and power, *be* unto him that sitteth upon the throne, and unto the Lamb for ever and ever.

14 And the four beasts said, Amen. And the four *and* twenty elders fell down and worshipped him that liveth for ever and ever.

6 AND I saw when the Lamb opened one of the seals, and I heard, as it were the noise of thunder, one of the four beasts saying, Come and see.

2 And I saw, and behold a white horse: and he that sat on him had a bow; and a crown was given unto him: and he went forth conquering, and to conquer.

3 And when he had opened the second seal, I heard the second beast say, Come and see.

4 And there went out another horse *that was* red: and *power* was given to him that sat thereon to take peace from the earth, and that they should kill one another: and there was given unto him a great sword.

5 And when he had opened the third seal, I heard the third beast say, Come and see. And I beheld, and lo a black horse; and he that sat on him had a pair of balances in his hand.

6 And I heard a voice in the midst of the four beasts say, A measure of wheat for a penny, and three measures of barley for a penny; and *see* thou hurt not the oil and the wine.

7 And when he had opened the fourth seal, I heard the voice of the fourth beast say, Come and see.

8 And I looked, and behold a pale horse: and his name that sat on him was Death, and Hell followed with him. And power was given unto them over the fourth part of the earth, to kill with sword, and with hunger, and with death, and with the beasts of the earth.

9 And when he had opened the fifth seal, I saw under the altar the souls of them that were slain for the word of God, and for the testimony which they held:

10 And they cried with a loud voice, saying, How long, O Lord, holy and true, dost thou not judge and avenge our blood on them that dwell on the earth?

11 And white robes were given unto every one of them; and it was said unto them, that they should rest yet for a little season, until their fellowservants also and their brethren, that should be killed as they *were*, should be fulfilled.

12 And I beheld when he had opened the sixth seal, and, lo, there was a great earthquake; and the sun became black as sackcloth of hair, and the moon became as blood;

13 And the stars of heaven fell unto the earth, even as a fig tree casteth her untimely figs, when she is shaken of a mighty wind.

14 And the heaven departed as a scroll when it is rolled together; and every mountain and island were moved out of their places.

15 And the kings of the earth, and the great men, and the rich men, and the chief captains, and the mighty men, and every bondman, and every free man, hid themselves in the dens and in the rocks of the mountains;

16 And said to the mountains and rocks, Fall on us, and hide us from the face of him that sitteth on the throne, and from the wrath of the Lamb:

17 For the great day of his wrath is come; and who shall be able to stand?

7 AND after these things I saw four angels standing on the four corners of the earth, holding the four winds of the earth, that the wind should not blow on the earth, nor on the sea, nor on any tree.

2 And I saw another angel ascending from the east, having the seal of the living God: and he cried with a loud voice to the four angels, to whom it was given to hurt the earth and the sea,

3 Saying, Hurt not the earth, neither the sea, nor the trees, till we have sealed the servants of our God in their foreheads.

4 And I heard the number of them which were sealed: and there were sealed an hundred and forty and four thousand of all the tribes of the children of Is'ra-el.

5 Of the tribe of Ju'da *were* sealed twelve thousand. Of the tribe of Reu'ben *were* sealed

twelve thousand. Of the tribe of Gad *were* sealed twelve thousand.

6 Of the tribe of A'ser *were* sealed twelve thousand. Of the tribe of Nep'tha-lim *were* sealed twelve thousand. Of the tribe of Ma-nas'-ses *were* sealed twelve thousand.

7 Of the tribe of Sim'e-on *were* sealed twelve thousand. Of the tribe of Le'vi *were* sealed twelve thousand. Of the tribe of Is'sa-char *were* sealed twelve thousand.

8 Of the tribe of Zab'u-lon *were* sealed twelve thousand. Of the tribe of Jo'seph *were* sealed twelve thousand. Of the tribe of Ben'ja-min *were* sealed twelve thousand.

9 After this I beheld, and, lo, a great multitude, which no man could number, of all nations, and kindreds, and people, and tongues, stood before the throne, and before the Lamb, clothed with white robes, and palms in their hands;

10 And cried with a loud voice, saying, Salvation to our God which sitteth upon the throne, and unto the Lamb.

11 And all the angels stood round about the throne, and *about* the elders and the four beasts, and fell before the throne on their faces, and worshipped God,

12 Saying, Amen: Blessing, and glory, and wisdom, and thanksgiving, and honour, and power, and might, *be* unto our God for ever and ever. Amen.

13 And one of the elders answered, saying unto me, What are these which are arrayed in white robes? and whence came they?

14 And I said unto him, Sir, thou knowest. And he said to me, These are they which came out of great tribulation, and have washed their robes, and made them white in the blood of the Lamb.

15 Therefore are they before the throne of God, and serve him day and night in his temple: and he that sitteth on the throne shall dwell among them.

16 They shall hunger no more, neither thirst any more; neither shall the sun light on them, nor any heat.

17 For the Lamb which is in the midst of the throne shall feed them, and shall lead them unto living fountains of waters: and God shall wipe away all tears from their eyes.

8 AND when he had opened the seventh seal, there was silence in heaven about the space of half an hour.

2 And I saw the seven angels which stood before God; and to them were given seven trumpets.

3 And another angel came and stood at the altar, having a golden censer; and there was given unto him much incense, that he should offer *it* with the prayers of all saints upon the golden altar which was before the throne.

4 And the smoke of the incense, *which came* with the prayers of the saints, ascended up before God out of the angel's hand.

5 And the angel took the censer, and filled it with fire of the altar, and cast *it* into the earth: and there were voices, and thunderings, and lightnings, and an earthquake.

6 And the seven angels which had the seven trumpets prepared themselves to sound.

7 The first angel sounded, and there followed hail and fire mingled with blood, and they were cast upon the earth: and the third part of trees was burnt up, and all green grass was burnt up.

8 And the second angel sounded, and as it were a great mountain burning with fire was

cast into the sea: and the third part of the sea became blood;

9 And the third part of the creatures which were in the sea, and had life, died; and the third part of the ships were destroyed.

10 And the third angel sounded, and there fell a great star from heaven, burning as it were a lamp, and it fell upon the third part of the rivers, and upon the fountains of waters;

11 And the name of the star is called Wormwood: and the third part of the waters became wormwood; and many men died of the waters, because they were made bitter.

12 And the fourth angel sounded, and the third part of the sun was smitten, and the third part of the moon, and the third part of the stars; so as the third part of them was darkened, and the day shone not for a third part of it, and the night likewise.

13 And I beheld, and heard an angel flying through the midst of heaven, saying with a loud voice, Woe, woe, woe, to the inhabiters of the earth by reason of the other voices of the trumpet of the three angels, which are yet to sound!

9 AND the fifth angel sounded, and I saw a star fall from heaven unto the earth: and to him was given the key of the bottomless pit.

2 And he opened the bottomless pit; and there arose a smoke out of the pit, as the smoke of a great furnace; and the sun and the air were darkened by reason of the smoke of the pit.

3 And there came out of the smoke locusts upon the earth: and unto them was given power, as the scorpions of the earth have power.

4 And it was commanded them that they should not hurt the grass of the earth, neither any green thing, neither any tree; but only those men which have not the seal of God in their foreheads.

5 And to them it was given that they should not kill them, but that they should be tormented five months: and their torment *was* as the torment of a scorpion, when he striketh a man.

6 And in those days shall men seek death, and shall not find it; and shall desire to die, and death shall flee from them.

7 And the shapes of the locusts *were* like unto horses prepared unto battle; and on their heads *were* as it were crowns like gold, and their faces *were* as the faces of men.

8 And they had hair as the hair of women, and their teeth were as *the teeth* of lions.

9 And they had breastplates, as it were breastplates of iron; and the sound of their wings *was* as the sound of chariots of many horses running to battle.

10 And they had tails like unto scorpions, and there were stings in their tails: and their power *was* to hurt men five months.

11 And they had a king over them, *which is* the angel of the bottomless pit, whose name in the He'brew tongue *is* A-bad'don, but in the Greek tongue hath *his* name A-poll'yon.

12 One woe is past; *and,* behold, there come two woes more hereafter.

13 And the sixth angel sounded, and I heard a voice from the four horns of the golden altar which is before God,

14 Saying to the sixth angel which had the trumpet, Loose the four angels which are bound in the great river Eu-phra'tes.

15 And the four angels were loosed, which were prepared for an hour, and a day, and a month, and a year, for to slay the third part of men.

16 And the number of the army of the horsemen *were* two hundred thousand thousand: and I heard the number of them.

17 And thus I saw the horses in the vision, and them that sat on them, having breastplates of fire, and of jacinth, and brimstone: and the heads of the horses *were* as the heads of lions; and out of their mouths issued fire and smoke and brimstone.

18 By these three was the third part of men killed, by the fire, and by the smoke, and by the brimstone, which issued out of their mouths.

19 For their power is in their mouth, and in their tails: for their tails *were* like unto serpents, and had heads, and with them they do hurt.

20 And the rest of the men which were not killed by these plagues yet repented not of the works of their hands, that they should not worship devils, and idols of gold, and silver, and brass, and stone, and of wood: which neither can see, nor hear, nor walk:

21 Neither repented they of their murders, nor of their sorceries, nor of their fornication, nor of their thefts.

10 AND I saw another mighty angel come down from heaven, clothed with a cloud: and a rainbow *was* upon his head, and his face *was* as it were the sun, and his feet as pillars of fire:

2 And he had in his hand a little book open: and he set his right foot upon the sea, and *his* left *foot* on the earth,

3 And cried with a loud voice, as *when* a lion roareth: and when he had cried, seven thunders uttered their voices.

4 And when the seven thunders had uttered their voices, I was about to write: and I heard a voice from heaven saying unto me, Seal up those things which the seven thunders uttered, and write them not.

5 And the angel which I saw stand upon the sea and upon the earth lifted up his hand to heaven,

6 And sware by him that liveth for ever and ever, who created heaven, and the things that therein are, and the earth, and the things that therein are, and the sea, and the things which are therein, that there should be time no longer:

7 But in the days of the voice of the seventh angel, when he shall begin to sound, the mystery of God should be finished, as he hath declared to his servants the prophets.

8 And the voice which I heard from heaven spake unto me again, and said, Go *and* take the little book which is open in the hand of the angel which standeth upon the sea and upon the earth.

9 And I went unto the angel, and said unto him, Give me the little book. And he said unto me, Take *it,* and eat it up; and it shall make thy belly bitter, but it shall be in thy mouth sweet as honey.

10 And I took the little book out of the angel's hand, and ate it up; and it was in my mouth sweet as honey: and as soon as I had eaten it, my belly was bitter.

11 And he said unto me, Thou must prophesy again before many peoples, and nations, and tongues, and kings.

11 AND there was given me a reed like unto a rod: and the angel stood, saying, Rise, and measure the temple of God, and the altar, and them that worship therein.

2 But the court which is without the temple leave out, and measure it not; for it is given

unto the Gen'tiles: and the holy city shall they tread under foot forty and two months.

3 And I will give power unto my two witnesses, and they shall prophesy a thousand two hundred and threescore days, clothed in sackcloth.

4 These are the two olive trees, and the two candlesticks standing before the God of the earth.

5 And if any man will hurt them, fire proceedeth out of their mouth, and devoureth their enemies: and if any man will hurt them, he must in this manner be killed.

6 These have power to shut heaven, that it rain not in the days of their prophecy: and have power over waters to turn them to blood, and to smite the earth with all plagues, as often as they will.

7 And when they shall have finished their testimony, the beast that ascendeth out of the bottomless pit shall make war against them, and shall overcome them, and kill them.

8 And their dead bodies shall lie in the street of the great city, which spiritually is called Sod'om and E'gypt, where also our Lord was crucified.

9 And they of the people and kindreds and tongues and nations shall see their dead bodies three days and an half, and shall not suffer their dead bodies to be put in graves.

10 And they that dwell upon the earth shall rejoice over them, and make merry, and shall send gifts one to another; because these two prophets tormented them that dwelt on the earth.

11 And after three days and an half the Spirit of life from God entered into them, and they stood upon their feet; and great fear fell upon them which saw them.

12 And they heard a great voice from heaven saying unto them, Come up hither. And they ascended up to heaven in a cloud; and their enemies beheld them.

13 And the same hour was there a great earthquake, and the tenth part of the city fell, and in the earthquake were slain of men seven thousand: and the remnant were affrighted, and gave glory to the God of heaven.

14 The second woe is past; and, behold, the third woe cometh quickly.

15 And the seventh angel sounded; and there were great voices in heaven, saying, The kingdoms of this world are become the kingdoms of our Lord, and of his Christ; and he shall reign for ever and ever.

16 And the four and twenty elders, which sat before God on their seats, fell upon their faces, and worshipped God,

17 Saying, We give thee thanks, O Lord God Almighty, which art, and wast, and art to come; because thou hast taken to thee thy great power, and hast reigned.

18 And the nations were angry, and thy wrath is come, and the time of the dead, that they should be judged, and that thou shouldest give reward unto thy servants the prophets, and to the saints, and them that fear thy name, small and great; and shouldest destroy them which destroy the earth.

19 And the temple of God was opened in heaven, and there was seen in his temple the ark of his testament: and there were lightnings, and voices, and thunderings, and an earthquake, and great hail.

12 AND there appeared a great wonder in heaven; a woman clothed with the sun,

and the moon under her feet, and upon her head a crown of twelve stars:

2 And she being with child cried, travailing in birth, and pained to be delivered.

3 And there appeared another wonder in heaven; and behold a great red dragon, having seven heads and ten horns, and seven crowns upon his heads.

4 And his tail drew the third part of the stars of heaven, and did cast them to the earth: and the dragon stood before the woman which was ready to be delivered, for to devour her child as soon as it was born.

5 And she brought forth a man child, who was to rule all nations with a rod of iron: and her child was caught up unto God, and to his throne.

6 And the woman fled into the wilderness, where she hath a place prepared of God, that they should feed her there a thousand two hundred and threescore days.

7 And there was war in heaven: Mi'chael and his angels fought against the dragon; and the dragon fought and his angels,

8 And prevailed not; neither was their place found any more in heaven.

9 And the great dragon was cast out, that old serpent, called the Dev'il, and Sa'tan, which deceiveth the whole world: he was cast out into the earth, and his angels were cast out with him.

10 And I heard a loud voice saying in heaven, Now is come salvation, and strength, and the kingdom of our God, and the power of his Christ: for the accuser of our brethren is cast down, which accused them before our God day and night.

11 And they overcame him by the blood of the Lamb, and by the word of their testimony; and they loved not their lives unto the death.

12 Therefore rejoice, ye heavens, and ye that dwell in them. Woe to the inhabiters of the earth and of the sea! for the devil is come down unto you, having great wrath, because he knoweth that he hath but a short time.

13 And when the dragon saw that he was cast unto the earth, he persecuted the woman which brought forth the man child.

14 And to the woman were given two wings of a great eagle, that she might fly into the wilderness, into her place, where she is nourished for a time, and times, and half a time, from the face of the serpent.

15 And the serpent cast out of his mouth water as a flood after the woman, that he might cause her to be carried away of the flood.

16 And the earth helped the woman, and the earth opened her mouth, and swallowed up the flood which the dragon cast out of his mouth.

17 And the dragon was wroth with the woman, and went to make war with the remnant of her seed, which keep the commandments of God, and have the testimony of Je'sus Christ.

13 AND I stood upon the sand of the sea, and saw a beast rise up out of the sea, having seven heads and ten horns, and upon his horns ten crowns, and upon his heads the name of blasphemy.

2 And the beast which I saw was like unto a leopard, and his feet were as the feet of a bear, and his mouth as the mouth of a lion: and the dragon gave him his power, and his seat, and great authority.

3 And I saw one of his heads as it were wounded to death; and his deadly wound was

healed: and all the world wondered after the beast.

4 And they worshipped the dragon which gave power unto the beast: and they worshipped the beast, saying, Who is like unto the beast? who is able to make war with him?

5 And there was given unto him a mouth speaking great things and blasphemies; and power was given unto him to continue forty and two months.

6 And he opened his mouth in blasphemy against God, to blaspheme his name, and his tabernacle, and them that dwell in heaven.

7 And it was given unto him to make war with the saints, and to overcome them: and power was given him over all kindreds, and tongues, and nations.

8 And all that dwell upon the earth shall worship him, whose names are not written in the book of life of the Lamb slain from the foundation of the world.

9 If any man have an ear, let him hear.

10 He that leadeth into captivity shall go into captivity: he that killeth with the sword must be killed with the sword. Here is the patience and the faith of the saints.

11 And I beheld another beast coming up out of the earth; and he had two horns like a lamb, and he spake as a dragon.

12 And he exerciseth all the power of the first beast before him, and causeth the earth and them which dwell therein to worship the first beast, whose deadly wound was healed.

13 And he doeth great wonders, so that he maketh fire come down from heaven on the earth in the sight of men,

14 And deceiveth them that dwell on the earth, by the means of those miracles which he had power to do in the sight of the beast; saying to them that dwell on the earth, that they should make an image to the beast, which had the wound by a sword, and did live.

15 And he had power to give life unto the image of the beast, that the image of the beast should both speak, and cause that as many as would not worship the image of the beast should be killed.

16 And he causeth all, both small and great, rich and poor, free and bond, to receive a mark in their right hand, or in their foreheads:

17 And that no man might buy or sell, save he that had the mark, or the name of the beast, or the number of his name.

18 Here is wisdom. Let him that hath understanding count the number of the beast: for it is the number of a man; and his number is Six hundred threescore and six.

14 AND I looked, and, lo, a Lamb stood on the mount Si'on, and with him an hundred forty and four thousand, having his Father's name written in their foreheads.

2 And I heard a voice from heaven, as the voice of many waters, and as the voice of a great thunder: and I heard the voice of harpers harping with their harps:

3 And they sung as it were a new song before the throne, and before the four beasts, and the elders: and no man could learn that song but the hundred and forty and four thousand, which were redeemed from the earth.

4 These are they which were not defiled with women; for they are virgins. These are they which follow the Lamb whithersoever he goeth. These were redeemed from among men, being the firstfruits unto God and to the Lamb.

5 And in their mouth was found no guile: for they are without fault before the throne of God.

6 And I saw another angel fly in the midst of heaven, having the everlasting gospel to preach unto them that dwell on the earth, and to every nation, and kindred, and tongue, and people,

7 Saying with a loud voice, Fear God, and give glory to him; for the hour of his judgment is come: and worship him that made heaven, and earth, and the sea, and the fountains of waters.

8 And there followed another angel, saying, Bab'y-lon is fallen, is fallen, that great city, because she made all nations drink of the wine of the wrath of her fornication.

9 And the third angel followed them, saying with a loud voice, If any man worship the beast and his image, and receive his mark in his forehead, or in his hand,

10 The same shall drink of the wine of the wrath of God, which is poured out without mixture into the cup of his indignation; and he shall be tormented with fire and brimstone in the presence of the holy angels, and in the presence of the Lamb:

11 And the smoke of their torment ascendeth up for ever and ever: and they have no rest day nor night, who worship the beast and his image, and whosoever receiveth the mark of his name.

12 Here is the patience of the saints: here are they that keep the commandments of God, and the faith of Je'sus.

13 And I heard the voice from heaven saying unto me, Write, Blessed are the dead which die in the Lord from henceforth: Yea, saith the Spirit, that they may rest from their labours; and their works do follow them.

14 And I looked, and behold a white cloud, and upon the cloud one sat like unto the Son of man, having on his head a golden crown, and in his hand a sharp sickle.

15 And another angel came out of the temple, crying with a loud voice to him that sat on the cloud, Thrust in thy sickle, and reap: for the time is come for thee to reap; for the harvest of the earth is ripe.

16 And he that sat on the cloud thrust in his sickle on the earth; and the earth was reaped.

17 And another angel came out of the temple which is in heaven, he also having a sharp sickle.

18 And another angel came out from the altar, which had power over fire; and cried with a loud cry to him that had the sharp sickle, saying, Thrust in thy sharp sickle, and gather the clusters of the vine of the earth; for her grapes are fully ripe.

19 And the angel thrust in his sickle into the earth, and gathered the vine of the earth, and cast it into the great winepress of the wrath of God.

20 And the winepress was trodden without the city, and blood came out of the winepress, even unto the horse bridles, by the space of a thousand and six hundred furlongs.

15 AND I saw another sign in heaven, great and marvellous, seven angels having the seven last plagues; for in them is filled up the wrath of God.

2 And I saw as it were a sea of glass mingled with fire: and them that had gotten the victory over the beast, and over his image, and over his mark, and over the number of his name, stand on the sea of glass, having the harps of God.

3 And they sing the song of Mo'ses the servant of God, and the song of the Lamb, saying,

Great and marvellous *are* thy works, Lord God Almighty; just and true *are* thy ways, thou King of saints.

4 Who shall not fear thee, O Lord, and glorify thy name? for *thou* only *art* holy: for all nations shall come and worship before thee; for thy judgments are made manifest.

5 And after that I looked, and, behold, the temple of the tabernacle of the testimony in heaven was opened:

6 And the seven angels came out of the temple, having the seven plagues, clothed in pure and white linen, and having their breasts girded with golden girdles.

7 And one of the four beasts gave unto the seven angels seven golden vials full of the wrath of God, who liveth for ever and ever.

8 And the temple was filled with smoke from the glory of God, and from his power; and no man was able to enter into the temple, till the seven plagues of the seven angels were fulfilled.

16 AND I heard a great voice out of the temple saying to the seven angels, Go your ways, and pour out the vials of the wrath of God upon the earth.

2 And the first went, and poured out his vial upon the earth; and there fell a noisome and grievous sore upon the men which had the mark of the beast, and *upon* them which worshipped his image.

3 And the second angel poured out his vial upon the sea; and it became as the blood of a dead *man*: and every living soul died in the sea.

4 And the third angel poured out his vial upon the rivers and fountains of waters; and they became blood.

5 And I heard the angel of the waters say, Thou art righteous, O Lord, which art, and wast, and shalt be, because thou hast judged thus.

6 For they have shed the blood of saints and prophets, and thou hast given them blood to drink; for they are worthy.

7 And I heard another out of the altar say, Even so, Lord God Almighty, true and righteous *are* thy judgments.

8 And the fourth angel poured out his vial upon the sun; and power was given unto him to scorch men with fire.

9 And men were scorched with great heat, and blasphemed the name of God, which hath power over these plagues: and they repented not to give him glory.

10 And the fifth angel poured out his vial upon the seat of the beast; and his kingdom was full of darkness; and they gnawed their tongues for pain,

11 And blasphemed the God of heaven because of their pains and their sores, and repented not of their deeds.

12 And the sixth angel poured out his vial upon the great river Eu-phra'tes; and the water thereof was dried up, that the way of the kings of the east might be prepared.

13 And I saw three unclean spirits like frogs *come* out of the mouth of the dragon, and out of the mouth of the beast, and out of the mouth of the false prophet.

.14 For they are the spirits of devils, working miracles, *which* go forth unto the kings of the earth and of the whole world, to gather them to the battle of that great day of God Almighty.

15 Behold, I come as a thief. Blessed *is* he that watcheth, and keepeth his garments, lest he walk naked, and they see his shame.

16 And he gathered them together into a place called in the He'brew tongue Ar-ma-ged'-don.

17 And the seventh angel poured out his vial into the air; and there came a great voice out of the temple of heaven, from the throne, saying, It is done.

18 And there were voices, and thunders, and lightnings; and there was a great earthquake, such as was not since men were upon the earth, so mighty an earthquake, *and* so great.

19 And the great city was divided into three parts, and the cities of the nations fell: and great Bab'y-lon came in remembrance before God, to give unto her the cup of the wine of the fierceness of his wrath.

20 And every island fled away, and the mountains were not found.

21 And there fell upon men a great hail out of heaven, *every stone* about the weight of a talent: and men blasphemed God because of the plague of the hail; for the plague thereof was exceeding great.

17 AND there came one of the seven angels which had the seven vials, and talked with me, saying unto me, Come hither; I will shew unto thee the judgment of the great whore that sitteth upon many waters:

2 With whom the kings of the earth have committed fornication, and the inhabitants of the earth have been made drunk with the wine of her fornication.

3 So he carried me away in the spirit into the wilderness: and I saw a woman sit upon a scarlet coloured beast, full of names of blasphemy, having seven heads and ten horns.

4 And the woman was arrayed in purple and scarlet colour, and decked with gold and precious stones and pearls, having a golden cup in her hand full of abominations and filthiness of her fornication:

5 And upon her forehead *was* a name written, MYSTERY, BAB'Y-LON THE GREAT, THE MOTHER OF HARLOTS AND ABOMINATIONS OF THE EARTH.

6 And I saw the woman drunken with the blood of the saints, and with the blood of the martyrs of Je'sus: and when I saw her, I wondered with great admiration.

7 And the angel said unto me, Wherefore didst thou marvel? I will tell thee the mystery of the woman, and of the beast that carrieth her, which hath the seven heads and ten horns.

8 The beast that thou sawest was, and is not; and shall ascend out of the bottomless pit, and go into perdition: and they that dwell on the earth shall wonder, whose names were not written in the book of life from the foundation of the world, when they behold the beast that was, and is not, and yet is.

9 And here *is* the mind which hath wisdom. The seven heads are seven mountains, on which the woman sitteth.

10 And there are seven kings: five are fallen, and one is, *and* the other is not yet come; and when he cometh, he must continue a short space.

11 And the beast that was, and is not, even he is the eighth, and is of the seven, and goeth into perdition.

12 And the ten horns which thou sawest are ten kings, which have received no kingdom as yet; but receive power as kings one hour with the beast.

13 These have one mind, and shall give their power and strength unto the beast.

14 These shall make war with the Lamb, and

the Lamb shall overcome them: for he is Lord of lords, and King of kings: and they that are with him *are* called, and chosen, and faithful.

15 And he saith unto me, The waters which thou sawest, where the whore sitteth, are peoples, and multitudes, and nations, and tongues.

16 And the ten horns which thou sawest upon the beast, these shall hate the whore, and shall make her desolate and naked, and shall eat her flesh, and burn her with fire.

17 For God hath put in their hearts to fulfil his will, and to agree, and give their kingdom unto the beast, until the words of God shall be fulfilled.

18 And the woman which thou sawest is that great city, which reigneth over the kings of the earth.

18 AND after these things I saw another angel come down from heaven, having great power and the earth was lightened with his glory.

2 And he cried mightily with a strong voice, saying, Bab'y-lon the great is fallen, is fallen, and is become the habitation of devils, and the hold of every foul spirit, and a cage of every unclean and hateful bird.

3 For all nations have drunk of the wine of the wrath of her fornication, and the kings of the earth have committed fornication with her, and the merchants of the earth are waxed rich through the abundance of her delicacies.

4 And I heard another voice from heaven, saying, Come out of her, my people, that ye be not partakers of her sins, and that ye receive not of her plagues.

5 For her sins have reached unto heaven, and God hath remembered her iniquities.

6 Reward her even as she rewarded you, and double unto her double according to her works: in the cup which she hath filled fill to her double.

7 How much she hath glorified herself, and lived deliciously, so much torment and sorrow give her: for she saith in her heart, I sit a queen, and am no widow, and shall see no sorrow.

8 Therefore shall her plagues come in one day, death, and mourning, and famine; and she shall be utterly burned with fire: for strong *is* the Lord God who judgeth her.

9 And the kings of the earth, who have committed fornication and lived deliciously with her, shall bewail her, and lament for her, when they shall see the smoke of her burning,

10 Standing afar off for the fear of her torment, saying, Alas, alas that great city Bab'y-lon, that mighty city! for in one hour is thy judgment come.

11 And the merchants of the earth shall weep and mourn over her; for no man buyeth their merchandise any more:

12 The merchandise of gold, and silver, and precious stones, and of pearls, and fine linen, and purple, and silk, and scarlet, and all thyine wood, and all manner vessels of ivory, and all manner vessels of most precious wood, and of brass, and iron, and marble,

13 And cinnamon, and odours, and ointments, and frankincense, and wine, and oil, and fine flour, and wheat, and beasts, and sheep, and horses, and chariots, and slaves, and souls of men.

14 And the fruits that thy soul lusted after are departed from thee, and all things which were dainty and goodly are departed from thee, and thou shalt find them no more at all.

15 The merchants of these things, which were made rich by her, shall stand afar off for the fear of her torment, weeping and wailing,

16 And saying, Alas, alas that great city, that was clothed in fine linen, and purple, and scarlet, and decked with gold, and precious stones, and pearls!

17 For in one hour so great riches is come to nought. And every shipmaster, and all the company in ships, and sailors, and as many as trade by sea, stood afar off,

18 And cried when they saw the smoke of her burning, saying, What *city is* like unto this great city!

19 And they cast dust on their heads, and cried, weeping and wailing, saying, Alas, alas that great city, wherein were made rich all that had ships in the sea by reason of her costliness! for in one hour is she made desolate.

20 Rejoice over her, *thou* heaven, and *ye* holy apostles and prophets; for God hath avenged you on her.

21 And a mighty angel took up a stone like a great millstone, and cast *it* into the sea, saying, Thus with violence shall that great city Bab'y-lon be thrown down, and shall be found no more at all:

22 And the voice of harpers, and musicians, and of pipers, and trumpeters, shall be heard no more at all in thee; and no craftsman, of whatsoever craft *he be*, shall be found any more in thee; and the sound of a millstone shall be heard no more at all in thee;

23 And the light of a candle shall shine no more at all in thee; and the voice of the bridegroom and of the bride shall be heard no more at all in thee: for thy merchants were the great men of the earth; for by thy sorceries were all nations deceived.

24 And in her was found the blood of prophets, and of saints, and of all that were slain upon the earth.

19 AND after these things I heard a great voice of much people in heaven, saying, Al-le-lu'ia; Salvation, and glory, and honour, and power, unto the Lord our God:

2 For true and righteous *are* his judgments: for he hath judged the great whore, which did corrupt the earth with her fornication, and hath avenged the blood of his servants at her hand.

3 And again they said, Al-le-lu'ia. And her smoke rose up for ever and ever.

4 And the four and twenty elders and the four beasts fell down and worshipped God that sat on the throne, saying, Amen; Al-le-lu'ia.

5 And a voice came out of the throne, saying, Praise our God, all ye his servants, and ye that fear him, both small and great.

6 And I heard as it were the voice of a great multitude, and as the voice of many waters, and as the voice of mighty thunderings, saying, Al-le-luia: for the Lord God omnipotent reigneth.

7 Let us be glad and rejoice, and give honour to him: for the marriage of the Lamb is come, and his wife hath made herself ready.

8 And to her was granted that she should be arrayed in fine linen, clean and white: for the fine linen is the righteousness of saints.

9 And he saith unto me, Write, Blessed *are* they which are called unto the marriage supper of the Lamb. And he saith unto me, These are the true sayings of God.

10 And I fell at his feet to worship him. And he said unto me, See *thou do it* not: I am thy fellowservant, and of thy brethren that have the testimony of Je'sus: worship God: for the testimony of Je'sus is the spirit of prophecy.

11 And I saw heaven opened, and behold a white horse; and he that sat upon him *was* called Faithful and True, and in righteousness he doth judge and make war.

12 His eyes *were* as a flame of fire, and on his head *were* many crowns; and he had a name written, that no man knew, but he himself.

13 And he *was* clothed with a vesture dipped in blood: and his name is called The Word of God.

14 And the armies *which were* in heaven followed him upon white horses, clothed in fine linen, white and clean.

15 And out of his mouth goeth a sharp sword, that with it he should smite the nations: and he shall rule them with a rod of iron: and he treadeth the winepress of the fierceness and wrath of Almighty God.

16 And he hath on *his* vesture and on his thigh a name written, KING OF KINGS, AND LORD OF LORDS.

17 And I saw an angel standing in the sun; and he cried with a loud voice, saying to all the fowls that fly in the midst of heaven, Come and gather yourselves together unto the supper of the great God;

18 That ye may eat the flesh of kings, and the flesh of captains, and the flesh of mighty men, and the flesh of horses, and of them that sit on them, and the flesh of all *men, both* free and bond, both small and great.

19 And I saw the beast, and the kings of the earth, and their armies, gathered together to make war against him that sat on the horse, and against his army.

20 And the beast was taken, and with him the false prophet that wrought miracles before him with which he deceived them that had received the mark of the beast, and them that worshipped his image. These both were cast alive into a lake of fire burning with brimstone.

21 And the remnant were slain with the sword of him that sat upon the horse, which *sword* proceeded out of his mouth: and all the fowls were filled with their flesh.

20 AND I saw an angel come down from heaven, having the key of the bottomless pit and a great chain in his hand.

2 And he laid hold on the dragon, that old serpent, which is the Dev'il, and Sa'tan, and bound him a thousand years,

3 And cast him into the bottomless pit, and shut him up, and set a seal upon him, that he should deceive the nations no more, till the thousand years should be fulfilled: and after that he must be loosed a little season.

4 And I saw thrones, and they sat upon them, and judgment was given unto them: and *I saw* the souls of them that were beheaded for the witness of Je'sus, and for the word of God, and which had not worshipped the beast, neither his image, neither had received *his* mark upon their foreheads, or in their hands; and they lived and reigned with Christ a thousand years.

5 But the rest of the dead lived not again until the thousand years were finished. This *is* the first resurrection.

6 Blessed and holy *is* he that hath part in the first resurrection: on such the second death hath no power, but they shall be priests of God and of Christ, and shall reign with him a thousand years.

7 And when the thousand years are expired, Sa'tan shall be loosed out of his prison,

8 And shall go out to deceive the nations which are in the four quarters of the earth, Gog and Ma'gog, to gather them together to battle: the number of whom *is* as the sand of the sea.

9 And they went up on the breadth of the earth, and compassed the camp of the saints about, and the beloved city: and fire came down from God out of heaven and devoured them.

10 And the devil that deceived them was cast into the lake of fire and brimstone, where the beast and the false prophet *are*, and shall be tormented day and night for ever and ever.

11 And I saw a great white throne, and him that sat on it, from whose face the earth and the heaven fled away; and there was found no place for them.

12 And I saw the dead, small and great, stand before God; and the books were opened: and another book was opened, which is *the book* of life: and the dead were judged out of those things which were written in the books, according to their works.

13 And the sea gave up the dead which were in it; and death and hell delivered up the dead which were in them: and they were judged every man according to their works.

14 And death and hell were cast into the lake of fire. This is the second death.

15 And whosoever was not found written in the book of life was cast into the lake of fire.

21 AND I saw a new heaven and a new earth: for the first heaven and the first earth were passed away; and there was no more sea.

2 And I John saw the holy city, new Je-ru'sa-lem, coming down from God out of heaven, prepared as a bride adorned for her husband.

3 And I heard a great voice out of heaven saying, Behold, the tabernacle of God *is* with men, and he will dwell with them, and they shall be his people, and God himself shall be with them, *and be* their God.

4 And God shall wipe away all tears from their eyes; and there shall be no more death, neither sorrow, nor crying, neither shall there be any more pain: for the former things are passed away.

5 And he that sat upon the throne said, Behold, I make all things new. And he said unto me, Write: for these words are true and faithful.

6 And he said unto me, It is done. I am Al'pha and O'me-ga, the beginning and the end. I will give unto him that is athirst of the fountain of the water of life freely.

7 He that overcometh shall inherit all things; and I will be his God, and he shall be my son.

8 But the fearful, and unbelieving, and the abominable, and murderers, and whoremongers, and sorcerers, and idolaters, and all liars, shall have their part in the lake which burneth with fire and brimstone: which is the second death.

9 And there came unto me one of the seven angels which had the seven vials full of the seven last plagues, and talked with me, saying, Come hither, I will shew thee the bride, the Lamb's wife.

10 And he carried me away in the spirit to a great and high mountain, and shewed me that great city, the holy Je-ru'sa-lem, descending out of heaven from God,

11 Having the glory of God: and her light *was* like unto a stone most precious, even like a jasper stone, clear as crystal;

12 And had a wall great and high, *and* had twelve gates, and at the gates twelve angels, and names written thereon, which are *the*

names of the twelve tribes of the children of Is'ra-el:

13 On the east three gates; on the north three gates; on the south three gates; and on the west three gates.

14 And the wall of the city had twelve foundations, and in them the names of the twelve apostles of the Lamb.

15 And he that talked with me had a golden reed to measure the city, and the gates thereof, and the wall thereof.

16 And the city lieth foursquare, and the length is as large as the breadth: and he measured the city with the reed, twelve thousand furlongs. The length and the breadth and the height of it are equal.

17 And he measured the wall thereof, an hundred *and* forty *and* four cubits, *according to* the measure of a man, that is, of the angel.

18 And the building of the wall of it was *of* jasper: and the city *was* pure gold, like unto clear glass.

19 And the foundations of the wall of the city *were* garnished with all manner of precious stones. The first foundation *was* jasper; the second, sapphire; the third, a chalcedony; the fourth, an emerald;

20 The fifth, sardonyx; the sixth, sardius; the seventh, chrysolyte; the eighth, beryl; the ninth, a topaz; the tenth, a chrysoprasus; the eleventh, a jacinth; the twelfth, an amethyst.

21 And the twelve gates *were* twelve pearls; every several gate was of one pearl: and the street of the city *was* pure gold, as it were transparent glass.

22 And I saw no temple therein: for the Lord God Almighty and the Lamb are the temple of it.

23 And the city had no need of the sun, neither of the moon, to shine in it: for the glory of God did lighten it, and the Lamb *is* the light thereof.

24 And the nations of them which are saved shall walk in the light of it: and the kings of the earth do bring their glory and honour into it.

25 And the gates of it shall not be shut at all by day: for there shall be no night there.

26 And they shall bring the glory and honour of the nations into it.

27 And there shall in no wise enter into it any thing that defileth, neither *whatsoever* worketh abomination, or *maketh* a lie: but they which are written in the Lamb's book of life.

22 AND he shewed me a pure river of water of life, clear as crystal, proceeding out of the throne of God and of the Lamb.

2 In the midst of the street of it, and on either side of the river, *was there* the tree of life, which bare twelve *manner of* fruits, *and* yielded her fruit every month: and the leaves of the tree *were* for the healing of the nations.

3 And there shall be no more curse: but the throne of God and of the Lamb shall be in it; and his servants shall serve him:

4 And they shall see his face; and his name *shall be* in their foreheads.

5 And there shall be no night there; and they need no candle, neither light of the sun; for the Lord God giveth them light: and they shall reign for ever and ever.

6 And he said unto me, These sayings *are* faithful and true: and the Lord God of the holy prophets sent his angel to shew unto his servants the things which must shortly be done.

7 Behold, I come quickly: blessed *is* he that keepeth the sayings of the prophecy of this book.

8 And I John saw these things, and heard *them*. And when I had heard and seen, I fell down to worship before the feet of the angel which shewed me these things.

9 Then saith he unto me, See *thou do it* not: for I am thy fellowservant, and of thy brethren the prophets, and of them which keep the sayings of this book: worship God.

10 And he saith unto me, Seal not the sayings of the prophecy of this book: for the time is at hand.

11 He that is unjust, let him be unjust still: and he which is filthy, let him be filthy still: and he that is righteous, let him be righteous still: and he that is holy, let him be holy still.

12 And, behold, I come quickly; and my reward *is* with me, to give every man according as his work shall be.

13 I am Al'pha and O'me-ga, the beginning and the end, the first and the last.

14 Blessed *are* they that do his commandments, that they may have right to the tree of life, and may enter in through the gates into the city.

15 For without *are* dogs, and sorcerers, and whoremongers, and murderers, and idolaters, and whosoever loveth and maketh a lie.

16 I Je'sus have sent mine angel to testify unto you these things in the churches. I am the root and the offspring of Da'vid, *and* the bright and morning star.

17 And the Spirit and the bride say, Come. And let him that heareth say, Come. And let him that is athirst come. And whosoever will, let him take the water of life freely.

18 For I testify unto every man that heareth the words of the prophecy of this book, If any man shall add unto these things, God shall add unto him the plagues that are written in this book:

19 And if any man shall take away from the words of the book of this prophecy, God shall take away his part out of the book of life, and out of the holy city, and *from* the things which are written in this book.

20 He which testifieth these things saith, Surely I come quickly. Amen. Even so, come, Lord Je'sus.

21 The grace of our Lord Je'sus Christ *be* with you all. Amen.

THE END OF THE NEW TESTAMENT.

HELPS
TO
BIBLE STUDY

A Short History of the Holy Bible

The Age of the Bible

The Holy Bible is not only the greatest and best of all books. Its history has been very difficult to trace, yet the same divine guidance that set its authors to work to write it has made Christians delve into the mists of the past to learn all about it. We find out more about it every day through the research of learned men, and things that are now hidden from us regarding it doubtless will be revealed in the course of time.

As to its authors and age, however, we know a very great deal. It was written by about forty different men and as it comes to us it took about sixteen hundred years to compose. We know pretty accurately that Moses began it about the year 1500 B. C. and that John, who wrote the last book, Revelation, finished it about the year 90 A. D., which estimate fills out the sixteen centuries.

The Bible gets its name from a Greek word which means "the little books." Gradually, in the course of many years, this word came to stand for something more than "little books," of which the Big Book was composed. It came to mean "the book," the "holy book," and finally it came to mean just what it means today—the Holy Book of Books.

This wonderful work is composed of two parts—the Old Testament and the New Testament. The Old Testament has in it thirty-nine books or parts. It contains God's account of the creation of the world, a history of the Jewish people and God's dealings with them, a number of books written by the great Jewish prophets in which are foretold the things that happen in the New Testament, as well as a number of beautiful books of purely a religious character, such as the Psalms.

The men who wrote the Old Testament left off work on it about four hundred years before Jesus Christ was born. The New Testament begins with the birth of Jesus and covers a period of about seventy-five years down to the time when the faith of Christianity was being extended by the men Jesus Himself chose to go out into the world and tell about it. The New Testament contains twenty-seven books, four of which are specially known as Gospels, because they tell particularly of the life of Jesus. The word "gospel" means "good tidings" or "good news," because of the tidings of salvation that it brings to those who read it.

Formation of the Bible and Languages

The student of the Bible must not think that the Book as he reads it is its original form. The men who wrote it did so with much labor, just as letters are now written, and on the things which were used by them just as we use paper. Not until the great art of printing was discovered was it possible to get a Bible such as we have. Instead readers of the Bible used many thousands of written pages, kept carefully bound together. Of these there were many copies, but not nearly enough to go around among those who wished to possess a copy.

The men who wrote the Bible used two or three different languages. In the Old Testament the older most were written in Hebrew, while portions were written in Aramaic, a language somewhat similar to Hebrew. The New Testament was written in a form of the Greek language. From these languages the Bible has been translated into almost every known tongue.

The growth of the Bible from two collections of smaller books into one grand whole was very slow, but God so directed the minds of men that they finally did the work and did it well. This was called forming the canon of Scripture. Canon is a word which means rod or rule. The term applied to the Bible means that it is the rule or form of God's word to mankind; in other words, the way God wants man to read what God has to say to him.

The canon of the Old Testament was formed first. This was done by the Jews

1

themselves, probably about four hundred years before Christ's time. Their learned men gathered together all the nation's sacred writings and under divine guidance made one work of them. After Jesus died began the preparation of the New Testament by the men God directed to do the work. Then these were also gathered together and councils of religious and wise men discussed them. It took several hundred years to get them arranged in their present form.

Of course, there have been many different translations of the Bible. The first ones were made into Greek and Latin. From the best of these—one called the Septuagint, made at Alexandria, Egypt, about 270 B. C. to 150 B. C.—became an important source document.

The chapter and verse subdivisions of the Bible, the descriptive headings of chapters and the presence of italics, or sloping letters, in the text, did not exist in the original. The division into chapters, which was for greater ease of reading and quotation, was made in the thirteenth century by Cardinal Hugo or Archbishop Langton.

At a later period, probably 1551, one Robert Stephens made the division into verses. They are very imperfect and sometimes greatly obscure the meaning. The presence of italics is due to the fact that in many instances it was necessary to introduce words to make clear a meaning which could not be translated easily, or to supply dificiencies due to differences in language.

What the Books of the Bible Contain

The Holy Bible is divided into two great parts, called the Old Testament and the New Testament. Each is complete and distinct in itself as far as the subjects treated are concerned, but through both run God's revelation of Himself to man, His promise of salvation, His laws and wishes for man to follow.

The Books of the Old Testament

The thirty-nine books of the Old Testament are divided into four sub-divisions— the Pentateuch, the historical books, the poetical books and the prophetical books.

The Pentateuch contains the earliest Hebrew history and the Hebrew law as laid down by Moses. It consists of the five books of Genesis, Exodus, Leviticus, Numbers and Deuteronomy.

The historical books contain the further history of the Hebrews up to the time the writing of the Old Testament ceased. They consist of twelve books: Joshua, Judges, Ruth, 1 Samuel, 2 Samuel, 1 Kings, 2 Kings, 1 Chronicles, 2 Chronicles, Ezra, Nehemiah and Esther.

The poetical books contain such of the poetry and philosophy of the Hebrews as has been preserved. They consist of five books: Job, the Psalms, Proverbs, Ecclesiastes and the Song of Solomon, also known as the Canticles.

The prophetical books contain the warnings and utterance of the Hebrew prophets. There are seventeen of them—five major prophets and twelve minor prophets. The major ones are Isaiah, Jeremiah, Lamentations, Ezekiel and Daniel. The minor ones are Hosea, Joel, Amos, Obadiah, Jonah, Micah, Nahum, Habakkuk, Zephaniah, Haggai, Zechariah and Malachi.

The Pentateuch Books

GENESIS, as its name implies, tells of the beginning of things, how the world was made and man placed upon it, of the fall of man through sin in yielding to temptation, of God's original promise to man of salvation through righteousness. It also tells of the dispersion of man through the Flood and the beginning of the history of the Hebrews. Genesis contains fifty chapters and was written by Moses about 1500 B. C.

EXODUS gets its name from the fact that it tells of the departure or exodus of the Hebrews from Egypt. It also tells of the wanderings of the Hebrews in the wilderness and of the giving of the Law to the Israelites by God through Moses. It was written almost certainly by Moses about the year 1485 B. C. and contains forty chapters.

LEVITICUS is a continuation of the book of Exodus. It takes its name from the fact that it contains the ceremonial and religious law, the performance of which was entrusted to the tribe of the Levites. It contains twenty-seven chapters and was apparently written by Moses about the year 1470 B. C.

NUMBERS is so named because it specially tells of the census or numbering of the Hebrews. It also tells of the history of the Hebrews on their journeyings after leaving Egypt. It contains thirty-six chapters and apparently was written by Moses about 1460 B. C.

DEUTERONOMY, the last book of the Pentateuch, gets its name from the fact that it contains a second account of the giving of the Law. It exhorts to obedience. It contains also an account of the death of Moses, within sight of the Promised Land. The book contains thirty-four chapters and was written partially by Moses and partially by Joshua. The date of writing is about 1450 B. C.

The Historical Books

JOSHUA. This book begins the historical books. It tells of the entrance of the Israelites into the Promised Land and the conquest of it. It contains twenty-four chapters and was written partly by Joshua and partly by some unknown author, about 1410 B. C.

JUDGES is to the Old Testament what the Acts of the Apostles is to the New. It tells of the troubled times through which the Israelites passed after the death of Joshua and the raising up by God of leaders and reformers for the ruling and leading of the nation. It brings the student up to the time of Eli and probably was written largely by Samuel. It contains twenty-one chapters and covers a period of about three hundred years.

RUTH contains some history of great value regarding the early ancestry of Jesus, but is chiefly remarkable for the story of Naomi and of Ruth and Boaz. It contains only four chapters and its author and date are unknown.

SAMUEL. These two books take their name from the great prophet-judge. Both contain historical matter of great importance, including the careers of Eli and Samuel, the last of the Judges, and the first two kings of the Hebrews, Saul and David. Samuel wrote a part of the first book, while it is probable that Nathan and Jeremiah had a large share in the authorship of both of them. The first book contains thirty-one chapters and the second twenty-four.

KINGS. These two books continue the history of the Hebrews so far as the independent kingdom of Israel is concerned. The narrative runs from the death of David, through the greatness of the reign of Solomon and the wickedness of the kings that followed him, down to the destruction of Jerusalem and the first two Captivities. A period of about 425 years is covered. Both books may have been written by Jeremiah. The first contains twenty-two chapters and the second twenty-five.

CHRONICLES. These two books are really Hebrew national religious records. But they also contain a history of the kingdom of Judah and many important family records. The authors of the books, which contain twenty-nine and thirty-six chapters respectively, are believed to have been Ezra and Daniel.

EZRA takes up the history of the Jews, beginning with the return from the Captivity, and goes over a period of about eighty years, telling of the rebuilding of the Temple at Jerusalem and the religious reformation of the people. The author,

Ezra, was one of the greatest of the Jewish historians. The book contains ten chapters.

NEHEMIAH is a companion book to Ezra, continuing the history of the Jews after the Captivity. Its author, Nehemiah, was also a great Jewish historian. The book contains thirteen chapters.

ESTHER takes its name from its principal figure, the beautiful Hebrew queen of King Ahasuerus. It tells of her elevation to the throne and how she overthrew the conspiracy formed by Haman for the slaughter of the Jews. It contains ten chapters.

The Poetical Books

JOB. This is the first of the poetical books, and one of the most remarkable books of the whole Bible and has been the subject of much debate among Bible scholars. It is the story of Job, a patriarch, who was tested by God. It is full of great beauty and wisdom. In many ways it reminds the reader of Bunyan's "Pilgrim's Progress." Its authorship and date of writing are unknown. It contains forty-two chapters.

THE PSALMS form another of the Bible's wonderful Books. The book is really a manual for devotional reading, no matter what the condition of the reader's mind or what his needs. Every form of sorrow, joy, repentance, aspiration, prayer, or hope finds expression in one or another of the Psalms. Persons learned in Bible lore have divided the book into four parts, as follows: Davidic Psalms, or psalms attributed to David, 1 to 72 inclusive; Asaphic Psalms, or psalms attributed to Asaph, 73 to 89 inclusive; Psalms of the Captivity, or psalms written in prophecy of or during the Captivity, 90 to 106 inclusive; and Psalms of the Restoration, or psalms written in prophecy of or during the Restoration, 107 to 150 inclusive. All the psalms are poems. Their authorship doubtless includes many men, among them being Moses, David, Asaph, Ezra, Nehemiah and Jeremiah. The book contains one hundred and fifty chapters.

PROVERBS is a book of wisdom, a collection of wise sayings, attributed to Solomon, but probably only collected by him. It contains thirty-one chapters.

ECCLESIASTES is a companion book to Proverbs. Its title means "the preacher." Like Proverbs, it has been attributed to Solomon. It contains twelve chapters.

THE SONG OF SOLOMON is another of the Bible's remarkable poems. It has been regarded as telling in allegory of the love between Christ and His Church. It contains eight chapters and is doubtfully attributed to Solomon.

The Prophetical Books

ISAIAH. The first of the prophetical books of the Bible, which cover a period of four centuries. It takes its name from its author, the greatest of all the Hebrew prophets. This is the first book of the Old Testament in which there is a clear and undoubted reference to the coming of Jesus. In fact, the entire book is particularly rich in prophecy regarding the Lord Jesus Christ. Isaiah contains sixty-six chapters and was written about 700 B. C.

JEREMIAH gets its title from its supposed author, the prophet of that name. He takes the Hebrews to task for their worship of false gods and their sins, exhorts them to repentance and makes several prophecies regarding Jesus. The book contains fifty-two chapters.

LAMENTATIONS is also by Jeremiah. It is remarkable for its poetic beauty and arrangement. The theme is sorrow and lamentation for the sins of the Hebrews. It contains five chapters.

EZEKIEL gets its name from its author, Ezekiel, the Prophet of the Captivity. It is wonderfully rich in prophecy, foretelling the coming of Christ. It is to the Old Testament what Revelation is to the New. It contains forty-eight chapters.

DANIEL gets its name from its author, who was a man of princely rank. It is half history and half prophecy. In it is the story of Nebuchadnezzar. The book contains twelve chapters.

HOSEA is the first of the minor prophetical books. It is full of rebuke to the Jews for their wickednesses. The book contains fourteen chapters.

JOEL gets its name from its author, of whom little is known save that he lived about 830 B. C. He calls the people to repentance and foretells the coming of the Holy Spirit. The book contains three chapters.

AMOS follows much the same lines as Joel. The book contains nine chapters.

OBADIAH is the shortest of the prophetical books. It contains only one chapter.

JONAH tells the remarkable account of the prophet who tried to evade his mission, was swallowed by a huge fish, cast out and, finally, through fear of God, made to perform his duty. This is the first book of the Bible wherein is shown the thought of spreading the faith of God among other peoples than the Jews—in other words, the foreign missionary spirit. The book contains four chapters.

MICAH is remarkable for the fact that in it is foretold the birth of Jesus in Bethlehem. The book contains seven chapters.

NAHUM has much of the beautiful thought of Isaiah. Little is known of its author. The book contains three chapters.

HABAKKUK takes its name from its author, who is regarded as the prophet of faith. The Apostle Paul evidently was a deep student of this book, which contains three chapters, written in conversational form.

ZEPHANIAH was written by a prophet who was of royal blood. He particularly foretells the day of wrath and the reward of the good. The book contains three chapters.

HAGGAI takes its name from its author and contains two chapters.

ZECHARIAH contains many allusions to the coming of Jesus, even foretelling the entry into Jerusalem on an ass's colt, the betrayal and the sum of money Judas received for it. The book contains fourteen chapters.

MALACHI is the last book of the Old Testament and contains more prophesies regarding Christ. It contains four chapters.

The New Testament: Division into Four Parts

Like the Old Testament, the New Testament is divided into four parts—the historical books, which include the four Gospels and the Acts of the Apostles; the epistles of Paul; the general epistles; and Revelation, a prophetical book.

The historical books are the Gospels of Matthew, Mark, Luke, and John, and the Acts of the Apostles.

The epistles of Paul are Romans, 1 Corinthians, 2 Corinthians, Galatians, Ephesians, Philippians, Colossians, 1 Thessalonians, 2 Thessalonians, 1 Timothy, 2 Timothy, and Philemon.

The author of Hebrews is not known.

The general epistles are James, 1 Peter, 2 Peter, 1 John, 2 John, 3 John, and Jude.

The prophetical book is Revelation.

The Historical Books

The historical books of the New Testament differ from those of the Old Testament in that they tell of the life of Jesus and the spread of the faith He founded from the Jews, to whom He gave it first, to the other races of the earth, known as the Gentiles, by the men He commanded to do the work.

The first three of the four Gospels are called synoptical gospels, because they give a synopsis, or general view, of Christ's life. The fourth Gospel, that of John, is called the doctrinal Gospel, because it teaches specifically the doctrine of the divine nature of Christ as the Son of God. Four different points of view are expressed in the Gospels and to each of them interpreters of Scripture have assigned a symbol, based upon Ezekiel 1: 4–10. The Acts has often been called the Gospel of the Holy Spirit.

MATTHEW was the Gospel written for the Jews. It shows Jesus as the Messiah and King, in whom were fulfilled all the great Old Testament prophecies. Matthew, its author, was a Jew and a man of humble birth. It was written about A. D. 60. It has twenty-eight chapters.

MARK was the Gospel written for the Gentiles, especially the Romans. It sets forth character of Jesus as the Son of man. Mark, who wrote it, worked about the year A. D. 63, and probably obtained his facts from Peter. It contains sixteen chapters.

LUKE was the Gospel written for the Greeks. Its author was Luke, who seems to have been a physician of Gentile birth. He appears to have written under the guidance of Paul about the year A. D. 60. He especially sets forth the sacrificial character of Jesus as the Savior and Redeemer. This Gospel is peculiarly rich in matter not contained in the other Gospels. It contains twenty-four chapters and its symbol is an ox.

JOHN was the Gospel which may be said to have been directed to all mankind. John, its author, was the youngest of the apostles, and has been honored with the title of "the disciple whom Jesus loved." His Gospel is probably the greatest of all. It was written later than the others (probably about the year A. D. 85) and dwells upon Jesus as the Lord and Word made flesh. It contains twenty-one chapters.

THE ACTS OF THE APOSTLES takes its name from the fact that it is a history of the doings of the apostles for the first generation after the crucifixion of Jesus. It sets forth the coming of the Holy Spirit and the spread of the church under Peter and Paul. It was written by Luke. It contains twenty-eight chapters and was written about A. D. 63.

The Pauline Epistles

ROMANS. The epistles of Paul are very wonderful pieces of writing. As they are arranged in the Bible they begin with Romans. This was written to the Romans who were Christians and lays stress upon the "righteousness which is by faith." It exhorts its readers to lay aside racial differences and come together on a common basis as believers on Christ. It was written probably while Paul was at Corinth about the year A. D. 58, and contains sixteen chapters.

CORINTHIANS. These two books were written to the Christians at Corinth in Greece. In the latter Paul gives considerable autobiography. The first contains sixteen and the second thirteen chapters.

GALATIANS was written to the Christians of Galatia, in Asia Minor. Its chief theme is the freedom of the Gospel as opposed to the bondage of the law. It contains six chapters.

EPHESIANS takes its name from the fact that it was written to the people of Ephesus. In it Paul describes his ideal church and the work of each individual in it, with Jews and Gentiles as one body, with Christ as the common head. It contains six chapters and was written while Paul was in prison at Rome.

PHILIPPIANS was written to the church at Philippi. It gives thanks for the kindnesses bestowed upon the writer and offers good advice. It was written from prison in Rome and contains four chapters.

COLOSSIANS, written to the church at Colossi, dwells on the completeness of the church in Christ and gives warnings against heresies. It contains four chapters.

THESSALONIANS. These two books were probably the earliest of the Pauline epistles. They are full of the second coming of Christ and sound advice for their readers. They contain five and three chapters respectively.

TIMOTHY. These two books are letters written to Paul's helper and disciple, Timothy. Both are beautiful examples of pastoral wisdom. The last seems to have been written upon the eve of Paul's martyrdom, as is shown in the fourth chapter. They contain six and four chapters respectively.

TITUS is a letter in very much the same style as those to Timothy. It contains three chapters.

PHILEMON was written to a person of that name. It is remarkable because it shows the wonderfully sympathetic and just nature of Paul. It contains but one chapter.

HEBREWS is a doctrinal epistle, which particularly calls attention to the priesthood of Jesus Christ. It contains fourteen chapters.

The General Epistles

JAMES. This is the first of the general epistles and takes its name from its author. It is a great exhortation to patience and piety. It contains five chapters.

PETER. These two books take their name from that of their author. Their special themes are patience under persecution and holiness in living. They contain five and three chapters respectively.

JOHN. These three books are the work of that same "beloved disciple" who wrote the last Gospel. They are letters of a type highly spiritual. They contain five, one, and one chapters respectively.

JUDE takes its name from its author and is an admonition to all Christians to stand firm in the faith. It contains but one chapter.

The Prophetical Book

REVELATION is the title of the last book in the Bible. It was written by John, the author of the Gospel and Epistles that bear his name. It is the only truly prophetical book in the New Testament and is of very great beauty. It is full of a symbolism that is not always intelligible to its readers, which is strong proof of its prophetical character. Its theme is the end of all present mundane things and the coming of "the new heaven and the new earth." It contains twenty-two chapters.

CHART OF THE LIFE OF JESUS CHRIST

Ancestry	On one side God himself. On the other every phase of character, every human tendency represented in his genealogy.
Preparations for his coming	Universal peace. One empire. One language generally known. The Jews with the Scriptures in all lands. A general awakening.
Birth of Jesus about December, B.C. 5 Childhood and Youth	Home training. Bible study. Schooling. Different languages. Travel to Jerusalem. Great religious meetings. Village life. Work at a trade. Knowledge of his country's history and hopes. A perfect and beautiful character.
Preparations for his ministry	John the Baptist. Baptism. The Holy Spirit. The Voice from God. Temptation.
A.D. 27 Judea First Year — Year of Beginnings	John's ministry of preparation began six months before Jesus began to preach, continued through the first year and three months into the second year. First disciples. First miracle. First discourse. First reform. First Samaritan disciple. Healing of the nobleman's son.
A.D. 28 Galilee Second Year — Year of Principles	Imprisonment of John the Baptist, March The Pool of Bethesda. Organization. Choosing apostles. Sermon on the Mount. Miracles proving his authority and illustrating his work. Forgiveness of Sins. Seeking the lost. Life from the dead. The light of the world. Warnings and invitations. Parables. The year in which Jesus laid down and worked out many of the fundamental principles and truths of his kingdom.
A.D. 29 Galilee/Perea 2-3 months Third Year — Year of Development	The Death of John the Baptist in March. Increasing opposition. Feeding the five thousand. Miracles: The dropsical man, the ten lepers, blind Bartimeus. The transfiguration. At the feast of tabernacles. Discourses in the Temple. Healing of one born blind. The good shepherd. Parables: The great supper, the lost sheep, the lost coin, the prodigal son, the unjust steward, the rich man and Lazarus, the pounds.
A.D. 30 Perea Last three months Jan. Feb. March	Raising of Lazarus. Miracles. Parables. Instructions. Children. Zaccheus.
Saturday April 1 – Saturday April 8 Last Week	Anointed at Bethany. Triumphal entry. Cleansing the Temple. Last great day of public teaching. Rest at Bethany. Passover/The Lord's Supper. The trial. The crucifixion. The burial. In the tomb.
Sunday April 9 – Thursday May 18 Resurrection Days	Forty days. Eleven appearances, between April 9 and May 18. A.D. 30. The Ascension, Thursday, May 18 from Mount of Olives.
The Ever-Living Saviour	Return through the Holy Spirit. A Saviour in heaven. Ever abiding with his people. Coming again in his kingdom. A universal king, the world redeemed.

THE HARMONY OF THE LIFE OF CHRIST

THE MIRACLES OF OUR LORD

THE PARABLES OF OUR LORD

THE APOSTLES AND THEIR HISTORY.

	NAME.	SURNAME.	PARENTS.	HOME.	BUSINESS.	WRITINGS.	WORK.	DEATH.
1	SIMON.	Peter Cephas} = *Rock*.	Jonah.	*Early Life:* Bethsaida. *Later:* Capernaum.	Fisherman.	1 Peter. 2 Peter.	A missionary among the Jews, as far as Babylon, 1 Pet. 5:13. Probably = Rome.	*Trad.:* Crucified head downward, at Rome.
2	ANDREW.		Jonah.	*Early Life:* Bethsaida. *Later:* Capernaum.	Fisherman.		*Tradition:* Preached in Scythia, Greece, and Asia Minor.	*Trad.:* Crucified on St. Andrew's cross (x).
3	JAMES the greater or elder.	Boanerges, or *Sons of Thunder*.	Zebedee and Salome.		Fisherman.		Preached in Jerusalem and Judea.	Beheaded by Herod, A.D. 41, at Jerusalem.
4	JOHN, the beloved disciple.			Bethsaida and afterward in Jerusalem.	Fisherman.	Gospel. 3 Epistles. Revelation.	Labored among the churches of Asia Minor, especially Ephesus.	Banished to Patmos, A.D. 95. Recalled. Died a natural death. *Trad.*
5	JAMES the less or younger.		Alpheus or Cleophas and Mary.	Galilee.			Preached in Palestine and Egypt.	*Trad.:* Crucified in Egypt; or thrown from a pinnacle.
6	JUDE.	Same as Thaddeus and Lebbeus.		Galilee.		Epistle.	Preached in Assyria and Persia. *Trad.*	Martyred in Persia. *Trad.*

THE APOSTLES AND THEIR HISTORY (Continued).

	NAME.	SURNAME.	PARENTS.	HOME.	BUSINESS.	WRITINGS.	WORK.	DEATH.
7	PHILIP.			Bethsaida.			Preached in Phrygia.	Died martyr at Hierapolis in Phrygia. *Trad.*
8	BARTHOLOMEW.	Nathaniel.		Cana of Galilee.				Flayed to death. *Trad.*
9	MATTHEW.	Levi.	Alpheus.	Capernaum.	Tax-collector.	Gospel.		*Trad.:* Died a martyr in Ethiopia.
10	THOMAS.	Didymus.		Galilee.			Claimed by the Syrian Christians as the founder of their church; perhaps also in Persia and India.	
11	SIMON.	The Cananæan, or *Zelotes.*		Galilee.				*Trad.:* Shot by arrows while at prayer.
12	JUDAS.	Iscariot.		Kerioth of Judea.			Betrayed the Lord Jesus.	*Trad.:* Crucified. Suicide.

REDI-REFERENCE

ANXIETY AND WORRY

Psalm 16:11; 37:1, 7; 43:5; Proverbs 16:7; Isaiah 41:10; Matthew 6:31-34; Philippians 4:6-9, 19; II Thessalonians 3:3; I Peter 5:7

ASSURANCE OF SALVATION

Matthew 24:35; John 5:24; 6:37; 10:27-30; 20:31; Romans 8:16, 31, 35-39; Hebrews 13:5; I John 5:11-13

BATTLE OF ARMAGEDDON

Revelation 14:14-20; 16:16

BEATITUDES

Matthew 5:3-12; Luke 20:23

BEREAVEMENT AND LOSS

Deuteronomy 31:8; Psalm 23; 27:10; 119:50

CHRISTIAN FELLOWSHIP

Psalm 122:1, 9; Matthew 18:20; John 13:34; Acts 2:42, 46; I Corinthians 1:9; Hebrews 10:24-25; I John 1:3, 7

CHRISTIAN'S ARMOR

Ephesians 6:11-18

COMFORT

Psalm 23; Lamentations 3:21-26; Matthew 5:4; 11:28-30; John 14:16-18; Romans 15:4; II Corinthians 1:3-5; II Thessalonians 2:16-17

CONFIDENCE

Psalm 27:3; Proverbs 3:26; 14:26; Isaiah 30:15; Galatians 6:9; Ephesians 3:11-12; Philippians 1:6; Hebrews 10:35; I Peter 2:9

CROWNS

I Corinthians 9:25; I Thessalonians 2:19-20; II Timothy 4:8; James 1:12; I Peter 5:2-4; Revelation 2:10

DANGER

Psalm 23:4; 32:7; 34:7, 17, 19; 91:1-2, 11; 121:1-8; Isaiah 43:2; Romans 14:8

DEATH

Psalm 23:4; 116:15; Romans 14:8; II Corinthians 5:1; Philippians 1:21; I Thessalonians 5:9-10; II Timothy 4:7-8; Hebrews 9:27; Revelation 21:4

DEITY OF CHRIST

Matthew 26:63-64; John 1:1-14, 18; 10:30; 14:9; 16:15; 17:10; 20:28; Romans 9:5; Colossians 1:15-19; 2:9; Titus 2:13; Hebrews 1:3, 8; I John 5:20

DIFFICULTIES

Romans 8:28; II Corinthians 4:17; Hebrews 5:8; 12:7, 11; Revelation 3:19

DISAPPOINTMENT

Psalm 43:5; 55:22; 126:6; John 14:27; II Corinthians 4:8-10

DISCOURAGEMENT

Joshua 1:9; Psalm 27:14; 43:5; John 14:1-3, 27; 16:33; 19:25-27; Colossians 1:5; Hebrews 4:16; I Peter 1:3-9; I John 5:14; Revelation 22:1-4

DIVORCE

Deuteronomy 24:1-4; Matthew 5:31-32; 19:3-12; Mark 10:2-12; Luke 16:18; I Corinthians 7:10-15

DOUBTFUL THINGS

Romans 14:1-23; I Corinthians 8:9, 13; Philippians 2:15; Colossians 3:2, 5-10, 17; I Thessalonians 5:22; Titus 2:12-14; James 4:4; I John 2:15-17

EXTERNAL PRESSURES

Joshua 1:9; Psalm 37:5; Romans 8:28; II Corinthians 12:9; I Peter 5:7; I John 5:4-5

FAITH

Romans 4:3; 10:17; Ephesians 2:8-9; Hebrews 11:1, 6; 12:2; James 1:3-6; I Peter 1:7

FEAR

Psalm 27:1; 56:11; 91:1-2; 121:1-8; Proverbs 3:25; 29:25; Isaiah 51:12; John 14:27; Romans 8:28-29, 31, 35-39; Philippians 4:19; II Timothy 1:7; I John 4:18; Jude 24-25

FORGIVENESS OF SIN

Psalm 32:5; 51; 103:3, 12; Proverbs 28:13; Isaiah 1:18; 55:7; James 5:15-16; I John 1:9

FORGIVING OTHERS

Proverbs 18:19; Matthew 5:44-47; 6:12, 14; 18:15-35; Mark 11:25-26; Luke 17:3-4; Ephesians 4:32; Colossians 3:13

FRIENDS AND FRIENDLINESS
Proverbs 18:24; John 13:35; 15:13-14; Galatians 6:1, 10

FRUIT OF THE SPIRIT
Galatians 5:22-23

GENEROSITY
I Chronicles 29:9; Psalm 37:21; Luke 6:38; Matthew 5:42; Proverbs 3:9-10; II Corinthians 9:6-7

GOD'S CARE
Psalm 31:19-20; 34:17-19; 91:1-2; Nahum 1:7; Ephesians 3:20; Philippians 4:19; I Peter 5:7; I John 4:16; Jude 24

GOLDEN RULE
Matthew 7:12; Luke 6:31

GREAT WHITE THRONE
Revelation 20:11-15

GROWING SPIRITUALLY
Ephesians 3:17-19; Colossians 1:9-11; 3:16; I Timothy 4:15; II Timothy 2:15; I Peter 2:2; II Peter 1:5-8; 3:18

GUIDANCE
Psalm 32:8; Isaiah 30:21; 58:11; Luke 1:79; John 16:13

GUILT
Psalm 32:1-2; Romans 8:1; II Corinthians 5:21; Ephesians 1:7; Colossians 2:9-17; Titus 3:5

HELL
Matthew 5:22; 13:42, 50; 18:8-9; 22:13; 25:41, 46; Mark 9:48; Jude 7

HELP AND CARE
II Chronicles 16:9; Psalm 34:7; 37:5, 24; 55:22; 91:4; Isaiah 50:9; 54:17; Hebrews 4:16; 13:5-6; I Peter 5:7

HOLY SPIRIT
Acts 5:3-4; I Corinthians 3:16; 6:19; 12:4-6; II Corinthians 13:14; I Peter 1:2

HONESTY
Romans 13:13; I Thessalonians 4:11-12; Hebrews 13:18; I Peter 2:11-12

HUMILITY
Proverbs 22:4; Micah 6:8; Acts 20:19; Romans 12:3; Philippians 2:3-4; I Peter 5:5-6

HUSBANDS
Genesis 18:19; Proverbs 23:13-14; I Corinthians 7:3; Ephesians 5:23-29; 6:4; I Peter 3:7

JESUS—
SAVIOUR OF THE WORLD
Matthew 1:21; Luke 19:10; John 3:16; 14:6; Acts 4:12; Romans 5:8; Ephesians 1:7; I John 5:12

JUDGMENT SEAT OF CHRIST
Matthew 6:2-4; 25:14-30; Luke 19:11-27; Romans 14:10-12; I Corinthians 3:9-15; II Corinthians 5:10; II Timothy 4:8

KINGDOM AGE
Isaiah 11:6-9; 14:7-8; 25:8-9; Revelation 20:1-6

LAKE OF FIRE
Revelation 20:14-15

LIBERTY
John 8:32, 36; Romans 6:6-7, 17-22; 7:6; 8:2; 14:1-23; I Corinthians 8:1-13; Galatians 2:21; 5:1, 13-14; Colossians 3:17; I Timothy 4:4

LIVING THE CHRISTIAN LIFE
Psalm 119:9-11; John 15:7; II Corinthians 5:17; Colossians 2:6; I Peter 2:2; I John 1:7

LONELINESS
Psalm 23; 27:10; 91:11; Isaiah 41:10; Matthew 28:20; Hebrews 13:5-6

LORD'S PRAYER
Matthew 6:9-15, Luke 11:1-13; I Corinthians 11:17-34

LORDSHIP
Luke 6:46; Romans 6:13-16; 10:9-10; 12:1-2; I Corinthians 6:19-20; Philippians 2:9-11

LOVE
John 3:16; 15:9-14; Romans 5:8; 8:35-39; I Corinthians 13; I John 3:1

MARK OF THE BEAST
Revelation 13

MARRIAGE SUPPER OF THE LAMB
Revelation 19:7-10

MAN'S NEED OF SALVATION
Isaiah 64:6; Romans 3:10, 23; 5:12; 6:23; Hebrews 9:27; I John 1:10

NATIONAL RESPONSIBILITIES
Psalm 33:12; Proverbs 14:34; 29:18; Romans 13:1-7; I Timothy 2:1-3; I Peter 2:13-17

NEW HEAVEN AND EARTH
Isaiah 65:17-25; Revelation 21-22

OBEDIENCE

I Samuel 15:22; Psalm 111:10; 119: 2;
Ecclesiastes 12:13; Isaiah 1:19-20; Matthew
6:24; John 14:15, 21; Romans 6:16;
II Corinthians 10:5; James 2:10; I John 3:22

OCCULT

Leviticus 20:27; Deuteronomy 18:9-12; I Samuel
28:7-12; II Kings 21:6; Isaiah 8:19; 19:3;
47:13-14; Acts 19:18-20; James 4:7

OCCUPATION

Genesis 2:15; Proverbs 14:23; Ecclesiastes 9:10;
Romans 12:11-13; Ephesians 4:28;
II Thessalonians 3:10-12

ONE HUNDRED & FORTY-FOUR THOUSAND

Revelation 7:4-8

OVERCOMING TEMPTATION

Isaiah 41:10; Matthew 26:41; I Corinthians
10:13; Philippians 1:6; II Thessalonians 3:3;
James 4:7; I Peter 2:9

PARADISE AND HADES

Numbers 16:33; Luke 16:22-26; 23:43

PARENTS AND CHILDREN

Exodus 20:12; Psalm 148:12-13; Proverbs 1:8-9;
6:20-23; 23:22, 26; 28:7; Ephesians 6:1-4;
Colossians 3:20-21; I Timothy 4:12; 5:4

PERSECUTION

Matthew 5:10-11; 10:22; Acts 5:41; 9:16;
Romans 8:17; II Timothy 3:12; Hebrews 11:25;
James 1:2-4; I Peter 2:20

PEACE

Isaiah 26:3-4; John 14:27; 16:33; Romans 5:1;
Philippians 4:4-9; Colossians 3:15

PLAN OF SALVATION

Isaiah 55:7; John 1:12; 3:3; 5:24; Romans
10:9-10, 13; Ephesians 2:8-9; Titus 3:5-7;
I John 5:11-13; Revelation 3:20

POWER OVER SATAN

James 4:7; I John 4:4

PRAISE AND GRATITUDE

Deuteronomy 8:10; I Samuel 12:24;
II Chronicles 20; Psalm 34:1-4; 50:23; 51:15;
63:2-7; 100:4; 107:8; 139:14; 147:1; 150;
Ephesians 5:18-20; Philippians 4:4-6; Colossians
3:15-17; I Thessalonians 5:18; Hebrews 13:15;
I Peter 1:6-9

PRAYER

Psalm 10:17; 18:3; 86:5, 7; 145:18; Jeremiah
33:3; Joel 2:32; Matthew 7:7-8; 21:22; John
14:13-14; 15:7; Romans 10:9-13; Ephesians
6:18; Hebrews 4:14-16; James 5:16; I John
5:14-15

PROVISION

Psalm 23; 34:10; 37:3-4; 84:11; Isaiah 58:11;
Matthew 6:33; II Corinthians 9:8; Ephesians
3:20; I Peter 1:3-5; II Peter 1:3-4

PURITY

Philippians 2:14-15; I Timothy 5:22; James
3:17; 4:8; I John 3:3

RAPTURE

I Corinthians 15:51-57; I Thessalonians 4:13-18

RETURN OF CHRIST

Luke 21:34-36; Acts 1:11; I Thessalonians
4:13-18; Titus 2:13; II Peter 3:8-14; I John
3:2-3

REWARDS

I Corinthians 3:11-15; Ephesians 5:27; 6:8;
II Thessalonians 2:14; II Timothy 4:8; I John
3:1-2; Jude 24

SATAN

Isaiah 14:12-15; Ezekiel 28:12-19; James 4:7;
II Peter 2:9; I John 4:4

SEAL JUDGMENTS

Revelation 6-7

SELF-IMAGE

I Samuel 16:7; Psalm 138:8; 139:14-16;
Philippians 1:6; Hebrews 12:2

SELF-CONTROL

Proverbs 4:23-26; Romans 13:14; I Corinthians
9:25; 16:13; I Timothy 6:11-12; II Timothy
2:3-5

SEX AND MARRIAGE

Proverbs 5:18-19; Song of Solomon;
I Corinthians 7; Ephesians 5:18-6:3;
I Thessalonians 4:1-7; Hebrews 13:4; I Peter
3:1-9

SICKNESS

Psalm 41:3; 103:3; Matthew 4:23; John 11:4;
James 5:13-15

SIN

Isaiah 53:5-6; 59:1-2; John 8:34; Romans 3:23;
6:23; Galatians 6:7-8

SIGNS OF THE TIMES

Physical Signs

Isaiah 35:1-2; Ezekiel 36:30; 38:14-16; 44:1-2; Daniel 11:40; 12:4; Matthew 24:7; 24:15; Luke 21:25-26; II Thessalonians 2:4; James 5:1-3; Revelation 11:1-2

Social Signs

Genesis 6:5; 13:13; 19:4-5; Deuteronomy 28:63-67; Ezekiel 34:11-13; 36:24; 38-39; Zechariah 12:2-3; Matthew 24:6, 9-10, 12, 37-39; Mark 7:21, 23; Luke 17:28-30; 21:24, 25, 29-33; 28:30; II Timothy 3:1-5; Revelation 9:13-21; 21:8; 22:15

Religious Signs

Daniel 8:23-25; 11:36-45; Joel 2:28-29; Matthew 24:5, 11, 13-14, 34; II Thessalonians 2:4-8; I Timothy 4:1; II Timothy 4:3-4; II Peter 2:1-2; 3:3-4; I John 5:19; Revelation 12:12; 13:1-18

SOCIAL RESPONSIBILITIES

Proverbs 19:17; Matthew 5:13-15; 10:42; Luke 3:10-11; Galatians 6:1-5; I John 3:17-18

SORROW

Job 5:17-18; Proverbs 10:22; Isaiah 53:4; Matthew 11:28-30; John 16:22; II Corinthians 1:3-5; 4:17-18; 6:10; I Thessalonians 4:13; I Peter 1:7; 4:12-13; Revelation 21:4

SPIRITUAL GIFTS

Romans 12:6-8; I Corinthians 12:14; Ephesians 4:11-12; I Peter 4:10

STRENGTH

Deuteronomy 33:25; Psalm 27:14; 28:7; Isaiah 40:29, 31; 41:10; II Corinthians 12:9; Philippians 4:13

STUDY

Psalm 19:7-11; 119:9, 11, 18; Acts 20:32; II Timothy 3:15-17; Hebrews 4:12; I Peter 2:2

SUFFERING

Romans 8:18; II Corinthians 1:5; Philippians 1:29; 3:10; II Timothy 2:12; I Peter 1:6-7; 2:19; 4:12-13, 16; 5:10

TEMPTATION

Psalm 94:17-18; Proverbs 28:13; Matthew 26:41; I Corinthians 10:12-13; Hebrews 2:18, 4:14-16; James 1:2-3, 12, 14; 4:7; I Peter 1:6; II Peter 2:9; I John 4:4; Jude 24

TEN COMMANDMENTS

Exodus 20

THOSE WHO HAVEN'T HEARD

John 6:45; 12:32; 16:8; Romans 1:19-20; 2:15, 18

TRIBULATION PERIOD

Daniel 9:24-27; Revelation 11:2-3; 13:5

TRUMPET JUDGMENTS

Revelation 8-9

TRUSTING

Psalm 5:11; 18:2; 37:5; Proverbs 3:5-6; Isaiah 12:2; 26:3

TWO WITNESSES

Revelation 11:3-12

UNPARDONABLE SIN

Matthew 12:22-32; Mark 3:22-30; Luke 11:14-23, 12:10; Hebrews 10:26; I John 5:16-17

VIAL JUDGMENTS

Revelation 16

VICTORY

II Chronicles 32:8; Romans 8:37; I Corinthians 15:57; II Corinthians 2:14; II Timothy 2:19; I John 5:4; Revelation 3:5; 21:7

WILL OF GOD

Psalm 37:4; 91:1-2; Proverbs 3:5-6; 4:26; Romans 14:5; Galatians 6:4; Ephesians 5:14-21; Philippians 2:12-13; I Thessalonians 4:3; I Peter 3:17

WITNESSING

Psalm 66:16; Proverbs 11:30; Matthew 5:16; Mark 5:19; Luke 24:48; Acts 1:8; Romans 1:16; II Corinthians 5:18-20; I Peter 3:15; 4:11

WIVES

Proverbs 11:6; 12:4; 14:1; 22:6, 15; 29:15; 31:10-31; I Timothy 3:11; Titus 2:3-5; I Peter 3:1-6

FAVORITE BIBLE STORIES

BIBLE DICTIONARY

AAR'ON (*mountaineer or enlightener*). Son of Amram and Jochebed, and elder brother of Moses and Miriam, Num. 26:59. Direct descendant of Levi by both parents. Called "the Levite," Ex. 4:14, when chosen as the "spokesman" of Moses. Married Elisheba, daughter of the prince of Judah, and had four sons, Nadab, Abihu, Eleazar, and Ithamar, Ex. 6:23. Eighty-three years old when introduced in the Bible. Mouthpiece and encourager of Moses before the Lord and the people of Israel, and in the Court of the Pharaoh, Ex. 4:30; 7:2. Miracle worker of the Exodus, Ex. 7:19. Helped Hur to stay the weary hands of Moses in the battle with Amalek, Ex. 17:9-12. In a weak moment yielded to idolatry among his people and incurred the wrath of Moses, Ex. 32. Consecrated to the priesthood by Moses, Ex. 29. Anointed and sanctified, with his sons, to minister in the priest's office, Ex. 40. Murmured against Moses at the instance of Miriam, but repented and joined Moses in prayer for Miriam's recovery, Num. 12. His authority in Israel vindicated by the miracle of the rod, Num. 17. Died on Mt. Hor, at age of one hundred and twenty-three years, and was succeeded in the priesthood by his son Eleazar, Num. 20:22-29. Office continued in his line till time of Eli. Restored to house of Eleazar by Solomon, 1 Kgs. 2:27.

A'BRA-HAM and **A'BRAM** (*father of a multitude*). Son of Terah, a dweller in Ur of the Chaldees, Gen. 11:25-31. Founder of the Jewish nation. Migrated from Chaldea to Haran. Moved thence to Canaan, to Egypt and back to Canaan, where he settled amid the oak-groves of Mamre. There confirmed in the thrice repeated promise that his seed should become a mighty nation, and his name changed from Abram to Abraham. Died, aged 175 years, and was buried in the tomb of Machpelah, Gen. 12.-26.

AD'AM (*red earth*). A city of Reuben, on Jordan, Josh. 3:16.

AD'AM (*red earth*). Used generically for man and woman, and translated *man*

in Gen. 1:26, 27; 5:1; Job 20:29; 21:33; Ps. 68:18; 76:10.

AD'AM (*red earth*). The first man. Creative work of the sixth day. Placed in the "Garden of Eden." Tempted to eat of the forbidden fruit, fell under God's disfavor, and driven out of the Garden subject to the curse of sorrow and toil. Died at age of 930 years. Gen. 1:26, etc.; 2.-5.

A'MOS (*weighty*). One of the lesser prophets. Lived during reigns of Uzziah and Jeroboam II., Amos 1:1-7; 7:14-15. His book is 30th of O. T. It rebukes the sins of Israel and closes with God's promise. Book abounds in rural allusions.

AN'DREW (*manly*). An Apostle of Christ, John 1:35-40; Matt. 4:18. Brother of Simon Peter, native of Bethsaida, and fisherman. Original disciple of John the Baptist, Mark 13:3; John 4:6-13; 12:22.

AN'GEL (*messenger*). A messenger, 2 Sam. 2:5; Luke 7:24. In a spiritual sense, a messenger of God, Gen. 24:7; Heb. 1:14. Nature, Matt. 18:10. Number, 1 Kgs. 22:19; Matt. 26:53; Heb. 12:22. Strength, Ps. 103:20; Rev. 5:2. Activity, Isa. 6:2-6. Appearance, Matt. 28:2-4; Rev. 10:1, 2. Office, Isa. 6:1-3; Rev. 6:11; Matt. 13:49; 16:27; 24:31.

AN'TI-OCH (*after Antiochus*). (1) Capital of the Greek kings of Syria, on the Orontes. First Gentile church founded there, and disciples first called Christians there; Acts 11:19-21, 26. (2) A city of Pisidia, Acts 13:14. Starting point of the persecutions which followed Paul all through Asia Minor, Acts 14.

A-POL'LOS (*belonging to Apollo*). A learned Jew and Christian convert of Alexandria, who became a preacher and friend of Paul, Acts 18:24-28; 1 Cor. 3:6-9; Tit. 3:13.

ATH'ENS (*city of Athena, or Minerva*). Capital of Attica and chief seat of Grecian learning and civilization. Situate in S. E. part of the Grecian Peninsula, five miles from its seaport, the Piræus. Paul preached on its Areopagus or Mars' Hill, Acts 17:19-22, and founded a church there.

AU-GUS'TUS (*venerable*). Caius Julius Cæsar Octavianus, grand-nephew of, and heir to, Julius Cæsar. Made first emperor of Rome B.C. 27, with title of Augustus. During his reign Christ was born, Luke 2:1. Died A.D. 14, aged 76 years.

BAR'NA-BAS (*son of comfort*). Joseph or Joses, a convert of Cyprus, and companion of Paul, Acts 4:36; 9:27; 11:25, 26; 15:22-39.

BAR-THOL'O-MEW (*son of Tolmai*). One of the twelve apostles, Matt. 10:3; Mark 3:18; Luke 6:14; Acts 1:13; perhaps Nathanael in John 1:45.

BETH'-LE-HEM, BETH'LE-HEM (*house of bread*). (1) A town of Palestine, six miles S. of Jerusalem. First called Ephrath or Ephratah, Gen. 35: 16-19; 48:7. Called Bethlehem-judah after the conquest, Judg. 17:7. Home of Ruth, Ruth 1:19. Birthplace of David, 1 Sam. 17:12. Here Christ was born, Matt. 2:1, 2; Luke 2:15-18. (2) A town in Zebulun, Josh. 19:15.

CHRIST. The Anointed; the Messiah. A title of Jesus, the Saviour: at first with the article, "The Christ;" later, as part of a proper name, "Jesus Christ." [JESUS.]

COR'INTH (*ornament*). Anciently Ephyra; capital of Achaia. Destroyed by Rome, B.C. 146. Rebuilt by Julius Cæsar, B.C. 46, as a Roman colony. Paul founded a church there, Acts 18:1; 20: 2, 3.

DA-MAS'CUS. A city of Asia, 133 miles N. E. of Jerusalem, Gen. 14:15; 15:2. Adjacent region called "Syria of Damascus," 2 Sam. 8:5. Taken by David, 2 Sam. 8:6; and by Jeroboam, 2 Kgs. 14:28. Scene of Paul's conversion, Acts 9:1-27; 22:1-16.

DA'VID (*well-beloved*). Youngest son of Jesse, 1 Sam. 16:8-12, born at Bethlehem. Anointed king by Samuel, 1 Sam. 16:13. Re-anointed at Hebron, 2 Sam. 2:4. United his kingdom and raised it to great strength and splendor. Died at the age of 70, B.C. 1015, after a reign of seven and a half years over

Judah and thirty-three years over the entire kingdom of Israel. History told in 1 Sam. 16. to 1 Kgs. 2.

DIS-CI'PLE (*learner*). Follower of Christ, Matt. 10:24; of John, Matt. 9:14. Applied specially to the twelve, Matt. 10:1; 11:1; 20:17.

E'GYPT (*Coptic land*). Northeastern country of Africa; the Hebrew "Mizraim," Gen. 10:6, and "Land of Ham," Ps. 105:23, 27. Bondage place of Israelites, Ex. 1.-14. Noted for Nile river, rich soil and gigantic ruins. Ancient religion monotheistic, with sun as central object; and attributes of nature in form of trinities. Vast temples and numerous priests. Kings called Pharaohs, who perpetuated their reins in obelisks, temples, sculptures, sphinxes, pyramids, etc. In intimate commerce with Hebrews, 1 Kgs. 3:1. Conquered Judea, 1 Kgs. 14:25, 26. Frequently mentioned in Scripture.

E-LI'JAH (*God is God*). (1) The prophet; Elias in N. T., Matt. 17:3. A Tishbite of Gilead; appears suddenly; is fed by ravens; restores the widow's son, 1 Kgs. 17:1-24; invokes fire on the prophets of Baal, 18:17-40; anoints Hazael, Jehu, and Elisha, 19.; denounces Ahab and Jezebel, 21:17-24; is translated in a chariot of fire, 2 Kgs. 2.; reappears on the mount of Transfiguration, Luke 9:28-35. (2) A son of Harim, Ez. 10:21.

EPH'E-SUS (*desirable*). Capital of Ionia, on the Ægean Sea. Noted for its commerce, learning, and architecture. Paul visited it, Acts 18:1-20, and founded a church there, to which he addressed one of his best epistles, Acts 19:1-10; 20:17-38.

E-PIS'TLE (*sending to*). In O. T. a letter, 2 Sam. 11:14; 2 Kgs. 5:5, 6; 2 Chr. 21:12; Ez. 4:6-11. In N. T., a formal tract containing Christian doctrine and salutary advice.

E-VAN'GEL-IST (*publisher of glad tidings*). One of the four writers of the gospels Matthew, Mark, Luke and John. A preacher of the gospel inferior in authority to the Apostles, Acts 8:14-19, and apparently to the prophets, Eph. 4:11, yet superior to the pastor and teacher, Acts 21:8; Eph. 4:11; 2 Tim.

4:5. A travelling and corresponding missionary, Acts 20:4, 5.

E-ZE'KI-EL (*strength of God*). One of the four greater prophets; carried captive to Babylon B.C. 598; entered the prophetic calling in fifth year of his captivity, Ezek. 1:1-3. Chapters 1.-24. of his book contain predictions before the fall of Jerusalem, and 25.-48. predictions after that event. The visions of the Temple, 40.-48. are a unique feature of the book.

EZ'RA (*help*). The famous scribe and priest, resident at Babylon, who returned to Jerusalem with his countrymen, B.C. 458, where he began instant reforms. He collected and revised the previous O. T. writings and largely settled the O. T. canon. His book, 15th of O. T., tells the story of the return and the establishment of a new order of things at Jerusalem and in Judea.

GA-LA'TIA (*land of the Galli, Gauls*). A central province of Asia Minor, and part of Paul's missionary field, Acts 16:6; 17:23; 2 Tim. 4:10.

GAL'I-LEE (*circle*). Originally the circuit containing the 20 towns given by Solomon to Hiram, Josh. 20:7; 1 Kgs. 9:11; 2 Kgs. 15:29. In time of Christ, one of the largest provinces of Palestine, in which he spent the greater part of his life and ministry. Luke 13:1; 23:6; John 1:43-47; Acts 1:11.

GETH-SEM'A-NE (*oil press*). Scene of Christ's agony and betrayal, at the foot of Olivet, near Jerusalem, Matt. 26:36-56; Mark 14:26-52; Luke 22:39-49; John 18:1-13.

GO-LI'ATH (*splendor*). The Philistine giant who defied the army of Israel, 1 Sam. 17:4-54. Another Goliath in 2 Sam. 21:19-22.

GREECE, GREEKS, GRE'CIANS. The well known country in S. E. of Europe, called also Hellas. Javan in O. T., Gen. 10:2-5; Isa. 46:19; Ezek. 27:13, 19; but direct in Dan. 8:21; 10:20; 11:2; Joel 3:6; Acts 20:2. Greek the original N. T. language.

HA-BAK'KUK (*embrace*). A minor prophet during reigns of Jehoiakim and Josiah. His book, thirteenth of the prophetic, denounces Chaldea, and concludes with a striking poem and prayer.

HAG'GA-I (*festive*). A minor prophet. His book, fifteenth of the prophetic, exhorts the Jews to crown the work of Zerubbabel.

HE'BREWS. "Abram the Hebrew," Gen. 14:13, that is, *eber*, the one who had "passed over" the Euphrates, westward. Hence, "seed" or descendants of Abraham. Among themselves, preferably, Israelites, from Gen. 32:28. Jews, *i.e.* Judahites, Judeans, after the captivity.

HER'OD (*heroic*). (1) Herod the Great, tetrarch of Judea, B.C. 41; King of Judea, B.C. 41-4; liberal, yet tyrannical and cruel. Issued murderous edict against children of Bethlehem, Matt. 2:16. (2) Herod Antipas, son of former; tetrarch of Galilee and Perea, B.C. 4-A.D. 39; murderer of John the Baptist, Matt. 14:1; Luke 3:19; 23:7-15; Acts 13:1. (3) Herod Philip, son of Herod the Great. Married Herodias, Matt. 14:3; Mark 6:17; Luke 3:19. Lived and died in private life. (4) Herod Philip II., son of Herod the Great, and tetrarch of Batanea, Ituraea, etc., B.C. 4-A.D. 34, Luke 3:1. (5) Herod Agrippa I., grandson of Herod the Great; tetrarch of Galilee; king of his grandfather's realm, A.D., 37-44, Acts 12:1-19. (6) Herod Agrippa II., son of former, and king of consolidated tetrarchies, A.D. 50-100, Acts 25:13-27; 26:1-28.

HIGH PRIEST. Chief priest, Aaron being the first. Originally a life office, limited to a line or family, Ex. 28:1; Lev. 21:10; Num. 3:32; 20:8; Deut. 10:6.

HO-SE'A (*help*). First of minor prophets. Prophetic career, B.C. 784-725, in Israel. Denounces the idolatries of Israel and Samaria. Style obscure.

I'SAAC (*laughter*). Son of Abraham, Gen. 17:17-22. Second of the patriarchs, and father of Jacob and Esau, Gen. 21.-35.

I-SA'IAH (*salvation of Jehovah*). Son of Amoz, Isa. 1:1, and first of greater prophets. His book, 23d of O. T., covers sixty years of prophecy, Isa. 1:1, at Jerusalem. It reproves the sins of the Jews and other nations, and foreshadows the coming of Christ. Called "prince of prophets." Poetically for Israel, Am. 7:9, 16.

IS'RA-EL (*who prevails with God*). Name given to Jacob, Gen. 32:28; 35:10; became national, Ex. 3:16; narrowed to northern kingdom after the revolt of the ten tribes from Judah, 1 Sam. 11:8; 2 Sam. 20:1; 1 Kgs. 12:16, with Shechem as capital, 1 Kgs. 12:25, and Tirzah as royal residence, 14:17; afterwards, capital at Samaria, 16:24. Kingdom lasted 254 years, with 19 kings, B.C. 975-721, when it fell a prey to the Assyrians. The returned of Israel blended with those of Judah.

JA'COB (*supplanter*). Son of Isaac and second born twin with Esau, Gen. 25:24-34. Bought Esau's birthright, fled to Padan-aram, married Rachel and Leah, wandered to Hebron, name changed to Israel, drifted to Egypt, where he died, aged 147 years, Gen. 25.-50.

JAMES (*Jacob*). (1) "The Greater" or "Elder," son of Zebedee and brother of John, Matt. 4:21, 22. A fisherman of Galilee, called to the Apostolate about A.D. 28, and styled Boanerges, Matt. 10:2, 3; Mark 3:14-18; Luke 6:12-16; Acts 1:13. Labored at Jerusalem. Beheaded by Herod, A.D. 44. (2) "The Less," another Apostle, son of Alphæus, Matt. 10:3; Mark 3:18; Luke 6:15. (3) Christ's brother, or more likely cousin, and identical with James the Less, Gal. 1:19. Compare Matt. 13:55; Mark 6:3; Acts 12:17. Resident at Jerusalem and author of The Epistle of James, written before A.D. 62 to the scattered Jews, urging good works as the groundwork and evidence of faith.

JE-HOSH'A-PHAT (*judged of God*). (1) Recorder under David and Solomon, 2 Sam. 8:16; 1 Kgs. 4:3. (2) A trumpeter, 1 Chr. 15:24. (3) Solomon's purveyor, 1 Kgs. 4:17. (4) Father of Jehu, 2 Kgs. 9:2-14. (5) Valley of Cedron, or else a visionary spot, Joel 3:2-12. (6) Son and successor of Asa on throne of Judah, B.C. 914-890. A God-fearing king, in close alliance with Israel, 1 Kgs. 15:24; 2 Kgs. 8:16; 2 Chr. 17.-21. 50.

JE-HO'VAH. "He that is." "I am," Ex. 3:14. The self-existent and eternal one. Hebrew word for God, generally rendered "Lord." Not pronounced; but Adonai, "Lord," or Elohim, "God," substituted, Ex. 6:3. [GOD.]

JER''E-MI'AH (*exalted*). (1) Second of greater prophets. His prophecies cover reins of Josiah, Jehoiakim, and Zedekiah, B.C. 628-586, and constitute the 24th O. T. book. Life one of vicissitude. Prophecies noted for boldness and beauty, and chiefly denunciative of Judah and her policy. Withdrew to Egypt, where he probably died. (2) Seven others in O. T., 2 Kgs. 23:31; 1 Chr. 12:4-13; 5:24; Neh. 10:2; 12:1, 12, 34; Jer. 35:3.

JE-RU'SA-LEM (*place of peace*). Capital of Hebrew monarchy and of kingdom of Judah, 24 miles west of Jordan and 37 east of the Mediterranean. "Salem," Ps. 76:2, and perhaps, Gen. 14:18. "Jebus," Judg. 19:10, 11. "Jebussalem," Jerusalem, Josh. 10:1. "City of David," Zion, 1 Kgs. 8:1; 2 Kgs. 14:20. "City of Judah," 2 Chr. 25:28. "City of God," Ps. 46:4. "City of the great King," Ps. 48:2. "The holy city," Neh. 11:1. Captured and rebuilt by David, and made his capital, 2 Sam. 5:6-13; 1 Chr. 11:4-9. Destroyed by Nebuchadnezzar, B.C. 588. Rebuilt by returned captives. Captured by Alexander the Great, B.C. 332; by Antiochus, B.C. 203; by Rome, B.C. 63.

JE'SUS CHRIST. Jesus the Saviour; Christ, or Messiah, the anointed. Jesus the Christ. Name given to the long promised prophet and king, Matt. 11:3; Acts 19:4. Only begotten of God. Born of Mary at Bethlehem, B.C. 5; reared at Nazareth, baptized at age of 30, Luke 3:23. Ministerial career, extending over Galilee, Judea, and Perea, began A.D. 27 and ended with the crucifixion, April 7, A.D. 30. Matthew, Mark, and Luke record his Galilean ministry; John his Judean ministry. The four gospels embrace Christ's biography.

JOB (*persecuted*). (1) The pious and wealthy patriarch of Uz, whose poem constitutes the 18th O. T. book, and first of the poetical. It is a dramatic narrative of his life of vicissitude, the gist being, whether goodness can exist irrespective of reward. Poetry noted for its sublimity, pathos, and beauty. Authorship disputed. Oldest of sacred writings.

(2) Son of Issachar, Gen. 46:13. Jashub, 1 Chr. 7:1.

JO'EL (*Jehovah his God*). (1) Son of Pethuel and second of minor prophets. Probably of Judah and Contemporary with Uzziah, B.C. 810-758. His book, 29th of O. T., depicts calamities, rises into exhortation, and foreshadows the Messiah. (2) Son of Samuel, 1 Sam. 8:2. (3) Others in 1 Chr. 4:35; 5:4, 8, 12; 6:36; 7:3; 11:38; 15:7; 23:8; 27:20; 2 Chr. 29:12; Ez. 10:43; Neh. 11:9.

JOHN (*God's gift*). Johanan, contraction of Jehohanan. (1) Kinsman of the high priest, Acts 4:6. (2) Hebrew name of Mark, Acts 12:25; 13:5; 15:37. (3) John the Baptist, son of Zacharias. Birth foretold, Luke 1. Born about six months before Christ. Retired to wilderness. Emerged to preach and baptize. Baptized Jesus, Matt. 3. Imprisoned by Herod, Luke 3:1-22. Beheaded, Matt. 14:1-12. (4) John, Apostle and Evangelist; son of Zebedee, Matt. 4:21; a fisherman of Galilee, Luke 5:1-10; a favorite apostle, noted for zeal and firmness, John 13:23; 19:26; 20:2; 21:7. He remained at Jerusalem till about A.D. 65, when he went to Ephesus. Banished to Patmos, and released A.D. 96. His writings, doubtless done at Ephesus, are the fourth Gospel, giving Christ's ministry in Judea; his three epistles, and Revelation. (5) A frequent name among the Maccabees, 1 Macc.

JO'NAH (*dove*). Son of Amittai. Commissioned to denounce Nineveh. His book, 32d of O. T. and 5th of minor prophets, narrates his refusal, escape from drowning, final acceptance and successful ministry. Its lesson is God's providence over all nations.

JON'A-THAN (*God-given*). (1) A Levite, Judg. 17:7-13; 18. (2) Eldest son of Saul, and friend of David, 1 Sam. 13: 2, 3; 18:1-4; 19:1-7; 20. Fell in battle of Gilboa. David's lament, 2 Sam. 1:17-27. (3) Others in 2 Sam. 15:27, 36; 21:20, 21; 23:32; 1 Chr. 2:32, 33; 27:32; Ez. 8:6; 10:15; Neh. 12:11, 14, 35; Jer. 37:15, 20; 40:8.

JOR'DAN (*descender*). Chief river of Palestine, rising in the Anti-Libanus range, flowing southward, enlarging into Sea of Galilee, emptying into Dead Sea. A swift, narrow, yet fordable stream,

with an entire course of about 200 miles, Gen. 13:10; Josh. 2:7; Judg. 3:28; 2 Sam. 10:17; Matt. 3:13.

JO'SEPH (*increase*). (1) Son of Jacob and Rachel, Gen. 37:3; sold into Egypt; promoted to high office by the Pharaoh; rescued his family from famine; settled them in Goshen; died at advanced age; bones carried back to Shechem, Gen. 37.-50. (2) An Isaacharite, Num. 13:7. (3) Two who returned, Ez. 10:42; Neh. 12:14. (4) Three of Christ's ancestors, Luke 3:24, 26, 30. (5) Husband of Mary, and a carpenter at Nazareth, Matt. 1:19; 13:55; Luke 3: 23; John 1:45. (6) Of Arimathea, a member of the Sanhedrim, who acknowledged Christ, Matt. 27:57-59; Mark 15:43; Luke 23:51. (7) The apostle Barsabas, substituted for Judas, Acts 1:23. (8) Frequent name in Apoc.

JU'DAH (*praise*). (1) Fourth son of Jacob, Gen. 29:35; 37:26-28; 43:3-10; 44:14-34. His tribe the largest, Num. 1:26, 27. Allotted the southern section of Canaan, Josh. 15:1-63. (2) Kingdom of, formed on disruption of Solomon's empire, out of Judah, Benjamin, Simeon, and part of Dan, with Jerusalem as capital, B.C. 975. Had 19 kings, and lasted for 389 years, till reduced by Nebuchadnezzar, B.C. 586. Outlived its rival, Israel, some 135 years. (3) City of Jerusalem, 2 Chr. 25:28. (4) A town in Naphtali, Josh. 19:34. (5) Persons in Ez. 3:9; 10:23; Neh. 11:9.

JU'DAS. Greek form of Judah. (1) Judah, Matt. 1:2, 3. (2) Iscariot, or of Kerioth. Betrayer of Christ, Matt. 10:4; Mark 3:19; Luke 6:16; John 6:71; 12: 6; 13:29. (3) Man of Damascus, Acts 9:11. (4) Barsabas, chief among the brethren, and prophet, Acts 15:22, 32. (5) A Galilean apostate, Acts 5:37. (6) Frequent name in Apoc.

JUDE, Jude 1:1. Judas, brother of James the Less, Luke 6:16; John 14:22; Acts 1:13; Matt. 13:55. Thaddæus, Lebbæus, Matt. 10:3; Mark 3:18. An Apostle and author of the epistle which bears his name, 26th N. T. book. Written about A.D. 65. Place not known.

JUDG'ES. Governors of Israel between Joshua and the kings. They were called to God, elective or usurpative. Qualification, martial or moral prowess.

Rule arbitrary. Fifteen are recorded. Period, B.C. 1400 - 1091, about 310 years. Book of Judges, 7th of O. T., probably compiled by Samuel. Its history is that of a tumultuous period, completing Joshua's conquests and leading to legitimate kingly rule.

LA'VER (*wash*). Brazen vessel holding water for priestly washings—hands, feet, and the sacrifices. Ex. 30:18-21; 38:8; 1 Kgs. 7:38-40; 2 Chr. 4:6.

LAW (*rule*). In Scripture, reference is nearly always to the Hebrew civil, moral, and ceremonial law, Matt. 5:17; John 1:17; Acts 25:8.

LEB'A-NON (*white*). Two mountain ranges running N. E., between which was Cœlo-Syria. The western is Libanus, or Lebanon proper. The eastern is Anti-Libanus, and skirted Palestine on the north, Deut. 1:7; Josh. 1:4. Many scripture allusions, Isa. 10:34; Jer. 22:23.

LE'VI (*joined*). (1) Third son of Jacob, Gen. 29:34; avenged Dinah's wrong, 34:25-31; cursed, 49:5-7; went to Egypt, Ex. 6:16; blessed, Ex. 32: 25-28. (2) Two of Christ's ancestors, Luke 3:24, 29. (3) Original name of Matthew, Mark 2:14; Luke 5:27, 29; compare Matt. 9:9.

LE'VITES. Descendants of Levi, Ex. 6:16-25; Lev. 25:32, etc.; Num. 35:2-8; Josh. 21:3. In above, the tribe is meant. But Levites came to mean the priestly branch, *i.e.*, descendants of Aaron, Josh. 3:3; 1 Kgs. 8:4; Ez. 2:70; John 1:19. Three Levitical lines, Kohathite, Gershonite, Merarite, Num. 3:17. Assigned 48 cities among the other tribes, Num. 35.

LORD (*loaf-guardian*). Jehovah, LORD, Gen. 15:4; Ps. 7., 100. Adonai, Lord, Christ, The Lord, Our Lord. Supreme ruler, and not the Saxon dignitary.

LORD'S SUP'PER. Substitute for the O. T. Paschal feast. Instituted by Christ the night before the crucifixion, as a reminder of his covenant with mankind, Matt. 26:19; Mark 14:16; Luke 22:13. "Breaking of bread," Acts 2:42; 20:7. "Communion," 1 Cor. 10:16. "Lord's Supper," only in 1 Cor. 11:20.

LUKE (*luminous*). Evangelist and physician, Col. 4:14; 2 Tim. 4:11. Author of third gospel and of Acts of the Apostles.

MAL'A-CHI (*God's messenger*). Last of minor prophets. Nothing known of nativity or lineage. Contemporary with Nehemiah, B.C. 445-433. His book foretells the coming of Christ and John the Baptist.

MARK (*polite, shining*). John Mark, Acts 12:12, 25; 15:37. John, Acts 13:5, 13. Mark, Acts 15:39. Convert of Peter, 1 Pet. 5:13. Companion of Paul, Col. 4:10. Author of second Gospel, which was probably written in Rome.

MA'RY (*rebellion*). Greek form of Miriam. (1) The bethrothed of Joseph and mother of Christ, Matt. 1:18-25; 12:46; Mark 6:3; Luke 8:19; John 2: 1-5; 19:26; Acts 1:14. (2) Wife of Cleophas, Matt. 27:56, 61; 28:1-9; Mark 16:1-8; Luke 24:1-10. (3) Mother of John Mark, Acts 12:12; Col. 4:10. (4) Sister of Martha and Lazarus, Luke 10: 41, 42; John 11, 12. (5) Mary Magdalene; *i.e.*, of Magdala, Matt. 28:1-10; Mark 16:1-10; Luke 24:10; John 20: 1-18. (6) A Roman convert, Rom. 16:6.

MAT'THEW (*gift of God*). Contraction of Mattathias. The Apostle and Evangelist. Levi in Luke, 5:27-29. Son of Alphæus, Mark 2:14. Tax-collector at Capernaum when called, Matt. 9:9. His gospel is first of N. T. Its original claimed to be the Hebrew, or Syro-Chaldaic, of Palestine. Time of writing placed at A.D. 60-66. Gist, to establish Jesus as O. T. Messiah.

MER'CY SEAT. Lid of the ark, Ex. 25:17-22; hence, covering, or atonement for sin, Heb. 9:5.

MI'CAH (*God-like*). (1) The erratic Ephraimite whose story is told in Judg. 17., 18. (2) Sixth of the minor prophets. Prophesied B.C. 750-698. He foretells the destruction of Samaria and Jerusalem, and prefigures the Messiah. (3) A Reubenite, 1 Chr. 5:5. (4) Grandson of Jonathan, 1 Chr. 8:34, 35. (5) A Levite, 1 Chr. 23:20. (6) Father of Abdon, 2 Chr. 24:20.

MIR'A-CLE (*wonderful*). In scripture, a supernatural event, Num. 22:28; 1 Kgs. 17:6; Matt. 9:18-33; 14:25.

MO'AB (*of his father*). Son of Lot by his daughter, and progenitor of the Moabites. The country lay east of the Dead Sea and south of the Arnon, Num.

21:13-15; 22.; Judg. 11:18. Though idolatrous, worshipping Chemosh, they were a strong, progressive people, holding Israel subject, Judg. 3:12-14; but finally subdued, 15-30; 2 Sam. 8:2; Isa. 15., 16.; Jer. 48.; Ruth 1., 2.

MO'SES (*drawn out*). The great leader and lawgiver of the Hebrews. Son of Amram, a Levite. Born in Egypt, about B.C. 1571. Adopted by Pharaoh's daughter, liberally educated, fled to Midian, Ex. 2. Called to lead the Exode, Ex. 3.-19. Promulgated the law, Ex. 20.-40.; Lev.; Num.; Deut. Died on Nebo, aged 120 years. Reputed author of Pentateuch and Job.

NA'HUM (*comforter*). Seventh of minor prophets. Probably an exile in Assyria. Approximate time of prophecy, B.C. 726-698. It relates to the fall of Nineveh. Noted for vigor and beauty.

NA'THAN (*given*). (1) Distinguished prophet, and royal adviser and biographer of David and Solomon, 2 Sam. 7:2-17; 12:1-22; 1 Kgs. 9:8-45; 1 Chr. 29:29; 2 Chr. 9:29. (2) A son of David, 1 Chr. 3:5; Luke 3:31. (3) Father of one of David's warriors, 2 Sam. 23:36. (4) A returned captive, Ez. 8:16.

NAZ'A-RETH (*separated*). A town of Galilee, now En-nazirah. Home of Jesus, Matt. 4:13; Mark 1:9; Luke 1:26; 4:16, 29; John 1:45, 46.

NE-HE-MI'AH (*consolidation*). (1) The Hebrew captive who returned, as leader of his people, to rebuild Jerusalem and administer its affairs. His book, 16th of O. T., B.C. 445-433, tells of his work. (2) Leader of returning captives, Ez. 2:2; Neh. 7:7. (3) An assistant wall-builder, Neh. 3:16.

NIC''O-DE'MUS (*people's victor*). The Pharisee ruler and timid convert who assisted at Christ's sepulture, John 3:1-10; 7:50; 19:39.

NILE (*dark blue*). The great river of Egypt, worshipped as a god, famous for its annual and fertilizing overflows and its many mouths. Name not mentioned in scripture, but alluded to as "the river," Gen. 41:1; Ex. 2:3; 7:21; "the river of Egypt," Gen. 15:18; "flood of Egypt," Am. 8:8; Sihor, "black," Josh. 13:3; Shihor, "dark blue," 1 Chr. 13:5;

"Nachal of Egypt," "river of Cush," etc.

NIN'E-VEH (*dwelling of Ninus*). Capital of Assyria, on river Tigris. Founded by Asshur, Gen. 10:11. At height of its wealth and splendor during time of Jonah and Nahum, and burden of their prophecies. Taken by Medes about B.C. 750, and destroyed by combined Medes and Babylonians, B.C. 606, Jonah; Nah. 1.-3.; Zeph. 2:13. Among the ruins of Nineveh, which was supposed to embrace Nimrud and other suburbs, have been discovered many palaces and temples, and a richly sculptured obelisk whose references are to Syria and Israel.

NO'AH (*rest*). (1) Ninth in descent from Adam, Gen. 5:28-32. Chosen to build the ark, Gen. 6:8-22. Saved from the flood, with his three sons, Shem, Ham, and Japheth, Gen. 7., 8. Repeopled the earth, Gen. 9., 10. Died at age of 950 years. (2) A daughter of Zelophehad, Num. 26:33.

O''BA-DI'AH (*servant of God*). (1) A Judahite, 1 Chr. 3:21. (2) A chief of Issachar, 1 Chr. 7:3. (3) Son of Azel, 1 Chr. 8:38. (4) A Levite, 1 Chr. 9:16. (5) A Gadite, 1 Chr. 12:9. (6) A court officer under Ahab, 1 Kgs. 18:3-16. (7) A teacher of the law, 2 Chr. 17:7. (8) Others, in 1 Chr. 27:19; 2 Chr. 34:12; Ez. 8:9; Neh. 10:5; 12:25. (9) Fourth of minor prophets. Prophesied after capture of Jerusalem. His book, 31st of O. T., is a denunciation of Edom. Nothing known of his history.

PAL''ES-TI'NA, PAL'ES-TINE (*land of sojourners*). Philistia, land of the Philistines, Ps. 40:8; 83:7. Palestina, Ex. 15:14; Isa. 14:29, 31. Palestine, Joel 3:4. Canaan, Gen. 12:5; Ex. 15:15; Holy Land, Zech. 2:12. The indefinitely bounded region promised to Abraham, lying between the Mediterranean Sea and Jordan River and Dead Sea. It also embraced the Hebrew settlements beyond Jordan, Gen. 15:18; 17:8; Num. 24:2-12; Deut. 1:7.

PAR'A-BLE (*comparison*). Allegorical representation of something real in nature or human affairs, whence a moral is drawn. A favorite method of Oriental teaching, 2 Sam. 12:1-4; Isa. 5:1-7. Christ spoke over 30 parables, Matt. 13:3-8; 24-30, 31, 32, and elsewhere in Gospels.

PASS'O-VER (*passing over*). First of three great Jewish feasts, instituted in honor of the "passing over" of the Hebrew households by the destroying angel, Ex. 12., 13:3-10; 23:14-19; Lev. 23: 4-14. Called the "feast of unleavened bread." The Christian Passover is "The Lord's Supper," eucharist, Matt. 27:62; Luke 22:1-20; John 19:42.

PAUL (*small*). In Hebrew, Saul. Born at Tarsus in Cilicia, of Benjamite parents, about the beginning of 1st century; a Pharisee in faith; a tent-maker by trade, Phil. 3:5; Acts 18:3; 21:39; 23:6. Studied law with Gamaliel at Jerusalem; persecuted early Christians; converted near Damascus, Acts 5:34; 7:58; 9:1-22. Commissioned an apostle to the Gentiles, Acts 26:13-20. Carried the gospel to Asia Minor, Greece, and Rome. Author of fourteen epistles, amplifying the Christian faith. Supposably a martyr at Rome, A.D. 68.

PEN'TA-TEUCH (*five-fold book*). Greek name for the first five O. T. books, or books of Moses. Called Torah, "the law," by Hebrews.

PEN'TE-COST (*fiftieth day*). The Hebrew harvest-home festival, celebrated on fiftieth day from the Passover, or on the date of the giving of the law at Sinai, Ex. 23:16; 34:22; Lev. 23: 15-22; Num. 28. In the Christian Church, Pentecost is celebrated seven weeks after Easter, to commemorate the day in Acts 2:1-14.

PE'TER (*stone, rock*). Simon, or Simeon; son of Jonas, Matt. 16:17; Acts 15:14. A fisherman, resident at Capernaum, Matt. 8:14; called, Matt. 4:18-20; name changed to Peter, John 1:42. Founder of Christian Church among the Jews, Acts 2.; spokesman of the apostles, Acts 10.; author of two epistles; a probable martyr at Rome. His first epistle is dated from Babylon; his second is his valedictory. Both are advisory and exhortatory.

PHA'RAOH (*sun-king*). General name of Egyptian kings. Only a few are definitely named in the Bible. Different ones alluded to are, Gen. 12:15; 41.;

Ex. 1:8; 5:1; 1 Chr. 4:18; 1 Kgs. 11: 18-22; 9:16; 2 Kgs. 18:21; Pharaohnechoh, 2 Kgs. 23:29; Pharaoh-hophra, Jer. 37:5-8.

PHIL'IP (*lover of horses*). (1) The apostle of Bethsaida, of whom little is known, Matt. 10:3; Mark 3:18; Luke 6:14; John 6:5-9; Acts 1:13. (2) The evangelist and deacon, resident at Cæsarea, and preacher throughout Samaria, Acts 6:5; 8:5-13; 21:8-10. (3) The tetrarch. [HEROD.] (4) Husband of Herodias, Matt. 14:3. [HEROD.] (5) Governor of Jerusalem under Antiochus, and regent of Syria, 2 Macc. 5:22. (6) Philip V., king of Macedonia, 1 Macc. 8:5. (7) King of Macedonia, B.C. 360-336, and father of Alexander the Great, 1 Macc. 1:1.

PHŒ-NI'CIA (*land of palm-trees*). Phenica in Acts 21:2. Phenice in Acts 11:19; 15:3. In O. T. referred to as Tyre and Sidon, or coasts of Tyre and Sidon. The small coast country north of Palestine, noted for its commercial enterprise, learning, and skill in arts. Included in the Land of Promise but never conquered, Josh. 13:4-6. David and Solomon employed its sailors and artisans, 2 Sam. 5:11; 1 Kgs. 5.

PI'LATE (*spear-armed*). Pontius Pilate in Matt. 27:2. Sixth Roman procurator of Judea, A.D. 26-36. Official residence at Cæsarea, with judicial visits to other places. Christ was brought before him at Jerusalem for judgment. He found no guilt, but lost his moral courage in the presence of the mob. Eventually banished to Gaul, Luke 23:1-7; John 18:27-40; 19.

PLAGUE (*blow*). Pestilential disease, Lev. 13:2-8; 26:25. Any calamitous visitation, Mark 5:29; Luke 7:21. The judgments of God on Egypt are called plagues. They were (1) Nile changed to blood, Ex. 7:14-25. (2) Visitation of frogs, Ex. 8:1-15. (3) Lice, Ex. 8:16-19. (4) Flies, Ex. 8:20-32. (5) Murrain, Ex. 9:1-7. (6) Boils, Ex. 9: 8-12. (7) Hail, Ex. 9:13-35. (8) Locusts, Ex. 10:1-20. (9) Darkness, Ex. 10:21-28. (10) Smiting of the firstborn, Ex. 12:29, 30.

PRIEST (*presbyter, elder*). Representative of man in things appertaining to God. Assistants of Moses as mediator,

Ex. 24:5. Function of priesthood conferred on Levites, Ex. 28. Priests divided into regular courses, 1 Chr. 24:1-19; 2 Chr. 23:8; Luke 1:5.

PROPH'ET (*speaking beforehand*). Who tells the future under God's inspiration. The prophetic order embraced political, as well as spiritual, advisers and warners. The books of seventeen—four greater and thirteen lesser prophets —are comprised in the O. T. Christ is the preeminent and eternal prophet, Luke 24:27, 44.

PSALMS (*play a stringed instrument*). In Hebrew, "Praises." The collection of one hundred and fifty lyrics which compose the nineteenth O. T. book. The liturgical hymnbook of the Hebrews, and accepted by early Christians. Authorship of seventy of them ascribed to David. The most perfect specimens of Hebrew poetry extant.

RED SEA. The arm of Gulf of Aden which separates Egypt from Arabia. "The sea," Ex. 14:2, 9, 16, 21, 28; 15: 1-19; Josh. 24:6, 7. "Egyptian sea," Isa. 11:15. "Sea of Suph," *weedy* or *reedy sea,* translated "Red Sea," Ex. 10:19; 13:18; 15:4; 23:31; Num. 21:4. In N. T., the Greek "Erythrean," or Red Sea, Acts 7:36. At its head it separates into gulfs of Akaba and Suez, the latter of which the Israelites crossed.

REV"E-LA'TION (*veil drawn back*). (1) Scripturally, revealing truth through divine agency or by supernatural means, 2 Cor. 12:1-7. (2) Book of Revelation, or Apocalypse; last of N. T. books; written by the Apostle John, about A.D. 95-97, probably at Ephesus. It is a record of his inspired visions while a prisoner on the island of Patmos. Its aim is much disputed, but it is seemingly a prophetic panorama of church history to the end of time.

ROME, RO'MANS. First mentioned in Bible in 1 Macc. 1:10, when Rome was pushing her conquests in Palestine and Syria. The capital, Rome, is on the Tiber, about 15 miles from the sea. Founded B.C. 752. Governed by kings till B.C. 509; then by consuls till Augustus Cæsar became emperor, B.C. 30. At the Christian era Rome was virtual mistress of the civilized world. Empire declined rapidly after removal of capital to Constantinople by Constantine, A.D. 328. Gospel early introduced among Romans, but Christians persecuted till time of Constantine. Palestine was ruled from Rome by kings, procurators, governors, or proconsuls. Paul wrote his celebrated epistle to the Romans from Corinth, about A.D. 58, to show that Jew and Gentile were alike subject to sin and in equal need of justification and sanctification.

SAB'BATH (*rest*). Rest day, or seventh of the week, Gen. 2:2, 3. Became a Mosaic institution for rest and festal occasions, Ex. 16:23-30; 20:8-11; Lev. 19:3, 30; 23:3; 25:4-9; Deut. 5:12-15. Day for consulting prophets, 2 Kgs. 4: 23. A day of teaching and joy, Neh. 8: 1-12; Hos. 2:11. A whole week of time is implied in Matt. 28:1; Mark 16:1; Luke 24:1; John 20:1; Acts 20:7; 1 Cor. 16:2. Among Christians, the day after the Hebrew Sabbath, or seventh-day, gradually and till fully established, became the Sabbath, or first-day, in commemoration of the resurrection of Christ. Hence, "The Lord's Day," John 20:26; Acts 20:6-11; 1 Cor. 16:2; Rev. 1:10.

SAB'BATH DAY'S JOURNEY. Travel on the Sabbath was limited, Ex. 16:29. Custom seemed to sanction 2000 paces from the walls of a city as sufficient for all needs on the day of rest, Acts 1:12.

SAD'DU-CEES (*disciples of Zadok*). A Jewish sect, supposably Zadokites, 1 Kgs. 1:32-45, whose chief tenets were (1) rejection of the divinity of the Mosaic oral law and traditions; (2) rejection of the later O. T. books, but acceptance of the Mosaic teachings; (3) denial of angel and spiritual existence, and consequent immortality of the soul; (4) belief in the absolute moral freedom of man. Their hatred of Christianity was as bitter as that of the Pharisees, Matt. 3:7; Mark 12:18; Luke 20:27; Acts 4:1; 5:17; 23:6-10. Though composed of men of position, the sect was never very numerous nor influential, and it disappeared from history after the first century of the Christian era.

SALT SEA. The Dead Sea. "Sea of the plain," Deut. 4:49; 2 Kgs. 14:25.

"Salt sea," Deut. 3:17; Josh. 3:16; 12:3. "East sea," Ezek. 47:18; Joel 2:20; Zech. 14:8. "The sea," Ezek. 47:8. "Vale of Siddim," Gen. 14:3. "Sodomitish sea," 1 Esdr. 5:7. Title "Dead Sea" not found among Hebrew writers, but introduced by Greek authors. Situate 16 miles E. of Jerusalem; 46 miles long by 10 wide; 1300 feet below the level of the Mediterranean; waters intensely salt; receives waters of Jordan from the north; no outlet.

SA-MA′RI-A (*watch mountain*). (1) The kingdom of Samaria, synonymous with the kingdom of Israel, lay to the north of Judah. It varied in size at different times, but in general embraced the territory of the ten revolting tribes on either side of the Jordan, 1 Kgs. 13:32. Named from its capital, Samaria. In N. T. times, Samaria was one of the three subdivisions of Palestine, lying between Judea on the south and Galilee on the north. (2) Capital of the kingdom of Samaria or Israel, and located 30 miles north of Jerusalem. Founded by Omri, king of Israel, about B.C. 925, and called Samaria, after Shemer, from whom he bought the ground, 1 Kgs. 16:23, 24. It became a beautiful and strong city and remained the capital till Shalmaneser, the Assyrian, destroyed it and the empire, B.C. 721, 2 Kgs. 18:9-12. Herod rebuilt it and restored much of its ancient splendor, naming it Sebaste in honor of Augustus, who gave it to him. Philip preached the gospel there, Acts 8:5-9. It is now a modest village called Sebastiyeh, which perpetuates the name Sebaste, and is noted for its many ruins, chief of which is the famous colonnade, 3000 feet in length, 100 columns of which are still standing. Respecting the city the prophecy, Mic. 1:6, has been literally fulfilled.

SAM′SON (*sunlike*). Son of Manoah, of Dan, and judge of Israel for 20 years, Judg. 13:3-25. Noted for his great strength, marvellous exploits, and moral weakness. Contrary to the wishes of his parents, and to the law as laid down in Ex. 34:16, Deut. 7:3, he married a Philistine woman of Timnath, whom he deserted on account of her treachery, Judg. 14. Wishing to return to her, and finding her given to another, he wreaked his vengeance on the Philistines by burning their crops and slaughtering great numbers of them, Judg. 15:1-8. He was surrounded by 3000 of his enemies, while he dwelt on the rock Etam, and surrendered to them, but burst his bands, and routed them with great slaughter, Judg. 15:9-19. Again he was surrounded by enemies in Gaza, but escaped by carrying away the gates of the city. The secret of his strength was finally detected by Delilah, and he was imprisoned and made blind. He finally killed himself and numerous enemies by pulling down the pillars of the house in which they were feasting, Judg. 16.

SAM′U-EL (*God hath heard*). Son of Elkanah and Hannah, celebrated Hebrew prophet and last of the judges, 1 Sam. 1:19-28. Educated under Eli, 1 Sam. 3:4-14, and became his successor in the prophetic office. His sons proved so recreant that the people demanded a king, and Samuel anointed Saul, and resigned his authority to him, 1 Sam. 12. He also anointed David, Saul's successor, 1 Sam. 16:13. He died at Ramah, 1 Sam. 25:1. The two books which bear his name, the 9th and 10th of O. T., are called also First and Second Books of Kings. They were originally one book and contain the lives of Samuel, Saul, and David. The authorship is ascribed to a period subsequent to the secession of the ten tribes, and it is clearly an authorship different from Kings, for in Kings there are many references to the law, while in Samuel there are none. In Kings the Exile is alluded to; it is not so in Samuel. The plans of the two works vary; Samuel is biographical, Kings annalistic.

SAN′HE-DRIM, SAN′HE-DRIN (*seated together*). The supreme council of the Jewish nation, whose germ was in the seventy elders, Num. 11:16, 17, and further development in Jehoshaphat's tribunal, 2 Chr. 19:8-11. In full power after the captivity, and lasted till A.D. 425. The "great Sanhedrim" was composed of 71 priests, scribes, and elders, and presided over by the high priest. The "lesser Sanhedrims" were provincial courts in the towns, and composed of 23 members appointed by the "great Sanhedrim." The word usually appears as "council" in

N. T., Matt. 5:22; Mark 14:55; John 11:47; Acts 4:5-7. The members of the Sanhedrim embraced the three classes, priests, elders, and scribes. After the Roman conquest it had no control of the death power, but the confirmation and execution of capital sentences rested with the Roman procurator. Thus it was that while the Sanhedrim condemned Christ for blasphemy, he was not brought under the Roman judgment of death till accused by the Jews of treason, Matt. 26:65, 66; John 18:31; 19:12. The stoning of Stephen, Acts 7:57-59, was either due to mob excitement, or else illegal.

SA'RAH (*princess*). (1) Wife of Abraham and mother of Isaac, Gen. 11:29; 21:2, 3. Name changed from Sarai to Sarah, Gen. 17:15, 16. At Abraham's request she passed herself off as his sister during their sojourn in Egypt, Gen. 12:10-20, which angered the Pharaoh and led to their banishment. Relentless toward Hagar (whom she had given to Abraham as a concubine) when she bore Ishmael, and caused her to be banished to the desert, Gen. 16:5-16; deceitful when Isaac was promised, Gen. 18:15; cruel again toward Hagar on the occasion of Isaac's weaning, causing her to be banished finally from the household, Gen. 21:9-21. Commended for her faith, Heb. 11:11; and obedience, 1 Pet. 3:6. Died at age of 127 years and buried at Machpelah, Gen. 23. (2) Daughter of Asher, Num. 26:46.

SA'TAN (*adversary*). In O. T. a common noun, meaning enemy or adversary in general, 1 Sam. 29:4; 2 Sam. 19:22; except in Job 1:6, 12; 2:1; Zech. 3:1, where the word becomes a proper noun, and spiritual representative of evil. In N. T. sense, chief of the evil spirits; great adversary of man; the devil, Matt. 4:10; 25:41; Rev. 20, and elsewhere. Called also "the prince of this world;" "the wicked one;" "the tempter;" and in Rev. 12:9, the old serpent, the devil, and Satan.

SAUL (*wished*). (1) An early king of Edom, Gen. 36:37, 38. Shaul in 1 Chr. 1:48, 49. (2) A Benjamite, son of Kish, and first king of Israel. Anointed by Samuel; reigned b.c. 1095-1055; slain with his sons at Gilboa. His versatile career is described in 1 Sam. 9.-31. He stands in Bible history for the stature, strength, and ruggedness of character so essential to judges in times of danger or necessary reform, and for the bravery, generalship and self-confidence of one called on to institute a new empire. Of boundless ambition and erratic judgment, he usurped the priestly function, and drew the reproaches of the aged prophet Samuel, who had surrendered his line in anointing him. The announcement that royalty could not be perpetuated in his family drove him to inexcusable follies, yet with the courage of youth he fought his last despairing battle with the Philistines, and finished his course on his own sword. (3) Hebrew name of Paul, Acts 13:9.

SCRIBE (*writer*). The Hebrew scribe or writer appears to have been at first a court or military official, Ex. 5:6; Judg. 5:14; then secretary or recorder, for kings, priests, and prophets, 2 Sam. 8:17; 20:25; finally a secretary of state, doctor, or teacher, Ez. 7:6. Scribes became a class or guild, copyists and expounders of the law, and through their innovations fell under the same denunciations as priests and Pharisees, Matt. 23:1-33; Mark 7:5-13; Luke 5:30.

SERPENT (*creeper*). The Hebrew original embraces the entire serpent genus. Serpents numerous and venomous in Bible lands. The word appears in Scripture under various names; adder, supposably the cerastes, Gen. 49:17; asp, or cobra, Deut. 32:33; cockatrice, Jer. 8:17; viper, Job 20:16. Subtile, Gen. 3:1; wise, Matt. 10:16; poisonous, Prov. 23:32; sharp-tongued, Ps. 140:3; charmed, Ps. 58:5; emblem of wickedness, Matt. 23:33; cruelty, Pa. 58:4; treachery, Gen. 49:17; the devil, Rev. 12:9-15; fiery serpents sent as a punishment, Num. 21:6; sight of "brazen serpent," an antidote for poison of bite, Num. 21:8, 9; "fiery flying serpent," a probable allusion to dragon, Isa. 14:29.

SEV'EN. A favorite, and often symbolic, number among Hebrews, Gen. 2:2; 7:2; 41:2, 3. Used as a round number, 1 Sam. 2:5; Matt. 12:45. Type of abundance and completeness, Gen. 4:15, 24; Matt. 18:21, 22. These references, and other places, show a seventh day and seventh year sabbath and a seven times seventh year of Jubilee; also sacrificial animals limited to seven, and the golden candlesticks. Seven priests with seven trumpets surrounded Jericho for seven days, and seven times on the seventh day. In the Apocalypse we find seven churches, seven candlesticks, seven stars, seven seals, seven trumpets, seven vials, seven plagues, seven angels.

SHE'BA (*oath*). (1) Son of Bichri, a Benjamite, who revolted from David and was beheaded, 2 Sam. 20:1-22. (2) A Gadite chief, 1 Chr. 5:13. (3) A descendant of Ham, Gen. 10:7; 1 Chr. 1:9. (4) Son of Joktan, Gen. 10:28. (5) Son of Jokshan, Gen. 25:3; 1 Chr. 1:32. (6) The kingdom of Sheba, whose queen visited Solomon, 1 Kgs. 10:1-13; 2 Chr. 9:1-12. This country has been variously located in Africa, in Arabia, on the Persian Gulf, and in Arabia, on the Red Sea. The burden of authority identifies it with Yemen or Arabia Felix, on the Red Sea, and peopled by descendants of Sheba, son of Joktan. (7) A town in Simeon, Josh. 19:2. Probably the Shema of Josh. 15:26.

SHEEP. An important animal among Hebrews, and a main source of wealth. Shepherd's occupation highly respectable, Gen. 4:2; Ex. 3:1; 1 Sam. 16:11; Job 42:12, though odious to Egyptians. Used for sacrifices, Ex. 20:24; 29:38; Lev. 9:3; for food, 1 Sam. 25:18. Wool used for clothing, Lev. 13:47. Skins used for tabernacle coverings, Ex. 25:5. Paid as tribute, 2 Kgs. 3:4. Sheep and shepherd employed much figuratively, 2 Chr. 18:16; Ps. 119:176; Matt. 9:36; John 10:11; Heb. 13:20. The common sheep of Syria and Palestine was the broad-tailed variety.

SHEP'HERD (*herder of sheep*). A highly honorable occupation among pastoral Hebrews, engaged in by both sexes, Gen. 29:6; 30:29-35; Ex. 2:16-22. Often arduous and dangerous employment, Gen. 31:40; 1 Sam. 17:34. Equipment consisted of a sheepskin mantle, a scrip or wallet, a sling and crook. He led the flock to pasture in the morning, tended them by day and folded and watched them at night, Job 30:1; Luke 2:8; John 10:4. The office of sheep-master or chief shepherd was one of great trust as well as honor, 2 Kgs. 3:4; Heb.

13:20; 1 Pet. 5:4. It was the shepherd's duty to count the sheep daily and to tithe them, and he was held responsible for lost ones, Gen. 31:38, 39; Ex. 22:12, 13; Lev. 27:32; Jer. 33:13. Shepherd is used figuratively for Jehovah in Ps. 80:1; Jer. 31:10; for kings, Ezek. 34:10; in N. T. for Christ, John 10:11; Heb. 13:20; 1 Pet. 5:4. It is applied also to teachers in the synagogue and to those who preside over it. Hence pastor and minister of the gospel.

SI'LAS (*Silvanus, woody*). An eminent member of the early Christian church. Written Silvanus in Paul's epistles. Resided at Jerusalem as teacher, but accompanied Paul on his tours, and was his fellow-prisoner at Philippi. Said to have been bishop of Corinth, Acts 15:22, 32-34, 40; 17:14; 18:5; 2 Cor. 1:19; 1 Thess. 1:1.

SIM'E-ON (*who hears*). (1) Son of Jacob and Leah, Gen. 29:33. For the crime in Gen. 34:25-30 his father denounced him, Gen. 49:5-7. His tribe was small, Num. 1:22, 23; 26:14, and their inheritance a scattered portion of Canaan, Josh. 19:1-9. (2) Son of Judah in genealogy of Christ, Luke 3:30. (3) Simon Peter, Acts 15:14. (4) a venerable and pious Jew who blessed the child Jesus in the temple, Luke 2:25-35. (5) Simeon Niger, Acts 13:1. [NIGER.]

SI'MON (*Simeon*). (1) Several distinguished Jews bore this name during the Maccabean period. (2) A native of Samaria and famous sorcerer, who professed Christ for mercenary purposes, Acts 8:9-24. (3) Simon Peter, Matt. 4:18. [PETER.] (4) Simon the Canaanite, or Simon Zelotes, was a member of the party of the Zealots who advocated the Jewish ritual, and an apostle, Matt. 10:4. (5) Simon the brother of Jesus, Matt. 13:55; Mark 6:3. (6) Simon the Pharisee, in whose house a woman anointed the feet of Jesus, Luke 7:36-50. (7) Simon, the leper of Bethany, Matt. 26:6. (8) Simon of Cyrene, who was compelled to bear Christ's cross, Matt. 27:32; Mark 15:21; Luke 23:26. (9) The tanner of Joppa with whom Peter lodged, Acts 9:43. (10) Simon the father of Judas Iscariot, John 6:71; 13:2, 26.

SI'NAI (*bushy*). The peninsula of

Sinai lies between the two great arms of the Red Sea, Gulf of Akba on the east, and Gulf of Suez on the west. This region contains the mountain system of Horeb or Sinai, on one of whose mounts, or peaks, God appeared to Moses in the burning bush, Ex. 3:1-5, amid whose surrounding wilderness the wandering Israelites encamped, Ex. 19:1, 2, and from whose cloud-obscured heights the law was delivered to Moses, Ex. 19:3-25; 20.-40.; Lev. The numbering also took place there, Num. 1.-10.:1-12. The peninsula is a triangle whose base extends from the head of Suez to Akaba. This base is pierced by the plateau of Tih, the "desert of wandering," south of which are those tumultous mountain clusters above mentioned, central among which is Mount Sinai. The coast ranges along Akaba and Suez are systematic and elevated. The region was a dependency of Egypt from earliest times, but became subject to Rome.

SOL'O-MON (*peaceful*). Last of David's sons by Bathsheba. Named Jedidiah, "beloved of God," by Nathan, 1 Chr. 3:5; 2 Sam. 12:25. Placed in Nathan's care. Secured the throne according to David's pledge, 1 Kgs. 1:13-53, and much to the consternation of Adonijah, the legal successor. Reigned forty years, B.C. 1015-975. Confirmed his father's conquests, built the palace and temple, extended commerce, contracted favorable alliances, grew famous for wisdom, raised his kingdom to great wealth, splendor, and power, mingled justice with cruelty, endorsed true and false worship, encouraged literature, and wrote largely himself, fell a prey to the sensualities of his time and position, died leaving his kingdom under the eclipse of faction and on the edge of decay, 1 Kgs. 2.-11.; 2 Chr. 1.-9.

SPAIN. Anciently the whole peninsula of southwestern Europe, embracing Spain and Portugal; known to Greeks as Iberia and to Romans as Hispania. If identical with Tarshish, then known to Hebrews in Solomon's time; certainly to Phœnicians. Known to Paul, who contemplated a visit to it, Rom. 15:24-28. Christianity early introduced there.

SPIR'IT (*breath*). The breath, 2 Thess. 2:8. The vital principle, Eccl. 8:8.

Elsewhere, the soul. [SOUL.] Holy Spirit, or Ghost, is the third person in the Trinity, 2 Cor. 13:14; Acts 15:28. Though Holy Spirit and Holy Ghost are synonymous in meaning, preference is given to the latter form in the Scriptures, Matt. 1:18; John 1:33; Acts 2:4; Rom. 5:5, and elsewhere, the former being used only four times.

STE'PHEN (*crown*). Chief of the first seven deacons, and first Christian martyr. A Greek convert of strong faith and great eloquence. Arrested and tried before the Sanhedrim, but stoned to death by an angry mob, before he had time to finish his defence. The date of his martyrdom is fixed at about A.D. 37. It was followed by the conversion of Saul, who was present at the stoning, and a bitter persecutor of early Christians at the time, Acts 6:5-15; 7., 8:1-3.

SYN'A-GOGUE (*led together*). The Jewish assembly for social and religious purposes seems to have had its origin during the captivity, or to have been an outgrowth of it, Ez. 8:15; Neh. 8:2; 9:1. The casual, or house, assemblages soon ran into regular congregations, with suitable buildings and stated meetings, at requisite points. These were the synagogues, often elaborate and costly, presided over by a chief, or rabbi, assisted by a council of elders, Mark 5:22, 35; Luke 4:20; John 16:2; Acts 18:8.

SYR'I-A. The Hebrew Aram. So indefinitely bounded at different times as to have been associated with Assyria (whence its name) and Babylon. More definitely the country to the north of Canaan, extending from the Tigris to the Mediterranean, and northward to the Taurus ranges. Damascus was the capital, and centre of wealth, learning, and power. Joshua subdued its petty kings, Josh. 11:2-18; David reduced it to submission, 2 Sam. 8., 10. During Solomon's reign it became independent, 1 Kgs. 11:23-25. The earliest recorded settlers in Syria were Hittites and other Hamitic races. The Shemitic element entered it from the southeast under Abraham and Chedorlaomer. After Syria became independent it was a persistent enemy of the Jews, 1 Kgs. 15:18-20; 20., 22.; 2 Kgs. 6:8-33; 7., 9:14, 15; 10:32, 33; 13:3, 14-25. The attempt of the Syrian king to ally Israel with him for the overthrow of Judah led Ahaz to call in the help of Assyria, and Syria was soon merged into the great Assyrian empire. It was conquered by Alexander the Great, B.C. 333, and finally fell to the lot of Seleucus Nicator, who made it the central province of his empire, with the capital at Antioch. The Syriac language was closely allied to the Hebrew.

TAB'ER-NA-CLE (*little shed or tent*). Tent of Jehovah, or movable sanctuary, which Moses was directed to erect in the wilderness, Ex. 25:8. Its plan, materials, and furnishings are described in Ex. 25:9-40; 26., 27. It could be readily taken down and set up and accompanied the Israelites during their wanderings, Ex. 40:38. During the conquest it was stationed at Gilgal, Josh. 4:19; 9:6; 10:15; and at Ebal, Josh. 8:30-35. After the conquest it was set up at Shiloh, Josh. 18:1, where it remained during the time of the Judges and where the ark was captured by the Philistines, 1 Sam. 4:17, 22. Sometime after the return of the ark it was taken to Jerusalem and placed in a new tabernacle, and finally in the temple, 2 Sam. 6:17; 1 Chr. 15:1, but the old structure was still venerated, as long as it remained at Shiloh. It was afterwards removed to Nob, 1 Sam. 21:1-9, and in the reign of David to Gibeon, 1 Chr. 16:39; 21:29, where it was at the beginning of Solomon's reign. Some suppose that the tabernacle and its furniture were moved into Solomon's temple when it was completed.

TAL'ENT (*weight*). A Hebrew weight and denomination for money, equal to 3,000 shekels, or 93¾ pounds of silver, and varying in value from $1,550 to $2,000, Ex. 38:25; Matt. 18:24. The Attic, or Greek talent, was worth about $1,200; the Roman great talent, $500; the Roman small talent, $375.

TAR'SUS (*wing*). Chief city of Cilicia, Asia Minor, on river Cydnus, six miles from the Mediterranean. Birthplace of Paul and rival of Athens and Alexandria in literature and fine arts, Acts 9:11, 30; 11:25; 21:39; 22:3. At the mouth of the Cydnus were fine docks, and Tarsus had, at one time, considerable commercial importance. Some would identify it with Tarshish. It was founded by the Assyrian, Sardanapalus, and was captured by the Romans and made a free city. It is now represented by Tersons, a mean Turkish city with a fluctuating population.

TEM'PLE. (1) Solomon's temple erected at Jerusalem on Mount Moriah. David proposed to transform the tabernacle into a permanent temple at Jerusalem, and collected much material, but its construction was forbidden by the prophet Nathan, 1 Chr. 17.; 2 Sam. 7:7-29. Solomon completed the work after David's plans and with the assistance of Hiram, king of Tyre. He began to build in the fourth year of his reign, B.C. 1012, and finished and dedicated it B.C. 1005, 1 Chr. 21., 22., 28:11-19; 29:4-7; 1 Kgs. 6.-8.; 2 Chr. 3.-7. This costly and imposing structure, for the age, was pillaged several times during the Eastern invasions, and was finally destroyed during the last siege of Jerusalem by Nebuchadnezzar, B.C. 588. (2) The temple of Zerubbabel was begun in B.C. 534, by the returned captives under the lead of Zerubbabel and the patronage of King Cyrus of Persia. Owing to discords and direct opposition it was not completed till B.C. 515. It was much inferior to the first in cost and beauty, though one third larger in dimensions. It was partially destroyed by Antiochus Epiphanes, B.C. 163, and restored by Judas Maccabeus, Ez. 3.-6.; 2 Macc. 10:1-9. (3) Herod the Great removed the decayed temple of Zerubbabel and began the erection of a new one B.C. 17. This gorgeous and costly structure was not completed till the time of Herod Agrippa II., A.D. 64. It was of marble, after Græco-Roman designs, and was destroyed by the Romans under Titus, A.D. 70, thus verifying Mark 13:2.

THES"SA-LO-NI'CA. Ancient Thermæ, "hot springs;" now Salonika. Enlarged by Cassander and called Thessalonica after his wife, daughter of Alexander the Great. An important city of Macedonia, at the head of the Gulf of Thessalonica, or Thermæ. Paul visited it during his second tour and founded a strong church there, to whose members he wrote two epistles, Acts 17:1-9.

THOM'AS (*twin*). The cautious, susceptible, even doubtful, apostle, whose name, in Greek, was Didymus, "twin," Matt. 10:3; Mark 3:18; Luke 6:15; John 11:16; 14:5, 6; 20:24-29; Acts 1:13.

TIM'O-THY (*honoring God*). Son of Eunice, a Jewess, by a Gentile father. Born in Derbe or Lystra, Lycaonia, Acts 16:1; 2 Tim. 1:5. Converted by Paul and became a close friend and valuable assistant, Rom. 16:21; Heb. 13:23. Recipient of two of Paul's epistles, 15th and 16th N. T. books. The first was written to him while at Ephesus, probably from Macedonia, and about A.D. 65. The second seems to have been written from Rome some three years later. They are called pastoral epistles, because devoted to description of church work and earnest exhortation to faithfulness.

TITHE (*tenth*). One tenth of all produce of lands and herds was set apart, under the Levitical law, for the support of the Levites, and a tenth of their tenth went to the priests. There was tithe regulations among other nations, Gen. 14:20; 28:22; Lev. 27:30-33; Num. 18:21-32; Deut. 12:17, 18; 14:22-27. The Pharisees tithed their mint, anise, cummin, and rue, Matt. 23:23.

TI'TUS (*pleasant*). A distinguished Grecian who became a Christian convert and a companion of Paul in his trials and on his missionary tours, Tit. 1:4; Gal. 2:3-5; 2 Cor. 8:6, 16, 23. Entrusted with many important commissions, 2 Cor. 12:18; 2 Tim. 4:10; Tit. 1:5. Paul wrote an epistle to Titus, the 17th N. T. book, about A.D. 65, designed to instruct him in his ministerial duties in Crete, which were arduous, on account of the immorality of the people.

TONGUES. "And the whole earth was of one language, and of one speech," Gen. 11:1. Confusion of tongues and dispersion of peoples coincident, Gen. 11:7-9. "New tongues," Mark 16:17, is the first notice of a gift specially characteristic of the first outpouring of the Spirit. Ten days afterward the promise was fulfilled in the Pentecostal phenomenon, Acts 2:1-13.

TYRE (*rock*). The celebrated commercial city of Phœnicia on the Mediterranean coast. It fell to the lot of Asher, but was never conquered, Josh. 19:29. In intimate commercial relation with Hebrews, and King Hiram furnished and artificers and material for the temple and royal houses at Jerusalem, 2 Sam. 5:11; 1 Kgs. 5:1; 7:13; 9:11-14; 1 Chr. 14:1; 2 Chr. 2:2-18. The city was denounced by the prophets, Isa. 23:1-17; Jer. 27:3; Ezek. 26:3-21. It resisted the five-year siege of Shalmaneser and the thirteen-year siege of Nebuchadnezzar, but fell before that of Alexander. Referred to in N. T., Matt. 11:21, 22; 15:21; Mark 7:24. Paul visited it, Acts 21:3, 4.

UR (*light, region*). (1) Place where Abraham lived with his father Terah and his wife Sarah, before they started for the land of Canaan, Gen. 11:28, 31. Mentioned in Gen. 15:7, as of the Chaldees, and Acts 7:2, as in Mesopotamia. (2) Father of Eliphal, one of David's guard, 1 Chr. 11:35. Called Ahasbai in 2 Sam. 23:34.

ZAC-CHÆ'US (*just*). The rich chief among publicans, resident at Jericho, who climbed a tree to see Jesus pass, was invited down, became the host of Jesus, and was converted, Luke 19:1-10.

ZACH"A-RI'AS (*remembered by Jehovah*). Greek form of Zachariah. (1) The name is borne by many priests and laymen in the books of Esdras. (2) Father of John the Baptist and husband of Elizabeth. He was a priest of the course of Abia, or Abijah, 1 Chr. 24:10, and probably lived at Hebron, Luke 1:5-25, 57-80. (3) Son of Barachias, who was slain between the temple and the altar, Matt. 23:35; Luke 11:51.

ZEB'E-DEE (*God's portion*). A fisherman of Galilee, husband of Salome, and father of the apostles James the Great and John, Matt. 4:21; 27:56; Mark 1:19, 20; 15:40. His home is located at or near Bethsaida, and he appears to have been able to employ help in his occupation, Mark 1:20.

ZECH"A-RI'AH (*memory of God*). Son of Benechiah, Zech. 1:1; of Iddo, Ez. 5:1. Eleventh of the minor prophets and contemporary of Haggai, born in Babylon during the captivity, returned with Zerubbabel, Ez. 5:1; 6:14. The time of his prophecies is reckoned as between B.C. 520 and 518, during the period of building the second temple, whose completion was largely due to his energies as priest and prophet. His book, 38th of O. T., is divided into two parts. Chapters 1.-8. contain hopeful visions of the restored Hebrew state, exhortations to turn to Jehovah, warnings against God's enemies. Chapters 9.-14. are prophetic of the future fortunes of the theocracy, the conversion of Israel, the glorification of God's kingdom and of the coming of the Messiah. The style of the book is obscure. Many critics attribute the authorship of the second division of the book to Jeremiah. (2) A Reubenite chief, at time of the captivity by Tiglath-pileser, 1 Chr. 5:7. (3) A Korhite Levite, keeper of one of the doors of the tabernacle, 1 Chr. 9:21. (4) A son of Jehiel, 1 Chr. 9:37. (5) A Levite of the second order, one of the temple musicians, 1 Chr. 15:18, 20. (6) A priest who blew the trumpet before the ark on its return, 1 Chr. 15:24. (7) A Kohathite Levite, 1 Chr. 24:25. (8) A Merarite Levite, 1 Chr. 26:11. (9) A Manassite, 1 Chr. 27:21. (10) A prince of Judah in reign of Jehoshaphat, 2 Chr. 17:7. (11) Father of Jahaziel, 2 Chr. 20:14. (12) A son of Jehoshaphat, 2 Chr. 21:2. (13) Son of the high priest Jehoiada, in reign of Joash king of Judah, 2 Chr. 24:20, and probably same as the Zacharias of Matt. 23:35. (14) A prophet and royal coun-

sellor in reign of Uzziah, 2 Chr. 16:5. (15) Father of Abijah, mother of King Hezekiah, 2 Chr. 29:1. (16) A member of the family of Asaph in time of Hezekiah, 2 Chr. 29:13. (17) A Kohathite Levite in the reign of Josiah, 2 Chr. 34:12. (18) One of the temple rulers in reign of Josiah, 2 Chr. 35:8. (19) Nine priests, Levites and returned captives in Ez. 8:3, 11, 16; 10:26; Neh. 8:4; 11:4, 5, 12; 12:16, 35, 41. (20) A witness for Isaiah, Isa. 8:2.

ZI'ON (*mount, sunny*). Zion or Sion in its literal and restricted sense was the celebrated mount in Jerusalem, the highest and southernmost or southwestern-most of the city. It was the original hill of the Jebusites, Josh. 15:63. After David became king, he captured it, "the stronghold of Zion," from the Jebusites, dwelt in the fort there, and greatly enlarged and strengthened its fortifications, calling it "the city of David," 2 Sam. 5:6-9; 1 Chr. 11:5-8. Despite David's prestige the name of Zion still clung to it, 1 Kgs. 8:1; 2 Kgs. 19:21, 31; 2 Chr. 5:2. The O. T. poets and prophets exalted the word Zion by frequent use and gave it a sacred turn, so that in time it came to type a sacred capital, Ps. 2:6; holy place, Ps. 137:2; 149:2; Isa. 30:19; God's chosen people, Ps. 51:18; 87:5; the Christian church, Heb. 12:22; the heavenly city, Rev. 14:1.

PALESTINE IN THE TIME OF JESUS

Dashed blue lines equate intermittent streams.

Kilometers 0 10 20 30 40

Statute Miles 0 10 20 30

© Copyright 1983 by HOLMAN BIBLE PUBLISHERS
All rights reserved. International copyright secured

A B C D E

1

•Sidon

ABILENE

SYRIA

PHOENICIA

Mt. Lebanon

Leontes River

Mt. Hermon

•Tyre

•Caesarea Philippi

2

Cadasa•

•Thella

•Ecdippa

Sepph•   •Jamnith

•Sogane

Ptolemais,
Acco•

GALILEE

•Chorazin
•Bethsaida?

Gennesaret•   •Capernaum

Cana•   Magdala•   Sea of   •Gergesa

Galilee

Yarmuk River

3

Sepphoris•

Tiberias•
Ammathus•

Hippus•

•Abila

Nazareth•

•Philoteria

Japhia•

•Nain

•Gadara

•Dora

4

Capercotnei,
Kefar Otnay•

Caesarea,
Strato's Tower•

Scythopolis•

•Pella

•Narbata

Ginae•

Jordan River

DECAPOLIS

5

SAMARIA

•Aenon?

•Agrippina?

•Samaria

Gerasa

Sychar•
Shechem•

Ammathus•   •Ragaba

Jabbok River

Apollonia•

Plain of Sharon

•Coreae

Joppa•

•Antipatris   Acrabeta•

•Tower of Aphek

Gerasa•

•Alexandrium

•Zia

Phasaelis•

•Gadora

6

Adida•

•Thamna

Archelais•

PEREA

Lydda, Lod•

Gophna•   Ephraim•

•Philadelphia

•Sappho   Rama•

•Neara

•Bethennabris

Emmaus,   Gabaon•

Jericho•

•Abila, Abel

Jamnia•

Nicopolis•   Jerusalem•   Mt. of Olives

•Livias, Julias,
Beth-ramatha

Ramat Rahel•   •Bethany   Qumran

•Essene community

7

Bethletepha•   Bethlehem•

Hyrcania

•Medeba

JUDEA   •Herodium

•Baaras

Ascalon•

Tekoa•

•Machaerus

Beror Hayil   •Betogabris

Callirrhoe•

•Anthedon   •Belzedek?

Lake Asphaltitis
(Dead Sea, Salt Sea)

•Dibon

•Gaza   •Adora   Hebron•   Engedi•

Arnon River

8

IDUMEA

Masada•

Areopolis•

•Raphia

•Arad

NABATAEANS

Beersheba•

•Malatha   En Boqeq•

9

Charachmoba•

•Elusa

•Zoar

Zered River

The Great Sea
(Mediterranean Sea)

N

Ernie Couch
CONSULTX